…HE…

DETERMINE TO WHICH OF THE FOUR PATTERNS YOUR CHARACTER BELONGS	Right	Wrong
◧ 1 Characters that can be divided into left and right parts	相 4-5 八 1-1 順 1-11 扱 3-3	片 1-3 用 1-4 可 3-2 多 3-3
⬒ 2 Characters that can be divided into top and bottom parts	二 1-1 寺 3-3 古 2-3 春 5-4	万 1-2 考 4-2 聞 8-4 坐 4-3
◘ 3 Characters that can be divided by an enclosure element	進 3-8 広 3-2 問 8-3 国 3-5	入 1-1 呉 4-3 名 3-3 為 5-4
■ 4 Characters that cannot be classified under patterns ◧1, ⬒2, or ◘3	雨 8-1 丘 5-2 中 4-3 与 3-4	刀 2-1 日 4-1 水 4-3
IF A CHARACTER CAN BE CLASSIFIED UNDER MORE THAN ONE PATTERN, SELECT THE ONE THAT FOLLOWS THE NATURAL CONSTRUCTION OF THE CHARACTER	児 ⬒2-5-2 箱 ⬒2-6-9	児 ◧1-2-5 箱 ◧1-7-8

HOW TO DIVIDE THE CHARACTER

DIVIDE THE CHARACTER INTO TWO PARTS AT THE FIRST DIVISION POINT	Right	Wrong
◧ Going from left to right, divide at the first space	明 4-4 小 1-2 扱 3-3	小 2-1 街 9-3
⬒ Going from top to bottom, divide at the first space, horizontal line, or frame element, whichever comes first	三 1-2 脅 2-8 赤 3-4 古 2-3	三 2-1 脅 6-4 赤 2-5 下 1-2
◘ Going from the outside toward the inside, divide after the first enclosure element	度 3-6 進 3-8 閉 8-3 目 3-2	度 7-2 磨 11-5
DO NOT VIOLATE THE PRINCIPLE OF ELEMENT INTEGRITY 1. Never break through strokes 2. Never break through indivisible units 3. Never make unnatural divisions	凶 ◘3-2-2 情 ◧1-3-8 気 ◘3-4-2	凶 ◧1-1-4 情 ◧1-1-10 気 ⬒2-2-4

HOW TO SUBCLASSIFY THE SOLID PATTERN

DETERMINE TO WHICH OF THE FOUR SOLID SUBPATTERNS YOUR CHARACTER BELONGS	Right	Wrong
1 Characters that contain a top line	雨 8-1 下 3-1 耳 6-1 果 8-1	刀 2-1 千 3-1 垂 8-1 丘 5-1
2 Characters that contain a bottom line	上 3-2 丘 5-2 垂 8-2	山 3-2 包 5-2 者 8-2
3 Characters that contain a through line	中 4-3 東 8-3 毛 4-3	水 4-3 寸 3-3 午 4-3 弟 7-3
4 Characters that do not contain a top line, bottom line, or through line	与 3-4 大 3-4 寿 7-4	糸 6-4 久 3-4 友 4-4 劣 6-4
IF A CHARACTER CAN BE CLASSIFIED UNDER MORE THAN ONE SUBPATTERN, THE SUBPATTERN WITH THE SMALLEST NUMBER TAKES PRECEDENCE	王 4-1 己 3-1 酉 7-1 果 8-1 出 5-2 生 5-2 甲 5-1	王 4-2 己 3-2 酉 7-2 果 8-3 出 5-3 生 5-3 甲 5-3

See **SYSTEM OF KANJI INDEXING BY PATTERNS** on p. 106a for details.

NTC's NEW JAPANESE-ENGLISH CHARACTER Dictionary

新漢英字典

NTC's NEW JAPANESE-ENGLISH CHARACTER Dictionary

新漢英字典

In association with
Kenkyusha Limited

Editor in Chief Jack Halpern

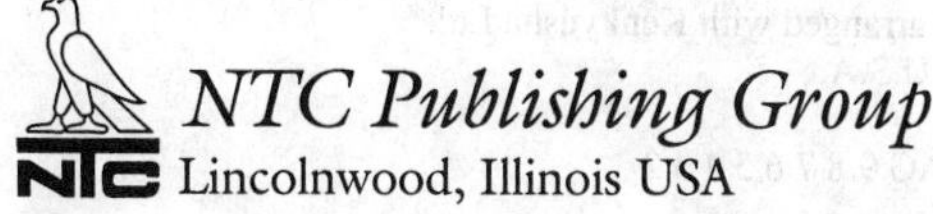

NTC's New Japanese-English Character Dictionary

1997 Printing

NTC's New Japanese-English Character Dictionary is published by National Textbook Company, a division of NTC Publishing Group, 4255 West Touhy Avenue, Lincolnwood (Chicago), Illinois 60646-1975 U.S.A.

Printed in the U.S.A.

6 7 8 9 AG 9 8 7 6 5 4 3 2

To Michal

Neither is a dictionary a bad book to read.
There is no cant in it,
no excess of explanation,
and it is full of suggestion,—
the raw material of possible poems and histories.

Ralph Waldo EMERSON (1860)

又、辞書も決して其れを読むに悪い書物ではない。
辞書には虚飾も無く、
冗漫な説明も無く、
示唆に富んでゐる、——
詩となり、歴史となり得る素材なのである。

ラルフ・ワルドー・エマソン(1860年)

CONTENTS 目次

APPENDIXES 付録

INDEXES 索引

EDITORIAL STAFF

Editor in Chief

Jack Halpern

Showa Women's University
Institute of Modern Culture

Editorial Consultants

Kusuo Hitomi	President of Showa Women's University
Eleanor H. Jorden	Professor/Distinguished Fellow, Johns Hopkins University and Mary Donlon Alger Professor of Linguistics Emeritus, Cornell University
Masaaki Nomura	Professor of Japanese at Center for Japanese Language, Waseda University
Akiyasu Todo	formerly Professor of Chinese Literature at University of Tokyo and Waseda University

Associate Editors

Masato Asada	M.A., University of Tokyo
Michael Carr	Ph.D., University of Arizona
Chikasada Harada	Professor, Showa Women's University
Yukio Ishikawa	M.A., Keio University
Tomoko Kaneko	Assistant Professor, Showa Women's University
Masako Nakamura	B.A., Hiroshima University

Editorial Assistants

Harumi Iida, Takane Ito, JeanPaul Jenack, Keith Johnson, Yoshikazu Kawakami, Ryoun Kobayashi, Christine Lamarre, Peter H. Liu, Russell Marcus, Susumu Miyazawa, Yuko Momose, Kimiko Morishita, Ryoko Murase, Tazuko Nagae, Setsuo Nara, Harumi Nishimoto, Aki Ono, Junko Osaki, Jack Plimpton, Meryl Schaffer, Junko Suzuki, Kazuko Suzuki, Yuriko Takagi, Hiroko Takahashi, Noriko Yamamoto, Tsuneo Yatagai, Tadashi Yumiketa

Keyboarding

Michal Halpern, Yoshie Miura, Taeko Moriguchi, Haruko Oasa, Kumiko Suga, Nobuko Suzuki, Keiko Uchida, Chieko Yokoe, Toshiko Yoshida

Programming and Computer Consultants

Shoichi Fujita, Yasuhiro Hasegawa, Koki Kondo, Toshio Otsuka

Secretarial and Clerical Assistants

Junko Higuchi, Keiko Ikuta, Miyuki Masuda, Hikaru Matsumoto, Keiko Matsuoka, Keiko Matsushima, Teruko Miyake, Kumiko Nakagawa, Sachiko Shibata, Kazuto Shioiri, Chieko Takahata, Mitsuko Yanagisawa

編集スタッフ

編集長

春遍雀來（ハル ベン・ジャック）

昭和女子大学
近代文化研究所

編集顧問

E. ジョーデン	ジョンズ・ホプキンズ大学教授／研究員 コーネル大学言語学名誉教授
藤堂明保	元東京大学教授・早稲田大学客員教授
野村雅昭	早稲田大学日本語研究教育センター教授
人見楠郎	昭和女子大学学長

編集員

浅田正人	東京大学文学修士
石川幸雄	慶應義塾大学文学修士
マイケル・カー	アリゾナ大学言語学博士
金子朝子	昭和女子大学助教授
中村雅子	広島大学教育学学士
原田親貞	昭和女子大学教授

編集協力者

飯田晴巳　伊藤たかね　大崎順子　大野亜紀　川上義和　小林陵雲
メリル・シェイファー　ジョンポール・ジャネック　キース・ジョンソン
鈴木和子　鈴木淳子　高木百合子　高橋裕子　永江多鶴子　奈良節夫
西本晴美　ジャック・プリントン　ラッセル・マーカス　宮沢進
村瀬良子　百瀬侑子　森下貴美子　谷田貝常夫　山本典子　弓桁正
クリスティーヌ・ラマール　劉丕

コンピュータ入力

打田恵子　大麻治子　菅久美子　鈴木宣子　春遍美晴　三浦淑江
森口栲子　横江智恵子　吉田敏子

プログラミング・コンピュータ顧問

大塚敏夫　近藤光輝　長谷川康弘　藤田彰一

事務員

活田恵子　塩入和人　柴田幸子　高畑千枝子　中川久美子　樋口順子
増田美由紀　松岡恵子　松島敬子　松本光　三宅照子　柳沢光子

ARE YOU IN A HURRY?

No sensible person would attempt to operate a sophisticated device like a computer without first reading the instruction manual. Yet many people think nothing of using a sophisticated tool like a comprehensive dictionary without as much as a glance at the front matter.

This dictionary has been carefully designed to be as user-friendly as possible. For example, a visually attractive layout makes the organization of character entries mostly self-explanatory. Nevertheless, you cannot expect to use it to the best advantage without some kind of preparation.

TO DERIVE MAXIMUM BENEFIT FROM THIS DICTIONARY, WE STRONGLY URGE YOU TO READ THE FRONT MATTER.

If you choose to ignore this advice, please remember this: this dictionary is not just a tool for looking up unknown characters and words—its primary aim is to help you gain an in-depth understanding of kanji. By skipping the front matter, you not only deprive yourself of access to the wealth of information that the dictionary contains, but will also be unable to take full advantage of the numerous features that make it a powerful learning aid.

IF YOU ARE IN A HURRY, AT THE VERY LEAST BE SURE TO READ THE SECTIONS LISTED BELOW.

1. INTRODUCTION (p. 25a): Discusses the aims of the dictionary and summarizes its main features.
2. EXPLANATORY CHART (p. 153a): Shows the various parts of the character entry.
3. SYSTEM OF KANJI INDEXING BY PATTERNS (p. 106a): Explains how to quickly locate character entries. If you are in a hurry, at least read **§ 2.1** and the charts inside the front and back covers.
4. FEATURES OF THIS DICTIONARY (p. 61a): Describes the dictionary's features and explains how these can benefit the learner. At the very least, be sure to read **§ 2. Understanding.**
5. GUIDE TO THE DICTIONARY (p. 159a): Describes the format and conventions used in the dictionary. You need not read all the details. We recommend that you at least read **§ 1. Character Entries,** **§ 2. Main Entries,** **§ 10.** COMPOUNDS **Section,** and, if possible, **§ 20. Character Meanings.**

FOREWORD

An isolated island country lying off the eastern edge of the continental land mass of Asia, Japan has, since ancient times, developed a distinctive culture and history of her own while maintaining relations with her Asian neighbors. Chinese characters, which were introduced to Japan from ancient China, gave birth to a new set of phonetic characters known as kana. Although both these forms of script have thereafter been used side by side to write the Japanese language, the Chinese characters have always played a central role, serving as the chief medium of communicating ideas in a broad spectrum of fields ranging from philosophy and scholarship to the literary arts and ethics.

The introduction of Chinese characters made it possible for the Japanese to learn about religious ideas from the Buddhist classics and gave them a new means for expressing subtle emotional nuances. Eventually evolved a script, unprecedented in history, in which kana and kanji blend to produce a powerful means of conveying meaning in a concise and effective manner. The adoption of advanced Western thought, culture, social institutions, and technology that took place during the rapid modernization after the Meiji Restoration gave rise to a need for coining countless neologisms to express new concepts. Such items as 文明 *bunmei* 'civilization', 経済 *keizai* 'economics', and 手続 *tetsuzuki* 'procedure' are only a few examples of the innumerable words whose coinage was made possible by the word-forming ability of Chinese characters.

This uniquely Japanese writing system, while playing a role as a most beneficial and distinctly *human* medium of communication, has blossomed into a treasure of Japanese culture and tradition. In this manner, the Chinese characters have served as an extremely convenient set of symbols—the central pillar of the evolution of Japan's culture; in fact, they are the very symbol of Japan's membership in the "Kanji Sphere of Culture"—a community of nations sharing a common heritage based on Chinese characters.

Though Japan has experienced many ups and downs during the period of more than one hundred years that has elapsed since the Meiji Restoration, she has successfully pulled through to attain a high level of economic growth, and now even stands at the forefront of science and technology. As Japan has come to occupy an important position in world affairs, a rapidly increasing number of people and nations in every corner of the globe are turning to her as a focus of intense interest and active concern. This trend, which is likely to accelerate as the world undergoes increased internationalization, is clearly apparent in the sharp rise, both at home and abroad, in the number of people studying Japanese in recent years. As Japan heads into the twenty-first century, organizations engaged in Japanese language education are vigorously preparing to accommodate the growing demand by training more teachers, improving teaching methods, developing improved teaching materials, and implementing Japanese language proficiency examinations.

All this notwithstanding, one of the central problems in Japanese language education today is, as pointed out by Shigeko Miyazaki, the executive director of the Association for Japanese-Language Teaching, the almost total lack of truly effective dictionaries for learners. A mere translated version of existing Japanese-Japanese dictionaries is hardly adequate for meeting the needs of the foreign student. More than anything else, there is now an urgent need for the publication of effective dictionaries that squarely address these needs.

The original motive force for the compilation of this dictionary sprung from the editor's own arduous experiences in struggling with traditional methods of rote memorization and the excessive burden which these place on the memory. Based on voluminous data sources and modern linguistic theory, this work is designed to meet the special needs of the non-Japanese student, while serving as a scholarly accurate, useful work of reference even for native Japanese.

This dictionary also introduces a new method of looking up characters known as the System of Kanji Indexing by Patterns (SKIP), which enables one to locate entries rapidly without previous knowledge of kanji elements. Character meanings and compound words are arranged in a manner that shows how each character functions as a word-building element, and an analysis of the differences between homophones (word pronounced alike but written differently) and kanji synonyms is presented. We are confident that students of Japanese using this dictionary will make rapid progress in their studies by deepening their knowledge and understanding of kanji, and will be completely gratified with its effectiveness.

In accordance with the founding principles of Showa Women's University, we endeavor to educate women to be "aware, intelligent, and fair-minded." Over the long years of our existence, we have striven to cultivate young women that will play an important role in society and, at the same time, have endeavored to contribute to research on and the advancement of culture. The Institute for the Study of Modern Culture, which is affiliated with the university and has been actively engaged in promoting cultural research, recognized that kanji is the key to the healthy growth of Japanese culture and literature. The Institute recognized the import of the new dictionary, and consequently proceeded, under the direction of Jack Halpern as editor in chief, to embark upon the long years of research necessary for its compilation.

To bring a project of this magnitude and complexity to successful completion required a high degree of scholarly expertise, the latest computer photocomposition technology, and advanced system design and software engineering. Furthermore, the layout and design of the dictionary had to be carefully executed to achieve maximum ease of use while satisfying a broad spectrum of diversified needs. To accomplish these objectives required an inestimable number of man-hours, painstaking labor, and capital funding on a major scale. If not for these coordinated efforts, this work would not have seen the light of day.

On this day, as we present the world with this new work, it is our duty to record our everlasting gratitude to Jack Halpern, the chief editor and central figure responsible for seeing this project through, for his outstanding achievement in producing a work that represents a significant departure from traditional character dictionary lexicography. It is our great fortune that Jack Halpern, who eagerly devoted himself to the project while overcoming innumerable difficulties, should have become captivated by the rhythmical tones of the Japanese language and so intrigued by the Chinese characters as to embark upon their serious study. The day will surely come when he will be widely recognized for promoting the study of kanji throughout the world.

I would like to express my heartfelt appreciation to the distinguished scholars that served as editorial consultants, including Professor Eleanor Jorden, Professor Akiyasu Todo, Professor Masaaki Nomura, Professor Chikasada Harada, and others for their most valuable advice and cooperation. Sincere gratitude also goes to the Dictionary Department of Kenkyusha as well as to the technical staff engaged in computer photocomposition at the Toppan Printing Company for rendering their outstanding efforts. I also wish to sincerely thank the many organizations, foundations, and individuals who have made financial contributions to the project for their unlimited understanding and moral support.

I am convinced that this dictionary will make a major contribution to both the teaching and learning of Japanese. It is, furthermore, my earnest hope that this work will help promote understanding of Japan among the people of the world, and thereby stimulate further international economic and cultural exchange.

KUSUO HITOMI
President of Showa Women's University

March 21, 1990
Tokyo

序　言

アジア大陸の東端に位置し、かつ島国である我が日本は、古来、時に応じて近隣諸国との交流を持ちながらも、独自の歴史を展開し特有の文化を創造してきた。古代中国から日本に伝来した漢字は、後に仮名という独特の文字を新たに生み出し、この二つの文字体系を組み合わせて用いられてはきたが、やはり漢字は思想、学問、文芸、道徳等、諸々の方面に於ける最も重要な情報伝達手段として中心的な役割を担い続けてきたのである。

漢字の伝来以来、日本人は漢字を通して神仏の加護について学び、細やかな感情表現に対する手段を与えられ、古今東西他に類を見ないほど瞬間的に意味を伝達できる「漢字仮名混じり文」を生み出すに至った。明治維新以来の急激な近代化の要請に伴い、欧米の進んだ文化、社会制度、技術、思想の導入に迫られ、新概念を表現するため、漢字による新造語が無数に産出された。文明、経済、手続…等の造語例を挙げれば枚挙に暇がないが、漢字の造語機能が新造語の発達を支えてきたのである。

我が国独特のこの文字体系は、非常に有益かつ人間的な情報用具としての役割を果たしつつ、日本の伝統と文化の中で素晴らしい花を開かせてきたと言えよう。このように、漢字はきわめて便利な図形であり、日本文化進展の大黒柱であり、日本がまさしく「漢字文化圏」に属している証しでもある。

明治維新後100年余を経過した今日、幾多の曲折がありながらも既に経済的に高度成長を達成し、さらに新しい先端技術を開拓し、世界でも重要な地位を占めるようになった日本に対し、興味や関心を強め、熱い眼差しを向けている世界の国々や人々は、今や激増の一途をたどっている。この傾向は、近年我が国の内外に於ける日本語学習者の急増の現象ともなって確実に現われており、国際化時代の進展と共に、加速化する要素が強い。21世紀に向けて関係機関は今や本腰を入れて、日本語教員の養成、その教育内容、教育方法、教育材料等の開発、日本語能力検定試験、日本語教育機関の充実など、受け入れ体制の整備を急いでいる。

それにもかかわらず、国際日本語普及協会常務理事の宮崎茂子女史によると、現在の日本語教育界で中心となる問題の一つは、実用的な学習辞典がほとんどないということである。従来から存在する漢和字典や国語辞典の翻訳版と言うだけでは日本語学習字典としては決して充分ではない。何よりもまず、外国人の側で求めている条件を満たした効率の優れた辞書を刊行することが緊急に要請されているのである。

このたび刊行する本字典の編纂は、そもそも外国人である編者が日本語を習得した時に、きわめて過大な記憶力に頼らざるを得なかったという、かつての苦い経験に端を発したものであった。豊富な調査データと最新の言語学理論を基に、外国人学習者自身の要望に応えるために完成させたものであり、外国人はもとより、我々日本人にとっても学術的に信頼できる、有用なものである。また、漢字を全く知らなくても引ける「字型式検字法」と称する新検字法を導入し、漢字特有の造語機能に従った字義の記述と熟語の分類、同訓異字の使い分け、類義漢字の用法の分析等を加えることにより、日本語学習者は漢字の知識と理解を飛躍的に広げ、かつ深めることができ、利用する全ての人が必ずや満足を見出すものとなっていると確信している。

我が昭和女子大学は、建学の精神にのっとり「目覚めたる婦人、正しき婦人、思慮ある力強き婦人」の育成を目指し、広く世のために奉仕し役立つ人材を世に送ることに長年精進してきた一方、文化の研究と向上に尽力してきた。後者については付設の近代文化研究所に於て取り組んできているが、特に日本の文化・文学の発展に於ける鍵とも言える漢字の重要性に鑑み、本字典編纂の意義の深さを確認し、編集長の春遍雀來氏を中心に多年に亘って研究活動に全力を集注してきた。

本字典編纂の作業に当たっては、庬大な原稿の量と編集の複雑さから言っても、専門性の高い学識、先端のコンピュータ写植技術、高度なシステム設計及びソフトウェア技術等が必要であり、使い易さを目指すためには、レイアウトにも特に念を入れる必要があった。しかも、取り扱っている対象が広範囲に亘っているので、これらを完成するには庬大な時間と労力及び多額の資金を要し、これら一連の総力の結集によって初めて出版が可能となったのである。そのどれ一つを欠いても、本書が日の目を見ることはなかったであろう。

本日ようやく上梓の日を迎えるに当たり、自らの寝食を忘れて研究に没頭し、あらゆる困難な条件を克服しながら企画を推進し、かつて見ることのなかった辞書編纂上の新機軸を開発しながらこの大業を完成させた、編集長であり、実質的刊行責任者である春遍雀來氏の功績を永久に書き留めなければならない。かつて日本語の響きに心を打たれ、漢字のとりこになったという春遍雀來氏によって、漢字学習の世界的普及が大いに促進されたと認められる日が到来するものと確信している。

それに加え、編集顧問のE・ジョーデン先生、藤堂明保先生、野村雅昭先生、原田親貞先生等の諸先生から賜わった多大なご高配、貴重なご助言と甚大なるご労力に対して、厚く感謝の意を表明すると共に、出版元の研究社辞書編集部と凸版印刷のコンピュータ写植技術者の方々の並々ならぬお骨折りに対し深く敬意を表する。また、資金面で限りなき理解とご支援をお寄せ下さった各方面の団体、財団、個人の方々に厚くお礼を申し上げる次第である。

本字典は、日本語の習得にとっても、教育にとっても必ずや大きな役割を果たすものと信じている。しかもさらに、世界の人々の対日理解を深め、ひいては経済、文化等各般に亘る国際交流の橋渡しに役立てて戴ければ幸甚の至りである。

平成2年3月21日　　昭和女子大学学長　人　見　楠　郎
東京

ACKNOWLEDGMENTS

The **NEW JAPANESE-ENGLISH CHARACTER DICTIONARY** is a collaborative effort produced through the enthusiastic cooperation of some 100 staff members, part-time assistants, and outside consultants over a period of about sixteen years. First and foremost, I wish to extend my heartfelt gratitude to Professor Kusuo Hitomi, President of Showa Women's University, whose personal support and concern for the project has seen it through the most difficult times both financially and logistically, and to Professor Masaaki Nomura of the Center for Japanese Language at Waseda University, whose valuable advice helped establish editorial policy for the selection of entries and compound words.

Special recognition is due to the distinguished scholars, editorial consultants, and editors without whose generous contributions this dictionary would not have seen the light of day. Dr. Michael Carr, Professor Chikasada Harada, and Assistant Professor Tomoko Kaneko critically proofread the entire manuscript. Professor Eleanor H. Jorden, a world authority on Japanese language studies, has made valuable suggestions, while internationally renowned kanji scholar Professor Akiyasu Todo and Japanese language authority Professor Haruhiko Kindaichi have offered their warm recommendations.

Special thanks are due to Masato Asada, Masako Nakamura, Toshiko Yoshida, Chieko Yokoe, Ryoko Murase, Kimiko Morishita and other editors for their years of devotion to the arduous tasks of semantic analysis, compilation of data, and the meticulous checking of sources. In addition, dozens of consultants, computer programmers, keyboard operators, and secretarial and clerical personnel have worked on the project at one time or another during its sixteen years of progress.

I also wish to thank the many organizations and individuals that have made substantial contributions to the dictionary, especially the staff members in charge of the project at Kenkyusha and the Toppan Printing Company, without whose computer photocomposition technology the publication of this dictionary would not have been possible, and those who have contributed to the scholarly accuracy of the dictionary or have assisted in other ways, including Kokugo Mondai Kyogikai president Nobutane Kiuchi, The Japan Foundation, The National Language Research Institute, Japan Research Corporation chairman Kazuo Noda, Association for Japanese-Language Teaching executive director Shigeko Miyazaki, and Professor Takao Suzuki. Thanks are also due to Ryoun Kobayashi, an expert calligrapher who has written the cursive and semicursive style characters for this dictionary.

To bring a project of this magnitude to successful completion required large-scale contributions and financial assistance from many quarters. I wish to express my deep appreciation to the approximately 150 individuals, private organizations, corporations, and foundations who recognized the import of the dictionary and have selflessly offered continuous support without seeking personal returns. The following individuals and organizations have made the most substantial financial contributions:

Masaharu Ando
The Bank of Tokyo Ltd.
Chubu Electric Power Co., Inc.
The Dai-ichi Kangyo Bank, Ltd.
Daiwa Securities Co., Ltd.
Epson Hanbai Corporation Ltd.
Foundation of International Education
The Fuji Bank, Ltd.
Takao Fujinami
Shoichi Fujita
Fujitsu Ltd.
Futaba Corporation
Atsuo Hashimoto
Hitachi Ltd.
Teruko Horiuchi
IBM Japan, Ltd.
Iona International Corporation
Sonoko Ishii
Takao Ishii
Japan Petroleum Consultants, Ltd.
Kano Shojuan
The Kansai Electric Power Co., Inc.
Toshinaga Karasawa
Kenkyusha Limited
Kokugo Mondai Kyogikai
Kokusai Denshin Denwa Co.
Matsushita Electric Industrial Company, Ltd.
The Mitsubishi Bank, Ltd.
Mitsubishi Electric Corporation
The Mitsui Bank, Ltd.
Mobil Sekiyu Kabushiki Kaisha
Masaki Nakajima
Yoko Nakayama
NEC Corporation
New Japan Securities Co., Ltd.
The Nikko Securities Co.,Ltd.
Nippon Life Insurance Co.
Nippon Telegraph and Telephone Corporation
Nippon Unicar Company, Ltd.
Nissan Motor Co., Ltd.
The Nomura Foundation
Nomura Securities Co., Ltd.
PHP Institute International, Inc.
Recruit Shuppan Co, Ltd.
Rocco Shuppan, Ltd.
The Saitama Bank, Ltd.
The Sanwa Bank, Ltd.
Sasakawa Peace Foundation
Sharp Corporation
Shiseido Co., Ltd.
Showa Leasing Co., Ltd.
Showa Women's University
SUMITOMO 3M Limited
Toshimasa Tabuchi
Kaoru Takahashi
Tohoku Electric Power Co., Inc.
Tokio Marine Kagami Memorial Foundation
The Tokyo Electric Power Co., Inc.
Toshiba Corporation
The Toyota Foundation
Wako Securities Co., Ltd.
Yamaichi Securities Co., Ltd.

I also wish to express my sincere thanks to Vice Chairman Sohei Nakayama and First Subcommittee Chairman Naohiro Amaya, both of the National Council on Educational Reform, who have given their wholehearted support and assistance in raising funds for the project, and to Kiyotaka Kurokawa, Yasuo Ushioda, Yoichiro Yamamura, and Russell Marcus for their active cooperation in the fund-raising effort and for their continuous moral support.

I am indebted to the following dictionaries and reference works as well as to the hundreds of other dictionaries, encyclopedias, books, magazines, and newspapers that were used as sources or for reference in the compilation of this dictionary.

Beijing Waiguo Xueyuan. *The Chinese-English Dictionary*. Hong Kong: Shangwuyinshuguan, 1979.
Ishii Shōji. *Jōyō Kanwa Jiten*. Tokyo: Gakushukenkyusha, 1976.
Katō Jōken, et al. *Kadokawa Jigen Jiten*. Tokyo: Kadokawa Shoten, 1983.
Kenbō Hidetoshi, et al. *Sanseidō Kokugo Jiten*. Tokyo: Sanseido, 1974.
Kindaichi Haruhiko, et al. *Gakken Kokugo Daijiten*. Tokyo: Gakushukenkyusha, 1978.
Koine Yoshio, et al. *New English-Japanese Dictionary*. Tokyo: Kenkyusha, 1980.
Lin Yutang. *Lin Yutang's Chinese-English Dictionary of Modern Usage*. Hong Kong: The Chinese University of Hong Kong, 1972.
Masuda Kō, et al. *New Japanese-English Dictionary*. Tokyo: Kenkyusha, 1974.
Morohashi Tetsuji. *Daikanwa Jiten*. Tokyo: Taishukan Shoten, 1955.
The National Language Research Institute. *A Study of Uses of Chinese Characters in Modern Newspapers*. Tokyo: Bunshōdō, 1976.
Nelson, Andrew N. *The Modern Reader's Japanese-English Character Dictionary*. Tokyo: Charles E. Tuttle Company Publishers, 1974.
Nihon Kokugo Daijiten. Tokyo: Shogakkan, 1972.
Takebe Yoshiaki. *Kanji no Yōhō*. Tokyo: Kadokawa Shoten, 1979.
Tōdō Akiyasu. *Gakken Kanwa Daijiten*. Tokyo: Gakushukenkyusha, 1978.
Yamada Tadao, et al. *Shinmeikai Kokugo Jiten*. Tokyo: Sanseido, 1981.
Yamada Toshio, et al. *Kadokawa Shinkokugo Jiten*. Tokyo: Kadokawa Shoten, 1981.

Finally, to my wife Michal, who for long years devoted superhuman efforts to the project and has seen it through the most difficult times, goes my everlasting gratitude and appreciation.

March 21, 1990
Niiza-shi, Saitama

JACK HALPERN, *Editor in Chief*

謝　辞

『新漢英字典』は、16年の年月を掛け、約100名のスタッフ、非常勤助手ならびに外部顧問の熱心な協力によって生まれたものである。まず誰よりも昭和女子大学学長人見楠郎先生に衷心からの感謝を表明したい。資金面や事業面に於て、非常に困難な状況にあった時、先生のご厚意とご支援によって、窮地を脱し得たことが幾度あったか知れない。また、本字典の親字及び熟語の選択基準を決定するに当たっては、早稲田大学日本語研究教育センターの野村雅昭教授から貴重なご助言を戴いた。先生のご好意に対して深く感謝する次第である。

本字典に多大な寄与をして下さった著名な学者、編集顧問、編集員の寛大なご協力なしには本字典は日の目を見ることがなかったであろうと思われ、格別の謝意を表したい。マイケル・カー博士、原田親貞教授、金子朝子助教授には全原稿に目を通して批評を加えて戴いた。日本語研究の世界的権威であるE・ジョーデン教授からは有益なご提言を戴き、また、国際的に著名な漢字学者の藤堂明保教授ならびに日本語学の権威である金田一春彦教授からは温かいご推薦を戴いた。

さらに、浅田正人、中村雅子、吉田敏子、横江智恵子、村瀬良子、森下貴美子の各氏ならびにその他編集協力者は、長年に亘って根気強く意味分析、資料収集、出典の緻密な調査作業に当たられた。ここに厚くお礼を申し上げたい。この他、顧問、プログラマー、入力者、事務員として幾多の人々がこの16年間の様々な時期に関わりを持たれた。

また、本字典出版のために重要な貢献をして下さった諸団体、個人の方々へも謝辞を呈したい。特に本企画担当の任に当たられた研究社のスタッフの方々と、凸版印刷株式会社のコンピュータ写植の技術によって本字典の刊行が可能となった。さらに、国語問題協議会会長木内信胤氏、国際交流基金、国立国語研究所、日本総合研究所理事長野田一夫氏、国際日本語普及協会常務理事宮崎茂子氏及び鈴木孝夫教授の各氏からは、本字典の学問的正確さやその他の面でご助力を戴き、深く感謝を申し上げる。なお、草行書体を書いて下さった書家小林陵雲氏に感謝の言葉を申し上げたい。

この種の厖大な規模を有する企画を完成させるためには、各方面からの莫大な寄付や財政援助を必要とした。本字典の重要性を認め、個人的な見返りを期待することなく無欲の援助を続けて下さった約150の個人、民間団体、会社、財団に対し、ここに衷心より厚くお礼申し上げる。以下に挙げる個人、団体は中でもとりわけ資金面で多大な寄与をして下さった方々である。（敬称略）

安藤正春
イオナインターナショナル（株）
石井園子
石井孝夫
エプソン販売（株）
叶匠寿庵
唐沢利長
関西電力（株）
（株）研究社
国語問題協議会
国際教育財団
国際電信電話（株）
国際PHP研究所
（株）埼玉銀行
笹川平和財団
（株）三和銀行
（株）資生堂
シャープ（株）
昭和女子大学
昭和リース（株）
新日本証券（株）
住友3M（株）
（株）第一勧業銀行
大和證券（株）
高橋馨
田淵俊正
中部電力（株）
東京海上各務記念財団
（株）東京銀行
東京電力（株）
（株）東芝
東北電力（株）
トヨタ財団
中島正樹
中山葉子
日興證券（株）
日産自動車（株）
日本アイ・ビー・エム（株）
日本生命保険
日本石油コンサルタント
日本電気（株）
日本電信電話（株）
日本ユニカー（株）
野村財団
野村證券（株）
橋本敦生
（株）日立製作所
（株）富士銀行
藤田彰一
富士通（株）
藤波孝生
双葉電子工業（株）
堀内照子
松下電器産業（株）
（株）三井銀行
（株）三菱銀行
三菱電機（株）
モービル石油（株）
山一證券（株）
リクルート出版（株）
（株）六興出版
和光証券（株）

臨時教育審議会会長代理中山素平氏及び同第一部会長天谷直弘氏からは、本企画の資金調達に対し熱心なご支援とご助力を与えられ、また、黒川清孝、潮田保雄、山村洋一郎ならびにラッセル・マーカスの諸氏からも、積極的なお骨折りと絶えざる精神的ご支援を賜わったことに対して厚くお礼を申し上げる次第である。

以下に記す辞典、参考文献を始めとして、その他編纂に当たって本字典のために出典及び参考資料として用いた数百の辞典、百科辞典、書物、雑誌、新聞等の刊行物に負うところは大である。

石井庄司『常用漢和辞典』、学習研究社、1976
加藤常賢、他『角川字源辞典』、角川書店、1983
金田一春彦、他『学研国語大辞典』、学習研究社、1978
見坊豪紀、他『三省堂国語辞典』、三省堂、1974
小稲義男、他『新英和大辞典』、研究社、1980
国立国語研究所『現代新聞の漢字』、文唱堂、1976
武部良明『漢字の用法』、角川書店、1979
藤堂明保『学研漢和大字典』、学習研究社、1978
『日本国語大辞典』、小学館、1972
ネルソン A.『最新漢英辞典』、タトル社、1974
北京外国語学院『中英辞典』、香港：商務印書館、1979
増田綱、他『新和英大辞典』、研究社、1974
諸橋轍次『大漢和辞典』、大修館書店、1955
林語堂『林語堂當代漢英詞典』、香港：香港中文大學、1972
山田忠雄、他『新明解国語辞典』、三省堂、1981
山田俊雄、他『角川新国語辞典』、角川書店、1981

最後に、長年に亘って超人的な努力を傾け、困難の時期を共に乗り越えてきてくれた妻ミハルに永遠の感謝と称賛の念を捧げたいと思う。

平成2年3月21日
埼玉県新座市

編集長　春遍雀來（ハル ベン・ジャック）

INTRODUCTION

The **NEW JAPANESE-ENGLISH CHARACTER DICTIONARY** is a totally new reference work designed to enable the learner to gain an in-depth understanding of how Chinese characters are used in contemporary Japanese.

Normally, the student faces the task of learning countless compound words as unrelated units. A unique feature of this dictionary that helps overcome this difficulty is the presentation of a central or **core meaning**, a concise English keyword that defines the most dominant meaning of each character, followed by detailed character meanings that clearly show how a few thousand basic building blocks are combined to form the several hundred thousand compounds in Japanese.

To further aid the learner, clear, complete, and accurate character meanings, illustrated by numerous compounds and examples, are grouped around the core meaning in a logically-structured manner that allows them to be conceived as an integrated unit. To make the dictionary a tool of real precision, it also provides full guidance for distinguishing between easily confused characters (synonyms and homophones).

Another unique feature is the introduction of SKIP, a new indexing system that enables the user to locate entries as quickly and as accurately as in alphabetical dictionaries. Since the system can be learned in a very short time and does not require prior knowledge of kanji elements, this dictionary is an extremely convenient and easy-to-use reference tool.

Various other features distinguish this as the most in-depth Japanese-English character dictionary ever compiled.

JAPANESE TODAY

The emergence of Japan as an economic and industrial superpower in the last third of the twentieth century has had a major impact on her role in world affairs. With the increasingly important role Japan is playing in the international arena, cross-cultural communications in the political, industrial, and commercial spheres have grown to unprecedented proportions. Language is an indispensable instrument for understanding the culture and mentality of any people; in the case of Japan, with her markedly different cultural traditions and patterns of behavior, the role it plays is even greater.

Japanese is often considered a difficult language. Some characteristics which justify this classification are its grammatical structure, which is radically different from that of the European languages, its complicated levels of formality, and what could be safely termed the most complex writing system devised by man. Although much of the so-called difficulty is based on a myth created and perpetuated by the Japanese themselves, it is nevertheless true that on the whole the non-Japanese learner must invest considerably more time and effort to master Japanese than many other foreign languages.

As Japan heads into the twenty-first century, the Japanese language is rapidly becoming an important medium of communication for a growing number of people. Statistics show that the number of Japanese language students in the world has been rising very rapidly. A survey conducted by the Agency of Cultural Affairs has shown that the total number of overseas students learning Japanese at schools and educational institutions in Japan has nearly quadrupled over a period of ten years, while the number outside Japan has increased eightfold in the same period. Moreover, there is clear evidence that the actual numbers exceed by far the official figures.

Whatever the actual figures may be, it is clear that the demand for Japanese language studies is growing at an unchecked pace. More than ever before, businessmen, students, diplomats, and scientists are faced with an urgent need to communicate with Japan in her own tongue. Although the Japanese government has set into motion various plans aimed at expanding facilities for the training of teachers, establishing Japanese language programs at institutions of higher learning, and so on, the fact remains that the number of available teachers and effective learning aids lags far behind the actual demand.

THE STUDY OF KANJI

The Japanese script is composed of two phonetic syllabaries, called *hiragana* and *katakana*, and thousands of Chinese characters, called *kanji*. Chinese characters have three basic properties: form, sound, and meaning. Many characters are of complex shape, some having more than twenty or even thirty strokes. Each character may be pronounced according to its Chinese derived *on* reading, or one of several native Japanese *kun* readings, and each reading may have numerous meanings. Moreover, since many words are pronounced the same but written differently, the Japanese script is highly complex and requires considerable effort to learn.

The question might well be asked: Does one really need to learn thousands of characters in order to master Japanese? The answer is, especially for the intermediate and advanced student, a very definite yes. There is a limit beyond which the student of the spoken language cannot progress unless he or she acquires proficiency in the written language. Despite the difficulties posed by the complex shapes and multiple readings, the effort to learn the characters is well worthwhile, for they provide a firm basis for the effective mastery of the bulk of the Japanese vocabulary. A knowledge of kanji actually accelerates, rather than impedes, progress in learning the language.

Chinese characters have the ability to generate hundreds of thousands of compound words from a basic stock of a few thousand units. They form a network of interrelated parts that function as an integrated system, not as an arbitrary set of disconnected symbols. Though this fact is, on the whole, recognized by educators, it has been largely disregarded in the development of kanji teaching programs and the compilation of character dictionaries. The traditional approach has been, and still is, to teach kanji more or less by rote, character by character, in the order in which they appear in the textbook lessons, often based on vague notions about their frequency of use.

In Japan, schoolchildren are subjected to an intense cycle of memorization, drilling, and testing. The emphasis is placed on how to write the characters correctly, paying scrupulous attention to minute details of form and stroke order, or on the rote memorization of compounds, while the meanings and functions of individual characters are mostly ignored. Although these methods have succeeded, by brute force, in achieving what is perhaps the highest literacy rate in the world, their lack of innovation and sheer dullness will hardly motivate the non-Japanese student.

Teaching materials are, for the most part, also based on this traditional approach. Although a number of good textbooks have been developed for mastering the spoken language, and various manuals for the study of the written language are available, the only Japanese-English character dictionary[1] in general use in the postwar period is already a quarter of a century old. A smaller dictionary, published before the war, is totally out-of-date and inadequate for modern needs. More serious, however, than the problems of up-to-dateness and scope is the failure of current and past works to systematically address that most elusive, yet undoubtedly most important, aspect of Chinese characters —their meanings, especially their meanings as word-building elements.

Kanji textbooks and dictionaries for non-Japanese users avoid the problem by limiting their treatment to compound words and independent words; the emphasis is almost entirely on form and sound, while the more difficult aspect of character meanings is virtually disregarded or lightly passed over. To make matters worse, existing character dictionaries, including those for native speakers, often list old or archaic meanings, while newer meanings are often inaccurate or entirely left out.

This lack of effective tools to overcome the formidable language barrier posed by the Japanese script has been one of the principal reasons that the number of foreigners to have truly mastered the language is still small. Never before has the time been so ripe, nor the need been so urgent, for the publication of a character dictionary that offers a systematic solution to the special problems of the non-Japanese student.

NEW CONCEPT DICTIONARY

The publication of a new character dictionary is an event of some importance in the world of Japanese language studies. The goals of the editors of the **NEW JAPANESE-ENGLISH CHARACTER DICTIONARY** have been set high: to create a completely new work that enables the learner to gain an in-depth understanding of the meanings and functions of all the high-frequency characters in contemporary Japanese.

The principal function of any dictionary is, needless to say, to enable the user to look up unknown items. Although this dictionary does accomplish that task most effectively, it does not aim to be a mere lookup tool. Rather, its primary aim is to serve as a reference tool of real precision, a powerful and practical learning aid that promotes understanding and stimulates a desire to learn. A mere com-

1. As opposed to word dictionaries, compound dictionaries, or textooks purporting to be dictionaries. Although various books on the market use the words "character dictionary" or "kanji dictionary" as part of their titles, most of these are actually study books that list characters along with a few examples, not dictionaries in the ordinary sense.

pilation of countless forms, readings, and compound words is of little value to the learner unless their significance and their relation to one another are properly understood. This dictionary not only accurately records the linguistic facts about kanji, but also strives to present them in a manner that gives the student insight into how they function as a system.

To achieve these aims, the dictionary departs from tradition in three important ways: (1) the presentation of clear, complete, and accurate character meanings arranged in a manner that shows how they are interrelated, (2) the introduction of a new indexing system that enables the user to locate entries with great speed and facility, and (3) the presentation of precise distinctions between closely related characters (synonyms and homophones). Many other features, such as full guidance on reading and writing and a wealth of reference data, distinguish this as the most in-depth Japanese-English character dictionary ever compiled.

Based on a systematic approach and firm theoretical foundation, the new work was produced by making full use of the most recent advances in linguistic science, computational lexicography, and photocomposition technology. From its inception, the work was designed to meet the needs of a broad range of users, including the beginner, intermediate, and advanced student, the teacher, the linguist, and the of developer teaching materials and courseware.

CHARACTER MEANING

Perhaps the most significant contribution of this dictionary is the in-depth manner in which it treats meaning. Not only are the character meanings accurate and complete, but they include many meanings that have never appeared in any other dictionary. The principal features that contribute to clarity of meaning are (1) the core meaning, (2) clear and accurate character meanings, (3) the ordering of senses in a manner that shows their interrelatedness, (4) the numerous compounds and examples that illustrate each sense, and (5) articles that describe how compounds are formed from their constituent parts. Each of these features is briefly described below.

1. Core Meaning

A striking feature of this dictionary is the presentation of a central or **core meaning.** This is a concise English keyword that provides a clear grasp of the central or most fundamental concept that links the principal senses of a character into one conceptual unit (e.g., 越 GO BEYOND). This is a feature unique to this dictionary that has been highly praised by scholars and educators as a powerful and effective learning aid.

2. Order of Senses

Traditionally, character dictionaries order meanings historically. Although this approach may be of value to the scholar, it is not necessarily useful to the student, since it does not reflect contemporary usage, and does not promote understanding. A possible alternative is the statistical approach, in which senses are ordered by frequency of occurrence. Even if such statistics were available, this would not be a useful system because it ignores the semantic relationships between individual senses.

This dictionary makes a significant departure from traditional character-dictionary lexicography by presenting meanings in a manner sometimes referred to as the *psychologistic approach;* i. e., the meanings are presented in a cogent order that clearly shows their interrelatedness. A keyword representing a dominant sense serves as the basis of organization, and the various senses are grouped in clusters in a manner that allows them to be conceived as a logically-structured, integrated unit. In adopting this policy we follow the precedent set by the *American Heritage Dictionary,* which is highly regarded by its users for this feature.

3. Character Meanings

Precisely-worded character meanings and a system of labels show exactly how each character functions as a word or word element. The meanings are presented in a manner that shows how the hundreds of thousands of compounds in Japanese can be generated from a basic stock of a few thousand characters. The functions of each character as a prefix, suffix, abbreviation, phonetic substitute, etc. are indicated, while the meanings of independent words are clearly distinguished from those of word elements. Moreover, a detailed analysis of the word-building function of one-character *kun* words and word elements is presented in English for the first time.

4. Compounds and Examples

The senses of each character are normally illustrated by numerous high-frequency compounds that provide maximally useful examples of each sense. Unlike conventional character dictionaries, the compounds are not restricted to those in which the entry character occurs in the initial position, and are arranged in a manner that clearly shows how they are formed from their constituent parts. This arrangement enables the user to easily infer the meanings of other compounds not found in the dictionary.

5. Compound Formation

The formation of a compound word is normally self-evident from the manner in which the compounds are grouped by meaning. When this is not obvious, a compound formation article describes how the compound is formed from its constituent parts; that is, how its constituent characters contribute to the meaning of the whole.

NEW INDEXING SYSTEM

In this dictionary, we depart from tradition by introducing a new scheme for classifying Chinese characters, the **System of Kanji Indexing by Patterns** (SKIP), which is based on the direct recognition of visual patterns—a new concept that ensures maximum lookup speed with minimum effort. With the help of simple rules, each character is unambiguously classified under one of four easy-to-identify geometrical patterns: ◧ 1 left-right, ⬒ 2 up-down, ◻ 3 enclosure, and ■ 4 solid. Within each group the characters are further subdivided into progressively smaller subgroups until each is assigned its own position.

One might well ask why there is a need for a new system. The answer is that the lack of an efficient classification scheme has long been a source of frustration to learners and native speakers alike. The traditional method of looking up characters presupposes a knowledge of kanji elements known as radicals. Looking up by radicals is a time-consuming, laborious, and unreliable process that may require weeks of practice to learn. Although many alternative systems have been devised, none have achieved the speed and simplicity required to meet the practical needs of the learner.

The system introduced here—designed from its inception for efficiency, speed, and ease of use—enables the user to locate entries as quickly and as accurately as in alphabetical dictionaries. It is a product of seven years of computer-assisted research and experimentation on how kanji elements are intuitively perceived and classified. Since the system can be learned in a very short time and does not require prior knowledge of kanji elements, it has been praised by Japanese language educators as a major breakthrough in Chinese character lexicography.

PRECISE DISTINCTIONS

A unique feature of this dictionary, presented here for the first time in any language, is the complete guidance it offers for the precise distinctions between **kanji synonyms.** Kanji synonym groups are presented along with English keywords in about 4650 synonym articles. Comparing these keywords, such as 推 INFER, 憶 SPECULATE, 測 CONJECTURE, and 察 GUESS, reveals both their differences and their similarities, and helps the student understand the different shades of meaning.

To further aid the learner, an appendix lists all the synonym groups for quick reference. This can be used as a simple version of a kanji thesaurus, and is also useful for looking up an unknown character from its meaning, rather than from its form or reading.

In addition, this dictionary provides, for the first time in English, ample information on the discrimination of homophones (such as *aku* written 開く 'open', 空く 'become vacant', and 明く 'regain sight') and orthographic variants (interchangeable forms such as 稀 *ki* and 希 *ki*). The approximately 600 usage notes enable the user to study the differences and similarities between the meanings of about 1410 homophones. Since these differences, which are a source of confusion to Japanese and non-Japanese alike, are often quite subtle, this feature should prove to be of enormous value to the student.

OTHER FEATURES

1. Six Lookup Methods

A major feature of this dictionary is the speed and facility with which entries can be looked up. Although we have departed from the traditional method of ordering characters, we have not overlooked the needs of the traditionally oriented user. The user has a choice of six different methods of locating entries:

1. **By pattern**: the **Pattern Index** allows characters to be quickly located from their geometrical patterns.
2. **By scanning**: a powerful shortcut allows characters of high stroke-count to be located almost instantaneously without counting strokes.
3. **By reading**: the **On-Kun Index** lists the characters alphabetically by both their *on* and *kun* readings.
4. **By radical**: the **Radical Index** lists the characters by their traditional radicals.
5. **By meaning**: the **List of Kanji Synonym Groups** arranges the characters in semantic groups listed alphabetically by their headwords.
6. **Directly**: a direct method allows characters to be located from their geometrical patterns without the use of any index.

2. Reading

The following ten features make this dictionary a convenient reference tool for reading both contemporary and prewar Japanese. The user can look up (1) unknown characters and their meanings with great speed and (2) unknown compounds and their meanings. The character entry includes (3) a wide range of character forms, (4) separate entries for nonstandard forms, (5) easily confused forms, (6) calligraphic and typeface styles, and (7) a wide range of character readings, while (8) the relative importance of readings is indicated. In addition, (9) all Japanese words and examples are romanized, and (10) the Chinese forms and readings are given.

3. Writing

The following eleven features make this

dictionary an excellent guide for writing Japanese: (1) detailed stroke order diagrams, (2) stroke order principles, (3) the three principal calligraphic styles, (4) stroke-count data, (5) stroke counting principles, (6) appendix on kana orthography, (7) indication of standard *okurigana*, (8) *okurigana* rules, (9) detailed information on orthographic variants, and full guidance on (10) the discrimination of homophones and on (11) kanji synonyms. These features enable learners to write the characters in the proper form, and to express themselves with clarity and precision.

4. Entry-Head Data

At the head of each entry is a wealth of useful information. This includes a full range of character readings, including standard Chinese, a full range of character forms, including simplified Chinese, three calligraphic styles, stroke order diagrams, and information on the function of the entry character as a radical.

5. Labeling System

A labeling system including status, subject, functional, and orthographic labels provides guidance on etymology, style, function, level of formality, etc. Thanks to these labels, which are absent in other character dictionaries, basic and frequent meanings are clearly distinguished from rare and archaic ones.

6. Degree of Importance

Although meanings are given up to the advanced level and beyond, the degree of importance of each character sense is indicated by various typographical differences and status labels for four levels of study. In addition, the relative importance of character readings and the degree of importance (frequency of occurrence and grade) of each character are indicated. For these reasons, the beginner and advanced student can use the dictionary with equal facility.

7. Cross-Reference Network

A systematic network of cross-references directs the user to a wealth of useful information. This includes cross-references from each member to every other member of synonym and homophone groups; cross-references to orthographic variants, usage notes, and compound formation articles; and other miscellaneous cross-references.

8. Reference Data

To round out a practical and useful reference work, especially for the more advanced student and the developer of teaching materials, eleven appendixes give the user quick access to a wealth of valuable reference data. This includes frequency lists, historical tables, rules for *okurigana*, kana charts, a list of kanji synonyms, and others.

9. Design Features

Another feature of this dictionary is a layout that is both visually attractive and easy to use. Typographical design with the aid of computer phototypesetting technology was used to achieve a harmonious blend of a wide range of type sizes and styles. Thanks to the consistent use of such typographical devices, the organization of the entry is mostly self-explanatory, quickly leading the user to the desired item.

* * *

Various other features round this out as a highly useful dictionary for learners. Modern linguistic theory was effectively integrated with information processing technology to produce a work that can be used by the beginner and advanced student with equal ease. For the first time, the student of Japanese has at his or her fingertips a wealth of information on kanji that is linguistically accurate, easy to use, and totally geared to his or her practical needs.

序　説

『新漢英字典』は、現代の日本語の漢字の用法が学習者に徹底的に理解されるよう工夫されており、きわめて斬新な漢字字典である。

通例、日本語の学習者は、無数の熟語を相互関係の理解なしに覚える課題を課せられている。本字典は、この困難を克服するために独自の特長を持っている。つまり、各字の「中心義」、即ち各漢字の最も中心的な意味を一個の簡潔な英語語句で表わし、次いで詳細な字義を掲げて、数千の基本的な造語成分の組み合わせによって数十万の熟語がどのように作り出されるかを明らかにしているのである。

さらに、学習者の便宜を図って、明快・完全かつ正確な字義に多数の熟語及び用例を付し、字義は中心義を核として合理的に配列されており、統合的な一体として把握できるように工夫した。本字典を真に正確な道具として役立てるために、間違え易い漢字（類義漢字・同訓異字語）の使い分けについての豊富な解説も行っている。

本字典のもう一つの独自の特長は、SKIPと呼ぶ新検字法であり、アルファベット順と同程度の速度で、確実に必要な項目が検索できる。この検字法は、短時間で習得できる上、漢字の要素に関する予備知識を必要としないので、本字典は非常に便利かつ利用し易い参考の書となっている。

その他、本字典には様々な特長があり、既存の字典と一線を画する最も充実した漢英字典であると言えよう。

今日の日本語

日本は、20世紀の後半30年間に経済大国、工業大国として目覚しい発展を遂げ、世界情勢に対して大きな影響力を持つ国となった。国際舞台に於ける日本の役割がますます重要になるにつれ、政治、産業及び通商の各方面での異文化間交流も、これまでになく活発になってきている。他民族の文化や国民性を理解する上で、言語は欠くべからざる手段であるが、日本のように文化の伝統も人々の行動様式もきわめて特殊な国の場合、言語の果たす役割は一層重要なものである。

日本語は難しい言語だとよく言われる。欧米の言語とは文章構造が根本的に異なる上、敬卑表現の使い分けが一筋縄ではゆかず、文字体系も人類史上最も複雑であると言っても過言ではない。確かに、日本人自身が日本語は難しいという神話を創り出し、広めてきた嫌いは多分にある。とは言え、事実、外国人が日本語を学ぶ場合、他の外国語を学ぶのに比べて遥かに多くの時間と労力を費やさなくてはならないのは否めない事実である。

21世紀を間近に控えた今、日本語はますます多くの人々にとって重要な意思疎通の手段になってきている。各種統計によると、世界各国に於ける日本語学習者人口は急増してきている。文化庁の調査によれば、日本国内の学校及び各種教育機関で外国人の日本語学習者の数は10年間でほぼ4倍に、また海外の学習者数は同じ期間に8倍にも達しているという。しかも、これは公式発表の数値に過ぎず、実際の数値はこれを遥かに上回っていることは確かである。

実際の数値はさておいて、日本語学習の需要が激増しているのは紛れのない事実である。ビジネスマン、学生、外交官及び科学者は、従来にも増して、日本人との意思交流を日本語で行う必要性に迫られているのである。日本政府は日本語教師養成機関を増設したり、高等教育機関に日本語課程を設置するなどの計画に着手したが、教師数、効果的教材に対する実際の要請から遥かに立ち遅れているのが実情である。

漢字の学習

日本語の文字体系は、「平仮名」及び「片仮名」と呼ばれる2種類の表音音節文字、及び「漢字」と呼ばれる数千の中国伝来の文字から構成されている。漢字には形・音・義の三つの基本的な特性がある。漢字の多くは複雑な字形をしており、画数が20画から30画に及ぶものもある。各字には中国伝来の「音読み」と、日本本来の「訓読み」があり、各読みに対して多くの意味があり得る。しかも、発音は同じでも表記が異なる語が多数あるために、日本語の表記はきわめて複雑で、習得するにはかなりの努力が必要である。

果たして、何千という漢字を覚えなくては日本語は使いこなせないものであろうか。答えは確固として、然りである。とりわけ、中級・上級の学習者は、どうしても漢字を覚えなくてはならない。話し言葉を学習する場合でも、書き言葉を習得しない限り、あるレベル以上に上達することは不可能であろう。複雑な字形と多数の読みという難関はあるにもかかわらず、漢字習得の努力は必ず報われる。日本語の厖大な語彙を効果的に習得するためのしっかりした土台が出来るからである。漢字の知識は日本語学習を阻害するどころか、逆に、上達を大いに促すのである。

漢字は数千字の基本的な構成単位を組み合わせることによって無数の熟語が作り出せるのである。漢字は相互に関連のある記号体系であり、単にばらばらな記号を寄せ集めたものではない。

教育関係者はかねてからこの点に気付いてはいたが、漢字教育課程の開発や字典の編纂に当たっては概ねこれを等閑にしてきたと言えよう。使用頻度といった大雑把な把握を手掛かりにして教科書に漢字を順に登場させ、一字一字いわば丸暗記させるのが、昔も今も漢字教育の普通のやり方である。

日本の生徒は、「暗記、反復練習、試験」の繰り返しで漢字を覚えていく。細やかな神経を払って、決められた字形や筆順に従って一点一画の間違いもないように正しく漢字を書くことや、熟語を丸暗記することに重点が置かれており、個々の漢字の意味、機能の説明にはほとんど力点が置かれていない。この方式は遮二無二詰め込むことでそれなりの効果を挙げ、お蔭で日本は恐らく世界で最高の識字率を維持してきたことは事実だが、こうした旧態依然の退屈そのもののやり方では、外国人学習者の学習意欲が殺がれるのではあるまいか。

教材もまた、概ねこの従来の方式にのっとって作られている。最近では話し言葉学習用の優れた教科書がいくつか編纂され、書き言葉を習得するための学習書も何種類か手に入るようになった。しかし、熟語の辞典あるいは自称「漢字字典」の学習書を除けば、戦後一般に使用されてきた唯一の漢英字典[1]も刊行されてから既に四半世紀を経過している。戦前に出版された小字典もあるにはあるが、今や時代遅れであり、現代の要請には到底応えきれない。しかも、既存の字典には、古さや規模の問題以上に重大な欠陥がある。それは漢字の字義、特に造語成分としての字義という捕え所がないがきわめて重要な側面を体系的に取り上げていないことである。

外国人向けの漢字教科書及び字典類は、対象を熟語や自立語に限定することによって、どうやらこの問題を避けてきた。字形と読みに専ら重点を置き、意味という大事な側面は事実上無視するか、あるいは極く表面的な説明で済ませてきたのである。さらに拙いことには、既存の字典類は日本人向けのものも含めて、古典的な字義が掲載されていることが多く、新しい字義は記述が不正確であったり、全く掲載されていなかったりというものもしばしば見られるのである。

日本語を真に使いこなせる外国人が未だに数少ないのは、「漢字」という難関を克服するための効果的な手段がないのが主要な理由であると言っても過言ではあるまい。今や、外国人の日本語学習者特有の諸問題に対する体系的な解決が切実に求められており、その要請に応え得る字典を刊行する機はまさに熟していると言えよう。

1. ここで言う「漢英字典」(character dictionary) とは、いわゆる辞典、熟語辞典あるいは自称「漢字字典」の学習書とは異なる。「character dictionary」または「kanji dictionary」と銘打っている数冊のものは市販されているが、その多くは数個の熟語例を付けて漢字を羅列している学習書であり、通常「字典」と呼ばれるものではない。

斬新な字典

日本語研究の分野に於て新しい漢字字典を刊行することは、一大事業と言えよう。本字典は高い目標を掲げた。即ち、現代の日本語に於ける使用頻度の高い全ての漢字の字義と機能が充分に理解できる字典を全く新しい構想に基づいて編み出す、というものであった。

辞書というものの中心となる目的は、当然のことながら、未知の項目を引くことである。本字典は、見事にこの目的を果たしてはいるが、単なる検索手段を狙っているのではない。むしろ、主な狙いは学習者の理解を深め、学習意欲を刺激するような真に正確な参考手段として、また強力で実用的な学習道具として役立てることなのである。字体や読みや熟語等を単に寄せ集めたところで、それらの意義や相互関連が正しく理解されない限り、学習者にとって価値が高いとは言い難い。本字典は、漢字に関わる語学上の情報を単に正確に収録しただけでなく、学習者に漢字体系の仕組みが理解できるよう、努力を払ったのである。

以上の主旨に鑑み、本字典は従来の字典と三つの重要な点で異なる。即ち、(1) 相互関連が分かるような配列で明快・完全・正確な字義が提示されている、(2) 必要項目が迅速かつ容易に引ける新しい検字法を採用している、(3) 関連性の深い漢字（類義漢字、同訓異字語）の明確な使い分けを示している、の3点である。さらに、日本語の読み書きに関する詳細な手引きになる点、参考データが豊富である点など、本字典ならではの特長が幾つもあり、従来の字典と一線を画する最も充実した漢英字典である。

編纂に当たっては、体系的手法及び堅固な理論的基盤に立ちつつ、最新の言語学理論、コンピュータ支援辞書編纂手法、及び写植技術を大幅に活用した。本字典は、発想の段階から、初級、中級、上級学習者は勿論のこと、教師、言語学者、教材やコースウエアの作成者まで含む様々の要請に応えるべく構想を練ったものである。

字義

本字典の最大の貢献は漢字の意味を徹底的に追求した点であると言えよう。各字の字義を正確かつ完全に記述するだけではなく、既存の字典に出現したことのない字義も数多く記載した。本字典は、(1) 中心義、(2) 明快かつ正確な字義、(3) 字義の相互関連が理解できるような字義配列順、(4) 各字義を例示する数多くの熟語及び用例、(5) 熟語の成立ち、という五つの特長によって字義が明確に把握できる仕組みになっている。各特長について以下に略説する。

1. 中心義

字義の中核となる「中心義」を掲げた点が本字典独自の大きな特長である。中心義は、簡潔な英語の語句を用いて、漢字の主要な字義を一個の概念単位にまとめ上げ、漢字の中心的な、あるいは最も基本的な概念を把握させるものである（例：越 GO BEYOND）。この特長は、非常に効果的な学習補助手段として、学者・教育関係者の高い評価を受けている。

2. 字義の配列順

従来の字典では、字義の配列は歴史的順序に従っている。この方式は学者には価値があるものの、現代の用法を反映しておらず、また理解を深める助けともなり難いために、学習者にとっては必ずしも有り難いものではない。これに代わる方式として字義の出現頻度順に配列することも考えられるが、たとえ出現頻度の統計が入手できたとしても、意味相互の関連を無視するため、やはり有効とは言えない。

本字典は敢えて字典編纂の伝統的手法から脱して、「psychologistic approach（合理重視方式）」とも呼ばれる方式に基づいて字義を配列することにした。即ち、字義間の相互関連がはっきり理解できるような、心理的に無理のない順序で字義を配列するのである。また、各字の最も中心的な意味を表わす英語の代表語を字義展開の中核にして各字義を小グループにまとめ、体系的に配列した。これによって字義全体を論理的に関連性を持つ統合体として把握できるのである。この方針を採用するに当たり、その点で高く評価されている『アメリカン・ヘリテイジ・ディクショナリー』の前例に倣った。

3. 字義

字義の明確な記述及び各種表示は、各字の語または語素としての機能を正確に示している。字義は、数千の基本的な漢字から無数の熟語が出来上がる仕組みが良く分かるように表示されている。各字について接頭辞、接尾辞、略語、宛て字等の機能を示すと共に、自立語としての意味と造語成分としての意味を明確に区別して記述した。また、一字からなる字訓語の造語機能を本格的に分析し、英語で解説したのは初の試みである。

4. 熟語及び用例

ほとんどの字義に対して、使用頻度が高く、各字義が最も良く理解できる多数の熟語及び用例を掲げた。従来の字典と異なり、親字が熟語及び用例の語頭に位置しないものも収録されている。造語成分がどのように結合して熟語を構成しているかが良く分かるように配列したため、本字典に収録されていない熟語についても容易に意味を類推することができる。

5. 熟語の成立ち

熟語は、意味ごとに配列されているため、その成立ちは一目瞭然であるのが普通である。成立ちが理解し難い語については解説を添え、熟語がその構成要素からどのように出来ているのかを明らかにしている。つまり、各字が熟語全体にどう関係しているかが理解できるのである。

新検字法

本字典は従来の検字法から離れ、「字型式検字法」（SKIP）と名付ける新しい漢字分類方式を採用している。基本となる構想は、パターン（字型）の視覚的認識に基づいており、最小限の労力で最大限に迅速な検索を可能にする、全く新しい検字法である。各字は簡単な規則に従って識別し易い4種類のパターン（字型）のいずれかに分類される。4種類の字型とは、(1) ◧左右型、(2) ⬒上下型、(3) ◘囲み型、(4) ■全体型である。各字型の中で順次下位グループへの分類が行われ、最後には各字の位置が決まる。

果たして、新しい検字法が必要なものであろうか。実際問題として、効率の高い検字法がないのが、外国人・日本人を問わず長年不満の種であった。従来の検字法で必要な項目を引き出すには、部首と呼ばれる漢字構成要素に関する予備知識がなくてはならない。部首による漢字検索法は使いこなすのに何週間も掛かる上、時間も労力も掛かり、しかも確実性に欠ける。部首検索に代わる方式も数多く考案されてはいるが、いずれも検索速度と使い易さの点で学習者の実際的要請を満たすに至っていないのが現状である。

本字典で採用した字型式検字法は、発想当初から効率、速度及び使い易さに主眼が置かれており、アルファベット順と同程度の速度で確実に必要な項目を検索できる。本検字法は、漢字の構成要素が直観的にいかに知覚され、分類されるかを7年に亘り、コンピュータを用いて研究、実験を重ねてきた賜物である。この方式は、短時間で使いこなせるようになる上、漢字の構成要素に関する予備知識も必要としないので、漢字字典編纂上の画期的進歩として日本語教育関係者の称讃を受けているのである。

正確な使い分け

本字典は、「類義漢字」の正確な使い分けの本格的な手引きとなっており、これは日本人向けのものも含め、これまで同様の試みがなされたことのない独自の特長である。本字典で扱われる類義漢字の項目は約4650に上り、各字に対して英語の代表語を付した。例えば、推 infer、憶 speculate、測 conjecture、察 guessのような代表語を比較することによって、各字相互の相違点も共通点も明らかになり、意味上のニュアンスの違いを理解する上でも大きな助けとなる。

本字典は、類義漢字系列を網羅した一覧表を巻末に付し、学習者の便宜を図った。この付録は簡易な類義漢字辞典としても役立ち、字形や読みではなく、意味を起点にして未知の漢字の検索にも利用できる。

さらに、本字典は、英文では初めて、同訓（同音）異字語（例えば「開く」open 、「空く」become vacant 、「明く」regain sight）及び書き換え漢字（例えば、「稀」と「希」のように互換性のある漢字）の使い分けについて充分な解説を加えた。約600項目に及ぶ同訓異字語について使い分けの解説を付けておいたので、学習者は約1410の同訓（同音）異字語の意味の相違点、共通点を理解できる。同訓異字語のニュアンスの違いはきわめて微妙である場合が多く、外国人学習者だけでなく、日本人にとっても紛らわしいものであるため、この特長が大いに役立つはずである。

その他の特長

1. 6種類の検索法

必要な項目を迅速かつ容易に検索できるのが本字典の大きな特長である。見出し字の配列は新しい検字法に基づいてはいるが、従来の検字法に慣れた向きへの配慮も怠ってはいない。以下の6種類の検索法のいずれによっても必要な項目を探し出せる。

1. **字型による検索**。漢字の図形的特徴に着目した「字型索引」により、見出し字を迅速に検索できる。
2. **早引き検索**。画数を数えずに、画数の多い見出し字を即座に検索できる強力な早引き法である。
3. **読みによる検索**。「音訓索引」には、見出し字が音訓のアルファベット順に配列してある。
4. **部首による検索**。「部首索引」には、見出し字が従来の部首別に配列してある。
5. **意味による検索**。「類義漢字系列一覧」には、類似の意味を持つ漢字系列が見出しとなる代表語のアルファベット順に配列してある。
6. **直接検索**。索引を使わずに字型により見出し字を直接引くことができる。

2. 読み

本字典は、次の10の特長により、戦前及び今日の日本語を読むに当たって非常に便利な参考書として役立つ。利用者は、(1) 未知の漢字とその意味を迅速に検索できる、(2) 未知の熟語とその意味を検索できる。親字項目には、(3) 各種の字体、(4) 非標準字体の別個項目、(5) 間違え易い字形、(6) 書体及び印刷体、及び (7) 各種の読みが含まれている他に、(8) 読みの重要度が示されている。さらに、(9) 日本語の語・用例は全てローマ字で表記されており、(10) 中国字体とその読みも掲げられている。

3. 書き

本字典は、次の11の特長により、日本語を書くに当たって、優れた手引きとして役立つ。即ち、(1) 詳細な筆順図解、(2) 漢字の書き方の解説 (巻末)、(3) 三大書体、(4) 画数情報、(5) 画数の数え方の解説 (巻末)、(6) 仮名表記に関する付録、(7) 送り仮名表示、(8) 送り仮名の付け方 (巻末)、(9) 漢字表記の詳細記述、(10) 同訓異字語、及び (11) 類義漢字の詳細な使い分け、の11点である。以上の特長によって学習者は正確な字体の漢字を書くことができ、しかも明快かつ厳密に文章を表現することができるのである。

4. 見出し部データ

各項目の見出し部には、有用な情報が多く盛り込まれており、中国語標準読みを含む各種の読み、中国の簡体字を含む各種の字体、三大書体、筆順、及び親字の部首字素としての機能に関する情報を網羅した。

5. 表示体系

位相表示、分野表示、機能表示及び表記表示を含む表示体系は、字源、文体、機能、敬卑等を指示する。他の字典には見られないこれらの表示は、基本的な字義やよく使われる字義、希な字義、古語的字義をはっきりと区別する役割を果たすのである。

6. 重要度

本字典は、上級以上の学習者に必要な字義を掲げると共に、各種の活字体、位相表示によって、四つの学習レベルに応じて、字義の重要度を示している。さらに、読みの重要度ならびに各字の重要度（使用頻度及び種別）が示されている。そのため、初心者、上級者を問わず本字典を容易に活用できるのである。

7. 相互参照網

体系的な相互参照網によって、豊富かつ有用な情報を参照することができる。これは、類義漢字系列及び同訓異字語グループ間のどの字からも他の字が見付け出せる相互参照や書換え漢字・同訓異字語使い分け解説・熟語の成立ち解説等の様々な相互参照を含む。

8. 参考資料

実用的参考書としてより完全に役立つために、主として上級学習者及び教材作成者を対象に、使用頻度表、各種参考表、送り仮名の付け方、五十音表、類義漢字系列一覧など、11の巻末付録が添えられている。これらによって、使用者は、豊富で貴重な参考資料をいつでも迅速に参照できるのである。

9. デザインの特長

読み易さ及び使い易さに重点を置いたレイアウトを採用したのも本字典の特長の一つである。コンピュータ写植技術により、多種類の活字号数や活字体等を併用し、全体的に調和の取れたデザインとなっている。こうした印刷技術を駆使したお蔭で、親字項目の構成は一見して理解し得るものとなっており、利用者は必要な項目を迅速に見つけ出せる。

＊＊＊

その他の様々な特長によって、本字典は真に有用な学習字典となっている。最新の言語理論と情報処理技術を有効に駆使した結果、初心者、上級者を問わず、利用し易いものになっている。日本語の学習者は、本字典にして初めて、言語学的に正確で使い易く、実際的な要請に的確に応える漢字情報の宝庫を手にすることができるのである。

EDITORIAL POLICY AND COMPILATION METHODS

COVERAGE

This dictionary offers a comprehensive treatment of the meanings and functions of the high-frequency characters and compounds used in present-day Japanese. The basic aim was to cover all the character meanings current in Modern Japanese, which refers to the language since the Meiji Restoration in 1868, with particular emphasis on contemporary usage and newspapers. Basically, this is a dictionary of characters rather than of words. It does not attempt to provide an exhaustive list of the hundreds of thousands of compounds and tens of thousands of characters that exist or have existed since antiquity. Rather, the emphasis has been placed on the practical needs of the learner.

The dictionary presents 4421 entry characters and approximately 60,000 senses for some 42,200 words, word elements, and illustrative examples. The entry characters, which were selected on the basis of frequency statistics, include all the characters approved in the official Jōyō Kanji (characters in common use) and Jinmei Kanji (characters used in names) lists, high-frequency unapproved characters, almost all phonetically replaced characters (including rare ones), radicals and their variants, nonstandard forms for main-entry characters, and cross-reference entries for rapid retrieval. This covers about 99% of the characters used in contemporary Japanese, especially newspapers, and is adequate for meeting the needs of learners up to and including the advanced level.

A characteristic feature of Chinese characters is their ability to form countless compound words by affixation; that is, to form new words by the addition of a suffix or prefix to a base. For example, the suffix –済 *-zumi* 'completed' is attached to 点検 *tenken* 'inspection' to yield 点検済 *tenkenzumi* 'inspection completed'. Since it would be impossible, even in principle, to cover all such potential combinations, the policy adopted here was to indicate the meanings of each character as an affix, followed by a few typical high-frequency examples carefully selected with a view to enabling the user to infer the meanings of words formed along a similar pattern but not found in the dictionary; e.g., 校正済 *kōseizumi* 'proofreading completed'.

The compounds and examples were selected on the basis of (1) their ability to illustrate the entry character's meaning and (2) frequency statistics. In principle, all high-frequency compounds in contemporary usage have been included, but only typical examples are given for the potentially innumerable words formed by affixation and derivation and for proper names. Characters and words that are infrequent or that appear only in classical Japanese or in technical literature have generally been omitted, but we have not hesitated to include archaic or rare items, accompanied by proper status labels, when these have been deemed useful for understanding a character or illustrating a meaning.

Many two-character *on* compounds are turned into verbs by adding する *suru,* into noun adjectives by adding な *na,* into adverbs by adding に *ni,* and so on. To include all these combinations would require far too much space. Our general guideline has been in line with our overall policy of including items that are most useful to the learner. Thus sometimes the verb, sometimes the noun, sometimes both forms, appear, normally based on their ability to illustrate the character meaning in question.

The primary emphasis in this dictionary has been completeness in terms of quality, rather than comprehensiveness in terms of quantity. It would, of course, have been easy to include many more words, such as technical terms, derived words, place names, and so on. But this would only increase the bulk of the dictionary, which is already bulky enough, and go against our aim of providing an effective tool for learning character meanings, not an exhaustive list of words.

SOURCES

The primary source for the selection of characters and compounds for this dictionary has been the frequency statistics published by The National Language Research Institute in a survey entitled *A Study of Uses of Chinese Characters in Modern Newspapers*, which is based on a corpus of one million characters. Widely recognized as the standard in the field, this survey includes detailed statistics on every aspect of the use of characters and compounds in contemporary Japanese newspapers. Masaaki Nomura, head of the survey project, was kind enough to offer his advice and guidance in analyzing and interpreting the data in a manner useful to the learner. This was supplemented by other statistical surveys, contemporary books, magazines, and signboards.

The sources for determining character meanings were compound words found in (1) the statistical surveys mentioned above, (2) the living language itself, extracted from contemporary newspapers, magazines, etc., and (3) dozens of character dictionaries and other reference works published in Japan, America, and China.

Although statistical data and other dictionaries served as our guidelines, the final authority in the selection of an item was the evidence of the living language itself. This analysis of statistics combined with actual field observations has led to some very interesting results. For example, we have found that the heavy reliance of existing character dictionaries and textbooks on classical Chinese sources has resulted in their inclusion of many old and archaic meanings, while newer meanings are often inaccurate or totally missing. Many of the high-frequency compounds and character meanings listed in this dictionary have never appeared in *any* character dictionary, including unabridged works for native speakers. On rare occasions, we even discovered common characters and character readings that have never been recorded.

Examples of unrecorded character meanings and compound words abound. This is especially true of, but by no means limited to, the use of characters as abbreviations, which has been largely ignored in existing works. For example, character dictionaries report that 雀 means 'sparrow' and has an *on* reading of *jaku* and a *kun* reading of *suzume*. In actual fact, 雀 is frequently used as an abbreviation of 麻雀 *mājan* with the meaning 'mahjong' in many common compounds such as 雀卓 *jantaku* 'mahjong board', 雀荘 *jansō* 'mahjong club', and so on. Neither the reading *jan*, nor the meaning 'mahjong', nor any of these compounds, are recorded in any of the twenty-five major Japanese-Japanese and Japanese-English character dictionaries and kanji textbooks on the market.

An example of a character that is not found in any dictionary, and, for inexplicable reasons, not even found in the Jōyō Kanji list, is 〇. This extremely common character, whose principal meaning is 'zero', has a form, a meaning, and *on* and *kun* readings, just like any other character. This is not the place for a theoretical discussion of whether 〇 is a kanji or not, but there is no doubt that it does function as a full-fledged kanji when used as a numeral. Moreover, many common abbreviated forms of characters, such as 门 for 門, are not found in most other character dictionaries.

In this manner, users of character dictionaries are often presented with inaccurate, incomplete, or outdated information. It can thus be said that an important contribution of this dictionary is the presentation of accurate and up-to-date information, especially many meanings that have never appeared in previous works.

COMPILATION METHODS

There are two traditions in dictionary-making: the *prescriptive* approach, which aims to establish standards of proper usage, and the *descriptive* approach, which aims to objectively report what established usage is. Traditionally, character dictionaries have often been compiled by scholars in the humanities on the basis of classical Chinese sources, or by copying old and archaic meanings from other dictionaries, with little or no attention given to contemporary sources and modern lexicographic methods.

This dictionary is firmly committed to the descriptive approach and modern linguistic theory. It aims to record usage as it actually occurs in the living language, not to maintain the purity of the language by prescribing standards, nor to report the results of previous works. Although hundreds of dictionaries and reference sources were consulted, the character meanings were extracted from actual occurrences in compound words, not merely on the authority of other dictionaries.

The compilation project was carried out through an interdisciplinary effort. Advice and guidance from experts in software development and Japanese language scholars from the United States and Japan helped establish standard procedures for analyzing meaning and the processing of data. Great pains have been taken to ensure accuracy and up-to-dateness, while paying an immense amount of attention to detail. The basic guideline was to strive for clarity and thoroughness at all times.

Each meaning was written afresh, the result of an exhaustive semantic analysis, and revised by experts in Japanese, English, and Chinese. The meanings were analyzed by such techniques as componential analysis and the study of near-synonyms. The denotation, connotation, and range of application of each sense were carefully studied and compared, with the aim of achieving a structured presentation in which the character meaning is divided by numbered divisions and subdivisions to give the various senses a clear and cogent order.

The chief editor coordinated the work flow during every stage of the project, methodically checked every line of manuscript, and was personally involved in analyzing the meaning of each entry character. This, and the extensive use of computers, has ensured a high level of accuracy, a systematic network of cross-references, and the implementation of lexicographic policy in a uniform and consistent manner.

The analysis of character meanings was inseparably linked to the analysis of kanji synonyms. As Ladislav Zgusta, the world-renowned authority on lexicography, has pointed out, the study of near-synonyms and the analysis of their differences is one of the most outstanding duties of the lexicographer, because, he asserts, one cannot really know the precise meaning of a word if it is not examined in comparison and in contrast with its near-synonyms.

In this dictionary, the analysis of character meanings was firmly based on such a policy. Not only was each meaning carefully analyzed into its single senses, but the connotation and range of application of each component of the meaning and its semantic relationships to other members of the same synonym group were analyzed and compared. The analysis of kanji synonyms thus served as an extremely powerful technique for establishing character meanings of high precision and clarity.

Although this dictionary is committed to the descriptive approach, there is one area, the discrimination of *kun* homophones, in which this approach does not always work. The Japanese writing system is now in a state of transition. For many *kun* homophones, no universally-accepted orthography exists. Theoretically, the choice should be based on meaning, but in fact it is often governed by personal preferences. As not enough data are available at this time to make a truly descriptive analysis, we have based our approach on a mixture of prescription and description, with emphasis on the latter.

COMPUTER EDITING

This is the first kanji dictionary to be edited and produced entirely by computer. Every important stage of the work, from editing, proofreading, and general data processing to phototypesetting and work flow management was carried out with the aid of six personal computers and wordprocessors, and a state-of-the-art mainframe computerized photocomposition system. Approximately 700 computer programs were written over a period of five years specifically for proofreading and processing the data for this dictionary.

The production of this dictionary is the first step in a series of computer-edited applications for the study of kanji. It is being utilized as a standard source of data for many useful teaching and learning aids such as learner's dictionaries and reference manuals, software packages such as CAI/CAL courseware, electronic learning machines, and so on. Four projects are under way as of 1989: a German version of this dictionary, a concise edition of this dictionary, the world's first Japanese-English dictionary of kanji synonyms, and a software package for studying kanji.

HISTORY OF PROJECT

Years of struggling with self-study using traditional methods of rote memorization inspired the chief editor to embark upon the compilation of a new dictionary based on a systematic approach. He began the work with the help of two assistants while residing in Kobe in 1974. Lack of funds have brought the project to a halt several times. In 1980 a donation by Konosuke Matsushita enabled the project to proceed in earnest. This was followed by grants from Showa Women's University and the Toyota Foundation, and donations from many private individuals and organizations. In June 1981, the editor joined the Institute for the Study of Modern Culture of Showa Women's University as a research fellow, and thereafter the university has been providing assistance and cooperation. Since that time, the work proceeded with a permanent staff of about ten and many outside consultants.

From its inception through publication, the dictionary has cost more than 1.6 million US dollars and required over sixty-six man-years for compiling, editing, keyboarding, proofreading, and data processing. This does not include the time of the editors and clerical assistants of the publisher, nor the time of the computer programmers and personnel involved in photocomposition, printing, and other production tasks. In all, some 100 persons have contributed in one way or another to the completion of this project over a period of sixteen years.

Even before publication, the work attracted much attention in Japanese language educational circles because it is the first systematic treatment of kanji based on semantic analysis and modern linguistics. Scholars well versed in Chinese, Japanese, and English linguistics, experienced lexicographers, as well as other experts, have directly contributed to the accuracy of its contents, and Japanese language authorities in the U.S. and Japan have confirmed its scholarly accuracy and lent their enthusiastic support and recommendations.

The dictionary project has also benefited from the official and unofficial support of various government-related agencies and officials. Japan's former Prime Minister Yasuhiro Nakasone praised the new work and offered his encouragement. The Japan Foundation, a government-funded agency, has recognized the dictionary project under the Assistance Program for the Development of Japanese-Language Teaching Resources. The project has also received the wholehearted support of members of the National Council on Educational Reform, a government organ, and the cooperation of scholars from The National Language Research Institute, an agency of the Japanese Ministry of Education.

***

As is often the case in dictionary compiling, one must strike a balance between theoretical considerations and the practical needs of the user. The lexicographer must walk a fine line between the consistent application of policy and the realistic presentation of useful information. In an undertaking of such magnitude, despite all efforts, some errors are inevitable. No one is more aware of this than the chief editor himself, who encourages users to suggest corrections or additions for future editions.

In hindsight, it is easy to criticize the inadequacy or incompleteness of a work based on new principles. However, we are confident that any minor errors, omissions, or inaccuracies will be far outweighed by the work's overall significance as a seminal contribution to Japanese language studies.

編集方針及び編纂方法

収録範囲

本字典は現代の日本語に於て使用頻度の高い漢字及び熟語の意味と機能に対して包括的な解説を行っている。基本的な主旨は現代日本語（明治維新以降）で使用される漢字の全ての字義を網羅し、現在の一般的用法及び新聞に於ける用法に重点を置いた。本字典は基本的に語の辞典ではなく、字の字典である。現存する、あるいはかつて存在した無数の熟語、何万もの漢字を網羅することを目的としていない。主眼はあくまでも学習者の実際の要請に応えることである。

本字典の見出し字は4421に及んでおり、約42,200語・語素・用例に対して、おおよそ6万の意味を記載した。見出し字は使用頻度の統計に基づいて厳選し、常用漢字、人名漢字はもとより、使用頻度の高い表外字、同音置換字のほぼ全て（希なものも含む）、部首とその変形、本親字の非標準字体、及び検索を迅速にするための相互参照項目を含んでいる。これによって、現代の日本語、特に新聞記事に使用する漢字の約99%が網羅されており、上級も含めて学習者の要請に充分応え得るものである。

漢字の特徴の一つは接辞を添加することによって無数の熟語が作れることである。つまり、語基に接頭辞や接尾辞を付けることによって新しい熟語が出来るのである。例えば、「点検」という語に「-済」という接尾辞を添加すれば、「点検済」という熟語が出来上がる。このような結合による熟語を全て網羅することは、事実上、不可能であるため、本字典は各字の接辞としての意味を明記し、使用頻度の高い代表的な用例を厳選して記載する方針を採った。従って、本字典に収録されていないが、「校正済」のように、類似の合成によって出来た熟語の意味も類推できる。

熟語及び用例の選択に当たっては、(1) 見出し字の字義を反映する好例であるか否か、及び (2) 使用頻度の統計値を取捨の基準とした。原則として、現代の日本語に於て頻度の高い熟語を網羅した。但し、接辞添加や派生によって形成される無数の熟語及び固有名詞は代表例に限っている。希にしか使用されない漢字や熟語及び古典や専門文献にのみ使用される漢字や熟語は概ね省いたが、漢字の理解に役立つ、あるいは字義の具体例として適切であるとみなした場合は、古典語や使用頻度の低い語でも、敢えてその旨を位相表示した上で収録した。

二字からなる字音語の多くは、「する」を添加して動詞に、「な」を添加して形容動詞に、あるいは「に」を添加して副詞に転化するが、これら全てを収録するには厖大な紙面が必要となる。ここでも、やはり「学習者に最も役立つものを収録する」という基本方針を貫いた。従って、本字典では、見出し字の字義を良く反映する用例であるか否かという基準に照らして、動詞を収録する場合、名詞を収録する場合、双方を収録する場合などがある。

本字典は量的包括性と言うより、質的充実に重点を置いた。無論、技術用語、派生語、地名等多数の語を収録して語数を増やすのは容易であるが、それでは無数の語彙を余すところなく羅列して既に大部となっている字典をいたずらに肥大させるだけであり、字義学習の効果的手段を提供するという主旨に反することになるのである。

典拠資料

本字典が収録すべき漢字及び熟語の選択に当たって中心的な資料としたのは、国立国語研究所編纂の『現代新聞の漢字』である。これは100万字を対象に、現代日本の新聞に見られる漢字及び熟語の用法に関して各種の詳細な統計調査を行ったものであり、この分野の標準となる調査データとして広く定評を得ている。この実態調査の責任者である野村雅昭先生からは、この調査データをどのように分析、解釈したら日本語学習者にとって役立つかについて貴重な助言を戴いた。これ以外に他の統計的実態調査、現代の書籍、雑誌、看板等も参考にした。

字義の記述に当たっては、(1) 上記の実態調査、(2) 現代の新聞、雑誌等から抽出した生きた日本語、及び (3) 日本、米国、中国で刊行されている数多くの字典及びその他の参考文献を典拠とした。

統計データや既存の辞書を参考にしたのは事実であるが、掲載事項を採用するに当たって最終的拠り所となったのは、現に使われている日本語そのものである。統計的分析と実地観察を総合した結果、きわめて興味深い発見をすることもあった。例えば、既存の字典や学習書は漢文に依拠する余り、もはや使われなくなっている古い意味を幾つも記載する一方で、新しい意味の記述は不正確であったり、全く欠落していることがある。また、本字典に掲載されている使用頻度の高い熟語や字義のうち、日本人向けの大字典を含めて、いずれの字典にも収録されていないものが少なくない。希にはこれまで一度も収録されていない極く普通の漢字と読みすら発見した。

既存の字典に収録されていない字義や熟語は枚挙に暇がない。その筆頭が略語である。これは決して略語に限ったことではないが、特に略語はこれまで無視される傾向が強かった。例えば、既存の字典によると、「雀」の字義は「スズメ」で、音読みは「ジャク」、訓読みは「すずめ」となっている。しかし実際には、「雀」は「麻雀」の略語としてよく使い、「雀卓」「雀荘」等の熟語にも登場する。ところが既存の25種類の主要な漢和字典・漢英字典類・漢字学習書のいずれを見ても、「麻雀」の意味はおろか、「ジャン」という読みならびに上記の熟語さえ収録されていない。

既存のいずれの字典にも収録されておらず、どういう訳か常用漢字表にさえ登場しない字の例としては、「〇」が挙げられる。非常によく使われるこの字の主要な意味は「ゼロ」であり、他の漢字と同様に、字形、字義及び音訓を持っている。「〇」が漢字であるか否かを学問的に論じるのはここでの本分ではないが、「〇」が数詞として立派に漢字の機能を果たしているのは確かである。また、「門」を「门」と書くなどの略字体は、これまではたいがいの字典に収録されていなかった。

このように、字典の使用者はしばしば不正確な、あるいは不完全な、あるいはまた時代遅れの情報を与えられているのである。その意味で、本字典がこれまで収録されたことのない多くの字義を含めて、正確かつ最新の情報を提供しているのは、重要な功績と見なし得るであろう。

編纂方法

辞書編纂の基本的立場は伝統的に大きく二つに分けられる。正しい用法の基準を確立することを目的とする「規範的立場」と、現実の用法を客観的に記述することを目的とする「記述的立場」である。既存の漢字字典の多くは、中国の古典を典拠として人文科学分野の学者が編纂したもの、あるいは既存の字典に収録されている古い意味をそのまま転載したものであり、現代の資料や最新の辞書編纂手法は概ね無視されてきたと言って良い。本字典はあくまでも記述的立場と最新の言語学理論にのっとっている。また、本字典の主旨は、規範を押し付けて言葉の純粋性を護ることでもなければ、既存の業績を踏襲することでもない。むしろ生きた言葉に見られる実際の用法を記述する点にある。数百冊の辞書及び参考資料を参考にしたことは事実であるが、各字の字義は熟語の実際例から抽出したものであり、単に他の辞書の権威に依拠したものではない。

本字典の編纂作業は学際的な協力の下で進められた。米国・日本の日本語研究者及びソフトウェア開発の専門家の助言もあり、意味分析及びデータ処理の標準的な手順が確立されたのである。正確さと新しさを確保するよう、最大の努力を払う一方、細部に亘って周到綿密を窮めた。編纂の基本方針は、常に明快さ、完全さに徹することにあった。

各字の意味は、徹底的な意味分析に基づいて新たに書き改めたものであり、日本語、英語、中国語の専門家の校閲を経ている。字義の分析に際しては、成分分析、類義語分析等の手法を利用した。個々の字義の明示的意味、暗示的意味及び適用範囲の慎重な分析及び比較検討を重ねた結果、字義を区分番号によって階層的に分類し、明確かつ心理的に無理のない順序に配列した。

編集長は、編纂企画の各段階で作業の進行を調整し、草稿の隅々まで入念に目を通し、直に親字一つ一つの意味分析に当たった。加えて、コンピュータの広範な活用のお蔭で、本字典の高度の正確さ、体系的な相互参照網、さらに一貫した編集方針の遂行が可能となった。

字義の分析と類義漢字の分析は密接に結び付いている。辞書学の世界的権威であるラディスラウ・ズグスタ（Ladislav Zgusta）が指摘する通り、語の厳密な意味を知るには、その類義語と比較対照して吟味することが不可欠であり、従って、類義語の研究及びその相違点の分析は、辞書編纂者にとって最も重要な使命の一つと言って良いであろう。

本字典は、あくまでもこの方針にのっとって字義の分析を行った。各字の個義を緻密に分析しただけでなく、個々の意味成分の暗示的意味（ニュアンス）及びその適用範囲を分析し、さらに各成分と、同類義漢字系列に属する他の漢字との意味関係をも分析・比較した。このように、字義を厳密にかつ明確に記述する上で、類義漢字の分析はきわめて有効な手段として役立った。

本字典は記述的立場を貫いているが、同訓異字語の使い分けに限り、この視点を使っての処理が必ずしも有効とは限らない。日本語の表記体系は現在過渡期にあり、同訓異字語については一般に認められている正書法が確立していない。理論的には意味によって使い分ければ良いのであるが、実際は個人の好みに委ねられている場合が多い。現時点では、本格的な記述的分析をするに足るデータが存在しないため、記述的立場に重点を置きつつ規範的視点も併用した。

コンピュータ編集

本字典は漢字字典としては初めて、編集及び印刷の過程を完全にコンピュータによって行った。編集、校正及び一般的なデータ処理から写植、作業の流れ管理に至るまでの作業の各重要段階で6台のパーソナル・コンピュータとワードプロセッサ、ならびにメインフレームコンピュータによる最新の写植システムを活用した。5年間に亘って本字典の校正及びデータ処理のために開発された専用プログラムは、ほぼ700本に及ぶ。

本字典は、コンピュータによる一連の漢字学習教材作成のための第一弾である。本書のデータは、基礎資料として、学習字典、参考書などからCAI／CALコースウェアのようなソフトウェア・パッケージや電子学習機等まで、各種の有益な教材、学習参考資料を開発することに役立っている。1989年現在、本字典のドイツ語版とコンサイス版、世界初の和英類義漢字辞典の刊行、漢字学習のためのソフトウェア・パッケージの開発、という四つの計画が進行中である。

本企画の経緯

編集長は、丸暗記という従来の学習法で長年独習を続けた挙句、体系的視点に基づいて新字典を編纂してみたいと思い立った。神戸在住中の1974年に、助手2人の協力を得て作業を開始した。

資金難で作業が頓座したことも何度かあるが、1980年、松下幸之助氏より寄付を得て作業は本格化した。次いで昭和女子大学、トヨタ財団、各方面の民間団体及び個人の方々の寄付を仰ぎ、1981年6月、編集長は昭和女子大学近代文化研究所の研究員となり、以後、同大学の支援、協力を受けてきた。以来10名前後の常任スタッフ及び多数の外部顧問の協力で作業は続行した。

そもそもの発端から刊行に至るまで、本字典に掛かった費用は160万米ドル（約2億円）を超え、編纂作業、編集、コンピュータ入力、校正、データ処理に要した時間は、延べにしておよそ66人年以上に相当する。この数字には出版社の編集者・事務員の作業時間は含まれず、写植、印刷、製作等に携わったコンピュータ・プログラマーやその関係者の作業時間も含まれていない。16年に及ぶ作業期間中に何等かの形で本企画に寄与された方々の数は100名前後に上る。

本字典は、意味分析と最新の言語学理論に基づいた初の体系的漢字字典であるため、刊行されないうちから日本語教育界の注目を集めてきた。中国語、日本語、英語の言語学に精しい学者、熟練した辞書編纂者など、専門家諸氏は内容の正確さを期するため直接寄与され、また、日本・米国に於ける日本語研究の諸権威の方々は学問的正確さを確認して下さるなど、多大の支援と推薦を下さった。

また、本企画には諸官庁からも公式、非公式の支援が寄せられた。中曽根元総理大臣からは、画期的業績に対する激励を戴いた。また、外務省国際交流基金からは、本字典の日本語教材開発事業としての価値を認められている。さらに、政府の諮問機関である臨時教育審議会からは暖かい支援を受け、文部省所属の国立国語研究所からは協力が寄せられた。

＊＊＊

辞書を編纂するとなると、理論的配慮と使用者の実践的な要請との兼ね合いを図らなくてはならないことが往々にしてある。辞書編纂者は、一貫した方針を貫きながらも、現実に即した有益な情報を提供するという、危うい綱渡りをしなければならない。これほどの壮図ともなれば、万全の注意を払ったつもりでも、多少の過誤が生ずるのは避け難い。編集長はこの事実を誰よりも痛感しており、今後の改訂に備えて、読者からの訂正・追加を期待するものである。

斬新な発想に基づく著作物が出来上がってからその不備を指摘するのはたやすいが、しかし、我々編纂者一同、たとえ瑣末な誤りや欠落、不正確な部分があるにせよ、本字典が全体として、今後の日本語研究へ多大な貢献をするであろうと確信する次第である。

OUTLINE OF JAPANESE WRITING SYSTEM

1. THE ORIGIN OF CHINESE CHARACTERS

1.1 The Birth of a Pictographic Script

Until recently, it was believed that the earliest examples of Chinese characters were those found in oracle bones used in divination rites dating back to the eighteenth century B.C. However, excavations made in China in 1986 have shown that at that time the Chinese characters had already had a history of 1200 years, which means that the Chinese script first appeared almost 5000 years ago.

The earliest characters were simple pictures of the things they represented. Although all the principal writing systems of the world began with pictures, these were in almost all cases simplified to abstract symbols that were eventually used for their sound values, giving rise to the major alphabet systems of the world. This happened everywhere but in China, where the primary function of the characters has always been to express both meaning and sound, rather than just sound.

Typical Pictographs

Early Forms	Modern Character	Meaning
 [illegible] → [illegible]	木	tree, wood
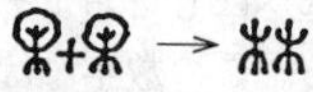 [illegible] → [illegible]	林	woods
 [illegible] → [illegible]	森	forest
 [illegible] → [illegible]	本	root, origin
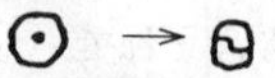 [illegible] → [illegible]	日	sun
 [illegible] → [illegible]	月	moon
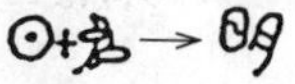 [illegible] → [illegible]	明	bright
 [illegible] → [illegible]	山	mountain
 [illegible] → [illegible]	鳥	bird
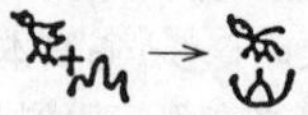 [illegible] → [illegible]	島	island

The table shows examples of early character forms and their modern counterparts. The earliest characters were pictographs, which were simple pictures of things. Pictographs may be combined to form new characters, especially characters that express complex or abstract ideas. Thus 木 'tree' is combined with 木 to give 林 'woods' while three trees give 森 'forest'; a line added to the bottom of a tree gives 本, which means 'root' or 'origin'; and so on.

The shapes of the characters underwent a great deal of change over the several thousand years of their history. Many calligraphic styles, character forms, and typeface styles have evolved over the years; furthermore, the character forms were simplified as a result of various language reforms in China and Japan. The chart below shows various forms and styles for the characters 楽 and 女.

Character Forms and Styles

Tortoise-shell writing	[illegible]	[illegible]
Bronze inscription	[illegible]	[illegible]
Seal style	[illegible]	[illegible]
Ancient square style	女	樂
Square style	女	楽
Semicursive style	女	樂
Cursive style	[illegible]	[illegible]
Simplified handwritten abbreviation	[illegible]	[illegible]
Ming typeface	女	楽
Gothic typeface	女	楽
Traditional form	女	樂
Alternative form	—	—
Handwritten abbreviation	—	—
Modern Chinese	女	乐

1.2 Formation of Chinese Characters

Traditionally, Chinese characters are classified into six categories known as 六書 *rikusho*. Introduced some 1900 years ago in the Chinese classic dictionary 説文解字 *setsumon kaiji*, these have played a central role in Chinese lexicography. The first four categories are based on the character formation process; the last two are based on usage.

1. **Pictographs** (象形文字 *shōkei moji*) are simple hieroglyphs that are rough sketches of the things they represent. Example: [illegible] (modern 目 *moku*) 'eye'.
2. **Simple Ideographs** (指事文字 *shiji moji*) suggest the meanings of abstract ideas, such as numerals and directions. Example: 三 *san* 'three'.
3. **Compound Ideographs** (会意文字 *kaii moji*) consist of two or more elements each of which contributes to the meaning of the whole. Example: 休 *kyū* 'rest' (person 人 resting under a tree 木).
4. **Phonetic-Ideographic Characters** (形声文字 *keisei moji*) consist of one element that roughly expresses meaning (usually called the **radical**), and another element that represents sound and often also meaning. Example: 茎 *kei* 'stem, stalk' consists of 艹 'plants' and 圣 *kei* 'straight', i.e., the straight part of a plant.
5. **Derivative Characters** (転注文字 *tenchū moji*) are characters used in an extended, derived, or figurative sense. Example: 令 *rei* changed from its original meaning 'command, order' to 'person who gives orders' to 'administrator, governor'.
6. **Phonetic Loans** (仮借文字 *kasha moji*) are characters borrowed to represent words phonetically without direct relation to their original meanings, or to characters used er-

roneously. Example: 豆 *tō* originally referred to an ancient sacrificial vessel, but is now used in the borrowed sense of 'bean'.

The great majority of characters are phonetic–ideographic (type 4 above). 民, for example, originally a picture of an eye pierced by a needle (𠬝), represented a slave blinded by his master to keep him from escaping, but later changed to 'ignorant masses' or 'people' in general. As a phonetic–ideographic element in the formation of other characters, it represents the sound *min* and has a basic meaning of 'sightlessness' or 'darkness'. For example, 民 (abbreviated to 氏) is combined with 日 'sun' to give 昏 'darkness, dusk'; 眠 'sleep' consists of an eye (目) in a state of sightlessness (民). An interesting example is 婚 'marriage', which consists of 女 'woman' + 昏 'darkness'. According to one theory, this is because wedding ceremonies were held at night.[1] In this way, a basic unit like 民 contributes its shape, its reading, and its meaning to the formation of other characters.

The table below shows several groups of characters that share the basic element 目 'eye':

Typical Atom in Periodic Table of Chinese Characters

Atom	Formation	Molecule	Reading	Basic Meaning	Compounds
目	[illegible] → [illegible] → [illegible] → 目		*moku*	eye	
	目 + 儿 (legs)	見	*ken*	see	現 規 硯 蜆
	目 + 木 (tree)	相	*sō*	face each other	想 霜 箱 湘 廂
	目 + ㄴ (object) + 十 (straight)	直	*choku*	straight	植 殖 値 置 埴
	直 + 心 (heart)	悳	*toku*	virtuous	德 聽 廳
	目 + 斤 (visor)	盾	*jun*	shield	循 楯 遁

Groups of characters sharing the same "molecule" element are closely interrelated.[2] They share three important features: (1) they share a basic element of the same **shape**, (2) they have more or less the same **reading**, and (3) they share a **meaning** on the character formation level. Chinese characters thus consist of logically interrelated parts that form a systematic body of symbols to express meaning and sound.

In addition to the six traditional categories, there is a seventh one limited to a

1. Another theory claims that in China's less enlightened days a man would go out in the stealth of night (昏) and kidnap a woman (女) to make her his wife. This savage practice was abandoned, but 婚 stays on as a reminder of the curious customs of a bygone age.
2. A full discussion of such groups can be found in 漢字の再発見 *kanji no saihakken* ('Rediscovering Chinese Characters'), Shōdensha (祥伝社), 1987, by Jack Halpern, which introduces a method of ordering these groups in a scheme called the "Atomic Theory of Chinese Characters."

small number of characters coined in Japan. When the Japanese could not find an appropriate character to represent a particular word, they sometimes created new characters, called 国字 *kokuji* 'national characters', on the model of the Chinese ones. Most of these have only *kun* readings (Japanese-derived pronunciations); some, such as 働 *dō* 'work', have both *on* (Chinese-derived pronunciations) and *kun* readings, while others, such as 腺 *sen* 'gland', have only *on* readings. In rare instances, as in the case of 腺, a character created in Japan was "exported" back to Chinese.

2. INTRODUCTION OF CHINESE CHARACTERS TO JAPAN

2.1 Early Stages

In the early centuries of the Christian era, the Japanese did not have a writing system of their own. As the Japanese began to interact with the Chinese, they adopted Chinese institutions and adapted them to their own needs. Chinese characters were introduced to Japan via the Korean peninsula in the fourth century A.D. In the next two centuries, Chinese books on philosophy and Buddhism were brought to Japan and studied by the Japanese aristocracy.

Initially, the Japanese used the characters for writing in authentic Chinese or a hybrid Japanese-Chinese style. A good example of the latter is the 古事記 *kojiki* (Ancient Chronicles) written in 712. Since the Japanese did not have their own script, they soon began to use the characters to write the Japanese language as well. In the early stages, they employed the characters purely for their phonetic values. For example, the native Japanese word *yama* 'mountain' was written 也麻, with the first character representing *ya* and the second *ma*. This method of writing is referred to as 万葉仮名 *man'yōgana* because it was used extensively in the 万葉集 *man'yōshū*, an eighth-century anthology of Japanese poems.

Because of the markedly different linguistic structures of Chinese and Japanese, the Chinese characters were not well-suited for writing Japanese. Whereas classical Chinese is basically a monosyllabic language with no inflected words, Japanese is a polysyllabic language with various elements attached to the stems of words to express grammatical meanings.

2.2 *On* and *Kun* Readings

These circumstances led to an extremely interesting method of writing Japanese: the Chinese characters were used for their meanings. The characters were used to write words of Chinese origin, or to write native Japanese words with Chinese characters representing the same or similar meanings. The grammatical elements continued to be written phonetically, but eventually the characters used for their phonetic values were simplified, giving rise to two sets of syllabic scripts, *hiragana* and *katakana*, in which each character represents a syllable. For example, the character 安 *an* 'peaceful' gave rise to the hiragana character あ *a*, whereas 阿 *a* was simplified to the katakana character ア *a* (See **Appendix 4**).

Characters used to represent meaning were pronounced in two ways: (1) the 音読み *on'yomi* or 'phonetic reading' and (2) the 訓読み *kun'yomi* or 'explanatory reading'. This phonetic duality of the Chinese characters is fundamental to the nature of the Japanese script. Let us briefly examine how it arose.

In the first method, which is often called the "Sino-Japanese reading" or "Chinese-derived pronunciation," the characters represent Chinese-derived words or word elements. This method of reading the characters will be referred to as the ***on* reading**. The reading assigned to each character was a rough approximation of the original Chinese pronunciation. For example, the character 山 'mountain' was assigned the reading *san* based on its old Chinese pronunciation (modern Chinese is *shān*). *On* readings are found more frequently in compound words (e.g. 連山 *renzan* 'mountain range') than in independent words (e.g. 天 *ten* 'heaven').

Since the Japanese often had native words to express the meanings represented by Chinese characters, they began to associate the characters not only with Chinese words but also with purely Japanese words. 山 'mountain', for example, was used to represent the native Japanese word *yama* 'mountain' with no regard to its Chinese-derived reading *san*. This method of reading the characters will be referred to as the ***kun* reading**.

Originally, the *kun* reading was a kind of explanation assigned to a character that was used to interpret its meaning in a Chinese text. In other words, it was a native Japanese word that was essentially a translation of the concept represented by the Chinese character. Over the years, certain words became so well established as the translation for a given character that they were considered to be the standard reading or readings for that character. In this manner, 山 acquired the reading *yama*, which eventually became established as its standard accepted pronunciation along with its *on* reading *san*.

A distinctive feature of Chinese characters as used in Japanese is their multiple readings. Since the characters entered Japan over different historical periods and originated from different geographical regions, many characters have acquired several *on* and/or *kun* readings. In extreme cases, a character may have more than 100 readings (生 has over 200).

On and *kun* readings may be combined in four possible ways: *on-on*, *kun-kun*, *on-kun*, and *kun-on*. Unfortunately, there is no reliable rule for determining if a character is to be read in the *on* or *kun*, or for deciding which of several possible readings to select in a particular instance. A rough guideline is that *on-on* or *kun-kun* readings are used in compounds, and *kun* readings in independent words, but there are many exceptions. For example, 毎朝 *maiasa* 'every morning' is an *on-kun* compound, though 毎 has the *kun* reading *goto* and 朝 the *on* reading *chō*.

2.3 Classification of *On* Readings

Traditionally, *on* readings are classified into four types:

1. 漢音 ***kan'on*** 'Han reading', the most frequent and the most productive *on* reading, was introduced to Japan during the seventh and eighth centuries. It is based on the pronunciation current during the Tang Dynasty in northwestern China. Example: 行 *kō*.

2. 呉音 ***goon*** 'Wu reading', which is commonly assumed to originate from the Wu region in the lower Yangtze River area near Shanghai, was introduced up to the sixth and seventh centuries along with Buddhist writings. It is used mostly in Buddhist terms. Example: 行 *gyō*.

3. 唐音 ***tōon*** 'Tang reading' was introduced between the thirteenth century and the Edo period. It is based on the pronunciation current in the Song Dynasty and after, and is used mostly

for borrowed words and technological terms. Example: 行 *an*.

4. **慣用音** ***kan'yōon*** 'popular reading' developed as a result of erroneous pronunciations that came into popular use and gained general acceptance. Example: 立 *ritsu*.

During the compilation of this dictionary, several types of *on* readings that cannot be classified under the traditional categories were found. (The terms used to describe these categories were coined by the editor.)

1. **中音** ***chūon*** 'modern Chinese reading' is an *on* reading based on modern Chinese. 荘, for example, is pronounced *chan* in such words as 一荘 *īchan* 'a game of mahjong', on the basis of its Mandarin pronunciation *yīzhuāng*.

2. **外音** ***gaion*** 'foreign reading' is an *on* reading derived from foreign languages other than Chinese. For example, 仙 *sen* is pronounced *sento* in the sense of 'cent'. Particularly interesting is a growing trend to create readings based on English, such as 高技 *haiteku* 'high technology'.

3. **和音** ***waon*** 'Japanese reading' is an *on* reading assigned to *kokuji* (characters coined in Japan) on the model of Chinese characters. For example, 働 'to work' is a character coined in Japan but has a "Chinese-derived" reading of *dō*, which is the reading of its principal component 動 'move'.

2.4 Special Uses

In addition to the standard *on* and *kun* readings, there are a few special ways in which characters can be used. The most important of these are:

1. **当て字** ***ateji*** 'phonetic substitutes' refers to characters used phonetically with little or no relation to their meanings. These are often used to transliterate Sanskrit Buddhist terms, such as 阿修羅 *ashura* 'Asura' (fighting demon), and other foreign words such as 倶楽部 *kurabu* 'club'.

2. **熟字訓** ***jukujikun*** 'special reading' refers to a reading of a word consisting of two or more characters assigned to a single word on the basis of its meaning without direct relation to the normal readings of each constituent character. For example, 大人 'adult' consists of 大 'big', normally pronounced *dai* or *ōkii*, and 人 'human being', normally pronounced *jin* or *hito*, but together they function as a single unit pronounced *otona*.

2.5 Language Reforms

Shortly after World War II, the Japanese government implemented language reforms aimed at limiting the number of characters and simplifying their forms, among other things. At the same time, kana orthography underwent extensive reforms to reflect actual pronunciation. For example, the sound *kyū* was historically written by such combinations as きう and きふ, but is now written きゅう. Large-scale language reforms also took place in China to limit the number of characters and drastically simplify their forms. As a result, many modern Chinese forms are totally different from their corresponding traditional and modern Japanese forms. For example, the traditional form of 發 *hatsu* 'start; emit' was simplified to 発 in Japanese but to 发 in Chinese.

We will not dwell on China, but briefly examine the language reforms that took place in Japan. In 1946, a list of characters known as 当用漢字 *tōyō kanji* was published, in which the number of characters was limited to 1850. Various amendments and additions followed in the ensuing years. In 1948, for example, an appendix listing 881 characters to be learned in the first six years of compulsory schooling was published, and the number of readings of many characters was reduced. In 1949, the forms of many characters were greatly simplified, while in 1951 a supplementary list of 92 characters was approved for use in personal names, bringing the total to 1942.

In spite of these changes, there was much dissatisfaction among the public, who wanted the number of characters increased. In 1973, 28 more characters for general use were added, while in 1976, 28 name characters were approved, followed by an additional 54 in 1981 and 118 in 1990. Meanwhile, cultural organizations and the public at large pressed for greater freedom in the use of Chinese characters in general, as a result of which an expanded list of 1945 characters known as 常用漢字 *jōyō kanji* was published in 1981. This brought the total number of name characters to 2229.

The general trend to increase the number of characters took place in the schools as well. In 1977, the number of characters to be learned during the six years of compulsory schooling was increased to 996, and in 1989 this number was again increased to 1006 in line with the Ministry of Education's policy to place greater emphasis on reading and writing.

Currently (early 1990), the most important official lists approved by the Japanese government as part of the postwar language reforms are:

1. **Jōyō Kanji** The 常用漢字表 *jōyō kanji hyō,* or "List of Characters in Common Use," is an official list (published in 1981) of 1945 characters widely used in the mass media, government and general publications, and education.
2. **Education Kanji** The 学年別漢字配当表 *gakunenbetsu kanji haitōhyō,* or "List of Characters Classified by School Grade," is an official list of 1006 characters that must be learned in the first six years of compulsory schooling. The list, which is commonly referred to as 教育漢字 *kyōiku kanji* ("Education Kanji"), was promulgated on March 15, 1989. Although it has become official on this date, it will not be fully implemented until 1992. During the transition period, the old list of 996 characters published in 1977 will be used alongside with the new one. The number of characters taught in each grade is as follows:

Grade	1977 List	1989 List
First	76	80
Second	145	160
Third	195	200
Fourth	195	200
Fifth	195	185
Sixth	190	181
Total	996	1006

The principal change introduced in the new list was the moving of 60 characters from higher to lower grades. For example, fourteen third-grade characters have become second-grade characters. In addition, twenty new characters were added to the list, while ten characters were deleted, as shown below:

Additions (20)	皿昔笛豆箱札松巣束梅 桜枝飼夢激盛装誕並暮
Deletions (10)	歓称壱勧兼釈需是俗弐

See **Appendix 10. Jōyō Kanji List** for a full listing of the Education Kanji.

3. **Jinmei Kanji** The 人名用漢字 *jinmeiyō kanji*, or "Name Characters," is an official list (published in 1981) of 166 characters approved for use in personal names in addition to the Jōyō Kanji list. In April 1990, 118 name characters were added, bringing the total to 284. (There was not enough time to incorporate these changes into the present edition.)

The promulgation of the Jōyō/Tōyō Kanji lists made it necessary to adopt various measures to ensure their smooth implementation. One problem was that it became impossible to write certain common words that included characters not in the official list. To solve this problem, the government published a list of simpler characters and words, called 同音の漢字による書きかえ *dōon no kanji ni yoru kakikae*, that may be used to replace the characters not in the list. These characters, which we will call **phonetic replacement characters,** have the same sound, and, often, the same (or a similar) meaning as the characters being replaced. The latter will be called **phonetically replaced characters.**

For example, the character 繫 (phonetically replaced character) in 連繫 *renkei* 'connection, linking, contact' was replaced by 係 (phonetic replacement character), which has the same *on* reading and is similar to it in meaning, so that the word is now written 連係. In addition to the 170 phonetic replacement characters appearing in the aforementioned list, there are many others which are in common use but do not appear in the list. For example, 混 replaces 渾 in the word 渾沌 *konton* 'chaos'.

3. CHINESE CHARACTERS IN JAPANESE

3.1 The Japanese Script

The Japanese writing system is composed of two syllabic scripts, called 平仮名 **hiragana** and 片仮名 **katakana,** and thousands of Chinese characters, called 漢字 **kanji.** The three scripts basically have different functions. Hiragana is used mostly to write grammatical elements, such as inflectional verb endings, and sometimes for writing native Japanese words. For example, in 見た *mita* the kanji 見 represents the stem of the verb 見る *miru* 'see' and た *ta* is a verb ending for forming the past tense. The kana endings attached to a kanji base or stem are called 送り仮名 *okurigana*. Katakana is used mostly to write Western loanwords, such as プリンター *purintā* 'printer', and onomatopoeic words, such as カチッと *kachitto* 'with a click'.

Kanji are used to write the core of the Japanese vocabulary. This includes words, especially nouns, of Chinese origin and words coined in Japan on the Chinese model, such as 山脈 *sanmyaku* 'mountain range', as well as native Japanese words, such as 山 *yama* 'mountain'. Kanji have three basic properties: form, sound, and meaning. Each character may be pronounced according to its Chinese derived *on* reading, or one of several native Japanese *kun* readings, and each reading may have numerous meanings associated with it.

A running Japanese text consists of a mixture of kanji and kana, with the latter normally outnumbering the former. For example:

漢字を組み合わせることによって多数の熟語が作り出せます。

Kanji o kumiawaseru koto ni yotte tasū no jukugo ga tsukuridasemasu.

Numerous compound words can be formed by combining Chinese characters.

In the above sentence, particles such as を *o* (object marker), as well as verb endings(-わせる *-waseru* in 組み合わせる *kumiawaseru* 'combine'), are written in hiragana, whereas nouns, such as 熟語 *jukugo* 'compound word', are written in kanji. Hiragana characters serve as natural borderlines that help the reader segment the text into meaningful units. For this reason, a Japanese text is easier to read than a running Chinese text, which consists of Chinese characters only.

3.2 Functions of Kanji

One of the most important characteristics of Chinese characters is their ability to convey meaning. Just how they do this is the subject of a vast literature full of conflicting theories. Chinese characters have been described by such terms as *logographic* (symbols for words), *ideographic* (symbols for ideas), and *morphographic* (symbols for morphemes). Scholars disagree over the precise terminology and function of the characters.

According to one extreme view, the characters convey meaning phonetically and their ideographic nature is nothing but a myth. According to another view, the characters can convey meaning directly; that is, with little or no dependence on their pronunciations. Alphabetic symbols, on the other hand, are one step removed from that which is ultimately represented because they normally stand for the sounds of speech, which are in turn associated with meaning. Various other theories take intermediate positions between these two extremes. The whole question is highly controversial, but it is generally accepted that, whatever linguistic units the characters actually correspond to, their essential nature is to convey both meaning and sound, not just sound.

Another important characteristic of Chinese characters is their high productivity. By combining a stock of a few thousand characters, countless compound words are generated. 戦 *sen* 'war', for example, is combined with other characters to form numerous compound words related to war, such as 戦友 *sen'yū* 'comrade-in-arms' and many others. Chinese characters in Japanese function much the same way as Latin and Greek roots do in English. Each character has one or more distinct meanings, and often functions as a highly productive word-building element.

hydrophobia	(Greek)	恐水病	*kyōsuibyō*	fear-water-illness
aquarium	(Latin)	水族館	*suizokukan*	water-family-building
waterwheel	(Anglo-Saxon)	水車	*mizuguruma*	water-wheel

In English, the relationship between the above words is somewhat obscured by the fact that the concept of water is expressed in three different written forms, i.e., *hydr*, *aqua*, and *water*. In Japanese, on the other hand, although 水 has different phonetic forms, i.e., an *on* reading of *sui* and a *kun* reading of *mizu,* it has only one *graphic* form, i.e., 水. The kanji thus provides a *visual link* that transcends the different pronunciations. This ability of kanji to represent a given meaning with little or no dependence on their pronunciations is perhaps one the most distinctive features of the Japanese script.

A further characteristic of Chinese characters is their *semantic transparency*. As each component of a compound word conveys a distinct meaning, the meaning of the resulting word is often self-evident. For example, 好奇心 "like + strangeness + heart (mind)" means 'curiosity', 貧血症 "little + blood + illness" means 'anemia', and 閉所恐怖症 "closed + place + fear + illness" means 'claustrophobia'. Once the meanings of the components are known, relatively little effort is needed to learn these words.

Finally, Japanese has a large number of *homophones* (words that sound the same but are written differently). *Kōki* and *kikō,* for instance, represent about a dozen words in common use, and there are many more less frequent ones. Since each character has a distinct form (and meaning), kanji serve to distinguish such words from each other. Thus, 機構 *kikō* 'mechanism' is easily distinguished from 帰港 *kikō* 'returning to the harbor'.

In summary, the principal features of the Japanese script are:

1. The Japanese writing system consists of three scripts, each of which has a different function. Each kanji has a form, sound, and meaning.
2. One of the most important characteristics of kanji is their ability to convey meaning.
3. Kanji can be combined with each other to form numerous compound words.
4. Kanji provide a visual link that transcends their different pronunciations.
5. Compound words are often semantically transparent; that is, their meanings are more or less evident from their components.
6. Since each character has a distinct form (and meaning), kanji serve to distinguish homophones from each other.

3.3 Word-Formation

Languages differ in the processes by which they form new words. The Japanese language is *agglutinative;* that is, it forms words by putting together basic elements, called *morphemes*, that retain their original forms and meanings with little change during the combination process. A morpheme is a distinctive linguistic unit of relatively stable meaning that cannot be divided into smaller meaningful parts. As a rule, each Chinese character represents one morpheme.

Compounding and *derivation* are among the most important word-formation processes in Japanese. Compounding consists of combining two or more words or word elements having their own lexical meaning (having a substantial meaning of their own) to produce a new unit that functions as a single word. Since the Chinese characters are extremely productive in their ability to generate new words, compounding plays a major role in Japanese word-formation. By combining a stock of a few thousand characters, hundreds of thousands of compound words are created.

Traditionally, a compound word is considered to be a combination of two or more free words, such as *headwaiter*, which consists of *head* and *waiter*. In Japanese, a compound may be any combination of free words, combining forms, and affixes that together function as a single word. The resulting compound is distinct from, but related to, its constituent components. For example, the compound 造船所 *zōsenjo* 'shipyard' consists of the free word 造船 'shipbuilding' (造 'make; build' + 船 'ship') followed by the suffix 所 'place' (see FEATURES OF THIS DICTIONARY **§ 7.1 Character Functions** for more details).

Derivation refers to creating a new word by adding to a stem a word element such as a suffix that expresses grammatical meaning but has no lexical meaning. For example, the noun 黒 *kuro* 'black' is combined with the adjective-forming suffix い *i* to form the adjective 黒い *kuroi* 'black'. Derivation should not be confused with *inflection*, which consists of adding word endings or modifying the form of a word in order to indicate various grammatical functions, such as tense. The resulting word is another *form* of the original word, not a new word in itself. For example, the last syllable of the verb 帰る *kaeru* 'to return' is inflected to yield 帰れ *kaere,* the imperative form. Inflectional word endings in Japanese are usually written in hiragana.

The precise distinctions between compounding, derivation, and inflection involve complex theoretical problems that need not concern the nonspecialist.

3.4 Meaning of Kanji

As we have seen above, kanji may be read in one of two ways: the *on* reading and the *kun* reading. For each reading, a character may function as an independent word (any free word that can be used on its own) or as a word element (bound form used only in combinations). Since a character may have a different sense associated with each reading and each function, the meaning of a character can be said to operate on four distinct but related levels:

1. as an *on* independent word (as 明 *mei* 'discernment' in 先見の明 *senken no mei* 'foresight')
2. as an *on* word element (as 明 'clear, obvious' in 明確な *meikaku na* 'clear, distinct')
3. as an independent *kun* word (as 明るい *akarui* 'bright, light')
4. as a *kun* word element (as -明け 'end' in 忌明け *imiake* 'end of mourning').

Each character may have numerous meanings on one or more of the four levels, and the levels may interact in a complex way. On each level, the characters may be combined in various ways, such as bound + free, bound + bound, free + free, etc., and may have several, sometimes a dozen or more, different meanings. Each character may have several *on* and *kun* readings, and each reading may have several derived words associated with it, which in turn have many meanings; or the character may function as a word element with one or more meanings.

In some cases, on each level the meanings are totally different; in others, they may be similar but not quite the same. Often there is partial overlapping of some meanings but total inequality of others. For example, the *on* word element 山 *san* and the independent *kun* word as well as *kun* word element 山 *yama* share the meaning 'mountain', but the *on* word element *san* also means 'Buddhist temple', as in 本山 *honzan* 'head temple', a meaning which is not shared by *yama*.

Generally, the more common a character is, the more numerous are its meanings and the more complex is the relationship between them. An extreme example is 上 *jō* 'up; go up'. This dictionary lists a total of 114 meanings for 上, subdivided into 16 subentries. It has 27 meanings as an *on* word element, 3 meanings as an independent *on* word, 17 meanings for 5 *kun* word elements and 67 meanings for 9 independent *kun* words. Although 上 is a very long entry and is hardly typical, many characters do have more than ten meanings.

***

The Japanese script is now in a state of flux, and is being constantly adapted to the needs of the times. In this brief outline we have only touched upon its most important aspects, especially the role of Chinese characters, to the extent deemed necessary for using this dictionary effectively.

FEATURES OF THIS DICTIONARY

The primary aim of this dictionary is to serve as an effective reference tool to help the learner of Japanese gain an in-depth understanding of kanji. Its many features meet the needs of a broad range of users—the student, the reader, the writer, the educator, and the scholar. See the **INTRODUCTION** for a full discussion of dictionary aims.

The aim of the sections that follow is to show how to make effective use of the features of this dictionary. To take full advantage of these features, keep in mind that although this dictionary is an efficient tool for looking up unknown characters and their meanings, using it merely as a means for locating items in isolation will deprive the user of access to the wealth of information it presents. To derive maximum benefit from the dictionary, remember that the meanings of characters and words form a network of closely-linked, interrelated units. In order to see how individual characters and words relate to one another, you should (1) consult relatively large parts of an entry at the time, such as all the meanings in a given section, and (2) occasionally consult other relevant entries by using the extensive network of cross-references.

Since this dictionary is a work of reference, it should not be used in isolation, but in conjunction with other learning aids such as readers and textbooks, or as a supplement to a classroom program. Although the study of kanji is a time-consuming task that requires diligence, we are confident that application of a systematic approach with the help of this dictionary as a reference tool will lead to satisfactory results.

The features of this dictionary are classified into six broad categories, which are briefly described below:

1. **FINDING**: A new indexing system makes this dictionary an efficient tool for **finding** characters with great speed and facility. The user has a choice of six methods of looking up entries.
2. **UNDERSTANDING**: Many features enable the learner to gain an in-depth **understanding** of the meanings and functions of kanji. These features clearly show how a few thousand building blocks are combined to form the countless compounds in Japanese.
3. **READING**: This dictionary is a convenient tool for **reading** Japanese because it enables the user to quickly look up a large variety of character readings, styles, forms,

and meanings.

4. **WRITING**: This dictionary is an excellent manual for **writing** because of the full guidance it provides on stroke order, stroke counting, and calligraphic styles, and the various features that help the student compose texts with clarity and precision.
5. **DISCRIMINATING**: This dictionary serves as an effective learning aid because of the complete guidance it provides for **discriminating** between easily confused characters such as synonyms, homophones, and orthographic variants.
6. **REFERRING**: A wealth of supplementary data and an extensive network of cross-references make this dictionary an invaluable tool for **referring.**

The first four categories, described in **PART I: GENERAL FEATURES** below, are general features useful to the beginner and advanced student alike. The last two categories, described in **PART II: ADVANCED FEATURES** on p. 87a, are advanced features that are particularly useful to the advanced student and scholar. For convenience of explanation, some advanced features are treated in **PART I**, accompanied by appropriate comments indicating their status as advanced features. The most important features are summarized in the chart below, which provides an overview of how this dictionary can benefit the learner of Japanese.

CHART OF DICTIONARY FEATURES

	FEATURES	BENEFITS
1. FINDING	1. Quick lookup method 2. Cross-references 3. Six lookup methods: by pattern by scanning by reading by radical by meaning directly 4. System of guides 5. Finding compounds and words 6. Readable layout and design 7. Extensive cross-reference network	A new indexing system makes this dictionary an efficient tool for **finding** characters with great speed and facility. The user has a choice of six methods of looking up character entries, while the cross-references at incorrect locations practically eliminate dead-end searching. Moreover, a system of guides facilitates the speedy location of entries, and a readable layout and extensive cross-reference network quickly lead to a wealth of useful information.
2. UNDERSTANDING	1. Core meanings 2. Character meanings 3. Interrelatedness of meaning 4. Logical ordering of senses 5. Importance of character senses 6. Explanatory glosses 7. English equivalents	A number of unique features enable the learner to gain an in-depth **understanding** of the meanings and functions of kanji in Japanese. The core meaning, a concise keyword that defines the most dominant character meaning, is followed by detailed meanings grouped in a manner that allows them to be conceived as an integrated unit. Numer-

	FEATURES	BENEFITS
	8. Supplementary information 9. Cross-references in equivalent 10. Numerous compounds and examples 11. Compounds with entry character in all positions 12. Compounds ordered by sense 13. Compound formation 14. Character functions 15. Labeling system 16. Synonym articles 17. Usage notes 18. Radicals 19. Character etymology	ous compounds and examples, supplemented by articles describing how they are formed, illustrate each meaning in a wide range of contexts. To help the student learn new words, the function of each character as a word or word element is indicated, accompanied by various glosses and cross-references. A system of labels provides practical guidance on function, usage, status, and orthography, clearly distinguishing frequent meanings from rare and archaic ones. Since the degree of importance is indicated for each character sense, the beginner and advanced student can use the dictionary with equal ease. Understanding is further enhanced by articles showing the distinctions between synonyms and homophones and by character etymologies.
3. READING	1. Looking up unknown characters 2. Looking up unknown compounds 3. Numerous character forms 4. Entries for nonstandard forms 5. Easily confused forms 6. Calligraphic and typeface styles 7. Numerous character readings 8. Importance of readings 9. Full romanization 10. Chinese forms and readings	The dictionary is a convenient tool for **reading** both contemporary and prewar Japanese because it enables the user to quickly look up a large variety of character readings, styles, and forms as well as the meanings and readings of unknown characters and compounds. Easily confused forms are cross-referenced, while all Japanese words and examples are romanized in a manner that shows their formation. Moreover, the Chinese form and reading are given for each character.
4. WRITING	1. Stroke order diagrams 2. Stroke order principles 3. Three calligraphic styles 4. Stroke-count data 5. Stroke counting	The dictionary is an excellent manual for **writing** the characters because of the full guidance it provides on stroke order, stroke counting, and calligraphic styles. This enables the student to write the characters in the proper form and propor-

	FEATURES	BENEFITS
	principles 6. Kana orthography 7. *Okurigana* affixes 8. *Okurigana* rules 9. Orthographic variants 10. Synonym articles 11. Usage notes	tion and is a prerequisite for studying calligraphy. Other features help the student write with clarity and precision by showing the fine distinctions between orthographic variants, homophones, and kanji synonyms, and by providing full guidance on kana orthography.
5. DISCRIMINATING	1. Synonym articles 2. Synonym headwords 3. Synonym keywords 4. Cross-references to synonyms 5. Simple kanji thesaurus 6. Usage notes 7. Orthographic labels 8. Cross-references to homophones 9. Examples in usage notes 10. Supplementary notes 11. Easily confused forms 12. Orthographic variants	The dictionary provides complete guidance for **discriminating** between easily confused characters, which serves as an effective learning aid. It shows the precise differences and similarities between kanji synonyms, homophones, easily confused forms, and orthographic variants so as to help the student understand shades of meaning and write with clarity and precision. This is enhanced by a network of cross-references, which helps quickly locate any member of a homophone or synonym group and also serves as a simple kanji thesaurus.
6. REFERRING	1. Eleven appendixes: • Kanji patterns • Strokes counting • Writing kanji • Kana and romanization • *Okurigana* rules • Radicals • Historical tables • Place name abbreviations • Core meanings by frequency • Jōyō Kanji list • Kanji synonyms 2. Extensive cross-reference network 3. Frequency statistics 4. Character grade	A wealth of supplementary data and an extensive network of cross-references make this dictionary an invaluable tool for **referring.** Eleven appendixes give the advanced student, the educator, and the scholar quick access to a valuable source of reference data. Frequency statistics and other data help the teacher compile graded lessons.

The above features are described in detail in the sections that follow. The introduction to each section presents an overview, and discusses the nature of the problems faced by the learner. Various cross-references direct the user to other relevant sections, especially to the GUIDE TO THE DICTIONARY on p. 159a, which is abbreviated to "GUIDE." Whereas the GUIDE deals mostly with format and presentation details, the aim here is to show how and why the information is useful, with emphasis on the practical needs of the learner. To distinguish dictionary features and technical terms specific to this dictionary, they are set in **sanserif boldface** when necessary.

PART I: GENERAL FEATURES

The purpose of PART I is to describe in detail the features of this dictionary that are useful to both the beginner and advanced student. The advanced features are described in PART II: ADVANCED FEATURES on p. 87a. For convenience, the chart on p. 62a summarizes the most important features.

1. FINDING

The lack of an efficient scheme for ordering Chinese characters has long posed a major obstacle to learners attempting to look up entries in character dictionaries. The main problem is that one cannot look up a character without already knowing something about it, such as its radical or reading. Neither the traditional radical system, nor the various alternative systems, have achieved the speed and simplicity required to meet the practical needs of dictionary users. Another problem is that current and past character dictionaries lack a systematic cross-reference network that directs the user's attention to closely-related characters.

This dictionary serves as an efficient tool for **finding** items with great speed and facility. The following features are designed to attain this end:

Summary of Features

General Features	1. A quick method for looking up characters by patterns. 2. Cross-reference entries at incorrect locations. 3. Six lookup methods: by pattern, by scanning, by reading, by radical, by meaning, directly. 4. A system of guides for speedy location of entries. 5. Finding compounds and independent words. 6. A readable layout and design.
Advanced Features	7. An extensive network of cross-references.

1.1 Finding Entry Characters

1.1.1 Quick Lookup Method A major feature of this dictionary is the new scheme it introduces for looking up characters with speed and facility. In addition, a cross-reference system practically eliminates dead-end searching by placing characters at locations where they might be mistakenly looked for. See SYSTEM OF KANJI INDEXING BY PATTERNS on p. 106a for details.

1.1.2 Six Lookup Methods We hope that the user will familiarize him/herself with the new classification scheme (SKIP) introduced here, since it offers a speedy and efficient lookup method. Although we have departed from the traditional method of ordering characters, we have not overlooked the needs of the traditionally oriented user. This dictionary offers six different methods of locating entries, which are listed below. This allows the user to choose the lookup method most appropriate to the situation or most suited to his or her personal preferences.

1. **By pattern**: the **Pattern Index** allows characters to be quickly located from their geometrical patterns. See SYSTEM OF KANJI INDEXING BY PATTERNS on p. 106a for details.
2. **By scanning**: a powerful shortcut allows characters of high stroke-count to be located almost instantaneously without counting strokes. See SYSTEM OF KANJI INDEXING BY PATTERNS § 3.2 SCAN **Method** for details.
3. **By reading**: the **On-Kun Index** lists the characters alphabetically by both their *on* and *kun* readings. See **On-Kun Index** on p. 1895 for details.
4. **By radical**: the **Radical Index** lists the characters by their traditional radicals and additional strokes. See **How to Use the Radical Index** on p. 1929 for details.
5. **By meaning**: the **List of Kanji Synonym Groups** arranges the characters in semantic groups listed alphabetically by their headwords. See **Appendix 11. List of Kanji Synonym Groups** on p. 1824 for details.
6. **Directly**: a direct method allows characters to be located from their geometrical patterns without the use of any index. See SYSTEM OF KANJI INDEXING BY PATTERNS **§ 3.1.3 Direct Method** for details.

1.1.3 System of Guides The various guides in the outer corners and margins of the page facilitate the speedy location of character entries. These are of six kinds: the pattern guide, the subsection guide, the margin guide, the subgroup guide, the entry number guide, and the page number. See SYSTEM OF KANJI INDEXING BY PATTERNS **§ 2.8 SKIP Guides** and GUIDE **§ 1.1 Guides** for details.

1.2 Finding Words

Each sense of a character or subentry headword is normally accompanied by numerous compounds and examples, which are grouped under the senses which they illustrate. To find a compound or example, follow the procedure below:

1. Locate the entry for the first character of the desired compound, word, or word element by one of the methods described in **§ 1.1.2 Six Lookup Methods.**

2. Look for *on* compounds in the COMPOUNDS section, independent *on* words in the INDEPENDENT section, *kun* words and compounds in the KUN section, and words having special readings in the SPECIAL READINGS section. If you do not know the type or the reading of your compound or word, scan through these sections until you locate it.

3. Within each section, the compounds and examples are arranged according to a scheme described in **GUIDE § 21. Compounds and Examples.** It is not necessary to know all the details of this scheme since the number of compounds or words within a given grouping is often small enough for the desired item to be quickly located by visual scanning.
4. If you cannot locate a compound at the entry for its first character, look for it at the entry for its second or third characters.

Example: FIND THE COMPOUND 残酷 *zankoku*

STEP 1	Locate the entry for the first character of 残酷 at 残 943.
STEP 2	Since 残酷 is an *on* compound, look for it in the COMPOUNDS section.
STEP 3	残酷な 'cruel' is found under sense ❷ 'ruthless', which is the sense that it illustrates.

Example: FIND THE COMPOUND 食べ物 *tabemono*

STEP 1	Locate the entry for the first character of 食べ物 at 食 2075.
STEP 2	Since 食べ物 is a *kun* compound, look for it in the KUN section.
STEP 3	Since 食べ物 is an example of 食べる, look for it under the subentry ta(beru), where it appears among several other compounds.

1.3 Design Features

An additional feature of the dictionary that helps the user find items is its **readable layout** and typographical design. Computer phototypesetting technology was used to achieve a harmonious blend of a wide range of type sizes, styles, and identifying labels. Thanks to the consistent use of such typographical devices, the organization of the entry is mostly self-explanatory, leading the user quickly and directly to the desired item.

1.4 Cross-Reference Network

An extensive **network of cross-references** directs the user to a wealth of information useful to both the learner and the educator. See **§ 6.2 Cross-Reference Network** for details.

2. UNDERSTANDING

The learner of Japanese must not only learn the complex shapes and many readings of numerous characters, but must also understand their meanings in the formation of compound words. Failure to do so would result in enormous inefficiency, since one would face the laborious task of memorizing countless words as unrelated units.

The most important feature of this dictionary is the in-depth manner in which it treats meaning. Past works have largely limited their treatment to character forms, readings, and compound words. This dictionary includes many unique features that enable the learner to gain a full, systematic **understanding** of the meanings and functions of each character. The most important of these are listed below:

Summary of Features

General Features	1. Core meanings given by concise English keywords. 2. Clear, complete, and accurate character meanings. 3. Interrelatedness of meaning. 4. Senses ordered in a logical manner. 5. Importance of character senses. 6. Explanatory glosses. 7. English equivalents. 8. Supplementary glosses and notes. 9. Cross-References in equivalent. 10. Numerous compounds and examples. 11. Compounds with entry character in all positions. 12. Compounds and examples ordered by sense. 13. Compound formation and etymology.
Advanced Features	14. Functions of characters as words or word elements. 15. System of labels. 16. Articles discriminate between kanji synonyms. 17. Usage notes discriminate between homophones. 18. Detailed information on radicals. 19. Character etymology.

2.1 Character Meaning

The meaning associated with a single character may be quite complex, for the following reasons:

1. A character may have meanings on as many as four distinct but interrelated levels: i.e., as an *on* word element, as an *on* free word, as a *kun* word element, and as a *kun* free word.
2. The levels may interact in a complex way, from partial or absolute equivalence to total nonequivalence.
3. On each level a character may have several, sometimes numerous, meanings.
4. On each level a character may have a variety of grammatical and other functions.

Since a character may thus have a large number of meanings that interact in a complex way and, furthermore, since the range of meaning represented by a single character may branch out into apparently unrelated directions, it would be burdensome to memorize the many meanings and usages of each character without understanding their interrelationships. This is not unlike trying to learn the English vocabulary without knowing the meanings of such prefixes as *un–* in *unmarried* and *semi–* in *semiannual*.

In this dictionary, we have made every effort to present meanings in a manner that helps the learner understand these relations. The **core meaning**, a concise English keyword that defines the most dominant meaning of each character, is followed by clear, complete, and accurate **character meanings** arranged in an order and format that show how compound words are formed from their constituents. The character meanings consist of sense division numbers, various labels and glosses, the English equivalent, and cross-references, and are followed by numerous compounds and examples that illustrate each sense. When necessary, these are supplemented by compound formation articles that show how compound words are formed from their constituent parts. The precisely-worded equivalents and the system of labels show how each character functions as a combining form, a prefix, a suffix, an abbreviation, a counter, etc.

The meanings of free words (independent *on* and *kun* words) are distinguished from those of word elements by treating them in separate sections. The COMPOUNDS section treats *on* word elements, while the INDEPENDENT section treats independent *on* words. The KUN section treats both independent *kun* words and *kun* word elements, and includes various labels and typographical devices to distinguish these categories. Thanks to this arrangement, the meanings and functions of a character on each of the four levels can be easily distinguished from each other.

These features, which enable the user to gain a systematic, in-depth understanding of character meanings, are described in detail below. To properly understand the material covered here, it is desirable to first read the **OUTLINE OF JAPANESE WRITING SYSTEM** on p. 50a.

2.2 Core Meaning

2.2.1 Concise English Keyword A unique highlight of this dictionary is the presentation of a **core meaning** or meanings. This is a concise English keyword that provides a clear grasp of the central or most fundamental concept linking the principal senses of a character into one conceptual unit. This is the first character dictionary in any language to present such a feature, which has been praised by scholars and educators as a powerful learning aid.

Consider the following four ideas: (1) fix, (2) detain, (3) reserve, and (4) pay attention to. On the surface, they appear to have little in common with each other; in fact, they represent four senses associated with one of the core meanings of 留, as shown below:

留 Core Meaning: ▶**KEEP**
2580

❶ cause to remain in a given place or condition:
- ⓐ **KEEP** in place, **KEEP** from moving, **KEEP** in position
- ⓑ **KEEP** in custody, detain
- ⓒ **KEEP** for future use, leave behind
- ⓓ **KEEP** in mind, pay attention to

By grasping that the central concept, or core meaning, represented by 留 is **KEEP**, it is immediately clear that such seemingly unrelated ideas as "pay attention to" and "detain" are merely variants of a single basic concept. Seen from this point of view, that is, as an expansion from a core or central concept, the four ideas are integrated into a single conceptual unit.

The core meaning is useful to the learner in five ways:

1. It serves as a concise English keyword that conveys the character's most fundamental or most important meaning.

2. It shows how the principal meanings of a character are linked to each other as well as to a single central concept; that is, it serves as the central pivot that links the various meanings into an integrated conceptual unit. The core meaning provides a visual reinforcement of the basic notion that links or relates the various senses to

one another.

3. It provides the user with an instant grasp of the meaning and function of the character as a word-building element. This is because (*a*) the core meaning usually represents the sense that is used most frequently in the formation of compounds, and (*b*) the part of speech of the core meaning often reflects the grammatical function of the character as a word element.

4. It is easy to memorize. Since the core meaning conveys the essence of the character in one concise thought, it leaves a lasting impression upon the mind.

5. It enables the user to grasp the fine differences and similarities between kanji synonyms.

Let us consider how this helps the user understand the meanings of 破:

破 Core Meaning: ▶**BREAK**
1150

❶ⓐ [original meaning] **BREAK**, smash
ⓑ **BREAK** through, penetrate
ⓒ **BREAK** out (of jail), escape
❷ **BREAK** the enemy, defeat
❸ⓐ (act contrary to) **BREAK** (as a promise), breach, violate
ⓑ **BREAK** with (the moral conventions), be exceptional
❹ **BREAK** down, go to pieces, go broke

It is obvious at a glance that the core meaning **BREAK** conveys the essential meaning of 破 in one concise, easy-to-remember keyword. Without it, it would be most difficult to perceive such widely differing notions as "penetrate" and "escape" as variants of the same central concept. The repeated use of **BREAK** in distinct, but interrelated, senses reveals both the differences and similarities between the various senses, and makes it easy to perceive them as an integrated unit.

Furthermore, comparing the core meaning of 破 with those of the other members of the synonym group listed in the SYNONYMS section, such as 壊 BREAK DOWN, 折 BREAK OFF, 裂 SPLIT, 砕 CRUSH UP, and 崩 CRUMBLE, clearly reveals both the differences and similarities between these characters, and helps the learner understand their different shades of meaning (see **§ 5.1.2 Powerful Learning Aid** for details). In addition, for the convenience of the learner and the developer of teaching materials, an appendix lists the core meanings in order of frequency of occurrence. See **Appendix 9. Core Meanings Arranged by Frequency** for details.

In conclusion, the core meaning is a powerful learning tool. It may be perceived as a highly-concentrated thought package that leaves a lasting impression on the mind. It promotes a quicker and fuller understanding of the meaning of each character, and makes the principal senses of the character easier to memorize by linking them to one fundamental concept. The core meaning appeals to the learner's powers of association without resorting to monotonous rote memorization. Consequently, it should prove to be of enormous value to the student of Japanese.

See **GUIDE § 9. CORE Section** for format details.

2.2.2 Theoretical Considerations

Because of the very important role that the core meaning plays as a feature of this dictionary, it may be of interest to the user to know some of the underlying theoretical principles.

The core meaning is not an objectively observable linguistic unit. Rather, it is a psychological unit, a basic notion of a character's meaning that conveys, in the famous linguist Edward Sapir's words, its "conceptual kernel." Linguistically, it is not normally possible to isolate any sense of a word or character that will, by a process of logical deduction, make it possible to derive all its other senses. Often, it is not even possible to trace the origin of each sense historically and show how the individual senses relate to the character's original meaning. The core meaning is thus not necessarily the original meaning of the character, though it often is.

The core meaning is often the direct, psychologically most dominant, meaning—the meaning that might occur to a native speaker if presented with the character in isolation. However, psychological dominance is not the only factor, since the popular meaning associated with a character by the average Japanese may differ considerably from the linguistic facts. Even more important is its ability to show the interrelatedness between the various senses and its frequency of occurrence (although in exceptional cases the core meaning may be archaic—see GUIDE **§ 24.2 Etymological Labels**).

The table below shows the relationship between the senses of BRIGHT, the English term representing the core meaning of 明, the *on* word element 明 *mei,* and the independent *kun* word 明るい *akarui.*

Typical words and word elements represented by 明:		English term representing core meaning of 明
明 *mei*	明るい *akarui*	BRIGHT
❶ⓐ [original meaning] bright, brilliant, light ⓑ (of colors) bright, light ⓒ (of cheerful disposition) bright, cheerful ❷ⓐ light ⓑ be lighted ❸ⓐ clear-sighted, bright, discerning, intelligent, wise ⓑ eyesight ❹ⓐ (free from doubt) clear, lucid, distinct, evident, obvious, explicit, manifest ⓑ make clear, clarify, throw light on, prove, demonstrate ❺ (unclouded) clear, transparent, translucent ❻ [also prefix] next, the coming (day or year) ❼ Ming Dynasty (1368–1644 A.D.) ⋮	❶ bright, light ❷ light (color) ❸ clear, uncorrupt ❹ (of cheerful disposition) bright, cheerful ❺ (full of promise) bright, promising ❻ be well versed in	❶ full of light ❷ brilliant in color ❸ glorious, splendid ❹ promising ❺ cheerful ❻ intelligent, smart

The English term for the core meaning of a character may be viewed as the center of a circle representing that term's area of meaning. Another circle or circles represent the area of meaning of the words or word elements that can be written with that character, as illustrated in the diagram below:

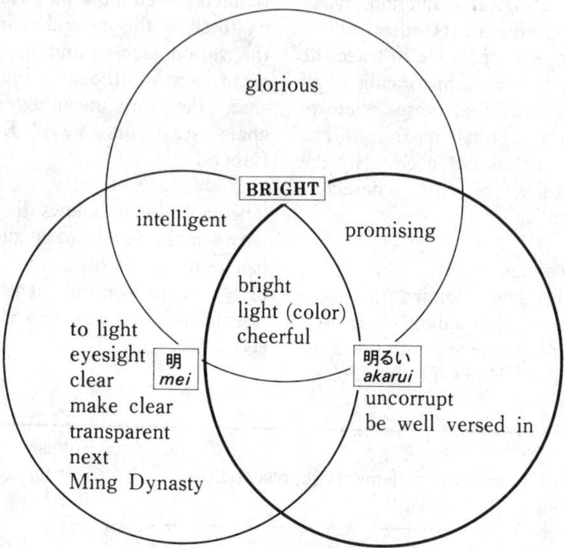

The core meaning is often given by the English term (in this case *bright*) for which the area of overlap is greatest. Although the meanings of a Japanese word (as 明るい *akarui*) or word element (as 明 *mei*) may differ from those of the English term in various details, the central concept they represent is essentially the same. That is, the differences are in the meanings lying toward the outlines of the circles, rather than towards their centers. 明 *mei* and BRIGHT, for instance, perfectly coincide in their most basic meanings, such as 'brilliant in light', but other senses, such as 'Ming Dynasty', are totally different and thus fall out of the area of overlap.

The core meanings were established by performing an exhaustive analysis of the lexical meaning and word-building function of each character. Each meaning component was carefully analyzed and compared with those of the other members of the same synonym group in order to determine the most precise English term for conveying the meaning, function, and subtle nuances of the character in contrast with those of other closely related characters. Based on a firm theoretical foundation, the core meaning is a highly useful abstraction and effective learning aid.

2.3 Character Meanings

2.3.1 Interrelatedness of Meaning

One of the principal objectives of this dictionary is to provide the user with a clear understanding of the meanings and functions of each character. The manner in which the character meanings are presented greatly contributes to this end by showing the **interrelatedness of meaning** between individual character senses. Four features are designed to achieve this aim:

1. The repeated appearance of a **core meaning** in the English equivalent

shows how the various senses of the character resemble and differ from each other by providing a visual link between them. See **§ 2.2 Core Meaning** for details.

2. The overall organization and **ordering of senses** in a manner that shows their interrelatedness. See **§ 2.3.2 Order of Senses** for details.

3. The subdivision of meanings by a system of **sense division numbers,** letters, and semicolons establishes a logical hierarchy between them. See GUIDE **§ 20.4 Sense Division** for details.

4. The **explanatory glosses,** which show how the various senses differ from one another. See **§ 2.3.4 Explanatory Gloss** for details.

These devices show both the differences and similarities between the senses; they help integrate the senses so that the user can learn them as a structured unit, rather than as an arbitrary list.

2.3.2 Order of Senses Traditionally, Chinese character dictionaries present character senses historically. Meanings appear in chronological order, beginning with the original meaning of the character. Although this approach may be of great value to the scholar, it is not necessarily the most useful one to the learner. The historical approach has two major drawbacks: (1) it does not normally reflect contemporary usage, since archaic and old senses often appear first, and (2) the order of presentation does not promote an understanding of how the meanings are interrelated.

An alternative method of ordering senses is the statistical approach. An inherent difficulty with this approach is the lack of data on the frequency of occurrence of specific senses. Even if such data were available, this would not be a useful system because it is based solely upon frequency of occurrence and ignores the semantic relationships between individual senses.

This dictionary makes a significant departure from traditional character–dictionary lexicography by presenting meanings in a manner sometimes referred to as the *psychologistic approach;* that is, the meanings are presented in a **cogent order that clearly shows their interrelatedness.** An English keyword (usually a core meaning) representing a dominant sense of the character serves as the basis of organization, and the various senses are grouped in clusters in a manner that allows them to be conceived as a logically-structured, psychologically integrated unit. In the example below, the various senses of 取る cluster around the core meaning TAKE, which is the central concept that links them together:

取る *toru* Core Meaning: ▶**TAKE**	
Arbitrary List	Expansion from Core Meaning
seize	ⓐ TAKE, take hold of
remove, delete	ⓑ TAKE off, take away
kill	ⓒ TAKE a life
eat, have	ⓓ TAKE a meal, have, eat
subscribe to, buy	ⓔ TAKE (in) a newspaper, magazine, etc.
harvest, reap	ⓕ TAKE in crops
charge	ⓖ TAKE money for

Although 取る has several distinct senses, they are presented in a manner that clearly shows their differences and similarities. This manner of presentation greatly facilitates understanding and reduces the burden of memorization. On the other hand, if the senses were arranged as shown in the left column, they would appear to be an arbitrary list of unrelated items, rather than as a structured unit. See also GUIDE **§ 20.3 Order of Senses.**

2.3.3 Importance of Character Senses Most existing character dictionaries are based on classical Chinese sources, and thus often list rare and archaic meanings. Since they do not normally include labels or other devices to distinguish these categories, the user has no way of knowing whether a meaning is common, rare, archaic, or obsolete. This could be a serious obstacle to the learner, especially the beginner, who may waste time and effort in learning advanced meanings.

A useful feature of this dictionary is the indication of the **degree of importance** of each character sense. Although meanings are given up to the advanced level and beyond, various typographical differences and **temporal labels** indicate the degree of importance for different types of users. The devices used for indicating degree of importance establish a hierarchy of *relative* importance between the individual senses of a specific character; they do not aim to be an absolute measure of the importance, or of the frequency of occurrence, of a character sense in relation to other characters.

The degree of importance is divided into four levels, listed below in descending order of importance. See also GUIDE **§ 20.5 Importance of Character Senses** for an illustration of the four levels.

Level 1	**Core Meaning**
	The most important sense, which is essential for the beginner, provides a basic understanding of the character (see **§ 2.2 Core Meaning**).
Level 2	**Boldface Equivalent**
	Signifies that the importance or frequency of occurrence of a character sense as an *on* word element is sufficiently high to merit study by the learner at the beginner to intermediate levels. These are the most useful character meanings to the learner, the ones that are essential for a practical course of self–study or a classroom program.
Level 3	**Lightface Equivalent**
	Signifies that a character sense as an *on* word element is sufficiently important to merit study by the learner at the intermediate to advanced levels or by the scholar. Although these meanings are not so frequent, they are current in contemporary Japanese and should be learned by the student interested in acquiring standard proficiency in the language.

Level 4	Temporal Labels
	Less important senses, such as rare, archaic, and obsolete ones, are indicated by the temporal labels. These are of primary interest to advanced students and scholars (see GUIDE **§ 24.3 Temporal Labels**).

The indication of degree of importance allows the user to easily distinguish between basic, advanced, rare, and archaic meanings. For the beginner, this establishes a hierarchy of importance for learning the senses of most frequent occurrence. For the advanced student and scholar, it isolates the more unusual senses that may be useful in reading classical literature or conducting research. This manner of presentation enables both the beginner and the advanced student to use the dictionary with equal ease, and helps the compiler of teaching materials to prepare graded lessons. This dictionary thus serves both as practical learning tool and as a useful teaching aid.

2.3.4 Explanatory Gloss In order to improve the user's understanding of character meanings, the English equivalents are often accompanied by **explanatory glosses.** These are of two kinds: (1) the subject guide phrase and (2) the explanation or definition. The **subject guide phrase** is a brief parenthetical phrase that restricts the range of application of the equivalent to a specific domain, such as the typical or only subject of an intransitive verb. The **explanation** is a description, rather than a translation, of the meaning or grammatical function. The **definition** resembles a full lexicographic definition in a monolingual dictionary.

The primary function of these glosses is to restrict, explain, define, supplement, or clarify the meaning conveyed by the equivalent. Their secondary function is to eliminate any ambiguity that might arise from equivalents that have more than one sense in English. This is especially effective in character entries in which the core meaning is repeatedly used as the first word of the equivalent in different senses in order to show how the individual character senses interrelate:

引
181

❶ⓐ [original meaning] (pull toward one) ——— explanatory gloss
draw, pull, haul, tug ——— equivalent
ⓑ (extend in length) draw out, stretch

⋮

❷ⓐ (cause to move, as by leading) **draw (toward), draw in, call in**
ⓑ draw a person to act: entice, induce, seduce

⋮

In the example, the word *draw* is used in different senses, while the glosses in parentheses pinpoint its precise meaning as an equivalent of 引. Thus, while the repeated use of the core meaning shows the *similarity* between the senses, the explanatory glosses show the *differences* between them. See GUIDE **§ 20.6 Explanatory Gloss** for format details.

2.3.5 The Equivalent **Equivalent** refers to synonymous or nearly synonymous words or phrases that are an English translation of the meaning of a Japanese word or word element (see example in § **2.3.4** above). The equivalent, which is the most important part of the character meaning, is presented in a manner that enables the learner to get a full understanding of each character's meaning and function. A system of sense division numbers, semicolons, and commas is used to present the equivalent in a logical and organized manner.

The equivalent shows how the character meanings are related to each other through a core meaning or keyword, as well as how the meanings are related to the meanings of other characters belonging to the same synonym group. See **§ 2.2 Core Meaning** and **§ 5.1 Discriminating Synonyms** for details. It may include various parenthetical adjuncts, as in "follow (a person's instructions)," that indicate a typical object of a transitive verb, or in other ways help clarify or supplement the meaning. See also GUIDE **§ 20.7 The Equivalent.**

2.3.6 Supplementary Information

The **supplementary gloss** supplements the equivalent by restricting its level of formality or social context, by describing its grammatical function, or by occasionally providing encyclopedic information such as dates, places, and so on:

唄
400

ⓑ [usu. 歌う *utau*] recite, sing—used esp. in reference to traditional Japanese songs

Furthermore, **supplementary notes** provide additional information on usage, orthography, character readings, etc. See GUIDE **§ 20.8 Supplementary Gloss** and GUIDE **§ 19.2.2 Supplementary Note** for details.

2.3.7 Cross-References An equivalent or supplementary gloss is sometimes followed by various **cross-references**, which direct the user to other locations in the dictionary for further useful information. See GUIDE **§ 20.9 Cross-References** for details.

2.4 Compounds and Examples

2.4.1 Numerous Compounds and Examples **Compound** or **compound word** refers to a combination of two or more words or word elements having their own lexical meaning that together function as a single word. **Example** is a word other than a compound, or a phrase or sentence, which usually illustrates the use of a free word. A compound or example consists of a Japanese word or phrase, a romanized transcription, and an English equivalent:

Compound: 金庫破り *kinkoyaburi* safecracking; safecracker

Example: 戸を破る *to o yaburu* break a door

The ability of characters to be combined with each other to form countless compound words is one of their most important functions. Numerous compounds and examples normally illustrate each character sense. Their aim is twofold: (1) to provide high-frequency, maximally useful examples for understanding the meanings and functions of each character as a component of compound words, and (2) to enable the reader to look up unknown compounds.

Unlike other character dictionaries, the compounds are not restricted to those in which the entry character occurs in the initial position, but include also those in which it appears in the medial or final positions. For example, the entry character 吹 in the example in **§ 2.4.2** below appears in the initial position in 吹奏 *suisō* but in the final position in 鼓吹 *kosui*. This arrangement helps illustrate the word-building function of the entry character in a wide variety of contexts.

2.4.2 Order of Compounds Traditionally, character dictionaries arrange the compounds within a character entry by stroke order or by reading. Such systems are geared to help the user locate a compound quickly. The ordering in this dictionary is more complex, since the primary emphasis is on helping the learner understand character meanings. The compounds and examples are grouped together under the meanings which they illustrate.

The compounds and examples in main entries are subdivided into groups according to the following criteria: by section, by subentry, by sense, by position of entry character, and by type. This arrangement is fully explained in GUIDE **§ 21.3 Order of Compounds,** but it is not necessary for the general user to know all the details. The important point is that the compounds and examples illustrating a particular sense (main sense or subsense) are all listed together under the same main sense:

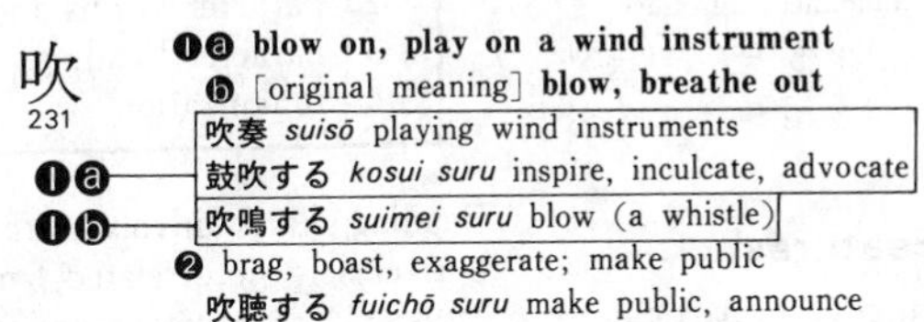

吹
231

❶ⓐ **blow on, play on a wind instrument**
ⓑ [original meaning] **blow, breathe out**

吹奏 *suisō* playing wind instruments
鼓吹する *kosui suru* inspire, inculcate, advocate
吹鳴する *suimei suru* blow (a whistle)

❷ brag, boast, exaggerate; make public
吹聴する *fuichō suru* make public, announce

This format has two important advantages: (1) it enables the user to know the specific sense in which the entry character is used within each compound, that is, its meaning and function as a word element, and (2) it makes it easy to infer the meanings of other compounds formed along a similar pattern but not found in the dictionary. When this arrangement does not make it sufficiently clear how a specific compound is formed, the formation or etymology of that compound is explained separately (see **§ 2.5 Compound Formation**).

2.5 Compound Formation

The formation of a compound word is normally self-evident from the manner in which the compounds are grouped by meaning (see **§ 2.4.2 Order of Compounds** for details). When this is not obvious, that is, when the relationship between the components is not clear, it is shown in one of three ways:

1. A COMPOUND FORMATION **article** describes the etymology (origin or development) of the compound and/or explains how its constituent characters contribute to the meaning of the whole:

以
41

COMPOUND FORMATION

以心伝心 *ishindenshin*
以心伝心 'silent [tacit] understanding, empathy', is to convey (伝) one's thoughts or feelings (心) by means of (以 ❷) thoughts (not words).

Understanding the role of each component also provides interesting sidelights on the historical circumstances that gave rise to the concept represented by the word. The entry for each constituent character includes (when relevant) a cross-reference note pointing to the entry where the compound formation article appears. See GUIDE **§ 18.** COMPOUND FORMATION **Section** for format details.

2. A **parenthetical phrase** enclosed in double quotation marks sometimes provides a literal, character-by-

character translation of the meaning of each component:

眠
1147

冬眠 *tōmin* hibernation ("winter sleep")

3. The **original meaning** of a compound word is sometimes given by an etymological label:

披
305

披露する *hirō suru* announce, introduce; [original meaning, now archaic] open one's heart

2.6 Advanced Features

A number of features are particularly useful to the advanced student or scholar wishing to gain a deeper understanding of each character:

1. The indication of **function** for each character meaning, which helps the user learn new words more effectively. See **§ 7.1 Character Functions** for details.

2. A **system of labels** provides practical guidance on the style and usage associated with each sense. See **§ 7.2 System of Labels** for details.

3. Understanding is enhanced by **synonym articles** that show the precise distinctions between **kanji synonyms** (such as 測 CONJECTURE and 察 GUESS). See **§ 5.1 Discriminating Synonyms** for details.

4. To help the student understand the differences between closely related words, **usage notes** show the precise distinctions between **homophones**, or words that are pronounced alike but written differently. See **§ 5.2 Discriminating Homophones** for details.

5. To help the learner gain a deeper understanding of character meaning, the dictionary gives the **etymology** of characters and compound words and presents detailed information on **radicals**. See **§ 2.5 Compound Formation** and **§ 7.3 Character Etymology** for details.

3. READING

Reading kanji involves three distinct, but closely interrelated, mental processes: (1) recognizing and decoding the form of the character, (2) identifying the reading of the character, i.e., deciding which of the several *on* and *kun* readings applies to the word in question, and (3) associating the character with a particular meaning. Since kanji can be combined with each other to form countless compound words, the ability to read the characters benefits the student by accelerating his or her progress in learning new vocabulary items. In fact, there is a limit beyond which the student of the spoken language cannot progress without acquiring a firm knowledge of the written language.

The student learning how to read Japanese faces several difficulties. First is the large number of Chinese characters in comparison with alphabetic systems. Although the total number of characters that exist or have existed is said to be about 80,000, only several thousand of these have been used at any one time. To read contemporary Japanese, a knowledge of about 2000 characters is adequate for most purposes. A second problem is the complex shape of the characters and the large variety of character forms and styles. A third difficulty is that each character may have several readings, and there is no reliable way to determine which reading applies in a particular instance.

This dictionary presents ten features that make it a convenient reference tool for **reading** both contemporary and prewar Japanese. The features listed below enable the user to quickly and efficiently look up a large variety of character readings, styles, and forms as well as the meanings and readings of unknown characters and compounds. This is the first character dictionary for non-Japanese users to present such a wide range of character forms and styles in a single volume.

Summary of Features

General Features	1. A new scheme for looking up unknown characters. 2. Looking up unknown compounds. 3. A wide range of character forms. 4. Separate entries for nonstandard forms. 5. Easily confused forms. 6. Calligraphic and typeface styles. 7. A wide range of character readings. 8. Indication of the importance of readings. 9. All Japanese words and examples are romanized.
Advanced Features	10. Chinese forms and readings.

3.1 Quick Lookup Method

A major feature of this dictionary that makes it convenient for the reader is a new scheme for looking up characters with great speed. This enables the user to easily locate unknown characters, compounds, and their meanings. See SYSTEM OF KANJI INDEXING BY PATTERNS on p. 106a for details.

3.2 Character Forms and Styles

This dictionary presents a wide variety of character forms, calligraphic styles, and typeface styles needed for reading contemporary and classical Japanese. This includes the standard form, three kinds of nonstandard forms, the Chinese form, the three principal calligraphic styles, and the Ming and Gothic typefaces. The character forms are presented in a logical order, and various symbols and typefaces distinguish one category from another, as illustrated below:

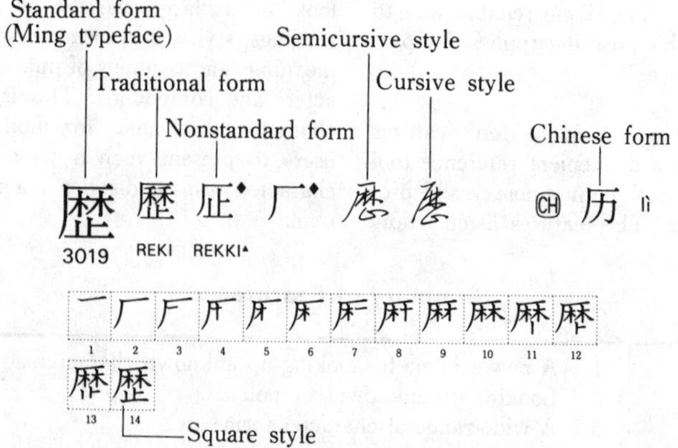

The character form is a theoretical construct—an abstraction based on various shapes that, in theory, has no physical identity. In the chart below, it is represented by thin strokes without embellishments. When a character is actually printed or written as a visual sign, it appears in a specific calligraphic or typeface style, such as the square style or the Ming typeface. A difference in calligraphic or typeface style is considered a difference in design, rather than a difference in character form. For example, 歴 and 歴, the Ming and Gothic typeface styles of 歴, are different *styles* of the standard form, whereas 歷 and 圧, the traditional form and handwritten abbreviation, are considered different *forms* of it.

Character Forms and Typeface Styles

Character Form	Standard Form		Nonstandard Forms (Ming typeface)			Modern Chinese
	Ming	Gothic	Traditional	Alternative	Handwritten	
歴	歴	歴	歷	—	圧 厂	历

Calligraphic Styles

Character Form	Square	Semicursive	Cursive
歴	歴	歴	歴

3.2.1 Character Forms Character form (字体 *jitai*) refers to the skeletal framework or delineation of the figure formed by a character. To ensure high accuracy and avoid duplicating the mistakes of existing works, the character forms in this dictionary were researched and methodically checked by experts. Three kinds of character forms are given:

1. The **standard form** is the form given for characters in the official Jōyō Kanji and Jinmei Kanji lists (approved characters). It is widely used in the mass media, government publications, education, literature, and so on. The ability to recognize this form is essential for reading contemporary Japanese.

2. The **nonstandard form** refers to a variant form other than the standard form of approved characters, and to a variant form other than the traditional form of unapproved characters. Nonstandard forms are of primary interest to advanced students. Three kinds of nonstandard forms are given:

   The **traditional form** (正字 *seiji*) is the full unsimplified form (orthodox form) introduced by the Chinese dictionary 康熙字典 *kōki jiten* in 1716. This was the standard form used in all publications in both China and Japan before language reforms were implemented, and is still the current standard in Hong Kong, Taiwan, and among overseas Chinese. This form is also used in certain publications in Japan, especially classical literature. A knowledge of this form is essential for reading prewar publications and classical Chinese.

   The **alternative form** (異体字 *itaiji*) is a variant form other than the traditional form. This includes the 俗字 *zokuji*, the "vernacular form," 略字 *ryakuji*, the "simplified form," and other character forms that are neither standard nor traditional but exist, or have existed, alongside the standard and traditional ones. The list of alternative forms is not exhaustive, but all important ones, both past and present, have been included.

   The **handwritten abbreviation** (筆写略字 *hissha-ryakuji*) is a simplified character form used in handwriting. This is not a different calligraphic style, nor is it a simplified variant in which the strokes have been run together (崩し字 *kuzushiji*)—it is a different character form in its own right. The handwritten abbreviation is restricted almost exclusively to handwriting, but may occasionally be found in print or on signboards.

   The nonstandard forms are listed along with their core meanings as separate entries at their own SKIP locations with a cross-reference to their corresponding standard forms. This is convenient when reading prewar literature, as it eliminates the need for looking up the standard form.

3. The **Chinese form** is described in **§ 7.4 Chinese.**

See GUIDE **§ 3.1 Character Forms** and GUIDE **§ 27. Nonstandard Entries** for format details.

3.2.2 Easily Confused Forms The great majority of characters have distinct graphic forms that are easily distinguished from each other. Some characters, however, are so similar in form that they are often confused by the learner and even by the native speaker. For example, 未 *mi* 'not yet' closely resembles 末 *matsu* 'termination', 幣 *hei* 'currency' closely resembles 弊 *hei* 'evil practice', etc. Such characters are often unrelated in meaning and pronunciation but are very similar in form. To aid the learner, they are identified by a cross-reference in the NOTE section:

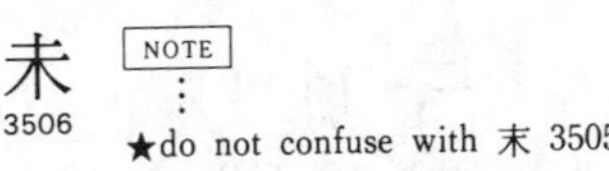

See also **§ 5. Discriminating** and GUIDE **§ 19.2.2 Supplementary Note.**

3.2.3 Calligraphic Styles **Calligraphic style** (書体 *shotai*) refers to the various styles of handwriting. Characters in the three principal calligraphic styles are given. The cursive and semicursive styles were written by expert calligraphers specifically for this dictionary. For the square style, a typeface based on handwriting was used or special fonts were made when unavailable. Calligraphic styles are of primary interest to advanced students.

1. The **square style** (楷書 *kaisho*) is the standard handwritten style used for official and formal purposes, education, and whenever clarity and unambiguity are required. Each stroke is written separately to produce a clearly legible form. The square style is similar to the Ming typeface, but differs from it in various details.

2. The **semicursive style** (行書 *gyōsho*), the most widely used calligraphic style, is used in writing letters, personal memos, and the like. The strokes are loosely joined together in a smooth movement of the brush or pen.

3. The **cursive style** (草書 *sōsho*) is used mostly for artistic effect, and is no longer very common. The character form is greatly simplified and the strokes are joined in a continuous smooth movement of the brush or pen to achieve great writing speed.

See GUIDE **§ 3.2 Calligraphic Styles** for format details.

3.2.4 Typeface Styles **Typeface style** (印刷体 *insatsutai*) refers to a uniform style or design of the character type. The two principal typeface styles are given:

1. The **Ming typeface** (明朝体 *minchōtai*) is the standard, most common kanji typeface in Japan. It is characterized by thick vertical strokes, thin horizontal strokes, and triangular serifs at the ends of horizontal strokes. The Ming typeface originated in carved woodblocks that were used for printing during the Ming dynasty in China (1368–1644 A.D.). This typeface is similar to the square style, but differs from it in various details.

2. The **Gothic typeface** (ゴシック体 *goshikkutai*), which is used in all compounds and examples, is the Japanese equivalent of boldface. Characterized by thick smooth strokes and clean edges, this is the second most common kanji typeface in Japan:

歴 歴史
3019

See GUIDE **§ 3.3 Typeface Styles** for format details.

3.3 Character Readings

A distinctive feature of Japanese is that each character may have one or more **readings**. This refers to one of several sequences of speech sounds associated with a character; that is, to the Chinese-derived pronunciation, or *on* reading, and the native Japanese pronunciation, or *kun* reading. The entry-head data presents all contemporary readings, as well as important historical and archaic ones when necessary:

行 行 り　CH 行 xíng háng
212　KŌ GYŌ AN i(ku) yu(ku) -yu(ki) -yuki -i(ki)
-iki okona(u)

The readings are presented in a logical order by type of reading and degree of importance. Various symbols and typefaces distinguish approved readings from unapproved ones, *on* from *kun*, and other categories. The pronunciation of each reading is given by the romanized transcription, with parentheses indicating kana endings (*okurigana*).

3.3.1 Kinds of Readings

Seven kinds of character readings are given. The first three are of interest to all users; the last four are of primary interest to the intermediate and advanced student.

1. The **principal reading** (主読み *shuyomi*) is the most common or representative character reading, and is used in this dictionary as a key for classifying characters in various lists and indexes.

2. The ***on* reading** (音読み *on'yomi*) is the Chinese-derived reading of a character. The entry-head data lists all approved *on* readings and a wide range of unapproved ones, from the traditional 漢音 *kan'on* 'Han reading' and 呉音 *goon* 'Wu reading' to the unconventional 外音 *gaion* 'foreign reading'. Although approved readings are distinguished from unapproved ones, the other categories are not marked in any special way since this is not a historical dictionary.

3. The ***kun* reading** (訓読み *kun'yomi*) is the native Japanese reading of a character. All approved *kun* readings and a wide range of unapproved ones are given, with *okurigana* shown in parentheses. Hyphens distinguish words from word elements.

4. **Special readings** (熟字訓 *jukujikun*) that can be isolated as independent readings in their own right, such as 凹 *boko* in 凸凹 *dekoboko* 'unevenness, etc.', are similar to ordinary readings and are so treated. Technically speaking, such readings are not really "special," but they are so marked because that is how they are classified in the Jōyō Kanji list. See also **§ 7.1.6 Special Readings.**

5. The **unapproved reading** (表外音訓 *hyōgai onkun*) is an *on* or *kun* reading not listed in the Jōyō Kanji list but sufficiently common to merit inclusion in the dictionary. The distinction between approved and unapproved readings applies only to characters in the Jōyō Kanji list. Although the treatment of unapproved readings is not exhaustive, a sufficiently wide range of readings has been included to meet the needs of the advanced student.

6. The **name reading** (名乗り *nanori*) is used only in the writing of personal, family, and place names but not in ordinary words. Many ordinary *on* and *kun* readings, such as 山 *yama* in 山本 *yamamoto,* can be used to write names, but the name readings are used exclusively in names. Name readings are given for all characters in the official Jinmei Kanji list. See also **§7.1.7 Names.**

7. The **Chinese reading** is described in **§ 7.4 Chinese.**

See GUIDE **§ 4. Character Readings** for format details and OUTLINE OF JAPANESE WRITING SYSTEM **§ 2. Introduction of Chinese Characters to Japan.**

3.3.2 Importance of Readings

The relative importance of readings is shown by distinguishing unapproved readings from approved ones by a superscript solid triangle ▲. This establishes a hierarchy of importance between the readings, and enables the beginner and intermediate student to ignore the unapproved readings while concentrating on the more important approved ones.

3.4 Romanization

Some educators maintain that it is best to avoid romanization and use kana to indicate pronunciation. In this dictionary, we have adopted romanization in order to make it accessible to users who cannot read kana, such as complete beginners, students of Chinese, or researchers and linguists using the dictionary for reference.

There are three important systems for romanizing Japanese: the Hepburn system (ヘボン式 *hebonshiki*), the Kunrei system (訓令式 *kunreishiki*), and the Nippon system (日本式 *nipponshiki*). The system adopted here is the Hepburn system, with the slight modifications introduced in Kenkyusha's *New Japanese-English Dictionary* (see **Appendix 4. Kana and Romanization** for details). Although this system has some built-in problems that make it less than ideal for pedagogical purposes, we have adopted it because it is the best known and most widely used system, and because English speakers, the primary target of this dictionary, find it particularly easy to learn.

All Japanese words and examples are followed by romanized transcriptions showing their pronunciations. Romanization is also used for character readings, subentry headings, and so on. Romanized transcriptions are set in easy-to-read sanserif typeface in order to distinguish them from other explanatory matter. Word division in romanized transcriptions closely reflects the function of, and the semantic relationship between, word and sentence components, as shown below:

一騎当千の武者 *ikki-tōsen no musha* matchless warrior, match for a thousand

See GUIDE **§ 29. Romanization** for format details.

4. WRITING

There are two aspects in learning how to write Japanese: (1) learning how to write the characters, and (2) learning how to compose texts. The serious student will no doubt want to learn how to write the language. The ability to write kanji will make it easier to memorize them and will provide preliminary knowledge for the study of calligraphy.

The student learning how to write Japanese faces several difficulties: the large number of characters and their complex shapes and many variations; the need to learn the correct stroke order; a high degree of variation in kana and kanji orthography; and the large number of easily confused homophones (words sounding alike but written differently).

This dictionary presents eleven features that make it an excellent guide for **writing.** The first five features help the student write the characters in the proper form and proportion; the last six aid the student compose texts with greater clarity and precision.

Summary of Features

General Features	1. Detailed stroke order diagrams. 2. An appendix on stroke order principles. 3. The three principal calligraphic styles. 4. Stroke-count data. 5. An appendix on stroke counting principles. 6. An appendix on kana orthography. 7. Indication of *okurigana* affixes. 8. An appendix on *okurigana* rules.
Advanced Features	9. Detailed information on orthographic variants. 10. Articles discriminate between kanji synonyms. 11. Usage notes discriminate between homophones.

4.1 Stroke Order

To write a character in the proper form and proportion, it is important to learn the correct **stroke order** (筆順 *hitsujun* or 書き順 *kakijun*). A knowledge of stroke order is essential for learning how to write the characters and is a prerequisite for studying calligraphy. It is also an effective way to master stroke counting. The following information is given on stroke order:

1. **Stroke order diagrams,** in which the last frame shows the full character in the standard square style, are given:

   光 2391 | 1 丨 2 丨丨 3 ⺌ 4 ⺌ 5 ⺌ 6 光

   Thoroughly researched for accuracy, these diagrams were prepared by experts specifically for this dictionary. For the convenience of the user, the order of writing is presented stroke-by-stroke, regardless of the number of strokes. Unlike other reference works, no attempt has been made to save space by cross-referencing to other entries. If there is more than one way to write the character (e.g. 必), only the standard stroke order is shown. See also GUIDE **§ 6. Stroke Order Diagram.**

2. A knowledge of the **stroke order principles** should enable one to write most characters correctly without referring to the stroke order diagrams. These are explained in detail in **Appendix 3. How to Write Kanji.**

4.2 Calligraphic Styles

Calligraphy is a highly developed art form with a long tradition in both China and Japan, but it is not necessary to learn it to be able to write Japanese. Though this dictionary is not a manual on calligraphy, it does help the user interested in the subject by (1) presenting the three main calligraphic styles, i.e., the square, semicursive, and cursive styles, and (2) by providing detailed guidance on stroke order, a knowledge of which is a prerequisite for studying calligraphy. Calligraphy is of primary interest to advanced students. See **§ 4.1 Stroke Order** and **§ 3.2.3 Calligraphic Styles** for details.

4.3 Stroke Counting

To write the characters correctly, the student must be aware of where one stroke ends and the next one begins; in other words, he or she must know how to count strokes. The ability to count strokes is also essential for using character dictionaries effectively. The following guidance is provided on stroke counting:

1. The **reference data box** gives the **stroke-count data** for the entry character. The stroke-count of nonstandard entries can be determined from the **margin guide**. See GUIDE **§ 7.3 Strokes** for format details.

2. The **principles of stroke counting** are explained in **Appendix 2. How to Count Strokes,** along with charts to help speed up the counting process.

3. Difficult-to-count characters are cross-referenced at *incorrect* stroke-count locations (see SYSTEM OF KANJI INDEXING BY PATTERNS **§ 2.6 Cross-References** for details).

4.4 Kana Orthography

One difficulty faced by the student of written Japanese is its variable kana orthography; that is, the variation in the kana endings, called *okurigana* (送り仮名), that are attached to a kanji base or stem. For example, *yuki-* 'bound for' is written either 行き or 行, depending on editorial policy or personal preference. This dictionary provides the following guidance on kana orthography:

1. The kana systems and kana orthography are described in **Appendix 4. Kana and Romanization**.

2. The entry-head data indicates in parentheses the standard ***okurigana*** **affixes** of *kun* readings in conformity with the official rules published by the Ministry of Education. The compounds and examples throughout the dictionary also conform to the official rules when applicable. Important nonstandard variations are shown when necessary.

3. The official **rules for affixing *okurigana*** are explained in detail in **Appendix 5. Rules for Okurigana.**

4.5 Advanced Features

A number of features are particularly useful to the advanced student learning how to write Japanese:

1. The dictionary provides full guidance on **orthographic variants** (such as 替える *kaeru* 'replace' and 換える *kaeru* 'exchange'). This helps the student write with greater precision. See **§ 5.4 Discriminating Variants** for details.

2. This dictionary helps the student write with greater clarity and precision by showing the distinctions between **kanji synonyms** (such as 測 CONJECTURE and 察 GUESS). See **§ 5.1 Discriminating Synonyms** for details.

3. A characteristic of Japanese that may pose considerable difficulties to the student is the large number of **homophones,** or words that are pronounced alike but written differently (such as 開く *aku* 'open' and 空く *aku* 'become vacant'). This dictionary helps the student write with greater precision by showing the differences and similarities between such words. See **§ 5.2 Discriminating Homophones** for details.

PART II: ADVANCED FEATURES

The purpose of **PART II** is to describe in detail the features of this dictionary that are particularly useful to the advanced student and scholar. Beginners may safely skip this section. The general features are described in **PART I: GENERAL FEATURES** on p. 65a. For convenience, the chart on p. 62a summarizes the most important features.

5. DISCRIMINATING

Each kanji in Japanese may have one or more forms, readings, and meanings. If the forms, readings, or meanings of one character resemble or are interchangeable with those of another, confusion may arise. Four kinds of problems may occur:

1. Identity or similarity in **meaning** (*synonyms*), e.g., 形 *kei* 'shape' and 状 *jō* 'form'.
2. Identity in **sound** (*homophones*): identical reading but different form and/or meaning, e.g., 開く *aku* 'open' and 空く *aku* 'become vacant'.
3. Similarity in **form**, e.g., 未 *mi* 'not yet' and 末 *matsu* 'termination'.
4. Interchangeability of **form** (*orthographic variants*): interchangeable forms that are identical in reading and/or meaning, e.g., 希 *ki* 'rare' and 稀 *ki* 'rare'.

A unique feature of this dictionary is the in-depth manner in which it treats the differences and similarities between similar, identical, or interchangeable items like the above. The various features listed below make the dictionary an excellent guide for **discriminating** between such easily confused items, thereby helping the student understand shades of meaning and write with clarity and precision.

Summary of Features

1. Articles discriminate between kanji synonyms.
2. Synonym headwords.
3. Synonym keywords.
4. Cross-references to synonyms group members.
5. Simple kanji thesaurus.
6. Usage notes discriminate between homophones.
7. Orthographic labels.
8. Cross-references to homophone group members.
9. Examples in usage notes.
10. Supplementary notes.
11. Discrimination of easily confused forms.
12. Detailed information on orthographic variants.

5.1 Discriminating Synonyms

The words of a language form a closely-linked network of interdependent units. The meaning of a word or expression cannot really be understood unless its relationships with other closely related words are taken into account. The student of a foreign language is often faced with choosing between words of similar, but not identical, meaning. In English, for example, such words as *kill*, *murder*, and *execute* share the meaning of 'put to death', but they differ considerably in usage and connotation. The ability to distinguish between such words not only allows one to gain a fuller understanding of their individual shades of meaning, but also helps the student write with greater clarity and precision.

A special feature of this dictionary, presented here for the first time, is the complete guidance it offers for the precise distinctions between **kanji synonyms**, or characters of similar meaning. Since a proper understanding of the meanings of each character is essential for the effective mastery of the Japanese vocabulary, this will be of considerable benefit to the serious student. The kanji synonyms serve as a powerful learning aid for the following reasons:

1. They show the differences and similarities between closely-related characters.
2. They act as a network of cross-references for quickly locating any synonym group member.
3. They act as a simple kanji thesaurus.
4. They provide the educator with a valuable source of reference data.

Below is a description of the various features designed to achieve these aims.

5.1.1 SYNONYMS Section The SYNONYMS section lists groups of kanji synonyms along with their English keywords in a single **synonyms article** for the principal senses of each main entry character:

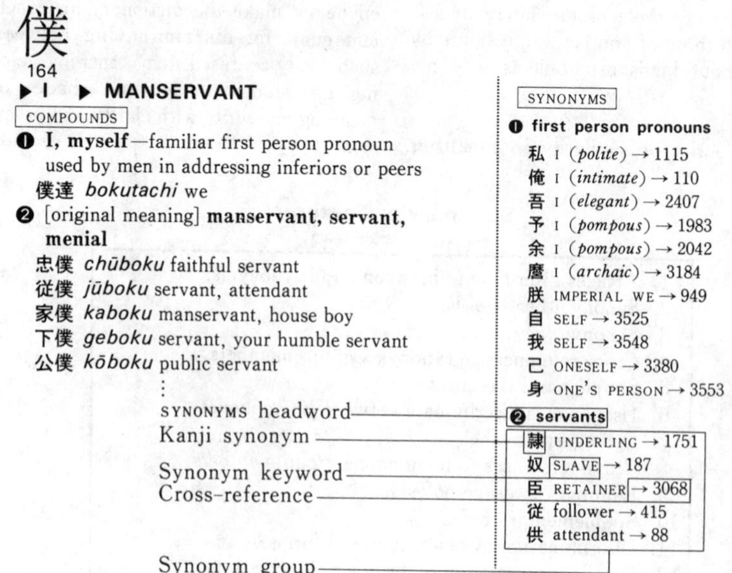

The SYNONYMS section consists of the following elements:

1. **Kanji synonyms** or **synonyms** as used here basically refers to two or more characters, usually *on* word elements, that share a basic meaning, or whose meanings are included in that of a more general term. For example, 私 and 俺 above share the meaning 'I', whereas 奴 and 臣 are included in the meaning of the headword **servants.** See GUIDE **§ 15.3 Semantic Relationships** for details.

2. **Synonym group** refers to a group of two or more kanji synonyms. The SYNONYMS section for a particular entry character includes all the members of that group, except for the entry character itself. Since most characters have more than one sense, it follows that a given character can belong to more than one synonym group; that is, a different group may exist for each principal sense of a character. In the example above, 僕 belongs to the **first person pronouns** group for sense ❶ and to the **servants** group for sense ❷.

3. The **SYNONYMS headword**, which appears at the beginning of each synonym group, is a concise English word or phrase selected to express the semantic relationship (usually the shared meaning) between the members of that group. In the example above, the headword **servants** is a general term that includes the meanings of all the group members. For example, both *slaves* and *retainers* are kinds of servants. The numbers preceding the headwords point to the sense number to which that group corresponds.

4. The **synonym keyword** following each group member is a concise English equivalent that most aptly represents the particular character sense relevant to that group. Small capitals indicate that the keyword is identical with the character's core meaning. In establishing the keywords, the denotation, connotation, and range of application of each character were carefully analyzed and compared so that the keywords reflect the fine differences between group members while enabling the user to quickly grasp the meaning of each.

5. The **cross-reference** consists of an arrow → followed by a numeral that refers to the entry number where that character appears as a main entry. The kanji synonyms thus act as a network of cross-references for quickly locating any member of a synonym group from any of the others. By consulting these entries and studying their character meanings and compounds, the user can acquire a fuller understanding of each group member.

See GUIDE **§ 15. SYNONYMS Section** for format details.

5.1.2 Powerful Learning Aid As we have seen, the SYNONYMS headwords show how the members of a synonym group *resemble* each other, while the keywords show how they *differ* from each other. Together, they serve as a powerful learning tool. Let us see how this helps the learner gain an in-depth understanding of the character 破:

破 ▶ **BREAK**
1150

COMPOUNDS

❶ⓐ [original meaning] BREAK, smash
ⓑ BREAK through, penetrate
ⓒ BREAK out (of jail), escape
❷ BREAK the enemy, defeat
❸ⓐ (act contrary to) BREAK (as a promise), breach, violate
ⓑ BREAK with (the moral conventions), be exceptional
❹ BREAK down, go to pieces, go broke
⋮

SYNONYMS

❶ⓐ **break**
壊 BREAK DOWN → 756
折 BREAK OFF → 253
割る crack → 1816
裂 SPLIT → 2687
砕 CRUSH UP → 1134
崩 CRUMBLE → 2296
ⓑ **penetrate**
貫 PENETRATE → 2460
透 PASS THROUGH → 3108
❷ **win**
勝 WIN → 1005
克 OVERCOME → 2046
征 CONQUER → 293

In the above table, the core meaning and English equivalents show that the central concept represented by 破 is BREAK. Referring to sense ❶ⓐ of the SYNONYMS section, which corresponds to sense ❶ⓐ of the COMPOUNDS section, we find the headword **break**, which indicates the meaning *shared* by the group members. By comparing the individual keywords, such as 壊 BREAK DOWN, 折 BREAK OFF, and 裂 SPLIT, we can see how they *differ* from each other. Studying the core meaning, English equivalents, headwords, and keywords together, rather than in isolation, provides a good understanding of the distinctive features of each group member.

To gain an even deeper understanding, turn to the entry numbers indicated by the cross-references, where detailed character meanings and illustrative examples for each group member appear. The table below brings these together for ready reference:

Basic Concept: BREAK			
Character	**Keyword**	**English Equivalent**	**Typical Compounds**
破 *ha*	BREAK	break, smash	破壊する *hakai suru* break (down), destroy, wreck
壊 *kai*	BREAK DOWN	break down, destroy, smash; (of a dam) burst	倒壊する *tōkai suru* collapse, be destroyed, crumble
折 *setsu*	BREAK OFF	(separate through the application of a sudden bending force) break off (as a branch), break (a bone), snap (in two), split	骨折 *kossetsu* bone fracture
割る *waru*	crack	ⓐ crack, break ⓑ split, chop (wood)	コップを割る *koppu o waru* crack [break] a glass
裂 *retsu*	SPLIT	ⓐ (separate or become separated into pieces) split, tear, crack ⓑ crack, fissure	破裂 *haretsu* explosion, bursting
砕 *sai*	CRUSH UP	crush up, break into pieces, smash	破砕する *hasai suru* crush, smash, crack to pieces
崩 *hō*	CRUMBLE	crumble, collapse	崩壊する *hōkai suru* collapse, crumble, break down, cave in

Comparing the meanings and examples for each group member shows their subtle differences in connotation (nuances) and range of application. For example, whereas 破 means to break in general, 折 implies the application of a sudden force to such things as branches and bones, 崩 denotes breaking into small pieces, and so on. See also **§2.2.1 Concise English Keyword.**

5.1.3 Simple Kanji Thesaurus The SYNONYMS sections and **Appendix 11. List of Kanji Synonym Groups** make it possible to use this dictionary as a **simple kanji thesaurus.** This helps the student composing texts in Japanese select the word most appropriate to the context so as to achieve greater clarity of expression, and, to a limited extent, makes it possible to locate characters from their meanings (see **Appendix 11** for details).

Consulting the entries for the various members of a synonym group will often lead to many words that are synonymous or closely related to the meaning expressed by the SYNONYMS headword. There are two ways to do this: (1) consulting the cross-references in the SYNONYMS sections, and (2) consulting **Appendix 11,** which lists the synonym groups alphabetically by their headwords. For example, to find Japanese synonyms for *break*, consult the entries for each group member indicated by the cross-references (entry numbers) in the SYNONYMS section for 破 (or in the **break** group in **Appendix 11**), where such words as 破壊 *hakai* 'breaking (down)', 破砕 *hasai* 'crushing', 崩壊 *hōkai* 'collapse', etc., can be found.

Admittedly, consulting several entries in this way is a laborious task. However, since the thesaurus function of this dictionary is only incidental to its main purpose as a learning aid, this is only to be expected. The synonym data appearing here will, in fact, serve as the basis for the first kanji thesaurus ever compiled, as well as for various software applications and computer-aided research on kanji semantic fields.

＊＊＊

In conclusion, studying the meanings of closely related characters together, rather than as isolated units, stimulates the interest of the learner and increases learning effectiveness. Moreover, the kanji synonyms help the student write with greater precision, and provide the educator and scholar with a valuable source of reference data.

5.2 Discriminating Homophones

One characteristic of Japanese is the existence of a large number of *homophones*, or words that are pronounced the same but written differently and usually differing in meaning. *Kōki* and *kikō*, for instance, each represent about a dozen words in common use, and the only way to distinguish between such compounds as 機構 *kikō* 'mechanism' and 帰港 *kikō* 'returning to the harbor' is through the characters. This is not unlike *principal* and *principle* in English, which are pronounced the same but have different meanings depending on their spellings.

Although *on* homophones like the above may occasionally cause confusion in the spoken language, they are easily distinguished in the written language. Since each character has a distinct form and meaning, and since the meanings of *on* homophones are normally unrelated to each other, such words are not likely to be confused as long as they are written in kanji.

On the other hand, the abundance of *kun* homophones is a source of confusion to Japanese and non-Japanese alike. Not only can each character have many *kun* readings, but many *kun* words can be written with a bewildering variety of characters. In extreme cases, such as the word *sasu*, a *kun* word can be written in dozens of ways, though only several of these are in common use. Unlike *on* homophones, the majority of *kun* homophones are often very close or even identical in meaning and thus easily confused. Study the table below:

Easily Distinguished		**Easily Confused**	
	hashi		*noboru*
橋	bridge	上る	go up (steps, a hill)
端	end, edge	登る	climb, scale
箸	chopsticks	昇る	ascend, rise (up to the sky)

Although the meanings of some *kun* homophones, such as *hashi* in the above table, are far apart and easily distinguished, in many other cases the differences may be subtle and a source of confusion. For example, *noboru* can be written in the three ways shown in the table, which are closely related and easily confused.

Another problem with *kun* homophones is their variable orthography. Two or more characters are often partially or completely interchangeable in some senses but not in others. For example, 解ける *tokeru* and 溶ける *tokeru* are interchangeable in the sense of 'melt, thaw' but not in the sense of 'come loose', which is always written 解ける. On the other hand, the meanings of some homophones are identical or are so similar that no meaningful distinction can be made between them. For example, **yawarakai** 'soft, subdued; gentle' is written 柔らかい or 軟らかい with exactly the same meaning. This is similar to the variant spellings of such English words as *judgment* and *judgement*, which are identical in meaning.

A further difficulty is that the distinctions between independent *kun* words do not necessarily apply to word elements. For example, although 換える **kaeru** 'exchange' is supposedly distinguished from 替える **kaeru** 'replace', the word **ryōgae** 'exchange of money' is written 両替, not 両換, as might be expected.

Because of these complications, students, especially students learning how to write Japanese, are often at a loss when attempting to select a character for a particular context. For many *kun* homophones, a universally-accepted orthography simply does not exist. Theoretically, the choice of character should be based on meaning, but in fact it is often governed by personal preferences.

To compound these difficulties, the complex problems inherent in *kun* homophones have been mostly ignored by existing reference works. Even dictionaries for native Japanese speakers often disagree over the correct character for a particular meaning. In extreme cases, the meanings of a group of homophones are lumped together in a single article without any indication of how to differentiate between them.

To summarize, homophones in Japanese present the following difficulties:

1. There are many homophones in Japanese.
2. The differences between homophones are often subtle and confusing.
3. There are numerous orthographic variants.
4. Usage is sometimes contrary to expectations.
5. Writing in Japanese often involves uncertainty over orthography.
6. The treatment of homophones in existing reference works is inadequate.

The serious student of Japanese will eventually have to tackle the problems related to homophones. Since each character has a distinct meaning, it follows that an effective way to distinguish between homophones is to understand the meaning of each character. Although we have done everything possible to simplify this task, a certain amount of confusion is, ultimately, unavoidable, since the relative abundance of homophones is inherent to the nature of the Japanese script.

To help the student overcome the special problems posed by homophones in Japanese, this dictionary provides thorough and complete guidance on the discrimination of all one-character *kun* homophones in current use, and a small number of other kinds of easily-confused homophones. Below is a description of the various features designed to achieve this aim.

5.2.1 Usage Notes A feature of enormous value to the student, appearing here for the first time in English, is the presentation of **usage notes**. These conveniently bring together in a single article the meanings for every member of a homophone group, along with other information that helps discriminate between them. The usage notes show precisely in which sense each homophone is used:

丘
3495

USAGE

oka

丘

[sometimes also 岡] hill, hillock, mound

岡

① [usu. 丘] hill, hillock, mound—used chiefly in proper names

② [sometimes also 傍-] [in compounds] outsider, third party, bystander

陸

land, shore

傍-

[usu. 岡] outsider, third party, bystander

★丘 and 岡 have the same meaning. The former is used in both common nouns and place names, while the latter is used chiefly in the writing of proper names.

HOMOPHONES

oka ⇨ 岡 2997 陸 543 傍 147

By comparing the English equivalents, the user can accurately grasp the differences and similarities in shades of meaning and in usage between easily confused homophones. The homophones treated in the USAGE section are mostly independent *kun* words and word elements that are etymologically related, but easily confused compounds (both *on* and *kun*) and synonyms are sometimes also included. See **GUIDE § 16. USAGE Section** for format details.

5.2.2 Orthographic Labels The **orthographic labels** indicate the degree of interchangeability between orthographic variants and show in which sense(s) these variants are interchangeable. In the above example, 丘 and 岡 are interchangeable in the sense of 'hill', but not in the sense of 'outsider'. Since orthographic variation is a source of much confusion, these labels will prove most useful to the user attempting to interpret or produce Japanese texts. See also **§ 5.4 Discriminating Variants.**

5.2.3 Cross-References The usage notes appear only at the entry for the most important member of a homophone group. The HOMOPHONES and NOTE sections act as a network of **cross-references** that enables the user to immediately identify the existence of other group members, and to quickly locate the compounds and examples for each. By studying the compounds and examples for each group member, the user can get a fuller understanding of how each is used. See **GUIDE § 17. HOMOPHONES Section** and **GUIDE § 19. NOTE Section** for details.

5.2.4 Illustrative Examples The usage notes do not normally include compounds and examples, which can be located at their appropriate entries through the cross-references. Sometimes, however, **illustrative examples** appear in the USAGE section itself in order to further clarify the differences between easily confused homophones. See also **GUIDE § 16.2.3 Illustrative Examples.**

5.2.5 Supplementary Notes The equivalents in a usage note are sometimes followed by **supplementary notes**, which provide additional information on differences in usage. In the above example, the supplementary note (preceded by ★) discusses the usage of 丘 and 岡.

* * *

In conclusion, the usage notes and other features described above serve as an effective learning aid. They enable the user to study the differences and similarities between the meanings of easily confused words, thereby providing a better understanding of each. They also help the user write with greater clarity and precision by helping him or her select the character most appropriate to a particular context. Since the differences between homophones, which are often quite subtle, are a source of confusion to Japanese and non-Japanese alike, these features should prove to be of enormous value to the student.

5.3 Discriminating Forms

Characters having **easily confused forms,** such as 未 and 末, are identified by cross-references in the NOTE section. See **§3.2.2 Easily Confused Forms** for details.

5.4 Discriminating Variants

A characteristic of the Japanese script that the learner must deal with is its variable orthography; that is, the many words that can be written with different character combinations. For example, 盲 is interchangeable with 妄 in such compounds as 妄想 (＝盲想) *mōsō* 'wild idea', but not in 盲従 *mōjū* 'blind obedience'. Two or more characters that are partially or completely interchangeable in this manner are referred to as **orthographic variants.** One such variant is often a **phonetically replaced character,** which refers to the characters that are now replaced by the **phonetic replacement characters** (see OUTLINE OF JAPANESE WRITING SYSTEM **§2.5 Language Reforms** for details).

Another kind of orthographic variation is the alternation between the kana and kanji scripts. For example, *neko* 'cat' may be written in kanji (猫), hiragana (ねこ), or katakana (ネコ). This aspect of orthography is not treated in this dictionary since it is a dictionary of characters, not of words.

An important feature of this dictionary is the full guidance it provides for discriminating between orthographic variants. This is particularly useful to the advanced student, since a knowledge of the differences and similarities between orthographic variants helps write with greater precision. The **orthographic labels** (enclosed in square brackets) indicate the orthographic variant(s) of a word or word element:

箱
2711

【hako 箱】
①ⓐ [sometimes also 函] [also suffix] box, case, chest, bin
ⓑ counter for boxes
② *slang* railway car
③ *slang* shamisen

函
3001

❶ [now usu. 箱 *hako*] [original meaning] box, case, mailbox
❷ [now also 関 *kan* 3328] used phonetically for *han* (in Chinese)
❸ abbrev. of 函館 *hakodate*, name of a city in Hokkaido

The orthographic labels serve three purposes:

1. To indicate the degree of interchangeability between orthographic variants. The labels also indicate whether the variants are interchangeable in contemporary Japanese, or over historical periods. In the example above, the labels indicate that 箱 *hako* is common while 函 *hako* is unusual.
2. To specify the sense(s) in which the orthographic variants are interchangeable. For example, 箱 *hako* and 函 *hako* are interchangeable in the sense of 'box', but not in the sense of 'counter for boxes'.
3. To serve as a cross-reference to the orthographic variants of the entry character, enabling the user to study their differences and similarities.

The meanings and format of the orthographic labels, which are mostly self-explanatory, are explained in detail in GUIDE **§22. Orthographic Labels.**

6. REFERRING

One problem with current and past character dictionaries is their lack of a systematic cross-reference network; that is, they fail to systematically bring to the user's attention the various relations (such as similarity in sound, form, and meaning) that exist between characters. This deprives learners of a means to deepen their knowledge by studying the differences and similarities between closely-related characters.

To round out a practical reference work, an extensive network of cross-references and eleven appendixes provide the user with a wealth of useful information and supplementary data in readily accessible form. This enhances the user's understanding and is invaluable to the advanced student, the educator, and the scholar. The following features make this dictionary an invaluable tool for **referring**:

Summary of Features

1. Eleven appendixes with detailed supplementary data.
2. An extensive network of cross-references.
3. Frequency statistics for main entry characters.
4. Grade of character.

In addition, various items in the entry-head data, such as the nonstandard forms, calligraphic styles, and stroke-count data, as well as miscellaneous items such as the degree of importance for each character sense, also serve as useful reference data.

Compilers of textbooks and developers of kanji curricula, teaching materials, or courseware will find this material particularly useful. For example, information on frequency of occurrence helps in compiling graded lessons based on actual statistics, while the indication of degree of importance for character senses facilitates the preparation of materials in which the characters are used only in their most frequent senses. Teachers will no doubt find many other ways to utilize such information in a manner most suitable to their specific needs.

6.1 Appendixes

The eleven **appendixes** listed below give the user quick access to a valuable source of supplementary data. See the introduction to each appendix for a detailed description.

1. **SKIP Rules: Theory and Practice**: a practical and theoretical description of how to identify, divide, and subclassify characters according to SKIP rules.
2. **How to Count Strokes**: explains the principles of stroke counting, which help one write the characters correctly.
3. **How to Write Kanji**: explains the principles of stroke order, which enable one to write most characters correctly without referring to the stroke order diagrams.
4. **Kana and Romanization**: presents charts and descriptions of hiragana, katakana, and romanization.
5. **Rules for Okurigana**: explains the official rules for affixing *okurigana* to aid the student learning to write.

6. **The Radicals**: describes the radical system and presents a detailed **Radical Chart,** which helps in understanding etymology and in using other dictionaries.
7. **Historical Tables**: presents various historical tables, such as the signs of the zodiac, which are useful for reading historical texts.
8. **Abbreviations of Place Names**: lists abbreviations of country and other place names for reference.
9. **Core Meanings Arranged by Frequency**: lists all main entry characters in order of frequency of occurrence along with their core meanings for ready reference.
10. **Jōyō Kanji List**: presents the official list of Jōyō Kanji classified by school grade for quick reference.
11. **List of Kanji Synonym Groups**: lists all the synonym groups together for quick reference, which makes it possible to look up characters from their meanings and serves as a simple kanji thesaurus.

6.2 Cross-Reference Network

An extensive **network of cross-references** directs the user to a wealth of information useful to both the learner and the educator. For convenience, the cross-references are briefly described below, followed by parenthetical references to where they are described in detail:

1. Radical variants and simplified forms are cross-referenced to their parent radicals (GUIDE **§ 8.2.2**).
2. All synonym group members are cross-referenced to each other (GUIDE **§ 15.2.2**).
3. Equivalents in usage articles are sometimes replaced by a cross-reference (GUIDE **§ 16.2.2**).
4. All homophone group members are cross-referenced to each other (GUIDE **§ 17.**).
5. Cross-reference notes point to usage notes, compound formation articles, easily confused characters, etc. (GUIDE **§ 19.**).
6. Character meanings are sometimes cross-referenced to other entries or entry parts (GUIDE **§ 20.9**).
7. Cross-references may follow or replace compounds (GUIDE **§ 21.4**).
8. Orthographic labels point to orthographic variants of the entry character (GUIDE **§ 22.**).
9. Nonstandard entries are cross-referenced to their corresponding standard forms (GUIDE **§ 27.**).
10. Cross-reference entries at incorrect SKIP locations point to correct locations (GUIDE **§ 28.**).
11. "Lost-radical" characters in the **Radical Index** are cross-referenced to their traditional locations (**How to Use the Radical Index** on p. 1929).
12. Cross-references at incorrect SKIP locations in the **Pattern Index** point to correct locations (SYSTEM OF KANJI INDEXING BY PATTERNS **§ 2.6 Cross-References**).

6.3 Character Importance

The **degree of importance** of the entry character is indicated by the frequency and the grade. This enables the student to know the relative importance of each character, and helps the teacher compile graded lessons. The degree of importance is also given for character meanings (**§ 2.3.3 Importance of Character Senses**) and character readings (**§ 3.3.2**

Importance of Readings).

6.3.1 Frequency The **frequency** is a number from 1 to 2135 that expresses the relative frequency of occurrence of a character in Modern Japanese; this normally, but not necessarily, indicates the ranking of each character in decreasing order of importance. It is presented as follows:

1. The frequency of main entry characters is given in the reference data box; the frequency of other characters is not given since it is so low as to be insignificant (GUIDE § 7.5).

絹 1361 | Freq 1185

2. **Appendix 9. Core Meanings Arranged by Frequency** lists all main entry characters in order of frequency.

6.3.2 Grade The **grade** is a classification that indicates the entry type, status, or school grade for each character. It is presented as follows:

1. The reference data box gives the grade of the entry character (GUIDE § 7.4).

絹 1361 | Grade Jōyō-6

2. **Appendix 10. Jōyō Kanji List** lists the official Jōyō Kanji by school grade.

7. OTHER ADVANCED FEATURES

This dictionary includes many features to help the learner understand the meanings and functions of each character. Most of these are described in detail in **§ 2. Understanding.** This section focuses on a number of features that are particularly useful to the advanced student or scholar wishing to gain a deeper understanding. It also describes how students of Japanese who are also interested in Chinese can benefit from the dictionary. The following features are described in the sections below:

Summary of Features

1. Functions of characters as words or word elements.
2. System of labels.
3. Detailed information on radicals.
4. Character etymology.
5. Chinese forms and readings.

7.1 Character Functions

Each character may, in addition to one or more meanings, have various grammatical and syntactic **functions.** One of the most important characteristics of kanji is their role as **word elements;** that is, their ability to form countless compound words by being combined with each other. New words can be formed by adding an **affix** (suffix or prefix) to a base, or by joining **combining forms** with each other. For example, the suffix -済 *-zumi* 'completed' is attached to 点

検 *tenken* 'inspection' to yield 点検済 *tenkenzumi* 'inspection completed'.

Another important function of kanji is as a **free word**, which is any word that can be used independently. Other functions include abbreviations, function words, counters, units, titles, numerals, and phonetic substitutes. Affixes, combining forms, and free words can be combined with each other in various ways, the most important of which are shown below:

combining form + combining form	外＋人→外人	*gaijin*	foreigner
combining form + free word	来＋年→来年	*rainen*	next year
free word + suffix	外国＋人→外国人	*gaikokujin*	foreigner
prefix + free word	明＋年度→明年度	*myōnendo*	next year
free word + free word	日本＋料理→日本料理	*nihon-ryōri*	Japanese cuisine

A useful feature of this dictionary is the indication of function for each character meaning. A system of labels, typographical devices, and the entry layout clearly distinguish the meanings of free words from the meanings of word elements, as well as other categories. A detailed analysis of the word-building function of one-character *kun* words and word elements is presented here for the first time in English.

Free words, combining forms, and affixes are basically distinct functional categories, but a character in any given sense may act in more than one of these capacities. Sometimes, a character may function as an affix in one sense and as a free word in another; at others, its meaning as a free word may be the same as its meaning as a combining form. Function and meaning may interact in other ways as well, all of which are indicated. For example, 著 acts as a combining form in the sense of 'author, write', as a suffix in the sense of 'authored by', and as a free word in the sense of 'literary work':

著
2300

❶ⓐ **author, write, publish** —— equivalent of a combining form
ⓑ [suffix] **authored by, by** —— equivalent of a suffix
著作する *chosaku suru* write, author
⋮
三島由紀夫著 *mishima yukio-cho* authored by Mishima Yukio

INDEPENDENT
【**cho** 著】literary work, book —— equivalent of a free word
...の著 *...no cho* book written by...

The fourteen character functions indicated in this dictionary are described in the sections that follow. Explanations of how each functional category is identified and detailed definitions of terms can be found in **GUIDE § 20.10** and **§ 20.11**.

Note that because of the special characteristics of the Japanese language, the terms used for describing function in this dictionary differ somewhat from their standard usage. Although the definitions have been applied with extreme caution, the dividing line between different categories is a fine one. Particularly, because of the existence of borderline cases, the difference between free words, combining forms, and affixes involves complex theoretical problems that make it impractical to provide a rigorous definition that renders them mutually exclusive one hundred percent of the time.

A detailed knowledge of character function is not always necessary for the beginner. However, it could be very useful in that it helps one learn new words more effectively by clearly showing the role of each character in the formation of compound words, and in that it enables the learner to easily infer the meanings of compound words not listed in the dictionary.

7.1.1 Free Words **Free word** refers to any independent word; that is, any independent *on* or *kun* word that can be freely combined with other words in a sentence. In the example in **§7.1** above, 著 is a free word meaning 'literary work'. Although free words often also function as word elements, these functions are clearly distinguished by treating independent *on* and *kun* words as separate subentries in the INDEPENDENT and KUN sections, respectively. See **GUIDE § 20.10.1 Free Words** for format details.

7.1.2 Combining Forms **Combining form** refers to a part of a word that is not an affix and that can form a new word by combining with one or more words or parts of a word. Combining forms and affixes are thus mutually exclusive. As the combining form is extremely common, it is not marked in any special way. Any meaning in the COMPOUNDS section and any KUN headword may function as a combining form, unless specifically indicated otherwise. In the example in **§7.1** above, 著 acts as a combining form meaning 'author, write'.

The function of characters as combining forms is of major importance in the formation of words in Japanese. As an *on* word element, a combining form corresponds to a single character; as a *kun* word element, it corresponds to a single character with or without *okurigana* endings. Normally, the part left after a combining form is removed from a compound word (e.g., 外人 *gaijin* 'foreigner') is a one-character combining form (外 *gai* 'foreign'). If the remaining part is a free word consisting of two or more characters (e.g., 外国 *gaikoku* 'foreign country' from 外国人 *gaikokujin* 'foreigner'), then the part removed (人 *jin* 'person') is an affix, not a combining form. See **GUIDE § 20.10.2 Combining Forms** for format details.

7.1.3 Affixes **Affix** refers to a part of a word added to a base (word or word element having its own lexical meaning) to form a new word. **Verbal affix** is a part of a word added to a base to form a new word, usually a *kun* verb. To qualify as a verbal affix, either the form itself or the base to which it is added must be a verb. For example, in 読み終わる *yomiowaru* 'finish reading', the verbal affix 終わる itself is a verb; in 取り組む *torikumu* 'grapple, tackle (a problem)' the verbal affix 取り itself is not a verb but the form 組む to which it is attached is.

Affixes added to the beginning of a word are called **prefixes**; those added to the end of a word are **suffixes.** Affixes include titles, counters, units, and certain function words, but exclude combining forms. Whereas combining forms are normally unmarked, affixes and verbal affixes are specifically identified by a label or some other means, as illustrated below:

古
2002

【furu- 古-】 [prefix] old, secondhand
古新聞 *furushinbun* old newspapers

What distinguishes an affix from a combining form is that the part of the word that remains after the affix is removed is, in principle, an independent unit in its own right, usually a free word consisting of two or more characters. The exception to this are titles, counters, units, and certain function words, in which the remaining part may consist of one character. See GUIDE **§20.10.3 Affixes** for format details.

7.1.4 Abbreviations **Abbreviation** refers to a single character used as a shortened form of a compound word, usually represented by its first constituent character. The first character of a compound is often used to represent the entire compound, as 大 for 大学 in the example below:

大
3416

❹ⓐ abbrev. of 大学 *daigaku*: **university, college**
⋮
大卒 *daisotsu* university graduate

Abbreviations are a concise means of conveying meaning, especially when used to create new compound words that might otherwise be long and cumbersome. Although abbreviations play an active role in the formation of many compounds, they have been practically ignored by other character dictionaries. This dictionary treats abbreviations rather comprehensively, and includes most of the ones in current use.

Abbreviations could be of ordinary compound words, as in 三本間 *sanponkan* 'between third and home base', where 三 stands for 三塁 *sanrui* 'third base' and 本 stands for 本塁 *honrui* 'home base', and in 入園 *nyūen* 'entering kindergarten', where 園 stands for 幼稚園 *yōchien* 'kindergarten'. Abbreviations could also be of place names, especially of city and country names, as 阪 for 大阪 *ōsaka* in 来阪 *raihan* 'coming to Osaka'. See GUIDE **§20.11.4 Abbreviations** for format details.

7.1.5 Counters **Counter** refers to a form, normally used as a suffix, that is added to a numeral to count objects, people, or abstract things:

杯
857

ⓑ **counter for cupfuls, glassfuls, bowlfuls or spoonfuls**
⋮
茶二杯 *cha nihai* two cups of tea

Counters are very common in Japanese, and often have no English equivalents. A counter indicates the characteristic of the thing being counted. The pronunciation of a counter may change according to the previous syllable, such has 杯 in 一杯 *ippai*, 二杯 *nihai*, 三杯 *sanbai*, etc.

7.1.6 Special Readings **Special reading** refers to a reading of a word consisting of two or more characters assigned to a single word on the basis of its meaning without direct relation to the normal readings of each constituent character:

大
3416

SPECIAL READINGS
大人 *otona* adult

In the example, both characters function as a single unit pronounced *otona*. Compound words having special readings appear together in the SPECIAL READINGS section. All the special readings appearing in the Jōyō Kanji list have been included, as well as other important ones that are not in the list. See also GUIDE **§ 20.11.11 Special Readings** and GUIDE **§ 13. SPECIAL READINGS Section.**

7.1.7 Names **Name reading** refers to a reading used only in the writing of personal, family, and place names. These are given for the 166 characters in the official Jinmei Kanji list published in 1981. Typical name examples appear in the NAMES section, which includes further information about the name, i.e., place name, female name, etc. See also GUIDE **§ 14. NAMES Section.**

7.1.8 Miscellaneous Functions
Other miscellaneous functions are indicated: (1) various **grammatical and syntactic functions,** (2) **numerals** (words or word elements expressing a number), (3) **function words** (words or word elements that show grammatical relationships), (4) **units** (forms representing units of measurement, weight, etc.), (5) **titles** (suffixes used as titles of courtesy), (6) **phonetic substitutes** (characters used for transliterating foreign words), and (7) **symbols** (characters used as symbols that have no pronunciation). These are described in GUIDE **§ 20.11 Miscellaneous Character Functions.**

7.2 System of Labels

Existing character dictionaries and textbooks often include obsolete, archaic, and rare meanings without any indication to that effect. While this dictionary lists both archaic and current meanings, a system of labels and typographical devices indicate the temporal status, etymology, orthography, style, function, level of formality, etc., for each sense. These labels clearly distinguish basic and frequent meanings from rare and archaic ones, and provide the user with practical guidance on the style and usage associated with each sense. The labels are of four major types: orthographic, functional, status, and subject.

7.2.1 Orthographic Labels The **orthographic labels** indicate the orthographic variants of a word or word element. See **§ 5.4 Discriminating Variants** and GUIDE **§ 22. Orthographic Labels** for format details.

7.2.2 Functional Labels The **functional labels** indicate the various grammatical and syntactic functions associated with a sense:

炎
2420
❸ [also suffix] **inflammation, -itis**
:
虫垂炎 *chūsuien* appendicitis

In addition to one or more meanings, each character may have various linguistic functions. Knowing these functions helps the student learn new words more effectively since it explains the character's role in the formation of compounds (see **§ 7.1 Character Functions** for details). Functional labels are of the following types:

1. The **part-of-speech label** indicates part of speech. Part-of-speech labels are given mostly when the part of speech is not already evident from the wording of the equivalent. Typical labels: *particle*, *vt* (transitive verb).

2. The **usage label** indicates how a word or word element is used, especially its syntactic function and the grammatical construction in which it normally appears. Typical labels: [in the form of...], [followed by...].

3. The **word-formation label** indicates the function of a form as a word element (affix or combining form). Typical labels: [prefix], [suffix], [also suffix], [verbal suffix], [in compounds].

4. Miscellaneous functional labels indi-

cate various functions of the character as a word or word element. Typical labels: [auxiliary], [emphatic].

See GUIDE **§23. Functional Labels** for details on label format and meanings.

7.2.3 Status Labels The **status labels** restrict a sense to a particular time, level of style, or level of formality:

晃 ● [archaic] dazzling, brilliant
2450

The complex levels of formality and diversified levels of style in Japanese pose considerable difficulties to the learner. The status labels are very useful because they distinguish basic and frequent meanings from rare and archaic ones, and show the appropriate context and degree of respect associated with a sense. They are of the following types:

1. The **etymological label**. See **§7.3.2 Original Meaning** for details.
2. The **temporal labels** restrict a sense to a particular time. They are of three kinds: [rare], [archaic], and [obsolete].
3. The **stylistic labels** restrict a sense to a particular level of style. They include *literary, elegant, colloq, slang,* and *vulgar*.
4. The **formality labels** restrict a sense to a particular level of formality. They include [honorific], [humble], [polite], and [belittling].

See GUIDE **§24. Status Labels** for details on label format and meanings.

7.2.4 Subject Labels The **subject labels** identify the field to which the sense applies, usually a branch of science:

粒 ⓑ *phys* grain, particle
1328 ⋮
素粒子 *soryūshi* elementary particle

See GUIDE **§25. Subject Labels** for details on label format and meanings.

7.3 Character Etymology

To help the learner gain a deeper understanding of character meaning, this dictionary presents information on the etymology of characters. This information can be classified into three groups: radicals, original meaning, and *kokuji*. The etymology of compounds is treated in the **compound formation articles** (see **§2.5 Compound Formation** for details).

7.3.1 Radicals A **radical** is a frequently recurring graphic component used for classifying Chinese characters into groups sharing a common element. A knowledge of radicals helps the user understand character etymology, and is useful for looking up characters in dictionaries and reference works based on the radical system. The following information is presented on radicals:

1. The RADICAL section describes the function of the entry character as a radical:

乙
3339
RADICAL 5
Standard form: 乙 *otsu* 'hook' (九 乞 乾)
Variant: 乚 *re* (乱 乳 也)
Description: used for character classification

It shows such details as the radical number, standard and variant forms, the radical name in Japanese and English, typical characters in which the radical appears, a description of the radical's meaning and function, and cross-references from variants to parent radicals. See GUIDE **§8. RADICAL Section** for format details.

2. The reference data box gives the **radical and radical number** for the entry character. See GUIDE **§ 7.2 Radical** for format details.

3. The traditional radicals of **"lost-radical" characters** are shown in the **Radical Index** (see p. 1929 for details).

4. An appendix describes the radical system and includes a detailed radical chart. See **Appendix 6. The Radicals** for details.

5. The **Radical Index** enables the user to look up characters by their radicals and is accompanied by various descriptions and charts about radicals.

7.3.2 Original Meaning The **original meaning**, which is the first meaning associated with a character after its formation in ancient China (rarely Japan), is often shown by an etymological label:

休 52 ❶❷ [original meaning] **rest, repose, relax**

The original meaning does not necessarily appear first, nor does it necessarily coincide with, the character's core meaning. Since this is not a historical dictionary, the treatment of original meanings is not exhaustive. It often appears when it is necessary to clarify the meaning of the character or to show the interrelatedness between its various senses. See also GUIDE **§ 24.2 Etymological Labels.**

7.3.3 *Kokuji* This dictionary shows if a character is of Chinese origin or if it is one of the small number of characters of Japanese origin (*kokuji*):

働 153 Ⓒⓗ none (国字)

See also **OUTLINE OF JAPANESE WRITING SYSTEM § 1.2 Formation of Chinese Characters** and GUIDE **§ 5.4 *Kokuji*.**

7.4 Chinese

Many students of Japanese are also interested in Chinese, and vice versa. Such students often seek learning materials or reference tools to help them learn both the Japanese and Chinese forms and readings together, or to enable them to take advantage of their knowledge of one system to learn the other.

Learning the forms and readings of both languages together has some advantages: the learner can compare their differences and similarities, and thus know which forms and readings of one language correspond to which of the other. On the other hand, it also presents certain difficulties. As a result of the extensive language reforms that took place in the People's Republic of China, many Chinese characters underwent major simplifications to the point where they are no longer recognizable from their traditional or modern Japanese forms.

Another problem is that there is often no straightforward, one-to-one correspondence between the Japanese and Chinese forms. Sometimes, two Chinese forms correspond to a single Japanese form, and vice versa, or the correspondence depends on meaning. For example, 發 and 髮, originally two distinct characters, have merged in Chinese into the single form 发, as shown below:

Traditional	Japanese	Chinese	Meaning
發	発 *hatsu*	发 fā	start; emit
髮	髪 *hatsu*	发 fà	hair

To aid the student learning both languages, this dictionary presents the Chinese forms and readings for each Japanese form:

錬 錬 錬 练 ㊥ 炼 链 liàn
1741 REN ne(ru)▲

The following information is presented:

1. The **Chinese form**, which is often a simplified form (簡体字 *kantaiji*) significantly different from the Japanese form, is the official form(s) used in the People's Republic of China.

2. The **Chinese reading**, which is transcribed in the official Pinyin system of romanization, is the pronunciation of the character in the People's Republic of China.

3. The **traditional form**, which is in standard use in Hong Kong, Taiwan, and among overseas Chinese (see § 3.2.1 **Character Forms** for details).

4. The correspondence between the Chinese and Japanese forms is shown on a character-by-character basis.

This is, to our knowledge, the first dictionary for learners of Japanese to include detailed information on Chinese forms and readings, and to show the correspondence between the Japanese and Chinese forms on a character-by-character basis, rather than the correspondence for simplified radicals and other elements. See GUIDE § 5. **Chinese** for format details.

SYSTEM OF KANJI INDEXING BY PATTERNS

QUICK GUIDE TO SKIP

The **System of Kanji Indexing by Patterns** (SKIP) can be used to locate character entries with great speed and little effort. If you are in a hurry to know the bare essentials of the system, do as follows:

1. Read section **§ 2.1 Overview of SKIP** on p. 113a.
2. Refer to the charts inside the front and back covers.

To get a more thorough understanding, carefully read the sections below. Pay special attention to **§ 3.1 SKIP Method,** which gives detailed instructions for locating entries.

1. INTRODUCTION

1.1 Historical Background

The lack of an efficient system for ordering Chinese characters has long been a source of frustration to learners and even native speakers of Chinese and Japanese, posing a major obstacle to the effective use of character dictionaries. The traditional method of looking up characters presupposes a knowledge of kanji elements known as **radicals.** Looking up by radicals is a time-consuming, laborious, and unreliable process that may require weeks of practice to learn. Although many alternative systems have been devised, none have achieved the speed and simplicity required to meet the practical needs of the learner.

1.1.1 The Radical System The traditional radical system is based on a table consisting of 214 elements plus about 150 variants used for classifying the characters into groups in Chinese character dictionaries (see **Appendix 6** for details). The radical system is complex and difficult to master. To use it effectively requires much experience, some knowledge of character etymology, the ability to identify the original radical from its variants, and familiarity with old character forms. Even experienced users must often resort to guesswork and repeated false attempts. The main reasons that the traditional radical system is difficult to use are:

1. A radical may have several variants of totally different form and/or stroke-count. Often, the variant cannot be recognized without prior knowledge. For example, 氵 is a three-stroke variant of the four-stroke 'water' radical 水.
2. Some radicals have almost exactly the same forms, and are easily confused. For example, 匚 (Radical 22) is the radical of 匠, while 匸 (Radical 23) is the radical of 匹.
3. Since some radicals have totally disappeared from the modern forms of characters, a knowledge of old forms is sometimes necessary. For example, 医 is classified under 酉 according to its old form 醫.
4. A character often includes several radical elements and one must choose between them; e.g., 副 consists of the four elements 一, 口, 田, and 刂, all of which are radicals.
5. A character that is itself a radical sometimes includes other radicals. For example, the 高 radical includes three radical elements: 亠, 口, and 冂.
6. The radical is sometimes "embedded" in the character and is difficult to identify. For example, 乙 is the radical of 也.
7. The radical sometimes appears in unpredictable positions. For example, the radical of characters with 禾 in the left position is usually 禾, but the radical of 和 is 口.

Although various attempts have been made to simplify and improve the system, it is basically cumbersome and difficult to use. Nevertheless, the time-honored radical system, which is in widespread use in character dictionaries and reference works, is important and should be learned by the serious student of Chinese or Japanese.

1.1.2 Alternative Systems To overcome the problems inherent in the radical system, numerous alternative systems have been devised throughout the long history of Chinese and Japanese lexicography. The most important of these can be classified into six types, which are briefly described below. The list includes the radical system for comparison purposes.

1. **Traditional Radical System** The traditional method of ordering entries in character dictionaries lists the characters according to their historical radicals and additional strokes. To use it effectively requires much experience, some knowledge of character etymology, familiarity with the 214 radicals and their variants, and a knowledge of old forms. Its main advantage is its widespread use in character dictionaries and reference works.

2. **Simplified Radical Systems** Since the traditional radical system is cumbersome, many attempts have been made to simplify it by such devices as (1) reducing the number of radicals, (2) basing the radical on new rather than old character forms, and (3) assigning the radical in a consistent manner. A good example of this is the Radical Priority System introduced in Andrew Nelson's well-known character dictionary. These simplified systems are a considerable improvement over the historical radicals. Their chief disadvantage is that the user must become familiar with yet another set of radicals, and their lack of standardization—every dictionary uses a somewhat different variation.

3. **Reading Indexes** The most widespread of these are the On-Kun index and romanized index, which list the characters phonetically by their *on* and *kun* readings for Japanese and their Mandarin pronunciations for

Chinese. This type of index suffers from two major drawbacks: (1) the user must have prior knowledge of the character's reading, and (2) dozens or even hundreds of entries may appear under a common reading such as *kō*.

4. **Stroke-Count Indexes** Most Japanese character dictionaries include a stroke-count index, which lists the characters by total stroke-count. These indexes are difficult to use because (1) many characters, sometimes over 500, appear in the same stroke-count section, (2) they require the user to count strokes accurately—no cross-references appear at incorrect locations, and (3) finding an entry is very slow. The characters are often further classified by radical, which requires familiarity with the radical system. The only advantage of this index is that, if one has patience, it serves as a last resort when all other means fail.

5. **Character and Stroke Form Systems** Many systems classify the characters on the basis of form. They usually define a table of elements based on various criteria such as stroke form or structure, strokes position, or structure of character parts (such as the top or corners). Some systems, such as the well-known Four Corner System, assign a numerical code to each character, and are fairly efficient once learned. Their main disadvantage is that they presuppose a knowledge of character form and/or stroke structure, which the beginner does not have, and often require one to memorize complex rules.

6. **Stroke Order Systems** Some systems classify the characters on the basis of stroke order. Although there are general stroke order principles, such as "first left then right," the rules are not strict enough to serve as a basis for an efficient lookup system. The main disadvantage of these systems is that they presuppose a knowledge of stroke order, which makes them unsuitable for learners.

One might well ask why, with so many systems in existence, is there a need for yet another system. The answer is that past and existing systems often suffer from a number of serious drawbacks, the most important of which are as follows:

1. Locating an entry can be a time-consuming, laborious process.
2. Some systems are difficult to learn, sometimes requiring rote memorization of many complex elements and weeks of practice.
3. Prior knowledge of kanji, such as of radicals, stroke order, stroke form, character reading, etc., is often required. In effect, the user is unable to look up a character without already knowing something about it.
4. Poor cross-referencing often requires going back and forth between entries.
5. Some systems are unreliable and inconsistent, requiring guesswork and repeated false attempts.
6. Poor entry distribution between subgroups. Some indexes may have hundreds of entries in one subsection.

Because of these drawbacks, previous systems are inadequate for meeting the practical needs of the learner.

1.2 System of Kanji Indexing by Patterns

1.2.1 New Indexing System To overcome the shortcomings of the traditional methods of ordering characters, this dictionary introduces a new scheme, called the **System of Kanji Indexing by**

Patterns or **SKIP**, that can be used to locate entries as quickly and as accurately as in alphabetical dictionaries. The system, which can be learned in a very short time, is based on a new concept: **the direct identification of geometrical patterns.** With the help of simple rules, each character is unambiguously classified under one of four easy-to-identify **patterns**: ◧ 1 left-right, ⬒ 2 up-down, ◻ 3 enclosure, and ■ 4 solid. For example, 相 is classified under pattern ◧ 1 since it can be divided into left and right parts (木 and 目).

Classification by patterns is not merely a variation of an existing system—it is, as we shall see below, a new *type* of lookup system based on an entirely new idea. The user need only identify the *pattern* formed by visual elements, and needs no prior knowledge of the character or its constituents.

Characters belonging to the first three patterns, the **divisible characters**, are arranged in ascending order of hyphenated numerals that indicate stroke-count. The first numeral indicates the number of strokes in the shaded segment of the pattern symbol, and the second the number of strokes in the nonshaded segment. The pattern number followed by these hyphenated numerals is referred to as the **SKIP number** for that character. The SKIP number for the **indivisible characters** (pattern ■ 4) is formed according to a somewhat different principle.

The character entries are ordered by their SKIP numbers. Locating a character is simply matter of determining its SKIP number and then finding the corresponding entry. To locate a divisible character, identify the pattern to which it belongs to determine the first part of the SKIP number, then divide it and count the strokes of each part to determine the second and third parts of that number. For example, 相 can be divided into left and right parts and is thus classified under pattern ◧ 1. Since it contains four strokes in the **shaded part** (木) and five strokes in the **blank part** (目), its SKIP number is ◧ 1-4-5.

To achieve maximum lookup speed, characters sharing the same SKIP number are further subdivided into progressively smaller groups, while characters that may be difficult to locate are systematically cross-referenced at locations where they might be mistakenly looked for.

1.2.2 Advantages of SKIP The **System of Kanji Indexing by Patterns** is a great improvement over its predecessors. To overcome the six shortcomings of traditional lookup systems listed in **§ 1.1.2** above, SKIP offers the following six advantages:

1. **Entries can be located with great speed and little effort.** Once the system has been mastered, the user can look up entries as quickly and as effortlessly as in alphabetically arranged dictionaries. The experienced user can often locate an entry in less than twenty seconds.

2. **The basic principles of the system can be learned in a few minutes.** Since SKIP rules are based on intuition, they are easy to learn in a short time. Tests have confirmed that after only ten to fifteen minutes of learning the rules, beginners can locate entries with an accuracy of 90 to 100 per cent. Although it may take some time to master the finer details, this is a small price to pay considering the total amount of time saved in looking up entries over the many years during which the dictionary is used.

3. **No prior knowledge of kanji elements is required.** The system relies on the direct identification of the *pattern* formed by kanji elements, not the *forms* of the elements themselves.

Thus no prior knowledge of the character or its constituents, such as its radical, reading, stroke order, or stroke form is needed.

4. **A cross-reference system practically eliminates dead-end searching** by placing difficult-to-find characters at locations where they might be mistakenly looked for.

5. **The system is reliable and logically consistent.** The user need not engage in guesswork and repeated false attempts. A proper understanding and application of the rules will always lead to the correct location on the first try.

6. **The distribution of characters among the four patterns is fairly uniform.** Moreover, there is no overconcentration of characters in the subdivisions into which each pattern section is divided.

As should be clear from the above, since no prior knowledge of the character or its constituents is required, one need not waste time in learning to recognize the *shapes* of an arbitrary set of elements—the user need only identify the *arrangement* of elements in relation to each other. In this sense, classification by patterns is intrinsically different from other systems—it is not merely a new variation of an existing system.

SKIP is a product of seven years of computer-assisted research and experimentation on how kanji elements are intuitively perceived in terms of their parts.[1] Since the system can be learned in a very short time and is easy to use, it has been praised by educators as an important breakthrough in Chinese character lexicography. At the very least, it represents a radical departure from all traditional systems for ordering characters in both China and Japan.

1.2.3 SKIP Rules Since the rules for classifying characters by patterns are essentially simple, it is often possible to identify the pattern correctly even with only a superficial knowledge of the rules. Inevitably, a small number of characters will be difficult to locate even if you know the rules. To eliminate dead-end searching, many of these problem characters are systematically cross-referenced at one or more locations where they might be mistakenly looked for.

Intuition and cross-references, however, cannot be relied upon all the time. To use the system effectively, a knowledge of the rules is necessary. In the initial stages, a brief glance at the pattern chart inside the back covers, which has been designed as an aid to locating entries without a detailed knowledge of the rules, will no doubt be most helpful. Once you become familiar with the rules and gain a little experience, you should normally be able to quickly locate a desired entry without referring to the chart.

In addition to the overall description of the system presented here, **Appendix 1** gives an in-depth, lengthy description that includes many interesting facts on the structure of kanji patterns. However, since the system is basically simple, it is not necessary for the general user to understand all the details. The reader may well wonder why, then, are such

1. Although SKIP has been designed primarily as a lookup system for character dictionaries, it has other potential applications. The most important of these include a kanji input system for computers and wordprocessors (patent pending); *structural description* rules for generating characters from a small set of elements; miscellaneous products such as road guides that classify place names by patterns; and as a basis for a collating sequence for sorting kanji data. The commercial utilization of SKIP (patent pending) in any form is strictly forbidden without the written permission of the publisher or copyright owner.

lengthy explanations necessary. The answer is twofold.

First, since SKIP allows entries to be looked up with great speed, it is likely to be widely adopted as a new classification scheme in future character dictionaries. We have thus felt it necessary, for reference purposes, to present a full treatment of all the theoretical and practical aspects of the system.

Second, as is well known, explaining in words the precise procedure for performing a simple action is often far more difficult than doing it. A facetious illustration of this is a condensed version of an excessively elaborate description of how to pronounce the *wh* in *when*: "...a voiceless glottal fricative (aspirate) followed by a voiceless labiovelar glide or bilabial (dorsovelar) semivowel produced with the lips... by directing a stream of breath... partially obstructed by the epiglottis, then causing the stream to glide between the pharingopalatine and glossopalatine arches... by continuously obstructing the stream with the velum and labia..." How much easier *wh* is to pronounce than it is to describe! The same can be said of SKIP. Describing it is far more difficult than using it.

1.3 Pattern Selection Criteria

The four SKIP patterns were selected on the basis of a study of the structure and geometrical properties of kanji elements, and an investigation of how combinations of such elements are intuitively perceived in terms of their parts. There are many other ways in which characters could conceivably be classified by patterns, such as triangular divisions (e.g. 春 under ◩), division into three parts (e.g. 指 under ◫), etc. Our computer-aided research has shown that the SKIP patterns are ideally suited as a scheme for ordering entries in character dictionaries for the following reasons:

1. They are in harmony with the way the characters are intuitively perceived.
2. They often coincide with etymologically meaningful parts.
3. The distribution of characters among the four patterns and their subdivisions is fairly uniform.

Each of these is discussed in greater detail below.

1.3.1 Psychologistics of Pattern Recognition There are countless ways in which combinations of visual elements may be perceived. Even a simple figure like a square can be divided up in numerous ways:

1. Four line segments of equal-length: 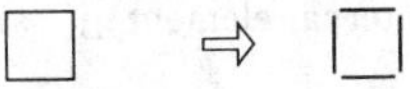
2. Four **L**-shaped components: 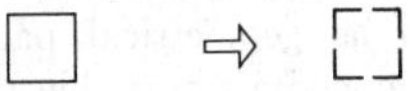
3. Many short line segments: 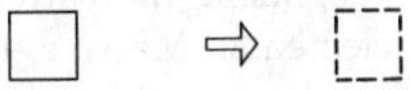
4. Two **U**-shaped components:

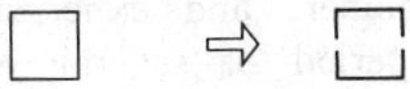

Dozens of other divisions are possible. The larger the components into which a structure is divided, the simpler is the relationship between them. Dividing into smaller parts results in more complex relations. That a structure can be broken up into certain parts does not mean that it has been assembled from those parts. In fact, no division is intrinsically superior to any other—all are equally arbitrary. The best division is the one that most aptly describes the figure for a particular purpose. However, some divisions are more "intuitive" than others. For example, most people perceive a square as consisting of four line segments—few would regard it as a combination of **L**-shapes.

The perceptual principles of organizing groups of elements into larger units form a fascinating branch of psychology. This is not the place to discuss these principles in detail. The point is that Chinese characters, many of which are of highly complex structure, can be divided in countless ways, but only some of these will seem "natural"—that is, will be in harmony with the way the character is *intuitively* perceived. "Intuitively" here refers to the manner in which the absolute majority of people tend to perceive a character in terms of its parts. For example, most people perceive 宗 as consisting of 宀 and 示 stacked one over another; 国 as consisting of 囗 enclosing the internal element 玉; and so on.

SKIP rules are based on an extensive analysis of how the characters are intuitively perceived as geometrical patterns. We have developed a set of objective criteria that closely reflect the *psychologistic* principles of recognizing the patterns formed by kanji elements. Massive volumes of kanji pattern data were analyzed by computer and subjected to many tests with both beginners and experienced users over a period of several years. The result of these efforts is a set of accurate and reliable rules that are, on the one hand, in close harmony with intuition, and, on the other, strike a good balance between component size and simplicity of relationship between parts.

Although we have done everything possible to ensure that the rules reflect intuition, some exceptions are inevitable. For example, some people may find it more natural to divide 真 into 直 and 六, rather than into 十 and 具. That a small number of divisions conflict with intuition is a small price to pay considering the speed, consistency, and ease with which characters can be located by following the rules.

Since SKIP rules are based on intuition, it follows that they are easy to learn in a short time. It also follows that most people will tend to intuitively divide characters according to these rules even if they do not know them. In conclusion, the firm psychological basis of SKIP patterns makes them well suited for lexicographic classification.

1.3.2 Etymological Integrity A second reason for adopting SKIP patterns is their etymological integrity; that is, dividing a character by SKIP rules often yields etymologically meaningful parts such as radicals, which are usually familiar kanji elements contributing to the character's meaning. For example, 休 *kyū* 'rest', which is classified under pattern ◧ 1, is a left-right character divided into 亻 'human being' and 木 *moku* 'tree', both of which are radicals.

However, it is important to note that SKIP rules do not *depend* on radicals or etymology; etymological integrity is merely a by-product that may be of benefit to the user familiar with the radical system. Since division by patterns is based on a precise set of rules, the division of many characters will of course not conform to division by radicals. For example, SKIP rules call for dividing 勝 into 月 and 券, whereas division by radicals gives 朕 and 力, a far less obvious division.

1.3.3 Uniform Distribution A third reason for adopting SKIP patterns is that the distribution of the character entries among the four patterns is fairly uniform. There is no overconcentration of characters under any one pattern, as shown in the table below:

Pattern	Percentage of entries	Percentage of occurrences
◧ 1	54	36
⬒ 2	28	20
◘ 3	11	11
■ 4	7	33

Although the percentage of total entries shows a high concentration of characters in the left-right and up-down patterns, the percentage of *occurrence* of characters in newspapers[2] is much more evenly distributed. For example, left-right characters account for about 54% of the entries in this dictionary, but only for approximately 36% of character occurrences. This means that although the actual number of left-right characters is large, the probability of encountering such a character is only 36%. On the other hand, although the percentage of solid characters is only 7%, the probability of encountering them is 33% because of the many high frequency characters that are included in that category. Thus, in terms of percentage of occurrence, the character entries are fairly evenly distributed.

In addition, there is no overconcentration of characters in the subdivisions (subsections and subgroups) into which each pattern section is divided. This means that the final stage of searching for an entry, which requires locating the character by visual scanning, is speedy and efficient.

2. DESCRIPTION OF THE SYSTEM

2.1 Overview of SKIP

The central idea of the **System of Kanji Indexing by Patterns** is the classification of characters into four major categories on the basis of easy-to-identify geometrical **patterns**: ◧ 1 **left-right** (相), ⬒ 2 **up-down** (字), ◘ 3 **enclosure** (進), and ■ 4 **solid** (下).

SKIP	Acronym of "**System of Kanji Indexing by Patterns.**" A system of classifying characters by geometrical patterns used for the rapid location of entries in this dictionary.

Characters belonging to the first three categories, referred to as the **divisible characters**, are arranged in ascending order of hyphenated numerals called the **subsection number.** The first numeral indicates the number of strokes in the

2. Based on a survey of JIS characters by Shiratori et al (1981).

shaded part, which corresponds to the shaded segment of the **pattern symbol,** and the second the number of strokes in the **blank part,** which corresponds to the nonshaded segment. The **pattern number** followed by the subsection number is referred to as the **SKIP number.**

To locate a divisible character, first identify the pattern to which it belongs to determine the first part of the SKIP number, then divide it and count the strokes of each part to determine the second and third parts of that number (the subsection number). For example, 格 can be divided into left and right parts and is thus classified under pattern ◧1. Since it contains four strokes in the shaded part (木) and six strokes in the blank part (各), its SKIP number is ◧1-4-6. It thus appears under pattern ◧1, subsection 4-6, along with other characters that share the same SKIP number such as 時 and 脂.

Divisible characters in the same **subsection** are divided into **subgroups** containing a shared element (such as 日 and 月), called the **subgroup element,** for maximum lookup speed. The characters within each subgroup are further subdivided into progressively smaller groups until each character is assigned its own position.

Characters that cannot be divided by SKIP rules, called the **indivisible characters,** are classified under pattern ■4, solid. These are arranged by total stroke-count and subclassified into four **solid subpatterns** on the basis of easy-to-identify lines: ⬒1 **top line** (下), ⬓2 **bottom line** (上), ◫3 **through line** (中), and □4 **others** (人). The first part of the subsection number for these characters represents their total stroke-counts, and the second part represents the number of the solid subpattern. 下, for example, is a three-stroke character containing a top line, and is thus classified under pattern ■4, subsection 3-1 (SKIP number ■4-3-1).

The character entries in the main part of the dictionary are ordered according to the above scheme. To attain greater lookup speed and flexibility, they are also listed in exactly the same order in the **Pattern Index.** Thus, once you have determined the SKIP number, you have a choice of two lookup methods: (1) locating the entry in the **Pattern Index,** or (2) locating the entry directly without using the index. In addition, there is a special shortcut called the **SCAN method** that makes it possible to locate entries quickly without determining their SKIP numbers.

Although SKIP rules are simple, a small number of characters may be difficult to locate. To eliminate dead-end searching, many of these are systematically cross-referenced at one or more locations where they might be mistakenly looked for. Moreover, various guides printed in the outer corners and margins of the page facilitate the rapid location of entries to achieve maximum lookup speed.

The above overview describes the most important elements of the system. Since it is essentially simple, you should be able to look up entries even on the basis of this brief description. Sections **§ 2.2** through **§ 7.** below explain in detail how to look up entries, summarize the rules for identifying the pattern and dividing the character, and define technical terms. **Appendix 1** presents a far more detailed description of the rules, but the descriptions here should normally be sufficient for gaining an adequate understanding without referring to the appendix.

It is most important that you acquire a clear understanding of the various terms used in a technical sense, particularly the term **division point.** The definitions of technical terms are enclosed in boxes, while terms appearing in the text are printed in **sanserif boldface** whenever it is necessary to draw attention to them, especially the first time they are used in a topic of discussion. All SKIP terms are briefly defined in **§ 7. Glossary,** while a detailed description of important terms appears in **Appendix 1. § 1. Definitions of Pattern Terminology.** To distinguish SKIP rules from ordinary text, the principal rules are set in sanserif boldface **CAPITAL LETTERS** and SMALL CAPITALS, while subrules are set in sanserif lowercase.

2.2 SKIP Patterns

The **System of Kanji Indexing by Patterns** classifies the characters into four major categories on the basis of easy-to-identify geometrical **patterns**: ◧ 1 left-right, ⬒ 2 up-down, □ 3 enclosure, and ■ 4 solid. Each pattern is identified by a **pattern symbol** and **pattern number.** The charts below illustrate and define the various parts and terms associated with SKIP patterns.

Structure of SKIP Patterns

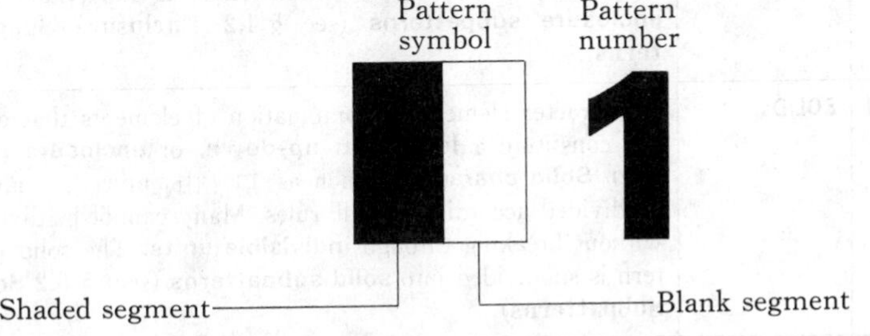

Pattern	A configuration of character elements that characterizes the four major character groups in the SKIP classification scheme; i.e., ◧ 1 **left-right,** ⬒ 2 **up-down,** □ 3 **enclosure,** and ■ 4 **solid.**
Pattern number	A number that identifies one of the four patterns in the SKIP classification scheme; i.e., 1 = ◧, 2 = ⬒, 3 = □, and 4 = ■.
Pattern symbol	A symbol that identifies one of the four patterns in the SKIP classification scheme; i.e., ◧ = 1, ⬒ = 2, □ = 3, and ■ = 4. The shaded segment of the first three pattern symbols corresponds to the **shaded part** of the **divisible characters,** and the nonshaded segment to the **blank part** of these characters.

The table below briefly describes the four SKIP patterns. Rules on how to identify each pattern are given in § 4. **How to Identify the Pattern.** The technical terms appearing in the table are fully explained in **Appendix 1.**

◧ 1	LEFT-RIGHT	A configuration of character elements placed side by side. The elements are separated from each other by a **space** (保). The left-right pattern is basically of vertical construction.
⬒ 2	UP-DOWN	A configuration of character elements stacked more or less one on top of the other. The elements are separated from each other by a **space** (示), a **horizontal line** (赤), or a **frame element** (古). Although the up-down pattern is basically of horizontal construction, triangular (合) and diagonal (多) divisions are also allowed.
□ 3	ENCLOSURE	A configuration of character elements in which an exterior element encloses the rest of a character on two or more sides. The **enclosure element** may be separated from the rest of the character by a **space** (広), or may be in full physical contact (田) with it. The enclosure pattern, which is basically of rectangular construction, is subdivided into **enclosure subpatterns** (see **§ 4.2 Enclosure Subpatterns**).
■ 4	SOLID	A character element or combination of elements that does not constitute a **left-right, up-down,** or **enclosure pattern. Solid characters,** such as 口, 由, and 求, cannot be divided according to SKIP rules. Many cannot be divided without breaking through **indivisible units.** The solid pattern is subdivided into **solid subpatterns** (see **§ 6.2 Solid Subpatterns**).

The chart below has been carefully designed to provide you with a good understanding of SKIP patterns and subpatterns. Since these are intuitively easy to identify, a glance at the chart will often enable you to locate a character even without a detailed knowledge of SKIP rules. For ready reference, this chart also appears inside the back covers.

SKIP Patterns

No.	Pattern	Classification	Examples
1	LEFT-RIGHT	clear space	相 4-5 代 2-3 情 3-8 八 1-1 川 1-2 州 2-4 順 1-11 傾 2-11
		conceptual space	扱 3-3 級 6-3 歡 11-4 街 3-9 町 5-2 翻 12-6 髄 10-9 伺 2-5
2	UP-DOWN	clear space	示 1-4 二 1-1 三 1-2 言 1-6 公 2-2 谷 2-5 父 2-2 多 3-3
		conceptual space	芳 3-4 合 2-4 響 11-9 桑 2-8 系 1-6 雀 4-7 券 6-2 春 5-4
		horizontal line	寺 3-3 空 3-5 文 2-2 亭 2-7 忘 2-5 学 5-3 索 4-6 義 3-10
		frame element	古 2-3 点 2-7 免 2-6 早 4-2 尭 2-6 当 3-3 南 2-7 支 2-2
3	ENCLOSURE		進 3-8 辻 4-2 起 7-3 延 3-5 魅 8-7 直 1-7 匕 1-1 止 2-2
			句 2-4 載 6-7 刀 1-1 司 1-4 可 2-3 戒 4-3 鳥 7-4 馬 6-4
			麻 3-8 圧 2-3 尾 3-4 病 5-5 石 2-3 考 4-2 着 7-5 斗 2-2
			間 8-4 岡 2-6 風 2-7 向 3-3 肉 4-2 凶 2-2 山 2-1 画 2-6
			医 2-5 臣 3-4 匿 2-9 丑 2-2
			回 3-3 国 3-5 田 3-2 日 3-1 目 3-2 四 3-2 罒 3-2
4	SOLID	1 top line	下 3-1 耳 6-1 雨 8-1 子 3-1 凸 5-1 口 3-1 亜 7-1 爾 14-1
		2 bottom line	上 3-2 七 2-2 亡 3-2 丘 5-2 由 5-2 自 6-2 坐 7-2 重 9-2
		3 through line	中 4-3 十 2-3 手 4-3 本 5-3 求 7-3 乗 9-3 毛 4-3 粛 11-3
		4 others	人 2-4 九 2-4 女 3-4 火 4-4 犬 4-4 成 6-4 寿 7-4 為 9-4

As should be clear from the chart, a pattern is essentially a spatial arrangement of elements. It is important to understand that it is the *position* of the elements in relation to each other, *not their forms*, that determines the pattern. For example, 休 consists of two elements, 亻 and 木, placed side by side and thus constitutes a left-right pattern. The shape of the element 亻, or the fact that it is a radical, is totally irrelevant. Any other elements arranged in a similar manner would equally qualify as a left-right pattern. The pattern is thus independent of the character's form, radical, reading, stroke-order, stroke-count, etc. Thus, the user need only identify the *arrangement* of the elements, not their *forms*.

2.3 Divisible and Indivisible Characters

From the point of view of SKIP rules, the characters are divided into two major groups: **divisible** and **indivisible.** The divisible characters are divided into two parts: the **shaded part,** which corresponds to the shaded segment of the **pattern symbol,** and the **blank part,** which corresponds to the nonshaded segment. The rules for dividing the divisible characters are described in **§5. How to Divide the Character.**

Characters that cannot be divided are referred to as **indivisible** or **solid characters.** These are subclassified according to a principle described in **§6. How to Subclassify the Solid Pattern.**

Divisible characters	Characters that can be divided according to SKIP rules; i.e., characters classified under patterns ◧ 1, ⬒ 2, and ▣ 3, such as 相, 字, and 広.
Indivisible characters	Characters that cannot be divided according to SKIP rules; i.e., characters classified under pattern ■ 4, such as 雨, 本, and 九.

Structure of Divisible Characters

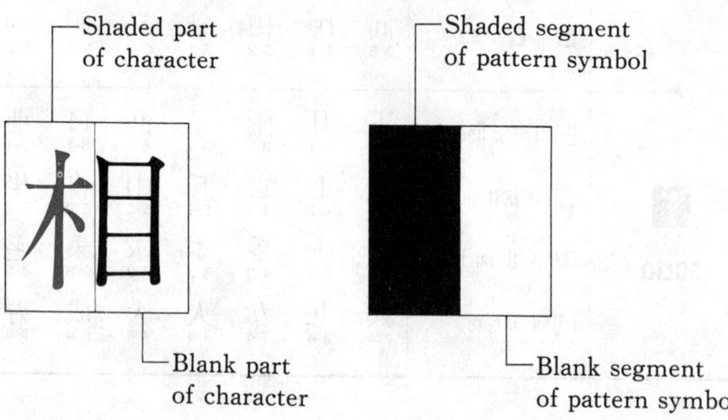

Structure of Indivisible Characters

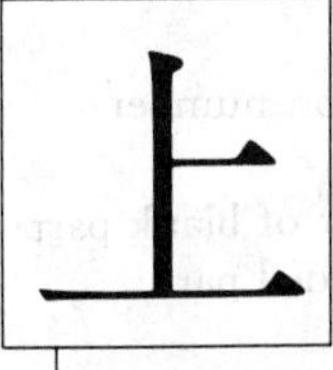

The entire character is a single indivisible unit.

The solid pattern symbol is completely shaded.

Shaded Part	The part of a **divisible character** corresponding to the shaded segment of the **pattern symbol**; i.e., the part removed at the first **division point**. For example, 木 is the shaded part of 相 (SKIP number ◧1-4-5). The stroke-count of this part corresponds to the second part of the **SKIP number** and the first part of the **subsection number**.
Blank Part	The part of a **divisible character** corresponding to the blank segment of the **pattern symbol**; i.e., the part remaining after the shaded part is removed. For example, 目 is the blank part of 相 (SKIP number ◧1-4-5). The stroke-count of this part corresponds to the third part of the **SKIP number** and the second part of the **subsection number**.

2.4 SKIP Number

The **SKIP Number** consists of a **pattern symbol** followed by hyphenated numerals used to locate characters according to SKIP rules. The second and third parts of this number are called the **subsection number.** Since the entries of this dictionary are ordered according to the SKIP number, it is important to get a thorough understanding of how it is formed.

SKIP number	A **pattern symbol** followed by hyphenated numerals consisting of three parts; for the divisible characters, (1) the **pattern number**, (2) the stroke-count of the **shaded part**, and (3) the stroke-count of the **blank part**; for the indivisible characters, (1) the **pattern number**, (2) the total stroke-count, and (3) the **solid subpattern number**. For example, 相 is classified under pattern ◧1 and divided into 木 (shaded part, 4 strokes) and 目 (blank part, 5 strokes), giving a SKIP number of ◧1-4-5. 下 is a three-stroke solid character containing a **top line** (solid subpattern ⬒1), giving a SKIP number of ■4-3-1.
Subsection number	Hyphenated numerals used to identify a **subsection** and corresponding to the second and third parts of the SKIP number. For example, the subsection number for 相 (SKIP number ◧1-4-5) is 4-5. This number helps quickly locate a desired subsection in the **Pattern Index** or in the main part of the dictionary.

SKIP Number of Divisible Characters

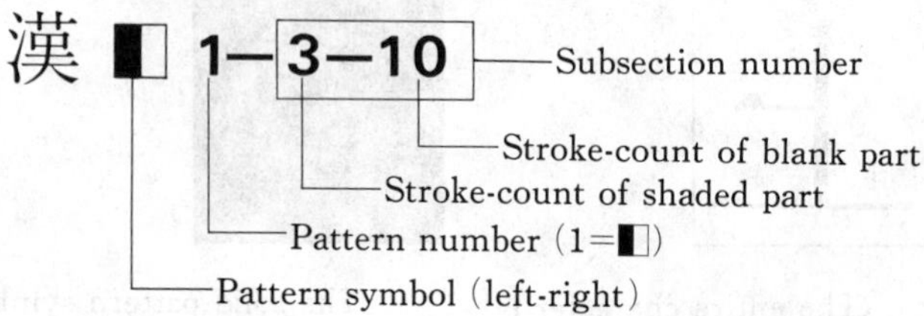

The principle for forming the SKIP number for the divisible characters is as follows:

1. The first part consists of the pattern symbol and the pattern number under which the character is classified; i.e., ◨ 1, ⬒ 2, or ◘ 3.
2. The second part indicates the stroke-count of the shaded part and corresponds to the first part of the subsection number.
3. The third part indicates the stroke-count of the blank part and corresponds to the second part of the subsection number.

SKIP Number of Indivisible Characters

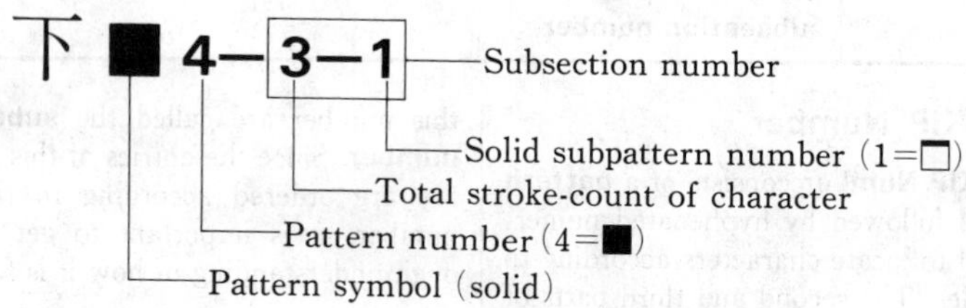

The principle for forming the SKIP number for the indivisible characters is as follows:

1. The first part consists of the pattern symbol and the pattern number for the solid pattern; i.e., ■ 4.
2. The second part indicates the total stroke-count of the character and corresponds to the first part of the subsection number.
3. The third part indicates the number of the solid subpattern under which the character is subclassified; i.e., □ 1, □ 2, □ 3, or □ 4 (see **§ 6.2** for details). It corresponds to the second part of the subsection number.

The table below shows the relationship between the SKIP number and the subsection number:

SKIP Number and Subsection Number

		SKIP Number	Subsection Number
Divisible characters	漢 安 度	◧ 1-3-10 ⬒ 2-3-3 □ 3-3-6	3-10 3-3 3-6
Indivisible characters	下 上 中 丸	■ 4-3-1 ■ 4-3-2 ■ 4-4-3 ■ 4-3-4	3-1 3-2 4-3 3-4

2.5 Classification Scheme

2.5.1 Order of Entries The order of entries in this dictionary is based on a new classification scheme. The characters are grouped into four major categories on the basis of geometrical **patterns**: ◧ 1 left-right, ⬒ 2 up-down, □ 3 enclosure, and ■ 4 solid. The characters within each category are divided into **subsections,** which are in turn subdivided into **subgroups.** The subgroups are further subdivided according to various classification keys into progressively smaller groups until each character is assigned its own position. The chart below shows the most important of these subdivisions (see § **2.7 Pattern Index** for a more detailed chart).

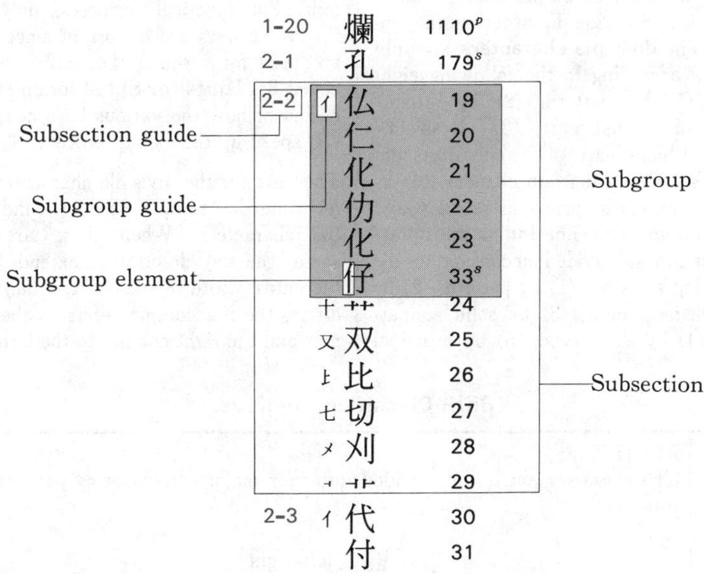

Subsection	A subdivision of the main part of the dictionary or of the **Pattern Index** in which the divisible characters are classified by **subgroup element** and the indivisible characters are classified by **entry type**. The subsections are arranged in ascending order of hyphenated numerals referred to as the **subsection number** (see **§ 2.4**). Each subsection is headed by a **subsection guide** for quick reference.
Subgroup	A subdivision of a **subsection** in which a group of **divisible characters** share a common **subgroup element.** Each subgroup is headed by a **subgroup guide,** which indicates the **subgroup element** for quick reference.
Subgroup element	The shared element of a **subgroup,** which corresponds to the **shaded part** of a divisible character. For example, 忄 is the subgroup element for the subgroup consisting of 怖 怪 怜 etc. Many subgroup elements, like 忄 above, are also radicals; others, like 君 in 群, are not. The subgroup elements that are radicals, which are ordered by their radical numbers, precede those that are not.

2.5.2 Classification Keys The complete scheme of SKIP classification keys is shown in the chart below. *Key* refers to any item, such as stroke-count, that is used as a criterion in ordering the entries. The **divisible characters** are subdivided according to the following eight keys: (1) by pattern, (2) by stroke-count of shaded part, (3) by stroke-count of blank part, (4) by enclosure subpattern, (5) by subgroup element, (6) by entry type, (7) by principal reading, and (8) by frequency. The **indivisible characters** are subdivided according to the following six keys: (1) by pattern, (2) by total stroke-count, (3) by solid subpattern, (4) by entry type, (5) by principal reading, and (6) by frequency.

The chart below is given for reference only—there is no need to understand all the details. For practical purposes, only the first three keys are important since they are used for forming the SKIP number. See **§ 3.3 Hints for Speed** for an explanation of how the various keys can help you speed up the lookup process.

The keys for the divisible characters differ somewhat from those for the indivisible characters. When these are the same, the key description extends over the entire width of the chart; when they differ, the left column refers to the former and the right column to the latter.

SKIP Classification Keys

❶	BY PATTERN: The character entries are divided into four major categories by **pattern number**: 1. ◧ 1 left-right 2. ⬒ 2 up-down 3. ◻ 3 enclosure 4. ■ 4 solid

	◧ 1 ⬒ 2 ▣ 3	■ 4
❷	**BY STROKE-COUNT OF SHADED PART:** Divisible characters classified under the same pattern are arranged in ascending order of the stroke-counts of their **shaded parts.**	**BY TOTAL STROKE-COUNT:** Indivisible characters are arranged in ascending order of their total stroke-counts.
❸	**BY STROKE-COUNT OF BLANK PART:** Divisible characters whose shaded parts have the same stroke-counts are arranged in ascending order of the stroke-counts of their **blank parts.**	
❹	**BY ENCLOSURE SUBPATTERN:** Divisible characters classified under pattern ▣ 3 whose blank parts have the same stroke-counts are grouped into eleven categories by **enclosure subpattern**: 1. two sides: ◻ ◻ ◻ ◻ 2. three sides: ◻ ◻ ◻ ◻ 3. four sides: ◻ ◻ ◻	**BY SOLID SUBPATTERN:** Indivisible characters sharing the same total stroke-count are grouped into four categories by **solid subpattern**: 1. ◻ 1 top line 2. ◻ 2 bottom line 3. ◻ 3 through line 4. ◻ 4 others
❺	**BY SUBGROUP ELEMENT:** Divisible characters whose blank parts have the same stroke-count (and, for pattern ▣ 3, which also share the same enclosure subpattern) are divided into **subgroups** by **subgroup element.** These are arranged in the following order: 1. Those that are **radicals** by their **radical numbers (Appendix 6).** 2. Those that are not radicals by their stroke-counts and SKIP numbers.	
❻	**BY ENTRY TYPE:** Divisible characters sharing the same subgroup element are divided into six groups by **entry type**:	Indivisible characters classified under the same solid subpattern are divided into six groups by **entry type**:
	1. standard entries 2. nonstandard entries 3. single-character cross-references for standard entries 4. single-character cross-references for nonstandard entries 5. multiple-character cross-references for standard entries 6. multiple-character cross-references for nonstandard entries.	

❼	**BY PRINCIPAL READING:** Characters of the same entry type are ordered alphabetically by their **principal readings** (GUIDE §4.2).
❽	**BY FREQUENCY:** Characters sharing the same principal reading are ordered by their **frequency** of occurrence (GUIDE §7.5).

2.6 Cross-References

Finding entries by SKIP rules is normally speedy and reliable. However, difficulties may arise in unusual cases, such as characters whose patterns are difficult to identify, or characters whose stroke-counts are difficult to count. For example, 児 is an up-down character that may be mistakenly classified as a left-right character by dividing it into 丿 and 旧, whereas 子 is a three-stroke element that may be incorrectly counted as a two-stroke element.

Characters like the above are systematically placed at one or more *incorrect* SKIP locations—that is, locations where they might be mistakenly looked for—and are followed by a cross-reference to their corresponding correct locations. To ensure maximum usefulness and accuracy, the kinds of mistakes likely to occur were systematically analyzed and tested, and a network of **cross-reference entries** was generated and checked by computer.

Cross-reference entry	A character entry in the main part of the dictionary or in the **Pattern Index** appearing at an **incorrect location** with a cross-reference to the corresponding correct location.

The cross-references greatly enhance the value of the system, since they practically eliminate dead-end searching. Moreover, they inform you of the kind of mistake you have made; that is, whether you have arrived at an incorrect pattern classification, an incorrect stroke-count, or both. This helps you learn from your mistakes and thus avoid similar ones.

Cross-reference entries appear in both the main part of the dictionary and in the **Pattern Index** (see chart in §2.7 **Pattern Index**). In the explanations below, the example on the left refers to the former and the one on the right to the latter.

2.6.1 Cross-Reference Types Cross-reference entries are of two kinds:

1. **Single-character** cross-reference entries are cross-references for one character at an incorrect location. The correct location is indicated by the entry number to be referred to:

5-2 穴	究	incorrect classification ⇨ see 2203	5-2	季	2554[S]
				穴 究	2203[P]
				立 辛	2038[P]

In the example, 究 appears under the incorrect classification ▀ 2-5-2, and the cross-reference points to 2203, the entry number under the correct classification ▀ 2-3-4. Cross-references are also given for nonstandard forms. In the main part, the corresponding standard form is shown in parentheses; in the index, nonstandard forms are listed but not marked in any special way:

1-12	临	incorrect classification ⇨ see 162 (nonstandard for 臨 1630)	1-12	愉惰etc⇨▌3-9[p] 临 162[p] 煙煩 ⇨▌4-9[p]

2. **Multiple-character** cross-reference entries are cross-references for a group of two or more characters of similar structure (pattern classification or stroke-count) at an incorrect location. The correct location is indicated by the pattern and subsection number to be referred to:

1-8	恒悔 etc.	incorrect classification ⇨ see ▌3-6	1-8 1-9	畑炮 ⇨▌4-5[p] 恒悔etc⇨▌3-6[p] 門 1165[p]

If the group consists of two characters, both are given. If the group consists of three or more characters, the first two are given and are followed by etc. This indicates that the other members of the group have the same structure as the first two and can also be found at the same correct location. In the example above, etc. indicates that, in addition to 恒 and 悔, other left-right characters sharing the subgroup element 忄, such as 恢 and 恰, can also be found at the correct location ▌3-6.

2.6.2 Incorrect Locations **Incorrect location** refers to a location where a character might be mistakenly looked for. Incorrect locations are of two kinds: (1) locations under an incorrect pattern classification, and (2) locations under an incorrect stroke-count. On rare occasions, an incorrect location may be a combination of both types:

1-15	憐	incorrect classification／stroke count ⇨ see 731	1-14 1-15	憤憐etc⇨▌3-12[p] 憐 731[ps] 憾憶etc⇨▌3-13[p]

In the main part of the dictionary, the kind of incorrect location is indicated by the brief description preceding the arrow ⇨; in the index, by the following superscript symbols:

- *p* incorrect pattern classification
- *s* incorrect stroke-count
- *ps* incorrect pattern classification and incorrect stroke-count

2.7 Pattern Index

The key to using this dictionary effectively is the **Pattern Index,** which allows you to quickly locate a character from its pattern. This section describes the physical layout of the index, and explains the various symbols and guides. The guides are designed to help you locate entries with maximum speed. Detailed instructions for locating character entries by means of this index can be found under **§ 3.1.2 Index Method** and **§ 3.2 SCAN Method.** The gist of the **Index Method** is as follows:

1. Determine the **SKIP number** of your character.
2. Determine the **entry number** by locating your character in the **Pattern Index.** Use the **subsection guides** and **subgroup guides.**
3. Locate your character entry from the entry number.

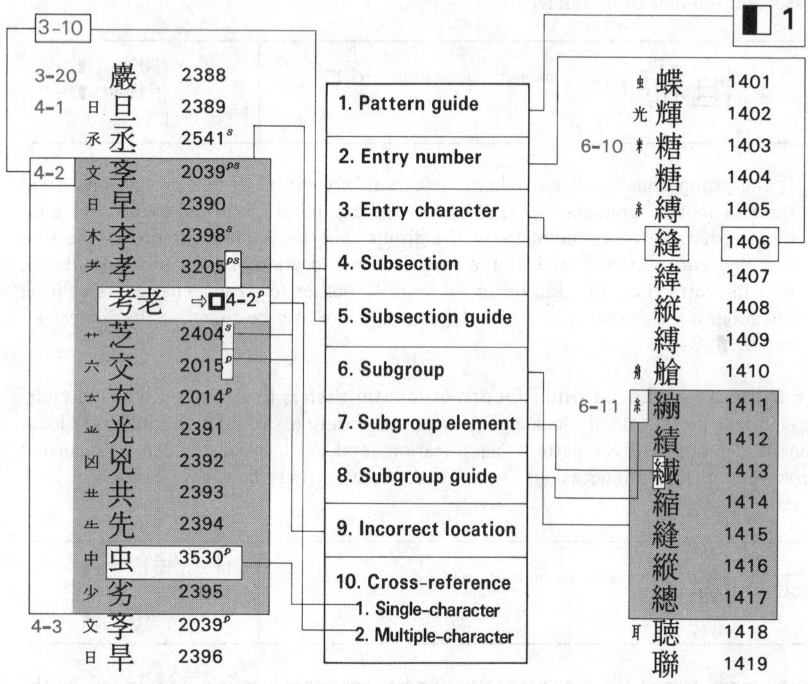

1. Pattern guide	A guide in the upper, outer corner of a page that indicates the **pattern** and **pattern number** for that page (see **§ 2.2**).
2. Entry number	A serial number that uniquely identifies the numbered character entries of the dictionary. After locating the entry number of your character in the index, turn the pages of the dictionary until you find the corresponding character entry.

3. Entry character	The character that heads an index entry.
4. Subsection	A subdivision of the main part of the dictionary or of the **Pattern Index** (see § **2.5.1**). The subsections are arranged in ascending order of their **subsection numbers** (see § **2.4**).
5. Subsection guide	1. Boldface numerals in the upper corner of a page that indicate the **subsection number** for that page. The upper-right guide indicates the subsection number for the first subsection, while the upper-left guide indicates the subsection number for the last subsection in that page. Together, they indicate the subsection number range for the two pages. 2. Red hyphenated numerals in the left part of **Pattern Index** column that indicate the subsection number for each subsection. Scanning through the subsection guides enables you to quickly locate the subsection number corresponding to your character.
6. Subgroup	A subdivision of a **subsection** in which a group of **divisible characters** share a common **subgroup element** (see § **2.5.1**).
7. Subgroup element	The shared element of a **subgroup,** which corresponds to the **shaded part** of a **divisible character** (see § **2.5.1**).
8. Subgroup guide	A guide to the left of the character column in the **Pattern Index** that indicates the **subgroup element**. Scanning through the subgroup guides enables you to quickly locate the one corresponding to the **shaded part** of your character.
9. Incorrect location	Location where a character might be mistakenly looked for (see § **2.6.2**): *p* incorrect pattern classification *s* incorrect stroke-count *ps* incorrect pattern classification and incorrect stroke-count
10. Cross-reference entry	An entry in the **Pattern Index** appearing at an **incorrect location** with a cross-reference to the corresponding correct location (see § **2.6**). These are of two kinds: 1. Cross-reference for a single character. 2. Cross-references for a group of two or more characters.

2.8 SKIP Guides

One feature that makes the **System of Kanji Indexing by Patterns** convenient to the user is a **system of guides.** The various guides printed in the outer corners and margins of the page have been carefully designed and laid out to facilitate the speedy location of entries. They are particularly useful for finding an entry directly from its **SKIP number** without consulting the **Pattern Index** (see **§ 3.1.3 Direct Method** for details).

The guides in the main part of the dictionary are of the following kinds: (1) the pattern guide, (2) the subsection guide, (3) the margin guide, (4) the subgroup guide, and (5) the entry number guide. These and other relevant elements are illustrated and described below. For a description of the guides in the **Pattern Index,** see **§ 2.7 Pattern Index.**

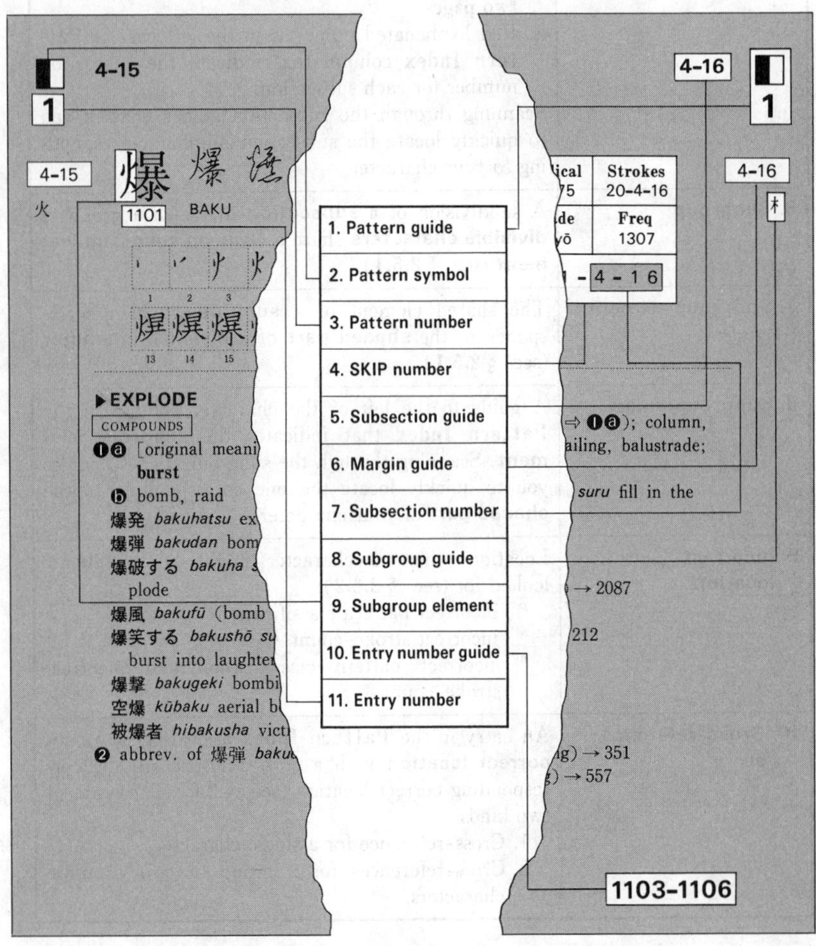

1. Pattern guide	A guide in the upper, outer corner of a page that indicates the **pattern** and **pattern number** for that page (see § 2.2).
2. Pattern symbol	A symbol that identifies one of the four patterns in the SKIP classification scheme (see § **2.2**).
3. Pattern number	A number that identifies one of the four patterns in the SKIP classification scheme (see § **2.2**).
4. SKIP number	A **pattern symbol** followed by hyphenated numerals used to locate characters according to SKIP rules (see § **2.4**).
5. Subsection guide	Boldface numerals in the upper corner of a page that indicate the **subsection number** for that page. The pattern guide and subsection guide in the upper left of the page indicate the SKIP number for the first entry character in a left-hand page, while those in the upper right indicate the SKIP number for the last entry character in a right-hand page. Together, they indicate the SKIP number range for the two pages and serve as a convenient aid when flipping through the pages in search of a desired entry.
6. Margin guide	A guide in the outer margin of a page that consists of a frame enclosing the **subsection number** for each entry character. It can be used in conjunction with, or independently of, the subsection guide to locate a desired subsection number.
7. Subsection number	Hyphenated numerals corresponding to the second and third parts of the SKIP number (see § **2.4**).
8. Subgroup guide	A guide in the outer margin of a page that indicates the **subgroup element** for each entry character. This guide helps quickly locate the character once the desired SKIP number range has been reached.
9. Subgroup element	The shared element of a **subgroup**, which corresponds to the **shaded part** of a **divisible character** (see § **2.5.1**).
10. Entry number guide	Boldface numerals or hyphenated boldface numerals in the lower, outer corner of a page that indicate the **entry number** or range of entry numbers for that page. This guide quickly helps locate a character whose entry number is known.
11. Entry number	A boldface serial number that uniquely identifies the numbered character entries of the dictionary (see also GUIDE § **1.4 Entry Number**).

3. INSTRUCTIONS FOR USE

There are two methods of locating entries by SKIP rules:

1. The **SKIP Method** consists of determining the **SKIP number** of your character then locating it in the main part of the dictionary. This is the method recommended for ordinary use.
2. The **SCAN Method** is a special shortcut that enables you to locate a character without determining its SKIP number. This method is only effective for characters containing elements of high stroke-count.

The sections below present detailed instructions for locating entries by the above methods. To use these instructions effectively, be sure you understand the material covered in **§ 2. Description of the System.** Although the instructions are very thorough, don't be overwhelmed by the details. Remember that the system is essentially simple—with just a little practice, you should be able to find entries with great speed and little effort.

3.1 SKIP Method

Finding an entry by the **SKIP Method** consists of two major steps:

1. Determine the **SKIP number** of your character.
2. Locate the character entry in the main part of the dictionary.

Once you know the SKIP number of your character, locating the character entry is a straightforward, largely mechanical process. To make the system as flexible as possible, there are two ways to do this: (1) the **Index Method,** by which you first find the entry number of your character in the **Pattern Index,** and (2) the **Direct Method,** by which you locate your character entry directly from its SKIP number. The second method is on the average faster than the first (see **§ 3.3 Hints for Speed** for details).

3.1.1 How to Determine the SKIP Number To locate a character by the SKIP Method, you must first determine its SKIP number. Since determining this number quickly is the key to using the system effectively, you should get a thorough understanding of how it is formed (see **§ 2.4 SKIP Number**). The gist of the method is a follows:

> Identify the **pattern** to get the first part of the SKIP number. To get the second and third parts, count the strokes of the **shaded part** and **blank part** of the divisible characters, or count the total stroke-count and determine the **solid subpattern** of the indivisible characters.

The chart below gives detailed instructions for determining the SKIP number, and includes references to other sections that explain each step in greater detail. Understanding this chart is of crucial importance, so study carefully the examples appearing right after the chart. For quick reference, this chart also appears inside the front covers.

How to Determine the SKIP Number

<table>
<tr><th colspan="3">DETERMINE THE SKIP NUMBER OF YOUR CHARACTER.</th></tr>
<tr><td>STEP 1</td><td colspan="2">IDENTIFY PATTERN
Determine to which of the four patterns your character belongs to get the first part of the SKIP number (the pattern number). If your character belongs to pattern ◧ 1, ⬒ 2, or ◘ 3, carry out the steps in the left column; if it belongs to pattern ■ 4, carry out the steps in the right column.
REFERENCE: §4. How to Identify the Pattern</td></tr>
<tr><td></td><td>◧ 1 ⬒ 2 ◘ 3</td><td>■ 4</td></tr>
<tr><td>STEP 2</td><td>DIVIDE CHARACTER
Divide the character into two parts at the first division point.
REFERENCE: §5. How to Divide the Character</td><td>OMIT
(Since solid characters cannot be divided, go to STEP 3.)
REFERENCE: §6. How to Subclassify the Solid Pattern</td></tr>
<tr><td>STEP 3</td><td>COUNT STROKES OF SHADED PART
Count the strokes of the shaded part to get the second part of the SKIP number.
REFERENCE: Appendix 2. How to Count Strokes</td><td>DETERMINE TOTAL STROKE-COUNT
Determine the total stroke-count of your character to get the second part of the SKIP number.
REFERENCE: Appendix 2. How to Count Strokes</td></tr>
<tr><td>STEP 4</td><td>COUNT STROKES OF BLANK PART
Count the strokes of the blank part to get the third part of the SKIP number.
REFERENCE: Appendix 2. How to Count Strokes</td><td>IDENTIFY SOLID SUBPATTERN
Determine to which of the four solid subpatterns your character belongs to get the third part of the SKIP number. Select from: ⍐ 1, ⍗ 2, ⎅ 3, or □ 4.
REFERENCE: §6. How to Subclassify the Solid Pattern</td></tr>
</table>

Example: DETERMINE THE SKIP NUMBER OF 棚.

<table>
<tr><td>STEP 1</td><td>IDENTIFY PATTERN</td><td>Since 棚 can be divided into left and right parts, we identify it as belonging to pattern ◧ 1, left-right. This gives the first part of the SKIP number as 1:

棚 → ◧ 1</td></tr>
<tr><td>STEP 2</td><td>DIVIDE CHARACTER</td><td>Dividing 棚 into two parts at the first division point yields 木, the shaded part, and 朋, the blank part:

棚 = 木 + 朋</td></tr>
</table>

STEP 3	COUNT STROKES OF SHADED PART	Counting the strokes of the **shaded part** (木) yields a stroke-count of 4. This gives the second part of the SKIP number as 4: 棚 ◧ 1-4-
STEP 4	COUNT STROKES OF BLANK PART	Counting the strokes of the **blank part** (朋) yields a stroke-count of 8. This gives the third part of the SKIP number as 8: 棚 → ◧ 1-4-8
		SKIP number of 棚: ◧ 1-4-8

Example: DETERMINE THE SKIP NUMBER OF 下.

STEP 1	IDENTIFY PATTERN	Since 下 cannot be divided into parts, we identify it as an **indivisible character** belonging to pattern ■ 4, solid. This gives the first part of the SKIP number as 4: 下 → ■ 4
STEP 2	OMIT	(Since 下 cannot be divided, go to STEP 3.)
STEP 3	DETERMINE TOTAL STROKE-COUNT	Counting the strokes of the entire character yields a stroke-count of 3. This gives the second part of the SKIP number as 3: 下 ■ 4-3-
STEP 4	IDENTIFY SOLID SUBPATTERN	Since 下 contains a line on top, we identify it as a **solid character** belonging to subpattern ▔ 1, **top line.** This gives the third part of the SKIP number as 1: 下 ■ 4-3-1
		SKIP number of 下: ■ 4-3-1

3.1.2 Index Method After determining the SKIP number of your character, you must locate it in the main part of the dictionary. The surest way to do this is by the **Index Method,** the gist of which is as follows:

> Flip through the **Pattern Index** until you locate the **pattern number** and **subsection number** for your character. Scan the **subgroup guides** to locate your **shaded part,** then find your character and its **entry number.** Finally, turn the pages of the dictionary until you find your entry number.

The chart below gives detailed instructions for locating character entries by the Index Method.

<table>
<tr><th colspan="3">DETERMINE THE ENTRY NUMBER IN THE PATTERN INDEX, THEN LOCATE YOUR CHARACTER ENTRY.</th></tr>
<tr><td>STEP 1</td><td colspan="2">LOCATE PATTERN
Turn the pages of the Pattern Index until you locate the pattern number (the first part of the SKIP number) which corresponds to your character. Use the pattern guides in the upper, outer corners of the pages.
REFERENCE: §2.7 Pattern Index</td></tr>
<tr><td rowspan="2">STEP 2</td><td colspan="2">LOCATE SUBSECTION
Continue turning the pages until you locate the subsection number (the second and third parts of the SKIP number) which corresponds to your character. Use the red subsection guides in the left part of the column.
REFERENCE: §2.7 Pattern Index</td></tr>
<tr><td>1 2 3</td><td>4</td></tr>
<tr><td>STEP 3</td><td>LOCATE SUBGROUP
Scan the column of subgroup guides until you locate the one which corresponds to the shaded part of your character.
REFERENCE: §2.7 Pattern Index</td><td>OMIT
(Since solid characters cannot be divided, they are not grouped by subgroup elements.)</td></tr>
<tr><td>STEP 4</td><td colspan="2">DETERMINE ENTRY NUMBER
Scan the column of characters until you locate your character and its entry number.</td></tr>
<tr><td>STEP 5</td><td colspan="2">LOCATE ENTRY CHARACTER
Turn the pages of the dictionary until you locate the one which includes your entry number, then scan that page until you locate your entry character. Use the entry number guides in the lower, outer corners of the pages.
REFERENCE: §2.8 SKIP Guides</td></tr>
</table>

3.1.3 Direct Method After determining the SKIP number of your character, there is a second method for locating your entry in the main part of the dictionary. This is called the **Direct Method**, and is usually faster than the **Index Method**. The gist of this method is as follows:

Turn the pages of the dictionary (*without* referring to the **Pattern Index**) until you locate the **pattern number** and **subsection number** for your character. Scan the **subgroup guides** to locate your **shaded part**, then continue flipping the pages until you locate your character.

The chart below gives detailed instructions for locating character entries by the Direct Method.

<table>
<tr><th colspan="3">LOCATE YOUR CHARACTER ENTRY DIRECTLY FROM ITS SKIP NUMBER.</th></tr>
<tr><td>STEP 1</td><td colspan="2">LOCATE PATTERN
Turn the pages of the dictionary until you locate the pattern number (the first part of the SKIP number) which corresponds to your character. Use the pattern guides in the upper, outer corners of the pages.
REFERENCE: § 2. 8 SKIP Guides</td></tr>
<tr><td rowspan="2">STEP 2</td><td colspan="2">LOCATE SUBSECTION
Continue turning the pages until you locate the subsection number (the second and third parts of the SKIP number) which corresponds to your character. Use the subsection guides in the upper, outer corners of the pages.
REFERENCE: § 2. 8 SKIP Guides</td></tr>
<tr><td>◧ 1 ⬒ 2 ◻ 3</td><td>■ 4</td></tr>
<tr><td>STEP 3</td><td>LOCATE SUBGROUP
Continue turning the pages until you locate the subgroup guide which corresponds to the shaded part of your character.
HINT: Subgroup elements that are radicals are ordered by radical number.
REFERENCES: § 2. 8 SKIP Guides
§ 2. 5 Classification Scheme
§ 3. 3 Hints for Speed</td><td>OMIT
Since solid characters are not grouped by subgroup element, go to STEP 4.</td></tr>
<tr><td>STEP 4</td><td colspan="2">LOCATE CHARACTER
Continue turning the pages until you locate your character entry.
HINT: The divisible characters in a given subgroup and the indivisible characters in a given subsection are further classified by entry type and ordered alphabetically by their principal readings.
REFERENCES: § 2. 5 Classification Scheme
§ 3. 3 Hints for Speed</td></tr>
</table>

3.2 SCAN Method

3.2.1 A Powerful Shortcut To locate an entry by the **SKIP Method,** you must first count the strokes of the character's components to determine its SKIP number. For characters of few strokes this does not pose much of a problem, but for elements of high stroke-count it could be time-consuming. While mastering the techniques explained in **Appendix 2. How to Count Strokes** helps, counting strokes is nevertheless an error-prone, laborious task.

The **SCAN Method** is a powerful shortcut that makes it possible to dispense with counting the strokes of elements of high stroke-count. Since characters containing such elements are relatively few and appear close together, you need only to find the approximate location of your character and then scan the vicinity to locate it. For complex characters, this is much faster than counting strokes to determine the SKIP number. Don't bother learning the SCAN Method unless it suits your taste—any entry can always be found reliably with the SKIP Method.

The SCAN Method is used for locating **divisible characters** whose shaded or blank parts have high stroke-counts. Basically, "high stroke-count" refers to 12 or more strokes. It is not sufficient for the *total* stroke-count of a character to be high; one of its *parts* must have 12 or more strokes. For example, although 償 (blank part 15 strokes) is ideally suited for this method, 騎 (total 18 strokes) is not since neither 馬 (10 strokes) nor 奇 (8 strokes) has 12 strokes.

The higher the stroke-count is, the shorter the "scanning distance" and the better the method works. If the shaded part has, say, 15 or more strokes, you can locate your character almost instantaneously. For pattern ◘ 3, which has relatively few entries, you can even use this method for stroke-counts of 11 or 10.

Finding a character by the SCAN Method consists of three basic steps:

1. **Selecting the SCAN Method** The SCAN Method has two variations: **SCAN Method A** for characters whose *shaded* parts have high stroke-counts, and **SCAN Method B** for those whose *blank* parts have high stroke-counts. Be sure not confuse the two. To select the SCAN Method, decide whether it is the shaded part or the blank part that has a high stroke-count (12 or more). Don't actually count the strokes—just make a rough "guesstimate."

2. **Finding the Approximate Location** To find a divisible character by the SCAN Method, you must first determine the **approximate location** from where to begin the search. The optimal approximate location is the vicinity where the **subsection numbers** begin with or end in 14, as explained in the table below:

Approximate Locations

Scan Method A	The vicinity where the subsection numbers **begin with 14;** i.e., 14-1, 14-2, 14-3, etc. A quick way to find it is to use the **pattern guides** to locate the beginning of the *next* pattern section and work your way backwards to 14.
Scan Method B	The subsection number that begins with the stroke-count of your shaded part and **ends in 14;** i.e., 1-14, 2-14, 3-14, etc. If there is no subsection number ending in 14, go to the nearest one, such as to one ending in 13 or 12.

Both kinds of approximate location are illustrated in the chart entitled **Scanning the Pattern Index** in **§ 3.2.2** below. In both cases, use the **subsection guides** (hyphenated numerals indicating the subsection number) to quickly find your subsection.

Fourteen serves as the standard stroke-count for the approximate location. If your stroke-count seems higher than 14, you may save time by beginning the search a little further ahead, such as at 16 or higher; if it seems lower than 14, by going back a little to the vicinity of 13 or 12. With a little practice, you should soon be able to find the approximate location in a few seconds.

3. **Scanning** After establishing the approximate location, you can quickly locate your character by **scanning.** This can be broken down into the following steps:

   1. Scan the **subgroup guides** until you locate the one corresponding to the shaded part of your character.
   2. Scan the entry characters within that **subgroup** until you locate your character.
   3. If your character is not in that subgroup, repeat the first two steps until you find it.

Scanning may sound complicated on paper, but is actually very simple to do. There is no need to think of it as consisting of distinct steps. Essentially, all you do is swiftly move from one subgroup to another using the subgroup guides as visual signposts. If you wish, you may scan the entry characters directly without using the subgroup guides. This could work well for high stroke-counts, since the "scanning distance" is short.

Scanning can also be used to find a character for which you have miscounted the number of strokes when determining the SKIP number (see **§ 3.3 Hints for Speed**).

3.2.2 Instruction Charts The charts below present precise instructions for locating a divisible character by scanning. Essentially, you just turn to the approximate location (subsection number beginning with or ending in 14) and scan until you locate your character. For example, to find 彎 you turn to the subsection numbers beginning with 14 and scan until you find it in subsection 19-3.

The instructions for locating an entry by the SCAN Method can be carried out in two ways:

1. **Determine the entry number of your character in the Pattern Index and then find your character entry.** This is similar to the **Index Method** (see **§ 3.1.2**) used for finding entries by the SKIP Method, but when using the SCAN Method there is no need to determine the subsection number since you locate your subsection by finding the approximate location and then scanning.
2. **Locate your entry directly in the main part of the dictionary without using the Pattern Index.** This is similar to the **Direct Method** (see **§ 3.1.3**) used for finding entries by the SKIP Method, but when using the SCAN Method there is no need to determine the subsection number since you locate your subsection by finding the approximate location and then scanning.

Whether to use the **Pattern Index** or not is largely a matter of personal taste. See **§ 3.3 Hints for Speed** for details.

Selecting the SCAN Method

INSTRUCTIONS	EXAMPLE: Find 襲 and 像
❶ IDENTIFY PATTERN See **§4. How to Identify the Pattern** for details.	襲: Since 襲 can be divided into up-down parts, we identify it as belonging to pattern ▀ 2. 像: Since 像 can be divided into left-right parts, we identify it as belonging to pattern ▌ 1.
❷ DIVIDE CHARACTER If your character belongs to pattern ▌ 1, ▀ 2, or □ 3, divide the character into two parts. See **§5. How to Divide the Character** for details.	襲: Dividing 襲 into up-down parts yields 龍, the shaded part, and 衣, the blank part. 像: Dividing 像 into left-right parts yields 亻, the shaded part, and 象, the blank part.
❸ SELECT SCAN METHOD If the stroke-count of the shaded part seems high, use **SCAN Method A.** If the stroke-count of the blank part seems high, use **SCAN Method B.**	襲: Since the stroke-count of the shaded part 龍 seems high (in this case 16), select SCAN Method A. 像: Since the stroke-count of the blank part 象 seems high (in this case 12), select SCAN Method B.

SCAN Method A: High Shaded Count

INSTRUCTIONS	EXAMPLE: Find 襲
❶ FIND APPROXIMATE LOCATION Using the **pattern** and **subsection guides,** turn to your pattern section and go to the vicinity where the **subsection numbers** begin with 14; i.e., 14-1, 14-2, 14-3, etc.	Turn to the subsection numbers beginning with 14 under pattern ▀ 2. This can be done quickly by finding the beginning of the pattern □ 3 section and working your way backwards.
❷ LOCATE CHARACTER BY SCANNING Using the **subgroup guides,** scan until you locate your character.	Scanning the subgroup guides quickly leads you to 龍, the shaded part of 襲. You then easily locate your character in subsection 16-6.

Scanning the Pattern Index

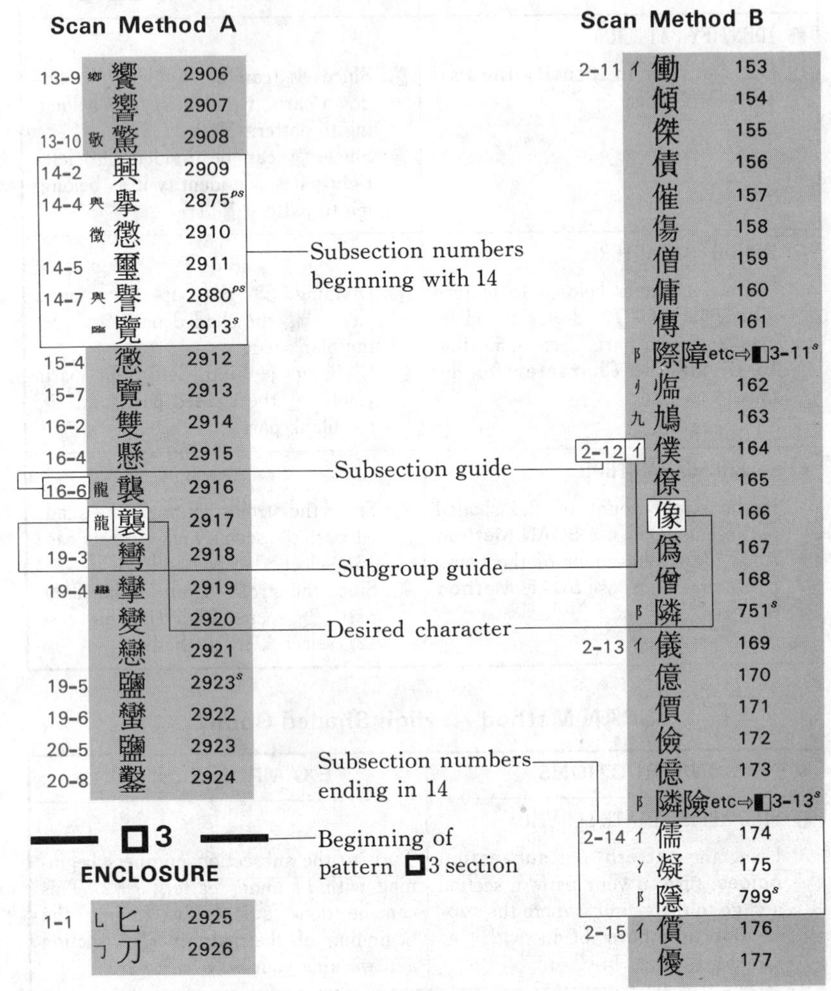

SCAN Method B: High Blank Count

	INSTRUCTIONS	EXAMPLE: Find 像
❶	DETERMINE STROKE-COUNT Count the exact number of strokes of the shaded part of your character.	Counting the strokes of the shaded part 亻 yields a stroke-count of 2.
❷	FIND APPROXIMATE LOCATION Using the **pattern** and **subsection guides**, turn to your pattern section and go to the **subsection number** that begins with the stroke-count of the shaded part and ends in 14; i.e., 1-14, 2-14, 3-14, etc.	Using the subsection guides, turn to the subsection number beginning with 2, the stroke-count of the shaded part 亻, and ending in 14, i.e., subsection 2-14 under pattern ▀ 2.
❸	LOCATE CHARACTER BY SCANNING Using the **subgroup guides**, scan until you locate your character.	Scanning the subgroup guides quickly leads you to 亻, the shaded part of 像. You then easily locate your character in subsection 2-12.

The above charts apply only to the divisible characters. A similar technique can be used for locating an indivisible character. If your character has a high stroke-count, say 10 or more, simply turn to the very end of the **Pattern Index** or of the main part of the dictionary, and search the vicinity until you find it. As there are very few characters of this kind, you should find your entry almost immediately.

3.3 Hints for Speed

Every effort has been made to eliminate guesswork and make SKIP an efficient and reliable lookup system. Below are various time-saving hints and shortcuts that will help you locate entries with maximum speed and minimum effort. To use these hints effectively, refer also to the chart in **§2.5.2 Classification Keys.**

1. **Pattern Identification** Since SKIP rules are based on intuition, you can often identify the correct pattern at once by merely looking at the character. When in doubt, your best guide will be the SKIP patterns chart appearing inside the back covers. This chart has been designed to help you quickly identify the pattern without thinking about the rules.

2. **Counting Strokes** The ability to count strokes quickly and accurately will help you determine the SKIP number faster. Although many cross-references appear at locations where you might mistakenly look for your character, it will be worth your while to learn the stroke counting techniques explained in **Appendix 2. How to Count Strokes.** Particularly effective is memorizing the stroke-counts of high-frequency radicals and difficult-to-count elements.

3. **SKIP vs. SCAN** The **SKIP Method** (**§3.1**), in which you must first determine the SKIP number, is a safe method that works reliably all the time. It is the method that you should nor-

mally use in most of your dictionary work. The **SCAN Method** (§ **3.2**), on the other hand, is much more limited in scope. Its main advantage is that it dispenses with the need for counting the strokes of complex elements. For characters containing parts of 12 or more strokes (e.g. 襲), it could be considerably faster than the SKIP Method, but for characters containing parts of medium stroke-count (say 12 or 13) it is inefficient or totally useless. In conclusion: if you want a reliable, safe method free of guesswork, use the SKIP Method. If you prefer a rough, speedy shortcut, use the SCAN Method when appropriate.

4. **Scanning** If you cannot find your character from its SKIP number, there is a good chance that you have miscounted the number of strokes by one stroke. Rather than count again, you might save time by looking for your character in the next or in the previous subsection. For example, if you look for 暗 under ◧ 1-4-10 and cannot find it, try at the previous subsection ◧ 1-4-9 or at the next subsection ◧ 1-4-11 (see **§ 3.2 SCAN Method**).

5. **Index vs. Direct** The main advantage of the **Direct Method** (§ **3.1.3**) is that it dispenses with the need for searching through the **Pattern Index.** When using the SKIP Method, the Direct Method is usually faster, sometimes considerably faster, than the **Index Method** (§ **3.1.2**), but for some characters the reverse may be true. A distinct advantage of the Index Method is its high reliability; once you locate the entry number of your character in the index, you can find your entry with great speed and no hesitation. When using the SCAN Method, the difference in speed between the two methods is not very great. Try both and use the one that best suits your personal taste.

6. **SKIP Guides** Be sure to make full use of the various **SKIP guides** (§ **2.8**), which are designed to facilitate speedy lookup. Particularly useful are the **subsection guides** (printed in red in the **Pattern Index**) and the **subgroup guides,** which help you swiftly move from one **subsection** or **subgroup** to another.

7. **Enclosure Subpatterns** Although the enclosure characters are grouped by **enclosure subpattern** (§ **4.2**), you may totally disregard this when looking for your entry. The enclosure pattern constitutes a single category, just like the left-right or up-down pattern.

8. **Subgroup Elements** The divisible characters in a given **subsection** are grouped by **subgroup element** (§ **2.5.1**). If you are using the Index Method, you can quickly locate your subgroup element without worrying about their order. Since the number of subgroup elements in a given subsection is small, you can quickly locate your element by skimming through the **subgroup guides** of the **Pattern Index.** If, on the other hand, you are using the Direct Method, you may speed up the search by keeping in mind that the subgroup elements that are radicals appear in order of their radical numbers. Ignore this feature if you do not know the radical system really well.

9. **Entry Types** The divisible characters in a given **subgroup** and the indivisible characters in a given **subsection** are further classified by **entry type** (see GUIDE **§ 1.6 Types of Entries**). The entries that you are most likely to look for—the standard entries—appear first, and the nonstandard and cross-reference entries, which are the least needed, fol-

low. This is not something that you need to be consciously aware of (except possibly when deliberately searching for a nonstandard form)—it is merely an auxiliary device that automatically speeds up the lookup process.

10. **Principal Reading** Characters of the same entry type are ordered alphabetically by their **principal readings**, which is usually the most common *on* reading (see GUIDE **§4.2 Principal Reading**). If you know the reading of your character, this may help you find it more quickly, especially when using the Direct Method.

11. **Frequency** Characters sharing the same principal reading are ordered by their **frequency** of occurrence (see GUIDE **§7.5**), so that the more frequent characters appear first. This may slightly contribute to lookup speed if you are looking for a high-frequency character.

4. HOW TO IDENTIFY THE PATTERN

4.1 Pattern Identification

To locate a character according to SKIP rules, the first task you face is to determine to which of the four patterns your character belongs. The **pattern number** will constitute the first part of the three-part **SKIP number** of your character. For example, 宙 is classified under the up-down pattern ▀ 2, so the first part of its SKIP number is 2. See **§2.4 SKIP Number** for details.

To identify the pattern, just *look* at the character (or imagine it in your mind's eye) and decide to which pattern it belongs. Most of the time, your intuition will lead you to the correct classification at once. For example, 好, 充, and 尾 look like they belong to patterns ◧ 1, ▀ 2, and ◘ 3 respectively, while 下 and 曲 look like they are indivisible and therefore belong to pattern ■ 4. If you have trouble classifying your character, a glance at the pattern chart inside the back covers should usually enable you to easily identify the pattern without referring to the rules given below.

In actual practice, you normally identify the pattern of a character and divide it or subclassify it more or less simultaneously. When you see a character like 相, for example, you identify it as a left-right pattern, and, at the same time, decide that it can be divided into 木 and 目. Nevertheless, for the sake of clarity and convenience of presentation, pattern identification and character division are treated here as separate topics (**§4.3** and **§5.3** respectively).

A formal statement of the rules for identifying the pattern is given in **§4.3** below. Each rule is explained in greater detail in **Appendix 1. §2. How to Identify the Pattern.**

4.2 Enclosure Subpatterns

To make it easier to identify the **enclosure pattern**, it is desirable to understand the concepts **enclosure element** and **enclosure subpattern**.

Enclosure element	A completely exterior element enclosing the rest of a character on two or more sides. The enclosure pattern is subdivided into **enclosure subpatterns.**
Enclosure subpattern	One of the eleven groups into which the enclosure pattern is subdivided according to the number of sides of the enclosure element and its position along the exterior of the character.
Enclosure subpattern symbol	A symbol that identifies one of the eleven enclosure subpatterns.

The enclosure subpatterns are illustrated in the chart below:

Enclosure Subpatterns

Sides	Subpattern Symbol	Examples
2		進
		句
		麻
		斗
3		閉
		凶
		医
4		丑
		団
		目
		四

It is important to keep in mind that the enclosure pattern constitutes a single category, just like the left–right or up–down pattern. Any enclosure character, regardless of its subpattern, is classified under the enclosure pattern, and it is not necessary to be particularly aware of the subpattern. The subpattern symbols are merely visual aids that help describe the structure of enclosure elements.

Some enclosure elements may be difficult to identify. If you have trouble, refer to **Appendix 1. § 1.7 Enclosure Element** for a more detailed description, and to the charts inside the front and back covers.

4.3 Pattern Identification Rules

❶ DETERMINE TO WHICH OF THE FOUR PATTERNS YOUR CHARACTER BELONGS	Right	Wrong
1 CHARACTERS THAT CAN BE DIVIDED INTO LEFT AND RIGHT PARTS		
(*a*) The resulting parts must be separated by a **space.**	相 4-5　八 1-1　順 1-11	片 1-3　用 1-4　隹 2-6
(*b*) The resulting division must be more or less vertical.	体 2-5　吹 3-4　扱 3-3	可 3-2　延 3-5　多 3-3

▬ 2 CHARACTERS THAT CAN BE DIVIDED INTO TOP AND BOTTOM PARTS (*a*) The resulting parts must be separated by a **space, horizontal line,** or **frame element.** (*b*) The resulting division need not be horizontal.	二 1-1 寺 3-3 古 2-3 会 2-4 字 3-3 春 5-4	万 1-2 考 4-2 間 8-4 坐 4-3 凶 2-2
□ 3 CHARACTERS THAT CAN BE DIVIDED BY AN **ENCLOSURE ELEMENT** (*a*) The resulting parts may be separated by a **space** or be in full physical contact. (*b*) The resulting division must be more or less rectangular.	進 3-8 問 8-3 国 3-5 可 2-3 広 3-2 凶 2-2	入 1-1 伺 3-4 呉 4-3 吹 4-3 名 3-3 為 5-4
■ 4 CHARACTERS THAT CANNOT BE CLASSIFIED UNDER **PATTERNS** ◧ 1, ▬ 2, OR □ 3	雨 8-1 丘 5-2 中 4-3 与 3-4	刀 2-1 日 4-1 水 4-3
❷ IF A CHARACTER CAN BE CLASSIFIED UNDER MORE THAN ONE PATTERN, SELECT THE ONE THAT FOLLOWS THE NATURAL CONSTRUCTION OF THE CHARACTER	児 ▬ 2-5-2 箱 ▬ 2-6-9	児 ◧ 1-2-5 箱 ◧ 1-7-8
❸ DO NOT VIOLATE THE PRINCIPLE OF ELEMENT INTEGRITY 1. NEVER BREAK THROUGH STROKES 2. NEVER BREAK THROUGH **INDIVISIBLE UNITS** 3. NEVER MAKE **UNNATURAL DIVISIONS**	口 ■ 4-3-1 情 ◧ 1-3-8 箱 ▬ 2-6-9	口 ▬ 2-1-3 情 ◧ 1-1-10 箱 ◧ 1-7-8

5. HOW TO DIVIDE THE CHARACTER

5.1 Character Division

Once you have determined to which of the four patterns your character belongs, you must divide it or subclassify it in order to determine the second and third parts of the **SKIP number.** Characters that can be divided into two or more parts are classified under the first three patterns, i.e., ◧ 1, ▬ 2, and □ 3. This section explains how to divide these **divisible characters.** Characters that cannot be classified under the above patterns are subclassified according to a different principle described in **§ 6.1 Subclassification of Solid Pattern.**

The imaginary line that divides the character splits it into a pattern whose shape roughly resembles the pattern symbol.

The divisible characters are divided into two parts: the **shaded part** and the **blank part**. The second part of the SKIP number indicates the stroke-count of the former, whereas the third part indicates that of the latter. For example, 相 is divided into 木 (4 strokes) and 目 (5 strokes), giving a SKIP number of ◧ 1-4-5. See **§ 2.4 SKIP Number** for details.

In the great majority of cases, you should have no problem in identifying the pattern and, at the same time, deciding at which point to divide the character. Sometimes, however, you may identify a character as belonging to a particular pattern but not be sure at which point the division should be made. That is, some characters, like 川, 三, and 磨, may contain several points at which a division could conceivably be made.

To divide such characters correctly and without hesitation, it is important that you get a clear understanding of the concept of **division points**. A brief description of these is given in § **5.2** below, while a more thorough treatment can be found in **Appendix 1. § 1. Definitions of Pattern Terminology.** The most important thing to remember is: **if there is more than one way to divide a character, divide at the first division point.**

When dividing a character, be sure not to violate the principle of **element integrity.** This rule prohibits breaking through strokes or **indivisible units.** For example, you must not divide characters like 口 into 丨 and ⼕, or characters like 情 into ⼂ and 情. It also prohibits making **unnatural divisions.** For example, 闘 should be classified under ◻ 3, and not be divided into left and right parts, i.e., 丨 and 鬪. See **Appendix 1. § 3.8 Element Integrity** for details.

A formal statement of the rules for dividing the divisible characters is given in **§ 5.3** below. Each rule is explained in greater detail in **Appendix 1. § 3. How to Divide the Character.**

5.2 Division Points

The first rule for dividing the pattern is: DIVIDE THE CHARACTER INTO TWO PARTS AT THE FIRST **DIVISION POINT**. That is, if there are several ways in which a character can be divided, always divide at the *first* place possible.

Division point	A **space, horizontal line, frame element,** or **enclosure element** at which it may be possible to divide a character.

A division point is not necessarily the point at which a character is actually divided according to SKIP rules. Whether a character can or cannot be divided at a given point depends on its structure and the particular SKIP rule applying to it. Each division point is defined below, followed by a reference to the section where it is described in detail.

	Examples
1. **Space** ⇨ **Appendix 1. § 1.1 Space** **A gap or breaking point between elements.** Division by space applies to patterns ◧ 1, ⬒ 2, and ◻ 3.	川 1-2 州 2-4 傾 2-11 三 1-2 言 1-6 公 2-2 街 3-9 町 5-2 翻 12-6 桑 2-8 系 1-6 雀 4-7
2. **Horizontal Line** ⇨ **Appendix 1. § 1.3 Horizontal Line** **A horizontal, or almost horizontal, stroke not intersected by any other strokes.** Division by horizontal line applies only to pattern ⬒ 2.	寺 3-3 空 3-5 文 2-2 亭 2-7 学 5-3 義 3-10
3. **Frame Element** ⇨ **Appendix 1. § 1.6 Frame Element** **A combination of strokes or stroke segments forming a figure enclosed on two, three, or four sides.** Division by frame element applies only to pattern ⬒ 2.	古 2-3 免 2-6 早 4-2 当 3-3 南 2-7 支 2-2
4. **Enclosure Element** ⇨ **Appendix 1. § 1.7 Enclosure Element** **A completely exterior element that encloses the rest of a character on two or more sides.** Division by enclosure element applies only to pattern ◻ 3.	進 3-8 旬 2-4 麻 3-8 間 8-4 医 2-5 回 3-3

5.3 Character Division Rules

MAIN RULES	Right	Wrong
❶ **DIVIDE THE CHARACTER INTO TWO PARTS AT THE FIRST DIVISION POINT**		
◧ GOING FROM LEFT TO RIGHT, DIVIDE AT THE FIRST **SPACE**		
Divide at the first **clear or conceptual space.**	明 4-4 小 1-2 扱 3-3	小 2-1 街 9-3

⬒ GOING FROM TOP TO BOTTOM, DIVIDE AT THE FIRST **SPACE, HORIZONTAL LINE,** OR **FRAME ELEMENT,** WHICHEVER COMES FIRST		
(*a*) Divide at the first **clear** or **conceptual space.**	三 1-2 会 2-4 脅 2-8	三 2-1 会 3-3 脅 6-4
(*b*) Divide after the first **horizontal line.** The horizontal line, along with its side, top, and end **attachments,** goes to the top.	赤 3-4 空 3-5 業 5-8 年 2-4	赤 2-5 空 5-3 業 8-5
(*c*) Divide at the first point where the first **frame element** is encountered.	古 2-3 当 3-3 南 2-7 早 4-2 呂 4-3 免 6-2	
(*d*) When dividing by **horizontal line** or by **frame element,** each part must have at least two strokes.	京 2-6 方 2-2 午 2-2 予 2-2	下 1-2 亡 2-1 了 1-1 白 1-4
◻ GOING FROM THE OUTSIDE TOWARD THE INSIDE, DIVIDE AFTER THE FIRST **ENCLOSURE ELEMENT**		
Separate the first **enclosure element** from the rest of the character, whether it is separated from it by a **clear** or **conceptual space,** or is in full physical contact with it.	度 3-6 進 3-8 閉 8-3 目 3-2	度 7-2 磨 11-5
❷ **DO NOT VIOLATE THE PRINCIPLE OF ELEMENT INTEGRITY** 1. NEVER BREAK THROUGH STROKES 2. NEVER BREAK THROUGH **INDIVISIBLE UNITS** 3. NEVER MAKE **UNNATURAL DIVISIONS**	凶 ◻3-2-2 情 ◧1-3-8 気 ◻3-4-2 漢 ◧1-3-10	凶 ◧1-1-4 情 ◧1-1-10 気 ⬒2-2-4 漢 ⬒2-4-9
COROLLARIES ❶ EACH PART MUST HAVE AT LEAST ONE STROKE ❷ THE **SHADED PART** MUST NOT BE FURTHER DIVISIBLE UNDER THE SAME **PATTERN**	門 ◧1-4-4 口 ■4-3-1 測 ◧1-3-9 順 ◧1-1-11	門 ◻3-8-0 口 ◻3-3-0 測 ◧1-10-2 順 ◧1-3-9

6. HOW TO SUBCLASSIFY THE SOLID PATTERN

6.1 Subclassification of Solid Pattern
6.2 Solid Subpatterns
6.3 Pattern Subclassification Rules

6.1 Subclassification of Solid Pattern

Characters that cannot be divided according to SKIP rules are referred to as **indivisible** or **solid characters** and are classified under pattern ■4. The second and third parts of the **SKIP number** of the divisible characters, i.e., the characters classified under patterns ◧1, ⬒2, or ▣3, are determined by dividing the character into two parts and counting the strokes of each part. Since the solid characters are, by definition, indivisible, a different principle is required for subclassifying them.

The indivisible characters are arranged in ascending order of their total stroke-counts and are subclassified into four **solid subpatterns** (see **§6.2** below). The second part of the SKIP number indicates the total stroke-count of the character, whereas the third part indicates one of the four solid subpatterns. 下, for example, is a three-stroke character containing a **top line** (subpattern ▔1), giving a SKIP number of ■4-3-1. See **§2.4 SKIP Number** for details.

6.2 Solid Subpatterns

The solid pattern is classified into four **solid subpatterns** on the basis of easy to identify lines located on the top, at the bottom, or in the middle of a character.

Solid subpattern	One of the four groups into which the solid characters are subdivided according to the presence or absence of prominent lines; i.e., ▔1 **top line,** ▁2 **bottom line,** ⎅3 **through line,** and □4 **others.**
Solid subpattern number	A number that identifies one of the four solid subpatterns; i.e., 1=▔, 2=▁, 3=⎅, and 4=□.
Solid subpattern symbol	A symbol that identifies one of the four solid subpatterns; i.e., ▔=1, ▁=2, ⎅=3, and □=4.

A formal definition of each subpattern is given below. Refer to **Appendix 1. §1.8 Solid Subpatterns** for a detailed description.

Solid Subpattern		Examples
▔ 1	**Top Line** A horizontal, or almost horizontal, stroke or stroke segment extending across the very top of a solid character.	下 3-1, 耳 6-1, 雨 8-1, 子 3-1, 久 3-1, 凸 5-1, 口 3-1, 亜 7-1, 爾 14-1
▁ 2	**Bottom Line** A horizontal, or almost horizontal, stroke or stroke segment extending across the very bottom of a solid character.	七 2-2, 上 3-2, 亡 3-2, 丘 5-2, 由 5-2, 自 6-2, 血 6-2, 垂 8-2, 重 9-2

◫ 3	**Through Line** A perfectly vertical stroke or stroke segment intersecting another stroke of a solid character and extending over its entire, or almost its entire, length.	中 4-3 十 2-3 手 4-3 本 5-3 米 6-3 車 7-3 求 7-3 乗 9-3 粛 11-3
□ 4	**Others** Solid characters that cannot be classified under subpatterns ⬒ 1, ⬓ 2, or ◫ 3.	人 2-4 九 2-4 女 3-4 火 4-4 犬 4-4 史 5-4 成 6-4 舟 6-4 為 9-4

6.3 Pattern Subclassification Rules

	Right	Wrong
❶ **DETERMINE TO WHICH OF THE FOUR SOLID SUBPATTERNS YOUR CHARACTER BELONGS**		
⬒ 1 CHARACTERS THAT CONTAIN A **TOP LINE**	雨 8-1 下 3-1 耳 6-1 果 8-1	刀 2-1 千 3-1 垂 8-1 丘 5-1
⬓ 2 CHARACTERS THAT CONTAIN A **BOTTOM LINE**	上 3-2 丘 5-2 垂 8-2	山 3-2 包 5-2 者 8-2
◫ 3 CHARACTERS THAT CONTAIN A **THROUGH LINE**	中 4-3 東 8-3 毛 4-3	水 4-3 寸 3-3 午 4-3 弟 7-3
□ 4 CHARACTERS THAT DO NOT CONTAIN A **TOP LINE, BOTTOM LINE, OR THROUGH LINE**	与 3-4 大 3-4 寿 7-4	糸 6-4 久 3-4 友 4-4 劣 6-4
❷ **IF A CHARACTER CAN BE CLASSIFIED UNDER MORE THAN ONE SUBPATTERN, THE SUBPATTERN WITH THE SMALLEST NUMBER TAKES PRECEDENCE**	王 4-1 己 3-1 酉 7-1 果 8-1 出 5-2 生 5-2 甲 5-1	王 4-2 己 3-2 酉 7-2 果 8-3 出 5-3 生 5-3 甲 5-3

7. GLOSSARY

To use the SKIP classification scheme effectively, it is important to get a clear understanding of the various terms used in a technical sense. These terms have been selected to render their meanings as self-evident as possible. The glossary below conveniently brings all SKIP terms together for quick reference. The brief definitions given here should be sufficient for most purposes. Detailed explanations of important terms can be found in **Appendix 1. § 1. Definitions of Pattern Terminology.**

The headwords, which are followed by their Japanese equivalents in parentheses, are arranged in alphabetical order and followed by a definition and examples in square brackets. At the end of each entry is an arrow ⇨ followed by a reference to a more detailed explanation of that term. The technical terms used within the definitions are printed in **boldface,** which indicates that these terms can be found at their own alphabetical locations in the glossary.

attachment (付随物)
one or more usually short strokes, stroke segments, or elements in physical contact, or almost in physical contact, with the main body of an element [字 年 軍]
⇨ Appendix 1. §1.5 Attachment

blank part (白部・従部)
the part of a **divisible character** corresponding to the blank segment of the **pattern symbol;** i.e., the part remaining after the **shaded part** is removed [従 単 医]
⇨ §2.3 Divisible and Indivisible Characters

bottom line (下線)
a horizontal, or almost horizontal, stroke or stroke segment extending across the very bottom of a **solid** character [世 由 丘]
⇨ Appendix 1. §1.8.1 Top Line and Bottom Line

branch (枝)
a stroke or stroke segment that abuts with other strokes or stroke segments at a point of **tangential contact** [古 京 井]
⇨ Appendix 1. §1.2 Tangential Contact

clear space (完全空白)
a clearly visible gap, especially one formed by parallel strokes or elements [三 川 公]
⇨ Appendix 1. §1.1.1 Clear Space

conceptual space (疑似空白)
a natural breaking point where one would expect a gap; i.e., a gap that may not be visible because the elements are crowded closely together [桑 矛 春]
⇨ Appendix 1. §1.1.2 Conceptual Space

cross-reference entry (相互参照項目)
a character entry or an entry in the **Pattern Index** appearing at an *incorrect* SKIP location with a cross-reference to the corresponding correct location
⇨ §2.6 Cross-References

divisible characters (可分漢字)
characters that can be divided according to SKIP rules; i.e., characters classified under **patterns** ◧1, ⬒2, or ◘3 [相 字 広]
⇨ §2.3 Divisible and Indivisible Characters

division point (可分点)
a **space** [川 芳], **horizontal line** [文 忘], **frame element** [古 当], or **enclosure element** [送 凶] at which it may be possible to divide a character
⇨ Appendix 1. §3.2 Division Points

element integrity (字形素分割禁止)
a principle that consists of three parts: (1) Never break through strokes, (2) Never break through **indivisible units,** and (3) Never make **unnatural divisions**
⇨ Appendix 1. §3.8 Element Integrity

enclosure (囲み型)
⇨ **enclosure pattern**

enclosure element (囲み要素)
a completely exterior element enclosing the rest of a character on two or more sides [広 同 団]
⇨ Appendix 1. §1.7 Enclosure Element

enclosure pattern (囲み型)
a configuration of character elements in which an exterior element encloses the rest of a character on two or more sides (pattern ◘3) [進 可 医 田]
⇨ §2.2 SKIP Patterns

enclosure subpattern (囲み型副パターン)
one of the eleven groups into which the **enclosure pattern** is subdivided according to the number of sides of the **enclosure element** and its position along the exterior of the character
⇨ §4.2 Enclosure Subpatterns

enclosure subpattern symbol (囲み型副パターン記号)
a symbol that identifies one of the eleven **enclosure subpatterns**; i.e., ◘ ◘ ◘ ◘ ◘ ◘ ◘ ◘ ◘ ◘ ◘
⇨ §4.2 Enclosure Subpatterns

end attachment (端部付随物)
one or more relatively short strokes or stroke segments in physical contact, or almost in physical contact, with the end of the main body of an element [軍 岩 字]
⇨ Appendix 1. §1.5.2 Side and End Attachments

entry number (親字番)
a serial number that uniquely identifies the numbered character entries of

the dictionary

⇨ § 2.8 SKIP Guides

entry number guide (親字番案内)

boldface numerals in the lower, outer corner of a page that indicate the **entry number** or range of entry numbers for that page

⇨ § 2.8 SKIP Guides

frame element (枠要素)

a combination of strokes or stroke segments forming a figure enclosed on two, three, or four sides [古 早 肖]

⇨ Appendix 1. § 1.6 Frame Element

horizontal line (横線)

a horizontal, or almost horizontal, stroke not intersected by any other strokes [赤 学 業]

⇨ Appendix 1. § 1.3 Horizontal Line

independent element (独立要素)

a stroke or combination of strokes that intersect or come in **tangential contact** with each other and that form a self-contained unit [桑 系 名]

⇨ Appendix 1. § 1.4 Independent Element

indivisible characters (不可分漢字)

characters that cannot be divided according to SKIP rules; i.e., characters classified under pattern ■ 4 [雨 本 九]

⇨ § 2.3 Divisible and Indivisible Characters

indivisible unit (不可分字形素)

a combination of strokes regarded as an indivisible whole [尺 口 情]

⇨ Appendix 1. § 3.8 Element Integrity

left-right (左右型)

⇨ **left-right pattern**

left-right pattern (左右型)

a configuration of character elements placed side by side (pattern ◧ 1) [川 保 殴]

⇨ § 2.2 SKIP Patterns

margin guide (欄外案内)

a guide in the outer margin of a page that consists of a frame enclosing the **subsection number** for each entry character

⇨ § 2.8 SKIP Guides

natural construction (自然構成)

an arrangement of character elements that is in harmony with the way a character is intuitively perceived as a combination of certain constituent parts

⇨ Appendix 1. § 2.7 Pattern Priority

others (その他)

solid characters that cannot be classified under **subpatterns** ⬒ 1, ⬓ 2, or ◫ 3 [人 大 寿]

⇨ Appendix 1. § 1.8.3 Others

pattern (パターン・字型・型)

a configuration of character elements that characterizes the four major character groups in the SKIP classification scheme; i.e., ◧ 1 **left-right,** ⬒ 2 **up-down,** ▣ 3 **enclosure,** and ■ 4 **solid**

⇨ § 2.2 SKIP Patterns

pattern guide (パターン案内)

a guide in the upper, outer corner of a page that indicates the **pattern** and **pattern number** for that page

⇨ § 2.8 SKIP Guides

pattern number (パターン番号)

a number that identifies one of the four **patterns** in the SKIP classification scheme; i.e., 1 = ◧, 2 = ⬒, 3 = ▣, and 4 = ■

⇨ § 2.2 SKIP Patterns

pattern symbol (パターン記号)

a symbol that identifies one of the four **patterns** in the SKIP classification scheme; i.e., ◧ = 1, ⬒ = 2, ▣ = 3, and ■ = 4

⇨ § 2.2 SKIP Patterns

shaded part (黒部・主部)

the part of a **divisible character** corresponding to the shaded segment of the **pattern symbol;** i.e., the part removed at the first **division point** [相 安 回]

⇨ § 2.3 Divisible and Indivisible Characters

side attachment (側部付随物)

one or more relatively short strokes or stroke segments in physical contact, or almost in physical contact, with the side of the main body of an element [年 台 句]

⇨ Appendix 1. § 1.5.2 Side and End Attachments

SKIP (「字型式検字法」の略称)

acronym of "**System of Kanji Indexing by Patterns**"

⇨ § 2.1 Overview of SKIP

SKIP number (SKIP番号)

a **pattern symbol** followed by hyphenated numerals consisting of three parts; for the **divisible characters,** (1) the **pattern number,** (2) the stroke-count of the **shaded part,** and (3) the stroke-count of the **blank part;** for the **indivisible characters,** (1) the **pattern number,** (2) the total stroke-count, and (3) the **solid subpattern number** [相: ◧ 1-4-5]

⇨ § 2.4 SKIP Number

solid (全体型)

⇨ **solid pattern**

solid pattern (全体型)

a character element or combination of elements that does not constitute a **left-right, up-down,** or **enclosure pattern** (pattern ■ 4) [下 由 本 力]

⇨ § 2.2 SKIP Patterns

solid subpattern (全体型副パターン)

one of the four groups into which the **solid** characters are subdivided according to the presence or absence of prominent lines; i.e., ⊤ 1 **top line,** ⊥ 2 **bottom line,** ⊞ 3 **through line,** and □ 4 **others**

⇨ § 6.2 Solid Subpatterns

solid subpattern number (全体型副パターン番号)

a number that identifies one of the four **solid subpatterns;** i.e., 1 = ⊤, 2 = ⊥, 3 = ⊞, and 4 = □

⇨ § 6.2 Solid Subpatterns

solid subpattern symbol (全体型副パターン記号)

a symbol that identifies one of the four **solid subpatterns**; i.e., ⊤ = 1, ⊥ = 2, ⊞ = 3, and □ = 4

⇨ § 6.2 Solid Subpatterns

space (空白・スペース)

a gap [三 小] or breaking point [会 桑] between elements

⇨ Appendix 1. § 1.1 Space

stroke (点画・画)

a character element such as a dot or line segment traditionally written with one sweep of the brush or pen [正 口 弓 主]

⇨ Appendix 1. § 3.8 Element Integrity, Appendix 2. How to Count Strokes

subgroup (下位グループ)

a subdivision of a **subsection** in which a group of **divisible characters** share a common **subgroup element**

⇨ § 2.5 Classification Scheme

subgroup element (主字素・字素)

the shared element of a **subgroup,** which corresponds to the **shaded part** of a **divisible character** [阪 岸 奔]

⇨ § 2.5 Classification Scheme

subgroup guide (主字素案内)

1. a guide in the outer margin of a page that indicates the **subgroup element** for each entry character

   ⇨ § 2.8 SKIP Guides
2. a guide to the left of the character column in the **Pattern Index** that indicates the **subgroup element** for that **subgroup**

   ⇨ § 2.7 Pattern Index

subpattern (副パターン)

1. ⇨ **enclosure subpattern**
2. ⇨ **solid subpattern**

subpattern number (副パターン番号)

⇨ **solid subpattern number**

subpattern symbol (副パターン記号)

1. ⇨ **enclosure subpattern symbol**
2. ⇨ **solid subpattern symbol**

subsection (下位部)

a subdivision of the main part of the dictionary or of the **Pattern Index** in which the **divisible characters** are classified by **subgroup element** and the **indivisible characters** are classified by entry type

⇨ § 2.5 Classification Scheme

subsection guide (下位部案内)

1. boldface numerals in the upper corner of a page that indicate the **subsection number** for that page
2. red hyphenated numerals in the left part of the **Pattern Index** column that indicate the **subsection number** for each **subsection**

⇨ § 2.8 SKIP Guides, ⇨ § 2.7 Pattern Index

subsection number (下位部番号)

hyphenated numerals used to identify a **subsection** and corresponding to the second and third parts of the SKIP

number
⇨ § 2.4 SKIP Number

System of Kanji Indexing by Patterns (字型式検字法)
a system of classifying characters by geometrical **patterns** used for the rapid location of entries in this dictionary
⇨ § 2.1 Overview of SKIP

tangential contact (枝点接触)
full physical contact between strokes or stroke segments that join at one point without intersecting [口 年 美]
⇨ Appendix 1. § 1.2 Tangential Contact

three-branch tangential contact (三枝点接触)
tangential contact in which three **branches** (strokes or stroke segments) join at one point [文 年]
⇨ Appendix 1. § 1.2 Tangential Contact

through line (通線)
a perfectly vertical stroke or stroke segment intersecting another stroke of a **solid** character and extending over its entire, or almost its entire, length [中 才 我]
⇨ Appendix 1. § 1.8.2 Through Line

top attachment (上部付随物)
one or more usually short strokes, stroke segments, or elements in physical contact, or almost in physical contact, with the top of the main body of an element [字 骨 學]
⇨ Appendix 1. § 1.5.1 Top Attachment

top line (上線)
a horizontal, or almost horizontal, stroke or stroke segment extending across the very top of a **solid** character [里 疋 平]
⇨ Appendix 1. § 1.8.1 Top Line and Bottom Line

two-branch tangential contact (二枝点接触)
tangential contact in which two **branches** (strokes or stroke segments) join at one point [口 弓 宀]
⇨ Appendix 1. § 1.2 Tangential Contact

unnatural division (不自然分割)
division of a character in a manner that is in conflict with the way it is intuitively perceived as a combination of certain constituent parts [漢 箱 導]
⇨ Appendix 1. § 3.8 Element Integrity

up-down (上下型)
⇨ **up-down pattern**

up-down pattern (上下型)
a configuration of character elements stacked more or less one on top of the other (pattern ⬒2) [京 音 当 早]
⇨ § 2.2 SKIP Patterns

EXPLANATORY CHART

The **Explanatory Chart** shows the various parts of the character entry. The boldface numerals refer to the section numbers of the **GUIDE TO THE DICTIONARY** on p. 159a, where the format of each section is explained in detail. Since the various conventions are mostly self-explanatory, a quick glance at this chart should normally be sufficient without further reference to the **GUIDE**.

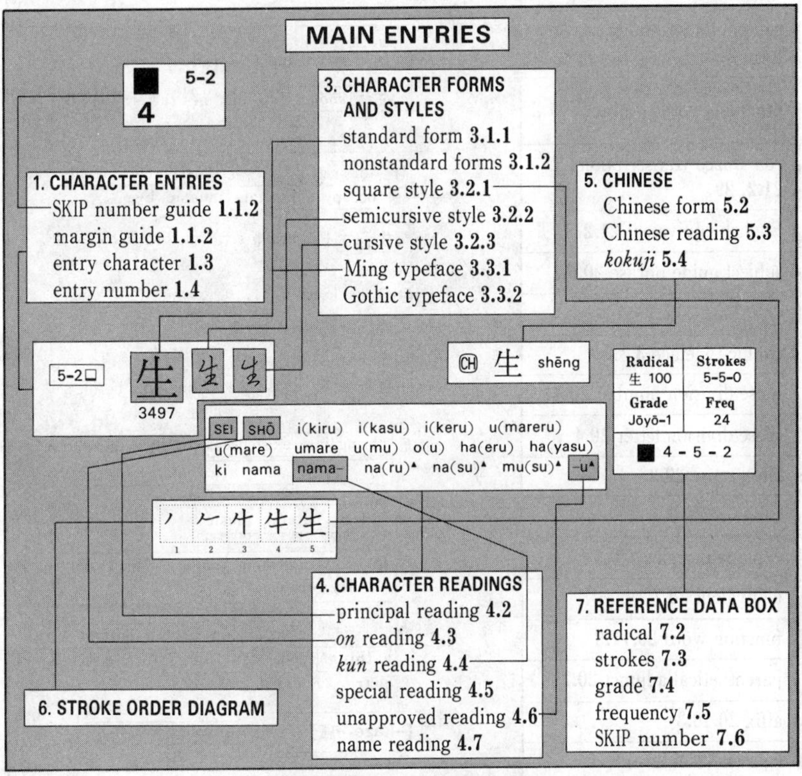

MAIN ENTRIES

■ 5-2
4

1. CHARACTER ENTRIES
SKIP number guide **1.1.2**
margin guide **1.1.2**
entry character **1.3**
entry number **1.4**

3. CHARACTER FORMS AND STYLES
standard form **3.1.1**
nonstandard forms **3.1.2**
square style **3.2.1**
semicursive style **3.2.2**
cursive style **3.2.3**
Ming typeface **3.3.1**
Gothic typeface **3.3.2**

5. CHINESE
Chinese form **5.2**
Chinese reading **5.3**
kokuji **5.4**

5-2□ 生 生 生
3497

Ⓒ 生 shēng

Radical	Strokes
生 100	5-5-0
Grade	**Freq**
Jōyō-1	24
■ 4 - 5 - 2	

SEI SHŌ i(kiru) i(kasu) i(keru) u(mareru)
u(mare) umare u(mu) o(u) ha(eru) ha(yasu)
ki nama nama- na(ru)▲ na(su)▲ mu(su)▲ -u▲

丿 𠂉 牛 牛 生
1 2 3 4 5

4. CHARACTER READINGS
principal reading **4.2**
on reading **4.3**
kun reading **4.4**
special reading **4.5**
unapproved reading **4.6**
name reading **4.7**

6. STROKE ORDER DIAGRAM

7. REFERENCE DATA BOX
radical **7.2**
strokes **7.3**
grade **7.4**
frequency **7.5**
SKIP number **7.6**

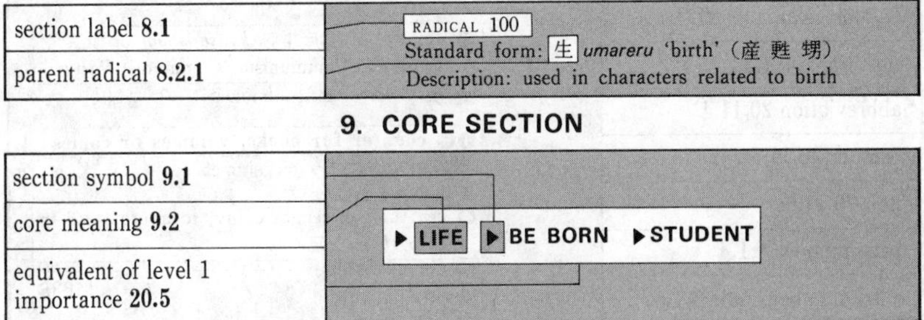

10. COMPOUNDS SECTION

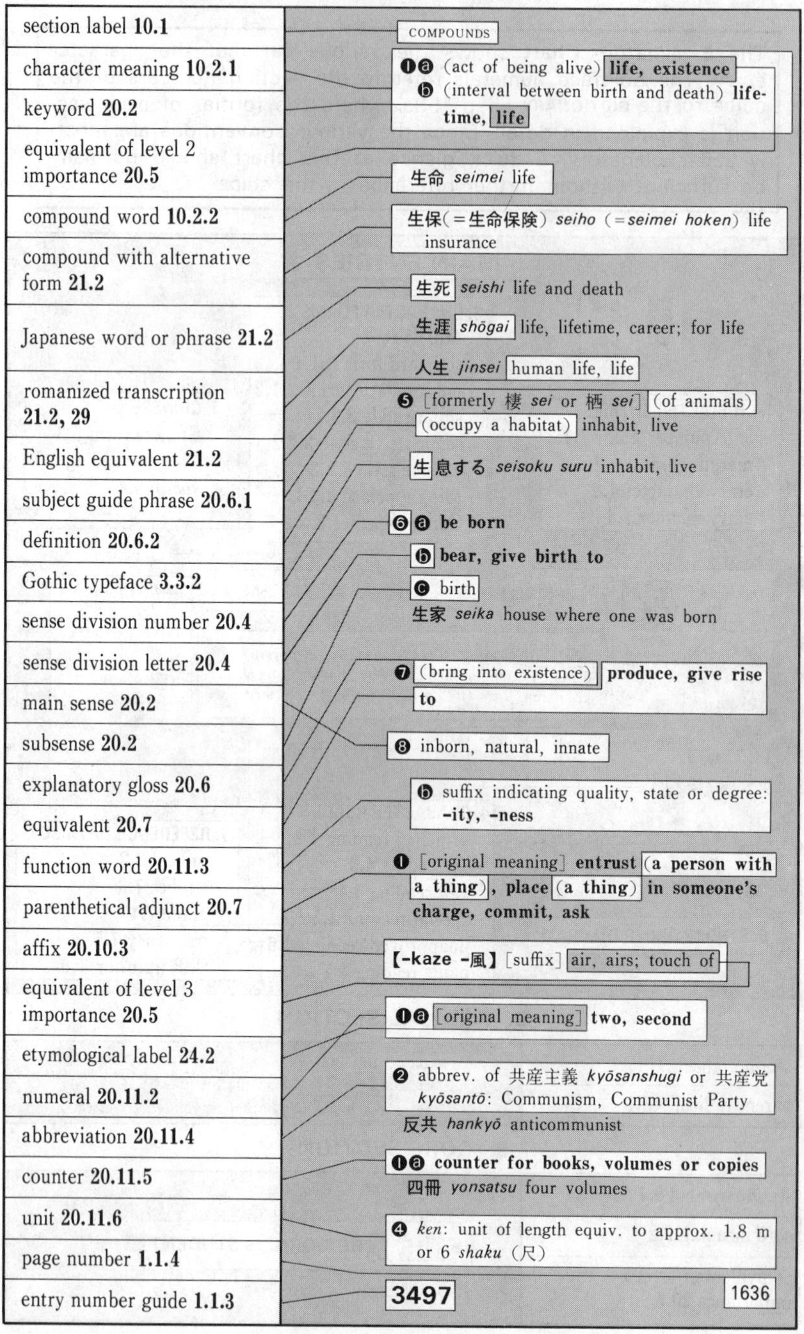

- section label **10.1**
- character meaning **10.2.1**
- keyword **20.2**
- equivalent of level 2 importance **20.5**
- compound word **10.2.2**
- compound with alternative form **21.2**
- Japanese word or phrase **21.2**
- romanized transcription **21.2, 29**
- English equivalent **21.2**
- subject guide phrase **20.6.1**
- definition **20.6.2**
- Gothic typeface **3.3.2**
- sense division number **20.4**
- sense division letter **20.4**
- main sense **20.2**
- subsense **20.2**
- explanatory gloss **20.6**
- equivalent **20.7**
- function word **20.11.3**
- parenthetical adjunct **20.7**
- affix **20.10.3**
- equivalent of level 3 importance **20.5**
- etymological label **24.2**
- numeral **20.11.2**
- abbreviation **20.11.4**
- counter **20.11.5**
- unit **20.11.6**
- page number **1.1.4**
- entry number guide **1.1.3**

COMPOUNDS

❶ⓐ (act of being alive) **life, existence**
ⓑ (interval between birth and death) **lifetime, life**

生命 *seimei* life

生保（＝生命保険） *seiho* （＝*seimei hoken*） life insurance

生死 *seishi* life and death

生涯 *shōgai* life, lifetime, career; for life

人生 *jinsei* human life, life

❺ ［formerly 棲 *sei* or 栖 *sei*］ (of animals) (occupy a habitat) inhabit, live

生息する *seisoku suru* inhabit, live

❻ⓐ **be born**

ⓑ **bear, give birth to**

ⓒ birth

生家 *seika* house where one was born

❼ (bring into existence) **produce, give rise to**

❽ inborn, natural, innate

ⓑ suffix indicating quality, state or degree: **-ity, -ness**

❶ ［original meaning］ **entrust (a person with a thing), place (a thing) in someone's charge, commit, ask**

【-kaze -風】 ［suffix］ air, airs; touch of

❶ⓐ ［original meaning］ **two, second**

❷ abbrev. of 共産主義 *kyōsanshugi* or 共産党 *kyōsantō*: Communism, Communist Party

反共 *hankyō* anticommunist

❶ⓐ **counter for books, volumes or copies**

四冊 *yonsatsu* four volumes

❹ *ken*: unit of length equiv. to approx. 1.8 m or 6 *shaku* （尺）

3497 1636

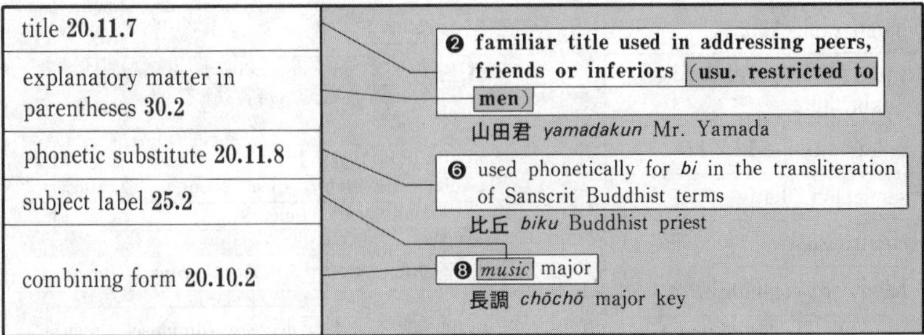

title 20.11.7
explanatory matter in parentheses 30.2
phonetic substitute 20.11.8
subject label 25.2
combining form 20.10.2
❷ familiar title used in addressing peers, friends or inferiors (usu. restricted to men)
山田君 yamadakun Mr. Yamada
❻ used phonetically for bi in the transliteration of Sanscrit Buddhist terms
比丘 biku Buddhist priest
❽ music major
長調 chōchō major key

11. INDEPENDENT SECTION

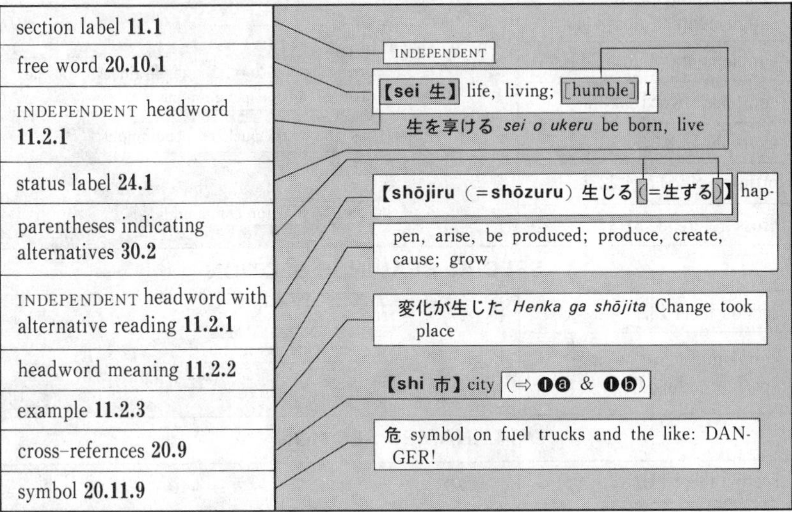

section label 11.1
free word 20.10.1
INDEPENDENT headword 11.2.1
status label 24.1
parentheses indicating alternatives 30.2
INDEPENDENT headword with alternative reading 11.2.1
headword meaning 11.2.2
example 11.2.3
cross-refernces 20.9
symbol 20.11.9
INDEPENDENT
【sei 生】 life, living; [humble] I
生を享ける sei o ukeru be born, live
【shōjiru (＝shōzuru) 生じる (＝生ずる)】 happen, arise, be produced; produce, create, cause; grow
変化が生じた Henka ga shōjita Change took place
【shi 市】 city (⇨ ❶ⓐ & ❶ⓑ)
危 symbol on fuel trucks and the like: DANGER!

12. KUN SECTION

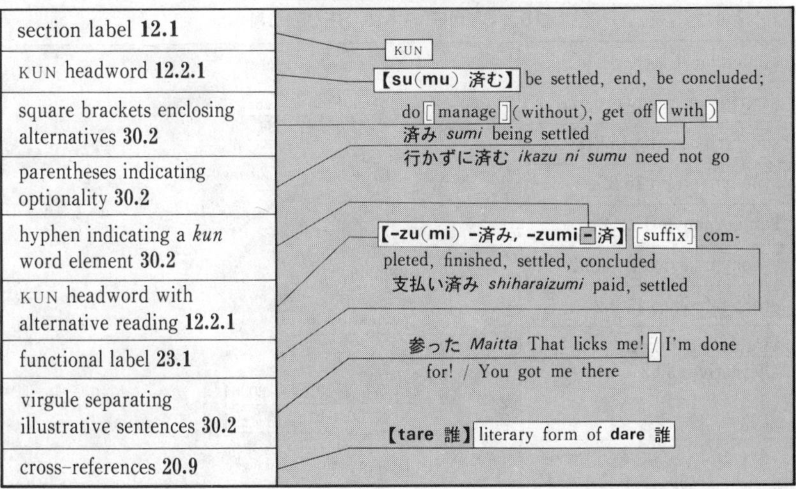

section label 12.1
KUN headword 12.2.1
square brackets enclosing alternatives 30.2
parentheses indicating optionality 30.2
hyphen indicating a kun word element 30.2
KUN headword with alternative reading 12.2.1
functional label 23.1
virgule separating illustrative sentences 30.2
cross-references 20.9
KUN
【su(mu) 済む】 be settled, end, be concluded; do [manage] (without), get off (with)
済み sumi being settled
行かずに済む ikazu ni sumu need not go
【-zu(mi) -済み, -zumi -済】 [suffix] completed, finished, settled, concluded
支払い済み shiharaizumi paid, settled
参った Maitta That licks me! / I'm done for! / You got me there
【tare 誰】 literary form of dare 誰

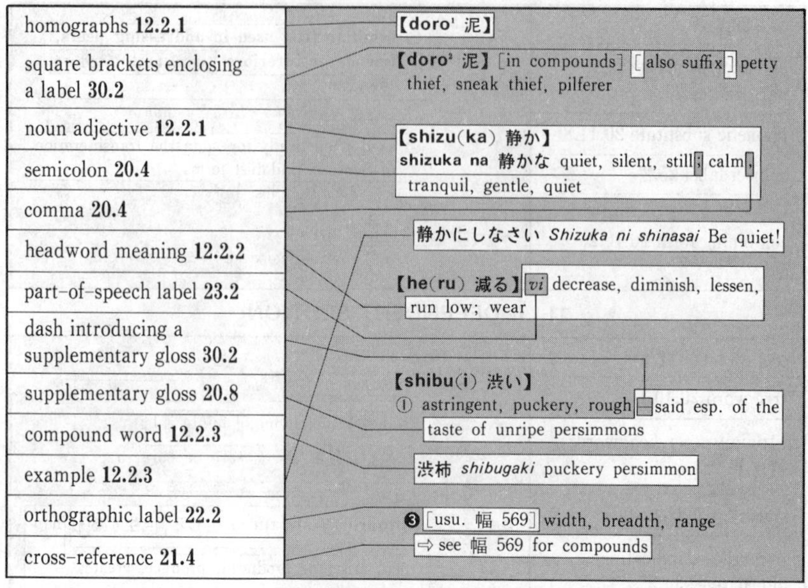
homographs 12.2.1
square brackets enclosing a label 30.2
noun adjective 12.2.1
semicolon 20.4
comma 20.4
headword meaning 12.2.2
part-of-speech label 23.2
dash introducing a supplementary gloss 30.2
supplementary gloss 20.8
compound word 12.2.3
example 12.2.3
orthographic label 22.2
cross-reference 21.4
【doro¹ 泥】
【doro² 泥】[in compounds] [also suffix] petty thief, sneak thief, pilferer
【shizu(ka) 静か】
shizuka na 静かな quiet, silent, still; calm, tranquil, gentle, quiet
静かにしなさい Shizuka ni shinasai Be quiet!
【he(ru) 減る】 vi decrease, diminish, lessen, run low; wear
【shibu(i) 渋い】
① astringent, puckery, rough —said esp. of the taste of unripe persimmons
渋柿 shibugaki puckery persimmon
❸ [usu. 幅 569] width, breadth, range
⇨ see 幅 569 for compounds

13. SPECIAL READINGS SECTION

section label 13.1
compound word having special reading 13.2
SPECIAL READINGS
芝生 shibafu lawn, turf
生憎▲ ainiku unfortunately, unluckily; I am sorry, but...

14. NAMES SECTION

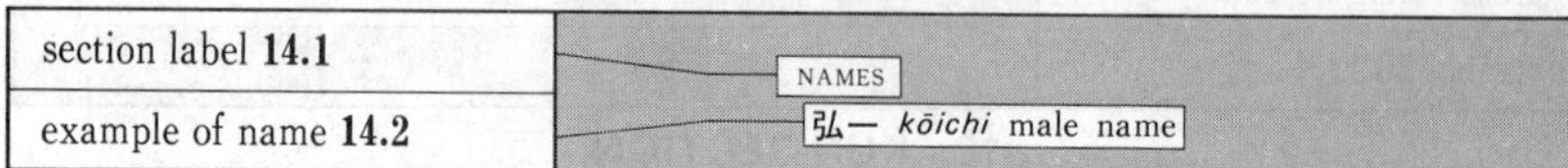
section label 14.1
example of name 14.2
NAMES
弘一 kōichi male name

15. SYNONYMS SECTION

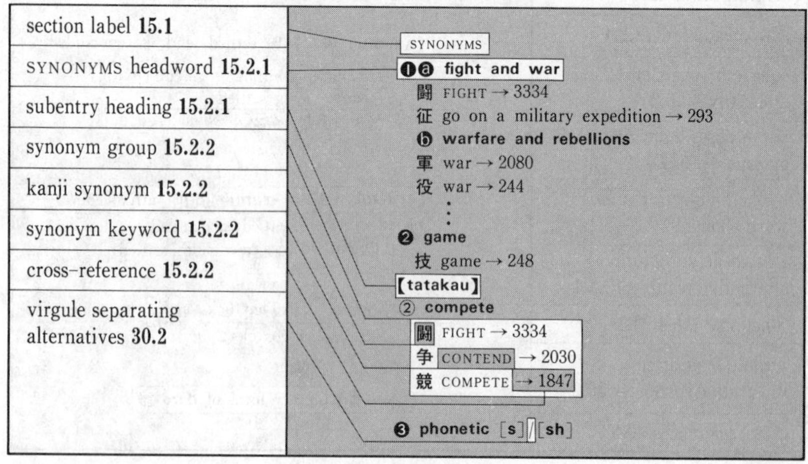
section label 15.1
SYNONYMS headword 15.2.1
subentry heading 15.2.1
synonym group 15.2.2
kanji synonym 15.2.2
synonym keyword 15.2.2
cross-reference 15.2.2
virgule separating alternatives 30.2
SYNONYMS
❶ⓐ fight and war
闘 FIGHT → 3334
征 go on a military expedition → 293
ⓑ warfare and rebellions
軍 war → 2080
役 war → 244
❷ game
技 game → 248
【tatakau】
② compete
闘 FIGHT → 3334
争 CONTEND → 2030
競 COMPETE → 1847
❸ phonetic [s]/[sh]

16. USAGE SECTION

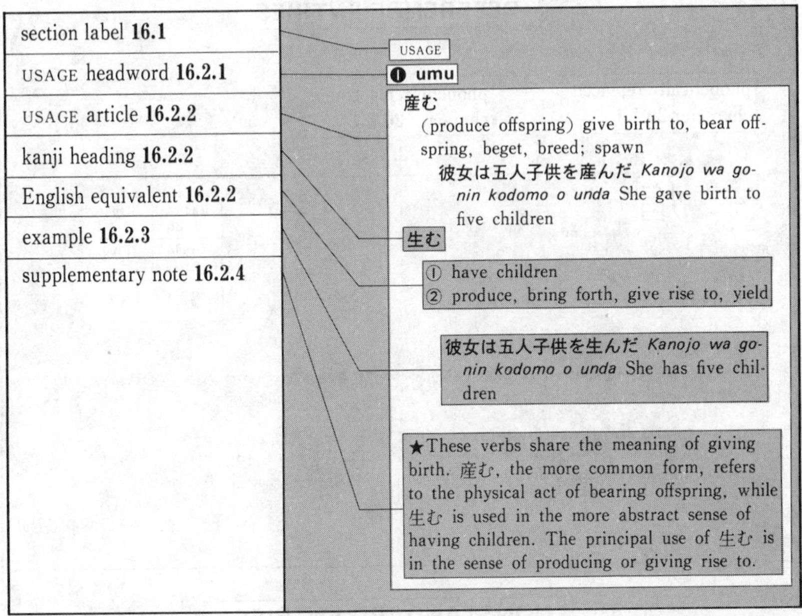
section label 16.1
USAGE headword 16.2.1
USAGE article 16.2.2
kanji heading 16.2.2
English equivalent 16.2.2
example 16.2.3
supplementary note 16.2.4
USAGE
❶ umu
産む
(produce offspring) give birth to, bear offspring, beget, breed; spawn
彼女は五人子供を産んだ Kanojo wa go-nin kodomo o unda She gave birth to five children
生む
① have children
② produce, bring forth, give rise to, yield
彼女は五人子供を生んだ Kanojo wa go-nin kodomo o unda She has five children
★These verbs share the meaning of giving birth. 産む, the more common form, refers to the physical act of bearing offspring, while 生む is used in the more abstract sense of having children. The principal use of 生む is in the sense of producing or giving rise to.

17. HOMOPHONES SECTION

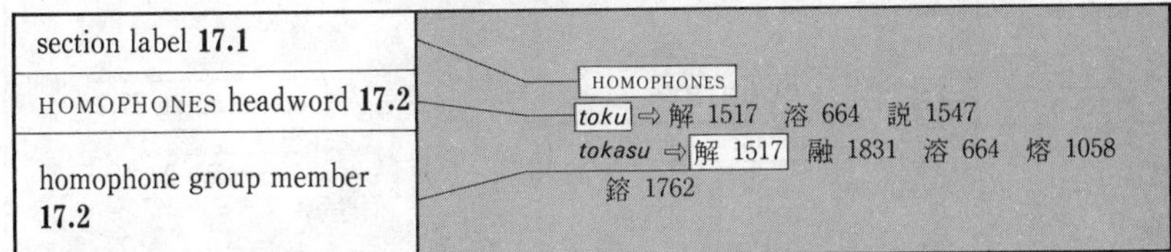
section label 17.1
HOMOPHONES headword 17.2
homophone group member 17.2
HOMOPHONES
toku ⇨ 解 1517 溶 664 説 1547
tokasu ⇨ 解 1517 融 1831 溶 664 熔 1058 鎔 1762

18. COMPOUND FORMATION SECTION

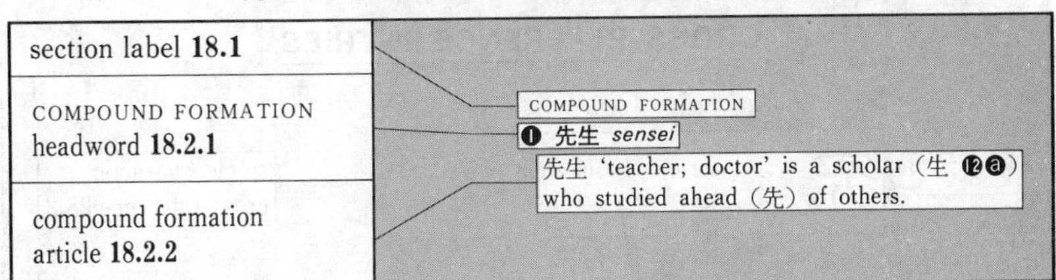
section label 18.1
COMPOUND FORMATION headword 18.2.1
compound formation article 18.2.2
COMPOUND FORMATION
❶ 先生 sensei
先生 'teacher; doctor' is a scholar (生 ⓬ⓐ) who studied ahead (先) of others.

19. NOTE SECTION

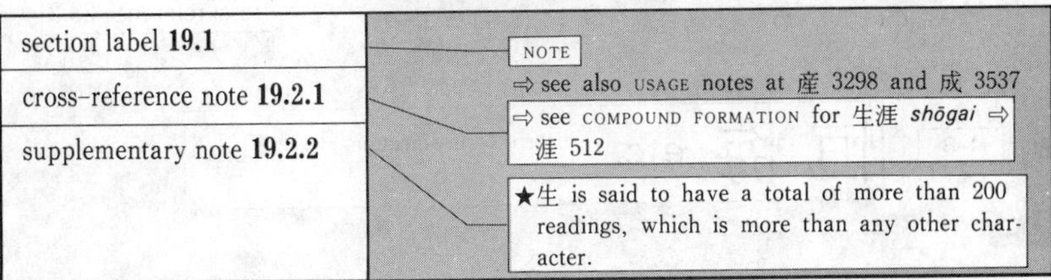
section label 19.1
cross-reference note 19.2.1
supplementary note 19.2.2
NOTE
⇨ see also USAGE notes at 産 3298 and 成 3537
⇨ see COMPOUND FORMATION for 生涯 shōgai ⇨ 涯 512
★生 is said to have a total of more than 200 readings, which is more than any other character.

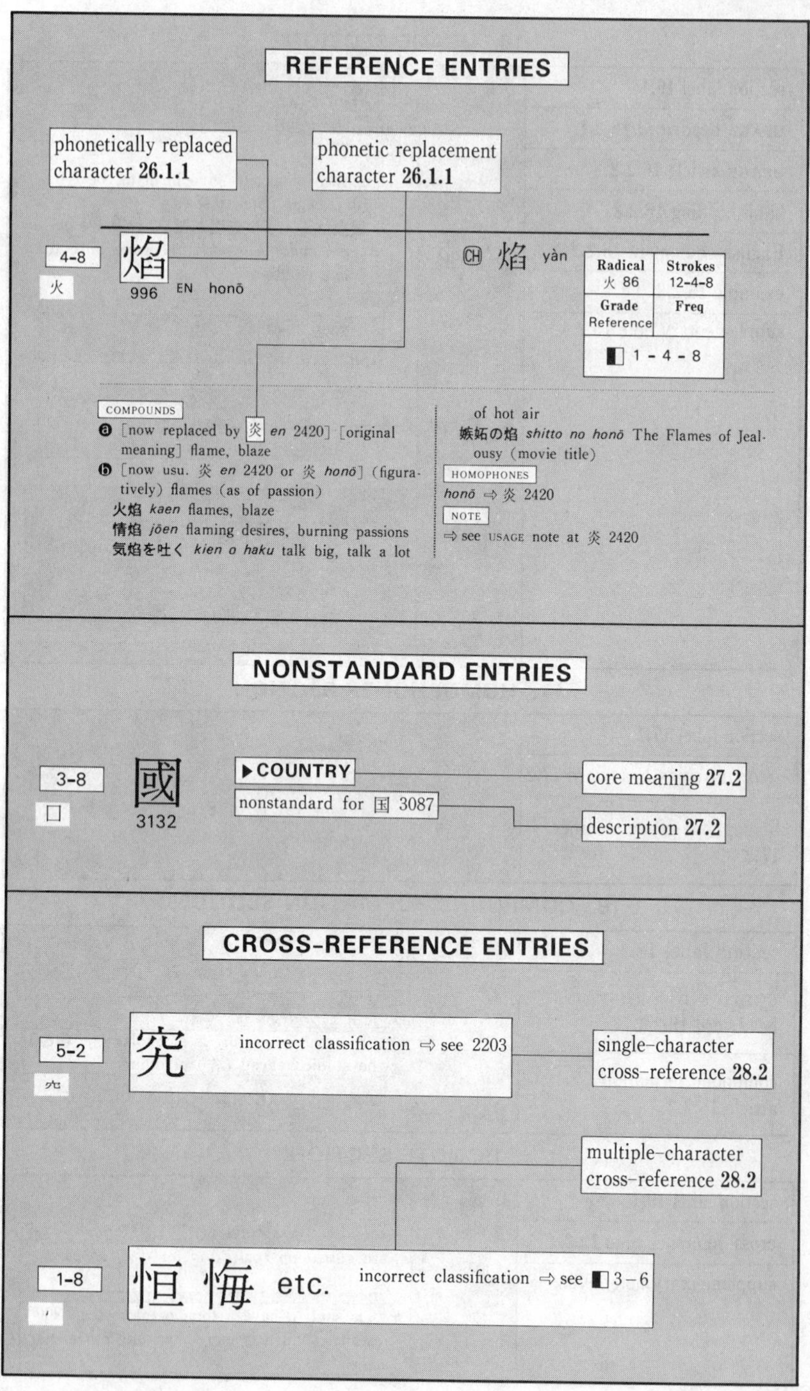

REFERENCE ENTRIES
phonetically replaced character 26.1.1
phonetic replacement character 26.1.1
4-8
火
焰
996
EN hono
CH 焰 yàn
Radical 火 86
Strokes 12-4-8
Grade Reference
Freq
1 - 4 - 8
COMPOUNDS
a [now replaced by 炎 en 2420] [original meaning] flame, blaze
b [now usu. 炎 en 2420 or 炎 honō] (figuratively) flames (as of passion)
火焰 kaen flames, blaze
情焰 jōen flaming desires, burning passions
気焰を吐く kien o haku talk big, talk a lot of hot air
嫉妬の焰 shitto no honō The Flames of Jealousy (movie title)
HOMOPHONES
honō ⇨ 炎 2420
NOTE
⇨ see USAGE note at 炎 2420
NONSTANDARD ENTRIES
3-8
口
國
3132
▶COUNTRY
nonstandard for 国 3087
core meaning 27.2
description 27.2
CROSS-REFERENCE ENTRIES
5-2
穴
究
incorrect classification ⇨ see 2203
single-character cross-reference 28.2
multiple-character cross-reference 28.2
1-8
恒 悔 etc.
incorrect classification ⇨ see 3-6

GUIDE TO THE DICTIONARY

The aim of this GUIDE TO THE DICTIONARY is to present a detailed description of the main body of the dictionary. This consists of explanations of the format, order, and manner of presentation of the various parts of the character entry, descriptions of the various labels, glosses, and abbreviations, definitions of technical terms, and other conventions. The GUIDE deals mostly with the technical details of the presentation, with primary emphasis on format. How and why this information is useful is treated in FEATURES OF THIS DICTIONARY on p. 61a.

Since the various conventions of this dictionary have been designed to be mostly self–explanatory, it is not necessary for the general user to acquire a thorough understanding of all the details presented here. Normally, a glance at the **Explanatory Chart** on p. 153a should be sufficient. Much of the information here is of value to the scholar interested in theoretical details, although the general user could greatly benefit from it as well. The most important sections are **§ 1. Character Entries, § 2. Main Entries, § 10. COMPOUNDS Section,** and **§ 20. Character Meanings.**

Unless otherwise indicated, the explanations in the GUIDE apply to **main entries.** Other types of entries are described in sections **§ 26.** through **§ 28.** Each convention is described in detail under its appropriate section. Those conventions that apply throughout the dictionary are described in **§ 30. Other Conventions.**

A network of cross–references directs the user to other relevant sections. To understand the explanations properly, a knowledge of the technical terms specific to this dictionary is required. These are set in **sanserif boldface** at the place where they are formally introduced, and occasionally at other places as necessary.

1. CHARACTER ENTRIES

1.1 Guides

1.1.1 General Description The various **guides** printed in the outer corners and margins of the page have been carefully designed and laid out in order to facilitate the speedy location of character entries:

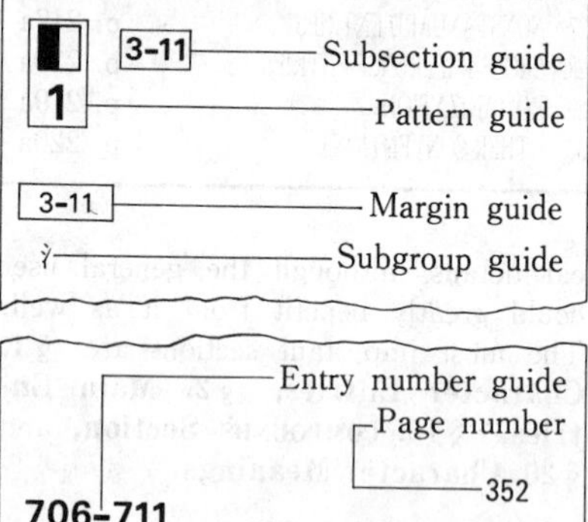

1.1.2 SKIP Guides The following guides are particularly useful for finding a character entry directly from its **SKIP number** without consulting the **Pattern Index**:

1. The **pattern guide** in the upper, outer corner of a page indicates the **pattern** and **pattern number** for that page.
2. The **subsection guide** in the upper corner of a page consists of boldface numerals that indicate the **subsection number** for that page.
3. The **margin guide** in the outer margin of a page consists of a frame enclosing the subsection number for each entry character.
4. The **subgroup guide** in the outer margin of a page indicates the **subgroup element** for each entry character.

See SYSTEM OF KANJI INDEXING BY PATTERNS § 2.8 **SKIP Guides** for details.

1.1.3 Entry Number Guide The **entry number guide** in the lower, outer corner of a page consists of boldface numerals or hyphenated boldface numerals that indicate the entry number or range of entry numbers for that page. This guide helps quickly locate a character whose entry number is known. See also **§ 1.4 Entry Number.**

1.1.4 Page Number The **page number** in the main body of the dictionary and in the back matter consists of boldface numerals centered at the bottom of each page; in the front matter, the page numbers are followed by the letter *a*. Entry numbers, not page numbers, are used in cross-references to character entries.

1.2 Character Entry

The matter between the heavy black lines across the page is the **character entry.** This consists of the entry character followed by the entry-head data and other explanatory matter; that is, it is the entire article of explanatory matter for an entry character. The entry-head data is printed across the page in single column format, while the explanatory matter that follows is set in two columns separated by a dotted line.

1.3 Entry Character

The large character heading the character entry is the **entry character.** It is set in Ming type, the most common kanji typeface in Japan. The entry character is the subject of all explanatory matter that follows within that entry. For Jōyō Kanji and Jinmei Kanji characters in main entries, it represents the officially approved standard form:

10-4 歌——Entry character
哥 1825

Other entry characters, except for cross-references, are given in the traditional form. See also **§ 3.1 Character Forms.**

1.4 Entry Number

The boldface numeral below each numbered entry character is the **entry number**. This is a serial number that uniquely identifies the numbered character entries of the dictionary and is used throughout the main body of the dictionary, the appendixes, and the indexes for reference and cross-reference. The entry number is given for all character entries, except for cross-reference entries, which are unnumbered. See also **§ 1.6 Types of Entries.**

1.5 Order of Entries

The order of entries in this dictionary is based on a new method of classifying characters according to geometrical patterns. This classification scheme, called **System of Kanji Indexing by Patterns** (SKIP), unequivocally assigns a position to each character. The characters are divided into four major groups: ◧ 1 left-right, ⬒ 2 up-down, ◻ 3 enclosure, and ■ 4 solid. See SYSTEM OF KANJI INDEXING BY PATTERNS **§ 2.5 Classification Scheme** for details.

1.6 Types of Entries

This dictionary contains a total of 4421 numbered and unnumbered character entries. These are classified according to their function and manner of treatment into the following four types: (1) main entry, (2) reference entry, (3) nonstandard entry, and (4) cross-reference entry. The layout and manner of presentation of the explanatory matter are different for each entry type. The four types are briefly described below:

1. The 2135 **main entry** characters include the 1945 characters in the official Jōyō Kanji list, the 166 in the Jinmei Kanji (name characters) list of 1981, and 24 high-frequency unapproved characters (characters not listed in the Jōyō Kanji and Jinmei Kanji lists). Main entry characters get full treatment and include all the features described herein. The main entry is described in detail in sections **§ 2.** through **§ 25.** For information on the Jōyō Kanji and Jinmei Kanji lists, see OUTLINE OF JAPANESE WRITING SYSTEM **§ 2.5 Language Reforms.**

2. The 472 **reference entry** characters are all unapproved characters. These include the principal **phonetically replaced characters** in contemporary Japanese; i.e., the 170 characters that are now replaced by the official **phonetic replacement characters,** and another 157 phonetically replaced characters that are not in the official list. The remaining reference entries consist of 145 characters that are radicals or radical variants but are not included in the main entry or nonstandard entry characters. The treatment of reference entries is more restricted in scope than that of main entry characters. See **§ 26. Reference Entries** for details.

3. The 980 **nonstandard entry** characters include 873 traditional forms (full unsimplified forms), 82 alternative forms (variant forms other than the traditional form), and 25 handwritten abbreviations (simplified forms used in handwriting). These appear at their own SKIP locations with a cross-reference to their corresponding standard forms. See **§ 27. Nonstandard Entries** for details.

4. The 834 **cross-reference** entry characters include 746 single-character and 88 multiple-character cross-reference entries at a location where they might be mistakenly looked for under an incorrect pattern classification or incorrect stroke-count. They appear at their own *incorrect* SKIP locations with a cross-reference to the character entry at the correct location. See **§ 28. Cross-Reference Entries** for details.

2. MAIN ENTRIES

2.1 Entry Description

The most frequently used characters in Japanese are treated as **main entries.** These include all the characters listed in the Jōyō Kanji and Jinmei Kanji lists and high-frequency unapproved characters:

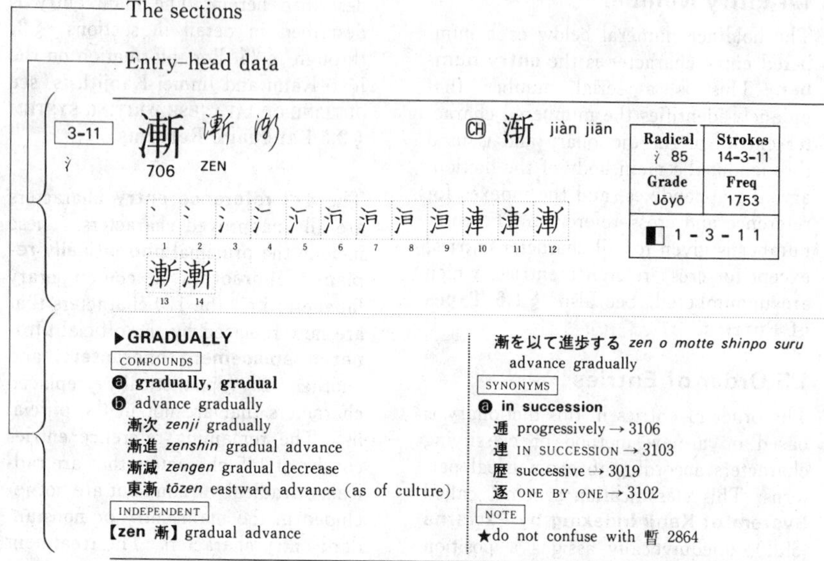

Main entry characters get full treatment and include the full range of features presented in this dictionary. Main entries can be distinguished from other types of character entries by the words "Jōyō," "Non-Jōyō," or "Names" in the reference data box, and can be easily recognized by the presence of core meanings and the organization of the explanatory matter into sections. The main entry is described in detail in sections § 2. through § 25.

2.2 Entry Format

The main entry consists of the entry-head data, printed across the page in single column format, and the explanatory matter, which is organized into sections and set in two columns separated from each other by a dotted line.

2.2.1 Entry-Head Data The **entry-head data** of main entries consists of the entry character (**§ 1.3**), the entry number (**§ 1.4**), the standard form (**§ 3.1.1**), nonstandard forms (**§ 3.1.2**), calligraphic styles (**§ 3.2**), typeface styles (**§ 3.3**), Chinese (**§ 5.**), character readings (**§ 4.**), the stroke order diagram (**§ 6.**), and the reference data box

(§7.). Each item is described in the section indicated by the cross-reference in parentheses.

2.2.2 The Sections The explanatory matter of main entries is subdivided into twelve parts referred to as **sections,** which appear in the order listed below. Not every entry includes every section—only those sections required for describing the entry character are given.

Section Label	Description
RADICAL	The RADICAL section describes the function of the entry character as a radical. See **§ 8. RADICAL Section** for details.
▶	The CORE section lists the core meaning or meanings of the entry character. See **§ 9. CORE Section** for details.
COMPOUNDS	The COMPOUNDS section, subdivided by sense division numbers and letters, lists the meanings of the entry character as an *on* word element. Each meaning is nearly always accompanied by compounds and examples and their English equivalents. See **§ 10. COMPOUNDS Section** for details.
INDEPENDENT	The INDEPENDENT section, subdivided into subentries, lists the meanings of the entry character as an independent *on* word. Each meaning is often accompanied by examples and their English equivalents. See **§ 11. INDEPENDENT Section** for details.
KUN	The KUN section, subdivided into subentries, lists the meanings of the entry character as a *kun* word or word element. Each meaning is usually accompanied by compounds and examples and their English equivalents. See **§ 12. KUN Section** for details.
SPECIAL READINGS	The SPECIAL READINGS section lists compound words having special readings and their English equivalents. See **§ 13. SPECIAL READINGS Section** for details.
NAMES	The NAMES section lists examples of names and their English descriptions. See **§ 14. NAMES Section** for details.
SYNONYMS	The SYNONYMS section, subdivided into synonym groups, lists groups of kanji synonyms and their English keywords for the principal senses of main entry characters. See **§ 15. SYNONYMS Section** for details.
USAGE	The USAGE section, subdivided into usage notes, discriminates between the meanings of homophones (rarely synonyms) by bringing together their English equivalents into a single article. See **§ 16. USAGE Section** for details.

HOMOPHONES	The HOMOPHONES section lists groups of homophones and their entry numbers for cross-reference. See **§ 17. HOMOPHONES Section** for details.
COMPOUND FORMATION	The COMPOUND FORMATION section, subdivided into compound formation articles, describes how a compound word is formed from its constituent parts and/or gives its etymology. See **§ 18. COMPOUND FORMATION Section** for details.
NOTE	The NOTE section consists of various cross-references and/or explanatory notes. See **§ 19. NOTE Section** for details.

3. CHARACTER FORMS AND STYLES

3.1 Character Forms

Character form refers to the skeletal framework or delineation of the figure formed by a character. The entry-head data includes character forms of three kinds: the standard form, the nonstandard forms, and the Chinese form.

3.1.1 Standard Form The large character set in Ming type at the head of main entry characters appearing in the Jōyō Kanji and Jinmei Kanji lists (approved characters) is the **standard form**:

This form is sanctioned for official purposes and is widely used as the standard form in most contemporary publications.

3.1.2 Nonstandard Forms The character(s) sometimes appearing immediately to the right of a main entry character are the **nonstandard forms.** These are set in Ming type in a size somewhat smaller than the main entry character:

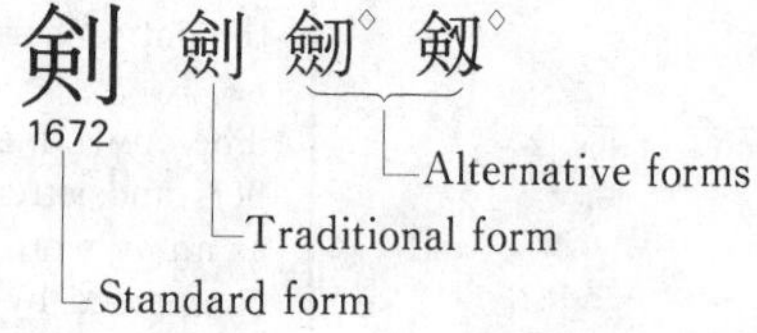

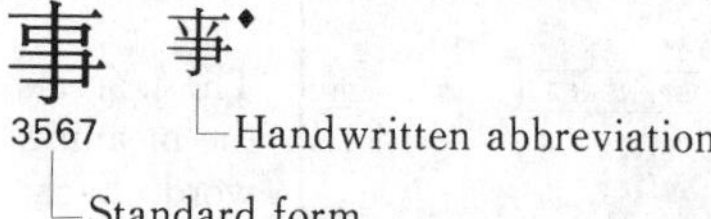

Nonstandard form refers to a variant form other than the standard form of approved characters, and to a variant form other than the traditional form of unapproved characters. Three kinds of nonstandard forms are given: the traditional form, the alternative forms, and the handwritten abbreviation, in that order.

1. **Traditional form** is the full unsimplified form (orthodox form) introduced by the Chinese dictionary 康熙字典 *kōki jiten* in 1716. It is always given if it differs from the standard form of main entry characters.

2. **Alternative forms,** marked by a superscript diamond symbol ◇, refers to variant forms other than the traditional form.

3. The **handwritten abbreviation,** marked by a superscript solid dia-

mond symbol ◆, is a simplified form used in handwriting.

Nonstandard forms are only given for main entry characters. If a main entry character is not followed by a nonstandard form, no common nonstandard form exists. See also § 27. **Nonstandard Entries.**

3.1.3 Chinese Form The character(s) appearing immediately to the right of the symbol Ⓒⓗ is the **Chinese form.** See § 5. **Chinese** for details.

3.2 Calligraphic Styles

Calligraphic style refers to the various styles of handwriting. Three calligraphic styles are given: the square style, the semicursive style, and the cursive style.

3.2.1 Square Style The character given in the last frame of the stroke order diagram is in the **square style.** Each stroke is written separately to produce a clearly legible form:

化 ノ イ イ' 化
21 1 2 3 4

The square style is given for all main entry characters, and for all reference and nonstandard entry characters that are used as radicals.

3.2.2 Semicursive Style The character immediately to the right of the nonstandard form(s) or, if no nonstandard form is given, of a main entry character, is a calligraphic variant in the **semicursive style.** The strokes are loosely joined together in a smooth movement of the brush or pen:

化 化 化
21

The semicursive style is given for all main entry characters.

3.2.3 Cursive Style The character immediately to the right of the semicursive style is a calligraphic variant in the **cursive style.** The character form is greatly simplified and the strokes are joined in a continuous smooth movement of the brush or pen:

化 化 化
21

The cursive style is given for all main entry characters.

3.3 Typeface Styles

Typeface style refers to a uniform style or design of the character type. The two principal styles are given: the Ming typeface and the Gothic typeface.

3.3.1 Ming Typeface The large entry character at the head of each character entry is set in **Ming type.** This typeface is characterized by thick vertical strokes, thin horizontal strokes, and triangular serifs at the ends of horizontal strokes:

19

The Ming typeface is given for all entry characters.

3.3.2 Gothic Typeface Entry characters appearing in the compounds and examples are set in **Gothic type.** This typeface is characterized by thick smooth strokes and clean edges:

仏 仏陀 *budda* Buddha
19

The Gothic typeface appears in all main and reference entries that include compounds or examples.

4. CHARACTER READINGS

4.1 General Description

The romanized transcription immediately to the right of the entry number is the **reading** or readings of the entry character in Japanese; the Chinese reading follows the Chinese form:

 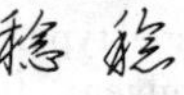 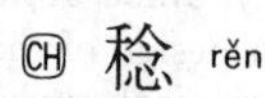 rěn
1207 NEN JIN mino(ru) NAMES toshi naru nari minoru

Reading refers to an established sequence of speech sounds, usually of Chinese or native Japanese origin, associated with a character. **Approved readings** are those listed in the Jōyō Kanji list; **unapproved readings** are those that are not. The Japanese readings appear in the following order: the principal reading; approved, special, and unapproved *on* readings; approved, special, and unapproved *kun* readings; and name readings. The Chinese readings appear in descending order of frequency or importance. Character readings are given for all main and reference entry characters, except for reference entry characters that are used only as a radical and have no readings.

4.2 Principal Reading

The **principal reading,** the first character reading given, is the most common or representative reading of a character. It is used as a key of classification in ordering the characters in various character lists and indexes. The principal reading is nearly always the *on* reading, but for characters that do not have an *on* reading, the *kun* reading is used. For Jōyō Kanji characters, the principal reading is, with a few minor exceptions, identical with the first reading listed in the Jōyō Kanji list.

4.3 *On* Reading

The ***on* reading,** set in sanserif small capitals, is the Sino-Japanese or Chinese-derived reading of a character. Approved *on* readings are unmarked; unapproved ones are marked by a superscript solid triangle ▲:

金 KIN KON GON▲ kane kana- -gane
2057

The *on* reading is presented in the following format:

1. Approved *on* readings are listed in the order in which they appear in the Jōyō Kanji list; unapproved ones, in descending order of importance.

2. A small number of *on* readings are preceded by a hyphen, which indicates that the reading is a variant of an approved *on* reading used only in certain words for euphony; e.g., the reading *-nō* for 応 as a variant of *ō* in the word 反応 *hannō*. The hyphen does not indicate that the character functions only as a suffix.

4.4 *Kun* Reading

The ***kun* reading,** set in sanserif lowercase, is the native Japanese reading of a character. Approved *kun* readings are unmarked; unapproved ones are marked by a small superscript solid triangle ▲:

中 CHŪ naka uchi▲ ata(ru)▲
3451

The *kun* reading is presented in the following format:

1. Approved *kun* readings, along with

readings derived from them, are listed in the order in which they appear in the Jōyō Kanji list; unapproved ones, in descending order of importance. The order of the *kun* readings corresponds exactly to that of the KUN headwords in the KUN section.

Kun readings that are directly derived from approved *kun* readings, such as the noun 掛け ***kake*** from the verb 掛ける ***kakeru*** 'set, put on, etc.', or *kun* readings that are identical with an approved or a derived *kun* reading but differ from it only in *okurigana*, such as the suffix -行き *-yuki* 'bound for' written without the ending き, i.e., -行, are given immediately after the reading from which they are derived:

掛 493 KAI▲ KEI▲ ka(keru) -ka(keru) ka(ke) -ka(ke) -ga(ke) ka(karu) -ka(karu) -ga(karu) ka(kari) -ga(kari) kakari -gakari

Although such readings are not listed in the Jōyō Kanji list, they are not considered unapproved readings since they are merely variants of approved *kun* readings, not independent readings in their own right.

2. *Okurigana* (kana endings) conforming to the official rules published by the Ministry of Education is shown in parentheses. See **Appendix 5. Rules for Okurigana** for details.
3. If a *kun* reading is preceded or followed by a hyphen, it functions only as a word element.
4. If two *kun* readings have exactly the same written form, they are marked by small superscript numerals:

代 30 DAI TAI ka(waru) ka(wari) -ga(wari) ka(eru) yo shiro[1] shiro[2]

See also § 12.2.1 KUN **Headword.**

4.5 Special Reading

The **special reading** is a reading of a word consisting of two or more characters assigned to a single word on the basis of its meaning without direct relation to the normal readings of each character. Since the pronunciation of each character cannot be isolated as a distinct reading, these are not given in the entry-head data but are treated in the SPECIAL READINGS section.

In exceptional cases, a component of what is normally considered a special reading can be isolated as an independent *on* or *kun* reading in its own right. For example, the 凹 in 凸凹 ***dekoboko*** 'unevenness, etc.' can be isolated as having the reading ***boko*** in the sense of concave. Such a reading is similar to an ordinary *kun* reading and is so treated in this dictionary. In the list of character readings, it is marked by a small superscript asterisk * :

凹 3482 Ō kubo(mu)▲ boko*

See also **§ 13. SPECIAL READINGS Section.**

4.6 Unapproved Reading

The **unapproved reading,** marked by a superscript solid triangle ▲, is an *on* or *kun* reading that is not listed in the Jōyō Kanji list but is sufficiently common to merit inclusion in the dictionary:

氷 39 HYŌ kōri hi kō(ru)▲

Unapproved readings are listed in descending order of importance. The distinction between approved and unapproved readings applies only to characters in the Jōyō Kanji list.

4.7 Name Reading

The **name reading** or readings, which appear immediately to the right of the symbol NAMES, are used only in the writing of personal, family, and place names but not in ordinary words:

鎌 REN kama NAMES KEN kata kane
1760

The name reading is presented in the following format:

1. In the list of name readings, *on* readings, if any, are given first, followed by *kun* readings. Within each category the readings are, generally, listed in descending order of frequency or importance.
2. If a reading can be used in both names and ordinary words, it is listed among the regular readings, not the name readings. For example, the reading *tane* of 胤 is used in both words and names and thus appears to the left of the symbol NAMES, but *kazu* is only used in names and thus appears to the right of the symbol:

   胤 IN tane NAMES tsugi tsugu
   17 kazu

3. Sometimes, the same reading appears on both sides of the symbol NAMES. This indicates that the reading on the left, which is used as a word, differs in *okurigana* from the reading on the right, which is used only in names:

   遥 YŌ haru(ka) NAMES haruka
   3141

Name readings are given for all Jinmei Kanji that have such readings. See also **OUTLINE OF JAPANESE WRITING SYSTEM § 2.5 Language Reforms.**

4.8 Chinese Reading

The romanized transcription following the Chinese form(s) is the **Chinese reading.** See **§ 5. Chinese** for details.

5. CHINESE

5.1 General Description

The matter following the symbol CH (for "Chinese") is the **Chinese form** and **Chinese reading**:

臨 臨◆ CH 临 lín
1630 RIN nozo(mu)

An entry character may have more than one Chinese form and/or Chinese reading corresponding to it. If one or more forms have the same reading or readings, those readings follow the form(s) to which they apply:

沈 CH 沉 chén 沈 shěn
261

In the example, the reading chén applies to 沉 and the reading shěn applies to 沈. The Chinese form(s) and Chinese reading(s) are given for all main and reference entry characters, except for reference entry characters that are used only as a radical but not as a word or word element.

5.2 Chinese Form

The **Chinese form** is the official form or forms used in the People's Republic of China. This is often a simplified form significantly different from the Japanese form, but sometimes, as in the example below, both forms are the same or the differences are very slight:

字 ⒸⒽ 字 zì
2172

5.3 Chinese Reading

The romanized transcription following the Chinese form(s) is the **Chinese reading**. This is the reading or readings of the character in Mandarin; that is, the standard pronunciation of the character in the People's Republic of China. The Chinese readings are transcribed in the official Pinyin system of romanization. The tones are indicated by the standard diacritic marks, as illustrated below:

first tone	ā
second tone	á
third tone	ǎ
fourth tone	à
neutral tone	a

5.4 *Kokuji*

Characters that were made in Japan on the model of Chinese characters are referred to as ***kokuji***. This is indicated by the characters "国字" in parentheses, as illustrated below:

峠 ⒸⒽ none（国字）
358

If the entry character is a *kokuji* not used in Chinese, this is indicated by the word "none" and no Chinese form or reading is given. If the entry character is a rare instance of a *kokuji* that has been borrowed into Chinese, the corresponding Chinese form and reading appear:

腺 ⒸⒽ 腺 xiàn（国字）
1035

6. STROKE ORDER DIAGRAM

The dotted box consisting of sequentially numbered frames and appearing below the entry character is the **stroke order diagram**. This shows the correct order in which the strokes of the entry character should be written:

価 ノ 亻 亻 亻 佰 価 価 価
87 1 2 3 4 5 6 7 8

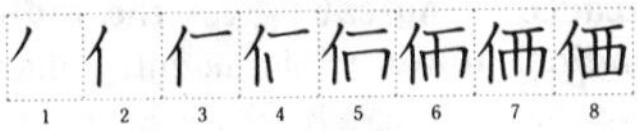

The order of writing is presented stroke by stroke; that is, each frame contains one more stroke than the previous frame, with the tiny numeral under the frame indicating the position of that stroke in the sequence. The last frame contains the full character in the standard square style. The stroke order diagram is given for all main entry characters, and for all reference and nonstandard entry characters that are used as radicals.

7. REFERENCE DATA BOX

7.1 General Description
7.2 Radical
7.3 Strokes
7.4 Grade
7.5 Frequency
7.6 SKIP Number

7.1 General Description

The framed box in the right part of the entry-head data of a character entry is the **reference data box**. This gives numerical data for reference and classification purposes:

輸
1607

Radical	Strokes
車 159	16-7-9
Grade	**Freq**
Jōyō-5	360
◧ 1 - 7 - 9	

The reference data box consists of (1) the radical, (2) the strokes, (3) the grade, (4) the frequency, and (5) the SKIP number. It appears in all main and reference entries, and in all nonstandard entries that are used as a radical.

7.2 Radical

The frame of the reference data box headed "**Radical**" gives the **radical** and **radical number** for the entry character:

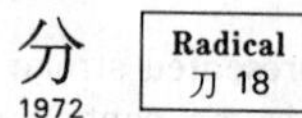

The radical, set in Ming type, is often the parent radical in its full traditional form. The radical number is a serial number from 1 to 214 traditionally assigned to each radical and widely used in character dictionaries and reference works for identification. The radical is presented in the following format:

1. If the form of the radical as it actually appears within the entry character (the actual form) differs considerably from the parent radical, then a variant form identical with, or closely resembling, the actual form is given:

   列 824 | Radical 刂 18

2. The radical given for "lost-radical" characters is a new radical based on the simplified form of the entry character. To distinguish the new radical, the radical number is followed by a superscript triangle $^{\triangle}$:

   会 2020 | Radical 人 $9^{\triangle}$

   The traditional radical of lost-radical characters (in this case 日 based on the old form 會) is not shown in the reference data box, but can be determined by looking the character up in the **Radical Index.**

See also **Appendix 6. The Radicals.**

7.3 Strokes

The frame of the reference data box headed "**Strokes**" gives the **stroke structure** for the entry character:

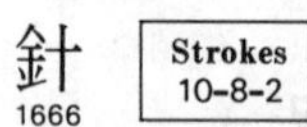

The hyphenated numeral consists of (1) the total stroke-count, (2) the stroke-count of the radical portion, and (3) the stroke-count of the nonradical portion. The total of the second and third parts equals the first part.

The total stroke-count of nonstandard entries that do not have reference data boxes can be determined by adding the two numerals of the **margin guide** for patterns ◧1, ⬒2, and ☐3. For pattern ■4, it is indicated by the first numeral of the margin guide.

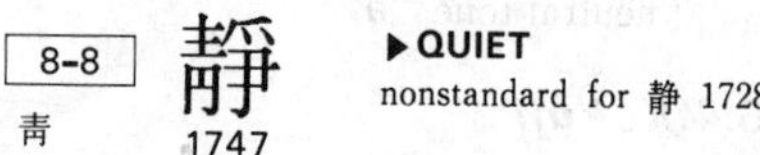

The total of the margin guide numerals above is 16, which is the total stroke-count of 靜.

7.4 Grade

The frame of the reference data box headed "**Grade**" gives the classification of the entry character:

針 1666 | Grade Jōyō-6

The characters are divided into the seven mutually exclusive categories described below:

Jōyō-+ number	A main entry character that is in the Education Kanji list; that is, a character taught in the first six years of compulsory schooling. The number from 1 to 6 following the hyphen corresponds to one of the six elementary school grades during which the character is taught.

Jōyō — A main entry character that is in the Jōyō Kanji list but is not included in the Education Kanji list; that is, a character taught in grades 7 to 9.

Non-Jōyō — A main entry character that is not in the Jōyō Kanji list.

Names — A main entry character that is in the Jinmei Kanji list.

Reference — A reference entry character that is a phonetically replaced character or that is a radical which is also used as a word or word element. See also **§ 26. Reference Entries.**

Radical — A reference entry character that is used only as a radical but not as a word or word element. See also **§ 26. Reference Entries.**

Variant — A nonstandard entry character that is also a radical or radical variant. See also **§ 27. Nonstandard Entries.**

For information on the Jōyō Kanji list and language reforms, see **OUTLINE OF JAPANESE WRITING SYSTEM § 2.5 Language Reforms.**

7.5 Frequency

The frame of the reference data box headed "**Freq**" gives the **frequency** of the entry character. This indicates the frequency of occurrence of the character in Modern Japanese:

針
1666

Freq
504

In the example, "504" means that the entry character is the 504th most frequently used main entry character. The frequency of use is only given for main entry characters. For other entry types the frequency frame is left blank. See also **Appendix 9. Core Meanings Arranged by Frequency.**

7.6 SKIP Number

The bottom frame of the reference data box gives the **SKIP number** for the entry character. This consists of the **pattern symbol** followed by hyphenated numerals used to locate characters according to SKIP rules:

針
1666

◧ 1 - 8 - 2

See SYSTEM OF KANJI INDEXING BY PATTERNS **§ 2.4 SKIP Number** for details.

8. RADICAL SECTION

8.1 Section Description
8.2 Section Format

8.1 Section Description

The matter headed by the label RADICAL is the **RADICAL section.** This describes the function of the entry character as a radical:

3368

RADICAL 9
Standard form: 人 *hito* 'person' (仄 以 來)
Left variant: 亻 *ninben* (仏 仁 代)
Top variant: 𠆢 *hitoyane* (今 令 会)
Description: used in characters related to human beings

The section label is followed by the radical number. This is a serial number from 1 to 214 traditionally assigned to each radical and widely used in character dictionaries and reference works for identification. The RADICAL section is given for every entry character that functions as a radical or radical variant. All such entries also contain a stroke order diagram and reference data box. See also §7.2 **Radical** and **Appendix 6. The Radicals.**

8.2 Section Format

8.2.1 Parent Radical The RADICAL section for an entry character that is one of the 214 traditional radicals in its parent form consists of (1) the standard form, (2) the variants, and (3) the description:

Standard Form: Consists of (*a*) the parent radical in Ming type in its full traditional form, (*b*) the radical name in italics (the most common name(s) of the radical in Japanese), (*c*) the English "name" of the parent radical enclosed in single quotation marks, and (*d*) examples in parentheses of characters in which the parent radical appears as a radical.

Variants: Consists of (*a*) a caption, such as "Left variant" or "Enclosure," that indicates the position in which the radical normally appears within the character, (*b*) the variant(s) in Ming type (simplified form of radical or one that differs considerably from parent radical), (*c*) the variant name in italics (the most common name(s) of the variant(s) in Japanese), and (*d*) examples in parentheses of characters in which the variant appears as a radical.

Descrip-tion: An explanation of the meaning or function of the radical as a character-forming element.

NOTE: Certain radicals are used mostly in their variant forms and the characters in which the parent form appears may be quite rare. In such cases, the characters given as examples may not appear in the dictionary as character entries in their own right.

8.2.2 Radical Variants Radical variants appear at their own SKIP locations. The RADICAL section for an entry character that is a radical variant consists of (1) a brief description and (2) a cross-reference to the parent radical, as illustrated below:

亻
3373

RADICAL 9
ninben, variant of 人 *hito* 'person'
⇨ see 人 3368 for radical description

Characters that are simplified forms of radicals but are not used as radicals in their own right are likewise cross-referenced:

3125

RADICAL 200
simplified form not used as radical
⇨ see 麻 3130 for radical description

9. CORE SECTION

9.1 Section Description

The matter headed by the symbol ▶ is the **CORE section.** This lists the core meaning or meanings of the entry character. The **core meaning,** set in boldface capitals, is a concise English keyword that represents the most fundamental or most important concept linking the principal senses of a character:

単 ▶SINGLE
2256

The CORE section is given for all main and nonstandard entries.

9.2 Section Format

The CORE section consists of one or more core meanings, each headed by the symbol ▶. When there are two or more core meanings, these are listed in descending order of importance. Normally, the core meaning applies to both *on* and *kun* words or word elements, but if the *kun* meaning is dominant and the *on* meaning uncommon, it may apply only to the *kun* meanings. Sometimes, as in the example below, one core applies to the *on* and the other to the *kun*:

係
97

▶CONNECT ▶PERSON IN CHARGE

COMPOUNDS

[formerly also 繫 2902]

❶ⓐ (have a relationship with) **connect, be connected with, relate to, interrelate**

⋮

KUN

⋮

【kakari 係】

[sometimes also 掛]

ⓐ person in charge, official in charge, clerk

10. COMPOUNDS SECTION

10.1 Section Description

The matter headed by the label COMPOUNDS is the **COMPOUNDS section.** In main entries, this lists the meanings of the entry character as an *on* word element. Each meaning is nearly always accompanied by compounds and examples and their English equivalents:

弘
192

COMPOUNDS

❶ **disseminate, spread, teach** (**esp. Buddhism**)

弘報(＝広報) *kōhō* (public) information, public relations

弘法 *guhō* spreading Buddhist teachings

❷ⓐ great, grand

ⓑ [original meaning, now rare] extensive, broad, vast

弘誓 *guzei* Buddha's great vows

弘大な *kōdai na* grand, magnificent, vast

弘遠な *kōen na* vast and far-reaching

The section label COMPOUNDS is merely an identifying symbol—it should not be interpreted to mean that the COMPOUNDS section lists only compound words. In fact, this is the most important section of the entry and usually contains the most useful information about the entry character, especially its meanings as an *on* word element.

The COMPOUNDS section is given for all main entries and reference entries whose main entry character is used as an *on* word element (which is almost all of them). The explanations below apply only to main entries. The COMPOUNDS section of reference entries, described in **§ 26. Reference Entries,** is organized somewhat differently.

10.2 Section Format

The COMPOUNDS section consists of (1) the character meanings and (2) the compounds and examples. These appear in an order that shows their semantic interrelatedness, with the compounds and examples following the sense which they illustrate.

10.2.1 Character Meaning The meaning of the entry character as an *on* word element (combining form or affix) is given by the English equivalent:

詩
1524

ⓐ [also suffix] [original meaning] **poetry, poem, verse**
ⓑ Chinese poetry [poem]

If a meaning has more than one sense, these are subdivided by sense division numbers and the degree of importance is indicated for each sense. It often includes various labels, glosses, and cross-references. These and the equivalent are described in **§ 20. Character Meanings** and in sections **§ 22.** through **§ 25.**

10.2.2 Compounds and Examples

Compounds and examples, grouped by meaning, almost always accompany each sense. These are usually compound words, but a phrase or sentence may occasionally be given:

詩
1524

詩人 *shijin* poet
詩情 *shijō* poetic sentiment, poetical interest
⋮

See **§ 21. Compounds and Examples** for details.

11. INDEPENDENT SECTION

11.1 Section Description 11.2 Section Format

11.1 Section Description

The matter headed by the label INDEPENDENT is the **INDEPENDENT section.** This lists the meanings of the entry character as an independent *on* word. Each meaning is often accompanied by examples and their English equivalents:

2429

INDEPENDENT
【hyō 表】 table, chart, diagram, schedule, tabular form; list
　表にする *hyō ni suru* tabulate; make a list of
【hyōsuru 表する】 express, manifest; pay (one's respects)

Independent *on* word refers to a one-character *on* word, with or without particles, auxiliaries, or inflections, that can be used on its own. Words consisting of one character terminating in the auxiliary verb -する *-suru* or one of its variants, i.e., -ずる *-zuru*, -じる *-jiru*, and -す *-su*, or in a function word such as -なる *-naru* or -たる *-taru*, are treated as separate independent *on* words. Thus, 表 and 表する in the example above are treated as separate independent *on* words.

Independent *on* words terminating in an inflection of する *suru* or one of its variants, or in a function word such as a particle, may appear in the examples under their original forms, but if such words have independent meanings that are unrelated to or that cannot be directly derived from their original forms, they are treated as INDEPENDENT headwords in their own right:

上
3404

【jō 上】 first class, the best; first book [volume]; (marking on gift wrapper) With one's compliments
　上の *jō no* first, best, excellent

乙
3339

【otsu 乙】 the second, B; the latter; second calendar sign; bass (in traditional Japanese music)
【otsu na 乙な】 queer, strange, odd; smartish, chic; nice, fanciful, delicate; romantic

The INDEPENDENT section is given for all main entries whose entry character is used as an independent *on* word. Independent words are also given for reference entries, which are described in **§ 26. Reference Entries.**

11.2 Section Format

The INDEPENDENT section is subdivided into parts referred to as **subentries.** Each independent *on* word is treated under one subentry. This consists of (1) the INDEPENDENT headword, (2) the headword meaning, and (3) the examples. The order of subentries follows that of the *on* readings given in the entry-head data (see **§ 4.3 *On* Reading**). INDEPENDENT headwords terminating in a particle or an auxiliary follow the form from which they originate. For example, 期する *kisuru,* which terminates in the auxiliary verb する *suru,* follows 期 *ki.*

11.2.1 INDEPENDENT Headword

The matter enclosed in heavy black square brackets 【】 at the head of a subentry is the **INDEPENDENT headword.** This consists of a boldface romanized transcription of an independent *on* word and the Japanese word in Gothic type:

明
855

【mei 明】 discernment, insight; eyesight

⋮

【min 明】 Ming Dynasty

The term **subentry headword** refers to an INDEPENDENT headword, a KUN headword, or to both collectively. The INDEPENDENT headword is presented in the following format:

1. If an INDEPENDENT headword has two or more readings or written forms, the alternative readings and/or forms follow in parentheses and are preceded by an equal sign. The first alternative is usually more common than the second.

難
1838

【nanjiru（=nanzuru）難じる(=難ずる)】
criticize unfavorably, blame, reproach

2. In the rare cases that a character is used as a symbol that has no pronunciation, such as 危 for "DANGER," no transcription is given.

11.2.2 Headword Meaning

The meaning of an INDEPENDENT headword as an independent *on* word is given by the English equivalent:

学
2555

【gaku 学】 studies, learning

The meaning is sometimes subdivided by sense division numbers and may include various labels, glosses, and cross-references. These and the equivalent are described in **§ 20. Character Meanings** and in sections **§ 22.** through **§ 25.** If the meaning consists of numbered senses, these appear flush left in the line immediately below the INDEPENDENT headword:

別
1117

【betsu 別】
① distinction, difference
⋮
② another thing, an extra
⋮
③ exception

11.2.3 The Examples

Examples, grouped by meaning, often accompany each INDEPENDENT headword. These consist of an INDEPENDENT headword terminating in a particle or an inflection of the auxiliary verb する *suru* or one its variants, or of a phrase or sentence:

負
2091

【fu 負】
負の *fu no* negative

窮
2358

【kyūsuru 窮する】 be in extremity, come to an extreme, be in distress, be in want [need]

窮すれば通ず *Kyūsureba tsūzu* Necessity is the mother of invention

See **§21. Compounds and Examples** for details.

12. KUN SECTION

12.1 Section Description 12.2 Section Format

12.1 Section Description

The matter headed by the label KUN is the **KUN section.** This lists the meanings of the entry character as a *kun* word or word element. Each meaning is usually accompanied by compounds and examples and their English equivalents:

123

KUN

【osa(meru) 修める】
① cultivate, pursue, practice, study; master, complete
学を修める *gaku o osameru* pursue knowledge [one's studies]
② order (one's life)
身を修める *mi o osameru* order one's life
【osa(maru) 修まる】 govern oneself, conduct oneself well
素行が修まらない *sokō ga osamaranai* conduct oneself loosely, be dissolute

The KUN section is given for all main entries whose main entry character is used as a *kun* word or word element. *Kun* words are also given for reference entries, which are described in **§26. Reference Entries.**

12.2 Section Format

The KUN section is subdivided into parts referred to as **subentries**. Each *kun* word or word element is treated under one subentry. This consists of (1) the KUN headword, (2) the headword meaning, and (3) the compounds and examples. The order of subentries follows that of the *kun* readings given in the entry–head data (see **§4.4 *Kun* Reading**).

12.2.1 KUN Headword The matter enclosed in heavy black square brackets 【】 at the head of a subentry is the **KUN headword.** This consists of a boldface romanized transcription of a *kun* word or word element and the Japanese word or word element in Gothic type:

 **【osa(meru) 修める】**
123 ⋮
【osa(maru) 修まる】

The term **subentry headword** refers to an INDEPENDENT headword, a KUN headword, or to both collectively. The KUN headword is presented in the following format:

1. The parentheses in the romanized transcription indicate *okurigana* (kana endings) in conformity with the official rules published by the Ministry of Education. See **Appendix 5. Rules for Okurigana** for details.
2. If a KUN headword has two readings or written forms, the second reading and/or form follows the first and is separated from it by a comma. The first form is in standard orthography and is usually more common than the second. The second form is usually a variant of the first with different kana endings:

522

【-zu(mi) -済み, -zumi -済】 [suffix] completed, finished, settled, concluded

Sometimes, the two alternatives differ slightly in pronunciation due to voicing or euphonic change:

 **【kata 潟, -gata -潟】**
745

3. If two *kun* words or word elements have exactly the same written form and the same reading but differ in function, they are treated as separate headwords and are distinguished by small superscript numerals. One of these *homographs* functions as a free *kun* word and/or word element:

泥
326

【doro¹ 泥】
① mud, mire, slush, dirt
泥沼 *doronuma* bog; swamp (of difficulties)
⋮
② unclassified compounds
泥棒 *dorobō* thief, crook

The other functions only as a word element, which is indicated by the functional label "[in compounds]":

泥
326

【doro² 泥】 [in compounds] [also suffix] petty thief, sneak thief, pilferer
泥縄 *doronawa* expediency coming too late (like making a rope after finding the thief)

4. If a *kun* word is a noun adjective, the KUN headword in the heavy black square brackets **【】** does not include な *na*, the attributive form of the copula だ *da*. The KUN headword is followed on the next line by a secondary headword in boldface (but not in brackets) that does include な *na*, which is used when the word functions as an attributive adjective:

静
1728

【shizu(ka) 静か】
shizuka na 静かな quiet, silent, still; calm, tranquil, gentle, quiet

Noun adjectives can also be used as adverbs by replacing な *na* with に *ni*.

5. If a KUN headword includes a hyphen, it functions only as a word element (affix or combining form) in all its senses. The position of the hyphen indicates whether the form is used in the final or in the initial position:

上
3404

【-a(geru) -上げる】
① up, upward
⋮
③ honorific verbal suffix

In the example, -上げる functions as a word element in the final position. See also **§ 20.10.4 Free Words Versus Word Elements.**

12.2.2 Headword Meaning

The meaning of a KUN headword as a *kun* word or word element is given by the English equivalent:

攻
242

【se(meru) 攻める】 attack, take the offensive

The meaning is sometimes subdivided by sense division numbers and may include various labels, glosses, and cross-references. These and the equivalent are described in **§ 20. Character Meanings** and in sections **§ 22.** through **§ 25.** If the meaning consists of numbered senses, these appear flush left in the line immediately below the KUN headword:

推
504

【o(su) 推す】
① infer, deduce, conjecture, surmise, guess
⋮
② recommend, propose, nominate

12.2.3 Compounds and Examples

Compounds and examples, grouped by meaning, usually accompany each sense of a KUN headword. These consist of compound words, inflected or derived forms of the KUN headword, a KUN headword terminating in a particle or auxiliary, or a phrase or sentence:

静
1728
【shizu(maru) 静まる】
⋮
静まり返る *shizumarikaeru* become still as death
寝静まる *neshizumaru* fall fast asleep
嵐が静まった *Arashi ga shizumatta* The storm has abated

See **§21. Compounds and Examples** for details.

13. SPECIAL READINGS SECTION

13.1 Section Description

The matter headed by the label [SPECIAL READINGS] is the **SPECIAL READINGS section.** This lists compound words having special readings and their English equivalents:

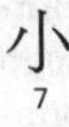
7
[SPECIAL READINGS]
小豆 *azuki* adzuki bean
小波▲ *sazanami* ripples, wavelets

A **special reading** is a reading of a word consisting of two or more characters assigned to a single word on the basis of its meaning without direct relation to the normal readings of each constituent character. *Approved* special readings are those listed in the appendix to the Jōyō Kanji list; *unapproved* special readings are those that are not. Since the pronunciation of each character cannot normally be isolated as a distinct reading, these are not listed in the entry-head data as character readings but are treated in the SPECIAL READINGS section.

The SPECIAL READINGS section appears in all main entries whose entry characters are used in common compound words having special readings. In reference entries, such words appear in the COMPOUNDS section. See also **§4.5 Special Reading.**

13.2 Section Format

All compound words having approved special readings and frequently used compound words with unapproved special readings are listed together in the SPECIAL READINGS section. Those with approved special readings are given first, followed by those with unapproved ones. A superscript triangle ▲ following the Japanese word indicates that the special reading in question is unapproved:

明
855
明日 *asu* tomorrow
明日▲ *ashita* tomorrow

See also **§21. Compounds and Examples.**

14. NAMES SECTION

14.1 Section Description

The matter headed by the label [NAMES] is the **NAMES section.** This lists examples of names and their English descriptions:

鳩
163
[NAMES]
鳩山 *hatoyama* surname
鳩彦 *yasuhiko* male name

The NAMES section gives name examples for the **name readings** (readings used only in the writing of names) for the 166 characters in the Jinmei Kanji list of 1981. See also **§4.7 Name Reading.**

14.2 Section Format

Name examples are listed together in the NAMES section. These appear in the same order as the corresponding character readings are listed in the entry-head data. An English description of the name replaces what would normally be the equivalent. This explains how the name is used; i.e., as a surname, male or female first name, place name, and so on, or as a combination of these:

敦
1693

敦 *ton* (=*atsushi*) male name
敦子 *atsuko* female name
敦賀 *tsuruga* surname also place name

See also **§21. Compounds and Examples.**

15. SYNONYMS SECTION

15.1 Section Description

The matter headed by the label SYNONYMS is the **SYNONYMS section.** This lists groups of kanji synonyms and their English keywords for the principal senses of main entry characters:

1787

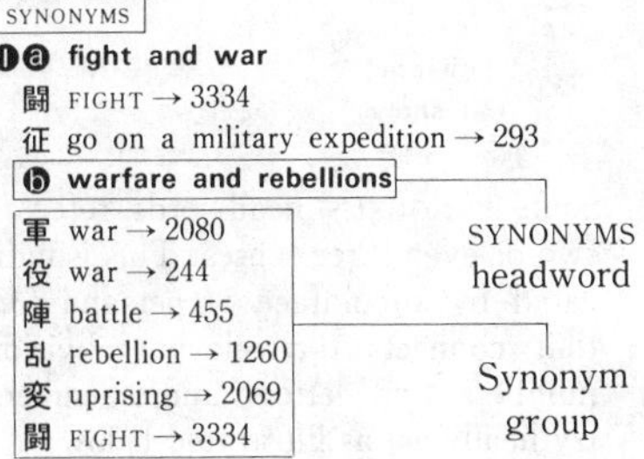

SYNONYMS
❶ⓐ fight and war
闘 FIGHT → 3334
征 go on a military expedition → 293
ⓑ warfare and rebellions
軍 war → 2080
役 war → 244
陣 battle → 455
乱 rebellion → 1260
変 uprising → 2069
闘 FIGHT → 3334
SYNONYMS headword
Synonym group

❷ **game**
技 game → 248
【tatakau】
② **compete**
闘 FIGHT → 3334
争 CONTEND → 2030
競 COMPETE → 1847

Synonym, or **kanji synonym,** is used in a broad sense that includes several categories of correlated characters; i.e., *synonyms* (terms that share the same basic meaning), *hyponyms* (specific terms included in a more general term), and, rarely, *complementaries* (terms of mutually exclusive meaning). As a rule, **kanji synonyms** refers to the relationship between word-building elements, especially *on* word elements. Important independent *kun* words are sometimes included, but independent *on* words are quite rare.

The SYNONYMS section has two principal aims:

1. To enable the user to study the differences and similarities of synonym group members by (*a*) indicating the semantic relationship (usually the shared meaning) between them and by (*b*) bringing together their English keywords into a single article.

2. To act as a network of cross-references that enables the user to quickly locate the meanings and the compounds or examples for any member of a synonym group from any of the others. This allows the user to acquire a full understanding of the differences in meaning between closely related characters, and to use the dictionary as a simple kanji thesaurus.

The SYNONYMS section is given for all principal senses of main entry characters that are semantically related to another main entry character (which is almost all of them). See also **Appendix 11. List of Kanji Synonym Groups.**

15.2 Section Format

Each group of synonyms is treated in a separate subsection. This consists of (1) the SYNONYMS headword and (2) the synonym group. The synonym groups are listed in the same order as the senses to which they apply originally appear in that character entry.

15.2.1 SYNONYMS Headword The boldface matter heading a synonym group is the **SYNONYMS headword.** This is an English word or phrase that concisely expresses the semantic relationship (usually the shared meaning) between the members of a synonym group. The SYNONYMS headwords refer to a main sense or subsense in the COMPOUNDS, KUN, or INDEPENDENT sections of that character entry, as explained below:

1. If a SYNONYMS headword refers to a sense in the COMPOUNDS section, it is preceded by dark-circled numbers and letters that point to the senses to which that synonym group applies:

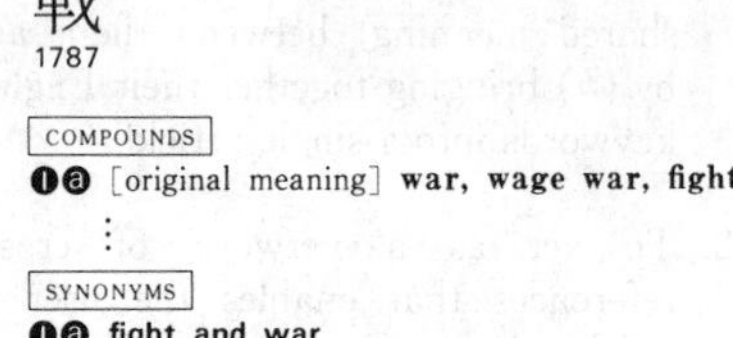

In the example, the headword **fight and war** applies to sense ❶ⓐ in the COMPOUNDS section.

2. If a SYNONYMS headword refers to a subentry headword (KUN or INDEPENDENT headword), it is preceded by a boldface subentry heading (enclosed in heavy black square brackets 【】) and clear-circled numbers and letters that point to the senses of the subentry headword to which that synonym group applies:

In the example, the group applies to sense ② of the KUN headword **tataka(u)**. The subentry heading is identical with the subentry headword to which it points, but *okurigana* endings are not shown.

3. If a SYNONYMS headword refers to an unnumbered sense, it is headed by the division number zero. If the sense referred to is in the COMPOUNDS section, the zero is represented by a solid black circle ●:

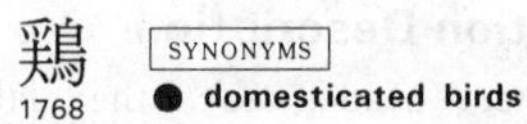

If the sense referred to is in the KUN or INDEPENDENT sections, the zero is represented by a clear circle ○ (except when the headword is preceded by an ampersand):

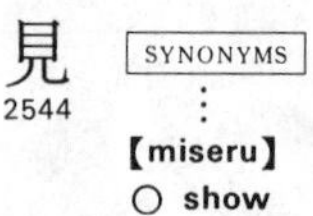

4. Some SYNONYMS headwords refer to two or even three senses. This is indicated by a boldface ampersand (**&**) that connects the relevant division numbers and letters and/or subentry headings, as illustrated below:

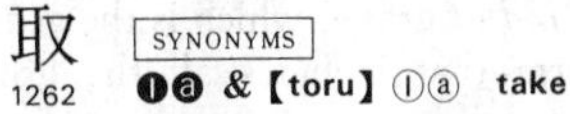

取 SYNONYMS
1262 ❶ⓐ & 【toru】 ①ⓐ take

In the example, the headword **take** applies to sense ❶ⓐ of 取 in the COMPOUNDS section and to sense ①ⓐ of **to(ru)** in the KUN section.

5. Sometimes two synonym groups apply to the same sense; that is, a particular sense relates equally well to two distinct synonym groups. This is shown by repeating the relevant division number and/or letter:

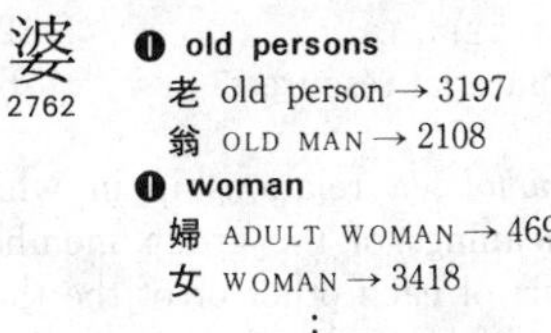

婆
2762
❶ **old persons**
老 old person → 3197
翁 OLD MAN → 2108
❶ **woman**
婦 ADULT WOMAN → 469
女 WOMAN → 3418
⋮

Sometimes one synonym group applies to all the subsenses of a main sense and another group to only one subsense of that main sense:

子
3390

❹ **nominalizers**
所 PARTICLE OF NOMINALIZATION → 851
⋮
ⓑ **particle**
粒 GRAIN → 1328

In the example, the **nominalizers** group applies to all of sense ❹, including subsenses ❹ⓐ and ❹ⓑ, while the **particle** group applies only to subsense ❹ⓑ.

15.2.2 Synonym Group Two or more *on* word elements or subentry headwords that are semantically related, especially those that share the same basic meaning, are referred to as a **synonym group.** The SYNONYMS section for a particular entry character includes all the members of that group, except for the entry character itself. A member of a synonym group is a **synonym group member.** This consists of (1) the kanji synonym, (2) the synonym keyword, and (3) the cross-reference. The synonym group members are normally presented in descending order of semantic relatedness:

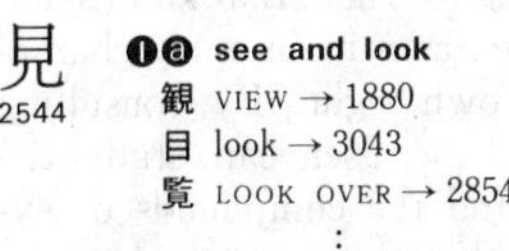

見
2544
❶ⓐ **see and look**
観 VIEW → 1880
目 look → 3043
覧 LOOK OVER → 2854
⋮

1. The **kanji synonym** is a Japanese word or word element in Gothic type that is a member of a synonym group. In the case of *kun* words or word elements, it includes *okurigana* endings and hyphens identical with the subentry headword to which it applies:

上 SYNONYMS
3404
⋮
立てる STAND → 1992
拾う PICK UP → 379

2. The **synonym keyword** is a concise English equivalent that most aptly represents that sense of a kanji synonym which is relevant to that synonym group. This is usually identical with one of the core meanings, or with an English keyword that is not a core meaning, of the entry character for that kanji synonym. Small capitals and lowercase are used to distinguish synonym keywords that are core meanings from those that are not:

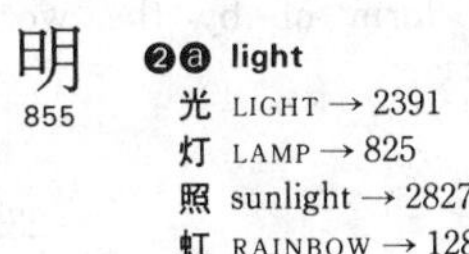

明
855
❷ⓐ **light**
光 LIGHT → 2391
灯 LAMP → 825
照 sunlight → 2827
虹 RAINBOW → 1285

In the example, the keyword "LIGHT" represents the core meaning of 光, so it is set in small capitals, whereas the keyword "sunlight," which is the sense of 照 that is relevant to the **light** group, is not a core meaning of 照 so it is set in lowercase.

3. The **cross-reference** consists of an arrow → followed by an entry number referring to where that kanji synonym appears as a main entry character in its own right. By consulting that entry, the user can study the meanings and the compounds or examples for that character.

15.3 Semantic Relationships

Various semantic relationships (sense relations) exist among the individual synonym group members and between the members and the SYNONYMS headword. The main relationships are (1) class-inclusion, (2) synonymy, (3) part-whole, and (4) complementarity. These are not mutually exclusive categories; in some cases they may partially or even wholly overlap. The various relationships are not distinguished by any formal means such as special typefaces or symbols. However, the phrasing or grammatical number of the SYNONYMS headword may identify or hint at the type of relationship, as explained below:

1. *Class-inclusion* or *kind of*, a relationship in which the SYNONYMS headword (*superordinate word*) is a general term that includes the meanings of the specific terms (class members or *hyponyms*) represented by the individual group members, is often indicated by a SYNONYMS headword in the plural form or by the words "kinds of":

graves

墓	GRAVE	2332
墳	TUMULUS	719
陵	IMPERIAL MAUSOLEUM	544
塚	grave mound	556

In the example, each group member is a *kind of* grave, which is the general term that includes all the group members.

2. *Synonymy*, a relationship in which the group members share a basic meaning or are similar or identical in meaning, is often indicated by a SYNONYMS headword given in the singular form:

matter

質	MATTER	2808
物	substance	874
材	MATERIAL	836
料	MATERIALS	1292
資	material resources	2695

3. *Part-whole*, a relationship in which the meanings of the group members are part of each other or of the thing represented by the SYNONYMS headword, is often indicated by a headword in the form "parts of..." or "...parts":

parts of towns

区	WARD	2963
街	CITY QUARTER	576
町	town section (*cho*)	1113
丁	TOWN SUBSECTION (*chome*)	3348
字	village or town section	2172

4. *Complementarity* is a relationship in which the meanings of the group members contrast with each other and are mutually exclusive:

siblings

妹	YOUNGER SISTER	278
姉	OLDER SISTER	280
兄	OLDER BROTHER	2154
弟	YOUNGER BROTHER	2044

Groups of complementary characters, which are similar to antonyms (words of opposite meaning) are, in principle, not given, except for special cases in which it was necessary to draw attention to closely-related characters.

16. USAGE SECTION

16.1 Section Description

The matter headed by the label USAGE is the **USAGE section.** This discriminates between the meanings of homophones (rarely synonyms) by bringing together their English equivalents into a single article:

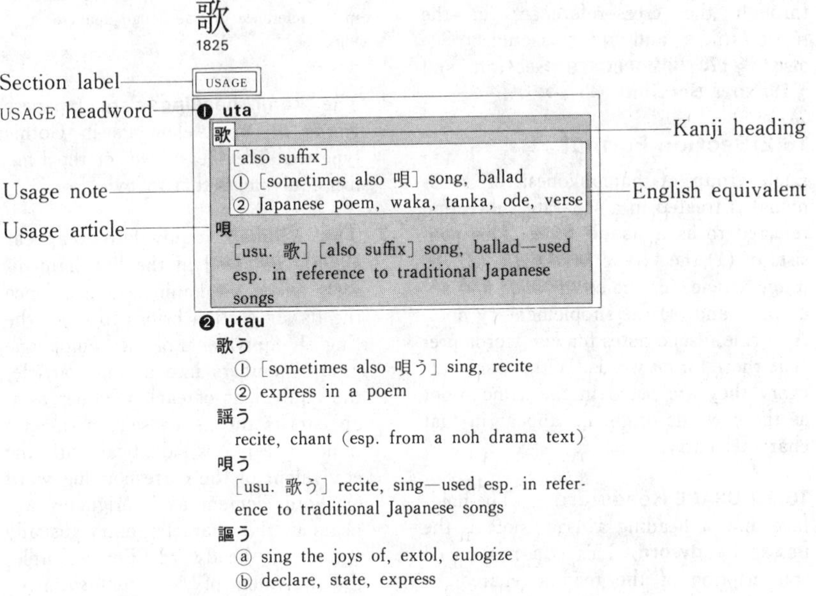

歌
1825
Section label
USAGE
USAGE headword
❶ uta
Kanji heading
歌
[also suffix]
① [sometimes also 唄] song, ballad
② Japanese poem, waka, tanka, ode, verse
English equivalent
Usage note
Usage article
唄
[usu. 歌] [also suffix] song, ballad—used esp. in reference to traditional Japanese songs
❷ utau
歌う
① [sometimes also 唄う] sing, recite
② express in a poem
謡う
recite, chant (esp. from a noh drama text)
唄う
[usu. 歌う] recite, sing—used esp. in reference to traditional Japanese songs
謳う
ⓐ sing the joys of, extol, eulogize
ⓑ declare, state, express

Homophones as used in this dictionary refers to words or word elements, often etymologically related, that are pronounced alike but written differently and often have different meanings. The term refers mostly to *kun* homophones that are subentry headwords or their derivatives. A group of such words is referred to as a **homophone group.**

The purpose of the USAGE section is to enable the user to study the differences and similarities between the meanings of the members of homophone (and synonym) groups. These are of the following kinds:

1. Independent *kun* words or word elements (KUN headwords or their derivatives) that are pronounced the same but written differently. These usually, but not always, differ in meaning. For example, ***aku*** is written in three ways—明く, 開く, and 空く—that differ in meaning.

2. Easily confused compound words, either *on* or *kun*, or independent *on* words that are pronounced the same but are written differently and have different meanings; e.g., 制作 ***seisaku*** 'production (of a film)' and 製作 ***seisaku*** 'manufacture'.

3. A small number of easily confused synonymous words or word elements that are similar in meaning but are written and pronounced differently;

e.g., 森 *mori* 'thick woods' and 林 *hayashi* 'small woods'.

The USAGE section appears only in main entries. As a rule, a usage note appears at the entry for the most common or important group member. It can be located from the other relevant group members through the cross-references in the HOMOPHONES and NOTE sections. See also **§17. HOMOPHONES Section** and **§19. NOTE Section.**

16.2 Section Format

Each group of homophones (or synonyms) is treated in a separate subsection referred to as a **usage note.** This consists of (1) the USAGE headword, (2) the usage article, (3) the compounds and examples, and (4) the supplementary note. As a rule, usage notes for *kun* words precede those for *on* words. Within each category they are listed in the same order as these words originally appear in that character entry.

16.2.1 USAGE Headword The boldface matter heading a usage note is the **USAGE headword.** This is a romanized transcription of the reading shared by the members of the homophone group treated in that usage note. *Okurigana* endings are not shown in the USAGE headword. When there are two or more usage notes, the USAGE headwords are numbered sequentially by dark-circled numbers:

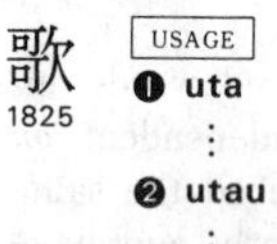

16.2.2 Usage Article The meanings of each member of a homophone (or synonym) group are given by the **usage article.** This consists of (1) the kanji headings and (2) the English equivalents:

1825

歌
[also suffix]
① [sometimes also 唄] song, ballad
② Japanese poem, waka, tanka, ode, verse
唄
[usu. 歌] [also suffix] song, ballad—used esp. in reference to traditional Japanese songs

1. The **kanji headings** are Japanese words or word elements in Gothic type that are the subject of the English equivalents that follow.

2. The **English equivalents** appear slightly indented in the line immediately below the kanji headings. Since the USAGE section brings together the English equivalents of the homophone group members into a single article, the equivalent of each member as it appears in the USAGE section is, with minor exceptions, identical with the equivalent of the corresponding word or word element as it originally appears in the character entry, usually as a KUN headword. For example, the equivalent of 点す *tomosu* in the USAGE section below is identical with the equivalent of the KUN headword **tomo(su).**

Sometimes, the equivalent of a word treated in the USAGE section is identical with that of another word appearing elsewhere in the same USAGE section. To save space in cases of long equivalents, the words "same as" introduce a cross-reference to the word with which it shares its meaning:

2084

tomosu
点す
[sometimes also 灯す] light (a lamp),

set alight, turn on (a light)
灯す
[usu. 点す] same as 点す

The equivalent is often subdivided by sense division numbers and accompanied by various labels and glosses. These and the equivalent are described in **§20. Character Meanings** and in sections **§22.** through **§25.**

16.2.3 Illustrative Examples

Usage notes are not normally accompanied by compounds and examples. The compounds and examples for the group member that includes the entry character itself can be found in the appropriate section (usually the KUN section) of that character entry, while those for the other group members can be located through the cross-references in the HOMOPHONES section (see **§17. HOMOPHONES Section** for details). In exceptional cases, additional illustrative examples appear in the USAGE section to further clarify the differences between easily confused homophones:

産
3298

❶ umu
産む
(produce offspring) give birth to, bear offspring, beget, breed; spawn
彼女は五人子供を産んだ *Kanojo wa gonin kodomo 'o unda* She gave birth to five children
生む
① have children
② produce, bring forth, give rise to, yield
彼女は五人子供を生んだ *Kanojo wa gonin kodomo o unda* She has five children

16.2.4 Supplementary Note

The matter preceded by the symbol ★ is the **supplementary note.** This is a comment or article that sometimes appears in a usage note and supplements the English equivalent(s). It may include an analysis of the usage of various examples and explain their differences and similarities:

止
2941

❹ -tomeru
-止める
⋮
-留める
⋮
★Both forms are used in compounds in the sense of kill, but -留める is preferred in the word 仕留める *shitomeru* 'kill, shoot dead'. *Tomeru* is not used independently in this sense.

Sometimes, as in the case of synonym groups, a supplementary note appears immediately after a USAGE headword and the equivalent is omitted:

2492

愛 ai　恋 ren
★Though both 恋 and 愛 mean love, the former is mostly restricted to love between man and woman while the latter is a general term roughly equivalent to the English word *love.*

17. HOMOPHONES SECTION

17.1 Section Description 17.2 Section Format

17.1 Section Description

The matter headed by the label HOMOPHONES is the **HOMOPHONES section.** This lists groups of homophones and their entry numbers for cross-reference:

歌　HOMOPHONES
1825
uta ⇨ 唄 400
utau ⇨ 謡 1597　唄 400　謳 1632

The terms **homophones** and **homo-**

phone group are defined in **§16. USAGE Section.** The HOMOPHONES sections form a network of cross-references that enables one to quickly locate information about any member of a homophone group from any of the others. This can be useful in two principal ways:

1. The HOMOPHONES section appears at each member of a group of homophones whose meanings are discriminated in a usage note and acts as a cross-reference to every other member. This enables the user to locate the compounds and examples for each group member.

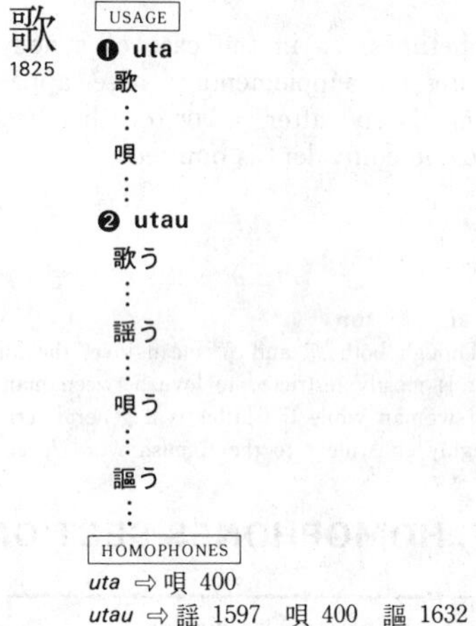

For example, the usage notes for *uta* and *utau* shown above appear in the USAGE section of 歌. The compounds and examples for 歌う are found in the KUN section of 歌 itself under the headword **uta(u)**, while those for 謳う, 唄う, and 謡う can be located through the cross-reference in the HOMOPHONES section of 歌.

2. The HOMOPHONES section acts as a cross-reference to characters in orthographic labels that are not followed by their entry numbers:

For example, the orthographic label "[sometimes also 唄う]" does not include the entry number, since the latter is found in the HOMOPHONES section. See also **§22. Orthographic Labels.**

The HOMOPHONES section appears in all main and reference entries whose entry characters are members of *kun* homophone groups (groups consisting partially or entirely of KUN headwords or their derivatives). See also **§16. USAGE Section.**

17.2 Section Format

Each homophone group is listed on a separate line. It consists of (1) the HOMOPHONES headword and (2) the homophone group members:

歌 1825 *utau* ⇨ 謡 1597 唄 400 謳 1632

As a rule, the homophone groups appear in the same order as the words or word elements that correspond to the HOMOPHONES headwords originally appear in that character entry. The HOMOPHONES section is presented in the following format:

1. The **HOMOPHONES headword** is a word heading a homophone group. It consists of an italicized transcription of the reading shared by the members of that group, and is followed by an arrow ⇨ that introduces the group members. The HOMOPHONES head-

word refers to a word or word element within that character entry, usually a KUN headword, with which it is identical in form, including hyphens, but *okurigana* endings are not shown.

2. The **homophone group member** is a member of a homophone group. It consists of the character in Ming type, without *okurigana* endings or hyphens, followed by its entry number. Sometimes one member of a homophone group may be a *kun* word written with two characters while the other members are written with one character. In such cases, the member with two characters is shown in full along with *okurigana* endings and entry numbers separated by a comma are given for both characters:

幸
2216

HOMOPHONES

⋮

shiawase ⇨ 倖せ 118 仕合わせ 34, 2019

18. COMPOUND FORMATION SECTION

18.1 Section Description

The matter headed by the label COMPOUND FORMATION is the **COMPOUND FORMATION section.** This describes how a compound word is formed from its constituent parts and/or gives its etymology:

得
477

COMPOUND FORMATION

❶ 得意 *tokui*
得意 'one's forte, etc.' is to satisfactorily achieve (得 ❸ⓑ) one's desires (意) and take pride in one's achievements.

❷ 説得 *settoku*
説得する 'persuade' is to persuade (説) a person so as to achieve (得 ❸ⓑ) one's ends.

Normally, the formation of a compound word is self-evident because the compounds and examples are grouped by meaning (see **§ 21. Compounds and Examples**). In some cases, however, the semantic relationship between the constituent parts may be obscure. The purpose of the COMPOUND FORMATION section is to explain how the constituent characters of such compound words are combined to yield the meaning of the whole. This is done by explaining the meaning or function of each component, or by presenting a brief etymology (origin and/or development) of the compound word.

The COMPOUND FORMATION section appears only in main entries that contain compound words whose formation may not be clear. As a rule, a compound formation article appears at the entry for the character most relevant to the discussion of that article. It can be located from the other relevant characters through the cross-references in the NOTE section. See also **§ 19. NOTE Section.**

18.2 Section Format

The formation and/or etymology of each compound word or group of related compound words are treated in a separate subsection. This consists of (1) the COMPOUND FORMATION headword and (2) the compound formation article. The compound formation articles appear in the same order as the words corresponding to the COMPOUND FORMATION headwords originally appear in that character entry.

18.2.1 COMPOUND FORMATION Headword The matter heading a compound formation article is the **COMPOUND FORMATION headword.** This is the Japanese compound word or words in Gothic type followed by an italicized transcription that is the subject of the compound formation article that follows. It consists of the compound word proper without particles or the auxiliary verb する *suru*. When there are two or more compound formation articles, the COMPOUND FORMATION headwords are numbered sequentially by dark-circled numbers:

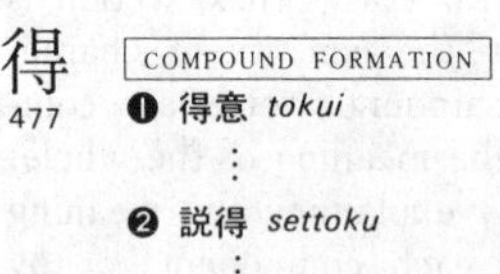

Sometimes, two or three compound words are treated in the same compound formation article. In such cases, the COMPOUND FORMATION headword consists of the relevant compound words:

正
3484

COMPOUND FORMATION
正弦 *seigen* **余弦** *yogen*

18.2.2 Compound Formation Article The matter appearing immediately below the COMPOUND FORMATION headword is the **compound formation article.** This is an explanation of the formation and/or etymology of a compound word whose formation may not be clear:

取
1262

関取 *sekitori*
関取 'ranking sumo wrestler' is a sumo wrestler (関) who acquired (取る ②ⓐ) a high rank.

Sense division numbers and letters within the article, often in parentheses, refer to the relevant sense in the COMPOUNDS or KUN sections. In the example in § 18.1 above, "得❸ⓑ" refers to sense ❸ⓑ in the COMPOUNDS section of 得; in the example immediately above, "取る ②ⓐ" refers to sense ②ⓐ under the subentry headword **to(ru)** in the KUN section of 取.

19. NOTE SECTION

19.1 Section Description
19.2 Section Format

19.1 Section Description

The matter headed by the label NOTE is the **NOTE section.** This consists of various cross-references and/or explanatory notes:

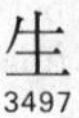
3497

NOTE
⇨ see also USAGE notes at 産 3298 and 成 3537
⇨ see COMPOUND FORMATION for 生涯 *shōgai* ⇨ 涯 512
★生 is said to have a total of more than 200 readings, which is more than any other character.

The NOTE section appears in all main and reference entries that require cross-references or supplementary remarks.

19.2 Section Format

The NOTE section consists of (1) the cross-reference note and (2) the supplementary note, in that order.

19.2.1 Cross-Reference Note The matter introduced by the arrow ⇨ is the **cross-reference note.** This directs the user to another character entry that should be consulted for further information. Cross-reference notes are of three kinds:

1. A cross-reference to a usage note:

朝
1695
⇨ see USAGE note at 旭 2977

A cross-reference beginning with "see also" indicates that the entry character appears in a usage note both at its own character entry and at the entry cross-referenced to:

次
54

⇨ see also USAGE note at 接 500

2. A cross-reference to a compound formation article:

話
1527

⇨ see COMPOUND FORMATION for
閑話休題 *kanwakyūdai* ⇨ 閑 3322
挿話 *sōwa* ⇨ 挿 431

3. Miscellaneous cross-references, such as to another NOTE section:

把
249

⇨ see also NOTE at 羽 226.

19.2.2 Supplementary Note The matter introduced by the symbol ★ is the **supplementary note.** This supplements the information provided by the other explanatory matter. Supplementary notes are of two kinds:

1. A supplementary remark on the usage, form, orthography, reading, etc., of the entry character:

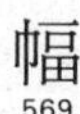
569

★Though 幅 and 巾 3409 are distinct characters, the latter is also used as an abbreviation of the former.

2. A warning directing attention to characters of similar form that are easily confused. These are cross-referenced to each other, as illustrated below:

部
1676

NOTE
★do not confuse with 陪 539

539

NOTE
★do not confuse with 部 1676

20. CHARACTER MEANINGS

20.1 General Description

The detailed presentation of character meanings is one of the principal features of this dictionary. Meanings are given for each character as an *on* word element in the COMPOUNDS section, for the headwords in the INDEPENDENT, KUN, and USAGE sections, and for the compounds and examples that usually accompany each sense. As a rule, everything that applies to the meanings of *on* word elements and the various headwords also applies to the meanings of the compounds and examples, but the latter are not divided by sense division numbers, nor are they treated in as much detail.

The meanings consist of sense division numbers, various labels and glosses, the English equivalent, and cross-references, which are presented in the following order: sense division numbers, orthographic labels, functional labels, status labels, subject labels, explanatory glosses, the equivalent, supplementary glosses, and cross-references. These are described in detail below, except for the labels, which are described in sections **§ 22.** through **§ 25.** The applicability of the labels and glosses to the individual senses as well as the various conventions that apply throughout the dictionary are treated in **§ 30. Other Conventions.**

20.2 Definitions of Terms

Following are definitions of some important terms related to character meanings:

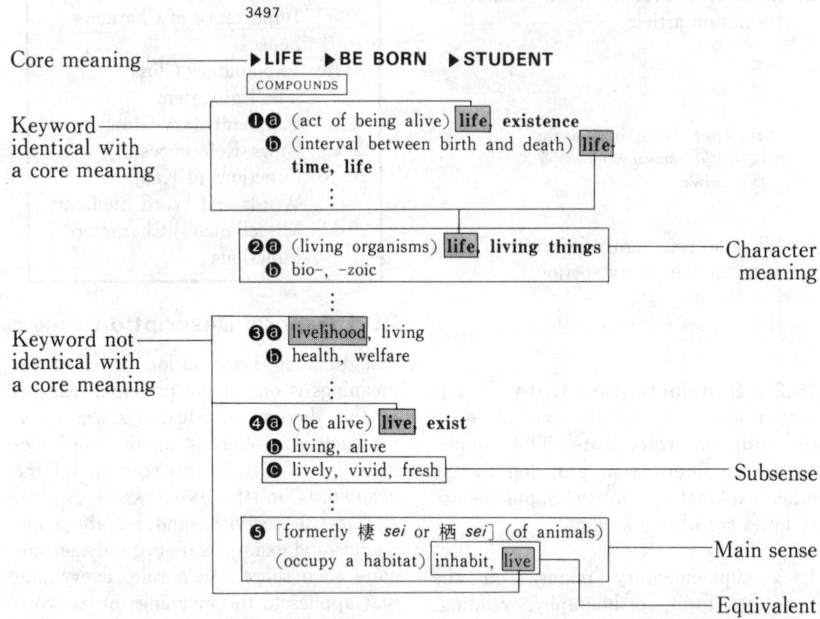

1. **Free word** or **word** refers to any independent word; that is, any word that can be used on its own (**§ 20.10.1**). This includes (1) independent *on* words, (2) independent *kun* words, and (3) most compound words.

2. **Word element** refers to any form used only in combinations; that is, any **combining form** or **affix**. This includes (1) ***on* word elements,** (2) **KUN headwords** (**§ 12.2.1**) that are used only in combinations, and (3) **compound words** (**§ 21.1**) not used on their own. ***On* word element**, a frequently used term, always refers to an element pronounced in the *on* reading that is used in the formation of compounds. *On* word elements are treated only in the COMPOUNDS section.

3. **Subentry headword** refers to (1) an independent *on* word acting as an **INDEPENDENT headword** (**§ 11.2.1**), (2) a *kun* word or word element acting as a **KUN headword** (**§ 12.2.1**), or (3) to both collectively.

4. **Meaning** or **character meaning** is a broad term used rather loosely; in addition to its use as an ordinary English word, it often refers to an equivalent along with other explanatory matter such as labels and glosses.

5. **Sense** refers to one of the meanings

of a word or word element. A sense may be further subdivided by sense division letters and/or semicolons into **subsenses**. The term **main sense** is used when it is necessary to distinguish a principal sense from a subsense. **Sense** unqualified may refer to either a main sense or a subsense.

6. **Equivalent** or **English equivalent** (§ 20.7) refers to synonymous or nearly synonymous words or phrases that are an English translation of a Japanese word or word element.

7. **Keyword** or **English keyword** is a concise English equivalent that most aptly represents the most fundamental concept of a sense or group of senses of an *on* word element or a subentry headword. Keywords are often, but not always, identical with a **core meaning** (§ 9.1) or with a **synonym keyword** (§ 15.2.2). In the example above, *life*, which is common to senses ❶ and ❷, is a keyword of 生 that is identical with one of its core meanings, whereas *live* or one of its derivatives, which is common to senses ❹ and ❺, is a keyword of 生 that is not identical with one of its core meanings.

When unqualified, **sense** and **equivalent** may apply to any word or word element; that is, to any meaning appearing in the dictionary. When it is necessary to restrict these terms to a particular kind of meaning, this is made clear by the context or by a qualifying phrase such as "sense of an *on* word element," "equivalent of a subentry headword," and so on.

20.3 Order of Senses

When an *on* word element or a subentry headword has more than one sense, the senses are arranged in an order that shows their semantic interrelatedness. The senses are arranged *psychologically;* that is, an English keyword, often a core meaning, serves as the basis of organization, and the various senses are grouped in clusters in a manner that shows their interrelatedness:

2029

▶**COLOR**

COMPOUNDS

❶ⓐ [also suffix] **color, coloring**
ⓑ counter for colors

⋮

❷ⓐ (facial expression) **color, complexion, countenance, look**
ⓑ good looks (of a woman), beauty

⋮

❸ [also suffix]
ⓐ (characteristic feature) **color, character, feature**
ⓑ (political tendency) coloring

In the example, the core meaning "COLOR" serves as the basis of organization and shows the interrelatedness between the senses. The senses of a compound or example are normally given in order of descending frequency or importance:

上
3404

上下 *jōge* upper and lower parts [sides], high and low; going up and down, rise and fall; first and second volumes

20.4 Sense Division

The meaning of an *on* word element or subentry headword having more than one sense is often subdivided by a system of sense division numbers, letters, and semicolons, as explained below. The senses of compounds and examples are subdivided by semicolons, but not by sense division numbers and letters.

1. Main senses are numbered sequentially by **sense division numbers.** When a numbered, or sometimes unnumbered, sense has two or more

semantically related subsenses, these are headed by **sense division letters.**

2. In the COMPOUNDS section, numbered senses are headed by dark-circled sense division numbers (as ❶❷❸ and so on) or letters (as ⓐⓑⓒ and so on), or by a combination of such numbers and letters:

雷
2791

❶ⓐ [original meaning] **thunder**
ⓑ lightning
⋮
❷ explosive device, mine, torpedo

If there is only one main sense that is not subdivided into subsenses, it is identified by a solid black circle ● that represents the theoretical sense division number zero:

煮
2785

● [original meaning] (cook by boiling) **boil, cook**

3. In the KUN and INDEPENDENT sections, numbered senses are headed by clear-circled sense division numbers (as ① ② ③ and so on) or letters (as ⓐ ⓑ ⓒ and so on), or by a combination of such numbers and letters. The sense division number zero is not used in these sections.

卑
2642

【iya(shii) 卑しい】
① [formerly also 賤しい] (low in social status) mean, lowly, humble, inferior in position
⋮
② [formerly also 賤しい]
ⓐ (of poor appearance) mean, shabby, seedy
ⓑ (lacking elevating human qualities) mean, base, vulgar, despicable

4. Numbered and unnumbered senses may be further subdivided by commas and/or semicolons. The comma, used to separate synonyms or near-synonyms, indicates the smallest degree of semantic difference, while the semicolon usually indicates a somewhat greater degree of difference:

字
2172

❶ⓐ **character, letter; type; word**

In unnumbered senses, the semicolon may indicate a semantic difference equivalent to a difference between one numbered sense and another:

明
855

【a(kari) 明かり】 light, glimmer; lamp; proof

5. Labels and glosses that apply to a particular numbered sense appear after the sense division number or letter to which they apply. In unnumbered senses, such information applies until the first semicolon or to the entire sense, depending on the context. See **§ 30.5 Applicability of Labels and Glosses** for details.

20.5 Importance of Character Senses

The **degree of importance** of each character sense is indicated by various typographical devices and labels:

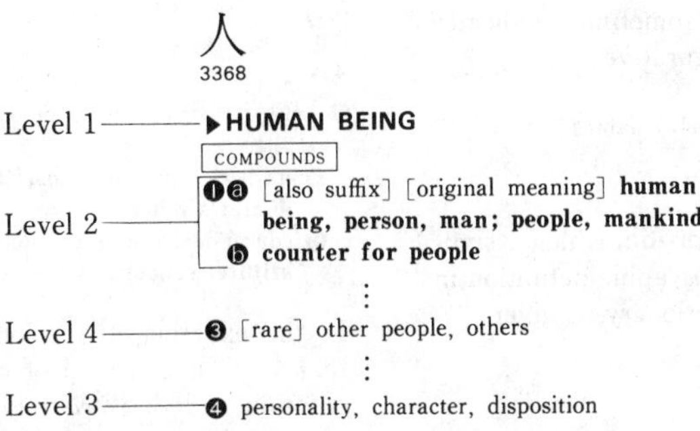

The degree of importance is divided into four levels, listed below in descending order of importance:

Level 1: Core Meaning—The most important sense, which is essential for the beginner (see **§ 9. CORE Section**).

Level 2: Boldface Equivalent — An English equivalent in the COMPOUNDS section printed in boldface signifies that the importance or frequency of occurrence of the sense in question is sufficiently high to merit study by the learner at the beginner to intermediate levels. The equivalent, along with its parenthetical adjuncts, is set in boldface; explanatory matter such as labels and glosses is set in lightface.

Level 3: Lightface Equivalent — An English equivalent in the COMPOUNDS section printed in lightface signifies that the sense in question is sufficiently important to merit study by the learner at the intermediate to advanced levels or by the scholar.

Level 4: Temporal Labels—Less important senses, such as rare, archaic, and obsolete ones, are indicated by the temporal labels (see **§ 24.3 Temporal Labels**).

20.6 Explanatory Gloss

The lightface matter often following the labels and preceding the equivalent is the **explanatory gloss**. This is an English word or phrase that restricts, explains, defines, supplements, or clarifies the meaning conveyed by the equivalent. Explanatory glosses are of two kinds: the subject guide phrase and the explanation or definition.

20.6.1 Subject Guide Phrase The **subject guide phrase** is a brief parenthetical phrase beginning with the word "of" that restricts the range of application of the equivalent to a specific subject. Specifically, it indicates an only or typical subject of an intransitive verb, or a typical or only noun that can be modified by an adjective given in the equivalent:

伸 ❷ (of stock prices) **rise**
70

20.6.2 Explanation or Definition

A word or phrase enclosed in parentheses or followed by a colon often precedes the equivalent and serves as an explanation or definition:

1. The **explanation** is a description, rather than a translation, of the meaning or grammatical function of a word or word element. It often helps eliminate the senses of a multisense word, usually the first word of the equivalent, that do not apply:

心 ❸ⓐ (central part) **heart, center, core**
11

An explanation sometimes indicates that a sense is figurative:

炎
2420

ⓑ (figuratively) **flames (as of passion)**

2. Sometimes a **definition**, which is similar to a full lexicographic definition in a monolingual dictionary, is given:

折
253

【o(ru) 折る】
① (separate through the application of a sudden bending force) break off (as a branch), break (a bone), snap (in two), split

The explanations and definitions are presented in the following format:

1. Explanations and definitions are normally enclosed in parentheses. Sometimes a parenthetical word or phrase preceding an equivalent may be an optional part of the equivalent itself, not an explanation or definition:

体
71

ⓐ **(characteristic) form, shape**
ⓑ (outer appearance) **form, appearance**

In subsense ⓐ, "(characteristic)" is an optional part of the equivalent that may be omitted (see § 30.2); in subsense ⓑ, "(outer appearance)" acts as an explanatory gloss.

2. Sometimes a colon is used instead of parentheses to separate an explanation or definition from the equivalent. The function of this colon is to coordinate the definition or explanation with the equivalent that follows the colon, especially when the former includes the meaning of the latter. It is often used when an explanation or definition is an expansion from a core meaning:

院
454

❶ [also suffix] institution or organization, esp.:
ⓐ medical institution: **hospital, clinic, doctor's office**
ⓑ educational institution: **academy, institute, school**

In the example, the colon indicates that *hospital* is a kind of medical institution and that *academy* is a kind of educational institution.

20.7 The Equivalent

The matter following an explanatory gloss or a label is the **equivalent** or **English equivalent**. This refers to synonymous or nearly synonymous words or phrases that are an English translation of a Japanese word or word element. Equivalents of *on* word elements are set in lightface or boldface depending upon their degree of importance (§ 20.5). All other equivalents are set in lightface:

守
2173

❶ⓐ **protect (from, against), defend, guard, watch over**
ⓑ guard, keeper

The equivalent is presented in the following format:

1. If a word or word element has no precise English equivalent, such as in the case of culture-bound terms or function words such as particles, an explanation replaces the equivalent:

荘
2262

ⓑ **suffix after names of villas, inns or apartment houses**

An explanation may include brief encyclopedic information, especially in reference to culture-bound terms:

荘
2262

❺ used in the formation of the names of former feudal villages (farm villages that were formerly manors) ⇨ see also 庄 3051 ❶

2. A definition sometimes replaces the equivalent of culture-bound terms:

矛
2008

● [original meaning] **ancient Chinese weapon resembling a halberd or spear**

3. Word elements in some compounds are used in a sense that is vague or unknown, with little or no relation to the character's meaning. In such cases the equivalent is omitted and the compounds are grouped under the heading "unclassified compounds":

当
2177

❾ **unclassified compounds**
弁当 *bentō* box lunch, lunch, picnic lunch
芸当 *geitō* feat, trick, stunt

4. The first word of an equivalent of an *on* word element or a subentry headword is often identical with a core meaning or another English keyword. It is sometimes modified by a qualifying word or phrase, around which the senses are grouped in clusters in a manner that shows their interrelatedness:

力
3371

▶**POWER**
COMPOUNDS
❶ⓐ [also suffix] [original meaning] **muscular power, physical strength, force, might**
ⓑ military power, armed force
ⓒ (power in general) **power to influence, strength, influence, authority**
⋮
❷ⓐ (source of energy) **power, energy; motive power**
ⓑ *phys* **force**
⋮
❸ⓐ [also suffix] (ability to do or act) **power, ability, faculty**

In the example, the keyword *power* (in this case the core meaning of 力), modified by such words as "muscular" or such glosses as "(source of energy)," shows how the individual senses are related to one central concept.

5. The equivalent may include various parenthetical adjuncts. These indicate a typical or only object of a transitive verb, a generic example of a class of things, a subject of a verb, or other miscellaneous items that help clarify or supplement the equivalent:

託
1455

❶ [original meaning] **entrust** (**a person with a thing**), **place** (**a thing**) **in someone's charge, commit, ask**

If the item in a parenthetical adjunct is a typical one in its class, it may be preceded by the word "as," but the omission of the latter does not indicate that the item is necessarily the only one in its class:

丁
3348

ⓑ **servings** (**as of cutlet, noodles, etc.**)

Note that some parentheses indicate optional parts of the equivalent (**§ 30.2**), not parenthetical adjuncts.

6. An equivalent may sometimes be separated into two parts by a colon. The function of this colon is to coordinate the two parts when the meaning of the first part includes, or is another way of phrasing, the meaning of the second part:

斤
2949

❶ **catty, *kin*: unit of weight equiv. to 600 g or 160 momme (匁)**

異
2584

❷ **not ordinary: strange, unusual, abnormal, unorthodox, extraordinary, exceptional, peculiar**

7. The equivalent is often subdivided by sense division numbers and accompanied by various labels, glosses, and cross-references. See also **§ 20.1 General Description.**

8. An equivalent of a compound or example is sometimes followed by a parenthetical phrase enclosed in double quotation marks. This is a literal, character-by-character translation that clarifies the meaning of each component character when this is not self-evident:

忘
2036

忘年会 *bōnenkai* year-end party ("forget the year party")

20.8 Supplementary Gloss

The lightface matter sometimes following the equivalent is the **supplementary gloss.** Introduced by a dash, this typically consists of a phrase, beginning with "said of" or "used in," that supplements the equivalent by restricting its range of application, level of formality, and so on, by describing its grammatical function, or by providing encyclopedic information about it:

渋
513

【shibu(i) 渋い】
① astringent, puckery, rough—said esp. of the taste of unripe persimmons

惣
2780

❸ eldest son, eldest child—used esp. in names

Sometimes, a supplementary gloss is a brief parenthetical phrase similar to an explanatory gloss that explains the preceding equivalent in order to eliminate the senses of a multisense equivalent that do not apply:

心
11

❷ [also suffix] [original meaning] **heart** (the organ)

20.9 Cross-References

The equivalent or supplementary gloss is sometimes followed by a **cross-reference** to a location that should be referred to for further information:

1. A long equivalent in the INDEPENDENT or KUN sections may occasionally be replaced by a cross-reference that points to an equivalent in the COMPOUNDS section with which it is identical in meaning. This consists of an arrow followed by a number or letter in parentheses, or a combination of these connected by an ampersand, that points to the relevant sense division number or numbers:

分
1972

【fun 分】 minute (⇨ ❾ⓐ & ❾ⓑ); *fun* (⇨ ⓮)

The example indicates that 分 *fun* means 'minute' in senses ❾ⓐ and ❾ⓑ and '*fun*' in sense ⓮ of the COMPOUNDS section.

2. Sometimes, a cross-reference in parentheses containing an arrow refers to an appendix:

丑
3433

● second sign of the Oriental zodiac: the Ox—(time) 1-3 a.m., (direction) NNE, (season) December (of the lunar calendar) (⇨ see APPENDIX 7)

3. Less frequently, an arrow followed by "see" refers to a meaning in another

character entry:

荘
2262

ⓑ used in the formation of the names of former feudal villages (farm villages that were formerly manors) ⇨ see also 庄 3051 ❶

4. An equivalent of a KUN headword is sometimes replaced by a cross-reference to another KUN headword with which it is identical in meaning. This is usually the case when a KUN headword has a more common variant that differs from it in style or grammatical function but not in meaning. A difference in stylistic level or grammatical function is indicated by a cross-reference including the words "form of":

660

【horo(bu) 滅ぶ】[sometimes also 亡ぶ] literary form of **horobiru 滅びる**

In the example, 滅ぶ is the literary form of 滅びる, with which it is identical in meaning. Synonymous words are indicated by a cross-reference beginning with the words "same as":

尊 **【tōto(i) 尊い】** same as **tattoi 尊い**
2324

20.10 Functions of Kanji as Words and Word Elements

The **function** of a character as a free word and word element is indicated by various typographical and other devices, as described below. The general user not interested in technical details may skip this and the next sections (**§20.10** and **§20.11**). See also **§20.2 Definitions of Terms.**

20.10.1 Free Words **Free word** or **word** refers to any independent word; that is, any word that can be used on its own. This includes (1) independent *on* words, (2) independent *kun* words, and (3) most compound words. Free words can be identified as follows:

1. Any INDEPENDENT headword functions as a free word (independent *on* word):

511

INDEPENDENT

【eki 液】 liquid, fluid; secretion; juice, sap

See also **§11. INDEPENDENT Section.**

2. Any KUN headword functions as a free word (independent *kun* word), unless specifically indicated that it functions only as a word element:

493

【ka(kari) 掛かり】
① expenses
掛かりが嵩む *Kakari ga kasamu* Expenses get heavy
【-ga(karu) -掛かる】
① resemble
芝居掛かった *shibaigakatta* theatrical, affected, pompous

In the example, the headword *kakari* is a free word, whereas the headword *-gakaru* includes a hyphen, which signifies that it functions as a combining form in the final position, not as a free word.

3. Most compounds and one-word examples function as free words. Some compounds, as in the example below, are used only as word elements:

士
3405

同士 *dōshi* fellow (as in **学生同士** *gakuseidōshi* 'fellow students')

20.10.2 Combining Forms Combining form refers to a part of a word that is not an affix and that can form a new word by combining with one or more words or parts of a word. The category *combining form* excludes the category *affix*. Combining forms can be identified as follows:

1. Any *on* word element functions as a combining form in any of its senses, unless a label indicates that in a given sense it is used only as an affix:

別
1117

❷ⓐ (divide by differences) **separate (into groups), sort, classify, distinguish**
ⓑ [suffix] **classified by**

上
3404

❶ⓐ **upper part, top; up, above**
ⓑ [also prefix] **upper, higher, outer**

In the first example, sense ❷ⓐ functions only as a combining form, whereas sense ❷ⓑ is used only as a suffix; in the second example, sense ❶ⓑ is used both as a prefix and as a combining form.

2. Any KUN headword may function as a combining form in any of its senses, unless a label or hyphen indicates that it is used only as an affix:

著
2300

【arawa(su) 著す】 author, write, publish
書き著す *kakiarawasu* publish (a book)

In the example, 著す can be used as a combining form, as in 書き著す, as well as a free word.

3. A KUN headword functioning as a combining form may be preceded or followed by a hyphen. See **§12.2.1 KUN Headword** for details.

4. If a sense of a KUN headword is preceded by the label "[in compounds]," that headword is used in that sense only as a combining form (not as an affix or free word) which may appear in the initial or in the final position:

丸
3417

【maru² 丸】
① [in compounds] round, circular, spherical
丸顔 *marugao* round face, moon face
⋮
② [also prefix] complete(ly), total(ly), perfect(ly)

In the example, the label "[in compounds]" indicates that 丸 functions as a combining form, as in 丸顔.

See also **§23.4 Word-Formation Labels.**

20.10.3 Affixes **Affix** refers to a part of a word added to a base (word or word element having its own lexical meaning) to form a new word. **Verbal affix** is a part of a word added to a base to form a new word, usually a *kun* verb. If an affix or verbal affix is added to the beginning of a word, it is a **prefix** or **verbal prefix**; if it is added to the end of a word, it is a **suffix** or **verbal suffix.**

An affix is normally a single character added to a two-character, often Chinese-derived, compound word. However, counters, units, titles, and various function words normally function as affixes and may be attached to one-character words. The categories *affix* and *verbal affix* exclude the category *combining form*. Affixes and verbal affixes can be identified as follows:

1. Affixes and verbal affixes are identified by a word-formation label such

as "[suffix]," "[prefix]," "[verbal suffix]," and so on, or by a phrase such as "suffix after...". These indicate that the sense or senses in question are used only as an affix or verbal affix, *not* as a combining form:

著 ⓑ [suffix] **authored by, by**
2300

2. Although combining forms and affixes are functionally distinct, mutually exclusive categories, a combining form or a free word can sometimes also function as an affix or verbal affix in a given sense or senses. This is indicated by a word-formation label beginning with "also," such as "[also suffix]," "[also prefix]," and "[also prefix and suffix]":

泥
326

【doro² 泥】 [in compounds] [also suffix] petty thief, sneak thief, pilferer
泥縄 *doronawa* expediency coming too late (like making a rope after finding the thief)
こそ泥 *kosodoro* sneak, pilferer
自動車泥 *jidōshadoro* auto [car] thief

In the example, 泥 functions as a suffix in such combinations as 自動車泥, but as a combining form in such words as 泥縄.

3. A KUN headword functioning as an affix or verbal affix is often preceded or followed by a hyphen. See **§ 12.2.1 KUN Headword** for details.

See also **§ 23.4 Word-Formation Labels.**

20.10.4 Free Words Versus Word Elements Some forms may function exclusively as word elements, others as free words only, and yet others both as free words and as word elements. The relationship between free words and word elements is explained below:

1. Any entry character functions as an *on* word element in all senses given in the COMPOUNDS section.

2. If an *on* word element in a given sense functions as an independent *on* word as well, that sense also appears in the INDEPENDENT section, and vice versa:

明
855

COMPOUNDS
⋮
❸ⓐ **clear-sighted, bright, discerning, intelligent, wise**
ⓑ eyesight
⋮
INDEPENDENT
【mei 明】 discernment, insight; eyesight

For example, in sense ❸ⓐ 'clear-sighted, etc.', 明 is used only as a combining form, but in sense ❸ⓑ 'eyesight', which also appears in the INDEPENDENT section, it is used both as an independent *on* word and as a combining form. On the other hand, in the sense 'discernment, insight', which does not appear in the COMPOUNDS section, 明 is used only as an independent *on* word, not as an *on* word element.

3. A KUN headword or one of its senses functions only as a *kun* word element, that is, it cannot be used as a free word, if (1) the KUN headword includes a hyphen, (2) a label, such as "[suffix]," "[verbal prefix]," and so on, indicates that it functions only as an affix or verbal affix, or (3) it includes the label "[in compounds]":

853

【-(p)pana(shi) -っ放し】
[sometimes also -放し *-hanashi*] [verbal suffix] *colloq*

In the example, the hyphen and the label "[verbal suffix]" indicate that -っ放し is used only as a word element (verbal suffix).

4. A KUN headword may function as a free word or as a word element, unless specifically indicated that it functions only as a word element:

指
378

【sa(su) 指す】
①ⓐ point to, point at, indicate
ⓑ aim at, have in view
⋮
【-sa(shi) -指し】 [suffix] player (of shogi)

For example, 指す is used as a free word or as a combining form, but -指し is used only as a suffix; that is, it is not used as a free word or as a combining form.

20.11 Miscellaneous Character Functions

20.11.1 Grammatical and Syntactic Functions

Various **grammatical and syntactic functions**, such as part of speech, are indicated by the functional labels. See **§23. Functional Labels** for details.

20.11.2 Numerals

An English equivalent consisting of a number indicates that a word or word element functions as a **numeral**. This refers to a word or word element expressing a number:

二 ❶❷ [original meaning] **two, second**
1922

The function of a character as a numeral is the same as its function as an ordinary noun.

20.11.3 Function Words

Function word refers to a word or word element whose primary function is to show grammatical relationships. This is usually a grammatical element used in forming compound words, particles, and so on:

性
299

ⓑ suffix indicating quality, state or degree: **-ity, -ness**

Since function words cannot usually be translated, an explanation, rather than an English equivalent, is normally given:

如
207

❷ **suffix added to modifiers (noun adjectives or adverbs) to express a state**

20.11.4 Abbreviations

The words "abbrev. of" indicate that a word or word element functions as an **abbreviation.** This is a shortened form of a compound word, usually represented by its first constituent character. If the abbreviation has an English equivalent, the latter is preceded by a colon:

共
2393

❷ abbrev. of 共産主義 *kyōsanshugi* or 共産党 *kyōsantō*: Communism, Communist Party

If the abbreviation is of a former place name, it is usually presented in the form illustrated below:

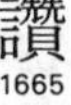
1665

❸ abbrev. of 讃岐 *sanuki*, old name for Kagawa Prefecture

Sometimes, the use of a character as an abbreviation becomes so well established that it can be considered to be an integral part of its meaning. This is often the case with characters used to abbreviate well-known country names or cities in Japan. In such cases, the meaning is given directly and its origin as an abbreviation is not indicated:

日
3027

❺ⓐ **Japan**

20.11.5 Counters The words "counter for" indicate that a word element functions as a **counter**. This is a form, normally used as a suffix, that is added to a numeral and is used for counting objects, people, or abstract things. Since counters cannot usually be translated, an explanation, rather than an English equivalent, is normally given:

冊
3483

❶ⓐ **counter for books, volumes or copies**

20.11.6 Units The words "unit of" indicate that a word element functions as a **unit**. This is a form, often used as a suffix, that represents a unit of measurement, weight, or volume, a monetary unit, and so on, used in China or Japan. The English equivalent or Japanese-derived loanword for the unit is normally followed by a colon and a full definition or explanation:

間
3323

❹ *ken*: unit of length equiv. to approx. 1.8 m or 6 *shaku* (尺)

Sometimes the meaning of a unit may be explained in a parenthetical gloss preceding the equivalent:

度
3100

❷ⓐ (unit of angular measure, latitude, longitude, etc.) **degree**
ⓑ (unit of temperature or humidity) **degree**

20.11.7 Titles A phrase including the word "title," usually preceded by a qualifier that shows the level of formality, indicates that a word element functions as a **title**. This is a suffix, usually added to the names of people, that functions as a title of courtesy on various levels of formality. Since titles cannot usually be translated, an explanation, rather than an English equivalent, is given:

君
3206

❷ **familiar title used in addressing peers, friends or inferiors (usu. restricted to men)**

20.11.8 Phonetic Substitutes The words "used phonetically for" indicate that a word element functions as a **phonetic substitute**. Phonetic substitutes are usually used to transliterate foreign words, typically Sanskrit Buddhist terms, with little or no relation to the character's meaning:

比
26

❻ used phonetically for *bi* in the transliteration of Sanscrit Buddhist terms

Sometimes, phonetic substitutes are used to represent grammatical elements that are usually written in hiragana, without direct relation to their meanings:

相
900

❻ⓐ used phonetically for *sō*
ⓑ function word indicating appearance
相場 *sōba* market price; estimation
可哀相な *kawaisō na* poor, pitiable, pathetic
悲し相な顔 *kanashisō na kao* sad-looking face

20.11.9 Symbols An explanation of an independent *on* word beginning with the word "symbol" indicates that in the sense in question the character functions as a **symbol**. This refers to the rare cases that a character is used as a symbol that has no pronunciation:

危
3199

INDEPENDENT

危 symbol on fuel trucks and the like: DANGER!

20.11.10 Names The function of characters in the writing of names is indicated as follows:

1. The entry-head data lists the name readings of Jinmei Kanji. See **§4.7 Name Reading** for details.

2. The NAMES section lists examples of names. See **§14. NAMES Section** for details.

3. The function of a character as an abbreviation of a place name is indicated. See **§20.11.4 Abbreviations** for details.

4. Sometimes, a sense is used exclusively or predominantly in the writing of names. This is indicated in the English explanation or by a gloss:

阪
271

【saka 阪】 slope, incline, hill—now used almost exclusively in the writing of names
大阪 *ōsaka* Osaka

20.11.11 Special Readings The function of characters as components of compound words having special readings is indicated as follows:

1. The entry-head data lists the special readings that can be isolated as independent readings in their own right. See **§4.5 Special Reading** for details.

2. The SPECIAL READINGS section of main entries and the COMPOUNDS section of reference entries list compound words having special readings. See **§13. SPECIAL READINGS Section** for details.

21. COMPOUNDS AND EXAMPLES

21.1 General Description

Each sense of an *on* word element or a subentry headword is usually illustrated by compounds and examples. **Compound** or **compound word** refers to a combination of two or more words or word elements having their own lexical meaning that together function as a single word:

携
648

携帯する *keitai suru* carry, bring with one, equip oneself with
携行する *keikō suru* carry along, bring

Example refers to a word other than a compound (including derived and inflected words) or to an illustrative phrase or sentence:

携
648

杖を携える *tsue o tazusaeru* carry a stick in one's hand

Compounds and examples of various parts of speech, such as nouns (高級 *kōkyū*) and noun adjectives (高等な *kōtō na*), are given. The choice of a particular part of speech is often arbitrary, with primary consideration given to the word's ability to illustrate the sense in question. With minor exceptions, all main and reference entry characters include compounds and examples. The explanations below apply to the COMPOUNDS, INDEPENDENT, and KUN sections. See **§ 13. SPECIAL READINGS Section** and **§ 14. NAMES Section** for a description of the compounds and examples in those sections.

21.2 Format of Compounds

The compounds and examples consist of (1) the Japanese word or phrase, (2) the romanized transcription, and (3) the English equivalent:

生
3497

写生する *shasei suru* sketch [draw] from nature; portray

1. The **Japanese word or phrase** is printed in Gothic type in a mixture of kana and kanji (rarely also numerals or roman letters), normally in conformity with the standard rules of orthography. If a compound or example has two or more written forms, the alternative forms follow in parentheses and are preceded by an equal sign. The equal sign does not imply that both alternatives are used with equal frequency. Normally, such parenthetical alternatives are only given when an orthographic label does not precede the sense under which the compound or example is classified, or when such a label does not apply to that particular compound or example:

奇
2217

❶ [formerly also 畸 1198]
ⓐ **unusual, strange, odd, extraordinary, queer, eccentric**
ⓑ deformity, malformation
奇異な *kii na* unusual, strange
奇人 *kijin* eccentric (person), queer [odd] fellow
奇妙な *kimyō na* strange, queer, odd
奇跡(＝奇蹟) *kiseki* miracle, wonder

In the example, 奇蹟, which is an alternative form of 奇跡, is shown in parentheses since the label "[formerly also 畸]" does not apply to 奇跡; that is, 畸 cannot replace 奇 in 奇跡.

2. The **romanized transcription** in italics of the pronunciation of a Japanese word or phrase is given in the modified Hepburn system of romanization. If a compound or example has two or more readings, the alternative readings follow in parentheses and are preceded by an equal sign:

生
3497

一生懸命(＝一所懸命)に *isshōkenmei* (＝*isshokenmei*) *ni* for life, with all one's might

On rare occasions, such as in the case of certain abbreviations used in newspapers, no transcription is given since the word cannot be pronounced:

保
96

保無(＝保守系無所属 *hoshukei mushozoku*) conservative without party affiliation

In the example, 保無 has no pronunciation, but the full form from which it is abbreviated is pronounced as shown.

3. The lightface **English equivalent** of a compound or example appears immediately after the romanized transcription. It is not divided by sense division numbers. The equivalent is sometimes accompanied by various labels and glosses. These and the equivalent are described in **§ 20. Character Meanings** and in sections **§ 22.** through **§ 25.**

21.3 Order of Compounds

The compounds and examples are grouped by meaning in a manner that shows how they are formed from their constituent parts. In the COMPOUNDS, INDEPENDENT, and KUN sections of main entries, they are subdivided into groups that appear in the following order:

1. **By section**: *on* compounds and examples appear in the COMPOUNDS section, independent *on* words in the INDEPENDENT section, and *kun* compounds and examples in the KUN section.
2. **By subentry**: in the INDEPENDENT and KUN sections, the compounds and examples are grouped by subentry headword; that is, the compounds and examples illustrating a particular subentry headword are grouped together under that headword:

選
3169

COMPOUNDS
❶ⓐ [original meaning] **choose, select, elect**
ⓑ [also suffix] selection, anthology
選択する *sentaku suru* select, choose
選抜 *senbatsu* selection, choice
⋮
INDEPENDENT
【sen 選】 selection, choice
選に入る *sen ni hairu* be chosen, be selected
KUN
【era(bu) 選ぶ】 choose, prefer, select; elect
上手に選ぶ *jōzu ni erabu* make a good choice
選ばれる *erabareru* be elected

In the example, 選に入る appears in the INDEPENDENT section under *sen*, 選ばれる appears in the KUN section under *erabu*, and so on.

3. **By sense**: within the same section or subentry, compounds and examples illustrating a particular sense (main sense or subsense) are grouped together under the same main sense. If a main sense is divided into subsenses, the compounds and examples do not appear immediately after each subsense that they illustrate; rather, they are all listed together under the same main sense and subdivided into groups in the order of the subsenses to which they apply:

In the example, 気圧, 気温, and 大気 illustrate subsense ❷ⓐ, so they are grouped together, while 気運 and 景気 illustrate subsense ❷ⓑ and are grouped together.

4. **By position of entry character**: compounds and examples illustrating a specific subsense, or, if there are no subsenses, a specific main sense, usually appear in the following order: (*a*) those consisting of one-character words, with or without *okurigana* or auxiliaries, (*b*) those in which the entry character appears in the initial position, and (*c*) those in which the entry character does not appear in the initial position.

In the previous example, 気圧 and 気温, which illustrate sense ❷ⓐ and have 気 in the initial position, appear first, and are followed by 大気, in which 気 is in the final position. Next appears 気運, which illustrates sense ❷ⓑ with 気 again in the initial position. In this manner, a shift of the entry character to the initial position signals the beginning of the next subsense group.

5. **By type**: within the same position group, compounds usually precede examples:

油
341

【abura 油】 oil, animal oil, vegetable oil
  油絵 *aburae* oil painting
  油気 *aburake* greasiness, oiliness
  油を売る *abura o uru* loaf, idle away one's time

The ordering criteria and manner of organization of compounds and examples in reference entries are described in **§ 26. Reference Entries.**

21.4 Cross-References

On rare occasions, the compounds and examples are followed, or completely replaced, by a cross-reference to another location where compounds and examples illustrating the sense in question appear:

巾
3409

❸ [usu. 幅 569] width, breadth, range
  ⇨ see 幅 569 for compounds

22. ORTHOGRAPHIC LABELS

22.1 Label Description

The lightface matter in square brackets sometimes appearing at the beginning of a sense is the **orthographic label.** This indicates the orthographic variant(s) of a word or word element:

2053

❷ [sometimes also 妄 2016] (not based on reason) **blind, reckless, aimless**

Orthographic variants refers to two or more characters that are partially or completely interchangeable in a given sense. For example, 盲 is interchangeable with 妄 in certain compounds but not in others. One variant is often a **phonetically replaced character,** while the other is a **phonetic replacement character.** See **§ 26.1.1 Phonetically Replaced Characters** for details.

Orthographic labels serve three purposes: (1) to indicate the degree of interchangeability between orthographic variants, (2) to specify the sense in which such variants are interchangeable, and (3) to serve as a cross-reference to the orthographic variants of the entry character, enabling the user to study their differences and similarities.

22.2 Explanation of Labels

The meanings of the orthographic labels, which are mostly self-evident, are explained below. The word *now* refers to Modern Japanese, especially in the postwar period, and implies that orthographic usage differs from the prewar period. The word *formerly* refers especially to Japanese in the prewar period, and implies that orthographic usage differs in the postwar period. The meaning of *archaic* is explained in **§ 24.3 Temporal Labels.** The entry character in which the orthographic label shown in the **Label** column appears is designated by *A;* the character within the orthographic label is designated by *B*. That is, the orthographic label being explained appears in the character entry for *A*.

Label	Explanation
[rarely also *B*]	*A* is common; *B* is extremely rare or archaic
[sometimes also *B*]	(1) *A* is common; *B* is unusual or rare (2) *A* is now common; *B* is now also sometimes used
[also *B*]	*A* and *B* are more or less equally common
[now also *B*]	(1) *A* and *B* are used interchangeably in some compounds and examples (2) *A* and *B* are now more or less equally common
[usu. *B*]	*A* is unusual or rare; *B* is common
[now usu. *B*]	(1) *B* replaces *A* in most compounds and examples (2) *B* is now common
[formerly *B*]	*A* is now common; *A* was not formerly used, or B may formerly have been used in all compounds and examples
[formerly also *B*]	*A* is now common; *A* and *B* have both been used, or *B* may formerly have been used in some compounds and examples
[now replaced by *B*]	*A* may now be replaced by *B* in all compounds and examples
[now always *B*]	*A* is extremely rare or archaic; *B* is common

22.3 Label Format

1. An orthographic label often applies to all the compounds and examples classified under that sense, but sometimes it applies to only some compounds and examples, as described in the explanation for each label:

   風
   3007

   ❿ [formerly also 諷 *fū* 1594] insinuate, hint, satirize
   風刺 *fūshi* satire, sarcasm
   風喩 *fūyu* hint, insinuation, allegory

   諷
   1594

   ❶ [now replaced by 風 3007] insinuate, hint, satirize
   諷刺 *fūshi* satire, sarcasm
   諷喩 *fūyu* hint, insinuation, allegory
   諷する *fūsuru* insinuate, hint, satirize

   In the entry for 風, the label indicates that 風 is now commonly used but that 諷 may formerly have been used in some compounds and examples. In the entry for 諷, the label indicates that 諷 may now be replaced by 風 in all compounds and examples, not just those given.

2. An italicized reading following an orthographic variant indicates that the characters are interchangeable only for that reading:

   誹
   1572

   ● [now also 非 *hi* 889] [original meaning] slander, calumniate, defame

   If an orthographic variant of an *on* word element is not followed by a reading, the *on* reading in the entry-head data applies. For orthographic variants accompanying a KUN headword, the reading of that KUN headword applies:

   1100 KŌ
   ⋮
   ❶ [now replaced by 広 3035] [original meaning] vast, spacious, open

遇
3135
【a(u) 遇う】 [also 遭う] (come upon, esp. by accident) meet with, encounter, be confronted

In the first example, 曠 is replaced by its orthographic variant 広 for the reading *kō*, which is the only *on* reading given in the entry-head data. In the second example, the reading of the KUN headword *au* applies; that is, 遇う and 遭う are interchangeable for the reading *au*.

3. If a word or word element has two or more orthographic variants, the orthographic labels are combined appropriately to show the relationship of the entry character to each of its orthographic variants, as illustrated below:

幸
2216
【shiawa(se) 幸せ】 [also 仕合わせ, formerly also 倖せ] happiness, blessing; good fortune

4. The character within an orthographic label is often followed by its entry number, which acts as a cross-reference to where it appears as an entry character in its own right:

注
325
❺ [formerly also 註 1499] **write down, take notes of, record**

To save space, orthographic variants of KUN headwords are not normally followed by their entry numbers, since these appear in the HOMOPHONES section. See § 17. **HOMOPHONES Section** for details.

23. FUNCTIONAL LABELS

23.1 Label Description

The lightface matter sometimes preceding the equivalent is the **functional label.** This indicates various grammatical and syntactic functions associated with a sense:

此
823
ⓐ *pronoun* this
ⓑ *demonstrative* this

大
3416
ⓑ [prefix] (before place names) Great, Greater

Functional labels are of four kinds: part-of-speech, usage, word-formation, and miscellaneous. These are sometimes combined with each other or with a status label, or are modified in some other way:

大
3416
❻ [honorific prefix]
ⓐ great, honorable
ⓑ Imperial

23.2 Part-of-Speech Labels

The **part-of-speech label,** set in italics, indicates part of speech. The meaning of each label is explained below:

demonstrative	function word that refers to something in terms of distance from the speaker
particle	particle or postposition
pronoun	pronoun
vi	intransitive verb
vi & vt	intransitive verb and transitive verb
vt	transitive verb

Part of speech and other grammatical functions are usually made clear by the wording of the equivalent and the glosses, or by miscellaneous functional labels. Part-of-speech labels appear mostly when it is necessary to eliminate ambiguity for a sense whose part of speech is not already self-evident:

601

【he(ru) 減る】 *vi* decrease, diminish, lessen, run low; wear

⋮

【he(rasu) 減らす】 *vt* decrease, reduce, lessen, shorten, cut

23.3 Usage Labels

The **usage label,** enclosed in square brackets, indicates how a word or word element is used, especially its syntactic function and the grammatical construction in which it normally appears. Usage labels apply mostly to free words, especially KUN headwords. The usage labels do not have a fixed form. Typical labels, which may be modified in some way, are explained below:

[in the form of...]	Indicates the form in which the word is normally used: 付 31 **【tsu(keru) 付ける】** ⋮ ⑪ [in the form of 付けて *tsukete*] refer to, relate to, connect with
[followed by...] [following the...]	Indicates the form that the word is followed by Indicates the form that the word normally follows: 見 2544 **【mi(ru) 見る】** ⋮ ⑥ [following the TE-form of verbs]
[in negative constructions]	Used in negative constructions: 優 177 **【sugu(reru) 優れる】** ⋮ ② [usu. in negative constructions] be fine, feel well

Miscellaneous usage labels	Indicate grammatical constructions or other contexts in which the word is normally used: 様 1052 **【sama 様】** ⋮ ④ [often preceded by お- *o*- or 御- *go*-] suffix for forming polite phrases

23.4 Word-Formation Labels

The **word-formation label**, enclosed in square brackets, indicates the function of a form as a word element (affix or combining form). The absence of a word-formation label before the equivalent of an *on* word element indicates that the character functions as a combining form in that sense. The absence of such a label before the equivalent of a KUN headword indicates that that headword functions as an independent *kun* word that may also function as a combining form in that sense. Word-formation labels do not appear in the INDEPENDENT section or in the compounds and examples. The meaning of each label is explained below. The terms used in the explanations are defined in **§ 20.10.**

[prefix]	used only as prefix; not used as combining form or free word
[also prefix]	prefix also used as combining form or free word
[suffix]	used only as suffix; not used as combining form or free word
[also suffix]	suffix also used as combining form or free word
[also prefix and suffix]	prefix also used as suffix
[verbal prefix]	used only as verbal prefix
[verbal suffix]	used only as verbal suffix
[in compounds]	*kun* word element used only as combining form; not used as affix or free word

Other word-formation labels, such as "[also verbal suffix]," "[mainly in compounds]," and the like, sometimes appear. The meanings of these labels correspond to the meanings of the standard word-formation labels listed above. The example below illustrates a typical word-formation label:

限
398
❺ [also suffix] **limit, bounds**

Word-formation labels are sometimes combined with each other or with other labels:

回
3055
【-mawa(su) -回す】 [emphatic verbal suffix] about, around

Word-formation is often indicated by the wording of the equivalent, in which case the label is omitted:

年
2035
❺ **suffix indicating the chronological order of years in a given era**

23.5 Miscellaneous Functional Labels

Miscellaneous functional labels, enclosed in square brackets, indicate various functions of the character as a word or word element:

[auxiliary]	a function word that functions as an adjunct to another word
[emphatic...]	a form that gives additional emphasis

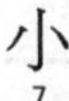
7

【ko- 小-】

⋮

③ [emphatic preceding adjectives or verbs] a little, slightly, very

24. STATUS LABELS

24.1 Label Description

The lightface matter in square brackets or italics sometimes preceding the equivalent is the **status label.** This restricts the sense to a particular time, level of style, or level of formality:

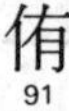
91

● [archaic] urge someone to eat or drink, assist with a meal

Status labels are of four kinds: etymological, temporal, stylistic, and formality. Status is sometimes indicated by the wording of the equivalent, in which case the status label is omitted:

2224

❷ honorific term used in reference to the Emperor or Buddha

Status labels are sometimes combined with each other or with a functional label:

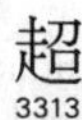
3313

❸ [original meaning, now archaic] jump over (an obstacle), cross over

24.2 Etymological Labels

The **etymological label,** enclosed in square brackets, indicates that the sense in question is the first to appear historically. There is only one kind of etymological label:

[original meaning]	indicates that the sense is the first meaning of the character after its formation in ancient China (rarely in Japan).

An etymological label is sometimes combined with a temporal label, as illustrated below:

[original meaning, now rare]
[original meaning, now archaic]
[original meaning, now obsolete]

The original meaning sometimes coincides with a core meaning, in which case it is also the most important, or one of the most important, meanings of the character:

象 **▶PHENOMENON ▶ELEPHANT**
2134

⋮

❹ [original meaning] **elephant**

⋮

Though etymological labels appear quite often, the treatment of original meanings is not exhaustive. An etymological label is likely to appear when it helps clarify the meaning of the character or the interrelatedness between senses, even if that meaning is rare or archaic:

894

❶ⓐ [original meaning, now rare] (emitting

light) luminous, bright, shining
ⓑ (enjoying the glory of enlightened rule) **enlightened, glorious, illustrious**

Sometimes, an etymological label is given for one of the senses of a compound word to help clarify how its constituent characters relate to each other:

3100

支度する *shitaku suru* arrange, prepare; [original meaning, now archaic] measure, estimate

24.3 Temporal Labels

The **temporal label**, enclosed in square brackets, restricts the accompanying sense to a particular time. This label refers only to the word or word element it accompanies, not to the thing represented. The absence of a temporal label indicates that the sense is current in Modern Japanese. This refers to the language in contemporary usage, especially since the Meiji Restoration in 1868, and does not include words and constructions used only in classical Japanese. The Meiji Restoration marks a period of transition, rather than a precise temporal boundary, for distinguishing between modern and archaic Japanese. The meaning of each label is explained below:

[rare]	Indicates that the sense is of infrequent occurrence in Modern Japanese. This label applies only to ordinary words or word elements in current use, not to technical terms, nor to archaic or obsolete ones:  958 ⓒ [rare] death penalty (in ancient China) imposed on an offender and his whole family
[archaic]	Indicates that the sense was used before the Meiji Restoration, especially in the classics and classical Chinese, or in ordinary usage during or before the Edo period:  383 ● [archaic] truly, really, utterly
[obsolete]	Indicates that the sense is not used in Modern Japanese and only rarely, if ever, in the classics. This label always appears in conjunction with an etymological label:  2021 ❷ⓐ [original meaning, now obsolete] stand on tiptoe

A temporal label is sometimes combined with an etymological label, as illustrated below. This means that the sense in question is an original meaning whose temporal status is as indicated by the second part of the label:

[original meaning, now rare]
[original meaning, now archaic]
[original meaning, now obsolete]

24.4 Stylistic Labels

The **stylistic label**, set in italics, restricts the accompanying sense to a particular level of style. Since style is more likely to apply to free words, rather than word elements, stylistic labels appear mostly with KUN and INDEPENDENT headwords, not *on* word elements. The absence of a stylistic label indicates that the sense in question is of neutral style. The meaning of each label is explained below:

literary	Indicates a style of language found in literature, particularly belles-letters. It does not refer merely to the written language as opposed to the spoken language, nor does it restrict the sense to classical Japanese literature: 猫 619 **【nao 猫】** ⋮ ③ *literary* as, just like, no more...than
elegant	Indicates a style of language associated with poetry, such as haiku or tanka, which is unlikely to be used in the standard language: 浦 437 **【ura 浦】** ① *elegant* seaside, seashore
colloq	The label *colloq* for "colloquial" indicates a style of language characteristic of the spoken language: 伝 44 **【den 伝】** *colloq* way, manner, trick
slang	Indicates a style of speech used between intimate friends, the family circle, and so on. It is used in extremely informal contexts, often in facetious figures of speech: 図 3071 **【zu 図】** ⋮ ③ *slang* expectation, intention
vulgar	Appears with a small number of senses or words associated with social taboo: 穴 2159 **【ketsu 穴】** *vulgar* ass, fanny; tail end

Other terms that do not appear in the stylistic labels, such as "pompous" and "intimate," may be used to indicate stylistic level:

2042

【yo 余】
⋮
② [also 予 1983] I, myself, the present writer—historically used as a formal first person pronoun but now only used pompously

24.5 Formality Labels

The **formality label**, enclosed in square brackets, restricts the accompanying sense to a particular level of formality. Since level of formality is more likely to apply to free words, rather than to word elements, formality labels are given mostly for KUN and INDEPENDENT headwords. The absence of a formality label in a subentry headword indicates neutrality; that is, neither respect nor humility. Unless indicated otherwise, subentry headwords appear in their *dictionary form* and are of neutral formality. The meaning of each label is explained below:

[honorific]	Indicates a level of language in which respect is shown by elevating the status of the grammatical subject: 高 2097 ❻ [honorific] your, your honorable
[humble]	Indicates a level of language in which respect is shown through humility; that is, by lowering the status of the subject: 拙 315 ❷ [humble] my humble, my poor
[polite]	Indicates a level of language used in standard polite conversation; that is, the *desu-masu* style: 氏 2951 **【shi 氏】** [polite] third person pronoun,
[belittling]	Indicates a level of language used to show contempt or abuse by lowering the status of the person addressed: 輩 2807 **【yakara 輩】** [belittling] fellows, guys; family; kinsmen

Other terms that do not appear in the formality labels, such as "neutral," may be used to indicate level of formality:

氏
2951

SYNONYMS

:

【shi】

○ **third person pronouns**

彼 THIRD PERSON PRONOUN (*neutral*) → 290

Formality labels are sometimes combined with functional labels:

大
3416

❻ [honorific prefix]

ⓐ great, honorable

Level of formality is often indicated by the wording of the equivalent or explanation, in which case the formality label is omitted:

共
2393

【-domo -共】 belittling or humble plural suffix

25. SUBJECT LABELS

25.1 Label Description

The lightface matter in italics sometimes preceding the equivalent is the **subject label.** This identifies the field to which the sense applies, usually a branch of science:

長 ⓐ *music* major
2556

The appearance of a subject label does not imply that the sense is never used in fields other than the one indicated by the label.

25.2 Label Format

The subject label is often an abbreviation, as *chem* for "chemistry." Subject label abbreviations are listed with their full forms in **Abbreviations and Symbols** on p. 225a. Typical examples are given below:

門 ⓑ *biol* phylum, division, subkingdom
888

元 ⓑ *math* **element, dimension**
1929

Two or three subject labels are sometimes combined with each other and separated by a comma:

相 ⓑ *chem*, *astron*, *phys* phase
900

26. REFERENCE ENTRIES

26.1 Entry Description

The most frequently used characters in Japanese, including all those listed in the Jōyō Kanji and Jinmei Kanji lists, are treated as **main entries,** which include the full range of features presented in this dictionary. In addition, the dictionary includes other characters of lesser importance referred to as **reference entries.** The treatment of reference entry characters is more restricted in scope than that of main entry characters.

996 EN honō

CH 焰 yàn

Radical	Strokes
火 86	12-4-8
Grade	**Freq**
Reference	
◧ 1 - 4 - 8	

COMPOUNDS

ⓐ [now replaced by 炎 *en* 2420] [original meaning] flame, blaze

ⓑ [now usu. 炎 *en* 2420 or 炎 *honō*] (figuratively) flames (as of passion)
火焰 *kaen* flames, blaze
情焰 *jōen* flaming desires, burning passions
気焰を吐く *kien o haku* talk big, talk a lot of hot air
嫉妬の焰 *shitto no honō* The Flames of Jealousy (movie title)

HOMOPHONES

honō ⇨ 炎 2420

NOTE

⇨ see USAGE note at 炎 2420

Reference entries can be distinguished from other types of character entries by the words "Reference" or "Radical" in the reference data box, and be easily recognized by the absence of core meanings. Reference entry characters are of two kinds: (1) the principal phonetically replaced characters in Modern Japanese, and (2) some radicals and their variants.

26.1.1 Phonetically Replaced Characters The reference entry characters include the principal **phonetically replaced characters** in Modern Japanese; i.e., the characters that are now replaced by the **phonetic replacement characters** in the official list published by the government, and other commonly used phonetically replaced characters that are not in the official list. Phonetically replaced characters always have a corresponding phonetic replacement character or characters. Phonetically replaced characters are of three kinds:

1. Those replaced by characters in the official list that have the same *on* reading, e.g., 鄭 *tei* replaced by 丁 *tei*.
2. Those replaced by characters not in the official list that have the same *on* reading, e.g., 芯 *shin* replaced by 心 *shin*.
3. Those replaced by characters not in the official list that have the same *kun* reading, e.g., 唄 *uta* replaced by 歌 *uta*.

The reference entries for phonetically replaced characters always contain a cross-reference to their corresponding phonetic replacement characters. The cross-reference appears in an orthographic label and/or in the HOMOPHONES or NOTE section:

400

COMPOUNDS

⋮

❷ⓐ [usu. 歌 *uta*] [also suffix] song, ballad

ⓑ [usu. 歌う *utau*] recite, sing—used esp. in reference to traditional Japanese songs

⋮

HOMOPHONES

uta ⇨ 歌 1825

utau ⇨ 歌 1825 謡 1597 謳 1632

NOTE

⇨ see USAGE note at 歌 1825

26.1.2 Radicals and Their Variants The reference entry characters also include characters that are **radicals** or **radical variants** but are not listed as main entry characters. Most of these characters, which are used only as radicals but not as words or word elements in their own right, contain only the RADICAL section:

歹

3445

RADICAL 78

Standard form: 歹 *gatsuhen* 'death' (死 残 殊)

Description: used in characters related to death or serious injury

The remaining characters, which are used both as radicals and as words or word elements in their own right, contain both the COMPOUNDS and RADICAL sections:

鼎

3585

RADICAL 206

Standard form: 鼎 *kanae* 'ritual cauldron'

Description: used in characters related to ritual cauldrons or tripod vessels

COMPOUNDS

❶ [original meaning] tripod cauldron

鼎の軽重を問う *kanae no keichō o tou* weigh one's ability, call one's ability into question

⋮

26.2 Entry Format

The organization of reference entries is similar to that of main entries. The entry-head data is printed across the page in single column format, and the explanatory matter is organized into sections and set in two columns separated from each other by a dotted line.

26.2.1 Entry-Head Data The **entry-head data** of reference entries consists of the entry character (§ **1.3**), the entry number (§ **1.4**), typeface styles (§ **3.3**), Chinese (§ **5.**), character readings (§ **4.**), and the reference data box (§ **7.**). Each item is described in the section indicated by the cross-reference in parentheses.

26.2.2 The Sections The explanatory matter of reference entries is subdivided into four parts referred to as **sections**, which appear in the order listed below. Not every entry includes every section—only those sections required for describing the entry character are given.

Section Label	Description
RADICAL	The RADICAL section describes the function of the entry character as a radical. See **§ 8. RADICAL Section** for details.
COMPOUNDS	The COMPOUNDS section, subdivided by sense division numbers and letters, lists all the meanings of the entry character, regardless of function or reading. Each meaning is usually accompanied by compounds and examples and their English equivalents. See **§ 26.3 COMPOUNDS Section** for details.
HOMOPHONES	The HOMOPHONES section lists groups of homophones and their entry numbers for cross-reference. See **§ 17. HOMOPHONES Section** for details.
NOTE	The NOTE section consists of various kinds of cross-references and/or explanatory notes. See **§ 19. NOTE Section** for details.

26.3 COMPOUNDS Section

The matter headed by the label COMPOUNDS is the COMPOUNDS section. In reference entries, this section lists all the meanings of the entry character, regardless of function or reading. That is, the meanings of *on* word elements, independent *on* words, *kun* words and word elements, and compound words having special readings are all treated in the same section. Each meaning is usually subdivided by sense division numbers and letters and accompanied by compounds and examples and their English equivalents:

1820

COMPOUNDS

❶ⓐ [original meaning] become tame [domesticated]

ⓑ [now also 順 *jun* 18] tame, domesticate

馴れた *nareta* tame, domesticated

馴染む *najimu* become familiar; grow accustomed; get (clothing) to fit

馴致する *junchi suru* tame, habituate; lead to

馴化 *junka* acclimation

馴らす *narasu* tame, domesticate

馴らし手 *narashite* tamer

馴鹿 *tonakai* reindeer

The COMPOUNDS section is given for all reference entries whose main entry character is used as a word or word element (which is almost all of them).

26.3.1 Character Meaning

The meaning of the entry character as a word or word element, regardless of its function or reading, is given by the English equivalent:

1605

COMPOUNDS

ⓐ wager, bet money
ⓑ [usu. 懸ける *kakeru*] stake (one's life), risk

The meaning is usually subdivided by sense division numbers and may include various labels, glosses, and cross-references. These and the equivalent are described in **§ 20. Character Meanings** and in sections **§ 22.** through **§ 25.**

26.3.2 Compounds and Examples

Compounds and examples, grouped by meaning, usually accompany each sense. These consist of compound words, free words, inflected and derived words, a word followed by a particle or auxiliary, or a phrase or sentence:

3017

❷ⓐ [usu. 飽きる *akiru*] grow tired of, lose interest in
ⓑ be disgusted with, detest, dislike
厭世観 *enseikan* pessimism
厭戦 *ensen* war-weariness
厭き厭きする *akiaki suru* be sick (of), be bored (with)
厭離 *onri Buddhism* depart from (in disdain)
厭う *itou* dislike; be disgusted with; take (good) care of
危険を厭わない *kiken o itowanai* do not mind running a risk

The order of the compounds and examples in reference entries is similar to that of main entries except for some minor details. The main difference is that in reference entries the compounds and examples are all grouped together in one section—the COMPOUNDS section—whereas in main entries they are grouped into sections by type of reading. In reference entries, the compounds and examples are subdivided into groups that appear in the following order:

1. **By sense**: compounds and examples illustrating a particular sense (main sense or subsense) are grouped together under the same main sense.

2. **By type of reading**: *on* compounds and examples, independent *on* words, *kun* compounds and examples, and special-reading compound words are grouped together, in that order.

3. **By position of entry character**: within the same readings group, the compounds and examples are usually grouped by entry character position.

4. **By type**: within the same position group, compounds usually precede examples.

See **§ 21. Compounds and Examples** for details.

27. NONSTANDARD ENTRIES

27.1 Entry Description

The nonstandard forms of main entry characters are treated as separate entries referred to as **nonstandard entries.** These appear along with their core meanings at their own SKIP locations with a cross-reference to their corresponding standard forms:

▶COUNTRY
nonstandard for 国 3087
3132

Nonstandard form refers to a variant form other than the standard form of approved characters, and to a variant form other than the traditional form of unapproved characters. This includes the traditional form (full unsimplified form), the alternative forms (variant forms other than the traditional form), and the handwritten abbreviation (simplified form used in handwriting).

Nonstandard entries can be distinguished from other types of character entries by the words "nonstandard for..." in the line below the core meaning(s), and by the absence of explanatory matter organized into sections. See also **§ 3.1.2 Nonstandard Forms.**

27.2 Entry Format

The nonstandard entry is printed across the page in single column format. All nonstandard entries consist of (1) the entry-head data, (2) the core meaning(s), and (3) the description:

1. The entry-head data of all nonstandard entries consists of the entry character (**§ 1.3**), the entry number (**§ 1.4**), and the Ming typeface (**§ 3.3.1**). Each item is described in the section indicated by the cross-reference in parentheses. Other explanatory matter, such as readings, meanings, and compounds and examples can be found under the main entry for the corresponding standard form.

2. The core meaning or meanings, preceded by the symbol ▶, are given for each nonstandard entry.

3. A brief description indicates the type of nonstandard form and includes a cross-reference to the corresponding standard form, as illustrated below.

Traditional or alternative forms:

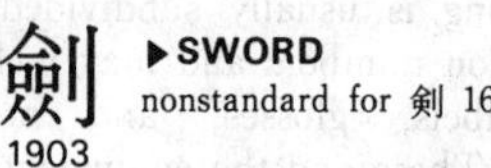

▶SWORD
nonstandard for 剣 1672
1903

Handwritten abbreviation:

▶AFFAIR **▶ABSTRACT THING**
handwritten abbreviation for 事 3567
3556

Nonstandard forms that are also radicals or radical variants include, in addition to the items described above, the reference data box (**§ 7.**), the stroke order diagram (**§ 6.**), and the RADICAL section (**§ 8.**). Each item is described in the section indicated by the cross-references in parentheses.

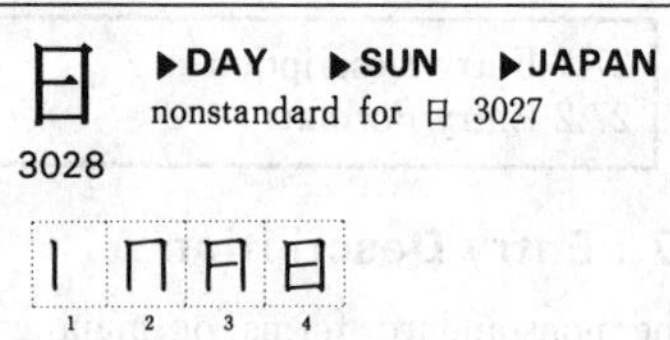

▶DAY **▶SUN** **▶JAPAN**
nonstandard for 日 3027
3028

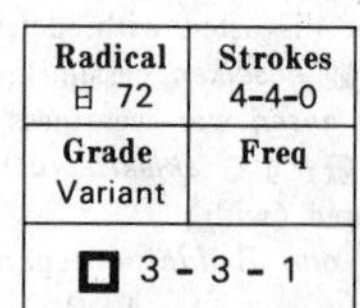

Radical 日 72	Strokes 4-4-0
Grade Variant	Freq
■ 3 - 3 - 1	

RADICAL 72
Standard form: 日 *hi* 'sun'
Variant: 日 *hi* (明 春 星)
Description: used in characters related to the sun, sunlight or time

28. CROSS-REFERENCE ENTRIES

28.1 Entry Description

Character entries appearing at an *incorrect* SKIP location with a cross-reference to the character entry at the correct location are referred to as **cross-reference entries**:

5-2 究 incorrect classification ⇨ see 2203

穴

Cross-reference entries can be distinguished from other types of character entries by the words "incorrect classification..." or "incorrect stroke count ...", and by the absence of entry numbers and explanatory matter organized into sections.

28.2 Entry Format

The cross-reference entry is printed across the page in single column format. It consists of (1) the entry character, (2) a description of the incorrect location, and (3) the correct location. Cross-reference entries are of two kinds: **single-character** and **multiple-character.** See SYSTEM OF KANJI INDEXING BY PATTERNS **§2.6 Cross-References** for details.

29. ROMANIZATION

29.1 Romanization System

The italicized matter following Japanese words or word elements is the **romanized transcription**. This is a representation of the Japanese pronunciation by means of the roman alphabet:

2308 **一喜一憂** *ikkiichiyū*

The romanization system employed is the widely used Hepburn system, with the slight modifications adopted in Kenkyusha's *New Japanese-English Dictionary*. This system is described in **Appendix 4. Kana and Romanization.**

29.2 Typeface Styles

1. Romanized transcriptions of compounds and examples are set in easy-to-read sanserif italics to distinguish them from other explanatory matter:

   剪
   2306 **枝を剪る** *eda o kiru* prune a tree

2. Subentry headwords and other romanized headings are set in boldface sanserif roman:

   喜
   2308 **【yoroko(bu) 喜ぶ】**

3. Romanized transcriptions, including transcriptions of proper nouns, are normally set in lowercase:

   東
   3568 **東名高速道路** *tōmei kōsokudōro* Tokyo-Nagoya Expressway

   Capitals are used only for the first letter of the first word of a sentence or part of a sentence:

   事
   3567
   彼は学校を遅刻する事が有る *Kare wa gakkō*

o chikoku suru koto ga aru He is sometimes late for school

4. In special contexts, such as the presentation of character readings in the entry-head data and the **On-Kun Index,** roman capitals are used to identify *on* readings while roman lowercase is used to identify *kun* readings:

2273 KA KE ie ya uchi▲

29.3 Word Division

There is no universally-accepted convention for the division of words in romanized Japanese. Different works spell compound words either solid, hyphenated, or open (separated by a space). The policy adopted here is designed to closely reflect the function of, and the semantic relationship between, word and sentence components. The main principles are explained below:

1. Free words, including particles and auxiliaries that are not an integral part of the word, are normally treated as independent units and separated by a space:

事 3567 **事を分ける** *koto o wakeru* reason with (a person)

2. Free words consisting of one character plus the auxiliary verb する *suru* or one of its variants (such as -ずる *-zuru*), or another function word that forms an integral part of the word, are treated as a single unit and spelled solid:

処 3031 **【shosuru 処する】**

3. Two-character compounds followed by する *suru* are treated as two words:

処 3031 **対処する** *taisho suru* cope [deal] with, meet

4. Word elements are normally written solid as part of the word in which they appear:

港 605 **貿易港** *bōekikō* trade port

Sometimes, as when a suffix applies to more than one word, this relation is shown by a hyphen:

著 2300 **三島由紀夫著** *mishima yukio-cho* authored by Mishima Yukio

5. Compounds are normally written solid. If a four-character compound consists of two independent two-character compounds, these are separated by a space or a hyphen, depending on the degree of relatedness between them:

133 **標準偏差** *hyōjun hensa* standard deviation

However, four-character compounds are written solid if they express an integrated semantic unit:

東 3568 **東西南北** *tōzainanboku* north, south, east and west

30. OTHER CONVENTIONS

30.1 General Description

A wide range of typeface styles and sizes and other typographical conventions ensure maximum ease of use of the dictionary. The various conventions are, for the most part, self-explanatory. Each convention is described in detail in the relevant sections in this **GUIDE TO THE DICTIONARY**. Those conventions that apply throughout the dictionary, especially those that are not explained elsewhere, are described below.

30.2 Punctuation Marks

The punctuation marks described below are used in special ways. They are also used as in ordinary writing, along with other punctuation marks. Punctuation marks do not normally appear in romanized transcriptions.

1. Parentheses ( ) are used (*a*) to enclose *okurigana* of *kun* readings, (*b*) to enclose explanatory glosses (**§ 20.6**) and miscellaneous explanatory matter, especially in the equivalent (**§ 20.7**); (*c*) to indicate that words or parts of words may be included or left out, i.e., *pick* (*up*) is the same as *pick* or *pick up;* and (*d*) to indicate alternative Japanese forms or readings, e.g., 世論 *seron* (=*yoron*).

2. Square brackets [ ] are used (*a*) to enclose most labels (**§ 22.** through **§ 24.**); and (*b*) to indicate alternatives, i.e., *pick* [*take*] *up* is the same as *pick up* or *take up*.

3. The virgule / is used (*a*) to occasionally indicate alternatives, especially in cross-reference entries and the SYNONYMS section; and (*b*) to separate illustrative sentences:

沙
266

❸ **phonetic** [**s**]/[**sh**]

免
2067

御免なさい *Gomen nasai* I'm sorry / Excuse me

4. The dash — is used to introduce a supplementary gloss (**§ 20.8**):

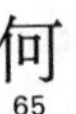
65

【nani, nan 何】 what, which, whatever—used also in the formation of various interrogative pronouns

5. The hyphen - is used indicate that a KUN headword is used as a word element (**§ 12.2.1**):

回
3055

【-mawa(shi) -回し】 turning, rotating

6. Single quotation marks ‘ ’ are often used to enclose the meanings of Japanese words when these appear within an explanatory text:

154

COMPOUND FORMATION

傾国 *keikoku*

傾国 ‘beautiful woman; courtesan’ derives

⋮

7. Semicolons (;) and commas (,) are used to separate synonyms or near-synonyms of a sense (**§ 20.4**):

147

KUN

【katawa(ra) 傍ら】 besides, while; side

8. Periods do not appear after illustrative sentences:

3551

又遊びに来て下さい *Mata asobi ni kite kudasai* Come and see me again

30.3 Typeface Styles

The principal typeface styles used in the dictionary are summarized below:

1. The equivalents and other English explanatory matter are set in lightface roman. Equivalents of level-one

importance are set in boldface roman:

玉
3477

❶ⓐ **gem, jewel(ry), precious stone**
ⓑ [original meaning] jade

2. Core meanings, headwords, most headings, character readings, and various other items are set in sanserif roman:

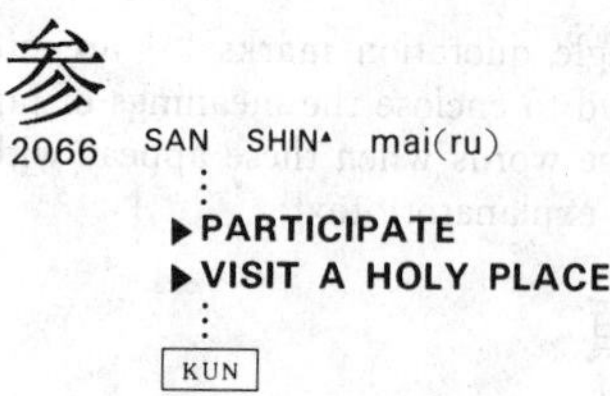

3. Japanese compounds and examples are set in Gothic type. The entry character and other explanatory matter in Japanese, such as orthographic labels, are set in Ming type:

生
3497

② [formerly also 活ける] arrange (flowers)
生け花 *ikebana* flower arrangement

4. Romanized transcriptions are normally set in sanserif italics:

生 生徒 *seito* pupil, student
3497

5. Section names and labels, and some cross-references, are set in small capitals:

早 NOTE
2390 ⇨ see also USAGE note at 小 7

30.4 Omission of Function Words

To save space, some function words (words that have grammatical function) that do not affect meaning have been omitted from the English equivalents and other explanatory matter:

1. Articles, especially the definite article *the*, are usually omitted unless such an omission changes the meaning or is extremely unidiomatic:

太
2152
太陽 *taiyō* sun
⋮
太閤 *taikō* father of the Imperial adviser; Toyotomi Hideyoshi

2. The word *to* is usually omitted from the infinitives of verbs. The status of a word as a verb is made clear by context, a gloss, or a part-of-speech label:

走 ❸ **travel by vehicle or craft, drive, sail**
2194

折 ⓑ (weaken, as in spirit) break down, (cause to) lose heart
253

30.5 Applicability of Labels and Glosses

A label or gloss appears before the matter to which it applies, as explained below:

1. A label or gloss that applies to a particular sense (main sense or subsense) appears before the equivalent to which it applies. The information applies from the point where it appears, which is usually right after a

sense division number or letter, but may be in the middle of an equivalent:

皇
2566

❶ⓐ **emperor, sovereign**
ⓑ **related to the emperor, imperial**
⋮
❹ [formerly 惶 *kō* 581] be afraid, be anxious; be flurried

呉
2549

【ku(reru) 呉れる】 give (to the speaker); give (to an inferior, animal or plant); [following the TE-form of verbs] do something for (the benefit of the speaker)

In the first example, the label "[formerly 惶 *kō* 581]" applies only to sense ❹, not to any other sense; in the second example, the gloss "[following the TE-form of verbs]" applies up to the end of the sense starting from the point where it appears.

2. If a label or gloss applies to an entire section, subentry, compound, or example, it precedes all the senses. If it applies to all the subsenses of a main sense, it precedes the first subsense division letter:

付
31

COMPOUNDS

[sometimes also 附 347]
❶ⓐ **attach, append, add to, affix**
ⓑ **attached, additional, supplementary**
⋮
❺ adjacent, near to
付近 *fukin* neighborhood, environs, vicinity

人
3368

❷ [suffix]
ⓐ **person of specific geographical origin, nationality or race**
ⓑ person of certain category, as the performer of an action or holder of an occupation: **-er** (**as in *manager***)

In the first example, the label "[sometimes also 附 347]" applies to all the senses in the COMPOUNDS section; in the second example, the label "[suffix]" applies to all the subsenses of sense ❷, i.e., ❷ⓐ and ❷ⓑ.

3. A label or gloss in an unnumbered sense normally applies up to the end of that sense, but may apply up to the first semicolon, depending on context.

怖
296

【kowa(i) 怖い】 [also 恐い] fearful, scary, uncanny; be afraid

畝
1465

【une 畝】 [original meaning] ridge, furrow; rib, cord (of textiles)

In the first example, the label "also [恐い]" applies to the entire sense; in the second example, the label "[original meaning]" applies up to the first semicolon, that is, it does not apply to *rib* and *cord*.

4. A label normally applies to all the compounds and examples listed under the sense (main sense or subsense) where that label appears, as well as to the compounds and examples that can be classified under that sense but that do not appear in the dictionary:

2049

❶ [formerly also 稀 *ki, ke* 1189] (not frequent) **rare, uncommon, unusual, scarce**
希書 *kisho* rare book
希元素 *kigenso* rare element

希少な *kishō na* scarce, rare
希有な *keu* (=*kiyū*) *na* rare, unusual, uncommon
古希 *koki* three score and ten, seventy years of age

In the example, the label "[formerly also 稀 *ki, ke* 1189]" applies to all the compound words listed, as well as to such words as 希世の *kisei no* 'uncommon, rare', which, although not listed, can also be classified under sense ❶. However, if such a label does not apply to an individual compound, an alternative form in parentheses or a label accompanies the equivalent of that compound.

30.6 Miscellaneous Conventions

1. Japanese words and phrases are normally written in a mixture of kanji and kana according to the standard rules of orthography. Except for special contexts, *okurigana* endings conform to the official rules published by the Japanese government.
2. Character forms in the Jōyō Kanji and Jinmei Kanji lists normally appear in the standard form. Other characters are normally given in the traditional form.
3. In principle, American English and spellings are used in the equivalents and other explanatory matter.
4. Some common abbreviations are used in the equivalents, labels, and other explanatory matter:

abbrev.	abbreviation
approx.	approximately
equiv.	equivalent
esp.	especially
usu.	usually

All abbreviations, especially those used in the subject labels, are listed with their full forms in **Abbreviations and Symbols** on p. 225a.

ABBREVIATIONS AND SYMBOLS

ABBREVIATIONS

abbrev.	abbreviation
A.D.	anno Domini
a.m.	ante meridiem
anat	anatomy
approx.	approximately
astron	astronomy
B.C.	before Christ
biol	biology
bot	botany
chem	chemistry
cm	centimeter
colloq	colloquial
elec	electricity
ENE	east-northeast
equiv.	equivalent
ESE	east-southeast
esp.	especially
etc.	etcetera
Freq	frequency
g	gram
geol	geology
gram	grammar
GUIDE	GUIDE TO THIS DICTIONARY (p. 159a)
hist	historical
in.	inch
kg	kilogram
km	kilometer
m	meter
math	mathematics
mg	milligram
mm	millimeter
NNE	north-northeast
NNW	north-northwest
p.	page
phys	physics
p.m.	post meridiem
psychol	psychology
sq.	square
sq.m	square meter
SSE	south-southeast
SSW	south-southwest
usu.	usually
vi	intransitive verb
vs.	versus
vt	transitive verb
WNW	west-northwest
WSW	west-southwest

SKIP SYMBOLS AND ABBREVIATIONS

etc.	in cross-reference entries, other characters of similar structure
p	incorrect pattern classification (in **Pattern Index**)
ps	incorrect pattern classification and stroke-count (in **Pattern Index**)
s	incorrect stroke-count (in **Pattern Index**)
SKIP	System of Kanji Indexing by Patterns
◧1	left-right pattern
⬒2	up-down pattern
▣3	enclosure pattern
■4	solid pattern
□1	top line (solid subpattern)
□2	bottom line (solid subpattern)
◫3	through line (solid subpattern)
□4	others (solid subpattern)

⇨ **SYSTEM OF KANJI INDEXING BY PATTERNS** on p. 106a

SYMBOLS IN ENTRY-HEAD DATA

Ⓒⓗ	Chinese forms and readings
( )	encloses *okurigana* of *kun* readings
1, 2	*kun* readings of exactly the same form
◇	alternative form
◆	handwritten abbreviation
–	*kun* reading used as word element
*	special reading that can be isolated
▲	unapproved reading
△	new radical based on simplified character form

⇨ GUIDE **§2.2.1 Entry-Head Data** on p. 162a

OTHER SYMBOLS AND MARKS

【 】	encloses subentry headwords (KUN and INDEPENDENT headwords)
❶ ❷···	numbered sense of COMPOUNDS section
ⓐ ⓑ··· (black)	numbered subsense of COMPOUNDS section
① ②···	numbered sense of subentry headwords
ⓐ ⓑ···	numbered subsense of subentry headwords
●	unnumbered sense of COMPOUNDS section
○	in SYNONYMS section, points to unnumbered sense of subentry headwords
▴	unapproved special reading in SPECIAL READINGS section
★	supplementary note in USAGE and NOTE sections
⇨, →	introduces cross-references
§	precedes section numbers in cross-references
=	precedes alternative forms/readings
( )	encloses ① *okurigana* endings, ② explanatory glosses, ③ optional omissions (*A* (*B*) = *A* or *AB*), ④ alternative forms/readings
[ ]	encloses ① most labels, ② alternatives (*A* [*B*] *C* = *AC* or *BC*)
/	① sometimes indicates alternatives, ② separates sentences
—	introduces supplementary glosses
-	KUN headword used as word element
‘ ’	encloses English equivalents in explanatory text
:	coordinates two parts of an English equivalent

SECTION LABELS

RADICAL	RADICAL section
▶	CORE section
COMPOUNDS	COMPOUNDS section
KUN	KUN section
INDEPENDENT	INDEPENDENT section
SPECIAL READINGS	SPECIAL READINGS section
NAMES	NAMES section
SYNONYMS	SYNONYMS section
USAGE	USAGE section
HOMOPHONES	HOMOPHONES section
COMPOUND FORMATION	COMPOUND FORMATION section
NOTE	NOTE section

⇨ **GUIDE** **§ 2.2.2 The Sections** on p. 163a

JAPANESE-ENGLISH CHARACTER DICTIONARY

漢　英　字　典

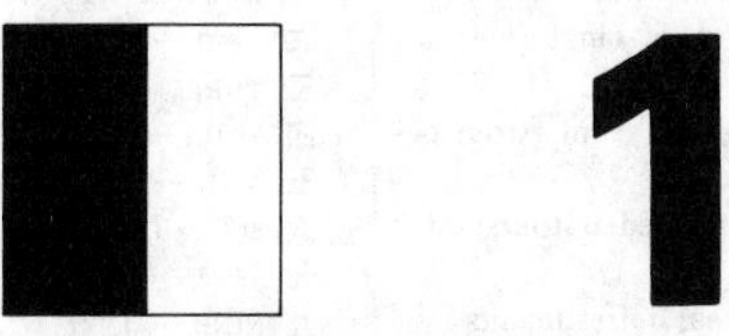

LEFT–RIGHT

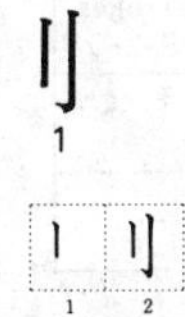

Radical	Strokes
刂 18	2-2-0
Grade	**Freq**
Radical	
◧ 1 - 1 - 1	

1-1 丨

RADICAL 18

rittō, variant of 刀 *katana* 'sword'

⇨ see 刀 2926 for radical description

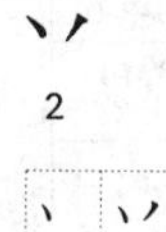

Radical	Strokes
丷 12	2-2-0
Grade	**Freq**
Radical	
◧ 1 - 1 - 1	

1-1 丶

RADICAL 12

variant of 八 *hachigashira* 'eight'

⇨ see 八 2928 for radical description

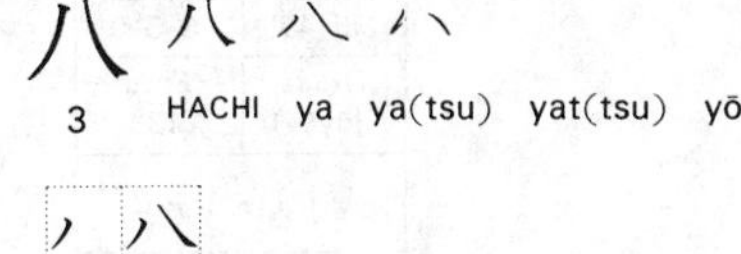

八 八 八 八

3 HACHI ya ya(tsu) yat(tsu) yō

Ⓒ 八 bā

Radical	Strokes
八 12	2-2-0
Grade	**Freq**
Jōyō-1	40
◧ 1 - 1 - 1	

1-1 丿

RADICAL 12

hachi, variant of 八 *hachigashira* 'eight'

⇨ see 八 2928 for radical description

▶EIGHT

COMPOUNDS

● **eight, eighth**

八十 *hachijū* 80

八面 *hachimen* eight faces

八苦 *hakku* the eight sufferings (of Buddhism)

尺八 *shakuhachi* bamboo flute

INDEPENDENT

【**hachi** 八】 eight

KUN

【**ya** 八】 [in compounds] many, varied

八重桜 *yaezakura* double flowered cherry tree
八百屋 *yaoya* greengrocer's; jack-of-all-trades
八百長 *yaochō* rigged affair, fixed game
【ya(tsu) 八つ】 eight; 2 o'clock (in former time system)
八つ切り *yatsugiri* cutting into eight parts; octavo
八つ当たり *yatsuatari* unjustified outburst of anger
お八つ *oyatsu* afternoon tea, refreshments
【yat(tsu) 八つ】 eight; eight years old
【yō 八】 [in compounds] eight; many
八日 *yōka* eight days; 8th of the month

SYNONYMS
● **small numbers**
一 ONE → 3341
二 TWO → 1922
三 THREE → 1924
四 FOUR → 3044
五 FIVE → 3436
六 SIX → 1965
七 SEVEN → 3362
九 NINE → 3369
十 TEN → 3365

NOTE
⇨ see COMPOUND FORMATION for 尺八 *shakuhachi* ⇨ 尺 3440

1-1
丿

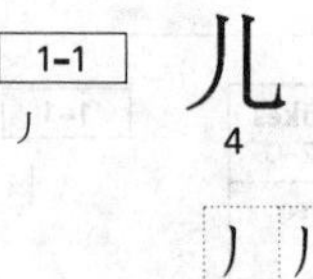

Radical	Strokes
儿 10	2-2-0
Grade	**Freq**
Radical	
1 - 1 - 1	

RADICAL 10
Standard form: 儿 *ninnyō* or *hitoashi* 'legs' (元 兆 兢)
Description: used for character classification

1-2

⺌
5

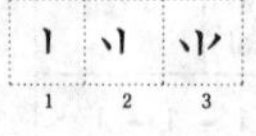

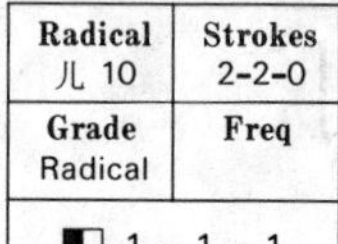

Radical	Strokes
⺌ 42	3-3-0
Grade	**Freq**
Radical	
1 - 1 - 2	

RADICAL 42
naogashira, variant of 小 *chiisai* 'small'
⇨ see 小 7 for radical description

1-2
丿

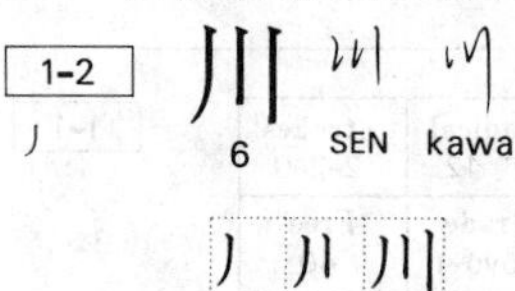

川 6 SEN kawa

CH 川 chuān

Radical	Strokes
川 47	3-3-0
Grade	**Freq**
Jōyō-1	136
1 - 1 - 2	

RADICAL 47
sanbongawa, variant of 巛 *magarigawa* 'river'
⇨ see 巛 9 for radical description

▶**RIVER**

COMPOUNDS
❶ⓐ [original meaning] **river**
ⓑ [rare] counter for rivers
河川 *kasen* rivers
山川 *sansen* mountains and rivers
三川 *sansen* three rivers
❷ unclassified compounds
川柳 *senryū* short humorous verse, satirical poem

KUN
【kawa 川】
[sometimes also 河]
ⓐ river, stream, brook
ⓑ suffix after names of (esp. Japanese) rivers
川上 *kawakami* upstream, upriver

川瀬 *kawase* rapids, shallows of a river
小川 *ogawa* brook, streamlet
江戸川 *edogawa* Edo River

SPECIAL READINGS

川原(＝河原) *kawara* dry riverbed, river beach

SYNONYMS

❶ⓐ **rivers and streams**
河 RIVER → 336
江 large river → 221
渓 mountain stream → 516
流 stream → 441

USAGE

kawa

川
[sometimes also 河]
ⓐ river, stream, brook
ⓑ suffix after names of (esp. Japanese) rivers

河
[usu. 川]
ⓐ river, stream
ⓑ suffix after names of (esp. foreign) rivers

HOMOPHONES

kawa ⇨ 河 336

NOTE

⇨ see COMPOUND FORMATION for 川柳 *senryū* ⇨ 柳 899

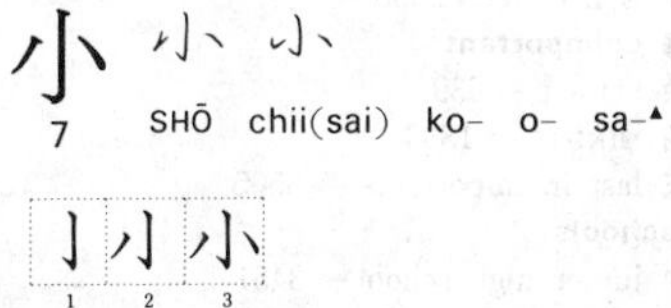

7 SHŌ chii(sai) ko- o- sa-▲

CH 小 xiǎo

Radical	Strokes
小 42	3-3-0
Grade	**Freq**
Jōyō-1	65
1 - 1 - 2	

1-2 丿

RADICAL 42

Standard form: 小 *chiisai* 'small' (少 尖 尠)
Top variant: ⺌ *naogashira* (当 尚)
Top variant: ⺍ *tsu* (単 営 巣)
Description: used in characters related to smallness

▶SMALL

COMPOUNDS

❶ⓐ [also prefix] [original meaning] (less in size, extent or quantity) **small, little, minor, short, tiny, miniature, minute**
ⓑ (less in intensity) small, slight
小国 *shōkoku* small nation, lesser power
小説 *shōsetsu* novel, story, fiction
小史 *shōshi* short history
小額 *shōgaku* small denomination
小アジア *shō-ajia* Asia Minor
小規模 *shōkibo* small scale
小東京 *shō-tōkyō* miniature Tokyo, epitome of Tokyo
大小 *daishō* large and small; size; long and short swords
縮小する *shukushō suru* reduce, curtail, cut down
中小企業 *chūshō kigyō* small-to-medium-sized enterprises
最小 *saishō* the smallest, minimum
小破 *shōha* slight damage

❷ⓐ (less in importance) **small, minor, petty**
ⓑ (of low rank) small, petty, lesser, lower
ⓒ small-minded, narrow-minded, timid
小前提 *shōzentei* minor premise
小事 *shōji* trifle
小委 *shōi* subcommittee
小学校 *shōgakkō* elementary [primary] school
過小評価する *kashō-hyōka suru* underestimate, underrate
小市民 *shōshimin* lower middle class
小身 *shōshin* humble position
小心な *shōshin na* timid, coward
小主観 *shōshukan* small ego

❸ⓐ abbrev. of 小学校 *shōgakkō*: **elementary school, grade school**
ⓑ **suffix after names of elementary schools**
小一 *shōichi* first-year student of an elementary school
同小 *dōshō* the above-mentioned elementary school
佃小 *tsukudashō* Tsukuda Elementary School

❹ [humble] my little, my humble, our humble
小生 *shōsei* I
小社 *shōsha* my company; little shrine
小店 *shōten* my little shop

❺ junior, younger, young, little
小弟 *shōtei* my foolish brother; I
小児 *shōni* little child, infant
小ケネディー *shō-kenedī* Kennedy Jr.

❻ urine
小用 *shōyō* urination; small matter

小水 *shōsui* urine, urination

INDEPENDENT

【shō 小】 smallness; small size, small; short month; child
大は小を兼ねる *Dai wa shō o kaneru* The greater serves for the lesser
小の月 *shō no tsuki* month with 30 days or less
小二十円 *shō nijūen* 20 yen for children

KUN

【chii(sai) 小さい】 small, little, tiny; minute, fine; trifling, petty; slight; young, little
小さな *chiisa na* noun adjective form of 小さい *chiisai*

【ko- 小-】
[also prefix]
①ⓐ (less in size or quantity) small, little, short
ⓑ (less in intensity) small, light, slight
小形の *kogata no* small-sized, tiny
小物 *komono* small articles, gadget
小鳥 *kotori* small [little] bird
小麦 *komugi* wheat
小唄 *kouta* ditty, ballad
小屋 *koya* cottage, hut, cabin; playhouse
小切手 *kogitte* check
小口 *koguchi* small lot, small sum [amount]; end, edge
小幅 *kohaba* single breadth, narrow range
小雪 *koyuki* light snowfall
小声 *kogoe* low voice, whisper
②ⓐ (of secondary importance) secondary, sub-
ⓑ [belittling] small, petty, little
小売り *kouri* retail, sale in small quantities
小分け *kowake* subdivision
小僧 *kozō* priestling; servant boy; kid, brat
小役人 *koyakunin* petty official
③ [emphatic preceding adjectives or verbs] a little, slightly, very
小戻す *komodosu* (of the market) rally a little
小恥ずかしい *kohazukashii* a little shameful
小高い *kodakai* slightly elevated
④ nearly, almost
小一時間 *koichijikan* nearly one hour

【o- 小-】 little, nice; a little
小川 *ogawa* brook, streamlet
小琴 *ogoto* small koto
小父さん *ojisan* man; Mister, Uncle
小暗い *ogurai* dusky

【sa- 小-】 [also prefix] *elegant* little, nice
小百合 *sayuri* lily
小夜曲 *sayokyoku* serenade

SPECIAL READINGS

小豆 *azuki* adzuki bean
小波▲ *sazanami* ripples, wavelets

SYNONYMS

❶ⓐ small and tiny
豆- miniature → 1943
微 SLIGHT → 639
細 MINUTE → 1333
寸 A BIT OF → 2935

❷ⓐ unimportant
微 SLIGHT → 639
細 MINUTE → 1333
末 last in importance → 3505

❸ schools
中 junior high school → 3451
園 kindergarten → 3156
高 high school → 2097
校 SCHOOL → 929
学 EDUCATIONAL INSTITUTION → 2555
塾 PRIVATE SCHOOL → 2860
大 UNIVERSITY → 3416
院 INSTITUTION → 454

❹ humble prefixes
弊 our [my] humble → 2884
拙 my humble → 315
愚 my foolish → 2834

USAGE

sa-
小-
[also prefix] *elegant* little, nice
早-
young, supple

HOMOPHONES

ko- ⇨ 子 3390 児 2546 娘 406 仔 33
sa- ⇨ 早 2390

NOTE

⇨ see also USAGE note at 子 3390

1-2

忄
8

Stroke order: 1 2 3

Radical	Strokes
忄 61	3-3-0
Grade	**Freq**
Radical	

1-1-2

RADICAL 61

risshinben, variant of 心 *kokoro* 'heart'
⇨ see 心 11 for radical description

巛

9

巛 (stroke order: 1 2 3)

Radical	Strokes
巛 47	3-3-0
Grade	**Freq**
Radical	
1 - 1 - 2	

1-2 く

RADICAL 47
Standard form: 巛 *magarigawa* 'river' (巡)
Variant: 川 *sanbongawa* (州)
Description: used for character classification

少

incorrect classification ⇨ see 3467

1-3 丿

水

10 SUI mizu mizu–

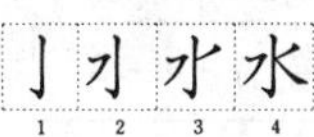

Ⓒⓗ 水 shuǐ

Radical	Strokes
水 85	4-4-0
Grade	**Freq**
Jōyō-1	145
1 - 1 - 3	

1-3 ㇇

RADICAL 85
Standard form: 水 *mizu* 'water' (永 沓 氷)
Left variant: 氵 *sanzui* (決 演 法)
Bottom variant: 氺 *shitamizu* (泰 求 滕)
Description: used in characters related to water flow, liquids or water bodies

▶WATER

COMPOUNDS

❶ [also suffix]
 ⓐ [original meaning] **water, cold water**
 ⓑ body of water, waters
 ⓒ the fifth of the five elements: water (⇨ see APPENDIX 7)
 水道 *suidō* water service [supply]; channel
 水準 *suijun* level, standard; water level
 海水 *kaisui* seawater
 地下水 *chikasui* underground water
 水産物 *suisanbutsu* marine products
 水域 *suiiki* water area, waters

❷ [also suffix] (liquid or water solution) water, lotion, liquid, fluid; soda
 水銀 *suigin* mercury, quicksilver
 石灰水 *sekkaisui* lime water
 化粧水 *keshōsui* toilet water [lotion]

❸ **hydrogen**
 水素 *suiso* hydrogen
 水爆 *suibaku* hydrogen bomb
 炭水化物 *tansuikabutsu* carbohydrates

❹ **Wednesday**
 水曜日 *suiyōbi* Wednesday
 月水金 *gessuikin* Mondays, Wednesdays and Fridays

❺ Mercury
 水星 *suisei* Mercury

INDEPENDENT

【sui 水】 Wednesday; shaved ice; the fifth of the five elements: water

KUN

【mizu 水】
①ⓐ water, cold water
 ⓑ [in compounds] liquid, watery
 水洗い *mizuarai* washing with water
 水着 *mizugi* bathing [swimming] suit
 雨水 *amamizu* rainwater
 水飴 *mizuame* glutinous starch syrup
② *sumo* break
 水入りの相撲 *mizuiri no sumō* sumo match with a break
③ damper, wet blanket, barrier
 水を注す *mizu o sasu* pour water (into); estrange (people); throw cold water

【mizu- 水-】 [prefix] water
 水資源 *mizushigen* water resources
 水仕事 *mizushigoto* scrubbing and washing, kitchen work
 水商売 *mizushōbai* bar and restaurant business; chancy trade

SYNONYMS

❶ⓐ **kinds of water**
 湯 HOT WATER → 612

汽 STEAM → 264
氷 ICE → 39
❷ **liquid**
液 LIQUID → 511
汁 fluid → 195
❸ **lighter elements**
酸 OXYGEN → 1563
窒 NITROGEN → 2288
塩 chlorine → 631
臭 bromine → 2633
硫 SULFUR → 1184
炭 carbon → 2257
❹ **days of the week**
木 Thursday → 3450
金 Friday → 2057
土 Saturday → 3403
日 Sunday → 3027
月 Monday → 2956
火 Tuesday → 3463

USAGE

mizu
水
①ⓐ water, cold water
ⓑ [in compounds] liquid, watery
② *sumo* break
③ damper, wet blanket, barrier

瑞-
young and fresh, vigorous

HOMOPHONES

mizu ⇨ 瑞 1027

1-3

11 SHIN kokoro -gokoro

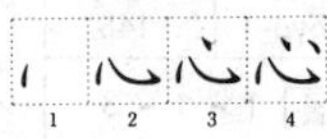

CH 心 xīn

Radical	Strokes
心 61	4-4-0
Grade	Freq
Jōyō-2	133
1 - 1 - 3	

RADICAL 61

Standard form: 心 *kokoro* 'heart' (必 忍 恥)
Left variant: 忄 *risshinben* (性 情 悩)
Bottom variant: 㣺 *shitagokoro* (恭 慕)
Description: used in characters related to emotions, thought or intellect

▶**HEART**

COMPOUNDS

❶ⓐ **heart, mind, spirit, feelings, emotions, thoughts**
ⓑ [also suffix] sense, motive
心情 *shinjō* one's heart, one's feelings
心身 *shinshin* mind and body
心理 *shinri* mental state, mentality; psychology
心配 *shinpai* anxiety, concern, worry, uneasiness; good offices
心境 *shinkyō* frame of mind, mental attitude [state]
心中 *shinchū* heart, mind, true motives
心中 *shinjū* lovers' suicide, double suicide
関心 *kanshin* concern, interest
安心する *anshin suru* have one's heart at ease, feel easy, be relieved
熱心 *nesshin* enthusiasm, zeal, fervor, earnestness
感心する *kanshin suru* admire, be deeply impressed
初心 *shoshin* one's original intention [object]
良心 *ryōshin* conscience
決心する *kesshin suru* make up one's mind, decide
苦心 *kushin* pains, efforts, hard work
以心伝心 *ishindenshin* silent [tacit] understanding, empathy
孝心 *kōshin* filial devotion [affection]
好奇心 *kōkishin* curiosity
愛国心 *aikokushin* patriotism, nationalism
公徳心 *kōtokushin* sense of public duty, public spirit

❷ [also suffix] [original meaning] **heart** (the organ)
心臓 *shinzō* heart
心電図 *shindenzu* electrocardiogram
心不全 *shinfuzen* heart failure
狭心症 *kyōshinshō* angina pectoris
衝心 *shōshin* heart failure
脂肪心 *shibōshin* fatty heart

❸ⓐ (central part) **heart, center, core**
ⓑ [formerly also 腎 *jin* 2832] heart of a matter, vital point
ⓒ (machine part) center
中心 *chūshin* center, middle
都心 *toshin* heart [center] of a city
核心 *kakushin* core, heart
重心 *jūshin* center of gravity, centroid
遠心力 *enshinryoku* centrifugal force
外心 *gaishin* circumcenter, outer center
肝心な *kanjin na* vital, essential, main
心棒 *shinbō* axle, shaft, arbor

心無し研削 *shinnashi kensaku* centerless grinding
❹ [usu. 芯 2423] core (of fruit); wick; lead (of a pencil); padding
心抜き器 *shinnukiki* corer
花心 *kashin* center of a flower
灯心 *tōshin* (lamp) wick
替え心 *kaeshin* spare lead
帯心 *obishin* sash padding

INDEPENDENT

【shin 心】
① heart, core; vitality; marrow
心から *shin kara* from the bottom of one's heart; by nature
心は良い男 *shin wa yoi otoko* a good man at heart
心が疲れる *shin ga tsukareru* tired to the bone; be mentally fatigued
② [usu. 芯 2423] core (of fruit); wick; lead (of a pencil); padding
林檎の心 *ringo no shin* core of an apple
蠟燭の心 *rōsoku no shin* wick of a candle
鉛筆の心 *enpitsu no shin* lead of a pencil
心を入れる *shin o ireru* pad (a sash)

KUN

【kokoro 心】
①ⓐ [also suffix] heart, mind, spirit, soul; thoughts, ideas
ⓑ attention, mind, interest
心構え *kokorogamae* mental attitude; preparation
心当たりが有る *kokoroatari ga aru* have an idea [a clue]
真心 *magokoro* sincerity, true heart
子供心 *kodomogokoro* child's naive [juvenile] mind
心を配る *kokoro o kubaru* give attention
心する *kokorosuru* mind, take care, be attentive
心掛ける *kokorogakeru* bear in mind; try, endeavor, intend
② (emotional state) heart, feelings, emotion
心を動かす *kokoro o ugokasu* move one's heart; impress, touch (a person's heart)
心残りだ *kokoronokori da* feel sorry, regret
心細い *kokorobosoi* helpless, forlorn; lonely
心安い *kokoroyasui* intimate, familiar
心持ち *kokoromochi* feeling, mood; slightly
心行く迄 *kokoroyuku made* to one's heart's content
気心 *kigokoro* temper, disposition
恋心 *koigokoro* one's love
③ⓐ (true) heart, wholeheartedness, sincerity
ⓑ (generous disposition) sympathy, heart, consideration
心から *kokoro kara* from the bottom of one's heart
心尽くし *kokorozukushi* kindness, consideration, solicitude
心を向ける *kokoro o mukeru* turn one's thoughts to
心無い *kokoronai* thoughtless; cruel; inconsiderate
心遣い *kokorozukai* consideration, anxiety
手心を加える *tegokoro o kuwaeru* use one's discretion, take into consideration
④ⓐ mind, intention, will, inclination
ⓑ frame of mind, mood
心積もり *kokorozumori* intention, expectation
下心 *shitagokoro* underlying motive, secret intention
⑤ meaning, essence; answer (to a riddle)
心得 *kokoroe* knowledge, information; instructions
歌の心 *uta no kokoro* true meaning of a poem, spirit of a poem

【-gokoro -心】 spirit, soul; disposition, turn of mind
大和心 *yamatogokoro* the Japanese spirit
歌心 *utagokoro* poetic turn of mind, feel for poetry

SPECIAL READINGS

心地 *kokochi* feeling, mood

SYNONYMS

❶ⓐ psyche
腹 heart → 1034
衷 INNER HEART → 2575
襟 inner mind → 1252
胸 breast → 951
懐 BOSOM → 763
神 MIND → 912
気 SPIRIT (consciousness) → 3194
精 SPIRIT (mind) → 1366
霊 SPIRIT (soul) → 2805
魂 SOUL, spirit → 1063

❷ internal organs
肺 LUNG → 916
胃 STOMACH → 2561
腸 INTESTINES → 1033
肝 LIVER → 841
胆 GALLBLADDER → 919

❸ⓐ middle
央 CENTER → 3509
核 NUCLEUS → 927
中 MIDDLE → 3451

❹ central parts
仁 kernel → 20
核 NUCLEUS → 927

【kokoro】
② feeling
気 spirits → 3194
情 EMOTION → 482
感 SENSE (feeling) → 2835

USAGE
shin
心
① heart, core; vitality; marrow
② [usu. 芯] core (of fruit); wick; lead (of a pencil); padding
芯
[sometimes also 心] core (of fruit); wick; lead (of a pencil); padding

NOTE
⇨ see COMPOUND FORMATION for
以心伝心 *ishindenshin* ⇨ 以 41
衝心 *shōshin* ⇨ 衝 725

1-3 小 12

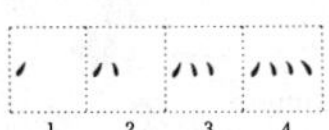

Radical	Strokes
小 61	4-4-0
Grade	**Freq**
Radical	
1-1-3	

RADICAL 61
shitagokoro, variant of 心 *kokoro* 'heart'
⇨ see 心 11 for radical description

1-3 灬 13

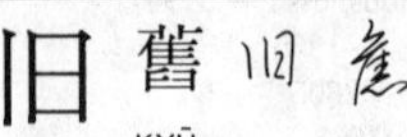

Radical	Strokes
灬 86	4-4-0
Grade	**Freq**
Radical	
1-1-3	

RADICAL 86
rekka, variant of 火 *hi* 'fire'
⇨ see 火 3463 for radical description

1-3 火 incorrect classification ⇨ see 3463

1-4 旧 舊 14 KYŪ Ⓒⓗ 旧 jiù

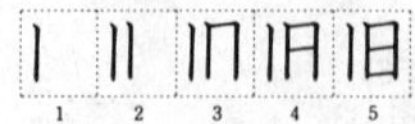

Radical	Strokes
日 72△	5-4-1
Grade	**Freq**
Jōyō-5	761
1-1-4	

▶FORMER

COMPOUNDS
❶ⓐ [also prefix] **former, ex-, old-time, old**
ⓑ old, ancient, antique, old-fashioned, bygone
旧夫 *kyūfu* former husband
旧居 *kyūkyo* former residence
旧軍人 *kyūgunjin* ex-soldier
旧制 *kyūsei* old system, old style
旧株 *kyūkabu* old stock
旧弊な *kyūhei na* old-fashioned, conservative
旧式 *kyūshiki* old style, old type
新旧の *shinkyū no* old and new
復旧する *fukkyū suru* be restored, recover
懐旧 *kaikyū* longing for the old days
❷ old acquaintance
故旧 *kokyū* old acquaintance
❸ old calendar, lunar calendar
旧暦 *kyūreki* old [lunar] calendar
旧正月 *kyūshōgatsu* New Year's Day in the lunar calendar

INDEPENDENT
【kyū 旧】 old things, original or former state, old times; old [lunar] calendar; old stock
旧に復する *kyū ni fukusuru* be restored to the former state
【kyū no 旧の】 old, former
旧の三月 *kyū no sangatsu* March according

to the old calendar

SYNONYMS

❶ⓐ former

元 former → 1929
故 OLD (earlier time) → 1141
前 previous → 2266
先 former → 2394
既 ALREADY → 1166

ⓑ old

故 OLD (of the past) → 1141
古 OLD (not new) → 2002
老 OLD (not young) → 3197

❸ calendars

新 new calendar → 1784
暦 CALENDAR → 3018

必

15 HITSU kanara(zu)

丶 ソ 必 必 必 (1 2 3 4 5)

 必 bì

Radical	Strokes
心 61	5-4-1
Grade	**Freq**
Jōyō-4	264
1 - 1 - 4	

1-4

▶WITHOUT FAIL

COMPOUNDS

❶ [original meaning] **without fail, certainly, surely; inevitable**

必須の *hissu no* indispensable, essential
必要 *hitsuyō* need, necessity
必死 *hisshi* inevitable death; desperation
必需 *hitsuju* necessary
必然性 *hitsuzensei* inevitability, necessity
必至の *hisshi no* inevitable, necessary
必勝 *hisshō* certain victory

❷ must, required, compulsory, worthwhile

必読書 *hitsudokusho* must book
必見の物 *hikken no mono* something that deserves attention; a must
必修科目 *hisshū kamoku* required subject

INDEPENDENT

【hissuru 必する】 warrant, guarantee

KUN

【kanara(zu) 必ず】 without fail, certainly, surely, invariably, always, necessarily

必ずしも *kanarazushimo* not always, not all

SYNONYMS

❶ certain

確 CERTAIN → 1228

❷ need and necessity

要 required → 2635
須 MUST → 574
需 DEMAND → 2797
入 necessary → 3370
用 needed for (a specific use) → 2976

忙

incorrect classification ⇨ see 214

1-5

州

incorrect classification ⇨ see 57

1-5

灯

incorrect classification ⇨ see 825

1-5

児

incorrect classification ⇨ see 2546

1-6

承

incorrect classification ⇨ see 16

1-6

1-6 快 incorrect classification ⇨ see 245

1-7 承 16 SHŌ uketamawa(ru) u(keru)▲

CH 承 chéng

Radical	Strokes
手 64	8-4-4
Grade	Freq
Jōyō-5	845
1-1-7	

▶**AGREE TO**

COMPOUNDS

❶ **agree to, consent, accept**

承諾する *shōdaku suru* consent, assent, agree, accept

承知する *shōchi suru* consent [agree] to; permit; forgive; know, understand

承認 *shōnin* approval, recognition

承服 *shōfuku* consent, acceptance

了承 *ryōshō* acknowledgment, understanding

❷ **succeed to, take over, inherit; receive**

承継 *shōkei* succession

承前 *shōzen* continued (from the previous text)

継承する *keishō suru* succeed to, accede to, inherit

伝承 *denshō* tradition, legend

❸ second stanza in a Chinese quatrain

起承転結 *kishōtenketsu* introduction, development, turn and conclusion (of a Chinese quatrain)

KUN

【uketamawa(ru) 承る】[humble] hear, listen to, be told; know, understand; receive (a command)

承りましょう *Uketamawarimashō* I'll listen to you respectfully

承れば *uketamawareba* from what I am told

【u(keru) 承ける】[usu. 受ける] inherit, get

親の気質を承ける *oya no kishitsu o ukeru* inherit one's parent's disposition

SYNONYMS

❶ **agree and approve**

諾 CONSENT → 1568

認 RECOGNIZE → 1546

肯 ASSENT → 2417

容 tolerate → 2277

可 APPROVE → 2969

賛 APPROVE OF → 2809

❷ **succeed**

継 SUCCEED → 1360

嗣 inherit → 1719

HOMOPHONES

ukeru ⇨ 受 2421 享 2051 請 1576

NOTE

⇨ see USAGE note at 受 2421

1-7 炉 炊 incorrect classification ⇨ see 4-4

1-7 性 怪 etc. incorrect classification ⇨ see 3-5

1-8 胤 17 IN tane NAMES tsugi tsugu kazu

CH 胤 yìn

Radical	Strokes
月 130	9-4-5
Grade	Freq
Names	2053
1-1-8	

▶**PROGENY**

COMPOUNDS

❶ⓐ **progeny, descendant, posterity**

ⓑ descent, lineage

落胤 *rakuin* illegitimate child, love child

後胤 *kōin* descendant, scion

皇胤 *kōin* [archaic] Imperial descendant [posterity]

胤裔 *in'ei* [archaic] descendant, successor
❷ [original meaning, now archaic] succeed to, inherit

KUN

【tane 胤】 [now usu. 種] paternal blood, offspring
胤違い *tanechigai* half brother, half sister

NAMES

胤信 *tanenobu* male name
胤雄 *kazuo* male name

SYNONYMS

❶ⓐ descendant
孫 GRANDCHILD, descendant → 410
末 posterity → 3505

HOMOPHONES

tane ⇨ 種 1218

NOTE

⇨ see USAGE note at 種 1218

畑 炮

incorrect classification ⇨ see ◧ 4–5 | 1-8 ˏ

恒 悔 etc.

incorrect classification ⇨ see ◧ 3–6 | 1-8 ˏ

閂

incorrect classification ⇨ see 1165 | 1-9 |

帰

incorrect classification ⇨ see 130 | 1-9 ˏ

烟

incorrect classification ⇨ see 944
(nonstandard for 煙 1021) | 1-9 ˏ

悩 悟 etc.

incorrect classification ⇨ see ◧ 3–7 | 1-9 ˏ

情 惨 etc.

incorrect classification ⇨ see ◧ 3–8 | 1-10 ˏ

順 順 順

18 JUN

CH 顺 shùn

1-11 丿

Radical	Strokes
頁 181	12-9-3
Grade	**Freq**
Jōyō-4	812
◧ 1 - 1 - 1 1	

Stroke order: 丿 丿丨 川 川一 川ア 川厂 川丙 川丙 川百 川有 川頁 順 (1–12)

▶ORDER ▶OBEY

COMPOUNDS

❶ [also suffix] **order, sequence, turn**
順番 *junban* order, turn
順序 *junjo* order, sequence; system, procedure
順位 *jun'i* order, rank, precedence
順順に *junjun ni* in order, in turn
筆順 *hitsujun* stroke order (in writing Chinese characters)
道順 *michijun* route, itinerary
手順 *tejun* procedure, program, process
先着順 *senchakujun* order of arrival
年齢順に *nenreijun ni* by priority of age
ABC順に *ē-bī-shī-jun ni* in alphabetical order
❷ⓐ [also 遵 3167] **obey, follow, submit to**
ⓑ obedient, gentle
ⓒ [also 馴 1820] tame, domesticate
順守する *junshu suru* observe, obey, follow, conform to
順法 *junpō* law observance

随順する *zuijun suru* obey meekly, faithfully follow (one's master)
順逆 *jungyaku* obedience and disobedience, right or wrong
恭順 *kyōjun* obedience, submission
温順 *onjun* obedience, gentleness, docility
順応 *junnō* adaptation, accommodation, adjustment
順化 *junka* acclimation

❸ **favorable, satisfactory, right**

順調 *junchō* favorable condition, smooth progress
順風 *junpū* favorable wind
順当な *juntō na* proper, right, reasonable
順境 *junkyō* favorable circumstances [condition]

INDEPENDENT

【jun 順】 order, sequence, turn
順に *jun ni* in order, by turns

SYNONYMS

❶ **order**

序 ORDER (sequence／arrangement) → 3065
次 order (sequence) → 54
番 NUMERICAL ORDER → 2748
秩 ORDER (methodical arrangement) → 1158

❷ⓐ **obey**

遵 OBEY → 3167
従 FOLLOW → 415
守 observe → 2173
隷 be subordinate to → 1751

❸ **good**

好 FAVORABLE → 208
良 GOOD → 3558
善 GOOD → 2325
佳 FINE → 86
美 BEAUTIFUL → 2264

1-11 焼 焰 incorrect classification ⇨ see ▐ 4－8

1-11 愉 惰 etc. incorrect classification ⇨ see ▐ 3－9

1-12 臨 incorrect classification ⇨ see 162 (nonstandard for 臨 1630)

1-12 煙 煩 incorrect classification ⇨ see ▐ 4－9

1-12 慎 慨 etc. incorrect classification ⇨ see ▐ 3－10

1-13 慣 慢 etc. incorrect classification ⇨ see ▐ 3－11

1-13 煽 熄 incorrect classification ⇨ see ▐ 4－10

1-14 憤 憐 etc. incorrect classification ⇨ see ▐ 3－12

1-15 憐 incorrect classification／stroke count ⇨ see 731

憾 憶 etc.	incorrect classification ⇨ see ◧ 3－13	1-15 ㇀
燃 燈 etc.	incorrect classification ⇨ see ◧ 4－12	1-15 ㇀
燥	incorrect classification ⇨ see 1087	1-16 ㇀
燻	incorrect classification ⇨ see 1098	1-17 ㇀
爆	incorrect classification ⇨ see 1101	1-18 ㇀
懷	incorrect classification ⇨ see 804 (nonstandard for 懐 763)	1-18 ㇀
鬪	incorrect classification ⇨ see 3338 (nonstandard for 闘 3334)	1-19 丨
爐	incorrect classification ⇨ see 1104 (nonstandard for 炉 869)	1-19 ㇀
爛	incorrect classification ⇨ see 1110	1-20 ㇀
孔	incorrect stroke count ⇨ see 179	2-1 子

仏 佛 仏 佛　　Ⓒⓗ 佛 fó fú

19　BUTSU　FUTSU▲　hotoke

Stroke order: ノ 亻 仏 仏 (1 2 3 4)

Radical	Strokes
亻 9	4-2-2
Grade	**Freq**
Jōyō-5	604
◧ 1 - 2 - 2	

2-2 亻

▶**BUDDHA** ▶**FRANCE**

COMPOUNDS

❶ⓐ **Buddha, Sakyamuni**

ⓑ **Buddhism**

ⓒ [also suffix] Buddhist image

仏陀 *budda* Buddha

神仏 *shinbutsu* gods and Buddha; Shinto and Buddhism

仏教 *bukkyō* Buddhism

念仏 *nenbutsu* Buddhist invocation, prayer to Amitabha

仏像 *butsuzō* image of Buddha; Buddhist statue

仏壇 *butsudan* family Buddhist altar

石仏 *sekibutsu* stone Buddhist image

三尊仏 *sanzonbutsu* image of the three honorable ones

❷ⓐ **France**

ⓑ **French (language)**
仏印 *futsuin* French Indochina
日仏 *nichifutsu* Japan and France
仏文学 *futsubungaku* French literature
仏英辞典 *futsuei jiten* French-English dictionary
❸ the deceased, departed soul
成仏する *jōbutsu suru* enter Nirvana, attain Buddhahood; die

INDEPENDENT

【butsu 仏】 Buddha; Buddhism
【futsu 仏】 France

KUN

【hotoke 仏】 Buddha; Buddhist image; the deceased, departed soul
仏様 *hotokesama* Buddha; deceased person

SYNONYMS

❶ⓐ Buddha
釈 Sakyamuni → 1484
ⓑ religions and sects
法 Buddha's teachings → 333
禅 ZEN → 1032
儒 CONFUCIANISM → 174
道 Taoism → 3134
ⓒ images
像 IMAGE → 166
偶 figure → 132
❷ⓐ European countries
英 ENGLAND → 2238
独 GERMANY → 395
伊 ITALY → 49
西 Spain → 3520
蘭 Holland → 2383
露 Russia → 2818

2-2
亻

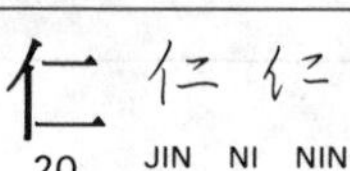

20 JIN NI NIN▲

CH 仁 rén

Radical	Strokes
亻 9	4-2-2
Grade	**Freq**
Jōyō-6	1342
1 - 2 - 2	

▶BENEVOLENCE

COMPOUNDS

❶ **benevolence, the perfect virtue, humaneness, compassion, kindness, love, mercy** (a basic Confucian precept)
仁愛 *jin'ai* benevolence, charity
仁術 *jinjutsu* benevolent act
仁義礼智信 *jingireichishin* the five Confucian virtues (benevolence, justice, courtesy, wisdom and sincerity)
仁徳 *jintoku* benevolence, goodness
仁義 *jingi* humanity and justice; moral code; formal greeting among gamblers
❷ benevolent personage
仁者 *jinsha* man of virtue
御仁 *gojin* personage
❸ kernel, core; karyosome
杏仁 *kyōnin* apricot stone
核仁 *kakujin* nucleus
❹ two (people)
仁王(＝二王) *niō* the two Deva kings

INDEPENDENT

【jin 仁】 benevolence (⇨ ❶); nucleolus
身を殺して仁を為す *mi o koroshite jin o nasu* do an act of benevolence at the sacrifice of oneself

SYNONYMS

❶ tender feelings for others
慈 compassion → 2339
情 sympathy → 482
悲 mercy → 2775
哀 PITY → 2068
❸ central parts
核 NUCLEUS → 927
心 core → 11

化 化 化 化 ㊥ 化 huà

21 KA KE ba(keru) ba(kasu)

ノ イ イ' 化
1 2 3 4

Radical	Strokes
ヒ 21	4-2-2
Grade	**Freq**
Jōyō-3	103
◧ 1 - 2 - 2	

2-2 亻

▶**CHANGE INTO**

COMPOUNDS

❶ⓐ **change into, transform into, turn into, convert**

ⓑ change (a person) for the better, convert, influence

化石 *kaseki* fossil, fossil remains; petrifaction
化成 *kasei* chemical synthesis, transformation
化合 *kagō* chemical combination
消化 *shōka* digestion; assimilation; consumption
同化 *dōka* assimilation
変化 *henka* change, transformation, variety; declension
文化 *bunka* culture
感化する *kanka suru* influence, exert influence, inspire
教化する *kyōka suru* enlighten, educate, civilize

❷ [also suffix]

ⓐ (cause to become) **-ize, -ify, make into**

ⓑ (become) **-ize, become transformed, turn into**

強化 *kyōka* strengthening, intensification, buildup, reinforcement
液化 *ekika* liquefaction
浄化する *jōka suru* purify, cleanse
近代化 *kindaika* modernization
コンピュータ化 *konpyūtaka* computerization
酸化 *sanka* oxidation
激化する *gekika* (=*gekka*) *suru* intensify, become aggravated
悪化する *akka suru* worsen, aggravate, deteriorate
軟化 *nanka* softening; weakening (of the market)

❸ **change [transform] oneself into, take the form of; disguise oneself**

化粧品 *keshōhin* cosmetics
化身 *keshin* Buddhist incarnation, reincarnation
権化 *gonge* incarnation, embodiment
変化 *henge* goblin, ghost

❹ abbrev. of 化学 *kagaku*: chemistry

化工 *kakō* chemical engineering
化繊 *kasen* synthetic fiber

INDEPENDENT

【kasuru (=kasu) 化する(=化す)】 change into, transform into; convert (by virtuous example), influence

徳を以て化する *toku o motte kasuru* influence by means of one's virtue

KUN

【ba(keru) 化ける】 change [transform] oneself into, take the form of; disguise oneself

お化け *obake* apparition, specter, ghost
女に化ける *onna ni bakeru* change into a woman, assume the shape of a woman

【ba(kasu) 化かす】 bewitch, deceive; transfigure

狐に化かされる *kitsune ni bakasareru* be deceived by a fox

SYNONYMS

❶ & ❷ **change and replace**

変 CHANGE → 2069
更 change → 3541
改 change → 243
易 change → 2411
遷 undergo transition → 3170
転 turn into → 1480
換 EXCHANGE → 587
交 INTERCHANGE → 2015
替 REPLACE → 2783
代 SUBSTITUTE → 30
迭 ALTERNATE → 3077

❸ **disguise**

装 dress up → 2685

COMPOUND FORMATION

文化 *bunka*

文化 'culture' is influencing (化 ❶ⓑ) by means of culture (文).

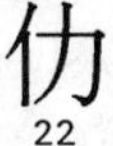

22

▶**WORK**

handwritten abbreviation for 働 153

2-2 亻

2-2 亻

化 23

▶CHANGE INTO
nonstandard for 化 21

2-2 亻

仔

incorrect stroke count ⇨ see 33

2-2 十

艹 24

Radical	Strokes
艹 140	4-4-0
Grade	**Freq**
Radical	
1 - 2 - 2	

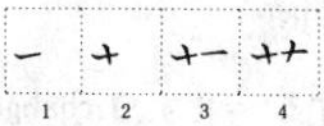

RADICAL 140
kusakanmuri, variant of 艸 *kusa* 'plants'
⇨ see 艸 209 for radical description

2-2 又

双 雙 双 叏 25

sō futa

CH 双 shuāng

Radical	Strokes
又 29△	4-2-2
Grade	**Freq**
Jōyō	1077
1 - 2 - 2	

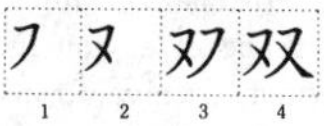

▶SET OF TWO

COMPOUNDS

❶ⓐ [original meaning] **set of two (identical things such as hands), pair, both, two**
ⓑ **counter for pairs**
双肩 *sōken* both shoulders
双生児 *sōseiji* twins
双方 *sōhō* both sides [parties]
双眼鏡 *sōgankyō* binoculars
一双 *issō* a pair
❷ comparison, match
双璧 *sōheki* two matchless authorities [jewels]
無双 *musō* matchless, peerless
❸ [also 叢 2621] crowd together, meet in large numbers
双書(＝総書) *sōsho* series, library

INDEPENDENT
【sō 双】 pair
双の手 *sō no te* both hands

KUN
【futa 双】 [in compounds] set of two, pair
双子 *futago* twins
双葉 *futaba* bud, cotyledon

SYNONYMS
❶ **two**
対 pair → 831
偶 COUPLE → 132
両 BOTH → 3518
二 TWO → 1922
弐 TWO (in legal documents) → 3195

HOMOPHONES
futa ⇨ 二 1922

NOTE
⇨ see USAGE note at 二 1922

比

26 HI kura(beru)

Stroke order: 一 ⺊ ⺊⺊ 比 (1 2 3 4)

CH 比 bǐ

Radical	Strokes
比 81	4-4-0
Grade	**Freq**
Jōyō-5	499
◧ 1 - 2 - 2	

2-2
⺊

RADICAL 81
Standard form: 比 *kuraberu* or *hi* 'compare' (毘)
Description: used for character classification

▶**COMPARE**

COMPOUNDS

❶ⓐ **compare (with), contrast**
ⓑ [also 譬 2903] compare to, liken
ⓒ (something of comparable standing) comparison, match, equal
比較 *hikaku* comparison
対比する *taihi suru* contrast, compare
比喩 *hiyu* simile, metaphor, allegory
比類 *hirui* parallel, equal, match
無比の *muhi no* incomparable, matchless, unparalleled
❷ [original meaning] rank, line up
比翼 *hiyoku* wings abreast; single garment made to look double
比肩する *hiken suru* equal, rank with, compare favorably
❸ [also suffix] **ratio**
比例 *hirei* proportion, ratio
比率 *hiritsu* ratio, percentage
正比 *seihi* direct ratio
容積比 *yōsekihi* volume ratio
❹ [also prefix] (of physical constants) specific
比熱 *hinetsu* specific heat
比重 *hijū* specific gravity, density; relative importance
比電荷 *hidenka* specific charge
❺ Philippines
比島 *hitō* the Philippines
比日 *hinichi* the Philippines and Japan
❻ used phonetically for *bi* in the transliteration of Sanscrit Buddhist terms
比丘 *biku* Buddhist priest

INDEPENDENT

【**hi 比**】comparison, match, equal; ratio; the Philippines
比を見ない *hi o minai* be unique [unrivaled]
比を求める *hi o motomeru* obtain the ratio
【**hisuru 比する**】compare

KUN

【**kura(beru) 比べる**】[sometimes also 較べる] compare, contrast
比べ物にならない *kurabemono ni naranai* be no match for
背比べ *seikurabe* comparison of statures

SYNONYMS

❶ⓐ **compare**
較 COMPARE → 1536
校 COLLATE → 929
照 check against → 2827
対 OPPOSE (contrast) → 831
参 refer → 2066
❷ **arrange**
並 LINE UP → 2246
列 arrange in a row → 824
陳 lay out (for exhibit) → 540
羅 spread out → 2622
揃える arrange properly → 590
整 PUT IN ORDER → 2871
理 put in order → 970
❸ **rate**
率 RATE → 2118
割 rate → 1816
歩 percentage → 2416
❺ **Asian countries**
印 India → 828
越 Vietnam → 3314
泰 Thailand → 2583
鮮 Korea → 1877
華 CHINA → 2283
日 JAPAN → 3027

USAGE

kuraberu
比べる
[sometimes also 較べる] compare, contrast
較べる
[usu. 比べる] compare, contrast

HOMOPHONES

kuraberu ⇨ 較 1536

2-2
七

切 切 切 切

Ⓒ 切 qiē qiè

27 SETSU SAI ki(ru) -ki(ru) ki(ri) -ki(ri) -gi(ri) ki(reru) -ki(reru) ki(re) -ki(re) -gi(re)

Radical	Strokes
刀 18	4-2-2
Grade	**Freq**
Jōyō-2	197
1 - 2 - 2	

一 七 切 切
1 2 3 4

▶**CUT**

COMPOUNDS

❶ [formerly also 截 *setsu* 3301] [original meaning] **cut, sever**
切断する *setsudan suru* cut (off), sever
切開 *sekkai* incision, section
切除する *setsujo suru* cut off, excise
切腹 *seppuku* hara-kiri, suicide by disembowelment
半切 *hansetsu* half size

❷ⓐ **keen, acute, intense**
ⓑ eager, earnest, ardent
切実に *setsujitsu ni* acutely, keenly, earnestly; sincerely, heartily
痛切な *tsūsetsu na* keen, acute, poignant
切望 *setsubō* earnest desire, eager wish
切切と *setsusetsu to* eagerly, earnestly, with emotion

❸ⓐ **in close contact, fitting closely, to the point**
ⓑ urgent, pressing, close
親切な *shinsetsu na* kind, friendly, obliging
適切な *tekisetsu na* appropriate, adequate, proper
懇切な *konsetsu na* kind, cordial; exhaustive
切迫した *seppaku shita* urgent, pressing, imminent
切羽詰まって *seppa-tsumatte* under the pressure of necessity
大切な *taisetsu na* important, weighty; valuable

❹ everything, all
一切の *issai no* all, entire, whole
合切 *gassai* all (together), altogether

INDEPENDENT

【setsu 切】 label on switches: OFF
切一入 *setsu-nyū* OFF-ON (marking on switches)

【setsunaru 切なる】 earnest, eager; keen, acute

【setsu ni 切に】 earnestly, eagerly, fervently

【setsunai 切ない】 painful, trying, distressing

KUN

【ki(ru) 切る】

①ⓐ cut, slice, carve
ⓑ [formerly also 伐る] cut down (trees), fell, chop down
ⓒ [formerly also 剪る] prune, trim, shear
ⓓ [formerly also 截る] cut (flat things such as cloth or paper)
切り離す *kirihanasu* cut [chop] off, sever, detach
切手 *kitte* postage stamp
切符 *kippu* ticket
切り倒す *kiritaosu* fell (a tree)

② [formerly 斬る] cut (a person) with a sword, cut down, kill
試し切り *tameshigiri* trying out a new sword (on someone)
裏切る *uragiru* betray, turn traitor, double-cross

③ (separate from the main body) cut off, break away
切符を切る *kippu o kiru* punch a ticket, rip off a coupon
封切り *fūkiri* release, first run, premiere

④ perform an action as if by cutting
波を切る *nami o kiru* cut one's way through the waves
踏切 *fumikiri* railroad crossing
皮切り *kawakiri* beginning, start

⑤ⓐ (discontinue an action) cut off, pause, break off, turn off, hang up
ⓑ cut [sever] connection with
切り替える *kirikaeru* switch, change, renew
思い切る *omoikiru* resign oneself to, give up; resolve, determine
打ち切る *uchikiru* put an end to, break off, finish
縁切り *enkiri* severing off connections

⑥ cut off [divide] by or as if by a partition
締切(=〆切) *shimekiri* closing day, deadline; Closed, No Entrance
仕切る *shikiru* partition, divide, mark off; settle accounts; *sumo* toe the mark

⑦ fall short of, be below
千円を切る *sen'en o kiru* be less than 1000 yen

⑧ perform an action boldly
切り札 *kirifuda* trump (card), last resort
踏み切る *fumikiru* make a bold start, take a plunge; take off; *sumo* step out of the ring
見得を切る *mie o kiru* pose, assume a posture; make a defiant [proud] gesture

⑨ drain (water)
水切り *mizukiri* drainer; cutwater, forefoot; ducks and drakes

【-ki(ru) -切る】
[verbal suffix]
① finish, be through
読み切る *yomikiru* finish reading, read through
②ⓐ perform an action thoroughly
ⓑ perform an action decisively
張り切る *harikiru* be in high spirits, be enthusiastic; stretch to the full
疲れ切る *tsukarekiru* be tired out, be exhausted
言い切る *iikiru* declare, assert; finish saying

【ki(ri) 切り】 limits, bounds, end; the lowest [worst]; last part (of a noh or kabuki play); last piece (on a noh or kabuki program)
切りが無い *kiri ga nai* be endless [boundless]
ピンから切り迄 *pin kara kiri made* of all sorts, of a wide range
大切り *ōgiri* last piece on the program; close, conclusion; large chop

【-ki(ri) -切り】 cutter
缶切り *kankiri* can opener
爪切り *tsumekiri* nail clipper [nipper]

【-gi(ri) -切り】 [also suffix] way of cutting
微塵切りにする *mijingiri ni suru* cut into fine pieces
四つ切り *yotsugiri* cutting in four; quarter

【ki(reru) 切れる】
① be cut off, break, snap, burst, collapse
切れた縄 *kireta nawa* broken rope
切れ端 *kirehashi* fragment, scrap
② be cut [injured], become fissured
切れ目 *kireme* rift, gap, break; end, pause, interval
手が切れた *Te ga kireta* I cut my hand
③ wear, be worn out
裾が切れる *suso ga kireru* get frayed at the hem
擦り切れる *surikireru* wear out, become seedy
④ break off, be interrupted
途切れる *togireru* break, pause, be interrupted
息切れする *ikigire suru* get short [out] of breath, be winded
⑤ cut [sever] connection with
手切れ *tegire* severance of connections; solatium for severing connections
⑥ run out, expire, terminate
期限が切れた *Kigen ga kireta* The term has expired
ガソリンが切れる *gasorin ga kireru* run out of gas
⑦ cut (well), be keen, be sharp
切れるナイフ *kireru naifu* sharp knife
⑧ sharp, smart, able
切れる男 *kireru otoko* able [competent] man
⑨ fall short of, be below
元値が切れる *motone ga kireru* be below the cost

【-ki(reru) -切れる】 [verbal suffix] be able to do, be able to finish
飲み切れますか *Nomikiremasu ka* Can you drink it all up?
やり切れない *yarikirenai* be unbearable, be too much
食べ切れない程のパン *tabekirenai hodo no pan* more bread than one can eat

【ki(re) 切れ】 sharpness, cutting quality; cloth; piece, bit, strip, slice
切れ味 *kireaji* sharpness, cutting quality
切れが悪い *kire ga warui* be dull [blunt]; thick, viscous
切れの帽子 *kire no bōshi* cloth hat
切れ切れの *kiregire no* fragmentary, intermittent
板切れ *itakire* piece of wood, scrap lumber

【-ki(re) -切れ】 counter for strips or slices
ケーキ一切れ *kēki hitokire* a piece of cake
二切れのパン *futakire no pan* two slices of bread

【-gi(re) -切れ】
[also suffix]
① expiration of, depletion of
品切れ *shinagire* absence [exhaustion] of stock
時間切れ *jikangire* expiration of the allotted time
② fragments from writings by famous historical figures
高野切れ *kōyagire* fragments from the old literary work kept at Koyasan

SYNONYMS

❶ cut
断 CUT OFF → 1492
裁 CUT OUT → 3299
割 cut with a knife → 1816
剖 DISSECT → 1670
刈る CLIP → 28
伐 CUT DOWN → 42
削 CUT BY CHIPPING → 1448

❷ⓐ extreme in degree
痛 bitter(ly) → 3285
酷 SEVERE → 1562
厳 SEVERE → 3289
激 intense → 776
極 EXTREME → 1017
甚 EXTREMELY → 2643
超 super- → 3313
強 STRONG → 475
重 HEAVY → 3573
高 HIGH → 2097
深 DEEP → 524
大 BIG → 3416

ⓑ eager
懇 EARNEST → 2899
篤 DEVOTED → 2716

熱 HOT → 2866

USAGE

❶ **kiru**

切る

①ⓐ cut, slice, carve
ⓑ [formerly also 伐る] cut down (trees), fell, chop down
ⓒ [formerly also 剪る] prune, trim, shear
ⓓ [formerly also 截る] cut (flat things such as cloth or paper)
② [formerly 斬る] cut (a person) with a sword, cut down, kill
③ (separate from the main body) cut off, break away
④ perform an action as if by cutting
⑤ⓐ (discontinue an action) cut off, pause, break off, turn off, hang up
ⓑ cut [sever] connection with
⑥ cut off [divide] by or as if by a partition
⑦ fall short of, be below
⑧ perform an action boldly
⑨ drain (water)

伐る

[now usu. 切る] cut down (trees), fell, chop down

剪る

[now usu. 切る] prune, trim, shear

截る

[now usu. 切る] cut (flat things such as cloth or paper)

斬る

① [now usu. 切る] cut (a person) with a sword, cut down, kill
② criticize severely, attack

❷ **-gire**

-切れ

[also suffix]
① expiration of, depletion of
② fragments from writings by famous historical figures

-裂れ

[also suffix] fragment (of old textile), strip

HOMOPHONES

kiru ⇨ 伐 42　剪 2306　截 3301　斬 1482
-gire ⇨ 裂 2687

COMPOUND FORMATION

大切 *taisetsu*

大切な 'important, etc.' originally referred to a state of extreme (大) urgency (切 ❸ⓑ).

2-2 メ

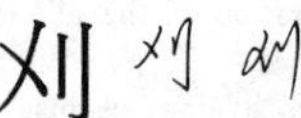

28　GAI▲　KAI▲　ka(ru)

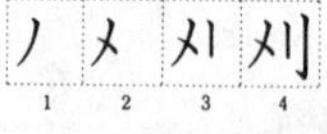

Ⓒⓗ 刈 yì

Radical	Strokes
刂 18	4-2-2
Grade	**Freq**
Jōyō	1640
1-2-2	

▶**CLIP**

COMPOUNDS

● [original meaning] **clip, crop, mow, cut down**

刈除する *kaijo suru* [rare] mow, cut off, remove

KUN

【**ka(ru) 刈る**】

ⓐ (cut grass, hair or the like by sharp instrument) clip, crop, cut, shear, mow, prune, trim

ⓑ reap, crop, harvest

刈り込む *karikomu* prune
刈り取る *karitoru* mow, cut down, reap, harvest
刈り立ての *karitate no* newly mown, newly cropped (head), just clipped
草刈り *kusakari* mowing, mower
羊毛を刈る *yōmō o karu* shear sheep
刈り入れ *kariire* harvest, reap
稲刈り *inekari* rice reaping

SYNONYMS

【**karu**】

ⓐ **cut**

伐 CUT DOWN → 42
削 CUT BY CHIPPING → 1448
切 CUT → 27
断 CUT OFF → 1492
裁 CUT OUT → 3299
割 cut with a knife → 1816
剖 DISSECT → 1670

ⓑ **harvest**

穫 HARVEST → 1251
摘 PICK → 694
採 PICK → 499

USAGE

karu

刈る

ⓐ (cut grass, hair or the like by sharp instrument) clip, crop, cut, shear, mow, prune, trim
ⓑ reap, crop, harvest

狩る

hunt
駆る
① drive (a car), urge (a horse) on, spur on
② prompt, inspire

HOMOPHONES
karu ⇨ 狩 397 駆 1823

艹

29

Radical	Strokes
艹 140	4-4-0
Grade	**Freq**
Radical	
◧ 1-2-2	

2-2

RADICAL 140
kusakanmuri, variant of 艸 *kusa* 'plants'
⇨ see 艸 209 for radical description

代 代 代

Ⓒⓗ 代 dài

30 DAI TAI ka(waru) ka(wari) -ga(wari) ka(eru) yo shiro[1] shiro[2]

Radical	Strokes
亻 9	5-2-3
Grade	**Freq**
Jōyō-3	84
◧ 1-2-3	

2-3 亻

▶**SUBSTITUTE** ▶**GENERATION** ▶**CHARGE**

COMPOUNDS

❶ⓐ [original meaning] **substitute, replace, represent, act for another, alternate**
ⓑ substitute, deputy, representative, proxy
代用する *daiyō suru* substitute, use for another
代行する *daikō suru* act for another, execute (business) for another
代表する *daihyō suru* represent, stand for; typify
代理人 *dairinin* representative, deputy, proxy
代議 *daigi* popular representation
代打 *daida* pinch-hitting; pinch hitter
代替エネルギー *daitai energī* alternative [substitute] energy
代謝(=新陳代謝) *taisha* (=*shinchintaisha*) metabolism; renewal, regeneration
交代する *kōtai suru* relieve (a person), take turns, alternate
師範代 *shihandai* acting instructor
城代 *jōdai* deputy castellan, keeper of the castle

❷ⓐ **generation, lifetime**
ⓑ counter for generations, descendants or reign periods
ⓒ suffix for range of a person's age in ten-year periods: -ies
代代 *daidai* generation after generation
世代 *sedai* generation
一代 *ichidai* one generation, lifetime
初代 *shodai* first generation, founder
四代目の店主 *yondaime no tenshu* shopkeeper of the fourth generation
徳川三代家光 *tokugawa sandai iemitsu* Iemitsu, third in the Tokugawa line
二十代の男 *nijūdai no otoko* man in his twenties

❸ⓐ **age, era, times**
ⓑ suffix indicating years spanning a specific period: **-ies, the...-hundreds**
ⓒ geological era
時代 *jidai* age, era, period; antiquity
現代 *gendai* present age, modern times, today
古代 *kodai* ancient times, antiquity, remote ages
年代 *nendai* age, era, period; date
千九百年代 *senkyūhyakunen dai* the 1900's
中生代 *chūseidai* Mesozoic era

❹ [also suffix] (price charged) **charge, fare, rate, fee, price, rent**
代金 *daikin* charge, fee, price
ホテル代 *hoterudai* charge for staying at a hotel
無代 *mudai* free of charge
タクシー代 *takushīdai* taxi fare
地代 *jidai* land rent, rental
部屋代 *heyadai* room rent

❺ abbrev. of 代表電話 *daihyō denwa*: main telephone number
大代465-1111 *daidai yon-roku-go no ichi-ichi-ichi-ichi* Contact 465-1111 (main number)

INDEPENDENT

【**dai 代**】generation; charge, fee, bill
親の代 *oya no dai* one's parents' generation
代が変わる *dai ga kawaru* be succeeded, change hands
お代を払う *odai o harau* pay the bill

KUN

【**ka(waru) 代わる**】substitute, be substituted for (a person), take the place of
代わる代わる *kawarugawaru* by turns, alternately
父親に代わって言う *chichioya ni kawatte iu* speak for one's father
...に代わって *...ni kawatte* for..., in place of..., instead of...
機械が人力に代わる *Kikai ga jinryoku ni kawaru* Machinery takes the place of human labor

【**ka(wari) 代わり**】
①ⓐ substitution, substitute
ⓑ substitute, deputy, proxy
父の代わりとして *chichi no kawari to shite* in place of one's father
身代わり *migawari* substitution; substitute, stand-in; scapegoat
② compensation, exchange
歩く代わりに走る *aruku kawari ni hashiru* run instead of walk
お代わり *okawari* second helping
③ though...on the other hand
高価な代わりに持ちが良い *Kōka na kawari ni mochi ga yoi* Though it is expensive, on the other hand it will last a long time

【**-ga(wari) -代わり**】[suffix] substitute, replacement
住所録代わり *jūshorokugawari* substitute for an address book

【**ka(eru) 代える**】substitute, use in place of, replace (something) with (another)
代え *kae* substitute, proxy
...に代えて *...ni kaete* instead of..., in place of...
BさんをAさんに代える *bī-san o ē-san ni kaeru* substitute Mr. A for Mr. B

【**yo 代**】
① era of rule, age
大正の代 *taishō no yo* Taisho era
明治天皇の代に *meiji tennō no yo ni* under the rule of Emperor Meiji
② reign, rule
君が代 *kimigayo* Imperial reign; title of Japanese national anthem

【**shiro[1] 代**】cost, charge; rice seedling; material, ingredient
薬の代 *kusuri no shiro* cost of medicine
飲み代 *nomishiro* drinking money
苗代 *nawashiro* bed for rice seedlings, rice nursery
代物 *shiromono slang* thing, stuff; business; guy

【**shiro[2] 代**】
[in compounds]
① margin, blank, allowance
糊代 *norishiro* overlap width; margin to paste up
研削代 *kensakushiro* grinding allowance
② substitute, symbol
身の代金 *minoshirokin* ransom
御霊代 *mitamashiro* something worshiped as a symbol for the spirit of the dead
③ share, portion
取り代 *torishiro* one's share, portion

SYNONYMS

❶ⓐ substitute
摂 ACT AS REGENT → 650
ⓐ change and replace
替 REPLACE → 2783
迭 ALTERNATE → 3077
交 INTERCHANGE → 2015
換 EXCHANGE → 587
転 turn into → 1480
遷 undergo transition → 3170
化 CHANGE INTO, -ize → 21
変 CHANGE → 2069
更 change → 3541
改 change → 243
易 change → 2411
❷ⓐ generation
世 generation → 3496
❸ⓐ long time periods
世 AGE → 3496
紀 ERA → 1276
時 TIME → 924
期 period → 1704
朝 dynastic period → 1695
❹ fee and price
賃 CHARGES → 2694
銭 money paid → 1725
料 FEE → 1292
費 EXPENSE → 2607
価 PRICE → 87
値 price → 109

HOMOPHONES

kawaru ⇨ 替 2783 換 587 変 2069
kawari ⇨ 替 2783 換 587 変 2069
kaeru ⇨ 替 2783 換 587 変 2069
kae ⇨ 替 2783 換 587 変 2069
yo ⇨ 世 3496

NOTE

⇨ see USAGE notes at 変 2069 and 台 2005 and 世 3496
⇨ see COMPOUND FORMATION for 代謝(＝新陳代謝) *taisha* (＝*shinchintaisha*) ⇨ 謝 1620

付付け

31 FU tsu(keru) -tsu(keru) -zu(keru) tsu(ke) tsu(ke)- -tsu(ke) -zu(ke) -zuke tsu(ku) -zu(ku) tsu(ki) -tsu(ki) -tsuki -zu(ki) -zuki

ノ 亻 仁 付 付 (1 2 3 4 5)

CH 付 fù

Radical	Strokes
亻 9	5-2-3
Grade	**Freq**
Jōyō-4	326
1 - 2 - 3	

2-3 亻

▶ATTACH

COMPOUNDS

[sometimes also 附 347]

❶ⓐ **attach, append, add to, affix**
ⓑ **attached, additional, supplementary**
ⓒ [original meaning] **attach itself to, stick to, adhere to**

付記する *fuki suru* add, write in addition
添付する *tenpu suru* attach, append, annex
貼付する *chōfu* (=*tenpu*) *suru* stick, paste, append
付録 *furoku* appendix, supplement
付言 *fugen* postscript, additional remarks
付図 *fuzu* attached map, appended figure [graph]
付則 *fusoku* additional rules, bylaw
付着する *fuchaku suru* adhere [cling] to, agglutinate; cohere

❷ be attached to, belong to, be affiliated with; be incidental to

付属する *fuzoku suru* be attached to, belong to
付随する *fuzui suru* accompany, be incidental to, be annexed to
付帯の *futai no* incidental, accessory, collateral

❸ abbrev. of 付属校 *fuzokukō* or 付属病院 *fuzoku byōin*: attached [affiliated] school, hospital in affiliation

東大付 *tōdaifu* school attached to Tokyo University

❹ⓐ **deliver, hand over, grant**
ⓑ entrust, commit to

付与する *fuyo suru* give, grant, allow, bestow
寄付する *kifu suru* contribute, donate
交付 *kōfu* delivery, grant, transfer, service
給付する *kyūfu suru* make a presentation, grant, pay
送付する *sōfu suru* send, remit
配付する *haifu suru* distribute, deal out
付託する *futaku suru* commit to, refer to, submit to

❺ adjacent, near to

付近 *fukin* neighborhood, environs, vicinity

INDEPENDENT

【fu 付(=附)】 appendix; supplement

付年表 *fu nenpyō* appendix: chronological table

【fusuru 付する(=附する)】 attach, append, add to, affix; commit [submit] to, refer to; consign to, dispose of

KUN

【tsu(keru) 付ける】

[sometimes also 附ける]

① attach, affix, stick, fasten, add (on), append; set, put (one thing on another)

付け加える *tsukekuwaeru* add
着付け *kitsuke* dressing, fitting
コップに口を付ける *koppu ni kuchi o tsukeru* put one's lips to a glass

② apply, put on

薬を付ける *kusuri o tsukeru* apply medicine

③ leave a mark on

染みを付ける *shimi o tsukeru* stain, blot, smudge

④ write, make an entry

帳簿に付ける *chōbo ni tsukeru* enter in a book

⑤ⓐ give, impart, direct (one's attention)
ⓑ set (a price)

元気を付ける *genki o tsukeru* give courage to, encourage
裏付け *urazuke* guarantee, endorsement; support, backing; substantiation, proof
貸し付け *kashitsuke* loaning
値段を高く付ける *nedan o takaku tsukeru* put a high price on

⑥ provide (a person) with an attendant, place a person in attendance (on)

護衛を付ける *goei o tsukeru* provide (a person) with a bodyguard

⑦ follow, trail, shadow

後を付ける *ato o tsukeru* follow, tag along

⑧ kindle, set (fire)

付け木 *tsukegi* spill (piece of wood for lighting)

⑨ load, put on, dish up

干し草を付けた馬 *hoshikusa o tsuketa uma* horse loaded with hay

⑩ settle, bring to terms

話を付ける *hanashi o tsukeru* settle a matter; negotiate, arrange

⑪ [in the form of 付けて *tsukete*] refer to, relate to, connect with

それに付けても *sore ni tsukete mo* in this

connection
⑫ unclassified compounds
受付 *uketsuke* receipt, reception, acceptance; receptionist, information clerk; information office [desk]

【-tsu(keru) -付ける】
① be accustomed [used] to
読み付けている *yomitsukete iru* be accustomed to reading
② perform an action vigorously [vehemently]
叱り付ける *shikaritsukeru* scold away, rebuke strongly, bawl out
③ perceive, detect
聞き付ける *kikitsukeru* hear, catch (the sound)

【-zu(keru) -付ける】 [verbal suffix] give, impart, provide with
位置付ける *ichizukeru* locate, position
関係付ける *kankeizukeru* connect with, relate to

【tsu(ke) 付け】 bill; account, credit
付けを払う *tsuke o harau* pay a bill
付けで買う *tsuke de kau* buy on credit

【tsu(ke)- 付け-】
①ⓐ attached, fixed
ⓑ external (medicine)
付け紐 *tsukehimo* sash attached to child's clothes
付け薬 *tsukegusuri* external medicine
② false (mustache), sham
付け髭 *tsukehige* false mustache [beard]

【-tsu(ke) -付け】 one's favorite, accustomed
行き付けの場所 *ikitsuke no basho* one's favorite place

【-zu(ke) -付け, -zuke -付】
① attaching, affixing
糊付け *norizuke* pasting
② [suffix] dated
八日付 *yōkazuke* dated the eighth

【tsu(ku) 付く】
[sometimes also 附く]
①ⓐ attach itself to, stick (to), adhere (to); be connected with
ⓑ come in contact with, touch, reach
結び付き *musubitsuki* connection, relation, alliance
近付く *chikazuku* approach, near, get near; get acquainted
追い付く *oitsuku* overtake, catch up with
② be attached to, belong to, join, associate with; take up the cause of
付き合う *tsukiau* keep company with, get along with
敵に付く *teki ni tsuku* take the side of the enemy
③ gain (weight, power), become proficient, grow (wise)
肉が付く *niku ga tsuku* gain [put on] weight
④ attend on, go with, accompany
付き添う *tsukisou* accompany, attend on, escort
⑤ be installed, be built
電話が付いた *Denwa ga tsuita* A telephone was installed
⑥ be written, be registered
帳面に付いている *chōmen ni tsuite iru* be written [entered] in a book
⑦ be perceived [detected]
目に付く *me ni tsuku* catch one's eye, attract one's attention
気付く *kizuku* notice, become aware of, find out
⑧ catch fire, be ignited
火が付く *hi ga tsuku* catch fire, be ignited
⑨ take (root)
根が付く *ne ga tsuku* take [strike] root
⑩ cost, amount to
安く付く *yasuku tsuku* come cheaper
⑪ be lucky
付いている *tsuite iru* be in luck
⑫ be settled, be established
話が付く *hanashi ga tsuku* come to terms, reach agreement

【-zu(ku) -付く】
[verbal suffix]
① gain
調子付く *chōshizuku* warm up; be elated, be puffed up
② be absorbed in
演劇付く *engekizuku* be absorbed in a play
③ become
元気付く *genkizuku* become heightened in spirits, get encouraged; recover one's strength

【tsu(ki) 付き】
① ability to stick, impression (quality of printing)
付きが良い *tsuki ga yoi* stay well (on)
② attendant, escort; attendance
お付き *otsuki* attendant; attendance
③ ease of kindling
火付きが悪い *hitsuki ga warui* be slow to kindle
④ luck
付きが変わった *Tsuki ga kawatta* My luck changed

【-tsu(ki) -付き, -tsuki -付】
[also suffix]
① with, including
バス付きの部屋 *basutsuki no heya* room with bath
期限付きの *kigentsuki no* with a fixed time, with a deadline
② appearance, state, condition
顔付き *kaotsuki* face, countenance; expression, look

目付き *metsuki* look in one's eyes, expression

【-zu(ki) -付き, -zuki -付】[suffix] attached to

大使館付き武官 *taishikanzuki bukan* military officer attached to the embassy

SYNONYMS

❶ⓐ & ❶ⓑ add to

附 ATTACH → 347
加 ADD → 38
追 add → 3096
添 ADD TO → 529

❶ⓒ stick

附 attach itself to → 347
着 STICK → 3316

❹ⓐ transfer

附 deliver → 347
渡 hand over → 611
譲 CEDE → 1649

USAGE

❶ tsukeru

付ける

[sometimes also 附ける]

① attach, affix, stick, fasten, add (on), append; set, put (one thing on another)
② apply, put on
③ leave a mark on
④ write, make an entry
⑤ⓐ give, impart, direct (one's attention)
ⓑ set (a price)
⑥ provide (a person) with an attendant, place a person in attendance (on)
⑦ follow, trail, shadow
⑧ kindle, set (fire)
⑨ load, put on, dish up
⑩ settle, bring to terms
⑪ [in the form of 付けて *tsukete*] refer to, relate to, connect with
⑫ unclassified compounds

附ける

[usu. 付ける] same as 付ける

着ける

① (cause to arrive) bring (a vehicle or boat) alongside, put ashore, berth
② put on clothes, don, wear, be dressed
③ (place a person in a position) settle, settle [seat] a person, situate, steady
④ set about, start, commence

就ける

① install [place] a person in a position
② [formerly 即ける] enthrone
③ make (a person) study under (a teacher)

即ける

[now usu. 就ける] enthrone

点ける

light, turn [switch] on

漬ける

① pickle (vegetables), salt, preserve
② immerse, steep, soak, dip

❷ -zuke

-付け

① attaching, affixing
② [suffix] dated

-漬け

[also suffix]
ⓐ pickles
ⓑ pickling with, preserving in

❸ tsuku

付く

[sometimes also 附く]

①ⓐ attach itself to, stick (to), adhere (to); be connected with
ⓑ come in contact with, touch, reach
② be attached to, belong to, join, associate with; take up the cause of
③ gain (weight, power), become proficient, grow (wise)
④ attend on, go with, accompany
⑤ be installed, be built
⑥ be written, be registered
⑦ be perceived [detected]
⑧ catch fire, be ignited
⑨ take (root)
⑩ cost, amount to
⑪ be lucky
⑫ be settled, be established

附く

[usu. 付く] same as 付く

着く

①ⓐ arrive at, reach, come to hand
ⓑ (succeed in touching) reach, come in contact with, touch
② (come to rest in a position) settle, settle [seat] oneself, become situated, settle down (in a place)

就く

①ⓐ set about a task, set out, enter upon, take up (a position), assume (office), enter (a business)
ⓑ set out, start, leave
② [formerly 即く] ascend to (the throne)
③ study under (a teacher)

即く

① [now usu. 就く] ascend to (the throne)
② be in immediate [close] contact, be based on

点く

be lighted, be switched on, go on

HOMOPHONES

tsukeru ⇨ 附 347 着 3316 就 1694 即 1120 点 2084 漬 702

-zuke ⇨ 漬 702

tsuku ⇨ 附 347 着 3316 就 1694 即 1120 点 2084

2-3
亻

仙 32 SEN SENTO▲

ノ 亻 仆 仙 仙 (1 2 3 4 5)

CH 仙 xiān

Radical	Strokes
亻 9	5-2-3
Grade	**Freq**
Jōyō	1137
1-2-3	

▶**IMMORTAL MOUNTAIN FAIRY**

COMPOUNDS

❶ⓐ **transcendent immortal fairy living in the mountains and capable of performing miracles, Taoist immortal, supernatural being**
ⓑ **hermit, recluse**
仙人 *sennin* immortal mountain fairy; hermit, unworldly person
仙術 *senjutsu* fairy magic
仙境 *senkyō* fairyland, enchanted land
神仙 *shinsen* supernatural being
酒仙 *shusen* hermit who enjoys drinking; son of Bacchus
❷ master (as of an art)
歌仙 *kasen* master [major] poet
❸ cent
五十仙 *gojussento* 50 cents
❹ unclassified compounds
仙骨 *senkotsu* sacrum
水仙 *suisen* narcissus

SYNONYMS

❶ **religious persons**
聖 SAINT → 2830

2-3
亻

仔 33 SHI ko

CH 仔 zǐ zǎi zī

Radical	Strokes
亻 9	5-2-3
Grade	**Freq**
Reference	
1-2-3	

COMPOUNDS

❶ [now usu. 子 *ko*] offspring, youngling; puppy; cub; roe
仔犬 *koinu* puppy
❷ [now usu. 子 *shi*] minute, fine, small
仔細 *shisai* particulars; reasons, circumstances

HOMOPHONES

ko ⇨ 子 3390 児 2546 娘 406 小 7

NOTE

⇨ see USAGE note at 子 3390

2-3
亻

仕 34 SHI JI tsuka(eru)

ノ 亻 仁 什 仕 (1 2 3 4 5)

CH 仕 shì

Radical	Strokes
亻 9	5-2-3
Grade	**Freq**
Jōyō-3	472
1-2-3	

▶**SERVE** ▶**DO**

COMPOUNDS

❶ **serve (under), take service under, enter the government service**
仕官 *shikan* entering the government service; find service with (a lord)
奉仕 *hōshi* attendance, service
出仕する *shusshi suru* enter the service of; attend (one's office)
❷ used for *shi* as the second (continuative) base of the verb *suru*: **do**
仕事 *shigoto* work, employment, business
仕立て *shitate* tailoring, dressmaking
仕方 *shikata* way, method, means
仕手 *shite* doer; protagonist in a noh drama; operator, speculator
仕組み *shikumi* construction; arrangement; plan, plot
仕上げ *shiage* finish, elaboration, completion
仕返し *shikaeshi* doing over, tit for tat, revenge
仕合わせ *shiawase* [also 幸せ, formerly also 倖せ] happiness, blessing; good fortune
給仕 *kyūji* office boy, page (boy), waiter; ser-

vice at table

INDEPENDENT

【shi 仕】 government service

仕を致す *shi o itasu* leave the government service

KUN

【tsuka(eru) 仕える】 serve (under), take service under, enter the service of the shogunate

宮仕え *miyazukae* court service

夫に良く仕える *otto ni yoku tsukaeru* be devoted [attentive] to one's husband

神に仕える *kami ni tsukaeru* serve God

二君に仕えず *nikun ni tsukaezu* not serve two masters

SYNONYMS

❶ work

勤める serve (in an office) → 1818

働 WORK → 153

稼 WORK (for a living) → 1230

労 LABOR → 2548

❷ do and act

為 DO → 3577

致す DO HUMBLY → 1316

行 ACT → 212

作 WORK → 68

HOMOPHONES

shiawase ⇨ 幸せ 2216 倖せ 118

仕合わせ 34, 2019

NOTE

⇨ see USAGE note at 幸 2216

⇨ see COMPOUND FORMATION for 仕合わせ *shiawase* ⇨ 合 2019

他 他 他

35 TA hoka▲

ノ イ 仆 他 他 (1 2 3 4 5)

Ⓒⓗ 他 tā

Radical	Strokes
亻 9	5-2-3
Grade	**Freq**
Jōyō-3	465
1-2-3	

2-3 亻

▶OTHER

COMPOUNDS

❶ⓐ [also prefix] **other, another**

ⓑ others, other people

他方 *tahō* other side [hand]

他意 *tai* other intention, secret purpose, ulterior motive

他人 *tanin* another person, other people; stranger

他国 *takoku* foreign countries, another province

他年 *tanen* some other year, some day

他府県 *tafuken* other prefectures

他殺 *tasatsu* homicide, murder

排他的な *haitateki na* exclusive, clannish

❷ transitive verb

自他 *jita* oneself and others; transitive and intransitive

INDEPENDENT

【ta 他】 others, other people; other things, the rest

他の言に惑わされる *ta no gen ni madowasareru* be led astray by others' opinion

その他 *sono ta* the others, the rest

KUN

【hoka 他】 [also 外] something other than, the rest

他の *hoka no* other, another, different, else

他ならぬ *hokanaranu* nothing but, no other than

山田他 *yamada hoka* Yamada and others [et al.]

SYNONYMS

❶ⓐ other

余 other → 2042

別 ANOTHER → 1117

HOMOPHONES

hoka ⇨ 外 186

NOTE

⇨ see USAGE note at 外 186

仏

36

▶INDIVIDUAL ▶GENERAL COUNTER

handwritten abbreviation for 個 117

2-3 亻

2-3 冫

氷

37

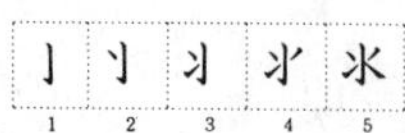

Radical	Strokes
水 85	5-5-0
Grade	Freq
Radical	
◧ 1 - 2 - 3	

RADICAL 85

shitamizu, variant of 水 *mizu* 'water'

⇨ see 水 10 for radical description

2-3 力

加

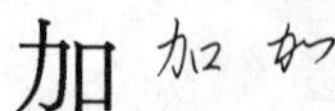

38 KA kuwa(eru) kuwa(waru)

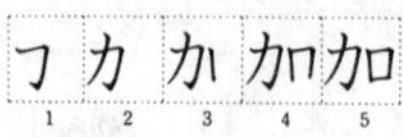

CH 加 jiā

Radical	Strokes
力 19	5-2-3
Grade	Freq
Jōyō-4	177
◧ 1 - 2 - 3	

▶**ADD**

COMPOUNDS

❶ⓐ **add, append**

ⓑ **add to, increase**

ⓒ *math* **add, sum up**

加速度 *kasokudo* acceleration

加味する *kami suru* tinge with, add to

追加する *tsuika suru* add, append, supplement

増加 *zōka* increase, gain, rise

加算 *kasan* addition

加減 *kagen* addition and subtraction; degree, extent; adjustment

❷ affect, influence, inflict

加工 *kakō* processing, manufacturing

加害者 *kagaisha* assailant, assaulter

❸ **join, take part in, participate**

加盟 *kamei* participation, affiliation

加入金 *kanyūkin* admission fee

加担(=荷担) *katan* assistance, support, participation

参加する *sanka suru* participate, join, take part in

❹ used phonetically for *ka*, esp. in place names, as:

ⓐ Canada

ⓑ California

日加 *nikka* Japan and Canada

加州 *kashū* State of California

INDEPENDENT

【**ka 加**】 addition, plus; Canada

KUN

【**kuwa(eru) 加える**】 *vt* add, append; add, sum up, increase; include, count in; inflict (an injury on), give

付け加える *tsukekuwaeru* add

五に六を加えよ *Go ni roku o kuwaeyo* Add six to five

仲間に加える *nakama ni kuwaeru* include in the circle

圧力を加える *atsuryoku o kuwaeru* press, apply pressure to

【**kuwa(waru) 加わる**】 *vi* join in, participate; gain (in), grow, increase

会議に加わる *kaigi ni kuwawaru* take part in a conference

暑さが加わる *atsusa ga kuwawaru* get hotter

SYNONYMS

❶ⓐ **add to**

追 add → 3096

添 ADD TO → 529

付 ATTACH → 31

附 ATTACH → 347

ⓑ **increase**

増 INCREASE → 677

殖 MULTIPLY → 994

倍 DOUBLE → 108

ⓒ **add**

足す add → 2188

❸ **participate and join**

参 PARTICIPATE → 2066

与 take part in → 3421

入 ENTER → 3370

❹ⓐ **North American countries**

米 AMERICA → 3529

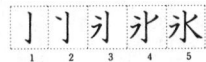

氷 氵 氷

39 HYŌ kōri hi kō(ru)▲

CH 冰 bīng

Radical	Strokes
水 85	5-4-1
Grade	**Freq**
Jōyō-3	1213
◧ 1 - 2 - 3	

2-3 冫

▶ICE

COMPOUNDS

ⓐ ice

ⓑ turn into ice, freeze

氷晶 *hyōshō* ice crystal
氷河 *hyōga* glacier
氷山 *hyōzan* iceberg
氷雪 *hyōsetsu* ice and snow
樹氷 *juhyō* trees covered with ice
製氷 *seihyō* ice making
氷点 *hyōten* freezing point
氷結する *hyōketsu suru* freeze, congeal

KUN

【kōri 氷】[also suffix] ice, shaved ice
氷枕 *kōrimakura* ice pillow
氷水 *kōrimizu* ice water; shaved ice
氷菓子 *kōrigashi* frozen sweet, ice candy
ぶっ欠き氷 *bukkakigōri* chipped ice

【hi 氷】ice, hail
氷雨 *hisame elegant* hail; chilly rain (esp. in autumn)

【kō(ru) 氷る】[now usu. 凍る] freeze
⇨ see 凍 129 for compounds

SYNONYMS

ⓐ **kinds of frozen water**
雪 SNOW → 2759

ⓐ **kinds of water**
水 WATER → 10
湯 HOT WATER → 612
汽 STEAM → 264

HOMOPHONES

kōru ⇨ 凍 129

NOTE

⇨ see USAGE note at 凍 129
★do not confuse with 永 1937

癶

40

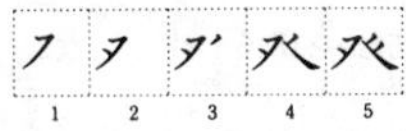

Radical	Strokes
癶 105	5-5-0
Grade	**Freq**
Radical	
◧ 1 - 2 - 3	

2-3 ヲ

RADICAL 105

Standard form: 癶 *hatsugashira* 'spread legs' (発 登 癸)
Description: used for character classification

以 以 以

41 I mot(te)▲

CH 以 yǐ

Radical	Strokes
人 9	5-2-3
Grade	**Freq**
Jōyō-4	139
◧ 1 - 2 - 3	

2-3 レ

▶TO THE...OF ▶BY MEANS OF

COMPOUNDS

❶ directional preposition placed before localizers to indicate the point of reference in compounds related to direction, time or range: **to the...of, -ward**

以東 *itō* to the east of, eastward
以上 *ijō* or more than, not less than; beyond; the above-mentioned; now that; that's all
以来 *irai* as of, since then, from that time on
以下 *ika* or less than, not more than, under; and downward; the following
以外に *igai ni* except for, excluding
以内 *inai* within, less than
以前 *izen* before, ago, since
以降 *ikō* on and after, hereafter
以後 *igo* after this, from now on, in future; after that, thereafter

❷ by means of, with, using
以心伝心 *ishindenshin* silent [tacit] understanding, empathy
❸ reason, cause
所以 *yuen* (=*shoi*) reason; way of doing

KUN

【mot(te) 以て】 with, by means of; because of; with this
以てする *motte suru* do by the use of
小刀を以て殺す *kogatana o motte korosu* kill (a person) with a knife
山高きを以て *yama takaki o motte* because the mountain is high
以て瞑すべし *Motte meisubeshi* You ought to be content with this
以ての外 *motte no hoka* outrageous, preposterous, scandalous

SYNONYMS

❶ direction indicators
自 from → 3525
来 since → 3551
迄 UP TO → 3201
-向け (bound) for → 3052
-行き bound for → 212
至 to → 2182

COMPOUND FORMATION

以心伝心 *ishindenshin*
以心伝心 'silent [tacit] understanding, empathy', is to convey (伝) one's thoughts or feelings (心) by means of (以 ❷) thoughts (not words).

NOTE

⇨ see COMPOUND FORMATION for 所以 *yuen* ⇨ 所 851

2-4
亻

伐 伐 伐
42 BATSU ki(ru)▲

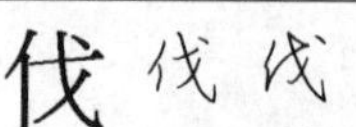

CH 伐 fá

Radical	Strokes
亻 9	6-2-4
Grade	**Freq**
Jōyō	1846
1 - 2 - 4	

▶CUT DOWN

COMPOUNDS

❶ cut down (trees), fell, chop down
伐採する *bassai suru* lumber, fell, deforest
伐木 *batsuboku* felling, cutting, logging
濫伐(=乱伐)する *ranbatsu suru* deforest indiscriminately, cut down [fell] trees recklessly
盗伐 *tōbatsu* secret felling of trees
❷ cut down (one's enemies), strike down, send a punitive expedition against, attack
殺伐な *satsubatsu na* bloody, savage, warlike
征伐 *seibatsu* subjugation, conquest
討伐 *tōbatsu* suppression (of a rebellion), punitive expedition

KUN

【ki(ru) 伐る】 [now usu. 切る] cut down (trees), fell, chop down
木を伐る *ki o kiru* fell a tree

SYNONYMS

❶ cut
切 CUT → 27
刈る CLIP → 28
断 CUT OFF → 1492
裁 CUT OUT → 3299
割 cut with a knife → 1816
剖 DISSECT → 1670
削 CUT BY CHIPPING → 1448
❷ conquer and suppress
討 SUPPRESS BY ARMED FORCE → 1456
征 CONQUER → 293
鎮 QUELL → 1759
靖 PACIFY → 1208

HOMOPHONES

kiru ⇨ 切 27 剪 2306 截 3301 斬 1482

NOTE

⇨ see USAGE note at 切 27

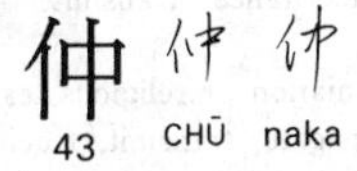

43 CHŪ naka

ノ イ 亻 仆 仲 仲
1 2 3 4 5 6

CH 仲 zhòng

Radical	Strokes
亻 9	6-2-4
Grade	**Freq**
Jōyō-4	873
◧ 1 - 2 - 4	

2-4 亻

▶**INTERMEDIARY**
▶**PERSONAL RELATIONS**

COMPOUNDS

❶ **intermediary, middleman, mediator**
仲介者 *chūkaisha* intermediary, mediator, agent
仲裁人 *chūsainin* arbitrator, mediator

❷ occupying an intermediate position:
ⓐ middle [second-month] of a season
ⓑ middle [second-born] brother
仲秋(=中秋) *chūshū* mid-autumn, August according to the old calendar
仲兄 *chūkei* second brother
伯仲する *hakuchū suru* be equal to

KUN

【naka 仲】

① personal relations, relationship, (familiar) terms, fellowship, friendship
仲が良い *naka ga yoi* be on good terms
仲間 *nakama* company, fellow, comrade, associate
仲直り *nakanaori* reconciliation
恋仲 *koinaka* love relationship

② intermediary, go-between
仲に入る *naka ni hairu* act as an intermediary
仲買人 *nakagainin* broker
仲立ち *nakadachi* intermediation
仲居 *nakai* parlormaid, waitress

③ [in compounds] inner, middle
仲見世通り *nakamisedōri* shopping street in the precincts of a shrine [temple]

SPECIAL READINGS

仲人 *nakōdo* go-between, matchmaker

SYNONYMS

❶ **mediating and mediators**
介 MEDIATE → 1967
紹 INTRODUCE → 1335
媒 INTERMEDIATE → 564

❷ **between**
中 MIDDLE → 3451
間 BETWEEN → 3323
際 inter- → 714

【naka】

① **personal relations**
縁 RELATION → 1386
交 INTERCOURSE → 2015
好 friendship → 208

HOMOPHONES

naka ⇨ 中 3451

COMPOUND FORMATION

❶ 伯仲 *hakuchū*
伯仲する 'be equal to' is a situation where it is difficult to determine which is the first-born brother (伯) and which is the second-born brother (仲 ❷ⓑ).

❷ 仲居 *nakai*
仲居 'parlormaid, waitress' is a person who is (居) an intermediary (仲 *naka* ②) between the customer and the kitchen.

NOTE

⇨ see USAGE note at 中 3451

伝 傳 伝 傳

44 DEN tsuta(waru) tsuta(eru) tsuta(u) -zuta(i) tsute▲

ノ イ 亻 仁 伝 伝
1 2 3 4 5 6

CH 传 chuán zhuàn

Radical	Strokes
亻 9	6-2-4
Grade	**Freq**
Jōyō-4	482
◧ 1 - 2 - 4	

2-4 亻

▶**TRANSMIT**

COMPOUNDS

❶ⓐ (convey from one person or place to another) **transmit, convey, pass on, communicate, initiate**
ⓑ (pass down by inheritance) **transmit, hand down**
ⓒ (disseminate information or religious teachings) **spread, propagate, transmit, teach**
ⓓ [original meaning] transmit by stages, relay
伝達する *dentatsu suru* transmit, convey, communicate; propagate
伝染 *densen* contagion, infection, communication (of a disease)

伝言 *dengon* verbal message, word
伝授する *denju suru* instruct, initiate
中国伝来の *chūgoku-denrai no* imported [transmitted] from China
直伝 *jikiden* direct initiation
伝統 *dentō* tradition, convention
伝説 *densetsu* legend, folk tale
伝承する *denshō suru* hand down, tell from generation to generation
以心伝心 *ishindenshin* silent [tacit] understanding, empathy
遺伝 *iden* hereditary transmission
伝道 *dendō* gospel preaching, missionary work, evangelism
宣伝 *senden* publicity, propaganda; advertisement
駅伝 *ekiden* post-horse, stagecoach; long-distance relay race

❷ *phys* transmit, conduct, convey
伝導 *dendō* conduction, transmission
伝声管 *denseikan* voice pipe, speaking tube

❸ⓐ [also suffix] biography
ⓑ tale, story, fable
伝記 *denki* biography
列伝 *retsuden* series of biographies
ナポレオン伝 *naporeonden* life of Napoleon
外伝 *gaiden* supplementary story; lateral biography

❹ [also suffix] commentary, exposition
古事記伝 *kojikiden* commentary on Kojiki (Ancient Chronicles)

INDEPENDENT

【den 伝】 *colloq* way, manner, trick
いつもの伝で *itsumo no den de* as usual, as is often the case

KUN

【tsuta(waru) 伝わる】 be transmitted [conveyed], spread, be propagated; be handed down, go [come] down, descend; go along, follow
ニュースが伝わった *Nyūsu ga tsutawatta* The news went around
代代伝わる *daidai tsutawaru* be transmitted [handed down] from generation to generation
屋根を伝わって歩く *yane o tsutawatte aruku* walk over the roof

【tsuta(eru) 伝える】
①ⓐ (convey from one person or place to another) transmit, convey, pass on, communicate, initiate
ⓑ (pass down by inheritance) transmit, hand down
ⓒ (disseminate information or religious teachings) spread, propagate, transmit, teach
命令を伝える *meirei o tsutaeru* pass the word
言い伝え *iitsutae* tradition, legend
キリスト教を伝える *kirisutokyō o tsutaeru* introduce Christianity
② *phys* transmit, conduct, convey
熱を伝える *netsu o tsutaeru* conduct heat

【tsuta(u) 伝う】 go along, follow
伝って登る *tsutatte noboru* climb up, shin up

【-zuta(i) -伝い】 [also suffix] along
川伝いに *kawazutai ni* along a river
磯伝いに *isozutai ni* along the beach
海岸伝い *kaiganzutai* along the coast

【tsute 伝】 intermediary, introducer, connection
良い伝が有る *yoi tsute ga aru* have a good connection

SPECIAL READINGS

伝馬船 *tenmasen* lighter, jolly (boat)
手伝う *tetsudau* help, assist, lend a hand

SYNONYMS

❶ⓐ & ❶ⓑ transmit and deliver
逓 RELAY → 3106
届ける DELIVER → 3078
達 deliver → 3139
ⓒ make widely known
布 SPREAD → 2973
流 spread → 441
広 spread → 3035
弘 DISSEMINATE (esp. Buddhism) → 192
及 REACH TO → 3385
❸ⓐ history
歴 PERSONAL HISTORY → 3019
史 HISTORY → 3510
ⓐ records
史 HISTORY → 3510
譜 SYSTEMATIC RECORD → 1637
録 RECORD → 1742
記 written account → 1453
誌 records → 1548

COMPOUND FORMATION

伝統 *dentō*
伝統 'tradition, convention' is that which is handed down (伝 ❶ⓑ) through one's ancestry or lineage (統).

NOTE

⇨ see COMPOUND FORMATION for
遺伝 *iden* ⇨ 遺 3166
以心伝心 *ishindenshin* ⇨ 以 41

伏 伏 伏

45 FUKU fu(seru) fu(su)

ノ イ 仁 付 伏 伏
1 2 3 4 5 6

CH 伏 fú

Radical	Strokes
亻 9	6-2-4
Grade	Freq
Jōyō	1364
1-2-4	

2-4 亻

▶**PROSTRATE**

COMPOUNDS

❶ [original meaning] **prostrate (oneself), fall prostrate, lie down, bend down**
平伏する *heifuku suru* prostrate oneself (before), kiss the ground
起伏 *kifuku* ups and downs, undulations
倒伏 *tōfuku* falling down

❷ [also 服 878] **submit to, yield to**
屈伏 *kuppuku* submission, surrender
降伏 *kōfuku* surrender, submission
折伏 *shakubuku* preaching down

❸ **lie in concealment, hide**
伏兵 *fukuhei* ambush, troops in ambush
伏線 *fukusen* preparation, foreshadow
雌伏 *shifuku* remaining in obscurity, lying low, biding one's time
潜伏 *senpuku* concealment, hiding; latency
埋伏歯 *maifukushi* impacted tooth

INDEPENDENT

【fukusuru 伏する】 prostrate; yield to
威に伏する *i ni fukusuru* yield to power

KUN

【fu(seru) 伏せる】
①ⓐ turn downward, lay upside down, turn over
ⓑ put something over (another)
ⓒ lay under the ground
身を伏せる *mi o fuseru* lie face down
説き伏せる *tokifuseru* argue down, persuade, convince
鶏に籠を伏せる *niwatori ni kago o fuseru* coop hens
待ち伏せる *machibuseru* lie in wait, ambush, conceal oneself in ambush
② keep secret
伏せ字 *fuseji* omission, blank, asterisk

【fu(su) 伏す】 prostrate, fall prostrate, lie down, bend down
伏し目 *fushime* downcast look
ひれ伏す *hirefusu* prostrate oneself before a person

SYNONYMS

❶ **lie down**
寝る lie down → 2329

❷ **submit and surrender**
服 SUBMIT → 878
屈 bend in submission → 3079
降 surrender → 458

❸ **hide**
隠 HIDE → 713
潜 LURK → 746
匿 CONCEAL → 3011
忍 perform by stealth → 2212

USAGE

fuseru

伏せる
①ⓐ turn downward, lay upside down, turn over
ⓑ put something over (another)
ⓒ lay under the ground
② keep secret

臥せる
① lie down
② be confined to one's bed, be sick in bed

HOMOPHONES

fuseru ⇨ 臥 1440

伎

46 GI KI

CH 伎 jì

Radical	Strokes
亻 9	6-2-4
Grade	Freq
Reference	
1-2-4	

2-4 亻

COMPOUNDS

❶ [now also 技 *gi* 248] [original meaning] skill, ability, craft, art
伎倆(=技量) *giryō* skill, ability, capacity

❷ actor, performer
伎楽 *gigaku* ancient mask show
歌舞伎 *kabuki* kabuki

2-4
亻

伍

47 GO NAMES kumi atsumu

丿 亻 仁 仃 伍 伍
1 2 3 4 5 6

CH 伍 wǔ

Radical	Strokes
亻 9	6-2-4
Grade	**Freq**
Names	2103
1 - 2 - 4	

▶RANK

COMPOUNDS

❶ⓐ rank, file, line

ⓑ (members of the same group) ranks, rank and file, squad, group

隊伍 *taigo* ranks, line array, formation

落伍(=落後)する *rakugo suru* straggle, drop out of line, fall out of the ranks

先頭伍 *sentōgo* leading file

伍長 *gochō* corporal; foreman

❷ five—used in legal documents and checks

金伍千円也 *kin gosen'en nari* five thousand yen

❸ [archaic]

ⓐ military unit of five soldiers (in Zhou Dynasty China)

ⓑ unit of administration consisting of five houses

伍伯 *gohaku* leader of a military unit of five soldiers

INDEPENDENT

【go 伍】five (⇒❷); military unit of five soldiers; rank, file, line

伍を重ねる *go o kasaneru* double the ranks

【gosuru 伍する】rank with, associate with

NAMES

永伍 *eigo* male name

伍子 *kumiko* female name

SYNONYMS

❶ⓐ linear arrangements

列 ROW → 824

行 LINE (esp. of print) → 212

欄 COLUMN → 1103

ⓑ groups

班 SQUAD → 946

軍 team → 2080

群 GROUP (of any kind) → 1540

組 group (of people) → 1337

陣 lineup → 455

連 set → 3103

族 common-interest group (*slang*) → 958

党 PARTY → 2581

隊 PARTY (organized group) → 625

団 BODY → 3053

❷ five

五 FIVE → 3436

2-4
亻

仰

48 GYŌ KŌ ao(gu) ō(se) os(sharu)▲

丿 亻 亻 仃 仰 仰
1 2 3 4 5 6

CH 仰 yǎng

Radical	Strokes
亻 9	6-2-4
Grade	**Freq**
Jōyō	1569
1 - 2 - 4	

▶LOOK UP

COMPOUNDS

❶ [original meaning] **look up, face upward**

仰視する *gyōshi suru* look up

仰角 *gyōkaku* angle of elevation

仰臥 *gyōga* lying face up

仰天する *gyōten suru* be astounded

❷ look up to, respect, revere

仰望する *gyōbō suru* look up to, revere

信仰する *shinkō suru* believe in, have faith

KUN

【ao(gu) 仰ぐ】look up, face upward; look up to, respect; turn to, ask for; drink

仰ぎ見る *aogimiru* look up

仰向け *aomuke* facing upward

師と仰ぐ *shi to aogu* look up to (a person) as one's preceptor

助言を仰ぐ *jogen o aogu* ask for advice

毒を仰ぐ *doku o aogu* take poison

【ō(se) 仰せ】statement, wishes or command of a superior

仰せに従って *ōse ni shitagatte* in obedience to your wishes, as you say

仰せつかる *ōsetsukaru* be ordered, be appointed

【os(sharu) 仰しゃる】honorific verb equiv. to 言う *iu*: say, tell, speak, talk; call

お名前は何と仰しゃいますか *Onamae wa nan to osshaimasu ka* What is your name, sir?

SYNONYMS

❶ see and look

望 LOOK AFAR → 2742

眺 LOOK OUT OVER → 1171
顧 LOOK BACK → 1900
覧 LOOK OVER → 2854
観 VIEW → 1880
目 look → 3043
見 SEE → 2544
視 REGARD → 972
看 WATCH → 3220
察 INSPECT → 2347

❷ **respect**
敬 RESPECT → 1701
欽 REVERE → 1690
崇 REVERENCE → 2297
尚 VALUE HIGHLY → 2233
重 set value on → 3573
拝 WORSHIP → 303
慕 ADORE → 2353
尊 HONOR → 2324

伊

49 I NAMES kore tada yoshi

CH 伊 yī

Radical	Strokes
亻 9	6-2-4
Grade	**Freq**
Names	1971
◧ 1-2-4	

2-4 亻

▶PHONETIC [i] ▶ITALY

COMPOUNDS

❶ **used phonetically for *i*, esp. in proper names**
伊太利 *itarī* Italy
伊呂波 *iroha* iroha, the Japanese syllabary [alphabet]

❷ⓐ **Italy**
ⓑ Italian (language)
日独伊 *nichidokui* Japan, Germany and Italy
駐伊 *chūi* stationed in Italy
日伊辞典 *nichii-jiten* Japanese-Italian dictionary

❸ [archaic]
ⓐ this
ⓑ he

❹ unclassified compounds
伊達者 *datesha* dandy, coxcomb, beau

INDEPENDENT

【i 伊】Italy

NAMES

伊豆 *izu* place name
伊勢 *ise* place name
伊東 *itō* surname also place name
伊藤 *itō* surname
伊沢 *izawa* surname
伊部 *korebe* surname

SYNONYMS

❶ **phonetic [i]**
斐 PHONETIC [i] → 2776

❷ⓐ **European countries**
英 ENGLAND → 2238
独 GERMANY → 395
仏 FRANCE → 19
西 Spain → 3520
蘭 Holland → 2383
露 Russia → 2818

仮 假

50 KA KE kari kari-

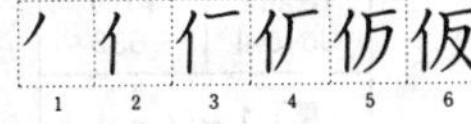

CH 假 jiǎ

Radical	Strokes
亻 9	6-2-4
Grade	**Freq**
Jōyō-5	1295
◧ 1-2-4	

2-4 亻

▶TEMPORARY

COMPOUNDS

❶ **temporary, provisional, transient**
仮設の *kasetsu no* provisional, temporary; hypothetical
仮眠 *kamin* nap, doze
仮定 *katei* assumption, supposition
仮説 *kasetsu* hypothesis
仮称 *kashō* temporary name
仮寓 *kagū* temporary residence
仮死 *kashi* suspended animation, apparent death
仮性近視 *kasei-kinshi* false nearsightedness, pseudomyopia

❷ **fake, false, sham, feigned, pseudo**
仮面 *kamen* mask, disguise
仮装 *kasō* disguise, fancy dress
仮名 *kamei* pseudonym, alias
仮病 *kebyō* feigned illness

❸ borrow, avail oneself of, allow

仮借無き *kashakunaki* merciless(ly)

KUN

【**kari** 仮】provisional, temporary; assumed

仮に *kari ni* provisionally, tentatively; for example; supposing that

仮の親 *kari no oya* expedient parent, foster parent

仮の名 *kari no na* assumed name, alias

【**kari-** 仮-】[also prefix] temporary, provisional

仮橋 *karibashi* temporary bridge

仮住まい *karizumai* temporary residence

仮契約 *karikeiyaku* provisional contract

仮溶接 *kariyōsetsu* tack welding

SPECIAL READINGS

仮名(＝仮字▲) *kana* kana, Japanese syllabary

SYNONYMS

❶ **temporary**

暫 for the time being → 2864

❷ **false**

虚 FALSE → 3237

偽 sham → 131

擬 imitation → 788

義 artificial → 2338

2-4

亻

件

51 KEN kudan▲

1 2 3 4 5 6

CH 件 jiàn

Radical	Strokes
亻 9	6-2-4
Grade	**Freq**
Jōyō-5	256
1 - 2 - 4	

▶MATTER

COMPOUNDS

ⓐ **matter, affair, case, incident, item**

ⓑ **counter for cases or affairs**

一件 *ikken* matter, affair, item

用件 *yōken* matter (of business), things to be done

人件費 *jinkenhi* personnel expenses, labor cost

条件 *jōken* condition; item, proviso

事件 *jiken* affair, incident, case, event

案件 *anken* matter, case, item

要件 *yōken* important matter; necessary condition

別件 *bekken* separate case, another matter

件数 *kensū* number of cases or items

五十件 *gojikken* 50 cases, 50 items

INDEPENDENT

【**ken** 件】matter, affair, case

例の件 *rei no ken* the matter you have been talking about

KUN

【**kudan** 件】the aforesaid matter

件の一件 *kudan no ikken* the aforesaid matter, the matter in question

SYNONYMS

ⓐ **affair**

儀 affair → 169

事 AFFAIR → 3567

ⓑ **general counters**

個 GENERAL COUNTER → 117

箇 COUNTER FOR ITEMS → 2700

点 counter for articles → 2084

丁 MISCELLANEOUS COUNTER → 3348

2-4

亻

休

52 KYŪ yasu(mu) yasu(maru) yasu(meru)

1 2 3 4 5 6

CH 休 xiū

Radical	Strokes
亻 9	6-2-4
Grade	**Freq**
Jōyō-1	636
1 - 2 - 4	

▶REST

COMPOUNDS

❶ⓐ [original meaning] **rest, repose, relax**

ⓑ abbrev. of 休暇 *kyūka* or 休業 *kyūgyō*: **holiday, vacation, suspension of business, day off**

休憩 *kyūkei* rest, repose

休息 *kyūsoku* rest, repose

休養 *kyūyō* rest, recuperation, relaxation

休止 *kyūshi* pause, standstill, dormancy; rest

休日 *kyūjitsu* holiday, day off

休暇 *kyūka* holiday, vacation

休業 *kyūgyō* suspension of business

休火山 *kyūkazan* dormant volcano

本日休診 *honjitsu kyūshin* Office Closed Today (sign at doctor's office)

連休 *renkyū* consecutive holidays

週休 *shūkyū* weekly holiday

定休 *teikyū* regular holiday
臨休 *rinkyū* extra [special] holiday
産休 *sankyū* maternity leave
❷ **suspend, discontinue; cancel**
休演する *kyūen suru* suspend performance
休会 *kyūkai* adjournment, recess (of the Diet)
休戦 *kyūsen* truce, armistice
休講 *kyūkō* cancellation of lecture (for the day)
運休 *unkyū* suspension of (bus) service
閑話休題 *kanwakyūdai* to return to the subject
❸ tranquil, peaceful
休戚 *kyūseki* weal and woe

INDEPENDENT

【kyūsu 休す】 cease, come to an end
万事休す *Banji kyūsu* It's all up [over] (with us) / Nothing can be done now

KUN

【yasu(mu) 休む】 rest, take a rest, repose; suspend, discontinue; be absent; go to bed, retire
休み *yasumi* rest, recess; suspension; vacation, holiday; absence
昼休み *hiruyasumi* noon recess, lunch break
夏休み *natsuyasumi* summer vacation
お休みなさい *oyasuminasai* good night

【yasu(maru) 休まる】 [sometimes also 安まる] feel rested; be set at ease
体が休まる *karada ga yasumaru* be [feel] rested

【yasu(meru) 休める】 rest, give a rest; suspend; set (a person's mind) at ease; lay land fallow
骨休め *honeyasume* relaxation, recreation
気休め *kiyasume* soothing, consolation

SYNONYMS

❶ⓐ **rest**
息 rest → 2647
憩 TAKE A REST → 2890
ⓑ **holiday**
暇 leave of absence → 1012
❷ **discontinue**
停 suspend → 139
止 STOP → 2941
断 CUT OFF → 1492
廃 ABOLISH → 3146
絶 BREAK OFF → 1353

USAGE

yasumaru
休まる
[sometimes also 安まる] feel rested; be set at ease
安まる
[usu. 休まる] feel rested; be set at ease

HOMOPHONES

yasumaru ⇨ 安 2171

NOTE

⇨ see COMPOUND FORMATION for 閑話休題 *kanwakyūdai* ⇨ 閑 3322

任 任 任

53 NIN maka(seru) maka(su)

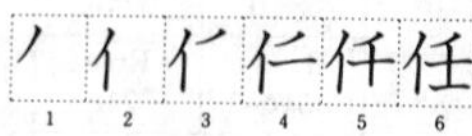

CH 任 rèn rén

Radical	Strokes
亻 9	6-2-4
Grade	**Freq**
Jōyō-5	270
1 - 2 - 4	

2-4 亻

▶OFFICE ▶LEAVE TO

COMPOUNDS

❶ⓐ **office, duties, official post**
ⓑ **duty, responsibility**
ⓒ take a duty upon oneself, assume responsibility
任期 *ninki* one's term of office
就任 *shūnin* assumption of office, inauguration
辞任 *jinin* resignation
留任 *ryūnin* remaining in office
赴任する *funin suru* proceed to a new post
解任 *kainin* release from office, dismissal, discharge
任務 *ninmu* duty, part, function; mission
責任 *sekinin* responsibility, liability
重任 *jūnin* heavy responsibility, important duty; reappointment
担任する *tannin suru* be in charge of, take (a class) under one's charge
歴任する *rekinin suru* hold various posts successively
❷ person holding an office
主任 *shunin* person in charge, head, chief
後任 *kōnin* successor, replacement
❸ⓐ **appoint (to an office), nominate, place**
ⓑ appointment, nomination
任命 *ninmei* appointment, nomination
任用する *nin'yō suru* appoint, employ
選任する *sennin suru* select and appoint, assign [nominate] a person to a post
常任 *jōnin* permanent appointment
❹ⓐ **leave (up) to, entrust to, entrust with**
ⓑ leave a matter to take its own course,

leave a person to himself, leave alone
任意の *nin'i no* optional, voluntary, discretionary
委任する *inin suru* entrust, delegate, commit
信任 *shinnin* confidence, trust, credence
一任する *ichinin suru* leave (a matter) to (a person), entrust (a person) with the task (of)
任侠 *ninkyō* chivalrous spirit, siding with the weak
放任する *hōnin suru* leave (a matter) to take its own course, leave (a person) to himself

❺ profess [claim] to be, pose
自任 *jinin* pretension

INDEPENDENT

【nin 任】 office, duties, official post; duty, responsibility; person of sufficient competence for the task
任を果たす *nin o hatasu* fulfill [discharge] one's duty [duties]
その任ではない *sono nin de wa nai* not be fit for the task

【ninjiru (＝ninzuru) 任じる(＝任ずる)】 appoint, nominate, place; take a duty upon oneself, assume responsibility; profess [claim] to be, pose

KUN

【maka(seru) 任せる】 leave (up) to, entrust to, entrust with; leave a matter to take its own course, leave a person to himself, leave alone
運を天に任せる *un o ten ni makaseru* resign oneself to one's fate, leave to chance
人任せ *hitomakase* leaving matters up to others

【maka(su) 任す】 same as **makaseru 任せる**
万事君に任す *Banji kimi ni makasu* I leave everything in your hands

SYNONYMS

❶ⓐ **work and employment**
務 DUTY → 1173
役 SERVICE (esp. public) → 244
勤 SERVICE (employment) → 1818
業 WORK → 2612
職 EMPLOYMENT → 1425
労 LABOR → 2548
ⓑ **responsibility**
務 DUTY → 1173
責 RESPONSIBILITY → 2467
分 one's part → 1972
❸ⓐ **appoint**
補 appoint → 1194
挙 NOMINATE → 2456
❹ⓐ **commit**
委 COMMIT → 2553
託 ENTRUST → 1455
預 DEPOSIT → 1042
嘱 CHARGE WITH → 718

2-4

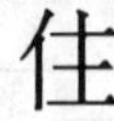

incorrect stroke count ⇨ see 77
(nonstandard for 住 64)

亻

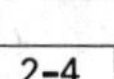

2-4

冫

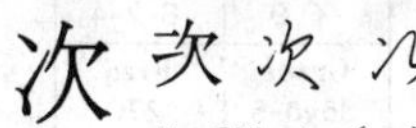

54 JI SHI tsu(gu) tsugi

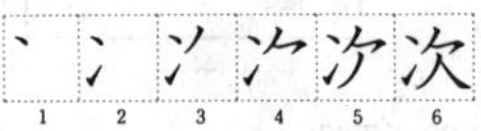

Ⓒⓗ 次 cì

Radical	Strokes
欠 76	6-4-2
Grade	**Freq**
Jōyō-3	216
1 - 2 - 4	

▶NEXT

COMPOUNDS

❶ [also prefix] **next, following, subsequent**
次回 *jikai* next time
次期 *jiki* next term
次号 *jigō* next issue
次週 *jishū* next week
次年度 *jinendo* next (fiscal) year

❷ next in order or rank:
ⓐ **second**
ⓑ **secondary, sub-, vice, deputy, assistant**
次男 *jinan* second son
次位 *jii* second rank, second place
次類 *jirui* subgenus
次官 *jikan* vice-minister, undersecretary
次長 *jichō* assistant director
次席 *jiseki* next in rank, associate
副次的な *fukujiteki na* secondary

❸ⓐ **order, sequence, arrangement**
ⓑ *math* (degree) order, degree
ⓒ **suffix indicating numerical order or number of times**
次第 *shidai* order; circumstances, reasons; as soon as
順次 *junji* order, turn; gradually
序次 *joji* order, sequence
席次 *sekiji* order of seats, seating precedence; class standing
目次 *mokuji* table of contents
次元 *jigen* dimension

高次の *kōji no* of high order
二次方程式 *niji hōteishiki* quadratic equation, equation of the second degree
一次の *ichiji no* first, primary; *math* linear, of the first degree
第二次世界大戦 *dainiji sekai taisen* World War II
❹ *chem* prefix indicating a low state of oxidation or low oxygen content: hypo–, sub–
次亜硫酸 *jiaryūsan* hyposulfurous acid
次酸化炭素 *jisanka-tanso* carbon suboxide
❺ [rare]
ⓐ lodge, take a rest
ⓑ inn, post town
旅次 *ryoji* inn, hotel

KUN

【tsu(gu) 次ぐ】 rank next to, come next [after]
相次ぐ *aitsugu* succeed one another
取り次ぐ *toritsugu* act as agent; transmit; answer the door

【tsugi 次】
① next, following
次次に *tsugitsugi ni* one after another, in succession
② post town
東海道五十三次 *tōkaidō gojūsantsugi* fifty-three stages on the Tokaido highway in former Japan

SYNONYMS

❶ **next**
明 next → 855
翌 THE FOLLOWING → 2668
来 the coming → 3551
❷ⓐ **second**
乙 SECOND → 3339
中 MIDDLE → 3451
後 AFTER (latter) → 361
ⓑ **subordinate**
副 SECONDARY → 1776
従 subordinate → 415
亜 SUB– → 3540
準 QUASI– → 2856
半 semi– → 3501
准 JUNIOR → 127
助 assistant → 1121
❸ⓐ **order**
順 ORDER (sequence) → 18
序 ORDER (sequence／arrangement) → 3065
番 NUMERICAL ORDER → 2748
秩 ORDER (methodical arrangement) → 1158
ⓒ **kinds of numbers**
–目 ordinal number suffix → 3043
第 ORDINAL NUMBER PREFIX → 2660
番 No. → 2748
号 NUMBER (numerical designation) → 2153
員 fixed number → 2269
数 NUMBER (mathematical unit) → 1790

USAGE

tsugi
次
① next, following
② post town
継ぎ
a patch

HOMOPHONES

tsugu ⇨ 継 1360 接 500 注 325
tsugi ⇨ 継 1360

NOTE

⇨ see also USAGE note at 接 500

冴 55 **▸CRISP AND CLEAR** 2-4 冫
nonstandard for 冴 79

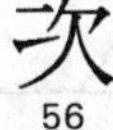
56 **▸NEXT** 2-4 冫
nonstandard for 次 54

防阪 incorrect stroke count ⇨ see ◧ 3–4 2-4 阝

2-4 刂

州 州 州 — 57

SHŪ SU▲ su

Stroke order: 1 丶 2 丿 3 小 4 州 5 州 6 州

Ⓒⓗ 州 zhōu

Radical	Strokes
川 47	6-3-3
Grade	**Freq**
Jōyō-3	515
1-2-4	

▶STATE

COMPOUNDS

❶ⓐ **state (as of the U.S. or Brazil), province (of Canada)**
ⓑ **suffix after names of states**
州政府 *shūseifu* state government
州立大学 *shūritsu-daigaku* state-run college
州都 *shūto* state capital
テキサス州 *tekisasushū* State of Texas
リオ・デ・ジャネイロ州 *rio de janeiro-shū* State of Rio de Janeiro

❷ⓐ (unit of administration in former Japan) province
ⓑ unit of administration in ancient China roughly equiv. to modern province
信州 *shinshū* Shinshu, Shinano
本州 *honshū* Honshu (the main island of Japan)

❸ [formerly also 洲 *shū* 391] continent
豪州 *gōshū* Australia
六大州 *rokudaishū* the Six Continents

INDEPENDENT

【shū 州】 state
州の花 *shū no hana* state flower

KUN

【su 州】 [formerly also 洲] sandbar, shallows, shoal
三角州 *sankakusu* delta
砂州 *sasu* sandbar, sandbank
座州する *zasu suru* strand, run aground

SYNONYMS

❶ **territorial divisions**
県 PREFECTURE → 2641
府 URBAN PREFECTURE → 3082
道 district of Hokkaido → 3134
都 METROPOLIS OF TOKYO → 1686
省 province in China → 2449
郡 COUNTY → 1466

【su】
○ **shoals**
瀬 SHALLOWS → 806
礁 REEF → 1243
○ **elevations in water**
島 ISLAND → 3310
礁 REEF → 1243

USAGE

su
州
[formerly also 洲] sandbar, shallows, shoal
洲
[now usu. 州] sandbar, shallows, shoal

HOMOPHONES

su ⇨ 洲 391

NOTE

★州 has two *on* readings, *shū* and *su* (the latter is not in the Jōyō Kanji list), and the *kun* reading *su*. Although *su* is both an *on* and *kun* reading, only the *kun* is used.

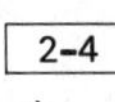

收 — 58

▶TAKE IN

nonstandard for 収 198

2-5 亻

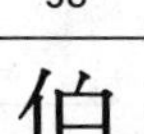

伯 伯 伯 — 59

HAKU

Stroke order: 1 丿 2 亻 3 亻' 4 作 5 伯 6 伯 7 伯

Ⓒⓗ 伯 bó bǎi

Radical	Strokes
亻 9	7-2-5
Grade	**Freq**
Jōyō	1612
1-2-5	

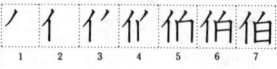

▶OLDER SIBLING OF PARENT
▶COUNT

COMPOUNDS

❶ **older sibling of one's parent, uncle, aunt**
伯父 *hakufu* (=*oji*) uncle (older than one's parent)
伯母 *hakubo* (=*oba*) aunt (older than one's parent)

❷ firstborn brother, older brother

伯仲する *hakuchū suru* be equal to

❸ⓐ **count, earl**

ⓑ **title after names of counts or earls**

伯爵 *hakushaku* count, earl

前島伯 *maejimahaku* Count Maejima

❹ⓐ master of an art

ⓑ title after names of artists

画伯 *gahaku* great artist, master painter

❺ abbrev. of 伯耆 *hōki*, old name for west Tottori Prefecture

伯備線 *hakubisen* Hakubi Line (West Tottori–Okayama Railway)

❻ Brazil

日伯 *nippaku* Japan and Brazil

❼ [rare] horse trader

伯楽 *hakuraku* horse trader

INDEPENDENT

【haku 伯】 count

SPECIAL READINGS

伯父 *oji* uncle (older than one's parent)

伯母 *oba* aunt (older than one's parent)

SYNONYMS

❶ **siblings of parents**

叔 YOUNGER SIBLING OF PARENT → 1272

❸ **noblemen**

侯 marquis → 98

公 duke → 1974

子 viscount → 3390

男 baron → 2542

NOTE

⇨ see COMPOUND FORMATION for 伯仲 *hakuchū* ⇨ 仲 43

60 HAN BAN tomona(u)

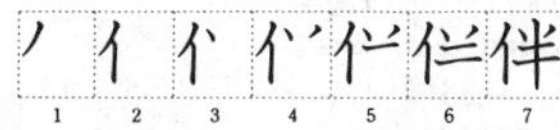

CH 伴 bàn

Radical	Strokes
亻 9	7-2-5
Grade	**Freq**
Jōyō	1057
◧ 1 - 2 - 5	

2-5 亻

▶ACCOMPANY

COMPOUNDS

❶ (go along with) **accompany, go with, attend on**

伴奏 *bansō* accompaniment

伴食大臣 *banshoku-daijin* nominal [figurehead] minister

お相伴 *oshōban* participation

同伴する *dōhan suru* accompany, go with

随伴する *zuihan suru* attend, accompany, follow

❷ [original meaning] companion, mate

伴侶 *hanryo* companion

KUN

【tomona(u) 伴う】 (go together with) accompany, go with, attend; (occur together with) accompany, go hand in hand with, follow

友達を伴って *tomodachi o tomonatte* accompanied by a friend

相伴う *aitomonau* accompany, go hand in hand

時勢に伴って *jisei ni tomonatte* in step with the times

SYNONYMS

❶ **accompany**

添 accompany → 529

陪 ACCOMPANY A SUPERIOR → 539

侍 ATTEND UPON → 85

従 FOLLOW → 415

随 FOLLOW → 627

位 位 位

61 I kurai[1] kurai[2] gurai

ノ 亻 亻' 亻' 亻+ 亻立 位

1 2 3 4 5 6 7

CH 位 wèi

Radical	Strokes
亻 9	7-2-5
Grade	**Freq**
Jōyō-4	441
◧ 1 - 2 - 5	

2-5 亻

▶RANK ▶POSITION

COMPOUNDS

❶ [also suffix] **rank, place, grade, position, station**

地位 *chii* position, status, post, social standing

順位 *jun'i* order, rank, precedence

上位 *jōi* higher rank, precedence

優位 *yūi* superiority, predominant position

首位 *shui* first place, leading position

学位 *gakui* academic degree

第一位 *daiichii* first place, foremost rank

正二位 *shōnii* senior grade of second rank

❷ [original meaning] **position, location,**

place; direction
位置 *ichi* position, place
機位 *kii* position of aircraft
方位 *hōi* direction, bearing
転位 *ten'i* transposition, displacement
定位 *teii* normal position; orientation
❸ⓐ decimal place, digit
ⓑ suffix after decimal places
百位 *hyakui* the hundreds (digit)
小数第五位 *shōsū daigoi* five decimal places
❹ level, standard of quality
水位 *suii* water level
単位 *tan'i* unit
品位 *hin'i* dignity, grace, nobility; grade, quality
❺ term of respect
各位 *kakui* gentlemen, sirs
❻ *theology* person, hypostasis
三位一体 *sanmi-ittai* the Trinity
❼ⓐ spirits of the dead
ⓑ counter for spirits
先祖の位牌 *senzo no ihai* ancestral tablet

KUN

【**kurai**[1] 位】rank, grade; dignity; the throne; decimal place
位の高い人 *kurai no takai hito* person of high rank
位する *kuraisuru* rank, be ranked; be located
位に就く *kurai ni tsuku* ascend to the throne
一の位 *ichi no kurai* the units

【**kurai**[2], **gurai** 位】
① about, approximately
十分位 *jippun-gurai* about ten minutes
これ位の大きさ *kore kurai no ōkisa* about this size
② particle indicating comparison or extent: as...as, like
これ位 *kore gurai* this much
東京タワー位高い *tōkyō tawā gurai takai* as high as Tokyo Tower
どの位? *dono kurai* how much?
お前位馬鹿な奴はいない *Omae gurai baka na yatsu wa inai* It would be hard to find an idiot like you
③ at least
お礼位言っても良さそうだ *Orei gurai itte mo yosasō da* He might at least thank me
④ particle indicating that speaker thinks lightly of subject; sooner...than; at all
バスを使う位なら自転車に乗ろう *Basu o tsukau kurai nara jitensha ni norō* I'd just as soon ride my bike as take the bus

SYNONYMS

❶ **class**
階 RANK → 624
身 social status → 3553
格 STATUS → 926
級 GRADE → 1279
段 grade → 1144
等 CLASS → 2682
流 class → 441
層 STRATUM → 3161
❷ **places and positions**
所 PLACE → 851
処 place → 3031
場 PLACE (for specific activity) → 558
地 PLACE (particular location) → 204
席 meeting place → 3113
点 POINT → 2084
座 place → 3116

【**gurai**】
① **approximately**
-頃 ABOUT → 144
-方 about → 1963
-程 ...or thereabouts → 1190
辺り thereabouts → 3029
約 APPROXIMATELY → 1280
概 GENERAL → 1048
大 in substance → 3416

2-5
亻

62 ITSU

Ⓒⓗ 佚 yì

Radical	Strokes
亻 9	7-2-5
Grade	Freq
Reference	
1-2-5	

COMPOUNDS

[now replaced by 逸 3120]
❶ lost, missing
佚書 *issho* lost book
散佚する *san'itsu suru* be lost and scattered
❷ indulge in idle pleasure
安佚 *an'itsu* (idle) ease, idleness, indolence

似

63 JI ni(ru)

ノ 亻 仆 化 仏 似 似

Radical	Strokes
亻 9	7-2-5
Grade	**Freq**
Jōyō-5	1172
1 - 2 - 5	

CH 似 sì shì

2-5 亻

▶RESEMBLE

COMPOUNDS

● [original meaning] **resemble, be similar**

類似する *ruiji suru* resemble, be alike, be similar

酷似 *kokuji* close resemblance

相似 *sōji* similarity, resemblance

近似する *kinji suru* approximate to, resemble closely

疑似コレラ *giji-korera* suspected case of cholera, para-cholera

KUN

【ni(ru) 似る】 resemble, be alike, be similar

似せる *niseru* imitate, copy; forge

似顔 *nigao* likeness, portrait

似通う *nikayou* resemble closely

似合う *niau* befit, suit; match well

不似合い *funiai* inaptitude, incongruity

SPECIAL READINGS

真似▲ *mane* imitation, mimicry

SYNONYMS

● **resemble**

類 be similar → 1807

住

64 JŪ su(mu) su(mau) -zu(mai)

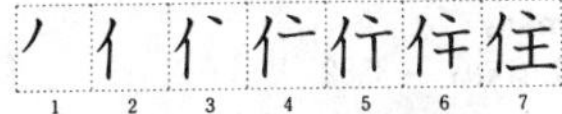

Radical	Strokes
亻 9	7-2-5
Grade	**Freq**
Jōyō-3	280
1 - 2 - 5	

CH 住 zhù

2-5 亻

▶LIVE

COMPOUNDS

❶ⓐ **live, reside, dwell, inhabit**

ⓑ **housing, residence, house, dwelling**

住民 *jūmin* residents, dwellers

住居 *jūkyo* house, dwelling, residence

住所 *jūsho* one's dwelling, address

住職 *jūshoku* Buddhist priest, chief priest

在住する *zaijū suru* live, reside, dwell

居住する *kyojū suru* live, dwell, reside

移住する *ijū suru* migrate, immigrate; move

住宅 *jūtaku* housing, dwelling house, residence

公住 *kōjū* apartment house built by the Japan Housing Corporation

衣食住 *ishokujū* food, clothing and shelter, the necessities of life

❷ abbrev. of 住職 *jūshoku*: Buddhist priest

先住 *senjū* previous priest; previous resident

❸ [original meaning] stop (an action), stand

行住座臥 *gyōjūzaga* the four cardinal behaviors (walking, stopping [standing], sitting and lying); daily life

INDEPENDENT

【jū 住】 living; dwelling, shelter

KUN

【su(mu) 住む】 (of people) live, reside, dwell

住み家 *sumika* residence

住み着く *sumitsuku* settle, take up residence

【su(mau) 住まう】 dwell, live, reside in

住まい *sumai* living; dwelling, house

【-zu(mai) -住まい】

ⓐ [suffix] living

ⓑ dwelling, residence

団地住まい *danchizumai* living in a housing complex

仮住まい *karizumai* temporary residence

SYNONYMS

❶ⓐ **reside**

居 RESIDE → 3080

生 inhabit → 3497

植 colonize → 990

ⓑ **houses**

居 residence → 3080

邸 STATELY RESIDENCE → 1131

宅 DWELLING HOUSE → 2174

戸 HOUSEHOLD → 1930

家 HOUSE → 2273

屋 HOUSE → 3098

軒 house → 1459

USAGE

sumu

住む

(of people) live, reside, dwell

棲む
(of animals) inhabit, live

HOMOPHONES
sumu ⇨ 棲 989

2-5
亻

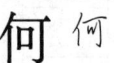

何 65

KA nani nan nani- nan-

CH 何 hé

Radical	Strokes
亻 9	7-2-5
Grade	**Freq**
Jōyō-2	446
1 - 2 - 5	

1 2 3 4 5 6 7

▶**WHAT** ▶**HOW MANY**

COMPOUNDS

● **what, which**

幾何学 *kikagaku* geometry
誰何する *suika suru* challenge (an unknown person), ask a person's identity

KUN

【**nani, nan** 何】 what, which, whatever—used also in the formation of various interrogative pronouns

何が何だか分からない *nani ga nan da ka wakaranai* don't know what's what
何時ですか *Nanji desu ka* What time is it?
何言ってるんだ *Nani itterunda* What's the idea [story]?
何か *nanika* something, some, any
何等 *nanra* what, whatever; (not) any
何で *nande* why, what for
何者 *nanimono* who, what kind of man
何故 *naniyue* why, how
何事 *nanigoto* whatever, what

【**nani-, nan-** 何-】
[also prefix]
① how many
何度 *nando* how many degrees; how many times
何人 *nannin* how many people
② several, some, odd
何十 *nanjū* several tens
何時間 *nanjikan* several hours

SPECIAL READINGS

何故▲ *naze* why, for what reason
如何▲ *ikaga* how; what
如何▲(=奈何▲) *ikan* what; how
如何に▲ *ika ni* how, in what way

SYNONYMS

● **interrogatives**

奈 interrogative forming element → 2219
那 interrogative forming element → 843
誰 WHO → 1578

【**nani-**】
① **how many**
幾 HOW MANY → 3582
② **some**
数 several → 1790
幾- SOME → 3582

COMPOUND FORMATION

幾何学 *kikagaku*

幾何学 'geometry' derives from 幾何, which originally meant 'how many'. The Chinese used these characters to phonetically transliterate the word *geometry*.

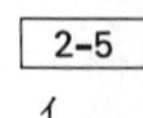
2-5
亻

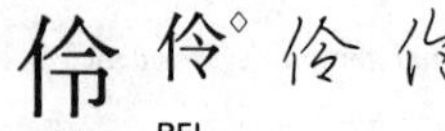

伶 66

REI

CH 伶 líng

Radical	Strokes
亻 9	7-2-5
Grade	**Freq**
Names	2131
1 - 2 - 5	

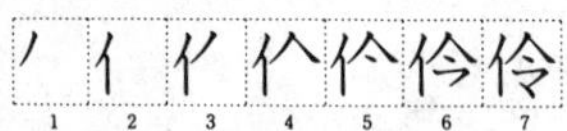

▶**MUSICIAN**

COMPOUNDS

❶ [original meaning] **musician, court musician, performer of court music, minstrel; actor**

伶人 *reijin* minstrel, court musician
伶官 *reikan* court musician
伶優 *reiyū* actor

❷ [now always 怜 298] clever, quick-witted, bright, nimble

伶俐(=怜悧) *reiri* cleverness, sagacity

NAMES

伶子 *reiko* female name

SYNONYMS

❶ **performers**

優 ACTOR → 177
俳 actor → 112

佐 佐 佐

67 SA

CH 佐 zuǒ

Radical	Strokes
亻 9	7-2-5
Grade	Freq
Jōyō	258
1 - 2 - 5	

2-5 亻

ノ 亻 仁 什 佐 佐 佐
1 2 3 4 5 6 7

▶ASSIST ▶FIELD OFFICER

COMPOUNDS

❶ **assist, aid, second**
佐幕派 *sabakuha* supporters of the shogun
補佐(=輔佐)する *hosa suru* assist, help
❷ (military officer or rank below 将 *shō* 460 (general officer) and above 尉 *i* 1685 (company officer) roughly equiv. to colonel or major (U.S. ranking)) **field officer**
佐官 *sakan* field officer
大佐 *taisa* (army) colonel, (navy) captain
中佐 *chūsa* (army) lieutenant colonel, (navy) commander
少佐 *shōsa* (army) major, (navy) lieutenant commander

SYNONYMS

❶ **help**
補 assist → 1194
輔 ASSIST → 1559
助 HELP → 1121
佑 HELP (said esp. of God) → 74
祐 DIVINE HELP → 915
援 AID → 586
済 RELIEVE → 522
❷ **military officers and ranks**
尉 COMPANY OFFICER → 1685
曹 SERGEANT → 2746
将 GENERAL OFFICER → 460
督 COMMANDER → 2796
帥 COMMANDER IN CHIEF → 1290

作 作 作

68 SAKU SA tsuku(ru) tsuku(ri) -zuku(ri)

CH 作 zuò zuō zuó

Radical	Strokes
亻 9	7-2-5
Grade	Freq
Jōyō-2	112
1 - 2 - 5	

2-5 亻

ノ 亻 亻 仐 作 作 作
1 2 3 4 5 6 7

▶MAKE ▶WORK

COMPOUNDS

❶ⓐ **make, produce, manufacture**
ⓑ something made; make
作成する *sakusei suru* make, produce, draw up, frame, prepare
製作 *seisaku* manufacture, production
工作 *kōsaku* handicraft; construction, building; maneuvering
試作 *shisaku* trial manufacture
家作 *kasaku* house for rent
造作 *zōsaku* fixtures; features
❷ⓐ **compose (a literary or musical work), create, write**
ⓑ [also suffix] (**literary or artistic**) **work, composition, production**
ⓒ [suffix] made by, authored [composed] by, produced by
作品 *sakuhin* (piece of) work, performance, product
作家 *sakka* writer, novelist, author
作曲する *sakkyoku suru* compose, write music
作者 *sakusha* author, writer, playwright
作文 *sakubun* composition, essay; writing
原作 *gensaku* original (work)
名作 *meisaku* masterpiece, fine work
創作 *sōsaku* creation, production; fiction writing
大作 *taisaku* monumental [great] work, major work
傑作 *kessaku* masterpiece, magnum opus; blunder
代表作 *daihyōsaku* representative work
川端康成作 *kawabata yasunari-saku* written [authored] by Kawabata Yasunari
❸ⓐ **work, do, perform, function**
ⓑ action, behavior
作業 *sagyō* work, operation
作用 *sayō* action, operation, function; effect
操作する *sōsa suru* operate, manipulate, handle
作法 *sahō* manners, etiquette, decorum
動作 *dōsa* action, movement; bearing, behavior
発作 *hossa* fit, attack, seizure
造作無く *zōsa-naku* without difficulty
❹ⓐ **raise crops, cultivate, farm**
ⓑ [also suffix] crop, harvest, yield

作物 *sakumotsu* crops
作付 *sakuzuke* planting
耕作 *kōsaku* cultivation, farming
連作 *rensaku* repeated cultivation; story made up by several writers working on it in turn
輪作 *rinsaku* rotation of crops
畑作 *hatasaku* dry field farming, dry field crop
作柄 *sakugara* harvest, crop; quality (of an artistic production)
稲作 *inasaku* rice crop; raising rice plants
豊作 *hōsaku* good [abundant] harvest
平年作 *heinensaku* average crop

❺ contrive, scheme
作戦 *sakusen* tactics, strategy; (military) operations, maneuvers
作為 *sakui* artificiality, intention; commission (of a crime)

❻ promote, arouse, awaken
作興する *sakkō suru* promote; awaken, arouse, enhance
振作 *shinsaku* promotion, enhancement, awakening

INDEPENDENT

【saku 作】(literary or artistic) work, composition, production; authorship; crop, harvest, yield
会心の作 *kaishin no saku* work after one's heart
作が悪い *saku ga warui* have a poor crop

KUN

【tsuku(ru) 作る】
①ⓐ make (out of materials), form, prepare
ⓑ [sometimes also 創る] create, bring into being
ⓒ make (as a document), make out, compose, frame, draw up
ⓓ form (an organization), organize, found, establish
ⓔ prepare food, cook; slice (raw fish)
形作る *katachizukuru* form, shape, make, mold
作り出す *tsukuridasu* make, turn out, create
詩を作る *shi o tsukuru* compose a poem
新内閣を作る *shinnaikaku o tsukuru* form a new Cabinet
刺身を作る *sashimi o tsukuru* slice (raw fish)
② raise crops, cultivate, grow, till
庭で作った野菜 *niwa de tsukutta yasai* vegetables grown in one's yard
③ foster, cultivate (a person's character), build up
良い習慣を作る *yoi shūkan o tsukuru* cultivate a good habit
④ make [touch] up, apply cosmetics; trim
酷く作った顔 *hidoku tsukutta kao* face with heavy makeup
⑤ make up (a story), invent, fabricate
作り話 *tsukuribanashi* fable, fiction
作り泣き *tsukurinaki* make-believe crying

【tsuku(ri) 作り】
① make, physique, features
顔の作り *kao no tsukuri* features of the face
② makeup
濃い作り *koi tsukuri* heavy makeup
③ *sashimi*, sliced raw flesh (esp. of fish)
お作り *otsukuri sashimi*, sliced raw flesh (esp. of fish)

【-zuku(ri) -作り】
① (build of the body) make, physique
細作りの人 *hosozukuri no hito* slender person
② suffix indicating material composition
粘土作りの *nendozukuri no* made of clay
③ affectation, pretense
若作りにする *wakazukuri ni suru* make oneself up to look younger
④ sliced raw fish, *sashimi*
生け作り(＝活け作り) *ikezukuri* freshly-killed fish served whole with its meat cut in slices

SYNONYMS

❶ⓐ make
造 MAKE → 3110
成 FORM → 3537
工 MANUFACTURE → 3381
製 MANUFACTURE → 2803
産 PRODUCE → 3298
調 PREPARE → 1567
組む ASSEMBLE → 1337
構 CONSTRUCT → 1049

❷ⓐ create
創 CREATE → 1815
生 produce → 3497
発 START → 2565
起 generate → 3307

ⓐ compose
著 AUTHOR → 2300
書く WRITE → 2658
筆 write → 2677

❸ⓐ do and act
行 ACT → 212
為 DO → 3577
仕 DO → 34
致す DO HUMBLY → 1316

❹ⓐ farm and plant
耕 TILL → 1308
農 farm, FARMING → 2698
培 CULTIVATE → 464
栽 PLANT (saplings) → 3297
植 PLANT → 990

USAGE

❶ tsukuru
作る

①ⓐ make (out of materials), form, prepare
ⓑ [sometimes also 創る] create, bring into being
ⓒ make (as a document), make out, compose, frame, draw up
ⓓ form (an organization), organize, found, establish
ⓔ prepare food, cook; slice (raw fish)
② raise crops, cultivate, grow, till
③ foster, cultivate (a person's character), build up
④ make [touch] up, apply cosmetics; trim
⑤ make up (a story), invent, fabricate

造る
①ⓐ make (as an object that requires time and skill), manufacture, fabricate, fashion
ⓑ build (ships or buildings), construct
② make (wine), brew
③ coin, mint

創る
[usu. 作る] create, bring into being

❷ **tsukuri**
作り
① make, physique, features
② makeup
③ *sashimi*, sliced raw flesh (esp. of fish)

造り
ⓐ making, building, constructing (as buildings or ships)
ⓑ make, structure, construction

❸ **-zukuri**
-作り
① (build of the body) make, physique
② suffix indicating material composition
③ affectation, pretense
④ sliced raw fish, *sashimi*

-造り
[also suffix]
ⓐ make, structure; style of building
ⓑ building, constructing, developing

HOMOPHONES
tsukuru ⇨ 造 3110 創 1815
tsukuri ⇨ 造 3110
-zukuri ⇨ 造 3110

伺 伺 伺
69 SHI ukaga(u)

ノ イ 亻 们 伺 伺 伺
1 2 3 4 5 6 7

CH 伺 sì cì

Radical	Strokes
亻 9	7-2-5
Grade	**Freq**
Jōyō	1822
1-2-5	

2-5
亻

▶**INQUIRE**

COMPOUNDS
[humble]
❶ **inquire [ask] after (a person's health)**
奉伺する *hōshi suru* inquire after (someone's health)
❷ⓐ **call on (a superior), pay a visit**
ⓑ wait upon, attend on, serve
伺候する *shikō suru* pay one's respects, make a courtesy call; wait upon (a nobleman)

KUN
【ukaga(u) 伺う】
[humble]
①ⓐ (put a question) inquire (about), ask
ⓑ (request information) inquire [ask] after (a person's health)
伺い *ukagai* question, inquiry; consulting the oracle; call, visit
御意見を伺う *goiken o ukagau* ask the opinion of (a superior)
伺いを立てる *ukagai o tateru* inquire of, ask for someone's opinion; invoke an oracle
暑中伺い *shochūukagai* inquiry after a person's health in the hot season
② call on (a superior), call at, pay a visit
何時お伺いしましょうか *Itsu oukagai shimashō ka* When shall I call on you?
③ hear, be told
...と伺った *...to ukagatta* I heard that...

SYNONYMS
❷ⓐ **visit**
寄 call at → 2291
訪 VISIT → 1468
参 VISIT A HOLY PLACE → 2066

【ukagau】
①ⓐ **inquire**
尋ねる INQUIRE → 2322
諮 CONSULT → 1596
質 query → 2808
聞く ask → 3326
問 QUESTION → 3320
詰 question closely → 1521

2-5 亻

伸 70

SHIN no(biru) no(basu) no(beru) no(su)▲

CH 伸 shēn

Radical	Strokes
亻 9	7-2-5
Grade	Freq
Jōyō	666
1 - 2 - 5	

▶**STRETCH**

COMPOUNDS

❶ⓐ [original meaning] **stretch, elongate, extend, spread**
ⓑ expand, grow, develop
伸縮 *shinshuku* expansion and contraction
伸張 *shinchō* expansion, elongation
伸展する *shinten suru* expand, extend
❷ (of stock prices) **rise**
急伸 *kyūshin* sudden rise (said esp. of stock prices), jump
続伸する *zokushin suru* continue to rise
❸ [sometimes also 申 3507] say, mention
追伸 *tsuishin* postscript

KUN

【no(biru) 伸びる】
vi
①ⓐ stretch, lengthen, extend, spread
ⓑ expand, increase, grow, develop, advance
伸び *nobi* stretching, elongation; development, growth; spread (as of paint)
背伸び *senobi* stretching one's back
伸び悩む *nobinayamu* be held in check, fail to grow
伸び率 *nobiritsu* growth rate; coefficient of extension
伸び伸び *nobinobi* at ease
② spread (as of paint)
良く伸びるクリーム *yoku nobiru kurīmu* well-spreading cream
③ be exhausted, be knocked out
殴られて伸びる *nagurarete nobiru* be knocked out cold

【no(basu) 伸ばす】
vt
①ⓐ stretch, elongate, extend, spread
ⓑ expand, let grow, develop
引き伸ばす *hikinobasu* stretch out, elongate; enlarge (photographs)
才能を伸ばす *sainō o nobasu* develop one's ability
② straighten
体を伸ばす *karada o nobasu* stretch (unbend) oneself
③ dilute
スープを伸ばす *sūpu o nobasu* thin soup with water
④ knock out
伸ばしてしまえ *Nobashite shimae* Knock him out!

【no(beru) 伸べる】
[also 延べる]
ⓐ extend, stretch out (one's arm)
ⓑ spread out (bedding)
手を差し伸べる *te o sashinoberu* extend one's arm, hold out one's hand
床を伸べる *toko o noberu* spread [make] a bed

【no(su) 伸す】 gain influence, rise in power; go further, extend one's journey; stretch, spread; *slang* knock out, send (a person) sprawling
党勢を伸す *tōsei o nosu* extend the strength of a party
伸し上がる *noshiagaru* stand on tiptoe; raise oneself to (a higher position); act important

SPECIAL READINGS

欠伸▲ *akubi* yawn

SYNONYMS

❶ⓐ **expand**
延 EXTEND → 3073
拡 ENLARGE → 309
広げる spread (out) → 3035
張 SPREAD → 474
膨 EXPAND → 1084
脹 SWELL → 1003
ⓑ **grow**
展 UNFOLD → 3111
発 develop → 2565
成 grow up → 3537
長 grow (up) → 2556
生 grow → 3497
育 grow → 2050

USAGE

❶ **nobiru**
伸びる
vi
①ⓐ stretch, lengthen, extend, spread
ⓑ expand, increase, grow, develop, advance
② spread (as of paint)
③ be exhausted, be knocked out
延びる
vi
① extend (in space or time), be extended,

be prolonged
② be postponed, be delayed

❷ **nobi**

伸び
①ⓐ stretching, elongation
ⓑ development, growth
② spread (as of paint)

延び
① extension
② postponement

❸ **nobasu**

伸ばす
vt
①ⓐ stretch, elongate, extend, spread
ⓑ expand, let grow, develop
② straighten
③ dilute
④ knock out

延ばす
vt
① extend (in space or time), prolong, spread
② postpone, delay, defer

❹ **nobinobi**

伸び伸び
at ease

延び延び
repeated delays, dragging on and on

❺ **noberu**

伸べる
[also 延べる]
ⓐ extend, stretch out (one's arm)
ⓑ spread out (bedding)

延べる
① [also 伸べる]
ⓐ extend, stretch out (one's arm)
ⓑ spread out (bedding)
② postpone, delay

HOMOPHONES

nobiru ⇨ 延 3073
nobi ⇨ 延 3073
nobasu ⇨ 延 3073
noberu ⇨ 延 3073

体 體 躰° 体 䏝

71 TAI TEI karada

ⒸⒽ 体 tǐ tī

Radical	Strokes
亻 9△	7-2-5
Grade	**Freq**
Jōyō-2	107
◧ 1 - 2 - 5	

2-5 亻

Stroke order: ノ 亻 仁 什 休 体 体 (1 2 3 4 5 6 7)

▶BODY ▶FORM

COMPOUNDS

❶ⓐ [also suffix] (physical organism) **body, corpse**
ⓑ counter for dead bodies [corpses]
体力 *tairyoku* physical strength, strength of one's body
体質 *taishitsu* physical constitution
体内 *tainai* interior of the body
体操 *taisō* gymnastics, physical exercise
体重 *taijū* body weight
体育 *taiiku* physical training [education]
身体 *shintai* body
人体 *jintai* human body
一体 *ittai* one body; a style, a form; (why, what) on earth, (what, why) in the world
自体 *jitai* one's own body; itself
全体 *zentai* whole (body), whole span
肉体 *nikutai* body, flesh
焼死体 *shōshitai* charred body
遺体 *itai* remains, body, corpse
脂肪体 *shibōtai* corpus adiposum
死体三体 *shitai santai* three corpses

❷ abbrev. of 体育 *taiiku*: physical education
体協 *taikyō* Japan Amateur Sports Association
国体 *kokutai* National Athletic Meet

❸ⓐ (main part, esp. of a vehicle) **body, framework**
ⓑ (main or essential part) **substance, reality, real thing**
車体 *shatai* car body, chassis; frame (of a bicycle)
機体 *kitai* fuselage, body (of an airplane); machine
解体 *kaitai* dismantling (a machine), scrapping; dissolution, disorganization; dissection
体言 *taigen* indeclinable parts of speech in Japanese, substantive
主体 *shutai* main part; subject
実体 *jittai* substance, essence
本体 *hontai* substance, thing itself; object of worship; main part
大体 *daitai* outline, substance; generally, roughly, on the whole

❹ [also suffix]
ⓐ (physical object or mass) **body, object, substance**
ⓑ *geometry* body, solid body, figure
体積 *taiseki* (cubic) volume, capacity
物体 *buttai* body, physical solid, object, substance

固体 *kotai* solid, solid matter
気体 *kitai* gas, vapor, gaseous body
天体 *tentai* heavenly body
有機体 *yūkitai* organism, organic body
立体 *rittai* solid (body), cube
六面体 *rokumentai* hexahedron
❺ (organized entity) body, organization
団体 *dantai* group, party, body, corps; corporation, organization
自治体 *jichitai* self-governing body [community]
組織体 *soshikitai* body, organization
❻ [also suffix]
ⓐ (**characteristic**) **form, shape**
ⓑ (outer appearance) **form, appearance**
ⓒ (manner of expression) style, form
ⓓ (mode of existence) form, system
体系 *taikei* system, organization
字体 *jitai* form of a character, type
具体的な *gutaiteki na* concrete, definite, specific
正体 *shōtai* one's natural [true] shape; consciousness
体貌 *taibō* appearance
体裁 *teisai* decency, form, style, appearance
風体 *fūtei* (=*fūtai*) appearance, looks; posture
世間体 *sekentei* appearance (in the eyes of society), decency
職人体の男 *shokunintei no otoko* man of workmanlike appearance
文体 *buntai* (literary) style
書体 *shotai* penmanship style, calligraphic style
ですます体 *desumasutai desu-masu* style (in Japanese grammar)
政体 *seitai* form [system] of government
❼ learn from experience
体得する *taitoku suru* realize, learn (from experience), comprehend, master
体験する *taiken suru* experience, go through, (actually) feel
❽ counter for images of Buddhist or Shinto deities
仏像二体 *butsuzō nitai* two images of Buddha
❾ *math* field
実数体 *jissūtai* real number field

INDEPENDENT

【tai 体】 body; form, style; substance, essence; *math* field
体を交わす *tai o kawasu* dodge, parry
体を成す *tai o nasu* take form [shape]

【taisuru 体する】 bear in mind, obey, comply with
社長の意を体する *shachō no i o taisuru* comply with the wishes of the company president

【tei 体】 appearance, air; condition, state
然有らぬ体で *saaranu tei de* with a nonchalant air
中止の体 *chūshi no tei* state of standstill

KUN

【karada 体】 body, physique; health
体造り *karadazukuri* physical culture
体付き *karadatsuki* one's figure
体が強い *karada ga tsuyoi* have a strong constitution, be in good health

SYNONYMS

❶ **body**
身 BODY (esp. vs. mind) → 3553
肉 FLESH → 3200
❸ⓑ **essential content**
実 substance → 2225
味 contents → 274
❹ⓐ **object**
物 THING → 874
品 ARTICLE → 2248
ⓑ **bodies**
塊 LUMP → 632
球 BALL → 969
❺ **organized bodies**
団 BODY → 3053
協 association → 93
会 SOCIETY → 2020
組 union → 1337
労 workers' union → 2548
連 federation → 3103
講 fraternity → 1619
院 INSTITUTION → 454
❻ⓐ **form**
状 FORM (external) → 272
形 SHAPE → 846
姿 FIGURE → 2636
ⓑ **appearance**
容 APPEARANCE → 2277
姿 FIGURE → 2636
相 PHASE → 900
色 COLOR → 2029
風 air → 3007

但 72 TAN▲ tada(shi)

CH 但 dàn

Radical	Strokes
亻 9	7-2-5
Grade	Freq
Jōyō	1811
1-2-5	

2-5 亻

Stroke order: ノ 亻 亻 们 但 但 但 (1 2 3 4 5 6 7)

▶**PROVIDED THAT**

COMPOUNDS

● abbrev. of 但馬 *tajima*, old name for north Hyogo Prefecture

播但線 *bantansen* Bantan Line (railway in Hyogo Prefecture)

KUN

【tada(shi) 但し】 provided that, on condition that, however, but, only

但し書き *tadashigaki* proviso, conditional clause

但し付き *tadashitsuki* conditional

但し…に就いてはこの限りではない *Tadashi...ni tsuite wa kono kagiri de wa nai* Provided that the same shall not apply to...

彼は約束はする、但し履行はせぬ *Kare wa yakusoku wa suru, tadashi rikō wa senu* He makes promises, but he does not keep them

SYNONYMS

【tàdashi】

○ **conditional conjunctions**

然し however → 2782

低 73 TEI hiku(i) hiku(meru) hiku(maru)

CH 低 dī

Radical	Strokes
亻 9	7-2-5
Grade	Freq
Jōyō-4	477
1-2-5	

2-5 亻

Stroke order: ノ 亻 亻 仫 住 低 低 (1 2 3 4 5 6 7)

▶**LOW**

COMPOUNDS

❶ⓐ [original meaning] (having little height) **low**

ⓑ lower, bring down

低地 *teichi* low ground, lowlands

低空 *teikū* low altitude

高低 *kōtei* high and low

低下する *teika suru* fall, sink, lower, go down

低頭 *teitō* bowing low

❷ [also prefix]

ⓐ (below average in degree) **low**

ⓑ low-priced, inexpensive

低音 *teion* low-pitched sound, bass

低温 *teion* low temperature

低能 *teinō* low intelligence

低気圧 *teikiatsu* low pressure, atmospheric depression

最低の *saitei no* lowest

低価 *teika* low price

低廉な *teiren na* cheap, inexpensive

低賃金 *teichingin* low wages

❸ (of inferior social standing) low, humble, vulgar

低級 *teikyū* low grade, low class, vulgar

低俗な *teizoku na* vulgar

❹ [formerly 彽 294] linger, wander

低回(=彽徊)する *teikai suru* linger, loiter, wander

INDEPENDENT

【tei 低】 low

高より低へ *kō yori tei e* from high to low

KUN

【hiku(i) 低い】 low, short (stature); (of inferior social standing) low, humble; in a low voice [key]

低くする *hikuku suru* lower, bring down

身長の低い人 *shinchō no hikui hito* short person

【hiku(meru) 低める】 lower, bring down

【hiku(maru) 低まる】 be lowered, come down

SYNONYMS

❶ⓐ **low**

下 lower → 3378

ⓑ **lower**

下 bring down → 3378

❷ⓐ **less in degree**

薄 THIN → 2370

浅 SHALLOW → 389

微 SLIGHT → 639

軽 LIGHT → 1515

弱 WEAK → 1167

ⓑ **inexpensive**

安 INEXPENSIVE → 2171
廉 CHEAP → 3153
❸ **lowly**
下 of low rank → 3378
卑 MEAN → 2642

2-5
亻

佑 佑 佑
74 YŪ U NAMES suke tasuku

ノ 亻 亻 仕 什 佑 佑
1 2 3 4 5 6 7

CH 佑 yòu

Radical	Strokes
亻 9	7-2-5
Grade	**Freq**
Names	2088
1 - 2 - 5	

▶HELP

COMPOUNDS

ⓐ [original meaning] **help, succor, protect** —said esp. of God

ⓑ [also 祐 915] divine help, heavenly assistance [protection]

佑助 *yūjo* help, divine help

天佑 *ten'yū* grace of Heaven, providential help

NAMES

佑介 *yūsuke* male name

佑次郎 *yūjirō* male name

佑山 *sukeyama* place name

SYNONYMS

● **help**

祐 DIVINE HELP → 915
助 HELP → 1121
援 AID → 586
佐 ASSIST → 67
補 assist → 1194
輔 ASSIST → 1559
済 RELIEVE → 522

2-5
亻

75

▶BUDDHA ▶FRANCE
nonstandard for 仏 19

2-5
亻

76

▶ACCOMPANY
nonstandard for 伴 60

2-5
亻

77

▶LIVE
nonstandard for 住 64

2-5
亻

78

▶MUSICIAN
nonstandard for 伶 66

2-5
冫

冴 冴 冴
79 GO sa(eru) NAMES sae saeru

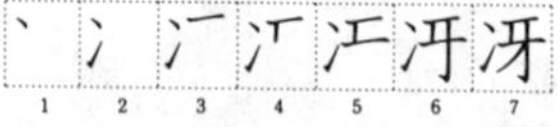

CH 冱 hù

Radical	Strokes
冫 15	7-2-5
Grade	**Freq**
Names	2076
1 - 2 - 5	

▶CRISP AND CLEAR

COMPOUNDS

● [original meaning] ice-cold, freezing; freeze

冴寒 *gokan* [rare] extreme cold

KUN

【sa(eru) 冴える】

①ⓐ be crisp and clear, be crystal-clear (as on an ice-cold winter night), be bright, be vivid

ⓑ be clearheaded, be wide-awake, be fresh

冴え返る *saekaeru* be exceedingly clear; be keenly cold

冴えた色 *saeta iro* bright color

冴え冴えした顔 *saezae shita kao* fresh com-

plexion, cheerful look
頭の冴え *atama no sae* bright intelligence
眼が冴える *me ga saeru* be wakeful, be wide-awake
② be ice-cold, be chilly
冴えた夜 *saeta yoru* crisp and cold night
③ become skilled, be dexterous
腕の冴え *ude no sae* skill, dexterity

NAMES

冴子 *saeko* female name

SYNONYMS

【saeru】
①ⓐ **clear**
朗 CLEAR (sky) → 1325
明 CLEAR (unclouded) → 855
清 CLEAR (liquid) → 523
澄 LIMPID → 740
透 TRANSPARENT → 3108

冷 冷 冷 冷

80

lěng

REI tsume(tai) hi(eru) hi(ya) hi(yayaka) hi(yasu) hi(yakasu) sa(meru) sa(masu)

Radical	Strokes
冫 15	7-2-5
Grade	**Freq**
Jōyō-4	780
◧ 1 - 2 - 5	

2-5 冫

Stroke order: 1 2 3 4 5 6 7

▶COLD

COMPOUNDS

❶ⓐ cold, chilled
ⓑ [original meaning] **cool, chill, refrigerate**
冷気 *reiki* cold air; cold, chill
冷害 *reigai* damage from cold weather
冷水 *reisui* cold water
寒冷 *kanrei* cold, coldness, chilliness
冷房 *reibō* air conditioning
冷凍 *reitō* freezing, cold storage
冷却 *reikyaku* cooling, refrigeration
冷蔵庫 *reizōko* refrigerator
水冷 *suirei* water cooling
❷ coldhearted, dispassionate
冷酷な *reikoku na* cruel, unfeeling, coldhearted
冷血な *reiketsu na* cold-blooded, coldhearted, heartless
冷笑 *reishō* derisive smile, sneer
冷評 *reihyō* sarcasm, sneer, jeer
冷静な *reisei na* cool, calm, cool-headed, dispassionate

KUN

【tsume(tai) 冷たい】 cold (to the touch), chilly; coldhearted, cold-blooded
冷たさ *tsumetasa* coldness; coldheartedness
冷たい戦争 *tsumetai sensō* cold war
【hi(eru) 冷える】 *vi* cool down, grow cold; feel chilly
冷え *hie* chilling
冷え込む *hiekomu* get colder, get chilled
冷え症 *hieshō* oversensitivity to cold
寝冷え *nebie* cold [chill] caught while sleeping
【hi(ya) 冷や】 cool drinking water; cold sake; [in compounds] cold, chilled
お冷や一杯 *ohiya ippai* a glass of water
冷や飯 *hiyameshi* cold rice; cold treatment [shoulder]
冷や汗 *hiyaase* cold sweat
【hi(yayaka) 冷ややか】
hiyayaka na 冷ややかな cold, chilly; frigid, indifferent
冷ややかさ *hiyayakasa* coldness; frigidity, indifference
冷ややかな態度 *hiyayaka na taido* cold attitude
【hi(yasu) 冷やす】 cool, chill, refrigerate
冷やし中華 *hiyashichūka* chilled Chinese noodles
頭を冷やす *atama o hiyasu* cool one's head
【hi(yakasu) 冷やかす】 banter, chaff, jeer at; window-shop, browse
冷やかし *hiyakashi* banter, chaff, raillery; window-shopping, browsing
【sa(meru) 冷める】
vi
ⓐ cool off, get cold
ⓑ cool down, subside, flag, be dampened
スープが冷めた *Sūpu ga sameta* The soup has cooled
興冷め *kyōzame* being wet-blanketed; skeleton at the feast
【sa(masu) 冷ます】
vt
① cool, let cool
熱冷まし *netsusamashi* antifebrile, antipyretic
② dampen, spoil
興を冷ます *kyō o samasu* spoil a person's pleasure, be a wet-blanket

SYNONYMS

❶ⓐ cold
寒 COLD (weather) → 2311
涼 COOL → 521
ⓑ **reduce the temperature**

凍 FREEZE → 129

HOMOPHONES

sameru ⇨ 覚 2604

samasu ⇨ 覚 2604

NOTE

⇨ see USAGE note at 覚 2604

2-5 冫

冷 81

▶**COLD**

nonstandard for 冷 80

2-5 子

孤

incorrect stroke count ⇨ see 356

2-5 阝

阻 附 etc.

incorrect stroke count ⇨ see ◧ 3–5

2-5 丿

児

incorrect classification ⇨ see 2546

2-6 亻

侮 侮 侮 侮 82

BU anado(ru)

ノ 亻 亻' 亻'' 仁 仢 侮 侮 (stroke order 1–8)

Ⓒ 侮 wǔ

Radical	Strokes
亻 9	8-2-6
Grade	**Freq**
Jōyō	1862
◧ 1 - 2 - 6	

▶**INSULT**

COMPOUNDS

ⓐ [original meaning] **insult, humiliate, make a fool of**

ⓑ despise, disdain, hold in contempt, make light of

侮辱する *bujoku suru* insult, treat with contempt

侮言 *bugen* words of insult

侮蔑 *bubetsu* contempt, scorn

軽侮する *keibu suru* look down upon, despise, disdain

KUN

【anado(ru) 侮る】 despise, disdain, hold in contempt, make light of

侮り *anadori* contempt, scorn

侮り難い敵 *anadorigatai teki* formidable enemy

SYNONYMS

ⓐ **disgrace**

辱 HUMILIATE → 2736

汚 defile → 222

恥 SHAME → 1313

ⓑ **disdain**

軽 make light of → 1515

2-6 亻

併 併 併 併 83

HEI awa(seru)

ノ 亻 亻' 亻'' 亻'' 亻'' 併 併 (stroke order 1–8)

Ⓒ 并 bìng bīng

Radical	Strokes
亻 9	8-2-6
Grade	**Freq**
Jōyō	892
◧ 1 - 2 - 6	

▶**TOGETHER**

COMPOUNDS

❶ [also 並 2246] **together, collectively, simultaneously, side by side**

併用する *heiyō suru* use together [jointly]

併発 *heihatsu* concurrence

併記する *heiki suru* line up together (in writing)

併呑 *heidon* annexation, merger

併殺 *heisatsu* double play

❷ [original meaning] **join together, combine, unite**

合併する *gappei suru* combine, unite, merge
兼併する *kenpei suru* join together, unite

KUN

【awa(seru) 併せる】[sometimes also 合わせる] (bring two or more things together) join together, combine, merge
併せて *awasete* collectively, all together; in addition, besides
併せ持つ *awasemotsu* own (something) as well
二つの会社を併せる *futatsu no kaisha o awaseru* merge two companies

SYNONYMS

❶ together
並 side by side → 2246
同 together → 2987
共 JOINT → 2393
兼 CONCURRENTLY → 2286

❷ combine
括 LUMP TOGETHER → 376
総 integrate → 1379
統 UNITE → 1352
結 TIE → 1348
合 COMBINE → 2019

HOMOPHONES

awaseru ⇨ 合 2019 会 2020 遭 3159

NOTE

⇨ see USAGE note at 合 2019

依 依 依

84 I E yo(ru)▲

CH 依 yī

Radical	Strokes
亻 9	8-2-6
Grade	**Freq**
Jōyō	1071
1-2-6	

2-6 亻

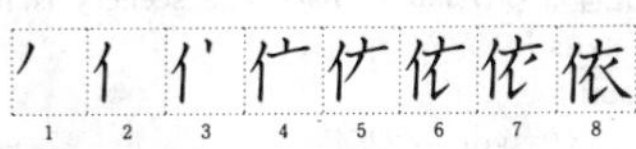

▶DEPEND ON

COMPOUNDS

❶ⓐ depend on, rely on
ⓑ be based on
依存する *izon* (=*ison*) *suru* depend on, rely on
依嘱する *ishoku suru* entrust with
依頼する *irai suru* request, make a request; entrust, commission; rely on, depend on
帰依 *kie* faith, devotion; conversion
依拠 *ikyo* basis, grounds; dependence
依願退職 *igan-taishoku* retirement at one's own request

❷ as it used to be
依然として *izen to shite* as ever, as before

KUN

【yo(ru) 依る】
① depend on, rely on, hang on
成功は忍耐の如何に依る *Seikō wa nintai no ikan ni yoru* Success depends upon perseverance
② do by (means of), resort to, have recourse to
彼らの助力に依って *karera no joryoku ni yotte* by dint of their help

SYNONYMS

❶ⓐ rely on
頼 RELY ON → 1615

HOMOPHONES

yoru ⇨ 拠 312 因 3054 由 3499 寄 2291

NOTE

⇨ see USAGE note at 因 3054

侍 侍 侍

85 JI samurai habe(ru)▲

CH 侍 shì

Radical	Strokes
亻 9	8-2-6
Grade	**Freq**
Jōyō	1713
1-2-6	

2-6 亻

ノ	亻	仁	仕	仕	佳	侍	侍
1	2	3	4	5	6	7	8

▶ATTEND UPON ▶SAMURAI

COMPOUNDS

● attend upon, wait upon, serve
侍女 *jijo* lady attendant
侍従 *jijū* chamberlain
侍医 *jii* court physician, personal physician
陪侍 *baiji* attending on the nobility; retainer
近侍 *kinji* attendant

KUN

【samurai 侍】[also suffix] samurai, warrior; man of resolution and ability
若侍 *wakazamurai* young samurai
犬侍 *inuzamurai* shameless [depraved] samurai

田舎侍 *inakazamurai* country samurai
【**habe(ru) 侍る**】attend upon, wait upon, serve
美女を侍らす *bijo o haberasu* be waited upon by a beauty

SYNONYMS

● **accompany**
陪 ACCOMPANY A SUPERIOR → 539
従 FOLLOW → 415
随 FOLLOW → 627
伴 ACCOMPANY → 60
添 accompany → 529

【**samurai**】
○ **soldiers and warriors**
武 warrior → 3210
士 MILITARY MAN → 3405
卒 private → 2055
兵 SOLDIER → 2551

2-6
亻

佳

86 KA

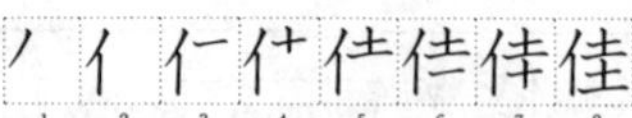

CH 佳 jiǎ

Radical	Strokes
亻 9	8-2-6
Grade	**Freq**
Jōyō	1575
1 - 2 - 6	

▶**FINE**

COMPOUNDS

❶ (of superior quality) **fine, good, excellent**
佳作 *kasaku* fine work
佳境 *kakyō* most interesting part, climax
佳品 *kahin* choice [excellent] article
佳味 *kami* fine [good] taste; delicious food
❷ [original meaning] (of pleasing appearance) **fine(-looking), beautiful**
佳人 *kajin* beautiful woman
佳麗 *karei* beauty
佳景 *kakei* fine [beautiful] view
絶佳の *zekka no* superb (landscape)
❸ [also 嘉 2340] happy, auspicious, lucky, good
佳節 *kasetsu* happy [auspicious] occasion
佳辰 *kashin* happy [auspicious] occasion

INDEPENDENT

【**ka 佳**】beauty, superbness
風光佳なり *Fūkō ka nari* The scenery is fine

SYNONYMS

❶ **good**
美 BEAUTIFUL → 2264
好 FAVORABLE → 208
順 favorable → 18
良 GOOD → 3558
善 GOOD → 2325
❷ **beautiful**
美 BEAUTIFUL → 2264
瑶 EXQUISITE → 1026
麗 OF GRACEFUL BEAUTY → 2151
艶 CHARMING → 1908
妙 of marvelous beauty → 239
華 MAGNIFICENT → 2283
絢 GORGEOUS → 1347
斐 florid → 2776

2-6
亻

価 價

87 KA atai

ノ 亻 亻一 亻冖 亻帀 亻丙 価 価
1 2 3 4 5 6 7 8

CH 价 jià jiè jie

Radical	Strokes
亻 9	8-2-6
Grade	**Freq**
Jōyō-5	269
1 - 2 - 6	

▶**PRICE** ▶**VALUE**

COMPOUNDS

❶ [original meaning] (monetary value) **price, cost**
価格 *kakaku* price, cost
物価 *bukka* prices (of commodities)
高価な *kōka na* expensive, high-priced
米価 *beika* price of rice
定価 *teika* fixed [set] price
❷ [also suffix] **value, worth, merit**
価値 *kachi* value, merit
評価する *hyōka suru* evaluate, appraise
声価 *seika* reputation, fame
栄養価 *eiyōka* nutritive value
❸ⓐ valence
ⓑ counter for valence
数価 *sūka* valence
原子価 *genshika* (atomic) valence
多価 *taka* polyvalence
二価の *nika no* divalent

KUN

【atai 価】price, cost
価千金の *atai senkin no* priceless, invaluable

SYNONYMS

❶ **fee and price**
値 price → 109
料 FEE → 1292
代 CHARGE → 30
賃 CHARGES → 2694
銭 money paid → 1725
費 EXPENSE → 2607
❷ **value**
値 VALUE → 109

HOMOPHONES

atai ⇨ 値 109

NOTE

⇨ see USAGE note at 値 109

供

供 供 (CH) 供 gōng gòng

88 KYŌ KU KŪ▲ GU▲ sona(eru) tomo -domo

Radical	Strokes
亻 9	8-2-6
Grade	**Freq**
Jōyō-6	467
◧ 1-2-6	

2-6 亻

Stroke order: 1 2 3 4 5 6 7 8

▶OFFER

COMPOUNDS

❶ⓐ (put at another's disposal) **offer, present, submit**
ⓑ **supply, deliver, furnish**
供覧 *kyōran* display, show
提供する *teikyō suru* offer, tender; sponsor (a show)
試供品 *shikyōhin* sample, specimen
供給する *kyōkyū suru* supply, furnish, provide
供与する *kyōyo suru* offer, present, submit
供出 *kyōshutsu* delivery of allotment to the government
供米 *kyōmai* delivery of rice to the government; rice delivered to the government
❷ [original meaning] **offer (sacrifices to a god), dedicate, sacrifice**
供物 *kumotsu* offering
供養 *kuyō* memorial service
供米 *kumai* rice offered to a god
供御 *kugo* emperor's meal
人身御供 *hitomigokū* human sacrifice, victim
❸ confess, depose
供述 *kyōjutsu* testimony, statement; confession
自供する *jikyō suru* confess, depose
❹ [formerly 饗 2906] treat, provide dinner for, entertain, banquet
供応 *kyōō* treat, feast, banquet
供宴 *kyōen* banquet, feast, dinner
❺ accompany, follow, go with
供奉する *gubu suru* accompany, be in attendance

INDEPENDENT

【kyōsuru 供する】offer, present, submit; furnish, provide

KUN

【sona(eru) 供える】offer (to a god), make an offering
供え *sonae* offering
供え物 *sonaemono* offering
墓に花を供える *haka ni hana o sonaeru* offer flowers on a tomb
【tomo 供】attendant, retinue
供回り *tomomawari* train of attendants, retinue
お供する *otomosuru* go with, accompany, follow
【-domo -供】plural suffix—now used only in 子供 *kodomo* without implying plurality
子供 *kodomo* child, kid; son, daughter

SYNONYMS

❶ⓐ & ❷ **offer**
献 OFFER (esp. to a superior) → 1785
納 offer (as to a god) → 1300
提 PRESENT → 591
貢 offer tribute → 2281
奉 DEDICATE → 2559
ⓑ **supply**
給 SUPPLY → 1350
納 deliver goods to a customer → 1300
【tomo】
○ **servants**
従 follower → 415
臣 RETAINER → 3068
僕 MANSERVANT → 164
奴 SLAVE → 187
隷 UNDERLING → 1751

HOMOPHONES

sonaeru ⇨ 備 146
sonae ⇨ 備 146
tomo ⇨ 友 2952 共 2393
-domo ⇨ 共 2393

NOTE

⇨ see USAGE notes at 備 146 and 友 2952 and 共 2393

2-6 例 例 例
亻
89 REI tato(eru)

ノ 亻 仁 仃 仴 伢 例 例
1 2 3 4 5 6 7 8

CH 例 lì

Radical	Strokes
亻 9	8-2-6
Grade	**Freq**
Jōyō-4	490
1 - 2 - 6	

▶EXAMPLE

COMPOUNDS

❶ⓐ [also suffix] (something representative) **example, instance, case**

ⓑ **previous example, precedent**

例題 *reidai* example, exercise

例文 *reibun* illustrative sentence, example (sentence)

一例 *ichirei* example, instance, case, illustration

範例 *hanrei* example

実例 *jitsurei* example, instance, concrete case

用例 *yōrei* example, illustration (of the use of a word)

特例 *tokurei* special case [example]; exception

具体例 *gutairei* concrete example

例外 *reigai* exception

類例 *ruirei* similar example, parallel

先例 *senrei* precedent, former example

前例 *zenrei* precedent; above example

判例 *hanrei* (judicial) precedent

❷ⓐ **established practice, custom, usage**

ⓑ **regular, usual, established**

恒例 *kōrei* regular ceremony, established custom

慣例 *kanrei* custom, usage, precedent

家例 *karei* family usage [practice, custom]

常例 *jōrei* usual practice, common usage, established custom

例会 *reikai* regular meeting

例年 *reinen* normal year, average year

例日 *reijitsu* regular day

例刻 *reikoku* regular time

❸ conventions, rules

条例 *jōrei* regulations, rules, law

凡例 *hanrei* introductory remarks, explanatory notes, legend

❹ put side by side, compare

比例 *hirei* proportion, ratio

INDEPENDENT

【**rei 例**】example, instance; precedent; practice, custom, habit

例を挙げる *rei o ageru* cite an example

例に無く *rei ni naku* unusually, contrary to one's habit

KUN

【**tato(eru) 例える**】illustrate, give an example

例えば *tatoeba* for example

SYNONYMS

❶ **example**

型 TYPE → 2638

❷ⓐ **custom**

慣 HABITUAL PRACTICE → 685

習 CUSTOM → 2667

風 manners → 3007

俗 popular custom → 104

癖 HABIT → 3290

弊 EVIL PRACTICE → 2884

ⓑ **constant**

常 REGULAR → 2590

恒 CONSTANT → 367

定 fixed → 2229

USAGE

tatoeru

例える

illustrate, give an example

譬える

[also 喩える] compare to, liken, speak figuratively

喩える

[also 譬える] compare to, liken, speak figuratively

HOMOPHONES

tatoeru ⇨ 譬 2903 喩 553

使 使 使 は

㊥ 使 shǐ

90 SHI tsuka(u) tsuka(i) -tsuka(i) -zuka(i)

丿 亻 亻 仁 佢 佢 使 使 (1 2 3 4 5 6 7 8)

Radical	Strokes
亻 9	8-2-6
Grade	**Freq**
Jōyō-3	226
◧ 1 - 2 - 6	

2-6 亻

▶USE ▶ENVOY

COMPOUNDS

❶ⓐ use, make use of, employ
ⓑ abbrev. of 使用者 *shiyōsha*: employer
使用する *shiyō suru* use, employ, apply
使途 *shito* how money is spent
使役 *shieki* employment, service; *gram* causative
行使する *kōshi suru* use, employ, exercise
駆使する *kushi suru* use freely, have good command of
労使 *rōshi* labor and management

❷ⓐ [also suffix] **envoy, messenger, emissary, ambassador, delegate**
ⓑ servant
使節 *shisetsu* envoy, ambassador
使者 *shisha* messenger
使命 *shimei* mission, appointed task
大使 *taishi* ambassador
特使 *tokushi* special envoy [messenger]
天使 *tenshi* angel
遣唐使 *kentōshi* Japanese envoy to Tang China
使丁 *shitei* servant

KUN

【tsuka(u) 使う】
①ⓐ use, make use of, employ, handle
ⓑ employ, keep (in one's employ)
使い古す *tsukaifurusu* wear out (a thing) by use
使いこなす *tsukaikonasu* manage, handle, acquire command of
使い分ける *tsukaiwakeru* use properly, know how to use properly
使い物にならない *tsukaimono ni naranai* be no use
使い手 *tsukaite* user, consumer; (fencing) master
魔法使い *mahōtsukai* magician, sorcerer
人を使う *hito o tsukau* employ, take a person in one's service
② [usu. 遣う] spend, use (time or money)
金を使う *kane o tsukau* spend money

【tsuka(i) 使い】 mission, errand; messenger, emissary
使いをやる *tsukai o yaru* send a messenger

【-tsuka(i), -zuka(i) -使い】
[also suffix]
① trainer, tamer
蛇使い *hebitsukai* snake charmer
象使い *zōtsukai* elephant trainer
② servant, employee
小間使い *komazukai* lady's maid, housemaid
召し使い *meshitsukai* servant

SYNONYMS

❶ⓐ use
用 EMPLOY → 2976

❷ⓐ agents
偵 SPY → 138

【tsukau】
①ⓑ employ
雇 EMPLOY → 1956
用 EMPLOY → 2976
役 press into service → 244

USAGE

❶ tsukau
使う
①ⓐ use, make use of, employ, handle
ⓑ employ, keep (in one's employ)
② [usu. 遣う] spend, use (time or money)
遣う
① [sometimes also 使う] spend, use (time or money)
② be anxious, worry
③ use (language properly), spell
④ manipulate

❷ -tsukai
-使い
[also suffix]
① trainer, tamer
② servant, employee
-遣い
① spending, spending money
② worrying, being anxious
③ use (of language), spelling
④ manipulating

HOMOPHONES

tsukau ⇨ 遣 3152
-tsukai ⇨ 遣 3152

COMPOUND FORMATION

使命 *shimei*
使命 'mission, appointed task' refers to the orders (命) or duties assigned to an envoy (使 ❷ⓐ).

NOTE
⇨ see COMPOUND FORMATION for 使節 *shise-tsu* ⇨ 節 2691

2-6 亻

侑 91

YŪ NAMES atsumu susumu yuki

CH 侑 yòu

Radical	Strokes
亻 9	8-2-6
Grade	**Freq**
Names	2133
1-2-6	

Stroke order: 1 2 3 4 5 6 7 8

▶URGE TO EAT

COMPOUNDS

● [archaic] urge someone to eat or drink, assist with a meal

侑觴 *yūshō* urging one to drink more good wine during a banquet

侑食 *yūshoku* dining with a superior, assisting at dinner

NAMES

侑子 *yūko* female name

侑 *susumu* male name

SYNONYMS

● **urge**

勧 URGE → 1857

催 PRESS FOR → 157

促 HASTEN → 103

誘 INDUCE → 1550

励 ENCOURAGE → 1119

2-6 亻

使 92

▶USE ▶ENVOY

nonstandard for 使 90

2-6 亻

隹

incorrect classification ⇨ see 3566

2-6 ⺊

協 93

KYŌ

CH 协 xié

Radical	Strokes
十 24	8-2-6
Grade	**Freq**
Jōyō-4	186
1-2-6	

Stroke order: 1 2 3 4 5 6 7 8

▶COOPERATE

COMPOUNDS

❶ⓐ [original meaning] **cooperate, collaborate, work together; be in harmony**

ⓑ [also suffix] abbrev. of 協会 *kyōkai* and 協同組合 *kyōdōkumiai*: **association, cooperative**

協力する *kyōryoku suru* cooperate, collaborate, work together

協同 *kyōdō* cooperation, collaboration, association

協調 *kyōchō* cooperation, harmony

協賛 *kyōsan* support, cooperation

協奏曲 *kyōsōkyoku* concerto

協会 *kyōkai* association, society

世界ボクシング協 *sekai bokushingu-kyō* World Boxing Association

農協 *nōkyō* agricultural cooperative

生協 *seikyō* cooperative association [society]

日米協 *nichibeikyō* Japan United States Cultural Exchange Association

❷ⓐ **reach an agreement, agree upon, make an agreement**

ⓑ abbrev. of 協議会 *kyōgikai*: conference, council

協議 *kyōgi* conference, deliberation

協議会 *kyōgikai* conference, council

協商 *kyōshō* entente, agreement

協約 *kyōyaku* pact, convention, agreement

協定 *kyōtei* agreement, pact

妥協 *dakyō* compromise, agreement, understanding

経協 *keikyō* Management Conference

SYNONYMS

❶ⓐ **cooperate**

携 join hands → 648

調 harmonize → 1567
ⓑ **organized bodies**
会 SOCIETY → 2020
団 BODY → 3053
体 BODY → 71
組 union → 1337
労 workers' union → 2548
連 federation → 3103

講 fraternity → 1619
院 INSTITUTION → 454
❷ⓐ **promise**
締 CONCLUDE (a treaty) → 1393
契 MAKE AN AGREEMENT → 2639
約 PROMISE → 1280
盟 ALLIANCE → 2794
誓 VOW → 2754

挍 94

2-6 扌

▶**COOPERATE**
handwritten abbreviation for 協 93

孤

2-6 子

incorrect stroke count ⇨ see 356

限 降

2-6 阝

incorrect stroke count ⇨ see ◧3-6

便 便 便 便 95

2-7 亻

BEN BIN tayo(ri)

Ⓒⓗ 便 biàn pián

Radical	Strokes
亻 9	9-2-7
Grade	**Freq**
Jōyō-4	792
◧ 1 - 2 - 7	

Stroke order: 1 2 3 4 5 6 7 8 9

▶**CONVENIENT** ▶**POST** ▶**EXCRETA**

COMPOUNDS

❶ⓐ [original meaning] **convenient, expedient, handy**
ⓑ convenient time for an action, opportunity, chance
便利な *benri na* convenient, handy, useful
便宜 *bengi* convenience, facility
便覧 *benran* (= *binran*) handbook, manual
便法 *benpō* convenient method, shortcut, expedient
不便な *fuben na* inconvenient
方便 *hōben* expedient, instrument
便乗する *binjō suru* take advantage of an opportunity; go on board
❷ⓐ (postal material) **post, mail, letter**
ⓑ [also suffix] **postal service, postal delivery, mail**
便箋 *binsen* letter paper, stationery, writing paper
郵便 *yūbin* mail service, mail, postal matter
別便 *betsubin* separate post
航空便 *kōkūbin* airmail
第一便 *daiichibin* first delivery
❸ (feces or urine) **excreta, excrement, feces, urine**
便所 *benjo* lavatory, bathroom
便秘 *benpi* constipation
便器 *benki* toilet bowl, urinal
大便 *daiben* feces, excrement
小便 *shōben* urine
❹ⓐ [also suffix] **transportation service, flight**
ⓑ counter for public transport runs or flights
定期便 *teikibin* regular service
下り便 *kudaribin* outbound train, down train
貨物便で *kamotsubin de* by freight
日航五百便 *nikkō gohyakubin* JAL flight No. 500
一日三便 *ichinichi sanbin* three flights [runs] per day
❺ relax, rest, be at ease
便衣 *ben'i* convenient clothes, ordinary clothes
❻ [archaic] flatter, curry favor
便佞 *bennei* flattery, adulation

INDEPENDENT

【**ben 便**】
① convenience, facilities, accommodation
便を図る *ben o hakaru* administer to the convenience of, provide facilities
交通の便 *kōtsū no ben* transportation facilities
②ⓐ feces, excrement
ⓑ abbrev. of 便所 *benjo*: toilet
便をする *ben o suru* evacuate the bowels

【bensuru 便する】 make convenient, provide facilities
【benjiru (=benzuru) 便じる(=便ずる)】 serve the purpose, will do
【bin 便】 post, mail; postal service; opportunity, chance; flight
次の便 *tsugi no bin* next post; next flight
便の有り次第 *bin no arishidai* on the first opportunity

KUN

【tayo(ri) 便り】 news, tidings; correspondence, letter, communication
花便り *hanadayori* news [first tidings] of the cherry blossoms
便りをする *tayori o suru* write a letter

SYNONYMS

❶ⓐ **suitable**
適 SUITABLE → 3160
当 proper → 2177
宜 RIGHT → 2223
❷ **mail**
郵 MAIL → 1687
❸ **excreta**
尿 URINE → 3064
汗 SWEAT → 220

2-7
亻

保 

96 HO HŌ▲ tamo(tsu)

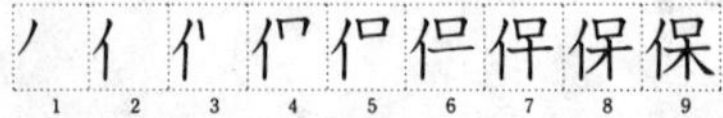

Ⓒⓗ 保 bǎo

Radical	Strokes
亻 9	9-2-7
Grade	**Freq**
Jōyō-5	173
◧ 1-2-7	

▶**PRESERVE**

COMPOUNDS

❶ⓐ (maintain unchanged) **preserve, maintain, keep, conserve, retain, hold**
ⓑ (maintain in good condition) **preserve, keep up, maintain**
保持する *hoji suru* maintain, preserve, retain
保有する *hoyū suru* possess, maintain
留保する *ryūho suru* reserve, withhold, keep back
確保する *kakuho suru* secure, make sure of, ensure
保存する *hozon suru* preserve, conserve, maintain, store, keep
保管する *hokan suru* take custody [charge] of, keep
保温 *hoon* keeping warm, heat insulation
保安 *hoan* preservation of public peace
保健 *hoken* (preservation of) health, sanitation
保全 *hozen* integrity, preservation
保線 *hosen* track maintenance
❷ⓐ [original meaning] (maintain in safety) **preserve, protect, defend, shield, guard**
ⓑ **care for, look after; nurse, suckle**
保護する *hogo suru* protect, safeguard, preserve, look after
保身 *hoshin* self-protection
保母 *hobo* nurse, kindergarten teacher
保育(=哺育) *hoiku* nurture, upbringing; lactation, nursing
❸ⓐ **insure, guarantee, ensure**
ⓑ abbrev. of 保険 *hoken*: **insurance**
保険 *hoken* insurance
保証する *hoshō suru* (assume responsibility for) guarantee, vouch for, certify
保障する *hoshō suru* (ensure that an undesirable condition does not occur) guarantee, secure, ensure
安保(=安全保障条約) *anpo* (=*anzen hoshō jōyaku*) Japan-U.S. Security Treaty
担保 *tanpo* security, mortgage
生保(=生命保険) *seiho* (=*seimei hoken*) life insurance
損保(=損害保険) *sonpo* (=*songai hoken*) damage insurance
❹ abbrev. of 保守 *hoshu*: the conservatives
保革 *hokaku* conservatives and reformists
保無(=保守系無所属 *hoshukei mushozoku*) conservative without party affiliation
❺ shop employee, shop
酒保 *shuho* canteen, PX
❻ unit of ten houses in a neighborhood
隣保館 *rinpokan* settlement house
❼ [also 堡 *ho, hō* 2821] fort
橋頭保 *kyōtoho* (=*kyōtōhō*) bridgehead, beachhead

INDEPENDENT

【hosuru 保する】 guarantee, secure

KUN

【tamo(tsu) 保つ】 (maintain unchanged) preserve, keep, maintain, hold; (maintain in good condition) preserve, maintain, support, sustain
命を保つ *inochi o tamotsu* preserve life
平和を保つ *heiwa o tamotsu* maintain [preserve] peace

SYNONYMS

❶ **preserve**

留 KEEP → 2580
持 uphold → 374
❷ **protect**
護 PROTECT → 1648
守 PROTECT → 2173
衛 GUARD → 760
警 GUARD AGAINST → 2893
防 defend → 270
番 WATCH → 2748
看 CARE FOR → 3220

USAGE
hoshō suru
保証する
(assume responsibility for) guarantee, vouch for, certify
保障する
(ensure that an undesirable condition does not occur) guarantee, secure, ensure

NOTE
⇨ see COMPOUND FORMATION for 保険 *hoken* ⇨ 険 542

係 係 係

97 KEI kaka(ru) kakari -gakari kaka(waru)▲

Ⓒⓗ 系 xì

Radical	Strokes
亻 9	9-2-7
Grade	**Freq**
Jōyō-3	241
1-2-7	

2-7 亻

Stroke order: 1 2 3 4 5 6 7 8 9

▶**CONNECT** ▶**PERSON IN CHARGE**

COMPOUNDS
[formerly also 繫 2902]
❶ⓐ (have a relationship with) **connect, be connected with, relate to, interrelate**
ⓑ connection, relation
係累 *keirui* family ties, dependents
係争 *keisō* dispute, contention; lawsuit
係属 *keizoku* pendency (of a legal case); relationship
関係 *kankei* relation, relationship, connection
連係 *renkei* connection, linking, contact
係数 *keisū math* coefficient
❷ **connect, tie up, fasten, moor**
係留 *keiryū* mooring, anchorage
係船 *keisen* mooring a ship

KUN
【kaka(ru) 係る】
① affect, concern, involve
面目に係る問題 *menboku ni kakaru mondai* problem concerning one's honor
② *gram* modify
係り *kakari* relation, connection (esp. in grammar)
係り結び *kakarimusubi* relation, connection (esp. in grammar)
副詞は動詞に係る *Fukushi wa dōshi ni kakaru* Adverbs modify verbs
③ is the work of, is done by
これは浅田氏に係る小説だ *Kore wa asadashi ni kakaru shōsetsu da* This novel is the work of Mr. Asada
【kakari 係】
[sometimes also 掛]
ⓐ person in charge, official in charge, clerk
ⓑ charge, duty, post
係員 *kakariin* clerk in charge
係長 *kakarichō* chief clerk
係官 *kakarikan* official in charge
係の人 *kakari no hito* person in charge
係をする *kakari o suru* be in charge
【-gakari -係】[sometimes also -掛] [suffix]
person in charge, official in charge, clerk
案内係 *annaigakari* clerk at the information desk
会計係 *kaikeigakari* accountant, treasurer
受付係 *uketsukegakari* reception clerk
【kaka(waru) 係わる】
[also 関わる]
① be concerned in, be involved
係わり *kakawari* relation, connection
事件に係わる *jiken ni kakawaru* be involved in a case
② influence (adversely), affect
命に係わる *inochi ni kakawaru* be threatening to one's life, be a matter of life and death

SYNONYMS
❶ⓐ **relate**
関 CONCERN → 3328
絡 INTERLINK → 1351
渉 HAVE RELATIONS WITH → 526
連 LINK → 3103
❷ **join**
接 join → 500
連 LINK → 3103
結 TIE → 1348
縛 BIND → 1405
束 TIE UP → 3554
【kakari】
ⓐ &【-gakari】 **person in charge**
-方 person in charge → 1963
員 MEMBER (of a staff) → 2269

USAGE
kakawaru

係わる
［also 関わる］
① be concerned in, be involved
② influence (adversely), affect
関わる
［also 係わる］ same as 係わる
拘わる
adhere to, stick to

HOMOPHONES
kakaru ⇨ 掛 493 懸 2915 架 2569 繋 2902 罹 2619
kakari ⇨ 掛 493
-gakari ⇨ 掛 493
kakawaru ⇨ 関 3328 拘 310

NOTE
⇨ see also USAGE note at 掛 493

2-7
亻

侯 侯 俟

98 KŌ

Stroke order: ノ 亻 亻 仁 伫 伫 俣 侯 侯 (1–9)

CH 侯 hóu hòu

Radical	Strokes
亻 9	9-2-7
Grade	**Freq**
Jōyō	1921
1 - 2 - 7	

▶**FEUDAL LORD**

COMPOUNDS
❶ⓐ **feudal lord, daimyo**
ⓑ **honorific title after names of feudal lords［daimyos］**
諸侯 *shokō* feudal lords
王侯 *ōkō* princess, royalty, crowned heads
仙台侯 *sendaikō* Lord of Sendai
❷ⓐ marquis
ⓑ title after names of marquises
侯爵 *kōshaku* marquis
黒田侯 *kurodakō* Marquis Kuroda

INDEPENDENT
【kō 侯】lord, daimyo; marquis

SYNONYMS
❶ **nobility**
公 nobleman → 1974
爵 RANK OF NOBILITY → 2524
❷ **noblemen**
公 duke → 1974
伯 COUNT → 59
子 viscount → 3390
男 baron → 2542

NOTE
★do not confuse with 候 119

2-7
亻

俚

99 RI

CH 俚 lǐ

Radical	Strokes
亻 9	9-2-7
Grade	**Freq**
Reference	
1 - 2 - 7	

COMPOUNDS
● ［now also 里 3542］［original meaning］ rural, rustic, vulgar
俚謡 *riyō* ballad, folk song
俚言 *rigen* dialect; slang
俚諺 *rigen* traditional［folk］saying, proverb
俚耳 *riji* public ears

2-7
亻

信 信 信

100 SHIN

Stroke order: ノ 亻 亻 仁 仁 信 信 信 信 (1–9)

CH 信 xìn

Radical	Strokes
亻 9	9-2-7
Grade	**Freq**
Jōyō-4	230
1 - 2 - 7	

▶**BELIEVE** ▶**MESSAGE**

COMPOUNDS
❶ⓐ **believe, trust, have confidence in**
ⓑ **believe in (God), have faith**
信託 *shintaku* trust
信用 *shin'yō* trust, credit, confidence
信頼 *shinrai* reliance, confidence, trust
自信 *jishin* self-confidence

不信 *fushin* distrust, discredit
確信 *kakushin* firm belief, conviction
信仰 *shinkō* faith, belief, conviction
信者 *shinja* believer, adherent
信心深い *shinjinbukai* religious, devout
信教 *shinkyō* religion, faith
❷ [original meaning] fidelity, faith, sincerity
信義 *shingi* fidelity, faith, loyalty
威信 *ishin* prestige, dignity, authority
背信 *haishin* breach of faith [trust], betrayal
❸ⓐ **message, signal, news, tidings**
ⓑ **written communication or message, letter, telegram**
信号 *shingō* signal; traffic light
受信 *jushin* reception (of radio waves); receipt of a message
混信 *konshin* jamming, interference, cross talk
交信 *kōshin* exchange of messages, communications
花信 *kashin* tidings of flowers, information about flowers for viewing
通信 *tsūshin* correspondence, communication, information
返信 *henshin* reply, answer
短信 *tanshin* brief note [letter], brief message
私信 *shishin* private note [letter]
電信 *denshin* telegraph, telegram
❹ abbrev. of 信用 *shin'yō* or 信託 *shintaku*: credit, trust
信金 *shinkin* credit union [guild]
投信 *tōshin* investment trust
❺ abbrev. of 信濃 *shinano*, old name for Nagano Prefecture
信州 *shinshū* Shinshu, Shinano
信越 *shin'etsu* Nagano and Niigata

INDEPENDENT

【shin 信】 trust, credit, confidence; fidelity, faith, sincerity
信を問う *shin o tou* make an appeal to the confidence of

【shinjiru (=shinzuru) 信じる(=信ずる)】 believe, trust; believe in, have faith in

SYNONYMS

❷ **fidelity**
実 faithfulness → 2225
誠 SINCERITY → 1523
忠 LOYALTY → 2433
義 faith → 2338
孝 FILIAL PIETY → 3205
悌 BROTHERLY LOVE → 424
操 constancy → 769
節 moral integrity → 2691
❸ⓐ **information**
報 information → 1698
ⓑ **written communications**
電 telegram → 2790
状 LETTER → 272
文 LETTER → 1962
書 letter → 2658

侵 侵 侵 侵

101 SHIN oka(su)

Stroke order: ノ 亻 亻 亻 亻 亻 亻 侵 侵 (1–9)

CH 侵 qīn

Radical	Strokes
亻 9	9-2-7
Grade	**Freq**
Jōyō	947
1 - 2 - 7	

2-7 亻

▶INVADE

COMPOUNDS

ⓐ (enter by force) **invade, raid**
ⓑ (intrude upon) **invade, infringe on, violate**
侵略 *shinryaku* invasion, aggression
侵入 *shinnyū* invasion, raid, trespass, intrusion
侵犯 *shinpan* invasion; violation
不可侵条約 *fukashin jōyaku* nonaggression treaty
侵食 *shinshoku* infringement, violation
侵害 *shingai* infringement, violation

KUN

【oka(su) 侵す】
ⓐ (enter by force) invade, raid
ⓑ (intrude upon) invade, infringe on, violate
国境を侵す *kokkyō o okasu* invade the frontier district, violate the border
権利を侵す *kenri o okasu* infringe upon someone's right

SYNONYMS

ⓐ **attack**
襲 RAID → 2917
攻 ATTACK → 242
撃 STRIKE → 2863
爆 bomb → 1101

USAGE

okasu
侵す
ⓐ (enter by force) invade, raid
ⓑ (intrude upon) invade, infringe on, violate
犯す

① offend against, violate, infringe upon, commit (a crime), sin against
② rape, violate, deflower

冒す
①ⓐ risk, brave, defy
ⓑ (risk the danger of using a great person's name) assume (another's name); bear
② affect, attack, afflict

HOMOPHONES

okasu ⇨ 犯 196 冒 2434

NOTE

⇨ see also USAGE note at 浸 442
★do not confuse with 浸 442

2-7
亻

俊 俊 俊

102 SHUN

ノ 亻 𠆢 ... 俊 (strokes 1–9)

Ⓒ 俊 jùn

Radical	Strokes
亻9	9-2-7
Grade	Freq
Jōyō	1324
1-2-7	

▶BRILLIANT PERSON

COMPOUNDS

❶ⓐ [original meaning] **brilliant [talented] person, genius**
ⓑ [sometimes also 駿 1832] **brilliant, talented, bright**

俊秀 *shunshū* genius, prodigy
俊才 *shunsai* genius, person of exceptional talent
俊英 *shun'ei* talent, genius; gifted person
俊傑 *shunketsu* genius, hero
俊童 *shundō* brilliant boy, infant prodigy
俊敏な *shunbin na* keen, quick-witted

❷ [also 駿 1832] swift-footed, fleet-footed

俊足 *shunsoku* fleet speed; fast runner; brilliant person

SYNONYMS

❶ⓐ **wise and talented persons**

秀 genius → 2545
才 person of talent → 3410
通 well-informed → 3109
博 DOCTOR → 151
賢 wise man → 2839
哲 sage → 2738

ⓑ **intelligent and wise**

聡 SHARP-WITTED → 1384
明 clear-sighted → 855
敏 NIMBLE → 1322
鋭 SHARP → 1730
哲 SAGACIOUS → 2738
伶 CLEVER → 298
慧 INTELLIGENT → 2810
賢 WISE → 2839
智 wise → 2784

2-7
亻

促 促 促

103 SOKU unaga(su)

ノ 亻 亻 ... 促 (strokes 1–9)

Ⓒ 促 cù

Radical	Strokes
亻9	9-2-7
Grade	Freq
Jōyō	1027
1-2-7	

▶HASTEN

COMPOUNDS

❶ (cause to act with haste) **hasten, urge, hurry, press (for)**

促進する *sokushin suru* promote, spur on, facilitate
促成栽培 *sokusei saibai* forcing culture ("fast-grow cultivation")
催促する *saisoku suru* press for, urge, demand
督促状 *tokusokujō* demand note, dunning letter [note]

❷ shorten, contract

促音 *sokuon* assimilated sound (double consonant represented by っ in Japanese)

KUN

【unaga(su) 促す】 hasten, accelerate, stimulate; urge, press, call for

発達を促す *hattatsu o unagasu* accelerate development
注意を促す *chūi o unagasu* call a person's attention (to)

SYNONYMS

❶ **urge**

催 PRESS FOR → 157
勧 URGE → 1857

誘 INDUCE → 1550
励 ENCOURAGE → 1119
侑 URGE TO EAT → 91

❶ **hurry**
急 HURRY → 2092

俗 俗 俗

104 ZOKU

Ⓒ 俗 sú

Radical	Strokes
亻 9	9-2-7
Grade	**Freq**
Jōyō	1461
◧ 1 - 2 - 7	

2-7 亻

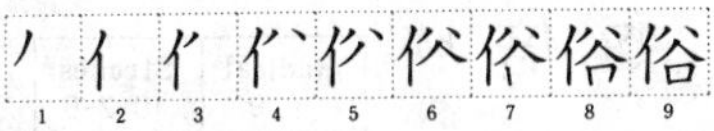

▶POPULAR

COMPOUNDS

❶ⓐ **popular, folk, common**
ⓑ **vulgar, low**
俗説 *zokusetsu* common saying, popular version
俗称 *zokushō* popular [common] name
俗習 *zokushū* popular custom, usage
俗語 *zokugo* slang
通俗 *tsūzoku* popularity, conventionality
俗っぽい *zokuppoi* common, vulgar
俗悪 *zokuaku* vulgarity, inelegance
低俗な *teizoku na* vulgar
❷ [original meaning] **popular custom, folk custom, folkways, convention**
風俗 *fūzoku* manners, customs; popular [public] morals
習俗 *shūzoku* manners and customs, folkways
民俗 *minzoku* folk customs, folkways
良俗 *ryōzoku* good custom
❸ⓐ **worldly, mundane; worldliness**
ⓑ secular
俗事 *zokuji* worldly affairs
俗人 *zokujin* layman, man of the world
俗情 *zokujō* worldly-mindedness, worldliness
俗世間 *zokuseken* the workaday world
脱俗 *datsuzoku* unworldliness
世俗の *sezoku no* common, worldly
俗名 *zokumyō* secular name
還俗 *genzoku* return to secular life, secularization

INDEPENDENT

【zoku 俗】 worldliness, vulgarity; laity
俗に *zoku ni* commonly, vulgarly

SYNONYMS

❶ⓐ **public**
公 PUBLIC → 1974
ⓑ **vulgar and unrefined**
卑 MEAN → 2642
里 rural → 3542
粗 COARSE → 1329
野 rustic → 1485
蛮 barbaric → 2129
❷ **custom**
風 manners → 3007
習 CUSTOM → 2667
例 established practice → 89
慣 HABITUAL PRACTICE → 685
癖 HABIT → 3290
弊 EVIL PRACTICE → 2884
❸ⓐ **worldly**
世 worldly → 3496

便

105

▶CONVENIENT ▶POST ▶EXCRETA

nonstandard for 便 95

2-7 亻

侮

106

▶INSULT

nonstandard for 侮 82

2-7 亻

侵

107

▶INVADE

nonstandard for 侵 101

2-7 亻

孫

incorrect stroke count ⇨ see 410

2-7 子

2-7 阝

陥

incorrect stroke count ⇨ see 548
(nonstandard for 陥 457)

2-7 阝

院 除 etc.

incorrect stroke count ⇨ see 3−7

2-8 亻

倍 倍 倍 倍

108 BAI

CH 倍 bèi

Radical	Strokes
亻 9	10-2-8
Grade	**Freq**
Jōyō-3	810
1-2-8	

丿 亻 亻' 亻亠 亻立 亻立 亻立 倍 倍 倍
1 2 3 4 5 6 7 8 9 10

▶**TIMES** ▶**DOUBLE**

COMPOUNDS

❶ **times, -fold**
倍数 *baisū* multiple
倍率 *bairitsu* magnification, magnifying power; rate of competition (in examinations)
三倍 *sanbai* three times, triple
数倍 *sūbai* several times (as large)

❷ⓐ **double**
ⓑ double, multiply, increase
倍増 *baizō* redoubling
倍額 *baigaku* double amount
倍加 *baika* doubling
人一倍働く *hitoichibai hataraku* work twice as hard as others
倍大 *baidai* double size

INDEPENDENT

【**bai** 倍】double
倍にして返す *bai ni shite kaesu* repay double the original amount
【**baisuru** 倍する】double, be doubled; increase

SYNONYMS

❶ **-fold**
重 -fold → 3573

❷ⓐ **compound**
複 COMPOUND → 1222
重 DUPLICATE → 3573

ⓑ **increase**
増 INCREASE → 677
殖 MULTIPLY → 994
加 add to → 38

2-8 亻

値 値 値

109 CHI ne atai

CH 值 zhí

Radical	Strokes
亻 9	10-2-8
Grade	**Freq**
Jōyō-6	320
1-2-8	

丿 亻 亻一 亻十 亻広 亻冇 亻有 値 値 値
1 2 3 4 5 6 7 8 9 10

▶**VALUE**

COMPOUNDS

ⓐ **value, worth, merit**
ⓑ [also suffix] *math* **value**
価値 *kachi* value, merit
数値 *sūchi* numerical value
絶対値 *zettaichi* absolute value
平均値 *heikinchi* mean value

KUN

【**ne** 値】[also suffix] price, cost
値が張る *ne ga haru* be expensive
値段 *nedan* price
値上げ *neage* price hike
高値 *takane* high price
仕入れ値 *shiirene* cost price

【**atai** 値】
ⓐ value, worth, merit
ⓑ *math* value
値する *ataisuru* be worth, deserve, merit
一読の値が有る *ichidoku no atai ga aru* be worth reading
Xの値 *ekkusu no atai* value of x

SYNONYMS

● **value**
価 VALUE → 87

【**ne**】
○ **fee and price**
費 EXPENSE → 2607
価 PRICE → 87
料 FEE → 1292

代 CHARGE → 30
賃 CHARGES → 2694
銭 money paid → 1725

USAGE

atai

値

ⓐ value, worth, merit
ⓑ *math* value

価

price, cost

HOMOPHONES

atai ⇨ 価 87

俺

110 EN ore

CH 俺 ǎn

Radical	Strokes
亻 9	10-2-8
Grade	Freq
Non-Jōyō	1803
◧ 1 - 2 - 8	

2-8 亻

丿 亻 亻 仆 仆 佧 侤 俺 俺 俺
1 2 3 4 5 6 7 8 9 10

▶I

KUN

【ore 俺】 I—intimate first person pronoun used by men; though usu. expressing intimacy, it sometimes has vulgar overtones

俺達 *oretachi* we

俺が俺がの連中 *ore ga ore ga no renchū* ego-driven men

SYNONYMS

【ore】

○ **first person pronouns**

僕 I (*familiar*) → 164
私 I (*polite*) → 1115
吾 I (*elegant*) → 2407
予 I (*pompous*) → 1983
余 I (*pompous*) → 2042
麿 I (*archaic*) → 3184
朕 IMPERIAL WE → 949
自 SELF → 3525
我 SELF → 3548
己 ONESELF → 3380
身 ONE'S PERSON → 3553

俱

111 GU KU tomo(ni)

CH 俱 jù

Radical	Strokes
亻 9	10-2-8
Grade	Freq
Reference	
◧ 1 - 2 - 8	

2-8 亻

COMPOUNDS

❶ [now usu. 共に *tomoni*] [original meaning] together

俱発 *guhatsu* concurrence (of offenses)

俱する(=具する) *gusuru* possess; take (retainers) with (one), be followed by

俱に天を戴かず *tomoni ten o itadakazu* cannot live together under the canopy of heaven

❷ used phonetically for *ku*

俱楽部 *kurabu* club

俱梨伽羅紋紋 *kurikara monmon* tattoo

俱舎宗 *kushashū* Kusha Sect

HOMOPHONES

tomoni ⇨ 共 2393

NOTE

⇨ see USAGE note at 共 2393

俳

112 HAI

CH 俳 pái

Radical	Strokes
亻 9	10-2-8
Grade	Freq
Jōyō-6	1207
◧ 1 - 2 - 8	

2-8 亻

丿 亻 仆 付 付 付 俳 俳 俳 俳
1 2 3 4 5 6 7 8 9 10

▶HAIKU

COMPOUNDS

❶ **haiku, 17-syllable poem**

俳句 *haiku* haiku

俳人 *haijin* haiku poet

俳壇 *haidan* haiku world

俳諧(＝誹諧) *haikai haikai*, (humorous) haiku

❷ [original meaning] **actor**

俳優 *haiyū* actor, actress

❸ [archaic] jest, joke

俳謔 *haigyaku* joke

SYNONYMS

❶ **poetry**

句 HAIKU → 2967

歌 Japanese poetry → 1825

詩 POETRY → 1524

❷ **performers**

優 ACTOR → 177

伶 MUSICIAN → 66

2-8 亻

倣 倣 倣

113 HŌ nara(u)

CH 仿 fǎng

Radical	Strokes
亻 9	10-2-8
Grade	**Freq**
Jōyō	1889
1 - 2 - 8	

▶COPY AFTER

COMPOUNDS

● **copy after, copy from, imitate**

模倣(＝摸倣)する *mohō suru* imitate, copy

KUN

【nara(u) 倣う】 copy after, copy from, imitate, follow an example

前例に倣う *zenrei ni narau* follow [copy after] a precedent

以下これに倣う *Ika kore ni narau* The undermentioned to follow this example

SYNONYMS

● **imitate**

擬 IMITATE → 788

模 pattern after → 1050

象 represent → 2134

肖 MODEL → 2205

HOMOPHONES

narau ⇨ 習 2667

NOTE

⇨ see USAGE note at 習 2667

2-8 亻

俸 俸 俸

114 HŌ

CH 俸 fèng

Radical	Strokes
亻 9	10-2-8
Grade	**Freq**
Jōyō	1904
1 - 2 - 8	

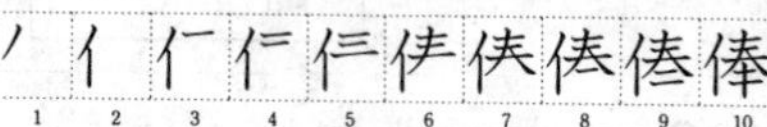

▶SALARY

COMPOUNDS

● **salary, pay**

俸給 *hōkyū* salary, pay

俸禄 *hōroku* retainer's stipend, official pay [salary]

年俸 *nenpō* annual salary

減俸 *genpō* salary cut

五号俸 *gogōhō* fifth grade salary

増俸 *zōhō* increase in salary, raise

INDEPENDENT

【hō 俸】 salary, pay

俸を食む *hō o hamu* receive a salary

SYNONYMS

● **pay and earnings**

給 PAY → 1350

賃 WAGE → 2694

料 FEE → 1292

禄 RETAINER'S STIPEND → 1002

収 income → 198

俵 俵 俵
115 HYŌ tawara

1 2 3 4 5 6 7 8 9 10

CH 俵 biào

Radical	Strokes
亻 9	10-2-8
Grade	**Freq**
Jōyō-5	1413
◧ 1 - 2 - 8	

2-8 亻

▶STRAW SACK

COMPOUNDS

ⓐ **straw sack [bag], sack**

ⓑ counter for sackfuls or straw bags

土俵 *dohyō* sumo (wrestling) ring; sandbag

俵数 *hyōsū* number of straw sacks [bags]

二俵 *nihyō* two straw sacks

INDEPENDENT

【hyō 俵】 straw sack

KUN

【tawara 俵】 straw sack [bag]; sumo ring

米俵 *komedawara* (straw) rice bag

SYNONYMS

ⓐ **bags**

袋 BAG → 2588

包 wrapper → 2966

胞 MEMBRANOUS SAC → 917

倹 儉 倹 倹
116 KEN tsuma(shii)▲

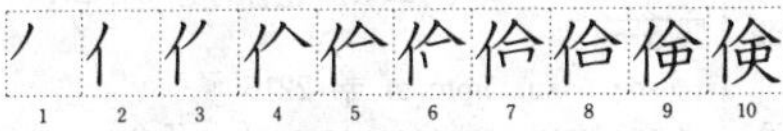

1 2 3 4 5 6 7 8 9 10

CH 俭 jiǎn

Radical	Strokes
亻 9	10-2-8
Grade	**Freq**
Jōyō	1871
◧ 1 - 2 - 8	

2-8 亻

▶FRUGAL

COMPOUNDS

❶ **frugal, thrifty, economical, sparing**

倹約 *ken'yaku* economy, frugality, thrift

勤倹 *kinken* diligence and thrift

節倹 *sekken* economy, frugality, thrift

❷ modest, humble, unpretentious

恭倹 *kyōken* respectfulness and modesty

KUN

【tsuma(shii) 倹しい】 frugal, economical, thrifty, sparing

倹しさ *tsumashisa* frugality

倹しく暮す *tsumashiku kurasu* live frugally

SYNONYMS

❶ **economizing and economy**

節 economize → 2691

省 SAVE → 2449

個 个◇ 𠆣◆ 個 個
117 KO KA▲

1 2 3 4 5 6 7 8 9 10

CH 个 gè gě

Radical	Strokes
亻 9	10-2-8
Grade	**Freq**
Jōyō-5	554
◧ 1 - 2 - 8	

2-8 亻

▶INDIVIDUAL ▶GENERAL COUNTER

COMPOUNDS

❶ [sometimes also 箇 *ko* 2700] [original meaning] **individual, single unit, single person or thing**

個個に *koko ni* individually, separately

個有の *koyū no* peculiar, inherent, characteristic

個室 *koshitsu* private room, single room

個別的に *kobetsuteki ni* individually, severally, singly

個人 *kojin* individual

個性 *kosei* individuality

個展 *koten* personal exhibition

各個 *kakko* one by one

❷ **general counter for things or articles**

個数 *kosū* number of articles

一個 *ikko* one, a piece

林檎三個 *ringo sanko* three apples

十個 *jikko* ten articles

❸ [usu. 箇 *ka* 2700] item, place

個所 *kasho* place, spot, point; part

個条書き *kajōgaki* itemization

INDEPENDENT

【ko 個】individual

個と全 *ko to zen* individual and the whole

SYNONYMS

❶ **one**

単 SINGLE → 2256

一 ONE → 3341

壱 ONE (in legal documents) → 2197

片- ONE OF TWO → 3461

隻 ONE OF A PAIR → 2755

❷ **general counters**

箇 COUNTER FOR ITEMS → 2700

点 counter for articles → 2084

件 counter for cases → 51

丁 MISCELLANEOUS COUNTER → 3348

NOTE

⇨ see USAGE note at 箇 2700

2-8

亻

倖

118 KŌ shiawa(se)

CH 幸 xìng

Radical	Strokes
亻 9	10-2-8
Grade	**Freq**
Reference	
1 - 2 - 8	

COMPOUNDS

[now replaced by 幸 *kō* 2216]

❶ⓐ [original meaning] good fortune, good luck

ⓑ happiness, well-being, felicity

薄倖 *hakkō* unhappiness; sad fate, misfortune

射倖心 *shakōshin* speculative spirit

僥倖 *gyōkō* good fortune, luck, lucky chance

倖せ *shiawase* [now usu. 幸せ or 仕合わせ] happiness, blessing; good fortune

❷ [archaic] be in the good graces of (one's ruler); bestow favor upon

倖臣 *kōshin* favorite courtier

HOMOPHONES

shiawase ⇨ 幸せ 2216 仕合わせ 34, 2019

NOTE

⇨ see USAGE note at 幸 2216

⇨ see COMPOUND FORMATION for 仕合わせ *shiawase* → 2019

2-8

亻

候 候 候

119 KŌ sōrō

CH 候 hòu

Radical	Strokes
亻 9	10-2-8
Grade	**Freq**
Jōyō-4	737
1 - 2 - 8	

▶SEASON ▶SEASONAL WEATHER

COMPOUNDS

❶ **season, time of year**

候鳥 *kōchō* migratory bird

時候 *jikō* season, time of the year

❷ **seasonal weather, climate, weather**

天候 *tenkō* weather

気候 *kikō* climate, weather; season

測候所 *sokkōjo* weather station

❸ **indication, sign, symptom; condition**

兆候(=徴候) *chōkō* symptom, sign; omen

症候 *shōkō* symptom

❹ **wait, await**

候補 *kōho* candidacy, candidate

候補者 *kōhosha* candidate, applicant

❺ inquire after, greet

斥候 *sekkō* scout, patrol, reconnoitering soldier

伺候する *shikō suru* pay one's respects, make a courtesy call; wait upon (a nobleman)

INDEPENDENT

【kō 候】season, time of year; seasonal weather

厳寒の候 *genkan no kō* the coldest season [weather]

KUN

【sōrō 候】classical verbal suffix equiv. to *-masu*

候文 *sōrōbun* epistolary style (i.e., the style employing the *sōrō* form)

候調 *sōrōchō* epistolary style

書き候 *kakisōrō* (have the honor) to write

居候 *isōrō* hanger-on, parasite

SYNONYMS

❶ **time periods**

季 SEASON (quarter) → 2554

節 SEASON OF THE YEAR → 2691

期 TERM → 1704

間 INTERVAL → 3323

刻 POINT OF TIME → 1267
般 period of time → 1317
暇 FREE TIME → 1012
頃 TIME → 144
時 TIME → 924
❷ **weather**
天 weather → 3442
晴 FINE WEATHER → 981
❸ **signs**
徴 SYMPTOM → 683
症 symptom (of a disease) → 3280
気 sign → 3194
兆 OMEN → 225

COMPOUND FORMATION
居候 *isōrō*
居候 'hanger-on, parasite' was formerly the polite form of 居る *iru* 'be', which was extended to mean 'one who is always around, one who feeds on others'. 候 *sōro* is a classical verbal suffix indicating politeness.

NOTE
⇨ see COMPOUND FORMATION for
候補者 *kōhosha* ⇨ 補 1194
測候所 *sokkōjo* ⇨ 測 610
★do not confuse with 侯 98

倫 倫 倫
120 RIN

Ⓒⓗ 伦 lún

Radical	Strokes
亻 9	10-2-8
Grade	**Freq**
Jōyō	1732
1 - 2 - 8	

2-8 亻

ノ 亻 亻 亻 伶 伶 伶 倫 倫 倫
1 2 3 4 5 6 7 8 9 10

▶**MORALS**
COMPOUNDS
❶ⓐ **morals, ethics, moral rules, code of conduct**
ⓑ human relations, esp. as conceived by feudal ethics
倫理 *rinri* ethics, morals, code of conduct
倫理学 *rinrigaku* ethics, moral philosophy
不倫な *furin na* immoral, illicit
人倫 *jinrin* humanity, morality; human relations
破倫 *harin* immorality; incest
五倫 *gorin* moral rules to govern the five human relations; the five cardinal principles of morality
❷ peer, match, equal
比倫 *hirin* peer, match, equal
絶倫の *zetsurin no* matchless, peerless
❸ used phonetically for *ron*
倫敦 *rondon* London

INDEPENDENT
【rin 倫】peer, equal
倫を絶する *rin o zessuru* incomparably excellent

SYNONYMS
❶ⓐ **moral principles**
道 the way of moral conduct → 3134

倆
121 RYŌ

Ⓒⓗ 俩 liǎ liǎng

Radical	Strokes
亻 9	10-2-8
Grade	**Freq**
Reference	
1 - 2 - 8	

2-8 亻

COMPOUNDS
● [now replaced by 量 2471] skill
技倆(＝伎倆) *giryō* skill, ability, capacity

2-8
亻

借 借 借
122 SHAKU ka(riru)

ノ 亻 仁 什 艹 借 借 借 借 借
1 2 3 4 5 6 7 8 9 10

CH 借 jiè

Radical	Strokes
亻 9	10-2-8
Grade	**Freq**
Jōyō-4	888
1-2-8	

▶**BORROW**

COMPOUNDS

❶ **borrow, get a loan**
借金する *shakkin suru* borrow money, run into debt
借用 *shakuyō* borrowing, loan
借家 *shakuya* house for rent, rented house
借款 *shakkan* loan
貸借 *taishaku* lending and borrowing, debt and credit, loan
拝借する *haishaku suru* borrow
賃借する *chinshaku suru* hire, lease

❷ by way of a makeshift, temporarily
借問す *Shakumon su* Let me ask you...
仮借無き *kashakunaki* merciless(ly)

KUN

【**ka(riru) 借りる**】borrow, get a loan; hire, rent; buy on credit
借り *kari* borrowing; debt, loan
借り集める *kariatsumeru* borrow money from many people
借り出す *karidasu* borrow, make a loan of
間借り *magari* renting a room

SYNONYMS

❶ **lend and borrow**
貸 LEND → 2600
債 DEBT → 156
融 finance → 1831

2-8
亻

修 修 修
123 SHŪ SHU osa(meru) osa(maru)

ノ 亻 亻 亻 亻 攸 俢 修 修 修
1 2 3 4 5 6 7 8 9 10

CH 修 xiū

Radical	Strokes
亻 9	10-2-8
Grade	**Freq**
Jōyō-5	627
1-2-8	

▶**CULTIVATE** ▶**REPAIR**

COMPOUNDS

❶ **cultivate (one's intellect or character), improve oneself, foster, pursue, study, train, practice**
修養する *shūyō suru* cultivate one's mind, improve oneself
修道院 *shūdōin* monastery, convent
修了 *shūryō* completion (of a course)
修行 *shugyō* training, study; ascetic practices
修験者 *shugenja* ascetic (living in the mountains)
研修 *kenshū* study and training
履修 *rishū* completion (of a course), taking (a course)
必修の *hisshū no* required, compulsory

❷ **repair, mend, rectify**
修正 *shūsei* amendment, revision, correction; retouch
修理 *shūri* repair, mending
修復 *shūfuku* restoration
修繕する *shūzen suru* mend, repair
改修する *kaishū suru* repair, improve
補修 *hoshū* repair, mending

❸ [original meaning] trim, decorate
修飾する *shūshoku suru* decorate, ornament; *gram* modify
修辞法 *shūjihō* rhetoric

❹ compile, edit
修史 *shūshi* compilation of a history
監修 *kanshū* (editorial) supervision

❺ used phonetically for *shu* in the transliteration of Sanscrit Buddhist terms
阿修羅 *ashura Asura* (fighting demon)

❻ perform (religious rites)
修祓 *shūfutsu* (=*shūbatsu*) expel [exorcise] evil spirits (by Shinto rituals)

INDEPENDENT

【**shūsuru 修する**】perform (religious rites)
法会を修する *hōe o shūsuru* perform a Buddhist mass

KUN

【**osa(meru) 修める**】
① cultivate, pursue, practice, study; master, complete
学を修める *gaku o osameru* pursue knowledge [one's studies]
② order (one's life)
身を修める *mi o osameru* order one's life

【**osa(maru) 修まる**】govern oneself, conduct

oneself well
素行が修まらない *sokō ga osamaranai* conduct oneself loosely, be dissolute

SYNONYMS

❶ **cultivate**
養 FOSTER (one's intellect) → 2365
練 TRAIN → 1375
錬 REFINE → 1741
鍛 train → 1755
磨 POLISH → 3181
琢 POLISH → 971

❷ **repair**
繕 MEND → 1423
直す FIX → 2932

❺ **phonetic** [s]/[sh]
須 phonetic [shu] → 574
西 phonetic [su] → 3520
相 phonetic [sō] → 900
沙 phonetic [sha] → 266
遮 phonetic [sha] → 3158
世 phonetic [se] → 3496

HOMOPHONES

osameru ⇨ 納 1300 収 198 治 335
osamaru ⇨ 納 1300 収 198 治 335

NOTE

⇨ see USAGE note at 納 1300
⇨ see COMPOUND FORMATION for 履修 *rishū* ⇨ 履 3171

倒

124 TŌ tao(reru) -dao(re) tao(su)

CH 倒 dǎo dào

Radical	Strokes
亻 9	10-2-8
Grade	**Freq**
Jōyō	1104
1 - 2 - 8	

2-8 亻

Stroke order: 1 2 3 4 5 6 7 8 9 10

▶TOPPLE

COMPOUNDS

❶ⓐ **topple, tumble down, fall over, fall, collapse**
ⓑ **cause to topple, overturn, overthrow, knock down**
倒木 *tōboku* fallen tree
倒壊する *tōkai suru* collapse, be destroyed, crumble
卒倒する *sottō suru* faint, fall unconscious, swoon
転倒する *tentō suru* tumble, fall down; invert, reverse; upset
倒産 *tōsan* insolvency, bankruptcy; breech birth
倒閣する *tōkaku suru* overthrow the cabinet
倒幕 *tōbaku* overthrowing the shogunate
打倒する *datō suru* overthrow, knock down, defeat

❷ⓐ **upside-down, inverted**
ⓑ turn upside down
倒立 *tōritsu* handstand
倒影 *tōei* inverted image
倒錯 *tōsaku* perversion, inversion
倒置 *tōchi* turning upside down; *gram* inversion

❸ indicates emphasis of action
圧倒する *attō suru* overwhelm, overpower, crush
罵倒する *batō suru* denounce, condemn, abuse
傾倒する *keitō suru* devote oneself to, set one's mind toward; admire
抱腹絶倒する *hōfukuzettō suru* double up with laughter

❹ unclassified compounds
面倒な *mendō na* troublesome, worrisome; difficult

KUN

【tao(reru) 倒れる】
① fall over, topple, tumble down, collapse
後に倒れる *ushiro ni taoreru* fall backward
② succumb, break down, fall senseless
③ⓐ go to ruin
ⓑ go bankrupt
共倒れ *tomodaore* falling together, joint bankruptcy
内閣が倒れた *Naikaku ga taoreta* The cabinet was overthrown
④ [formerly 斃れる] fall down dead, perish, die
行き倒れ *ikidaore* person dying [dead] on the street

【-dao(re) -倒れ】
① bad debt, loss, financial ruin
貸し倒れ *kashidaore* irrecoverable debt
食い倒れ *kuidaore* bringing ruin upon oneself by extravagance in food
② showy but worthless, deceptive
看板倒れ *kanbandaore* gorgeous in appearance but poor in substance

【tao(su) 倒す】
① bring down, fell, knock down, throw to the ground
押し倒す *oshitaosu* push down
②ⓐ overthrow, ruin
ⓑ defeat
拝み倒す *ogamitaosu* entreat (a person) into

consent, win over by persuasive entreaty
③ [formerly 斃す] kill
④ fail to pay
踏み倒す *fumitaosu* trample down; bilk, shirk payment
⑤ [in compounds] make a show of, sham
見掛け倒し *mikakedaoshi* deceptive appearance, mere show

SYNONYMS

❶ **descend and fall**
落 FALL → 2318
墜 DROP DOWN → 2881
降 DESCEND → 458
下 go down → 3378
ⓑ **overturn**
転 turn [roll] over → 1480
覆 OVERTURN → 2726
翻 TURN OVER → 1897
反 turn over → 2945
❷ⓐ **opposite**
逆 REVERSE → 3091
反 COUNTER → 2945
対 OPPOSITE → 831

USAGE

❶ **taoreru**
倒れる
① fall over, topple, tumble down, collapse
② succumb, break down, fall senseless
③ⓐ go to ruin
ⓑ go bankrupt
④ [formerly 斃れる] fall down dead, perish, die
斃れる
[now usu. 倒れる] fall down dead, perish, die
❷ **taosu**
倒す
① bring down, fell, knock down, throw to the ground
②ⓐ overthrow, ruin
ⓑ defeat
③ [formerly 斃す] kill
④ fail to pay
⑤ [in compounds] make a show of, sham
斃す
[now usu. 倒す] kill

HOMOPHONES

taoreru ⇨ 斃 2891
taosu ⇨ 斃 2891

2-8
亻
倍
125

▶**TIMES** ▶**DOUBLE**
nonstandard for 倍 108

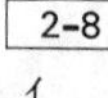
2-8
亻
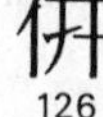
併
126

▶**TOGETHER**
nonstandard for 併 83

2-8
亻
偶

incorrect stroke count ⇨ see 132

2-8
亻

健

incorrect stroke count ⇨ see 134

2-8
冫
准 准 准
127 JUN

Ⓒⓗ 准 zhǔn

Radical	Strokes
冫 15	10-2-8
Grade	**Freq**
Jōyō	1682
1-2-8	

1 2 3 4 5 6 7 8 9 10

▶**JUNIOR**

COMPOUNDS

❶ [also prefix] (of secondary rank) **junior, assistant**
准教員 *junkyōin* junior [assistant] teacher
准尉 *jun'i* warrant officer
准看護婦 *junkangofu* practical nurse
❷ grant permission, permit, sanction, authorize, allow
批准 *hijun* ratification

SYNONYMS

❶ **subordinate**

助 assistant → 1121
副 SECONDARY → 1776
次 secondary → 54
従 subordinate → 415
亜 SUB- → 3540
準 QUASI- → 2856
半 semi- → 3501
❷ **permit**
許 PERMIT → 1470
免 license → 2067
允 GIVE CONSENT → 1982

凌

128 RYŌ shino(gu)

CH 凌 líng

Radical	Strokes
冫 15	10-2-8
Grade	**Freq**
Reference	
1-2-8	

2-8 冫

COMPOUNDS

❶ rise high, soar aloft
凌雲の *ryōun no* rising up high; rising in the world
凌霄花 *nōzenkazura* great trumpet flower, *Campsis chinensis*
❷ [now also 陵 *ryō* 544] insult, offend
凌辱する *ryōjoku suru* insult, disgrace; rape
❸ⓐ [now also 陵 *ryō* 544] outdo, surpass
ⓑ get through, pull over
壮者を凌ぐ *sōsha o shinogu* put young men to shame
年末を凌ぐ *nenmatsu o shinogu* pull through the year end

凍 凍 冻

129 TŌ kō(ru) kogo(eru) i(teru)▲ shi(miru)▲

CH 冻 dòng

Radical	Strokes
冫 15	10-2-8
Grade	**Freq**
Jōyō	1254
1-2-8	

2-8 冫

▶FREEZE

COMPOUNDS

ⓐ (turn solid because of cold) **freeze, congeal**
ⓑ (be harmed by cold or frost) freeze, be frostbitten
凍結 *tōketsu* freezing
冷凍 *reitō* freezing, cold storage
不凍港 *futōkō* ice-free port
凍死する *tōshi suru* freeze to death
凍害 *tōgai* frost damage
凍傷 *tōshō* frostbite

KUN

【kō(ru) 凍る】 [formerly also 氷る] freeze, congeal
凍り付く *kōritsuku* freeze
【kogo(eru) 凍える】 be frozen, be chilled
凍え死ぬ *kogoeshinu* freeze to death
【i(teru) 凍てる】 *literary* freeze
凍て付く *itetsuku* freeze
【shi(miru) 凍みる】 freeze, congeal

SYNONYMS

ⓐ **reduce the temperature**
冷 cool → 80
ⓐ **solidify and coagulate**
固 solidify → 3086
凝 CONGEAL → 175
結 form into a mass → 1348

USAGE

kōru
凍る
[formerly also 氷る] freeze, congeal
氷る
[now usu. 凍る] freeze

HOMOPHONES

kōru ⇨ 氷 39
shimiru ⇨ 染 2572 滲 703

NOTE

⇨ see also USAGE note at 染 2572

隅

incorrect stroke count ⇨ see 623

2-8 阝

2-8 阝 **随** incorrect stroke count ⇨ see 627

2-8 阝 **陸 険** etc. incorrect stroke count ⇨ see ◧3-8

2-8 刂 **帰 歸 帰 㷖**

130 KI kae(ru) kae(su)

CH 归 guī

Radical	Strokes
刂 18△	10-2-8
Grade	**Freq**
Jōyō-2	399
◧ 1-2-8	

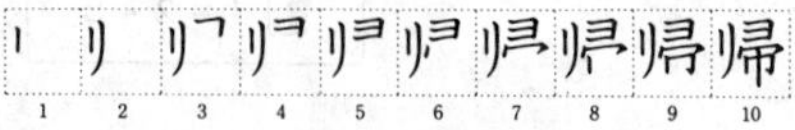

1 2 3 4 5 6 7 8 9 10

▶RETURN

COMPOUNDS

❶ **return, come back, go back, take one's leave**

帰着する *kichaku suru* return, come back; arrive at, result in
帰還する *kikan suru* return, come home, be repatriated
帰国する *kikoku suru* return to one's country
帰京 *kikyō* returning to Tokyo
帰路 *kiro* homeward journey, return circuit
帰宅する *kitaku suru* come [return] home
復帰する *fukki suru* return, be restored, revert

❷ⓐ **settle in place, conclude**
ⓑ settle in one place, be brought together, unite

帰結 *kiketsu* conclusion, end, result
帰一する *kiitsu suru* be united into one
帰納法 *kinōhō* inductive method

❸ follow, yield to, pledge allegiance to

帰順 *kijun* submission, return to allegiance
帰化 *kika* naturalization
帰依 *kie* faith, devotion; conversion

INDEPENDENT

【ki 帰】 returning
【kisuru 帰する】 come to, result in, attribute; fall into

KUN

【kae(ru) 帰る】
[sometimes also 還る]
ⓐ return (to one's original position), come back, come home
ⓑ go back [home], take one's leave

帰り道 *kaerimichi* the way back, return trip
日帰りする *higaeri suru* return on the same day, make a day's trip
家に帰る *ie ni kaeru* come back home
帰れ *Kaere* Get out! / Go home!

【kae(su) 帰す】 let (someone) return, see out, send (someone) home, dismiss

生徒を帰す *seito o kaesu* dismiss the pupils

SYNONYMS

❶ **return**

還 RETURN → 3180
回 turn back → 3055
戻る RETURN → 1942
復 RETURN TO → 575

❷ **settle**

着 settle (down) → 3316
落 be concluded → 2318

USAGE

kaeru

帰る
[sometimes also 還る]
ⓐ return (to one's original position), come back, come home
ⓑ go back [home], take one's leave

還る
[usu. 帰る] same as 帰る

返る
① be restored to, return to (the original state)
② be given back

反る
vi turn over, become overturned

HOMOPHONES

kaeru ⇨ 還 3180 返 3060 反 2945
kaesu ⇨ 返 3060 反 2945

NOTE

⇨ see also USAGE note at 返 3060

偽 僞 偽 伪

131 GI itsuwa(ru) nise

ノ イ イ' 伊 伊 伊 偽 偽 偽 偽 偽
1 2 3 4 5 6 7 8 9 10 11

CH 伪 wěi

Radical	Strokes
イ 9	11-2-9
Grade	**Freq**
Jōyō	1512
1-2-9	

2-9 イ

▶**FALSIFY**

COMPOUNDS

ⓐ [original meaning] **falsify, forge, deceive**
ⓑ **falsehood, lie**
ⓒ false, forged
偽造 *gizō* forgery, fabrication
偽証 *gishō* perjury
真偽 *shingi* truth or falsehood; authenticity
虚偽 *kyogi* falsehood, lie, fallacy
偽善 *gizen* hypocrisy
偽名 *gimei* false name
偽印 *giin* false [forged] seal

KUN

【itsuwa(ru) 偽る】
ⓐ (state untruthfully) falsify, misrepresent, lie
ⓑ [formerly also 詐る] (cause to believe a falsehood) falsify, deceive, cheat
ⓒ feign, pretend
偽り *itsuwari* lie, falsehood, fabrication
大学生と身分を偽る *daigakusei to mibun o itsuwaru* misrepresent oneself as a university student

【nise 偽】 [also prefix] sham, imitation, fake, forgery
偽物 *nisemono* sham, imitation, fake, forgery
偽札 *nisesatsu* counterfeit paper money
偽君子 *nisekunshi* sham gentleman

SYNONYMS

ⓐ **deceive**
欺 DECEIVE → 1703
詐 SWINDLE → 1502
惑 mislead → 2786
拐 defraud → 308

【nise】
○ **false**
擬 imitation → 788
仮 fake → 50
虚 FALSE → 3237
義 artificial → 2338

USAGE

itsuwaru
偽る
ⓐ (state untruthfully) falsify, misrepresent, lie
ⓑ [formerly also 詐る] (cause to believe a falsehood) falsify, deceive, cheat
ⓒ feign, pretend
詐る
[now usu. 偽る] (cause to believe a falsehood) falsify, deceive, cheat

HOMOPHONES

itsuwaru ⇨ 詐 1502

偶 偶 偶

132 GŪ tama▲

ノ イ イ 仴 仴 但 但 倡 偶 偶 偶
1 2 3 4 5 6 7 8 9 10 11

CH 偶 ǒu

Radical	Strokes
イ 9	11-2-9
Grade	**Freq**
Jōyō	1573
1-2-9	

2-9 イ

▶**BY CHANCE** ▶**COUPLE**

COMPOUNDS

❶ **by chance, accidentally, by coincidence, unexpectedly**
偶然に *gūzen ni* by chance, accidentally, by coincidence
偶発的な *gūhatsuteki na* accidental, contingent
偶詠 *gūei* impromptu poem, poem written at the moment of inspiration
偶成の *gūsei no* fortuitous, contingent
偶感 *gūkan* random thoughts, chance impressions

❷ⓐ **couple, pair**
ⓑ mate, spouse
偶力 *gūryoku* couple (of forces)
対偶 *taigū* contrapositive; spouse, companion
配偶者 *haigūsha* spouse, mate
❸ *math* even, even number
偶数 *gūsū* even number
奇偶 *kigū* odd and even numbers
❹ [original meaning] (wooden) figure, idol, image
偶像 *gūzō* idol, image
土偶 *dogū* earthen [clay] figure

KUN

【tama 偶】 rare occasion

偶に *tama ni* occasionally, on rare occasions

偶偶 *tamatama* by chance, accidentally

SYNONYMS

❷ⓐ two

対 pair → 831

両 BOTH → 3518

双 SET OF TWO → 25

二 TWO → 1922

弐 TWO (in legal documents) → 3195

❹ images

像 IMAGE → 166

仏 Buddhist image → 19

2-9

亻

偏 偏 偏 偏

133 HEN katayo(ru)

ⒸⒽ 偏 piān

Radical	Strokes
亻 9	11-2-9
Grade	**Freq**
Jōyō	1507
◧ 1-2-9	

ノ 亻 亻 亻 亻 伊 伊 偏 偏 偏 偏
1 2 3 4 5 6 7 8 9 10 11

▶ONE-SIDED

COMPOUNDS

❶ⓐ [original meaning] (occurring on one side) **one-sided, uneven, unbalanced**

ⓑ (favoring one side) **one-sided, biased, partial, unfair, prejudiced**

偏頭痛 *henzutsū* headache on one side, migraine

偏在 *henzai* uneven distribution

偏食 *henshoku* unbalanced diet

偏執狂 *henshitsukyō* (=*henshūkyō*) monomaniac

偏見 *henken* prejudice, biased view, narrow view

偏重する *henchō suru* attach too much importance, overemphasize

偏愛 *hen'ai* partiality, favoritism

❷ⓐ (deviating from normal) **eccentric, deviating**

ⓑ (deviating from circular) **eccentric**

偏屈 *henkutsu* eccentricity, obstinacy, narrow-mindedness

標準偏差 *hyōjun hensa* standard deviation

偏心 *henshin* eccentricity

❸ [sometimes also 扁 3005] left-side radical of Chinese characters, left radical

偏旁 *henbō* left and right radicals

人偏 *ninben ninben*, 'person' radical (亻)

❹ countryside

偏土 *hendo* remote region

INDEPENDENT

【hen 偏】 left-side radical of Chinese characters

「偏」の偏は人偏と言う *Hen no hen wa ninben to iu* The left-side radical of 偏 is called *ninben*

【hensuru 偏する】 be one-sided, be partial; deviate

KUN

【katayo(ru) 偏る】

ⓐ be one-sided, be prejudiced, be partial, be unfair

ⓑ deviate

偏った考え *katayotta kangae* partial [one-sided] view, prejudice

偏り *katayori* deviation, offset; polarization

偏りシリンダー *katayorishirindā* offset cylinder

SYNONYMS

❶ⓐ one side

片- one side → 3461

ⓑ inclining toward

傾 incline toward → 154

USAGE

katayoru

偏る

ⓐ be one-sided, be prejudiced, be partial, be unfair

ⓑ deviate

片寄る

concentrate on one side [place], go aside

HOMOPHONES

katayoru ⇨ 片寄る 3461, 2291

NOTE

⇨ see COMPOUND FORMATION for 偏執狂 *henshitsukyō* (=*henshūkyō*) ⇨ 執 1680

健 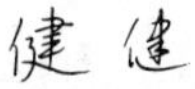

134 KEN suko(yaka)

ⒸⒽ 健 jiàn

Radical	Strokes
亻 9	11-2-9
Grade	**Freq**
Jōyō-4	614
◧ 1 - 2 - 9	

2-9 亻

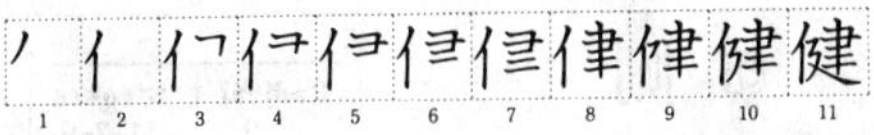

▶ROBUST

COMPOUNDS

❶ (strong and in good health) **robust, healthy, sound, strong**

健康な *kenkō na* healthy, sound, well

健保(＝健康保険) *kenpo* (＝*kenkō hoken*) health insurance

健在だ *kenzai da* be well, be in good health

健全 *kenzen* health, soundness

健脚の *kenkyaku no* strong in walking

強健な *kyōken na* robust, healthy, strong

保健 *hoken* (preservation of) health, sanitation

穏健な *onken na* moderate, temperate, sound

剛健な *gōken na* strong and sturdy, virile; manly

❷ be strong in, be good at

健筆 *kenpitsu* powerful [facile] pen

健忘 *kenbō* forgetfulness, short memory

健闘する *kentō suru* fight bravely; make strenuous efforts

KUN

【suko(yaka) 健やか】

sukoyaka na 健やかな healthy, sound

健やかな体 *sukoyaka na karada* healthy [sound] body

SPECIAL READINGS

健気な▲ *kenage na* praiseworthy, admirable; brave

SYNONYMS

❶ **healthy**

生 health → 3497

康 HEALTHY → 3124

❶ **strong**

康 HEALTHY → 3124

丈 STOUT → 3419

壮 VIGOROUS → 224

強 STRONG → 475

偲

135 SAI SHI shino(bu)

ⒸⒽ 偲 sī cāi

Radical	Strokes
亻 9	11-2-9
Grade	**Freq**
Reference	
◧ 1 - 2 - 9	

2-9 亻

COMPOUNDS

❶ recall, recollect, remember, reminisce

故人を偲ぶ *kojin o shinobu* think of the dead

昔を偲ばせる品 *mukashi o shinobaseru shina* things reminiscent of bygone days

❷ [archaic] talented

HOMOPHONES

shinobu ⇨ 忍 2212

NOTE

⇨ see USAGE note at 忍 2212

脩 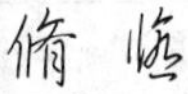

136 SHŪ NAMES osamu osa naga nobu haru

ⒸⒽ 脩 xiū

Radical	Strokes
月 130	11-4-7
Grade	**Freq**
Names	2122
◧ 1 - 2 - 9	

2-9 亻

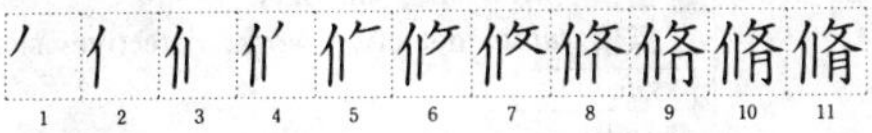

▶DRIED MEAT

COMPOUNDS

❶ⓐ [original meaning] **dried meat**

ⓑ **dried meat or ham as gift to teacher in lieu of salary in ancient times**

束脩 *sokushū* tuition; ham as gift to teacher in lieu of tuition

❷ [rare] long

脩竹 *shūchiku* tall bamboo

NAMES

脩 *osamu* male name
脩夫 *nobuo* male name

SYNONYMS

❶ **meat**
肉 FLESH → 3200
身 meat → 3553

2-9
亻

側 側 側

137 SOKU kawa gawa▲ soba▲

CH 侧 cè zhāi zè

Radical	Strokes
亻 9	11-2-9
Grade	**Freq**
Jōyō-4	198
1 - 2 - 9	

ノ 亻 亻 们 们 俱 俱 俱 俱 側 側
1 2 3 4 5 6 7 8 9 10 11

▶SIDE

COMPOUNDS

❶ⓐ (one of two or more opposing parts) **side, part**
ⓑ (lateral surface) **side, flank**
右側 *usoku* (=*migigawa*) right side
側聞(=仄聞)する *sokubun suru* learn by hearsay
側面 *sokumen* side, flank
側壁 *sokuheki* side wall
船側 *sensoku* side of a ship
❷ surroundings, vicinity
側近者 *sokkinsha* close associate, aide
君側 *kunsoku* vicinity of a lord

KUN

【**kawa** 側】[also suffix] side, part; row
西側 *nishigawa* west side; west European countries and America
内側 *uchigawa* inside, interior
裏側 *uragawa* back [reverse, other] side, wrong side
敵側 *tekigawa* enemy's side
反対側 *hantaigawa* opposite side; opponents' side
消費者側 *shōhishagawa* consumers' side
この側 *kono kawa* this row
【**gawa** 側】side, part; vicinity; those around one; case (of a watch)
どちらの側 *dochira no gawa* which side
側の者 *gawa no mono* people around one
銀側の時計 *gingawa no tokei* silver watch
【**soba** 側】[sometimes also 傍] side, vicinity
側に *soba ni* by the side of
側女 *sobame* mistress, concubine

SYNONYMS

❶ **side**
方 side → 1963
辺 -side → 3029
面 side → 2087
傍 BESIDE → 147
横 SIDEWAYS → 1066

USAGE

soba
側
[sometimes also 傍] side, vicinity
傍
[usu. 側] side, vicinity

HOMOPHONES

soba ⇨ 傍 147

2-9
亻

偵 偵 偵

138 TEI

CH 侦 zhēn

Radical	Strokes
亻 9	11-2-9
Grade	**Freq**
Jōyō	1765
1 - 2 - 9	

ノ 亻 亻 亻 亻 偵 偵 偵 偵 偵 偵
1 2 3 4 5 6 7 8 9 10 11

▶SPY

COMPOUNDS

❶ **spy, detect, scout, investigate**
偵察 *teisatsu* scouting, reconnaissance
偵知 *teichi* [rare] spying, investigating
内偵する *naitei suru* make secret inquiries, scout
❷ [original meaning] **spy**
密偵 *mittei* spy, emissary
探偵 *tantei* detective work; detective, sleuth

SYNONYMS

❶ **spy**
探 spy on → 505
❷ **agents**
使 ENVOY → 90

停 停 停

139 TEI to(meru)▲ to(maru)▲

CH 停 tíng

Radical	Strokes
亻 9	11-2-9
Grade	**Freq**
Jōyō-4	720
1-2-9	

2-9 亻

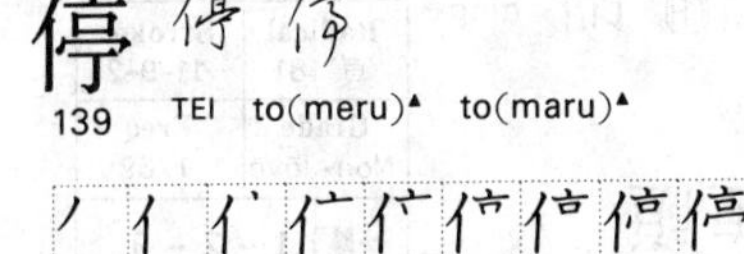

▶**HALT**

COMPOUNDS

❶ⓐ (make a temporary stop) **halt, pause, stop**

ⓑ be at a standstill, remain inactive

停留する *teiryū suru* halt, stop

停止 *teishi* stop, halt; suspension

停車 *teisha* stoppage (of a vehicle)

停滞 *teitai* stagnation, accumulation; arrearage

❷ abbrev. of 停留所 *teiryūjo*: stopping place, stop, station

バス停 *basutei* bus stop

電停 *dentei* tram stop

❸ **suspend, discontinue**

停学 *teigaku* suspension from school

停職 *teishoku* suspension from office

停戦 *teisen* cease-fire, armistice

停電 *teiden* stoppage of electric power, power failure

調停する *chōtei suru* mediate, arbitrate, make peace

❹ [formerly 碇 1202] anchor

停泊する *teihaku suru* anchor, moor

KUN

【to(meru) 停める】 [now usu. 止める] (bring a vehicle to a temporary halt) stop (a bus or train), bring to a halt, brake

車を停める *kuruma o tomeru* bring a car to a halt

【to(maru) 停まる】 [now usu. 止まる] (of vehicles) roll to a stop, stop (at a station)

停まらずに行く *tomarazu ni iku* run without stopping, run past

SYNONYMS

❶ⓐ **stop**

止 STOP → 2941

駐 park → 1826

❷ **places for landing or stopping**

駅 STATION → 1822

港 PORT → 605

津 HARBOR (*elegant*) → 390

❸ **discontinue**

休 suspend → 52

止 STOP → 2941

断 CUT OFF → 1492

廃 ABOLISH → 3146

絶 BREAK OFF → 1353

HOMOPHONES

tomeru ⇨ 止 2941 留 2580 泊 331

tomaru ⇨ 止 2941 留 2580 泊 331

NOTE

⇨ see USAGE note at 止 2941

偏

140

▶**ONE-SIDED**

nonstandard for 偏 133

2-9 亻

偉

141

▶**GREAT**

nonstandard for 偉 148

2-9 亻

條

142

▶**ARTICLE**

nonstandard for 条 2200

2-9 亻

假

143

▶**TEMPORARY**

nonstandard for 仮 50

2-9 亻

2-9 匕

頃 頃 頃 — CH 顷 qǐng

144 KEI koro goro -goro

Radical	Strokes
頁 181	11-9-2
Grade	**Freq**
Non-Jōyō	1769
1-2-9	

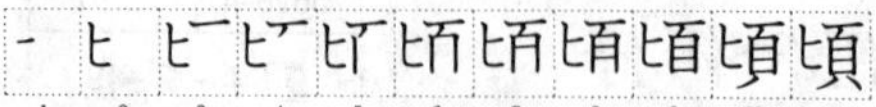

▶TIME ▶ABOUT

COMPOUNDS

● [archaic] moment, instant, short time
頃刻 *keikoku* short moment

KUN

【koro, goro 頃】

①ⓐ time, approximate time
ⓑ right time (for doing something)
この頃 *kono goro* now, these days; lately
もう彼が帰る頃だ *Mō kare ga kaeru koro da* It's about time for him to come home
食べ頃 *tabegoro* right time for eating
② [in compounds] convenience, suitability
頃合いの *koroai no* suitable, handy
手頃な *tegoro na* handy, convenient
③ unclassified compounds
身頃 *migoro* body of a garment

【-goro -頃】 [also suffix] about, around, toward
十八世紀の終わり頃 *jūhasseiki no owarigoro* toward the end of the eighteenth century
八時頃 *hachijigoro* about eight o'clock

SYNONYMS

● **short time periods**
瞬 INSTANT → 1247
秒 SECOND → 1137
分 MINUTE → 1972
時 hour → 924
暫 SHORT WHILE → 2864

【koro】

①ⓐ **time periods**
般 period of time → 1317
暇 FREE TIME → 1012
時 TIME → 924
刻 POINT OF TIME → 1267
間 INTERVAL → 3323
期 TERM → 1704
節 SEASON OF THE YEAR → 2691
季 SEASON (quarter) → 2554
候 SEASON (time of year) → 119

【-goro】

○ **approximately**
位 about → 61
-方 about → 1963
-程 ...or thereabouts → 1190
辺り thereabouts → 3029
約 APPROXIMATELY → 1280
概 GENERAL → 1048
大 in substance → 3416

2-9 阝

階 隊 etc.

incorrect stroke count ⇨ see 3-9

2-9 丁

頂 頂 頂 — CH 顶 dǐng

145 CHŌ itada(ku) itadaki

Radical	Strokes
頁 181	11-9-2
Grade	**Freq**
Jōyō-6	1310
1-2-9	

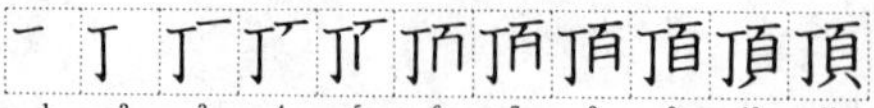

▶SUMMIT ▶RECEIVE HUMBLY

COMPOUNDS

❶ⓐ (highest part) **summit, top, peak, apex, vertex**
ⓑ (mountain top) **summit, peak**
頂点 *chōten* apex, peak
絶頂 *zetchō* summit, peak, climax
有頂天 *uchōten* exaltation, ecstasy
山頂 *sanchō* summit
頂上 *chōjō* summit, peak, top; climax
登頂する *tōchō suru* climb to the summit
❷ⓐ [original meaning] top of the head, crown
ⓑ head
頭頂 *tōchō anat* vertex, parietal
円頂 *enchō* tonsured head; priest; round top
❸ **receive humbly, accept with thanks**
頂戴する *chōdai suru* [humble] receive, accept, take; eat, drink

KUN

【itada(ku) 頂く】
[sometimes also 戴く]
① [humble]
ⓐ receive humbly, accept with thanks, be given, be favored with
ⓑ eat, drink
ⓒ trouble someone to do something, have something done

頂き *itadaki* windfall, unexpected gain; unauthorized borrowing
頂けない *itadakenai* unapprovable, dissatisfactory
頂き物 *itadakimono* gift, present
有り難く頂く *arigataku itadaku* accept (a thing) with thanks
この本を頂いても良いですか *Kono hon o itadaite mo ii desu ka* Can I have this book?
酒も煙草も頂きます *Sake mo tabako mo itadakimasu* I both drink and smoke
十分頂きました *Jūbun itadakimashita* I have had enough
今晩来て頂きたい *Konban kite itadakitai* I hope you will come this evening
お茶を入れて頂けませんか *Ocha o irete itadakemasen ka* May I trouble you for a cup of tea?

② have over, be presided over by, live under (a ruler)
指導者として頂く *shidōsha to shite itadaku* have (a person) as one's leader
彼らは女王を頂く *Karera wa joō o itadaku* They have a queen over them

③ wear (a crown); be crowned (with snow)
雪を頂いた山 *yuki o itadaita yama* snow-crowned mountain

【itadaki 頂】 summit, peak, top

SYNONYMS

❶ⓐ tops
上 upper part → 3404
頭 HEAD → 1604
ⓑ high parts of mountains
峰 PEAK → 411
嶺 RIDGE → 2376
峠 MOUNTAIN PASS → 358
❸ receive
戴 RECEIVE HUMBLY → 3302
拝 have the honor to receive → 303
受 RECEIVE → 2421
享 ENJOY → 2051
領 receive → 1224
収 TAKE IN → 198
納 ACCEPT → 1300

USAGE

itadaku
頂く
[sometimes also 戴く]
① [humble]
ⓐ receive humbly, accept with thanks, be given, be favored with
ⓑ eat, drink
ⓒ trouble someone to do something, have something done
② have over, be presided over by, live under (a ruler)
③ wear (a crown); be crowned (with snow)
戴く
[usu. 頂く] same as 頂く

HOMOPHONES

itadaku ⇨ 戴 3302

備 備 備

146 BI sona(eru) sona(waru)

CH 备 bèi

Radical	Strokes
亻 9	12-2-10
Grade	**Freq**
Jōyō-5	317
1-2-10	

2-10 亻

Stroke order: 1 2 3 4 5 6 7 8 9 10 11 12

▶PROVIDE

COMPOUNDS

❶ⓐ [original meaning] **provide for [against], prepare for [against], get ready**
ⓑ preparations, preparedness
備考 *bikō* explanatory note, remarks (for reference)
備蓄 *bichiku* saving for [against] emergency, storing
準備する *junbi suru* provide for [against], prepare for [against]
予備 *yobi* reserve, spare; preparation, preliminaries
警備 *keibi* guard, defense
軍備 *gunbi* military preparations, armaments
防備 *bōbi* defense, defensive preparations

❷ⓐ provide (with), equip, fit
ⓑ be provided with, be equipped with
備品 *bihin* fixtures, furnishings
設備する *setsubi suru* equip [provide] (with)
整備 *seibi* maintenance, servicing, preparation
装備 *sōbi* equipment, outfit
完備した *kanbi shita* fully-equipped, perfect,

complete
具備する *gubi suru* be endowed [equipped] with, possess
❸ old name for south Okayama and east Hiroshima prefectures
備後 *bingo* old name for east Hiroshima Prefecture

KUN

【sona(eru) 備える】
①ⓐ provide for, make preparations for, stock
ⓑ provide with, furnish
備え *sonae* provision, preparation; defense
万一に備える *man'ichi ni sonaeru* provide against contingencies
備え付ける *sonaetsukeru* provide with, furnish, fit with
② possess, be endowed with
資格を備える *shikaku o sonaeru* have a qualification (for)

【sona(waru) 備わる】 *vi* be provided [furnished] with; be possessed of, be endowed with
名実共に備わる *meijitsu tomoni sonawaru* live up to one's name
自然に備わる人格 *shizen ni sonawaru jinkaku* one's natural dignity

SYNONYMS

❶ⓐ prepare
調 PREPARE → 1567
❷ equip and install
設 SET UP → 1471
装 FIT OUT → 2685
架 LAY ACROSS → 2569
敷 LAY → 1870
据える INSTALL → 497

USAGE

❶ sonaeru
備える
①ⓐ provide for, make preparations for, stock
ⓑ provide with, furnish
② possess, be endowed with
供える
offer (to a god), make an offering
❷ sonae
備え
① provision, preparation
② defense
供え
offering

HOMOPHONES

sonaeru ⇨ 供 88
sonae ⇨ 供 88

2-10
亻

傍 傍 傍 傍 CH 旁 páng 傍 bàng

147 BŌ katawa(ra) waki▲ oka-▲ hata▲ soba▲

Stroke order: 1 2 3 4 5 6 7 8 9 10 11 12

Radical	Strokes
亻 9	12-2-10
Grade	**Freq**
Jōyō	1580
1-2-10	

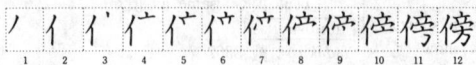

▶BESIDE

COMPOUNDS

● [sometimes also 旁 2095] **beside, by, by the side, nearby; side**
傍観者 *bōkansha* bystander, onlooker
傍系の *bōkei no* collateral, subsidiary, affiliated
傍受 *bōju* interception, tapping
傍線 *bōsen* side line, underline
傍聴 *bōchō* hearing; attendance
傍若無人な *bōjakubujin na* overbearing, arrogant, audacious
路傍 *robō* roadside, wayside
近傍 *kinbō* neighborhood

KUN

【katawa(ra) 傍ら】 besides, while; side
勉強の傍ら音楽を聞く *benkyō no katawara ongaku o kiku* listen to music while studying
傍らに寄る *katawara ni yoru* step aside

【waki 傍】 [now usu. 脇]
①ⓐ side
ⓑ the other way, another place
傍に置く *waki ni oku* lay aside
傍視 *wakimi* looking aside
② supporting actor [role]
傍役 *wakiyaku* supporting actor [role]

【oka- 傍-】 [usu. 岡] outsider, third party, bystander
傍目八目 *okame hachimoku* Onlookers can see [read] the game far better than the players themselves

【hata 傍】 bystander, outsider
傍の者達 *hata no monotachi* bystanders, onlookers

【soba 傍】 [usu. 側] side, vicinity
傍に *soba ni* by the side of

SYNONYMS

● near
沿 ALONG → 328
近 NEAR → 3061

隣 neighboring → 781
● side
側 SIDE → 137
方 side → 1963
辺 -side → 3029
面 side → 2087
横 SIDEWAYS → 1066
【katawara】
○ additionally
並びに and also → 2246
及び and → 3385
亦 ALSO → 2011
又 also, and → 3351
尚 STILL → 2233
更に furthermore → 3541
且つ AS WELL → 3485
兼 CONCURRENTLY → 2286

USAGE

waki
傍
［now usu. 脇］
①ⓐ side
ⓑ the other way, another place
② supporting actor ［role］
脇
① ［formerly also 傍］
ⓐ side
ⓑ the other way, another place
② ［formerly also 傍］ supporting actor ［role］
③ ［also 腋］
ⓐ armpit
ⓑ armhole
腋
［also 脇］
ⓐ armpit
ⓑ armhole

HOMOPHONES

waki ⇨ 脇 952 腋 1004
oka- ⇨ 岡 2997 丘 3495 陸 543
hata ⇨ 端 1221
soba ⇨ 側 137

NOTE

⇨ see also USAGE notes at 丘 3495 and 端 1221 and 側 137

偉 偉 偉 偉

148 I era(i)

CH 伟 wěi

Radical	Strokes
亻 9	12-2-10
Grade	Freq
Jōyō	1419
◧ 1-2-10	

2-10 亻

Stroke order: 1 2 3 4 5 6 7 8 9 10 11 12

▶GREAT

COMPOUNDS

ⓐ (of superior character) **great, grand**
ⓑ ［original meaning］ (of large size) great, towering
偉大な *idai na* great, mighty, grand
偉人 *ijin* great man
偉業 *igyō* great work ［achievement］
偉勲 *ikun* great achievement
偉観 *ikan* grand sight
魁偉な *kaii na* gigantic, large-boned and impressive
偉丈夫 *ijōfu* towering ［great］ man; hero

INDEPENDENT

【i 偉】 ［rare］ greatness
偉とするに足る *I to suru ni taru* Credit is due to one

KUN

【era(i) 偉い】
①ⓐ great, grand; famous, eminent
ⓑ ［sometimes also 豪い］ remarkable, extraordinary
偉さ *erasa* greatness; remarkableness
偉い人 *erai hito* great man, extraordinary character
お偉方 *oeragata* dignitary, exalted personalities
偉がる *eragaru* be self-important, be conceited
偉物 *erabutsu* extraordinary ［able］ character
② ［sometimes also 豪い］ awful, serious
ど偉い *doerai* terrible, very serious

SYNONYMS

ⓐ **great**
大 BIG → 3416
宏 GRAND (large in scale) → 2202
壮 GRAND (having grandeur) → 224
豪 MAGNIFICENT → 2140
雄 HEROIC → 1008

USAGE

erai
偉い
①ⓐ great, grand; famous, eminent
ⓑ ［sometimes also 豪い］ remarkable, extraordinary
② ［sometimes also 豪い］ awful, serious
豪い
［usu. 偉い］
① remarkable, extraordinary
② awful, serious

HOMOPHONES
erai ⇨ 豪 2140

2-10 亻 **傍** 149

▶BESIDE
nonstandard for 傍 147

2-10 亻 **傑** 150

▶OUTSTANDING PERSON
nonstandard for 傑 155

2-10 十 **博** 博 博 博 151 HAKU BAKU

CH 博 bó

Radical	Strokes
十 24	12-2-10
Grade	**Freq**
Jōyō-4	788
1-2-10	

Stroke order: 1–12

▶EXTENSIVE ▶DOCTOR

COMPOUNDS

❶ **extensive (knowledge), wide (learning), well-informed, learned**
博士 *hakushi* doctor, Ph.D.
博物学 *hakubutsugaku* natural history
博覧 *hakuran* extensive reading, wide knowledge
博覧会 *hakurankai* exhibition, fair, exposition
博愛主義 *hakuaishugi* philanthropy, humanity
博識 *hakushiki* extensive knowledge
博学 *hakugaku* extensive learning, erudition, wide knowledge
該博な *gaihaku na* extensive (knowledge), profound (learning)

❷ abbrev. of 博士 *hakushi*: **doctor, Ph.D.**
医博 *ihaku* doctor of medicine, M.D.
文博 *bunhaku* doctor of literature

❸ abbrev. of 博覧会 *hakurankai*: exposition, expo
万博 *banpaku* world fair
宇宙博 *uchūhaku* Space Expo

❹ gamble
博徒 *bakuto* gambler
賭博 *tobaku* gambling

INDEPENDENT

【hakusuru 博する】 gain, win, enjoy
名声を博する *meisei o hakusuru* earn fame, achieve reputation

SPECIAL READINGS

博士 *hakase* expert, learned man; doctor, Ph.D.

SYNONYMS

❶ **wide and extensive**
広 WIDE → 3035
紘 WIDE-RANGING → 1298
浩 VAST → 438
洸 VAST (expanse of water) → 387

❷ **wise and talented persons**
秀 genius → 2545
才 person of talent → 3410
通 well-informed person → 3109
賢 wise man → 2839
俊 BRILLIANT PERSON → 102
哲 sage → 2738

❸ **public display**
展 exhibition → 3111

2-10 十 **博** 152

▶EXTENSIVE ▶DOCTOR
nonstandard for 博 151

2-10 阝 **隔 隙** etc. incorrect stroke count ⇨ see 3-10

働 仂 働 働

CH none（国字）

153 DŌ hatara(ku)

Radical	Strokes
亻 9	13-2-11
Grade	**Freq**
Jōyō-4	423
1-2-11	

2-11 亻

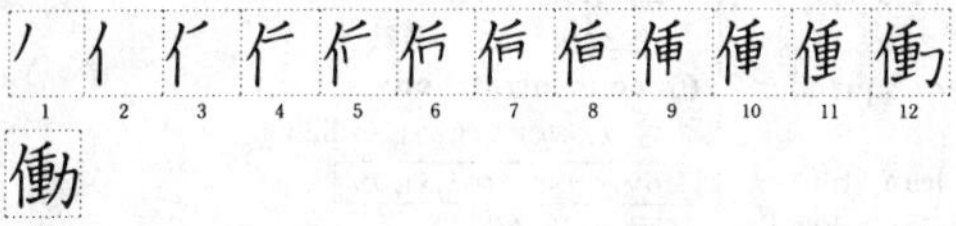

▶**WORK**

COMPOUNDS

ⓐ [original meaning] **work, labor, serve**

ⓑ work for, act, be active

労働 *rōdō* (manual) labor, toil

稼働(＝稼動) *kadō* working, work; operation (of a machine)

実働時間 *jitsudō-jikan* actual working hours

重労働 *jūrōdō* heavy labor

共働 *kyōdō biol* coaction

協働 *kyōdō* cooperation

働き掛ける *hatarakikakeru* work on someone; begin to work

下働き *shitabataraki* subordinate work; underworker

共働き *tomobataraki* working together (for a living), working in double harness

悪事を働く *akuji o hataraku* do evil, commit a crime

ブレーキが働く *Burēki ga hataraku* The brakes function

KUN

【**hatara(ku)** 働く】work, labor; do, act, commit; operate, function

働き *hataraki* work, labor; activity, function; ability, talent

働き手 *hatarakite* worker, breadwinner

SYNONYMS

ⓐ **work**

稼 WORK (for a living) → 1230

労 LABOR → 2548

勤める serve (in an office) → 1818

仕 SERVE → 34

傾 傾 傾

CH 倾 qīng

154 KEI katamu(ku) katamu(keru) kashi(geru)▲

Radical	Strokes
亻 9	13-2-11
Grade	**Freq**
Jōyō	831
1-2-11	

2-11 亻

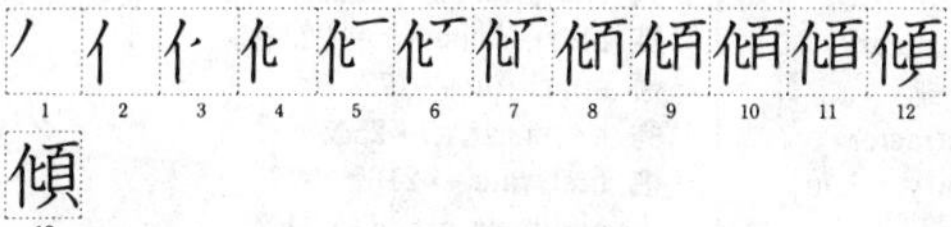

▶**INCLINE**

COMPOUNDS

❶ⓐ [original meaning] **incline, lean, tilt, slant**

ⓑ inclination, tilt

傾斜する *keisha suru* incline, slant, tilt

傾度 *keido* inclination

傾角 *keikaku* (angle of) inclination

前傾 *zenkei* forward inclination [tilt]

❷ⓐ **incline toward, be inclined to, tend to, lean to**

ⓑ (trend toward) inclination, tendency

傾向 *keikō* tendency, trend; disposition

左傾 *sakei* tendency [inclination] to the left

右傾する *ukei suru* lean to the right

❸ devote oneself to, concentrate on

傾倒する *keitō suru* devote oneself to, set one's mind toward; admire

傾聴 *keichō* listening closely

傾注 *keichū* devotion, concentration

❹ topple, bring down, cause the downfall of

傾城 *keisei* courtesan, harlot; beautiful woman

傾国 *keikoku* beautiful woman; courtesan

KUN

【**katamu(ku)** 傾く】*vi* incline, lean, tilt, slant; incline toward, be inclined to, tend to; decline, be sinking; decline, fall

傾き *katamuki* inclination, slope; tendency, trend

悪に傾く *aku ni katamuku* be inclined to evil

日が西に傾く *Hi ga nishi ni katamuku* The sun declines westward

傾いた家運 *katamuita kaun* fortunes on the wane [decline]

【**katamu(keru)** 傾ける】*vt* incline, lean, tilt,

slant; devote oneself to, concentrate on; ruin, squander
首を傾ける *kubi o katamukeru* incline one's head
愛情を傾ける *aijō o katamukeru* fix one's affection on
身代を傾ける *shindai o katamukeru* squander one's fortunes
【**kashi(geru) 傾げる**】*vt* incline, lean, tilt
首を傾げる *kubi o kashigeru* put one's head on one side

SYNONYMS

❶ⓐ **obliqueness and inclining**
斜 OBLIQUE → 1486
❷ⓐ **inclining toward**
偏 ONE-SIDED → 133
ⓑ **tendency**
向 tendency → 3052
性 NATURE → 299
勢 trend → 2857
潮 TIDE → 739
流 CURRENT → 441
❸ **concentrate on**
注 CONCENTRATE → 325

COMPOUND FORMATION

傾国 *keikoku*
傾国 'beautiful woman; courtesan' derives from an ancient Chinese legend of a beautiful siren that brought on the downfall (傾 ❹) of a nation (国) with her voluptuous charms.

2-11
亻

傑 155 KETSU

Ⓒⓗ 杰 jié

Radical	Strokes
亻 9	13-2-11
Grade	**Freq**
Jōyō	1565
▮ 1-2-11	

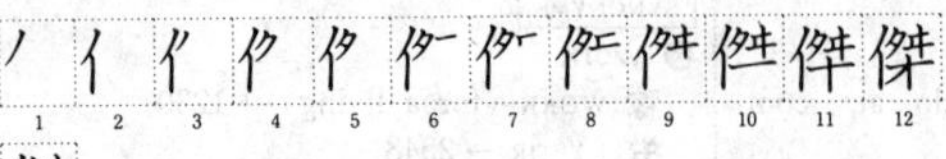

▶ **OUTSTANDING PERSON**

COMPOUNDS

❶ [original meaning] **outstanding person, hero, great man, master**
傑物 *ketsubutsu* great man, outstanding figure
豪傑 *gōketsu* hero, great [extraordinary] man
女傑 *joketsu* heroine, lady of character
怪傑 *kaiketsu* man of extraordinary talent, wonder man
英傑 *eiketsu* great man, hero, master mind
❷ **outstanding, remarkable, extraordinary**
傑作 *kessaku* masterpiece, magnum opus; blunder
傑出する *kesshutsu suru* excel, stand out
傑人 *ketsujin* outstanding person

SYNONYMS

❶ **great persons**
豪 GREAT MAN → 2140
雄 hero → 1008
匠 CRAFTSMAN → 2990
聖 great master → 2830
❷ **excellent and superior**
逸 exceptional → 3120
英 DISTINGUISHED → 2238
優 SUPERIOR → 177
秀 EXCELLENT → 2545
名 first-rate → 2169
上 of upper grade → 3404
絶 without match → 1353
卓 PROMINENT → 2064
快 splendid → 245
妙 MARVELOUS → 239
❷ **conspicuous**
卓 PROMINENT → 2064
著 CONSPICUOUS → 2300
顕 MANIFEST → 1806

債 債 債

156 SAI

丿 亻 仁 仕 仹 佳 倩 倩 債 債 債 債 債

CH 债 zhài

Radical	Strokes
亻 9	13-2-11
Grade	Freq
Jōyō	707
◧ 1-2-11	

2-11
亻

▶DEBT ▶BOND

COMPOUNDS

❶ **debt, liability**

債権 *saiken* credit, claim
債務 *saimu* debt, obligation, liabilities
負債 *fusai* debt, liabilities
減債 *gensai* partial payment of a debt

❷ [also suffix] **bond, debenture, loan**

債券 *saiken* bond, debenture
社債 *shasai* debenture, corporation bond
国債 *kokusai* national bonds; national debt [loan]
起債 *kisai* floatation of a loan, issue of bonds
公債 *kōsai* public bond; public loan

SYNONYMS

❶ **lend and borrow**

借 BORROW → 122
貸 LEND → 2600
融 finance → 1831

❷ **securities**

株 STOCK → 935

催 催 催

157 SAI moyō(su)

丿 亻 亻 亻 亻 亻 亻 亻 亻 亻 催 催 催

CH 催 cuī

Radical	Strokes
亻 9	13-2-11
Grade	Freq
Jōyō	743
◧ 1-2-11	

2-11
亻

▶HOLD AN EVENT ▶PRESS FOR

COMPOUNDS

❶ **hold an event [a meeting], give (a dinner), sponsor**

催事場 *saijijō* event hall
開催する *kaisai suru* hold an event, open (an exhibition)
共催 *kyōsai* joint auspices, cosponsorship
主催 *shusai* sponsorship, promotion

❷ⓐ **press for, urge, hasten**

ⓑ excite, stimulate, arouse, induce

催促する *saisoku suru* press for, urge, demand
催告 *saikoku* notification, demand
催涙弾 *sairuidan* tear-gas bomb
催眠 *saimin* hypnotism
催淫剤 *saiinzai* aphrodisiac

KUN

【moyō(su) 催す】 hold an event [a meeting], give (a dinner), put on (a show); feel like

催し *moyōshi* event, festivities, function, gathering; auspices; opening, holding (a meeting)
会を催す *kai o moyōsu* hold a meeting
涙を催す *namida o moyōsu* be moved to tears

SYNONYMS

❶ **hold an event**

挙 hold a function → 2456

❷ⓐ **urge**

促 HASTEN → 103
勧 URGE → 1857
誘 INDUCE → 1550
励 ENCOURAGE → 1119
侑 URGE TO EAT → 91

2-11 傷 傷 伤 ㊥ 伤 shāng

亻 158 SHŌ kizu ita(mu) ita(meru)

Radical	Strokes
亻 9	13-2-11
Grade	**Freq**
Jōyō-6	633
1 - 2 - 11	

ノ 亻 亻' 𠆢 作 佇 佴 佴 偟 傷 傷 傷 傷
1 2 3 4 5 6 7 8 9 10 11 12 13

▶**WOUND**

COMPOUNDS

❶ⓐ [also suffix] **wound, injury, bruise, scar**
ⓑ **wound, injure, hurt; damage**
傷病 *shōbyō* injuries and sickness
負傷する *fushō suru* be injured [wounded], get hurt
重傷 *jūshō* heavy [serious] wound, severe injury
打撲傷 *dabokushō* bruise, contusion
傷害 *shōgai* injury, bodily harm
殺傷 *sasshō* killing and wounding
損傷 *sonshō* damage, injury
❷ be grieved at heart, be wounded, be pained
傷心 *shōshin* heartbreak, grief
感傷 *kanshō* sentiment, sentimentality
愁傷 *shūshō* grief, lamentation, condolence
❸ slander, abuse
中傷 *chūshō* slander, libel

KUN

【kizu 傷】
① wound, injury, bruise, scar
傷口 *kizuguchi* wound
傷跡(=傷痕) *kizuato* scar, cicatrix
傷付ける *kizutsukeru* wound, injure, damage; hurt (a person's feelings), disgrace (one's family name)
傷付く *kizutsuku* get injured, be wounded [bruised]; be (emotionally) hurt
擦り傷 *kasurikizu* bruise, scratch, graze
古傷 *furukizu* old wound, scar; past misdeed
② [formerly also 疵] defect, flaw, crack, fault, weak point
傷物 *kizumono* defective article; deflowered girl

【ita(mu) 傷む】
① be damaged, be spoiled, wear out
傷み *itami* damage, injury, bruise; wear; rot
傷んだ家 *itanda ie* damaged house
② rot, spoil
傷んだトマト *itanda tomato* rotten tomatoes

【ita(meru) 傷める】 damage, spoil
花を傷める *hana o itameru* spoil a flower

SPECIAL READINGS

火傷▲ *yakedo* (=*kashō*) burn

SYNONYMS

❶ⓐ **injury**
創 wound (cut) → 1815
-擦れ sore → 790
ⓑ **harm and damage**
損 damage → 651
害 HARM, damage → 2272
❷ **grieve**
悼 MOURN → 485
慨 DEPLORE → 641
嘆 SIGH → 630
悲 feel sad → 2775

USAGE

kizu

傷
① wound, injury, bruise, scar
② [formerly also 疵] defect, flaw, crack, fault, weak point

疵
[now usu. 傷] defect, flaw, crack, fault, weak point

HOMOPHONES

kizu ⇨ 疵 3282
itamu ⇨ 痛 3285 悼 485
itameru ⇨ 痛 3285

NOTE

⇨ see also USAGE note at 痛 3285

僧

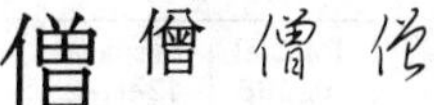

159 SŌ

CH 僧 sēng

Radical	Strokes
亻 9	13-2-11
Grade	**Freq**
Jōyō	1332
◧ 1 - 2 - 1 1	

2-11 亻

Stroke order: ノ 亻 亻 亻' 亻'' 亻' 伃 俤 倆 倆 僧 僧 僧 (1–13)

▸BONZE

COMPOUNDS

ⓐ [also suffix] [original meaning] **bonze, Buddhist monk, priest**

ⓑ [original meaning] *saṃgha*, Buddhist order or community

僧侶 *sōryo* bonze, Buddhist priest
僧職 *sōshoku* priesthood
僧院 *sōin* monastery, temple
禅僧 *zensō* Zen priest [monk]
尼僧 *nisō* nun, sister; (Buddhist) priestess
小僧 *kozō* priestling; servant boy; kid, brat
破戒僧 *hakaisō* sinful priest, depraved monk
僧伽 *sōgya saṃgha*

INDEPENDENT

【sō 僧】 monk, priest, bonze
僧になる *sō ni naru* become a monk

SYNONYMS

ⓐ **clergymen**
坊 Buddhist priest → 233
尼 BUDDHIST NUN → 3033
父 FATHER → 1973

傭

160 YŌ yato(u)

CH 佣 yōng yòng

Radical	Strokes
亻 9	13-2-11
Grade	**Freq**
Reference	
◧ 1 - 2 - 1 1	

2-11 亻

COMPOUNDS

[now usu. 雇う *yatou*]

ⓐ [now also 用 *yō* 2976] hire, employ

ⓑ hire (as a boat), charter

傭兵 *yōhei* mercenary soldier, hireling
傭人 *yōnin* employee
雇傭する *koyō suru* employ, hire
傭(=雇) *yatoi* government employee
傭船 *yōsen* chartered ship

HOMOPHONES

yatou ⇨ 雇 1956
yatoi ⇨ 雇 1956

NOTE

⇨ see USAGE note at 雇 1956
★do not confuse with 庸 3128

傳

161

▸TRANSMIT

nonstandard for 伝 44

2-11 亻

際 障 etc.

incorrect stroke count ⇨ see ◧ 3 – 11

2-11 阝

临

162

▸BE PRESENT AT

handwritten abbreviation for 臨 1630

2-11 刂

2-11 九

鳩 163 KYŪ hato NAMES yasu

CH 鸠 jiū

Radical	Strokes
鳥 196	13-11-2
Grade	Freq
Names	2014
1-2-11	

1 2 3 4 5 6 7 8 9 10 11 12 13

▶PIGEON

COMPOUNDS

❶ **pigeon, dove, carrier pigeon**
鳩舎 *kyūsha* pigeon house
鳩信 *kyūshin* communication by carrier pigeon

❷ huddle like pigeons, herd together
鳩首する *kyūshu suru* go into a huddle

KUN

【hato 鳩】[also suffix] pigeon, dove
鳩派 *hatoha* doves, soft-liners
伝書鳩 *denshobato* carrier [homing] pigeon

NAMES

鳩山 *hatoyama* surname
鳩彦 *yasuhiko* male name

SYNONYMS

❶ **domesticated birds**
鶏 CHICKEN → 1768

2-12 亻

僕 164 BOKU shimobe▲

CH 仆 pú pū

Radical	Strokes
亻 9	14-2-12
Grade	Freq
Jōyō	1405
1-2-12	

1 2 3 4 5 6 7 8 9 10 11 12 13 14

▶I ▶MANSERVANT

COMPOUNDS

❶ **I, myself**—familiar first person pronoun used by men in addressing inferiors or peers
僕達 *bokutachi* we

❷ [original meaning] **manservant, servant, menial**
忠僕 *chūboku* faithful servant
従僕 *jūboku* servant, attendant
家僕 *kaboku* manservant, house boy
下僕 *geboku* servant, your humble servant
公僕 *kōboku* public servant

INDEPENDENT

【boku 僕】 I (⇨ ❶)
僕の *boku no* my

KUN

【shimobe 僕】 manservant, servant
忠実な僕 *chūjitsu na shimobe* faithful servant

SYNONYMS

❶ **first person pronouns**
私 I (*polite*) → 1115
俺 I (*intimate*) → 110
吾 I (*elegant*) → 2407
予 I (*pompous*) → 1983
余 I (*pompous*) → 2042
麿 I (*archaic*) → 3184
朕 IMPERIAL WE → 949
自 SELF → 3525
我 SELF → 3548
己 ONESELF → 3380
身 ONE'S PERSON → 3553

❷ **servants**
隷 UNDERLING → 1751
奴 SLAVE → 187
臣 RETAINER → 3068
従 follower → 415
供 attendant → 88

NOTE

★do not confuse with 撲 733

僚 165 RYŌ

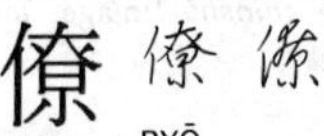

㊥ 僚 liáo

Radical	Strokes
亻 9	14-2-12
Grade	**Freq**
Jōyō	778
1 - 2 - 12	

2-12 亻

▶COLLEAGUE

COMPOUNDS

❶ [original meaning] **colleague, associate, co-worker, companion**

僚友 *ryōyū* comrade, colleague, fellow worker
僚機 *ryōki* consort plane
同僚 *dōryō* colleague, associate, comrade, fellow official

❷ **official**

閣僚 *kakuryō* cabinet members
官僚 *kanryō* government official(s); bureaucracy, officialdom
幕僚 *bakuryō* staff, staff officer

SYNONYMS

❶ **friends and associates**

友 FRIEND → 2952
朋 COMRADE → 880
輩 FELLOW → 2807

❷ **officials**

吏 OFFICIAL → 3536
官 GOVERNMENT OFFICIAL → 2226
司 officiator → 2931
役 executive → 244
事 officer → 3567

像 166 ZŌ

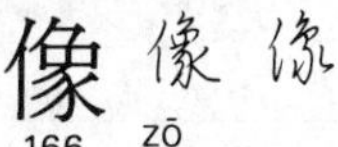

㊥ 像 xiàng

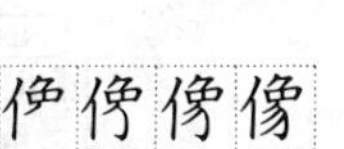

Radical	Strokes
亻 9	14-2-12
Grade	**Freq**
Jōyō-5	963
1 - 2 - 12	

2-12 亻

▶IMAGE

COMPOUNDS

❶ⓐ **optical image**

ⓑ [also suffix] **mental image, image**

ⓒ *math* image

影像 *eizō* image; shadow, phantom
映像 *eizō* (TV) picture, image; reflection
画像 *gazō* portrait, likeness
現像する *genzō suru* develop (film)
実像 *jitsuzō* real image
虚像 *kyozō* virtual image
心像 *shinzō* mental image
想像する *sōzō suru* imagine
日本人の外人像 *nihonjin no gaijinzō* the Japanese image of foreigners
鏡像 *kyōzō* reflected image; *math* image by inversion

❷ [also suffix] (sculptured or painted likeness) **image, likeness, figure, statue; picture, portrait**

仏像 *butsuzō* image of Buddha; Buddhist statue
肖像 *shōzō* portrait, likeness
マリア像 *mariazō* image of the Virgin Mary
銅像 *dōzō* bronze statue [image]
自画像 *jigazō* self-portrait

INDEPENDENT

【zō 像】image, statue; optical image; *math* image

自由の女神の像 *jiyū no megami no zō* Statue of Liberty

SYNONYMS

❶ⓐ **image**

影 SHADOW → 1889

❷ **images**

仏 Buddhist image → 19
偶 figure → 132

USAGE

zō 像 象

★像 is easily confused with 象, to which it is similar in shape, sound and meaning. 像, always read *zō*, has the core meaning IMAGE, i.e., a reduplication of appearance such as an optical image or a sculptured likeness. 象 refers to the outer appearance or manifestation of a thing, i.e., 'phenomenon', in which sense it is always read *shō*. In the sense of elephant, 象 is always read *zō*. Both characters share the meaning 'mental image', as in the 心像 *shinzō* 'mental image' and 心象 *shinshō* 'image, mental picture'.

2-12
亻

167

▶FALSIFY
nonstandard for 偽 131

2-12
亻

168

▶BONZE
nonstandard for 僧 159

2-12
阝

incorrect stroke count ⇨ see 751
(nonstandard for 隣 781)

2-13
亻

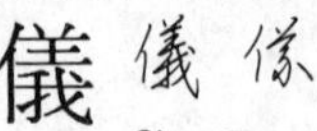
169 GI

Radical	Strokes
亻 9	15-2-13
Grade	**Freq**
Jōyō	1219
1-2-13	

1 2 3 4 5 6 7 8 9 10 11 12 13 14 15

▶CEREMONY

COMPOUNDS

❶ⓐ ceremony, rite, ritual
ⓑ [original meaning] (polite behavior) **ceremony**
儀式 *gishiki* ceremony, rite, ritual
婚儀 *kongi* wedding ceremony
葬儀 *sōgi* funeral service [rites]
礼儀 *reigi* etiquette, courtesy, propriety, manners
行儀 *gyōgi* manners, behavior

❷ⓐ [suffix] (miniature representation) **model, globe**
ⓑ (example to be followed) model, paragon
地球儀 *chikyūgi* globe (of the world)
儀典 *giten* formality, (diplomatic) rite
律儀 *richigi* honesty, faithfulness, loyalty

❸ [suffix] measuring instrument, apparatus (esp. for astronomical applications)
経緯儀 *keiigi* theodolite
水準儀 *suijungi* leveling instrument, surveyor's level

❹ⓐ affair, matter, case
ⓑ [suffix] as for
余儀 *yogi* another method; another problem
難儀 *nangi* hardship, trouble
私儀 *watakushigi* as for me, I

INDEPENDENT

【gi 儀】 ceremony; affair, matter, case
婚礼の儀 *konrei no gi* wedding ceremony
其の儀に就いて *sono gi ni tsuite* about the matter

SYNONYMS

❶ⓐ ceremonies and festivities
式 CEREMONY → 3049
典 formal ceremony → 2627
礼 RITE → 818
斎 religious ritual → 2115
会 Buddhist ceremony → 2020
祭 FESTIVAL → 2672
ⓑ etiquette
礼 ETIQUETTE → 818
❷ⓐ prototype
型 TYPE → 2638
❸ machines and tools
鏡 OPTICAL INSTRUMENT → 1766
器 INSTRUMENT → 2713
具 IMPLEMENT → 2552
械 MECHANICAL CONTRIVANCE → 961
機 MACHINE → 1076
❹ⓐ affair
事 AFFAIR → 3567
件 MATTER → 51

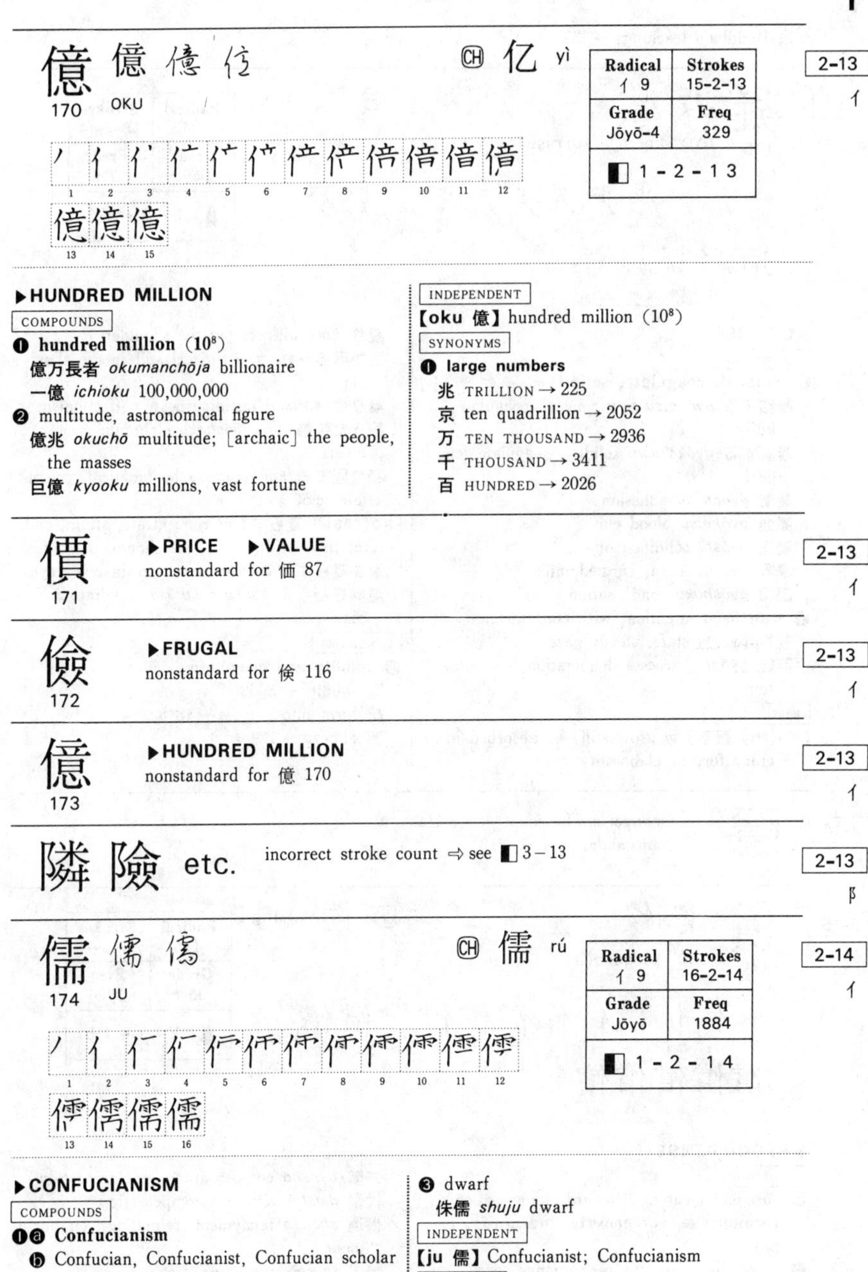

億 170 OKU — CH 亿 yì

Radical	Strokes
亻 9	15-2-13
Grade	**Freq**
Jōyō-4	329
◧ 1-2-13	

2-13 亻

▶**HUNDRED MILLION**

COMPOUNDS

❶ **hundred million** (10⁸)

億万長者 *okumanchōja* billionaire

一億 *ichioku* 100,000,000

❷ multitude, astronomical figure

億兆 *okuchō* multitude; [archaic] the people, the masses

巨億 *kyooku* millions, vast fortune

INDEPENDENT

【**oku 億**】 hundred million (10⁸)

SYNONYMS

❶ **large numbers**

兆 TRILLION → 225

京 ten quadrillion → 2052

万 TEN THOUSAND → 2936

千 THOUSAND → 3411

百 HUNDRED → 2026

價 171 ▶**PRICE** ▶**VALUE**

nonstandard for 価 87 — 2-13 亻

儉 172 ▶**FRUGAL**

nonstandard for 倹 116 — 2-13 亻

憶 173 ▶**HUNDRED MILLION**

nonstandard for 億 170 — 2-13 亻

隣 險 etc. — incorrect stroke count ⇨ see ◧ 3-13 — 2-13 阝

儒 174 JU — CH 儒 rú

Radical	Strokes
亻 9	16-2-14
Grade	**Freq**
Jōyō	1884
◧ 1-2-14	

2-14 亻

▶**CONFUCIANISM**

COMPOUNDS

❶ⓐ **Confucianism**

ⓑ Confucian, Confucianist, Confucian scholar

儒教 *jukyō* Confucianism

儒仏 *jubutsu* Confucianism and Buddhism

儒者 *jusha* Confucianist

❷ learned scholars

大儒 *daiju* great scholar

❸ dwarf

侏儒 *shuju* dwarf

INDEPENDENT

【**ju 儒**】 Confucianist; Confucianism

SYNONYMS

❶ⓐ **religions and sects**

道 Taoism → 3134

仏 Buddhism → 19

禅 ZEN → 1032

法 Buddha's teachings → 333

2-14
冫

凝 凝 凝
175 GYŌ ko(ru) ko(rasu)

CH 凝 níng

Radical	Strokes
冫 15	16-2-14
Grade	**Freq**
Jōyō	1715
■ 1-2-14	

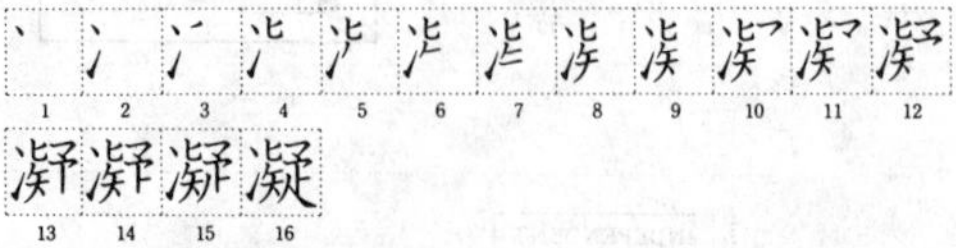

▶CONGEAL

COMPOUNDS

❶ **congeal, coagulate, solidify**
凝結する *gyōketsu suru* congeal, coagulate, solidify
凝固する *gyōko suru* solidify, coagulate, congeal
凝着 *gyōchaku* adhesion
凝血 *gyōketsu* blood clot
凝脂 *gyōshi* solidified oil
凝乳 *gyōnyū* curd, curdled milk
凝縮 *gyōshuku* condensation
❷ with fixed attention, with concentration
凝視 *gyōshi* stare, steady gaze
凝議 *gyōgi* (earnest) deliberation, consultation

KUN

【ko(ru) 凝る】 *vi* grow stiff; be absorbed in, be crazy for; be elaborate
凝り *kori* stiffness (in the shoulders)
肩が凝る *kata ga koru* feel stiff in the shoulders
凝り性 *korishō* fastidiousness, perfectionism
凝った装飾 *kotta sōshoku* elaborate ornaments
凝り固まる *korikatamaru* be fanatical; coagulate, clot
【ko(rasu) 凝らす】 *vt* concentrate, strain, elaborate; have stiffness (in the shoulders)
瞳を凝らす *hitomi o korasu* strain one's eyes
趣向を凝らす *shukō o korasu* elaborate a plan

SYNONYMS

❶ **solidify and coagulate**
固 solidify → 3086
結 form into a mass → 1348
凍 FREEZE → 129

2-14
阝

隱

incorrect stroke count ⇨ see 799
(nonstandard for 隠 713)

2-15
亻

償 償 償
176 SHŌ tsuguna(u)

CH 偿 cháng

Radical	Strokes
亻 9	17-2-15
Grade	**Freq**
Jōyō	1024
■ 1-2-15	

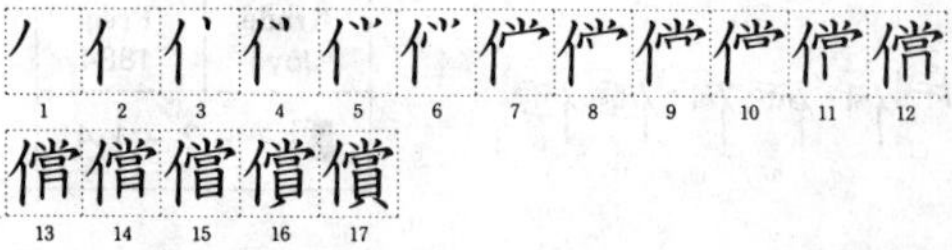

▶RECOMPENSE

COMPOUNDS

ⓐ [original meaning] (award compensation) **recompense, compensate, indemnify, repay**
ⓑ (meet by payment) **recompense, pay**
償却 *shōkyaku* repayment, refundment
報償 *hōshō* recompense, compensation
補償 *hoshō* compensation, indemnity
賠償 *baishō* indemnity, compensation, recompense
弁償 *benshō* compensation, indemnification
代償 *daishō* vicarious compensation
償還 *shōkan* repayment, refunding, reimbursement
無償 *mushō* gratuitous, free

KUN

【tsuguna(u) 償う】 recompense, make up for, atone for
償い *tsugunai* recompense, indemnity, atone-

ment
損失を償う *sonshitsu o tsugunau* recompense for a loss

SYNONYMS

ⓐ **compensate**
賠 COMPENSATE → 1582
酬 RECIPROCATE → 1539
報 REQUITE → 1698

ⓑ **pay**
払う PAY → 194
納 PAY (to the authorities) → 1300
済 settle accounts → 522
支 pay out → 1979
賦 INSTALLMENT → 1583

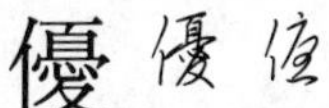
優 　Ⓒ𝐇 优 yōu

177 YŪ U▲ yasa(shii) sugu(reru) masa(ru)▲

Radical	Strokes
亻 9	17-2-15
Grade	**Freq**
Jōyō-6	455
▐ 1-2-15	

2-15 亻

▶**SUPERIOR** ▶**ACTOR**

COMPOUNDS

❶ⓐ (far above average) **superior, excellent, dominant, predominant**
ⓑ *math* superior, major
ⓒ (school mark) Excellent, A
優秀な *yūshū na* excellent, superior, best
優良品 *yūryōhin* excellent articles
優等生 *yūtōsei* honor student, prize pupil
優越 *yūetsu* superiority, supremacy
優勝する *yūshō suru* win the victory [championship]
優先 *yūsen* preference, priority
優勢 *yūsei* superiority, lead, predominance
優性形質 *yūsei keishitsu* dominant character
優弧 *yūko* superior [major] arc
全優の学生 *zen'yū no gakusei* straight A student

❷ **actor, actress, performer**
俳優 *haiyū* actor, actress
女優 *joyū* actress
名優 *meiyū* great actor
声優 *seiyū* radio actor; dialogue speaker (in dubbing)

❸ **kindly, gracious, gentle, kind, cordial**
優遇 *yūgū* favorable treatment, warm reception
優待する *yūtai suru* treat kindly, receive hospitably, give special consideration

❹ graceful, elegant, delicate
優美な *yūbi na* graceful, elegant, refined
優雅 *yūga* elegance, grace
優艶な *yūen na* beautiful, charming

❺ slowly, leisurely
優柔不断 *yūjūfudan* indecisiveness, vacillation

❻ used phonetically for *u*, esp. in the transliteration of Sanscrit Buddhist terms
優曇華 *udonge Udumbara*, name of a legendary tree which is thought to blossom once in 3000 years

INDEPENDENT

【yū 優】 superiority; (school mark) Excellent, A
【yū ni 優に】 well, sufficiently, amply, fully; in a graceful manner
優に三時間は掛かる *Yū ni sanjikan wa kakaru* It takes a good three hours

KUN

【yasa(shii) 優しい】
①ⓐ gentle, tender, sweet
ⓑ kindhearted, kind
優男 *yasaotoko* man of gentle manners
優しい声 *yasashii koe* soft voice
優しくする *yasashiku suru* be kind to, treat kindly
② graceful, delicate

【sugu(reru) 優れる】
[formerly also 勝れる]
① be superior to, be excellent, be better than, surpass
優れて *sugurete* exceedingly, conspicuously, by far
優れた学者 *sugureta gakusha* eminent scholar
② [usu. in negative constructions] be fine, feel well
気分が優れない *kibun ga sugurenai* not feel well

【masa(ru) 優る】 [now usu. 勝る] excel, be better than, surpass
優るとも劣らない *masaru tomo otoranai* not at all inferior to

SYNONYMS

❶ⓐ **excellent and superior**
秀 EXCELLENT → 2545
英 DISTINGUISHED → 2238
傑 outstanding → 155
逸 exceptional → 3120
名 first-rate → 2169

上 of upper grade → 3404
絶 without match → 1353
卓 PROMINENT → 2064
快 splendid → 245
妙 MARVELOUS → 239
❷ **performers**
俳 actor → 112
伶 MUSICIAN → 66
❸ **kind**
渥 GRACIOUS → 600
厚 KIND → 3003
篤 cordial → 2716
懇 cordial → 2899
慈 AFFECTIONATE → 2339
温 warmhearted → 608
❹ **elegant**
雅 ELEGANT → 1197
淑 GRACEFUL → 527
粋 REFINED → 1293
彬 REFINED AND GENTLE → 960
【yasashii】
①ⓐ **gentle**
穏 MILD → 1235
柔 SOFT → 2088

USAGE

❶ **yasashii**
優しい
①ⓐ gentle, tender, sweet
ⓑ kindhearted, kind
② graceful, delicate
易しい
easy, simple
❷ **sugureru**
優れる
［formerly also 勝れる］
① be superior to, be excellent, be better than, surpass
② ［usu. in negative constructions］ be fine, feel well
勝れる
［now usu. 優れる］ same as 優れる

HOMOPHONES

yasashii ⇨ 易 2411
sugureru ⇨ 勝 1005
masaru ⇨ 勝 1005

NOTE

⇨ see also USAGE note at 勝 1005

2-20
亻
儼
178 GEN

Ⓒⓗ 俨 yǎn

Radical	Strokes
亻 9	22-2-20
Grade	**Freq**
Reference	
1-2-20	

COMPOUNDS

● ［now replaced by 厳 3289］ majestic, solemn, dignified-looking

儼然たる *genzentaru* solemn, grave, majestic, stern

3-1
子
孔
179 KŌ ana▲

Ⓒⓗ 孔 kǒng

Radical	Strokes
子 39	4-3-1
Grade	**Freq**
Jōyō	1691
1-3-1	

▶**OPEN HOLE**

COMPOUNDS

❶ ［also suffix］ **open or bottomless hole, opening, aperture**
鼻孔 *bikō* nostrils
気孔 *kikō* pore, stoma
瞳孔 *dōkō* pupil
穿孔 *senkō* perforation, punching; rupture
排水孔 *haisuikō* scupper (hole); osculum
❷ Confucius, Confucianism, Confucian
孔子 *kōshi* Confucius
孔門 *kōmon* Confucian school
❸ peacock
孔雀 *kujaku* peacock

INDEPENDENT

【kō 孔】 open hole
孔を穿つ *kō o ugatsu* pierce a hole

KUN

【ana 孔】 ［usu. 穴］ open or bottomless hole, opening, aperture, perforation
針の孔 *hari no ana* needle's eye
毛孔 *keana* pores (of the skin)

SYNONYMS

❶ **holes and cavities**

穴 HOLE → 2159
口 MOUTH → 3382
坑 PIT → 236
溝 CHANNEL → 659
堀 DITCH → 467
凹 concavity → 3482
洞 CAVE → 380

❷ **Confucius and Confucianists**

子 the Master (Confucius) → 3390
孟 MENCIUS → 2220

HOMOPHONES

ana ⇨ 穴 2159

NOTE

⇨ see USAGE note at 穴 2159

幻 幻 幻

180 GEN maboroshi

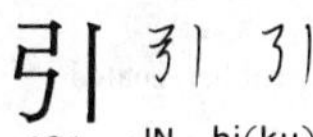

Ⓒⓗ 幻 huàn

Radical	Strokes
幺 52	4-3-1
Grade	**Freq**
Jōyō	1526
◧ 1 - 3 - 1	

3-1 幺

▶PHANTOM

COMPOUNDS

❶ **phantom, phantasm, fantasy, illusion, hallucination, vision**

幻像 *genzō* phantom, vision, illusion
幻肢 *genshi* phantom limb
幻影 *gen'ei* vision, phantom, illusion
幻想 *gensō* fantasy, illusion
幻覚 *genkaku* illusion, hallucination
幻聴 *genchō* auditory hallucination
幻滅 *genmetsu* disillusionment
変幻自在の *hengen-jizai no* ever-changing, phantasmagoric

❷ bewitch, bewilder, create an illusion

幻術 *genjutsu* magic, witchcraft
幻惑 *genwaku* bewitching, fascination
夢幻 *mugen* dream; vision; fantasy

KUN

【maboroshi 幻】 phantom, apparition, phantasm; illusion, hallucination, vision, dream
幻を追う *maboroshi o ou* pursue phantoms

SYNONYMS

❶ **illusory mental images**

夢 DREAM → 2336

❷ **charm**

魅 CHARM → 3329

引 引 引

181 IN hi(ku) hi(ki) hi(ki)- -bi(ki) hi(keru)

㇇	㇇	弓	引
1	2	3	4

Ⓒⓗ 引 yǐn

Radical	Strokes
弓 57	4-3-1
Grade	**Freq**
Jōyō-2	210
◧ 1 - 3 - 1	

3-1 弓

▶DRAW

COMPOUNDS

❶ⓐ [original meaning] (pull toward one) **draw, pull, haul, tug**
ⓑ (extend in length) draw out, stretch

引力 *inryoku* gravitation
引航する *inkō suru* tug, tow
牽引する *ken'in suru* pull, draw, haul
強引な *gōin na* overbearing, coercive
延引 *en'in* delay, postponement

❷ⓐ (cause to move, as by leading) **draw (toward), draw in, call in**
ⓑ draw a person to act: entice, induce, seduce
ⓒ lead, guide, take along

引火する *inka suru* ignite, catch fire
引見する *inken suru* receive, favor (a person) with an interview
我田引水 *gaden'insui* seeking one's own interests
吸引 *kyūin* suction, absorption, aspiration; attraction
誘引 *yūin* enticement, inducement, attraction
引率する *insotsu suru* lead, command
引導 *indō* guidance; address to a departed soul
引致 *inchi* arrest, custody

❸ **quote, cite, refer to**

引用 *in'yō* quotation, citation
引照 *inshō* reference
引喩 *in'yu* allusion
索引 *sakuin* index

❹ withdraw, retire

引退する *intai suru* retire, go into retirement

❺ take upon oneself, accept
引責する *inseki suru* take responsibility upon oneself
❻ introduction, foreword
小引 *shōin* brief foreword

KUN

【hi(ku) 引く】
①ⓐ draw, pull, haul, tug; drag, trail
ⓑ (cause to retreat) draw in, pull in
引 *hiku* PULL (marking on doors)
引っ張る *hipparu* pull, draw; drag
引き上げる *hikiageru* draw [pull] up; promote; increase
引き出す *hikidasu* draw out; lure out
引き分け *hikiwake* draw; drawn game [match]
引き摺る *hikizuru* drag along; trail
弓を引く *yumi o hiku* draw a bow
船を引く *fune o hiku* tow a boat
手を引く *te o hiku* wash one's hands of; lead by the hand
② [formerly also 惹く]
ⓐ draw (attention or sympathy), attract, catch
ⓑ catch (a cold)
引き付ける *hikitsukeru* attract, charm, keep at hand; have a convulsive fit
客引き *kyakuhiki* touting; tout, barker, pander
注意を引く *chūi o hiku* draw attention
風邪を引いている *kaze o hiite iru* have a cold
③ⓐ draw (off) (water), tap, conduct, lead (a stream through a field)
ⓑ lay on (gas or water), install (a telephone)
川から水を引く *kawa kara mizu o hiku* draw water off a river
電話を引く *denwa o hiku* install a telephone
④ draw (a line or diagram)
図面を引く *zumen o hiku* draw a plan
⑤ draw lots
福引き *fukubiki* lottery
⑥ [also 退く]
ⓐ retreat, withdraw
ⓑ retire, resign
駆け引き *kakehiki* bargaining; tactics
後へ引く *ato e hiku* retreat, recede
役所を引く *yakusho o hiku* leave office, resign one's post in an office
⑦ [also 退く] subside, abate, go down
熱が引いた *Netsu ga hiita* The fever has abated
⑧ subtract, deduct, deduce; allow discount
引き算 *hikizan* subtraction
三引く二は一 *San hiku ni wa ichi* Three minus two equals one
割引 *waribiki* discount, reduction
⑨ quote, cite, refer to
例を引く *rei o hiku* cite an example
⑩ look up, consult (a dictionary)
生き字引 *ikijibiki* walking dictionary
⑪ lay on, apply, oil
油を引く *abura o hiku* oil
⑫ succeed to, take over
引き継ぐ *hikitsugu* take over, hand over; succeed to, inherit
引き受ける *hikiukeru* undertake; answer for, guarantee
引き取る *hikitoru* take over, receive; retire
皇室の血を引いている *kōshitsu no chi o hiite iru* be descended from the Imperial House
⑬ lift, steal
万引き *manbiki* shoplifting; shoplifter
⑭ unclassified compounds
取り引き *torihiki* transaction, dealings

【hi(ki) 引き】
① [sometimes also 抽-] drawing
引き出し *hikidashi* drawer; withdrawal (of money)
② patronage, backing, pull
良い引きが有る *yoi hiki ga aru* have a strong pull

【hi(ki)- 引き-】 [sometimes 引っ *hit-* or 引ん *hin-*] emphatic verbal prefix
引き払う *hikiharau* clear out, move out
引っ捕らえる *hittoraeru* capture, arrest, seize
引ん剝く *hinmuku* peel, strip

【-bi(ki) -引き】
[also suffix]
① coated with
ゴム引きの *gomubiki no* rubber-coated
② discount
一割引き *ichiwaribiki* 10% off

【hi(keru) 引ける】 *vi* close, be over, break up; feel small, become self-conscious
引け *hike* defeat, reverse; close (esp. of stock market)
引け時 *hikedoki* closing time (of school)
学校が引けてから *gakkō ga hikete kara* after school
引け目を感じる *hikeme o kanjiru* feel small, feel inferior
気が引ける *ki ga hikeru* feel small, become self-conscious

SYNONYMS

❶ⓐ pull
抽 DRAW OUT → 302
抜 PULL OUT → 246
控える HOLD BACK → 495
寄せる DRAW NEAR → 2291
❷ⓒ lead and escort
率 LEAD → 2118
導 GUIDE → 2888
連 take along → 3103
❸ quote

挙 cite → 2456

【hiku】

⑧ **subtract**

減 subtract → 601

控 HOLD BACK → 495

USAGE

❶ **hiku**

引く

①ⓐ draw, pull, haul, tug; drag, trail

ⓑ (cause to retreat) draw in, pull in

② [formerly also 惹く]

ⓐ draw (attention or sympathy), attract, catch

ⓑ catch (a cold)

③ⓐ draw (off) (water), tap, conduct, lead (a stream through a field)

ⓑ lay on (gas or water), install (a telephone)

④ draw (a line or diagram)

⑤ draw lots

⑥ [also 退く]

ⓐ retreat, withdraw

ⓑ retire, resign

⑦ [also 退く] subside, abate, go down

⑧ subtract, deduct, deduce; allow discount

⑨ quote, cite, refer to

⑩ look up, consult (a dictionary)

⑪ lay on, apply, oil

⑫ succeed to, take over

⑬ lift, steal

⑭ unclassified compounds

弾く

play on (stringed instruments)

退く

[also 引く]

①ⓐ retreat, withdraw

ⓑ retire, resign

② subside, abate, go down

惹く

[now usu. 引く]

ⓐ draw (attention or sympathy), attract, catch

ⓑ catch (a cold)

挽く

① grind (meat or coffee)

② saw, cut with a saw

③ turn (a potter's wheel)

轢く

run over (with a vehicle), knock down

❷ **hiki**

引き

① [sometimes also 抽-] drawing

② patronage, backing, pull

抽-

[usu. 引き] drawing

HOMOPHONES

hiku ⇨ 弾 572 退 3094 惹 2493 挽 427 轢 1662

hiki ⇨ 抽 302

NOTE

⇨ see also USAGE note at 上 3404

⇨ see COMPOUND FORMATION for 駆け引き *kakehiki* ⇨ 駆 1823

 叱 𠮟

182 SHITSU shika(ru)

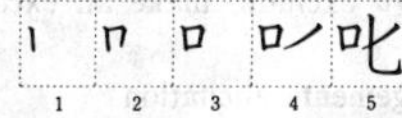

Ⓒⓗ 叱 chi

Radical	Strokes
口 30	5-3-2
Grade	**Freq**
Non-Jōyō	1969
◧ 1 - 3 - 2	

3-2 口

▶**SCOLD**

COMPOUNDS

● [original meaning] **scold, reprehend, reproach**

叱咤する *shitta suru* scold, give a scolding; command

叱責する *shisseki suru* reproach, scold, reprove

叱正 *shissei* correction (of errors)

KUN

【shika(ru) 叱る】 scold, rebuke, reprove, call down, bawl out

叱られる *shikarareru* be scolded [reproved]

叱り付ける *shikaritsukeru* scold away, rebuke strongly, bawl out

SYNONYMS

● **blame and accuse**

責 BLAME → 2467

詰 REPRIMAND → 1521

難 find fault with → 1838

批 CRITICIZE → 250

劾 EXPOSE CRIMES → 1266

弾 impeach → 572

3-2
口

叮
183 TEI

Ⓒ 叮 丁 dīng

Radical	Strokes
口 30	5-3-2
Grade	**Freq**
Reference	
1 - 3 - 2	

COMPOUNDS

● [now replaced by 丁 3348] courteous

叮嚀(＝丁寧)な *teinei na* polite, courteous

3-2
口

叫
184

▶**SHOUT**
nonstandard for 叫 201

3-2
土

切
185

▶**CUT**
nonstandard for 切 27

3-2
夕

外 外 外
186 GAI GE soto hoka hazu(su) hazu(reru) to-▲

Ⓒ 外 wài

Radical	Strokes
夕 36	5-3-2
Grade	**Freq**
Jōyō-2	110
1 - 3 - 2	

ノ ク タ 外 外
1 2 3 4 5

▶**OUTSIDE**

COMPOUNDS

❶ⓐ (outer side) **outside, exterior; out, outer**
ⓑ [also suffix] (beyond the boundary) **outside, without, beyond**
外部の *gaibu no* outside, outer, external
外野 *gaiya* outfield; outsiders
外角 *gaikaku* outside corner; external angle
外見 *gaiken* outward appearance
外科 *geka* (department of) surgery
外出 *gaishutsu* going out, outing
意外な *igai na* unexpected, unforeseen, surprising
郊外 *kōgai* suburbs, outskirts
案外 *angai* contrary to one's expectations, unexpectedly
以外に *igai ni* except for, excluding
内外 *naigai* inside and outside; approximately
海外 *kaigai* overseas, abroad
...の範囲外に *...no han'igai ni* beyond the scope of...
予想外の *yosōgai no* unexpected, unforeseen
❷ⓐ **foreign, external**
ⓑ abbrev. of 外務省 *gaimushō*: Ministry of Foreign Affairs
外国 *gaikoku* foreign country
外人 *gaijin* foreigner, alien
外為 *gaitame* foreign exchange
外交 *gaikō* diplomacy, foreign relations
外務 *gaimu* foreign affairs
外貨 *gaika* foreign currency [money]; foreign [imported] goods
在外の *zaigai no* overseas
外相 *gaishō* Minister of Foreign Affairs
❸ leave out, exclude
除外する *jogai suru* exclude, make an exception of
疎外 *sogai* estrangement, alienation
❹ maternal, mother's
外祖父 *gaisofu* maternal grandfather
外姓 *gaisei* mother's family name
❺ unorthodox, unofficial, off-the-record
外道 *gedō* heresy, paganism, pagan
外史 *gaishi* unofficial history

KUN

【soto 外】 outside, exterior; open air, outdoors
家の外 *ie no soto* outside the house
外側 *sotogawa* exterior, outside
外回り *sotomawari* circumference, periphery; outside work; outer track (of a two-way belt line)
外で遊ぶ *soto de asobu* play outdoors

【hoka 外】
① [also 他] something other than, the rest
外の *hoka no* other, another, different, else

外ならぬ *hokanaranu* nothing but, no other than
山田外 *yamada hoka* Yamada and others [et al.]
② some other place, outside
外で *hoka de* elsewhere, somewhere else
外を探す *hoka o sagasu* search somewhere else
③ outside, beyond, besides; except, but
恋は思案の外 *Koi wa shian no hoka* Love and reason do not go together
その外 *sono hoka* besides, in addition; the rest, others
そうする外は無い *Sō suru hoka wa nai* There is nothing for it but to do so

【hazu(su) 外す】 take off, remove, undo, detach; miss, let go, fail; avoid, dodge, slip away; leave out, exclude
眼鏡を外す *megane o hazusu* take off one's glasses
取り外す *torihazusu* remove, dismantle
機会を外す *kikai o hazusu* miss a chance
席を外している *seki o hazushite iru* be not at one's desk
予定から外す *yotei kara hazusu* exclude from the schedule

【hazu(reru) 外れる】
① come off, get out of place, slip out, be separated
ボタンが外れている *botan ga hazurete iru* be unbuttoned
② miss, go wide, fail
外れ *hazure* end, verge; miss, failure
並外れの *namihazure no* out of the common, far above the average
③ be contrary to, be against
道理に外れた *dōri ni hazureta* contrary to reason

【to- 外-】 outside, outer
外様 *tozama* one not included in the favored group, outsider; outside daimyo

SYNONYMS

❶ outside
表 SURFACE → 2429
面 FACE → 2087
❷ⓐ foreign
異 foreign → 2584
【hazusu】
○ eliminate
脱 REMOVE → 973
去 take away → 2156
除 RID OF → 456
省 leave out → 2449
却 ELIMINATE → 1118
削 cross out → 1448
抹 wipe off → 313
撤 WITHDRAW → 738
排 EXCLUDE → 490
払う CLEAR AWAY → 194
【hazureru】
① come off
脱 get out of place → 973
② deviate
逸 deviate → 3120

USAGE

hoka
外
① [also 他] something other than, the rest
② some other place, outside
③ outside, beyond, besides; except, but
他
[also 外] something other than, the rest

HOMOPHONES

hoka ⇨ 他 35

NOTE

⇨ see COMPOUND FORMATION for
案外 *angai* ⇨ 案 2270
外為 *gaitame* ⇨ 為 3577

奴 187

奴 ぬ

DO yatsu▲ yakko▲

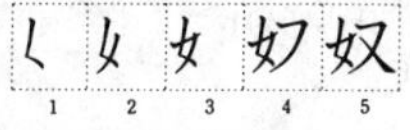

Ⓒⓗ 奴 nú

Radical	Strokes
女 38	5-3-2
Grade	**Freq**
Jōyō	1757
◧ 1-3-2	

3-2 女

▶SLAVE ▶GUY

COMPOUNDS

❶ slave, serf, manservant, menial
奴隷 *dorei* slave, servant
農奴 *nōdo* serf
黒奴 *kokudo* black slave
❷ derogatory suffix for persons performing a menial action
売国奴 *baikokudo* traitor
守銭奴 *shusendo* miser, slave of money
❸ fellow, guy
奴輩 *dohai* fellows, guys

KUN

【yatsu 奴】
slang
①ⓐ guy, fellow, chap
ⓑ thing; things, matter
奴等 *yatsura* those guys, they

黒い奴 *kuroi yatsu derogatory* nigger; black one
② third person pronoun
【**yakko** 奴】servant, footman; guy, fellow, chap; tofu [bean curd] cut in cubes
奴さん *yakkosan* guy, fellow, chap; footman, attendant

SPECIAL READINGS
彼奴▲ *aitsu* that guy, he, she; that one

SYNONYMS
❶ **servants**
僕 MANSERVANT → 164
隷 UNDERLING → 1751
臣 RETAINER → 3068
従 follower → 415
供 attendant → 88
【**yatsu**】
Ⓘⓐ **fellow**
漢 FELLOW → 657
輩 FELLOW (*belittling*) → 2807
徒 fellows → 416
棒 tough guy → 983
坊 COLLOQUIAL PERSON SUFFIX → 233
屋 colloquial person suffix → 3098
物 character → 874
② **third person pronouns**
彼 THIRD PERSON PRONOUN (*neutral*) → 290
氏 third person pronoun (*polite*) → 2951

3-2
女

好

incorrect stroke count ⇨ see 208

3-2
工

巧 巧 巧

188 KŌ taku(mi) taku(mu)▲ uma(i)▲

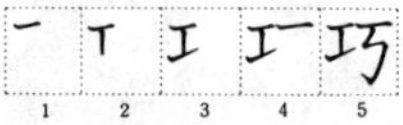

Ⓒⓗ 巧 qiǎo

Radical	Strokes
工 48	5-3-2
Grade	**Freq**
Jōyō	1395
◧ 1-3-2	

▶**SKILLFUL**

COMPOUNDS
● **skillful, ingenious, clever**
巧妙な *kōmyō na* skillful, ingenious, clever
巧拙 *kōsetsu* skill, dexterity, workmanship
巧者 *kōsha* skillful [ingenious] person
巧言 *kōgen* flattery
技巧 *gikō* art, craftsmanship, technical skill; trick
精巧な *seikō na* elaborate, exquisite, ingenious
悧巧(=利口)な *rikō na* clever, bright, sharp, shrewd

INDEPENDENT
【**kō** 巧】skillfulness, dexterity
巧を誇る *kō o hokoru* be of excellent workmanship

KUN
【**taku(mi)** 巧み】skill, dexterity, ingenuity
巧みな *takumi na* skillful, clever, cunning
巧みな手段 *takumi na shudan* clever trick
【**taku(mu)** 巧む】[in negative constructions] contrive
巧まぬ技巧 *takumanu gikō* artless art
【**uma(i)** 巧い】[also 上手い or 旨い] skillful, clever; splendid, excellent
巧さ *umasa* skillfulness, ingenuity
英語が巧い *eigo ga umai* speak English well
巧い絵 *umai e* excellent picture [painting]

SYNONYMS
● **skillful**
能 able → 1323

USAGE
takumi
巧み
skill, dexterity, ingenuity
匠
artisan; woodworker, carpenter

HOMOPHONES
takumi ⇨ 匠 2990
umai ⇨ 旨い 2024 甘い 3494
上手い 3404, 3456

NOTE
⇨ see also USAGE note at 旨 2024
★do not confuse with 功 189

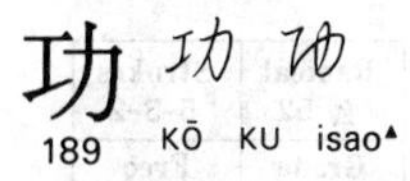

功 功 㓛
189 KŌ KU isao▲

一 丅 工 玏 功
1 2 3 4 5

Ⓒⓗ 功 gōng

Radical	Strokes
力 19	5-2-3
Grade	**Freq**
Jōyō-4	702
1 - 3 - 2	

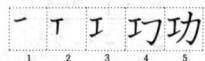

3-2 工

▶**MERIT**

COMPOUNDS

ⓐ **merit(s), meritorious deed [service]**
ⓑ **success, achievement, result, fruit**

功績 *kōseki* meritorious deed, achievement
功労 *kōrō* meritorious deed, (distinguished) services
功名 *kōmyō* great exploit; distinction, fame
功罪 *kōzai* merits and demerits
功徳 *kudoku* virtue, merits of one's pious acts
功力 *kuriki* merits [influence] of one's pious acts or religious practice
年功 *nenkō* long service, years' [long] experience
勲功 *kunkō* distinguished services, merit
戦功 *senkō* merit of war
功利主義 *kōrishugi* utilitarianism
成功 *seikō* success

INDEPENDENT

【**kō 功**】merit(s), meritorious deed [service]; success, achievement, result, fruit
功を争う *kō o arasou* claim credit, contend for distinction
功を奏する *kō o sōsuru* succeed

KUN

【**isao 功**】[also 勲] *elegant* meritorious service, merit

SYNONYMS

ⓐ **accomplishment**
績 ACHIEVEMENTS → 1412
勲 MERITORIOUS SERVICE → 2869

HOMOPHONES

isao ⇨ 勲 2869

NOTE

⇨ see USAGE note at 勲 2869
★do not confuse with 巧 188

刊 刊 刋
190 KAN

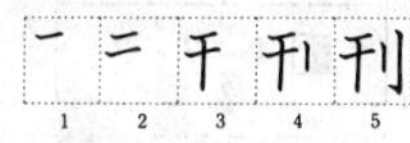

一 二 干 刊 刊
1 2 3 4 5

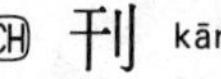

Ⓒⓗ 刊 kān

Radical	Strokes
リ 18	5-2-3
Grade	**Freq**
Jōyō-5	1050
1 - 3 - 2	

3-2 干

▶**PUBLISH**

COMPOUNDS

ⓐ [also suffix] **publish**
ⓑ **publication, edition, issue**

刊行 *kankō* publication
発刊 *hakkan* publication, issue
未刊の *mikan no* unpublished
既刊の *kikan no* already published
隔月刊 *kakugetsukan* published bimonthly
創刊号 *sōkangō* inaugural number, first issue
週刊 *shūkan* weekly publication, weekly
朝刊 *chōkan* morning edition [paper]
夕刊 *yūkan* evening edition [paper]

INDEPENDENT

【**kan 刊**】published by [in]...
昭和三年刊 *shōwa sannen kan* published in 1928

SYNONYMS

ⓐ **print and publish**
版 PUBLISHING → 872
植 typeset → 990
刷 PRINT → 1273
印 print → 828
載 PUT IN PRINT → 3300
掲 display in writing → 494

ⓑ **editions**
版 edition → 872
訂 revision → 1442
刷 printing → 1273

3-2
幺

幼 幼 幼

191 YŌ osana(i)

Stroke order: 1 2 3 4 5

Ⓒⓗ 幼 yòu

Radical	Strokes
幺 52	5-3-2
Grade	**Freq**
Jōyō-6	1038
1 - 3 - 2	

▶**VERY YOUNG**

COMPOUNDS

❶ⓐ **very young, infant**
ⓑ **infantile, immature**

幼児 *yōji* young child, infant
幼女 *yōjo* baby girl
幼時 *yōji* childhood, infancy
幼年 *yōnen* infancy, childhood
幼稚な *yōchi na* childish, infantile, crude
幼稚園 *yōchien* kindergarten

❷ [original meaning] **young child, child**

長幼 *chōyō* young and old
老幼 *rōyō* old people and children

INDEPENDENT

【**yō 幼**】abbrev. of 幼稚園 *yōchien*: kindergarten; infancy

KUN

【**osana(i) 幼い**】very young, infant; childish, infantile

幼子 *osanago* baby, infant, child
幼心 *osanagokoro* child's mind; innocent heart

SYNONYMS

❶ **young**

稚 CHILDISH → 1206
若 YOUNG → 2241
弱 young → 1167
少 young → 3467
青 youthful → 2430

❷ **child**

児 CHILD (of any age) → 2546
子 CHILD → 3390
童 CHILD (young person) → 2130
坊 SONNY → 233

3-2
弓

弘 弘 弘

192 KŌ GU NAMES hiro hiroshi hiromu mitsu

Stroke order: 1 2 3 4 5

Ⓒⓗ 弘 hóng

Radical	Strokes
弓 57	5-3-2
Grade	**Freq**
Names	1978
1 - 3 - 2	

▶**DISSEMINATE**

COMPOUNDS

❶ **disseminate, spread, teach (esp. Buddhism)**

弘報(=広報) *kōhō* (public) information, public relations
弘法 *guhō* spreading Buddhist teachings

❷ⓐ great, grand
ⓑ [original meaning, now rare] extensive, broad, vast

弘誓 *guzei* Buddha's great vows
弘大な *kōdai na* grand, magnificent, vast
弘遠な *kōen na* vast and far-reaching

NAMES

弘一 *kōichi* male name
弘 *hiroshi* male name
弘前 *hirosaki* place name
昭弘 *akihiro* male name

SYNONYMS

❶ **make widely known**

布 SPREAD → 2973
流 spread → 441
伝 spread → 44
広 spread → 3035
及 REACH TO → 3385

NOTE

⇨ see USAGE note at 広 3035

193 DA DĀSU▲ u(tsu) u(chi)-

Ⓒⓗ 打 dǎ dá

Radical	Strokes
扌 64	5-3-2
Grade	**Freq**
Jōyō-3	146
◧ 1 - 3 - 2	

3-2 扌

▶**STRIKE**

COMPOUNDS

❶ [also prefix] [original meaning] **strike, hit, beat**
打撃 *dageki* blow, strike; batting, hitting
打撲 *daboku* blow, stroke
打診 *dashin* sounding, tapping; percussion
打電 *daden* sending a telegram
打楽器 *dagakki* percussion instrument, traps
殴打する *ōda suru* give a blow, beat, strike

❷ *baseball*
ⓐ **hit, bat**
ⓑ [also suffix] **hit, base hit**
打線 *dasen* batting line-up
打者 *dasha* batter, hitter
打席 *daseki* batter's box; one's turn at bat
安打 *anda* safe hit, base hit
代打 *daida* pinch-hitting; pinch hitter
打率 *daritsu* batting average
長打 *chōda* long hit
本塁打 *honruida* home run
適時打 *tekijida* timely hit

❸ **used in verbal compounds to add euphony**
打開 *dakai* break, development, a new turn
打倒する *datō suru* overthrow, knock down, defeat
打算 *dasan* calculation, self-interest, selfishness
打破する *daha suru* break down, overthrow, abolish

❹ dozen
三打 *sandāsu* three dozen

INDEPENDENT

【**da** 打】*baseball* batting
打のチーム *da no chīmu* team excellent in batting

KUN

【**u(tsu)** 打つ】
①ⓐ strike, hit, beat, give a blow, thrash
ⓑ (of a clock) strike (the hour)
ⓒ (impress upon) strike, move, impress
打ち込む *uchikomu* strike [drive] into, ram down; devote oneself to, be absorbed in
打ち上げる *uchiageru* launch, shoot up; (of waves) dash, wash up [ashore]; finish, close
鞭打つ *muchiutsu* whip, lash, give the rod; spur on
三時を打つ *sanji o utsu* strike three
心を打つ *kokoro o utsu* impress (a person), touch (a person's) heart

② perform an action by striking, as:
ⓐ drive in (a nail), affix
ⓑ cut off (a person's head)
ⓒ water, sprinkle
ⓓ play (as a game of go)
ⓔ till (the soil)
ⓕ make something by striking
銘打つ *meiutsu* engrave an inscription; call [designate] itself
打ち首 *uchikubi* decapitation, beheading
打ち水 *uchimizu* watering, sprinkling
碁を打つ *go o utsu* play (a game of) go
田を打つ *ta o utsu* till [plow] a rice paddy
刀を打つ *katana o utsu* temper [forge] a sword

③ perform an action (as if by striking), as:
ⓐ send (a telegram)
ⓑ pay (money on a contract)
ⓒ perform, run
電報を打つ *denpō o utsu* send a telegram
手付けを打つ *tetsuke o utsu* advance money (on a contract)
芝居を打つ *shibai o utsu* give [present] a play; play a trick, put up a false show
仕打ち *shiuchi* (unfavorable) treatment, (cool) attitude

④ [usu. 撃つ, sometimes also 討つ] attack, strike, assault
不意を打つ *fui o utsu* make a surprise attack, take (a person) unawares
挟み打ち *hasamiuchi* attack on both sides [flanks], pincer attack
追い打ち *oiuchi* attacking the routed enemy, pursuit

【**u(chi)-** 打ち-】verbal prefix adding euphony or emphasis
打ち出す *uchidasu* set out [forth], work out, hammer out; strike out, emboss; announce
打ち切る *uchikiru* put an end to, break off, finish
打ち合わせ *uchiawase* preliminary [previous] arrangement, preliminaries
打ち消す *uchikesu* deny, negate, contradict
打ち明ける *uchiakeru* confide in (someone), reveal, disclose

SYNONYMS

❶ **strike**

撃 STRIKE → 2863
当てる HIT → 2177
拍 BEAT (strike repeatedly) → 304
撲 DEAL A BLOW → 733
殴 BEAT (strike a person) → 886

USAGE

utsu

打つ

①ⓐ strike, hit, beat, give a blow, thrash
ⓑ (of a clock) strike (the hour)
ⓒ (impress upon) strike, move, impress
② perform an action by striking, as:
ⓐ drive in (a nail), affix
ⓑ cut off (a person's head)
ⓒ water, sprinkle
ⓓ play (as a game of go)
ⓔ till (the soil)
ⓕ make something by striking
③ perform an action (as if by striking), as:
ⓐ send (a telegram)
ⓑ pay (money on a contract)
ⓒ perform, run
④ [usu. 撃つ, sometimes also 討つ] attack, strike, assault

撃つ

① fire, shoot, discharge
② [sometimes also 打つ or 討つ] attack, strike, assault

討つ

① kill (with a sword or spear)
②ⓐ suppress by armed force, put down [attack] the enemy, send a punitive expedition
ⓑ [usu. 撃つ, sometimes also 打つ] attack, strike, assault

HOMOPHONES

utsu ⇨ 撃 2863 討 1456

3-2 扌

払 拂

194 FUTSU hara(u) -hara(i) -bara(i)

一 十 扌 払 払 (1 2 3 4 5)

Ⓒⓗ 拂 fú

Radical	Strokes
扌 64	5-3-2
Grade	**Freq**
Jōyō	711
1 - 3 - 2	

▶**CLEAR AWAY** ▶**PAY**

COMPOUNDS

❶ [original meaning] **clear away, sweep away, wipe away**

払拭する *fusshoku suru* wipe out, sweep off
払底 *futtei* shortage

❷ clear up, dawn

払暁 *futsugyō* dawn

KUN

【hara(u) 払う】

①ⓐ (remove something undesirable) clear away, sweep away, brush off, prune
ⓑ [also verbal suffix] (drive off) clear out, drive away, expel, exorcise

払い除ける *harainokeru* brush off, sweep away
払い落とす *haraiotosu* shake off, brush off
足払い *ashibarai* tripping up
取り払う *toriharau* clear away, remove
追い払う(＝追っ払う) *oiharau* (＝*opparau*) drive away, expel, exorcise
露払い *tsuyuharai* herald; heralding, ushering
厄払い *yakubarai* exorcism
焼き払う *yakiharau* clear away by burning, reduce to ashes

② (dispose of supplies on hand) clear out, sell off, dispose of

払い下げる *haraisageru* sell, dispose of

③ (clear a debt) pay, settle accounts

払い *harai* payment; account, bill
払い戻す *haraimodosu* pay back
払い込む *haraikomu* pay in, pay up
勘定を払う *kanjō o harau* pay a bill, settle one's account

④ pay (attention), give heed

注意を払う *chūi o harau* pay attention (to)

⑤ (go away) clear out, leave, quit

引き払う *hikiharau* clear out, move out
出払う *deharau* be all out

【-hara(i), -bara(i) -払い】

① [also suffix] payment, settlement

支払い *shiharai* payment, payout, defrayment
延べ払い *nobebarai* deferred payment
分割払い *bunkatsubarai* payment in installments

② emphatic verbal suffix

酔っ払い *yopparai* drunkard, boozer
掻っ払い *kapparai* pilferer; pilfering

SYNONYMS

❶ **clean and wash**

掃 SWEEP → 503
清 CLEAR → 523
粛 PURGE → 3581
浄 cleanse → 382
洗 WASH → 388
濯 RINSE → 793

浴 BATHE → 445
【harau】
①ⓐ **eliminate**
排 EXCLUDE → 490
撤 WITHDRAW → 738
除 RID OF → 456
外す take off → 186
脱 REMOVE → 973
去 take away → 2156
省 leave out → 2449
却 ELIMINATE → 1118
削 cross out → 1448
抹 wipe off → 313
ⓑ **drive out**
駆 drive away → 1823
退 cause to retreat → 3094
追 chase away → 3096
逐 DRIVE OUT → 3102
斥 EXPEL → 2972
排 EXCLUDE → 490
③ **pay**
納 PAY (to the authorities) → 1300
済 settle accounts → 522
支 pay out → 1979
賦 INSTALLMENT → 1583
償 RECOMPENSE → 176

 incorrect stroke count ⇨ see 823 3-2 止

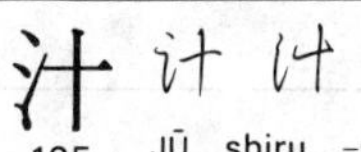

195 JŪ shiru -shiru

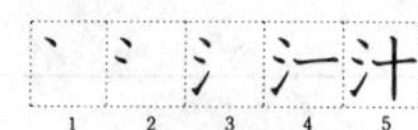

Ⓒⓗ  zhī

Radical	Strokes
氵 85	5-3-2
Grade	**Freq**
Jōyō	1443
1 - 3 - 2	

3-2 氵

▶**JUICE** ▶**SOUP**

COMPOUNDS

❶ⓐ **juice, sap**
ⓑ **soup, broth**
汁液 *jūeki* juice
果汁 *kajū* fruit juice
一汁一菜 *ichijū-issai* simple meal
肉汁 *nikujū* meat juice, gravy
❷ [original meaning] fluid, body fluid, liquid
胆汁 *tanjū* bile, gall
墨汁 *bokujū* India ink, black writing fluid

KUN

【**shiru** 汁】 juice, sap; soup, gravy; pus; profit yielded through another person's effort
蜜柑の汁 *mikan no shiru* mandarin orange juice
澄まし汁 *sumashijiru* clear soup
甘い汁を吸う *amai shiru o suu* make a good thing out of (something)
【**-shiru** -汁】 [suffix] soup
味噌汁 *misoshiru miso* soup
野菜汁 *yasaijiru* vegetable soup

SYNONYMS

❶ **drinks**
乳 MILK → 1438
酒 ALCOHOLIC DRINK → 444
茶 TEA → 2259
❷ **liquid**
液 LIQUID → 511
水 WATER → 10

犯 犯 犯

196 HAN BON▲ oka(su)

Ⓒⓗ 犯 fàn

Radical	Strokes
犭 94	5-3-2
Grade	**Freq**
Jōyō-5	619
1 - 3 - 2	

3-2 犭

▶**OFFENSE**

COMPOUNDS

❶ⓐ [also suffix] **offense, crime**
ⓑ counter for offenses
犯罪 *hanzai* offense, crime
犯行 *hankō* criminal act, crime, offense
防犯 *bōhan* crime prevention
初犯 *shohan* first offense
過失犯 *kashitsuhan* careless offense
前科三犯 *zenka sanpan* previously convicted three times
❷ⓐ **offend against, violate, infringe**

ⓑ [also suffix] **offender, criminal**
犯則 *hansoku* transgression, violation (of the law)
侵犯 *shinpan* invasion; violation
違犯(＝違反) *ihan* violation (of the law), infringement; breach
不犯 *fubon* strict observance of the Buddhist commandment that all priests should be celibate
犯人 *hannin* criminal, offender
戦犯 *senpan* war criminal
共犯 *kyōhan* accomplice, confederate, partner, associate
殺人犯 *satsujinhan* murderer
知能犯 *chinōhan* intellectual criminal

KUN

【oka(su) 犯す】
① offend against, violate, infringe upon, commit (a crime), sin against
犯し難い *okashigatai* dignified
法を犯す *hō o okasu* violate the law
罪を犯す *tsumi o okasu* commit a crime
② rape, violate, deflower
女を犯す *onna o okasu* rape a girl

SYNONYMS

❶ **crimes and offenses**
罪 CRIME → 2610
凶 atrocious crime → 2961
❷ⓐ **violate**
違 VIOLATE → 3151
破 BREAK → 1150
反 act contrary to → 2945
背 go against → 2573

HOMOPHONES

okasu ⇨ 侵 101 冒 2434

NOTE

⇨ see USAGE note at 侵 101

3-2 比 incorrect stroke count ⇨ see 26
匕

3-2 以 incorrect classification ⇨ see 41
𠂉

3-2 北 北 北 197 HOKU kita
丬

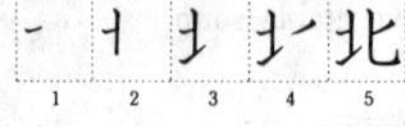

Ⓒ北 běi

Radical	Strokes
匕 21	5-2-3
Grade	**Freq**
Jōyō-2	100
◧ 1 - 3 - 2	

▶NORTH

COMPOUNDS

❶ **north**
北部 *hokubu* north, northern part
北欧 *hokuō* Northern Europe, Scandinavia
北爆 *hokubaku* bombing the North (Vietnam)
北東 *hokutō* northeast
北極 *hokkyoku* North Pole
北緯 *hokui* north latitude
北方 *hoppō* north, northward; northern district
❷ [original meaning] turn one's back on
敗北 *haiboku* defeat, setback
❸ abbrev. of 北海道 *hokkaidō*: Hokkaido district
北大 *hokudai* Hokkaido University

KUN

【kita 北】 [also prefix] north
北口 *kitaguchi* north exit
北側 *kitagawa* north side, north bank
北半球 *kitahankyū* Northern Hemisphere

SYNONYMS

❶ **cardinal points**
東 EAST → 3568
西 WEST → 3520
南 SOUTH → 2082

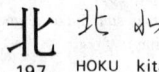

収 收 収 収

198 SHŪ osa(meru) osa(maru)

丨 刂 丩 収 収
1 2 3 4 5

CH 收 shōu

Radical	Strokes
又 29△	5-2-3
Grade	**Freq**
Jōyō-6	387
◧ 1 - 3 - 2	

3-2 丩

▶TAKE IN

COMPOUNDS

❶ⓐ take in, gather in, absorb

ⓑ collect materials and record [write down]

ⓒ [formerly also 蒐 2506] **collect**

収容する *shūyō suru* accommodate, receive (guests)

収納 *shūnō* storing; harvesting; receipt

収穫 *shūkaku* harvest; harvesting

収着 *shūchaku* sorption

吸収 *kyūshū* absorption, assimilation; merger

買収 *baishū* buying up, purchasing; bribing

回収する *kaishū suru* collect, recover; withdraw

収録する *shūroku suru* collect, record, write down

収集する *shūshū suru* collect, gather, accumulate

徴収する *chōshū suru* collect taxes [payment]

❷ⓐ (take possession of, esp. in payment) **take in, receive, accept**

ⓑ take possession by force, confiscate, seize

ⓒ [original meaning] take in a prisoner, take into custody

収入 *shūnyū* income, earnings, receipts

収益 *shūeki* profit, earnings, proceeds, returns

収賄 *shūwai* acceptance of a bribe, corruption

収得する *shūtoku suru* take possession of

領収 *ryōshū* receipt

収用 *shūyō* expropriation

押収する *ōshū suru* seize, confiscate

没収 *bosshū* confiscation, seizure, forfeiture

接収 *sesshū* requisition, takeover, seizure

収監する *shūkan suru* confine in jail, imprison

❸ income, receipts, revenue

収支 *shūshi* incomings and outgoings, earnings and expenses

増収 *zōshū* increased income [revenue]; increased yield

月収 *gesshū* monthly income

税収 *zeishū* yield of taxes, tax revenues

❹ shrink; converge

収縮する *shūshuku suru* contract, shrink

収斂する *shūren suru* be astringent, contract; converge

収差 *shūsa* aberration

収束 *shūsoku* convergence

❺ bring to order [settlement]

収拾する *shūshū suru* get under control, save (the situation)

KUN

【osa(meru) 収める】

①ⓐ gain, obtain, reap

ⓑ achieve, attain

勝利を収める *shōri o osameru* win, gain a victory

成果を収める *seika o osameru* achieve success

② collect materials and record [write down]

情報を収めた本 *jōhō o osameta hon* book containing the information

③ [also 納める] put (back) in place, replace

元の所へ収める *moto no tokoro e osameru* put (a thing) back in its place

④ [also 納める] accept

どうぞお収め下さい *Dōzo oosame kudasai* Please accept it

【osa(maru) 収まる】

① be put (back) in place, be restored

箱に収まる *hako ni osamaru* be stored in a box

②ⓐ be settled, be brought to a settlement

ⓑ calm down (as of the wind)

収まり *osamari* conclusion, end, settlement

争いが収まる *arasoi ga osamaru* be settled

台風が収まった *Taifū ga osamatta* The typhoon spent itself out

SYNONYMS

❶ⓐ take in

摂 TAKE IN → 650

喫 INGEST → 551

吸 SUCK → 202

❶ⓑ & ❶ⓒ gather

採 GATHER → 499

集 COLLECT → 2771

❷ⓐ get

獲 obtain → 779

得 ACQUIRE → 477

拾 PICK UP → 379

取 TAKE → 1262

ⓐ receive

受 RECEIVE → 2421

享 ENJOY → 2051
領 receive → 1224
納 ACCEPT → 1300
戴 RECEIVE HUMBLY → 3302
頂 RECEIVE HUMBLY → 145
拝 have the honor to receive → 303
❺ take forcibly
拐 KIDNAP → 308
奪 ROB → 2343
❸ pay and earnings
禄 RETAINER'S STIPEND → 1002
俸 SALARY → 114
料 FEE → 1292
賃 WAGE → 2694
給 PAY → 1350

HOMOPHONES
osameru ⇨ 納 1300 治 335 修 123
osamaru ⇨ 納 1300 治 335 修 123

NOTE
⇨ see USAGE notes at 納 1300 and 徴 683

3-2
卩

卯 卯 卯

199 BŌ u NAMES akira shigeru

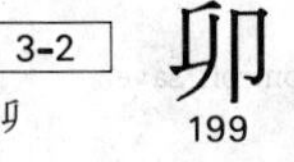

CH 卯 mǎo

Radical	Strokes
卩 26	5-2-3
Grade	Freq
Names	2071
1-3-2	

▶THE HARE

COMPOUNDS
● fourth sign of the Oriental zodiac: the Hare—(time) 5–7 a.m., (direction) east, (season) February (of the lunar calendar) (⇨ see APPENDIX 7)
卯月 *bōgetsu* second month of the lunar calendar

KUN
【u 卯】fourth sign of the Oriental zodiac: the Hare (⇨ ●)
卯月 *uzuki* fourth month (of the lunar calendar), April
卯の花 *unohana* flower of the deutzia; bean curd refuse

NAMES
卯月 *uzuki* surname
卯三郎 *usaburō* male name

3-2
卩

印

incorrect stroke count ⇨ see 828

3-3
口

吃

200 KITSU domo(ru)

CH 吃 chī

Radical	Strokes
口 30	6-3-3
Grade	Freq
Reference	
1-3-3	

COMPOUNDS
❶ [original meaning] stammer, stutter
吃音 *kitsuon* stammering, dysphemia
吃りながら *domorinagara* stammering(ly), stuttering(ly)
❷ [now replaced by 喫 *kitsu* 551] be subjected to, suffer, incur
吃驚する *kikkyō suru* be astonished
吃水 *kissui* draft, sea gauge
❸ [now replaced by 喫 *kitsu* 551] urgent, pressing
吃緊の *kikkin no* very important, urgent

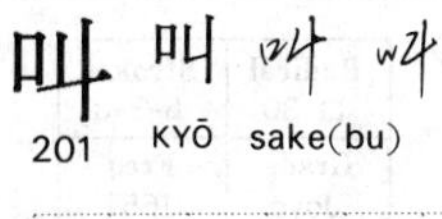

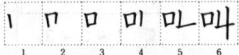

201 KYŌ sake(bu)

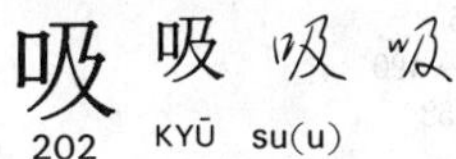

Ⓒⓗ 叫 jiào

Radical	Strokes
口 30	6-3-3
Grade	**Freq**
Jōyō	1238
◧ 1 - 3 - 3	

3-3 口

▶**SHOUT**

COMPOUNDS

● [original meaning] **shout, cry (out), shriek, scream, yell**
叫喚 *kyōkan* shout, cry, scream
叫号する *kyōgō suru* [rare] cry aloud
絶叫する *zekkyō suru* exclaim, ejaculate, scream, shout

KUN

【**sake(bu) 叫ぶ**】 shout, scream, cry; advocate
叫び *sakebi* shout, cry, scream
叫び声 *sakebigoe* shout, outcry
泣き叫ぶ *nakisakebu* cry, scream, wail
改革を叫ぶ *kaikaku o sakebu* cry loudly for a reform

SYNONYMS

● **shout**
号 holler → 2153
喝 SHOUT AT → 461
喚 call out → 550
呼 CALL → 273
鳴 CRY → 674

吸 吸 吸 吸

202 KYŪ su(u)

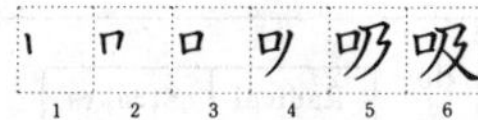

Ⓒⓗ 吸 xī

Radical	Strokes
口 30	6-3-3
Grade	**Freq**
Jōyō-6	1224
◧ 1 - 3 - 3	

3-3 口

▶**SUCK** ▶**BREATHE IN**

COMPOUNDS

❶ [original meaning] **suck, suck in, absorb**
吸収 *kyūshū* absorption, assimilation; merger
吸着 *kyūchaku* adsorption
吸引する *kyūin suru* suck (in), absorb, aspirate; attract
吸塵 *kyūjin* dust vacuuming
吸血鬼 *kyūketsuki* vampire
吸盤 *kyūban* sucker, sucking disk

❷ **breathe in, inhale**
吸入する *kyūnyū suru* inhale, breath in; suck (in); imbibe
吸気 *kyūki* inhalation of air; air breathed in
呼吸 *kokyū* breathing, respiration

KUN

【**su(u) 吸う**】 inhale, breathe in; smoke; suck, sip, absorb; draw
吸い殻 *suigara* cigarette butt
煙草を吸う *tabako o suu* smoke a cigarette
吸い出す *suidasu* suck [draw] out; aspirate
吸い物 *suimono* Japanese style soup

SYNONYMS

❶ **take in**
喫 INGEST → 551
摂 TAKE IN → 650
収 TAKE IN → 198

❷ **breathe and blow**
呼 breathe out → 273
吹 BLOW → 231
息 BREATH → 2647
気 breath → 3194

3-3 **吐** 吐 吐

口 203 TO ha(ku)

丨 ㄇ 口 口一 叶 吐
1 2 3 4 5 6

Ⓒⓗ 吐 tǔ tù

Radical	Strokes
口 30	6-3-3
Grade	**Freq**
Jōyō	1657
◧ 1 - 3 - 3	

▶**SPEW**

COMPOUNDS

❶ [original meaning] **spew, vomit**

吐出 *toshutsu* spew, vomit, disgorge
吐血 *toketsu* vomiting blood
吐息 *toiki* sigh, long breath
嘔吐 *ōto* vomiting
音吐朗朗と *onto-rōrō to* in a clear voice

❷ (spew out words) express, speak out

吐露する *toro suru* express one's mind

KUN

【**ha(ku) 吐く**】spew, vomit; exhale; emit, send forth; express, utter, give vent to; confess, own

吐き出す *hakidasu* spew, vomit, disgorge
吐き気 *hakike* nausea
息を吐く *iki o haku* exhale, breathe out
煙を吐く *kemuri o haku* emit smoke
意見を吐く *iken o haku* give one's opinion
私が彼を吐かせてやる *Watashi ga kare o hakasete yaru* I will have it out of him

SYNONYMS

❶ **discharge from mouth**

吹 BLOW → 231

❶ **emit**

噴 SPOUT → 717
放 radiate → 853
出 PUT OUT → 3498
発 EMIT → 2565
排 DISCHARGE → 490
射 SHOOT → 1458

3-3 **地** 地 地

土 204 CHI JI

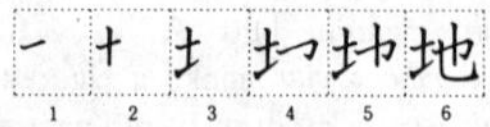

Ⓒⓗ 地 dì de

Radical	Strokes
土 32	6-3-3
Grade	**Freq**
Jōyō-2	33
◧ 1 - 3 - 3	

▶**GROUND** ▶**PLACE**

COMPOUNDS

❶ [also suffix]

ⓐ (solid surface of the earth) **ground, earth, land**

ⓑ (functionally distinguished tract) **land, ground, soil**

地面 *jimen* surface, ground, land
地下の *chika no* underground, subterranean
地震 *jishin* earthquake
地上に *chijō ni* on the ground; on earth
地階 *chikai* basement, cellar
地図 *chizu* map, atlas
地理 *chiri* geographical features, topography; geography
地盤 *jiban* ground, foundation, base
土地 *tochi* land
高地 *kōchi* high ground, plateau, heights
湿地 *shitchi* damp ground, swamp
耕地 *kōchi* arable land, farm land
扇状地 *senjōchi* alluvial delta
地主 *jinushi* landlord, landowner
地目 *chimoku* classification of land category
地価 *chika* price [value] of land
宅地 *takuchi* land for housing, residential land
敷地 *shikichi* (building) site, (plot of) ground, lot
空き地 *akichi* unoccupied ground, vacant lot
分譲地 *bunjōchi* (building) lots for sale

❷ⓐ [original meaning] (surface of the world, as distinguished from heaven) **earth**

ⓑ **Earth, the Earth**

地獄 *jigoku* hell; inferno
天地 *tenchi* heaven and earth; top and bottom
大地 *daichi* ground, earth, solid earth
地球 *chikyū* the Earth
地殻 *chikaku* crust (of the earth)
地軸 *chijiku* axis of the earth
地動説 *chidōsetsu* heliocentric [Copernican] theory
地磁気 *chijiki* terrestrial magnetism

❸ⓐ [also suffix] (particular location) **place, grounds, position**

ⓑ [also suffix] (particular region) **place, lo-**

cality, region, district

ⓒ of that place or region

ⓓ abbrev. of 地方 *chihō*: district

地点 *chiten* spot, point, place

各地 *kakuchi* every place, various parts [areas] (of the country)

基地 *kichi* base

団地 *danchi* (public) housing development

現地 *genchi* actual place [locale]

当地 *tōchi* this place [locality], here

番地 *banchi* lot [house] number, address

余地 *yochi* room, space, margin

墓地 *bochi* graveyard, cemetery, burial grounds

爆心地 *bakushinchi* center of explosion

地元 *jimoto* local end, local area

産地 *sanchi* place of production; place of birth

辺地 *henchi* remote place

寒冷地 *kanreichi* cold [northern] district

遠隔地 *enkakuchi* distant place

地酒 *jizake* locally brewed sake

地卵 *jitamago* homegrown eggs, local eggs

地唄 *jiuta* ballad, folk song

地裁 *chisai* district court

❹ (main surface or background, as in a painting) **ground, background**

地金 *jigane* ore; ground metal; one's true character

地肌 *jihada* one's skin; surface of the ground; texture

地色 *jiiro* ground color

白地 *shiroji* white (back)ground

下地 *shitaji* ground work, prearrangement; grounding, making

無地 *muji* solid color

❺ⓐ **one's ground, one's stand, one's place, one's position**

ⓑ state of one's emotions

地位 *chii* position, status, post, social standing

地歩 *chiho* one's stand, foothold, position

見地 *kenchi* standpoint, viewpoint

窮地 *kyūchi* predicament, difficult situation, dilemma

実地 *jitchi* actuality, reality; practice

境地 *kyōchi* state, stage; field, ground

心地 *kokochi* feeling, mood

意地 *iji* nature, disposition; will power, backbone

❻ **natural, in its natural [original] form, inherent**

地力 *jiriki* one's own strength

地声 *jigoe* natural voice

地髪 *jigami* natural hair

地味な *jimi na* plain, sober, unpretentious

地道な *jimichi na* steady, straight, fair

素地 *soji* inclination, makings; grounding, foundation

生地(=素地) *kiji* one's true color [character]; (plain) cloth, texture; unglazed pottery

❼ [also suffix] **fabric, texture, cloth, material**

服地 *fukuji* cloth, dress material, clothing fabric

裏地 *uraji* lining (cloth), material for lining

厚地 *atsuji* thick cloth

織地 *oriji* fabric, texture

タオル地 *taoruji* toweling

プリント地 *purintoji* printed cloth

❽ descriptive [narrative] part (as opposed to dialogue); choric part (in noh or *utai* singing)

地謡 *jiutai* chorus in *utai* singing

INDEPENDENT

【chi 地】

①ⓐ (solid surface of the earth) ground, earth, land

ⓑ (surface of the world, as distinguished from heaven) earth

足を地に付けて *ashi o chi ni tsukete* with one's feet planted on the ground, with steady steps

地の果て *chi no hate* end of the earth

② (particular location) place, grounds, position

地の利 *chi no ri* vantage ground, advantageous position

景勝の地 *keishō no chi* place of scenic beauty

③ lower place, bottom

天と地 *ten to chi* top and bottom; heaven and earth

【ji 地】

① (solid surface of the earth) ground, earth, land

地を均す *ji o narasu* level the ground

② (particular region) place, locality, region, district

地の卵 *ji no tamago* farm-fresh eggs, local eggs

③ captured territory in the game of go

④ (main surface or background, as in a painting) ground, background

地を赤で塗る *ji o aka de nuru* paint the ground in red

⑤ descriptive [narrative] part (as opposed to dialogue); choric part (in noh or *utai* singing)

地の文 *ji no bun* descriptive [narrative] part

⑥ fabric, texture, cloth, material

地の詰んだ *ji no tsunda* of close texture

⑦ natural form, original condition

地が出る *ji ga deru* show one's true colors, betray oneself

⑧ actuality, reality

地で行く *ji de iku* carry (a story) into actual practice

SYNONYMS

❶ **land and soil**

陸 LAND → 543
土 SOIL → 3403
壌 ARABLE SOIL → 755
泥 MUD → 326

❸ⓐ **places and positions**

場 PLACE (for specific activity) → 558
所 PLACE → 851
処 place → 3031
席 meeting place → 3113
位 POSITION → 61
点 POINT → 2084
座 place → 3116

ⓑ **areas and localities**

方 locality → 1963
辺 VICINITY → 3029
域 BOUNDED AREA → 465
区 DISTRICT → 2963
領 TERRITORY → 1224
帯 BELT → 2582
圏 SPHERE → 3148

❺ⓐ **standpoint**

立 standpoint → 1992

❻ **natural**

野 wild → 1485
粗 crude → 1329
原 in the original state → 3009

❼ **fabric**

布 CLOTH → 2973

3-3 夕

舛
205

ノ ク タ タ' タ匚 舛
1 2 3 4 5 6

Radical	Strokes
舛 136	6-6-0
Grade	**Freq**
Radical	
1 - 3 - 3	

RADICAL 136

Standard form: 舛 *masu* 'dancing' (舜)
Bottom variant: 舛 *maiashi* (舞)
Description: used for character classification

3-3 女

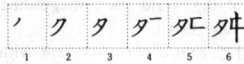

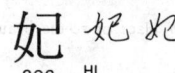

妃 妃 妃
206 HI

Ⓒⓗ 妃 fēi

く 女 女 女' 女ⁿ 妃
1 2 3 4 5 6

Radical	Strokes
女 38	6-3-3
Grade	**Freq**
Jōyō	1677
1 - 3 - 3	

▶**PRINCESS**

COMPOUNDS

● (wife of a member of the Imperial or Royal family) **princess, queen, empress; consort (as of an emperor)**

妃殿下 *hidenka* Her Imperial Highness
王妃 *ōhi* queen, empress
后妃 *kōhi* queen consort, empress, queen
親王妃 *shinnōhi* Imperial princess

INDEPENDENT

【hi 妃】princess, consort (one rank below the empress)

SYNONYMS

● **wives of rulers**

后 EMPRESS → 2981
室 wife (esp. of persons of rank) → 2254

如 如 如

207 JO NYO goto(shi)▲

㊥ 如 rú

Radical	Strokes
女 38	6-3-3
Grade	Freq
Jōyō	1459
1-3-3	

3-3 女

▶AS

COMPOUNDS

❶ **as, like, as if, such as**

如上の *jojō no* above-mentioned
如実に *nyojitsu ni* truly, realistically
如是 *nyoze* thus, so, like this
如来 *nyorai* Buddha
不如意の *funyoi no* contrary to one's wishes, hard up, pressed for money

❷ **suffix added to modifiers (noun adjectives or adverbs) to express a state**

突如 *totsujo* suddenly, unexpectedly
欠如 *ketsujo* lack, shortage
躍如たる *yakujotaru* vivid, graphic, lifelike

KUN

【**goto(shi)** 如し】 like, as, as if
如く *gotoku* like, as if
...の如し *...no gotoshi* be like, be as if, seem

SPECIAL READINGS

如何▲ *ikaga* how; what
如何▲(＝奈何▲) *ikan* what; how
如何に▲ *ika ni* how, in what way

SYNONYMS

❶ **similar**

-通り as → 3109
様 like → 1052
類 similar → 1807
云 SUCH → 1931

❷ **modifier suffixes**

然 MODIFIER FORMING SUFFIX → 2782
爾 adjective suffix → 3587
的 ADJECTIVAL SUFFIX → 1125

好 好 好

208 KŌ kono(mu) su(ku) yo(i)▲ i(i)▲

㊥ 好 hǎo hào

Radical	Strokes
女 38	6-3-3
Grade	Freq
Jōyō-4	343
1-3-3	

3-3 女

▶LIKE ▶FAVORABLE

COMPOUNDS

❶ [original meaning] **like, be fond of, love**

好学 *kōgaku* love of learning
好物 *kōbutsu* favorite dish
好角家 *kōkakuka* sumo fan, wrestling enthusiast
愛好者 *aikōsha* lover (of music), fan
同好会 *dōkōkai* association of like-minded persons; club

❷ⓐ [also prefix] **favorable, good, fine**
ⓑ good-looking, beautiful

好調 *kōchō* favorable [good] condition
好機 *kōki* favorable opportunity, good chance
好況 *kōkyō* brisk market, prosperity
好意 *kōi* goodwill, favor, kindness
好感 *kōkan* good feeling, good impression
好評 *kōhyō* favorable criticism [comment], public favor
好影響 *kōeikyō* favorable influence
好都合な *kōtsugō na* favorable, fortunate
絶好の *zekkō no* splendid, grand, best, golden
好男子 *kōdanshi* handsome man
恰好(＝格好) *kakkō* suitability, moderateness (in price); shape, form; appearance, manner

❸ friendship, friendly relations

好誼 *kōgi* warm friendship
親好 *shinkō* friendship, good fellowship
友好的な *yūkōteki na* friendly, fraternal

KUN

【**kono(mu)** 好む】 like, be fond of, prefer
好み *konomi* taste, liking; choice; wish; fashion
好ましい *konomashii* desirable, welcome, nice, pleasant

【**su(ku)** 好く】 like, be fond of, love
好き *suki* liking, fondness; fancy; taste
好きだ *suki da* like, be fond of, love
好き好む *sukikonomu* like, be fond of
好き嫌い *sukikirai* likes and dislikes, taste
物好き *monozuki* curiosity, eccentricity; curiosity seeker

【yo(i) 好い】[now usu. 良い] same as **yoi** 良い 3558
お人好し *ohitoyoshi* good natured person; credulous person
⇨ see 良 3558 for other compounds
【i(i) 好い】[now usu. 良い] colloquial form of **yoi** 好い
好い加減 *iikagen* moderate, right; random, not thorough, vague

SYNONYMS
❶ **love and like**
愛 LOVE → 2492
恋 LOVE (the opposite sex) → 2098
❷ⓐ **good**
順 favorable → 18
良 GOOD → 3558
善 GOOD → 2325
佳 FINE → 86
美 BEAUTIFUL → 2264
❸ **personal relations**
交 INTERCOURSE → 2015
仲 PERSONAL RELATIONS → 43
縁 RELATION → 1386

HOMOPHONES
yoi ⇨ 良 3558 善 2325
ii ⇨ 良 3558

NOTE
⇨ see USAGE note at 良 3558

3-3 屮

艸
209

Radical	Strokes
艸 140	6-6-0
Grade	**Freq**
Radical	
■ 1 - 3 - 3	

RADICAL 140
Standard form: 艸 *kusa* 'plants'
Top variants: 艹 艹 艹 *kusakanmuri* (花 芯 蔑)
Description: used in characters related to plants or their qualities

---

3-3 工

巧
incorrect stroke count ⇨ see 188

3-3 巾

帆 帆 帆 帆
210 HAN ho

CH 帆 fān

Radical	Strokes
巾 50	6-3-3
Grade	**Freq**
Jōyō	1764
■ 1 - 3 - 3	

▶**SAIL**

COMPOUNDS
❶ [original meaning] **sail, canvas**
帆船 *hansen* sailing vessel, sailboat
機帆船 *kihansen* motor-powered sailboat
順風満帆 *junpūmanpan* smooth sailing, sailing before the wind
❷ⓐ sail, set sail
ⓑ sailboat
帆走 *hansō* sailing by boat
出帆 *shuppan* sailing, departure
帰帆 *kihan* returning sailboat
孤帆 *kohan* solitary sailboat

KUN
【**ho** 帆】sail
帆影 *hokage* sight of a sail
帆柱(=檣) *hobashira* mast
帆掛け船 *hokakebune* sailing ship, sailboat
帆前船 *homaesen* sailing ship
白帆 *shiraho* white sail

3-3 巾

帆
211

▶**SAIL**
nonstandard for 帆 210

行 行 り

㊥ 行 xíng háng

212 KŌ GYŌ AN i(ku) yu(ku) -yu(ki) -yuki -i(ki) -iki okona(u)

Radical	Strokes
行 144	6-6-0
Grade	**Freq**
Jōyō-2	21
▐ 1 - 3 - 3	

1 2 3 4 5 6

RADICAL 144
Standard form: 行 *gyō* 'road'
Enclosure: 行 *gyōgamae* (術 衛 街)
Description: used in characters related to roads or paths

▶GO ▶ACT ▶LINE

COMPOUNDS

❶ⓐ **go, walk, travel**
ⓑ [also suffix] trip, journey
行進する *kōshin suru* march, parade
行列 *gyōretsu* procession, queue; matrix
徐行 *jokō* going slowly
旅行 *ryokō* travel, trip
歩行 *hokō* walk, walking
流行 *ryūkō* fashion; prevalence
平行 *heikō* parallelism, parallel; going side by side; occurring together
行幸 *gyōkō* Imperial visit
行脚 *angya* pilgrimage; walking tour; tour
箱根行 *hakonekō* trip to Hakone
❷ⓐ (perform an action) **act, do, carry out, perform, conduct**
ⓑ (something done) **act, action, deed**
行動 *kōdō* action, conduct, behavior
行為 *kōi* act, deed, conduct, transaction
行政 *gyōsei* administration
行事 *gyōji* event, function
実行 *jikkō* practice, action; execution
非行 *hikō* delinquency, misdeed, misdemeanor
悪行 *akugyō* misdeed, wicked act
❸ (personal behavior) **conduct, behavior**
行儀 *gyōgi* manners, behavior
品行 *hinkō* (moral) conduct, behavior, deportment
言行 *genkō* speech and conduct
奇行 *kikō* eccentric conduct
❹ⓐ **line (esp. of print), row**
ⓑ counter for lines or columns
行間 *gyōkan* between the lines
行数 *gyōsū* linage, number of lines
行中 *gyōchū* in the middle of a line
別行 *betsugyō* separate line, another row
三行 *sangyō* three lines
❺ religious austerities, self-discipline, asceticism
行者 *gyōja* ascetic, pilgrim, devotee
修行 *shugyō* training, study; ascetic practices
苦行 *kugyō* asceticism, hard spiritual exercises
❻ business establishment, firm
銀行 *ginkō* bank
洋行 *yōkō* foreign firm (in preliberation China)
興行 *kōgyō* public entertainment, show business
❼ publish
刊行する *kankō suru* publish
発行する *hakkō suru* publish, issue; issue (bank notes)
単行本 *tankōbon* separate volume, independent volume
❽ⓐ abbrev. of 銀行 *ginkō*: bank
ⓑ counter for banks
行員 *kōin* bank clerk
行務 *kōmu* bank business
当行 *tōkō* our bank
三行 *sankō* three banks
❾ *gyosho*, semicursive style of Chinese characters
行書 *gyōsho* semicursive style of Chinese characters
行体 *gyōtai* semicursive characters
❿ party, suite
一行 *ikkō* party, suite
⓫ abbrev. of 行政 *gyōsei*: administration
行革(＝行政改革) *gyōkaku* (＝*gyōsei kaikaku*) administrative reform
行官庁 *gyōkanchō* Administrative Management Agency
⓬ [also suffix] a style of Chinese poetry
琵琶行 *biwakō* Biwa Song
⓭ one of the five natural elements (or phases) that constitute the universe in Chinese philosophy
五行 *gogyō* the five elements
諸行 *shogyō* all earthly things
⓮ [original meaning] crossroads, road
行程 *kōtei* distance, journey
⓯ designed for carrying while walking, portable
行火 *anka* bed warmer, foot warmer
行灯 *andon* paper-enclosed oil lantern

INDEPENDENT

【kō 行】 party, suite; journey; a style of Chi-

nese poetry
行を共にする *kō o tomoni suru* join the party
【gyō 行】 line (esp. of print), row; religious austerities, asceticism; *gyosho* (⇨ ❾)
行を改める *gyō o aratameru* start a new paragraph
朝夕の行 *asayū no gyō* morning and evening services
【gyōzuru 行ずる】 train; practice asceticism

KUN

【i(ku) 行く】
① go, proceed, leave for; attend; visit
行き着く *ikitsuku* arrive at, get to
行き先 *ikisaki* (=*yukisaki*) one's destination
行き過ぎる *ikisugiru* go too far, go to extremes
②ⓐ go [fare] (well), turn out
ⓑ go well, turn out well, proceed satisfactorily
ⓒ *slang* ejaculate, come
旨く行かない *umaku ikanai* go badly, be unsuccessful
満足が行く *manzoku ga iku* be satisfied
③ [following the TE-form of verbs]
ⓐ auxiliary indicating change in progress: turn, grow
ⓑ auxiliary indicating continuation of action: go on, continue
段段夜が明けて行った *Dandan yo ga akete itta* Night melted into day
どうにか食って行く *dōnika kutte iku* manage to keep body and soul together
【yu(ku) 行く】 literary form of **iku** 行く
行き帰り *yukikaeri* going and returning, both ways
行方 *yukue* one's whereabouts
【-yu(ki) -行き, -yuki -行】 [suffix] bound for, for
東京行きの列車 *tōkyōyuki no ressha* train (bound) for Tokyo
【-i(ki) -行き, -iki -行】 [suffix] bound for, for
大阪行 *ōsakaiki* for Osaka
【okona(u) 行う】 act, do, perform; practice, carry out; hold (a meeting)
行い *okonai* act, action, deed; conduct, behavior
行われる *okonawareru* be done, be practiced; take place

SYNONYMS

❶ⓐ go and come
往 GO ON → 292
出 go to → 3498
参 go somewhere → 2066
来 COME → 3551
通 go to and from → 3109
向 head toward → 3052
赴 PROCEED TO → 3303
ⓑ journey
旅 TRAVEL → 922
遊 tour → 3142
巡 tour around → 3047
❷ⓐ do and act
為 DO → 3577
仕 DO → 34
致す DO HUMBLY → 1316
作 WORK → 68
ⓐ execute
執 EXECUTE → 1680
履 FULFILL → 3171
施 CARRY OUT → 891
践 IMPLEMENT → 1535
果たす effect → 3560
遂 ACCOMPLISH → 3138
ⓑ acts
挙 NOTEWORTHY ACT → 2456
業 deed → 2612
❸ behavior
挙 deportment → 2456
動 behavior → 1778
❹ⓐ linear arrangements
列 ROW → 824
伍 RANK → 47
欄 COLUMN → 1103
❽ⓐ bank
銀 bank → 1722
【-yuki】
○ direction indicators
至 to → 2182
-向け (bound) for → 3052
迄 UP TO → 3201
以 TO THE...OF → 41
自 from → 3525
来 since → 3551

USAGE

yuku
行く
literary form of **iku** 行く
逝く
depart this life, pass away, die

HOMOPHONES

yuku ⇨ 逝 3104

NOTE

⇨ see also USAGE note at 平 3478

行 213

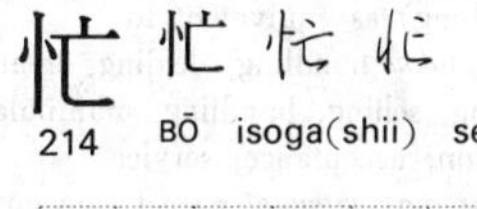

Radical	Strokes
行 144	6-6-0
Grade	**Freq**
Radical	
◧ 1 - 3 - 3	

3-3 彳

RADICAL 144

gyōgamae, variant of 行 *gyō* 'road'

⇨ see 行 212 for radical description

忙 忙 忙 忙 214 BŌ isoga(shii) sewa(shii)▲

Ⓒ忙 máng

Radical	Strokes
忄 61	6-3-3
Grade	**Freq**
Jōyō	1288
◧ 1 - 3 - 3	

3-3 忄

▶**BUSY**

COMPOUNDS

● **busy, occupied**

忙殺される *bōsatsu sareru* be very busily occupied, be worked to death

多忙な *tabō na* busy

繁忙である *hanbō de aru* be busy, be fully occupied

INDEPENDENT

【**bō** 忙】 busyness

忙を厭わず *bō o itowazu* despite one's busyness

KUN

【**isoga(shii)** 忙しい】 busy, occupied, engaged

忙しさ *isogashisa* busyness

仕事で忙しい *shigoto de isogashii* be busy with one's work

【**sewa(shii)** 忙しい】 restless, fidgety; busy

忙しさ *sewashisa* busyness

忙しげな *sewashige na* looking restless

気忙しい *kizewashii* restless, fidgety, fussy

SYNONYMS

● **busy**

繁 bustling → 2853

慌てる FLURRIED → 580

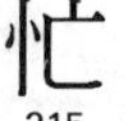

215

▶**BUSY**

nonstandard for 忙 214

3-3 忄

扣 216 KŌ

Ⓒ扣 kòu

Radical	Strokes
扌 64	6-3-3
Grade	**Freq**
Reference	
◧ 1 - 3 - 3	

3-3 扌

COMPOUNDS

❶ [now replaced by 控 495] hold back part of something, deduct, subtract

扣除 *kōjo* (tax) deduction, subtraction

❷ button

3-3 扌

扱 扱 扱 扱

217 SHŌ▲ atsuka(u) atsuka(i)

Ⓒⓗ 扱 chā

Radical	Strokes
扌 64	6-3-3
Grade	**Freq**
Jōyō	857
1 - 3 - 3	

▶HANDLE

KUN

【atsuka(u) 扱う】

① [original meaning] (manipulate with the hands) handle, manipulate, work

粗末に扱う *somatsu ni atsukau* handle (a thing) roughly

機械を扱う *kikai o atsukau* work a machine, handle a tool

上手に扱う *jōzu ni atsukau* handle skillfully

②ⓐ (deal with) handle (a matter), deal with, treat, manage

ⓑ (trade in) handle (goods), deal in

問題を扱う *mondai o atsukau* deal with [handle] a matter

取り扱う *toriatsukau* handle, deal with, treat; deal in; handle, manipulate, operate; conduct; accept, take in

薬を扱う *kusuri o atsukau* deal in medicines

扱わない品 *atsukawanai shina* goods not in one's line

③ (treat a person in a particular way) handle, receive, entertain

人を公平に扱う *hito o kōhei ni atsukau* deal justly with a person

【atsuka(i) 扱い】

① [also suffix] (manipulation with the hands) handling, manipulation, operation

扱い方 *atsukaikata* how to handle, way with (an animal)

ボール扱いが巧い *bōruatsukai ga umai* be good at handling a ball

②ⓐ [also suffix] (dealing with a matter) handling, managing, processing

ⓑ [suffix] handling (something) as, regarding (something) as equivalent to

取り扱い *toriatsukai* handling, dealing, treatment; trading, selling; handling, manipulation, operation; acceptance, service

小荷物扱い *konimotsuatsukai* parcel consignment

出席扱い *shussekiatsukai* regard as equivalent to attendance

他人扱いにする *tanin atsukai ni suru* treat (a person) as a stranger

③ treatment of a person, reception, service

客扱い *kyakuatsukai* hospitality, entertainment; service

SYNONYMS

【atsukau】

① **handle**

操 MANIPULATE → 769

揮 WIELD → 589

運 control movement skillfully → 3140

②ⓐ **deal with**

処 DEAL WITH → 3031

措 dispose of → 502

置 take proper steps → 2608

③ **treat and welcome**

遇 TREAT → 3135

待 treat → 364

款 treat cordially → 1700

接 receive → 500

迎 WELCOME → 3059

3-3 氵

池 池 池

218 CHI ike

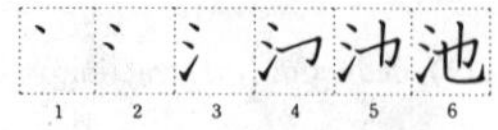

Ⓒⓗ 池 chí

Radical	Strokes
氵 85	6-3-3
Grade	**Freq**
Jōyō-2	704
1 - 3 - 3	

▶POND

COMPOUNDS

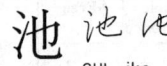

❶ⓐ [also suffix] [original meaning] **pond, pool**

ⓑ **reservoir**

池畔 *chihan* edge of a pond

池沼 *chishō* ponds and swamps

養殖池 *yōshokuchi* fish pond

貯水池 *chosuichi* reservoir

用水池 *yōsuichi* reservoir

電池 *denchi* electric cell, battery

❷ inkstone well

墨池 *bokuchi* inkstone well, inkhorn

KUN

【ike 池】pond, pool; reservoir; inkstone well
溜め池 *tameike* reservoir, irrigation pond, cistern
古池 *furuike* old pond

SYNONYMS

❶ⓐ **lakes and marshes**
湖 LAKE → 604
潟 LAGOON → 745
沼 MUDDY POND → 339
沢 MARSH → 267

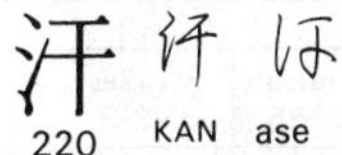
219 HAN

CH 泛 fàn

Radical	Strokes
氵 85	6-3-3
Grade	**Freq**
Reference	
◧ 1 - 3 - 3	

3-3 氵

COMPOUNDS

❶ⓐ overall, general, universal, versatile
ⓑ [prefix] pan-
汎論 *hanron* general remarks; outline
汎愛 *han'ai* philanthropy
汎用型コンピュータ *han'yōgata konpyūta* mainframe computer
汎神論 *hanshinron* pantheism
汎アメリカ主義 *han-amerikashugi* Pan-Americanism
❷ [now replaced by 範 2709] extensive, wide-ranging
広汎な *kōhan na* extensive, wide-ranging, comprehensive

汗 汗 ほ
220 KAN ase

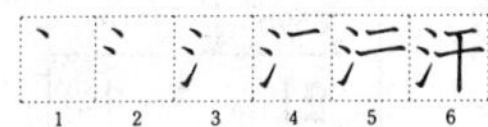

CH 汗 hàn hán

Radical	Strokes
氵 85	6-3-3
Grade	**Freq**
Jōyō	1416
◧ 1 - 3 - 3	

3-3 氵

▶**SWEAT**

COMPOUNDS

❶ **sweat, perspiration**
汗腺 *kansen* sweat gland
汗顔 *kangan* sweating from shame
汗血 *kanketsu* sweat and blood
発汗する *hakkan suru* perspire, sweat
冷汗 *reikan* cold sweat
❷ [rare] khan, chieftain
ジンギス汗 *jingisukan* Genghis Khan

KUN

【ase 汗】sweat, perspiration
汗掻き(=汗っ掻き) *asekaki* (=*asekkaki*) one who perspires freely, great sweater
汗臭い *asekusai* smelling of sweat
汗だくで *asedaku de* bathed in perspiration, dripping with sweat
汗ばむ *asebamu* become slightly sweaty
汗を掻く *ase o kaku* sweat, perspire
冷や汗 *hiyaase* cold sweat

SYNONYMS

❶ **bodily secretions**
涙 TEAR → 440
精 sperm → 1366
乳 MILK → 1438
❶ **excreta**
尿 URINE → 3064
便 EXCRETA → 95

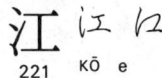

3-3 氵

江 221 KŌ e

Stroke order: 1 2 3 4 5 6

CH 江 jiāng

Radical	Strokes
氵 85	6-3-3
Grade	**Freq**
Jōyō	540
1 - 3 - 3	

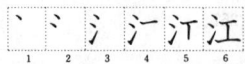

▶**INLET**

COMPOUNDS

ⓐ [original meaning] **large river**·
ⓑ suffix after names of large rivers
ⓒ Yangtze River (name of longest river in Asia)

江上 *kōjō* bank of a large river
江山 *kōzan* [rare] rivers and mountains
江湖 *kōko* general public, the world ("rivers and lakes")
揚子江 *yōsukō* Yangtze River
江河 *kōga* Yangtze and Yellow rivers
長江 *chōkō* Yangtze River, Changjiang River

KUN

【e 江】 inlet, cove
入り江 *irie* inlet, cove, creek

SYNONYMS

ⓐ & ⓑ **rivers and streams**
川 RIVER → 6
河 RIVER → 336
渓 mountain stream → 516
流 stream → 441

【e】
○ **inlets and bays**
浦 coastal indentation → 437
湾 BAY → 613
峡 narrows → 357

3-3 氵

汚 222 O kega(su) kega(reru) kega(rawashii) yogo(su) yogo(reru) kitana(i)

Stroke order: 1 2 3 4 5 6

CH 污 wū

Radical	Strokes
氵 85	6-3-3
Grade	**Freq**
Jōyō	1205
1 - 3 - 3	

▶**DIRTY**

COMPOUNDS

❶ⓐ **dirty, contaminated, defiled**
ⓑ (make or become unclean) **dirty, soil, defile; become dirty, become defiled**

汚水 *osui* dirty [filthy] water, sewage
汚物 *obutsu* dirt, filth, impurities
汚染 *osen* pollution, contamination

❷ (bring dishonor upon) **defile, disgrace, corrupt, dishonor**

汚職 *oshoku* (official) corruption, bribery
汚名 *omei* bad name, ill fame, disgrace
汚点 *oten* disgrace, flaw; stain, blot
汚濁 *odaku* (=*ojoku*) corruption

KUN

【kega(su) 汚す】 (bring dishonor upon) defile, disgrace, dishonor, desecrate; [humble] be given a position
名声を汚す *meisei o kegasu* defile one's reputation
女を汚す *onna o kegasu* defile [deflower] a woman
末席を汚す *masseki o kegasu* have the honor of being a member

【kega(reru) 汚れる】 (become unclean) become dirty, become defiled, be stained; (be contrary to honor or rules) be defiled, get corrupted, be stained
汚れ *kegare* dirt, uncleanliness; impurity, disgrace
汚れた手 *kegareta te* dirty hand, (blood-) stained hand
汚れた一生 *kegareta isshō* dirty [sinful] life

【kega(rawashii) 汚らわしい】 dirty, filthy; detestable
汚らわしい身形 *kegarawashii minari* dirty getup [appearance]
見るのも汚らわしい *miru no mo kegarawashii* be detestable to look at

【yogo(su) 汚す】 (make unclean) make dirty, soil, defile; (bring dishonor upon) defile, corrupt, dishonor
服を汚す *fuku o yogosu* soil one's clothes
面汚し *tsurayogoshi* disgrace, shame

【yogo(reru) 汚れる】 (become unclean) become dirty, become defiled
汚れ *yogore* dirt, filth
汚れ物 *yogoremono* laundry

【kitana(i) 汚い】 (unclean) dirty, soiled; (contrary to honor or rules) dirty, foul, base, ob-

scene; niggardly
汚らしい *kitanarashii* dirty-looking, squalid
汚いやり方 *kitanai yarikata* dirty trick
口汚い *kuchigitanai* foulmouthed
金に汚い *kane ni kitanai* stingy, mean [greedy] about money

SYNONYMS

❶ⓐ dirty

濁 TURBID → 774

❶ⓑ &【yogosu】 dirty

染 contaminate → 2572

❷ disgrace

辱 HUMILIATE → 2736
侮 INSULT → 82
恥 SHAME → 1313

汐 汐 汐

223 SEKI shio

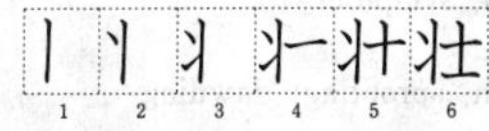

CH 汐 xī

Radical	Strokes
氵 85	6-3-3
Grade	**Freq**
Names	2107
1 - 3 - 3	

3-3 氵

▶TIDE

COMPOUNDS

ⓐ tide, ebb tide
ⓑ [original meaning, now archaic] evening tide
潮汐 *chōseki* ebb and flow, tide

KUN

【shio 汐】
[usu. 潮]
①ⓐ tide, current
ⓑ seawater
汐干狩り *shiohigari* shell gathering (at low tide)
汐汲み *shiokumi* drawing water from the sea; person who draws water from the sea
② tide (in the archaic sense of 'favorable occasion'), opportunity, chance

汐合い *shioai* chance, opportunity

NAMES

汐見 *shiomi* surname
汐留 *shiodome* place name

SYNONYMS

ⓐ running water

潮 TIDE → 739
流 CURRENT → 441
瀬 rapids → 806
滝 WATERFALL → 661
洪 FLOOD → 386
渦 WHIRLPOOL → 603

HOMOPHONES

shio ⇨ 潮 739

NOTE

⇨ see USAGE note at 潮 739

壮 壮 壮 壮

224 SŌ

丨 丬 丬 丬一 壮 壮
1 2 3 4 5 6

CH 壮 zhuàng

Radical	Strokes
士 33	6-3-3
Grade	**Freq**
Jōyō	1434
1 - 3 - 3	

3-3 丬

▶VIGOROUS ▶GRAND

COMPOUNDS

❶ⓐ vigorous, robust, strong, able-bodied, energetic
ⓑ [original meaning] vigorous young man, prime of life
壮健な *sōken na* vigorous, healthy, robust
強壮な *kyōsō na* robust, strong, vigorous
壮年 *sōnen* prime of life
壮丁 *sōtei* young man of conscription age
少壮 *shōsō* youth

❷ⓐ (having grandeur) **grand, magnificent, splendid**

ⓑ heroic, ambitious, brave, dauntless
壮観 *sōkan* grand sight, magnificent view
壮大な *sōdai na* grand, magnificent, grandiose
壮麗な *sōrei na* grand, magnificent, splendid, imposing
豪壮な *gōsō na* grand, magnificent, splendid
宏壮な *kōsō na* grand, magnificent, imposing
壮烈な *sōretsu na* heroic, brave
壮挙 *sōkyo* grand scheme, heroic [daring] attempt
壮士 *sōshi* desperado, brave, swashbuckler
壮途 *sōto* ambitious embarkment
勇壮な *yūsō na* brave, heroic

悲壮な *hisō na* pathetic, tragic

INDEPENDENT

【sō 壮】 vigor; lofty ambition, courage
壮とする *sō to suru* admire [approve of] a person's courage

SYNONYMS

❶ⓐ **strong**
強 STRONG → 475
丈 STOUT → 3419
健 ROBUST → 134
康 HEALTHY → 3124
❷ⓐ **great**
宏 GRAND (large in scale) → 2202
偉 GREAT (of superior character) → 148
大 BIG → 3416
豪 MAGNIFICENT → 2140
雄 HEROIC → 1008
ⓑ **brave**
雄 HEROIC → 1008
豪 bold and restrained → 2140
敢 bold → 1706
赳 VALIANT → 3308
勇 BRAVE → 2089
義 chivalrous → 2338

3-3 丬

兆 兆 兆

225 CHŌ kiza(su) kiza(shi)

Ⓒⓗ 兆 zhào

Radical	Strokes
儿 10	6-2-4
Grade	**Freq**
Jōyō-4	1322
1-3-3	

丿 丬 丬 兆 兆 兆
1 2 3 4 5 6

▶**OMEN** ▶**TRILLION**

COMPOUNDS

❶ **omen, sign, indication, symptom; foreboding**
兆候(＝徴候) *chōkō* symptom, sign; omen
前兆 *zenchō* omen, sign
吉兆 *kitchō* good omen, lucky sign
❷ⓐ **trillion** (10^{12})
ⓑ astronomical figure, multitude
八兆円 *hatchōen* eight trillion yen
億兆 *okuchō* multitude; [archaic] the people, the masses
❸ [original meaning, now obsolete] line pattern on the back of a tortoise shell used for divination in ancient China

INDEPENDENT

【chō 兆】 omen, sign; trillion (10^{12})
不吉の兆有り *fukitsu no chō ari* have an ill omen

KUN

【kiza(su) 兆す】 show signs [symptoms] of
【kiza(shi) 兆し】 omen, sign, symptom
凶事の兆し *kyōji no kizashi* omen of disaster

SYNONYMS

❶ **signs**
症 symptom (of a disease) → 3280
徴 SYMPTOM → 683
候 indication → 119
気 sign → 3194
❷ⓐ **large numbers**
京 ten quadrillion → 2052
億 HUNDRED MILLION → 170
万 TEN THOUSAND → 2936
千 THOUSAND → 3411
百 HUNDRED → 2026

USAGE

❶ **kizasu**
兆す
show signs [symptoms] of
萌す
germinate, sprout; spring up, dawn
❷ **kizashi**
兆し
omen, sign, symptom
萌し
germination, sprouting; dawning

HOMOPHONES

kizasu ⇨ 萌 2301
kizashi ⇨ 萌 2301

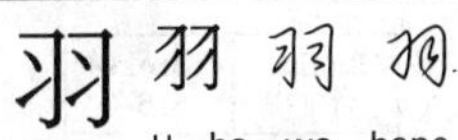

226 u ha wa hane

Ⓒ羽 yǔ

Radical	Strokes
羽 124	6-6-0
Grade	Freq
Jōyō-2	725
1-3-3	

3-3 羽

1 2 3 4 5 6

RADICAL 124

variant of 羽 *hane* 'wing'

⇨ see 羽 227 for radical description

▶FEATHER ▶WING

COMPOUNDS

❶ [original meaning] **feather, plumage**

羽毛 *umō* feathers, plumage, down

❷ **wing (of birds or insects), ala**

羽翼 *uyoku* wings; assistance

羽化 *uka* emergence (of insects)

❸ abbrev. of 出羽 *dewa*, old name for west Tohoku district

奥羽 *ōu* Ou, old name for Tohoku district

❹ [rare] fifth note of the pentatonic scale (⇨ see APPENDIX 7)

INDEPENDENT

【u 羽】[rare] fifth note of the pentatonic scale

KUN

【ha 羽】

① feather, plumage

羽衣 *hagoromo* robe of feathers

② wing, ala

羽蟻 *haari* winged ant

羽音 *haoto* flapping [whirring] of wings

③ used phonetically for *ha*

羽織 *haori* Japanese half coat, *haori*

【wa 羽】 counter for birds or rabbits

一羽 *ichiwa* one bird [rabbit]

三羽 *sanba* three birds [rabbits]

【hane 羽】 feather, plume; wing, ala; [also 羽根] fan, blade

羽布団 *hanebuton* feather quilt

SYNONYMS

❶ **hair**

毛 HAIR (of any kind) → 3453

髪 HAIR (on the head) → 2846

❷ **wings**

翼 WING (of birds or aircraft) → 2720

葉 plane → 2321

【wa】

○ **counters for animals**

匹 COUNTER FOR ANIMALS → 2962

頭 counter for large animals → 1604

COMPOUND FORMATION

羽化 *uka*

羽化 'emergence (of insects)' is the process of becoming transformed (化) into a winged (羽 ❷) creature.

NOTE

★The pronunciation of 羽 *wa* when used as a bird counter depends on the preceding syllable as follows: 一羽 *ichiwa*, 二羽 *niwa*, 三羽 *sanba*, 四羽 *yonwa*, 五羽 *gowa*, 六羽 *rokuwa* (=*roppa*), 七羽 *nanawa*, 八羽 *hachiwa* (=*happa*), 九羽 *kyūwa*, 十羽 *jūwa* (=*jippa*).

羽

227

▶FEATHER ▶WING

nonstandard for 羽 226

Radical	Strokes
羽 124	6-6-0
Grade	Freq
Variant	
1-3-3	

3-3 羽

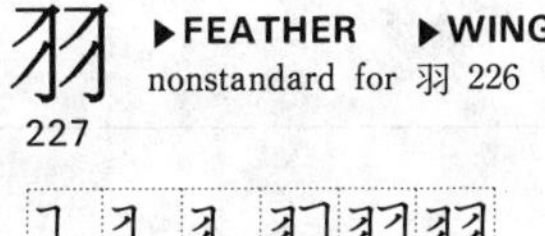

1 2 3 4 5 6

RADICAL 124

Standard form: 羽 *hane* 'wing' (翰 翳 翅)

Variant: 羽 *hane* (習 翁 翔)

Description: used in characters related to wings, feathers or related actions

3-3
⺮

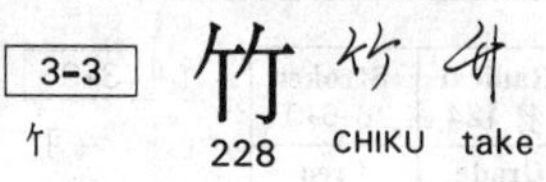

228 CHIKU take

ⒸⒽ 竹 zhú

Radical	Strokes
竹 118	6-6-0
Grade	**Freq**
Jōyō-1	825
■ 1-3-3	

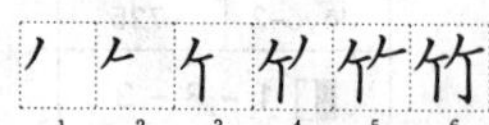

1 2 3 4 5 6

RADICAL 118

Standard form: 竹 *take* 'bamboo'

Top variant: ⺮ *takekanmuri* (第 策 答)

Description: used in characters related to bamboo or bamboo products

▶**BAMBOO**

COMPOUNDS

❶ **bamboo**

竹馬の友 *chikuba no tomo* childhood friend, old playmate

竹材 *chikuzai* bamboo

竹林 *chikurin* bamboo grove

❷ bamboo writing tablets used for recording history in ancient China

竹簡 *chikukan* bamboo writing strip

竹帛 *chikuhaku* history

❸ [rare] bamboo wind instruments, as: flute, pipe, *sho* (Japanese mouth organ)

糸竹 *shichiku* musical instruments

KUN

【take 竹】 bamboo

竹細工 *takezaiku* bamboo work

竹製 *takesei* made of bamboo

竹馬 *takeuma* (=*chikuba*) stilts

SPECIAL READINGS

竹刀 *shinai* bamboo sword

SYNONYMS

❶ **bamboo**

笹 BAMBOO GRASS → 2663

❷ **writing strips**

簡 bamboo writing strips → 2721

COMPOUND FORMATION

竹馬 *takeuma* (=*chikuba*) 竹馬の友 *chikuba no tomo*

竹馬 'stilts' are so called because they resemble a bamboo (竹 ❶) horse (馬). 竹馬の友 'childhood friend, old playmate' refers to friends (友) that used to play together with stilts.

3-3
⺮

⺮

229

Radical	Strokes
⺮ 118	6-6-0
Grade	**Freq**
Radical	
■ 1-3-3	

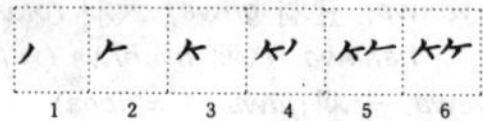

1 2 3 4 5 6

RADICAL 118

takekanmuri, variant of 竹 *take* 'bamboo'

⇨ see 竹 228 for radical description

3-3
⾅

臼 incorrect stroke count ⇨ see 845

230 GIN

1 2 3 4 5 6 7

Ⓒⓗ 吟 yín

Radical	Strokes
口 30	7-3-4
Grade	**Freq**
Jōyō	1743
1 - 3 - 4	

▶**RECITE**

COMPOUNDS

❶ⓐ **recite (a poem), chant, intone**

ⓑ compose (a poem)

ⓒ [also suffix] poem

吟詠 *gin'ei* reciting [chanting] a poem; poem

吟唱(=吟誦)する *ginshō suru* recite, chant

詩吟 *shigin* reciting Chinese poems

苦吟 *kugin* laborious composition

沈吟 *chingin* painstaking elaboration on one's poem; groaning in distress

病中吟 *byōchūgin* poems composed in one's sickbed

❷ examine carefully

吟味する *ginmi suru* examine closely, scrutinize

❸ moan, groan

呻吟する *shingin suru* moan, groan

INDEPENDENT

【**gin** 吟】 recital, chanting (a poem); poem

【**ginjiru** (=**ginzuru**) 吟じる(=吟ずる)】 recite, chant (a poem); compose (a poem)

SYNONYMS

❶ⓐ **recite**

詠 RECITE POETRY → 1500

唱 chant → 462

読 READ → 1541

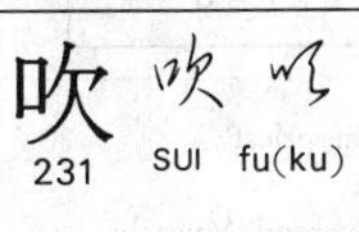

231 SUI fu(ku)

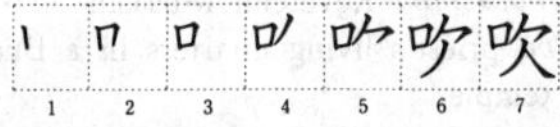

Ⓒⓗ 吹 chuī

Radical	Strokes
口 30	7-3-4
Grade	**Freq**
Jōyō	914
1 - 3 - 4	

▶**BLOW**

COMPOUNDS

❶ⓐ **blow on, play on a wind instrument**

ⓑ [original meaning] **blow, breathe out**

吹奏 *suisō* playing wind instruments

鼓吹する *kosui suru* inspire, inculcate, advocate

吹鳴する *suimei suru* blow (a whistle)

❷ brag, boast, exaggerate; make public

吹聴する *fuichō suru* make public, announce

KUN

【**fu(ku)** 吹く】

①ⓐ blow, breathe out

ⓑ blow (as a trumpet), play on a wind instrument

吹き込む *fukikomu* blow into, breathe into

笛吹き *fuefuki* flute player

② (of wind) blow

吹き荒れる *fukiareru* blow violently

③ (of germs or buds) sprout

芽吹く *mebuku* bud

④ brag

ほら吹き *horafuki* boaster, braggart

SPECIAL READINGS

息吹 *ibuki* breath

吹雪 *fubuki* snowstorm

SYNONYMS

❶ⓐ **play music**

弾 play on (stringed instruments) → 572

奏 PLAY MUSIC → 2577

ⓑ **discharge from mouth**

吐 SPEW → 203

ⓑ **breathe and blow**

呼 breathe out → 273

吸 BREATHE IN → 202

息 BREATH → 2647

気 breath → 3194

USAGE

fuku

吹く

①ⓐ blow, breathe out

ⓑ blow (as a trumpet), play on a wind instrument

② (of wind) blow

③ (of germs or buds) sprout

④ brag

噴く

spout, emit, spurt, gush out

HOMOPHONES

fuku ⇨ 噴 717

COMPOUND FORMATION

鼓吹 *kosui*
鼓吹 was originally a kind of ancient military or court music in which drums (鼓) and wind instruments (吹 ❶ⓐ) were used. 鼓吹する 'inspire, inculcate, advocate' derives from the idea of drumming up or rousing a person's emotions.

3-4
口

吸
232

▶SUCK ▶BREATHE IN
nonstandard for 吸 202

3-4
口

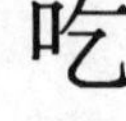

incorrect stroke count ⇨ see 200

3-4
口

incorrect stroke count ⇨ see 202

3-4
土

坊 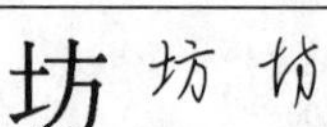
233 BŌ BOT-

Ⓒⓗ 坊 fāng fáng

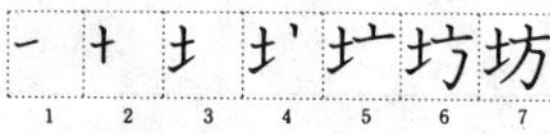

Radical	Strokes
土 32	7-3-4
Grade	**Freq**
Jōyō	1196
◧ 1 - 3 - 4	

▶SONNY
▶COLLOQUIAL PERSON SUFFIX

COMPOUNDS

❶ **sonny, boy, sonny boy**
坊や *bōya* sonny, sonny boy, boy
坊ちゃん *botchan* sonny, boy; Master Darling; greenhorn, baby
凸坊 *dekobō* beetle-browed boy; mischievous boy, imp

❷ **colloquial suffix indicating endearment, intimacy or derision, as the English "Jimmy boy" for James or such nicknames as "fatso" for a fat person**
赤ん坊 *akanbō* baby
春坊 *harubō* nickname for such names as Haruo or Haruko
朝寝坊 *asanebō* late riser, sleepy head
けちん坊 *kechinbō* miser, niggard, stingy fellow
食いしん坊 *kuishinbō* glutton
風来坊 *fūraibō* wanderer, vagabond, hobo
見栄坊 *miebō* fop, swell, dude, coxcomb

❸ colloquial suffix for children's games or various actions
隠れん坊 *kakurenbō* hide-and-seek
通せん坊 *tōsenbō* barring (a person's) way
立ちん坊 *tachinbō* being kept standing

❹ⓐ **Buddhist priest [monk], bonze**
ⓑ title after names of Buddhist priests
ⓒ [also suffix] priest's residence
坊主 *bōzu* Buddhist priest [monk], bonze; shaven head; sonny, sonny boy, boy
坊さん *bōsan* Buddhist priest
御坊 *gobō* Reverend
武蔵坊 *musashibō* Reverend Musashi
僧坊 *sōbō* priest's living quarters in a Buddhist temple
宿坊 *shukubō* priest's quarters; visitor's lodgings in a temple
本因坊 *hon'inbō* Honinbo Lodge in Jakko Temple; grand champion of go

❺ city quarter, streets
坊間 *bōkan* all over town

INDEPENDENT

【bō 坊】Buddhist priest [monk], bonze; priest's residence
師の坊 *shi no bō* master priest
坊の主 *bō no aruji* master of the priest's quarters

SYNONYMS

❶ **child**
幼 young child → 191
童 CHILD (young person) → 2130
子 CHILD → 3390
児 CHILD (of any age) → 2546

❷ **fellow**
屋 colloquial person suffix → 3098
物 character → 874
棒 tough guy → 983
奴 GUY → 187
漢 FELLOW → 657
輩 FELLOW (*belittling*) → 2807
徒 fellows → 416

❹ⓐ **clergymen**
僧 BONZE → 159
尼 BUDDHIST NUN → 3033
父 FATHER → 1973

NOTE
⇨ see COMPOUND FORMATION for 赤ん坊 *akanbō* ⇨ 赤 2193

坂 坂 坂

234 HAN saka

Ⓒⓗ 坂 bǎn

Radical	Strokes
土 32	7-3-4
Grade	**Freq**
Jōyō-3	646
◧ 1 - 3 - 4	

3-4 土

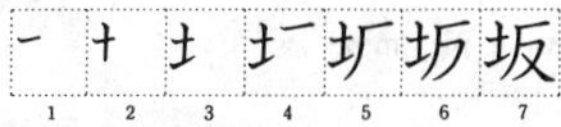

1 2 3 4 5 6 7

▶SLOPE

COMPOUNDS
● [original meaning] **slope, incline, hill**
急坂 *kyūhan* steep hill [slope]
登坂 *tohan* climbing a slope [hill]

KUN
【**saka** 坂】 slope, incline, hill
坂道 *sakamichi* slope
上り坂 *noborizaka* ascent, upward slope

SYNONYMS
● **hills**
阪 slope → 271
丘 HILL → 3495
岡 HILL → 2997
台 heights → 2005
塚 MOUND → 556
陵 high mound → 544

USAGE
saka
坂
slope, incline, hill
阪
slope, incline, hill
★Both forms have the same meaning, but the latter is now used almost exclusively in the writing of names.

HOMOPHONES
saka ⇨ 阪 271

均 均 均

235 KIN nara(su)▲

Ⓒⓗ 均 jūn

Radical	Strokes
土 32	7-3-4
Grade	**Freq**
Jōyō-5	822
◧ 1 - 3 - 4	

3-4 土

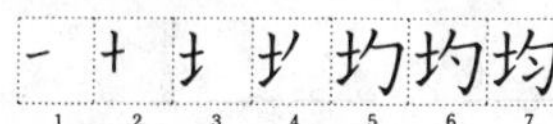

1 2 3 4 5 6 7

▶EVEN

COMPOUNDS
ⓐ **even, uniform, equal, same, symmetrical, well-balanced**
ⓑ [original meaning] make even, level
均一な *kin'itsu na* uniform, equal, even
均等の *kintō no* equal, uniform
均質 *kinshitsu* homogeneity
均分 *kinbun* equal division
均勢 *kinsei* balance [equilibrium] of power, uniformity
均整(＝均斉) *kinsei* symmetry
均衡 *kinkō* balance, equilibrium
平均 *heikin* average, (arithmetical) mean; equilibrium, balance

KUN
【**nara(su)** 均す】
① level, make even, roll
土を均す *tsuchi o narasu* level the ground
② average
均し *narashi* average

SYNONYMS
ⓐ **same and uniform**
斉 UNIFORM → 2054
平 equal → 3478
等 EQUAL → 2682
同 SAME → 2987
一 same → 3341

HOMOPHONES
narasu ⇨ 慣 685 馴 1820

NOTE
⇨ see USAGE note at 慣 685

3-4 土

坑 坑 坑

236 KŌ

一 十 土 圵 圹 圹 坑
1 2 3 4 5 6 7

CH 坑 kēng

Radical	Strokes
土 32	7-3-4
Grade	**Freq**
Jōyō	1725

1 - 3 - 4

▶PIT

COMPOUNDS

❶ⓐ pit (of a mine), mine-pit, mine
ⓑ [original meaning] pit, shaft
坑口 *kōkō* pithead, minehead
坑外で *kōgai de* out of the pit
坑夫 *kōfu* miner
坑内 *kōnai* mine-pit, shaft
坑底 *kōtei* mine-pit bottom
鉱坑 *kōkō* mine, shaft, pit
炭坑 *tankō* coal-mine, coal pit
坑道 *kōdō* tunnel, pit; (mine) level; shaft
❷ [rare] bury alive
坑儒 *kōju* burying Confucian scholars alive

INDEPENDENT

【kō 坑】 mine-pit, mine

SYNONYMS

❶ⓐ mine
鉱 MINE → 1709
山 mine → 2940
ⓑ holes and cavities
穴 HOLE → 2159
孔 OPEN HOLE → 179
口 MOUTH → 3382
堀 DITCH → 467
溝 CHANNEL → 659
凹 concavity → 3482
洞 CAVE → 380

3-4 夕

舛

237

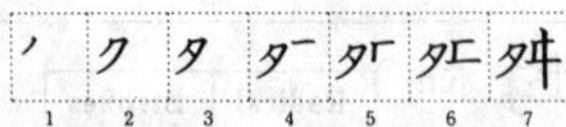

Radical	Strokes
舛 136	7-7-0
Grade	**Freq**
Radical	

1 - 3 - 4

RADICAL 136

maiashi, variant of 舛 *masu* 'dancing'
⇨ see 舛 205 for radical description

3-4 女

妨 妨 妨

238 BŌ samata(geru)

く 女 女 女' 女 妨 妨
1 2 3 4 5 6 7

CH 妨 fáng fāng

Radical	Strokes
女 38	7-3-4
Grade	**Freq**
Jōyō	1404

1 - 3 - 4

▶HINDER

COMPOUNDS

● hinder, interfere with, disturb, obstruct, impede
妨害する *bōgai suru* disturb, hinder, obstruct, hamper, impede, interfere
妨害放送 *bōgai hōsō* radio jamming

KUN

【samata(geru) 妨げる】 hinder, interfere with, disturb, obstruct, impede; preclude
妨げ *samatage* hindrance, obstruction, disturbance
睡眠を妨げる *suimin o samatageru* disturb one's sleep
重任を妨げない *Jūnin o samatagenai* Reappointment is not precluded

SYNONYMS

● obstruct and hinder
障 hinder → 715
阻 OBSTRUCT → 348
遮 INTERRUPT → 3158
害 stand in the way → 2272

妙 妙 妙

239 MYŌ tae▲

く 女 女 女丨 女小 女小 妙 (stroke order 1–7)

Ⓒⓗ 妙 miào

Radical	Strokes
女 38	7-3-4
Grade	Freq
Jōyō	1002
◧ 1 - 3 - 4	

3-4 女

▶MARVELOUS

COMPOUNDS

❶ⓐ (causing wonder) **marvelous, wonderful, miraculous**

ⓑ [original meaning] **of marvelous beauty, exquisite, charming, subtle**

ⓒ (of incredible excellence) **marvelous, superb, excellent; adroit, ingenious**

妙薬 *myōyaku* miracle drug, golden remedy
絶妙な *zetsumyō na* miraculous, exquisite, superb
妙法蓮華経 *myōhōrengekyō* Lotus Sutra
妙味 *myōmi* subtle charm, beauty
美妙な *bimyō na* elegant, exquisite
微妙な *bimyō na* subtle, delicate
妙案 *myōan* bright idea, excellent plan
妙技 *myōgi* wonderful skill; stunt
巧妙な *kōmyō na* skillful, ingenious, clever

❷ (arousing marvel) **strange, odd, queer, singular**

奇妙な *kimyō na* strange, queer, odd
珍妙な *chinmyō na* queer, odd, fantastic

❸ youthful, young and beautiful

妙齢の *myōrei no* young, blooming

INDEPENDENT

【myō 妙】 mystery, miracle, wonder; cleverness, adroitness; strangeness

妙な *myō na* strange, queer, funny
造化の妙 *zōka no myō* the mystery of creation
妙を得ている *myō o ete iru* clever, skillful
妙に思う *myō ni omou* think strange

KUN

【tae 妙】

taenaru 妙なる exquisite, excellent; delicate; charming

妙なる調べ *taenaru shirabe* sweet tune, enchanting melody

SYNONYMS

❶ⓐ **miraculous**
魔 magic(al) → 3187

ⓑ **beautiful**
艶 CHARMING → 1908
麗 OF GRACEFUL BEAUTY → 2151
瑶 EXQUISITE → 1026
佳 FINE → 86
美 BEAUTIFUL → 2264
華 MAGNIFICENT → 2283
絢 GORGEOUS → 1347
斐 florid → 2776

ⓒ **excellent and superior**
快 splendid → 245
卓 PROMINENT → 2064
絶 without match → 1353
優 SUPERIOR → 177
秀 EXCELLENT → 2545
英 DISTINGUISHED → 2238
傑 outstanding → 155
逸 exceptional → 3120
名 first-rate → 2169
上 of upper grade → 3404

❷ **abnormal**
奇 UNUSUAL → 2217
変 ABNORMAL → 2069
怪 MYSTERIOUS → 297
異 not ordinary → 2584
珍 curious → 909

妊 姙° 妊 妊

240 NIN hara(mu)▲

く 女 女 女' 女二 女壬 妊 (stroke order 1–7)

Ⓒⓗ 妊 rèn

Radical	Strokes
女 38	7-3-4
Grade	Freq
Jōyō	1707
◧ 1 - 3 - 4	

3-4 女

▶BECOME PREGNANT

COMPOUNDS

ⓐ [original meaning] **become pregnant, conceive**

ⓑ **pregnant, expectant**

妊娠する *ninshin suru* become pregnant, conceive
避妊 *hinin* contraception
懐妊 *kainin* pregnancy, conception
不妊 *funin* sterility

妊婦 *ninpu* pregnant woman
妊産婦 *ninsanpu* pregnant women and nursing mothers

KUN

【hara(mu) 妊む】 become pregnant, conceive
子供を妊む *kodomo o haramu* become pregnant, conceive

SYNONYMS

● **conceive**
娠 CONCEIVE → 408

3-4
女

incorrect stroke count ⇨ see 280

3-4
女

姉

incorrect stroke count ⇨ see 282
(nonstandard for 姉 280)

3-4
山

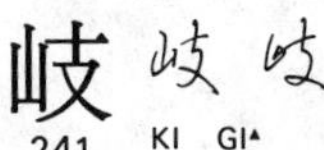

241 KI GI▲

Ⓒ 岐 岐 qí

Radical	Strokes
山 46	7-3-4
Grade	**Freq**
Jōyō	1349
1 - 3 - 4	

丨 屮 山 山一 山十 山ケ 岐
1 2 3 4 5 6 7

▶DIVERGE

COMPOUNDS

❶ⓐ diverge, branch off, ramify, fork
ⓑ [original meaning] **forked road, branch road**
分岐 *bunki* divergence, ramification, forking
分岐点 *bunkiten* junction
多岐 *taki* many branches, many divergences
岐路 *kiro* forked road, crossroad
❷ abbrev. of 岐阜県 *gifuken*: Gifu Prefecture
三岐代表 *sangi daihyō* representative of Gifu and Mie prefectures

SYNONYMS

❶ⓐ diverge
分 branch off → 1972
ⓑ ways and routes
辻 CROSSROADS → 3192
道 WAY (path) → 3134
途 WAY (route) → 3107
路 ROAD → 1533
筋 wayside → 2678
通り street → 3109
街 city street → 576
径 PATH → 291
軌 TRACK → 1445
線 LINE → 1392

3-4
工

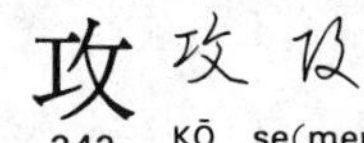

242 KŌ se(meru)

Ⓒ 攻 gōng

Radical	Strokes
攵 66	7-4-3
Grade	**Freq**
Jōyō	530
1 - 3 - 4	

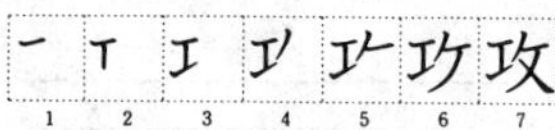

▶ATTACK

COMPOUNDS

❶ⓐ attack, take the offensive
ⓑ attack, offensive, offense
攻撃 *kōgeki* attack, assault; criticism; *baseball* batting
攻勢 *kōsei* offensive, aggression
攻略 *kōryaku* capture, conquest; invasion
正攻法 *seikōhō* regular tactics for attack
攻守 *kōshu* offense and defense; batting and fielding
速攻 *sokkō* swift attack
反攻 *hankō* counterattack, counteroffensive
❷ specialize, study
攻究 *kōkyū* investigation, research
専攻する *senkō suru* major in, specialize in

INDEPENDENT

【kō 攻】 *baseball* batting

KUN

【se(meru) 攻める】 attack, take the offensive
攻め *seme* [also suffix] attack, offensive, bombardment; batting

攻め込む *semekomu* attack and invade
攻め滅ぼす *semehorobosu* attack and overthrow, utterly destroy
質問攻め *shitsumonzeme* barrage of questions

SYNONYMS

❶ **attack**
撃 STRIKE → 2863
襲 RAID → 2917
侵 INVADE → 101
爆 bomb → 1101

❷ **learn and study**
研 RESEARCH → 1132
学 STUDY → 2555
考 study → 3196
習 LEARN → 2667
究 STUDY EXHAUSTIVELY → 2203

USAGE

❶ **semeru**
攻める
attack, take the offensive
責める
① blame, condemn, censure, accuse, criticize, reproach
② torture, persecute
③ urge, press; tease

❷ **seme**
攻め
① [also suffix] attack, offensive, bombardment
② batting
責め
① responsibility
② blame
③ [also suffix] torture, persecution

HOMOPHONES

semeru ⇨ 責 2467
seme ⇨ 責 2467

改

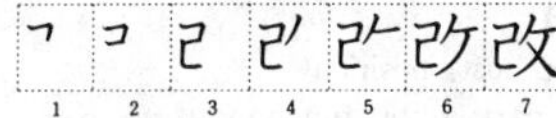

243 KAI arata(meru) arata(maru)

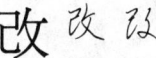

Ⓒⓗ 改 gǎi

Radical	Strokes
攵 66	7-4-3
Grade	**Freq**
Jōyō-4	257
1 - 3 - 4	

3-4 己

▶REFORM

COMPOUNDS

❶ⓐ **reform, renew, rectify, correct, revise, amend**
ⓑ **change, convert, modify**
ⓒ **redo, renew**
改善する *kaizen suru* improve, ameliorate
改新 *kaishin* renovation, reformation
改革 *kaikaku* reform, reformation
改正 *kaisei* revision, amendment
改名 *kaimei* changing a name
改行する *kaigyō suru* change lines [paragraphs]
改選 *kaisen* reelection
改葬 *kaisō* reburial

❷ examine, inspect
改札 *kaisatsu* ticket examination

KUN

【arata(meru) 改める】 reform, rectify, correct; renew, redo; change, alter; revise, improve; examine
改めて *aratamete* again, over again, anew; formally
悔い改める *kuiaratameru* repent, be penitent
稿を改める *kō o aratameru* rewrite a manuscript
切符を改める *kippu o aratameru* examine tickets

【arata(maru) 改まる】 be renewed, be renovated; change, be improved, be reformed; stand on ceremony, become formal
年が改まる *Toshi ga aratamaru* The new year comes round
改まった *aratamatta* formal, ceremonious

SYNONYMS

❶ⓐ **reform**
革 REFORM → 2448
更 RENEW → 3541
新 make new → 1784

ⓐ **correct**
矯 RECTIFY → 1241
匡 RECTIFY → 2989
正 RIGHT → 3484
直す correct → 2932
訂 REVISE → 1442

ⓑ **change and replace**
変 CHANGE → 2069
更 change → 3541
易 change → 2411
化 CHANGE INTO, -ize → 21
遷 undergo transition → 3170
転 turn into → 1480
換 EXCHANGE → 587
交 INTERCHANGE → 2015
替 REPLACE → 2783
代 SUBSTITUTE → 30
迭 ALTERNATE → 3077

ⓒ **repeating and repetition**

-換える redo → 587
-直す repetition suffix → 2932
-返す do over → 3060
再 ANOTHER TIME → 3519
又 AGAIN → 3351
復 repeat → 575
重 DUPLICATE → 3573
畳 reduplicate → 2592

3-4
彳

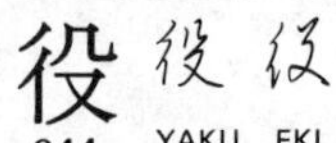

244 YAKU EKI

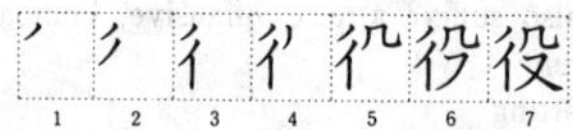

CH 役 yì

Radical	Strokes
彳 60	7-3-4
Grade	**Freq**
Jōyō-3	294
1-3-4	

▶ **SERVICE**

COMPOUNDS

❶ⓐ **service, public service, duty, official post, office**
ⓑ **executive, officer, public servant, official, director, person in charge**
役所 *yakusho* public [government] office
役場 *yakuba* public office
役柄 *yakugara* nature [quality] of one's office, one's position
役目 *yakume* duty, function; role
役員 *yakuin* officer, leader, director
下役 *shitayaku* subordinate official
助役 *joyaku* assistant official; deputy mayor; deputy station-master
重役 *jūyaku* director, executive
取締役 *torishimariyaku* director
❷ⓐ **press into service, enlist one's service, employ**
ⓑ **unpaid service, exacted labor, work, corvée**
ⓒ **military service, army duty**
使役 *shieki* employment, service; *gram* causative
労役 *rōeki* labor, work, toil
雑役 *zatsueki* miscellaneous services, odd jobs
懲役 *chōeki* penal servitude, imprisonment with hard labor
役務 *ekimu* labor, service
役牛 *ekigyū* work cattle
兵役 *heieki* military service
退役する *taieki suru* retire from military service
予備役 *yobieki* service in the first reserve
❸ **service, serviceability, usefulness, utility**
役立つ *yakudatsu* be of use, serve a purpose
役立てる *yakudateru* put to use, make use of, turn to account
❹ [also suffix] **role, part, cast**
役割 *yakuwari* casting of parts; part, role
役者 *yakusha* actor, actress
配役 *haiyaku* cast (of a play)
悪役 *akuyaku* villain (of the piece)
主役 *shuyaku* leading part, starring role
顔役 *kaoyaku* influential man, boss
メフィストフェレス役 *mefisutoferesuyaku* part of Mephistopheles
❺ war, battle, expedition
戦役 *sen'eki* war, battle
❻ scoring hand of cards or mahjong tiles
手役 *teyaku* hand of cards which scores as it is
❼ [also 軛 *yaku* 1481] yoke
共役 *kyōeki math* conjugation

INDEPENDENT

【yaku 役】
①ⓐ office, post, position
ⓑ role, part; duty, function
役に就く *yaku ni tsuku* assume office, be appointed to a post
役を勤める *yaku o tsutomeru* hold an office; act (as), play the part (of)
オセロの役を演じる *osero no yaku o enjiru* act [play] the part of Othello
仲人の役を買って出る *nakōdo no yaku o katte deru* offer one's service as a matchmaker
② serviceability, usefulness, utility, help
役に立つ *yaku ni tatsu* be useful, be helpful
役に立たない *yaku ni tatanai* be useless, be of no avail
③ scoring hand of cards or mahjong tiles
【eki 役】 war, battle, expedition
西南の役 *seinan no eki* the Satsuma Rebellion

SYNONYMS

❶ⓐ & ❷ⓑ work and employment
勤 SERVICE (employment) → 1818
務 DUTY → 1173
任 OFFICE → 53
業 WORK → 2612
職 EMPLOYMENT → 1425
労 LABOR → 2548
ⓑ officials
官 GOVERNMENT OFFICIAL → 2226
吏 OFFICIAL → 3536
僚 official → 165
司 officiator → 2931

事 officer → 3567
❷ⓐ **employ**
雇 EMPLOY → 1956
用 EMPLOY → 2976
使う employ → 90
❸ **benefit**
用 use(ful) → 2976
為 SAKE → 3577
益 BENEFIT → 2285

利 ADVANTAGE → 1114
❺ **warfare and rebellions**
戦 WAR → 1787
軍 war → 2080
陣 battle → 455
乱 rebellion → 1260
変 uprising → 2069
闘 FIGHT → 3334

徃

incorrect stroke count ⇨ see 295
(nonstandard for 往 292)

3-4 彳

快 快 快

245 KAI kokoroyo(i)

Ⓒⓗ 快 kuài

Radical 忄 61	Strokes 7-3-4
Grade Jōyō-5	Freq 1011

◧ 1 - 3 - 4

3-4 忄

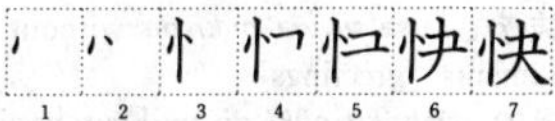

▶**PLEASANT**

COMPOUNDS

❶ [original meaning] **pleasant, agreeable, comfortable, delightful, jolly**
快感 *kaikan* agreeable sensation, comfort
快適な *kaiteki na* comfortable, pleasant, agreeable
快楽 *kairaku* pleasure, enjoyment
快削鋼 *kaisakukō* free-cutting steel
愉快な *yukai na* pleasant, delightful, joyful
不快な *fukai na* unpleasant, disagreeable
❷ [also prefix] splendid, fine, good
快挙 *kaikyo* brilliant achievement, heroic deed [feat]
快晴 *kaisei* fine weather, fair and clear weather
快男児 *kaidanji* fine fellow, spirited fellow
❸ **fast, speedy, rapid, quick**
快速 *kaisoku* high speed; fast (local) train
快走 *kaisō* fast running, fast sailing
快足の *kaisoku no* quick of foot, fast
特快 *tokkai* special fast (local) train
軽快な *keikai na* light, nimble, quick; cheerful
❹ [formerly also 恢 366] recover, convalesce
快方 *kaihō* convalescence
快復 *kaifuku* recovery (from illness)
全快 *zenkai* complete recovery
❺ sharp
快刀 *kaitō literary* sharp sword

INDEPENDENT

[kai 快] pleasure, delight, enjoyment
快を貪る *kai o musaboru* enjoy oneself to the full

KUN

[kokoroyo(i) 快い] pleasant, agreeable, comfortable, delightful, refreshing
快さ *kokoroyosa* pleasantness, comfortableness
快く *kokoroyoku* cheerfully, comfortably; gladly, willingly

SYNONYMS

❶ **pleased and pleasant**
朗 CHEERFUL → 1325
楽 pleasurable → 2826
愉 PLEASED → 582
悦 DELIGHTED → 418
嬉しい GLAD → 722
喜 HAPPY → 2308
歓 JOYOUS → 1867
欣 JOYFUL → 852
❷ **excellent and superior**
妙 MARVELOUS → 239
卓 PROMINENT → 2064
絶 without match → 1353
優 SUPERIOR → 177
秀 EXCELLENT → 2545
英 DISTINGUISHED → 2238
傑 outstanding → 155
逸 exceptional → 3120
名 first-rate → 2169
上 of upper grade → 3404
❸ **fast**
疾 fast → 3279
速 QUICK → 3105
早 QUICK → 2390
迅 SWIFT → 3046
急 rapid → 2092
敏 NIMBLE → 1322
即 IMMEDIATE → 1120

❹ **cure and recover**
癒 HEAL → 3291
治 CURE → 335
医 cure → 2993
療 TREAT → 3288

3-4
扌

抜 抜 抜 拔 ㊥ 拔 bá

246 BATSU nu(ku) -nu(ku) nu(ki) nu(keru) nu(kasu) nu(karu)

Radical	Strokes
扌 64	7-3-4
Grade	**Freq**
Jōyō	654
1 - 3 - 4	

▶**PULL OUT** ▶**STAND OUT**

COMPOUNDS

❶ [original meaning] **pull out, draw out, extract, remove**
抜歯 *basshi* tooth extraction
抜糸 *basshi* removal [extraction] of stitches
抜刀 *battō* drawing a sword; drawn sword
抜本的な *bapponteki na* radical, drastic
不抜の *fubatsu no* indomitable, unswerving
❷ single out, select, pick out, extract, excerpt
抜擢 *batteki* selection, choice
抜粋 *bassui* extract, excerpt, selection
選抜する *senbatsu suru* select, choose, pick out
❸ **stand out** [**above**], **rise above, surpass, excel**
抜群の *batsugun no* preeminent, outstanding
奇抜な *kibatsu na* novel, unconventional, extraordinary
卓抜する *takubatsu suru* excel, surpass, stand high, be distinguished
海抜 *kaibatsu* above sea level

KUN

【nu(ku) 抜く】
①ⓐ pull out, draw out, extract
ⓑ remove, take out (a stain)
ⓒ leave out, omit, skip
引き抜く *hikinuku* pull [draw] out, extract; single [pick] out, choose, recruit
色抜き *ironuki* decolorization
手を抜く *te o nuku* scamp [skimp] one's work, cut corners
② single out, select, pick out, extract, excerpt
抜き刷り *nukizuri* offprint
③ outstrip, surpass, excel
抜きん出る *nukinderu* excel, stand out, be preeminent
④ pierce, shoot through
踏み抜く *fuminuku* tread (a nail) into the sole of one's foot; tread through (the floor)

【-nu(ku) -抜く】
[verbal suffix]
① perform an action to the end, stick it out
生き抜く *ikinuku* live through
踊り抜く *odorinuku* dance away
② be in a complete state of (distress)
困り抜く *komarinuku* be in great trouble

【nu(ki) 抜き】
[also suffix]
① leaving out, omission
挨拶は抜きで *aisatsu wa nuki de* without compliments [greetings]
夕食抜きで *yūshoku nuki de* without having supper
② beating (in a match)
五人抜き *goninnuki* beating five opponents in a row

【nu(keru) 抜ける】 come [fall] out [off], escape; leave, quit, withdraw, be left out, be missing; be dull-witted, be mentally deficient; go by [through], pass through; [in compounds] surpass, excel
抜け毛 *nukege* fallen hair, combings
会を抜ける *kai o nukeru* withdraw from a society [meeting]
一行抜けている *Ichigyō nukete iru* A line is left out
彼は抜けている *Kare wa nukete iru* He is a bit soft in his head
抜け道 *nukemichi* byroad, secret passage; loophole, excuse
ずば抜けた *zubanuketa* outstanding, prominent, distinguished

【nu(kasu) 抜かす】 leave out, omit, skip; *slang* have the impudence to say
二頁抜かす *nipēji nukasu* skip two pages
何を抜かす *Nani o nukasu* None of your cheek!

【nu(karu) 抜かる】 commit a blunder, make a slip
抜かり *nukari* slip, blunder, oversight

SYNONYMS

❶ **pull**
引 DRAW → 181
抽 DRAW OUT → 302
控える HOLD BACK → 495
寄せる DRAW NEAR → 2291
❷ **choose**
摘 pick out → 694

採 PICK → 499
択 SELECT → 255
選 CHOOSE → 3169
❸ **excel**
超 SURPASS → 3313
勝 EXCEL → 1005
越 GO BEYOND → 3314
【nuku】
①ⓒ **omit**
脱 leave out by mistake → 973
漏 omit → 701
欠 missing → 1987
NOTE
⇨ see COMPOUND FORMATION for 抜群 *batsugun* ⇨ 群 1540

扶 
247 FU tasu(keru)▲

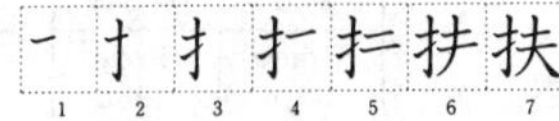

Ⓒⓗ 扶 fú

Radical	Strokes
扌 64	7-3-4
Grade	Freq
Jōyō	1629
◧ 1 - 3 - 4	

3-4 扌

▶LEND SUPPORT TO
COMPOUNDS
ⓐ **lend support to, support, hold up, sustain**
ⓑ [original meaning, now archaic] support with the hand, hold up
扶養する *fuyō suru* support, maintain
扶助する *fujo suru* support, sustain
扶育 *fuiku* bringing up (children)
KUN
【tasu(keru) 扶ける】[now usu. 助ける] help, aid, assist
扶け起こす *tasukeokosu* help a person to his [her] feet
家計の扶け *kakei no tasuke* assistance in supporting a family
SYNONYMS
ⓐ **support**
擁 SUPPORT → 770
支 SUPPORT → 1979
賛 back up → 2809
HOMOPHONES
tasukeru ⇨ 助 1121
NOTE
⇨ see USAGE note at 助 1121

技 技 技 技
248 GI waza

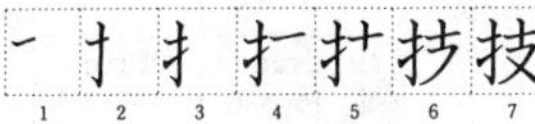

Ⓒⓗ 技 jì

Radical	Strokes
扌 64	7-3-4
Grade	Freq
Jōyō-5	433
◧ 1 - 3 - 4	

3-4 扌

▶SKILL
COMPOUNDS
❶ [sometimes also 伎 46] [original meaning] **skill, ability, craft, art**
技術 *gijutsu* technique, art, skill; technology
技能 *ginō* skill, ability, capacity
技師 *gishi* engineer, technician
技量 *giryō* skill, ability, capacity
技巧 *gikō* art, craftsmanship, technical skill; trick
競技 *kyōgi* match, contest, game; sporting event
演技 *engi* acting, performance
特技 *tokugi* one's special ability [talent], one's special skill [art]
実技 *jitsugi* practical technique [skill]
❷ game, sport, pastime
球技 *kyūgi* ball game
国技 *kokugi* national sport game
INDEPENDENT
【gi 技】 skill, ability, craft, art
入神の技 *nyūshin no gi* skill of superhuman level
KUN
【waza 技】
① skill, ability, craft, art
技を磨く *waza o migaku* improve one's skill
② *judo*
ⓐ trick
ⓑ half point
SYNONYMS
❶ **art**
術 PRACTICAL ART → 476
芸 ART → 2209

道 the way of an art → 3134
❶ **skill**
腕 skill → 1006
能 ABILITY → 1323
力 POWER → 3371
才 TALENT → 3410
❷ **game**
戦 match → 1787

USAGE

waza

技
① skill, ability, craft, art
② *judo*
ⓐ trick
ⓑ half point

業
work, act, deed

HOMOPHONES

waza ⇨ 業 2612

3-4
扌

把 把 把

249 HA WA

1 2 3 4 5 6 7

CH 把 bǎ bà

Radical	Strokes
扌 64	7-3-4
Grade	**Freq**
Jōyō	1956
1 - 3 - 4	

▶GRIP

COMPOUNDS

❶ⓐ [original meaning] **grip, grasp, seize, hold**
ⓑ a grip, a handle
把握する *haaku suru* grip, grasp; understand, grasp
把持する *haji suru* grasp, hold, grip
把手 *hashu* (=*totte*) handle, grip
❷ counter for bundles or sheaves
薪二把 *takigi niwa* two bundles of firewood

SYNONYMS

❶ⓐ **take**
握 GRASP → 585
執 SEIZE → 1680
捕 CATCH → 429
取 TAKE → 1262
持 HOLD → 374
ⓑ **handles**
手 handle → 3456
柄 HANDLE → 897

NOTE

★As a counter for bundles, 把 is read *wa*, *ba* or *pa* depending on the preceding syllable ⇨ see also NOTE at 羽 226.

3-4
扌

批 批 批

250 HI

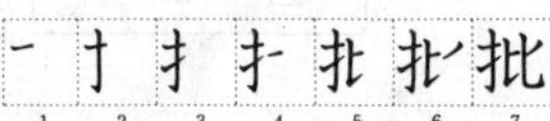

1 2 3 4 5 6 7

CH 批 pī

Radical	Strokes
扌 64	7-3-4
Grade	**Freq**
Jōyō-6	667
1 - 3 - 4	

▶CRITICIZE

COMPOUNDS

❶ **criticize, comment, review**
批評 *hihyō* criticism, comment
批難(=非難) *hinan* criticism, blame
批評家 *hihyōka* critic, reviewer
批判 *hihan* criticism, comment
批議する *higi suru* blame, criticize
❷ ratify, sanction
批准 *hijun* ratification
批准書 *hijunsho* instrument of ratification

SYNONYMS

❶ **comment upon**
評 COMMENT → 1501
❶ **blame and accuse**
難 find fault with → 1838
責 BLAME → 2467
叱 SCOLD → 182
詰 REPRIMAND → 1521
劾 EXPOSE CRIMES → 1266
弾 impeach → 572

抒 251 JO

CH 抒 shū

Radical	Strokes
扌 64	7-3-4
Grade	Freq
Reference	
◧ 1 - 3 - 4	

3-4 扌

COMPOUNDS

● [now replaced by 叙 1446] describe, narrate, depict, explain

抒情 *jojō* description of feelings, lyricism
抒情詩 *jojōshi* lyric poem [poetry]

抗 抗 抗 252 KŌ

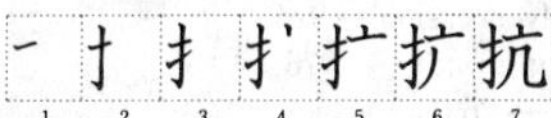

CH 抗 kàng

Radical	Strokes
扌 64	7-3-4
Grade	Freq
Jōyō	687
◧ 1 - 3 - 4	

3-4 扌

▶**RESIST**

COMPOUNDS

ⓐ [original meaning] **resist, defy, oppose**
ⓑ [prefix] anti-
抗争 *kōsō* dispute, resistance
抗議 *kōgi* protest, remonstrance, objection
反抗 *hankō* resistance, opposition, defiance
抵抗する *teikō suru* resist, oppose, defy
対抗する *taikō suru* oppose, antagonize, rival; counteract
不可抗力 *fukakōryoku* act of god, irresistible force
抗日 *kōnichi* anti-Japanese
抗生物質 *kōsei busshitsu* antibiotic
抗ヒスタミン剤 *kōhisutaminzai* antihistamine

INDEPENDENT

【kōsuru 抗する】 resist, defy

SYNONYMS

ⓐ **resist**
抵 RESIST → 319
耐 WITHSTAND → 1282
対 OPPOSE → 831
反 COUNTER → 2945
逆 rebel → 3091

折 折 お 253 SETSU o(ru) ori o(ri) -o(ri) o(reru)

CH 折 zhé shé zhē

Radical	Strokes
扌 64	7-3-4
Grade	Freq
Jōyō-4	766
◧ 1 - 3 - 4	

3-4 扌

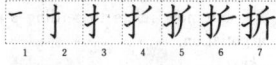

一 十 扌 扌 扩 折 折 (1 2 3 4 5 6 7)

▶**BREAK OFF** ▶**FOLD**

COMPOUNDS

❶ⓐ (separate through the application of a sudden bending force) **break off (as a branch), break (a bone), snap (in two), split**
ⓑ (weaken, as in spirit) break down, (cause to) lose heart
折半 *seppan* halving
折衷 *setchū* compromise, eclecticism
骨折 *kossetsu* bone fracture
折衝 *sesshō* negotiation, parley
挫折する *zasetsu suru* fail, be frustrated [baffled]
❷ **fold**
折角 *sekkaku* with much trouble; specially
❸ **bend**
曲折 *kyokusetsu* bending, winding; zigzags
屈折 *kussetsu* bending, turn; refraction
❹ turn (to the right or left)
右折する *usetsu suru* turn to the right
左折する *sasetsu suru* turn to the left
❺ chastise, criticize severely
折檻する *sekkan suru* chastise, correct, spank (a naughty boy)
❻ die
夭折 *yōsetsu* premature death

KUN

【o(ru) 折る】

① (separate through the application of a sudden bending force) break off (as a branch), break (a bone), snap (in two), split
歯を一本折る *ha o ippon oru* break a tooth
へし折る *heshioru* smash, shatter
② fold
折り重ねる *orikasaneru* fold back [up]
折り紙 *origami* folded paper; the art of paper folding
③ bend, turn back
折り曲げる *orimageru* bend, double, turn up [down]
折り返し運転 *orikaeshi unten* shuttle service
④ yield, give in
折り合い *oriai* mutual relations; compromise
⑤ break off, quit
筆を折る *fude o oru* break off writing

【ori 折, o(ri) 折り】

① occasion, time, chance, opportunity
折折 *oriori* sometimes, occasionally, once in a while
折悪しくして *oriashiku shite* inopportunely, unseasonably
折りに触れて *ori ni furete* on opportunity, occasionally
時折 *tokiori* sometimes, occasionally
② small wooden box
折り箱 *oribako* small wooden box
折り詰め *orizume* food packed in a small wooden box
菓子折り *kashiori* box of cakes

【-o(ri) -折り】

① counter for number of foldings
二つ折り判の本 *futatsuoriban no hon* books in folio
② counter for small boxes of food
寿司一折り *sushi hitoori* a box of sushi

【o(reru) 折れる】 *vi* break, snap; be folded, be doubled; turn (to the right or left); give in, yield
ぽきんと折れる *pokinto oreru* snap, break with a snap
折れ目 *oreme* crease, fold
折れ曲がる *oremagaru* be folded
左に折れる *hidari ni oreru* turn to the left
折れ合う *oreau* make concessions, come to an agreement

SYNONYMS

❶ⓐ break
破 BREAK → 1150
壊 BREAK DOWN → 756
割る crack → 1816
裂 SPLIT → 2687
砕 CRUSH UP → 1134
崩 CRUMBLE → 2296

❷ &【oru】② fold
畳む FOLD UP → 2592

❸ &【oru】③ bend
屈 BEND → 3079
曲 CURVE → 3527

【ori】

① occasions
際 OCCASION → 714
時 timely occasion → 924
機 OPPORTUNITY → 1076
節 time → 2691

USAGE

oru

折る
① (separate through the application of a sudden bending force) break off (as a branch), break (a bone), snap (in two), split
② fold
③ bend, turn back
④ yield, give in
⑤ break off, quit

織る
weave

HOMOPHONES

oru ⇨ 織 1422

COMPOUND FORMATION

❶ 折衝 *sesshō*
折衝 'negotiation, parley' originally referred to breaking (折 ❶ⓑ) the brunt of an enemy attack (衝), but now refers to settling a dispute by negotiation.

❷ 折角 *sekkaku*
折角 'with much trouble; specially' originally referred to folding (折 ❷) the corners (角) of one's hood in ancient China. How it acquired its current meaning is not clear.

NOTE

★do not confuse with 析 862

抄 抄 抄

254 SHŌ

CH 抄 chāo

Radical	Strokes
扌 64	7-3-4
Grade	**Freq**
Jōyō	1825
1 - 3 - 4	

3-4 扌

▶**EXCERPT**

COMPOUNDS

❶ⓐ **excerpt, extract, abridge, select**
ⓑ [also suffix] **excerpt, selection, summary, abridgment**
抄出する *shōshutsu suru* take excerpts
抄録 *shōroku* quotation, summary
抄訳 *shōyaku* abridged translation
抄本 *shōhon* extract, abstract
平家物語抄 *heikemonogatarishō* Abridged Version of the Historic Romance of the Taira Family
❷ⓐ annotate, append notes
ⓑ [suffix] annotation, commentary
抄物 *shōmono* (=*shōmotsu*) commentary
史記抄 *shikishō* Commentary on Shiki
❸ copy, transcribe
手抄 *shushō* manual copying; excerption; excerpt
❹ manufacture paper
抄紙 *shōshi* paper making

INDEPENDENT

【shō 抄】 excerpt
【shōsuru 抄する】 excerpt, quote

SYNONYMS

❶ⓐ **abridge**
要 SUMMARIZE → 2635
約 CONTRACT → 1280
略 omit → 1169

択 擇 択 擇

255 TAKU

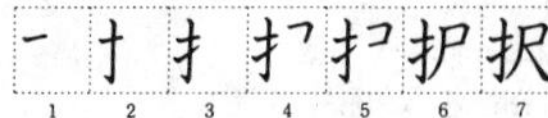

CH 择 zé zhái

Radical	Strokes
扌 64	7-3-4
Grade	**Freq**
Jōyō	1314
1 - 3 - 4	

3-4 扌

▶**SELECT**

COMPOUNDS

● [original meaning] **select, choose, pick out**
選択する *sentaku suru* select, choose
採択する *saitaku suru* adopt, select
二者択一 *nisha-takuitsu* choosing an alternative

SYNONYMS

● **choose**
選 CHOOSE → 3169
採 PICK → 499
摘 pick out → 694
抜 single out → 246

投 投 投

256 TŌ na(geru) -na(ge)

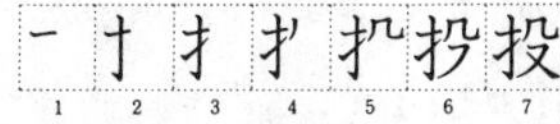

CH 投 tóu

Radical	Strokes
扌 64	7-3-4
Grade	**Freq**
Jōyō-3	227
1 - 3 - 4	

3-4 扌

▶**THROW** ▶**SEND IN**

COMPOUNDS

❶ⓐ [original meaning] **throw, cast, throw down**
ⓑ throwing, throw
ⓒ throw oneself into (a river, etc. to commit suicide)
ⓓ *baseball* **pitch, pitching**
投下 *tōka* throwing down, dropping, airdrop; investment
投棄する *tōki suru* abandon, give up, throw away
投石 *tōseki* throwing stones
投擲する *tōteki suru* throw

第一投 *daiittō* first throw
投身 *tōshin* suicide by drowning or jumping from a high place
投手 *tōshu* pitcher
投球 *tōkyū* throwing a ball, pitching
投打 *tōda* pitching and batting
力投 *rikitō* all-out pitching
好投 *kōtō* good [nice] pitching
完投する *kantō suru* pitch a whole game
❷ abbrev. of 投手 *tōshu*: pitcher
投飛 *tōhi* pitcher's fly
❸ project (an image), cast
投影 *tōei* cast shadow; projection
❹ⓐ **send in [to], submit, deliver**
ⓑ submit oneself, surrender
投書 *tōsho* contribution, letter (from a reader)
投稿 *tōkō* contribution (to a magazine)
投票する *tōhyō suru* vote, cast a ballot
投資 *tōshi* investment
投入する *tōnyū suru* invest; throw into
投降する *tōkō suru* surrender (to the enemy)
❺ prescribe (medicine)
投薬 *tōyaku* prescription, medication
投与する *tōyo suru* prescribe medicine, administer (medicine)
❻ fit in with, agree with, be suited to the occasion
投合 *tōgō* agreement, coincidence
投機 *tōki* speculation, venture
❼ stay over, stop over
投宿する *tōshuku suru* put up at a hotel

INDEPENDENT

【**tō 投**】 pitching strength
投に優る *tō ni masaru* surpass in pitching strength
【**tōjiru (=tōzuru) 投じる(=投ずる)**】 throw, cast, pitch; send in [to]; launch into, join; invest, spend on; catch on, hit, seize on the situation

KUN

【**na(geru) 投げる**】 throw, cast, pitch; throw [give] up, abandon; sell at a loss
投げ *nage* throw, throwing; giving up; shake-out
投げ飛ばす *nagetobasu* fling away
身投げ *minage* suicide by drowning or jumping from a high place
投げ出す *nagedasu* throw out; throw [give] up, abandon, leave off
投げ売り *nageuri* bargain [sacrifice] sale
【**-na(ge) -投げ**】 [also suffix] *sports* throw, throwing
ハンマー投げ *hanmānage* hammer throw
背負い投げ *seoinage* back throw
上手投げ *uwatenage sumo* trick of throwing the opponent over oneself; *baseball* overhand throw

SPECIAL READINGS

投網 *toami* casting net

SYNONYMS

❶ⓐ **throw**
放 toss → 853
❹ⓐ **send**
送 SEND → 3093
回 send round → 3055
遣 DISPATCH → 3152
派 DISPATCH → 381

3-4
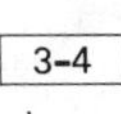

抑 257

YOKU osa(eru)

CH 抑 yì

Radical	Strokes
扌 64	7-3-4
Grade	**Freq**
Jōyō	1305
1-3-4	

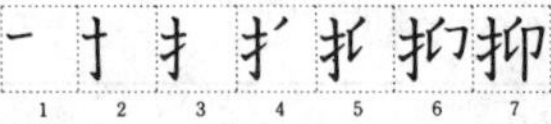

▶**SUPPRESS**

COMPOUNDS

❶ⓐ (hold down) **suppress, repress, restrain**
ⓑ (put down forcibly) suppress, bring under control
抑制する *yokusei suru* control, suppress, inhibit
抑止する *yokushi suru* deter, check, hold back
抑留 *yokuryū* detainment, detention, internment, arrest
抑圧する *yokuatsu suru* oppress, repress, suppress
抑鬱 *yokuutsu* depression, dejection
❷ lower, tone down
抑揚 *yokuyō* rising and falling (of tones), intonation

KUN

【**osa(eru) 抑える**】
①ⓐ (hold down) suppress, repress, restrain, control, hold down; check, curb, stop; keep back, withhold
ⓑ (put down forcibly) suppress, subdue, bring under control
抑え *osae* check, defense, suppression; control
抑え難い *osaegatai* irrepressible, uncontrollable

反乱を抑える *hanran o osaeru* stifle a rebellion
② catch, arrest
警官に抑えられる *keikan ni osaerareru* be caught by a policeman

SYNONYMS

❶ⓐ **restrain**
制 CONTROL (restrain) → 1274
禁 PROHIBIT → 2795
限 LIMIT → 398
束 TIE UP → 3554
縛 BIND → 1405
控える HOLD BACK → 495
渋る hang [hold] back → 513

HOMOPHONES

osaeru ⇨ 押 314
osae ⇨ 押 314

NOTE

⇨ see USAGE note at 押 314

258

▶SKILL
nonstandard for 技 248

3-4 扌

扱
259

▶HANDLE
nonstandard for 扱 217

3-4 扌

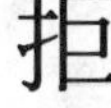

incorrect stroke count ⇨ see 311

3-4 扌

扱

incorrect stroke count ⇨ see 217

3-4 扌

没 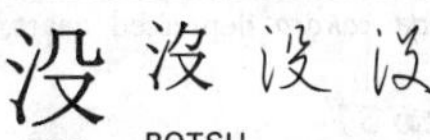
260 BOTSU

CH 没 méi mò

Radical	Strokes
氵 85	7-3-4
Grade	**Freq**
Jōyō	1430
1 - 3 - 4	

3-4 氵

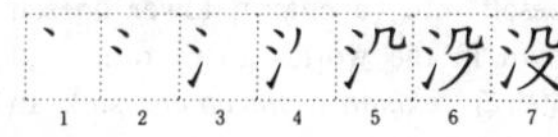
1 2 3 4 5 6 7

▶SINK

COMPOUNDS

❶ⓐ [original meaning] **sink into the water, submerge; sink below the horizon**
ⓑ **sink into the ground, subside, fall in**
水没する *suibotsu suru* sink, submerge
沈没する *chinbotsu suru* sink, go to the bottom
日没 *nichibotsu* sunset
埋没する *maibotsu suru* be buried; fall into oblivion
陥没する *kanbotsu suru* sink, fall, cave in
❷ⓐ disappear, vanish, go out of sight, hide
ⓑ make disappear, hide, efface
出没する *shutsubotsu suru* make frequent appearances; haunt
没却する *bokkyaku suru* discard and ignore, lose sight of (an objective)
没我 *botsuga* selflessness
❸ be sunk in thought, become absorbed in
没頭する *bottō suru* be absorbed in
没入する *botsunyū suru* be immersed in (one's work), be absorbed in
❹ [formerly also 歿 868] **die, perish**
没後 *botsugo* after one's death
没年 *botsunen* year of death
戦没する *senbotsu suru* be killed in action
❺ [prefix] lacking in, not, un-
没常識 *botsujōshiki* lack of common sense
没個性 *botsukosei* lack of individuality
❻ reject, discard
没書 *bossho* rejected manuscript
❼ confiscate
没収 *bosshū* confiscation, seizure, forfeiture

INDEPENDENT

【botsu 没】 rejected manuscript; [formerly also 歿 *botsu*] indicates date of death
没にする *botsu ni suru* reject (a manuscript), turn down (a proposal)
昭和三年没 *shōwa sannen botsu* died 1928
【bossuru 没する】 sink, be immersed in; sink below the horizon; disappear, hide; ignore

(someone's merits); reject; confiscate; [formerly also 歿する *bossuru*] die

SYNONYMS

❶ⓐ sink
沈 SINK → 261
潜 SUBMERGE → 746
ⓑ collapse
陥 FALL IN → 457
落 FALL → 2318
崩 CRUMBLE → 2296
❷ⓐ disappear
消 disappear → 443
❹ die
死 DIE → 3521
亡 DECEASE → 3402
殉 DIE A MARTYR → 941
去 pass away → 2156
逝 DEPART THIS LIFE → 3104
枯 WITHER → 898
❺ terms of negation
欠 LACK → 1987
無 WITHOUT (nonexistence) → 2135
非 IS NOT (contrariety) → 889
不 NOT (negation) → 3434
否 OR NOT → 2406
未 NOT YET → 3506

NOTE

⇨ see USAGE note at 不 3434

3-4 沈 沈 沈 Ⓒⓗ 沉 chén 沈 shěn
氵
261 CHIN JIN▲ shizu(mu) shizu(meru)

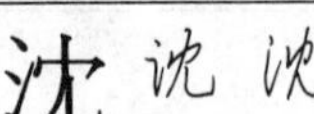

Radical	Strokes
氵 85	7-3-4
Grade	**Freq**
Jōyō	1242
1-3-4	

▶SINK

COMPOUNDS

❶ⓐ sink, submerge, go down
ⓑ [original meaning] **(cause to) sink, submerge**
沈没する *chinbotsu suru* sink, go to the bottom
沈下 *chinka* subsidence, sinking
沈澱 *chinden* precipitation, settlement
沈滞 *chintai* stagnation, dullness
浮沈 *fuchin* rise and fall, ebb and flow; ups and downs
撃沈する *gekichin suru* attack and sink a ship
❷ⓐ be sunk in thought, become absorbed in
ⓑ (sink into depression) **depressed, melancholy**
沈潜する *chinsen suru* sink into deep thought; sink to the depths
沈思 *chinshi* meditation, deep thought
沈鬱な *chin'utsu na* melancholy, gloomy
❸ⓐ quiet, calm, tranquil
ⓑ quiet, still
沈静 *chinsei* stillness, tranquility, slackness
沈着 *chinchaku* composure, self-possession
沈黙 *chinmoku* silence, reticence, taciturnity
❹ kind of aromatic tree
沈丁花 *jinchōge* (=*chinchōge*) (sweet-smelling) daphne

KUN

【shizu(mu) 沈む】 sink, submerge, go down; set; sink into depression, be downcast; be losing (in a game of mahjong)
船が沈んだ *Fune ga shizunda* A ship sank
日が沈む *Hi ga shizumu* The sun sets
沈んだ心 *shizunda kokoro* depressed heart, low spirits

【shizu(meru) 沈める】
ⓐ sink, send to the bottom, submerge
ⓑ sink oneself into (a chair), lower oneself
ⓒ sink down in the world, go to ruin
敵艦を沈める *tekikan o shizumeru* sink an enemy ship
椅子に身を沈める *isu ni mi o shizumeru* sink into a chair
苦界に身を沈める *kugai ni mi o shizumeru* (sink into the brothel) become a prostitute

SYNONYMS

❶ sink
没 SINK → 260
潜 SUBMERGE → 746
❷ⓑ sad and depressed
陰 gloomy → 541
愁 MELANCHOLY → 2829
哀 sorrowful → 2068
悲 SAD → 2775
寂 LONESOME → 2290
惨 MISERABLE → 483

HOMOPHONES

shizumeru ⇨ 鎮 1759 静 1728

NOTE

⇨ see USAGE note at 静 1728

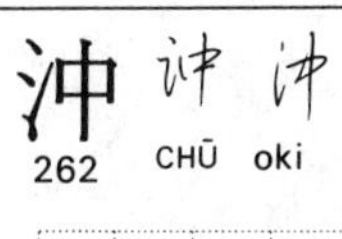

262 CHŪ oki

CH 沖 chōng chòng

Radical	Strokes
氵 85	7-3-4
Grade	**Freq**
Jōyō	762
◧ 1 - 3 - 4	

3-4 氵

▶**OFFING**

COMPOUNDS

❶ rise straight to heaven, soar to the skies
沖天 *chūten* rising to heaven
❷ wash away
沖積層 *chūsekisō* alluvium

INDEPENDENT

【**chūsuru 沖する**】rise straight to heaven

KUN

【**oki 沖**】[also suffix] offing, offshore, open sea
沖合い *okiai* offing, offshore
沖釣り *okizuri* offshore fishing
二キロ沖 *nikirooki* two kilometers offshore

SYNONYMS

【**oki**】
○ **sea**
海 SEA → 384
洋 OCEAN → 392

263 KETSU ki(meru) -gi(me) ki(maru)

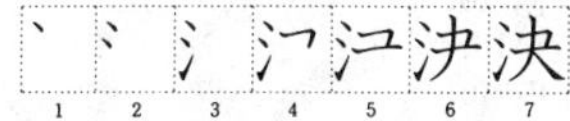

CH 決 jué

Radical	Strokes
氵 85	7-3-4
Grade	**Freq**
Jōyō-3	80
◧ 1 - 3 - 4	

3-4 氵

▶**DECIDE**

COMPOUNDS

❶ⓐ (make up one's mind) **decide, determine, fix**
ⓑ (pronounce judgment) **decide, resolve, settle**
ⓒ decision
決定 *kettei* decision, settlement, conclusion
決意 *ketsui* resolution, determination
決心 *kesshin* determination, resolution, decision
解決 *kaiketsu* solution, settlement
決算 *kessan* settlement of accounts
決勝 *kesshō* decision (of a contest)
決議 *ketsugi* resolution, decision
判決 *hanketsu* judicial decision, judgment, sentence
可決する *kaketsu suru* approve [adopt] a bill
裁決 *saiketsu* decision, ruling
多数決 *tasūketsu* decision by majority
❷ decisively, resolutely
決行 *kekkō* decisive action
決然たる *ketsuzentaru* decisive, resolute, determined
❸ [original meaning] break, burst, rip—said esp. of dikes
決壊 *kekkai* rip, break
決裂 *ketsuretsu* breakdown, rupture
❹ [formerly also 蹶 1643] spring to one's feet, rouse oneself
決起する *kekki suru* rise to action, spring up
❺ [formerly also 訣 1469] separate, part, bid farewell
決別 *ketsubetsu* separation, farewell
❻ [formerly also 訣 1469] secrets (as of an art), knack
秘決 *hiketsu* secret, key

INDEPENDENT

【**ketsu 決**】decision, vote
決を採る *ketsu o toru* take a vote
【**kessuru 決する**】come to a decision, be settled; break, give way (as of dikes)
【**kesshite 決して**】never, by no means, not at all

KUN

【**ki(meru) 決める**】
[sometimes also 極める]
① decide, determine, fix
自分で決める *jibun de kimeru* decide by oneself
② agree upon, arrange
取り決め *torikime* decision, agreement
③ (bring to a conclusion) settle, conclude
決め付ける *kimetsukeru* scold, take (a person) to task
決め手 *kimete* decisive factor, clincher; trump card, winning move
【**-gi(me) -決め**】[usu. -極め] indicates peri-

ods of time (esp. months)
【ki(maru) 決まる】
[sometimes also 極まる]
① be decided [fixed], be settled, be arranged
決まり *kimari* settlement, conclusion; rule, regulation; custom
十五日と決まっている *Jūgonichi to kimatte iru* The date is fixed for the 15th of the month
② be certain [sure], be a matter of course
雨が降るに決まっている *Ame ga furu ni kimatte iru* It is sure to rain
行かないに決まっている *Ikanai ni kimatte iru* Of course I won't go

SYNONYMS
❶ⓐ decide
定 FIX → 2229
断 RESOLVE → 1492
ⓑ judge
判 JUDGE → 1122
裁 JUDGE → 3299
鑑 APPRAISE → 1773
評 evaluate → 1501
審 TRY → 2360
視 REGARD → 972
❷ resolutely
断 resolutely → 1492
敢 BOLDLY → 1706

USAGE
❶ kimeru
決める
[sometimes also 極める]
① decide, determine, fix
② agree upon, arrange
③ (bring to a conclusion) settle, conclude
極める
[usu. 決める] same as 決める
❷ -gime
-決め
[usu. -極め] indicates periods of time (esp. months)
-極め
[sometimes also -決め] same as -決め
❸ kimaru
決まる
[sometimes also 極まる]
① be decided [fixed], be settled, be arranged
② be certain [sure], be a matter of course
極まる
[usu. 決まる] same as 決まる

HOMOPHONES
kimeru ⇨ 極 1017
-gime ⇨ 極 1017
kimaru ⇨ 極 1017

3-4
氵
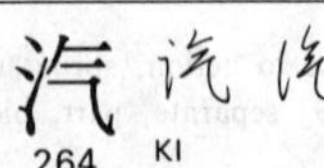
264 KI

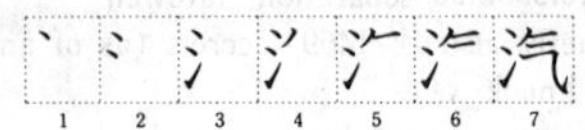

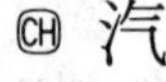
CH 汽 qì

Radical	Strokes
氵 85	7-3-4
Grade	**Freq**
Jōyō-2	1641

1 - 3 - 4

▶STEAM

COMPOUNDS
● steam, vapor
汽車 *kisha* (steam) train
汽船 *kisen* steamship
汽圧 *kiatsu* steam pressure
汽罐 *kikan* boiler
汽笛 *kiteki* steam whistle
汽水 *kisui* brackish water

SYNONYMS
● gas and vapor
気 GAS → 3194
空 AIR → 2227
● kinds of water
湯 HOT WATER → 612
水 WATER → 10
氷 ICE → 39

汲

265 KYŪ ku(mu)

Ⓒⓗ 汲 jí

Radical	Strokes
氵 85	7-3-4
Grade	**Freq**
Reference	
◧ 1 - 3 - 4	

3-4 氵

COMPOUNDS

❶ [original meaning] draw (water), scoop up, ladle, pump

汲汲としている *kyūkyū to shite iru* think only of, be absorbed in

汲み取る *kumitoru* draw up; take into consideration

汲み立ての *kumitate no* freshly drawn

汲み干す *kumihosu* drain out, pump dry

水汲み *mizukumi* drawing water

❷ consider, sympathize with

意を汲む *i o kumu* enter into a person's feelings

HOMOPHONES

kumu ⇨ 酌 1461

NOTE

⇨ see USAGE note at 酌 1461

沙

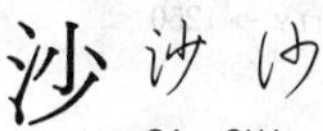

266 SA SHA

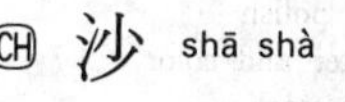

Radical	Strokes
氵 85	7-3-4
Grade	**Freq**
Names	2083
◧ 1 - 3 - 4	

3-4 氵

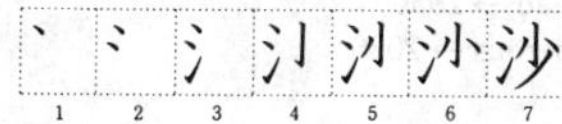

▶SAND

COMPOUNDS

❶ [now usu. 砂 *sa* 1133]

ⓐ [original meaning] **sand (of granular constitution), tiny gravel or pebbles**

ⓑ **sandy plain, the sands**

沙丘 *sakyū* sand dune, sand hill

沙漠 *sabaku* desert

❷ wash, sift, sort

沙汰 *sata* instructions; notice, tidings, rumor; affair

御無沙汰しております *Gobusata shite orimasu* I haven't seen you for a long time

❸ used phonetically for *sha*, esp. in the transliteration of Sanscrit Buddhist terms

沙弥 *shami* Buddhist novice, *śrāmaṇera*|

沙門 *shamon* wandering Buddhist monk

沙翁 *saō* Shakespeare

NAMES

美沙子 *misako* female name

SYNONYMS

❶ⓐ **sand**

砂 SAND (fine) → 1133

❸ **phonetic** [s]/[sh]

遮 phonetic [sha] → 3158

世 phonetic [se] → 3496

須 phonetic [shu] → 574

修 phonetic [shu] → 123

西 phonetic [su] → 3520

相 phonetic [sō] → 900

COMPOUND FORMATION

沙汰 *sata*

沙汰 'instructions, etc.' originally meant to sift out (沙 ❷) impurities from rice by washing (汰), and was extended to mean distinguishing between good and evil. When a superior makes a judgment to determine good or evil, he informs or instructs his subordinates to that effect. By this roundabout logic, 沙汰 came to mean instructions or tidings, giving rise to the expression 御無沙汰しております *gobusata shite orimasu*, literally "I have not (無) presented you with my humble (御) tidings (沙汰) or greetings," i.e., I have not seen you for a long time.

3-4 氵

沢 澤 沢 沢

267 TAKU sawa

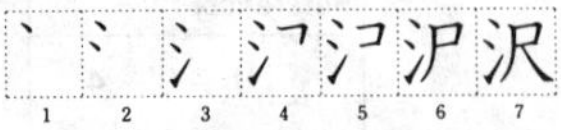

CH 泽 zé

Radical	Strokes
氵 85	7-3-4
Grade	**Freq**
Jōyō	417
1 - 3 - 4	

▶**MARSH**

COMPOUNDS

❶ [original meaning] **marsh, swamp**
沼沢 *shōtaku* marsh, swamp
❷ **plentiful, abundant**
沢山 *takusan* large quantity, plenty, abundance
潤沢 *juntaku* abundance, plenty
贅沢 *zeitaku* luxury, extravagance
❸ luster, gloss, brightness
光沢 *kōtaku* luster, gloss, polish
色沢 *shikitaku* [rare] luster and color
❹ favor, benefit, grace, blessing
恩沢 *ontaku* favor, benefit
徳沢 *tokutaku* grace, blessing
余沢 *yotaku* blessings, benefits

KUN

【**sawa** 沢】 marsh, swamp; valley, dale
沢辺 *sawabe* edge of a swamp
沢地 *sawachi* marshy land
一ノ倉沢 *ichinokurasawa* Ichinokura Valley

SYNONYMS

❶ **lakes and marshes**
沼 MUDDY POND → 339
湖 LAKE → 604
池 POND → 218
潟 LAGOON → 745
❷ **many**
豊 PLENTIFUL → 2697
穣 YIELDING ABUNDANTLY → 1250
裕 ABUNDANT → 1195
富 RICH → 2310
多 MANY → 2170
万 myriad → 2936
百 numerous → 2026
❸ **luster**
艶 gloss → 1908

3-4 氵

没

268

▶**SINK**
nonstandard for 没 260

3-4 氵

汚

incorrect stroke count ⇨ see 222

3-4 氵

注

incorrect stroke count ⇨ see 342
(nonstandard for 注 325)

3-4 犭

狂 狂 狂

269 KYŌ kuru(u) kuru(oshii)

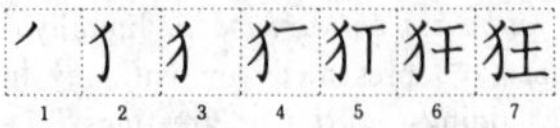

CH 狂 kuáng

Radical	Strokes
犭 94	7-3-4
Grade	**Freq**
Jōyō	1353
1 - 3 - 4	

▶**CRAZY**

COMPOUNDS

❶ [original meaning] **crazy, mad, insane**
狂気の *kyōki no* insane, mad, crazy
狂人 *kyōjin* lunatic, maniac
狂犬病 *kyōkenbyō* rabies
狂的な *kyōteki na* insane, fanatic
発狂する *hakkyō suru* go mad, become insane [crazy]
❷ [suffix] (enthusiastic fan) **maniac, fanatic, fan, enthusiast**
殺人狂 *satsujinkyō* homicidal maniac
映画狂 *eigakyō* cinema enthusiast, movie fan
窃盗狂 *settōkyō* kleptomaniac
偏執狂 *henshitsukyō* (=*henshūkyō*) monomaniac

❸ raging, wild, furious
狂奔する *kyōhon suru* rush around, run madly about, run wild; make frantic efforts, be very busy (in)
狂喜 *kyōki* wild joy, ecstasy
❹ comical, funny, jocular, humorous
狂言 *kyōgen* noh farce, comic interlude in a noh drama; kabuki play; sham, put-up job
狂歌 *kyōka* comic [satirical] tanka

KUN

【kuru(u) 狂う】 become insane [crazy], go mad; become crazy about (someone); go wild, rave; get out of order, be upset; warp, get warped
狂い死に *kuruijini* death in madness
女に狂う *onna ni kuruu* run mad after a girl
荒れ狂う風 *arekuruu kaze* raving wind
時計が狂っている *Tokei ga kurutte iru* My watch is not right
番狂わせ *bankuruwase* upsetting of arrangements, upset, surprise
狂い *kurui* warp, deviation; aberration

【kuru(oshii) 狂おしい】 driving mad, distracting; bordering on insanity
狂おしい思い *kuruoshii omoi* maddening thought

SYNONYMS

❷ **mania and maniacs**
魔 maniac → 3187
痴 infatuated → 3286
熱 fever → 2866
❸ **extreme in power**
激 VIOLENT → 776
荒 WILD → 2260
烈 VEHEMENT → 2652
猛 FIERCE → 537

NOTE

⇨ see COMPOUND FORMATION for 偏執狂 *henshitsukyō* (= *henshūkyō*) ⇨ 執 1680

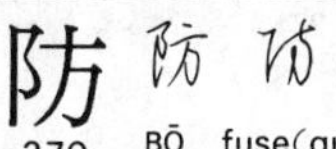

270 BŌ fuse(gu)

Ⓒⓗ 防 fáng

Radical	Strokes
阝 170	7-3-4
Grade	**Freq**
Jōyō-5	292
◧ 1 - 3 - 4	

3-4 阝

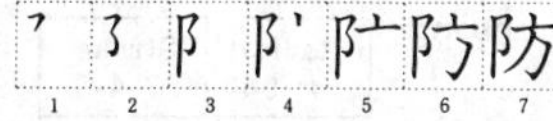

▶**PREVENT**

COMPOUNDS

❶❸ **prevent, hold in check, keep away, shut out**
ⓑ **preventing, -proof, anti-**
防止する *bōshi suru* prevent, hold in check
防除 *bōjo* pest control, extermination
消防 *shōbō* fire fighting, prevention and extinction of fires
予防 *yobō* prevention, protection, precaution
防火 *bōka* fire prevention, fireproof
防水布 *bōsuifu* waterproof cloth
防虫剤 *bōchūzai* insecticide, vermicide
防腐剤 *bōfuzai* antiseptic
❷❸ **defend, guard against, protect, resist**
ⓑ **defense**
防衛する *bōei suru* defend, protect, safeguard, shield
防備 *bōbi* defense, defensive preparations
防御 *bōgyo* defense, protection, safeguard
国防 *kokubō* national defense
❸ [original meaning] dike
堤防 *teibō* bank, embankment, dike
❹ abbrev. of 周防 *suō*, old name for east Yamaguchi Prefecture
防府 *hōfu* Hofu city

INDEPENDENT

【bō 防】 defense, protection

KUN

【fuse(gu) 防ぐ】 [formerly also 禦ぐ] prevent, keep off, ward off; defend, protect, resist
伝染を防ぐ *densen o fusegu* prevent infection
侵略を防ぐ *shinryaku o fusegu* defend against an invasion

SYNONYMS

❶ **prevent**
止 STOP → 2941
❷ **protect**
守 PROTECT → 2173
護 PROTECT → 1648
衛 GUARD → 760
警 GUARD AGAINST → 2893
番 WATCH → 2748
保 PRESERVE → 96
看 CARE FOR → 3220
❸ **embankment**
堤 EMBANKMENT → 560

USAGE

fusegu
防ぐ
[formerly also 禦ぐ] prevent, keep off, ward off; defend, protect, resist
禦ぐ
[now usu. 防ぐ] same as 防ぐ

HOMOPHONES

fusegu ⇨ 禦 2870

3-4 阝

阪 阪 阪

271 HAN saka

(stroke order: 1–7)

CH 阪 bǎn

Radical	Strokes
阝 170	7-3-4
Grade	**Freq**
Non-Jōyō	397

1 - 3 - 4

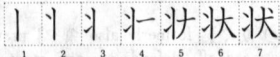

▶OSAKA

COMPOUNDS

❶ **Osaka**

阪神 *hanshin* Hanshin, Osaka and Kobe
阪大 *handai* Osaka University
阪急デパート *hankyū depāto* Hankyu Department Store
来阪する *raihan suru* come to Osaka

❷ [original meaning] slope, incline, hill

KUN

【saka 阪】 slope, incline, hill—now used almost exclusively in the writing of names
大阪 *ōsaka* Osaka

SYNONYMS

❶ **Kansai cities**

神 Kobe → 912
京 KYOTO → 2052

❷ **hills**

坂 SLOPE → 234
丘 HILL → 3495
岡 HILL → 2997
台 heights → 2005
塚 MOUND → 556
陵 high mound → 544

HOMOPHONES

saka ⇨ 坂 234

NOTE

⇨ see USAGE note at 坂 234

3-4 丬

状 状 状 状

272 JŌ

(stroke order: 1–7)

CH 状 zhuàng

Radical	Strokes
犬 94	7-4-3
Grade	**Freq**
Jōyō-5	365

1 - 3 - 4

▶FORM ▶CONDITION ▶LETTER

COMPOUNDS

❶ⓐ [original meaning] **(external) form, shape, appearance**

ⓑ [also suffix] **-form, in the form of, -shaped, -like**

形状 *keijō* shape, form, configuration
環状の *kanjō no* ring-shaped, circular
波状 *hajō* wave, undulation
球状 *kyūjō* shape of a globe, globular shape
帯状の *obijō* (=*taijō*) *no* belt-shaped
ガス状の *gasujō no* gaseous, gasiform
液状の *ekijō no* liquefied

❷ **(actual) condition, state, situation, circumstances**

状態 *jōtai* state, condition, appearance, situation, aspect
状況 *jōkyō* state of affairs, conditions, circumstances
現状 *genjō* present condition
商状 *shōjō* market condition
症状 *shōjō* symptom
病状 *byōjō* condition of a disease [patient]
罪状 *zaijō* offense, charges

❸ [also suffix]

ⓐ **letter, note, card**

ⓑ **official document [paper], official letter, certificate, warrant**

書状 *shojō* letter, note
賞状 *shōjō* certificate of merit
招待状 *shōtaijō* letter of invitation
年賀状 *nengajō* New Year's card
公開状 *kōkaijō* open letter
信任状 *shinninjō* credentials, letter of credence
免状 *menjō* license, diploma
令状 *reijō* warrant, writ
遺言状 *yuigonjō* will, testament

❹ describe, narrate

白状 *hakujō* confession
名状する *meijō suru* describe

INDEPENDENT

【jō 状】 condition, state; letter, epistle
この状持参の者 *kono jō jisan no mono* the person bearing this letter

SYNONYMS

❶ **form**

体 FORM (characteristic) → 71

形 SHAPE → 846
姿 FIGURE → 2636
❷ **states and situations**
況 CONDITIONS → 337
景 business conditions → 2470
態 STATE → 2847
勢 course of events → 2857
境 SITUATION → 676
局 current situation → 3063
情 ACTUAL CONDITIONS → 482
訳 circumstances → 1473
調 TONE → 1567

様 MODE → 1052
相 PHASE → 900
❸ⓐ **written communications**
文 LETTER → 1962
書 letter → 2658
信 written communication → 100
電 telegram → 2790
ⓑ **certificates**
証 CERTIFICATE → 1506
券 CERTIFICATE → 2630
免 license → 2067

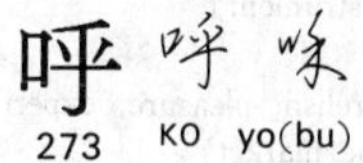

273 KO yo(bu)

1 2 3 4 5 6 7 8

Ⓒⓗ 呼 hū

Radical	Strokes
口 30	8-3-5
Grade	**Freq**
Jōyō-6	580
1 - 3 - 5	

3-5 口

▶**CALL**

COMPOUNDS

❶ (cry out in a loud voice) **call, call out to**
呼応する *koō suru* hail to each other, act in concert
呼号する *kogō suru* cry out, proclaim
指呼する *shiko suru* beckon
点呼 *tenko* roll call
歓呼する *kanko suru* cheer, cry out
❷ (attach a name to) call, name
呼称する *koshō suru* call, name
称呼 *shōko* appellation, designation
❸ [original meaning] **breathe out, exhale**
呼吸する *kokyū suru* breathe, respire
呼気 *koki* exhalation

KUN

【yo(bu) 呼ぶ】
①ⓐ (cry out) call, call out to
ⓑ (summon) call, send for, invite
呼び掛ける *yobikakeru* call to; appeal to
呼び出し *yobidashi* call, calling out, summons
呼び寄せる *yobiyoseru* call, summon, send for, call together
医者を呼ぶ *isha o yobu* call the doctor
② call, give a name to
呼び名 *yobina* given name, popular name
③ bring about, give rise to
呼び起こす *yobiokosu* awake, arise; call to mind

SYNONYMS

❶ **shout**
喚 call out → 550
喝 SHOUT AT → 461
号 holler → 2153
叫 SHOUT → 201
鳴 CRY → 674
❷ **name**
言う call → 1941
称 name → 1160
❸ **breathe and blow**
吹 BLOW → 231
吸 BREATHE IN → 202
息 BREATH → 2647
気 breath → 3194
【yobu】
①ⓑ **call and invite**
喚 CALL → 550
召 SUMMON → 2001
招 INVITE → 316

3-5

口

味 味 味

274 MI aji aji(wau)

丨 ㄇ 口 口一 口二 口+ 味 味
1 2 3 4 5 6 7 8

Ⓒ 味 wèi

Radical	Strokes
口 30	8-3-5
Grade	**Freq**
Jōyō-3	341
1-3-5	

▶**TASTE**

COMPOUNDS

❶ **taste, flavor**
味覚 *mikaku* sense of taste
調味 *chōmi* seasoning, flavoring
風味 *fūmi* flavor, taste

❷ⓐ (quality of attracting interest) **taste, interest, flavor, charm, beauty**
ⓑ **taste, savor, appreciate, enjoy**
趣味 *shumi* hobby, interest, taste
興味 *kyōmi* interest
妙味 *myōmi* subtle charm, beauty
味読する *midoku suru* appreciate a book
吟味 *ginmi* close examination, scrutiny

❸ⓐ suffix attached to the stem of adjectives or words inflected like adjectives: a dash of, a flavor, a touch, a tinge
ⓑ suffix of nominalization like −さ *-sa* or *−ness*
赤味 *akami* a tinge of red
滑稽味が有る *kokkeimi ga aru* tinged with humor
深味 *fukami* depth, profundity
嫌味 *iyami* disagreeableness

❹ⓐ tasty food, nourishment; condiments
ⓑ counter for foods or condiments
味噌 *miso miso*, bean paste; flattery
滋味 *jimi* savoriness; rich food, nourishment
七味 *shichimi shichimi* (a kind of spice)

❺ **contents, substance; meaning**
正味の *shōmi no* net, full, clear
意味 *imi* meaning, intention, significance, purport

❻ feeling, sensation
気味 *kimi* feeling, sensation; a touch [tinge] (of)
地味な *jimi na* plain, sober, unpretentious

❼ companion, fellow, mate
味方 *mikata* friend, ally, one's side
一味 *ichimi* fellow conspirators, gang

❽ used phonetically for *mi*
三味線 *shamisen* shamisen (Japanese three-stringed musical instrument)

KUN

【aji 味】 taste, flavor; relish, pleasure; experience; sentiment (of the market)
味な *aji na* clever, witty, strange
味付け *ajitsuke* seasoning
後味 *atoaji* aftertaste
味気無い *ajikenai* (=*ajikinai*) wearisome, insipid
文学の味 *bungaku no aji* the pleasures of literature
女の味を知る *onna no aji o shiru* have carnal knowledge (of a woman)
場味 *baaji* market sentiment

【aji(wau) 味わう】 taste, savor; appreciate, enjoy
味わい *ajiwai* taste, flavor
味わい知る *ajiwaishiru* taste and know
読書の面白味を味わう *dokusho no omoshiromi o ajiwau* appreciate the pleasures of reading

SYNONYMS

❷ⓐ **flavor and elegance**
趣 FLAVOR → 3317
風 elegance → 3007
品 refinement → 2248

❺ **essential content**
実 substance → 2225
体 substance → 71

COMPOUND FORMATION

正味 *shōmi*
正味の 'net, full, clear' refers to the correct (正) content (味 ❺), i.e., the net amount, as in 正味重量 *shōmi-jūryō* 'net weight'.

坪

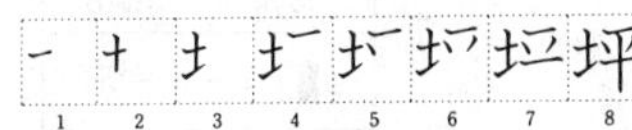

275 HEI▲ tsubo

CH 坪 píng

Radical	Strokes
土 32	8-3-5
Grade	Freq
Jōyō	1552
1-3-5	

3-5 土

▶TSUBO

COMPOUNDS

● [original meaning, now obsolete] level ground

KUN

【tsubo 坪】

tsubo:

ⓐ unit of sq. measure equiv. to approx. 3.3 sq.m or 36 sq. *shaku* (尺), used esp. for measuring land area

ⓑ unit of cubic measure equiv. to approx. 6000 liters or 216 cubic *shaku* (尺), used esp. for measuring earth

十坪 *totsubo* 10 *tsubo*

建て坪 *tatetsubo* floor space

SYNONYMS

【tsubo】

ⓐ **area units**

歩 *bu* (3.3 sq.m) → 2416

畝 *SE* (0.99 ares) → 1465

反 *tan* (9.9 ares) → 2945

町 *cho* (99.2 ares) → 1113

坪

276

▶TSUBO

nonstandard for 坪 275

3-5 土

姆

277 BO uba

CH 姆 mǔ

Radical	Strokes
女 38	8-3-5
Grade	Freq
Reference	
1-3-5	

3-5 女

COMPOUNDS

● [now replaced by 母 *bo* 3475] wet nurse, amah

保姆 *hobo* nurse, kindergarten teacher

妹

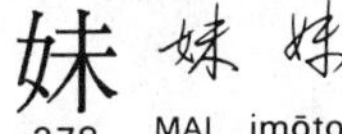

278 MAI imōto

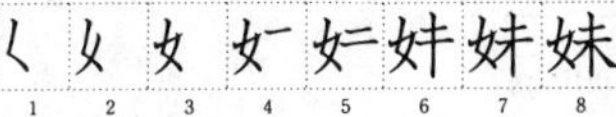

CH 妹 mèi

Radical	Strokes
女 38	8-3-5
Grade	Freq
Jōyō-2	1204
1-3-5	

3-5 女

▶YOUNGER SISTER

COMPOUNDS

● [original meaning] **younger sister**

姉妹 *shimai* (=*kyōdai*) sisters

義妹 *gimai* sister-in-law

弟妹 *teimai* younger brothers and sisters

実妹 *jitsumai* one's true (younger) sister

令妹 *reimai* your younger sister

KUN

【imōto 妹】 younger sister

妹娘 *imōtomusume* younger daughter

妹分 *imōtobun* protégée

SYNONYMS

● **siblings**

姉 OLDER SISTER → 280

兄 OLDER BROTHER → 2154

弟 YOUNGER BROTHER → 2044

3-5 女

姓 姓 姓

279 SEI SHŌ

㇛ 𡿨 女 女 女 妌 姓 姓 姓
1 2 3 4 5 6 7 8

㊥ 姓 xìng

Radical	Strokes
女 38	8-3-5
Grade	**Freq**
Jōyō	1648
1 - 3 - 5	

▶SURNAME

COMPOUNDS

❶ⓐ **surname, family name**
ⓑ surname conferred by emperor in ancient times
姓名 *seimei* full name
同姓 *dōsei* same surname
旧姓 *kyūsei* one's former name, née
改姓する *kaisei suru* change one's family name
百姓 *hyakushō* farmer, peasant
氏姓制度 *shisei seido* former naming system

❷ clan, cast
四姓 *shisei* the four castes (of India)
百姓 *hyakusei* common people

INDEPENDENT

【sei 姓】 surname, family name
姓が変わる *sei ga kawaru* assume a new surname

SYNONYMS

❶ **name**
氏 FAMILY NAME → 2951
名 NAME → 2169
称 APPELLATION → 1160
題 TITLE → 3337
銘 name (inscribed by maker) → 1724
号 DESIGNATION → 2153

COMPOUND FORMATION

百姓 *hyakushō*
百姓 'farmer, peasant' originally meant 100 (百) surnames (姓 ❶ⓐ), i.e., the masses or peasantry.

3-5 女

姉 姉° 姉 姉

280 SHI ane

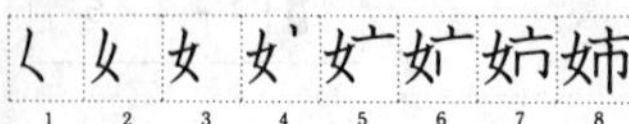

㊥ 姊 zǐ

Radical	Strokes
女 38	8-3-5
Grade	**Freq**
Jōyō-2	1360
1 - 3 - 5	

▶OLDER SISTER

COMPOUNDS

❶ **older sister**
姉妹 *shimai* (=*kyōdai*) sisters
実姉 *jisshi* one's true (older) sister
義姉 *gishi* older sister-in-law
令姉 *reishi* your older sister
同母姉 *dōboshi* uterine sisters, sisters of the same mother

❷ title of respect for female peers or seniors
諸姉 *shoshi* you (feminine plural), you ladies
貴姉 *kishi* term of respect in addressing ladies or another's older sister

KUN

【ane 姉】 older sister
姉上 *aneue* older sister

SPECIAL READINGS

姉さん *nēsan* older sister; waitress, girl; miss

SYNONYMS

❶ **siblings**
妹 YOUNGER SISTER → 278
兄 OLDER BROTHER → 2154
弟 YOUNGER BROTHER → 2044

3-5 女

始 281

SHI haji(meru) -haji(meru) haji(maru)

CH 始 shǐ

Radical	Strokes
女 38	8-3-5
Grade	Freq
Jōyō-3	437
1 - 3 - 5	

▶**BEGIN**

COMPOUNDS

❶ **begin, start, open**

始動 *shidō* starting (machines)

始業式 *shigyōshiki* opening ceremony of the school term

開始する *kaishi suru* begin, commence, open

創始する *sōshi suru* initiate, create, found

❷ⓐ **beginning, inception, start, origin**

ⓑ (source of something) beginning, origin; first, starting

始末する *shimatsu suru* manage, deal with, dispose of; put in order

年始 *nenshi* beginning of the year; New Year's greetings

終始 *shūshi* from beginning to end, always

原始的な *genshiteki na* primitive, primeval

始発 *shihatsu* first departure; starting station

KUN

【haji(meru) 始める】 *vt* begin, open, start, originate; set about, embark on

始め *hajime* (act or point of commencement) beginning, start; (source) beginning, origin

始めて *hajimete* begin and... (TE-form of 始める *hajimeru*)

手始め *tehajime* beginning, start, outset

御用始め *goyōhajime* resumption of office business after the New Year recess

【-haji(meru) -始める】 [verbal suffix] begin to perform an action

雨が降り始めた *Ame ga furihajimeta* It has begun to rain

勉強し始める *benkyō shihajimeru* begin to study

【haji(maru) 始まる】 *vi* begin, commence, start, open; originate; arise, break out

始まり *hajimari* beginning

始まらない *Hajimaranai* It's no use

SYNONYMS

❶ **begin**

-出す begin to do → 3498

-掛ける start doing → 493

発 START → 2565

起 start → 3307

就 SET ABOUT → 1694

開 OPEN → 3321

創 initiate → 1815

肇 ORIGINATE → 2799

❷ **beginnings**

初 beginning → 1116

緒 OUTSET → 1378

序 INTRODUCTORY PART → 3065

端 start → 1221

元 ORIGIN → 1929

本 origin → 3502

根 ROOT → 930

源 SOURCE → 656

HOMOPHONES

hajime ⇨ 初 1116

hajimete ⇨ 初 1116 甫 3549

COMPOUND FORMATION

始末 *shimatsu*

始末する 'manage, deal with, etc.' is to deal with something from beginning (始 ❷ⓐ) to end (末).

NOTE

⇨ see USAGE note at 初 1116

姉 282

3-5 女

▶**OLDER SISTER**

nonstandard for 姉 280

孤 283

3-5 子

▶**SOLITARY**

nonstandard for 孤 356

3-5
山

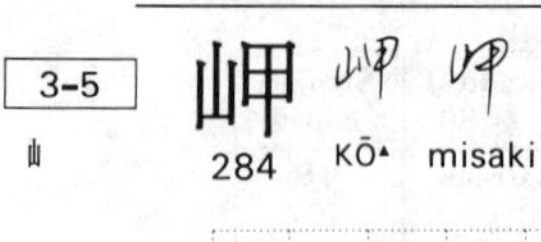

284 KŌ▲ misaki

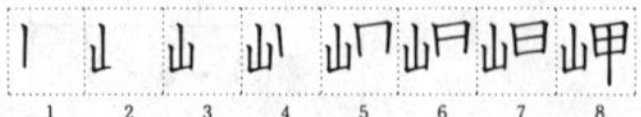

Ⓒ 岬 jiǎ

Radical	Strokes
山 46	8-3-5
Grade	**Freq**
Jōyō	1714
◧ 1 - 3 - 5	

▶**CAPE**

COMPOUNDS

❶ **cape, promontory**

岬角 *kōkaku* [rare] promontory; *anat* promontory

❷ [original meaning, now archaic] ravine, glen

KUN

【**misaki** 岬】

ⓐ cape, promontory, headland

ⓑ suffix after names of capes

潮岬 *shionomisaki* Cape Shio

三浦岬 *miuramisaki* Miura Point, headland of Miura

SYNONYMS

❶ **points of land**

崎 PROMONTORY → 472

3-5
山

285 SO

Ⓒ 岨 jū

Radical	Strokes
山 46	8-3-5
Grade	**Freq**
Reference	
◧ 1 - 3 - 5	

COMPOUNDS

ⓐ [now replaced by 阻 348] steep

ⓑ [original meaning, now archaic] steep mountain, rocky mountain

嶮岨(＝険阻)な *kenso na* steep (mountain pass), precipitous

3-5
巾

286 CHŌ JŌ

Ⓒ 帖 tiē tiě tiè

Radical	Strokes
巾 50	8-3-5
Grade	**Freq**
Reference	
◧ 1 - 3 - 5	

COMPOUNDS

❶ [now also 帳 *chō* 473] notebook, book, register

手帖 *techō* pocketbook, memo

画帖 *gajō* picture album

❷ model of calligraphy for copying

法帖 *hōjō* copybook printed from the works of old masters of calligraphy

❸ counter for quires (of paper), folding screens, volumes of Japanese books, etc.

和紙三帖 *washi sanjō* three quires of Japanese paper

❹ [usu. 畳 *jō* 2592] counter for tatami or (straw) mats

六帖の部屋 *rokujō no heya* six-mat room

弦 287 GEN tsuru

CH 弦 xián

Radical	Strokes
弓 57	8-3-5
Grade	Freq
Jōyō	1523
◧ 1 - 3 - 5	

3-5 弓

▶**STRING**

COMPOUNDS

❶ [formerly also 絃 1330]

ⓐ **string or chord of a musical instrument**

ⓑ counter for strings [chords]

ⓒ [original meaning] bowstring

弦楽器 *gengakki* stringed instruments
調弦 *chōgen* tuning
一弦琴 *ichigenkin* one-stringed instrument, monochord
三弦 *sangen* three-stringed instrument, shamisen

❷ **string instrument, the strings**

弦楽 *gengaku* string music
弦歌 *genka* singing and (string) music
管弦 *kangen* wind and string instruments

❸ *geometry* chord; hypotenuse

弦材 *genzai civil engineering* chord member
補弦 *hogen* supplementary chord
正弦 *seigen* sine (of an angle)

❹ quarter (of the moon)

弦月 *gengetsu* crescent moon
上弦 *jōgen* first quarter, dichotomy
下弦の月 *kagen no tsuki* waning moon

INDEPENDENT

【gen 弦】 string (of musical instrument); *geometry* chord; bowstring
ギターの弦 *gitā no gen* guitar string [chord]

KUN

【tsuru 弦】 bowstring
弦音 *tsuruoto* sound of a vibrating bowstring
弓弦 *yumizuru* (= *yuzuru*) bowstring

SYNONYMS

❶ⓐ **ropes and lines**

線 LINE → 1392
索 cable → 2455
鎖 CHAIN → 1761
組 braid → 1337
緒 cord → 1378
縄 ROPE (esp. of straw) → 1388
綱 ROPE (esp. of fiber) → 1372

❷ **musical instrument**

管 wind instrument → 2701

❸ **lines and line segments**

径 DIAMETER → 291
辺 side → 3029
弧 ARC → 360
線 LINE → 1392

NOTE

⇨ see COMPOUND FORMATION for
正弦 *seigen* ⇨ 正 3484
余弦 *yogen* ⇨ 正 3484

弥 288 MI BI iya ya NAMES hisa hisashi wataru mitsu

彌 弥 彌

CH 弥 mí

Radical	Strokes
弓 57	8-3-5
Grade	Freq
Names	1987
◧ 1 - 3 - 5	

3-5 弓

▶**PHONETIC** [mi]

COMPOUNDS

❶ **used phonetically for *mi*, esp. in the transliteration of Sanscrit Buddhist terms**

弥勒 *miroku* Maitreya (a bodhisattva)
阿弥陀 *amida* Amitabha; lottery; wearing a hat on the back of the head

❷ fill up, patch up

弥縫 *bihō* patching up

❸ [original meaning, now rare] reach for, extend, pervade, spread

弥久 *bikyū* extending over a long time

KUN

【iya 弥】 *elegant* all the more, increasingly
弥増す *iyamasu* increase all the more

【ya 弥】 [in compounds] all the more, increasingly
弥生 *yayoi* third month (of the lunar calendar), March

NAMES

弥生 *yayoi* surname also female name also place name
高弥 *takaya* male name

SYNONYMS

❶ **phonetic** [m]

摩 phonetic [ma] → 3175

3-5 弓

弧 289

▶**ARC**

nonstandard for 弧 360

3-5 彳

彼 290

HI kare kano ka(no)▲

CH 彼 bǐ

Radical	Strokes
彳 60	8-3-5
Grade	**Freq**
Jōyō	480
1-3-5	

▶**THIRD PERSON PRONOUN**

COMPOUNDS

❶ **third person pronoun, the other party, he, she**

彼我 *higa* he [she] and I, they and we, both sides

❷ that, the other

彼岸 *higan* equinoctial week; the other shore

KUN

【**kare** 彼】 he; boyfriend, lover

彼等 *karera* they

彼氏 *kareshi* he; lover, beau

【**kano** 彼】 [in compounds] third person pronoun

彼女 *kanojo* she; one's sweetheart

【**ka(no)** 彼の】 *literary* that

彼の地 *kano chi* that place, there

SYNONYMS

❶ & 【**kare**】 **third person pronouns**

氏 third person pronoun (*polite*) → 2951

奴 third person pronoun (*slang*) → 187

❷ **this and that**

之 this → 3420

是 this → 2436

爾 THAT → 3587

本 THIS → 3502

今 THIS (week, etc.) → 1968

当 THE PRESENT → 2177

該 the said → 1519

同 the same → 2987

3-5 彳

径 291

徑 圣° 径 𢓊

KEI

CH 径 jìng

Radical	Strokes
彳 60	8-3-5
Grade	**Freq**
Jōyō-4	1382
1-3-5	

▶**PATH** ▶**DIAMETER**

COMPOUNDS

❶ [original meaning] **(narrow) path, footpath, shortcut**

径路 *keiro* path; process

捷径 *shōkei* path, lane

山径 *sankei* mountain path

小径 *shōkei* path, lane

❷ **diameter**

直径 *chokkei* diameter

半径 *hankei* radius, semidiameter

口径 *kōkei* caliber, bore; diameter

❸ straight, direct

直情径行 *chokujōkeikō* straightforwardness

INDEPENDENT

【**kei** 径】 diameter

径の大きい *kei no ōkii* of large diameter

SYNONYMS

❶ **ways and routes**

軌 TRACK → 1445

線 LINE → 1392

道 WAY (path) → 3134

途 WAY (route) → 3107

路 ROAD → 1533

筋 wayside → 2678

通り street → 3109

街 city street → 576

辻 CROSSROADS → 3192

岐 forked road → 241

❷ **width**

幅 WIDTH → 569

員 girth → 2269

❷ **lines and line segments**

弦 chord → 287

辺 side → 3029
弧 ARC → 360
線 LINE → 1392

往 往 往 往 ㊥ 往 wǎng wàng

292 Ō

Radical	Strokes
彳 60	8-3-5
Grade	**Freq**
Jōyō-5	1241
◧ 1 - 3 - 5	

3-5 彳

丿 彡 彳 彳' 彳亠 行 往 往
1 2 3 4 5 6 7 8

▶GO ON

COMPOUNDS

❶ⓐ **go on, proceed, move ahead, go by**
ⓑ go on to the next world, pass away
往復 *ōfuku* going and returning; round trip
往来 *ōrai* come-and-go, traffic; road, street
往診 *ōshin* doctor's visit to a patient, house call
右往左往する *uōsaō suru* go this way and that
一往(=一応) *ichiō* once; in outline; tentatively; for the time being
往生する *ōjō suru* pass away; be at a loss
❷ **bygone days, ancient days**
往時 *ōji* bygone days
往古より *ōko yori* from ancient times, from times immemorial
既往症 *kiōshō* previous illness, medical history
❸ now and then
往往 *ōō* sometimes; often

SYNONYMS

❶ⓐ **go and come**
行 GO → 212
出 go to → 3498
参 go somewhere → 2066
来 COME → 3551
通 go to and from → 3109
向 head toward → 3052
赴 PROCEED TO → 3303
❷ **old times**
昔 FORMER TIMES → 2432

NOTE

⇨ see COMPOUND FORMATION for 一応（=一往）*ichiō* ⇨ 応 3066

征 ㊥ 征 zhēng

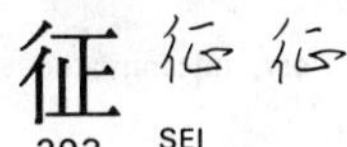

293 SEI

Radical	Strokes
彳 60	8-3-5
Grade	**Freq**
Jōyō	1438
◧ 1 - 3 - 5	

3-5 彳

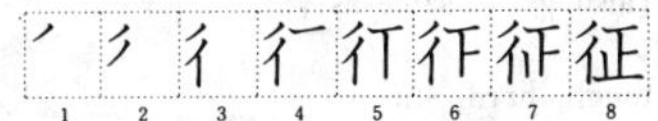

▶CONQUER

COMPOUNDS

❶ **conquer, subjugate (the enemy), attack, assault, invade**
征服 *seifuku* conquest, subjugation
征伐 *seibatsu* subjugation, conquest
征討 *seitō* subjugation, conquest
❷ⓐ **go on a military expedition, go to war, go to the front, lead a punitive force, invade**
ⓑ military expedition, expeditionary force
征夷大将軍 *seii-taishōgun* Commander in chief of the Expeditionary Force Against the Barbarians
遠征 *ensei* (punitive) expedition, invasion; tour
出征する *shussei suru* go to war
外征 *gaisei* foreign expedition
❸ [original meaning] go on a journey, travel
征途に上る *seito ni noboru* go on a military expedition; start on a journey

INDEPENDENT

【seisuru 征する】 attack the rebellious, subjugate

SYNONYMS

❶ **conquer and suppress**
討 SUPPRESS BY ARMED FORCE → 1456
伐 CUT DOWN → 42
鎮 QUELL → 1759
靖 PACIFY → 1208
❶ **win**
克 OVERCOME → 2046
勝 WIN → 1005
破 BREAK → 1150
❷ⓐ **fight and war**
戦 WAR → 1787

闘 FIGHT → 3334

3-5
亻

秖
294 TEI

CH 秖 dī chí

Radical	Strokes
亻 60	8-3-5
Grade	Freq
Reference	
1 - 3 - 5	

COMPOUNDS

● [now replaced by 低 73] linger, wander
低徊(＝低回)する *teikai suru* linger, loiter, wander
低徊趣味(＝低回趣味) *teikai shumi* dilettantism

3-5
亻

徃
295

▶ **GO ON**
nonstandard for 往 292

3-5
忄

怖
296 FU kowa(i) kowa(garu) o(jiru)▲

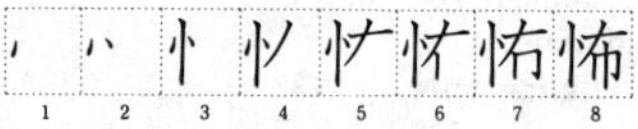

CH 怖 bù

Radical	Strokes
忄 61	8-3-5
Grade	Freq
Jōyō	1511
1 - 3 - 5	

▶ **FEARFUL**

COMPOUNDS

● [original meaning] **fear, be afraid of**
畏怖 *ifu* awe, fear, dread, fright
恐怖 *kyōfu* fear

KUN

【kowa(i) 怖い】[also 恐い] fearful, scary, uncanny; be afraid
怖さ *kowasa* fear, dreadfulness
怖怖 *kowagowa* timidly, gingerly
怖い顔 *kowai kao* angry look, grim face
犬が怖い *inu ga kowai* be afraid of dogs

【kowa(garu) 怖がる】[also 恐がる] be afraid of, be frightened
怖がり *kowagari* timidity; coward

【o(jiru) 怖じる】be frightened, be scared
怖じ気 *ojike* fear, fright
物怖じ *monooji* timidity

SYNONYMS

● & **【kowai】** **fear**
恐 FEAR → 2650

USAGE

❶ **kowai**

怖い
[also 恐い] fearful, scary, uncanny; be afraid

恐い
[also 怖い] same as 怖い

強い
tough, hard, stiff

❷ **kowagaru**

怖がる
[also 恐がる] be afraid of, be frightened

恐がる
[also 怖がる] same as 怖がる

HOMOPHONES

kowai ⇨ 恐 2650 強 475
kowagaru ⇨ 恐 2650

怪 怪 怪

297 KAI KE▲ aya(shii) aya(shimu)

Ⓒⓗ 怪 guài

Radical	Strokes
忄 61	8-3-5
Grade	Freq
Jōyō	1304
◧ 1 - 3 - 5	

3-5 忄

▶MYSTERIOUS

COMPOUNDS

❶ [also prefix] **mysterious, strange, unusual, suspicious, suspicious-looking**

怪奇 *kaiki* mystery, wonder
怪異な *kaii na* mysterious, marvelous, grotesque
怪盗 *kaitō* mysterious thief
怪聞 *kaibun* strange rumor, scandal
怪事件 *kaijiken* mystery case
怪文書 *kaibunsho* mysterious document; subversive literature
怪人物 *kaijinbutsu* mysterious person

❷ exceptional; extraordinary man

怪力 *kairiki* Herculean strength
怪傑 *kaiketsu* man of extraordinary talent, wonder man

❸ **monster, ghost, goblin, demon**

怪獣 *kaijū* monster; beast
怪物 *kaibutsu* monster; ghost, goblin, bogey; mysterious figure
怪談 *kaidan* ghost story
妖怪 *yōkai* ghost, apparition, phantom, goblin

❹ used phonetically for *ke*

怪我 *kega* injury, wound; accident

INDEPENDENT

【kai 怪】 mystery, wonder; apparition, specter
怪中の怪 *kaichū no kai* mystery of mysteries
【ke 怪】 evil spirit
物の怪 *mono no ke* evil spirit, specter; supernatural thing

KUN

【aya(shii) 怪しい】 doubtful; suspicious; strange, mysterious; uncanny; clumsy, awkward
怪しげな *ayashige na* questionable, doubtful, suspicious
怪しい手付きで *ayashii tetsuki de* with clumsy hands, clumsily
【aya(shimu) 怪しむ】 suspect, be suspicious; doubt; wonder, marvel
怪しむに足りない *ayashimu ni tarinai* It is no wonder (that)

SYNONYMS

❶ **abnormal**
奇 UNUSUAL → 2217
妙 strange → 239
異 not ordinary → 2584
珍 curious → 909
変 ABNORMAL → 2069

❸ **supernatural and evil beings**
魔 DEMON → 3187
鬼 DEVIL → 2657
霊 SPIRIT → 2805
精 SPIRIT → 1366

【ayashimu】
○ **doubt**
疑 DOUBT → 1565

怜 怜 怜 怜

298 REI REN NAMES sato satoshi

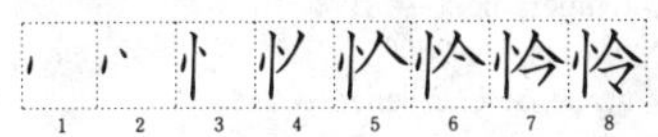

Ⓒⓗ 怜 lián

Radical	Strokes
忄 61	8-3-5
Grade	Freq
Names	2089
◧ 1 - 3 - 5	

3-5 忄

▶CLEVER

COMPOUNDS

● [rarely also 伶 *rei* 66] **clever, quick-witted, bright, nimble**

怜悧(=伶俐) *reiri* cleverness, sagacity

NAMES

怜子 *reiko* (=*satoko*) female name
怜 *satoshi* male name

SYNONYMS

● **intelligent and wise**
哲 SAGACIOUS → 2738
明 clear-sighted → 855
聡 SHARP-WITTED → 1384
俊 brilliant → 102
鋭 SHARP → 1730
敏 NIMBLE → 1322
慧 INTELLIGENT → 2810

賢 WISE → 2839 | 智 wise → 2784

3-5
忄

性 性 性
299 SEI SHŌ saga▲

Stroke order: 1 2 3 4 5 6 7 8

CH 性 xìng

Radical	Strokes
忄 61	8-3-5
Grade	**Freq**
Jōyō-5	234
1 - 3 - 5	

▶NATURE ▶SEX ▶-ITY

COMPOUNDS

❶ⓐ [original meaning] **one's nature, inherent nature, innate quality, character, temperament, disposition**
ⓑ [suffix] **nature, propensity towards, habit**
性格 *seikaku* character, personality
性質 *seishitsu* nature, temperament, character; (characteristic) property, quality
性悪な *shōwaru na* ill-natured
性向 *seikō* inclination, disposition
個性 *kosei* individuality
天性 *tensei* nature, one's innate disposition
根性 *konjō* nature, spirit, temper; will power; guts
習性 *shūsei* habit, (one's) way
肥満性 *himanshō* tendency to be obese
苦労性 *kurōshō* worry habit, pessimistic nature

❷ⓐ **essential nature (of things), intrinsic quality, natural property, characteristic**
ⓑ suffix indicating quality, state or degree: **-ity, -ness**
ⓒ *Buddhism* nature; that which belongs to a substance independent of external influences
性能 *seinō* performance, capacity, efficiency
性質 *seishitsu* nature, temperament, character; (characteristic) property, quality
属性 *zokusei* attribute, property
人間性 *ningensei* human nature, humanity
慢性の *mansei no* chronic
生産性 *seisansei* productivity
可能性 *kanōsei* possibility
安定性 *anteisei* stability
アルカリ性 *arukarisei* alkalinity
爆発性 *bakuhatsusei* explosiveness
仏性 *busshō* Buddha nature

❸ⓐ (male or female classification) **sex**
ⓑ (sexual intercourse) **sex, sexuality, sexual desire**
ⓒ gender
性別 *seibetsu* distinction of sex; gender
男性 *dansei* male, man
性欲 *seiyoku* sexual desire, lust
性行為 *seikōi* sexual act, intercourse
性教育 *seikyōiku* sex education
中性 *chūsei* neuter gender
女性名詞 *josei-meishi* feminine noun

INDEPENDENT

【sei 性】
①ⓐ one's nature, disposition
ⓑ essential nature, inherent quality
人の性は善なり *Hito no sei wa zen nari* Man is naturally good
水の性 *mizu no sei* properties of water
②ⓐ (male or female classification) sex
ⓑ (sexual intercourse) sex, sexuality, sexual desire
ⓒ gender
性の区別 *sei no kubetsu* distinction of the sexes
性の自由 *sei no jiyū* sexual freedom

【shō 性】
①ⓐ nature, disposition, temperament, character
ⓑ *Buddhism* nature (⇨ ❷ⓒ)
性の悪い犬 *shō no warui inu* ill-tempered dog, vicious dog
性に合う *shō ni au* be congenial, agree with one
② quality, state
性の良い *shō no yoi* of good quality

KUN

【saga 性】 one's nature, one's way, custom
女の性 *onna no saga* the ways of women

SYNONYMS

❶ⓐ & ❷ⓐ nature and character
気 temperament → 3194
質 QUALITY → 2808
品 grade of excellence → 2248
柄 CHARACTER → 897
格 (good) character → 926
ⓑ tendency
向 tendency → 3052
勢 trend → 2857
傾 inclination → 154
潮 TIDE → 739
流 CURRENT → 441
❷ⓑ nominalizers
子 NOUN SUFFIX → 3390
事 nominalization word → 3567

所 PARTICLE OF NOMINALIZATION → 851
❸ⓑ **sex**
情 (illicit) love → 482
春 love → 2576

色 lust → 2029

NOTE

⇨ see COMPOUND FORMATION for 慢性 *mansei* ⇨ 慢 686

怜 300

3-5 忄

▶**CLEVER**
nonstandard for 伶 298

拇 301 BO

3-5 扌

Ⓒⓗ 拇 mǔ

Radical	Strokes
扌 64	8-3-5
Grade	Freq
Reference	
◧ 1 - 3 - 5	

COMPOUNDS

● [now also 母 3475] [original meaning] thumb

拇指 *boshi* thumb
拇印 *boin* thumbprint

抽 302 CHŪ hiki-▲

3-5 扌

一 十 扌 扌 扣 抽 抽 抽 (1–8)

Ⓒⓗ 抽 chōu

Radical	Strokes
扌 64	8-3-5
Grade	Freq
Jōyō	1415
◧ 1 - 3 - 5	

▶**DRAW OUT**

COMPOUNDS

● [original meaning] **draw out, extract**
抽出する *chūshutsu suru* extract, abstract, educe
抽選(=抽籤) *chūsen* drawing of lots
抽象的 *chūshōteki* abstract

KUN

【**hiki- 抽-**】[usu. 引き] drawing
抽出し *hikidashi* (desk) drawer

SYNONYMS

● **pull**

引 DRAW → 181
抜 PULL OUT → 246
控える HOLD BACK → 495
寄せる DRAW NEAR → 2291

HOMOPHONES

hiki- ⇨ 引 181

NOTE

⇨ see USAGE note at 引 181
⇨ see COMPOUND FORMATION for 抽象 *chūshō* ⇨ 象 2134

拝 303 HAI oga(mu)

3-5 扌

一 十 扌 扌 扌 扌 扌 拝 (1–8)

Ⓒⓗ 拜 bài

Radical	Strokes
扌 64	8-3-5
Grade	Freq
Jōyō-6	1396
◧ 1 - 3 - 5	

▶**WORSHIP** ▶**HUMBLY**

COMPOUNDS

❶ⓐ (render religious reverence to) **worship, pay reverence to, pay one's respects**
ⓑ (feel an adoring reverence for) **worship, adore**

拝殿 *haiden* front shrine, hall of worship
参拝する *sanpai suru* worship, pay reverence at, visit a shrine [temple]
礼拝 *reihai* (=*raihai*) worship; church service
拝金 *haikin* money worship, worship of mammon

拝外的な *haigaiteki na* proforeign, xenophilous
崇拝 *sūhai* worship, adoration
❷ bow in veneration, make a bow
拝礼 *hairei* worship
遥拝する *yōhai suru* worship from afar
三拝九拝する *sanpai-kyūhai suru* kowtow, bow many times
❸ⓐ **humbly, respectfully, reverentially**—honorific term expressing humility in reference to an action of the speaker
ⓑ **honorific term used in salutations**
拝見する *haiken suru* have the honor of seeing, see, look at, inspect
拝借する *haishaku suru* borrow
拝聴する *haichō suru* listen attentively [respectfully]
拝受する *haiju suru* receive [accept] (humbly)
拝啓 *haikei* Dear Sir, Dear Madam
拝復 *haifuku* in reply to your letter; Dear Sir, Dear Madam
❹ [humble]
ⓐ have the honor to receive
ⓑ have the honor to see [meet]
拝命 *haimei* receiving an official appointment
拝領する *hairyō suru* receive (from a superior), be bestowed
拝眉する *haibi suru* have the pleasure of seeing (a person)
拝顔の栄 *haigan no ei* honor of seeing (a person)

INDEPENDENT

【hai 拝】 term of humility used after one's name (chiefly males) in letters
山本太郎拝 *yamamoto tarō-hai* your humble servant Taro Yamamoto

【haisuru 拝する】
① bow in veneration, make a bow
神前に拝する *shinzen ni haisuru* bow to a god in veneration
② [humble]
ⓐ have the honor to receive
ⓑ have the honor to see
大命を拝する *taimei o haisuru* receive an Imperial command
お顔を拝する *okao o haisuru* have the honor to see his (Majesty's) face

KUN

【oga(mu) 拝む】 bow in veneration, make a bow, worship; pay one's respects with joined hands, entreat, solicit; [humble] see, have a look
伏し拝む *fushiogamu* kneel down and worship, drop to one's knees
拝み倒す *ogamitaosu* entreat (a person) into consent, win over by persuasive entreaty
拝ませる *ogamaseru* let a person have a look; allow to worship

SYNONYMS

❶ⓐ **pray and worship**
祈 PRAY → 875
願 pray → 1845
崇 REVERENCE → 2297
斎 OBSERVE RELIGIOUS ABSTINENCE → 2115
ⓑ **respect**
慕 ADORE → 2353
重 set value on → 3573
尚 VALUE HIGHLY → 2233
崇 REVERENCE → 2297
仰 look up to → 48
欽 REVERE → 1690
敬 RESPECT → 1701
尊 HONOR → 2324
❷ **bow**
礼 courtesy bow → 818
❸ⓐ **humble**
謙 HUMBLE → 1617
ⓐ **respectful**
奉 reverentially → 2559
謹 RESPECTFULLY → 1618
恭 RESPECTFUL → 2459
❹ⓐ **receive**
戴 RECEIVE HUMBLY → 3302
頂 RECEIVE HUMBLY → 145
受 RECEIVE → 2421
享 ENJOY → 2051
領 receive → 1224
収 TAKE IN → 198
納 ACCEPT → 1300

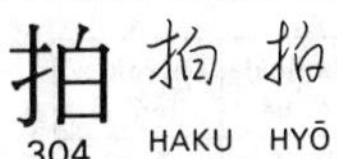
304 HAKU HYŌ

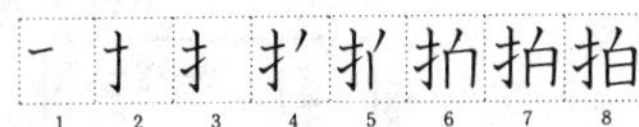

Ⓒ 拍 pāi

Radical	Strokes
扌 64	8-3-5
Grade	**Freq**
Jōyō	1407
◧ 1 - 3 - 5	

3-5 扌

▶**BEAT**

COMPOUNDS

❶ [also 搏 *haku* 646] [original meaning] (strike repeatedly or rhythmically) **beat, clap (one's hands), throb**
拍手 *hakushu* applause, clapping
拍車 *hakusha* spur, rowel spur
拍動 *hakudō* pulsation, pulsebeat
脈拍 *myakuhaku* pulse, pulsation

❷ⓐ **beat, rhythm, time**
ⓑ counter for beats or number of syllables in Japanese words
拍子 *hyōshi* time, beat, rhythm; chance, the moment
手拍子 *tebyōshi* beating time with the hand; careless move
三拍子 *sanbyōshi* simple triple time
三拍 *sanpaku* three beats, three syllables

INDEPENDENT

【**haku** 拍】 beat
拍を数える *haku o kazoeru* count beats

SYNONYMS

❶ **strike**
打 STRIKE → 193
撃 STRIKE → 2863
当てる HIT → 2177
撲 DEAL A BLOW → 733
殴 BEAT (strike a person) → 886

❷ **musical elements**
律 RHYTHM → 363
韻 RHYME → 1811
調 TONE → 1567
呂 ancient musical note → 2187

披 披 披
305 HI

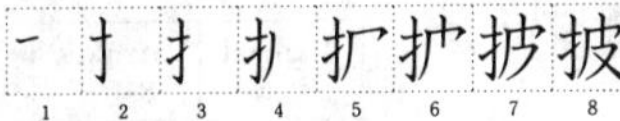

Ⓒ 披 pī

Radical	Strokes
扌 64	8-3-5
Grade	**Freq**
Jōyō	1410
◧ 1 - 3 - 5	

3-5 扌

▶**OPEN OUT**

COMPOUNDS

❶ **open out (one's heart), reveal**
披講 *hikō* introduction of poems at a poetry party
披露する *hirō suru* announce, introduce; [original meaning, now archaic] open one's heart
披瀝する *hireki suru* express (one's opinion), reveal (one's thoughts)
お披露目(＝お広め) *ohirome* début

❷ [original meaning] open and read, unseal, unfold, unroll
披見する *hiken suru* open and read, peruse (a letter)
直披 *chokuhi* (＝*jikihi*) confidential letter

SYNONYMS

❶ **reveal**
発 reveal → 2565
露 EXPOSE → 2818
暴 disclose → 2515
顕 MANIFEST → 1806
現 cause to appear → 968

❷ **open**
展 UNFOLD → 3111
開 OPEN → 3321

3-5 扌

抱 抱 抱 抱

306 HŌ da(ku) ida(ku) kaka(eru)

一 十 扌 扌 扚 抅 抅 抱

1 2 3 4 5 6 7 8

CH 抱 bào

Radical	Strokes
扌 64	8-3-5
Grade	**Freq**
Jōyō	1143
1-3-5	

▶**HUG**

COMPOUNDS

❶ [formerly also 捧 491] [original meaning] **hug, embrace, hold in one's arms, enfold**

抱擁する *hōyō suru* embrace, hug, hold in one's arms

抱卵 *hōran* incubation

抱腹絶倒する *hōfukuzettō suru* double up with laughter

介抱する *kaihō suru* nurse, care for

❷ (harbor a thought or feeling) **hug, cherish, entertain**

抱懐する *hōkai suru* harbor, cherish, entertain

抱負 *hōfu* aspiration, ambition

辛抱 *shinbō* patience, endurance, forbearance

KUN

【**da(ku) 抱く**】 hug, embrace, hold in one's arms

抱き合う *dakiau* hug, embrace

抱き締める *dakishimeru* embrace closely, cuddle, hug

【**ida(ku) 抱く**】 harbor (suspicion), entertain (hope), cherish, hug (a belief); hold in one's arms, hug

疑いを抱く *utagai o idaku* harbor suspicion

【**kaka(eru) 抱える**】 hold in one's arms; employ, hire

抱え *kakae* armful; employee

抱え込む *kakaekomu* hold in one's arm, take upon oneself

抱き抱える *dakikakaeru* hold, carry, embrace (in one's arms)

召し抱える *meshikakaeru* employ, engage

SYNONYMS

❶ **embrace**

擁 embrace → 770

❷ **hold in the mind**

持 HOLD → 374

懐 embosom → 763

3-5 扌

抛

307 HŌ nageu(tsu)

CH 抛 pāo

Radical	Strokes
扌 64	8-3-5
Grade	**Freq**
Reference	
1-3-5	

COMPOUNDS

[now replaced by 放 *hō* 853]

ⓐ [original meaning] toss, throw, let fly

ⓑ toss away, throw away, cast away

抛物線 *hōbutsusen* parabola

抛棄 *hōki* abandonment, resignation

抛擲する *hōteki suru* abandon, give up, quit

抛つ *nageutsu* fling away, abandon

3-5 扌

拐 拐° 拐 拐

308 KAI

一 十 扌 扌 扣 扣 拐 拐

1 2 3 4 5 6 7 8

CH 拐 guǎi

Radical	Strokes
扌 64	8-3-5
Grade	**Freq**
Jōyō	1962
1-3-5	

▶**KIDNAP**

COMPOUNDS

❶ **kidnap, abduct**

拐取する *kaishu suru* abduct (legal term)

誘拐 *yūkai* kidnapping, abduction

❷ **defraud, swindle, abscond**

拐帯 *kaitai* abscondence with money

SYNONYMS

❶ **take forcibly**

奪 ROB → 2343

収 take possession by force → 198

❷ **deceive**

惑 mislead → 2786

詐 SWINDLE → 1502

欺 DECEIVE → 1703

偽 FALSIFY → 131

拡 擴 拡 拡

309 KAKU hiro(garu)▲ hiro(geru)▲

一 十 扌 扌 扩 扩 拡 拡 (1 2 3 4 5 6 7 8)

Ⓒ𝐇 扩 kuò

Radical	Strokes
扌 64	8-3-5
Grade	**Freq**
Jōyō-6	688
◧ 1 - 3 - 5	

3-5 扌

▶ **ENLARGE**

COMPOUNDS

● [original meaning] **enlarge, expand, magnify, widen, extend**

拡大する *kakudai suru* magnify, enlarge, expand

拡張する *kakuchō suru* expand, extend, enlarge

拡散 *kakusan* scattering, diffusion

拡声器 *kakuseiki* (loud)speaker, microphone

拡充 *kakujū* expansion, amplification

軍拡 *gunkaku* expansion of armaments

KUN

【hiro(garu) 拡がる】

[usu. 広がる] *vi*

ⓐ spread out, stretch, unfold

ⓑ expand, extend

ⓒ spread, reach, go about

拡がり *hirogari* extent, expanse, stretch, spread

火が燃え拡がった *Hi ga moehirogatta* The fire spread

【hiro(geru) 拡げる】

[usu. 広げる] *vt*

①ⓐ spread (out), outstretch

ⓑ unfold, unroll, open

地図を拡げる *chizu o hirogeru* spread a map

拡げた腕 *hirogeta ude* outstretched arms

繰り拡げる *kurihirogeru* roll out, unfold, spread out; develop

② widen, enlarge, expand, extend

SYNONYMS

● **expand**

広げる spread (out) → 3035

張 SPREAD → 474

膨 EXPAND → 1084

脹 SWELL → 1003

伸 STRETCH → 70

延 EXTEND → 3073

HOMOPHONES

hirogaru ⇨ 広 3035

hirogeru ⇨ 広 3035

NOTE

⇨ see USAGE note at 広 3035

拘 拘 拘

310 KŌ kaka(waru)▲

一 十 扌 扌 扚 扚 拘 拘 (1 2 3 4 5 6 7 8)

Ⓒ𝐇 拘 jū

Radical	Strokes
扌 64	8-3-5
Grade	**Freq**
Jōyō	1464
◧ 1 - 3 - 5	

3-5 扌

▶ **ARREST**

COMPOUNDS

❶ [sometimes also 勾 2942] [original meaning] **arrest, detain, confine**

拘留 *kōryū* penal detention up to 30 days

拘禁する *kōkin suru* detain, confine, imprison

拘置 *kōchi* detention, confinement, arrest

拘束 *kōsoku* restriction, restraint, binding

拘引 *kōin* arrest, custody

❷ restrain, restrict the freedom of

拘泥する *kōdei suru* adhere to (laws and rules), stick to (conventions)

KUN

【kaka(waru) 拘わる】 adhere to, stick to

...にも拘わらず *...ni mo kakawarazu* in spite of..., regardless of...

SYNONYMS

❶ **imprison and confine**

禁 confine → 2795

留 keep in custody → 2580

置 place in custody → 2608

❶ **catch a criminal**

逮 CATCH A CRIMINAL → 3123
捕 CATCH → 429

HOMOPHONES
kakawaru ⇨ 係 97 関 3328

NOTE
⇨ see USAGE note at 係 97

3-5 扌

拒 拒 拒 拒

311 KYO koba(mu)

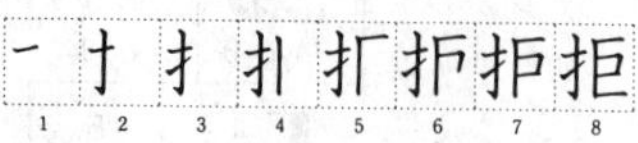

Ⓒⓗ 拒 jù

Radical	Strokes
扌 64	8-3-5
Grade	**Freq**
Jōyō	1118
1 - 3 - 5	

▶REFUSE

COMPOUNDS

❶ **refuse, reject, deny**
拒絶する *kyozetsu suru* refuse, reject, deny
拒否する *kyohi suru* deny, reject
拒止 *kyoshi* refusal
峻拒 *shunkyo* flat refusal, stern rejection

❷ resist, repel
抗拒する *kōkyo suru* resist, oppose

KUN

【koba(mu) 拒む】 refuse, decline, deny; prevent
支払いを拒む *shiharai o kobamu* refuse payment, decline to pay
入場を拒む *nyūjō o kobamu* deny (a person) admission

SYNONYMS

❶ **refuse and reject**
断る refuse → 1492
否 SAY NO → 2406
却 reject → 1118

3-5 扌

拠 據 拠 拠

312 KYO KO yo(ru)▲

Ⓒⓗ 据 jù jū

Radical	Strokes
扌 64	8-3-5
Grade	**Freq**
Jōyō	882
1 - 3 - 5	

▶GROUNDS

COMPOUNDS

❶ **grounds, base, basis, foundation; authority**
拠点 *kyoten* strongpoint, base
根拠 *konkyo* grounds, basis, authority
本拠 *honkyo* base, stronghold, headquarters
論拠 *ronkyo* grounds [basis] of an argument
典拠 *tenkyo* authority
証拠 *shōko* proof, evidence

❷ occupy, take possession of, hold one's ground
拠守 *kyoshu* defense
占拠 *senkyo* occupation, exclusive possession
割拠する *kakkyo suru* hold one's own ground

❸ [also 醵 *kyo* 1655] contribute money to a common purpose
拠出 *kyoshutsu* donation, contribution
拠金 *kyokin* contribution, subscription

KUN

【yo(ru) 拠る】
① be based on, be grounded on
辞書に拠れば *jisho ni yoreba* based on [according to] the dictionary
② occupy (a fortress), hold
天険に拠る *tenken ni yoru* hold a mountain fortress

SYNONYMS

❶ **basis**
本 BASIS → 3502
基 BASE → 2673
素 ELEMENT → 2458
礎 foundation → 1248
底 BOTTOM → 3084
根 ROOT → 930

❷ **occupy**
占 OCCUPY → 2003
領 take possession of → 1224
専 take exclusive possession of → 2644

HOMOPHONES
yoru ⇨ 依 84 因 3054 由 3499 寄 2291

NOTE
⇨ see USAGE note at 因 3054

抹 抹 抹

313 MATSU

(CH) 抹 mǒ mò mā

Radical	Strokes
扌 64	8-3-5
Grade	**Freq**
Jōyō	1957
1 - 3 - 5	

3-5 扌

一 十 扌 扌 扌 扌 抹 抹 (strokes 1–8)

▶**WIPE**

COMPOUNDS

❶ⓐ (remove by rubbing) **wipe off, wipe out, erase, strike out**

ⓑ (spread over) wipe over [on], coat with, paint over

抹殺する *massatsu suru* erase, strike out; deny, ignore; do away with, liquidate

抹消する *masshō suru* erase, strike out

塗抹する *tomatsu suru* coat with, pain over

一抹 *ichimatsu* a touch of, a tinge of

❷ pulverize, powder

抹茶 *matcha* powdered tea

抹香 *makkō* incense powder, incense

抹香臭い *makkō kusai* sound religious, smack of religion

SYNONYMS

❶ⓐ **eliminate**

削 cross out → 1448

却 ELIMINATE → 1118

省 leave out → 2449

脱 REMOVE → 973

去 take away → 2156

外す take off → 186

除 RID OF → 456

撤 WITHDRAW → 738

排 EXCLUDE → 490

払う CLEAR AWAY → 194

ⓑ **spread**

塗 APPLY ON A SURFACE → 2841

舗 PAVE → 1735

敷く LAY → 1870

布 SPREAD → 2973

散 SCATTER → 1702

❷ **break into small pieces**

砕 CRUSH UP → 1134

押 押 押

314 Ō o(su) o(shi)- o(t)- o(saeru)

 yā

Radical	Strokes
扌 64	8-3-5
Grade	**Freq**
Jōyō	523
1 - 3 - 5	

3-5 扌

一 十 扌 扌 扣 扣 押 押 (strokes 1–8)

▶**PUSH**

COMPOUNDS

❶ⓐ [original meaning] **push or press downward**

ⓑ (fix a seal) **seal, stamp**

ⓒ seal, signature

押下する *ōka suru* depress, press down (a computer key)

押印する *ōin suru* seal, affix a seal

押捺 *ōnatsu* sealing (a document)

花押 *kaō* signature, written seal

❷ **perform an action by force, take by force**

押収 *ōshū* seizure, confiscation

押送する *ōsō suru* transfer (a convict), escort

❸ to rhyme

押韻 *ōin* rhyme, rhyming

KUN

【o(su) 押す】

①ⓐ (force to move) push, press, thrust, shove

ⓑ [formerly also 圧す] press down, press; compress, squash

押し *oshi* pushing, push; self-confidence, impudence; fall (in prices)

押 *osu* PUSH (marking on doors)

押し上げる *oshiageru* push up, boost

押し返す *oshikaesu* push back, force back

押し釦 *oshibotan* push-button

押し屋 *oshiya* commuter train packer

後押し *atooshi* pushing; support, backing

押しも押されもせぬ *oshi mo osare mo senu* of established reputation

押し潰す *oshitsubusu* squash, crush, flatten

② (force to act) push [force] oneself; push a person (to do something)

押して *oshite* forcibly, by compulsion; importunately

押し売り *oshiuri* coercive touting, importunate peddling [peddler]

押し問答 *oshimondō* bandying words, haggling, argument

中押し *chūoshi* one-sided game, victory by a wide margin (in go)
病気を押して行く *byōki o oshite iku* go in spite of illness
③ fix a seal, stamp
スタンプを押す *sutanpu o osu* stamp
④ overwhelm, have an edge over
⑤ perform an action though it is not necessary, make doubly sure
念を押す *nen o osu* call attention to, make sure of, emphasize
駄目を押す *dame o osu* make sure
⑥ put (gold) leaf over, gild
手押し *teoshi* hand gilding
⑦ (of prices) sag, drop, fall
押し目 *oshime* weakness, relapse, scale-down

【o(shi)- 押し-】
[verbal prefix]
① push (oneself or others) to perform an action
押し付ける *oshitsukeru* press against; force, compel
押し通す *oshitōsu* push through, carry it through, hold out to the end
押し切る *oshikiru* have one's own way, push one's way through
押し掛ける *oshikakeru* force oneself upon (a person), go uninvited
② emphatic verbal prefix
押し並べて *oshinabete* generally
押し隠す *oshikakusu* conceal, cover up
押し黙る *oshidamaru* keep silent, clam up
押し寄せる *oshiyoseru* advance on, rush for, push to one side

【o(t)- 押っ-】 emphatic verbal prefix
押っ立てる *ottateru* raise, set up
押っ始める *oppajimeru* begin

【o(saeru) 押さえる】
① press down, hold down, force down
押さえ *osae* weight, paperweight; rear guard
押さえ込む *osaekomu* immobilize, pin down
② stop up, cover
耳を押さえる *mimi o osaeru* hold one's ears
③ⓐ seize (goods), distrain, levy distress on
ⓑ seize, secure
差し押さえ *sashiosae* attachment, seizure, distraint
証拠を押さえる *shōko o osaeru* seize [secure] evidence

SYNONYMS

❶ⓐ push
突く THRUST → 2230
圧 apply pressure → 2970
ⓑ mark
印 imprint → 828
画 mark off → 3000

【osu】
①ⓐ **force to move**
駆 DRIVE → 1823
推 propel → 504
② **compel and press**
強 force → 475
圧 PRESSURE → 2970
迫 PRESS → 3074

USAGE

❶ osu
押す
①ⓐ (force to move) push, press, thrust, shove
ⓑ [formerly also 圧す] press down, press; compress, squash
② (force to act) push [force] oneself; push a person (to do something)
③ fix a seal, stamp
④ overwhelm, have an edge over
⑤ perform an action though it is not necessary, make doubly sure
⑥ put (gold) leaf over, gild
⑦ (of prices) sag, drop, fall
推す
① infer, deduce, conjecture, surmise, guess
② recommend, propose, nominate
圧す
[now usu. 押す] press down, press; compress, squash

❷ oshi
押し
① pushing, push
② self-confidence, impudence
③ fall (in prices)
圧し
① pressing down
② weight
③ authority, commanding presence

❸ osaeru
押さえる
① press down, hold down, force down
② stop up, cover
③ⓐ seize (goods), distrain, levy distress on
ⓑ seize, secure
抑える
①ⓐ (hold down) suppress, repress, restrain, control, hold down; check, curb, stop; keep back, withhold
ⓑ (put down forcibly) suppress, subdue, bring under control
② catch, arrest

❹ osae
押さえ
① weight, paperweight
② rear guard
抑え
ⓐ check, defense, suppression
ⓑ control

HOMOPHONES
osu ⇨ 推 504 圧 2970
oshi ⇨ 圧 2970
osaeru ⇨ 抑 257
osae ⇨ 抑 257

拙 拙 拙

315 SETSU tsutana(i)▲

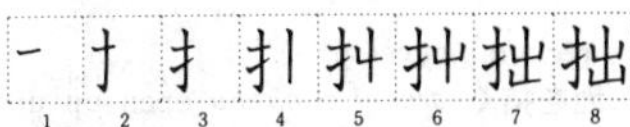

Ⓒ 拙 zhuō

Radical	Strokes
扌 64	8-3-5
Grade	Freq
Jōyō	1696
1-3-5	

3-5 扌

▶**CLUMSY**

COMPOUNDS

❶ **clumsy, unskillful**
拙劣な *setsuretsu na* clumsy, awkward, unskillful
拙速主義 *sessokushugi* rough-and-ready method
巧拙 *kōsetsu* skill, dexterity, workmanship

❷ [humble] my humble, my poor
拙者 *sessha* I
拙宅 *settaku* my home, my humble abode

INDEPENDENT

【setsu 拙】 clumsiness; [humble] I
巧と拙 *kō to setsu* skillfulness and clumsiness

KUN

【tsutana(i) 拙い】 clumsy, unskillful; incompetent, inexperienced; unfortunate (in war)
拙い文章 *tsutanai bunshō* poor writing

SYNONYMS

❷ **humble prefixes**
小 my little (*humble*) → 7
弊 our [my] humble → 2884
愚 my foolish → 2834

招 招 招

316 SHŌ mane(ku)

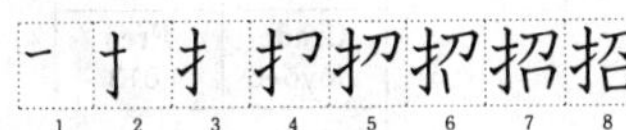

Ⓒ 招 zhāo

Radical	Strokes
扌 64	8-3-5
Grade	Freq
Jōyō-5	715
1-3-5	

3-5 扌

▶**INVITE**

COMPOUNDS

ⓐ **invite**
ⓑ [original meaning] beckon (with the hand), call
招待 *shōtai* invitation
招宴 *shōen* invitation to a party; party
招請国 *shōseikoku* inviting country, host nation
招集する *shōshū suru* call, summon, convene
招致 *shōchi* summons, invitation
招聘 *shōhei* invitation; engagement

INDEPENDENT

【shōjiru (=shōzuru) 招じる(=請じる, 招ずる, 請ずる)】 invite; usher in

KUN

【mane(ku) 招く】 invite; beckon, call; engage (someone's services); bring about, incur, cause
招き *maneki* invitation, engagement
災いを招く *wazawai o maneku* bring calamity upon oneself

SYNONYMS

● **call and invite**
召 SUMMON → 2001
呼ぶ CALL → 273
喚 CALL → 550

3-5 扌

拓 拓 拓

317 TAKU hira(ku)▲

CH 拓 tuò tà

Radical	Strokes
扌 64	8-3-5
Grade	**Freq**
Jōyō	1320
1-3-5	

▶**OPEN UP**

COMPOUNDS

❶ **open up (farmland or new frontiers), clear land, reclaim, develop**

拓殖 *takushoku* colonization, exploitation

開拓 *kaitaku* reclamation, opening up, clearing; exploitation

干拓 *kantaku* land reclamation by drainage

❷ copy by rubbing, make rubbings from inscriptions on stone

拓本 *takuhon* rubbed copy

魚拓 *gyotaku* fish print

❸ abbrev. of 拓殖 *takushoku*: colonization

拓大 *takudai* Takushoku University

拓銀 *takugin* Takushoku Bank

KUN

【**hira(ku)** 拓く】[usu. 開く] open up (land), clear, reclaim, develop

荒れ地を拓く *arechi o hiraku* open up unbroken land

自分の道を拓く *jibun no michi o hiraku* hew one's way out

SYNONYMS

❶ **reclaim**

墾 RECLAIM → 2896

開 OPEN → 3321

❷ **copy**

写 COPY → 2000

謄 TRANSCRIBE → 1093

複 duplicate → 1222

HOMOPHONES

hiraku ⇨ 開 3321 啓 2763

NOTE

⇨ see USAGE note at 開 3321

3-5 扌

担 擔 担 擔

318 TAN katsu(gu) nina(u)

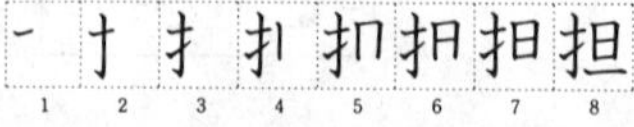

CH 担 dān dàn

Radical	Strokes
扌 64	8-3-5
Grade	**Freq**
Jōyō-6	613
1-3-5	

▶**BEAR ON SHOULDER** ▶**UNDERTAKE**

COMPOUNDS

❶ [original meaning] **bear [carry] on one's shoulder, shoulder, bear**

担架 *tanka* stretcher

❷ **undertake (a task), take (a job) upon oneself**

担当する *tantō suru* undertake, be in charge of

担保 *tanpo* security, mortgage

担任する *tannin suru* be in charge of, take (a class) under one's charge

負担 *futan* burden, charge, responsibility

分担 *buntan* partial charge, allotment

❸ assist, help

加担(=荷担) *katan* assistance, support, participation

KUN

【**katsu(gu)** 担ぐ】shoulder, carry [bear] on one's shoulder; have as (president of), have (a person) over; be superstitious; take in, play a trick on

担ぎ *katsugi* carrier

担ぎ上げる *katsugiageru* carry up

担ぎ屋 *katsugiya* superstitious person; black-market peddler

...を担いで *...o katsuide* with (a person) at the head

【**nina(u)** 担う】bear [carry] on one's shoulder, shoulder; undertake, take upon oneself

担い手 *ninaite* bearer, carrier

責任を担う *sekinin o ninau* shoulder responsibility

SYNONYMS

❶ **bear**

負 BEAR (on the back) → 2091

荷 carry on shoulder → 2282

支 SUPPORT → 1979

❷ **undertake**

負 BEAR → 2091

抵 319 TEI

Ⓒⓗ 抵 dǐ

Radical	Strokes
扌 64	8-3-5
Grade	Freq
Jōyō	1277
1-3-5	

3-5 扌

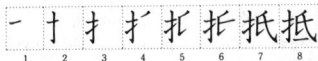

▶RESIST

COMPOUNDS

❶ **resist, withstand, oppose, stand up to**
抵抗する *teikō suru* resist, oppose, defy

❷ **be equivalent to, correspond to**
抵当 *teitō* mortgage, security

❸ [formerly also 牴 908 or 觝 1498] collide with, touch
抵触 *teishoku* conflict; contradiction; incompatibility

❹ generally, mostly
大抵 *taitei* generally, mostly, for the most part

SYNONYMS

❶ **resist**
抗 RESIST → 252
耐 WITHSTAND → 1282
対 OPPOSE → 831
反 COUNTER → 2945
逆 rebel → 3091

拔 320

▶PULL OUT ▶STAND OUT
nonstandard for 抜 246

3-5 扌

拂 321

▶CLEAR AWAY ▶PAY
nonstandard for 払 194

3-5 扌

抱 322

▶HUG
nonstandard for 抱 306

3-5 扌

拐 323

▶KIDNAP
nonstandard for 拐 308

3-5 扌

拒 324

▶REFUSE
nonstandard for 拒 311

3-5 扌

注 325 CHŪ soso(gu) sa(su)▲ tsu(gu)▲

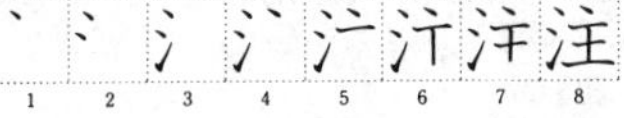

Ⓒⓗ 注 zhù

Radical	Strokes
氵 85	8-3-5
Grade	Freq
Jōyō-3	392
1-3-5	

3-5 氵

▶POUR ▶CONCENTRATE

COMPOUNDS

❶ **pour, pour into, pour on, inject**
注入する *chūnyū suru* pour into, inject
注水 *chūsui* flooding; douche
注射 *chūsha* injection, shot
注油 *chūyu* oiling, lubrication

❷ abbrev. of 注射 *chūsha*: injection, shot
筋注 *kinchū* intramuscular injection
静注 *jōchū* intravenous injection

❸ **concentrate (on), pay attention to**
注意 *chūi* attention, care, advice
注目 *chūmoku* attention, notice
注視 *chūshi* steady gaze, close observation

傾注 *keichū* devotion, concentration

❹ [formerly also 註 1499]

ⓐ **annotate, explain with notes**

ⓑ **annotation, explanatory notes, comment**

注釈 *chūshaku* annotation, note, comment
注解 *chūkai* annotation, explanatory notes
注記 *chūki* annotation, commentary
頭注 *tōchū* headnote
脚注 *kyakuchū* footnote
評注 *hyōchū* commentary, notes and comments

❺ [formerly also 註 1499] **write down, take notes of, record**

注進する *chūshin suru* inform, make a report
注文する *chūmon suru* order, place an order; request

❻ [formerly also 註 1499] abbrev. of 注文 *chūmon*: order

発注する *hatchū suru* place an order
受注する *juchū suru* receive an order

INDEPENDENT

【chū 注(=註)】 annotation, explanatory note, comment

【chūsuru 注する(=註する)】 annotate, comment

KUN

【soso(gu) 注ぐ】 pour into, pour on; irrigate, sprinkle; flow into (the sea); concentrate (on), pay attention to

注ぎ込む *sosogikomu* pour into, instill
注意を注ぐ *chūi o sosogu* pay attention
力を注ぐ *chikara o sosogu* concentrate one's effort (on something)

【sa(su) 注す】

① [usu. 差す] pour (into), fill up

器に水を注す *utsuwa ni mizu o sasu* fill a pitcher with water

② [usu. 差す] color

【tsu(gu) 注ぐ】 pour out, pour in, fill

注ぎ込む *tsugikomu* pour in [into]; invest in
注ぎ口 *tsugiguchi* spout

SYNONYMS

❶ **flow and drip**

流 FLOW → 441
濫 overflow → 801
漏 LEAK → 701
滴 DROP → 705
泌 SECRETE → 332

❸ **concentrate on**

傾 devote oneself to → 154

❹ⓐ **explain**

解 CLARIFY → 1517
講 expound → 1619
釈 ELUCIDATE → 1484
説 EXPLAIN → 1547
明 make clear → 855

ⓑ **explanatory remarks**

評 COMMENT → 1501

HOMOPHONES

sasu ⇨ 差 3311 指 378 刺 1275 挿 431 射 1458 止 2941
tsugu ⇨ 接 500 継 1360 次 54

NOTE

⇨ see USAGE notes at 差 3311 and 接 500
⇨ see COMPOUND FORMATION for 注文 *chūmon* ⇨ 文 1962

3-5
氵

泥 泥 泥

326 DEI doro[1] doro[2]

Ⓒⓗ 泥 ní nì

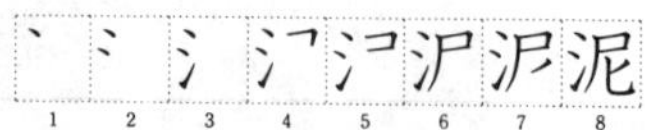

Radical	Strokes
氵 85	8-3-5
Grade	**Freq**
Jōyō	1412
1 - 3 - 5	

▶MUD

COMPOUNDS

❶ⓐ [original meaning] **mud, mire**

ⓑ something with the consistency of mud

泥土 *deido* mud, mire
泥水 *deisui* (=*doromizu*) muddy water, liquid mud
泥濘 *deinei* mud, slush, mire; muddy road
雲泥の差 *undei no sa* great difference (as between clouds and mud)
泥炭 *deitan* peat
金泥 *kindei* (=*kondei*) gold paint

❷ lose one's senses

泥酔する *deisui suru* get dead drunk

❸ stick to (old traditions), adhere

拘泥する *kōdei suru* adhere to (laws and rules), stick to (conventions)

INDEPENDENT

【dei 泥】 mud

泥の像 *dei no zō* mud image

KUN

【doro[1] 泥】

① mud, mire, slush, dirt

泥沼 *doronuma* bog; swamp (of difficulties)
泥んこ *doronko* mud, morasses of mud
顔に泥を塗る *kao ni doro o nuru* fling mud at, bring disgrace [dishonor] on

② unclassified compounds

泥棒 *dorobō* thief, crook
【**doro² 泥**】[in compounds] [also suffix] petty thief, sneak thief, pilferer
泥縄 *doronawa* expediency coming too late (like making a rope after finding the thief)
こそ泥 *kosodoro* sneak, pilferer
自動車泥 *jidōshadoro* auto [car] thief

SYNONYMS

❶ⓐ land and soil
土 SOIL → 3403
壌 ARABLE SOIL → 755
地 GROUND → 204
陸 LAND → 543

【**doro²**】
○ thieves
盗 thief → 2670
賊 BANDIT → 1530

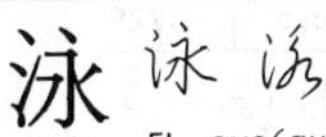

327 EI oyo(gu)

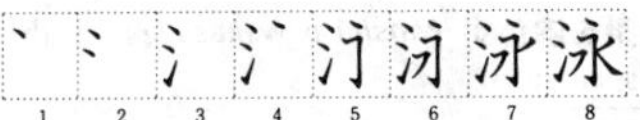

Ⓒⓗ 泳 yǒng

Radical	Strokes
氵 85	8-3-5
Grade	**Freq**
Jōyō-3	1088
◧ 1 - 3 - 5	

3-5 氵

▶SWIM

COMPOUNDS

ⓐ [original meaning] **swim**
ⓑ swimming
泳法 *eihō* swimming style
水泳 *suiei* swimming
競泳 *kyōei* swimming race
背泳 *haiei* backstroke
継泳 *keiei* relay swimming

KUN

【**oyo(gu) 泳ぐ**】 swim; (figuratively) swim, get along
泳ぎ *oyogi* swimming
平泳ぎ *hiraoyogi* breast stroke
人波を泳ぐ *hitonami o oyogu* wade through a crowd
時流に乗って泳ぐ *jiryū ni notte oyogu* swim with the current

SYNONYMS

ⓐ move through water
渉 wade → 526

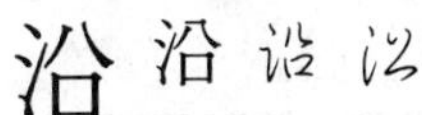

328 EN so(u) -zo(i)

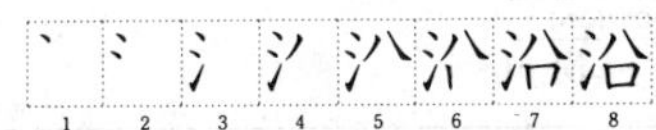

Ⓒⓗ 沿 yán yàn

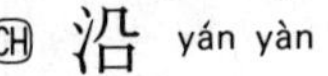

Radical	Strokes
氵 85	8-3-5
Grade	**Freq**
Jōyō-6	1286
◧ 1 - 3 - 5	

3-5 氵

▶ALONG

COMPOUNDS

❶ along, alongside
沿道 *endō* along the route
沿線の *ensen no* along a railway line
沿海 *enkai* coast, shore
沿岸 *engan* coast, shore
❷ follow (a tradition)
沿革 *enkaku* history, annals

KUN

【**so(u) 沿う**】
ⓐ lie along (a river), follow along
ⓑ be in line with (a policy)
路線に沿って *rosen ni sotte* along the route [line]
対外政策に沿って *taigai seisaku ni sotte* in line with the foreign policy
【**-zo(i) -沿い**】 [also suffix] along
川沿いに *kawazoi ni* along the riverside
山沿いの地方 *yamazoi no chihō* mountainous region
南岸沿い *nanganzoi* along the southern coast

SYNONYMS

❶ near
傍 BESIDE → 147
近 NEAR → 3061
隣 neighboring → 781

USAGE

sou
沿う
ⓐ lie along (a river), follow along
ⓑ be in line with (a policy)
添う
① accompany, go along with, stay with
② marry
③ meet (someone's wishes), suit

④ add to, increase

HOMOPHONES

sou ⇨ 添 529

COMPOUND FORMATION

沿革 *enkaku*

沿革 'history, annals' is following (沿 ❷) a tradition and reforming (革) it, i.e., the annals of change.

3-5
氵

沸 329

FUTSU wa(ku) wa(kasu)

Ⓒⓗ 沸 fèi

Radical	Strokes
氵 85	8-3-5
Grade	**Freq**
Jōyō	1728
1-3-5	

▶BOIL

COMPOUNDS

● (undergo boiling) **boil**

沸騰する *futtō suru* boil, seethe, bubble
沸点 *futten* boiling point
煮沸 *shafutsu* boiling

KUN

【wa(ku) 沸く】

vi

① boil, grow hot
沸きが早い *waki ga hayai* quick to warm up
沸き上がる *wakiagaru* boil up; break out, arise; seethe, be in uproar

② boil over (with excitement), seethe, be excited
沸き返る *wakikaeru* seethe, be in uproar; boil up

【wa(kasu) 沸かす】

vt

① boil, make hot
湯沸かし *yuwakashi* kettle, water heater

② excite, stimulate
観衆を沸かす *kanshū o wakasu* excite the spectators

SYNONYMS

● **cook**

煮 BOIL (cook by boiling) → 2785
炊 COOK → 870
蒸 STEAM → 2334
焼く cook by fire → 997
揚げる fry in deep fat → 593

USAGE

waku

沸く
vi
① boil, grow hot
② boil over (with excitement), seethe, be excited

湧く
① spring forth, gush out
② take form, appear; grow, spring up
③ breed (teemingly), be hatched

HOMOPHONES

waku ⇨ 湧 615

3-5
氵

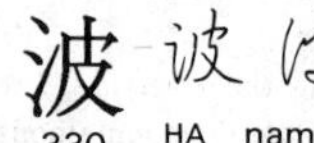

波 330

HA nami

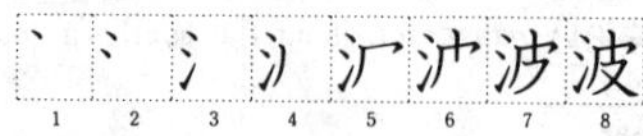

Ⓒⓗ 波 bō

Radical	Strokes
氵 85	8-3-5
Grade	**Freq**
Jōyō-3	579
1-3-5	

▶WAVE

COMPOUNDS

❶ⓐ [also suffix] [original meaning] **wave**
ⓑ *phys* **wave**

波浪 *harō* waves, billows
波紋 *hamon* ripple; stir, sensation
波止場 *hatoba* wharf, quay
波瀾(=波乱) *haran* disturbance, troubles; fluctuation
風波 *fūha* wind and waves, rough seas, storm
波動 *hadō* wave motion, undulation
電磁波 *denjiha* electromagnetic waves
電波 *denpa* electromagnetic waves, radio waves
短波 *tanpa* shortwave
音波 *onpa* sound waves
光波 *kōha* light waves

❷ⓐ something that occurs in waves
ⓑ counter for events occurring in waves
ⓒ spread like waves
寒波 *kanpa* cold wave

第三波スト *daisanpa suto* the third wave of strikes
波及する *hakyū suru* be propagated; extend, spread; affect
❸ⓐ used phonetically for *ha* and closely-related sounds
ⓑ Poland
波羅蜜 *haramitsu pāramitā*, entrance into Nirvana
日波 *nippo* Japan and Poland

KUN

【nami 波】 wave, billow, ripple; fluctuations, rise and fall; wave motion, undulation; wrinkles

波乗り *naminori* surfriding, surfing
津波 *tsunami* tsunami, tidal wave
人波 *hitonami* surging crowd
波打つ *namiutsu* undulate, heave, surge; be wavy
横波 *yokonami* side wave; *phys* transverse wave
老いの波 *oi no nami* wrinkles

SYNONYMS

❶ waves
浪 BILLOW → 439
❸ⓐ phonetic [ha]
巴 phonetic [ha] → 3438

泊 洦 泊

331 HAKU to(maru) to(meru)

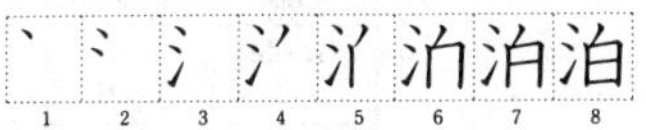

Ⓒⓗ 泊 bó pō

Radical	Strokes
氵 85	8-3-5
Grade	**Freq**
Jōyō	1191
◧ 1 - 3 - 5	

3-5 氵

▶STAY OVERNIGHT

COMPOUNDS

❶ⓐ stay overnight, lodge, stay at
ⓑ counter for number of overnight stays
宿泊 *shukuhaku* lodging
外泊 *gaihaku* staying out overnight
民泊 *minpaku* private residence temporarily taking lodgers
一泊 *ippaku* overnight stay
三泊四日の旅 *sanpaku-yokka no tabi* trip of four days and three nights
❷ stay at anchor, anchor a ship
泊地 *hakuchi* anchorage, berth
停泊 *teihaku* anchorage, mooring
仮泊 *kahaku* temporary anchoring
❸ simple, plain
淡泊(＝淡白)な *tanpaku na* light (color, taste); plain, simple; indifferent
❹ [original meaning] shallow body of water
漂泊する *hyōhaku suru* roam, drift about, wander
梁山泊 *ryōzanpaku* gathering place of ambitious men

INDEPENDENT

【haku 泊】 overnight stay
泊を重ねる *haku o kasaneru* stay long

KUN

【to(maru) 泊まる】
① stay overnight, lodge, stay at
泊まり *tomari* stopover, stay; night duty; anchorage
素泊まり *sudomari* staying overnight without board
② stay at anchor
港に泊まる *minato ni tomaru* stay at anchor
③ be on night duty
泊まり番 *tomariban* night duty

【to(meru) 泊める】
① lodge, give shelter, accommodate
友達を泊める *tomodachi o tomeru* put a friend up for the night
② anchor a ship

SYNONYMS

❶ⓐ stay
宿 LODGE → 2293
在 reside temporarily → 2984
屯 STATION TROOPS → 3457
駐 STATIONED → 1826
留 STAY → 2580
滞 STAY → 663

HOMOPHONES

tomaru ⇨ 止 2941 留 2580 停 139
tomari ⇨ 止 2941
tomeru ⇨ 止 2941 留 2580 停 139

COMPOUND FORMATION

梁山泊 *ryōzanpaku*
梁山泊 'gathering place of ambitious men' refers to a shallow body of water (泊 ❹) near Mt. Ryozan (梁山), since ambitious men would gather there.

NOTE

⇨ see USAGE note at 止 2941

3-5
氵

泌 泌 泌

332 HITSU HI

丶 氵 氵 氵 汈 汉 泌 泌
1 2 3 4 5 6 7 8

CH 泌 mì bì

Radical	Strokes
氵 85	8-3-5
Grade	**Freq**
Jōyō	1806
1-3-5	

▶**SECRETE**

COMPOUNDS

● [original meaning] **secrete**
泌尿器 *hinyōki* urinary organs
分泌 *bunpitsu* (=*bunpi*) secretion
内分泌腺 *naibunpisen* endocrine gland

SYNONYMS

● **flow and drip**
滴 DROP → 705
漏 LEAK → 701
濫 overflow → 801
注 POUR → 325
流 FLOW → 441

3-5
氵

法 法 法

333 HŌ HAT- HOT- FURAN▲ nori▲

丶 氵 氵 氵 汁 注 法 法
1 2 3 4 5 6 7 8

CH 法 fǎ

Radical	Strokes
氵 85	8-3-5
Grade	**Freq**
Jōyō-4	126
1-3-5	

▶**LAW** ▶**METHOD**

COMPOUNDS

❶ⓐ [also suffix] **law, rule, act, code of laws**
ⓑ law(s) (as of an art), principle, rule
ⓒ abbrev. of 法学(部) *hōgaku(bu)*: law (department)
法律 *hōritsu* law
法令 *hōrei* laws and ordinances, statute
法学 *hōgaku* law, jurisprudence
法廷 *hōtei* law court
法的 *hōteki* legal, legalistic
法規 *hōki* laws and regulations
法案 *hōan* bill, legislative proposal
法人 *hōjin* legal person, corporation
法典 *hōten* code of laws, statute
法度 *hatto* law, ordinance, prohibition
憲法 *kenpō* constitution, constitutional law
違法の *ihō no* illegal, unlawful
刑法 *keihō* criminal law, penal code
国際法 *kokusaihō* international laws
農地法 *nōchihō* Agricultural Land Law
騒音防止法 *sōon bōshi-hō* Noise Abatement Act
法則 *hōsoku* law, rule
画法 *gahō* laws [canons] of painting
法博 *hōhaku* Doctor of Law
❷ laws of propriety, rules of etiquette
作法 *sahō* manners, etiquette, decorum
礼法 *reihō* courtesy, etiquette, manners
❸ [also suffix] **method, way, manner, system, process, technique**
方法 *hōhō* method, way; system; scheme, means; process, procedure; plan
手法 *shuhō* technique, mechanism, style
療法 *ryōhō* method of treatment, cure, remedy
製法 *seihō* method of manufacture, process of preparation, recipe
生活法 *seikatsuhō* way of life, art of living
教授法 *kyōjuhō* method of teaching
銅アンモニア法 *dōanmoniahō* cuprous ammoniacal process
❹ⓐ **Buddha's teachings, Buddha's doctrine, dharma, Buddhism; religious tenets**
ⓑ religious rites, ceremony, service
法王 *hōō* Pope
法主 *hossu* (=*hōshu, hosshu*) high priest (of a Buddhist sect)
仏法 *buppō* Buddhism
説法 *seppō* (Buddhist) sermon, preaching, moralizing
法事 *hōji* (Buddhist) memorial service
法要 *hōyō* (Buddhist) memorial service
❺ [suffix] *gram* mood
仮定法 *kateihō* subjunctive mood
不定法 *futeihō* infinitive mood
❻ franc
百法 *hyakufuran* 100 francs
❼ model
法帖 *hōjō* copybook printed from the works of old masters of calligraphy

INDEPENDENT

【hō 法】

① law, rule, regulation
法を守る *hō o mamoru* observe the law
② method, way
旨い法を考え出す *umai hō o kangaedasu* devise a crack method
③ Buddha's teachings, dharma
法を説く *hō o toku* preach the truth
④ manners, etiquette
法に適う *hō ni kanau* conform to the rules of etiquette
⑤ reason
そんな法は無い *Sonna hō wa nai* That's against reason / That's absurd
⑥ divisor, modulus, modulo
六は五を法として十一と合同である *Roku wa go o hō to shite jūichi to gōdō de aru* Six is congruent to eleven, modulo five
⑦ *gram* mood
法と時制 *hō to jisei* mood and tense

KUN

【**nori** 法】law, rule, regulation; model, pattern; religious doctrine; sacred teachings of Buddha
法を越える *nori o koeru* violate the laws of nature

SYNONYMS

❶ⓐ & ❶ⓑ laws and rules
律 LAW → 363
典 CANON → 2627
憲 CONSTITUTION → 2368
令 ordinance → 1995
則 RULE → 1444
矩 RULE → 1148
規 REGULATION → 978
紀 discipline → 1276

❸ way and style
途 WAY → 3107
方 WAY → 1963
流 STYLE → 441
式 STYLE → 3049
調 TONE → 1567
様 MODE → 1052
風 MANNER → 3007

❹ⓐ religions and sects
仏 Buddhism → 19
禅 ZEN → 1032
儒 CONFUCIANISM → 174
道 Taoism → 3134

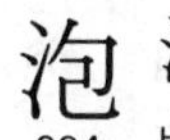

泡 泡 泡 (CH) 泡 pào pāo

334 HŌ awa

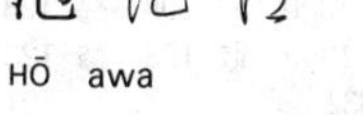

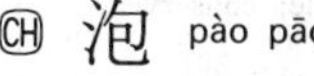

Radical	Strokes
氵 85	8-3-5
Grade	**Freq**
Jōyō	1793
◧ 1-3-5	

3-5 氵

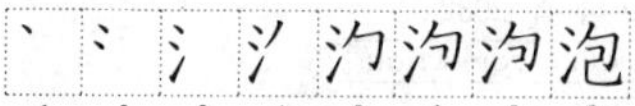

▶BUBBLE

COMPOUNDS

● [original meaning] **bubble, foam**
泡沫 *hōmatsu* bubble, foam, froth
泡沫会社 *hōmatsugaisha* bubble company, fly-by-night concern
発泡 *happō* foaming, effervescence
気泡 *kihō* air bubble, bubble
水泡 *suihō* bubble, foam

KUN

【**awa** 泡】bubble, foam
泡立つ *awadatsu* bubble, foam
泡盛 *awamori* millet brandy
石鹸の泡 *sekken no awa* lather, soapsuds

SYNONYMS

● small water masses
滴 DROP → 705

治 治 治 (CH) 治 zhì

335 JI CHI osa(meru) osa(maru) nao(ru) nao(su)

Stroke order: 1–8

Radical	Strokes
氵 85	8-3-5
Grade	**Freq**
Jōyō-4	180
◧ 1-3-5	

3-5 氵

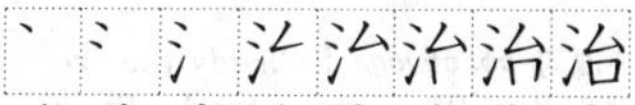

▶GOVERN ▶CURE

COMPOUNDS

❶ⓐ govern, administer, rule over, reign over
ⓑ government, rule, administration
治国 *chikoku* government
治世 *chisei* reign, rule, regime, dynasty
自治 *jichi* self-government, autonomy
統治 *tōchi* rule, government, reign
明治 *meiji* Meiji era

治下の *chika no* under the rule of
政治 *seiji* government, administration, politics
内治 *naichi* (=*naiji*) home administration
法治 *hōchi* constitutional government
文治 *bunchi* civil administration
❷ bring under control, manage, control
治具 *jigu* jig
治産 *chisan* property management
治水 *chisui* flood control
❸ **public order, peace**
治安 *chian* public peace and order
治乱 *chiran* war and peace
治平 *chihei* peace and tranquility
退治 *taiji* subjugation, subdual; extermination; crusade
❹ⓐ **cure, treat, heal**
ⓑ cure, recovery
治療 *chiryō* medical treatment [cure]
治癒 *chiyu* healing, cure, recovery
主治医 *shujii* physician in charge
不治の *fuji no* incurable, fatal
根治 *konji* (=*konchi*) complete [radical] cure
湯治 *tōji* hot spring cure, taking healing baths

INDEPENDENT

【jisuru 治する】 cure, heal; rule; conserve
【chi 治】 peace, public order
治に居て乱を忘れず *Chi ni ite ran o wasurezu* We must not forget war in peace

KUN

【osa(meru) 治める】
ⓐ govern, rule over, reign over, manage
ⓑ bring under control, put down, suppress, pacify, quell
国を治める *kuni o osameru* govern a country, manage a state
暴動を治める *bōdō o osameru* quell a disturbance
【osa(maru) 治まる】
① be in peace, be governed well
国が治まる *Kuni ga osamaru* Peace reigns in the country
② be cured, be relieved (of pain)
痛みが治まる *Itami ga osamaru* A pain is cured
【nao(ru) 治る】 be cured, get well, recover
治り *naori* recovery
傷が治った *Kizu ga naotta* The wound has healed up
【nao(su) 治す】 cure, heal
風邪を治す *kaze o naosu* cure a cold

SYNONYMS

❶ⓐ **govern**
統 rule → 1352
ⓑ **government**
政 POLITICAL ADMINISTRATION → 1142
❸ **peace**
安 public peace → 2171
和 PEACE → 1130
❹ **cure and recover**
医 cure → 2993
癒 HEAL → 3291
快 recover → 245
療 TREAT → 3288

HOMOPHONES

osameru ⇨ 納 1300 収 198 修 123
osamaru ⇨ 納 1300 収 198 修 123
naoru ⇨ 直 2932
naosu ⇨ 直 2932

COMPOUND FORMATION

治具 *jigu*
治具 'jig' is a phonetic rendering of *jig*, i.e., a device for holding or guiding (治 ❷) a tool (具).

NOTE

⇨ see USAGE notes at 直 2932 and 納 1300
⇨ see COMPOUND FORMATION for 明治 *meiji* ⇨ 明 855

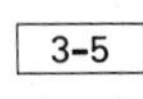
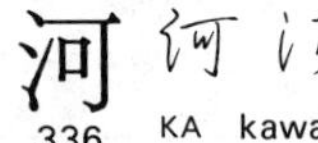
336 KA kawa

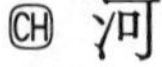
hé

Radical	Strokes
氵 85	8-3-5
Grade	**Freq**
Jōyō-5	723
◧ 1 - 3 - 5	

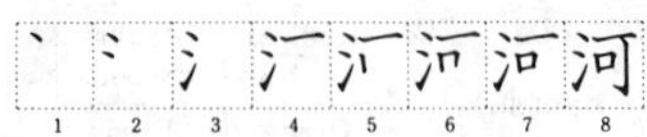

▶**RIVER**

COMPOUNDS

❶ [original meaning] **river, large river**
河川 *kasen* rivers
河流 *karyū* stream
河口 *kakō* river mouth, estuary
河岸 *kashi* riverside; fish market
運河 *unga* canal
銀河 *ginga* Milky Way; galaxy
暴虎馮河 *bōkohyōga* foolhardy courage
❷ the Yellow River, the Huanghe River
河北 *kahoku* north of the Yellow River; Hebei (Province)
黄河 *kōga* the Yellow River

KUN

【kawa 河】
[usu. 川]
ⓐ river, stream

ⓑ suffix after names of (esp. foreign) rivers
河底 *kawazoko* riverbed
アマゾン河 *amazongawa* Amazon River

SPECIAL READINGS

河原 *kawara* dry riverbed, river beach
河童▲ *kappa* water sprite, *kappa*; excellent swimmer
河豚▲ *fugu fugu*, globefish, swellfish

SYNONYMS

❶ **rivers and streams**

川 RIVER → 6
江 large river → 221
渓 mountain stream → 516
流 stream → 441

HOMOPHONES

kawa ⇨ 川 6

NOTE

⇨ see USAGE note at 川 6
⇨ see COMPOUND FORMATION for 暴虎馮河 *bōkohyōga* ⇨ 暴 2515

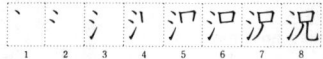

況 况 况

337 KYŌ

` ﾝ 氵 氵' 氵冂 氵口 沪 況
1 2 3 4 5 6 7 8

CH 况 kuàng

Radical	Strokes
氵 85	8-3-5
Grade	**Freq**
Jōyō	601
1 - 3 - 5	

3-5 氵

▶CONDITIONS

COMPOUNDS

❶ **conditions, condition, situation, state of affairs**
状況 *jōkyō* state of affairs, conditions, circumstances
戦況 *senkyō* war situation, progress of a battle
近況 *kinkyō* recent condition [situation]
実況 *jikkyō* actual conditions
概況 *gaikyō* general condition [situation], outlook
好況 *kōkyō* brisk market, prosperity
市況 *shikyō* market conditions, tone of the market
不況 *fukyō* depression, slump, recession
盛況 *seikyō* prosperity, boom, success

❷ compare
比況 *hikyō* comparison

SYNONYMS

❶ **states and situations**

景 business conditions → 2470
状 CONDITION → 272
態 STATE → 2847
勢 course of events → 2857
境 SITUATION → 676
局 current situation → 3063
情 ACTUAL CONDITIONS → 482
訳 circumstances → 1473
調 TONE → 1567
様 MODE → 1052
相 PHASE → 900

 泣 泣

338 KYŪ na(ku)

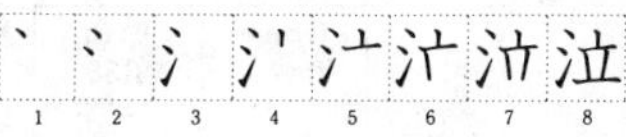
1 2 3 4 5 6 7 8

CH 

Radical	Strokes
氵 85	8-3-5
Grade	**Freq**
Jōyō-4	1117
1 - 3 - 5	

3-5 氵

▶CRY

COMPOUNDS

● [original meaning] **cry, weep, sob**
泣訴する *kyūso suru* implore with tears in one's eyes
号泣する *gōkyū suru* wail, lament
感泣する *kankyū suru* weep with emotion, be moved to tears

KUN

【na(ku) 泣く】 cry, weep, sob
泣き *naki* weeping, lamenting
泣き顔 *nakigao* tear-stained face
泣き叫ぶ *nakisakebu* cry, scream, wail
咽び泣く *musebinaku* sob, be choked with tears

SYNONYMS

● **cry and sigh**

嘆 SIGH → 630

USAGE

naku

泣く
cry, weep, sob

鳴く
(of animals, birds or insects) cry, chirp,

ululate, howl, yelp, meow

HOMOPHONES
naku ⇨ 鳴 674

3-5 氵

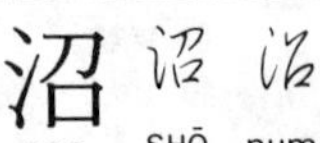

339 SHŌ numa

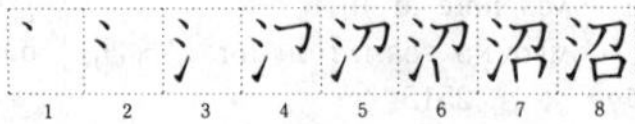

(CH) 沼 zhǎo

Radical	Strokes
氵 85	8-3-5
Grade	Freq
Jōyō	1120
1 - 3 - 5	

▶MUDDY POND

COMPOUNDS

● [original meaning] **muddy pond, low-lying lake, swamp, marsh, bog**

沼沢 *shōtaku* marsh, swamp
沼気 *shōki* marsh gas, methane
湖沼 *koshō* lakes and marshes
沼地 *numachi* swampland, bogland, marshland
泥沼 *doronuma* bog; swamp (of difficulties)
長沼 *naganuma* Lake Naganuma

KUN

【**numa** 沼】muddy pond, low-lying lake, swamp, marsh, bog; suffix after name of muddy ponds

SYNONYMS

● **lakes and marshes**

沢 MARSH → 267
湖 LAKE → 604
池 POND → 218
潟 LAGOON → 745

3-5 氵

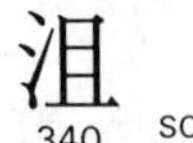

340 SO

(CH) 沮 jǔ jù

Radical	Strokes
氵 85	8-3-5
Grade	Freq
Reference	
1 - 3 - 5	

COMPOUNDS

[now replaced by 阻 348]

❶ (prevent the progress or passage of) obstruct, impede, hinder, check

沮止 *soshi* obstruction, check, hindrance
沮害 *sogai* obstruction, check, impediment, hindrance

❷ be dejected, lose heart

沮喪 *sosō* loss of spirit, dejection

3-5 氵

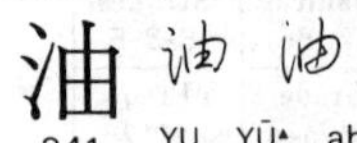

341 YU YŪ* abura

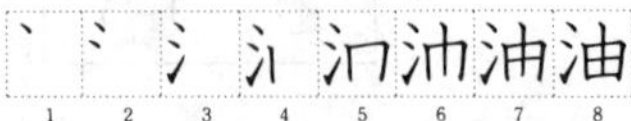

(CH) 油 yóu

Radical	Strokes
氵 85	8-3-5
Grade	Freq
Jōyō-3	638
1 - 3 - 5	

▶OIL

COMPOUNDS

❶ [also suffix]

ⓐ **oil, animal oil, vegetable oil**

ⓑ (petroleum or petroleum derivative) **oil, petroleum**

油脂 *yushi* fats and oils
油断 *yudan* negligence, carelessness, inattentiveness
醤油 *shōyu* soy sauce
サラダ油 *saradayu* (=*saradaabura*) salad oil
オリーブ油 *orībuyu* olive oil
石油 *sekiyu* petroleum, oil
重油 *jūyu* heavy [thick] oil
灯油 *tōyu* kerosene, lamp oil
原油 *gen'yu* crude oil
潤滑油 *junkatsuyu* lubricant, lubricating oil

❷ abundantly

油然と *yūzen to* gushingly, copiously

KUN

【**abura** 油】oil, animal oil, vegetable oil

油絵 *aburae* oil painting

油気 *aburake* greasiness, oiliness
油を売る *abura o uru* loaf, idle away one's time
油を絞る *abura o shiboru* extract oil by pressing; give a person a severe talking-to
胡麻油 *gomaabura* sesame (seed) oil
大豆油 *daizuabura* soy bean oil

SYNONYMS

❶ⓐ fats and oils
脂 FAT → 954
肪 ANIMAL FAT → 877
ⓐ seasonings
酢 VINEGAR → 1516
塩 SALT → 631
糖 SUGAR → 1403
ⓑ kinds of fuel
炭 COAL, CHARCOAL → 2257
薪 FIREWOOD → 2374

USAGE

abura
油
oil, animal oil, vegetable oil
脂
[formerly also 膏] fat, grease, lard, blubber; greasy substance
膏
[now usu. 脂] fat, grease; greasy substance

HOMOPHONES

abura ⇨ 脂 954 膏 2141

COMPOUND FORMATION

油断 *yudan*
油断 'negligence, carelessness, inattentiveness', a Buddhist term found in the Nirvana Sutra, is derived from an ancient tale of a monarch that has his retainer hold a pot full of oil so as to test his powers of concentration. If the retainer should be so careless as to let even a single drop of oil (油 ❶ⓐ) spill, he would have his life cut off (断), that is, he would be put to death. In this way, 油断 came to signify carelessness or inattentiveness.

注 342

▶POUR ▶CONCENTRATE
nonstandard for 注 325

3-5 氵

沿 343

▶ALONG
nonstandard for 沿 328

3-5 氵

泡 344

▶BUBBLE
nonstandard for 泡 334

3-5 氵

狗 345

KU inu

CH 狗 gǒu

Radical	Strokes
犭 94	8-3-5
Grade	**Freq**
Reference	
1-3-5	

3-5 犭

COMPOUNDS

❶ [original meaning] dog (esp. of small variety)
走狗 *sōku* running dog; dupe, tool, cat's paw
羊頭狗肉 *yōtōkuniku* using a better name to sell inferior goods, crying wine and selling vinegar
天狗 *tengu tengu*, long-nosed goblin; braggart
狗尾草 *enokorogusa* foxtail, *Setaria viridis*
❷ [now usu. 犬 *inu*]
ⓐ dog (esp. of small variety)
ⓑ spy
喪家の狗 *sōka no inu* feeling lost like a stray dog
警察の狗 *keisatsu no inu* police spy

HOMOPHONES

inu ⇨ 犬 3464 戌 3535

NOTE

⇨ see USAGE note at 犬 3464
⇨ see COMPOUND FORMATION for 羊頭狗肉 *yōtōkuniku* ⇨ 羊 2183

3-5
阝

阿

346 A o- omone(ru)

1 2 3 4 5 6 7 8

CH 阿 ā ē

Radical	Strokes
阝 170	8-3-5
Grade	**Freq**
Names	1983
1 - 3 - 5	

▶**PHONETIC** [a]

COMPOUNDS

❶ⓐ **used phonetically for *a*, esp. in the transliteration of names, foreign words or Sanscrit Buddhist terms**
ⓑ the letter *a* (in esoteric Buddhism symbolizes the unity of the world)
阿片 *ahen* opium
阿弥陀 *amida* Amitabha; lottery; wearing a hat on the back of the head
阿修羅 *ashura Asura* (fighting demon)
阿字 *aji* the letter *a* (in esoteric Buddhism)
阿吽 *aun* alpha and omega; inhalation and exhalation
❷ flatter, fawn upon, toady, favor
阿諛 *ayu* flattery
阿世 *asei* [rare] timeserving
❸ fool, simpleton
阿呆 *ahō* fool, idiot
❹ prefix for conveying intimacy
阿兄 *akei* my dear brother
阿Q正伝 *akyūseiden* The True Life of Ah-Q
❺ Africa
南阿共和国 *nan'a kyōwakoku* Republic of South Africa
❻ abbrev. of 阿波 *awa*, old name for Tokushima Prefecture
阿南市 *ananshi* Anan City
❼ [archaic] hook-shaped object, bent
❽ [original meaning, now archaic] recesses of a mountain

INDEPENDENT

【a 阿】 the letter *a* (in esoteric Buddhism *a* is mother of all sounds and represents the unity of the world)

KUN

【o- 阿-】 [also 御-] prefix for conveying intimacy, esp. before names of women
阿父様 *otōsama* Father
阿国 *okuni* Okuni (female name)
【omone(ru) 阿る】 flatter, fawn upon, toady
大衆に阿る *taishū ni omoneru* sell out to the masses

NAMES

阿波 *awa* place name
阿部 *abe* surname
阿蘇 *aso* place name

SYNONYMS

❶ⓐ **phonetic** [a]
亜 PHONETIC [a] → 3540
❺ **continents**
亜 Asia → 3540
欧 EUROPE → 887
米 AMERICA → 3529
豪 Australia → 2140

HOMOPHONES

o- ⇨ 御 577

NOTE

⇨ see USAGE note at 御 577

3-5
阝

附

347 FU tsu(keru)▲ tsu(ku)▲

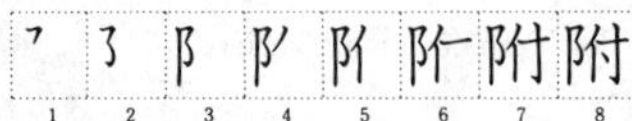
1 2 3 4 5 6 7 8

CH 附 fù

Radical	Strokes
阝 170	8-3-5
Grade	**Freq**
Jōyō	1906
1 - 3 - 5	

▶**ATTACH**

COMPOUNDS

[usu. 付]
❶ⓐ [original meaning] **attach, append, add to, affix**
ⓑ **attached, additional, supplementary**
ⓒ **attach itself to, stick to, adhere to**
添附する *tenpu suru* attach, append, annex
附着する *fuchaku suru* adhere [cling] to, agglutinate; cohere
❷ be attached to, belong to, be affiliated with
附属する *fuzoku suru* be attached to, belong to
❸ abbrev. of 附属校 *fuzokukō* and 附属病院 *fuzoku byōin*: attached [affiliated] school, hospital in affiliation
赤十字附 *sekijūjifu* school attached to the Japan Red Cross Society

❹ⓐ **deliver, hand over, grant**
ⓑ entrust, commit to
交附する *kōfu suru* deliver, grant, hand (a ticket) to (a person)
寄附する *kifu suru* contribute, donate
❺ adjacent, near to
附近 *fukin* neighborhood, environs, vicinity

INDEPENDENT
【fu 附(=付)】 appendix; supplement
【fusuru 附する(=付する)】 attach, append, add to, affix; commit [submit] to, refer to; consign to, dispose of

KUN
【tsu(keru) 附ける】 [usu. 付ける] same as **tsukeru 付ける** 31
【tsu(ku) 附く】 [usu. 付く] same as **tsuku 付く** 31

SYNONYMS
❶ⓐ & ❶ⓑ add to
付 ATTACH → 31
加 ADD → 38
追 add → 3096
添 ADD TO → 529
ⓒ stick
付 attach itself to → 31
着 STICK → 3316
❹ⓐ transfer
付 deliver → 31
渡 hand over → 611
譲 CEDE → 1649

HOMOPHONES
tsukeru ⇨ 付 31 着 3316 就 1694 即 1120 点 2084 漬 702
tsuku ⇨ 付 31 着 3316 就 1694 即 1120 点 2084

NOTE
⇨ see USAGE note at 付 31

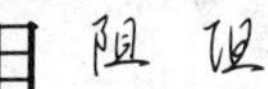

阻

348 SO haba(mu)

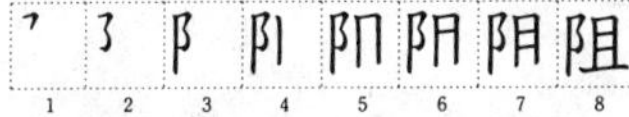

CH 阻 zǔ

Radical	Strokes
阝 170	8-3-5
Grade	**Freq**
Jōyō	1253
◧ 1-3-5	

3-5 阝

▶**OBSTRUCT**

COMPOUNDS
❶ [formerly also 沮 340] (prevent the progress or passage of) **obstruct, impede, hinder, check**
阻害する *sogai suru* obstruct, check, impede, hinder
阻止 *soshi* obstruction, check, hindrance
❷ [formerly also 沮 340] be dejected, lose heart
阻喪 *sosō* loss of spirit, dejection
❸ separate, isolate
阻隔 *sokaku* separation, estrangement
❹ [formerly also 岨 285] steep
険阻(=嶮岨)な *kenso na* steep (mountain pass), precipitous

KUN
【haba(mu) 阻む】 obstruct, impede, hinder, check, prevent
道を阻む *michi o habamu* obstruct one's way
成長を阻む *seichō o habamu* hinder [check] the growth of (plants)

SPECIAL READINGS
悪阻▲ *tsuwari* (=*oso*) morning sickness

SYNONYMS
❶ obstruct and hinder
妨 HINDER → 238
障 hinder → 715
遮 INTERRUPT → 3158
害 stand in the way → 2272

咲 咲 咲 咲

349 SHŌ▲ sa(ku) -zaki

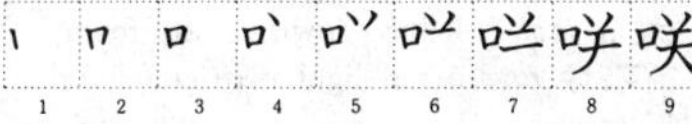

CH 笑 xiào

Radical	Strokes
口 30	9-3-6
Grade	**Freq**
Jōyō	1339
◧ 1-3-6	

3-6 口

▶**BLOOM**

COMPOUNDS
● [original meaning, now obsolete] laugh, smile

KUN
【sa(ku) 咲く】 bloom, blossom, flower; effloresce
咲き渡る *sakiwataru* bloom over a wide area

早咲き *hayazaki* early blooming, early flowering
狂い咲く *kuruizaku* bloom out of season
文化が花と咲く *Bunka ga hana to saku* Fine arts effloresce
【-zaki -咲】 suffix indicating state of florescence
五分咲き *gobuzaki* half-florescent

SYNONYMS
【saku】
○ **sprout and bloom**
萌 GERMINATE → 2301

3-6 口

咲 350

▶BLOOM
nonstandard for 咲 349

3-6 土

垣 351

EN▲ kaki

Stroke order: 1–9

CH 垣 yuán

Radical	Strokes
土 32	9-3-6
Grade	**Freq**
Jōyō	1491
1-3-6	

▶FENCE

COMPOUNDS
● [original meaning] **fence, wall**
垣牆 *enshō* [archaic] fence, hedge

KUN
【kaki 垣】 [formerly also 牆] [also suffix] fence, wall, hedge; barrier
垣根 *kakine* fence, hedge
生け垣 *ikegaki* hedge, quickset
石垣 *ishigaki* stone wall
四つ目垣 *yotsumegaki* lattice fence

SYNONYMS
● **fences and walls**
塀 FENCE (for screening) → 557
壁 WALL → 2895
囲い enclosure → 3069
欄 railing → 1103

USAGE
kaki
垣
[formerly also 牆] [also suffix] fence, wall, hedge; barrier
牆
[now usu. 垣] [also suffix] fence, wall

HOMOPHONES
kaki ⇨ 牆 1088

3-6 土

城 352

JŌ shiro

Stroke order: 1–9

CH 城 chéng

Radical	Strokes
土 32	9-3-6
Grade	**Freq**
Jōyō-6	657
1-3-6	

▶CASTLE

COMPOUNDS
❶ⓐ (fortified building) **castle, fort, fortress, citadel, stronghold**
ⓑ (fortified stately residence) castle, palace
ⓒ **suffix after names of castles**
城塞(=城砦) *jōsai* fortress, stronghold, citadel
城壁 *jōheki* castle wall, rampart
城下町 *jōkamachi* castle town, fief capital
城郭 *jōkaku* castle, fortress; castle walls, enclosure
籠城 *rōjō* confinement, keeping inside; holding a castle, sustaining a siege
牙城 *gajō* stronghold, inner citadel
落城 *rakujō* fall of a castle
築城 *chikujō* castle construction
城主 *jōshu* lord of a castle
王城 *ōjō* Imperial castle, royal palace
大阪城 *ōsakajō* Osaka Castle
❷ [original meaning] fortified town, city wall (in China)
城市 *jōshi* fortified town, castle town
不夜城 *fuyajō* red-light district, city that never sleeps
京城 *keijō* Seoul
万里の長城 *banri no chōjō* Great Wall of China

KUN
【shiro 城】 castle, fort, citadel; (place of priva-

cy) castle
自分の城に閉じ籠もる *jibun no shiro ni tojikomoru* keep in one's own castle
城跡 *shiroato* ruins of a castle
根城 *nejiro* stronghold, citadel; base of operations

SYNONYMS
❶ⓐ & ❶ⓒ **strongholds**
塁 SMALL FORT → 2593

姻 353 IN

CH 姻 yīn

Radical	Strokes
女 38	9-3-6
Grade	**Freq**
Jōyō	1877
1-3-6	

3-6 女

▶MARRIAGE

COMPOUNDS
ⓐ **marriage**
ⓑ relative by marriage
婚姻 *kon'in* marriage, matrimony
姻族 *inzoku* relatives by marriage
姻戚 *inseki* relatives by marriage, in-laws

SYNONYMS
ⓐ **marrying and marriage**
縁 marriage relation → 1386
婚 MARRY → 470
嫁 WED A MAN → 635
ⓑ **family and relations**
縁 RELATION → 1386
親 RELATIVES → 1799
族 FAMILY → 958
家 FAMILY → 2273
門 family → 888
氏 clan → 2951

姫 354

▶DAUGHTER OF NOBLE BIRTH
nonstandard for 姫 407

3-6 女

姙 355

▶BECOME PREGNANT
nonstandard for 妊 240

3-6 女

孤 356 KO

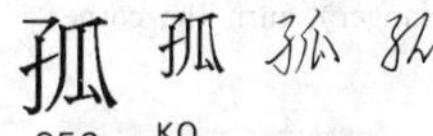

CH 孤 gū

Radical	Strokes
子 39	9-3-6
Grade	**Freq**
Jōyō	1400
1-3-6	

3-6 子

▶SOLITARY

COMPOUNDS
❶ⓐ **solitary, lone, isolated**
ⓑ lonely
孤独の *kodoku no* solitary, lonely, alone
孤立 *koritsu* isolation
孤客 *kokaku* lone traveler
孤島 *kotō* solitary island
孤軍 *kogun* lone [isolated] force, forlorn force
孤城 *kojō* solitary [isolated] castle
孤愁 *koshū* lonely contemplation
❷ [original meaning] orphan
孤児 *koji* orphan

INDEPENDENT
【**ko** 孤】 orphan; loneliness
幼にして孤となる *yō ni shite ko to naru* be orphaned in one's babyhood
徳は孤ならず *Toku wa ko narazu* The good will not long remain lonely

SYNONYMS
❶ⓐ **alone**
独 ALONE → 395
❷ **offspring**
子 CHILD → 3390
嫡 LEGITIMATE CHILD → 680
息 son → 2647
男 son → 2542
惣 eldest son → 2780

娘 DAUGHTER → 406
女 daughter → 3418
姫 DAUGHTER OF NOBLE BIRTH → 407

NOTE
★do not confuse with 弧 360

3-6
山

峡 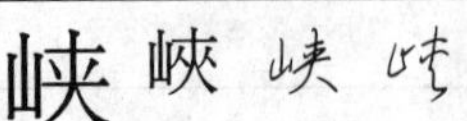

357 KYŌ

CH 峡 xiá

Radical	Strokes
山 46	9-3-6
Grade	Freq
Jōyō	1844
1-3-6	

丨 ㄣ 山 山 山 山 山 峡 峡
1 2 3 4 5 6 7 8 9

▶**GORGE**

COMPOUNDS

❶ⓐ **gorge, ravine, glen**
ⓑ suffix after names of gorges or valleys
峡谷 *kyōkoku* gorge, ravine, canyon, valley
峡間 *kyōkan* between the mountains; ravine
山峡 *sankyō* (=*yamakai*) gorge, ravine, glen
黒部峡 *kurobekyō* Kurobe Canyon
❷ **narrows, strait**
峡湾 *kyōwan* fjord
海峡 *kaikyō* straits, narrows, channel, sound
地峡 *chikyō* isthmus

SYNONYMS

❶ **valley**
渓 RAVINE → 516
谷 VALLEY → 2043
❷ **inlets and bays**
湾 BAY → 613
浦 coastal indentation → 437
江 INLET → 221

3-6
山

峠 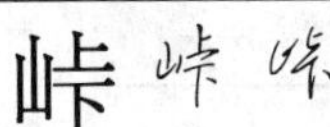

358 tōge

CH none (国字)

Radical	Strokes
山 46	9-3-6
Grade	Freq
Jōyō	1644
1-3-6	

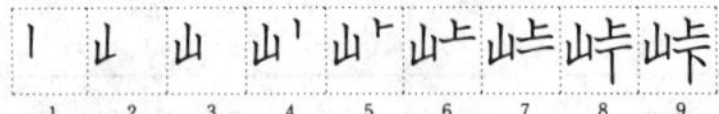

1 2 3 4 5 6 7 8 9

▶**MOUNTAIN PASS**

KUN

【tōge 峠】
①ⓐ mountain pass, ridge
ⓑ suffix after names of mountain passes
峠を越える *tōge o koeru* cross a pass, pass over the peak
峠道 *tōgemichi* road over a mountain pass
碓氷峠 *usuitōge* Usui Pass
② crisis, climax, height, turning point
峠を越す *tōge o kosu* the worst is over, pass the peak of (danger), turn the corner

SYNONYMS

【tōge】
① **high parts of mountains**
嶺 RIDGE → 2376
峰 PEAK → 411
頂 SUMMIT → 145

3-6
干

359

▶**SHAPE**
nonstandard for 形 846

弧 弧 弧 弧

360 KO

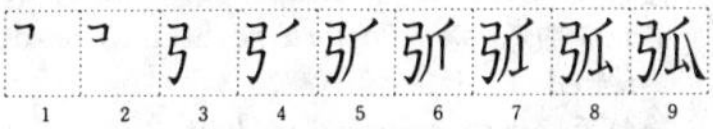

ㄱ ㄱ 弓 弓 弓 弧 弧 弧 弧

1 2 3 4 5 6 7 8 9

Ⓒⓗ 弧 hú

Radical	Strokes
弓 57	9-3-6
Grade	**Freq**
Jōyō	1842
◧ 1 - 3 - 6	

3-6 弓

▶ARC

COMPOUNDS

❶ⓐ **arc**

ⓑ *math* **arc**

弧状の *kojō no* arc-shaped
括弧 *kakko* parentheses, brackets
弧線 *kosen* arc (of a circle)
弧形 *kokei* arc
円弧 *enko* circular arc; arc of a circle
劣弧 *rekko* minor arc

❷ [original meaning, now archaic] wooden bow

INDEPENDENT

【ko 弧】 arc; *math* arc
弧を描く *ko o egaku* describe an arc

SYNONYMS

❶ **lines and line segments**
弦 chord → 287
径 DIAMETER → 291
辺 side → 3029
線 LINE → 1392

NOTE

★do not confuse with 孤 356

後 後 後

361 GO KŌ nochi ushi(ro) ushiro ato oku(reru)

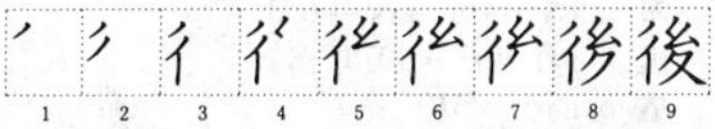

ノ ㇰ 彳 彳 彳 彳 彳 後 後

1 2 3 4 5 6 7 8 9

Ⓒⓗ 后 hòu

Radical	Strokes
彳 60	9-3-6
Grade	**Freq**
Jōyō-2	32
◧ 1 - 3 - 6	

3-6 彳

▶AFTER

COMPOUNDS

❶ [sometimes also 后 *go* 2981] [also suffix] (subsequent in time) **after, afterwards, later, subsequent**

後遺症 *kōishō* sequela, aftereffect (of a disease)
後任 *kōnin* successor, replacement
直後 *chokugo* immediately after
生後 *seigo* after birth
今後 *kongo* after this, from now on
以後 *igo* after this, from now on, in future; after that, thereafter
午後 *gogo* afternoon
老後 *rōgo* one's old age
十年後 *jūnengo* ten years after [hence]
終戦後の *shūsengo no* postwar

❷ (subsequent in order) **after, latter, second**

後者 *kōsha* the latter
後半 *kōhan* latter half, second half
後期 *kōki* latter period
後場 *goba* afternoon session [market]
後半生 *kōhansei* latter half of one's life
後手 *gote* moving second (in a board game); rear guard
最後の *saigo no* last, final

❸ afteryears, future generations, posterity

後世 *kōsei* future life, life to come
後事 *kōji* future affairs, affairs after one's death
後裔 *kōei* descendant, scion, offspring
後継者 *kōkeisha* successor, inheritor, heir
後続 *kōzoku* succession

❹ [also prefix] (behind in space) **after-, rear, back, hind**

後部 *kōbu* back part, rear
後援 *kōen* support, backing
後退する *kōtai suru* retreat, recede
後甲板 *kōkanpan* afterdeck
後頭部 *kōtōbu* back (part) of the head
前後 *zengo* before and after; order, sequence
背後 *haigo* back, rear
落後(＝落伍)する *rakugo suru* straggle, drop out of line, fall out of the ranks

❺ [original meaning] fall behind, fall back, lag behind, be backwards

後進国 *kōshinkoku* underdeveloped countries
後配株 *kōhaikabu* deferred stock
後家 *goke* widow

INDEPENDENT

【go 後】 after, afterward, later; since; abbrev. of 午後 *gogo*: afternoon
その後 *sono go* after that, afterward
後四時 *go yoji* 4 p.m.

KUN

【nochi 後】[also suffix] after, afterwards, later; after death; future
- 後程 *nochihodo* afterwards, later
- その後 *sono nochi* since then, thereafter
- 二週間後に *nishūkan nochi ni* two weeks hence
- 後添い *nochizoi* one's second wife
- 後の世 *nochi no yo* after ages, posterity; future life

【ushi(ro) 後ろ, ushiro 後】 back, rear
- 後ろから *ushiro kara* from behind
- 後ろ足 *ushiroashi* hind leg
- 後ろ姿 *ushirosugata* sight of one's back
- 後ろ楯 *ushirodate* backing, protection; supporter
- 後ろめたく思う *ushirometaku omou* have a guilty conscience
- 後ろ暗い事 *ushirogurai koto* shady [questionable] matters

【ato 後】

①ⓐ [also suffix] (subsequent in time) after, afterward, later, subsequent
ⓑ (subsequent in order) after, latter, next, following
ⓒ after death
- 後の *ato no* later, subsequent; the next [following]; back
- 後で *ato de* after, afterwards, later, later on
- 髭剃り後 *higesoriato* after shaving
- 三日後に *mikkaato ni* three days after [later]
- 後払い *atobarai* deferred payment
- 後書き *atogaki* postscript, afterword
- 後回し *atomawashi* deferment, postponement
- 後作 *atosaku* second crop
- 後を弔う *ato o tomurau* perform religious rites for the repose of a soul

② back, rear
- 後足 *atoashi* hind leg
- 後戻りする *atomodori suru* go backward, move back, turn back; retrograde

③ⓐ descendant, posterity
ⓑ future
- 源氏の後 *genji no ato* descendant of the Genji family
- 後後 *atoato* distant future

④ⓐ rest, remainder
ⓑ and, and also
- 後金 *atokin* rest of the payment
- 後十分 *ato jippun* ten minutes more
- 鉛筆と後消しゴム *enpitsu to ato keshigomu* pencil and also eraser

⑤ consequences, results, conclusion
- 後を濁す *ato o nigosu* leave a bad impression behind
- 後を引く *ato o hiku* The effects linger [remain]

【oku(reru) 後れる】

ⓐ fall behind, fall back, be outstripped, be backwards
ⓑ outlive
- 後れ *okure* backwardness, lag; failure, defeat
- 後れを取る *okure o toru* be beaten, be defeated
- 後れ毛 *okurege* straggling hair
- 手後れ *teokure* being too late
- 死に後れる *shiniokureru* outlive, survive

SYNONYMS

❶ **after**
余 after → 2042

❷ **second**
次 second → 54
乙 SECOND → 3339
中 MIDDLE → 3451

❸ **future**
来 coming generations → 3551

❹ **rear**
背 BACK → 2573
裏 REAR → 2138
尻 tail end → 3032
尾 TAIL → 3062

❺ **be late and delay**
遅 be late → 3133
滞 fall into arrears → 663
延 POSTPONE → 3073
猶 DELAY → 619

USAGE

❶ **ato**

後

①ⓐ [also suffix] (subsequent in time) after, afterward, later, subsequent
ⓑ (subsequent in order) after, latter, next, following
ⓒ after death
② back, rear
③ⓐ descendant, posterity
ⓑ future
④ⓐ rest, remainder
ⓑ and, and also
⑤ consequences, results, conclusion

跡

①ⓐ (mark left by something) trace(s), track, mark, footprint, trail, sign
ⓑ (sign of former presence) ruins, remains, aftermath
② succession
③ inheritance, headship of a family

❷ **okureru**

後れる

ⓐ fall behind, fall back, be outstripped, be backwards
ⓑ outlive

遅れる

ⓐ be late, be tardy, be delayed

ⓑ (of clocks) go slow, lose

❸ **okure**

後れ

① backwardness, lag

② failure, defeat

遅れ

ⓐ being late

ⓑ (of clocks) going slow

HOMOPHONES

ato ⇨ 跡 1534

okureru ⇨ 遅 3133

okure ⇨ 遅 3133

徊

362 KAI

Ⓒⓗ 徊 huái

Radical	Strokes
彳 60	9-3-6
Grade	**Freq**
Reference	
◧ 1-3-6	

3-6 彳

COMPOUNDS

● [now also 回 3055] [original meaning] move to and fro, walk around

低徊(＝低回)する *teikai suru* linger, loiter, wander

徘徊する *haikai suru* loiter, wander about

律

律 律

363 RITSU RICHI RETSU▲

Ⓒⓗ 律 lǜ

Radical	Strokes
彳 60	9-3-6
Grade	**Freq**
Jōyō-6	982
◧ 1-3-6	

3-6 彳

丿 ㇒ 彳 彳 彳 彳 彳 律 律

1 2 3 4 5 6 7 8 9

▶**LAW** ▶**RHYTHM**

COMPOUNDS

❶ⓐ [also suffix] **law, rule, statute, regulation; commandment**

ⓑ [suffix] **law (of nature), principle**

ⓒ (bind by law) control, restrain

律令 *ritsuryō* ancient laws

律儀 *richigi* honesty, faithfulness, loyalty

法律 *hōritsu* law

規律 *kiritsu* order, discipline; regulation, law

不文律 *fubunritsu* unwritten law [rule]

道徳律 *dōtokuritsu* moral law

戒律 *kairitsu* commandments, precepts

黄金律 *ōgonritsu* golden rule

因果律 *ingaritsu* law of cause and effect, principle of causality

自然律 *shizenritsu* natural law

自律 *jiritsu* self-control, self-restraint

❷ **rhythm, tone, pitch**

律動 *ritsudō* rhythm, rhythmic movement

一律 *ichiritsu* uniformity, equality

旋律 *senritsu* melody

調律 *chōritsu* tuning

韻律 *inritsu* rhythm, meter, measure

❸ stanza of eight lines in Chinese poetry

律詩 *risshi* stanza of eight lines in Chinese poetry

❹ name of pentatonic music scale used in Japanese court music (D-E-G-A-B)

呂律 *roretsu* articulation

INDEPENDENT

【ritsu 律】 law, rule, statute, regulation, commandment; poetic form (⇨ ❸); pentatonic scale (⇨ ❹)

【rissuru 律する】 apply a rule to, judge, measure

SYNONYMS

❶ⓐ **laws and rules**

法 LAW → 333

典 CANON → 2627

憲 CONSTITUTION → 2368

令 ordinance → 1995

則 RULE → 1444

矩 RULE → 1148

規 REGULATION → 978

紀 discipline → 1276

ⓑ **principle**

理 BASIC PRINCIPLE → 970

❷ **musical elements**

韻 RHYME → 1811

拍 BEAT → 304

調 TONE → 1567

呂 ancient musical note → 2187

COMPOUND FORMATION

一律 *ichiritsu*

一律 'uniformity, equality' originally referred to the same (一) or uniform tone (律 ❷).

3-6 亻

待 364

TAI ma(tsu) -ma(chi)

CH 待 dài dāi

Radical	Strokes
亻 60	9-3-6
Grade	**Freq**
Jōyō-3	370
1-3-6	

▶WAIT

COMPOUNDS

❶ⓐ wait

ⓑ wait for, await, expect, look forward to

待機する *taiki suru* wait for an opportunity, stand ready
待避する *taihi suru* take shelter; shunt
待命 *taimei* waiting for orders
待望の *taibō no* hoped-for, long-awaited
期待 *kitai* expectation, anticipation, hope

❷ treat, entertain, receive

待遇する *taigū suru* treat, receive, entertain
接待する *settai suru* receive (guests), welcome; offer, serve, entertain
招待 *shōtai* invitation
優待する *yūtai suru* treat kindly, receive hospitably, give special consideration
歓待する *kantai suru* give a cordial [warm] reception, entertain

KUN

【ma(tsu) 待つ】
ⓐ wait
ⓑ wait for, expect, look forward to
待ち *machi* waiting, waiting time
待たせる *mataseru* keep (a person) waiting
待ち合わせる *machiawaseru* wait, meet by appointment
待ちくたびれる *machikutabireru* get tired of waiting
待ち伏せ *machibuse* ambush
待ち望む *machinozomu* expect, look forward to

【-ma(chi) -待ち】 [suffix] wait, waiting
信号待ち *shingōmachi* waiting for a traffic light
キャンセル待ち *kyanserumachi* waiting for a cancellation (on a flight)

SYNONYMS

❶ⓐ wait
控える be in waiting → 495

ⓑ expect
期 EXPECT → 1704

❷ treat and welcome
遇 TREAT → 3135
扱う HANDLE → 217
款 treat cordially → 1700
接 receive → 500
迎 WELCOME → 3059

3-6 忄

悔 365

KAI ku(iru) ku(yamu) kuya(shii)

CH 悔 huǐ

Radical	Strokes
忄 61	9-3-6
Grade	**Freq**
Jōyō	1851
1-3-6	

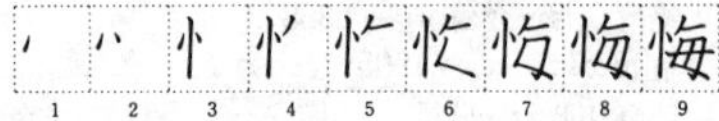

▶REPENT

COMPOUNDS

● repent, regret, be sorry

悔悛 *kaishun* repentance, penitence
悔恨 *kaikon* regret, repentance
悔悟 *kaigo* repentance, remorse
後悔する *kōkai suru* be sorry, regret, repent

KUN

【ku(iru) 悔いる】 repent, regret, be sorry
悔い *kui* regret, repentance
悔い改める *kuiaratameru* repent, be penitent

【ku(yamu) 悔やむ】 repent, regret, lament; condole
悔やまれる失策 *kuyamareru shissaku* regrettable misstep
お悔やみ *okuyami* condolence, visit of condolence

【kuya(shii) 悔しい】 [also 口惜しい] vexing, mortifying, regrettable
悔しさ *kuyashisa* vexation, chagrin, regret
悔し泣き *kuyashinaki* crying from vexation, tears of regret

SYNONYMS

● regret
惜 REGRET → 484
恨 regret → 369
憾 STRONGLY REGRET → 764

USAGE

kuyashii

悔しい

[also 口惜しい] vexing, mortifying, regrettable

口惜しい

[also 悔しい] vexing, mortifying, regrettable

HOMOPHONES

kuyashii ⇨ 口惜しい 3382, 484

恢

366 KAI

CH 恢 huī

Radical	Strokes
忄 61	9-3-6
Grade	Freq
Reference	
◧ 1 - 3 - 6	

3-6 忄

COMPOUNDS

❶ [now replaced by 回 3055 or 快 245] recover, restore

恢復(＝回復) *kaifuku* recovery, restoration; rehabilitation

恢復(＝快復) *kaifuku* recovery (from illness)

❷ great, extensive, vast

天網恢恢疎にして漏らさず *Tenmō kaikai so ni shite morasazu* Heaven's net has large meshes, but nothing escapes

恒 㤚 恒 恒

367 KŌ

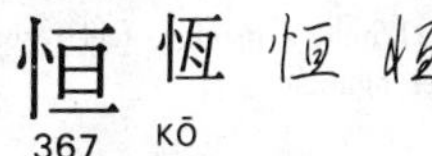

CH 恒 héng

Radical	Strokes
忄 61	9-3-6
Grade	Freq
Jōyō	1363
◧ 1 - 3 - 6	

3-6 忄

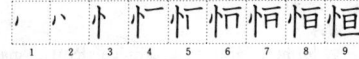

▸**CONSTANT**

COMPOUNDS

❶ⓐ [original meaning] **constant, unchanging, fixed**

ⓑ regular, established

恒常 *kōjō* constancy

恒産 *kōsan* fixed property

恒数 *kōsū* constant (in science)

恒星 *kōsei* fixed star

恒例 *kōrei* regular ceremony, established custom

❷ permanent, lasting

恒久 *kōkyū* perpetuity, permanency

SYNONYMS

❶ **constant**

定 fixed → 2229

常 REGULAR → 2590

例 regular → 89

❷ **of long duration**

久 OF LONG DURATION → 3384

永 ETERNAL → 1937

長 LONG → 2556

恰

368 KŌ KAT- CHŌ ataka(mo)

CH 恰 qià

Radical	Strokes
忄 61	9-3-6
Grade	Freq
Reference	
◧ 1 - 3 - 6	

3-6 忄

COMPOUNDS

ⓐ [original meaning] just, exactly

ⓑ [formerly also 宛も *atakamo*] as if, just as, just like

恰好(＝格好) *kakkō* suitability, moderateness (in price); shape, form; appearance, manner

恰度 *chōdo* [now usu. 丁度] just, exactly; as if

恰も好し *atakamo-yoshi* luckily, fortunately

HOMOPHONES

atakamo ⇨ 宛 2222

NOTE

⇨ see USAGE note at 宛 2222

3-6 ↑

恨 𢙴 𢚩
369 KON ura(mu) ura(meshii)

Stroke order: 1 2 3 4 5 6 7 8 9

Ⓒ 恨 hèn

Radical	Strokes
忄 61	9-3-6
Grade	**Freq**
Jōyō	1860
1-3-6	

▶**HOLD A GRUDGE**

COMPOUNDS

❶ⓐ hold a grudge, hate, feel bitter against

ⓑ grudge, hatred

遺恨 *ikon* grudge, rancor, ill will
怨恨 *enkon* grudge, enmity
多情多恨 *tajōtakon* sensibility

❷ regret

恨事 *konji* regrettable matter
悔恨 *kaikon* regret, repentance
痛恨 *tsūkon* deep regret, great sorrow

KUN

【ura(mu) 恨む】

ⓐ [formerly also 怨む] hold a grudge, feel resentment, feel bitter against
ⓑ blame, reproach

恨み *urami* grudge, hatred, malice
逆恨み *sakaurami* unjustified resentment through misunderstanding
恨み言 *uramigoto* grudge; reproach
我が身を恨む *wagami o uramu* blame oneself

【ura(meshii) 恨めしい】

ⓐ [formerly also 怨めしい] resentful, reproachful, indignant
ⓑ regrettable

恨めし気に *urameshige ni* reproachfully
彼が金を貸してくれないのが恨めしかった *Kare ga kane o kashite kurenai no ga urameshikatta* I thought it cruelly unkind of him not to lend me money

SYNONYMS

❶ hate and dislike

嫌 DISLIKE → 636
忌む ABHOR → 2207
憎 HATE → 687
悪 hate → 2745

❷ regret

惜 REGRET → 484
憾 STRONGLY REGRET → 764
悔 REPENT → 365

USAGE

❶ uramu

恨む

ⓐ [formerly also 怨む] hold a grudge, feel resentment, feel bitter against
ⓑ blame, reproach

怨む

[now usu. 恨む] hold a grudge, feel resentment, feel bitter against

憾む

be sorry for, regret

❷ urami

恨み

[formerly also 怨み] grudge, hatred, malice

怨み

[now usu. 恨み] grudge, hatred, malice

憾み

regret, matter for regret

❸ urameshii

恨めしい

ⓐ [formerly also 怨めしい] resentful, reproachful, indignant
ⓑ regrettable

怨めしい

[now usu. 恨めしい] resentful, reproachful, indignant

HOMOPHONES

uramu ⇨ 怨 2570 憾 764
urami ⇨ 怨 2570 憾 764
urameshii ⇨ 怨 2570

3-6 ↑

恆
370

▶**CONSTANT**
nonstandard for 恒 367

3-6 ↑

悖

incorrect stroke count ⇨ see 420

按
371 AN

CH 按 àn

Radical	Strokes
扌 64	9-3-6
Grade	Freq
Reference	
◧ 1 - 3 - 6	

3-6
扌

COMPOUNDS

❶ [original meaning] press down with the hand, rub with the hand
按摩 *anma* massage; massager, masseur, masseuse
按腹 *anpuku* ventral massage
❷ [now also 案 2270] according to
按分する *anbun suru* divide [distribute] proportionally
按配(＝按排)する *anbai suru* arrange, distribute; adjust
❸ examine, consider
按ずる *anzuru* investigate, consider

NOTE

⇨ see USAGE note at 案 2270

挑
372 CHŌ ido(mu)

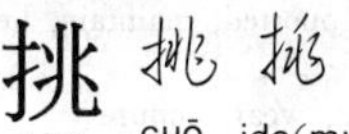

1 2 3 4 5 6 7 8 9

CH 挑 tiāo tiǎo

Radical	Strokes
扌 64	9-3-6
Grade	Freq
Jōyō	1217
◧ 1 - 3 - 6	

3-6
扌

▶PROVOKE

COMPOUNDS

● [original meaning] **provoke, arouse, instigate, stir up, challenge**
挑戦 *chōsen* challenge, defiance
挑発する *chōhatsu suru* provoke, incite, excite, stimulate

KUN

【ido(mu) 挑む】 challenge, defy, dare; make advances to
戦いを挑む *tatakai o idomu* challenge (a person) to a fight

SYNONYMS

● **incite**
唆 INSTIGATE → 402
扇 FAN → 1950
激 excite → 776
奮 ROUSE UP → 2367
振 arouse to action → 430
動 MOVE → 1778
起 rise to action → 3307

拷
373 GŌ

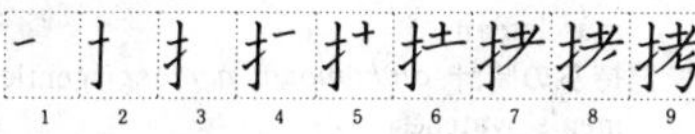

1 2 3 4 5 6 7 8 9

CH 拷 kǎo

Radical	Strokes
扌 64	9-3-6
Grade	Freq
Jōyō	1885
◧ 1 - 3 - 6	

3-6
扌

▶TORTURE

COMPOUNDS

● **torture, flog, beat**
拷問 *gōmon* torture; rack; third degree
拷問台 *gōmondai* rack, instrument of torture
拷器 *gōki* [archaic] instruments of torture

SYNONYMS

● **torture and oppress**
責める torture → 2467
虐 treat cruelly → 3218
迫 oppress → 3074

3-6
扌

持 持 㧗

374 JI mo(tsu) -mo(chi) mo(teru)

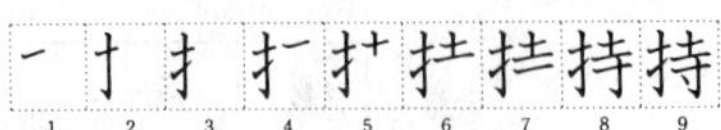

Ⓒ 持 chí

Radical	Strokes
扌 64	9-3-6
Grade	**Freq**
Jōyō-3	162
1 - 3 - 6	

▶**HOLD**

COMPOUNDS

❶ [original meaning] **hold, grasp, have; have with one**
持参する *jisan suru* bring [take] with one, carry
把持 *haji* grasp, hold, grip
捧持する *hōji suru* hold up, bear, present
支持する *shiji suru* support, maintain, back up
所持する *shoji suru* have (money) about one; possess

❷ remain or cause to remain in a given condition:
ⓐ **hold out, hold up, last, endure**
ⓑ uphold, preserve, maintain, observe
持続する *jizoku suru* continue, last; maintain
持久 *jikyū* endurance, sustenance, persistence
持病 *jibyō* chronic illness
保持する *hoji suru* maintain, preserve, retain
維持 *iji* maintenance, upkeep, preservation
護持する *goji suru* defend, protect; uphold
持戒 *jikai* observance of the Buddhist commandments
矜持 *kyōji* (=*kinji*) pride, dignity

❸ⓐ **hold in one's possession, possess, have**
ⓑ **hold on to one's opinion, adhere to**
持薬 *jiyaku* favorite medicine
享持する *kyōji suru* secure rights and profits
住持 *jūji* chief priest (of a temple)
持論 *jiron* pet theory
堅持する *kenji suru* maintain firmly, hold fast to
固持する *koji suru* persist in, adhere to

❹ draw, drawn game (of go)
持碁 *jigo* drawn game of go

INDEPENDENT

【**ji** 持】draw, drawn game (of go)

KUN

【**mo(tsu)** 持つ】
①ⓐ hold, take, have
ⓑ have with one, carry
持ち上げる *mochiageru* raise, lift up; flatter
持ち出す *mochidasu* take out, carry out; run away with; advance (one's opinion); begin to have
持ち越す *mochikosu* carry forward, bring over, defer
持ち掛ける *mochikakeru* propose, offer (a suggestion)

②ⓐ hold in one's possession: have, possess, own, bear
ⓑ hold (an opinion), have, harbor, cherish
持ち主 *mochinushi* owner, proprietor
持ち船 *mochibune* one's own ship
手持ち *temochi* holdings
意見を持つ *iken o motsu* hold an opinion

③ⓐ hold (out), be supported, maintain, keep up
ⓑ hold up, last long, wear, endure
持ち *mochi* wear, durability, life; draw
持ち直す *mochinaosu* improve, rally, recover
身を持ち崩す *mi o mochikuzusu* ruin oneself
長持ちする *nagamochi suru* last [keep] long, endure
この財布は五年持った *Kono saifu wa gonen motta* This purse has lasted me five years

④ⓐ take charge of
ⓑ bear (expenses), stand, pay
受け持つ *ukemotsu* have [take] charge of
掛け持ちする *kakemochi suru* hold two or more positions concurrently
持ち分 *mochibun* quota, one's share; holdings
費用を持つ *hiyō o motsu* bear the expenses

【**-mo(chi)** -持ち】
①ⓐ person who has something, possessor
ⓑ suitable for carrying on one's person, designed for
金持ち *kanemochi* wealthy [rich] person
子持ち *komochi* motherhood, maternity
力持ち *chikaramochi* man of great strength, muscleman
男持ちの時計 *otokomochi no tokei* gentlemen's watches

② [suffix] charge, expense
会社持ち *kaishamochi* at company expense

③ state (of a person's feeling)
気持ち *kimochi* feeling, sensation, mood
心持ち *kokoromochi* feeling, mood; slightly
面持ち *omomochi* look, countenance, face

【**mo(teru)** 持てる】be made much of, be welcomed, be popular

SYNONYMS

❶ **hold**
提 carry in hand → 591
携 CARRY IN HAND → 648

❶ **take**
取 TAKE → 1262
把 GRIP → 249
握 GRASP → 585
執 SEIZE → 1680
捕 CATCH → 429
❷ⓐ **continue**
続 CONTINUE → 1362
継 SUCCEED → 1360
連 IN SUCCESSION → 3103
ⓑ **preserve**
保 PRESERVE → 96
留 KEEP → 2580

❸ⓐ **possess**
有 HAVE → 2983
属 BELONG TO → 3145
蔵 own → 2364
享 ENJOY → 2051
具 possess → 2552
ⓑ **hold in the mind**
抱 HUG → 306
懐 embosom → 763

NOTE
⇨ see COMPOUND FORMATION for 維持 *iji* ⇨ 維 1370

挌

375 KAKU

CH 挌 gé

Radical	Strokes
扌 64	9-3-6
Grade	**Freq**
Reference	
◧ 1 - 3 - 6	

3-6 扌

COMPOUNDS
● [now replaced by 格 926] [original meaning] strike, hit, fight
挌闘する *kakutō suru* grapple, fight hand to hand

NOTE
★do not confuse with 格 926

括 括 括

376 KATSU kuku(ru)▲

CH 括 kuò guā

Radical	Strokes
扌 64	9-3-6
Grade	**Freq**
Jōyō	1540
◧ 1 - 3 - 6	

3-6 扌

一 1 十 2 扌 3 扌 4 扩 5 扦 6 拆 7 括 8 括 9

▶LUMP TOGETHER

COMPOUNDS
● **lump together, lump, sum up, draw together**
括弧 *kakko* parentheses, brackets
括約筋 *katsuyakukin* sphincter
一括する *ikkatsu suru* lump together, sum up
総括的 *sōkatsuteki* all-inclusive, all-embracing
概括する *gaikatsu suru* summarize, sum up, generalize
包括する *hōkatsu suru* include, comprehend, comprise
統括する *tōkatsu suru* generalize

KUN
【**kuku(ru)** 括る】 fasten, make fast; bundle up, tie up; lump together, sum up
括り付ける *kukuritsukeru* fasten (a person) to
引っ括る *hikkukuru* tie up
首を括る *kubi o kukuru* hang oneself
締め括り *shimekukuri* completion, summing up; supervision

SYNONYMS
● **combine**
総 integrate → 1379
併 join together → 83
統 UNITE → 1352
結 TIE → 1348
合 COMBINE → 2019

3-6 扌

挟 挾 挟 挟 (CH) 夹 jiā gā 挟 xié

377 KYŌ hasa(mu) hasa(maru) wakibasa(mu)▲

Radical	Strokes
扌 64	9-3-6
Grade	**Freq**
Jōyō	1947
1-3-6	

一 十 扌 扌 扌 扌 扌 挟 挟
1 2 3 4 5 6 7 8 9

▶**HOLD BETWEEN**

COMPOUNDS

❶ **hold between, pinch**
挟瞼器 *kyōkenki* entropion forceps
挟撃 *kyōgeki* attack on both sides, pincer movement
挟殺 *kyōsatsu baseball* rundown
❷ [original meaning, now archaic] hold under the arm
挟書 *kyōsho* possession of books

KUN

【hasa(mu) 挟む】
①ⓐ hold between, hold
ⓑ pinch, nip
テーブルを挟んで話し合う *tēburu o hasande hanashiau* hold a conversation across the table
箸で漬け物を挟む *hashi de tsukemono o hasamu* hold a pickle with chopsticks
紙挟み *kamibasami* paper clip, paper holder
ペンを唇に挟む *pen o kuchibiru ni hasamu* nip a pen between one's lips
② [formerly also 挿む] put (something) between, insert, interpose
挟み込む *hasamikomu* insert
雑誌に挟む *zasshi ni hasamu* place in a magazine
口を挟む *kuchi o hasamu* interject, cut into (a conversation)

【hasa(maru) 挟まる】 get between, lie between, be caught in
指がドアに挟まる *yubi ga doa ni hasamaru* one's fingers are caught in a door

【wakibasa(mu) 挟む】 hold under the arm
泰山を挟んで北海を超ゆ *Taizan o wakibasande hokkai o koyu* carry Taishan Mountain under one's arm and leap over the north sea

SYNONYMS

❶ **contain and include**
包 ENCOMPASS → 2966
容 CONTAIN (have within) → 2277
含 CONTAIN (have as a part) → 2041

USAGE

hasamu
挟む
①ⓐ hold between, hold
ⓑ pinch, nip
② [formerly also 挿む] put (something) between, insert, interpose
挿む
[now usu. 挟む] put (something) between, insert, interpose
鋏む
snip, clip

HOMOPHONES

hasamu ⇨ 挿 431 鋏 1731

3-6 扌

指 指 指 (CH) 指 zhǐ zhī zhí

378 SHI yubi sa(su) -sa(shi)

Radical	Strokes
扌 64	9-3-6
Grade	**Freq**
Jōyō-3	233
1-3-6	

一 十 扌 扌 扌 指 指 指 指
1 2 3 4 5 6 7 8 9

▶**FINGER** ▶**POINT**

COMPOUNDS

❶ⓐ [original meaning] **finger**
ⓑ counter for fingers
指紋 *shimon* fingerprint
指圧 *shiatsu shiatsu*, acupressure
五指 *goshi* the five fingers
❷ⓐ **point (to), point out, indicate, show**
ⓑ **direct, instruct**
指定する *shitei suru* designate, appoint
指示する *shiji suru* instruct, point out; indicate, point to
指摘する *shiteki suru* point out
指数 *shisū* index (number); exponent
指名する *shimei suru* nominate, designate, name
指南 *shinan* instruction, teaching; instructor, teacher
指導する *shidō suru* guide, lead, instruct
指揮者 *shikisha* conductor; commander

指令 *shirei* order, instruction
❸ play or manipulate the pieces of board games, esp. shogi (Japanese chess)
指了図 *shiryōzu* end game position

KUN

【yubi 指】 finger, toe
指輪 *yubiwa* (finger) ring
人指し指 *hitosashiyubi* index finger
親指 *oyayubi* thumb
足の指 *ashi no yubi* toe

【sa(su) 指す】
①ⓐ point to, point at, indicate
ⓑ aim at, have in view
方向を指す *hōkō o sasu* point to a direction
指し図 *sashizu* directions
目指す(=目差す) *mezasu* aim for, have an eye on
頂上を目指す *chōjō o mezasu* set out for the summit
② appoint, nominate; finger, accuse
名指し *nazashi* nomination, calling names
③ play board games (esp. shogi)
指し手 *sashite* shogi move, shogi player
早指しチェス *hayazashi-chesu* blitz chess

【-sa(shi) -指し】 [suffix] player (of shogi)
将棋指し *shōgisashi* shogi player

SYNONYMS

❶ **hand and arm**
掌 PALM → 2602
手 HAND → 3456
腕 ARM → 1006
❷ⓐ **indicate**
示 SHOW → 1936
標 MARK → 1064
宛てる ADDRESS → 2222
ⓑ **instruct**
訓 INSTRUCT → 1454

HOMOPHONES

sasu ⇨ 差 3311 刺 1275 挿 431 注 325 射 1458 止 2941
-sashi ⇨ 差 3311 刺 1275 止 2941

NOTE

⇨ see USAGE note at 差 3311

拾

379 SHŪ JŪ hiro(u)

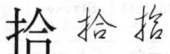

Ⓒⓗ 拾 shí

Radical	Strokes
扌 64	9-3-6
Grade	**Freq**
Jōyō-3	1449
1 - 3 - 6	

3-6 扌

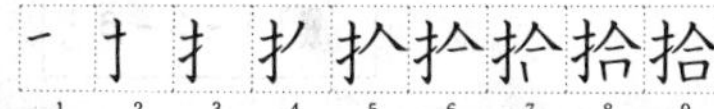

▶ **PICK UP**

COMPOUNDS

❶ [original meaning] **pick up, gather**
拾得する *shūtoku suru* pick up, find
拾遺 *shūi* gleaning
収拾する *shūshū suru* get under control, save (the situation)
❷ ten—used in legal documents and checks
金拾万円 *kin jūman'en* one hundred thousand yen

INDEPENDENT

【jū 拾】 ten (⇨ ❷)

KUN

【hiro(u) 拾う】 pick up, gather; find; (acquire something hard to get) get hold of, gain; pick out, select
拾い上げる *hiroiageru* pick up; pick out
拾い集める *hiroiatsumeru* gather
石を拾う *ishi o hirou* pick up a stone
拾い物 *hiroimono* thing picked up [found]; bargain
命拾い *inochibiroi* narrow escape (from death), close shave
拾い出す *hiroidasu* pick out, select
拾い読みする *hiroiyomi suru* read here and there, skim through

SYNONYMS

❶ **get**
得 ACQUIRE → 477
獲 obtain → 779
収 TAKE IN → 198
取 TAKE → 1262
❷ **ten**
十 TEN → 3365

【hirou】
○ **raise**
揚 RAISE HIGH → 593
掲 PUT UP → 494
挙 RAISE → 2456
上 raise → 3404
起 raise up → 3307
立てる STAND → 1992

挺

incorrect stroke count ⇨ see 428

3-6 扌

3-6
氵

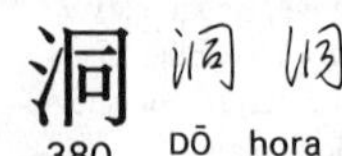
380 DŌ hora

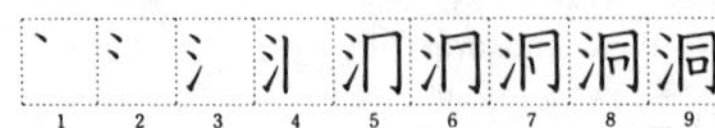

Ⓒⓗ 洞 dòng

Radical	Strokes
氵 85	9-3-6
Grade	Freq
Jōyō	1679
1-3-6	

▶**CAVE**

COMPOUNDS

❶ [also suffix] [original meaning] **cave, cavern, grotto; cavity, tunnel**
洞窟 *dōkutsu* cavern, cave
洞穴 *dōketsu* cave, den, excavation
空洞 *kūdō* cave, cavern, hollow
風洞 *fūdō* wind tunnel
鐘乳洞 *shōnyūdō* limestone cave [grotto]

❷ see through, penetrate, have an insight into
洞察 *dōsatsu* insight, penetration

KUN

【hora 洞】 cave, cavern, den
洞穴 *horaana* cave, cavern, den

SYNONYMS

❶ **holes and cavities**
凹 concavity → 3482
穴 HOLE → 2159
孔 OPEN HOLE → 179
口 MOUTH → 3382
坑 PIT → 236
堀 DITCH → 467
溝 CHANNEL → 659

3-6
氵

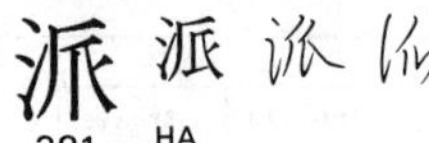
381 HA

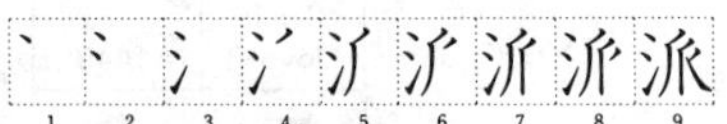

Ⓒⓗ 派 pài

Radical	Strokes
氵 85	9-3-6
Grade	Freq
Jōyō-6	251
1-3-6	

▶**SECT** ▶**DISPATCH**

COMPOUNDS

❶ⓐ [also suffix] **sect, faction, party; school; clique, group**
ⓑ **religious sect, denomination**
派閥 *habatsu* clique, faction, coterie
一派 *ippa* sect, denomination; school; party
党派 *tōha* party, faction, clique
左派 *saha* left wing, left faction
流派 *ryūha* school
学派 *gakuha* school, sect
古典派 *kotenha* the classical school
田中派 *tanakaha* Tanaka faction
宗派 *shūha* religious sect, denomination
真宗大谷派 *shinshū ōtani-ha* Otani sect of Shinshu

❷ⓐ branch off, diverge, derive
ⓑ [original meaning] branch, offshoot
派生する *hasei suru* derive from, stem from
分派 *bunpa* branch, sect, denomination

❸ **dispatch, send**
派出する *hashutsu suru* send out, dispatch
派米する *habei suru* dispatch to the U.S.
派遣する *haken suru* dispatch, send
派兵 *hahei* dispatch of troops
特派員 *tokuhain* special correspondent; delegate

❹ unclassified compounds
派手な *hade na* showy, flashy, gaudy
立派な *rippa na* fine, excellent, admirable

INDEPENDENT

【ha 派】 sect, faction; group
彼の派 *kare no ha* his sect [faction]
【hasuru 派する】 send, dispatch

SYNONYMS

❶ **parties and sects**
流 school → 441
翼 WING → 2720
系 faction → 1944
門 (religious) sect → 888
宗 RELIGIOUS SECT (esp. Buddhist) → 2228
党 PARTY → 2581
閥 CLIQUE → 3325

❸ **send**
遣 DISPATCH → 3152
回 send round → 3055
送 SEND → 3093
投 SEND IN → 256

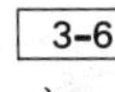

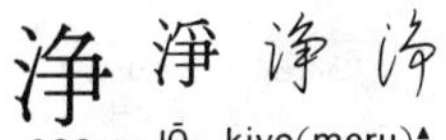

382 JŌ kiyo(meru)▲

Ⓒⓗ 浄 jìng

Radical	Strokes
氵 85	9-3-6
Grade	**Freq**
Jōyō	1510
◧ 1-3-6	

3-6 氵

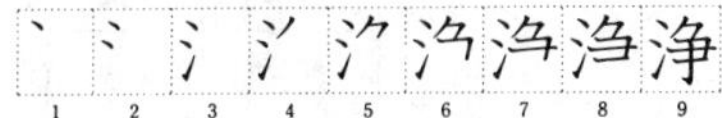

1 2 3 4 5 6 7 8 9

▶**CLEAN**

COMPOUNDS

❶ⓐ **clean, pure, unstained**
ⓑ **cleanse, purify**
ⓒ [formerly 滌 *deki, jō* 696] **wash, cleanse**
清浄な *seijō na* pure, clean
浄化 *jōka* purification, cleansing
浄書 *jōsho* clean copy
浄水場 *jōsuijō* water purification plant
洗浄 *senjō* washing, irrigation

❷ *Buddhism* pure, sacred
浄土 *jōdo* pure land, (Buddhist) paradise
浄土宗 *jōdoshū Jodo* sect (of Buddhism)
浄瑠璃 *jōruri joruri*, ballad drama; clear lapis lazuli

KUN

【kiyo(meru) 浄める】
①ⓐ [usu. 清める] (rid of dirt or impurities) cleanse, purify
ⓑ [sometimes also 清める] (rid of moral taint) purify, purge
② [usu. 清める] exorcise
⇨ see 清 523 for compounds

SYNONYMS

❶ⓐ **clean and purified**
清 clean → 523
純 PURE → 1297
潔 IMMACULATE → 744
粋 REFINED (free from impurities) → 1293
精 refined (purified) → 1366

❶ⓑ & ❶ⓒ **clean and wash**
粛 PURGE → 3581
清 CLEAR → 523
払 CLEAR AWAY → 194
掃 SWEEP → 503
洗 WASH → 388
濯 RINSE → 793
浴 BATHE → 445

HOMOPHONES

kiyomeru ⇨ 清 523

NOTE

⇨ see USAGE note at 清 523

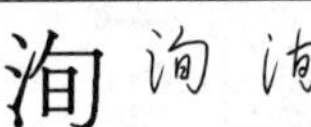

383 JUN NAMES makoto nobu

Ⓒⓗ 洵 xún

Radical	Strokes
氵 85	9-3-6
Grade	**Freq**
Names	2132
◧ 1-3-6	

3-6 氵

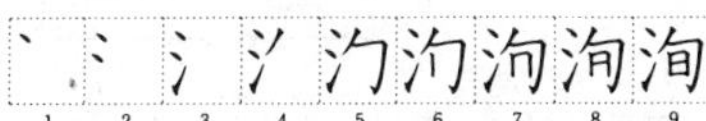

1 2 3 4 5 6 7 8 9

▶**TRULY**

COMPOUNDS

● [archaic] truly, really, utterly
洵美 *junbi* truly beautiful, exquisite

NAMES

洵子 *junko* female name
洵 *makoto* male name

SYNONYMS

● **true**
真 TRUE → 2111
実 REAL → 2225
本 real → 3502
正 genuine → 3484
現 ACTUAL → 968

3-6
氵

海 海 海 海

384 KAI umi

(CH) 海 hǎi

Radical	Strokes
氵 85	9-3-6
Grade	**Freq**
Jōyō-2	144
1-3-6	

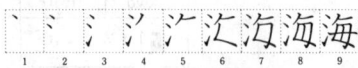

▶**SEA**

COMPOUNDS

❶ⓐ **sea, ocean**
ⓑ (large landlocked body of water) sea, large lake
ⓒ **suffix after names of seas**
海洋 *kaiyō* ocean, sea
海外 *kaigai* overseas, abroad
海水浴 *kaisuiyoku* sea bathing
海岸 *kaigan* seashore, (sea) coast, beach
海軍 *kaigun* navy
航海 *kōkai* voyage, ocean navigation
南海 *nankai* southern sea; South Seas
カスピ海 *kasupikai* Caspian Sea
日本海 *nihonkai* Japan Sea
❷ⓐ a sea of, a vast collection of
ⓑ as vast as the sea
樹海 *jukai* (abundant) leafage ("sea of trees")
言海 *genkai* dictionary, wordbook
海容 *kaiyō* magnanimous forgiveness
❸ abbrev. of 海軍 *kaigun*: navy
海相 *kaishō* Navy Minister

INDEPENDENT

【**kai** 海】 sea; marine

KUN

【**umi** 海】 sea, ocean; lake
海辺 *umibe* seaside, beach, seashore
荒海 *araumi* rough sea, stormy sea

SPECIAL READINGS

海女 *ama* woman diver
海原 *unabara* sea, ocean
海老▲ *ebi* lobster, shrimp

SYNONYMS

❶ **sea**
洋 OCEAN → 392
沖 OFFING → 262

3-6
氵

活 活 活

385 KATSU i(kiru)▲ i(kasu)▲ i(keru)▲

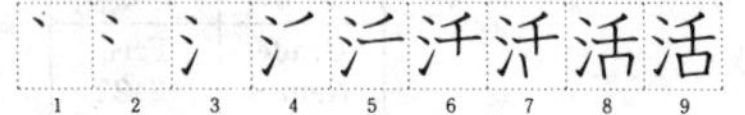

(CH) 活 huó

Radical	Strokes
氵 85	9-3-6
Grade	**Freq**
Jōyō-2	225
1-3-6	

▶**ACTIVE** ▶**LIVE**

COMPOUNDS

❶ⓐ **active, lively, live, energetic, moving**
ⓑ activity, energy, vitality
活動 *katsudō* activity, action; function
活躍する *katsuyaku suru* be active in, be actively engaged
活発な *kappatsu na* lively, active
活性 *kassei* activity
活気 *kakki* vigor, spirit, animation
活況 *kakkyō* activity, briskness, prosperity
活写する *kassha suru* describe vividly, paint a lively picture of
活火山 *kakkazan* active volcano
敏活 *binkatsu* quickness, alacrity
不活性化 *fukasseika* inactivation
部活 *bukatsu* club activity
❷ abbrev. of 活動写真 *katsudō shashin*: motion picture
活弁 *katsuben* film interpreter, movie reciter
日活 *nikkatsu* Nikkatsu Corporation
❸ⓐ (not fixed) **live, movable**
ⓑ *elec* live
活字 *katsuji* movable type, printing type
活版 *kappan* printing, typography
活軸 *katsujiku* live axle
活線 *kassen* live wire
❹ⓐ **live, be alive**
ⓑ **let live, keep alive**
ⓒ (having life) live, living, alive
ⓓ life
活路 *katsuro* means of escape, way out
復活する *fukkatsu suru* revive, come to life again, be resurrected
活殺 *kassatsu* life and death
活仏 *katsubutsu* living Buddha; grand Lama
死活 *shikatsu* life and/or death
❺ (pass one's life) **live, lead one's life**
生活 *seikatsu* life, existence; livelihood
自活 *jikatsu* self-support

❻ [formerly 闊 3333] broad-minded, generous
快活(=快闊)な *kaikatsu na* cheerful, lively, lighthearted

INDEPENDENT

【katsu 活】 *judo* resuscitation; living, life
活を入れる *katsu o ireru* apply the art of resuscitation
活を求める *katsu o motomeru* try to find a way out

KUN

【i(kiru) 活きる】 [now usu. 生きる] be enlivened
その一語で文章が活きる *Sono ichigo de bunshō ga ikiru* That single word gives life to the style

【i(kasu) 活かす】
[now usu. 生かす]
① make the most of
学問を活かして使う *gakumon o ikashite tsukau* put one's knowledge to practical use
② put life [vividness] into, vivify
絵を活かす *e o ikasu* put life into a painting

【i(keru) 活ける】 [now usu. 生ける] arrange (flowers)
活け花 *ikebana* flower arrangement

SYNONYMS

❶ⓐ active
動 dynamic → 1778

❹ⓐ & ❹ⓑ & ❺ live
暮らす LIVE (pass one's life) → 2354
生 live (be alive) → 3497

HOMOPHONES

ikiru ⇨ 生 3497
ikasu ⇨ 生 3497
ikeru ⇨ 生 3497 埋 403

NOTE

⇨ see USAGE note at 生 3497

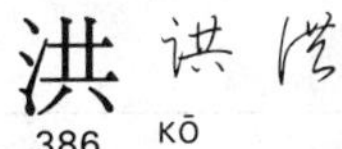

386 KŌ

hóng

Radical	Strokes
氵 85	9-3-6
Grade	**Freq**
Jōyō	1905
1-3-6	

3-6 氵

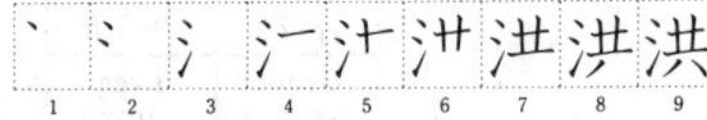

1 2 3 4 5 6 7 8 9

▶FLOOD

COMPOUNDS

❶ [original meaning] **flood, inundation**
洪水 *kōzui* flood, inundation
洪積世 *kōsekisei* diluvial epoch
❷ great, grand, vast
洪大な *kōdai na* great, immense
❸ [rare] Hungary
日洪親善 *nikkō-shinzen* goodwill between Japan and Hungary

SYNONYMS

❶ running water
渦 WHIRLPOOL → 603
流 CURRENT → 441
潮 TIDE → 739
汐 TIDE → 223
瀬 rapids → 806
滝 WATERFALL → 661

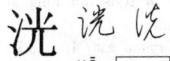

洸 洸 洸

387 KŌ NAMES hiro hiroshi takeshi

CH 洸 guāng

Radical	Strokes
氵 85	9-3-6
Grade	**Freq**
Names	2127
1-3-6	

3-6 氵

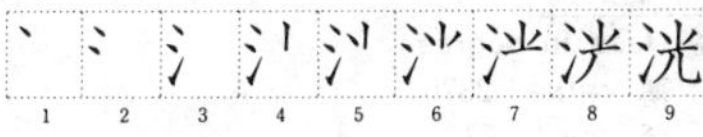

1 2 3 4 5 6 7 8 9

▶VAST

COMPOUNDS

[archaic]
ⓐ vast and deep like an expanse of water
ⓑ glittering like water; surge of water
洸洋 *kōyō* great expanse of water; unfathomable, incoherent
洸洸 *kōkō* brave, valiant; surge (of water)

NAMES

洸 *kō* male name
洸江 *hiroe* female name

SYNONYMS

ⓐ wide and extensive
浩 VAST → 438
博 EXTENSIVE → 151
紘 WIDE-RANGING → 1298
広 WIDE → 3035

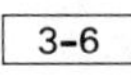
3-6

氵

洗 洗 洗

388 SEN ara(u)

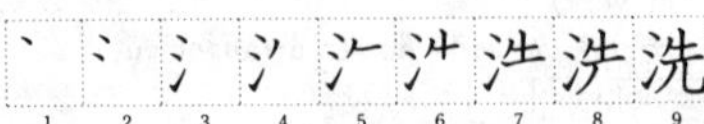

Ⓒⓗ 洗 xǐ xiǎn

Radical	Strokes
氵 85	9-3-6
Grade	Freq
Jōyō-6	1028
1 - 3 - 6	

▶ **WASH**

COMPOUNDS

● [original meaning] **wash, clean**

洗浄 *senjō* washing, irrigation
洗顔 *sengan* washing one's face
洗剤 *senzai* detergent, cleanser
洗礼 *senrei* baptism
洗面所 *senmenjo* washroom; bathroom
洗濯 *sentaku* laundering, washing
洗練 *senren* refinement, polishing, elegance
水洗 *suisen* flushing, washing

KUN

【ara(u) 洗う】 wash, cleanse, bathe, rinse; inquire, probe

手洗い *tearai* washstand, toilet

SYNONYMS

● **clean and wash**

濯 RINSE → 793
浴 BATHE → 445
浄 cleanse → 382
粛 PURGE → 3581
清 CLEAR → 523
払 CLEAR AWAY → 194
掃 SWEEP → 503

3-6

氵

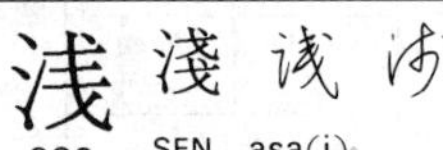

浅 淺 浅 浅

389 SEN asa(i)

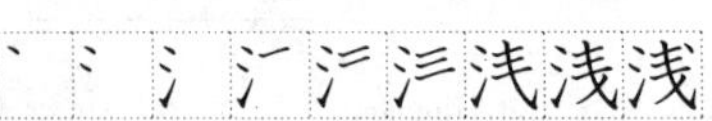

Ⓒⓗ 浅 qiǎn jiān

Radical	Strokes
氵 85	9-3-6
Grade	Freq
Jōyō-4	955
1 - 3 - 6	

▶ **SHALLOW**

COMPOUNDS

❶ [original meaning] (not deep) **shallow**

浅海 *senkai* shallow sea
深浅 *shinsen* depth

❷ (lacking profundity) **shallow, superficial**

浅薄 *senpaku* shallowness, superficiality, flimsiness
浅学 *sengaku* superficial knowledge
浅慮 *senryo* indiscretion, imprudence, thoughtlessness
浅才 *sensai* lack of ability, incompetence

❸ light-colored, pale

浅紅 *senkō* light red
浅緑 *senryoku* (=*asamidori*) light green

❹ slightly

浅酌低唱する *senshakuteishō suru* get slightly intoxicated and hum a tune

KUN

【asa(i) 浅い】 shallow; superficial; light, pale; short (day); close (connection); slight (wound)

浅瀬 *asase* shoal, shallows
浅はかな *asahaka na* frivolous, thoughtless
考えの浅い人 *kangae no asai hito* shallow-brained person
浅黒い *asaguroi* dark-complexioned, tanned, swarthy
会社は創立以来日がまだ浅い *Kaisha wa sōritsu irai hi ga mada asai* It is not long since the firm was established
春はまだ浅い *Haru wa mada asai* It is still early spring

SYNONYMS

❷ **less in degree**

薄 THIN → 2370
低 LOW → 73
微 SLIGHT → 639
軽 LIGHT → 1515
弱 WEAK → 1167

❸ **light-colored**

淡 LIGHT → 528
薄い pale → 2370
鈍- DULL → 1689

390 SHIN tsu

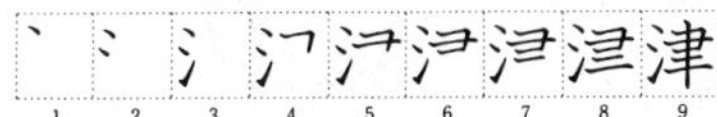

Ⓒⓗ 津 jīn

Radical	Strokes
氵 85	9-3-6
Grade	**Freq**
Jōyō	691
◧ 1 - 3 - 6	

3-6 氵

▶**HARBOR**

COMPOUNDS

● overflow, be replete

興味津津と *kyōmi-shinshin to* of absorbing [great] interest

KUN

【tsu 津】 *elegant* harbor, ferry

津津浦浦に *tsutsu-uraura ni* throughout the land, in every harbor and every bay

津波 *tsunami* tsunami, tidal wave

SYNONYMS

【tsu】

○ **places for landing or stopping**

港 PORT → 605

駅 STATION → 1822

停 stopping place → 139

391 SHŪ su

Ⓒⓗ 洲 zhōu

Radical	Strokes
氵 85	9-3-6
Grade	**Freq**
Reference	
◧ 1 - 3 - 6	

3-6 氵

COMPOUNDS

❶ [now usu. 州 *su*] [original meaning] sandbar, shallows, shoal

座洲する *zasu suru* strand, run aground

❷ [now replaced by 州 *shū* 57] continent, state

六大洲 *rokudaishū* the Six Continents

HOMOPHONES

su ⇨ 州 57

NOTE

⇨ see USAGE note at 州 57

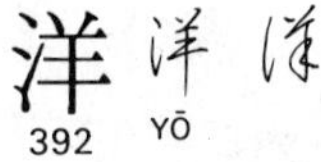

392 YŌ

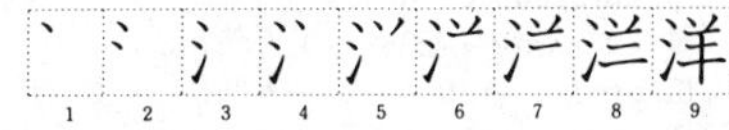

Ⓒⓗ 洋 yáng

Radical	Strokes
氵 85	9-3-6
Grade	**Freq**
Jōyō-3	427
◧ 1 - 3 - 6	

3-6 氵

▶**OCEAN** ▶**WESTERN**

COMPOUNDS

❶ⓐ **ocean, sea**

ⓑ suffix after names of oceans

ⓒ as wide or vast as the ocean

洋上 *yōjō* in the ocean, on the sea

海洋 *kaiyō* ocean, sea

大洋 *taiyō* ocean

太平洋 *taiheiyō* Pacific Ocean

インド洋 *indoyō* Indian Ocean

洋洋たる *yōyōtaru* vast, boundless

❷ⓐ [also prefix] **Western, European, foreign**

ⓑ **the West, the Occident**

洋風 *yōfū* Western [foreign] style

洋画 *yōga* foreign film; Western painting

洋服 *yōfuku* (Western) clothes

洋品 *yōhin* haberdashery

洋裁 *yōsai* foreign-style dressmaking

洋酒 *yōshu* foreign wine [liquors]

西洋 *seiyō* the West, the Occident

❸ abbrev. of 洋間 *yōma*: Western style room

和洋 *wayō* Japanese and Western style rooms

INDEPENDENT

【yō 洋】 half of the world, eastern or western hemisphere

洋の東西を問わず *yō no tōzai o towazu* both in the Occident and the Orient, in all parts of the world

SYNONYMS

❶ⓐ & ❶ⓑ **sea**
海 SEA → 384
沖 OFFING → 262
❷ **west**
西 the West → 3520

3-6
氵

派
393

▶SECT ▶DISPATCH
nonstandard for 派 381

3-6
氵

流
394

▶FLOW ▶CURRENT ▶STYLE
nonstandard for 流 441

3-6
氵

浮

incorrect stroke count ⇨ see 435

3-6
犭

独 獨 独 犳
395 DOKU hito(ri)

Ⓒⓗ 独 dú

Radical	Strokes
犭 94	9-3-6
Grade	**Freq**
Jōyō-5	468
1 - 3 - 6	

▶ALONE ▶GERMANY

COMPOUNDS

❶ⓐ **alone, by oneself, single, sole, solo**
ⓑ act arbitrarily, act without the advice of others
独走 *dokusō* running alone; easy victory, walkover
独演 *dokuen* solo recital
独奏する *dokusō suru* play solo, play alone
独立 *dokuritsu* independence, self-reliance
独学 *dokugaku* self-study, self-teaching
独身 *dokushin* single life; celibacy
独占 *dokusen* exclusive possession, monopoly
独裁 *dokusai* dictatorship, autocracy
単独の *tandoku no* single, independent, sole, lone
孤独の *kodoku no* solitary, lonely, alone
独断 *dokudan* arbitrary decision, dogmatism
独善 *dokuzen* self-righteousness
❷ⓐ **Germany**
ⓑ **German (language)**
西独 *seidoku* West Germany
独文 *dokubun* German literature
和独辞典 *wadoku jiten* Japanese-German dictionary

INDEPENDENT

【doku 独】 Germany

KUN

【hito(ri) 独り】
ⓐ alone, solitary, by oneself
ⓑ single, unmarried
独りぼっちの *hitoribotchi no* solitary
独り旅 *hitoritabi* traveling alone, solitary journey
独り者 *hitorimono* single [unmarried] man [woman]

SYNONYMS

❶ⓐ **alone**
孤 SOLITARY → 356
ⓑ **acting arbitrarily**
横 arbitrary → 1066
専 arrogate to oneself → 2644
❷ⓐ **European countries**
英 ENGLAND → 2238
仏 FRANCE → 19
伊 ITALY → 49
西 Spain → 3520
蘭 Holland → 2383
露 Russia → 2818

USAGE

hitori
独り
ⓐ alone, solitary, by oneself
ⓑ single, unmarried
一人
ⓐ one person
ⓑ only (child, son or daughter)

HOMOPHONES

hitori ⇨ 一人 3341, 3368

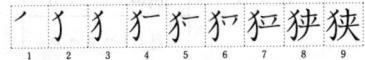

狭 狭 狭 狭

396 KYŌ sema(i) seba(meru) seba(maru)

CH 狭 xiá

Radical	Strokes
犭 94	9-3-6
Grade	**Freq**
Jōyō	1311
◧ 1 - 3 - 6	

3-6 犭

丿 犭 犭 犭 犭 犭 狂 狭 狭
1 2 3 4 5 6 7 8 9

▶NARROW

COMPOUNDS

ⓐ [original meaning] **narrow, constricted**
ⓑ (of limited scope) **narrow, limited, restricted**
ⓒ narrow, contract

狭小な *kyōshō na* narrow, cramped, small-sized
狭窄 *kyōsaku* stricture, stenosis
広狭 *kōkyō* width and narrowness, width
狭量な *kyōryō na* narrow-minded
狭義 *kyōgi* narrow meaning
偏狭な *henkyō na* narrow-minded, intolerant; parochial
狭心症 *kyōshinshō* angina pectoris

KUN

【sema(i) 狭い】 narrow, small, tight; (of limited scope) narrow (minded), limited, restricted
狭苦しい *semakurushii* narrow and close, cramped
狭き門 *semakimon* narrow gate; school [position] hard to enter [get]
狭い部屋 *semai heya* small room
視野の狭い *shiya no semai* narrow-minded, shortsighted

【seba(meru) 狭める】 *vt* narrow, contract, reduce
範囲を狭める *han'i o sebameru* narrow down the range

【seba(maru) 狭まる】 *vi* become narrow, narrow, contract
視界が狭まった *Shikai ga sebamatta* Visibility became poor

狩 狩 狩

397 SHU ka(ru) ka(ri) -ga(ri)

CH 狩 shòu

Radical	Strokes
犭 94	9-3-6
Grade	**Freq**
Jōyō	1524
◧ 1 - 3 - 6	

3-6 犭

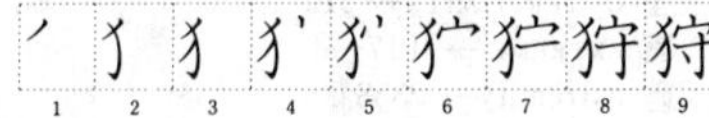

▶HUNT

COMPOUNDS

❶ [original meaning] **hunt**
狩猟 *shuryō* hunting, hunt
狩猟期 *shuryōki* hunting season
❷ [archaic] Imperial visit to the countryside
巡狩 *junshu* Imperial visit

KUN

【ka(ru) 狩る】 hunt
狩人 *karyūdo* hunter
狩り込み *karikomi* roundup
狩り出す *karidasu* hunt out, round up
狩り集める *kariatsumeru* muster, gather

【ka(ri) 狩り】 hunting, hunt, chase
狩りに行く *kari ni iku* go hunting

【-ga(ri) -狩り】
[also suffix]
① hunting; roundup
熊狩り *kumagari* bear hunting
暴力団狩り *bōryokudangari* roundup of gangsters
② gathering (fruits)
葡萄狩り *budōgari* grape picking
潮干狩り *shiohigari* shell gathering (at low tide)
③ viewing
紅葉狩り *momijigari* viewing autumn leaves

SYNONYMS

❶ **hunt and fish**
猟 HUNTING → 538
獲 CATCH GAME → 779
漁 FISH → 698
釣 ANGLE → 1674

HOMOPHONES

karu ⇨ 刈 28 駆 1823

NOTE

⇨ see USAGE note at 刈 28

3-6
阝

限 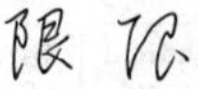

398 GEN kagi(ru) kagi(ri) -kagi(ri)

1 2 3 4 5 6 7 8 9

Ⓒⓗ 限 xiàn

Radical	Strokes
阝 170	9-3-6
Grade	**Freq**
Jōyō-5	440
◧ 1 - 3 - 6	

▶LIMIT

COMPOUNDS

❶ⓐ [original meaning] **limit, set a limit, restrict**
ⓑ [also suffix] **limit, bounds**
限定する *gentei suru* limit, restrict, define
制限する *seigen suru* restrict, limit
局限する *kyokugen suru* localize, limit, set limits to
時限爆弾 *jigen-bakudan* time bomb
限度 *gendo* limit, bounds
限界 *genkai* boundary, limit, bounds
期限 *kigen* time limit, term
上限 *jōgen* upper limit, maximum
権限 *kengen* power, authority; competence (of law)
門限 *mongen* closing-time, lockup
無限の *mugen no* infinite, endless, unfathomable
最小限 *saishōgen* minimum
❷ [suffix] period, hour (in school)
第一限 *daiichigen* first period

KUN

【kagi(ru) 限る】 limit, restrict (to); be the best, be the only way
日を限る *hi o kagiru* put a time-limit on
...とは限らない *...to wa kagiranai* be not always [necessarily]...
その手に限る *Sono te ni kagiru* That's the best way
【kagi(ri) 限り】 limit, limits, bound; as far (much) as possible
限り無い *kagirinai* unlimited, limitless
限り有る *kagiriaru* limited, finite
出来る限り *dekiru kagiri* as far as possible
【-kagi(ri) -限り】 [suffix] insofar as, this time only
今度限り *kondo kagiri* for this once only

SYNONYMS

❶ⓐ **restrain**
制 CONTROL (restrain) → 1274
禁 PROHIBIT → 2795
抑 SUPPRESS → 257
束 TIE UP → 3554
縛 BIND → 1405
控える HOLD BACK → 495
渋る hang [hold] back → 513
ⓑ **extreme**
涯 OUTER LIMITS → 512
極 EXTREME → 1017
窮 extremity → 2358
果て end → 3560

3-6
阝

降

399

▶DESCEND
nonstandard for 降 458

3-7
口

唄

400 BAI uta uta(u)

Ⓒⓗ 呗 bài bei

Radical	Strokes
口 30	10-3-7
Grade	**Freq**
Reference	
◧ 1 - 3 - 7	

COMPOUNDS

❶ song in praise of Buddha's virtues
梵唄 *bonbai* song in praise of Buddha's virtues
❷ⓐ [usu. 歌 *uta*] [also suffix] song, ballad
ⓑ [usu. 歌う *utau*] recite, sing—used esp. in reference to traditional Japanese songs
小唄 *kouta* ditty, ballad
子守唄 *komoriuta* lullaby

HOMOPHONES

uta ⇨ 歌 1825
utau ⇨ 歌 1825 謡 1597 謳 1632

NOTE

⇨ see USAGE note at 歌 1825

哺

401 HO

CH 哺 bǔ

Radical	Strokes
口 30	10-3-7
Grade	**Freq**
Reference	
1 - 3 - 7	

3-7 口

COMPOUNDS

● nurse, suckle

哺乳類 *honyūrui* Mammalia

哺育(＝保育)する *hoiku suru* nurture, bring up; suckle, nurse

唆

402 SA sosonoka(su)

CH 唆 suō

Radical	Strokes
口 30	10-3-7
Grade	**Freq**
Jōyō	1440
1 - 3 - 7	

3-7 口

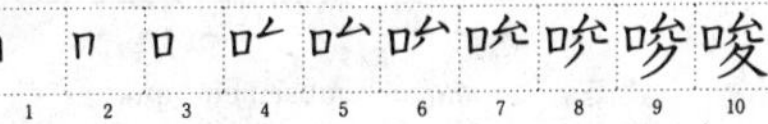

▶INSTIGATE

COMPOUNDS

● [original meaning] **instigate, incite, abet**

教唆 *kyōsa* instigation, incitement

示唆する *shisa suru* suggest, hint

KUN

【**sosonoka(su) 唆す**】 instigate, egg on, abet, incite

唆し *sosonokashi* instigation

人に悪事を唆す *hito ni akuji o sosonokasu* entice a person to do something wrong

SYNONYMS

● **incite**

挑 PROVOKE → 372

扇 FAN → 1950

激 excite → 776

奮 ROUSE UP → 2367

振 arouse to action → 430

動 MOVE → 1778

起 rise to action → 3307

埋

403 MAI u(meru) u(maru) u(moreru) uzu(meru)▲ uzu(maru)▲ i(keru)▲

CH 埋 mái mán

Radical	Strokes
土 32	10-3-7
Grade	**Freq**
Jōyō	1256
1 - 3 - 7	

3-7 土

▶BURY

COMPOUNDS

● [original meaning] **bury, embed**

埋葬 *maisō* burial, interment

埋蔵物 *maizōbutsu* buried treasure

埋没する *maibotsu suru* be buried; fall into oblivion

埋線 *maisen* underground cable

埋設する *maisetsu suru* put [lay] underground

埋め立てる *umetateru* reclaim, fill in

埋め合わせる *umeawaseru* make amends, compensate for

穴埋めする *anaume suru* fill a gap, make up a loss

KUN

【**u(meru) 埋める**】 *vt* bury, embed; fill up; make up for

土に埋める *tsuchi ni umeru* bury in the ground

生き埋め *ikiume* being buried alive

【**u(maru) 埋まる**】 *vi* be filled up, be buried under, be embedded

雪に埋まった小道 *yuki ni umatta komichi* lane buried deep in snow

【**u(moreru) 埋もれる**】 *vi* be buried, be buried in oblivion, live in obscurity

埋もれ木 *umoregi* bogwood

【**uzu(meru) 埋める**】 *vt* bury

骨を埋める *hone o uzumeru* die in (a foreign land)

【**uzu(maru) 埋まる**】 *vi* be filled up (with)

花で埋まる *hana de uzumaru* be filled up with flowers

【i(keru) 埋ける】 bury; bury coals in ashes

SYNONYMS

● **bury**

葬 bury (a corpse) → 2320

HOMOPHONES

ikeru ⇨ 生 3497 活 385

NOTE

⇨ see USAGE note at 生 3497

3-7 土

城 404

▶CASTLE

nonstandard for 城 352

3-7 女

娯 405

GO

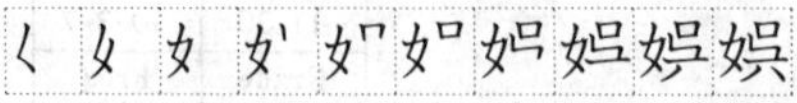

1 2 3 4 5 6 7 8 9 10

Ⓒⓗ 娯 yú

Radical	Strokes
女 38	10-3-7
Grade	**Freq**
Jōyō	1547
1-3-7	

▶ENJOYMENT

COMPOUNDS

ⓐ **enjoyment, amusement, merriment, pleasure**

ⓑ [original meaning] enjoy [amuse] oneself, be merry; amuse, give pleasure to

娯楽 *goraku* amusement, pastime

娯楽街 *gorakugai* amusement quarter

娯楽室 *gorakushitsu* recreation room

SYNONYMS

ⓐ **pleasure**

興 AMUSEMENT → 2909

楽 PLEASURE → 2826

3-7 女

娘 406

JŌ▲ musume ko▲

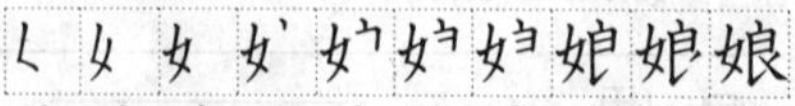

1 2 3 4 5 6 7 8 9 10

Ⓒⓗ 娘 niáng

Radical	Strokes
女 38	10-3-7
Grade	**Freq**
Jōyō	964
1-3-7	

▶DAUGHTER ▶GIRL

COMPOUNDS

● [original meaning] **girl, beautiful maiden**

娘子軍 *jōshigun* Amazons, Amazonian troops

KUN

【musume 娘】

① daughter

一人娘 *hitori musume* only daughter

② [also suffix] girl, maiden

娘心 *musumegokoro* girlish innocence

小娘 *komusume* young girl, lass

箱入り娘 *hakoirimusume* innocent [naive] girl of a good family

花売り娘 *hanaurimusume* flower girl

【ko 娘】 [also 子 or コ] girl, gal

良い娘だ *Ii ko da* She's a nice [good-looking] girl [gal]

SYNONYMS

【musume】

① **offspring**

女 daughter → 3418

姫 DAUGHTER OF NOBLE BIRTH → 407

子 CHILD → 3390

孤 orphan → 356

嫡 LEGITIMATE CHILD → 680

息 son → 2647

男 son → 2542

惣 eldest son → 2780

② **woman**

嬢 YOUNG LADY → 758

女 WOMAN → 3418

婦 ADULT WOMAN → 469

婆 OLD WOMAN → 2762

雌 FEMALE → 1055

HOMOPHONES

ko ⇨ 子 3390 児 2546 仔 33 小 7

NOTE

⇨ see USAGE note at 子 3390

姫 姫 姫 姫

407 KI▲ hime hime-

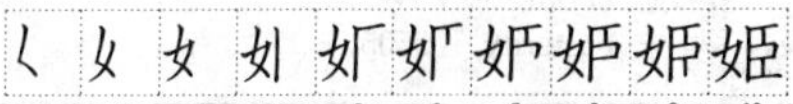

CH 姫 jī

Radical	Strokes
女 38	10-3-7
Grade	Freq
Jōyō	1500
◧ 1 - 3 - 7	

3-7 女

▶DAUGHTER OF NOBLE BIRTH

COMPOUNDS

❶ concubine, mistress (of a nobleman)

寵姫 *chōki* one's favorite mistress

❷ charming girl

美姫 *biki* beautiful maiden, beauty

KUN

【hime 姫】

①ⓐ daughter [young lady] of noble [gentle] birth, princess

ⓑ courtesy title after names of young ladies of noble birth

姫君 *himegimi* princess, highborn young lady

姫様 *himesama* daughter of a nobleman

姫宮 *himemiya* princess

千姫 *senhime* Princess Sen

シンデレラ姫 *shindererahime* Cinderella

② *elegant* girl, charming girl

歌姫 *utahime* songstress, chanteuse

舞姫 *maihime* dancing girl, dancer

【hime- 姫-】 [prefix] small, little, pretty

姫小松 *himekomatsu* small pine

SYNONYMS

【hime】

① **offspring**

娘 DAUGHTER → 406

女 daughter → 3418

子 CHILD → 3390

孤 orphan → 356

嫡 LEGITIMATE CHILD → 680

息 son → 2647

男 son → 2542

惣 eldest son → 2780

娠 娠 娠

408 SHIN

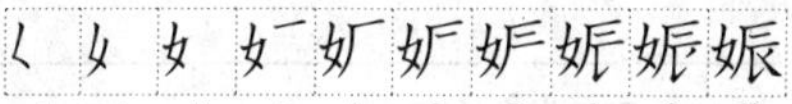

CH 娠 shēn

Radical	Strokes
女 38	10-3-7
Grade	Freq
Jōyō	1759
◧ 1 - 3 - 7	

3-7 女

▶CONCEIVE

COMPOUNDS

● [original meaning] **conceive, become pregnant**

妊娠 *ninshin* pregnancy, conception

SYNONYMS

● **conceive**

妊 BECOME PREGNANT → 240

娯

409

▶ENJOYMENT

nonstandard for 娯 405

3-7 女

孫 孫 孫

410 SON mago

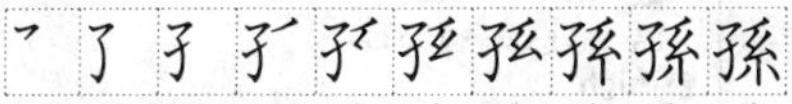

CH 孙 sūn

Radical	Strokes
子 39	10-3-7
Grade	Freq
Jōyō-4	1303
◧ 1 - 3 - 7	

3-7 子

▶GRANDCHILD

COMPOUNDS

❶ [original meaning] **grandchild**

皇孫 *kōson* Imperial grandchild

嫡孫 *chakuson* heir of the eldest son

王孫 *ōson* royal grandson

❷ **descendant**

子孫 *shison* descendant, offspring

天孫 *tenson* descendant of a god

KUN

【**mago** 孫】grandchild; [in compounds] secondary

孫娘 *magomusume* granddaughter

孫弟子 *magodeshi* disciples of one's disciples

孫引き *magobiki* reference to secondary sources

SYNONYMS

❶ & ❷ **descendant**

胤 PROGENY → 17

末 posterity → 3505

3-7

山

峰 峯° 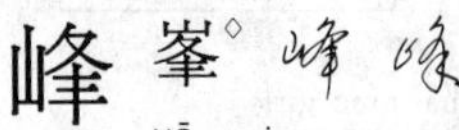

411 HŌ mine

CH 峰 fēng

Radical	Strokes
山 46	10-3-7
Grade	**Freq**
Jōyō	1362
1-3-7	

▶PEAK

COMPOUNDS

ⓐ [also suffix] (mountain with pointed summit) **peak, high mountain**

ⓑ [original meaning] (pointed summit of a mountain) **peak, summit, mountaintop**

峰頭 *hōtō* [rare] summit of a peak

主峰 *shuhō* main peak

連峰 *renpō* mountain range, series of mountain peaks

未踏峰 *mitōhō* unclimbed mountain

高峰 *kōhō* lofty peak, high mountain

最高峰 *saikōhō* highest peak; highest authority

KUN

【**mine** 峰】(summit or vicinity of a summit) peak, summit, ridge; high mountain; back of a sword

峰峰 *minemine* peaks

峰伝いに *minezutai ni* along the ridges

峰続き *minetsuzuki* succession of peaks

峰打ち *mineuchi* striking with the back of a sword

SYNONYMS

ⓐ **mountains**

岳 HIGH MOUNTAIN → 2557

山 MOUNTAIN → 2940

ⓑ **high parts of mountains**

頂 SUMMIT → 145

嶺 RIDGE → 2376

峠 MOUNTAIN PASS → 358

3-7

山

峻 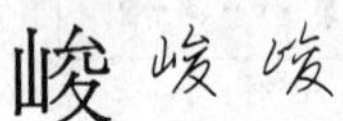

412 SHUN NAMES taka takashi chika toshi

CH 峻 jùn

Radical	Strokes
山 46	10-3-7
Grade	**Freq**
Names	2099
1-3-7	

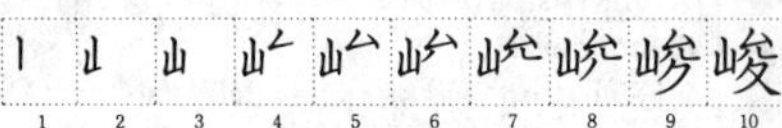

▶STERN

COMPOUNDS

[rarely also 駿 1832]

❶ **stern, strict, severe, uncompromising**

峻厳な *shungen na* strict, stern, rigorous, severe

峻拒する *shunkyo suru* refuse flatly, reject sternly

峻別 *shunbetsu* sharp distinction, strict discrimination

峻下剤 *shungezai* drastic aperient

❷ (esp. of mountains) high and steep, rising sharply, precipitous, towering, lofty

峻険な *shunken na* steep, precipitous

峻嶺 *shunrei* steep peak, high rugged mountain

急峻な *kyūshun na* steep, sharp

NAMES

峻 *shun* male name

峻雄 *takao* male name

SYNONYMS

❶ **strict**

厳 strict → 3289

酷 SEVERE → 1562

❷ **high**

高 HIGH → 2097

喬 TALL → 2488

❷ **steep**

険 STEEP → 542

急 steep → 2092

峽 413

▶**GORGE**
nonstandard for 峡 357

3-7 山

徐 徐 徐 414

JO omomu(roni)▲

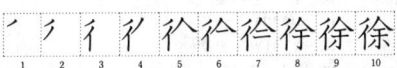

Ⓒ𝐇 徐 xú

Radical	Strokes
亻 60	10-3-7
Grade	**Freq**
Jōyō	1561
◧ 1 - 3 - 7	

3-7 亻

Stroke order: ノ ク 彳 彳 彳 彳 彳 彳 徐 徐 (1–10)

▶**SLOWLY**

COMPOUNDS

● **slowly, gently, quietly**
徐徐に *jojo ni* slowly, gradually
徐行する *jokō suru* go slowly
緩徐曲 *kanjokyoku adagio*

KUN

【**omomu(roni)** 徐ろに】slowly, quietly; patiently
徐ろに時機を待つ *omomuroni jiki o matsu* wait patiently for an opportunity

SYNONYMS

● **slow**
遅 SLOW → 3133
慢 SLUGGISH → 686
緩 SLACK → 1389

従 従 従 従 415

JŪ SHŌ JU shitaga(u) shitaga(eru)

Ⓒ𝐇 从 cóng cōng

Radical	Strokes
亻 60	10-3-7
Grade	**Freq**
Jōyō-6	648
◧ 1 - 3 - 7	

3-7 亻

Stroke order: ノ ク 彳 彳 彳 彳 彳 彳 徉 従 (1–10)

▶**FOLLOW**

COMPOUNDS

❶ⓐ (go after) **follow, accompany, attend on**
ⓑ **follower, attendant, servant, vassal**
従軍する *jūgun suru* follow [join] the army, go to the front
随従する *zuijū suru* follow the lead of, play second fiddle to
追従する *tsuijū suru* follow, be servile to; imitate
従者 *jūsha* follower, attendant, squire
従僕 *jūboku* servant, attendant
主従 *shujū* (=*shūjū*) master and servant, lord and vassal
侍従 *jijū* chamberlain

❷ (act in accordance with) **follow (a person's instructions), comply with, obey, observe, submit to**
従順な *jūjun na* submissive, obedient, docile
服従する *fukujū suru* obey, submit to
盲従する *mōjū suru* follow blindly
屈従 *kutsujū* servile submission, subservience
追従 *tsuishō* flattery, sycophancy

❸ (take up as main work) **follow an occupation, engage in, be engaged in**
従事する *jūji suru* engage in, be engaged in
従業する *jūgyō suru* be employed, be in service
専従者 *senjūsha* full time worker

❹ⓐ [also prefix] **subordinate, second grade, secondary**
ⓑ accessory
従属する *jūzoku suru* be subordinate, depend
従的な *jūteki na* subordinate, secondary
従節 *jūsetsu* subordinate clause
従三位 *jusanmi* second grade of the third rank of honor
従因 *jūin* secondary cause
従犯 *jūhan* participation in crime, accessory
従物 *jūbutsu* accessory (thing)

❺ next in kin
従兄 *jūkei* (=*itoko*) older cousin

❻ since, from
従来の *jūrai no* former, old, existing
従前の *jūzen no* previous, former

❼ in proportion to, in accordance
従価税 *jūkazei ad valorem* duty

❽ lax, easy
従容たる *shōyōtaru* composed, calm, tranquil

❾ from north to south
合従 *gasshō* alliance of states against a powerful enemy

INDEPENDENT

【jū 従】subordinate, secondary; vassal, attendant

従たる *jūtaru* secondary, subordinate, incidental, junior, accessory

KUN

【shitaga(u) 従う】

①ⓐ (go after) follow, accompany, attend on

ⓑ [in the form of 従って *shitagatte*] (result as a consequence) follow, result in

付き従う *tsukishitagau* follow, accompany

従って *shitagatte* therefore, consequently, accordingly

②ⓐ follow (a person's advice), obey, abide by, conform to; follow (a precedent)

ⓑ comply with, accede to

忠告に従う *chūkoku ni shitagau* follow [act upon] advice

...に従って *...ni shitagatte* in accordance with...; in proportion to...

③ yield to, submit

征服者に従う *seifukusha ni shitagau* submit to a conqueror

【shitaga(eru) 従える】be attended by, take along; conquer, subjugate

家来二人従えて *kerai futari shitagaete* attended by two retainers

SYNONYMS

❶ⓐ follow and pursue

追 CHASE → 3096
随 FOLLOW → 627

ⓐ accompany

随 FOLLOW → 627
侍 ATTEND UPON → 85
陪 ACCOMPANY A SUPERIOR → 539
伴 ACCOMPANY → 60
添 accompany → 529

ⓑ servants

供 attendant → 88
臣 RETAINER → 3068
僕 MANSERVANT → 164
奴 SLAVE → 187
隷 UNDERLING → 1751

❷ obey

順 OBEY → 18
遵 OBEY → 3167
守 observe → 2173
隷 be subordinate to → 1751

❹ⓐ subordinate

副 SECONDARY → 1776
次 secondary → 54
亜 SUB- → 3540
準 QUASI- → 2856
半 semi- → 3501
准 JUNIOR → 127
助 assistant → 1121

NOTE

★do not confuse with 徒 416

3-7 彳

徒 徒 徒

416 TO itazura▲ ada▲

丿 彡 彳 彳一 彳十 彳土 彳土 彳作 徒 徒
1 2 3 4 5 6 7 8 9 10

CH 徒 tú

Radical	Strokes
彳 60	10-3-7
Grade	Freq
Jōyō-4	747
1-3-7	

▶FOLLOWER

COMPOUNDS

❶ [also suffix] (adherent) **follower, believer, disciple, pupil**

信徒 *shinto* believer, devotee; the faithful
十二使徒 *jūnishito* the Twelve Apostles
学徒 *gakuto* student, follower
生徒 *seito* pupil, student
仏教徒 *bukkyōto* Buddhist

❷ⓐ fellows, companions, gang, party

ⓑ fellow, person

徒党 *totō* clique, faction, conspirators
暴徒 *bōto* rioters, mobsters, insurgents
博徒 *bakuto* gambler

❸ⓐ vain, futile, wasted, worthless

ⓑ empty, empty-handed

徒労 *torō* vain effort, lost labor
徒食 *toshoku* idle life
徒手体操 *toshu-taisō* free standing exercises

❹ [original meaning] go on foot, walk, run

徒歩 *toho* walking, going on foot
徒競走 *tokyōsō* foot race

❺ punish, sentence to labor

徒刑 *tokei* penal servitude
囚徒 *shūto* prisoner, convict

INDEPENDENT

【to 徒】party, gang, set; follower, disciple

無頼の徒 *burai no to* gang of rowdies
学問の徒 *gakumon no to* student, scholar

KUN

【itazura 徒】uselessness, idleness

徒に *itazura ni* in vain, uselessly, aimlessly, idly

【ada 徒】[in compounds] vain, empty, fruitless; ephemeral; fickle, frivolous

徒な *ada na* vain, futile
徒桜 *adazakura* ephemeral cherry blossom
徒し心 *adashigokoro* fickle heart

SYNONYMS

❶ **students and followers**

弟 disciple → 2044
門 pupil → 888
生 STUDENT → 3497
卒 graduate student → 2055
学 scholar → 2555

❷ **fellow**

輩 FELLOW (*belittling*) → 2807
漢 FELLOW → 657
奴 GUY → 187
棒 tough guy → 983
坊 COLLOQUIAL PERSON SUFFIX → 233
屋 colloquial person suffix → 3098
物 character → 874

❸ⓐ **vain**

空 EMPTY → 2227
虚 without substance → 3237

❹ **walk**

歩 WALK → 2416
脚 move on foot → 974
足 travel on foot → 2188
踏 TREAD → 1587

HOMOPHONES

itazura ⇨ 悪戯 2745, 1875

NOTE

⇨ see USAGE note at 戯 1875
★do not confuse with 従 415

3-7 彳

徑 417

▶**PATH** ▶**DIAMETER**
nonstandard for 径 291

3-7 忄

悦 悦 悦 悦 418

ETSU yoroko(bu)▲ yoroko(basu)▲

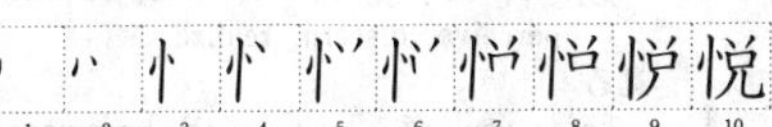

Ⓒⓗ 悦 yuè

Radical	Strokes
忄 61	10-3-7
Grade	**Freq**
Jōyō	1625
1 - 3 - 7	

▶**DELIGHTED**

COMPOUNDS

ⓐ [original meaning] **delighted, pleased, happy**

ⓑ [archaic] please, delight, make happy

悦楽 *etsuraku* pleasure, joy
喜悦 *kietsu* delight, rapture, joy
満悦 *man'etsu* great joy, rapture
愉悦 *yuetsu* joy
法悦 *hōetsu* religious exultation; ecstasy

INDEPENDENT

【**etsu 悦**】delight, joy, rapture
一人悦に入る *hitori etsu ni iru* chuckle with delight, be pleased with oneself

KUN

【**yoroko(bu) 悦ぶ**】[now usu. 喜ぶ] *vi* be happy [glad], be delighted
悦び *yorokobi* [now usu. 喜び] joy, delight
悦ばしい *yorokobashii* joyful, delightful, gratifying

【**yoroko(basu) 悦ばす**】[now usu. 喜ばす] *vt* please, gladden, make happy
親を悦ばす *oya o yorokobasu* make one's parents happy
目を悦ばす *me o yorokobasu* feast one's eyes (on)

SYNONYMS

ⓐ **pleased and pleasant**

愉 PLEASED → 582
嬉しい GLAD → 722
喜 HAPPY → 2308
歓 JOYOUS → 1867
欣 JOYFUL → 852
快 PLEASANT → 245
楽 pleasurable → 2826
朗 CHEERFUL → 1325

HOMOPHONES

yorokobu ⇨ 喜 2308
yorokobi ⇨ 喜 2308 慶 3173
yorokobasu ⇨ 喜 2308

NOTE

⇨ see USAGE note at 喜 2308

3-7 ↑

悟

419 GO sato(ru)

CH 悟 wù

Radical	Strokes
↑ 61	10-3-7
Grade	**Freq**
Jōyō	1398
1 - 3 - 7	

1 2 3 4 5 6 7 8 9 10

▶AWAKE TO

COMPOUNDS

❶ⓐ awake to, become aware of, realize, comprehend

ⓑ become aware of one's sins, repent

悟了 *goryō* complete comprehension

覚悟する *kakugo suru* be ready [prepared] for; be resigned; make up one's mind

悔悟 *kaigo* repentance, remorse

❷ⓐ awake to the Truth, become enlightened, attain satori

ⓑ spiritual awakening, enlightenment, satori

悟道 *godō* spiritual enlightenment; philosophy; (Buddhist) enlightenment

悟入する *gonyū suru* enter (Buddhist) enlightenment

❸ wisdom, intelligence, reason

悟性 *gosei* wisdom, reason

大悟 *taigo* great wisdom

KUN

【sato(ru) 悟る】

① be spiritually awakened, attain (Buddhist) enlightenment [satori]

悟り *satori* satori, spiritual awakening

② [formerly 覚る] awake to, be aware of, perceive, discern, realize

悟り *satori* satori, spiritual awakening; [formerly 覚り] comprehension, understanding

悟りが早い *satori ga hayai* be quick to understand

SYNONYMS

❶ⓐ know and understand

了 COMPREHEND → 3350

諒 UNDERSTAND → 1575

解 understand → 1517

分かる understand → 1972

得 gain understanding of → 477

知 KNOW → 1127

通 know thoroughly → 3109

❶ⓐ & ❷ⓐ awake

覚 awake → 2604

USAGE

❶ satoru

悟る

① be spiritually awakened, attain (Buddhist) enlightenment [satori]

② [formerly 覚る] awake to, be aware of, perceive, discern, realize

覚る

[now usu. 悟る] awake to, be aware of, perceive, discern, realize

❷ satori

悟り

① satori, spiritual awakening

② [formerly 覚り] comprehension, understanding

覚り

[now usu. 悟り] comprehension, understanding

HOMOPHONES

satoru ⇨ 覚 2604

satori ⇨ 覚 2604

3-7 ↑

悖

420 HAI moto(ru)

CH 悖 bèi

Radical	Strokes
↑ 61	10-3-7
Grade	**Freq**
Reference	
1 - 3 - 7	

COMPOUNDS

● [now replaced by 背 *hai* 2573] go against, be contrary to

悖徳 *haitoku* immorality, corruption, lapse from virtue

悖る *motoru* go against, deviate from

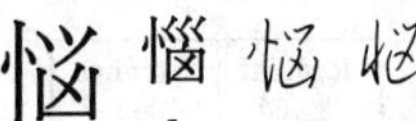

421 NŌ naya(mu) naya(masu)

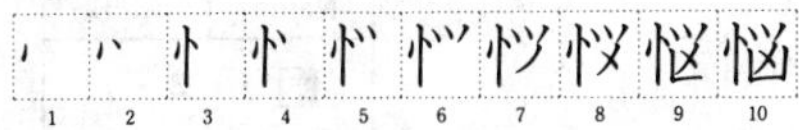

Ⓒⓗ 恼 nǎo

Radical	Strokes
忄 61	10-3-7
Grade	**Freq**
Jōyō	945
◧ 1-3-7	

3-7 忄

▶**SUFFER**

COMPOUNDS

ⓐ [original meaning] **suffer, be distressed**
ⓑ cause suffering, afflict
ⓒ **suffering, distress, pain, trouble, affliction**

悩乱 *nōran* worry, anguish
懊悩 *ōnō* agony, anguish, trouble
悩殺する *nōsatsu suru* fascinate, enchant
苦悩 *kunō* suffering, distress, anguish
煩悩 *bonnō* worldly desires, carnal desires

KUN

【naya(mu) 悩む】 *vi* be troubled, be worried; suffer, be distressed
悩み *nayami* troubles, worries, suffering, anguish
悩ましい *nayamashii* distressful, full of cares and vexations; seductive, alluring
伸び悩む *nobinayamu* be held in check, fail to grow

【naya(masu) 悩ます】 *vt* afflict, torment; trouble, annoy, harass
頭を悩ます *atama o nayamasu* rack one's brains

SYNONYMS

● **trouble and suffering**
苦 SUFFERING → 2243
窮 BE IN EXTREMITY → 2358
困 BE IN TROUBLE → 3070
痛 PAIN → 3285
辛 HARD → 2038
煩 VEXED → 1022
難 DIFFICULT → 1838

悧

422 RI

Ⓒⓗ 俐 lì

Radical	Strokes
忄 61	10-3-7
Grade	**Freq**
Reference	
◧ 1-3-7	

3-7 忄

COMPOUNDS

● [now also 利 1114] sharp, keen, clever
悧巧(=利口)な *rikō na* clever, bright, sharp, shrewd
怜悧(=伶俐) *reiri* cleverness, sagacity

悄

423 SHŌ

Ⓒⓗ 悄 qiǎo qiāo

Radical	Strokes
忄 61	10-3-7
Grade	**Freq**
Reference	
◧ 1-3-7	

3-7 忄

COMPOUNDS

● [now usu. 消 443] become disheartened, become dispirited; be worried
悄然たる *shōzentaru* dejected, dispirited
悄気る *shogeru* be disheartened, be dispirited

3-7 忄

悌 悌 悌

424 TEI DAI NAMES tomo yasu yasushi yoshi

CH 悌 tì

Radical	Strokes
忄 61	10-3-7
Grade	**Freq**
Names	2052
1 - 3 - 7	

丶 丷 忄 忄 忄 忄 忄 悄 悌 悌 (1–10)

▶BROTHERLY LOVE

COMPOUNDS

ⓐ [original meaning] **brotherly love, obedience to one's older brother**

ⓑ serving one's elders, obedience to one's seniors

孝悌 *kōtei* filial piety and brotherly love

悌順 *teijun* [archaic] obedience

NAMES

悌三 *teizō* male name

悌夫 *tomoo* male name

悌成 *yasunari* male name

SYNONYMS

ⓐ **fidelity**

孝 FILIAL PIETY → 3205

忠 LOYALTY → 2433

義 faith → 2338

誠 SINCERITY → 1523

実 faithfulness → 2225

信 fidelity → 100

操 constancy → 769

節 moral integrity → 2691

3-7 忄

悅

425

▶DELIGHTED

nonstandard for 悦 418

3-7 忄

悔

426

▶REPENT

nonstandard for 悔 365

3-7 忄

惇

incorrect stroke count ⇨ see 486

3-7 扌

挽

427 BAN hi(ku)

CH 挽 wǎn

Radical	Strokes
扌 64	10-3-7
Grade	**Freq**
Reference	
1 - 3 - 7	

COMPOUNDS

❶ [original meaning] pull strongly, tug, draw

挽回 *bankai* retrieval, recovery, restoration

❷ mourn

挽歌 *banka* elegy, funeral song

❸ grind (meat or coffee)

挽き肉 *hikiniku* ground [minced] meat

挽き立てのコーヒー *hikitate no kōhī* freshly-ground coffee

❹ saw, cut with a saw

木挽き歌 *kobikiuta* sawyer's song

❺ turn (a potter's wheel)

HOMOPHONES

hiku ⇨ 引 181 弾 572 退 3094 惹 2493 轢 1662

NOTE

⇨ see USAGE note at 引 181

挺

428 CHŌ TEI

CH 挺 tǐng

Radical	Strokes
扌 64	10-3-7
Grade	Freq
Reference	
1 - 3 - 7	

3-7 扌

COMPOUNDS

❶ [now also 丁 *chō* 3348] counter for long objects such as guns, oars, guitars, palanquins or candles

ピストル五挺 *pisutoru gochō* five pistols

ギター三挺 *gitā sanchō* three guitars

❷ volunteer bravely

挺身 *teishin* volunteering

挺進する *teishin suru* go ahead of

空挺部隊 *kūtei butai* airborne troops

挺する(＝挺す) *teisuru* (＝*teisu*) volunteer bravely

捕 捕 捕

429 HO to(raeru) to(rawareru) to(ru) tsuka(maeru) tsuka(maru)

CH 捕 bǔ

Radical	Strokes
扌 64	10-3-7
Grade	Freq
Jōyō	576
1 - 3 - 7	

3-7 扌

一 1 ｜ 2 扌 3 扌 4 扩 5 捐 6 捐 7 捐 8 捕 9 捕 10

▶**CATCH**

COMPOUNDS

❶ⓐ **catch, seize, grasp**

ⓑ (capture by force) **catch, capture, arrest**

捕獲する *hokaku suru* catch (fish); capture (a ship), seize

捕捉する *hosoku suru* catch, seize, capture; apprehend; understand

捕球 *hokyū* a catch (in baseball)

捕手 *hoshu* catcher

逮捕 *taiho* arrest, capture

捕鯨 *hogei* whaling

捕虜 *horyo* prisoner of war, captive

❷ *baseball* catcher

捕逸 *hoitsu* catcher passed ball

INDEPENDENT

【**ho** 捕】*baseball* catcher

KUN

【**to(raeru)** 捕らえる】

①ⓐ catch, seize, grasp

ⓑ (capture by force) catch, capture, arrest

袖を捕らえる *sode o toraeru* catch a person by the sleeve

泥棒を捕らえる *dorobō o toraeru* arrest a thief

引っ捕らえる *hittoraeru* capture, arrest, seize

② [formerly also 捉える] (take hold as if with the hand) grasp (an idea), seize (an opportunity)

捕らえ所の無い *toraedokoro no nai* elusive, subtle, slippery

【**to(rawareru)** 捕らわれる】

①ⓐ be caught, be arrested

ⓑ [also 囚われる] be imprisoned, be taken captive

捕らわれ *toraware* captivity, imprisonment

敵に捕らわれる *teki ni torawareru* be caught by the enemy

② [also 囚われる] adhere to (tradition), be swayed by

捕らわれた考え *torawareta kangae* conventional ideas, prejudiced opinion

【**to(ru)** 捕る】catch, take, seize

捕り物 *torimono* capture, arrest

魚を捕る *sakana o toru* catch fish

分捕る *bundoru* loot, grab

【**tsuka(maeru)** 捕まえる】arrest, nab, capture, catch

犯人を捕まえる *hannin o tsukamaeru* arrest the culprit

【**tsuka(maru)** 捕まる】be caught, be arrested

取っ捕まる *tottsukamaru* be caught

SYNONYMS

❶ⓐ **take**

執 SEIZE → 1680

握 GRASP → 585

把 GRIP → 249

取 TAKE → 1262

持 HOLD → 374

ⓑ **catch a criminal**

逮 CATCH A CRIMINAL → 3123

拘 ARREST → 310

USAGE

❶ **toraeru**

捕らえる

①ⓐ catch, seize, grasp
ⓑ (capture by force) catch, capture, arrest
② [formerly also 捉える] (take hold as if with the hand) grasp (an idea), seize (an opportunity)

捉える
[now usu. 捕らえる] (take hold as if with the hand) grasp (an idea), seize (an opportunity)

❷ **torawareru**
捕らわれる
①ⓐ be caught, be arrested
ⓑ [also 囚われる] be imprisoned, be taken captive
② [also 囚われる] adhere to (tradition), be swayed by

囚われる
[also 捕らわれる]
① be imprisoned, be taken captive
② adhere to (tradition), be swayed by

❸ **tsukamaeru**
捕まえる
arrest, nab, capture, catch
摑まえる
catch, seize, grasp, get hold of

❹ **tsukamaru**
捕まる
be caught, be arrested
摑まる
hold fast to, cling to

HOMOPHONES

toraeru ⇨ 捉 433
torawareru ⇨ 囚 3042
toru ⇨ 取 1262 採 499 撮 737 執 1680
tsukamaeru ⇨ 摑 690
tsukamaru ⇨ 摑 690

NOTE

⇨ see also USAGE note at 取 1262

3-7
扌

振 振 振

430 SHIN fu(ru) bu(ru) fu(ri) -bu(ri) fu(ruu)

CH 振 zhèn

Radical	Strokes
扌 64	10-3-7
Grade	**Freq**
Jōyō	728
1-3-7	

▶**SWING**

COMPOUNDS

❶ⓐ [original meaning] **swing, oscillate, vibrate**
ⓑ *baseball* **swing**
振動 *shindō* vibration
振幅 *shinpuku* amplitude (of vibration)
強振する *kyōshin suru* swing hard
三振 *sanshin* strikeout

❷ⓐ arouse to action, rouse up
ⓑ **rise, prosper, thrive**
振作する *shinsaku suru* promote, enhance, stimulate
振興 *shinkō* promotion, furtherance, rousing
不振 *fushin* dullness, depression, stagnation, slump

INDEPENDENT

【shin 振】 abbrev. of 三振 *sanshin*: strikeout

KUN

【fu(ru) 振る】
①ⓐ wave, shake; swing, oscillate
ⓑ brandish, wield, flourish
ⓒ sprinkle, cast
手を振る *te o furu* wave one's hand
振り子 *furiko* pendulum
振り袖 *furisode* long sleeved kimono
② yaw, wag
台風が進路を北に振った *Taifū ga shinro o kita ni futta* The typhoon changed course to the north
③ reject, refuse; jilt, ditch
振られる *furareru* get the mitten, be kicked out
④ give (a role), cast (a part)
役を割り振る *yaku o warifuru* assign a role to an actor
⑤ draw, issue, remit
振り替え *furikae* change, transfer
振り込み *furikomi* bank transfer
⑥ unclassified compounds
振る舞う *furumau* behave oneself; entertain, treat

【bu(ru) 振る】 assume an air of, pretend, affect
厭に振っている *iya ni butte iru* reek of affectation
上品振る *jōhinburu* be prudish
学者振る *gakushaburu* assume the air of a scholar, be pedantic

【fu(ri) 振り】 swing, shake, wave; dress, personal appearance; show, make-believe, pretense; posture, gesture, action; counter for Japanese swords
人の振り見て我が振り直せ *Hito no furi mite waga furi naose* Correct your conduct by observing that of others

寝た振りをする *neta furi o suru* pretend to be asleep
振り付け *furitsuke* dance composition, choreography
身振りで示す *miburi de shimesu* express by gestures

【-bu(ri) -振り】
[also suffix]
① [sometimes also っ振り *-ppuri*] manner, way, style
枝振り *edaburi* shape of a tree, ramifications
男っ振り *otokoppuri* man's looks; public estimation
飲みっ振りが良いね *Nomippuri ga ii ne* You can really down it, eh!
② after a lapse of
久し振りに *hisashiburi ni* after a long time [interval]
三年振りに帰省する *sannenburi ni kisei suru* come home after three years' absence
③ size, amount
大振りの *ōburi no* large, of a larger size

【fu(ruu) 振るう】
①ⓐ [formerly also 揮う] wield, brandish, manipulate, master
ⓑ wield (authority), exercise, exhibit (one's powers)
ⓒ shake
槍を振るう *yari o furuu* wield a spear
腕を振るう *ude o furuu* display one's ability, exercise one's talent
振るい落とす *furuiotosu* shake off
②ⓐ be in high spirits, be invigorated
ⓑ flourish, thrive, be prosperous
軍の士気が振るう *Gun no shiki ga furuu* The morale of the army is high
振るわない *furuwanai* be dull, be in a bad way
振るった *furutta* original, striking, extraordinary

SYNONYMS

❶ⓐ shake
震 QUAKE → 2806
揺 SHAKE → 594
❷ⓐ incite
起 rise to action → 3307
動 MOVE → 1778
奮 ROUSE UP → 2367
激 excite → 776
扇 FAN → 1950
挑 PROVOKE → 372
唆 INSTIGATE → 402
ⓑ prospering and prosperity
隆 PROSPER → 545
興 RISE TO PROSPERITY → 2909
栄 FLOURISH → 2574
繁 THRIVE → 2853
盛 PROSPEROUS → 2675
昌 PROSPERING → 2414

USAGE

furuu
振るう
①ⓐ [formerly also 揮う] wield, brandish, manipulate, master
ⓑ wield (authority), exercise, exhibit (one's powers)
ⓒ shake
②ⓐ be in high spirits, be invigorated
ⓑ flourish, thrive, be prosperous
揮う
[now usu. 振るう] wield, brandish, manipulate, master
震う
tremble, quiver, shudder
奮う
rouse up, rouse oneself, arouse

HOMOPHONES

furuu ⇨ 揮 589 震 2806 奮 2367

挿 挿 挿° 挿 挿

431 sō sa(su) hasa(mu)▲

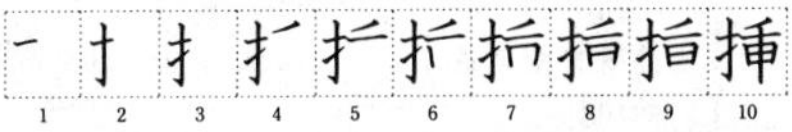

Ⓒⓗ 插 chā

Radical	Strokes
扌 64	10-3-7
Grade	**Freq**
Jōyō	1943
◧ 1 - 3 - 7	

3-7
扌

▶INSERT

COMPOUNDS

● [original meaning] **insert, put into, stick between**
挿入する *sōnyū suru* insert, put into
挿話 *sōwa* anecdote
挿画 *sōga* illustration (in a book)
挿花 *sōka* flower arrangement

KUN

【sa(su) 挿す】
ⓐ insert, put into, stick between
ⓑ insert seedlings, plant
挿し絵 *sashie* illustration (in a book)
挿し木 *sashiki* cutting; cuttage
花瓶に花を挿す *kabin ni hana o sasu* put flowers in a vase

【hasa(mu) 挿む】 [now usu. 挟む] put (some-

thing) between, insert, interpose
本に栞を挿む *hon ni shiori o hasamu* put a bookmark between the pages of a book

SYNONYMS
● **put in**
入 PUT IN → 3370
-込む cause to move inward → 3030

HOMOPHONES
sasu ⇨ 指 378 差 3311 刺 1275 注 325
射 1458 止 2941
hasamu ⇨ 挟 377 鋏 1731

COMPOUND FORMATION
挿話 *sōwa*
挿話 'anecdote' refers to an inserted (挿) story (話).

NOTE
⇨ see USAGE notes at 差 3311 and 挟 377

3-7 扌

搜 搜 搜 搜

432 SŌ saga(su)

一 十 扌 扌 扩 扫 押 押 搜 搜 (1–10)

CH 搜 sōu

Radical	Strokes
扌 64	10-3-7
Grade	**Freq**
Jōyō	605
1-3-7	

▶**LOOK FOR**

COMPOUNDS
● [original meaning] **look for, search**
搜査 *sōsa* criminal investigation, search
搜索 *sōsaku* search, investigation
博搜 *hakusō* searching far and wide

KUN
【**saga(su) 搜す**】[also 探す] look for (a lost object), search for, hunt for
搜し物 *sagashimono* looking for something lost; thing to look for
宝搜し *takarasagashi* treasure hunt
本を搜す *hon o sagasu* look for a book

SYNONYMS
● **seek**
索 SEARCH FOR → 2455
探 SEARCH → 505
求 SEEK → 3550
猟 hunt for → 538

USAGE
sagasu
搜す
[also 探す] look for (a lost object), search for, hunt for
探す
[also 搜す] search for (something desired), search about, look for

HOMOPHONES
sagasu ⇨ 探 505

3-7 扌

捉

433 SOKU tora(eru)

CH 捉 zhuō

Radical	Strokes
扌 64	10-3-7
Grade	**Freq**
Reference	
1-3-7	

COMPOUNDS
❶ⓐ [original meaning, now archaic] grasp, clutch, catch
ⓑ capture, catch
捕捉 *hosoku* seizure, capture; apprehension; understanding
❷ [now usu. 捕らえる *toraeru*] (take hold as if with the hand) grasp (an idea), seize (an opportunity)
捉え所の無い *toraedokoro no nai* elusive, subtle
意味を捉える *imi o toraeru* grasp the meaning

HOMOPHONES
toraeru ⇨ 捕 429

NOTE
⇨ see USAGE note at 捕 429

3-7 扌

挾

434

▶**HOLD BETWEEN**
nonstandard for 挟 377

拷 incorrect stroke count ⇨ see 373

浮 浮 浮 浮 CH 浮 fú

435 FU u(ku) u(kareru) u(kabu) u(kaberu)

Radical	Strokes
氵 85	10-3-7
Grade	**Freq**
Jōyō	983
1-3-7	

▶FLOAT

COMPOUNDS

❶ [original meaning] **float, rise to the surface**

浮沈 *fuchin* rise and fall, ebb and flow; ups and downs
浮上する *fujō suru* surface, rise [float] to the surface
浮揚 *fuyō* floating
浮力 *furyoku* buoyancy, lift
浮標 *fuhyō* (marker) buoy
浮遊 *fuyū* floating, suspension

❷ **floating, transient, insecure, insubstantial**

浮浪者 *furōsha* vagabond, loafer, hobo
浮動する *fudō suru* fluctuate; float, waft
浮説 *fusetsu* wild rumor, speculation
浮言 *fugen* unfounded report, wild rumor
浮生 *fusei* transient life

❸ thoughtless, flippant, fickle

浮薄な *fuhaku na* frivolous, fickle, insincere
浮華 *fuka* empty show, frivolity, levity

KUN

【u(ku) 浮く】 *vi* float, rise to the surface; feel (one's teeth) loose, be set on edge; become buoyant; frivolous, flippant, insecure; be left over, be saved

浮き *uki* float; buoy, life buoy
浮き彫り *ukibori* relief, embossed carving
浮き上がる *ukiagaru* float, rise to the surface
浮き草 *ukikusa* floating weed
歯の浮く様な音 *ha no uku yō na oto* noise that sets one's teeth on edge
浮き浮きと *ukiuki to* buoyantly, cheerfully
浮き名を流す *ukina o nagasu* get a reputation as a philanderer
浮き世 *ukiyo* transitory world, fleeting life
浮き足立つ *ukiashidatsu* begin to waver [falter], lose confidence

【u(kareru) 浮かれる】 *vi* become buoyant, be gay, be in high spirits; be on the spree

浮かれ男 *ukareotoko* playboy
花に浮かれる *hana ni ukareru* be intoxicated with the blossoms

【u(kabu) 浮かぶ】 float, rise to the surface; loom up, appear; come across one's mind; rest in peace

水に浮かぶ泡 *mizu ni ukabu awa* bubbles on the water
微笑の浮かんだ唇 *hohoemi no ukanda kuchibiru* lips with a flickering smile
心に浮かぶ *kokoro ni ukabu* come across one's mind
浮かばれない *ukabarenai* cannot rest in peace, turn in one's grave

【u(kaberu) 浮かべる】 *vt* float, set afloat; express, show; call to mind

ボートを浮かべる *bōto o ukaberu* launch a boat
微笑を浮かべて *bishō o ukabete* with a smile
思い浮かべる *omoiukaberu* call to mind

SPECIAL READINGS

浮気 *uwaki* inconstancy; love affair; fickleness
浮付く *uwatsuku* be fickle, be flippant, be restless

SYNONYMS

❶ **float**

漂 DRIFT → 699

3-7 氵

浜 濱 浜 濵

436 HIN hama

Ⓒⓗ 滨 bīn

Radical	Strokes
氵 85	10-3-7
Grade	**Freq**
Jōyō	545
1 - 3 - 7	

▶**BEACH**

COMPOUNDS

❶ **beach, seashore, coast**

海浜 *kaihin* seashore, seaside, beach

❷ Yokohama

京浜 *keihin* Tokyo and Yokohama

KUN

【**hama** 浜】 beach, seashore, coast; *slang* Yokohama; captured stone in the game of go

浜辺 *hamabe* beach, seashore

砂浜 *sunahama* sandy beach, sands

浜風 *hamakaze* beach wind

浜茄子 *hamanasu* sweet brier

浜伝いに *hamazutai ni* along the beach

浜っ子 *hamakko* native of Yokohama

SYNONYMS

❶ **shores and watersides**

岸 SHORE → 2236

畔 WATERSIDE → 1145

-辺 -side → 3029

浦 SEASIDE → 437

渚 STRAND → 525

磯 ROCKY BEACH → 1242

❷ **Kanto cities**

京 TOKYO → 2052

東 Tokyo → 3568

都 METROPOLIS OF TOKYO → 1686

3-7 氵

浦 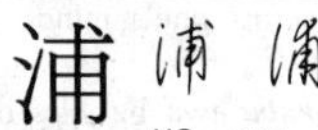

437 HO ura

Ⓒⓗ 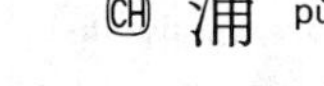 pǔ

Radical	Strokes
氵 85	10-3-7
Grade	**Freq**
Jōyō	841
1 - 3 - 7	

▶**SEASIDE**

COMPOUNDS

● [original meaning] **shore, coast, seaside, water's edge**

曲浦 *kyokuho* winding coast [beach]

KUN

【**ura** 浦】

① *elegant* seaside, seashore

浦風 *urakaze* sea breeze

浦人 *urabito* seaside dweller

浦里 *urazato* village by the sea

津津浦浦に *tsutsu-uraura ni* throughout the land, in every harbor and every bay

② coastal indentation, inlet, small bay

浦曲 *urawa* coastal indentations

SYNONYMS

【**ura**】

① **shores and watersides**

岸 SHORE → 2236

浜 BEACH → 436

-辺 -side → 3029

畔 WATERSIDE → 1145

渚 STRAND → 525

磯 ROCKY BEACH → 1242

② **inlets and bays**

江 INLET → 221

湾 BAY → 613

峡 narrows → 357

浩 浩 浩 浩

438 KŌ NAMES hiro hiroshi yutaka

CH 浩 hào

Radical	Strokes
氵 85	10-3-7
Grade	**Freq**
Names	1990
◧ 1 - 3 - 7	

3-7 氵

1 2 3 4 5 6 7 8 9 10

▶**VAST**

COMPOUNDS

ⓐ **vast (like an expanse of water), extensive, immense, great**

ⓑ vast (amount), huge (quantity); numerous

浩然たる *kōzentaru* vast; magnanimous

浩瀚な *kōkan na* bulky, voluminous

NAMES

浩二 *kōji* male name

浩子 *hiroko* female name

浩 *hiroshi* (=*yutaka*) male name

SYNONYMS

ⓐ **wide and extensive**

洸 VAST (expanse of water) → 387

博 EXTENSIVE → 151

紘 WIDE-RANGING → 1298

広 WIDE → 3035

ⓑ **big and huge**

巨 HUGE → 3039

太 GREAT → 2152

大 BIG → 3416

浪 浪 浪

439 RŌ

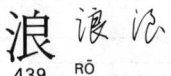

CH 浪 làng

Radical	Strokes
氵 85	10-3-7
Grade	**Freq**
Jōyō	1371
◧ 1 - 3 - 7	

3-7 氵

1 2 3 4 5 6 7 8 9 10

▶**BILLOW** ▶**WANDER**

COMPOUNDS

❶ **billow, large wave, wave**

波浪 *harō* waves, billows

風浪 *fūrō* wind and waves, heavy seas

❷ **wander, roam, ramble, drift about**

浪浪 *rōrō* wandering

浪人 *rōnin* lordless samurai, *ronin*; unsuccessful examinee; jobless person

放浪する *hōrō suru* wander about, roam

浮浪者 *furōsha* vagabond, loafer, hobo

流浪する *rurō suru* wander [roam] about from place to place

❸ abbrev. of 浪人 *rōnin*: student waiting for another chance to be enrolled in a university

三浪 *sanrō* unsuccessful examinee waiting for the third chance to be enrolled in a university

❹ wasteful, extravagant, unrestrained

浪費 *rōhi* waste, extravagance

❺ abbrev. of 浪花 *naniwa*, old name of Osaka

浪曲 *rōkyoku naniwabushi*, form of traditional Japanese vaudeville

❻ used phonetically for *rō*

浪漫主義 *rōmanshugi* romanticism

SPECIAL READINGS

浪花▲ *naniwa* old name for Osaka

SYNONYMS

❶ **waves**

波 WAVE → 330

❷ **wander**

遊 move about freely → 3142

漂 drift about → 699

流 drift → 441

3-7
氵

涙 涙 涙 涙

440 RUI namida

CH 泪 lèi

Radical	Strokes
氵 85	10-3-7
Grade	**Freq**
Jōyō	1271
1-3-7	

▶TEAR

COMPOUNDS

● [original meaning] **tear, tears**

涙腺 *ruisen* lachrymal gland
涙嚢 *ruinō* lachrymal sac, dacryocyst
落涙する *rakurui suru* shed tears
催涙ガス *sairui-gasu* tear gas
暗涙に咽ぶ *anrui ni musebu* shed silent tears

KUN

【**namida** 涙】 tear, tears; sympathy; a mere particle of, a modicum of
涙ぐむ *namidagumu* be moved to tears
涙を呑む *namida o nomu* choke back one's tears, pocket an insult
涙雨 *namidaame* sprinkling rain
嬉し涙 *ureshinamida* tears of joy
涙金 *namidakin* small sum of consolation money
雀の涙程の補助金 *suzume no namida hodo no hojokin* a mere particle of subsidy

SYNONYMS

● **bodily secretions**
汗 SWEAT → 220
精 sperm → 1366
乳 MILK → 1438

3-7
氵

流 流 流 流

441 RYŪ RU naga(reru) naga(re) naga(su) -naga(su)

CH 流 liú

Radical	Strokes
氵 85	10-3-7
Grade	**Freq**
Jōyō-3	301
1-3-7	

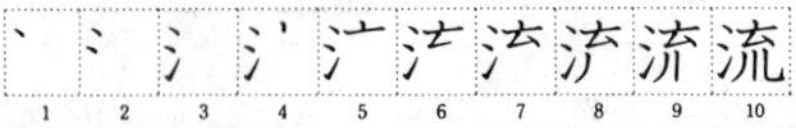

▶FLOW ▶CURRENT ▶STYLE

COMPOUNDS

❶ⓐ [original meaning] **flow, stream, run**
ⓑ **let flow, spill out, discharge, shed**
ⓒ be swept away by the flow, drift

流動する *ryūdō suru* flow, circulate, be liquid
流出 *ryūshutsu* outflow, effusion
漂流する *hyōryū suru* drift, be adrift
合流する *gōryū suru* flow together; join, unite
流血 *ryūketsu* bloodshed
放流 *hōryū* discharge; stocking (a river) with (fish)
流失する *ryūshitsu suru* be washed away
流木 *ryūboku* driftwood
浮流 *furyū* floating, drifting

❷ flowing, fluent

流暢に *ryūchō ni* fluently, flowingly, smoothly
流麗な *ryūrei na* fluent, flowing

❸ⓐ (water or air flow) **current, stream, flow**
ⓑ (body of running water) **stream, river**
ⓒ (general tendency) **current, drift, trend**

海流 *kairyū* ocean current
気流 *kiryū* air [atmospheric] current, air stream
暖流 *danryū* warm current
上流 *jōryū* upper stream (of a river); upper class
潮流 *chōryū* tide, current; tendency, trend
急流 *kyūryū* rapid stream, swift current; swift-running river; rapids
本流 *honryū* main course (of a river), main stream
分流 *bunryū* distributary, river branch
時流 *jiryū* fashion [current] of the times, general drift of affairs
主流 *shuryū* main current, mainstream
底流 *teiryū* bottom current, undercurrent

❹ electric current

電流 *denryū* electric current
交流 *kōryū* alternating current; interchange
整流 *seiryū* rectification

❺ⓐ **spread, be disseminated, be circulated, pervade**
ⓑ spreading of false rumors

流通 *ryūtsū* circulation of money or goods; flow of water; ventilation
流布 *rufu* circulation, dissemination, spread
流行する(＝流行る) *ryūkō suru* (＝*hayaru*) be fashionable, be in vogue; prevail
流説 *ryūsetsu* groundless rumor, false report

❻ drift, wander

流民 *rumin* (=*ryūmin*) roaming [wandering] people, displaced persons
流浪 *rurō* vagrancy
流離する *ryūri suru* wander alone in a strange country

❼ cast out, banish, exile
流罪 *ruzai* banishment, exile
流刑 *rukei* deportation, banishment

❽ be abandoned before completion, prove abortive
流会 *ryūkai* adjournment of a meeting, be called off (due to lack of attendance)
流産 *ryūzan* miscarriage, abortion

❾ characteristic or institutionalized style:
ⓐ [also suffix] **style, way, mode, manner, form, fashion**
ⓑ [also suffix] **school, style, system**
ⓒ counter for schools
自己流 *jikoryū* one's own style, one's way of doing things
三島流の *mishimaryū no* in the style of Mishima
流派 *ryūha* school
流儀 *ryūgi* school, style, system, method
草月流 *sōgetsuryū* Sogetsu school of flower arrangement

❿ class, order, rate, grade
中流 *chūryū* middle class
一流大学 *ichiryū-daigaku* first-rate university
二流の出版社 *niryū no shuppansha* second-rate publisher

⓫ members of the same group or profession
女流文学者 *joryū bungakusha* lady of letters

⓬ bloodline, descent
嫡流 *chakuryū* lineage of the eldest son; orthodox school

⓭ [also 旒 *ryū* 1009] counter for flags
旗二流 *hata niryū* two flags

KUN

【naga(reru) 流れる】 flow, run; pass (time); drift away, float; wander, drift, stray; be called off; be forfeited
流れ込む *nagarekomu* flow into, stream in; wander into (town)
時が流れる *Toki ga nagareru* Time flows
流れ星 *nagareboshi* shooting star, meteor
流れ者 *nagaremono* vagrant
会が流れた *Kai ga nagareta* The meeting was called off

【naga(re) 流れ】
①ⓐ flowing, flow, current, stream
ⓑ (body of running water) stream, river
ⓒ stream, flow (of things or people)
川流れ *kawanagare* being carried away by a current
急な流れ *kyū na nagare* rapid stream, swiftly running river
車の流れ *kuruma no nagare* flow of cars
音楽の流れ *ongaku no nagare* flow of music
流れ作業 *nagaresagyō* assembly-line system
②ⓐ descent, lineage
ⓑ school, style
平家の流れ *heike no nagare* the Heike line
三島の流れを汲む *mishima no nagare o kumu* belong to Mishima's school (of literature)
③ suspension, postponement
会合をお流れにする *kaigō o onagare ni suru* postpone a meeting
④ forfeiture, foreclosure
質流れの時計 *shichinagare no tokei* unredeemed (pawned) watch
⑤ counter for flags
旗二流れ *hata futanagare* two flags

【naga(su) 流す】
①ⓐ let flow, spill, drain
ⓑ set adrift, float
ⓒ wash, scrub (one's back)
流し *nagashi* sink; bath attendant; strolling musician; cruising taxi
流し込む *nagashikomu* pour into; wash down
涙を流す *namida o nagasu* shed tears
流し網 *nagashiami* drift net
背中を流す *senaka o nagasu* rinse one's back
② exile, banish
島流し *shimanagashi* exile
罪人を流す *zainin o nagasu* exile a criminal
③ forfeit, foreclose
質草を流す *shichigusa o nagasu* forfeit a pawned article
④ cruise along, stroll
タクシーが流す *Takushī ga nagasu* Taxis cruise along
⑤ spread, broadcast
ラジオ番組で流す *rajio bangumi de nagasu* broadcast on a radio program
噂を流す *uwasa o nagasu* spread rumors
⑥ suspend, abort
総会を流す *sōkai o nagasu* call off a general meeting

【-naga(su) -流す】 [verbal suffix] ignore, do and disregard
聞き流す *kikinagasu* let something go in one ear and out the other
受け流す *ukenagasu* ward off, elude; turn aside (a joke)

SYNONYMS

❶ **flow and drip**
注 POUR → 325
濫 overflow → 801
漏 LEAK → 701
滴 DROP → 705
泌 SECRETE → 332

❷ **smooth**
暢 FLUENT → 1226
滑 SMOOTH → 658

❸ⓐ **running water**

潮 TIDE → 739
汐 TIDE → 223
瀬 rapids → 806
滝 WATERFALL → 661
洪 FLOOD → 386
渦 WHIRLPOOL → 603
ⓑ **rivers and streams**
渓 mountain stream → 516
川 RIVER → 6
河 RIVER → 336
江 large river → 221
ⓒ **tendency**
潮 TIDE → 739
向 tendency → 3052
性 NATURE → 299
勢 trend → 2857
傾 inclination → 154
❹ **electricity and magnetism**
電 ELECTRICITY → 2790
磁 MAGNETISM → 1214
❺ⓐ **make widely known**
布 SPREAD → 2973
伝 spread → 44
広 spread → 3035
弘 DISSEMINATE (esp. Buddhism) → 192
及 REACH TO → 3385
❻ **wander**
漂 drift about → 699
浪 WANDER → 439
遊 move about freely → 3142
❾ⓐ **way and style**
式 STYLE → 3049
調 TONE → 1567
法 METHOD → 333
途 WAY → 3107
方 WAY → 1963
様 MODE → 1052
風 MANNER → 3007
ⓑ **parties and sects**
派 SECT → 381
翼 WING → 2720
系 faction → 1944
門 (religious) sect → 888
宗 RELIGIOUS SECT (esp. Buddhist) → 2228
党 PARTY → 2581
閥 CLIQUE → 3325
❿ **class**
等 CLASS → 2682
級 GRADE → 1279
段 grade → 1144
位 RANK → 61
階 RANK → 624
身 social status → 3553
格 STATUS → 926
層 STRATUM → 3161

3-7 氵

  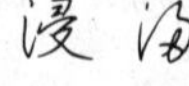

442 SHIN hita(su) hita(ru)

CH 浸 jìn

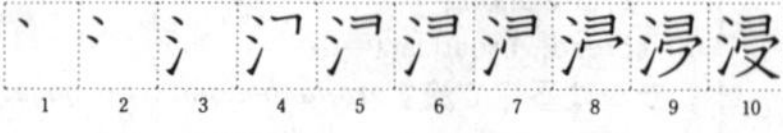

Radical	Strokes
氵 85	10-3-7
Grade	**Freq**
Jōyō	1496
1-3-7	

▶**SOAK**

COMPOUNDS

❶ⓐ [original meaning] **soak, immerse**
ⓑ [formerly also 滲 703] **permeate, infiltrate, penetrate; ooze, seep**
浸水 *shinsui* inundation, submergence
浸透 *shintō* permeation, penetration
浸潤 *shinjun* permeation, infiltration
浸出 *shinshutsu* percolation, exudation, effusion

❷ gradual, gradually
浸食 *shinshoku* erosion, corrosion

KUN

【hita(su) 浸す】 *vt* soak, dip, steep, immerse; drench, moisten
浸し物 *hitashimono* boiled greens flavored with soy
布を染料に浸す *nuno o senryō ni hitasu* soak cloth in a dye
水浸し *mizubitashi* submergence; being waterlogged
牛乳に浸したパン *gyūnyū ni hitashita pan* bread dunked in milk

【hita(ru) 浸る】 *vi* be soaked in, dip in; be addicted to, be indulged in
風呂の湯に浸る *furo no yu ni hitaru* soak in a bathtub, sink into a hot bath
幸福に浸る *kōfuku ni hitaru* swim in bliss
入り浸り *iribitari* frequenting; staying long

SYNONYMS

❶ **moisten**
漬ける immerse → 702
潤 moisten → 742

USAGE

shinshoku
浸食
erosion, corrosion
侵食
infringement, violation

NOTE

★do not confuse with 侵 101

消 消 消 㳺 Ⓒⓗ 消 xiāo

443 SHŌ ki(eru) ke(su)

Radical	Strokes
氵 85	10-3-7
Grade	**Freq**
Jōyō-3	332
◧ 1-3-7	

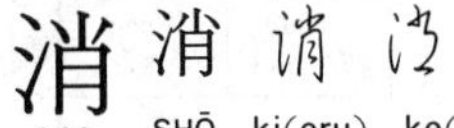

▶**EXTINGUISH** ▶**SPEND**

COMPOUNDS

❶ (put out a light or fire) **extinguish, put out; switch off**
消防 *shōbō* fire fighting, prevention and extinction of fires
消火 *shōka* fire fighting
消灯する *shōtō suru* turn off the lights

❷ⓐ (wipe out of existence) **extinguish, eliminate, remove from, obliterate**
ⓑ **disappear, vanish**
消化 *shōka* digestion; assimilation; consumption
消毒 *shōdoku* disinfection, sterilization
消音 *shōon* silencing (a machine)
消臭剤 *shōshūzai* deodorant
消却する *shōkyaku suru* efface; erase
消磁 *shōji* demagnetization
解消する *kaishō suru* liquidate, annul, solve; be liquidated, be solved
抹消する *masshō suru* erase, strike out
消息 *shōsoku* (personal) news, movements; letter
消失する *shōshitsu suru* disappear, vanish; die away
消滅する *shōmetsu suru* become extinct, disappear

❸ⓐ **spend, use up, consume; become spent out**
ⓑ [formerly also 銷 1732] spend (time), pass
消費する *shōhi suru* consume, spend
消耗する *shōmō suru* consume, exhaust, use up
消夏 *shōka* summering
消光する *shōkō suru* pass one's time

❹ negative
消極的な *shōkyokuteki na* negative

❺ [formerly also 銷 1732 or 悄 423] become disheartened, become dispirited; be worried
消然(＝悄然)たる *shōzentaru* dejected, dispirited
意気消沈(＝意気銷沈)する *iki-shōchin suru* be dispirited, be disheartened

KUN

【ki(eru) 消える】 *vi* be extinguished, go [die] out; disappear, vanish, melt away, wear out [away]
消えた火 *kieta hi* dead fire
立ち消え *tachigie* going out; flickering out
消え去る *kiesaru* vanish, disappear

【ke(su) 消す】 *vt* (put out a light or fire) extinguish, put out; switch off; (wipe out of existence) extinguish, eliminate, remove from, obliterate; cancel, annul
消し止める *keshitomeru* put out, extinguish
消しゴム *keshigomu* eraser
インク消し *inkukeshi* ink eraser
消し印 *keshiin* postmark, (postal) cancellation
取り消す *torikesu* cancel, nullify, annul

SYNONYMS

❶ **extinguish**
滅 go out → 660

❷ⓐ **destroy**
滅 DESTROY → 660
亡 perish → 3402
ⓑ **disappear**
没 disappear → 260

❸ⓐ **consume**
費 expend → 2607
尽 EXHAUST → 3050
耗 WEAR AWAY → 1309

NOTE

⇨ see COMPOUND FORMATION for 消息 *shōsoku* ⇨ 息 2647

3-7 氵

酒 酒 酒

444 SHU sake saka-

Ⓒⓗ 酒 jiǔ

Radical	Strokes
酉 164	10-7-3
Grade	**Freq**
Jōyō-3	903
1-3-7	

丶 冫 氵 汀 沂 沔 沔 洒 酒 酒
1 2 3 4 5 6 7 8 9 10

▶ALCOHOLIC DRINK

COMPOUNDS

ⓐ [also suffix] [original meaning] **alcoholic drink, wine, liquor, beer**

ⓑ **sake, rice wine**

酒造 *shuzō* sake brewing; distilling
酒家 *shuka* wine shop, pub; heavy drinker
酒宴 *shuen* banquet, drinking bout
飲酒 *inshu* drinking (alcoholic drinks)
洋酒 *yōshu* foreign wine [liquors]
醸造酒 *jōzōshu* brewage, liquor
清酒 *seishu* (refined) sake

KUN

【sake 酒, saka- 酒-】 sake, rice wine; alcoholic drink, wine, liquor, beer
お酒 *osake* sake, rice wine; alcoholic drink, wine, liquor, beer
酒癖が悪い *sakeguse ga warui* be a bad drunk
酒飲み *sakenomi* drinker
酒屋 *sakaya* sake dealer, liquor store
酒場 *sakaba* bar, barroom, pub, tavern
酒盛り *sakamori* drinking bout, merrymaking
甘酒 *amazake* sweet rice wine

SPECIAL READINGS

お神酒 *omiki* sacred wine [sake]; sake

SYNONYMS

● **drinks**
茶 TEA → 2259
汁 JUICE, SOUP → 195
乳 MILK → 1438

3-7 氵

浴 浴 浴

445 YOKU a(biru) a(biseru)

Ⓒⓗ 浴 yù

Radical	Strokes
氵 85	10-3-7
Grade	**Freq**
Jōyō-4	1095
1-3-7	

1 2 3 4 5 6 7 8 9 10

▶BATHE

COMPOUNDS

❶ [original meaning] **bathe**
浴場 *yokujō* bath, bathhouse
浴槽 *yokusō* bathtub
浴室 *yokushitsu* bathroom
入浴する *nyūyoku suru* bathe, take a bath

❷ⓐ [suffix] **bath, bathing**
ⓑ (liquid or container for immersion) bath
海水浴 *kaisuiyoku* sea bathing
日光浴 *nikkōyoku* sunbath
冷水浴 *reisuiyoku* cold-water bath
塩浴 *en'yoku* salt bath

INDEPENDENT

【yoku 浴】 bath (⇨❷)
【yokusuru 浴する】 bask in, be favored with

KUN

【a(biru) 浴びる】 *vi* bathe, take a bath; be bathed (in sunlight); be washed (by the waves); be under fire; be charged with (a crime); be covered (with dust)
水浴びする *mizuabi suru* bathe in cold water
【a(biseru) 浴びせる】 *vt* pour (water) on; subject to, shower (abuse) upon, deluge with
非難を浴びせる *hinan o abiseru* heap abuse upon (a person)

SPECIAL READINGS

浴衣 *yukata* (=*yokui*) informal summer kimono, *yukata*

SYNONYMS

❶ **clean and wash**
洗 WASH → 388
濯 RINSE → 793
浄 cleanse → 382
粛 PURGE → 3581
清 CLEAR → 523
払 CLEAR AWAY → 194
掃 SWEEP → 503

❷ⓐ **baths**
湯 hot bath → 612
泉 hot spring → 2567

浮 446
▶FLOAT
nonstandard for 浮 435
3-7 氵

海 447
▶SEA
nonstandard for 海 384
3-7 氵

浩 448
▶VAST
nonstandard for 浩 438
3-7 氵

浸 449
▶SOAK
nonstandard for 浸 442
3-7 氵

消 450
▶EXTINGUISH ▶SPEND
nonstandard for 消 443
3-7 氵

涉 451
▶HAVE RELATIONS WITH
nonstandard for 涉 526
3-7 氵

淳
incorrect stroke count ⇨ see 514
3-7 氵

狹 452
▶NARROW
nonstandard for 狭 396
3-7 犭

猛
incorrect stroke count ⇨ see 537
3-7 犭

陛 453
HEI
CH 陛 bi
3-7 阝

Radical	Strokes
阝 170	10-3-7
Grade	Freq
Jōyō-6	1358
1-3-7	

Stroke order: 1–10

▶IMPERIAL PALACE STEPS

COMPOUNDS

● [original meaning] **imperial palace steps, steps leading to the imperial palace hall**

陛下 *heika* His [Her, Your] Majesty; [original meaning] at the palace steps

陛衛 *heiei* [archaic] Imperial guard

天皇陛下 *tennōheika* His Majesty the Emperor, His Imperial Majesty

SYNONYMS

● **steps**

段 STEP → 1144

階 stairs → 624

NOTE

★do not confuse with **階** 624

3-7 阝

院 454 IN

Ⓒⓗ 院 yuàn

Radical	Strokes
阝 170	10-3-7
Grade	Freq
Jōyō-3	211
1-3-7	

▶ **INSTITUTION**

COMPOUNDS

❶ [also suffix] institution or organization, esp.:
ⓐ medical institution: **hospital, clinic, doctor's office**
ⓑ educational institution: **academy, institute, school**
院長 *inchō* hospital director; academy president
病院 *byōin* hospital
医院 *iin* clinic
入院する *nyūin suru* be hospitalized
退院 *taiin* discharge from a hospital
養老院 *yōrōin* institution for the aged
院生 *insei* graduate student
学院 *gakuin* institute, academy
孤児院 *kojiin* orphanage
大学院 *daigakuin* graduate school
美容院 *biyōin* beauty shop [parlor]

❷ [also suffix] legislative institution or body: **House, Diet, Congress, Parliament**
院内 *innai* inside the House [Diet]
上院 *jōin* Upper House
議院 *giin* House, Diet Chamber
両院 *ryōin* both Houses
参議院 *sangiin* House of Councilors, Upper House
衆議院 *shūgiin* House of Representatives, Lower House

❸ religious institution: monastery, (Buddhist) temple
寺院 *jiin* temple
尼僧院 *nisōin* nunnery, convent
修道院 *shūdōin* monastery, convent

❹ⓐ ex-Emperor, cloistered Emperor; palace of ex-Emperor
ⓑ honorific suffix after names of ex-Emperors
院政 *insei* government by cloistered Emperor
後鳥羽院 *gotobain* ex-Emperor Gotoba

❺ honorific suffix after posthumous Buddhist names
保善院 *hozen'in* Hozen of Blessed Memory

INDEPENDENT

【in 院】 institution; House of Representatives, House of Councilors; palace of ex-Emperor
院の内外 *in no naigai* legislative circles

SYNONYMS

❶ **organized bodies**
会 SOCIETY → 2020
協 association → 93
団 BODY → 3053
体 BODY → 71
組 union → 1337
労 workers' union → 2548
連 federation → 3103
講 fraternity → 1619

ⓑ **schools**
学 EDUCATIONAL INSTITUTION → 2555
校 SCHOOL → 929
塾 PRIVATE SCHOOL → 2860
大 UNIVERSITY → 3416
高 high school → 2097
中 junior high school → 3451
小 elementary school → 7
園 kindergarten → 3156

❷ **legislature**
議 LEGISLATIVE BODY → 1647
会 assembly → 2020

❸ **places of worship**
堂 temple building → 2589
塔 pagoda → 561
寺 BUDDHIST TEMPLE → 2164
社 Shinto shrine → 840
宮 SHINTO SHRINE → 2274
教 church → 1493

陣 陣 陣
455 JIN

Ⓒⓗ 阵 zhèn

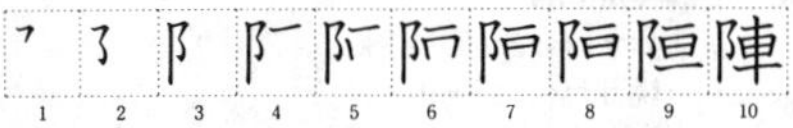

Radical	Strokes
⻖ 170	10-3-7
Grade	**Freq**
Jōyō	796
◧ 1-3-7	

3-7 ⻖

▶**BATTLE FORMATION** ▶**CAMP**

COMPOUNDS

❶ⓐ **battle formation, battle array, troop deployment, battle position, battlefield**
ⓑ **battle, war**
ⓒ battle troops, army
陣形 *jinkei* battle formation
陣容 *jin'yō* battle formation; members of a group
陣立て *jindate* battle array
円陣 *enjin* circular formation, circle
西陣織 *nishijin'ori Nishijin* brocade
陣没 *jinbotsu* death in battle
先陣 *senjin* advance guard, vanguard
陣頭 *jintō* head of an army
❷ **army camp, encampment, position**
陣営 *jin'ei* camp, quarters
陣地 *jinchi* encampment, position
退陣する *taijin suru* decamp, withdraw
論陣を張る *ronjin o haru* argue about, take a firm stand
❸ [suffix] (group of persons performing a common action) **lineup, corps, camp, group**
報道陣 *hōdōjin* reportorial camp, press corps
教授陣 *kyōjujin* professorate, faculty, group of professors
❹ occurring in spells
陣痛 *jintsū* labor pains
一陣の風 *ichijin no kaze* gust of wind

INDEPENDENT

【jin 陣】camp, encampment; battle formation, battle position; battle
陣を張る *jin o haru* pitch camp
陣を立て直す *jin o tatenaosu* redeploy troops
夏の陣 *natsu no jin* summer battle

SYNONYMS

❶ⓑ **warfare and rebellions**
戦 WAR → 1787
軍 war → 2080
役 war → 244
乱 rebellion → 1260
変 uprising → 2069
闘 FIGHT → 3334
❷ **camps**
営 BARRACKS → 2603
❸ **groups**
組 group (of people) → 1337
群 GROUP (of any kind) → 1540
連 set → 3103
族 common-interest group (*slang*) → 958
党 PARTY → 2581
隊 PARTY (organized group) → 625
団 BODY → 3053
伍 ranks → 47
班 SQUAD → 946
軍 team → 2080

COMPOUND FORMATION

西陣織 *nishijin'ori*
西陣 originally referred to the western (西) battlefield (陣 ❶ⓐ) in Kyoto. Since the area is well known as a textile district, 西陣織 '*Nishijin* brocade' refers to a type of brocade (織) from that area.

NOTE

★do not confuse with 陳 540

除 除 除
456 JO JI nozo(ku) -yo(ke)▲

Ⓒⓗ 除 chú

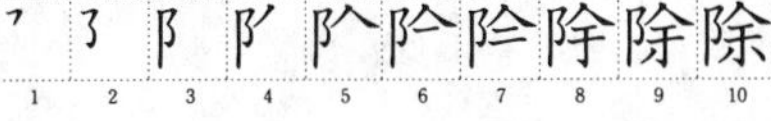

Radical	Strokes
⻖ 170	10-3-7
Grade	**Freq**
Jōyō-6	643
◧ 1-3-7	

3-7 ⻖

▶**RID OF**

COMPOUNDS

❶ **rid of, clear away, remove, eliminate**
除去する *jokyo suru* rid of, remove, eliminate
除雪する *josetsu suru* get rid of snow, remove snow
除外 *jogai* exclusion, exception
解除する *kaijo suru* remove [lift] (a ban), cancel; release, acquit
掃除 *sōji* cleaning
排除 *haijo* exclusion, removal, elimination
削除する *sakujo suru* delete, eliminate, cancel

控除 *kōjo* (tax) deduction, subtraction
❷ get rid of the old in favor of the new
除夜 *joya* New Year's Eve
❸ *math* divide
除数 *josū* divisor
乗除 *jōjo* multiplication and division

INDEPENDENT

【jo 除】 *math* division
【josuru 除する】 exclude; *math* divide

KUN

【nozo(ku) 除く】 rid of, remove; abolish, cancel; exclude, omit
取り除く *torinozoku* get rid of, remove, take away
月曜日を除いて *getsuyōbi o nozoite* excepting Mondays
【-yo(ke) -除け】 protection, keeping off; charm, amulet
霜除け *shimoyoke* shelter against frost
弾除け *tamayoke* protection against bullets; charm against bullets

SYNONYMS

❶ **eliminate**
外す take off → 186
脱 REMOVE → 973
去 take away → 2156
省 leave out → 2449
撤 WITHDRAW → 738
排 EXCLUDE → 490
払う CLEAR AWAY → 194
却 ELIMINATE → 1118
削 cross out → 1448
抹 wipe off → 313
❸ **divide**
割る DIVIDE → 1816

3-7
阝

陥 陥 陥 陥

457 KAN ochii(ru) otoshii(reru)

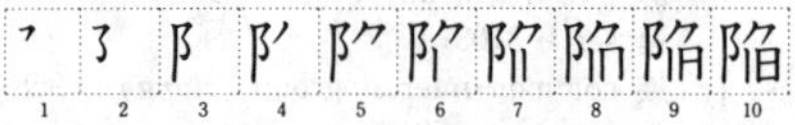

CH 陷 xiàn

Radical	Strokes
阝 170	10-3-7
Grade	**Freq**
Jōyō	1551
1-3-7	

▶**FALL IN**

COMPOUNDS

❶ⓐ [original meaning] **fall in, cave in, collapse, sink**
ⓑ cause to fall into (a trap)
陥没する *kanbotsu suru* sink, fall, cave in
陥入する *kannyū suru* subside, fall [cave] in, collapse
陥落する *kanraku suru* fall in, cave in; surrender
陥穽 *kansei* pitfall, trap; plot
❷ fall, surrender
失陥 *shikkan* fall, surrender of one's land
❸ defect, fault
欠陥 *kekkan* defect, fault, deficiency

KUN

【ochii(ru) 陥る】 *vi* fall into, be led into, lapse into; fall (as of a castle), be reduced; fall in, sink
誤りに陥る *ayamari ni ochiiru* fall into error
罪に陥る *tsumi ni ochiiru* slide into sin
穴に陥る *ana ni ochiiru* fall in a pit
【otoshii(reru) 陥れる】 *vt* entrap, entice, lead into; capture, carry (a castle)
人を陥れる *hito o otoshiireru* entrap a person
困難に陥れる *konnan ni otoshiireru* put (a person) in a fix
城を陥れる *shiro o otoshiireru* carry a castle

SYNONYMS

❶ⓐ **collapse**
落 FALL → 2318
崩 CRUMBLE → 2296
没 SINK → 260
❸ **faults and flaws**
難 fault → 1838
短 shortcoming → 1182
欠 incompleteness → 1987

降 降 降 降 ㊥ 降 jiàng xiáng

458 KŌ GŌ▲ o(riru) o(rosu) fu(ru) fu(ri) kuda(ru)▲ kuda(su)▲

Radical	Strokes
⻖ 170	10-3-7
Grade	**Freq**
Jōyō-6	686
◧ 1-3-7	

� 1 2 3 4 5 6 7 8 9 10

▶**DESCEND**

COMPOUNDS

❶ move from a higher to a lower place:
ⓐ [original meaning] **descend, fall, come down, drop**
ⓑ descend from heaven: **fall, come down**—said of atmospheric moisture such as rain
ⓒ **alight, get off**
降下する *kōka suru* descend, fall, drop
滑降 *kakkō* descent (in skiing)
昇降する *shōkō suru* ascend and descend, go up and down
沈降する *chinkō suru* precipitate, subside
降雨 *kōu* rainfall, rain
降雪 *kōsetsu* snowfall, snow
降車する *kōsha suru* alight, get off, get down
乗降 *jōkō* boarding and alighting, getting on and off
❷ⓐ descend upon the earth, make an appearance
ⓑ cause to descend upon, invoke (a divinity)
降誕 *kōtan* birth, nativity; advent
降臨 *kōrin* advent, descent
降神 *kōshin* spiritism, spiritualism
❸ⓐ cause to descend to lower status, demote, reduce the rank or power of
ⓑ descend to lower status, degrade oneself
降等 *kōtō* demotion
降給 *kōkyū* reduction in pay
降嫁 *kōka* marriage of an Imperial princess to a subject
❹ⓐ **surrender, submit to**
ⓑ cause to surrender, conquer
降参する *kōsan suru* surrender, submit, yield
降伏(=降服) *kōfuku* surrender, submission
降魔 *gōma* conquering the devil
❺ onward, afterward
以降 *ikō* on and after, hereafter

KUN

【**o(riru) 降りる**】
①ⓐ (dismount) alight, get off, disembark
ⓑ (come down from a high place) alight, land, swoop
ⓒ (of frost or rain) fall, come down
乗り降り *noriori* boarding and alighting
飛び降りる *tobioriru* jump off (a moving vehicle), jump down
舞い降りる *maioriru* fly down, alight
② retire (from a position), withdraw, drop out (of a program), quit

【**o(rosu) 降ろす**】
① set (a passenger) down, discharge, unload
乗客を降ろす *jōkyaku o orosu* discharge passengers
② demote, deprive (someone) of (his) role
主役から降ろす *shuyaku kara orosu* relieve someone of the leading role

【**fu(ru) 降る**】 fall, come down, rain—said of atmospheric moisture such as rain or snow
降らす *furasu* send (rain), shed
降り懸かる *furikakaru* fall upon, come in one's way, impend upon

【**fu(ri) 降り**】 fall, rainfall, snowfall
土砂降り *doshaburi* pouring rain, downpour
雪降り *yukifuri* snowfall

【**kuda(ru) 降る**】 surrender, submit to
軍門に降る *gunmon ni kudaru* surrender, capitulate

【**kuda(su) 降す**】 [usu. 下す] subjugate, subdue; defeat, beat

SYNONYMS

❶ⓐ **descend and fall**
下 go down → 3378
落 FALL → 2318
墜 DROP DOWN → 2881
倒 TOPPLE → 124
ⓒ **get off**
下 get down → 3378
❹ⓐ **submit and surrender**
服 SUBMIT → 878
伏 submit → 45
屈 bend in submission → 3079

HOMOPHONES

oriru ⇨ 下 3378
orosu ⇨ 下 3378 卸 1447
kudaru ⇨ 下 3378
kudasu ⇨ 下 3378

NOTE

⇨ see USAGE note at 下 3378

3-7 ⻖

陞

459 SHŌ

Ⓒⓗ 升 shēng

Radical	Strokes
⻖ 170	10-3-7
Grade	**Freq**
Reference	
◧ 1 - 3 - 7	

COMPOUNDS

● [now replaced by 昇 2415] ascend to a higher rank, rise in rank, be promoted

陞叙 *shōjo* promotion, advancement

陞進する *shōshin suru* be promoted, rise in rank

陞任 *shōnin* promotion, advancement

3-7 ⻖

陥

incorrect stroke count ⇨ see 548 (nonstandard for 陷 457)

3-7 丬

将 將 将 㸓

460 SHŌ masa(ni)▲

Ⓒⓗ 将 jiāng jiàng

Radical	Strokes
寸 41	10-3-7
Grade	**Freq**
Jōyō-6	500
◧ 1 - 3 - 7	

丨	丨	丬	丬	丬	丬	丬	丬	将	将
1	2	3	4	5	6	7	8	9	10

▶GENERAL OFFICER

COMPOUNDS

❶ⓐ **general officer, general, admiral, commander; leader**

ⓑ leading person, superior

将軍 *shōgun* commander, general
将校 *shōkō* officer, commissioned officer
将兵 *shōhei* officers and men
将官 *shōkan* general, admiral
陸将 *rikushō* lieutenant general, general officer
大将 *taishō* admiral, general; old chap
武将 *bushō* commander, warlord
将棋 *shōgi* shogi, Japanese chess
王将 *ōshō* king (in shogi)
主将 *shushō* captain
女将 *joshō* (=*okami*) mistress, proprietress, landlady

❷ **on the verge of, be about to happen**

将来 *shōrai* future; in the future

❸ take, bring

将来する *shōrai suru* invite, introduce; bring about, give rise to, cause

INDEPENDENT

【**shō** 将】 commander, general, leader

将中に将たる *shōchū ni shōtaru* being a leader among leaders

KUN

【**masa(ni)** 将に】 be about to, on the verge of

将に滅びんとしている *masani horobin to shite iru* be on the brink of ruin

SYNONYMS

❶ⓐ **military officers and ranks**

督 COMMANDER → 2796
帥 COMMANDER IN CHIEF → 1290
佐 FIELD OFFICER → 67
尉 COMPANY OFFICER → 1685
曹 SERGEANT → 2746

❷ **on the verge of**

-際 on the verge of → 714
臨 on the point of → 1630
-掛かる be on the verge of → 493

HOMOPHONES

masani ⇨ 正 3484 当 2177

NOTE

⇨ see USAGE note at 正 3484

3-7 亻

修 候

incorrect classification ⇨ see ◧ 2-8

鄉 incorrect stroke count ⇨ see 549 3-7 纟

喝 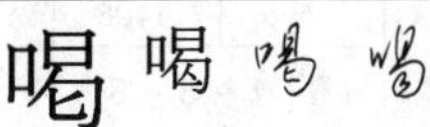

461 KATSU

Ⓒⓗ 喝 hē hè

Radical	Strokes
口 30	11-3-8
Grade	Freq
Jōyō	1958
1-3-8	

3-8 口

▶ **SHOUT AT**

COMPOUNDS

❶ **shout at, roar, bark, bellow, bawl, bawl out**

喝采 *kassai* applause, cheers

喝破する *kappa suru* shout someone down, declare, pronounce

一喝 *ikkatsu* thundering cry, roar

大喝する *daikatsu suru* shout in a thunderous voice

❷ shout threats at someone, intimidate, threaten

恐喝する *kyōkatsu suru* threaten, menace

恫喝 *dōkatsu* threat, intimidation

INDEPENDENT

【**katsu 喝**】 shouting in Zen meditation to awaken trainees

【**kassu 喝す**】 shout threats at someone

SYNONYMS

❶ **shout**

叫 SHOUT → 201

号 holler → 2153

喚 call out → 550

呼 CALL → 273

鳴 CRY → 674

❷ **threaten**

嚇 INTIMIDATE → 784

威 THREATEN BY FORCE → 3578

脅 THREATEN → 2109

唱 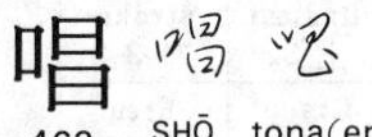

462 SHŌ tona(eru)

Ⓒⓗ 唱 chàng

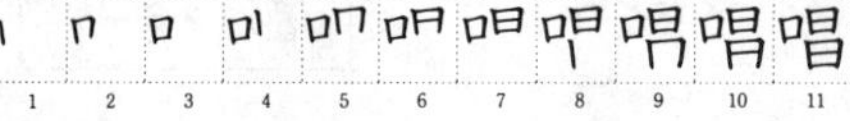

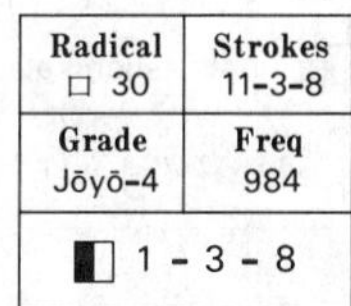

Radical	Strokes
口 30	11-3-8
Grade	Freq
Jōyō-4	984
1-3-8	

3-8 口

▶ **SING**

COMPOUNDS

❶ⓐ [original meaning] **sing, chant**

ⓑ song

合唱 *gasshō* chorus

独唱する *dokushō suru* sing solo

唱歌 *shōka* song

❷ [formerly also 誦 1549] **chant, recite, intone**

唱和する *shōwa suru* chant [cheer] in chorus

吟唱する *ginshō suru* recite, chant

暗唱する *anshō suru* recite from memory

詠唱する *eishō suru* chant

三唱 *sanshō* cheering (banzai) three times

❸ **advocate, preach**

唱導 *shōdō* advocacy

提唱する *teishō suru* advocate, propose

KUN

【**tona(eru) 唱える**】 chant, recite, repeat; cry, cheer; advocate, set forth, preach; quote (prices)

念仏を唱える *nenbutsu o tonaeru* chant [repeat] the name of Buddha

主戦論を唱える *shusenron o tonaeru* advocate war

SYNONYMS

❶ⓐ **sing**

歌 sing → 1825

❷ **recite**

吟 RECITE → 230

詠 RECITE POETRY → 1500

読 READ → 1541

❸ **advocate**

説 preach → 1547

3-8 口

唯 唯 唯

463 YUI I tada▲

CH 唯 wéi wěi

Radical	Strokes
口 30	11-3-8
Grade	**Freq**
Jōyō	1408

1 - 3 - 8

丨 ㄇ 口 口' 口' 口' 口'' 口'' 口'' 唯 唯

1 2 3 4 5 6 7 8 9 10 11

▶**ONLY**

COMPOUNDS

❶ [rarely also 惟 *yui* 481] **only, sole, one and only**

唯一の *yuiitsu no* the only, the sole

唯一無二の *yuiitsu-muni no* the one and only, unique

唯心論 *yuishinron* idealism, spiritualism

唯美主義 *yuibishugi* aestheticism

唯物主義 *yuibutsushugi* materialism

❷ yes

唯唯諾諾として *ii-dakudaku to shite* willingly, readily

KUN

【**tada** 唯】[also 只] only, just, merely, solely

唯一度 *tada ichido* only once

唯そこへ行きさえすれば良い *tada soko e iki sae sureba yoi* have [need] only to go there

SYNONYMS

❶ **only**

一 one and only → 3341

USAGE

tada

唯

[also 只] only, just, merely, solely

只

① no charge

② ordinariness, plainness

③ doing nothing, being idle

只-

① free of charge, cost-free, for nothing

② ordinary, common, plain

③ [also 唯] only, just, merely, solely

HOMOPHONES

tada ⇨ 只 2155

3-8 土

培 培 培 培

464 BAI tsuchika(u)

CH 培 péi

Radical	Strokes
土 32	11-3-8
Grade	**Freq**
Jōyō	1504

1 - 3 - 8

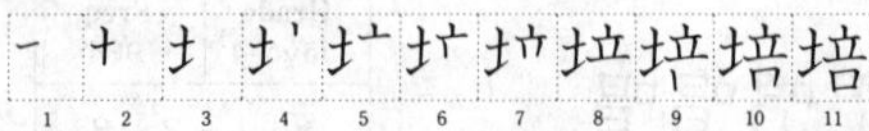

1 2 3 4 5 6 7 8 9 10 11

▶**CULTIVATE**

COMPOUNDS

ⓐ [original meaning] (work the earth to grow vegetation) **cultivate, raise, grow**

ⓑ (grow microorganisms) cultivate, culture

栽培 *saibai* cultivation, raising, growing

培養 *baiyō* cultivation, culture, incubation

培地 *baichi* culture medium

KUN

【**tsuchika(u)** 培う】 raise, grow; cultivate, foster

異境に培われた花 *ikyō ni tsuchikawareta hana* flower grown in a foreign land

愛国心を培う *aikokushin o tsuchikau* foster a patriotic spirit

SYNONYMS

ⓐ **farm and plant**

栽 PLANT (saplings) → 3297

植 PLANT → 990

耕 TILL → 1308

作 raise crops → 68

農 farm, FARMING → 2698

域 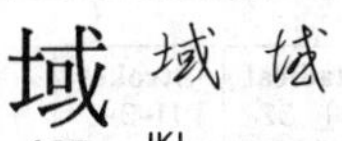
465 IKI

Ⓒ 域 yù

Radical	Strokes
土 32	11-3-8
Grade	**Freq**
Jōyō-6	609
◧ 1-3-8	

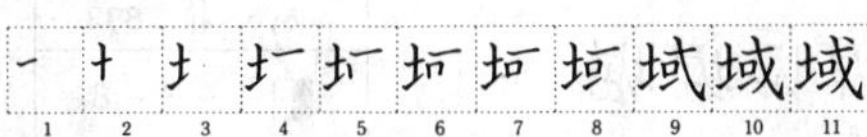

▶**BOUNDED AREA**

COMPOUNDS

❶ [also suffix]

ⓐ **bounded area, region, limits, zone, district**

ⓑ (scope of something) area, range

域内の *ikinai no* within the area
地域 *chiiki* region, area
水域 *suiiki* water area, waters
区域 *kuiki* zone, area; limits
海域 *kaiiki* sea area
全域 *zen'iki* the whole area, entire region
聖域 *seiiki* holy [sacred] precincts, sanctuary
領域 *ryōiki* territory, domain, sphere, province; *math* domain
音域 *on'iki* compass, (singing) range
職域 *shokuiki* range of one's work [occupation]
暴風域 *bōfūiki* storm area

❷ land, country

異域 *iiki* foreign land

INDEPENDENT

【**iki** 域】 level, stage, confines
名人の域に達する *meijin no iki ni tassuru* reach the stage of a master

SYNONYMS

❶ⓐ **areas and localities**
辺 VICINITY → 3029
地 PLACE → 204
方 locality → 1963
区 DISTRICT → 2963
領 TERRITORY → 1224
帯 BELT → 2582
圏 SPHERE → 3148

ⓑ **range**
範 range → 2709
程 EXTENT → 1190
圏 SPHERE → 3148
野 FIELD → 1485
界 field (*phys*) → 2563
場 field (*phys*, *psychol*) → 558

466 KI saki sai

Ⓒ 埼 qí

Radical	Strokes
土 32	11-3-8
Grade	**Freq**
Reference	
◧ 1-3-8	

COMPOUNDS

❶ⓐ [now usu. 崎 *saki*] promontory, cape

ⓑ suffix after names of promontories or capes

犬吠埼 *inubōsaki* Cape Inubosaki

❷ abbrev. of 埼玉 *saitama*: Saitama Prefecture

埼銀 *saigin* Saitama Bank

HOMOPHONES

saki ⇨ 崎 472

NOTE

⇨ see USAGE note at 崎 472

3-8 土

堀 堀 堀

467 KUTSU▲ hori

CH 堀 kū

Radical	Strokes
土 32	11-3-8
Grade	**Freq**
Jōyō	893
1 - 3 - 8	

▶**DITCH**

COMPOUNDS

● [original meaning, now obsolete] dig

KUN

【hori 堀】

① ditch, canal

堀川 *horikawa* canal
堀割り *horiwari* canal, ditch
用水堀 *yōsuibori* irrigation ditch
釣り堀 *tsuribori* fishing pond, fishpond

② [formerly also 濠] moat

堀端 *horibata* edge of the moat
外堀 *sotobori* outer moat

SYNONYMS

【hori】

① **holes and cavities**

坑 PIT → 236
穴 HOLE → 2159
孔 OPEN HOLE → 179
口 MOUTH → 3382
溝 CHANNEL → 659
凹 concavity → 3482
洞 CAVE → 380

USAGE

hori

堀
① ditch, canal
② [formerly also 濠] moat

濠
[now usu. 堀] moat

HOMOPHONES

hori ⇨ 濠 792

NOTE

★do not confuse with 掘 496

3-8 土

堷

468

▶**CULTIVATE**

nonstandard for 培 464

3-8 女

婦 婦 婦 妇

469 FU

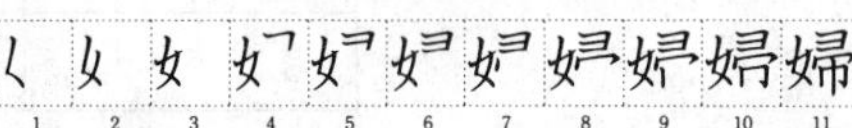

CH 妇 fù

Radical	Strokes
女 38	11-3-8
Grade	**Freq**
Jōyō-5	511
1 - 3 - 8	

▶**ADULT WOMAN**

COMPOUNDS

❶ⓐ **adult woman, woman, lady**

ⓑ [original meaning] **married woman, wife, housewife**

婦人 *fujin* woman, lady, female
婦警 *fukei* policewoman
裸婦 *rafu* nude woman
主婦 *shufu* housewife
夫婦 *fūfu* husband and wife, married couple
新婦 *shinpu* bride

❷ⓐ [also suffix] **woman worker, working [career] woman**

ⓑ abbrev. of 看護婦 *kangofu*: nurse

娼婦 *shōfu* prostitute, harlot
看護婦 *kangofu* nurse
掃除婦 *sōjifu* charwoman, cleaning woman
婦長 *fuchō* chief nurse

INDEPENDENT

【fu 婦】 daughter-in-law

SYNONYMS

❶ⓐ **woman**

女 WOMAN → 3418
嬢 YOUNG LADY → 758
娘 GIRL → 406
婆 OLD WOMAN → 2762
雌 FEMALE → 1055

ⓑ **wives**

妻 WIFE → 2558
奥 wife → 2824
内 wife → 3466
室 wife (esp. of persons of rank) → 2254
嫡 legitimate wife → 680
嫁 BRIDE → 635
寡 widow → 2344

❷ⓐ workers and professionals
孃 (unmarried) female worker → 758
夫 MAN LABORER → 3460
匠 CRAFTSMAN → 2990
工 workman → 3381
手 OCCUPATION SUFFIX → 3456
屋 colloquial occupation suffix → 3098
員 MEMBER (of a staff) → 2269
人 person of certain category → 3368
者 person who → 3211
師 profession suffix → 1326
士 PROFESSION SUFFIX → 3405
客 skilled person → 2250
家 professional → 2273

婚 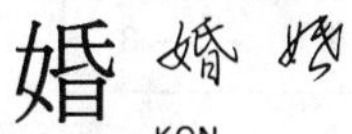
470 KON

Ⓒⓗ 婚 hūn

Radical	Strokes
女 38	11-3-8
Grade	**Freq**
Jōyō	781
◧ 1 - 3 - 8	

3-8 女

▶MARRY

COMPOUNDS

ⓐ marry, wed
ⓑ [original meaning] **marriage, wedding**
婚姻 *kon'in* marriage, matrimony
婚礼 *konrei* wedding ceremony
婚約 *kon'yaku* engagement, betrothal
結婚 *kekkon* marriage
求婚 *kyūkon* proposal of marriage
再婚 *saikon* remarriage, second marriage
離婚 *rikon* divorce
新婚の *shinkon no* newly wedded
婚儀 *kongi* wedding ceremony
金婚 *kinkon* golden wedding
近親婚 *kinshinkon* consanguineous marriage

SYNONYMS

● marrying and marriage
姻 MARRIAGE → 353
嫁 WED A MAN → 635
縁 marriage relation → 1386

471

▶ADULT WOMAN
nonstandard for 婦 469

3-8 女

娯

incorrect stroke count ⇨ see 405

3-8 女

崎 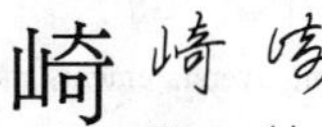
472 KI▴ saki

Ⓒⓗ 崎 qí

Radical	Strokes
山 46	11-3-8
Grade	**Freq**
Jōyō	489
◧ 1 - 3 - 8	

3-8 山

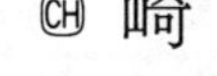

▶PROMONTORY

COMPOUNDS

❶ promontory, cape
崎陽 *kiyō* [archaic] Nagasaki
❷ [rare] steep
崎崖 *kigai* steepness of a mountain

KUN

【saki 崎】
ⓐ [formerly also 埼] promontory, cape
ⓑ suffix after names of promontories or capes
州崎 *susaki* sandbar
御前崎 *omaezaki* Cape Omaezaki

SYNONYMS

❶ points of land
岬 CAPE → 284

USAGE

saki
崎
ⓐ [formerly also 埼] promontory, cape
ⓑ suffix after names of promontories or capes
埼
ⓐ [now usu. 崎] promontory, cape
ⓑ suffix after names of promontories or capes

HOMOPHONES
saki ⇨ 埼 466

3-8 巾

帳 悵 帐
473 CHŌ tobari▲

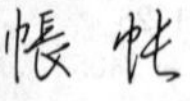

CH 帐 zhàng

Radical	Strokes
巾 50	11-3-8
Grade	**Freq**
Jōyō-3	1113
1 - 3 - 8	

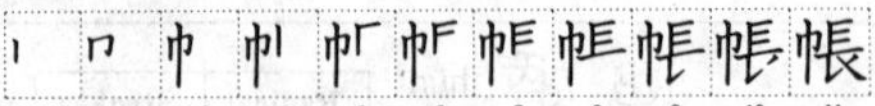

1 丨 2 冂 3 巾 4 巾' 5 巾' 6 巾F 7 巾E 8 巾E 9 帳 10 帳 11 帳

▶NOTEBOOK

COMPOUNDS

❶ [formerly also 帖 286] [also suffix] **notebook, book, register, account book, album**

帳面 *chōmen* notebook, account book, register
帳簿 *chōbo* account book, ledger, register
帳尻 *chōjiri* balance of accounts
手帳 *techō* pocketbook, memo
日記帳 *nikkichō* diary
通帳 *tsūchō* bankbook, passbook

❷ [original meaning] drapery, drop curtain, curtain
几帳 *kichō* screen
緞帳 *donchō* thick curtain, drop curtain
開帳する *kaichō suru* unveil a Buddhist image; gamble

❸ net
蠅帳 *haichō* fly-net cupboard

KUN

【tobari 帳】 veil, curtain
夜の帳 *yoru no tobari* veil of darkness

SPECIAL READINGS

蚊帳 *kaya* mosquito net

SYNONYMS

❶ **notebook**
簿 RECORD BOOK → 2727
籍 REGISTER → 2731

❷ **curtain**
幕 CURTAIN → 2335

3-8 弓

張 張 张
474 CHŌ ha(ru) -ha(ri) -ba(ri)

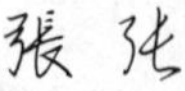

CH 张 zhāng

Radical	Strokes
弓 57	11-3-8
Grade	**Freq**
Jōyō-5	436
1 - 3 - 8	

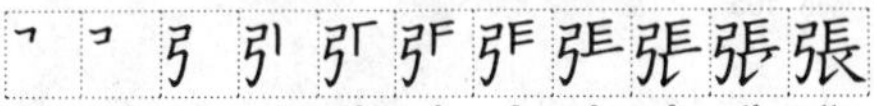

1 ㇕ 2 ㇕ 3 弓 4 弓' 5 弓' 6 弓F 7 弓F 8 弓E 9 張 10 張 11 張

▶SPREAD ▶STRAIN

COMPOUNDS

❶ (open to the full extent) **spread (out), extend (over), stretch**
拡張 *kakuchō* expansion, extension, enlargement
膨張(=膨脹) *bōchō* expansion, swelling; growth, increase
伸張 *shinchō* expansion, elongation
出張する *shutchō suru* travel on official business

❷ⓐ [original meaning] **strain, stretch, be tense, tighten**
ⓑ tension
張力 *chōryoku* tension, tensile strength
緊張 *kinchō* tension, strain
等張の *tōchō no* isotonic

❸ **insist, persist**
主張する *shuchō suru* insist on, assert, maintain
誇張 *kochō* exaggeration, overstatement, magnification

❹ⓐ counter for bows or stringed instruments
ⓑ counter for curtains, screens or nets
琴一張 *koto itchō* one koto (Japanese harp)
幕二張 *maku nichō* two curtains
一張羅 *itchōra* one's Sunday best; only suit one has

❺ unclassified compounds
張本人 *chōhonnin* originator, perpetrator

KUN

【ha(ru) 張る】
① (open to the full extent) spread (out), extend over, stretch
縄張り *nawabari* roping off; one's sphere of influence, one's territory
翼を張る *tsubasa o haru* spread the wings
②ⓐ strain, stretch, tighten
ⓑ be stretched [tightened], become taut
ⓒ be under strain, be tense, be anxious; be

enthusiastic
張り *hari* tension; will power, pluck
引っ張る *hipparu* pull, draw; drag
糸を張る *ito o haru* stretch a string
張り裂ける *harisakeru* burst (open), break, split
乳が張る *Chichi ga haru* The breasts swell
頬張る *hōbaru* cram one's mouth (with food)
突っ張る *tsupparu* become taut; thrust (one's opponent); stick to (one's opinion), insist on; *slang* be delinquent
気が張る *ki ga haru* feel nervous
欲を張る *yoku o haru* lust for
張り詰めた *haritsumeta* high-strung, tense
張り切る *harikiru* be in high spirits, be enthusiastic; stretch to the full
③ [also 貼る]
ⓐ stick, paste; apply to
ⓑ cover, line
張り付ける *haritsukeru* stick on, paste
タイルを張る *tairu o haru* tile a floor
④ stick out, project
張り出す *haridasu* project, jut out
角張った顔 *kakubatta kao* squarish face
⑤ keep watch, guard
張り込む *harikomu* look out for, ambush
見張る *miharu* watch, guard
⑥ⓐ insist, persist
ⓑ display, demonstrate
頑張る *ganbaru* persist, be tenacious, hold out
意地を張る *iji o haru* be obstinate
威張る *ibaru* put on airs, be haughty; boast, brag
見栄を張る *mie o haru* show off
⑦ hold, give (a banquet), run, manage
世帯を張る *shotai o haru* keep [set up] house
⑧ *slang* slap, smack
張り倒す *haritaosu* knock down
⑨ rival, compete
張り合う *hariau* compete, challenge
向こうを張る *mukō o haru* vie with one's opponent

【-ha(ri) -張り】 counter for bows, stringed instruments or paper lanterns
弓三張り *yumi mihari* three bows

【-ba(ri) -張り】
① [suffix] fashion, manner
川端張りの小説 *kawabatabari no shōsetsu* novel written in imitation of Kawabata's
② [also suffix] [sometimes also 貼り] covered with, lined with
絹張り *kinubari* lined with silk
③ unit for expressing the power of a bow in terms of number of persons

SYNONYMS

❶ **expand**
広げる spread (out) → 3035
膨 EXPAND → 1084
脹 SWELL → 1003
拡 ENLARGE → 309
伸 STRETCH → 70
延 EXTEND → 3073

❷ⓐ **tighten**
緊 TIGHTEN → 2838
締める TIGHTEN → 1393

USAGE

❶ **haru**
張る
① (open to the full extent) spread (out), extend over, stretch
②ⓐ strain, stretch, tighten
ⓑ be stretched [tightened], become taut
ⓒ be under strain, be tense, be anxious; be enthusiastic
③ [also 貼る]
ⓐ stick, paste; apply to
ⓑ cover, line
④ stick out, project
⑤ keep watch, guard
⑥ⓐ insist, persist
ⓑ display, demonstrate
⑦ hold, give (a banquet), run, manage
⑧ *slang* slap, smack
⑨ rival, compete

貼る
[also 張る]
ⓐ stick, paste; apply to
ⓑ cover, line

❷ **-bari**
-張り
①[suffix] fashion, manner
②[also suffix] [sometimes also 貼り] covered with, lined with
③ unit for expressing the power of a bow in terms of number of persons

-貼り
[usu. -張り] [also suffix] covered with, lined with

HOMOPHONES

haru ⇨ 貼 1510
-bari ⇨ 貼 1510

COMPOUND FORMATION

出張 *shutchō*
出張する 'travel on official business' originally meant to go out (出) on a military expedition and pitch or set up (張 ❶) tents as a temporary battle position.

NOTE

⇨ see COMPOUND FORMATION for
主張 *shuchō* ⇨ 主 1938
威張る *ibaru* ⇨ 威 3578

頑張る *ganbaru* ⇨ 頑 1040

3-8
弓

強 强 強 強 (CH) 强 qiáng qiǎng jiàng

475 KYŌ GŌ tsuyo(i) tsuyo(maru) tsuyo(meru) shi(iru) kowa(i)▲

Radical	Strokes
弓 57	11-3-8
Grade	**Freq**
Jōyō-2	108
1-3-8	

▶**STRONG**

COMPOUNDS

❶ⓐ (having great strength) **strong, powerful; robust**

ⓑ [formerly also 彊 *kyō* 2714] (capable of enduring) **strong, hard, solid, tough**

強力な *kyōryoku na* strong, powerful, mighty
強者 *kyōsha* strong man
強大な *kyōdai na* mighty, powerful, strong
強敵 *kyōteki* powerful enemy [rival]
強国 *kyōkoku* powerful country
強力(＝剛力) *gōriki* Herculean strength; mountain carrier [guide]
屈強な *kukkyō na* strong, sturdy, robust
強壮な *kyōsō na* robust, strong, vigorous
強固な *kyōko na* firm, stable, solid, strong
強硬な *kyōkō na* firm (attitude), unbending; drastic (measure)
強情な *gōjō na* obstinate, headstrong
強膜 *kyōmaku* sclera

❷ (of great intensity) **strong, severe, intense**

強度 *kyōdo* intensity; strength
強風 *kyōfū* strong [high] wind
強震 *kyōshin* severe earthquake
強打 *kyōda* heavy blow, slug; hitting (the ball) hard
強烈な *kyōretsu na* intense, severe

❸ **strengthen, intensify**

強化 *kyōka* strengthening, intensification, buildup, reinforcement
強心剤 *kyōshinzai* cardiotonic drug
強調する *kyōchō suru* emphasize, stress
増強する *zōkyō suru* reinforce, augment
補強する *hokyō suru* reinforce, strengthen

❹ **force, compel, coerce**

強制する *kyōsei suru* compel, force
強行 *kyōkō* forcing, enforcement
強要 *kyōyō* coercion, extortion
強引な *gōin na* overbearing, coercive
強訴 *gōso* direct petition
強姦 *gōkan* rape
強盗 *gōtō* robbery
勉強 *benkyō* study; selling cheap; [rare] diligence

❺ [suffix] a little over

五キロ強 *gokirokyō* a little over 5 kg [km]

INDEPENDENT

【kyō 強】 strength, might; the strong
弱を以て強に当たる *jaku o motte kyō ni ataru* attacking strength by means of [with] weakness

KUN

【tsuyo(i) 強い】 strong, mighty, powerful; robust; intense, violent, strong; hard, tough; be strong (in); brave, stout
強さ *tsuyosa* strength, power, tenacity
力強い *chikarazuyoi* powerful, vigorous, reassuring
強気 *tsuyoki* strong feeling [market]
粘り強い *nebarizuyoi* tenacious, sticky; persistent
強味 *tsuyomi* one's strength, one's forte
強い心 *tsuyoi kokoro* stout heart [mind]

【tsuyo(maru) 強まる】 become strong, gain strength

【tsuyo(meru) 強める】 strengthen, intensify; emphasize; lay stress on; reinforce
語を強める *go o tsuyomeru* put stress on a word

【shi(iru) 強いる】 force, compel, press
無理強い *murijii* forcing, compulsion, coercion

【kowa(i) 強い】 tough, hard, stiff
情が強い *jō ga kowai* be hardheaded, be stubborn

SYNONYMS

❶ⓐ **strong**
壮 VIGOROUS → 224
丈 STOUT → 3419
健 ROBUST → 134
康 HEALTHY → 3124

ⓑ **hard**
剛 TOUGH → 1673
硬 HARD → 1183
堅 FIRM → 2823
固 SOLID → 3086

❷ **extreme in degree**
超 super- → 3313
重 HEAVY → 3573
高 HIGH → 2097
深 DEEP → 524
大 BIG → 3416
甚 EXTREMELY → 2643
切 keen → 27

痛 bitter(ly) → 3285
極 EXTREME → 1017
激 intense → 776
厳 SEVERE → 3289
酷 SEVERE → 1562
❹ **compel and press**
迫 PRESS → 3074
押す PUSH → 314
圧 PRESSURE → 2970

HOMOPHONES

kowai ⇨ 怖 296 恐 2650

COMPOUND FORMATION

勉強 *benkyō*

勉強 'study, etc.' is to force (強 ❹) oneself to make efforts (勉), that is, to work diligently or study hard.

NOTE

⇨ see USAGE note at 怖 296

術 術 術 術 476 JUTSU sube▲

CH 术 shù zhú

Radical	Strokes
行 144	11-6-5
Grade	**Freq**
Jōyō-5	348
◧ 1 - 3 - 8	

3-8 彳

Stroke order: 1–11

▶PRACTICAL ART

COMPOUNDS

❶ⓐ **practical art, technique, skill**
ⓑ **technical art, technique, technology**
美術 *bijutsu* art, fine arts
芸術 *geijutsu* art, the arts
手術 *shujutsu* surgical operation
戦術 *senjutsu* tactics, strategy
奇術 *kijutsu* conjuring tricks, jugglery
医術 *ijutsu* art of medicine
催眠術 *saiminjutsu* hypnotism, mesmerism
用兵術 *yōheijutsu* tactics, strategy
術語 *jutsugo* technical term, terminology
技術 *gijutsu* technique, art, skill; technology
学術 *gakujutsu* science, learning; arts and sciences
❷ magic, witchcraft
魔術 *majutsu* magic, sorcery, witchcraft
幻術 *genjutsu* magic, witchcraft
❸ artifice, stratagem, trick
術策 *jussaku* artifice, stratagem, trick
術中に *jutchū ni* in the trap, entrapped
❹ [also suffix] abbrev. of 手術 *shujutsu*: surgical operation
術後の *jutsugo no* postoperative
開腹術 *kaifukujutsu* laparotomy

INDEPENDENT

【jutsu 術】 practical art, technique, skill; means, way; magic, witchcraft; artifice, stratagem, trick
護身の術 *goshin no jutsu* art of self-defense
術が尽きる *jutsu ga tsukiru* be at one's wit's end
術を使う *jutsu o tsukau* practice magic
術を授ける *jutsu o sazukeru* teach tricks to

KUN

【sube 術】 means, way
為す術も無く *nasu sube mo naku* at one's wit's end

SYNONYMS

❶ **art**
技 SKILL → 248
芸 ART → 2209
道 the way of an art → 3134

得 得 得 477 TOKU e(ru) u(ru)

CH 得 dé děi de

Radical	Strokes
彳 60	11-3-8
Grade	**Freq**
Jōyō-4	321
◧ 1 - 3 - 8	

3-8 彳

Stroke order: 1–11

▶ACQUIRE ▶GAIN

COMPOUNDS

❶ (obtain possession of) **acquire, obtain, gain**
獲得する *kakutoku suru* get, acquire, obtain
取得する *shutoku suru* acquire, gain; purchase
❷ⓐ (obtain as profit) **gain, earn, profit**
ⓑ (something earned) **gain, profit**
所得 *shotoku* income, earnings
損得 *sontoku* advantage and disadvantage, loss and gain
利得 *ritoku* profit, benefit, gain
両得 *ryōtoku* double gain

❸ⓐ **gain understanding of, comprehend, realize**
ⓑ **gain one's end, attain one's goal, achieve satisfaction**
習得する *shūtoku suru* learn, master, acquire (an art)
体得する *taitoku suru* realize, learn (from experience), comprehend, master
納得 *nattoku* assent, consent, understanding
得意 *tokui* one's forte; pride; customer
得道する *tokudō suru* attain salvation
得心する *tokushin suru* consent to, be convinced of, be satisfied
説得する *settoku suru* persuade
❹ advantage, benefit
買い得品 *kaidokuhin* good bargain
ごね得だ *Gonedoku da* It pays to make trouble

INDEPENDENT

【toku 得】 gain, profit; advantage, benefit
得な *toku na* profitable, advantageous, economical
得になる *toku ni naru* bring profit, do (a person) good
【tokusuru 得する】 profit, gain, benefit

KUN

【e(ru) 得る】
① [sometimes also 獲る] acquire, get, gain, obtain, win
得難い *egatai* hard to get, rare
見得 *mie* [sometimes also 見え] pose, posture
勝ち得る *kachieru* achieve, win, gain
心得る *kokoroeru* know, understand, give consent
② can, be able to
...せざるを得ない *...sezaru o enai* cannot help (doing)
【u(ru) 得る】
① literary form of **eru** 得る
得る所が有る *uru tokoro ga aru* get benefit from
② [verbal suffix] can, be able to
...し得る *...shiuru* can, be able to
有り得る *ariuru* possible, likely

SYNONYMS

❶ **get**
獲 obtain → 779
収 TAKE IN → 198
取 TAKE → 1262
拾 PICK UP → 379
❷ⓑ **profit**
益 PROFIT → 2285
利 PROFIT → 1114
❸ⓐ **know and understand**
分かる understand → 1972
解 understand → 1517
諒 UNDERSTAND → 1575
了 COMPREHEND → 3350
知 KNOW → 1127
通 know thoroughly → 3109
悟 AWAKE TO → 419

USAGE

eru
得る
① [sometimes also 獲る] acquire, get, gain, obtain, win
② can, be able to
獲る
① catch game, hunt, fish
② [usu. 得る] acquire, get, gain, obtain, win

HOMOPHONES

eru ⇨ 獲 779
mie ⇨ 見え 2544 見栄 2544, 2574 見得 2544, 477

COMPOUND FORMATION

❶ 得意 *tokui*
得意 'one's forte, etc.' is to satisfactorily achieve (得 ❸ⓑ) one's desires (意) and take pride in one's achievements.
❷ 説得 *settoku*
説得する 'persuade' is to persuade (説) a person so as to achieve (得 ❸ⓑ) one's ends.

NOTE

⇨ see also USAGE note at 見 2544

3-8 彳 御 478

▶**GENERAL HONORIFIC TERM**
nonstandard for 御 577

3-8 彳 從 479

▶**FOLLOW**
nonstandard for 従 415

術 480

▶PRACTICAL ART

nonstandard for 術 476

3-8 亻

惟 481

惟 惟 惟 — CH 惟 wéi

I YUI omo(nmiru) kore NAMES tada yoshi nobu

Radical	Strokes
忄 61	11-3-8
Grade	**Freq**
Names	2116
1 - 3 - 8	

3-8 忄

▶MEDITATE

COMPOUNDS

❶ **meditate, ponder, think**

思惟 *shii* thinking, speculation

❷ [now always 唯 *yui* 463] only

惟一の *yuiitsu* (=*yuitsu*) *no* the only, the sole

KUN

【**omo(nmiru)** 惟んみる】 reflect, meditate

つらつら惟んみるに *tsuratsura omonmiru ni* on careful reflection, I find that...

【**kore** 惟】 [archaic] emphatic adverb

弁明惟努めたい *Benmei kore tsutometai* Well, I shall explain myself

NAMES

惟章 *koreaki* male name

惟俊 *tadatoshi* male name

SYNONYMS

❶ **think and consider**

量 weigh → 2471

省 INTROSPECT → 2449

勘 take into consideration → 1777

慮 CONSIDER → 3266

想 CONCEIVE → 2828

思 THINK → 2564

考 THINK → 3196

存 hold an opinion → 2982

案 think out → 2270

HOMOPHONES

kore ⇨ 是 2436 之 3420 此 823

NOTE

⇨ see USAGE note at 是 2436

情 482

情 情 情 — CH 情 qíng

JŌ SEI nasa(ke)

Radical	Strokes
忄 61	11-3-8
Grade	**Freq**
Jōyō-5	261
1 - 3 - 8	

3-8 忄

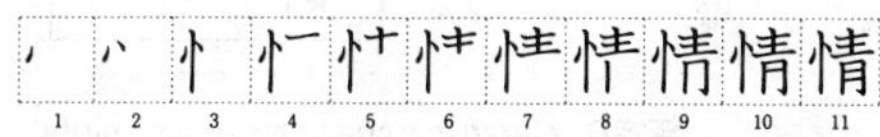

▶EMOTION ▶ACTUAL CONDITIONS

COMPOUNDS

❶ [original meaning] **emotion, feeling, sentiment, passion**

情緒 *jōcho* emotion, feeling

情操 *jōsō* sentiment

激情 *gekijō* violent emotion, passion

感情 *kanjō* feelings, emotion, sentiment

友情 *yūjō* friendship, fellowship

表情 *hyōjō* expression, look

❷ **sympathy, compassion, kindness**

同情 *dōjō* sympathy, compassion

人情 *ninjō* human feelings, humanity, sympathy

❸ⓐ love, affection

ⓑ (illicit) love, love affair, lovemaking, sexual desire

愛情 *aijō* love, affection

情死 *jōshi* double love suicide

情事 *jōji* love affair, romance

情交 *jōkō* sexual intercourse, illicit intercourse

❹ **actual conditions, actual facts, real circumstances**

情勢 *jōsei* state of things, situation

情報 *jōhō* information, intelligence, report, news

情況 *jōkyō* conditions, circumstances

事情 *jijō* circumstances, conditions, situation

実情 *jitsujō* actual circumstances, real state of affairs

❺ taste, elegance

情趣 *jōshu* mood, sentiment, artistic effects, charms

風情 *fuzei* appearance, air, taste, elegance

❻ obstinacy

強情な *gōjō na* obstinate, headstrong

INDEPENDENT

【jō 情】

①ⓐ emotion, feelings, sentiment, heart
ⓑ affection, love, passion, sexual desire
ⓒ sympathy, compassion, kindness
ⓓ faithfulness, good faith

情の深い人 *jō no fukai hito* kindhearted person
親の情 *oya no jō* parental love
情の籠もった *jō no komotta* sympathetic, warmhearted

② actual facts, real circumstances

情を明かす *jō o akasu* disclose the true facts

③ obstinacy

情を張る *jō o haru* be obstinate

KUN

【nasa(ke) 情け】 sympathy, kindness, mercy; love; taste

情け深い *nasakebukai* compassionate, kindhearted
情け無い *nasakenai* unfeeling, cruel; pitiful, wretched; shameful
情けを交わす *nasake o kawasu* have sexual intercourse

SYNONYMS

❶ feeling

感 SENSE (feeling) → 2835
心 HEART → 11
気 spirits → 3194

❷ tender feelings for others

慈 compassion → 2339
仁 BENEVOLENCE → 20
悲 mercy → 2775
哀 PITY → 2068

❸ⓐ love

愛 LOVE → 2492
恋 LOVE (for the opposite sex) → 2098
艶 ROMANCE → 1908

ⓑ sex

春 love → 2576
色 lust → 2029
性 SEX → 299

❹ states and situations

局 current situation → 3063
境 SITUATION → 676
勢 course of events → 2857
状 CONDITION → 272
況 CONDITIONS → 337
景 business conditions → 2470
態 STATE → 2847
訳 circumstances → 1473
調 TONE → 1567
様 MODE → 1052
相 PHASE → 900

3-8 忄

惨 惨 惨 惨

483 SAN ZAN miji(me)

CH 惨 cǎn

Radical	Strokes
忄 61	11-3-8
Grade	**Freq**
Jōyō	1397
1-3-8	

Stroke order: 1 2 3 4 5 6 7 8 9 10 11

▶MISERABLE ▶CRUEL

COMPOUNDS

❶ miserable, wretched, pitiable, tragic; terrible, horrible, disastrous

惨事 *sanji* disaster, tragic incident, catastrophe
惨状 *sanjō* pitiful situation
惨禍 *sanka* terrible disaster, crushing calamity
惨劇 *sangeki* tragedy, tragic event
惨憺たる *santantaru* pitiable, wretched, miserable, terrible, horrible
惨敗 *zanpai* miserable defeat
悲惨な *hisan na* miserable, wretched, tragic, pitiable
凄惨な *seisan na* ghastly, gruesome, lurid

❷ [usu. 残 *zan* 943] **cruel, ruthless, atrocious**

惨殺する *zansatsu suru* murder cruelly, slaughter, butcher
惨酷 *zankoku* cruelty, atrocity, brutality
無惨な *muzan na* cruel, atrocious; pitiful, tragic, miserable

INDEPENDENT

【san 惨】 misery, wretchedness

惨たる光景 *santaru kōkei* disastrous scene

KUN

【miji(me) 惨め】

mijime na 惨めな miserable, pitiable, tragic

惨めな思いをする *mijime na omoi o suru* feel miserable

SYNONYMS

❶ sad and depressed

寂 LONESOME → 2290
沈 depressed → 261
陰 gloomy → 541
愁 MELANCHOLY → 2829
哀 sorrowful → 2068
悲 SAD → 2775

❷ cruel

虐 CRUEL → 3218

酷 SEVERE → 1562 残 RUTHLESS → 943	凶 ATROCIOUS → 2961

惜 惜 惜

484 SEKI o(shii) o(shimu)

CH 惜 xī

Radical	Strokes
忄 61	11-3-8
Grade	**Freq**
Jōyō	1406
◧ 1 - 3 - 8	

3-8 忄

▶**REGRET**

COMPOUNDS

❶ **regret, lament**

惜別 *sekibetsu* parting regrets
惜敗 *sekihai* regrettable defeat
哀惜 *aiseki* lamentation, grief

❷ value highly, hold dear

愛惜 *aiseki* reluctance (to part)

KUN

【**o(shii) 惜しい**】 regrettable, disappointing; precious, valuable; too good (for)

惜しさ *oshisa* unwillingness to lose [part with]
惜し気無く *oshige naku* unsparingly, generously, lavishly
それは惜しい *Sore wa oshii* That's a pity!
命が惜しい *Inochi ga oshii* Life is dear
まだ捨てるには惜しい *mada suteru ni wa oshii* still too good to throw away

【**o(shimu) 惜しむ**】 grudge, be sparing of; regret; be reluctant; value

惜しみ無く *oshiminaku* freely, without stint
出し惜しみする *dashioshimi suru* grudge, be stingy
惜しむべき *oshimubeki* regrettable, lamentable
別れを惜しむ *wakare o oshimu* loathe to part with
時間を惜しむ *jikan o oshimu* value time
口惜しい(＝悔しい) *kuyashii* vexing, mortifying, regrettable

SYNONYMS

❶ **regret**

恨 regret → 369
憾 STRONGLY REGRET → 764
悔 REPENT → 365

HOMOPHONES

kuyashii ⇨ 悔しい 365 口惜しい 3382, 484

NOTE

⇨ see USAGE note at 悔 365

悼 悼 悼

485 TŌ ita(mu)

CH 悼 dào

Radical	Strokes
忄 61	11-3-8
Grade	**Freq**
Jōyō	1864
◧ 1 - 3 - 8	

3-8 忄

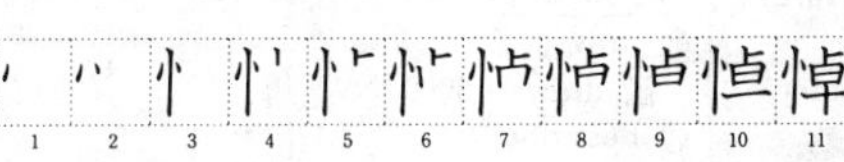

▶**MOURN**

COMPOUNDS

● **mourn, grieve, lament**

悼辞 *tōji* message of condolence
哀悼する *aitō suru* condole, mourn, grieve
追悼 *tsuitō* mourning

KUN

【**ita(mu) 悼む**】 mourn, grieve over, be grieved at

死を悼む *shi o itamu* mourn over the death of

SYNONYMS

● **mourn and mourning**

弔 CONDOLE → 3432
喪 MOURNING → 2825
忌 MOURNING → 2207

● **grieve**

傷 grieve → 158
慨 DEPLORE → 641
嘆 SIGH → 630
悲 feel sad → 2775

HOMOPHONES

itamu ⇨ 痛 3285 傷 158

NOTE

⇨ see USAGE note at 痛 3285

3-8 忄

惇 486

惇 惇 惇

TON NAMES atsushi atsu makoto toshi

CH 惇 dūn

Radical	Strokes
忄 61	11-3-8
Grade	Freq
Names	2130
1 - 3 - 8	

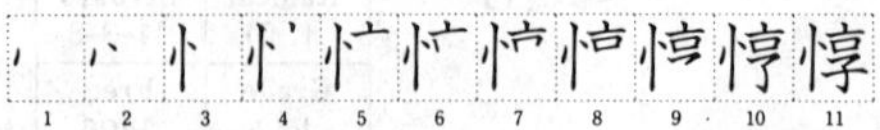

▶**SINCERE**

COMPOUNDS

❶ [rare] sincere, honest, solid

惇厚な *tonkō na* sincere and kindhearted, honest and simple

惇朴(=惇樸)な *tonboku na* simple and honest

❷ [archaic] cordial, kind, warm, friendly

惇睦な *tonboku na* cordial and friendly

NAMES

惇 *atsushi* (=*ton*) male name

SYNONYMS

❶ **purehearted**

敦 HONEST → 1693

直 straightforward → 2932

廉 INCORRUPT → 3153

潔 IMMACULATE → 744

清 clean → 523

淳 PUREHEARTED → 514

純 PURE → 1297

3-8 忄

情 487

▶**EMOTION** ▶**ACTUAL CONDITIONS**

nonstandard for 情 482

3-8 扌

描 488

描 描 描

BYŌ ega(ku) ka(ku)▲

CH 描 miáo

Radical	Strokes
扌 64	11-3-8
Grade	Freq
Jōyō	1012
1 - 3 - 8	

一 十 扌 扌 扌 扌 扌 措 描 描 描 (1–11)

▶**DEPICT**

COMPOUNDS

❶ [original meaning] (represent in a picture) **depict, draw, paint**

描画する *byōga suru* draw a picture, paint

素描 *sobyō* (rough) sketch

点描 *tenbyō* sketch

実物描写 *jitsubutsu byōsha* model drawing

❷ (represent in words) **depict, describe**

描写 *byōsha* depiction, description; portrayal; drawing

描出 *byōshutsu* depiction, description; portrayal; drawing

KUN

【ega(ku) 描く】

① [sometimes also 画く] (represent in a picture) depict, draw, paint

油絵を描く *aburae o egaku* paint in oil

② (represent in words) depict, describe

描き出す *egakidasu* delineate, depict, portray

思い描く *omoiegaku* imagine, figure, see

【ka(ku) 描く】 draw, paint

絵描き *ekaki* painter, artist

SYNONYMS

❶ **draw**

画 draw → 3000

❷ **describe**

叙 DESCRIBE → 1446

写 portray → 2000

USAGE

egaku

描く

① [sometimes also 画く] (represent in a picture) depict, draw, paint

② (represent in words) depict, describe

画く

[usu. 描く] draw, paint

HOMOPHONES

egaku ⇨ 画 3000

kaku ⇨ 書 2658

NOTE

⇨ see also USAGE note at 書 2658

掩

489 EN ō(u)

CH 掩 yǎn

Radical	Strokes
扌 64	11-3-8
Grade	**Freq**
Reference	
1 - 3 - 8	

3-8 扌

COMPOUNDS

❶ [original meaning] cover, hide, conceal
掩蔽 *enpei* cover, obscuration
掩蓋 *engai* cover; gun apron

❷ [now usu. 覆う *ōu*]
ⓐ cover, veil
ⓑ hide, conceal, screen
棺を掩う *kan o ōu* cover the coffin
顔を掩う *kao o ōu* cover one's face

❸ [now also 援 *en* 586] cover, protect
掩護する *engo suru* cover, protect, shelter
掩壕 *engō* cover trench

HOMOPHONES

ōu ⇨ 覆 2726 被 1163 蓋 2503 蔽 2523

NOTE

⇨ see USAGE note at 覆 2726

排

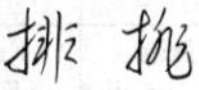

490 HAI

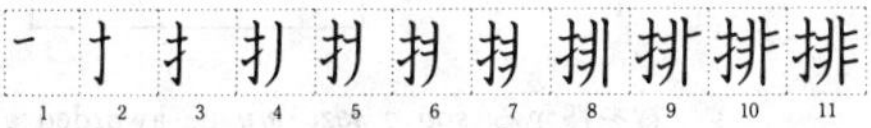

CH 排 pái pǎi

Radical	Strokes
扌 64	11-3-8
Grade	**Freq**
Jōyō	1171
1 - 3 - 8	

3-8 扌

▶EXCLUDE ▶DISCHARGE

COMPOUNDS

❶ⓐ [original meaning] **exclude, expel, reject, drive out**
ⓑ anti-
排除 *haijo* exclusion, removal, elimination
排斥する *haiseki suru* expel, reject, exclude, ostracize
排他的な *haitateki na* exclusive, clannish
排外的 *haigaiteki* antiforeign, exclusive

❷ (put out, esp. undesirable substances) **discharge, exhaust, drain, excrete**
排出 *haishutsu* discharge, exhaust, evacuation
排水 *haisui* drainage, draining; (of ships) displacement
排気 *haiki* exhaust, used steam; exhaustion, evacuation
排尿 *hainyō* urination

❸ [usu. 配 1460] arrange, put in order
排列 *hairetsu* arrangement, disposition
按排する *anbai suru* arrange, distribute; adjust

INDEPENDENT

【haisuru 排する】 exclude, expel, reject, drive out; push open

SYNONYMS

❶ⓐ **drive out**
斥 EXPEL → 2972
追 chase away → 3096
退 cause to retreat → 3094
駆 drive away → 1823
逐 DRIVE OUT → 3102
払う clear out → 194

ⓑ **eliminate**
払う CLEAR AWAY → 194
撤 WITHDRAW → 738
除 RID OF → 456
外す take off → 186
脱 REMOVE → 973
去 take away → 2156
省 leave out → 2449
却 ELIMINATE → 1118
削 cross out → 1448
抹 wipe off → 313

❷ **emit**
出 PUT OUT → 3498
放 radiate → 853
発 EMIT → 2565
射 SHOOT → 1458
噴 SPOUT → 717
吐 SPEW → 203

3-8
扌

捧

491 HŌ sasa(geru)

Ⓒⓗ 捧 pěng

Radical	Strokes
扌 64	11-3-8
Grade	**Freq**
Reference	
◧ 1 - 3 - 8	

COMPOUNDS

ⓐ [now also 奉 *hō* 2559 or 抱 *hō* 306] [original meaning] hold in both hands

ⓑ offer respectfully

捧持(=奉持)する *hōji suru* hold up, bear

捧腹絶倒(=抱腹絶倒)する *hōfuku-zettō suru* double up with laughter

捧呈する *hōtei suru* dedicate, present, offer (to a high personage)

捧げる *sasageru* lift up, hold up; present, offer; devote, sacrifice

捧げ物 *sasagemono* offering, sacrifice

3-8
扌

授 挍 授

492 JU sazu(keru) sazu(karu)

Ⓒⓗ 授 shòu

Radical	Strokes
扌 64	11-3-8
Grade	**Freq**
Jōyō-5	532
◧ 1 - 3 - 8	

一 十 扌 扩 扩 扩 扩 扩 护 挼 授
1 2 3 4 5 6 7 8 9 10 11

▶CONFER

COMPOUNDS

❶ **confer, grant, award; give, hand over**

授与する *juyo suru* grant, give, confer

授賞 *jushō* awarding a prize

授産 *jusan* providing with work, giving employment

授受 *juju* giving and receiving

授乳 *junyū* breast-feeding

❷ **teach, instruct, initiate**

授業 *jugyō* teaching, instruction; lesson

教授 *kyōju* teaching; professor

伝授 *denju* instruction, initiation

口授 *kōju* oral instruction

KUN

【**sazu(keru)** 授ける】 confer, grant, award; give, hand over

学位を授ける *gakui o sazukeru* award a degree

...の秘伝を授ける *...no hiden o sazukeru* initiate into the secrets of

【**sazu(karu)** 授かる】 be gifted with, be granted; be taught

賞を授かる *shō o sazukaru* be awarded a prize

SYNONYMS

❶ **give**

与 GIVE → 3421

上 give (to superior or others) → 3404

下 give (to inferior or speaker) → 3378

呉れる give (to speaker) → 2549

賜 DEIGN TO GIVE → 1585

贈 PRESENT A GIFT → 1634

賄 BRIBE → 1529

呈 PRESENT → 2189

進 present to a superior → 3121

❷ **teach**

教 TEACH → 1493

育 educate → 2050

練 TRAIN → 1375

訓 INSTRUCT → 1454

諭 ADMONISH → 1598

導 GUIDE → 2888

迪 EDIFY → 3076

啓 ENLIGHTEN → 2763

掛 掛 掛

493 KAI▲ KEI▲ ka(keru) -ka(keru) ka(ke) -ka(ke) -ga(ke) ka(karu) -ka(karu) -ga(karu) ka(kari) -ga(kari) kakari -gakari

CH 挂 guà

Radical	Strokes
扌 64	11-3-8
Grade	**Freq**
Jōyō	1292
1-3-8	

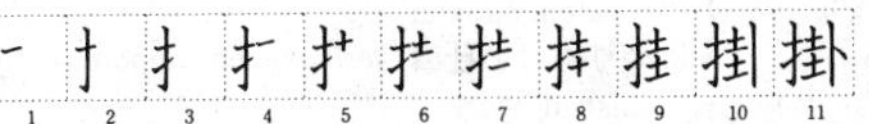

▶**SET** ▶**HANG**

COMPOUNDS

● [original meaning] **hang, suspend**
掛留 *keiryū music* suspension

KUN

【**ka(keru)** 掛ける】

①ⓐ set, put on, put over, spread
ⓑ set against, put up against, fasten
ⓒ set on a scale, weigh
ⓓ (set on one's head or shoulders) wear, put on
掛け布団 *kakebuton* covering quilt
薦を掛ける *komo o kakeru* spread a mat
薬罐を掛ける *yakan o kakeru* put a kettle on (the stove)
梯子を掛ける *hashigo o kakeru* set a ladder up against
掛け小屋 *kakegoya* lean-to; temporary theater
計りに掛ける *hakari ni kakeru* weigh on a scale
眼鏡を掛ける *megane o kakeru* wear glasses
ショールを掛ける *shōru o kakeru* put a shawl on

② set one's body down, sit, sit down
掛け心地 *kakegokochi* feel of a chair
腰掛け *koshikake* chair, seat, bench, stool
腰を掛ける *koshi o kakeru* sit down

③ pour, sprinkle
掛け汁 *kakejiru* dressing, gravy
振り掛ける *furikakeru* sprinkle, spatter
水を掛ける *mizu o kakeru* sprinkle water on (something)

④ set going, set in motion, turn on, start, operate; phone
火を掛ける *hi o kakeru* set fire
レコードを掛ける *rekōdo o kakeru* play a record
仕掛け *shikake* device, mechanism
電話を掛ける *denwa o kakeru* make a phone call, telephone

⑤ⓐ set before, present, pose
ⓑ set (a tax) on, lay, impose
お目に掛ける *ome ni kakeru* show to someone, present
舞台に掛ける *butai ni kakeru* put on stage
謎を掛ける *nazo o kakeru* pose a riddle
持ち掛ける *mochikakeru* propose, offer (a suggestion)
見せ掛け *misekake* outward appearance
掛け金 *kakekin* installment; premium
掛け値 *kakene* overcharge, inflated price; exaggeration
税金を掛ける *zeikin o kakeru* place a tax on
保険を掛ける *hoken o kakeru* insure (something)

⑥ exert influence on, impose
迷惑を掛ける *meiwaku o kakeru* impose trouble
心配を掛ける *shinpai o kakeru* cause someone to worry
面倒を掛ける *mendō o kakeru* put someone to trouble

⑦ hang, hang up, suspend
掛け物 *kakemono* hanging scroll
掛け看板 *kakekanban* hanging sign
カーテンを掛ける *kāten o kakeru* hang up a curtain

⑧ fasten onto, affix
掛け時計 *kakedokei* wall clock
引っ掛ける *hikkakeru* hang on, hook; throw on; trap, cheat; have a drink
フックに掛ける *fukku ni kakeru* hang on a hook

⑨ fasten (one's mind) upon
気に掛ける *ki ni kakeru* have one's mind upon, take to heart
願を掛ける *gan o kakeru* make a wish (to a god)

⑩ lock, close
掛け金 *kakegane* (window) latch
錠を掛ける *jō o kakeru* fasten a lock

⑪ speak, call out
掛け声 *kakegoe* shout to mark time, shout of encouragement
掛け合い *kakeai* dialogue, duet; bargaining
気合いを掛ける *kiai o kakeru* raise a shout, cheer on
話し掛ける *hanashikakeru* call out to someone, accost

⑫ entrust someone to (a physician), put under medical treatment
医者に掛ける *isha ni kakeru* entrust to a doctor (for treatment)

⑬ spend (time or money)
時間を掛ける *jikan o kakeru* spend time (on

doing something)
お金を掛ける *okane o kakeru* spend money (on something)
⑭ raise
帆を掛ける *ho o kakeru* raise a sail
⑮ multiply
掛け算 *kakezan* multiplication
八掛ける二 *hachi kakeru ni* 2 times 8
⑯ mate (animals), cross (plants or animals)
二つの植物を掛け合わせて新種を作る *Futatsu no shokubutsu o kakeawasete shinshu o tsukuru* Make a new plant by crossing two others
⑰ pun, play on words
掛け詞 *kakekotoba* play on words (as a poetic device)
これは書名に掛けた謳い文句だ *Kore wa shomei ni kaketa utai monku da* This slogan plays on the name [title] of the book

【-ka(keru) -掛ける】
① [verbal suffix]
ⓐ start doing, begin to do; be about to do
ⓑ perform an action partway
走り掛ける *hashirikakeru* start running
死に掛ける *shinikakeru* be dying
言い掛けて止める *iikakete yameru* stop in the middle of a sentence
② emphatic verbal suffix, somewhat vague in meaning, used to emphasize the action of the doer upon the object, e.g., latch on to, close in on, attach, etc.
詰め掛ける *tsumekakeru* crowd (a house); throng to (a door)
押し掛ける *oshikakeru* force oneself upon (a person), go uninvited
追い掛ける(＝追っ掛ける) *oikakeru* (＝*okkakeru*) chase, run after
見掛ける *mikakeru* catch sight of
心掛ける *kokorogakeru* bear in mind; try, endeavor, intend
出掛ける *dekakeru* go out, set off; be about to go out

【ka(ke) 掛け】
① noodles in broth
掛けうどん *kakeudon* thick noodles in broth
② credit, installment
掛けにする *kake ni suru* give credit
掛け買い *kakegai* credit purchase
掛け売り *kakeuri* credit sale

【-ka(ke) -掛け】
[also suffix]
① rack, hanger
帽子掛け *bōshikake* hat rack
タオル掛け *taorukake* towel rack
衣紋掛け *emonkake* coat hanger
② garment, cover
テーブル掛け *tēburukake* tablecloth
肩掛け *katakake* shawl
前掛け *maekake* apron
③ dish prepared with broth or dressing on it
葛掛け *kuzukake* food dressed with liquid starch
④ half-finished, in the process of
食べ掛けのバナナ *tabekake no banana* half-eaten banana
やり掛けの仕事 *yarikake no shigoto* unfinished work

【-ga(ke) -掛け】
① half-done, in the process of, about to
寝掛けに *negake ni* when half-asleep
起き掛けに *okigake ni* when half-awake
帰り掛けに *kaerigake ni* on the way home
② 10 percent
八掛け *hachigake* 80%
③ multiple of, times as large
二つ掛け *futatsugake* two times
④ suffix indicating sitting capacity
三人掛けのベンチ *sanningake no benchi* bench for three persons
⑤ [suffix] vs., uneven match
五人掛け *goningake* five against one
⑥ [suffix] wearing, clad
浴衣掛けで *yukatagake de* wearing a *yukata*

【ka(karu) 掛かる】
① hang, be suspended
壁に掛かる *kabe ni kakaru* hang on the wall
② be set over, cover
そこに布団が掛かっている *Soko ni futon ga kakatte iru* The quilt is spread over there
霧が地面に掛かっている *Kiri ga jimen ni kakatte iru* Fog covers the ground
③ splash
掛かり湯 *kakariyu* fresh bathwater to pour over oneself
私のズボンに水が掛かった *Watakushi no zubon ni mizu ga kakatta* My trousers were splashed with water
④ lean against
伸し掛かる *noshikakaru* lean on (a person), bear down on
寄り掛かる *yorikakaru* lean against something
梯子が壁に掛かっている *Hashigo ga kabe ni kakatte iru* The ladder is leaning against the wall
⑤ⓐ be caught, be trapped
ⓑ be caught (on one's mind), weigh
罠に掛かる *wana ni kakaru* caught in a trap
引っ掛かる *hikkakaru* be caught, catch on; get entangled; be trapped
心に掛かる *kokoro ni kakaru* weigh on one's mind
娘の事が気掛かりだ *Musume no koto ga kigakari da* I am anxious about my daughter
⑥ set about, apply oneself to, be engaged in
仕事に掛かる *shigoto ni kakaru* get to work
用意に掛かる *yōi ni kakaru* set about prepara-

tions
取り掛かる *torikakaru* commence, undertake
仕事に掛かり切りになる *shigoto ni kakarikiri ni naru* give one's whole time to the job
⑦ⓐ depend upon, hinge upon
ⓑ involve, concern
責任は彼に掛かる *Sekinin wa kare ni kakaru* Responsibility rests with him
金が有るか無いかに掛かる *kane ga aru ka nai ka ni kakaru* depend on whether or not there is money
子供に掛かる *kodomo ni kakaru* depend on one's children
掛かり合い *kakariai* involvement
手掛かり *tegakari* something to rely on, clue
⑧ consult (a doctor)
掛かり付けの医者 *kakaritsuke no isha* family physician [doctor]
⑨ start, start operating, work
エンジンが掛かる *Enjin ga kakaru* The engine starts
電話が掛かって来る *denwa ga kakatte kuru* get a phone call
⑩ appear (at a theater)
今映画が掛かっている *Ima eiga ga kakatte iru* A film is now being shown
⑪ require, cost; weigh
時間が掛かる *jikan ga kakaru* take time
余り金が掛からない *Amari kane ga kakaranai* It doesn't cost very much
目方はどの位掛かりますか *Mekata wa dono kurai kakarimasu ka* How much does it weigh?
⑫ attack, fall upon
襲い掛かる *osoikakaru* assault, pounce upon, sweep down on (a person)
飛び掛かる *tobikakaru* spring upon
敵に掛かる *teki ni kakaru* assail the enemy
⑬ approach, come near
山道に掛かる *yamamichi ni kakaru* come to a mountain path
⑭ [formerly 繫る] anchor, moor

【-ka(karu) -掛かる】
[verbal suffix]
① be on the verge of
死に掛かる *shinikakaru* be dying
② happen to (do something)
来掛かる *kikakaru* happen to come by
通り掛かる *tōrikakaru* happen to pass by

【-ga(karu) -掛かる】
① resemble
芝居掛かった *shibaigakatta* theatrical, affected, pompous
② tinged with
藍色掛かった生地 *aiirogakatta kiji* cloth tinged with indigo

【ka(kari) 掛かり】
① expenses
掛かりが嵩む *Kakari ga kasamu* Expenses get heavy
② scale, scope
大掛かりな *ōgakari na* large-scale, extensive
③ engagement, catching on
歯車の掛かりが悪い *Haguruma no kakari ga warui* The gears are improperly engaged
④ attack

【-ga(kari) -掛かり】
① [suffix] combined, in a group of
一家掛かりで *ikkagakari de* with the whole family
五人掛かりで運ぶ *goningakari de hakobu* be carried by five people
② [suffix] requiring (a period of time)
三年掛かりの仕事 *sannengakari no shigoto* job requiring three years
③ [also suffix] resembling
能掛かり *nōgakari* resembling a noh performance
④ be entrusted to, depend on
親掛かりの *oyagakari no* dependent on one's parents

【kakari 掛】
[usu. 係]
ⓐ person in charge (of a post, esp. in a government agency or railway company)
ⓑ charge, duty, post
掛長 *kakarichō* chief clerk
掛の人 *kakari no hito* official in charge

【-gakari -掛】 [usu. -係] [suffix] person in charge (of a post, esp. in a government agency or railway company)
出札掛 *shussatsugakari* ticket agent

SYNONYMS

【kakeru】
① **put**
置 PLACE → 2608
措 DISPOSE → 502
据える INSTALL → 497
④ **set in motion**
駆 DRIVE → 1823
動 MOVE → 1778
⑦ **hang**
懸 SUSPEND → 2915
釣り- suspended → 1674
垂 HANG DOWN → 3565
⑮ **multiply**
乗 multiply → 3576

【-kakeru】
①ⓐ **begin**
-出す begin to do → 3498
始 BEGIN → 281
発 START → 2565
起 start → 3307
就 SET ABOUT → 1694
開 OPEN → 3321
創 initiate → 1815

肇 ORIGINATE → 2799

【-kakaru】

① **on the verge of**

将 on the verge of → 460

-際 on the verge of → 714

臨 on the point of → 1630

USAGE

❶ **kakeru**

掛ける

①ⓐ set, put on, put over, spread
ⓑ set against, put up against, fasten
ⓒ set on a scale, weigh
ⓓ (set on one's head or shoulders) wear, put on
② set one's body down, sit, sit down
③ pour, sprinkle
④ set going, set in motion, turn on, start, operate; phone
⑤ⓐ set before, present, pose
ⓑ set (a tax) on, lay, impose
⑥ exert influence on, impose
⑦ hang, hang up, suspend
⑧ fasten onto, affix
⑨ fasten (one's mind) upon
⑩ lock, close
⑪ speak, call out
⑫ entrust someone to (a physician), put under medical treatment
⑬ spend (time or money)
⑭ raise
⑮ multiply
⑯ mate (animals), cross (plants or animals)
⑰ pun, play on words

架ける

lay (a bridge or wire) across, build across, span (a river) with (a bridge), bridge
★ *kakeru* in the sense of span or bridge is correctly written 架ける, not 掛ける. This is in spite of the fact that *kakehashi* 'suspension bridge' is normally written 掛け橋.

懸ける

① [sometimes also 賭ける] stake (one's life), risk
② offer [set] a prize
③ [in compounds] be (greatly) different from, be far apart

賭ける

ⓐ wager, bet money
ⓑ [usu. 懸ける] stake (one's life), risk

駆ける

gallop, run quickly, dash

翔る

soar, fly

★掛ける is a complicated word with many meanings. Make a careful study of the equivalents and examples. In the sense of hang or suspend, 掛ける, *not* 懸ける, is correct. This is in spite of the fact that 懸 means to suspend or hang when used in compounds, as for example in 懸垂 *kensui* 'suspension, etc.'

❷ **kake**

掛け

① noodles in broth
② credit, installment

賭け

bet, wager

❸ **kakaru**

掛かる

① hang, be suspended
② be set over, cover
③ splash
④ lean against
⑤ⓐ be caught, be trapped
ⓑ be caught (on one's mind), weigh
⑥ set about, apply oneself to, be engaged in
⑦ⓐ depend upon, hinge upon
ⓑ involve, concern
⑧ consult (a doctor)
⑨ start, start operating, work
⑩ appear (at a theater)
⑪ require, cost; weigh
⑫ attack, fall upon
⑬ approach, come near
⑭ [formerly 繋る] anchor, moor

懸かる

① be suspended in midair (as of the moon), hang
② have a prize offered, have a reward (set on one's head)

架かる

span, (of cables) be laid across, be built across

係る

① affect, concern, involve
② *gram* modify
③ is the work of, is done by

繋る

[now usu. 掛かる] anchor, moor

罹る

ⓐ fall ill, contract (a disease)
ⓑ suffer (from a calamity)

★掛かる is the intransitive form of 掛ける and shares most of its meanings. Study the equivalents and examples under *kakaru* above. Note that 掛かる is to hang in the sense of being snagged or caught on something, whereas 懸かる means to be suspended in midair.

❹ **kakari**

掛かり

① expenses
② scale, scope
③ engagement, catching on
④ attack

掛
[usu. 係]
ⓐ person in charge (of a post, esp. in a government agency or railway company)
ⓑ charge, duty, post

係り
relation, connection (esp. in grammar)
★Note that 係り, *not* 係かり or 係, is the correct form here.

係
[sometimes also 掛]
ⓐ person in charge, official in charge, clerk
ⓑ charge, duty, post

❺ -gakari

-掛かり
① [suffix] combined, in a group of
② [suffix] requiring (a period of time)
③ [also suffix] resembling
④ be entrusted to, depend on

-掛
[usu. -係] [suffix] person in charge (of a post, esp. in a government agency or railway company)

-係
[sometimes also -掛] [suffix] person in charge, official in charge, clerk

★Note how the meanings of *kakari* and *-gakari* vary in accordance with the different *okurigana* inflections.

HOMOPHONES

kakeru ⇨ 架 2569 懸 2915 賭 1605 駆 1823 翔 1357
kake ⇨ 賭 1605
kakaru ⇨ 懸 2915 架 2569 係 97 繋 2902 罹 2619
kakari ⇨ 係 97
-gakari ⇨ 係 97

掲 掲 掲 掲

494 KEI kaka(geru)

CH 揭 jiē

Radical	Strokes
扌 64	11-3-8
Grade	**Freq**
Jōyō	1148
◧ 1 - 3 - 8	

3-8
扌

一 十 扌 扌 打 抈 抈 押 揭 揭 掲
1 2 3 4 5 6 7 8 9 10 11

▶PUT UP

COMPOUNDS

❶ put up, display, hoist, raise
掲揚する *keiyō suru* hoist, put up, fly (a flag)
掲示する *keiji suru* put up a notice [bulletin]

❷ display in writing, mention, show
掲載する *keisai suru* publish, insert, print
前掲の *zenkei no* shown above, aforementioned

KUN

【kaka(geru) 掲げる】 put up, display, hoist, raise; display in writing, mention, carry, publish
国旗を掲げる *kokki o kakageru* hoist the national flag
上に掲げた費用 *ue ni kakageta hiyō* the expenses mentioned above

SYNONYMS

❶ display
展 DISPLAY → 3111
陳 lay out (for exhibit) → 540

❶ raise
揚 RAISE HIGH → 593
挙 RAISE → 2456
上 raise → 3404
起 raise up → 3307
立てる STAND → 1992
拾う PICK UP → 379

❷ print and publish
載 PUT IN PRINT → 3300
版 PUBLISHING → 872
刊 PUBLISH → 190
刷 PRINT → 1273
印 print → 828
植 typeset → 990

3-8 控 控 控 控 ⒸⒽ 控 kòng
扌
495 KŌ hika(eru) hika(e)

Radical	Strokes
扌 64	11-3-8
Grade	**Freq**
Jōyō	1130
1 - 3 - 8	

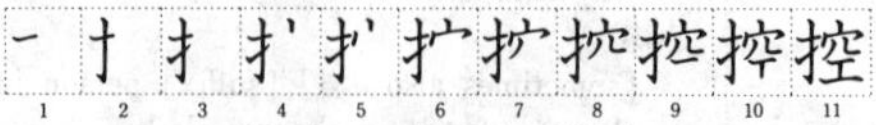

▶**HOLD BACK**

COMPOUNDS

❶ [formerly 扣 216] **hold back part of something, deduct, subtract**
控除 *kōjo* (tax) deduction, subtraction
❷ [original meaning] (keep in check) **hold back, keep**
❸ **accuse in court, charge, sue**
控訴 *kōso* (intermediate) appeal

KUN

【hika(eru) 控える】
① (keep in check) hold back, keep
馬を控える *uma o hikaeru* hold back a horse
②ⓐ (refrain from) hold back (from), restrain oneself, refrain
ⓑ be moderate, be sparing
差し控える *sashihikaeru* be moderate in; withhold, desist from, refrain from
手控える *tebikaeru* hang [hold] back, hold off, refrain
食べ物を控える *tabemono o hikaeru* be temperate in eating
控え目な *hikaeme na* modest, temperate, reserved
③ be in waiting, wait
別の間に控える *betsu no ma ni hikaeru* wait in another room
④ note down, write down, take notes
電話番号を控える *denwa bangō o hikaeru* jot down a phone number
⑤ have (something at hand)
選挙を控えて *senkyo o hikaete* with the election around the corner

【hika(e) 控え】
① note, memo; counterfoil, stub
控え書き *hikaegaki* notes, memo
捕り物控え *torimonohikae* detective's memoirs
領収書の控え *ryōshūsho no hikae* counterfoil of a receipt
② duplicate, copy
控えを取る *hikae o toru* take a copy of
控え見本 *hikaemihon* duplicate sample
③ waiting; reserve, substitute, alternate
控えの間 *hikae no ma* antechamber, anteroom
控え室 *hikaeshitsu* anteroom, waiting room
控えの力士 *hikae no rikishi* sumo wrestler waiting at the ringside
控え選手 *hikaesenshu* reserve, substitute player
④ prop, stay
主控え *shubikae* mainstay

SYNONYMS

❶ **subtract**
減 subtract → 601
引く subtract → 181
❸ **sue**
告 accuse of → 2409
訴 SUE → 1507
訟 LITIGATE → 1472

【hikaeru】
① **pull**
引 DRAW → 181
抽 DRAW OUT → 302
抜 PULL OUT → 246
寄せる DRAW NEAR → 2291
② **restrain**
渋る hang [hold] back → 513
禁 PROHIBIT → 2795
制 CONTROL (restrain) → 1274
限 LIMIT → 398
抑 SUPPRESS → 257
束 TIE UP → 3554
縛 BIND → 1405
③ **wait**
待 WAIT → 364
④ **write**
記 WRITE DOWN → 1453
紀 record in writing → 1276
録 RECORD → 1742
登 register → 2595
写 COPY → 2000
書 WRITE → 2658
筆 write → 2677

掘 掘 掘

496 KUTSU ho(ru)

(CH) 掘 jué

Radical	Strokes
扌 64	11-3-8
Grade	Freq
Jōyō	1208
1-3-8	

3-8 扌

一 十 扌 扌 扌 扩 扩 扩 护 掘 掘
1 2 3 4 5 6 7 8 9 10 11

▶DIG

COMPOUNDS

ⓐ [original meaning] **dig, excavate**

ⓑ **dig out, dig up, excavate**

掘削する *kussaku suru* dig out, excavate
採掘 *saikutsu* mining
試掘 *shikutsu* prospecting, trial digging
掘進する *kusshin suru* excavate, tunnel
発掘する *hakkutsu suru* dig, excavate

KUN

【ho(ru) 掘る】

ⓐ dig, bore, excavate
ⓑ dig up, dig out, unearth

掘り返す *horikaesu* turn up (the soil), tear up (a road)
掘り下げる *horisageru* dig down; investigate, probe, delve into
露天掘り *rotenbori* open-air [strip] mining

SYNONYMS

● **dig**

削 excavate → 1448

USAGE

horu

掘る
ⓐ dig, bore, excavate
ⓑ dig up, dig out, unearth

彫る
ⓐ (cut so as to form designs or figures) engrave, carve, chisel
ⓑ tattoo

HOMOPHONES

horu ⇨ 彫 1683

NOTE

★do not confuse with 堀 467

据 据 据

497 KYO▲ su(eru) su(waru)

(CH) 据 jù jū

Radical	Strokes
扌 64	11-3-8
Grade	Freq
Jōyō	1110
1-3-8	

3-8 扌

一 十 扌 扌 扌 护 护 护 护 据 据
1 2 3 4 5 6 7 8 9 10 11

▶INSTALL

COMPOUNDS

❶ pinch, pick

拮据 *kikkyo* assiduity, diligence, hard toil; [archaic] pinching

❷ [original meaning, now archaic] sit down

KUN

【su(eru) 据える】

① (set in position) install, place in position, fix, mount, set up; set (a table); lay (a foundation)

据え付ける *suetsukeru* install, equip, fit
据え置き *sueoki* leaving (a thing) as it stands; deferred savings
据え膳 *suezen* meal set before one; women's advances
見据える *misueru* fix one's eyes, look hard

②ⓐ install a person in a post, place, appoint
ⓑ install a person in a seat, seat (a person)

後釜に据える *atogama ni sueru* install (a person) in (someone's) place
上座に据える *kamiza ni sueru* give (a guest) the seat of honor
腰を据える *koshi o sueru* settle oneself (in a place)

【su(waru) 据わる】 be set

目が据わって *me ga suwatte* with set eyes
腹の据わった男 *hara no suwatta otoko* man with plenty of guts

SYNONYMS

【sueru】

① **put**

置 PLACE → 2608
掛ける SET → 493
措 DISPOSE → 502

① **equip and install**

敷 LAY → 1870
架 LAY ACROSS → 2569
装 FIT OUT → 2685
設 SET UP → 1471
備 PROVIDE → 146

HOMOPHONES

suwaru ⇨ 座 3116 坐 3547

NOTE
⇨ see USAGE note at 座 3116

3-8 扌

掠

498 RYAKU kasu(meru) kasu(ru) kasu(reru)

CH 掠 lüè

Radical	Strokes
扌 64	11-3-8
Grade	**Freq**
Reference	
1 - 3 - 8	

COMPOUNDS

❶ⓐ [now replaced by 略 *ryaku* 1169] plunder, pillage, rob
ⓑ cheat
掠奪 *ryakudatsu* pillage, plunder, looting
侵掠する *shinryaku suru* invade, aggress (against)
奪掠 *datsuryaku* pillage, plunder, looting
掠め取る *kasumetoru* rob, cheat
人目を掠めて *hitome o kasumete* by stealth, on the sly
❷ graze, brush past; skim
水面を掠める *suimen o kasumeru* skim over the water
掠る *kasuru* graze; squeeze, exploit
❸ become hoarse [husky]
声が掠れる *koe ga kasureru* become hoarse

3-8 扌

採 採 採 採

499 SAI to(ru)

CH 采 cǎi cài

Radical	Strokes
扌 64	11-3-8
Grade	**Freq**
Jōyō-5	789
1 - 3 - 8	

一 十 扌 扌 扌 扌 扌 扌 扌 採 採
1 2 3 4 5 6 7 8 9 10 11

▶PICK ▶GATHER

COMPOUNDS

❶ⓐ [original meaning] **pick, pluck, gather**
ⓑ **gather (something useful), collect, mine, extract**
採取 *saishu* picking, collecting, harvesting
採綿器 *saimenki* cotton picker
伐採 *bassai* lumbering, lumber-felling, deforestation
採集 *saishū* collecting, gathering
採掘 *saikutsu* mining
採炭 *saitan* coal mining
採油 *saiyu* drilling for oil, oil extraction
採血 *saiketsu* blood collecting [gathering]
採算 *saisan* (commercial) profit
採点 *saiten* marking, grading, rating
採録する *sairoku suru* transcribe, record
❷ **pick (out), select, adopt**
採用 *saiyō* adoption, acceptance; employment, appointment
採択する *saitaku suru* adopt, select
採決 *saiketsu* ballot taking, vote, roll call

KUN

【to(ru) 採る】
①ⓐ gather, collect, extract (oil), produce (wine out of grapes)
ⓑ admit (light)
山菜を採る *sansai o toru* gather edible wild plants
葡萄からワインを採る *budō kara wain o toru* make wine from grapes
明かり採り *akaritori* skylight, dormer, transom
②ⓐ pick (out), choose, prefer
ⓑ adopt, take, engage
採り上げる *toriageru* adopt, accept, listen to
可否を採る *kahi o toru* take the ayes and noes
新卒者を採る *shinsotsusha o toru* engage a new graduate

SYNONYMS

❶ⓐ **harvest**
摘 PICK → 694
穫 HARVEST → 1251
刈る reap → 28
ⓑ **gather**
収 collect → 198
集 COLLECT → 2771
❷ **choose**
摘 pick out → 694
択 SELECT → 255
選 CHOOSE → 3169
抜 single out → 246

HOMOPHONES
toru ⇨ 取 1262 捕 429 執 1680 撮 737

NOTE
⇨ see USAGE note at 取 1262

接 接 接 接
500 SETSU tsu(gu)

㊥ 接 jiē

Radical	Strokes
扌 64	11-3-8
Grade	Freq
Jōyō-5	555
◧ 1-3-8	

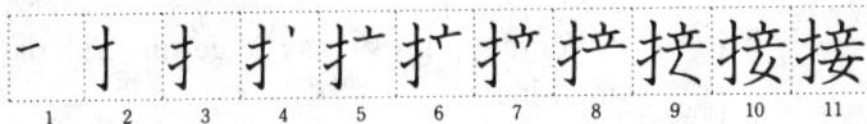

▶**CONTACT**

COMPOUNDS

❶ **contact, touch, come in contact with**
接触 *sesshoku* contact, touch
接種 *sesshu* vaccination, inoculation
接点 *setten* point of contact, contact
接線(＝切線) *sessen* tangent
接吻 *seppun* kiss
隣接 *rinsetsu* contiguity, adjacency

❷ bring into contact:
ⓐ **join, connect**
ⓑ weld, welding
接合 *setsugō* joining, union
接続 *setsuzoku* connection, joining
接着 *setchaku* adhesion, gluing
溶接 *yōsetsu* welding
融接 *yūsetsu* fusion welding
鍛接 *tansetsu* forge welding

❸ come close to, approach
接近する *sekkin suru* approach, draw near, come close
直接に *chokusetsu ni* directly
間接的な *kansetsuteki na* indirect, roundabout

❹ⓐ **receive (guests), welcome, meet**
ⓑ receive, accept
接待する *settai suru* receive (guests), welcome; offer, serve, entertain
面接 *mensetsu* interview
応接 *ōsetsu* reception
接収する *sesshū suru* requisition, take over, seize
接受する *setsuju suru* receive

INDEPENDENT

【**setsu 接**】(of electical appliances) on, in contact

【**sessuru 接する**】come in contact, touch; adjoin, be contiguous; receive, see; receive, be in receipt of; meet with, encounter

KUN

【**tsu(gu) 接ぐ**】
ⓐ join, piece together, set (a broken bone), splice (ropes)
ⓑ graft (trees)
骨接ぎ *honetsugi* bonesetting
接ぎ木 *tsugiki* grafting, grafted tree
木に竹を接ぐ *ki ni take o tsugu* graft a bamboo shoot on a tree, sew a fox's skin to the lion's

SYNONYMS

❶ **touch**
触 TOUCH → 1518
当てる apply → 2177

❷ **join**
係 CONNECT → 97
連 LINK → 3103
結 TIE → 1348
縛 BIND → 1405
束 TIE UP → 3554

❸ **approach**
寄る DRAW NEAR → 2291
近 NEAR → 3061
迫 PRESS → 3074

❹ⓐ **treat and welcome**
款 treat cordially → 1700
待 treat → 364
遇 TREAT → 3135
迎 WELCOME → 3059
扱う HANDLE → 217

USAGE

tsugu
接ぐ
ⓐ join, piece together, set (a broken bone), splice (ropes)
ⓑ graft (trees)
継ぐ
① succeed (to), accede; inherit
② couple, link, relay
③ patch (up)
④ add to, replenish, feed
次ぐ
rank next to, come next [after]
注ぐ
pour out, pour in, fill

HOMOPHONES
tsugu ⇨ 継 1360 次 54 注 325

3-8
扌

捨 捨 捨 捨

501 SHA su(teru)

CH 捨 shě

Radical	Strokes
扌 64	11-3-8
Grade	**Freq**
Jōyō-6	1152
1 - 3 - 8	

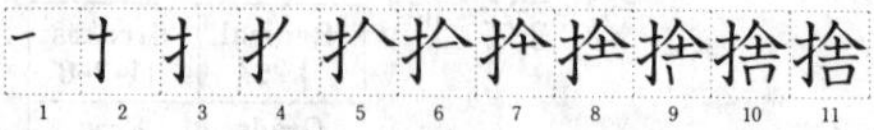

一 十 扌 扌 扌 扌 拎 拎 拎 捨 捨
1 2 3 4 5 6 7 8 9 10 11

▶**DISCARD**

COMPOUNDS

❶ⓐ **discard, reject, cast away**
ⓑ give up, abandon
取捨 *shusha* adoption or rejection, choice
用捨 *yōsha* adoption or rejection, choice
四捨五入 *shishagonyū* rounding (to the nearest integer)
捨身 *shashin* becoming a priest; risking one's life for others
❷ give alms, dispense charity
喜捨する *kisha suru* give alms, donate

KUN

【**su(teru)** 捨てる】
① [sometimes also 棄てる]
ⓐ discard, throw away, cast aside
ⓑ abandon, desert, discard, forsake, give up
ごみ捨て *gomisute* dumping refuse; garbage pit, dumping ground
捨て子 *sutego* foundling, abandoned child; abandoning one's child
見捨てる *misuteru* forsake, desert
② leave unattended
捨てて置く *sutete oku* leave something as it is
③ [in compounds] act as if getting rid of something
言い捨てる *iisuteru* say (something) over one's shoulder

SYNONYMS

❶ **discard and abandon**
棄 ABANDON → 2137

USAGE

suteru
捨てる
① [sometimes also 棄てる]
ⓐ discard, throw away, cast aside
ⓑ abandon, desert, discard, forsake, give up
② leave unattended
③ [in compounds] act as if getting rid of something
棄てる
[usu. 捨てる]
ⓐ discard, throw away, cast aside
ⓑ abandon, desert, discard, forsake, give up

HOMOPHONES

suteru ⇨ 棄 2137

3-8
扌

措 措 措

502 SO o(ku)▲

CH 措 cuò

Radical	Strokes
扌 64	11-3-8
Grade	**Freq**
Jōyō	830
1 - 3 - 8	

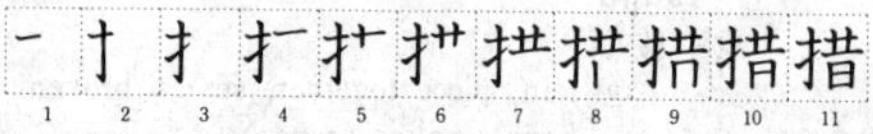

一 十 扌 扌 扌 扌 拌 拌 措 措 措
1 2 3 4 5 6 7 8 9 10 11

▶**DISPOSE**

COMPOUNDS

❶ (put in the right position) **dispose, place, arrange**
措定する *sotei suru* suppose, assume
措辞 *soji* phraseology, wording
措辞法 *sojihō* syntax
❷ (deal with) **dispose of, take steps, manage**
措置 *sochi* measure, step, action
❸ behavior, deportment
措止 *soshi* demeanor, behavior
挙措 *kyoso* behavior, manner
❹ unclassified compounds
窮措大 *kyūsodai* poor student [scholar]

KUN

【**o(ku)** 措く】
① desist from, discontinue
賞賛して措かない *shōsan shite okanai* extol, applaud highly
② except, set apart, lay aside
措いて *oite* except, no other
ここを措いて道は無い *Koko o oite michi wa nai* There is no other alternative

SYNONYMS

❶ **put**
置 PLACE → 2608
掛ける SET → 493

据える INSTALL → 497
❷ **deal with**
扱う HANDLE → 217
処 DEAL WITH → 3031
置 take proper steps → 2608

USAGE

oite
措いて
except, no other
於て
① in, at, on (in reference to time or place)
② as for, on one's part

HOMOPHONES

oku ⇨ 置 2608 擱 789
oite ⇨ 於 854

COMPOUND FORMATION

措辞 *soji* 措定 *sotei*
The meaning of 措 in Japanese is rather vague. 措 originally meant to put or arrange, which explains the formation of 措辞 'phraseology, wording', to place (措 ❶) words (辞) in the proper position. 措定する 'suppose, assume', a philosophical term, is, literally, to place (措 ❶) in a fixed (定) position.

NOTE

⇨ see also USAGE note at 置 2608

掃 掃 掃 掃

503 sō ha(ku)

Ⓒⓗ 扫 sǎo sào

Radical	Strokes
扌 64	11-3-8
Grade	**Freq**
Jōyō	1163
◧ 1 - 3 - 8	

3-8 扌

一 十 扌 扌 扫 扫 扫 掃 掃 掃 掃
1 2 3 4 5 6 7 8 9 10 11

▶**SWEEP**

COMPOUNDS

❶ [original meaning] **sweep, sweep away, brush, clean up**
掃除 *sōji* cleaning
掃射する *sōsha suru* sweep with fire, mow down
掃海 *sōkai* mine sweeping
清掃 *seisō* cleaning
❷ [formerly also 剿 1858] exterminate, wipe out
掃滅する *sōmetsu suru* wipe out, annihilate
掃討する *sōtō suru* wipe out (the enemy), clear
一掃する *issō suru* clean out, wipe out, dispel, eradicate

KUN

【ha(ku) 掃く】
① sweep, brush, clean up
掃き出す *hakidasu* sweep out
掃き集める *hakiatsumeru* sweep up together
② [also 刷く] brush, apply with a brush
紅を掃く *beni o haku* give [have] a brush of rouge (to one's cheeks)
③ gather silkworms
掃き立て *hakitate* being newly-swept; gathering silkworms from the egg paper

SYNONYMS

❶ **clean and wash**
払 CLEAR AWAY → 194
清 CLEAR → 523
粛 PURGE → 3581
浄 cleanse → 382
洗 WASH → 388
濯 RINSE → 793
浴 BATHE → 445

USAGE

haku
掃く
① sweep, brush, clean up
② [also 刷く] brush, apply with a brush
③ gather silkworms
刷く
[also 掃く] brush, apply with a brush

HOMOPHONES

haku ⇨ 刷 1273

3-8 扌

推 推 推

504 SUI o(su)

CH 推 tuī

Radical	Strokes
扌 64	11-3-8
Grade	**Freq**
Jōyō-6	622
1-3-8	

一 十 才 扌 扌 扌 扌 扌 推 推 推
1 2 3 4 5 6 7 8 9 10 11

▶INFER

COMPOUNDS

❶ **infer, deduce, conjecture, surmise, guess**
推定する *suitei suru* presume, infer
推理 *suiri* reasoning, inference
推測 *suisoku* conjecture, supposition
推察する *suisatsu suru* guess, conjecture, infer, imagine
推論 *suiron* reasoning, inference, induction, deduction
類推 *ruisui* analogy
邪推する *jasui suru* suspect without reason, mistrust

❷ **recommend, propose, nominate**
推薦する *suisen suru* recommend, nominate
推挙する *suikyo suru* recommend, nominate

❸ **propel, drive, push**
推進する *suishin suru* propel, drive; promote
推力 *suiryoku* thrust, driving force
推薬 *suiyaku* propellant

❹ change in succession
推移 *suii* transition, change

KUN

【o(su) 推す】
① infer, deduce, conjecture, surmise, guess
推して *oshite* by conjecture [deduction]
推し量る *oshihakaru* conjecture, surmise, guess
② recommend, propose, nominate
会長に推す *kaichō ni osu* recommend (a person) for the post of president

SYNONYMS

❶ **conjecture**
憶 SPECULATE → 765
測 CONJECTURE → 610
察 GUESS → 2347

❷ **recommend**
薦 RECOMMEND → 2373

❸ **force to move**
駆 DRIVE → 1823
押す PUSH → 314

HOMOPHONES

osu ⇨ 押 314 圧 2970

NOTE

⇨ see USAGE note at 押 314

3-8 扌

探 探 探

505 TAN sagu(ru) saga(su)

CH 探 tàn

Radical	Strokes
扌 64	11-3-8
Grade	**Freq**
Jōyō-6	1232
1-3-8	

一 十 才 扌 扌 扌 扌 扌 扌 探 探
1 2 3 4 5 6 7 8 9 10 11

▶PROBE ▶SEARCH

COMPOUNDS

❶ⓐ **probe, search into, explore, inquire**
ⓑ **search, look for**
探求 *tankyū* quest, search, pursuit
探究 *tankyū* investigation, search, inquiry
探査 *tansa* inquiry, investigation
探測 *tansoku* sounding, probing
探訪 *tanbō* (private) inquiry
探検(=探険) *tanken* exploration, expedition
探索 *tansaku* search, quest; inquiry, investigation
探鉱 *tankō* prospecting
探照灯 *tanshōtō* searchlight

❷ⓐ spy on, trace, detect
ⓑ [rare] spy
探偵 *tantei* detective work; detective, sleuth
探知 *tanchi* detection
独探 *dokutan* German spy

❸ visit, view, appreciate
探勝 *tanshō* sightseeing
探鳥 *tanchō* bird-watching

KUN

【sagu(ru) 探る】 probe, search into, explore
探り *saguri* sounding, probing; probe, stylet; spy
探り出す *saguridasu* spy out
手探り *tesaguri* groping

【saga(su) 探す】 [also 捜す] search for (something desired), search about, look for
探し回る *sagashimawaru* search about for
職探し *shokusagashi* job hunting

SYNONYMS

❶ⓐ **investigate and examine**

検 EXAMINE → 986
診 EXAMINE A PATIENT → 1504
調 INVESTIGATE → 1567
査 LOOK INTO → 2437
審 EXAMINE CAREFULLY → 2360
験 TEST → 1833
勘 CHECK → 1777
討 STUDY → 1456
察 INSPECT → 2347
究 STUDY EXHAUSTIVELY → 2203
閲 REVIEW → 3330
糾 INQUIRE INTO → 1278

ⓑ **seek**

捜 LOOK FOR → 432
索 SEARCH FOR → 2455
求 SEEK → 3550
猟 hunt for → 538

❷ⓐ **spy**

偵 SPY → 138

HOMOPHONES

sagasu ⇨ 捜 432

NOTE

⇨ see USAGE note at 捜 432

控 506

▶HOLD BACK
nonstandard for 控 495

3-8 扌

採 507

▶PICK ▶GATHER
nonstandard for 採 499

3-8 扌

接 508

▶CONTACT
nonstandard for 接 500

3-8 扌

捨 509

▶DISCARD
nonstandard for 捨 501

3-8 扌

掃 510

▶SWEEP
nonstandard for 掃 503

3-8 扌

挽

incorrect stroke count ⇨ see 427

3-8 扌

插

incorrect stroke count ⇨ see 598
(nonstandard for 挿 431)

3-8 扌

揷

incorrect stroke count ⇨ see 599
(nonstandard for 挿 431)

3-8 扌

3-8
氵

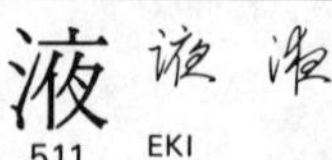

液 511 EKI

Ⓒⓗ 液 yè

Radical	Strokes
氵 85	11-3-8
Grade	**Freq**
Jōyō-5	1203
1 - 3 - 8	

丶 冫 氵 氵' 氵亠 氵广 氵疒 氵疒 液 液 液
1 2 3 4 5 6 7 8 9 10 11

▶**LIQUID**

COMPOUNDS

[also suffix]

ⓐ [original meaning] **liquid, fluid**

ⓑ **solution**

ⓒ bodily secretion, juice

液体 *ekitai* liquid, fluid
廃液 *haieki* waste fluid
血液 *ketsueki* blood
乳液 *nyūeki* milky lotion; latex
溶液 *yōeki* solution, solvent
消毒液 *shōdokueki* antiseptic solution
胃液 *ieki* gastric juice

INDEPENDENT

【eki 液】 liquid, fluid; secretion; juice, sap
液を絞る *eki o shiboru* squeeze the juice (from)

SYNONYMS

ⓐ **liquid**

汁 fluid → 195
水 WATER → 10

3-8
氵

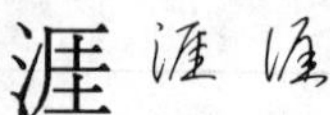

涯 512 GAI

Ⓒⓗ 涯 yá

Radical	Strokes
氵 85	11-3-8
Grade	**Freq**
Jōyō	1574
1 - 3 - 8	

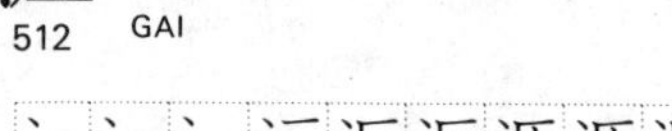

丶 冫 氵 氵一 氵厂 氵厂 氵厓 氵厓 涯 涯 涯
1 2 3 4 5 6 7 8 9 10 11

▶**OUTER LIMITS**

COMPOUNDS

❶ **outer limits, end, bound**

生涯 *shōgai* life, lifetime, career; for life
際涯 *saigai* limits, end, extremity
天涯 *tengai* far-off land (as remote as the horizon)

❷ [original meaning, now rare] water's edge, bank

水涯 *suigai* water's edge

SYNONYMS

❶ **extreme**

限 LIMIT → 398
極 EXTREME → 1017
窮 extremity → 2358
果て end → 3560

❶ **edges and boundaries**

縁 EDGE → 1386
端 edge → 1221
辺 border → 3029
境 BOUNDARY → 676
界 BOUNDS → 2563
際 VERGE → 714

COMPOUND FORMATION

生涯 *shōgai*

生涯 'life, etc.' denotes the limits (涯 ❶) of one's life (生), i.e., the period from birth to death.

3-8
氵

渋 澁 渋 渋

渋 513 JŪ shibu shibu(i) shibu(ru)

Ⓒⓗ 涩 sè

Radical	Strokes
氵 85	11-3-8
Grade	**Freq**
Jōyō	889
1 - 3 - 8	

丶 冫 氵 氵丨 氵卜 氵止 氵止 渋 渋 渋 渋
1 2 3 4 5 6 7 8 9 10 11

▶**NOT GO SMOOTHLY** ▶**ASTRINGENT**

COMPOUNDS

❶ⓐ [original meaning] **not go smoothly, make poor progress**

ⓑ difficult (to understand), abstruse

渋滞 *jūtai* delay, retardation, stagnation
苦渋 *kujū* distress, affliction
難渋 *nanjū* suffering, hardship

晦渋な *kaijū na* ambiguous, obscure, equivocal
❷ glum, sullen
渋面 *jūmen* sullen face

KUN

【**shibu** 渋】 astringent juice (of unripe persimmons), persimmon tannin
渋紙 *shibugami* tanned paper
茶渋 *chashibu* tea incrustations

【**shibu(i)** 渋い】
① astringent, puckery, rough—said esp. of the taste of unripe persimmons
渋柿 *shibugaki* puckery persimmon
渋い酒 *shibui sake* rough wine
② glum, sullen, wry
渋い顔をしている *shibui kao o shite iru* look sullen, be grim-faced
③ subdued, quiet, sober (color); refined, elegant
渋い色 *shibui iro* sober [quiet] color
渋い着物 *shibui kimono* tasteful dress
④ stingy, parsimonious
やり方が渋い *Yarikata ga shibui* He has stingy ways

【**shibu(ru)** 渋る】
① hang [hold] back, hesitate, be reluctant
渋渋 *shibushibu* reluctantly, grudgingly
言い渋る *iishiburu* be reluctant [unwilling] to say
答えを渋る *kotae o shiburu* hesitate to answer, be reluctant to answer
② suffer from loose bowels with a gripping pain
渋り腹 *shiburibara* painful loose bowels

SYNONYMS

❶ⓐ **stagnate**
滞 STAGNATE → 663

【**shibui**】
① **unsavory tastes**
酸 sour → 1563
辛 PUNGENT → 2038
苦 BITTER → 2243

【**shiburu**】
① **restrain**
控える HOLD BACK → 495
禁 PROHIBIT → 2795
制 CONTROL (restrain) → 1274
限 LIMIT → 398
抑 SUPPRESS → 257
束 TIE UP → 3554
縛 BIND → 1405

淳

514 JUN NAMES atsu atsushi kiyo kiyoshi makoto sunao

CH 淳 chún

Radical	Strokes
氵 85	11-3-8
Grade	Freq
Names	2012
1-3-8	

3-8 氵

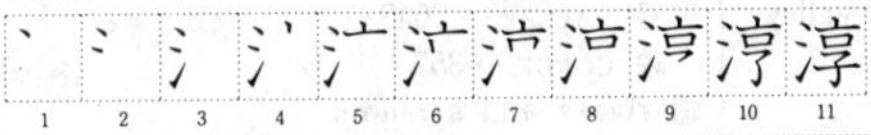

▶PUREHEARTED

COMPOUNDS

● purehearted, simple, innocent
淳良な *junryō na* simple and kind, innocent
淳朴(＝純朴) *junboku* simplicity and honesty

NAMES

淳子 *junko* female name
淳三郎 *junzaburō* male name

SYNONYMS

● **purehearted**
純 PURE → 1297
清 clean → 523
潔 IMMACULATE → 744
廉 INCORRUPT → 3153
敦 HONEST → 1693
惇 SINCERE → 486
直 straightforward → 2932

渇

515 KATSU kawa(ku)

CH 渴 kě

Radical	Strokes
氵 85	11-3-8
Grade	Freq
Jōyō	1859
1-3-8	

3-8 氵

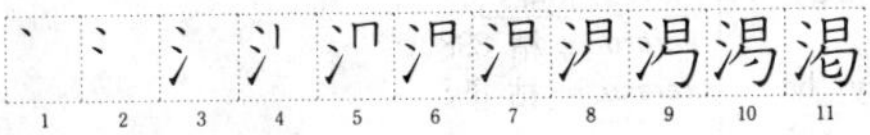

▶RUN DRY ▶THIRST

COMPOUNDS

❶ [original meaning] **run dry, dry up**
渇水 *kassui* water shortage
枯渇する *kokatsu suru* dry up, run dry; be exhausted, be depleted

❷ⓐ **thirst, be thirsty; thirst**
ⓑ thirst for, long for, crave
渇死する *kasshi suru* [archaic] die of thirst
飢渇 *kikatsu* hunger and thirst
渇望する *katsubō suru* thirst for, long for, crave
渇仰 *katsugō* adoration

INDEPENDENT

【katsu 渇】 thirst
渇を癒やす *katsu o iyasu* quench one's thirst
【kassuru 渇する】 be thirsty; dry up; thirst [long] for

KUN

【kawa(ku) 渇く】 be thirsty, thirst
渇き *kawaki* thirst
喉が渇く *nodo ga kawaku* be thirsty

SYNONYMS

❶ **dry**
燥 DRY UP → 1087
干 DRY → 3379
乾 DRY → 1679
❷ⓐ **hunger and thirst**
餓 STARVED → 1734
飢 STARVE → 1668
ⓑ **wish and desire**
慕 yearn for → 2353
懐 LONG FOR → 763
欲 DESIRE → 1475
求 SEEK → 3550
希 ASPIRE → 2049
望 HOPE → 2742
願 WISH → 1845

HOMOPHONES

kawaku ⇨ 乾 1679
kawaki ⇨ 乾 1679

NOTE

⇨ see USAGE note at 乾 1679

3-8
氵

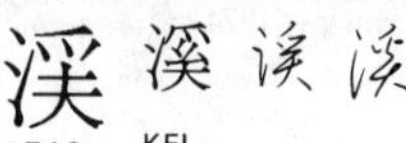

516 KEI

(CH) 溪 xī qī

Radical	Strokes
氵 85	11-3-8
Grade	Freq
Jōyō	1706
1 - 3 - 8	

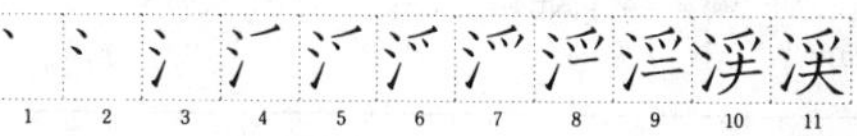

▶**RAVINE**

COMPOUNDS

ⓐ [also suffix] **ravine, valley**
ⓑ [original meaning] mountain stream, valley stream
渓谷 *keikoku* ravine, valley, canyon
渓間 *keikan* ravine
雪渓 *sekkei* snowy valley [ravine]
耶馬渓 *yabakei* Yabakei Valley
渓流 *keiryū* mountain stream
渓声 *keisei* sound of a valley stream

SYNONYMS

ⓐ **valley**
谷 VALLEY → 2043
峡 GORGE → 357
ⓑ **rivers and streams**
流 stream → 441
川 RIVER → 6
河 RIVER → 336
江 large river → 221

3-8
氵

517 KO ka(reru) ka(rasu)

(CH) 涸 hé

Radical	Strokes
氵 85	11-3-8
Grade	Freq
Reference	
1 - 3 - 8	

COMPOUNDS

● [now also 枯 *ko* 898] [original meaning] dry up, run dry
涸渇する *kokatsu suru* dry up, run dry; be exhausted, be depleted
涸れる *kareru* dry up, run dry, be exhausted
涸らす *karasu* dry up, exhaust

HOMOPHONES

kareru ⇨ 枯 898
karasu ⇨ 枯 898

NOTE

⇨ see USAGE note at 枯 898

淆

518 KŌ

CH 淆 xiáo

Radical	Strokes
氵 85	11-3-8
Grade	**Freq**
Reference	
1 - 3 - 8	

3-8 氵

COMPOUNDS

● [now replaced by 交 2015] [original meaning] intermingle, mix, blend

混淆する *konkō suru* mix up, jumble together

混 混 混

519 KON ma(jiru) -ma(jiri) ma(zaru) ma(zeru) ko(mu)▲

CH 混 hùn hún

Radical	Strokes
氵 85	11-3-8
Grade	**Freq**
Jōyō-5	838
1 - 3 - 8	

3-8 氵

▶**MIX**

COMPOUNDS

❶ⓐ (combine or cause to combine into an indistinguishable mass) **mix, blend, mingle**

ⓑ suffix indicating fabric of mixed composition

混血 *konketsu* mixed-blood, racial mixture
混合 *kongō* mixing, mixture
混声合唱 *konsei-gasshō* mixed chorus
混紡 *konbō* mixed spinning
混浴 *kon'yoku* mixed bathing
二十パーセント麻混の綿 *nijuppāsento asakon no men* cotton mixed with 20% hemp

❷ **mixed up, confused, disorderly, chaotic**

混雑 *konzatsu* confusion, disorder, congestion
混乱 *konran* disorder, confusion, chaos
混同 *kondō* confusion; mixing
混迷 *konmei* confusion, bewilderment
混沌 *konton* [sometimes also 渾沌] chaos

❸ [also 渾 606] unified in an integrated whole, entire, complete

混然一体となる *konzen'ittai to naru* be joined together, form a complete whole

❹ [formerly 昏 2418] lose consciousness, faint

混迷 *konmei* stupor, unconsciousness

KUN

【ma(jiru) 混じる】 *vi* be blended, get mixed (with the constituents blending into each other)

混じり合う *majiriau* be blended, be mixed together
混じり気 *majirike* a dash of (something), impurity

【-ma(jiri) -混じり】 [also suffix] mingling of

雨混じりの雪 *amemajiri no yuki* snow mingled with rain
鼻歌混じりで働く *hanautamajiri de hataraku* work while humming a tune

【ma(zaru) 混ざる】 same as **majiru 混じる**

混ざり物 *mazarimono* impurity

【ma(zeru) 混ぜる】

vt

ⓐ (combine together into a single mass) blend, mix, adulterate

ⓑ mix by stirring, scramble, toss, churn

混ぜ合わす *mazeawasu* mix together; blend, compound
混ぜ返す *mazekaesu* banter, make fun of (what a person says)
掻き混ぜる(＝掻き交ぜる) *kakimazeru* mix by stirring, mix up, scramble, toss, churn

【ko(mu) 混む】 [usu. 込む] be crowded, be congested, be packed

混み合う *komiau* be crowded, be packed, be jammed
人混み *hitogomi* crowd [throng] (of people)

SYNONYMS

❶ⓐ **mix**

交 intermingle → 2015
雑 MIXED → 1385
錯 MIXED UP → 1743

❷ **disordered**

錯 MIXED UP → 1743
雑 mixed up → 1385
乱 DISORDERED → 1260
紛 CONFUSED → 1296

USAGE

❶ **majiru**

混じる

vi be blended, get mixed (with the constituents blending into each other)

交じる

vi be mingled, be mixed, intermingle (with

the constituents remaining distinct)
★混じる and 交じる are often used interchangeably.

❷ **mazaru**
混ざる
same as 混じる *majiru*
交ざる
same as 交じる *majiru*

❸ **mazeru**
混ぜる
vt
ⓐ (combine together into a single mass) blend, mix, adulterate
ⓑ mix by stirring, scramble, toss, churn
交ぜる
vt (combine together, with the constituents remaining distinct) mix, shuffle

HOMOPHONES
majiru ⇨ 交 2015
mazaru ⇨ 交 2015
mazeru ⇨ 交 2015
komu ⇨ 込 3030

NOTE
⇨ see also USAGE note at 込 3030

3-8
氵

淋
520 RIN sabi(shii) sami(shii)

CH 淋 lín lìn

Radical	Strokes
氵 85	11-3-8
Grade	**Freq**
Reference	
◧ 1-3-8	

COMPOUNDS
❶ [usu. 寂しい *sabishii, samishii*]
ⓐ lonesome, lonely, desolate, deserted
ⓑ scarce, scanty
淋しがる *sabishigaru* feel lonely, miss someone
懐が淋しい *futokoro ga sabishii* have a scanty supply of money
❷ gonorrhea
淋病 *rinbyō* gonorrhea
淋菌 *rinkin* gonococcus
❸ used phonetically for *rin*
淋巴 *rinpa* lymph
❹ [original meaning] drip (with sweat), drench, pour
淋漓たる *rinritaru* brimming, dripping

HOMOPHONES
sabishii ⇨ 寂 2290
samishii ⇨ 寂 2290

NOTE
⇨ see USAGE note at 寂 2290

3-8
氵

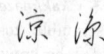

涼 
521 RYŌ suzu(shii) suzu(mu)

1 2 3 4 5 6 7 8 9 10 11

CH 涼 liáng liàng

Radical	Strokes
氵 85	11-3-8
Grade	**Freq**
Jōyō	1554
◧ 1-3-8	

▶**COOL**

COMPOUNDS
❶ⓐ **cool, refreshing**
ⓑ the cool, cool evening air
涼気 *ryōki* cool air
涼風 *ryōfū* cool breeze
涼味 *ryōmi* coolness, cool
清涼な *seiryō na* cool, refreshing
冷涼 *reiryō* coolness
納涼 *nōryō* enjoying the evening cool
❷ [also 寥 2346] desolate, deserted, empty
荒涼たる *kōryōtaru* desolate, dreary

INDEPENDENT
【ryō 涼】 the cool, the evening cool
涼を取る *ryō o toru* enjoy the cool breeze

KUN
【suzu(shii) 涼しい】 cool, refreshing
涼しさ *suzushisa* coolness
涼しい顔 *suzushii kao* nonchalant (unruffled) air
【suzu(mu) 涼む】 cool oneself, enjoy the cool breeze
涼み *suzumi* cooling oneself, enjoying the cool air
涼み台 *suzumidai* bench

SYNONYMS
❶ⓐ **cold**
冷 COLD → 80
寒 COLD (weather) → 2311

済 濟 済 済

522 SAI SEI▲ su(mu) -zu(mi) -zumi su(manai) su(masu) -su(masu)

㊥ 済 jì jǐ

Radical	Strokes
氵 85	11-3-8
Grade	**Freq**
Jōyō-6	273
◧ 1 - 3 - 8	

▶**SETTLE** ▶**RELIEVE**

COMPOUNDS

❶ⓐ **settle accounts, pay back, clear**
ⓑ **settle, conclude, finish**
返済する *hensai suru* repay, reimburse
決済 *kessai* settlement of accounts
弁済 *bensai* repayment, payment, settlement
既済の *kisai no* paid up, already settled
完済 *kansai* full payment, liquidation
未済の *misai no* unsettled, unpaid, outstanding; unfinished

❷ **relieve, aid, save, redeem**
済民 *saimin* relieving the sufferings of the people
済度 *saido Buddhism* salvation
経済 *keizai* economy, economics
救済する *kyūsai suru* relieve, help, save, deliver
共済 *kyōsai* mutual aid

❸ numerous
多士済済 *tashi-seisei* (=*tashi-saisai*) galaxy of intellectuals

KUN

【**su(mu)** 済む】 be settled, end, be concluded; do [manage] (without), get off (with)
済み *sumi* being settled
行かずに済む *ikazu ni sumu* need not go
少しの損で済む *sukoshi no son de sumu* get off with a little loss

【**-zu(mi)** -済み, **-zumi** -済】 [suffix] completed, finished, settled, concluded
支払い済み *shiharaizumi* paid, settled
点検済み *tenkenzumi* inspection completed, checked up
使用済みの切手 *shiyōzumi no kitte* used stamps

【**su(manai)** 済まない】 inexcusable, unpardonable
済みません *Sumimasen* Excuse me / I am sorry

【**su(masu)** 済ます】 settle, finish, bring to a conclusion, get through with; make shift, manage (with), make (a thing) do [serve the purpose]
勘定を済ます *kanjō o sumasu* pay one's bill
仕事を済ます *shigoto o sumasu* finish one's work
無しで済ます *nashi de sumasu* do without

【**-su(masu)** -済ます】 [also -澄ます] [verbal suffix] perform an action well [perfectly]
成り済ます *narisumasu* successfully impersonate

SYNONYMS

❶ⓐ **pay**
払う PAY → 194
納 PAY (to the authorities) → 1300
支 pay out → 1979
賦 INSTALLMENT → 1583
償 RECOMPENSE → 176
ⓑ **end**
了 FINISH → 3350
-上げる completion suffix → 3404
完 COMPLETE → 2201
結 CONCLUDE → 1348
終 END → 1336
絶 COME TO AN END → 1353
閉 CLOSE → 3319
❷ **rescue**
救 SAVE → 1497
❷ **help**
助 HELP → 1121
佑 HELP (said esp. of God) → 74
祐 DIVINE HELP → 915
援 AID → 586
佐 ASSIST → 67
補 assist → 1194
輔 ASSIST → 1559

HOMOPHONES

-*sumasu* ⇨ 澄 740

NOTE

⇨ see USAGE note at 澄 740
⇨ see COMPOUND FORMATION for 経済 *keizai* ⇨ 経 1331

3-8 清 清 清 清 ⓒⒽ 清 qīng

氵

523 SEI SHŌ SHIN▲ kiyo(i) kiyo(maru) kiyo(meru)

Radical	Strokes
氵 85	11-3-8
Grade	**Freq**
Jōyō-4	624
1-3-8	

▶**CLEAR**

COMPOUNDS

❶ⓐ (of liquids) **clear, unmixed**
ⓑ (of the weather) clear
清水 *seisui* pure [clear] water
清流 *seiryū* clear [limpid] stream
清酒 *seishu* (refined) sake
血清 *kessei* serum
河清 *kasei* clearing of the river water
清澄な *seichō na* clear, lucid; serene
清秋 *seishū* clear fall (weather)
❷ (of sounds) unvoiced, voiceless
清音 *seion* unvoiced sound
清子音 *seishiin* voiceless consonant
❸ⓐ (rid of impurities) **clear, clean**
ⓑ **clear up, settle (a debt)**
清掃 *seisō* cleaning
六根清浄 *rokkon-shōjō* purification of one's self through detachment from the senses
清算 *seisan* settlement, liquidation; clearing (off)
粛清 *shukusei* purge, purging, liquidation
❹ⓐ (free from dirt or impurities) **clean, pure, neat**
ⓑ (free from moral taint) **clean, honest, pure, honorable**
清潔 *seiketsu* cleanliness, neatness, purity
清浄 *seijō* purity, cleanness
清書 *seisho* fair [clean] copy
清純な *seijun na* pure (and innocent)
清楚な *seiso na* neat and clean, tidy, trim
清濁 *seidaku* purity and impurity; good and evil
清廉 *seiren* integrity, honesty, uprightness
清貧 *seihin* honest [honorable] poverty
清教徒 *seikyōto* Puritan
❺ cool, refreshing, clean
清新の *seishin no* fresh, new
清涼な *seiryō na* cool, refreshing
清風 *seifū* cool [refreshing] breeze
清清する *seisei suru* feel refreshed, feel relieved
❻ quiet, tranquil
清閑 *seikan* quiet, tranquility
清聴 *seichō* your kind attention (to my talk)
❼ Qing Dynasty, Manchu Dynasty (1644-1912 A.D.)
清国 *shinkoku* China under the Manchus
日清戦争 *nisshin sensō* the Sino-Japanese War (of 1894-95)

INDEPENDENT

【shin 清】 Qing Dynasty, Manchu Dynasty

KUN

【kiyo(i) 清い】 (free from dirt or impurities) clean, pure, neat; (free from moral taint) clean, honest, pure, honorable
清らかな *kiyoraka na* same as **kiyoi 清い**
清い月影 *kiyoi tsukikage* clear moon, beautiful moonlight
清い愛 *kiyoi ai* pure [platonic] love

【kiyo(maru) 清まる】 be purified, be cleansed
心が清まる *kokoro ga kiyomaru* feel purified

【kiyo(meru) 清める】
①ⓐ [sometimes also 浄める] (rid of dirt or impurities) cleanse, purify
ⓑ [usu. 浄める] (rid of moral taint) purify, purge
清め *kiyome* purification, ablution
② [sometimes also 浄める] exorcise
身を清める *mi o kiyomeru* cleanse oneself

SPECIAL READINGS

清水 *shimizu* spring water

SYNONYMS

❶ⓐ **clear**
明 CLEAR (unclouded) → 855
朗 CLEAR (sky) → 1325
冴える CRISP AND CLEAR → 79
澄 LIMPID → 740
透 TRANSPARENT → 3108
❸ **clean and wash**
浄 cleanse → 382
粛 PURGE → 3581
払 CLEAR AWAY → 194
掃 SWEEP → 503
洗 WASH → 388
濯 RINSE → 793
浴 BATHE → 445
❹ⓐ **clean and purified**
浄 CLEAN → 382
純 PURE → 1297
潔 IMMACULATE → 744
粋 REFINED (free from impurities) → 1293
精 refined (purified) → 1366
ⓑ **purehearted**
純 PURE → 1297
淳 PUREHEARTED → 514
潔 IMMACULATE → 744

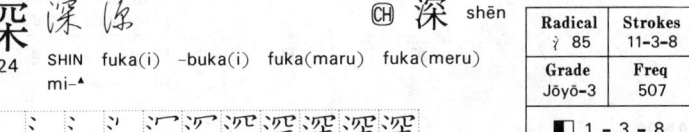

廉 INCORRUPT → 3153
敦 HONEST → 1693
惇 SINCERE → 486
直 straightforward → 2932
❼ **later Chinese dynasties**
明 Ming Dynasty → 855
元 Yuan Dynasty → 1929
唐 TANG DYNASTY → 3115

USAGE

kiyomeru

清める
①ⓐ [sometimes also 浄める] (rid of dirt or impurities) cleanse, purify
ⓑ [usu. 浄める] (rid of moral taint) purify, purge
② [sometimes also 浄める] exorcise

浄める
①ⓐ [usu. 清める] (rid of dirt or impurities) cleanse, purify
ⓑ [sometimes also 清める] (rid of moral taint) purify, purge
② [usu. 清める] exorcise

HOMOPHONES

kiyomeru ⇨ 浄 382

深 524

SHIN fuka(i) -buka(i) fuka(maru) fuka(meru) mi-▲

CH 深 shēn

Radical	Strokes
氵 85	11-3-8
Grade	**Freq**
Jōyō-3	507
1-3-8	

3-8 氵

▶**DEEP**

COMPOUNDS

❶ⓐ [original meaning] (extending downward) **deep**
ⓑ (extending inward) **deep, distant, inmost, secluded**
ⓒ depth
深海 *shinkai* deep sea
深耕 *shinkō* deep plowing
深部 *shinbu* deep part, depth
深呼吸 *shinkokyū* deep breathing
深山幽谷に *shinzan-yūkoku ni* deep in the mountains
深窓 *shinsō* secluded inner room
水深 *suishin* depth of water

❷ⓐ (difficult to fathom) **deep, profound, unfathomable, innermost**
ⓑ (of great intensity) **deep, intense, extreme, profound**
ⓒ [also prefix] **deep-colored, dark**
ⓓ **in the deep [dead] of night, late at night**
深遠 *shin'en* profundity, depth
深奥 *shin'ō* esoteric doctrines, mysteries, depth
深刻な *shinkoku na* serious, grave, keen, poignant
深甚なる *shinjinnaru* deep, extreme
深謝 *shinsha* deep gratitude, sincere apology
深緑 *shinryoku* dark [deep] green
深紅色 *shinkōshoku* deep crimson, scarlet
深夜 *shin'ya* dead of night, midnight
深更 *shinkō* dead of night, midnight

❸ (characterized by deep friendship) intimate, close, friendly, kind
深交 *shinkō* close friendship
深切(＝親切) *shinsetsu* kindness

KUN

【fuka(i) 深い】 deep, inmost, distant; profound, deep; intense, profound; deep-colored, dark; late (in the season); close, intimate; thick, dense
深さ *fukasa* depth; profundity
深み *fukami* depth, the deep; profundity
奥深い *okubukai* (＝*okufukai*) deep, profound; esoteric
深い愛情 *fukai aijō* deep affection
深い関係 *fukai kankei* close connection
深緑色 *fukamidoriiro* dark [deep] green
深い霧 *fukai kiri* thick [dense] fog

【-buka(i) -深い】 [also suffix] deep, intense
根深い *nebukai* deep-rooted, ingrained
興味深い *kyōmibukai* of great interest

【fuka(maru) 深まる】 *vi* deepen, become deeper
秋が深まって冬になった *Aki ga fukamatte fuyu ni natta* Autumn deepened into winter

【fuka(meru) 深める】 *vt* deepen, heighten, intensify, strengthen
理解を深める *rikai o fukameru* cultivate a better understanding

【mi- 深-】 [also prefix] indicates elegance or euphony
深山 *miyama* mountain recesses
深雪 *miyuki* deep snow

SYNONYMS

❶ⓑ **inner**
奥 inner → 2824
幽 QUIET AND SECLUDED → 3008

❷ⓐ **profound**
奥 inmost → 2824
幽 deep hidden → 3008

玄 PROFOUND → 1991
ⓑ **extreme in degree**
高 HIGH → 2097
大 BIG → 3416
重 HEAVY → 3573
強 STRONG → 475
超 super- → 3313
甚 EXTREMELY → 2643
切 keen → 27
痛 bitter(ly) → 3285
極 EXTREME → 1017
激 intense → 776
厳 SEVERE → 3289
酷 SEVERE → 1562
ⓒ **dark-colored**
暗 DARK → 1010
濃 dark → 777

3-8
氵

渚 渚 渚 渚

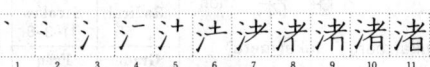

525 SHO nagisa

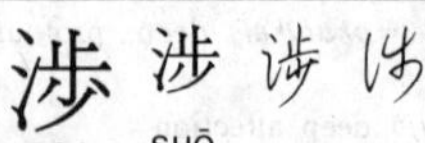

CH 渚 zhǔ

Radical	Strokes
氵 85	11-3-8
Grade	Freq
Names	2080
1 - 3 - 8	

▶**STRAND**

COMPOUNDS

❶ **strand, beach, waterside, shore**
渚畔 *shohan* [archaic] waterside, shore
❷ [original meaning, now archaic] sand bar in a river
汀渚 *teisho* water's edge; sand bar

KUN

【**nagisa** 渚】strand, beach, waterside, shore
渚伝い *nagisazutai* along the shore

NAMES

渚 *nagisa* surname also female name

SYNONYMS

❶ **shores and watersides**
磯 ROCKY BEACH → 1242
浦 SEASIDE → 437
岸 SHORE → 2236
浜 BEACH → 436
-辺 -side → 3029
畔 WATERSIDE → 1145

3-8
氵

渉 渉 渉 渉

526 SHŌ

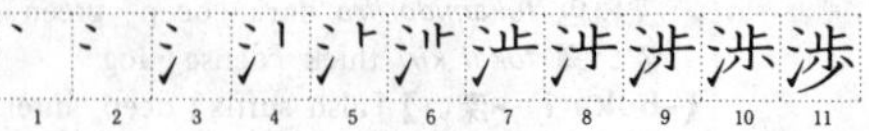

CH 涉 shè

Radical	Strokes
氵 85	11-3-8
Grade	Freq
Jōyō	717
1 - 3 - 8	

▶**HAVE RELATIONS WITH**

COMPOUNDS

❶ **have relations [connections] with, relate, interrelate**
渉外 *shōgai* public relations
交渉 *kōshō* negotiation, bargaining, discussion
干渉 *kanshō* interference, intervention
❷ [original meaning] wade (across water), ford
渉禽類 *shōkinrui* wading birds
徒渉 *toshō* wading, fording
❸ wander about in search for something
渉猟 *shōryō* searching far and wide (for); extensive reading

SYNONYMS

❶ **relate**
関 CONCERN → 3328
係 CONNECT → 97
絡 INTERLINK → 1351
連 LINK → 3103
❷ **cross**
渡 CROSS → 611
越 GO BEYOND → 3314
❷ **move through water**
泳 SWIM → 327

淑 㳙 𣳡

527 SHUKU shito(yaka)▲

(CH) 淑 shū

Radical	Strokes
氵 85	11-3-8
Grade	**Freq**
Jōyō	1775
1 - 3 - 8	

3-8 氵

Stroke order: 丶 冫 氵 氵 汁 汁 汁 汁 洙 淑 淑 (1–11)

▶GRACEFUL

COMPOUNDS

❶ (of women) **graceful, gentle and kind, refined, fair**

淑徳 *shukutoku* feminine grace, womanly virtues

淑女 *shukujo* lady, gentlewoman

貞淑 *teishuku* chastity, female virtue

❷ adore, respect

私淑する *shishuku suru* adore, look up to

KUN

【shito(yaka) 淑やか】

shitoyaka na 淑やかな graceful, gentle, modest

淑やかさ *shitoyaka sa* grace, gentleness, modesty

SYNONYMS

❶ **elegant**

優 graceful → 177

雅 ELEGANT → 1197

粋 REFINED → 1293

彬 REFINED AND GENTLE → 960

淡 淡 淡

528 TAN awa(i)

(CH) 淡 dàn

Radical	Strokes
氵 85	11-3-8
Grade	**Freq**
Jōyō	1487
1 - 3 - 8	

3-8 氵

Stroke order: 丶 冫 氵 氵 氵 氵 氵 淡 淡 淡 淡 (1–11)

▶LIGHT

COMPOUNDS

❶ⓐ [also prefix] **light-colored, faint, pale**

ⓑ light-flavored, plain, not flavored

淡色 *tanshoku* light color

淡彩 *tansai* light color

淡紅色 *tankōshoku* pink, rose pink

濃淡 *nōtan* light and shade

淡白(=淡泊)な *tanpaku na* light (color, taste); plain, simple; indifferent

❷ indifferent, unconcerned, disinterested

淡淡たる *tantantaru* indifferent, unconcerned

冷淡な *reitan na* cool, indifferent

❸ (not saline) fresh (water)

淡水 *tansui* fresh water

淡湖 *tanko* freshwater lake

KUN

【awa(i) 淡い】 light (color, flavor), faint; fleeting, transitory

淡さ *awasa* faintness, lightness

淡雪 *awayuki* light snow

淡い悲しみ *awai kanashimi* fleeting sorrow

SYNONYMS

❶ⓐ **light-colored**

浅 light → 389

薄い pale → 2370

鈍- DULL → 1689

添 添 添 添

529 TEN so(eru) so(u)

(CH) 添 tiān

Radical	Strokes
氵 85	11-3-8
Grade	**Freq**
Jōyō	1354
1 - 3 - 8	

3-8 氵

Stroke order: 丶 冫 氵 汇 汇 汘 沃 添 添 添 添 (1–11)

▶ADD TO

COMPOUNDS

❶ **add to, append, affix, accompany**

添加する *tenka suru* add, annex, append

添削 *tensaku* correction

添付する *tenpu suru* attach, append, annex

添書 *tensho* accompanying letter

❷ **accompany, go along with, attend on**

添乗員 *tenjōin* (escort) courier, tour conductor

KUN

【**so(eru)** 添える】 add to, attach to, accompany; garnish

添え物 *soemono* addition, supplement; garnishing

添え書き *soegaki* postscript, additional writing

介添え *kaizoe* assistance; helper, assistant, best man or bridesmaid

力添え *chikarazoe* aid, help, assistance

手紙を添える *tegami o soeru* attach a letter to

パセリを添える *paseri o soeru* garnish (a dish) with parsley

【**so(u)** 添う】

① accompany, go along with, stay with

添い寝 *soine* sleeping with (one's child)

付き添い *tsukisoi* attendance; attendant, escort

② marry

連れ添う *tsuresou* be man and wife, be married to

③ meet (someone's wishes), suit

人の要求に添う *hito no yōkyū ni sou* meet one's demands

④ add to, increase

趣が添う *omomuki ga sou* add color to

SYNONYMS

❶ **add to**

追 add → 3096

加 ADD → 38

付 ATTACH → 31

附 ATTACH → 347

❷ **accompany**

伴 ACCOMPANY → 60

陪 ACCOMPANY A SUPERIOR → 539

侍 ATTEND UPON → 85

従 FOLLOW → 415

随 FOLLOW → 627

HOMOPHONES

sou ⇨ 沿 328

NOTE

⇨ see USAGE note at 沿 328

3-8 氵 淨 530

▶**CLEAN**

nonstandard for 浄 382

3-8 氵 淚 531

▶**TEAR**

nonstandard for 涙 440

3-8 氵 淸 532

▶**CLEAR**

nonstandard for 清 523

3-8 氵 淺 533

▶**SHALLOW**

nonstandard for 浅 389

3-8 氵 添 534

▶**ADD TO**

nonstandard for 添 529

3-8 氵 渡

incorrect stroke count ⇨ see 611

3-8 氵 游

incorrect stroke count ⇨ see 614

猫 猫 猫 猫

535 BYŌ neko

㊥ 猫 māo máo

Radical	Strokes
犭 94	11-3-8
Grade	**Freq**
Jōyō	1742
◧ 1 - 3 - 8	

3-8 犭

丿 犭 犭 犭一 犭十 犭艹 犭艹 猫 猫 猫 猫
1 2 3 4 5 6 7 8 9 10 11

▶**CAT**

COMPOUNDS

● [original meaning] **cat**

猫額大の土地 *byōgakudai no tochi* narrow strip of land

愛猫家 *aibyōka* cat lover

KUN

【neko 猫】 [also suffix] cat; feline, catlike; clay foot warmer; wheelbarrow; *slang* geisha girl

猫科 *nekoka* cat family, Felidae

子猫 *koneko* kitten

ペルシャ猫 *perushaneko* Persian cat

猫背 *nekoze* stoop, bent back

猫撫で声で *nekonadegoe de* in a soft coaxing voice

猫被り *nekokaburi* hypocrisy, false modesty; hypocrite, wolf in a lamb's skin

SYNONYMS

● **domesticated mammals**

犬 DOG → 3464

牛 CATTLE → 3452

馬 HORSE → 3296

豚 PIG → 976

羊 SHEEP → 2183

猪 猪 猪 猪

536 CHO inoshishi i

㊥ 猪 zhū

Radical	Strokes
犭 94	11-3-8
Grade	**Freq**
Names	2007
◧ 1 - 3 - 8	

3-8 犭

丿 犭 犭 犭一 犭十 犭土 犭耂 犭者 猪 猪 猪
1 2 3 4 5 6 7 8 9 10 11

▶**WILD BOAR**

COMPOUNDS

ⓐ [original meaning] **wild boar, boar**

ⓑ as daring and reckless as a wild boar

野猪 *yacho* wild boar

猪突 *chototsu* recklessness, foolhardiness

KUN

【inoshishi 猪】 wild boar; reckless fellow, daredevil

猪武者 *inoshishimusha* foolhardy warrior; hotspur

【i 猪】 [in compounds] wild boar

猪首 *ikubi* bull neck

NAMES

猪木 *inoki* surname

猪苗代 *inawashiro* place name

SYNONYMS

ⓐ **swine**

亥 THE BOAR → 2012

豚 PIG → 976

ⓐ **undomesticated mammals**

象 ELEPHANT → 2134

熊 BEAR → 2848

虎 TIGER → 3212

鹿 DEER → 3126

猿 MONKEY → 669

鯨 WHALE → 1882

USAGE

i

猪

[in compounds] wild boar

亥

twelfth sign of the Oriental zodiac: the Boar

HOMOPHONES

i ⇨ 亥 2012

3-8 犭

猛 猛 猛

537 MŌ

CH 猛 měng

Radical	Strokes
犭 94	11-3-8
Grade	**Freq**
Jōyō	1284

1 - 3 - 8

Stroke order: 1 2 3 4 5 6 7 8 9 10 11

▶FIERCE

COMPOUNDS

❶ⓐ [original meaning] (having a ferocious nature) **fierce, violent, savage, ferocious**

ⓑ [also prefix] (extremely severe) **fierce, violent; heavy, hard, intensive**

猛犬 *mōken* fierce [ferocious] dog
猛獣 *mōjū* fierce [savage] animal [beast]
獰猛な *dōmō na* fierce, ferocious
猛烈な *mōretsu na* violent, vehement, fierce
猛然と *mōzen to* fiercely
猛毒 *mōdoku* deadly poison
猛爆 *mōbaku* heavy bombing
猛襲 *mōshū* fierce attack
猛練習 *mōrenshū* hard training

❷ brave

猛将 *mōshō* brave general, brave warrior
勇猛な *yūmō na* daring, brave, valiant

SPECIAL READINGS

猛者 *mosa* stalwart; veteran

SYNONYMS

❶ⓐ **violent**

暴 VIOLENT → 2515
荒い WILD → 2260

ⓑ **extreme in power**

烈 VEHEMENT → 2652
激 VIOLENT → 776
荒 WILD → 2260
狂 raging → 269

3-8 犭

猟 獵 猟 猟

538 RYŌ

CH 猎 liè

Radical	Strokes
犭 94	11-3-8
Grade	**Freq**
Jōyō	1690

1 - 3 - 8

Stroke order: 1 2 3 4 5 6 7 8 9 10 11

▶HUNTING

COMPOUNDS

❶ [original meaning] **hunting, shooting**

猟季 *ryōki* hunting season
猟銃 *ryōjū* hunting gun
猟犬 *ryōken* hound, hunting dog
狩猟 *shuryō* hunting, hunt
銃猟 *jūryō* shooting, hunting
禁猟 *kinryō* prohibition of shooting [hunting]

❷ hunt for, search for, seek

猟奇 *ryōki* bizarrerie hunting
猟色 *ryōshoku* lewdness, debauchery
渉猟 *shōryō* searching far and wide (for); extensive reading

INDEPENDENT

【ryō 猟】 hunting, shooting; game
猟をする *ryō o suru* hunt, shoot

SYNONYMS

❶ **hunt and fish**

狩 HUNT → 397
獲 CATCH GAME → 779
漁 FISH → 698
釣 ANGLE → 1674

❷ **seek**

求 SEEK → 3550
捜 LOOK FOR → 432
索 SEARCH FOR → 2455
探 SEARCH → 505

陪 陪 陪 陪

539 BAI

Ⓒⓗ 陪 péi

Radical	Strokes
阝 170	11-3-8
Grade	**Freq**
Jōyō	1881
1-3-8	

3-8 阝

▶ACCOMPANY A SUPERIOR

COMPOUNDS

❶ **accompany a superior, perform an action in the company of a superior, keep company with a person of rank, attend upon**

陪席 *baiseki* sitting with one's superior

陪従する *baijū suru* wait upon, attend on, accompany

陪食 *baishoku* dining with a superior

陪乗する *baijō suru* ride in the same carriage [car] (with a superior), attend on (one's superior) in the same carriage

陪審 *baishin* jury

陪侍 *baiji* attending on the nobility; retainer

❷ retainer's retainer, rear vassal

陪臣 *baishin* rear vassal, vassal's vassal, daimyo's retainer

SYNONYMS

❶ **accompany**

伴 ACCOMPANY → 60

添 accompany → 529

侍 ATTEND UPON → 85

従 FOLLOW → 415

随 FOLLOW → 627

COMPOUND FORMATION

陪審 *baishin*

陪審 'jury' refers to a group of people attending on (陪 ❶) the judge and aiding him in trying (審).

NOTE

★do not confuse with 部 1676

陳 陳 陳

540 CHIN

Ⓒⓗ 陈 chén

Radical	Strokes
阝 170	11-3-8
Grade	**Freq**
Jōyō	1267
1-3-8	

3-8 阝

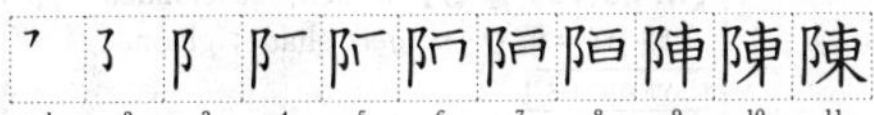

▶SET FORTH

COMPOUNDS

❶ **set forth, state, explain, declare**

陳情 *chinjō* petition, appeal

陳述する *chinjutsu suru* state, set forth, declare, expound

陳謝 *chinsha* apology

開陳する *kaichin suru* state, express (one's opinion)

❷ [original meaning] **lay out (for exhibit), put on display, spread out**

陳列する *chinretsu suru* exhibit, display

出陳 *shutchin* submitting (something) to an exhibition

❸ old, stale

陳腐な *chinpu na* old-fashioned, trite, worn-out

新陳代謝（＝代謝）*shinchintaisha* (＝*taisha*) metabolism; renewal, regeneration

❹ Chen Dynasty (557-589 A.D.)

INDEPENDENT

【chin 陳】 Chen Dynasty

【chinzuru 陳ずる】 state, declare, expound

SYNONYMS

❶ **speak and say**

述 STATE → 3075

弁 SPEAK ELOQUENTLY → 2004

申す SPEAK HUMBLY → 3507

語る TELL → 1543

談 TALK → 1569

口 give mouth to → 3382

話 SPEAK → 1527

言 SAY → 1941

云 say → 1931

❷ **display**

展 DISPLAY → 3111

掲 PUT UP → 494

❷ **arrange**

列 arrange in a row → 824

羅 spread out → 2622

揃える arrange properly → 590

整 PUT IN ORDER → 2871

理 put in order → 970

並 LINE UP → 2246

比 rank → 26

NOTE
⇨ see COMPOUND FORMATION for 代謝(=新陳代謝) *taisha* (=*shinchintaisha*) ⇨ 謝 1620
★do not confuse with 陣 455

3-8
阝

陰 陰 陰

541 IN kage kage(ru)

CH 阴 yīn

Radical	Strokes
阝 170	11-3-8
Grade	**Freq**
Jōyō	1355
1-3-8	

1 2 3 4 5 6 7 8 9 10 11

▶SHADE

COMPOUNDS

❶ **shade**
陰影 *in'ei* shadow
緑陰 *ryokuin* shade of trees
樹陰 *juin* [rare] shade of a tree

❷ [original meaning] shaded or north side of a mountain; south side of a stream
山陰 *san'in* shaded or north side of a mountain; Sanin District

❸ⓐ shaded, dark
ⓑ become cloudy, be overcast
陰湿な *inshitsu na* dark and damp, dampish
夜陰 *yain* darkness of the night, shades of night
陰晴 *insei* fine weather and cloudy weather

❹ in the shades, hidden, secret, unseen
陰謀 *inbō* scheme, plot, conspiracy
陰徳 *intoku* secret charity

❺ **gloomy, melancholy, dejected**
陰気 *inki* gloominess, cheerlessness
陰鬱 *in'utsu* gloominess, melancholy
陰惨 *insan* sadness and gloom

❻ sex [reproductive] organ, esp. the female genital organ
陰部 *inbu* private parts, sex organ
陰唇 *inshin* labium
陰茎 *inkei* penis

❼ yin: the female and passive principle in Chinese dualistic philosophy representing negative concepts such as femininity, moon, darkness, earth, etc.
陰陽 *in'yō* yin and yang, positive and negative, active and passive

❽ⓐ **negative**
ⓑ *elec* **negative pole**
陰性 *insei* negative, dormant
陰電気 *indenki* negative electricity

❾ moon
陰暦 *inreki* lunar calendar
太陰 *taiin* moon

❿ time
光陰 *kōin* time, Father Time

INDEPENDENT

【in 陰】 yin (⇨ ❼); concealed, gloomy
陰に陽に *in ni yō ni* openly and covertly, implicitly and explicitly

KUN

【kage 陰】
① [formerly also 蔭] shade
日陰 *hikage* the shade
② [formerly also 蔭]
ⓐ back side, reverse side
ⓑ behind the scenes
戸の陰に隠れる *to no kage ni kakureru* hide behind a door
陰で *kage de* behind one's back
陰口 *kageguchi* backbiting
③ [also 蔭] [in the form of お陰 *okage*] grace, favor
お陰で *okage de* thanks to; due to
お陰様で助かりました *Okagesama de tasukarimashita* Thank you for your kind assistance

【kage(ru) 陰る】 darken, be clouded
陰り(=翳り) *kageri* shade; gloom

SYNONYMS

❶ **shadow**
影 SHADOW → 1889

❸ⓐ **dark**
暗 DARK → 1010
黒 BLACK → 2740

❺ **sad and depressed**
沈 depressed → 261
愁 MELANCHOLY → 2829
哀 sorrowful → 2068
悲 SAD → 2775
寂 LONESOME → 2290
惨 MISERABLE → 483

❻ **genitals**
胎 WOMB → 918
恥 private parts → 1313

❼ **yin and yang**
陽 yang → 626

❽ⓐ **negative**
負 negative → 2091

❾ **moon**
月 MOON → 2956

USAGE

kageri
陰り
[formerly also 翳り] shade; gloom

翳り
[now usu. 陰り] shade; gloom

HOMOPHONES

kage ⇨ 蔭 2517 影 1889

kageri ⇨ 翳 2874

NOTE

⇨ see also USAGE note at 影 1889

険 險 険 険

542 KEN kewa(shii)

CH 险 xiǎn

Radical	Strokes
阝 170	11-3-8
Grade	**Freq**
Jōyō-5	615
◧ 1-3-8	

3-8 阝

Stroke order: 1 2 3 4 5 6 7 8 9 10 11

▶**DANGER** ▶**STEEP**

COMPOUNDS

❶ⓐ **danger, risk, hazard**
ⓑ **dangerous, risky, hazardous**
危険な *kiken na* dangerous
保険 *hoken* insurance
険悪な *ken'aku na* dangerous, threatening, serious
冒険 *bōken* adventure, risk
探険(=探検) *tanken* exploration, expedition

❷ⓐ [formerly also 嶮] **steep, precipitous**
ⓑ [original meaning] steep [inaccessible] place, steep pass, stronghold
険路 *kenro* steep pass
険阻(=嶮岨) *kenso* steepness, precipice
峻険な *shunken na* steep, precipitous
天険 *tenken* natural stronghold

❸ sinister, vicious
陰険な *inken na* sly, crafty, treacherous

❹ (figuratively) sharp (look), stern (expression)
険相 *kensō* uncanny look

INDEPENDENT

【**ken** 険】[formerly also 嶮 759] steep place, impregnable pass, stronghold; stern expression
アルプスの険 *arupusu no ken* steep pass in the Alps
険の有る目 *ken no aru me* sharp look

KUN

【**kewa(shii)** 険しい】(sharply inclined and difficult to climb) steep, precipitous; craggy; severe, grim, fierce, angry
険しさ *kewashisa* steepness; severity, grimness
険しい山 *kewashii yama* steep [craggy] mountain
険しい顔 *kewashii kao* grim face

SYNONYMS

❶ **danger**
危 DANGEROUS → 3199

❷ **steep**
急 steep → 2092
峻 high and steep → 412

COMPOUND FORMATION

保険 *hoken*
保険 'insurance' means to guarantee (保) against hazards (険 ❶ⓐ).

陸 陸 陸

543 RIKU ROKU▲ oka▲

CH 陆 lù

Radical	Strokes
阝 170	11-3-8
Grade	**Freq**
Jōyō-4	582
◧ 1-3-8	

3-8 阝

Stroke order: 1 2 3 4 5 6 7 8 9 10 11

▶**LAND**

COMPOUNDS

❶ (solid ground of the earth, as distinguished from the sea) **land, shore**
陸地 *rikuchi* land
陸上 *rikujō* land, ground; shore; track and field
陸橋 *rikkyō* overland bridge
陸兵 *rikuhei* land troops
陸岸 *rikugan* shore, land
陸軍 *rikugun* army
陸上自衛隊 *rikujō jieitai* Ground Self Defense Forces
大陸 *tairiku* continent
上陸 *jōriku* landing, disembarkation
着陸 *chakuriku* landing, alighting

❷ abbrev. of 陸軍 *rikugun* or 陸上自衛隊 *rikujō jieitai*: army, Ground Self Defense Forces
陸相(=陸軍大臣) *rikushō* (=*rikugun daijin*) Minister of War

陸大 *rikudai* Military Staff College
❸ continuously
陸続と *rikuzoku to* continuously, successively
❹ six—used in legal documents and checks
陸萬円也 *rokuman'en nari* sum of sixty thousand yen
❺ abbrev. of 陸奥 *mutsu*, old name for northeast Tohoku district
陸前 *rikuzen* Rikuzen (old name for Miyagi Prefecture)
❻ brilliant, vivid
光彩陸離たる *kōsai-rikuritaru* brilliant, dazzling

INDEPENDENT
【**riku 陸**】land, shore; six (⇨ ❹)
陸を行く *riku o iku* go by land, travel overland

KUN
【**oka 陸**】land, shore
陸釣り *okazuri* angling from the shore
陸稲 *okabo* (=*rikutō*) rice grown in a dry field

SYNONYMS
❶ **land and soil**
地 GROUND → 204
土 SOIL → 3403
壌 ARABLE SOIL → 755
泥 MUD → 326
❹ **six**
六 SIX → 1965

HOMOPHONES
oka ⇨ 丘 3495 岡 2997 傍 147

NOTE
⇨ see USAGE note at 丘 3495

3-8
阝

陵 陵 陵

544 RYŌ misasagi

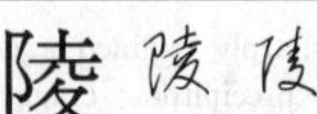

CH 陵 líng

Radical	Strokes
阝 170	11-3-8
Grade	**Freq**
Jōyō	1890
1 - 3 - 8	

▶**IMPERIAL MAUSOLEUM**

COMPOUNDS
❶ [also suffix] **imperial mausoleum, imperial tomb**
陵墓 *ryōbo* imperial tomb
御陵 *goryō* imperial mausoleum
皇陵 *kōryō* imperial mausoleum
仁徳陵 *nintokuryō* Mausoleum of Emperor Nintoku
❷ [original meaning] **high mound, hillock**
丘陵 *kyūryō* hill, hillock
高陵土 *kōryōdo* kaolin, porcelain clay
❸ [also 凌 128] surpass, outdo
陵駕する *ryōga suru* excel, surpass, outdo
❹ [also 凌 128] insult, offend
陵辱 *ryōjoku* insult; rape

INDEPENDENT
【**ryō 陵**】imperial mausoleum, imperial tomb

KUN
【**misasagi 陵**】imperial mausoleum, imperial tomb

SYNONYMS
❶ **graves**
墳 TUMULUS → 719
墓 GRAVE → 2332
塚 grave mound → 556
❷ **hills**
塚 MOUND → 556
丘 HILL → 3495
岡 HILL → 2997
台 heights → 2005
坂 SLOPE → 234
阪 slope → 271

3-8
阝

隆 隆 隆 隆

545 RYŪ

CH 隆 lóng lōng

Radical	Strokes
阝 170	11-3-8
Grade	**Freq**
Jōyō	1228
1 - 3 - 8	

▶**PROSPER**

COMPOUNDS
❶ **prosper, rise to prosperity, flourish**
隆隆たる *ryūryūtaru* prosperous, thriving; brawny
隆盛 *ryūsei* prosperity
隆昌 *ryūshō* prosperity
隆運 *ryūun* prosperity, good fortune

興隆 *kōryū* prosperity, rise
❷ⓐ **protuberant, elevated, bulging**
ⓑ elevate
隆起 *ryūki* protuberance, elevation
隆鼻術 *ryūbijutsu* plastic surgery of the nose

SYNONYMS

❶ **prospering and prosperity**
振 rise → 430
興 RISE TO PROSPERITY → 2909
栄 FLOURISH → 2574
繁 THRIVE → 2853
盛 PROSPEROUS → 2675
昌 PROSPERING → 2414
❷ⓐ **protrude and protruding**
突 protruding → 2230
凸 CONVEX → 3486
起 RISE → 3307
出る stick out → 3498

陶 陶 陶 546 TŌ

CH 陶 táo yáo

Radical	Strokes
阝 170	11-3-8
Grade	**Freq**
Jōyō	1521
◧ 1 - 3 - 8	

3-8 阝

Stroke order: 1–11

▶POTTERY

COMPOUNDS

❶ **pottery, ceramics, earthenware**
陶器 *tōki* pottery, porcelain, chinaware
陶芸 *tōgei* ceramic art
陶磁器 *tōjiki* porcelain, pottery, ceramics
陶工 *tōkō* potter, ceramist
❷ contented, happy, entranced
陶酔 *tōsui* intoxication; fascination, rapture
鬱陶しい *uttōshii* gloomy, depressing; dull, cloudy
❸ influence a person, educate
陶冶 *tōya* training, education

INDEPENDENT

【tō 陶】 pottery, china, ceramics
陶の人形 *tō no ningyō* ceramic figurine

SYNONYMS

❶ **ceramics ware**
磁 porcelain → 1214
窯 ceramics → 2361

陪 547 **▶ACCOMPANY A SUPERIOR**
nonstandard for 陪 539

3-8 阝

陥 548 **▶FALL IN**
nonstandard for 陥 457

3-8 阝

隅 incorrect stroke count ⇨ see 623

3-8 阝

随 incorrect stroke count ⇨ see 627

3-8 阝

脩 條 incorrect classification ⇨ see ◧ 2－9

3-8 亻

悠 incorrect classification ⇨ see 2741

3-8 亻

3-8 纟

郷 郷 鄉 ㄋ

549 KYŌ GŌ sato▲

Ⓒⓗ 乡 xiāng

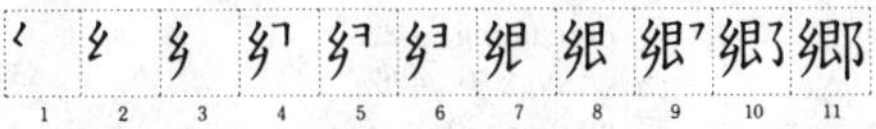

Radical	Strokes
阝 163	11-3-8
Grade	**Freq**
Jōyō-6	1064
1-3-8	

▶**HOMETOWN**

COMPOUNDS

❶ **hometown, homeland, native place, birthplace**

郷里 *kyōri* one's old home, native place
郷土 *kyōdo* one's birthplace
郷愁 *kyōshū* homesickness, nostalgia
故郷 *kokyō* hometown, birthplace
愛郷心 *aikyōshin* love of one's hometown
同郷人 *dōkyōjin* person from the same province [town, village]
帰郷する *kikyō suru* go [come] home

❷ⓐ the country, countryside, rural district
ⓑ village, hamlet
ⓒ *go*: former unit of administration smaller than 郡 *gun* and larger than 村 *mura*

郷士 *gōshi* country samurai
在郷者 *zaigōsha* countryman, rustic
郷俗 *kyōzoku* village customs
郷村 *gōson* villages
郷邑 *kyōyū* village, hamlet
白川郷 *shirakawagō* Shirakawa Village

❸ (figuratively) land, district

異郷 *ikyō* strange land, away from home
理想郷 *risōkyō* ideal land, Utopia, earthly paradise
桃源郷 *tōgenkyō* Shangri-la

INDEPENDENT

【**kyō** 郷】 hometown, homeland, birthplace
【**gō** 郷】 the country, countryside; village, hamlet

KUN

【**sato** 郷】 [usu. 里] hometown, one's birthplace
故郷(=古里) *furusato* hometown, birthplace

SYNONYMS

❶ **villages and towns**
里 hamlet → 3542
庄 FEUDAL VILLAGE → 3051
村 VILLAGE → 834
町 TOWN → 1113

❷ⓐ **the country**
里 COUNTRYSIDE → 3542
郊 SUBURB → 1286
辺 BORDERLAND → 3029

HOMOPHONES

sato ⇨ 里 3542

NOTE

⇨ see USAGE note at 里 3542

3-9 口

喚 喚 唤

550 KAN wame(ku)▲

Ⓒⓗ 唤 huàn

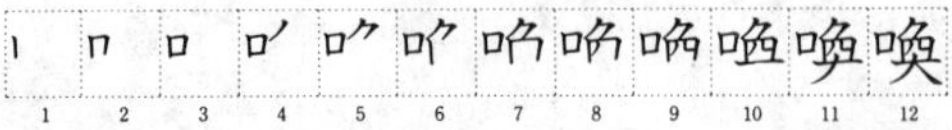

Radical	Strokes
口 30	12-3-9
Grade	**Freq**
Jōyō	1833
1-3-9	

▶**CALL**

COMPOUNDS

❶ⓐ **call, call to, summon**
ⓑ (elicit) call out, arouse

喚問 *kanmon* summons
召喚する *shōkan suru* summon, cite, subpoena
喚起する *kanki suru* awaken, rouse, arouse

❷ [original meaning] **call out, scream, shout, yell**

喚声 *kansei* shout, yell, scream, clamor
叫喚 *kyōkan* shout, cry, scream

KUN

【**wame(ku)** 喚く】 cry, scream, shout
喚き声 *wamekigoe* shout, yell, outcry
喚き立てる *wamekitateru* bawl out, yell

SYNONYMS

❶ⓐ **call and invite**
呼ぶ CALL → 273
召 SUMMON → 2001
招 INVITE → 316

❷ **shout**
叫 SHOUT → 201
号 holler → 2153
喝 SHOUT AT → 461
呼 CALL → 273
鳴 CRY → 674

喫 喫 喫 喫

551 KITSU

Ⓒ 吃 chī

Radical	Strokes
口 30	12-3-9
Grade	**Freq**
Jōyō	1394
◧ 1 - 3 - 9	

3-9 口

Stroke order: 1 丶 2 ⺆ 3 口 4 口⁻ 5 ... 12 喫

▶INGEST

COMPOUNDS

❶ (introduce into one's body) **ingest, eat, drink, inhale, swallow**

喫飯 *kippan* [rare] eating, taking a meal

喫茶店 *kissaten* coffee shop, tea house

喫煙 *kitsuen* smoking

満喫する *mankitsu suru* have enough, enjoy fully

❷ [formerly also 吃 200] be subjected to, suffer, incur

喫驚する *kikkyō suru* be astonished

喫水 *kissui* draft, sea gauge

❸ [formerly also 吃 200] urgent, pressing

喫緊事 *kikkinji* urgent [pressing] matter

INDEPENDENT

【kissuru 喫する】 suffer, sustain; take

惨敗を喫する *zanpai* (= *sanpai*) *o kissuru* sustain a crushing defeat

SYNONYMS

❶ **ingest**

服 take → 878

食 EAT → 2075

飲 DRINK → 1692

❶ **take in**

吸 SUCK → 202

摂 TAKE IN → 650

収 TAKE IN → 198

喰

552 ku(u) ku(rau)

Ⓒ none (国字)

Radical	Strokes
口 30	12-3-9
Grade	**Freq**
Reference	
◧ 1 - 3 - 9	

3-9 口

COMPOUNDS

❶ *colloq*

ⓐ [original meaning] eat (greedily), devour

ⓑ [now usu. 食う *kuu*] get (as a slap in the face)

一口喰う *hitokuchi kuu* take a bite, have a munch

飯を喰う *meshi o kuu* devour a meal

びんたを喰う *binta o kuu* get slapped in the face

❷ *vulgar*

ⓐ eat (greedily), devour

ⓑ [now usu. 食らう *kurau*] get (as a slap in the face)

面喰らう *menkurau* be confused, be bewildered

一発喰らわす *ippatsu kurawasu* give a blow

HOMOPHONES

kuu ⇨ 食 2075

kurau ⇨ 食 2075

NOTE

⇨ see USAGE note at 食 2075

喩

553 YU tato(eru)

Ⓒ 喻 yù

Radical	Strokes
口 30	12-3-9
Grade	**Freq**
Reference	
◧ 1 - 3 - 9	

3-9 口

COMPOUNDS

ⓐ metaphor, simile, allegory

ⓑ [also 譬える *tatoeru*] compare to, liken, speak figuratively

比喩 *hiyu* simile, metaphor, allegory

直喩 *chokuyu* simile

暗喩 *an'yu* metaphor

諷喩 *fūyu* hint, insinuation, allegory

引喩 *in'yu* allusion
喩え *tatoe* metaphor, simile, allegory
死を眠りに喩える *shi o nemuri ni tatoeru* compare death to sleep

HOMOPHONES
tatoeru ⇨ 例 89 譬 2903

NOTE
⇨ see USAGE note at 例 89

3-9 口 喝 554 ▶**SHOUT AT**
nonstandard for 喝 461

3-9 口 喫 555 ▶**INGEST**
nonstandard for 喫 551

3-9 土 塚 塚 塚 塚 556 CHŌ▲ tsuka -zuka Ⓒ 塚 zhǒng

Radical	Strokes
土 32	12-3-9
Grade	**Freq**
Jōyō	876
1-3-9	

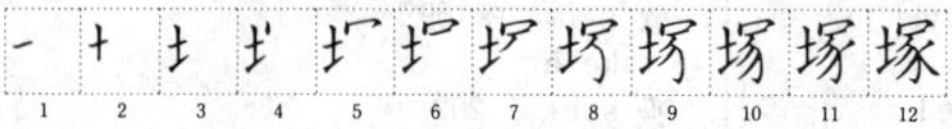

▶**MOUND**

KUN
【**tsuka** 塚, **-zuka** -塚】
① mound, hillock, heap
塚を築く *tsuka o kizuku* pile up a mound
蟻塚 *arizuka* anthill
貝塚 *kaizuka* shell heap, shell mound; kitchen midden
一里塚 *ichirizuka* milepost, milestone
② grave mound, tumulus; grave
塚穴 *tsukaana* grave

SYNONYMS
【**tsuka**】
① **hills**
陵 high mound → 544
丘 HILL → 3495
岡 HILL → 2997
台 heights → 2005
坂 SLOPE → 234
阪 slope → 271
② **graves**
墳 TUMULUS → 719
陵 IMPERIAL MAUSOLEUM → 544
墓 GRAVE → 2332

3-9 土 塀 塀 塀 塀 557 HEI Ⓒ none（国字）

Radical	Strokes
土 32	12-3-9
Grade	**Freq**
Jōyō	1948
1-3-9	

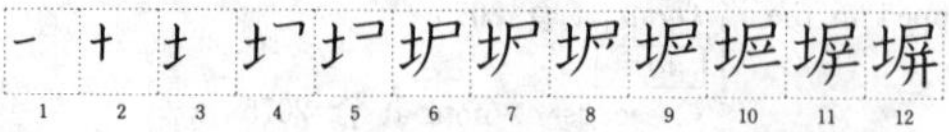

▶**FENCE**

COMPOUNDS
● [also suffix] [original meaning] **fence (for screening), wall, board fence, enclosure**
土塀 *dobei* mud wall, plaster wall
板塀 *itabei* board fence, wooden wall
煉瓦塀 *rengabei* brick wall
ブロック塀 *burokkubei* concrete (block) wall

INDEPENDENT
【**hei** 塀】fence (for screening), wall, board fence, enclosure
塀を巡らす *hei o megurasu* surround with a wall, fence in

SYNONYMS
● **fences and walls**
垣 FENCE (for partitioning) → 351
壁 WALL → 2895
囲い enclosure → 3069
欄 railing → 1103

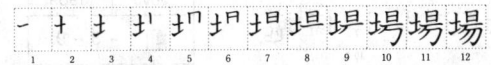

場 場 𫷂 (CH) 场 cháng chǎng

558 JŌ ba

Radical	Strokes
土 32	12-3-9
Grade	**Freq**
Jōyō-2	34
◧ 1 - 3 - 9	

▶**PLACE**

COMPOUNDS

❶ⓐ [also suffix] place or chamber for specific activity: **place, hall, room, house; plant**
ⓑ **stage, scene**
会場 *kaijō* place of meeting, site
式場 *shikijō* hall of ceremony, stateroom
工場 *kōjō* factory, plant, workshop
劇場 *gekijō* theater
入場 *nyūjō* entrance, admission
出場する *shutsujō suru* take part, participate
試験場 *shikenjō* examination hall [room]; laboratory
登場する *tōjō suru* come on stage; appear

❷ⓐ [also suffix] place or open area for conducting activities such as sports: **ground(s), field, arena, course**
ⓑ site for conducting religious services
球場 *kyūjō* baseball ground, ball park
戦場 *senjō* battlefield, front
運動場 *undōjō* playground, sports field
ゴルフ場 *gorufujō* golf links, golf course
競輪場 *keirinjō* cycle racing track [course]
斎場 *saijō* funeral hall; site of a religious service

❸ market, exchange
市場 *shijō* market, mart
上場する *jōjō suru* list (stocks)

INDEPENDENT

【jō 場】 place, spot

KUN

【ba 場】

①ⓐ [also suffix] place, spot, site; ground
ⓑ space, room
場所 *basho* place, spot, site; space, room
現場 *genba* actual spot; job site, building site
職場 *shokuba* place of work, workshop
立場 *tachiba* standpoint
酒場 *sakaba* bar, barroom, pub, tavern
遊び場 *asobiba* playground
停車場 *teishaba* station
その場で *sono ba de* then and there; on the spot, on that occasion
場を取る *ba o toru* occupy much space
広場 *hiroba* square, open space

② occasion, moment; situation
場合 *baai* occasion, situation, circumstances, case
夏場 *natsuba* summertime

③ *theater* scene
場面 *bamen* scene; situation
二幕三場 *nimaku sanba* Act 2, Scene 3

④ market, exchange; session; trading floor
市場 *ichiba* market, marketplace
相場 *sōba* market price; estimation

⑤ *phys*, *psychol* field
磁場 *jiba* magnetic field
力の場 *chikara no ba* field of force

SYNONYMS

❶ⓐ **places and positions**
所 PLACE → 851
処 place → 3031
地 PLACE (particular location) → 204
席 meeting place → 3113
位 POSITION → 61
点 POINT → 2084
座 place → 3116

❷ⓐ **sports fields**
庭 COURT → 3114
野 baseball field → 1485

❸ **market**
市 MARKET → 1993

【ba】

③ **parts of plays**
幕 act → 2335

⑤ **range**
界 field (*phys*) → 2563
野 FIELD → 1485
圏 SPHERE → 3148
域 area → 465
範 range → 2709
程 EXTENT → 1190

NOTE

⇨ see COMPOUND FORMATION for 相場 *sōba* ⇨ 相 900

3-9
土

堪 堪 堪

559 KAN TAN▲ ta(eru) tama(ru)▲

CH 堪 kān

Radical	Strokes
土 32	12-3-9
Grade	Freq
Jōyō	1909
1-3-9	

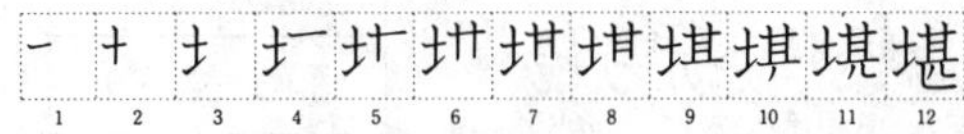

▶ **ENDURE**

COMPOUNDS

❶ **endure, bear, tolerate**
堪忍(＝勘忍)する *kannin suru* have patience, bear with; forgive, pardon

❷ competent, fit for
堪能 *kannō* (＝*tannō*) skillful, proficient
不堪 *fukan* [rare] incompetence

KUN

【ta(eru) 堪える】
①ⓐ [sometimes also 耐える] endure, bear, stand, tolerate
ⓑ bear (a burden), hold out, stand
堪え忍ぶ *taeshinobu* endure, bear up, tolerate, put up with
堪え難い *taegatai* unbearable
不幸に堪える *fukō ni taeru* bear up under misfortune
遺憾に堪えない *ikan ni taenai* be really regrettable
② be fit for, be competent, be equal to
仕事に堪える *shigoto ni taeru* be fit for work

【tama(ru) 堪る】 [usu. in negative constructions] can(not) stand, be (un)able to put up with
堪らない *tamaranai* cannot stand, be unbearable; cannot help (doing)

SYNONYMS

❶ **bear and endure**
忍 BEAR → 2212
耐 WITHSTAND → 1282

USAGE

taeru
堪える
①ⓐ [sometimes also 耐える] endure, bear, stand, tolerate
ⓑ bear (a burden), hold out, stand
② be fit for, be competent, be equal to
耐える
ⓐ (resist physical forces) withstand, resist, be proof against
ⓑ [usu. 堪える] endure, bear, tolerate

HOMOPHONES

taeru ⇨ 耐 1282

NOTE

★do not confuse with 勘 1777

3-9
土

堤 堤 堤

560 TEI tsutsumi

CH 堤 dī

Radical	Strokes
土 32	12-3-9
Grade	Freq
Jōyō	1420
1-3-9	

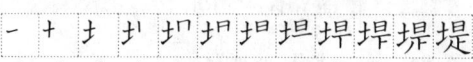

一 十 土 扌 扣 坦 坦 垾 埕 埕 堤 堤
1 2 3 4 5 6 7 8 9 10 11 12

▶ **EMBANKMENT**

COMPOUNDS

● [also suffix] [original meaning] **embankment, dike, bank**
堤防 *teibō* bank, embankment, dike
突堤 *tottei* pier, breakwater
築堤 *chikutei* embankment, bank; building an embankment
防潮堤 *bōchōtei* tide embankment, seawall
防波堤 *bōhatei* breakwater

KUN

【tsutsumi 堤】 embankment, dike, bank
堤を築く *tsutsumi o kizuku* build an embankment

SYNONYMS

● **embankment**
防 dike → 270

塔 561 TŌ

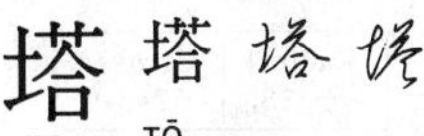

CH 塔 tǎ

Radical	Strokes
土 32	12-3-9
Grade	Freq
Jōyō	1489
1-3-9	

3-9 土

▶**TOWER**

COMPOUNDS

❶ [also suffix] **tower**

鉄塔 *tettō* steel tower; pylon
テレビ塔 *terebitō* television tower
管制塔 *kanseitō* control tower
エッフェル塔 *efferutō* Eiffel Tower

❷ⓐ [also suffix] **pagoda**
ⓑ [original meaning] dagoba, stupa

卒塔婆 *sotoba* (=*sotōba*) wooden grave tablet; stupa, dagoba
仏塔 *buttō* pagoda, Buddhist pagoda
堂塔 *dōtō* temple buildings, temple
五重の塔 *gojū no tō* five-storied pagoda

INDEPENDENT

【tō 塔】 tower; pagoda

SYNONYMS

❶ **tall buildings**

楼 TALL BUILDING → 1019
閣 TALL MAGNIFICENT BUILDING → 3327
台 observatory → 2005

❷ⓐ **places of worship**

堂 temple building → 2589
寺 BUDDHIST TEMPLE → 2164
社 Shinto shrine → 840
宮 SHINTO SHRINE → 2274
院 monastery → 454
教 church → 1493

NOTE

★do not confuse with 搭 592

堺 562

▶**WORLD** ▶**BOUNDS**
nonstandard for 界 2563

3-9 土

壻 563

▶**SON-IN-LAW**
nonstandard for 婿 566

3-9 土

媒 564 BAI

CH 媒 méi

Radical	Strokes
女 38	12-3-9
Grade	Freq
Jōyō	1763
1-3-9	

3-9 女

▶**INTERMEDIATE**

COMPOUNDS

ⓐ **intermediate, mediate, act as a go-between; act as a medium**
ⓑ [original meaning] go-between, matchmaker

媒介 *baikai* mediation, intervention, intermediation
媒質 *baishitsu* medium
媒体 *baitai* medium
媒染剤 *baisenzai* mordant
触媒 *shokubai* catalyst, catalyzer
霊媒 *reibai* (spiritualistic) medium
媒酌人 *baishakunin* go-between, matchmaker

SYNONYMS

ⓐ **mediating and mediators**

介 MEDIATE → 1967
紹 INTRODUCE → 1335
仲 INTERMEDIARY → 43

3-9
女

媚
565 BI ko(biru)

CH 媚 méi

Radical	Strokes
女 38	12-3-9
Grade	Freq
Reference	
1-3-9	

COMPOUNDS

❶ fawn upon; curry favor with
媚態 *bitai* coquetry
媚薬 *biyaku* aphrodisiac, love potion
権力に媚びる *kenryoku ni kobiru* be obsequious to power

❷ [now also 美 *bi* 2264] beautiful, charming, fascinating
風光明媚の地 *fūkō-meibi no chi* place of scenic beauty

3-9
女

婿 壻 聟° 婿 婿
566 SEI muko

CH 婿 xù

Radical	Strokes
女 38	12-3-9
Grade	Freq
Jōyō	1887
1-3-9	

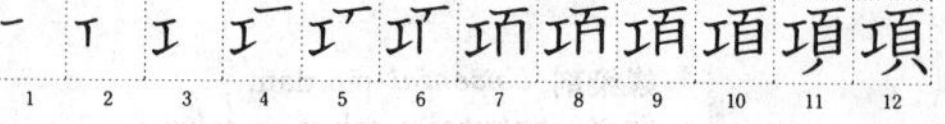

▶**SON-IN-LAW**

COMPOUNDS

● [original meaning] **son-in-law**
女婿 *josei* son-in-law
令婿 *reisei* your son-in-law

KUN

【**muko** 婿】 son-in-law; bridegroom, husband
娘婿 *musumemuko* son-in-law
婿入する *mukoiri suru* marry into the family of one's bride
花嫁花婿 *hanayome hanamuko* bride and groom

SYNONYMS

● **in-laws**
嫁 daughter-in-law → 635

3-9
川

順
incorrect classification ⇨ see 18

3-9
工

項 項 项
567 KŌ unaji▲

CH 项 xiàng

Radical	Strokes
頁 181	12-9-3
Grade	Freq
Jōyō	912
1-3-9	

一 丅 工 工' 工' 工丆 項 項 項 項 項 項
1 2 3 4 5 6 7 8 9 10 11 12

▶**CLAUSE**

COMPOUNDS

❶ [also suffix] **clause, subsection, item, paragraph**
項目 *kōmoku* clause, item, provision
事項 *jikō* matters, facts; articles, items
別項 *bekkō* separate paragraph, another clause
要項 *yōkō* important points; gist
条項 *jōkō* articles (and clauses), terms
第九条第二項 *daikyūjō dainikō* Section 9, Subsection 2

❷ *math* term, member
多項式 *takōshiki* polynomial
同類項 *dōruikō* similar terms, like terms
方程式の一項 *hōteishiki no ikkō* member of an equation

❸ [original meaning, now rare] nape
項領 *kōryō* neck, collar

INDEPENDENT

【**kō** 項】 clause, subsection, item, paragraph; *math* term, member
項に分かつ *kō ni wakatsu* itemize, paragraph

KUN

【unaji 項】nape

SYNONYMS

❶ **parts of writing**

目 ITEM → 3043
箇 item → 2700
条 ARTICLE → 2200
款 ARTICLE → 1700
節 paragraph → 2691
段 passage → 1144
章 CHAPTER → 2117

❸ **neck**

首 NECK → 2265

帽 568 BŌ

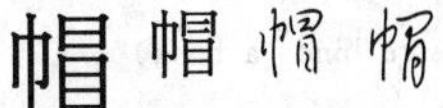

Ⓒ 帽 mào

Radical	Strokes
巾 50	12-3-9
Grade	**Freq**
Jōyō	1462
◧ 1 - 3 - 9	

3-9 巾

▶HEADGEAR

COMPOUNDS

● [also suffix] [original meaning] **headgear, hat, cap**

帽子 *bōshi* cap, hat
帽章 *bōshō* badge on a cap
学帽 *gakubō* school cap
制帽 *seibō* regulation [school] cap
脱帽 *datsubō* taking off one's cap [hat]; submission
ベレー帽 *berēbō* beret (cap)
無帽の *mubō no* hatless
登山帽 *tozanbō* climber's hat

SYNONYMS

● **headgear**

冠 CROWN → 2081

幅 569 FUKU haba

Ⓒ 幅 fú

Radical	Strokes
巾 50	12-3-9
Grade	**Freq**
Jōyō	628
◧ 1 - 3 - 9	

3-9 巾

▶WIDTH

COMPOUNDS

❶ [sometimes also 巾 3409] **width, breadth, range**

幅員 *fukuin* width [extent] of roads or ships
増幅 *zōfuku* amplification
振幅 *shinpuku* amplitude (of vibration)
全幅 *zenpuku* overall width, extreme breadth (of a ship), wing span

❷ⓐ scroll, scroll picture

ⓑ counter for scrolls or picture scrolls

画幅 *gafuku* hanging picture, picture scroll
掛け軸二幅 *kakejiku nifuku* two scrolls

❸ border, exterior

辺幅 *henpuku* outer appearance

INDEPENDENT

【**fuku** 幅】scroll, scroll picture

KUN

【**haba** 幅】[also suffix] width, breadth, range; influence, power; difference (in price)

幅広い *habahiroi* wide, broad
幅跳び *habatobi* broad jump
大幅に *ōhaba ni* sharply, by a large margin
小幅 *kohaba* single breadth, narrow range
横幅 *yokohaba* breadth
幅利き *habakiki* man of influence
値幅 *nehaba* difference (in price)

SYNONYMS

❶ **width**

員 girth → 2269
径 DIAMETER → 291

COMPOUND FORMATION

増幅 *zōfuku*

増幅 'amplification' is to increase (増) the range (幅 ❶).

NOTE

★Though 幅 and 巾 3409 are distinct characters, the latter is also used as an abbreviation of the former.

3-9
巾

幀

570 TEI

CH 帧 zhèng

Radical	Strokes
巾 50	12-3-9
Grade	Freq
Reference	
▮ 1 - 3 - 9	

COMPOUNDS

● [now replaced by 丁 3348] bookbinding

装幀する *sōtei suru* bind (a book)

3-9
巾

帽

571

▶**HEADGEAR**
nonstandard for 帽 568

3-9
弓

弾

彈 弹 弾

572

CH 弹 dàn tán

DAN hi(ku) -hi(ki) hazu(mu) tama haji(ku)▲ haji(keru)▲

Radical	Strokes
弓 57	12-3-9
Grade	Freq
Jōyō	862
▮ 1 - 3 - 9	

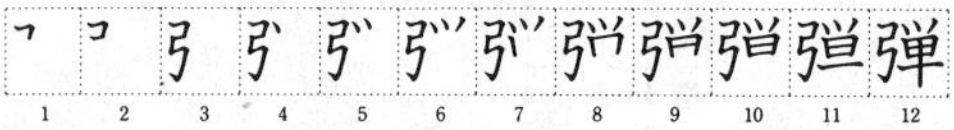

▶**PROJECTILE** ▶**SPRING BACK**

COMPOUNDS

❶ [also suffix] **projectile, bullet, shell, missile, (cannon) ball, bomb**
弾丸 *dangan* shot, bullet, shell
弾薬 *dan'yaku* ammunition
弾頭 *dantō* warhead
弾道弾 *dandōdan* ballistic missile
爆弾 *bakudan* bomb
砲弾 *hōdan* cannonball, shell
銃弾 *jūdan* bullet, shot
散弾 *sandan* shot
実弾 *jitsudan* ball cartridge, live ammunition; money
不発弾 *fuhatsudan* unexploded shell

❷ counter for steps, measures or stages
第一弾 *daiichidan* first step

❸ **spring back (to the original shape), resile**
弾性 *dansei* elasticity, resilience
弾力性 *danryokusei* elasticity, resilience; flexibility, adaptability
弾機 *danki* (=*bane*) spring

❹ⓐ impeach, censure
ⓑ put down, suppress
弾劾 *dangai* impeachment, denunciation, accusation
糾弾 *kyūdan* impeachment, censure
弾圧 *dan'atsu* oppression, suppression
指弾 *shidan* rejection, disdain

❺ [original meaning] **play on (stringed instruments)**
弾奏 *dansō* playing on stringed instruments
連弾 *rendan* four handed performance (on the piano)

INDEPENDENT

【danzuru (=danjiru) 弾ずる(=弾じる)】 play on stringed instruments

KUN

【hi(ku) 弾く】 play on (stringed instruments)
弾き手 *hikite* player, performer
弾き語り *hikigatari* reciting to one's own accompaniment
爪弾く *tsumabiku* pluck the strings (of a guitar)

【-hi(ki) -弾き】 [suffix] player
ベートーベン弾き *bētōbenhiki* Beethoven player
バイオリン弾き *baiorinhiki* violinist

【hazu(mu) 弾む】 spring back (from a surface), bounce, rebound, bound; be animated, be spurred on; invest in, fork out (generously), treat oneself to; breathe hard
弾み *hazumi* spring, bound; momentum, impulse, force; chance
気分が弾む *kibun ga hazumu* cheer up
チップを弾む *chippu o hazumu* tip generously
息を弾ませる *iki o hazumaseru* pant

【tama 弾】 bullet, shot, shell
鉄砲弾(=鉄砲玉) *teppōdama* gunshot, bullet; lost [truant] messenger; bull's-eye

【haji(ku) 弾く】 *vt* fillip, flip; repel, reject; use an abacus
弾き *hajiki* repellence; *slang* gun
爪弾き *tsumahajiki* fillip; ostracism; black sheep (of a family)

ters; amusement quarters
商店街 *shōtengai* shopping center
中国人街 *chūgokujingai* Chinatown
住宅街 *jūtakugai* residential quarter
歓楽街 *kanrakugai* amusement center [quarter]
銀天街 *gintengai* Gintengai Shopping Center
❷ [original meaning] city street, thoroughfare, crossroads
街道 *kaidō* thoroughfare, highway
街頭 *gaitō* street
街灯 *gaitō* street lamp

KUN

【machi 街】 (busy) city quarter(s), city streets
街の女 *machi no onna* streetwalker
街角 *machikado* street corner
街着 *machigi* street clothes
商人街 *shōninmachi* business street
北野街 *kitanomachi* Kitano shopping center

SYNONYMS

❶ **parts of towns**
区 WARD → 2963
町 town section (*chō*) → 1113
丁 TOWN SUBSECTION (*chōme*) → 3348
字 village or town section → 2172
❷ **ways and routes**
通り street → 3109
道 WAY (path) → 3134
途 WAY (route) → 3107
路 ROAD → 1533
筋 wayside → 2678
辻 CROSSROADS → 3192
岐 forked road → 241
径 PATH → 291
軌 TRACK → 1445
線 LINE → 1392

HOMOPHONES

machi ⇨ 町 1113

NOTE

⇨ see USAGE note at 町 1113

御 御 御 御

577 GYO GO on- o-▲ mi-▲

CH 御 yù

Radical	Strokes
彳 60	12-3-9
Grade	**Freq**
Jōyō	836
1 - 3 - 9	

3-9 彳

Stroke order: ノ ク 彳 彳 彳 彳 彳 彳 彳 彳 御 御 (1–12)

▶GENERAL HONORIFIC TERM

COMPOUNDS

❶ⓐ [also prefix] **general honorific term for conveying respect**
ⓑ **general honorific prefix attached to Sino-Japanese compounds to convey humility**
ⓒ honorific suffix conveying respect for persons, esp. for members of another's family
御用 *goyō* your order, your business
御飯 *gohan* boiled rice; meal
御存じの方 *gozonji no kata* your acquaintance
御意 *gyoi* your will, your pleasure
御馳走 *gochisō* feast, treat
御成功 *goseikō* your success
御両親 *goryōshin* your (honorable) parents
御自身 *gojishin* yourself; himself, herself
御案内申し上げます *Goannai mōshiagemasu* I shall be pleased to show you the way
御説明致します *Gosetsumei itashimasu* I beg to explain
母御 *hahago* your mother
嫁御 *yomego* bride
女御 *nyōgo* court lady
❷ [also prefix] [honorific] imperial, emperor's
御所 *gosho* old imperial palace
御物 *gyobutsu* (=*gomotsu*) imperial property
御製 *gyosei* emperor's poem or song
御苑 *gyoen* Imperial garden
御用邸 *goyōtei* imperial villa
崩御 *hōgyo* demise [death] of an emperor
❸ [formerly also 馭 *gyo* 1814 or 禦 *gyo* 2870]
ⓐ handle (affairs), control, manage
ⓑ [original meaning] handle a horse well, train a horse
制御する *seigyo suru* control, govern, suppress
統御 *tōgyo* rule, control, management
御者 *gyosha* coachman, driver
❹ [formerly also 禦 *gyo* 2870] resist, keep out, ward off
防御する *bōgyo suru* defend, protect, safeguard

INDEPENDENT

【gyosuru 御する】 handle, control, manage; [formerly also 馭する] handle a horse well, train a horse

KUN

【on- 御-】 honorific prefix for conveying a greater degree of respect than *o-*
御身 *onmi* you [him]; your [his] honorable body

御大 *ontai* boss, governor
御中 *onchū* Messrs.

【o- 御-】

①ⓐ general honorific prefix for conveying respect or politeness

ⓑ general honorific prefix for conveying humility

御顔 *okao* your (honorable) face
御日様 *ohisama* sun
御美しい事 *Outsukushii koto* How beautiful!
御玉 *otama* ladle; egg
御会い出来て嬉しゅう御座います *Oai dekite ureshū gozaimasu* I'm delighted to have the honor of seeing you

② [also 阿-] prefix for conveying intimacy, esp. before names of women

御花さん *ohanasan* Ohana

【mi- 御-】 honorific prefix—used esp. in reference to religious matters or the emperor

主の御名 *shu no mina* the Lord's name
明治天皇の御代 *meiji tennō no miyo* reign of Emperor Meiji

SYNONYMS

❶ⓐ honorific prefixes

貴 YOUR HONORABLE → 2606
尊 your honorable → 2324
令 your honorable → 1995

USAGE

❶ o-

御-

①ⓐ general honorific prefix for conveying respect or politeness

ⓑ general honorific prefix for conveying humility

② [also 阿-] prefix for conveying intimacy, esp. before names of women

阿-

[also 御-] prefix for conveying intimacy, esp. before names of women

❷ gyosuru

御する

ⓐ handle, control, manage

ⓑ [formerly also 馭する] handle a horse well, train a horse

馭する

[now replaced by 御する] handle a horse well, train a horse

HOMOPHONES

o- ⇨阿 346

NOTE

⇨ see COMPOUND FORMATION for 御馳走 *gochisō* ⇨走 2194

3-9
彳

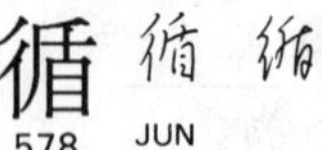

578 JUN

ⒸⒽ 循 xún

Radical	Strokes
彳 60	12-3-9
Grade	**Freq**
Jōyō	1579
1 - 3 - 9	

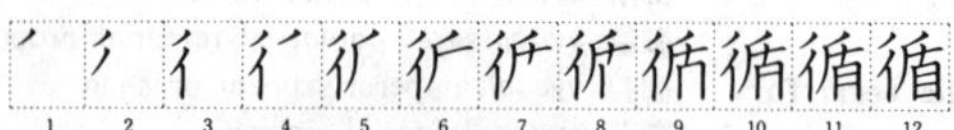

▶CIRCULATE

COMPOUNDS

❶ circulate, go round

循環 *junkan* circulation, rotation; cycle

❷ [original meaning] follow (rules or customs), abide by

因循 *injun* conservatism; vacillation, indecision

SYNONYMS

❶ turn

巡 MAKE THE ROUNDS → 3047
回 TURN ROUND → 3055
転 TURN → 1480
旋 GYRATE → 957

3-9
忄

惰 惰 惰

579 DA

ⒸⒽ 惰 duò

Radical	Strokes
忄 61	12-3-9
Grade	**Freq**
Jōyō	1867
1 - 3 - 9	

1 2 3 4 5 6 7 8 9 10 11 12

▶LAZY

COMPOUNDS

❶ [original meaning] **lazy, indolent, idle**

惰気 *daki* indolence, inactivity, laziness
惰眠 *damin* indolence, idle slumber, inactivity
怠惰 *taida* laziness, idleness

❷ inertia; force of habit

惰性 *dasei* inertia, momentum; force of habit
惰力 *daryoku* inertia, momentum; force of habit

SYNONYMS

❶ **lazy**

怠 REMISS → 2085

慢 SLUGGISH → 686

❷ **motion**

動 motion → 1778

慌 慌 慌 慌

580 KŌ awa(teru) awa(tadashii)

Ⓒ慌 huāng

Radical	Strokes
忄 61	12-3-9
Grade	**Freq**
Jōyō	1853
◧ 1 - 3 - 9	

3-9 忄

▶FLURRIED

COMPOUNDS

● frightened

恐慌 *kyōkō* panic, scare, alarm

KUN

【awa(teru) 慌てる】 be flurried [fluttered], be confused, be in a hurry

慌てふためく *awatefutameku* be all in a flurry, hurry-scurry, act helter-skelter

慌てて *awatete* in confusion, in hot haste

慌て者 *awatemono* flutterer, scatterbrain, bustling fellow

大慌て *ōawate* total fluster, hot haste

【awa(tadashii) 慌ただしい】 flurried, confused; busy, bustling, hurried

慌ただしさ *awatadashisa* flurry, rush, restlessness

慌ただしい一生 *awatadashii isshō* fleeting life

SYNONYMS

【awateru】

○ **busy**

忙 BUSY → 214

繁 bustling → 2853

NOTE

★do not confuse with 荒 2260

惶

581 KŌ

Ⓒ惶 huáng

Radical	Strokes
忄 61	12-3-9
Grade	**Freq**
Reference	
◧ 1 - 3 - 9	

3-9 忄

COMPOUNDS

● [now replaced by 皇 2566] be afraid, be anxious; be flurried

蒼惶(=倉皇)として *sōkō to shite* in great haste

愉 愉 愉 愉

582 YU tano(shii)▲ tano(shimu)▲

Ⓒ愉 yú

Radical	Strokes
忄 61	12-3-9
Grade	**Freq**
Jōyō	1745
◧ 1 - 3 - 9	

3-9 忄

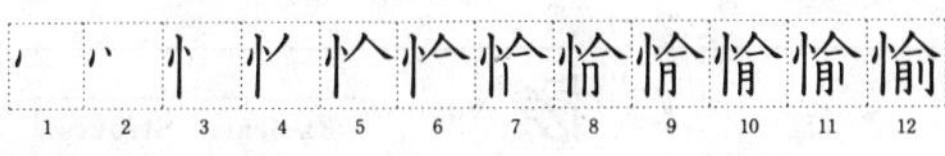

▶PLEASED

COMPOUNDS

● [original meaning] **pleased, delighted, happy, cheerful, joyful**

愉快な *yukai na* pleasant, delightful, joyful

愉悦 *yuetsu* joy

愉色 *yushoku* pleased look, cheerful expression

愉楽 *yuraku* pleasure, joy

不愉快な *fuyukai na* unpleasant, disagreeable, cheerless

KUN

【tano(shii) 愉しい】 [usu. 楽しい] pleasurable, pleasant, enjoyable, merry

愉しさ *tanoshisa* pleasure, joy; pleasantness

愉しげな *tanoshige na* joyous, merry, pleasant, happy, gay

【tano(shimu) 愉しむ】 [usu. 楽しむ] take pleasure in, enjoy (oneself)

愉しみ *tanoshimi* pleasure, enjoyment; amusement, diversion, hobby

SYNONYMS

● **pleased and pleasant**
悦 DELIGHTED → 418
快 PLEASANT → 245
楽 pleasurable → 2826
朗 CHEERFUL → 1325
嬉しい GLAD → 722
喜 HAPPY → 2308
歓 JOYOUS → 1867
欣 JOYFUL → 852

HOMOPHONES

tanoshii ⇨ 楽 2826
tanoshimu ⇨ 楽 2826
tanoshimi ⇨ 楽 2826

NOTE

⇨ see USAGE note at 楽 2826

3-9 忄

惱 583

▶SUFFER
nonstandard for 悩 421

3-9 忄

愉 584

▶PLEASED
nonstandard for 愉 582

3-9 扌

握 握 握 585

AKU nigi(ru)

Ⓒⓗ 握 wò

一 十 扌 扌 扌 扌 扌 扌 扌 扌 握 握
1 2 3 4 5 6 7 8 9 10 11 12

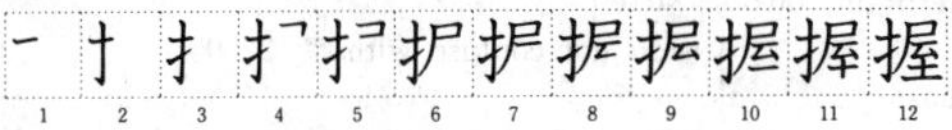

Radical	Strokes
扌 64	12-3-9
Grade	**Freq**
Jōyō	1373
1-3-9	

▶GRASP

COMPOUNDS

ⓐ **grasp, seize, clasp, hold**
ⓑ **seize (power), hold (the reins of government)**
握力 *akuryoku* grasping power
握手 *akushu* handshake, handshaking
一握 *ichiaku* a handful (of sand)
把握する *haaku suru* grip, grasp; understand, grasp
掌握する *shōaku suru* hold, seize, grasp, command

KUN

【nigi(ru) 握る】
①ⓐ grasp, seize, clasp, seize
ⓑ seize (power), hold (the reins of government)
握り *nigiri* grasp, grip; handle; rice ball, hand-rolled sushi
握り締める *nigirishimeru* squeeze, grip, clasp
権力を握る *kenryoku o nigiru* seize power
② make hand-rolled sushi balls
握り飯 *nigirimeshi* rice ball
寿司を握る *sushi o nigiru* make hand-rolled sushi

SYNONYMS

ⓐ **take**
把 GRIP → 249
執 SEIZE → 1680
捕 CATCH → 429
取 TAKE → 1262
持 HOLD → 374

3-9 扌

援 援 援 援 586

EN

Ⓒⓗ 援 yuán

一 十 扌 扌 扌 扌 扌 扌 扌 扌 援 援
1 2 3 4 5 6 7 8 9 10 11 12

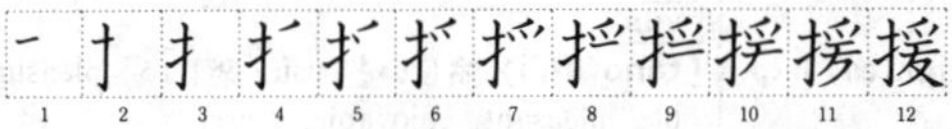

Radical	Strokes
扌 64	12-3-9
Grade	**Freq**
Jōyō	519
1-3-9	

▶AID

COMPOUNDS

❶ⓐ [original meaning] **aid, help out, give a hand, give support**
ⓑ [formerly 掩 489] cover, protect
援助 *enjo* aid, assistance, help
援軍 *engun* relieving force, reinforcements
支援 *shien* support, backing, aid
応援 *ōen* aid, reinforcement; support; cheering

後援する *kōen suru* give support [backing]
援護 *engo* support, protection; covering
❷ cite, quote, invoke (the law)
援用する *en'yō suru* quote, invoke

SYNONYMS

❶ⓐ help
助 HELP → 1121
佑 HELP (said esp. of God) → 74
祐 DIVINE HELP → 915
佐 ASSIST → 67
補 assist → 1194
輔 ASSIST → 1559
済 RELIEVE → 522

換 換 换

587 KAN ka(eru) -ka(eru) ka(waru)

CH 换 huàn

Radical	Strokes
扌 64	12-3-9
Grade	**Freq**
Jōyō	823
◧ 1 - 3 - 9	

3-9 扌

一 十 扌 扌 扌 扌 扚 扚 扚 换 換 換
1 2 3 4 5 6 7 8 9 10 11 12

▶EXCHANGE

COMPOUNDS

● exchange, interchange, change, turn, convert; take the place of, replace
換気 *kanki* ventilation
換金する *kankin suru* cash (a check), turn into money
換算する *kanzan suru* convert, change, exchange
変換 *henkan* change, conversion, transformation
転換 *tenkan* conversion, switchover, turnabout
互換性 *gokansei* interchangeability, compatibility
交換する *kōkan suru* exchange, interchange, barter, substitute

KUN

【ka(eru) 換える】[sometimes also 替える] exchange, interchange, trade, barter, change (money), convert
換え *kae* rate of exchange
本を金に換える *hon o kane ni kaeru* exchange a book for money
ドルを円に換える *doru o en ni kaeru* convert dollars into yen
十ドル札を換える *jūdorusatsu o kaeru* get change for a ten-dollar bill
本と時計を換える *hon to tokei o kaeru* swap a watch for a book
引き換える *hikikaeru* exchange, change, convert
一リットル百円換えで買う *ichirittoru hyakuengae de kau* purchase at 100 yen per liter

【-ka(eru) -換える】[verbal suffix] redo, renew, change
書き換える *kakikaeru* rewrite, renew (a bill), transfer
作り換える *tsukurikaeru* remake, reconstruct
乗り換える *norikaeru* change (trains), transfer

【ka(waru) 換わる】 be exchanged, become interchanged, be converted, change
換わり *kawari* exchange
段ボールがお金に換わる *Danbōru ga okane ni kawaru* Cardboard can be traded in for money

SYNONYMS

● change and replace
交 INTERCHANGE → 2015
替 REPLACE → 2783
代 SUBSTITUTE → 30
迭 ALTERNATE → 3077
転 turn into → 1480
遷 undergo transition → 3170
化 CHANGE INTO, -ize → 21
変 CHANGE → 2069
更 change → 3541
改 change → 243
易 change → 2411

【-kaeru】
○ repeating and repetition
改 redo → 243
-直す repetition suffix → 2932
-返す do over → 3060
再 ANOTHER TIME → 3519
又 AGAIN → 3351
復 repeat → 575
重 DUPLICATE → 3573
畳 reduplicate → 2592

HOMOPHONES

kaeru ⇨ 替 2783 代 30 変 2069
kae ⇨ 替 2783 代 30 変 2069
kawaru ⇨ 替 2783 代 30 変 2069
kawari ⇨ 替 2783 代 30 変 2069

NOTE

⇨ see USAGE note at 変 2069

3-9
扌

揆
588 KI

Ⓒⓗ 揆 kuí

Radical	Strokes
扌 64	12-3-9
Grade	**Freq**
Reference	
◧ 1 - 3 - 9	

COMPOUNDS

❶ plot, plan

一揆 *ikki* riot, uprising, revolt

❷ [also 軌 1445] way of doing

揆を一にする *ki o itsu ni suru* have the same way of doing

❸ [original meaning, now archaic] conjecture, estimate

NOTE

⇨ see USAGE note at 軌 1445

3-9
扌

揮 揮 揮
589 KI furu(u)▲

Ⓒⓗ 挥 huī

Radical	Strokes
扌 64	12-3-9
Grade	**Freq**
Jōyō-6	988
◧ 1 - 3 - 9	

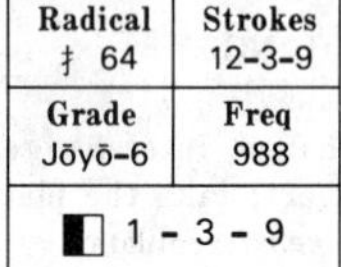

▶WIELD

COMPOUNDS

❶ⓐ [original meaning] **wield, brandish, wave**

ⓑ wield the writing brush, write

指揮者 *shikisha* conductor; commander

揮毫する *kigō suru* write, draw, paint

❷ **wield (one's power), display (one's abilities)**

発揮する *hakki suru* display, exhibit, demonstrate

❸ scatter, sprinkle, wipe away

揮発する *kihatsu suru* volatilize

揮発油 *kihatsuyu* gasoline

KUN

【furu(u) 揮う】[now usu. 振るう] wield, brandish, manipulate, master

筆を揮う *fude o furuu* drive a quill [pen], wield the writing brush

SYNONYMS

❶ **handle**

操 MANIPULATE → 769

扱う HANDLE → 217

運 control movement skillfully → 3140

❷ **express**

表 EXPRESS → 2429

HOMOPHONES

furuu ⇨ 振 430 震 2806 奮 2367

NOTE

⇨ see USAGE note at 振 430

3-9
扌

揃 揃 揃
590 SEN soro(eru) soro(u) soro(i) -zoro(i)

Ⓒⓗ 揃 jiǎn

Radical	Strokes
扌 64	12-3-9
Grade	**Freq**
Non-Jōyō	1967
◧ 1 - 3 - 9	

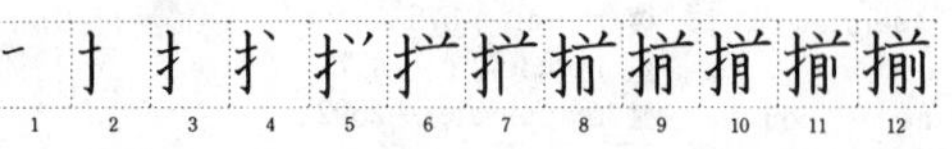

▶MAKE UNIFORM

KUN

【soro(eru) 揃える】

① make uniform [even], act in line [concert]

高さを揃える *takasa o soroeru* make all of uniform height

歩調を揃える *hochō o soroeru* keep step with

口を揃えて *kuchi o soroete* unanimously, in chorus

② arrange properly, put in order

靴を揃える *kutsu o soroeru* arrange the shoes

③ have a complete set of, assort

家具を揃える *kagu o soroeru* have a suite of furniture

取り揃える *torisoroeru* assort; gather, put together

一揃え *hitosoroe* a set [suit]
品揃え *shinazoroe* full stock of goods
④ collect, gather, put together
首を揃える *kubi o soroeru* get together
数を揃える *kazu o soroeru* have a complete set of, make up the number
【soro(u) 揃う】 be uniform [even], be in concert, match; become complete, make a pair [set]; get together, assemble, be all present
揃わない *sorowanai* uneven, unequal, odd; incomplete
条件が揃う *jōken ga sorou* satisfy the requirements
揃った蔵書 *sorotta zōsho* good collection of books
揃って *sorotte* in a body, all together; all alike
【soro(i) 揃い】
① uniformity, sameness
揃いの *soroi no* uniform, of the same pattern
②ⓐ counter for sets or suits
ⓑ set, pair
ⓒ [in compounds] assembly (of one sort), array
食器一揃い *shokki hitosoroi* a table service
お揃いで *osoroi de* in a body, all together; hand in hand
揃い踏み *soroibumi sumo* stamping on the ring in unison
勢揃いする *seizoroi suru* assemble in full force, muster
【-zoro(i) -揃い】 [suffix] assembly (of one sort), array
傑作揃い *kessakuzoroi* full array of masterpieces

SYNONYMS

【soroeru】
① **fit**
合 FIT → 2019
適 suit → 3160
② **arrange**
整 PUT IN ORDER → 2871
理 put in order → 970
列 arrange in a row → 824
陳 lay out (for exhibit) → 540
羅 spread out → 2622
並 LINE UP → 2246
比 rank → 26

提 提 提

591 TEI CHŌ▲ DAI▲ sa(geru)

CH 提 tí dī

Radical	Strokes
扌 64	12-3-9
Grade	**Freq**
Jōyō-5	355
◧ 1 - 3 - 9	

3-9 扌

Stroke order: 一 十 扌 扌 扣 扣 担 担 捍 捍 掦 提 (1–12)

▶**PRESENT**

COMPOUNDS

❶ (bring before a person, as for consideration) **present, bring forward, offer, tender, propose**
提案 *teian* proposition, proposal, suggestion
提出する *teishutsu suru* present, submit, turn in
提供する *teikyō suru* offer, tender; sponsor (a show)
提言 *teigen* proposal, suggestion
提示する *teiji suru* present, exhibit
提訴する *teiso suru* present a case to (the court), file an action
提議 *teigi* proposition, proposal, motion
前提 *zentei* premise, presupposition
❷ **carry in hand**
提琴 *teikin* violin
提灯 *chōchin* paper lantern
❸ help each other
提携 *teikei* cooperation, tie-up
❹ control, manage
提督 *teitoku* admiral
❺ used phonetically for *dai* in the transliteration of Sanscrit Buddhist terms
菩提 *bodai* Bodhi

KUN

【sa(geru) 提げる】 carry in hand, take (a thing) with (a person)
手提げ袋 *tesagebukuro* handbag

SYNONYMS

❶ **offer**
供 OFFER (to a person or god) → 88
献 OFFER (esp. to a superior) → 1785
納 offer (as to a god) → 1300
貢 offer tribute → 2281
奉 DEDICATE → 2559
❷ **hold**
携 CARRY IN HAND → 648
持 HOLD → 374

HOMOPHONES

sageru ⇨ 下 3378

NOTE

⇨ see USAGE note at 下 3378

3-9 扌

搭 搭 搭 搭

592 TŌ

CH 搭 dā

Radical	Strokes
扌 64	12-3-9
Grade	**Freq**
Jōyō	1949
1 - 3 - 9	

一 十 扌 扌 扌 扌 扌 扌 扌 搭 搭 搭

1 2 3 4 5 6 7 8 9 10 11 12

▶**BOARD**

COMPOUNDS

❶ **board, get on, embark**

搭乗する *tōjō suru* board, get on a plane, embark

❷ **load on board (a ship or vehicle)**

搭載する *tōsai suru* load, embark

SYNONYMS

❶ **get on**

乗 GET ON → 3576

❷ **load**

載 LOAD → 3300

積む load → 1236

NOTE

★do not confuse with 塔 561

3-9 扌

揚 揚 揚

593 YŌ a(geru) -a(ge) a(garu)

CH 扬 yáng

Radical	Strokes
扌 64	12-3-9
Grade	**Freq**
Jōyō	1017
1 - 3 - 9	

一 十 扌 扌 扌 扌 扌 扌 扌 揚 揚 揚

1 2 3 4 5 6 7 8 9 10 11 12

▶**RAISE HIGH** ▶**EXALT**

COMPOUNDS

❶ⓐ (cause to rise high) **raise high, lift, hoist, elevate, fly; rise, fly**

ⓑ raise one's voice, declare in public

揚力 *yōryoku* lift, lifting power

揚抗比 *yōkōhi* lift-drag ratio

揚炭機 *yōtanki* coal hoist

掲揚する *keiyō suru* hoist, put up, fly (a flag)

飛揚 *hiyō* flying, flight

揚言する *yōgen suru* profess, declare in public, proclaim

抑揚 *yokuyō* rising and falling (of tones), intonation

❷ⓐ (raise to a higher level of dignity) **exalt, extol, praise, enhance, uplift**

ⓑ (raise one's spirits) **be exalted, be in high spirits**

称揚する *shōyō suru* praise, admire, exalt, extol

発揚する *hatsuyō suru* exalt, raise, enhance

高揚(＝昂揚)する *kōyō suru* exalt, enhance, uplift; surge up

意気揚揚と *ikiyōyō to* exultantly, in exalted spirits, proudly

❸ land, unload, disembark

揚陸料 *yōrikuryō* landing charge

KUN

【a(geru) 揚げる】

① (cause to rise high or float in the air) raise (a flag), send up, hoist, lift, fly (a kite), shoot up (fireworks)

旗を揚げる *hata o ageru* raise [hoist] a flag

凧揚げ *takoage* kite-flying

② fry in deep fat

揚げ *age* fried bean curd

揚げ物 *agemono* fried food, a fry

魚を揚げる *sakana o ageru* fry fish

③ land, unload, disembark

陸揚げ *rikuage* landing, unloading

引き揚げる *hikiageru* withdraw, leave, return, repatriate

【-a(ge) -揚げ】

ⓐ [also suffix] fried food, fry

ⓑ fried bean curd

精進揚げ *shōjin'age* fried vegetables

油揚げ *aburaage* fried bean curd

【a(garu) 揚がる】

① (rise high or float in the air) (of kites or flags) be up, fly, be flying; (of fireworks) be shot up, be set off

旗が揚がっている *Hata ga agatte iru* The flag is up

② be fried, fry

③ (of appearance) stand out, improve

風采が揚がらない *fūsai ga agaranai* make a poor appearance

④ become elated, get into high spirits

意気が揚がっている *iki ga agatte iru* be in high spirits

SYNONYMS

❶ⓐ raise
揭 PUT UP → 494
挙 RAISE → 2456
上 raise → 3404
起 raise up → 3307
立てる STAND → 1992
拾う PICK UP → 379

❷ⓐ praise
賞 express admiration → 2618
賛 PRAISE → 2809
美 regard as beautiful → 2264
褒 COMMEND → 2144
嘉 commend (esp. an inferior) → 2340
彰 PROCLAIM MERITS → 1860
称 acclaim → 1160
頌 EULOGIZE → 1045

ⓑ elated
高 high-spirited → 2097
昂 high-spirited → 2412
奮 roused up → 2367

【ageru】

② cook
焼く cook by fire → 997
蒸 STEAM → 2334
炊 COOK → 870
煮 BOIL (cook by boiling) → 2785
沸 BOIL (undergo boiling) → 329

【-age】

ⓐ cooked dishes
-焼き roasted, baked or fried food → 997
-煮 boiled food → 2785

HOMOPHONES

ageru ⇨ 上 3404 挙 2456
-age ⇨ 上 3404
agaru ⇨ 上 3404 挙 2456

NOTE

⇨ see USAGE note at 上 3404

揺 搖 揺 揺 — 594

Ⓒⓗ 揺 yáo

3-9 扌

YŌ yu(reru) yu(ru) yu(ragu) yu(rugu) yu(suru) yu(saburu) yu(suburu)

Radical	Strokes
扌 64	12-3-9
Grade	**Freq**
Jōyō	1522
◧ 1 - 3 - 9	

Stroke order: 1–12

▶SHAKE

COMPOUNDS

● [original meaning] **shake, sway, rock**
揺動 *yōdō* titubation; shaking, swinging
揺籃 *yōran* cradle
動揺 *dōyō* shaking, trembling; restlessness, uneasiness, disquiet

KUN

【yu(reru) 揺れる】 shake, sway, vibrate, rock, swing
揺れ *yure* shaking, vibration, tremor
揺れ動く *yureugoku* rock; sway, vacillate
大揺れ *ōyure* severe quake; turbulence

【yu(ru) 揺る】 jolt, jog, be rocked
揺り返し *yurikaeshi* aftershock, after quake
揺り起こす *yuriokosu* shake up, wake by shaking
揺り籠 *yurikago* swinging cot, cradle
バスに揺られる *basu ni yurareru* be jolted along in a bus

【yu(ragu) 揺らぐ】 *vi* swing, sway, shake, fluctuate
揺らめく *yurameku* flicker, quiver, waver, sway
決心が揺らぐ *kesshin ga yuragu* one's resolution wavers

【yu(rugu) 揺るぐ】 shake, waver
揺るぎ無い *yuruginai* firm, solid, steady
揺るがす *yurugasu* shake, swing, sway, shock

【yu(suru) 揺する】 shake, rock, joggle, swing, roll
貧乏揺すり *binbōyusuri* nervous shaking of the body

【yu(saburu) 揺さぶる】 shake, jolt, jerk
揺さぶり *yusaburi* shaking; shaking up (one's adversary)

【yu(suburu) 揺すぶる】 shake, swing, joggle, jolt
木を揺すぶる *ki o yusuburu* shake a tree (for fruit)

SYNONYMS

● shake
震 QUAKE → 2806
振 SWING → 430

描 — 595

3-9 扌

▶DEPICT

nonstandard for 描 488

3-9 扌 **援** 596

▶AID
nonstandard for 援 586

3-9 扌 **掲** 597

▶PUT UP
nonstandard for 掲 494

3-9 扌 **揷** 598

▶INSERT
nonstandard for 挿 431

3-9 扌 **插** 599

▶INSERT
nonstandard for 挿 431

3-9 扌 **搜**

incorrect stroke count ⇨ see 652
(nonstandard for 捜 432)

3-9 氵 **渥** 600 AKU NAMES atsu atsushi

CH 渥 wò

Radical	Strokes
氵 85	12-3-9
Grade	**Freq**
Names	2034
1-3-9	

1 2 3 4 5 6 7 8 9 10 11 12

▶GRACIOUS

COMPOUNDS

❶ **gracious, cordial, benevolent**
優渥な *yūaku na* gracious (words of the Emperor)
❷ [archaic] glossy, shining with a beautiful luster
渥然たる *akuzentaru* glossy
❸ [archaic] be moistened, soak wet; moisten
渥地 *akuchi* marshland

NAMES

渥美 *atsumi* surname also female name also place name
渥 *atsushi* male name

SYNONYMS

❶ **kind**
優 kindly → 177
温 warmhearted → 608
慈 AFFECTIONATE → 2339
篤 cordial → 2716
懇 cordial → 2899
厚 KIND → 3003

3-9 氵 **減** 601 GEN he(ru) he(rasu)

CH 减 jiǎn

Radical	Strokes
氵 85	12-3-9
Grade	**Freq**
Jōyō-5	483
1-3-9	

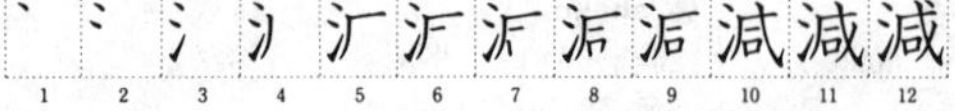

1 2 3 4 5 6 7 8 9 10 11 12

▶DECREASE

COMPOUNDS

❶ⓐ [original meaning] (grow or cause to grow less) **decrease, reduce, lessen**
ⓑ [also suffix] **decrease, reduction, fall**
減少する *genshō suru* decrease, reduce, lessen
減税 *genzei* reduction of taxes, tax cut
減速 *gensoku* speed reduction
減配 *genpai* reduction in a dividend; smaller ration
減点 *genten* demerit mark
削減 *sakugen* curtailment, reduction

満 満 満 満

607 MAN mi(chiru) mi(tsu) mi(tasu)

Ⓒⓗ 満 mǎn

Radical	Strokes
氵 85	12-3-9
Grade	**Freq**
Jōyō-4	557
1-3-9	

Stroke order: 1 2 3 4 5 6 7 8 9 10 11 12

▶**FULL**

COMPOUNDS

❶ⓐ (filled to capacity) **full**
ⓑ (to the maximum extent) **full**
ⓒ (complete) **full, whole, entire, perfect**
ⓓ [prefix] full, fully—said of a person's age or period of time
満員 *man'in* full to capacity
満塁 *manrui* full bases
満満の *manman no* full of, brimming with
満腹の *manpuku no* full, satiated
肥満した *himan shita* fat, obese, corpulent
満月 *mangetsu* full moon
満開 *mankai* full bloom
満潮 *manchō* high tide, high water
満載 *mansai* full load
未満の *miman no* less than
満点 *manten* full marks, perfect score
満面 *manmen* whole face
満座 *manza* the whole assembly
満三歳だ *mansansai da* be a full three years old
満二年 *manninen* a full two years

❷ⓐ [original meaning] **fill, fill up, be filled**
ⓑ **reach the full extent, expire**
ⓒ fulfill, carry out
充満する *jūman suru* be full, be filled with, overflow
金満家 *kinmanka* man of wealth, millionaire
満期 *manki* expiration (of a term)
満了 *manryō* expiration, due
満願 *mangan* completion [fulfillment] of a vow

❸ **satisfied**
満足 *manzoku* satisfaction, contentment
満喫する *mankitsu suru* have enough, enjoy fully
不満 *fuman* dissatisfaction, discontent
円満な *enman na* perfect, harmonious, well-rounded

❹ Manchuria
満州 *manshū* Manchuria
満蒙 *manmō* Manchuria and Mongolia

INDEPENDENT

【man 満】 fullness; age in full
満を持する *man o jisuru* watch in readiness for a golden opportunity
年齢を満で数える *nenrei o man de kazoeru* count age in full

KUN

【mi(chiru) 満ちる】
① be filled, be full of
満ち足りる *michitariru* be content, have enough, be happy
光に満ちた空 *hikari ni michita sora* sky suffused with light
② reach the full extent:
ⓐ expire, mature
ⓑ (of tides) rise, (of the moon) wax
任期が満ちた *Ninki ga michita* One's term of office has expired
満ち潮 *michishio* high tide, high water
満ち欠け *michikake* waxing and waning (of the moon)

【mi(tsu) 満つ】 [in negative constructions] reach the limit (in numbers)
...に満たない *...ni mitanai* less than...

【mi(tasu) 満たす】
[sometimes also 充たす]
① fill (up), pack
水を満たす *mizu o mitasu* fill (a glass) with water
② fill, fulfill, satisfy, meet (the demand)
腹を満たす *hara o mitasu* satisfy one's appetite
条件を満たす *jōken o mitasu* answer the requirement

SYNONYMS

❶ⓐ & ❶ⓑ full
飽 SATIATED → 1715
ⓒ **all**
丸 complete(ly) → 3417
一 all in one → 3341
全 WHOLE → 2022
万 all → 2936
皆 ALL → 2445
都 all → 1686
完 COMPLETE → 2201
総 TOTAL → 1379
諸 VARIOUS → 1577
毎 EVERY → 2034
各 EACH → 2168
❷ⓐ & ❷ⓑ fill
充 FILL → 2014
詰める STUFF → 1521
❸ **suffice**

足 SUFFICE → 2188

USAGE

mitasu

満たす

[sometimes also 充たす]

① fill (up), pack

② fill, fulfill, satisfy, meet (the demand)

充たす

[usu. 満たす] same as 満たす

HOMOPHONES

mitasu ⇨ 充 2014

3-9

氵

温 溫 温 𣴎

608 ON atata(ka) atata(kai) atata(maru) atata(meru)

CH 温 wēn

Radical	Strokes
氵 85	12-3-9
Grade	**Freq**
Jōyō-3	800
1 - 3 - 9	

1	2	3	4	5	6	7	8	9	10	11	12
丶	冫	氵	氵	汩	汩	泪	泪	温	温	温	温

▶WARM

COMPOUNDS

❶ [also prefix] **warm, hot, temperate**

温暖な *ondan na* warm, mild

温泉 *onsen* hot spring

温水プール *onsui pūru* heated swimming pool

温室 *onshitsu* greenhouse

温度 *ondo* temperature

温和な *onwa na* (of the weather) mild, temperate

温湿布 *onshippu* hot compress

❷ [also suffix] **temperature, heat, warmth**

気温 *kion* (atmospheric) temperature

低温 *teion* low temperature

保温 *hoon* keeping warm, heat insulation

海水温 *kaisuion* seawater temperature

❸ warmhearted, kindly, gentle

温和(＝穏和)な *onwa na* gentle, mild, genial

温厚な *onkō na* gentle, courteous

温情 *onjō* warm feeling, kindliness, warmheartedness

❹ review

温古知新 *onkochishin* learning from the past

❺ take good care of

温存する *onzon suru* preserve, retain

INDEPENDENT

【on 温】 warm temper, gentle temper

KUN

【atata(ka) 温か】

atataka na 温かな same as **atatakai** 温かい

【atata(kai) 温かい】

① warm (to the touch), lukewarm

温かい御飯 *atatakai gohan* warm rice

② heartwarming, warm (feeling or atmosphere)

温かい歓迎 *atatakai kangei* warm reception

【atata(maru) 温まる】

① (of objects or persons) warm oneself, take warmth, get warm, be heated

日光に温まる *nikkō ni atatamaru* bask in the sun, sun oneself

② be heartwarming

心温まる *kokoroatatamaru* heartwarming

【atata(meru) 温める】

① (raise the temperature of a thing) warm, heat

コーヒーを温める *kōhī o atatameru* warm up coffee

② nurse (an idea), let (an idea) mellow

アイディアを温める *aidia o atatameru* nurse an idea in one's mind

③ renew (an old friendship)

SYNONYMS

❶ **hot**

暖 WARM (esp. weather) → 1011

暑い HOT (weather) → 2473

熱 HOT → 2866

炎 scorching → 2420

❸ **kind**

渥 GRACIOUS → 600

優 kindly → 177

慈 AFFECTIONATE → 2339

篤 cordial → 2716

懇 cordial → 2899

厚 KIND → 3003

【atatameru】

① **raise the temperature**

暖 WARM (the air) → 1011

熱 HEAT → 2866

HOMOPHONES

atatakai ⇨ 暖 1011

atatamaru ⇨ 暖 1011

atatameru ⇨ 暖 1011

NOTE

⇨ see USAGE note at 暖 1011

湿 濕

CH 湿 shī

609 SHITSU shime(ru) shime(su)

Radical	Strokes
氵 85	12-3-9
Grade	**Freq**
Jōyō	1516
◧ 1 - 3 - 9	

3-9 氵

▶**DAMP**

COMPOUNDS

❶ⓐ [original meaning] **damp, moist, wet, humid**

ⓑ dampness, moisture, humidity

湿地 *shitchi* damp ground, swamp

湿布 *shippu* wet compress

湿気 *shikke* (=*shikki*) moisture, dampness, humidity

湿電池 *shitsudenchi* wet cell

湿度 *shitsudo* humidity

乾湿 *kanshitsu* dryness and moisture, humidity

防湿 *bōshitsu* dampproofing, prevention of moisture

❷ itch

湿疹 *shisshin* eczema

KUN

【**shime(ru) 湿る**】 get damp, get wet

湿り *shimeri* dampness, moisture, humidity; rain

湿った *shimetta* damp, moist, wet

【**shime(su) 湿す**】 damp, dampen, wet, moisten

タオルを湿す *taoru o shimesu* dampen a towel

SYNONYMS

❶ⓐ **wet**

潤 MOIST → 742

USAGE

shimeru

湿る

get damp, get wet

-染める

permeate with fluid or smoke

HOMOPHONES

shimeru ⇨ 染 2572

測 测

CH 测 cè

610 SOKU haka(ru)

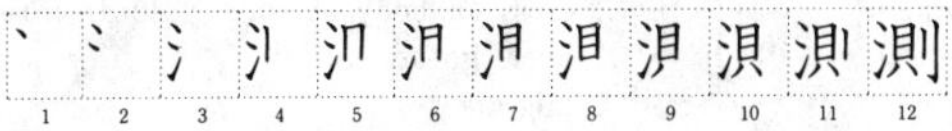

Radical	Strokes
氵 85	12-3-9
Grade	**Freq**
Jōyō-5	794
◧ 1 - 3 - 9	

3-9 氵

▶**MEASURE** ▶**CONJECTURE**

COMPOUNDS

❶ⓐ [original meaning] **measure, gauge, survey, fathom**

ⓑ observe

測定する *sokutei suru* measure, gauge

測量 *sokuryō* measurement, surveying

測深 *sokushin* sounding

測候所 *sokkōjo* weather station

観測 *kansoku* observation

天測 *tensoku* astronomical observation

❷ **conjecture, surmise, suppose, presume, presuppose; expect; estimate**

推測 *suisoku* conjecture, supposition

予測 *yosoku* estimate, forecast, prediction

不測の *fusoku no* unexpected, unforeseen

憶測 *okusoku* conjecture, speculation, guess

KUN

【**haka(ru) 測る**】 (measure the physical dimensions of) measure, gauge (length, depth, distance or area)

標高を測る *hyōkō o hakaru* measure the height of (a mountain)

SYNONYMS

❶ⓐ **measure**

量 measure → 2471

❷ **conjecture**

憶 SPECULATE → 765

推 INFER → 504

察 GUESS → 2347

HOMOPHONES

hakaru ⇨ 量 2471 計 1441 図 3071 謀 1593 諮 1596

COMPOUND FORMATION

測候所 *sokkōjo*

測候所 'weather station' is a place (所) for observing (測 ❶ⓑ) the weather (候).

NOTE

⇨ see USAGE note at 計 1441

3-9 氵

渡 渡 渡

611 TO wata(ru) -wata(ru) wata(su)

CH 渡 dù

Radical	Strokes
氵 85	12-3-9
Grade	**Freq**
Jōyō	588
1-3-9	

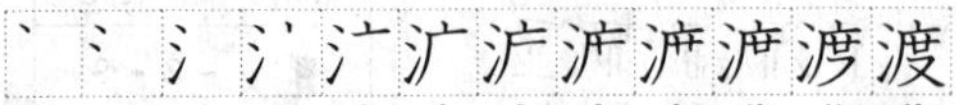

▶**CROSS**

COMPOUNDS

❶ [original meaning] **cross (a body of water), ford, cross over, go overseas, go across**
渡航 *tokō* crossing, passage, voyage
渡米 *tobei* going to America
渡河 *toka* wading [fording] a river
渡来 *torai* importation, influx

❷ go through (life), pass
渡世 *tosei* livelihood, subsistence
過渡期 *katoki* transitional period [stage]

❸ hand over, transfer, turn over
譲渡する *jōto suru* transfer, hand over

KUN

【wata(ru) 渡る】
① cross (a body of water), ford, cross over, go across
渡り *watari* passage, transit; migration; mutual arrangement, negotiation
綱渡り *tsunawatari* tightrope walking [walker]
② migrate
渡り鳥 *wataridori* migratory bird
渡り者 *watarimono* migratory worker
③ go through (life), pass
世渡り *yowatari* living, subsistence
④ be transferred, be handed over, be supplied
人手に渡る *hitode ni wataru* fall into another's hands
不渡り *fuwatari* dishonor, nonpayment

【-wata(ru) -渡る】 [verbal suffix] reach all over, spread, extend
晴れ渡る *harewataru* clear up
染み渡る(＝滲み渡る) *shimiwataru* penetrate, pervade, spread

【wata(su) 渡す】 carry across (a river); hand over, deliver, transfer; build, span (a bridge)
渡し *watashi* ferry (crossing); ferry(boat); [also suffix] delivery
渡し船 *watashibune* ferryboat
言い渡す *iiwatasu* announce, tell; sentence; order
手渡す *tewatasu* hand over (to), give, deliver
引き渡す *hikiwatasu* deliver, turn over, surrender

SYNONYMS

❶ **cross**
渉 wade → 526
越 GO BEYOND → 3314

❸ **transfer**
譲 CEDE → 1649
付 deliver → 31
附 deliver → 347

USAGE

wataru
渡る
① cross (a body of water), ford, cross over, go across
② migrate
③ go through (life), pass
④ be transferred, be handed over, be supplied
亘る
extend over, extend for, range, span, last

HOMOPHONES

wataru ⇨ 亘 1939

3-9 氵

湯 湯 湯

612 TŌ yu

CH 汤 tāng

Radical	Strokes
氵 85	12-3-9
Grade	**Freq**
Jōyō-3	1131
1-3-9	

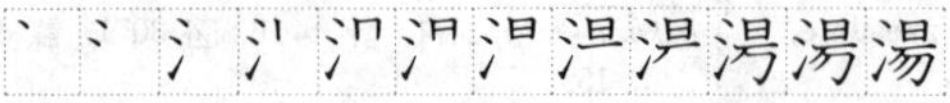

▶**HOT WATER**

COMPOUNDS

❶ [original meaning] **hot water, boiling water**
給湯 *kyūtō* hot water supply
熱湯 *nettō* boiling water

❷ **hot bath, hot spring**
湯治 *tōji* hot spring cure, taking healing baths
入湯 *nyūtō* taking a hot bath

錢湯 *sentō* public bath, bathhouse
❸ [also suffix] medical decoction, infusion
薬湯 *yakutō* infusion, decoction, medical bath
葛根湯 *kakkontō* antifebrile infusion

KUN

【yu 湯】
① hot water
湯気 *yuge* steam, vapor
茶の湯 *chanoyu* tea ceremony
② hot bath, hot spring; bathhouse, public bath
湯船 *yubune* bathtub
湯殿 *yudono* bathroom
湯屋 *yuya* public bath house

SYNONYMS

❶ **kinds of water**
水 WATER → 10
汽 STEAM → 264
氷 ICE → 39
❷ **baths**
浴 bath → 445
泉 hot spring → 2567

湾 灣 湾 [variant]

613 WAN

CH 湾 wān

Radical	Strokes
氵 85	12-3-9
Grade	**Freq**
Jōyō	931

1 - 3 - 9

3-9 氵

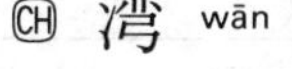
1 2 3 4 5 6 7 8 9 10 11 12

▶BAY

COMPOUNDS

❶ⓐ [original meaning] **bay, gulf, inlet**
ⓑ **suffix after names of bays and gulfs**
湾口 *wankō* bay entrance
湾内 *wannai* inside the bay
港湾局 *kōwankyoku* Port and Harbor Authority
東京湾 *tōkyōwan* Tokyo Bay
メキシコ湾 *mekishikowan* Gulf of Mexico
❷ [formerly also 彎 2918] curve
湾曲 *wankyoku* curve, crook, bend
湾入する *wannyū suru* curve in

INDEPENDENT

【**wan** 湾】 bay, gulf, inlet

SYNONYMS

❶ **inlets and bays**
浦 coastal indentation → 437
江 INLET → 221
峡 narrows → 357

游

614 YŪ

CH 游 yóu

Radical	Strokes
氵 85	12-3-9
Grade	**Freq**
Reference	

1 - 3 - 9

3-9 氵

COMPOUNDS

● [now usu. 遊 3142] [original meaning] swim
游泳 *yūei* swimming
回游 *kaiyū* migration (of fish)
浮游する *fuyū suru* waft, float

湧

615 YŪ YŌ wa(ku)

CH 涌 yǒng

Radical	Strokes
氵 85	12-3-9
Grade	**Freq**
Reference	

1 - 3 - 9

3-9 氵

COMPOUNDS

❶ [original meaning] spring forth, gush out
湧出 *yūshutsu* welling, gushing
湧水 *yūsui* [rare] welling of water
湧き出る *wakideru* well up, spring forth
❷ take form, appear; grow, spring up
湧き上がる *wakiagaru* arise
降って湧く *futte waku* take place unexpectedly
❸ breed (teemingly), be hatched

ぼうふらが湧いた *Bōfura ga waita* Mosquito larvae have hatched

HOMOPHONES

waku ⇨ 沸 329

NOTE

⇨ see USAGE note at 沸 329

3-9 氵

渴 616

▶RUN DRY ▶THIRST

nonstandard for 渇 515

3-9 氵

港 617

▶PORT

nonstandard for 港 605

3-9 氵

渚 618

▶STRAND

nonstandard for 渚 525

3-9 犭

猶 619

猶 猶 犹

YŪ YU▲ nao▲

CH 犹 yóu

丿 犭 犭 犭 犭' 犭ᅩ 犭ᅶ 犭ᅶ 犭酉 犭酋 猶 猶

1 2 3 4 5 6 7 8 9 10 11 12

Radical	Strokes
犭 94	12-3-9
Grade	**Freq**
Jōyō	1664
1 - 3 - 9	

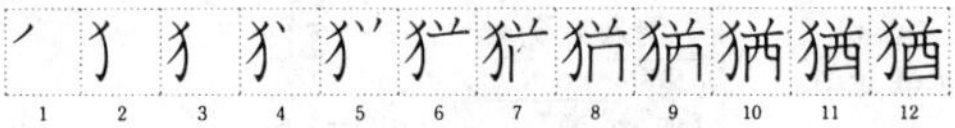

▶DELAY

COMPOUNDS

❶ **delay, put off, postpone; waver, dally**

猶予する *yūyo suru* postpone, delay, extend; hesitate

執行猶予 *shikkō yūyo* stay of execution, probation, suspended sentence

❷ just, like

猶子 *yūshi* nephew ("like a son")

❸ Jew, Jewish

猶太 *yudaya* Judea, Jewish people

日猶同祖論 *nichiyū-dōsoron* hypothesis that Jews and Japanese are of common ancestry

KUN

【nao 猶】

[usu. 尚]

①ⓐ (in increasing degree) still (more), all the more

ⓑ further, in addition, by the way

猶の事 *nao no koto* all the more, still more

猶良い *nao yoi* still better

猶一層悪い事は *nao issō warui koto wa* what is worse still

②ⓐ still, yet

ⓑ even, still

春猶浅し *Haru nao asashi* Spring is not yet far advanced

昼猶暗い *hiru nao kurai* be dark even in the daytime

③ *literary* as, just like, no more...than

鯨の魚にあらざるは猶馬の魚にあらざるが如し *Kujira no sakana ni arazaru wa nao uma no sakana ni arazaru ga gotoshi* A whale is no more a fish than a horse is

SYNONYMS

❶ **be late and delay**

延 POSTPONE → 3073

遅 be late → 3133

後 fall behind → 361

滞 fall into arrears → 663

HOMOPHONES

nao ⇨ 尚 2233

NOTE

⇨ see USAGE note at 尚 2233

3-9 犭

猫 620

▶CAT

nonstandard for 猫 535

621

▶WILD BOAR
nonstandard for 猪 536

3-9 犭

猶
622

▶DELAY
nonstandard for 猶 619

3-9 犭

隅 隅 隅
623 GŪ sumi

Ⓒⓗ 隅 yú

Radical	Strokes
阝 170	12-3-9
Grade	**Freq**
Jōyō	1602
◧ 1 - 3 - 9	

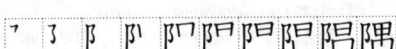

3-9 阝

1 2 3 4 5 6 7 8 9 10 11 12

▶NOOK

COMPOUNDS

● [original meaning] **nook, corner**
一隅 *ichigū* corner, nook

KUN

【sumi 隅】 nook, corner; angle
隅隅 *sumizumi* every nook and corner
片隅 *katasumi* corner, nook
隅から隅まで *sumi kara sumi made* every nook and corner
隅木 *sumiki* angle rafter, angle [corner] block
隅に置けない *sumi ni okenai* be witty and knowing

SYNONYMS

● **corners**
角 corner → 2047
圭 SHARP CORNER → 2165

階 階 階
624 KAI kizahashi▲

Ⓒⓗ  jiē

Radical	Strokes
阝 170	12-3-9
Grade	**Freq**
Jōyō-3	379
◧ 1 - 3 - 9	

3-9 阝

1 2 3 4 5 6 7 8 9 10 11 12

▶FLOOR ▶RANK

COMPOUNDS

❶ⓐ **floor, story**
ⓑ **counter for floors**
地階 *chikai* basement, cellar
各階 *kakukai* every floor
三階 *sangai* third floor
❷ **stairs, flight of stairs, steps, staircase**
階段 *kaidan* steps, flight of stairs
階下 *kaika* lower floor, downstairs
階梯 *kaitei* step, ladder; stepping-stone; guide
❸ **rank, order, grade, class**
階級 *kaikyū* class, estate; rank, grade
階層 *kaisō* social stratum, class; tier
位階 *ikai* court rank
段階 *dankai* grade, rank, step, stage

INDEPENDENT

【kai 階】 floor; stairs, steps; *geol* stage
下の階 *shita no kai* lower floor

KUN

【kizahashi 階】 stairs, steps

SYNONYMS

❶ **floor**
層 story → 3161
❷ **steps**
段 STEP → 1144
陛 IMPERIAL PALACE STEPS → 453
❸ **class**
位 RANK → 61
身 social status → 3553
格 STATUS → 926
級 GRADE → 1279
段 grade → 1144
等 CLASS → 2682
流 class → 441
層 STRATUM → 3161

NOTE

★do not confuse with 陛 453

3-9 阝

隊 隊 隊 隊

625 TAI

CH 队 duì

Radical	Strokes
阝 170	12-3-9
Grade	Freq
Jōyō-4	396
1-3-9	

Stroke order: 1–12

▶**PARTY**

COMPOUNDS

❶ [also suffix] (organized group of people) **party, group, troop, company, band**

隊員 *taiin* member of the group
一隊 *ittai* party (of mountaineers), company (of soldiers), gang, troop, squad
楽隊 *gakutai* musical band
デモ隊 *demotai* demonstrators
捜索隊 *sōsakutai* search party
親衛隊 *shin'eitai* bodyguards; groupies

❷ (organized group of troops) **party, army unit, corps, body of troops**

隊長 *taichō* captain, leader, commander
隊形 *taikei* battle formation, disposition of troops
軍隊 *guntai* army, troops
部隊 *butai* unit, corps, party, squad
連隊 *rentai* regiment
中隊 *chūtai* company, squadron
兵隊 *heitai* soldier; troops
艦隊 *kantai* squadron, fleet
自衛隊 *jieitai* Self Defense Forces
警官隊 *keikantai* police force [squad]
分遣隊 *bunkentai* detachment
別動隊 *betsudōtai* detached party [column]

INDEPENDENT

【**tai** 隊】 party, company, corps
隊を組む *tai o kumu* form a party, line up

SYNONYMS

❶ **groups**

党 PARTY → 2581
団 BODY → 3053
伍 ranks → 47
班 SQUAD → 946
軍 team → 2080
群 GROUP (of any kind) → 1540
組 group (of people) → 1337
陣 lineup → 455
連 set → 3103
族 common-interest group (*slang*) → 958

❷ **armed forces**

勢 forces → 2857
兵 the military → 2551
軍 ARMY → 2080

3-9 阝

陽 陽 陽

626 YŌ hi▲

CH 阳 yáng

Radical	Strokes
阝 170	12-3-9
Grade	Freq
Jōyō-3	1042
1-3-9	

Stroke order: 1–12

▶**SUN**

COMPOUNDS

❶ⓐ **sun, sunlight**

ⓑ sunny, bright

陽光 *yōkō* sunshine, sunlight, sun
陽暦 *yōreki* solar calendar
太陽 *taiyō* sun
落陽 *rakuyō* setting sun
春陽 *shun'yō* spring sunshine
陽気な *yōki na* cheerful, bright, sunny

❷ [original meaning] sunny or south side of a mountain; north side of a stream

山陽 *san'yō* south side of a mountain; Sanyo district
漢陽 *kan'yō* Hanyang (city in China)

❸ yang: the masculine and active principle in Chinese dualistic philosophy representing positive concepts such as masculinity, sun, light, heaven, etc.

陰陽 *in'yō* yin and yang, positive and negative, active and passive

❹ⓐ **positive**

ⓑ *elec* **positive, positive pole**

陽性 *yōsei* positivity
陽画 *yōga* positive photographic print
陽子 *yōshi* proton
陽極 *yōkyoku* positive pole, anode
陽電気 *yōdenki* positive electricity

❺ male genitals

陽物 *yōbutsu* phallus, penis

❻ openly, ostensibly, explicitly

陽報 *yōhō* open reward, rewarding openly

INDEPENDENT

【yō 陽】yang (⇨ ❸); open, explicit
陰と陽 *in to yō* the positive and the negative
陰に陽に *in ni yō ni* openly and covertly, implicitly and explicitly

KUN

【hi 陽】[usu. 日] sun, sunlight
夕陽 *yūhi* setting sun

SYNONYMS

❶ⓐ sun
日 SUN → 3027
旭 RISING SUN → 2977
❸ yin and yang
陰 yin → 541
❹ positive
正 positive → 3484

HOMOPHONES

hi ⇨ 日 3027

NOTE

⇨ see USAGE note at 日 3027

随 隨 随 (cursive)

627 ZUI

CH 随 suí

Radical	Strokes
阝 170	12-3-9
Grade	**Freq**
Jōyō	1343
1-3-9	

3-9 阝

Stroke order: 1 2 3 4 5 6 7 8 9 10 11 12

▶FOLLOW

COMPOUNDS

❶ⓐ (go after) **follow, attend (on), accompany**
ⓑ (comply with) follow, obey
随行する *zuikō suru* attend on, accompany, follow
随員 *zuiin* attendants, retinue
付随の *fuzui no* accompanying, incidental
随従する *zuijū suru* follow the lead of, play second fiddle to
随順する *zuijun suru* obey meekly, faithfully follow (one's master)
追随する *tsuizui suru* follow (in the wake of)
❷ let (oneself) do (as one pleases), let things take their natural course
随筆 *zuihitsu* essay; stray notes
随意に *zuii ni* voluntarily, at will
随想 *zuisō* occasional thoughts
随分 *zuibun* extremely, considerably ("as much as one pleases")
❸ irrespective of time or place
随時に *zuiji ni* anytime, as occasion calls
随所に *zuisho ni* everywhere

SYNONYMS

❶ⓐ follow and pursue
追 CHASE → 3096
従 FOLLOW → 415
ⓐ accompany
従 FOLLOW → 415
侍 ATTEND UPON → 85
陪 ACCOMPANY A SUPERIOR → 539
伴 ACCOMPANY → 60
添 accompany → 529
❷ let do
放 LET GO → 853

COMPOUND FORMATION

随筆 *zuihitsu*
随筆 'essay; stray notes' is, literally, something written (筆) in a manner that one pleases (随 ❷); that is, without following specific rules.

隆

628

▶PROSPER
nonstandard for 隆 545

3-9 阝

隊

629

▶PARTY
nonstandard for 隊 625

3-9 阝

鄉

incorrect stroke count ⇨ see 673
(nonstandard for 郷 549)

3-9 阝

3-10 口

嘆 嘆 嘆 嘆　Ⓒ叹 tàn

630 TAN nage(ku) nage(kawashii)

Radical	Strokes
口 30	13-3-10
Grade	Freq
Jōyō	1447
1-3-10	

1 2 3 4 5 6 7 8 9 10 11 12 13

▶**SIGH**

COMPOUNDS

[formerly also 歎 1869]

❶ [original meaning] **sigh (in grief or despair), grieve, lament**

嘆息 *tansoku* sigh

嘆願 *tangan* entreaty, appeal

悲嘆 *hitan* grief, sorrow, lamentation

慨嘆 *gaitan* deploring, regret

❷ **sigh in admiration, exclaim, admire, praise**

嘆声 *tansei* sigh, lamentation; sigh of admiration

詠嘆 *eitan* exclamation, admiration

賛嘆 *santan* praise, admiration

驚嘆 *kyōtan* admiration, wonder

感嘆する *kantan suru* admire, be struck with admiration

INDEPENDENT

【tan 嘆(=歎)】 sigh, grief, lamentation

髀肉の嘆を託つ *hiniku no tan o kakotsu* fret from forced idleness

【tanjiru (=tanzuru) 嘆じる(=歎じる, 嘆ずる, 歎ずる)】 grieve, lament; sigh in admiration

KUN

【nage(ku) 嘆く】 [formerly also 歎く] sigh (in grief or despair), grieve, lament; deplore

嘆き *nageki* grief, lamentation

嘆き悲しむ *nagekikanashimu* grieve and moan

政治の腐敗を嘆く *seiji no fuhai o nageku* deplore the corruption of politics

【nage(kawashii) 嘆かわしい】 lamentable, deplorable, regrettable

嘆かわしい事態 *nagekawashii jitai* deplorable situation

SYNONYMS

❶ **grieve**

慨 DEPLORE → 641

悼 MOURN → 485

傷 grieve → 158

悲 feel sad → 2775

❶ **cry and sigh**

泣 CRY → 338

❷ **feel deeply**

感 feel deeply → 2835

動 be moved → 1778

USAGE

❶ **nageku**

嘆く

[formerly also 歎く] sigh (in grief or despair), grieve, lament; deplore

歎く

[now usu. 嘆く] same as 嘆く

❷ **nageki**

嘆き

[formerly also 歎き] grief, lamentation

歎き

[now usu. 嘆き] grief, lamentation

HOMOPHONES

nageku ⇨ 歎 1869

nageki ⇨ 歎 1869

3-10 土

塩 鹽 塩 塩　Ⓒ盐 yán

631 EN shio

Radical	Strokes
土 32△	13-3-10
Grade	Freq
Jōyō-4	1026
1-3-10	

1 2 3 4 5 6 7 8 9 10 11 12 13

▶**SALT**

COMPOUNDS

❶ [original meaning] **salt**

塩分 *enbun* salt, salinity

塩水 *ensui* salt water

食塩 *shokuen* table salt

天然塩 *tennen'en* natural salt
❷ [also suffix] chemical salt, base, alkali
塩基 *enki* base
炭酸塩 *tansan'en* carbonate
中性塩 *chūseien* neutral salt
❸ [also suffix] **chlorine, chloride compound**
塩酸 *ensan* hydrochloric acid
塩素 *enso* chlorine
塩化 *enka* chloridation, salification

INDEPENDENT

【en 塩】 chemical salt, base, alkali

KUN

【shio 塩】 salt
塩味 *shioaji* salty taste, seasoning
塩辛い *shiokarai* salty
塩水 *shiomizu* salt water
塩加減をする *shiokagen o suru* season with salt

SPECIAL READINGS

塩梅▲ *anbai* seasoning, flavoring; taste, flavor; condition, state

SYNONYMS

❶ **seasonings**
糖 SUGAR → 1403
酢 VINEGAR → 1516
油 OIL → 341
❸ **lighter elements**
臭 bromine → 2633
水 hydrogen → 10
酸 OXYGEN → 1563
窒 NITROGEN → 2288
硫 SULFUR → 1184
炭 carbon → 2257

塊 塊 塊 3-10 土

632 KAI katamari

Ⓒⓗ 块 kuài

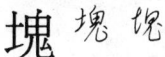

Radical	Strokes
土 32	13-3-10
Grade	**Freq**
Jōyō	1856
◧ 1-3-10	

Stroke order: 1 一 2 十 3 土 4 圠 5 圠 6 坘 7 坘 8 坲 9 坤 10 坤 11 塊 12 塊 13 塊

▶LUMP

COMPOUNDS

● **lump, mass; ingot; nugget**
塊土 *kaido* lump of earth
塊鉱 *kaikō* lump ore
地塊 *chikai* block, landmass
金塊 *kinkai* nugget, gold ingot

KUN

【katamari 塊】
① [usu. 固まり] lump, mass, clod; ingot
血の塊 *chi no katamari* clot of blood
② [sometimes also 固まり] group, crowd, cluster
③ [usu. 固まり] devotee, worshiper; incarnation (of selfishness), personification
欲の塊 *yoku no katamari* lump of avarice, incarnation of selfishness
拝金主義の塊 *haikinshugi no katamari* money worshiper

SYNONYMS

● **bodies**
体 BODY → 71
球 BALL → 969

HOMOPHONES

katamari ⇨ 固 3086

NOTE

⇨ see USAGE note at 固 3086

塚 3-10 土

633

▶MOUND
nonstandard for 塚 556

塔 3-10 土

634

▶TOWER
nonstandard for 塔 561

3-10 女

嫁 嫁 嫁

635 KA yome totsu(gu)

CH 嫁 jià

Radical	Strokes
女 38	13-3-10
Grade	Freq
Jōyō	1497
▮ 1-3-10	

▶WED A MAN ▶BRIDE

COMPOUNDS

❶ **wed a man, marry into a family**

降嫁 *kōka* marriage of an Imperial princess to a subject

再嫁 *saika* second marriage

❷ **bride**

惣嫁(＝総嫁) *sōka* streetwalker (in the Edo period)

❸ impute, blame (someone else)

転嫁する *tenka suru* impute, lay the blame on another

INDEPENDENT

【kasuru 嫁する】 wed a man; impute, blame (someone else)

KUN

【yome 嫁】

ⓐ bride, (young) wife

ⓑ daughter-in-law

嫁入る *yomeiru* marry a man, wed

花嫁 *hanayome* bride

兄嫁 *aniyome* sister-in-law, older brother's wife

嫁いびり *yomeibiri* bullying a young wife

【totsu(gu) 嫁ぐ】 wed, marry a man, get married

嫁ぎ先 *totsugisaki* family a woman has married into

SYNONYMS

❶ **marrying and marriage**

婚 MARRY → 470

姻 MARRIAGE → 353

縁 marriage relation → 1386

❷ **wives**

妻 WIFE → 2558

奥 wife → 2824

内 wife → 3466

室 wife (esp. of persons of rank) → 2254

嫡 legitimate wife → 680

婦 married woman → 469

寡 widow → 2344

【yome】

ⓑ **in-laws**

婿 SON-IN-LAW → 566

NOTE

⇨ see COMPOUND FORMATION for 惣嫁 *sōka* ⇨ 惣 2780

3-10 女

嫌 嫌 嫌 嫌

636 KEN GEN kira(u) kira(i) iya

CH 嫌 xián

Radical	Strokes
女 38	13-3-10
Grade	Freq
Jōyō	1936
▮ 1-3-10	

(stroke order: 1–13)

▶DISLIKE

COMPOUNDS

❶ **dislike, hate, detest**

嫌悪 *ken'o* hatred, dislike, repugnance

嫌忌 *kenki* dislike, aversion

機嫌 *kigen* [sometimes also 譏嫌] mood, temper, disposition; health

❷ suspect

嫌疑 *kengi* suspicion

KUN

【kira(u) 嫌う】 dislike, have an aversion to

交際を嫌う *kōsai o kirau* shun society

所嫌わず *tokoro kirawazu* no matter where, indiscriminately

夫に嫌われる *otto ni kirawareru* lose one's husband's love

【kira(i) 嫌い】

①ⓐ dislike, aversion, antipathy

ⓑ [suffix] have a dislike for; person having a dislike for something

嫌いな *kirai na* distasteful, disagreeable, repugnant

嫌いだ *kirai da* dislike, do not like
毛嫌い *kegirai* prejudiced aversion
好き嫌い *sukikirai* likes and dislikes, taste
雨が嫌い *ame ga kirai* dislike rain
食わず嫌い *kuwazugirai* prejudice against (some food); aversion without even trying
人間嫌い *ningengirai* misanthropist, man-hater; misanthropy, dislike for mankind

② undesirable tendency, tinge of (something to be criticized)
行き過ぎの嫌いが有る *yukisugi no kirai ga aru* tend to go too far

【iya 嫌】
iya na 嫌な [formerly also 厭な] disagreeable, repulsive
嫌がる *iyagaru* dislike, hate
嫌な気持 *iya na kimochi* unpleasant feeling
嫌気が差す *iyake ga sasu* feel dislike for
嫌嫌(＝厭厭) *iyaiya* grudgingly, unwillingly; (of children) shaking of the head in refusal

SYNONYMS

❶ **hate and dislike**
憎 HATE → 687
忌む ABHOR → 2207
悪 hate → 2745
恨 HOLD A GRUDGE → 369

USAGE

❶ **iya**
嫌な
[formerly also 厭な] disagreeable, repulsive
厭な
[now usu. 嫌な] disagreeable, repulsive
否
ⓐ no
ⓑ being unwilling, wanting to say no

❷ **iyaiya**
嫌嫌
[also 厭厭]
ⓐ grudgingly, unwillingly
ⓑ (of children) shaking of the head in refusal
厭厭
[also 嫌嫌] same as 嫌嫌
否否
definitely [absolutely] not

HOMOPHONES

iya ⇨ 厭 3017 否 2406

NOTE

⇨ see COMPOUND FORMATION for 機嫌 *kigen* ⇨ 機 1076

媾

637 KŌ

ⒸⒽ 媾 gòu

Radical	Strokes
女 38	13-3-10
Grade	**Freq**
Reference	
◧ 1-3-10	

3-10
女

COMPOUNDS

❶ [now replaced by 講 1619] make peace, come to terms
媾和 *kōwa* peace, reconciliation

❷ [original meaning, now rare] have sexual intercourse
交媾 *kōkō* sexual union

嫌

638

▸DISLIKE
nonstandard for 嫌 636

3-10
女

3-10 亻

微 微 微 微

639 BI kasu(ka)▲

CH 微 wēi

Radical	Strokes
亻 60	13-3-10
Grade	Freq
Jōyō	1186
1-3-10	

Stroke order: 1 2 3 4 5 6 7 8 9 10 11 12 13

▶**SLIGHT**

COMPOUNDS

❶ [also prefix]

ⓐ (of very small size) **slight, minute, small, tiny, microscopic, fine**

ⓑ (of very small quantity) **slight, very little**

微細な *bisai na* minute, fine; detailed, minute; delicate, subtle

微生物 *biseibutsu* microorganism

微粒子 *biryūshi* (minute) particle, corpuscle

微調整 *bichōsei* minute adjustment; fine tuning

顕微鏡 *kenbikyō* microscope

微微たる *bibitaru* slight, small, insignificant

微量 *biryō* slight amount, extremely small quantity

微少 *bishō* minute quantity

❷ⓐ (of low intensity) **slight, weak, faint**

ⓑ lose vigor, become weak

微笑 *bishō* smile

微震 *bishin* slight earthquake

微温 *bion* lukewarmness, tepidity

微光 *bikō* faint light

微弱な *bijaku na* feeble, weak; faint, slight

微妙な *bimyō na* subtle, delicate

衰微 *suibi* decline, decay

❸ⓐ (of little importance or influence) slight, insignificant, beneath notice, mean, humble

ⓑ [humble] my humble, my poor

微賤 *bisen* low rank, humble station

軽微な *keibi na* slight, little, insignificant

微力 *biryoku* one's poor ability, the little one can do

微意 *bii* small token (of gratitude), my (humble) feelings

❹ unnoticed, concealed

微行 *bikō* traveling incognito

機微 *kibi* niceties, delicate signs, inner workings

❺ [rare] 1/1,000,000

二微 *nibi* 2/1,000,000

INDEPENDENT

【bi 微】 minuteness; insignificance; [rare] 1/1,000,000

微に入り細を穿つ *bi ni iri sai o ugatsu* go into the minutest details

KUN

【kasu(ka) 微か】

kasuka na 微かな faint, weak; dim, vague; scanty, slight

微かな笑み *kasuka na emi* faint smile

微かに見える *kasuka ni mieru* be seen dimly

SYNONYMS

❶ⓐ small and tiny

細 MINUTE → 1333

寸 A BIT OF → 2935

小 SMALL → 7

豆- miniature → 1943

ⓑ few

寸 A BIT OF → 2935

薄 meager → 2370

乏 SCANTY → 1933

寡 FEW → 2344

少 LITTLE → 3467

❷ⓐ less in degree

軽 LIGHT → 1515

弱 WEAK → 1167

低 LOW → 73

薄 THIN → 2370

浅 SHALLOW → 389

❸ⓐ unimportant

細 MINUTE → 1333

小 SMALL → 7

末 last in importance → 3505

NOTE

★do not confuse with 徵 683

3-10 亻

微

640

▶**SLIGHT**

nonstandard for 微 639

慨 641 GAI

ⒸⒽ 慨 kǎi

Radical	Strokes
忄 61	13-3-10
Grade	**Freq**
Jōyō	1663
1-3-10	

3-10 忄

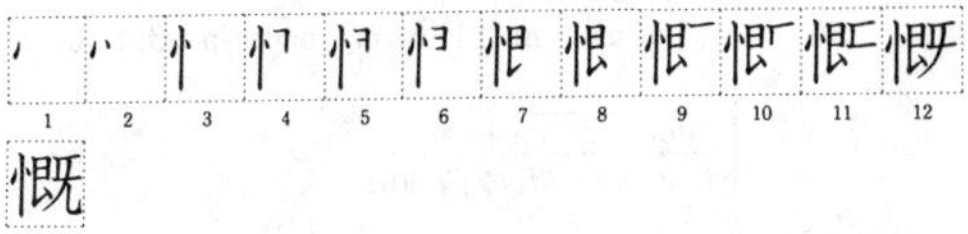

▶DEPLORE

COMPOUNDS

ⓐ **deplore, lament, regret, grieve**
ⓑ **resent, be indignant, be angry**

慨歎する *gaitan suru* deplore, lament, regret
慨然と *gaizen to* deploringly; indignantly
慨世 *gaisei* concern for the public welfare
感慨 *kangai* deep [profound] emotion
慷慨 *kōgai* patriotic lamentation, deploration; righteous indignation
憤慨 *fungai* resentment, indignation

INDEPENDENT

【gaisuru 慨する】 deplore, lament

SYNONYMS

ⓐ **grieve**
嘆 SIGH → 630
悼 MOURN → 485
傷 grieve → 158
悲 feel sad → 2775

ⓑ **anger**
憤 INDIGNATION → 730
怒 GET ANGRY → 2571

NOTE

★do not confuse with 概 1048

慄 642 RITSU

ⒸⒽ 栗 lì

Radical	Strokes
忄 61	13-3-10
Grade	**Freq**
Reference	
1-3-10	

3-10 忄

COMPOUNDS

● [rarely also 栗 2649] [original meaning] tremble with fear, shudder

慄然として *ritsuzen to shite* with horror
戦慄する *senritsu suru* shudder, shiver

慎 643 SHIN tsutsushi(mu)

ⒸⒽ 慎 shèn

Radical	Strokes
忄 61	13-3-10
Grade	**Freq**
Jōyō	1023
1-3-10	

3-10 忄

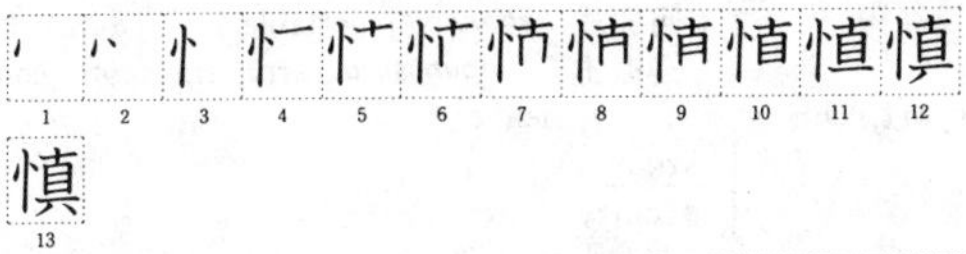

▶PRUDENT

COMPOUNDS

● **prudent, discreet, careful**

慎重 *shinchō* prudence, discretion, circumspection
謹慎 *kinshin* house arrest, domiciliary confinement; penitence
戒慎する *kaishin suru* be cautious, be discreet

KUN

【tsutsushi(mu) 慎む】

ⓐ be prudent, be discreet, be careful
ⓑ restrain oneself, abstain from, be moderate

慎み *tsutsushimi* prudence, modesty, self-control
慎み深い *tsutsushimibukai* discreet, prudent, modest
口を慎む *kuchi o tsutsushimu* be careful in

speech
酒を慎む *sake o tsutsushimu* abstain from drinking

SYNONYMS

● **careful**
謹 carefully → 1618
精 meticulous → 1366

USAGE

tsutsushimu

慎む
ⓐ be prudent, be discreet, be careful
ⓑ restrain oneself, abstain from, be moderate

謹む
[usu. in TE-form] be respectful, be humble

HOMOPHONES

tsutsushimu ⇨ 謹 1618

3-10 忄

慌 644

▶ **FLURRIED**
nonstandard for 慌 580

3-10 忄

愼 645

▶ **PRUDENT**
nonstandard for 慎 643

3-10 扌

搏 646 HAKU

CH 搏 bó

Radical	Strokes
扌 64	13-3-10
Grade	Freq
Reference	
1-3-10	

COMPOUNDS

● [now also 拍 304] [original meaning] beat, clap, throb

搏動 *hakudō* pulsation, pulsebeat
脈搏 *myakuhaku* pulse, pulsation

3-10 扌

搬 搬 搬 647 HAN

CH 搬 bān

Radical	Strokes
扌 64	13-3-10
Grade	Freq
Jōyō	1654
1-3-10	

1 2 3 4 5 6 7 8 9 10 11 12 13

▶ **CARRY**

COMPOUNDS

● [original meaning] **carry, transport, convey**
搬送 *hansō* conveyance
搬出する *hanshutsu suru* carry out
搬入する *hannyū suru* carry in
搬送波 *hansōha* carrier wave
可搬式 *kahanshiki* portable
運搬する *unpan suru* carry, transport, convey, deliver

SYNONYMS

● **carry**
運 CARRY → 3140
輸 TRANSPORT → 1607

携 攜 携 携

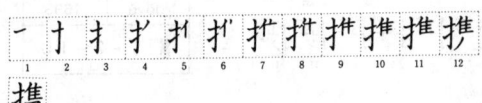

648 KEI tazusa(eru) tazusa(waru)

CH 携 xié

Radical	Strokes
扌 64	13-3-10
Grade	**Freq**
Jōyō	1330
◧ 1-3-10	

3-10 扌

▶CARRY IN HAND

COMPOUNDS

❶ **carry in hand, carry (along) on one's person**

携帯する *keitai suru* carry, bring with one, equip oneself with

携行する *keikō suru* carry along, bring

携帯カメラ *keitai kamera* hand camera

必携 *hikkei* indispensableness; handbook, manual

❷ **join hands, work together, act in concert**

提携する *teikei suru* cooperate with, act in concert with, tie up with

連携 *renkei* cooperation, league, concert

KUN

【tazusa(eru) 携える】 carry in one's hand; take a thing [person] with one

杖を携える *tsue o tazusaeru* carry a stick in one's hand

手を携えて *te o tazusaete* hand in hand

妻子を携える *saishi o tazusaeru* be accompanied by one's family

【tazusa(waru) 携わる】 participate in; concern oneself in

教育に携わる人人 *kyōiku ni tazusawaru hitobito* those who participate in education

SYNONYMS

❶ **hold**

提 carry in hand → 591

持 HOLD → 374

❷ **cooperate**

協 COOPERATE → 93

調 harmonize → 1567

搾 搾 搾

649 SAKU shibo(ru)

CH 搾 zhà

Radical	Strokes
扌 64	13-3-10
Grade	**Freq**
Jōyō	1863
◧ 1-3-10	

3-10 扌

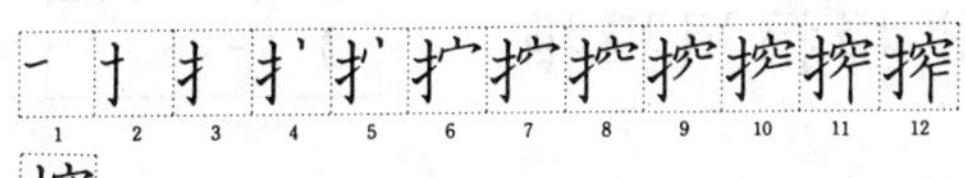

▶SQUEEZE

COMPOUNDS

ⓐ [original meaning] **squeeze, extract, press**

ⓑ (obtain by force) squeeze, extort, exploit

搾乳 *sakunyū* milking

搾油 *sakuyu* oil expression [extraction]

圧搾する *assaku suru* press, compress

搾取する *sakushu suru* exploit, sweat, squeeze (money out of a person)

KUN

【shibo(ru) 搾る】

①ⓐ squeeze, press, squash, extract

ⓑ squeeze (money from), sweat, screw

搾り *shibori* squeezing

搾り滓 *shiborikasu* strained lees [draff]

搾り立てのオレンジジュース *shiboritate no orenji-jūsu* fresh orange juice

搾り取る *shiboritoru* squeeze, extract; squeeze (money from), sweat

② scold, reprimand

油を搾る *abura o shiboru* press oil; give a sound scolding

SYNONYMS

ⓐ **squeeze**

絞る WRING → 1349

圧 apply pressure → 2970

HOMOPHONES

shiboru ⇨ 絞 1349

shibori ⇨ 絞 1349

NOTE

⇨ see USAGE note at 絞 1349

3-10
扌

摂 攝 摂 摂

650 SETSU

CH 摄 shè

Radical	Strokes
扌 64	13-3-10
Grade	**Freq**
Jōyō	1693
1-3-10	

▶TAKE IN ▶ACT AS REGENT

COMPOUNDS

❶ **take in, ingest, absorb, assimilate**

摂取する *sesshu suru* take (in), ingest, absorb

摂動 *setsudō* (gravitational) perturbation

包摂する *hōsetsu suru* connote, subsume

カロリーの摂取量 *karorī no sesshuryō* caloric intake

❷ **act as regent, represent, act as deputy; carry on in addition to**

摂政 *sesshō* regency; regent

摂関家 *sekkanke* line of regents

兼摂する *kensetsu suru* hold an additional post

❸ conserve one's health

摂生 *sessei* preservation of one's health

❹ regulate

摂理 *setsuri* providence

❺ centigrade

摂氏 *sesshi* centigrade

INDEPENDENT

【**sessuru** 摂する】 act as regent; carry on in addition to

SYNONYMS

❶ **take in**

収 TAKE IN → 198

喫 INGEST → 551

吸 SUCK → 202

❷ **substitute**

代 SUBSTITUTE → 30

3-10
扌

損 損 損

651 SON soko(nau) -soko(nau) soko(neru) -soko(neru)

CH 损 sǔn

Radical	Strokes
扌 64	13-3-10
Grade	**Freq**
Jōyō-5	997
1-3-10	

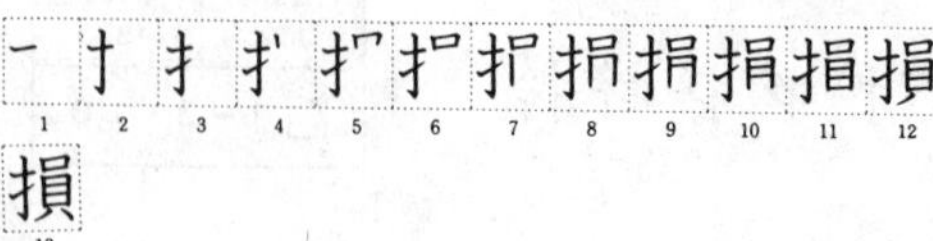

▶LOSS

COMPOUNDS

❶ⓐ **loss**

ⓑ *elec* loss

ⓒ **lose, suffer loss**

損失 *sonshitsu* loss

損益 *son'eki* profit and loss; advantage and disadvantage

全損 *zenson* total loss

駒損 *komason* (=*komazon*) loss of material (in shogi)

損率 *sonritsu* loss factor

損流 *sonryū* loss current

欠損 *kesson* deficit, deficiency; loss

❷ disadvantage

損得 *sontoku* advantage and disadvantage, loss and gain

骨折り損 *honeorizon* waste of labor, vain efforts

❸ **damage, harm**

損害 *songai* damage, harm

損傷 *sonshō* damage, injury

破損 *hason* damage, breakdown

毀損(=棄損) *kison* damage, injury, waste

❹ [original meaning] decrease

損耗 *sonmō* (=*sonkō*) wear, waste, loss

INDEPENDENT

【**son** 損】 loss; damage; disadvantage

損になる *son ni naru* do not pay

損な条件 *son na jōken* unfavorable conditions

【**sonsuru** 損する】 lose, suffer loss

【**sonjiru** (=**sonzuru**) 損じる(=損ずる)】 lose; damage; [verbal suffix] fail to (do), fail in (doing)

読み損じる *yomisonjiru* fail to read correctly

KUN

【**soko(nau)** 損なう】 harm, hurt, injure, damage

損 健康を損なう *kenkō o sokonau* lose one's health

【**-soko(nau)** -損なう】
[verbal suffix]
① fail to (do), fail in (doing)
映画を見損なう *eiga o misokonau* fail to see a film
② come near (doing), make a narrow escape
溺れ損なう *oboresokonau* come near being drowned

【**soko(neru)** 損ねる】 same as **sokonau** 損なう
機嫌を損ねる *kigen o sokoneru* offend, displease, hurt (a person's) feelings

【**-soko(neru)** -損ねる】 same as **-sokonau** -損なう

SYNONYMS

❶ **losing and loss**
失 LOSE → 3511
逸 LET SLIP → 3120
喪 lose → 2825
❸ **harm and damage**
害 HARM, damage → 2272
傷 WOUND → 158
【**-sokonau**】
① **fail**
落 fall through → 2318
敗 fail → 1476

捜
652

▶**LOOK FOR**
nonstandard for 捜 432

3-10 扌

搭
653

▶**BOARD**
nonstandard for 搭 592

3-10 扌

搖
654

▶**SHAKE**
nonstandard for 揺 594

3-10 扌

摸

incorrect stroke count ⇨ see 691

3-10 扌

雌

incorrect stroke count ⇨ see 1055

3-10 止

漠 漠 漠 漠
655 BAKU

㊥ 漠 mò

Radical	Strokes
氵 85	13-3-10
Grade	**Freq**
Jōyō	1760
◧ 1-3-10	

3-10 氵

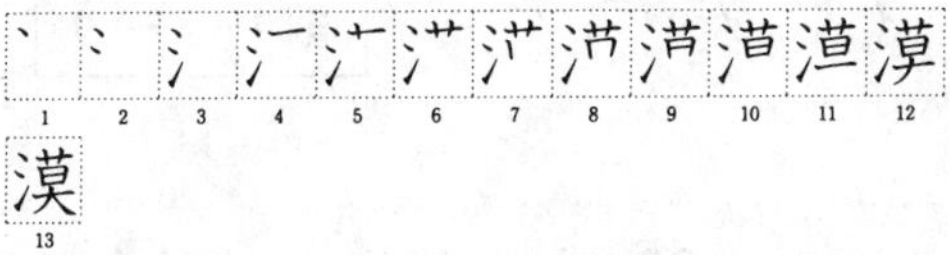

▶**DESERT** ▶**OBSCURE**

COMPOUNDS

❶ **desert**
漠北 *bakuhoku* north of the Gobi Desert, Outer Mongolia
砂漠 *sabaku* desert
❷ as vast or boundless as the desert
茫漠たる *bōbakutaru* vast, boundless; obscure, vague
広漠たる *kōbakutaru* vast, wide, boundless
❸ **obscure, vague**
漠然たる *bakuzentaru* obscure, vague, hazy
空漠たる考え *kūbakutaru kangae* vague [loose] ideas; idle thoughts
❹ lonesome, dreary
索漠たる *sakubakutaru* dreary, bleak, desolate

INDEPENDENT

【**baku to shita** 漠とした】 *literary* obscure;

vast

SYNONYMS

❶ **uncultivated expanses of land**

原 PLAIN → 3009
野 FIELD → 1485

3-10
氵

源 656 GEN minamoto

CH 源 yuán

Radical	Strokes
氵 85	13-3-10
Grade	**Freq**
Jōyō-6	807
1-3-10	

1 2 3 4 5 6 7 8 9 10 11 12 13

▶**SOURCE**

COMPOUNDS

❶ⓐ [also suffix] **source, origin, beginning, root**

ⓑ [original meaning] (place where water originates) source (of a river), fountainhead

源泉 *gensen* fountainhead, source
根源 *kongen* root, origin, source
起源 *kigen* origin, beginning
語源 *gogen* derivation of a word, etymology
資源 *shigen* resources
財源 *zaigen* revenue source, financial resources
震源 *shingen* earthquake [seismic] center
栄養源 *eiyōgen* source of nutrients
源流 *genryū* source (of a stream)
水源 *suigen* source [head] (of a stream), fountainhead

❷ abbrev. of 源氏 *genji*: the Genji Family, the Minamotos

源平 *genpei* Genji and Heike clans; two opposing sides

KUN

【**minamoto** 源】source, fountainhead, origin

河の源 *kawa no minamoto* fountainhead
その源は明らかではない *Sono minamoto wa akiraka de wa nai* It is of obscure origin

SYNONYMS

❶ⓐ **beginnings**

根 ROOT → 930
元 ORIGIN → 1929
本 origin → 3502
緒 OUTSET → 1378
序 INTRODUCTORY PART → 3065
端 start → 1221
始 beginning → 281
初 beginning → 1116

ⓑ **water sources**

泉 SPRING → 2567
井 WELL → 3454

3-10
氵

漢 657 KAN

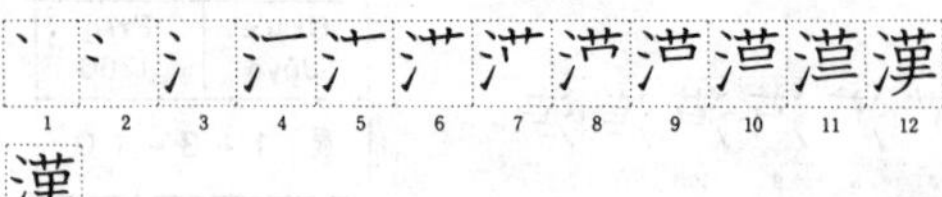

CH 汉 hàn

Radical	Strokes
氵 85	13-3-10
Grade	**Freq**
Jōyō-3	1393
1-3-10	

1 2 3 4 5 6 7 8 9 10 11 12 13

▶**CHINESE** ▶**FELLOW**

COMPOUNDS

❶ⓐ (of ancient China or its people) **Chinese; old name for China, ancient China**

ⓑ **Han Dynasty** (206 B.C.-220 A.D.)

漢土 *kando* China
漢方薬 *kanpōyaku* Chinese (herbal) medicine
漢民族 *kanminzoku* Chinese people, Han race
漢朝 *kanchō* Han Dynasty
前漢 *zenkan* Former Han

❷ⓐ **Chinese (language), classical Chinese**

ⓑ **kanji, Chinese character, logograph**

漢語 *kango* Chinese word, Chinese expression
漢文 *kanbun* Chinese classics, Chinese writing
漢字 *kanji* Chinese characters, kanji
漢詩 *kanshi* classical Chinese poetry [poem]
漢和辞典 *kanwa jiten* Chinese-Japanese character dictionary
漢英辞典(=漢英字典) *kan'ei jiten* Japanese-English character dictionary, kanji dictio-

nary
漢プリ *kanpuri* kanji printer
単漢選択キー *tankan-sentakukī* single character selector button (in kanji word processors)
❸ [also suffix] **fellow, man**
好漢 *kōkan* nice fellow
痴漢 *chikan* molester of women, masher
熱血漢 *nekketsukan* hot-blooded man
大食漢 *taishokukan* great eater, glutton
❹ⓐ [original meaning] name of tributary of the Yangtze River: Han River
ⓑ Milky Way
漢水 *kansui* Han River
銀漢 *ginkan* Milky Way

INDEPENDENT

【kan 漢】 Han Dynasty

SYNONYMS

❶ⓐ China
華 CHINA → 2283
支 China → 1979
中 People's Republic of China → 3451
台 Taiwan → 2005
唐 Cathay → 3115
呉 KINGDOM OF WU → 2549
ⓑ earlier Chinese dynasties
晋 JIN DYNASTY → 2656
周 Zhou Dynasty → 2998
商 Shang Dynasty → 2116
夏 Xia Dynasty → 2113
❷ⓐ Chinese
中 Modern Chinese → 3451
ⓑ characters
字 CHARACTER → 2172
文 LETTER → 1962
❸ fellow
輩 FELLOW (*belittling*) → 2807
徒 fellows → 416
奴 GUY → 187
棒 tough guy → 983
坊 COLLOQUIAL PERSON SUFFIX → 233
屋 colloquial person suffix → 3098
物 character → 874

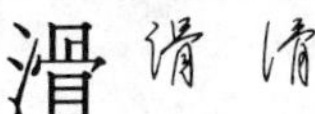

658 KATSU KOTSU▴ sube(ru) name(raka)

Ⓒⓗ 滑 huá

Radical	Strokes
氵 85	13-3-10
Grade	**Freq**
Jōyō	1374
◧ 1-3-10	

3-10 氵

▶SLIDE ▶SMOOTH

COMPOUNDS

❶ slide, glide, slip
滑走する *kassō suru* glide, volplane; slide
滑空機 *kakkūki* glider, sailplane
滑車 *kassha* pulley, block, tackle
❷ smooth
滑脱 *katsudatsu* adaptation to circumstances
滑剤 *katsuzai* lubricant
円滑な *enkatsu na* smooth, harmonious
潤滑 *junkatsu* lubrication
❸ speak smoothly and glibly, crack jokes
滑稽な *kokkei na* funny, jocular, humorous; laughable, ridiculous

KUN

【sube(ru) 滑る】
① slide, glide, skate
滑り *suberi* sliding, slipping
滑り台 *suberidai* (playground) slide; launching platform
横滑り *yokosuberi* skid, skidding
② [formerly also 辷る] slip
滑り落ちる *suberiochiru* slip off
口が滑る *kuchi ga suberu* make a slip of the tongue
③ [formerly also 辷る] flunk an (entrance) examination
滑り止め *suberidome* tire chains; creepers; taking the entrance examination to a university as a safety measure in case one fails at other universities

【name(raka) 滑らか】
nameraka na 滑らかな smooth, glassy
滑らかに *nameraka ni* smoothly

SYNONYMS

❶ move
動 MOVE → 1778
運 MOVE → 3140
移 SHIFT → 1177
転 remove → 1480
遷 TRANSFER → 3170
繰る SHIFT ONWARD → 1427
❷ smooth
暢 FLUENT → 1226
流 flowing → 441

USAGE

suberu
滑る

① slide, glide, skate
② [formerly also 辷る] slip
③ [formerly also 辷る] flunk an (entrance) examination

辷る
[now usu. 滑る]
① slip
② flunk an (entrance) examination

HOMOPHONES
suberu ⇨ 辷 3191

3-10
氵

溝 659

KŌ mizo

Ⓒⓗ 沟 gōu

Radical	Strokes
氵 85	13-3-10
Grade	**Freq**
Jōyō	1616
◧ 1-3-10	

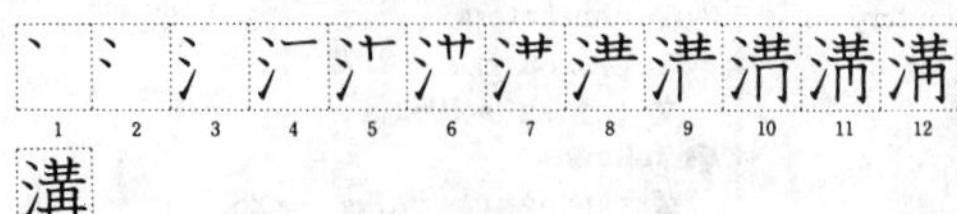

▶**CHANNEL**

COMPOUNDS

❶ [original meaning] **channel, ditch, gutter, canal, trench**
溝渠 *kōkyo* ditch, sewer, canal
側溝 *sokkō* channel, ditch, gutter
排水溝 *haisuikō* waterway, drainage, canal
下水溝 *gesuikō* ditch
海溝 *kaikō* sea trench

❷ [archaic] one hundred nonillion (10^{32})

KUN

【**mizo 溝**】 channel, ditch, drain, gutter; groove, slot; gap, gulf
溝掘り機 *mizohoriki* ditching machine
溝形鋼 *mizogatakō* channel (type of section steel)
溝レール *mizorēru* grooved rail
溝が有る *mizo ga aru* be estranged

SYNONYMS

❶ **holes and cavities**
堀 DITCH → 467
坑 PIT → 236
凹 concavity → 3482
洞 CAVE → 380
穴 HOLE → 2159
孔 OPEN HOLE → 179
口 MOUTH → 3382

3-10
氵

滅 660

METSU horo(biru) horo(bu) horo(bosu)

Ⓒⓗ 灭 miè

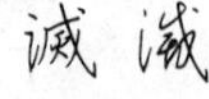

Radical	Strokes
氵 85	13-3-10
Grade	**Freq**
Jōyō	1346
◧ 1-3-10	

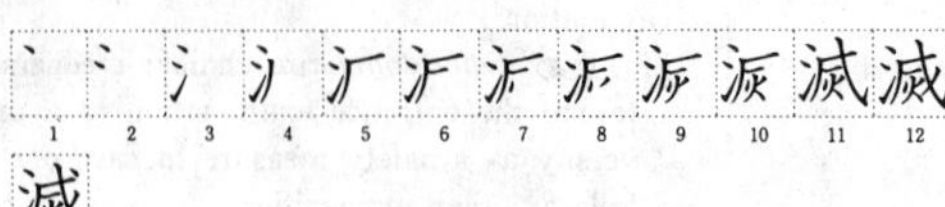

▶**DESTROY**

COMPOUNDS

❶ⓐ **destroy, ruin, annihilate, wipe out**
ⓑ **meet with destruction, go to ruin, cease to exist**
滅菌 *mekkin* sterilization
撃滅する *gekimetsu suru* destroy, exterminate
絶滅 *zetsumetsu* extermination, eradication; extinction
滅亡 *metsubō* ruin, downfall
消滅 *shōmetsu* extinction, disappearance
不滅 *fumetsu* immortality, indestructibility, imperishability
全滅 *zenmetsu* annihilation, total destruction
潰滅(＝壊滅) *kaimetsu* destruction, annihilation
死滅 *shimetsu* extinction, annihilation, destruction
自滅 *jimetsu* natural decay; self-destruction, self-ruin
破滅 *hametsu* ruin, destruction, wreck, collapse, downfall

❷ go out, be extinguished
点滅する *tenmetsu suru* (of light) go [come] on and off; turn [switch] on and off
明滅する *meimetsu suru* flicker, blink

❸ unreasonable, excessive, reckless, extreme
滅法 *meppō* extraordinarily, unreasonably
滅多な *metta na* reckless, careless

❹ death of a priest or Buddha, entering Nir-

vana
滅度 *metsudo* extinguishing illusion and passing over to Nirvana
入滅 *nyūmetsu* entering Nirvana, death of a saint
仏滅 *butsumetsu* Buddha's death; most unlucky day

INDEPENDENT

【metsu 滅】 label on switches: OFF
【messuru 滅する】 be destroyed, perish; destroy

KUN

【horo(biru) 滅びる】 [sometimes also 亡びる] go to ruin, meet with destruction, cease to exist; be overthrown
滅びて行く民族 *horobite iku minzoku* dying race
【horo(bu) 滅ぶ】 [sometimes also 亡ぶ] literary form of **horobiru 滅びる**
【horo(bosu) 滅ぼす】 [sometimes also 亡ぼす] destroy, ruin, annihilate; overthrow
敵を滅ぼす *teki o horobosu* destroy the enemy

SYNONYMS

❶ **destroy**
亡 perish → 3402
消 EXTINGUISH → 443
❷ **extinguish**
消 EXTINGUISH → 443
❸ **rash**
妄 RASH → 2016
盲 BLIND → 2053
暴 unrestrained → 2515
荒 WILD → 2260
濫 EXCESSIVE → 801
乱 excessive → 1260

USAGE

❶ **horobiru**
滅びる
[sometimes also 亡びる] go to ruin, meet with destruction, cease to exist; be overthrown
亡びる
[usu. 滅びる] same as 滅びる
❷ **horobu**
滅ぶ
[sometimes also 亡ぶ] literary form of 滅びる *horobiru*
亡ぶ
[usu. 滅ぶ] literary form of 亡びる *horobiru*
❸ **horobosu**
滅ぼす
[sometimes also 亡ぼす] destroy, ruin, annihilate; overthrow
亡ぼす
[usu. 滅ぼす] destroy, ruin, annihilate; overthrow

HOMOPHONES

horobiru ⇨ 亡 3402
horobu ⇨ 亡 3402
horobosu ⇨ 亡 3402

滝 瀧 滝 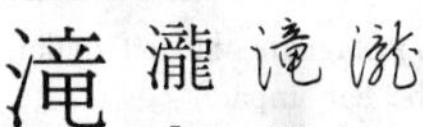 Ⓒⓗ 泷 lóng shuāng 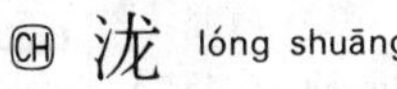

661 RŌ▲ taki

Radical	Strokes
氵 85	13-3-10
Grade	**Freq**
Jōyō	1293
▐ 1-3-10	

3-10 氵

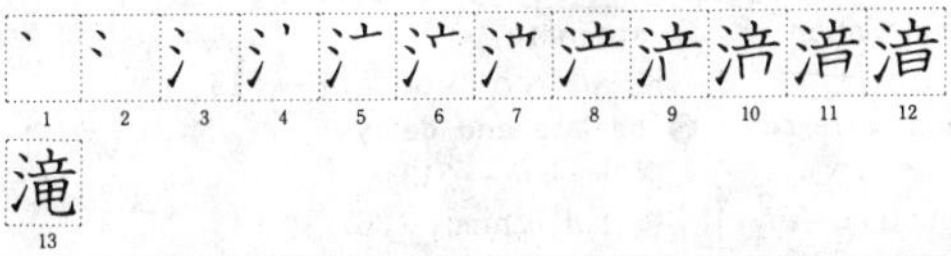

(stroke order 1–13)

▶**WATERFALL**

KUN

【taki 滝】 waterfall, falls, cascade
滝壺 *takitsubo* pool below a waterfall
滝川 *takigawa* rapids
雄滝(＝男滝) *odaki* greater waterfall (of the two)

SYNONYMS

【taki】
○ **running water**
流 CURRENT → 441
潮 TIDE → 739
汐 TIDE → 223
瀬 rapids → 806
洪 FLOOD → 386
渦 WHIRLPOOL → 603

3-10 氵

溜
662 RYŪ ta(maru) ta(meru)

Ⓒ 溜 liū liù

Radical	Strokes
氵 85	13-3-10
Grade	**Freq**
Reference	
1-3-10	

COMPOUNDS

❶ [now replaced by 留 *ryū* 2580] distill
- 蒸溜 *jōryū* distillation
- 分溜 *bunryū* fraction, fractional distillation
- 乾溜 *kanryū* dry distillation

❷ (of water) accumulate
- 溜飲 *ryūin* water brash, sour stomach
- 溜飲が下がる *ryūin ga sagaru* be cured of water brash; have one's grudge satisfied

❸ⓐ accumulate, heap up
ⓑ collect (stamps)
ⓒ store (esp. water)
- 溜め *tame* sink, cesspool; manure sink
- ごみ溜め *gomitame* garbage, pit
- 切手を溜める *kitte o tameru* collect stamps

❹ run up (a bill), leave undone
- 家賃を溜める *yachin o tameru* let the rent fall into arrears

HOMOPHONES

tameru ⇨ 貯 1509

NOTE

⇨ see USAGE note at 貯 1509

3-10 氵

滞
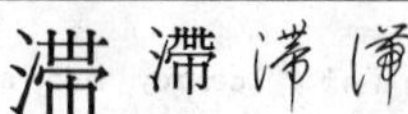
663 TAI todokō(ru)

Ⓒ 滞 zhì

Radical	Strokes
氵 85	13-3-10
Grade	**Freq**
Jōyō	1109
1-3-10	

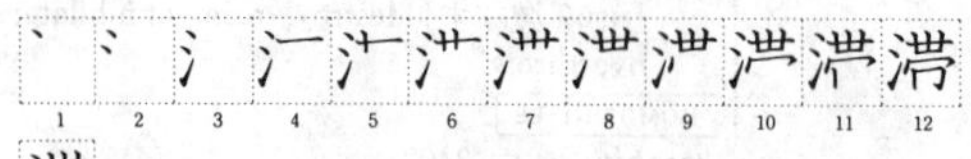

▶STAGNATE ▶STAY

COMPOUNDS

❶ [original meaning] **stagnate, be at [in] a standstill, be blocked up, be retarded, congest**
- 滞貨 *taika* freight congestion; accumulation of stocks
- 停滞 *teitai* stagnation, accumulation; arrearage
- 渋滞 *jūtai* delay, retardation, stagnation
- 沈滞 *chintai* stagnation, dullness
- 遅滞 *chitai* delay, retardation

❷ fall into arrears, leave unpaid
- 滞納 *tainō* nonpayment, delinquency (in payment)
- 延滞 *entai* arrear, arrearage

❸ (remain in a given place) **stay, remain, sojourn**
- 滞在 *taizai* stay, sojourn
- 滞留 *tairyū* sojourn, stay
- 滞米 *taibei* staying in America
- 滞欧 *taiō* staying in Europe
- 滞空 *taikū* staying [remaining] in the air

KUN

【todokō(ru) 滞る】 stagnate, be left undone; fall into arrears, be left unpaid
- 滞り *todokōri* hitch, hindrance; arrearage

SYNONYMS

❶ **stagnate**
- 渋 NOT GO SMOOTHLY → 513

❷ **be late and delay**
- 遅 be late → 3133
- 後 fall behind → 361
- 延 POSTPONE → 3073
- 猶 DELAY → 619

❸ **remain**
- 留 STAY → 2580
- 残 REMAIN → 943
- 余 REMAINING → 2042

❸ **stay**
- 留 STAY → 2580
- 駐 STATIONED → 1826
- 屯 STATION TROOPS → 3457
- 在 reside temporarily → 2984
- 泊 STAY OVERNIGHT → 331
- 宿 LODGE → 2293

溶 溶 溶

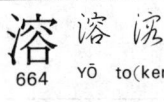

664 YŌ to(keru) to(kasu) to(ku)

Ⓒⓗ 溶 róng

Radical	Strokes
氵 85	13-3-10
Grade	**Freq**
Jōyō	1638
◧ 1 - 3 - 10	

3-10 氵

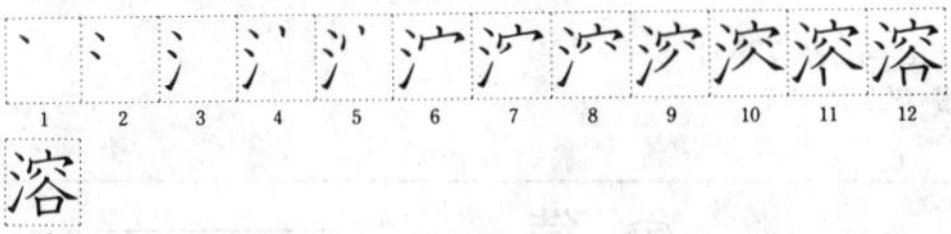

1 2 3 4 5 6 7 8 9 10 11 12 13

▶DISSOLVE ▶MELT

COMPOUNDS

❶ (pass or cause to pass into solution) **dissolve**

溶解 *yōkai* dissolution, liquefaction; melting, fusion
溶液 *yōeki* solution, solvent
溶媒 *yōbai* solvent
溶血 *yōketsu* hemolysis
水溶性の *suiyōsei no* water soluble

❷ [formerly 熔 1058 or 鎔 1762] (change or cause to change from solid to liquid, esp. by heat) **melt**

溶融 *yōyū* melting, fusion
溶接 *yōsetsu* welding
溶岩 *yōgan* lava
溶鉱炉 *yōkōro* smelting [blast] furnace

❸ [rare] having much water

溶溶たる *yōyōtaru* overflowing with water; vast, spacious

KUN

【to(keru) 溶ける】

vi

① (pass into solution) dissolve

塩は水に溶ける *Shio wa mizu ni tokeru* Salt dissolves in water

②ⓐ [formerly 熔ける or 鎔ける] (of metals) melt (up), fuse, smelt

ⓑ [formerly 融ける, usu. 解ける] (esp. of snow or ice) melt, thaw

火で溶ける *hi de tokeru* melt in the fire
溶け込む *tokekomu* melt into, fuse into

【to(kasu) 溶かす】

vt

① (cause to pass into solution or to turn liquid) dissolve, melt, liquefy

砂糖を水に溶かす *satō o mizu ni tokasu* dissolve sugar in water

② [formerly 熔かす or 鎔かす] melt (up) (metals), fuse, smelt

鉄を溶かす *tetsu o tokasu* melt [fuse] iron

【to(ku) 溶く】

vt

① (cause to pass into solution) dissolve (paint)

絵の具を溶く *enogu o toku* dissolve colors

② whip an egg

溶きほぐす *tokihogusu* whip an egg

SYNONYMS

❶ & ❷ liquefy

解 DISSOLVE → 1517
融 FUSE → 1831

HOMOPHONES

tokeru ⇨ 解 1517 融 1831 熔 1058 鎔 1762
tokasu ⇨ 解 1517 融 1831 熔 1058 鎔 1762 梳 964
toku ⇨ 解 1517 説 1547 梳 964

NOTE

⇨ see USAGE note at 解 1517

滋

665

▶NOURISH

nonstandard for 滋 602

3-10 氵

渓

666

▶RAVINE

nonstandard for 渓 516

3-10 氵

溝

667

▶CHANNEL

nonstandard for 溝 659

3-10 氵

3-10 氵

溫 668

▶**WARM**
nonstandard for 温 608

3-10 氵

滿

incorrect stroke count ⇨ see 709
(nonstandard for 満 607)

3-10 犭

猿 669

EN saru

CH 猿 yuán

Radical	Strokes
犭 94	13-3-10
Grade	**Freq**
Jōyō	1655
1-3-10	

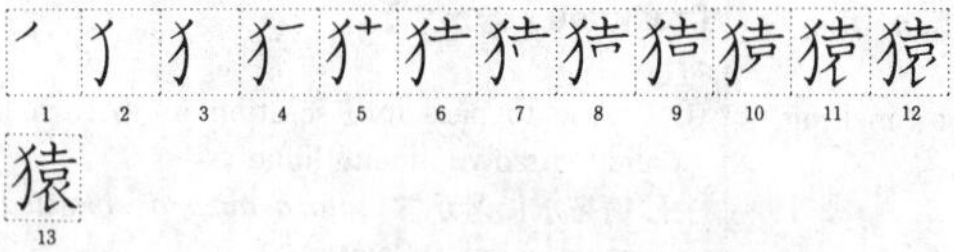

▶**MONKEY**

COMPOUNDS

● [original meaning] **monkey, ape**
猿人 *enjin* ape-man
類人猿 *ruijin'en* anthropoid, troglodyte
犬猿 *ken'en* dog and monkey
犬猿の仲である *ken'en no naka de aru* lead a cat and dog life; be at enmity

KUN

【saru 猿】
① monkey, ape
猿真似 *sarumane* blind imitation
猿芝居 *sarushibai* monkey show; shallow-minded trick
猿回し *sarumawashi* monkey showman, monkey show
日本猿 *nihonzaru* Japan monkey
山猿 *yamazaru* wild monkey; countryman, rustic
② sly person
猿知恵 *sarujie* shallow cunning
③ⓐ door bolt
ⓑ fastener

SYNONYMS

● **monkey**
申 the Monkey → 3507
● **undomesticated mammals**
鹿 DEER → 3126
猪 WILD BOAR → 536
象 ELEPHANT → 2134
熊 BEAR → 2848
虎 TIGER → 3212
鯨 WHALE → 1882

USAGE

saru
猿
① monkey, ape
② sly person
③ⓐ door bolt
ⓑ fastener
申
ninth sign of the Oriental zodiac: the Monkey

HOMOPHONES

saru ⇨ 申 3507

3-10 阝

隙 670

GEKI suki su(ku) su(kasu)

CH 隙 xì

Radical	Strokes
阝 170	13-3-10
Grade	**Freq**
Reference	
1-3-10	

COMPOUNDS

❶ⓐ [original meaning] gap, interval, opening, space
ⓑ [also 透き *suki*] gap, interval
間隙 *kangeki* gap, interval
空隙 *kūgeki* opening, crevice, gap, void
塡隙 *tengeki* caulking
隙 *geki* gap, interval
隙 *suki* gap, interval
隙間 *sukima* gap, opening; crack, crevice
❷ⓐ [now usu. 透く *suku*] leave a gap
ⓑ [now usu. 透かす *sukasu*] leave a space

[opening], thin (out)
隙かさず *sukasazu* without a moment's delay
隙いた枝 *suita eda* thinned branches
❸ chance, unguarded moment
隙を見付ける *suki o mitsukeru* seize an opportunity
隙を窺う *suki o ukagau* watch for an unguarded moment

HOMOPHONES
suki ⇨ 透 3108
suku ⇨ 透 3108 空 2227
sukasu ⇨ 透 3108 空 2227

NOTE
⇨ see USAGE note at 透 3108

隔 隔 隔 隔 ⒸⒽ 隔 gé

671 KAKU heda(teru) heda(taru)

Radical	Strokes
⻏ 170	13-3-10
Grade	**Freq**
Jōyō	1493
◧ 1-3-10	

3-10 ⻏

Stroke order: 1–13

▶APART

COMPOUNDS

❶ **apart, separated, distant**
隔世 *kakusei* distant age
隔絶する *kakuzetsu suru* be separated, be isolated
遠隔の *enkaku no* distant, remote, far
❷ⓐ [original meaning] **partition, screen, interpose; separate, set apart**
ⓑ partition; septum
隔壁 *kakuheki* partition, bulkhead; septum
隔膜 *kakumaku* partition; diaphragm
隔離する *kakuri suru* isolate, segregate
横隔膜 *ōkakumaku* diaphragm; midriff
間隔 *kankaku* interval, space
中隔 *chūkaku* septum
縦隔 *jūkaku* mediastinum
❸ estrange, alienate
隔意 *kakui* reserve, alienation
疎隔 *sokaku* estrangement, alienation
❹ **alternate, every other**
隔日 *kakujitsu* alternate days
隔週に *kakushū ni* biweekly
隔年の *kakunen no* every other year

KUN

【**heda(teru) 隔てる**】separate, set apart; partition, screen, interpose; estrange, alienate
隔て *hedate* partition; distinction, reserve, estrangement
別け隔て *wakehedate* discrimination, favoritism

【**heda(taru) 隔たる**】be apart [separated], be distant; become estranged from
隔たり *hedatari* distance, interval; gap, difference; estrangement
懸け隔たる *kakehedataru* be far apart; be different from

SYNONYMS

❶ **distant**
離 separated → 1836
遠 DISTANT → 3150
遥 FAR → 3141
悠 far-off → 2741
遼 FARAWAY → 3168
❷ⓐ **separate**
離 SEPARATE → 1836
別 SEPARATE → 1117
割 DIVIDE → 1816
分 DIVIDE → 1972
解 TAKE APART → 1517
析 ANALYZE → 862

672

▶APART
nonstandard for 隔 671

3-10 ⻏

673

▶HOMETOWN
nonstandard for 郷 549

3-10 ⻓

3-11 口

鳴 674

MEI na(ku) na(ru) na(rasu)

Ⓒ鸣 míng

Radical	Strokes
鳥 196	14-11-3
Grade	**Freq**
Jōyō-2	1133
1-3-11	

▶CRY ▶SOUND

COMPOUNDS

❶ⓐ [original meaning] (of birds and animals) **cry, howl**
ⓑ cry out, shout
鶏鳴 *keimei* cockcrowing
悲鳴 *himei* shriek, scream

❷ **sound, ring, roar**
鳴動 *meidō* rumbling
共鳴 *kyōmei* resonance
雷鳴 *raimei* thunderclap
吹鳴 *suimei* blowing (a whistle)
奏鳴曲 *sōmeikyoku* sonata

KUN

【**na(ku)** 鳴く】(of animals, birds or insects) cry, chirp, ululate, howl, yelp, meow
鳴き声 *nakigoe* cry, song, chirping
鳴き交わす *nakikawasu* cry [howl] to each other, exchange wooing cries
長鳴き *naganaki* long crowing [warbling]

【**na(ru)** 鳴る】*vi* sound, ring, roar, resound
鳴り *nari* sound, ringing
鳴り響く *narihibiku* reverberate, echo, resound
鳴り渡る *nariwataru* resound [echo] far and wide
鳴り物 *narimono* musical instruments; music, fanfare
高鳴る *takanaru* ring high, roar; (of one's heart) throb violently
耳鳴り *miminari* buzzing in the ears, tinnitus

【**na(rasu)** 鳴らす】*vt* ring, sound, chime; be famous; complain of, air one's grievances
掻き鳴らす *kakinarasu* thrum, strum
作家として鳴らす *sakka to shite narasu* be very popular as a writer
非を鳴らす *hi o narasu* denounce publicly, cry against

SYNONYMS

❶ **shout**
叫 SHOUT → 201
号 holler → 2153
喝 SHOUT AT → 461
喚 call out → 550
呼 CALL → 273

❷ **make sound or noise**
響 REVERBERATE → 2878
騒 CLAMOR → 1835

HOMOPHONES

naku ⇨ 泣 338

NOTE

⇨ see USAGE note at 泣 338

3-11 口

嘆 675

▶SIGH

nonstandard for 嘆 630

3-11 土

境 676

KYŌ KEI sakai

Ⓒ境 jìng

Radical	Strokes
土 32	14-3-11
Grade	**Freq**
Jōyō-5	727
1-3-11	

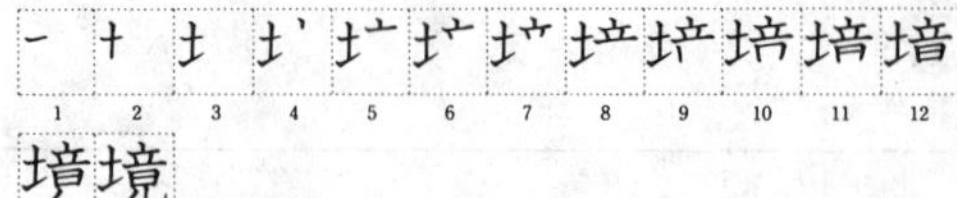

▶BOUNDARY ▶SITUATION

COMPOUNDS

❶ [formerly also 疆 *kyō* 1430] [original meaning] **boundary, border, frontier**
境界 *kyōkai* boundary, border
境域 *kyōiki* boundary; precincts, grounds
境内 *keidai* grounds [premises] (of a shrine or temple)

国境 *kokkyō* (national) boundary [border]
越境 *ekkyō* border transgression, violation of the border
辺境 *henkyō* frontier (district), remote region, border(land)
県境 *kenkyō* prefectural border
❷ region, place, country, land
秘境 *hikyō* unexplored regions
異境 *ikyō* foreign country, strange land
仙境 *senkyō* fairyland, enchanted land
❸ **situation, condition(s), state**
境遇 *kyōgū* one's lot, circumstances, situation in life
境地 *kyōchi* state, stage; field, ground
環境 *kankyō* environment, surroundings, circumstances
心境 *shinkyō* frame of mind, mental attitude [state]
逆境 *gyakkyō* adversity, adverse [unfavorable] circumstances
進境 *shinkyō* progress, improvement

INDEPENDENT

【kyō 境】 region, place; state of mind
無人の境 *mujin no kyō* uninhabited land
無我の境 *muga no kyō* state of complete self-effacement

KUN

【sakai 境】 boundary, border; place, region
境目 *sakaime* border, boundary line; crisis
国境 *kunizakai* (national, state or provincial) boundary [border]
見境 *misakai* distinction, discrimination
生死の境 *seishi no sakai* between life and death
境を異にする *sakai o koto ni suru* live in different worlds

SYNONYMS

❶ **edges and boundaries**
界 BOUNDS → 2563
辺 border → 3029
縁 EDGE → 1386
端 edge → 1221
際 VERGE → 714
涯 OUTER LIMITS → 512
❸ **states and situations**
局 current situation → 3063
状 CONDITION → 272
況 CONDITIONS → 337
景 business conditions → 2470
勢 course of events → 2857
態 STATE → 2847
情 ACTUAL CONDITIONS → 482
訳 circumstances → 1473
調 TONE → 1567
様 MODE → 1052
相 PHASE → 900

増 増 増 増

677 zō ma(su) ma(shi) fu(eru) fu(yasu)

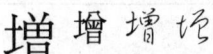

CH 増 zēng

Radical	Strokes
土 32	14-3-11
Grade	**Freq**
Jōyō-5	282
1-3-11	

3-11 土

Stroke order: 1 2 3 4 5 6 7 8 9 10 11 12 13 14

▶**INCREASE**

COMPOUNDS

❶ⓐ [original meaning] (grow or cause to grow in quantity or number) **increase, multiply, augment**
ⓑ [also suffix] **increase, rise**
増加する *zōka suru* increase, multiply, rise
増産 *zōsan* production increase
増税 *zōzei* tax increase
増員する *zōin suru* increase the staff [personnel]
増進する *zōshin suru* promote, improve, advance
増幅 *zōfuku* amplification
増大する *zōdai suru* increase, enlarge, enhance
増減 *zōgen* increase and decrease, rise and fall
急増 *kyūzō* sudden [rapid] increase
自然増 *shizenzō* natural increase
❷ grow impudent, become arrogant
増長する *zōchō suru* grow presumptuous

INDEPENDENT

【zō 増】 increase
五割の増 *gowari no zō* increase of 50%

KUN

【ma(su) 増す】 [sometimes also 益す] *vi & vt* increase, augment, multiply
増し刷り *mashizuri* additional printing, reprinting
信用が増す *shin'yō ga masu* gain more confidence

【ma(shi) 増し】 [also suffix] increase, addition; one by one
水増し予算 *mizumashi yosan* budget of padded [empty] figures

割増し料金 *warimashi-ryōkin* extra charge
日増しに *himashi ni* day by day
増しな *mashi na* less objectionable, better, preferable

【**fu(eru) 増える**】*vi* (grow in number or in quantity) increase, accrue, multiply
体重が増える *taijū ga fueru* gain weight
量が増える *ryō ga fueru* gain in quantity

【**fu(yasu) 増やす**】*vt* (cause to grow in number or quantity) increase, add
人手を増やす *hitode o fuyasu* add to the staff

SYNONYMS

❶ **increase**
殖 MULTIPLY → 994
倍 DOUBLE → 108
加 add to → 38

USAGE

❶ **masu**
増す
[sometimes also 益す] *vi* & *vt* increase, augment, multiply
益す
[usu. 増す] *vi* & *vt* increase, augment, multiply

❷ **fueru**
増える
vi (grow in number or in quantity) increase, accrue, multiply
殖える
vi (increase of its own accord) multiply, increase, propagate—said esp. of wealth or living things

❸ **fuyasu**
増やす
vt (cause to grow in number or quantity) increase, add
殖やす
vt (cause to multiply of its own accord) multiply, increase, propagate, augment—said esp. of wealth or living things

HOMOPHONES

masu ⇨ 益 2285
fueru ⇨ 殖 994
fuyasu ⇨ 殖 994

NOTE

⇨ see COMPOUND FORMATION for 増幅 *zōfuku* ⇨ 幅 569

3-11
土

678

▶**FENCE**
nonstandard for 塀 557

3-11
土

679

▶**BOUNDARY** ▶**SITUATION**
nonstandard for 境 676

3-11
女

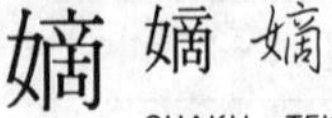
680 CHAKU TEKI▲

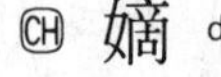
dí

Radical	Strokes
女 38	14-3-11
Grade	**Freq**
Jōyō	1893
1-3-11	

Stroke order: 1 2 3 4 5 6 7 8 9 10 11 12 13 14

▶**LEGITIMATE CHILD**

COMPOUNDS

❶ⓐ **legitimate child, heir, successor**
ⓑ [original meaning] **legitimate wife, legal wife**
嫡子 *chakushi* legitimate child
廃嫡 *haichaku* disinheritance
嫡男 *chakunan* heir, eldest son; legitimate son
嫡出 *chakushutsu* legitimacy (of birth)
嫡妻 *chakusai* legitimate wife
嫡室 *chakushitsu* legitimate wife

❷ in direct line (of descent); orthodox
嫡流 *chakuryū* lineage of the eldest son; orthodox school

SYNONYMS

❶ⓐ **offspring**
子 CHILD → 3390
孤 orphan → 356
息 son → 2647
男 son → 2542
惣 eldest son → 2780
娘 DAUGHTER → 406
女 daughter → 3418
姫 DAUGHTER OF NOBLE BIRTH → 407
ⓐ **inheritors**

嗣 HEIR → 1719
❺ **wives**
妻 WIFE → 2558
奥 wife → 2824
内 wife → 3466
室 wife (esp. of persons of rank) → 2254
婦 married woman → 469
嫁 BRIDE → 635
寡 widow → 2344

嫡

681

▶**LEGITIMATE CHILD**
nonstandard for 嫡 680

3-11 女

嶋

682

▶**ISLAND**
nonstandard for 島 3310

3-11 山

徴

徴 徴 𢕟 Ⓒ 征 zhēng 徵 zhǐ

683 CHŌ CHI▲ shirushi▲

Radical	Strokes
彳 60	14-3-11
Grade	**Freq**
Jōyō	932
◧ 1-3-11	

3-11 彳

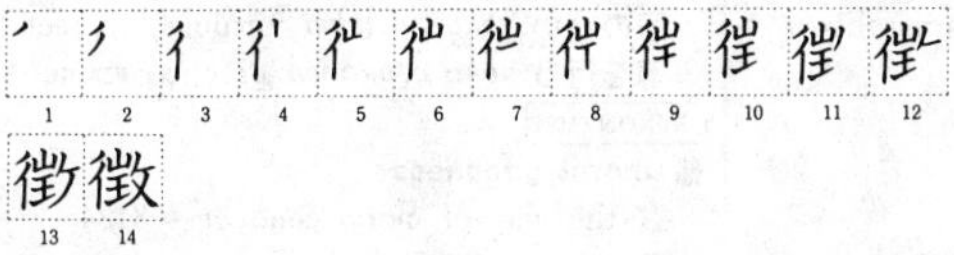

▶**LEVY** ▶**SYMPTOM**

COMPOUNDS

❶ (collect taxes or payment) **levy, collect, impose**
徴収する *chōshū suru* collect taxes [payment]
徴税 *chōzei* tax collection
追徴する *tsuichō suru* collect in addition
課徴金 *kachōkin* surcharge (on imports)
❷ⓐ (enlist troops) **levy, conscript, recruit**
ⓑ (collect by force) requisition, commandeer
徴兵 *chōhei* conscription, enlistment, draft
徴募 *chōbo* recruitment
徴集する *chōshū suru* levy, recruit
徴発 *chōhatsu* commandeering, requisition
❸ⓐ (evidence of a fact or event) **symptom, sign, indication, omen**
ⓑ evidence, proof
徴候 *chōkō* symptom, sign; omen
徴証 *chōshō* token, sign
象徴 *shōchō* symbol
明徴 *meichō* clarification
❹ **characteristic, character, feature**
特徴 *tokuchō* distinctive feature, characteristic
標徴 *hyōchō biol* diagnostic character, distinguishing mark
性徴 *seichō biol* sexual character
❺ [rare] fourth note of the pentatonic scale (⇨ see APPENDIX 7)

INDEPENDENT

【chō 徴】 symptom, sign, indication
【chōsuru 徴する】 judge by [from], refer to; solicit, seek
【chi 徴】 [rare] fourth note of the pentatonic scale

KUN

【shirushi 徴】
① effectiveness (of medicine)
② symptom, sign, indication
地震の徴 *jishin no shirushi* signs of an earthquake

SYNONYMS

❶ **impose**
課 impose → 1573
❷ **enlist**
募 RAISE → 2316
❸ⓐ **signs**
症 symptom (of a disease) → 3280
兆 OMEN → 225
候 indication → 119
気 sign → 3194

USAGE

chōshū suru
徴収する
collect taxes [payment]
徴集する
levy, recruit

HOMOPHONES

shirushi ⇨ 印 828

NOTE

⇨ see also USAGE note at 印 828
★do not confuse with 徵 639

3-11 彳

徳 徳 徳 徳

684 TOKU

CH 徳 dé

Radical	Strokes
彳 60	14-3-11
Grade	**Freq**
Jōyō-5	844
1-3-11	

▶**VIRTUE**

COMPOUNDS

❶ⓐ (moral excellence) **virtue, morality**

ⓑ (act of moral excellence) **virtue, virtuous deed**

徳行 *tokkō* virtuous deeds, goodness
徳義 *tokugi* morality, sincerity
道徳 *dōtoku* morality, morals
悪徳 *akutoku* vice, corruption, immorality
公徳 *kōtoku* public morality
美徳 *bitoku* virtue, good deed

❷ act of kindness, favor

徳沢 *tokutaku* grace, blessing
徳政 *tokusei* benevolent administration
報徳 *hōtoku* requital of a person's kindness

❸ⓐ profit, winnings

ⓑ benefits

徳用な *tokuyō na* economical
徳分 *tokubun* profits, winnings
余徳 *yotoku* benefits (that descend to posterity of a man of great virtue)

INDEPENDENT

【**toku** 徳】(moral excellence) virtue, morality; (act of moral excellence) virtue, virtuous act; power of commending love and respect; benefits

徳の高い *toku no takai* virtuous, respectable
徳を行う *toku o okonau* practice virtue

SYNONYMS

❶ **moral goodness**

道 the way of moral conduct → 3134
善 GOOD → 2325
義 RIGHTEOUSNESS → 2338

❷ **favor**

恵 FAVOR → 2659
恩 GRACE → 2655

3-11 忄

慣 慣 慣

685 KAN na(reru) na(rasu)

CH 惯 guàn

Radical	Strokes
忄 61	14-3-11
Grade	**Freq**
Jōyō-5	1202
1-3-11	

▶**HABITUAL PRACTICE**

COMPOUNDS

❶ **habitual [usual, established] practice, custom, habit, usual way, convention**

慣行 *kankō* habitual [usual] practice
慣例 *kanrei* custom, usage, precedent
習慣 *shūkan* custom, habit

❷ **grow accustomed to, get used to, become habituated**

慣用 *kan'yō* common use, usage

❸ remain in present state

慣性 *kansei* inertia

KUN

【**na(reru)** 慣れる】[also suffix] grow accustomed to, get used to, become inured to, become experienced in

慣れ *nare* habituation, practice, experience
慣れた *nareta* practiced, experienced, familiar
慣れ親しむ *nareshitashimu* get used to, become familiar with
見慣れる *minareru* get used to seeing
場慣れ *banare* experience, poise in a critical situation

【**na(rasu)** 慣らす】inure, habituate, accustom, make used to

足慣らし(＝足馴らし) *ashinarashi* walking practice, warming up
使い慣らす *tsukainarasu* accustom oneself to using (a thing), train
体を寒さに慣らす *karada o samusa ni narasu* inure oneself to cold

SYNONYMS

❶ **custom**

例 established practice → 89

習 CUSTOM → 2667
風 manners → 3007
俗 popular custom → 104
癖 HABIT → 3290
弊 EVIL PRACTICE → 2884

USAGE

❶ **nareru**
慣れる
[also suffix] grow accustomed to, get used to, become inured to, become experienced in
馴れる
① become tame [domesticated]
② [in compounds] become overfamiliar with

❷ **narasu**
慣らす
inure, habituate, accustom, make used to
馴らす
tame, domesticate
均す
① level, make even, roll
② average

HOMOPHONES

nareru ⇨ 馴 1820
narasu ⇨ 馴 1820 均 235

慢

686 MAN

CH 慢 màn

Radical	Strokes
忄 61	14-3-11
Grade	**Freq**
Jōyō	1411
◧ 1 - 3 - 1 1	

3-11 忄

1 2 3 4 5 6 7 8 9 10 11 12 13 14

▶ARROGANT ▶SLUGGISH

COMPOUNDS

❶ **arrogant, supercilious, haughty, conceited, proud**
慢心 *manshin* self-conceit; pride
自慢 *jiman* pride, self-praise, vanity
高慢な *kōman na* haughty, arrogant, proud
傲慢な *gōman na* arrogant, haughty, insolent
我慢 *gaman* patience, endurance; self-restraint

❷ (slow to act) **sluggish, slow, dragging**
慢性の *mansei no* chronic
緩慢な *kanman na* slack, slow-moving, dull, inactive

❸ [original meaning] (lacking in vigor) sluggish, lazy, idle
怠慢な *taiman na* negligent, inattentive, remiss

INDEPENDENT

【manjiru (=manzuru) 慢じる(=慢ずる)】 be self-conceited, swell with pride

SYNONYMS

❶ **boasting and arrogance**
誇 BOAST → 1522

❷ **slow**
緩 SLACK → 1389
徐 SLOWLY → 414
遅 SLOW → 3133

❸ **lazy**
惰 LAZY → 579
怠 REMISS → 2085

COMPOUND FORMATION

❶ **我慢** *gaman*
我慢 'patience, etc.' originally meant self (我) conceit (慢 ❶).

❷ **慢性** *mansei*
慢性の 'chronic' refers to a disease that has the quality (性) of dragging on and on (慢 ❷).

NOTE

★do not confuse with 漫 700

3-11 忄

憎 憎 憎 憎

687 ZŌ niku(mu) niku(i) niku(rashii) niku(shimi)

CH 憎 zēng

Radical	Strokes
忄 61	14-3-11
Grade	**Freq**
Jōyō	1718
1-3-11	

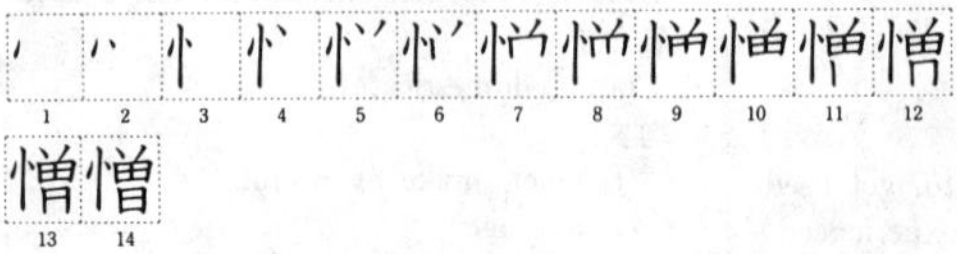

▶**HATE**

COMPOUNDS

ⓐ [original meaning] **hate, detest**

ⓑ hate, hatred

憎悪 *zōo* abhorrence, hatred

愛憎 *aizō* love and hate

KUN

【**niku(mu) 憎む**】 hate, detest, abhor

憎まれ口 *nikumareguchi* offensive [abusive] language

憎まれっ子 *nikumarekko* bad [naughty] child

【**niku(i) 憎い**】 hateful, abominable

憎さ *nikusa* hatefulness, hatred

憎憎しい *nikunikushii* hateful, detestable

生憎 *ainiku* unfortunately, unluckily; I am sorry, but...

小面憎い *kozuranikui* saucy, cheeky, pert

【**niku(rashii) 憎らしい**】 hateful, horrible, provoking

小憎らしい *konikurashii* saucy; provoking

【**niku(shimi) 憎しみ**】 hatred, enmity

SYNONYMS

● **hate and dislike**

悪 hate → 2745

忌む ABHOR → 2207

嫌 DISLIKE → 636

恨 HOLD A GRUDGE → 369

3-11 忄

慨

688

▶**DEPLORE**

nonstandard for 慨 641

3-11 忄

慘

689

▶**MISERABLE** ▶**CRUEL**

nonstandard for 惨 483

3-11 扌

摑

690 KAKU tsuka(mu) tsuka(maeru) tsuka(maru)

CH 掴 guāi guó

Radical	Strokes
扌 64	14-3-11
Grade	**Freq**
Reference	
1-3-11	

COMPOUNDS

ⓐ [original meaning] grasp, grip, clutch

ⓑ catch, seize, grasp, get hold of

ⓒ hold fast to, cling to

摑み取り *tsukamidori* taking (as much as one can hold) by the hand

鳥を摑まえる *tori o tsukamaeru* catch a bird

吊り革に摑まる *tsurikawa ni tsukamaru* cling to a strap

HOMOPHONES

tsukamaeru ⇨ 捕 429

tsukamaru ⇨ 捕 429

NOTE

⇨ see USAGE note at 捕 429

摸

691 MO MŌ

CH 摸 mō mó

Radical	Strokes
扌 64	14-3-11
Grade Reference	Freq
◧ 1-3-11	

3-11 扌

COMPOUNDS

❶ [now replaced by 模 *mo* 1050] pattern after, imitate, copy, model upon
摸写する *mosha suru* copy, trace, reproduce
摸倣する *mohō suru* imitate, copy
摸造 *mozō* imitation, counterfeit
摸擬試験 *mogi shiken* sham [trial] examination
摸する *mosuru* copy, imitate
❷ [now usu. 模 *mo* 1050] [original meaning] grope, feel about [for], search
摸牌する *mōpai suru* identify a piece by touch in a mahjong game
暗中摸索 *anchū mosaku* groping in the dark

摧

692 SAI

CH 摧 cuī

Radical	Strokes
扌 64	14-3-11
Grade Reference	Freq
◧ 1-3-11	

3-11 扌

COMPOUNDS

● [now replaced by 砕 1134] crush up, break into pieces, smash
破摧する *hasai suru* crush, smash, crack to pieces
玉摧する *gyokusai suru* die but never surrender

摺

693 SHŌ su(ru)

CH 折 zhé

Radical	Strokes
扌 64	14-3-11
Grade Reference	Freq
◧ 1-3-11	

3-11 扌

COMPOUNDS

❶ⓐ rub against
ⓑ print by rubbing
摺り足 *suriashi* shuffling walk
引き摺る *hikizuru* drag along; trail
スプーン摺り切り一杯 *supūn surikiri ippai* level spoonful
石摺り *ishizuri* print from stone, rubbing, rubbed copy
❷ [original meaning, now archaic] fold
摺本 *shōhon* folded book

HOMOPHONES

suru ⇨ 擦 790 磨 3181 刷 1273

NOTE

⇨ see USAGE note at 擦 790

3-11 扌

摘 摘 摘 摘

694 TEKI tsu(mu)

Ⓒ 摘 zhāi

Radical	Strokes
扌 64	14-3-11
Grade	**Freq**
Jōyō	962
◧ 1-3-11	

Stroke order: 1 2 3 4 5 6 7 8 9 10 11 12 13 14

▶PICK

COMPOUNDS

❶ [original meaning] **pick (flowers), pluck, gather**

摘果 *tekika* thinning out superfluous fruit

摘出する *tekishutsu suru* extract, excise, remove; point out

❷ⓐ (choose the best part) **pick out, select, make an extract**

ⓑ **point out (a person's mistakes), expose**

摘要 *tekiyō* summary

摘記する *tekki suru* summarize, epitomize

摘発する *tekihatsu suru* expose, lay bare, disclose

指摘する *shiteki suru* point out

KUN

【tsu(mu) 摘む】

① pick (flowers), pluck, gather

摘み取る *tsumitoru* pick, pluck

摘み草 *tsumikusa* gathering wild greens

茶摘み *chatsumi* tea-picking

②ⓐ nip

ⓑ [also 剪む] cut (one's hair), trim

芽を摘む *me o tsumu* nip the buds; nip something in the bud

髪を摘む *kami o tsumu* have one's hair cut [trimmed]

SYNONYMS

❶ **harvest**

採 PICK → 499

穫 HARVEST → 1251

刈る reap → 28

❷ⓐ **choose**

採 PICK → 499

択 SELECT → 255

選 CHOOSE → 3169

抜 single out → 246

USAGE

tsumu

摘む

① pick (flowers), pluck, gather

②ⓐ nip

ⓑ [also 剪む] cut (one's hair), trim

剪む

[also 摘む] cut (one's hair), trim

HOMOPHONES

tsumu ⇨ 剪 2306

3-11 扌

摘

695

▶PICK

nonstandard for 摘 694

3-11 扌

携

incorrect stroke count ⇨ see 648

3-11 氵

696 DEKI TEKI JŌ

Ⓒ 涤 dí

Radical	Strokes
氵 85	14-3-11
Grade	**Freq**
Reference	
◧ 1-3-11	

COMPOUNDS

● [now replaced by 浄 *jō* 382] wash, cleanse

洗滌する *sendeki* (=*senjō*) *suru* wash, irrigate

演 演 演
697 EN

Ⓒⓗ 演 yǎn

Radical	Strokes
氵 85	14-3-11
Grade	**Freq**
Jōyō-5	220
◧ 1-3-11	

3-11 氵

▶PERFORM

COMPOUNDS

❶ⓐ perform, act, enact, play, entertain
ⓑ performance, acting, enactment, play
演劇 *engeki* drama, play
演出 *enshutsu* production (of a play); representation
演技 *engi* acting, performance
演奏 *ensō* musical performance
演芸 *engei* performance, entertainments
主演する *shuen suru* play the leading part
上演する *jōen suru* put on stage
出演する *shutsuen suru* appear on stage, perform, play
開演 *kaien* raising the curtain, commencing a performance
共演 *kyōen* coacting, costarring
公演 *kōen* public performance
初演 *shoen* first performance, premier
❷ⓐ make a speech, lecture, expound
ⓑ speech, lecture
演説 *enzetsu* (public) speech, address, oration
講演 *kōen* lecture
演題 *endai* subject of a speech, speech title
❸ practice, exercise
演習 *enshū* exercise, practice; military maneuvers; seminar
演算 *enzan* mathematical operation
❹ deduce
演繹 *en'eki* deduction, deductive reasoning

INDEPENDENT

【enjiru (=enzuru) 演じる(=演ずる)】 perform, play, act
ロミオを演じる *romio o enjiru* act the part of Romeo

SYNONYMS

❶ⓑ performance
劇 DRAMA → 1904
芸 entertainment → 2209
❷ speak in public
講 LECTURE → 1619

漁 漁 漁
698 GYO RYŌ asa(ru)▲

Ⓒⓗ 渔 yú

Radical	Strokes
氵 85	14-3-11
Grade	**Freq**
Jōyō-4	714
◧ 1-3-11	

3-11 氵

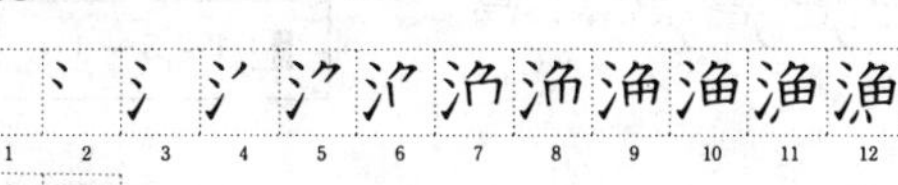

▶FISH

COMPOUNDS

❶ⓐ [original meaning] **fish, angle**
ⓑ [also suffix] **fishing, fishery**
漁業 *gyogyō* fishing industry
漁船 *gyosen* fishing boat
漁獲 *gyokaku* fishing; haul [catch] (of fish)
漁場 *gyojō* fishing ground, fishery
漁師 *ryōshi* fisherman
禁漁 *kinryō* prohibition of fishing
出漁する *shutsuryō suru* go (off) fishing
鮭漁 *sakeryō* salmon fishing
延縄漁 *haenawaryō* longline fishing
❷ catch, haul
大漁 *tairyō* large catch
不漁 *furyō* poor catch [haul]
❸ fish for, search for, hunt for
漁色 *gyoshoku* debauchery, philandering

INDEPENDENT

【ryō 漁】 fishing, fishery, fishing excursion; catch, haul

KUN

【asa(ru) 漁る】 [also verbal suffix] fish for, search for, hunt for
漁り *asari* search, rummaging search; fishing
掃き溜めを漁る *hakidame o asaru* pick a garbage dump, rummage a dustbin
買い漁る *kaiasaru* hunt for, go round shop-

ping

SYNONYMS

❶ **hunt and fish**
釣 ANGLE → 1674

猟 HUNTING → 538
狩 HUNT → 397
獲 CATCH GAME → 779

3-11
氵

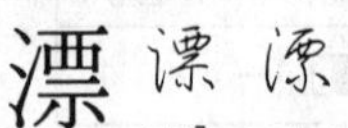

漂 699 HYŌ tadayo(u)

CH 漂 piāo piǎo piào

Radical	Strokes
氵 85	14-3-11
Grade	**Freq**
Jōyō	1610
1-3-11	

1 2 3 4 5 6 7 8 9 10 11 12 13 14

▶**DRIFT**

COMPOUNDS

❶ⓐ [original meaning] **drift, float**
ⓑ drift about, roam, wander
漂流する *hyōryū suru* drift, be adrift
漂着 *hyōchaku* drifting ashore
浮漂 *fuhyō* floating
漂泊 *hyōhaku* roaming, drifting about, wandering
漂浪 *hyōrō* [rare] wandering
漂然(＝飄然)と *hyōzen to* aimlessly, unexpectedly

❷ bleach
漂白 *hyōhaku* bleaching, decoloration

KUN

【tadayo(u) 漂う】 drift, be adrift; float, waft; waver, flicker, play
漂う小舟 *tadayou kobune* drifting boat
芳香が漂う *Hōkō ga tadayou* Fragrance floats in the air
唇に微笑を漂わせて *kuchibiru ni bishō o tadayowasete* with a smile on one's lips

SYNONYMS

❶ⓐ **float**
浮 FLOAT → 435
ⓑ **wander**
流 drift → 441
浪 WANDER → 439
遊 move about freely → 3142

3-11
氵

漫 700 MAN

CH  màn

Radical	Strokes
氵 85	14-3-11
Grade	**Freq**
Jōyō	1335
1-3-11	

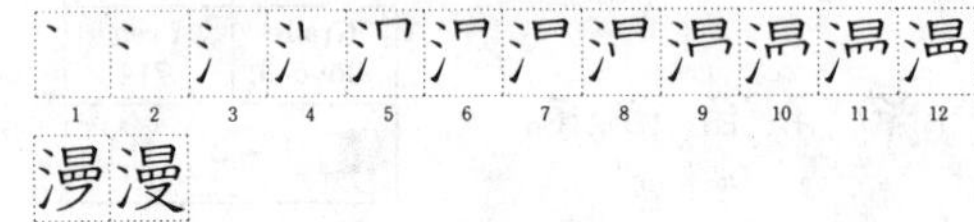

1 2 3 4 5 6 7 8 9 10 11 12 13 14

▶**RAMBLING** ▶**COMIC**

COMPOUNDS

❶ **rambling, random, discursive, desultory, aimless, unrestrained, casual**
漫遊する *man'yū suru* make a leisurely tour
漫文 *manbun* random notes
漫然たる *manzentaru* rambling, random, desultory
漫歩する *manpo suru* ramble, saunter
散漫な *sanman na* desultory, vagrant, vague
放漫 *hōman* laxity, looseness, indiscretion
冗漫な *jōman na* diffuse, verbose, prolix

❷ **comic, idle**
漫画 *manga* cartoon, comic strip
漫才 *manzai* comic dialogue, comic backchat, *manzai*
漫談 *mandan* idle talk, comic chat
漫楽 *mangaku manzai* accompanied by music
漫研(＝漫画研究会) *manken* (＝*manga kenkyūkai*) comic book [cartoon] research group

❸ [original meaning] vast, endless, boundless
漫漫たる *manmantaru* vast, boundless
爛漫たる *ranmantaru* in full bloom; in profusion

❹ used phonetically for *man* in the transliteration of foreign words
浪漫主義 *rōmanshugi* romanticism

SYNONYMS

❶ **unrestrained**

散 unrestrained → 1702
❷ **comic**
戯 sportive → 1875

NOTE
★do not confuse with 慢 686

漏 701

RŌ mo(ru) mo(reru) mo(rasu)

CH 漏 lòu

Radical	Strokes
氵 85	14-3-11
Grade	**Freq**
Jōyō	1703
1-3-11	

3-11 氵

1 2 3 4 5 6 7 8 9 10 11 12 13 14

▶LEAK

COMPOUNDS

❶ⓐ [original meaning] **leak**
ⓑ (of secrets) **leak (out), be disclosed, be divulged**
漏出 *rōshutsu* leak
漏水 *rōsui* water leakage
漏電 *rōden* short circuit, leakage
歯槽膿漏 *shisōnōrō* pyorrhea alveolaris
漏洩 *rōei* leakage, disclosure

❷ **omit, leave out**
遺漏 *irō* omission, oversight, neglect
脱漏 *datsurō* omission
疎漏 *sorō* carelessness, inadvertence, oversight

❸ water clock
漏刻 *rōkoku* water clock

KUN

【mo(ru) 漏る】 *vi* leak, be leaky
漏り *mori* leak, leakage
雨漏り *amamori* leak in the roof, leaking of rain

【mo(reru) 漏れる】 *vi* leak; (of secrets) leak, be disclosed, be divulged; find vent [expression]; be omitted, be left out
漏れ *more* leak, leakage; omission, oversight
ガス漏れ *gasumore* gas leak
口から漏れる *kuchi kara moreru* pass from one's lips
漏れ無く *morenaku* without omission, in full
招待に漏れる *shōtai ni moreru* be left out of an invitation

【mo(rasu) 漏らす】 *vt* let leak; express, give vent to; reveal, disclose
小便を漏らす *shōben o morasu* wet one's pants
秘密を漏らす *himitsu o morasu* betray [reveal] a secret

SYNONYMS

❶ⓐ **flow and drip**
滴 DROP → 705
泌 SECRETE → 332
流 FLOW → 441
注 POUR → 325
濫 overflow → 801

❷ **omit**
脱 leave out by mistake → 973
抜く leave out → 246
欠 missing → 1987

漬 702

SHI▲ tsu(keru) tsu(karu) -zu(ke) -zuke

CH 渍 zì

Radical	Strokes
氵 85	14-3-11
Grade	**Freq**
Jōyō	1808
1-3-11	

3-11 氵

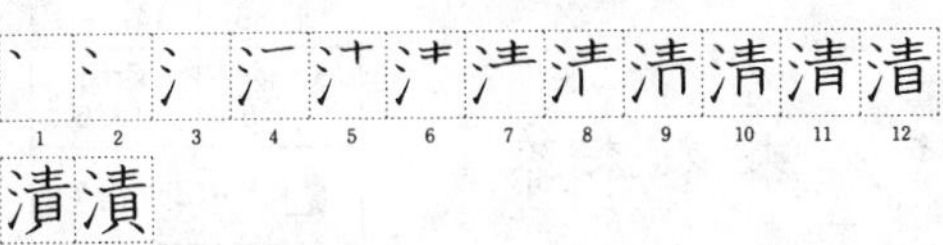

1 2 3 4 5 6 7 8 9 10 11 12 13 14

▶PICKLE

KUN

【tsu(keru) 漬ける】
vt
① pickle (vegetables), salt, preserve
漬け物 *tsukemono* pickles, pickled vegetable
漬け菜 *tsukena* pickled [salted] greens
菜を漬ける *na o tsukeru* pickle greens
梅を塩に漬ける *ume o shio ni tsukeru* salt plums; preserve plums in salt
② immerse, steep, soak, dip
手を水に漬ける *te o mizu ni tsukeru* immerse

[dip] one's hand in water
衣服を良く漬けて置け *Ifuku o yoku tsukete oke* Give the clothes a thorough soak
【tsu(karu) 漬かる】 *vi* be immersed [steeped], soak, be soaked in, be submerged; (of pickles) be seasoned, be salted
湯に漬かる *yu ni tsukaru* have a dip in the bath tub
白菜が良く漬かっている *Hakusai ga yoku tsukatte iru* The Chinese cabbage is well seasoned [salted]
【-zu(ke) -漬け, -zuke -漬】
[also suffix]
ⓐ pickles
ⓑ pickling with, preserving in
千枚漬け *senmaizuke* pickled sliced radishes
松前漬け *matsumaezuke* Matsumae pickles
塩漬け *shiozuke* salted [corned] food; pickling with salt
味噌漬け *misozuke* vegetables preserved in *miso*; preserving in *miso*
ホルマリン漬け *horumarinzuke* specimen preserved in formalin

SYNONYMS
【tsukeru】
① **preservatize**
薫 smoke → 2371
② **moisten**
浸 SOAK → 442
潤 moisten → 742
【-zuke】
ⓐ **preserved foods**
-干し dried food → 3379

HOMOPHONES
tsukeru ⇨ 付 31 附 347 着 3316 就 1694 即 1120 点 2084
-zuke ⇨ 付 31

NOTE
⇨ see USAGE note at 付 31

3-11

滲

703 SHIN shi(miru) niji(mu)

Ⓒ 渗 shèn

Radical	Strokes
氵 85	14-3-11
Grade	**Freq**
Reference	
1 - 3 - 1 1	

COMPOUNDS
❶ⓐ [now replaced by 浸 *shin* 442] [original meaning] permeate, infiltrate, penetrate; ooze, seep
ⓑ blot, spread, run, blur; ooze, be saturated with (as of blood, tears or sweat)
滲透する *shintō suru* permeate, penetrate
滲出 *shinshutsu* percolation, exudation, effusion
滲炭鋼 *shintankō* cement steel
滲み易いインク *nijimiyasui inku* ink that runs easily
額に汗を滲ませて *hitai ni ase o nijimasete* with a sweating brow
❷ [also 染みる *shimiru*]
ⓐ soak into, permeate
ⓑ penetrate (to the bone), come home to one's heart
ⓒ smart from irritation
滲み込む *shimikomu* soak into, permeate

HOMOPHONES
shimiru ⇨ 染 2572 凍 129

NOTE
⇨ see USAGE note at 染 2572

3-11

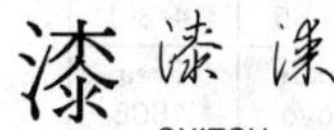

漆

704 SHITSU urushi

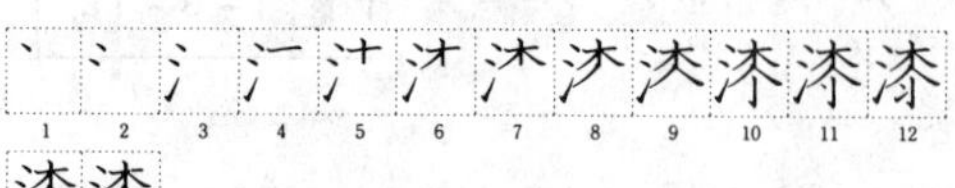

Ⓒ 漆 qī

Radical	Strokes
氵 85	14-3-11
Grade	**Freq**
Jōyō	1875
1 - 3 - 1 1	

▶LACQUER

COMPOUNDS
❶ [original meaning] **(Japanese or Chinese) lacquer, varnish, japan, *urushi***
漆器 *shikki* lacquer ware
漆工 *shikkō* lacquer work, japanner
❷ (as black as lacquer) pitch-black
漆黒 *shikkoku* pitch black

❸ unclassified compounds
漆喰 *shikkui* plaster, stucco

KUN

【urushi 漆】
① Japanese lacquer, varnish, japan, *urushi*
漆塗り *urushinuri* lacquering, japanning; lacquer ware
② Japanese lacquer [varnish] tree
漆かぶれ *urushikabure* lacquer poisoning

SYNONYMS

❶ **pigments**
墨 INDIA INK → 2753
藍 INDIGO → 2381
❷ **black colors**
黒 BLACK → 2740
【urushi】
② **trees**
桑 MULBERRY → 2112
梓 CATALPA → 962
桂 AROMATIC TREE, katsura tree → 928
桐 PAULOWNIA → 937
楠 CAMPHOR TREE → 1018
槙 PODOCARPUS → 1051
杉 CRYPTOMERIA → 832
松 PINE → 864
楓 MAPLE → 1015
柳 WILLOW → 899
桜 CHERRY → 931

滴 滴 滴 滴

705 TEKI shizuku shitata(ru)

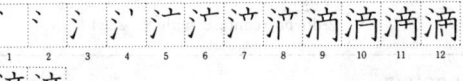

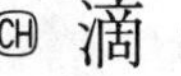

Radical	Strokes
氵 85	14-3-11
Grade	**Freq**
Jōyō	1797
◧ 1-3-11	

3-11 氵

Stroke order: 1–12

13 14

▶DROP

COMPOUNDS

❶ **drop, drip, trickle**
滴下する *tekika suru* drip, trickle
滴水 *tekisui* water dripping
点滴 *tenteki* falling drops of water; intravenous infusion
❷ⓐ [original meaning] (liquid globule) **drop**
ⓑ counter for drops
水滴 *suiteki* water drop
雨滴 *uteki* raindrops
数滴 *sūteki* several drops
一滴 *itteki* a drop

KUN

【shizuku 滴】
[also 雫]
ⓐ (liquid globule) drop
ⓑ counter for drops
露の滴 *tsuyu no shizuku* dewdrop
一滴 *hitoshizuku* a drop
【shitata(ru) 滴る】 drip, drop, trickle
滴り *shitatari* dripping; drop, trickle
滴り落ちる *shitatariochiru* trickle down

SYNONYMS

❶ **flow and drip**
漏 LEAK → 701
泌 SECRETE → 332
流 FLOW → 441
注 POUR → 325
濫 overflow → 801
❷ⓐ **small water masses**
泡 BUBBLE → 334

USAGE

shizuku
滴
[also 雫]
ⓐ (liquid globule) drop
ⓑ counter for drops
雫
[also 滴] same as 滴

HOMOPHONES

shizuku ⇨ 雫 2760

3-11 氵

漸 ZEN

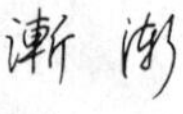

706

CH 渐 jiàn jiān

Radical	Strokes
氵 85	14-3-11
Grade	Freq
Jōyō	1753
1 - 3 - 1 1	

▶**GRADUALLY**

COMPOUNDS

ⓐ **gradually, gradual**

ⓑ advance gradually

漸次 *zenji* gradually

漸進 *zenshin* gradual advance

漸減 *zengen* gradual decrease

東漸 *tōzen* eastward advance (as of culture)

INDEPENDENT

【**zen** 漸】 gradual advance

漸を以て進歩する *zen o motte shinpo suru* advance gradually

SYNONYMS

ⓐ **in succession**

逓 progressively → 3106

連 IN SUCCESSION → 3103

歴 successive → 3019

逐 ONE BY ONE → 3102

NOTE

★do not confuse with 暫 2864

3-11 氵

漠

707

▶**DESERT** ▶**OBSCURE**

nonstandard for 漠 655

3-11 氵

漢

708

▶**CHINESE** ▶**FELLOW**

nonstandard for 漢 657

3-11 氵

滿

709

▶**FULL**

nonstandard for 満 607

3-11 氵

滯

710

▶**STAGNATE** ▶**STAY**

nonstandard for 滞 663

3-11 氵

滴

711

▶**DROP**

nonstandard for 滴 705

3-11 氵

潟

incorrect stroke count ⇨ see 745

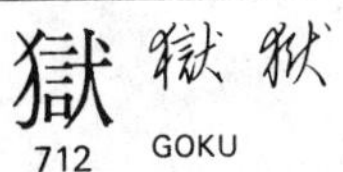

712 GOKU

CH 狱 yù

Radical	Strokes
犬 94	14-4-10
Grade	**Freq**
Jōyō	1598
◧ 1-3-11	

3-11 犭

▶**PRISON**

COMPOUNDS

❶ **prison, jail**

獄中記 *gokuchūki* diary written in prison
獄衣 *gokui* prison uniform
獄死 *gokushi* death in prison
出獄 *shutsugoku* release from prison
牢獄 *rōgoku* prison, jail
脱獄 *datsugoku* prison break, jailbreak

❷ hell

地獄 *jigoku* hell; inferno
煉獄 *rengoku* purgatory

❸ lawsuit, litigation

疑獄 *gigoku* criminal case, scandal
大獄 *taigoku* wholesale arrest, roundup

INDEPENDENT

【**goku** 獄】prison, jail
獄を破る *goku o yaburu* break prison

SYNONYMS

❶ **prison**

監 prison → 2852

❷ **posthumous worlds**

幽 world of the dead → 3008
天 HEAVEN → 3442

隠 隠 隠 隠

713 IN ON▲ kaku(su) kaku(shi)- kaku(reru)

CH 隐 yǐn

Radical	Strokes
阝 170	14-3-11
Grade	**Freq**
Jōyō	1495
◧ 1-3-11	

3-11 阝

▶**HIDE**

COMPOUNDS

❶ⓐ [original meaning] (conceal from sight) **hide, conceal**
ⓑ hidden from view, concealed, secret
ⓒ become hidden from view, disappear

隠蔽する *inpei suru* conceal, cover up, hide
隠匿 *intoku* concealment; misprision
隠語 *ingo* secret language, jargon
隠密 *onmitsu* secrecy, privacy; detective, spy
隠花植物 *inka shokubutsu* cryptogamic plant
隠滅する *inmetsu suru* extinction, destruction
隠見(＝隠顕) *inken* appearance and disappearance

❷ retire from the world, live in seclusion

隠居 *inkyo* retirement; person retired from active life
隠棲 *insei* secluded life

❸ feel pity, have compassion

惻隠の情 *sokuin no jō* pity, compassion

KUN

【**kaku(su)** 隠す】*vt* hide, conceal; hide (a matter from someone), keep secret

隠し持つ *kakushimotsu* carry (something) under cover
覆い隠す *ōikakusu* cover, mask

【**kaku(shi)-** 隠し-】[prefix] hidden, concealed, secret

隠し事 *kakushigoto* secret
隠し芸 *kakushigei* hidden talent; parlor trick
隠しカメラ *kakushikamera* hidden [spy] camera
隠し財源 *kakushizaigen* secret resources
隠し場所 *kakushibasho* place for concealment

【**kaku(reru)** 隠れる】*vi* hide, hide [conceal] oneself, disappear, be hidden from sight; be unknown [anonymous]; retire from the world; [honorific] pass away

隠れ伏す *kakurefusu* lie concealed
隠れん坊 *kakurenbō* hide-and-seek
隠れ蓑 *kakuremino* invisible cloak; pretext
雲隠れする *kumogakure suru* vanish behind clouds; disappear, run away
隠れ道 *kakuremichi* hidden path
隠れも無い *kakure mo nai* well-known
野に隠れる *no ni kakureru* retire from public

service

SYNONYMS

❶ⓐ hide

伏 lie in concealment → 45
潜 LURK → 746
匿 CONCEAL → 3011
忍 perform by stealth → 2212

ⓑ secret and private

秘 SECRET → 1159
密 SECRET → 2292
暗 in the dark → 1010
私 PRIVATE → 1115
内 not public → 3466

3-11
阝

際 際 際

714 SAI kiwa -giwa

Ⓒ𝐇 际 jì

Radical	Strokes
阝 170	14-3-11
Grade	**Freq**
Jōyō-5	286
1-3-11	

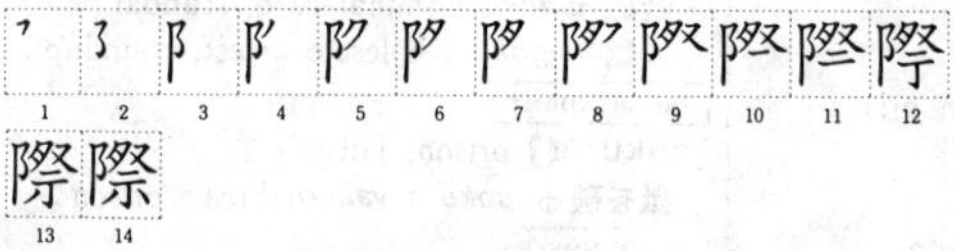

▶VERGE ▶OCCASION

COMPOUNDS

❶ verge, brink, edge

際限 *saigen* limits, end, bounds
際涯 *saigai* limits, end, extremity
金輪際 *konrinzai* never; *Buddhism* deepest bottom of the earth
天際 *tensai* horizon

❷ occasion, time

実際の *jissai no* true, real; actual; practical

❸ have relations, have social intercourse

交際 *kōsai* association, friendship, intercourse

❹ inter-, between, among

国際的な *kokusaiteki na* international
学際的 *gakusaiteki* interdisciplinary
州際通商委員会 *shūsai tsūshō iinkai* Interstate Commerce Commission

❺ occur unexpectedly

際会する *saikai suru* meet, face, confront

❻ degree, rank

分際 *bunzai* one's social position [standing]

INDEPENDENT

【sai 際】 occasion, time; when

あの際に *ano sai ni* on that occasion
食事の際に *shokuji no sai ni* when eating

KUN

【kiwa 際】 verge, edge, brink, side; occasion, time when something is about to happen, critical moment

際立つ *kiwadatsu* be conspicuous, be prominent
際どい *kiwadoi* dangerous, risky, hairbreadth
水際 *mizugiwa* beach, waterside
窓際の席 *madogiwa no seki* window seat
...の際に *...no kiwa ni* at the edge of; at the moment of
際物 *kiwamono* seasonal articles; temporary

【-giwa -際】 on the verge of, on the point of

間際 *magiwa* on the verge of, just before, on the point of
死に際に *shinigiwa ni* on the verge of death

SYNONYMS

❶ edges and boundaries

縁 EDGE → 1386
端 edge → 1221
辺 border → 3029
境 BOUNDARY → 676
界 BOUNDS → 2563
涯 OUTER LIMITS → 512

❷ occasions

折 occasion → 253
時 timely occasion → 924
機 OPPORTUNITY → 1076
節 time → 2691

❹ between

間 BETWEEN → 3323
中 MIDDLE → 3451
仲 intermediate → 43

【-giwa】

○ on the verge of

将 on the verge of → 460
臨 on the point of → 1630
-掛かる be on the verge of → 493

障 障 障 ⻖

715 SHŌ sawa(ru)

Ⓒⓗ 障 zhàng

Radical	Strokes
⻖ 170	14-3-11
Grade	**Freq**
Jōyō-6	647
1-3-11	

3-11 ⻖

▶**HINDRANCE**

COMPOUNDS

❶ⓐ **hindrance, obstruction, obstacle, barrier**

ⓑ [original meaning] **hinder, obstruct, block, screen**

障子 *shōji* paper sliding-door, *shoji*

故障 *koshō* malfunction, breakdown; physical disorder; hindrance, obstacle, accident; objection, protest

支障 *shishō* hindrance, obstacle, difficulty

万障 *banshō* all hindrances, all obstacles

排障器 *haishōki* obstruction guard

罪障 *zaishō* sins

障壁 *shōheki* barrier, obstacle; wall

障壁 *shōheki* [formerly also 牆壁] fence, wall; barrier

障害 *shōgai* obstacle, hindrance; (physical) disorder

❷ defend, protect; keep away, shut out

保障する *hoshō suru* (ensure that an undesirable condition does not occur) guarantee, secure, ensure

KUN

【**sawa(ru)** 障る】

① hinder, interfere with

障り *sawari* hindrance, obstacle; harm, bad effect; sickness

差し障り *sashisawari* obstacle, offense

月の障り *tsuki no sawari* menses

② affect, harm, jar on

体に障る *karada ni sawaru* affect one's health

SPECIAL READINGS

気障▲ *kiza* affectation

SYNONYMS

❶ⓐ **obstacle**

関 BARRIER → 3328

ⓑ **obstruct and hinder**

妨 HINDER → 238

阻 OBSTRUCT → 348

害 stand in the way → 2272

遮 INTERRUPT → 3158

HOMOPHONES

sawaru ⇨ 触 1518

sawari ⇨ 触 1518

NOTE

⇨ see USAGE notes at 保 96 and 触 1518

障

716

▶**HINDRANCE**

nonstandard for 障 715

3-11 ⻖

噴 噴 噴 ⻖

717 FUN fu(ku)

Ⓒⓗ 喷 pēn pèn

Radical	Strokes
口 30	15-3-12
Grade	**Freq**
Jōyō	1597
1-3-12	

3-12 口

▶**SPOUT**

COMPOUNDS

● [original meaning] **spout, emit, spurt, gush out**

噴出 *funshutsu* spouting, gushing

噴水 *funsui* jet (of water), fountain

噴火山 *funkazan* volcano

噴霧器 *funmuki* sprayer, vaporizer, atomizer

噴射 *funsha* jet, jet propulsion

噴飯する *funpan suru* burst out laughing

KUN

【**fu(ku)** 噴く】 spout, emit, spurt, gush out

噴き出す *fukidasu* spout, spurt, gush out; break into laughter

SYNONYMS

● **emit**

吐 SPEW → 203
射 SHOOT → 1458
排 DISCHARGE → 490
発 EMIT → 2565
出 PUT OUT → 3498
放 radiate → 853

HOMOPHONES

fuku ⇨ 吹 231

NOTE

⇨ see USAGE note at 吹 231

3-12 口

嘱 嘱 嘱 嘱

718 SHOKU

Ⓒⓗ 嘱 zhǔ

Radical	Strokes
口 30	15-3-12
Grade	**Freq**
Jōyō	1756
1-3-12	

▶CHARGE WITH

COMPOUNDS

[sometimes also 属 3145]

❶ [original meaning] **charge (a person) with (a job), ask someone to do something; entrust**

嘱託する *shokutaku suru* entrust with
委嘱する *ishoku suru* charge, commission [entrust] with

❷ fasten one's attention upon

嘱目する *shokumoku suru* pay attention to

SYNONYMS

❶ **commit**

託 ENTRUST → 1455
預 DEPOSIT → 1042
委 COMMIT → 2553
任 LEAVE TO → 53

❶ **request**

頼 ASK → 1615
訴 APPEAL TO → 1507
請 REQUEST → 1576
要 REQUIRE → 2635
願 ASK A FAVOR → 1845
求 SEEK → 3550

3-12 土

墳 墳 墳 墳

719 FUN

Ⓒⓗ 坟 fén

Radical	Strokes
土 32	15-3-12
Grade	**Freq**
Jōyō	1874
1-3-12	

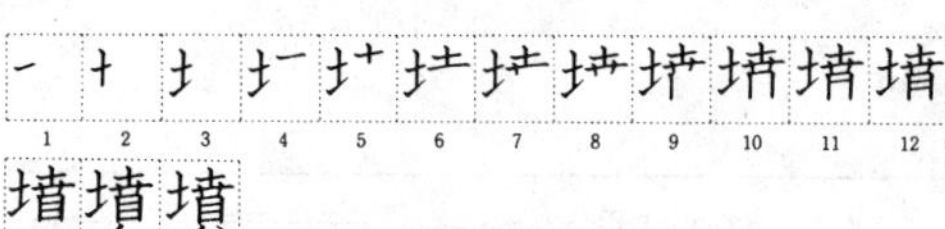

▶TUMULUS

COMPOUNDS

● **tumulus, grave mound, tomb**

墳墓 *funbo* grave, tomb
古墳 *kofun* tumulus, ancient tomb, old mound
円墳 *enpun* burial mound

SYNONYMS

● **graves**

陵 IMPERIAL MAUSOLEUM → 544
墓 GRAVE → 2332
塚 grave mound → 556

720 KYO

Ⓒⓗ 墟 xū

Radical	Strokes
土 32	15-3-12
Grade	Freq
Reference	
◧ 1-3-12	

3-12 土

COMPOUNDS

● [now also 虚 3237] [original meaning] ruins

廃墟 *haikyo* ruins, remains

壿

721

▶**INCREASE**

nonstandard for 増 677

3-12 土

嬉 嬉 嬉

722 KI ure(shii)

Ⓒⓗ 嬉 xī

Radical	Strokes
女 38	15-3-12
Grade	Freq
Non-Jōyō	1968
◧ 1-3-12	

3-12 女

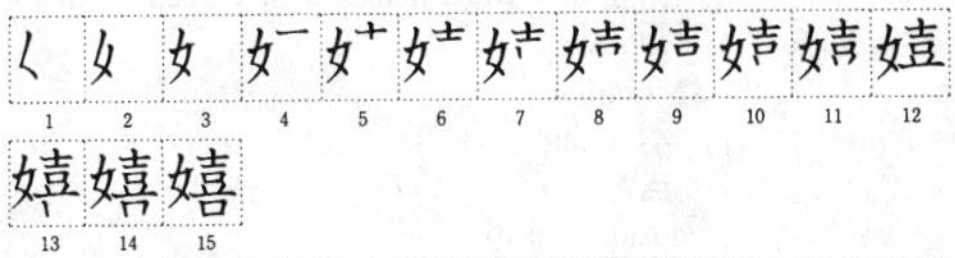

▶**GLAD**

COMPOUNDS

● [original meaning] be merry, play, sport

嬉嬉として *kiki to shite* merrily, joyfully

嬉戯する *kigi suru* frisk, frolic

KUN

【ure(shii) 嬉しい】 glad, pleased, happy, delighted; joyful, delightful

嬉しさ *ureshisa* joy, delight, gladness

嬉しそうな *ureshisō na* delightful, glad-looking

SYNONYMS

【ureshii】

○ **pleased and pleasant**

喜 HAPPY → 2308

愉 PLEASED → 582

悦 DELIGHTED → 418

歓 JOYOUS → 1867

欣 JOYFUL → 852

楽 pleasurable → 2826

快 PLEASANT → 245

朗 CHEERFUL → 1325

723 MAN HAN BAN hata

Ⓒⓗ 幡 fān

Radical	Strokes
巾 50	15-3-12
Grade	Freq
Reference	
◧ 1-3-12	

3-12 巾

COMPOUNDS

● *patākā*: pendant streamer hung before a temple in honor of Buddha

八幡 *hachiman* God of War, *Hachiman*

幢幡 *dōban* hanging-banner used as ornament in Buddhist temples

HOMOPHONES

hata ⇨ 旗 1047

NOTE

⇨ see USAGE note at 旗 1047

彈

724

▶**PROJECTILE** ▶**SPRING BACK**

nonstandard for 弾 572

3-12 弓

3-12 亻

衝 衝 衝
725 SHŌ tsu(ku)▲

CH 冲 chōng chòng

Radical	Strokes
行 144	15-6-9
Grade	Freq
Jōyō	835
1-3-12	

1 2 3 4 5 6 7 8 9 10 11 12 13 14 15

▶COLLIDE

COMPOUNDS

❶ **collide, dash [run] against, crash**
衝突する *shōtotsu suru* collide (with), crash (into); conflict [clash] (with)
衝撃 *shōgeki* impact, shock, impulse
衝動 *shōdō* impulse, urge
衝心 *shōshin* heart failure
衝天 *shōten* high spirits
緩衝 *kanshō* buffer
❷ important position, strategic place, hub, focus
要衝 *yōshō* key point, strategic position
❸ attack, strike
折衝 *sesshō* negotiation, parley
❹ [original meaning, now archaic] thoroughfare, avenue

INDEPENDENT

【shō 衝】 important position, focus; *astron* opposition
攻撃の衝に当たる *kōgeki no shō ni ataru* bear the brunt of an attack
世界交通の衝 *sekai-kōtsū no shō* focus of the trade routes of the world

KUN

【tsu(ku) 衝く】
① [usu. 突く] attack, strike at
中堅を衝く *chūken o tsuku* strike [attack] at the center [heart]
② [usu. 突く] brave, face courageously
嵐を衝いて進む *arashi o tsuite susumu* proceed in the face of a storm
③ [usu. 突く] stimulate (the senses), be pungent
鼻を衝く *hana o tsuku* assail the nostrils
④ unclassified compounds
衝立て *tsuitate* single-leaf screen

SYNONYMS

❶ **collide**
突 DASH → 2230
当たる HIT → 2177

HOMOPHONES

tsuku ⇨ 突 2230

COMPOUND FORMATION

❶ 衝心 *shōshin*
衝心 'heart failure' is a collision or crash (衝 ❶) of the heart (心).
❷ 衝天 *shōten*
衝天 'high spirits' is to be in spirits so high as to crash (衝 ❶) or soar into the sky (天).

NOTE

⇨ see USAGE note at 突 2230
⇨ see COMPOUND FORMATION for 折衝 *sesshō* ⇨ 折 253

3-12 彳

徹 徹 徹
726 TETSU

CH 彻 chè

Radical	Strokes
彳 60	15-3-12
Grade	Freq
Jōyō	980
1-3-12	

1 2 3 4 5 6 7 8 9 10 11 12 13 14 15

▶GO THROUGH

COMPOUNDS

❶ **go through [with], be thorough, be exhaustive**
徹底的 *tetteiteki* thorough, exhaustive
貫徹する *kantetsu suru* carry through, go through with, accomplish, attain
一徹な *ittetsu na* obstinate, stubborn
透徹した *tōtetsu shita* lucid, clear, penetrating
❷ all through, throughout
徹夜 *tetsuya* all night vigil [sitting]
徹宵 *tesshō* all night long, throughout the night

INDEPENDENT

【tessuru 徹する】 go through (with), be thorough, devote oneself to; penetrate, pierce

SYNONYMS

❶ **accomplish**

遂 ACCOMPLISH → 3138
達 ATTAIN → 3139
成 ACHIEVE → 3537
破 carry through with → 1150

❷ **throughout**

通 through → 3109
終 from beginning to end → 1336
中 throughout → 3451

NOTE

★do not confuse with 撤 738

徵 727 **▶LEVY ▶SYMPTOM** 3-12 彳

nonstandard for 徵 683

衞 728 **▶GUARD** 3-12 彳

nonstandard for 衛 760

德 729 **▶VIRTUE** 3-12 彳

nonstandard for 徳 684

憤 730 FUN ikidō(ru) 3-12 忄

CH 愤 fèn

Radical	Strokes
忄 61	15-3-12
Grade	**Freq**
Jōyō	1660
◧ 1-3-12	

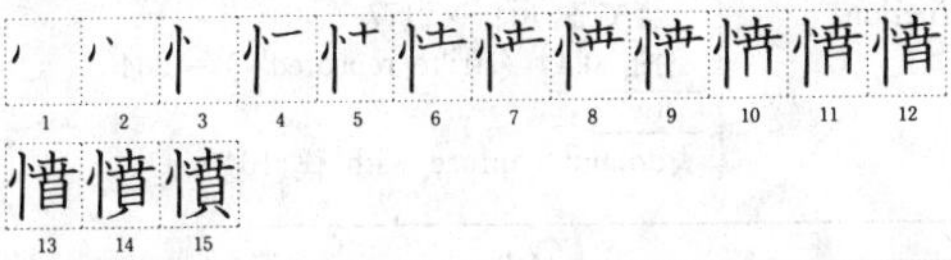

▶INDIGNATION

COMPOUNDS

❶ⓐ **indignation, resentment, exasperation, rage**

ⓑ **be indignant, resent, be angry**

憤怒 *fundo* (=*funnu*) anger, rage, resentment
公憤 *kōfun* public indignation [resentment]
義憤 *gifun* righteous indignation
憤激する *fungeki suru* be inflamed by anger, flare up
憤慨 *fungai* resentment, indignation
憤然と *funzen to* indignantly, in a rage
憤死する *funshi suru* die in a fit of anger
悲憤 *hifun* indignation, resentment

❷ [also 奮 2367] rise to action, be stirred
発憤する *happun suru* be stimulated, be inspired, be roused

KUN

【ikidō(ru) 憤る】 be indignant, resent, be angry
憤り *ikidōri* indignation, resentment
時世を憤る *jisei o ikidōru* be indignant at the times

SYNONYMS

❶ **anger**

慨 resent → 641
怒 GET ANGRY → 2571

憐 731 REN awa(remu) 3-12 忄

CH 怜 lián

Radical	Strokes
忄 61	15-3-12
Grade	**Freq**
Reference	
◧ 1-3-12	

COMPOUNDS

● [now usu. 哀れむ *awaremu*] pity, sympathize, feel compassion
憐憫(=憐愍) *renbin* compassion, mercy

憐情 *renjō* pity, compassion
哀憐 *airen* pity, compassion, affection
可憐な *karen na* cute, sweet, pretty; tiny
憐れみ *awaremi* pity, compassion

HOMOPHONES
awaremu ⇨ 哀 2068

NOTE
⇨ see USAGE note at 哀 2068

3-12
忄

憎 732

▶HATE
nonstandard for 憎 687

3-12
扌

撲 733

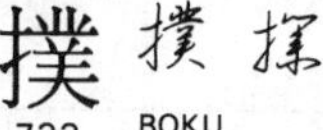

BOKU

CH 扑 pū

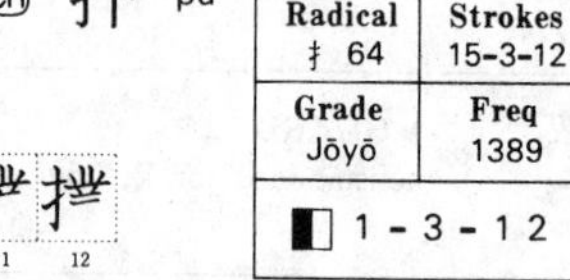

Radical	Strokes
扌 64	15-3-12
Grade	**Freq**
Jōyō	1389

1 - 3 - 12

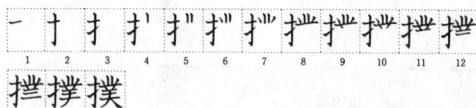

一 十 扌 扌' 扌'' 扌'' 扌''' 扌丵 扌丵 扌丵 扌丵 扌丵 扌丵 撲 撲
1 2 3 4 5 6 7 8 9 10 11 12 13 14 15

▶DEAL A BLOW

COMPOUNDS
● [original meaning] **deal [give] a blow, beat, strike forcefully, strike a blow**
撲殺 *bokusatsu* clubbing to death
撲滅 *bokumetsu* eradication, destruction
打撲 *daboku* blow, stroke

SPECIAL READINGS
相撲 *sumō* sumo wrestling

SYNONYMS
● **strike**
殴 BEAT (strike a person) → 886
打 STRIKE → 193
撃 STRIKE → 2863
当てる HIT → 2177
拍 BEAT (strike repeatedly) → 304

NOTE
★do not confuse with 僕 164

3-12
扌

撥 734

HATSU BACHI ha(neru)

CH 拨 bō

Radical	Strokes
扌 64	15-3-12
Grade	**Freq**
Reference	

1 - 3 - 12

COMPOUNDS
❶ [now replaced by 発 *hatsu* 2565] [original meaning] rebound, repel, repulse
反撥 *hanpatsu* repulsion, repelling; rally (of the market); opposition
❷ [now replaced by 発 *hatsu* 2565] stir, stir up
挑撥 *chōhatsu* provocation, incitement, excitement, stimulation
❸ pluck (the strings); plectrum, pick
撥弦 *hatsugen* plucking string instrument
撥 *bachi* plectrum, pick
❹❺ flip, splash
❺ strike, knock down
車に撥ねられる *kuruma ni hanerareru* be struck by a car
❺ reject, turn down
試験で撥ねられる *shiken de hanerareru* get flunked in an examination
❻ sweep up (in brush stroke of kanji)
❼ pronounce ん *n* as a syllabic consonant
撥音 *hatsuon* syllabic nasal in Japanese (ん)
撥ねる *haneru* pronounce ん *n* as a syllabic consonant

HOMOPHONES
haneru ⇨ 跳 1532

NOTE
⇨ see USAGE note at 跳 1532

撈

735 RŌ

Ⓒ 捞 lāo

Radical	Strokes
扌 64	15-3-12
Grade	**Freq**
Reference	
◧ 1 - 3 - 12	

3-12 扌

COMPOUNDS

● [now replaced by 労 2548] [original meaning] drag for, dredge up, fish for

漁撈 *gyorō* fishing, fishery

撒

736 SAN SATSU ma(ku)

Ⓒ 撒 sā sǎ

Radical	Strokes
扌 64	15-3-12
Grade	**Freq**
Reference	
◧ 1 - 3 - 12	

3-12 扌

COMPOUNDS

● [now replaced by 散 *san* 1702] [original meaning] (cause to) scatter, sprinkle, disperse

撒水 *sansui* (=*sassui*) water sprinkling

撒布する *sanpu* (=*sappu*) *suru* scatter, sprinkle, spray

撒く *maku* scatter, sprinkle; give (someone) the slip

撮 撮 撮

737 SATSU to(ru) -do(ri)

Ⓒ 撮 cuō zuǒ

Radical	Strokes
扌 64	15-3-12
Grade	**Freq**
Jōyō	1159
◧ 1 - 3 - 12	

3-12 扌

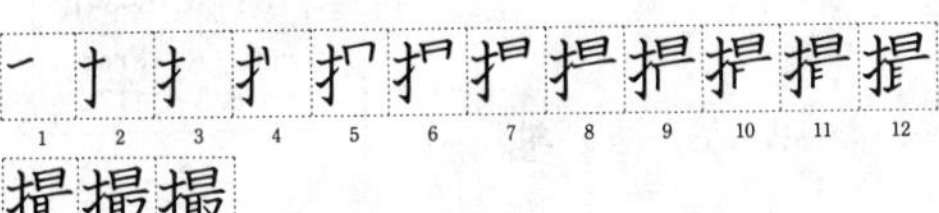

▶**PHOTOGRAPH**

COMPOUNDS

❶ **photograph, take a picture, film**

撮影 *satsuei* photographing, shooting (of a movie)

撮像管 *satsuzōkan* image pick up [camera] tube

特撮 *tokusatsu* trick work

❷ⓐ [original meaning] pinch, take with fingers, gather

ⓑ [archaic] a pinch, a slight amount

撮要 *satsuyō* compendium, summary, outline

撮土 *satsudo* a pinch of earth, small area

KUN

【**to(ru) 撮る**】 photograph, shoot, film, videotape

写真を撮る *shashin o toru* take a picture

隠し撮り *kakushidori* sneaking a shot

【**-do(ri) -撮り**】 counter for number of shots [pictures] available in a film

十二枚撮りのフィルム *jūnimaidori no firumu* film for 12 shots

SYNONYMS

❶ **photograph**

写 shoot → 2000

HOMOPHONES

toru ⇨ 取 1262 採 499 執 1680 捕 429

-dori ⇨ 取 1262

NOTE

⇨ see USAGE note at 取 1262

3-12
扌

撤 撤 撤
738 TETSU

Ⓒⓗ 撤 chè

Radical	Strokes
扌 64	15-3-12
Grade	**Freq**
Jōyō	1180
1-3-12	

一 十 扌 扌 扌 扌 扌 扌 揹 揹 揹 揹 揹 揹 撤
1 2 3 4 5 6 7 8 9 10 11 12 13 14 15

▶WITHDRAW

COMPOUNDS

❶ [original meaning] (take back) **withdraw, remove, take away**
撤去 *tekkyo* removal, dismantlement (of a building); evacuation (of an army)
撤回 *tekkai* withdrawal, retraction
撤廃 *teppai* abolition, removal

❷ (move back) **withdraw, retreat, evacuate**
撤退 *tettai* withdrawal, evacuation, pullout
撤兵する *teppei suru* withdraw troops
撤収する *tesshū suru* withdraw, pull out

SYNONYMS

❶ **eliminate**
排 EXCLUDE → 490
払う CLEAR AWAY → 194
除 RID OF → 456
外す take off → 186
脱 REMOVE → 973
去 take away → 2156
省 leave out → 2449
却 ELIMINATE → 1118
削 cross out → 1448
抹 wipe off → 313

❷ **leave and set forth**
退 RETREAT → 3094
去 GO AWAY → 2156
離 leave → 1836
発 START → 2565
出 GO OUT → 3498

NOTE

★do not confuse with 徹 726

3-12
氵

潮 潮 潮 潮
739 CHŌ shio ushio▲

Ⓒⓗ 潮 cháo

Radical	Strokes
氵 85	15-3-12
Grade	**Freq**
Jōyō-6	1175
1-3-12	

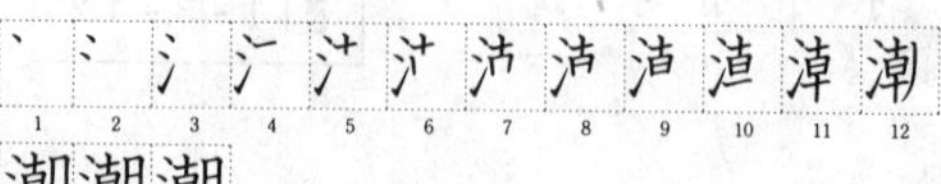

▶TIDE

COMPOUNDS

❶ⓐ [original meaning] **tide, current**
ⓑ (ocean water in motion) tide, seawater
潮汐 *chōseki* ebb and flow, tide
干潮 *kanchō* ebb tide
満潮 *manchō* high tide, high water
潮流 *chōryū* tide, current; tendency, trend
潮音 *chōon* [rare] sound of waves

❷ⓐ (stream of events) tide, tendency, trend, drift
ⓑ (extreme condition) tide, situation
風潮 *fūchō* tide, trend, tendency
思潮 *shichō* trend of thought
最高潮 *saikōchō* climax, acme

❸ menses
初潮 *shochō* beginning of menstrual function

KUN

【shio 潮】 [sometimes also 汐]
①ⓐ tide, current
ⓑ seawater
潮干狩り *shiohigari* shell gathering (at low tide)
引き潮 *hikishio* ebb tide, low water
血潮 *chishio* blood
潮風 *shiokaze* sea breeze, briny air
② tide (in the archaic sense of 'favorable occasion'), opportunity, chance
潮時 *shiodoki* time of ebb and flow; good chance, favorable opportunity

【ushio 潮】 tide; seawater
潮の如く押し寄せる *ushio no gotoku oshiyoseru* surge, rush like a flood

SYNONYMS

❶ⓐ **running water**
汐 TIDE → 223
流 CURRENT → 441

瀬 rapids → 806
滝 WATERFALL → 661
洪 FLOOD → 386
渦 WHIRLPOOL → 603
❷ⓐ **tendency**
流 CURRENT → 441
向 tendency → 3052
性 NATURE → 299
勢 trend → 2857
傾 inclination → 154

USAGE

shio

潮
[sometimes also 汐]
①ⓐ tide, current
ⓑ seawater
② tide (in the archaic sense of 'favorable occasion'), opportunity, chance

汐
[usu. 潮] same as 潮

HOMOPHONES

shio ⇨ 汐 223

澄 渣 𣲶 740

CHŌ su(mu) su(masu) -su(masu)

Ⓒⓗ 澄 chéng dèng

Radical	Strokes
氵 85	15-3-12
Grade	**Freq**
Jōyō	1578
◧ 1-3-12	

3-12 氵

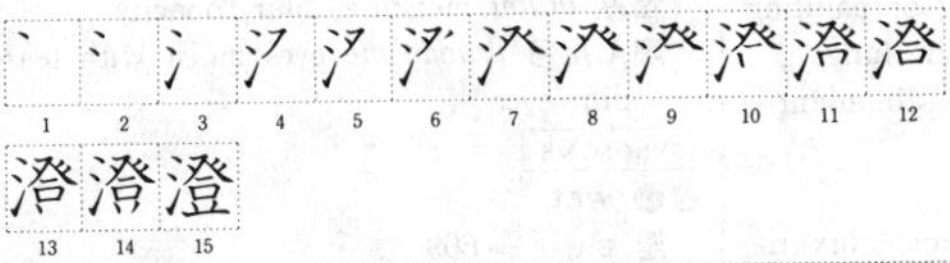

▶LIMPID

COMPOUNDS

● **limpid, clear, transparent, lucid, serene**
清澄な *seichō na* clear, lucid; serene
明澄な *meichō na* unclouded, clear, limpid

KUN

【su(mu) 澄む】 *vi* clear, become clear
澄み切った *sumikitta* perfectly clear
澄んだ水 *sunda mizu* limpid water

【su(masu) 澄ます】 *vi* look grave, look unconcerned; put on airs; *vt* strain (as one's ears); clear (water), make clear
澄まし顔 *sumashigao* smug face
耳を澄ます *mimi o sumasu* strain one's ears
澄まし汁 *sumashijiru* clear soup

【-su(masu) -澄ます】 [also -済ます] [verbal suffix] perform an action well [perfectly]
研ぎ澄ます *togisumasu* sharpen [grind] well
見澄ます *misumasu* observe carefully, watch intently

SYNONYMS

● **clear**
透 TRANSPARENT → 3108
清 CLEAR (liquid) → 523
明 CLEAR (unclouded) → 855
朗 CLEAR (sky) → 1325
冴える CRISP AND CLEAR → 79

USAGE

-sumasu

-澄ます
[also -済ます] [verbal suffix] perform an action well [perfectly]

-済ます
[also -澄ます] [verbal suffix] same as -澄ます

HOMOPHONES

-sumasu ⇨ 済 522

潑 741

HATSU

Ⓒⓗ 泼 pō

Radical	Strokes
氵 85	15-3-12
Grade	**Freq**
Reference	
◧ 1-3-12	

3-12 氵

COMPOUNDS

● [now also 発 2565] lively, energetic
潑剌たる *hatsuratsutaru* lively, sprightly, vivid
活潑な *kappatsu na* lively, active

3-12 氵

潤 㵎 注

742 JUN uruo(u) uruo(su) uru(mu)

CH 润 rùn

Radical	Strokes
氵 85	15-3-12
Grade	Freq
Jōyō	1636
1-3-12	

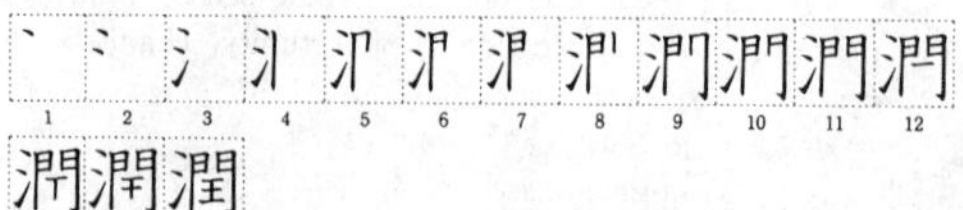

▶**MOIST**

COMPOUNDS

❶ⓐ **moist, wet**

ⓑ **moisten, be moistened, ooze, be wet**

湿潤な *shitsujun na* moist, damp, wet

潤滑油 *junkatsuyu* lubricant, lubricating oil

潤筆料 *junpitsuryō* fee for writing or painting

肺浸潤 *haishinjun* infiltration of the lungs

❷ⓐ enrich, make prosperous; rich, abundant

ⓑ gain, profit; favor

潤沢 *juntaku* abundance, plenty

豊潤な *hōjun na* rich and prosperous, luxurious

利潤 *rijun* profit, returns

❸ embellish

潤色 *junshoku* rhetorical flourishes

KUN

【uruo(u) 潤う】be moistened, be wet, be damp; receive benefits, profit, be made rich, become prosperous

潤い *uruoi* moisture, dampness; gain, profit; tastefulness

【uruo(su) 潤す】wet, moisten, dip. irrigate; profit, enrich, make prosperous

喉を潤す *nodo o uruosu* appease one's thirst

【uru(mu) 潤む】be moist [wet] (with tears); be dimmed, become turbid, be clouded

潤み *urumi* moisture, blur, opacity

潤んだ目 *urunda me* eyes moist with tears; dim eyes

SYNONYMS

❶ⓐ **wet**

湿 DAMP → 609

ⓑ **moisten**

浸 SOAK → 442

漬ける immerse → 702

COMPOUND FORMATION

潤筆料 *junpitsuryō*

潤筆料 'fee for writing or painting' is a fee (料) for moistening (潤 ❶ⓑ) one's brush (筆).

3-12 氵

潰

743 KAI tsubu(su) tsubu(reru) tsui(eru)

CH 溃 kuì huì

Radical	Strokes
氵 85	15-3-12
Grade	Freq
Reference	
1-3-12	

COMPOUNDS

❶ⓐ [usu. 壊 *kai* 756] [original meaning] break down, destroy, collapse; (of a dam) burst

ⓑ fester, ulcerate

崩潰する *hōkai suru* collapse, crumble, break down, cave in

倒潰 *tōkai* collapse, destruction, crumbling

全潰 *zenkai* complete collapse

決潰 *kekkai* rip, break

潰す *tsubusu* crush, smash, batter, squash; scrap, junk; butcher, kill; ruin, wreck; pass, kill (time)

潰れる *tsubureru* be crushed [smashed], be battered, break; be worn down, wear away; collapse, be ruined

潰瘍 *kaiyō* ulcer

❷ [now usu. 壊 *kai* 756] be routed, be utterly defeated

潰走する *kaisō suru* be routed, stampede

潰滅する *kaimetsu suru* be destroyed, be annihilated

潰える *tsuieru* be routed, be utterly defeated; collapse

HOMOPHONES

tsuieru ⇨ 費 2607

NOTE

⇨ see USAGE note at 費 2607

潔 潔 潔 潔

744 KETSU isagiyo(i)

CH 洁 jié

Radical	Strokes
氵 85	15-3-12
Grade	**Freq**
Jōyō-5	1409
◧ 1-3-12	

3-12 氵

▶IMMACULATE

COMPOUNDS

❶ⓐ (free from stain) **immaculate, clean, pure, spotless**

ⓑ (free from moral blemish) **immaculate, pure, upright**

潔癖 *keppeki* love of cleanliness, fastidiousness

清潔な *seiketsu na* clean, neat, pure

不潔な *fuketsu na* unclean, dirty, impure, maculate

潔白な *keppaku na* innocent, pure, upright

純潔な *junketsu na* purehearted, immaculate, innocent

貞潔 *teiketsu* chastity and purity

❷ concise, brief

簡潔な *kanketsu na* brief, concise

KUN

【isagiyo(i) 潔い】 gallant, brave, manly, resolute

潔さ *isagiyosa* manliness, resolute composure

潔く *isagiyoku* bravely, manfully; frankly, with good grace

潔しとしない *isagiyoshi to shinai* be too proud (to do), find it against one's conscience (to do)

SYNONYMS

❶ⓐ clean and purified

浄 CLEAN → 382

清 clean → 523

純 PURE → 1297

粋 REFINED (free from impurities) → 1293

精 refined (purified) → 1366

ⓑ purehearted

純 PURE → 1297

淳 PUREHEARTED → 514

清 clean → 523

廉 INCORRUPT → 3153

敦 HONEST → 1693

惇 SINCERE → 486

直 straightforward → 2932

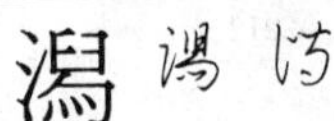

745 SEKI▲ kata -gata

Radical	Strokes
氵 85	15-3-12
Grade	**Freq**
Jōyō	1043
◧ 1-3-12	

3-12 氵

▶LAGOON

COMPOUNDS

● tideland

KUN

【kata 潟, -gata -潟】

①ⓐ lagoon

ⓑ suffix after names of lagoons

八郎潟 *hachirōgata* Lagoon Hachiro

② beach at ebb tide

干潟 *higata* beach at ebb tide

③ [also suffix] inlet, creek

難波潟 *naniwagata* Naniwa Bay (old name for Osaka Bay)

SYNONYMS

【kata】

① lakes and marshes

湖 LAKE → 604

池 POND → 218

沼 MUDDY POND → 339

沢 MARSH → 267

3-12 氵

潜 潜 潜 潜

746 SEN hiso(mu) mogu(ru)

CH 潜 qián

Radical	Strokes
氵 85	15-3-12
Grade	Freq
Jōyō	1235
1-3-12	

▶SUBMERGE ▶LURK

COMPOUNDS

❶ⓐ [original meaning] **submerge, dive**

ⓑ abbrev. of 潜水艦 *sensuikan*: submarine

潜水 *sensui* diving

潜水艦 *sensuikan* submarine

潜航 *senkō* submarine voyage, underwater navigation

原潜 *gensen* nuclear submarine

❷ submerge oneself in thought, concentrate

潜心 *senshin* meditation

沈潜する *chinsen suru* sink into deep thought; sink to the depths

❸ⓐ **lurk, hide, lie concealed; be latent**

ⓑ latent

潜伏 *senpuku* concealment, hiding; latency

潜入 *sennyū* infiltration

潜行する *senkō suru* travel in disguise; move [travel] under water

潜在の *senzai no* latent, potential

潜熱 *sennetsu* latent heat

潜像 *senzō* latent image

KUN

【hiso(mu) 潜む】 lurk in, lie concealed; be latent

潜んでいる力 *hisonde iru chikara* latent power, potentiality

【mogu(ru) 潜る】 dive into, submerge; get in, crawl in; lie low

潜り *moguri* diving; unlicensed (person)

潜り込む *mogurikomu* get in, crawl into

SYNONYMS

❶ⓐ **sink**

没 SINK → 260

沈 SINK → 261

ⓑ **boats and ships**

艦 WARSHIP → 1435

船 SHIP → 1341

舶 OCEANGOING SHIP → 1340

舟 SMALL BOAT → 3538

艇 BOAT → 1365

隻 COUNTER FOR SHIPS → 2755

❸ⓐ **hide**

伏 lie in concealment → 45

隠 HIDE → 713

匿 CONCEAL → 3011

忍 perform by stealth → 2212

3-12 氵

潮

747

▶TIDE

nonstandard for 潮 739

3-12 氵

澁

748

▶NOT GO SMOOTHLY ▶ASTRINGENT

nonstandard for 渋 513

3-12 氵

潔

749

▶IMMACULATE

nonstandard for 潔 744

3-12 氵

潛

750

▶SUBMERGE ▶LURK

nonstandard for 潜 746

3-12 阝

隣

751

▶NEIGHBOR

nonstandard for 隣 781

隨 incorrect stroke count ⇨ see 783
(nonstandard for 随 627)

3-12 阝

噸
752 TON

Ⓒⓗ 吨 dūn (国字)

Radical	Strokes
口 30	16-3-13
Grade	**Freq**
Reference	
1-3-13	

3-13 口

COMPOUNDS

[now also 屯 3457]

ⓐ [original meaning] ton, tonnage

ⓑ shipping ton

十六噸 *jūrokuton* 16 tons

英噸 *eiton* British [long] ton

噸数 *tonsū* tonnage

噴
753

▶**SPOUT**

nonstandard for 噴 717

3-13 口

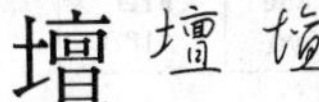

壇
754 DAN TAN

Ⓒⓗ 坛 tán

Radical	Strokes
土 32	16-3-13
Grade	**Freq**
Jōyō	1285
1-3-13	

3-13 土

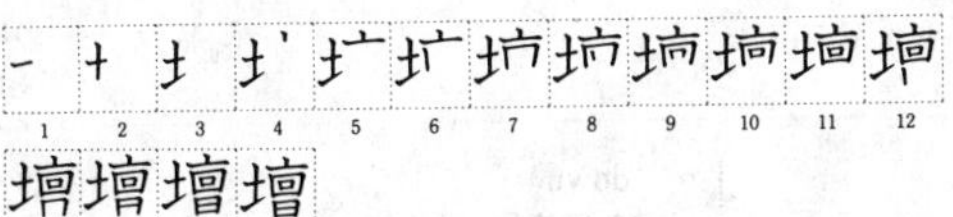

▶**PLATFORM**

COMPOUNDS

❶ⓐ **platform, raised floor, stage, dais**

ⓑ [original meaning] platform for religious rites, altar

壇上 *danjō* on the platform, on the stage

壇場 *danjō* stage

演壇 *endan* platform, rostrum

花壇 *kadan* flower bed

教壇 *kyōdan* teacher's platform, rostrum

戒壇 *kaidan* ordination platform (in temples)

仏壇 *butsudan* family Buddhist altar

祭壇 *saidan* altar

❷ **circles, world**

文壇 *bundan* literary circles, world of literature

俳壇 *haidan* haiku world

画壇 *gadan* artists' world, painting circles

詩壇 *shidan* poetical circles, world of poetry

劇壇 *gekidan* stage, theatrical world

土壇場 *dotanba* the last moment

INDEPENDENT

【**dan** 壇】 platform, raised floor, stage, dais; altar

壇に登る *dan ni noboru* get on the platform

SYNONYMS

❶ **flat supports**

台 STAND → 2005

座 SEAT → 3116

棚 SHELF → 984

架 rack → 2569

床 BED → 3067

❷ **circles**

界 WORLD → 2563

NOTE

⇨ see COMPOUND FORMATION for 土壇場 *dotanba* ⇨ 土 3403

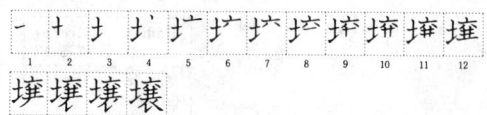

3-13 壤 壤 壤 壤 ㊥ 壌 rǎng
土
755 JŌ

Radical	Strokes
土 32	16-3-13
Grade	**Freq**
Jōyō	1778
1-3-13	

1 2 3 4 5 6 7 8 9 10 11 12 13 14 15 16

▶ARABLE SOIL

COMPOUNDS

ⓐ [original meaning] **arable soil, (loose or loamy) soil, fertile soil, earth, loam**

ⓑ earth, land

土壌 *dojō* soil, earth

天壌 *tenjō* heaven and earth

SYNONYMS

● **land and soil**

土 SOIL → 3403

地 GROUND → 204

陸 LAND → 543

泥 MUD → 326

3-13 壊 壊 壊 壊 ㊥ 坏 huài pī
土
756 KAI kowa(su) kowa(reru)

Radical	Strokes
土 32	16-3-13
Grade	**Freq**
Jōyō	1168
1-3-13	

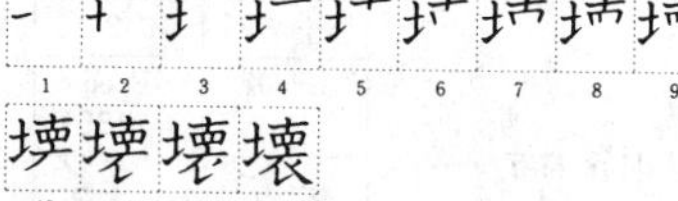

1 2 3 4 5 6 7 8 9 10 11 12 13 14 15 16

▶BREAK DOWN

COMPOUNDS

❶ [sometimes also 潰 743] **break down, destroy, smash;** (of a dam) **burst**

破壊する *hakai suru* break (down), destroy, wreck

崩壊 *hōkai* collapse, crumbling, breakdown, cave-in

全壊 *zenkai* complete collapse

決壊 *kekkai* rip, break

倒壊する *tōkai suru* collapse, be destroyed, crumble

❷ [formerly also 潰 743] be routed, be utterly defeated

壊滅 *kaimetsu* destruction, annihilation

壊乱する *kairan suru* corrupt, demoralize

KUN

【**kowa(su) 壊す**】*vt* break (down), destroy, smash, take apart; spoil, mar, upset

取り壊し *torikowashi* demolition, pulling down

ぶち壊す *buchikowasu* destroy, demolish, smash; spoil, upset

【**kowa(reru) 壊れる**】*vi* break (down), be broken; get out of order; be broken off, fall through, be upset

壊れ物 *kowaremono* fragile article, breakables; broken article

壊れた時計 *kowareta tokei* broken clock

縁談が壊れた *Endan ga kowareta* The match was broken off

SYNONYMS

❶ **break**

破 BREAK → 1150

折 BREAK OFF → 253

割る crack → 1816

裂 SPLIT → 2687

砕 CRUSH UP → 1134

崩 CRUMBLE → 2296

3-13 墳
土
757

▶TUMULUS

nonstandard for 墳 719

孃

758 JŌ

CH 娘 niáng

Radical	Strokes
女 38	16-3-13
Grade	**Freq**
Jōyō	1669
1-3-13	

3-13 女

▶YOUNG LADY

COMPOUNDS

❶ⓐ **unmarried young lady, girl, mademoiselle**

ⓑ [also suffix] (**unmarried**) **female worker**

ⓒ daughter

令孃 *reijō* daughter; young lady

老孃 *rōjō* spinster

交換孃 *kōkanjō* telephone operator

案内孃 *annaijō* usherette

愛孃 *aijō* one's beloved daughter

❷ title after names of unmarried young ladies: Miss

良子孃 *yoshikojō* Miss Yoshiko

INDEPENDENT

【jō 孃】 young lady; daughter

お孃さん *ojōsan* young lady; your daughter

SYNONYMS

❶ⓐ **woman**

娘 GIRL → 406

女 WOMAN → 3418

婦 ADULT WOMAN → 469

婆 OLD WOMAN → 2762

雌 FEMALE → 1055

ⓑ **workers and professionals**

婦 woman worker → 469

夫 MAN LABORER → 3460

匠 CRAFTSMAN → 2990

工 workman → 3381

手 OCCUPATION SUFFIX → 3456

屋 colloquial occupation suffix → 3098

員 MEMBER (of a staff) → 2269

人 person of certain category → 3368

者 person who → 3211

師 profession suffix → 1326

士 PROFESSION SUFFIX → 3405

客 skilled person → 2250

家 professional → 2273

❷ **titles of address**

氏 COURTESY TITLE → 2951

兄 familiar title (seniors) → 2154

君 FAMILIAR TITLE (peers) → 3206

様 FORMAL TITLE → 1052

殿 FORMAL HONORIFIC TITLE → 1792

師 honorific title (clergymen) → 1326

公 honorific title (noblemen) → 1974

759 KEN

xiǎn

Radical	Strokes
山 46	16-3-13
Grade	**Freq**
Reference	
1-3-13	

3-13 山

COMPOUNDS

[now replaced by 険 542]

ⓐ [original meaning] steep, precipitous

ⓑ steep [inaccessible] place, steep pass, stronghold

嶮岨(＝険阻) *kenso* steepness, precipice

峻嶮な *shunken na* steep, precipitous

天嶮 *tenken* natural stronghold

アルプスの嶮 *arupusu no ken* steep pass in the Alps

3-13
彳

衛 衛 衛◇ 衛 衛 (CH) 卫 wèi

760 EI E▲

Radical	Strokes
行 144	16-6-10
Grade	**Freq**
Jōyō-5	336
1-3-13	

1 2 3 4 5 6 7 8 9 10 11 12 13 14 15 16

▶**GUARD**

COMPOUNDS

❶ⓐ **guard, defend, escort, protect, preserve**

ⓑ **guard, keeper**

衛生 *eisei* hygiene, sanitation, preservation of health

護衛 *goei* guard, escort

自衛 *jiei* self-defense, self-protection

防衛 *bōei* defense, protection

紅衛兵 *kōeihei* Red Guards

近衛兵 *konoehei* personal guard

守衛 *shuei* guard, doorkeeper

前衛 *zen'ei* advance guard, vanguard; forward player

警衛 *keiei* guard, patrol, escort

❷ [original meaning] revolve, go round, orbit

衛星 *eisei* satellite; moon

SYNONYMS

❶ⓐ **protect**

警 GUARD AGAINST → 2893

守 PROTECT → 2173

護 PROTECT → 1648

防 defend → 270

番 WATCH → 2748

保 PRESERVE → 96

看 CARE FOR → 3220

3-13
彳

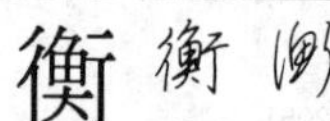

761 KŌ

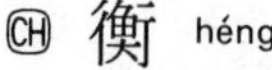

Radical	Strokes
行 144	16-6-10
Grade	**Freq**
Jōyō	1584
1-3-13	

▶**BALANCE**

COMPOUNDS

❶ⓐ **balance, equilibrium**

ⓑ **balanced, stable**

平衡 *heikō* equilibrium, balance

均衡 *kinkō* balance, equilibrium

❷ⓐ **scales, weighing machine**

ⓑ beam [arm] of a scale

度量衡 *doryōkō* weights and measures

権衡 *kenkō* scales; balance, equilibrium

❸ weigh, consider

銓衡(＝選考)する *senkō suru* select, screen

❹ horizontal, crosswise

連衡 *renkō* lateral league of six states (in Chinese history); Japanese Confederation of Labor

SYNONYMS

❷ **measuring devices**

計 meter → 1441

尺 rule → 3440

3-13
彳

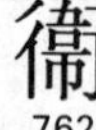

762

▶**GUARD**

nonstandard for 衛 760

懐 懐 懐 㤜 (CH) 怀 huái

763 KAI futokoro natsu(kashii) natsu(kashimu) natsu(ku) natsu(keru)

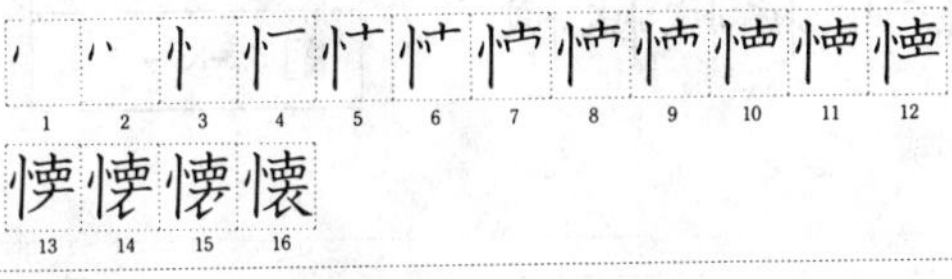

Radical	Strokes
忄 61	16-3-13
Grade	**Freq**
Jōyō	1658
◧ 1-3-13	

3-13 忄

▶**BOSOM** ▶**LONG FOR**

COMPOUNDS

❶ (underside of garment covering chest) **bosom, pocket**
懐中 *kaichū* one's pocket
❷ⓐ [original meaning] (place in the bosom) embosom, carry in the bosom
ⓑ (harbor a thought) **embosom, cherish, harbor**
懐炉 *kairo* pocket heater
懐胎 *kaitai* conception, becoming pregnant
懐妊 *kainin* pregnancy, conception
懐疑 *kaigi* doubt, skepticism, disbelief
抱懐する *hōkai suru* harbor, cherish, entertain
❸ (thoughts cherished in one's heart) bosom, heart, feelings
本懐 *honkai* one's long-cherished desire [object]
虚心担懐 *kyoshintankai* frankness, candidness
述懐 *jukkai* effusion of one's thoughts (and feelings), reminiscence
❹ **long for, miss, yearn, be attached to, be filled with nostalgia**
懐旧 *kaikyū* longing for the old days
懐古 *kaiko* yearning for the old days
懐郷 *kaikyō* nostalgia, homesickness
追懐 *tsuikai* recollection, reminiscence

KUN

【futokoro 懐】 bosom, breast; heart, mind; one's pocket, one's purse
自然の懐 *shizen no futokoro* bosom of Nature
内懐 *uchibutokoro* inside pocket; bosom; one's real intention
懐銭 *futokorozeni* pocket money
懐が寂しい *futokoro ga sabishii* have a scanty supply of money
【natsu(kashii) 懐かしい】 dear, beloved, longed-for, old; long for, miss
懐かしさ *natsukashisa* yearning, longing, nostalgia
人懐かしい *hitonatsukashii* miss people, long for others' presence
【natsu(kashimu) 懐かしむ】 long [pine] for, yearn after, miss
昔を懐かしむ *mukashi o natsukashimu* view the past with nostalgia
【natsu(ku) 懐く】 become attached to; be tamed
人懐っこい(=人懐こい) *hitonatsukkoi* (=*hitonatsukoi*) be affable, be sociable, love company; (of animals) take kindly to men
【natsu(keru) 懐ける】 make (another) attached to one, win a person's heart, win over; tame, domesticate
手懐ける *tenazukeru* bring (a person or animal) round, gain over to one's side; influence with money

SYNONYMS

❶ **garment parts**
袖 SLEEVE → 1164
襟 COLLAR → 1252
❷ⓑ **hold in the mind**
抱 HUG → 306
持 HOLD → 374
❸ **psyche**
胸 breast → 951
襟 inner mind → 1252
衷 INNER HEART → 2575
心 HEART → 11
腹 heart → 1034
神 MIND → 912
気 SPIRIT (consciousness) → 3194
精 SPIRIT (mind) → 1366
霊 SPIRIT (soul) → 2805
魂 SOUL, spirit → 1063
❹ **wish and desire**
慕 yearn for → 2353
渇 thirst for → 515
欲 DESIRE → 1475
求 SEEK → 3550
希 ASPIRE → 2049
望 HOPE → 2742
願 WISH → 1845

3-13 忄

憾 憾 憾

764 KAN ura(mu)▲

CH 憾 hàn

Radical	Strokes
忄 61	16-3-13
Grade	**Freq**
Jōyō	1651
1-3-13	

1 2 3 4 5 6 7 8 9 10 11 12 13 14 15 16

▶STRONGLY REGRET

COMPOUNDS

● [original meaning] **strongly regret, be sorry for, be dissatisfied**

遺憾な *ikan na* regrettable

KUN

【ura(mu) 憾む】 be sorry for, regret

憾み *urami* regret, matter for regret

それは片手落ちの憾みが有る *Sore wa katate-ochi no urami ga aru* I'm sorry to say so, but it may not be quite fair

SYNONYMS

● **regret**

惜 REGRET → 484

恨 regret → 369

悔 REPENT → 365

HOMOPHONES

uramu ⇨ 恨 369 怨 2570

urami ⇨ 恨 369 怨 2570

NOTE

⇨ see USAGE note at 恨 369

3-13 忄

憶 憶 憶 憶

765 OKU

CH 忆 yì

Radical	Strokes
忄 61	16-3-13
Grade	**Freq**
Jōyō	1653
1-3-13	

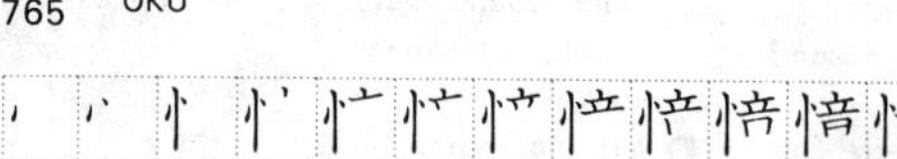

13 14 15 16

▶SPECULATE ▶REMEMBER

COMPOUNDS

❶ [formerly 臆 1092] (engage in conjectural thought) **speculate, conjecture, guess, infer**

憶説 *okusetsu* hypothesis, speculation

憶測 *okusoku* conjecture, speculation, guess

憶断 *okudan* jumping to hasty conclusions

❷ **remember, recall, recollect**

記憶 *kioku* memory, recollection

追憶 *tsuioku* recollection, retrospection

❸ [usu. 臆 1092] fear, feel timid

憶病 *okubyō* cowardice, timidity

SYNONYMS

❶ **conjecture**

推 INFER → 504

測 CONJECTURE → 610

察 GUESS → 2347

❷ **remember**

覚える COMMIT TO MEMORY → 2604

記 commit to memory → 1453

追 reminisce → 3096

顧 LOOK BACK → 1900

3-13 忄

憤

766

▶INDIGNATION

nonstandard for 憤 730

3-13 忄

憶

767

▶SPECULATE ▶REMEMBER

nonstandard for 憶 765

768 SEN hoshiimama

CH 擅 shàn

Radical	Strokes
扌 64	16-3-13
Grade Reference	Freq
◧ 1-3-13	

3-13 扌

COMPOUNDS

● [now also 専 *sen* 2644] [original meaning] arrogate to oneself, claim arbitrarily, do something on one's own authority

擅断 *sendan* arbitrary decision, arbitrariness

独擅場 *dokusenjō* one's unrivaled sphere of activity, one's monopoly

擅 *hoshiimama* self-indulgent, selfish; arbitrary

操 操 操

769 sō misao ayatsu(ru)

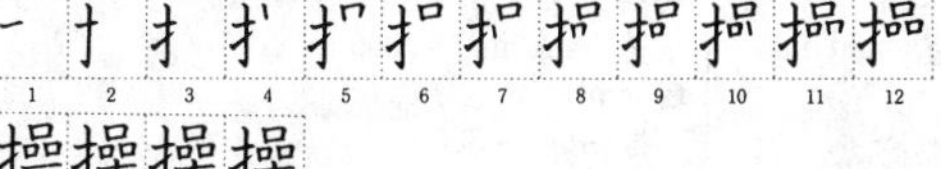

CH 操 cāo

Radical	Strokes
扌 64	16-3-13
Grade	Freq
Jōyō-6	948
◧ 1-3-13	

3-13 扌

▶**MANIPULATE**

COMPOUNDS

❶ⓐ **manipulate, handle, operate (a machine)**

ⓑ [original meaning] hold in the hand

操作 *sōsa* operation, manipulation, handling

操縦する *sōjū suru* manage, control; steer; pilot, fly

操業 *sōgyō* operation, work

操車 *sōsha* marshaling (in a classification yard)

操舵 *sōda* steering

❷ exercise, drill

体操 *taisō* gymnastics, physical exercise

❸ⓐ constancy, integrity, fidelity, moral principles

ⓑ chastity

情操 *jōsō* sentiment

節操 *sessō* constancy, fidelity, integrity, honor

操守 *sōshu* preserving one's chastity, adhering to moral principles

貞操 *teisō* chastity, virginity

KUN

【misao 操】 constancy, fidelity; chastity

操を守る *misao o mamoru* preserve one's chastity; adhere to one's principles

【ayatsu(ru) 操る】

ⓐ (operate skillfully with the hands) manipulate, handle, work, operate (a machine); steer (a ship)

ⓑ (influence skillfully) manipulate, pull strings, mastermind

操り *ayatsuri* manipulation; puppet

操り人形 *ayatsuriningyō* puppet

巧みに操る *takumi ni ayatsuru* manipulate, maneuver

英語を操る *eigo o ayatsuru* have a good command of English

世論を操る *seron o ayatsuru* manipulate public opinion

SYNONYMS

❶ⓐ **handle**

扱う HANDLE → 217

揮 WIELD → 589

運 control movement skillfully → 3140

❸ⓐ **fidelity**

節 moral integrity → 2691

信 fidelity → 100

実 faithfulness → 2225

誠 SINCERITY → 1523

悌 BROTHERLY LOVE → 424

孝 FILIAL PIETY → 3205

義 faith → 2338

忠 LOYALTY → 2433

ⓑ **chastity**

貞 CHASTE → 2083

3-13 扌

擁 770 YŌ

Ⓒ 拥 yōng

Radical	Strokes
扌 64	16-3-13
Grade	Freq
Jōyō	1506
1-3-13	

▶**SUPPORT**

COMPOUNDS

❶ **support, protect**

擁立する *yōritsu suru* give backing to, support, help (to the throne)

擁護する *yōgo suru* protect, defend, support, safeguard

❷ [original meaning] **embrace, hold in one's arms, hug**

抱擁する *hōyō suru* embrace, hug, hold in one's arms

INDEPENDENT

【**yōsuru** 擁する】 possess; have a person as the leader; embrace, hold in one's arms

巨富を擁する *kyofu o yōsuru* possess enormous wealth

SYNONYMS

❶ **support**

支 SUPPORT → 1979

扶 LEND SUPPORT TO → 247

賛 back up → 2809

❷ **embrace**

抱 HUG → 306

3-13 扌

擄 771

▶**GROUNDS**

nonstandard for 拠 312

3-13 扌

擇 772

▶**SELECT**

nonstandard for 択 255

3-13 扌

擔 773

▶**BEAR ON SHOULDER** ▶**UNDERTAKE**

nonstandard for 担 318

3-13 氵

濁 774 DAKU JOKU▲ nigo(ru) nigo(su)

Ⓒ 浊 zhuó

Radical	Strokes
氵 85	16-3-13
Grade	Freq
Jōyō	1647
1-3-13	

▶**TURBID**

COMPOUNDS

❶ **turbid, muddy, cloudy, impure**

濁流 *dakuryū* muddy stream

濁度 *dakudo* turbidity

濁酒 *dakushu* unrefined sake

混濁した *kondaku shita* turbid, thick, muddy, cloudy

清濁 *seidaku* purity and impurity; good and evil

水質汚濁 *suishitsuodaku* water pollution

❷ corrupt, depraved

濁世 *jokuse Buddhism* corrupt world, the world of man

汚濁 *odaku* (=*ojoku*) corruption

❸ voiced, sonant

濁音 *dakuon* voiced sound, sonant

濁点 *dakuten* voiced consonant marks (as in だ)

KUN

【nigo(ru) 濁る】*vi* become turbid [muddy, impure]; be vague; be in disorder; be voiced
濁り *nigori* turbidity, muddiness; voiced sound; unrefined sake
濁り水 *nigorimizu* muddy water
濁り酒 *nigorizake* unrefined sake
濁った頭 *nigotta atama* vague head
濁った世の中 *nigotta yononaka* this corrupt world
濁り点 *nigoriten* voiced consonant marks

【nigo(su) 濁す】*vt* make turbid [muddy], make cloudy; speak ambiguously, not commit oneself
立つ鳥後を濁さず *Tatsu tori ato o nigosazu* It is an ill bird that fouls its own nest
お茶を濁す *ocha o nigosu* temporize, make do
言葉を濁す *kotoba o nigosu* not commit oneself

SYNONYMS

❶ **dirty**
汚 DIRTY → 222

澱

775 DEN ori

CH 淀 diàn

Radical	Strokes
氵 85	16-3-13
Grade	**Freq**
Reference	
1-3-13	

3-13 氵

COMPOUNDS

ⓐ [now also 殿 *den* 1792] settle, precipitate
ⓑ settlings, sediment
澱粉 *denpun* starch
沈澱 *chinden* precipitation, settlement
酒の澱 *sake no ori* sediment of wine, lees

激

776 GEKI hage(shii)

CH 激 jī

Radical	Strokes
氵 85	16-3-13
Grade	**Freq**
Jōyō-6	565
1-3-13	

3-13 氵

▶**VIOLENT**

COMPOUNDS

❶ⓐ (acting with extreme force) **violent, fierce, vehement**
ⓑ sudden, rapid
激烈な *gekiretsu na* vehement, furious, violent, severe
激戦 *gekisen* fierce [hard-fought] battle; hot contest
激突 *gekitotsu* crash, collision
激情 *gekijō* violent emotion, passion
激変(=劇変) *gekihen* sudden change, upheaval
激増 *gekizō* sudden [rapid] increase
急激な *kyūgeki na* sudden, abrupt

❷ [sometimes also 劇 1904] (of great intensity) **intense, violent, severe, strong**
激化 *gekika* (=*gekka*) intensification, aggravation
激賞 *gekishō* high praise, unbounded admiration
激痛(=劇痛) *gekitsū* violent [intense] pain
過激派 *kagekiha* extreme Radicals

❸ [formerly also 戟 1696] excite, stimulate, stir up
激励 *gekirei* encouragement
感激する *kangeki suru* be deeply moved
憤激する *fungeki suru* be inflamed by anger, flare up
刺激する *shigeki suru* stimulate, excite

INDEPENDENT

【gekisuru 激する】get excited, be agitated, be enraged

KUN

【hage(shii) 激しい】
[sometimes also 烈しい]
① (acting with extreme force) violent, fierce, vehement
激しさ *hageshisa* intensity, severity
激しい風 *hageshii kaze* strong wind
② (of great intensity) intense, violent, severe
激しい競争 *hageshii kyōsō* hot competition

SYNONYMS

❶ⓐ **extreme in power**
荒 WILD → 2260
狂 raging → 269
烈 VEHEMENT → 2652
猛 FIERCE → 537
ⓑ **sudden**
急 SUDDEN → 2092
暴 sudden → 2515
突 abruptly → 2230
❷ **extreme in degree**
酷 SEVERE → 1562
厳 SEVERE → 3289
極 EXTREME → 1017
痛 bitter(ly) → 3285
切 keen → 27
甚 EXTREMELY → 2643
超 super- → 3313
強 STRONG → 475
重 HEAVY → 3573
高 HIGH → 2097
深 DEEP → 524
大 BIG → 3416
❸ **incite**
奮 ROUSE UP → 2367
振 arouse to action → 430
起 rise to action → 3307
動 MOVE → 1778
挑 PROVOKE → 372
唆 INSTIGATE → 402
扇 FAN → 1950

USAGE

hageshii
激しい
[sometimes also 烈しい]
① (acting with extreme force) violent, fierce, vehement
② (of great intensity) intense, violent, severe
烈しい
[usu. 激しい] same as 激しい

HOMOPHONES

hageshii ⇨ 烈 2652

3-13
氵

濃 
777 NŌ ko(i)

Ⓒ 浓 nóng

Radical	Strokes
氵 85	16-3-13
Grade	**Freq**
Jōyō	1212
1-3-13	

1 2 3 4 5 6 7 8 9 10 11 12
13 14 15 16

▶THICK

COMPOUNDS

❶ [also prefix] **thick, concentrated, dense, heavy**
濃厚な *nōkō na* thick, dense, heavy, rich
濃度 *nōdo* density
濃縮 *nōshuku* concentration
濃霧 *nōmu* dense [thick] fog
濃密な *nōmitsu na* thick; crowded
濃硫酸 *nōryūsan* concentrated sulfuric acid
❷ [also prefix] **dark-colored, deep, rich**
濃紺 *nōkon* dark blue, navy blue
濃グレー *nōgurē* dark gray
濃淡 *nōtan* light and shade
濃緑色 *nōryokushoku* dark green
❸ abbrev. of 美濃 *mino*, old name for south Gifu Prefecture
濃尾平野 *nōbi heiya* Nobi Plain

KUN

【ko(i) 濃い】 thick, concentrated, dense; strong; thick-haired; intimate, thick; dark-colored, deep
濃さ *kosa* depth (of color); thickness, strength (as of coffee)
濃いスープ *koi sūpu* thick soup
濃い仲である *koi naka de aru* bound by love, be thick (with)
濃紫 *komurasaki* dark purple

SYNONYMS

❶ **dense**
密 CLOSE → 2292
❷ **dark-colored**
暗 DARK → 1010
深 DEEP → 524

3-13
氵

澤
778

▶MARSH
nonstandard for 沢 267

獲 獲 獲 狻

779 KAKU e(ru)

CH 获 huò

Radical	Strokes
犭 94	16-3-13
Grade	Freq
Jōyō	1164
1-3-13	

3-13 犭

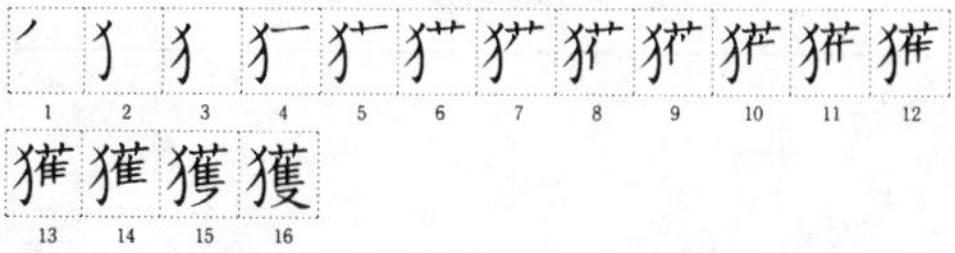

▶**CATCH GAME**

COMPOUNDS

❶ [original meaning] **catch game, fish, hunt, capture**

漁獲 *gyokaku* fishing; haul [catch] (of fish)
捕獲する *hokaku suru* catch (fish); capture (a ship), seize
乱獲 *rankaku* reckless fishing, excessive hunting
収獲 *shūkaku* game; (good) result
鹵獲する *rokaku suru* capture, seize, plunder

❷ **obtain, get, acquire**

獲得する *kakutoku suru* get, acquire, obtain

KUN

【e(ru) 獲る】

① catch game, hunt, fish
獲物 *emono* game, spoils, catch, capture; good luck, prize

② [usu. 得る] acquire, get, gain, obtain, win
地位を獲る *chii o eru* acquire a position

SYNONYMS

❶ **hunt and fish**

狩 HUNT → 397
猟 HUNTING → 538
漁 FISH → 698
釣 ANGLE → 1674

❷ **get**

収 TAKE IN → 198
得 ACQUIRE → 477
拾 PICK UP → 379
取 TAKE → 1262

HOMOPHONES

eru ⇨ 得 477

NOTE

⇨ see USAGE note at 得 477
★do not confuse with 穫 1251

獨

780

▶**ALONE** ▶**GERMANY**

nonstandard for 独 395

3-13 犭

隣 隣 鄰° 隣 隣

781 RIN tona(ru) tonari

CH 邻 lín

Radical	Strokes
阝 170	16-3-13
Grade	Freq
Jōyō	1015
1-3-13	

3-13 阝

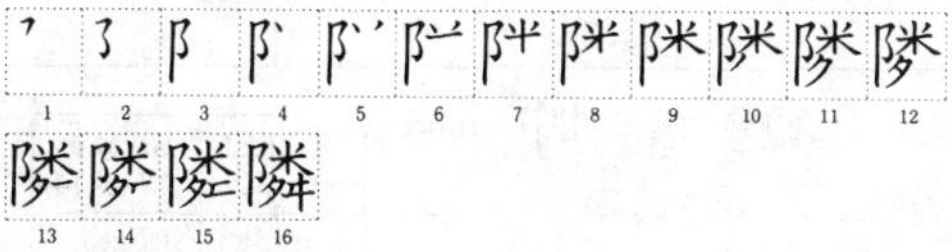

▶**NEIGHBOR**

COMPOUNDS

❶ⓐ (live or be situated close by) **neighbor, adjoin**
ⓑ **neighboring, adjoining, adjacent**
ⓒ (houses or villages located near another) neighbor

隣接した *rinsetsu shita* neighboring, adjoining, adjacent
隣国 *rinkoku* neighboring country
隣家 *rinka* neighboring house
隣村 *rinson* neighboring village
隣人 *rinjin* neighbor
近隣 *kinrin* neighborhood
善隣政策 *zenrin seisaku* Good Neighbor Policy

❷ [archaic] unit of administration in Zhou Dynasty China consisting of five households

KUN

【tona(ru) 隣る】 neighbor, adjoin
隣り合う *tonariau* adjoin, be next door to each other
隣り合わせの *tonariawase no* adjoining

【tonari 隣】 neighboring house, next door;

next-door neighbor; next seat
隣の *tonari no* neighboring, adjacent
隣近所 *tonarikinjo* neighborhood
隣に住む *tonari ni sumu* live next door

SYNONYMS
❶ⓑ **near**
近 NEAR → 3061
傍 BESIDE → 147
沿 ALONG → 328

3-13 阝

險 782

▶DANGER ▶STEEP
nonstandard for 険 542

3-13 阝

隨 783

▶FOLLOW
nonstandard for 随 627

3-14 口

嚇 784

KAKU odo(kasu)▲

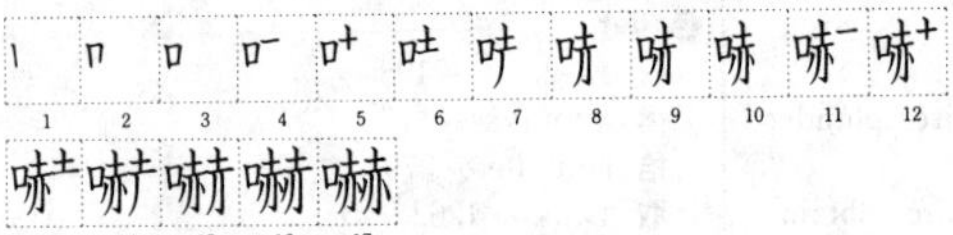

CH 吓 xià hè

Radical	Strokes
口 30	17-3-14
Grade	**Freq**
Jōyō	1931
1-3-14	

▶INTIMIDATE

COMPOUNDS
❶ **intimidate, frighten, threaten, scare**
威嚇する *ikaku suru* intimidate, threaten, menace
恐嚇(=脅嚇) *kyōkaku* [rare] intimidation, threat
❷ [also 赫 1557] [original meaning] explode with anger, be enraged
嚇怒する *kakudo suru* be greatly enraged, get furious

KUN
【odo(kasu) 嚇かす】
[now usu. 脅かす]
ⓐ threaten, menace, intimidate
ⓑ startle
嚇かして金を取る *odokashite kane o toru* scare money out of (a person)

SYNONYMS
❶ **threaten**
喝 shout threats at → 461
脅 THREATEN → 2109
威 THREATEN BY FORCE → 3578

HOMOPHONES
odokasu ⇨ 脅 2109 威 3578

NOTE
⇨ see USAGE note at 脅 2109

3-14 口

嚀 785

NEI

CH 宁 咛 níng

Radical	Strokes
口 30	17-3-14
Grade	**Freq**
Reference	
1-3-14	

COMPOUNDS
● [now replaced by 寧 2345] courteous, polite
叮嚀(=丁寧)な *teinei na* polite, courteous

3-14 弓

彌 786

▶PHONETIC [mi]
nonstandard for 弥 288

徽 787 KI

CH 徽 huī

Radical	Strokes
彳 60	17-3-14
Grade	**Freq**
Reference	
1 - 3 - 14	

3-14 彳

COMPOUNDS

● [now replaced by 記 1453] emblem, badge

徽章 *kishō* emblem, insignia

擬 擬 擬 788 GI

CH 拟 nǐ

Radical	Strokes
扌 64	17-3-14
Grade	**Freq**
Jōyō	1735
1 - 3 - 14	

3-14 扌

一 1 亅 2 扌 3 扌 4 扌 5 扌 6 扌 7 扌 8 扌 9 扌 10 扌 11 扌 12 扌 13 扌 14 扌 15 扌 16 擬 17

▶**IMITATE**

COMPOUNDS

❶ⓐ [original meaning] **imitate, copy, mimic, model after**

ⓑ [also prefix] imitation, dummy, pseudo

擬装 *gisō* camouflage, disguise

擬似 *giji* false, dummy, pseudo

擬声語 *giseigo* onomatopoeic word

擬人 *gijin* personification, impersonation

擬製 *gisei* imitation, forgery

模擬の *mogi no* imitation, sham, mock, simulated

擬毛 *gimō* imitation wool

擬古典的な *gikotenteki na* pseudoclassic

擬爆弾 *gibakudan* dummy bomb

❷ feign, pretend

擬勢 *gisei* sham display of forces

INDEPENDENT

【**gisuru** 擬する】 point (a gun) at, aim; nominate for office; imitate, mimic; liken, compare

後継内閣の首班に擬せられている *kōkei-naikaku no shuhan ni giserarete iru* be considered as head of the incoming Cabinet

SYNONYMS

❶ⓐ **imitate**

倣 COPY AFTER → 113

模 pattern after → 1050

象 represent → 2134

肖 MODEL → 2205

ⓑ **false**

偽 sham → 131

虚 FALSE → 3237

仮 fake → 50

義 artificial → 2338

COMPOUND FORMATION

擬声語 *giseigo*

擬声語 'onomatopoeic word' is a word (語) that imitates (擬 ❶ⓐ) a sound (声).

擱 789 KAKU o(ku)

CH 搁 gē gé

Radical	Strokes
扌 64	17-3-14
Grade	**Freq**
Reference	
1 - 3 - 14	

3-14 扌

COMPOUNDS

❶ lay down (one's pen)

筆を擱く *fude o oku* lay down one's pen, stop writing

❷ run aground

擱座する *kakuza suru* run aground; be stalled

HOMOPHONES

oku ⇨ 置 2608 措 502

NOTE

⇨ see USAGE note at 置 2608

3-14
扌

擦 擦 擦

CH 擦 cā

790 SATSU su(ru) su(reru) -zu(re) kosu(ru)▲ kosu(reru)▲

Radical	Strokes
扌 64	17-3-14
Grade	**Freq**
Jōyō	1857
▮ 1-3-14	

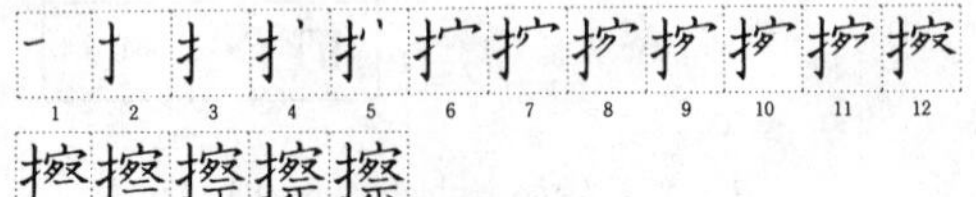

▶**RUB**

COMPOUNDS

● [original meaning] **rub**

擦過傷 *sakkashō* abrasion, scratch
摩擦する *masatsu suru* rub, chafe
摩擦 *masatsu* friction; rubbing, chafing
塗擦剤 *tosatsuzai* liniment

KUN

【su(ru) 擦る】
vt
①ⓐ rub, chafe
ⓑ strike
擦り傷 *surikizu* scratch, abrasion
頰擦り *hōzuri* nestling one's cheek to another's
マッチを擦る *matchi o suru* strike a match
② lose, forfeit
身代を擦る *shindai o suru* lose a person's fortune

【su(reru) 擦れる】 *vi* rub, chafe, brush; wear, be worn; become sophisticated
擦れ合う *sureau* rub against each other, jostle with
衣擦れ *kinuzure* rustling (of clothes)
擦れ違う *surechigau* pass by each other, brush past
擦れて薄くなる *surete usuku naru* wear thin
擦れっ枯らし *surekkarashi* worldly-wise impudence, person dead to all sense of shame

【-zu(re) -擦れ】
[also suffix]
① sore
靴擦れ *kutsuzure* shoe sore
床擦れ *tokozure* bedsores
② sophistication
人擦れ *hitozure* sophistication
悪擦れ *waruzure* over-sophistication

【kosu(ru) 擦る】 *vt* rub, scour, scrub, scrape
擦り付ける *kosuritsukeru* rub on, smear; nuzzle against
擦り落とす *kosuriotosu* rub off, scrape off

【kosu(reru) 擦れる】 *vi* be rubbed
木の葉の擦れる音 *konoha no kosureru oto* rustling of leaves

SYNONYMS

● **polish and rub**
摩 RUB AGAINST → 3175
磨 POLISH → 3181
研 GRIND → 1132
削 CUT BY CHIPPING → 1448

【-zure】
① **injury**
傷 WOUND → 158
創 wound (cut) → 1815

USAGE

suru
擦る
vt
①ⓐ rub, chafe
ⓑ strike
② lose, forfeit
磨る
polish, file, rub down
摺る
ⓐ rub against
ⓑ print by rubbing
刷る
print, put in print

HOMOPHONES

suru ⇨ 磨 3181 摺 693 刷 1273

擡

791 TAI mota(geru)

CH 抬 tái

Radical	Strokes
扌 64	17-3-14
Grade Reference	Freq
1-3-14	

3-14 扌

COMPOUNDS

● [now also 台 *tai* 2005] [original meaning] raise (one's head), lift

擡頭する *taitō suru* raise one's head; come to the fore

擡げる *motageru* lift, raise (one's head)

擴

incorrect stroke count ⇨ see 800
(nonstandard for 拡 309)

3-14 扌

濠

792 GŌ hori

CH 濠 háo

Radical	Strokes
氵 85	17-3-14
Grade Reference	Freq
1-3-14	

3-14 氵

COMPOUNDS

❶ [now usu. 堀 *hori*] [original meaning] moat

濠 *gō* moat

内濠 *uchibori* inner moat

❷ [now replaced by 豪 *gō* 2140] Australia

濠洲(=豪州) *gōshū* Australia

HOMOPHONES

hori ⇨ 堀 467

NOTE

⇨ see USAGE note at 堀 467

濯 濯 濯 濯

793 TAKU

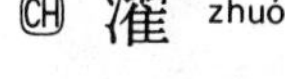

CH 濯 zhuó

Radical	Strokes
氵 85	17-3-14
Grade	Freq
Jōyō	1818
1-3-14	

3-14 氵

1 2 3 4 5 6 7 8 9 10 11 12 13 14 15 16 17

▶RINSE

COMPOUNDS

● [original meaning] **rinse, wash, wash out**

洗濯する *sentaku suru* launder, wash

洗濯機 *sentakuki* washing machine

SYNONYMS

● **clean and wash**

洗 WASH → 388

浴 BATHE → 445

浄 cleanse → 382

粛 PURGE → 3581

清 CLEAR → 523

払 CLEAR AWAY → 194

掃 SWEEP → 503

濱

794

▶BEACH

nonstandard for 浜 436

3-14 氵

3-14 氵

濟 795

▶SETTLE ▶RELIEVE
nonstandard for 済 522

3-14 氵

濕 796

▶DAMP
nonstandard for 湿 609

3-14 氵

濯 797

▶RINSE
nonstandard for 濯 793

3-14 氵

濫

incorrect stroke count ⇨ see 801

3-14 犭

獲 798

▶CATCH GAME
nonstandard for 獲 779

3-14 阝

隱 799

▶HIDE
nonstandard for 隠 713

3-15 扌

擴 800

▶ENLARGE
nonstandard for 拡 309

3-15 氵

濫 801 RAN

CH 滥 làn

Radical	Strokes
氵 85	18-3-15
Grade	**Freq**
Jōyō	1910
1-3-15	

▶**EXCESSIVE**

COMPOUNDS

❶ [also 乱 1260] **excessive, indiscriminate, extravagant, inordinate, haphazard, reckless**

濫造 *ranzō* excessive production, careless manufacture
濫伐 *ranbatsu* indiscriminate deforestation, overcutting of forests
濫費 *ranpi* extravagance, money wasting
濫用する *ran'yō suru* abuse, use to excess
紙幣の濫発 *shihei no ranpatsu* excessive [reckless] issue of bank notes

❷ [original meaning] **overflow, flow over, inundate**

氾濫する *hanran suru* overflow, flood

❸ set afloat

濫觴 *ranshō* genesis, origin

SYNONYMS

❶ **rash**

乱 excessive → 1260
荒 WILD → 2260
暴 unrestrained → 2515
妄 RASH → 2016
盲 BLIND → 2053
滅 unreasonable → 660

❶ **exceeding and excess**

余 EXCESS → 2042
剰 SURPLUS → 1779
冗 REDUNDANT → 1976
過 EXCEED → 3137
超 SURPASS → 3313

越 GO BEYOND → 3314
❷ **flow and drip**
流 FLOW → 441
注 POUR → 325
漏 LEAK → 701
滴 DROP → 705
泌 SECRETE → 332

獵 3-15 犭
802
▶**HUNTING**
nonstandard for 猟 538

壞 3-16 土
803
▶**BREAK DOWN**
nonstandard for 壊 756

懷 3-16 忄
804
▶**BOSOM** ▶**LONG FOR**
nonstandard for 懐 763

瀕 3-16 氵
805 HIN

Ⓒⓗ 濒 bīn

Radical	Strokes
氵 85	19-3-16
Grade	**Freq**
Reference	
◧ 1-3-16	

COMPOUNDS
● [rarely also 頻 1758] on the verge of
瀕死 *hinshi* on the verge of death
瀕する *hinsuru* be on the verge of

瀬 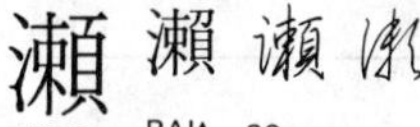 3-16 氵
806 RAI▲ se

 lài

Radical	Strokes
氵 85	19-3-16
Grade	**Freq**
Jōyō	951
◧ 1-3-16	

(stroke order 1–19)

▶**SHALLOWS**
COMPOUNDS
● [original meaning] **rapids**
KUN
【se 瀬】
①ⓐ shallows, shoal
ⓑ rapids, torrent, swift current
瀬戸 *seto* strait, channel
浅瀬 *asase* shoal, shallows
早瀬 *hayase* rapids, swift current
瀬を下る *se o kudaru* descend the rapids
②ⓐ standpoint, one's ground
ⓑ occasion, opportunity
立つ瀬 *tatsuse* one's ground, one's position
逢瀬 *ōse* meeting, date
年の瀬 *toshi no se* closing days of the year

SYNONYMS
【se】
①ⓐ **shoals**
州 sandbar → 57
礁 REEF → 1243
ⓑ **running water**
潮 TIDE → 739
汐 TIDE → 223
流 CURRENT → 441
滝 WATERFALL → 661
洪 FLOOD → 386
渦 WHIRLPOOL → 603

3-16 瀝 807 REKI
氵

CH 沥 lì

Radical	Strokes
氵 85	19-3-16
Grade Reference	Freq
1-3-16	

COMPOUNDS

[now also 歴 3019]
ⓐ [original meaning] drip, trickle
ⓑ pour

瀝青炭 *rekiseitan* bituminous coal
披瀝する *hireki suru* express (one's opinion), reveal (one's thoughts)

3-16 瀨 808
氵
▶**SHALLOWS**
nonstandard for 瀬 806

3-16 瀧 809
氵
▶**WATERFALL**
nonstandard for 滝 661

3-17 壤 810
土
▶**ARABLE SOIL**
nonstandard for 壌 755

3-17 孃 811
女
▶**YOUNG LADY**
nonstandard for 嬢 758

3-18 攜 812
扌
▶**CARRY IN HAND**
nonstandard for 携 648

3-18 攝 813
扌
▶**TAKE IN** ▶**ACT AS REGENT**
nonstandard for 摂 650

3-20 黴 814 BAI kabi ka(biru)
彳

CH 霉 méi

Radical	Strokes
黑 203	23-12-11
Grade Reference	Freq
1-3-20	

COMPOUNDS

● [now also 梅 *bai* 925] mold, mildew, fungus
黴毒 *baidoku* syphilis

黴菌 *baikin* bacterium, germ
黴雨 *baiu* rainy season (of early summer)
黴びる *kabiru* become musty, mildew

3-21 囑 815
口
▶**CHARGE WITH**
nonstandard for 嘱 718

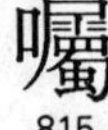

3-22 氵

灣 816

▶**BAY**

nonstandard for 湾 613

4-1 木

札 817 札 札

SATSU fuda

Ⓒⓗ 札 zhá

Radical	Strokes
木 75	5-4-1
Grade	**Freq**
Jōyō-4	803
1-4-1	

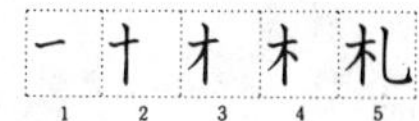

▶**TAG**

COMPOUNDS

❶ⓐ **tag, plate, placard**

ⓑ **ticket**

ⓒ [original meaning] thin wooden tablet used for writing in ancient China

標札(=表札) *hyōsatsu* nameplate, doorplate

門札 *monsatsu* doorplate, nameplate

鑑札 *kansatsu* license, certificate

検札 *kensatsu* examination of tickets

改札口 *kaisatsuguchi* ticket barrier [gate], wicket

❷ [also suffix] **bill, paper money, bank note**

札入れ *satsuire* billfold, wallet

札束 *satsutaba* bundle of (bank) notes, wad of bills

贋札 *gansatsu* (=*nisesatsu*) counterfeit paper money, forged note

千円札 *sen'ensatsu* 1000-yen bill

❸ tender, bid

入札する *nyūsatsu suru* tender, bid

落札 *rakusatsu* successful bid

❹ document, certificate; letter

一札 *issatsu* document, paper; bond

INDEPENDENT

【satsu 札】 bill, paper money, bank note

札を崩す *satsu o kuzusu* change a note

KUN

【fuda 札】

① [also suffix] tag, tab, label, card, placard; billboard

札を付ける *fuda o tsukeru* put a tag on, label

値札 *nefuda* price tag [mark, label]

手札 *tefuda* visiting card, card

守り札 *mamorifuda* paper charm

名札 *nafuda* nameplate

立て札 *tatefuda* bulletin board

質札 *shichifuda* pawn ticket

② playing card

切り札 *kirifuda* trump (card), last resort

③ tender, bill

入れ札 *irefuda* tender, bid

SYNONYMS

❶ **labels and slips**

券 TICKET → 2630

票 SLIP → 2669

符 tally → 2661

節 token → 2691

❷ **money**

幣 CURRENCY → 2885

貨 MONEY (legal tender), coin → 2465

銭 MONEY → 1725

金 MONEY → 2057

-玉 coin suffix → 3477

銀 SILVER → 1722

財 finance → 1457

資 RESOURCES → 2695

4-1 礻

礼 818 禮 礼 礼

REI RAI

Ⓒⓗ 礼 lǐ

Radical	Strokes
礻 113	5-4-1
Grade	**Freq**
Jōyō-3	1079
1-4-1	

▶**ETIQUETTE** ▶**RITE**

COMPOUNDS

❶ⓐ **etiquette, courtesy, propriety, manners, ceremony**

ⓑ [also suffix] **courtesy bow, salutation**

礼儀 *reigi* etiquette, courtesy, propriety, manners

礼節 *reisetsu* courtesy, etiquette

礼式 *reishiki* etiquette, manner

失礼 *shitsurei* impoliteness, rudeness; bad manners; I beg your pardon / Good-by

礼砲 *reihō* salute gun

一礼 *ichirei* bow, greeting; courtesy
敬礼 *keirei* salutation, salute, bow
栄誉礼 *eiyorei* salute of guards of honor
❷ [also suffix] [original meaning] **rite, ceremony, ritual, religious service**
礼典 *reiten* ceremony, ritual, rite
礼服 *reifuku* ceremonial dress
婚礼 *konrei* wedding ceremony
洗礼 *senrei* baptism
朝礼 *chōrei* morning gathering
立太子礼 *rittaishirei* ceremonial of instituting the Crown Prince
❸ show respect to, treat politely
礼拝 *reihai* (=*raihai*) worship; church service
礼遇 *reigū* honorable treatment
礼讃(=礼賛)する *raisan suru* worship, adore, glorify
❹ⓐ **thanks, gratitude, appreciation**
ⓑ **monetary gift, remuneration, reward**
礼状 *reijō* letter of thanks
礼金 *reikin* reward, fee, honorarium
謝礼 *sharei* remuneration, reward; thanks
返礼 *henrei* return present; return call

INDEPENDENT

【rei 礼】
① bow, salutation
礼をする *rei o suru* salute, make a bow; reward, remunerate
② etiquette, courtesy, propriety
礼を失する *rei o shissuru* be impolite [disrespectful]
③ⓐ thanks, appreciation
ⓑ reward, return present
お礼 *orei* thanks, appreciation; reward; gift, return present

SYNONYMS

❶ⓐ **etiquette**
儀 CEREMONY → 169
ⓑ **bow**
拝 bow in veneration → 303
❷ **ceremonies and festivities**
式 CEREMONY → 3049
儀 CEREMONY → 169
典 formal ceremony → 2627
斎 religious ritual → 2115
会 Buddhist ceremony → 2020
祭 FESTIVAL → 2672
❹ⓐ **thanking and gratitude**
謝 THANK → 1620
恩 DEBT OF GRATITUDE → 2655
ⓑ **monetary gifts**
謝 monetary gift of thanks → 1620

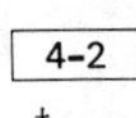
4-2
木

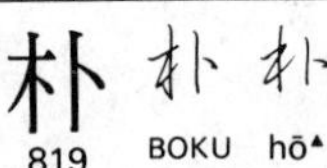
819 BOKU hō▲

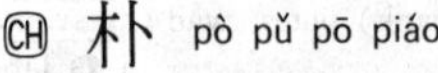
Ⓒ朴 pò pǔ pō piáo

Radical	Strokes
木 75	6-4-2
Grade	**Freq**
Jōyō	1558
1-4-2	

▶ **SIMPLE**

COMPOUNDS

❶ **simple, unadorned, plain**
朴訥 *bokutotsu* rugged honesty
朴直な *bokuchoku na* simple and honest, artless, naive
素朴な *soboku na* simple, naive, artless
質朴な *shitsuboku na* simple, plain, unsophisticated
敦朴(=敦樸)な *tonboku na* [archaic] honest and simple
❷ unsociable
朴念仁 *bokunenjin* quiet unsociable person

KUN

【hō 朴】*Magnolia hypoleuca* (tree used for the supports of clogs)
朴の木 *hō no ki Magnolia hypoleuca*

SYNONYMS

❶ **plain and simple**
単 simple (uncomplicated) → 2256
素 PLAIN → 2458

机 机 机 820 KI tsukue

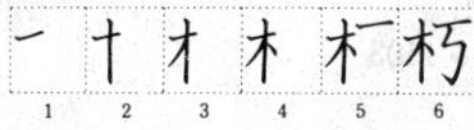

ⒸⒽ 几 jī

Radical	Strokes
木 75	6-4-2
Grade	Freq
Jōyō-6	1566
◧ 1 - 4 - 2	

4-2 木

▶**DESK**

COMPOUNDS

● **desk, table**

机上 *kijō* top of desk; academic, theoretical
机辺 *kihen* around the desk [table]
机下(＝几下) *kika* under the desk

KUN

【**tsukue** 机】[also suffix] desk, table

机でする仕事 *tsukue de suru shigoto* desk work [job]
勉強机 *benkyōzukue* (writing) desk
事務机 *jimuzukue* office desk

SYNONYMS

● **tables and stands**

卓 TABLE → 2064
台 STAND → 2005

朽 朽 朽 821 KYŪ ku(chiru)

一 十 才 木 朽 朽

ⒸⒽ 朽 xiǔ

Radical	Strokes
木 75	6-4-2
Grade	Freq
Jōyō	1781
◧ 1 - 4 - 2	

4-2 木

▶**DECAY**

COMPOUNDS

● [original meaning] **decay, rot**

朽廃する *kyūhai suru* decay, be dilapidated [ruined]
腐朽 *fukyū* deterioration, decay
老朽 *rōkyū* superannuation, decrepitude
不朽の *fukyū no* immortal, undecaying, eternal

KUN

【**ku(chiru)** 朽ちる】decay, rot; remain in obscurity

朽ち葉 *kuchiba* decayed leaves
朽ち果てる *kuchihateru* decay completely, rot away; rust away; rusticate oneself

SYNONYMS

● **decay**

枯 WITHER → 898
腐 ROT → 3162

权 822 ▶**RIGHT** ▶**POWER**
nonstandard for 権 1065

4-2 木

此 823 SHI ko(re) ko(no)

ⒸⒽ 此 cǐ

Radical	Strokes
止 77	6-4-2
Grade	Freq
Reference	
◧ 1 - 4 - 2	

4-2 止

COMPOUNDS

ⓐ *pronoun* this

ⓑ *demonstrative* this

此処 *koko* here, this place
此奴 *koitsu* this fellow, this guy
此岸 *shigan* this world [life]
此の世界 *kono sekai* this world

HOMOPHONES

kore ⇨ 之 3420 是 2436 惟 481

NOTE

⇨ see USAGE note at 是 2436

4-2 歹

列 列 歹

824 RETSU RE▲

CH 列 liè

Radical	Strokes
刂 18	6-2-4
Grade	**Freq**
Jōyō-3	837
1 - 4 - 2	

▶**ROW**

COMPOUNDS

❶ⓐ [also suffix] **row, line, file, rank; series**
ⓑ counter for rows
行列 *gyōretsu* procession, queue; matrix
系列 *keiretsu* order, succession; series
戦列 *senretsu* line of battle
序列 *joretsu* rank, grade, order
等差数列 *tōsasūretsu* arithmetical progression [series]
パラフィン列 *parafinretsu* paraffin series
三列 *sanretsu* three rows [lines]

❷ **arrange in a row, line up**
列車 *ressha* (railway) train
列島 *rettō* archipelago
列挙 *rekkyo* enumeration, listing
整列する *seiretsu suru* stand in a row, line up
陳列する *chinretsu suru* exhibit, display

❸ attend, participate
列席 *resseki* attendance, presence
参列する *sanretsu suru* attend, be present, participate

❹ many, numerous
列国 *rekkoku* the powers, all nations
列強 *rekkyō* the great powers

❺ used phonetically for *re* or similar sounds in the transliteration of foreign words
列寧 *rēnin* Lenin

INDEPENDENT

【retsu 列】 row, line, file, rank; column (of a matrix)
列を作る *retsu o tsukuru* form a line [row]

SYNONYMS

❶ⓐ **linear arrangements**
行 LINE (esp. of print) → 212
伍 RANK → 47
欄 COLUMN → 1103

❷ **arrange**
陳 lay out (for exhibit) → 540
羅 spread out → 2622
並 LINE UP → 2246
比 rank → 26
揃える arrange properly → 590
整 PUT IN ORDER → 2871
理 put in order → 970

4-2 火

灯 燈 灯 灯

825 TŌ hi ho-▲ tomoshibi▲ tomo(su)▲

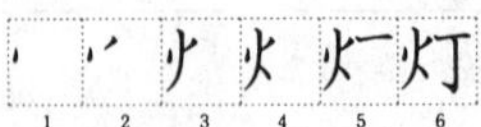

CH 灯 dēng

Radical	Strokes
火 86	6-4-2
Grade	**Freq**
Jōyō-4	1261
1 - 4 - 2	

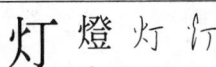

▶**LAMP**

COMPOUNDS

ⓐ [also suffix] [original meaning] **lamp, light, lantern**
ⓑ counter for lamps or lights
灯台 *tōdai* lighthouse; oil-lamp stand
灯火 *tōka* light, lamplight
灯油 *tōyu* kerosene, lamp oil
電灯 *dentō* lamp, electric light
街灯 *gaitō* street lamp
尾灯 *bitō* taillight
蛍光灯 *keikōtō* fluorescent lamp [light]
五十灯 *gojittō* 50 lamps

INDEPENDENT

【tō 灯】 lamp, light, lantern

KUN

【hi 灯】 (source of illumination) light, lantern, lamp
灯を付ける *hi o tsukeru* turn on the light

【ho- 灯-】 [also 火-] fire
灯影 *hokage* (=*tōei*) firelight in the dark; shadows by the firelight

【tomoshibi 灯】 [also 灯し火] light, lamp, flame
風前の灯 *fūzen no tomoshibi* candle flickering before the wind; extremely precarious position

【tomo(su) 灯す】 [usu. 点す] light (a lamp), set alight, turn on (a light)
松明を灯す *taimatsu o tomosu* kindle a torch

SPECIAL READINGS

提灯▲ *chōchin* paper lantern

行灯▲ *andon* paper-enclosed oil lantern

SYNONYMS

ⓐ **light**

光 LIGHT → 2391

明 light → 855

照 sunlight → 2827

虹 RAINBOW → 1285

HOMOPHONES

hi ⇨ 火 3463

ho- ⇨ 火 3463

tomosu ⇨ 点 2084

NOTE

⇨ see USAGE notes at 火 3463 and 点 2084

邪

incorrect stroke count ⇨ see 838
(nonstandard for 邪 1124)

4-2 牙

牝

826 HIN mesu me- men

Ⓒⓗ 牝 pìn

Radical	Strokes
牛 93	6-4-2
Grade	Freq
Reference	
◧ 1 - 4 - 2	

4-2 牛

COMPOUNDS

● [usu. 雌 *mesu, me-, men*] [original meaning] (of animals) female

牝馬 *hinba* [rare] mare

牝犬 *mesuinu* female dog, bitch

牝牛 *meushi* cow

牝鳥(=牝鶏) *mendori* hen

HOMOPHONES

mesu ⇨ 雌 1055

me- ⇨ 雌 1055 女 3418

men ⇨ 雌 1055

NOTE

⇨ see USAGE note at 雌 1055

肌 肌 𠘨

827 KI▲ hada

Ⓒⓗ 肌 jī

Radical	Strokes
月 130	6-4-2
Grade	Freq
Jōyō	1794
◧ 1 - 4 - 2	

4-2 月

▶**SKIN**

COMPOUNDS

● [original meaning] **skin (of the human body)**

肌膚 *kifu* skin

肌骨 *kikotsu* skin and bones

KUN

【hada 肌】

[formerly also 膚]

①ⓐ skin, body

ⓑ surface; grain (of wood)

肌身 *hadami* body

肌着 *hadagi* underwear

肌を許す *hada o yurusu* surrender one's chastity to a man

赤肌 *akahada* abraded skin

山肌 *yamahada* surface of a mountain

美しい肌の材 *utsukushii hada no zai* wood of fine grain

②ⓐ disposition, temperament

ⓑ [suffix] turn of mind

肌が合わない *hada ga awanai* cannot go together (with)

学者肌 *gakushahada* scholarly bent of mind

SYNONYMS

● **kinds of skin**

膚 SKIN (of the human body) → 3265

皮 SKIN (of any kind) → 3037

革 LEATHER → 2448

USAGE

hada

肌

[formerly also 膚]

①ⓐ skin, body

ⓑ surface; grain (of wood)

②ⓐ disposition, temperament

ⓑ [suffix] turn of mind

膚

[now replaced by 肌] same as 肌

HOMOPHONES
hada ⇨ 膚 3265

4-2 那 incorrect stroke count ⇨ see 843

4-2

印 印 印 印

828 IN shirushi -jirushi shiru(su)▲

CH 印 yìn

Radical	Strokes
卩 26	6-2-4
Grade	Freq
Jōyō-4	724
1-4-2	

1 2 3 4 5 6

▶MARK ▶SEAL

COMPOUNDS

❶ (visible sign) **mark, imprint, sign**
烙印 *rakuin* brand
❷ⓐ [original meaning] imprint, impress, make a mark
ⓑ imprint on the mind, make an impression
印字 *inji* printing, typing
印刻 *inkoku* engraving
印象 *inshō* impression
❸ **print**
印刷 *insatsu* printing
印行する *inkō suru* print and publish
影印 *eiin* phototype process, photoengraving
❹ [also suffix] **seal, stamp; seal impression**
印鑑 *inkan* personal seal
印税 *inzei* royalty (on a book)
印紙 *inshi* (revenue) stamp
調印 *chōin* signing, sealing; signature
消印 *keshiin* postmark, (postal) cancellation mark
封印 *fūin* (stamped) seal
押印する *ōin suru* seal, affix a seal
刻印 *kokuin* carved seal, stamp
ゴム印 *gomuin* rubber stamp
偽造印 *gizōin* forged seal
❺ India
印綿(=印棉) *inmen* Indian raw cotton
日印関係 *nichiin kankei* Japan-India relations

INDEPENDENT

【in 印】 seal, stamp; *Buddhism* hand signs; India
印を押す *in o osu* affix one's seal
印を結ぶ *in o musubu* make symbolic signs [gestures] with the fingers
【insuru 印する】 print, impress

KUN

【shirushi 印】
① mark, sign; symbol
目印 *mejirushi* mark, sign, landmark
矢印 *yajirushi* arrow (mark)
② token (of appreciation)
感謝の印 *kansha no shirushi* token of appreciation
③ proof
...の印として *...no shirushi to shite* as proof of...
【-jirushi -印】 trademark, brand
雪印 *yukijirushi* Snow Brand
【shiru(su) 印す】 mark, inscribe

SYNONYMS

❶ **marks and signs**
標 MARK (identifying sign) → 1064
跡 TRACE → 1534
紋 print → 1299
符 SYMBOL → 2661
号 SIGN → 2153
❷ **mark**
押 seal → 314
画 mark off → 3000
❸ **print and publish**
刷 PRINT → 1273
植 typeset → 990
刊 PUBLISH → 190
版 PUBLISHING → 872
載 PUT IN PRINT → 3300
掲 display in writing → 494
❹ **seals**
判 personal seal → 1122
璽 IMPERIAL SEAL → 2911
❺ **Asian countries**
比 Philippines → 26
越 Vietnam → 3314
泰 Thailand → 2583
鮮 Korea → 1877
華 CHINA → 2283
日 JAPAN → 3027

USAGE

shirushi
印
① mark, sign; symbol
② token (of appreciation)
③ proof
徴

① effectiveness (of medicine)
② symptom, sign, indication

HOMOPHONES

shirushi ⇨ 徴 683

shirusu ⇨ 記 1453

NOTE

⇨ see also USAGE note at 記 1453

印 829

▶MARK ▶SEAL

nonstandard for 印 828

4-2 E

刑 刑 ＊ 830 KEI

(CH) 刑 xíng

Radical	Strokes
刂 18	6-2-4
Grade	**Freq**
Jōyō	764
◧ 1-4-2	

一 二 于 开 刑 刑 (1 2 3 4 5 6)

4-2 开

▶PENALTY

COMPOUNDS

ⓐ [also suffix] **penalty, punishment, sentence**
ⓑ [original meaning] punish, torture
刑罰 *keibatsu* penalty, punishment
刑期 *keiki* prison term
刑事 *keiji* (police) detective
刑務所 *keimusho* prison
刑法 *keihō* criminal law, penal code
処刑 *shokei* execution, punishment
求刑する *kyūkei suru* demand a sentence (for the accused)
死刑 *shikei* capital punishment, death penalty
絞首刑 *kōshukei* death [execution] by hanging

INDEPENDENT

【kei 刑】 penalty, punishment, sentence
刑に服する *kei ni fukusuru* serve a sentence, endure a penalty
【keisuru 刑する】 sentence

SYNONYMS

ⓐ **punishment**
罰 PUNISHMENT → 2613
懲 CHASTISE → 2910
処 DEAL WITH (lawbreakers) → 3031

邦

incorrect stroke count ⇨ see 847

4-2 丰

対 對 対 ＊ 831 TAI TSUI

(CH) 对 duì

Radical	Strokes
寸 41	7-3-4
Grade	**Freq**
Jōyō-3	49
◧ 1-4-3	

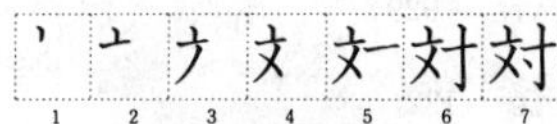

4-3 文

▶OPPOSITE ▶OPPOSE

COMPOUNDS

❶ⓐ **opposite, facing each other, opposed, opposing**
ⓑ [original meaning] **face (each other), confront**
対談 *taidan* talk, tête-à-tête, interview; personal negotiation
対話 *taiwa* dialogue, conversation
対岸 *taigan* opposite bank [shore]
対座する *taiza suru* sit opposite each other
対辺 *taihen* opposite side
対局 *taikyoku* game of go [shogi]
対面する *taimen suru* meet, face
相対 *sōtai* relativity

❷ⓐ **oppose, confront (each other), counter**
ⓑ [also prefix] **counter-, opposite, contra-, anti-**
ⓒ abbrev. of 対策 *taisaku*: countermeasure
対立 *tairitsu* opposition, antagonism
対抗 *taikō* opposition, antagonism, rivalry; counteraction
対決 *taiketsu* confrontation, showdown
対戦 *taisen* waging war; competition
反対する *hantai suru* oppose, object (to)
敵対 *tekitai* hostility, antagonism

対策 *taisaku* countermeasure, counterplan
対案 *taian* counterproposal
対語 *tsuigo* (=*taigo*) antonym
対潜水艦の *taisensuikan no* antisubmarine
失対 *shittai* measure against unemployment
選対本部 *sentai honbu* election headquarters

❸ (place in opposition and compare) **oppose, contrast**
対象 *taishō* object (of study), subject, target
対照 *taishō* contrast, comparison; control
対比する *taihi suru* contrast, compare
対等 *taitō* equality, parity
対称的な *taishōteki na* symmetrical
絶対の *zettai no* absolute
相対性理論 *sōtaisei riron* theory of relativity

❹ [also prefix] **toward, to, in relation to, versus**
対米 *taibei* with [toward] America
対日感情 *tainichi kanjō* feeling [sentiment] toward Japan
対外の *taigai no* foreign; outside
対中国関係 *taichūgoku kankei* relations with China

❺ⓐ **cope with, treat, receive**
ⓑ answer, reply
対処する *taisho suru* cope [deal] with, meet
対応する *taiō suru* correspond to, answer to; be equivalent; deal [cope] with
応対 *ōtai* reception (of visitors); address

❻ⓐ (two things of the same kind) **pair, couple, set**
ⓑ counter for pairs
対偶 *taigū* pair; antithesis
対句 *tsuiku* couplet, antithesis
一対 *ittsui* a pair

❼ⓐ equal, even
ⓑ used phonetically for the transliteration of the English word *tie*
対価 *taika* compensation, equivalent value
対スコア *taisukoa* tie score

INDEPENDENT

【tai 対】
① the opposite, one of a pair
白の対は黒 *Shiro no tai wa kuro* The opposite of white is black
②ⓐ versus, against, to (in competitions or transactions)
ⓑ *math* to (in ratios)
原告対被告 *genkoku tai hikoku* plaintiff versus defendant
二対一 *ni tai ichi* two to one
③ⓐ *colloq* equal terms
ⓑ tie (⇨ ❼ⓑ)
対で勝負する *tai de shōbu suru* play a game on equal terms
④ annex building in old Japanese palace-style house

【taisuru 対する】
① face (each other), confront
丘に対する部屋 *oka ni taisuru heya* room facing a hill
② toward, to, in relation to
彼は人に対して親切だ *Kare wa hito ni taishite shinsetsu da* He is kind to others
③ⓐ oppose, confront (each other), counter
ⓑ as opposed to, in opposition to, against
全力で敵に対する *zenryoku de teki ni taisuru* fight against the enemy with all one's might
口語体に対する文語体 *kōgotai ni taisuru bungotai* literary style as opposed to colloquial style
④ treat, receive, address
寛容を以て人に対する *kan'yō o motte hito ni taisuru* treat others with magnanimity

【tsui 対】 (two things of the same kind) pair, couple, set
対になる *tsui ni naru* form a pair

SYNONYMS

❶ⓐ & ❷ⓑ opposite
反 COUNTER → 2945
逆 REVERSE → 3091
倒 upside-down → 124
ⓑ face
面 FACE → 2087
向 TURN TOWARD → 3052
❷ⓐ resist
反 COUNTER → 2945
逆 rebel → 3091
抗 RESIST → 252
抵 RESIST → 319
耐 WITHSTAND → 1282
❸ compare
照 check against → 2827
参 refer → 2066
比 COMPARE → 26
較 COMPARE → 1536
校 COLLATE → 929
❻ two
偶 COUPLE → 132
両 BOTH → 3518
双 SET OF TWO → 25
二 TWO → 1922
弐 TWO (in legal documents) → 3195

COMPOUND FORMATION

絶対 *zettai*
絶対の 'absolute' refers to something without match (絶); that is, to something that cannot compared in contrast (対 ❸) to something else.

NOTE

⇨ see COMPOUND FORMATION for
相対 *sōtai* ⇨ 相 900
対象 *taishō* ⇨ 象 2134

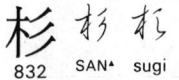

杉 杉 杉
832 SAN▲ sugi

一 十 才 木 木' 杉 杉
1 2 3 4 5 6 7

Ⓒⓗ 杉 shān shā

Radical	Strokes
木 75	7-4-3
Grade	**Freq**
Jōyō	884
◧ 1 - 4 - 3	

4-3 木

▶CRYPTOMERIA

COMPOUNDS

● **cryptomeria, Japanese [Japan] cedar, sugi**
老杉 *rōsan* [archaic] old cryptomeria

KUN

【sugi 杉】 cryptomeria, Japanese [Japan] cedar, sugi
杉林 *sugibayashi* cryptomeria forest
杉並木 *suginamiki* avenue of cryptomerias
杉箸 *sugibashi* cryptomeria [sugi] chopsticks
杉垣 *sugigaki* cryptomeria hedge

SYNONYMS

● **trees**
槙 PODOCARPUS → 1051
松 PINE → 864
楠 CAMPHOR TREE → 1018
桐 PAULOWNIA → 937
桂 AROMATIC TREE, katsura tree → 928
梓 CATALPA → 962
桑 MULBERRY → 2112
漆 Japanese lacquer tree → 704
楓 MAPLE → 1015
柳 WILLOW → 899
桜 CHERRY → 931

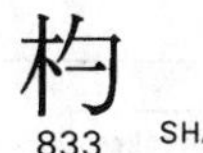
833 SHAKU

Ⓒⓗ  sháo

Radical	Strokes
木 75	7-4-3
Grade	**Freq**
Reference	
◧ 1 - 4 - 3	

4-3 木

COMPOUNDS

● [rarely also 勺 2933] dipper, ladle, spoon
杓子 *shakushi* dipper, (wooden) ladle
杓文字 *shamoji* rice scoop
柄杓 *hishaku* ladle, dipper, scoop
杓 *shaku* dipper, ladle

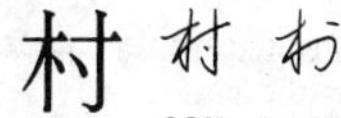
834 SON mura

Ⓒⓗ 村 cūn

Radical	Strokes
木 75	7-4-3
Grade	**Freq**
Jōyō-1	218
◧ 1 - 4 - 3	

4-3 木

▶VILLAGE

COMPOUNDS

ⓐ [also suffix] [original meaning] **village, hamlet; rural district**
ⓑ (unit of local administration) village
ⓒ counter for villages
村落 *sonraku* village, hamlet
農村 *nōson* farm village, agricultural community
漁村 *gyoson* fishing village
無医村 *muison* doctorless village
一宮村 *ichinomiyason* Ichinomiya Village
村長 *sonchō* village mayor
市町村 *shichōson* cities, towns and villages; municipalities
六か村 *rokkason* six villages

INDEPENDENT

【son 村】 (unit of local administration) village

KUN

【mura 村】
ⓐ [also suffix] village, hamlet
ⓑ (unit of local administration) village
ⓒ suffix after names of villages
村人 *murabito* villager
村里 *murazato* villages
村八分 *murahachibu* village ostracism
八木村 *yagimura* Yagi Village

SYNONYMS

● **villages and towns**

里 hamlet → 3542

庄 FEUDAL VILLAGE → 3051

郷 HOMETOWN → 549

町 TOWN → 1113

4-3 木

杜

835 TO TŌ ZU mori

Ⓒ 杜 dù

Radical 木 75	Strokes 7-4-3
Grade Reference	Freq
1 - 4 - 3	

COMPOUNDS

❶ [now replaced by 途 *to* 3107] shut out, stop, prevent

杜絶する *tozetsu suru* be stopped, be interrupted, cease

❷ careless

杜撰な *zusan na* careless, slipshod, faulty

杜漏な *zurō na* careless, negligent

❸ Chinese family name: Du

杜甫 *to ho* Du Fu (famous Chinese poet)

杜詩 *toshi* poems of Du Fu

杜氏 *tōji* chief brewer at a sake brewery (so called after the name of sake's alleged inventor)

❹ [usu. 森 *mori*] thick woods, forest

鎮守の杜 *chinju no mori* grove of the village shrine

HOMOPHONES

mori ⇨ 森 2475

NOTE

⇨ see USAGE note at 森 2475

4-3 木

材 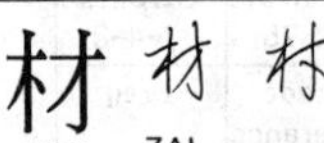

836 ZAI

Ⓒ 材 cái

Radical 木 75	Strokes 7-4-3
Grade Jōyō-4	Freq 599
1 - 4 - 3	

▶TIMBER ▶MATERIAL

COMPOUNDS

❶ [original meaning] **timber, lumber, wood**

材木 *zaimoku* timber, lumber, wood, logs

木材 *mokuzai* wood, timber, lumber

良材 *ryōzai* good timber

製材業 *seizaigyō* lumbering [sawing] industry

❷ⓐ [also suffix] **material, raw material**

ⓑ (**written**) **materials, data**

材質 *zaishitsu* material properties; lumber quality

材料 *zairyō* material, matter, stuff; factor, element

素材 *sozai* material; subject matter

鋼材 *kōzai* steel materials, structural steel

資材 *shizai* materials

教材 *kyōzai* teaching materials [aids]

取材 *shuzai* collection of data [materials], gathering of news

❸ⓐ **ability, talent**

ⓑ man of ability, capable person

材器 *zaiki* talent, ability

人材 *jinzai* (man of) talent, capable man

適材 *tekizai* man fit for the post

INDEPENDENT

【zai 材】 timber, lumber; material; ability, talent

有為の材 *yūi no zai* man of talent

SYNONYMS

❶ **kinds of wood**

木 WOOD → 3450

薪 FIREWOOD → 2374

❷ⓐ **matter**

料 MATERIALS → 1292

資 material resources → 2695

質 MATTER → 2808

物 substance → 874

4-3 木

朽 

incorrect stroke count ⇨ see 821

837 ▶VIGOROUS ▶GRAND
nonstandard for 壮 224

邪
838 ▶EVIL
nonstandard for 邪 1124

牡
839 BO osu o- on

Ⓒⓗ 牡 mǔ

Radical	Strokes
牛 93	7-4-3
Grade	**Freq**
Reference	
◧ 1 - 4 - 3	

COMPOUNDS

● [usu. 雄 *osu, o-, on*] [original meaning] (of animals) male
牡丹 *botan* peony, *Paeonia suffruticosa*
牡猫 *osuneko* tomcat
牡牛 *oushi* bull, steer
牡鳥(=牡鶏) *ondori* rooster
牡蠣 *kaki* oyster

HOMOPHONES

osu ⇨ 雄 1008
o- ⇨ 雄 1008 男 2542
on ⇨ 雄 1008

NOTE

⇨ see USAGE note at 雄 1008

社 社 社 社
840 SHA yashiro

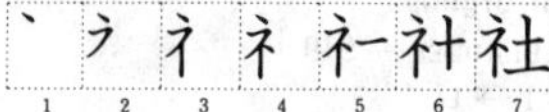

Ⓒⓗ 社 shè

Radical	Strokes
礻 113	7-4-3
Grade	**Freq**
Jōyō-2	48
◧ 1 - 4 - 3	

▶COMPANY ▶SOCIETY

COMPOUNDS

❶ⓐ [also suffix] **company, firm, corporation; office**
ⓑ counter for companies
社員 *shain* staff member, employee
社長 *shachō* president (of a company)
社団 *shadan* corporation, association
会社 *kaisha* company, corporation, firm
公社 *kōsha* public corporation
入社 *nyūsha* entering [joining] a company
本社 *honsha* head office, this office; head shrine, this shrine
新聞社 *shinbunsha* newspaper office
出版社 *shuppansha* publishing company
二十二社 *nijūnisha* 22 companies

❷ⓐ **society, community, the public, the world**
ⓑ **social, socialism; Socialist Party**
ⓒ abbrev. of 社会科 *shakaika*: social studies, civics
社会 *shakai* society, the world
社交 *shakō* social intercourse, society
民社党 *minshatō* Democratic Socialist Party
倫社 *rinsha* ethics and civics

❸ **Shinto shrine**
社殿 *shaden* Shinto shrine
神社 *jinja* Shinto shrine
総社(=惣社) *sōja* shrine enshrining several gods
寺社 *jisha* shrines and temples
出雲大社 *izumotaisha* The Grand Shrine of Izumo

❹ [original meaning] tutelary deity
社稷 *shashoku* the State (tutelary deity and god of grain)

❺ tribe
蕃社 *bansha* aborigines' village

INDEPENDENT

【**sha** 社】company, office; Socialist Party
社の方針 *sha no hōshin* company policy
社・共 *sha-kyō* Social and Communist Parties

KUN

【**yashiro** 社】Shinto shrine
村のお社 *mura no oyashiro* village shrine

SYNONYMS

❶ **places of business**

店 SHOP (of any kind) → 3085
舗 SHOP (esp. traditional) → 1735
屋 SMALL SHOP → 3098

❷ⓐ **society**

世 WORLD → 3496
公 PUBLIC → 1974

❸ **places of worship**

宮 SHINTO SHRINE → 2274
寺 BUDDHIST TEMPLE → 2164
堂 temple building → 2589
塔 pagoda → 561
院 monastery → 454
教 church → 1493

NOTE

⇨ see COMPOUND FORMATION for 物社 *sōja* ⇨ 物 2780

4-3
月

肝 841 KAN kimo

Ⓒⓗ 肝 gān

Radical	Strokes
月 130	7-4-3
Grade	**Freq**
Jōyō	1454
1-4-3	

▶LIVER

COMPOUNDS

❶ [original meaning] **liver**

肝臓 *kanzō* liver
肝油 *kan'yu* liver oil
肝炎 *kan'en* hepatitis

❷ heart, mind

肝胆相照らす間柄である *Kantan-aiterasu aidagara de aru* be quite in sympathy with each other
肝銘(=感銘) *kanmei* deep impression
心肝 *shintan* the heart

❸ **main part, essence**

肝腎(=肝心)な *kanjin na* vital, essential, main
肝要な *kan'yō na* important, vital, essential, necessary

INDEPENDENT

【kan 肝】 liver

KUN

【kimo 肝】 liver; inner heart; pluck, guts, courage, nerve

肝に銘じる *kimo ni meijiru* be deeply impressed
肝っ玉 *kimottama* pluck, courage
肝を冷やす *kimo o hiyasu* be struck with terror

SYNONYMS

❶ **internal organs**

胆 GALLBLADDER → 919
心 HEART → 11
肺 LUNG → 916
胃 STOMACH → 2561
腸 INTESTINES → 1033

4-3
月

肛 842 KŌ

Ⓒⓗ 肛 gāng

Radical	Strokes
月 130	7-4-3
Grade	**Freq**
Non-Jōyō	1966
1-4-3	

▶ANUS

COMPOUNDS

● [original meaning] **anus**

肛門 *kōmon* anus
肛門科 *kōmonka* proctology; proctology clinic
脱肛 *dakkō* prolapse of the anus

SYNONYMS

● **buttocks**

尻 BUTTOCKS → 3032

那 那 那 那

843 NA NAMES tomo yasu

CH 那 nà nǎ nèi nā

Radical	Strokes
阝 163	7-3-4
Grade	Freq
Names	1984
◧ 1 - 4 - 3	

4-3 冄

Stroke order: ㇆ ヨ ヨ 月 月' 那 那 (1–7)

▶PHONETIC [na]

COMPOUNDS

❶ **used phonetically for *na*, esp. in the transliteration of Sanscrit Buddhist terms or names**

旦那 *danna* master, husband, patron, protector; sir; [original meaning] donor

刹那 *setsuna* moment, instant; *kṣaṇa* (1/75 of a second)

❷ [also 奈 2219] element for forming interrogative words

那辺 *nahen* where?

NAMES

那須 *nasu* surname also place name

那覇 *naha* place name

SYNONYMS

❶ **phonetic** [na]

奈 PHONETIC [na] → 2219

❷ **interrogatives**

奈 interrogative forming element → 2219

何 WHAT → 65

誰 WHO → 1578

844

▶PHONETIC [na]

nonstandard for 那 843

4-3 冄

臼

845

Radical	Strokes
臼 134	7-7-0
Grade	Freq
Radical	
◧ 1 - 4 - 3	

4-3 E

Stroke order: ノ 亻 臼 臼 臼 臼 臼 (1–7)

RADICAL 134

variant of 臼 *usu* 'mortar'

⇨ see 臼 3528 for radical description

形 形° 形 形

846 KEI GYŌ kata -gata katachi nari▲

CH 形 xíng

Radical	Strokes
彡 59	7-3-4
Grade	Freq
Jōyō-2	404
◧ 1 - 4 - 3	

4-3 开

Stroke order: 一 二 于 开 开' 形 形 (1–7)

▶SHAPE

COMPOUNDS

❶ⓐ [also suffix] [original meaning] **shape, material form, figure**

ⓑ appearance, look, condition

形状 *keijō* shape, form, configuration

形態(=形体) *keitai* shape, form, structure, morphology

形式 *keishiki* form, model, formality

図形 *zukei* figure, diagram

体形 *taikei* form, figure

球形 *kyūkei* globular shape

変形する *henkei suru* change shape, transform

人形 *ningyō* doll

長方形 *chōhōkei* rectangle

半月形の *hangetsukei no* semicircular, crescent-shaped

形勢 *keisei* situation, state of affairs; prospects

形相 *gyōsō* features, look, aspect

❷ appear in visible form, manifest

形成する *keisei suru* form, make up, mold

形容する *keiyō suru* qualify, modify

❸ body
形骸 *keigai* ruin, wreck, mere skeleton

KUN

【kata 形】
①ⓐ shape, form; pattern, design
ⓑ marks, traces
形どる *katadoru* [usu. 象る] model after, represent
形が崩れる *kata ga kuzureru* lose shape, get out of shape
花形 *hanagata* floral pattern; star, lion; leading, popular, favorite
形見 *katami* keepsake, memento
② security, pledge
借金の形 *shakkin no kata* security for a loan
手形 *tegata* promissory note; hand print
【-gata -形】 [also suffix] -shaped
卵形の *tamagogata no* egg-shaped
弓形の *yumigata no* arched, crescent-shaped
【katachi 形】
① shape, form
形作る *katachizukuru* form, shape, make, mold
② [formerly also 貌] appearance, looks, figure
顔形 *kaokatachi* features, looks
【nari 形】 shape, form, figure; stature, size; appearance, dress, outfit, getup
弓形になる *yuminari ni naru* become bow-shaped, bend backward
大きな形をして *ōkina nari o shite* for all one's stoutness
身形 *minari* dress, outfit, getup, appearance

SYNONYMS

❶ⓐ form
状 FORM (external) → 272
体 FORM (characteristic) → 71
姿 FIGURE → 2636

USAGE

katachi
形
① shape, form
② [formerly also 貌] appearance, looks, figure
貌
[now usu. 形]
ⓐ appearance, looks, figure
ⓑ aspect, condition

HOMOPHONES

kata ⇨ 型 2638
katadoru ⇨ 象 2134
-gata ⇨ 型 2638
katachi ⇨ 貌 1556

NOTE

⇨ see also USAGE notes at 型 2638 and 象 2134

4-3
扌

邦 邦 邦 邦

847 HŌ

Ⓒⓗ 邦 bāng

Radical	Strokes
阝 163	7-3-4
Grade	**Freq**
Jōyō	969
1-4-3	

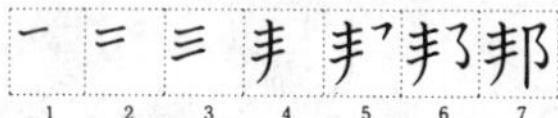

▶STATE ▶JAPAN

COMPOUNDS

❶ⓐ state, country, nation
ⓑ [original meaning] domain, territory
邦家 *hōka* one's country, the state
隣邦 *rinpō* neighboring country
盟邦 *meihō* ally, allied powers
東邦 *tōhō* eastern country, Oriental nation; the Orient
友邦 *yūhō* friendly nation, ally
連邦 *renpō* federation, confederation, union
本邦 *honpō* this [our] country
異邦人 *ihōjin* foreigner, alien
邦土 *hōdo* realm, country
❷ⓐ Japan, our country
ⓑ Japanese (language)
邦人 *hōjin* Japanese, fellow countryman
邦楽 *hōgaku* Japanese music
邦画 *hōga* Japanese film [movie]; Japanese painting
邦訳 *hōyaku* translation into Japanese
邦字新聞 *hōji shinbun* Japanese-language newspaper

SYNONYMS

❶ⓐ country
国 COUNTRY → 3087
土 land → 3403
❷ⓐ Japan
和 JAPAN → 1130
日 JAPAN → 3027
国 Japanese → 3087

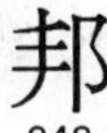

848 ▶STATE ▶JAPAN
nonstandard for 邦 847

4-3 扌

卵 卯 卵

849 RAN tamago

ⒸⒽ 卵 luǎn

Radical	Strokes
卩 26	7-2-5
Grade	**Freq**
Jōyō-6	1259
◧ 1-4-3	

4-3 卩

▶EGG

COMPOUNDS

ⓐ [original meaning] **egg; spawn, roe**
ⓑ ovum
卵殻 *rankaku* eggshell
卵黄 *ran'ō* yolk
鶏卵 *keiran* (hen's) egg
産卵 *sanran* egg-laying, spawning
卵子 *ranshi* ovum, ovule, egg
卵巣 *ransō* ovary
排卵 *hairan* ovulation

INDEPENDENT

【ran 卵】 ovum

KUN

【tamago 卵】
①ⓐ [also 玉子] egg
ⓑ spawn, roe
卵焼き *tamagoyaki* fried egg, omelette
② (an expert) in the making
文士の卵 *bunshi no tamago* hatching writer

SYNONYMS

ⓐ **early states of animal life**
胎 FETUS → 918
ⓑ **reproductive cells**
精 sperm → 1366

USAGE

tamago
卵
①ⓐ [also 玉子] egg
ⓑ spawn, roe
② (an expert) in the making
玉子
[also 卵] egg

HOMOPHONES

tamago ⇨ 玉子 3477, 3390

所

850 ▶PLACE ▶PARTICLE OF NOMINALIZATION
nonstandard for 所 851

4-4 戸

所 所 所 所

851 SHO tokoro -tokoro dokoro toko▲

ⒸⒽ 所 suǒ

Radical	Strokes
戸 63	8-4-4
Grade	**Freq**
Jōyō-3	114
◧ 1-4-4	

4-4 戸

▶PLACE
▶PARTICLE OF NOMINALIZATION

COMPOUNDS

❶ⓐ [sometimes also 処 *sho* 3031] (portion of space) **place, spot, point, part**
ⓑ [also suffix] **place for specific purpose, dwelling place, facilities, quarters**
場所 *basho* place, spot, site; space, room
箇所(=個所) *kasho* place, spot, point; part
住所 *jūsho* one's dwelling, address
近所 *kinjo* neighborhood
名所 *meisho* noted place, sights, scenic place
余所(=他所) *yoso* another place, strange parts
一所懸命(=一生懸命)に *isshokenmei* (=*isshōkenmei*) *ni* for life, with all one's might
出所 *shussho* origin, source; release from prison
便所 *benjo* lavatory, bathroom
停留所 *teiryūjo* (bus) stop, station
休憩所 *kyūkeijo* resting room [place], lounge
❷ [also suffix]
ⓐ place for conducting specific activities: **office, bureau, organization, institu-**

tion, institute, agency
❺ place equipped with facilities for specific task: **plant, station, factory, facilities**
所長 *shochō* head, chief, manager
役所 *yakusho* public [government] office
入所する *nyūsho suru* enter (an institute); be put in prison
事務所 *jimusho* office, one's place of business
研究所 *kenkyūjo* (=*kenkyūsho*) research laboratory [institute]
裁判所 *saibansho* court of justice, courthouse
保健所 *hokenjo* public health center
発電所 *hatsudensho* power plant, generating station
造船所 *zōsenjo* dock yard, shipbuilding yard
製作所 *seisakusho* factory, works, plant
❸❹ **particle of nominalization, function word for turning verbs into nouns**
❺ function word indicating the passive voice
所以 *yuen* (=*shoi*) reason; way of doing
所有する *shoyū suru* have, own, possess
所属する *shozoku suru* belong to, be attached to
所得 *shotoku* income, earnings
所望 *shomō* desire, wish
所信 *shoshin* one's belief, one's opinion
所在 *shozai* whereabouts, position, situation
所轄 *shokatsu* jurisdiction
所定の *shotei no* fixed, prescribed, stated
❹ point, feature
短所 *tansho* shortcoming, defect
急所 *kyūsho* vital part; vital point, tender spot

INDEPENDENT

【sho 所】 place for specific activity or task (⇨❷): office, institution; plant, station
所の事情 *sho no jijō* circumstances of the office

KUN

【tokoro 所】
①ⓐ place, spot, site; part; room, space; district
ⓑ one's place, one's house, one's address
所所 *tokorodokoro* here and there, at places
所を替える *tokoro o kaeru* change places, change sides
居所 *idokoro* one's address [residence], one's whereabouts
台所 *daidokoro* kitchen
所書き *tokorogaki* one's address
②ⓐ time, moment
ⓑ occasion, case
早い所 *hayai tokoro* promptly
今の所 *ima no tokoro* at present
書いている所だ *Kaite iru tokoro da* I am writing now
彼は今来た所だ *Kare wa ima kita tokoro da* He has just arrived
所構わず *tokoro kamawazu* irrespective of the occasion, indiscriminately
③ point, feature
詩人らしい所 *shijinrashii tokoro* something of a poet
強い所 *tsuyoi tokoro* strong point
④ extent
...所では *...tokoro de wa* so far as...
倍でも安い所だ *Bai demo yasui tokoro da* It would be cheap even at twice the sum
⑤ passage, part
面白い所 *omoshiroi tokoro* interesting passage
⑥ⓐ function word equiv. to relative pronoun: what, thing that, which, who
ⓑ [in the form of 所となる *tokoro to naru*] function word indicating the passive voice
彼の言う所 *kare no iu tokoro* what he says
私が愛する所の女性 *watakushi ga aisuru tokoro no josei* the woman whom I love
人の好む所となる *hito no konomu tokoro to naru* be liked by people
⑦ⓐ when, upon, even if
ⓑ [in the form of 所が *tokoro ga*] but, however, on the contrary
ⓒ [in the form of 所で *tokoro de*] well, now, by the way, incidentally
問い合わせた所、嘘だと分かった *Toiawaseta tokoro, uso da to wakatta* On inquiry, the report proved false
損をした所で *son o shita tokoro de* even if one loses
所が失敗した *Tokoro ga shippai shita* Nevertheless, I failed
所で猫は好きですか *Tokoro de neko wa suki desu ka* By the way, do you like cats?

【-tokoro -所】
① counter for places
三所 *mitokoro* three places
② *literary* counter for people
宮様お二所 *miyasama ofutatokoro* two Imperial princes

【dokoro 所】
① anything but, far from; not to mention
失望する所か *shitsubō suru dokoro ka* far from being disappointed
暑い所の騒ぎじゃない *Atsui dokoro no sawagi ja nai* "Hot" isn't the word
② [suffix] place, point
掴み所 *tsukamidokoro* hold, grip; point
聞き所 *kikidokoro* most important part, finest passage
拠り所 *yoridokoro* grounds, foundation, authority
③ [suffix] producing center
お茶所 *ochadokoro* tea-growing district, tea producing center

【toko 所】 colloquial form of **tokoro 所**

851

僕ん所 *bokuntoko* at my place
早い所片付けよう *Hayai toko katazukeyō* Let's finish up quickly

SPECIAL READINGS

所以▲ *yuen* reason; way of doing

SYNONYMS

❶ **places and positions**
処 place → 3031
場 PLACE (for specific activity) → 558
地 PLACE (particular location) → 204
席 meeting place → 3113
位 POSITION → 61
点 POINT → 2084
座 place → 3116
❷ⓐ **public offices**
局 public service office → 3063
署 PUBLIC-SERVICE STATION → 2609
公 public office → 1974
府 government office → 3082
庁 GOVERNMENT AGENCY → 3034
省 MINISTRY → 2449
❸ⓐ **nominalizers**
事 nominalization word → 3567
子 NOUN SUFFIX → 3390
性 -ITY → 299

USAGE

tokoro
所
①ⓐ place, spot, site; part; room, space; district
ⓑ one's place, one's house, one's address
②ⓐ time, moment
ⓑ occasion, case
③ point, feature
④ extent
⑤ passage, part
⑥ⓐ function word equiv. to relative pronoun: what, thing that, which, who
ⓑ [in the form of 所となる *tokoro to naru*] function word indicating the passive voice
⑦ⓐ when, upon, even if
ⓑ [in the form of 所が *tokoro ga*] but, however, on the contrary
ⓒ [in the form of 所で *tokoro de*] well, now, by the way, incidentally

処
place (for a specific purpose, as eating or resting)

HOMOPHONES

tokoro ⇨ 処 3031

COMPOUND FORMATION

所以 *yuen*
所以 'reason; way of doing' is a combination of 以 and 所 ❸ⓐ, which functions as a particle of nominalization. 以 here is actually a verb turned into a noun by means of 所.

NOTE

⇨ see COMPOUND FORMATION for 一生懸命(=一所懸命) *isshōkenmei* (=*isshokenmei*) ⇨ 生 3497

852 KIN GON NAMES yasushi yoshi

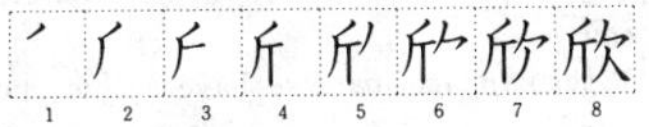

CH 欣 xīn

Radical	Strokes
欠 76	8-4-4
Grade	**Freq**
Names	2056
◧ 1-4-4	

4-4 斤

▶**JOYFUL**

COMPOUNDS

ⓐ [original meaning] **joyful, glad, happy**
ⓑ joyfully, gladly
欣悦 *kin'etsu* gladness, joy
欣然と *kinzen to* joyfully, gladly
欣喜雀躍する *kinkijakuyaku suru* dance [jump] for joy
欣快 *kinkai* great pleasure
欣懐する *kinkai suru* think happily of
欣求浄土 *gongujōdo* seeking rebirth in the Pure Land

NAMES

欣也 *kin'ya* male name
欣秀 *yoshihide* male name

SYNONYMS

ⓐ **pleased and pleasant**
歓 JOYOUS → 1867
喜 HAPPY → 2308
嬉しい GLAD → 722
悦 DELIGHTED → 418
愉 PLEASED → 582
朗 CHEERFUL → 1325
快 PLEASANT → 245
楽 pleasurable → 2826

4-4 放 放 𣃗 ㊥ 放 fàng

方

853 HŌ hana(su) -(p)pana(shi) hana(tsu) hana(reru) hō(ru)▲

Radical	Strokes
攵 66	8-4-4
Grade	Freq
Jōyō-3	250
1-4-4	

丶 亠 ㇇ 方 方 㫃 㫃 放 (1 2 3 4 5 6 7 8)

▶**LET GO**

COMPOUNDS

❶ⓐ (set free) **let go, release, free**
ⓑ send away, exile
放流する *hōryū suru* discharge; stock (a river) with (fish)
放牧 *hōboku* pasturage, grazing
放課後 *hōkago* after school
解放する *kaihō suru* release, set free
釈放する *shakuhō suru* release, liberate, discharge, acquit
放逐する *hōchiku suru* expel, banish, expatriate
放校 *hōkō* expulsion from school
追放する *tsuihō suru* banish, purge, exile

❷ⓐ **let things go, let alone, leave as it is**
ⓑ **let oneself go, do as one pleases**
放任する *hōnin suru* leave (a matter) to take its own course, leave (a person) to himself
放置する *hōchi suru* leave alone, neglect, leave as it is
放心 *hōshin* absence of mind, abstraction
開放する *kaihō suru* open, leave open
放談 *hōdan* random [irresponsible] talk
放蕩する *hōtō suru* live fast, throw one's money away
放浪 *hōrō* wandering, roaming
奔放な *honpō na* wild, extravagant; free-spirited
したい放題 *shitai-hōdai* as one pleases, at will
野放図な *nohōzu na* unrestrained, unruly

❸ⓐ (give off in all directions) **radiate, emit, emanate, broadcast**
ⓑ **let out, discharge, excrete**
放射する *hōsha suru* radiate, emit, emanate
放光 *hōkō* emission of light
放映 *hōei* telecasting
放送 *hōsō* broadcasting
民放 *minpō* commercial broadcast
放水 *hōsui* discharge, drainage
放屁 *hōhi* breaking wind

❹ [formerly 抛 307]
ⓐ toss, throw, let fly
ⓑ toss away, throw away, cast away
放物線 *hōbutsusen* parabola
放棄 *hōki* abandonment, resignation
放擲する *hōteki suru* abandon, give up, quit

❺ set off, set fire to
放火する *hōka suru* set fire to

KUN

【hana(su) 放す】
ⓐ (set free) let go, release, free, turn loose
ⓑ (release one's hold) let go (one's hold of), leave go
放し飼い *hanashigai* grazing; letting (a dog) run free
見放す *mihanasu* desert, abandon, give up
手放す *tebanasu* release [let go] one's hold

【-(p)pana(shi) -っ放し】
[sometimes also -放し *-hanashi*] [verbal suffix] *colloq*
① leaving something as it is
やりっ放し *yarippanashi* leaving alone, negligence
開けっ放す *akeppanasu* leave open
掛けっ放しにする *kakeppanashi ni suru* leave (the radio) on
② performing successively
勝ちっ放し *kachippanashi* winning straight victories, making a clean score

【hana(tsu) 放つ】 emit, give out, send forth; discharge, fire, let fly; set free, release; set fire
芳香を放つ *hōkō o hanatsu* give out [off] fragrance
言い放つ *iihanatsu* declare, avow, venture to say
一発放つ *ippatsu hanatsu* have a shot; break wind

【hana(reru) 放れる】 free oneself of, get free
狼が鎖を放れた *Ōkami ga kusari o hanareta* The wolf freed itself of its chain

【hō(ru) 放る】 throw, toss, fling, cast; throw up, neglect
放り出す *hōridasu* throw out; dismiss, expel
放って置く *hōtte oku* neglect, leave alone
放ったらかす *hottarakasu* neglect, let aside

SYNONYMS

❶ⓐ **release**
釈 release → 1484
❷ **let do**
随 let do → 627
❸ **emit**
発 EMIT → 2565
出 PUT OUT → 3498
排 DISCHARGE → 490
射 SHOOT → 1458

噴 SPOUT → 717
吐 SPEW → 203
❹ⓐ **throw**
投 THROW → 256

HOMOPHONES
hanasu ⇨ 離 1836
hanareru ⇨ 離 1836
NOTE
⇨ see USAGE note at 離 1836

於

854 O oi(te) o(keru)

Ⓒ于 yú 於 yū wū

Radical	Strokes
方 70	8-4-4
Grade	Freq
Reference	
◧ 1-4-4	

4-4 方

COMPOUNDS
❶ in, at, on (in reference to time or place)
東京に於て *tōkyō ni oite* in Tokyo
❷ as for, on one's part
その点に於て *sono ten ni oite* on that point, in that respect
❸ [in the form of に於ける *ni okeru*] to
水の魚に於けるは空気の人に於けるが如し *Mizu no sakana ni okeru wa kūki no hito ni okeru ga gotoshi* Water is to fish what air is to man

HOMOPHONES
oite ⇨ 措 502
NOTE
⇨ see USAGE note at 措 502

明 明 明 明

855 MEI MYŌ MIN▲ a(kari) aka(rui) aka(rumu) aka(ramu) aki(raka) a(keru) -a(ke) a(ku) a(kuru) a(kasu)

Ⓒ明 míng

Radical	Strokes
日 72	8-4-4
Grade	Freq
Jōyō-2	89
◧ 1-4-4	

4-4 日

丨	冂	日	日	明	明	明	明
1	2	3	4	5	6	7	8

▶BRIGHT ▶CLEAR

COMPOUNDS
❶ⓐ [original meaning] **bright, brilliant, light**
ⓑ (of colors) **bright, light**
ⓒ (of cheerful disposition) bright, cheerful
明月 *meigetsu* bright moon, full moon; harvest moon
明星 *myōjō* Venus
明暗 *meian* light and dark; contrast
照明 *shōmei* illumination, lighting
鮮明な *senmei na* vivid, clear
明色 *meishoku* bright [light] color
明度 *meido* lightness, value of color
明朗な *meirō na* cheerful, bright; clean (politics)
❷ⓐ light
ⓑ be lighted
灯明 *tōmyō* votive light offered (as to a god); stand for votive light; candlestand
明滅する *meimetsu suru* flicker, blink
❸ⓐ **clear-sighted, bright, discerning, intelligent, wise**
ⓑ eyesight
明哲 *meitetsu* wisdom, sagacity; wise man
明察 *meisatsu* discernment, insight
賢明な *kenmei na* wise, intelligent; sensible
聡明な *sōmei na* sagacious, wise, sharp, mentally acute
不明 *fumei* lack of sagacity [foresight], ignorance; missing persons
発明する *hatsumei suru* invent, devise
失明 *shitsumei* loss of eyesight
❹ⓐ (free from doubt) **clear, lucid, distinct, evident, obvious, explicit, manifest**
ⓑ **make clear, clarify, throw light on, prove, demonstrate**
明確な *meikaku na* clear, precise, distinct
明治 *meiji* Meiji era
明記する *meiki suru* write clearly, specify
表明 *hyōmei* manifestation, demonstration
不明な *fumei na* obscure, unknown
自明の理 *jimei no ri* self-evident truth, axiom
公明正大な *kōmei-seidai na* fair, just
文明 *bunmei* civilization, culture
証明 *shōmei* proof, evidence, verification
説明する *setsumei suru* explain, illustrate

❺ (unclouded) clear, transparent, translucent
明澄な *meichō na* unclouded, clear, limpid
透明度 *tōmeido* transparency, degree of clearness
❻ [also prefix] next, the coming (day or year)
明日 *myōnichi* (=*ashita, asu*) tomorrow
明晩 *myōban* tomorrow night
明年度 *myōnendo* next (fiscal) year
❼ Ming Dynasty (1368–1644 A.D.)
明朝 *minchō* Ming Dynasty
明朝体 *minchōtai* Ming-style typeface
❽ daybreak, dawn
黎明 *reimei* dawn, daybreak
未明 *mimei* early dawn, the gray of the morning
❾ⓐ abbrev. of 明治 *meiji*: Meiji era
ⓑ abbrev. of 明治大学 *meiji daigaku*: Meiji University
明初 *meisho* first year of Meiji era
明大 *meidai* Meiji University
早明戦 *sōmeisen* Waseda-Meiji (baseball) game
❿ divinity, God
神明 *shinmei* deity, God
⓫ this world
幽明 *yūmei* this and the other world

INDEPENDENT

【mei 明】 discernment, insight; eyesight
先見の明 *senken no mei* foresight, power of seeing into the future
明を失う *mei o ushinau* lose one's eyesight
【min 明】 Ming Dynasty

KUN

【a(kari) 明かり】 light, glimmer; lamp; proof
明かり障子 *akarishōji* paper screen door for admitting light
薄明かり *usuakari* faint light, half-light of early morning
【aka(rui) 明るい】 bright, light; light (color); clear, uncorrupt; (of cheerful disposition) bright, cheerful; (full of promise) bright, promising; be well versed in
明るさ *akarusa* brightness; cheerfulness
明るい政治 *akarui seiji* clean politics
彼は文学に明るい *Kare wa bungaku ni akarui* He is well-read in literature
【aka(rumu) 明るむ】 brighten; be cheered up
明るみに出す *akarumi ni dasu* bring to light, make public
空が明るむ *Sora ga akarumu* The sky brightens
【aka(ramu) 明らむ】 brighten
【aki(raka) 明らか】
akiraka na 明らかな clear, distinct, apparent, obvious, unquestionable; bright, cheerful
明らかにする *akiraka ni suru* clarify; disclose, make public
明らかな事実 *akiraka na jijitsu* obvious fact
【a(keru) 明ける】
① dawn, become light, break
明け *ake* dawn; expiration
夜明け *yoake* dawn, daybreak
② (of the new year) begin, open
明けましておめでとうございます *Akemashite omedetō gozaimasu* Happy New Year
年明け *toshiake* beginning of the year
③ expire, be over
冬が明けた *Fuyu ga aketa* Winter is over
④ [in compounds] disclose, reveal
打ち明ける *uchiakeru* confide in (someone), reveal, disclose
【-a(ke) -明け】 [also suffix] end, expiration
忌み明け *imiake* end of mourning
連休明け *renkyūake* end of vacation
【a(ku) 明く】
① one's eyes open, regain sight
目が明く *me ga aku* regain sight
② be settled, be put in order
埒が明かない *rachi ga akanai* remain unsettled, make no progress
③ (of clothing) be opened (at the back)
背の明いた服 *se no aita fuku* garment open at the back
【a(kuru) 明くる】 next, following
明くる日 *akuru hi* the following day
【a(kasu) 明かす】
① [also suffix] spend (the night), stay up all night (doing something)
飲み明かす *nomiakasu* drink the night away
夜を語り明かす *yo o katariakasu* talk the night away
② disclose, reveal
秘密を明かす *himitsu o akasu* disclose a secret

SPECIAL READINGS

明日 *asu* tomorrow
明日▲ *ashita* tomorrow

SYNONYMS

❶ⓐ bright
昭 LUMINOUS → 894
蛍 fluorescent → 2591
晃 DAZZLING → 2450
ⓑ vivid
鮮 VIVID → 1877
❷ⓐ light
光 LIGHT → 2391
灯 LAMP → 825
照 sunlight → 2827
虹 RAINBOW → 1285
❸ⓐ intelligent and wise
聡 SHARP-WITTED → 1384
哲 SAGACIOUS → 2738
賢 WISE → 2839
智 wise → 2784

慧 INTELLIGENT → 2810
怜 CLEVER → 298
俊 brilliant → 102
鋭 SHARP → 1730
敏 NIMBLE → 1322
❹ⓐ **evident**
鮮 VIVID → 1877
亮 LUCID → 2071
顕 MANIFEST → 1806
ⓑ **explain**
説 EXPLAIN → 1547
釈 ELUCIDATE → 1484
講 expound → 1619
解 CLARIFY → 1517
注 annotate → 325
❺ **clear**
朗 CLEAR (sky) → 1325
冴える CRISP AND CLEAR → 79
清 CLEAR (liquid) → 523
澄 LIMPID → 740
透 TRANSPARENT → 3108
❻ **next**
次 NEXT → 54
来 the coming → 3551
翌 THE FOLLOWING → 2668
❼ **later Chinese dynasties**
唐 TANG DYNASTY → 3115
元 Yuan Dynasty → 1929
清 Qing Dynasty → 523

USAGE

❶ **akeru**
明ける
① dawn, become light, break
② (of the new year) begin, open
③ expire, be over
④ [in compounds] disclose, reveal
空ける
① empty, clear, vacate, clear out
② leave space, make room
③ bore, make a hole
④ free oneself (to do), make spare time
開ける
open, unlock
❷ **aku**
明く
① one's eyes open, regain sight
② be settled, be put in order
③ (of clothing) be opened (at the back)
空く
① become vacant, become vacated [empty]
② become available for use
③ become free [unoccupied]
④ have (a hole or aperture) in, (a gap) is open
開く
ⓐ open, become open
ⓑ (of a shop) open, begin

HOMOPHONES

akaramu ⇨ 赤 2193
akeru ⇨ 空 2227 開 3321
aku ⇨ 空 2227 開 3321

COMPOUND FORMATION

❶ 明治 *meiji*
明治 'Meiji era' literally means clear and impartial (明 ❹ⓐ) governing (治). It is the name of the Japanese era from 1868 to 1912.
❷ 文明 *bunmei*
文明 'civilization, culture' refers to the clear (明 ❹ⓐ) manifestation of learning or culture (文).

NOTE

⇨ see also USAGE note at 赤 2193

明
856

▶BRIGHT ▶CLEAR
nonstandard for 明 855

4-4
日

杯 盃◇
857 HAI sakazuki

ⒸⒽ 杯 bēi

Radical	Strokes
木 75	8-4-4
Grade	**Freq**
Jōyō	1063
◧ 1 - 4 - 4	

4-4
木

▶CUP

COMPOUNDS

❶ⓐ [original meaning] **wine cup, cup, glass, goblet**
ⓑ **counter for cupfuls, glassfuls, bowlfuls or spoonfuls**
杯盤 *haiban* glasses and plates
金杯 *kinpai* gold cup [goblet]
苦杯 *kuhai* bitter ordeal
祝杯 *shukuhai* a toast
乾杯 *kanpai* a toast
一杯 *ippai* a cup (as of tea), a glass (as of beer)
茶二杯 *cha nihai* two cups of tea

砂糖三杯 *satō sanbai* three spoons of sugar
❷ [also suffix] **prize cup, trophy**
賞杯 *shōhai* prize cup, trophy
賜杯 *shihai* trophy given by the Emperor [Prince]
デ杯 *dehai* Davis Cup
優勝杯 *yūshōhai* championship cup, trophy
❸ degree of fullness, capacity
一杯 *ippai* fullness
満杯 *manpai* full to capacity
❹ⓐ counter for ships
ⓑ counter for octopi or cuttlefish
舟二杯 *fune nihai* two boats
烏賊六杯 *ika roppai* six cuttlefish

INDEPENDENT

【hai 杯】 wine cup, wine glass, sake cup
杯を重ねる *hai o kasaneru* have one cup of sake after another

KUN

【sakazuki 杯】 wine cup, sake cup
杯を干す *sakazuki o hosu* drink the cup dry

SYNONYMS

❶ **vessels and receptacles**
鉢 BOWL → 1708
鍋 POT → 1752
盆 TRAY → 2079
皿 PLATE → 3474
盤 dish → 2851
❷ **prizes**
賞 PRIZE → 2618
章 decoration → 2117

4-4 木

板 板 板

858 HAN BAN ita

Stroke order: 1 2 3 4 5 6 7 8

CH 板 bǎn

Radical	Strokes
木 75	8-4-4
Grade	**Freq**
Jōyō-3	712
1 - 4 - 4	

▶BOARD ▶PLATE

COMPOUNDS

❶ [original meaning] (sheet of wood) **board, plank**
掲示板 *keijiban* notice board
黒板 *kokuban* blackboard
看板 *kanban* signboard, sign
甲板 *kanpan* (=*kōhan*) deck
❷ⓐ [also suffix] (sheet of hard material, esp. metal) **plate, sheet, slab, tablet**
ⓑ [sometimes also 鈑 *ban* 1688] sheet metal
ⓒ abbrev. of 投手板 *tōshuban*: pitcher's plate
鉄板 *teppan* iron [steel] plate
鋼板 *kōhan* steel plate
投手板 *tōshuban* pitcher's plate
板金 *bankin* sheet metal
ニッケル板 *nikkeruban* nickel plate
登板する *tōban suru* take the plate
❸ [usu. 版 *han* 872] printing block, wood block
板画 *hanga* woodcut print
板木 *hangi* (printing) block, woodcut

KUN

【ita 板】 board, plank; panel, plate; the boards, stage; *kamaboko* (boiled fish paste); cook versed in Japanese cooking
板切れ *itakire* piece of wood, scrap lumber
戸板 *toita* wooden door [shutter]
板に着く *ita ni tsuku* be at home (on the stage)

SYNONYMS

❶ & ❷ **boards and plates**
盤 BOARD → 2851

4-4 木

枚 枚 枚

859 MAI BAI▲

Stroke order: 1 2 3 4 5 6 7 8

CH 枚 méi

Radical	Strokes
木 75	8-4-4
Grade	**Freq**
Jōyō-6	754
1 - 4 - 4	

▶COUNTER FOR FLAT THINGS

COMPOUNDS

❶ⓐ **counter for thin flat things, as sheets (of paper), boards, leaves (of a book), pages, articles of clothing, panes, etc.**
ⓑ counter for order of precedence in sumo
枚数 *maisū* number of flat things
紙五枚 *kami gomai* five sheets of paper
十円切手五枚 *jūen-kitte gomai* five 10-yen

stamps
二枚上がった *nimai agatta* be promoted by two ranks in sumo
❷ enumerate, count one by one
枚挙する *maikyo suru* list, enumerate
大枚の金 *taimai no kane* large sum of money
INDEPENDENT
【bai 枚】*literary* gag
枚を銜む *bai o fukumu* (of a horse) be gagged
SYNONYMS
❶ⓐ **counters for flat things**
葉 counter for leaves → 2321
丁 counter for sheets → 3348
頁 counter for pages → 2086
通 counter for letters → 3109

枡

860 masu

CH none (国字)

Radical	Strokes
木 75	8-4-4
Grade	Freq
Reference	
◧ 1-4-4	

4-4 木

COMPOUNDS
[now usu. 升 *masu*]
❶ⓐ measure, measuring box
ⓑ box (seat)
枡目 *masume* measure; square (of graph paper)
五升枡 *goshōmasu* 5-*sho* measure
❷ square (as of graph paper)
枡形 *masugata* square (shape)
HOMOPHONES
masu ⇨ 升 3455
NOTE
⇨ see USAGE note at 升 3455

林 林 林 林

861 RIN hayashi

CH 林 lín

Radical	Strokes
木 75	8-4-4
Grade	Freq
Jōyō-1	410
◧ 1-4-4	

4-4 木

▶**FOREST**
COMPOUNDS
❶ⓐ [also suffix] [original meaning] **forest, woods, grove**
ⓑ forestry
林業 *ringyō* forestry
林道 *rindō* path through a forest, trail through the woods
林檎 *ringo* apple
森林 *shinrin* forest, woodland
山林 *sanrin* mountains and forests; forest on a mountain
杏林 *kyōrin* doctor
密林 *mitsurin* close thicket, dense forest, jungle
営林 *eirin* forest management
造林 *zōrin* afforestation, reforestation
原始林 *genshirin* primeval forest
農林 *nōrin* agriculture and forestry
❷ something resembling a forest in profusion
林立する *rinritsu suru* stand close together, bristle (with)
辞林 *jirin* dictionary
酒池肉林 *shuchinikurin* sumptuous feast
❸ circles, groups
芸林 *geirin* artists' circles
KUN
【hayashi 林】[also suffix] small woods, grove, thicket
松林 *matsubayashi* pine forest
雑木林 *zōkibayashi* thicket of assorted trees
SYNONYMS
❶ⓐ & 【hayashi】 **forest**
森 THICK WOODS → 2475
USAGE
林 hayashi　森 mori
★The difference between the words 林 *hayashi* and 森 *mori* is much like the difference between *woods* and *forest*. The latter is thicker and extends over a wide area. However, note that when 林 is used as a word element pronounced *rin*, it is closer to English *forest* than to *woods*.
NOTE
⇨ see COMPOUND FORMATION for 杏林 *kyōrin* ⇨ 杏 2397

4-4
木

析 析 析

862 SEKI

Ⓒⓗ 析 xī

Radical	Strokes
木 75	8-4-4
Grade	Freq
Jōyō	1326
1-4-4	

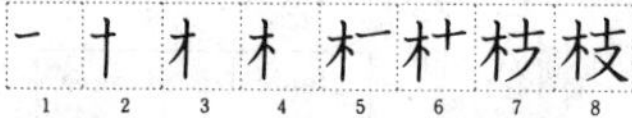

▶ANALYZE

COMPOUNDS

ⓐ (separate an abstract entity into parts) **analyze, dissect**

ⓑ (separate a material entity into parts) analyze, separate, dissect, divide

分析 *bunseki* analysis

解析 *kaiseki* analysis, analytical research

析出 *sekishutsu chem* separating, eduction

開析台地 *kaiseki daichi* dissected plateau

透析 *tōseki chem* dialysis

SYNONYMS

● **separate**

解 TAKE APART → 1517

分 DIVIDE → 1972

割 DIVIDE → 1816

別 SEPARATE → 1117

離 SEPARATE → 1836

隔 partition → 671

NOTE

★do not confuse with 折 253

4-4
木

枝 枝 枝

863 SHI eda

Ⓒⓗ 枝 zhī

Radical	Strokes
木 75	8-4-4
Grade	Freq
Jōyō-5	1098
1-4-4	

▶BRANCH

COMPOUNDS

❶ⓐ [original meaning] **branch, twig**

ⓑ [usu. 支 1979] (something structurally analogous to a branch) branch, offshoot

枝葉 *shiyō* branches and leaves; minor details

枝垂れ桜 *shidarezakura* weeping cherry

楊枝 *yōji* tooth pick

樹枝状の *jushijō no* arborescent

枝族(=支族) *shizoku* tribe, branch family

❷ [rare] counter for slender objects

長刀一枝 *chōtō isshi* one long sword

KUN

【eda 枝】 branch, twig; branch, offshoot, ramification

枝切り *edakiri* pruning

枝葉 *edaha* branches and leaves; minor details

枝分かれ *edawakare* branch, ramification

枝道 *edamichi* branch road, byway

枝毛 *edage* split hair

SYNONYMS

❶ⓐ **branches and twigs**

梢 TIP OF A TWIG → 963

4-4
木

松 松 松 松

864 SHŌ matsu

Ⓒⓗ 松 sōng

Radical	Strokes
木 75	8-4-4
Grade	Freq
Jōyō-4	260
1-4-4	

▶PINE

COMPOUNDS

● **pine**

松竹梅 *shōchikubai* pine-bamboo-plum; congratulatory tree decorations

松根油 *shōkon'yu* pine oil

青松 *seishō* green pine

KUN

【matsu 松】 pine

松林 *matsubayashi* pine forest

松葉 *matsuba* pine needle
松茸 *matsutake matsutake* mushroom
門松 *kadomatsu* pine decorations (for New Year's)

SYNONYMS

● **trees**
杉 CRYPTOMERIA → 832
槙 PODOCARPUS → 1051
楠 CAMPHOR TREE → 1018
桐 PAULOWNIA → 937
桂 AROMATIC TREE, katsura tree → 928
梓 CATALPA → 962
桑 MULBERRY → 2112
漆 Japanese lacquer tree → 704
楓 MAPLE → 1015
柳 WILLOW → 899
桜 CHERRY → 931

枢 樞 枢 枢

865 sū

Ⓒⓗ 枢 shū

Radical	Strokes
木 75	8-4-4
Grade	**Freq**
Jōyō	1723
◧ 1 - 4 - 4	

4-4 木

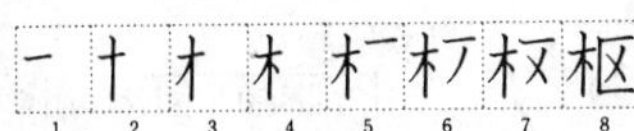

1 2 3 4 5 6 7 8

▶PIVOT

COMPOUNDS

ⓐ (central part) **pivot, center**
ⓑ [original meaning] pivot, hinged axis
枢要な *sūyō na* pivotal, cardinal
枢軸国 *sūjikukoku* the Axis Powers
枢機 *sūki* most important affairs (of state)
枢密 *sūmitsu* secret government affairs
中枢 *chūsū* pivot, center
枢軸 *sūjiku* central point, center; (mechanical) pivot, axis

SYNONYMS

ⓐ **essential part**
精 ESSENCE (essential part) → 1366
粋 essence (best part) → 1293
髄 essence (vital part) → 1842
幹 TRUNK → 1718
綱 ESSENTIAL POINTS → 1372
旨 PURPORT → 2024
要 summary → 2635

枠 枠 枠

866 waku

Ⓒⓗ none (国字)

Radical	Strokes
木 75	8-4-4
Grade	**Freq**
Jōyō	1941
◧ 1 - 4 - 4	

4-4 木

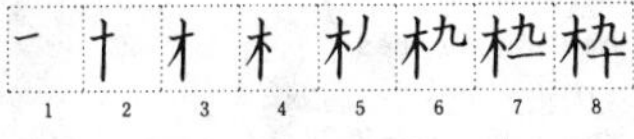

1 2 3 4 5 6 7 8

▶FRAME

KUN

【waku 枠】
①ⓐ frame, framework
ⓑ [original meaning] spool, reel
枠を付ける *waku o tsukeru* frame, set a frame
枠組み *wakugumi* framework, frame
窓枠 *madowaku* window frame, sash
糸枠 *itowaku* spool
② framework, limits, confines, bounds
枠に嵌まった *waku ni hamatta* stereotyped
枠内 *wakunai* within the limits [framework]

SYNONYMS

【waku】
① **frames**
格 framework → 926
額 picture frame → 1805

松

867

▶PINE
nonstandard for 松 864

4-4 木

柱

incorrect stroke count ⇨ see 902
(nonstandard for 柱 896)

4-4 木

4-4 歹

歿
868 BOTSU

CH 歿 没 mò

Radical	Strokes
歹 78	8-4-4
Grade	Freq
Reference	
1-4-4	

COMPOUNDS
[now replaced by 没 260]
ⓐ [original meaning] die, perish
ⓑ indicates date of death
戦歿する *senbotsu suru* be killed in action
死歿 *shibotsu* death, demise
病歿 *byōbotsu* death from sickness
歿する *bossuru* die
昭和三年歿 *shōwa sannen botsu* died 1928

4-4 火

炉 爐
869 RO

CH 炉 lú

Radical	Strokes
火 86	8-4-4
Grade	Freq
Jōyō	1695
1-4-4	

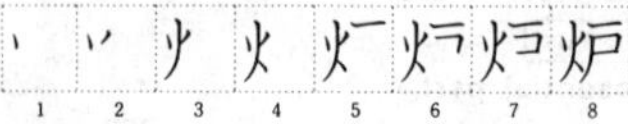

▶FURNACE

COMPOUNDS
❶ [also suffix]
ⓐ **furnace, kiln**
ⓑ reactor
高炉 *kōro* blast furnace
転炉 *tenro* rotary kiln
溶鉱炉 *yōkōro* smelting [blast] furnace
電気炉 *denkiro* electric furnace
反射炉 *hansharo* reverberatory furnace
乾燥炉 *kansōro* drying kiln
燃焼炉 *nenshōro* combustion furnace
炉心 *roshin* reactor core
原子炉 *genshiro* nuclear reactor
軽水炉 *keisuiro* light-water reactor

❷ [original meaning] **hearth, fireplace**
炉端 *robata* fireside
炉床 *roshō* hearth
暖炉 *danro* fireplace, stove
懐炉 *kairo* pocket heater
香炉 *kōro* incense burner
囲炉裏 *irori* hearth sunk in the floor

INDEPENDENT
【**ro** 炉】hearth, fireplace, fire; furnace, kiln
炉を囲む *ro o kakomu* sit around the fire

SYNONYMS
❶ⓐ **heating devices**
窯 KILN → 2361
缶 steam boiler → 2033

4-4 火

炊
870 SUI ta(ku) -da(ki)

CH 炊 chuī

Radical	Strokes
火 86	8-4-4
Grade	Freq
Jōyō	1798
1-4-4	

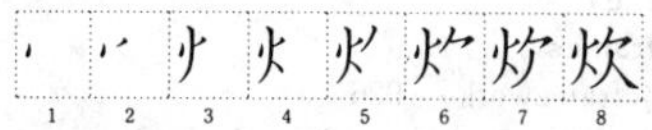

▶COOK

COMPOUNDS
● [original meaning] **cook, boil**
炊事 *suiji* cooking
炊婦 *suifu* cook, kitchenmaid
自炊 *jisui* cooking food for oneself

KUN
【**ta(ku)** 炊く】cook, boil
炊き込み御飯 *takikomigohan* rice seasoned and cooked with various ingredients
炊き出し *takidashi* distribution of boiled rice (in emergency)
飯炊き *meshitaki* cooking rice; kitchenmaid, cook
煮炊き *nitaki* cooking
【**-da(ki)** -炊き】suffix indicating cooking capacity
一リットル炊きの *ichirittorudaki no* having a cooking capacity of one liter

SYNONYMS
● **cook**
煮 BOIL (cook by boiling) → 2785
沸 BOIL (undergo boiling) → 329
蒸 STEAM → 2334
焼く cook by fire → 997
揚げる fry in deep fat → 593

USAGE
taku
炊く
cook, boil
焚く
burn, kindle, build a fire

HOMOPHONES
taku ⇨ 焚 2778

狀 ▶**FORM** ▶**CONDITION** ▶**LETTER** 4-4 片
871
nonstandard for 状 272

版 版 版 ㊥ 版 bǎn 4-4 片
872 HAN

Radical	Strokes
片 91	8-4-4
Grade	**Freq**
Jōyō-5	965

◧ 1 - 4 - 4

Stroke order: 丿 丿 𠂆 片 片 片 版 版 (1–8)

▶**PRINTING PLATE** ▶**PUBLISHING**

COMPOUNDS
❶ [sometimes also 板 858] [also suffix] **printing plate, printing block, wood block**
版木 *hangi* (printing) block, woodcut
版画 *hanga* woodcut print
活版 *kappan* printing, typography
凸版 *toppan* letterpress, relief printing
木版 *mokuhan* wood block printing, wood engraving
原色版 *genshokuban* heliotype
謄写版 *tōshaban* mimeograph
❷ **publishing, printing**
版行する *hankō suru* publish, print
版元 *hanmoto* publisher
版権 *hanken* copyright
出版 *shuppan* publishing; publication
再版する *saihan suru* reprint
❸ⓐ [also suffix] **edition, impression, printing**
ⓑ counter for editions
初版 *shohan* first edition
重版 *jūhan* second printing, reprint; second edition
地方版 *chihōban* local edition
決定版 *ketteiban* authoritative edition; last word
第二版 *dainihan* second edition
❹ household or population register
版図 *hanto* territory

INDEPENDENT
【**han** 版】printing block, plate; edition, impression, printing
版を改める *han o aratameru* revise an edition

SYNONYMS
❶ **printing plate**
梓 printing block → 962
❷ **print and publish**
刊 PUBLISH → 190
刷 PRINT → 1273
印 print → 828
植 typeset → 990
載 PUT IN PRINT → 3300
掲 display in writing → 494
❸ **editions**
刊 publication → 190
訂 revision → 1442
刷 printing → 1273

4-4 牛

牧 牧 牧

873 BOKU maki

CH 牧 mù

Radical	Strokes
牛 93	8-4-4
Grade	**Freq**
Jōyō-4	1187
◧ 1 - 4 - 4	

丿 𠂉 牛 牛 牜 牞 牧 牧
1 2 3 4 5 6 7 8

▶**PASTURE**

COMPOUNDS

❶ [original meaning] (put cattle to pasture) **pasture, tend cattle, herd, shepherd, raise cattle**

牧畜 *bokuchiku* livestock farming, cattle breeding
牧歌的な *bokkateki na* pastoral, idyllic
牧童 *bokudō* cowboy; shepherd
牧人 *bokujin* shepherd, herdsman
牧羊 *bokuyō* sheep farming
放牧する *hōboku suru* pasture, put to grass, graze
遊牧 *yūboku* nomadism

❷ (give guidance to) shepherd, lead, govern

牧師 *bokushi* pastor, minister, priest
牧民 *bokumin* [archaic] shepherding [governing] the people

❸ **pasture, grazing land, meadow**

牧場 *bokujō* stock farm, pasture
牧草 *bokusō* pasture, grass
牧野 *bokuya* pasture land, ranch
放牧地 *hōbokuchi* grazing land, pasture

KUN

【**maki** 牧】 pasture

牧場 *makiba* pasture, grazing land, meadow
牧を駈ける駒 *maki o kakeru koma* horse galloping in the pasture

SYNONYMS

❶ **raise and nourish**

飼 RAISE ANIMALS → 1716
養 FOSTER → 2365
育 RAISE → 2050
滋 NOURISH → 602

❸ **cultivated fields**

畑 FIELD → 905
園 GARDEN → 3156
田 RICE FIELD → 3041
甫 vegetable garden → 3549

4-4 牛

物 物 物

874 BUTSU MOTSU mono mono-

CH 物 wù

Radical	Strokes
牛 93	8-4-4
Grade	**Freq**
Jōyō-3	123
◧ 1 - 4 - 4	

丿 𠂉 牛 牛 牜 牞 物 物
1 2 3 4 5 6 7 8

▶**THING**

COMPOUNDS

❶ⓐ [also suffix] (inanimate material entity) **thing, object, article**
ⓑ (animate entity) **living thing, life**
ⓒ [also suffix] **commodity, goods, product**

物品 *buppin* goods, article, commodity
物体 *buttai* body, physical solid, object, substance
物的な *butteki na* material, physical
現物 *genbutsu* (actual) thing; spot goods
見物 *kenbutsu* sightseeing, visit
実物 *jitsubutsu* real thing, actual object, genuine article
風物 *fūbutsu* natural objects [features], scenery; scenes and manners
荷物 *nimotsu* baggage, load
書物 *shomotsu* book, volume
障害物 *shōgaibutsu* obstacle, hurdle
動物 *dōbutsu* animal
植物 *shokubutsu* plant, vegetation
生物 *seibutsu* living thing, life, organism
物価 *bukka* prices (of commodities)
物資 *busshi* commodities, goods, resources
物産 *bussan* product, produce
名物 *meibutsu* specialty, noted product
産物 *sanbutsu* product, produce
貨物 *kamotsu* freight, cargo, goods
穀物 *kokumotsu* grain, cereals
出版物 *shuppanbutsu* publication

❷ [also suffix] **substance, matter, material**

物質 *busshitsu* matter, substance
鉱物 *kōbutsu* mineral substance
毒物 *dokubutsu* poisonous substance, toxin
薬物 *yakubutsu* drugs, medicinal substances
化合物 *kagōbutsu* (chemical) compound
有機物 *yūkibutsu* organic matter
塩化物 *enkabutsu* chloride

❸ⓐ (abstract entity) **thing(s), matter, affair, something**
ⓑ **physical phenomena, material world, reality**
物情 *butsujō* public feeling
物騒な *bussō na* dangerous, insecure, disturbed
禁物 *kinmotsu* taboo, prohibited thing
物理 *butsuri* physics; natural law
物象 *busshō* material phenomena; science of inanimate nature
博物学 *hakubutsugaku* natural history
❹ (person distinguished by some characteristic) **character, person, man**
人物 *jinbutsu* character; person, figure
難物 *nanbutsu* hard character, person hard to please; hard nut to crack, difficulty
俗物 *zokubutsu* worldly(-minded) person, snob, worldling, Philistine
傑物 *ketsubutsu* great man, outstanding figure
❺ select according to one's judgment, judge
物色する *busshoku suru* look for, pick out
物議 *butsugi* public criticism [censure], public discussion
❻ die
物故 *bukko* death
❼ [usu. 勿 *mot-* 2943] used phonetically for *motsu*
物体 *mottai* air of importance, superior airs
物体無い *mottainai* wasteful; be more than one deserves
物怪の幸い *mokke no saiwai* piece of good luck, windfall

INDEPENDENT

【butsu 物】 *slang* loot, hot goods; abbrev. of 物理学 *butsurigaku*: physics
物を質入れする *butsu o shichiire suru* pawn hot goods

KUN

【mono 物】
①ⓐ [also suffix] (inanimate material entity) thing, object, article, something
ⓑ [also suffix] commodity, goods, product
ⓒ possession, property
物置き *monooki* storeroom
物陰 *monokage* place behind something
建物 *tatemono* building, structure
品物 *shinamono* article, thing, goods
本物 *honmono* real thing [stuff], genuine article; expert performance
贈り物 *okurimono* present, gift
織物 *orimono* cloth, textile, fabric
読み物 *yomimono* reading matter, book
洗濯物 *sentakumono* wash, washing, laundry
売り物 *urimono* article for sale, offerings
近海物 *kinkaimono* shorefish, inshore catch
ハウス物 *hausumono* vegetables grown in a hothouse
学校の物 *gakkō no mono* school property
② [also suffix] thing(s), matter, something, act
物語 *monogatari* story, tale, legend
物事 *monogoto* things, matter; everything
物知り *monoshiri* well-informed person, walking dictionary
物思い *monoomoi* reverie, meditation, anxiety
笑い物 *waraimono* object of ridicule, subject of derision
催し物 *moyōshimono* (program of) entertainments, amusements
買い物 *kaimono* shopping, marketing; purchase
捕り物 *torimono* capture, arrest
噴飯物 *funpanmono* something that makes one laugh, quite absurd thing
③ something, somebody, a success
物に成る *mono ni naru* come to good, prove successful
物の数に入らない *mono no kazu ni hairanai* be insignificant, be off the map
物ともせずに *mono to mo sezu ni* in defiance of, in the face of
大物 *ōmono* great man, big shot
④ reason, sense
物の分かった *mono no wakatta* sensible, fair-minded
物心 *monogokoro* judgment, discretion

【mono- 物-】 somehow, in some way or other
物凄い *monosugoi* ghastly, weird; terrible, tremendous
物足りない *monotarinai* be somehow unsatisfied, feel something wanting; be unsatisfactory
物悲しい *monoganashii* sad, melancholy

SYNONYMS

❶ⓐ object
品 ARTICLE → 2248
体 BODY → 71
ⓑ animal
生 LIFE → 3497
獣 BEAST → 1892
畜 LIVESTOCK → 2096
ⓒ merchandise
貨 GOODS → 2465
品 ARTICLE (of merchandise) → 2248
産 product → 3298
❷ matter
質 MATTER → 2808
材 MATERIAL → 836
料 MATERIALS → 1292
資 material resources → 2695
❸ⓐ abstract thing
事 ABSTRACT THING → 3567
ⓑ phenomenon
気 natural phenomenon → 3194

象 PHENOMENON → 2134
❹ **fellow**
屋 colloquial person suffix → 3098
坊 COLLOQUIAL PERSON SUFFIX → 233
棒 tough guy → 983
奴 GUY → 187
漢 FELLOW → 657
輩 FELLOW (*belittling*) → 2807
徒 fellows → 416

USAGE

mono
物
①ⓐ [also suffix] (inanimate material entity) thing, object, article, something
ⓑ [also suffix] commodity, goods, product
ⓒ possession, property
② [also suffix] thing(s), matter, something, act
③ something, somebody, a success
④ reason, sense

者
person, fellow, somebody

HOMOPHONES

mono ⇨ 者 3211

4-4
ネ

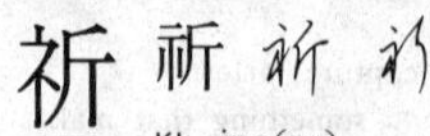
875 KI ino(ru)

Ⓒ祈 qí

Radical	Strokes
ネ 113	8-4-4
Grade	**Freq**
Jōyō	1492
1-4-4	

▶PRAY

COMPOUNDS

● [original meaning] **pray**
祈禱 *kitō* prayer
祈願する *kigan suru* pray, implore
祈念 *kinen* prayer

KUN

【**ino(ru) 祈る**】[formerly also 禱る] pray, wish for
祈り *inori* prayer
祈り求める *inorimotomeru* pray for

SYNONYMS

● **pray and worship**
願 pray → 1845
拝 WORSHIP → 303
崇 REVERENCE → 2297
斎 OBSERVE RELIGIOUS ABSTINENCE → 2115

USAGE

❶ **inoru**
祈る
[formerly also 禱る] pray, wish for
禱る
[now usu. 祈る] pray, wish for

❷ **inori**
祈り
[formerly also 禱り] prayer
禱り
[now usu. 祈り] prayer

HOMOPHONES

inoru ⇨ 禱 1253
inori ⇨ 禱 1253

4-4
ネ

祉
876 SHI

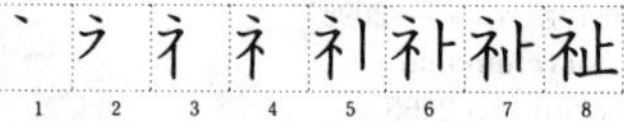

Ⓒ祉 zhǐ

Radical	Strokes
ネ 113	8-4-4
Grade	**Freq**
Jōyō	1365
1-4-4	

▶BLESSEDNESS

COMPOUNDS

● [original meaning] **blessedness, happiness**
祉福 *shifuku* [archaic] happiness, prosperity; blessedness and joy
福祉 *fukushi* welfare

SYNONYMS

● **happiness**
幸 HAPPINESS → 2216
福 FORTUNE → 1029

肪 877 BŌ

Ⓒ 肪 fáng

Radical	Strokes
月 130	8-4-4
Grade	**Freq**
Jōyō	1829
◧ 1 - 4 - 4	

4-4 月

丿 ⺆ 月 月 月' 月亠 肪 肪
1 2 3 4 5 6 7 8

▶**ANIMAL FAT**

COMPOUNDS

● [original meaning] **animal fat, fat**
脂肪 *shibō* fat, grease

SYNONYMS

● **fats and oils**
脂 FAT → 954
油 OIL → 341

服 878 FUKU

Ⓒ 服 fú fù

Radical	Strokes
月 74	8-4-4
Grade	**Freq**
Jōyō-3	733
◧ 1 - 4 - 4	

4-4 月

丿 ⺆ 月 月 月⁷ 肙 服 服
1 2 3 4 5 6 7 8

▶**CLOTHES** ▶**SUBMIT**

COMPOUNDS

❶ⓐ [also suffix] **clothes, clothing, dress, costume**
ⓑ put on clothes, don
服装 *fukusō* dress, garments, attire
服飾 *fukushoku* dress and its ornaments
洋服 *yōfuku* (Western) clothes
呉服 *gofuku* dry goods; drapery
制服 *seifuku* uniform, regulation uniform
衣服 *ifuku* clothes, dress, clothing
紳士服 *shinshifuku* men's suit
宇宙服 *uchūfuku* spacesuit
元服 *genpuku* ceremony of attaining manhood
❷ⓐ [also 伏 45] **submit to, yield to, surrender; obey, observe**
ⓑ cause to submit
服罪 *fukuzai* submitting to a sentence
服従 *fukujū* obedience, submission
屈服する *kuppuku suru* bend in submission, submit to, surrender, yield to
承服 *shōfuku* consent, acceptance
感服 *kanpuku* admiration, wonder
征服 *seifuku* conquest, subjugation
克服する *kokufuku suru* conquer, overcome, subjugate
❸ serve, discharge one's duties
服役 *fukueki* penal servitude; military service
服務 *fukumu* duty, public service
❹ⓐ **take (medicine or tea)**
ⓑ counter for packets of medicine, sips (of tea) or puffs (of smoke)
服用する *fukuyō suru* take (medicine)
服毒する *fukudoku suru* take poison
内服薬 *naifukuyaku* medicine for internal use
一服 *ippuku* a dose (of medicine); a puff [whiff] (of a cigarette); a sip (of tea); rest; lull, calm market
❺ appropriate, embezzle
着服する *chakufuku suru* embezzle, misappropriate
❻ mourning
服喪する *fukumo suru* go into mourning
除服する *jofuku suru* come out of mourning

INDEPENDENT

【fuku 服】 clothes, clothing, dress, costume
【fukusuru 服する】 submit to, yield; obey, observe; admit; serve, discharge one's duties; take, drink

SYNONYMS

❶ⓐ **clothing**
-着 wear → 3316
衣 GARMENT → 2013
装 DRESS → 2685
❷ **submit and surrender**
伏 submit → 45
屈 bend in submission → 3079
降 surrender → 458
❹ⓐ **ingest**
喫 INGEST → 551
飲 DRINK → 1692
食 EAT → 2075

NOTE

⇨ see COMPOUND FORMATION for 元服 *genpuku* ⇨ 元 1929

4-4
月

肥 肥 肥

879 HI ko(eru) koe ko(yasu) ko(yashi) futo(ru)▲

Ⓒⓗ 肥 féi

Radical	Strokes
月 130	8-4-4
Grade	Freq
Jōyō-5	1287
◧ 1-4-4	

丿 1 刀 2 月 3 月 4 月⁻ 5 月⁻ 6 月ᄀ 7 肥 8

▶**FATTEN**

COMPOUNDS

❶ **fatten, fat up, grow fat, make fat**
肥大した *hidai shita* fat, enlarged
肥満する *himan suru* become obese
肥馬 *hiba* fat horse
肥育 *hiiku* fattening

❷ⓐ **fatten the soil, fertilize, enrich**
ⓑ (of land) fat, fertile, rich
ⓒ **fertilizer**
施肥 *sehi* fertilization, manuring
肥沃な *hiyoku na* fertile, productive
肥料 *hiryō* fertilizer, manure
堆肥 *taihi* barnyard manure
金肥 *kinpi* chemical fertilizer

❸ old name for Nagasaki, Saga and Kumamoto prefectures
豊肥本線 *hōhi honsen* Hohi Main Line (Oita-Kumamoto Railway)

KUN

【ko(eru) 肥える】 fatten, grow fat, grow fertile; have a trained (eye or ear)
肥え太る *koefutoru* grow fat
耳が肥えている *mimi ga koete iru* have an ear for music

【koe 肥】 manure, fertilizer; night soil
肥汲み *koekumi* carrying night soil; night soil man
肥溜め *koedame* night soil vat

【ko(yasu) 肥やす】 manure, fertilize; fatten; enrich oneself
馬を肥やす *uma o koyasu* fatten a horse
私腹を肥やす *shifuku o koyasu* fill [stuff] one's own pocket by taking advantage of a position

【ko(yashi) 肥やし】 manure; night soil
肥やし桶 *koyashioke* night soil pail

【futo(ru) 肥る】 [usu. 太る] grow fat, fatten, gain weight
肥った *futotta* fat, stout, plump

SYNONYMS

❶ **fatten**
太る grow fat → 2152

HOMOPHONES

futoru ⇨ 太 2152

NOTE

⇨ see USAGE note at 太 2152

4-4
月

朋 朋 朋 朋

880 HŌ NAMES tomo

Ⓒⓗ 朋 péng

Radical	Strokes
月 74	8-4-4
Grade	Freq
Names	2028
◧ 1-4-4	

丿 1 刀 2 月 3 月 4 月丿 5 月刀 6 朋 7 朋 8

▶**COMRADE**

COMPOUNDS

❶ **comrade, friend, companion, mate, fellow**
朋友 *hōyū* friend, companion
朋輩 *hōbai* comrade, friend, associate

❷ clique, group
朋党 *hōtō* faction, clique

NAMES

朋子 *tomoko* female name
朋広 *tomohiro* male name

SYNONYMS

❶ **friends and associates**
友 FRIEND → 2952
輩 FELLOW → 2807
僚 COLLEAGUE → 165

股

881 KO mata

Ⓒⓗ 股 gǔ

Radical	Strokes
月 130	8-4-4
Grade	Freq
Reference	
1 - 4 - 4	

4-4 月

COMPOUNDS

● [original meaning] crotch (of the human body), thigh

股関節 *kokansetsu* coxa

股肱 *kokō* one's right-hand man, one's trusted henchman

四股 *shiko* stamping on the sumo ring

股旅 *matatabi* wandering life of a gambler

股に掛ける *mata ni kakeru* travel all over, be active in places widely apart

内股 *uchimata* inside of a thigh; pigeon-toe; throwing down the opponent with one's leg between his [her] legs (in judo)

HOMOPHONES

mata ⇨ 叉 3386

肢 䏻 彶

882 SHI

丿 1   冂 2   月 3   月 4   月一 5   月十 6   肢 7   肢 8

Ⓒⓗ 肢 zhī

Radical	Strokes
月 130	8-4-4
Grade	Freq
Jōyō	1952
1 - 4 - 4	

4-4 月

▶**LIMB**

COMPOUNDS

ⓐ [original meaning] (human or animal appendage) **limb, member, arm or leg**

ⓑ (subdivision) limb, branch

肢体 *shitai* limbs, members

下肢 *kashi* lower limbs, legs

四肢 *shishi* limbs, legs and arms

前肢 *zenshi* forelimb, front leg

多肢選択式試問 *tashi-sentakushiki-shimon* multiple-choice question

選択肢 *sentakushi* choices (of a multiple choice test)

SYNONYMS

ⓐ **limbs**

腕 ARM → 1006

脚 LEG → 974

胏

883

▶**LUNG**

nonstandard for 肺 916

4-4 月

服

884

▶**CLOTHES** ▶**SUBMIT**

nonstandard for 服 878

4-4 月

朋

885

▶**COMRADE**

nonstandard for 朋 880

4-4 月

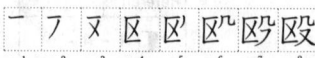

4-4 区

殴 毆 886 Ō nagu(ru)

CH 殴 ōu

Radical	Strokes
殳 79	8-4-4
Grade	**Freq**
Jōyō	1854
1 - 4 - 4	

▶**BEAT**

COMPOUNDS

● [original meaning] (strike a person) **beat (up), hit, strike, thrash**

殴打 *ōda* blow, beating
殴殺する *ōsatsu suru* beat to death

KUN

【nagu(ru) 殴る】 beat up, beat, hit, strike, thrash

殴り倒す *naguritaosu* knock down
殴り合う *naguriau* fight, exchange blows
殴り込み *nagurikomi* attack, raid
横殴り *yokonaguri* side sweep, side blow
書き殴る *kakinaguru* write [scribble] off

SYNONYMS

● **strike**

撲 DEAL A BLOW → 733
打 STRIKE → 193
撃 STRIKE → 2863
当てる HIT → 2177
拍 BEAT (strike repeatedly) → 304

4-4 区

欧 歐 887 Ō

CH 欧 ōu

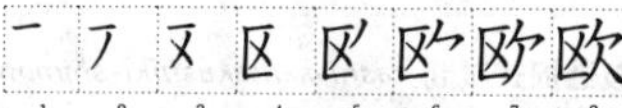

Radical	Strokes
欠 76	8-4-4
Grade	**Freq**
Jōyō	693
1 - 4 - 4	

▶**EUROPE**

COMPOUNDS

● **Europe**

欧州 *ōshū* Europe
欧米 *ōbei* Europe and America
欧亜 *ōa* Europe and Asia
欧文 *ōbun* foreign text
全欧 *zen'ō* the whole of Europe
西欧 *seiō* West Europe, the Occident
東欧 *tōō* East Europe

INDEPENDENT

【ō 欧】 Europe

SYNONYMS

● **continents**

米 AMERICA → 3529
豪 Australia → 2140
亜 Asia → 3540
阿 Africa → 346

4-4 门

門 门 888 MON kado

CH 门 mén

Radical	Strokes
門 169	8-8-0
Grade	**Freq**
Jōyō-2	435
1 - 4 - 4	

RADICAL 169

Standard form: 門 *mon* or *mongamae* 'gate' (間 開 関)
Description: used in characters related to gates, doors or outer enclosures

▶**GATE**

COMPOUNDS

❶ⓐ [also suffix] [original meaning] **gate, gateway, entrance, door**
ⓑ narrow orifice, esp. in the human body

門戸 *monko* door, entrance; school
門番 *monban* gatekeeper, janitor
正門 *seimon* main gate, main entrance
校門 *kōmon* school gate
通用門 *tsūyōmon* side door
門脈 *monmyaku* portal vein
肛門 *kōmon* anus

噴門 *funmon* cardia
❷ⓐ **field, branch, division**
ⓑ *biol* phylum, division, subkingdom
門外漢 *mongaikan* layman, outsider
専門 *senmon* specialty, profession
部門 *bumon* class, group, division, department, section; genus
仏門 *butsumon* Buddhism; priesthood
節足動物門 *sessoku-dōbutsumon* Arthropoda
❸ (from the idea of people gathering under the same gateway)
ⓐ (persons under same teacher) **pupil, disciple**
ⓑ **(religious) sect, branch, school**
門下生 *monkasei* disciple, pupil
門弟 *montei* pupil, disciple
入門する *nyūmon suru* become a pupil of, enter a private school
同門 *dōmon* fellow pupil
門徒 *monto* sectarian, follower, believer
破門 *hamon* excommunication, expulsion
宗門 *shūmon* religious sect
禅門 *zenmon* Zen sect
稲門 *tōmon* Waseda University
❹ family, clan
門閥 *monbatsu* (renowned) lineage, pedigree
名門 *meimon* distinguished [noted] family; prestigious establishment
一門 *ichimon* family, the whole clan
❺ counter for cannons
大砲三門 *taihō sanmon* three cannons

INDEPENDENT

【mon 門】
① gate, entrance, door
門を開ける *mon o akeru* open the gate
② (religious) sect, branch, school
A氏の門に入る *ēshi no mon ni hairu* study under Mr. A
③ *biol* phylum, division, subkingdom

KUN

【kado 門】 door, gate, gateway
門出 *kadode* departure, setting out
門口 *kadoguchi* front door, entrance, gateway
笑う門には福来たる *Warau kado ni wa fuku kitaru* Fortune comes to a merry home

SYNONYMS

❶ⓐ **doors**
戸 DOOR → 1930
扉 HINGED DOOR → 1955
口 entrance (or exit) → 3382
❷ⓐ **branch of study**
科 SUBJECT OF STUDY → 1138
学 branch of study → 2555
❸ⓐ **students and followers**
弟 disciple → 2044
徒 FOLLOWER → 416
生 STUDENT → 3497
卒 graduate student → 2055
学 scholar → 2555
ⓑ **parties and sects**
宗 RELIGIOUS SECT (esp. Buddhist) → 2228
系 faction → 1944
翼 WING → 2720
派 SECT → 381
流 school → 441
閥 CLIQUE → 3325
党 PARTY → 2581
❹ **family and relations**
家 FAMILY → 2273
族 FAMILY → 958
氏 clan → 2951
縁 RELATION → 1386
姻 relative by marriage → 353
親 RELATIVES → 1799

非

889 HI ara(zu)▲

Stroke order: 1 2 3 4 5 6 7 8

CH 非 fēi

Radical	Strokes
非 175	8-8-0
Grade	**Freq**
Jōyō-5	442
◧ 1 - 4 - 4	

4-4 ⺕

RADICAL 175

Standard form: 非 *arazu* 'not' (靠 靡)
Description: used for character classification

▶IS NOT

COMPOUNDS

❶ⓐ [also prefix] **is not, not, non-, un-, in-**—element of contrariety usu. placed before nouns
ⓑ unfavorable, unlucky
非常 *hijō* emergency, calamity
非鉄金属 *hitetsu-kinzoku* nonferrous metals
非番 *hiban* off duty
非情の *hijō no* coldhearted; inanimate
非礼 *hirei* impoliteness
非売品 *hibaihin* articles not for sale
非公式の *hikōshiki no* informal, unofficial
非金属 *hikinzoku* nonmetal

非科学的な *hikagakuteki na* unscientific
非運 *hiun* bad luck, misfortune
❷ⓐ **wrong, wrongdoing, mistake**
ⓑ **wrong, not right**
是非 *zehi* right and/or wrong; by all means, at any cost
前非 *zenpi* one's past folly [sin]
非行 *hikō* delinquency, misdeed, misdemeanor
非道い(=酷い) *hidoi* cruel, harsh, rough; severe, intense, heavy
❸ [sometimes also 誹 1572] slander, calumniate, defame
非難(=批難) *hinan* criticism, blame
非毀 *hiki* defamation
非議する *higi suru* criticize, censure

INDEPENDENT

【hi 非】 wrong, wrongdoing, mistake
非とする *hi to suru* condemn, denounce

KUN

【ara(zu) 非ず】 *literary* not
然に非ず *Sa ni arazu* Not so

SYNONYMS

❶ⓐ **terms of negation**
不 NOT (negation) → 3434
無 WITHOUT (nonexistence) → 2135
否 OR NOT → 2406
未 NOT YET → 3506
没 lacking in → 260
欠 LACK → 1987
❷ⓐ **wrongdoing and evil**
邪 wrong → 1124
罪 sin → 2610
悪 evil (something bad) → 2745
弊 evil(s) (something undesirable) → 2884

HOMOPHONES

hidoi ⇨ 酷い 1562 非道い 889, 3134

NOTE

⇨ see USAGE notes at 不 3434 and 酷 1562

4-5
手

拝 890

▶WORSHIP ▶HUMBLY
nonstandard for 拝 303

4-5
方

施 891

施 施

SHI SE hodoko(su)

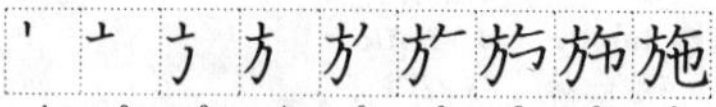
1 2 3 4 5 6 7 8 9

Ⓒⓗ 施 shī

Radical	Strokes
方 70	9-4-5
Grade	**Freq**
Jōyō	415
1-4-5	

▶CARRY OUT

COMPOUNDS

❶ **carry out, put into practice, enforce, execute, conduct**
施行する *shikō suru* enforce, execute, carry out
施工する *sekō* (=*shikō*) *suru* execute (a building contract), carry out
施術 *shijutsu* surgical operation
施策 *shisaku* enforcement of a policy
施政 *shisei* administration, government
実施する *jisshi suru* carry out, enforce, execute
❷ **give alms, give charity, dispense gratis, render services (to the needy)**
施薬 *seyaku* free medicine
施行する *segyō suru* give alms
施主 *seshu* chief mourner; donor, benefactor
施餓鬼 *segaki* service for the unmourned dead
布施 *fuse* alms
❸ **make, construct, equip**
施設 *shisetsu* equipment, facilities; institution, establishment
施条 *shijō* making lines; rifling a gun barrel
❹ apply, spread
施肥 *sehi* fertilization, manuring

KUN

【hodoko(su) 施す】
① conduct, perform, take (measures), carry out; apply
応急手当を施す *ōkyū-teate o hodokosu* give (a person) first aid
策を施す *saku o hodokosu* take measures
面目を施す *menboku o hodokosu* win honor, get credit
② give alms [charity], dispense (medicine) gratis, render services
施し *hodokoshi* alms, almsgiving

SYNONYMS

❶ **execute**
執 EXECUTE → 1680
履 FULFILL → 3171
践 IMPLEMENT → 1535
行 ACT → 212
果たす effect → 3560

遂 ACCOMPLISH → 3138
❷ **donate**
恵む give charity → 2659
寄 CONTRIBUTE → 2291
献 donate → 1785

映 映 昳

892 EI utsu(ru) utsu(su) ha(eru) -ba(e)

CH 映 yìng

Radical	Strokes
日 72	9-4-5
Grade	**Freq**
Jōyō-6	362
◧ 1-4-5	

4-5
日

丨 冂 月 日 日卜 日冖 日口 日中 映
1 2 3 4 5 6 7 8 9

▶REFLECT ▶PROJECT

COMPOUNDS

❶ **reflect, mirror, shine**
映射する *eisha suru* [rare] reflect, shine
反映 *han'ei* reflection
❷ **project (an image), screen (a film), show**
映像 *eizō* (TV) picture, image; reflection
映写 *eisha* projection
映画 *eiga* cinema, film, movie
上映する *jōei suru* screen, show, project
放映する *hōei suru* televise, telecast
❸ⓐ abbrev. of 映画 *eiga*: motion picture, movie, film
ⓑ abbrev. of 映画館 *eigakan* or 映画会社 *eigagaisha*: suffix after names of movie theaters or motion picture companies
映倫 *eirin* Motion Picture Code of Ethics Committee
映配 *eihai* film distributing company
銀映 *gin'ei* The Ginei Movie Theater
大映 *daiei* Daiei Motion Picture Company

INDEPENDENT

【eijiru (=eizuru) 映じる(=映ずる)】 be reflected, shine on; impress, appear (to)
水に映じる *mizu ni eijiru* be reflected in the water

KUN

【utsu(ru) 映る】
①ⓐ be reflected, be imaged, be mirrored
ⓑ be projected, be on (TV)
映り *utsuri* reflection; quality of a picture [film]; match, harmony
鏡に映る *kagami ni utsuru* be reflected in a mirror
② match, suit, be becoming
この色は良く映る *Kono iro wa yoku utsuru* The colors match well

【utsu(su) 映す】
① reflect, mirror
鏡に自分の姿を映す *kagami ni jibun no sugata o utsusu* reflect oneself in a mirror
② project (a motion picture)
映画をスクリーンに映す *eiga o sukurīn ni utsusu* project a motion picture on a screen
障子に影を映す *shōji ni kage o utsusu* project a shadow on a *shoji* (paper sliding-door)

【ha(eru) 映える】
① shine, excel in brilliance
照り映える *terihaeru* glow (in the sun), be lighted up
面映ゆい *omohayui* abashed, made self-conscious
② [also 栄える] look better [to advantage], go well with
映えない色 *haenai iro* dull color

【-ba(e) -映え】
① glow
夕映え *yūbae* evening [sunset] glow
② [also -栄え] looking better
代わり映えがしない *Kawaribae ga shinai* It's none the better for the change
③ [usu. -栄え] result, effect
出来映え *dekibae* result, effect, workmanship

SYNONYMS

❶ **shine and reflect**
照 ILLUMINATE → 2827
輝 SHINE BRILLIANTLY → 1402
光 shine → 2391
❷ **project**
写 project → 2000
❸ⓐ **motion picture**
画 film → 3000

USAGE

❶ **utsuri**
映り
①ⓐ reflection
ⓑ quality of a picture [film]
② match, harmony
写り
print, impression
移り
① change, transition
② return present
❷ **haeru**
映える
① shine, excel in brilliance
② [also 栄える] look better [to advantage], go well with
栄える

[also 映える] look better [to advantage], go well with
❸ **-bae**
-映え
① glow
② [also -栄え] looking better
③ [usu. -栄え] result, effect
-栄え
① [also -映え] looking better
② [sometimes also -映え] result, effect

HOMOPHONES
utsuru ⇨ 写 2000 移 1177
utsuri ⇨ 写 2000 移 1177
utsusu ⇨ 写 2000 移 1177
haeru ⇨ 栄 2574
-bae ⇨ 栄 2574

NOTE
⇨ see also USAGE note at 写 2000

4-5
日

昨
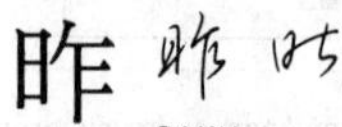
893 SAKU

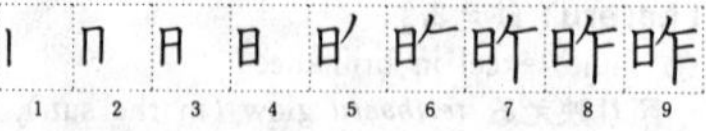

CH 昨 zuó

Radical	Strokes
日 72	9-4-5
Grade	**Freq**
Jōyō-4	288
1-4-5	

▶YESTERDAY ▶LAST

COMPOUNDS
❶ⓐ [also prefix] **yesterday, yesterday's**
ⓑ yesteryear
昨日 ***sakujitsu*** yesterday
昨晩 ***sakuban*** last night, last evening
昨紙 ***sakushi*** yesterday's paper
昨五月二日 ***saku-gogatsu futsuka*** yesterday, May 2
昨今 ***sakkon*** these days
❷ⓐ (most recent) **last (year, etc.)**
ⓑ [prefix] last year's, of last year
昨年 ***sakunen*** last year
昨春 ***sakushun*** last spring
一昨昨日 ***issakusakujitsu*** three days ago
昨昭和五十五年 ***saku-shōwa gojūgonen*** last year, 1980

SPECIAL READINGS
昨日 ***kinō*** yesterday
昨夜▲ ***yūbe*** last night, last evening
一昨日▲ ***ototoi*** day before yesterday

SYNONYMS
❶ⓐ **yesterday and today**
今 today → 1968
❷ⓐ **most recent**
去 last → 2156
先 last → 2394

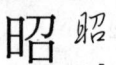

4-5
日

昭
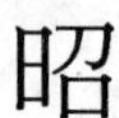
894 SHŌ

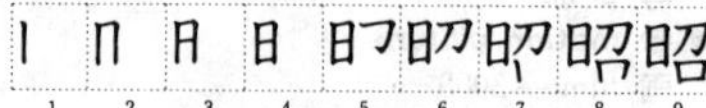

CH 昭 zhāo

Radical	Strokes
日 72	9-4-5
Grade	**Freq**
Jōyō-3	569
1-4-5	

▶LUMINOUS

COMPOUNDS
❶ⓐ [original meaning, now rare] (emitting light) luminous, bright, shining
ⓑ (enjoying the glory of enlightened rule) **enlightened, glorious, illustrious**
昭昭たる ***shōshōtaru*** [rare] bright, clear; obvious, plain
昭代 ***shōdai*** enlightened era, glorious reign
昭和 ***shōwa*** Showa era
❷ [archaic] (clearly intelligible) luminous, clear, obvious, evident
昭然たる ***shōzentaru*** clear, manifest
❸ abbrev. of 昭和 ***shōwa***: **Showa era**
昭電 ***shōden*** Showa Denko (name of a company)

INDEPENDENT
【**shō 昭**】abbrev. of 昭和 ***shōwa***: Showa era
昭五十六年 ***shō gojūrokunen*** fifty-sixth year of the Showa era (1981)

SYNONYMS
❶ **bright**
明 BRIGHT → 855
蛍 fluorescent → 2591
晃 DAZZLING → 2450

COMPOUND FORMATION
昭和 *shōwa*
昭和 'Showa era' refers to the era of enlightenment (昭 ❶ⓑ) and peace (和). It is the name of the Japanese era beginning in 1926.

旺
▶**DAY OF THE WEEK**
handwritten abbreviation for 曜 1096

895 | 4-5 日

柱 柱 柱 柱
896 CHŪ hashira

Ⓒ柱 zhù

Radical	Strokes
木 75	9-4-5
Grade	Freq
Jōyō-3	1313
1 - 4 - 5	

4-5 木

一 十 才 木 木 杧 杧 柱 柱 (1 2 3 4 5 6 7 8 9)

▶**PILLAR**

COMPOUNDS

❶ⓐ [original meaning] **pillar, post, column, pole**
ⓑ something shaped like a pillar
ⓒ *mining* pillar, post
石柱 *sekichū* stone pillar
円柱 *enchū* column, shaft, cylinder
電柱 *denchū* telegraph [telephone, electric] pole
門柱 *monchū* gate post, pier
氷柱 *hyōchū* icicle; block [square pillar] of ice
炭柱 *tanchū* coal pillar
鉱柱 *kōchū* pillar, rib
残柱 *zanchū* pillar
❷ [also suffix] *math* cylinder
柱面 *chūmen* cylindrical surface
直円柱 *chokuenchū* right cylinder
❸ something that supports like a pillar; mainstay, prop
支柱 *shichū* prop, stay, support
国家の柱石 *kokka no chūseki* pillar of state

INDEPENDENT

【chū 柱】 *math* cylinder

KUN

【hashira 柱】 [also suffix] pillar, post, column; prop, mainstay; adductor (of bivalves); counter for gods
柱時計 *hashiradokei* grandfather's clock
大黒柱 *daikokubashira* principal post, central pillar (of a house); prop, mainstay
貝柱 *kaibashira* adductor muscle
三柱の神 *mihashira no kami* three gods

SYNONYMS

❶ **supporting structures**
礎 FOUNDATION STONE → 1248

柄 柄 柄 柄
897 HEI gara[1] gara[2] e tsuka▲

Ⓒ柄 bǐng bìng

Radical	Strokes
木 75	9-4-5
Grade	Freq
Jōyō	953
1 - 4 - 5	

4-5 木

一 十 才 木 木 杧 柄 柄 柄 (1 2 3 4 5 6 7 8 9)

▶**CHARACTER** ▶**HANDLE**

COMPOUNDS

❶ [original meaning] **handle, handhold, grip**
柄杓 *hishaku* ladle, dipper, scoop
葉柄 *yōhei* leafstalk, stipe
❷ (ability to handle) authority, power
権柄 *kenpei* power, authority
横柄な *ōhei na* overbearing, arrogant
❸ (handling of a specific subject) topic
話柄 *wahei* subject, topic (of conversation)

KUN

【gara[1] 柄】
①ⓐ [in compounds] [also suffix] character, nature, quality, fineness, grade; social standing, status
ⓑ [suffix] considering the character of (the matter in question), in view of; in character, appropriate to
人柄 *hitogara* character, personality
役柄 *yakugara* nature [quality] of one's office, one's position
作柄 *sakugara* harvest, crop; quality (of an artistic production)
事柄 *kotogara* matter, affair, circumstances
身柄 *migara* one's person; social standing
間柄 *aidagara* relation, terms
家柄 *iegara* social standing of a family; lineage, descent; good family
身分柄 *mibungara* social standing, status
仕事柄 *shigotogara* character of work; because of [in connection with] one's work
時局柄 *jikyokugara* in view of the present sit-

uation
時節柄の贈り物 *jisetsugara no okurimono* seasonable gift
② [in compounds] pattern (on cloth), design, figure
柄物 *garamono* patterned cloth
花柄 *hanagara* flower pattern
③ [in compounds] physique, build
小柄 *kogara* small build, short stature
④ [in compounds] shaft
矢柄 *yagara* shaft of an arrow
【gara² 柄】
①ⓐ character (of a person), nature, breeding
ⓑ in character, becoming
柄の悪い *gara no warui* ill-bred
柄にも無く *gara ni mo naku* unlike one, out of one's way
彼はそんな事を言う柄じゃない *Kare wa sonna koto o iu gara ja nai* It's out of character of him to say such a thing
② pattern (on cloth), design, figure
流行の柄 *ryūkō no gara* pattern now in fashion
【e 柄】 handle, crank, grip, haft; shaft
柄の長い柄杓 *e no nagai hishaku* long-handled ladle
長柄 *nagae* long handle, long shaft
取り柄 *torie* merit, worth, recommendable feature
【tsuka 柄】 hilt, handle
柄頭 *tsukagashira* pommel

SYNONYMS

❶ &【e】 handles
手 handle → 3456
把 GRIP → 249
【gara¹】
①ⓐ **nature and character**
格 (good) character → 926
性 NATURE → 299
気 temperament → 3194
質 QUALITY → 2808
品 grade of excellence → 2248
ⓑ **aspect**
上 from the viewpoint of → 3404
面 side → 2087
② **pattern**
模 PATTERN (decorative design) → 1050
文 decorative pattern → 1962
様 pattern → 1052
紋 figure → 1299

USAGE

tsuka
柄
hilt, handle
束
① hand breadth
② short support
③ bulk (of a book)

HOMOPHONES

tsuka ⇨ 束 3554

COMPOUND FORMATION

❶ 事柄 *kotogara*
事柄 'matter, affair, circumstances' refers to the nature (柄 *gara*¹ ①ⓐ) of a matter (事).
❷ 取り柄 *torie*
取り柄 'merit, worth, recommendable feature' probably comes from the idea of something (柄 *e*) worthwhile holding on to (取).

4-5
木

枯

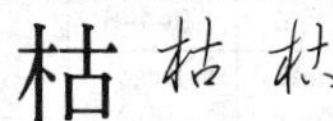

898 KO ka(reru) ka(rasu)

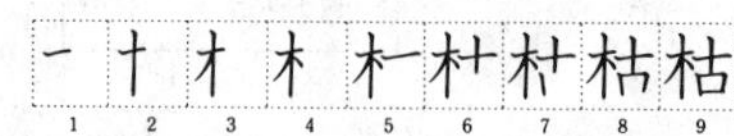

Ⓒⓗ 枯 kū

Radical	Strokes
木 75	9-4-5
Grade	**Freq**
Jōyō	1680
1 - 4 - 5	

▶WITHER

COMPOUNDS

❶ⓐ (of plants) (dry up and die) **wither, die**
ⓑ (loss vigor) **wither, decline**
枯死 *koshi* withering, dying
栄枯盛衰 *eikoseisui* prosperity and decline, rise and fall
❷ [formerly also 涸 517] **dry up, run dry**
枯渇 *kokatsu* drying up, running dry; exhaustion, depletion
❸ seasoned, refined
枯淡 *kotan* seasoned [refined] simplicity

KUN

【ka(reru) 枯れる】
① wither, die
枯れ葉 *kareha* dead [withered] leaf
枯れ野 *kareno* desolate [dreary] field
立ち枯れの *tachigare no* blighted, withered
夏枯れ *natsugare* summer inactivity, summer slump
② be seasoned
枯れた演技 *kareta engi* well-seasoned acting
【ka(rasu) 枯らす】
① kill, blight, let wither
木枯らし *kogarashi* cold wintry wind
② season

SYNONYMS

❶ⓐ decay

朽 DECAY → 821
腐 ROT → 3162
ⓐ **die**
死 DIE → 3521
没 die → 260
亡 DECEASE → 3402
去 pass away → 2156
逝 DEPART THIS LIFE → 3104
殉 DIE A MARTYR → 941

USAGE

❶ **kareru**
枯れる
① wither, die
② be seasoned
涸れる
dry up, run dry, be exhausted

❷ **karasu**
枯らす
① kill, blight, let wither
② season
涸らす
dry up, exhaust

HOMOPHONES

kareru ⇨ 涸 517
karasu ⇨ 涸 517

柳 柳 柳

899 RYŪ yanagi

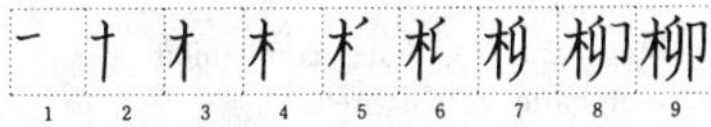

Ⓒⓗ 柳 liǔ

Radical	Strokes
木 75	9-4-5
Grade	**Freq**
Jōyō	1039
◧ 1 - 4 - 5	

4-5 木

▶WILLOW

COMPOUNDS

❶ [original meaning] **willow**
蒲柳 *horyū* purple willow; infirmity, delicate constitution
花柳 *karyū* geisha girls, courtesans; red-light district
花柳界 *karyūkai* red-light district
❷ as slender or graceful as a willow
柳眉 *ryūbi* beautiful eyebrows
❸ unclassified compounds
川柳 *senryū* short humorous verse, satirical poem

KUN

【**yanagi** 柳】 willow
柳腰 *yanagigoshi* slim waist

SYNONYMS

❶ **trees**
楓 MAPLE → 1015
松 PINE → 864
杉 CRYPTOMERIA → 832
槙 PODOCARPUS → 1051
楠 CAMPHOR TREE → 1018
桐 PAULOWNIA → 937
桂 AROMATIC TREE, katsura tree → 928
梓 CATALPA → 962
桑 MULBERRY → 2112
漆 Japanese lacquer tree → 704
桜 CHERRY → 931

COMPOUND FORMATION

❶ 花柳 *karyū*
花柳 'geisha girls, etc.' literally "blossoms (花) and willows (柳 ❶)," is a poetic term for courtesan.
❷ 川柳 *senryū*
川柳 'short humorous verse, satirical poem' derives from its originator's name and is unrelated to its constituent components 柳 'willow' and 川 'river'.

相 相 相

900 SŌ SHŌ ai-

一 十 才 木 札 机 相 相 相
1 2 3 4 5 6 7 8 9

Ⓒⓗ 相 xiāng xiàng

Radical	Strokes
目 109	9-5-4
Grade	**Freq**
Jōyō-3	58
◧ 1 - 4 - 5	

4-5 木

▶PHASE ▶MUTUAL ▶MINISTER

COMPOUNDS

❶ⓐ (outer appearance or state, esp. as indication of characteristic essence) **phase, looks, appearance, aspect, state, condition**
ⓑ *chem, astron, phys* phase
ⓒ *elec* phase; counter for phases
ⓓ *geol* facies
ⓔ [also suffix] *gram* aspect (of verbs)

様相 *yōsō* aspect, phase, condition
時代相 *jidaisō* phases of the times
貧相な *hinsō na* poor-looking
寝相 *nezō* one's sleeping posture
色相 *shikisō* color phase
世相 *sesō* phases [aspect] of life, social conditions
真相 *shinsō* truth, facts, real situation
諸相 *shosō* various aspects, various phases
実相 *jissō* real state of affairs
位相 *isō* phase, topology
気相 *kisō* gaseous phase
月相 *gessō* phase of the moon
分相機 *bunsōki* phase splitter
三相電動機 *sansō-dendōki* three-phase motor
層相 *sōsō* facies
進行相 *shinkōsō* progressive aspect

❷ⓐ **physiognomy**
ⓑ read a person's physiognomy; [original meaning] observe carefully
人相 *ninsō* looks, physiognomy
手相 *tesō* palmistry, lines of palm
骨相 *kossō* physique
家相 *kasō* physiognomy of a house
観相学 *kansōgaku* physiognomy

❸ **mutual, reciprocal; mutually**
相互の *sōgo no* mutual, reciprocal
相談 *sōdan* consultation
相当する *sōtō suru* correspond to, be proportionate; be suitable for, become
相違 *sōi* difference, disparity
相対 *sōtai* relativity
相応な *sōō na* suitable, fit; becoming; adequate
相殺 *sōsai* offset, cancellation
相関 *sōkan* mutual relationship, correlation
相似 *sōji* similarity, resemblance
相思相愛 *sōshisōai* mutual love

❹ [also suffix] **minister (of state), councilor**
首相 *shushō* prime minister
蔵相 *zōshō* Minister of Finance
文相 *bunshō* Minister of Education, Science and Culture
外相 *gaishō* Minister of Foreign Affairs
労働相 *rōdōshō* Minister of Labor

❺ succeed to, inherit
相続 *sōzoku* succession, descent
相伝 *sōden* inheritance

❻ⓐ used phonetically for *sō*
ⓑ function word indicating appearance
相場 *sōba* market price; estimation
可哀相な *kawaisō na* poor, pitiable, pathetic
悲し相な顔 *kanashisō na kao* sad-looking face

❼ abbrev. of 相模 *sagami*, old name for Kanagawa Prefecture
相鉄 *sōtetsu* Sagami Railway

INDEPENDENT

【sō 相】 aspect, phase; features; physiognomy; phase (⇨ ❶ⓑ & ❶ⓒ); *geol* facies; aspect (of verbs)
険悪の相 *ken'aku no sō* a wild look
相を見る *sō o miru* read (a person's) physiognomy

KUN

【ai- 相-】
[also prefix]
①ⓐ each other, mutually
ⓑ together
相性 *aishō* affinity, congeniality
相槌を打つ *aizuchi o utsu* make agreeable responses
相手 *aite* partner; opponent
相乗り *ainori* riding together
相合傘で *aiaigasa de* sharing the same umbrella
相棒 *aibō* pal, mate, companion
② emphatic verbal prefix
相変わらず *aikawarazu* as usual, as before
相次いで *aitsuide* in succession

SPECIAL READINGS

相撲 *sumō* sumo wrestling

SYNONYMS

❶ⓐ **appearance**
容 APPEARANCE → 2277
姿 FIGURE → 2636
体 FORM (outer appearance) → 71
色 COLOR → 2029
風 air → 3007
ⓒ **states and situations**
様 MODE → 1052
調 TONE → 1567
態 STATE → 2847
状 CONDITION → 272
況 CONDITIONS → 337
景 business conditions → 2470
勢 course of events → 2857
境 SITUATION → 676
局 current situation → 3063
情 ACTUAL CONDITIONS → 482
訳 circumstances → 1473
❸ **mutual**
互 RECIPROCAL → 3437
❹ **high officials**
宰 chief minister → 2275
❻ⓐ **phonetic** [s]/[sh]
西 phonetic [su] → 3520
修 phonetic [shu] → 123
須 phonetic [shu] → 574
世 phonetic [se] → 3496
遮 phonetic [sha] → 3158
沙 phonetic [sha] → 266

USAGE

ai

相-
[also prefix]
①ⓐ each other, mutually
ⓑ together
② emphatic verbal prefix

合い
① [in compounds]
ⓐ fitting
ⓑ prearranged, agreed upon
② [also 間] (space between) interval, space, opening
③ [also 間]
ⓐ (time between) interval, intermission
ⓑ between seasons
④ [also 間] [in compounds] mixed (blood)

間
[also 合い or 合]
① (space between) interval, space, opening
②ⓐ [also prefix] (time between) interval, intermission
ⓑ between seasons
③ [in compounds] mixed (blood)

HOMOPHONES

ai- ⇨ 合 2019 間 3323

COMPOUND FORMATION

❶ **相当** *sōtō*
相当する 'correspond to, etc.' means to correspond to (当) each other (相 ❸).

❷ **相対** *sōtai*
相対 'relativity' originally meant to face (対) each other (相 ❸).

❸ **相場** *sōba*
相場 'market price; estimation' consists of 相 ❻ⓐ, apparently used phonetically without relation to its meaning, and 場, in this case used in the sense of market.

柢

901 TEI

Ⓒⓗ 柢 dǐ

Radical	Strokes
木 75	9-4-5
Grade	**Freq**
Reference	
◧ 1 - 4 - 5	

4-5 木

COMPOUNDS

ⓐ [now replaced by 底 3084] bottom, basis, origin

ⓑ [original meaning, now archaic] root
根柢 *kontei* root, basis, foundation

柱

902

▶**PILLAR**
nonstandard for 柱 896

4-5 木

柄

903

▶**CHARACTER** ▶**HANDLE**
nonstandard for 柄 897

4-5 木

㭭

904

▶**MODE** ▶**FORMAL TITLE**
handwritten abbreviation for 様 1052

4-5 木

畑 畑 畑

905 hata hatake -batake

Ⓒⓗ none (国字)

Radical	Strokes
田 102	9-5-4
Grade	**Freq**
Jōyō-3	1141
◧ 1 - 4 - 5	

4-5 火

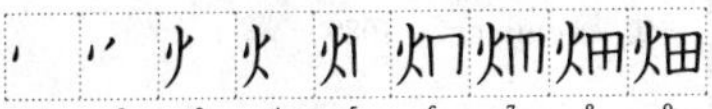

Stroke order: 丶(1) 丷(2) 少(3) 火(4) 灯(5) 炉(6) 畑(7) 畑(8) 畑(9)

▶**FIELD**

KUN

【**hata 畑**】[formerly also 畠] (plowed or cultivated) field, farm, vegetable garden, plantation
畑地 *hatachi* farmland

畑作 *hatasaku* dry field farming, dry field crop
田畑 *tahata* (=*denpata*) fields and rice paddies

【hatake 畑】
[formerly also 畠]
① (plowed or cultivated) field, farm, vegetable garden, plantation
畑を作る *hatake o tsukuru* cultivate a field, farm
② one's field, one's specialty
畑違いだ *hatakechigai da* be out of one's field

【-batake -畑】
① [also suffix] field, farm, vegetable garden, plantation
花畑 *hanabatake* flower garden
段段畑 *dandanbatake* terraced fields, terraced farm
コーヒー畑 *kōhībatake* coffee plantation
② [suffix] one's field, one's specialty
技術畑の人 *gijutsubatake no hito* man in the technical line, career technician

SYNONYMS

【hata】
○ & **【hatake】** ① **cultivated fields**
牧 PASTURE → 873
田 RICE FIELD → 3041
甫 vegetable garden → 3549
園 GARDEN → 3156

USAGE

❶ **hata**
畑
[formerly also 畠] (plowed or cultivated) field, farm, vegetable garden, plantation
畠
[now usu. 畑] same as 畑

❷ **hatake**
畑
[formerly also 畠]
① (plowed or cultivated) field, farm, vegetable garden, plantation
② one's field, one's specialty
畠
[now usu. 畑] same as 畑

HOMOPHONES

hata ⇨ 畠 2578
hatake ⇨ 畠 2578

4-5
火

906 HŌ

Ⓒⓗ 炮 páo pào bāo

Radical	Strokes
火 86	9-4-5
Grade	Freq
Reference	
1-4-5	

COMPOUNDS

❶ [original meaning] roast, bake
炮烙(=焙烙) *hōroku* parching pan, baking pan
❷ [now always 砲 1151] cannon

4-5
牛

牲 牲 牲

907 SEI

丿 𠂉 牛 牛 牛 牜 牪 牪 牲
1 2 3 4 5 6 7 8 9

Ⓒⓗ 牲 shēng

Radical	Strokes
牛 93	9-4-5
Grade	Freq
Jōyō	1333
1-4-5	

▶SACRIFICE

COMPOUNDS

❶ **sacrifice**
犠牲 *gisei* sacrifice
❷ [original meaning, now archaic] sacrificial animal, sacrifice

SYNONYMS

❶ **sacrifice**
犠 SACRIFICE → 1089

牴

908 TEI

CH 牴 dǐ

Radical	Strokes
牛 93	9-4-5
Grade	**Freq**
Reference	
1 - 4 - 5	

4-5 牛

COMPOUNDS

● [now replaced by 抵 319] collide with, touch

牴触 *teishoku* conflict; contradiction; incompatibility

珍

909 CHIN mezura(shii)

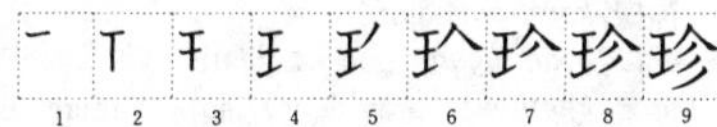

CH 珍 zhēn

Radical	Strokes
王 96	9-4-5
Grade	**Freq**
Jōyō	1182
1 - 4 - 5	

4-5 王

▶**RARE**

COMPOUNDS

❶ⓐ [original meaning] (of infrequent occurrence or unusual excellence) **rare, infrequent, precious**

ⓑ [also prefix] **curious, strange, queer, odd, funny**

珍味 *chinmi* food of delicate flavor, delicacy
珍品 *chinpin* rare article, curio
珍客 *chinkyaku* unexpected (but welcome) visitor
珍妙な *chinmyō na* queer, odd, fantastic
珍奇な *chinki na* novel, curious; rare; strange
珍現象 *chingenshō* strange phenomenon

❷ value highly, treasure

珍重する *chinchō suru* value highly, treasure

INDEPENDENT

【**chin** 珍】 rare phenomenon

珍中の珍 *chinchū no chin* black swan; rarity
珍な *chin na* curious, strange, marvelous, queer; rare

KUN

【**mezura(shii)** 珍しい】 rare, infrequent, unusual; uncommon, new, novel; precious (due to the rarity of the thing)

珍しさ *mezurashisa* rarity; novelty
珍しがる *mezurashigaru* think (it) a curiosity
物珍しげに *monomezurashige ni* curiously, with curious eyes

SYNONYMS

❶ⓐ **rare**

希 RARE → 2049

ⓑ **abnormal**

異 not ordinary → 2584
妙 strange → 239
奇 UNUSUAL → 2217
変 ABNORMAL → 2069
怪 MYSTERIOUS → 297

玲

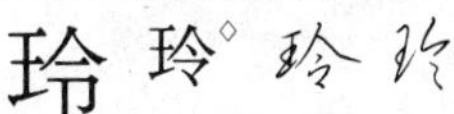

910 REI NAMES tama akira

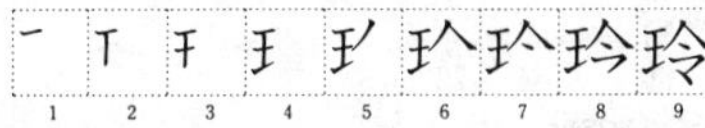

CH 玲 líng

Radical	Strokes
王 96	9-4-5
Grade	**Freq**
Names	2046
1 - 4 - 5	

4-5 王

▶**TINKLING OF JADES**

COMPOUNDS

❶ **tinkling of jades, sound of jewels**

玲玲 *reirei* [archaic] tinkling of jades

❷ brilliant, translucent, clear and bright

玲瓏たる *reirōtaru* brilliant, translucent, clear; sweetly ringing (as tinklings of jades)

NAMES

玲子 *reiko* female name
玲二 *reiji* male name

SYNONYMS

❶ **kinds of sound**
韻 melodious tone → 1811
響 reverberation → 2878
音 SOUND → 2070
声 VOICE → 2198

4-5
王
玲 911
▶**TINKLING OF JADES**
nonstandard for 玲 910

4-5
礻
神 神 神 神 912
SHIN JIN kami kan- kō-

CH 神 shén

Radical	Strokes
礻 113	9-4-5
Grade	**Freq**
Jōyō-3	259
1-4-5	

▶**GOD** ▶**MIND**

COMPOUNDS

❶ⓐ **god, God, deity, spirit**
ⓑ **Shinto deity, *kami***
神学 *shingaku* theology
神父 *shinpu* priest, Father
神仏 *shinbutsu* gods and Buddha; Shinto and Buddhism
多神教 *tashinkyō* polytheism
神宮 *jingū* Shinto shrine; Grand Shrine at Ise
神道 *shintō* Shinto, the Way of the Gods
神社 *jinja* Shinto shrine
❷ divine, sacred, godly, supernatural, mysterious
神秘的な *shinpiteki na* mysterious
神話 *shinwa* myth, mythology
神木 *shinboku* sacred tree
神童 *shindō* child prodigy
神聖な *shinsei na* holy, sacred, divine
❸ **mind, consciousness, spirit, soul**
神経 *shinkei* nerve; sensitivity; worry
神髄(＝真髄) *shinzui* essence, quintessence, soul
精神 *seishin* mind, soul, heart; intention, motive; the spirit (of something)
失神する *shisshin suru* lose consciousness, faint
色神 *shikishin* color sense (ability of color discrimination)
❹ Kobe
阪神 *hanshin* Hanshin, Osaka and Kobe

INDEPENDENT

【**shin** 神】 mind, spirit; divine power; abbrev. of 神道 *shintō*: Shinto
妙技神に入る *myōgi shin ni iru* be divinely skilled

KUN

【**kami** 神】 god, God, the Lord; deity; Shinto deity, *kami*; [in compounds] divine
神様 *kamisama* god, God
死に神 *shinigami* god of death
神業 *kamiwaza* providence, superhuman feat
神風 *kamikaze* providential [divine] wind; suicide plane, kamikaze
【**kan-** 神-】 god
神主 *kannushi* Shinto priest
【**kō-** 神-】 god
神神しい *kōgōshii* divine, solemn

SPECIAL READINGS

お神酒 *omiki* sacred wine [sake]; sake
神楽 *kagura* sacred (Shinto) music and dancing

SYNONYMS

❶ **god**
帝 the Supreme Being → 2073
天 HEAVEN → 3442
主 Lord → 1938
❷ **holy**
聖 HOLY → 2830
霊 miraculous → 2805
❸ **psyche**
気 SPIRIT (consciousness) → 3194
精 SPIRIT (mind) → 1366
霊 SPIRIT (soul) → 2805
魂 SOUL, spirit → 1063
心 HEART → 11
腹 heart → 1034
衷 INNER HEART → 2575
襟 inner mind → 1252
胸 breast → 951
懐 BOSOM → 763
❹ **Kansai cities**
阪 OSAKA → 271
京 KYOTO → 2052

COMPOUND FORMATION

神経 *shinkei*
神経 'nerve, etc.' is that which passes through (経) the body and mind (神 ❸).

祝 祝 祝 祝

913 SHUKU SHŪ iwa(u)

` ラ ネ ネ ネ 礻口 礻口 祀 祝
1 2 3 4 5 6 7 8 9

CH 祝 zhù

Radical	Strokes
礻 113	9-4-5
Grade	**Freq**
Jōyō-4	991
◧ 1 - 4 - 5	

4-5 礻

▶CELEBRATE

COMPOUNDS

❶ⓐ **celebrate**

ⓑ **congratulate, felicitate**

祝賀 *shukuga* celebration; congratulation

祝日 *shukujitsu* holiday, festival day

慶祝 *keishuku* celebration, congratulation

祝言 *shūgen* wedding

祝儀 *shūgi* celebration; congratulatory gift; tip

❷ⓐ **bless, pray, express good wishes**

ⓑ prayer

祝福 *shukufuku* blessing

祝禱 *shukutō* benediction, blessing

❸ [original meaning] priest (in ancient religions)

巫祝 *fushuku* ancient priest; shrine maiden

INDEPENDENT

【**shuku 祝**】celebration; congratulation

【**shukusuru 祝する**】celebrate; congratulate; wish good luck

KUN

【**iwa(u) 祝う**】celebrate, commemorate; congratulate, felicitate

祝い *iwai* celebration; congratulation

人の成功を祝う *hito no seikō o iwau* congratulate a person on his [her] success

祝い酒 *iwaizake* celebratory drink

SPECIAL READINGS

祝詞 *norito* Shinto ritual prayer

SYNONYMS

❶ **celebrating and congratulating**

慶 FELICITATION → 3173

賀 CONGRATULATE → 2599

寿 CONGRATULATIONS → 3557

祖 祖 祖 祖

914 SO

` ラ ネ ネ 礻 initial 初 礻冂 祖 祖
1 2 3 4 5 6 7 8 9

CH 祖 zǔ

Radical	Strokes
礻 113	9-4-5
Grade	**Freq**
Jōyō-5	1270
◧ 1 - 4 - 5	

4-5 礻

▶ANCESTOR

COMPOUNDS

❶ⓐ **ancestor, forefather**

ⓑ grandparent

祖先 *sosen* ancestor, forefather

祖国 *sokoku* one's native country

先祖 *senzo* forefather, ancestor

祖父母 *sofubo* grandparents

❷ **founder, originator**

開祖 *kaiso* founder, originator

元祖 *ganso* originator, pioneer

教祖 *kyōso* founder of a religion, head of a sect

INDEPENDENT

【**so 祖**】forefather, ancestor; founder, originator, father

医学の祖 *igaku no so* founder of medical science

SPECIAL READINGS

お祖父さん▲ *ojiisan* grandfather

お祖母さん▲ *obāsan* grandmother

4-5
ネ

祐 祐 祐 祐

Ⓒ祐 yòu

915 YŪ U NAMES suke sachi yoshi tasuku

1 2 3 4 5 6 7 8 9

Radical	Strokes
ネ 113	9-4-5
Grade	**Freq**
Names	2017
◧ 1 - 4 - 5	

▶DIVINE HELP

COMPOUNDS

ⓐ [also 佑 *yū* 74] [original meaning] **divine help, heavenly assistance [protection]**

ⓑ [also 右 *yū* 2975] help, assist

天祐 *ten'yū* grace of Heaven, providential help

神祐 *shin'yū* [rare] divine help, heavenly protection

祐筆 *yūhitsu* amanuensis, private secretary

NAMES

祐一 *yūichi* male name

康祐 *kōsuke* male name

SYNONYMS

● **help**

佑 HELP (said esp. of God) → 74

助 HELP → 1121

援 AID → 586

佐 ASSIST → 67

補 assist → 1194

輔 ASSIST → 1559

済 RELIEVE → 522

4-5
月

肺 肺 肺 肺

Ⓒ肺 fèi

916 HAI

1 2 3 4 5 6 7 8 9

Radical	Strokes
月 130	9-4-5
Grade	**Freq**
Jōyō-6	1646
◧ 1 - 4 - 5	

▶LUNG

COMPOUNDS

❶ⓐ [original meaning] **lung, lungs**

ⓑ [also prefix] pulmonary

肺臓 *haizō* lungs

肺活量 *haikatsuryō* lung breathing capacity

肺癌 *haigan* lung cancer

肺炎 *haien* pneumonia, inflammation of the lungs

肺結核 *haikekkaku* pulmonary tuberculosis

❷ innermost heart

肺肝 *haikan* [rare] innermost heart; lungs and liver

肺腑 *haifu* lungs; one's innermost heart

❸ aircraft engine

片肺飛行 *katahai hikō* one-engine flight

INDEPENDENT

【**hai** 肺】 lung, lungs; pulmonary disease, phthisis, tuberculosis

肺が弱い *hai ga yowai* have a weak chest

肺を病んでいる *hai o yande iru* suffer from tuberculosis

SYNONYMS

❶ **internal organs**

心 HEART → 11

胃 STOMACH → 2561

腸 INTESTINES → 1033

肝 LIVER → 841

胆 GALLBLADDER → 919

胞 胞 胞 佨

917 HŌ

丿 月 月 月 肞 肞 肑 胞 胞
1 2 3 4 5 6 7 8 9

ⒸⒽ 胞 bāo

Radical	Strokes
月 130	9-4-5
Grade	**Freq**
Jōyō	1719
◧ 1 - 4 - 5	

4-5
月

▶MEMBRANOUS SAC

COMPOUNDS

❶ **any small membranous sac such as a vesicle, theca, sac, sheath, capsule or cell**

胞子 *hōshi* spore
細胞 *saibō* cell
芽胞 *gahō* spore
小胞 *shōhō* vesicle
肺胞 *haihō* alveolus

❷ⓐ [original meaning] afterbirth, amnion
ⓑ womb
胞衣 *hōi* afterbirth
同胞 *dōhō* brothers; brethren, fellow countrymen

SPECIAL READINGS

同胞▲ *harakara* brothers; brethren, fellow countrymen

SYNONYMS

❶ **bags**
包 wrapper → 2966
袋 BAG → 2588
俵 STRAW SACK → 115

COMPOUND FORMATION

同胞 *dōhō*
同胞 'brothers, etc.' refers to persons of the same (同) womb (胞 ❷ⓑ) or mother.

胎 胎 佁

918 TAI

丿 月 月 月 肞 肞 胎 胎 胎
1 2 3 4 5 6 7 8 9

ⒸⒽ 胎 tāi

Radical	Strokes
月 130	9-4-5
Grade	**Freq**
Jōyō	1733
◧ 1 - 4 - 5	

4-5
月

▶FETUS ▶WOMB

COMPOUNDS

❶ [original meaning] **fetus, embryo**
胎児 *taiji* embryo, fetus
胎動 *taidō* quickening, fetal movement; indication
堕胎 *datai* abortion

❷ⓐ **womb, uterus**
ⓑ (figuratively) womb, origin, beginning
胎内 *tainai* interior of the womb
胎生 *taisei* viviparity
胎教 *taikyō* prenatal care
母胎 *botai* mother's womb
胚胎する *haitai suru* originate in, arise from

❸ conceive, become pregnant
懐胎 *kaitai* conception, becoming pregnant
受胎 *jutai* conception, fertilization

INDEPENDENT

【tai 胎】 womb

SYNONYMS

❶ **early states of animal life**
卵 EGG → 849

❷ⓐ **genitals**
陰 sex organ → 541
恥 private parts → 1313

4-5
月

胆 膽 胆 𦞂
919 TAN

丿 刀 月 月 月' 月⺈ 胆 胆 胆
1 2 3 4 5 6 7 8 9

CH 胆 dǎn

Radical	Strokes
月 130	9-4-5
Grade	**Freq**
Jōyō	1590
1 - 4 - 5	

▶**GALLBLADDER**

COMPOUNDS

❶ **gallbladder, gall**
胆嚢 *tannō* gall, gallbladder
胆汁 *tanjū* bile, gall
胆石 *tanseki* gallstone
❷ **pluck, guts, courage, nerve, gall**
胆力 *tanryoku* pluck, courage, nerve
大胆 *daitan* boldness, daring
豪胆 *gōtan* boldness, iron nerves
落胆 *rakutan* disappointment, discouragement
❸ one's inner heart, feelings
魂胆 *kontan* secret intention, ulterior motive
肝胆相照らす間柄である *Kantan-aiterasu aida-gara de aru* be quite in sympathy with each other

INDEPENDENT

【**tan** 胆】 pluck, guts, courage

SYNONYMS

❶ **internal organs**
肝 LIVER → 841
心 HEART → 11
肺 LUNG → 916
胃 STOMACH → 2561
腸 INTESTINES → 1033
❷ **courage**
勇 bravery → 2089

4-5
月

胞
920

▶**MEMBRANOUS SAC**
nonstandard for 胞 917

4-5
月

脉
921

▶**VEIN** ▶**PULSE**
nonstandard for 脈 953

4-6
方

旅 旅 旅 𣄃
922 RYO tabi

丶 亠 亣 方 方' 方⺈ 方ケ 旅 旅 旅
1 2 3 4 5 6 7 8 9 10

CH 旅 lǚ

Radical	Strokes
方 70	10-4-6
Grade	**Freq**
Jōyō-3	608
1 - 4 - 6	

▶**TRAVEL**

COMPOUNDS

❶ⓐ **travel, traveling, journey, trip**
ⓑ **travel, take a trip**
ⓒ **traveler**
旅行 *ryokō* travel, trip
旅券 *ryoken* passport
旅装 *ryosō* traveling outfit
旅費 *ryohi* traveling expenses
旅客 *ryokaku* traveler, passenger, tourist
旅館 *ryokan* Japanese inn
逆旅 *gekiryo* inn
❷ [original meaning] brigade, troops
旅団 *ryodan* brigade

KUN

【**tabi** 旅】 journey, traveling, travel, trip
旅する *tabisuru* travel, take a trip
旅人 *tabibito* traveler
旅路 *tabiji* journey
船旅 *funatabi* voyage

SYNONYMS

❶ⓐ & ❶ⓑ **journey**
行 trip → 212
遊 tour → 3142
巡 tour around → 3047

旅 923 ▶TRAVEL nonstandard for 旅 922

4-6 方

時 時 时 924 JI toki -doki

Ⓒ𝐇 时 shí

Radical	Strokes
日 72	10-4-6
Grade	Freq
Jōyō-2	17
◧ 1 - 4 - 6	

4-6 日

▶TIME

COMPOUNDS

❶ⓐ [original meaning] (continuous duration) **time, duration, interval**
ⓑ (specific time) **the time, o'clock, hour**
ⓒ [suffix] **time, at the time of, when**
時間 *jikan* time, period; hour
時刻 *jikoku* time; hour
同時の *dōji no* simultaneous
臨時の *rinji no* temporary, provisional, special
一時 *ichiji* for a time, temporarily; once; one o'clock
時限 *jigen* time limit, closing time; period, hour
八時 *hachiji* eight o'clock
何時ですか *Nanji desu ka* What time is it?
日時 *nichiji* date, time
昼食時 *chūshokuji* lunch time
出願時 *shutsuganji* (at the) time of application

❷ⓐ **time(s), age, period, season**
ⓑ (opportune moment) timely occasion, right time, opportunity
ⓒ current times, currently, present
時代 *jidai* age, era, period; antiquity
時勢 *jisei* trend of the times, spirit of the age
時期 *jiki* time, season
当時 *tōji* at that time, in those days; at the present time
時機 *jiki* opportunity, chance
時宜 *jigi* right time [occasion], proper time
時節 *jisetsu* season, times; occasion
時事 *jiji* current events
時価 *jika* current price

❸ at times, periodically
時習 *jishū* periodic reviewing

❹ⓐ **hour**
ⓑ counter for hours
時速 *jisoku* speed per hour
時給 *jikyū* payment by the hour
一時間 *ichijikan* one hour
五十時 *gojūji* 50 hours

❺ *gram* tense
時制 *jisei* tense
現在完了時 *genzaikanryōji* present perfect tense

KUN

[toki 時]

①ⓐ time, hour, moment
ⓑ times, age, the day
ⓒ (former unit of time) two-hour period
時が移る *Toki ga utsuru* Time elapses
一時 *hitotoki* time, while, moment
引け時 *hikedoki* closing time (of school)
時の *toki no* then, of the day
戦争の時 *sensō no toki* times of war
子の時 *ne no toki* midnight

②ⓐ right time, opportunity, occasion, case; season
ⓑ [also 秋] critical moment
時時 *tokidoki* sometimes, occasionally; each occasion
時を待つ *toki o matsu* wait for a favorable chance
時と場合によって *toki to baai ni yotte* should time and circumstances permit
丁度良い時に *chōdo yoi toki ni* just at the right moment
危急存亡の時 *kikyūsonbō no toki* crisis, critical moment

③ⓐ when
ⓑ in case of, if, in the event of
家に帰る時 *ie ni kaeru toki* when returning home
五時迄に帰らない時は *goji made ni kaeranai toki wa* if I don't come back till five o'clock

④ *gram* tense
法と時 *hō to toki* mood and tense

[-doki -時]

[suffix]

① time, proper time, season
食事時 *shokujidoki* mealtime
花見時 *hanamidoki* (cherry) blossom season

② suffix indicating time in former system of measuring time

九つ時 *kokonotsudoki* midnight, noon

SPECIAL READINGS

時計 *tokei* clock, watch
時雨 *shigure* late fall or early winter rain

SYNONYMS

❶ **time periods**
刻 POINT OF TIME → 1267
頃 TIME → 144
般 period of time → 1317
暇 FREE TIME → 1012
間 INTERVAL → 3323
期 TERM → 1704
節 SEASON OF THE YEAR → 2691
季 SEASON (quarter) → 2554
候 SEASON (time of year) → 119
❷ⓐ **long time periods**
代 age → 30
世 AGE → 3496
紀 ERA → 1276
期 period → 1704
朝 dynastic period → 1695
ⓑ **occasions**
際 OCCASION → 714
折 occasion → 253
機 OPPORTUNITY → 1076
節 time → 2691
❹ⓐ **short time periods**
分 MINUTE → 1972
秒 SECOND → 1137
瞬 INSTANT → 1247
頃 moment → 144
暫 SHORT WHILE → 2864

USAGE

toki
時
①ⓐ time, hour, moment
ⓑ times, age, the day
ⓒ (former unit of time) two-hour period
②ⓐ right time, opportunity, occasion, case; season
ⓑ [also 秋] critical moment
③ⓐ when
ⓑ in case of, if, in the event of
④ *gram* tense
秋
[also 時] critical moment

HOMOPHONES

toki ⇨ 秋 1139

4-6
木

梅 梅 梅 梅

925 BAI ume

Ⓒⓗ 梅 méi

Radical	Strokes
木 75	10-4-6
Grade	**Freq**
Jōyō-4	1018
1-4-6	

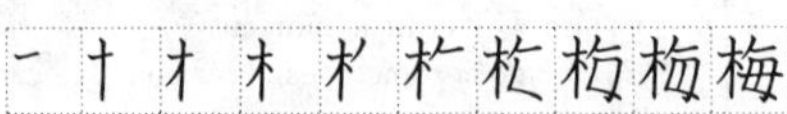

1 2 3 4 5 6 7 8 9 10

▶JAPANESE APRICOT

COMPOUNDS

❶ⓐ **Japanese apricot tree, *ume* tree; Japanese apricot, *ume***
ⓑ ***ume* blossom**
梅林 *bairin ume* grove
梅花 *baika ume* blossoms
梅雨(=黴雨) *baiu* rainy season (of early summer)
紅梅 *kōbai* red-blossomed Japanese apricot
観梅 *kanbai ume* blossom viewing
塩梅 *anbai* seasoning, flavoring; taste, flavor; condition, state
❷ rainy season (when the *ume* blossoms in Japan)
入梅 *nyūbai* beginning of the rainy season
❸ [formerly 黴 814] mold, mildew, fungus
梅毒 *baidoku* syphilis

KUN

【ume 梅】 Japanese apricot tree, *ume* tree; *ume* blossom; Japanese apricot (the fruit), *ume*
梅の実 *ume no mi* Japanese apricot, *ume*
梅見 *umemi ume* blossom viewing
梅干し *umeboshi* pickled *ume*
梅酒 *umeshu ume* [apricot] brandy

SPECIAL READINGS

梅雨 *tsuyu* rainy season (of early summer)

SYNONYMS

❶ⓐ **fruits and fruit trees**
杏 APRICOT → 2397
李 PLUM → 2398
桃 PEACH → 936
橘 MANDARIN → 1077
栗 CHESTNUT → 2649
梨 PEAR → 2744
ⓑ **flowering plants**
桜 cherry blossom → 931
菊 CHRYSANTHEMUM → 2303
葵 MALLOW → 2317
蓉 COTTON ROSE → 2337
芙 LOTUS → 2208
蘭 ORCHID → 2383
萩 *HAGI* → 2319
藤 WISTERIA → 2382

格 格 格

Ⓒ 格 gé

Radical	Strokes
木 75	10-4-6
Grade	**Freq**
Jōyō-5	354
◧ 1 - 4 - 6	

4-6 木

926 KAKU KŌ KYAKU▲ GŌ▲

▶**NORM** ▶**STATUS**

COMPOUNDS

❶ⓐ **norm, standard, model, pattern, rule, regulation**

ⓑ **ability to meet the norm, qualification, eligibility, competency, capacity**

ⓒ (make conform to the norm) rectify, correct, show the right way to

格外の *kakugai no* nonstandard, extraordinary, special
格別な *kakubetsu na* particular, exceptional
格式 *kakushiki* established form, formalities
規格 *kikaku* standard, norm
本格 *honkaku* fundamental rules, propriety
本格的な *honkakuteki na* full-scale, full-fledged; standard
語格 *gokaku* rules of grammar, usage
資格 *shikaku* qualifications, competence, capacity
合格する *gōkaku suru* pass (an examination), be found eligible [qualified]
失格する *shikkaku suru* be disqualified
格言 *kakugen* maxim, proverb

❷ **status, rank, capacity, standing, class, grade**

格上げする *kakuage suru* raise to higher status, promote to a higher rank
格式 *kakushiki* status, social standing
格付けする *kakuzuke suru* grade, rate, classify
昇格 *shōkaku* promotion in status
同格 *dōkaku* same status, equality; apposition
寺格 *jikaku* status of a Buddhist temple
リーダー格 *rīdākaku* capacity as a leader
価格 *kakaku* price, cost

❸ (degree of excellence) (**good**) **character, personality;** (**high**) **quality, distinction, style**

格差 *kakusa* difference in quality [price]
格安な *kakuyasu na* inexpensive, reasonable in price
格調 *kakuchō* tone, strain, style
人格 *jinkaku* character, personality
性格 *seikaku* character, personality
品格 *hinkaku* dignity, grace
風格の有る人物 *fūkaku no aru jinbutsu* man of distinctive character
厳格な *genkaku na* strict, stern, severe, rigorous

❹ⓐ framework, latticework, grid

ⓑ [formerly also 骼 *kaku* 1830] frame, build, physique

格子 *kōshi* latticework, lattice, grid
格天井 *gōtenjō* coffered ceiling
体格 *taikaku* physique, build
骨格 *kokkaku* frame, physique; framework, skeletal structure

❺ [also suffix] *gram* case

主格 *shukaku* nominative case
目的格 *mokutekikaku* objective case

❻ [also 恰 *kat-* 368] just, exactly

格好 *kakkō* suitability, moderateness (in price); shape, form; appearance, manner

❼ [formerly 挌 *kaku* 375] strike, hit, fight

格闘する *kakutō suru* grapple, fight hand to hand

❽ put away, store

格納 *kakunō* housing, hangar

❾ [also suffix] Imperial ordinance in Nara and Heian periods

弘仁格 *kōninkyaku* Ordinance of the Konin Era

❿ *logic* figure, schema

第二格 *dainikaku* second figure

⓫ investigate thoroughly, search to the very source

格物致知 *kakubutsuchichi* gaining a perfect knowledge of natural laws

⓬ [usu. 角 *kaku* 2047] unit of type size equiv. to one em quad

半格 *hankaku* en quad

INDEPENDENT

【**kaku 格**】norm, standard, rule; status, rank, capacity, class; *gram* case; *logic* figure, schema

格を上げる *kaku o ageru* raise the standard
格を守る *kaku o mamoru* observe the rules
格が上がる *kaku ga agaru* be promoted to a higher rank
...の格で *...no kaku de* in the capacity of, as
名詞の格 *meishi no kaku* case of a noun

SYNONYMS

❶ⓐ **model**

準 STANDARD → 2856
式 form → 3049
程 ESTABLISHED FORM → 1190
模 PATTERN → 1050

典 CANON → 2627
範 MODEL → 2709
❷ **class**
身 social status → 3553
階 RANK → 624
位 RANK → 61
級 GRADE → 1279
段 grade → 1144
等 CLASS → 2682
流 class → 441
層 STRATUM → 3161
❸ **nature and character**
柄 CHARACTER → 897
性 NATURE → 299
気 temperament → 3194
質 QUALITY → 2808
品 grade of excellence → 2248
❹ⓐ **frames**
枠 FRAME → 866
額 picture frame → 1805

COMPOUND FORMATION

❶ 格言 *kakugen*
格言 'maxim, proverb' is a saying (言) that shows one the right way (格 ❶ⓒ).
❷ 厳格 *genkaku*
厳格な 'strict, etc.' refers to the strictness (厳) of a person's character (格 ❸).

NOTE

★do not confuse with 挌 375

4-6
木

核 核 核 核

927 KAKU

Ⓒⓗ 核 hé hú

Radical	Strokes
木 75	10-4-6
Grade	**Freq**
Jōyō	516
1-4-6	

Stroke order: 一 十 木 木 木' 朩 朩 杉 核 核 (1–10)

▶NUCLEUS

COMPOUNDS

[also prefix and suffix]
❶ⓐ (central part) **nucleus, core**
ⓑ *biol, chem* **nucleus**
ⓒ [original meaning] kernel (of a fruit), putamen
核仁 *kakujin* nucleus
核家族 *kakukazoku* nucleus family
中核 *chūkaku* core, nucleus; kernel
核崩壊 *kakuhōkai* disintegration of a cell nucleus
核酸 *kakusan* nucleic acid
細胞核 *saibōkaku* nucleus (of a cell)
神経核 *shinkeikaku* neuron
結核 *kekkaku* tuberculosis
痔核 *jikaku* hemorrhoids
果核 *kakaku* putamen
❷ⓐ (central part of an atom) **nucleus**
ⓑ **nuclear, atomic**
ⓒ abbrev. of 核兵器 *kakuheiki*: nuclear weapons
核反応 *kakuhannō* nuclear reaction
核融合 *kakuyūgō* nuclear fusion
原子核 *genshikaku* atomic nucleus
核エネルギー *kakuenerugī* nuclear energy
核兵器 *kakuheiki* nuclear weapons
核防衛力 *kakubōeiryoku* nuclear defenses
核戦争 *kakusensō* nuclear war

INDEPENDENT

【**kaku** 核】 nucleus, kernel, core; nucleus (of a cell); atomic nucleus
核の傘 *kaku no kasa* nuclear umbrella

SYNONYMS

❶ **central parts**
仁 kernel → 20
心 core → 11
ⓐ **middle**
心 HEART → 11
央 CENTER → 3509
中 MIDDLE → 3451
❷ⓐ & ❷ⓑ **particle**
子 particle suffix → 3390
粒 GRAIN → 1328

桂 桂 桂

928 KEI katsura NAMES katsu yoshi

CH 桂 guì

Radical	Strokes
木 75	10-4-6
Grade	**Freq**
Names	1982
◧ 1 - 4 - 6	

4-6 木

▶AROMATIC TREE

COMPOUNDS

❶ **general term for aromatic trees, esp. cinnamon or cassia**

桂冠 *keikan* crown of laurel

肉桂 *nikkei* cinnamon tree

月桂樹 *gekkeiju* laurel

カシア桂皮 *kashiakeihi* cassia

❷ [rare] tree in the moon (according to ancient Chinese legend); moon

桂月 *keigetsu* [archaic] moon

月桂 *gekkei* laurel in the moon; moonlight

❸ name of chess piece in shogi (Japanese chess): *keima*, knight

桂馬 *keima keima*, knight

桂成り *keinari* knight promotion

INDEPENDENT

【kei 桂】 *keima* (⇨ ❸)

桂を落とす *kei o otosu* lose a knight

KUN

【katsura 桂】 katsura tree, katsura

桂男 *katsuraotoko* man in the moon

NAMES

桂三 *keizō* male name

桂子 *keiko* (=*yoshiko*) female name

桂 *katsura* surname also male name also female name

桂浜 *katsurahama* place name

SYNONYMS

❶ **& 【katsura】 trees**

梓 CATALPA → 962

桑 MULBERRY → 2112

漆 Japanese lacquer tree → 704

桐 PAULOWNIA → 937

楠 CAMPHOR TREE → 1018

槙 PODOCARPUS → 1051

杉 CRYPTOMERIA → 832

松 PINE → 864

楓 MAPLE → 1015

柳 WILLOW → 899

桜 CHERRY → 931

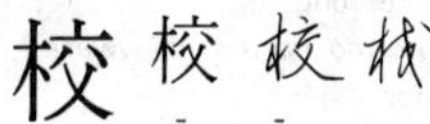

校 校 校 校

929 KŌ KYŌ▲

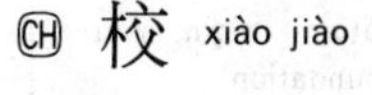

CH 校 xiào jiào

Radical	Strokes
木 75	10-4-6
Grade	**Freq**
Jōyō-1	168
◧ 1 - 4 - 6	

4-6 木

▶SCHOOL ▶COLLATE

COMPOUNDS

❶ⓐ [also suffix] **school**

ⓑ counter for schools

校長 *kōchō* principal, schoolmaster, rector

校舎 *kōsha* school building

校内 *kōnai* school grounds

校友 *kōyū* schoolmate, alumnus

校則 *kōsoku* school regulations

学校 *gakkō* school, college

母校 *bokō* one's alma mater, one's old school

登校 *tōkō* attending school

高校 *kōkō* senior high school

予備校 *yobikō* preparatory school

二十五校 *nijūgokō* 25 schools

❷ⓐ **collate, proofread, check, examine, revise**

ⓑ proof

ⓒ counter for proofs

校合する *kyōgō* (=*kōgō*) *suru* collate, examine and compare

校正 *kōsei* proofreading

校訂 *kōtei* revision

校正刷 *kōseizuri* galley proofs

校閲 *kōetsu* revision, reviewing, editing

校了 *kōryō* final proof

初校 *shokō* first proof

三校目 *sankōme* third proof

❸ commanding officer

将校 *shōkō* officer, commissioned officer

INDEPENDENT

【kō 校】 proofreading

校を重ねる *kō o kasaneru* proofread again and again

SYNONYMS

❶ **schools**

学 EDUCATIONAL INSTITUTION → 2555
塾 PRIVATE SCHOOL → 2860
院 INSTITUTION → 454
大 UNIVERSITY → 3416
高 high school → 2097
中 junior high school → 3451
小 elementary school → 7
園 kindergarten → 3156

❷ⓐ **revise**

訂 REVISE → 1442
閲 REVIEW → 3330

ⓑ **compare**

照 check against → 2827
対 OPPOSE (contrast) → 831
参 refer → 2066
比 COMPARE → 26
較 COMPARE → 1536

4-6
木

根 根 杦

930 KON ne -ne

Ⓒ 根 gēn

Radical	Strokes
木 75	10-4-6
Grade	**Freq**
Jōyō-3	496
1-4-6	

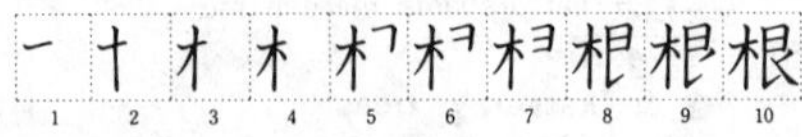

1 2 3 4 5 6 7 8 9 10

▶**ROOT**

COMPOUNDS

❶ [original meaning] **root (of a plant)**
根菜 *konsai* root crops
毛根 *mōkon* root of a hair
大根 *daikon* Japanese radish
球根 *kyūkon* bulb

❷ⓐ (primary source) **root, source, origin**
ⓑ (essential part) **root, basis, foundation**
ⓒ radically, completely
根源 *kongen* root, origin, source
語根 *gokon* root [origin] of a word
根本 *konpon* basis, foundation; origin, source
根底 *kontei* root, basis, foundation
根拠 *konkyo* grounds, basis, authority
根絶する *konzetsu suru* eradicate, exterminate, root out
根治する *konji* (=*konchi*) *suru* cure radically, be completely cured

❸ⓐ *math* root, radical
ⓑ *chem* radical
根号 *kongō* radical sign
平方根 *heihōkon* square root
水酸根 *suisankon* hydroxyl radical

❹ **perseverance, stamina, mental energy**
根気 *konki* perseverance, patience, energy
根性 *konjō* nature, spirit, temper; will power; guts
精根 *seikon* energy, vitality

❺ organ; sense organ (esp. in Buddhism)
男根 *dankon* penis
六根清浄 *rokkon-shōjō* purification of one's self through detachment from the senses

❻ *Buddhism*
ⓐ *indriya* (Sanscrit): powerful act capable of producing something
ⓑ character [nature] of man
機根 *kikon* capacity of the common people to understand the teachings of Buddhism

INDEPENDENT

【**kon** 根】 *math* root; radical; *chem* radical; perseverance, stamina, mental energy
根の良い *kon no yoi* persevering, enduring

KUN

【**ne** 根】 root; source, origin; basis, foundation; nature
根っ子 *nekko* root; stump, stub
根元 *nemoto* root; base
根強い *nezuyoi* deep-rooted
根付く *nezuku* take root
根も葉も無い噂 *ne mo ha mo nai uwasa* groundless rumor
根深い *nebukai* deep-rooted, ingrained
根はおとなしい *ne wa otonashii* be tender-hearted by nature
性根 *shōne* nature, disposition

【**-ne** -根】 used phonetically for *ne*, esp. for euphony
屋根 *yane* roof
羽根 *hane* fan, blade
垣根 *kakine* fence, hedge

SYNONYMS

❶ **supporting parts of plants**
株 stump → 935
幹 TRUNK → 1718
茎 STEM → 2242

❷ⓐ **beginnings**
源 SOURCE → 656
元 ORIGIN → 1929
本 origin → 3502
緒 OUTSET → 1378
序 INTRODUCTORY PART → 3065
端 start → 1221
始 beginning → 281
初 beginning → 1116

ⓑ **basis**

本 BASIS → 3502
底 BOTTOM → 3084
拠 GROUNDS → 312
礎 foundation → 1248
基 BASE → 2673
素 ELEMENT → 2458

桜 櫻 桜 桜
931 Ō sakura

Ⓒⓗ 櫻 yīng

Radical	Strokes
木 75	10-4-6
Grade	**Freq**
Jōyō-5	1125
◧ 1-4-6	

4-6 木

▶CHERRY

COMPOUNDS

ⓐ **cherry tree, (Japanese) flowering cherry, *sakura***

ⓑ **cherry blossom**

桜花 *ōka* cherry blossoms
桜桃 *ōtō* cherry
観桜 *kan'ō* cherry-blossom viewing

KUN

【**sakura** 桜】cherry tree, (Japanese) flowering cherry, *sakura*; cherry blossom; pink; horse meat

桜ん坊(=桜桃) *sakuranbo* cherry
山桜 *yamazakura* wild cherry tree
葉桜 *hazakura* cherry tree in leaf
桜色 *sakurairo* pink
桜貝 *sakuragai* carpenter's tellin, pink shell
桜肉 *sakuraniku* horse meat

SYNONYMS

ⓐ **trees**

柳 WILLOW → 899
楓 MAPLE → 1015
松 PINE → 864
杉 CRYPTOMERIA → 832
槙 PODOCARPUS → 1051
楠 CAMPHOR TREE → 1018
桐 PAULOWNIA → 937
桂 AROMATIC TREE, katsura tree → 928
梓 CATALPA → 962
桑 MULBERRY → 2112
漆 Japanese lacquer tree → 704

ⓑ **flowering plants**

梅 *ume* blossom → 925
菊 CHRYSANTHEMUM → 2303
葵 MALLOW → 2317
蓉 COTTON ROSE → 2337
芙 LOTUS → 2208
蘭 ORCHID → 2383
萩 *HAGI* → 2319
藤 WISTERIA → 2382

桟 棧 栈 桟
932 SAN

Ⓒⓗ 栈 zhàn

Radical	Strokes
木 75	10-4-6
Grade	**Freq**
Jōyō	1754
◧ 1-4-6	

4-6 木

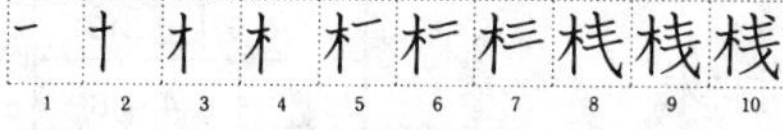

▶PLANK BRIDGE

COMPOUNDS

❶ **plank bridge, suspension bridge, plank passageway**

桟道 *sandō* plank road, plank bridge, suspension bridge
桟橋 *sanbashi* (landing) pier, jetty, wharf
桟梯子 *sanbashigo* gangway ladder

❷ **joist**

桟敷 *sajiki* reviewing stand, box, gallery

INDEPENDENT

【**san** 桟】crosspiece; frame; bolt (of a door)

桟を打ち付ける *san o uchitsukeru* nail a crosspiece (to)
障子の桟 *shōji no san* frame of a *shoji* (paper sliding-door)
戸の桟を外す *to no san o hazusu* unbolt the door

SPECIAL READINGS

桟敷 *sajiki* reviewing stand, box, gallery

SYNONYMS

❶ **bridges**

橋 BRIDGE → 1078

【**san**】

○ **shafts**

棒 ROD → 983
軸 AXLE → 1514
錘 SPINDLE → 1744

4-6 木

栖
933 SEI

(CH) 栖 qī xī

Radical	Strokes
木 75	10-4-6
Grade	Freq
Reference	
1 - 4 - 6	

COMPOUNDS

❶ [now replaced by 生 3497] (of animals) inhabit, live
❷ (of people) live, dwell, reside

栖息する *seisoku suru* inhabit, live
隠栖 *insei* secluded life
幽栖する *yūsei suru* live a quiet life in seclusion away from the masses

4-6 木

栓 栓 栓 栓
934 SEN

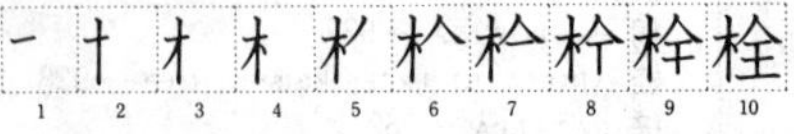

(CH) 栓 shuān

Radical	Strokes
木 75	10-4-6
Grade	Freq
Jōyō	1946
1 - 4 - 6	

▶STOPPER

COMPOUNDS

❶ⓐ [original meaning] **stopper, plug, cork, peg; door bolt**
ⓑ stopper, block up
栓抜き *sennuki* bottle opener, corkscrew
コルク栓 *korukusen* cork
脳血栓 *nōkessen* cerebral thrombosis
密栓する *missen suru* stopper tightly, seal hermetically
❷ [also suffix] stopcock, tap, faucet, spigot
水栓 *suisen* water tap, faucet
消火栓 *shōkasen* fire hydrant, fireplug

INDEPENDENT

【sen 栓】 stopper, cork, plug; stopcock, faucet, tap
瓶の栓 *bin no sen* bottle stopper
栓を抜く *sen o nuku* uncork a bottle
水道の栓 *suidō no sen* water spigot

SYNONYMS

❶ⓐ & ❷ stoppers
弁 VALVE → 2004

4-6 木

株 株 株
935 SHU▲ kabu

(CH) 株 zhū

Radical	Strokes
木 75	10-4-6
Grade	Freq
Jōyō-6	313
1 - 4 - 6	

▶STOCK

COMPOUNDS

● [original meaning] **stump, stub**
守株 *shushu* stupidity, lack of innovation

KUN

【kabu 株】
①ⓐ [also suffix] stock, stocks, shares
ⓑ counter for stocks or shares
ⓒ abbrev. of 株式会社 *kabushikigaisha*: joint stock corporation, Ltd., Inc.
株を買う *kabu o kau* buy stock
株式 *kabushiki* stocks, shares
株価 *kabuka* price of stocks
株券 *kabuken* share [stock] certificate
株主 *kabunushi* stockholder
株式会社 *kabushikigaisha* joint stock corporation
新株 *shinkabu* new stock
優先株 *yūsenkabu* preference shares
二百株 *nihyakkabu* 200 shares
山田製紙株 *yamadaseishi-kabu* Yamada Paper Manufacturing Company Ltd.
②ⓐ stump, stub
ⓑ root, plant
ⓒ counter for plants with roots
切り株 *kirikabu* stump
株分け *kabuwake* root division
レタス五株 *retasu gokabu* 5 heads of lettuce

③ assets, business practice, goodwill
商売の株 *shōbai no kabu* goodwill of a business
④ position, reputation
親分株 *oyabunkabu* position of boss [big shot]
⑤ one's forte, one's specialty
お株を取られる *okabu o torareru* be outdone, be beaten in one's own field

SYNONYMS

● & **【kabu】** ②ⓐ **supporting parts of plants**
幹 TRUNK → 1718
根 ROOT → 930
茎 STEM → 2242
【kabu】
①ⓐ **securities**
債 BOND → 156

COMPOUND FORMATION

守株 *shushu*
守株 is a classical Chinese allusion that originally meant to stay and keep watch (守) by a stump (株) in the hope of catching a hare. The reasoning behind this strange behavior is that since a hare had once accidentally dashed against the stump and died there, maybe another one would come by. This gave rise to the current meaning of 'stupidity, lack of innovation'.

NOTE

⇨ see COMPOUND FORMATION for 株式 *kabushiki* ⇨ 式 3049

桃 桃 桃

936 TŌ momo

CH 桃 táo

Radical	Strokes
木 75	10-4-6
Grade	**Freq**
Jōyō	1611
1-4-6	

4-6 木

一 十 才 木 札 札 村 桃 桃 桃 (1–10)

▶PEACH

COMPOUNDS

● [original meaning] **peach tree; peach**
桃花 *tōka* [rare] peach blossom
桃李 *tōri* peach and plum
桜桃 *ōtō* cherry
黄桃 *ōtō* yellow peach
扁桃腺 *hentōsen* tonsils

KUN

【momo 桃】 peach; peach tree
桃色 *momoiro* rose, pink
桃園 *momozono* peach orchard
桃割れ *momoware momoware* coiffure

SYNONYMS

● **fruits and fruit trees**
李 PLUM → 2398
杏 APRICOT → 2397
梅 JAPANESE APRICOT → 925
橘 MANDARIN → 1077
栗 CHESTNUT → 2649
梨 PEAR → 2744

桐 桐 桐

937 TŌ DŌ kiri NAMES hisa

CH 桐 tóng

Radical	Strokes
木 75	10-4-6
Grade	**Freq**
Names	2004
1-4-6	

4-6 木

一 十 才 木 札 机 机 桐 桐 桐 (1–10)

▶PAULOWNIA

COMPOUNDS

● **paulownia**
桐油 *tōyu* tung oil, (Chinese) wood oil
梧桐 *gotō* Chinese parasol (tree), phoenix tree

KUN

【kiri 桐】 paulownia
桐材 *kirizai* paulownia wood

NAMES

桐野 *kirino* surname
桐ヶ丘 *kirigaoka* place name

SYNONYMS

● **trees**
桂 AROMATIC TREE, katsura tree → 928
梓 CATALPA → 962
桑 MULBERRY → 2112
漆 Japanese lacquer tree → 704
桜 CHERRY → 931
柳 WILLOW → 899
楓 MAPLE → 1015
松 PINE → 864

杉 CRYPTOMERIA → 832
槙 PODOCARPUS → 1051
楠 CAMPHOR TREE → 1018

4-6 木

核 938

▶NUCLEUS
nonstandard for 核 927

4-6 木

校 939

▶SCHOOL ▶COLLATE
nonstandard for 校 929

4-6 木

栓 940

▶STOPPER
nonstandard for 栓 934

4-6 歹

殉 殉 殉 941 JUN

CH 殉 xùn

Radical	Strokes
歹 78	10-4-6
Grade	Freq
Jōyō	1786
1-4-6	

一 ㄏ 万 歹 歹 歹 歹 殉 殉 殉
1 2 3 4 5 6 7 8 9 10

▶DIE A MARTYR

COMPOUNDS

ⓐ **die a martyr, sacrifice oneself, die for a cause**
ⓑ follow (one's master) to the grave
殉教 *junkyō* martyrdom
殉職 *junshoku* dying at one's post
殉国 *junkoku* dying for one's country
殉難者 *junnansha* martyr, victim
殉死する *junshi suru* follow (one's master) by committing suicide

INDEPENDENT

【junjiru 殉じる】die a martyr

SYNONYMS

ⓐ **die**
死 DIE → 3521
没 die → 260
亡 DECEASE → 3402
去 pass away → 2156
逝 DEPART THIS LIFE → 3104
枯 WITHER → 898

4-6 歹

殊 殊 殊 942 SHU koto

CH 殊 shū

Radical	Strokes
歹 78	10-4-6
Grade	Freq
Jōyō	1282
1-4-6	

一 ㄏ 万 歹 歹 歹 歼 歼 殊 殊
1 2 3 4 5 6 7 8 9 10

▶SPECIAL

COMPOUNDS

● (exceptional) **special, distinguished, unusual, above others**
殊勲 *shukun* meritorious deeds, distinguished service
殊勝な *shushō na* laudable, praiseworthy
殊遇 *shugū* special favor
特殊な *tokushu na* special, unique

KUN

【koto 殊】[in compounds] specialness, distinctiveness

殊に *koto ni* especially, distinctly, exceptionally, above all
殊の外 *koto no hoka* exceedingly, beyond measure; unexpectedly
殊更に *kotosara ni* especially; intentionally, deliberately

SYNONYMS

● **special**
特 SPECIAL (distinct) → 945
別 special (distinct) → 1117
専 EXCLUSIVE → 2644

USAGE

koto

殊

[in compounds] specialness, distinctiveness

異

difference

HOMOPHONES

koto ⇨ 異 2584

残 殘 残 𣦸

943 ZAN noko(ru) noko(su)

Ⓒⓗ 残 cán

Radical	Strokes
歹 78	10-4-6
Grade	**Freq**
Jōyō-4	449
◧ 1-4-6	

4-6 歹

一 厂 万 歹 歹 歹 歹 残 残 残
1 2 3 4 5 6 7 8 9 10

▶**REMAIN** ▶**RUTHLESS**

COMPOUNDS

❶ **remain, linger, stay**

残余 *zan'yo* remainder, residue, remnant
残高 *zandaka* balance, remainder
残額 *zangaku* balance (of an account)
残業 *zangyō* overtime
残飯 *zanpan* leftover food [rice]
残雪 *zansetsu* lingering snow
残念 *zannen* regret, disappointment, chagrin

❷ [sometimes also 惨 483] **ruthless, cruel, brutal**

残酷な *zankoku na* cruel, ruthless, atrocious
残虐な *zangyaku na* cruel, atrocious, brutal, inhuman
残忍 *zannin* cruelty, atrocity, brutality
無残な *muzan na* cruel, atrocious; pitiful, tragic, miserable

❸ injure, destroy

廃残 *haizan* ruin, decline

INDEPENDENT

【zan 残】 remainder, balance

百円の残 *hyakuen no zan* balance of 100 yen

KUN

【noko(ru) 残る】 remain, linger, stay; be left over; survive; *sumo* remain in competition, stay in the ring

残り *nokori* remainder, remnant, residue, leavings
残り物 *nokorimono* leftovers, remains, scraps
生き残る *ikinokoru* survive, outlive
残った *Nokotta* Not yet!

【noko(su) 残す】 leave (behind), keep back; reserve, save; bequeath, hand down (to posterity); *sumo* remain in competition, stay in the ring; [in compounds] leave undone

食べ残し *tabenokoshi* leftover food
取り残す *torinokosu* leave (behind)
言い残す *iinokosu* leave word with, state in one's will; leave (something) unsaid, forget to mention

SPECIAL READINGS

名残 *nagori* parting; memory; remains

SYNONYMS

❶ **remain**

余 REMAINING → 2042
留 STAY → 2580
滞 STAY → 663

❷ **cruel**

惨 CRUEL → 483
虐 CRUEL → 3218
酷 SEVERE → 1562
凶 ATROCIOUS → 2961

【nokosu】

○ **leave**

遺 LEAVE BEHIND → 3166

NOTE

⇨ see COMPOUND FORMATION for 残念 *zannen* ⇨ 念 2059

烟

944

▶**SMOKE**

nonstandard for 煙 1021

4-6 火

4-6
牛

特 特 特
945 TOKU

CH 特 tè

Radical	Strokes
牜 93	10-4-6
Grade	**Freq**
Jōyō-4	215
1-4-6	

▶**SPECIAL**

COMPOUNDS

ⓐ (distinct among others) **special, peculiar, unique, exclusive**

ⓑ (surpassing what is common) special, extraordinary

特別の *tokubetsu no* special, particular; extraordinary
特色 *tokushoku* characteristic
特徴 *tokuchō* distinctive feature, characteristic
特価 *tokka* special price, bargain price
特集 *tokushū* special edition
特許 *tokkyo* patent; special permission; concession
特権 *tokken* privilege, exclusive right
特使 *tokushi* special envoy [messenger]
特定の *tokutei no* specific, particular
特殊な *tokushu na* special, unique
特急 *tokkyū* super-express
特大 *tokudai* extra large, oversize
独特 *dokutoku* peculiarity, uniqueness
特等 *tokutō* special class [grade]
奇特な *kitoku na* praiseworthy; benevolent

INDEPENDENT

【**toku** 特】special grade (of a product)
特に *toku ni* specially, particularly, especially

SYNONYMS

ⓐ **special**
別 special (distinct) → 1117
殊 SPECIAL (exceptional) → 942
専 EXCLUSIVE → 2644

4-6
王

班 班 班
946 HAN

CH 班 bān

Radical	Strokes
王 96	10-4-6
Grade	**Freq**
Jōyō-6	1315
1-4-6	

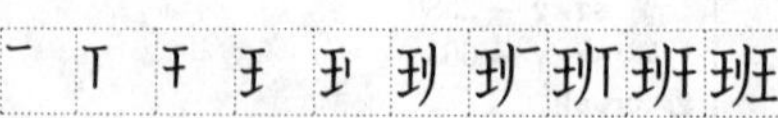

▶**SQUAD**

COMPOUNDS

❶ [also suffix] small group of individuals engaged in a common effort:
ⓐ **squad, group, party, team, crew**
ⓑ (military unit) squad, corps
班長 *hanchō* squad [group] leader
班員 *han'in* member of a group
取材班 *shuzaihan* data collecting party
三班 *sanpan* group 3
救護班 *kyūgohan* relief squad [party]
作業班 *sagyōhan* work party
第四中隊第二班 *daiyonchūtai dainihan* second squad of the fourth company

❷ [usu. 斑 1000] spot, speck
班点 *hanten* spot, speck

❸ order, seating order, precedence, ranking
班次 *hanji* precedence, ranking
首班 *shuhan* head (of state or of a cabinet), prime minister

❹ allot, distribute
班田 *handen hist* ancient farmland allotment

INDEPENDENT

【**han** 班】squad, group
三つの班に分ける *mittsu no han ni wakeru* divide into three groups

SYNONYMS

❶ⓐ **groups**
群 GROUP (of any kind) → 1540
組 group (of people) → 1337
陣 lineup → 455
連 set → 3103
族 common-interest group (*slang*) → 958
党 PARTY → 2581
隊 PARTY (organized group) → 625
団 BODY → 3053
伍 ranks → 47
軍 team → 2080

COMPOUND FORMATION

首班 *shuhan*
首班 'head, etc.' is the man who occupies the top or leading (首) seat or rank (班 ❸).

珠 珠 珠

947 SHU tama▲

CH 珠 zhū

Radical	Strokes
王 96	10-4-6
Grade	**Freq**
Jōyō	1635
1-4-6	

4-6 王

▶**PEARL**

COMPOUNDS

ⓐ **pearl**

ⓑ **something round like a pearl, bead**

珠玉 *shugyoku* jewel, gem

真珠 *shinju* pearl

珠算 *shuzan* calculation on the abacus

KUN

【**tama** 珠】[now usu. 玉] gem, jewel, precious stone, pearl; bead

珠暖簾 *tamanoren* bead curtain

SPECIAL READINGS

数珠 *juzu* (Buddhist) rosary

SYNONYMS

ⓐ **precious stones**

玉 GEM → 3477

瑛 TRANSPARENT GEM → 999

瑠 LAPIS LAZULI → 1060

璃 GLASSY SUBSTANCE → 1059

晶 CRYSTAL → 2474

HOMOPHONES

tama ⇨ 玉 3477 球 969 弾 572

NOTE

⇨ see USAGE note at 玉 3477

祥 祥 祥 祥

948 SHŌ

CH 祥 xiáng

Radical	Strokes
礻 113	10-4-6
Grade	**Freq**
Jōyō	1453
1-4-6	

4-6 礻

▶**AUSPICIOUS**

COMPOUNDS

❶ⓐ **auspicious, propitious, favorable**

ⓑ **auspicious omen, lucky sign**

不祥事 *fushōji* scandal, inauspicious event

吉祥 *kichijō* (=*kisshō*) auspicious omen

発祥 *hasshō* origin; appearance of auspicious omen

瑞祥 *zuishō* auspicious sign, good omen

❷ death or mourning anniversary

祥月 *shōtsuki* death month

SYNONYMS

❶ **good fortune**

瑞 AUSPICIOUS OMEN → 1027

禎 PROPITIOUS OMEN → 1031

吉 LUCKY → 2167

嘉 HAPPY → 2340

幸 GOOD FORTUNE → 2216

福 FORTUNE → 1029

朕 朕 朕 朕

949 CHIN

CH 朕 zhèn

Radical	Strokes
月 74	10-4-6
Grade	**Freq**
Jōyō	1933
1-4-6	

4-6 月

▶**IMPERIAL WE**

INDEPENDENT

【**chin** 朕】Imperial We—formal first person pronoun used chiefly by the Emperor of Japan

朕の *chin no* Our

朕が意 *chin ga i* Our will

SYNONYMS

【**chin**】

○ **first person pronouns**

麿 I (*archaic*) → 3184

余 I (*pompous*) → 2042

予 I (*pompous*) → 1983

吾 I (*elegant*) → 2407
私 I (*polite*) → 1115
僕 I (*familiar*) → 164
俺 I (*intimate*) → 110
自 SELF → 3525
我 SELF → 3548
己 ONESELF → 3380
身 ONE'S PERSON → 3553

4-6
月

胴 胴 胴

950 DŌ

CH 胴 dòng

Radical	Strokes
月 130	10-4-6
Grade	**Freq**
Jōyō	1460
■ 1 - 4 - 6	

丿 刀 月 月 月| 肌 肌 胴 胴 胴
1 2 3 4 5 6 7 8 9 10

▶TRUNK

COMPOUNDS

❶ [original meaning] **trunk (of the body), torso, abdomen**
胴体 *dōtai* trunk, body, torso, hull
胴巻き *dōmaki* bellyband
胴衣 *dōi* jacket, vest
胴上げ *dōage* tossing (a person in triumph)
❷ (main body of anything) trunk, body, main part
胴乱 *dōran* collecting [botanical] case
双胴機 *sōdōki* twin-fuselage plane
❸ used phonetically for *dō*
胴欲 *dōyoku* avarice, greed
胴元 *dōmoto* bookmaker (in gambling)

INDEPENDENT

【dō 胴】 trunk; main body of anything
胴が長い *dō ga nagai* have a long trunk
胴を着ける *dō o tsukeru* put on body armor

SYNONYMS

❶ **trunk parts**
腹 BELLY → 1034
腰 WAIST → 1036
胸 CHEST → 951
背 BACK → 2573
肩 SHOULDER → 1947

4-6
月

胸 胸 胸

951 KYŌ mune muna-

CH 胸 xiōng

Radical	Strokes
月 130	10-4-6
Grade	**Freq**
Jōyō-6	1051
■ 1 - 4 - 6	

丿 刀 月 月 月' 肑 肑 胸 胸 胸
1 2 3 4 5 6 7 8 9 10

▶CHEST

COMPOUNDS

❶ⓐ [original meaning] **chest, breast, thorax**
ⓑ breast height
胸囲 *kyōi* chest measurement
胸部 *kyōbu* breast, chest
胸骨 *kyōkotsu* breastbone
胸郭 *kyōkaku* thorax, chest
気胸 *kikyō* pneumothorax
胸壁 *kyōheki* chest wall; breast work
胸像 *kyōzō* bust
❷ (seat of emotions) **breast, (inmost) heart, mind, feelings**
胸裏 *kyōri* one's bosom, one's heart, one's feelings
胸中 *kyōchū* mind, heart, one's feelings, thoughts
度胸 *dokyō* courage, pluck, heart

KUN

【mune 胸, muna- 胸-】 chest, breast, thorax; heart, lungs; (seat of emotions) breast, bosom, heart
胸飾り *munekazari* brooch
胸板 *munaita* breast
胸毛 *munage* chest hair
胸焼け *muneyake* heartburn, sour stomach
胸を病む *mune o yamu* become consumptive
鳩胸 *hatomune* chicken [pigeon] breast
胸騒ぎ *munasawagi* uneasiness, (heart) flutter, emotional upset
胸を痛める *mune o itameru* worry oneself (about)

SYNONYMS

❶ⓐ **chest**
乳 breast → 1438
ⓐ **trunk parts**
腹 BELLY → 1034
胴 TRUNK → 950
腰 WAIST → 1036
背 BACK → 2573
肩 SHOULDER → 1947
❷ **psyche**

懐 BOSOM → 763
襟 inner mind → 1252
衷 INNER HEART → 2575
心 HEART → 11
腹 heart → 1034
神 MIND → 912
気 SPIRIT (consciousness) → 3194
精 SPIRIT (mind) → 1366
霊 SPIRIT (soul) → 2805
魂 SOUL, spirit → 1063

脇

952 KYŌ waki wake

CH 胁 xié

Radical	Strokes
月 130	10-4-6
Grade	**Freq**
Reference	
◧ 1 - 4 - 6	

4-6 月

COMPOUNDS

❶ [formerly also 傍 *waki* 147]
ⓐ side
ⓑ the other way, another place
脇腹 *wakibara* one's side, flank; illegitimate birth
関脇 *sekiwake* second champion sumo wrestler
脇見 *wakimi* looking aside

❷ [formerly also 傍 *waki* 147] supporting actor [role]
脇役 *wakiyaku* supporting actor [role]

❸ [also 腋 *waki* 1004]
ⓐ [original meaning] armpit
ⓑ armhole
脇毛 *wakige* hair of the armpit

HOMOPHONES

waki ⇨ 傍 147 腋 1004

NOTE

⇨ see USAGE note at 傍 147

脈

脈 脉◇ 脈 脈

953 MYAKU

CH 脉 mài mò

Radical	Strokes
月 130	10-4-6
Grade	**Freq**
Jōyō-4	1468
◧ 1 - 4 - 6	

4-6 月

▶**VEIN** ▶**PULSE**

COMPOUNDS

❶ [original meaning] (any blood vessel) **vein, artery, blood vessel**
脈管 *myakkan* blood vessel; duct
動脈 *dōmyaku* artery
静脈 *jōmyaku* vein

❷ⓐ **something resembling a vein in shape or structure**
ⓑ *geol* vein, seam
脈脈たる *myakumyakutaru* continuous, unbroken; pulsating forcefully
山脈 *sanmyaku* mountain range
葉脈 *yōmyaku* veins of a leaf
鉱脈 *kōmyaku* (mineral) vein, deposit, lode
水脈 *suimyaku* water vein; waterway

❸ (distinctive thread) vein, thread, line
脈絡 *myakuraku* logical connection, chain of reasoning
文脈 *bunmyaku* context
乱脈 *ranmyaku* disorder, confusion, chaos
人脈 *jinmyaku* line of connections
金脈 *kinmyaku* (questionable) financial connections; vein of gold

❹ **pulse, pulsation**
脈拍 *myakuhaku* pulse, pulsation
徐脈 *jomyaku* bradycardia
平脈 *heimyaku* regular pulse
不整脈 *fuseimyaku* arrhythmia

INDEPENDENT

【myaku 脈】 pulse, pulsation; hope
脈を取る *myaku o toru* take a pulse
まだ脈が有る *mada myaku ga aru* be not altogether hopeless

SYNONYMS

❶ **tubular passages**
管 PIPE → 2701
筒 TUBE → 2680
道 passage → 3134

❷ **line**
条 strip → 2200
筋 THREADLIKE STRUCTURE → 2678
線 LINE → 1392
棒 straight line → 983
軸 AXIS → 1514

❸ **reasoning**

筋 thread → 2678 | 理 REASON → 970

4-6 月

脂 954 SHI abura

CH 脂 zhī

Radical	Strokes
月 130	10-4-6
Grade	**Freq**
Jōyō	1418

1 - 4 - 6

▶FAT

COMPOUNDS

❶ [original meaning] **fat, grease, animal fat**

脂肪 *shibō* fat, grease

脂質 *shishitsu* lipid, fats

油脂 *yushi* fats and oils

脱脂粉乳 *dasshi-funnyū* skim milk

❷ resin

樹脂 *jushi* resin

❸ rouge, lipstick

脂粉 *shifun* cosmetics, rouge and powder

KUN

【abura 脂】[formerly also 膏] fat, grease, lard, blubber; greasy substance

脂ぎった *aburagitta* greasy, oily

脂が乗る *abura ga noru* be in good table quality; get into the swing of (as one's work)

脂性 *aburashō* fatty constitution

SYNONYMS

❶ **fats and oils**

肪 ANIMAL FAT → 877

油 OIL → 341

HOMOPHONES

abura ⇨ 油 341 膏 2141

NOTE

⇨ see USAGE note at 油 341

4-6 月

955

▶VEIN ▶PULSE

nonstandard for 脈 953

4-6 月

956

▶IMPERIAL WE

nonstandard for 朕 949

4-7 方

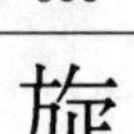
957 SEN

CH 旋 xuán xuàn

Radical	Strokes
方 70	11-4-7
Grade	**Freq**
Jōyō	1559

1 - 4 - 7

▶GYRATE

COMPOUNDS

❶ **gyrate, whirl, revolve, spiral, go around**

旋回 *senkai* revolution, rotation, circling, swiveling

旋転 *senten* gyration, whirling, revolution, rotation

旋盤 *senban* lathe

旋削 *sensaku* turning (on a lathe)

旋風 *senpū* whirlwind

旋律 *senritsu* melody

螺旋 *rasen* spiral, helix; screw

❷ render a service to, mediate

斡旋 *assen* good offices, services; mediation

周旋業 *shūsengyō* brokerage

❸ return, turn back

凱旋 *gaisen* triumphal return

SYNONYMS

❶ **turn**

転 TURN → 1480

回 TURN ROUND → 3055

巡 MAKE THE ROUNDS → 3047

循 CIRCULATE → 578

族 958 ZOKU

㊥ 族 zú

Radical	Strokes
方 70	11-4-7
Grade	**Freq**
Jōyō-3	577
1-4-7	

4-7 方

▶FAMILY

COMPOUNDS

❶ⓐ **family, kinsman; relatives**
ⓑ family of rank, nobility
ⓒ [rare] death penalty (in ancient China) imposed on an offender and his whole family

家族 *kazoku* family, household
遺族 *izoku* bereaved family
親族 *shinzoku* relative
一族 *ichizoku* kinsman, relative, one's (whole) family; race
血族 *ketsuzoku* blood relative
貴族 *kizoku* nobility, noble
皇族 *kōzoku* imperial family, royalty
族滅 *zokumetsu* putting an entire family to death

❷ **race, clan, tribe**
民族 *minzoku* race, people, nation
部族 *buzoku* tribe
種族 *shuzoku* race, tribe; family, genus; species
蛮族 *banzoku* savage tribe
アリアン族 *arianzoku* Aryan family
アイヌ族 *ainuzoku* the Ainu race

❸ⓐ [also suffix] class of things with common features, as a family of languages
ⓑ *math* family
ⓒ *chem* group (of elements)
語族 *gozoku* family of languages
水族館 *suizokukan* aquarium
関数族 *kansūzoku* family of functions
亜族 *azoku* subgroup (of the periodic table)
白金族 *hakkinzoku* platinum group

❹ [also suffix] *slang* (group of persons who share a common interest or engage in a common activity) **tribe, herd, clan, gang, set, clique**
雷族 *kaminarizoku* Thunder Herd, hot-rodders
暴走族 *bōsōzoku* motorcycle gang, hot-rodders
深夜族 *shin'yazoku* the night owls
社用族 *shayōzoku* expense-account spenders
ながら族 *nagarazoku* persons who do two things at the same time (as studying while watching TV)
団地族 *danchizoku* housing project dwellers

❺ [formerly also 簇 2719] form a cluster
族生する *zokusei suru* (of plants) grow in clusters

SYNONYMS

❶ⓐ **family and relations**
家 FAMILY → 2273
門 family → 888
氏 clan → 2951
縁 RELATION → 1386
姻 relative by marriage → 353
親 RELATIVES → 1799

❷ **people**
民 PEOPLE → 3036

❹ **groups**
連 set → 3103
党 PARTY → 2581
隊 PARTY (organized group) → 625
団 BODY → 3053
伍 ranks → 47
班 SQUAD → 946
軍 team → 2080
群 GROUP (of any kind) → 1540
組 group (of people) → 1337
陣 lineup → 455

晩 959

▶EVENING

nonstandard for 晩 979

4-7 日

4-7 木

彬 彬 彬

960 HIN NAMES akira aki yoshi

CH 彬 bīn

Radical	Strokes
彡 59	11-3-8
Grade	Freq
Names	2134
1-4-7	

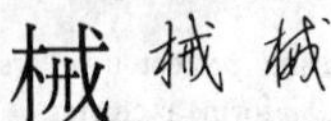

▶REFINED AND GENTLE

COMPOUNDS

● [rare] (having both appearance and substance) refined and gentle, handsome and solid in character, having a due combination of plainness and ornament

彬蔚 *hin'utsu* handsome, erudite and refined

文質彬彬 *bunshitsu-hinpin* refined, handsome and solid in character

NAMES

彬 *akira* male name

彬光 *akimitsu* male name

SYNONYMS

● **elegant**

粋 REFINED → 1293

雅 ELEGANT → 1197

淑 GRACEFUL → 527

優 graceful → 177

4-7 木

械 械 械

961 KAI kase▲

CH 械 xiè

Radical	Strokes
木 75	11-4-7
Grade	Freq
Jōyō-4	927
1-4-7	

▶MECHANICAL CONTRIVANCE

COMPOUNDS

● **mechanical contrivance, device, instrument, tool**

機械 *kikai* machine, mechanism

器械 *kikai* instrument, apparatus, appliance

KUN

【**kase** 械】[original meaning] fetters, shackles

足械 *ashikase* fetters, shackles, hobbles

SYNONYMS

● **machines and tools**

機 MACHINE → 1076

具 IMPLEMENT → 2552

器 INSTRUMENT → 2713

儀 measuring instrument → 169

鏡 OPTICAL INSTRUMENT → 1766

4-7 木

梓 梓 梓

962 SHI azusa

CH 梓 zǐ

Radical	Strokes
木 75	11-4-7
Grade	Freq
Names	2079
1-4-7	

▶CATALPA

COMPOUNDS

❶ **catalpa, catalpa tree, Japanese catalpa tree**

梓宮 *shikyū* [archaic] Emperor's coffin (so called because it was made of catalpa wood)

❷ printing block, woodcut; wood printing

上梓 *jōshi* publishing

❸ [archaic] carpentry, woodwork; cabinetmaker

梓匠 *shishō* woodworker, cabinetmaker

INDEPENDENT

【**shi** 梓】printing block

梓に上せる *shi ni noboseru* publish, bring (a book) into the world

KUN

【**azusa** 梓】catalpa, Japanese catalpa tree

梓弓 *azusayumi* catalpa bow

NAMES

梓 *azusa* surname also male name also female name

梓川 *azusagawa* place name

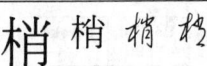

SYNONYMS

❶ **trees**

桑 MULBERRY → 2112
漆 Japanese lacquer tree → 704
桂 AROMATIC TREE, katsura tree → 928
桐 PAULOWNIA → 937
楠 CAMPHOR TREE → 1018
槙 PODOCARPUS → 1051
杉 CRYPTOMERIA → 832
松 PINE → 864
楓 MAPLE → 1015
柳 WILLOW → 899
桜 CHERRY → 931

❷ **printing plate**

版 PRINTING PLATE → 872

梢 梢 梢 梢

963 SHŌ kozue

Ⓒⓗ 梢 shāo

Radical	Strokes
木 75	11-4-7
Grade	Freq
Names	2078
1-4-7	

4-7 木

▶TIP OF A TWIG

COMPOUNDS

❶ⓐ [original meaning] **tip of a twig or branch**
ⓑ **tip, end**
末梢 *masshō* tip, end; tip of a twig; *anat* periphery
末梢神経 *masshō shinkei* peripheral nerve
❷ [archaic] rudder
梢子 *shōshi* boatman

KUN

【kozue 梢】 treetop, tip of a twig
松の梢 *matsu no kozue* top of a pine tree

NAMES

梢 *kozue* male name also female name

SYNONYMS

❶ⓐ **branches and twigs**
枝 BRANCH → 863
ⓑ **extremity**
末 end → 3505
先 point → 2394
端 END → 1221

梳

964 SO to(ku) to(kasu) su(ku) kezu(ru) kushikezu(ru)

Ⓒⓗ 梳 shū

Radical	Strokes
木 75	11-4-7
Grade	Freq
Reference	
1-4-7	

4-7 木

COMPOUNDS

ⓐ [original meaning] comb (one's hair)
ⓑ comb (one's hair)
梳毛 *somō* combed wool [yarn]
髪を梳かす *kami o tokasu* comb (one's hair)
羊毛を梳く *yōmō o suku* card wool

HOMOPHONES

toku ⇨ 解 1517 溶 664 説 1547
tokasu ⇨ 解 1517 融 1831 溶 664 熔 1058 鎔 1762

NOTE

⇨ see USAGE note at 解 1517

梅

965

▶JAPANESE APRICOT

nonstandard for 梅 925

4-7 木

梢

966

▶TIP OF A TWIG

nonstandard for 梢 963

4-7 木

4-7 火 焰 incorrect stroke count ⇨ see 996

4-7 爿 將 967 ▶**GENERAL OFFICER**
nonstandard for 将 460

4-7 王 現 968 GEN arawa(reru) arawa(su) Ⓒⓗ 现 xiàn

Radical	Strokes
王 96	11-4-7
Grade	**Freq**
Jōyō-5	81
1-4-7	

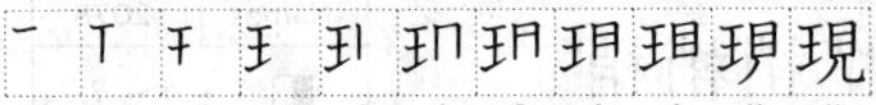

▶**ACTUAL** ▶**APPEAR**

COMPOUNDS

❶ⓐ [also prefix] (occurring at the present moment) **actual, present, current, existing, now**
ⓑ *Buddhism* present life, life in this world
現在 *genzai* present time, now; present tense; actually
現代 *gendai* present age, modern times, today
現行の *genkō no* present, existing, current, actual
現職 *genshoku* present post [office]; incumbent
現住所 *genjūsho* present address
現内閣 *gennaikaku* present cabinet
現世 *gense* this world, this life
過現未 *kagenmi* past, present and future, three temporal states of existence
❷ⓐ (existing in fact) **actual, real**
ⓑ on hand—said esp. of money
現実 *genjitsu* actuality, reality
現状 *genjō* present condition
現地 *genchi* actual place [locale]
現役 *gen'eki* active service
現場 *genba* actual spot; job site, building site
現金 *genkin* cash
❸ⓐ **appear, become visible, come into view, be revealed, materialize**
ⓑ cause to appear, show, reveal
現象 *genshō* phenomenon
出現する *shutsugen suru* appear, make an appearance, emerge
実現する *jitsugen suru* realize, materialize
表現する *hyōgen suru* express, represent, manifest; give expression to
現像 *genzō* developing (a film)
再現する *saigen suru* reenact, reproduce
顕現 *kengen* manifestation

INDEPENDENT

【gen 現】 actuality; abbrev. of 現在形 *genzaikei*: present tense; abbrev. of 現職 *genshoku*: incumbent
現に *gen ni* actually, really, as a matter of fact
無所属·現 *mushozoku gen* incumbent member (of the House of Representatives) without party affiliation

KUN

【arawa(reru) 現れる】
① appear, emerge, come out, become visible, materialize
現れ *araware* embodiment, materialization
雲間に現れた月 *kumoma ni arawareta tsuki* moon peeping from behind the clouds
② become known, attain distinction; be exposed [found out]
悪事が現れた *Akuji ga arawareta* The evil deed was discovered

【arawa(su) 現す】
① cause to appear, show, display, reveal
姿を現す *sugata o arawasu* make an appearance
② attain distinction, become famous
名を現す *na o arawasu* distinguish oneself

SYNONYMS

❶ⓐ **present**
今 PRESENT → 1968
当 THE PRESENT → 2177
❷ⓐ **true**
実 REAL → 2225
本 real → 3502
正 genuine → 3484
真 TRUE → 2111
洵 TRULY → 383
❸ⓐ **appear**
出 come out → 3498
顕 MANIFEST → 1806
ⓑ **reveal**

顕 MANIFEST → 1806
発 reveal → 2565
露 EXPOSE → 2818
暴 disclose → 2515
披 OPEN OUT → 305

HOMOPHONES
arawareru ⇨ 表 2429
araware ⇨ 表 2429
arawasu ⇨ 表 2429 著 2300

NOTE
⇨ see USAGE note at 表 2429

球 球 球

969 KYŪ tama

Ⓒ 球 qiú

Radical	Strokes
王 96	11-4-7
Grade	**Freq**
Jōyō-3	325
1-4-7	

4-7 王

一 丅 干 王 王一 玎 玎 玎 球 球 球
1 2 3 4 5 6 7 8 9 10 11

▶**BALL**

COMPOUNDS

❶ⓐ [original meaning] (spherical body) **ball, globe, sphere**
ⓑ [suffix] light bulb
球体 *kyūtai* sphere, globe
球形 *kyūkei* globular shape
球根 *kyūkon* bulb
地球 *chikyū* the Earth
眼球 *gankyū* eyeball
電球 *denkyū* light bulb
❷ⓐ **ball (in a sports game)**
ⓑ [also suffix] **manner of delivering a ball, esp. in baseball; ball**
ⓒ counter for number of pitches
球技 *kyūgi* ball game
硬球 *kōkyū* regulation ball
投球 *tōkyū* throwing a ball, pitching
好球 *kōkyū* good pitch
速球 *sokkyū* fast ball
内角球 *naikakkyū* inside ball, insider
四球 *shikyū* base on balls
第一球 *daiikkyū* first pitch
❸ⓐ **ball game, -ball**
ⓑ abbrev. of 野球 *yakyū*: **baseball**
野球 *yakyū* baseball
卓球 *takkyū* table tennis, ping-pong
庭球 *teikyū* tennis
球団 *kyūdan* baseball team
球場 *kyūjō* baseball ground, ball park

INDEPENDENT

【kyū 球】 globe, sphere, ball

KUN

【tama 球】
ⓐ ball (in a sports game)
ⓑ light bulb
球拾い *tamahiroi* picking up balls; poor (ball) player
釣り球 *tsuridama* deceptive pitch
電気の球 *denki no tama* electric [light] bulb

SYNONYMS

❶ⓐ **spherical object**
玉 spherical object → 3477
丸 round body → 3417
ⓐ **bodies**
塊 LUMP → 632
体 BODY → 71

HOMOPHONES
tama ⇨ 玉 3477 珠 947 弾 572

NOTE
⇨ see USAGE note at 玉 3477

理 理 理

970 RI kotowari▲

Ⓒ 理 lǐ

Radical	Strokes
王 96	11-4-7
Grade	**Freq**
Jōyō-2	106
1-4-7	

4-7 王

一 丅 干 王 玎 玎 玥 玾 理 理 理
1 2 3 4 5 6 7 8 9 10 11

▶**REASON** ▶**BASIC PRINCIPLE**

COMPOUNDS

❶ⓐ **reason, what is right and proper**
ⓑ (rational thought) **reason, logic, line of thought**
理想 *risō* ideal
理由 *riyū* reason, cause, ground
道理 *dōri* reason, right, justice, truth
合理的な *gōriteki na* rational, logical, reasonable
無理な *muri na* unreasonable, unjustifiable; impossible; forced; excessive; irrational

(equation)
理性 *risei* reason, reasoning power
理屈 *rikutsu* reason, logic; argument; pretext; theory
理不尽な *rifujin na* unreasonable, unjust, absurd
論理 *ronri* logic
条理 *jōri* reason, logic
❷ realize, appreciate, understand
理解する *rikai suru* understand, comprehend
❸ **basic principle(s) (as of a science), rationale of things, law, theory, doctrine**
理論 *riron* theory
原理 *genri* principle, theory
真理 *shinri* truth
定理 *teiri* theorem, proposition
心理 *shinri* mental state, mentality; psychology
生理 *seiri* physiological functions, physiology; menstruation
地理 *chiri* geographical features, topography; geography
哲理 *tetsuri* philosophy (of something)
❹ⓐ **natural science, physics**
ⓑ abbrev. of 物理学 *butsurigaku*: physics
ⓒ abbrev. of 理科 *rika*: science
理学 *rigaku* (physical) science
理科 *rika* science; science department
物理学 *butsurigaku* physics, physical science
理化学 *rikagaku* physics and chemistry
理工学部 *rikōgakubu* department [school] of science and engineering
❺ⓐ **manage, run**
ⓑ abbrev. of 理事会 *rijikai*: board of trustees
理事 *riji* director, trustee
管理する *kanri suru* administer, supervise, manage, exercise control [jurisdiction] over
処理する *shori suru* manage, deal with, dispose of; process, treat
総理大臣 *sōri-daijin* prime minister
代理 *dairi* representation; agency; proxy, deputy
料理する *ryōri suru* cook; handle, manage
受理する *juri suru* accept (a report)
安保理 *anpori* Security Council
❻ⓐ **put in order, arrange**
ⓑ cut (one's hair), dress
修理する *shūri suru* repair, mend
整理する *seiri suru* put in order, arrange; liquidate, disorganize; retrench; cut, dispose of
理容 *riyō* hairdressing
理髪 *rihatsu* haircut, hairdressing
❼ [original meaning] grain, texture, line, stripe
木理 *mokuri* grain of wood
大理石 *dairiseki* marble

INDEPENDENT

【ri 理】
①ⓐ reason, what is right and proper
ⓑ (rational thought) reason, logic, line of thought
理が非でも *ri ga hi demo* right or wrong, by fair means or foul
理の有る *ri no aru* justifiable
② principle, law, philosophy
陰陽の理 *onmyō no ri* principle of duality
③ truth
不変の理 *fuhen no ri* eternal truth
理外の理 *rigai no ri* transcendental reason

KUN

【kotowari 理】 *literary* reason, right, justice
彼がそう云うのも理だ *Kare ga sō iu no mo kotowari da* He may well say so

SYNONYMS

❶ⓐ **reason**
訳 SENSE → 1473
ⓑ **reasoning**
筋 thread → 2678
脈 VEIN → 953
❸ **principle**
律 LAW → 363
❺ⓐ **direct and supervise**
営 MANAGE → 2603
経 MANAGE → 1331
宰 PRESIDE → 2275
司 OFFICIATE → 2931
督 SUPERVISE → 2796
監 OVERSEE → 2852
掌 TAKE CHARGE OF → 2602
轄 EXERCISE JURISDICTION OVER → 1627
管 EXERCISE CONTROL → 2701
制 CONTROL → 1274
❻ⓐ **arrange**
整 PUT IN ORDER → 2871
揃える arrange properly → 590
羅 spread out → 2622
陳 lay out (for exhibit) → 540
列 arrange in a row → 824
比 rank → 26
並 LINE UP → 2246

NOTE

⇨ see COMPOUND FORMATION for
理屈 *rikutsu* ⇨ 屈 3079
論理 *ronri* ⇨ 論 1574
理不尽 *rifujin* ⇨ 尽 3050

琢 琢 琢 琢

971 TAKU NAMES aya taka

CH 琢 zhuó zuó

Radical	Strokes
王 96	11-4-7
Grade	**Freq**
Names	2060
◧ 1 - 4 - 7	

4-7 王

一 T Ŧ 王 王 王 玎 玡 琢 琢 琢
1 2 3 4 5 6 7 8 9 10 11

▶POLISH

COMPOUNDS

❶ **polish [improve] one's skills, cultivate one's mind**

切磋琢磨 *sessa-takuma* working hard together, assiduity in friendly rivalry

❷ [original meaning] polish (jade or jewels), carve

彫琢する *chōtaku suru* carve and polish; elaborate

NAMES

琢磨 *takuma* male name

琢之助 *takunosuke* male name

SYNONYMS

❶ **cultivate**

磨 POLISH → 3181
鍛 train → 1755
錬 REFINE → 1741
練 TRAIN → 1375
修 CULTIVATE → 123
養 FOSTER (one's intellect) → 2365

疎 疏

incorrect stroke count ⇨ see ◧ 5-7

4-7 𤴔

視 視 視 視

972 SHI

CH 视 shì

Radical	Strokes
見 147	11-7-4
Grade	**Freq**
Jōyō-6	457
◧ 1 - 4 - 7	

4-7 礻

丶 ラ ネ ネ 礻 礻 礻 礻 祖 視 視
1 2 3 4 5 6 7 8 9 10 11

▶REGARD

COMPOUNDS

❶ⓐ [original meaning] (look at attentively) **regard, look at, gaze**

ⓑ **inspect, watch over**

視聴者 *shichōsha* viewer, audience
視界 *shikai* field of vision, visibility
視野 *shiya* field of vision; one's mental horizon
視力 *shiryoku* eyesight
視覚 *shikaku* sense of sight
凝視する *gyōshi suru* stare, gaze at
注視する *chūshi suru* gaze steadily at, observe (a person) closely
視察 *shisatsu* inspection, observation
監視する *kanshi suru* watch, keep under observation, exercise surveillance
巡視 *junshi* inspection tour
警視庁 *keishichō* Metropolitan Police Office

❷ eyesight, vision

近視 *kinshi* nearsightedness, shortsightedness
乱視 *ranshi* astigmatism

❸ [also suffix] **regard as, consider**

軽視する *keishi suru* make light of, despise; neglect
敵視する *tekishi suru* regard as an enemy
無視する *mushi suru* ignore, disregard
重要視する *jūyōshi suru* regard as important, think much of

❹ [prefix] *astron* apparent

視地平 *shichihei* apparent horizon

SYNONYMS

❶ **see and look**

看 WATCH → 3220
察 INSPECT → 2347
見 SEE → 2544
目 look → 3043
観 VIEW → 1880
覧 LOOK OVER → 2854
眺 LOOK OUT OVER → 1171
望 LOOK AFAR → 2742
仰 LOOK UP → 48
顧 LOOK BACK → 1900

❸ **judge**

判 JUDGE → 1122
裁 JUDGE → 3299
鑑 APPRAISE → 1773
評 evaluate → 1501

審 TRY → 2360 | 決 DECIDE → 263

4-7
月

脱 脱 脱 脱

973 DATSU nu(gu) nu(geru)

ⒸⒽ 脱 tuō

Radical	Strokes
月 130	11-4-7
Grade	**Freq**
Jōyō	839
1-4-7	

丿 1 冂 2 月 3 月 4 月 5 月 6 月 7 肸 8 肸 9 脫 10 脱 11

▶REMOVE ▶ESCAPE FROM

COMPOUNDS

❶ⓐ [also prefix] **remove, eliminate, de- (as in *decarbonate*)**

ⓑ **remove (one's) clothes, take off, undress**

脱脂 *dasshi* fat removal
脱毛 *datsumō* removal of hair; falling out of hair
脱色 *dasshoku* decoloration
脱水 *dassui* dehydration
脱炭酸 *datsutansan* decarbonation
脱帽 *datsubō* taking off one's cap [hat]; submission
脱衣 *datsui* undressing
脱皮 *dappi* ecdysis; self-renewal

❷ⓐ **get out of place, come off**

ⓑ **leave out by mistake, omit; be left out, be omitted**

脱線 *dassen* derailment; deviation, aberration
脱肛 *dakkō* prolapse of the anus
脱臼 *dakkyū* dislocation
脱落する *datsuraku suru* be omitted; fall away [behind], drop out
脱漏 *datsurō* omission
逸脱 *itsudatsu* deviation, departure from the norm

❸ⓐ [also prefix] **escape from (an undesirable situation), get away from, extricate oneself from, withdraw from**

ⓑ extricate oneself from worldly affairs

脱税 *datsuzei* tax evasion
脱退 *dattai* withdrawal, secession
脱出 *dasshutsu* escape, extrication
脱走 *dassō* desertion, escape
脱獄 *datsugoku* prison break, jailbreak
脱却する *dakkyaku suru* get rid of; slough off
脱会 *dakkai* withdrawal (from an organization)
脱石油 *datsusekiyu* extrication from dependence on oil
離脱 *ridatsu* breakaway, separation, secession
脱俗 *datsuzoku* unworldliness
洒脱な *shadatsu na* free and easy, unconstrained
超脱 *chōdatsu* transcendency, detachment
解脱 *gedatsu Buddhism* deliverance (of one's soul), salvation

❹ lose one's strength

脱力感 *datsuryokukan* feeling of exhaustion
虚脱 *kyodatsu* (physical) collapse, prostration; absentmindedness

INDEPENDENT

【dassuru 脱する】 escape from, get away from, extricate oneself from; rise above

危険を脱する *kiken o dassuru* get out of danger
凡庸を脱する *bon'yō o dassuru* rise above mediocrity

KUN

【nu(gu) 脱ぐ】 *vt* remove (one's) clothes, take off, undress

脱ぎ捨てる *nugisuteru* throw off (clothes), kick off (boots)

【nu(geru) 脱げる】 *vi* (of clothes or footwear) come off, slip off

靴が脱げない *Kutsu ga nugenai* My shoes will not come off

SYNONYMS

❶ⓐ **eliminate**

去 take away → 2156
外す take off → 186
除 RID OF → 456
省 leave out → 2449
却 ELIMINATE → 1118
削 cross out → 1448
抹 wipe off → 313
撤 WITHDRAW → 738
排 EXCLUDE → 490
払う CLEAR AWAY → 194

❷ⓐ **come off**

外れる come off → 186

ⓑ **omit**

抜く leave out → 246
漏 omit → 701
欠 missing → 1987

❸ⓐ **escape**

逃 ESCAPE → 3095
亡 flee → 3402
走 run away → 2194

脚 腳◇ 脚 䏐

974 KYAKU KYA ashi

CH 脚 jiǎo jué

Radical	Strokes
月 130	11-4-7
Grade	Freq
Jōyō	1193
1-4-7	

4-7 月

丿 月 月 月 月 月 肚 肚 胠 胠 脚 (1–11)

▶**LEG**

COMPOUNDS

❶ⓐ [original meaning] **leg, foot**
ⓑ **move on foot, walk, run**
脚力 *kyakuryoku* strength of one's legs; walking ability
脚線美 *kyakusenbi* beauty of leg lines
馬脚 *bakyaku* horse's legs; one's true character
健脚の *kenkyaku no* strong in walking
行脚 *angya* pilgrimage; walking tour; tour
飛脚 *hikyaku* express messenger; postman (in former times)

❷ⓐ (leg-shaped support) **leg, base**
ⓑ counter for legged furniture
ⓒ foot, lower part, bottom
脚部 *kyakubu* leg (as of a table)
脚立 *kyatatsu* footstool; stepladder
三脚 *sankyaku* tripod
橋脚 *kyōkyaku* bridge pier
机二脚 *tsukue nikyaku* two desks
脚注 *kyakuchū* footnote
立脚する *rikkyaku suru* be based on

❸ bottom radical of Chinese characters, leg radical
偏旁冠脚 *henbōkankyaku* the radicals

❹ **plot of a play, script**
脚本 *kyakuhon* script, playbook, drama, scenario
脚色 *kyakushoku* dramatization

❺ social standing
失脚する *shikkyaku suru* lose one's social standing

INDEPENDENT

【**kyaku** 脚】 undercarriage (of an aircraft)

KUN

【**ashi** 脚】
① [also 足] (leg-shaped support) leg
三本脚の机 *sanbon'ashi no tsukue* three-legged table
② [also 足] movement, pace
雨脚 *amaashi* density of the falling rain; pace (of the approaching shower)
③ bottom radical of Chinese characters, leg radical
人脚 *hitoashi hitoashi*, 'bottom legs' radical (儿)

SYNONYMS

❶ⓐ **foot**
足 FOOT → 2188
ⓐ **limbs**
肢 LIMB → 882
腕 ARM → 1006
ⓑ **walk**
徒 go on foot → 416
歩 WALK → 2416
足 travel on foot → 2188
踏 TREAD → 1587

HOMOPHONES

ashi ⇨ 足 2188

NOTE

⇨ see USAGE note at 足 2188

脳 腦 脳 𦡀

975 NŌ

CH 脑 nǎo

Radical	Strokes
月 130	11-4-7
Grade	Freq
Jōyō-6	795
1-4-7	

4-7 月

丿 月 月 月 月 月 月 月 月 脳 脳 (1–11)

▶**BRAIN**

COMPOUNDS

❶ⓐ [also prefix] [original meaning] **brain**
ⓑ (intellectual capacity) **brain(s), intellect, mind**
脳髄 *nōzui* brain
脳炎 *nōen* brain inflammation, encephalitis
脳細胞 *nōsaibō* brain cells
大脳 *dainō* cerebrum
脳裏 *nōri* brain, mind, memory
頭脳 *zunō* brain; brains, head
首脳 *shunō* head, leader

❷ xylem, woody tissue
樟脳 *shōnō* camphor

INDEPENDENT

【**nō** 脳】 brain; brains

脳の損傷 *nō no sonshō* brain damage

SYNONYMS

❶ⓐ **head**

頭 HEAD → 1604

首 HEAD, NECK → 2265

COMPOUND FORMATION

樟脳 *shōnō*

樟脳 'camphor' refers to the woody substance (脳 ❷) obtained from the camphor tree (樟).

4-7 月

豚

976 TON buta

CH 豚 tún

Radical	Strokes
豕 152	11-7-4
Grade	**Freq**
Jōyō	1429
1-4-7	

1 2 3 4 5 6 7 8 9 10 11

▶PIG

COMPOUNDS

ⓐ [original meaning] **pig, hog, swine**

ⓑ pig [hog] meat, pork

ⓒ [humble] as worthless as a pig

豚舎 *tonsha* pigsty, pigpen

養豚 *yōton* swine keeping

豚カツ *tonkatsu* pork cutlet

豚児 *tonji* my (foolish) son

INDEPENDENT

【**ton** 豚】 pig; pork

KUN

【**buta** 豚】 pig, hog, swine, boar; pig [hog] meat, pork

豚小屋 *butagoya* hogpen

子豚 *kobuta* piglet

豚肉 *butaniku* pork, hog meat

豚箱 *butabako slang* police cell, jug

SPECIAL READINGS

河豚▲ *fugu fugu*, globefish, swellfish

SYNONYMS

ⓐ **swine**

猪 WILD BOAR → 536

亥 THE BOAR → 2012

ⓐ **domesticated mammals**

羊 SHEEP → 2183

牛 CATTLE → 3452

馬 HORSE → 3296

犬 DOG → 3464

猫 CAT → 535

4-7 月

脫

977

▶REMOVE ▶ESCAPE FROM

nonstandard for 脱 973

4-7 夫

規

978 KI

CH 规 guī

Radical	Strokes
見 147	11-7-4
Grade	**Freq**
Jōyō-5	434
1-4-7	

1 2 3 4 5 6 7 8 9 10 11

▶REGULATION

COMPOUNDS

❶ⓐ **regulation, rule, standard**

ⓑ **regulate, control**

規定 *kitei* regulations, rules; provisions

規則 *kisoku* rule, regulation

規約 *kiyaku* agreement, rules, bylaws

規律 *kiritsu* order, discipline; regulation, law

規範 *kihan* standard, norm, criterion

規格 *kikaku* standard, norm

法規 *hōki* laws and regulations

内規 *naiki* private rules [regulations], bylaws

校規 *kōki* school regulations

規制する *kisei suru* regulate, control

新規に *shinki ni* newly

❷ [original meaning] compass

規矩 *kiku* standard, rule; compass and ruler

規模 *kibo* scale, scope

定規 *jōgi* ruler, rule, square

SYNONYMS

❶ⓐ **laws and rules**

則 RULE → 1444

矩 RULE → 1148

紀 discipline → 1276

法 LAW → 333

律 LAW → 363

典 CANON → 2627

憲 CONSTITUTION → 2368

令 ordinance → 1995

NOTE

⇨ see COMPOUND FORMATION for 規模 *kibo* ⇨ 模 1050

晩 晩 晩 晩

979 BAN

CH 晩 wǎn

Radical	Strokes
日 72	12-4-8
Grade	**Freq**
Jōyō-6	1154
1-4-8	

4-8 日

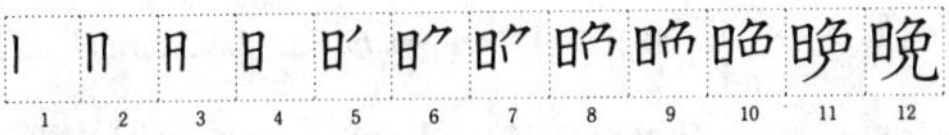

▶**EVENING**

COMPOUNDS

❶ **evening, night**

晩方 *bangata* toward evening
晩鐘 *banshō* evening bell, curfew (bell)
晩御飯 *bangohan* supper
毎晩 *maiban* every evening [night]
今晩 *konban* this evening, tonight
今晩は *konban wa* good evening

❷ⓐ (advanced) late, drawing toward the end, in the latter part

ⓑ **late in life**

晩春 *banshun* late spring
早晩 *sōban* sooner or later
晩学 *bangaku* late education
晩年 *bannen* late in life
晩婚 *bankon* late marriage

INDEPENDENT

【**ban** 晩】 evening, night
晩に *ban ni* in the evening

SYNONYMS

❶ **evening and night**

夕 EVENING → 3387
夜 NIGHT → 2056
宵 EARLY EVENING → 2276
暮 DUSK → 2354

❷ **late**

遅 LATE (delayed) → 3133

暁 暁 暁 暁

980 GYŌ akatsuki

CH 晓 xiǎo

Radical	Strokes
日 72	12-4-8
Grade	**Freq**
Jōyō	1678
1-4-8	

4-8 日

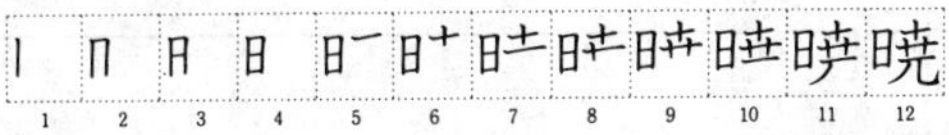

▶**DAWN**

COMPOUNDS

❶ [original meaning] **dawn, daybreak**

暁天 *gyōten* dawn
暁星 *gyōsei* morning star, Venus
今暁 *kongyō* at daybreak today

❷ be as clear as dawn, understand thoroughly

通暁する *tsūgyō suru* have a thorough knowledge of

KUN

【**akatsuki** 暁】 dawn, daybreak; in the event of

暁の空 *akatsuki no sora* dawning sky
成功の暁には *seikō no akatsuki ni wa* when one has succeeded

SYNONYMS

❶ **morning and dawn**

旦 DAYBREAK → 2389
朝 MORNING → 1695

4-8 日

晴 晴 晴 晴

981 SEI ha(reru) ha(re) ha(re)- -ba(re) ha(rasu)

CH 晴 qíng

Radical	Strokes
日 72	12-4-8
Grade	**Freq**
Jōyō-2	679

1-4-8

丨 冂 日 日 日一 日十 日丰 日圭 旪 晴 晴 晴
1 2 3 4 5 6 7 8 9 10 11 12

▶**FINE WEATHER**

COMPOUNDS

● [original meaning] **fine weather, fair weather, clear [cloudless] sky, bright sky**
晴天 *seiten* fine [fair] weather, cloudless sky
晴雨計 *seiukei* barometer
晴耕雨読 *seikōudoku* working in the field in fine weather and reading at home in rainy weather
晴曇 *seidon* fine and cloudy weather

KUN

【ha(reru) 晴れる】 clear up, become fine; cease to rain; be dispelled, be dissipated; be refreshed, be enlivened
晴れた空 *hareta sora* clear [cloudless] sky
晴れ上がる *hareagaru* clear up
疑いが晴れる *utagai ga hareru* be cleared of a charge
晴れやかな笑顔 *hareyaka na egao* beaming smile
【ha(re) 晴れ】 fine weather, clear sky; ceremonial [formal] occasion
晴れの日 *hare no hi* fine day; formal occasion
【ha(re)- 晴れ-】 formal, ceremonial, gala
晴れ着 *haregi* one's best (clothes), gala [holiday] dress
晴れ舞台 *harebutai* gala occasion
【-ba(re) -晴れ】 fine weather, bright sky
五月晴れ *satsukibare* fine weather in early summer [during the rainy season]
梅雨晴れ *tsuyubare* sunny spell during the rainy season
【ha(rasu) 晴らす】
① dispel (doubts or gloom), clear away
気晴らし *kibarashi* diversion, relaxation
疑いを晴らす *utagai o harasu* dispel doubts
② unclassified compounds
素晴らしい *subarashii* splendid, magnificent, wonderful, excellent
見晴らし *miharashi* view, outlook

SYNONYMS

● **weather**
天 weather → 3442
候 SEASONAL WEATHER → 119

4-8 日

晴

982

▶**FINE WEATHER**
nonstandard for 晴 981

4-8 木

棒 棒 棒

983 BŌ

CH 棒 bàng

Radical	Strokes
木 75	12-4-8
Grade	**Freq**
Jōyō-6	1369

1-4-8

一 十 才 木 木一 木二 木三 桂 栲 楱 棒 棒
1 2 3 4 5 6 7 8 9 10 11 12

▶**ROD**

COMPOUNDS

❶ⓐ [original meaning] **rod, stick, bar, pole, staff, club**
ⓑ rodlike, rod-shaped; bar of, stick of
ⓒ strike with a rod, hit with a club
棒状 *bōjō* cylinder or rod-shaped
棒高跳び *bōtakatobi* pole vault [jump]
棒術 *bōjutsu bojutsu* (art of using a stick as a weapon), cudgels
警棒 *keibō* policeman's club, nightstick
編み棒 *amibō* knitting needle
棍棒 *konbō* cudgel, club
鉄棒 *tetsubō* iron rod; horizontal bars
心棒 *shinbō* axle, shaft, arbor
延べ棒 *nobebō* ingot
棒温度計 *bōondokei* bar thermometer
痛棒 *tsūbō* severe attack, bitter criticism
❷ⓐ straight line, thick straight line
ⓑ **in a straight line, straight**
棒グラフ *bōgurafu* bar graph
棒立ち *bōdachi* standing erect
棒読み *bōyomi* reading without expression; reading a Chinese classical text without

translating it into Japanese
棒暗記 *bōanki* memorization word by word
❸ **tough guy, fellow, chum**
泥棒 *dorobō* thief, crook
用心棒 *yōjinbō* bodyguard, bouncer; bar, bolt
相棒 *aibō* pal, mate, companion
❹ unclassified compounds
箆棒な *berabō na* absurd, unreasonable, awful

INDEPENDENT

【bō 棒】rod, stick, bar, pole, staff, club, baton; straight line, dash; waste, futility; *bojutsu*
棒で殴る *bō de naguru* hit with a club
チョコレートの棒 *chokorēto no bō* bar of chocolate
棒を引く *bō o hiku* draw a line
棒に振る *bō ni furu* sacrifice, waste

SYNONYMS

❶ⓐ & ❶ⓑ shafts
桟 crosspiece → 932
軸 AXLE → 1514
錘 SPINDLE → 1744
❷ⓐ line
軸 AXIS → 1514
線 LINE → 1392
筋 THREADLIKE STRUCTURE → 2678
条 strip → 2200
脈 VEIN → 953
ⓑ straight
直 STRAIGHT → 2932
❸ fellow
奴 GUY → 187
漢 FELLOW → 657
輩 FELLOW (*belittling*) → 2807
徒 fellows → 416
坊 COLLOQUIAL PERSON SUFFIX → 233
屋 colloquial person suffix → 3098
物 character → 874

棚 棚 棚 棚

984 HŌ▲ tana -dana

Stroke order: 一 十 才 木 木 机 朋 朋 棚 棚 棚 棚 (1–12)

Ⓒⓗ 棚 péng

Radical	Strokes
木 75	12-4-8
Grade	**Freq**
Jōyō	1796
◧ 1 - 4 - 8	

4-8 木

▶**SHELF**

COMPOUNDS

❶ [original meaning] **shelf**
陸棚 *rikuhō* continental shelf
❷ [archaic] suspension bridge

KUN

【tana 棚, -dana -棚】
ⓐ [also suffix] shelf, rack, ledge, mantelpiece
ⓑ (natural shelflike structure) shelf, ledge (of rock)
ⓒ continental shelf
棚卸し(＝店卸し) *tanaoroshi* inventory
棚牡丹 *tanabota* windfall, godsend
棚上げする *tanaage suru* shelve (up), pigeonhole
棚引く *tanabiku* trail, hang [lie] over
書棚 *shodana* bookshelf
食器棚 *shokkidana* cupboard, sideboard
岩棚 *iwadana* ledge
大陸棚 *tairikudana* continental shelf
陸棚 *rikudana* continental shelf

SYNONYMS

❶ flat supports
架 rack → 2569
壇 PLATFORM → 754
座 SEAT → 3116
台 STAND → 2005
床 BED → 3067

HOMOPHONES

tana ⇨ 店 3085

NOTE

⇨ see USAGE note at 店 3085

棺 棺 棺

985 KAN

Stroke order: 一 十 才 木 木' 木' 木宀 杧 杧 棺 棺 棺 (1–12)

Ⓒⓗ 棺 guān

Radical	Strokes
木 75	12-4-8
Grade	**Freq**
Jōyō	1873
◧ 1 - 4 - 8	

4-8 木

▶**COFFIN**

COMPOUNDS

● [original meaning] **coffin, casket**
棺桶 *kan'oke* coffin, casket
石棺 *sekkan* sarcophagus
納棺する *nōkan suru* place a body in a coffin

出棺 *shukkan* carrying the coffin out of the house

INDEPENDENT

【kan 棺】 coffin, casket

棺に納める *kan ni osameru* lay in a coffin

SYNONYMS

● **containers**

槽 TANK → 1067
箱 BOX → 2711
籠 BASKET → 2734
袋 BAG → 2588
器 VESSEL → 2713
瓶 BOTTLE → 1344
缶 CAN → 2033

4-8
木

検 檢 検

986 KEN

CH 检 jiǎn

Radical	Strokes
木 75	12-4-8
Grade	**Freq**
Jōyō-5	297
1 - 4 - 8	

一 十 才 木 木' 木ᐟ 朴 柃 柃 枱 検 検
1 2 3 4 5 6 7 8 9 10 11 12

▶ **EXAMINE**

COMPOUNDS

❶ⓐ **examine, inspect, investigate, verify, test, check**

ⓑ **examination, inspection, test, -opsy**

検査 *kensa* inspection, examination, test

検討する *kentō suru* examine, study, investigate

検診 *kenshin* medical examination

検証 *kenshō* verification, identification; inspection

検察 *kensatsu* criminal investigation; prosecution

検事 *kenji* public prosecutor

検閲 *ken'etsu* censorship; inspection, review

検便 *kenben* stool examination

探検(＝探険) *tanken* exploration, expedition

点検 *tenken* inspection, examination

車検 *shaken* automobile inspection

三等検 *santōken* test for third-grade articles

生検 *seiken* biopsy

❷ **detect, search, measure**

検索する *kensaku suru* look up (a word in a dictionary), search for, refer to

検出する *kenshutsu suru* detect, find

検温 *ken'on* thermometry

検波 *kenpa* detection, demodulation

検流計 *kenryūkei* galvanometer

❸ abbrev. of 検察庁 *kensatsuchō*: public prosecutors office

地検 *chiken* district public prosecutors office

送検する *sōken suru* commit for trial, send to the prosecutors office

❹ restrict, restrain, regulate

検挙 *kenkyo* arrest, roundup

検束 *kensoku* arrest, custody

❺ [original meaning] put a seal on

検印 *ken'in* seal of approval

INDEPENDENT

【kensuru 検する】 examine, investigate; regulate

SYNONYMS

❶ⓐ **investigate and examine**

探 PROBE → 505
討 STUDY → 1456
察 INSPECT → 2347
究 STUDY EXHAUSTIVELY → 2203
閲 REVIEW → 3330
診 EXAMINE A PATIENT → 1504
調 INVESTIGATE → 1567
査 LOOK INTO → 2437
審 EXAMINE CAREFULLY → 2360
験 TEST → 1833
勘 CHECK → 1777
糾 INQUIRE INTO → 1278

ⓑ **examination**

試 examination (school test) → 1525

❷ **detect**

感 SENSE → 2835

棋 棊◦ 棋 枝

987 KI

Ⓒⓗ 棋 qí

Radical	Strokes
木 75	12-4-8
Grade	Freq
Jōyō	1155
◧ 1 - 4 - 8	

4-8 木

一 十 才 木 杧 杧 栱 栱 柤 棋 棋 棋
1 2 3 4 5 6 7 8 9 10 11 12

▶**SHOGI**

COMPOUNDS

ⓐ **shogi, Japanese chess; chess**
ⓑ go, Chinese checkers
棋士 *kishi* professional go [shogi] player
棋界 *kikai* go circles; shogi circles
棋譜 *kifu* record of a game of shogi [go]
棋道 *kidō* art of shogi [go]
将棋 *shōgi* shogi, Japanese chess
西洋将棋 *seiyō-shōgi* chess

SYNONYMS

ⓐ **board games**
碁 GO → 2699
雀 MAHJONG → 2469
局 board game → 3063

棉

988 MEN wata

Ⓒⓗ 棉 mián

Radical	Strokes
木 75	12-4-8
Grade	Freq
Reference	
◧ 1 - 4 - 8	

4-8 木

COMPOUNDS

[now replaced by 綿 *men, wata* 1373]
ⓐ cotton plant
ⓑ cotton fiber, cotton cloth, cotton wool
棉花 *menka* raw cotton, cotton wool
棉実油 *menjitsuyu* cottonseed oil
印棉 *inmen* Indian raw cotton

HOMOPHONES

wata ⇨ 綿 1373

NOTE

⇨ see USAGE note at 綿 1373

棲

989 SEI su(mu)

Ⓒⓗ 栖 qī xī

Radical	Strokes
木 75	12-4-8
Grade	Freq
Reference	
◧ 1 - 4 - 8	

4-8 木

COMPOUNDS

ⓐ [now replaced by 生 *sei* 3497] (of animals) inhabit, live
ⓑ (of people) live, dwell, reside
棲息する *seisoku suru* inhabit, live
水棲の *suisei no* aquatic, living in the water
両棲類 *ryōseirui* Amphibia, amphibian
棲む *sumu* (of animals) inhabit, live
鳥が棲む森 *tori ga sumu mori* woods inhabited by birds
同棲する *dōsei suru* live together, cohabit with
隠棲 *insei* secluded life
幽棲する *yūsei suru* live a quiet life in seclusion away from the masses

HOMOPHONES

sumu ⇨ 住 64

NOTE

⇨ see USAGE note at 住 64

4-8 木

植 植 植

990 SHOKU u(eru) u(waru)

CH 植 zhí

Radical	Strokes
木 75	12-4-8
Grade	Freq
Jōyō-3	981
1-4-8	

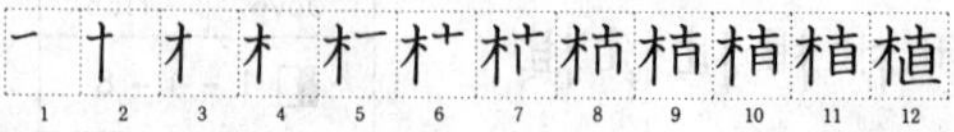

一 十 才 木 村 村 杧 枯 柿 植 植 植
1 2 3 4 5 6 7 8 9 10 11 12

▶**PLANT**

COMPOUNDS

❶ [original meaning] **plant**
植樹 *shokuju* tree planting
植栽 *shokusai* raising trees and plants
移植 *ishoku* transplanting

❷ **plant, plants, vegetation**
植物 *shokubutsu* plant, vegetation
植生 *shokusei* vegetation
動植物 *dōshokubutsu* animals and plants

❸ [sometimes also 殖 994] colonize, settle
植民地 *shokuminchi* colony, settlement
入植 *nyūshoku* settlement, immigration

❹ typeset, set in type
植字 *shokuji* typesetting, composition
誤植 *goshoku* typographical error, misprint
写植 *shashoku* phototypesetting

KUN

【**u(eru)** 植える】plant, raise, grow; typeset, set in type
植木 *ueki* garden plant, shrub, pot plant
田植え *taue* rice planting

【**u(waru)** 植わる】be planted

SYNONYMS

❶ **farm and plant**
栽 PLANT (saplings) → 3297
培 CULTIVATE → 464
耕 TILL → 1308
作 raise crops → 68
農 farm, FARMING → 2698

❷ **plants**
菜 VEGETABLE → 2305
栽 garden plant → 3297

❸ **reside**
住 LIVE → 64
居 RESIDE → 3080
生 inhabit → 3497

❹ **print and publish**
刷 PRINT → 1273
印 print → 828
刊 PUBLISH → 190
版 PUBLISHING → 872
載 PUT IN PRINT → 3300
掲 display in writing → 494

4-8 木

棟 棟 棟

991 TŌ mune muna-

CH 栋 dòng

Radical	Strokes
木 75	12-4-8
Grade	Freq
Jōyō	1767
1-4-8	

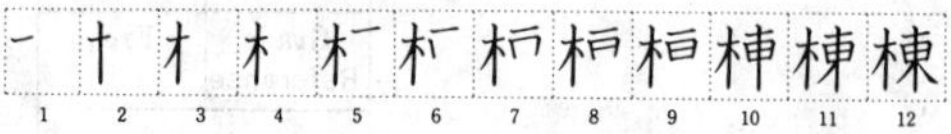

一 十 才 木 木 朩 杤 杤 栯 棟 棟 棟
1 2 3 4 5 6 7 8 9 10 11 12

▶**BLOCK**

COMPOUNDS

❶ⓐ [also suffix] (long building or part thereof) **block, building, ward**
ⓑ **counter for blocks of flats or buildings**
病棟 *byōtō* (hospital) ward
翼棟 *yokutō* wing (of a building)
研究室棟 *kenkyūshitsutō* research laboratory building, laboratory block
第三棟 *daisantō* Block No. 3

❷ [original meaning] **ridge, edge of a roof**
上棟式 *jōtōshiki* ceremony of raising the ridgepole

❸ chief, head, leader
棟梁 *tōryō* chief support, pillar (of a nation), chief, leader, foreman

KUN

【**mune** 棟】
① ridge, ridgepole
棟上げ *muneage* ridgepole raising
②ⓐ building, house
ⓑ counter for buildings or houses
別棟 *betsumune* another building, outhouse
一棟四戸建て *hitomune yonkodate* tenement house divided into four apartments
三棟 *mimune* three buildings [houses]

【**muna-** 棟-】ridge, ridgepole
棟瓦 *munagawara* ridge tile
棟木 *munagi* ridgepole

SYNONYMS

❶ **buildings**
舎 BUILDING → 2060
館 PUBLIC BUILDING → 1748

堂 HALL → 2589
閣 TALL MAGNIFICENT BUILDING → 3327
宇 large building → 2175
殿 PALACE → 1792
❷ **roof parts**
軒 EAVES → 1459
【mune】
②ⓑ **counters for houses**
軒 COUNTER FOR HOUSES → 1459
戸 counter for households → 1930

棚 992 4-8 木

▶SHELF
nonstandard for 棚 984

棧 993 4-8 木

▶PLANK BRIDGE
nonstandard for 桟 932

極 4-8 木

incorrect stroke count ⇨ see 1017

殖 994 4-8 歹

殖 殖 SHOKU fu(eru) fu(yasu)

Ⓒⓗ 殖 zhí

Radical	Strokes
歹 78	12-4-8
Grade	**Freq**
Jōyō	1589
1 - 4 - 8	

一 1, 𠂇 2, 歹 3, 歹 4, 歹 5, 歼 6, 歼 7, 殖 8, 殖 9, 殖 10, 殖 11, 殖 12

▶MULTIPLY

COMPOUNDS

❶ⓐ [original meaning] (produce offspring) **multiply, propagate, breed**
ⓑ (increase the quantity of, esp. wealth) **multiply, increase, make (money)**
増殖する *zōshoku suru* multiply, propagate, increase
繁殖する *hanshoku suru* breed, propagate, increase, multiply
生殖 *seishoku* reproduction, procreation, generation
殖産 *shokusan* increase of production; enhancement of one's fortune
利殖 *rishoku* moneymaking
❷ multitude, great deal
学殖 *gakushoku* scholarship, learning, knowledge
❸ [usu. 植 990] colonize, settle
殖民 *shokumin* colonization
拓殖 *takushoku* colonization, exploitation

KUN

【fu(eru) 殖える】 *vi* (increase of its own accord) multiply, increase, propagate—said esp. of wealth or living things
蝿が殖える *Hae ga fueru* Flies multiply
財産が殖える *zaisan ga fueru* become rich
【fu(yasu) 殖やす】 *vt* (cause to multiply of its own accord) multiply, increase, propagate, augment—said esp. of wealth or living things
貯金を殖やす *chokin o fuyasu* increase one's savings
家畜を殖やす *kachiku o fuyasu* breed cattle

SYNONYMS

❶ⓐ **give birth**
産 GIVE BIRTH → 3298
生 BE BORN → 3497
誕 BE BORN → 1579
ⓑ **increase**
増 INCREASE → 677
倍 DOUBLE → 108
加 add to → 38

HOMOPHONES

fueru ⇨ 増 677
fuyasu ⇨ 増 677

NOTE

⇨ see USAGE note at 増 677

殘 995 4-8 歹

▶REMAIN ▶RUTHLESS
nonstandard for 残 943

4-8
火

焰
996 EN honō

CH 焰 yàn

Radical	Strokes
火 86	12-4-8
Grade	Freq
Reference	
1 - 4 - 8	

COMPOUNDS

ⓐ [now replaced by 炎 *en* 2420] [original meaning] flame, blaze

ⓑ [now usu. 炎 *en* 2420 or 炎 *honō*] (figuratively) flames (as of passion)

火焰 *kaen* flames, blaze
情焰 *jōen* flaming desires, burning passions
気焰を吐く *kien o haku* talk big, talk a lot of hot air
嫉妬の焰 *shitto no honō* The Flames of Jealousy (movie title)

HOMOPHONES

honō ⇨ 炎 2420

NOTE

⇨ see USAGE note at 炎 2420

4-8
火

焼 燒 焼 𤏐
997 SHŌ ya(ku) ya(ki) ya(ki)- -ya(ki) ya(keru)

CH 烧 shāo

Radical	Strokes
火 86	12-4-8
Grade	Freq
Jōyō-4	672
1 - 4 - 8	

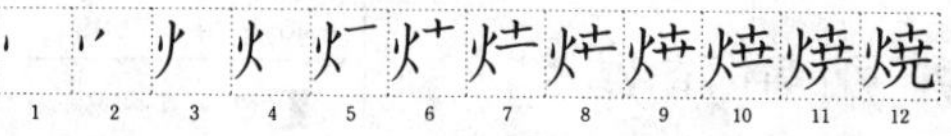

▶ **BURN**

COMPOUNDS

ⓐ [original meaning] (set or be set on fire) **burn, incinerate**

ⓑ **be burnt (down), be destroyed by fire**

焼却する *shōkyaku suru* destroy by fire, incinerate
焼身自殺 *shōshin jisatsu* suicide by fire, burning oneself to death
焼香する *shōkō suru* burn [offer] incense
焼夷弾 *shōidan* incendiary bomb
焼死 *shōshi* death by fire
全焼する *zenshō suru* be burnt down
半焼 *hanshō* partial destruction by fire
類焼する *ruishō suru* catch fire from next door

KUN

【ya(ku) 焼く】
vt

①ⓐ burn, set on fire, incinerate; scorch; cauterize
ⓑ bake (pottery), fire
ⓒ cremate

炭焼き *sumiyaki* charcoal making
焼き物 *yakimono* pottery, porcelain, earthenware
焼き場 *yakiba* crematory

② cook by fire: bake, roast, broil, grill, toast

焼き網 *yakiami* toasting grill, broiling grill

③ burn with jealousy, be envious

焼き餅 *yakimochi* jealousy; roast rice cake

④ print (photos)

焼き付け *yakitsuke* printing (photos)
焼き増し *yakimashi* extra prints

⑤ take the trouble to do something

余計な世話を焼く *yokei na sewa o yaku* poke one's nose (in) where one is not wanted

【ya(ki) 焼き】

① roasting, broiling; baking, toasting

焼きの足りない *yaki no tarinai* underfired

② annealing

焼き戻し *yakimodoshi* tempering
焼き入れ *yakiire* quenching, hardening
焼きを入れる *yaki o ireru* harden, temper; discipline; torture

③ figurative meaning

焼きが回る *yaki ga mawaru* become decrepit, become dull

【ya(ki)- 焼き-】 [also prefix] roasted, broiled, baked, parched

焼き芋 *yakiimo* baked sweet potato
焼き鳥 *yakitori* grilled chicken
焼き飯 *yakimeshi* frizzled [fried] rice
焼き豆腐 *yakidōfu* broiled bean curd

【-ya(ki) -焼き】
[also suffix]

① roasted, baked or fried food

鋤焼き *sukiyaki* sukiyaki
鉄板焼き *teppanyaki* meat and vegetables roasted on hot plate
目玉焼き *medamayaki* fried eggs, sunny side up

カルメ焼き *karumeyaki* brittle
② ware, pottery, porcelain
有田焼き *aritayaki* Arita ware [porcelain]
【ya(keru) 焼ける】
vi
①ⓐ burn, be burnt, be destroyed by fire; be scorched
ⓑ (of the sky) glow, burn
焼け跡 *yakeato* ruins of fire
日焼け *hiyake* suntan
夕焼け *yūyake* sunset glow
② be cooked by fire: be baked, be roasted, be broiled, be toasted
良く焼けた *yoku yaketa* well done, done brown
③ be jealous, burn with jealousy
焼けて堪まらない *Yakete tamaranai* How I envy him!
④ have heartburn
胸焼け *muneyake* heartburn, sour stomach
⑤ be subjected to (the trouble of doing something for someone)
世話の焼ける *sewa no yakeru* troublesome, annoying

SYNONYMS
● **burn**
燃 BURN (undergo combustion) → 1081
焦 SCORCH → 2770
【yaku】
② **cook**
揚げる fry in deep fat → 593
蒸 STEAM → 2334
炊 COOK → 870
煮 BOIL (cook by boiling) → 2785
沸 BOIL (undergo boiling) → 329
【yaki】
② **work metals**
鋳 CAST → 1729
鍛 FORGE → 1755
錬 REFINE (crude metals) → 1741
【-yaki】
① **cooked dishes**
-揚げ fried food → 593
-煮 boiled food → 2785

牒

incorrect stroke count ⇨ see 1025

4-8 片

雅
998

▶**ELEGANT**
nonstandard for 雅 1197

4-8 牙

瑛
999

瑛 瑛 瑛 Ⓒⓗ 瑛 yīng

EI NAMES YŌ aki akira teru

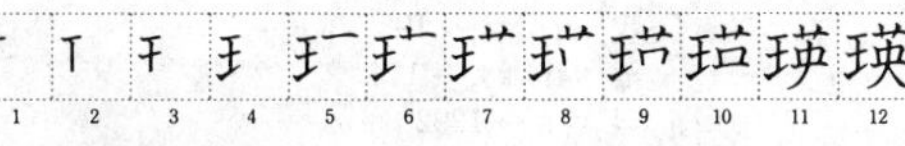

Radical 王 96	Strokes 12-4-8
Grade Names	Freq 2129
◧ 1-4-8	

4-8 王

▶**TRANSPARENT GEM**
COMPOUNDS
● [original meaning, now archaic] transparent gem, jewel
玉瑛 *gyokuei* transparent gem, crystal
NAMES
瑛子 *eiko* (=*akiko*) female name
瑛 *akira* male name
瑛代 *teruyo* female name

SYNONYMS
● **precious stones**
玉 GEM → 3477
珠 PEARL → 947
瑠 LAPIS LAZULI → 1060
璃 GLASSY SUBSTANCE → 1059
晶 CRYSTAL → 2474

4-8
王

斑

1000 HAN fu madara

CH 斑 bān

Radical	Strokes
文 67	12-4-8
Grade	Freq
Reference	
1 - 4 - 8	

COMPOUNDS

❶ [sometimes also 班 *han* 946] [also suffix] spot, speck

❷ spotted, streaked, variegated

斑点 *hanten* spot, speck

斑状組織 *hanjōsoshiki* porphyritic structure

大赤斑 *daisekihan* Jupiter's Great Red Spot

紫斑病 *shihanbyō* purpura

蒙古斑 *mōkohan* Mongolian spot

斑条 *hanjō* variegated streaks

斑入りの *fuiri no* variegated, spotted

斑牛 *madaraushi* brindled ox

4-8
王

琢

1001

▶**POLISH**

nonstandard for 琢 971

4-8
礻

禄 祿 禄 禄

1002 ROKU NAMES toshi yoshi

CH 禄 lù

`、 ラ ネ ネ ネ¬ ネヨ ネヨ 祁 祁 禄 禄 禄` (1–12)

Radical	Strokes
礻 113	12-4-8
Grade	Freq
Names	2051
1 - 4 - 8	

▶**RETAINER'S STIPEND**

COMPOUNDS

❶ (ration of rice paid to samurai in feudal Japan) **retainer's stipend, official pay, fief**

禄高 *rokudaka* amount of one's fief [stipend]

俸禄 *hōroku* retainer's stipend, official pay [salary]

微禄 *biroku* small stipend

❷ happiness, prosperity, wealth

禄命 *rokumei* one's lot

福禄寿 *fukurokuju* God of Wealth and Longevity

INDEPENDENT

【**roku** 禄】 retainer's stipend, fief (⇨ ❶)

四百石の禄 *yonhyakkoku no roku* fief of 400 *koku*

NAMES

禄郎 *rokurō* male name

禄夫 *yoshio* male name

SYNONYMS

❶ **pay and earnings**

収 income → 198

俸 SALARY → 114

料 FEE → 1292

賃 WAGE → 2694

給 PAY → 1350

4-8
月

脹 脹

1003 CHŌ ha(reru)▲ fuku(ramu)▲ fuku(reru)▲

CH 胀 zhàng

`丿 刀 月 月 月' 月⺁ 月⺁ 月F 月F 脹 脹 脹` (1–12)

Radical	Strokes
月 130	12-4-8
Grade	Freq
Jōyō	1932
1 - 4 - 8	

▶**SWELL**

COMPOUNDS

❶ **swell, expand, bulge**

膨脹(＝膨張) *bōchō* expansion, swelling; growth, increase

腫脹 *shuchō* swelling, puffiness

❷ [original meaning] have a swelled [full] stomach

脹満 *chōman* tympanites

KUN

【ha(reru) 脹れる】 swell, become swollen; tumefy
脹れ *hare* swelling, boil
脹れぼったい *harebottai* somewhat swollen, puffy
みみず脹れ *mimizubare* wale, welt
【fuku(ramu) 脹らむ】 [usu. 膨らむ] expand, swell (out), get big, become inflated
脹らみ *fukurami* swelling, bulge, puff
脹ら脛 *fukurahagi* calf
【fuku(reru) 脹れる】
[usu. 膨れる]
① expand, swell (out), get big, become inflated
脹れ上がる *fukureagaru* swell up
下脹れの *shimobukure no* full-cheeked, round-faced
② get sulky, sulk, fret, get peevish
脹れっ面 *fukurettsura* sulky look [face], sullen look

SYNONYMS

❶ **expand**
膨 EXPAND → 1084
張 SPREAD → 474
広げる spread (out) → 3035
拡 ENLARGE → 309
伸 STRETCH → 70
延 EXTEND → 3073

HOMOPHONES

fukuramu ⇨ 膨 1084
fukureru ⇨ 膨 1084

NOTE

⇨ see USAGE note at 膨 1084

腋

1004 EKI waki

Ⓒ 腋 yè

Radical	Strokes
月 130	12-4-8
Grade	**Freq**
Reference	
 1-4-8	

4-8 月

COMPOUNDS

[also 脇 *waki*]
ⓐ armpit
ⓑ armhole
腋窩腺 *ekikasen* axillary gland
腋毛 *wakige* hair of the armpit

HOMOPHONES

waki ⇨ 傍 147 脇 952

NOTE

⇨ see USAGE note at 傍 147

勝 勝 勝 勝

1005 SHŌ ka(tsu) -ga(chi) masa(ru) sugu(reru)▲

Ⓒ 胜 shèng shēng

Radical	Strokes
力 19	12-2-10
Grade	**Freq**
Jōyō-3	167
1-4-8	

4-8 月

1	2	3	4	5	6	7	8	9	10	11	12
丿	冂	月	月	月	月	月	月	胖	胖	勝	勝

▶**WIN** ▶**EXCEL**

COMPOUNDS

❶ⓐ **win, defeat**
ⓑ **win, victory**
ⓒ **counter for wins (in sports)**
勝者 *shōsha* winner
全勝する *zenshō suru* win all the games, make a clean sweep
優勝 *yūshō* victory, championship
勝利 *shōri* victory, triumph, win
勝敗 *shōhai* victory or defeat
勝負 *shōbu* victory or defeat; match, game
決勝戦 *kesshōsen* final round match, finals
大勝 *taishō* great [sweeping] victory
連勝 *renshō* straight victories
二勝三敗 *nishō sanpai* two wins and three defeats
❷ **excel, surpass, outdo**
殊勝な *shushō na* laudable, praiseworthy
❸ place of natural beauty
勝地 *shōchi* beauty spot
景勝 *keishō* picturesque scenery
名勝 *meishō* place of scenic beauty

INDEPENDENT

【shō 勝】 place of natural beauty
天下の勝 *tenka no shō* beautiful scenery

KUN

【ka(tsu) 勝つ】
①ⓐ win, defeat, triumph
ⓑ [formerly 克つ] control (oneself), overcome
勝ち *kachi* win, victory

勝ち取る *kachitoru* gain, win
赤が勝っている *aka ga katte iru* predominated by red
② unclassified compounds
勝手 *katte* one's own way; convenience; circumstances; kitchen

【-ga(chi) -勝ち】
[suffix]
① apt to, prone to; predominated by
病気勝ちだ *byōkigachi da* be prone to diseases
極端に走り勝ちだ *kyokutan ni hashirigachi da* be apt to go to extremes
② win, victory
逆転勝ちする *gyakutengachi suru* win after defeat seems certain

【masa(ru) 勝る】 [formerly also 優る] excel, be better than, surpass
男勝りの *otokomasari no* (of a woman) strong-minded, spirited
全てに於て勝る *subete ni oite masaru* excel in every respect

【sugu(reru) 勝れる】
[now usu. 優れる]
① be superior to, be excellent, be better than, surpass
勝れた業績 *sugureta gyōseki* outstanding achievement
② [usu. in negative constructions] be fine, feel well
気分が勝れない *kibun ga sugurenai* not feel well

SYNONYMS

❶ **win**
克 OVERCOME → 2046
征 CONQUER → 293
破 BREAK → 1150

❷ **excel**
抜 STAND OUT → 246
超 SURPASS → 3313
越 GO BEYOND → 3314

USAGE

❶ **katsu**
勝つ
①ⓐ win, defeat, triumph
ⓑ [formerly 克つ] control (oneself), overcome
② unclassified compounds
克つ
[now usu. 勝つ] control (oneself), overcome

❷ **masaru**
勝る
[formerly also 優る] excel, be better than, surpass
優る
[now usu. 勝る] excel, be better than, surpass

HOMOPHONES

katsu ⇨ 克 2046
masaru ⇨ 優 177
sugureru ⇨ 優 177

NOTE

⇨ see also USAGE note at 優 177

4-8
月

腕 腕 䏹

1006 WAN ude

Ⓒⓗ 腕 wàn

Radical	Strokes
月 130	12-4-8
Grade	**Freq**
Jōyō	1076
1-4-8	

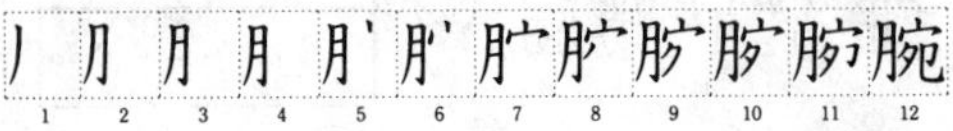

▶ARM

COMPOUNDS

❶ **arm**
腕章 *wanshō* armband, arm badge
腕力 *wanryoku* muscular strength
上腕 *jōwan* upper arm
左腕投手 *sawan tōshu* left-handed pitcher

❷ **skill, ability**
手腕 *shuwan* ability, skill
才腕 *saiwan* ability, skill
敏腕 *binwan* ability, capability

❸ unclassified compounds
腕白 *wanpaku* naughtiness, mischief

KUN

【ude 腕】 arm; skill, ability
腕時計 *udedokei* wrist watch
腕首 *udekubi* wrist
腕が良い *ude ga ii* be skilled, be able
腕前 *udemae* skill, ability, capacity
腕利き *udekiki* man of ability

SYNONYMS

❶ **hand and arm**
手 HAND → 3456
掌 PALM → 2602
指 FINGER → 378

❶ **limbs**
肢 LIMB → 882
脚 LEG → 974

❷ **skill**
技 SKILL → 248
能 ABILITY → 1323
力 POWER → 3371

才 TALENT → 3410

NOTE

⇨ see COMPOUND FORMATION for 腕前 *udemae* ⇨ 前 2266

勝 1007

▶**WIN** ▶**EXCEL**

nonstandard for 勝 1005

4-8 月

雄 1008

YŪ o- osu on▲

Ⓒⓗ 雄 xióng

Radical	Strokes
隹 172	12-8-4
Grade	**Freq**
Jōyō	587
◧ 1-4-8	

4-8 ナ

一 ナ 𠂇 厷 厷 𠫔 𠫔 𠫔 𦏺 𦏺 雄 雄
1 2 3 4 5 6 7 8 9 10 11 12

▶**MALE** ▶**HEROIC**

COMPOUNDS

❶ [original meaning] (of plants or animals) **male**

雄性 *yūsei* male characteristics, manliness
雄蕊 *yūzui* (=*oshibe*) stamen
雌雄 *shiyū* male and female; victory or defeat

❷ⓐ **heroic, manly, brave, bold**

ⓑ (impressive in scale) **heroic, grand, magnificent**

雄壮な *yūsō na* brave, heroic, gallant
雄姿 *yūshi* brave [imposing] figure
雄武 *yūbu* bravery
雄断 *yūdan* manly decision
雄弁な *yūben na* eloquent, fluent
雄渾な *yūkon na* magnificent, sublime; vigorous, bold
雄図 *yūto* ambitious enterprise, grand project
雄飛する *yūhi suru* launch out, embark upon (a career)
雄大な *yūdai na* grand, magnificent, heroic

❸ **hero, great man, great leader, master**

英雄 *eiyū* hero
両雄 *ryōyū* two great men
群雄 *gun'yū* rival leaders [barons]

❹ victory

雌雄を決する *shiyū o kessuru* fight a decisive battle

INDEPENDENT

【**yū** 雄】hero, great leader, master

一世の雄 *issei no yū* greatest hero [mastermind] of the age
私学の雄 *shigaku no yū* one of the leading private schools

KUN

【**o-** 雄-】

ⓐ (of plants) male
ⓑ manly, masculine
ⓒ [sometimes also 牡-] (of animals) male
ⓓ [also 男] the larger or stronger of two

雄花 *obana* male flower
雄雄しい *ooshii* manly, brave, heroic
雄牛 *oushi* bull, steer
雄滝 *odaki* the greater waterfall (of the two)

【**osu** 雄】[sometimes also 牡] (of animals) male

雄犬 *osuinu* male dog

【**on** 雄】[sometimes also 牡] (of animals) male

雄鳥(=雄鶏) *ondori* rooster

SYNONYMS

❶ **man**

男 MAN → 2542
郎 YOUNG MAN → 1289
夫 male adult → 3460
翁 OLD MAN → 2108

❷ⓐ **brave**

壮 heroic → 224
勇 BRAVE → 2089
赳 VALIANT → 3308
敢 bold → 1706
豪 bold and unrestrained → 2140
義 chivalrous → 2338

ⓑ **great**

豪 MAGNIFICENT → 2140
壮 GRAND (having grandeur) → 224
宏 GRAND (large in scale) → 2202
偉 GREAT (of superior character) → 148
大 BIG → 3416

❸ **great persons**

豪 GREAT MAN → 2140
傑 OUTSTANDING PERSON → 155
匠 CRAFTSMAN → 2990
聖 great master → 2830

USAGE

❶ **o**

雄-

ⓐ (of plants) male
ⓑ manly, masculine

ⓒ [sometimes also 牡-] (of animals) male
ⓓ [also 男] the larger or stronger of two

牡-
[usu. 雄-] (of animals) male

男
① *elegant* man, male
② [in compounds] the larger or stronger of two

❷ **osu**

雄
[sometimes also 牡] (of animals) male

牡
[usu. 雄] (of animals) male

❸ **on**

雄
[sometimes also 牡] (of animals) male

牡
[usu. 雄] (of animals) male

HOMOPHONES

o- ⇨ 牡 839 男 2542
osu ⇨ 牡 839
on ⇨ 牡 839

4-9
方

旒
1009 RYŪ

Ⓒⓗ 旒 liú

Radical	Strokes
方 70	13-4-9
Grade	Freq
Reference	
◧ 1 - 4 - 9	

COMPOUNDS

ⓐ flag, pennant

ⓑ [now also 流 441] counter for flags
旗二旒 *hata niryū* two flags

4-9
日

暗 暗 暗 暗
1010 AN kura(i)

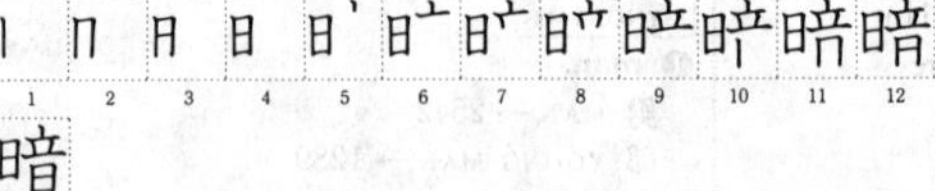

暗
13

Ⓒⓗ 暗 àn

Radical	Strokes
日 72	13-4-9
Grade	Freq
Jōyō-3	1001
◧ 1 - 4 - 9	

▶**DARK**

COMPOUNDS

❶ⓐ [formerly also 闇 3332] [original meaning] **dark, dim**
ⓑ [formerly also 闇 3332] **darkness**
ⓒ [also prefix] **dark-colored**
暗黒 *ankoku* darkness
暗室 *anshitsu* dark room
暗雲 *an'un* dark clouds
暗夜 *an'ya* dark night
暗中模索 *anchū-mosaku* groping in the dark
明暗 *meian* light and dark; contrast
暗色 *anshoku* dark color
暗赤色 *ansekishoku* dark red

❷ **in the dark, hidden, secret**
暗殺 *ansatsu* assassination
暗号 *angō* code, password
暗礁 *anshō* sunken rock, unknown reef; deadlock
暗黙の *anmoku no* tacit
暗示 *anji* hint, suggestion

❸ [formerly also 闇 3332] (lacking wisdom) dark, ignorant, foolish
暗愚な人人 *angu na hitobito* dark souls
暗黒時代 *ankoku jidai* the Dark Ages
暗君 *ankun* foolish ruler

❹ **from memory, by heart, by rote**
暗記する *anki suru* learn by heart, memorize
暗誦(＝暗唱)する *anshō suru* recite from memory
暗算 *anzan* mental arithmetic [calculation]

INDEPENDENT

【an 暗】 darkness
【an ni 暗に】 tacitly, by implication

KUN

【kura(i) 暗い】 dark, dim; (of colors) dark; (producing gloom) dark, dreary, dismal; (concealed) dark, shadowy, shady; be ignorant, be a stranger to
暗さ *kurasa* darkness; gloom
薄暗い *usugurai* gloomy, dim
暗い色 *kurai iro* dark color
暗い過去 *kurai kako* shadowy past
暗い気持になる *kurai kimochi ni naru* feel gloomy
世事に暗い *seji ni kurai* know little of the

world

SYNONYMS

❶ⓐ **dark**
黒 BLACK → 2740
陰 shaded → 541
ⓒ **dark-colored**
濃 dark → 777
深 DEEP → 524
❷ **secret and private**
秘 SECRET → 1159
密 SECRET → 2292
私 PRIVATE → 1115
内 not public → 3466
隠 hidden from view → 713
❸ **foolish**
愚 FOOLISH → 2834
痴 STUPID → 3286
鈍 DULL → 1689

暖 暖 暖 暖

1011 DAN NON▴ atata(ka) atata(kai) atata(maru) atata(meru)

Ⓒⓗ 暖 nuǎn

Radical	Strokes
日 72	13-4-9
Grade	**Freq**
Jōyō-6	1189
1-4-9	

4-9 日

1 2 3 4 5 6 7 8 9 10 11 12 13

▶WARM

COMPOUNDS

ⓐ **warm (esp. weather), mild, genial, temperate**
ⓑ [formerly also 煖 *dan* 1020] **warm (the surrounding air), warm up, heat**
暖流 *danryū* warm current
暖地 *danchi* warm district, region of mild climate
暖冬 *dantō* mild winter
暖衣飽食 *dan'ihōshoku* warm clothes and plenty to eat
温暖な *ondan na* warm, mild
暖房 *danbō* heating
暖炉 *danro* fireplace, stove
暖気 *danki* warmth, warm weather
暖簾 *noren* shop curtain, *noren*; credit, reputation

INDEPENDENT

【dan 暖】 warmth, heat
暖を取る *dan o toru* warm oneself

KUN

【atata(ka) 暖か】
atataka na 暖かな same as **atatakai** 暖かい
暖かみ *atatakami* warmth
暖かな毛布 *atataka na mōfu* warm blanket
【atata(kai) 暖かい】
①ⓐ (of weather) warm, mild, genial, temperate
ⓑ warm (color)
暖かさ *atatakasa* warmth
今日は暖かい *Kyō wa atatakai* It is warm today
暖かい色 *atatakai iro* warm color
② warmhearted, kindhearted, sympathetic
暖かい人 *atatakai hito* warmhearted person
【atata(maru) 暖まる】 (surrounding air rises in temperature) get warm, be warmed, warm
暖まった空気 *atatamatta kūki* warmed air
【atata(meru) 暖める】 (warm up the surrounding air) warm, warm up, heat
部屋を暖める *heya o atatameru* heat the room

SYNONYMS

ⓐ **hot**
温 WARM → 608
暑い HOT (weather) → 2473
熱 HOT → 2866
炎 scorching → 2420
ⓑ **&【atatameru】 raise the temperature**
温める WARM (a thing) → 608
熱 HEAT → 2866

USAGE

❶ **atatakai**
暖かい
①ⓐ (of weather) warm, mild, genial, temperate
ⓑ warm (color)
② warmhearted, kindhearted, sympathetic
温かい
① warm (to the touch), lukewarm
② heartwarming, warm (feeling or atmosphere)

★Note the difference between sense ② of 暖かい and 温かい, roughly equivalent to the difference between *warmhearted* and *heartwarming*. Study the equivalents and examples carefully, as these words are easily confused by Japanese and foreigners alike. There is no difference between the forms *atatakai* and *atataka na*, except that the former is an adjective and the latter a noun adjective.

❷ **atatamaru**
暖まる
(surrounding air rises in temperature) get warm, be warmed, warm
温まる
① (of objects or persons) warm oneself, take warmth, get warm, be heated
② be heartwarming
❸ **atatameru**
暖める
(warm up the surrounding air) warm, warm up, heat
温める
① (raise the temperature of a thing) warm, heat
② nurse (an idea), let (an idea) mellow
③ renew (an old friendship)

HOMOPHONES
atatakai ⇨ 温 608
atatamaru ⇨ 温 608
atatameru ⇨ 温 608

COMPOUND FORMATION
暖簾 *noren*
暖簾 'shop curtain, etc.' originally referred to a reed screen (簾) used in warming (暖 ⓑ) taverns or restaurants. *no* is a corrupt form of the reading *non*.

NOTE
⇨ see COMPOUND FORMATION for 暖房 *danbō* ⇨ 房 1946

4-9
日
暇
1012 KA hima itoma▲

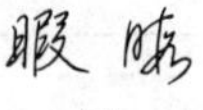

CH 假 jià 暇 xiá

Radical	Strokes
日 72	13-4-9
Grade	**Freq**
Jōyō	1501
◧ 1 - 4 - 9	

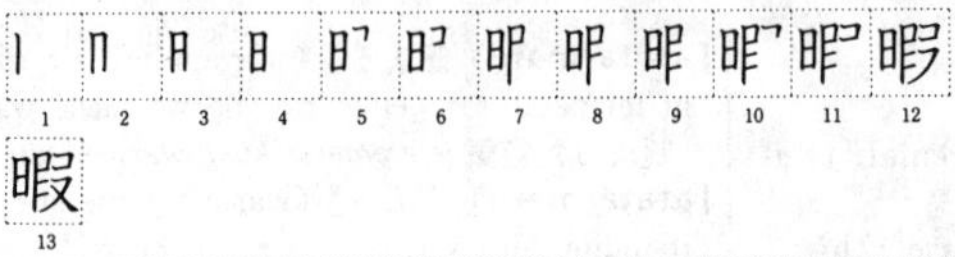

▶FREE TIME

COMPOUNDS
ⓐ **free time, spare time, leisure**
ⓑ **leave of absence, vacation**
余暇 *yoka* leisure, spare time
寸暇 *sunka* moment's leisure
休暇 *kyūka* holiday, vacation
賜暇 *shika* leave of absence, furlough
請暇 *seika* request for leave of absence; leave of absence

KUN
【**hima** 暇】 free time, spare time, leisure; dullness, slackness; dismissal, discharge
暇潰し *himatsubushi* time killer; waste of time
暇が無い *hima ga nai* have no (free) time, be busy
暇な商売 *hima na shōbai* dull business
暇が出る *hima ga deru* be discharged
【**itoma** 暇】 time to spare; dismissal; farewell
暇も無く *itoma mo naku* without losing time (to do)
永のお暇になる *naga no oitoma ni naru* be dismissed
暇乞い *itomagoi* leave-taking, farewell visit

SYNONYMS
ⓐ **leisure**
閑 LEISURE → 3322
ⓐ **time periods**
時 TIME → 924
頃 TIME → 144
般 period of time → 1317
刻 POINT OF TIME → 1267
間 INTERVAL → 3323
期 TERM → 1704
節 SEASON OF THE YEAR → 2691
季 SEASON (quarter) → 2554
候 SEASON (time of year) → 119
ⓑ **holiday**
休 holiday → 52

4-9
日
暿
1013
▶DARK
nonstandard for 暗 1010

4-9
日
煖
1014
▶WARM
nonstandard for 暖 1011

楓 楓 枫

CH 枫 fēng

1015 FŪ kaede

Radical	Strokes
木 75	13-4-9
Grade	Freq
Names	2113
1-4-9	

4-9 木

Stroke order: 1–13

▶**MAPLE**

COMPOUNDS

❶ **maple, maple tree**

楓林 *fūrin* maple grove

観楓会 *kanpūkai* maple-leaf viewing

❷ [rare] liquidambar (kind of tree)

楓属 *fūzoku* genus *Liquidambar*

楓子香 *fūshikō* galbanum

INDEPENDENT

【fū 楓】[rare] liquidambar, *Liquidambar formosana*

KUN

【kaede 楓】maple, maple tree

楓糖 *kaedetō* maple sugar

NAMES

楓 *kaede* female name

SYNONYMS

❶ **trees**

柳 WILLOW → 899

松 PINE → 864

杉 CRYPTOMERIA → 832

槙 PODOCARPUS → 1051

楠 CAMPHOR TREE → 1018

桐 PAULOWNIA → 937

桂 AROMATIC TREE, katsura tree → 928

梓 CATALPA → 962

桑 MULBERRY → 2112

漆 Japanese lacquer tree → 704

桜 CHERRY → 931

楯

CH 楯 dùn shǔn

1016 JUN tate

Radical	Strokes
木 75	13-4-9
Grade	Freq
Reference	
1-4-9	

4-9 木

COMPOUNDS

● [usu. 盾 *tate*] shield, escutcheon

楯突く *tatetsuku* oppose, defy, rebel

法律を楯に取って *hōritsu o tate ni totte* on the authority of law

HOMOPHONES

tate ⇨ 盾 3006

NOTE

⇨ see USAGE note at 盾 3006

極 極 极

CH 极 jí

1017 KYOKU GOKU kiwa(meru) kiwa(maru) kiwa(mari) kiwa(mi) ki(meru)▲ -gi(me)▲ ki(maru)▲

Radical	Strokes
木 75	13-4-9
Grade	Freq
Jōyō-4	597
1-4-9	

4-9 木

Stroke order: 1–13

▶**EXTREME** ▶**POLE**

COMPOUNDS

❶ⓐ [also suffix] (utmost or exceedingly great) **extreme, utmost, maximum, ultimate, highest, ultra-, hyper-**

ⓑ **extreme, utmost point, extremity, limit**

ⓒ **reach the extreme, go to extremes**

極端な *kyokutan na* extreme; radical
極限 *kyokugen* utmost limits, limit
極右 *kyokuu* extreme right
極東 *kyokutō* Far East
極度 *kyokudo* highest degree, extreme
極超短波 *gokuchōtanpa* ultrashort waves
極刑 *kyokkei* capital punishment, extreme penalty
極力 *kyokuryoku* to the utmost, to the best of one's power
窮極の *kyūkyoku no* ultimate, extreme
至極 *shigoku* very, most, exceedingly, extremely
積極的な *sekkyokuteki na* positive, active

❷ⓐ geographical pole
ⓑ magnetic pole, electrical pole, electrode
極光 *kyokkō* aurora
極地 *kyokuchi* polar regions, pole
極距離 *kyokukyori* polar distance
北極 *hokkyoku* North Pole
エヌ極 *enukyoku* magnetic north pole
多極化 *takyokuka* multipolarization
陽極 *yōkyoku* positive pole, anode

❸ Imperial throne [rank]
大極殿 *daigokuden* Council Hall in the Imperial Palace

❹ discern, ascertain
極印 *gokuin* hallmark; brand of villainy

❺ [archaic] quindecillion (10^{48})

INDEPENDENT

【kyoku 極】 extreme, extremity, height, climax, zenith; (magnetic or geographical) pole
混乱の極に達する *konran no kyoku ni tassuru* come to extreme disorder

【goku 極(＝極く)】 extremely, very, most
極小さい *goku chiisai* very small
極希な *goku mare na* extremely rare

KUN

【kiwa(meru) 極める】
[also 窮める]
ⓐ carry to extremity, go to extremes, be extremely (cruel)
ⓑ go to the extreme [end], reach an extreme, go to the highest point
極めて *kiwamete* extremely, very
口を極めて誉める *kuchi o kiwamete homeru* be lavish in another's praise
暴虐を極める *bōgyaku o kiwameru* act with extreme violence
惨状を極める *sanjō o kiwameru* present a very terrible [miserable] sight
貧困を極める *hinkon o kiwameru* be reduced to extreme poverty, be extremely poor
極め付きの品 *kiwametsuki no shina* article of certified genuineness
見極める *mikiwameru* see through, discern; ascertain, grasp
山頂を極める *sanchō o kiwameru* reach the summit

【kiwa(maru) 極まる】 [also suffix] reach an extreme (state or point), be extremely (dangerous)
感極まる *kankiwamaru* be overcome with emotion
危険極まる *kikenkiwamaru* extremely dangerous

【kiwa(mari) 極まり】
[sometimes also 窮まり] extremity, limit
極まり無い *kiwamarinai* extremely, in the extreme
痛快極まり無い *tsūkaikiwamarinai* be extremely thrilling

【kiwa(mi) 極み】 height, apex, utmost
栄華の極み *eiga no kiwami* apex of prosperity

【ki(meru) 極める】
[usu. 決める]
① decide, determine, fix
② agree upon, arrange
③ (bring to a conclusion) settle, conclude
⇨ see 決 263 for compounds

【-gi(me) -極め】 [sometimes also -決め] indicates periods of time (esp. months)
月極め駐車場 *tsukigime chūshajō* parking lot rented on a monthly basis

【ki(maru) 極まる】
[usu. 決まる]
① be decided [fixed], be settled, be arranged
② be certain [sure], be a matter of course
⇨ see 決 263 for compounds

SYNONYMS

❶ⓐ most
至 utmost → 2182
最 MOST → 2472
ⓐ extreme in degree
甚 EXTREMELY → 2643
酷 SEVERE → 1562
厳 SEVERE → 3289
激 intense → 776
痛 bitter(ly) → 3285
切 keen → 27
超 super- → 3313
強 STRONG → 475
重 HEAVY → 3573
高 HIGH → 2097
深 DEEP → 524
大 BIG → 3416
ⓑ extreme
窮 extremity → 2358
限 LIMIT → 398
涯 OUTER LIMITS → 512
果て end → 3560

USAGE

❶ **kiwameru**

極める
[also 窮める]
ⓐ carry to extremity, go to extremes, be extremely (cruel)
ⓑ go to the extreme [end], reach an extreme, go to the highest point

窮める
① [also 極める]
ⓐ carry to extremity, go to extremes, be extremely (cruel)
ⓑ go to the extreme [end], reach an extreme, go to the highest point
② [usu. 究める] investigate thoroughly, study exhaustively, master

究める
[sometimes also 窮める] investigate thoroughly, study exhaustively, master

❷ **kiwamaru**

極まる
[also suffix] reach an extreme (state or point), be extremely (dangerous)

窮まる
[sometimes also 谷まる]
ⓐ come to an end, terminate
ⓑ come to the end of one's tether, be at a loss

谷まる
[usu. 窮まる] same as 窮まる

❸ **kiwamari**

極まり
[sometimes also 窮まり] extremity, limit

窮まり
[now usu. 極まり] extremity, limit

❹ **kiwami**

極み
height, apex, utmost

窮み
extremity, end, limit

HOMOPHONES

kiwameru ⇨ 窮 2358 究 2203
kiwamaru ⇨ 窮 2358 谷 2043
kiwamari ⇨ 窮 2358
kiwami ⇨ 窮 2358
kimeru ⇨ 決 263
-gime ⇨ 決 263
kimaru ⇨ 決 263

NOTE

⇨ see also USAGE note at 決 263

楠 楠 楠

1018 NAN kusu kusunoki

CH 楠 nán

Radical	Strokes
木 75	13-4-9
Grade	**Freq**
Names	2019
1 - 4 - 9	

4-9
木

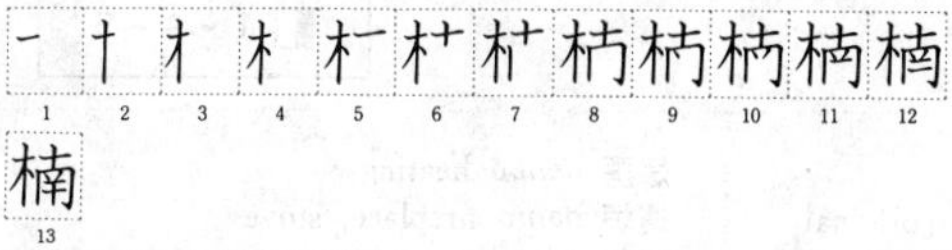

Stroke order: 1 一 2 十 3 才 4 木 5 木一 6 木十 7 木十 8 柿 9 柿 10 柄 11 楠 12 楠 13 楠

▶**CAMPHOR TREE**

KUN

【**kusu** 楠】camphor tree
楠の木 *kusunoki* camphor tree
【**kusunoki** 楠】camphor tree

NAMES

楠本 *kusumoto* surname
楠木 *kusunoki* surname

SYNONYMS

【**kusu**】
○ **trees**
桐 PAULOWNIA → 937
桂 AROMATIC TREE, katsura tree → 928
梓 CATALPA → 962
桑 MULBERRY → 2112
漆 Japanese lacquer tree → 704
槙 PODOCARPUS → 1051
杉 CRYPTOMERIA → 832
松 PINE → 864
楓 MAPLE → 1015
柳 WILLOW → 899
桜 CHERRY → 931

4-9 木

楼 樓 楼 楼
1019 RŌ

CH 楼 lóu

Radical	Strokes
木 75	13-4-9
Grade	Freq
Jōyō	1834
1 - 4 - 9	

一 十 才 木 木 木' 木'' 桝 桝 楼 楼 楼 楼
1 2 3 4 5 6 7 8 9 10 11 12 13

▶**TALL BUILDING**

COMPOUNDS

❶ [original meaning] **tall building, tower, storied building; watchtower, lookout**
楼閣 *rōkaku* multistoried building
鐘楼 *shōrō* bell tower, belfry
望楼 *bōrō* watchtower, observation tower, lookout
五層楼 *gosōrō* five-storied building [tower]
高楼 *kōrō* lofty [high] building; skyscraper
登楼する *tōrō suru* go into a tall building; visit a brothel
摩天楼 *matenrō* skyscraper

❷ suffix after names of tall buildings, inns, restaurants, etc.
山水楼 *sansuirō* Sansuiro (name of an exclusive restaurant)

INDEPENDENT

【rō 楼】tall building, tower; lookout, belvedere
楼に登る *rō ni noboru* go up a tower

SYNONYMS

❶ **tall buildings**
塔 TOWER → 561
閣 TALL MAGNIFICENT BUILDING → 3327
台 observatory → 2005

4-9 火

煖
1020 DAN

CH 暖 nuǎn

Radical	Strokes
火 86	13-4-9
Grade	Freq
Reference	
1 - 4 - 9	

COMPOUNDS

● [now replaced by 暖 *dan* 1011] [original meaning] warm, warm up, heat
煖房 *danbō* heating
煖炉 *danro* fireplace, stove
煖気 *danki* warmth, warm weather

4-9 火

煙 煙 烟° 煙 煙
1021 EN kemu(ru) kemuri kemu(i)

CH 烟 yān

Radical	Strokes
火 86	13-4-9
Grade	Freq
Jōyō	1054
1 - 4 - 9	

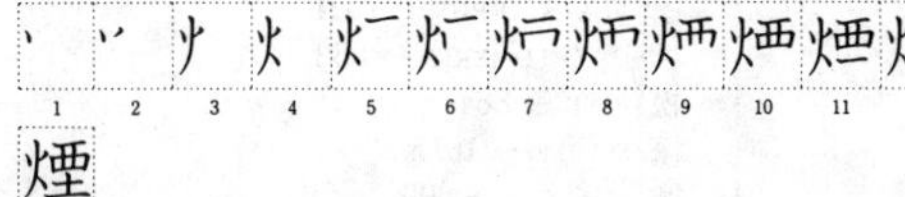

▶**SMOKE**

COMPOUNDS

❶ⓐ **smoke**
ⓑ smokelike substance such as soot
煙突 *entotsu* chimney, smokestack
煙幕 *enmaku* smoke screen
煤煙 *baien* soot and smoke
油煙 *yuen* lamp soot [smoke]

❷ **smoking, cigarettes**
禁煙 *kin'en* NO SMOKING; giving up smoking
喫煙 *kitsuen* smoking
嫌煙権 *ken'enken* right to dislike smoking
節煙 *setsuen* moderation in smoking

KUN

【kemu(ru) 煙る】smoke; be hazy
【kemuri 煙】smoke, fumes
煙になる *kemuri ni naru* vanish in thin air

雪煙 *yukikemuri* smoky snow flakes
【**kemu(i) 煙い**】smoky
煙たい *kemutai* smoky; feeling awkward

SPECIAL READINGS

煙草▲ *tabako* tobacco, cigarette

SYNONYMS

❶ⓐ products of combustion
灰 ASH → 2979
殻 cinders → 1490
炭 CHARCOAL → 2257

煩 

1022 HAN BON wazura(u) wazura(wasu)

CH 烦 fán

Radical	Strokes
火 86	13-4-9
Grade	**Freq**
Jōyō	1908
◧ 1 - 4 - 9	

4-9 火

▶VEXED

COMPOUNDS

❶ [original meaning] **vexed, annoyed, irritated, troubled, worried**
煩悶 *hanmon* anguish, worry
煩悩 *bonnō* worldly desires, carnal desires

❷ **vexatious, intricate, confused, entangled**
煩雑な *hanzatsu na* vexatious, troublesome, intricate
煩瑣な *hansa na* vexatious, troublesome, complicated
煩労 *hanrō* trouble, pains

INDEPENDENT

【**han 煩**】trouble
煩を避ける *han o sakeru* spare the trouble (of doing)

KUN

【**wazura(u) 煩う**】worry about, feel anxious, be vexed
煩い *wazurai* worry, agony, vexation
煩わしい *wazurawashii* vexatious, troublesome, complicated
思い煩う *omoiwazurau* worry about, be vexed

【**wazura(wasu) 煩わす**】trouble, bother, give trouble; annoy, pester, vex
人手を煩わす *hitode o wazurawasu* trouble a person
心を煩わす *kokoro o wazurawasu* worry oneself over

SYNONYMS

❶ trouble and suffering
難 DIFFICULT → 1838
辛 HARD → 2038
痛 PAIN → 3285
苦 SUFFERING → 2243
悩 SUFFER → 421
窮 BE IN EXTREMITY → 2358
困 BE IN TROUBLE → 3070

❷ complex
繁 complicated → 2853

HOMOPHONES

wazurau ⇨ 患 2747
wazurai ⇨ 患 2747

NOTE

⇨ see USAGE note at 患 2747

煉

1023 REN ne(ru)

CH 炼 liàn

Radical	Strokes
火 86	13-4-9
Grade	**Freq**
Reference	
◧ 1 - 4 - 9	

4-9 火

COMPOUNDS

❶ⓐ [now also 錬 *ren* 1741] [original meaning] refine (crude metals), smelt; work metals, temper

ⓑ [now also 練 *ren* 1375] refine (one's skills), purify
煉丹術 *rentanjutsu* art of making elixirs, alchemy
精煉する *seiren suru* refine (metals), smelt (copper); temper
煉獄 *rengoku* purgatory
洗煉された *senren sareta* refined, polished
試煉 *shiren* trial, test, probation

❷ [now also 練 *ren* 1375 or 練る *neru*] knead
煉乳 *rennyū* condensed milk
煉炭 *rentan* (charcoal or coal) briquette

煉瓦 *renga* brick

HOMOPHONES

neru ⇨ 練 1375 錬 1741

NOTE

⇨ see USAGE note at 練 1375

4-9 火

煙 1024

▶SMOKE

nonstandard for 煙 1021

4-9 片

牒 1025 CHŌ

Ⓒⓗ 牒 dié

Radical	Strokes
片 91	13-4-9
Grade	**Freq**
Reference	
1 - 4 - 9	

COMPOUNDS

❶ [now replaced by 丁 3348] [original meaning] wooden placard, label, tag

符牒 *fuchō* sign; secret price tag; password

❷ official notice

通牒 *tsūchō* notification, circular

4-9 王

瑶 瑤 1026 YŌ NAMES tama

Ⓒⓗ 瑶 yáo

Radical	Strokes
王 96	13-4-9
Grade	**Freq**
Names	2128
1 - 4 - 9	

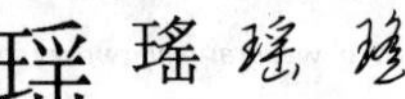

▶EXQUISITE

COMPOUNDS

❶ⓐ [rare] exquisite, beautiful like a gem, glittering, splendid; ornamented with gems

ⓑ [original meaning, now archaic] beautiful white gem

瑶台 *yōdai* beautiful building ornamented with gems; fairyland

瑶顔 *yōgan* exquisite countenance, beautiful face

❷ [archaic] fairyland, place where immortal wizards live

瑶池 *yōchi* place where immortals live; beautiful pond

❸ [archaic] [honorific] your (esp. in reference to letters)

瑶緘 *yōkan* your letter

NAMES

瑶子 *yōko* (= *tamako*) female name

SYNONYMS

❶ⓐ **beautiful**

美 BEAUTIFUL → 2264
佳 FINE → 86
絢 GORGEOUS → 1347
華 MAGNIFICENT → 2283
斐 florid → 2776
妙 of marvelous beauty → 239
艶 CHARMING → 1908
麗 OF GRACEFUL BEAUTY → 2151

瑞 瑞 瑞 ㊥ 瑞 ruì

1027 ZUI SUI mizu- NAMES tama

Radical	Strokes
王 96	13-4-9
Grade	Freq
Names	2013
◧ 1 - 4 - 9	

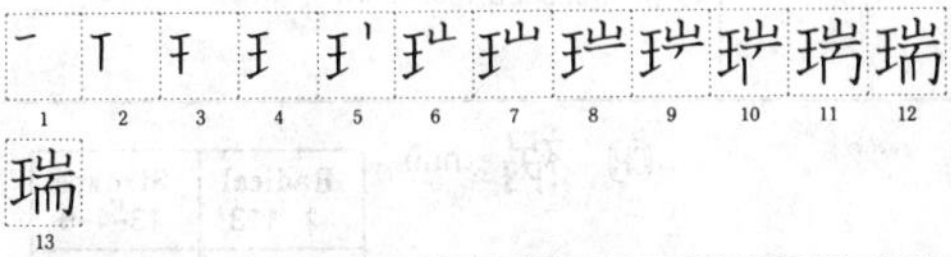

4-9 王

一 丅 干 王 王' 王ᵎ 王ᵎᵎ 王山 王屮 王耑 瑞 瑞 瑞
1 2 3 4 5 6 7 8 9 10 11 12 13

▶AUSPICIOUS OMEN

COMPOUNDS

❶ⓐ **auspicious [good] omen, luck sign**
ⓑ **auspicious, propitious, good**
奇瑞 *kizui* auspicious [good] omen
瑞祥 *zuishō* auspicious sign, good omen
瑞兆 *zuichō* auspicious sign, good omen
瑞雲 *zuiun* auspicious clouds

❷ [rare]
ⓐ Switzerland
ⓑ Sweden
瑞西 *suisu* Switzerland
瑞典 *suēden* Sweden

❸ [original meaning, now obsolete] jade tablet used as a token of authority in ancient China

KUN

[mizu- 瑞-] young and fresh, vigorous
瑞瑞しい *mizumizushii* young and fresh, fresh-looking, juicy
瑞穂の国 *mizuho no kuni* Land of Vigorous Rice Plants, Japan

NAMES

瑞男 *tamao* male name
瑞穂 *mizuho* male name also female name also place name

SYNONYMS

❶ **good fortune**
祥 AUSPICIOUS → 948
嘉 HAPPY → 2340
吉 LUCKY → 2167
禎 PROPITIOUS OMEN → 1031
幸 GOOD FORTUNE → 2216
福 FORTUNE → 1029

HOMOPHONES

mizu- ⇨ 水 10

NOTE

⇨ see USAGE note at 水 10

瑛 **▶TRANSPARENT GEM**

1028 nonstandard for 瑛 999

4-9 王

福 福 福 福 ㊥ 福 fú

1029 FUKU

Radical	Strokes
礻 113	13-4-9
Grade	Freq
Jōyō-3	466
◧ 1 - 4 - 9	

4-9 礻

丶 ㇇ 礻 礻 礻一 礻冖 礻冂 礻口 礻𠮛 礻畐 福 福 福
1 2 3 4 5 6 7 8 9 10 11 12 13

▶FORTUNE

COMPOUNDS

ⓐ (**good**) **fortune, blessing, good luck, prosperity, happiness**
ⓑ (riches) fortune, wealth
福徳 *fukutoku* fortune, happiness and prosperity
福利 *fukuri* public welfare, well-being, prosperity
福祉 *fukushi* welfare
福音 *fukuin* gospel, good news
祝福 *shukufuku* blessing
大福 *daifuku* great fortune, good luck; rice cake stuffed with bean jam
禍福 *kafuku* fortune and misfortune
幸福な *kōfuku na* happy; blessed, fortunate
裕福な *yūfuku na* rich, wealthy

INDEPENDENT

[fuku 福] (good) fortune, blessing, good luck, prosperity, happiness
福は内!鬼は外! *Fuku wa uchi, oni wa soto* Fortune in, Devils out!

SYNONYMS
ⓐ **good fortune**
幸 GOOD FORTUNE → 2216
吉 LUCKY → 2167
嘉 HAPPY → 2340
祥 AUSPICIOUS → 948
瑞 AUSPICIOUS OMEN → 1027
禎 PROPITIOUS OMEN → 1031
ⓑ **happiness**
幸 HAPPINESS → 2216
祉 BLESSEDNESS → 876

4-9
ネ

禍 禍 禍 禍

1030 KA wazawai▲

CH 祸 huò

Radical	Strokes
ネ 113	13-4-9
Grade	Freq
Jōyō	1618
1-4-9	

▶**CALAMITY**

COMPOUNDS
ⓐ [original meaning] **calamity, misfortune, disaster, evil**
ⓑ slip, accident
禍福 *kafuku* fortune and misfortune
禍根 *kakon* root of evil
災禍 *saika* accident, natural calamity, disaster, misfortune
黄禍 *kōka* Yellow Peril
水禍 *suika* flood disaster; drowning
惨禍 *sanka* terrible disaster, crushing calamity
舌禍 *zekka* unfortunate slip of the tongue
交通禍 *kōtsūka* traffic accident

INDEPENDENT
【ka 禍】 calamity, misfortune, disaster
風雨の禍 *fūu no ka* disaster caused by wind and rain

KUN
【wazawai 禍】 [now usu. 災い] calamity, misfortune, disaster, evil, serious trouble
禍する *wazawaisuru* be the ruin of
口は禍の元 *Kuchi wa wazawai no moto* Out of the mouth comes evil

SYNONYMS
ⓐ **misfortune and disaster**
厄 MISFORTUNE → 2947
凶 BAD LUCK → 2961
災 NATURAL CALAMITY → 2206
難 DISASTER → 1838

HOMOPHONES
wazawai ⇨ 災 2206

NOTE
⇨ see USAGE note at 災 2206

4-9
ネ

禎 禎 禎 禎

1031 TEI NAMES sada tadashi yoshi sachi tomo

CH 祯 zhēn

Radical	Strokes
ネ 113	13-4-9
Grade	Freq
Names	2066
1-4-9	

▶**PROPITIOUS OMEN**

COMPOUNDS
[archaic]
ⓐ propitious omen
ⓑ happiness
禎祥 *teishō* good omen

NAMES
禎次 *teiji* male name
禎子 *sadako* female name
禎利 *yoshitoshi* male name

SYNONYMS
ⓐ **good fortune**
瑞 AUSPICIOUS OMEN → 1027
祥 AUSPICIOUS → 948
嘉 HAPPY → 2340
吉 LUCKY → 2167
幸 GOOD FORTUNE → 2216
福 FORTUNE → 1029

禅 禪 禅 祥 — 1032 ZEN

Ⓒⓗ 禅 chán shàn

Radical	Strokes
⺬ 113	13-4-9
Grade	**Freq**
Jōyō	1595
◧ 1-4-9	

4-9 ⺬

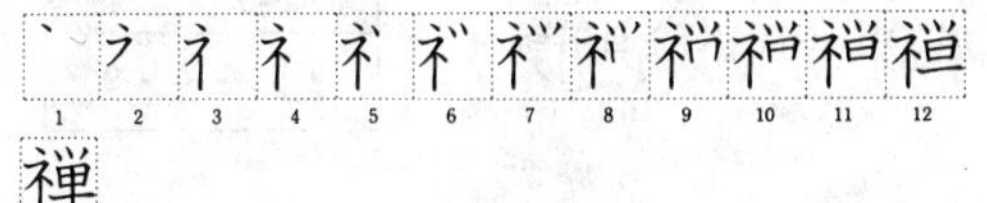

禅 13

▶ZEN

COMPOUNDS

❶ⓐ **Zen Buddhism, Chan**

ⓑ Zen meditation, dhyana

禅宗 *zenshū* Zen sect

禅僧 *zensō* Zen priest [monk]

禅寺 *zendera* Zen temple

禅定 *zenjō* Samadhi, meditative concentration

座禅 *zazen* Zen meditation

❷ abdicate (the throne)

禅譲 *zenjō* abdication

❸ [original meaning, now archaic] ancient Chinese sacrificial ritual

封禅 *hōzen* ancient Chinese sacrificial ritual

INDEPENDENT

【**zen 禅**】Zen Buddhism; Zen meditation

SYNONYMS

❶ **religions and sects**

仏 Buddhism → 19

法 Buddha's teachings → 333

儒 CONFUCIANISM → 174

道 Taoism → 3134

腸 腸 𦛜 — 1033 CHŌ harawata▲

Ⓒⓗ 肠 cháng

Radical	Strokes
月 130	13-4-9
Grade	**Freq**
Jōyō-4	1621
◧ 1-4-9	

4-9 月

丿 1 冂 2 月 3 月 4 月' 5 ... 腸 12 腸 13

▶INTESTINES

COMPOUNDS

❶ⓐ [original meaning] **intestines, entrails, bowels**

ⓑ [prefix] intestinal, enteric

腸炎 *chōen* enteritis

胃腸 *ichō* stomach and intestines [bowels]

小腸 *shōchō* small intestine

脱腸 *datchō* enterocele

盲腸 *mōchō* cecum, appendix

灌腸(＝浣腸)する *kanchō suru* give an enema

腸結核 *chōkekkaku* intestinal tuberculosis

腸チフス *chōchifusu* typhoid fever

❷ mind, heart

断腸 *danchō* heartbreak

INDEPENDENT

【**chō 腸**】intestines, entrails, bowels

腸の病気 *chō no byōki* bowel disease

KUN

【**harawata 腸**】entrails, bowels, guts; placenta (of a melon); mind, heart

腸の腐った男 *harawata no kusatta otoko* man with a corrupt heart

SYNONYMS

❶ **internal organs**

胃 STOMACH → 2561

心 HEART → 11

肺 LUNG → 916

肝 LIVER → 841

胆 GALLBLADDER → 919

4-9 月

腹 1034 FUKU hara

CH 腹 fù

Radical	Strokes
月 130	13-4-9
Grade	Freq
Jōyō-6	1223
1 - 4 - 9	

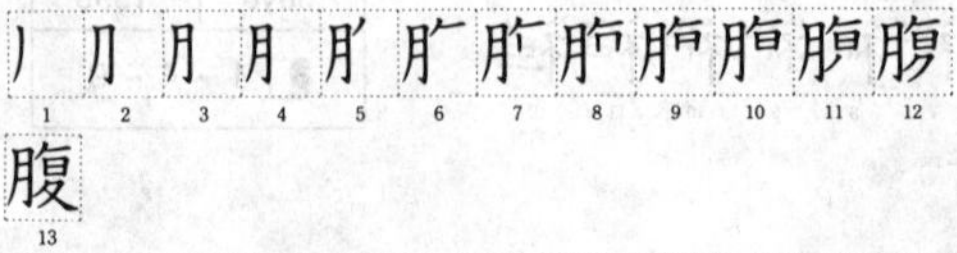

丿 1 月 2 月 3 月 4 月' 5 月'' 6 肸 7 肸 8 胪 9 胪 10 腹 11 腹 12 腹 13

▶**BELLY**

COMPOUNDS

❶ⓐ [original meaning] **belly, abdomen, stomach, bowels**

ⓑ (uterus) belly, womb

腹部 *fukubu* abdomen, belly

腹痛 *fukutsū* stomachache, abdominal pain

満腹 *manpuku* full belly, satiety

切腹 *seppuku* hara-kiri, suicide by disembowelment

空腹 *kūfuku* empty stomach, hunger

同腹の *dōfuku no* uterine (brothers)

❷ something shaped like a belly, thickest or widest part

船腹 *senpuku* bottoms; shipping, tonnage; freight space

中腹に *chūfuku ni* halfway up the mountain

❸ⓐ **heart, mind, intention**

ⓑ guts, courage

腹案 *fukuan* plan, scheme, idea

腹心 *fukushin* trusted friend, trusted retainer

剛腹 *gōfuku* magnanimity

立腹する *rippuku suru* get angry, lose one's temper

KUN

【**hara** 腹】belly, abdomen; bowels; stomach; womb; (counter for the young) litter (of animals); roe (of fish); (thickest part) belly; heart, mind, *hara*; intention, guts; temper

腹一杯 *haraippai* full stomach

下腹 *shitahara* abdomen

腹違い *harachigai* (born) of a different mother, half-blooded

船の腹 *fune no hara* belly of a boat

樽の腹 *taru no hara* belly of a cask; midsection of a barrel

腹黒い *haraguroi* blackhearted, malicious

太っ腹な *futoppara na* generous, large-minded, big-hearted

腹を立てる *hara o tateru* get angry, take offense

SYNONYMS

❶ⓐ **trunk parts**

胸 CHEST → 951

胴 TRUNK → 950

腰 WAIST → 1036

背 BACK → 2573

肩 SHOULDER → 1947

❸ⓐ **psyche**

心 HEART → 11

衷 INNER HEART → 2575

襟 inner mind → 1252

胸 breast → 951

懐 BOSOM → 763

神 MIND → 912

気 SPIRIT (consciousness) → 3194

精 SPIRIT (mind) → 1366

霊 SPIRIT (soul) → 2805

魂 SOUL, spirit → 1063

NOTE

⇨ see COMPOUND FORMATION for 立腹 *rippuku* ⇨ 立 1992

4-9 月

腺 1035 SEN

CH 腺 xiàn (国字)

Radical	Strokes
月 130	13-4-9
Grade	Freq
Non-Jōyō	1800
1 - 4 - 9	

丿 1 月 2 月 3 月 4 月' 5 月' 6 肑 7 肑 8 肑 9 腺 10 腺 11 腺 12 腺 13

▶**GLAND**

COMPOUNDS

● [also suffix] [original meaning] **gland**

腺熱 *sen'netsu* glandular fever

腺病質 *senbyōshitsu* lymphatic temperament, scrofulousness

甲状腺 *kōjōsen* thyroid gland
乳腺 *nyūsen* mammary gland
唾液腺 *daekisen* salivary gland
内分泌腺 *naibunpisen* endocrine gland
リンパ腺 *rinpasen* lymphatic gland

INDEPENDENT

【sen 腺】 gland

腰 腰 腰 𦞂 Ⓒⓗ 腰 yāo

1036 YŌ koshi

Radical	Strokes
月 130	13-4-9
Grade	**Freq**
Jōyō	1160

1-4-9

4-9 月

丿 1 ⺆ 2 月 3 月 4 月⁻ 5 月⺈ 6 月⺊ 7 胚 8 腘 9 腘 10 腰 11 腰 12 腰 13

▶WAIST

COMPOUNDS

● [original meaning] **waist, hips, loin, pelvic region**
腰部 *yōbu* waist, hips
腰間 *yōkan* hips
腰痛 *yōtsū* lumbago, pain in the hips
腰囲 *yōi* hip measurement
細腰 *saiyō* slender hips

KUN

【koshi 腰】
①ⓐ waist, hips, loin, pelvic region
ⓑ (middle part) waist; (of garments) waist, hips
ⓒ lower part (of a wall)
腰骨 *koshibone* hipbone, innominate bone
腰を掛ける *koshi o kakeru* sit down
足腰 *ashikoshi* legs and loins
腰巻 *koshimaki* loincloth
腰上げ *koshiage* tuck at the waist
腰張りをする *koshibari o suru* paper the lower part (of a wall)
障子の腰 *shōji no koshi* lower part of a *shoji* (paper sliding-door)
② [also suffix] stick-to-itiveness, tenacity, perseverance
腰が強い *koshi ga tsuyoi* take a firm stand, be firm
弱腰 *yowagoshi* weak attitude
物腰 *monogoshi* movements, (polite) bearing, mien
話の腰を折る *hanashi no koshi o oru* butt in, interfere
本腰を入れる *hongoshi o ireru* set about in earnest
③ sticky, glutinous; stiff, retaining shape (of clothes)
この餅は腰が有る *Kono mochi wa koshi ga aru* This *mochi* is glutinous
布地の腰が強い *Nunoji no koshi ga tsuyoi* The cloth is stiff
④ counter for objects attached to the waist, as swords, *hakama* (divided skirt), etc.
太刀二腰 *tachi futakoshi* two swords
⑤ third verse of a waka poem
腰折れ *koshiore* poor poem; stooped over (old people)

SYNONYMS

● **trunk parts**
胴 TRUNK → 950
腹 BELLY → 1034
胸 CHEST → 951
背 BACK → 2573
肩 SHOULDER → 1947

脚 1037 **▶LEG**
nonstandard for 脚 974

4-9 月

腦 1038 **▶BRAIN**
nonstandard for 脳 975

4-9 月

腰 1039 **▶WAIST**
nonstandard for 腰 1036

4-9 月

4-9 元

頑 1040 GAN

CH 顽 wán

Radical	Strokes
頁 181	13-9-4
Grade	**Freq**
Jōyō	1951
1 - 4 - 9	

一 二 テ 元 ... 頑 (1–13)

▶STUBBORN

COMPOUNDS

ⓐ **stubborn, obstinate; hardheaded, thick-headed**

ⓑ (unyielding) **stubborn, firm, tenacious**

頑固な *ganko na* stubborn, obstinate, bigoted
頑強な *gankyō na* stubborn, unyielding
頑丈な *ganjō na* solid, firm; strong
頑健 *ganken* robust health
頑張る *ganbaru* persist, be tenacious, hold out

INDEPENDENT

【gan to shite 頑として】 stubbornly, firmly

SYNONYMS

● **firm and obstinate**

硬 hard-line → 1183
毅 RESOLUTE → 1866
剛 TOUGH → 1673
堅 FIRM → 2823
固 FIRM, stiff → 3086
確 firm → 1228

COMPOUND FORMATION

頑張る *ganbaru*

頑張る 'persist, etc.' derives from, and is a new way of writing, the expression 我に張る *ga ni haru* 'to insist on one's way'.

4-9 扌

瓶 1041

▶BOTTLE

nonstandard for 瓶 1344

4-9 予

預 1042 YO azu(keru) azu(karu)

CH 预 yù

Radical	Strokes
頁 181	13-9-4
Grade	**Freq**
Jōyō-5	1073
1 - 4 - 9	

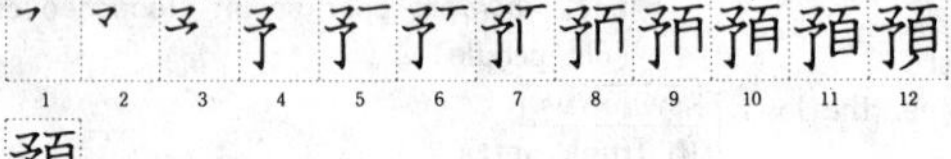

▶DEPOSIT

COMPOUNDS

❶ **deposit**

預金 *yokin* deposit, bank account
預託する *yotaku suru* deposit
預貸率 *yotairitsu* loan-deposit ratio
預貯金 *yochokin* deposits and savings, bank account
預血する *yoketsu suru* deposit blood (in a blood bank)

❷ [usu. 予 1983] previously, in advance

預言 *yogen* prophecy (in Christianity)

KUN

【azu(keru) 預ける】 deposit, entrust, leave with; leave (a child) in the care of

預け *azuke* custody, keeping
預け金 *azukekin* key money
預け入れる *azukeireru* make a deposit

【azu(karu) 預かる】

① receive on deposit, take charge of, keep

預かり *azukari* custody; undecided match, draw, tie
保護預かり *hogoazukari* safe deposit

② refrain from (doing something)

批評は暫く預かる *Hihyō wa shibaraku azukaru* I refrain from commenting on it now

③ leave (a game) undecided

預かりにする *azukari ni suru* call off (a game) as a draw

SYNONYMS

❶ **commit**

託 ENTRUST → 1455
委 COMMIT → 2553
任 LEAVE TO → 53

囑 CHARGE WITH → 718

USAGE

azukaru

預かる

① receive on deposit, take charge of, keep

② refrain from (doing something)

③ leave (a game) undecided

与る

① participate in, take part in, share in

② enjoy, receive

HOMOPHONES

azukaru ⇨ 与 3421

NOTE

⇨ see also USAGE note at 予 1983

頒 頒 頒 頒

1043 HAN waka(tsu)▲

CH 颁 bān

Radical	Strokes
頁 181	13-9-4
Grade	**Freq**
Jōyō	1916
◧ 1 - 4 - 9	

4-9 分

Stroke order: 1–13

▶DISTRIBUTE WIDELY

COMPOUNDS

❶ **distribute widely, circulate, promulgate**

頒布 *hanpu* distribution, circulation

頒価 *hanka* distribution price

頒行 *hankō* [rare] distribution, circulation, promulgation

❷ [archaic] mottled, streaked

頒白 *hanpaku* grayish hair

KUN

【**waka(tsu)** 頒つ】[usu. 分かつ] distribute (things among people)

実費でお頒ちします *Jippi de owakachi shimasu* It will be offered at actual cost

SYNONYMS

❶ **distribute**

配 DISTRIBUTE → 1460

分 DIVIDE → 1972

HOMOPHONES

wakatsu ⇨ 分 1972

NOTE

⇨ see USAGE note at 分 1972

頒

1044

▶DISTRIBUTE WIDELY

nonstandard for 頒 1043

4-9 分

頌 頌 頌 頌

1045 SHŌ JU NAMES tsugu nobu

CH 颂 sòng

Radical	Strokes
頁 181	13-9-4
Grade	**Freq**
Names	2111
◧ 1 - 4 - 9	

4-9 公

Stroke order: 1–13

▶EULOGIZE

COMPOUNDS

❶ⓐ **eulogize, extol, praise highly**

ⓑ poem of eulogy, hymn of praise

頌徳 *shōtoku* eulogy

頌歌 *shōka* anthem, carol, hymn of praise

❷ celebrate, congratulate

頌春 *shōshun* Happy New Year

❸ [now always 誦 *shō* 1549] [original meaning] recite

INDEPENDENT

【**shō** 頌】eulogy, panegyric

【**shōsuru** 頌する】eulogize, extol, praise highly

NAMES

正頌 *masatsugu* male name

SYNONYMS

❶ⓐ **praise**

揚 EXALT → 593

賛 PRAISE → 2809

美 regard as beautiful → 2264

褒 COMMEND → 2144
嘉 commend (esp. an inferior) → 2340
彰 PROCLAIM MERITS → 1860
称 acclaim → 1160
賞 express admiration → 2618

4-9
公

頌
1046

▶EULOGIZE
nonstandard for 頌 1045

4-10
方

旗 旗 旗
1047 KI hata

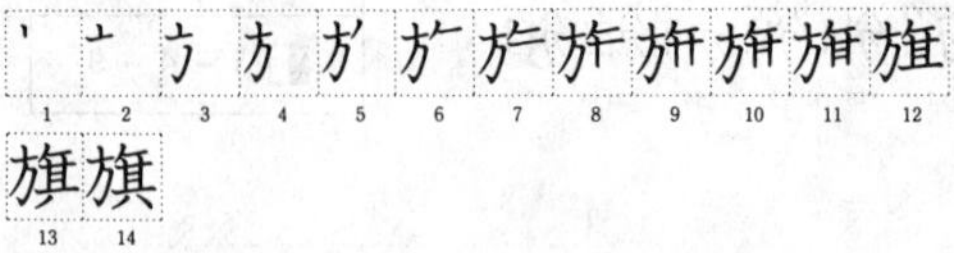

CH 旗 qí

Radical	Strokes
方 70	14-4-10
Grade	**Freq**
Jōyō-4	1100
1-4-10	

▶FLAG

COMPOUNDS

❶ⓐ **flag, banner, standard, ensign**
ⓑ [suffix] **flag, emblem**
旗艦 *kikan* flagship
旗手 *kishu* standard bearer
国旗 *kokki* national flag
反旗を翻す *hanki o hirugaesu* raise the standard of revolt, rise in revolt
星条旗 *seijōki* the Stars and Stripes
国連旗 *kokurenki* United Nations Emblem
日章旗 *nisshōki* Rising Sun flag
❷ [also 麾 3174] command
旗下の *kika no* under one's command, under the banner (of)

KUN

【hata 旗】 flag, banner, standard, ensign
旗揚げ *hataage* raising an army; launching business
手旗 *tebata* semaphore [hand] flag

USAGE

hata
旗
flag, banner, standard, ensign
幡
patākā: pendant streamer hung before a temple in honor of Buddha

HOMOPHONES

hata ⇨ 幡 723

4-10
木

概 概 概 概
1048 GAI ōmu(ne)▲

CH 概 gài

Radical	Strokes
木 75	14-4-10
Grade	**Freq**
Jōyō	1300
1-4-10	

▶GENERAL

COMPOUNDS

❶ⓐ **general, on the whole, approximate, rough**
ⓑ **general outline**
ⓒ generalize
概論 *gairon* outline, general remarks
概算 *gaisan* approximation, rough estimate [calculation]
概況 *gaikyō* general condition [situation], outlook
概念 *gainen* general idea, concept
概略 *gairyaku* outline, summary; roughly, approximately
概要 *gaiyō* outline, summary, synopsis
一概に *ichigai ni* unconditionally; wholly, indiscriminately
大概 *taigai* generally, mostly; probably, maybe
概括する *gaikatsu suru* summarize, sum up, generalize
❷ manner of carrying [conducting] oneself, looks
気概 *kigai* spirit, pluck

INDEPENDENT

【**gai** 概】 manner of carrying [conducting] oneself
将軍の概が有る *shōgun no gai ga aru* look like a commander
【**gaishite** 概して】 generally, on the whole, as a rule

KUN

【**ōmu(ne)** 概ね】 generally, on the whole, approximately, roughly

SYNONYMS

❶ⓐ **approximately**
約 APPROXIMATELY → 1280
大 in substance → 3416
-頃 ABOUT → 144
位 about → 61
-方 about → 1963
-程 ...or thereabouts → 1190
辺り thereabouts → 3029

NOTE

★do not confuse with 慨 641

構 構 構 𣘺

1049 KŌ kama(eru) kama(u)

Ⓒⓗ 构 gòu

Radical 木 75	Strokes 14-4-10
Grade Jōyō-5	Freq 411
1-4-10	

4-10 木

一 十 才 木 木一 木+ 木艹 木卄 桝 桝 構 構 構 構 (1–14)

▶CONSTRUCT ▶MIND

COMPOUNDS

❶ⓐ [original meaning] (build by assembling parts) **construct, frame, assemble, form, compose**
ⓑ **structure, framework, construction, fabrication**
構成 *kōsei* composition, construction, formation, organization
構造 *kōzō* structure, construction, framework
構築する *kōchiku suru* construct, build
構文 *kōbun* sentence construction, syntax
機構 *kikō* mechanism, structure; system, organization; frame, framework
結構 *kekkō* structure, construction; quite, well enough, fairly well; all right; no thank you
虚構 *kyokō* fabrication, fiction
❷ plan constructively, frame, contrive, devise
構想する *kōsō suru* conceive, contrive; plan
構図 *kōzu* design, plot, plan
❸ premises, enclosure
構内 *kōnai* premises, compound, grounds
構外 *kōgai* out of the premises

KUN

【**kama(eru)** 構える】 set up (a house), take up, keep; assume a posture, make ready
構え *kamae* structure, construction, style; posture, attitude; enclosure radical (of Chinese characters), embracing radical
居を構える *kyo o kamaeru* take up one's residence
銃を構えて *jū o kamaete* ready with a rifle leveled
待ち構える *machikamaeru* wait eagerly for, be on the watch for
心構え *kokorogamae* mental attitude; preparation
二段構え *nidangamae* two-stage preparation
【**kama(u)** 構う】
① mind, care about, be concerned about
構わない *kamawanai* do not care [mind], be indifferent (to)
人が何と言おうと構わない *Hito ga nan to iō to kamawanai* I don't care what people say about me
② care for; entertain
どうぞお構い無く *Dōzo okamai naku* Please don't trouble yourself (on my account)
③ meddle in, butt in
私の事を構わないでくれ *Watashi no koto o kamawanaide kure* Leave me [let me be] alone!
④ tease, molest
犬を構う *inu o kamau* tease a dog

SYNONYMS

❶ⓐ **make**
組む ASSEMBLE → 1337
調 PREPARE → 1567
作 MAKE → 68
造 MAKE → 3110
成 FORM → 3537
工 MANUFACTURE → 3381
製 MANUFACTURE → 2803
産 PRODUCE → 3298
ⓑ **structure**
造り MAKE → 3110
【**kamau**】
① **worry**
憂 BE ANXIOUS → 2145

配 concern oneself → 1460
虞 FEARS (of undesirable event) → 3254

4-10 木

模 模 模 模

1050 MO BO

CH 模 mó mú

Radical	Strokes
木 75	14-4-10
Grade	**Freq**
Jōyō-6	639
1-4-10	

▶PATTERN

COMPOUNDS

❶ (something worthy of imitation) **pattern, model, norm, exemplar**
模範 *mohan* model, pattern, example
模型 *mokei* model, pattern, mold
模式標本 *moshiki-hyōhon* type specimen

❷ [formerly also 摸 *mo* 691] **pattern after, imitate, copy, model upon**
模造 *mozō* imitation, counterfeit
模擬の *mogi no* imitation, sham, mock, simulated
模倣する *mohō suru* imitate, copy
模写する *mosha suru* copy, trace, reproduce

❸ (decorative design) **pattern, design, figure**
模様 *moyō* pattern, design; appearance, circumstances
規模 *kibo* scale, scope

❹ [formerly also 摸 *mo* 691] grope, feel about [for], search
模索 *mosaku* groping

❺ vague, dim, indistinct
模糊 *moko* dimness, vagueness

INDEPENDENT

【**mosuru** 模する(=摸する)】 copy, imitate

SYNONYMS

❶ **model**
範 MODEL → 2709
典 CANON → 2627
程 ESTABLISHED FORM → 1190
式 form → 3049
準 STANDARD → 2856
格 NORM → 926

❷ **imitate**
象 represent → 2134
肖 MODEL → 2205
倣 COPY AFTER → 113
擬 IMITATE → 788

❸ **pattern**
文 decorative pattern → 1962
柄 pattern (on cloth) → 897
様 pattern → 1052
紋 figure → 1299

COMPOUND FORMATION

規模 *kibo*

規模 'scale, scope' originally referred to the shape or pattern (模 ❸) of an object drawn with the aid of a compass (規). This came to signify the overall structure or scale of things.

4-10 木

槙 槙 槙 槙

1051 TEN SHIN maki

CH 槙 zhěn diān

Radical	Strokes
木 75	14-4-10
Grade	**Freq**
Names	2120
1-4-10	

▶PODOCARPUS

COMPOUNDS

● cedar or related trees
柏槙 *byakushin* juniper

KUN

【**maki** 槙】 podocarpus; cedar, white cedar
犬槙 *inumaki* podocarpus, *Podocarpus macrophyllus*

NAMES

槙子 *makiko* female name
槙枝 *makieda* surname

SYNONYMS

【**maki**】

○ **trees**
杉 CRYPTOMERIA → 832
楠 CAMPHOR TREE → 1018

桐 PAULOWNIA → 937	松 PINE → 864
桂 AROMATIC TREE, katsura tree → 928	楓 MAPLE → 1015
梓 CATALPA → 962	柳 WILLOW → 899
桑 MULBERRY → 2112	桜 CHERRY → 931
漆 Japanese lacquer tree → 704	

様 樣 杧◆ 様 様

Ⓒⓗ 样 yàng

1052 YŌ sama zama▲

Radical	Strokes
木 75	14-4-10
Grade	Freq
Jōyō-3	550
◧ 1-4-10	

4-10 木

一 十 才 木 木' 木'' 木'' 栏 栏 样 样 样 样 様

1 2 3 4 5 6 7 8 9 10 11 12 13 14

▶MODE ▶FORMAL TITLE

COMPOUNDS

❶ⓐ (manner of doing) **mode, method, way, manner, style**

ⓑ [verbal suffix] **way of doing**

様式 *yōshiki* mode, manner; style, order
今様の *imayō no* modern, up to date
各人各様 *Kakujin kakuyō* So many men, so many ways
唐様 *karayō* Chinese style [design]
同様に *dōyō ni* similarly
泳ぎ様 *oyogiyō* way of swimming
仕様が無い *shiyō ga nai* have no choice; it is no use; cannot bear

❷ (manner of being) **mode, state, aspect, appearance**

様相 *yōsō* aspect, phase, condition
様子 *yōsu* situation, aspect, circumstances; appearance, looks; sign, indication
様態 *yōtai* mode
異様な *iyō na* strange, odd, singular

❸ⓐ variety, sort, kind

ⓑ [suffix] **like, such as**

一様 *ichiyō* uniformity, equality
多様な *tayō na* various, manifold
左様 *sayō* such; yes; let me see
歯ブラシ様の物 *haburashiyō no mono* something resembling a toothbrush

❹ pattern, figure

模様 *moyō* pattern, design; appearance, circumstances
文様 *mon'yō* pattern, design

INDEPENDENT

【yō 様】

① way, manner, mode, method
この様に *kono yō ni* in this way

② like, as
天使の様な少女 *tenshi no yō na shōjo* angel of a girl
雪の様に白い *yuki no yō ni shiroi* white as snow

③ kind, sort, the like (of something)
彼はどの様な人ですか *Kare wa dono yō na hito desu ka* What sort of person is he?

④ⓐ appearance, looks
ⓑ it appears that, it seems
雨の様だ *Ame no yō da* It looks like rain

⑤ in order to, so that
風邪を引かない様にセーターを着た *Kaze o hikanai yō ni sētā o kita* I put on a sweater so as not to catch a cold

⑥ that, thus
彼に電話する様に言った *Kare ni denwa suru yō ni itta* I told him to telephone
邪魔をしない様に *Jama o shinai yō ni* Leave me alone!
長生きなさいます様に *Nagaiki nasaimasu yō ni* May you live long!
最近煙草を吸う様になった *Saikin tabako o suu yō ni natta* I started smoking recently

KUN

【sama 様】

① state, situation; appearance
有り様 *arisama* condition, state of affairs; sight

② kind, sort
様様な *samazama na* various, manifold

③ formal title: Mr., Miss, Mrs., Ms., Esq.
山本様 *yamamotosama* Mr. Yamamoto
貴様 *kisama* [belittling] you; [original meaning] sir, madam

④ [often preceded by お- *o-* or 御- *go-*] suffix for forming polite phrases
お気の毒様 *Okinodokusama* I am sorry
御苦労様 *Gokurōsama* I thank you for your kind efforts

【zama 様】

① state, plight, appearance, spectacle
様を見ろ *Zama o miro* Serves you right!

② [suffix]
ⓐ when, as soon as
ⓑ way of doing

ⓒ direction
妻の方を振り向き様、彼は黙れと叫んだ *Tsuma no hō o furimukizama, kare wa damare to sakenda* "Shut up!" cried he, turning to his wife
生き様 *ikizama* way of life, form of existence
後ろ様に倒れる *ushirozama ni taoreru* fall backward

SYNONYMS

❶ **way and style**
風 MANNER → 3007
方 WAY → 1963
途 WAY → 3107
法 METHOD → 333
流 STYLE → 441
式 STYLE → 3049
調 TONE → 1567

❷ **states and situations**
相 PHASE → 900
調 TONE → 1567
態 STATE → 2847
状 CONDITION → 272
況 CONDITIONS → 337
景 business conditions → 2470
勢 course of events → 2857
境 SITUATION → 676
局 current situation → 3063
情 ACTUAL CONDITIONS → 482
訳 circumstances → 1473

❸ⓐ **kinds and types**
種 VARIETY → 1218
類 KIND → 1807
色 kind → 2029
属 genus → 3145
品 category → 2248
般 SORT → 1317
型 TYPE → 2638

ⓑ **similar**
如 AS → 207
-通り as → 3109
云 SUCH → 1931
類 similar → 1807

❹ **pattern**
模 PATTERN (decorative design) → 1050
文 decorative pattern → 1962
柄 pattern (on cloth) → 897
紋 figure → 1299

【sama】

③ **titles of address**
殿 FORMAL HONORIFIC TITLE → 1792
氏 COURTESY TITLE → 2951
兄 familiar title (seniors) → 2154
君 FAMILIAR TITLE (peers) → 3206
嬢 Miss → 758
師 honorific title (clergymen) → 1326
公 honorific title (noblemen) → 1974

4-10 木

搆 1053

▶CONSTRUCT ▶MIND
nonstandard for 構 1049

4-10 木

槙 1054

▶PODOCARPUS
nonstandard for 槇 1051

4-10 止

雌 1055

SHI me- mesu men▲

Ⓒ 雌 cí

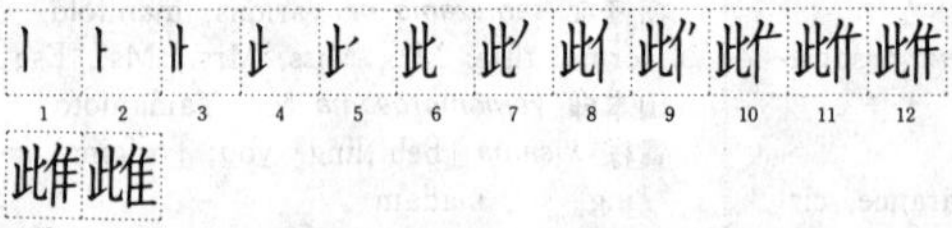

Radical	Strokes
隹 172	14-8-6
Grade	**Freq**
Jōyō	1841
1-4-10	

▶FEMALE

COMPOUNDS

❶ [original meaning] (of plants or animals) **female**
雌雄 *shiyū* male and female; victory or defeat
雌蕊 *shizui* pistil

❷ weak, retiring, inferior
雌伏する *shifuku suru* remain in obscurity, lie low, bide one's time

KUN

【me- 雌-】
ⓐ (of plants) female
ⓑ [sometimes also 牝-] (of animals) female
ⓒ [also 女] the weaker or smaller of two
雌花 *mebana* female flower
雌蕊 *meshibe* pistil
雌捻子(＝雌螺子) *meneji* female screw

雌牛 *meushi* cow
雌滝 *medaki* the smaller waterfall (of the two)
【mesu 雌】[sometimes also 牝] (of animals) female
雌の狐 *mesu no kitsune* vixen, bitch fox
雌犬 *mesuinu* female dog, bitch
【men 雌】[sometimes also 牝] (of animals) female
雌鳥(＝雌鶏) *mendori* hen

SYNONYMS

❶ **woman**
女 WOMAN → 3418
婦 ADULT WOMAN → 469
嬢 YOUNG LADY → 758
娘 GIRL → 406
婆 OLD WOMAN → 2762

USAGE

❶ **me**
雌-
ⓐ (of plants) female
ⓑ [sometimes also 牝-] (of animals) female
ⓒ [also 女] the weaker or smaller of two
牝-
[usu. 雌] (of animals) female
女
① *elegant* the fair sex, woman, female
② [in compounds] the weaker or smaller of two

❷ **mesu**
雌
[sometimes also 牝] (of animals) female
牝
[usu. 雌] (of animals) female

❸ **men**
雌
[sometimes also 牝] (of animals) female
牝
[usu. 雌] (of animals) female

HOMOPHONES

me- ⇨ 牝 826 女 3418
mesu ⇨ 牝 826
men ⇨ 牝 826

煽

1056 SEN ao(ru) oda(teru)

Ⓒⓗ 煽 扇 shān

Radical	Strokes
火 86	14-4-10
Grade	Freq
Reference	
◧ 1-4-10	

4-10 火

COMPOUNDS

● [now replaced by 扇 *sen* 1950] (move to action) fan, stir up, instigate
煽動する *sendō suru* instigate, agitate
煽情的な *senjōteki na* inflammatory, lascivious
煽る *aoru* fan, flap; fan, stir up, instigate
煽り *aori* influence; gust (of wind)
煽てる *odateru* stir up, instigate, incite; flatter

熄

1057 SOKU

Ⓒⓗ 熄 xī

Radical	Strokes
火 86	14-4-10
Grade	Freq
Reference	
◧ 1-4-10	

4-10 火

COMPOUNDS

● [now replaced by 息 2647] [original meaning] go out, die out
終熄する *shūsoku suru* cease, come to an end

4-10
火

熔

1058 YŌ to(keru) to(kasu)

Ⓒⓗ 熔 róng

Radical	Strokes
火 86	14-4-10
Grade	Freq
Reference	
1-4-10	

COMPOUNDS

ⓐ [now replaced by 溶 *yō* 664] (change or cause to change from solid to liquid, esp. by heat) melt

ⓑ [now usu. 溶ける *tokeru*] *vi* (of metals) melt (up), fuse, smelt

ⓒ [now usu. 溶かす *tokasu*] *vt* melt (up) (metals), fuse, smelt

熔解する *yōkai suru* melt, fuse
熔融 *yōyū* melting, fusion
熔接する *yōsetsu suru* weld
熔鉱炉 *yōkōro* smelting [blast] furnace
熔銑 *yōsen* molten iron
熔岩 *yōgan* lava
鉄を熔かす *tetsu o tokasu* melt [fuse] iron

HOMOPHONES

tokeru ⇨ 解 1517 融 1831 溶 664 鎔 1762
tokasu ⇨ 解 1517 融 1831 溶 664 鎔 1762 梳 964

NOTE

⇨ see USAGE note at 解 1517

4-10
王

璃 璃 璃

1059 RI NAMES aki

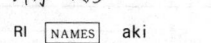

Ⓒⓗ 璃 lí

Radical	Strokes
王 96	14-4-10
Grade	Freq
Names	2118
1-4-10	

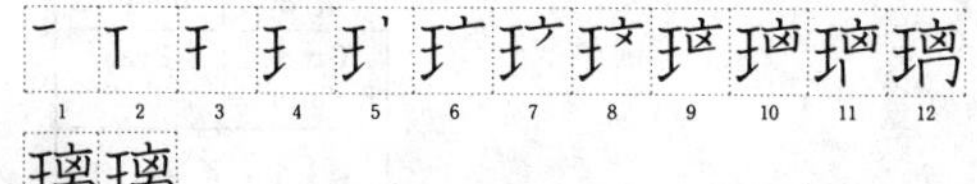

▶GLASSY SUBSTANCE

COMPOUNDS

● **glassy substance, glass; crystal**
瑠璃(＝琉璃) *ruri* lapis lazuli, lapis lazuli blue; [archaic] glass
玻璃 *hari* crystal; glass
浄瑠璃 *jōruri joruri*, ballad drama; clear lapis lazuli

NAMES

瑠璃子 *ruriko* female name
璃子 *akiko* female name

SYNONYMS

● **precious stones**
瑠 LAPIS LAZULI → 1060
晶 CRYSTAL → 2474
玉 GEM → 3477
珠 PEARL → 947
瑛 TRANSPARENT GEM → 999

4-10
王

瑠 瑠 瑠

1060 RU RYŪ NAMES ruri

Ⓒⓗ 琉 liú

Radical	Strokes
王 96	14-4-10
Grade	Freq
Names	2090
1-4-10	

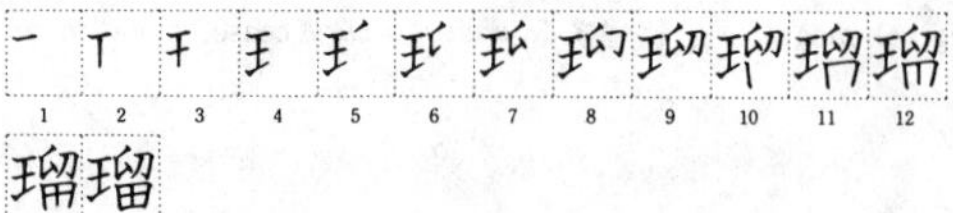

▶LAPIS LAZULI

COMPOUNDS

ⓐ (kind of gemstone) **lapis lazuli**
ⓑ (variant of blue) lapis lazuli, lapis lazuli blue
瑠璃(＝琉璃) *ruri* lapis lazuli, lapis lazuli blue; [archaic] glass
瑠璃色 *ruriiro* lapis lazuli blue, bright blue

瑠璃唐草 *rurikarakusa* baby blue-eyes (name of plant)
浄瑠璃 *jōruri joruri*, ballad drama; clear lapis lazuli

NAMES

瑠璃子 *ruriko* female name
瑠子 *ruriko* female name

SYNONYMS

ⓐ **precious stones**
璃 GLASSY SUBSTANCE → 1059
晶 CRYSTAL → 2474
玉 GEM → 3477
珠 PEARL → 947
瑛 TRANSPARENT GEM → 999

ⓑ **blue and purple colors**
碧 DEEP BLUE → 2836
青 BLUE → 2430
紺 DARK BLUE → 1332
藍 INDIGO → 2381
紫 PURPLE → 2688

NOTE

★Though 瑠 and 琉 are distinct characters, they have the same meanings and may be used interchangeably. However, *ryūkyū*, another name for Okinawa, is usu. written 琉球.

瑤 1061 — 4-10 王

▶EXQUISITE
nonstandard for 瑶 1026

膜 1062 — 4-10 月

膜 膜 膜 MAKU

Ⓒⓗ 膜 mó

Radical	Strokes
月 130	14-4-10
Grade	**Freq**
Jōyō	1791

▮ 1-4-10

▶MEMBRANE

COMPOUNDS

● [also suffix] [original meaning] **membrane, film**
膜状の *makujō no* membranous, filmy
粘膜 *nenmaku* mucous membrane
角膜 *kakumaku* cornea
腹膜 *fukumaku* peritoneum
鼓膜 *komaku* eardrum
細胞膜 *saibōmaku* cellular membrane
イオン交換膜 *ion kōkan-maku* ion exchange membrane

INDEPENDENT

【**maku** 膜】 membrane, film
膜が張る *Maku ga haru* A film is formed

魂 1063 — 4-10 云

魂 魂 KON tamashii tama▲

Ⓒⓗ 魂 hún

Radical	Strokes
鬼 194	14-10-4
Grade	**Freq**
Jōyō	1637

▮ 1-4-10

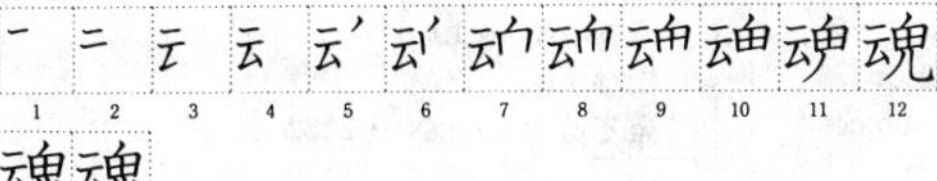

▶SOUL

COMPOUNDS

❶ [original meaning] **soul, spirit**
魂魄 *konpaku* soul, spirit, ghost
霊魂 *reikon* spirit, soul
英魂 *eikon* departed spirit

❷ **spirit, heart**
魂胆 *kontan* secret intention, ulterior motive
闘魂 *tōkon* fighting spirit
心魂 *shinkon* one's soul [heart]
商魂 *shōkon* commercial enthusiasm, salesmanship

KUN

【**tamashii** 魂】 soul, spirit
魂を入れ替える *tamashii o irekaeru* reform (oneself), turn over a new leaf
面魂 *tsuradamashii* determined expression, plucky countenance

【tama 魂】[also 霊] soul, spirit, ghost
魂送り *tamaokuri* sending off the spirits of the dead
人魂 *hitodama* spirit of a dead person

SYNONYMS

❶ & ❷ **psyche**
霊 SPIRIT (soul) → 2805
精 SPIRIT (mind) → 1366
気 SPIRIT (consciousness) → 3194
神 MIND → 912
懐 BOSOM → 763
心 HEART → 11
腹 heart → 1034
衷 INNER HEART → 2575
襟 inner mind → 1252
胸 breast → 951

USAGE

tama
魂
[also 霊] soul, spirit, ghost
霊
[also 魂] soul, spirit, ghost

HOMOPHONES

tama ⇨ 霊 2805

4-11
木

標 標 標

1064 HYŌ

Ⓒ 标 biāo

Radical 木 75	Strokes 15-4-11
Grade Jōyō-4	Freq 742
1-4-11	

一 十 才 木 木 木 杆 標 標 標 標 標 標 標 標
1 2 3 4 5 6 7 8 9 10 11 12 13 14 15

▶**MARK**

COMPOUNDS

❶ⓐ (identifying sign) **mark, sign, symbol, label, inscription**
ⓑ (something serving as a guide) **mark, landmark, signpost, indication**
標章 *hyōshō* ensign, emblem, mark
標札(=表札) *hyōsatsu* nameplate, doorplate
商標 *shōhyō* trademark
墓標 *bohyō* grave post, grave marker, gravestone
指標 *shihyō* index, indication
音標 *onpyō* phonetic sign
浮標 *fuhyō* (marker) buoy
座標 *zahyō* coordinates
里程標 *riteihyō* milestone, milepost
境界標 *kyōkaihyō* boundary mark
❷ (something aimed at) **mark, target, standard**
標的 *hyōteki* target, mark
標準 *hyōjun* standard, norm, criterion
目標 *mokuhyō* mark, target, goal, object
❸ **mark, indicate, designate**
標示する *hyōji suru* post up, declare, demonstrate
標語 *hyōgo* slogan, motto, catch word
標本 *hyōhon* specimen, sample
標高 *hyōkō* elevation, (height) above the sea
標記する *hyōki suru* mark; write a title
標題 *hyōdai* title, headline, caption

INDEPENDENT

【hyō 標】 post, sign post; mark, target

SYNONYMS

❶ⓐ **marks and signs**
印 MARK (visible sign) → 828
跡 TRACE → 1534
紋 print → 1299
符 SYMBOL → 2661
号 SIGN → 2153
❷ **target**
的 TARGET → 1125
目 aim → 3043
❸ **indicate**
示 SHOW → 1936
指 POINT → 378
宛てる ADDRESS → 2222

NOTE

⇨ see USAGE note at 表 2429

権 權 权° 権 権

1065 KEN GON

CH 权 quán

Radical	Strokes
木 75	15-4-11
Grade	**Freq**
Jōyō-6	222
1-4-11	

4-11 木

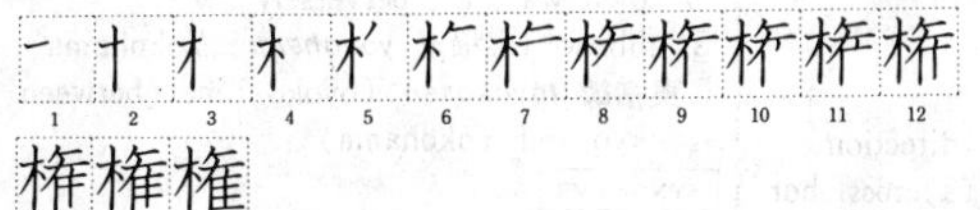

13 14 15

▶**RIGHT** ▶**POWER**

COMPOUNDS

❶ [also suffix] **right, privilege, claim**
権利 *kenri* right; authority; privilege
権限 *kengen* power, authority; competence (of law)
債権 *saiken* credit, claim
職権 *shokken* official [legal] authority
特権 *tokken* privilege, exclusive right
有権者 *yūkensha* elector, voter; holder of a right
棄権 *kiken* abstention from voting, abandoning one's right
人権 *jinken* human rights
男女同権 *danjo-dōken* equal rights for men and women
所有権 *shoyūken* ownership, proprietary rights
参政権 *sanseiken* suffrage, right to vote

❷ **power to control, ability to exact obedience, authority**
権威 *ken'i* authority, power
権力 *kenryoku* power, authority, influence
権勢 *kensei* power, influence, authority
政権 *seiken* political power, administrative power
実権 *jikken* real power
制海権 *seikaiken* command of the sea, naval supremacy

❸ temporary, transient—said esp. of Buddhist incarnation
権現 *gongen* incarnation of Buddha; Tokugawa Ieyasu
権化 *gonge* incarnation, embodiment

❹ scheme, expediency
権謀 *kenbō* artifice, wiles, trick

❺ [original meaning] balance weight
権衡 *kenkō* scales; balance, equilibrium

INDEPENDENT

【ken 権】 power, authority
兵馬の権 *heiba no ken* military power

SYNONYMS

❷ **power and authority**
勢 POWER (to influence) → 2857
威 MIGHT → 3578
力 POWER → 3371
覇 SUPREMACY → 2730

横 横 横 横

1066 Ō yoko

CH 横 héng hèng

Radical	Strokes
木 75	15-4-11
Grade	**Freq**
Jōyō-3	374
1-4-11	

4-11 木

1 2 3 4 5 6 7 8 9 10 11 12 13 14 15

▶**SIDEWAYS**

COMPOUNDS

❶ⓐ **sideways, horizontal, across, crosswise, transverse, lateral, latitudinal**
ⓑ place sideways, lay across, lay down
横転する *ōten suru* roll, fall down sidelong; barrel roll
横断する *ōdan suru* cross, traverse
横隔膜 *ōkakumaku* diaphragm; midriff
縦横に *jūō ni* vertically and horizontally, in all directions; freely
横臥する *ōga suru* lie on one's side, repose

❷ **arbitrary, perverse, despotic, tyrannical, overbearing**
横暴な *ōbō na* arbitrary, tyrannical, despotic
横着な *ōchaku na* impudent, brazen; idle, lazy
横領 *ōryō* seizure, embezzlement, usurpation
横行する *ōkō suru* be rampant, overrun, swagger, strut
横柄な *ōhei na* overbearing, arrogant
専横 *sen'ō* arbitrariness, despotism

❸ unnatural
横死 *ōshi* unnatural [violent] death
❹ overflow
横溢する *ōitsu suru* be filled with (vitality), overflow with

KUN

【yoko 横】
①ⓐ side, flank, width; transverse direction
ⓑ [in compounds] side(ways), (a)cross, horizontal, lateral
横から *yoko kara* from one's side
横書きする *yokogaki suru* write laterally, write from left to right
横文字 *yokomoji* letters written in lateral lines; European [Western] language
横綱 *yokozuna* (grand) champion sumo wrestler
横たわる *yokotawaru* lie (down)
横這い *yokobai* crawling sideways; remain at the same level
横風 *yokokaze* side wind
横糸 *yokoito* [also 緯糸 or 緯] woof
横投げ *yokonage* throwing sideways
② [in compounds] arbitrary, perverse, wrong
横槍 *yokoyari* interruption
横取り *yokodori* usurpation
横車を押す *yokoguruma o osu* have one's own way, act perversely
③ abbrev. of 横浜 *yokohama*: Yokohama
東横線 *tōyokosen* Toyoko Line (between Tokyo and Yokohama)

SYNONYMS

❶ⓐ side
側 SIDE → 137
方 side → 1963
辺 -side → 3029
面 side → 2087
傍 BESIDE → 147
❷ acting arbitrarily
独 act arbitrarily → 395
専 arrogate to oneself → 2644

HOMOPHONES

yokoito ⇨ 緯 1407 横糸 1066, 2179
緯糸 1407, 2179

NOTE

⇨ see USAGE note at 緯 1407

4-11
木

槽 槽 槽

1067 SŌ fune▲

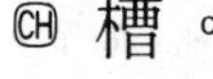

Ⓒⓗ 槽 cáo

Radical	Strokes
木 75	15-4-11
Grade	**Freq**
Jōyō	1816
1-4-11	

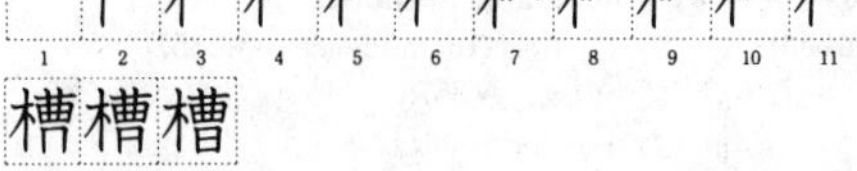

▶TANK

COMPOUNDS

ⓐ [also suffix] **tank, vat, tub**
ⓑ tank or tub-shaped cavity
油槽 *yusō* oil tank
浴槽 *yokusō* bathtub
貯水槽 *chosuisō* water tank
水槽 *suisō* water tank
浄化槽 *jōkasō* tank for purifying water
歯槽 *shisō* alveolus, socket of a tooth

KUN

【fune 槽】 [also 船] tub, tank, vessel
湯槽 *yubune* bathtub

SYNONYMS

ⓐ containers
棺 COFFIN → 985
箱 BOX → 2711
籠 BASKET → 2734
袋 BAG → 2588
器 VESSEL → 2713
瓶 BOTTLE → 1344
缶 CAN → 2033

HOMOPHONES

fune ⇨ 船 1341 舟 3538

NOTE

⇨ see USAGE note at 船 1341

4-11
木

槪

1068

▶GENERAL
nonstandard for 概 1048

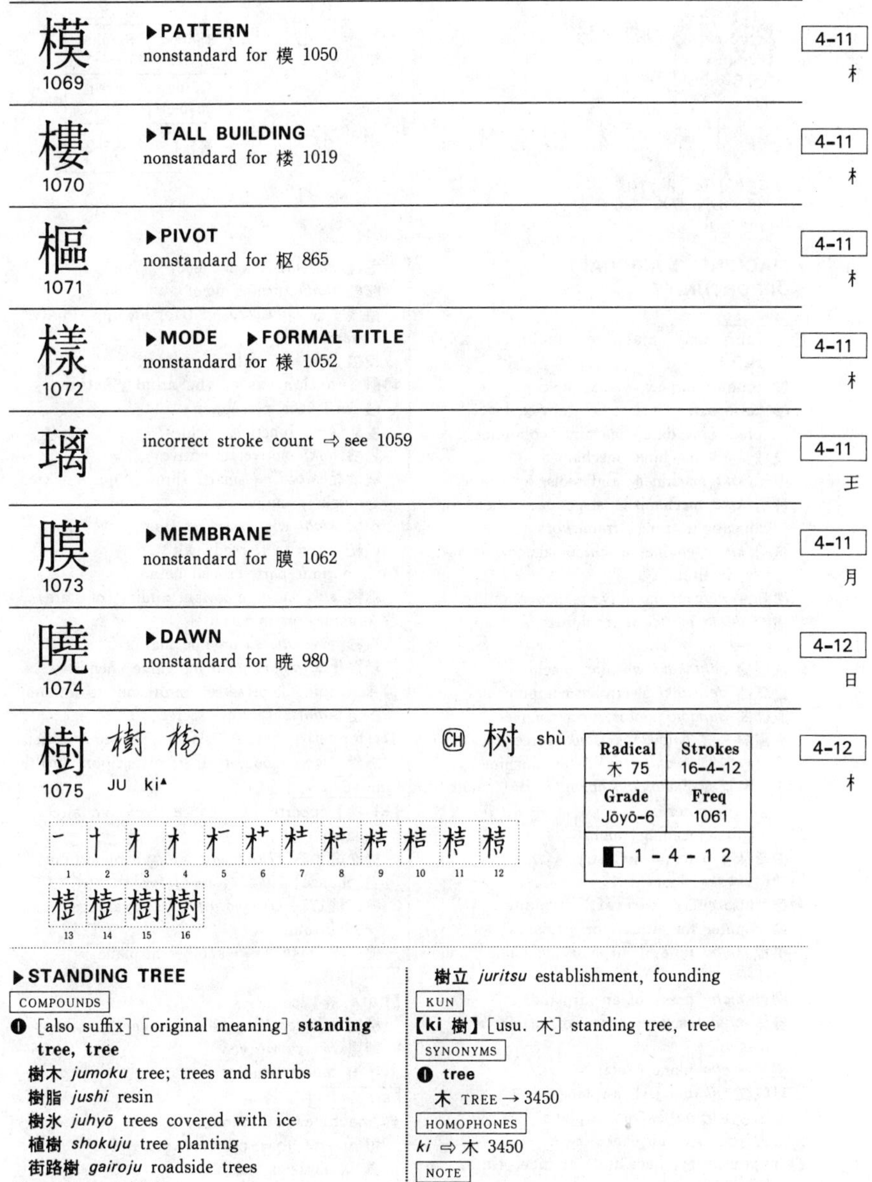

模 1069
▶PATTERN
nonstandard for 模 1050
4-11 木

樓 1070
▶TALL BUILDING
nonstandard for 楼 1019
4-11 木

樞 1071
▶PIVOT
nonstandard for 枢 865
4-11 木

樣 1072
▶MODE ▶FORMAL TITLE
nonstandard for 様 1052
4-11 木

璃
incorrect stroke count ⇨ see 1059
4-11 王

膜 1073
▶MEMBRANE
nonstandard for 膜 1062
4-11 月

曉 1074
▶DAWN
nonstandard for 暁 980
4-12 日

樹 1075
JU ki▲
CH 树 shù
4-12 木

Radical	Strokes
木 75	16-4-12
Grade	**Freq**
Jōyō-6	1061

1-4-12

1 2 3 4 5 6 7 8 9 10 11 12 13 14 15 16

▶**STANDING TREE**

COMPOUNDS

❶ [also suffix] [original meaning] **standing tree, tree**

樹木 *jumoku* tree; trees and shrubs
樹脂 *jushi* resin
樹氷 *juhyō* trees covered with ice
植樹 *shokuju* tree planting
街路樹 *gairoju* roadside trees

❷ set up, establish

樹立 *juritsu* establishment, founding

KUN

【ki 樹】[usu. 木] standing tree, tree

SYNONYMS

❶ **tree**

木 TREE → 3450

HOMOPHONES

ki ⇨ 木 3450

NOTE

⇨ see USAGE note at 木 3450

4-12 木

機 機 機 機

㊥ 机 jī

1076 KI hata

Radical	Strokes
木 75	16-4-12
Grade	**Freq**
Jōyō-4	101
1-4-12	

▶MACHINE ▶AIRCRAFT ▶OPPORTUNITY

COMPOUNDS

❶ⓐ [also suffix] **machine, machinery, apparatus**
ⓑ counter for heavy machinery
ⓒ [also suffix] (electronic device for processing data) machine, computer
機械 *kikai* machine, mechanism
機器 *kiki* machinery and tools, apparatus
機構 *kikō* mechanism, structure; system, organization; frame, framework
機関 *kikan* engine, machine; agency, facilities, institution
機動性 *kidōsei* mobility, maneuverability
電機 *denki* electrical machinery and appliances
洗濯機 *sentakuki* washing machine
電算機 *densanki* electronic computer
原動機 *gendōki* motor, prime mover
発電機三機 *hatsudenki sanki* three dynamos
8ビット機 *hachibittoki* 8-bit machine
IBM互換機 *aibīemu gokanki* IBM compatible computer
❷ [original meaning] loom
機業 *kigyō* textile industry
織機 *shokki* loom
❸ⓐ [also suffix] **aircraft, airplane**
ⓑ counter for aircraft or airplanes
機種 *kishu* type of airplane [machine], model
機首 *kishu* nose (of an airplane)
機体 *kitai* fuselage, body (of an airplane); machine
機長 *kichō* plane captain
日航機 *nikkōki* JAL airplane
ジェット機 *jettoki* jet airplane
五機 *goki* five airplanes
❹ **opportunity, occasion, chance, time, crucial point**
機会 *kikai* opportunity, occasion
機運 *kiun* opportunity, chance
時機 *jiki* opportunity, chance
好機 *kōki* favorable opportunity, good chance
契機 *keiki* opportunity, chance; *philosophy* moment
危機 *kiki* crisis, emergency
転機 *tenki* turning point
待機する *taiki suru* wait for an opportunity, stand ready
投機 *tōki* speculation, venture
❺ⓐ **function (as of the mind), action**
ⓑ wit, keen perception
機能 *kinō* function, faculty
動機 *dōki* motive, incentive
機敏な *kibin na* smart, shrewd, quick-witted; quick, prompt
機智 *kichi* wit, resources, tact
機転 *kiten* tact, ready wit
❻ important part, crucial point
枢機 *sūki* most important affairs (of state)
❼ organic, organic matter
有機物 *yūkibutsu* organic matter
無機化学 *mukikagaku* inorganic chemistry
❽ something kept secret or difficult to fathom
機密 *kimitsu* secrecy, secret
❾ [formerly 譏 1638] slander, censure, criticize
機嫌 *kigen* mood, temper, disposition; health

INDEPENDENT

【ki 機】 opportunity, chance, occasion; aircraft, airplane
機を逸する *ki o issuru* miss an opportunity [chance]
機に乗じる *ki ni jōjiru* take advantage of an opportunity
他の機 *hoka no ki* another airplane

KUN

【hata 機】 loom
機織り *hataori* weaving; weaver; grasshopper
機屋 *hataya* weaver
手機 *tebata* handloom

SYNONYMS

❶ **machines and tools**
械 MECHANICAL CONTRIVANCE → 961
具 IMPLEMENT → 2552
器 INSTRUMENT → 2713
儀 measuring instrument → 169
鏡 OPTICAL INSTRUMENT → 1766
❸ⓐ **aircraft and spacecraft**
空 aircraft → 2227
船 spaceship → 1341
❹ **occasions**

際 OCCASION → 714
折 occasion → 253
時 timely occasion → 924
節 time → 2691
❺ⓐ **potency**
能 action → 1323
効 EFFECT → 1265
験 efficacy → 1833

COMPOUND FORMATION
❶ **機動性** *kidōsei*
機動性 'mobility, maneuverability' originally referred to the capacity (性) of a machine 機 ❶ⓐ) in action (動).
❷ **機嫌** *kigen*
機嫌 'mood, etc.' was formerly written 譏嫌, meaning slander (譏 or 機 ❾) and dislike (嫌).

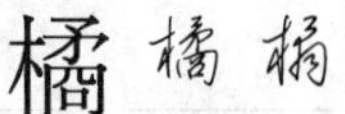

橘

1077 KITSU tachibana

CH 桔 橘 jú

Radical	Strokes
木 75	16-4-12
Grade	**Freq**
Names	2035
◧ 1-4-12	

4-12 木

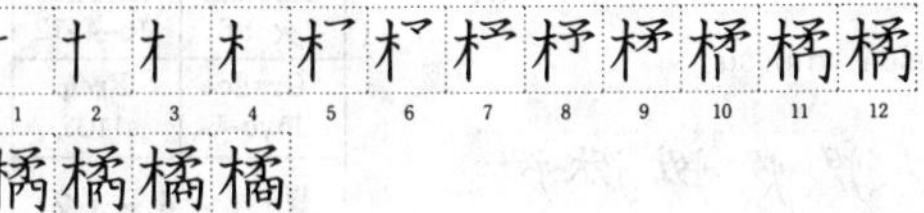

1 2 3 4 5 6 7 8 9 10 11 12 13 14 15 16

▶MANDARIN

COMPOUNDS
● **mandarin orange, tangerine; citrus fruit; mandarin tree**
柑橘類 *kankitsurui* citrus fruits, oranges

KUN
【tachibana 橘】 mandarin tree; kind of mandarin orange

NAMES
橘川 *kikkawa* surname
橘 *tachibana* surname

SYNONYMS
● **fruits and fruit trees**
桃 PEACH → 936
李 PLUM → 2398
杏 APRICOT → 2397
梅 JAPANESE APRICOT → 925
栗 CHESTNUT → 2649
梨 PEAR → 2744

橋

1078 KYŌ hashi

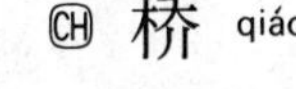

CH 桥 qiáo

Radical	Strokes
木 75	16-4-12
Grade	**Freq**
Jōyō-3	339
◧ 1-4-12	

4-12 木

1 2 3 4 5 6 7 8 9 10 11 12 13 14 15 16

▶BRIDGE

COMPOUNDS
ⓐ [also suffix] [original meaning] **bridge**
ⓑ *anat* pons
橋梁 *kyōryō* bridge
橋脚 *kyōkyaku* bridge pier
架橋 *kakyō* bridge building
鉄橋 *tekkyō* iron bridge
歩道橋 *hodōkyō* pedestrian bridge
脳橋 *nōkyō* pons

INDEPENDENT
【kyō 橋】 *anat* pons

KUN
【hashi 橋】 [also suffix] bridge
橋渡し *hashiwatashi* mediation, good offices
釣り橋 *tsuribashi* suspension bridge
丸木橋 *marukibashi* log bridge
吉野川橋 *yoshinogawa-bashi* Yoshinogawa Bridge

SYNONYMS
ⓐ **bridges**
桟 PLANK BRIDGE → 932

USAGE
hashi
橋
[also suffix] bridge
端
① end, extremity, tip
② edge, margin, brink, border; side
③ beginning

④ unwanted piece, scrap, fragment
箸
chopsticks

HOMOPHONES
hashi ⇨ 端 1221 箸 2708

4-12 木 **機** 1079

▶MACHINE ▶AIRCRAFT ▶OPPORTUNITY
nonstandard for 機 1076

4-12 木 **横** 1080

▶SIDEWAYS
nonstandard for 横 1066

4-12 火 **燃** 1081 NEN mo(eru) mo(yasu) mo(su)

Ⓒ 燃 rán

Radical	Strokes
火 86	16-4-12
Grade	Freq
Jōyō-5	1102
1 - 4 - 1 2	

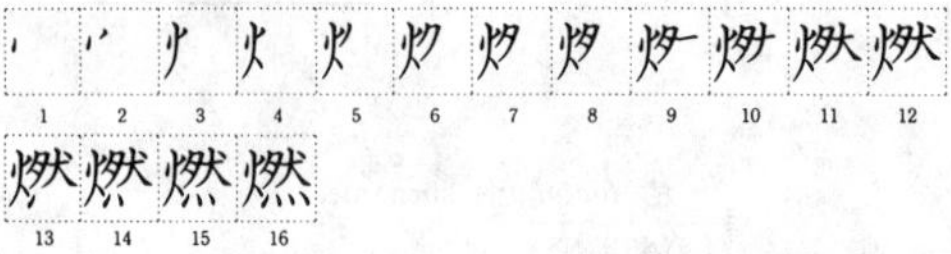

1 2 3 4 5 6 7 8 9 10 11 12 13 14 15 16

▶BURN

COMPOUNDS

● **burn, undergo combustion**
燃焼 *nenshō* combustion, burning
燃料 *nenryō* fuel
可燃性 *kanensei* combustibility
内燃機関 *nainenkikan* internal combustion engine
再燃する *sainen suru* revive, come to the fore again

KUN

【mo(eru) 燃える】
vi
ⓐ burn, undergo combustion, blaze
ⓑ burn with emotion
燃え尽きる *moetsukiru* burn out [away], be burned up
燃え付く *moetsuku* catch fire

【mo(yasu) 燃やす】 *vt* burn
闘志を燃やす *tōshi o moyasu* burn with combativeness

【mo(su) 燃す】 colloquial equiv. of **moyasu** 燃やす

SYNONYMS

● **burn**
焼 BURN → 997
焦 SCORCH → 2770

USAGE

moeru
燃える
vi
ⓐ burn, undergo combustion, blaze
ⓑ burn with emotion
萌える
sprout, bud, burst into bud

HOMOPHONES
moeru ⇨ 萌 2301

4-12 火 **燒** 1082

▶BURN
nonstandard for 焼 997

4-12 火 **燈** 1083

▶LAMP
nonstandard for 灯 825

膨  (CH) 膨 péng

1084 BŌ fuku(ramu) fuku(reru)

Radical	Strokes
月 130	16-4-12
Grade	Freq
Jōyō	1450
1-4-12	

4-12 月

▶**EXPAND**

COMPOUNDS

❶ [original meaning] **expand, swell, bulge, inflate**

膨大 *bōdai* swelling, expansion

膨脹(＝膨張) *bōchō* expansion, swelling; growth, increase

膨隆する *bōryū suru* swell up

膨満する *bōman suru* be inflated

❷ [formerly 厖 3002] bulky, extensive

膨大な *bōdai na* bulky, massive, extensive

KUN

【fuku(ramu) 膨らむ】[sometimes also 脹らむ] expand, swell (out), get big, become inflated

膨らみ *fukurami* swelling, bulge, puff

膨らます *fukuramasu* cause to bulge, expand, dilate; raise

膨らし粉 *fukurashiko* baking powder

【fuku(reru) 膨れる】

[sometimes also 脹れる]

① expand, swell (out), get big, become inflated

青膨れ *aobukure* dropsical swelling

着膨れる *kibukureru* be thickly clad

② get sulky, sulk, fret, get peevish

膨れっ面 *fukurettsura* sulky look [face], sullen look

SYNONYMS

❶ **expand**

脹 SWELL → 1003

張 SPREAD → 474

広げる spread (out) → 3035

拡 ENLARGE → 309

伸 STRETCH → 70

延 EXTEND → 3073

USAGE

❶ **fukuramu**

膨らむ

[sometimes also 脹らむ] expand, swell (out), get big, become inflated

脹らむ

[usu. 膨らむ] same as 膨らむ

❷ **fukureru**

膨れる

[sometimes also 脹れる]

① expand, swell (out), get big, become inflated

② get sulky, sulk, fret, get peevish

脹れる

[usu. 膨れる] same as 膨れる

HOMOPHONES

fukuramu ⇨ 脹 1003

fukureru ⇨ 脹 1003

豫 1085

▶**IN ADVANCE**

nonstandard for 予 1983

4-12 予

檢 1086

▶**EXAMINE**

nonstandard for 検 986

4-13 木

4-13 火

燥 1087 SŌ

CH 燥 zào

Radical	Strokes
火 86	17-4-13
Grade	**Freq**
Jōyō	1544
1-4-13	

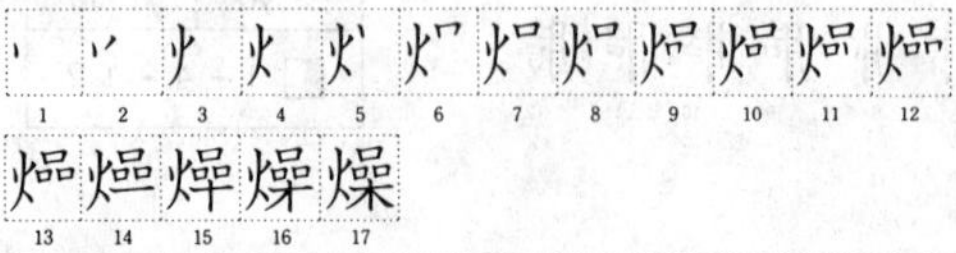

▶**DRY UP**

COMPOUNDS

❶ [original meaning] (become very dry, esp. by the action of heat) **dry up, parch, desiccate**

乾燥する *kansō suru* dry up, desiccate, become parched [dry]
枯燥する *kosō suru* dry up, parch
高燥地 *kōsōchi* high and dry ground
無味乾燥な *mumi-kansō na* dry as dust, insipid

❷ [formerly 躁 1652] restless, impatient, rash, impetuous

焦燥 *shōsō* fretfulness, impatience

SYNONYMS

❶ **dry**
渇 RUN DRY → 515
乾 DRY → 1679
干 DRY → 3379

❷ **impatient**
焦 BE IMPATIENT → 2770

4-13 爿

牆 1088 SHŌ kaki

CH 墙 qiáng

Radical	Strokes
爿 90	17-4-13
Grade	**Freq**
Reference	
1-4-13	

COMPOUNDS

ⓐ [now replaced by 障 *shō* 715] [original meaning] fence, wall

ⓑ [now usu. 垣 *kaki* 351] [also suffix] fence, wall

牆壁 *shōheki* fence, wall; barrier

HOMOPHONES

kaki ⇨ 垣 351

NOTE

⇨ see USAGE note at 垣 351

4-13 牛

犠 1089 GI

CH 牺 xī

Radical	Strokes
牛 93	17-4-13
Grade	**Freq**
Jōyō	1210
1-4-13	

▶**SACRIFICE**

COMPOUNDS

❶ⓐ **sacrifice**

ⓑ *baseball* **sacrifice**

犠牲 *gisei* sacrifice
犠打 *gida* sacrifice, sacrifice batting
犠飛 *gihi* sacrifice fly

❷ [original meaning, now archaic] (sacrificial animal offered to a deity) sacrifice

犠牛 *gigyū* sacrificial bullock
供犠 *kugi* (=*kyōgi*) sacrificial animal, sacrifice

SYNONYMS

❶ **sacrifice**
牲 SACRIFICE → 907

4-13 王

環 環 環 环

1090 KAN wa▲

CH 环 huán

Radical	Strokes
王 96	17-4-13
Grade	Freq
Jōyō	929
1-4-13	

一 丅 干 王 王' 王⁻ ... 環 (stroke order 1–17)

▶RING ▶SURROUND

COMPOUNDS

❶ⓐ **ring, circle, loop**

ⓑ *chem* ring, cycle

ⓒ cycle

環状の *kanjō no* ring-shaped, circular

環状線 *kanjōsen* belt line

環指 *kanshi* ring finger

環礁 *kanshō* atoll

一環 *ikkan* link; part

金環食 *kinkanshoku* annular eclipse

環化 *kanka* cyclization

ベンゼン環 *benzenkan* benzene ring

生活環 *seikatsukan* life cycle

❷ **surround, encircle; around**

環境 *kankyō* environment, surroundings, circumstances

環海 *kankai* surrounding seas

循環 *junkan* circulation, rotation; cycle

❸ abbrev. of 環状線 *kanjōsen*: belt line

環七 *kannana* Loop 7 (name of a Tokyo road)

INDEPENDENT

【kan 環】*chem* ring; cycle

KUN

【wa 環】[usu. 輪] ring, circle, link

指環 *yubiwa* (finger) ring

SYNONYMS

❶ⓐ **circular objects**

輪 WHEEL, RING → 1589

車 WHEEL → 3552

盤 DISK → 2851

❷ **surround**

囲む ENCLOSE → 3069

包 ENCOMPASS → 2966

HOMOPHONES

wa ⇨ 輪 1589

NOTE

⇨ see USAGE note at 輪 1589

4-13 王

環

1091

▶RING ▶SURROUND

nonstandard for 環 1090

4-13 月

臆

1092 OKU

CH 臆 yì

Radical	Strokes
月 130	17-4-13
Grade	Freq
Reference	
1-4-13	

COMPOUNDS

❶ [now replaced by 憶 765]

ⓐ (engage in conjectural thought) speculate, conjecture, guess, infer

ⓑ [original meaning] thoughts, feelings

臆説 *okusetsu* hypothesis, speculation

臆測 *okusoku* conjecture, speculation, guess

臆断 *okudan* jumping to hasty conclusions

胸臆 *kyōoku* one's inmost thoughts [feelings]

❷ [sometimes also 憶 765] fear, feel timid

臆病 *okubyō* cowardice, timidity

臆する *okusuru* fear, feel timid

4-13 月

謄 謄 謄 謄 ⓒⓗ 誊 téng

1093 TŌ

Radical	Strokes
言 149	17-7-10
Grade	Freq
Jōyō	1883
1-4-13	

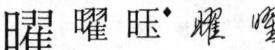

▶**TRANSCRIBE**

COMPOUNDS

● [original meaning] (make an exact copy of an original text) **transcribe, copy, duplicate (a document)**

謄本 *tōhon* certified copy, transcript; copy of the domiciliary register

謄写 *tōsha* copy, reproduction, mimeograph

謄写版 *tōshaban* mimeograph

SYNONYMS

● **copy**

写 COPY → 2000

複 duplicate → 1222

拓 copy by rubbing → 317

NOTE

★do not confuse with 騰 1106

4-13 月

膽

1094

▶**GALLBLADDER**

nonstandard for 胆 919

4-13 月

1095

▶**TRANSCRIBE**

nonstandard for 謄 1093

4-14 日

曜 曜 旺♦ 曜 曜 ⓒⓗ 曜 yào

1096 YŌ

Radical	Strokes
日 72	18-4-14
Grade	Freq
Jōyō-2	818
1-4-14	

▶**DAY OF THE WEEK**

COMPOUNDS

❶ **day of the week, -day**

曜日 *yōbi* day of the week

七曜 *shichiyō* seven days of the week; [archaic] sun, moon and five planets

日曜日 *nichiyōbi* Sunday

木曜日 *mokuyōbi* Thursday

水曜日 *suiyōbi* Wednesday

七曜表 *shichiyōhyō* calendar

❷ⓐ [original meaning] luminous, bright

ⓑ [archaic] luminous heavenly body

黒曜石 *kokuyōseki* obsidian, volcanic glass

曜霊 *yōrei* literary term for the sun

SYNONYMS

❶ **days**

日 DAY → 3027

昼 DAYTIME → 3097

旦 first day → 2389

4-14 日

1097

▶**DAY OF THE WEEK**

nonstandard for 曜 1096

曠 incorrect stroke count ⇨ see 1100 | 4–14 日

燻 ㊥ 熏 xūn xùn | 4–14 火

1098 KUN ibu(su) ibu(ru) kusu(buru) kuyu(rasu)

Radical	Strokes
火 86	18–4–14
Grade Reference	Freq
◧ 1-4-14	

COMPOUNDS

● [now also 薫 *kun* 2371] [original meaning] smoke, fumigate, fume
燻製 *kunsei* smoking (fish or meat)
燻蒸する *kunjō suru* fumigate, smoke
燻し *ibushi* fumigation; oxidization (of metal)

臟 incorrect stroke count ⇨ see 1102 | 4–14 月

曝 ㊥ 曝 pù 暴 bào | 4–15 日

1099 BAKU sara(su)

Radical	Strokes
日 72	19–4–15
Grade Reference	Freq
◧ 1-4-15	

COMPOUNDS

ⓐ [original meaning] expose to the sun
ⓑ [now also 暴 *baku* 2515] disclose, divulge, expose
曝書 *bakusho* airing of books
曝す *sarasu* expose; bleach
曝露 *bakuro* exposure, disclosure

曠 ㊥ 旷 kuàng | 4–15 日

1100 KŌ

Radical	Strokes
日 72	19–4–15
Grade Reference	Freq
◧ 1-4-15	

COMPOUNDS

❶ [now replaced by 広 3035] [original meaning] vast, spacious, open
曠野 *kōya* vast plain, prairie
❷ unexcelled, unrivaled, unprecedented
曠古の *kōko no* historic, unprecedented
曠世の *kōsei no* unparalleled, matchless
❸ neglect
曠職 *kōshoku* neglect of official duty

4-15
火

爆

1101 BAKU

Ⓒⓗ 爆 bào

Radical	Strokes
火 86	19-4-15
Grade	**Freq**
Jōyō	430
1-4-15	

1 2 3 4 5 6 7 8 9 10 11 12 13 14 15 16 17 18 19

▶EXPLODE

COMPOUNDS

❶ⓐ [original meaning] **explode, detonate, burst**

ⓑ bomb, raid

爆発 *bakuhatsu* explosion, blast; eruption

爆弾 *bakudan* bomb

爆破する *bakuha suru* blast, blow up, explode

爆風 *bakufū* (bomb or explosion) blast

爆笑する *bakushō suru* roar with laughter, burst into laughter

爆撃 *bakugeki* bombing, bombardment

空爆 *kūbaku* aerial bombing

被爆者 *hibakusha* victim of atomic air raid

❷ abbrev. of 爆弾 *bakudan*: bomb

原爆 *genbaku* atomic bomb

水爆 *suibaku* hydrogen bomb

SYNONYMS

❶ⓐ **explode**

発 discharge → 2565

ⓑ **attack**

撃 STRIKE → 2863

襲 RAID → 2917

攻 ATTACK → 242

侵 INVADE → 101

❷ **projectiles and bombs**

雷 explosive device → 2791

弾 PROJECTILE → 572

丸 round projectile → 3417

矢 ARROW → 2009

4-15
月

臓

臟 臓

1102 ZŌ

Ⓒⓗ 脏 zàng

Radical	Strokes
月 130	19-4-15
Grade	**Freq**
Jōyō-6	1194
1-4-15	

1 2 3 4 5 6 7 8 9 10 11 12 13 14 15 16 17 18 19

▶INTERNAL ORGAN

COMPOUNDS

● [original meaning] **internal organ, viscus**

臓器 *zōki* internal organs, viscera

臓物 *zōmotsu* entrails, giblets

内臓 *naizō* viscera, internal organs

心臓 *shinzō* heart

肝臓 *kanzō* liver

五臓 *gozō* the five viscera (liver, lungs, heart, kidneys and spleen)

SYNONYMS

● **organ**

器 organ → 2713

官 organ → 2226

4–16 木

欄 欄 㯗 㯗

1103 RAN

Ⓒⓗ 栏 lán

Radical	Strokes
木 75	20–4–16
Grade	**Freq**
Jōyō	1307
◧ 1-4-16	

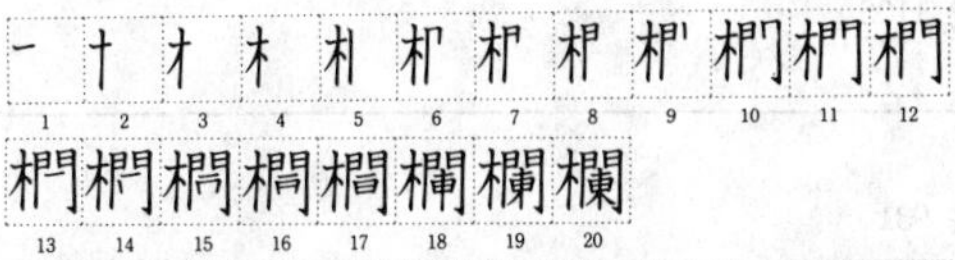

▶COLUMN

COMPOUNDS

❶ [also suffix]

ⓐ **column (as of a newspaper or periodical), section, page**

ⓑ (section of written material) **column, blank column, blank, space**

本欄 *honran* this column
広告欄 *kōkokuran* advertisement column
スポーツ欄 *supōtsuran* sports section [page]
欄外 *rangai* margin
空欄 *kūran* blank column, blank
登記番号欄 *tōki-bangōran* registry number column

❷ railing, balustrade, handrail
欄干 *rankan* railing, handrail, balustrade
高欄 *kōran* balustrade, handrail

❸ file (of a chessboard)
ビショップ欄 *bishoppuran* bishop file

INDEPENDENT

【ran 欄】 column, section (⇨ ❶ⓐ); column, blank column (⇨ ❶ⓑ); railing, balustrade; file (of a chessboard)
欄に記入する *ran ni kinyū suru* fill in the blank (column)

SYNONYMS

❶ⓐ parts of periodicals
面 page (of a newspaper) → 2087

ⓑ linear arrangements
行 LINE (esp. of print) → 212
列 ROW → 824
伍 RANK → 47

❷ fences and walls
囲い enclosure → 3069
垣 FENCE (for partitioning) → 351
塀 FENCE (for screening) → 557
壁 WALL → 2895

4–16 火

爐

1104

▶FURNACE
nonstandard for 炉 869

4–16 牛

犧

1105

▶SACRIFICE
nonstandard for 犠 1089

4–16 月

騰 騰 騰 騰

1106 TŌ

Ⓒⓗ 腾 téng

Radical	Strokes
馬 187	20–10–10
Grade	**Freq**
Jōyō	1289
◧ 1-4-16	

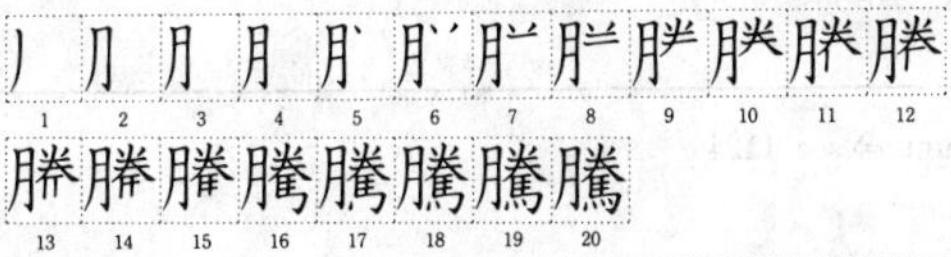

▶RISE

COMPOUNDS

● [original meaning] **rise, jump up, advance**—said esp. of prices
騰貴 *tōki* rise (in prices)
騰落 *tōraku* rise and fall, fluctuations
高騰(=昂騰) *kōtō* steep rise (in prices), jump
暴騰 *bōtō* sudden (price) rise
沸騰 *futtō* boiling, seething, bubbling

SYNONYMS

● ascend
上 go up → 3404
昇 ASCEND → 2415

登 CLIMB → 2595

NOTE
★do not confuse with 謄 1093

4-16 月 騰 1107
▶**RISE**
nonstandard for 騰 1106

4-17 木 櫻 1108
▶**CHERRY**
nonstandard for 桜 931

4-17 木 欄 1109
▶**COLUMN**
nonstandard for 欄 1103

4-17 火 爛 1110 RAN tada(reru)

Ⓒ 烂 làn

Radical	Strokes
火 86	21-4-17
Grade	Freq
Reference	
1-4-17	

COMPOUNDS
❶ [now also 乱 *ran* 1260] overripe, rotten
爛熟する *ranjuku suru* become overripe; attain full maturity
腐爛する *furan suru* ulcerate, decompose
❷ bright, brilliant
爛爛たる *ranrantaru* glaring, flaming, blazing
絢爛たる *kenrantaru* gorgeous, dazzling; flowery (speech)
桜花爛漫 *Ōka ranman* The cherry blossoms are in full glory
爛たる *rantaru* bright, brilliant
❸ break out in sores, be inflamed, be ulcerated
爛れた皮膚 *tadareta hifu* inflamed skin

4-18 木 權 1111
▶**RIGHT** ▶**POWER**
nonstandard for 権 1065

4-18 月 臟
incorrect stroke count ⇨ see 1112
(nonstandard for 臓 1102)

4-19 月 臟 1112
▶**INTERNAL ORGAN**
nonstandard for 臓 1102

5-2 牙 邪
incorrect stroke count ⇨ see 1124

5-2 田

町 町 町

1113 CHŌ machi

CH 町 tǐng dīng

Radical	Strokes
田 102	7-5-2
Grade	**Freq**
Jōyō-1	148
1 - 5 - 2	

丨 1 冂 2 冂 3 冊 4 田 5 田一 6 町 7

▶**TOWN**

COMPOUNDS

❶ⓐ **town, city**

ⓑ (unit of local administration) **town**

ⓒ **suffix after names of towns**

町人 *chōnin* tradesman (in Edo period), townsman, townsfolk

町家 *chōka* town house; tradesman's house

町長 *chōchō* town headman [manager]

町名 *chōmei* town name

町立の *chōritsu no* established by the town

市町村 *shichōson* cities, towns and villages; municipalities

小山町 *oyamachō* town of Oyama

❷ⓐ (subdivision in the Japanese addressing system) **town section, *cho***

ⓑ **suffix after names of town sections (*cho*)**

町会 *chōkai* town block association

一宮町 *ichinomiyachō* Ichinomiya-cho

❸ street, lane

横町 *yokochō* bystreet, sideway

❹ *cho*:

ⓐ unit of sq. measure equiv. to approx. 99.2 ares or 10 *tan* (反)

ⓑ [sometimes also 丁 3348] former unit of length equiv. to approx. 109 m or 60 *ken* (間)

町歩 *chōbu* hectare

二町 *nichō* two *cho*

INDEPENDENT

【**chō 町**】 town (⇨ ❶ⓑ); town section, *cho* (⇨ ❷ⓐ); *cho* (⇨ ❹)

町の方針 *chō no hōshin* policies of the town [*cho*]

KUN

【**machi 町**】

① [also suffix]

ⓐ town

ⓑ (unit of local administration) town

ⓒ suffix after names of towns

町へ行く *machi e iku* go to town

町工場 *machikōba* town factory

港町 *minatomachi* port town

温泉町 *onsenmachi* spa town, hot spring resort

町役場 *machiyakuba* town office

水上町 *minakamimachi* town of Minakami

②ⓐ (subdivision in the Japanese addressing system) *machi*, town section

ⓑ suffix after names of town sections (*machi*)

信濃町 *shinanomachi* Shinanomachi

③ [usu. 街] (busy) city quarter(s), city streets

町筋 *machisuji* street

町並み *machinami* rows of stores and houses on a street

下町 *shitamachi* (downtown) business quarters, old part of Tokyo

SYNONYMS

❶ **cities and towns**

市 CITY → 1993

京 CAPITAL → 2052

都 METROPOLIS → 1686

❶ **villages and towns**

村 VILLAGE → 834

里 hamlet → 3542

庄 FEUDAL VILLAGE → 3051

郷 HOMETOWN → 549

❷ **parts of towns**

丁 TOWN SUBSECTION (*chome*) → 3348

区 WARD → 2963

街 CITY QUARTER → 576

字 village or town section → 2172

❹ⓐ **area units**

反 *tan* (9.9 ares) → 2945

畝 *SE* (0.99 ares) → 1465

歩 *bu* (3.3 sq.m) → 2416

坪 *TSUBO* (3.3 sq.m) → 275

ⓑ **length units**

里 LEAGUE, *ri* (3.4 km) → 3542

丈 *jo* (3.03 m) → 3419

間 *ken* (1.8 m) → 3323

尋 fathom (1.8 m) → 2322

米 meter → 3529

尺 *SHAKU* (30.3 cm) → 3440

寸 *sun* (3.03 cm) → 2935

USAGE

machi

町

① [also suffix]

ⓐ town

ⓑ (unit of local administration) town

ⓒ suffix after names of towns

②ⓐ (subdivision in the Japanese address-

ing system) *machi*, town section
ⓑ suffix after names of town sections (*machi*)
③ [usu. 街] (busy) city quarter(s), city streets

街
(busy) city quarter(s), city streets

HOMOPHONES
machi ⇨ 街 576

5-2 禾

1114 RI ki(ku)

CH 利 lì

Radical	Strokes
刂 18	7-2-5
Grade	**Freq**
Jōyō-4	252

1-5-2

▶ADVANTAGE ▶PROFIT

COMPOUNDS

❶ⓐ **advantage, benefit, superiority, convenience, expediency**
ⓑ **be of advantage to, benefit**
利点 *riten* advantage, point in favor
有利な *yūri na* advantageous, favorable; profitable
権利 *kenri* right; authority; privilege
便利 *benri* convenience, handiness, usefulness
利用する *riyō suru* utilize, make use of, avail oneself of

❷ⓐ **profit, gains, advantage, benefit**
ⓑ [also suffix] **interest (on money)**
利益 *rieki* profit, gains; benefit
利食い *rigui* profit taking
利得 *ritoku* profit, benefit, gain
営利 *eiri* profit, gain
利子 *rishi* interest
利息 *risoku* interest
複利 *fukuri* compound interest
六分半利 *rokubuhanri* 6.5% bonds

❸ⓐ sharp(-edged), keen
ⓑ [formerly also 悧 422] sharp, keen, clever
利刀 *ritō* sharp sword
鋭利な *eiri na* sharp, keen; acute, sharp, clever
利口(=悧巧)な *rikō na* clever, bright, sharp, shrewd

❹ victory
勝利 *shōri* victory, triumph, win

❺ used phonetically for *ri*
砂利 *jari* gravel, fine gravel, ballast
仏舎利 *busshari* Buddha's ashes
伊太利 *itarī* Italy

INDEPENDENT

【ri 利】advantage, profit; interest; victory
地の利 *chi no ri* vantage ground, advantageous position

【risuru 利する】profit, benefit (by)

KUN

【ki(ku) 利く】
① work (well), function (properly)
利き *kiki* function, efficacy
耳が利く *mimi ga kiku* have a sharp ear
左利き *hidarikiki* left-handedness; left-hander; drinker, wine lover
② speak (esp. as a mediator)
口利き *kuchikiki* mediation; mediator, mouthpiece

SYNONYMS

❶ **benefit**
益 BENEFIT → 2285
為 SAKE → 3577
用 use(ful) → 2976
役 SERVICE → 244

❷ⓐ **profit**
益 PROFIT → 2285
得 GAIN → 477
ⓑ **interest and dividend**
子 interest → 3390
配 dividend → 1460

HOMOPHONES

kiku ⇨ 効 1265
kiki ⇨ 効 1265

NOTE

⇨ see USAGE note at 効 1265

私 私 私

1115 SHI watakushi watashi▲

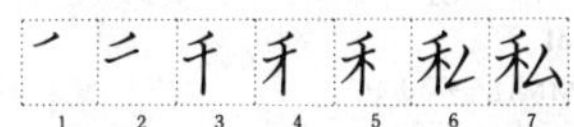

CH 私 sī

Radical	Strokes
禾 115	7-5-2
Grade	Freq
Jōyō-6	203
1-5-2	

5-2 禾

▶**PRIVATE** ▶**I**

COMPOUNDS

❶ⓐ [also suffix] [original meaning] (pertaining to a particular person) **private, personal**

ⓑ (intimate) private, clandestine, secret, confidential

ⓒ illicit, illegal

私的な *shiteki na* private, personal
私学 *shigaku* private [nongovernmental] school [college, university]
私鉄 *shitetsu* nongovernmental [private] railroad line
私物 *shibutsu* private property
私立の *shiritsu* (=*watakushiritsu*) *no* private, nongovernmental
私書箱 *shishobako* post office box (P.O.B.)
私生活 *shiseikatsu* one's private life
公私 *kōshi* public and private
私語 *shigo* secret talk, whispering
私生児 *shiseiji* illegitimate child, bastard child
私通 *shitsū* illicit intercourse

❷ selfish

私腹を肥やす *shifuku o koyasu* fill [stuff] one's own pocket by taking advantage of a position
公平無私な *kōhei-mushi na* fair and disinterested, impartial

KUN

【watakushi 私】

① I, myself—polite first person pronoun
私達 *watakushitachi* we
私小説 *watakushishōsetsu* (=*shishōsetsu*) first person novel, private [real] life novel

② privateness, privacy; partiality
私事 *watakushigoto* personal affairs
私する *watakushisuru* think only of oneself, possess oneself

【watashi 私】 I, myself—polite first person pronoun (formerly used esp. by women)
私の *watashi no* my

SYNONYMS

❶ⓐ & ❶ⓑ secret and private
内 not public → 3466
秘 SECRET → 1159
密 SECRET → 2292
暗 in the dark → 1010
隠 hidden from view → 713

【watakushi】

① first person pronouns
僕 I (*familiar*) → 164
俺 I (*intimate*) → 110
吾 I (*elegant*) → 2407
予 I (*pompous*) → 1983
余 I (*pompous*) → 2042
麿 I (*archaic*) → 3184
朕 IMPERIAL WE → 949
自 SELF → 3525
我 SELF → 3548
己 ONESELF → 3380
身 ONE'S PERSON → 3553

初 初 初

1116 SHO haji(me) haji(mete) hatsu hatsu- ui- -so(meru) -zo(me)

丶 ラ ネ ネ ネ 初 初
1 2 3 4 5 6 7

CH 初 chū

Radical	Strokes
刀 18	7-2-5
Grade	Freq
Jōyō-4	275
1-5-2	

5-2 ネ

▶**FIRST**

COMPOUNDS

❶ⓐ **first, initial, original**

ⓑ [prefix] **first**

初回 *shokai* first time; first inning
初日 *shonichi* first day, opening day
初版 *shohan* first edition
初代 *shodai* first generation, founder
初任給 *shoninkyū* initial salary
初志 *shoshi* original aim [intention]
初対面 *shotaimen* first meeting

❷ⓐ [also suffix] **beginning, origin, early stages**

ⓑ **beginning stages, first steps**

最初 *saisho* first, outset, beginning
当初の *tōsho no* original, initial, first

初期 *shoki* early days, early stage, beginning; early, initial
初夏 *shoka* early summer
初歩 *shoho* first steps, rudiments, the ABCs (of)
初級 *shokyū* beginner's class, junior course
初心者 *shoshinsha* beginner

KUN

【haji(me) 初め】
① (initial period) beginning (of the month), outset, first stage, early period
初めは *hajime wa* at first; originally
年度初め *nendo hajime* beginning of the (fiscal) year
② including, as well as, not to speak of
田中氏初め六人 *tanakashi hajime rokunin* Mr. Tanaka and five others

【haji(mete) 初めて】 for the first time; not...until
初めての *hajimete no* first, first-time
初めまして *Hajimemashite* I am glad to meet you
健康は失って初めてその価値が分かる *Kenkō wa ushinatte hajimete sono kachi ga wakaru* We don't know the value of health till we lose it

【hatsu 初】 the first, first time
初に *hatsu ni* for the first time
初の成功 *hatsu no seikō* the first success

【hatsu- 初-】 [also prefix] first, early, new, inaugural; first (of the new year or season)
初恋 *hatsukoi* first love
初舞台 *hatsubutai* one's first appearance on stage, debut
初日の出 *hatsuhinode* first sunrise of the year

【ui- 初-】 first
初陣 *uijin* one's first battle
初孫 *uimago* (=*hatsumago*) first grandchild
初初しい *uiuishii* innocent, naive, fresh

【-so(meru) -初める】 [verbal suffix] begin to (occur); for the first time
咲き初める *sakisomeru* begin to bloom

【-zo(me) -初め】 [verbal suffix] performing an action for the first time (of the year)
書き初め *kakizome* New Year's writing

SYNONYMS

❶ **first**
甲 FIRST → 3481

❶ **original**
原 ORIGINAL → 3009
本 original → 3502
素 primary → 2458

❷ **beginnings**
始 beginning → 281
緒 OUTSET → 1378
序 INTRODUCTORY PART → 3065
端 start → 1221
元 ORIGIN → 1929
本 origin → 3502
根 ROOT → 930
源 SOURCE → 656

USAGE

❶ **hajime**
初め
① (initial period) beginning (of the month), outset, first stage, early period
② including, as well as, not to speak of
始め
① (act or point of commencement) beginning, start
② (source) beginning, origin

❷ **hajimete**
初めて
for the first time; not...until
始めて
begin and... (TE-form of 始める *hajimeru*)
甫めて
literary barely, just

HOMOPHONES

hajime ⇨ 始 281
hajimete ⇨ 始 281 甫 3549
-someru ⇨ 染 2572
-zome ⇨ 染 2572

NOTE

⇨ see also USAGE note at 染 2572

5-2
另

別 別 㓣

1117 BETSU waka(reru) wa(keru)▲

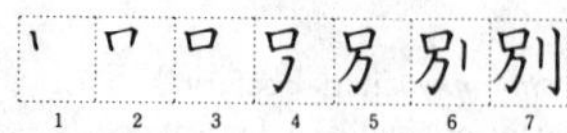

Ⓒⓗ 別 bié biè

Radical	Strokes
刂 18	7-2-5
Grade	**Freq**
Jōyō-4	278
1-5-2	

▶SEPARATE ▶ANOTHER

COMPOUNDS

❶ⓐ [original meaning] (part company) **separate, part from, be separated**
ⓑ parting company
ⓒ (be apart) **separate, separated**
別離 *betsuri* separation, parting
別居 *bekkyo* separation, limited divorce
別辞 *betsuji* farewell address, parting words
離別 *ribetsu* parting, separation; divorce

告別 *kokubetsu* leave taking, farewell
別荘 *bessō* villa, country cottage
別冊 *bessatsu* separate volume, extra issue
別館 *bekkan* annex, extension, outbuilding
別巻 *bekkan* separate volume, extra issue
別間 *betsuma* separate room, special room
別別に *betsubetsu ni* separately, individually, respectively
別送 *bessō* separate post

❷ⓐ (divide by differences) **separate (into groups), sort, classify, distinguish**
ⓑ [suffix] **classified by**
差別 *sabetsu* discrimination
個別的に *kobetsuteki ni* individually, severally, singly
区別する *kubetsu suru* distinguish; classify, divide
分別する *bunbetsu suru* classify, distinguish; divide, separate
分別 *funbetsu* discretion, prudence, judgment, good sense
判別する *hanbetsu suru* distinguish, discriminate
類別 *ruibetsu* classification
戸別 *kobetsu* each house
職業別電話帳 *shokugyōbetsu-denwachō* classified telephone directory
府県別人口 *fukenbetsu-jinkō* population classified by prefectures

❸ⓐ [also prefix] **another, different, distinct**
ⓑ (distinct among others) **special, particular**
別個の *bekko no* another, different; separate
別種 *besshu* another kind, distinct species
別人 *betsujin* another [different] person
別世界 *bessekai* another world [planet]
別段の *betsudan no* particular, special
別格 *bekkaku* extra status
特別の *tokubetsu no* special, particular; extraordinary
格別な *kakubetsu na* particular, exceptional

INDEPENDENT

【betsu 別】
① distinction, difference
男女の別 *danjo no betsu* distinction of sex
② another thing, an extra
別の本 *betsu no hon* another [different] book
③ exception
別にする *betsu ni suru* set aside [apart]
【besshite 別して】 especially, particularly

KUN

【waka(reru) 別れる】
ⓐ separate, part from, bid farewell
ⓑ separate (from one's spouse), divorce
別れ *wakare* separation, parting, leave-taking, farewell
別れ別れに *wakarewakare ni* separately, apart
別れ話 *wakarebanashi* talk about divorce
死に別れる *shiniwakareru* be separated from (one's spouse) by death
【wa(keru) 別ける】 [usu. 分ける] (cause to separate) part, separate, set aside
別けても *waketemo* above all, in particular

SYNONYMS

❶ⓐ **part company**
離 SEPARATE → 1836
❷ⓐ **separate**
離 SEPARATE → 1836
隔 partition → 671
割 DIVIDE → 1816
分 DIVIDE → 1972
解 TAKE APART → 1517
析 ANALYZE → 862
❸ⓐ **other**
他 OTHER → 35
余 other → 2042
ⓑ **special**
特 SPECIAL (distinct) → 945
殊 SPECIAL (exceptional) → 942
専 EXCLUSIVE → 2644

HOMOPHONES

wakareru ⇨ 分 1972
wakare ⇨ 分 1972
wakeru ⇨ 分 1972

NOTE

⇨ see USAGE note at 分 1972

却 卻° 却 却

1118 KYAKU kae(tte)▲

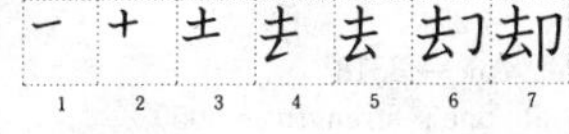

Ⓒ 却 què

Radical	Strokes
卩 26	7-2-5
Grade	**Freq**
Jōyō	1222
◨ 1-5-2	

5-2
去

▶ELIMINATE

COMPOUNDS

❶ **eliminate, exclude, remove, get rid of**—used as the second element in verbal compounds similar to *off* in *kill off*
除却する *jokyaku suru* exclude, eliminate
脱却する *dakkyaku suru* get rid of; slough off
消却する *shōkyaku suru* efface; erase
忘却する *bōkyaku suru* forget
焼却する *shōkyaku suru* destroy by fire, incin-

erate
売却する *baikyaku suru* sell off, dispose of by sale
償却する *shōkyaku suru* repay, refund
❷ **reject, turn down, decline**
却下する *kyakka suru* reject, dismiss, turn down
棄却する *kikyaku suru* turn down, reject, renounce
❸ retreat, step back
退却する *taikyaku suru* retreat
❹ return
返却する *henkyaku suru* return

KUN

【kae(tte) 却って】 on the contrary, rather

SYNONYMS

❶ **eliminate**
抹 wipe off → 313
削 cross out → 1448
省 leave out → 2449
脱 REMOVE → 973
去 take away → 2156
外す take off → 186
除 RID OF → 456
撤 WITHDRAW → 738
排 EXCLUDE → 490
払う CLEAR AWAY → 194
❷ **refuse and reject**
拒 REFUSE → 311
断る refuse → 1492
否 SAY NO → 2406

5-2 氐

incorrect stroke count ⇨ see 1131

5-2 厉

励 勵

1119 REI hage(mu) hage(masu)

CH 励 lì

Radical	Strokes
力 19	7-2-5
Grade	**Freq**
Jōyō	1230
1-5-2	

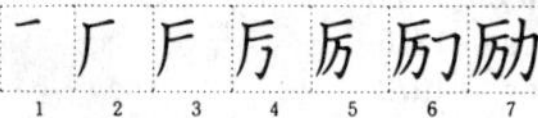

1 2 3 4 5 6 7

▶ENCOURAGE

COMPOUNDS

❶ (impart confidence or spirit) **encourage, cheer up, inspire**
奨励 *shōrei* encouragement, promotion, stimulation, incitement
激励する *gekirei suru* encourage, urge, cheer up
督励 *tokurei* urging (one's subordinates)
❷ *elec* excite
励磁電流 *reiji-denryū* exciting current
励振管 *reishinkan* exciter tube
他励 *tarei* separate excitation
❸ [original meaning] **make efforts, work hard at, be diligent**
励行する *reikō suru* observe strictly, carry out
励声 *reisei* straining one's voice
精励 *seirei* diligence, industry
勉励 *benrei* diligence, industry
奮励 *funrei* strenuous efforts [exertions]

KUN

【hage(mu) 励む】 strive for, make efforts, be diligent
励み *hagemi* encouragement, incentive
勉強に励む *benkyō ni hagemu* work hard at one's lessons

【hage(masu) 励ます】 encourage, urge, cheer up; raise [strain] (one's voice)
励まし *hagemashi* encouragement, stimulation
病人を励ます *byōnin o hagemasu* cheer up an invalid
声を励ます *koe o hagemasu* raise one's voice

SYNONYMS

❶ **urge**
勧 URGE → 1857
催 PRESS FOR → 157
促 HASTEN → 103
誘 INDUCE → 1550
侑 URGE TO EAT → 91
❸ **exert oneself**
勤 work diligently → 1818
努 EXERT → 2547
勉 ENDEAVOR → 3318
尽 use all one's strength → 3050
精 put one's heart into → 1366

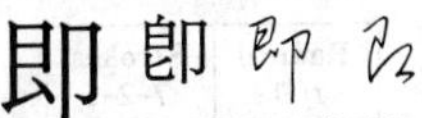

Ⓒⓗ 即 jí

1120 SOKU tsu(ku)▲ tsu(keru)▲ sunawa(chi)▲

Radical	Strokes
卩 26	7-2-5
Grade	Freq
Jōyō	1081
1-5-2	

5-2 艮

▶**IMMEDIATE**

COMPOUNDS

❶ⓐ immediate, prompt, instant, on the spot

ⓑ [original meaning] be in immediate [close] contact

即死 *sokushi* instant death, death on the spot
即売 *sokubai* sale on the spot, spot sale
即時 *sokuji* immediately, promptly
即刻 *sokkoku* immediately, instantly
即座に *sokuza ni* immediately, promptly, at once
即効 *sokkō* immediate effect
即答 *sokutō* prompt answer
即金 *sokkin* immediate cash, ready cash
一触即発 *isshokusokuhatsu* touch-and-go situation, hair-trigger crisis
即応する *sokuō suru* meet, adopt oneself to, conform to
不即不離の *fusokufuri no* neutral, middle-of-the-road

❷ same (day, etc.)
即日 *sokujitsu* same day

❸ namely, that is
色即是空 *Shikisokuzekū* Matter is void / Form [Matter] is nonsubstantial

❹ ascend (the throne)
即位する *sokui suru* ascend the throne

INDEPENDENT

【soku 即】 namely, that is, i.e.; immediately, on the spot
生即死 *Sei soku shi* Life is death
即実行せよ *Soku jikkō seyo* Do it immediately

【sokusuru 即する】 conform to, agree with; be in immediate [close] contact, be based on

KUN

【tsu(ku) 即く】
① [now usu. 就く] ascend to (the throne)
位に即く *kurai ni tsuku* ascend to the throne
② be in immediate [close] contact, be based on
即かず離れずの態度 *tsukazu hanarezu no taido* neutral attitude

【tsu(keru) 即ける】 [now usu. 就ける] enthrone
王位に即ける *ōi ni tsukeru* place on the throne

【sunawa(chi) 即ち】
ⓐ namely, that is, i.e.
ⓑ nothing but, precisely
救世主即ちキリスト *kyūseishu sunawachi kirisuto* the Savior, that is, Christ

SYNONYMS

❶ⓐ immediate
直 straight away → 2932

ⓐ fast
敏 NIMBLE → 1322
迅 SWIFT → 3046
急 rapid → 2092
快 fast → 245
疾 fast → 3279
速 QUICK → 3105
早 QUICK → 2390

USAGE

❶ sunawachi
即ち
ⓐ namely, that is, i.e.
ⓑ nothing but, precisely
乃ち
ⓐ thereupon, whereupon, accordingly
ⓑ and then

❷ sokusuru
即する
ⓐ conform to, agree with
ⓑ be in immediate [close] contact, be based on
則する
conform to the rules, follow precedent

HOMOPHONES

tsuku ⇨ 就 1694 着 3316 付 31 附 347 点 2084
tsukeru ⇨ 就 1694 着 3316 付 31 附 347 点 2084 漬 702
sunawachi ⇨ 乃 2927

NOTE

⇨ see also USAGE notes at 付 31 and 速 3105
⇨ see COMPOUND FORMATION for 即座 *sokuza* ⇨ 座 3116

5-2 助 助 𠬝 (CH) 助 zhù

且

1121 JO tasu(keru) tasu(karu) suke

Radical	Strokes
力 19	7-2-5
Grade	Freq
Jōyō-3	364
1-5-2	

丨 冂 月 月 且 助 助
1 2 3 4 5 6 7

▶HELP

COMPOUNDS

❶ⓐ [original meaning] **help, aid, assist**
ⓑ (act of helping) help, aid
ⓒ save, rescue, relieve
助手 *joshu* assistant, helper
助成 *josei* fostering; aid, assistance
援助 *enjo* aid, assistance, help
補助 *hojo* assistance, support, aid
一助 *ichijo* help, aid
天助 *tenjo* Heaven's help
助命 *jomei* sparing a person's life
救助 *kyūjo* rescue, relief

❷ [also prefix] **assistant, auxiliary**
助詞 *joshi gram* postpositional particle
助役 *joyaku* assistant official; deputy mayor; deputy station-master
助教授 *jokyōju* assistant [associate] professor
助監督 *jokantoku* assistant director [manager]
助動詞 *jodōshi* auxiliary verb

KUN

【tasu(keru) 助ける】
① [formerly also 扶ける] help, aid, assist
助け *tasuke* aid, rescue, relief
助け合う *tasukeau* help each other
手助け *tedasuke* help, assistance
② save, rescue, relieve
助け出す *tasukedasu* rescue (a person) from [out of], deliver [extricate] (a person) from

【tasu(karu) 助かる】 be helped, be rescued, be spared
大助かり *ōdasukari* big help

【suke 助】
① helping, assisting; assistant vaudevillian
助太刀する *sukedachi suru* help (a person in a fight), back up
助っ人 *suketto colloq* helper, backer, supporter
② *colloq* suffix for derisive nicknames
飲み助 *nomisuke* drunkard
雲助 *kumosuke* reckless and dishonest cab-driver or palanquin bearer
③ *slang* broad, chick
助番 *sukeban* leader of a group of delinquent girls
助平 *sukebei* lewd person; Peeping Tom

SYNONYMS

❶ help
佑 HELP (said esp. of God) → 74
祐 DIVINE HELP → 915
援 AID → 586
佐 ASSIST → 67
補 assist → 1194
輔 ASSIST → 1559
済 RELIEVE → 522

❷ subordinate
准 JUNIOR → 127
副 SECONDARY → 1776
次 secondary → 54
従 subordinate → 415
亜 SUB- → 3540
準 QUASI- → 2856
半 semi- → 3501

USAGE

tasukeru
助ける
① [formerly also 扶ける] help, aid, assist
② save, rescue, relieve
扶ける
[now usu. 助ける] help, aid, assist

HOMOPHONES

tasukeru ⇨ 扶 247

判 判 判 わ

1122 HAN BAN waka(ru)▲

Ⓒⓗ 判 pàn

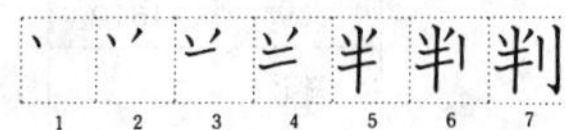

Radical	Strokes
刂 18	7-2-5
Grade	**Freq**
Jōyō-5	276
◧ 1 - 5 - 2	

5-2 半

▶JUDGE

COMPOUNDS

❶ⓐ (pass legal judgment) **judge, hand down a decision, pronounce sentence**

ⓑ (decide upon critically) **judge, decide, distinguish, differentiate**

判決 *hanketsu* judicial decision, judgment, sentence
判事 *hanji* judge
判例 *hanrei* (judicial) precedent
裁判 *saiban* trial, judgment, decision
公判 *kōhan* (public) trial [hearing]
判断する *handan suru* judge, decide; interpret, foretell, read
判定する *hantei suru* judge, decide
批判する *hihan suru* criticize, comment
評判 *hyōban* fame, reputation
審判 *shinpan* (=*shinban*) refereeing, judgment; referee, umpire

❷ puzzle out, solve, decipher

判読 *handoku* decipherment, interpretation

❸ obvious, clear

判明する *hanmei suru* become clear, be confirmed
判然と *hanzen to* clearly, distinctly, plainly

❹ **personal seal, seal, stamp, chop; seal impression**

判子 *hanko* handstamp, seal; seal impression
盲判 *mekuraban* undeliberated endorsement
血判 *keppan* seal of blood

❺ [also suffix] format, size (of books or paper)

菊判 *kikuban* small octavo, medium octavo
二つ折り判 *futatsuoriban* folio

❻ [in compounds] former oval Japanese gold coin

大判 *ōban* large oval Japanese gold coin
小判 *koban* smaller sized oval Japanese gold coin

INDEPENDENT

【han 判】 personal seal, seal, chop; stamp, seal impression; format, size (of books or paper)
判を押す *han o osu* affix a seal

【hanjiru 判じる】 judge, decide; puzzle out, decipher; guess, interpret

【ban 判】 format, size

KUN

【waka(ru) 判る】
[usu. 分かる, sometimes also 解る]

①ⓐ (grasp the meaning of) understand, comprehend, see

ⓑ (be sympathetic toward) understand, show understanding for (another's feelings)

判り *wakari* understanding
判り難い *wakarinikui* hard to understand, incomprehensible, unintelligible
物判りの良い *monowakari no yoi* understanding; sensible

②ⓐ know, tell, recognize

ⓑ be made known, be brought to light

先の事は判らない *saki no koto wa wakaranai* cannot tell what will happen in the future
身元が判る *mimoto ga wakaru* be identified

③ appreciate

音楽が判る *ongaku ga wakaru* have appreciation [an ear] for music

SYNONYMS

❶ **judge**

裁 JUDGE → 3299
鑑 APPRAISE → 1773
評 evaluate → 1501
審 TRY → 2360
決 DECIDE → 263
視 REGARD → 972

❹ **seals**

印 SEAL → 828
璽 IMPERIAL SEAL → 2911

HOMOPHONES

wakaru ⇨ 分 1972 解 1517

NOTE

⇨ see USAGE note at 分 1972

判

1123

▶JUDGE

nonstandard for 判 1122

5-2 半

5-3
牙

邪 邪 邪 邪

1124 JA yokoshi(ma)▲

Ⓒⓗ 邪 xié

Radical	Strokes
阝 163	8-3-5
Grade	**Freq**
Jōyō	1670
◧ 1 - 5 - 3	

▶**EVIL**

COMPOUNDS

❶ⓐ (morally bad) **evil, wicked, bad, unjust, heretical, wrong**
ⓑ (causing harm) evil
ⓒ wrong, evil
邪悪 *jaaku* wickedness, vice
邪心 *jashin* wicked heart, evil design
邪道 *jadō* evil course; heresy
邪魔 *jama* hindrance, obstruction, impediment
無邪気 *mujaki* innocence, simplicity
正邪の区別 *seija no kubetsu* discrimination between right and wrong
❷ *baseball* foul
邪飛 *jahi* foul fly

INDEPENDENT

【ja 邪】 wrong, injustice, unrighteousness
邪は正に勝たず *Ja wa sei ni katazu* Virtue triumphs over vice

KUN

【yokoshi(ma) 邪ま】
yokoshima na 邪まな evil, wicked, vicious; unjust; dishonest
邪まな心 *yokoshima na kokoro* evil heart

SPECIAL READINGS

風邪 *kaze* (=*fūja*) (common) cold

SYNONYMS

❶ⓐ **evil**
悪 BAD → 2745
凶 ATROCIOUS → 2961
ⓒ **wrongdoing and evil**
非 wrong(doing) → 889
罪 sin → 2610
悪 evil (something bad) → 2745
弊 evil(s) (something undesirable) → 2884

NOTE

⇨ see COMPOUND FORMATION for 邪魔 *jama* ⇨ 魔 3187

5-3
白

的 的 的 的

1125 TEKI mato

丿 ⺅ 白 白 白 白 的 的

Ⓒⓗ 的 dì dí de

Radical	Strokes
白 106	8-5-3
Grade	**Freq**
Jōyō-4	37
◧ 1 - 5 - 3	

▶**TARGET** ▶**ADJECTIVAL SUFFIX**

COMPOUNDS

❶ⓐ **target, mark, bull's eye**
ⓑ right on target, accurate
標的 *hyōteki* target, mark
射的 *shateki* target practice, shooting
目的 *mokuteki* object, purpose
的中する *tekichū suru* hit the mark, hit (on) it
的確な *tekikaku na* precise, accurate, exact
❷ **suffix for forming adjectives from nouns or word elements**—used to express resemblance, relation or the like (similar to English *-tic* or *-al*)
劇的な *gekiteki na* dramatic
歴史的 *rekishiteki* historical
合理的な *gōriteki na* rational, logical, reasonable
法的 *hōteki* legal, legalistic
私的な *shiteki na* private, personal
規則的 *kisokuteki* systematic, regular
知的 *chiteki* intellectual, mental
国際的な *kokusaiteki na* international
❸ suffix indicating endearment or derision—often attached to a person's name (similar to *boy* in *Jimmy Boy*)
権的 *gonteki* nickname for 権兵衛 *gonbē*

KUN

【mato 的】 target, mark; object, target
的外れの *mato hazure no* out of focus; off the point
的に達しない *mato ni tasshinai* fall short of the mark

SYNONYMS

❶ⓐ **target**
標 MARK → 1064
目 aim → 3043
❷ **modifier suffixes**
爾 adjective suffix → 3587
如 modifier suffix → 207

然 MODIFIER FORMING SUFFIX → 2782

的 ▶TARGET ▶ADJECTIVAL SUFFIX
1126
nonstandard for 的 1125

5-3 白

知 1127 CHI shi(ru) shi(raseru)

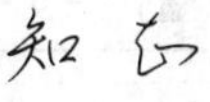

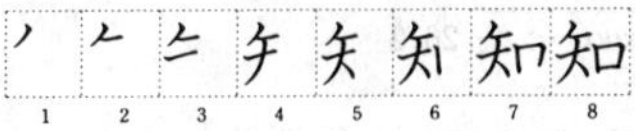

CH 知 zhī

Radical	Strokes
矢 111	8-5-3
Grade	**Freq**
Jōyō-2	208
1-5-3	

5-3 矢

▶KNOW

COMPOUNDS

❶ⓐ **know, be aware of, understand; perceive, recognize**
ⓑ [formerly also 智 2784] **knowledge, wisdom, intelligence, intellect**
ⓒ [formerly 智 2784] wise, clever, resourceful
知識 *chishiki* knowledge
知覚 *chikaku* perception, sensation
周知の *shūchi no* known to all, universally known
承知する *shōchi suru* consent [agree] to; permit; forgive; know, understand
探知 *tanchi* detection
知恵 *chie* wisdom, intelligence, sagacity
知能 *chinō* intelligence, mental capacity
知覚知 *chikakuchi* knowledge by acquaintance
知情意 *chijōi* intellect, emotion and volition
知将 *chishō* resourceful general
❷ **let know, inform**
通知する *tsūchi suru* notify, inform, let know
告知する *kokuchi suru* notify, announce
❸ⓐ come to know, become acquainted with
ⓑ acquaintance, friend
知人 *chijin* acquaintance, friend
旧知 *kyūchi* old friend
❹ govern, rule
県知事 *kenchiji* prefectural governor

INDEPENDENT

【chi 知(=智)】 wisdom, intellect, intelligence, sense; stratagem
知余って勇足らず *chi amatte yū tarazu* be too sagacious to be bold

KUN

【shi(ru) 知る】 know, be aware of, understand; perceive, recognize, feel; infer; become acquainted with; be concerned with; reign, govern
知らん顔 *shirankao* feigned ignorance, unconcerned air
知れ渡る *shirewataru* become widely known
物知り *monoshiri* well-informed person, walking dictionary
高が知れている *taka ga shirete iru* not amount to much
知り合い *shiriai* acquaintance
それは僕の知った事じゃない *Sore wa boku no shitta koto ja nai* It's no concern of mine
知ろし召す *shiroshimesu* reign

【shi(raseru) 知らせる】 let know, inform, tell, report
知らせ *shirase* information, notice, report

SYNONYMS

❶ⓐ **know and understand**
通 know thoroughly → 3109
得 gain understanding of → 477
解 understand → 1517
分かる understand → 1972
諒 UNDERSTAND → 1575
了 COMPREHEND → 3350
悟 AWAKE TO → 419
ⓐ **perceive**
覚 PERCEIVE → 2604
感 FEEL → 2835
認 RECOGNIZE → 1546
ⓑ **wisdom**
智 WISDOM → 2784
慧 prajna (transcendental wisdom) → 2810
哲 PHILOSOPHY → 2738
識 KNOWLEDGE → 1639
ⓑ **learning and knowledge**
識 KNOWLEDGE → 1639
学 learning → 2555
文 culture → 1962
業 studies → 2612
❷ **inform and communicate**
報 INFORM → 1698
通 COMMUNICATE → 3109
告 NOTIFY → 2409
届ける give notice → 3078
達 issue a notice → 3139
申 REPORT → 3507
宣 PROCLAIM → 2252

5-3 礻

祀

1128 SHI matsu(ru)

CH 祀 sì

Radical	Strokes
示 113	8-5-3
Grade	Freq
Reference	
1-5-3	

COMPOUNDS

[now usu. 祭る *matsuru*]

ⓐ worship as god, deify

ⓑ enshrine

祭祀 *saishi* religious service; festival

先祖を祀る *senzo o matsuru* worship one's ancestors

HOMOPHONES

matsuru ⇨ 祭 2672

NOTE

⇨ see USAGE note at 祭 2672

5-3 礻

社

1129

▶COMPANY ▶SOCIETY

nonstandard for 社 840

5-3 禾

和 和 和

1130 WA O yawa(ragu) yawa(rageru) nago(mu) nago(yaka)

CH 和 hé hè huó huò hú

Radical	Strokes
口 30	8-3-5
Grade	Freq
Jōyō-3	166
1-5-3	

一 二 千 禾 禾 禾 和 和 (1 2 3 4 5 6 7 8)

▶HARMONIOUS ▶PEACE ▶JAPAN

COMPOUNDS

❶ⓐ **harmonious, in accord, peaceful, friendly**

ⓑ [original meaning] harmonize, sing in harmony

和気 *waki* harmonious atmosphere

和合 *wagō* harmony, concord; union

調和 *chōwa* harmony, accord, agreement, symmetry

共和制 *kyōwasei* republicanism

昭和 *shōwa* Showa era

和声 *wasei* harmony, concord, consonance

❷ **peace**

和平 *wahei* peace

和解する *wakai suru* make peace, come to terms

平和 *heiwa* peace, harmony

講和 *kōwa* peace, reconciliation

❸ gentle, mild, soft

緩和する *kanwa suru* ease, relieve, alleviate

温和(=穏和)な *onwa na* gentle, mild, genial

柔和な *nyūwa na* gentle, mild, tender, meek

❹ⓐ **Japan, Japanese**

ⓑ Japanese (language)

和服 *wafuku* Japanese clothes, kimono

和歌 *waka* Japanese poem, tanka

和食 *washoku* Japanese-style food

和訳 *wayaku* Japanese translation

漢和辞典 *kanwa jiten* Chinese-Japanese character dictionary

❺ sum, total

総和 *sōwa* sum total, lump sum

代数的和 *daisūtekiwa* algebraic sum

❻ mix

混和 *konwa* mixture, mingling

中和 *chūwa* neutralization; counteraction (of poison)

❼ used phonetically for *o*

和尚 *oshō* Buddhist priest [abbot] in charge of a temple

INDEPENDENT

【**wa** 和】 harmony, accord; peace; sum

夫婦の和 *fūfu no wa* concord between husband and wife, conjugal harmony

和を結ぶ *wa o musubu* make peace

二と三の和は五 *Ni to san no wa wa go* The sum of two and three is five

KUN

【**yawa(ragu)** 和らぐ】 *vi* soften; abate, lessen; calm down

和らぎ *yawaragi* abatement, alleviation; peacefulness

寒さが和らいだ *Samusa ga yawaraida* The cold has decreased its severity

【**yawa(rageru)** 和らげる】 *vt* soften, tone down, calm; lessen, mitigate, relieve

苦痛を和らげる *kutsū o yawarageru* relieve a

person's pain
【nago(mu) 和む】 be softened, become lukewarm
心が和む *kokoro ga nagomu* feel relaxed
【nago(yaka) 和やか】
nagoyaka na 和やかな peaceful, mild, gentle
和やかな家庭 *nagoyaka na katei* harmonious [happy] family

SPECIAL READINGS

大和 *yamato* Yamato (old name for Japan)
大和魂 *yamatodamashii* the Japanese spirit
日和 *hiyori* weather

SYNONYMS

❶ⓐ familiar and friendly
睦 FRIENDLY → 1199
懇 FAMILIAR → 2899
親 INTIMATE → 1799
密 CLOSE → 2292
近 NEAR → 3061
❷ peace
安 public peace → 2171
治 public order → 335
❹ⓐ Japan
邦 JAPAN → 847
日 JAPAN → 3027
国 Japanese → 3087
❺ total
総 TOTAL → 1379
計 total → 1441

NOTE

⇨ see COMPOUND FORMATION for 昭和 *shōwa* ⇨ 昭 894

邸

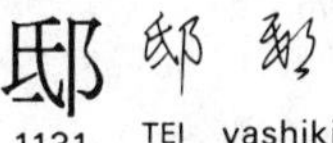

1131 TEI yashiki▲

dǐ

Radical	Strokes
⻏ 163	8-3-5
Grade	**Freq**
Jōyō	1174
◧ 1-5-3	

5-3 氐

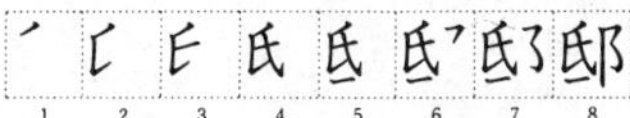

1 2 3 4 5 6 7 8

▶STATELY RESIDENCE

COMPOUNDS

ⓐ stately residence, mansion, official residence, villa, house
ⓑ suffix for forming names of residences or mansions
ⓒ [original meaning, now obsolete] residence where feudal lords used to lodge when in the capital
邸宅 *teitaku* residence, mansion
公邸 *kōtei* official residence
官邸 *kantei* official residence
私邸 *shitei* one's private residence
別邸 *bettei* villa, country residence
徳川公爵邸 *tokugawakōshaku-tei* mansion of Prince Tokugawa
山本氏邸 *yamamotoshi-tei* Mr. Yamamoto's residence

KUN

【yashiki 邸】 [now usu. 屋敷] mansion, residence

SYNONYMS

● mansions
館 stately mansion → 1748
荘 VILLA → 2262
● houses
居 residence → 3080
住 housing → 64
宅 DWELLING HOUSE → 2174
戸 HOUSEHOLD → 1930
家 HOUSE → 2273
屋 HOUSE → 3098
軒 house → 1459

USAGE

yashiki
邸
[now usu. 屋敷] mansion, residence
屋敷
① [sometimes also 邸] mansion, residence
② residential lot

HOMOPHONES

yashiki ⇨ 屋敷 3098, 1870

矩

incorrect stroke count ⇨ see 1148

5-4 矢

5-4 石

研 1132 KEN to(gu)

CH 研 yán

Radical	Strokes
石 112	9-5-4
Grade	**Freq**
Jōyō-3	431
1 - 5 - 4	

1 2 3 4 5 6 7 8 9

▶**GRIND** ▶**RESEARCH**

COMPOUNDS

❶ [original meaning] **grind, polish**

研磨する *kenma suru* grind, polish; study hard, brush up
研削 *kensaku* grinding
研米機 *kenmaiki* rice polisher

❷ⓐ **research, study (hard), investigate**

ⓑ abbrev. of 研究所 *kenkyūsho* or 研究会 *kenkyūkai*: research institute, laboratory, research society

研究 *kenkyū* research, study
研修 *kenshū* study and training
研鑽 *kensan* study
技研 *giken* technical research institute
癌研 *ganken* Cancer Research Institute

KUN

【to(gu) 研ぐ】 sharpen, grind, whet, polish; wash (rice)

研ぎ *togi* grinding, polish, sharpening
研ぎ石 *togiishi* whetstone, knife sharpener
研ぎ澄ます *togisumasu* sharpen [grind] well

SYNONYMS

❶ **polish and rub**

削 CUT BY CHIPPING → 1448
磨 POLISH → 3181
摩 RUB AGAINST → 3175
擦 RUB → 790

❷ⓐ **learn and study**

究 STUDY EXHAUSTIVELY → 2203
学 STUDY → 2555
考 study → 3196
習 LEARN → 2667
攻 specialize → 242

5-4 石

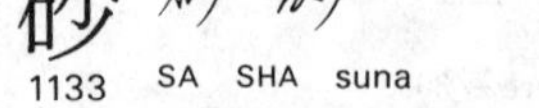

砂 1133 SA SHA suna

CH 砂 沙 shā

Radical	Strokes
石 112	9-5-4
Grade	**Freq**
Jōyō-6	1006
1 - 5 - 4	

1 2 3 4 5 6 7 8 9

▶**SAND**

COMPOUNDS

[sometimes also 沙 *sa* 266]

ⓐ **sand (of fine constitution)**

ⓑ **sandy, granular**

砂漠 *sabaku* desert
砂丘 *sakyū* sand dune, sand hill
砂岩 *sagan* sandstone
砂州(＝砂洲) *sasu* sandbar, sandbank
土砂 *dosha* earth and sand
砂糖 *satō* sugar
砂金 *sakin* gold dust
砂鉄 *satetsu* iron sand

KUN

【suna 砂】 sand, grit

砂地 *sunaji* sandy place
砂浜 *sunahama* sandy beach, sands
砂場 *sunaba* sandbox

SPECIAL READINGS

砂利 *jari* gravel, fine gravel, ballast

SYNONYMS

ⓐ **sand**

沙 SAND (granular) → 266

砕 碎 砕 碎

1134 SAI kuda(ku) kuda(keru)

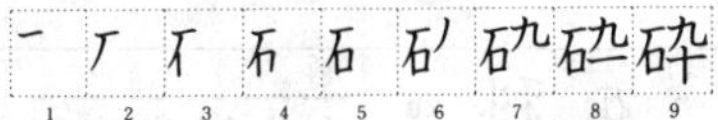

Ⓒⓗ 碎 suì

Radical	Strokes
石 112	9-5-4
Grade	**Freq**
Jōyō	1571
1-5-4	

5-4 石

▶CRUSH UP

COMPOUNDS

❶ [formerly also 摧 692] [original meaning] **crush up, break into pieces, smash**
- 砕岩機 *saiganki* rock crusher
- 砕氷船 *saihyōsen* ice breaker
- 砕石 *saiseki* quarrying
- 破砕する *hasai suru* crush, smash, crack to pieces
- 粉砕する *funsai suru* pulverize, shatter, smash, crush
- 爆砕する *bakusai suru* blast, blow to pieces
- 玉砕 *gyokusai* death for honor

❷ exert oneself to the utmost, rack one's brain
- 粉骨砕身する *funkotsusaishin suru* do one's best, exert oneself

KUN

【kuda(ku) 砕く】 *vt* crush, smash, break into pieces, shatter; rack (one's brains); explain plainly
- 打ち砕く *uchikudaku* break to pieces, smash, crush; baffle, frustrate
- 噛み砕く *kamikudaku* crunch; simplify, explain plainly

【kuda(keru) 砕ける】 *vi* be crushed, be broken, be smashed; break down, buckle, give way; become softened, become complaisant, get friendly; be easy [plain]
- 砕け散る *kudakechiru* be smashed up
- 腰砕け *koshikudake* breaking down in the middle of a bout; weakening of one's attitude
- 砕けた態度 *kudaketa taido* friendly attitude
- 砕けた文章 *kudaketa bunshō* plain [informal] writing

SYNONYMS

❶ **break into small pieces**
- 抹 pulverize → 313

❶ **break**
- 裂 SPLIT → 2687
- 割る crack → 1816
- 破 BREAK → 1150
- 壊 BREAK DOWN → 756
- 折 BREAK OFF → 253
- 崩 CRUMBLE → 2296

1135 **▶PRAY**

nonstandard for 祈 875

5-4 示

1136 **▶BLESSEDNESS**

nonstandard for 祉 876

5-4 示

秒 秒 秒

1137 BYŌ

Ⓒⓗ 秒 miǎo

Radical	Strokes
禾 115	9-5-4
Grade	**Freq**
Jōyō-3	826
1-5-4	

5-4 禾

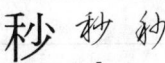

▶SECOND

COMPOUNDS

❶ⓐ (unit of time) **second**

ⓑ (unit of angular measure) second

ⓒ **counter for seconds**

ⓓ (brief while) second, moment
- 秒速 *byōsoku* speed per second
- 秒針 *byōshin* second hand
- 秒時計 *byōdokei* stop watch
- 三十五秒 *sanjūgobyō* 35 seconds
- 二分三十秒 *nifun sanjūbyō* 2′30″
- 寸秒 *sunbyō* a moment, a second

❷ [original meaning, now archaic] beard of grain

INDEPENDENT

【byō 秒】 second

SYNONYMS

❶ⓐ short time periods

頃 moment → 144

瞬 INSTANT → 1247

分 MINUTE → 1972

時 hour → 924

暫 SHORT WHILE → 2864

5-4 禾

科 1138 KA

CH 科 kē

Radical	Strokes
禾 115	9-5-4
Grade	**Freq**
Jōyō-2	425
1 - 5 - 4	

▶SUBJECT OF STUDY

COMPOUNDS

❶ [also suffix] **subject of study, branch of academic study, subdivision of a discipline**

科目 *kamoku* school subject; subdivision, items

教科 *kyōka* school subject; course of study, curriculum

学科 *gakka* school subject; course of study

理科 *rika* science; science department

分科会 *bunkakai* sectional subcommittee

百科事典 *hyakka-jiten* encyclopedia

社会科 *shakaika* social studies

❷ [also suffix] **course (of study), department (of a university or hospital)**

内科 *naika* (department of) internal medicine

外科 *geka* (department of) surgery

歯科 *shika* dentistry

本科 *honka* regular course [department]

文科 *bunka* literary department

小児科 *shōnika* (department of) pediatrics

❸ **study systematically**

科学 *kagaku* science

❹ *biol* family

科名 *kamei* family name

猫科 *nekoka* cat family, Felidae

❺ⓐ punishment, sentence

ⓑ **offense, criminal record**

科料 *karyō* police fine, minor fine

前科 *zenka* previous offense, criminal record

罪科 *zaika* offense, crime, guilt; punishment

❻ rule, law

金科玉条 *kinkagyokujō* golden rule

❼ acting, performance

科白 *kahaku* (=*serifu*) speech, words (in a play); one's remarks

❽ civil examinations in ancient China

科挙 *kakyo* ancient Chinese higher civil service examinations

INDEPENDENT

【ka 科】 course (of study), department (of a university or hospital); *biol* family

彼とは科が違う *Kare to wa ka ga chigau* He is not in the same department

この科の植物 *kono ka no shokubutsu* plant of this family

【kasuru 科する】 inflict (a punishment), impose (a penalty)

SYNONYMS

❶ branch of study

学 branch of study → 2555

門 field → 888

❷ units of learning

課 LESSON → 1573

講 LECTURE → 1619

5-4 禾

秋 1139 SHŪ aki toki▴

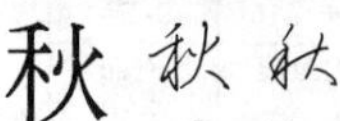

CH 秋 qiū

Radical	Strokes
禾 115	9-5-4
Grade	**Freq**
Jōyō-2	585
1 - 5 - 4	

▶AUTUMN

COMPOUNDS

❶ [original meaning] **autumn, fall**

秋分 *shūbun* autumnal equinox

秋思 *shūshi* lonely feeling of fall

晩秋 *banshū* late fall

今秋 *konshū* this [next] autumn

春秋 *shunjū* spring and autumn; years, age; Chronicles of Lu

春夏秋冬 *shunkashūtō* four seasons, all (the)

year round
❷ years, time
千秋 *senshū* a thousand years, many years

KUN

【**aki** 秋】 autumn, fall
秋風 *akikaze* autumn breeze
【**toki** 秋】 [also 時] critical moment
危急存亡の秋 *kikyūsonbō no toki* crisis, critical moment

SYNONYMS

❶ **cold seasons**
冬 WINTER → 2157
寒 coldest season → 2311

HOMOPHONES

toki ⇨ 時 924

NOTE

⇨ see USAGE note at 時 924

衿

1140 KIN eri

Ⓒⓗ 衿 jīn

Radical	Strokes
衤 145	9-5-4
Grade	**Freq**
Reference	
◧ 1 - 5 - 4	

5-4 衤

COMPOUNDS

[also 襟 *eri*]
ⓐ [original meaning] collar, lapel, neck
ⓑ nape
衿裏 *eriura* lining of the collar
半衿 *han'eri* neckpiece (on a kimono)

HOMOPHONES

eri ⇨ 襟 1252

NOTE

⇨ see USAGE note at 襟 1252

故

1141 KO yue

Ⓒⓗ 故 gù

Radical	Strokes
攵 66	9-4-5
Grade	**Freq**
Jōyō-5	401
◧ 1 - 5 - 4	

5-4 古

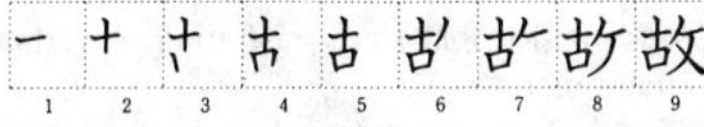

▶**OLD** ▶**THE LATE**

COMPOUNDS

❶ⓐ (of an earlier time) **old, former**
ⓑ (of the past) **old, of old, ancient**
ⓒ things of old, tradition
故郷 *kokyō* hometown, birthplace
故国 *kokoku* one's native land [country]
故旧 *kokyū* old acquaintance
故事 *koji* tradition; historical fact, origin
故実 *kojitsu* ancient customs
故老(=古老) *korō* elder, old man; old-timer
温故知新 *onkochishin* Exploring the old [past] one comes to understand the new [present]
典故 *tenko* authentic precedent
❷ⓐ [prefix] **the late, deceased**
ⓑ die
故川田氏 *ko-kawadashi* the late Mr. Kawada
故人 *kojin* the deceased
物故する *bukko suru* die
❸ **incident, affair, event, occurrence**
故障 *koshō* malfunction, breakdown; physical disorder; hindrance, obstacle, accident; objection, protest
事故 *jiko* accident, incident, trouble
世故 *seko* worldly affairs
❹ intentional, on purpose
故意 *koi* intention, purpose, bad faith
故買 *kobai* buying stolen goods
❺ reason, cause, grounds
縁故 *enko* relation, connection; relative

KUN

【**yue** 故】
ⓐ reason, cause, grounds
ⓑ circumstances
故に *yue ni* therefore, accordingly
...の故に *...no yue ni* on account of..., by reason of...
故有って *yue atte* for a certain reason; owing to unavoidable circumstances

SPECIAL READINGS

何故▲ *naze* why, for what reason

SYNONYMS

❶ⓐ **former**
旧 FORMER → 14
元 former → 1929
前 previous → 2266
先 former → 2394

既 ALREADY → 1166
ⓑ **old**
旧 old → 14
古 OLD (not new) → 2002
老 OLD (not young) → 3197
❷ⓐ **dead**
亡 deceased → 3402
❸ **incident**
事 AFFAIR → 3567
変 unexpected event → 2069
【yue】
ⓐ **cause and reason**
訳 reason → 1473
為 because → 3577
因 CAUSE → 3054
由 REASON → 3499

5-4
正

政 政 政

1142 SEI SHŌ matsurigoto man▲

一 丅 下 正 正 正 正' 政 政 政
1 2 3 4 5 6 7 8 9

Ⓒ 政 zhèng

Radical	Strokes
攵 66	9-4-5
Grade	**Freq**
Jōyō-5	36
1-5-4	

▶**POLITICAL ADMINISTRATION**

COMPOUNDS

❶ⓐ [also suffix] **political administration, government**
ⓑ form of government, government system
政府 *seifu* government, administration
政治 *seiji* government, administration, politics
政権 *seiken* political power, administrative power
政策 *seisaku* policy, political measures
政令 *seirei* government ordinance, cabinet order
行政 *gyōsei* administration
内政 *naisei* domestic administration, internal affairs
郵政 *yūsei* postal system
国政 *kokusei* (national) administration, government
施政 *shisei* administration, government
民政 *minsei* civil administration [government]
摂政 *sesshō* regency; regent
東京都政 *tōkyōtosei* government of Tokyo Metropolis
共和政 *kyōwasei* republicanism
❷ **politics, political affairs**
政党 *seitō* political party
政界 *seikai* political world
政局 *seikyoku* political situation
政経 *seikei* politics and economics
❸ management (of one's affairs), administration
家政 *kasei* household management
財政 *zaisei* public finance, financial affairs

KUN

【matsurigoto 政】 administration, government, affairs of state
政を執る *matsurigoto o toru* administer the affairs of state
【man 政】 [in compounds] political administration, government
政所 *mandokoro* administrative office (in the shogunate government); titled lady

SYNONYMS

❶ⓐ **government**
治 government → 335

5-4
⺧

叛

1143 HAN HON somu(ku)

Ⓒ 叛 pàn

Radical	Strokes
又 29	9-2-7
Grade	**Freq**
Reference	
1-5-4	

COMPOUNDS

ⓐ [now replaced by 反 *han* 2945] [original meaning] rebel, revolt
ⓑ [usu. 背く *somuku*] go against, disobey, rebel against, violate
叛乱 *hanran* rebellion, revolt
叛逆 *hangyaku* revolt, rebellion, mutiny
叛旗 *hanki* flag [standard] of revolt
叛徒 *hanto* rebels, insurgents
謀叛 *muhon* rebellion, revolt, treason
親に叛く *oya ni somuku* disobey one's parent(s)

HOMOPHONES

somuku ⇨ 背 2573

NOTE
⇨ see USAGE note at 背 2573

段 1144 DAN TAN▲

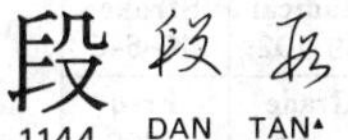

Ⓒⓗ 段 duàn

Radical	Strokes
殳 79	9-4-5
Grade	Freq
Jōyō-6	315
◧ 1-5-4	

5-4

▶ **STEP**

COMPOUNDS

❶ⓐ **step, stair, rung**
ⓑ **counter for steps**
段丘 *dankyū* terrace, bench (in geography)
階段 *kaidan* steps, flight of stairs
石段 *ishidan* stone steps
百段 *hyakudan* 100 steps

❷ⓐ (division or level) **step, stage, level**
ⓑ counter for steps or stages
段階 *dankai* grade, rank, step, stage
値段 *nedan* price
一段と *ichidan to* greater, more, further
格段の相違 *kakudan no sōi* marked difference
多段式ロケット *tadanshiki roketto* multistage rocket
二段ベッド *nidan-beddo* double bunk

❸ (step in a ranking system) **grade, degree or rank in go, karate, judo or various martial arts** (higher than 級 *kyū*)
段違い *danchigai* different class, different level; widely apart
初段 *shodan* first degree black belt (as in karate)
有段者 *yūdansha* grade holder
五段 *godan* fifth grade (as in karate)

❹ (means to an end) **step, measure**
段取り *dandori* program, plan, step, course of action
手段 *shudan* means, way, step
算段 *sandan* contrivance, management

❺ subdivision of a literary or artistic work:
ⓐ passage (of a text or music), paragraph
ⓑ act, scene (of a play)
段落 *danraku* end of a paragraph, conclusion
段物 *danmono* musical [dramatic] piece in several acts
忠臣蔵六段目 *chūshingura rokudanme* Sixth Act of "Chushingura"

❻ⓐ column (of print), rank
ⓑ counter for columns (of print)
全段 *zendan* whole page (of a newspaper)
二段組 *nidangumi* double column setting

❼ case, occasion
普段(=不断)の *fudan no* usual, ordinary, everyday, habitual
別段の *betsudan no* particular, special

❽ [now usu. 反 *tan* 2945] *tan*: unit of sq. measure equiv. to approx. 9.9 ares or 300 *bu* (歩)

INDEPENDENT

【dan 段】
① step, stair, rung
梯子の段 *hashigo no dan* rung of a ladder
② (division or level) step, stage, level
五の段の九九 *go no dan no kuku* the five times table
③ grade, degree (⇨ ❸)
段を取る *dan o toru* obtain a degree (in judo); get a black belt
④ subdivision of a literary or artistic work:
ⓐ passage (of a text or music), paragraph
ⓑ act, scene
物語の最後の段 *monogatari no saigo no dan* last part of a story
⑤ column (of print)
⑥ case, occasion
いざと云う段になると *iza to iu dan ni naru to* when the matter comes to a crisis

【tan 段】 *tan* (⇨ ❽)

SYNONYMS

❶ **steps**
階 stairs → 624
陛 IMPERIAL PALACE STEPS → 453

❸ **class**
級 GRADE → 1279
位 RANK → 61
階 RANK → 624
身 social status → 3553
格 STATUS → 926
等 CLASS → 2682
流 class → 441
層 STRATUM → 3161

❹ **means**
手 means → 3456
策 MEASURE → 2679

❺ⓐ **parts of writing**
節 paragraph → 2691
章 CHAPTER → 2117
款 ARTICLE → 1700
条 ARTICLE → 2200
項 CLAUSE → 567

目 ITEM → 3043 | 箇 item → 2700

5-5
田

畔 畔 畔 畔
1145 HAN aze▲

CH 畔 pàn

Radical	Strokes
田 102	10-5-5
Grade	**Freq**
Jōyō	1700
1 - 5 - 5	

丨 冂 冊 田 田 田` 田'' 田⺌ 田⺌ 畔
1 2 3 4 5 6 7 8 9 10

▶WATERSIDE

COMPOUNDS

❶ **waterside, water's edge, bank, shore**
湖畔 *kohan* lake shore, lakeside
河畔 *kahan* riverside, banks of a river
池畔 *chihan* edge of a pond
橋畔 *kyōhan* approach to a bridge
吉野川畔 *yoshinogawahan* the banks of Yoshino River
❷ [original meaning] ridge between rice fields

KUN

【aze 畔】 ridge between rice fields
畔道 *azemichi* footpath between rice fields

SYNONYMS

❶ **shores and watersides**
-辺 -side → 3029
浜 BEACH → 436
岸 SHORE → 2236
浦 SEASIDE → 437
渚 STRAND → 525
磯 ROCKY BEACH → 1242

5-5
田

1146

▶WATERSIDE
nonstandard for 畔 1145

5-5
目

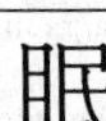

眠 眠 眠
1147 MIN nemu(ru) nemu(i)

CH 眠 mián

Radical	Strokes
目 109	10-5-5
Grade	**Freq**
Jōyō	1294
1 - 5 - 5	

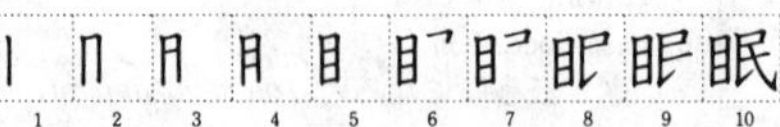

1 2 3 4 5 6 7 8 9 10

▶SLEEP

COMPOUNDS

● [original meaning] **sleep**
睡眠 *suimin* sleep, slumber
催眠術 *saiminjutsu* hypnotism, mesmerism
不眠 *fumin* sleeplessness, insomnia
冬眠 *tōmin* hibernation ("winter sleep")
安眠 *anmin* quiet sleep, peaceful slumber
永眠 *eimin* eternal sleep, death

KUN

【nemu(ru) 眠る】 sleep; die; lie idle
眠り *nemuri* sleep, slumber, nap
眠り込む *nemurikomu* fall asleep
安らかに眠れ *Yasuraka ni nemure* May rest in peace the deceased
眠っている金 *nemutte iru kane* money lying idle

【nemu(i) 眠い】 sleepy
眠気 *nemuke* sleepiness

SYNONYMS

● **sleep**
睡 SLEEP → 1200
寝 GO TO SLEEP → 2329

矩 矩 矩 矩

1148 KU kane NAMES nori tsune tadashi

CH 矩 jǔ

Radical	Strokes
矢 111	10-5-5
Grade	**Freq**
Names	2110
◧ 1 - 5 - 5	

5-5 矢

▶**RULE**

COMPOUNDS

❶ⓐ (established standard) **rule, standard, criterion**

ⓑ (measuring tool) carpenter's square, rule, ruler

矩則 *kusoku* rule, standard

規矩 *kiku* standard, rule; compass and ruler

❷ square, rectangle

矩形 *kukei* rectangle

❸ *astron* quadrature

矩象 *kushō* quadrature

INDEPENDENT

【**ku 矩**】 *astron* quadrature

KUN

【**kane 矩**】 carpenter's square, metal measure; regular *shaku* (尺) (approx. 12 in.)

矩尺(＝曲尺) *kanejaku* carpenter's square; regular *shaku* (尺) (approx. 12 in.)

NAMES

規矩男 *kikuo* male name

矩夫 *tsuneo* male name

矩次 *noritsugu* male name

SYNONYMS

❶ⓐ **laws and rules**

則 RULE → 1444

規 REGULATION → 978

紀 discipline → 1276

法 LAW → 333

律 LAW → 363

典 CANON → 2627

憲 CONSTITUTION → 2368

令 ordinance → 1995

NOTE

★do not confuse with 短 1182

矩

1149

▶**RULE**

nonstandard for 矩 1148

5-5 矢

破 破 破

1150 HA yabu(ru) yabu(reru)

CH 破 pò

Radical	Strokes
石 112	10-5-5
Grade	**Freq**
Jōyō-5	600
◧ 1 - 5 - 5	

5-5 石

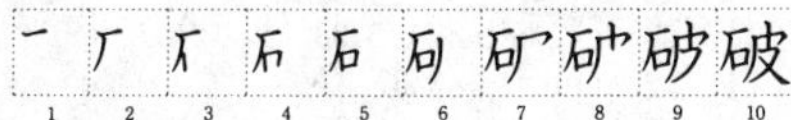

▶**BREAK**

COMPOUNDS

❶ⓐ [original meaning] **break, smash**

ⓑ **break through, penetrate**

ⓒ break out (of jail), escape

破壊する *hakai suru* break (down), destroy, wreck

破片 *hahen* fragment, broken piece, scrap

破損 *hason* damage, breakdown

破砕する *hasai suru* crush, smash, crack to pieces

破滅 *hametsu* ruin, destruction, wreck, collapse, downfall

爆破 *bakuha* blasting, blowing up, explosion

難破 *nanpa* shipwreck

打破する *daha suru* break down, overthrow, abolish

突破する *toppa suru* break [smash] through; surmount; exceed

看破する *kanpa suru* see through, penetrate, read (another's thoughts)

破牢 *harō* jailbreak

破獄 *hagoku* jailbreak

❷ **break the enemy, defeat**

撃破する *gekiha suru* defeat, rout; destroy

論破する *ronpa suru* refute, defeat in argument

連破する *renpa suru* defeat one's enemy in succession

❸ⓐ (act contrary to) **break** (**as a promise**), **breach, violate**

ⓑ break with (the moral conventions), be exceptional

破棄 *haki* breaking (a treaty), annulment

破談 *hadan* cancellation, breaking off
破約 *hayaku* breach of contract
破格の *hakaku no* exceptional, unconventional; irregular, contrary to usage
破廉恥 *harenchi* shamelessness, infamy, impudence
破門 *hamon* excommunication, expulsion
❹ **break down, go to pieces, go broke**
破局 *hakyoku* collapse, catastrophe
破綻 *hatan* failure, rupture; bankruptcy
破産する *hasan suru* go bankrupt, go broke
❺ **carry through with, perform an action to the end**
読破する *dokuha suru* read through
走破する *sōha suru* run [cover] the whole distance
描破する *byōha suru* depict thoroughly
❻ second part of a traditional Japanese performance
序破急 *johakyū* artistic modulations in traditional Japanese performances; opening, middle and climax [end]

INDEPENDENT

【ha 破】 second part of a traditional Japanese performance

KUN

【yabu(ru) 破る】
①ⓐ break, smash, destroy
ⓑ tear, rip
戸を破る *to o yaburu* break a door
紙を破る *kami o yaburu* tear (up) paper
② (force one's way) break through, penetrate, break out (of jail)
囲みを破る *kakomi o yaburu* break through a siege
見破る *miyaburu* see through, penetrate, read (another's thoughts)
金庫破り *kinkoyaburi* safecracking; safecracker
③ break the enemy, defeat
敵を破る *teki o yaburu* defeat one's enemy
④ (surpass) break (a record)
記録を破る *kiroku o yaburu* break the record
⑤ⓐ (act contrary to) break (a promise), breach, violate
ⓑ break with (the moral conventions), be exceptional
規則を破る *kisoku o yaburu* violate the rules
型破りの *katayaburi no* extraordinary, uncommon
⑥ baffle, thwart, frustrate
スト破り *sutoyaburi* strikebreaker, scab; strikebreaking

【yabu(reru) 破れる】
① tear, be torn, rip open
破れ目 *yabureme* rent, tear, split
② be ruined
国破れて *kuni yaburete* with one's country in ruins
③ be baffled, be frustrated
破れた夢 *yabureta yume* shattered dream

SYNONYMS

❶ⓐ **break**
壊 BREAK DOWN → 756
折 BREAK OFF → 253
割る crack → 1816
裂 SPLIT → 2687
砕 CRUSH UP → 1134
崩 CRUMBLE → 2296
ⓑ **penetrate**
貫 PENETRATE → 2460
透 PASS THROUGH → 3108
❷ **win**
勝 WIN → 1005
克 OVERCOME → 2046
征 CONQUER → 293
❸ⓐ **violate**
違 VIOLATE → 3151
犯 offend against → 196
反 act contrary to → 2945
背 go against → 2573
❹ **degenerate**
堕 DEGENERATE → 2822
衰 DECLINE → 2100
落 FALL → 2318
❺ **accomplish**
達 ATTAIN → 3139
遂 ACCOMPLISH → 3138
成 ACHIEVE → 3537
徹 GO THROUGH → 726

USAGE

yabureru
破れる
① tear, be torn, rip open
② be ruined
③ be baffled, be frustrated
敗れる
be defeated, be beaten, lose

HOMOPHONES

yabureru ⇨ 敗 1476

砲 砲 砲 砲 ㊥ 炮 pào

1151 HŌ

一 丆 𠂇 石 石 石' 矿 矽 砲 砲
1 2 3 4 5 6 7 8 9 10

Radical	Strokes
石 112	10-5-5
Grade	**Freq**
Jōyō	1142
1 - 5 - 5	

5-5 石

▶HEAVY GUN

COMPOUNDS

❶ [rarely also 炮 906]
ⓐ [also suffix] **heavy gun, gun, artillery, ordnance**
ⓑ **cannon**
砲火 *hōka* gunfire
砲声 *hōsei* sound of firing, roar of cannon
砲術 *hōjutsu* gunnery, artillery
祝砲 *shukuhō* feu de joie, artillery [gun] salute
鉄砲 *teppō* gun, firearm
銃砲 *jūhō* firearm
重砲 *jūhō* heavy gun
発砲する *happō suru* fire, discharge (a gun)
対戦車砲 *taisenshahō* antitank gun
砲丸 *hōgan* cannon ball
大砲 *taihō* gun, cannon, artillery
❷ suffix after names of main batters
ON砲 *ō-enu-hō* Oh and Nagashima (famous baseball stars)
❸ [original meaning, now obsolete] catapult

INDEPENDENT

【**hō 砲**】 cannon; artillery, guns

SYNONYMS

❶ **weapons for shooting**
銃 GUN (portable firearm) → 1723
火 firearms → 3463
弓 BOW → 3383

砲 1152 **▶HEAVY GUN** nonstandard for 砲 1151 — 5-5 石

祕 1153 **▶SECRET** nonstandard for 秘 1159 — 5-5 示

神 1154 **▶GOD ▶MIND** nonstandard for 神 912 — 5-5 示

祝 1155 **▶CELEBRATE** nonstandard for 祝 913 — 5-5 示

祖 1156 **▶ANCESTOR** nonstandard for 祖 914 — 5-5 示

祐 1157 **▶DIVINE HELP** nonstandard for 祐 915 — 5-5 示

5-5 禾

秩 秩 秩

1158 CHITSU

CH 秩 zhì

Radical	Strokes
禾 115	10-5-5
Grade	Freq
Jōyō	1327
1-5-5	

丿 二 千 禾 禾 禾 秆 秆 秩 秩
1 2 3 4 5 6 7 8 9 10

▶ **ORDER**

COMPOUNDS

❶ **order, methodical arrangement**

秩序 *chitsujo* order, discipline; method, system

❷ [rare] fief, retainer's stipend, salary

秩禄 *chitsuroku* official salary

SYNONYMS

❶ **order**

序 ORDER (sequence／arrangement) → 3065

順 ORDER (sequence) → 18

次 order (sequence) → 54

番 NUMERICAL ORDER → 2748

5-5 禾

秘 祕 秘 秘

1159 HI hi(meru)

CH 秘 mì bì

Radical	Strokes
禾 115	10-5-5
Grade	Freq
Jōyō-6	1022
1-5-5	

丿 二 千 禾 禾 禾 秒 秘 秘 秘
1 2 3 4 5 6 7 8 9 10

▶ **SECRET**

COMPOUNDS

❶ⓐ [original meaning] (without the knowledge of others) **secret, private, clandestine, hidden**

ⓑ (something kept secret) **secret, secrecy**

ⓒ [original meaning] (beyond human understanding) secret, mysterious, abstruse

秘密 *himitsu* secret, mystery; privacy

秘術 *hijutsu* secret (art); the best of one's skill

秘訣 *hiketsu* secret, key

秘伝 *hiden* secret, mystery

秘宝 *hihō* (hidden) treasure

秘書 *hisho* secretary; treasured book

黙秘する *mokuhi suru* keep silent, keep secret

極秘 *gokuhi* strict secrecy, top secret

部外秘の *bugaihi no* restricted

神秘 *shinpi* mystery

❷ constipated

秘結 *hiketsu* constipation, costiveness

便秘 *benpi* constipation

INDEPENDENT

【hi 秘】 secret

秘中の秘 *hichū no hi* top secret, secret of secrets

【hisuru 秘する】 keep secret, conceal, hide

KUN

【hi(meru) 秘める】 keep secret, conceal, hide

秘め事 *himegoto* secret

心に秘める *kokoro ni himeru* keep to oneself

SYNONYMS

❶ⓐ & ❶ⓑ secret and private

密 SECRET → 2292

暗 in the dark → 1010

私 PRIVATE → 1115

内 not public → 3466

隠 hidden from view → 713

NOTE

⇨ see COMPOUND FORMATION for 秘書 *hisho* ⇨ 書 2658

称 稱 称 称 Ⓒⓗ 称 chēng chèn chèng

1160 SHŌ tata(eru)▲

Radical	Strokes
禾 115	10-5-5
Grade	**Freq**
Jōyō	1090
1 - 5 - 5	

5-5 禾

▶**APPELLATION**

COMPOUNDS

❶ⓐ **appellation, name, title**

ⓑ **name, call, designate, entitle**

称号 *shōgō* title, degree
名称 *meishō* appellation, name, title
通称 *tsūshō* popular [common] name
俗称 *zokushō* popular [common] name
愛称 *aishō* nickname, pet name
総称 *sōshō* generic name, general term
呼称する *koshō suru* call, name
誇称する *koshō suru* boast, exaggerate
自称する *jishō suru* profess oneself (to be someone), call [style] oneself

❷ acclaim, commend, praise, admire

称賛(＝賞賛) *shōsan* laudation, praise, admiration, commendation
称揚 *shōyō* praise, admiration, exaltation

❸ symmetrical, matching

対称 *taishō* symmetry

❹ *gram* person

一人称 *ichininshō* first person
他称 *tashō* third person

INDEPENDENT

【**shō 称**】name, title, designation; fame
【**shōsuru 称する**】name, designate; pretend, claim; acclaim, praise
病と称する *yamai to shōsuru* feign illness, pretend to be ill

KUN

【**tata(eru) 称える**】praise, extol
誉め称える *hometataeru* admire, applaud, praise

SYNONYMS

❶ⓐ **name**

名 NAME → 2169
号 DESIGNATION → 2153
題 TITLE → 3337
姓 SURNAME → 279
氏 FAMILY NAME → 2951
銘 name (inscribed by maker) → 1724

ⓑ **name**

呼 CALL → 273
言う call → 1941

❷ **praise**

彰 PROCLAIM MERITS → 1860
賞 express admiration → 2618
揚 EXALT → 593
頌 EULOGIZE → 1045
賛 PRAISE → 2809
美 regard as beautiful → 2264
褒 COMMEND → 2144
嘉 commend (esp. an inferior) → 2340

租 租 租 Ⓒⓗ 租 zū

1161 SO

Radical	Strokes
禾 115	10-5-5
Grade	**Freq**
Jōyō	1701
1 - 5 - 5	

5-5 禾

▶**LAND TAX**

COMPOUNDS

❶ **land tax, crop tax, taxes**

租税 *sozei* taxes, taxation
租庸調 *soyōchō* taxes in kind or service (former tax system), corvée
田租 *denso* rice field tax
地租 *chiso* land tax
免租 *menso* tax exemption
貢租 *kōso* tribute, annual tax

❷ rent, lease (land or a house)

租借する *soshaku suru* lease
租界 *sokai* concession, settlement

SYNONYMS

❶ **tax**

税 TAX → 1191
貢 TRIBUTE → 2281
賦 levy → 1583

5-5 立 **竝** ▶**LINE UP**
nonstandard for 並 2246
1162

5-5 ネ **被** 被 被 Ⓒ 被 bèi
1163 HI kōmu(ru) ō(u)▲ kabu(ru)▲ kabu(seru)▲

Radical	Strokes
ネ 145	10-5-5
Grade	**Freq**
Jōyō	782

1 - 5 - 5

▶**BE SUBJECTED TO**

COMPOUNDS

❶ⓐ **be subjected to, undergo, suffer**
ⓑ **auxiliary verb for forming the passive voice similar to the English *be***
被害 *higai* damage, harm
被弾 *hidan* being bombed
被災 *hisai* suffering, affection
被傭者(=被用者) *hiyōsha* employee
被爆者 *hibakusha* victim of atomic air raid
被告人 *hikokunin* defendant
被保険者 *hihokensha* insured person
被選挙権 *hisenkyoken* eligibility for election
❷ⓐ **cover, envelope; wear**
ⓑ cover(ing), clothing
被覆 *hifuku* covering, coating
被膜 *himaku* tunic, capsule
被服 *hifuku* clothing
外被 *gaihi* outer cover
法被 *happi* (workman's) livery coat
花被 *kahi* perianth, floral envelope

KUN

【kōmu(ru) 被る】[also 蒙る] be subjected to, undergo, receive, sustain
損害を被る *songai o kōmuru* suffer a loss
恩恵を被る *onkei o kōmuru* share in the benefit
【ō(u) 被う】[usu. 覆う] cover, veil
被い *ōi* cover, mantle
雪で被われる *yuki de ōwareru* be covered with snow
【kabu(ru) 被る】 put on headgear, wear; pour (as water) on oneself, be covered with; take upon oneself; *photography* be fogged
猫被り *nekokaburi* hypocrisy, false modesty; hypocrite, wolf in a lamb's skin
引っ被る *hikkaburu* pull (a thing) over one's head
泥を被る *doro o kaburu* be covered with mud; take another's fault upon oneself
【kabu(seru) 被せる】 cover, put (a thing) on, plate (a thing) with, pour, dash (water) on; pin (a crime) on, frame
土を被せる *tsuchi o kabuseru* cover with earth
歯に金を被せる *ha ni kin o kabuseru* crown a tooth with gold
押っ被せる *okkabuseru* put a thing on top of another

SYNONYMS

❶ⓐ **be subjected to**
受 be subjected to → 2421
❷ⓐ **cover and wrap**
覆 COVER → 2726
包 WRAP → 2966
【kaburu】
○ **wear and put on**
履く put on footwear → 3171
着 PUT ON → 3316
装 DRESS → 2685
帯 WEAR (esp. at the belt) → 2582

USAGE

kōmuru
被る
[also 蒙る] be subjected to, undergo, receive, sustain
蒙る
[also 被る] same as 被る

HOMOPHONES

kōmuru ⇨ 蒙 2505
ōu ⇨ 覆 2726 蓋 2503 掩 489 蔽 2523

NOTE

⇨ see also USAGE note at 覆 2726

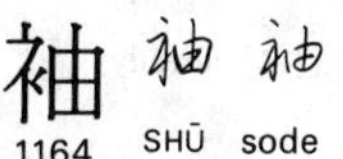

1164 SHŪ sode

CH 袖 xiù

Radical	Strokes
礻 145	10-5-5
Grade	**Freq**
Non-Jōyō	1787
◧ 1 - 5 - 5	

5-5 礻

1 2 3 4 5 6 7 8 9 10

▶**SLEEVE**

COMPOUNDS

● [original meaning] **sleeve**

袖手傍観する *shūshu-bōkan suru* look on with folded arms [with one's hands in one's sleeves], remain a passive onlooker

袖珍本 *shūchinbon* pocket-size book

領袖 *ryōshū* leader, chief

KUN

【**sode** 袖】[also suffix] sleeve; wing (as of a building)

袖口 *sodeguchi* edge of a sleeve; cuff, sleeve band, wristband

長袖の *nagasode no* long-sleeved

七分袖 *shichibusode* three-quarter sleeves

元禄袖 *genrokusode* short and round sleeves of a kimono

舞台の左右の袖 *butai no sayū no sode* wings of a stage

片袖机 *katasodezukue* desk with a wing

SYNONYMS

● **garment parts**

襟 COLLAR → 1252

懐 BOSOM → 763

COMPOUND FORMATION

領袖 *ryōshū*

領袖 'leader, chief' refers to the collar (領) and sleeve (袖), which are the most prominent parts of one's garment.

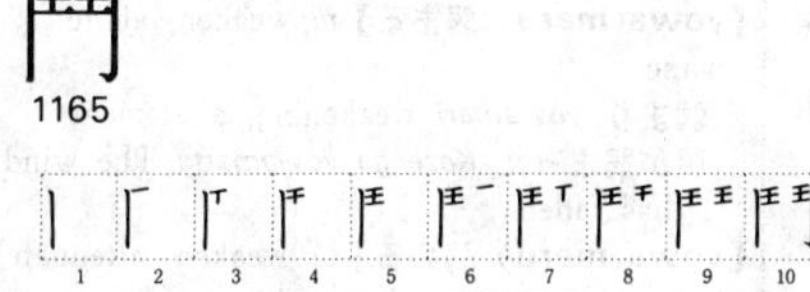

1165

Radical	Strokes
鬥 191	10-10-0
Grade	**Freq**
Radical	
◧ 1 - 5 - 5	

5-5 鬥

1 2 3 4 5 6 7 8 9 10

RADICAL 191

Standard form: 鬥 *tōgamae* 'fight' (鬨 鬪 鬧)

Description: used in characters related to fighting

既 既 既 既

1166 KI sude(ni)

CH 既 jì

Radical	Strokes
无 71	10-5-5
Grade	**Freq**
Jōyō	1329
◧ 1 - 5 - 5	

5-5 艮

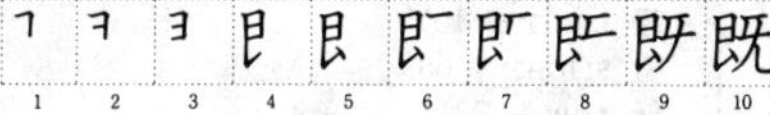

1 2 3 4 5 6 7 8 9 10

▶**ALREADY**

COMPOUNDS

❶ [also prefix] **already, previous**

既刊の *kikan no* already published

既婚の *kikon no* already married

既存の *kison no* existing

既定の *kitei no* fixed, prearranged

既往症 *kiōshō* previous illness, medical history

既知数 *kichisū* known quantity

既報 *kihō* previous report

既製品 *kiseihin* ready-made goods

既発表の *kihappyō no* already published

❷ finish

皆既日食 *kaiki-nisshoku* total lunar eclipse

KUN

【**sude(ni)** 既に】

①ⓐ [formerly also 已に] already

ⓑ previously

彼は既に出発していた *Kare wa sudeni shuppatsu shite ita* He had already started

既に申した様に *sudeni mōshita yō ni* as I have previously stated

② itself, in itself

その事が既に *sono koto ga sudeni* the fact itself, the very fact

SYNONYMS

❶ **former**

先 former → 2394
前 previous → 2266
旧 FORMER → 14
元 former → 1929
故 OLD (earlier time) → 1141

USAGE

sudeni

既に
①ⓐ [formerly also 已に] already
ⓑ previously
② itself, in itself

已に
[now usu. 既に] already

HOMOPHONES

sudeni ⇨ 已 3377

5-5
弓

弱 弱 弱 弱

1167 JAKU yowa(i) yowa(ru) yowa(maru) yowa(meru)

CH 弱 ruò

Radical	Strokes
弓 57	10-3-7
Grade	**Freq**
Jōyō-2	769
1-5-5	

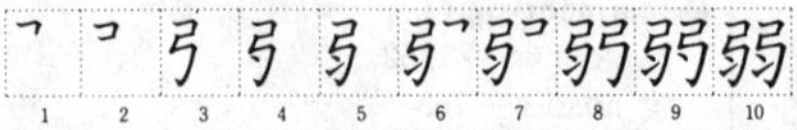

▶**WEAK**

COMPOUNDS

❶ⓐ [also prefix] [original meaning] (lacking strength) **weak, feeble**
ⓑ [also prefix] (lacking force) **weak**
ⓒ weaken

弱点 *jakuten* weak point
弱肉強食 *jakunikukyōshoku* law of the jungle (the strong prey on the weak)
虚弱な *kyojaku na* weak, feeble, sickly
弱震 *jakushin* weak earthquake, minor tremor
弱毒 *jakudoku* weak poison
弱電器 *jakudenki* light electrical appliance
弱酸性 *jakusansei* slight acidity
衰弱する *suijaku suru* weaken, lose vigor

❷ [also 若 2241] young

弱年 *jakunen* youth, early age
弱冠 *jakkan* 20 years old; youth

❸ [suffix] a little less than

一マイル弱 *ichimairujaku* a little less than a mile

INDEPENDENT

【**jaku** 弱】 weakness, feebleness; the weak

弱を以て強に当たる *jaku o motte kyō ni ataru* attacking strength by means of [with] weakness

KUN

【**yowa(i)** 弱い】 weak, feeble; fragile, frail, invalid; (lacking competence) weak, poor, unskilled

弱さ *yowasa* weakness
弱火 *yowabi* low fire, gentle heating
弱味 *yowami* weak point, sore spot
ひ弱な *hiyowa na* weak, delicate, sickly
数字に弱い *sūji ni yowai* not good with figures

【**yowa(ru)** 弱る】 *vi* weaken, wane; be debilitated [emaciated]; be embarrassed, be in a fix

弱り果てる *yowarihateru* be worn out; be helpless
大弱りの *ōyowari no* very much annoyed

【**yowa(maru)** 弱まる】 *vi* weaken, abate, wane

弱まり *yowamari* weakening, abatement
風が弱まった *Kaze ga yowamatta* The wind has fallen

【**yowa(meru)** 弱める】 *vt* weaken, attenuate, lower, soften, tone down, dilute

ガスを弱める *gasu o yowameru* turn down the gas
語気を弱める *goki o yowameru* soften one's voice

SYNONYMS

❶ⓐ **weak**

柔 SOFT → 2088

ⓑ **less in degree**

軽 LIGHT → 1515
微 SLIGHT → 639
低 LOW → 73
薄 THIN → 2370
浅 SHALLOW → 389

ⓒ **weaken**

衰 DECLINE → 2100

❷ **young**

若 YOUNG → 2241
少 young → 3467
青 youthful → 2430
幼 VERY YOUNG → 191
稚 CHILDISH → 1206

弱 1168

▶WEAK
nonstandard for 弱 1167

5-5 弓

略 1169

略 畧◇ 略 略 ㊥ 略 lüè

RYAKU

Radical	Strokes
田 102	11-5-6
Grade	**Freq**
Jōyō-5	868
◧ 1-5-6	

5-6 田

丨 冂 冊 田 田 田 町 畋 略 略 略
1 2 3 4 5 6 7 8 9 10 11

▶ABRIDGED ▶STRATEGY

COMPOUNDS

❶ⓐ **abridged, brief, concise**
ⓑ essentials, gist
略語 *ryakugo* abbreviation
略字 *ryakuji* simplified character; abbreviation
略文 *ryakubun* abridged sentence
略歴 *ryakureki* brief personal history
簡略な *kanryaku na* simple, brief, concise; informal
要略 *yōryaku* epitome, summary, outline
概略 *gairyaku* outline, summary; roughly, approximately

❷ⓐ **omit, leave out**
ⓑ informal
省略する *shōryaku suru* omit, abbreviate, abridge
中略 *chūryaku* ellipsis, omission (of interior parts)
略式の *ryakushiki no* informal, summary
略服 *ryakufuku* informal clothes [dress]

❸ **strategy, plan, tactics, scheme, stratagem**
計略 *keiryaku* stratagem, plan, scheme
戦略 *senryaku* strategy, stratagem
政略 *seiryaku* political tactics [maneuver], politicking
策略 *sakuryaku* artifice, stratagem, scheme
謀略 *bōryaku* stratagem, scheme, plot
党略 *tōryaku* party politics [tactics]

❹ [formerly also 掠 498] plunder, pillage
略奪 *ryakudatsu* pillage, plunder, looting
略取 *ryakushu* capture, occupation, plunder
侵略する *shinryaku suru* invade, aggress (against)
攻略 *kōryaku* capture, conquest; invasion

❺ supervise, plan
経略する *keiryaku suru* administer, rule

INDEPENDENT

【ryaku 略】 abbreviation, abridgment; omission; outline, summary
EはEASTの略である *ī wa īsuto no ryaku de aru* "E" is an abbreviation of "East"

【ryakusu 略す】 abbreviate, shorten; omit, leave out
略して *ryakushite* for short

SYNONYMS

❶ⓐ **short and shortened**
簡 simplified → 2721
短 SHORT → 1182

❷ⓐ **abridge**
約 CONTRACT → 1280
抄 EXCERPT → 254
要 SUMMARIZE → 2635

❸ **plans and planning**
策 SCHEME → 2679
謀 SCHEME → 1593
計 PLAN → 1441
画 DRAW UP A PLAN → 3000
案 PROPOSAL → 2270
企 PROJECT → 2021
図 systematic plan → 3071

❹ **steal and rob**
奪 ROB → 2343
取 TAKE → 1262
盗 STEAL → 2670
窃 STEAL → 2253

5-6 目

眸

1170 BŌ hitomi

Ⓒ 眸 móu

Radical	Strokes
目 109	11-5-6
Grade	**Freq**
Names	2112
1-5-6	

1 2 3 4 5 6 7 8 9 10 11

▶**EYE**

COMPOUNDS

ⓐ [original meaning] **eye, eyes**

ⓑ **pupil (of the eye)**

眸子 *bōshi* eye; pupil

双眸 *sōbō* both eyes

明眸 *meibō* bright eyes, beautiful eyes

一眸(＝一望) *ichibō* sweep of the eye

KUN

【hitomi 眸】

[usu. 瞳]

ⓐ pupil, the apple of one's eye

ⓑ one's eyes

黒い眸 *kuroi hitomi* (beautiful) dark eyes

NAMES

眸 *hitomi* male name also female name

SYNONYMS

● **eye**

眼 EYE → 1172

目 EYE → 3043

瞳 PUPIL → 1237

HOMOPHONES

hitomi ⇨ 瞳 1237

NOTE

⇨ see USAGE note at 瞳 1237

5-6 目

眺

1171 CHŌ naga(meru)

Ⓒ 眺 tiào

Radical	Strokes
目 109	11-5-6
Grade	**Freq**
Jōyō	1802
1-5-6	

1 2 3 4 5 6 7 8 9 10 11

▶**LOOK OUT OVER**

COMPOUNDS

● [original meaning] **look out over, look far and wide, look afar, gaze**

眺望 *chōbō* view, prospect, outlook

KUN

【naga(meru) 眺める】 look out over, look afar, gaze, look at, watch

眺め *nagame* view, scene; prospect, outlook

海を眺める *umi o nagameru* look out over the sea

月を眺める *tsuki o nagameru* gaze at the moon

SYNONYMS

● **see and look**

望 LOOK AFAR → 2742

覧 LOOK OVER → 2854

仰 LOOK UP → 48

顧 LOOK BACK → 1900

観 VIEW → 1880

視 REGARD → 972

看 WATCH → 3220

見 SEE → 2544

目 look → 3043

察 INSPECT → 2347

5-6 目

眼

1172 GAN GEN manako me▲

Ⓒ 眼 yǎn

Radical	Strokes
目 109	11-5-6
Grade	**Freq**
Jōyō-5	1149
1-5-6	

1 2 3 4 5 6 7 8 9 10 11

▶**EYE**

COMPOUNDS

❶ⓐ [original meaning] **eye**

ⓑ (small hole) eye, eyelet, loop

眼球 *gankyū* eyeball

眼科 *ganka* ophthalmology

碧眼 *hekigan* blue eyes
近眼 *kingan* nearsightedness
双眼鏡 *sōgankyō* binoculars
開眼 *kaigen* opening one's eyes to the truth, enlightenment
銃眼 *jūgan* loophole, eyelet
❷ what one sees, field of vision
眼界 *gankai* field of vision, sight
着眼する *chakugan suru* notice, aim at, have an eye to
❸ [also suffix] (power of discrimination) **eye, discernment, insight**
眼力 *ganriki* insight, power of observation
眼識 *ganshiki* insight, discrimination
審美眼 *shinbigan* an eye for the beautiful, aesthetic sense
❹ key point, gist
眼目 *ganmoku* main object [point], gist, essence
主眼 *shugan* prime object, central aim, gist
❺ [formerly 嵌 *gan* 2313] inlay, set in
象眼 *zōgan* inlaid work, inlaying

INDEPENDENT

【gan 眼】 eye
眼を付ける *gan o tsukeru* fasten one's eye on (a person)

KUN

【manako 眼】 eye
寝惚け眼 *nebokemanako* sleepy eyes; drowsy look
団栗眼 *dongurimanako* goggle eyes, round eyes

【me 眼】 [usu. 目] eye
眼鏡 *megane* (=*gankyō*) glasses, spectacles; judgment, insight

SYNONYMS

❶ **eye**
目 EYE → 3043
眸 EYE → 1170
瞳 PUPIL → 1237
❸ **discernment**
識 power of discrimination → 1639

HOMOPHONES

me ⇨ 目 3043 芽 2240

NOTE

⇨ see USAGE note at 目 3043

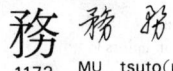

務 務 務

1173 MU tsuto(meru)

Ⓒⓗ 务 wù

Radical	Strokes
力 19	11-2-9
Grade	Freq
Jōyō-5	132

1-5-6

5-6 矛

▶DUTY

COMPOUNDS

❶ (task required by one's occupation) **duty, task, office, function**
任務 *ninmu* duty, part, function; mission
勤務 *kinmu* duty, service, work
職務 *shokumu* duty, duties, function
業務 *gyōmu* business, affairs, work, service
❷ (moral or legal obligations) duty, responsibility, obligation
義務 *gimu* duty, obligation
責務 *sekimu* responsibility and obligation, responsibility to do one's duty
債務 *saimu* debt, obligation, liabilities
❸ **affairs, business**
国務 *kokumu* duties of state, national affairs
外務 *gaimu* foreign affairs
事務 *jimu* business, clerical work, duties of an office
総務 *sōmu* general affairs; manager, director
公務 *kōmu* public service, official affairs
専務 *senmu* managing [executive] director
法務 *hōmu* judicial affairs; clerical duty

KUN

【tsuto(meru) 務める】
ⓐ discharge [perform] one's duties
ⓑ play [act, perform] (a part or role)
務め *tsutome* duty, task, responsibility
議長を務める *gichō o tsutomeru* act as chairman

SYNONYMS

❶ **work and employment**
任 OFFICE → 53
役 SERVICE (esp. public) → 244
勤 SERVICE (employment) → 1818
業 WORK → 2612
職 EMPLOYMENT → 1425
労 LABOR → 2548
❷ **responsibility**
任 duty → 53
責 RESPONSIBILITY → 2467
分 one's part → 1972
❸ **affairs**
事 affairs → 3567
用 THINGS TO DO → 2976

HOMOPHONES

tsutomeru ⇨ 勤 1818 努 2547 勉 3318

tsutome ⇨ 勤 1818

NOTE
⇨ see USAGE note at 勤 1818

5-6 石 研 1174 ▶GRIND ▶RESEARCH
nonstandard for 研 1132

5-6 石 硫 1175 ▶SULFUR
nonstandard for 硫 1184

5-6 示 祥 1176 ▶AUSPICIOUS
nonstandard for 祥 948

5-6 禾 移 1177 I utsu(ru) utsu(su)

CH 移 yí

Radical	Strokes
禾 115	11-5-6
Grade	**Freq**
Jōyō-5	629
1-5-6	

▶SHIFT

COMPOUNDS

ⓐ (change in position, time or state) **shift, move, change**

ⓑ **cause to shift, transfer, remove, move**

移行する *ikō suru* shift [switch] over
移動する *idō suru* move, shift, transfer
移転 *iten* transfer, removal; change of address
移植 *ishoku* transplanting
推移 *suii* transition, change
移住 *ijū* migration, immigration; move
移籍 *iseki* transfer of one's name in the register

KUN

【utsu(ru) 移る】

vi

① move (to a new house)
移り *utsuri* change, transition; return present
東京に移る *tōkyō ni utsuru* move to Tokyo

② shift, change, pass
移り変わり *utsurikawari* change, transition

③ be infected with; be contagious
燃え移る *moeutsuru* (of fire) spread, extend itself
下痢が移った *geri ga utsutta* be infected with diarrhea

④ (of odors) soak in
移り香 *utsuriga* lingering [absorbed] scent

【utsu(su) 移す】

vt

①ⓐ shift, move, transfer
ⓑ transfuse (liquids or colors)
ⓒ divert, turn, direct
移し替える *utsushikaeru* shift [move] (an object) to [into]
都会に移す *tokai ni utsusu* move (an object or person) to the city
口移し *kuchiutsushi* mouth-to-mouth feeding; conveying by word of mouth
計画を実行に移す *keikaku o jikkō ni utsusu* carry a plan into practice

② transmit (a disease)
風邪を移す *kaze o utsusu* give [transmit] a cold (to someone)

SYNONYMS

● **move**
転 remove → 1480
遷 TRANSFER → 3170
動 MOVE → 1778
運 MOVE → 3140
滑 SLIDE → 658
繰る SHIFT ONWARD → 1427

HOMOPHONES

utsuru ⇨ 写 2000 映 892
utsuri ⇨ 映 892 写 2000
utsusu ⇨ 写 2000 映 892

NOTE
⇨ see USAGE notes at 写 2000 and 映 892

疎 疎 疎

1178 SO uto(i) uto(mu) maba(ra)▲

Ⓒⓗ 疏 shū

Radical	Strokes
疋 103	12-5-7
Grade	**Freq**
Jōyō	1683
◧ 1-5-7	

5-7 疋

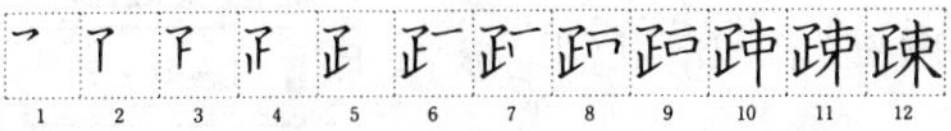

▶SPARSE ▶ESTRANGE

COMPOUNDS

❶ **sparse, thin, scattered, sporadic**
疎開 *sokai* dispersal, evacuation
疎密 *somitsu* sparseness and luxuriant growth
疎林 *sorin* sparse woods
過疎 *kaso* depopulation
空疎な *kūso na* empty, unsubstantial

❷ⓐ **estrange, alienate, neglect**
ⓑ **estranged, alienated, distant**
疎外 *sogai* estrangement, alienation
疎隔 *sokaku* estrangement, alienation
疎水性の *sosuisei no* hydrophobic
疎遠 *soen* estrangement, alienation, neglect

❸ negligent, careless
疎漏 *sorō* carelessness, inadvertence, oversight

❹ [formerly also 疏 1179]
ⓐ pass, let pass
ⓑ (cause water to pass) clear, dredge (a watercourse)
疎通 *sotsū* mutual understanding
疎水 *sosui* canal

❺ [formerly also 疏 1179] commentary on earlier commentary, sub-commentary, annotation
注疎 *chūso* detailed commentary

INDEPENDENT

【so 疎】 sparseness; estrangement
人口が疎である *jinkō ga so de aru* be sparsely populated

KUN

【uto(i) 疎い】 estranged, distant; ignorant of
去る者は日日に疎し *Saru mono wa hibi ni utoshi* Out of sight, out of mind
世事に疎い *seji ni utoi* know but little of the world

【uto(mu) 疎む】 neglect, shun, estrange, alienate
疎ましい *utomashii* disagreeable, offensive
疎んじる *utonjiru* neglect, shun, alienate
友達に疎んじられる *tomodachi ni utonjirareru* be treated distantly by one's friends

【maba(ra) 疎ら】
mabara na 疎らな sparse, thin, scattered, sporadic

SYNONYMS

❶ **rare and sparse**
粗 COARSE → 1329
薄い THIN → 2370
希 RARE → 2049

❷ **estrange**
離 separate from → 1836
遠 DISTANT → 3150

疏

1179 SO

Ⓒⓗ 疏 shū

Radical	Strokes
疋 103	12-5-7
Grade	**Freq**
Reference	
◧ 1-5-7	

5-7 疋

COMPOUNDS

❶ [now replaced by 疎 1178]
ⓐ pass, let pass
ⓑ (cause water to pass) clear, dredge (a watercourse)
意志の疏通 *ishi no sotsū* mutual understanding
疏水 *sosui* canal

❷ [now usu. 疎 1178] commentary on earlier commentary, sub-commentary, annotation
注疏 *chūso* detailed commentary

5-7 白

皓 皓 皓 皓

1180 KŌ NAMES akira teru aki hiro hiroshi

CH 皓 hào

Radical	Strokes
白 106	12-5-7
Grade	**Freq**
Names	2115
1-5-7	

1 2 3 4 5 6 7 8 9 10 11 12

▶**BRIGHT WHITE**

COMPOUNDS

● [original meaning] **bright white, sparkling white, beautifully white, pure white**

皓月 *kōgetsu* [archaic] bright white moon

皓礬 *kōban* white vitriol, zinc sulfate heptahydrate

明眸皓歯 *meibōkōshi* starry eyes and beautiful white teeth (said of beautiful women)

NAMES

皓一 *kōichi* male name

皓 *akira* male name

皓子 *teruko* female name

SYNONYMS

● **white colors**

白 WHITE → 3493

銀 SILVER → 1722

5-7 白

皓

1181

▶**BRIGHT WHITE**

nonstandard for 皓 1180

5-7 矢

短 短 短

1182 TAN mijika(i)

CH 短 duǎn

Radical	Strokes
矢 111	12-5-7
Grade	**Freq**
Jōyō-3	760
1-5-7	

1 2 3 4 5 6 7 8 9 10 11 12

▶**SHORT**

COMPOUNDS

❶ⓐ [also prefix] [original meaning] (not long) **short**

ⓑ (of short duration) **short, brief**

ⓒ shorten

短波 *tanpa* shortwave

短気 *tanki* short [hot] temper

短歌 *tanka* tanka, Japanese verse

短期大学 *tanki daigaku* junior college

短期間 *tankikan* short term, short time

短縮 *tanshuku* shortening, contraction, reduction

❷ shortcoming, defect

短所 *tansho* shortcoming, defect

一長一短 *itchō ittan* merits and demerits, strong and weak points

❸ abbrev. of 短期大学 *tanki daigaku*: junior college

栄養短 *eiyōtan* Junior College of Nutrition

❹ *music* minor

短調 *tanchō* minor key

ハ短調 *hatanchō* C minor

INDEPENDENT

【tan 短】 shortcoming, defect

短を補う *tan o oginau* remedy one's defects

KUN

【mijika(i) 短い】 short, brief

短過ぎる *mijikasugiru* too short

手短に *temijika ni* shortly, briefly

SYNONYMS

❶ⓐ **short and shortened**

簡 simplified → 2721

略 ABRIDGED → 1169

❷ **faults and flaws**

難 fault → 1838

陥 defect → 457

欠 incompleteness → 1987

NOTE

★do not confuse with 矩 1148

硬 硬 硬 硬

1183 KŌ kata(i)

Ⓒⓗ 硬 yìng

Radical	Strokes
石 112	12-5-7
Grade	**Freq**
Jōyō	1112
◧ 1 - 5 - 7	

5-7 石

一 ㄏ 不 石 石 石一 石厂 石冂 石再 石百 硬 硬 (1–12)

▶HARD

COMPOUNDS

❶ [original meaning] **hard, firm, tough, solid**
硬度 *kōdo* hardness
硬化する *kōka suru* harden, stiffen
硬貨 *kōka* coin, metallic currency
硬式 *kōshiki* hardball (baseball)
硬直 *kōchoku* stiffness, rigidity
硬骨 *kōkotsu* hard bone; firmness

❷ [formerly also 鞕 1878] **hard-line, stiff, unyielding, obdurate**
硬派 *kōha* hard-line elements, stalwart
硬軟両派 *kōnan-ryōha* stalwart and insurgent factions
強硬な *kyōkō na* firm (attitude), unbending; drastic (measure)

❸ immature, unrefined
生硬な *seikō na* crude, immature, unpolished

INDEPENDENT

【kō 硬】 hard
硬の芯 *kō no shin* hard pencil lead

KUN

【kata(i) 硬い】
① (resisting pressure) hard, tough, strong (esp. metals or stone)
硬さ *katasa* hardness
硬い石 *katai ishi* hard stone
②ⓐ stiff (style), uninteresting
ⓑ stiff (facial expression)
硬い文章 *katai bunshō* stiff style
硬い表情 *katai hyōjō* stiff expression

SYNONYMS

❶ **hard**
堅 FIRM → 2823
固 SOLID → 3086
剛 TOUGH → 1673
強 STRONG → 475

❷ **firm and obstinate**
頑 STUBBORN → 1040
剛 TOUGH → 1673
毅 RESOLUTE → 1866
堅 FIRM → 2823
固 FIRM, stiff → 3086
確 firm → 1228

HOMOPHONES

katai ⇨ 堅 2823 固 3086 難 1838

NOTE

⇨ see USAGE note at 固 3086

硫 硫 硫 硫

1184 RYŪ

Ⓒⓗ 硫 liú

Radical	Strokes
石 112	12-5-7
Grade	**Freq**
Jōyō	1437
◧ 1 - 5 - 7	

5-7 石

一 ㄏ 不 石 石 石' 石亠 石㐬 石㐬 石㐬 硫 硫 (1–12)

▶SULFUR

COMPOUNDS

● [original meaning] **sulfur**
硫酸 *ryūsan* sulfuric acid
硫安 *ryūan* ammonium sulfate
硫化する *ryūka suru* sulfurize
加硫 *karyū* vulcanization
脱硫 *datsuryū* desulfurization

SPECIAL READINGS

硫黄 *iō* sulfur

SYNONYMS

● **lighter elements**
炭 carbon → 2257
水 hydrogen → 10
酸 OXYGEN → 1563
窒 NITROGEN → 2288
塩 chlorine → 631
臭 bromine → 2633

5-7 石

硝 硝 硝 硝

1185 SHŌ

Ⓒⓗ 硝 xiāo

Radical	Strokes
石 112	12-5-7
Grade	Freq
Jōyō	1866
1-5-7	

Stroke order: 1 2 3 4 5 6 7 8 9 10 11 12

▶NITER

COMPOUNDS

● **niter, saltpeter, potassium nitrate**

硝石 *shōseki* saltpeter
硝酸 *shōsan* nitric acid
硝薬 *shōyaku* gunpowder
硝煙 *shōen* gunpowder smoke
硝化 *shōka* nitrification

SPECIAL READINGS

硝子▲ *garasu* glass

SYNONYMS

● **nitrogen**

窒 NITROGEN → 2288

5-7 石

硬

1186

▶HARD

nonstandard for 硬 1183

5-7 石

硝

1187

▶NITER

nonstandard for 硝 1185

5-7 示

視

1188

▶REGARD

nonstandard for 視 972

5-7 禾

稀

1189 KI KE mare

Ⓒⓗ 稀 xī

Radical	Strokes
禾 115	12-5-7
Grade	Freq
Reference	
1-5-7	

COMPOUNDS

❶ [now replaced by 希 *ki, ke* 2049 or 希 *mare*] (not frequent) rare, uncommon, unusual, scarce

稀代の *kitai* (=*kidai*) *no* uncommon, rare
稀有な *keu* (=*kiyū*) *na* rare, unusual, uncommon
稀少な *kishō na* scarce, rare
古稀 *koki* three score and ten, seventy years of age
稀な *mare na* rare, uncommon, scarce, unique

❷ [now replaced by 希 *ki* 2049]

ⓐ [original meaning] (thin in density) rare, rarefied, dilute, thin

ⓑ [also prefix] *chem* dilute

稀薄な *kihaku na* dilute, thin, rare, sparse
稀釈 *kishaku* dilution
稀硫酸 *kiryūsan* dilute sulfuric acid

HOMOPHONES

mare ⇨ 希 2049

NOTE

⇨ see USAGE note at 希 2049
⇨ see COMPOUND FORMATION for 古希 *koki* ⇨ 希 2049

程 程 程 程

1190 TEI hodo -hodo

㊥ 程 chéng

Radical	Strokes
禾 115	12-5-7
Grade	**Freq**
Jōyō-5	476
◧ 1 - 5 - 7	

5-7 禾

▶EXTENT ▶ESTABLISHED FORM

COMPOUNDS

❶ⓐ **extent, degree, range, limit**
ⓑ (range of distance) **extent, distance, range, mileage, journey**
程度 *teido* degree, extent, standard
射程 *shatei* shooting range
旅程 *ryotei* distance to be covered; plan of one's trip
航程 *kōtei* run (of a ship), sail; flight
マイル程 *mairutei* mileage
音程 *ontei* (musical) interval, distance (between tones)

❷ⓐ established form or mode of behavior: **rule, regulation, standard procedure, pattern**
ⓑ established order of doing things: **process, course**
ⓒ preestablished program of events: **schedule, program, plan, agenda, course of study**
規程 *kitei* official regulations, inner rules
方程式 *hōteishiki* equation
工程 *kōtei* process of manufacture, amount of work
過程 *katei* process, course
課程 *katei* course, curriculum
日程 *nittei* a day's program, order of the day
上程する *jōtei suru* introduce on the agenda, lay [introduce] a bill before the Diet

KUN

【hodo 程】
①ⓐ extent, degree, measure; limit
ⓑ extent [degree] of distance, time or quality
程良く *hodoyoku* properly, rightly, moderately
程を過ごす *hodo o sugosu* break bounds, go too far
どれ程 *dorehodo* how far; how long; how many [much]
左程 *sahodo* (not) much, (not) very
成程 *naruhodo* I see, really, indeed
程遠い *hodotōi* far (from), distant, fall far short of
先程 *sakihodo* some time ago, a little while ago
② one's position, one's social status
身の程 *minohodo* one's social position, one's own place
③ state of affairs
真偽の程 *shingi no hodo* whether it is true or not
④ *particle*
ⓐ as, as...as, (not) so...as
ⓑ the more [less]...the more [less]
僕は奴にそんな質問をする程馬鹿じゃない *Boku wa yatsu ni sonna shitsumon o suru hodo baka ja nai* I'm not so stupid as to ask him such a question
早ければ早い程良い *Hayakereba hayai hodo yoi* The sooner, the better

【-hodo -程】 ...or thereabouts, about, approximately
三週間程 *sanshūkanhodo* three weeks or thereabouts

SYNONYMS

❶ⓐ **degree**
度 DEGREE → 3100
分 relative degree → 1972
ⓑ **distance and interval**
距 DISTANCE → 1511
間 INTERVAL → 3323
ⓑ **range**
範 range → 2709
域 area → 465
圏 SPHERE → 3148
野 FIELD → 1485
界 field (*phys*) → 2563
場 field (*phys*, *psychol*) → 558

❷ⓐ **model**
式 form → 3049
準 STANDARD → 2856
格 NORM → 926
範 MODEL → 2709
典 CANON → 2627
模 PATTERN → 1050

【-hodo】
○ **approximately**
辺り thereabouts → 3029
-頃 ABOUT → 144
位 about → 61
-方 about → 1963
約 APPROXIMATELY → 1280
概 GENERAL → 1048
大 in substance → 3416

COMPOUND FORMATION

成程 *naruhodo*

成程 'I see, etc.' originally meant attaining (成) the greatest possible extent (程 *hodo* ① ⓐ), i.e., as much as possible. What this has to do with "I see" is quite a mystery.

5-7 禾

税 税 税 税

1191 ZEI

CH 税 shuì

Radical	Strokes
禾 115	12-5-7
Grade	**Freq**
Jōyō-5	371

◧ 1-5-7

▶**TAX**

COMPOUNDS

❶ [also suffix] **tax, duty**

- 税金 *zeikin* tax, duty; rates
- 税関 *zeikan* customhouse
- 租税 *sozei* taxes, taxation
- 課税 *kazei* taxation
- 脱税 *datsuzei* tax evasion
- 減税 *genzei* reduction of taxes, tax cut
- 納税 *nōzei* tax payment
- 所得税 *shotokuzei* income tax
- 間接税 *kansetsuzei* indirect tax

❷ dues, rates, fee

- 郵税 *yūzei* postage, postal rates
- 印税 *inzei* royalty (on a book)
- 入港税 *nyūkōzei* port dues [fees]

INDEPENDENT

【zei 税】 tax, duty

- 税を納める *zei o osameru* pay a tax
- 税を課する *zei o kasuru* impose a tax

SYNONYMS

❶ **tax**

- 租 LAND TAX → 1161
- 貢 TRIBUTE → 2281
- 賦 levy → 1583

5-7 禾

程

1192

▶**EXTENT** ▶**ESTABLISHED FORM**

nonstandard for 程 1190

5-7 禾

稅

1193

▶**TAX**

nonstandard for 税 1191

5-7 衤

補 補 補

1194 HO ogina(u)

CH 补 bǔ

Radical	Strokes
衤 145	12-5-7
Grade	**Freq**
Jōyō-6	471

◧ 1-5-7

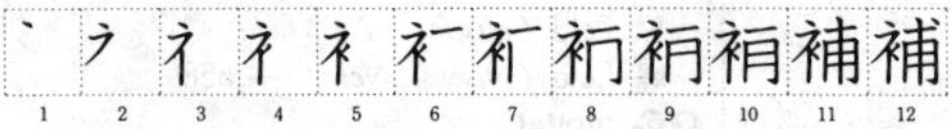

▶**SUPPLEMENT**

COMPOUNDS

❶ⓐ **supplement, make up for, compensate; replenish, supply**

ⓑ supplementary, extra

- 補足 *hosoku* supplement, replenishment
- 補遺 *hoi* supplement
- 補償する *hoshō suru* compensate, indemnify
- 補充する *hojū suru* supplement, replenish, recruit
- 補給 *hokyū* supply, replenishment
- 補欠 *hoketsu* filling a vacancy; substitute, alternate
- 補習 *hoshū* supplementary lessons
- 補則 *hosoku* supplementary rules

❷ (fill a vacancy) **appoint, assign, select**

- 補任する *honin suru* appoint to office
- 候補者 *kōhosha* candidate, applicant

❸ repair, mend

- 補修する *hoshū suru* repair, mend

❹ⓐ [formerly also 輔 1559] assist, aid; give guidance

ⓑ [suffix] assistant, aid, apprentice

- 補佐(＝輔佐)する *hosa suru* assist, help
- 補助する *hojo suru* assist, support, aid
- 補導する *hodō suru* guide, direct, lead; take into custody
- 書記補 *shokiho* assistant clerk

警部補 *keibuho* assistant inspector
外交官補 *gaikōkanho* probationary diplomat

INDEPENDENT

【**hosuru** 補する】 be appointed

KUN

【**ogina**(**u**) 補う】 supplement, make up for, compensate; replenish, supply
補い *oginai* supplement, replenishment, reparation
欠陥を補う *kekkan o oginau* make up for a fault
不足を補う *fusoku o oginau* replenish a shortage

SYNONYMS

❶ⓐ **supplement**
足 supplement → 2188
給 SUPPLY → 1350
充 fill up (a vacancy) → 2014
ⓑ **additional**
追 additional → 3096
副 accessory → 1776
❷ **appoint**
任 appoint → 53
挙 NOMINATE → 2456
❹ⓐ **help**
輔 ASSIST → 1559
佐 ASSIST → 67
助 HELP → 1121
援 AID → 586
佑 HELP (said esp. of God) → 74
祐 DIVINE HELP → 915
済 RELIEVE → 522
ⓑ **assistant**
丞 AIDE → 2541

COMPOUND FORMATION

候補者 *kōhosha*
候補者 'candidate, applicant' is a person (者) waiting (候) to be appointed (補 ❷).

裕 裕 裕

1195 YŪ

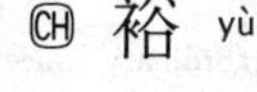

Radical	Strokes
衤 145	12-5-7
Grade	**Freq**
Jōyō	1325
1 - 5 - 7	

5-7 衤

▶**ABUNDANT**

COMPOUNDS

❶ **abundant, plentiful, ample**
裕福な *yūfuku na* rich, wealthy
余裕 *yoyū* surplus, margin, room; composure
富裕な *fuyū na* wealthy, rich
❷ tolerant, big-hearted
裕度 *yūdo elec* tolerance

SYNONYMS

❶ **many**
富 RICH → 2310
豊 PLENTIFUL → 2697
沢 plentiful → 267
穣 YIELDING ABUNDANTLY → 1250
多 MANY → 2170
万 myriad → 2936
百 numerous → 2026

裡

1196

▶**REAR**
nonstandard for 裏 2138

5-7 衤

雅 雅 雅

1197 GA miya(bi)▲

ⒸⒽ 雅 yǎ

Radical	Strokes
隹 172	13-8-5
Grade	**Freq**
Jōyō	1378
1 - 5 - 8	

5-8 牙

▶**ELEGANT**

COMPOUNDS

❶ⓐ **elegant, refined, graceful, artistic, sophisticated**
ⓑ proper and elegant, standard, classical
雅趣 *gashu* elegance, artistry, taste
雅号 *gagō* pen name, pseudonym
優雅な *yūga na* elegant, graceful, refined

風雅 *fūga* elegance, refinement, daintiness
雅楽 *gagaku* ceremonial court music
高雅な *kōga na* refined, elegant, chaste
❷ honorific prefix
雅兄 *gakei* polite word used in addressing a friend in a letter

INDEPENDENT

【**ga** 雅】 elegance, good taste

KUN

【**miya**(**bi**) 雅び】 elegance, gracefulness; refined taste
雅びやかな *miyabiyaka na* elegant, graceful, refined

SYNONYMS

❶ **elegant**
淑 GRACEFUL → 527
優 graceful → 177
粋 REFINED → 1293
彬 REFINED AND GENTLE → 960

5-8
田

畸
1198 KI

CH 畸 jī

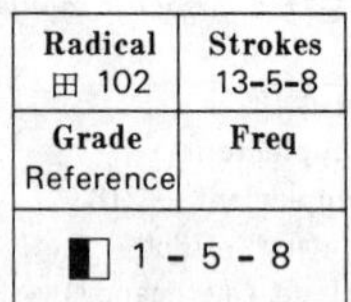

Radical	Strokes
田 102	13-5-8
Grade	Freq
Reference	
1 - 5 - 8	

COMPOUNDS

[now replaced by 奇 2217]
❶ unusual, strange, odd, extraordinary, queer, eccentric
畸人 *kijin* eccentric (person), queer [odd] fellow
❷ deformity, malformation
畸形 *kikei* deformity, malformation

5-8
目

睦
1199 BOKU mutsu(majii) mutsu(mu) NAMES mutsu chika yoshi

CH 睦 mù

Radical	Strokes
目 109	13-5-8
Grade	Freq
Names	2027
1 - 5 - 8	

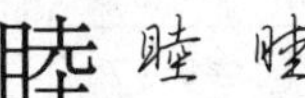

1 2 3 4 5 6 7 8 9 10 11 12 13

▶**FRIENDLY**

COMPOUNDS

ⓐ **friendly, harmonious, peaceful**
ⓑ [original meaning] live together in harmony
親睦 *shinboku* friendliness, amity, intimacy
和睦 *waboku* reconciliation, peace
敦睦な *tonboku na* [archaic] cordial and friendly, affectionate

KUN

【**mutsu**(**majii**) 睦まじい】 friendly, intimate, harmonious
【**mutsu**(**mu**) 睦む】 get along well together
睦言 *mutsugoto* lover's talk, whispered intimacies

NAMES

睦美 *mutsumi* female name
睦男 *mutsuo* male name
伴睦 *banboku* male name
睦子 *mutsuko* (=*chikako*) female name

SYNONYMS

ⓐ **familiar and friendly**
懇 FAMILIAR → 2899
親 INTIMATE → 1799
密 CLOSE → 2292
近 NEAR → 3061
和 HARMONIOUS → 1130

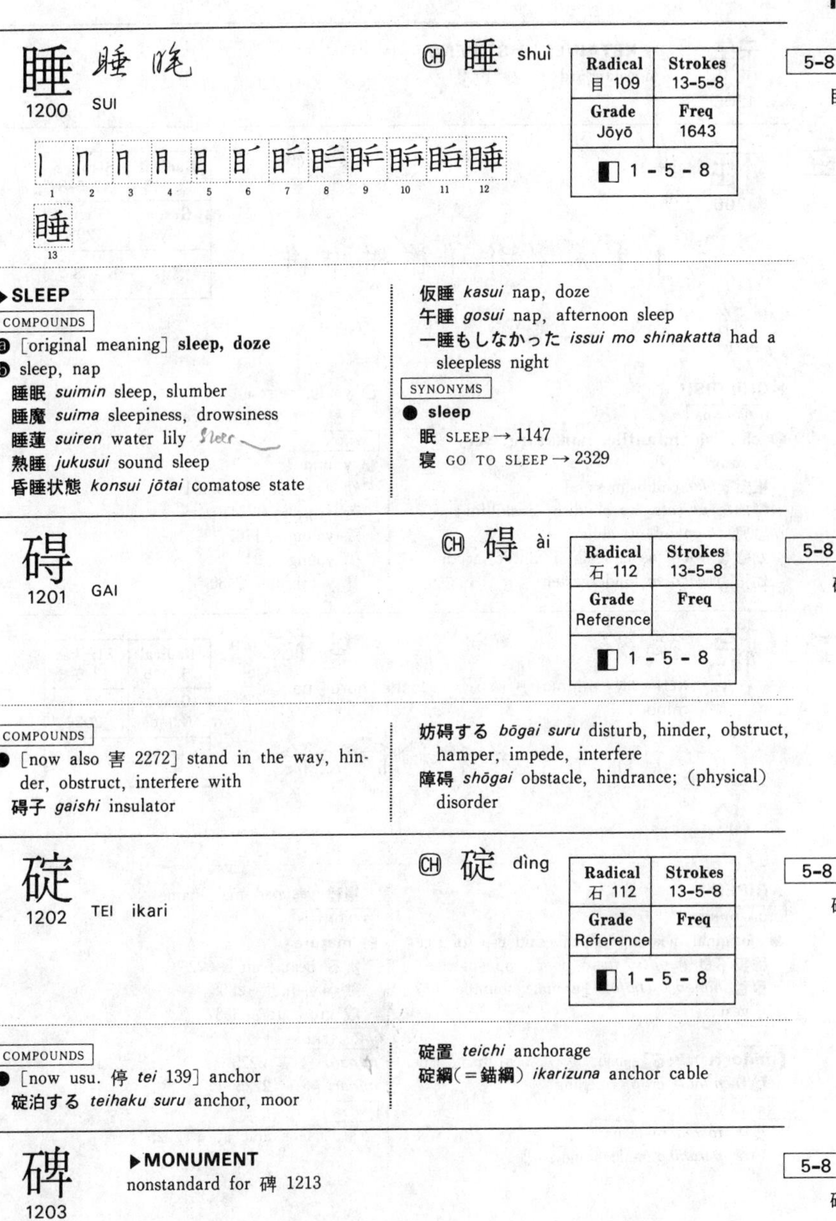

睡 1200 SUI

1 丨 2 冂 3 月 4 月 5 目 6 目′ 7 目⺁ 8 目⺧ 9 目乍 10 目乍 11 目垂 12 睡 13 睡

Ⓒⓗ 睡 shuì

Radical	Strokes
目 109	13-5-8
Grade	**Freq**
Jōyō	1643
◧ 1 - 5 - 8	

5-8 目

▶**SLEEP**

COMPOUNDS

ⓐ [original meaning] **sleep, doze**

ⓑ sleep, nap

睡眠 *suimin* sleep, slumber
睡魔 *suima* sleepiness, drowsiness
睡蓮 *suiren* water lily
熟睡 *jukusui* sound sleep
昏睡状態 *konsui jōtai* comatose state
仮睡 *kasui* nap, doze
午睡 *gosui* nap, afternoon sleep
一睡もしなかった *issui mo shinakatta* had a sleepless night

SYNONYMS

● **sleep**

眠 SLEEP → 1147
寝 GO TO SLEEP → 2329

碍 1201 GAI

Ⓒⓗ 碍 ài

Radical	Strokes
石 112	13-5-8
Grade	**Freq**
Reference	
◧ 1 - 5 - 8	

5-8 石

COMPOUNDS

● [now also 害 2272] stand in the way, hinder, obstruct, interfere with

碍子 *gaishi* insulator
妨碍する *bōgai suru* disturb, hinder, obstruct, hamper, impede, interfere
障碍 *shōgai* obstacle, hindrance; (physical) disorder

碇 1202 TEI ikari

Ⓒⓗ 碇 dìng

Radical	Strokes
石 112	13-5-8
Grade	**Freq**
Reference	
◧ 1 - 5 - 8	

5-8 石

COMPOUNDS

● [now usu. 停 *tei* 139] anchor

碇泊する *teihaku suru* anchor, moor
碇置 *teichi* anchorage
碇綱(＝錨綱) *ikarizuna* anchor cable

碑 1203

▶**MONUMENT**

nonstandard for 碑 1213

5-8 石

碎 1204

▶**CRUSH UP**

nonstandard for 砕 1134

5-8 石

5-8
禄
1205

▶RETAINER'S STIPEND
nonstandard for 禄 1002

5-8
稚 稚 稚
1206 CHI

CH 稚 zhì

Radical	Strokes
禾 115	13-5-8
Grade	**Freq**
Jōyō	1296
1-5-8	

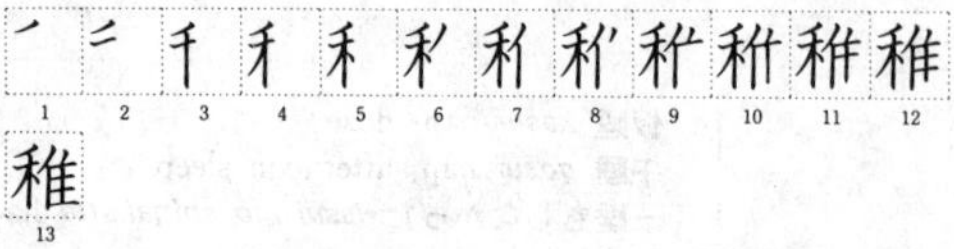

▶CHILDISH

COMPOUNDS

❶ **childish, infantile, immature; very young**
稚気 *chiki* childishness
稚拙な *chisetsu na* childish, unskillful
稚児 *chigo* infant, child
幼稚な *yōchi na* childish, infantile, crude
幼稚園 *yōchien* kindergarten

❷ young person
丁稚 *detchi* apprentice

SYNONYMS

❶ **young**
幼 VERY YOUNG → 191
若 YOUNG → 2241
弱 young → 1167
少 young → 3467
青 youthful → 2430

5-8
稔 稔 稔
1207 NEN JIN mino(ru) NAMES toshi naru nari minoru

CH 稔 rěn

Radical	Strokes
禾 115	13-5-8
Grade	**Freq**
Names	2026
1-5-8	

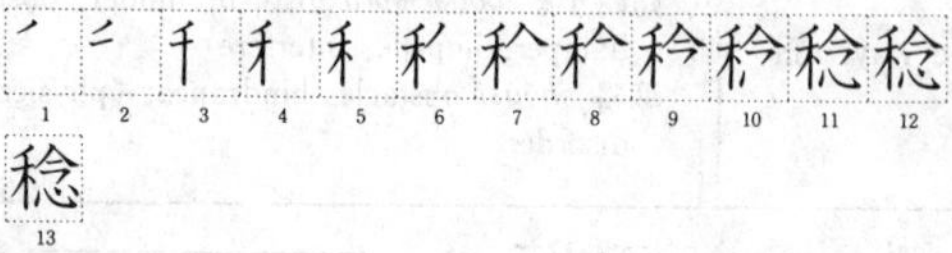

▶RIPEN

COMPOUNDS

● [original meaning] ripen—said esp. of rice
稔実不良 *nenjitsu furyō* poor crop (of rice)
豊稔 *hōnen* (=*hōjin*) [archaic] bumper harvest

KUN

【mino(ru) 稔る】 [usu. 実る] bear fruit, ripen
稔り *minori* crop, ripening

NAMES

稔男 *toshio* male name
稔彦 *naruhiko* male name
緩稔 *yasunari* male name

SYNONYMS

● **mature**
実る bear fruit → 2225
熟 MATURE → 2868
成 grow up → 3537

HOMOPHONES

minoru ⇨ 実 2225
minori ⇨ 実 2225

NOTE

⇨ see USAGE note at 実 2225

靖

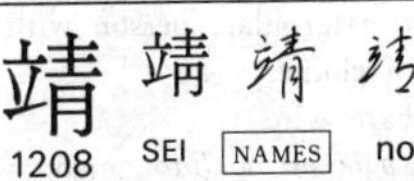

1208 SEI NAMES nobu yasu yasushi shizu osamu

Ⓒⓗ 靖 jìng

Radical	Strokes
青 174	13-8-5
Grade	**Freq**
Names	2008
◧ 1-5-8	

5-8 立

▶PACIFY

COMPOUNDS

ⓐ [archaic] pacify, quell, put down

ⓑ [original meaning, now archaic] peaceful, tranquil, quiet

靖国 *seikoku* pacifying the nation

閑靖 *kansei* quiet, tranquil

NAMES

靖子 *yasuko* female name

靖夫 *yasuo* male name

SYNONYMS

ⓐ **conquer and suppress**

鎮 QUELL → 1759

征 CONQUER → 293

討 SUPPRESS BY ARMED FORCE → 1456

伐 CUT DOWN → 42

靖

1209

▶PACIFY

nonstandard for 靖 1208

5-8 立

褐

1210 KATSU

Ⓒⓗ 褐 hè

Radical	Strokes
衤 145	13-5-8
Grade	**Freq**
Jōyō	1953
◧ 1-5-8	

5-8 衤

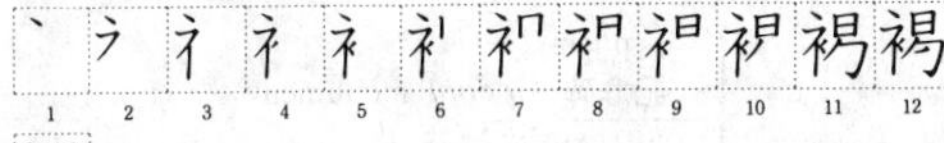

▶BROWN

COMPOUNDS

❶ **brown, dirty brown**

褐色 *kasshoku* brown

褐炭 *kattan* brown coal, lignite

褐藻 *kassō* brown algae

茶褐色 *chakasshoku* brown, liver brown

❷ [original meaning, now archaic] coarse cloth or garment

SYNONYMS

❶ **brown colors**

茶 light brown → 2259

裸

1211 RA hadaka

Ⓒⓗ 裸 luǒ

Radical	Strokes
衤 145	13-5-8
Grade	**Freq**
Jōyō	1729
◧ 1-5-8	

5-8 衤

▶NAKED

COMPOUNDS

ⓐ [original meaning] (without clothing) **naked, nude, bare**

ⓑ (without covering) naked, uncovered, bare

裸婦 *rafu* nude woman

裸体 *ratai* naked [nude] body, nudity

全裸の *zenra no* stark naked, nude

裸出 *rashutsu* exposure
裸眼 *ragan* naked eye
赤裸裸 *sekirara* nakedness, frankness

KUN

【hadaka 裸】 naked body; being uncovered [bare]; being penniless
裸の *hadaka no* naked, nude, bare, undressed
裸馬 *hadakauma* barebacked horse
素っ裸の *suppadaka no* stark naked, in one's bare skin
裸虫 *hadakamushi* caterpillar; person with scanty supply of clothes
裸線 *hadakasen* bare wire
裸一貫の人 *hadaka ikkan no hito* person with no property but his [her] own body

SPECIAL READINGS

裸足▲ *hadashi* barefoot, bare feet

SYNONYMS

● **naked**
素 bare → 2458

5-8 号

號

1212

▶**NUMBER** ▶**DESIGNATION** ▶**SIGN**

nonstandard for 号 2153

5-8 此

雌

incorrect classification／stroke count ⇨ see 1055

5-9 石

碑 碑 碑 碑

1213 HI ishibumi▲

CH 碑 bēi

Radical	Strokes
石 112	14-5-9
Grade	**Freq**
Jōyō	1617
1 - 5 - 9	

一 1 ㄏ 2 丆 3 石 4 石 5 石' 6 石' 7 矿 8 砷 9 砷 10 砷 11 砷 12 碑 13 碑 14

▶**MONUMENT**

COMPOUNDS

ⓐ **monument, stone monument**
ⓑ suffix after names of monuments
碑文 *hibun* epitaph, inscription
石碑 *sekihi* stone monument, tombstone
墓碑 *bohi* tombstone, gravestone
歌碑 *kahi* monument inscribed with a tanka poem
記念碑 *kinenhi* monument

INDEPENDENT

【hi 碑】 monument
新田義貞の碑 *nitta yoshisada no hi* monument in memory of Nitta Yoshisada

KUN

【ishibumi 碑】 stone monument

5-9 石

磁 磁 磁 磁

1214 JI

CH 磁 cí

Radical	Strokes
石 112	14-5-9
Grade	**Freq**
Jōyō-6	1830
1 - 5 - 9	

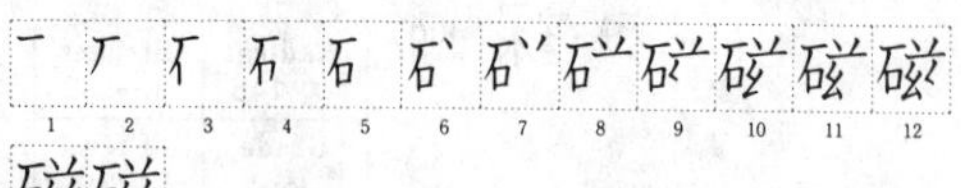

磁 13 磁 14

▶**MAGNETISM**

COMPOUNDS

❶ⓐ **magnetism**
ⓑ [also prefix] **magnetic**
ⓒ [original meaning] **magnet**
磁気 *jiki* magnetism
磁力線 *jiryokusen* line of magnetic force
磁場 *jiba* magnetic field
磁極 *jikyoku* magnetic pole
電磁波 *denjiha* electromagnetic waves
磁方位 *jihōi* magnetic bearing
磁石 *jishaku* magnet; compass
❷ porcelain, chinaware
陶磁器 *tōjiki* porcelain, pottery, ceramics
青磁 *seiji* celadon porcelain
白磁 *hakuji* white porcelain

SYNONYMS

❶ⓐ & ❶ⓑ electricity and magnetism
電 ELECTRICITY → 2790
流 electric current → 441

❷ ceramics ware
陶 POTTERY → 546
窯 ceramics → 2361

福 1215 ▶FORTUNE
nonstandard for 福 1029 5-9 礻

禍 1216 ▶CALAMITY
nonstandard for 禍 1030 5-9 礻

禎 1217 ▶PROPITIOUS OMEN
nonstandard for 禎 1031 5-9 礻

種 1218 種 種 (CH) 种 zhǒng zhòng chóng 5-9 禾

SHU tane -gusa▲

Radical	Strokes
禾 115	14-5-9
Grade	**Freq**
Jōyō-4	486
1-5-9	

Stroke order: 1–14

▶VARIETY ▶SEED

COMPOUNDS

❶ⓐ **variety, kind, type, sort, breed, race**
ⓑ counter for kinds, varieties or events (in sport programs)
種目 *shumoku* item; event (as a race)
各種の *kakushu no* each [every] kind, various
一種の *isshu no* a kind of, of a sort
機種 *kishu* type of airplane [machine], model
業種 *gyōshu* type of industry, category of business
職種 *shokushu* type of occupation, occupational category
品種 *hinshu* kind, variety, description, brand
人種 *jinshu* (human) race
第三種郵便物 *daisanshu yūbinbutsu* third-class mail matter
五種競技 *goshu kyōgi* pentathlon, five events
❷ⓐ [also suffix] *biol* **species, variety**
ⓑ *logic* species
亜種 *ashu* subspecies
変種 *henshu* variety; mutation
ホルスタイン種 *horusutain-shu* Holstein, Holstein-Friesian
種概念 *shugainen logic* species
❸ **seed**
種子 *shushi* seed, pit, stone
種皮 *shuhi* seed coat, testa
❹ [original meaning] sow, plant
播種 *hashu* sowing, planting
❺ vaccinate
種痘 *shutō* vaccination against smallpox
予防接種 *yobō sesshu* protective inoculation, vaccination
❻ breeding, reproduction
種畜 *shuchiku* breeding stock
断種 *danshu* castration, sterilization

INDEPENDENT

【shu 種】 kind, sort; *biol* species, variety; *logic* species
この種の *kono shu no* this kind of
種の起源 *shu no kigen* Origin of Species

KUN

【tane 種】
① seed, stone, kernel, pip
菜種 *natane* rapeseed, coleseed
②ⓐ kind, species, variety; quality
ⓑ breed, stock
変わり種 *kawaridane* novelty, exception, freak
種馬 *taneuma* stud horse, stallion
一粒種 *hitotsubudane* one's only child
③ [formerly also 胤] paternal blood, offspring
種違い *tanechigai* half brother, half sister
④ⓐ material, matter
ⓑ subject, topic, matter, news

料理の種を仕込む *ryōri no tane o shikomu* prepare for cooking
特種 *tokudane* exclusive news, scoop
⑤ cause, source, origin
悩みの種 *nayami no tane* cause of annoyance
⑥ trick, secret, gimmick
種明かし *taneakashi* exposure of a trick
【-gusa -種】［usu. -草］material, stuff
質種 *shichigusa* article for pawning
笑い種 *waraigusa* laughingstock

SYNONYMS

❶ⓐ kinds and types
様 variety → 1052
類 KIND → 1807
色 kind → 2029
般 SORT → 1317
型 TYPE → 2638
属 genus → 3145
品 category → 2248
❸ early states of plant life
苗 SEEDLING → 2237
芽 BUD → 2240

USAGE

tane
種
① seed, stone, kernel, pip
②ⓐ kind, species, variety; quality
ⓑ breed, stock
③［formerly also 胤］paternal blood, offspring
④ⓐ material, matter
ⓑ subject, topic, matter, news
⑤ cause, source, origin
⑥ trick, secret, gimmick
胤
［now usu. 種］paternal blood, offspring

HOMOPHONES

tane ⇨ 胤 17
-gusa ⇨ 草 2263

NOTE

⇨ see also USAGE note at 草 2263

5-9 禾

稲 稲 稲 稲

1219 TŌ ine ina-

Radical	Strokes
禾 115	14-5-9
Grade	**Freq**
Jōyō	921
1 - 5 - 9	

▶RICE PLANT

COMPOUNDS

● rice plant, rice
水稲 *suitō* paddy-rice plant, aquatic rice
陸稲 *rikutō* (=*okabo*) rice grown in a dry field
晩稲 *bantō* late growing rice

KUN

【ine 稲】 rice plant
稲刈り *inekari* rice reaping
【ina- 稲-】
① rice plant, rice
稲作 *inasaku* rice crop; raising rice plants
稲穂 *inaho* ear of rice
稲田 *inada* rice field
② lightning
稲妻 *inazuma* lightning
稲光 *inabikari* lightning

SYNONYMS

● rice
米 RICE → 3529
飯 COOKED RICE → 1691

COMPOUND FORMATION

稲妻 *inazuma*
稲妻 'lightning' consist of 稲 'rice plants' and 妻 'wife', which in this case means 'husband'. It originates from the belief that ears of rice are produced as a result of a spiritual union between lightning and rice plants.

5-9 禾

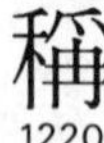
1220

▶APPELLATION
nonstandard for 称 1160

5-9 禾

incorrect stroke count ⇨ see 1233
(nonstandard for 稲 1219)

端 端 端

1221 TAN hashi ha[1] ha[2] hata -bata hana▲

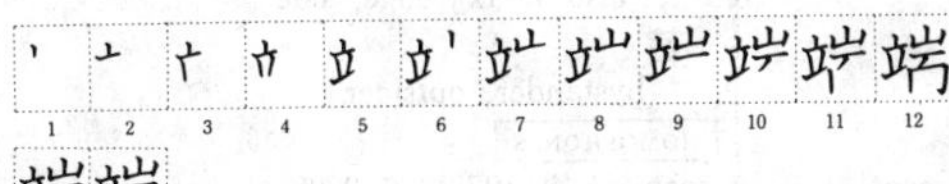

(CH) 端 duān

Radical	Strokes
立 117	14-5-9
Grade	**Freq**
Jōyō	897
1-5-9	

5-9 立

▶**END**

COMPOUNDS

❶ **end, extremity, tip**

端子 *tanshi* terminal
突端 *tottan* tip, point
両端 *ryōtan* both ends
先端(=尖端) *sentan* pointed end, tip; spearhead; vanguard
末端 *mattan* end, tip, termination
一端 *ittan* one end, edge, side; a part
極端 *kyokutan* extreme, extremity, pole
異端 *itan* heresy, paganism, heterodoxy

❷ **start, beginning, starting point, origin**

端緒 *tansho* (=*tancho*) beginning, start, first step; clue
端午 *tango* festival on the 5th of May (of the lunar calendar)
発端 *hottan* origin, beginning, outset
戦端を開く *sentan o hiraku* take up arms (against), open hostilities
途端に *totan ni* just as, just at the moment

❸ [original meaning] correct, proper, upright

端正な *tansei na* correct, just, proper
端然と *tanzen to* properly
端座(=端坐)する *tanza suru* sit upright [properly]
端麗な *tanrei na* graceful, elegant, handsome

❹ straight, direct

端的に *tanteki ni* directly, straightforwardly, frankly

❺ matter, event

多端 *tatan* many items; pressure of business
万端 *bantan* everything, all

INDEPENDENT

【tan 端】 start, beginning, origin
...に端を発する *...ni tan o hassuru* have its origin in...

KUN

【hashi 端】

① end, extremity, tip
紐の端 *himo no hashi* end of a string
両端 *ryōhashi* both ends

② edge, margin, brink, border; side
端端に *hashibashi ni* here and there, in some parts
道の端 *michi no hashi* edge of a street
右端 *migihashi* right side, right margin

③ beginning
端書き *hashigaki* preface, introduction

④ unwanted piece, scrap, fragment
端くれ *hashikure* fag end
木の端 *ki no hashi* fragment of wood

【ha[1] 端】 edge, border
山の端 *yama no ha* edge [brow] of mountain

【ha[2] 端】 [in compounds] odd thing, fragment, piece—historically sometimes interchangeable with 葉, as in the word *hagaki*, which is now always written 葉書
端数 *hasū* fraction, odd sum
端役 *hayaku* minor role [part]
半端 *hanpa* fragment, odd item; incompleteness
下っ端 *shitappa* underling, subordinate

【hata 端, -bata -端】 [also suffix] edge, side
池の端で *ike no hata de* near [by] the pond
道端 *michibata* roadside, wayside
海岸端 *kaiganbata* seaside

【hana 端】
[also 鼻]
① beginning
寝入り端に *neiribana ni* just when one has fallen asleep
② end, protruded point

SYNONYMS

❶ & **【hashi】** ① **extremity**
先 point → 2394
末 end → 3505
梢 tip → 963

❷ **beginnings**
緒 OUTSET → 1378
序 INTRODUCTORY PART → 3065
始 beginning → 281
初 beginning → 1116
元 ORIGIN → 1929
本 origin → 3502
根 ROOT → 930
源 SOURCE → 656

❸ **right**
正 RIGHT → 3484
是 RIGHT → 2436

【hashi】
② & **【hata】** **edges and boundaries**
縁 EDGE → 1386

辺 border → 3029
境 BOUNDARY → 676
界 BOUNDS → 2563
際 VERGE → 714
涯 OUTER LIMITS → 512

USAGE

❶ **ha**
端
[in compounds] odd thing, fragment, piece—historically sometimes interchangeable with 葉, as in the word *hagaki*, which is now always written 葉書
葉
[in compounds] fragment, piece—historically sometimes interchangeable with 端, as in the word *hagaki*, which is now always written 葉書

❷ **hata**
端
[also suffix] edge, side
傍
bystander, outsider

HOMOPHONES

hashi ⇨ 橋 1078 箸 2708
ha² ⇨ 葉 2321
hata ⇨ 傍 147
hana ⇨ 鼻 2706

NOTE

⇨ see also USAGE notes at 橋 1078 and 鼻 2706

5-9
衤

複 複 複

1222 FUKU

CH 复 fù

Radical	Strokes
衤 145	14-5-9
Grade	**Freq**
Jōyō-5	1020
1-5-9	

▶**COMPOUND**

COMPOUNDS

❶ⓐ **compound, double, multiple, complex, composite**
ⓑ doubles (as in tennis)
複合 *fukugō* compound, composite, complex
複利 *fukuri* compound interest
複視 *fukushi* polyopia
複葉機 *fukuyōki* biplane
複星 *fukusei* multiple star
複数 *fukusū* plural
複雑な *fukuzatsu na* complicated, complex, involved, intricate
単複 *tanpuku gram* singular and plural; singles and doubles (in tennis)

❷ **duplicate, copy**
複本(=副本) *fukuhon* duplicate, copy
複製 *fukusei* duplication, reproduction
複写 *fukusha* copy, duplication

❸ [original meaning, now archaic] lined garment
複衣 *fukui* lined garment

INDEPENDENT

【**fuku** 複】 plural; doubles (in tennis); place ticket (in horse racing)

SYNONYMS

❶ⓐ **compound**
倍 DOUBLE → 108
重 DUPLICATE → 3573

❷ **copy**
写 COPY → 2000
謄 TRANSCRIBE → 1093
拓 copy by rubbing → 317

5-9
衤

褐

1223

▶**BROWN**

nonstandard for 褐 1210

5-9
衤

褪

incorrect stroke count ⇨ see 1234

領 領◇ 领 𠃑

1224 RYŌ

Ⓒ 领 lǐng

Radical 頁 181	Strokes 14-9-5
Grade Jōyō-5	Freq 284
◧ 1 - 5 - 9	

▶TERRITORY

COMPOUNDS

❶ⓐ [also suffix] **territory, domain, possession, estate**

ⓑ fief, feudal estate, feudal manor

領土 *ryōdo* territory, domain

領内 *ryōnai* domains, territory

領海 *ryōkai* territorial water

領地 *ryōchi* territory, possession, dominion, domain; fief, feud

天領 *tenryō* imperial demesne; shogunal demesne

日本領 *nihonryō* Japanese territory

カンボジア領 *kanbojiaryō* Cambodian possession

領主 *ryōshu* lord of a fief [manor]

領民 *ryōmin* population of a fief

❷ⓐ (sphere of action) **territory, domain, area**

ⓑ area of the cerebral cortex

領域 *ryōiki* territory, domain, sphere, province; *math* domain

領分 *ryōbun* territory, domain; sphere of action

本領 *honryō* characteristic, one's specialty; one's line

運動領 *undōryō* motor area

❸ **take possession of, occupy, have jurisdiction over**

領有 *ryōyū* possession

占領する *senryō suru* capture, occupy, take possession of

横領する *ōryō suru* seize upon, embezzle, usurp

❹ **receive**

領収書 *ryōshūsho* receipt, voucher

受領 *juryō* receipt

拝領する *hairyō suru* receive (from a superior), be bestowed

❺ **leader, chief, head, administrator**

領事 *ryōji* consul, consular representative

大統領 *daitōryō* president

首領 *shuryō* leader, head, chief

❻ main point, essentials, outline

要領 *yōryō* gist, essentials; outline; procedure

綱領 *kōryō* essential [main] points, gist, outline; summary

❼ [usu. 了 3350] understand, comprehend

領承する *ryōshō suru* acknowledge, understand, note

❽ [original meaning] nape (of the neck), collar

領袖 *ryōshū* leader, chief

❾ counter for suits of armor or Japanese clothing

具足二領 *gusoku niryō* two suits of armor

INDEPENDENT

【**ryō 領**】 territory, domain

【**ryōsuru 領する**】 govern, rule over, possess, prevail

SYNONYMS

❶ⓐ **areas and localities**

区 DISTRICT → 2963

域 BOUNDED AREA → 465

帯 BELT → 2582

圏 SPHERE → 3148

辺 VICINITY → 3029

方 locality → 1963

地 PLACE → 204

ⓑ **feudal territorial divisions**

封 daimiate → 1287

荘 manor (in feudal Japan) → 2262

藩 FEUDAL DOMAIN → 2379

国 province (in former Japan) → 3087

❸ **occupy**

占 OCCUPY → 2003

拠 occupy → 312

専 take exclusive possession of → 2644

❹ **receive**

受 RECEIVE → 2421

享 ENJOY → 2051

収 TAKE IN → 198

納 ACCEPT → 1300

戴 RECEIVE HUMBLY → 3302

頂 RECEIVE HUMBLY → 145

拝 have the honor to receive → 303

❺ **leaders**

首 LEADER → 2265

頭 HEAD → 1604

長 CHIEF → 2556

王 KING → 3439

主 MASTER → 1938

NOTE
⇨ see COMPOUND FORMATION for 領袖 *ryōshū* ⇨ 袖 1164

5-9 令

領 1225

▶TERRITORY
nonstandard for 領 1224

5-9 申

暢 1226

暢 畅 — CH 畅 chàng

CHŌ NAMES itaru nobu noburu naga tōru

Radical	Strokes
日 72	14-4-10
Grade	**Freq**
Names	2054
◧ 1-5-9	

▶FLUENT

COMPOUNDS
● **fluent(ly), smooth(ly), free(ly), with ease**
暢達 *chōtatsu* fluency, facileness
流暢な *ryūchō na* fluent, flowing, smooth

SPECIAL READINGS
暢気な▲ *nonki na* easygoing, happy-go-lucky; free from care

NAMES
暢夫 *nobuo* male name
暢子 *nobuko* female name

SYNONYMS
● **smooth**
滑 SMOOTH → 658
流 flowing → 441

5-10 白

魄 1227

HAKU — CH 魄 pò tuò bó

Radical	Strokes
鬼 194	15-10-5
Grade	**Freq**
Reference	
◧ 1-5-10	

COMPOUNDS
❶ⓐ [now also 迫 3074] spirit, soul
ⓑ baser animal spirit of man
気魄 *kihaku* spirit, soul, vigor
魂魄 *konpaku* soul, spirit, ghost
❷ out of luck
落魄する *rakuhaku suru* be reduced to poverty
❸ [archaic] dark portion of the moon
死魄 *shihaku* waning moon

5-10 石

確 1228

確 確 — CH 确 què

KAKU tashi(ka) tashi(kameru)

Radical	Strokes
石 112	15-5-10
Grade	**Freq**
Jōyō-5	349
◧ 1-5-10	

▶CERTAIN

COMPOUNDS
ⓐ **certain, definite, positive, sure, reliable, accurate**
ⓑ (not easily moved) firm, solid, steadfast, sound
確認 *kakunin* confirmation, ascertainment
確実な *kakujitsu na* certain, sure, reliable; sound, solid
確証 *kakushō* certain [definite] proof, posi-

tive evidence, corroboration
確率 *kakuritsu* probability
確答 *kakutō* definite answer [reply]
正確な *seikaku na* accurate, precise, exact
明確な *meikaku na* clear, precise, distinct
的確な *tekikaku na* precise, accurate, exact
確保する *kakuho suru* secure, make sure of, ensure
確立する *kakuritsu suru* establish, build up
確信する *kakushin suru* believe firmly, be convinced
確執 *kakushitsu* (=*kakushū*) discord, strife
確定 *kakutei* decision, settlement; confirmation
確固たる *kakkotaru* firm, sure, resolute

INDEPENDENT

【kakutaru 確たる】 certain, definite, positive, sure, reliable
確たる証拠 *kakutaru shōko* certain [definite] evidence

KUN

【tashi(ka) 確か】 perhaps, probably, I suppose, if I remember correctly
確かな *tashika na* certain, definite, positive, sure, reliable, trustworthy; able, competent, sober, sane
確かそうだ *tashikasō da* probably so
確かな事実 *tashika na jijitsu* established [certain] fact
確かな筋 *tashika na suji* reliable source
気は確かだ *ki wa tashika da* be sane, be in one's senses

【tashi(kameru) 確かめる】 ascertain, make sure of, confirm, corroborate
確かめ *tashikame* confirmation, certification, ascertainment
真偽を確かめる *shingi o tashikameru* make sure of the truth

SYNONYMS

ⓐ certain
必 WITHOUT FAIL → 15

ⓐ exact
正 RIGHT → 3484
真 right → 2111

ⓑ firm and obstinate
固 FIRM, stiff → 3086
堅 FIRM → 2823
毅 RESOLUTE → 1866
剛 TOUGH → 1673
頑 STUBBORN → 1040
硬 hard-line → 1183

NOTE

⇨ see COMPOUND FORMATION for 確執 *kakushitsu* (=*kakushū*) ⇨ 執 1680

磁 1229

▶MAGNETISM
nonstandard for 磁 1214

5-10 石

稼 1230

KA kase(gu)

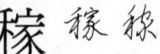

Ⓒⓗ 稼 jià

Radical	Strokes
禾 115	15-5-10
Grade	**Freq**
Jōyō	1792
◧ 1-5-10	

5-10 禾

1 2 3 4 5 6 7 8 9 10 11 12 13 14 15

▶WORK

COMPOUNDS

● work, work for a living, earn
稼働(=稼動) *kadō* working, work; operation (of a machine)
稼業 *kagyō* trade, business; work; occupation

KUN

【kase(gu) 稼ぐ】 work, work for a living, earn; gain a profitable situation
稼ぎ *kasegi* labor, work; earnings, income
稼ぎ手 *kasegite* breadwinner, supporter; good [hard] worker
稼ぎ取る *kasegitoru* earn by working
出稼ぎ *dekasegi* working away from home
共稼ぎ *tomokasegi* working together (for a living), working in double harness
点数を稼ぐ *tensū o kasegu* score points with (a person)
時間を稼ぐ *jikan o kasegu* gain time

SYNONYMS

● work
働 WORK → 153
労 LABOR → 2548
勤める serve (in an office) → 1818
仕 SERVE → 34

5-10 禾

稿 稿 稿

1231 KŌ

CH 稿 gǎo

Radical	Strokes
禾 115	15-5-10
Grade	**Freq**
Jōyō	1276
1-5-10	

1 2 3 4 5 6 7 8 9 10 11 12 13 14 15

▶MANUSCRIPT

COMPOUNDS

❶ [also suffix] **manuscript, draft, copy**

稿料 *kōryō* payment for a manuscript
原稿 *genkō* manuscript, draft, copy
寄稿 *kikō* contribution (to a newspaper)
草稿 *sōkō* outline, draft
遺稿 *ikō* posthumous work [manuscript]
投稿する *tōkō suru* contribute (an article)
脱稿する *dakkō suru* finish writing, complete (a novel)
決定稿 *ketteikō* final manuscript

❷ [original meaning, now archaic] straw, stalk of grain

稿人 *kōjin* straw figure

INDEPENDENT

【kō 稿】 manuscript, copy, draft

稿を改める *kō o aratameru* rewrite a manuscript

SYNONYMS

❶ **manuscript**

草 draft → 2263
案 draft → 2270

5-10 禾

穂 穂 穂 穂

1232 SUI ho

CH 穗 suì

Radical	Strokes
禾 115	15-5-10
Grade	**Freq**
Jōyō	1442
1-5-10	

1 2 3 4 5 6 7 8 9 10 11 12

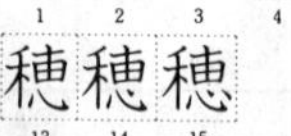

13 14 15

▶SPIKE

COMPOUNDS

● [original meaning] **spike, ear [head] of grain**

穂状の *suijō no* shaped like an ear of grain
出穂期 *shussuiki* sprouting season (of ears of grain)
花穂 *kasui* spike

KUN

【ho 穂】 spike, ear [head] of grain; something shaped like a spike, as the tip of a writing brush

穂波 *honami* waving heads (of grain)
稲穂 *inaho* ear of rice
落ち穂 *ochibo* gleanings
穂先 *hosaki* spike [ear] of grain; spike of a spear; tip of a writing brush

5-10 禾

稻

1233

▶RICE PLANT

nonstandard for 稲 1219

褪

1234 TAI TON a(seru)

CH 褪 tùn tuì

Radical	Strokes
衤 145	15-5-10
Grade	Freq
Reference	
1-5-10	

5-10 衤

COMPOUNDS

● [now replaced by 退 *tai* 3094] fade, discolor

褪色する *taishoku suru* fade, grow dull in color

褪紅色 *taikōshoku* pink

色褪せる *iroaseru* fade, grow dull in color

穏 穏 穏 穏

1235 ON oda(yaka)

CH 稳 wěn

Radical	Strokes
禾 115	16-5-11
Grade	Freq
Jōyō	1426
1-5-11	

5-11 禾

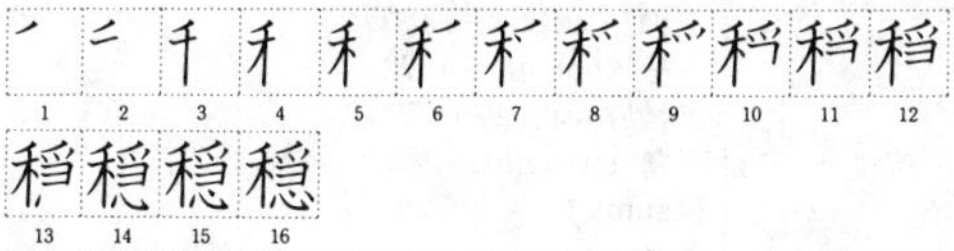

▶CALM ▶MILD

COMPOUNDS

❶ **calm, peaceful, quiet, tranquil, placid**

平穏な *heion na* calm, quiet, tranquil

安穏 *annon* peace, quiet, tranquility

不穏な *fuon na* disquieting, restless

❷ **mild, gentle, moderate, temperate**

穏健な *onken na* moderate, temperate, sound

穏和(=温和)な *onwa na* gentle, mild, genial

穏当な *ontō na* proper, reasonable, moderate

穏便な *onbin na* gentle, quiet, peaceable; private

KUN

【oda(yaka) 穏やか】

odayaka na 穏やかな calm, tranquil, peaceful; mild, gentle; moderate, reasonable

穏やかな海 *odayaka na umi* calm sea

穏やかな人 *odayaka na hito* mild [gentle] person

穏やかさ *odayakasa* mildness, gentleness

穏やかな風 *odayaka na kaze* gentle breeze

穏やかに話す *odayaka ni hanasu* talk quietly

穏やかな処置 *odayaka na shochi* moderate measure, reasonable step

SYNONYMS

❶ **calm and peaceful**

平 CALM → 3478

静 QUIET → 1728

泰 TRANQUIL → 2583

安 PEACEFUL → 2171

康 peaceful → 3124

寧 peaceful → 2345

❷ **gentle**

優しい gentle → 177

柔 SOFT → 2088

積 積 積

1236 SEKI tsu(mu) -zu(mi) tsu(moru) tsu(mori)

CH 积 jī

Radical	Strokes
禾 115	16-5-11
Grade	Freq
Jōyō-4	537
1-5-11	

5-11 禾

▶ACCUMULATE

COMPOUNDS

❶ⓐ [original meaning] **accumulate, pile up, heap up**

ⓑ accumulated, many

積載 *sekisai* loading, carrying

積極的に *sekkyokuteki ni* positively, actively
堆積 *taiseki* accumulation, pile, heap
蓄積 *chikuseki* accumulation, stockpiling
山積する *sanseki suru* form a (huge) pile
累積 *ruiseki* accumulation
積雪 *sekisetsu* (fallen) snow
積年 *sekinen* many years

❷ **size, volume, capacity, area**
面積 *menseki* area, square measure
体積 *taiseki* (cubic) volume, capacity
容積 *yōseki* capacity, volume, bulk

❸ *math* product
積算法 *sekisanhō* integration
相乗積 *sōjōseki* product (of A multiplied by B)

INDEPENDENT

【seki 積】 *math* product
AとBの積 *ē to bī no seki* product of A and B

KUN

【tsu(mu) 積む】
vt
① pile up, heap (up), stack
積み上げる *tsumiageru* pile [heap] up, accumulate
上積み *uwazumi* upper load, deck cargo; loading on top, overlaying
② load, ship, stow aboard
積み込む *tsumikomu* load (up), put on board, stow aboard
船積み *funazumi* shipment, shipping
③ accumulate, lay by, save, amass
積み立て *tsumitate* laying by, reserving, accumulation

【-zu(mi) -積み】
[suffix]
① shipment
汽船積み *kisenzumi* shipment by steamer
② capacity
九トン積み貨車 *kyūtonzumi-kasha* 9-ton freight car

【tsu(moru) 積もる】 *vi* accumulate, get accumulated, be piled up; estimate, calculate, measure
降り積もる *furitsumoru* (of snow) pile up
見積もる *mitsumoru* estimate

【tsu(mori) 積もり】 intention, purpose
行く積もりだ *iku tsumori da* intend to go

SYNONYMS

❶ⓐ **accumulate**
累 CUMULATE → 2585
重 pile up → 3573
盛る heap up → 2675

❷ **quantity and number**
量 QUANTITY → 2471
嵩 BULK → 2331
額 AMOUNT → 1805
分 content → 1972
数 NUMBER → 1790
勢 strength → 2857

【tsumu】
② **load**
載 LOAD → 3300
搭 load on board → 592

USAGE

tsumu
積む
① pile up, heap (up), stack
② load, ship, stow aboard
③ accumulate, lay by, save, amass
詰む
① be packed, become fine [close]
② be checkmated

HOMOPHONES

tsumu ⇨ 詰 1521

5-12
目

瞳 瞳 瞳 瞳

1237 DŌ TŌ hitomi NAMES akira

Ⓒⓗ 瞳 tóng

Radical	Strokes
目 109	17-5-12
Grade	**Freq**
Names	2038
1-5-12	

1 2 3 4 5 6 7 8 9 10 11 12 13 14 15 16 17

▶PUPIL

COMPOUNDS

● [original meaning] **pupil (of the eye)**
瞳孔 *dōkō* pupil
瞳子 *dōshi* pupil

KUN

【hitomi 瞳】
[sometimes also 眸]
ⓐ pupil
ⓑ one's eyes
瞳の *hitomi no* pupilary
瞳を凝らす *hitomi o korasu* strain one's eyes

NAMES

瞳子 *tōko* female name
瞳 *hitomi* male name also female name

SYNONYMS

● **eye**

眸 EYE → 1170
眼 EYE → 1172
目 EYE → 3043

USAGE

hitomi

瞳
[sometimes also 眸]
ⓐ pupil
ⓑ one's eyes

眸
[usu. 瞳]
ⓐ pupil, the apple of one's eye
ⓑ one's eyes

★Both these characters have the same meaning, but the latter has a more literary flavor.

HOMOPHONES

hitomi ⇨ 眸 1170

瞭

1238 RYŌ

Ⓒ 了 liǎo

Radical	Strokes
目 109	17-5-12
Grade	**Freq**
Reference	
◧ 1 - 5 - 12	

5-12 目

COMPOUNDS

ⓐ [rarely also 亮 2071] clear, obvious
ⓑ [original meaning] clearly visible

明瞭な *meiryō na* clear, plain, lucid
一目瞭然の *ichimokuryōzen no* quite obvious, as clear as day

矇

1239

▶**PUPIL**
nonstandard for 瞳 1237

5-12 目

瞬

1240

▶**INSTANT**
nonstandard for 瞬 1247

5-12 目

矯 矯 矯

1241 KYŌ ta(meru)

Ⓒ 矫 jiǎo

Radical	Strokes
矢 111	17-5-12
Grade	**Freq**
Jōyō	1901
◧ 1 - 5 - 12	

5-12 矢

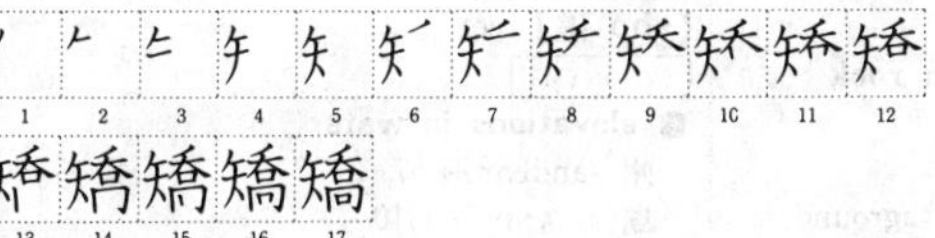

▶**RECTIFY**

COMPOUNDS

❶ **rectify, reform, correct, straighten out**
矯正 *kyōsei* correction, rectification
矯風 *kyōfū* moral reform
❷ extreme, eccentric
矯激な *kyōgeki na* radical, extreme, eccentric
奇矯 *kikyō* eccentricity
❸ pretend, feign, falsify
矯飾 *kyōshoku* pretense, affectation

KUN

【**ta(meru) 矯める**】
① straighten; correct, redress, remedy
枝を矯める *eda o tameru* straighten a branch
不正を矯める *fusei o tameru* redress injustice
② aim with one eye
矯めつ眇めつする *tametsu-sugametsu suru* scrutinize, scan

SYNONYMS

❶ **correct**
匡 RECTIFY → 2989
改 REFORM → 243
正 RIGHT → 3484
訂 REVISE → 1442
直す correct → 2932

5-12
石

磯 磯 磯 磯

1242 KI iso

CH 矶 jī

Radical	Strokes
石 112	17-5-12
Grade	**Freq**
Names	1997
1 - 5 - 1 2	

▶ROCKY BEACH

KUN

【iso 磯】

① rocky beach, beach, seashore

磯辺 *isobe* rocky beach, beach

磯巾着 *isoginchaku* sea anemone, seaflower

磯釣り *isozuri* fishing from rocks near the shore

磯伝いに *isozutai ni* along the beach

荒磯 *araiso* reefy coast, windswept and wave-beaten shore

② flank of a koto

NAMES

磯田 *isoda* surname

磯江 *isoe* female name

黒磯 *kuroiso* place name

SYNONYMS

【iso】

① **shores and watersides**

渚 STRAND → 525

浦 SEASIDE → 437

岸 SHORE → 2236

浜 BEACH → 436

-辺 -side → 3029

畔 WATERSIDE → 1145

5-12
石

礁 礁 礁

1243 SHŌ

CH 礁 jiāo

Radical	Strokes
石 112	17-5-12
Grade	**Freq**
Jōyō	1699
1 - 5 - 1 2	

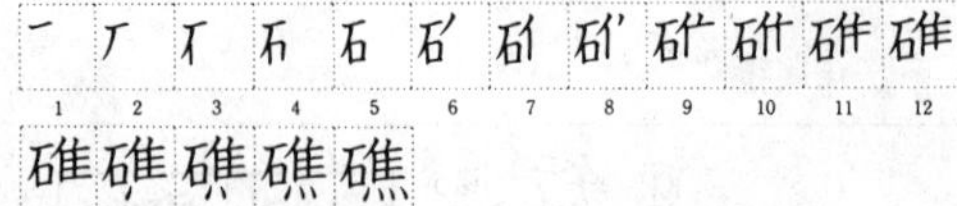

▶REEF

COMPOUNDS

● [original meaning] **reef, sunken rock**

岩礁 *ganshō* reef

珊瑚礁 *sangoshō* coral reef

座礁(＝坐礁)する *zashō suru* run aground, be stranded

環礁 *kanshō* atoll

暗礁 *anshō* sunken rock, unknown reef; deadlock

INDEPENDENT

【shō 礁】 reef

SYNONYMS

● **elevations in water**

州 sandbar → 57

島 ISLAND → 3310

● **shoals**

州 sandbar → 57

瀬 SHALLOWS → 806

5-12
石

礒

1244

▶ROCKY BEACH

nonstandard for 磯 1242

5-12
示

禪

1245

▶ZEN

nonstandard for 禅 1032

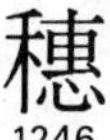

1246

▶SPIKE
nonstandard for 穂 1232

5-12
禾

瞬 瞬 瞬 瞬

1247 SHUN matata(ku)

Ⓒⓗ 瞬 shùn

Radical	Strokes
目 109	18-5-13
Grade	**Freq**
Jōyō	1255
◧ 1 - 5 - 1 3	

5-13
目

▶INSTANT

COMPOUNDS

❶ **instant, moment; in the twinkling of an eye**

瞬間 *shunkan* instant, moment, second
瞬時 *shunji* instant, moment; minute
一瞬 *isshun* instant, moment

❷ [original meaning] blink, wink

KUN

【matata(ku) 瞬く】 wink, blink; twinkle, flicker

瞬き *matataki* wink; twinkle (of stars)
瞬く間に *matataku ma ni* in the twinkling of an eye

SYNONYMS

❶ **short time periods**

頃 moment → 144
秒 SECOND → 1137
分 MINUTE → 1972
時 hour → 924
暫 SHORT WHILE → 2864

礎 礎 礎

1248 SO ishizue

Ⓒⓗ 础 chǔ

Radical	Strokes
石 112	18-5-13
Grade	**Freq**
Jōyō	1266
◧ 1 - 5 - 1 3	

5-13
石

▶FOUNDATION STONE

COMPOUNDS

ⓐ **foundation stone, cornerstone, foundation**

ⓑ (nonphysical support) **foundation, basis**

礎石 *soseki* foundation stone, cornerstone
礎材 *sozai* foundation materials
柱礎 *chūso* plinth
定礎 *teiso* laying of a foundation stone
基礎 *kiso* basis, foundation
国礎 *kokuso* pillar of state

KUN

【ishizue 礎】 foundation stone, cornerstone; foundation, basis, base

礎を築く *ishizue o kizuku* lay the foundation (for)

SYNONYMS

ⓐ **bottoms and bases**

盤 bedrock → 2851
床 BED → 3067
底 BOTTOM → 3084
下 lower part → 3378
基 BASE → 2673

ⓐ **supporting structures**

柱 PILLAR → 896

ⓑ **basis**

基 BASE → 2673
本 BASIS → 3502
素 ELEMENT → 2458
底 BOTTOM → 3084
根 ROOT → 930
拠 GROUNDS → 312

5-13 礻

禮
1249

▶ETIQUETTE ▶RITE
nonstandard for 礼 818

5-13 禾

穰 穰 穰 穰
1250 JŌ NAMES shige minoru yutaka

CH 穰 ráng

Radical	Strokes
禾 115	18-5-13
Grade	Freq
Names	2057
1-5-13	

▶YIELDING ABUNDANTLY

COMPOUNDS

❶ **yielding abundantly, abundant (harvest), luxuriant, plentiful**

豊穰 *hōjō* abundant crop, rich harvest

❷ [original meaning, now archaic] stalk of grain

❸ [archaic] ten octillion (10^{28})

NAMES

穰 *minoru* (= *yutaka*) male name

SYNONYMS

❶ **many**

豊 PLENTIFUL → 2697
沢 plentiful → 267
裕 ABUNDANT → 1195
富 RICH → 2310
多 MANY → 2170
万 myriad → 2936
百 numerous → 2026

5-13 禾

穫 穫 穫 穫
1251 KAKU

CH 获 huò

Radical	Strokes
禾 115	18-5-13
Grade	Freq
Jōyō	1591
1-5-13	

▶HARVEST

COMPOUNDS

● [original meaning] **harvest, reap, gather**

収穫する *shūkaku suru* harvest, gather in, reap

SYNONYMS

● **harvest**

刈る reap → 28
摘 PICK → 694
採 PICK → 499

NOTE

★do not confuse with 獲 779

襟 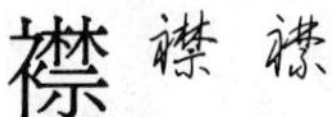

1252 KIN eri

CH 襟 jīn 

Radical	Strokes
衤 145	18-5-13
Grade	Freq
Jōyō	1944
1-5-13	

5-13 衤

▶**COLLAR**

COMPOUNDS

❶ **collar, lapel**

開襟シャツ *kaikin shatsu* wing-collared [open-neck] shirt

❷ inner mind, heart, bosom, thoughts

襟懐 *kinkai* inner thoughts, feelings

胸襟 *kyōkin* bosom, heart

KUN

【**eri 襟**】

[also 衿]

ⓐ collar, lapel, neck

ⓑ nape

襟巻き *erimaki* scarf, muffler

襟を正す *eri o tadasu* straighten oneself

詰め襟 *tsumeeri* stand-up collar

襟首 *erikubi* neck, back of neck

SYNONYMS

❶ **garment parts**

袖 SLEEVE → 1164

懐 BOSOM → 763

❷ **psyche**

衷 INNER HEART → 2575

胸 breast → 951

懐 BOSOM → 763

心 HEART → 11

腹 heart → 1034

神 MIND → 912

気 SPIRIT (consciousness) → 3194

精 SPIRIT (mind) → 1366

霊 SPIRIT (soul) → 2805

魂 SOUL, spirit → 1063

USAGE

eri

襟

[also 衿]

ⓐ collar, lapel, neck

ⓑ nape

衿

[also 襟] same as 襟

HOMOPHONES

eri ⇨ 衿 1140

礦 incorrect stroke count ⇨ see 1256

5-14 石

禱

1253 TŌ ino(ru)

CH 祷 dǎo

Radical	Strokes
示 113	19-5-14
Grade	Freq
Reference	
1-5-14	

5-14 示

COMPOUNDS

ⓐ [now usu. 祈る *inoru*] [original meaning] pray, wish for

ⓑ prayer

祈禱 *kitō* prayer

黙禱 *mokutō* silent prayer

禱り *inori* prayer

HOMOPHONES

inoru ⇨ 祈 875

inori ⇨ 祈 875

NOTE

⇨ see USAGE note at 祈 875

穫

1254

▶**HARVEST**

nonstandard for 穫 1251

5-14 禾

5-14 禾

穏 1255

▶CALM ▶MILD
nonstandard for 穏 1235

5-14 衤

襤

incorrect stroke count ⇨ see 1257

5-15 石

礦 1256 KŌ

CH 矿 kuàng

Radical	Strokes
石 112	20-5-15
Grade	Freq
Reference	
1-5-15	

COMPOUNDS
[now replaced by 鉱 1709]
❶ [original meaning] ore
礦石 *kōseki* ore, mineral
礦業 *kōgyō* mining (industry)

❷ⓐ mine
ⓑ suffix after names of mines
炭礦 *tankō* coal mine
夕張礦 *yūbarikō* Yubari Mine

5-15 衤

襤 1257 RAN

CH 襤 lán

Radical	Strokes
衤 145	20-5-15
Grade	Freq
Reference	
1-5-15	

COMPOUNDS
● [rarely also 藍 2381] [original meaning] rags, tattered clothes
襤褸 *ranru* (=*boro*) rags, tattered clothes

5-17 禾

穰 1258

▶YIELDING ABUNDANTLY
nonstandard for 穣 1250

6-1 糸

糺 1259

▶INQUIRE INTO
nonstandard for 糾 1278

6-1 舌

乱 1260 亂 乱 乿

RAN mida(reru) mida(ru) mida(su)

CH 乱 luàn

Radical	Strokes
乚 5	7-1-6
Grade	Freq
Jōyō-6	641
1-6-1	

ノ ニ 千 千 舌 舌 乱
1 2 3 4 5 6 7

▶DISORDERED

COMPOUNDS
❶ [also prefix]
ⓐ **disordered, confused, chaotic, boisterous, abusive, reckless**
ⓑ random
ⓒ [also 濫 801] **excessive, indiscriminate, extravagant, inordinate, haphazard, reckless**
乱雑 *ranzatsu* disorder, confusion
乱暴 *ranbō* violence, roughness; rape
乱闘 *rantō* free-for-all [confused] fight, me-

lee
乱気流 *rankiryū* turbulent air, turbulence
波乱(＝波瀾) *haran* disturbance, troubles; fluctuation
混乱 *konran* disorder, confusion, chaos
乱数 *ransū* random number
乱編成ファイル *ranhensei fairu* random file
乱読 *randoku* indiscriminate reading
乱用 *ran'yō* abuse, misuse, misappropriation
乱造 *ranzō* excessive production, careless manufacture
乱開発 *rankaihatsu* indiscriminate development

❷ⓐ **social disorder, disturbance**
ⓑ **rebellion, civil war, war, riot, revolt**
動乱 *dōran* upheaval, disturbance, agitation
戦乱 *senran* disturbances of war
反乱 *hanran* rebellion, revolt

❸ be corrupt, be demoralized
乱行 *rangyō* profligacy, debauchery, misconduct
淫乱 *inran* lewdness, lasciviousness

❹ [formerly 爛 1110] overripe, rotten
腐乱 *furan* ulceration, decomposition

INDEPENDENT

【ran 乱】 rebellion, civil war, war, riot, revolt, disturbance
乱を起こす *ran o okosu* rise in rebellion
応仁の乱 *ōnin no ran* Onin War (1467–1477)

KUN

【mida(reru) 乱れる】 be disordered, go out of order, be confused; be disturbed, be chaotic; be disheveled; be demoralized
乱れ *midare* disorder, disturbance, unrest
乱れ髪 *midaregami* disheveled hair
心が乱れる *kokoro ga midareru* lose one's composure

【mida(ru) 乱る】 *elegant* become disordered; put into disorder

【mida(su) 乱す】 put into disorder, throw into confusion, disturb; dishevel
掻き乱す *kakimidasu* throw into disorder

SYNONYMS

❶ⓐ **disordered**
紛 CONFUSED → 1296
錯 MIXED UP → 1743
混 mixed up → 519
雑 mixed up → 1385

ⓒ **rash**
濫 EXCESSIVE → 801
荒 WILD → 2260
暴 unrestrained → 2515
妄 RASH → 2016
盲 BLIND → 2053
滅 unreasonable → 660

❷ⓑ **warfare and rebellions**
戦 WAR → 1787
軍 war → 2080
役 war → 244
陣 battle → 455
変 uprising → 2069
闘 FIGHT → 3334

乳 incorrect stroke count ⇨ see 1438 | 6-1 孚

糾 ▶**INQUIRE INTO**
1261 nonstandard for 糺 1278 | 6-2 糸

取 1262

取 取 ㊥取 qǔ

SHU to(ru) to(ri) to(ri)- tori- -do(ri)

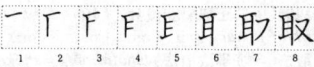

Radical	Strokes
又 29	8-2-6
Grade	**Freq**
Jōyō-3	184
◧ 1 - 6 - 2	

6-2 耳

Stroke order: 一 丅 F F E 耳 耳 取 (1–8)

▶**TAKE**

COMPOUNDS

❶ⓐ [original meaning] (grasp with the hands) **take, pick, gather**
ⓑ (bring into one's possession) **take, obtain, acquire, get, gather**
ⓒ take one of several, pick out, choose
ⓓ take away from, steal

採取 *saishu* picking, collecting, harvesting
摘取する *tekishu suru* pick, pluck up
取材する *shuzai suru* collect data [materials], gather news
取得する *shutoku suru* acquire, gain; purchase
摂取する *sesshu suru* take (in), ingest, absorb

二点先取する *niten senshu suru* take [score] the first two points of the game
聴取する *chōshu suru* listen to, give a hearing to
取捨する *shusha suru* take or leave, choose
詐取 *sashu* fraud, swindle
搾取 *sakushu* exploitation, sweating, squeezing

❷ face a challenge, come to grips with
進取の精神 *shinshu no seishin* progressive [enterprising] spirit

KUN

【to(ru) 取る】

①ⓐ take, take hold of, seize
ⓑ take off, take away, remove, delete, leave out
ⓒ take (a life) away, kill
ⓓ (ingest food) take, have, eat
ⓔ (secure by payment) take (in) (a newspaper), subscribe to; buy, order
ⓕ (take in crops) harvest, reap, gather
ⓖ (take money for) charge, ask
取り柄 *torie* merit, worth, recommendable feature
取り上げる *toriageru* take [pick] up; take away, confiscate; deliver a baby; accept, listen to; adopt (a proposal)
手に取る *te ni toru* take in one's hand
取り外す *torihazusu* remove, dismantle
帽子を取る *bōshi o toru* take off one's hat
蚊取り線香 *katorisenkō* mosquito-repellent incense
朝食を取る *chōshoku o toru* take breakfast
朝日新聞を取る *asahi shinbun o toru* take in [subscribe to] the *Asahi* (newspaper)
取り入れる *toriireru* take in; harvest; accept, adopt, introduce
食費を取る *shokuhi o toru* charge for one's meal

② get or cause to come into one's possession:
ⓐ take, receive, get, obtain, accept, acquire
ⓑ take possession of (a castle), seize, capture, conquer
ⓒ take away from, deprive, steal
ⓓ (reserve) take, book, engage
取り戻す *torimodosu* take back, regain, restore
関取 *sekitori* ranking sumo wrestler
受け取る *uketoru* receive, accept; understand
満点を取る *manten o toru* get full marks
連絡を取る *renraku o toru* get in touch with
城を取る *shiro o toru* take a castle
寝取る *netoru* steal another's wife [husband, lover]
席を取って置く *seki o totte oku* book [take] a seat

③ cause an abstract thing or action to shift towards oneself or elsewhere:
ⓐ take down (notes), write, record
ⓑ take on (responsibility), assume
ⓒ take (the meaning of a passage), make out, interpret
ⓓ take count, measure
ⓔ undergo, suffer
書き取る *kakitoru* write down, note down
ノートを取る *nōto o toru* note down, take notes
責任を取る *sekinin o toru* take responsibility for
気取る *kidoru* make an affected pose, assume airs
意味を取る *imi o toru* understand the meaning of, follow the sense
脈を取る *myaku o toru* take a pulse
不覚を取る *fukaku o toru* suffer a defeat

④ take (time), take up (space), require
手間を取る *tema o toru* take time, be detained
場所を取る *basho o toru* take up [occupy] space

【to(ri) 取り】 star performer; active partner in judo performances
頭取 *tōdori* (bank) president; greenroom manager

【to(ri)- 取り-, tori- 取-】

① emphatic verbal prefix implying that the action is performed with thoroughness and care
取り扱う *toriatsukau* handle, deal with, treat; deal in; handle, manipulate, operate; conduct; accept, take in
取り決める *torikimeru* make arrangements, agree upon
取り組む *torikumu* grapple, tackle (a problem)
取り調べ *torishirabe* investigation, inquiry
取り締まり *torishimari* control, management; supervisor
取り止めの無い *toritome no nai* wandering, incoherent, vague
取り立てて *toritatete* particularly

② transaction, dealings
取り引き *torihiki* transaction, dealings
公取委(＝公正取引委員会) *kōtorii* (＝*kōsei torihiki iinkai*) Fair Trade Commission
証取法(＝証券取引法) *shōtorihō* (＝*shōken torihiki-hō*) Securities and Exchange Act

③ abbrev. of 取り扱い *toriatsukai*: handling, operating
取説(＝取り扱い説明書) *torisetsu* (＝*toriatsukai-setsumeisho*) instruction manual

【-do(ri) -取り】

① arrangement, placement
間取り *madori* room arrangement
日取り *hidori* schedule

② manner, style

足取り *ashidori* one's manner of walking; trace (of a culprit's movement); (price) movement

SYNONYMS

❶ⓐ & 【toru】 ①ⓐ take

持 HOLD → 374
把 GRIP → 249
握 GRASP → 585
執 SEIZE → 1680
捕 CATCH → 429

ⓑ get

収 TAKE IN → 198
得 ACQUIRE → 477
獲 obtain → 779
拾 PICK UP → 379

ⓓ steal and rob

盗 STEAL → 2670
窃 STEAL → 2253
奪 ROB → 2343
略 plunder → 1169

USAGE

❶ toru

取る

①ⓐ take, take hold of, seize
ⓑ take off, take away, remove, delete, leave out
ⓒ take (a life) away, kill
ⓓ (ingest food) take, have, eat
ⓔ (secure by payment) take (in) (a newspaper), subscribe to; buy, order
ⓕ (take in crops) harvest, reap, gather
ⓖ (take money for) charge, ask

② get or cause to come into one's possession:
ⓐ take, receive, get, obtain, accept, acquire
ⓑ take possession of (a castle), seize, capture, conquer
ⓒ take away from, deprive, steal
ⓓ (reserve) take, book, engage

③ cause an abstract thing or action to shift towards oneself or elsewhere:
ⓐ take down (notes), write, record
ⓑ take on (responsibility), assume
ⓒ take (the meaning of a passage), make out, interpret
ⓓ take count, measure
ⓔ undergo, suffer

④ take (time), take up (space), require

採る

①ⓐ gather, collect, extract (oil), produce (wine out of grapes)
ⓑ admit (light)

②ⓐ pick (out), choose, prefer
ⓑ adopt, take, engage

執る

① perform (duties), conduct, transact, take (trouble)
② perform an action while holding an object (such as a pen)
③ persist in, insist on

捕る

catch, take, seize

撮る

photograph, shoot, film, videotape

❷ -dori

-取り

① arrangement, placement
② manner, style

-撮り

counter for number of shots [pictures] available in a film

HOMOPHONES

toru ⇨ 採 499 執 1680 捕 429 撮 737
-dori ⇨ 撮 737

COMPOUND FORMATION

関取 *sekitori*

関取 'ranking sumo wrestler' is a sumo wrestler (関) who acquired (取る ②ⓐ) a high rank.

NOTE

⇨ see COMPOUND FORMATION for 取り柄 *torie* ⇨ 柄 897

耴 1263

▶EMPLOYMENT

handwritten abbreviation for 職 1425

6-2 耳

耶

incorrect stroke count ⇨ see 1283

6-2 耳

臥

incorrect stroke count ⇨ see 1440

6-2 臣

6-2
至

到 到 到

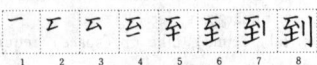

1264 TŌ ita(ru)▲

一 𠫔 厶 𠫓 至 至 到 到
1 2 3 4 5 6 7 8

Ⓒⓗ 到 dào

Radical	Strokes
刂 18	8-2-6
Grade	**Freq**
Jōyō	949
1 - 6 - 2	

▶**ARRIVE**

COMPOUNDS

❶ **arrive (at), reach, come to**

到着 *tōchaku* arrival

到達 *tōtatsu* arrival; attainment

到来 *tōrai* arrival, advent

殺到する *sattō suru* rush in, pour in; descend on

❷ reach [go to] the limit of

到底 *tōtei* after all, in the long run

到頭 *tōtō* at last, after all

❸ scrupulous, attentive

周到な *shūtō na* scrupulous, cautious, circumspect

精到な *seitō na* meticulous

KUN

【**ita(ru)** 到る】[usu. 至る] arrive at, reach, come to

目的地に到る *mokutekichi ni itaru* arrive at one's destination

SYNONYMS

❶ **arrive**

着 ARRIVE → 3316

至 COME TO → 2182

及 REACH TO → 3385

届く REACH → 3078

達 ATTAIN → 3139

HOMOPHONES

itaru ⇨ 至 2182

NOTE

⇨ see USAGE note at 至 2182

6-2
交

効 效 効 効

1265 KŌ ki(ku)

Ⓒⓗ 效 xiào

Radical	Strokes
力 19	8-2-6
Grade	**Freq**
Jōyō-5	669
1 - 6 - 2	

▶**EFFECT**

COMPOUNDS

ⓐ **effect, efficacy (esp. of drugs), virtue**

ⓑ (state of being operative or in force) **effect, effectiveness, validity**

効果 *kōka* effect, efficacy; result

効率 *kōritsu* efficiency

効能 *kōnō* effect, efficacy

即効 *sokkō* immediate effect

薬効 *yakkō* effect of a medicine

特効薬 *tokkōyaku* specific medicine

効力 *kōryoku* effect, efficacy; effect (as of a law), validity

有効な *yūkō na* effective, valid

無効 *mukō* invalidity, ineffectiveness

発効する *hakkō suru* become effective, take effect, come into force

INDEPENDENT

【**kō** 効】effect, efficacy, virtue

効が有る *kō ga aru* be efficacious, be beneficial to

KUN

【**ki(ku)** 効く】be effective, have an effect, produce a desired effect

効き *kiki* effectiveness (esp. of drugs)

効き目 *kikime* effect, efficacy

良く効く薬 *yoku kiku kusuri* very efficacious medicine

SYNONYMS

ⓐ **potency**

験 efficacy → 1833

能 action → 1323

機 function → 1076

USAGE

❶ **kiku**

効く

be effective, have an effect, produce a desired effect

利く

① work (well), function (properly)

② speak (esp. as a mediator)

❷ **kiki**

効き

effectiveness (esp. of drugs)

利き

function, efficacy

HOMOPHONES

kiku ⇨ 利 1114

kiki ⇨ 利 1114

郊

incorrect stroke count ⇨ see 1286

6-2 交

劾 劾 劾 劾

1266 GAI

Ⓒ劾 hé

Radical	Strokes
力 19	8-2-6
Grade	**Freq**
Jōyō	1917
◧ 1 - 6 - 2	

6-2 亥

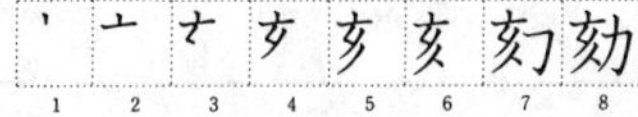

1 2 3 4 5 6 7 8

▶EXPOSE CRIMES

COMPOUNDS

● **expose (a person's) crimes or misdeeds, impeach, accuse; investigate crime**

劾奏する *gaisō suru* report an official's offense to the emperor

弾劾する *dangai suru* impeach, denounce, accuse

SYNONYMS

● **blame and accuse**

弾 impeach → 572

批 CRITICIZE → 250

難 find fault with → 1838

詰 REPRIMAND → 1521

叱 SCOLD → 182

責 BLAME → 2467

刻 刻 刻 刻

1267 KOKU kiza(mu) kiza(mi)

Ⓒ刻 kè

Radical	Strokes
刂 18	8-2-6
Grade	**Freq**
Jōyō-6	967
◧ 1 - 6 - 2	

6-2 亥

1 2 3 4 5 6 7 8

▶ENGRAVE ▶POINT OF TIME

COMPOUNDS

❶ [original meaning] (cut letters or designs on a surface) **engrave, carve, chisel**

刻印 *kokuin* carved seal, stamp

刻字 *kokuji* carving characters; carved characters

彫刻する *chōkoku suru* sculpt, carve, engrave

陰刻 *inkoku* white line

❷ⓐ **point of time, time, moment, hour**

ⓑ (period of time) time, interval

ⓒ two-hour period in former system of measuring time

刻限 *kokugen* time, appointed time

刻一刻 *kokuikkoku* moment by moment, hour by hour

時刻 *jikoku* time; hour

遅刻 *chikoku* tardiness, lateness

定刻 *teikoku* regular [appointed] time

即刻 *sokkoku* immediately, instantly

夕刻 *yūkoku* evening

上刻 *jōkoku* first third of a two-hour period

❸ division of a water clock

漏刻 *rōkoku* water clock

❹ cruel, severe

刻薄(=酷薄) *kokuhaku* cruelty, inhumanity

深刻な *shinkoku na* serious, grave, keen, poignant

INDEPENDENT

【koku 刻】 two-hour period (⇨ ❷ⓒ)

子の刻 *ne no koku* midnight

【kokusuru 刻する】 engrave

KUN

【kiza(mu) 刻む】 cut fine, chop up; engrave, carve; notch; (of a clock) tick (away)

刻み *kizami* notch, nick; shredded tobacco

刻み付ける *kizamitsukeru* engrave, inscribe

刻み出す *kizamidasu* carve out

小刻みに *kokizami ni* little by little, piecemeal

切り刻む *kirikizamu* cut, chop, mince

【kiza(mi) 刻み】

[in compounds]

ⓐ minced, shredded

ⓑ at equal intervals

刻み煙草 *kizamitabako* pipe tobacco; shredded tobacco

五分刻みで *gofunkizami de* every five minutes

SYNONYMS

❶ **form and carve**
彫 CARVE → 1683
塑 MODEL → 2843
鋳 CAST → 1729

❷ **time periods**
時 TIME → 924
頃 TIME → 144
暇 FREE TIME → 1012
般 period of time → 1317
間 INTERVAL → 3323
期 TERM → 1704
節 SEASON OF THE YEAR → 2691
季 SEASON (quarter) → 2554
候 SEASON (time of year) → 119

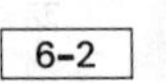
6-2
亥

劾
1268

▶EXPOSE CRIMES
nonstandard for 劾 1266

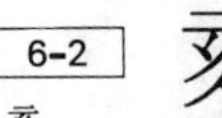
6-2
亥
刻
1269

▶ENGRAVE ▶POINT OF TIME
nonstandard for 刻 1267

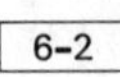
6-2
虍

剧
1270

▶DRAMA
handwritten abbreviation for 劇 1904

6-2
缶

卸
1271

▶WHOLESALE
nonstandard for 卸 1447

6-2
未
叔
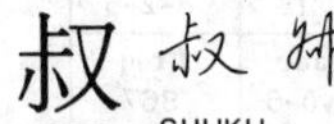
1272 SHUKU

Ⓒⓗ 叔 shū

Radical	**Strokes**
又 29	8-2-6
Grade	**Freq**
Jōyō	1891
1-6-2	

▶YOUNGER SIBLING OF PARENT

COMPOUNDS

❶ **younger sibling of one's parent, uncle, aunt**
叔父 *shukufu* (=*oji*) uncle (younger than one's parent)
叔母 *shukubo* (=*oba*) aunt (younger than one's parent)

❷ [archaic] third-born brother, younger brother
伯叔 *hakushuku* brothers

❸ [rare] declining, terminal
叔世 *shukusei* age of decline (said of a nation)

SPECIAL READINGS
叔父 *oji* uncle (younger than one's parent)
叔母 *oba* aunt (younger than one's parent)

SYNONYMS

❶ **siblings of parents**
伯 OLDER SIBLING OF PARENT → 59

6-2
有

郁

incorrect stroke count ⇨ see 1288

刷 刷 刷

1273 SATSU su(ru) -zu(ri) -zuri ha(ku)▲

CH 刷 shuā shuà

Radical	Strokes
刂 18	8-2-6
Grade	**Freq**
Jōyō-4	1351
1-6-2	

6-2 吊

Stroke order: 1 2 3 4 5 6 7 8

▶PRINT

COMPOUNDS

❶ⓐ print, put in print

ⓑ counter for printings

印刷 *insatsu* printing

縮刷する *shukusatsu suru* print in reduced size

増刷 *zōsatsu* additional printing, reprinting

第四版三刷 *daiyonhan sansatsu* fourth edition, third printing

❷ⓐ [original meaning] brush, scrub

ⓑ brush

刷新する *sasshin suru* reform, renovate, clean up

刷子 *sasshi* brush, commutator brush

KUN

【su(ru) 刷る】 print, put in print

刷り *suri* printing

刷り上げる *suriageru* finish printing, print off

【-zu(ri) -刷り, -zuri -刷】

ⓐ [suffix] printing

ⓑ counter for printings

校正刷り *kōseizuri* proofs

多色刷り *tashokuzuri* polychrome printing

第四刷 *daiyonzuri* fourth printing

【ha(ku) 刷く】 [also 掃く] brush, apply with a brush

刷毛 *hake* brush

紅を刷く *beni o haku* give [have] a brush of rouge (to one's cheeks)

SYNONYMS

❶ⓐ print and publish

印 print → 828

植 typeset → 990

刊 PUBLISH → 190

版 PUBLISHING → 872

載 PUT IN PRINT → 3300

掲 display in writing → 494

ⓑ editions

版 edition → 872

刊 publication → 190

訂 revision → 1442

HOMOPHONES

suru ⇨ 摺 693 擦 790 磨 3181

haku ⇨ 掃 503

NOTE

⇨ see USAGE notes at 擦 790 and 掃 503

郎

incorrect stroke count ⇨ see 1289

6-2 良

制 制 制

1274 SEI

CH 制 zhì

Radical	Strokes
刂 18	8-2-6
Grade	**Freq**
Jōyō-5	174
1-6-2	

6-2 朱

Stroke order: 1 2 3 4 5 6 7 8

▶SYSTEM ▶CONTROL

COMPOUNDS

❶ⓐ (organizational form) **system, organization, institution**

ⓑ [suffix] **system**

制度 *seido* system, organization, institution

体制 *taisei* system, structure, organization

市制 *shisei* city organization

税制 *zeisei* tax system

天皇制 *tennōsei* emperor system of Japan

六・三制 *rokusansei* the 6-3 school year system

❷ establish rules, enact, institute

制定する *seitei suru* establish, enact

制憲する *seiken suru* establish a constitution

制服 *seifuku* uniform, regulation uniform

❸ⓐ (hold in restraint) **control, restrain, restrict, suppress, inhibit**

ⓑ [prefix] anti-, -inhibiting

制止する *seishi suru* control, check, stop (a person) from (doing)

制限 *seigen* restriction, limit

制御する *seigyo suru* control, govern, suppress
抑制する *yokusei suru* control, suppress, inhibit
強制する *kyōsei suru* compel, force
制癌剤 *seiganzai* cancer-inhibiting drug
制酸薬 *seisan'yaku* gastric antacid
❹ⓐ (exercise authority) **control, regulate, dominate, command**
ⓑ have the upper hand, get the better of
制海権 *seikaiken* command of the sea, naval supremacy
管制塔 *kanseitō* control tower
統制する *tōsei suru* control, regulate
規制する *kisei suru* regulate, control
制勝する *seishō suru* win, chalk up a win
先制する *sensei suru* get a head start on
❺ make, produce (films)
制作 *seisaku* production (of a film), (literary) work
編制する *hensei suru* organize, form

INDEPENDENT

【sei 制】 system
【seisuru 制する】 control, govern; suppress, restrain; have the upper hand, get the better of

SYNONYMS

❶ **system**
系 SYSTEM → 1944
統 INTERCONNECTED SYSTEM → 1352
網 network → 1374
❸ⓐ **restrain**
禁 PROHIBIT → 2795
限 LIMIT → 398
抑 SUPPRESS → 257
束 TIE UP → 3554
縛 BIND → 1405
控える HOLD BACK → 495
渋る hang [hold] back → 513
❹ⓐ **direct and supervise**
管 EXERCISE CONTROL → 2701
轄 EXERCISE JURISDICTION OVER → 1627
掌 TAKE CHARGE OF → 2602
監 OVERSEE → 2852
督 SUPERVISE → 2796
司 OFFICIATE → 2931
宰 PRESIDE → 2275
営 MANAGE → 2603
理 manage → 970
経 MANAGE → 1331

NOTE

⇨ see USAGE note at 製 2803

6-2
朿

刺 刺 お

1275 SHI sa(su) sa(saru) sa(shi) sashi toge▲

Ⓒⓗ 刺 cì cī

Radical	Strokes
刂 18	8-2-6
Grade	**Freq**
Jōyō	959
1 - 6 - 2	

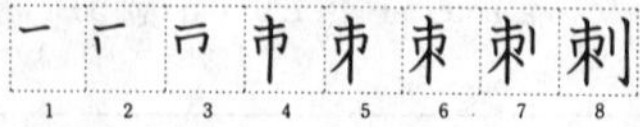

▶**STAB**

COMPOUNDS

❶ⓐ [original meaning] **stab, pierce, prick, thrust**
ⓑ **stab to death, assassinate**
ⓒ irritate
刺傷 *shishō* stab, pierced wound
刺繍 *shishū* embroidery
刺殺する *shisatsu suru* stab to death
刺客 *shikaku* assassin
刺激 *shigeki* stimulus; stimulation, excitation
❷ prickle, thorn, needle
刺状突起 *shijō-tokki* prickle (of plants)
有刺鉄線 *yūshitessen* barbed wire
❸ satirize, criticize
風刺 *fūshi* satire, sarcasm
❹ calling card
名刺 *meishi* calling [business] card

INDEPENDENT

【shi 刺】 calling card
刺を通じる *shi o tsūjiru* present one's card

KUN

【sa(su) 刺す】
①ⓐ stab, pierce, prick, thrust
ⓑ sting, bite
突き刺す *tsukisasu* stab, pierce, thrust
蜂に刺される *hachi ni sasareru* be stung by a bee
② sew, stitch
雑巾を刺す *zōkin o sasu* quilt a dustcloth
③ *baseball* catch (a runner) out
三塁で刺される *sanrui de sasareru* be put [thrown] out at third base
【sa(saru) 刺さる】 stick, be stuck
喉に刺さった骨 *nodo ni sasatta hone* bone stuck in one's throat
【sa(shi) 刺し, sashi 刺】
① stabbing, piercing, pricking
② stitch
刺し子 *sashiko* quilting
③ *sashimi*, sliced raw flesh (esp. of fish)
刺身 *sashimi sashimi*, sliced raw flesh (esp. of fish)

牛刺 *gyūsashi* sliced raw beef
【toge 刺】 thorn, prickle, barb; harshness, sarcasm
刺を抜く *toge o nuku* pull out a thorn
刺の有る言葉 *toge no aru kotoba* harsh language, stinging [barbed] words

SPECIAL READINGS

刺青▲ *irezumi* tattooing

SYNONYMS

❶ⓐ stab
突く THRUST → 2230
ⓑ kill
殺 KILL → 1324
絞 STRANGLE → 1349
窒 CHOKE → 2288
❷ needle
針 NEEDLE → 1666

HOMOPHONES

sasu ⇨ 差 3311 指 378 挿 431 注 325 射 1458 止 2941
sashi ⇨ 差 3311 指 378 止 2941

NOTE

⇨ see USAGE note at 差 3311

紀 1276 KI

ⒸⒽ 纪 jì jǐ

Radical	Strokes
糸 120	9-6-3
Grade	**Freq**
Jōyō-4	968
1-6-3	

6-3 糸

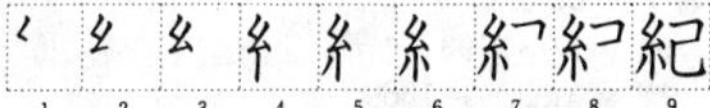

▶ERA

COMPOUNDS

❶ⓐ era, epoch, period of years, age
ⓑ [suffix] *geol* period
ⓒ age of a person
紀元 *kigen* era
世紀 *seiki* century
西紀 *seiki* Christian era
皇紀 *kōki* Imperial era
千年紀 *sennenki* millennium
デボン紀 *debonki* Devonian period
芳紀 *hōki* age of a young lady
❷ⓐ record [put down] in writing, record systematically, chronicle
ⓑ chronicle(s), annals, historical record
ⓒ abbrev. of 日本書紀 *nihonshoki*: Nihonshoki (Chronicles of Japan)
紀要 *kiyō* bulletin, proceedings
紀行 *kikō* travelogue
日本書紀 *nihonshoki* Nihonshoki (Chronicles of Japan)
記紀 *kiki* Kojiki and Nihonshoki
❸ discipline, morals, order, code of behavior
校紀 *kōki* school discipline
風紀 *fūki* public morals
綱紀 *kōki* law and order, official discipline
軍紀 *gunki* military discipline, troop morals
党紀 *tōki* party discipline
❹ abbrev. of 紀伊 *kii*, old name for Wakayama and south Mie prefectures
紀勢本線 *kisei honsen* Kisei Main Line (Wakayama-Mie Railway)

INDEPENDENT

【ki 紀】 *geol* period

SYNONYMS

❶ⓐ long time periods
世 AGE → 3496
代 age → 30
時 TIME → 924
朝 dynastic period → 1695
期 period → 1704
❷ⓐ write
記 WRITE DOWN → 1453
控える note down → 495
録 RECORD → 1742
登 register → 2595
写 COPY → 2000
書 WRITE → 2658
筆 write → 2677
❸ laws and rules
規 REGULATION → 978
矩 RULE → 1148
則 RULE → 1444
法 LAW → 333
律 LAW → 363
典 CANON → 2627
憲 CONSTITUTION → 2368
令 ordinance → 1995

NOTE

★do not confuse with 記 1453

6-3
糸

紅

1277 KŌ KU beni kurenai aka(i)▲

Ⓒ 红 hóng gōng

Radical	Strokes
糸 120	9-6-3
Grade	**Freq**
Jōyō-6	904
1 - 6 - 3	

1 2 3 4 5 6 7 8 9

▶CRIMSON

COMPOUNDS

❶ **crimson, deep red, red**

紅白 *kōhaku* red and white
紅海 *kōkai* Red Sea
紅葉 *kōyō* (=*momiji*) red leaves, crimson foliage, autumn tints
紅旗 *kōki* Red Flag
紅茶 *kōcha* black tea
紅衛兵 *kōeihei* Red Guards
深紅色 *shinkōshoku* deep crimson, scarlet
深紅 *shinku* crimson

❷ of a woman

紅涙 *kōrui* tears of a beautiful woman; tears of blood

KUN

【beni 紅】 rouge, lipstick; crimson, red
紅花 *benibana* safflower
口紅 *kuchibeni* lipstick, rouge
頬紅 *hōbeni* blusher
紅色 *beniiro* red, crimson

【kurenai 紅】 crimson, deep red, scarlet
薄紅 *usukurenai* light crimson, pink

【aka(i) 紅い】 [usu. 赤い] crimson, deep red
紅組 *akagumi* red team

SPECIAL READINGS

紅葉 *momiji* red leaves, crimson foliage, autumn tints; Japanese maple

SYNONYMS

❶ **red colors**

赤 RED → 2193
緋 SCARLET → 1369
朱 VERMILION → 3531
丹 CINNABAR → 3441
茜 MADDER → 2261

【beni】

○ **cosmetics**

粉 face powder → 1291

HOMOPHONES

akai ⇨ 赤 2193

NOTE

⇨ see USAGE note at 赤 2193

6-3
糸

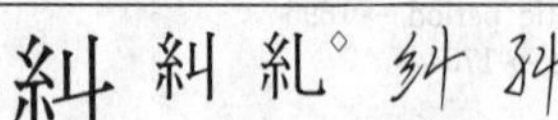

糾

1278 KYŪ tada(su)▲

Ⓒ 纠 jiū

Radical	Strokes
糸 120	9-6-3
Grade	**Freq**
Jōyō	1604
1 - 6 - 3	

1 2 3 4 5 6 7 8 9

▶INQUIRE INTO

COMPOUNDS

❶ **inquire into (esp. a crime), investigate into, examine**

糾明 *kyūmei* searching examination
糾弾 *kyūdan* impeachment, censure
糾問 *kyūmon* cross-examination, arraignment

❷ gather together

糾合する *kyūgō suru* gather together, muster, rally

❸ entangle

紛糾 *funkyū* complication, disorder, entanglement

KUN

【tada(su) 糾す】 inquire into, investigate into, examine
元を糾す *moto o tadasu* inquire into the origin, go to the bottom of an affair

SYNONYMS

❶ **investigate and examine**

勘 CHECK → 1777
験 TEST → 1833
審 EXAMINE CAREFULLY → 2360
査 LOOK INTO → 2437
調 INVESTIGATE → 1567
診 EXAMINE A PATIENT → 1504
検 EXAMINE → 986
探 PROBE → 505
討 STUDY → 1456
察 INSPECT → 2347
究 STUDY EXHAUSTIVELY → 2203
閲 REVIEW → 3330

HOMOPHONES

tadasu ⇨ 正 3484 質 2808

NOTE

⇨ see USAGE note at 正 3484

級 級 级 级

1279 KYŪ

CH 级 jí

Radical	Strokes
糸 120	9-6-3
Grade	Freq
Jōyō-3	573
1-6-3	

6-3 糸

▶GRADE

COMPOUNDS

❶ⓐ [also suffix] [original meaning] **grade, class, rank, degree, rating, level**

ⓑ grade or rank in go, judo or various martial arts (lower than 段 *dan*)

等級 *tōkyū* class, grade, rank, magnitude
特級品 *tokkyūhin* special grade article
階級 *kaikyū* class, estate; rank, grade
ライト級選手 *raitokyū senshu* lightweight boxer
初級 *shokyū* beginner's class, junior course
上級 *jōkyū* higher grade, advanced class, high class
高級 *kōkyū* high rank, high class [grade]
昇級 *shōkyū* promotion to a higher grade, advancement
第一級殺人 *daiikkyū satsujin* first degree murder
大使級会談 *taishikyū kaidan* ambassador-level conference
囲碁三級 *igo sankyū* third rank in the game of go

❷ **(school) grade, class, school year**

級友 *kyūyū* classmate
級長 *kyūchō* class president
学級 *gakkyū* class, grade
進級する *shinkyū suru* be promoted (to a higher grade)
同級 *dōkyū* same class [grade]
三年級 *sannenkyū* third year class

❸ decapitated head

首級 *shukyū* decapitated head

INDEPENDENT

【kyū 級】 grade, class
上の級に進む *ue no kyū ni susumu* move up to a higher grade

SYNONYMS

❶ⓐ **class**

段 grade → 1144
位 RANK → 61
階 RANK → 624
身 social status → 3553
格 STATUS → 926
等 CLASS → 2682
流 class → 441
層 STRATUM → 3161

❷ **class in school**

組 class → 1337

約 約 约 约

1280 YAKU

CH 约 yuē yāo

Radical	Strokes
糸 120	9-6-3
Grade	Freq
Jōyō-4	127
1-6-3	

6-3 糸

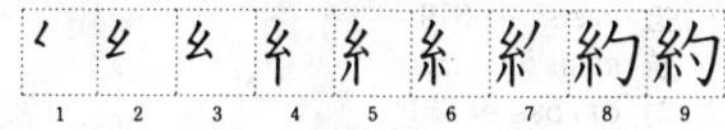

▶PROMISE ▶CONTRACT ▶APPROXIMATELY

COMPOUNDS

❶ⓐ **promise, make an agreement, conclude a treaty**

ⓑ **promise, agreement, contract, treaty**

約束 *yakusoku* promise, vow, pledge
契約 *keiyaku* contract, agreement
予約 *yoyaku* reservation, preengagement; subscription
公約 *kōyaku* public pledge [promise]
誓約 *seiyaku* vow, pledge, oath, swearing
約款 *yakkan* article, stipulation, provision, clause
条約 *jōyaku* treaty
婚約 *kon'yaku* engagement, betrothal
解約 *kaiyaku* dissolution [cancellation] of a contract

❷ⓐ [original meaning] **contract, abridge, summarize, shorten**

ⓑ *math* reduce

括約筋 *katsuyakukin* sphincter
制約 *seiyaku* restriction, limitation; condition
集約的な *shūyakuteki na* intensive
要約 *yōyaku* summary, abridged statement
約分 *yakubun* reduction of a fraction to lowest terms
公約数 *kōyakusū* common divisor

❸ economical, frugal
節約する *setsuyaku suru* economize, save
倹約する *ken'yaku suru* economize, be frugal [thrifty]

INDEPENDENT

【yaku 約】
① promise, vow
約を交わす *yaku o kawasu* exchange promises
② approximately, about
約百万円 *yaku hyakuman'en* approximately one million yen
約三年 *yaku sannen* about three years
③ abridgment, abbreviation

【yakusu 約す】 promise, vow, pledge; abridge, abbreviate, contract; *math* reduce

SYNONYMS

❶ promise
締 CONCLUDE (a treaty) → 1393
協 reach an agreement → 93
契 MAKE AN AGREEMENT → 2639
盟 ALLIANCE → 2794
誓 VOW → 2754

❷ⓐ contract and shrink
縮 SHRINK → 1414

ⓐ abridge
要 SUMMARIZE → 2635
抄 EXCERPT → 254
略 omit → 1169

【yaku】
② approximately
概 GENERAL → 1048
大 in substance → 3416
-頃 ABOUT → 144
位 about → 61
-方 about → 1963
-程 ...or thereabouts → 1190
辺り thereabouts → 3029

6-3

約 1281

▶PROMISE ▶CONTRACT ▶APPROXIMATELY
nonstandard for 約 1280

6-3
而

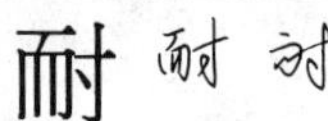

耐 1282

TAI ta(eru)

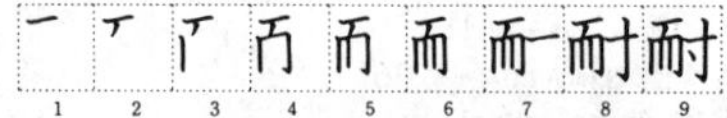

Ⓒⓗ 耐 nài

Radical	Strokes
而 126	9-6-3
Grade	**Freq**
Jōyō	1249
1 - 6 - 3	

▶WITHSTAND

COMPOUNDS

❶ⓐ (resist physical forces) **withstand, resist**
ⓑ [also prefix] **-proof, -resistant, -resisting**
耐火 *taika* fireproof
耐震 *taishin* earthquake-proof
耐熱 *tainetsu* heat-resisting
耐水 *taisui* waterproof
耐アルカリ性 *taiarukarisei* alkali resistance

❷ endure, bear, last
耐久 *taikyū* endurance, persistence; durability, life
耐乏 *taibō* austerity, voluntary privation
忍耐 *nintai* perseverance, patience, endurance

KUN

【ta(eru) 耐える】
ⓐ (resist physical forces) withstand, resist, be proof against
ⓑ [usu. 堪える] endure, bear, tolerate
火に耐える *hi ni taeru* be fireproof
重圧に耐える *jūatsu ni taeru* withstand pressures

SYNONYMS

❶ resist
抵 RESIST → 319
抗 RESIST → 252
対 OPPOSE → 831
反 COUNTER → 2945
逆 rebel → 3091

❶ⓑ & ❷ bear and endure
忍 BEAR → 2212
堪 ENDURE → 559

HOMOPHONES

taeru ⇨ 堪 559

NOTE

⇨ see USAGE note at 堪 559

1283 YA ka ya

Ⓒ耶 yé yē

Radical 耳 128	Strokes 9-6-3
Grade Names	Freq 2095
◧ 1 - 6 - 3	

6-3 耳

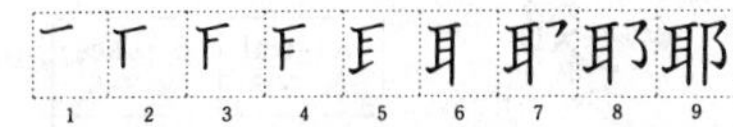

1 2 3 4 5 6 7 8 9

▶INTERROGATIVE PARTICLE

COMPOUNDS

❶ used phonetically for *Jesus*

耶蘇 *yaso* Jesus

❷ [archaic] father

耶嬢 *yajō* father and mother

KUN

【ka 耶】[formerly also 乎, now always か *ka*] interrogative particle

女子有り問うて曰く誰耶と *Joshi ari tōte iwaku tare ka to* A woman asked, "Who art thou?"

【ya 耶】[also 哉 or 也] classical rhetorical or exclamatory particle

安ぞ敢えて毒とせん耶 *Izukunzo aete doku to sen ya* How dare you regard it as poison?

NAMES

麻耶 *maya* female name

耶馬渓 *yabakei* place name

SYNONYMS

【ka】

○ classical particles

也 rhetorical particle → 3406

哉 EXCLAMATORY PARTICLE → 3294

USAGE

ka

耶

[formerly also 乎, now always か *ka*] interrogative particle

乎

[formerly also 耶, now always か *ka*] interrogative particle

HOMOPHONES

ya ⇨ 也 3406 哉 3294

ka ⇨ 乎 3504

NOTE

⇨ see also USAGE note at 也 3406

致

1284

▶BRING ABOUT ▶DO HUMBLY

nonstandard for 致 1316

6-3 至

虹 虹 虹

1285 KŌ niji

Ⓒ虹 hóng jiàng

Radical 虫 142	Strokes 9-6-3
Grade Names	Freq 2097
◧ 1 - 6 - 3	

6-3 虫

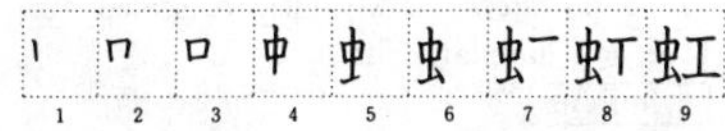

1 2 3 4 5 6 7 8 9

▶RAINBOW

COMPOUNDS

● **rainbow**

虹蜺 *kōgei literary* rainbow

虹彩 *kōsai* iris

白虹 *hakkō* [rare] white rainbow

KUN

【niji 虹】 rainbow

虹色 *nijiiro* rainbow colors

NAMES

虹子 *nijiko* female name

SYNONYMS

● **light**

照 sunlight → 2827

灯 LAMP → 825

明 light → 855

光 LIGHT → 2391

COMPOUND FORMATION

虹彩 *kōsai*

虹彩 'iris' literally refers to the colors (彩) of the rainbow (虹). The meaning of iris probably derives from the idea that the iris represents a rainbowlike display of eye colors. It may be an abbreviation of 虹彩膜 *kōsaimaku* 'rainbow-colored membrane', the Chinese term for iris.

6-3 开

形
incorrect classification ⇨ see 359
(nonstandard for 形 846)

6-3 交

郊
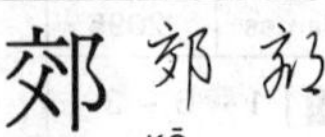
1286 KŌ

Ⓒ 郊 jiāo

Radical	Strokes
阝 163	9-3-6
Grade	**Freq**
Jōyō	1239

1 - 6 - 3

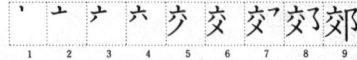

▶**SUBURB**

COMPOUNDS

● [original meaning] **suburb, outskirts, country**
郊外 *kōgai* suburbs, outskirts
郊野 *kōya* suburban fields
近郊 *kinkō* suburbs, outskirts
断郊競争 *dankō-kyōsō* cross-country race
西郊 *seikō* [rare] western suburb

SYNONYMS

● **the country**
里 COUNTRYSIDE → 3542
郷 the country → 549
辺 BORDERLAND → 3029

6-3 圭

封
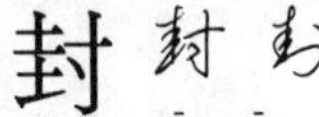
1287 FŪ HŌ

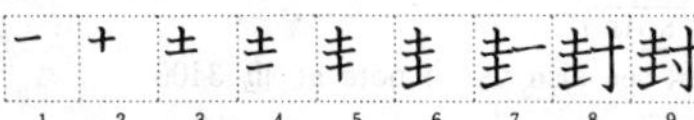

Ⓒ 封 fēng

Radical	Strokes
寸 41	9-3-6
Grade	**Freq**
Jōyō	1019

1 - 6 - 3

▶**SEAL**

COMPOUNDS

❶ **seal, seal off, block, enclose**
封印 *fūin* (stamped) seal
封鎖 *fūsa* blockade
封書 *fūsho* sealed letter
封殺 *fūsatsu baseball* force-out
密封する *mippū suru* seal hermetically, seal up
同封する *dōfū suru* enclose (in a letter)
❷ⓐ (invest with a fief or feudal estate) **enfeoff**
ⓑ (territory of a daimyo) daimiate, fief
封建制度 *hōken seido* feudalism
封地 *hōchi* daimiate, fief
封土 *hōdo* daimiate, fief
❸ *baseball* abbrev. of 封殺 *fūsatsu*: force-out, force play
二封 *nifū* two force-outs

INDEPENDENT

【fū 封】 seal, sealing, closing; abbrev. of 封殺 *fūsatsu*: *baseball* force-out
封を切る *fū o kiru* break the seal
【fūjiru (=fūzuru) 封じる(=封ずる)】 seal, glue up, fasten; enclose, block, seal off; shut up by incantation; bar, ban, prohibit
私は口を封じられている *Watakushi wa kuchi o fūjirarete iru* My lips are sealed
【hō 封】 daimiate, fief

SYNONYMS

❶ **close**
閉 CLOSE → 3319
鎖 lock up → 1761
❷ⓑ **feudal territorial divisions**
領 fief → 1224
荘 manor (in feudal Japan) → 2262
藩 FEUDAL DOMAIN → 2379
国 province (in former Japan) → 3087

郁 郁 郁

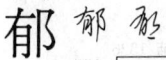

1288 IKU NAMES aya kaoru

ノ ナ オ 有 有 有 有⁷ 有阝 郁

1 2 3 4 5 6 7 8 9

Ⓒⓗ 郁 yù

Radical	Strokes
阝 163	9-3-6
Grade	**Freq**
Names	2030
◧ 1 - 6 - 3	

6-3 有

▶**AROMATIC**

COMPOUNDS

❶ **aromatic, rich in aroma, fragrant, sweet-smelling**

馥郁たる *fukuikutaru* sweet-smelling, fragrant

❷ teeming with culture, flourishing

郁郁たる *ikuikutaru* teeming with culture, flourishing; diffusing of aroma, aromatic

NAMES

郁子 *ikuko* female name

郁夫 *ikuo* (=*ayao*) male name

SYNONYMS

❶ **smell and fragrance**

薫 BALMY → 2371

芳 FRAGRANT → 2210

馨 PERFUME → 2879

気 smell → 3194

臭 BAD SMELL → 2633

香 SWEET SMELL → 2568

郎 郎 郎 郎

1289 RŌ

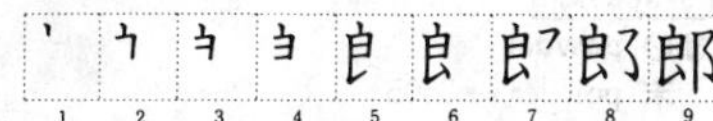

Ⓒⓗ 郎 láng

Radical	Strokes
阝 163	9-3-6
Grade	**Freq**
Jōyō	293
◧ 1 - 6 - 3	

6-3 良

▶**YOUNG MAN** ▶**MALE NAME SUFFIX**

COMPOUNDS

❶ *elegant* **young man, man; husband**

郎君 *rōkun* [rare] young nobleman, young lord

野郎 *yarō* guy, fellow, man, rascal

遊冶郎 *yūyarō* man of pleasure, libertine

新郎新婦 *shinrō shinpu* bride and bridegroom

❷ **suffix for forming male names, usu. indicating order of birth**

一郎 *ichirō* Ichiro (name of eldest son)

次郎 *jirō* Jiro (name of second son)

太郎 *tarō* Taro

❸ retainer, vassal, manservant

郎等(=郎党) *rōdō* retainers, vassals, followers

下郎 *gerō* servant; menial

女郎 *jorō* prostitute, courtesan

SYNONYMS

❶ **man**

男 MAN → 2542

雄 MALE → 1008

夫 male adult → 3460

翁 OLD MAN → 2108

❷ **name suffixes**

麿 CLASSICAL MALE NAME SUFFIX → 3184

彦 MALE NAME ELEMENT → 3295

-子 female name element → 3390

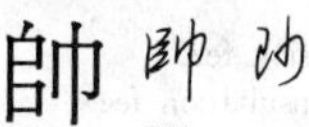

1290 SUI

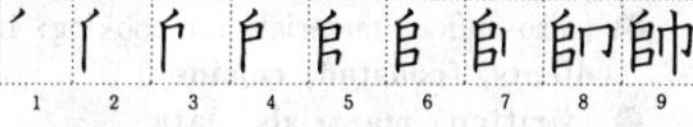

Ⓒⓗ 帅 shuài

Radical	Strokes
巾 50	9-3-6
Grade	**Freq**
Jōyō	1724
◧ 1 - 6 - 3	

6-3 自

▶**COMMANDER IN CHIEF**

COMPOUNDS

ⓐ **commander in chief, leader, general**

ⓑ [original meaning] command, lead troops

元帥 *gensui* marshal, general

将帥 *shōsui* commander

総帥 *sōsui* commander in chief

統帥 *tōsui* supreme command

SYNONYMS

ⓐ **military officers and ranks**

督 COMMANDER → 2796
将 GENERAL OFFICER → 460
佐 FIELD OFFICER → 67
尉 COMPANY OFFICER → 1685
曹 SERGEANT → 2746

NOTE
★do not confuse with 師 1326

6-4
*

粉 粉 粉 粉

1291 FUN ko kona deshimētoru▲

Ⓒⓗ 粉 fěn

Radical	Strokes
米 119	10-6-4
Grade	Freq
Jōyō-4	1097
1 - 6 - 4	

▶**POWDER**

COMPOUNDS

❶ⓐ [original meaning] **powder, dust**
ⓑ (grind to a powder) powder, pulverize
粉末 *funmatsu* powder
粉乳 *funnyū* powdered milk
鉄粉 *teppun* iron powder
精粉 *seifun* fine powder
粉砕 *funsai* pulverization
❷ (powdered meal) **flour, meal**
穀粉 *kokufun* grain [rice] flour
澱粉 *denpun* starch
米粉 *beifun* rice flour
製粉 *seifun* flour milling
❸ⓐ face powder, cosmetics
ⓑ apply face powder, make up
脂粉 *shifun* cosmetics, rouge and powder
紅粉 *kōfun* rouge and powder
粉飾 *funshoku* embellishment, makeup
❹ (color of powdered meal) white, white-washed
粉壁 *funpeki* white wall

KUN

【**ko** 粉】[also suffix] powder, dust; flour, meal
洗濯粉 *sentakuko* detergent
小麦粉 *komugiko* (wheat) flour
【**kona** 粉】powder, dust; flour, meal
粉薬 *konagusuri* powdered medicine
粉粉になる *konagona ni naru* go to pieces, break into fragments
【**deshimētoru** 粉】decimeter

SYNONYMS

❶ⓐ **powder**
末 powder → 3505
❷ **cereal**
穀 CEREAL → 1824
❸ⓐ **cosmetics**
紅 rouge → 1277
ⓑ **decorate**
粧 APPLY MAKEUP → 1345
飾 DECORATE → 1717
装 DRESS → 2685

6-4
*

料 料 料

1292 RYŌ

Radical	Strokes
斗 68	10-4-6
Grade	Freq
Jōyō-4	243
1 - 6 - 4	

▶**FEE** ▶**MATERIALS**

COMPOUNDS

❶ [also suffix]
ⓐ (charge for services) **fee, charge, rate, allowance**
ⓑ (payment received for services) **fee, remuneration**
料金 *ryōkin* charge, rate, fee, fare
無料 *muryō* no charge, free
送料 *sōryō* postage, carriage
手数料 *tesūryō* commission, (handling) fee, charge
使用料 *shiyōryō* rental fee
入場料 *nyūjōryō* admission fee
診察料 *shinsatsuryō* consultation fee
給料 *kyūryō* salary, pay, wages
❷ⓐ **materials, material, stuff, matter**
ⓑ [also suffix] materials for cooking: **ingredients, foodstuff, cuisine**
ⓒ (written) **materials, data**
材料 *zairyō* material, matter, stuff; factor, element
原料 *genryō* raw material
燃料 *nenryō* fuel
食料 *shokuryō* food, foodstuffs
清涼飲料水 *seiryō inryōsui* cooling drink

料理 *ryōri* cooking, cuisine; handling
料亭 *ryōtei* high-class restaurant, Japanese restaurant
調味料 *chōmiryō* seasoning, flavoring
資料 *shiryō* materials, data
史料 *shiryō* historical materials [records]
❸ conjecture, infer, consider
料簡 *ryōken* idea, thought, intention, discretion
思料(=思量)する *shiryō suru* consider carefully, think

INDEPENDENT

【ryō 料】 materials; fee, charge
研究の料 *kenkyū no ryō* research materials

SYNONYMS

❶ⓐ fee and price
代 CHARGE → 30
賃 CHARGES → 2694
銭 money paid → 1725
費 EXPENSE → 2607
価 PRICE → 87
値 price → 109
ⓑ pay and earnings
給 PAY → 1350
賃 WAGE → 2694
俸 SALARY → 114
禄 RETAINER'S STIPEND → 1002
収 income → 198
❷ matter
資 material resources → 2695
材 MATERIAL → 836
物 substance → 874
質 MATTER → 2808

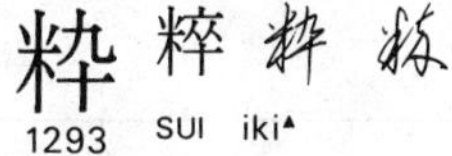

1293 SUI iki▲

CH 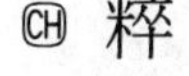 cuì

Radical	Strokes
米 119	10-6-4
Grade	**Freq**
Jōyō	1556
1 - 6 - 4	

6-4

▶REFINED

COMPOUNDS

❶ⓐ (free from impurities) **refined, pure, unmixed**
ⓑ (best part) **essence, quintessence**
純粋な *junsui na* pure, genuine; unalloyed, unmixed
生粋の *kissui no* trueborn, pure, genuine
精粋 *seisui* essence, purity
国粋 *kokusui* national characteristics
❷ (free from coarseness) **refined, sophisticated, polished, elegant, cultivated, tasteful**
粋人 *suijin* refined [romantic] man
粋狂(=酔狂) *suikyō* vagary, whim
無粋(=不粋)な *busui na* lacking in polish, inelegant; unromantic
❸ [formerly 萃 2479] gather, assemble
抜粋 *bassui* extract, excerpt, selection

INDEPENDENT

【sui 粋】 essence, pith, quintessence; refinement, cultivation; delicacy, considerateness
流行の粋 *ryūkō no sui* the cream [pink] of fashion
粋な人 *sui na hito* man of well-cultivated tastes
粋な裁き *sui na sabaki* delicate judgment

KUN

【iki 粋】 smartness, stylishness, chic
粋な *iki na* stylish, smart, chic
粋がる *ikigaru* try to appear smart

SYNONYMS

❶ⓐ clean and purified
精 refined (purified) → 1366
潔 IMMACULATE → 744
純 PURE → 1297
浄 CLEAN → 382
清 clean → 523
ⓑ essential part
精 ESSENCE (essential part) → 1366
髄 essence (vital part) → 1842
枢 PIVOT → 865
幹 TRUNK → 1718
綱 ESSENTIAL POINTS → 1372
旨 PURPORT → 2024
要 summary → 2635
❷ elegant
彬 REFINED AND GENTLE → 960
雅 ELEGANT → 1197
淑 GRACEFUL → 527
優 graceful → 177

1294

▶POWDER

nonstandard for 粉 1291

6-4

6-4 糸

紡 紡 紡
1295 BŌ tsumu(gu)

Ⓒ 纺 fǎng

Radical	Strokes
糸 120	10-6-4
Grade	**Freq**
Jōyō	1068

1 - 6 - 4

▶**SPIN**

COMPOUNDS

● [original meaning] **spin, make yarn**

紡糸 *bōshi* spinning; spun cotton [wool]
紡績 *bōseki* spinning
紡織 *bōshoku* spinning and weaving
紡錘 *bōsui* spindle
紡毛 *bōmō* carded wool
混紡 *konbō* mixed spinning
綿紡 *menbō* cotton spinning

KUN

【**tsumu(gu)** 紡ぐ】 spin, make yarn
綿を糸に紡ぐ *men o ito ni tsumugu* spin cotton into yarn

SYNONYMS

● **weave and sew**

績 spin → 1412
織 WEAVE → 1422
縫 SEW → 1406
編 KNIT → 1387
組 braid → 1337

6-4 糸

紛 紛 紛
1296 FUN magi(reru) -magi(re) magi(rasu) magi(rawasu) magi(rawashii)

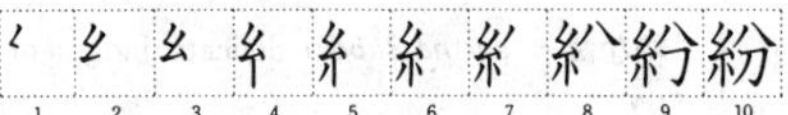

Ⓒ 纷 fēn

Radical	Strokes
糸 120	10-6-4
Grade	**Freq**
Jōyō	1004

1 - 6 - 4

▶**CONFUSED**

COMPOUNDS

ⓐ [original meaning] (in a jumbled state) **confused, tangled, disorderly**
ⓑ confusion, trouble

紛争 *funsō* conflict, strife
紛失 *funshitsu* loss
紛紛と *funpun to* confusedly; in profusion
紛乱 *funran* confusion, disorder
紛糾 *funkyū* complication, disorder, entanglement
内紛 *naifun* internal trouble [strife]; storm in a teacup

KUN

【**magi(reru)** 紛れる】 be confused with, get mixed with, be mistaken for; be diverted from
紛れ *magire* confusion
紛れ込む *magirekomu* get lost among, disappear in (the crowd)
闇に紛れて *yami ni magirete* under cover of night
気が紛れる *ki ga magireru* be diverted [distracted] from

【**-magi(re)** -紛れ】 [suffix] in a fit of, out of, taking advantage of
腹立ち紛れに *haradachimagire ni* in a fit of anger
どさくさ紛れに *dosakusamagire ni* taking advantage of the confusion

【**magi(rasu)** 紛らす】 divert, distract; beguile, evade, conceal
悲しみを紛らす *kanashimi o magirasu* divert one's mind from sorrow
冗談に紛らす *jōdan ni magirasu* turn it off as a joke

【**magi(rawasu)** 紛らわす】 same as **magirasu** 紛らす

【**magi(rawashii)** 紛らわしい】 confusing, misleading, ambiguous
紛らわしい名前 *magirawashii namae* confusing [misleading] name

SYNONYMS

ⓐ **disordered**

乱 DISORDERED → 1260
錯 MIXED UP → 1743
混 mixed up → 519
雑 mixed up → 1385

葉 LEAF → 2321
丁 sheet → 3348
頁 PAGE → 2086
面 page (of a newspaper) → 2087

❷ **periodicals**
報 bulletin → 1698
誌 MAGAZINE → 1548

紛 1303

▶**CONFUSED**
nonstandard for 紛 1296

6-4 糸

級 1304

▶**GRADE**
nonstandard for 級 1279

6-4 糸

紋 1305

▶**CREST**
nonstandard for 紋 1299

6-4 糸

納 1306

▶**PAY** ▶**ACCEPT** ▶**PUT AWAY**
nonstandard for 納 1300

6-4 糸

級

incorrect stroke count ⇨ see 1279

6-4 糸

缺 1307

▶**LACK**
nonstandard for 欠 1987

6-4 缶

耕 耕 耕 耕 1308

KŌ tagaya(su)

CH 耕 gēng

Radical	Strokes
耒 127	10-6-4
Grade	**Freq**
Jōyō-5	1474
1 - 6 - 4	

6-4 耒

Stroke order: 1 2 3 4 5 6 7 8 9 10

▶**TILL**

COMPOUNDS

❶ [original meaning] **till, plow**
耕作する *kōsaku suru* cultivate, plow, till
耕地 *kōchi* arable land, farm land
耕具 *kōgu* farm implements
耕運機 *kōunki* cultivator, tiller
農耕 *nōkō* farming
深耕 *shinkō* deep plowing
晴耕雨読 *seikōudoku* working in the field in fine weather and reading at home in rainy weather

❷ earn one's livelihood by writing [copying]
筆耕料 *hikkōryō* copying fee

KUN

【tagaya(su) 耕す】 till, plow, cultivate
耕し得る土地 *tagayashiuru tochi* arable land

SYNONYMS

❶ **farm and plant**
作 raise crops → 68
農 farm, FARMING → 2698
培 CULTIVATE → 464
栽 PLANT (saplings) → 3297
植 PLANT → 990

6-4 耗 耗 耗 耗 ㊥ 耗 hào

1309 MŌ KŌ

Radical	Strokes
耒 127	10-6-4
Grade	**Freq**
Jōyō	1784

1 - 6 - 4

一 二 三 丰 耒 耒 耒 耒 耗 耗

▶**WEAR AWAY**

COMPOUNDS

ⓐ **wear away, wear out, use up, consume**

ⓑ become worn out, become exhausted

摩耗する *mamō suru* wear away, wear out

減耗 *genmō* natural decrease

消耗する *shōmō suru* consume, exhaust, use up

損耗する *sonmō* (=*sonkō*) *suru* wear out, be wasted, be worn out

心神耗弱者 *shinshin-kōjakusha* feebleminded person

SYNONYMS

ⓐ **consume**

消 SPEND → 443

費 expend → 2607

尽 EXHAUST → 3050

ⓐ **decrease**

減 DECREASE → 601

削 cut down → 1448

縮 SHRINK → 1414

落 FALL → 2318

6-4 耘 ㊥ 耘 yún

1310 UN

Radical	Strokes
耒 127	10-6-4
Grade	**Freq**
Reference	

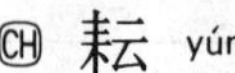

COMPOUNDS

● [now also 運 3140] [original meaning] weed, remove weeds

耕耘機 *kōunki* cultivator, tiller

6-4 耕 ▶**TILL**

1311 nonstandard for 耕 1308

6-4 秏 ▶**WEAR AWAY**

1312 nonstandard for 耗 1309

6-4 恥 耻◇ 恥 恥 ㊥ 耻 chǐ

1313 CHI ha(jiru) haji ha(jirau) ha(zukashii)

Radical	Strokes
心 61	10-4-6
Grade	**Freq**
Jōyō	1626

1 - 6 - 4

▶**SHAME**

COMPOUNDS

❶ⓐ **shame, disgrace, dishonor, humiliation**

ⓑ **feel [be] ashamed**

恥辱 *chijoku* disgrace, dishonor, shame

羞恥 *shūchi* shyness; sense of shame

厚顔無恥な *kōganmuchi na* shameless, unscrupulous

破廉恥 *harenchi* shamelessness, infamy, impudence

❷ private parts, pubic region

恥骨 *chikotsu* pubic bone, pubis

恥丘 *chikyū* mons pubis, mons veneris

恥部 *chibu* private parts; something to be ashamed of

KUN

【ha(jiru) 恥じる】feel ashamed
恥じ入る *hajiiru* feel quite ashamed
【haji 恥】shame, disgrace, humiliation
恥知らず *hajishirazu* shameless person
【ha(jirau) 恥じらう】be shy [coy], look abashed
恥じらい *hajirai* shyness
【ha(zukashii) 恥ずかしい】shy; ashamed; shameful, disgraceful
恥ずかしがる *hazukashigaru* be shy [coy], be abashed
気恥ずかしい *kihazukashii* feel ashamed, feel awkward

SYNONYMS

❶ **disgrace**
辱 HUMILIATE → 2736
侮 INSULT → 82
汚 defile → 222
❷ **genitals**
陰 sex organ → 541
胎 WOMB → 918

耻
1314

▶SHAME
nonstandard for 恥 1313

6-4 耳

聀
1315

▶EMPLOYMENT
handwritten abbreviation for 職 1425

6-4 耳

致 致 致 𢻰
1316 CHI ita(su)

㊥ 致 zhì

Radical	Strokes
至 133	10-6-4
Grade	**Freq**
Jōyō	885
◧ 1 - 6 - 4	

6-4 至

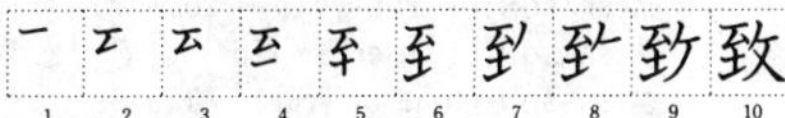

▶BRING ABOUT ▶DO HUMBLY

COMPOUNDS

❶ⓐ **bring about, cause to, lead to, incur**
ⓑ cause to reach an extreme
致死の *chishi no* lethal, fatal
致命的 *chimeiteki* fatal
一致 *itchi* accord, agreement
合致 *gatchi* agreement, concurrence
極致 *kyokuchi* culmination, acme
❷ⓐ [original meaning] **cause to come, invite, lure**
ⓑ cause to reach, send, forward
誘致 *yūchi* lure, enticement, attraction; bringing about
招致 *shōchi* summons, invitation
拉致する *rachi suru* take (a person) away, kidnap
送致 *sōchi* sending, forwarding
❸ good taste, elegance, grace
風致 *fūchi* taste, elegance
筆致 *hitchi* literary style; stroke of the brush, touch
❹ resign, retire
致仕 *chishi* resignation; seventy years of age

KUN

【ita(su) 致す】
① do humbly, perform an action (with humility)
致し方 *itashikata* way, method
これは如何致しましょうか *Kore wa ikaga itashimashō ka* What shall I do with this?
どう致しまして *Dō itashimashite* You are welcome
②ⓐ bring about, lead to, cause
ⓑ forward, send
人を死に致す *hito o shi ni itasu* cause the death of a person
不才の致す所 *fusai no itasu tokoro* be due to my incompetence
思いを致す *omoi o itasu* give one's thought to, think of
③ render (assistance), exert (oneself)
力を致す *chikara o itasu* make an effort, render assistance

SYNONYMS

❶ⓐ **cause**
誘 INDUCE → 1550
【itasu】
① **do and act**
為 DO → 3577
仕 DO → 34
行 ACT → 212
作 WORK → 68

6-4 舟

般 1317 HAN

1 2 3 4 5 6 7 8 9 10

CH 般 bān

Radical	Strokes
舟 137	10-6-4
Grade	Freq
Jōyō	551
1 - 6 - 4	

▶**SORT**

COMPOUNDS

❶ (things of the same category) **sort, kind, way**
一般の *ippan no* general, universal, widespread
全般の *zenpan no* whole, general, overall
万般 *banpan* all things, all affairs, all sorts of matters
百般の *hyappan no* all, every, all sorts of
諸般の *shohan no* various, several, all, every
❷ **period of time**
先般 *senpan* the other day, some time ago
今般 *konpan* now, recently
過般 *kahan* some time ago, recently
❸ used phonetically for *han* in the transliteration of 般若 *hannya Prajñā*
般若 *hannya* wisdom, prajna

SYNONYMS

❶ **kinds and types**
類 KIND → 1807
色 kind → 2029
属 genus → 3145
品 category → 2248
型 TYPE → 2638
種 VARIETY → 1218
様 variety → 1052
❷ **time periods**
頃 TIME → 144
暇 FREE TIME → 1012
時 TIME → 924
刻 POINT OF TIME → 1267
間 INTERVAL → 3323
期 TERM → 1704
節 SEASON OF THE YEAR → 2691
季 SEASON (quarter) → 2554
候 SEASON (time of year) → 119

6-4 舟

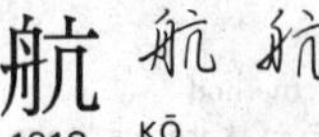

航 1318 KŌ

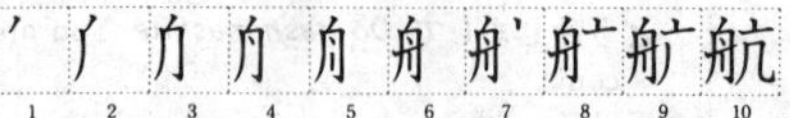

1 2 3 4 5 6 7 8 9 10

CH 航 háng

Radical	Strokes
舟 137	10-6-4
Grade	Freq
Jōyō-4	456
1 - 6 - 4	

▶**NAVIGATE**

COMPOUNDS

❶ⓐ (travel over water) **navigate, sail, cruise**
ⓑ navigation, voyage
航行 *kōkō* navigation, cruise
航法 *kōhō* navigation
航海 *kōkai* voyage, ocean navigation
潜航 *senkō* submarine voyage, underwater navigation
運航 *unkō* navigation; (airline or shipping) service
難航 *nankō* hard passage, rough going
欠航 *kekkō* suspension of (ferry or aircraft) service
密航 *mikkō* secret passage, stowing away

❷ⓐ (travel through the air) **navigate, fly**
ⓑ abbrev. of 航空 *kōkū*: flying, aviation
航空 *kōkū* aviation, aerial navigation
航空機 *kōkūki* aircraft, airplane
航宙 *kōchū* space flight
日航 *nikkō* Japan Airlines

INDEPENDENT

【**kōsuru** 航する】navigate, sail, cruise

SYNONYMS

❶ⓐ **travel by vehicle**
乗 RIDE → 3576
走 travel by vehicle → 2194
騎 RIDE ON HORSEBACK → 1834
❷ⓐ **fly**
飛 FLY → 3572
翔 SOAR → 1357

蚊 蚊 蚊 蚊

1319 BUN▲ ka

ⒸⒽ 蚊 wén

Radical	Strokes
虫 142	10-6-4
Grade	Freq
Jōyō	1711
1-6-4	

6-4 虫

▶**MOSQUITO**

COMPOUNDS

● [original meaning] **mosquito**
飛蚊症 *hibunshō* myodesopsia

KUN

【**ka** 蚊】[also suffix] mosquito
蚊の鳴く様な声 *ka no naku yō na koe* very thin [faint] voice
蚊取り線香 *katorisenkō* mosquito-repellent incense
蚊帳 *kaya* mosquito net
藪蚊 *yabuka* striped mosquito
小型赤家蚊 *kogata-akaieka Culex tritaeniorhynchus*

SYNONYMS

● **insects**
蛍 FIREFLY → 2591
蝶 BUTTERFLY → 1401
蚕 SILKWORM → 2457

䘇

1320

▶**MOSQUITO**
nonstandard for 蚊 1319

6-4 虫

效

1321

▶**EFFECT**
nonstandard for 効 1265

6-4 交

敏 敏 敏 敏

1322 BIN

ⒸⒽ 敏 mǐn

Radical	Strokes
攵 66	10-4-6
Grade	Freq
Jōyō	1345
1-6-4	

6-4 毎

▶**NIMBLE**

COMPOUNDS

❶ (physically agile) **nimble, agile, quick, alert**
敏速 *binsoku* quickness, agility, activity
敏捷な *binshō na* agile, nimble, quick; shrewd, smart
機敏 *kibin* smartness, shrewdness, sharpness; quickness, promptness

❷ (mentally agile) **nimble, clever, shrewd; keen, sharp**
敏感な *binkan na* sensitive
敏腕 *binwan* ability, capability
鋭敏な *eibin na* sharp, keen, sensitive

INDEPENDENT

【**bin** 敏】agility, alacrity, quickness
機を見るに敏なり *ki o miru ni bin nari* be quick at seizing an opportunity

SYNONYMS

❶ **fast**
即 IMMEDIATE → 1120
迅 SWIFT → 3046
急 rapid → 2092
快 fast → 245
疾 fast → 3279
速 QUICK → 3105
早 QUICK → 2390

❷ **intelligent and wise**
鋭 SHARP → 1730
聡 SHARP-WITTED → 1384
俊 brilliant → 102
明 clear-sighted → 855
哲 SAGACIOUS → 2738
怜 CLEVER → 298
慧 INTELLIGENT → 2810
賢 WISE → 2839
智 wise → 2784

6-4

⺈

能 能 㑺

1323 NŌ

Ⓒ 能 néng

Radical	Strokes
月 130	10-4-6
Grade	**Freq**
Jōyō-5	383
■ 1 - 6 - 4	

1 2 3 4 5 6 7 8 9 10

▶ABILITY

COMPOUNDS

❶ⓐ ability, capability
ⓑ able, skilled, skillful
能力 *nōryoku* ability, capacity, faculty
技能 *ginō* skill, ability, capacity
芸能 *geinō* public entertainment
才能 *sainō* talent, ability
万能 *bannō* omnipotence
有能な *yūnō na* able, competent
知能 *chinō* intelligence, mental capacity
本能 *honnō* instinct
能筆 *nōhitsu* skillful penmanship
能弁 *nōben* eloquence, oratory
能吏 *nōri* able official
❷ possible, can
可能性 *kanōsei* possibility
不能な *funō na* impossible; impotent
❸ⓐ action, function, effect, efficiency
ⓑ act upon, affect
能率 *nōritsu* efficiency
機能 *kinō* function, faculty
性能 *seinō* performance, capacity, efficiency
効能 *kōnō* effect, efficacy
能動的 *nōdōteki* active
❹ *phys* energy, power
放射能 *hōshanō* radioactivity
❺ noh play
能面 *nōmen* noh mask
脇能 *wakinō* minor piece in noh plays

INDEPENDENT

【nō 能】 ability, capability; noh play
能が無い *nō ga nai* have no merit
能を演ずる *nō o enzuru* play a noh drama

SYNONYMS

❶ⓐ skill
技 SKILL → 248
腕 skill → 1006
才 TALENT → 3410
力 POWER → 3371
ⓑ skillful
巧 SKILLFUL → 188
❷ possible
可 -ABLE → 2969
❸ⓐ potency
効 EFFECT → 1265
験 efficacy → 1833
機 function → 1076

6-4

⺨

殺 殺 殺 殺

1324 SATSU SAI SETSU koro(su) -goro(shi) so(gu)▲

Ⓒ 杀 shā

Radical	Strokes
殳 79	10-4-6
Grade	**Freq**
Jōyō-4	541
■ 1 - 6 - 4	

▶KILL

COMPOUNDS

❶ kill, murder
殺人 *satsujin* murder, homicide
殺生する *sesshō suru* destroy life, kill animals
殺害 *satsugai* (=*setsugai*) murder, killing, assassination
殺菌 *sakkin* sterilization, pasteurization
暗殺 *ansatsu* assassination
自殺 *jisatsu* suicide
謀殺 *bōsatsu* premeditated murder
射殺する *shasatsu suru* shoot to death
銃殺する *jūsatsu suru* shoot to death, execute by firing squad
❷ obliterate, wipe out
殺風景 *sappūkei* inelegance; lack of refinement
抹殺する *massatsu suru* erase, strike out; deny, ignore; do away with, liquidate
❸ dampen, reduce, cut down
減殺する *gensai suru* lessen, diminish, reduce
相殺する *sōsai suru* offset, cancel each other
❹ [emphatic auxiliary] entirely, utterly, completely
殺到する *sattō suru* rush in, pour in; descend on
悩殺する *nōsatsu suru* fascinate, enchant

KUN

【koro(su) 殺す】 kill, murder; bump off; mas-

sacre; pawn, waste; hold back (tears); *baseball* strike out
殺し *koroshi* killing, murder
殺し屋 *koroshiya* hired killer
締め殺す *shimekorosu* strangle to death
轢き殺す *hikikorosu* kill by running over
感情を殺す *kanjō o korosu* suppress one's emotions

【-goro(shi) -殺し】 [also suffix] killing, murder, -cide
人殺し *hitogoroshi* murder; murderer
幼児殺し *yōjigoroshi* infanticide
二人殺し *futarigoroshi* double murder

【so(gu) 殺ぐ】
[also 削ぐ]
① chip, cut off
殺がれた耳 *sogareta mimi* mutilated ear
②ⓐ diminish, reduce, dampen
ⓑ spoil
興を殺ぐ *kyō o sogu* spoil the fun of

SYNONYMS
❶ **kill**
刺 stab to death → 1275
絞 STRANGLE → 1349
窒 CHOKE → 2288

HOMOPHONES
sogu ⇨ 削 1448

NOTE
⇨ see USAGE note at 削 1448

朗 朗 朗

1325 RŌ hoga(raka)

Ⓒⓗ 朗 lǎng

Radical	Strokes
月 74	10-4-6
Grade	**Freq**
Jōyō-6	1402
1 - 6 - 4	

6-4 良

▶CHEERFUL ▶CLEAR

COMPOUNDS
❶ (marked by or conductive to cheer) **cheerful, bright, cheery**
朗報 *rōhō* cheering [good] news
明朗な *meirō na* cheerful, bright; clean (politics)
❷ⓐ **clear (voice), loud and clear, sonorous, loud, resonant**
ⓑ [original meaning] clear (sky), bright (moon)
朗詠 *rōei* reciting, chanting
朗吟する *rōgin suru* recite, sing
朗読 *rōdoku* reading aloud
朗朗たる *rōrōtaru* clear (and ringing), sonorous, resonant; bright (moon)
晴朗な *seirō na* clear, fair, serene

KUN
【hoga(raka) 朗らか】
hogaraka na 朗らかな cheerful, bright; clear (sky)
朗らかに笑う *hogaraka ni warau* laugh merrily, smile brightly

SYNONYMS
❶ **pleased and pleasant**
快 PLEASANT → 245
楽 pleasurable → 2826
愉 PLEASED → 582
悦 DELIGHTED → 418
嬉しい GLAD → 722
喜 HAPPY → 2308
歓 JOYOUS → 1867
欣 JOYFUL → 852
❷ⓐ **loud**
高い loud → 2097
騒 clamorous → 1835
ⓑ **clear**
明 CLEAR (unclouded) → 855
冴える CRISP AND CLEAR → 79
清 CLEAR (liquid) → 523
澄 LIMPID → 740
透 TRANSPARENT → 3108

6-4 自

師

1326 SHI

Ⓒⓗ 师 shī

Radical	Strokes
巾 50	10-3-7
Grade	**Freq**
Jōyō-5	475
1 - 6 - 4	

Stroke order: 1–10

▶MASTER

COMPOUNDS

❶ **master, teacher, instructor**

師範 *shihan* teacher, master, coach
師匠 *shishō* master, teacher
師事する *shiji suru* study under, look up to (a person) as one's teacher
師走 *shiwasu* December
教師 *kyōshi* teacher, instructor
講師 *kōshi* speaker, lecturer
恩師 *onshi* one's respected teacher, one's former teacher

❷ honorific title, esp. after names of clergymen or traditional artists

ホメイニ師 *homeinishi* the Ayatollah Khomeini
宝井馬琴師 *takarai bakin-shi* Master Bakin Takarai

❸ [also suffix] **member of a profession or performer of an action**

医師 *ishi* doctor, physician, surgeon
技師 *gishi* engineer, technician
牧師 *bokushi* pastor, minister, priest
絵師 *eshi* painter, artist
美容師 *biyōshi* beauty artist
ペテン師 *petenshi* swindler, finagler

❹ [original meaning] army

師団 *shidan* army division

❺ [rare] god (of natural phenomena)

風師 *fūshi* wind god

❻ [archaic] capital city

京師 *keishi* old city of Kyoto

INDEPENDENT

【shi 師】master, teacher, instructor

師と仰ぐ *shi to aogu* look up to (a person) as one's preceptor

SYNONYMS

❷ **titles of address**

公 honorific title (noblemen) → 1974
殿 FORMAL HONORIFIC TITLE → 1792
様 FORMAL TITLE → 1052
氏 COURTESY TITLE → 2951
兄 familiar title (seniors) → 2154
君 FAMILIAR TITLE (peers) → 3206
嬢 Miss → 758

❸ **workers and professionals**

家 professional → 2273
客 skilled person → 2250
士 PROFESSION SUFFIX → 3405
者 person who → 3211
人 person of certain category → 3368
員 MEMBER (of a staff) → 2269
屋 colloquial occupation suffix → 3098
手 OCCUPATION SUFFIX → 3456
婦 woman worker → 469
嬢 (unmarried) female worker → 758
夫 MAN LABORER → 3460
匠 CRAFTSMAN → 2990
工 workman → 3381

COMPOUND FORMATION

師走 *shiwasu*

According to one theory, 師走 'December' originally referred to a Buddhist monk (師 ❶) running around (走) at the end of the year.

NOTE

★do not confuse with 帥 1290

6-4 孝

incorrect stroke count ⇨ see 1493

粘 粘 粘

1327 NEN neba(ru)

Ⓒ 黏 nián 粘 zhān

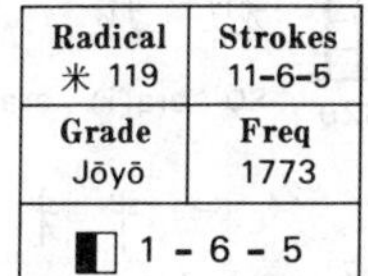

Radical	Strokes
米 119	11-6-5
Grade	**Freq**
Jōyō	1773
▌ 1 - 6 - 5	

6-5 米

▶**STICKY**

COMPOUNDS

● [original meaning] **sticky, glutinous, viscous, adhesive**

粘着性 *nenchakusei* stickiness, adhesion, viscosity
粘土 *nendo* clay
粘板岩 *nenbangan* clay rock, slate
粘膜 *nenmaku* mucous membrane
粘度 *nendo* viscosity
粘液 *nen'eki* mucus
粘性 *nensei* stickiness, viscidity

KUN

【neba(ru) 粘る】 be sticky, be glutinous; persevere

粘い *nebai* sticky
粘り *nebari* stickiness; tenacity
粘り強い *nebarizuyoi* tenacious, sticky; persistent
粘つく *nebatsuku* be sticky, be glutinous
粘っこい *nebakkoi* sticky; stiff, tenacious

粒 粒 粒

1328 RYŪ tsubu

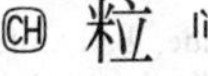

Ⓒ 粒 lì

Radical	Strokes
米 119	11-6-5
Grade	**Freq**
Jōyō	1499
▌ 1 - 6 - 5	

6-5 米

、 丷 丷 丬 半 米 米 籵 粁 粒 粒
1 2 3 4 5 6 7 8 9 10 11

▶**GRAIN**

COMPOUNDS

❶ⓐ (small particulate mass) **grain, granule**
ⓑ *phys* grain, particle
ⓒ counter for grains

粒子 *ryūshi* particle, grain
粒状の *ryūjō no* granular
顆粒 *karyū* granule
粒度 *ryūdo* particle size, grain size
粒径 *ryūkei* grain [particle] diameter
粒界 *ryūkai* grain boundary
素粒子 *soryūshi* elementary particle
米十粒 *kome jūryū* ten grains of rice

❷ [original meaning] grain (of rice), grain (of cereal)

粒粒辛苦 *ryūryū-shinku* assiduously, painstakingly
穀粒 *kokuryū* grain

KUN

【tsubu 粒】 grain, particle; drop; counter for grains or drops; each person or thing

粒粒の *tsubutsubu no* granulated, lumpy
米粒 *kometsubu* grain of rice
雨粒 *amatsubu* raindrop
一粒の涙 *hitotsubu no namida* one tear
粒揃い *tsubuzoroi* uniform excellence
粒選りの *tsubuyori no* the pick, the choice

SYNONYMS

❶ **particle**

子 particle suffix → 3390
核 NUCLEUS → 927

COMPOUND FORMATION

粒粒辛苦 *ryūryū-shinku*

粒粒辛苦 'assiduously, painstakingly' originally referred to working as strenuously (辛苦) as peasants did at growing rice grain (粒❷) by grain (粒❷).

6-5 米

粗 粗 粗 Ⓒ粗 cū

1329 SO ara(i) ara-

Radical	Strokes
米 119	11-6-5
Grade	**Freq**
Jōyō	1477
1-6-5	

Stroke order: 1 2 3 4 5 6 7 8 9 10 11

▶COARSE

COMPOUNDS

❶ (not fine) **coarse, rough, rugged**
粗密 *somitsu* roughness and fineness
粗布 *sofu* coarse cloth
精粗 *seiso* fineness or coarseness; minuteness or roughness

❷ⓐ (of inferior quality) **coarse, crude, inferior, poor, humble, shabby**—used esp. as a term of humility before items presented as gifts
ⓑ (of unrefined manner) coarse, crude, rude, rough, harsh
粗悪な *soaku na* coarse, crude, bad, inferior
粗品 *soshina* trifling gift, inferior goods
粗茶 *socha* coarse tea
粗末な *somatsu na* coarse, crude, inferior, humble
粗雑な *sozatsu na* coarse, rough, crude
粗暴な *sobō na* wild, rude

❸ (in the natural state) crude, raw, unrefined, unprocessed
粗製 *sosei* crude manufacture
粗鉱 *sokō* unprocessed ore
粗鋼 *sokō* crude steel

❹ careless, negligent
粗相 *sosō* carelessness, careless mistake, blunder
粗忽な *sokotsu na* careless, thoughtless, rash

INDEPENDENT

【so 粗】 coarseness, roughness
粗に過ぎる *so ni sugiru* be too rough

KUN

【ara(i) 粗い】
①ⓐ (not fine) coarse, rough, gross
ⓑ (not smooth) coarse, rough, rugged
ⓒ (not elaborate) coarse, rough, crude, gross
粗 *ara* fault, defect; bony parts (of a fish)
粗い網 *arai ami* coarse net
粗い肌 *arai hada* rough skin
粗い細工 *arai saiku* rough workmanship
② sparse, scattered
種を粗く播く *tane o araku maku* sow sparsely

【ara- 粗-】
①ⓐ [also 荒-] (not elaborate) coarse, rough, crude, gross
ⓑ (in the natural state) crude, raw, unrefined, unprocessed
粗筋 *arasuji* outline, summary
粗造り *arazukuri* rough work
粗金 *aragane* ore
② sparse, scattered
粗播き *aramaki* sparse sowing [seeding]

SYNONYMS

❶ **rare and sparse**
疎 SPARSE → 1178
薄い THIN → 2370
希 RARE → 2049

❷ⓐ **bad**
悪 BAD → 2745
劣 INFERIOR → 2395
下 of low grade → 3378
弊 shabby → 2884
駄 GOOD FOR NOTHING → 1821
廃 WASTE → 3146

ⓑ **vulgar and unrefined**
野 rustic → 1485
里 rural → 3542
俗 vulgar → 104
卑 MEAN → 2642
蛮 barbaric → 2129

❸ **natural**
野 wild → 1485
地 natural → 204
原 in the original state → 3009

HOMOPHONES

arai ⇨ 荒 2260
ara- ⇨ 荒 2260

NOTE

⇨ see USAGE note at 荒 2260

紘

1330 GEN

Ⓒⓗ 弦 xián

Radical	Strokes
糸 120	11-6-5
Grade	Freq
Reference	
1-6-5	

6-5 糸

COMPOUNDS

[now replaced by 弦 287]

❶ [original meaning]

ⓐ chord or string of a musical instrument

ⓑ counter for chords [strings]

紘楽器 *gengakki* stringed instruments

三紘 *sangen* three-stringed instrument, shamisen

❷ stringed instrument, the strings

紘歌 *genka* singing and (string) music

管紘楽 *kangengaku* orchestral music

経 經 圣° 经 徑

1331 KEI KYŌ he(ru) ta(tsu)▲ tateito▲

Ⓒⓗ 经 jīng

Radical	Strokes
糸 120	11-6-5
Grade	Freq
Jōyō-5	137
1-6-5	

6-5 糸

▶PASS THROUGH ▶MANAGE

COMPOUNDS

❶ⓐ (go through without stopping) **pass through, go through**

ⓑ **pass through an experience, experience**

ⓒ (of time) **pass, elapse**

経由する *keiyu suru* go via, pass through

神経 *shinkei* nerve; sensitivity; worry

経験 *keiken* experience

経歴 *keireki* personal history

経過する *keika suru* pass, elapse

❷ **manage (the affairs of an organization or a state), administer**

経世 *keisei* administration, government, conduct of state affairs

経理 *keiri* accounting

経済 *keizai* economy, economics

経営 *keiei* management

❸ abbrev. of 経済 *keizai*: **economics**

経企庁(＝経済企画庁) *keikichō* (＝*keizai kikaku-chō*) Economic Planning Agency

経団連(＝経済団体連合会) *keidanren* (＝*keizai dantai rengōkai*) Federation of Economic Organizations

政経 *seikei* politics and economics

❹ⓐ **religious classic, Buddhist scriptures, sutra**

ⓑ classical works; Chinese classics

経典 *kyōten* sacred books, scripture, sutras; Bible

経文 *kyōmon* sutras

阿弥陀経 *amidakyō* the Sukhavati sutra

仏経 *bukkyō* sutras

経史 *kyōshi* Chinese classics

❺ⓐ **periodic, regular, ordinary**

ⓑ period, menstruation

経常費 *keijōhi* ordinary expenditure

経費 *keihi* expense(s), cost(s), expenditure, upkeep

月経 *gekkei* menstruation

閉経 *heikei* menopause

❻ [original meaning] warp

整経機 *seikeiki* warping machine

❼ longitude

経度 *keido* longitude

西経 *seikei* west longitude

❽ *Chinese medicine* meridian; blood vessels

INDEPENDENT

【kei 経】 main plot (of a story)

【kyō 経】 sutra

KUN

【he(ru) 経る】 pass, elapse, go by; pass [go] through; pass [go] through, experience

十年を経て *jūnen o hete* after ten years

手続きを経る *tetsuzuki o heru* go through formalities

【ta(tsu) 経つ】 pass, elapse, go by

時間が経つ *Jikan ga tatsu* Time goes by

【tateito 経】 [also 縦糸 or 経糸] warp

SYNONYMS

❶ⓐ **pass**

通 PASS → 3109

過 PASS BY → 3137

ⓒ **elapse**

歴 pass → 3019

去 pass away → 2156

過 PASS BY → 3137
❷ **direct and supervise**
営 MANAGE → 2603
理 manage → 970
宰 PRESIDE → 2275
司 OFFICIATE → 2931
督 SUPERVISE → 2796
監 OVERSEE → 2852
掌 TAKE CHARGE OF → 2602
轄 EXERCISE JURISDICTION OVER → 1627
管 EXERCISE CONTROL → 2701
制 CONTROL → 1274
❹ⓐ **books**
典 STANDARD WORK → 2627
鑑 REFERENCE VOLUME → 1773
編 volume → 1387
巻 VOLUME → 2645
本 BOOK → 3502
書 BOOK → 2658
冊 bound book → 3483
籍 books → 2731
著 literary work → 2300
❻ **threads and fibers**
緯 woof → 1407
糸 THREAD → 2179
繊 FIBER → 1413
維 FIBER → 1370

❼ **latitude and longitude**
緯 LATITUDE → 1407

USAGE

tateito
経
［also 縦糸 or 経糸］ warp
縦糸
［also 経糸 or 経］ warp
経糸
［also 経 or 縦糸］ warp

HOMOPHONES

tatsu ⇨ 立 1992 建 3090 起 3307 発 2565
tateito ⇨ 縦糸 1408, 2179 経糸 1331, 2179

COMPOUND FORMATION

経済 *keizai*
経済 'economy, economics' is an abbreviation of 経国済民 *keikoku-saimin* 'administration and statesmanship', that is, administrating (経 ❷) the country (国) and relieving (済) the sufferings of the people (民). 経済 was coined in Japan by means of characters imported from China and then "exported" back to China.

NOTE

⇨ see also USAGE note at 立 1992
⇨ see COMPOUND FORMATION for 神経 *shinkei* ⇨ 神 912

6-5
糸

紺

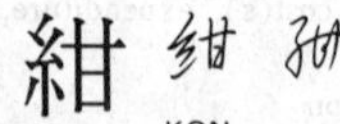

1332 KON

Ⓒⓗ 紺 gàn

Radical	Strokes
糸 120	11-6-5
Grade	**Freq**
Jōyō	1609

1 - 6 - 5

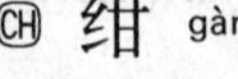

1 2 3 4 5 6 7 8 9 10 11

▶DARK BLUE

COMPOUNDS

● ［original meaning］ **dark blue, navy blue**
紺色 *kon'iro* dark blue, navy blue
紺地 *konji* dark blue ground; dark blue cloth
紺青 *konjō* Prussian blue, deep blue
紺屋 *kōya* (=*kon'ya*) dyer; dyer's shop
紫紺 *shikon* purplish blue
濃紺 *nōkon* dark blue, navy blue

INDEPENDENT

【**kon 紺**】 dark blue, navy blue
紺の背広 *kon no sebiro* blue business suit

SYNONYMS

● **blue and purple colors**
藍 INDIGO → 2381
紫 PURPLE → 2688
青 BLUE → 2430
碧 DEEP BLUE → 2836
瑠 LAPIS LAZULI (bright blue) → 1060

細 细 𦀊 ㊥ 细 xì

Radical	Strokes
糸 120	11-6-5
Grade	**Freq**
Jōyō-2	729
1 - 6 - 5	

6-5 糸

1333 SAI hoso(i) hoso(ru) koma(ka) koma(kai)

1 2 3 4 5 6 7 8 9 10 11

▶**SLENDER** ▶**MINUTE**

COMPOUNDS

❶ [also prefix] [original meaning] **slender, fine, thin, narrow**
細流 *sairyū* streamlet, brooklet, rivulet
細腰 *saiyō* slender hips
細動脈 *saidōmyaku* arteriole
毛細血管 *mōsai-kekkan* capillary vessel
繊細な *sensai na* delicate, fine, subtle

❷ⓐ (very small) **minute, fine, small, microscopic**
ⓑ (detailed) **minute, detailed, close, elaborate**
細胞 *saibō* cell
細菌 *saikin* bacteria, germ, microbe
細分する *saibun suru* subdivide, fractionate
微細な *bisai na* minute, fine; detailed, minute; delicate, subtle
細部 *saibu* details, particulars
細心 *saishin* carefulness, discretion
細工 *saiku* work, craftsmanship; artifice, tactics
詳細 *shōsai* details, particulars
明細 *meisai* particulars, details, specifics
精細な *seisai na* detailed, minute, exact

❸ (beneath notice) minute, minor, trifling, insignificant
細事 *saiji* minor details
細君 *saikun* wife
零細な *reisai na* small, trifling, petty
些細な *sasai na* trifling, slight, insignificant

INDEPENDENT

【sai 細】 minute details
微に入り細を穿つ *bi ni iri sai o ugatsu* go into the minutest details

KUN

【hoso(i) 細い】 slender; fine, thin; narrow; small, slight; sensitive, delicate
細い糸 *hosoi ito* fine thread
細長い *hosonagai* slender, linear, long and narrow
細面 *hosoomote* slender face
心細い *kokorobosoi* helpless, forlorn; lonely
神経が細い *shinkei ga hosoi* be oversensitive

【hoso(ru) 細る】 get thin, taper off; dwindle, be reduced
身が細る *mi ga hosoru* become thin, lose weight
先細り *sakibosori* tapering off [away]
食が細る *shoku ga hosoru* lose one's appetite

【koma(ka) 細か】
komaka na 細かな (very small) minute, fine, small; (detailed) minute, elaborate, close; thrifty, frugal, stingy
事細かに *kotokomaka ni* minutely, in detail

【koma(kai) 細かい】 same as **komaka na** 細かな
細かく *komakaku* finely, minutely
細かい金 *komakai kane* small change
細細した *komagoma shita* sundry
細かい指示 *komakai shiji* detailed instructions
神経が細かい *shinkei ga komakai* be sensitive, have delicate feeling
金銭に細かい *kinsen ni komakai* be scrimpy about money

SYNONYMS

❶ **thin**
薄 THIN → 2370
繊 FINE → 1413

❷ⓐ **small and tiny**
微 SLIGHT → 639
寸 A BIT OF → 2935
小 SMALL → 7
豆- miniature → 1943

ⓑ **detailed**
密 CLOSE → 2292
詳 DETAILED → 1526
精 meticulous → 1366

❸ **unimportant**
微 SLIGHT → 639
小 SMALL → 7
末 last in importance → 3505

6-5 糸

紳 绅 孙

1334 SHIN

CH 绅 shēn

Radical	Strokes
糸 120	11-6-5
Grade	**Freq**
Jōyō	1594
1 - 6 - 5	

▶GENTLEMAN

COMPOUNDS

❶ **gentleman, gentry; men of rank**

紳士 *shinshi* gentleman

紳商 *shinshō* merchant prince, rich merchant

貴紳 *kishin* men of rank, notables

❷ [original meaning, now archaic] ornamental sash worn by ancient Chinese noblemen

SYNONYMS

❶ **gentleman**

子 gentleman → 3390

士 man of learning and virtue → 3405

6-5 糸

紹 绍 孙

1335 SHŌ

CH 绍 shào

Radical	Strokes
糸 120	11-6-5
Grade	**Freq**
Jōyō	954
1 - 6 - 5	

▶INTRODUCE

COMPOUNDS

● **introduce, bring together**

紹介する *shōkai suru* introduce, present

紹介状 *shōkaijō* letter of introduction

SYNONYMS

● **mediating and mediators**

介 MEDIATE → 1967

媒 INTERMEDIATE → 564

仲 INTERMEDIARY → 43

6-5 糸

終 終 終 孙

1336 SHŪ o(waru) -o(waru) o(eru) tsui▲ tsui(ni)▲

CH 终 zhōng

Radical	Strokes
糸 120	11-6-5
Grade	**Freq**
Jōyō-3	291
1 - 6 - 5	

▶END

COMPOUNDS

❶ⓐ **end, come to an end, finish, terminate**

ⓑ **bring to an end, finish, complete**

ⓒ end one's life, die

終了する *shūryō suru* end, conclude, complete; expire

終結 *shūketsu* end, conclusion, termination

終戦 *shūsen* end of the war

終極の *shūkyoku no* ultimate, final

終業時間 *shūgyō jikan* closing hour

臨終 *rinjū* hour of death, one's last moment

❷ⓐ end, ending, finish

ⓑ [also prefix] **last, final, terminal**

最終 *saishū* last, the end; final

終始 *shūshi* from beginning to end, always

終点 *shūten* last stop, terminus

終盤戦 *shūbansen* end game

終列車 *shūressha* last train

終刊号 *shūkangō* final issue

❸ from beginning to end, all through, all

終日 *shūjitsu* all [throughout] the day

終身 *shūshin* all through life

終夜 *shūya* all night

KUN

【o(waru) 終わる】 *vi* end, come to an end, finish, terminate; end one's life, die

終わり *owari* end(ing), conclusion

終わり頃 *owarigoro* toward the end

【-o(waru) -終わる】 [verbal suffix] bring an action to an end, finish

読み終わる *yomiowaru* read through, finish reading

【o(eru) 終える】 *vt* end, finish, complete

し終える *shioeru* finish doing something

【tsui 終】 *elegant* the end

【tsui(ni) 終に】 [usu. 遂に] at last, at length, in the end, finally

SYNONYMS

❶ **end**

絶 COME TO AN END → 1353
閉 CLOSE → 3319
了 FINISH → 3350
済 SETTLE → 522
-上げる completion suffix → 3404
完 COMPLETE → 2201
結 CONCLUDE → 1348

❷ⓐ **ends**

尾 end → 3062
局 close → 3063
末 LAST PART → 3505

ⓑ **last**

末 last in time → 3505

❸ **throughout**

中 throughout → 3451
徹 all through → 726
通 through → 3109

HOMOPHONES

tsuini ⇨ 遂 3138

NOTE

⇨ see USAGE note at 遂 3138

組 組 組

1337 SO ku(mu) kumi -gumi

CH 组 zǔ

Radical	Strokes
糸 120	11-6-5
Grade	**Freq**
Jōyō-2	171
1 - 6 - 5	

6-5 糸

(Stroke order 1–11)

▶**ORGANIZE** ▶**ASSEMBLE**

COMPOUNDS

❶ⓐ **organize, form, arrange, unite**

ⓑ organization

組織する *soshiki suru* organize, form, set up; constitute, construct
組成 *sosei* composition, formation, construction
組閣する *sokaku suru* form a cabinet, organize a ministry
改組 *kaiso* reorganization (of a union)

❷ abbrev. of 組合 *kumiai*: **union**

日教組 *nikkyōso* Japan Teachers Union
労組 *rōso* labor union
職組 *shokuso* employees' union

❸ⓐ [original meaning] braid, plait

ⓑ to braid

編組機械 *henso kikai* knitting machinery

KUN

【ku(mu) 組む】

①ⓐ assemble, construct, put together, fit together

ⓑ unite, associate oneself with, organize

組み立てる *kumitateru* assemble, construct, erect
組み合わせる *kumiawaseru* combine, assort, join together, match
仕組み *shikumi* construction; arrangement; plan, plot
番組 *bangumi* (TV) program
団体を組む *dantai o kumu* form an organization
組んで事業をする *kunde jigyō o suru* join forces [tie up] (with others) in business
縁組 *engumi* marriage, (conjugal) union

② cross (one's legs); fold (one's arms)

足を組む *ashi o kumu* cross one's legs
手を組む *te o kumu* join hands together

③ grapple with

取り組む *torikumu* grapple, tackle (a problem)

④ typeset, compose

組み *kumi* typesetting, composition
組み版 *kumihan* typesetting, composition
活字を組む *katsuji o kumu* set type

⑤ braid

組み紐 *kumihimo* plaited cord (used with kimonos)
糸を組む *ito o kumu* braid string

【kumi 組】

①ⓐ group (of people), team, company, party, gang

ⓑ set (of tea cups), suit

組合 *kumiai* union, guild, association
組合頭 *kumiaigashira* group leader
組を作る *kumi o tsukuru* make up a party
赤組 *akagumi* red team
茶器組 *chakigumi* tea set

② [also suffix] (school) class

会話の組 *kaiwa no kumi* conversation class
一年三組 *ichinen sankumi* first-grade, class three

【-gumi -組】

[suffix]

① group, gang

三人組の強盗 *sanningumi no gōtō* gang of three robbers
四人組 *yoningumi* the Gang of Four

② company

大林組 *ōbayashigumi* Obayashi & Company

SYNONYMS

❶ⓐ organize
結 form → 1348
編 put together → 1387

❷ organized bodies
労 workers' union → 2548
体 BODY → 71
団 BODY → 3053
協 association → 93
会 SOCIETY → 2020
連 federation → 3103
講 fraternity → 1619
院 INSTITUTION → 454

❸ⓐ ropes and lines
緒 cord → 1378
縄 ROPE (esp. of straw) → 1388
綱 ROPE (esp. of fiber) → 1372
索 cable → 2455
鎖 CHAIN → 1761
線 LINE → 1392
弦 STRING → 287

ⓑ weave and sew
編 KNIT → 1387
縫 SEW → 1406
織 WEAVE → 1422
紡 SPIN → 1295
績 spin → 1412

【kumu】

①ⓐ make
構 CONSTRUCT → 1049
調 PREPARE → 1567
作 MAKE → 68
造 MAKE → 3110
成 FORM → 3537
工 MANUFACTURE → 3381
製 MANUFACTURE → 2803
産 PRODUCE → 3298

【kumi】

① groups
群 GROUP (of any kind) → 1540
陣 lineup → 455
連 set → 3103
族 common-interest group (*slang*) → 958
党 PARTY → 2581
隊 PARTY (organized group) → 625
団 BODY → 3053
伍 ranks → 47
班 SQUAD → 946
軍 team → 2080

② class in school
級 GRADE → 1279

NOTE

⇨ see COMPOUND FORMATION for 番組 *bangumi* ⇨ 番 2748

6-5 糸

1338

▶END
nonstandard for 終 1336

6-5 糸

統
1339

▶UNITE ▶INTERCONNECTED SYSTEM
nonstandard for 統 1352

6-5 舟

舶 舶 舶
1340 HAKU

Ⓒⓗ 舶 bó

Radical	Strokes
舟 137	11-6-5
Grade	**Freq**
Jōyō	1509
1-6-5	

Stroke order: 1 2 3 4 5 6 7 8 9 10 11

▶OCEANGOING SHIP

COMPOUNDS

❶ [original meaning] **oceangoing ship, ship, vessel**
舶用機関 *hakuyōkikan* marine engine
船舶 *senpaku* ship, vessel; craft

❷ import, ship
舶来 *hakurai* imported goods, foreign-made articles
舶載 *hakusai* ocean transportation; importation, imported goods

SYNONYMS

❶ boats and ships
船 SHIP → 1341
艦 WARSHIP → 1435
潜 submarine → 746
舟 SMALL BOAT → 3538
艇 BOAT → 1365
隻 COUNTER FOR SHIPS → 2755

船 船 船 船

1341 SEN fune funa- -bune

Ⓒⓗ 船 chuán

Radical	Strokes
舟 137	11-6-5
Grade	**Freq**
Jōyō-2	272
1 - 6 - 5	

Stroke order: 1 2 3 4 5 6 7 8 9 10 11

▶SHIP

COMPOUNDS

[also suffix]

ⓐ [original meaning] **ship, boat, vessel, seacraft**

ⓑ spaceship, airship

船舶 *senpaku* ship, vessel; craft
船長 *senchō* (ship) captain
汽船 *kisen* steamship
風船 *fūsen* balloon
造船 *zōsen* shipbuilding
商船 *shōsen* merchant ship, trading vessel
貨物船 *kamotsusen* freighter, cargo ship
宇宙船 *uchūsen* spaceship
軌道船 *kidōsen* orbiter
飛行船 *hikōsen* ship, airship

KUN

【fune 船】

① ship, boat, vessel, seacraft
船に乗る *fune ni noru* board a ship
② [also 槽] tub, tank, vessel
湯船 *yubune* bathtub

【funa- 船-】 [also 舟-] [also prefix] ship
船乗り *funanori* sailor, seaman
船旅 *funatabi* voyage
船火事 *funakaji* fire on a ship

【-bune -船】 [also -舟] [also suffix] ship, vessel
助け船 *tasukebune* lifeboat; help
乗り合い船 *noriaibune* ferryboat

SYNONYMS

ⓐ **boats and ships**

舶 OCEANGOING SHIP → 1340
艦 WARSHIP → 1435
潜 submarine → 746
舟 SMALL BOAT → 3538
艇 BOAT → 1365
隻 COUNTER FOR SHIPS → 2755

ⓑ **aircraft and spacecraft**

空 aircraft → 2227
機 AIRCRAFT → 1076

USAGE

❶ **fune**

船
① ship, boat, vessel, seacraft
② [also 槽] tub, tank, vessel

舟
small boat [craft], (row)boat

槽
[also 船] tub, tank, vessel

❷ **funa-**

船-
[also 舟-] [also prefix] ship

舟-
[also 船-] [also prefix] small boat

❸ **-bune**

-船
[also -舟] [also suffix] ship, vessel

-舟
[also -船] [also suffix] small boat

HOMOPHONES

fune ⇨ 舟 3538 槽 1067
funa- ⇨ 舟 3538
-bune ⇨ 舟 3538

船

1342

▶SHIP

nonstandard for 船 1341

6-5 虫

蛇 蛇 虵
1343 JA DA hebi

ⒸⒽ 蛇 shé yí

Radical	Strokes
虫 142	11-6-5
Grade	Freq
Jōyō	1937
▮ 1 - 6 - 5	

Stroke order: 1 2 3 4 5 6 7 8 9 10 11

▶SNAKE

COMPOUNDS

❶ [original meaning] **snake, serpent**
- **蛇蝎** *dakatsu* snake and scorpion, viper
- **蛇行する** *dakō suru* meander, zigzag
- **蛇足** *dasoku* superfluity, redundancy
- **蛇の目** *janome* umbrella with a snake's eye pattern; double circle pattern
- **大蛇** *daija* big snake, serpent

❷ objects shaped like a snake, as tubes, pipes or the like
- **蛇口** *jaguchi* faucet
- **蛇管** *jakan* hose
- **蛇腹** *jabara* bellows; cornice

INDEPENDENT

【ja 蛇】 snake, serpent
- **蛇の道は蛇** *Ja no michi wa hebi* One devil knows another

KUN

【hebi 蛇】 [also suffix] snake, serpent
- **蛇の様な** *hebi no yō na* snakelike, snaky, serpentine
- **蛇座** *hebiza* the Serpent (constellation)
- **毒蛇** *dokuhebi* poisonous snake
- **がらがら蛇** *garagarahebi* rattlesnake

SYNONYMS

❶ **snake**
- 巳 THE SERPENT → 3388

❶ **reptiles**
- 亀 TURTLE → 2128
- 竜 DRAGON → 2099

COMPOUND FORMATION

蛇足 *dasoku*

蛇足 'superfluity, redundancy' derives from an ancient Chinese tale of a group of servants that competed for getting a drink from their master. They held a contest in which the fastest one to draw a picture of a snake (蛇 ❶) was to be the winner. One of the contestants was so far ahead of the others that he added legs (足) to the snake, just for amusement. But since a snake has no legs, he wound up losing the contest. In this way, 蛇足 came to represent something "as superfluous as the legs on a snake."

6-5 并

瓶 瓶 甁 缾
1344 BIN kame▲

Radical	Strokes
瓦 98	11-5-6
Grade	Freq
Jōyō	1814
▮ 1 - 6 - 5	

Stroke order: 1 2 3 4 5 6 7 8 9 10 11

▶BOTTLE

COMPOUNDS

❶ⓐ [also suffix] **bottle, flask, decanter, vase, jar**

ⓑ counter for bottles
- **広口瓶** *hirokuchibin* widemouthed bottle, jar
- **花瓶** *kabin* flower vase
- **魔法瓶** *mahōbin* thermos bottle
- **徳用瓶** *tokuyōbin* economy bottle
- **二瓶** *futabin* two bottles

❷ kettle, teapot
- **鉄瓶** *tetsubin* iron kettle

INDEPENDENT

【bin 瓶】 bottle, flask, decanter

KUN

【kame 瓶】 earthenware pot, jar, vase

SYNONYMS

❶ⓐ **containers**
- 缶 CAN → 2033
- 器 VESSEL → 2713
- 袋 BAG → 2588
- 籠 BASKET → 2734
- 箱 BOX → 2711
- 槽 TANK → 1067
- 棺 COFFIN → 985

NOTE

⇨ see COMPOUND FORMATION for 魔法瓶 *mahōbin* ⇨ 魔 3187

粧 粧 粧

1345 SHŌ

Ⓒⓗ 妆 zhuāng

Radical	Strokes
米 119	12-6-6
Grade	**Freq**
Jōyō	1482
◧ 1-6-6	

6-6 米

丶 丷 䒑 半 米 米 米' 米⺈ 粁 粧 粧 粧
1 2 3 4 5 6 7 8 9 10 11 12

▶APPLY MAKEUP

COMPOUNDS

● [original meaning] **apply makeup [cosmetics], make up, adorn oneself**

化粧する *keshō suru* make up, put on make-up

美粧院 *bishōin* beauty shop

SYNONYMS

● **decorate**

粉 apply face powder → 1291

飾 DECORATE → 1717

装 DRESS → 2685

絵

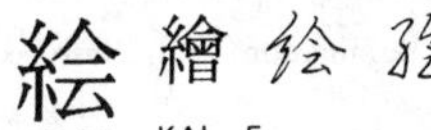

1346 KAI E

Ⓒⓗ 绘 huì

Radical	Strokes
糸 120	12-6-6
Grade	**Freq**
Jōyō-2	990
◧ 1-6-6	

6-6 糸

▶PICTURE

COMPOUNDS

● [sometimes also 画 *e* 3000] [also prefix and suffix] [original meaning] **picture, painting, drawing, sketch, illustration**

絵画 *kaiga* pictures, paintings, drawings

絵本 *ehon* picture book

絵描き *ekaki* painter, artist

絵の具 *enogu* coloring materials, colors, oils, paint

絵葉書 *ehagaki* picture postcard

絵日記 *enikki* diary with illustrations

油絵 *aburae* oil painting

浮世絵 *ukiyoe ukiyoe*, color print of everyday life in old Japan

INDEPENDENT

【e 絵】

ⓐ [sometimes also 画 *e* 3000] picture, painting, drawing, sketch, illustration, cut, (woodcut) print

ⓑ [usu. 画 *e* 3000] television field

絵の展覧会 *e no tenrankai* art exhibition

SYNONYMS

● **picture**

図 DRAWING → 3071

画 PICTURE → 3000

USAGE

e

絵

ⓐ [sometimes also 画] picture, painting, drawing, sketch, illustration, cut, (woodcut) print

ⓑ [usu. 画] television field

画

ⓐ [usu. 絵] [also suffix] picture, painting, drawing, sketch, illustration, cut, (woodcut) print

ⓑ [sometimes also 絵] television field

HOMOPHONES

e ⇨ 画 3000

絢 絢 絢

1347 KEN NAMES JUN aya

Ⓒⓗ 绚 xuàn

Radical	Strokes
糸 120	12-6-6
Grade	**Freq**
Names	2093
◧ 1-6-6	

6-6 糸

𠃋 幺 幺 糸 糸 糸 糸' 約 約 絢 絢 絢
1 2 3 4 5 6 7 8 9 10 11 12

▶GORGEOUS

COMPOUNDS

ⓐ **gorgeous, resplendent, brilliant, florid**

ⓑ [original meaning, now archaic] gorgeous pattern, beautiful design

絢爛たる *kenrantaru* gorgeous, dazzling; flow-

ery (speech)
絢文 *kenbun* colorful pattern

NAMES

絢子 *ayako* (=*junko*) female name

SYNONYMS

ⓐ **beautiful**
斐 florid → 2776
華 MAGNIFICENT → 2283
妙 of marvelous beauty → 239
艶 CHARMING → 1908
麗 OF GRACEFUL BEAUTY → 2151
瑶 EXQUISITE → 1026
美 BEAUTIFUL → 2264
佳 FINE → 86

6-6
糸

結 結 結

1348 KETSU KECHI▴ musu(bu) yu(u) yu(waeru)

CH 结 jié jiē

Radical	Strokes
糸 120	12-6-6
Grade	**Freq**
Jōyō-4	143
1 - 6 - 6	

▶**TIE** ▶**CONCLUDE**

COMPOUNDS

❶ⓐ [original meaning] **tie (up), bind, knot**
ⓑ (bring or come together closely) **tie, unite, join**
結髪 *keppatsu* hairdressing, hairdo
結縄 *ketsujō* knotting a rope
結束 *kessoku* unity, union
連結する *renketsu suru* connect, couple, link
直結する *chokketsu suru* connect directly with
結合する *ketsugō suru* unite, combine, join together
結婚 *kekkon* marriage
結縁 *kechien* making a connection (with Buddha)
締結する *teiketsu suru* conclude, contract
妥結 *daketsu* compromise, agreement, understanding

❷ⓐ **form into a mass, congeal, coagulate**
ⓑ **form (an organization), organize, set up**
結晶 *kesshō* crystallization, crystal; grain; fruit(s)
結核 *kekkaku* tuberculosis
結集 *kesshū* concentration, regimentation
凍結 *tōketsu* freezing
凝結する *gyōketsu suru* congeal, coagulate, solidify
結成する *kessei suru* form, organize
結構 *kekkō* structure, construction; quite, well enough, fairly well; all right; no thank you
結社 *kessha* association, society, fraternity
結団する *ketsudan suru* form into an organization

❸ⓐ (bring to an end) **conclude, close, finish, settle**
ⓑ concluding stanza in a Chinese quatrain
結論 *ketsuron* conclusion
結局 *kekkyoku* after all, finally, in conclusion
結末 *ketsumatsu* termination, end, close, conclusion
結語 *ketsugo* conclusion, concluding remarks
結願 *kechigan* expiration of one's vow term
終結する *shūketsu suru* end, close, terminate
完結する *kanketsu suru* complete, conclude, finish; be complete, be concluded, be finished
起承転結 *kishōtenketsu* introduction, development, turn and conclusion (of a Chinese quatrain)

❹ bear fruit, result in
結実する *ketsujitsu suru* bear fruit; be successful, achieve success
結果 *kekka* result, outcome, consequence

KUN

【musu(bu) 結ぶ】
①ⓐ tie (up), bind, knot
ⓑ (connect as if by tying) tie, join, link
紐を結ぶ *himo o musubu* tie a string
結び付ける *musubitsukeru* tie up, join together, link together
東京と大阪を結ぶ *tōkyō to ōsaka o musubu* link Tokyo with Osaka
手を結ぶ *te o musubu* join hands
② (settle a transaction) conclude, close, make (a contract)
国交を結ぶ *kokkō o musubu* enter into diplomatic relations
③ take form, result in
実を結ぶ *mi o musubu* bear fruit
夢を結ぶ *yume o musubu* fall asleep, sleep
④ (bring to an end) conclude, close, finish
結び *musubi* end, close, conclusion; [also suffix] knot, tie; uniting; *Japanese grammar* relation, connection; riceball
小結び *komusubi* third ranking sumo wrestler
⑤ set up, build
庵を結ぶ *iori o musubu* build oneself a hermitage

【yu(u) 結う】 dress (the hair), do up (one's

hair); tie (up), bind, fasten
髪結い *kamiyui* hairdresser; hairdressing
帯を結い上げる *obi o yuiageru* do up a sash
結納 *yuinō* ceremonial exchange of betrothal gifts; betrothal present [gift]
【yu(waeru) 結わえる】 tie (up), bind, fasten
縄を杭に結わえる *nawa o kui ni yuwaeru* tie [fasten] a rope to a post

SYNONYMS

❶ⓐ join
縛 BIND → 1405
束 TIE UP → 3554
連 LINK → 3103
係 CONNECT → 97
接 join → 500
ⓑ combine
統 UNITE → 1352
合 COMBINE → 2019

括 LUMP TOGETHER → 376
総 integrate → 1379
併 join together → 83
❷ⓐ solidify and coagulate
凝 CONGEAL → 175
固 solidify → 3086
凍 FREEZE → 129
ⓑ organize
組 ORGANIZE → 1337
編 put together → 1387
❸ⓐ end
終 END → 1336
絶 COME TO AN END → 1353
閉 CLOSE → 3319
了 FINISH → 3350
済 SETTLE → 522
-上げる completion suffix → 3404
完 COMPLETE → 2201

絞 絞 絞 絞

1349 KŌ shibo(ru) shi(meru) shi(maru)

CH 绞 jiǎo

Radical	Strokes
糸 120	12-6-6
Grade	**Freq**
Jōyō	1761
1-6-6	

6-6 糸

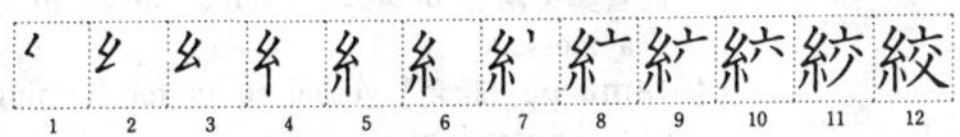

▶STRANGLE ▶WRING

COMPOUNDS

● strangle, strangulate, hang
絞殺する *kōsatsu suru* strangle, hang
絞首刑 *kōshukei* death [execution] by hanging
絞罪 *kōzai* hanging, execution by hanging

KUN

【shibo(ru) 絞る】
①ⓐ wring, wring out
ⓑ strain, rack (one's brains)
絞り *shibori* iris diaphragm; white spots on a dyed ground, tie-dyed fabrics; variegation, spots (in flowers)
お絞り *oshibori* wet towel, steamed towel
雑巾を絞る *zōkin o shiboru* wring a floorcloth
知恵を絞る *chie o shiboru* rack one's brains, think hard
② tighten, close tight, press
袋の口を絞る *fukuro no kuchi o shiboru* close a bag tight by pulling the drawstring
③ⓐ make narrow, focus; lower (the volume)
ⓑ narrow down to, focus on
議論を要点だけに絞る *giron o yōten dake ni shiboru* narrow an argument down
【shi(meru) 絞める】
① strangle, strangulate, wring
絞め殺す *shimekorosu* strangle to death
首を絞める *kubi o shimeru* strangle, wring the neck
② squeeze
羽交い絞め *hagaijime* pinioning
【shi(maru) 絞まる】 be strangled
首が絞まる *kubi ga shimaru* have one's neck wringed

SYNONYMS

● kill
窒 CHOKE → 2288
殺 KILL → 1324
刺 stab to death → 1275
【shiboru】
①ⓐ squeeze
搾 SQUEEZE → 649
圧 apply pressure → 2970

USAGE

❶ shiboru
絞る
①ⓐ wring, wring out
ⓑ strain, rack (one's brains)
② tighten, close tight, press
③ⓐ make narrow, focus; lower (the volume)
ⓑ narrow down to, focus on
搾る
①ⓐ squeeze, press, squash, extract
ⓑ squeeze (money from), sweat, screw
② scold, reprimand
❷ shibori
絞り
① iris diaphragm

②ⓐ white spots on a dyed ground, tie-dyed fabrics
ⓑ variegation, spots (in flowers)

搾り
squeezing

HOMOPHONES

shiboru ⇨ 搾 649

shibori ⇨ 搾 649
shimeru ⇨ 締 1393 〆 3372 閉 3319
shimaru ⇨ 締 1393 閉 3319

NOTE

⇨ see also USAGE note at 締 1393

6-6
糸

給 给 𢇁 Ⓒⓗ 给 gěi jǐ

1350 KYŪ tama(u)▲ tamo(u)▲ -tama(e)▲

Radical	Strokes
糸 120	12-6-6
Grade	**Freq**
Jōyō-4	546
1 - 6 - 6	

▶**SUPPLY** ▶**PAY**

COMPOUNDS

❶ⓐ (provide with something requisite) **supply, provide**
ⓑ [original meaning] (make up for a deficiency) **supply, supplement**
ⓒ *economics* supply
給水 *kyūsui* water supply
給油 *kyūyu* supply of oil
給食 *kyūshoku* (provision of) meals
支給 *shikyū* provision, supply; allowance, grant; payment
配給 *haikyū* distribution, supply; rationing
供給する *kyōkyū suru* supply, furnish, provide
補給 *hokyū* supply, replenishment
自給 *jikyū* self-supply, self-support
需給 *jukyū* supply and demand

❷ give, donate, grant
給血 *kyūketsu* donation of blood

❸ [also suffix] **pay, salary, wages**
給料 *kyūryō* salary, pay, wages
給与 *kyūyo* allowance, grant; pay, salary
給付する *kyūfu suru* make a presentation, grant, pay
月給 *gekkyū* monthly pay [salary]
俸給 *hōkyū* salary, pay
時間給 *jikankyū* payment by the hour
固定給 *koteikyū* regular pay, fixed salary
初任給 *shoninkyū* initial salary

❹ serve; servant
給仕 *kyūji* office boy, page (boy), waiter; service at table
女給 *jokyū* waitress, barmaid, hostess

INDEPENDENT

【kyūsuru 給する】 allow, grant; supply, provide

KUN

【tama(u), tamo(u) 給う】
① [sometimes also 賜う] [suffix] *literary* deign to (perform an action for an inferior)
天皇が立ち給う *Tennō ga tachitamau* His Majesty deigns to stand up
② [usu. 賜う] *literary* deign to give, bestow, grant, award
拝謁を給う *haietsu o tamau* deign to grant an audience
お言葉を給う *okotoba o tamau* deign to give a message

【-tama(e) -給え】 verbal suffix for forming polite imperatives
行き給え *Ikitamae* (=*Yukitamae*) Please go

SYNONYMS

❶ⓐ **supply**
供 supply → 88
納 deliver goods to a customer → 1300
ⓑ **supplement**
補 SUPPLEMENT → 1194
足 supplement → 2188
充 fill up (a vacancy) → 2014

❸ **pay and earnings**
賃 WAGE → 2694
料 FEE → 1292
俸 SALARY → 114
禄 RETAINER'S STIPEND → 1002
収 income → 198

USAGE

tamau
給う
① [sometimes also 賜う] [suffix] *literary* deign to (perform an action for an inferior)
② [usu. 賜う] *literary* deign to give, bestow, grant, award
賜う
① [sometimes also 給う] *literary* deign to give, bestow, grant, award
② [usu. 給う] [suffix] *literary* (perform an action for an inferior) deign to

HOMOPHONES

tamau ⇨ 賜 1585

絡 络 絡

1351 RAKU kara(mu) kara(maru)

CH 络 luò lào

Radical	Strokes
糸 120	12-6-6
Grade	**Freq**
Jōyō	870
1-6-6	

6-6 糸

▶INTERLINK ▶ENTWINE

COMPOUNDS

❶ **interlink, link, connect, join**

連絡 *renraku* connection, contact; communication

脈絡 *myakuraku* logical connection, chain of reasoning

短絡 *tanraku* short circuit

❷ [original meaning] **entwine, twine, intertwine**

籠絡する *rōraku suru* inveigle, ensnare, entice

交絡 *kōraku statistics* confounding, interrelationship

❸ *Chinese medicine* subsidiary meridians in the human body through which vital energy, blood and nutriments flow

KUN

【kara(mu) 絡む】 entwine, twine around, get caught; be involved; pick a fight

絡み *karami* entanglement; involvement, relationship

絡み合う *karamiau* intertwine, entwine, interlock

痰が絡む *Tan ga karamu* Phlegm sticks in the throat

金が絡んだ問題 *kane ga karanda mondai* matter involving money

【kara(maru) 絡まる】 entwine, twine around, get caught [entangled]

絡まり *karamari* entanglement

木に絡まる植物 *ki ni karamaru shokubutsu* creeping plant on trees

SYNONYMS

❶ **relate**

連 LINK → 3103

関 CONCERN → 3328

係 CONNECT → 97

渉 HAVE RELATIONS WITH → 526

❷ **wind and twine**

巻 ROLL UP → 2645

繰る REEL → 1427

統 統 統 統

1352 TŌ su(beru)

CH 统 tǒng

Radical	Strokes
糸 120	12-6-6
Grade	**Freq**
Jōyō-5	202
1-6-6	

6-6 糸

▶UNITE

▶INTERCONNECTED SYSTEM

COMPOUNDS

❶ **unite, unify, gather into one**

統一 *tōitsu* unity, coordination, standardization

統合する *tōgō suru* integrate, combine, unify

統計 *tōkei* statistics

統轄 *tōkatsu* general control, control and jurisdiction

❷ (unite under one rule) **rule, govern, command**

統治する *tōchi suru* rule, govern, reign over

統制 *tōsei* control, regulation

統率 *tōsotsu* leadership, command

総統 *sōtō* sovereign, highest post of the government

大統領 *daitōryō* president

❸ **interconnected system, lineage**

系統 *keitō* system; geological formation; lineage, ancestry

血統 *kettō* lineage, blood, bloodline

正統派 *seitōha* orthodox school

伝統 *dentō* tradition, convention

❹ [rare] counter for setnets

二統 *nitō* two setnets

❺ *geol* series

沖積統 *chūsekitō* alluvial series

INDEPENDENT

【tō 統】 *geol* series

KUN

【su(beru) 統べる】 unite, unify, gather into one; (unite under one rule) rule, govern, command

統べ合わせる *subeawaseru* unite, bring together

三軍を統べる *sangun o suberu* command three forces

SYNONYMS

❶ **combine**

合 COMBINE → 2019

結 TIE → 1348

括 LUMP TOGETHER → 376

総 integrate → 1379

併 join together → 83

❷ **govern**

治 GOVERN → 335

❸ **system**

系 SYSTEM → 1944

制 SYSTEM → 1274

網 network → 1374

NOTE

⇨ see COMPOUND FORMATION for 伝統 *dentō* ⇨ 伝 44

6-6

糸

絶 絕 绝 𦀚

1353 ZETSU ta(eru) ta(yasu) ta(tsu)

CH 绝 jué

Radical	Strokes
糸 120	12-6-6
Grade	**Freq**
Jōyō-5	815
1-6-6	

Stroke order: 1 2 3 4 5 6 7 8 9 10 11 12

▶**BREAK OFF** ▶**COME TO AN END**

COMPOUNDS

❶ⓐ **break off, discontinue, cut off, sever**

ⓑ cutoff, isolated

絶交 *zekkō* breaking off friendship [diplomatic relations]

絶縁 *zetsuen* breaking off relations; insulation, isolation

絶版になる *zeppan ni naru* go out of print

絶食 *zesshoku* fasting

断絶 *danzetsu* severance, rupture; discontinuation

中絶 *chūzetsu* interruption, discontinuance; abortion

根絶する *konzetsu suru* eradicate, exterminate, root out

絶海 *zekkai* distant seas

絶島 *zettō* lonely island

❷ **come to an end, cease to exist**

絶望 *zetsubō* despair, hopelessness

絶滅 *zetsumetsu* extermination, eradication; extinction

絶息する *zessoku suru* expire, die

気絶する *kizetsu suru* faint

杜絶(=途絶) *tozetsu* stoppage, interruption, cessation

❸ **without match, peerless, unparalleled**

絶対の *zettai no* absolute

絶賛 *zessan* great admiration

絶好の *zekkō no* splendid, grand, best, golden

絶妙な *zetsumyō na* miraculous, exquisite, superb

絶世の *zessei no* peerless, unequaled

絶景 *zekkei* superb view, picturesque scenery

絶唱 *zesshō* superb song [poem]

空前絶後 *kūzenzetsugo* the first and probably the last

❹ reject, decline, refuse

拒絶する *kyozetsu suru* refuse, reject, deny

謝絶 *shazetsu* declination, refusal

❺ Chinese quatrain poetry

絶句 *zekku* Chinese quatrain poetry; breaking off in one's speech

INDEPENDENT

【zessuru 絶する】 be beyond (as words or imagination)

想像を絶する *sōzō o zessuru* be beyond imagination, be unimaginable

KUN

【ta(eru) 絶える】 come to an end, cease to exist; become extinct

絶えず *taezu* constantly, always

絶え間 *taema* interval, gap

途絶える *todaeru* come to an end

通信が絶える *Tsūshin ga taeru* Correspondence has ceased

絶えてしまった種 *taete shimatta shu* extinct species

死に絶える *shinitaeru* die out, become extinct

【ta(yasu) 絶やす】 exterminate, extirpate, eradicate; allow to run out, run out of

鼠を絶やす *nezumi o tayasu* exterminate rats

酒を絶やす *sake o tayasu* run out of wine

【ta(tsu) 絶つ】

① break off, discontinue, cut off, sever

連絡を絶つ *renraku o tatsu* sever the connection

② exterminate, extirpate, eradicate

禍根を絶つ *kakon o tatsu* strike at the root of an evil

SYNONYMS

❶ⓐ **discontinue**

廃 ABOLISH → 3146

断 CUT OFF → 1492

止 STOP → 2941

休 suspend → 52

停 suspend → 139

❷ **end**
終 END → 1336
閉 CLOSE → 3319
了 FINISH → 3350
済 SETTLE → 522
-上げる completion suffix → 3404
完 COMPLETE → 2201
結 CONCLUDE → 1348
❷ **come to an end**
尽 be exhausted → 3050
❸ **excellent and superior**
妙 MARVELOUS → 239
快 splendid → 245
卓 PROMINENT → 2064
優 SUPERIOR → 177
秀 EXCELLENT → 2545
英 DISTINGUISHED → 2238
傑 outstanding → 155
逸 exceptional → 3120
名 first-rate → 2169
上 of upper grade → 3404

HOMOPHONES
tatsu ⇨ 断 1492 裁 3299

NOTE
⇨ see USAGE note at 断 1492
⇨ see COMPOUND FORMATION for 絶対 *zettai* ⇨ 対 831

絞 1354 — **▶STRANGLE ▶WRING** — 6-6 糸
nonstandard for 絞 1349

絲 1355 — **▶THREAD** — 6-6 糸
nonstandard for 糸 2179

絕 1356 — **▶BREAK OFF ▶COME TO AN END** — 6-6 糸
nonstandard for 絶 1353

翔 翔 翔 翔 1357 — 6-6 ⺷
SHŌ kake(ru) to(bu)

CH 翔 xiáng

Radical	Strokes
羽 124	12-6-6
Grade	Freq
Names	2100
1-6-6	

Stroke order: 1 2 3 4 5 6 7 8 9 10 11 12

▶SOAR

COMPOUNDS
● **soar, fly**
翔破する *shōha suru* complete a flight
飛翔 *hishō* flight, soaring
滑翔機 *kasshōki* sailplane, glider
競翔 *kyōshō* flying race (between pigeons)

KUN
【kake(ru) 翔る】 soar, fly
天翔る *amagakeru* ride the skies
飛び翔る *tobikakeru* soar, fly
【to(bu) 翔ぶ】 soar, fly
翔んでる *tonderu* groovy, far-out, flipped out

NAMES
翔 *shō* male name

SYNONYMS
● **fly**
飛 FLY → 3572
航 NAVIGATE → 1318

HOMOPHONES
kakeru ⇨ 駆 1823 掛 493 懸 2915 架 2569 賭 1605
tobu ⇨ 飛 3572 跳 1532

NOTE
⇨ see USAGE notes at 掛 493 and 飛 3572

翔 1358 — **▶SOAR** — 6-6 ⺷
nonstandard for 翔 1357

6-6 舟 **艇** incorrect stroke count ⇨ see 1365

6-6 虫 **蛔**
1359 KAI

CH 蛔 huí

Radical	Strokes
虫 142	12-6-6
Grade	Freq
Reference	
1 - 6 - 6	

COMPOUNDS

● [now replaced by 回 3055] [original meaning] roundworm, ascarid
蛔虫 *kaichū* roundworm, ascarid

6-7 糸 **継** 繼 継 𢇁
1360 KEI tsu(gu) mama-▲

CH 继 jì

Radical	Strokes
糸 120	13-6-7
Grade	Freq
Jōyō	887
1 - 6 - 7	

▶SUCCEED

COMPOUNDS

❶ⓐ (come after and take the place of) **succeed (to), accede, inherit**
ⓑ (come next or after) **succeed, continue, follow**
ⓒ **execute (a race) by relay**
継承する *keishō suru* succeed to, accede to, inherit
継嗣 *keishi* successor, heir, heiress
継投 *keitō* relieving the (starting) pitcher
後継 *kōkei* succession; successor, inheritor, heir
継続する *keizoku suru* continue, last, maintain
継起する *keiki suru* occur in succession
継走 *keisō* relay race
継泳 *keiei* relay swimming
継電器 *keidenki* (electric) relay
中継 *chūkei* relay, rebroadcasting
❷ step–; second (wife or husband)
継母 *keibo* stepmother
継夫 *keifu* second husband

KUN

【tsu(gu) 継ぐ】
① succeed (to), accede; inherit
家を継ぐ *ie o tsugu* succeed to a house
受け継ぐ *uketsugu* inherit, succeed to
跡継ぎ *atotsugi* successor, heir
引き継ぐ *hikitsugu* take over, hand over; succeed to, inherit
② couple, link, relay
継ぎ足す *tsugitasu* add to; extend, piece out
言葉を継ぐ *kotoba o tsugu* continue (to say)
③ patch (up)
継ぎ *tsugi* a patch
④ add to, replenish, feed
【mama- 継-】 step–
継母 *mamahaha* stepmother
継子 *mamako* stepchild

SYNONYMS

❶ⓐ **succeed**
承 succeed to → 16
嗣 inherit → 1719
ⓑ **continue**
続 CONTINUE → 1362
連 IN SUCCESSION → 3103
持 HOLD → 374
❷ **related by marriage**
義 -in-law → 2338

HOMOPHONES

tsugu ⇨ 接 500 次 54 注 325
tsugi ⇨ 次 54

NOTE

⇨ see USAGE notes at 接 500 and 次 54

絹 絹 絹

1361 KEN kinu

(CH) 绢 juàn

Radical	Strokes
糸 120	13-6-7
Grade	**Freq**
Jōyō-6	1185
◧ 1 - 6 - 7	

6-7 糸

▶SILK

COMPOUNDS

● [original meaning] **silk**

絹布 *kenpu* silk, silk cloth
絹糸 *kenshi* (=*kinuito*) silk thread
人絹 *jinken* artificial silk; rayon
正絹 *shōken* (pure) silk

KUN

【kinu 絹】 silk, silk fabrics

絹織物 *kinuorimono* silk fabrics [goods]
絹地 *kinuji* silk fabrics
絹糸 *kinuito* silk thread
薄絹 *usuginu* sheer silk

SYNONYMS

● **fabrics**

綾 TWILL → 1376
綿 COTTON → 1373
麻 HEMP → 3125
毛 wool → 3453
錦 BROCADE → 1738
紗 GAUZE → 1301
織 woven fabric → 1422

USAGE

kinu

絹
silk, silk fabrics

衣
elegant garment

HOMOPHONES

kinu ⇨ 衣 2013

続 續 続 続

1362 ZOKU tsuzu(ku) tsuzu(keru)

(CH) 续 xù

Radical	Strokes
糸 120	13-6-7
Grade	**Freq**
Jōyō-4	196
◧ 1 - 6 - 7	

6-7 糸

▶CONTINUE

COMPOUNDS

ⓐ [original meaning] **continue, follow, ensue, be adjacent**

ⓑ [prefix] **continuation, sequel, second series**

続行 *zokkō* continuation
続出する *zokushutsu suru* appear in succession
続落 *zokuraku* continuous drop (of stocks)
継続する *keizoku suru* continue, last, maintain
連続 *renzoku* continuation, succession, series
接続する *setsuzoku suru* connect, join
持続力 *jizokuryoku* tenacity
続近代文明論 *zoku-kindaibunmeiron* Later Thoughts on Modern Civilization

INDEPENDENT

【zoku 続】 continuation, sequel, second series

正と続 *sei to zoku* first and second series

KUN

【tsuzu(ku) 続く】 *vi* continue, go on, follow, ensue; be adjacent, lead to

続き *tsuzuki* continuation, sequel, second series; [also suffix] continuation (in time and space), succession, spell
晴天続き *seitentsuzuki* spell of fine weather
引き続く *hikitsuzuku* continue, last; occur in succession, ensue
続き物 *tsuzukimono* serial story
寝室に続く廊下 *shinshitsu ni tsuzuku rōka* corridor leading to the bedroom
手続き *tetsuzuki* procedure, formalities

【tsuzu(keru) 続ける】 *vt* [also verbal suffix] continue, keep up, go ahead

続け様に *tsuzukezama ni* successively, in a row
立て続けに *tatetsuzuke ni* in succession, on the trot
歩き続ける *arukitsuzukeru* keep walking

SYNONYMS

ⓐ **continue**

継 SUCCEED → 1360

連 IN SUCCESSION → 3103

持 HOLD → 374

6-7 糸

經 1363

▶**PASS THROUGH** ▶**MANAGE**

nonstandard for 経 1331

6-7 舌

辞 1364 辭 辞 辞

JI ya(meru)

Ⓒⓗ 辞 cí

Radical	Strokes
辛 160	13-7-6
Grade	**Freq**
Jōyō-4	852
1 - 6 - 7	

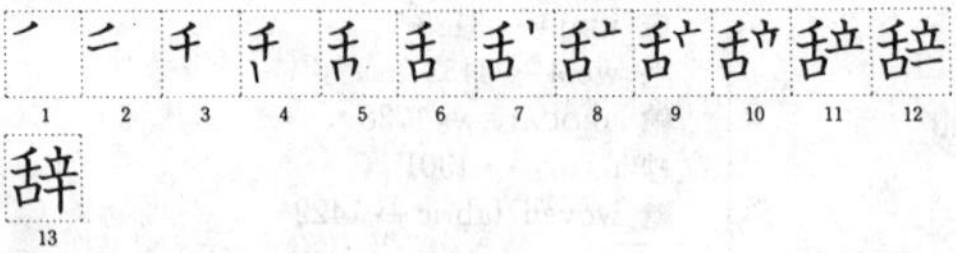

▶**WORD** ▶**RESIGN**

COMPOUNDS

❶ⓐ **word, term, phrase, expression, sentence**

ⓑ *gram* function word, particle

辞典 *jiten* dictionary

辞書 *jisho* dictionary

世辞 *seji* compliment

式辞 *shikiji* address

措辞 *soji* phraseology, wording

接辞 *setsuji* affix

❷ **resign, retire, quit**

辞職 *jishoku* resignation

辞表 *jihyō* (letter of) resignation

辞意 *jii* intention to resign

❸ decline, refuse

辞退 *jitai* declining, refusal

❹ leave, depart

辞去する *jikyo suru* leave, quit, retire

辞世 *jisei* passing away; death poem

❺ form of poetic prose in ancient China

楚辞 *soji* collection of poems by Qu Yuan and others, *Chuci*

INDEPENDENT

【**ji 辞**】formal message; word, expression; function word; form of poetic prose in ancient China

告別の辞 *kokubetsu no ji* parting [farewell] address

【**jisuru 辞する**】resign; decline; take one's leave

職を辞する *shoku o jisuru* resign one's post

KUN

【**ya(meru) 辞める**】resign, retire, quit

会社を辞める *kaisha o yameru* leave the company

SYNONYMS

❶ **words and expressions**

語 WORD → 1543

詞 WORDS → 1503

句 PHRASE → 2967

❷ **resign**

退 retire → 3094

USAGE

yameru

辞める

resign, retire, quit

罷める

[in the form of 罷めさせる *yamesaseru*] fire, discharge

止める

①ⓐ stop (performing an action), cease, discontinue

ⓑ give up, abandon, quit

② abolish, do away with

HOMOPHONES

yameru ⇨ 罷 2617 止 2941

NOTE

⇨ see COMPOUND FORMATION for 措辞 *soji* ⇨ 措 502

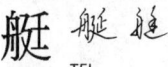

艇 1365 TEI

CH 艇 tǐng

Radical	Strokes
舟 137	13-6-7
Grade	**Freq**
Jōyō	1338
1-6-7	

6-7 舟

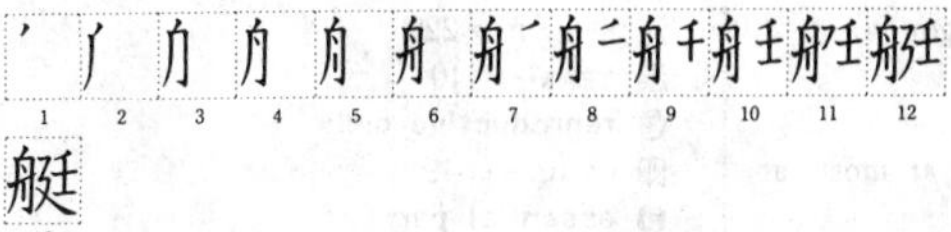

▶BOAT

COMPOUNDS

● [also suffix] [original meaning] **boat, small boat, light craft**
艇長 *teichō* coxswain, captain (of a submarine)
舟艇 *shūtei* boat, craft
短艇 *tantei* boat
競艇 *kyōtei* boat race
艦艇 *kantei* war vessels
警備艇 *keibitei* guardship
救命艇 *kyūmeitei* lifeboat

INDEPENDENT

【tei 艇】 small boat, boat

SYNONYMS

● **boats and ships**
舟 SMALL BOAT → 3538
船 SHIP → 1341
舶 OCEANGOING SHIP → 1340
艦 WARSHIP → 1435
潜 submarine → 746
隻 COUNTER FOR SHIPS → 2755

精 1366 SEI SHŌ

CH 精 jīng

Radical	Strokes
米 119	14-6-8
Grade	**Freq**
Jōyō-5	659
1-6-8	

6-8 米

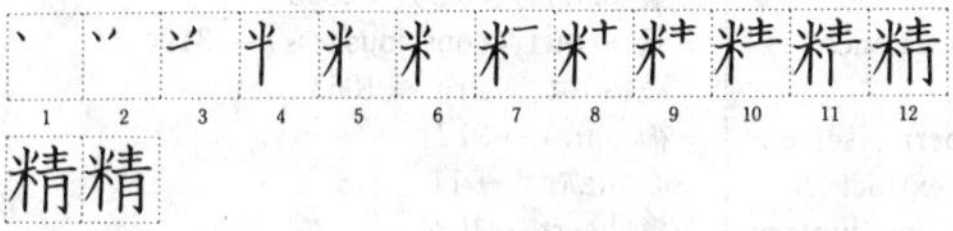

▶REFINE ▶ESSENCE ▶SPIRIT

COMPOUNDS

❶ⓐ **refine (crude materials), polish**
ⓑ (purified) **refined, fine**
ⓒ [original meaning] polish rice, clean
精錬 *seiren* refining, smelting; tempering
精製 *seisei* refining; careful manufacture
精糖 *seitō* refined sugar, sugar refining
精油 *seiyu* refined oil; essential oil, essence
精白 *seihaku* refining, polishing
精米 *seimai* rice polishing; polished [white] rice

❷ⓐ (essential part of a substance) essence, extract, spirit
ⓑ (essential substance of life) **sperm, semen**
酒精 *shusei* spirit of wine, alcohol
木精 *mokusei* wood alcohol; spirit of wood
糊精 *kosei* dextrin(e)
薄荷精 *hakkasei* essence of mint
精子 *seishi* sperm
精液 *seieki* semen, sperm
受精 *jusei* fertilization, impregnation; pollination
夢精 *musei* nocturnal emission, wet dream

❸ⓐ (essential part) **essence, quintessence, spirit**
ⓑ choice, picked, best
精髄 *seizui* essence, soul, spirit, pith
精華 *seika* flower, essence, glory
精肉 *seiniku* choice meat
精鋭 *seiei* best [pick] (of the aviators), choice (of an army)
精兵 *seihei* picked troops

❹ **meticulous, careful, elaborate, precise, exact, detailed, fine**
精査 *seisa* minute investigation, close inspection, careful examination
精選 *seisen* careful selection
精緻な *seichi na* minute, subtle, delicate, exquisite
精巧な *seikō na* elaborate, exquisite, ingenious
精密 *seimitsu* precision, accuracy, minuteness
精度 *seido* precision, accuracy
精算 *seisan* exact calculation; settlement of accounts
精通する *seitsū suru* be well versed in, have

thorough knowledge of
❺ⓐ (source of vital energy) **spirit, energy, vitality, vigor**
ⓑ (spiritual part of man) **spirit, mind, soul**
精力 *seiryoku* energy, vitality, vigor
精気 *seiki* spirit, energy, essence
精根 *seikon* energy, vitality
精精 *seizei* with all one's might; at most, at best
精一杯 *seiippai* with all one's might
精神 *seishin* mind, soul, heart; intention, motive; the spirit (of something)
精魂 *seikon* spirit, soul; vitality
❻ put one's heart into, be diligent
精励 *seirei* diligence, industry
精勤 *seikin* diligence, good attendance
精進 *shōjin* diligence, concentration, devotion; religious purification; abstinence from (eating) fish and meat
丹精(＝丹誠) *tansei* efforts, pains
無精 *bushō* indolence, laziness
❼ (supernatural being) spirit, sprite, fairy
精霊 *seirei* spirit of a dead person; spirit, sprite
妖精 *yōsei* fairy, elf, sprite

INDEPENDENT

【sei 精】
①ⓐ (essential part of a substance) essence, extract, spirit
ⓑ (essential substance of life) sperm, semen
バニラの精 *banira no sei* vanilla extract
精を漏らす *sei o morasu* have an involuntary emission of semen
② (source of vital energy) spirit, energy, vitality, vigor
精が尽きる *sei ga tsukiru* one's energy is gone, be exhausted
精を出す *sei o dasu* work hard [diligently]
③ (supernatural being) spirit, sprite, fairy
花の精 *hana no sei* spirit of a flower

SYNONYMS

❶ⓐ refine
錬 REFINE (crude metals) → 1741
留 distill → 2580
ⓑ clean and purified
粋 REFINED (free from impurities) → 1293
潔 IMMACULATE → 744
純 PURE → 1297
浄 CLEAN → 382
清 clean → 523
❷ⓑ bodily secretions
乳 MILK → 1438
汗 SWEAT → 220
涙 TEAR → 440
ⓑ reproductive cells
卵 ovum → 849
❸ⓐ essential part
粋 essence (best part) → 1293
髄 essence (vital part) → 1842
枢 PIVOT → 865
幹 TRUNK → 1718
綱 ESSENTIAL POINTS → 1372
旨 PURPORT → 2024
要 summary → 2635
❹ detailed
密 CLOSE → 2292
細 MINUTE → 1333
詳 DETAILED → 1526
❹ careful
謹 carefully → 1618
慎 PRUDENT → 643
❺ⓐ life energy
気 vital energy → 3194
ⓑ psyche
霊 SPIRIT (soul) → 2805
気 SPIRIT (consciousness) → 3194
魂 SOUL, spirit → 1063
神 MIND → 912
心 HEART → 11
腹 heart → 1034
衷 INNER HEART → 2575
襟 inner mind → 1252
胸 breast → 951
懐 BOSOM → 763
❻ exert oneself
尽 use all one's strength → 3050
勤 work diligently → 1818
励 make efforts → 1119
勉 ENDEAVOR → 3318
努 EXERT → 2547
❼ supernatural and evil beings
霊 SPIRIT → 2805
怪 monster → 297
魔 DEMON → 3187
鬼 DEVIL → 2657

6-8

精 1367

▶REFINE ▶ESSENCE ▶SPIRIT
nonstandard for 精 1366

6-8

粹 1368

▶REFINED
nonstandard for 粋 1293

緋 緋 緋

1369 HI NAMES ake

CH 绯 fēi

Radical	Strokes
糸 120	14-6-8
Grade	**Freq**
Names	2108
1 - 6 - 8	

6-8
糸

▶ **SCARLET**

COMPOUNDS

● **scarlet**

緋縅し *hiodoshi* scarlet-threaded suit of armor

緋鯉 *higoi* red carp, golden carp

INDEPENDENT

【**hi 緋**】 scarlet, cardinal

緋の衣 *hi no koromo* scarlet robe

NAMES

緋田 *akeda* surname

SYNONYMS

● **red colors**

紅 CRIMSON → 1277
赤 RED → 2193
朱 VERMILION → 3531
丹 CINNABAR → 3441
茜 MADDER → 2261

維 維 維

1370 I

CH 维 wéi

Radical	Strokes
糸 120	14-6-8
Grade	**Freq**
Jōyō	878
1 - 6 - 8	

6-8
糸

▶ **FIBER**

COMPOUNDS

❶ⓐ **fiber**

ⓑ [original meaning, now archaic] rope

纖維 *sen'i* fiber, textile

線維束 *sen'isoku* fascicle

維管束 *ikansoku* vascular bundle

❷ **tie up, hold together, maintain**

維持する *iji suru* maintain, keep (up), preserve

❸ **emphatic prefix**

維新 *ishin* renovation, restoration; Imperial Restoration of 1868

SYNONYMS

❶ⓐ **threads and fibers**

纖 FIBER → 1413
糸 THREAD → 2179
緯 woof → 1407
経 warp → 1331

COMPOUND FORMATION

❶ **維持** *iji*

維持する 'maintain, etc.' literally means to secure (維 ❷) something so as to hold (持) it in place.

❷ **維新** *ishin*

維新 'renovation, etc.' is to totally (維 ❸) reform or make new (新).

綺

1371 KI

CH 绮 qǐ

Radical	Strokes
糸 120	14-6-8
Grade	**Freq**
Reference	
1 - 6 - 8	

6-8
糸

COMPOUNDS

❶ [now also 奇 2217] beautiful, gorgeous, elegant

綺麗な *kirei na* beautiful, pretty; clean; fair

綺想曲 *kisōkyoku* caprice, capriccio
❷ fine thin silk with slanting weave
綺羅 *kira* fine clothes, gorgeous dress
❸ clever, amusing
綺談 *kidan* colorful story

6-8 糸

綱

1372 KŌ tsuna

Ⓒⓗ 纲 gāng

Radical	Strokes
糸 120	14-6-8
Grade	Freq
Jōyō	1135
1-6-8	

1 2 3 4 5 6 7 8 9 10 11 12 13 14

▶ESSENTIAL POINTS ▶ROPE

COMPOUNDS

❶ **essential [main] points, essence, gist, outline**
綱領 *kōryō* essential [main] points, gist, outline; summary
綱要 *kōyō* elements, essentials; outline
要綱 *yōkō* outline, gist; general plan
大綱 *taikō* outline, general features
❷ guiding principle, discipline, morals
綱紀 *kōki* law and order, official discipline
政綱 *seikō* political principle, policy
❸ *biol* class, -acea
亜綱 *akō* subclass
甲殻綱 *kōkakukō* Crustacea
❹ [original meaning] **rope (esp. headrope on a net)**

INDEPENDENT

【kō 綱】 *biol* class

KUN

【tsuna 綱】 rope (esp. of fiber), line, cord, cable; sumo grand championship
綱渡り *tsunawatari* tightrope walking [walker]
綱引き *tsunahiki* tug of war; forward puller (of a rickshaw)
手綱 *tazuna* bridle, reins
頼みの綱 *tanomi no tsuna* last ray of hope
綱を張る *tsuna o haru* be a grand champion
横綱 *yokozuna* (grand) champion sumo wrestler

SYNONYMS

❶ **essential part**
旨 PURPORT → 2024
要 summary → 2635
精 ESSENCE (essential part) → 1366
粋 essence (best part) → 1293
髄 essence (vital part) → 1842
枢 PIVOT → 865
幹 TRUNK → 1718
❷ **policy**
是 policy → 2436
策 policy → 2679
【tsuna】
○ **ropes and lines**
縄 ROPE (esp. of straw) → 1388
緒 cord → 1378
組 braid → 1337
索 cable → 2455
鎖 CHAIN → 1761
線 LINE → 1392
弦 STRING → 287

NOTE

★do not confuse with 網 1374

6-8 糸

綿

1373 MEN wata

Ⓒⓗ 绵 mián

Radical	Strokes
糸 120	14-6-8
Grade	Freq
Jōyō-5	987
1-6-8	

1 2 3 4 5 6 7 8 9 10 11 12 13 14

▶COTTON

COMPOUNDS

❶ [formerly also 棉 988]
ⓐ **cotton plant**
ⓑ **cotton fiber, cotton cloth, cotton wool**
綿花 *menka* raw cotton, cotton wool
原綿 *genmen* raw cotton
綿糸 *menshi* cotton yarn [thread]

綿羊(＝緬羊) *men'yō* sheep
綿紡 *menbō* cotton spinning
綿織物 *men'orimono* cotton goods
木綿 *momen* cotton, cotton cloth
梳綿機 *somenki* carding machine
印綿 *inmen* Indian raw cotton

❷ minute, fine
綿密な *menmitsu na* close, minute, detailed

❸ everlasting
綿綿たる *menmentaru* endless, continuous

KUN

【wata 綿】
[formerly also 棉]
ⓐ cotton plant
ⓑ cotton fiber, cotton cloth, cotton wool
綿の実 *wata no mi* cotton seed
綿繰り *watakuri* cotton ginning
綿菓子 *watagashi* cotton candy

SYNONYMS

❶ⓐ fiber-producing plants
麻 HEMP → 3125

ⓑ fabrics
麻 HEMP → 3125
毛 wool → 3453
錦 BROCADE → 1738
綾 TWILL → 1376
絹 SILK → 1361
紗 GAUZE → 1301
織 woven fabric → 1422

USAGE

wata
綿
[formerly also 棉]
ⓐ cotton plant
ⓑ cotton fiber, cotton cloth, cotton wool
棉
[now replaced by 綿] same as 綿

HOMOPHONES

wata ⇨ 棉 988

網

1374 MŌ ami

CH 网 wǎng

Radical	Strokes
糸 120	14-6-8
Grade	**Freq**
Jōyō	1281
1-6-8	

6-8
糸

▶**NET**

COMPOUNDS

❶ⓐ [original meaning] **net (for catching animals)**
ⓑ (reticulated fabric) **net, netting**
ⓒ catch with a net, capture everything
漁網 *gyomō* fishing net
鉄条網 *tetsujōmō* barbed wire entanglements
網状組織 *mōjō-soshiki* network, reticulum
網膜 *mōmaku* retina
網羅する *mōra suru* encompass, comprehend

❷ (something that entraps) net
天網 *tenmō* Heaven's net, Heaven's vengeance
法網 *hōmō* net of the law, justice

❸ [suffix] **network**
通信網 *tsūshinmō* communications network
鉄道網 *tetsudōmō* railway network
放送網 *hōsōmō* broadcasting network

KUN

【ami 網】 net, netting
網目 *amime* meshes (of a net)
金網 *kanaami* wire netting, screen
引き網 *hikiami* seine, dragnet

SYNONYMS

❶ⓐ & ❶ⓑ net
羅 bird net → 2622

❸ system
統 INTERCONNECTED SYSTEM → 1352
系 SYSTEM → 1944
制 SYSTEM → 1274

NOTE

★do not confuse with 綱 1372

6-8 糸

練 練 練 練

1375 REN ne(ru) ne(ri)-

(CH) 练 liàn

Radical	Strokes
糸 120	14-6-8
Grade	**Freq**
Jōyō-3	623
1-6-8	

1 2 3 4 5 6 7 8 9 10 11 12 13 14

▶TRAIN

COMPOUNDS

❶ⓐ [sometimes also 錬 1741] **train, practice, exercise, drill, discipline; refine**
ⓑ (make proficient) **train, drill**
ⓒ trained, experienced, skilled
練成 *rensei* training, drilling
練習 *renshū* practice, training
習練する *shūren suru* train, discipline
訓練 *kunren* training, drill
教練 *kyōren* military drill
練達 *rentatsu* skill, dexterity
未練 *miren* lingering affection, reluctance to give up
熟練した *jukuren shita* skilled, experienced, proficient

❷ [formerly 煉 1023]
ⓐ refine (one's skills), purify
ⓑ knead
洗練された *senren sareta* refined, polished
試練 *shiren* trial, test, probation
練乳 *rennyū* condensed milk
練炭 *rentan* (charcoal or coal) briquette

❸ [original meaning] (soften and whiten raw silk by boiling) gloss, boil off, soften
精練 *seiren* scouring; training

KUN

【ne(ru) 練る】
①ⓐ train, drill, exercise
ⓑ polish (one's style), refine
練り上げる *neriageru* train up, discipline
文を練る *bun o neru* polish one's style
② gloss, boil off, soften
練り絹 *neriginu* glossed silk
③ walk in procession
練り歩く *neriaruku* parade, march
④ [formerly 煉る] knead
練り *neri* kneading; gloss; tempering
⑤ [formerly 錬る] temper (metals), forge

【ne(ri)- 練り-】 [also prefix] paste
練り薬 *nerigusuri* medicated paste
練り製品 *neriseihin* fish paste

SYNONYMS

❶ⓐ **cultivate**
錬 REFINE → 1741
鍛 train → 1755
修 CULTIVATE → 123
養 FOSTER (one's intellect) → 2365
磨 POLISH → 3181
琢 POLISH → 971

ⓑ **teach**
訓 INSTRUCT → 1454
教 TEACH → 1493
授 teach → 492
育 educate → 2050
諭 ADMONISH → 1598
導 GUIDE → 2888
迪 EDIFY → 3076
啓 ENLIGHTEN → 2763

USAGE

❶ **neru**
練る
①ⓐ train, drill, exercise
ⓑ polish (one's style), refine
② gloss, boil off, soften
③ walk in procession
④ [formerly 煉る] knead
⑤ [formerly 錬る] temper (metals), forge
錬る
[now usu. 練る] temper, forge, refine, smelt
煉る
[now also 練る] knead

❷ **ren 練 錬**
★These two characters are often interchangeable in the sense of training or cultivating one's character, but 練 is usually preferred. In compounds related to metalworking, such as 鍛錬 *tanren* 'forging', only 錬 is used.

HOMOPHONES

neru ⇒ 錬 1741 煉 1023

COMPOUND FORMATION

❶ 未練 *miren*
未練 'lingering affection, reluctance to give up' originally meant unskilled or inexperienced; that is, a person who is not yet (未) sufficiently experienced or skilled (練 ❶ⓒ).

❷ 試練 *shiren*
試練 'trial, test, probation' is to have one's faith purified (練 ❷ⓐ) by being tried (試).

綾 绫 𦃇

1376 RYŌ aya

Ⓒⓗ 绫 líng

Radical	Strokes
糸 120	14-6-8
Grade	**Freq**
Names	2009
◧ 1 - 6 - 8	

6-8 糸

1 2 3 4 5 6 7 8 9 10 11 12 13 14

▶TWILL

COMPOUNDS

● [original meaning] **twilled silk**

綾羅 *ryōra* figured silk and thin silk; elaborated cloth

KUN

【aya 綾】

①ⓐ [in compounds] twill, twilled fabric
ⓑ twilled silk
ⓒ [in compounds] as beautiful or intricate as twilled silk

綾織り *ayaori* twill
綾錦 *ayanishiki* twill damask and brocade
綾取り *ayatori* cat's cradle
目も綾な *memoaya na* dazzlingly beautiful, brilliant

② [also 文] figure, design, pattern (as of cloth)

綾を成して *aya o nashite* in beautiful patterns

③ [also 文]
ⓐ figure of speech, rhetorical flourish
ⓑ intricate and subtle details, intricacies

言葉の綾 *kotoba no aya* figure of speech
事件の綾 *jiken no aya* web of the case

NAMES

綾部 *ayabe* surname also place name
綾子 *ayako* female name

SYNONYMS

【aya】

①ⓐ **fabrics**

絹 SILK → 1361
錦 BROCADE → 1738
綿 COTTON → 1373
麻 HEMP → 3125
毛 wool → 3453
紗 GAUZE → 1301
織 woven fabric → 1422

USAGE

aya

綾
①ⓐ [in compounds] twill, twilled fabric
ⓑ twilled silk
ⓒ [in compounds] as beautiful or intricate as twilled silk
② [also 文] figure, design, pattern (as of cloth)
③ [also 文]
ⓐ figure of speech, rhetorical flourish
ⓑ intricate and subtle details, intricacies

文
[also 綾]
① figure, design, pattern (as of cloth)
②ⓐ figure of speech, rhetorical flourish
ⓑ intricate and subtle details, intricacies

HOMOPHONES

aya ⇨ 文 1962

緑 綠 绿 𦀌

1377 RYOKU ROKU midori

Ⓒⓗ 绿 lü lù

Radical	Strokes
糸 120	14-6-8
Grade	**Freq**
Jōyō-3	1170
◧ 1 - 6 - 8	

6-8 糸

1 2 3 4 5 6 7 8 9 10 11 12 13 14

▶GREEN

COMPOUNDS

❶ⓐ [original meaning] **green, emerald**
ⓑ [prefix] greenish

緑色 *ryokushoku* green, verdure
緑茶 *ryokucha* green tea, Japanese tea
緑青 *rokushō* verdigris, copper [green] rust
葉緑素 *yōryokuso* chlorophyll
緑白色 *ryokuhakushoku* greenish white

❷ (abounding in growth) green, verdant

緑地帯 *ryokuchitai* green belt
緑化 *ryokka* tree planting, afforestation

緑土 *ryokudo* verdant area

KUN

【midori 緑】 green; verdure; *elegant* young leaves

緑色 *midoriiro* green

浅緑 *asamidori* (=*senryoku*) light green

緑に覆われた山 *midori ni ōwareta yama* mountain robed in verdure

緑の黒髪 *midori no kurokami* glossy black hair (of a young woman)

SYNONYMS

❶ green colors

青 GREEN → 2430

翠 JADE GREEN → 2705

NOTE

★do not confuse with 縁 1386

6-8 糸

緒 緒 緒 絃

1378 SHO CHO o itoguchi▲

Ⓒⓗ 绪 xù

Radical	Strokes
糸 120	14-6-8
Grade	**Freq**
Jōyō	1236
1-6-8	

▶OUTSET

COMPOUNDS

❶ outset, beginning, inception, first step, early stage

緒戦 *shosen* (=*chosen*) beginning of hostilities, early stage of a war

緒論 *shoron* introduction, preface

緒言 *shogen* (=*chogen*) foreword, preface

端緒 *tansho* (=*tancho*) beginning, start, first step; clue

❷ mental or emotional state

情緒 *jōcho* emotion, feeling

心緒 *shinsho* (=*shincho*) emotion; mind

❸ⓐ thread of events, line, lineage

ⓑ [original meaning, now archaic] end of a thread

由緒 *yuisho* history, lineage

一緒に *issho ni* together; at the same time; in a lump

❹ used phonetically for *sho*

内緒(=内証) *naisho* (=*naishō*) secrecy, privacy

INDEPENDENT

【sho (=cho) 緒】 beginning, inception

緒に就く *sho* (=*cho*) *ni tsuku* get underway, be started

KUN

【o 緒】 cord, strap, thong; string

臍の緒 *heso no o* umbilical cord

鼻緒 *hanao* clog thong, strap

緒締め *ojime* string-fastener

【itoguchi 緒】 [now usu. 糸口] beginning, first step; clue

緒を開く *itoguchi o hiraku* make a beginning; find a clue

SYNONYMS

❶ beginnings

序 INTRODUCTORY PART → 3065

端 start → 1221

始 beginning → 281

初 beginning → 1116

元 ORIGIN → 1929

本 origin → 3502

根 ROOT → 930

源 SOURCE → 656

【o】

○ ropes and lines

組 braid → 1337

縄 ROPE (esp. of straw) → 1388

綱 ROPE (esp. of fiber) → 1372

索 cable → 2455

鎖 CHAIN → 1761

線 LINE → 1392

弦 STRING → 287

USAGE

itoguchi

緒

[now usu. 糸口] beginning, first step; clue

糸口

[formerly also 緒] beginning, first step; clue

HOMOPHONES

itoguchi ⇨ 糸口 2179, 3382

COMPOUND FORMATION

一緒 *issho*

一緒に 'together, etc.' is "correctly" (but not actually) written 一所に 'in one place' and can probably be explained as one (一) thread or line (緒 ❸ⓐ) of events.

総 總 総 綛

1379 sō su(bete)▲

CH 总 zǒng

Radical	Strokes
糸 120	14-6-8
Grade	**Freq**
Jōyō-5	152
◧ 1-6-8	

1 2 3 4 5 6 7 8 9 10 11 12 13 14

▶**TOTAL** ▶**GENERAL**

COMPOUNDS

❶ⓐ [also prefix] **total, whole, combined, full, complete, gross**

ⓑ [formerly also 綜 1380] **integrate, unify, total**

総額 *sōgaku* total amount, sum total
総数 *sōsū* total (number)
総点 *sōten* sum total of one's marks
総体 *sōtai* the whole, all; on the whole, generally
総掛かり *sōgakari* combined efforts
総二階 *sōnikai* full two-story house
総予算 *sōyosan* complete budget
総量 *sōryō* gross weight [volume]
総計する *sōkei suru* total, sum up
総合する *sōgō suru* synthesize, integrate, put together
総括する *sōkatsu suru* generalize, summarize

❷ [formerly also 惣 2780] [also suffix] (applicable to the whole) **general, overall; ordinary**

総会 *sōkai* general meeting
総務 *sōmu* general affairs; manager, director
総選挙 *sōsenkyo* general election
総辞職 *sōjishoku* resignation en masse
総評(＝日本労働組合総評議会) *sōhyō* (＝*nihon rōdōkumiai sōhyōgikai*) General Council of Trade Unions of Japan
総菜 *sōzai* daily [household] dish, side dish
総社 *sōja* shrine enshrining several gods
総嫁 *sōka* streetwalker (in the Edo period)

❸ [formerly also 惣 2780]

ⓐ [also prefix] (of highest or supreme rank) **general, -general, supreme, head, -in-chief**

ⓑ exercise general control, supervise, manage

総長 *sōchō* president of a university, chancellor
総監 *sōkan* governor-general, inspector general
総裁 *sōsai* president, governor
総理 *sōri* president, prime minister
総統 *sōtō* sovereign, highest post of the government
総監督 *sōkantoku* general manager
総本山 *sōhonzan* sectarian headquarters temple
総領息子 *sōryō-musuko* eldest son

❹ [original meaning] tuft, fringe

総状花序 *sōjō-kajo* racemous inflorescence, raceme

❺ old name for Chiba Prefecture

総武線 *sōbusen* Sobu Line (Chiba–Tokyo Railway)
房総半島 *bōsō hantō* Boso Peninsula

INDEPENDENT

【**sōjite** 総じて】 generally, in general, as a rule

KUN

【**su(bete)** 総べて】

[also 凡て or 全て]

①ⓐ all, everything, the whole

ⓑ entirely, wholly

総べての *subete no* all, entire, whole

② generally, as a rule

SYNONYMS

❶ⓐ **total**
計 total → 1441
和 sum → 1130

ⓐ **all**
皆 ALL → 2445
都 all → 1686
万 all → 2936
全 WHOLE → 2022
一 all in one → 3341
満 FULL → 607
丸 complete(ly) → 3417
完 COMPLETE → 2201
諸 VARIOUS → 1577
毎 EVERY → 2034
各 EACH → 2168

ⓑ **combine**
括 LUMP TOGETHER → 376
統 UNITE → 1352
結 TIE → 1348
合 COMBINE → 2019
併 join together → 83

❷ **general**
惣 GENERAL → 2780

❸ⓐ **high-ranking**
高 HIGH → 2097
太 of highest rank → 2152

上 upper → 3404
貴 NOBLE → 2606

HOMOPHONES

subete ⇨ 凡 2938 全 2022

NOTE

⇨ see USAGE notes at 惣 2780 and 凡 2938

⇨ see COMPOUND FORMATION for
惣菜 *sōzai* ⇨ 惣 2780
惣社 *sōja* ⇨ 惣 2780
惣嫁 *sōka* ⇨ 惣 2780

6-8 糸

綜

1380 SŌ

CH 综 zōng zèng

Radical	Strokes
糸 120	14-6-8
Grade	Freq
Reference	
1 - 6 - 8	

COMPOUNDS

❶ [now replaced by 総 1379] integrate, unify, total
綜合する *sōgō suru* synthesize, integrate, put together
綜覧 *sōran* general survey; comprehensive bibliography
❷ intertwine
錯綜した *sakusō shita* complicated, intricate

6-8 糸

綴

1381 TEI TETSU to(jiru) tsuzu(ru)

CH 缀 zhuì

Radical	Strokes
糸 120	14-6-8
Grade	Freq
Reference	
1 - 6 - 8	

COMPOUNDS

❶ⓐ bind, file
ⓑ [original meaning] sew up, stitch together; mend
綴じて *tojite* in bound form
綴じ込み *tojikomi* file
綴じ本 *tojihon* bound book
点綴する *tentei* (=*tentetsu*) *suru* intersperse; dot
補綴 *hotei* (=*hotetsu*) mending; composing (poetry)
綴じ蓋 *tojibuta* mended lid
❷ⓐ (put words together correctly) compose, write
ⓑ spell
詩歌を綴る *shiika o tsuzuru* compose poetry
綴字 *teiji* (=*tsuzuriji*) spelling
綴り *tsuzuri* spelling, orthography; binding, patching

HOMOPHONES

tojiru ⇨ 閉 3319

NOTE

⇨ see USAGE note at 閉 3319

6-8 糸

綱

1382

▶**NET**
nonstandard for 網 1374

6-8 糸

緑

1383

▶**GREEN**
nonstandard for 緑 1377

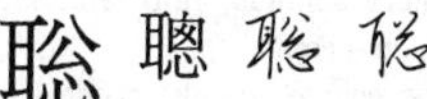

1384 SŌ sato(i) NAMES sato satoshi satoru aki akira toshi

CH 聪 cōng

Radical	Strokes
耳 128	14-6-8
Grade	Freq
Names	2047
1-6-8	

6-8 耳

▶SHARP-WITTED

COMPOUNDS

ⓐ **sharp-witted, quick-witted, clever, bright, astute, perceptive**

ⓑ [original meaning] sharp-eared, quick of hearing

聡明な *sōmei na* sagacious, wise, sharp, mentally acute

KUN

【**sato(i)** 聡い】 sharp-witted, quick-witted, clever

利に聡い *ri ni satoi* be wide-awake to one's interests

耳聡い *mimizatoi* sharp-[keen-]eared

NAMES

聡 *sō* (=*satoshi, satoru*) male name

聡子 *satoko* (=*akiko*) female name

SYNONYMS

ⓐ **intelligent and wise**

明 clear-sighted → 855
俊 brilliant → 102
鋭 SHARP → 1730
敏 NIMBLE → 1322
哲 SAGACIOUS → 2738
怜 CLEVER → 298
慧 INTELLIGENT → 2810
賢 WISE → 2839
智 wise → 2784

蝶 incorrect stroke count ⇨ see 1401

6-8 虫

號 incorrect stroke count ⇨ see 1212 (nonstandard for 号 2153)

6-8 号

雌 incorrect classification ⇨ see 1055

6-8 此

雑 雜 雑 雑

1385 ZATSU ZŌ

CH 杂 zá

Radical	Strokes
隹 172	14-8-6
Grade	Freq
Jōyō-5	820
1-6-8	

6-8 杂

▶MISCELLANEOUS ▶MIXED

COMPOUNDS

❶ [also prefix] **miscellaneous, various, sundry, motley**

雑多 *zatta* miscellaneous, various
雑誌 *zasshi* magazine, journal
雑用 *zatsuyō* miscellaneous business
雑費 *zappi* miscellaneous expenses
雑貨 *zakka* sundries, general cargo; miscellaneous goods
雑文家 *zatsubunka* miscellaneous writer, miscellanist
雑木 *zōki* miscellaneous trees
雑歌 *zōka* miscellaneous poems
雑所得 *zatsushotoku* miscellaneous [sundry] incomes

❷ⓐ [original meaning] **mixed, blended**
ⓑ **mixed up, disorderly, confused, intricate**
雑種 *zasshu* mixed breed, hybrid
雑居地 *zakkyochi* mixed residential quarter
雑然とした *zatsuzen to shita* promiscuous, disorderly
複雑な *fukuzatsu na* complicated, complex, involved, intricate
混雑した *konzatsu shita* confused, disorderly; congested
乱雑な *ranzatsu na* disorderly, confused
繁雑な *hanzatsu na* complicated, intricate, confused
煩雑な *hanzatsu na* vexatious, troublesome, intricate
錯雑 *sakuzatsu* complication, intricacy
❸ coarse, rough, low class, ordinary
雑草 *zassō* weed
雑音 *zatsuon* noise, jarring and grating; jamming; interference
雑巾 *zōkin* rag; mop
雑言 *zōgon* foul language, abuse
雑兵 *zōhyō* ordinary soldiers, rank and file
雑人 *zōnin* low-call people
粗雑な *sozatsu na* coarse, rough, crude

INDEPENDENT

【zatsu 雑】 miscellany
雑な *zatsu na* coarse, rough, crude
雑の部 *zatsu no bu* (=*zō no bu*) miscellany

SPECIAL READINGS

雑魚 *zako* small fish, small fry; lesser fry

SYNONYMS

❶ **various**
諸 VARIOUS → 1577
庶 MANIFOLD → 3127
❷ⓐ **mix**
錯 MIXED UP → 1743
混 MIX → 519
交 intermingle → 2015
ⓑ **disordered**
錯 MIXED UP → 1743
混 mixed up → 519
乱 DISORDERED → 1260
紛 CONFUSED → 1296

6-9
糸

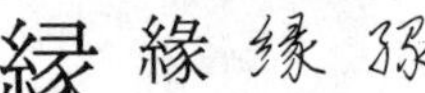
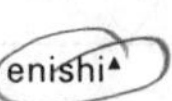
1386 EN -NEN fuchi heri▲ enishi▲

ⒸⒽ 

Radical	Strokes
糸 120	15-6-9
Grade	**Freq**
Jōyō	1283
1-6-9	

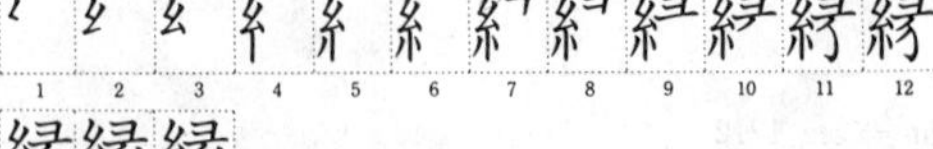

▶**RELATION** ▶**EDGE**

COMPOUNDS

❶ⓐ **relation (between persons), affinity, personal relations, connection, relationship**
ⓑ **family relation, relations, relative, kinsman**
縁故 *enko* relation, connection; relative
腐れ縁 *kusareen* unhappy yet inseparable relation; mismated marriage
因縁 *innen* connection, affinity; pretext; origin
絶縁 *zetsuen* breaking off relations; insulation, isolation
無縁の *muen no* unrelated; without relatives, having no surviving relatives
血縁 *ketsuen* blood relation
遠縁 *tōen* distant relation
❷ **marriage relation, marriage**
縁談 *endan* marriage proposal
縁組 *engumi* marriage, (conjugal) union
内縁の妻 *naien no tsuma* common-law wife
❸ *Buddhism*
ⓐ karma relation, predestination, fate, destiny
ⓑ indirect cause, contributory cause
宿縁 *shukuen* karma, destiny, fate
縁起 *engi* origin, history; omen, luck
因縁 *innen* karma, fate; direct and indirect causes
❹ⓐ **edge, margin**
ⓑ [original meaning] fringe, hem
縁辺 *enpen* border, edge; relations
外縁 *gaien* outer edge, brink
❺ (edge of building) veranda, porch, balcony
縁側 *engawa* veranda
縁先 *ensaki* edge of a veranda

INDEPENDENT

【en 縁】
①ⓐ relation, affinity, connection
ⓑ family relation, relative
縁が無い *en ga nai* have no relation to
縁を切る *en o kiru* sever connections; get a divorce
縁が遠い *en ga tōi* distantly related
② marriage relation, marriage

夫婦の縁を結ぶ *fūfu no en o musubu* get married

③ⓐ karma relation, fate, destiny, chance

ⓑ *Buddhism* indirect cause, contributory cause

不思議な縁で *fushigi na en de* by happy chance

④ veranda, porch, balcony

縁の下 *en no shita* space under the floor

縁の下の力持ち *en no shita no chikaramochi* thankless task; person who does a thankless task

KUN

【fuchi 縁】 edge, verge, brink, border, side; frame; hem, fringe

盆の縁 *bon no fuchi* edge of a tray

額縁 *gakubuchi* (picture) frame

縁取り *fuchidori* bordering, hemming

【heri 縁】 edge, verge; hem

【enishi 縁】 relation (between man and woman), affinity

SYNONYMS

❶ⓐ personal relations

仲 PERSONAL RELATIONS → 43

交 INTERCOURSE → 2015

好 friendship → 208

ⓑ family and relations

親 RELATIVES → 1799

姻 relative by marriage → 353

族 FAMILY → 958

家 FAMILY → 2273

門 family → 888

氏 clan → 2951

❷ marrying and marriage

姻 MARRIAGE → 353

婚 MARRY → 470

嫁 WED A MAN → 635

❸ⓐ fate and fortune

業 karma → 2612

命 fate → 2058

運 FORTUNE → 3140

❹ⓐ edges and boundaries

端 edge → 1221

辺 border → 3029

境 BOUNDARY → 676

界 BOUNDS → 2563

際 VERGE → 714

涯 OUTER LIMITS → 512

NOTE

★do not confuse with 緑 1377

編 編 编 𦅾

1387 HEN a(mu) -a(mi)

CH 编 biān

Radical	Strokes
糸 120	15-6-9
Grade	**Freq**
Jōyō-5	606
◧ 1 - 6 - 9	

6-9 糸

(Stroke order 1–15)

▶COMPILE ▶KNIT

COMPOUNDS

❶ⓐ compile, edit, compose

ⓑ compiled by, edited by

編集 *henshū* editing, compilation

編纂 *hensan* compilation, editing

編者 *hensha* (=*henja*) editor, compiler

編成する *hensei suru* form, compose, compile

浅田先生編 *asada sensei-hen* edited by Prof. Asada

❷ (bring together and arrange) put together, compile, organize, form, arrange

編制する *hensei suru* organize, form

編曲 *henkyoku* arrangement (of a melody)

改編する *kaihen suru* reorganize, remodel

❸ [formerly also 篇 2710]

ⓐ [also suffix] **volume, book, literary work; film**

ⓑ chapter, section, part, canto

ⓒ counter for chapters or parts

巨編 *kyohen* great literary work

長編 *chōhen* long section (as of a novel or a film)

予告編 *yokokuhen* preview

上編 *jōhen* first volume, Book I

続編 *zokuhen* sequel, supplementary volume

第一編 *daiippen* Chapter 1, Canto 1

❹ⓐ poem

ⓑ counter for poems

詩編 *shihen* Psalms

一編の詩 *ippen no shi* one poem

❺ [original meaning] **knit**

編組機械 *henso kikai* knitting machinery

❻ string for binding books of bamboo tablets

韋編 *ihen* leather cord

INDEPENDENT

【hen 編】 chapter, section, part

二の編 *ni no hen* Part 2

KUN

【a(mu) 編む】 knit, braid; compile, edit

編み機 *amiki* knitting machine

編み物 *amimono* knitting, knitted goods

本を編む *hon o amu* compile a book
【-a(mi) -編み】 [also suffix] knitting, knitted
機械編み *kikaiami* machine knitted
レース編み *rēsuami* lace knitting

SYNONYMS

❶ **compile**
集 edit → 2771
著 AUTHOR → 2300
❷ **organize**
組 ORGANIZE → 1337
結 form → 1348
❸ⓐ **books**
巻 VOLUME → 2645
鑑 REFERENCE VOLUME → 1773
典 STANDARD WORK → 2627
経 religious classic → 1331
本 BOOK → 3502
書 BOOK → 2658
冊 bound book → 3483
籍 books → 2731
著 literary work → 2300
❺ **weave and sew**
組 braid → 1337
縫 SEW → 1406
織 WEAVE → 1422
紡 SPIN → 1295
績 spin → 1412

NOTE

★Note the difference between the words 編成 and 編制, both *hensei*, under meanings ❶ and ❷ above.

6-9 糸

縄 繩 绳 𦀌

1388 JŌ nawa

Ⓒⓗ 绳 shéng

Radical	Strokes
糸 120	15-6-9
Grade	**Freq**
Jōyō	902
1-6-9	

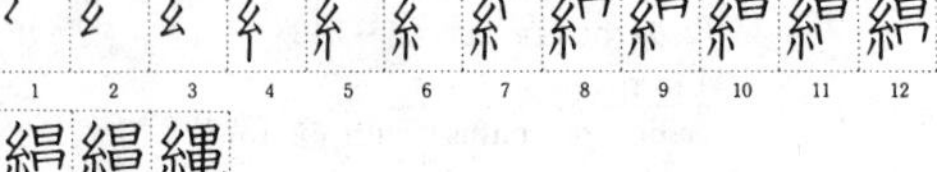

▶**ROPE**

COMPOUNDS

❶ⓐ [original meaning] **rope, straw rope, cord, spun yarn**
ⓑ inking line, inked string
縄文 *jōmon* straw-rope pattern
捕縄 *hojō* rope for binding criminals
自縄自縛に陥る *jijōjibaku ni ochiiru* be caught in one's own trap
縄墨 *jōboku* inked timber marking string; standard
❷ standard, norm
準縄 *junjō* level and inked string; rule, standard

KUN

【nawa 縄】 (straw) rope, cord, bonds
縄跳び *nawatobi* rope skipping, rope jumping
縄張り *nawabari* roping off; one's sphere of influence, one's territory
泥縄 *doronawa* expediency coming too late (like making a rope after finding the thief)

SYNONYMS

❶ⓐ **ropes and lines**
綱 ROPE (esp. of fiber) → 1372
緒 cord → 1378
組 braid → 1337
索 cable → 2455
鎖 CHAIN → 1761
線 LINE → 1392
弦 STRING → 287

緩 緩 緩 緩

Ⓒⓗ 缓 huǎn

1389 KAN yuru(i) yuru(yaka) yuru(mu) yuru(meru)

Radical	Strokes
糸 120	15-6-9
Grade	**Freq**
Jōyō	1156
◧ 1 - 6 - 9	

6-9 糸

▶**SLACK**

COMPOUNDS

❶ (reduce tension) **slack, slacken, loosen**

緩和 *kanwa* easing, relief, alleviation
緩衝弁 *kanshōben* cushion valve
弛緩 *shikan* relaxation; atony

❷ (not fast or lively) **slack, slow, sluggish**

緩慢な *kanman na* slack, slow-moving, dull, inactive
緩球 *kankyū* slow ball
緩行 *kankō* going slowly
緩急 *kankyū* fast and slow motion, high and low speed; emergency
緩下剤 *kangezai* laxative

KUN

【yuru(i) 緩い】 slack, loose; lenient, easy; gentle, slow; loose, watery (bowels)

緩さ *yurusa* slackness, looseness, lenience, gentleness
緩目の *yurume no* somewhat loose
緩い規則 *yurui kisoku* lenient regulations
緩いカーブ *yurui kābu* gentle curve
腹が緩い *hara ga yurui* have loose bowels

【yuru(yaka) 緩やか】

yuruyaka na 緩やかな slack, loose; lenient, easy; gentle, slow

緩やかさ *yuruyakasa* slackness, looseness, lenience, gentleness
緩やかな衣服 *yuruyaka na ifuku* loose garment
緩やかに進む *yuruyaka ni susumu* proceed slowly

【yuru(mu) 緩む】 *vi* slack(en), loosen, relax; be assuaged, abate, moderate, ease off

緩み *yurumi* slackness, looseness; slack
結び目が緩む *Musubime ga yurumu* A knot comes loose
気が緩んで *ki ga yurunde* in lack of vigilance

【yuru(meru) 緩める】 *vt* loosen, unloose, unfasten; ease (up), mitigate, moderate

手綱を緩める *tazuna o yurumeru* slack the reins
速度を緩める *sokudo o yurumeru* ease up the speed

SYNONYMS

❷ **slow**

慢 SLUGGISH → 686
徐 SLOWLY → 414
遅 SLOW → 3133

緬

Ⓒⓗ 缅 miǎn

1390 MEN

Radical	Strokes
糸 120	15-6-9
Grade	**Freq**
Reference	
◧ 1 - 6 - 9	

6-9 糸

COMPOUNDS

❶ fine thread

緬羊(＝綿羊) *men'yō* sheep
縮緬 *chirimen* crepe, silk crepe

❷ [rare] Burma

緬甸 *menden* Burma

6-9 糸

縅

1391 odo(shi)

CH none (国字)

Radical	Strokes
糸 120	15-6-9
Grade	Freq
Reference	
1-6-9	

COMPOUNDS

● [sometimes also 威し] [original meaning] braid or thread of Japanese armor
緋縅し鎧 *hiodoshiyoroi* scarlet-threaded suit of armor

HOMOPHONES

odoshi ⇨ 脅 2109 威 3578

NOTE

⇨ see USAGE note at 脅 2109

6-9 糸

線 線 𢘿

1392 SEN

CH 线 xiàn

Radical	Strokes
糸 120	15-6-9
Grade	Freq
Jōyō-2	238
1-6-9	

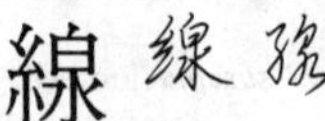

▶**LINE**

COMPOUNDS

❶ⓐ (continuous lengthwise mark) **line**
ⓑ (border, esp. between two surfaces) line
ⓒ *geometry* **line**
線画 *senga* line drawing, linework
線審 *senshin* linesman
直線 *chokusen* straight line
下線 *kasen* underline
戦線 *sensen* (war) front, battle line
前線 *zensen* front line, fighting front; *meteorology* front
水平線 *suiheisen* horizon
放物線 *hōbutsusen* parabola
❷ something resembling a line, as a ray or beam
線香 *senkō* stick of incense, joss stick
光線 *kōsen* ray (of light), beam
三味線 *shamisen* shamisen (Japanese three-stringed musical instrument)
打線 *dasen* batting line-up
伏線 *fukusen* preparation, foreshadow
放射線 *hōshasen* radiation, radioactive rays
❸ *elec* **line, wire, cable**
無線 *musen* radio, wireless
電線 *densen* electric wire
内線 *naisen* telephone extension; inner line
回線 *kaisen* circuit
電話線 *denwasen* telephone line
❹ (public transportation route) **line, track, route**
線路 *senro* (railway) line, track
路線 *rosen* route, way, line
沿線の *ensen no* along a railway line
脱線 *dassen* derailment; deviation, aberration
東海道線 *tōkaidōsen* Tokaido Line
二番線 *nibansen* Track No.2

INDEPENDENT

【sen 線】 line (⇨ ❶); *elec* line, wire, cable; something resembling a line; (course of action) line
線を引く *sen o hiku* draw a line
良い線を行く *ii sen o iku* be on the right track
線の太い人 *sen no futoi hito* strong-nerved person

SYNONYMS

❶ⓐ & ❶ⓑ line
筋 THREADLIKE STRUCTURE → 2678
条 strip → 2200
脈 VEIN → 953
棒 straight line → 983
軸 AXIS → 1514
ⓒ lines and line segments
弧 ARC → 360
弦 chord → 287
径 DIAMETER → 291
辺 side → 3029
❸ ropes and lines
索 cable → 2455
鎖 CHAIN → 1761
弦 STRING → 287
綱 ROPE (esp. of fiber) → 1372
縄 ROPE (esp. of straw) → 1388

緒 cord → 1378
組 braid → 1337
❹ **ways and routes**
軌 TRACK → 1445
径 PATH → 291
道 WAY (path) → 3134
途 WAY (route) → 3107
路 ROAD → 1533
筋 wayside → 2678
通り street → 3109
街 city street → 576
辻 CROSSROADS → 3192
岐 forked road → 241

締 締 締 締 ㊥ 缔 dì

1393 TEI shi(maru) shi(mari) shi(meru) -shi(me) -ji(me)

Radical	Strokes
糸 120	15-6-9
Grade	**Freq**
Jōyō	675
1-6-9	

6-9 糸

Stroke order: 1–15

▶CONCLUDE ▶TIGHTEN

COMPOUNDS

❶ⓐ unite two nations by reaching an agreement: **conclude (a treaty), contract, form (an alliance)**
ⓑ [archaic] unite in wedlock, marry
締結する *teiketsu suru* conclude, contract
締約 *teiyaku* conclusion of a treaty
締盟 *teimei* conclusion of a treaty of alliance
❷ [original meaning] tie together with a string, bind, connect
結締組織 *kettei soshiki* connective tissue

INDEPENDENT

【teisuru 締する】 conclude (a treaty), contract (a friendship)

KUN

【shi(maru) 締まる】
vi
①ⓐ tighten, become taut; be compact, be firm
ⓑ tighten one's belt, be frugal
締まった体格 *shimatta taikaku* well-knit frame, firm build
締まり屋 *shimariya* thrifty person, tightfisted person
② brace oneself up, become steady
引き締まる *hikishimaru* tighten, become tight; be braced up
③ (of the market) become firm
小締まり *kojimari* firmer tendency
④ [in compounds] exercise (tight) control over, regulate
取り締まる *torishimaru* manage, control, superintend

【shi(mari) 締まり】
① tightness, firmness, steadiness
締まりの無い *shimari no nai* loose, slack, lax
② fastening [locking] of a door
戸締まり *tojimari* fastening the doors

【shi(meru) 締める】
vt
①ⓐ tighten, tauten
ⓑ fasten, tie up, bind
ベルトを締める *beruto o shimeru* tighten one's belt
締め括る *shimekukuru* bind fast; settle, round off (a passage)
締め金 *shimegane* buckle, clasp, clamp
② exercise tight [rigid] control over, exercise close supervision; reprimand
締め上げる *shimeageru* screw up; put the screws on (a person)
元締め *motojime* manager, controller
③ [also 〆める] add up, sum up; close the account
締め *shime* summing up; *judo* choking [strangling] techniques
締めて *shimete* in all, all told
締め切り日 *shimekiribi* closing day, time limit, deadline
④ economize, save
家計を締める *kakei o shimeru* economize in the household
⑤ [also 〆める] [in compounds] fasten, lock (a door or window), shut
締め出す *shimedasu* shut the door on (a person), shut out
締め切り(=〆切) *shimekiri* closing day, deadline; Closed, No Entrance

【-shi(me), -ji(me) -締め】
① counter for reams or bundles of paper
紙二締め *kami futashime* two reams of paper
② *judo* choke, choking [strangling] techniques
片十字締め *katajūjijime* cross choke

SYNONYMS

❶ⓐ **promise**
協 reach an agreement → 93

契 MAKE AN AGREEMENT → 2639
約 PROMISE → 1280
盟 ALLIANCE → 2794
誓 VOW → 2754

【shimeru】

①ⓐ **tighten**
緊 TIGHTEN → 2838
張 STRAIN → 474

USAGE

❶ **shimaru**

締まる
vi
①ⓐ tighten, become taut; be compact, be firm
ⓑ tighten one's belt, be frugal
② brace oneself up, become steady
③ (of the market) become firm
④ [in compounds] exercise (tight) control over, regulate

閉まる
vi be shut, be closed, shut, close

絞まる
be strangled

★Note that when used independently the words 閉める and 閉まる mean to shut in the sense of moving into a closed position. 締, not used independently, appears in such compounds as 締め切る *shimekiru* 'fasten, shut up' and 戸締まり *tojimari* 'fastening the doors', and means to fasten or secure with a lock.

❷ **shimeru**

締める
vt
①ⓐ tighten, tauten
ⓑ fasten, tie up, bind
② exercise tight [rigid] control over, exercise close supervision; reprimand
③ [also メめる] add up, sum up; close the account
④ economize, save
⑤ [also メめる] [in compounds] fasten, lock (a door or window), shut

メめる
[also 締める]
① add up, sum up; close the account
② [in compounds] fasten, lock (a door or window), shut

閉める
vt (move into closed position) shut, close

絞める
① strangle, strangulate, wring
② squeeze

HOMOPHONES

shimaru ⇨ 閉 3319 絞 1349
shimeru ⇨ メ 3372 閉 3319 絞 1349

6-9 糸

縁 1394

▶RELATION ▶EDGE
nonstandard for 縁 1386

6-9 糸

編 1395

▶COMPILE ▶KNIT
nonstandard for 編 1387

6-9 糸

緯 1396

▶LATITUDE
nonstandard for 緯 1407

6-9 糸

緩 1397

▶SLACK
nonstandard for 緩 1389

6-9 糸

練 1398

▶TRAIN
nonstandard for 練 1375

6-9 糸

緒 1399

▶OUTSET
nonstandard for 緒 1378

1400

▶CONCLUDE ▶TIGHTEN
nonstandard for 締 1393

6-9 糸

縫

incorrect stroke count ⇨ see 1406

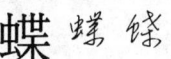

6-9 糸

蝶
1401 CHŌ

Ⓒ 蝶 dié

Radical	Strokes
虫 142	15-6-9
Grade	**Freq**
Names	2022
◧ 1 - 6 - 9	

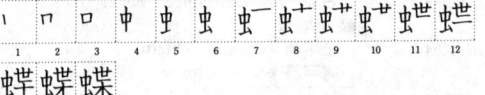

6-9 虫

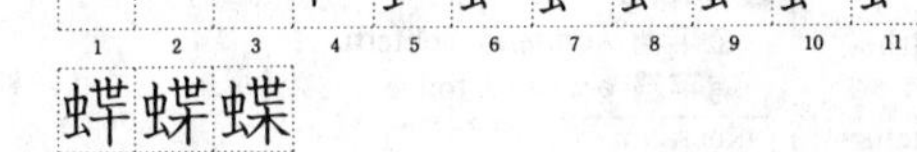

▶BUTTERFLY

COMPOUNDS

● [also suffix] [original meaning] **butterfly**
蝶蝶 *chōchō* butterfly
胡蝶 *kochō* butterfly
高山蝶 *kōzanchō* alpine butterfly
紋白蝶 *monshirochō* cabbage butterfly

INDEPENDENT

【**chō 蝶**】butterfly

NAMES

蝶子 *chōko* female name

SYNONYMS

● **insects**
蛍 FIREFLY → 2591
蚊 MOSQUITO → 1319
蚕 SILKWORM → 2457

1402 KI kagaya(ku)

Ⓒ 辉 huī

Radical	Strokes
車 159	15-7-8
Grade	**Freq**
Jōyō	1384
◧ 1 - 6 - 9	

6-9 光

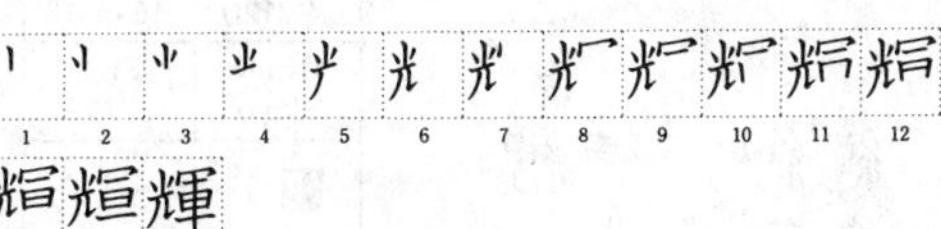

▶SHINE BRILLIANTLY

COMPOUNDS

● **shine brilliantly, glitter, sparkle, radiate**
輝線 *kisen* bright line
輝石 *kiseki* pyroxene, augite
輝度 *kido* brightness
輝輝 *kiki* brilliance
光輝有る *kōkiaru* shining, brilliant, glorious, splendid

KUN

【**kagaya(ku) 輝く**】shine brilliantly, glitter, gleam, sparkle, light up, brighten

輝き *kagayaki* brilliancy
輝き渡る *kagayakiwataru* shine out far and wide
輝かしい業績 *kagayakashii gyōseki* brilliant achievements, bright future
喜びに輝く目 *yorokobi ni kagayaku me* eyes sparkling with joy

SYNONYMS

● **shine and reflect**
光 shine → 2391
照 ILLUMINATE → 2827
映 REFLECT → 892

6-10 米

糖 糖 *糖* *糖*

1403 TŌ

CH 糖 táng

Radical	Strokes
米 119	16-6-10
Grade	**Freq**
Jōyō-6	1069
1-6-10	

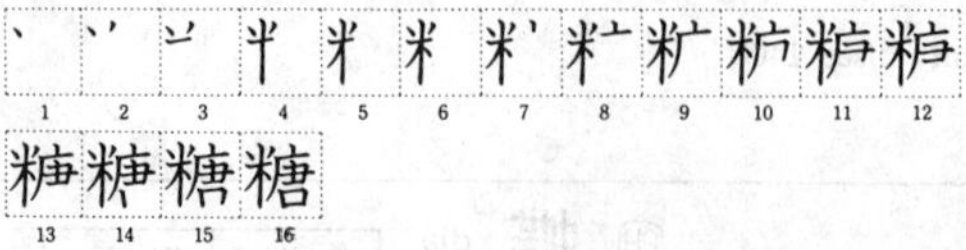

▶**SUGAR**

COMPOUNDS

❶ⓐ (sweet substance derived from sugar cane or beets) **sugar**

ⓑ [also suffix] (water-soluble sweet carbohydrate) **sugar**

ⓒ abbrev. of 製糖 *seitō*: sugar manufacturing

砂糖 *satō* sugar
グラニュー糖 *guranyūtō* granulated sugar
精糖 *seitō* refined sugar, sugar refining
製糖業 *seitōgyō* sugar manufacturing industry
糖分 *tōbun* sugar content
糖尿病 *tōnyōbyō* diabetes
果糖 *katō* fruit sugar, fructose
蔗糖 *shotō* sucrose
葡萄糖 *budōtō* grape sugar, dextrose
日糖 *nittō* Dai-Nippon Sugar, Inc.

❷ sweets

金平糖 *konpeitō* confetti
有平糖 *aruheitō* toffee

INDEPENDENT

【tō 糖】 sugar (⇨ ❶ⓑ)
血液中の糖 *ketsuekichū no tō* blood sugar

SYNONYMS

❶ⓐ **seasonings**

塩 SALT → 631
酢 VINEGAR → 1516
油 OIL → 341

6-10 米

糖

1404

▶**SUGAR**

nonstandard for 糖 1403

6-10 糸

縛 縛 *縛* *縛*

1405 BAKU shiba(ru)

CH 缚 fù

Radical	Strokes
糸 120	16-6-10
Grade	**Freq**
Jōyō	1848
1-6-10	

▶**BIND**

COMPOUNDS

❶ⓐ [original meaning] **bind, tie up**

ⓑ apprehension by binding, arrest

緊縛 *kinbaku* tight binding
就縛する *shūbaku suru* be put in bonds, come under arrest
捕縛する *hobaku suru* put in bonds, arrest

❷ (restrain as if with bonds) **bind, restrict, restrain**

束縛する *sokubaku suru* restrain, restrict, bind, fetter
呪縛 *jubaku* spell
自縄自縛に陥る *jijōjibaku ni ochiiru* be caught in one's own trap

INDEPENDENT

【baku 縛】 apprehension, arrest
縛に就く *baku ni tsuku* be put in bonds, come under arrest

KUN

【shiba(ru) 縛る】 bind, tie, fasten; (restrain as if with bonds) bind, restrict, restrain
きつく縛る *kitsuku shibaru* fasten tightly
縛り上げる *shibariageru* bind [tie] up
規則で縛る *kisoku de shibaru* restrict (a person) by rule
金縛りになっている *kanashibari ni natte iru* be bound hand and foot; be tied down with money

SYNONYMS

❶ⓐ **join**

束 TIE UP → 3554
結 TIE → 1348
連 LINK → 3103
係 CONNECT → 97
接 join → 500

❷ **restrain**

束 TIE UP → 3554
抑 SUPPRESS → 257
限 LIMIT → 398
禁 PROHIBIT → 2795
制 CONTROL (restrain) → 1274
控える HOLD BACK → 495
渋る hang [hold] back → 513

縫 縫 縫 縫

1406 HŌ nu(u)

Ⓒⓗ 缝 féng fèng

Radical	Strokes
糸 120	16-6-10
Grade	**Freq**
Jōyō	1243
◧ 1-6-10	

6-10 糸

▶SEW

COMPOUNDS

❶ [original meaning] **sew, stitch**

縫合する *hōgō suru* suture, stitch (a wound)
縫工 *hōkō* seamstress, tailor
裁縫 *saihō* sewing, needlework, dressmaking
天衣無縫 *ten'imuhō* perfect beauty with no trace of artifice

❷ mend, patch up

弥縫する *bihō suru* patch up, make shift

KUN

【nu(u) 縫う】 sew, stitch

縫い合わせる *nuiawaseru* sew up [together]
手縫いの *tenui no* hand-tailored[-sewed]
傷口を縫う *kizuguchi o nuu* sew up [suture] a wound

SYNONYMS

❶ **weave and sew**

編 KNIT → 1387
組 braid → 1337
織 WEAVE → 1422
紡 SPIN → 1295
績 spin → 1412

COMPOUND FORMATION

天衣無縫 *ten'imuhō*

天衣無縫 'perfect beauty with no trace of artifice' is being like a robe (衣) from heaven (天) without (無) the slightest trace of sewing (縫 ❶).

緯 緯 緯 緯

1407 I yokoito▲ nuki▲

Ⓒⓗ 纬 wěi

Radical	Strokes
糸 120	16-6-10
Grade	**Freq**
Jōyō	1562
◧ 1-6-10	

6-10 糸

▶LATITUDE

COMPOUNDS

❶ **latitude, lines of latitude**

緯度 *ido* latitude
緯線 *isen* parallels of latitude
経緯 *keii* latitude and longitude
北緯 *hokui* north latitude

❷ [original meaning] woof, weft

経緯 *keii* warp and woof; circumstances, details

❸ [rare] books about charms and omens circulated as appendixes to the Chinese classics

緯書 *isho* book of omens appended to Confucian Chinese classics

INDEPENDENT

【i 緯】 main plot (of a story)

KUN

【yokoito 緯】 [also 横糸 or 緯糸] woof
【nuki 緯】 woof

SYNONYMS

❶ **latitude and longitude**

経 longitude → 1331

❷ **threads and fibers**
経 warp → 1331
糸 THREAD → 2179
織 FIBER → 1413
維 FIBER → 1370

USAGE

yokoito
緯
[also 横糸 or 緯糸] woof
横糸
[also 緯糸 or 緯] woof
緯糸
[also 横糸 or 緯] woof

HOMOPHONES

yokoito ⇨ 横糸 1066, 2179 緯糸 1407, 2179

6-10
糸

縦 縦 縦 縦

1408 JŪ tate

CH 纵 zòng

Radical	Strokes
糸 120	16-6-10
Grade	Freq
Jōyō-6	1297
1-6-10	

1 2 3 4 5 6 7 8 9 10 11 12 13 14 15 16

▶**VERTICAL**

COMPOUNDS

❶ **vertical, lengthwise, perpendicular, longitudinal**
縦断 *jūdan* cutting vertically
縦横に *jūō ni* vertically and horizontally, in all directions; freely
縦貫する *jūkan suru* run through, traverse
縦走 *jūsō* running lengthwise; mountain range traversing
縦線 *jūsen* vertical line, bar (in music)

❷ self-indulgent, wayward, selfish, as one pleases
放縦 *hōjū* self-indulgence
操縦 *sōjū* management, controlling; steering; piloting, flying

KUN

【tate 縦】
① [formerly also 竪] length, height
縦の *tate no* vertical, longitudinal
縦書き *tategaki* vertical writing
縦縞 *tatejima* vertical stripes
② warp
縦糸 *tateito* [also 経糸 or 経] warp

SYNONYMS

❶ **vertical**
直 STRAIGHT → 2932
垂 perpendicular → 3565
立て- standing → 1992

HOMOPHONES

tate ⇨ 立 1992 建 3090 竪 2837
tateito ⇨ 経 1331 縦糸 1408, 2179
経糸 1331, 2179

NOTE

⇨ see USAGE notes at 立 1992 and 経 1331

6-10
糸

縛

1409

▶**BIND**
nonstandard for 縛 1405

6-10
舟

艙

1410 SŌ

CH 舱 cāng

Radical	Strokes
舟 137	16-6-10
Grade	Freq
Reference	
1-6-10	

COMPOUNDS

● [now replaced by 倉 2104] ship's hold, cabin
船艙 *sensō* hold (of a ship), hatch

綳 1411 HŌ

CH 绷 bēng běng

Radical	Strokes
糸 120	17-6-11
Grade	Freq
Reference	
1 - 6 - 11	

6-11 糸

COMPOUNDS

● [now replaced by 包 2966] [original meaning] bind up, strap up
綳帯 *hōtai* bandage, dressing

績 绩 𦄂 1412 SEKI

CH 绩 jī

Radical	Strokes
糸 120	17-6-11
Grade	Freq
Jōyō-5	698
1 - 6 - 11	

6-11 糸

▶ACHIEVEMENTS

COMPOUNDS

❶ **achievements, accomplishments, merit, results, record**
成績 *seiseki* results, record, achievement
実績 *jisseki* (actual) result, positive achievements
業績 *gyōseki* achievements; business results
功績 *kōseki* meritorious deed, achievement
戦績 *senseki* war record, military achievements; results, score
不成績 *fuseiseki* poor result, underachievement

❷ [original meaning] **spin thread, make yarn**
紡績 *bōseki* spinning

SYNONYMS

❶ **accomplishment**
功 MERIT → 189
勲 MERITORIOUS SERVICE → 2869

❷ **weave and sew**
紡 SPIN → 1295
織 WEAVE → 1422
縫 SEW → 1406
編 KNIT → 1387
組 braid → 1337

纖 繊 纎° 缄 𦇧 1413 SEN

CH 纤 xiān

Radical	Strokes
糸 120	17-6-11
Grade	Freq
Jōyō	1040
1 - 6 - 11	

6-11 糸

▶FINE ▶FIBER

COMPOUNDS

❶ⓐ **fine, slender**
ⓑ fine and delicate, slender and graceful
繊細な *sensai na* delicate, fine, subtle
繊毛 *senmō* cilia, fine hair
繊切り(＝千切り) *sengiri* long thin strips (of a vegetable)
繊指 *senshi* woman's slender fingers
繊手 *senshu* delicate hands

❷ [original meaning] **fiber, filament**
繊維 *sen'i* fiber, textile
繊条 *senjō* filament
化繊 *kasen* synthetic fiber
合繊 *gōsen* synthetic fiber

❸ [rare] 1/10,000,000
三繊 *sansen* 3/10,000,000

INDEPENDENT

【sen 繊】 long thin strips (of a vegetable); [rare] 1/10,000,000

大根を繊に切る *daikon o sen ni kiru* cut a radish into fine strips

SYNONYMS

❶ⓐ **thin**

細 SLENDER → 1333

薄 THIN → 2370

❷ **threads and fibers**

維 FIBER → 1370

糸 THREAD → 2179

緯 woof → 1407

経 warp → 1331

6-11 糸

縮 1414

SHUKU chiji(mu) chiji(maru) chiji(meru) chiji(reru) chiji(rasu)

CH 缩 suō sù

Radical	Strokes
糸 120	17-6-11
Grade	**Freq**
Jōyō-6	853
1-6-11	

1 2 3 4 5 6 7 8 9 10 11 12 13 14 15 16 17

▶**SHRINK**

COMPOUNDS

❶ⓐ [original meaning] (draw together) **shrink, contract**

ⓑ (make or become smaller) **shrink, reduce, shorten**

収縮 *shūshuku* contraction, shrinking

伸縮 *shinshuku* expansion and contraction

短縮 *tanshuku* shortening, contraction, reduction

縮小 *shukushō* reduction, curtailment, cut

縮減する *shukugen suru* reduce, diminish

軍縮 *gunshuku* reduction of armaments

濃縮する *nōshuku suru* concentrate

❷ (draw back) shrink (as with fear), curl up, recoil, wince

畏縮する *ishuku suru* shrink, flinch, wince

恐縮する *kyōshuku suru* feel much obliged, deeply appreciate; regret; feel embarrassed

KUN

【**chiji(mu)** 縮む】*vi* shrink, contract; cringe

縮み *chijimi* shrinkage; cotton crepe

縮み織り *chijimiori* cotton crepe, preshrunk cloth

伸び縮み *nobichijimi* expansion and contraction, flexibility

縮み上がる *chijimiagaru* cringe, wince, flinch

【**chiji(maru)** 縮まる】*vi* be shortened, be contracted

【**chiji(meru)** 縮める】*vt* contract, shorten, shrink

【**chiji(reru)** 縮れる】*vi* be wavy, curl; shrink, be wrinkled

縮れ毛 *chijirege* curly, wavy, or fuzzy hair

【**chiji(rasu)** 縮らす】*vt* curl, crinkle, crimp

SYNONYMS

❶ⓐ **contract and shrink**

約 CONTRACT → 1280

ⓑ **decrease**

減 DECREASE → 601

耗 WEAR AWAY → 1309

削 cut down → 1448

落 FALL → 2318

6-11 糸

縫 1415

▶**SEW**

nonstandard for 縫 1406

6-11 糸

縱 1416

▶**VERTICAL**

nonstandard for 縦 1408

6-11 糸

總 1417

▶**TOTAL** ▶**GENERAL**

nonstandard for 総 1379

聴 聽 聴 𦗟

1418 CHŌ ki(ku)

Ⓒℍ 听 tīng

Radical	Strokes
耳 128	17-6-11
Grade	Freq
Jōyō	970
1 - 6 - 1 1	

6-11 耳

▶**LISTEN**

COMPOUNDS

❶ⓐ [original meaning] **listen, hear**
ⓑ sense [capacity] of hearing
聴取する *chōshu suru* listen to, give a hearing to
聴衆 *chōshū* audience
聴講 *chōkō* lecture attendance
聴聞会 *chōmonkai* hearing
傍聴する *bōchō suru* hear, listen to; attend
視聴者 *shichōsha* viewer, audience
公聴会 *kōchōkai* public [open] hearing
傾聴 *keichō* listening closely
聴力 *chōryoku* power [sense] of hearing
難聴 *nanchō* hardness of hearing

❷ⓐ listen to (instructions), obey
ⓑ comply with, grant (permission)
聴従する *chōjū suru* follow advice
聴許 *chōkyo* permission

KUN

【ki(ku) 聴く】 listen (to), give an ear to
民の声を聴く *tami no koe o kiku* listen to the voice of the people

SYNONYMS

❶ⓐ **hear**
聞 HEAR → 3326

HOMOPHONES

kiku ⇨ 聞 3326 訊 1452

NOTE

⇨ see USAGE note at 聞 3326

聯

1419 REN

Ⓒℍ 联 lián

Radical	Strokes
耳 128	17-6-11
Grade	Freq
Reference	
1 - 6 - 1 1	

6-11 耳

COMPOUNDS

❶ [now replaced by 連 3103]
ⓐ (join together) link, join
ⓑ (connect as if by linking) link, connect, join, unite
聯立 *renritsu* alliance, coalition
聯句 *renku* linked verse
聯珠 *renju gobang*
聯絡 *renraku* connection, contact; communication
聯想 *rensō* association (of ideas)
聯合 *rengō* combination, union, alliance; association
聯邦 *renpō* federation, confederation, union
聯盟 *renmei* union, federation, league
聯隊 *rentai* regiment
関聯 *kanren* connection, relation, association

❷ⓐ couplet
ⓑ counter for stanzas [verses]
対聯 *tairen* distich, couplet
五聯の詩 *goren no shi* five-verse poem

聰

1420

▶**SHARP-WITTED**
nonstandard for 聡 1384

6-11 耳

臨

incorrect stroke count ⇨ see 1630

6-11 臣

6-12 米

糧 糧 糧

1421 RYŌ RŌ kate

CH 粮 liáng

Radical	Strokes
米 119	18-6-12
Grade	**Freq**
Jōyō	1273
1-6-12	

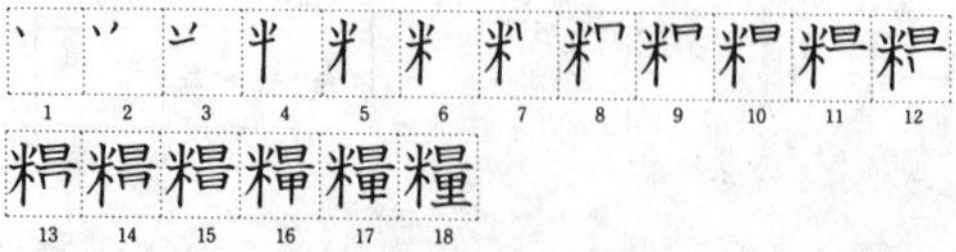

丶 丷 䒑 半 米 米 米 粐 粐 粐 粐 粐 粡 糧 糧 糧 糧 糧

1 2 3 4 5 6 7 8 9 10 11 12 13 14 15 16 17 18

▶FOOD PROVISIONS

COMPOUNDS

● **food provisions, food, foodstuffs**

糧食 *ryōshoku* provisions, food, rations
糧道 *ryōdō* supply of provisions
食糧 *shokuryō* provisions, food, foodstuffs
衣糧 *iryō* clothing and food
兵糧 *hyōrō* army provisions, food

KUN

【**kate** 糧】provisions, food; (figuratively) food, bread, pabulum
日日の糧 *hibi no kate* daily food
心の糧 *kokoro no kate* mental pabulum for thought

SYNONYMS

● **food**
食 FOOD, meal → 2075
飯 MEAL → 1691

6-12 糸

織 織 織 織

1422 SHOKU SHIKI o(ru) o(ri) ori -ori -o(ri)

CH 织 zhī

Radical	Strokes
糸 120	18-6-12
Grade	**Freq**
Jōyō-5	735
1-6-12	

𠃋 幺 幺 糸 糸 糸 糸 紵 紵 紵 綜 綜 綜 綜 綜 織 織 織

1 2 3 4 5 6 7 8 9 10 11 12 13 14 15 16 17 18

▶WEAVE

COMPOUNDS

❶ⓐ [original meaning] **weave**
ⓑ woven fabric, textile
織工 *shokkō* weaver
織機 *shokki* loom
織女星 *shokujosei* Vega
紡織 *bōshoku* spinning and weaving
染織 *senshoku* dyeing and weaving
製織 *seishoku* weaving
織布 *shokufu* woven fabric

❷ **organize**
組織 *soshiki* organization, system; constitution, construction; tissue

KUN

【**o(ru)** 織る】weave
織り込む *orikomu* interweave
織物 *orimono* cloth, textile, fabric
機織り *hataori* weaving; weaver; grasshopper

【**o(ri)** 織り, **ori** 織】texture, weave; weaving
織り目 *orime* texture
目の細かな織り *me no komaka na ori* fine texture
羽織 *haori* Japanese half coat, *haori*

【**-ori** -織, **-o(ri)** -織り】[also suffix] woven fabric, brocade
毛織 *keori* woolen fabric, woolen cloth
西陣織 *nishijin'ori Nishijin* brocade

SYNONYMS

❶ⓐ **weave and sew**
紡 SPIN → 1295
績 spin → 1412
縫 SEW → 1406
編 KNIT → 1387
組 braid → 1337

ⓑ **fabrics**
紗 GAUZE → 1301
絹 SILK → 1361
綾 TWILL → 1376
綿 COTTON → 1373
麻 HEMP → 3125
毛 wool → 3453
錦 BROCADE → 1738

HOMOPHONES

oru ⇒ 折 253

COMPOUND FORMATION

織女星 *shokujosei*
織女星 'Vega' is the star (星) of the weaver (織 ❶ⓐ) girl (女) in Chinese mythology.

NOTE
⇨ see USAGE note at 折 253

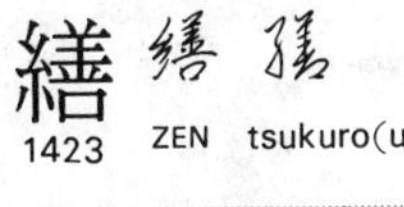

1423 ZEN tsukuro(u)

CH 缮 shàn

Radical	Strokes
糸 120	18-6-12
Grade	Freq
Jōyō	1858

1-6-12

6-12 糸

▶**MEND**

COMPOUNDS

● [original meaning] (fix and/or make whole) **mend, repair**

修繕する *shūzen suru* mend, repair
営繕 *eizen* building and repairs, maintenance

KUN

【tsukuro(u) 繕う】 mend, repair, darn; trim, tidy, adjust; cover up, smooth over, save

繕い *tsukuroi* mending, darning
身繕い *mizukuroi* tidying up oneself, grooming oneself
見繕う *mitsukurou* choose (a thing) at one's own discretion
繕い立てる *tsukuroitateru* put up a good front
取り繕う *toritsukurou* smooth over, temporize

SYNONYMS

● **repair**

修 REPAIR → 123
直す FIX → 2932

織 1424

▶**WEAVE**
nonstandard for 織 1422

6-12 糸

繩

incorrect stroke count ⇨ see 1428 (nonstandard for 縄 1388)

6-12 糸

職 職 聀 聀 職

1425 SHOKU SOKU

CH 职 zhí

Radical	Strokes
耳 128	18-6-12
Grade	Freq
Jōyō-5	311

1-6-12

6-12 耳

▶**EMPLOYMENT**

COMPOUNDS

❶ [also suffix]

ⓐ **employment, occupation, work, job**
ⓑ abbrev. of 職業 *shokugyō* or 職務 *shokumu*: employment, duty
ⓒ **post, office**

職業 *shokugyō* occupation, vocation, profession
職務 *shokumu* duty, duties, function
職場 *shokuba* place of work, workshop
職種 *shokushu* type of occupation, occupational category
職員 *shokuin* staff, employee, personnel
就職 *shūshoku* finding employment
退職 *taishoku* retirement, resignation
無職の *mushoku no* without occupation, unemployed
内職 *naishoku* side job
専門職 *senmonshoku* profession, professional job
職安 *shokuan* Public Employment Security Office
公職 *kōshoku* public office
現職 *genshoku* present post [office]; incumbent

管理職 *kanrishoku* administrative [manageri-al] position
汚職 *oshoku* (official) corruption, bribery
❷ [also suffix] craftsman, artisan
職人 *shokunin* craftsman, artisan
畳職 *tatamishoku* tatami maker
❸ knowledge
有職 *yūsoku* knowledge of ancient court prac-tices

INDEPENDENT

【**shoku** 職】 employment, occupation, work, job; post, office; (professional) skill

職を探す *shoku o sagasu* seek employment, hunt for a job
職を辞する *shoku o jisuru* resign one's post

SYNONYMS

❶ **work and employment**
業 WORK → 2612
労 LABOR → 2548
勤 SERVICE (employment) → 1818
役 SERVICE (esp. public) → 244
任 OFFICE → 53
務 DUTY → 1173

6-12 耳

職 ▶**EMPLOYMENT**
nonstandard for 職 1425
1426

6-13 糸

繰 1427 SŌ▲ ku(ru)[1] ku(ru)[2]

CH 缫 sāo 缲 qiāo

Radical	Strokes
糸 120	19-6-13
Grade	**Freq**
Jōyō	1167
1-6-13	

▶**REEL** ▶**SHIFT ONWARD**

COMPOUNDS

● **reel, wind**
繰糸機 *sōshiki* silk reeling machine

KUN

【**ku(ru)**[1] 繰る】
①ⓐ reel (silk off a cocoon); gin (cotton); spin
ⓑ reel in, reel up, wind, roll out
繰り綿 *kuriwata* ginned cotton
繰り取る *kuritoru* reel off
繰り出す *kuridasu* draw out; call out (troops), sally forth
手繰る *taguru* pull in hand over hand, draw in, reel in; retrace
掻い繰る *kaiguru* haul in hand over hand
雨戸を繰る *amado o kuru* roll open the shut-ters
② shift one by one, transfer in succession, per-form repeatedly:
ⓐ turn over (the pages of a book), look up [consult] (a dictionary or calendar)
ⓑ count one by one, reckon
辞書を繰る *jisho o kuru* consult a dictionary
指で日を繰る *yubi de hi o kuru* count the days on one's fingers

【**ku(ru)**[2] 繰る】
[in compounds]
①ⓐ shift onward to the next stage, move up, carry over
ⓑ shift (a plan) to the next phase
繰り上げる *kuriageru* advance, move up
繰り込み理論 *kurikomiriron* renormalization theory
繰り入れ金 *kuriirekin* transfer balance
繰り替える *kurikaeru* exchange; appropriate (money to some other purpose)
繰り延べる *kurinoberu* postpone, put off
繰り合わせる *kuriawaseru* make time, ar-range matters
② shift for, make shift, get along, manage
やり繰り *yarikuri* tiding over, makeshift, man-agement
資金繰り *shikinguri* raising funds
臍繰り *hesokuri* secret savings, pin money
③ⓐ perform an action repeatedly
ⓑ move [roll] back and forth (between the fingers)
繰り返す *kurikaesu* repeat, do over again
繰り言 *kurigoto* same story told over and over again; grumble
爪繰る *tsumaguru* finger, roll between the thumb and the fingers
乳繰り合う *chichikuriau* have a love intrigue, flirt
④ unclassified compounds
勘繰る *kanguru* guess at someone's true inten-tions, doubt

SYNONYMS

【kuru¹】

① **wind and twine**

巻 ROLL UP → 2645
絡 ENTWINE → 1351

【kuru²】

① **move**

移 SHIFT → 1177
遷 TRANSFER → 3170
転 remove → 1480
動 MOVE → 1778
運 MOVE → 3140
滑 SLIDE → 658

COMPOUND FORMATION

乳繰り合う *chichikuriau*

乳繰り合う 'have a love intrigue, flirt' is, literally, to roll (繰る *kuru²* ③ⓑ) a woman's breasts (乳) between one's fingers.

繩 1428

▶**ROPE**

nonstandard for 縄 1388

6-13 糸

繪 1429

▶**PICTURE**

nonstandard for 絵 1346

6-13 糸

疆 1430

KYŌ

Ⓒⓗ 疆 jiāng

Radical	Strokes
田 102	19-5-14
Grade	Freq
Reference	
◧ 1-6-13	

6-13 弓

COMPOUNDS

● [now usu. 境 676] [original meaning] boundary, border, frontier

辺疆 *henkyō* frontier (district), remote region, border(land)
新疆 *shinkyō* Sinkiang

繼 1431

▶**SUCCEED**

nonstandard for 継 1360

6-14 糸

艦

incorrect stroke count ⇨ see 1435

6-14 舟

纏 1432

TEN matsu(waru) mato(u) mato(meru) mato(maru)

Ⓒⓗ 缠 chán

Radical	Strokes
糸 120	21-6-15
Grade	Freq
Reference	
◧ 1-6-15	

6-15 糸

COMPOUNDS

❶ⓐ [original meaning] wind round, bind, tangle

ⓑ twine round, hang about; be related to

纏足 *tensoku* foot-binding
纏綿 *tenmen* entanglement, involvement
それに纏わる話 *sore ni matsuwaru hanashi* story related to it

❷ [now also 天 *ten* 3442] put on, be wrapped in

半纏 *hanten* short coat, workman's livery coat
纏う *matou* wear, put on; wind round

❸ⓐ collect, put together; summarize

ⓑ settle, conclude

纏める *matomeru* collect, put together; summarize; settle, conclude
纏め *matome* summary, conclusion

纏まる *matomaru* be collected; be settled, be in order

纏まり *matomari* settlement, conclusion; unity, coherence

6-15 糸 **纎** 1433

▶**FINE** ▶**FIBER**

nonstandard for 繊 1413

6-15 糸 **續** 1434

▶**CONTINUE**

nonstandard for 続 1362

6-15 舟 **艦** 艦 艦 1435 KAN

Ⓒ𝐇 舰 jiàn

Radical	Strokes
舟 137	21-6-15
Grade	**Freq**
Jōyō	1215
1-6-15	

▶**WARSHIP**

COMPOUNDS

● **warship, battleship**

艦船 *kansen* ships and warships
艦隊 *kantai* squadron, fleet
艦艇 *kantei* war vessels
艦長 *kanchō* captain of a warship
軍艦 *gunkan* warship

INDEPENDENT

【**kan 艦**】warship, battleship

艦と運命を共にする *kan to unmei o tomoni suru* go down with the ship

SYNONYMS

● **boats and ships**

船 SHIP → 1341
舶 OCEANGOING SHIP → 1340
潜 submarine → 746
舟 SMALL BOAT → 3538
艇 BOAT → 1365
隻 COUNTER FOR SHIPS → 2755

6-17 糸 **纖** 1436

▶**FINE** ▶**FIBER**

nonstandard for 繊 1413

6-18 缶 **罐** 1437

▶**CAN**

nonstandard for 缶 2033

7-1 孚 **乳** 乳 乳 乳 1438 NYŪ chichi chi

Ⓒ𝐇 乳 rǔ

Radical	Strokes
乚 5	8-1-7
Grade	**Freq**
Jōyō-6	933
1-7-1	

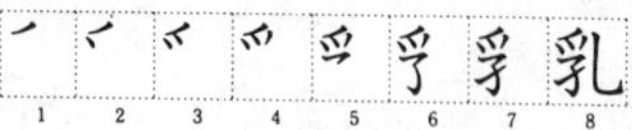

▶**MILK**

COMPOUNDS

❶ⓐ (mammalian secretion) **milk**
ⓑ (food product) **milk**
ⓒ milklike substance

母乳 *bonyū* mother's milk
牛乳 *gyūnyū* (cow's) milk
乳業 *nyūgyō* dairy industry
乳価 *nyūka* price of milk
粉乳 *funnyū* powdered milk
脱脂乳 *dasshinyū* nonfat milk
乳液 *nyūeki* milky lotion; latex
豆乳 *tōnyū* soybean milk

❷ **breast, breasts**

乳房 *nyūbō* (=*chibusa*) breast, nipple
乳癌 *nyūgan* breast cancer
乳頭 *nyūtō* nipple

❸ infancy
乳児 *nyūji* infant, baby, suckling
乳歯 *nyūshi* milk teeth

KUN

【chichi 乳】 milk; breast, breasts
乳牛 *chichiushi* (=*nyūgyū*) milch cow, dairy cattle
乳首 *chichikubi* (=*chikubi*) teat, nipple
乳繰り合う *chichikuriau* have a love intrigue, flirt

【chi 乳】 loop; [in compounds] milk; breast
旗に乳を付ける *hata ni chi o tsukeru* sew loops on a flag
乳飲み子 *chinomigo* baby, suckling

SPECIAL READINGS

乳母 *uba* wet nurse

SYNONYMS

❶ⓐ bodily secretions
精 sperm → 1366
汗 SWEAT → 220
涙 TEAR → 440

ⓑ dairy products
酪 DAIRY PRODUCTS → 1538

ⓑ drinks
汁 JUICE, SOUP → 195
酒 ALCOHOLIC DRINK → 444
茶 TEA → 2259

❷ chest
胸 CHEST → 951

NOTE

⇨ see COMPOUND FORMATION for 乳繰り合う *chichikuriau* ⇨ 繰 1427

乳
1439

▶MILK
nonstandard for 乳 1438

7-1 孚

臥
1440 GA fuse(ru)

CH 卧 wò

Radical	Strokes
臣 131	9-7-2
Grade	**Freq**
Reference	
◧ 1 - 7 - 2	

7-2 臣

COMPOUNDS

❶ [original meaning] lie down
仰臥 *gyōga* lying face up
行住座臥 *gyōjūzaga* the four cardinal behaviors (walking, stopping [standing], sitting and lying); daily life
臥する *gasuru* lie down

❷ be confined to one's bed, be sick in bed
病臥 *byōga* being sick in bed
風邪で臥っている *kaze de fusette iru* be laid up with a cold

HOMOPHONES

fuseru ⇨ 伏 45

NOTE

⇨ see USAGE note at 伏 45

計
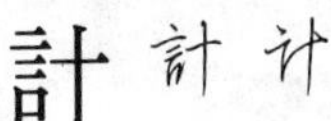
1441 KEI haka(ru) haka(rau)

CH 计 jì

Radical	Strokes
言 149	9-7-2
Grade	**Freq**
Jōyō-2	193
◧ 1 - 7 - 2	

7-2 言

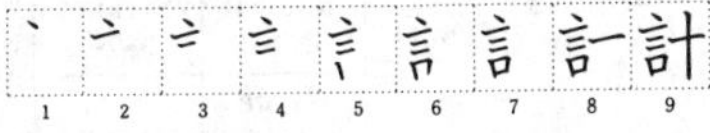

▶PLAN ▶COMPUTE

COMPOUNDS

❶ⓐ plan, design, devise, scheme
ⓑ plan, stratagem
計画 *keikaku* plan, project
設計 *sekkei* design, plan
計略 *keiryaku* stratagem, plan, scheme
妙計 *myōkei* ingenious trick, clever scheme
奸計 *kankei* vicious plan, crafty design

❷ compute, calculate, reckon, count, estimate
計算 *keisan* computation, calculation
計上する *keijō suru* sum up, appropriate (a sum for some purpose)
計量 *keiryō* measuring, weighing
推計する *suikei suru* estimate

統計 *tōkei* statistics
会計 *kaikei* account, finance; bill
集計 *shūkei* totalization, classified total

❸ [also suffix] **meter, gauge, measuring instrument**
計器 *keiki* meter, gauge; instrument
時計 *tokei* clock, watch
速度計 *sokudokei* speedometer
地震計 *jishinkei* seismometer
温度計 *ondokei* thermometer

❹ **total, sum total**
合計 *gōkei* sum total, total
総計 *sōkei* total, total amount
小計 *shōkei* subtotal

INDEPENDENT

【kei 計】 plan, scheme, plot, stratagem; total, sum total
国家百年の計 *kokka-hyakunen no kei* permanent national policy
計五万円 *kei goman'en* total 50,000 yen

KUN

【haka(ru) 計る】
① compute, calculate, estimate
所要時間を計る *shoyō jikan o hakaru* calculate the time required
② guess, surmise, fathom
計り知れない *hakarishirenai* unfathomable, inestimable
③ plan, design, scheme
国の将来を計る *kuni no shōrai o hakaru* plan [provide] for the future of the country
④ deceive, play upon, take in
計られる *hakarareru* be taken in

【haka(rau) 計らう】 see to, arrange, manage, dispose; talk together, discuss
計らい *hakarai* discretion, arrangement, disposition, good offices
見計らう *mihakarau* choose at one's own discretion; time (one's visit)

SYNONYMS

❶ **plans and planning**
画 DRAW UP A PLAN → 3000
案 PROPOSAL → 2270
企 PROJECT → 2021
図 systematic plan → 3071
謀 SCHEME → 1593
策 SCHEME → 2679
略 STRATEGY → 1169

❷ **calculate and count**
算 CALCULATE → 2702
数 count → 1790

❸ **measuring devices**
尺 rule → 3440
衡 scales → 761

❹ **total**
総 TOTAL → 1379
和 sum → 1130

USAGE

hakaru

計る
① compute, calculate, estimate
② guess, surmise, fathom
③ plan, design, scheme
④ deceive, play upon, take in

測る
(measure the physical dimensions of) measure, gauge (length, depth, distance or area)

量る
① (determine the weight or volume of) measure, weigh
② [in compounds] guess, surmise, fathom

図る
① strive for, work for, promote, look to, provide for, seek
② bring about, attempt
③ [in negative constructions] expect, look forward to

謀る
scheme, plot, conspire, contrive

諮る
consult, confer, ask (a person's) opinion

HOMOPHONES

hakaru ⇨ 測 610 量 2471 図 3071 謀 1593 諮 1596

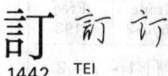

7-2 言

訂 1442 TEI

Ⓒⓗ 订 dìng

Radical	Strokes
言 149	9-7-2
Grade	**Freq**
Jōyō	1528
◧ 1-7-2	

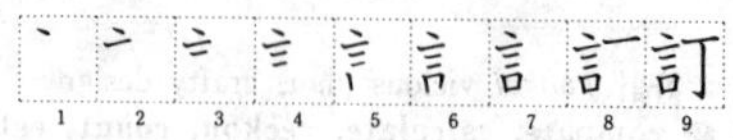

▶REVISE

COMPOUNDS

ⓐ **revise, correct, edit**
ⓑ revision, edition
ⓒ counter for revised editions

訂正する *teisei suru* correct, amend, revise
改訂する *kaitei suru* revise, edit
校訂する *kōtei suru* revise
新訂 *shintei* new revision
三訂版 *santeiban* third revised edition

INDEPENDENT

【teisuru 訂する】 revise, correct, amend

SYNONYMS

ⓐ **revise**

校 COLLATE → 929

閲 REVIEW → 3330

ⓐ **correct**

矯 RECTIFY → 1241

匡 RECTIFY → 2989

改 REFORM → 243

正 RIGHT → 3484

直す correct → 2932

ⓑ **editions**

版 edition → 872

刊 publication → 190

刷 printing → 1273

卻

1443

▶ELIMINATE

nonstandard for 却 1118

7-2 谷

則 则 𠟼

1444 SOKU notto(ru)▲

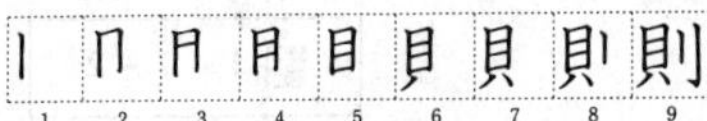

Ⓒⓗ 则 zé

Radical	Strokes
刂 18	9-2-7
Grade	**Freq**
Jōyō-5	833
◧ 1 - 7 - 2	

7-2 貝

▶RULE

COMPOUNDS

ⓐ [also suffix] **rule, regulation, principle, law**

ⓑ counter for rules or items

規則 *kisoku* rule, regulation

法則 *hōsoku* law, rule

鉄則 *tessoku* ironclad rule, immutable law

原則 *gensoku* principle, general rule

学則 *gakusoku* school regulations

教則 *kyōsoku* rules for teaching

反則 *hansoku* violation of rules, infringement, foul

罰則 *bassoku* penal regulations, punitive provisions

付則 *fusoku* additional rules, bylaw

自民党則 *jimintōsoku* rules of the Liberal Democratic Party

五則 *gosoku* five rules

INDEPENDENT

【sokusuru 則する】 conform to the rules, follow precedent

KUN

【notto(ru) 則る】 conform to the rules, follow, model

SYNONYMS

ⓐ **laws and rules**

矩 RULE → 1148

規 REGULATION → 978

紀 discipline → 1276

法 LAW → 333

律 LAW → 363

典 CANON → 2627

憲 CONSTITUTION → 2368

令 ordinance → 1995

NOTE

⇨ see USAGE note at 即 1120

1445 KI

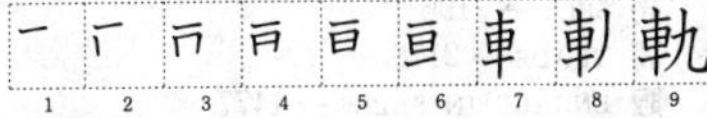

Ⓒⓗ 轨 guǐ

Radical	Strokes
車 159	9-7-2
Grade	**Freq**
Jōyō	1480
◧ 1 - 7 - 2	

7-2 車

▶TRACK

COMPOUNDS

❶ⓐ (wheel) **track, rut, path**

ⓑ **railway track**

軌跡 *kiseki* locus; tracks

軌道 *kidō* track, railway; planetary orbit; beaten track

軌条 *kijō* rails

❷ beaten track; model, paragon

常軌 *jōki* beaten track, proper course

❸ⓐ gauge of a railway track

ⓑ [original meaning] distance between the wheels of a carriage

広軌 *kōki* broad gauge

INDEPENDENT

【ki 軌(＝揆)】 way of doing
軌を一にする *ki o itsu ni suru* have the same way of doing

SYNONYMS

❶ **trace**
跡 TRACE → 1534
❶ **ways and routes**
線 LINE → 1392
径 PATH → 291
道 WAY (path) → 3134
途 WAY (route) → 3107
路 ROAD → 1533
筋 wayside → 2678
通り street → 3109
街 city street → 576
辻 CROSSROADS → 3192
岐 forked road → 241

USAGE

ki
軌
[also 揆] way of doing
揆
[also 軌] way of doing

7-2
余

叙 敍 叙

1446 JO

CH 叙 xù

Radical	Strokes
又 29△	9-2-7
Grade	**Freq**
Jōyō	1463
1-7-2	

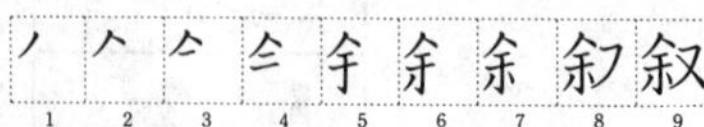
1 2 3 4 5 6 7 8 9

▶DESCRIBE

COMPOUNDS

❶ [formerly also 抒 251] **describe, narrate, depict, explain**
叙述 *jojutsu* description, depiction
叙説 *josetsu* explanation, interpretation
叙情詩 *jojōshi* lyric poem [poetry]
叙事 *joji* narration, description
自叙伝 *jijoden* autobiography
平叙文 *heijobun* declarative sentence
❷ confer (a rank) upon, bestow
叙位 *joi* conferment of a rank
叙勲 *jokun* decoration, bestowal of an order

INDEPENDENT

【josuru 叙する】 describe, depict; confer
男爵に叙せられる *danshaku ni joserareru* be conferred (a) baron

SYNONYMS

❶ **describe**
描 DEPICT → 488
写 portray → 2000

7-2
𠂉

卸 卸 卸

1447 SHA▲ oro(su) oroshi oro(shi)

CH 卸 xiè

Radical	Strokes
卩 26	9-2-7
Grade	**Freq**
Jōyō	1179
1-7-2	

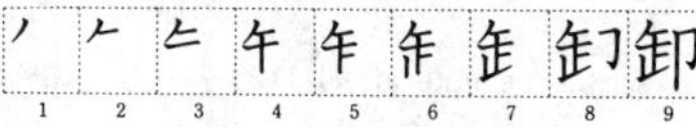
1 2 3 4 5 6 7 8 9

▶WHOLESALE

KUN

【oro(su) 卸す】 wholesale, sell wholesale
小売りに卸す *kouri ni orosu* sell wholesale to a retailer
【oroshi 卸, oro(shi) 卸し】 [also prefix and suffix] wholesale, wholesale trade; wholesaler
野菜を卸しで買う *yasai o oroshi de kau* buy vegetables wholesale
卸商 *oroshishō* wholesaler
卸売り *oroshiuri* wholesale
卸値 *oroshine* wholesale price
卸相場 *oroshisōba* wholesale price [market]
貴金属卸 *kikinzokuoroshi* wholesale [wholesaler] in precious metals
棚卸し(＝店卸し) *tanaoroshi* inventory

SYNONYMS

【orosu】
○ **sell and trade**
売 SELL → 2196
商 TRADE → 2116
販 ENGAGE IN SALES → 1477
貿 TRADE → 2601
易 EXCHANGE → 2411

USAGE

oroshi
卸
[also prefix and suffix] wholesale, wholesale trade; wholesaler
卸し

see comment below
下ろし
grated radish; vegetable grater
★卸し is a verbal gerund while 卸 is a noun. Both these forms are used in the sense of wholesaling. In the sense of grating vegetables, only 下ろし should be used. In the latter sense, *oroshi* is sometimes mistakenly written 卸し.

HOMOPHONES
orosu ⇨ 下 3378 降 458
oroshi ⇨ 下 3378

NOTE
⇨ see also USAGE note at 下 3378

削 削 削 削

1448 SAKU kezu(ru) so(gu)▲

Ⓒ 削 xiāo xuē

Radical	Strokes
刂 18	9-2-7
Grade	**Freq**
Jōyō	1372
◧ 1-7-2	

7-2
肖

丨 丷 ⺌ 𣥂 肖 肖 肖 肖丨 削
1 2 3 4 5 6 7 8 9

▶CUT BY CHIPPING

COMPOUNDS

❶ⓐ cut by chipping, whittle, cut metal (with a cutting tool), machine
ⓑ [formerly 鑿 2924] (cut a hole in) **excavate, drill**
切削 *sessaku* cutting, machining
研削 *kensaku* grinding
旋削 *sensaku* turning (on a lathe)
削岩機 *sakuganki* rock drill
削井 *sakusei* well drilling
掘削する *kussaku suru* dig out, excavate
開削 *kaisaku* excavation, cutting, digging
❷ⓐ cut down, whittle down, curtail
ⓑ cross out, strike off, delete, cancel
削減 *sakugen* curtailment, reduction
削除 *sakujo* deletion, elimination, cancellation
添削する *tensaku suru* correct, touch up ("add and delete")

KUN

【kezu(ru) 削る】 whittle, shave, sharpen, cut by chipping; cut down, whittle down, curtail; cross out, strike off, delete, cancel
削り屑 *kezurikuzu* shavings, chips
鉛筆削り *enpitsukezuri* pencil sharpener
荒削り *arakezuri* rough planing, roughing, machining
予算を削る *yosan o kezuru* curtail a budget
一字削る *ichiji kezuru* delete a letter
【so(gu) 削ぐ】
[also 殺ぐ]
① chip, cut off
鼻を削がれる *hana o sogareru* have one's nose mutilated [cut off]
②ⓐ diminish, reduce, dampen
ⓑ spoil
気勢を削ぐ *kisei o sogu* diminish [dampen] the spirit
興を削ぐ *kyō o sogu* spoil the fun of

SYNONYMS

❶ⓐ cut
切 CUT → 27
断 CUT OFF → 1492
裁 CUT OUT → 3299
割 cut with a knife → 1816
剖 DISSECT → 1670
刈る CLIP → 28
伐 CUT DOWN → 42
ⓐ polish and rub
研 GRIND → 1132
磨 POLISH → 3181
摩 RUB AGAINST → 3175
擦 RUB → 790
ⓑ dig
掘 DIG → 496
❷ⓐ decrease
減 DECREASE → 601
耗 WEAR AWAY → 1309
縮 SHRINK → 1414
落 FALL → 2318
ⓑ eliminate
抹 wipe off → 313
却 ELIMINATE → 1118
省 leave out → 2449
脱 REMOVE → 973
去 take away → 2156
外す take off → 186
除 RID OF → 456
撤 WITHDRAW → 738
排 EXCLUDE → 490
払う CLEAR AWAY → 194

USAGE

sogu
削ぐ
[also 殺ぐ]
① chip, cut off
②ⓐ diminish, reduce, dampen
ⓑ spoil
殺ぐ
[also 削ぐ] same as 削ぐ

HOMOPHONES
sogu ⇨ 殺 1324

7-2 肖

削 1449

▶CUT BY CHIPPING

nonstandard for 削 1448

7-2 皀

卽 1450

▶IMMEDIATE

nonstandard for 即 1120

7-2 君

郡

incorrect stroke count ⇨ see 1466

7-2 良

郎

incorrect stroke count ⇨ see 1467
(nonstandard for 郎 1289)

7-2 束

勅 1451

敕 勅 勅

CHOKU

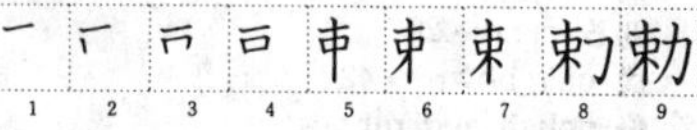

ⒸⒽ 敕 chì

Radical	Strokes
力 19	9-2-7
Grade	**Freq**
Jōyō	1895
1-7-2	

▶IMPERIAL DECREE

COMPOUNDS

ⓐ **imperial [royal] decree, imperial order [edict]**

ⓑ imperial

勅宣 *chokusen* imperial decree
勅語 *chokugo* imperial rescript
詔勅 *shōchoku* imperial edict
神勅 *shinchoku* oracle
勅使 *chokushi* imperial messenger
勅選 *chokusen* imperial nomination

INDEPENDENT

【choku 勅】 imperial decree [order]

SYNONYMS

ⓐ **imperial decree**

詔 IMPERIAL EDICT → 1505
宣 imperial proclamation → 2252

7-2 享

郭

incorrect stroke count ⇨ see 1678

7-3 言

訊 1452

JIN ki(ku)

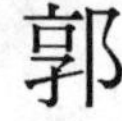

ⒸⒽ 讯 xùn

Radical	Strokes
言 149	10-7-3
Grade	**Freq**
Reference	
1-7-3	

COMPOUNDS

❶ [now replaced by 尋 *jin* 2322] interrogate, question

訊問する *jinmon suru* question, examine, interrogate

❷ [now usu. 聞く *kiku*] ask, inquire

道を訊く *michi o kiku* ask the way

HOMOPHONES

kiku ⇨ 聞 3326 聴 1418

NOTE

⇨ see USAGE note at 聞 3326

記 記 记 1453 KI shiru(su)

CH 记 jì

Radical	Strokes
言 149	10-7-3
Grade	Freq
Jōyō-2	159
1 - 7 - 3	

7-3 言

▶ **WRITE DOWN**

COMPOUNDS

❶ⓐ [original meaning] **write down, record, put down in writing**

ⓑ [also suffix] **written account, record, description**

記録 *kiroku* record, document, chronicle; (new) record
記者 *kisha* journalist, reporter; editor
記事 *kiji* news, article; account
記入 *kinyū* entry, record
記名する *kimei suru* sign one's name, register
明記する *meiki suru* write clearly, specify
登記 *tōki* registration, registry
下記の *kaki no* following, undermentioned
表記する *hyōki suru* write on a surface; write, express in writing
標記する *hyōki suru* mark; write a title
日記 *nikki* diary
手記 *shuki* note, memorandum; memoirs
伝記 *denki* biography
旅行記 *ryokōki* travel record, travel book
古事記 *kojiki* Kojiki (Ancient Chronicles)

❷ **commit to memory, memorize, remember, bear in mind**

記憶 *kioku* memory, recollection
記念日 *kinenbi* memorial day, anniversary
暗記 *anki* learning by heart, memorizing
銘記する *meiki suru* bear in mind, remember; inscribe, engrave
強記 *kyōki* good memory

❸ officer managing records and documents

書記 *shoki* clerk, secretary

❹ [formerly also 徽 787] sign, mark, emblem

記号 *kigō* symbol, mark, sign
記章 *kishō* medal, badge; emblem, insignia

❺ abbrev. of 古事記 *kojiki*: Kojiki (Ancient Chronicles)

記紀 *kiki* Kojiki and Nihonshoki

INDEPENDENT

【ki 記】 written account, description; record; used at the beginning of official records
思い出の記 *omoide no ki* one's memoirs
二月二十八日記 *nigatsu nijūhachinichi ki* recorded on February 28

【kisuru 記する】 record, write down

KUN

【shiru(su) 記す】 write down, record, put down in writing
書き記す *kakishirusu* write down, record, register

SYNONYMS

❶ⓐ **write**

紀 record in writing → 1276
控える note down → 495
録 RECORD → 1742
登 register → 2595
写 COPY → 2000
書 WRITE → 2658
筆 write → 2677

ⓑ **records**

録 RECORD → 1742
譜 SYSTEMATIC RECORD → 1637
誌 records → 1548
史 HISTORY → 3510
伝 biography → 44

❷ **remember**

覚える COMMIT TO MEMORY → 2604
憶 REMEMBER → 765
追 reminisce → 3096
顧 LOOK BACK → 1900

USAGE

shirusu

記す
write down, record, put down in writing

印す
mark, inscribe

HOMOPHONES

shirusu ⇨ 印 828

NOTE

⇨ see also USAGE note at 表 2429
★do not confuse with 紀 1276

7-3 言

訓 訓 訓

1454 KUN

ⒸⒽ 训 xùn

Radical	Strokes
言 149	10-7-3
Grade	Freq
Jōyō-4	976
1-7-3	

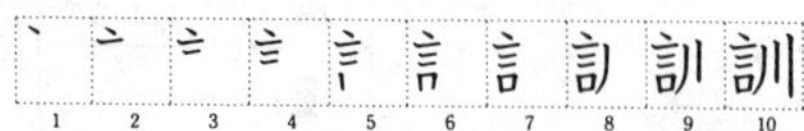

▶**INSTRUCT**

COMPOUNDS

❶ **instruct, teach, admonish**

訓練 *kunren* training, drill

訓辞 *kunji* admonitory speech

訓戒 *kunkai* admonition, warning

訓導 *kundō* old word for licensed elementary school teacher; instruction

❷ (give orders) **instruct, advise, order**

訓示 *kunji* instruction

訓令 *kunrei* instructions, (official) orders, directive

❸ precept, lesson, admonition, instruction, teachings

家訓 *kakun* family precepts

教訓 *kyōkun* lesson, precept, teachings

処生訓 *shoseikun* guiding motto for one's life

❹ **Japanese-derived pronunciation of kanji, *kun* reading**

訓読 *kundoku* (=*kun'yomi*) Japanese-derived pronunciation of kanji, *kun* reading

和訓 *wakun* Japanese reading of a Chinese character

❺ decipher, interpret, explain

訓解 *kunkai* explanation, interpretation

訓釈する *kunshaku suru* explain the meanings of old words

INDEPENDENT

【**kun** 訓】*kun* reading; precept, lesson, one's teachings

【**kunzuru** 訓ずる】read in the *kun*

SYNONYMS

❶ **teach**

諭 ADMONISH → 1598

導 GUIDE → 2888

迪 EDIFY → 3076

啓 ENLIGHTEN → 2763

教 TEACH → 1493

授 teach → 492

育 educate → 2050

練 TRAIN → 1375

❷ **instruct**

指 direct → 378

❸ **precept**

戒 commandment → 3204

7-3 言

託 託 讬

1455 TAKU kakotsu(keru)▲ kako(tsu)▲

ⒸⒽ 托 tuō

Radical	Strokes
言 149	10-7-3
Grade	Freq
Jōyō	1169
1-7-3	

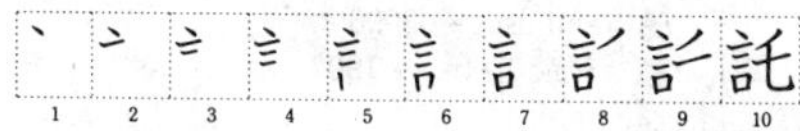

▶**ENTRUST**

COMPOUNDS

❶ [original meaning] **entrust (a person with a thing), place (a thing) in someone's charge, commit, ask**

託児所 *takujisho* day nursery

委託する *itaku suru* entrust with, charge with, consign

嘱託 *shokutaku* part-time employee

寄託する *kitaku suru* deposit, entrust

信託 *shintaku* trust

結託する *kettaku suru* conspire with, be in collusion with

供託金 *kyōtakukin* deposit money

屈託の無い *kuttaku no nai* free from worry, carefree

❷ express oneself indirectly; oracle

託宣 *takusen* (Buddhist or Shinto) oracle

神託 *shintaku* oracle

御託 *gotaku* repetitious talk; saucy speech, pretentious statement

❸ make a pretext of, give pretext

託言 *takugen* excuse, pretext, plea

仮託 *kataku* pretext, pretense, plea

INDEPENDENT

【**takusu** 託す】entrust (a person with a thing); anchor (one's hope); convey (one's feelings) in (verse)

KUN

【**kakotsu(keru)** 託ける】make a pretext of, use (a thing) as pretext

病気に託けて *byōki ni kakotsukete* under the

pretext of ill health

【kako(tsu) 託つ】 complain of, rail [repine] at

不遇を託つ *fugū o kakotsu* repine at one's hard lot

SYNONYMS

❶ **commit**

委 COMMIT → 2553
預 DEPOSIT → 1042
任 LEAVE TO → 53
嘱 CHARGE WITH → 718

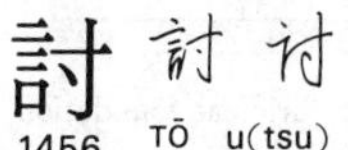

1456 TŌ u(tsu)

CH 讨 tǎo

Radical	Strokes
言 149	10-7-3
Grade	**Freq**
Jōyō-6	385
◧ 1-7-3	

7-3 言

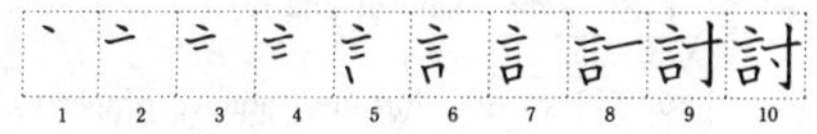

1 2 3 4 5 6 7 8 9 10

▶**STUDY**
▶**SUPPRESS BY ARMED FORCE**

COMPOUNDS

❶ (inquire into and examine closely) **study, scrutinize, examine, discuss**

討議 *tōgi* discussion, debate, deliberation
討論 *tōron* debate, discussion, argument
討究 *tōkyū* investigation, study
検討する *kentō suru* examine, study, investigate

❷ **suppress by armed force, put down [attack] the enemy, send a punitive expedition**

討伐 *tōbatsu* suppression (of a rebellion), punitive expedition
討幕する *tōbaku suru* attack the shogunate
討匪 *tōhi* suppression of bandits
掃討する *sōtō suru* wipe out (the enemy), clear
追討する *tsuitō suru* hunt down and kill
征討 *seitō* subjugation, conquest

KUN

【u(tsu) 討つ】

① kill (with a sword or spear)
敵討ち *katakiuchi* vendetta, revenge

②ⓐ suppress by armed force, put down [attack] the enemy, send a punitive expedition
ⓑ [usu. 撃つ, sometimes also 打つ] attack, strike, assault

敵を討つ *teki o utsu* quell the enemy
討ち入る *uchiiru* break into (a house to kill the master), raid
手討ち *teuchi* capital punishment given personally by a feudal lord
不意討ち *fuiuchi* surprise attack
夜討ち *youchi* night attack

SYNONYMS

❶ **investigate and examine**

検 EXAMINE → 986
探 PROBE → 505
察 INSPECT → 2347
究 STUDY EXHAUSTIVELY → 2203
閲 REVIEW → 3330
診 EXAMINE A PATIENT → 1504
調 INVESTIGATE → 1567
査 LOOK INTO → 2437
審 EXAMINE CAREFULLY → 2360
験 TEST → 1833
勘 CHECK → 1777
糾 INQUIRE INTO → 1278

❷ **conquer and suppress**

征 CONQUER → 293
伐 CUT DOWN → 42
鎮 QUELL → 1759
靖 PACIFY → 1208

HOMOPHONES

utsu ⇨ 撃 2863 打 193

NOTE

⇨ see USAGE note at 打 193

7-3
貝

財 財 財

1457 ZAI SAI

CH 財 cái

Radical	Strokes
貝 154	10-7-3
Grade	**Freq**
Jōyō-5	527
1 - 7 - 3	

1 2 3 4 5 6 7 8 9 10

▶WEALTH

COMPOUNDS

❶ⓐ **wealth, fortune, money; property, assets, goods, commodities**
ⓑ [suffix] goods, assets, property
財貨 *zaika* wealth, money and property; goods
財産 *zaisan* property, fortune, wealth
財布 *saifu* purse, wallet
私財 *shizai* private funds, private property
蓄財 *chikuzai* accumulation of wealth
資財 *shizai* property, fortune, assets
家財 *kazai* household effects [goods]
耐久消費財 *taikyū shōhizai* durable consumer goods
文化財 *bunkazai* cultural assets [properties]
❷ **finance, funds, revenue**
財界 *zaikai* business world, economic circles
財源 *zaigen* revenue source, financial resources
財政 *zaisei* public finance, financial affairs
財団法人 *zaidan hōjin* juridical foundation, juridical person
財務 *zaimu* financial affairs

INDEPENDENT

【zai 財】 wealth, fortune, money; property, goods
財を成す *zai o nasu* build a fortune

SYNONYMS

❶ⓐ **wealth**
産 property → 3298
富 riches → 2310
宝 TREASURE → 2224
❷ **money**
資 RESOURCES → 2695
金 MONEY → 2057
銭 MONEY → 1725
貨 MONEY (legal tender), coin → 2465
幣 CURRENCY → 2885
銀 SILVER → 1722
-玉 coin suffix → 3477
札 bill → 817

7-3
身

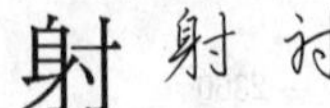

1458 SHA i(ru) sa(su)▲

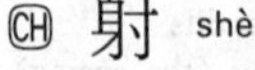

CH 射 shè

Radical	Strokes
寸 41	10-3-7
Grade	**Freq**
Jōyō-6	917
1 - 7 - 3	

1 2 3 4 5 6 7 8 9 10

▶SHOOT

COMPOUNDS

❶ⓐ **shoot, fire**
ⓑ [original meaning] shoot an arrow
射撃 *shageki* shooting, gunshot, firing
射的 *shateki* target practice, shooting
射程 *shatei* shooting range
射殺する *shasatsu suru* shoot to death
発射する *hassha suru* discharge, shoot, launch
高射砲 *kōshahō* antiaircraft gun, high-angle gun
❷ (emit forcefully) **shoot (out) (radiation or liquids), emit, radiate, discharge, eject**
射精 *shasei* ejaculation, seminal emission
放射する *hōsha suru* radiate, emit, emanate
日射 *nissha* insolation, solar radiation
反射 *hansha* reflection
直射日光 *chokusha-nikkō* direct rays of the sun
注射 *chūsha* injection, shot
❸ archery
射手 *shashu* archer
騎射 *kisha* shooting on horseback, equestrian archery

INDEPENDENT

【sha 射】 archery
射を学ぶ *sha o manabu* learn archery

KUN

【i(ru) 射る】 shoot (an arrow), let off (an arrow)
射止める *itomeru* shoot to death; win, acquire
射抜く *inuku* shoot through
【sa(su) 射す】 [now usu. 差す] shine on

障子に影が射す *Shōji ni kage ga sasu* A shadow is cast on the *shoji* (paper sliding-door)

SYNONYMS

❶ **shoot**

撃 fire → 2863

発 discharge → 2565

❷ **emit**

放 radiate → 853

出 PUT OUT → 3498

発 EMIT → 2565

排 DISCHARGE → 490

噴 SPOUT → 717

吐 SPEW → 203

HOMOPHONES

sasu ⇨ 差 3311 指 378 刺 1275 挿 431 注 325 止 2941

NOTE

⇨ see USAGE note at 差 3311

軒 1459 KEN noki

CH 轩 xuān

Radical	Strokes
車 159	10-7-3
Grade	**Freq**
Jōyō	1233
◧ 1 - 7 - 3	

7-3 車

▶**EAVES** ▶**COUNTER FOR HOUSES**

COMPOUNDS

❶ **eaves, canopy**

軒灯 *kentō* eaves lantern, door light

❷ⓐ **counter for houses**

ⓑ house

四軒 *yonken* four houses

一軒家 *ikken'ya* solitary house; private home

数軒 *sūken* several houses

軒別に *kenbetsu ni* house to house

❸ suffix after names of restaurants or shops

来来軒 *rairaiken* The Rairai (name of a Chinese restaurant)

東海軒 *tōkaiken* Tokai Restaurant

❹ rise high

意気軒高(=意気軒昂)として *ikikenkō to shite* in high spirits

❺ [original meaning, now archaic] chariot used by noblemen in ancient China

KUN

【**noki** 軒】eaves

軒下 *nokishita* under the eaves

軒先 *nokisaki* edge of the eaves, house frontage

軒並み *nokinami* row of houses; all round, across the board

SYNONYMS

❶ **roof parts**

棟 ridge → 991

❷ⓐ **counters for houses**

戸 counter for households → 1930

棟 counter for buildings → 991

ⓑ **houses**

家 HOUSE → 2273

屋 HOUSE → 3098

戸 HOUSEHOLD → 1930

宅 DWELLING HOUSE → 2174

居 residence → 3080

邸 STATELY RESIDENCE → 1131

住 housing → 64

配 1460 HAI kuba(ru)

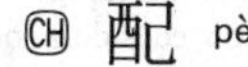

CH 配 pèi

Radical	Strokes
酉 164	10-7-3
Grade	**Freq**
Jōyō-3	319
◧ 1 - 7 - 3	

7-3 酉

▶**DISTRIBUTE**

COMPOUNDS

❶ **distribute, apportion, allot, allocate**

配達 *haitatsu* delivery

配給 *haikyū* distribution, supply; rationing

配本 *haihon* distribution of books

配付 *haifu* distribution, apportionment

配当する *haitō suru* allot

配役 *haiyaku* cast (of a play)

分配 *bunpai* division, distribution, allotment

❷ [sometimes also 排 490] **match, put in order, arrange**

配置 *haichi* arrangement; posting (of troops)

配合 *haigō* combination, distribution, arrange-

ment; harmony
配列 *hairetsu* arrangement, disposition
配色 *haishoku* color arrangement [scheme]
按配する *anbai suru* arrange, distribute; adjust
❸ⓐ match [join] in marriage, get married
ⓑ mate (animals), breed
配偶者 *haigūsha* spouse, mate
交配 *kōhai* mating
❹ **concern oneself with (a person's welfare), be concerned about**
配慮 *hairyo* consideration, care, concern
心配 *shinpai* anxiety, concern, worry, uneasiness; good offices
高配 *kōhai* your trouble, your good offices
手配 *tehai* arrangement, preparation; search instruction (by police)
❺ abbrev. of 配当 *haitō*: dividend
減配 *genpai* reduction in a dividend; smaller ration
無配の *muhai no* without dividend
❻ place under, subordinate
配下 *haika* subordinates, followers
支配する *shihai suru* control, manage, govern
采配 *saihai* baton (of command)
軍配 *gunbai* sumo umpire's fan; commander's fan (in old Japan); stratagem
❼ send a criminal to exile, banish
配流 *hairu* exile, banishment
配所 *haisho* place of exile
❽ used phonetically for *hai*
気配 *kehai* sign, indication

INDEPENDENT
【haisuru 配する】 allot, arrange; match; [archaic] exile

KUN
【kuba(ru) 配る】 distribute, apportion, allot, allocate; concern oneself with, attend to
トランプを配る *toranpu o kubaru* deal cards
心配り *kokorokubari* exerting care, attention

SYNONYMS
❶ **distribute**
頒 DISTRIBUTE WIDELY → 1043
分 DIVIDE → 1972
❹ **worry**
憂 BE ANXIOUS → 2145
構う MIND → 1049
虞 FEARS (of undesirable event) → 3254
❺ **interest and dividend**
利 interest → 1114
子 interest → 3390

7-3
酉

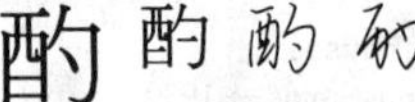

1461 SHAKU ku(mu)

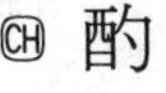 zhuó

Radical	Strokes
酉 164	10-7-3
Grade	**Freq**
Jōyō	1903
1-7-3	

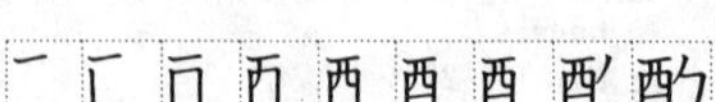

1 2 3 4 5 6 7 8 9 10

▶**POUR WINE**

COMPOUNDS
❶ [original meaning] **pour [serve] wine or sake, fill a person's cup; drink wine**
酌婦 *shakufu* barmaid, waitress
晩酌 *banshaku* evening drink
手酌 *tejaku* self-service in sake drinking
❷ weigh and consider, take into consideration
酌量 *shakuryō* consideration, extenuation
参酌する *sanshaku suru* take into consideration, make allowances for
媒酌 *baishaku* matchmaking

INDEPENDENT
【shaku 酌】 serving wine
お酌 *oshaku* serving wine
酌をする *shaku o suru* serve wine or sake; fill a person's cup

KUN
【ku(mu) 酌む】 drink, have a drink
酒を酌み交わす *sake o kumikawasu* drink together, help one another to sake

SYNONYMS
❶ **offer wine**
献 offer wine → 1785
酬 reciprocate wineglasses → 1539

USAGE
kumu
酌む
drink, have a drink
汲む
① draw (water), scoop up, ladle, pump
② consider, sympathize with

HOMOPHONES
kumu ⇨ 汲 265

1462

▶**DISTRIBUTE**
nonstandard for 配 1460

7-3 酉

酌
1463

▶**POUR WINE**
nonstandard for 酌 1461

7-3 酉

1464

Radical	Strokes
髟 190	10-10-0
Grade	**Freq**
Radical	
◧ 1 - 7 - 3	

7-3 髟

Stroke order: 一 ｢ F F 镸 镸 镸 髟 髟 髟 (1–10)

RADICAL 190
Standard form: 髟 *kamikanmuri* 'hair' (髪 鬚 髭)
Description: used in characters related to human hair

畝 畝 畝
1465 BŌ▲ se une

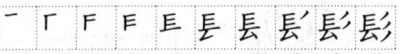

Ⓒⓗ 亩 mǔ

Radical	Strokes
田 102	10-5-5
Grade	**Freq**
Jōyō	1927
◧ 1 - 7 - 3	

7-3 亩

Stroke order: 1–10

▶***SE***

KUN

【se 畝】 *se*, are: unit of sq. measure equiv. to approx. 0.99 ares or 30 *bu* (歩), used esp. for measuring fields or farms
十畝 *jisse* approx. 10 ares
町段畝歩 *chōtansebu* units of sq. measure (for rice fields, forests, etc.)

【une 畝】 [original meaning] ridge, furrow; rib, cord (of textiles)
畝溝 *unemizo* furrow ridges
畝織 *uneori* rep, ribbed fabric

SYNONYMS

【se】
○ **area units**
反 *tan* (9.9 ares) → 2945
町 *cho* (99.2 ares) → 1113
歩 *bu* (3.3 sq.m) → 2416
坪 *TSUBO* (3.3 sq.m) → 275

郡 郡 郡
1466 GUN kōri▲

Ⓒⓗ 郡 jùn

Radical	Strokes
阝 163	10-3-7
Grade	**Freq**
Jōyō-4	772
◧ 1 - 7 - 3	

7-3 君

▶**COUNTY**

COMPOUNDS

❶ⓐ **county (of a Japanese prefecture or U.S. state), district, subprefecture**
ⓑ **suffix after names of counties**
郡部 *gunbu* counties; rural districts
郡長 *gunchō* head county official, district headman
郡制 *gunsei* county system
郡県 *gunken* counties and prefectures
名西郡 *myōzaigun* Myozai District

❷ prefecture in ancient China

INDEPENDENT

【gun 郡】 county, district

KUN

【kōri 郡】 unit of administration in former Japan

SYNONYMS
❶ **territorial divisions**
都 METROPOLIS OF TOKYO → 1686
道 district of Hokkaido → 3134
府 URBAN PREFECTURE → 3082
県 PREFECTURE → 2641
州 STATE → 57
省 province in China → 2449

7-3
良
郞
1467

▶**YOUNG MAN** ▶**MALE NAME SUFFIX**
nonstandard for 郎 1289

7-3
享
郭

incorrect stroke count ⇨ see 1678

7-4
言
訪 訪 访
1468 HŌ otozu(reru) tazu(neru) to(u)▲

CH 访 fǎng

Radical	Strokes
言 149	11-7-4
Grade	**Freq**
Jōyō-6	492
1 - 7 - 4	

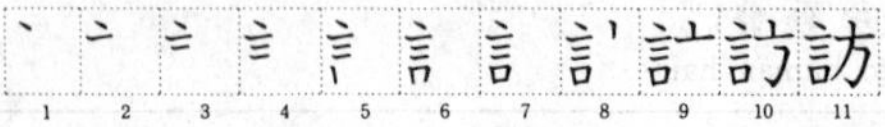

▶**VISIT**
COMPOUNDS
❶ⓐ **visit, call on**
ⓑ **visit, call**
訪問 *hōmon* visit
訪日 *hōnichi* visiting Japan, visit to Japan
訪米 *hōbei* visit to the United States
訪客 *hōkyaku* visitor
来訪する *raihō suru* visit, call
歴訪 *rekihō* round of calls
❷ inquire into, investigate
探訪する *tanbō suru* make inquiries, inquire into

KUN
【**otozu(reru) 訪れる**】visit, call on, pay a visit
訪れ *otozure* visit, call; advent, arrival
病院を訪れる *byōin o otozureru* visit at a hospital
【**tazu(neru) 訪ねる**】visit, call on, pay a visit
友人を訪ねる *yūjin o tazuneru* call on a friend
【**to(u) 訪う**】call on, visit

SYNONYMS
❶ **visit**
参 VISIT A HOLY PLACE → 2066
伺 call on → 69
寄 call at → 2291

HOMOPHONES
tazuneru ⇨ 尋 2322
tou ⇨ 問 3320

NOTE
⇨ see USAGE notes at 尋 2322 and 問 3320

7-4
言
訣
1469 KETSU

CH 诀 jué

Radical	Strokes
言 149	11-7-4
Grade	**Freq**
Reference	
1 - 7 - 4	

COMPOUNDS
[now also 決 263]
❶ separate, part, bid farewell
訣別 *ketsubetsu* separation, farewell
永訣 *eiketsu* last farewell
❷ secrets (as of an art), knack
秘訣 *hiketsu* secret, key

許 許 许

1470 KYO yuru(su) moto▲

CH 许 xǔ

Radical	Strokes
言 149	11-7-4
Grade	Freq
Jōyō-5	706
1 - 7 - 4	

7-4

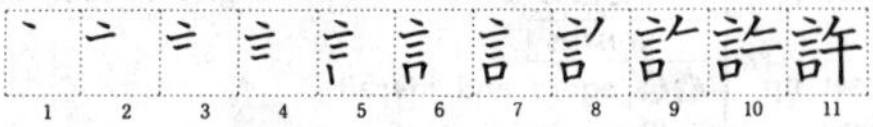

▶**PERMIT**

COMPOUNDS

ⓐ [original meaning] **permit, allow, approve, sanction**

ⓑ permission, license, authorization

許可 *kyoka* permission, approval, authorization

許容する *kyoyō suru* tolerate, allow, permit

許諾する *kyodaku suru* consent, approve, permit

黙許 *mokkyo* tacit permission

免許 *menkyo* license, permit

特許 *tokkyo* patent; special permission; concession

公許 *kōkyo* official permission, license

KUN

【yuru(su) 許す】

①ⓐ permit, allow, approve

ⓑ license, authorize

許し *yurushi* permission

結婚を許す *kekkon o yurusu* give permission to marry

時間の許す限り *jikan no yurusu kagiri* as long as time allows

開業を許す *kaigyō o yurusu* license to practice (law)

②ⓐ forgive, pardon, excuse

ⓑ exempt, exonerate, excuse from

過失を許す *kashitsu o yurusu* forgive (a person) for his [her] fault

それぱかりはお許し下さい *Sore bakari wa oyurushi kudasai* Please let me be excused from that

③ relax one's caution, let in on, yield to

心を許せる人 *kokoro o yuruseru hito* confidant, one's trusted friend

肌を許す *hada o yurusu* surrender one's chastity to a man

④ (let something unfavorable happen) allow, suffer, sustain

ヒットを許す *hitto o yurusu* allow a hit

⑤ admit, acknowledge

自他共に許す *jita tomoni yurusu* be acknowledged by oneself and others

【moto 許】 [now usu. 元] in the vicinity of, near (a person), with (someone), under (someone's roof)

手許 *temoto* at hand, within reach; cash at hand

国許 *kunimoto* one's home, one's birthplace

父母の許 *fubo no moto* under one's parents' roof

SPECIAL READINGS

許嫁▲(=許婚▲) *iinazuke* one's fiancé [fiancée], one's betrothed

SYNONYMS

ⓐ **permit**

免 license → 2067

准 grant permission → 127

允 GIVE CONSENT → 1982

【yurusu】

②ⓐ **forgive**

免 EXEMPT → 2067

赦 AMNESTY → 1478

HOMOPHONES

moto ⇨ 元 1929 下 3378 本 3502 基 2673 素 2458

NOTE

⇨ see USAGE note at 元 1929

設 設 设

1471 SETSU mō(keru)

CH 设 shè

Radical	Strokes
言 149	11-7-4
Grade	Freq
Jōyō-5	153
1 - 7 - 4	

7-4

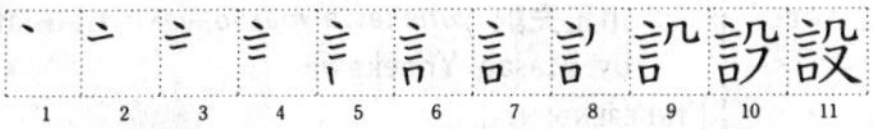

▶**SET UP**

COMPOUNDS

❶ⓐ (assemble and/or erect) **set up, install, erect, construct**

ⓑ (found) **set up (as an institution), establish, found**

設備 *setsubi* equipment, facilities

建設 *kensetsu* construction, building, erection

埋設する *maisetsu suru* put [lay] underground
施設 *shisetsu* equipment, facilities; institution, establishment
設立する *setsuritsu suru* establish, found, set up
設置する *setchi suru* establish, found, set up
設定 *settei* establishment, creation, fixation, setting up
開設 *kaisetsu* establishment, inauguration
創設 *sōsetsu* establishment, founding
特設する *tokusetsu suru* set up specially
私設の *shisetsu no* private

❷ (put forth) set up (plans), pose (a question)
設計 *sekkei* design, plan
設問する *setsumon suru* pose a question

KUN

【mō(keru) 設ける】 set up, establish, found; organize; prepare (seats), provide
設け *mōke* preparation, provision; establishment
工場を設ける *kōjō o mōkeru* set up a factory
席を設ける *seki o mōkeru* give a banquet

SYNONYMS

❶ⓐ equip and install
備 PROVIDE → 146
装 FIT OUT → 2685
架 LAY ACROSS → 2569
敷 LAY → 1870
据える INSTALL → 497

ⓐ build
建 BUILD (a building) → 3090
造 build (various structures) → 3110
築 CONSTRUCT → 2715

ⓑ found
立 ESTABLISH → 1992
置 found → 2608

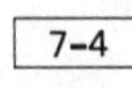
7-4

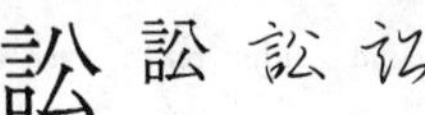
訟 訟 訟 訟

1472 SHŌ

Ⓒ讼 sòng

Radical	Strokes
言 149	11-7-4
Grade	Freq
Jōyō	1533
1-7-4	

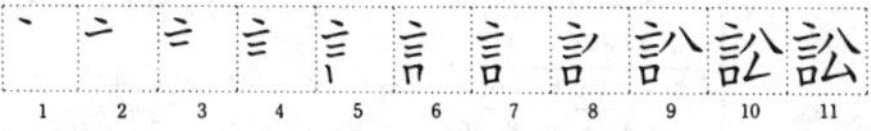

▶LITIGATE

COMPOUNDS

ⓐ litigate, bring a case to court, sue
ⓑ [rare] dispute, argue
訟務部 *shōmubu* Litigation Department (of the Ministry of Justice)
訴訟 *soshō* lawsuit, litigation
争訟 *sōshō* dispute

SYNONYMS

ⓐ sue
訴 SUE → 1507
控 accuse in court → 495
告 accuse of → 2409

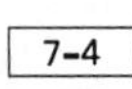
7-4

訳 譯 訳 译

1473 YAKU wake

Ⓒ译 yì

Radical	Strokes
言 149	11-7-4
Grade	Freq
Jōyō-6	1240
1-7-4	

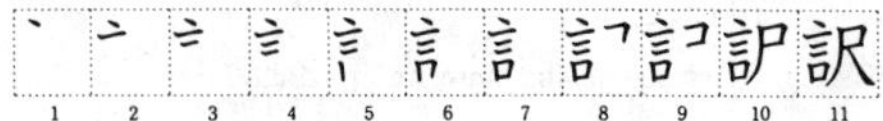

▶TRANSLATE ▶SENSE

COMPOUNDS

ⓐ [original meaning] **translate, interpret, render**
ⓑ [also suffix] **translation, rendering, version, interpretation**
ⓒ [suffix] translated by
訳者 *yakusha* translator
通訳 *tsūyaku* interpreting; interpreter
翻訳 *hon'yaku* translation, rendering
直訳 *chokuyaku* literal translation
新訳 *shin'yaku* new translation
和文英訳 *wabun-eiyaku* Japanese-English translation
日本語訳 *nihongoyaku* Japanese translation [version]
米川正夫訳 *yonekawa masao-yaku* translated by Masao Yonekawa

INDEPENDENT

【yaku 訳】 translation, rendering
巧い訳 *umai yaku* good translation
【yakusu 訳す】 translate
訳し難い *yakushigatai* difficult to translate

KUN

【wake 訳】

① sense, meaning

訳の分からない言葉 *wake no wakaranai kotoba* words that make no sense, meaningless words

② (good) sense, reason

訳の分かった人 *wake no wakatta hito* sensible man

訳知り *wakeshiri* person who knows the world; possessing an understanding about love affairs

③ reason, cause, ground(s)

訳も無く *wake mo naku* without reason, without cause

言い訳 *iiwake* apology, excuse, explanation

申し訳 *mōshiwake* excuse, apology, explanation

④ circumstances, matter, case

訳を説明する *wake o setsumei suru* explain the circumstances

どう云う訳だ *Dō iu wake da* What's the matter?

内訳 *uchiwake* items (of an account), details, breakdown

⑤ natural consequence

彼女が怒る訳だ *Kanojo ga okoru wake da* No wonder she got angry

⑥ [in negative constructions] trouble

訳無く *wakenaku* without difficulty, easily

SYNONYMS

ⓐ translate

翻 RENDER → 1897

【wake】

① meaning

義 MEANING → 2338
意 MEANING → 2136
旨 PURPORT → 2024
趣 PURPOSE → 3317

② reason

理 REASON → 970

③ cause and reason

故 reason → 1141
為 because → 3577
因 CAUSE → 3054
由 REASON → 3499

④ states and situations

情 ACTUAL CONDITIONS → 482
局 current situation → 3063
境 SITUATION → 676
勢 course of events → 2857
状 CONDITION → 272
況 CONDITIONS → 337
景 business conditions → 2470
態 STATE → 2847
調 TONE → 1567
様 MODE → 1052
相 PHASE → 900

1474

▶LITIGATE
nonstandard for 訟 1472

7-4 言

註

incorrect stroke count ⇨ see 1499

7-4 言

 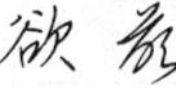
1475 YOKU hos(suru) ho(shii)

Ⓒⓗ 欲 yù

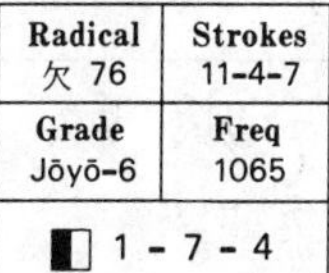

Radical	Strokes
欠 76	11-4-7
Grade	**Freq**
Jōyō-6	1065
◧ 1 - 7 - 4	

7-4 谷

1 2 3 4 5 6 7 8 9 10 11

▶DESIRE

COMPOUNDS

ⓐ [formerly also 慾 2862] [original meaning] **desire, craving; avarice, greed**

ⓑ **desire, wish, want, crave for**

欲情 *yokujō* sexual desire, craving, passion
食欲 *shokuyoku* appetite (for food)
物欲 *butsuyoku* worldly desires
性欲 *seiyoku* sexual desire, lust
意欲 *iyoku* volition, will, desire
知識欲 *chishikiyoku* intellectual thirst
欲念 *yokunen* desire, wish; passion
欲求 *yokkyū* want(s), desire, wish
欲望 *yokubō* desire, craving

INDEPENDENT

【yoku 欲(=慾)】 desire, craving; avarice, greed

欲の奴隷 *yoku no dorei* slave to avarice

KUN

【hos(suru) 欲する】 desire, wish, want, crave for

平和を欲する *heiwa o hossuru* desire [wish

for] peace

【ho(shii) 欲しい】 want, desire, wish for

欲しがる *hoshigaru* desire, want, wish for, covet

来て欲しくない *Kite hoshiku nai* I don't want you to come

SYNONYMS

ⓐ **will and intention**

志 AMBITION → 2199

意 MIND → 2136

図 intention → 3071

気 mind to do something → 3194

念 thought of doing something → 2059

趣 PURPOSE → 3317

ⓑ **wish and desire**

求 SEEK → 3550

渇 thirst for → 515

慕 yearn for → 2353

懐 LONG FOR → 763

希 ASPIRE → 2049

望 HOPE → 2742

願 WISH → 1845

7-4 貝

敗

1476 HAI yabu(reru)

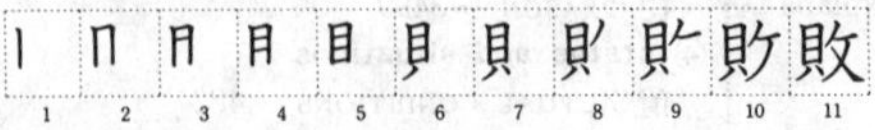

Ⓒ 败 bài

Radical	Strokes
攵 66	11-4-7
Grade	**Freq**
Jōyō-4	491

1 - 7 - 4

▶BE DEFEATED

COMPOUNDS

❶ⓐ **be defeated, lose**

ⓑ defeat

ⓒ counter for number of defeats

敗北 *haiboku* defeat, setback

敗軍 *haigun* defeated army

敗戦 *haisen* lost battle, defeat

勝敗 *shōhai* victory or defeat

連敗 *renpai* successive defeats

完敗 *kanpai* crushing defeat; complete failure

一勝二敗 *isshō nihai* one victory and two defeats

❷ **fail**

失敗 *shippai* failure, mistake

成敗 *seihai* success or failure

成敗 *seibai* punishment

❸ spoil, rot, be ruined

腐敗する *fuhai suru* rot, decay; become corrupt

INDEPENDENT

【hai 敗】 defeat

敗を取る *hai o toru* suffer a defeat

KUN

【yabu(reru) 敗れる】 be defeated, be beaten, lose

試合に敗れる *shiai ni yabureru* lose a game

SYNONYMS

❶ **lose**

負 LOSE → 2091

❷ **fail**

落 fall through → 2318

-損なう fail to (do) → 651

HOMOPHONES

yabureru ⇨ 破 1150

NOTE

⇨ see USAGE note at 破 1150

7-4 貝

販

1477 HAN

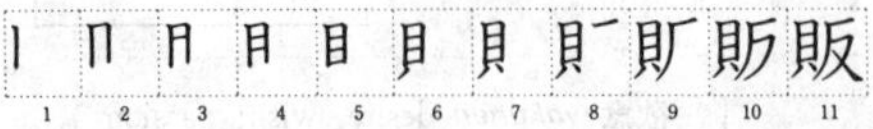

Ⓒ 贩 fàn

Radical	Strokes
貝 154	11-7-4
Grade	**Freq**
Jōyō	978

1 - 7 - 4

▶ENGAGE IN SALES

COMPOUNDS

ⓐ **engage in sales, deal in, sell, trade, market**

ⓑ abbrev. of 販売 *hanbai*: **sales**

販売する *hanbai suru* engage in sales, sell, market

販路 *hanro* market, outlet

市販 *shihan* marketing

再販 *saihan* resale

信販 *shinpan* sales on credit

自販 *jihan* automobile sales

SYNONYMS

● **sell and trade**

売 SELL → 2196

卸す WHOLESALE → 1447

商 TRADE → 2116
貿 TRADE → 2601
易 EXCHANGE → 2411

赦 1478 SHA

Ⓒⓗ 赦 shè

Radical	Strokes
赤 155	11-7-4
Grade	Freq
Jōyō	1828
1 - 7 - 4	

7-4 赤

▶AMNESTY

COMPOUNDS

ⓐ (forgive a crime or error) **amnesty, pardon, forgive, excuse**
ⓑ **amnesty, general pardon**
赦免 *shamen* pardon, amnesty, clemency
容赦 *yōsha* pardon, forgiveness, mercy
恩赦 *onsha* amnesty, general pardon
特赦 *tokusha* amnesty, special pardon
大赦 *taisha* amnesty, general amnesty

SYNONYMS

● **forgive**
免 EXEMPT → 2067
許す forgive → 1470

距

incorrect stroke count ⇒ see 1511

7-4 足

軟 1479 NAN yawa(raka) yawa(rakai)

一 ㄏ 𠄌 … (stroke order 1–11)

Ⓒⓗ 软 ruǎn

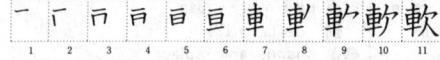

Radical	Strokes
車 159	11-7-4
Grade	Freq
Jōyō	1173
1 - 7 - 4	

7-4 車

▶SOFT

COMPOUNDS

❶ⓐ [original meaning] (not hard) **soft**
ⓑ (lacking vigor) soft, weak
軟化 *nanka* softening; weakening (of the market)
軟骨 *nankotsu* cartilage
柔軟な *jūnan na* soft, pliable, flexible
硬軟 *kōnan* hardness
軟弱 *nanjaku* weakness; effeminacy
軟調 *nanchō* weakness; bearish tone
軟着陸 *nanchakuriku* soft landing
❷ erotic, sexually wanton
軟文学 *nanbungaku* erotic literature
軟派 *nanpa* a flirt; moderate party

INDEPENDENT

【nan 軟】 softness

KUN

【yawa(raka) 軟らか】
yawaraka na 軟らかな [also 柔らかな]
① soft, tender
軟らかな土 *yawaraka na tsuchi* soft earth
② soft, subdued (color or light)
軟らかな光 *yawaraka na hikari* soft light
③ gentle, meek, mild
軟らかな風 *yawaraka na kaze* gentle breeze
【yawa(rakai) 軟らかい】
[also 柔らかい]
① soft, tender
軟らかい若葉 *yawarakai wakaba* soft young leaf
② gentle, meek
軟らかく話す *yawarakaku hanasu* speak gently
③ informal
軟らかい文章 *yawarakai bunshō* informal style

SYNONYMS

❶ⓐ **soft**
柔 SOFT (supple and yielding) → 2088
塑 plastic → 2843

HOMOPHONES

yawaraka ⇒ 柔 2088
yawarakai ⇒ 柔 2088

NOTE

⇒ see USAGE note at 柔 2088

7-4 車

転 轉 転 转 (CH) 转 zhuǎn zhuàn

1480 TEN koro(garu) koro(geru) koro(gasu) koro(bu)

Radical	Strokes
車 159	11-7-4
Grade	**Freq**
Jōyō-3	312
1 - 7 - 4	

一 𠄌 丙 両 亘 亘 車 車 軒 転 転
1 2 3 4 5 6 7 8 9 10 11

▶TURN

COMPOUNDS

❶ [original meaning] **turn, revolve, rotate**
回転する *kaiten suru* revolve, rotate, turn
自転 *jiten* rotation (of the earth)
運転する *unten suru* operate, drive, run

❷ [formerly also 顚 1843] **turn over, roll over, tumble down, fall over**
転倒する *tentō suru* tumble, fall down; invert, reverse; upset
転落する *tenraku suru* fall off, tumble down
転覆する *tenpuku suru* overturn, turn over, upset; overthrow
七転八倒する *shichitenhattō* (=*shichitenbattō, shittenbattō*) *suru* toss oneself about in great pain

❸ⓐ (undergo change) **turn into, turn, change, convert**
ⓑ **remove, move, change, transfer**
転化 *tenka* change, transformation, inversion
転換 *tenkan* conversion, switchover, turnabout
転向 *tenkō* turn, conversion, about-face
転義 *tengi* figurative meaning
変転 *henten* change, transition
好転 *kōten* take a turn for the better
一転 *itten* complete change; turn
逆転 *gyakuten* reversal, turnabout, inversion; reverse rotation
転居する *tenkyo suru* move, change one's residence
転職 *tenshoku* change of occupation
転転とする *tenten to suru* wander about; change hands; roll
移転する *iten suru* transfer, remove; move

❹ third stanza in a Chinese quatrain; the turn
起承転結 *kishōtenketsu* introduction, development, turn and conclusion (of a Chinese quatrain)

INDEPENDENT

【ten 転】 corruption (of a word's meaning)
【tenjiru 転じる】 turn round, turn; turn, shift; turn into, change; remove, be transferred

KUN

【koro(garu) 転がる】 *vi* roll over, tumble over
転がり込む *korogarikomu* role in; fall in one's way
【koro(geru) 転げる】 same as **korogaru 転がる**
転げ落ちる *korogeochiru* fall off, tumble down
【koro(gasu) 転がす】 *vt* roll; roll over, tumble over
車を転がす *kuruma o korogasu* drive a car
【koro(bu) 転ぶ】 *vi* tumble down, fall over
寝転ぶ *nekorobu* lie down

SYNONYMS

❶ **turn**
回 TURN ROUND → 3055
旋 GYRATE → 957
巡 MAKE THE ROUNDS → 3047
循 CIRCULATE → 578

❷ **overturn**
覆 OVERTURN → 2726
翻 TURN OVER → 1897
反 turn over → 2945
倒 TOPPLE → 124

❸ⓐ **change and replace**
化 CHANGE INTO, -ize → 21
遷 undergo transition → 3170
換 EXCHANGE → 587
交 INTERCHANGE → 2015
替 REPLACE → 2783
代 SUBSTITUTE → 30
迭 ALTERNATE → 3077
変 CHANGE → 2069
更 change → 3541
改 change → 243
易 change → 2411

ⓑ **move**
移 SHIFT → 1177
動 MOVE → 1778
運 MOVE → 3140
滑 SLIDE → 658
遷 TRANSFER → 3170
繰る SHIFT ONWARD → 1427

COMPOUND FORMATION

運転 *unten*
運転する 'operate, drive, run' is to put something in motion (運) and keep it rolling or moving (転 ❶).

軛

1481 YAKU kubiki

Ⓒ 轭 è

Radical	Strokes
車 159	11-7-4
Grade	**Freq**
Reference	
◧ 1 - 7 - 4	

7-4 車

COMPOUNDS

● [now also 役 *yaku* 244] [original meaning] yoke

共軛 *kyōyaku math* conjugation

斬

1482 ZAN ki(ru)

Ⓒ 斩 zhǎn

Radical	Strokes
斤 69	11-4-7
Grade	**Freq**
Reference	
◧ 1 - 7 - 4	

7-4 車

COMPOUNDS

❶ [now usu. 切る *kiru*] cut (a person) with a sword, cut down, kill

斬首 *zanshu* decapitation

斬新な *zanshin na* new, novel, original

斬り死に *kirijini* fighting (with a sword) to death

斬り掛かる *kirikakaru* stab at, assault with a sword

❷ criticize severely, attack

HOMOPHONES

kiru ⇨ 切 27 伐 42 剪 2306 截 3301

NOTE

⇨ see USAGE note at 切 27

酔

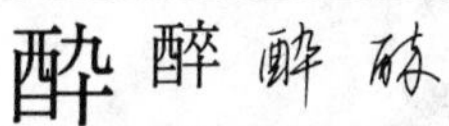

1483 SUI yo(u) yo(i)

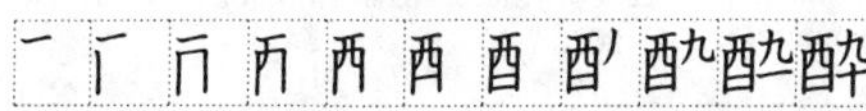

Ⓒ 醉 zuì

Radical	Strokes
酉 164	11-7-4
Grade	**Freq**
Jōyō	1366
◧ 1 - 7 - 4	

7-4 酉

▶BECOME INTOXICATED

COMPOUNDS

❶ **become intoxicated (with alcohol), get drunk**

酔態 *suitai* drunkenness, intoxication

酔漢 *suikan* drunkard, drunken fellow

泥酔した *deisui shita* dead-drunk

麻酔 *masui* anesthesia

❷ be intoxicated (with strong emotion), be infatuated, be fascinated

心酔 *shinsui* infatuation

陶酔 *tōsui* intoxication; fascination, rapture

KUN

【yo(u) 酔う】 get drunk [high], become intoxicated; be intoxicated (with delight), be in rapture; feel sick (as from riding in a vehicle)

酔っ払う *yopparau* get drunk

酔っ払い *yopparai* drunkard, boozer

酔い痴れる *yoishireru* be fuddled [drunk] (with)

【yo(i) 酔い】 [also suffix] drunkenness, intoxication; motion sickness

二日酔い *futsukayoi* hangover, morning after

船酔い *funayoi* seasickness

乗り物酔い *norimonoyoi* motion sickness

SYNONYMS

❶ **become stupefied**

麻 BECOME NUMB → 3125

7-4
釆

釈 釋 釈 釋

1484 SHAKU

CH 释 shì

Radical	Strokes
釆 165	11-7-4
Grade	**Freq**
Jōyō	1162
1-7-4	

1 2 3 4 5 6 7 8 9 10 11

▶ELUCIDATE

COMPOUNDS

❶ⓐ **elucidate, explain, interpret, explicate**
ⓑ elucidation, explanation, interpretation, commentary
ⓒ explain oneself, make an excuse, vindicate
解釈 *kaishaku* interpretation, explanation
注釈 *chūshaku* annotation, note, comment
会釈する *eshaku suru* salute, greet, bow slightly
語釈 *goshaku* definition of words
釈明する *shakumei suru* explain, vindicate; apologize

❷ **release, free**
釈放 *shakuhō* release, liberation, discharge, acquittal
保釈する *hoshaku suru* bail, let (a prisoner) out on bail

❸ⓐ clear up, dispel
ⓑ dissolve (in water)
釈然として *shakuzen to shite* with sudden illumination
希釈 *kishaku* dilution

❹ⓐ **Sakyamuni, Buddha**
ⓑ prefix preceding the name or posthumous name of a Buddhist
釈迦 *shaka* Sakyamuni, Gautama
釈典 *shakuten* Buddhist literature, Buddhist sutras
釈空海 *shakukūkai* Kukai (name of a Buddhist priest)

INDEPENDENT

【**shaku** 釈】 explanation, elucidation, interpretation
難解文の釈 *nankaibun no shaku* elucidation of a difficult passage

SYNONYMS

❶ⓐ **explain**
説 EXPLAIN → 1547
明 make clear → 855
講 expound → 1619
解 CLARIFY → 1517
注 annotate → 325

❷ **release**
放 LET GO → 853

❹ⓐ **Buddha**
仏 BUDDHA → 19

NOTE

⇨ see COMPOUND FORMATION for 会釈 *eshaku* ⇨ 会 2020

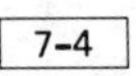
里

野 埜 野 埜

1485 YA no no-

CH 野 yě

Radical	Strokes
里 166	11-7-4
Grade	**Freq**
Jōyō-2	104
1-7-4	

▶FIELD

COMPOUNDS

❶ⓐ [original meaning] (**uncultivated**) **field, open country, wilderness**
ⓑ cultivated field
野外 *yagai* field, fields, open air
平野 *heiya* plain(s), open field
原野 *gen'ya* vast plain, wilderness, field
荒野 *kōya* wilderness, the wilds, wasteland
野菜 *yasai* vegetables, greens

❷ (sphere of action) **field, range, area**
分野 *bun'ya* field, sphere, area
視野 *shiya* field of vision; one's mental horizon
照射野 *shōshaya* irradiation field (of x rays)

❸ⓐ **baseball field**
ⓑ abbrev. of 野手 *yashu*: fielder
野球 *yakyū* baseball
内野 *naiya* infield
外野 *gaiya* outfield; outsiders
野選 *yasen* fielder's choice

❹ⓐ (growing or occurring in the field) **wild, undomesticated, savage**
ⓑ **rustic, unrefined, coarse, vulgar, savage**
野犬 *yaken* stray dog
野鳥 *yachō* wild fowl, wild bird
野性 *yasei* wild nature, uncouthness

野獣 *yajū* wild animal, wild game
野蛮な *yaban na* savage, barbarous, uncivilized
野趣 *yashu* charms of the countryside, rural beauty
野暮な *yabo na* unrefined, rustic, boorish
粗野な *soya na* rustic, rude, vulgar

❺ **nongovernmental, (party or people) outside the government**
野党 *yatō* opposition party
朝野 *chōya* government and people
在野の *zaiya no* out of office [power], in opposition

❻ audacious, inordinate
野心 *yashin* ambition, inordinate aspiration
野望 *yabō* ambition, designs, treason

INDEPENDENT

【ya 野】 (uncultivated) field, open country, wilderness; the opposition
虎を野に放つ *tora o ya ni hanatsu* let loose a tiger in the field
野に在る *ya ni aru* be in private life; be in opposition

KUN

【no 野】 [also suffix] (uncultivated) field, open country, plain
野の花 *no no hana* wild flowers
野原 *nohara* field, plain
野良 *nora* the fields
枯れ野 *kareno* desolate [dreary] field
武蔵野 *musashino* Musashi Plain

【no- 野-】
ⓐ [also prefix] wild, undomesticated
ⓑ (lacking restraint) wild, unruly
野菊 *nogiku* wild chrysanthemum; aster
野兎 *nousagi* hare
野葡萄 *nobudō* wild grape
野放しの *nobanashi no* untethered, loose, at grass, at large
野放図な *nohōzu na* unrestrained, unruly

SYNONYMS

❶ⓐ uncultivated expanses of land
原 PLAIN → 3009
漠 DESERT → 655

❷ range
界 field (*phys*) → 2563
場 field (*phys*, *psychol*) → 558
圏 SPHERE → 3148
域 area → 465
範 range → 2709
程 EXTENT → 1190

❸ⓐ sports fields
場 ground(s) → 558
庭 COURT → 3114

❹ⓐ natural
地 natural → 204
粗 crude → 1329
原 in the original state → 3009

ⓑ vulgar and unrefined
粗 COARSE → 1329
里 rural → 3542
俗 vulgar → 104
卑 MEAN → 2642
蛮 barbaric → 2129

斜 1486

SHA nana(me) hasu▲

(CH) 斜 xié

Radical	Strokes
斗 68	11-4-7
Grade	**Freq**
Jōyō	1630

◧ 1-7-4

7-4 余

Stroke order: 1–11

▶OBLIQUE

COMPOUNDS

● [also prefix] [original meaning] **oblique, diagonal, slanting, inclined, sloping, leaning, tilting**
斜線 *shasen* oblique line, slanting line, slash mark
斜面 *shamen* slope, slanting surface
斜影 *shaei* slanting shadow
斜滑降 *shakakkō* traversing (in skiing)
斜投影 *shatōei* oblique projection
傾斜 *keisha* inclination, slant, tilt
ピサの斜塔 *pisa no shatō* Leaning Tower of Pisa

INDEPENDENT

【sha 斜】 obliqueness, slant, inclination
斜に構える *sha ni kamaeru* couch (a sword); stand ready (to do)

KUN

【nana(me) 斜め】 [also prefix] obliqueness, slant, inclination; displeasure
斜めな *naname na* oblique, diagonal, slanting; displeased, cross
斜め応力 *nanameōryoku* oblique stress
斜め入射 *nanamenyūsha* oblique incidence
御機嫌斜めだ *gokigen-naname da* be in a bad temper

【hasu 斜】 slant, bias, obliquity
斜交いに *hasukai ni* obliquely, diagonally

SYNONYMS

● obliqueness and inclining
傾 INCLINE → 154

7-4
余
敍 1487
▶DESCRIBE
nonstandard for 叙 1446

7-4
杀
殺 1488
▶KILL
nonstandard for 殺 1324

7-4
每
敏 1489
▶NIMBLE
nonstandard for 敏 1322

7-4
壳
殼 1490 殼 殼 殼
KAKU kara gara

Ⓒⓗ 壳 ké qiào

Radical	Strokes
殳 79	11-4-7
Grade	**Freq**
Jōyō	1739
■ 1-7-4	

一 十 士 士 声 声 壳 壳 殼 殼 殼
1 2 3 4 5 6 7 8 9 10 11

▶SHELL

COMPOUNDS

ⓐ **shell (of any kind), crust**
ⓑ electron shell
殼頂 *kakuchō* umbo, apex of a shell
甲殼類 *kōkakurui* Crustacea
地殼 *chikaku* crust (of the earth)
卵殼 *rankaku* eggshell
原子のM殼 *genshi no emukaku* M shell

INDEPENDENT

【**kaku** 殼】shell, crust; electron shell
殼の内部 *kaku no naibu* inside of a shell

KUN

【**kara** 殼】
①ⓐ shell, crust
ⓑ husk, hull
殼を閉ざす *kara o tozasu* retire into one's shell, close up like an oyster
卵の殼 *tamago no kara* eggshell
貝殼 *kaigara* shell
豆殼 *mamegara* bean husk
② castoff skin, refuse
抜け殼 *nukegara* castoff skin; mere shadow of one's true self
【**gara** 殼】cinders, ashes
燃え殼 *moegara* cinders
石炭殼 *sekitangara* coal cinders
吸い殼 *suigara* cigarette butt

SYNONYMS

ⓐ **shells**
甲 SHELL (of animals) → 3481
貝 seashell → 2543
【**gara**】
○ **products of combustion**
灰 ASH → 2979
炭 CHARCOAL → 2257
煙 SMOKE → 1021

HOMOPHONES

kara ⇨ 空 2227

NOTE

⇨ see USAGE note at 空 2227
★do not confuse with 穀 1824

7-4
旡
旣 1491
▶ALREADY
nonstandard for 既 1166

断 斷 断

1492 DAN ta(tsu) kotowa(ru)

ⒸⒽ 断 duàn

Radical	Strokes
斤 69	11-4-7
Grade	**Freq**
Jōyō-5	448
1 - 7 - 4	

▶**CUT OFF** ▶**RESOLVE**

COMPOUNDS

❶ⓐ [original meaning] (detach by severing) **cut off, sever, cut apart**
ⓑ cut across, go through
断片 *danpen* fragment, piece
断面 *danmen* (cross) section, profile
断頭台 *dantōdai* guillotine
断裁機 *dansaiki* paper cutter
切断する *setsudan suru* cut (off), sever
横断 *ōdan* crossing, traversing

❷ⓐ (cause to discontinue) **cut off (the water supply), sever (a connection), break off (relations), discontinue**
ⓑ abstain from, give up
断絶 *danzetsu* severance, rupture; discontinuation
断交 *dankō* severing [breaking off] relations
断続的に *danzokuteki ni* intermittently, off and on
断水 *dansui* suspension of water supply
中断する *chūdan suru* interrupt, discontinue, suspend
遮断 *shadan* interception, interruption, blockade, isolation
油断 *yudan* negligence, carelessness, inattentiveness
断食 *danjiki* fasting
断念 *dannen* abandonment, relinquishment
禁断の木の実 *kindan no konomi* the forbidden fruit

❸ (make a firm decision or judgment) **resolve, decide, conclude**
断定 *dantei* decision, conclusion
断言 *dangen* (positive) assertion, declaration
断罪 *danzai* judgment of a crime
決断 *ketsudan* decision, determination, resolution
判断 *handan* judgment, decision
診断 *shindan* diagnosis
予断 *yodan* prediction, foregone conclusion

❹ resolutely, decisively, absolutely
断固たる *dankotaru* firm, conclusive, determined
断行する *dankō suru* carry out resolutely
断然 *danzen* resolutely, decisively

❺ permission, prior notice
無断で *mudan de* without permission; without notice [warning]

INDEPENDENT

【dan 断】 decision, judgment, ruling; OFF (marking for circuits)
断を下す *dan o kudasu* make a decision, pass judgment

【danzuru (=danjiru) 断ずる(=断じる)】 conclude; judge
断じて *danjite* decidedly, absolutely

KUN

【ta(tsu) 断つ】
① (detach by severing) cut off, sever, cut apart
断ち切る *tachikiru* cut off, disconnect
② (stop or interrupt the intended course) cut off, intercept
退路を断つ *tairo o tatsu* cut off the retreat
③ abstain from, give up
塩断ち *shiodachi* abstinence from salt as a vow

【kotowa(ru) 断る】 refuse, reject, decline; give notice beforehand, call attention to; obtain consent, ask for permission
断り *kotowari* refusal, declining; prohibition; notice, warning; permission; excuse, apology
申し出を断る *mōshide o kotowaru* turn down an offer
断る迄も無く *kotowaru made mo naku* needless to say
断らずに *kotowarazu ni* without permission

SYNONYMS

❶ⓐ **cut**
切 CUT → 27
裁 CUT OUT → 3299
割 cut with a knife → 1816
剖 DISSECT → 1670
刈る CLIP → 28
伐 CUT DOWN → 42
削 CUT BY CHIPPING → 1448

❷ⓐ **discontinue**
絶 BREAK OFF → 1353
廃 ABOLISH → 3146
止 STOP → 2941
休 suspend → 52
停 suspend → 139

❸ **decide**
決 DECIDE → 263
定 FIX → 2229

❹ **resolutely**
決 decisively → 263
敢 BOLDLY → 1706
【kotowaru】
○ **refuse and reject**
拒 REFUSE → 311
否 SAY NO → 2406
却 reject → 1118

USAGE

tatsu
断つ
① (detach by severing) cut off, sever, cut apart
② (stop or interrupt the intended course) cut off, intercept
③ abstain from, give up
絶つ
① break off, discontinue, cut off, sever
② exterminate, extirpate, eradicate
裁つ
cut out (a garment), cut (paper)

HOMOPHONES

tatsu ⇨ 絶 1353 裁 3299

NOTE

⇨ see COMPOUND FORMATION for 油断 *yudan* ⇨ 油 341

7-4 孝

教 教 教 教

1493 KYŌ oshi(eru) oso(waru)

Ⓒⓗ 教 jiào jiāo

Radical	Strokes
攵 66	11-4-7
Grade	**Freq**
Jōyō-2	97
1-7-4	

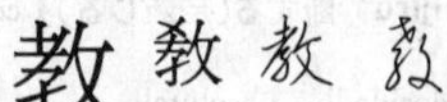

▶**TEACH** ▶**RELIGION**

COMPOUNDS

❶ [original meaning] **teach, instruct, educate**
教育 *kyōiku* education, teaching
教授する *kyōju suru* teach, instruct, give lessons
教師 *kyōshi* teacher, instructor
教室 *kyōshitsu* classroom, class
教養 *kyōyō* culture, education, cultivation
教科 *kyōka* school subject; course of study, curriculum
教材 *kyōzai* teaching materials [aids]
教訓 *kyōkun* lesson, precept, teachings
文教 *bunkyō* education, culture
❷ abbrev. of 教育 *kyōiku* or 教職員 *kyōshokuin*: education, school personnel
教委 *kyōi* Board of Education
日教組 *nikkyōso* Japan Teachers Union
❸ⓐ **religion, religious teachings, religious sect**
ⓑ **suffix after names of religions**
教会 *kyōkai* church
教祖 *kyōso* founder of a religion, head of a sect
宗教 *shūkyō* religion, faith, creed
殉教 *junkyō* martyrdom
布教する *fukyō suru* propagate (a religion)
仏教 *bukkyō* Buddhism
キリスト教 *kirisutokyō* Christianity
ユダヤ教 *yudayakyō* Judaism
❹ church
教区 *kyōku* parish
教籍 *kyōseki* church membership

KUN

【oshi(eru) 教える】 teach, instruct, educate; tell, show, inform; reveal, suggest
教え *oshie* teaching, education; lesson; teachings, religious teachings
教え込む *oshiekomu* inculcate, instill, train
教え子 *oshiego* one's (former) pupil
【oso(waru) 教わる】 be taught, learn, take lessons in, receive lessons
英語を教わる *eigo o osowaru* be taught English

SYNONYMS

❶ **teach**
授 teach → 492
育 educate → 2050
練 TRAIN → 1375
訓 INSTRUCT → 1454
諭 ADMONISH → 1598
導 GUIDE → 2888
迪 EDIFY → 3076
啓 ENLIGHTEN → 2763
❸ **religion**
宗 religion → 2228
道 the Way → 3134
❹ **places of worship**
院 monastery → 454
宮 SHINTO SHRINE → 2274
社 Shinto shrine → 840
寺 BUDDHIST TEMPLE → 2164
塔 pagoda → 561
堂 temple building → 2589

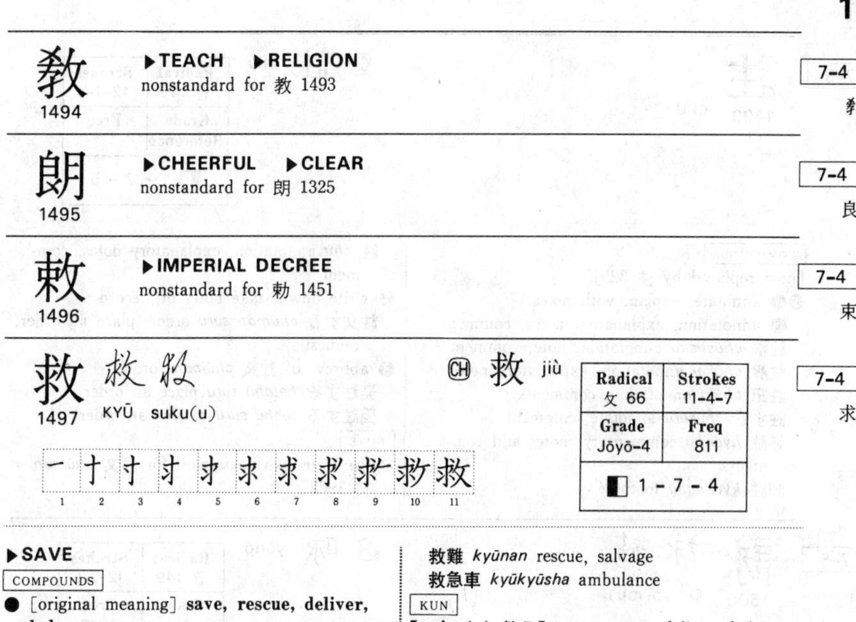

教 1494

▶TEACH ▶RELIGION
nonstandard for 教 1493

7-4 孝

朗 1495

▶CHEERFUL ▶CLEAR
nonstandard for 朗 1325

7-4 良

敕 1496

▶IMPERIAL DECREE
nonstandard for 勅 1451

7-4 束

救 救 救 1497 KYŪ suku(u)

Ⓒⓗ 救 jiù

Radical	Strokes
攵 66	11-4-7
Grade	**Freq**
Jōyō-4	811
◧ 1 - 7 - 4	

7-4 求

Stroke order: 一 十 才 才 求 求 求 求 求 救 救 (1 2 3 4 5 6 7 8 9 10 11)

▶SAVE

COMPOUNDS

● [original meaning] **save, rescue, deliver, help**

救済する *kyūsai suru* relieve, help, save, deliver
救命 *kyūmei* lifesaving
救出 *kyūshutsu* rescue, relief, deliverance
救世主 *kyūseishu* the Savior, the Messiah
救援 *kyūen* relief, rescue, help
救助 *kyūjo* rescue, relief
救難 *kyūnan* rescue, salvage
救急車 *kyūkyūsha* ambulance

KUN

【**suku(u)** 救う】 save, rescue, deliver, help, relieve
救い *sukui* rescue, relief, help, salvation
救い出す *sukuidasu* help out, rescue from
救い主 *sukuinushi* rescuer, Savior

SYNONYMS

● **rescue**
済 RELIEVE → 522

敦

incorrect stroke count ⇒ see 1693

7-4 享

觝 1498 TEI

Ⓒⓗ 觝 dǐ

Radical	Strokes
角 148	12-7-5
Grade	**Freq**
Reference	
◧ 1 - 7 - 5	

7-5 角

COMPOUNDS

● [now replaced by 抵 319] [original meaning] collide with, touch

觝触する *teishoku suru* conflict with; be contrary to; be incompatible with

7-5 言

註

1499 CHŪ

ⒸⒽ 註 zhù

Radical	Strokes
言 149	12-7-5
Grade	**Freq**
Reference	
◧ 1 - 7 - 5	

COMPOUNDS

[now replaced by 注 325]

❶ⓐ annotate, explain with notes

ⓑ annotation, explanatory notes, comment

註釈 *chūshaku* annotation, note, comment

註解 *chūkai* annotation, explanatory notes

註記 *chūki* annotation, commentary

註する *chūsuru* annotate, comment

評註 *hyōchū* commentary, notes and comments

脚註 *kyakuchū* footnote

註 *chū* annotation, explanatory notes, comment

❷ write down, take notes of, record

註文する *chūmon suru* order, place an order; request

❸ abbrev. of 註文 *chūmon*: order

発註する *hatchū suru* place an order

受註する *juchū suru* receive an order

NOTE

⇨ see COMPOUND FORMATION for 注文 *chūmon* ⇨ 文 1962

7-5 言

詠

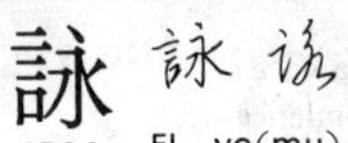

1500 EI yo(mu)

ⒸⒽ 咏 yǒng

Radical	Strokes
言 149	12-7-5
Grade	**Freq**
Jōyō	1849
◧ 1 - 7 - 5	

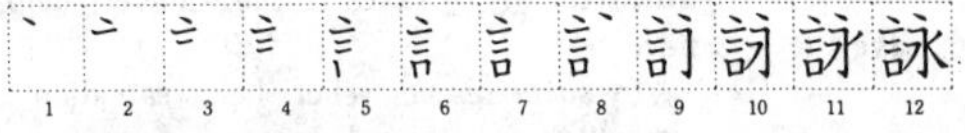

▶**RECITE POETRY**

COMPOUNDS

❶ [original meaning] **recite poetry, chant, sing**

詠唱 *eishō* chanting; aria

吟詠 *gin'ei* reciting [chanting] a poem; poem

朗詠 *rōei* reciting, chanting

❷ **write poetry, compose waka or haiku**

詠歌 *eika* composing poetry; Buddhist hymn

題詠 *daiei* poetry composed on a set theme

❸ poem, ode

詠草 *eisō* draft of a poem

❹ exclaim in admiration, praise

詠嘆(=詠歎) *eitan* exclamation, admiration

INDEPENDENT

【ei 詠】 poem

...の詠 *...no ei* poem written by...

【eijiru (=eizuru) 詠じる(=詠ずる)】 recite poetry; write poetry, compose waka or haiku

...を詠じた詩 *...o eijita shi* a poem about...

KUN

【yo(mu) 詠む】 compose (waka or haiku poems)

詠み人知らず *yomibito-shirazu* waka-composer unknown; author unknown

和歌を詠む *waka o yomu* compose a waka

SYNONYMS

❶ **recite**

吟 RECITE → 230

唱 chant → 462

読 READ → 1541

HOMOPHONES

yomu ⇨ 読 1541

NOTE

⇨ see USAGE note at 読 1541

評 評 評 讠平

1501 HYŌ

CH 评 píng

Radical	Strokes
言 149	12-7-5
Grade	**Freq**
Jōyō-5	484
◧ 1-7-5	

7-5 言

Stroke order: 1 2 3 4 5 6 7 8 9 10 11 12

▶COMMENT

COMPOUNDS

❶ⓐ **comment, criticize, review**

ⓑ [also suffix] **comment, criticism**

評論 *hyōron* comment, criticism, review
評判 *hyōban* fame, reputation
評釈 *hyōshaku* annotation, commentary
評者 *hyōsha* critic, reviewer
論評 *ronpyō* comment, criticism, review
批評する *hihyō suru* criticize, comment
好評 *kōhyō* favorable criticism [comment], public favor
定評 *teihyō* established reputation
書評 *shohyō* book reviews
下馬評 *gebahyō* gossip, advance rumor
映画評 *eigahyō* film review

❷ⓐ **evaluate, appraise, judge, decide by consultation**

ⓑ reputation

評価 *hyōka* evaluation, appraisal
評点 *hyōten* examination marks, rating
評定 *hyōtei* rating, evaluation
評議 *hyōgi* conference, consultation
評定 *hyōjō* conference, consultation
評決 *hyōketsu* decision, verdict
世評 *sehyō* public opinion; reputation

❸ abbrev. of 評議会 *hyōgikai*: council

総評(＝日本労働組合総評議会) *sōhyō* (＝*nihon rōdōkumiai sōhyōgikai*) General Council of Trade Unions of Japan

INDEPENDENT

【hyō 評】 comment, criticism; reputation
大方の評では *ōkata no hyō de wa* according to public opinion

【hyōsuru 評する】 comment, criticize

SYNONYMS

❶ⓐ **comment upon**
批 CRITICIZE → 250

ⓑ **explanatory remarks**
注 annotation → 325

❷ⓐ **judge**
判 JUDGE → 1122
裁 JUDGE → 3299
鑑 APPRAISE → 1773
審 TRY → 2360
決 DECIDE → 263
視 REGARD → 972

詐 詐 讠乍

1502 SA itsuwa(ru)▲

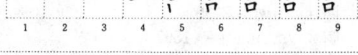

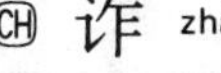

CH 诈 zhà

Radical	Strokes
言 149	12-7-5
Grade	**Freq**
Jōyō	1340
◧ 1-7-5	

7-5 言

Stroke order: 1 2 3 4 5 6 7 8 9 10 11 12

▶SWINDLE

COMPOUNDS

● **swindle, defraud, falsify, deceive; feign, pretend**

詐欺 *sagi* swindle, fraud
詐取 *sashu* fraud, swindle
詐称 *sashō* misrepresentation, false statement

KUN

【itsuwa(ru) 詐る】 [now usu. 偽る] (cause to believe a falsehood) falsify, deceive, cheat
詐って金を取る *itsuwatte kane o toru* obtain money by fraud

SYNONYMS

● **deceive**
欺 DECEIVE → 1703
惑 mislead → 2786
拐 defraud → 308
偽 FALSIFY → 131

HOMOPHONES

itsuwaru ⇨ 偽 131

NOTE

⇨ see USAGE note at 偽 131

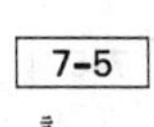

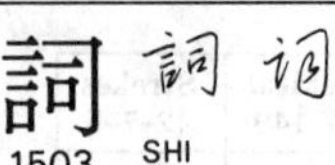

1503 SHI

CH 词 cí

Radical	Strokes
言 149	12-7-5
Grade	Freq
Jōyō-6	1588
1 - 7 - 5	

` 亠 ⺀ 亖 ⾔ 言 言 訁 訂 詞 詞 詞 (1–12)

▶WORDS

COMPOUNDS

❶ⓐ words, wording, lyrics, expressions

ⓑ [also suffix] **part of speech**

歌詞 *kashi* words [lyrics] of a song

祝詞 *shukushi* congratulations

賞詞(=頌詞) *shōshi* (words of) praise, eulogy

誓詞 *seishi* oath, pledge

作詞 *sakushi* writing lyrics

品詞 *hinshi* part of speech

動詞 *dōshi* verb

名詞 *meishi* noun

定冠詞 *teikanshi* definite article

前置詞 *zenchishi* preposition

❷ style of Chinese poetry usu. associated with the Song Dynasty

宋詞 *sōshi* Song poetry

INDEPENDENT

【shi 詞】 lyrics (of a popular song)

SPECIAL READINGS

祝詞 *norito* Shinto ritual prayer

台詞▲ *serifu* one's lines, words

SYNONYMS

❶ words and expressions

語 WORD → 1543

辞 WORD → 1364

句 PHRASE → 2967

7-5 言

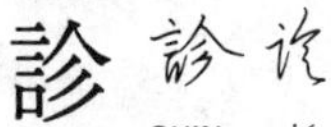

1504 SHIN mi(ru)

Radical	Strokes
言 149	12-7-5
Grade	Freq
Jōyō	1037
1 - 7 - 5	

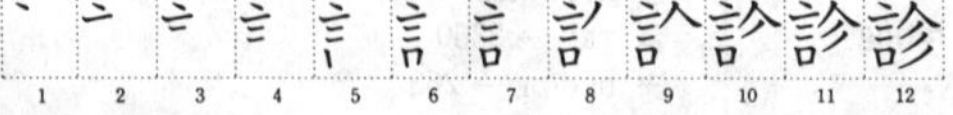

▶EXAMINE A PATIENT

COMPOUNDS

● examine a patient, diagnose

診察する *shinsatsu suru* examine (a patient)

診療 *shinryō* diagnosis and treatment

診断 *shindan* diagnosis

聴診器 *chōshinki* stethoscope

検診 *kenshin* medical examination

往診 *ōshin* doctor's visit to a patient, house call

本日休診 *honjitsu kyūshin* Office Closed Today (sign at doctor's office)

打診する *dashin suru* sound out, tap (a person's views); examine by percussion

KUN

【mi(ru) 診る】 examine (a patient)

脈を診る *myaku o miru* examine one's pulse

SYNONYMS

● investigate and examine

検 EXAMINE → 986

察 INSPECT → 2347

討 STUDY → 1456

探 PROBE → 505

究 STUDY EXHAUSTIVELY → 2203

閲 REVIEW → 3330

調 INVESTIGATE → 1567

査 LOOK INTO → 2437

審 EXAMINE CAREFULLY → 2360

験 TEST → 1833

勘 CHECK → 1777

糾 INQUIRE INTO → 1278

HOMOPHONES

miru ⇨ 見 2544 観 1880 看 3220

NOTE

⇨ see USAGE note at 見 2544

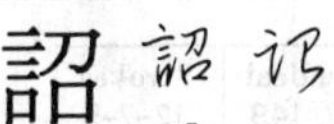

1505 SHŌ mikotonori

Ⓒⓗ 诏 zhào

Radical	Strokes
言 149	12-7-5
Grade	Freq
Jōyō	1896
◧ 1 - 7 - 5	

7-5 言

▶**IMPERIAL EDICT**

COMPOUNDS

● [original meaning] **imperial edict, imperial rescript**

詔令 *shōrei* imperial edict

詔勅 *shōchoku* imperial edict

詔書 *shōsho* imperial edict

大詔 *taishō* imperial rescript [mandate]

KUN

【**mikotonori** 詔】 imperial edict

SYNONYMS

● **imperial decree**

勅 IMPERIAL DECREE → 1451

宣 imperial proclamation → 2252

証 證 証 証

1506 SHŌ akashi▲

Ⓒⓗ 证 zhèng

Radical	Strokes
言 149	12-7-5
Grade	Freq
Jōyō-5	403
◧ 1 - 7 - 5	

7-5 言

▶**PROVE** ▶**CERTIFICATE**

COMPOUNDS

❶ⓐ [original meaning] **prove, testify, bear witness; guarantee**

ⓑ **proof, evidence, testimony**

証明 *shōmei* proof, evidence, verification

証言 *shōgen* testimony, verbal evidence

証人 *shōnin* witness, attestor

保証する *hoshō suru* (assume responsibility for) guarantee, vouch for, certify

実証 *jisshō* actual proof

証書 *shōsho* bond, deed; certificate

証拠 *shōko* proof, evidence

検証する *kenshō suru* verify, identify; inspect

確証する *kakushō suru* prove positively [definitely], corroborate

❷ⓐ [also suffix] **certificate, card, license**

ⓑ abbrev. of 証券 *shōken*: certificate of stock, securities, bond

免許証 *menkyoshō* license

会員証 *kaiinshō* membership card

証券 *shōken* bill, bond, securities

証取り法 *shōtorihō* Securities and Exchange Act

INDEPENDENT

【**shō** 証】 proof, evidence, testimony

証として *shō to shite* in proof of, in sign of

【**shōsuru** 証する】 prove, give evidence; bear witness

KUN

【**akashi** 証】 proof, evidence, vindication

身の証を立てる *mi no akashi o tateru* vindicate one's innocence

SYNONYMS

❷ⓐ **certificates**

券 CERTIFICATE → 2630

状 official document → 272

免 license → 2067

NOTE

⇨ see USAGE note at 保 96

7-5 言

訴 1507

SO utta(eru)

CH 诉 sù

Radical	Strokes
言 149	12-7-5
Grade	Freq
Jōyō	655
1-7-5	

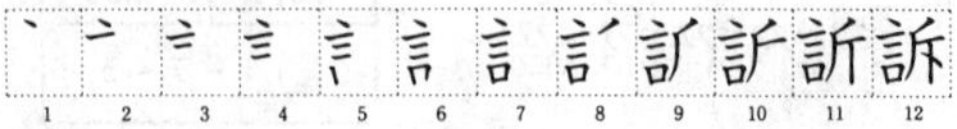

▶APPEAL TO ▶SUE

COMPOUNDS

❶ⓐ **appeal to a higher court**
ⓑ **sue, litigate, take legal action**
控訴 *kōso* (intermediate) appeal
上訴する *jōso suru* appeal to a higher court
訴訟 *soshō* lawsuit, litigation
訴願 *sogan* appeal, petition
訴状 *sojō* written complaint
起訴 *kiso* prosecution, indictment, litigation
告訴 *kokuso* legal action, complaint, accusation
公訴 *kōso* arraignment, prosecution
敗訴 *haiso* losing a suit [case]

❷ (try to deal with one's grievances by asking for sympathy) appeal to, entreat, implore
哀訴 *aiso* entreaty, complaint
愁訴する *shūso suru* entreat, implore, appeal

KUN

【utta(eru) 訴える】sue, appeal to the law, litigate; complain; appeal to (a sense of justice), resort to (violence); appeal to (the heart or the eye)
訴え *uttae* lawsuit, action, appeal, complaint
隣人を訴える *rinjin o uttaeru* sue one's neighbor
理性に訴える *risei ni uttaeru* appeal to one's reason
暴力に訴える *bōryoku ni uttaeru* resort to violence
貧者への援助を訴える *hinja e no enjo o uttaeru* appeal to people to help the poor
人に訴える力が無い *hito ni uttaeru chikara ga nai* be of little appeal to people

SYNONYMS

❶ⓑ **sue**
訟 LITIGATE → 1472
控 accuse in court → 495
告 accuse of → 2409

❷ **request**
請 REQUEST → 1576
頼 ASK → 1615
嘱 CHARGE WITH → 718
要 REQUIRE → 2635
願 ASK A FAVOR → 1845
求 SEEK → 3550

7-5 言

評 1508

▶COMMENT

nonstandard for 評 1501

7-5 貝

貯 1509

CHO ta(meru)▲ takuwa(eru)▲

CH 贮 zhù

Radical	Strokes
貝 154	12-7-5
Grade	Freq
Jōyō-4	1246
1-7-5	

▶LAY UP

COMPOUNDS

● [original meaning] **lay up (money or supplies), lay by, save, store up, lay in, stock**
貯金 *chokin* savings, deposit
貯蓄 *chochiku* savings
貯蔵する *chozō suru* store, preserve, set aside
貯水池 *chosuichi* reservoir
貯炭 *chotan* storing coal; stored coal
預貯金 *yochokin* deposits and savings, bank account
郵貯(＝郵便貯金) *yūcho* (＝*yūbin chokin*) postal [post-office] savings [deposit]

KUN

【ta(meru) 貯める】save (money), lay up (one's income)
金を貯める *kane o tameru* save money
【takuwa(eru) 貯える】[usu. 蓄える] store up, lay in stock, save, lay aside
貯え *takuwae* store, reserve, stock; savings

SYNONYMS

● **store**

蔵 STORE → 2364
蓄 STORE UP → 2333
納 PUT AWAY → 1300

USAGE

tameru
貯める
save (money), lay up (one's income)
溜める
①ⓐ accumulate, heap up
ⓑ collect (stamps)
ⓒ store (esp. water)
② run up (a bill), leave undone

HOMOPHONES

tameru ⇨ 溜 662
takuwaeru ⇨ 蓄 2333
takuwae ⇨ 蓄 2333

NOTE

⇨ see also USAGE note at 蓄 2333

貼

1510 TEN CHŌ ha(ru) -ba(ri)

CH 贴 tiē

Radical	Strokes
貝 154	12-7-5
Grade	**Freq**
Reference	
◧ 1-7-5	

7-5 貝

COMPOUNDS

ⓐ [also 張る *haru*] [original meaning] stick, paste; apply to
ⓑ [also 張る *haru*] cover, line
ⓒ [usu. -張り *-bari*] [also suffix] covered with, lined with
貼付する *chōfu* (=*tenpu*) *suru* stick, paste, append
貼り付ける *haritsukeru* stick on, paste
貼り合わせる *hariawaseru* paste together
床にタイルを貼る *yuka ni tairu o haru* tile a floor
絹貼り *kinubari* lined with silk

HOMOPHONES

haru ⇨ 張 474
-bari ⇨ 張 474

NOTE

⇨ see USAGE note at 張 474

距 距 距 距

1511 KYO

CH 距 jù

Radical	Strokes
足 157	12-7-5
Grade	**Freq**
Jōyō	1178
◧ 1-7-5	

7-5 𧾷

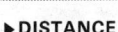

丨 ロ ロ 早 早 𧾷 𧾷 𧾷 𧾷 𧾷 距 距
1 2 3 4 5 6 7 8 9 10 11 12

▶**DISTANCE**

COMPOUNDS

❶ⓐ **distance, range, spacing**
ⓑ **be at a distance from, be apart**
角距 *kakkyo* angular distance
測距儀 *sokkyogi* range finder
輪距 *rinkyo* wheel track
高距 *kōkyo* elevation (above sea level)
距離 *kyori* distance, range; interval
❷ⓐ *anat* ankle
ⓑ [original meaning, now archaic] cockspur
距骨 *kyokotsu* anklebone, talus
距爪 *kyosō* cockspur

SYNONYMS

❶ⓐ **distance and interval**
間 INTERVAL → 3323
程 EXTENT → 1190

距

1512

▶**DISTANCE**
nonstandard for 距 1511

7-5 𧾷

躰

1513

▶**BODY** ▶**FORM**
nonstandard for 体 71

7-5 身

7-5
車

軸 軸 軸

1514 JIKU

CH 轴 zhóu zhòu

Radical	Strokes
車 159	12-7-5
Grade	Freq
Jōyō	1583
1 - 7 - 5	

一 ㄏ 亓 戸 百 亘 車 車 軋 軸 軸 軸
1 2 3 4 5 6 7 8 9 10 11 12

▶AXLE ▶AXIS

COMPOUNDS

❶ⓐ [original meaning] **axle, shaft, spindle**
ⓑ something resembling an axle in shape or function, as a scroll roller or pen holder
軸箱 *jikubako* axle box
車軸 *shajiku* wheel axle, axle
動軸 *dōjiku* driving axle
死軸 *shijiku* dead axle
軸木 *jikugi* splint; scroll roller
巻軸 *makijiku* scroll; scroll roller
ペン軸 *penjiku* penholder
❷ [also suffix]
ⓐ (line about which rotation occurs) **axis**
ⓑ *math* **axis**
ⓒ *optics* axis
ⓓ *anat* axis
軸線 *jikusen* axis, shaft line
地軸 *chijiku* axis of the earth
回転軸 *kaitenjiku* axis of revolution
左右軸 *sayūjiku* lateral axis
主軸 *shujiku* principal axis; main spindle [shaft]
座標軸 *zahyōjiku* coordinate axis
屈折軸 *kussetsujiku* axis of refraction
軸索 *jikusaku* axon, axis cylinder
❸ (central part) axis, center, pivot
枢軸 *sūjiku* central point, center; (mechanical) pivot, axis
新機軸 *shinkijiku* new departure, milestone, breakthrough
❹ⓐ scroll, scroll picture, *kakemono*
ⓑ counter for scrolls
軸物 *jikumono* scroll picture
掛け軸 *kakejiku* scroll
巻き物二軸 *makimono nijiku* two scrolls

INDEPENDENT

【**jiku** 軸】axle, shaft; holder; axis; *math* axis; *bot* axis, stem; scroll; *kakemono*; matchwood, matchstick
軸の *jiku no* axial
ペンの軸 *pen no jiku* penholder
茸の軸 *kinoko no jiku* stem of a mushroom
軸を掛ける *jiku o kakeru* hang a scroll picture

SYNONYMS

❶ **shafts**
棒 ROD → 983
桟 crosspiece → 932
錘 SPINDLE → 1744
❷ **line**
線 LINE → 1392
筋 THREADLIKE STRUCTURE → 2678
条 strip → 2200
脈 VEIN → 953
棒 straight line → 983

7-5
車

軽 輕 軽 轻

1515 KEI karu(i) karo(yaka)

CH 轻 qīng

Radical	Strokes
車 159	12-7-5
Grade	Freq
Jōyō-3	690
1 - 7 - 5	

一 ㄏ 亓 戸 百 亘 車 車 軒 軽 軽 軽
1 2 3 4 5 6 7 8 9 10 11 12

▶LIGHT

COMPOUNDS

❶ [also prefix] [original meaning] (not heavy) **light**
軽量 *keiryō* light weight
軽油 *keiyu* gas oil, light oil
軽金属 *keikinzoku* light metals
❷ⓐ (not intense) **light, slight**
ⓑ [also prefix] (not difficult or serious) **light, easy, simple**
軽震 *keishin* weak earthquake
軽傷 *keishō* slight injury
軽減する *keigen suru* reduce, lighten, mitigate
軽便 *keiben* convenience, simplicity
軽食 *keishoku* light meal, snack
軽易な *keii na* easy, light, simple
軽労働 *keirōdō* light labor
軽犯罪 *keihanzai* minor offense
軽音楽 *keiongaku* light music
❸ⓐ light-headed, frivolous, thoughtless, rash
ⓑ (moving quickly) light-footed, nimble,

agile, simple
軽率な *keisotsu na* rash, light-headed, careless
軽薄な *keihaku na* insincere, frivolous, flippant, fickle
軽快な *keikai na* light, nimble, quick; cheerful

❹ make light of, think little of
軽視する *keishi suru* make light of, despise; neglect
軽蔑 *keibetsu* contempt, disdain

KUN

【karu(i) 軽い】 (not heavy) light, lightweight; (not intense) light, slight; (not difficult or serious) light, easy, simple; light (taste); (not important) light, insignificant
軽さ *karusa* lightness
軽軽と *karugaru to* easily
身軽な *migaru na* light, agile, nimble
気軽な *kigaru na* lighthearted, cheerful; ready
手軽な *tegaru na* easy, light, plain
軽い犯罪 *karui hanzai* minor offense
尻軽な女 *shirigaru na onna* wanton girl

【karo(yaka) 軽やか】
karoyaka na 軽やかな light, nimble, airy

SYNONYMS

❷ⓐ less in degree
微 SLIGHT → 639
弱 WEAK → 1167
低 LOW → 73
薄 THIN → 2370
浅 SHALLOW → 389

ⓑ easy
簡 SIMPLE → 2721
易 EASY (without difficulty) → 2411
安 easy (without effort) → 2171

❹ disdain
侮 despise → 82

酢

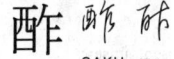

1516 SAKU su

Ⓒ 酢 zuò cù

Radical	Strokes
酉 164	12-7-5
Grade	**Freq**
Jōyō	1568
◧ 1 - 7 - 5	

7-5 酉

▶VINEGAR

COMPOUNDS

● [formerly also 醋 1591] [original meaning] **vinegar**
酢酸 *sakusan* acetic acid

KUN

【su 酢】 [also suffix] vinegar
酢の物 *sunomono* pickled dish
酢蛸 *sudako* (sliced and) pickled octopus
酢料理 *suryōri* pickled dish
醸造酢 *jōzōsu* brewed vinegar

SYNONYMS

● sour substances
酸 ACID → 1563

● seasonings
油 OIL → 341
塩 SALT → 631
糖 SUGAR → 1403

解

1517 KAI GE to(ku) to(kasu) to(keru) hodo(ku)▲ waka(ru)▲

Ⓒ 解 jiě jiè xiè

Radical	Strokes
角 148	13-7-6
Grade	**Freq**
Jōyō-5	191
◧ 1 - 7 - 6	

7-6 角

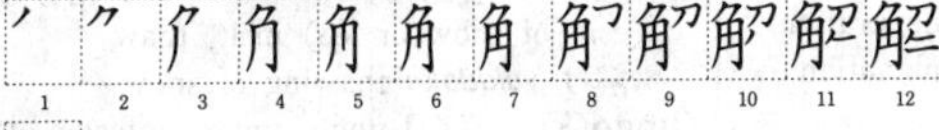

▶TAKE APART ▶DISSOLVE ▶CLARIFY

COMPOUNDS

❶ [original meaning] (break into component parts) **take apart, resolve, dissolve, separate, dissect**
解体 *kaitai* dismantling (a machine), scrapping; dissolution, disorganization; dissection
解剖 *kaibō* dissection, autopsy; analysis
解像力 *kaizōryoku* resolving power (of a lens)
解析 *kaiseki* analysis, analytical research
分解する *bunkai suru* take apart [to pieces]; analyze, decompose; be decomposed, break down
瓦解 *gakai* collapse, breakup, downfall

電解 *denkai* electrolysis
❷ **dissolve, melt, liquefy**
解凍 *kaitō* thawing, defrosting
溶解する *yōkai suru* dissolve, liquefy; melt, fuse
潮解 *chōkai* deliquescence
融解 *yūkai* fusion, melting
氷解する *hyōkai suru* melt away, be cleared [dispelled]
❸ⓐ (cause to disperse) **dissolve (a meeting), break up (an organization), dispel**
ⓑ (take away the binding power) **dissolve, cancel (a contract), release, lift (a ban)**
解散 *kaisan* breakup, dispersion; dissolution
解組する *kaiso suru* break up an organization
解放する *kaihō suru* release, set free
解消 *kaishō* liquidation, annulment, solution
解除 *kaijo* removal [lifting] (of a ban), cancellation; release, acquittal
解約 *kaiyaku* dissolution [cancellation] of a contract
解禁 *kaikin* removal of a ban; opening of the fishing [hunting] season
❹ untie, undo, unfasten
解纜 *kairan* unmooring, sailing off
❺ⓐ **release from office, discharge, dismiss**
ⓑ (release from pain) relieve, alleviate
解任する *kainin suru* release from office, dismiss, discharge
解雇する *kaiko suru* discharge, dismiss, fire
解毒剤 *gedokuzai* antidote
解熱 *genetsu* alleviation of fever
解脱 *gedatsu Buddhism* deliverance (of one's soul), salvation
緩解 *kankai* relief [remission] (of pain)
❻ⓐ **clarify, explain, elucidate, interpret**
ⓑ **explanation, commentary**
解説 *kaisetsu* explanation, commentary
解釈 *kaishaku* interpretation, explanation
解明する *kaimei suru* explain, elucidate
弁解 *benkai* explanation, vindication, justification, excuse
図解 *zukai* explanatory diagram, illustration
詳解 *shōkai* detailed [minute] explanation, full commentary
注解 *chūkai* annotation, explanatory notes
❼ⓐ **solve, find a solution, settle**
ⓑ **solution, answer**
解決 *kaiketsu* solution, settlement
解答する *kaitō suru* solve, answer
解法 *kaihō* solution, key to solution
和解 *wakai* reconciliation, amicable settlement
正解 *seikai* right answer, correct solution
❽ **understand, comprehend**
理解する *rikai suru* understand, comprehend
見解 *kenkai* opinion, view
了解 *ryōkai* understanding, comprehension; consent
誤解 *gokai* misunderstanding, misconception
難解な *nankai na* difficult, hard to understand
不可解な *fukakai na* incomprehensible, inexplicable, baffling

INDEPENDENT

【kai 解】 explanation, commentary; solution; *math* root (of an equation)
解を示す *kai o shimesu* show the solution
解と係数の関係 *kai to keisū no kankei* relation between the roots and coefficients
【kaisuru 解する】 understand, comprehend; interpret
人語を解する *jingo o kaisuru* understand human speech
善意に解する *zen'i ni kaisuru* take it in a favorable sense
【gesenai 解せない】 be beyond understanding

KUN

【to(ku) 解く】
① undo, unfasten, unloosen, unsew
解き放す *tokihanasu* set free
② dissolve, cancel, release, lift
禁を解く *kin o toku* lift [remove] a ban
③ solve, work out
謎解き *nazotoki* solution of a riddle
④ *literary* relieve (a person) of a post
任を解かれる *nin o tokareru* be relieved of one's post
【to(kasu) 解かす】 [formerly also 融かす] *vt* melt (snow or ice), thaw (out)
氷を解かす *kōri o tokasu* melt ice
【to(keru) 解ける】
vi
① come loose, come undone
靴紐が解けた *Kutsuhimo ga toketa* The shoestrings came untied
② be allayed, relent
③ be solved, be resolved, be cleared
解けない問題 *tokenai mondai* insoluble problem
④ [formerly 融ける, sometimes also 溶ける] (esp. of snow or ice) melt, thaw
雪解け *yukidoke* thawing of snow
【hodo(ku) 解く】 undo, untie, unfasten, loosen; unravel, unknit
結び目を解く *musubime o hodoku* undo a knot
【waka(ru) 解る】
[usu. 分かる, sometimes also 判る]
①ⓐ (grasp the meaning of) understand, comprehend, see
ⓑ (be sympathetic toward) understand, show understanding for (another's feelings)

解り *wakari* understanding
解り難い *wakarinikui* hard to understand, incomprehensible, unintelligible
物解りの良い *monowakari no ii* understanding; sensible
②ⓐ know, tell, recognize
ⓑ be made known, be brought to light
先の事は解らない *saki no koto wa wakaranai* cannot tell what will happen in the future
身元が解る *mimoto ga wakaru* be identified
③ appreciate
音楽が解る *ongaku ga wakaru* have an ear [appreciation] for music

SYNONYMS

❶ **separate**
割 DIVIDE → 1816
分 DIVIDE → 1972
析 ANALYZE → 862
別 SEPARATE → 1117
離 SEPARATE → 1836
隔 partition → 671

❷ **liquefy**
溶 DISSOLVE, MELT → 664
融 FUSE → 1831

❸ⓐ **disperse**
散 SCATTER → 1702

❺ⓐ **dismiss**
免 discharge → 2067
罷 DISMISS → 2617

❻ **explain**
釈 ELUCIDATE → 1484
明 make clear → 855
説 EXPLAIN → 1547
講 expound → 1619
注 annotate → 325

❼ **answer**
答 ANSWER → 2681
返 reply → 3060
応 RESPOND → 3066

❽ **know and understand**
諒 UNDERSTAND → 1575
了 COMPREHEND → 3350
分かる understand → 1972
得 gain understanding of → 477
知 KNOW → 1127
通 know thoroughly → 3109
悟 AWAKE TO → 419

USAGE

❶ **toku**
解く
① undo, unfasten, unloosen, unsew
② dissolve, cancel, release, lift
③ solve, work out
④ *literary* relieve (a person) of a post
説く
① explain
② preach, advocate; persuade
溶く
vt
① (cause to pass into solution) dissolve (paint)
② whip an egg
梳く
comb (one's hair)

❷ **tokasu**
解かす
[formerly also 融かす] *vt* melt (snow or ice), thaw (out)
融かす
[now usu. 解かす] *vt* melt (snow or ice), thaw (out)
溶かす
vt
① (cause to pass into solution or to turn liquid) dissolve, melt, liquefy
② [formerly 熔かす or 鎔かす] melt (up) (metals), fuse, smelt
熔かす
[now usu. 溶かす] *vt* melt (up) (metals), fuse, smelt
鎔かす
[now usu. 溶かす] *vt* melt (up) (metals), fuse, smelt
梳かす
comb (one's hair)

❸ **tokeru**
解ける
vi
① come loose, come undone
② be allayed, relent
③ be solved, be resolved, be cleared
④ [formerly 融ける, sometimes also 溶ける] (esp. of snow or ice) melt, thaw
融ける
[now usu. 解ける, sometimes also 溶ける] *vi* (esp. of snow or ice) melt, thaw
溶ける
vi
① (pass into solution) dissolve
②ⓐ [formerly 熔ける or 鎔ける] (of metals) melt (up), fuse, smelt
ⓑ [formerly 融ける, usu. 解ける] (esp. of snow or ice) melt, thaw
熔ける
[now usu. 溶ける] *vi* (of metals) melt (up), fuse, smelt
鎔ける
[now usu. 溶ける] *vi* (of metals) melt (up), fuse, smelt

HOMOPHONES

toku ⇨ 説 1547 溶 664 梳 964
tokasu ⇨ 融 1831 溶 664 熔 1058 鎔 1762 梳 964
tokeru ⇨ 融 1831 溶 664 熔 1058 鎔 1762
wakaru ⇨ 分 1972 判 1122

NOTE

⇨ see also USAGE note at 分 1972

7-6 角

触 觸 触 觸

Ⓒ 触 chù

1518 SHOKU fu(reru) sawa(ru)

Radical	Strokes
角 148	13-7-6
Grade	**Freq**
Jōyō	1165

1 - 7 - 6

ノ ク ⺈ 角 角 角 角 角 角 角 角 角 触 (strokes 1–13)

▶TOUCH

COMPOUNDS

❶ⓐ **touch, contact**

ⓑ **perceive by touching, feel**

接触 *sesshoku* contact, touch

一触即発 *isshokusokuhatsu* touch-and-go situation, hair-trigger crisis

感触 *kanshoku* (sense of) touch, feeling

触角 *shokkaku* feeler, antenna

触覚 *shokkaku* sense of touch

触媒 *shokubai* catalyst, catalyzer

❷ conflict with, violate

抵触する *teishoku suru* conflict with; be contrary to; be incompatible with

KUN

【fu(reru) 触れる】 touch, feel; come in contact with, meet; touch on, mention; conflict with, violate; announce, hawk

触れ *fure* proclamation, official notice; touch

手を触れるな *Te o fureru na* Hands off!

目に触れる *me ni fureru* catch the eye, attract attention

要点に触れる *yōten ni fureru* come to [touch on] the point

法に触れる *hō ni fureru* violate the law

触れ込み *furekomi* (exaggerated) introduction

【sawa(ru) 触る】

① touch, feel

触り *sawari* touch, feel; impression (of a person); most impressive passage, punch line

肌触り *hadazawari* touch, feel

② become involved in

触らぬ神に祟り無し *Sawaranu kami ni tatari nashi* Let sleeping dogs lie

寄ると触ると *yoru to sawaru to* whenever they come together

SYNONYMS

❶ **touch**

接 CONTACT → 500

当てる apply → 2177

USAGE

❶ **sawaru**

触る

① touch, feel

② become involved in

障る

① hinder, interfere with

② affect, harm, jar on

❷ **sawari**

触り

① touch, feel

② impression (of a person)

③ most impressive passage, punch line

障り

① hindrance, obstacle

②ⓐ harm, bad effect

ⓑ sickness

HOMOPHONES

sawaru ⇨ 障 715

sawari ⇨ 障 715

該 該 該 該

1519 GAI

Ⓒⓗ 该 gāi

Radical	Strokes
言 149	13-7-6
Grade	**Freq**
Jōyō	1698
◨ 1-7-6	

7-6 言

Stroke order: ` 一 ニ 三 言 言 言 言 言 訁 訁 該 該 (1–13)

▶CORRESPOND TO

COMPOUNDS

❶ⓐ **correspond to, conform to, apply to, fall under**

ⓑ [also prefix] **the said, the one in question, that**

該当する *gaitō suru* come under, be applicable to

当該 *tōgai* the said, the concerned

該案 *gaian* the said proposal

該問題 *gaimondai* the said problem, the matter in question

❷ inclusive, extensive

該博な *gaihaku na* extensive (knowledge), profound (learning)

SYNONYMS

❶ⓐ **correspond to**

準 apply correspondingly → 2856

当 be equivalent → 2177

ⓑ **this and that**

当 THE PRESENT → 2177

本 THIS → 3502

今 THIS (week, etc.) → 1968

同 the same → 2987

之 this → 3420

是 this → 2436

爾 THAT → 3587

彼 that → 290

詭

1520 KI

Ⓒⓗ  guǐ

Radical	Strokes
言 149	13-7-6
Grade	**Freq**
Reference	
◨ 1-7-6	

7-6 言

COMPOUNDS

● [now also 奇 2217] [original meaning] cheat, deceive, defraud

詭弁 *kiben* sophism, sophistry

詭計 *kikei* artifice, trick

詰 詰 詰

1521 KITSU tsu(meru) tsu(me) -zu(me) tsu(maru) tsu(mu)

Ⓒⓗ 诘 jié jí

Radical	Strokes
言 149	13-7-6
Grade	**Freq**
Jōyō	1122
◨ 1-7-6	

7-6 言

Stroke order: ` 一 ニ 三 言 言 言 言 言 計 計 詰 詰 (1–13)

▶REPRIMAND ▶STUFF

COMPOUNDS

❶ [original meaning] **reprimand, reprove, censure, rebuke**

詰責する *kisseki suru* [rare] reproach, reprove, reprimand

面詰する *menkitsu suru* reprimand (a person) personally

難詰する *nankitsu suru* blame, censure, reproach

❷ **question closely, press a person hard with questions, interrogate**

詰問する *kitsumon suru* cross-examine, cross-question, question closely

❸ [rare] cramped, confined

詰屈した *kikkutsu shita* rugged

KUN

【tsu(meru) 詰める】

①ⓐ (fill by packing closely) stuff, fill, pack into, cram; charge
ⓑ (fill an aperture) stuff (up), stop up, block up
詰に詰める *bin ni tsumeru* fill a bottle
詰め合わせ *tsumeawase* combination, assortment
詰め込む *tsumekomu* cram, stuff, pack
詰め物 *tsumemono* stuffing
息を詰める *iki o tsumeru* hold one's breath
② place close together; sit close; write close
詰め掛ける *tsumekakeru* crowd (a house); throng to (a door)
行間を詰める *gyōkan o tsumeru* crowd the lines
③ be stationed at, be on duty, attend office
詰めている *tsumete iru* be in attendance [on duty]
詰め所 *tsumesho* station, office, guardroom
④ shorten; cut down, reduce, economize
指を詰める *yubi o tsumeru* cut off a person's finger
暮らしを詰める *kurashi o tsumeru* cut down housekeeping expenses
⑤ checkmate, mate
王を詰める *ō o tsumeru* checkmate the king
⑥ keep doing, keep up, go on with
詰めて通う *tsumete kayou* frequent tirelessly
根を詰める *kon o tsumeru* strain one's nerve
⑦ finalize
問題を詰める *mondai o tsumeru* work toward a solution to a problem

【tsu(me) 詰め】

① stuffing, packing, stopper
②ⓐ final stage [move]
ⓑ checkmating
大詰め *ōzume* finale, end
詰め将棋 *tsumeshōgi* chess problem
③ edge, approach (of a bridge)
橋の西詰め *hashi no nishizume* western edge of a bridge

【-zu(me) -詰め】

① [also suffix]
ⓐ packed in, bottled in, boxed in
ⓑ filled with
缶詰め *kanzume* canned goods, canning; cooping-up, confining
箱詰めの *hakozume no* packed in a case; boxed (candies)
四百字詰め *yonhyakujizume* with 400 characters
② persisting in doing something
立ち詰めでいる *tachizume de iru* keep standing
理詰め *rizume* reasoning, cogent argument
③ [suffix] on duty at
本省詰め *honshōzume* service at the Head Office

【tsu(maru) 詰まる】

①ⓐ be stuffed, be full, be packed
ⓑ be stopped [plugged] up, be [get] blocked, get clogged
ぎっしり詰まっている *gisshiri tsumatte iru* be crammed, be packed full
鼻詰まり *hanazumari* nasal congestion
声を詰まらせて *koe o tsumarasete* in a chocked voice
② be shortened, become shorter; contract
詰まり *tsumari* in short, after all; blockade; stuffing; ultimate
それは洗うと詰まる *Sore wa arau to tsumaru* It shrinks when washed
③ [also suffix] be driven to a corner, be cornered; be hard up
言葉に詰まる *kotoba ni tsumaru* be at a loss for words
返答に詰まる *hentō ni tsumaru* be embarrassed for a reply
行き詰まる *ikizumaru* reach the limits, come to the end of one's tether
金詰まり *kanezumari* money distress, shortage of money

【tsu(mu) 詰む】

① be packed, become fine [close]
目の詰んだ *me no tsunda* fine(-grained), close
② be checkmated
詰み *tsumi* checkmate

SYNONYMS

❶ blame and accuse
責 BLAME → 2467
叱 SCOLD → 182
難 find fault with → 1838
批 CRITICIZE → 250
劾 EXPOSE CRIMES → 1266
弾 impeach → 572

❷ inquire
問 QUESTION → 3320
聞く ask → 3326
質 query → 2808
尋ねる INQUIRE → 2322
伺う INQUIRE (*humble*) → 69
諮 CONSULT → 1596

【tsumeru】

① **fill**
充 FILL → 2014
満 fill → 607

HOMOPHONES

tsumu ⇨ 積 1236

NOTE

⇨ see USAGE note at 積 1236

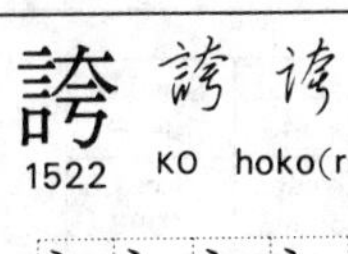

1522 KO hoko(ru)

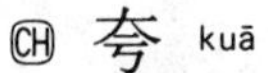

Radical	Strokes
言 149	13-7-6
Grade	**Freq**
Jōyō	1190
◧ 1 - 7 - 6	

7-6 言

1 2 3 4 5 6 7 8 9 10 11 12 13

▶**BOAST**

COMPOUNDS

ⓐ [original meaning] **boast, brag, be proud**

ⓑ **exaggerate, overstate**

誇称 *koshō* boasting, exaggeration
誇示 *koji* ostentation, display, showing off
誇色 *koshoku* proud countenance
誇張する *kochō suru* exaggerate, overstate, magnify
誇大 *kodai* exaggeration, magnification

KUN

【hoko(ru) 誇る】 boast, brag, take pride in, peacock oneself

誇り *hokori* pride
誇らしい *hokorashii* proud
誇り顔 *hokorigao* triumphant look
勝ち誇る *kachihokoru* be triumphant
咲き誇る *sakihokoru* be in all glory

SYNONYMS

ⓐ **boasting and arrogance**

慢 ARROGANT → 686

誠 誠 誠 诚

1523 SEI makoto

Ⓒ 诚 chéng

Radical	Strokes
言 149	13-7-6
Grade	**Freq**
Jōyō-6	1199
◧ 1 - 7 - 6	

7-6 言

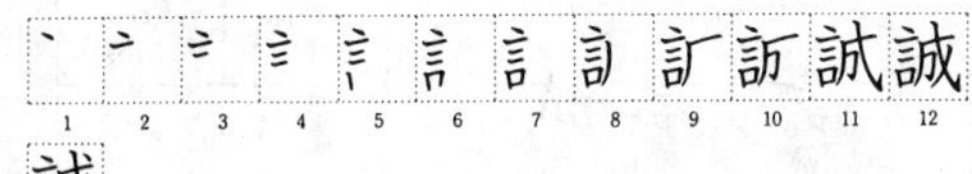

1 2 3 4 5 6 7 8 9 10 11 12 13

▶**SINCERITY**

COMPOUNDS

● **sincerity, true heart, honesty, fidelity**

誠実 *seijitsu* sincerity, honesty, faith
誠意 *seii* sincerity, good faith
忠誠 *chūsei* faithfulness, fidelity
至誠 *shisei* sincerity, devotion

KUN

【makoto 誠】

① sincerity, true heart, honesty, fidelity

誠を尽くす *makoto o tsukusu* do with sincerity

② [sometimes also 実 or 真] truth, reality

誠の *makoto no* true, genuine
誠に *makoto ni* truly, really; very, extremely
誠しやかに *makotoshiyaka ni* plausibly, with seeming truth
嘘か誠か *uso ka makoto ka* true or false

SYNONYMS

● **fidelity**

実 faithfulness → 2225
信 fidelity → 100
忠 LOYALTY → 2433
義 faith → 2338
操 constancy → 769
節 moral integrity → 2691
孝 FILIAL PIETY → 3205
悌 BROTHERLY LOVE → 424

USAGE

makoto

誠

① sincerity, true heart, honesty, fidelity
② [sometimes also 実 or 真] truth, reality

実

[usu. 誠, sometimes also 真] truth, reality

真

[usu. 誠, sometimes also 実] truth, reality

HOMOPHONES

makoto ⇨ 実 2225 真 2111

7-6 言

詩 詩 诗

1524 SHI

CH 诗 shī

Radical	Strokes
言 149	13-7-6
Grade	**Freq**
Jōyō-3	1093
1 - 7 - 6	

1 2 3 4 5 6 7 8 9 10 11 12 13

▶**POETRY**

COMPOUNDS

ⓐ [also suffix] [original meaning] **poetry, poem, verse**

ⓑ Chinese poetry [poem]

詩人 *shijin* poet
詩情 *shijō* poetic sentiment, poetical interest
詩集 *shishū* anthology of poems
詩的な *shiteki na* poetic
叙事詩 *jojishi* epic (poem), epic poetry
詩吟 *shigin* reciting Chinese poems
詩歌 *shiika* (=*shika*) Chinese and Japanese poetry; poems
唐詩 *tōshi* Tang poetry

INDEPENDENT

【shi 詩】 poetry, poem, lines, verse, rhyme; Chinese poetry [poem]
詩を作る *shi o tsukuru* compose a poem

SYNONYMS

ⓐ **poetry**
歌 Japanese poetry → 1825
俳 HAIKU → 112
句 HAIKU → 2967

7-6 言

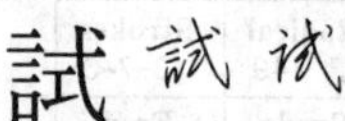

1525 SHI kokoro(miru) tame(su)

CH 试 shì

Radical	Strokes
言 149	13-7-6
Grade	**Freq**
Jōyō-4	389
1 - 7 - 6	

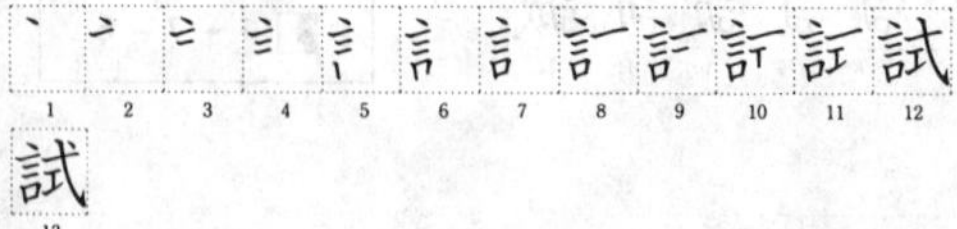

13

▶**TRY**

COMPOUNDS

❶ⓐ [original meaning] (attempt to do) **try, attempt**

ⓑ (test the quality of) **try, test, sample**

試案 *shian* tentative plan, draft
試作 *shisaku* trial manufacture
試算する *shisan suru* make a trial calculation
試写 *shisha* preview, private showing
試食 *shishoku* sampling (of food)
試験 *shiken* test, examination
試練 *shiren* trial, test, probation
試運転 *shiunten* test run

❷ abbrev. of 試験 *shiken*: examination, school test

入試 *nyūshi* entrance examination
追試 *tsuishi* supplementary examination
模試 *moshi* sham examination

❸ used phonetically for *shi*

試合 *shiai* match, game

KUN

【kokoro(miru) 試みる】 try, attempt, test
試み *kokoromi* trial, attempt, test
抵抗を試みる *teikō o kokoromiru* offer [put up] resistance

【tame(su) 試す】 try, test, experiment
試し *tameshi* trial, test, try
力を試す *chikara o tamesu* try one's strength

SYNONYMS

❶ **try**
験 TEST → 1833

❷ **examination**
検 examination → 986

COMPOUND FORMATION

試合 *shiai*

試合 'match, game' consists of 試 ❸, used phonetically for 為 *shi*, the verb stem of 為る *suru* 'to do'. It derives from 為合う *shiau* 'do something to each other'.

NOTE

⇨ see COMPOUND FORMATION for 試練 *shiren* ⇨ 練 1375

詳 詳 詳

1526 SHŌ kuwa(shii) tsumabi(raka)▲

Ⓒⓗ 详 xiáng

Radical	Strokes
言 149	13-7-6
Grade	**Freq**
Jōyō	1422
◧ 1-7-6	

7-6 言

▶**DETAILED**

COMPOUNDS

ⓐ **detailed, minute, full**

ⓑ [original meaning] explain [investigate] in detail

ⓒ know in detail

詳細 *shōsai* details, particulars
詳密な *shōmitsu na* minute, detailed, elaborate
詳察 *shōsatsu* careful observation
詳報 *shōhō* detailed report
詳論する *shōron suru* explain in detail
未詳の *mishō no* unknown
不詳 *fushō* unknown, unidentified

KUN

【**kuwa(shii) 詳しい**】 detailed, minute; complete, full; exact, accurate; know well (about), be (well) versed in

詳しさ *kuwashisa* detailedness; completeness; knowledge
詳しい話 *kuwashii hanashi* detailed account
この辺の地理に詳しい *kono hen no chiri ni kuwashii* know every inch of this neighborhood

【**tsumabi(raka) 詳らか**】

tsumabiraka na 詳らかな detailed; accurate; clearly known

詳らかでない *tsumabiraka de nai* be unknown
事情を詳らかにする *jijō o tsumabiraka ni suru* reveal the circumstances

SYNONYMS

ⓐ **detailed**

細 MINUTE → 1333
密 CLOSE → 2292
精 meticulous → 1366

話 話 話

1527 WA hana(su) hanashi

Ⓒⓗ 话 huà

Radical	Strokes
言 149	13-7-6
Grade	**Freq**
Jōyō-2	151
◧ 1-7-6	

7-6 言

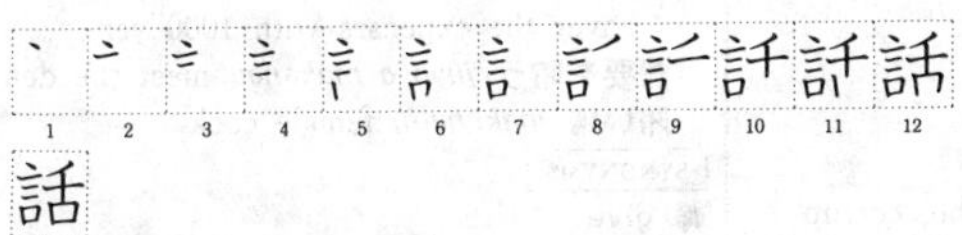

▶**SPEAK**

COMPOUNDS

❶ⓐ [original meaning] **speak, talk, converse**

ⓑ conversation, speech, talk

話者 *washa* speaker, narrator
会話 *kaiwa* conversation
対話 *taiwa* dialogue, conversation
電話 *denwa* telephone; phone call
談話 *danwa* talk, conversation
話題 *wadai* topic [subject] of conversation
世話 *sewa* help, aid, good offices; care; everyday affairs
閑話休題 *kanwakyūdai* to return to the subject

❷ⓐ **story, tale, fable**

ⓑ counter for stories

神話 *shinwa* myth, mythology
童話 *dōwa* nursery tale, fairy tale
民話 *minwa* folk tale, folk story
実話 *jitsuwa* true story
挿話 *sōwa* anecdote
第五話 *daigowa* story No.5

KUN

【**hana(su) 話す**】 speak, talk; tell; consult with

話し合う *hanashiau* discuss, talk over, consult with
事情を話す *jijō o hanasu* explain the situation

【**hanashi 話**】 [also suffix] talk, conversation, speech; chat; rumor, report; consultation, agreement

話の種 *hanashi no tane* topic of conversation
笑い話 *waraibanashi* funny [humorous] story

昔話 *mukashibanashi* legend, old tale
思い出話 *omoidebanashi* reminiscent talk

SYNONYMS

❶ⓐ speak and say
言 SAY → 1941
云 say → 1931
口 give mouth to → 3382
申す SPEAK HUMBLY → 3507
弁 SPEAK ELOQUENTLY → 2004
語る TELL → 1543
談 TALK → 1569
述 STATE → 3075
陳 SET FORTH → 540

❷ⓐ stories
談 account → 1569
語 tale → 1543
説 narrative → 1547

COMPOUND FORMATION

世話 *sewa*
世話 'help, aid, etc.' originally meant society (世) chat (話 ❶ⓑ) or daily gossip. It is not clear how this is related to its current meaning of helping or taking care.

NOTE

⇨ see COMPOUND FORMATION for
閑話休題 *kanwakyūdai* ⇨ 閑 3322
挿話 *sōwa* ⇨ 挿 431

7-6 言

該
1528

▶CORRESPOND TO
nonstandard for 該 1519

7-6 言

誕

incorrect stroke count ⇨ see 1579

7-6 貝

賄
1529 WAI makana(u)

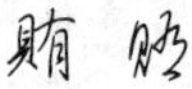

CH 贿 huì

Radical	Strokes
貝 154	13-7-6
Grade	**Freq**
Jōyō	1686
1-7-6	

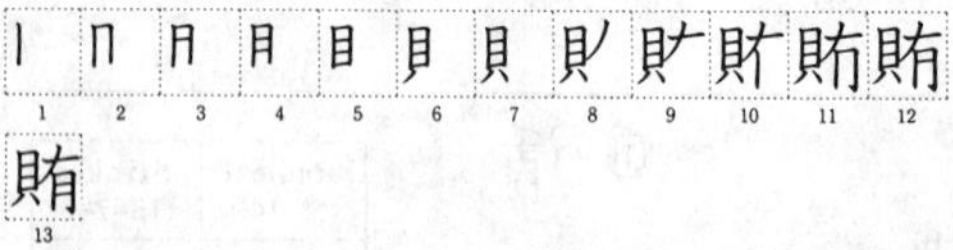

▶BRIBE

COMPOUNDS

● bribe
賄賂 *wairo* bribe, bribery
収賄 *shūwai* acceptance of a bribe, corruption
贈賄する *zōwai suru* bribe, corrupt
贈収賄 *zōshūwai* corruption, bribery

KUN

【makana(u) 賄う】 manage to cover (expenses), meet (the demand); provide meals [board], cater
賄い *makanai* board, meals; boarding, catering; cook
千円で賄う *sen'en de makanau* manage to cover the expenses with 1000 yen
需要を賄う *juyō o makanau* meet the demand
賄い婦 *makanaifu* female cook

SYNONYMS

● give
贈 PRESENT A GIFT → 1634
呈 PRESENT → 2189
進 present to a superior → 3121
賜 DEIGN TO GIVE → 1585
授 CONFER → 492
与 GIVE → 3421
上 give (to superior or others) → 3404
下 give (to inferior or speaker) → 3378
呉れる give (to speaker) → 2549

賊 1530 ZOKU

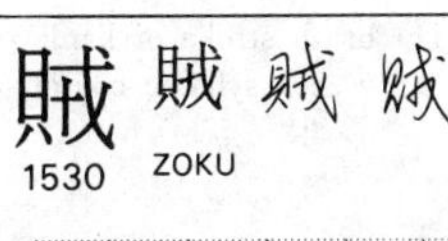

Ⓒⓗ 賊 zéi

Radical	Strokes
貝 154	13-7-6
Grade	**Freq**
Jōyō	1835
◧ 1-7-6	

7-6 貝

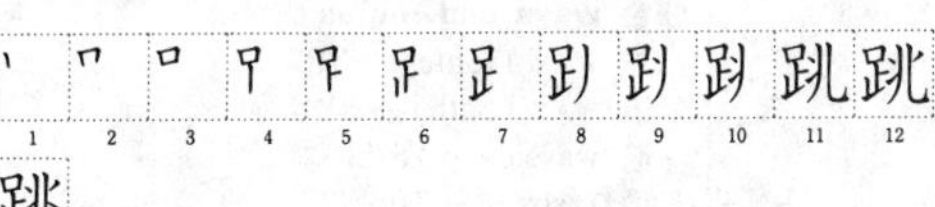

▶**BANDIT**

COMPOUNDS

❶ⓐ **bandit, robber, pirate, thief**
ⓑ **rebel, traitor, insurgent**
賊徒 *zokuto* bandit, robber; rebels, traitors
盗賊 *tōzoku* thief, robber, bandit
海賊 *kaizoku* pirate
山賊 *sanzoku* bandit, mountain robber
匪賊 *hizoku* bandit
賊軍 *zokugun* insurgents, rebel army
逆賊 *gyakuzoku* rebel, traitor, insurgent
国賊 *kokuzoku* traitor (to the country)

❷ [original meaning] harm, injure, kill
賊虐 *zokugyaku* damage and ill-treatment

INDEPENDENT

【zoku 賊】 thief, burglar; rebel, insurgent
賊を捕らえる *zoku o toraeru* arrest [catch] a thief
【zokusuru 賊する】 harm, hurt, kill

SYNONYMS

❶ⓐ **thieves**
盗 thief → 2670
泥 petty thief → 326

賊 1531

▶**BANDIT**
nonstandard for 賊 1530

7-6 貝

跳 1532 CHŌ ha(neru) to(bu) -to(bi)

Ⓒⓗ 跳 tiào

Radical	Strokes
足 157	13-7-6
Grade	**Freq**
Jōyō	1855
◧ 1-7-6	

7-6 𧾷

▶**JUMP**

COMPOUNDS

❶ [original meaning] **jump, leap, spring**
跳躍する *chōyaku suru* jump, leap, spring
跳馬 *chōba* long horse (vault)
反跳 *hanchō phys* recoil
❷ be rampant
跳梁 *chōryō* rampancy, domination; [original meaning] jumping about

KUN

【ha(neru) 跳ねる】
①ⓐ leap, spring, jump, hop
ⓑ bound, rebound, recoil
ⓒ (of the market) jump (to)
跳ね起きる *haneokiru* jump up, spring up
跳び跳ねる *tobihaneru* jump up and down, hop
跳ね返る *hanekaeru* rebound, bounce; (of the market) recover
② (of the theater) be over, close
【to(bu) 跳ぶ】
ⓐ jump, leap, spring
ⓑ jump [leap] over, vault
縄跳び *nawatobi* rope skipping, rope jumping
跳び過ぎる *tobisugiru* overleap, overjump
【-to(bi) -跳び】 [also suffix] jump
棒高跳び *bōtakatobi* pole vault [jump]
背面跳び *haimentobi* backward jump, Fosbury flop

SYNONYMS

❶ **jump**
躍 LEAP → 1658

USAGE

haneru
跳ねる
①ⓐ leap, spring, jump, hop

ⓑ bound, rebound, recoil
ⓒ (of the market) jump (to)
② (of the theater) be over, close
撥ねる
①ⓐ flip, splash
ⓑ strike, knock down
② reject, turn down
③ sweep up (in brush stroke of kanji)
④ pronounce ん *n* as a syllabic consonant

HOMOPHONES

haneru ⇨ 撥 734
tobu ⇨ 飛 3572 翔 1357

NOTE

⇨ see also USAGE note at 飛 3572

7-6
足

路 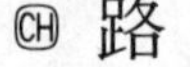

1533 RO RU▲ -ji michi▲

Ⓒⓗ 路 lù

Radical	Strokes
足 157	13-7-6
Grade	**Freq**
Jōyō-3	359

1-7-6

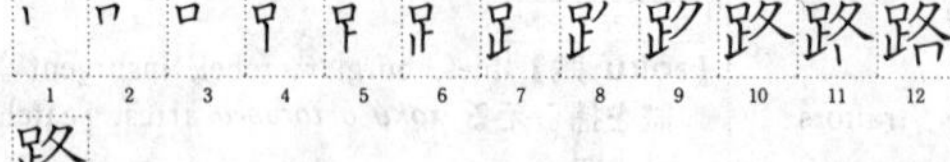

路
13

▶**ROAD**

COMPOUNDS

❶ⓐ [also suffix] **road, route, way**
ⓑ journey, traveling
路上 *rojō* on the road, road
路面 *romen* road surface
路線 *rosen* route, way, line
道路 *dōro* road, street, way
空路 *kūro* air route, airway
線路 *senro* (railway) line, track
通路 *tsūro* passage, pathway, alley, aisle
悪路 *akuro* bad road
滑走路 *kassōro* runway
路用 *royō* traveling expenses
路銀 *rogin* traveling expenses
❷ *elec* circuit, wire
回路 *kairo* (electric) circuit
短路 *tanro* short circuit
閉路 *heiro* closed circuit
断路 *danro* disconnection (of a wire)
❸ line of reasoning, logic
理路 *riro* reasoning, argument
❹ important position, high rank
要路 *yōro* important position, the authorities; important road
当路 *tōro* the authorities
❺ used phonetically for *ru*, esp. in the transliteration of foreign names
路加 *ruka* St. Luke

KUN

【-ji -路】
①ⓐ way (to), route—often used as suffix after names of provinces in old Japan
ⓑ suffix indicating number of days of a journey
旅路 *tabiji* journey
伊勢路 *iseji* way to Ise
五日路 *itsukaji* five days' journey
② suffix indicating age in tens of years
五十路 *isoji* 50 years old
【michi 路】[now usu. 道] road, avenue, boulevard
町を貫く路 *machi o tsuranuku michi* road passing through the town

SYNONYMS

❶ⓐ **ways and routes**
途 WAY (route) → 3107
道 WAY (path) → 3134
筋 wayside → 2678
通り street → 3109
街 city street → 576
辻 CROSSROADS → 3192
岐 forked road → 241
径 PATH → 291
軌 TRACK → 1445
線 LINE → 1392
❺ **phonetic [r]**
呂 PHONETIC [ro] → 2187
羅 PHONETIC [ra] → 2622

HOMOPHONES

michi ⇨ 道 3134

NOTE

⇨ see USAGE note at 道 3134

跡 迹° 跡 跡

1534 SEKI ato

Ⓒⓗ 迹 jī

Radical	Strokes
足 157	13-7-6
Grade	**Freq**
Jōyō	899
◧ 1 - 7 - 6	

7-6 足

▶TRACE

COMPOUNDS

❶ [formerly also 蹟 1635]

ⓐ (mark left by something) **trace(s), track, mark, footprint, trail**

ⓑ (sign of former presence) **traces, ruins, remains**

足跡 *sokuseki* footprint, footmark; the course of one's life, one's achievements
追跡 *tsuiseki* pursuit, chase, follow-up
軌跡 *kiseki* locus; tracks
航跡 *kōseki* wake, track; flight path, vapor trail
人跡 *jinseki* human traces
筆跡 *hisseki* handwriting, holograph
遺跡 *iseki* ruins, remains
史跡 *shiseki* historic spot [remains]
古跡 *koseki* historic remains, ruins

❷ sign, indication, phenomenon
奇跡 *kiseki* miracle, wonder

❸ traditional family name, status or property
門跡 *monzeki* status of a temple leading a Buddhist sect, esp. Honganji-Temple; priest-prince
名跡 *myōseki* family name

KUN

【ato 跡】

①ⓐ (mark left by something) trace(s), track, mark, footprint, trail, sign

ⓑ (sign of former presence) ruins, remains, aftermath

跡形も無く *atokata mo naku* without leaving any trace
傷跡 *kizuato* scar, cicatrix
足跡 *ashiato* footprint, footmark
跡始末(=後始末)する *atoshimatsu suru* settle, take remedial measures
城跡 *shiroato* ruins of a castle

② succession
跡を絶たない *ato o tatanai* (there) be no end to
跡を絶つ *ato o tatsu* put an end to, wipe out

③ inheritance, headship of a family
跡継ぎ *atotsugi* successor, heir
跡目 *atome* headship of a family, family property

SYNONYMS

❶ⓐ trace
軌 TRACK → 1445

ⓐ marks and signs
印 MARK (visible sign) → 828
標 MARK (identifying sign) → 1064
紋 print → 1299
符 SYMBOL → 2661
号 SIGN → 2153

HOMOPHONES

ato ⇨ 後 361

NOTE

⇨ see USAGE note at 後 361

践 踐 践 践

1535 SEN

Ⓒⓗ 践 jiàn

Radical	Strokes
足 157	13-7-6
Grade	**Freq**
Jōyō	1684
◧ 1 - 7 - 6	

7-6 足

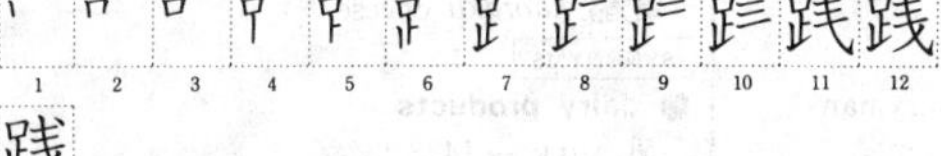

▶IMPLEMENT

COMPOUNDS

❶ (give practical effect to and ensure actual fulfillment) **implement, carry through, put in practice, carry out**

践言する *sengen suru* keep one's word
実践する *jissen suru* put in practice, implement

❷ accession (to the throne)
践祚 *senso* accession (to the throne)

❸ [archaic] step (upon), tread upon
践踏する *sentō suru* trample down

SYNONYMS

❶ **execute**
施 CARRY OUT → 891
執 EXECUTE → 1680
行 ACT → 212
履 FULFILL → 3171
果たす effect → 3560
遂 ACCOMPLISH → 3138

7-6 車

較 1536 KAKU KŌ▲ kura(beru)▲

Ⓒⓗ 较 jiào

Radical	Strokes
車 159	13-7-6
Grade	**Freq**
Jōyō	1257
1 - 7 - 6	

▶COMPARE

COMPOUNDS

● **compare**
較量 *kōryō* [rare] comparison
較差 *kakusa* (= *kōsa*) range
比較する *hikaku suru* compare with, draw a comparison

KUN

【kura(beru) 較べる】 [usu. 比べる] compare, contrast
大きさを較べる *ōkisa o kuraberu* compare the size

SYNONYMS

● **compare**
比 COMPARE → 26
校 COLLATE → 929
照 check against → 2827
対 OPPOSE (contrast) → 831
参 refer → 2066

HOMOPHONES

kuraberu ⇨ 比 26

NOTE

⇨ see USAGE note at 比 26

7-6 車

1537

▶COMPARE
nonstandard for 較 1536

7-6 酉

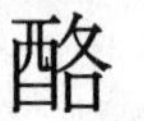
1538 RAKU

Ⓒⓗ 酪 lào

Radical	Strokes
酉 164	13-7-6
Grade	**Freq**
Jōyō	1748
1 - 7 - 6	

▶DAIRY PRODUCTS

COMPOUNDS

● **dairy products**
酪農 *rakunō* dairy farming
酪農家 *rakunōka* dairy farmer, dairyman
酪製品 *rakuseihin* dairy products
酪酸 *rakusan* butyric acid
乳酪 *nyūraku* dairy products
牛酪 *gyūraku* butter
乾酪 *kanraku* cheese

SYNONYMS

● **dairy products**
乳 MILK → 1438

1539 SHŪ muku(iru)▲

CH 酬 chóu

Radical	Strokes
酉 164	13-7-6
Grade	Freq
Jōyō	1607
◧ 1-7-6	

7-6 酉

▶RECIPROCATE

COMPOUNDS

❶ⓐ **reciprocate, requite, recompense; respond**

ⓑ **remuneration, reward**

応酬 *ōshū* response, reply; exchange

報酬 *hōshū* remuneration, reward; pay

❷ [original meaning] reciprocate [exchange] wineglasses, offer wine in return

献酬 *kenshū* exchange of sake cups

KUN

【muku(iru) 酬いる】

[now usu. 報いる]

ⓐ requite, repay

ⓑ recompense, reward

酬い *mukui* recompense, return

労に酬いる *rō ni mukuiru* recompense a person for his [her] labor

SYNONYMS

❶ⓐ **compensate**

報 REQUITE → 1698

償 RECOMPENSE → 176

賠 COMPENSATE → 1582

❷ **offer wine**

酌 POUR WINE → 1461

献 offer wine → 1785

HOMOPHONES

mukuiru ⇨ 報 1698

mukui ⇨ 報 1698

NOTE

⇨ see USAGE note at 報 1698

酵 incorrect stroke count ⇨ see 1561

7-6 酉

群 羣◇

1540 GUN mu(reru) mu(re) mura mura(garu)

CH 群 qún

Radical	Strokes
羊 123	13-6-7
Grade	Freq
Jōyō-5	827
◧ 1-7-6	

7-6 君

▶GROUP

COMPOUNDS

❶ⓐ [also suffix] **group (of any kind), crowd, flock, cluster, swarm**

ⓑ group (in U.S. Army or Air Force)

ⓒ *chem* group

群衆 *gunshū* crowd of people, multitude

群像 *gunzō art* group

魚群 *gyogun* school of fish

一群の羊 *ichigun no hitsuji* flock of sheep

抜群の *batsugun no* preeminent, outstanding

層群 *sōgun geol* group

子音群 *shiingun* consonant cluster

流星群 *ryūseigun* meteoric swarm

❷ⓐ form a group, cluster

ⓑ in groups, many

群生する *gunsei suru* grow gregariously [in crowds]

群集 *gunshū* crowd, mob; forming a large group (of people)

群島 *guntō* group of islands, archipelago

群落 *gunraku* many communities; cluster of plants

群発地震 *gunpatsu jishin* earthquake swarm

INDEPENDENT

【gun 群】 group, crowd (⇨ ❶)

群を成して *gun o nashite* in a group, in crowds, in swarms

KUN

【mu(reru) 群れる】 crowd together, throng,

flock together, swarm

人が群れる *hito ga mureru* be crowded with people

【mu(re) 群れ】 group, crowd, flock, swarm, herd

群れを成す *mure o nasu* form groups

羊の群れ *hitsuji no mure* flock of sheep

【mura 群】
[sometimes also 叢]
ⓐ [in compounds] group, crowd, flock
ⓑ counter for groups or flocks

群雀 *murasuzume* flock of sparrows

一群 *hitomura* a flock, a bunch

【mura(garu) 群がる】 [sometimes also 叢がる] crowd together, throng, flock together, swarm

蜂が群がる *hachi ga muragaru* be swarmed with bees

SYNONYMS

❶ **groups**

組 group (of people) → 1337
陣 lineup → 455
連 set → 3103
族 common-interest group (*slang*) → 958
党 PARTY → 2581
隊 PARTY (organized group) → 625
団 BODY → 3053
伍 ranks → 47
班 SQUAD → 946
軍 team → 2080

ⓐ **crowd**

衆 MULTITUDE → 2683

USAGE

❶ **mura**

群
[sometimes also 叢]
ⓐ [in compounds] group, crowd, flock
ⓑ counter for groups or flocks

叢
[usu. 群] same as 群

❷ **muragaru**

群がる
[sometimes also 叢がる] crowd together, throng, flock together, swarm

叢がる
[usu. 群がる] same as 群がる

HOMOPHONES

mura ⇨ 叢 2621
muragaru ⇨ 叢 2621

COMPOUND FORMATION

抜群 *batsugun*

抜群の 'preeminent, outstanding' is rising above (抜) the crowds (群 ❶ⓐ), i.e., to be extraordinary or outstanding.

7-7 言

読 讀 読 读

ⒸⒽ 读 dú dòu

1541 DOKU TOKU TŌ yo(mu) -yo(mi)

Radical	Strokes
言 149	14-7-7
Grade	**Freq**
Jōyō-2	513
▮ 1 - 7 - 7	

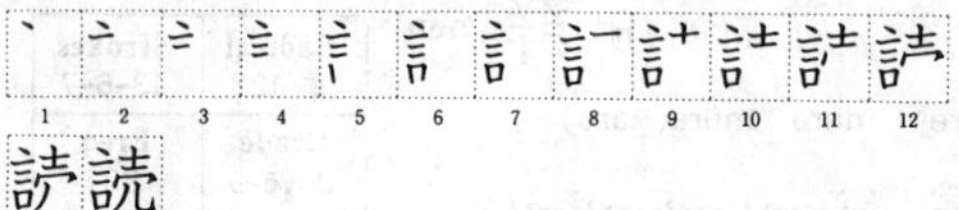

▶**READ**

COMPOUNDS

❶ⓐ **read**
ⓑ read (aloud), recite, chant

読者 *dokusha* reader, subscriber
読本 *tokuhon* reader, reading book
読書 *dokusho* reading a book, reading
読解力 *dokkairyoku* ability to read and understand
愛読書 *aidokusho* one's favorite book
熟読 *jukudoku* careful reading
朗読 *rōdoku* reading aloud
音読する *ondoku suru* read aloud

❷ reading or pronunciation of Chinese characters

音読 *ondoku* (=*on'yomi*) Chinese-derived pronunciation of kanji, *on* reading
訓読 *kundoku* (=*kun'yomi*) Japanese-derived pronunciation of kanji, *kun* reading

❸ division of text

読点 *tōten* comma
句読 *kutō* punctuation, pointing

KUN

【yo(mu) 読む】
①ⓐ read
ⓑ read (aloud), recite, chant

読み *yomi* reading; reading (of Chinese characters); judgment, foresight, insight
読み物 *yomimono* reading matter, book
読み手 *yomite* reader, subscriber; reciter
楽譜を読む *gakufu o yomu* read music
立ち読み *tachiyomi* browsing (in a bookstore)
読み上げる *yomiageru* read aloud, read off
経を読む *kyō o yomu* chant a sutra

② (interpret the meaning of) read, comprehend, divine, guess, estimate

読み取る *yomitoru* read (someone's) mind;

read (the calibration)
人の心を読む *hito no kokoro o yomu* guess what a person is thinking, read a person's thoughts
票読み *hyōyomi* estimation of the number of possible votes a person will get
【-yo(mi) -読み】 [suffix] reading (of Chinese characters)
重箱読み *jūbakoyomi* reading of a compound in which *on* and *kun* are mixed (in that order)
湯桶読み *yutōyomi* reading of a compound in which *kun* and *on* are mixed (in that order)

SPECIAL READINGS

読経 *dokyō* sutra chanting

SYNONYMS

❶ⓑ **recite**
吟 RECITE → 230
唱 chant → 462
詠 RECITE POETRY → 1500

USAGE

yomu
読む
①ⓐ read
ⓑ read (aloud), recite, chant
② (interpret the meaning of) read, comprehend, divine, guess, estimate
詠む
compose (waka or haiku poems)
★Note that although 詠 means to recite poetry as an element in the formation of *on* compounds, the word 詠む *yomu* is only used in the sense of composing (not reciting) poetry. Reciting poetry is expressed by 読む *yomu*.

HOMOPHONES

yomu ⇨ 詠 1500

誤 誤 誤 误

1542 GO ayama(ru) -ayama(ru)

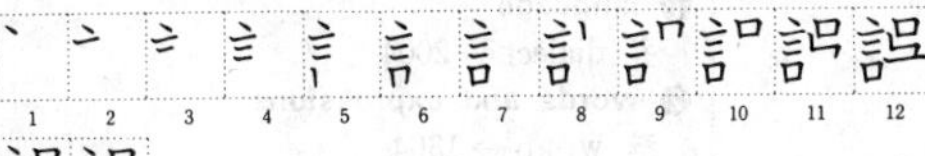

㊥ 误 wù

Radical	Strokes
言 149	14-7-7
Grade	**Freq**
Jōyō-6	1035
◧ 1-7-7	

7-7 言

▶MISTAKE

COMPOUNDS

ⓐ **mistake, err, make a mistake**
ⓑ [also prefix] **mistaken, mis-, incorrect, wrong**
ⓒ **mistake, error**
誤解 *gokai* misunderstanding, misconception
誤字 *goji* wrong character, misprint
誤報 *gohō* misinformation, incorrect report
誤算 *gosan* miscalculation; misjudgment
誤写 *gosha* error in copying
誤投下 *gotōka* accidental bombing
誤謬 *gobyū* mistake, error, fallacy
誤差 *gosa* error, aberration
錯誤 *sakugo* mistake, error
正誤 *seigo* correction of errors

KUN

【ayama(ru) 誤る】
① [formerly also 謬る] mistake, make a mistake, err
誤り *ayamari* mistake, error, slip
誤って *ayamatte* by mistake, accidentally
② mislead, lead astray
人を誤る *hito o ayamaru* mislead a person
【-ayama(ru) -誤る】 [verbal suffix] make a mistake in performing an action
言い誤る *iiayamaru* mistake, make a mistake in speaking
見誤る *miayamaru* fail to recognize [see], mistake

SYNONYMS

● **mistakes and mistaking**
-違える mis- → 3151
錯 mistaken → 1743
失 SLIP → 3511
過 error → 3137

HOMOPHONES

ayamaru ⇨ 謬 1631 謝 1620

NOTE

⇨ see USAGE note at 謝 1620

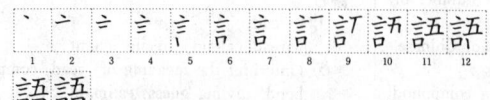

7-7 言

語 語 话

1543 GO kata(ru) kata(rau)

CH 语 yǔ yù

Radical	Strokes
言 149	14-7-7
Grade	**Freq**
Jōyō-2	265
1-7-7	

▶LANGUAGE ▶WORD ▶TELL

COMPOUNDS

❶ⓐ [also suffix] **language, speech**
ⓑ **suffix for forming names of languages**
語学 *gogaku* language study, linguistics
言語 *gengo* language, speech, words
国語 *kokugo* national language; Japanese
文語 *bungo* literary [written] language
敬語 *keigo* honorific language, polite speech
標準語 *hyōjungo* standard language [speech]
外国語 *gaikokugo* foreign language
英語 *eigo* English
日本語 *nihongo* Japanese

❷ [also suffix] **word, term, phrase**
語意 *goi* meaning of a word
語句 *goku* words and phrases
単語 *tango* word
用語 *yōgo* terminology; diction, wording; vocabulary
主語 *shugo* subject (word)
流行語 *ryūkōgo* word [phrase] in fashion, word [phrase] on everybody's lips

❸ [original meaning] **talk, speak**
語気 *goki* manner of speaking
語調 *gochō* tone (of voice), note, accent
私語 *shigo* secret talk, whispering

❹ tale, story, narrative, legend
落語 *rakugo rakugo*, Japanese-style comic story

INDEPENDENT

【**go** 語】word, term; speech, manner of speaking
語の意味 *go no imi* meaning of a word
ゲーテの語に曰く *gēte no go ni iwaku* according to Goethe
語を結ぶ *go o musubu* conclude one's speech

KUN

【**kata(ru)** 語る】
①ⓐ (express in words) tell, talk, speak
ⓑ tell (a story), narrate, relate
真実を語る *shinjitsu o kataru* speak the truth
語り手 *katarite* narrator, storyteller
語り伝える *kataritsutaeru* pass on (a story or tradition)
語り合う *katariau* talk together, have a chat with
語り *katari* narrative
語り草(=語り種) *katarigusa* story, topic
物語 *monogatari* story, tale, legend
② recite, chant
義太夫語り *gidayūkatari gidayu* reciter

【**kata(rau)** 語らう】talk together, chat; invite (to); conspire, plot together
語らい *katarai* talk, chat; lover's vow
語らうに友無く *katarau ni tomo naku* with no friend to talk to
仲間を語らって *nakama o kataratte* together with one's lot

SYNONYMS

❶ **language**
弁 dialect → 2004

❷ **words and expressions**
辞 WORD → 1364
詞 WORDS → 1503
句 PHRASE → 2967

❹ **stories**
話 story → 1527
談 account → 1569
説 narrative → 1547

【**kataru**】
① **speak and say**
談 TALK → 1569
弁 SPEAK ELOQUENTLY → 2004
申す SPEAK HUMBLY → 3507
口 give mouth to → 3382
話 SPEAK → 1527
言 SAY → 1941
云 say → 1931
述 STATE → 3075
陳 SET FORTH → 540

USAGE

❶ **kataru**
語る
①ⓐ (express in words) tell, talk, speak
ⓑ tell (a story), narrate, relate
② recite, chant
騙る
① deceive, cheat, swindle, defraud
② assume (another's) name

❷ **katari**
語り
narrative

騙り
fraud, swindle

HOMOPHONES
kataru ⇨ 騙 1841
katari ⇨ 騙 1841

誨
1544 KAI

Ⓒ诲 huì

Radical	Strokes
言 149	14-7-7
Grade	**Freq**
Reference	
◧ 1 - 7 - 7	

7-7 言

COMPOUNDS
● [now replaced by 戒 3204] [original meaning] instruct, teach
教誨 *kyōkai* exhortation, preaching

誡
1545 KAI

Ⓒ诫 jiè

Radical	Strokes
言 149	14-7-7
Grade	**Freq**
Reference	
◧ 1 - 7 - 7	

7-7 言

COMPOUNDS
[now replaced by 戒 *kai* 3204]
❶ caution against, admonish, warn, give warning
誡告 *kaikoku* caution, warning, reprimand
訓誡する *kunkai suru* admonish, warn
❷ commandment, *śīla*, precept
十誡 *jikkai* the Ten Commandments (of Moses)
❸ instruct, teach

NOTE
⇨ see USAGE note at 戒 3204

認 認 認 認
1546 NIN mito(meru)

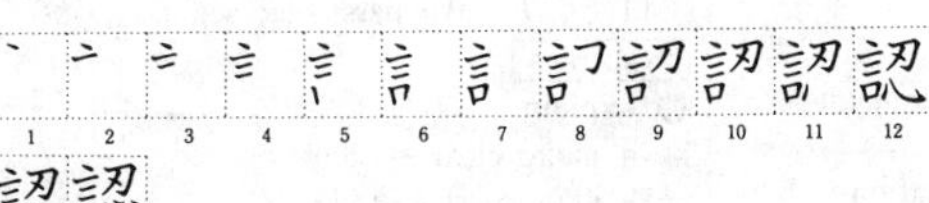

Ⓒ认 rèn

Radical	Strokes
言 149	14-7-7
Grade	**Freq**
Jōyō-6	306
◧ 1 - 7 - 7	

7-7 言

▶**RECOGNIZE**

COMPOUNDS
❶ [original meaning] (be aware of something perceived) **recognize, perceive, identify**
認識 *ninshiki* cognition, perception; understanding
誤認 *gonin* mistake, misconception, misunderstanding
確認 *kakunin* confirmation, ascertainment
❷ (approve or give permission for) **recognize, acknowledge, approve, admit**
認可する *ninka suru* approve, authorize, give permission
認定 *nintei* authorization, recognition, acknowledgment
認知 *ninchi* recognition, acknowledgment
承認 *shōnin* approval, recognition
公認 *kōnin* official recognition [approval], authorization, certification
黙認 *mokunin* tacit [silent] approval, toleration

KUN
【**mito(meru)** 認める】 recognize, acknowledge, approve, admit; judge, conclude; see, witness
認め *mitome* approval; private seal
認め難い *mitomegatai* unapprovable
誤りを認める *ayamari o mitomeru* admit to a mistake
必要と認める *hitsuyō to mitomeru* judge as necessary
人影を認める *hitokage o mitomeru* make out someone's figure

SYNONYMS

❶ **perceive**

覚 PERCEIVE → 2604
知 KNOW → 1127
感 FEEL → 2835

❷ **agree and approve**

可 APPROVE → 2969
賛 APPROVE OF → 2809
諾 CONSENT → 1568
承 AGREE TO → 16
肯 ASSENT → 2417
容 tolerate → 2277

7-7 言

説 説 説 说

1547 SETSU ZEI to(ku)

CH 说 shuō shuì yuè

Radical	Strokes
言 149	14-7-7
Grade	Freq
Jōyō-4	334
1-7-7	

1 2 3 4 5 6 7 8 9 10 11 12 13 14

▶**EXPLAIN** ▶**THEORY**

COMPOUNDS

❶ⓐ [original meaning] **explain**
ⓑ explanation, statement
説明 *setsumei* explanation, description
解説 *kaisetsu* explanation, commentary
演説 *enzetsu* (public) speech, address, oration
論説 *ronsetsu* discourse, dissertation; editorial
力説する *rikisetsu suru* emphasize, lay stress on, insist upon
概説 *gaisetsu* general statement, outline
序説 *josetsu* introduction
言説 *gensetsu* remark, statement

❷ preach, advocate; persuade
説教 *sekkyō* preaching, scolding
説法 *seppō* (Buddhist) sermon, preaching, moralizing
説得 *settoku* persuasion
遊説 *yūzei* electioneering tour; campaign speech

❸ⓐ [also suffix] (proposed explanation) **theory, doctrine**
ⓑ **opinion, view**
学説 *gakusetsu* theory
仮説 *kasetsu* hypothesis
新説 *shinsetsu* new theory [doctrine]; new opinion
地動説 *chidōsetsu* heliocentric [Copernican] theory
原子説 *genshisetsu* atomic theory
社説 *shasetsu* editorial (article)
自説 *jisetsu* one's own view
通説 *tsūsetsu* common opinion, popular view

❹ **narrative, story**
説話 *setsuwa* narrative, tale
小説 *shōsetsu* novel, story, fiction
伝説 *densetsu* legend, folk tale

❺ [also suffix] rumor
風説 *fūsetsu* rumor, hearsay
解散説 *kaisansetsu* rumor of dissolution

❻ style of Chinese poetry

INDEPENDENT

【**setsu** 説】theory, doctrine; opinion, view; rumor
説を立てる *setsu o tateru* put forward a theory
お説の通りです *Osetsu no tōri desu* I agree with you
...との説が有る *...to no setsu ga aru* Rumors hold that...

KUN

【**to(ku)** 説く】
① explain
説き明かす *tokiakasu* explain, solve; make clear
② preach, advocate; persuade
口説く *kudoku* persuade; seduce

SYNONYMS

❶ **explain**
明 make clear → 855
釈 ELUCIDATE → 1484
講 expound → 1619
解 CLARIFY → 1517
注 annotate → 325

❷ **advocate**
唱 advocate → 462

❸ⓐ **theory**
論 THEORY (systematic knowledge) → 1574
ⓑ **opinion**
論 opinion → 1574
観 VIEW (conception) → 1880
見 view (personal opinion) → 2544

❹ **stories**
話 story → 1527
談 account → 1569
語 tale → 1543

HOMOPHONES

toku ⇨ 解 1517 溶 664 梳 964

NOTE
⇨ see USAGE note at 解 1517

⇨ see COMPOUND FORMATION for 説得 *settoku* ⇨ 得 477

誌 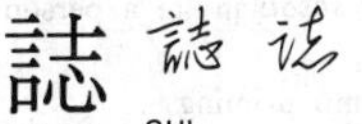
1548 SHI

CH 志 zhì

Radical	Strokes
言 149	14-7-7
Grade	**Freq**
Jōyō-6	1060
1-7-7	

7-7 言

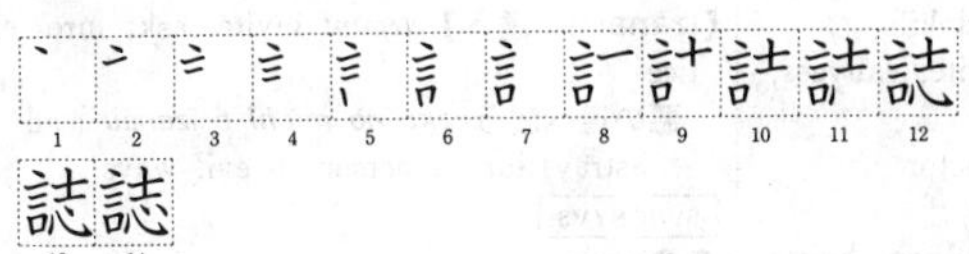

▶**MAGAZINE**

COMPOUNDS

❶ⓐ [also suffix] **magazine, periodical**
ⓑ **suffix after names of magazines or periodicals**
誌面 *shimen* page of a magazine
誌上で *shijō de* in a magazine
雑誌 *zasshi* magazine, journal
週刊誌 *shūkanshi* weekly magazine
ニューズウィーク誌 *nyūzuuīkushi* Newsweek
❷ⓐ [also suffix] records, document
ⓑ record, write down
日誌 *nisshi* diary
植物誌 *shokubutsushi* flora
地誌 *chishi* topography, geographical description
墓誌 *boshi* epitaph, inscription on a tomb

SYNONYMS

❶ **periodicals**
紙 newspaper → 1302
報 bulletin → 1698
❷ⓐ **records**
記 written account → 1453
録 RECORD → 1742
譜 SYSTEMATIC RECORD → 1637
史 HISTORY → 3510
伝 biography → 44

誦
1549 SHŌ JU ZU

CH 诵 sòng

Radical	Strokes
言 149	14-7-7
Grade	**Freq**
Reference	
1-7-7	

7-7 言

COMPOUNDS

● [now also 唱 *shō* 462, rarely also 頌 *shō* 1045] recite, read aloud, chant, intone
誦経 *zukyō* reciting [chanting] a sutra
暗誦する *anshō suru* recite from memory
吟誦 *ginshō* reciting (poetry), chanting
愛誦する *aishō suru* love to recite (a poem), read with pleasure
読誦する *dokuju suru* read aloud, recite, intone
誦する *shōsuru* recite, chant, read aloud
誦する *jusuru* recite, chant, read aloud

誘 誘 誘
1550 YŪ saso(u) izana(u)▲

CH 诱 yòu

Radical	Strokes
言 149	14-7-7
Grade	**Freq**
Jōyō	1128
1-7-7	

7-7 言

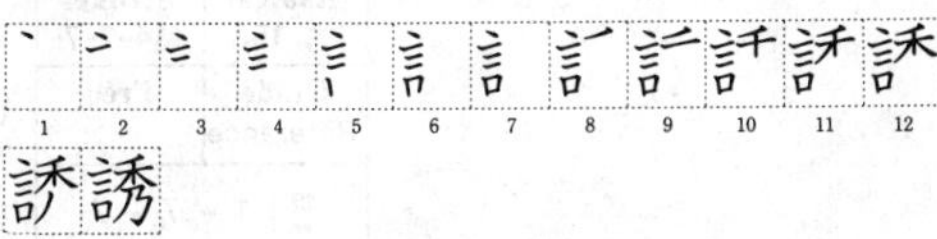

▶**INDUCE**

COMPOUNDS

❶ⓐ (move by persuasion) **induce, lure, tempt, entice, seduce; lead, guide**
ⓑ (produce by induction) induce
誘致する *yūchi suru* lure, entice, invite; bring

about, cause
誘惑 *yūwaku* temptation, seduction
誘引する *yūin suru* entice, induce, attract
誘導する *yūdō suru* induce, incite; guide, lead
誘拐 *yūkai* kidnapping, abduction
誘蛾灯 *yūgatō* luring lamp
誘殺する *yūsatsu suru* seduce and kill
勧誘する *kan'yū suru* induce, invite, canvass, persuade
誘電子 *yūdenshi* (electrical) inductor
誘爆 *yūbaku* induced explosion

❷ (stimulate the occurrence of) **induce, bring about, cause**
誘発する *yūhatsu suru* cause, induce, lead up to
誘起する *yūki suru* give rise to, lead to
誘因 *yūin* immediate cause, incentive

KUN

【saso(u) 誘う】 invite, ask; induce, provoke, cause; allure, tempt, entice, seduce
誘い *sasoi* temptation, allurement, enticement; invitation
芝居に誘う *shibai ni sasou* invite a person to the theater
誘い水 *sasoimizu* pump priming
誘い出す *sasoidasu* decoy, entice, lure away

【izana(u) 誘う】 *elegant* invite, ask; lure, entice
悪の道へ誘う *aku no michi e izanau* lead astray, lure a person to evil ways

SYNONYMS

❶ⓐ **urge**
勧 URGE → 1857
催 PRESS FOR → 157
促 HASTEN → 103
励 ENCOURAGE → 1119
侑 URGE TO EAT → 91

❷ **cause**
致 BRING ABOUT → 1316

7-7 言

誤 1551

▶MISTAKE
nonstandard for 誤 1542

7-7 言

認 1552

▶RECOGNIZE
nonstandard for 認 1546

7-7 言

誠 1553

▶SINCERITY
nonstandard for 誠 1523

7-7 言

說 1554

▶EXPLAIN ▶THEORY
nonstandard for 説 1547

7-7 言

誕 1555

▶BE BORN
nonstandard for 誕 1579

7-7 言

誇

incorrect stroke count ⇨ see 1522

7-7 豸

貌 1556

BŌ katachi

CH 貌 mào

Radical	Strokes
豸 153	14-7-7
Grade	**Freq**
Reference	
1-7-7	

COMPOUNDS

ⓐ [now usu. 形 *katachi*] [original meaning] appearance, looks, figure
ⓑ aspect, condition

容貌 *yōbō* looks, personal appearance
美貌 *bibō* good looks, pretty features
変貌 *henbō* transfiguration
顔貌 *kaokatachi* features, looks
全貌 *zenbō* full view, whole aspect

HOMOPHONES
katachi ⇨ 形 846

NOTE
⇨ see USAGE note at 形 846

賦

incorrect stroke count ⇨ see 1583

7-7 貝

赫

1557 KAKU

CH 赫 hè

Radical	Strokes
赤 155	14-7-7
Grade	**Freq**
Reference	
◧ 1 - 7 - 7	

7-7 赤

COMPOUNDS
❶ [now also 嚇 784] explode with anger, be enraged
赫怒する *kakudo suru* be greatly enraged, get furious
❷ brilliant, bright, glorious
赫赫たる *kakkakutaru* (=*kakukakutaru*) splendid, brilliant, glorious

---

踊

1558 YŌ odo(ru) odo(ri)

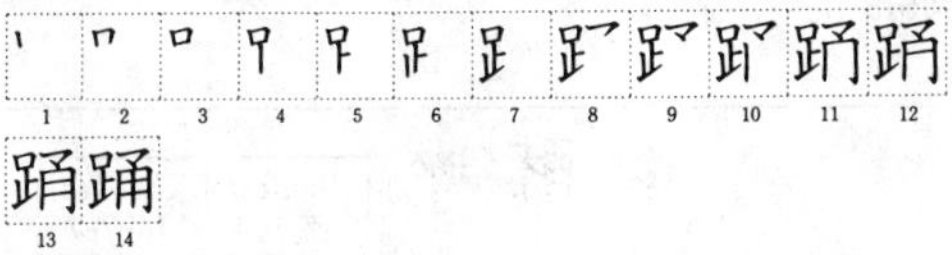

CH 踊 yǒng

Radical	Strokes
足 157	14-7-7
Grade	**Freq**
Jōyō	1114
◧ 1 - 7 - 7	

7-7 足

▶DANCE

COMPOUNDS
❶ **dance**
舞踊 *buyō* dancing, dance
民踊 *min'yō* folk dance
❷ [original meaning] leap up, jump up and down
踊躍する *yōyaku suru* leap with joy, jump about

KUN
【odo(ru) 踊る】 dance (energetically)
踊り手 *odorite* dancer
【odo(ri) 踊り】 [also suffix] dance, dancing
盆踊り *bon'odori* Bon Festival dance

SYNONYMS
❶ &【odoru】 dance

舞 DANCE (gracefully) → 2146

USAGE
❶ **odoru**
踊る
dance (energetically)
躍る
ⓐ leap, jump, bound
ⓑ (of one's heart) throb, leap
❷ **odori**
踊り
[also suffix] dance, dancing
躍り
leaping, jumping

HOMOPHONES
odoru ⇨ 躍 1658
odori ⇨ 躍 1658

7-7 車

輔 輔 輔

1559 HO FU NAMES suke tasuku

CH 辅 fǔ

Radical	Strokes
車 159	14-7-7
Grade	Freq
Names	2015
1-7-7	

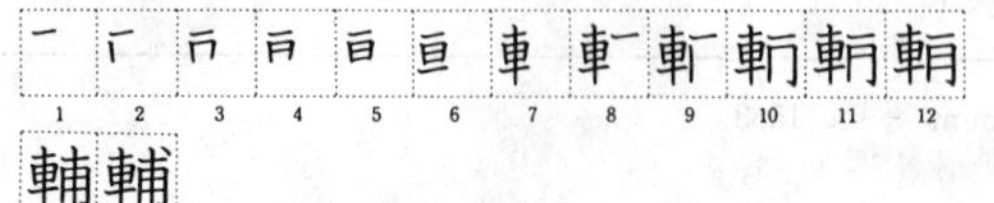

輔 輔

13 14

▶ **ASSIST**

COMPOUNDS

❶ [now usu. 補 1194] **assist, aid; give guidance**

輔佐 *hosa* assistance, aid; assistant; counselor, adviser

輔弼 *hohitsu* assistance, council

輔導 *hodō* guidance; custody

❷ [original meaning] wheel guard

唇歯輔車 *shinshi-hosha* mutual dependence

NAMES

輔治野 *fujino* surname

大輔 *daisuke* male name

SYNONYMS

❶ **help**

補 assist → 1194

佐 ASSIST → 67

助 HELP → 1121

佑 HELP (said esp. of God) → 74

祐 DIVINE HELP → 915

援 AID → 586

済 RELIEVE → 522

COMPOUND FORMATION

唇歯輔車 *shinshi-hosha*

唇歯輔車 'mutual dependence' is relying on one another like lips (唇) and teeth (歯) or as wheel guard (輔 ❷) and cart (車).

7-7 車

輕

1560

▶ **LIGHT**

nonstandard for 軽 1515

7-7 酉

酵 酵 酵

1561 KŌ

CH 酵 jiào

Radical	Strokes
酉 164	14-7-7
Grade	Freq
Jōyō	1727
1-7-7	

一 丆 亓 丙 西 西 酉 酉一 酉十 酉土 酉耂 酉考 酵 酵

1 2 3 4 5 6 7 8 9 10 11 12 13 14

▶ **FERMENT**

COMPOUNDS

ⓐ (something that causes fermentation) **ferment**

ⓑ (undergo fermentation) **ferment**

酵素 *kōso* ferment; enzyme

酵母 *kōbo* yeast; ferment

酵母菌 *kōbokin* yeast fungus

発酵 *hakkō* fermentation, zymosis

SYNONYMS

ⓑ **brew and ferment**

醸 BREW → 1654

酷 酷 酷 酷

1562 KOKU hido(i)▲

ⒸⒽ 酷 kù

Radical	Strokes
酉 164	14-7-7
Grade	Freq
Jōyō	1674
1-7-7	

7-7 酉

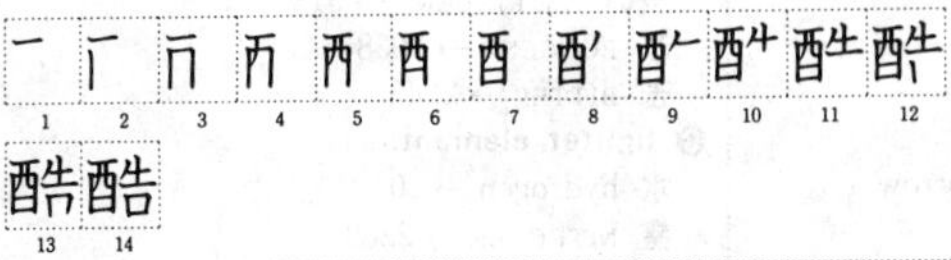

一 丆 冂 丙 西 西 酉 酉' 酉ᐩ 酉十 酉牛 酉告 酷 酷

1 2 3 4 5 6 7 8 9 10 11 12 13 14

▶**SEVERE**

COMPOUNDS

❶ **severe, harsh, cruel, brutal, merciless**

酷刑 *kokkei* severe punishment
酷評 *kokuhyō* severe criticism
酷薄(＝刻薄)な *kokuhaku na* cruel, inhumane
酷使する *kokushi suru* drive (a person) hard, abuse, sweat (one's workers), overwork
残酷な *zankoku na* cruel, ruthless, atrocious
苛酷(＝過酷)な *kakoku na* severe, harsh, cruel

❷ (of great intensity) **severe, intense**

酷寒 *kokkan* severe [intense] cold; depth of winter
酷暑 *kokusho* severe heat
酷似 *kokuji* close resemblance

INDEPENDENT

【**koku 酷**】severity, harshness, cruelty
酷な *koku na* severe, harsh, stringent, rigorous, strict; unfair
酷なやり方 *koku na yarikata* cruel act

KUN

【**hido(i) 酷い**】
[also 非道い]
① cruel, harsh, rough
酷さ *hidosa* harshness, severity
酷い仕打ち *hidoi shiuchi* cruel treatment
② severe, intense, heavy
酷く暑い *Hidoku atsui* It's awfully hot

SYNONYMS

❶ **cruel**

残 RUTHLESS → 943
惨 CRUEL → 483
虐 CRUEL → 3218
凶 ATROCIOUS → 2961

❶ **strict**

厳 strict → 3289
峻 STERN → 412

❷ **extreme in degree**

厳 SEVERE → 3289
激 intense → 776
極 EXTREME → 1017
痛 bitter(ly) → 3285
切 keen → 27
甚 EXTREMELY → 2643
超 super- → 3313
強 STRONG → 475
重 HEAVY → 3573
高 HIGH → 2097
深 DEEP → 524
大 BIG → 3416

USAGE

hidoi

酷い
[also 非道い]
① cruel, harsh, rough
② severe, intense, heavy

非道い
[also 酷い] same as 酷い

HOMOPHONES

hidoi ⇨ 非道い 889, 3134

酸 酸 酸

1563 SAN su(i)

ⒸⒽ 酸 suān

Radical	Strokes
酉 164	14-7-7
Grade	Freq
Jōyō-5	1260
1-7-7	

7-7 酉

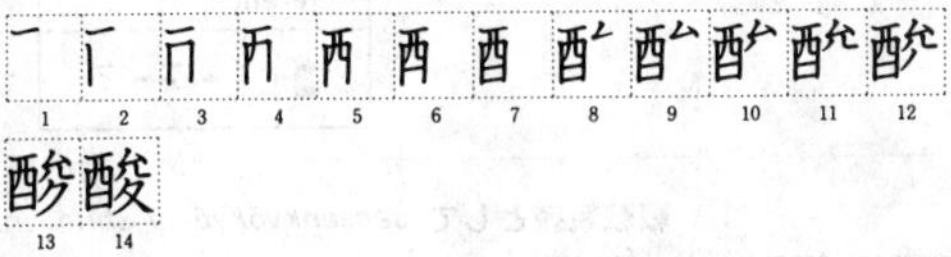

一 丆 冂 丙 西 西 酉 酉ᐩ 酉厶 酉𠆢 酉允 酸 酸 酸

1 2 3 4 5 6 7 8 9 10 11 12 13 14

▶**ACID** ▶**OXYGEN**

COMPOUNDS

❶ [also suffix] **acid, acidity**

酸性 *sansei* acidity
酸基 *sanki* acid radical
硫酸 *ryūsan* sulfuric acid
塩酸 *ensan* hydrochloric acid
胃酸 *isan* stomach acid

乳酸 *nyūsan* lactic acid
アミノ酸 *aminosan* amino acid
❷ sour, acid, tart
酸味 *sanmi* sourness
❸ **oxygen**
酸素 *sanso* oxygen
酸化 *sanka* oxidation
❹ sick at heart, grieved, distressed
酸鼻 *sanbi* extreme pain, deep sorrow

INDEPENDENT

【san 酸】 acid; sourness
酸とアルカリ *san to arukari* acid and alkali

KUN

【su(i) 酸い】 sour, acid
酸っぱい *suppai* sour

SYNONYMS

❶ **sour substances**
酢 VINEGAR → 1516
❷ **unsavory tastes**
渋い ASTRINGENT → 513
辛 PUNGENT → 2038
苦 BITTER → 2243
❸ **lighter elements**
水 hydrogen → 10
窒 NITROGEN → 2288
塩 chlorine → 631
臭 bromine → 2633
硫 SULFUR → 1184
炭 carbon → 2257

7-7 酉

酷 1564

▶SEVERE
nonstandard for 酷 1562

7-7 𠤕

疑 1565 GI utaga(u)

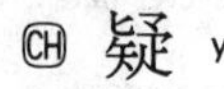

Ⓒⓗ 疑 yí

Radical	Strokes
疋 103	14-5-9
Grade	**Freq**
Jōyō-6	535
1 - 7 - 7	

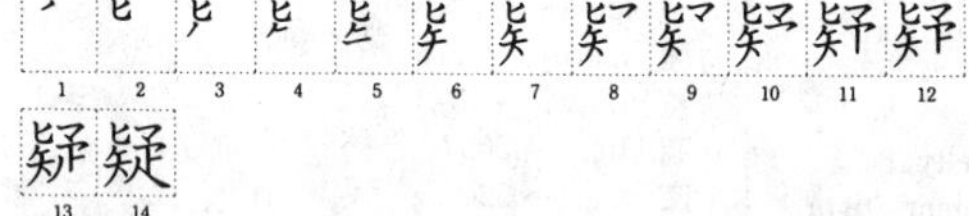

▶DOUBT

COMPOUNDS

❶ **doubt, suspect**
疑惑 *giwaku* doubt, suspicion
疑問 *gimon* question, problem, doubt
疑心 *gishin* doubt, suspicion, fear
半信半疑の *hanshin-hangi no* dubious, incredulous
懐疑 *kaigi* doubt, skepticism, disbelief
容疑 *yōgi* suspicion
❷ hesitate
遅疑する *chigi suru* hesitate, vacillate

INDEPENDENT

【gi 疑】 doubt, suspicion

KUN

【utaga(u) 疑う】 doubt, be suspicious, distrust
疑い *utagai* doubt, suspicion; question
疑わしい *utagawashii* doubtful, suspicious

SYNONYMS

❶ **doubt**
怪しむ suspect → 297

7-7 克

兢 1566 KYŌ

Ⓒⓗ 兢 jīng

Radical	Strokes
儿 10	14-2-12
Grade	**Freq**
Reference	
1 - 7 - 7	

COMPOUNDS

● [now replaced by 恐 2650] be in fear, tremble
戦戦兢兢として *sensenkyōkyō to shite* with fear and trembling

調える
① prepare, make ready, procure, raise (money)
② season, flavor
③ (bring to a conclusion) arrange, settle, conclude

整える
(put in order) arrange, tidy up, adjust (clothes), regulate

HOMOPHONES
totonou ⇨ 整 2871
totonoeru ⇨ 整 2871

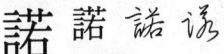

諾
1568 DAKU

CH 诺 nuò

Radical	Strokes
言 149	15-7-8
Grade	**Freq**
Jōyō	1548
1-7-8	

7-8 言

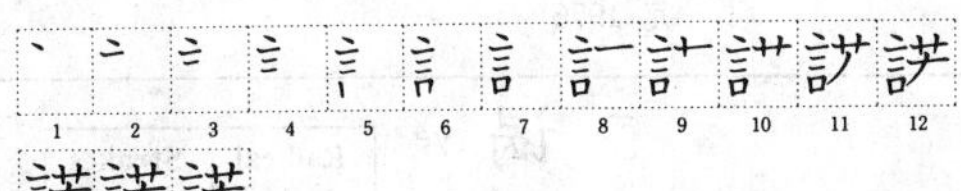

▶CONSENT

COMPOUNDS
❶ⓐ **consent (to), say yes, agree to, assent**
ⓑ yes, aye
受諾 *judaku* acceptance
承諾 *shōdaku* consent, assent, agreement, acceptation
応諾 *ōdaku* consent, assent
快諾 *kaidaku* ready consent
内諾 *naidaku* informal [private] consent
諾否 *dakuhi* definitive answer, yes or no
諾諾 *dakudaku* yes, yes
❷ Norway
日諾 *nichidaku* Japan and Norway

INDEPENDENT
【daku 諾】 *literary* consent
【dakusuru 諾する】 consent, say yes

SYNONYMS
❶ⓐ **agree and approve**
承 AGREE TO → 16
認 RECOGNIZE → 1546
可 APPROVE → 2969
賛 APPROVE OF → 2809
肯 ASSENT → 2417
容 tolerate → 2277
ⓑ **terms of assent**
然 SO → 2782

談
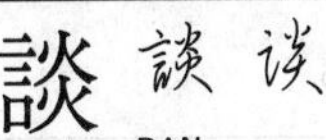
1569 DAN

CH  tán

Radical	Strokes
言 149	15-7-8
Grade	**Freq**
Jōyō-3	327
1-7-8	

7-8 言

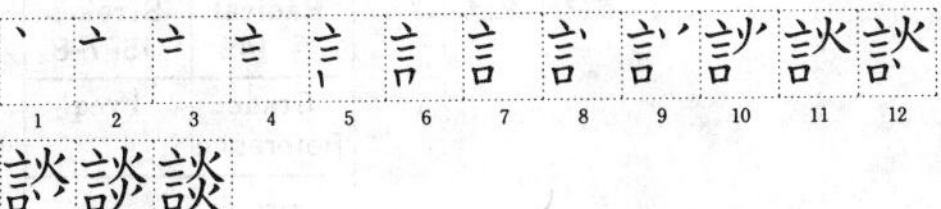

▶TALK

COMPOUNDS
❶ⓐ [original meaning] **talk, converse, speak, confer, discuss**
ⓑ [also suffix] **talk, conversation**
談合 *dangō* consultation, negotiation
談話 *danwa* talk, conversation
会談 *kaidan* conversation, talk, conference
相談する *sōdan suru* consult, talk over, confer
対談する *taidan suru* talk with, converse; negotiate in person with
懇談 *kondan* familiar talk [chat]
座談会 *zadankai* round table talk, symposium
冗談 *jōdan* joke
政談 *seidan* political talk
車中談 *shachūdan* informal talk given (as by a politician) aboard a train
❷ **account, story, tale**
怪談 *kaidan* ghost story
講談 *kōdan* storytelling, narration; historical narrative
冒険談 *bōkendan* account of an adventure; adventure story

INDEPENDENT
【dan 談】 *literary* talk, conversation; account
同日の談ではない *dōjitsu no dan de wa nai* not to be mentioned in the same breath

【danjiru (＝danzuru) 談じる(＝談ずる)】 talk about, discuss; negotiate with

SYNONYMS

❶ⓐ **speak and say**
語る TELL → 1543
口 give mouth to → 3382
話 SPEAK → 1527
言 SAY → 1941
云 say → 1931
弁 SPEAK ELOQUENTLY → 2004
申す SPEAK HUMBLY → 3507
述 STATE → 3075
陳 SET FORTH → 540

ⓑ **speech**
言 SPEECH → 1941
舌 TONGUE → 2186
口 MOUTH → 3382

❷ **stories**
語 tale → 1543
話 story → 1527
説 narrative → 1547

NOTE

⇨ see COMPOUND FORMATION for 冗談 *jōdan* ⇨ 冗 1976

7-8 言

謁 謁 謁 谒

1570 ETSU

CH 谒 yè

Radical	Strokes
言 149	15-7-8
Grade	**Freq**
Jōyō	1911
1-7-8	

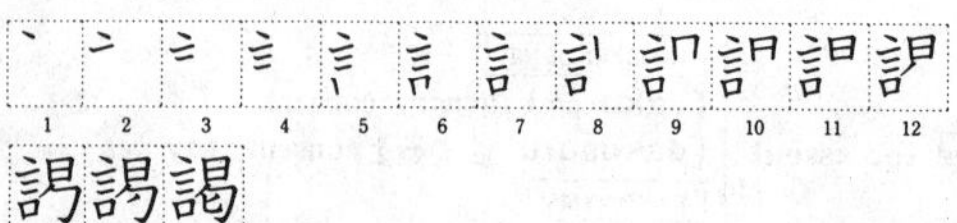

▶**BE GRANTED AN AUDIENCE**

COMPOUNDS

❶ **be granted [have] an audience with a superior, esp. a ruler or the Emperor**
謁見 *ekken* audience
拝謁 *haietsu* audience with the Emperor

❷ [original meaning, now archaic] beseech, beg, request
請謁する *seietsu suru* request, beseech; request an audience

INDEPENDENT

【etsu 謁】 audience (with the Emperor)
謁を賜わる *etsu o tamawaru* be granted an audience

【essuru 謁する】 be received in audience

SYNONYMS

❶ **meet**
見 SEE → 2544
会 MEET → 2020
遭 MEET WITH → 3159
遇 ENCOUNTER → 3135

7-8 言

誼

1571 GI yoshimi

CH 谊 yì

Radical	Strokes
言 149	15-7-8
Grade	**Freq**
Reference	
1-7-8	

COMPOUNDS

● [also 宜 *gi* 2223 or 義 *gi* 2338] friendship; favor, kindness
友誼(＝友宜) *yūgi* friendship, fellowship
交誼(＝交宜) *kōgi* friendship, amity
好誼(＝好宜) *kōgi* warm friendship
高誼(＝高宜) *kōgi* your kindness [favor]
恩誼(＝恩義) *ongi* obligation, debt of gratitude
情誼(＝情宜, 情義)を尽くす *jōgi o tsukusu* do (a person) a kindness
誼(＝誼み) *yoshimi* friendship; favor, kindness

誹

1572 HI HAI soshi(ru)

CH 诽 fěi

Radical	Strokes
言 149	15-7-8
Grade	**Freq**
Reference	
◧ 1 - 7 - 8	

7-8 言

COMPOUNDS

● [now also 非 *hi* 889] [original meaning] slander, calumniate, defame
誹謗 *hibō* slander, abuse
誹議する *higi suru* criticize, censure
誹諧(＝俳諧) *haikai haikai*, (humorous) haiku
誹る *soshiru* slander, libel, criticize

HOMOPHONES

soshiru ⇨ 譏 1638

課 課 课

1573 KA

CH 课 kè

Radical	Strokes
言 149	15-7-8
Grade	**Freq**
Jōyō-4	509
◧ 1 - 7 - 8	

7-8 言

1 2 3 4 5 6 7 8 9 10 11 12 13 14 15

▶**SECTION** ▶**LESSON**

COMPOUNDS

❶ [also suffix] **section, department (of a company or government office)**
課長 *kachō* section chief [head]
分課 *bunka* section, subdivision; dividing into sections
人事課 *jinjika* personnel section
会計課 *kaikeika* accounts [accounting] section
❷ⓐ **lesson, task**
ⓑ counter for lessons
課程 *katei* course, curriculum
課目(＝科目) *kamoku* school subject, course, curriculum
学課 *gakka* lesson, school work
日課 *nikka* daily lesson, daily task
放課後 *hōkago* after school
二課勉強する *nika benkyō suru* study two lessons
❸ **impose, levy**
課題 *kadai* task, assignment; problem
課税 *kazei* taxation
課徴金 *kachōkin* surcharge (on imports)
賦課 *fuka* levy, imposition, assessment
❹ [original meaning] evaluate, rate
考課 *kōka* evaluation, rating

INDEPENDENT

【ka 課】 section, department (of a company or government office); lesson, task
課の仕事 *ka no shigoto* job [responsibility] of a section
次の課 *tsugi no ka* next lesson
【kasuru 課する】 impose, levy

SYNONYMS

❶ **divisions of organizations**
部 department → 1676
局 BUREAU → 3063
❷ **units of learning**
科 course → 1138
講 LECTURE → 1619
❸ **impose**
徴 LEVY → 683

7-8 言

論 論 论

1574 RON

Ⓒ 论 lùn lún

Radical	Strokes
言 149	15-7-8
Grade	**Freq**
Jōyō-6	245
1-7-8	

1 2 3 4 5 6 7 8 9 10 11 12 13 14 15

▶**ARGUE** ▶**THEORY**

COMPOUNDS

❶ⓐ [original meaning] (put forth reasons) **argue, discuss, discourse, reason**

ⓑ (contend in argument) **argue, dispute**

ⓒ **argument, argumentation, debate**

論評 *ronpyō* comment, criticism, review
論説 *ronsetsu* discourse, dissertation; editorial
論理 *ronri* logic
評論 *hyōron* comment, criticism, review
理論 *riron* theory
言論 *genron* speech, discussion
推論 *suiron* reasoning, inference, induction, deduction
論議 *rongi* discussion, argument, debate
論争する *ronsō suru* dispute, argue
討論 *tōron* debate, discussion, argument
議論 *giron* argument, discussion
結論 *ketsuron* conclusion
反論 *hanron* counterargument, refutation
勿論 *mochiron* of course, no doubt, naturally

❷ [also suffix]

ⓐ (systematically organized knowledge) **theory, doctrine, system of thought**

ⓑ **opinion, view**

ⓒ **essay, treatise, comments**

進化論 *shinkaron* theory of evolution
音韻論 *on'inron* phonology
世論 *seron* (=*yoron*) public opinion
異論 *iron* different [dissenting] opinion; objection, dissent, protest
持論 *jiron* pet theory
時論 *jiron* current view, contemporary opinion; comments on current events
強硬論 *kyōkōron* hard line
論文 *ronbun* thesis, paper, treatise, dissertation
芸術論 *geijutsuron* essay on art
時事論 *jijiron* comments on current events

❸ [also suffix] **question, issue, problem**

論外な *rongai na* out of the question, beside the point
国防論 *kokubōron* the question of national defense
漢字制限論 *kanji-seigenron* the question of limiting the use of Chinese characters

❹ abbrev. of 論文 *ronbun*: thesis

卒論 *sotsuron* graduation thesis, dissertation

❺ The Analects of Confucius

論孟 *ronmō* The Confucian Analects and the Discourses of Mencius

INDEPENDENT

【ron 論】 argument, argumentation, debate; opinion, view

論より証拠 *Ron yori shōko* Proof is better than argument
論が分かれている *Ron ga wakarete iru* Opinion is divided

【ronjiru (=ronzuru) 論じる(=論ずる)】

① (contend in argument) argue, dispute

声高に論じる *kowadaka ni ronjiru* argue loudly

② (set forth one's opinion systematically) discuss, discourse, comment on, treat

文学を論じる *bungaku o ronjiru* discuss literature

③ consider, take into account

同列に論じる *dōretsu ni ronjiru* consider (something) in the same bracket

SYNONYMS

❶ **argue and discuss**

弁 argue (for) → 2004
議 DISCUSS → 1647
争 CONTEND → 2030

❷ⓐ **theory**

説 THEORY (proposed explanation) → 1547

ⓑ **opinion**

説 opinion → 1547
観 VIEW (conception) → 1880
見 view (personal opinion) → 2544

❸ **question**

問 QUESTION (inquiry) → 3320
題 PROBLEM → 3337

COMPOUND FORMATION

❶ 論理 *ronri*

論理 'logic' is the thread or chain of reasoning (理) of an argument (論 ❶ⓒ).

❷ 勿論 *mochiron*

勿論 'of course, etc.' is a state without (勿) argument (論 ❶ⓒ).

NOTE

★do not confuse with 諭 1598

諒 諒 谅

1575 RYŌ NAMES aki masa makoto

CH 谅 liàng

Radical	Strokes
言 149	15-7-8
Grade	**Freq**
Names	2109
◧ 1 - 7 - 8	

7-8 言

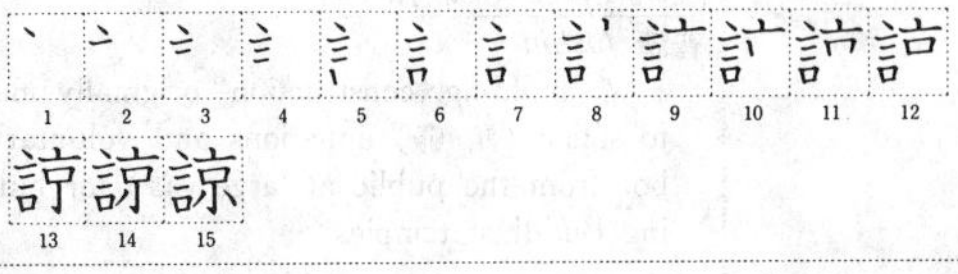

▶UNDERSTAND

COMPOUNDS

❶ [now usu. 了 3350]

ⓐ **understand, comprehend, know clearly**

ⓑ [rarely also 亮 2071] show understanding, be sympathetic, acknowledge, forgive

諒解 *ryōkai* understanding, comprehension; consent

諒承する *ryōshō suru* acknowledge, understand, note

諒察する *ryōsatsu suru* consider, take into account, sympathize with

❷ really, truly

諒闇 *ryōan* court [national] mourning

INDEPENDENT

【ryō 諒】[sometimes also 了 3350] understanding, comprehension

諒とする(=了とする) *ryō to suru* understand, appreciate, excuse

【ryōsuru 諒する】 understand, appreciate, excuse

NAMES

諒一 *ryōichi* (=*masakazu*) male name

諒 *makoto* male name

SYNONYMS

❶ **know and understand**

解 understand → 1517

了 COMPREHEND → 3350

分かる understand → 1972

得 gain understanding of → 477

悟 AWAKE TO → 419

知 KNOW → 1127

通 know thoroughly → 3109

COMPOUND FORMATION

諒闇 *ryōan*

諒闇 'court [national] mourning' originates from the idea of being truly (諒 ❷) dark (闇).

請 請 請 请

1576 SEI SHIN SHŌ▲ ko(u) u(keru)

CH 请 qǐng

Radical	Strokes
言 149	15-7-8
Grade	**Freq**
Jōyō	620
◧ 1 - 7 - 8	

7-8 言

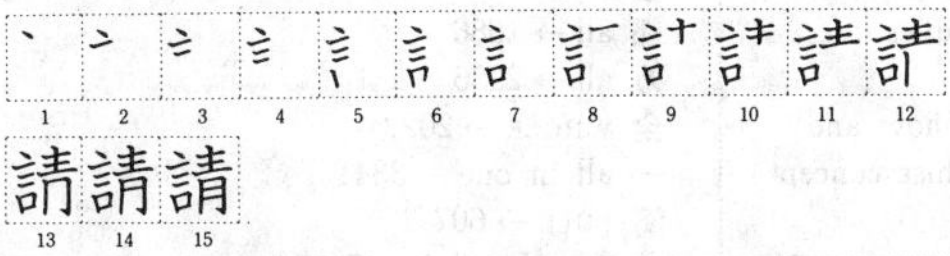

▶REQUEST

COMPOUNDS

❶ [original meaning] **request, ask, beg, solicit**

請求 *seikyū* demand, request, claim

請願 *seigan* petition

請訓 *seikun* request for instructions

申請 *shinsei* application, petition, request

要請する *yōsei suru* request, demand

懇請する *konsei suru* request earnestly, solicit, entreat

普請 *fushin* building, construction

❷ (request a person's presence) invite

招請 *shōsei* invitation

INDEPENDENT

【shōjiru (=shōzuru) 請じる(=招じる, 請ずる, 招ずる)】 invite; usher in

KUN

【ko(u) 請う】

ⓐ ask, request, solicit

ⓑ [also 乞う] beg

寄付を請う *kifu o kou* solicit donations

【u(keru) 請ける】

① undertake, take upon oneself

請け合う *ukeau* assure, guarantee; undertake

請け負う *ukeou* contract for, undertake

下請け *shitauke* subcontract

② redeem (pawned goods), ransom

請け出す *ukedasu* redeem, pay off, take out of pawn

SYNONYMS

❶ **request**

訴 APPEAL TO → 1507
頼 ASK → 1615
嘱 CHARGE WITH → 718
要 REQUIRE → 2635
願 ASK A FAVOR → 1845
求 SEEK → 3550

USAGE

kou

請う
ⓐ ask, request, solicit
ⓑ [also 乞う] beg

乞う
ⓐ [also 請う] beg
ⓑ [in compounds] solicit, pray for

HOMOPHONES

kou ⇨ 乞 1961
ukeru ⇨ 受 2421 享 2051 承 16

COMPOUND FORMATION

普請 *fushin*
普請 'building, construction' originally meant to solicit (請 ❶) donations and voluntary labor from the public at large (普) for building Buddhist temples.

NOTE

⇨ see also USAGE note at 受 2421

7-8 言

諸 諸 諸 诸

1577 SHO moro▲

Ⓒ 诸 zhū

Radical	Strokes
言 149	15-7-8
Grade	**Freq**
Jōyō-6	563
1-7-8	

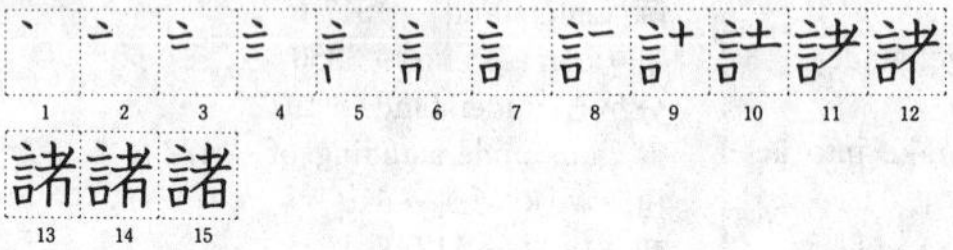

▶VARIOUS

COMPOUNDS

● [also prefix] **various, all kinds of; many, all**
諸説 *shosetsu* various views [theories]
諸島 *shotō* archipelago
諸派 *shoha* minor parties
諸君 *shokun* Ladies and Gentlemen, my friends, you
諸国 *shokoku* various [all] countries
諸般の *shohan no* various, several, all, every
諸問題 *shomondai* various [all] questions [problems]
諸行無常 *shogyōmujō* All things flow and nothing is permanent (a Buddhist concept)

KUN

【**moro** 諸】[in compounds] altogetherness, being all in one piece; both
諸に *moro ni* altogether, completely, bodily
諸共に *morotomo ni* altogether, one and all
諸諸の *moromoro no* various, diverse
諸手(＝両手) *morote* both hands

SYNONYMS

● **various**
庶 MANIFOLD → 3127
雑 MISCELLANEOUS → 1385

● **all**
毎 EVERY → 2034
各 EACH → 2168
皆 ALL → 2445
都 all → 1686
万 all → 2936
全 WHOLE → 2022
一 all in one → 3341
満 FULL → 607
丸 complete(ly) → 3417
完 COMPLETE → 2201
総 TOTAL → 1379

誰 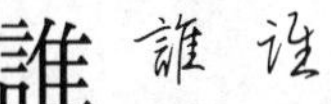

1578 SUI dare tare ta

CH 谁 shuí shéi

Radical	Strokes
言 149	15-7-8
Grade	**Freq**
Non-Jōyō	1741
1-7-8	

7-8 言

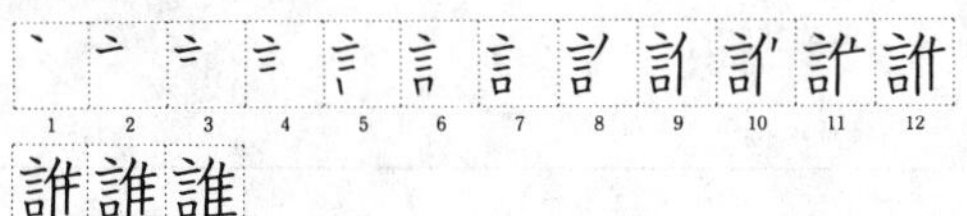

▶WHO

COMPOUNDS

● [original meaning] **who**

誰何する *suika suru* challenge (an unknown person), ask a person's identity

KUN

【dare 誰】 who; someone, somebody; anyone, anybody

誰の *dare no* whose

彼は誰ですか *Kare wa dare desu ka* Who is he?

誰か *dareka* someone, somebody

誰でも *daredemo* anyone, anybody

誰一人も *dare hitori mo* no one, nobody, none

【tare 誰】 literary form of **dare** 誰

誰彼 *tarekare* this or that person

【ta 誰】 *literary* who

誰が為に *ta ga tame ni* for whom

SYNONYMS

● **interrogatives**

何 WHAT → 65

那 interrogative forming element → 843

奈 interrogative forming element → 2219

誕 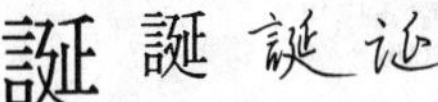

1579 TAN

CH 诞 dàn

Radical	Strokes
言 149	15-7-8
Grade	**Freq**
Jōyō-6	1359
1-7-8	

7-8 言

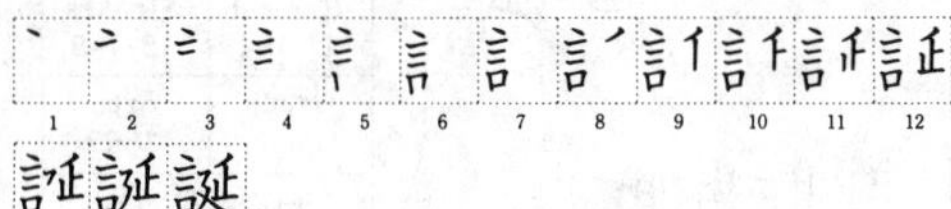

▶BE BORN

COMPOUNDS

❶ⓐ **be born**

ⓑ **birth**

誕生 *tanjō* birth, nativity

誕生日 *tanjōbi* birthday

誕辰 *tanshin* birthday

生誕 *seitan* birth, nativity

キリストの降誕 *kirisuto no kōtan* the Nativity, the Advent

❷ [original meaning] absurd, fantastic, deceitful

荒誕 *kōtan* wild talk, nonsense, lies

SYNONYMS

❶ **give birth**

生 BE BORN → 3497

産 GIVE BIRTH → 3298

殖 MULTIPLY → 994

諷

1580

▶TONE ▶INVESTIGATE ▶PREPARE

nonstandard for 調 1567

7-8 言

請

1581

▶REQUEST

nonstandard for 請 1576

7-8 言

諜

incorrect stroke count ⇨ see 1593

7-8 言

7-8 言
誤
incorrect stroke count ⇨ see 1542

7-8 言
誤
incorrect stroke count ⇨ see 1550

7-8 貝
賠 賠 賠 賠
1582 BAI

CH 赔 péi

Radical	Strokes
貝 154	15-7-8
Grade	**Freq**
Jōyō	1697
1 - 7 - 8	

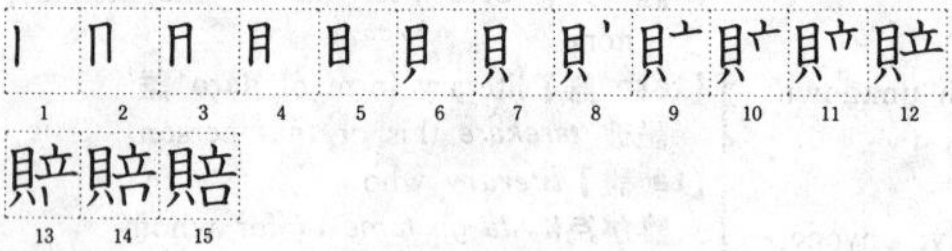

▶ **COMPENSATE**

COMPOUNDS

● [original meaning] **compensate, indemnify**

賠償する *baishō suru* indemnify, compensate, recompense

賠償金 *baishōkin* indemnity, reparation

賠責 *baiseki* liability insurance

自賠法 *jibaihō* Automobile Accident Compensation Act

SYNONYMS

● **compensate**

償 RECOMPENSE → 176

酬 RECIPROCATE → 1539

報 REQUITE → 1698

7-8 貝
賦 賦 賦
1583 FU BU▲

CH 赋 fù

Radical	Strokes
貝 154	15-7-8
Grade	**Freq**
Jōyō	1667
1 - 7 - 8	

▶ **INSTALLMENT**

COMPOUNDS

❶ **installment, payment by installment**

賦払い *bubarai* installment system, easy payment plan

月賦 *geppu* monthly installments

割賦 *kappu* (=*wappu*) payment by installments

❷ levy, levying, tax; exacted service

賦課する *fuka suru* levy, impose, assess

賦役 *fueki* slave labor, corvée, levy of labor

❸ⓐ natural endowment [gift]

ⓑ endow, give

天賦 *tenpu* natural gift

賦与 *fuyo* endowment

❹ ode, prose poem; descriptive prose interspersed with verse

詞賦 *shifu* Chinese poetry

早春賦 *sōshunfu* Ode to Early Spring

INDEPENDENT

【**fu 賦**】 ode, prose poem; descriptive prose interspersed with verse

【**fusuru 賦する**】 levy, allot; compose, write (a poem)

SYNONYMS

❶ **pay**

払う PAY → 194

納 PAY (to the authorities) → 1300

済 settle accounts → 522

支 pay out → 1979

償 RECOMPENSE → 176

❷ **tax**

貢 TRIBUTE → 2281

税 TAX → 1191

租 LAND TAX → 1161

1584 SEN iya(shii) iya(shimu) iya(shimeru) shizu

CH 贱 jiàn

Radical	Strokes
貝 154	15-7-8
Grade	**Freq**
Reference	
1 - 7 - 8	

7-8 貝

COMPOUNDS

❶ [now usu. 卑しい *iyashii*] (low in social status) mean, lowly, humble, inferior in position

賤民 *senmin* lowly people, outcasts
卑賤 *hisen* lowly position, humble condition
貴賤 *kisen* high and low, all ranks
下賤の *gesen no* of low birth, vulgar
賤しい稼業 *iyashii kagyō* mean occupation
賤の女 *shizu no me* woman of lowly birth

❷ [now usu. 卑しい *iyashii*]

ⓐ (of poor appearance) mean, shabby, seedy

ⓑ (lacking elevating human qualities) mean, base, vulgar, despicable

賤しい身形 *iyashii minari* shabby appearance
賤しい笑い *iyashii warai* mean smirk
賤業婦 *sengyōfu* prostitute

❸ [now usu. 卑しむ *iyashimu* or 卑しめる *iyashimeru*] despise, disdain, look down on, regard with contempt

賤称 *senshō* [rare] depreciatory name
賤しむべき *iyashimubeki* despicable
労働を賤しむ *rōdō o iyashimu* despise labor

❹ [original meaning, now archaic] inexpensive, cheap

HOMOPHONES

iyashii ⇨ 卑 2642
iyashimu ⇨ 卑 2642
iyashimeru ⇨ 卑 2642

NOTE

⇨ see USAGE note at 卑 2642

賜 賜 賜

1585 SHI tamawa(ru) tama(u)▲ tamo(u)▲

CH 赐 cì

Radical	Strokes
貝 154	15-7-8
Grade	**Freq**
Jōyō	1850
1 - 7 - 8	

7-8 貝

▶DEIGN TO GIVE

COMPOUNDS

ⓐ [original meaning] **deign to give, bestow, grant, award; be awarded, have the honor to receive**

ⓑ gift, boon

賜金 *shikin* money grant
賜杯 *shihai* trophy given by the Emperor [Prince]
賜暇 *shika* leave of absence, furlough
下賜する *kashi suru* grant, deign to give
恩賜 *onshi* Imperial gift

KUN

【tamawa(ru) 賜る】 deign to give, bestow, grant, award; be awarded, have the honor to receive

賜り物 *tamawarimono* gift, boon

【tama(u), tamo(u) 賜う】

① [sometimes also 給う] *literary* deign to give, bestow, grant, award

賜物 *tamamono* gift, boon; result, fruit
拝謁を賜う *haietsu o tamau* deign to grant an audience

② [usu. 給う] [suffix] *literary* (perform an action for an inferior) deign to

天皇が立ち賜う *Tennō ga tachitamou* His Majesty deigns to stand up

SYNONYMS

ⓐ **give**

授 CONFER → 492
与 GIVE → 3421
上 give (to superior or others) → 3404
下 give (to inferior or speaker) → 3378
呉れる give (to speaker) → 2549
贈 PRESENT A GIFT → 1634
賄 BRIBE → 1529
呈 PRESENT → 2189
進 present to a superior → 3121

HOMOPHONES

tamau ⇨ 給 1350

NOTE

⇨ see USAGE note at 給 1350

7-8 貝

賠

1586

▶**COMPENSATE**

nonstandard for 賠 1582

7-8 足

踏 踏 踏

1587

TŌ fu(mu) fu(maeru)

CH 踏 tà tā

Radical	Strokes
足 157	15-7-8
Grade	**Freq**
Jōyō	985
1 - 7 - 8	

▶**TREAD**

COMPOUNDS

❶ [original meaning] **tread (on), step on, stamp, trample**

踏破する *tōha suru* crush underfoot; travel on foot

未踏の *mitō no* untrodden, unexplored

舞踏(＝舞蹈) *butō* dancing

❷ go to the spot (to investigate something)

踏査 *tōsa* survey, investigation

❸ [formerly also 蹈 1626] follow, pursue

踏襲する *tōshū suru* follow, follow suit

❹ [formerly 沓 2419] crowded, confused

雑踏 *zattō* hustle and bustle, traffic jam

KUN

【**fu(mu) 踏む**】 step on, tread on, stamp; go through, finish; estimate, value; rhyme

踏み入れる *fumiireru* walk in on, tread upon

踏み切る *fumikiru* make a bold start, take a plunge; take off; *sumo* step out of the ring

足踏み *ashibumi* stepping, step, tread

踏切 *fumikiri* railroad crossing

【**fu(maeru) 踏まえる**】 step on, stand on; be based on

政府の方針を踏まえて *seifu no hōshin o fumaete* based on government policy

SYNONYMS

❶ **walk**

足 travel on foot → 2188

歩 WALK → 2416

徒 go on foot → 416

脚 move on foot → 974

7-8 足

踐

1588

▶**IMPLEMENT**

nonstandard for 践 1535

7-8 車

輪 輪 輪

1589

RIN wa

CH 轮 lún

Radical	Strokes
車 159	15-7-8
Grade	**Freq**
Jōyō-4	936
1 - 7 - 8	

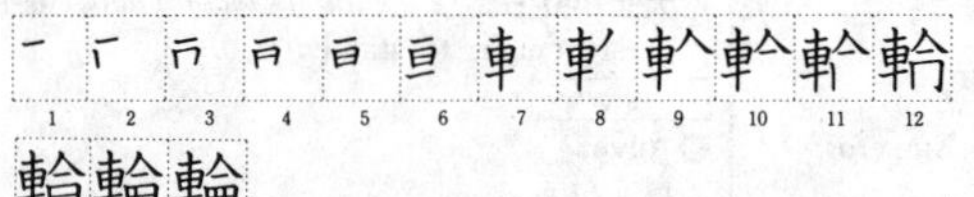

▶**WHEEL** ▶**RING**

COMPOUNDS

❶ⓐ [original meaning] **wheel**

ⓑ counter for wheels

車輪 *sharin* wheel

前輪 *zenrin* front wheel

二輪車 *nirinsha* two-wheeled vehicle, bicycle

一輪車 *ichirinsha* unicycle; wheelbarrow

❷ **wheeled vehicle, cycle, bicycle, automobile**

輪業 *ringyō* bicycle industry

輪禍 *rinka* automobile accident, traffic accident

輪タク *rintaku* pedicab, trishaw

競輪 *keirin* bicycle race

駐輪場 *chūrinjō* bicycle parking lot

❸ **ring, circle**

輪状の *rinjō no* ring-shaped, annular

輪形の *rinkei no* ring-shaped, circular

年輪 *nenrin* annual ring, growth ring

五輪のマーク *gorin no māku* the five-ring Olympic emblem
❹ⓐ corolla, flower
ⓑ counter for flowers
大輪の *tairin no* large-flowered
一輪の花 *ichirin no hana* a (single) flower
❺ take turns, rotate, alternate
輪転 *rinten* rotation
輪番 *rinban* turn, rotation
輪唱する *rinshō suru* troll, sing in a circular canon
輪読 *rindoku* reading by turns
❻ periphery, outline
輪郭 *rinkaku* contour, outline, profile

KUN

【wa 輪】
① [sometimes also 環] ring, circle, link
輪投げ *wanage* quoits, ringtoss
輪になって踊る *wa ni natte odoru* dance in a circle [ring]
指輪 *yubiwa* (finger) ring
② wheel

SYNONYMS

❶ & ❸ circular objects
車 WHEEL → 3552
環 RING → 1090
盤 DISK → 2851
❷ vehicle
車 VEHICLE → 3552
乗 vehicle → 3576
台 COUNTER FOR VEHICLES → 2005
❺ alternate
迭 ALTERNATE → 3077
交 INTERCHANGE → 2015

USAGE

wa
輪
① [sometimes also 環] ring, circle, link
② wheel
環
[usu. 輪] ring, circle, link

HOMOPHONES

wa ⇨ 環 1090

NOTE

★do not confuse with 輪 1607

輛
1590 RYŌ

Ⓒⓗ 辆 liàng

Radical	Strokes
車 159	15-7-8
Grade Reference	Freq
◧ 1 - 7 - 8	

7-8 車

COMPOUNDS

[now replaced by 両 3518]
ⓐ vehicle, railway car
ⓑ counter for railway cars
車輛 *sharyō* vehicle, car; rolling stock
三輛 *sanryō* three cars, three coaches

醋
1591 SAKU

Ⓒⓗ 醋 cù

Radical	Strokes
酉 164	15-7-8
Grade Reference	Freq
◧ 1 - 7 - 8	

7-8 酉

COMPOUNDS

● [now replaced by 酢 1516] [original meaning] vinegar
醋酸 *sakusan* acetic acid

醉
1592

▶BECOME INTOXICATED
nonstandard for 酔 1483

7-8 酉

7-9 言

謀 𫞏 课

1593 BŌ MU haka(ru) hakarigoto▲

13 14 15 16

CH 谋 móu

Radical	Strokes
言 149	16-7-9
Grade Jōyō	Freq 1348
1-7-9	

▶**SCHEME**

COMPOUNDS

❶ⓐ **scheme, plot, conspire, contrive**
ⓑ **scheme, plot, conspiracy, intrigue**
謀殺 *bōsatsu* premeditated murder
首謀者 *shubōsha* ringleader, mastermind
謀略 *bōryaku* stratagem, scheme, plot
謀反 *muhon* rebellion, revolt, treason
共謀 *kyōbō* conspiracy, collusion
陰謀 *inbō* scheme, plot, conspiracy
❷ⓐ plan, think ahead
ⓑ plan, strategy
謀臣 *bōshin* strategist, tactician; schemer
深謀 *shinbō* deeply laid plan
無謀 *mubō* recklessness, imprudence
参謀 *sanbō* staff officer, the staff; adviser, counselor

KUN

【haka(ru) 謀る】 scheme, plot, conspire, contrive
暗殺を謀る *ansatsu o hakaru* plot an assassination

【hakarigoto 謀】 scheme, plot, stratagem, conspiracy

SYNONYMS

❶ **plans and planning**
策 SCHEME → 2679
略 STRATEGY → 1169
図 systematic plan → 3071
企 PROJECT → 2021
計 PLAN → 1441
画 DRAW UP A PLAN → 3000
案 PROPOSAL → 2270

HOMOPHONES

hakaru ⇨ 計 1441 図 3071 諮 1596 量 2471 測 610

NOTE

⇨ see USAGE note at 計 1441

7-9 言

諷

1594 FŪ

CH 讽 fěng

Radical	Strokes
言 149	16-7-9
Grade Reference	Freq
1-7-9	

COMPOUNDS

❶ [now replaced by 風 3007] insinuate, hint, satirize
諷刺 *fūshi* satire, sarcasm
諷喩 *fūyu* hint, insinuation, allegory
諷する *fūsuru* insinuate, hint, satirize
❷ [archaic] recite, chant
諷誦 *fūju* reciting

7-9 言

謂

1595 I i(u)

CH 谓 wèi

Radical	Strokes
言 149	16-7-9
Grade Reference	Freq
1-7-9	

COMPOUNDS

● [usu. 言う *iu*] refer to, call—used chiefly in certain set expressions
謂わば *iwaba* as it were, so to call it
これを音素と謂う *Kore o onso to iu* To this is given the term "phoneme"
ここで船とは宇宙船を謂う *Koko de fune to wa uchūsen o iu* By "ship" here is meant

a spaceship
所謂 *iwayuru* what is called, so-called

HOMOPHONES

iu ⇨ 言 1941 云 1931

NOTE

⇨ see USAGE note at 言 1941

諮 諮 諮 谘

1596 SHI haka(ru)

CH 谘 zī

Radical	Strokes
言 149	16-7-9
Grade	**Freq**
Jōyō	1252
1-7-9	

7-9 言

▶CONSULT

COMPOUNDS

● **consult, confer, ask for advice, inquire**
諮問する *shimon suru* consult, inquire
諮議する *shigi suru* consult, confer

KUN

【**haka(ru)** 諮る】consult, confer, ask (a person's) opinion
委員会に諮る *iinkai ni hakaru* submit (a plan) to a committee for deliberation

SYNONYMS

● **inquire**
伺う INQUIRE (*humble*) → 69
尋ねる INQUIRE → 2322
質 query → 2808
聞く ask → 3326
問 QUESTION → 3320
詰 question closely → 1521

HOMOPHONES

hakaru ⇨ 謀 1593 図 3071 計 1441 量 2471 測 610

NOTE

⇨ see USAGE note at 計 1441

謡 謠 謡 谣

1597 YŌ utai uta(u)

CH 谣 yáo

Radical	Strokes
言 149	16-7-9
Grade	**Freq**
Jōyō	1458
1-7-9	

7-9 言

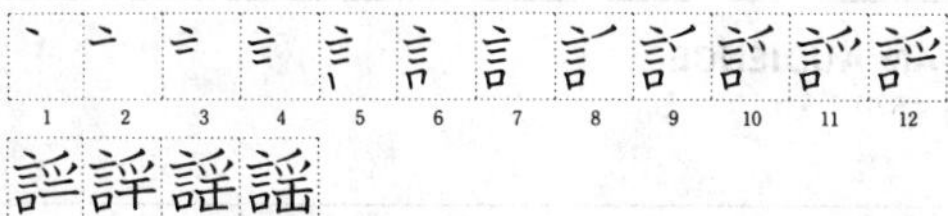

▶POPULAR SONG

COMPOUNDS

❶ⓐ **popular song, ballad, folk song**
ⓑ **chant in a noh drama**
俗謡 *zokuyō* popular song, ballad
民謡 *min'yō* folk song [ballad]
歌謡曲 *kayōkyoku* popular song
童謡 *dōyō* children's song, nursery rhyme
里謡 *riyō* ballad, folk song
謡曲 *yōkyoku* noh chant
❷ [original meaning, now archaic] sing

KUN

【**utai** 謡】*utai*, chanting of a noh text
謡物 *utaimono* an *utai* piece for recitation
【**uta(u)** 謡う】recite, chant (esp. from a noh drama text)
謡を謡う *utai o utau* recite an *utai*

SYNONYMS

❶ⓐ **music and songs**
歌 SONG → 1825
曲 MUSICAL COMPOSITION → 3527
節 tune → 2691
調べ melody → 1567
音 sound of music → 2070
楽 MUSIC → 2826

HOMOPHONES

utau ⇨ 歌 1825 唄 400 謳 1632

NOTE

⇨ see USAGE note at 歌 1825

7-9 言

諭 䛕 諭 谕

1598 YU sato(su)

CH 谕 yù

Radical	Strokes
言 149	16-7-9
Grade	**Freq**
Jōyō	1490
1-7-9	

▶**ADMONISH**

COMPOUNDS

ⓐ **admonish, give guidance, instruct, advise, persuade**

ⓑ official guidance, Imperial instructions, edict

諭旨 *yushi* official suggestion or instruction (to a subordinate)

教諭 *kyōyu* teacher, instructor

説諭 *setsuyu* admonition, reproof

訓諭 *kun'yu* [rare] admonition, caution, warning

勅諭 *chokuyu* Imperial instructions, Imperial mandate

KUN

【**sato(su) 諭す**】admonish, give guidance, instruct, advise; persuade, reason (with)

諭し *satoshi* guidance, admonition

教え諭す *oshiesatosu* give guidance

SYNONYMS

ⓐ **teach**

訓 INSTRUCT → 1454

導 GUIDE → 2888

迪 EDIFY → 3076

啓 ENLIGHTEN → 2763

教 TEACH → 1493

授 teach → 492

育 educate → 2050

練 TRAIN → 1375

ⓐ **warn**

告 advise → 2409

戒 CAUTION → 3204

警 WARN → 2893

NOTE

★do not confuse with 論 1574

7-9 言

諾

1599

▶**CONSENT**

nonstandard for 諾 1568

7-9 言

謁

1600

▶**BE GRANTED AN AUDIENCE**

nonstandard for 謁 1570

7-9 言

諮

1601

▶**CONSULT**

nonstandard for 諮 1596

7-9 言

諸

1602

▶**VARIOUS**

nonstandard for 諸 1577

7-9 言

䛕

1603

▶**ADMONISH**

nonstandard for 諭 1598

輸 輸 輸 𨏊

1607 YU SHU▲

CH 输 shū

Radical	Strokes
車 159	16-7-9
Grade	Freq
Jōyō-5	360
1 - 7 - 9	

7-9 車

▶TRANSPORT

COMPOUNDS

❶ⓐ [original meaning] (transfer by vehicle) **transport, ship, carry, convey**

ⓑ transfer

輸送する *yusō suru* transport, convey

運輸 *un'yu* transport(ation), conveyance

空輸 *kūyu* air transportation

輸出 *yushutsu* export

輸入 *yunyū* import, importation

輸血 *yuketsu* blood transfusion

❷ abbrev. of 輸入 *yunyū* or 輸出 *yushutsu*: **import, export**

輸銀 *yugin* import-export bank

禁輸 *kin'yu* embargo

直輸 *chokuyu* direct import [export]

密輸 *mitsuyu* smuggling, contraband trade

❸ [rare] lose, be defeated

輸贏 *yuei* (=*shuei*) gain or loss

INDEPENDENT

【yusuru 輸する】 transport, carry; give, yield; be defeated

SYNONYMS

❶ⓐ **carry**

搬 CARRY → 647

運 CARRY → 3140

NOTE

★do not confuse with 輪 1589

輸 1608

▶TRANSPORT

nonstandard for 輸 1607

7-9 車

辦 1609 BEN

CH 办 bàn

Radical	Strokes
辛 160	16-7-9
Grade	Freq
Reference	
1 - 7 - 9	

7-9 辛

COMPOUNDS

● [now replaced by 弁 2004] [original meaning] dispose of, manage, attend to

合辦 *gōben* joint management [venture]

辨 1610

nonstandard for 弁 2004

7-9 辛

頸 1611 KEI kubi

CH 颈 jǐng

Radical	Strokes
頁 181	16-9-7
Grade	Freq
Reference	
1 - 7 - 9	

7-9 巠

COMPOUNDS

[now usu. 首 *kubi*]

ⓐ [original meaning] neck

ⓑ narrow part, neck (of a bottle)

頸飾り *kubikazari* necklace

手頸 *tekubi* wrist

バイオリンの頸 *baiorin no kubi* neck of a violin

HOMOPHONES

kubi ⇨ 首 2265

NOTE

⇨ see USAGE note at 首 2265

7-9 穎 1612 EI

CH 颖 yǐng

Radical	Strokes
禾 115	16-5-11
Grade	**Freq**
Reference	
1-7-9	

COMPOUNDS

❶ distinguished, outstanding, talented, intelligent

穎才 *eisai* [now usu. 英才] talent, genius; gifted person, talented person

穎脱する *eidatsu suru* gain recognition, rise above one's fellows

❷ glume, awn

穎果 *eika* caryopsis

穎 *ei* glume, awn

7-9 頻 1613

▶**FREQUENTLY**

nonstandard for 頻 1758

7-9 頽 1614 TAI

CH 颓 tuí

Radical	Strokes
頁 181	16-9-7
Grade	**Freq**
Reference	
1-7-9	

COMPOUNDS

● [now also 退 *tai* 3094] decline, decay

頽勢 *taisei* one's declining fortunes, decay

頽廃 *taihai* degeneration, decadence, deterioration

頽唐 *taitō* decadence, decline

頽齢 *tairei* declining years

衰頽 *suitai* decline, decay, degeneration

7-9 頼 頼 頼 頼 1615 RAI tano(mu) tano(moshii) tayo(ru)

CH 赖 lài

Radical	Strokes
貝 154	16-7-9
Grade	**Freq**
Jōyō	785
1-7-9	

▶**RELY ON** ▶**ASK**

COMPOUNDS

❶ **rely on, depend on, trust**

信頼する *shinrai suru* rely on, have confidence, trust in

無頼漢 *buraikan* villain, scoundrel

❷ **ask, request**

頼信紙 *raishinshi* telegraph (application) blank

依頼する *irai suru* request, make a request; entrust, commission; rely on, depend on

KUN

【**tano(mu)** 頼む】 ask, request

頼み *tanomi* request, favor; reliance, dependence

頼み込む *tanomikomu* request earnestly

【**tano(moshii)** 頼もしい】 reliable, trustworthy; hopeful

【tayo(ru) 頼る】 rely on, depend on, trust
　頼り *tayori* reliance, dependence, trust; help, support
　頼り無い *tayorinai* unreliable, undependable; vague; helpless, forlorn

SYNONYMS

❶ **rely on**
　依 DEPEND ON → 84

❷ **request**
　請 REQUEST → 1576
　訴 APPEAL TO → 1507
　嘱 CHARGE WITH → 718
　要 REQUIRE → 2635
　願 ASK A FAVOR → 1845
　求 SEEK → 3550

1616

▶RELY ON　▶ASK
nonstandard for 頼 1615

7-9
束

謙 謙 謙 謙　Ⓒ 谦 qiān
1617　KEN

Radical	Strokes
言 149	17-7-10
Grade	**Freq**
Jōyō	1545
◧ 1-7-10	

7-10
言

1 2 3 4 5 6 7 8 9 10 11 12 13 14 15 16 17

▶HUMBLE

COMPOUNDS

● **humble, modest**
　謙遜 *kenson* humility, modesty
　謙虚な *kenkyo na* humble, modest
　謙譲 *kenjō* modesty, humility

SYNONYMS

● **humble**
　拝 HUMBLY → 303

謹 謹 謹 謹　Ⓒ 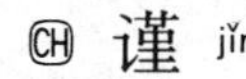 jǐn
1618　KIN　tsutsushi(mu)

Radical	Strokes
言 149	17-7-10
Grade	**Freq**
Jōyō	1780
◧ 1-7-10	

7-10
言

1 2 3 4 5 6 7 8 9 10 11 12 13 14 15 16 17

▶RESPECTFULLY

COMPOUNDS

❶ **respectfully, with respect, reverently; respectful**
　謹賀新年 *kingashinnen* Happy New Year
　謹呈する *kintei suru* present, make a present
　謹厳な *kingen na* stern, grave, solemn
　謹告する *kinkoku suru* inform with respect, announce respectfully
　謹啓 *kinkei* Dear Sirs, Gentlemen
　謹書 *kinsho* written, respectfully

❷ **carefully, attentively, cautiously**
　謹製 *kinsei* careful production
　謹聴する *kinchō suru* listen attentively
　謹慎 *kinshin* house arrest, domiciliary confinement; penitence

KUN

【tsutsushi(mu) 謹む】 [usu. in TE-form] be respectful, be humble
　謹んで *tsutsushinde* respectfully, reverently, humbly

SYNONYMS

❶ **respectful**
　恭 RESPECTFUL → 2459
　奉 reverentially → 2559
　拝 HUMBLY → 303

❷ **careful**
　慎 PRUDENT → 643
　精 meticulous → 1366

HOMOPHONES

tsutsushimu ⇨ 慎 643

NOTE

⇨ see USAGE note at 慎 643

7-10 言

講 講 講 𧫷 (CH) 讲 jiǎng

1619 KŌ

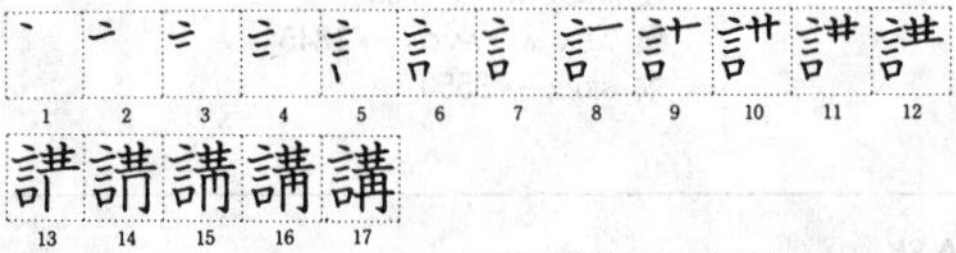

Radical	Strokes
言 149	17-7-10
Grade	Freq
Jōyō-5	670
1-7-10	

▶**LECTURE**

COMPOUNDS

❶ⓐ **lecture, speak in public**
ⓑ **lecture**
ⓒ counter for lectures
講演 *kōen* lecture
講師 *kōshi* speaker, lecturer
講堂 *kōdō* lecture hall, auditorium
講座 *kōza* lectureship, (professor's) chair; course of study
講壇 *kōdan* lecture platform
講読する *kōdoku suru* read and explain
開講する *kaikō suru* begin a series of one's lectures
受講する *jukō suru* attend lectures
近代文学十講 *kindai bungaku jikkō* Ten Lectures on Modern Literature
第二講 *dainikō* second lecture

❷ⓐ **expound, explain, interpret**
ⓑ **speak, tell**
講義 *kōgi* lecture
講話 *kōwa* lecture, discourse
講談 *kōdan* storytelling, narration; historical narrative

❸ study, practice
講習 *kōshū* short training course
講武 *kōbu* military training

❹ [formerly also 媾 637] make peace, come to terms
講和する *kōwa suru* make peace with, reconcile

❺ⓐ fraternity, religious association
ⓑ mutual financing association
講社 *kōsha* religious association, fraternity
講中 *kōjū* religious association (of non-Christians); club
恵比須講 *ebisukō* fête in honor of *Ebisu*
頼母子講 *tanomoshikō* mutual financing association

INDEPENDENT

【**kō 講**】mutual financing association
無尽の講 *mujin no kō* mutual financing association

【**kōjiru (=kōzuru) 講じる(=講ずる)**】lecture, give a lecture; devise, think out
手段を講じる *shudan o kōjiru* take steps [measures]

SYNONYMS

❶ⓐ **speak in public**
演 make a speech → 697
ⓑ **units of learning**
課 LESSON → 1573
科 course → 1138

❷ **explain**
釈 ELUCIDATE → 1484
説 EXPLAIN → 1547
明 make clear → 855
解 CLARIFY → 1517
注 annotate → 325

❺ **organized bodies**
院 INSTITUTION → 454
連 federation → 3103
労 workers' union → 2548
組 union → 1337
体 BODY → 71
団 BODY → 3053
協 association → 93
会 SOCIETY → 2020

謝 謝 訁 　 CH 谢 xiè

1620 SHA ayama(ru)

Radical 言 149	Strokes 17-7-10
Grade Jōyō-5	Freq 1188
◧ 1-7-10	

7-10 言

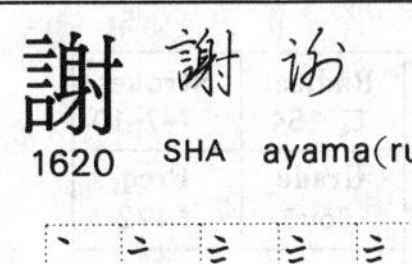

▶THANK ▶APOLOGIZE

COMPOUNDS

❶ⓐ **thank, be grateful**

ⓑ **monetary gift of thanks, remuneration, reward, fee**

謝恩 *shaon* expression of gratitude
感謝 *kansha* gratitude, thanks
謝礼 *sharei* remuneration, reward; thanks
月謝 *gessha* monthly fee
薄謝 *hakusha* small remuneration, small token of gratitude

❷ **apologize**

謝罪 *shazai* apology
陳謝 *chinsha* apology

❸ decline, refuse

謝絶する *shazetsu suru* decline, refuse

❹ fade, wither, atrophy

代謝(＝新陳代謝) *taisha* (＝*shinchintaisha*) metabolism; renewal, regeneration

❺ [formerly 藉 2529] console, solace

慰謝料 *isharyō* consolation money

INDEPENDENT

【**shasuru** 謝する】thank; apologize; decline

KUN

【**ayama(ru)** 謝る】apologize

謝り *ayamari* apology, excuse
平謝り *hiraayamari* humble apology

SYNONYMS

❶ⓐ **thanking and gratitude**

礼 thanks → 818
恩 DEBT OF GRATITUDE → 2655

ⓑ **monetary gifts**

礼 monetary gift → 818

USAGE

ayamaru

謝る
apologize

誤る
① [formerly also 謬る] mistake, make a mistake, err
② mislead, lead astray

謬る
[now usu. 誤る] mistake, make a mistake, err

HOMOPHONES

ayamaru ⇨ 誤 1542 謬 1631

COMPOUND FORMATION

代謝(＝新陳代謝) *taisha* (＝*shinchintaisha*)
代謝 'metabolism, etc.' is the replacing (代) of what has atrophied (謝 ❹).

謙

1621

▶**HUMBLE**
nonstandard for 謙 1617

7-10 言

講

1622

▶**LECTURE**
nonstandard for 講 1619

7-10 言

謠

1623

▶**POPULAR SONG**
nonstandard for 謡 1597

7-10 言

7-10 貝

購 購 購 購

1624 KŌ

CH 购 gòu

Radical	Strokes
貝 154	17-7-10
Grade	**Freq**
Jōyō	1472
1-7-10	

1 2 3 4 5 6 7 8 9 10 11 12 13 14 15 16 17

▶PURCHASE

COMPOUNDS

● [original meaning] **purchase, buy**

購買 *kōbai* purchase, buying
購読 *kōdoku* subscription
購入 *kōnyū* purchase, buying
購書 *kōsho* purchasing books; purchased books

SYNONYMS

● **buy**

買 BUY → 2598

7-10 貝

購

1625

▶PURCHASE

nonstandard for 購 1624

7-10 足

蹈

1626 TŌ

CH 蹈 dǎo

Radical	Strokes
足 157	17-7-10
Grade	**Freq**
Reference	
1-7-10	

COMPOUNDS

❶ [original meaning] step on, tread

舞蹈(=舞踏) *butō* dancing
蹈鞴 *tatara* foot bellows
蹈鞴を踏む *tatara o fumu* totter

❷ [now usu. 踏 1587] follow, pursue

蹈襲する *tōshū suru* follow, follow suit

7-10 車

轄 轄 轄 轄

1627 KATSU

CH 辖 xiá

Radical	Strokes
車 159	17-7-10
Grade	**Freq**
Jōyō	1650
1-7-10	

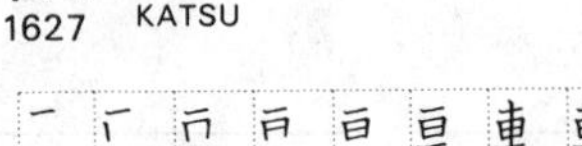

1 2 3 4 5 6 7 8 9 10 11 12 13 14 15 16 17

▶EXERCISE JURISDICTION OVER

COMPOUNDS

❶ **exercise [have] jurisdiction over, control, supervise, administer**

統轄 *tōkatsu* general control, control and jurisdiction
管轄 *kankatsu* jurisdiction, control
直轄 *chokkatsu* direct jurisdiction [control], immediate supervision
分轄 *bunkatsu* separate control [jurisdiction]
所轄 *shokatsu* jurisdiction

❷ [original meaning, now archaic] wedge

車轄 *shakatsu* linchpin

SYNONYMS

❶ **direct and supervise**

管 EXERCISE CONTROL → 2701
制 CONTROL → 1274
掌 TAKE CHARGE OF → 2602
監 OVERSEE → 2852
督 SUPERVISE → 2796
司 OFFICIATE → 2931
宰 PRESIDE → 2275

営 MANAGE → 2603
理 manage → 970

経 MANAGE → 1331

轄
1628

▶**EXERCISE JURISDICTION OVER**
nonstandard for 轄 1627

7-10 車

醜 醜 醜
1629 SHŪ miniku(i) shiko▲

CH 丑 chǒu

Radical	Strokes
酉 164	17-7-10
Grade	Freq
Jōyō	1837
1-7-10	

7-10 酉

一 丆 丙 丙 两 西 酉 酉′ 酉′ 酌 酌 酣 酣 酥 醜 醜 醜
1 2 3 4 5 6 7 8 9 10 11 12 13 14 15 16 17

▶**UGLY**

COMPOUNDS

❶ **ugly, bad-looking, unsightly**
醜悪な *shūaku na* ugly, repulsive
醜女 *shūjo* ugly woman
美醜 *bishū* beauty or ugliness
❷ disgraceful, dishonorable, indecent
醜行 *shūkō* disgraceful [scandalous] conduct
醜聞 *shūbun* scandal, ill fame
醜態 *shūtai* disgraceful behavior, shameful conduct

INDEPENDENT

【shū 醜】 ugliness; disgrace
醜と美 *shū to bi* ugliness and beauty

KUN

【miniku(i) 醜い】 ugly, bad-looking; ignoble, disgraceful, mean
醜さ *minikusa* ugliness
醜い女 *minikui onna* ugly [homely] woman
醜い争い *minikui arasoi* scandalous dispute
【shiko 醜】
[in compounds] *elegant*
ⓐ ugliness
ⓑ term of humility
醜女 *shikome* ugly woman
醜の御楯 *shiko-no-mitate* the humble shield of our Sovereign Lord

臨 临◆ 臨 臨
1630 RIN nozo(mu)

CH 临 lín

Radical	Strokes
臣 131	18-7-11
Grade	Freq
Jōyō-6	821
1-7-11	

7-11 臣

丨 𠃌 𠃌 𠂉 𠂉 𠂉 臣 臣′ 臣′ 臣′ 臣′ 臣′ 臨 臨 臨 臨 臨 臨
1 2 3 4 5 6 7 8 9 10 11 12 13 14 15 16 17 18

▶**BE PRESENT AT**

COMPOUNDS

❶ⓐ **be present at, be on the spot, attend, come to, visit**
ⓑ (of a ruler or superior) descend upon, come down upon, arrive
臨床医 *rinshōi* clinician
臨席 *rinseki* presence, attendance
臨場 *rinjō* presence, attendance; visit
臨検 *rinken* spot inspection, raid
臨在 *rinzai* presence
来臨 *rairin* attendance, presence; visit
君臨する *kunrin suru* reign, rule over, dominate

❷ⓐ **on the point of, on the verge of, face to face with**
ⓑ abbrev. of 臨時 *rinji*: temporary, provisional
臨時の *rinji no* temporary, provisional, special
臨終 *rinjū* hour of death, one's last moment
臨界点 *rinkaiten* critical point [temperature]
臨機応変 *rinkiōhen* adaptation to circumstances
臨休 *rinkyū* extra [special] holiday
❸ [original meaning] overlook, look down on, face
臨海学校 *rinkai-gakkō* seaside school

臨港の *rinkō no* facing [along] the harbor
❹ copy, imitate
臨写 *rinsha* copying

KUN

【nozo(mu) 臨む】
① be present at, be on the spot, attend, come to, visit
会合に臨む *kaigō ni nozomu* be present at a meeting
② come face to face, meet, be confronted with
別れに臨んで *wakare ni nozonde* at parting (with)
③ overlook, face, border on
海に臨んだホテル *umi ni nozonda hoteru* hotel on the sea

SYNONYMS

❶ⓐ attend
登 attend → 2595
出 appear → 3498
ⓐ exist and be
居 be present → 3080
在 BE → 2984
存 EXIST → 2982
有 exist → 2983
也 CLASSICAL COPULA → 3406
❷ⓐ on the verge of
-際 on the verge of → 714
将 on the verge of → 460
-掛かる be on the verge of → 493

HOMOPHONES

nozomu ⇨ 望 2742

NOTE

⇨ see USAGE note at 望 2742

7-11 言

謬
1631 BYŪ ayama(ru)

Ⓒⓗ 谬 miù

Radical	Strokes
言 149	18-7-11
Grade	Freq
Reference	
◧ 1-7-11	

COMPOUNDS

ⓐ [now usu. 誤る *ayamaru*] mistake, make a mistake, err
ⓑ wrong, mistaken, false
謬説 *byūsetsu* fallacy, mistaken opinion
謬見 *byūken* wrong view, mistaken notion
謬伝 *byūden* false report [rumor]
誤謬 *gobyū* mistake, error, fallacy

HOMOPHONES

ayamaru ⇨ 誤 1542 謝 1620

NOTE

⇨ see USAGE note at 謝 1620

7-11 言

謳
1632 Ō uta(u)

Ⓒⓗ 讴 ōu

Radical	Strokes
言 149	18-7-11
Grade	Freq
Reference	
◧ 1-7-11	

COMPOUNDS

❶ⓐ sing the joys of, extol, eulogize
ⓑ declare, state, express
謳歌する *ōka suru* glorify, eulogize, applaud
謳われる *utawareru* be famous for
謳い文句 *utaimonku* catchphrase, promotional line
❷ [original meaning, now archaic] sing a tune

HOMOPHONES

utau ⇨ 歌 1825 謡 1597 唄 400

NOTE

⇨ see USAGE note at 歌 1825

7-11 言

謹
1633

▶**RESPECTFULLY**
nonstandard for 謹 1618

贈 贈 贈 贈

1634 zō sō oku(ru)

CH 赠 zèng

Radical	Strokes
貝 154	18-7-11
Grade	Freq
Jōyō	999
1-7-11	

7-11 貝

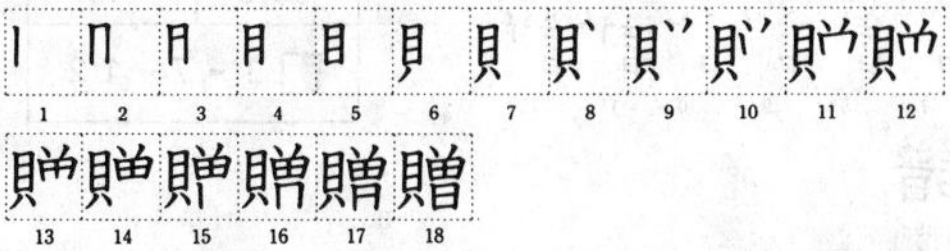

▶**PRESENT A GIFT**

COMPOUNDS

❶ **present a gift, give a present**
贈答品 *zōtōhin* present, gift
贈呈 *zōtei* presentation
贈与 *zōyo* donation, presentation
贈賄 *zōwai* bribery, corruption
寄贈 *kizō* (=*kisō*) donation, presentation

❷ confer a rank posthumously
贈位する *zōi suru* confer a posthumous rank
遺贈 *izō* testation, bequest

INDEPENDENT

【**zō 贈**】presentation; conferment
贈中村先生 *zō nakamura sensei* presented to Prof. Nakamura

KUN

【**oku(ru) 贈る**】
① present (a gift), give (a present)
贈り物 *okurimono* present, gift
花を贈る *hana o okuru* give flowers as a gift
② bestow on, confer upon
死後に位を贈る *shigo ni kurai o okuru* confer a posthumous rank

SYNONYMS

❶ **give**
呈 PRESENT → 2189
進 present to a superior → 3121
賄 BRIBE → 1529
賜 DEIGN TO GIVE → 1585
授 CONFER → 492
与 GIVE → 3421
上 give (to superior or others) → 3404
下 give (to inferior or speaker) → 3378
呉れる give (to speaker) → 2549

HOMOPHONES

okuru ⇨ 送 3093

NOTE

⇨ see USAGE note at 送 3093

蹟

1635 SEKI

CH 迹 jī

Radical	Strokes
足 157	18-7-11
Grade	Freq
Reference	
1-7-11	

7-11 足

COMPOUNDS

[now replaced by 跡 1534]

❶ⓐ [original meaning] (mark left by something) trace(s), track, mark, footprint, trail
ⓑ (sign of former presence) traces, ruins, remains
筆蹟 *hisseki* handwriting, holograph
手蹟 *shuseki* holograph, calligraphic specimen
真蹟 *shinseki* genuine handwriting
遺蹟 *iseki* ruins, remains
古蹟 *koseki* historic remains; ruins
史蹟 *shiseki* historic spot [remains]
旧蹟 *kyūseki* historic spot

❷ sign, indication, phenomenon
奇蹟 *kiseki* miracle, wonder

轉

1636

▶**TURN**
nonstandard for 転 1480

7-11 車

7-12 言

譜 譜 譜 谱

1637 FU

Ⓒⓗ 谱 pǔ

Radical	Strokes
言 149	19-7-12
Grade	**Freq**
Jōyō	1401
1-7-12	

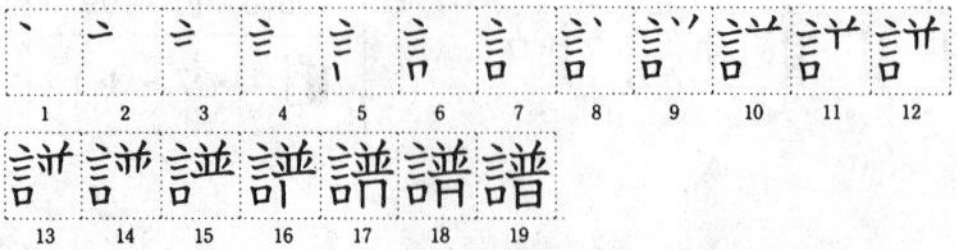

▶**SYSTEMATIC RECORD**

COMPOUNDS

❶ [also suffix] systematic record, as:
ⓐ **record, chronology, chart**
ⓑ **record of shogi, chess or go**
ⓒ **family record, genealogy**
年譜 *nenpu* chronological record
棋譜 *kifu* record of a game of shogi [go]
譜代 *fudai* successive generations; hereditary Tokugawa daimyo
系譜 *keifu* genealogy, family tree
家譜 *kafu* genealogy, pedigree
皇統譜 *kōtōfu* Imperial family record
❷ (musical record) **sheet music, musical score, notes**
楽譜 *gakufu* (sheet of) music, musical score
採譜 *saifu* recording a tune in musical notes
暗譜 *anpu* memorizing musical scores
五線譜 *gosenfu* staff notation
❸ [also suffix] album
花譜 *kafu* flower album

INDEPENDENT

【**fu** 譜】 sheet music, musical score
譜を読む *fu o yomu* read music

SYNONYMS

❶ & ❷ **records**
録 RECORD → 1742
記 written account → 1453
誌 records → 1548
史 HISTORY → 3510
伝 biography → 44

7-12 言

譏

1638 KI soshi(ru)

Ⓒⓗ 讥 jī

Radical	Strokes
言 149	19-7-12
Grade	**Freq**
Reference	
1-7-12	

COMPOUNDS

● [original meaning] slander, censure, criticize
譏誹 *kihi* [archaic] slander, abuse
譏嫌 *kigen* [now usu. 機嫌] mood, temper, disposition; health
譏る *soshiru* slander, libel, criticize

HOMOPHONES

soshiru ⇨ 誹 1572

NOTE

⇨ see COMPOUND FORMATION for 機嫌 *kigen* ⇨ 機 1076

7-12 言

識 識 識 谈

1639 SHIKI

Ⓒⓗ 识 shí zhì

Radical	Strokes
言 149	19-7-12
Grade	**Freq**
Jōyō-5	591
1-7-12	

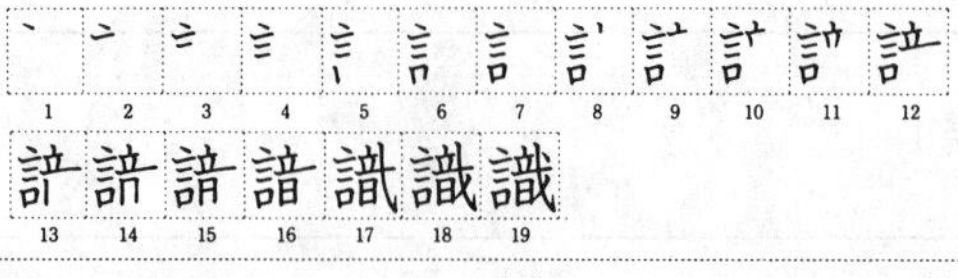

▶**DISCRIMINATE** ▶**KNOWLEDGE**

COMPOUNDS

❶ⓐ **discriminate, discern, recognize**
ⓑ **power of discrimination, discernment**
ⓒ *Buddhism* consciousness
識別する *shikibetsu suru* discriminate, dis-

cern, recognize
認識 *ninshiki* cognition, perception; understanding
鑑識する *kanshiki suru* identify, judge; discern
眼識 *ganshiki* insight, discrimination
意識する *ishiki suru* be conscious of, be aware of
六識 *rokushiki* six consciousnesses
❷ **(acquired) knowledge, sense, wisdom, learning**
識見 *shikiken* knowledge, judgment, discernment
知識 *chishiki* knowledge
常識 *jōshiki* common sense, common knowledge
良識 *ryōshiki* good sense
有識者 *yūshikisha* learned [informed, intellectual] people, the wise
学識 *gakushiki* learning, scholarship
❸ⓐ know, be acquainted with
ⓑ acquaintance
識字 *shikiji* teaching illiterate people how to read
面識 *menshiki* acquaintance
相識の *sōshiki no* mutually acquainted
❹ write down, record
識語 *shikigo* editor's note; preface; postscript
❺ landmark, sign
道路標識 *dōro hyōshiki* signpost

SYNONYMS
❶ⓐ **discriminate**
弁 distinguish → 2004
分 tell apart → 1972
ⓑ **discernment**
眼 EYE → 1172
❷ **wisdom**
智 WISDOM → 2784
慧 prajna (transcendental wisdom) → 2810
哲 PHILOSOPHY → 2738
知 knowledge → 1127
❷ **learning and knowledge**
知 knowledge → 1127
学 learning → 2555
文 culture → 1962
業 studies → 2612

識 1640
▶**DISCRIMINATE** ▶**KNOWLEDGE**
nonstandard for 識 1639
7-12 言

證 1641
▶**PROVE** ▶**CERTIFICATE**
nonstandard for 証 1506
7-12 言

贈 1642
▶**PRESENT A GIFT**
nonstandard for 贈 1634
7-12 貝

蹶 1643 KETSU
ⒸⒽ 蹶 jué juě

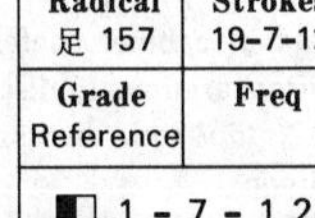

Radical	Strokes
足 157	19-7-12
Grade	Freq
Reference	
◧ 1-7-12	

7-12 足

COMPOUNDS
● [now also 決 263] spring to one's feet, rouse oneself
蹶起する *kekki suru* rise to action
蹶然と *ketsuzen to* with a spring, resolutely

瓣 1644
▶**VALVE**
nonstandard for 弁 2004
7-12 辛

7-12 酉

醱
1645 HATSU

Ⓒⓗ 酦 pō

Radical	Strokes
酉 164	19-7-12
Grade	**Freq**
Reference	
1 - 7 - 12	

COMPOUNDS

● [now replaced by 発 2565] brew, ferment

醱酵 *hakkō* fermentation, zymosis

7-13 角

觸
1646

▶**TOUCH**
nonstandard for 触 1518

7-13 言

議
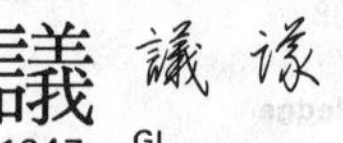

1647 GI

Ⓒⓗ 议 yì

Radical	Strokes
言 149	20-7-13
Grade	**Freq**
Jōyō-4	41
1 - 7 - 13	

▶**DISCUSS** ▶**LEGISLATIVE BODY**

COMPOUNDS

❶ⓐ [original meaning] (talk together) **discuss, consult**
ⓑ (conduct a formal discussion) **discuss, debate, deliberate, argue, propose**
議題 *gidai* topic for discussion
議決 *giketsu* decision, resolution
議事 *giji* proceedings, business
会議 *kaigi* conference, meeting, council
審議する *shingi suru* deliberate, consider, discuss
閣議 *kakugi* cabinet conference
議論 *giron* argument, discussion
討議する *tōgi suru* discuss, debate on, deliberate upon
論議する *rongi suru* discuss, argue, debate
不思議な *fushigi na* strange, mysterious, wonderful
衆議院 *shūgiin* House of Representatives, Lower House

❷ⓐ [also suffix] **legislative body, legislature**
ⓑ abbrev. of 議員 *giin*: **member of an assembly, assemblyman**
議会 *gikai* assembly, national assembly
議員 *giin* member of an assembly, assemblyman
議長 *gichō* chairman, president (of the senate)
議場 *gijō* assembly hall; the House
議院 *giin* House, Diet Chamber
区議 *kugi* ward assemblyman
都議 *togi* Metropolitan assemblyman

❸ proposal, proposition, opinion
議案 *gian* bill, measure
決議 *ketsugi* resolution, decision
異議 *igi* objection, complaint
建議 *kengi* proposal, suggestion

❹ criticize
誹議(=非議)する *higi suru* criticize, censure

INDEPENDENT

【gi 議】discussion, debate, deliberation, consultation; proposal
議に上る *gi ni noboru* come up for discussion
【gisuru 議する】discuss, examine, deliberate; consult, consider

SYNONYMS

❶ **argue and discuss**
争 CONTEND → 2030
論 ARGUE → 1574
弁 argue (for) → 2004

❷ⓐ **legislature**
会 assembly → 2020
院 House → 454

護 護 護 護

1648 GO mamo(ru)▲

㊥ 护 hù

Radical	Strokes
言 149	20-7-13
Grade	**Freq**
Jōyō-5	570
1-7-13	

7-13

言

1 2 3 4 5 6 7 8 9 10 11 12

13 14 15 16 17 18 19 20

▶PROTECT

COMPOUNDS

❶ [original meaning] **protect, safeguard, shield, defend**

護衛 *goei* guard, escort

護憲 *goken* safeguarding the constitution

護送 *gosō* safeguard, convoy, escort

護身術 *goshinjutsu* art of self-defense

護符 *gofu* charm, amulet

守護 *shugo* protection, guard, defense, safeguard

保護する *hogo suru* protect, safeguard, preserve, look after

援護 *engo* support, protection; covering

弁護する *bengo suru* defend, speak in defense of (another)

看護する *kango suru* nurse, attend on

擁護する *yōgo suru* protect, defend, support, safeguard

❷ used phonetically for *go*

護摩 *goma homa*, Buddhist rite of cedar-stick burning

KUN

【**mamo(ru) 護る**】[now usu. 守る] protect, defend, guard, watch over

身を護る *mi o mamoru* defend oneself

SYNONYMS

❶ **protect**

守 PROTECT → 2173

衛 GUARD → 760

警 GUARD AGAINST → 2893

防 defend → 270

番 WATCH → 2748

保 PRESERVE → 96

看 CARE FOR → 3220

HOMOPHONES

mamoru ⇨ 守 2173

NOTE

⇨ see USAGE note at 守 2173

譲 譲 譲 譲

1649 JŌ yuzu(ru)

㊥ 让 ràng

Radical	Strokes
言 149	20-7-13
Grade	**Freq**
Jōyō	1013
1-7-13	

7-13

言

1 2 3 4 5 6 7 8 9 10 11 12

13 14 15 16 17 18 19 20

▶CEDE

COMPOUNDS

❶ⓐ **cede, transfer, assign, give up, yield**

ⓑ sell, dispose of

譲渡 *jōto* transfer, conveyance

譲与 *jōyo* transfer

譲位 *jōi* abdication

委譲 *ijō* transfer, assignment

分譲 *bunjō* sale (of land) in lots, lotting-out

❷ concede, yield to, relinquish

譲歩 *jōho* concession, compromise

互譲 *gojō* mutual concessions, compromise

❸ modesty, humility

謙譲 *kenjō* modesty, humility

KUN

【**yuzu(ru) 譲る**】transfer, assign, give up, yield; sell, dispose of; concede, yield to, relinquish; leave, defer, postpone

譲り渡す *yuzuriwatasu* turn over, convey

親譲りの *oyayuzuri no* hereditary

安く譲る *yasuku yuzuru* sell (a thing) cheap

譲り合う *yuzuriau* compromise, concede

後日に譲る *gojitsu ni yuzuru* keep (the matter) for another occasion

SYNONYMS

❶ⓐ **transfer**

渡 hand over → 611

付 deliver → 31

附 deliver → 347

❷ compromise | 妥 COME TO TERMS → 2400

7-13 言

譜 1650

▶**SYSTEMATIC RECORD**

nonstandard for 譜 1637

7-13 言

譯 1651

▶**TRANSLATE** ▶**SENSE**

nonstandard for 訳 1473

7-13 𧾷

躁 1652 SŌ

ⒸⒽ 躁 zào

Radical	Strokes
足 157	20-7-13
Grade	**Freq**
Reference	
1-7-13	

COMPOUNDS

● [now also 燥 1087] [original meaning] restless, impatient, rash, impetuous

躁病 *sōbyō* mania

躁鬱病 *sōutsubyō* manic-depressive psychosis

狂躁(＝狂騒) *kyōsō* wild excitement

焦躁 *shōsō* fretfulness, impatience

7-13 辛

辮 1653 BEN

ⒸⒽ 辫 biàn

Radical	Strokes
糸 120	20-6-14
Grade	**Freq**
Reference	
1-7-13	

COMPOUNDS

● [now replaced by 弁 2004] pigtail, queue

辮髪 *benpatsu* pigtail, queue

7-13 酉

釀 釀 醸 醸 1654 JŌ kamo(su)

ⒸⒽ 酿 niàng

Radical	Strokes
酉 164	20-7-13
Grade	**Freq**
Jōyō	1779
1-7-13	

▶**BREW**

COMPOUNDS

● **brew, make alcoholic beverages**

醸造 *jōzō* brewing; distilling

醸母 *jōbo* yeast, leaven

醸成する *jōsei suru* brew; bring about

KUN

【**kamo(su) 醸す**】 brew; distill; cause, bring about

酒を醸す *sake o kamosu* brew sake

醸し出す *kamoshidasu* engender, bring about

物議を醸す *butsugi o kamosu* give rise to hostile comment

SYNONYMS

● **brew and ferment**

酵 FERMENT → 1561

醵

1655 KYO

Ⓒⓗ 醵 jù

Radical	Strokes
酉 164	20-7-13
Grade	**Freq**
Reference	
◧ 1-7-13	

7-13 酉

COMPOUNDS

● [now also 拠 312] contribute money to a common purpose

醵出 *kyoshutsu* donation, contribution
醵金 *kyokin* contribution, subscription

釋

1656

▶ELUCIDATE
nonstandard for 釈 1484

7-13 釆

護

1657

▶PROTECT
nonstandard for 護 1648

7-14 言

躍 躍 躍 躍

1658 YAKU odo(ru)

Ⓒⓗ 跃 yuè

Radical	Strokes
足 157	21-7-14
Grade	**Freq**
Jōyō	915
◧ 1-7-14	

7-14 ⻊

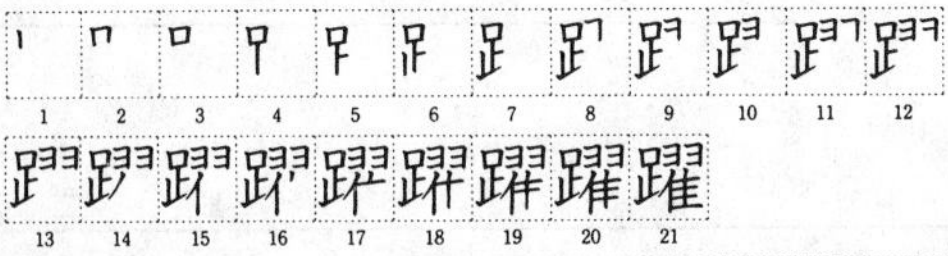

▶LEAP

COMPOUNDS

❶ [original meaning] **leap, jump up, spring**

躍進する *yakushin suru* make rapid progress, advance by leaps and bounds
飛躍 *hiyaku* leap, jump
一躍 *ichiyaku* at a bound, with a jump
跳躍する *chōyaku suru* jump, leap, spring

❷ **move as if leaping with excitement, stir, be active**

躍動する *yakudō suru* move lively, throb
躍如たる *yakujotaru* vivid, graphic, lifelike
躍起 *yakki* excitement, enthusiasm, desperation
活躍 *katsuyaku* (great) activity, action
暗躍 *an'yaku* secret maneuvers

KUN

【odo(ru) 躍る】

ⓐ leap, jump, bound
ⓑ (of one's heart) throb, leap

躍り *odori* leaping, jumping
躍り上がる *odoriagaru* spring up, leap to one's feet
躍り込む *odorikomu* jump into; rush into

SYNONYMS

❶ **jump**

跳 JUMP → 1532

HOMOPHONES

odoru ⇨ 踊 1558
odori ⇨ 踊 1558

NOTE

⇨ see USAGE note at 踊 1558

躍

1659

▶LEAP
nonstandard for 躍 1658

7-14 ⻊

辯

1660

▶SPEAK ELOQUENTLY
nonstandard for 弁 2004

7-14 辛

7-15
言

讀 1661

▶**READ**
nonstandard for 読 1541

7-15
車

轢 1662

REKI hi(ku)

CH 轹 lì

Radical	Strokes
車 159	22-7-15
Grade	**Freq**
Reference	
1-7-15	

COMPOUNDS

● [original meaning] run over (with a vehicle), knock down

轢死 *rekishi* being killed by a train or automobile

轢断する *rekidan suru* cut in two under train wheels

轢く *hiku* run over (with a vehicle), knock down

轢き逃げ *hikinige* hit-and-run

HOMOPHONES

hiku ⇨ 引 181 弾 572 退 3094 惹 2493 挽 427

NOTE

⇨ see USAGE note at 引 181

7-17
言

讓 1663

▶**CEDE**
nonstandard for 譲 1649

7-17
酉

釀 1664

▶**BREW**
nonstandard for 醸 1654

7-19
言

讚 1665

SAN

CH 赞 zàn

Radical	Strokes
言 149	26-7-19
Grade	**Freq**
Reference	
1-7-19	

COMPOUNDS

❶ [now usu. 賛 2809] [original meaning] praise, laud, admire, commend

讚嘆 *santan* praise, admiration

讚辞 *sanji* eulogy, praise, compliment

讚美歌 *sanbika* hymn, psalm

和讚 *wasan* Japanese translation of Buddhist hymns of praise

賞讚(＝称讚)する *shōsan suru* praise, laud, admire

❷ [now replaced by 賛 2809] legend or inscription on a picture

画讚 *gasan* legend [writing] on a picture

自画自讚 *jigajisan* painting with the eulogy written in by the artist himself; self-praise

讚 *san* legend or inscription on a picture; a style of Chinese poetry

❸ abbrev. of 讚岐 *sanuki*, old name for Kagawa Prefecture

土讚本線 *dosan honsen* Dosan Main Line (Kochi-Kagawa Railway)

1666 SHIN hari

ノ 𠆢 亼 今 全 全 余 金 金 針

1 2 3 4 5 6 7 8 9 10

CH 针 zhēn

Radical	Strokes
金 167	10-8-2
Grade	**Freq**
Jōyō-6	504
◧ 1 - 8 - 2	

8-2 金

▶**NEEDLE**

COMPOUNDS

❶ⓐ [original meaning] **needle**

ⓑ **needle-shaped object as the hand of clock or pointer of an instrument**

運針 *unshin* handling of a needle
針葉樹 *shin'yōju* conifer
長針 *chōshin* long [minute] hand
秒針 *byōshin* second hand
指針 *shishin* compass needle; indicator, pointer; hand; guiding principle
磁針 *jishin* magnetic needle
検針 *kenshin* inspection of a meter
羅針盤 *rashinban* compass
避雷針 *hiraishin* lightning rod

❷ [formerly also 鍼 1754] acupuncture

針術 *shinjutsu* acupuncture
針灸 *shinkyū* acupuncture and moxibustion

❸ direction, bearing

針路 *shinro* course, direction
方針 *hōshin* course, policy, plan

KUN

【**hari 針**】

①ⓐ [also suffix] needle

ⓑ needle-shaped object as the hand of a clock or pointer of an instrument

針仕事 *harishigoto* needlework, sewing
針山 *hariyama* pincushion
針箱 *haribako* needlecase, sewing box
針状の *harijō no* needle-shaped, pointed
針で刺す *hari de sasu* prick with a needle
縫い針 *nuibari* needle
木綿針 *momenbari* needle for cotton thread
鉤針 *kagibari* hook, crochet needle
針金 *harigane* wire
釣り針 *tsuribari* (fish)hook

② sting, sarcasm

針を含んだ言葉 *hari o fukunda kotoba* stinging [scathing] words

SYNONYMS

❶ **needle**

刺 prickle → 1275

USAGE

hari

針

①ⓐ [also suffix] needle

ⓑ needle-shaped object as the hand of a clock or pointer of an instrument

② sting, sarcasm

鍼

ⓐ acupuncture needle

ⓑ acupuncture

HOMOPHONES

hari ⇨ 鍼 1754

NOTE

⇨ see COMPOUND FORMATION for 羅針盤 *rashinban* ⇨ 羅 2622

釘

1667 TEI kugi

CH 钉 dīng dìng

Radical	Strokes
金 167	10-8-2
Grade	**Freq**
Reference	
◧ 1 - 8 - 2	

8-2 金

COMPOUNDS

❶ nail

釘頭 *teitō* nailhead
釘抜き *kuginuki* pincers, nail puller
釘付け *kugizuke* nailing; pegging; being stationary
釘を差す *kugi o sasu* remind (a person) of, give a warning

❷ [now replaced by 丁 *tei* 3348] book binding

装釘する *sōtei suru* bind (a book)

8-2
食

飢 飢 飢 飢

1668 KI u(eru)

㊥ 饥 jī

Radical	Strokes
食 184	10-8-2
Grade	**Freq**
Jōyō	1840
1-8-2	

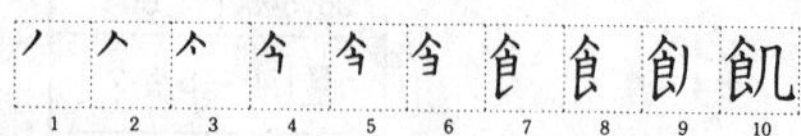

▶STARVE

COMPOUNDS

[formerly also 饑 1813]

ⓐ [original meaning] **starve, be hungry, famish**

ⓑ **year of famine**

飢餓 *kiga* starvation, hunger, famine
飢民 *kimin* starving people
飢渇 *kikatsu* hunger and thirst
飢饉 *kikin* famine, failure of crops; shortage

KUN

【u(eru) 飢える】

[formerly also 餓える]

ⓐ starve, be hungry, famish
ⓑ hunger [starve] for (love), thirst for (knowledge)

飢え *ue* hunger, starvation
飢え死に *uejini* (death by) starvation
愛に飢える *ai ni ueru* hunger [starve] for love

SYNONYMS

ⓐ **hunger and thirst**

餓 STARVED → 1734
渇 THIRST → 515

USAGE

ueru

飢える

[formerly also 餓える]
ⓐ starve, be hungry, famish
ⓑ hunger [starve] for (love), thirst for (knowledge)

餓える

[now usu. 飢える] same as 飢える

HOMOPHONES

ueru ⇨ 餓 1734

8-2
斉

剤 劑 剤 剤

1669 ZAI

㊥ 剂 jì

Radical	Strokes
刂 18	10-2-8
Grade	**Freq**
Jōyō	1377
1-8-2	

▶PREPARATION

COMPOUNDS

❶ⓐ [also suffix] [original meaning] **pharmaceutical preparation, drug, medicine**

ⓑ [also suffix] chemical preparation, chemical

薬剤 *yakuzai* medicine, drugs
調剤する *chōzai suru* prepare [compound] medicines
錠剤 *jōzai* pill, tablet
ビタミン剤 *bitaminzai* vitamin preparation
調合剤 *chōgōzai* preparation, mixture
消化剤 *shōkazai* digestive, peptic
鎮痛剤 *chintsūzai* anodyne, painkiller
洗剤 *senzai* detergent, cleanser
殺虫剤 *satchūzai* insecticide, vermicide
酸化防止剤 *sankabōshizai* antioxidant

❷ counter for doses

下剤二剤 *gezai nizai* two doses of a purgative preparation

SYNONYMS

❶ⓐ **medicines**

薬 DRUG → 2375
錠 PILL → 1737
丸 pill suffix → 3417

剖 剖 剖 剖

1670 BŌ

㊥ 剖 pōu

Radical	Strokes
刂 18	10-2-8
Grade	**Freq**
Jōyō	1845
1-8-2	

8-2 音

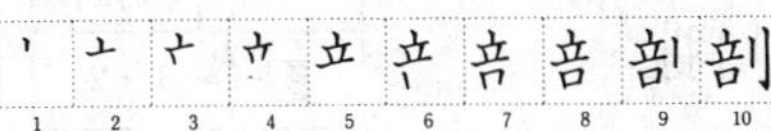

▶**DISSECT**

COMPOUNDS

● [original meaning] **dissect, cut open, split in two**

剖検 *bōken* autopsy, necropsy

解剖する *kaibō suru* dissect, anatomize, hold an autopsy; analyze

解剖学 *kaibōgaku* anatomy

SYNONYMS

● **cut**

割 cut with a knife → 1816

切 CUT → 27

断 CUT OFF → 1492

裁 CUT OUT → 3299

刈る CLIP → 28

伐 CUT DOWN → 42

削 CUT BY CHIPPING → 1448

部

incorrect stroke count ⇨ see 1676

8-2 音

剖

1671

▶**DISSECT**

nonstandard for 剖 1670

8-2 音

郭

incorrect stroke count ⇨ see 1678

8-2 享

剣 劍 劒 剱 剣 剣

1672 KEN tsurugi

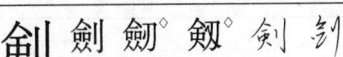

㊥ 剑 jiàn

Radical	Strokes
刂 18	10-2-8
Grade	**Freq**
Jōyō	1177
1-8-2	

8-2 㑒

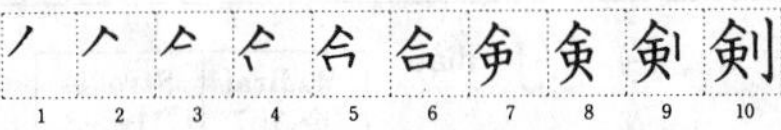

▶**SWORD**

COMPOUNDS

ⓐ [original meaning] **(double-edged) sword, sword, blade**

ⓑ **swordsmanship, fencing, *kendo***

刀剣 *tōken* sword

銃剣 *jūken* bayonet

真剣 *shinken* real sword; seriousness

手裏剣 *shuriken* throwing knife

剣道 *kendō* fencing, swordsmanship, *kendo*

剣客 *kenkyaku* swordsman, fencer

INDEPENDENT

【ken 剣】 sword (esp. double-edged), blade; bayonet; swordsmanship; sting (of a bee)

剣を抜く *ken o nuku* draw a sword

KUN

【tsurugi 剣】 sword (esp. double-edged)

剣の山を登る *tsurugi no yama o noboru* perform a hazardous deed

SYNONYMS

ⓐ **cutting instruments**

刀 SWORD (single-edged) → 2926

矛 HALBERD → 2008

鎌 SICKLE → 1760

刃 BLADE → 2929

8-2 岡

剛 剛 剛

1673 GŌ

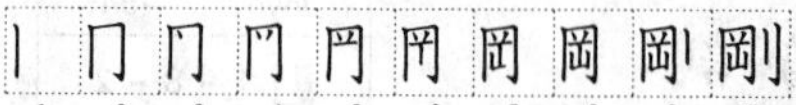

CH 刚 gāng

Radical	Strokes
刂 18	10-2-8
Grade	Freq
Jōyō	1749
1-8-2	

▶**TOUGH**

COMPOUNDS

❶ [original meaning] (hard and strong) **tough, strong, rigid, hard**

剛性 *gōsei* rigidity

剛体 *gōtai* rigid body

剛力(=強力) *gōriki* Herculean strength; mountain carrier [guide]

剛球 *gōkyū baseball* fast ball

金剛石 *kongōseki* diamond

❷ (of strong spirit) **tough, stout, resolute, brave**

剛毅な *gōki na* hardy, sturdy

剛健 *gōken* fortitude and vigor, sturdiness, virility; manliness

剛直 *gōchoku* moral courage, integrity

剛勇 *gōyū* bravery, prowess

INDEPENDENT

【gō 剛】 *literary* toughness, strength, hardiness

柔能く剛を制す *Jū yoku gō o seisu* Softness overcomes hardness / Soft words win hard hearts

SYNONYMS

❶ **hard**

強 STRONG → 475

硬 HARD → 1183

堅 FIRM → 2823

固 SOLID → 3086

❷ **firm and obstinate**

毅 RESOLUTE → 1866

頑 STUBBORN → 1040

硬 hard-line → 1183

堅 FIRM → 2823

固 FIRM, stiff → 3086

確 firm → 1228

8-2 者

都

incorrect stroke count ⇨ see 1686

8-2 垂

郵

incorrect stroke count ⇨ see 1687

8-3 金

釣 釣 釣 釣

1674 CHŌ tsu(ru) tsu(ri) tsu(ri)-

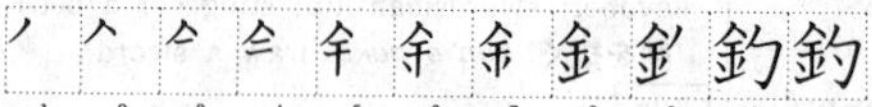

CH 钓 diào

Radical	Strokes
金 167	11-8-3
Grade	Freq
Jōyō	1144
1-8-3	

▶**ANGLE**

COMPOUNDS

● [original meaning] **angle, fish**

釣魚 *chōgyo* fishing, angling

釣果 *chōka* catch, haul

KUN

【tsu(ru) 釣る】

① angle, fish

釣り上げる *tsuriageru* fish up, land

② decoy, allure, take in

釣り出す *tsuridasu* fish out, draw out, decoy

【tsu(ri) 釣り】

① [also suffix] angling, rod fishing

釣り糸 *tsuriito* fishing line

釣り師 *tsurishi* angler

魚釣り *sakanatsuri* angling, fishing

鮪釣り *magurotsuri* tuna fishing

一本釣り *ipponzuri* pole-and-line fishing

② change (for money)

お釣り *otsuri* change

釣り銭 *tsurisen* change

【tsu(ri)- 釣り-】 [also 吊り] suspended, hanging

釣り橋 *tsuribashi* suspension bridge

釣り鐘 *tsurigane* hanging bell, temple bell

釣り合い *tsuriai* balance, equilibrium; propor-

tion
釣り下げる *tsurisageru* suspend from

SYNONYMS

● &【tsuru】① **hunt and fish**
漁 FISH → 698
猟 HUNTING → 538
狩 HUNT → 397
獲 CATCH GAME → 779

【tsuri-】
○ **hang**
懸 SUSPEND → 2915
掛ける HANG → 493
垂 HANG DOWN → 3565

USAGE

❶ **tsuru**
釣る
① angle, fish
② decoy, allure, take in
吊る
① hang, suspend, swing, sling
② lift by the loins (in sumo wrestling)
③ [formerly 攣る] cramp, have a cramp
④ [formerly 攣る] turn up, slant upward
攣る
[now usu. 吊る]
① cramp, have a cramp
② turn up, slant upward
❷ **tsuri**
釣り
① [also suffix] angling, rod fishing
② change (for money)
釣り-
[also 吊り] suspended, hanging
吊り
①ⓐ suspension, hanging
ⓑ [also 釣り-] suspended, hanging
② lifting by the loins (in sumo wrestling)

HOMOPHONES

tsuru ⇨ 吊 2163 攣 2919
tsuri ⇨ 吊 2163

鈎
1675

▶ANGLE
nonstandard for 釣 1674

8-3 金

彬

incorrect classification ⇨ see 960

8-3 林

部 部 部 部
1676 BU -be▲

ⒸⒽ 部 bù

Radical	Strokes
阝 163	11-3-8
Grade	**Freq**
Jōyō-3	42
1-8-3	

8-3 音

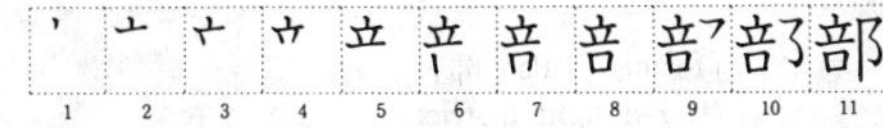

▶SECTION

COMPOUNDS

❶ⓐ [also suffix] **section, part, category, division, region**
ⓑ [original meaning, now archaic] divide in sections, divide in half
部分 *bubun* part, section, portion
部品 *buhin* parts, accessories
部門 *bumon* class, group, division, department, section; genus
部類 *burui* class, category, division
一部 *ichibu* part, portion, section; a copy (of a book)
北部 *hokubu* north, northern part
全部 *zenbu* all, the whole; wholly, entirely
内部 *naibu* interior, inner parts
上部 *jōbu* upper part [section], top; surface
中央部 *chūōbu* central part
心臓部 *shinzōbu* region of the heart
第三部 *daisanbu* Section 3
❷ⓐ section of Chinese character dictionary, radical of Chinese character
ⓑ counter for sections of Chinese character dictionaries
部首 *bushu* radical (of Chinese characters)
水部 *mizunobu* 'water' radical
❸ⓐ [also suffix] section or major subdivision of an organization: **department, division, section, faculty; military unit**
ⓑ club, group
部属 *buzoku* section, division
部長 *buchō* section chief, department head
部会 *bukai* section meeting
部下 *buka* subordinate
部隊 *butai* unit, corps, party, squad
幹部 *kanbu* executive, (managing) staff

学部 *gakubu* faculty, department
編集部 *henshūbu* editorial department [staff]
文学部 *bungakubu* department [faculty] of literature
営業部 *eigyōbu* business department, sales department
文化事業部 *bunka jigyō-bu* Cultural Affairs Department
野球部 *yakyūbu* baseball club
❹ **counter for copies of printed matter**
部数 *busū* number of copies, circulation
一部二百円 *ichibu nihyakuen* 200 yen per copy
❺ community
部落 *buraku* community, village, hamlet
部族 *buzoku* tribe

INDEPENDENT

【**bu 部**】 section, division, head; section (of a company), department, division; class, category
...の部に入る *...no bu ni hairu* fall under the heading of; be classed among

KUN

【**-be -部**】 hereditary clan engaged in specific profession in ancient Japan
語部 *kataribe* clan of professional reciters

SPECIAL READINGS

部屋 *heya* room, chamber

SYNONYMS

❶ⓐ **part**
分 PART → 1972
局 LIMITED PART → 3063
片 FRAGMENT → 3461
❸ⓐ **divisions of organizations**
課 SECTION → 1573
局 BUREAU → 3063
❹ **counters for books**
冊 COUNTER FOR BOOKS → 3483
巻 counter for volumes → 2645

NOTE

★do not confuse with 陪 539

8-3
音

部 1677

▶**SECTION**
nonstandard for 部 1676

8-3
享

郭 1678

KAKU kuruwa▲

CH 郭 guō

Radical	Strokes
阝 163	11-3-8
Grade	**Freq**
Jōyō	1632
1 - 8 - 3	

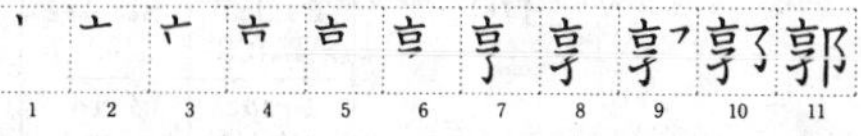

▶**OUTER ENCLOSURE**

COMPOUNDS

[formerly also 廓 3163]
❶ [original meaning] **outer enclosure [walls], outline, contour**
外郭 *gaikaku* outer block [enclosure]; outline, contour
城郭 *jōkaku* castle, fortress; castle walls, enclosure
輪郭 *rinkaku* contour, outline, profile
胸郭 *kyōkaku* thorax, chest
❷ district, red-light district
遊郭 *yūkaku* licensed quarters, red-light district
一郭 *ikkaku* a block
❸ open, wide, empty
郭清する *kakusei suru* purify, clean up, purge

KUN

【**kuruwa 郭**】
[formerly also 廓]
① red-light district
郭通いをする *kuruwagayoi o suru* frequent a house of ill fame
② area enclosed by earthwork

SYNONYMS

❶ **periphery**
周 PERIPHERY → 2998
囲 circumference → 3069

USAGE

kuruwa
郭
[formerly also 廓]
① red-light district
② area enclosed by earthwork
廓
[now usu. 郭] same as 郭

HOMOPHONES

kuruwa ⇨ 廓 3163

乾 乾 乾

1679 KAN KEN▲ kawa(ku) kawa(kasu) ho(su)▲ hi(ru)▲ inui▲

CH 干 gān 乾 qián

Radical	Strokes
乙 5	11-1-10
Grade	**Freq**
Jōyō	1392
1 - 8 - 3	

8-3 卓

▶DRY

COMPOUNDS

❶ⓐ [original meaning] **dry, dry up, desiccate**

ⓑ **dry, dried**

乾燥する *kansō suru* dry up, desiccate, become parched [dry]

乾杯する *kanpai suru* drink a toast, toast

乾枯する *kanko suru* completely dry up

乾物 *kanbutsu* dry provisions, groceries

乾パン *kanpan* cracker, hard biscuit

乾電池 *kandenchi* dry cell

乾溜(=乾留) *kanryū* dry distillation

❷ heaven (as opposed to earth)

乾坤 *kenkon* heaven and earth, universe

❸ first of the eight trigrams in the Book of Changes: northwest

❹ one of the four supplementary signs of the Oriental zodiac: northwest

乾位 *ken'i* [rare] northwest

KUN

【kawa(ku) 乾く】 *vi* dry (up), run dry

乾き *kawaki* drying, dryness

乾きの早い *kawaki no hayai* fast drying (clothes)

【kawa(kasu) 乾かす】 *vt* dry, desiccate

着物を乾かす *kimono o kawakasu* dry clothes

【ho(su) 乾す】

[now usu. 干す] *vt*

ⓐ draw off (liquids), drain off

ⓑ drink up, drain dry

池を乾す *ike o hosu* drain off a pond

干乾し *hiboshi* starving

飲み乾す *nomihosu* drink up

【hi(ru) 乾る】 [now usu. 干る] *vi* get dry, parch

乾物 *himono* dried fish

【inui 乾】 one of the four supplementary signs of the Oriental zodiac: northwest

SYNONYMS

❶ **dry**

干 DRY → 3379

燥 DRY UP → 1087

渇 RUN DRY → 515

USAGE

❶ **kawaku**

乾く

vi dry (up), run dry

渇く

be thirsty, thirst

❷ **kawaki**

乾き

drying, dryness

渇き

thirst

HOMOPHONES

kawaku ⇨ 渇 515

kawaki ⇨ 渇 515

hosu ⇨ 干 3379

hiru ⇨ 干 3379

NOTE

⇨ see also USAGE note at 干 3379

執 執 執

1680 SHITSU SHŪ to(ru)

CH 执 zhí

Radical	Strokes
土 32	11-3-8
Grade	**Freq**
Jōyō	909
1 - 8 - 3	

8-3 幸

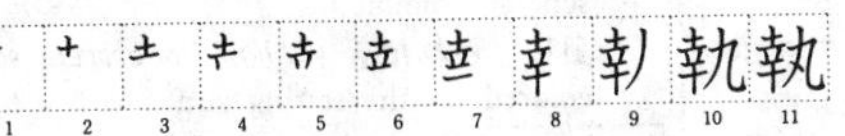

▶EXECUTE ▶SEIZE

COMPOUNDS

❶ (perform a specific task with care) **execute, carry out, perform, conduct**

執行する *shikkō suru* execute, perform, carry out

執務 *shitsumu* performance of one's official duties

執事 *shitsuji* steward, butler

中執(=中央執行委員会) *chūshitsu* (=*chūō shikkō iinkai*) Central Executive Committee

❷ⓐ seize, hold in hands; seize power

ⓑ **seize [hold] an object (such as a pen) and perform an action with**

ⓒ [original meaning] seize a criminal

執金鋼 *shikkongō* Diamond Holder (name of

a Buddhist celestial being)
執権 *shikken* regent
執筆 *shippitsu* writing
執刀する *shittō suru* perform an operation
❸ **adhere to, stick fast to, hold fast to, persist in**
執念 *shūnen* tenacity of purpose, vindictiveness, spite
執着する *shūchaku* (=*shūjaku*) *suru* be attached to; adhere to, hold fast to
執拗な *shitsuyō na* obstinate; tenacious, persistent
固執する *koshitsu* (=*koshū*) *suru* adhere to, persist in
確執 *kakushitsu* (=*kakushū*) discord, strife
偏執狂 *henshitsukyō* (=*henshūkyō*) monomaniac

KUN
【to(ru) 執る】
① perform (duties), conduct, transact, take (trouble)
執り行う *toriokonau* carry out, perform
事務を執る *jimu o toru* do [attend to] business
② perform an action while holding an object (such as a pen)
筆を執る *fude o toru* write, pen, draw
③ persist in, insist on
固く自説を執る *kataku jisetsu o toru* persist in one's views

SYNONYMS
❶ **execute**
施 CARRY OUT → 891
践 IMPLEMENT → 1535
履 FULFILL → 3171
遂 ACCOMPLISH → 3138
果たす effect → 3560
行 ACT → 212
❷ⓑ **take**
握 GRASP → 585
把 GRIP → 249
捕 CATCH → 429
取 TAKE → 1262
持 HOLD → 374
❸ **adhere to**
着 stick to → 3316

HOMOPHONES
toru ⇨ 取 1262 採 499 捕 429 撮 737

COMPOUND FORMATION
❶ 確執 *kakushitsu* (=*kakushū*)
確執 'discord, strife' originally meant firm (確) adherence (執 ❸) to one's own views. Since insisting on one's own opinion leads to an argument, 確執 came to denote discord or strife.
❷ 偏執狂 *henshitsukyō* (=*henshūkyō*)
偏執狂 'monomaniac' is a maniac (狂) who sticks to (執 ❸) only one thing (偏).

NOTE
⇨ see USAGE note at 取 1262

8-3
采

彩 彩 彩 彩

1681 SAI irodo(ru)

CH 彩 cǎi

Radical	Strokes
彡 59	11-3-8
Grade	**Freq**
Jōyō	1368
1-8-3	

▶BEAUTIFUL COLORING

COMPOUNDS
❶ⓐ **beautiful [brilliant] coloring, coloration, color, variegated colors**
ⓑ [original meaning] **color, paint**
色彩 *shikisai* color, coloring, hue, tinge
多彩な *tasai na* colorful, varicolored; variegated, diversified
五彩 *gosai* five beautiful colors
虹彩 *kōsai* iris
光彩 *kōsai* luster, brilliancy
彩色 *saishoku* coloring, painting
彩画 *saiga* painting, colored picture
彩管 *saikan* paintbrush
❷ (outward appearance) color, appearance
生彩 *seisai* life, vividness
異彩 *isai* conspicuousness, outstandingness

KUN
【irodo(ru) 彩る】 [also 色取る] color, paint, dye; make up
彩り *irodori* coloring, coloration, color scheme; makeup
夕日に彩られた空 *yūhi ni irodorareta sora* sky colored by the setting sun

SYNONYMS
❶ⓐ **color**
色 COLOR → 2029
ⓑ **color**
染 DYE → 2572

NOTE
⇨ see COMPOUND FORMATION for 虹彩 *kōsai* ⇨ 虹 1285

彩 ▶BEAUTIFUL COLORING
1682
nonstandard for 彩 1681

8-3 采

彫 彫 彫 彫
1683 CHŌ ho(ru) -bo(ri)

Ⓒⓗ 雕 diāo

Radical	Strokes
彡 59	11-3-8
Grade	**Freq**
Jōyō	1312

1-8-3

8-3 周

丿 冂 月 円 円 用 周 周 周 彫 彫
1 2 3 4 5 6 7 8 9 10 11

▶**CARVE**

COMPOUNDS

● [original meaning] (cut so as to form a desired shape or design) **carve, sculpt, engrave**
彫刻 *chōkoku* sculpture, carving, engraving
彫像 *chōzō* carved statue
彫金 *chōkin* metal carving, chasing
彫塑 *chōso* carving and modeling, plastic arts; clay model

KUN

【**ho(ru) 彫る**】
ⓐ (cut so as to form designs or figures) engrave, carve, chisel
ⓑ tattoo

彫り物 *horimono* carving; tattoo
木彫り *kibori* woodcarving
浮き彫り *ukibori* relief, embossed carving
【**-bo(ri) -彫り**】[suffix] carving, sculpture
鎌倉彫り *kamakurabori* carvings of the Kamakura style

SYNONYMS

● **form and carve**
刻 ENGRAVE → 1267
塑 MODEL → 2843
鋳 CAST → 1729

HOMOPHONES

horu ⇨ 掘 496

NOTE

⇨ see USAGE note at 掘 496

彫 ▶CARVE
1684
nonstandard for 彫 1683

8-3 周

尉 尉 尉
1685 I JŌ▲

Ⓒⓗ 尉 wèi yù

Radical	Strokes
寸 41	11-3-8
Grade	**Freq**
Jōyō	1645

1-8-3

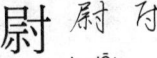

8-3 尸

フ コ 尸 尸 尸 层 层 层 尉 尉 尉
1 2 3 4 5 6 7 8 9 10 11

▶**COMPANY OFFICER**

COMPOUNDS

❶ (military officer or rank such as captain or lieutenant) **company officer**
尉官 *ikan* company officer
空軍大尉 *kūgun taii* air force captain
中尉 *chūi* first lieutenant (U.S. Army)
少尉 *shōi* second lieutenant
❷ (white-haired) old man (in a noh drama)
黒色尉 *kokushikijō* 'Old Black Joe' (a noh mask)

INDEPENDENT

【**jō 尉**】(white-haired) old man (in a noh drama)

SYNONYMS

❶ **military officers and ranks**
曹 SERGEANT → 2746
佐 FIELD OFFICER → 67
将 GENERAL OFFICER → 460
督 COMMANDER → 2796
帥 COMMANDER IN CHIEF → 1290

8-3 者

都 都 都

1686 TO TSU miyako

CH 都 dōu dū

Radical	Strokes
⻏ 163	11-3-8
Grade	**Freq**
Jōyō-3	111
1 - 8 - 3	

▶**METROPOLIS**
▶**METROPOLIS OF TOKYO**

COMPOUNDS

❶ **metropolis, capital**
都会 *tokai* city, town
都市 *toshi* cities, urban communities
都心 *toshin* heart [center] of a city
東京都 *tōkyōto* Metropolis of Tokyo
首都 *shuto* capital (city)
遷都 *sento* transfer of the capital

❷ⓐ **Metropolis of Tokyo, Tokyo**
ⓑ (of the Metropolis of Tokyo) **Metropolitan, Tokyo**
都立の *toritsu no* metropolitan, under control of the Tokyo Metropolitan government
都内で *tonai de* in Tokyo Metropolis
東都 *tōto* Tokyo Metropolis
都庁 *tochō* Tokyo Metropolitan Government Office
都電 *toden* Metropolitan Electric Railway
都議選 *togisen* Tokyo Assembly elections

❸ all, every, everything
都度 *tsudo* each time, whenever
都合 *tsugō* convenience, circumstances; in all, altogether, totally

❹ beautiful, elegant
都雅 *toga* elegance

❺ exercise control
都督 *totoku* governor general

INDEPENDENT

【to 都】Metropolis of Tokyo
都の *to no* Metropolitan, municipal

KUN

【miyako 都】capital; city
都落ち *miyakoochi* rustication

SYNONYMS

❶ **cities and towns**
京 CAPITAL → 2052
市 CITY → 1993
町 TOWN → 1113

❷ **Kanto cities**
京 TOKYO → 2052
東 Tokyo → 3568
浜 Yokohama → 436

❷ **territorial divisions**
道 district of Hokkaido → 3134
府 URBAN PREFECTURE → 3082
県 PREFECTURE → 2641
州 STATE → 57
省 province of China → 2449
郡 COUNTY → 1466

❸ **all**
皆 ALL → 2445
万 all → 2936
全 WHOLE → 2022
一 all in one → 3341
満 FULL → 607
丸 complete(ly) → 3417
完 COMPLETE → 2201
総 TOTAL → 1379
諸 VARIOUS → 1577
毎 EVERY → 2034
各 EACH → 2168

COMPOUND FORMATION

都合 *tsugō*
都合 'convenience, circumstances; in all, altogether, totally' refers to combining (合) everything (都 ❸) together.

8-3 垂

郵 郵 郵

1687 YŪ

CH 邮 yóu

Radical	Strokes
⻏ 163	11-3-8
Grade	**Freq**
Jōyō-6	851
1 - 8 - 3	

▶**MAIL**

COMPOUNDS

● (postal delivery system) **mail, post**
郵便 *yūbin* mail service, mail, postal matter
郵便局 *yūbinkyoku* post office
郵政 *yūsei* postal system
郵送 *yūsō* mailing
郵税 *yūzei* postage, postal rates
郵船 *yūsen* mail steamer
郵貯(＝郵便貯金) *yūcho* (＝*yūbin chokin*)

postal [post-office] savings [deposit]
郵袋 *yūtai* mailbag

INDEPENDENT

【yū 郵】 abbrev. of 郵便番号 *yūbin bangō*: postal code, zip code

郵100 *yū hyaku* zip code 100

SYNONYMS

● **mail**
便 POST → 95

鈑
1688 BAN

Ⓒⓗ 钣 bǎn

Radical	Strokes
金 167	12-8-4
Grade	**Freq**
Reference	
◧ 1 - 8 - 4	

8-4 金

COMPOUNDS

● [now usu. 板 858] sheet metal

鈑金 *bankin* sheet metal

鈍 鈍 鈍
1689 DON nibu(i) nibu(ru) nibu- nama(ru)▲ namaku(ra)▲

Ⓒⓗ 钝 dùn

Radical	Strokes
金 167	12-8-4
Grade	**Freq**
Jōyō	1601
◧ 1 - 8 - 4	

8-4 金

Stroke order: ノ(1) 𠆢(2) 亽(3) 今(4) 仐(5) 伞(6) 余(7) 金(8) 金一(9) 釒七(10) 釒匸(11) 鈍(12)

▶ **DULL**

COMPOUNDS

❶ⓐ [original meaning] (not sharp) **dull, blunt**
ⓑ (not intense) dull, slow
鈍器 *donki* dull weapon, blunt sword
鈍角 *donkaku* obtuse angle
鈍痛 *dontsū* dull pain
鈍行 *donkō* ordinary [slow] train

❷ (not agile) **dull, dull-witted, slow, stupid**
鈍才 *donsai* dullness, stupidity
鈍感 *donkan* thickheadedness
鈍重な *donjū na* dull-witted, phlegmatic
愚鈍 *gudon* stupidity, silliness

INDEPENDENT

【don 鈍】 dullness, slowness
鈍な *don na* dull, slow, stupid, dull-brained

KUN

【nibu(i) 鈍い】 dull, slow-witted, thickheaded; slow, sluggish; dull, blunt (sword); dim (light); dull (color)
鈍さ *nibusa* dullness, sluggishness
鈍い音 *nibui oto* thick sound
鈍い男 *nibui otoko* dolt, dullard

【nibu(ru) 鈍る】 *vi* become dull; weaken
決心が鈍る *kesshin ga niburu* waver in one's resolution
腕が鈍る *ude ga niburu* become less capable
鈍らす *niburasu vt* dull, blunt; weaken

【nibu- 鈍-】 [prefix] (of colors) dull
鈍黄色 *nibukiiro* dull yellow

【nama(ru) 鈍る】 (of cutlery) become dull, get blunted; be weakened, become less capable
体が鈍った *Karada ga namatta* The body has lost its former agility

【namaku(ra) 鈍ら】 dull blade; lazy fellow; good-for-nothing, useless (thing)

SYNONYMS

❷ **foolish**
痴 STUPID → 3286
暗 DARK → 1010
愚 FOOLISH → 2834

【nibu-】
○ **light-colored**
淡 LIGHT → 528
浅 light → 389
薄い pale → 2370

8-4 金

欽 欽 欽

1690 KIN NAMES yoshi hitoshi

CH 钦 qīn

Radical	Strokes
欠 76	12-4-8
Grade	**Freq**
Names	2055
1-8-4	

丿 𠆢 亼 仝 牟 金 金 金 釒 釒 欽 欽
1 2 3 4 5 6 7 8 9 10 11 12

▶**REVERE**

COMPOUNDS

❶ **revere, respect, adore, admire**

欽慕 *kinbo* admiration, adoration, reverence

❷ imperial, authorized by the emperor

欽定憲法 *kintei kenpō* constitution granted by the Emperor

NAMES

欽一 *kin'ichi* (=*yoshikazu*) male name

憲欽 *noriyoshi* male name

SYNONYMS

❶ **respect**

敬 RESPECT → 1701

仰 look up to → 48

崇 REVERENCE → 2297

尚 VALUE HIGHLY → 2233

重 set value on → 3573

拝 WORSHIP → 303

慕 ADORE → 2353

尊 HONOR → 2324

8-4 革

靴

incorrect stroke count ⇨ see 1781

8-4 食

飯 飯 飯 飯

1691 HAN meshi

CH 饭 fàn

Radical	Strokes
食 184	12-8-4
Grade	**Freq**
Jōyō-4	1086
1-8-4	

▶**COOKED RICE** ▶**MEAL**

COMPOUNDS

❶ **cooked rice, boiled rice**

御飯 *gohan* boiled rice; meal

炊飯器 *suihanki* rice cooker

赤飯 *sekihan* cooked rice and red beans

❷ⓐ **meal**

ⓑ food

飯店 *hanten* (high-class) Chinese restaurant; hotel (in Chinese)

飯場 *hanba* bunkhouse, workers' living quarters

夕飯 *yūhan* evening meal, supper

飯台 *handai* dining table

残飯 *zanpan* leftover food [rice]

KUN

【**meshi** 飯】 cooked rice, boiled rice; meal; livelihood

飯炊き *meshitaki* cooking rice; kitchenmaid, cook

飯粒 *meshitsubu* grain of boiled rice

焼き飯 *yakimeshi* frizzled [fried] rice

昼飯 *hirumeshi* lunch, midday meal

飯が食えない *meshi ga kuenai* cannot make a living

SYNONYMS

❶ **rice**

米 RICE → 3529

稲 RICE PLANT → 1219

❷ **food**

食 FOOD, meal → 2075

糧 FOOD PROVISIONS → 1421

飲 飲 飲 飲

1692 IN no(mu) -no(mi)

CH 饮 yǐn yìn

Radical	Strokes
食 184	12-8-4
Grade	**Freq**
Jōyō-3	979
1 - 8 - 4	

8-4 食

▶**DRINK**

COMPOUNDS

ⓐ **drink**

ⓑ [original meaning] **drink alcoholic beverages**

ⓒ **drink, beverage**

飲食 *inshoku* eating and drinking
飲酒 *inshu* drinking (alcoholic drinks)
愛飲する *aiin suru* be fond of drinking
飲料 *inryō* drink, beverage
溜飲 *ryūin* water brash, sour stomach

INDEPENDENT

【in 飲】[rare] drink (of sake); drinking (sake)

KUN

【no(mu) 飲む】

①ⓐ drink
ⓑ drink alcoholic beverages
飲み込む *nomikomu* swallow, gulp down; grasp, take in
飲み物 *nomimono* beverage
飲み屋 *nomiya* bar, tavern
② smoke
一服飲む *ippuku nomu* have a smoke

【-no(mi) -飲み】[suffix] drinker
大酒飲み *ōzakenomi* guzzler, boozer

SYNONYMS

● **ingest**
食 EAT → 2075
喫 INGEST → 551
服 take → 878

USAGE

nomu

飲む
①ⓐ drink
ⓑ drink alcoholic beverages
② smoke

呑む
①ⓐ swallow, gulp
ⓑ swallow (one's feelings), hold back
② accept
③ despise
④ conceal

HOMOPHONES

nomu ⇨ 呑 2410

敦 敦 敦

1693 TON NAMES atsu atsushi tsuru

CH 敦 dūn duì

Radical	Strokes
攵 66	12-4-8
Grade	**Freq**
Names	2061
1 - 8 - 4	

8-4 享

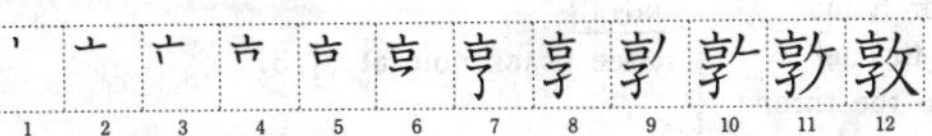

▶**HONEST**

COMPOUNDS

❶ [rare] honest, staunch, sincere, simple
敦厚な *tonkō na* sincere and kindhearted, honest and simple
敦朴(=敦樸)な *tonboku na* [archaic] honest and simple

❷ [archaic] cordial, warm, kind, kindhearted
敦睦な *tonboku na* cordial and friendly, affectionate

❸ used phonetically for *ton*
倫敦 *rondon* London

NAMES

敦 *ton* (=*atsushi*) male name
敦子 *atsuko* female name
敦賀 *tsuruga* surname also place name

SYNONYMS

❶ **purehearted**
惇 SINCERE → 486
直 straightforward → 2932
廉 INCORRUPT → 3153
潔 IMMACULATE → 744
清 clean → 523
淳 PUREHEARTED → 514
純 PURE → 1297

8-4
京

就 就 𥁕

1694 SHŪ JU tsu(ku) tsu(keru)

Ⓒ 就 jiù

Radical	Strokes
尢 43	12-3-9
Grade	Freq
Jōyō-6	859
1-8-4	

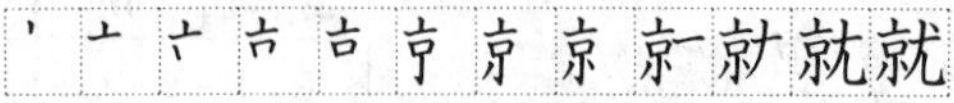

▶SET ABOUT

COMPOUNDS

❶ⓐ **set about a task, set out, proceed to do, set to, enter upon, launch into, take up (a position)**

ⓑ set out, go to

就職 *shūshoku* finding employment

就任 *shūnin* assumption of office, inauguration

就学する *shūgaku suru* enter school

就労する *shūrō suru* set to work, find employment

就航 *shūkō* (of ships) going into commission

就業 *shūgyō* employment, starting work

就寝する *shūshin suru* go to bed

就眠する *shūmin suru* go to sleep

去就 *kyoshū* one's course of action

❷ accomplish, achieve

成就 *jōju* accomplishment, achievement, attainment

KUN

【tsu(ku) 就く】

①ⓐ set about a task, set out, enter upon, take up (a position), assume (office), enter (a business)

ⓑ set out, start, leave

就いて *tsuite* about, concerning

職に就く *shoku ni tsuku* take up employment

帰途に就く *kito ni tsuku* leave for home

② [formerly 即く] ascend to (the throne)

位に就く *kurai ni tsuku* ascend to the throne

③ study under (a teacher)

先生に就く *sensei ni tsuku* study under (a teacher)

【tsu(keru) 就ける】

① install [place] a person in a position

役に就ける *yaku ni tsukeru* place someone in a position

② [formerly 即ける] enthrone

王位に就ける *ōi ni tsukeru* place on the throne

③ make (a person) study under (a teacher)

良い先生に就ける *yoi sensei ni tsukeru* have one study under a good teacher

SYNONYMS

❶ⓐ **begin**

始 BEGIN → 281

-出す begin to do → 3498

-掛ける start doing → 493

発 START → 2565

起 start → 3307

開 OPEN → 3321

創 initiate → 1815

肇 ORIGINATE → 2799

HOMOPHONES

tsuku ⇨ 付 31 着 3316 附 347 即 1120 点 2084

tsukeru ⇨ 付 31 附 347 着 3316 即 1120 点 2084 漬 702

NOTE

⇨ see USAGE note at 付 31

8-4
𠦝

朝 朝 朝 𠮷

1695 CHŌ asa

Ⓒ 朝 zhāo cháo

Radical	Strokes
月 74	12-4-8
Grade	Freq
Jōyō-2	248
1-8-4	

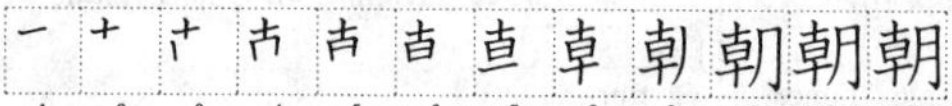

▶MORNING ▶DYNASTY

COMPOUNDS

❶ **morning, forenoon, morn**

朝刊 *chōkan* morning edition [paper]

朝食 *chōshoku* breakfast

早朝 *sōchō* early morning

一朝一夕に *itchō-isseki ni* in one day, in a short time

❷ [also suffix]

ⓐ **dynasty, reign, rule**

ⓑ **dynastic period, age**

王朝 *ōchō* dynasty, Imperial regime

清朝 *shinchō* Qing Dynasty, Manchu Dynasty

平安朝 *heianchō* Heian Period

❸ court, government

朝廷 *chōtei* Imperial Court

朝野 *chōya* government and people
朝貢する *chōkō suru* bring tribute
❹ⓐ North Korea, Korea
ⓑ Korean (language)
朝鮮 *chōsen* (North) Korea
日朝辞典 *nitchō jiten* Japanese–Korean dictionary
❺ country ruled by emperor (esp. Japan)
帰朝する *kichō suru* come back to one's country (Japan)
来朝する *raichō suru* come to Japan

INDEPENDENT

【chō 朝】 dynasty, reign; dynastic period; in office, in power
桓武天皇の朝 *kanmu tennō no chō* in the reign of Emperor Kanmu
【chōsuru 朝する】 proceed to the court

KUN

【asa 朝】 morning, forenoon, morn
朝方 *asagata* toward morning
朝日 *asahi* [sometimes also 旭] rising sun, morning sun; rays of the morning sun
朝早く *asahayaku* early in the morning
毎朝 *maiasa* every morning

SPECIAL READINGS

今朝 *kesa* this morning

SYNONYMS

❶ **morning and dawn**
暁 DAWN → 980
旦 DAYBREAK → 2389
❷ⓑ **long time periods**
期 period → 1704
世 AGE → 3496
代 age → 30
紀 ERA → 1276
時 TIME → 924
❸ **governments**
廷 COURT → 3058
宮 Imperial Court → 2274
幕 SHOGUNATE → 2335
官 GOVERNMENT → 2226
❹ⓐ **Korea**
鮮 Korea → 1877
韓 SOUTH KOREA → 1757

HOMOPHONES

asahi ⇨ 旭 2977 朝日 1695, 3027

NOTE

⇨ see USAGE note at 旭 2977

戟

1696 GEKI

Ⓒⓗ 戟 jǐ

Radical	Strokes
戈 62	12-4-8
Grade Reference	**Freq**
◧ 1 - 8 - 4	

8-4 卓

COMPOUNDS

❶ [now replaced by 激 776] stir up, stimulate, excite
刺戟する *shigeki suru* stimulate, excite
❷ [original meaning] halberd, two-pronged lance
剣戟 *kengeki* weapons, arms
戟 *geki* halberd, two-pronged lance

朝

1697 ▶**MORNING** ▶**DYNASTY**

nonstandard for 朝 1695

8-4 卓

乾

incorrect stroke count ⇨ see 1679

8-4 卓

8-4
幸

報 報 报

1698 HŌ muku(iru)

Ⓒⓗ 报 bào

Radical	Strokes
土 32	12-3-9
Grade	Freq
Jōyō-5	274
1-8-4	

一 十 土 ± 圭 圭 幸 幸 幸 幸 報 報 報
1 2 3 4 5 6 7 8 9 10 11 12

▶INFORM ▶REQUITE

COMPOUNDS

❶ⓐ **inform, report, announce, convey**
ⓑ **information, report, news**
ⓒ [also suffix] **bulletin, newspaper, magazine**
報道 *hōdō* news, report, information
報告する *hōkoku suru* report, inform
通報する *tsūhō suru* report, send information
一報 *ippō* information, notification
予報 *yohō* forecast, prediction
情報 *jōhō* information, intelligence, report, news
電報 *denpō* telegram
広報(=弘報) *kōhō* (public) information, public relations
公報 *kōhō* public [official] report [bulletin]
日報 *nippō* daily report, daily news
速報 *sokuhō* prompt report, news flash
官報 *kanpō* official gazette, official telegram
画報 *gahō* illustrated magazine
研究所報 *kenkyūshohō* research institute bulletin

❷ signal, warning
時報 *jihō* time signal; review
警報 *keihō* warning signal, alarm
大雨注意報 *ōame-chūihō* storm warning

❸ⓐ (make return for) **requite, return, repay; reward, recompense**
ⓑ (take revenge) requite, avenge, retaliate
報奨 *hōshō* reward, compensation
報恩 *hōon* repaying a kindness, gratitude
報酬 *hōshū* remuneration, reward; pay
返報 *henpō* requital, retaliation, revenge
報復 *hōfuku* retaliation, reprisal, revenge

INDEPENDENT

【hō 報】 information, news
報に接する *hō ni sessuru* get information, be informed of

【hōjiru (=hōzuru) 報じる(=報ずる)】 report, inform; return, requite

KUN

【muku(iru) 報いる】
① [formerly also 酬いる]
ⓐ requite, repay
ⓑ recompense, reward
報い *mukui* recompense, return; punishment, retribution
労に報いる *rō ni mukuiru* recompense a person for his [her] labor
② revenge oneself on, retaliate

SYNONYMS

❶ⓐ inform and communicate
通 COMMUNICATE → 3109
告 NOTIFY → 2409
届ける give notice → 3078
達 issue a notice → 3139
知 let know → 1127
申 REPORT → 3507
宣 PROCLAIM → 2252

ⓑ information
信 MESSAGE → 100

ⓒ periodicals
誌 MAGAZINE → 1548
紙 newspaper → 1302

❷ signal
号 signal → 2153

❸ⓐ compensate
酬 RECIPROCATE → 1539
償 RECOMPENSE → 176
賠 COMPENSATE → 1582

USAGE

❶ mukuiru
報いる
① [formerly also 酬いる]
ⓐ requite, repay
ⓑ recompense, reward
② revenge oneself on, retaliate
酬いる
[now usu. 報いる]
ⓐ requite, repay
ⓑ recompense, reward

❷ mukui
報い
ⓐ [formerly also 酬い] recompense, return
ⓑ punishment, retribution
酬い
[now usu. 報い] recompense, return

HOMOPHONES

mukuiru ⇨ 酬 1539
mukui ⇨ 酬 1539

NOTE

⇨ see also USAGE note at 広 3035

8-4 壳

殼 1699

▶SHELL
nonstandard for 殻 1490

8-4 款

款 款 款
1700 KAN

CH 款 kuǎn

Radical	Strokes
欠 76	12-4-8
Grade	**Freq**
Jōyō	1508
1-8-4	

一 十 士 圭 圭 耒 耒 崇 崇 款 款 款
1 2 3 4 5 6 7 8 9 10 11 12

▶ARTICLE

COMPOUNDS

❶ⓐ article, item, subsection
ⓑ counter for articles or subsections
定款 *teikan* articles of association, company contract
約款 *yakkan* article, stipulation, provision, clause
条款 *jōkan* article, stipulation, provision, clause
第二款 *dainikan* Article 2
❷ sum of money, funds
借款 *shakkan* loan
❸ [usu. 歓 1867] **treat cordially, have friendly relations with**
款待 *kantai* cordial [warm] reception
交款 *kōkan* exchange of cordialities
❹ inscription, seal
落款 *rakkan* sign and seal, signature

INDEPENDENT

【kan 款】 goodwill, cordiality; article, item, subsection
款を通ずる *kan o tsūzuru* form a close friendship; communicate secretly

SYNONYMS

❶ parts of writing
条 ARTICLE → 2200
項 CLAUSE → 567
目 ITEM → 3043
箇 item → 2700
節 paragraph → 2691
段 passage → 1144
章 CHAPTER → 2117
❸ treat and welcome
接 receive → 500
遇 TREAT → 3135
待 treat → 364
扱う HANDLE → 217
迎 WELCOME → 3059

8-4 苟

敬 敬 敬 敬
1701 KEI KYŌ▲ uyama(u)

CH 敬 jìng

Radical	Strokes
攵 66	12-4-8
Grade	**Freq**
Jōyō-6	1200
1-8-4	

一 十 艹 艹 芍 芍 苟 苟 苟 苟 敬 敬
1 2 3 4 5 6 7 8 9 10 11 12

▶RESPECT

COMPOUNDS

● respect, revere, honor
敬意 *keii* respect, regard, honor
敬称 *keishō* honorific title, term of respect
敬老 *keirō* respect for the aged
敬語 *keigo* honorific language, polite speech
敬遠する *keien suru* keep at a respectful distance; avoid
敬具 *keigu* Yours truly [respectfully]
敬服する *keifuku suru* have great admiration for
敬愛 *keiai* respect and affection, veneration
尊敬する *sonkei suru* respect, esteem, honor, revere
失敬な *shikkei na* disrespectful, rude, impolite
愛敬 *aikyō* (personal) charm, winsomeness, courtesy

INDEPENDENT

【keisuru 敬する】 respect, esteem, honor

KUN

【uyama(u) 敬う】 respect, revere, reverence, honor, venerate
敬い *uyamai* respect, reverence, veneration, honor, esteem
神を敬う *kami o uyamau* revere God

SYNONYMS

● respect

欽 REVERE → 1690
仰 look up to → 48
崇 REVERENCE → 2297
尚 VALUE HIGHLY → 2233
重 set value on → 3573
拝 WORSHIP → 303
慕 ADORE → 2353
尊 HONOR → 2324

8-4 昔

散 散 㪚

1702 SAN chi(ru) chi(rasu) -chi(rasu) chi(rakasu) chi(rakaru)

CH 散 sàn sǎn

Radical	Strokes
攵 66	12-4-8
Grade	**Freq**
Jōyō-4	549
1-8-4	

一 十 艹 廾 𠀍 𦉭 昔 昔 𣥋 𣥌 散 散
1 2 3 4 5 6 7 8 9 10 11 12

▶SCATTER

COMPOUNDS

❶ⓐ **scatter, disperse, break up**

ⓑ [formerly also 撒 *san, satsu* 736] [original meaning] (**cause to**) **scatter, sprinkle, adjourn** (**a meeting**), **disperse**

散乱 *sanran* dispersion, scattering
散発的な *sanpatsuteki na* sporadic
解散 *kaisan* breakup, dispersion; dissolution
拡散 *kakusan* scattering, diffusion
分散 *bunsan* dispersion, breakup, divergence; variance
四散する *shisan suru* scatter (in all directions)
一目散に *ichimokusan ni* at full [top] speed
散髪 *sanpatsu* haircut
散布 *sanpu* (=*sappu*) scattering, sprinkling, spraying
散水 *sansui* water sprinkling
散会する *sankai suru* break up, adjourn, disperse

❷ⓐ **unrestrained, free, carefree, relaxed, loose**

ⓑ **random, haphazard**

散歩 *sanpo* walk, (leisurely) stroll
散文 *sanbun* prose
閑散 *kansan* leisure, inactivity
散散に *sanzan ni* severely, terribly, unsparingly
散漫な *sanman na* desultory, vagrant, vague

❸ powdered medicine

散剤 *sanzai* powdered medicine
胃散 *isan* powder for the stomach

INDEPENDENT

【sanjiru (=sanzuru) 散じる(=散ずる)】
spend, squander; dispel, dissipate
家財を散じる *kazai o sanjiru* squander one's fortune
鬱を散じる *utsu o sanjiru* chase one's gloom away

KUN

【chi(ru) 散る】
vi
① scatter, disperse, break up, dissipate
散り散りに *chirijiri ni* scatteredly, separately
飛び散る *tobichiru* fly off, fly apart, scatter
② fall, be scattered [shed]; die
散る落葉 *chiru ochiba* falling leaves
南海に散る *nankai ni chiru* die in the south sea
③ run, spread, blur
この紙はインクが散る *Kono kami wa inku ga chiru* Ink runs [spreads] on this paper
④ resolve, be resolved
腫れ物が散った *Haremono ga chitta* The tumor has resolved
⑤ be distracted
気が散った *Ki ga chitta* My attention was distracted

【chi(rasu) 散らす】 *vt* scatter, disperse, strew, break up, dissipate; resolve; distract
散らし *chirashi* leaflet, handbill, flyer; uncaked *sushi*
追い散らす *oichirasu* drive away, scatter, rout
盲腸を散らす *mōchō o chirasu* resolve appendicitis
気を散らす *ki o chirasu* distract a person's attention

【-chi(rasu) -散らす】 verbal suffix indicating disorder or indiscretion
食い散らす *kuichirasu* eat untidily, eat a bit of everything
当たり散らす *atarichirasu* find fault with everybody, make oneself disagreeable

【chi(rakasu) 散らかす】 *vt* scatter (around), disarrange, leave untidy
部屋を散らかす *heya o chirakasu* litter a room (with things)

【chi(rakaru) 散らかる】 *vi* lie scattered about, be in disorder
散らかった紙屑 *chirakatta kamikuzu* scattered [littered] paper scraps

SYNONYMS

❶ⓐ **spread**
布 SPREAD → 2973
敷く LAY → 1870
舗 PAVE → 1735

塗 APPLY ON A SURFACE → 2841
抹 wipe over → 313
ⓑ **disperse**
解 DISSOLVE → 1517
❷ **unrestrained**
漫 RAMBLING → 700

欺 欺 欺

1703 GI azamu(ku)

Ⓒⓗ 欺 qī

Radical	Strokes
欠 76	12-4-8
Grade	**Freq**
Jōyō	1376
◧ 1 - 8 - 4	

8-4 其

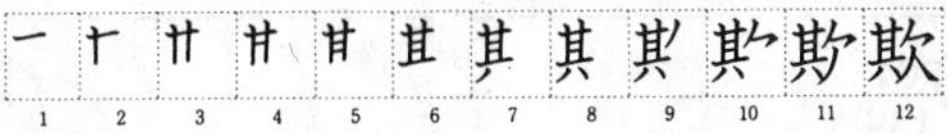

▶DECEIVE

COMPOUNDS

● [original meaning] **deceive, cheat, swindle**
欺瞞 *giman* deception, imposition
詐欺 *sagi* swindle, fraud

KUN

【azamu(ku) 欺く】 deceive, cheat, delude; be comparable to; outshine
欺き惑わす *azamukimadowasu* deceive and lead astray
花を欺く美人 *hana o azamuku bijin* woman as pretty as a flower

SYNONYMS

● **deceive**
詐 SWINDLE → 1502
偽 FALSIFY → 131
惑 mislead → 2786
拐 defraud → 308

期 期 期 期

1704 KI GO

Ⓒⓗ 期 qī

Radical	Strokes
月 74	12-4-8
Grade	**Freq**
Jōyō-3	120
◧ 1 - 8 - 4	

8-4 其

▶TERM ▶EXPECT

COMPOUNDS

❶ⓐ [also suffix] **term, school term, period, season, quarter; stage, phase; session**
ⓑ (deadline) **term, time limit, appointed day**
ⓒ inevitable moment
期間 *kikan* term, period
期末試験 *kimatsushiken* term-end examination
学期 *gakki* school term
時期 *jiki* time, season
第一期計画 *daiikki keikaku* first phase of a plan
初期 *shoki* early days, early stage, beginning; early, initial
上半期 *kamihanki* first half of the (fiscal) year
定期 *teiki* fixed term; fixed deposit; abbrev. of 定期券 *teikiken*: season [commuter] pass
期限 *kigen* time limit, term
延期する *enki suru* postpone, defer
任期 *ninki* one's term of office
満期 *manki* expiration (of a term)
最期 *saigo* one's last moments, death

❷ⓐ [also suffix] **period, age, time, occasion**
ⓑ geological age
青年期 *seinenki* adolescence
幼児期 *yōjiki* babyhood
平安後期 *heian kōki* late Heian period
画期的な *kakkiteki na* epoch-making, epochal
氷河期 *hyōgaki* ice age

❸ **expect, look forward to, anticipate, hope for**
期待する *kitai suru* expect, look forward to, anticipate, hope for
予期する *yoki suru* expect, anticipate, hope for
所期の *shoki no* expected, anticipated, hoped-for

❹ determine, decide; promise, pledge
期成 *kisei* resolution to carry out (a plan)

INDEPENDENT

【ki 期】 time, date, occasion
【kisuru 期する】 fix a date, determine; resolve; promise; expect, hope for
【go 期】 inevitable moment
【gosuru 期する】 wait expectantly for

SYNONYMS

❶ⓐ **time periods**
節 SEASON OF THE YEAR → 2691

季 SEASON (quarter) → 2554
候 SEASON (time of year) → 119
間 INTERVAL → 3323
時 TIME → 924
頃 TIME → 144
暇 FREE TIME → 1012
般 period of time → 1317
刻 POINT OF TIME → 1267

❷ⓐ **long time periods**
時 TIME → 924
代 age → 30
紀 ERA → 1276
世 AGE → 3496
朝 dynastic period → 1695
❸ **expect**
待 wait for → 364

8-4 其

朞
1705

▶TERM ▶EXPECT
nonstandard for 期 1704

8-4 𤔔

敢 敢 𢼸
1706 KAN a(ete)▲ a(enai)▲ a(ezu)▲

一 丅 工 干 于 盲 貢 貢 貢 䝦 敢 敢
1 2 3 4 5 6 7 8 9 10 11 12

CH 敢 gǎn

Radical	Strokes
攵 66	12-4-8
Grade	**Freq**
Jōyō	1744
1 - 8 - 4	

▶**BOLDLY**

COMPOUNDS

ⓐ **boldly, daringly, bravely, fearlessly, resolutely**
ⓑ **bold, daring, brave, fearless, resolute**
敢闘する *kantō suru* fight bravely
敢然(と) *kanzen (to)* boldly, bravely
敢行 *kankō* decisive [daring] action
果敢な *kakan na* bold, daring; resolute
勇敢な *yūkan na* brave, courageous, daring, heroic

KUN

【a(ete) 敢えて】 boldly, daringly; [in negative constructions] (not) at all
敢えてする *aete suru* dare [venture] to do
敢えて驚くには当たらない *Aete odoroku ni wa ataranai* There is nothing strange about it
【a(enai) 敢えない】 sad, tragic
敢えない最期 *aenai saigo* tragic death
敢え無く *aenaku* sadly, tragically
【a(ezu) 敢えず】 *literary* hardly finishing (doing), unable to do sufficiently
涙塞き敢えず *namida sekiaezu* unable to fight back tears
取り敢えず *toriaezu* as a temporary measure, for the present, in a hurry; first of all

SYNONYMS

ⓐ **resolutely**
断 resolutely → 1492
決 decisively → 263
ⓑ **brave**
勇 BRAVE → 2089
赳 VALIANT → 3308
豪 bold and unrestrained → 2140
雄 HEROIC → 1008
壮 heroic → 224
義 chivalrous → 2338

8-4 𠀎

𣪘
incorrect stroke count ⇨ see 1791

鉛 鉛 鉛 鉛

1707 EN namari

CH 铅 qiān yán

Radical	Strokes
金 167	13-8-5
Grade	Freq
Jōyō	1581
1 - 8 - 5	

8-5 金

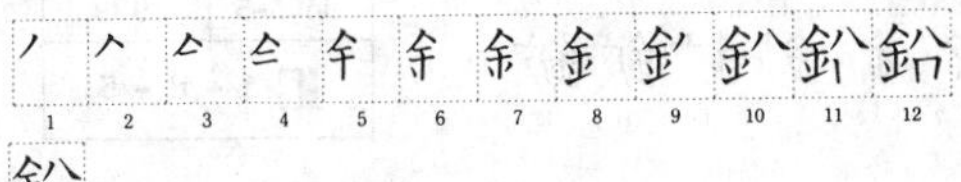

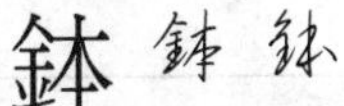

▶**LEAD**

COMPOUNDS

● [original meaning] **lead**

鉛毒 *endoku* lead poisoning

鉛筆 *enpitsu* pencil

鉛管 *enkan* lead pipe

加鉛ガソリン *kaen-gasorin* leaded gasoline

亜鉛 *aen* zinc

KUN

【namari 鉛】 lead

鉛色 *namariiro* lead color; livid

SYNONYMS

● **metals**

鉄 IRON → 1711

銅 COPPER → 1721

銀 SILVER → 1722

金 GOLD → 2057

鉢 鉢 鉢

1708 HACHI HATSU

CH 钵 bō

Radical	Strokes
金 167	13-8-5
Grade	Freq
Jōyō	1945
1 - 8 - 5	

8-5 金

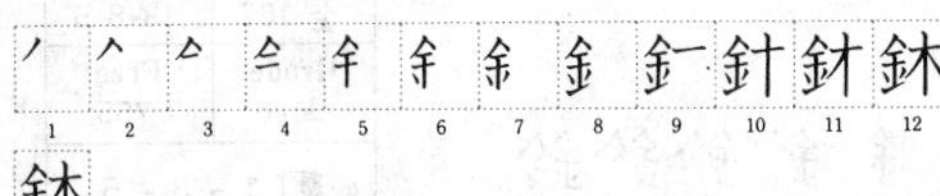

鉢 13

▶**BOWL**

COMPOUNDS

❶ⓐ **bowl, pot, basin**

ⓑ Buddhist priest's rice bowl

鉢物 *hachimono* food served in bowls; bonsai

菓子鉢 *kashibachi* bowl for confectioneries

鉄鉢 *teppachi* mendicant priest's begging bowl

托鉢 *takuhatsu* religious mendicancy, begging bonze

衣鉢 *ihatsu* (=*ehatsu*) mysteries (of Buddhism or an art)

❷ⓐ **flowerpot**

ⓑ counter for potted plants

鉢植え *hachiue* potted plant

植木鉢 *uekibachi* flowerpot

菊二鉢 *kiku futahachi* two flowerpots of chrysanthemums

❸ crown (of the head), brainpan, skull

鉢巻き *hachimaki* headband

鉢合わせ *hachiawase* bumping of heads; running into someone

INDEPENDENT

【hachi 鉢】 basin; flowerpot; crown (of the head), brainpan, skull

お鉢 *ohachi* rice tub; one's turn

鉢の花 *hachi no hana* flower in a pot

鉢の開いた頭 *hachi no hiraita atama* flat-crowned head

SYNONYMS

❶ⓐ **vessels and receptacles**

鍋 POT → 1752

杯 CUP → 857

盆 TRAY → 2079

皿 PLATE → 3474

盤 dish → 2851

COMPOUND FORMATION

❶ 托鉢 *takuhatsu*

托鉢 'religious mendicancy, begging bonze' represents a Buddhist bonze making rounds from house to house chanting sutra and holding out (托) his begging bowl (鉢 ❶ⓑ) for rice.

❷ 衣鉢 *ihatsu* (=*ehatsu*)

衣鉢 'mysteries (of Buddhism or an art)' represents the surplice (衣) and bowl (鉢 ❶ⓑ) that a Buddhist master would hand his disciple to symbolize initiation into the secrets of Buddhism. It is chiefly used in the expression 衣鉢を継ぐ *ihatsu o tsugu* 'have the mysteries of one master's art imparted to one'.

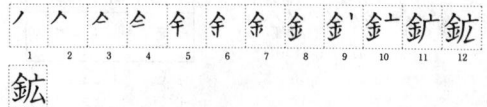

8-5 金

鉱 鑛 鉱 𨱎

㊥ 矿 kuàng

1709 KŌ

Radical	Strokes
金 167	13-8-5
Grade	**Freq**
Jōyō-5	939
1 - 8 - 5	

丿 人 亽 今 全 余 侌 金 釒 釒 鉱 鉱 鉱 (1–13)

▶**ORE** ▶**MINE**

COMPOUNDS

❶ [formerly also 礦 1256] [also suffix] [original meaning] **ore**

鉱石 *kōseki* ore, mineral
鉱床 *kōshō* ore deposit
鉱山 *kōzan* mine
鉱坑 *kōkō* mine, shaft, pit
金鉱 *kinkō* gold ore; gold mine
鉄鉱 *tekkō* iron ore
磁鉄鉱 *jitekkō* magnetite, loadstone

❷ⓐ **mine**
ⓑ suffix after names of mines
鉱業 *kōgyō* mining (industry)
炭鉱 *tankō* coal mine
夕張鉱 *yūbarikō* Yubari Mine

SYNONYMS

❶ **metal**
金 METAL → 2057

❷ **mine**
山 mine → 2940
坑 PIT → 236

8-5 金

鈴 鈴° 鈴 𨰻

㊥ 铃 líng

1710 REI RIN suzu

Radical	Strokes
金 167	13-8-5
Grade	**Freq**
Jōyō	755
1 - 8 - 5	

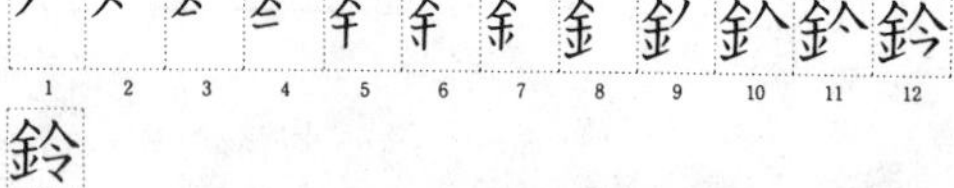

丿 人 亽 今 全 余 侌 金 釒 鈴 鈴 鈴 鈴 (1–13)

▶**BELL**

COMPOUNDS

● [original meaning] **bell (that jingles or rings)**

電鈴 *denrei* electric bell
振鈴 *shinrei* ringing bell, hand bell
予鈴 *yorei* the first bell
銀鈴 *ginrei* silver bell
風鈴 *fūrin* wind-bell
呼び鈴 *yobirin* (call) bell, doorbell

INDEPENDENT

【**rin** 鈴】 bell, doorbell
鈴を鳴らす *rin o narasu* ring a bell

KUN

【**suzu** 鈴】 bell (that jingles)
鈴蘭 *suzuran* lily of the valley
鈴虫 *suzumushi* "bell ring" insect (a kind of cricket)

SYNONYMS

● **bells**
鐘 BELL (that tolls) → 1769

鉄 鐵 鉃 銕

1711 TETSU kurogane▲

CH 铁 tiě

Radical	Strokes
金 167	13-8-5
Grade	Freq
Jōyō-3	295
1-8-5	

8-5 金

鉄 13

▶**IRON**

COMPOUNDS

❶ⓐ [original meaning] **iron**
ⓑ as hard or rigid as iron
鉄鋼 *tekkō* iron and steel
鉄板 *teppan* iron [steel] plate
鉄筋コンクリート *tekkin-konkurīto* reinforced concrete, ferroconcrete
鉄砲 *teppō* gun, firearm
鉄道 *tetsudō* railway
製鉄 *seitetsu* iron manufacture
非鉄金属 *hitetsu-kinzoku* nonferrous metals
鉄則 *tessoku* ironclad rule, immutable law
❷ iron blue, reddish black
鉄色 *tetsuiro* iron blue, reddish black
❸ abbrev. of 鉄道 *tetsudō*: **railway, railroad line**
国鉄 *kokutetsu* Japanese National Railways (defunct)
地下鉄 *chikatetsu* subway
私鉄 *shitetsu* nongovernmental [private] railroad line
電鉄 *dentetsu* electric railway
❹ blade, weapon
寸鉄 *suntetsu* short blade, small weapon; epigram, pithy saying

INDEPENDENT

【**tetsu** 鉄】iron; iron blue, reddish black
鉄の *tetsu no* ferrous, ferric
鉄のカーテン *tetsu no kāten* iron curtain

KUN

【**kurogane** 鉄】*elegant* iron

SYNONYMS

❶ⓐ **iron and steel**
鋼 STEEL → 1740
銑 PIG IRON → 1726
ⓐ **metals**
鉛 LEAD → 1707
銅 COPPER → 1721
銀 SILVER → 1722
金 GOLD → 2057
❸ **kinds of railway**
電 electric railway → 2790
車 railway car → 3552
両 counter for railway cars → 3518

鈆

1712

▶**LEAD**
nonstandard for 鉛 1707

8-5 金

銃

1713

▶**GUN**
nonstandard for 銃 1723

8-5 金

鈴

1714

▶**BELL**
nonstandard for 鈴 1710

8-5 金

8-5 食

飽 飽 飽 飽

1715 HŌ a(kiru) a(kasu) a(ku)▲

CH 饱 bǎo

Radical	Strokes
食 184	13-8-5
Grade	Freq
Jōyō	1839
1-8-5	

ノ 𠆢 𠆢 今 今 今 食 食 飠 飽 飽 飽 飽 (1–13)

▶SATIATED

COMPOUNDS

● [original meaning] (have a full stomach) **satiated, sated, satisfied, surfeited**

飽食する *hōshoku suru* satiate oneself, surfeit, eat one's fill
飽満 *hōman* satiety, surfeit
飽食暖衣 *hōshoku dan'i* being well fed and well clad
飽和 *hōwa* saturation

KUN

【a(kiru) 飽きる】
ⓐ [also suffix] be satiated, be surfeited, be fed up
ⓑ [sometimes also 厭きる] grow tired of, lose interest in
聞き飽きる *kikiakiru* be fed up listening to
快楽に飽きる *kairaku ni akiru* be satiated with pleasures
飽き *aki* weariness, tiresomeness
飽きっぽい *akippoi* be fickle [capricious], get soon wearied of
飽き飽きする *akiaki suru* be sick (of), be bored (with), be fed up

【a(kasu) 飽かす】 surfeit, satiate, spend unsparingly; tire, bore (a reader)
金に飽かして *kane ni akashite* regardless of expense, sparing no money
聴衆を飽かさない *chōshū o akasanai* hold the attention of the audience

【a(ku) 飽く】 *elegant* same as **akiru 飽きる**
飽かず *akazu* insatiably, without being bored
飽く迄 *akumade* to the last, stubbornly

SYNONYMS

● **full**
満 FULL → 607

USAGE

akiru
飽きる
ⓐ [also suffix] be satiated, be surfeited, be fed up
ⓑ [sometimes also 厭きる] grow tired of, lose interest in
厭きる
ⓐ [usu. 飽きる] grow tired of, lose interest in
ⓑ be disgusted with, detest, dislike

HOMOPHONES

akiru ⇨ 厭 3017

8-5 食

飼 飼 飼 飼

1716 SHI ka(u)

CH 饲 sì

Radical	Strokes
食 184	13-8-5
Grade	Freq
Jōyō-5	1347
1-8-5	

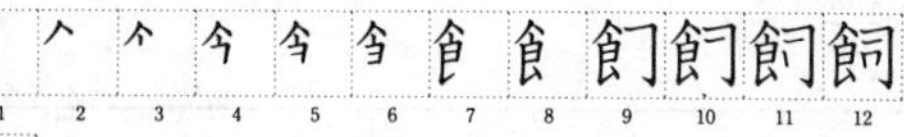

飼 (13)

▶RAISE ANIMALS

COMPOUNDS

● [original meaning] **raise animals, rear, breed, keep**

飼育する *shiiku suru* raise animals, breed, rear
飼養 *shiyō* breeding, raising
飼料 *shiryō* fodder

KUN

【ka(u) 飼う】 raise (animals), rear; keep (a dog), feed (cattle)
羊飼い *hitsujikai* shepherd
放し飼い *hanashigai* grazing; letting (a dog) run free
飼い犬 *kaiinu* house dog
飼い殺し *kaigoroshi* keeping (an employee) in service for life

SYNONYMS

● **raise and nourish**
牧 PASTURE → 873

育 RAISE → 2050
養 FOSTER → 2365
滋 NOURISH → 602

飾 飾 飾 飾

1717 SHOKU kaza(ru) kaza(ri)

Ⓒ饰 shì

Radical	Strokes
飠 184	13-8-5
Grade	**Freq**
Jōyō	1007
◧ 1 - 8 - 5	

8-5 飠

ノ 𠆢 亽 今 今 今 食 食 飠 飣 飾 飾 飾 (1–13)

▶**DECORATE**

COMPOUNDS

❶ⓐ [original meaning] **decorate, adorn, ornament, embellish**
ⓑ **decoration, ornament**
ⓒ hair ornament; hair
装飾する *sōshoku suru* ornament, adorn, decorate
修飾する *shūshoku suru* decorate, ornament; *gram* modify
電飾 *denshoku* decorative illumination
満艦飾の船 *mankanshoku no fune* full dress ship
服飾 *fukushoku* dress and its ornaments
落飾 *rakushoku* tonsure
❷ affect, be ostentatious, embellish
虚飾 *kyoshoku* ostentation, affectation, show
粉飾する *funshoku suru* embellish, color, rig

KUN

【kaza(ru) 飾る】 decorate, ornament, adorn, embellish; affect, be affected; exhibit, display; gloss over (one's defects)
着飾る *kikazaru* dress up
飾り立てる *kazaritateru* decorate gaudily, deck out
【kaza(ri) 飾り】 ornament, decoration; embellishment, display, ostentation
飾り気の無い *kazarike no nai* unaffected, plain
飾り窓 *kazarimado* show window, display window
首飾り *kubikazari* necklace

SYNONYMS

❶ⓐ & ❶ⓑ **decorate**
粧 APPLY MAKEUP → 1345
粉 apply face powder → 1291
装 DRESS → 2685

瓶 incorrect classification ⇨ see 1041
(nonstandard for 瓶 1344)

8-5 井

幹 幹 幹

1718 KAN miki

Ⓒ干 gàn

Radical	Strokes
干 51	13-3-10
Grade	**Freq**
Jōyō-5	668
◧ 1 - 8 - 5	

8-5 龺

一 十 𠂇 古 古 古 直 卓 卓 𠦝 𠦝 𠦝 幹 (1–13)

▶**TRUNK**

COMPOUNDS

❶ [original meaning] **tree trunk**
樹幹 *jukan* trunk, shaft
根幹 *konkan* basis, root; keynote; [original meaning] root and trunk
軀幹 *kukan* body, trunk, physique
❷ (main part of something) **trunk, main part**
幹線 *kansen* trunk line, main line
幹部 *kanbu* executive, (managing) staff
幹事 *kanji* manager, secretary; organizer
基幹 *kikan* mainstay, nucleus
主幹 *shukan* editor in chief
❸ ability, talent (in performing office work)
才幹 *saikan* ability, capability

KUN

【miki 幹】 tree trunk

SYNONYMS

❶ **supporting parts of plants**
株 stump → 935
根 ROOT → 930
茎 STEM → 2242
❷ **essential part**
枢 PIVOT → 865
精 ESSENCE (essential part) → 1366
粋 essence (best part) → 1293
髄 essence (vital part) → 1842
綱 ESSENTIAL POINTS → 1372
旨 PURPORT → 2024
要 summary → 2635

8-5 冊

嗣 嗣 嗣

1719 SHI

CH 嗣 sì

Radical	Strokes
口 30	13-3-10
Grade	**Freq**
Jōyō	1726
1 - 8 - 5	

▶HEIR

COMPOUNDS

❶ **heir, successor**
嗣子 *shishi* heir, successor
後嗣 *kōshi* heir, successor
令嗣 *reishi* your [his] heir
皇嗣 *kōshi* Imperial Heir, Crown Prince
❷ inherit, succeed
継嗣 *keishi* successor, heir, heiress

INDEPENDENT

【**shi** 嗣】 heir, successor
皇帝の嗣 *kōtei no shi* Emperor's heir

SYNONYMS

❶ **inheritors**
嫡 LEGITIMATE CHILD → 680
❷ **succeed**
継 SUCCEED → 1360
承 succeed to → 16

8-6 金

鉾

1720 BŌ hoko

CH 铧 móu

Radical	Strokes
金 167	14-8-6
Grade	**Freq**
Reference	
1 - 8 - 6	

COMPOUNDS

● decorative halberd
山鉾 *yamaboko* festival float mounted with a decorative halberd
蒲鉾 *kamaboko* steamed fish paste

HOMOPHONES

hoko ⇨ 矛 2008 戈 3462

NOTE

⇨ see USAGE note at 矛 2008

8-6 金

銅 銅 銅

1721 DŌ akagane▲

CH 铜 tóng

Radical	Strokes
金 167	14-8-6
Grade	**Freq**
Jōyō-5	1321
1 - 8 - 6	

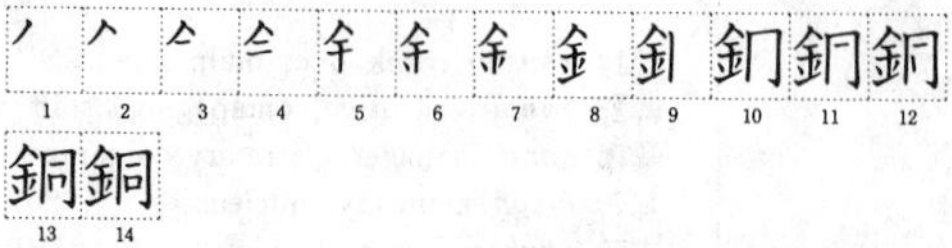

▶COPPER

COMPOUNDS

❶ [also prefix] [original meaning] **copper**
銅鉱 *dōkō* copper ore
銅線 *dōsen* copper wire
銅山 *dōzan* copper mine
銅貨 *dōka* copper coin, copper
銅相場 *dōsōba* market price of copper

青銅 *seidō* bronze
❷ bronze
銅像 *dōzō* bronze statue [image]
銅鐸 *dōtaku* bronze bell

INDEPENDENT

【dō 銅】 copper; abbrev. of 銅メダル *dōmedaru*: copper medal
銅の *dō no* copper

KUN

【akagane 銅】 [also 赤金] copper
銅の器 *akagane no utsuwa* copper vessel

SYNONYMS

❶ **metals**
鉄 IRON → 1711
鉛 LEAD → 1707
銀 SILVER → 1722
金 GOLD → 2057

USAGE

akagane
銅
[also 赤金] copper
赤金
[also 銅] copper

HOMOPHONES

akagane ⇨ 赤金 2193, 2057

銀 1722

GIN shirogane▲

Ⓒⓗ 银 yín

Radical	Strokes
金 167	14-8-6
Grade	Freq
Jōyō-3	363
1 - 8 - 6	

8-6

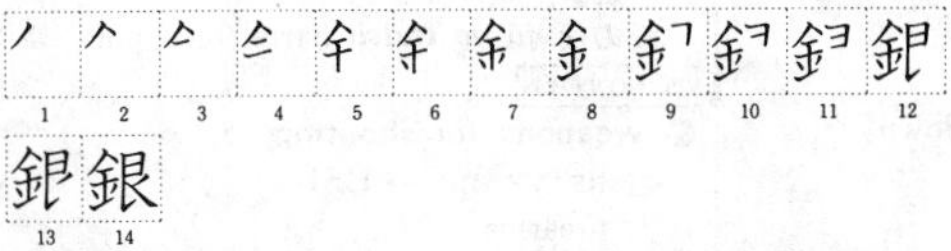

▶**SILVER**

COMPOUNDS

❶ⓐ **silver**
ⓑ (of silvery color) **silver**
銀貨 *ginka* silver coin
水銀 *suigin* mercury, quicksilver
純銀 *jungin* pure silver
硝酸銀 *shōsangin* silver nitrate
金銀 *kingin* gold and silver; money
銀色 *gin'iro* silver color, silveriness
銀婚式 *ginkonshiki* silver wedding
銀河 *ginga* Milky Way; galaxy
銀髪 *ginpatsu* silver hair
❷ (medium of exchange) **silver, silver coin, money, wages**
銀行 *ginkō* bank
銀座 *ginza* the Ginza; mint (during Edo period)
銀本位制 *ginhon'isei* silver standard
賃銀(＝賃金) *chingin* wages, pay
労銀 *rōgin* wages (for labor)
❸ abbrev. of 銀行 *ginkō*: **bank**
日銀 *nichigin* Bank of Japan
勧銀 *kangin* hypothecary bank
開銀 *kaigin* development bank
❹ name of chess piece in shogi (Japanese chess): *gin*, the Silver
銀将 *ginshō gin*
銀交換 *ginkōkan* exchange of *gins*
❺ *astron* galactic
銀経 *ginkei* galactic longitude

INDEPENDENT

【gin 銀】 silver; abbrev. of 銀メダル *ginmedaru*: silver medal; *gin* (⇨ ❹)
銀を取る *gin o toru* desilverize; capture a *gin*

KUN

【shirogane 銀】
[sometimes also 白金]
ⓐ silver
ⓑ silver coin

SYNONYMS

❶ⓐ **metals**
金 GOLD → 2057
銅 COPPER → 1721
鉄 IRON → 1711
鉛 LEAD → 1707
ⓑ **white colors**
皓 BRIGHT WHITE → 1180
白 WHITE → 3493
❷ **money**
金 MONEY → 2057
銭 MONEY → 1725
貨 MONEY (legal tender), coin → 2465
幣 CURRENCY → 2885
財 finance → 1457
資 RESOURCES → 2695
-玉 coin suffix → 3477
札 bill → 817
❸ **bank**
行 bank → 212

HOMOPHONES

shirogane ⇨ 白金 3493, 2057

NOTE
⇨ see USAGE note at 金 2057

⇨ see COMPOUND FORMATION for 銀座 *ginza* ⇨ 座 3116

8-6 金

銃 銃 銃 銃

1723 JŪ

Radical	Strokes
金 167	14-8-6
Grade	**Freq**
Jōyō	1103
1 - 8 - 6	

▶GUN

COMPOUNDS

[also suffix]

ⓐ (portable firearm) **gun, rifle, firearm**

ⓑ (something resembling a gun in shape or function) gun

銃声 *jūsei* sound of gunfire
銃撃 *jūgeki* shooting, gunning (down)
銃砲 *jūhō* firearm
拳銃 *kenjū* pistol, handgun
猟銃 *ryōjū* hunting gun
短銃 *tanjū* pistol
ライフル銃 *raifurujū* rifle
機関銃 *kikanjū* machine gun
鋲打ち銃 *byōuchijū* rivet gun

INDEPENDENT

【jū 銃】 gun, rifle
銃の筒 *jū no tsutsu* barrel of a gun

SYNONYMS

ⓐ **weapons for shooting**

砲 HEAVY GUN → 1151
火 firearms → 3463
弓 BOW → 3383

8-6 金

銘 銘 銘

1724 MEI

CH 铭 míng

Radical	Strokes
金 167	14-8-6
Grade	**Freq**
Jōyō	1138
1 - 8 - 6	

▶INSCRIPTION

COMPOUNDS

❶ [original meaning] (name or words inscribed on metal or stone) **inscription, epitaph (usu. written in classical Chinese)**

銘文 *meibun* inscription
碑銘 *himei* inscription, epitaph
墓碑銘 *bohimei* epitaph, inscription on a tombstone

❷ engrave on one's mind, bear in mind

銘記する *meiki suru* bear in mind, remember; inscribe, engrave
感銘 *kanmei* deep impression

❸ **name (inscribed by maker on finished product), appellation, signature**

銘刀 *meitō* sword inscribed by the sword smith
銘板 *meiban* nameplate (of machines)
銘柄 *meigara* brand name, brand, name
銘打つ *meiutsu* engrave an inscription; call [designate] itself
無銘の *mumei no* anonymous

❹ of well-known name, of noted brand, choice, superior

銘茶 *meicha* refined tea
銘酒 *meishu* choice [superior] sake

❺ motto

座右銘 *zayūmei* motto

INDEPENDENT

【mei 銘】 inscription, epitaph, signature; name, brand name, appellation; precept, motto, maxim
銘を刻む *mei o kizamu* engrave an inscription
座右の銘 *zayū no mei* (one's) motto

【meizuru 銘ずる】 impress, stamp, engrave

SYNONYMS

❶ **writing**

文 WRITINGS → 1962
筆 WRITING → 2677
書 writing(s) → 2658

❸ **name**
題 TITLE → 3337
号 DESIGNATION → 2153
称 APPELLATION → 1160
名 NAME → 2169
氏 FAMILY NAME → 2951
姓 SURNAME → 279

銭 銭 銭 銭

1725 SEN zeni

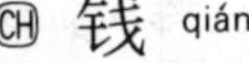

CH 钱 qián

Radical	Strokes
金 167	14-8-6
Grade	Freq
Jōyō-5	1052
1 - 8 - 6	

8-6

▶**MONEY**

COMPOUNDS

❶ⓐ **money, cash**
ⓑ **coin, copper coin**
金銭 *kinsen* money, cash
釣り銭 *tsurisen* change
無銭の *musen no* penniless, moneyless
守銭奴 *shusendo* miser, slave of money
賽銭 *saisen* money offering
バラ銭 *barasen* (small) change, loose coins
銅銭 *dōsen* copper coin
穴明き銭 *anaakisen* perforated coin

❷ money paid, charges, fee
銭湯 *sentō* public bath, bathhouse
木戸銭 *kidosen* gate money, admission fee
煙草銭 *tabakosen* tobacco money

❸ **sen:**
ⓐ **monetary unit equiv. to 1/100 of a yen** (円)
ⓑ former monetary unit equiv. to 1/1000 of a *kan* (貫)
二円五十銭 *nien gojussen* 2 yen 50 sen

INDEPENDENT

【sen 銭】 sen (⇨ ❸)

KUN

【zeni 銭】 money, cash; coin, copper coin
銭の取れる *zeni no toreru* worth the money
銭箱 *zenibako* cashbox
小銭 *kozeni* small money, small coin
[change]
日銭 *hizeni* daily income in cash
身銭 *mizeni* one's own money
銭入れ *zeniire* purse, till
銭亀 *zenigame* baby spotted turtle, young Japanese terrapin

SYNONYMS

❶ⓐ **money**
金 MONEY → 2057
貨 MONEY (legal tender), coin → 2465
幣 CURRENCY → 2885
銀 SILVER → 1722
財 finance → 1457
資 RESOURCES → 2695
-玉 coin suffix → 3477
札 bill → 817

❷ **fee and price**
賃 CHARGES → 2694
代 CHARGE → 30
料 FEE → 1292
費 EXPENSE → 2607
価 PRICE → 87
値 price → 109

❸ **Japanese money denominations**
円 YEN → 2955
厘 *RIN* → 3004
両 *ryo* → 3518
文 *mon* → 1962

8-6 釒

銑 銑 銑

1726 SEN

Ⓒⓗ 铣 xiǎn xǐ

Radical	Strokes
金 167	14-8-6
Grade	Freq
Jōyō	1922
1 - 8 - 6	

1 2 3 4 5 6 7 8 9 10 11 12 13 14

▶**PIG IRON**

COMPOUNDS

● **pig iron**

銑鉄 *sentetsu* pig iron

溶銑 *yōsen* molten iron

白銑 *hakusen* white pig iron

SYNONYMS

● **iron and steel**

鉄 IRON → 1711

鋼 STEEL → 1740

8-6 釒

銓

1727 SEN

Ⓒⓗ 铨 quán

Radical	Strokes
金 167	14-8-6
Grade	Freq
Reference	
1 - 8 - 6	

COMPOUNDS

● [now replaced by 選 *sen* 3169] [original meaning] weigh, evaluate

銓衡(＝選考)する *senkō suru* select, screen

8-6 青

静 靜 静 静

1728 SEI JŌ shizu- shizu(ka) shizu(maru) shizu(meru)

Ⓒⓗ 静 jìng

Radical	Strokes
青 174	14-8-6
Grade	Freq
Jōyō-4	685
1 - 8 - 6	

1 2 3 4 5 6 7 8 9 10 11 12 13 14

▶**QUIET**

COMPOUNDS

❶ⓐ [original meaning] (free from noise) **quiet, still, silent**

ⓑ (free of agitation) **quiet, calm, serene, tranquil**

ⓒ (make quiet) **quiet, calm, still**

静寂 *seijaku* silence, quietness, stillness

静聴する *seichō suru* listen quietly

沈静 *chinsei* stillness, tranquility, slackness

平静な *heisei na* calm, serene

冷静な *reisei na* cool, calm, cool-headed, dispassionate

鎮静する *chinsei suru* calm down, be tranquilized, subside; calm, tranquilize

❷ (motionless)

ⓐ **still, quiet, static, inactive**

ⓑ [prefix] static, statical

静止する *seishi suru* stand still, come to a standstill

静脈 *jōmyaku* vein

静座 *seiza* sitting quietly, meditation

静圧比 *seiatsuhi* static pressure ratio

静電気 *seidenki* static electricity

INDEPENDENT

【**sei 静**】 quiet, calm, stillness

静と動 *sei to dō* stillness and motion

KUN

【**shizu- 静-**】 quiet, calm

静けさ *shizukesa* stillness, silence, tranquility

静静と *shizushizu to* quietly, gently, calmly, slowly

【**shizu(ka) 静か**】

shizuka na 静かな quiet, silent, still; calm, tranquil, gentle, quiet

静かさ *shizukasa* quiet, calm

物静かな *monoshizuka na* quiet, still, calm
静かにしなさい *Shizuka ni shinasai* Be quiet!

【shizu(maru) 静まる】
ⓐ become quiet, grow still
ⓑ calm down, become tranquil, be lulled
静まり返る *shizumarikaeru* become still as death
寝静まる *neshizumaru* fall fast asleep
嵐が静まった *Arashi ga shizumatta* The storm has abated

【shizu(meru) 静める】
ⓐ (make quiet) quiet, calm, still
ⓑ (make calm) appease, calm, pacify
気を静める *ki o shizumeru* compose oneself, becalm one's feelings

SYNONYMS

❶ⓐ quiet
閑 QUIET → 3322
寂 quiet → 2290
幽 QUIET AND SECLUDED → 3008
粛 still → 3581
黙 SILENT → 2865

ⓑ calm and peaceful
泰 TRANQUIL → 2583
平 CALM → 3478
穏 CALM → 1235
安 PEACEFUL → 2171
康 peaceful → 3124
寧 peaceful → 2345

❷ⓐ not moving
止 still → 2941
定 fixed → 2229
固 FIRM → 3086

USAGE

❶ shizumaru
静まる
ⓐ become quiet, grow still
ⓑ calm down, become tranquil, be lulled
鎮まる
① be quelled, be suppressed, subside, be put down
② be alleviated, be relieved, be soothed
③ be enshrined

❷ shizumeru
静める
ⓐ (make quiet) quiet, calm, still
ⓑ (make calm) appease, calm, pacify
鎮める
① quell, suppress, put down, subdue, pacify
② alleviate (pain), relieve, allay, soothe
沈める
ⓐ sink, send to the bottom, submerge
ⓑ sink oneself into (a chair), lower oneself
ⓒ sink down in the world, go to ruin

HOMOPHONES

shizumaru ⇨ 鎮 1759
shizumeru ⇨ 鎮 1759 沈 261

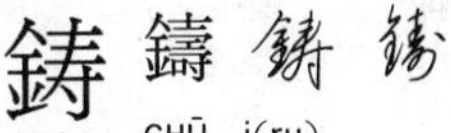

1729 CHŪ i(ru)

CH 铸 zhù

Radical	Strokes
金 167	15-8-7
Grade	**Freq**
Jōyō	1755
1-8-7	

8-7 金

▶CAST

COMPOUNDS

● [original meaning] **cast, mint, coin**
鋳鉄 *chūtetsu* iron casting
鋳造 *chūzō* casting, minting, coining
鋳金 *chūkin* casting
鋳鋼 *chūkō* cast steel
改鋳 *kaichū* recoinage, recasting

KUN

【i(ru) 鋳る】 cast, mint, coin
鋳物 *imono* cast metal, casting
鋳型 *igata* mold, cast, matrix, die
鋳直し *inaoshi* recasting

SYNONYMS

● form and carve
塑 MODEL → 2843
彫 CARVE → 1683
刻 ENGRAVE → 1267

● work metals
錬 REFINE (crude metals) → 1741
鍛 FORGE → 1755
焼き annealing → 997

8-7

金

鋭 鋭 鋭 鋭

1730 EI surudo(i)

Ⓒ 锐 ruì

Radical	Strokes
金 167	15-8-7
Grade	Freq
Jōyō	1197
1-8-7	

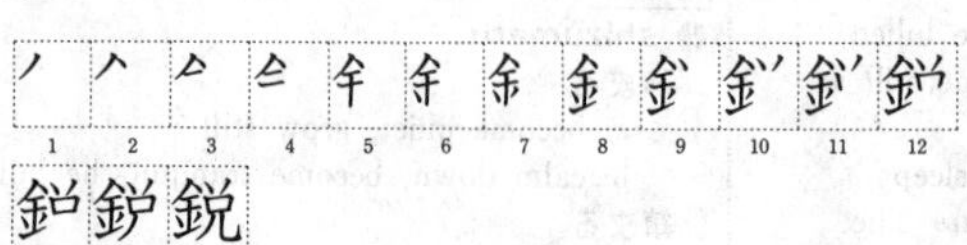

▶**SHARP**

COMPOUNDS

❶ⓐ [original meaning] (having an acute point) **sharp, pointed**

ⓑ (having an acute edge) **sharp, acute**

鋭鋒 *eihō* brunt (of an attack); incisive reasoning

先鋭(=尖鋭)な *sen'ei na* radical; acute, sharp

鋭利な *eiri na* sharp, keen; acute, sharp, clever

鋭角 *eikaku* acute angle

❷ **sharp-witted, quick, trenchant**

鋭敏な *eibin na* sharp, keen, sensitive

❸ vigorous, energetic, stinging

鋭気有る *eiki aru* spirited, dashing

鋭意 *eii* zeal

❹ **the choice, the best (esp. troops)**

鋭兵 *eihei* picked troops

新鋭な *shin'ei na* fresh picked

精鋭 *seiei* best [pick] (of the aviators), choice (of an army)

INDEPENDENT

【**ei** 鋭】 sharpness; vigor; (sharp) weapon

鋭を挫く *ei o kujiku* break the brunt

鋭を取る *ei o toru* take up a weapon

KUN

【**surudo(i)** 鋭い】 pointed, acute; sharp-witted, quick-witted, shrewd, keen, acute; violent, stinging, pungent

鋭さ *surudosa* sharpness, acuteness, poignancy

鋭いナイフ *surudoi naifu* sharp knife

頭の鋭い男 *atama no surudoi otoko* man of keen intelligence

鋭い批判 *surudoi hihan* sharp criticism

SYNONYMS

❶ **sharp**

先 pointed → 2394

❷ **intelligent and wise**

敏 NIMBLE → 1322

聡 SHARP-WITTED → 1384

俊 brilliant → 102

明 clear-sighted → 855

哲 SAGACIOUS → 2738

怜 CLEVER → 298

慧 INTELLIGENT → 2810

賢 WISE → 2839

智 wise → 2784

8-7

金

鋏

1731 KYŌ hasami hasa(mu)

Ⓒ 铗 jiá

Radical	Strokes
金 167	15-8-7
Grade	Freq
Reference	
1-8-7	

COMPOUNDS

❶ snip, clip

枝を鋏む *eda o hasamu* trim [prune] a tree

❷ⓐ scissors, shears

ⓑ punch

花鋏 *hanabasami* flower scissors

入鋏 *nyūkyō* (ticket) punching

HOMOPHONES

hasamu ⇨ 挟 377 挿 431

NOTE

⇨ see USAGE note at 挟 377

銷

1732 SHŌ

Ⓒⓗ 销 xiāo

Radical	Strokes
金 167	15-8-7
Grade	**Freq**
Reference	
◧ 1-8-7	

8-7 金

COMPOUNDS

[now replaced by 消 *shō* 443]

❶ become disheartened, become dispirited; be worried

意気銷沈する *iki-shōchin suru* be dispirited, be disheartened

❷ spend (time), pass

銷夏 *shōka* summering

❸ eliminate, cancel

銷却する *shōkyaku suru* efface; erase

鋭

1733

▶**SHARP**

nonstandard for 鋭 1730

8-7 金

餓 餓 餓 𩜁

1734 GA u(eru)▲

Ⓒⓗ 饿 è

Radical	Strokes
飠 184	15-8-7
Grade	**Freq**
Jōyō	1870
◧ 1-8-7	

8-7 飠

丿 人 𠆢 今 今 今 飠 飠 飠 飠 飢 飢 餓 餓 餓

1 2 3 4 5 6 7 8 9 10 11 12 13 14 15

▶**STARVED**

COMPOUNDS

● [original meaning] **starved, hungry**

餓死 *gashi* death from starvation

餓鬼 *gaki* hungry ghost; *slang* kid

飢餓 *kiga* starvation, hunger, famine

KUN

【u(eru) 餓える】

[now usu. 飢える]

ⓐ starve, be hungry, famish

ⓑ hunger [starve] for (love), thirst for (knowledge)

餓え死に *uejini* (death by) starvation

SYNONYMS

● **hunger and thirst**

飢 STARVE → 1668

渇 THIRST → 515

HOMOPHONES

ueru ⇨ 飢 1668

NOTE

⇨ see USAGE note at 飢 1668

舗 舗 舗 舖

1735 HO

Ⓒⓗ 铺 pū pù

Radical	Strokes
人 9▵	15-2-13
Grade	**Freq**
Jōyō	1593
◧ 1-8-7	

8-7 舎

丿 人 亼 亽 全 全 舎 舎 舎 舎 舗 舗 舗 舗 舗

1 2 3 4 5 6 7 8 9 10 11 12 13 14 15

▶**PAVE** ▶**SHOP**

COMPOUNDS

❶ **pave, lay**

舗装 *hosō* paving

舗道 *hodō* pavement, paved street

❷ [also suffix] **shop, store**—said esp. of shops having a long tradition

店舗 *tenpo* shop, store

老舗 *rōho* (=*shinise*) old [long-established] shop

名舗 *meiho* famous store, quality shop
本舗 *honpo* head office, main shop
薬舗 *yakuho* pharmacy, drugstore
新聞舗 *shinbunho* newspaper distributor
❸ counter for sheets
地図二舗 *chizu niho* two maps

SYNONYMS

❶ **spread**
塗 APPLY ON A SURFACE → 2841
敷く LAY → 1870
布 SPREAD → 2973
抹 wipe over → 313
散 SCATTER → 1702
❷ **places of business**
店 SHOP (of any kind) → 3085
屋 SMALL SHOP → 3098
社 COMPANY → 840

8-7 舎

舗 1736

▶PAVE ▶SHOP
nonstandard for 舗 1735

8-8 金

錠 1737 JŌ

CH 锭 dìng

Radical	Strokes
金 167	16-8-8
Grade	**Freq**
Jōyō	1665
1-8-8	

▶LOCK ▶PILL

COMPOUNDS

❶ [also suffix] **lock, padlock**
錠前 *jōmae* lock
手錠 *tejō* handcuffs
文字合わせ錠 *mojiawasejō* combination lock
❷ⓐ [also suffix] **pill, tablet**
ⓑ counter for pills
錠剤 *jōzai* pill, tablet
糖衣錠 *tōijō* sugar-coated pill
ビタミン錠 *bitaminjō* vitamin tablet [pill]
モヒ錠 *mohijō* tablet of morphine
二錠 *nijō* two pills

INDEPENDENT

【jō 錠】 lock
錠を掛ける *jō o kakeru* fasten a lock

SYNONYMS

❶ **locks and keys**
鍵 KEY → 1753
❷ **medicines**
剤 PREPARATION → 1669
薬 DRUG → 2375
丸 pill suffix → 3417

8-8 金

錦 1738 KIN nishiki NAMES kane

CH 锦 jǐn

Radical	Strokes
金 167	16-8-8
Grade	**Freq**
Names	2005
1-8-8	

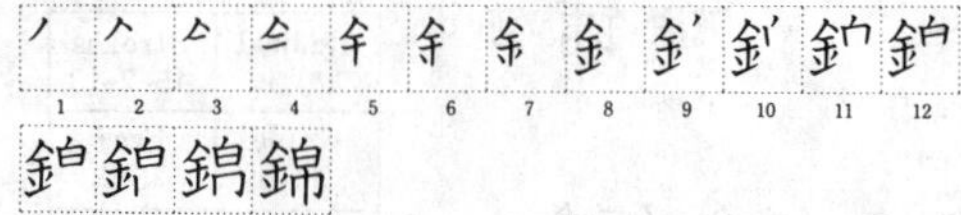

▶BROCADE

COMPOUNDS

❶ [original meaning] **brocade**
錦旗 *kinki* gold-brocade flag; pennant
❷ term of respect
錦地 *kinchi* your place of residence

KUN

【nishiki 錦】 (Japanese) brocade; fine dress
錦絵 *nishikie* color print
錦鯉 *nishikigoi* colored carp
毛織錦 *keorinishiki* woolen brocade

NAMES

錦一 *kin'ichi* male name
錦文 *kanefumi* male name
錦町 *nishikichō* place name

SYNONYMS

❶ **fabrics**
綾 TWILL → 1376

絹 SILK → 1361
綿 COTTON → 1373
麻 HEMP → 3125
毛 wool → 3453
紗 GAUZE → 1301
織 woven fabric → 1422

錮

1739 KO

(CH) 锢 gù

Radical	Strokes
金 167	16-8-8
Grade	**Freq**
Reference	
1 - 8 - 8	

8-8 金

COMPOUNDS

❶ [now replaced by 固 3086] imprison, hold in custody

禁錮 *kinko* imprisonment

❷ [original meaning, now obsolete] plug with molten metal

鋼

1740 KŌ hagane

(CH) 钢 gāng gàng

Radical	Strokes
金 167	16-8-8
Grade	**Freq**
Jōyō-6	806
1 - 8 - 8	

8-8 金

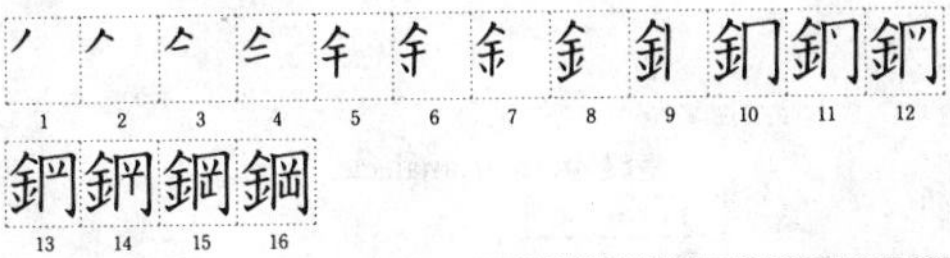

▶STEEL

COMPOUNDS

ⓐ [also suffix] [original meaning] **steel**

ⓑ hard like steel

鋼材 *kōzai* steel materials, structural steel
鋼板 *kōhan* steel plate
鋼管 *kōkan* steel pipe [tubing]
鋼線 *kōsen* steel wire
製鋼 *seikō* steel manufacture
鉄鋼 *tekkō* iron and steel
ステンレス鋼 *sutenresukō* stainless steel
鋼玉 *kōgyoku* corundum

INDEPENDENT

【kō 鋼】 steel

KUN

【hagane 鋼】 steel

鋼色 *haganeiro* steel blue

SYNONYMS

ⓐ **iron and steel**

鉄 IRON → 1711
銑 PIG IRON → 1726

錬

1741 REN ne(ru)▲

(CH) 炼 链 liàn

Radical	Strokes
金 167	16-8-8
Grade	**Freq**
Jōyō	1807
1 - 8 - 8	

8-8 金

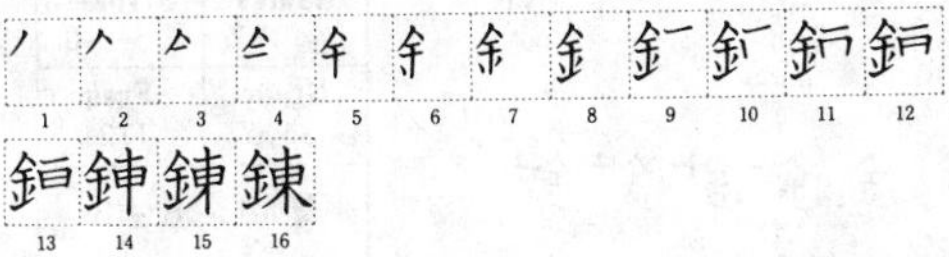

▶REFINE

COMPOUNDS

❶ [formerly also 煉 1023] [original meaning] **refine (crude metals), smelt; work metals, temper**

錬金術 *renkinjutsu* alchemy
錬鉄 *rentetsu* wrought iron
錬鋼 *renkō* wrought steel
精錬 *seiren* refining, smelting; tempering
製錬 *seiren* smelting
鍛錬する *tanren suru* temper, forge; train, discipline

❷ [usu. 練 1375] **refine one's mental and physical skills, train, cultivate, improve one's character**

錬成 *rensei* training, drilling

錬磨する *renma suru* train, practice, cultivate
修錬する *shūren suru* train, discipline

KUN

【ne(ru) 錬る】[now usu. 練る] temper, forge, refine, smelt

SYNONYMS

❶ **refine**
精 REFINE (crude materials) → 1366
留 distill → 2580

❶ **work metals**
鍛 FORGE → 1755
鋳 CAST → 1729

焼き annealing → 997

❷ **cultivate**
練 TRAIN → 1375
鍛 train → 1755
修 CULTIVATE → 123
養 FOSTER (one's intellect) → 2365
磨 POLISH → 3181
琢 POLISH → 971

HOMOPHONES

neru ⇨ 練 1375 煉 1023

NOTE

⇨ see USAGE note at 練 1375

8-8
金

録 錄 録 䘵

1742 ROKU

CH 录 lù

Radical 金 167	Strokes 16-8-8
Grade Jōyō-4	Freq 470
1-8-8	

ノ 𠆢 亼 今 全 余 伞 金 釗 鈩 鈩 鈩 録 録 録 録
1 2 3 4 5 6 7 8 9 10 11 12 13 14 15 16

▶RECORD

COMPOUNDS

❶ⓐ [original meaning] **record, write down, register**
ⓑ **record on tape**
記録する *kiroku suru* record, register, write down; set a record
収録する *shūroku suru* collect, record, write down
登録 *tōroku* registration
録音 *rokuon* sound recording
録画 *rokuga* videotaping

❷ [also suffix] **record, records; proceedings, annals**
目録 *mokuroku* catalog
付録 *furoku* appendix, supplement
会議録 *kaigiroku* minutes, proceedings
語録 *goroku* analects, sayings

SYNONYMS

❶ **write**
登 register → 2595
控える note down → 495
紀 record in writing → 1276
記 WRITE DOWN → 1453
写 COPY → 2000
書 WRITE → 2658
筆 write → 2677

❷ **records**
譜 SYSTEMATIC RECORD → 1637
記 written account → 1453
誌 records → 1548
史 HISTORY → 3510
伝 biography → 44

8-8
金

錯 錯 错

1743 SAKU SHAKU▲

CH 错 cuò

Radical 金 167	Strokes 16-8-8
Grade Jōyō	Freq 1721
1-8-8	

ノ 𠆢 亼 今 全 余 伞 金 金一 金十 金廾 金廾 錯 錯 錯 錯
1 2 3 4 5 6 7 8 9 10 11 12 13 14 15 16

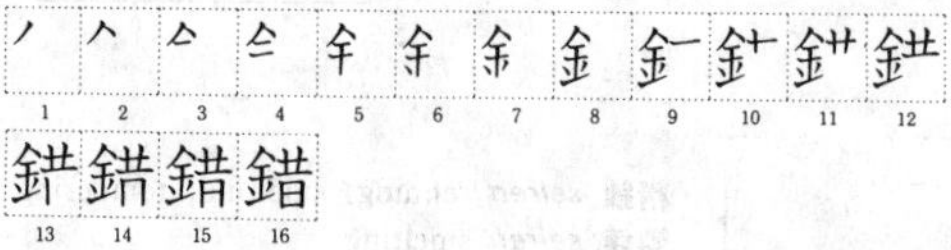

▶MIXED UP

COMPOUNDS

❶ⓐ **mixed up, intricate, confused, disordered, complicated**
ⓑ *chem* complex
錯雑 *sakuzatsu* complication, intricacy
錯綜 *sakusō* complication, intricacy
交錯した *kōsaku shita* mingled, entangled, complicated, intricate
錯イオン *sakuion* complex ion

❷ⓐ **mistaken, erroneous, wrong**
ⓑ **put in the wrong place, invert**
錯誤 *sakugo* mistake, error
錯覚 *sakkaku* false perception, mistaken idea, (optical) illusion
錯乱 *sakuran* distraction, derangement, confusion
錯角 *sakkaku* alternate interior angles
錯字症 *sakujishō* paragraphia
倒錯 *tōsaku* perversion, inversion
❸ unclassified compounds
介錯する *kaishaku suru* assist a person in committing hara-kiri

SYNONYMS

❶ⓐ **mix**
雑 MIXED → 1385
交 intermingle → 2015
混 MIX → 519
ⓐ **disordered**
混 mixed up → 519
雑 mixed up → 1385
乱 DISORDERED → 1260
紛 CONFUSED → 1296
❷ⓐ **mistakes and mistaking**
誤 MISTAKE → 1542
-違える mis- → 3151
失 SLIP → 3511
過 error → 3137

錘 1744

SUI tsumu omori▲

Ⓒⓗ 锤 chuí

Radical	Strokes
金 167	16-8-8
Grade	**Freq**
Jōyō	1923
1-8-8	

8-8 金

Stroke order: 1–16

▶SPINDLE

COMPOUNDS

❶ⓐ **spindle (for spinning)**
ⓑ **counter for spindles**
紡錘 *bōsui* spindle
休錘 *kyūsui* idle spindles
十万錘 *jūmansui* 100,000 spindles
❷ [original meaning] **weight, counterweight, plumb**
鉛錘 *ensui* plumb
平衡錘 *heikōsui* counterpoise, counterweight

KUN

【**tsumu** 錘】spindle
錘形の *tsumugata no* spindle-shaped, fusiform
【**omori** 錘】[also 重り] weight, plumb, sinker, plummet
糸に錘を付ける *ito ni omori o tsukeru* weight a line

SYNONYMS

❶ **shafts**
軸 AXLE → 1514
桟 crosspiece → 932
棒 ROD → 983
❷ **weight**
鎮 weight → 1759

HOMOPHONES

omori ⇨ 重 3573

NOTE

⇨ see USAGE note at 重 3573

錄 1745

8-8 金

▶RECORD

nonstandard for 録 1742

錢 1746

8-8 金

▶MONEY

nonstandard for 銭 1725

鍵

8-8 金

incorrect stroke count ⇨ see 1753

8-8 青

靜 1747

▶**QUIET**
nonstandard for 静 1728

8-8 食

館 館 舘° 1748

KAN yakata▲ tate▲

CH 馆 guǎn

Radical	Strokes
食 184	16-8-8
Grade	**Freq**
Jōyō-3	352
1-8-8	

▶**PUBLIC BUILDING**

COMPOUNDS

❶ⓐ [also suffix] **public building (esp. a large building for cultural activities), hall, edifice, pavilion**
ⓑ **building**
館長 *kanchō* director, superintendent
会館 *kaikan* hall, assembly hall
図書館 *toshokan* library
大使館 *taishikan* embassy
公民館 *kōminkan* public hall, citizen's hall
体育館 *taiikukan* gymnasium, gym
映画館 *eigakan* cinema house, movie theater
文明館 *bunmeikan* The Bunmeikan Theater
カナダ館 *kanadakan* The Canada Pavilion
館内 *kannai* in the building
本館 *honkan* this building; main building
別館 *bekkan* annex, extension, outbuilding
❷ⓐ [original meaning] inn, lodge
ⓑ **suffix after names of inns, hotels, restaurants or movie theaters**
旅館 *ryokan* Japanese inn
風月館 *fūgetsukan* The Fugetsukan Inn

INDEPENDENT

【**kan 館**】 cinema house, movie theater

KUN

【**yakata 館**】 stately mansion, palace, manor house
【**tate 館**】 fort
衣川の館 *koromogawa no tate* Fort of Koromogawa

SYNONYMS

❶ **buildings**
堂 HALL → 2589
舎 BUILDING → 2060
棟 BLOCK → 991
閣 TALL MAGNIFICENT BUILDING → 3327
宇 large building → 2175
殿 PALACE → 1792
❷ **temporary quarters**
亭 INN → 2072
宿 lodging → 2293
寮 DORMITORY → 2359
舎 temporary quarters → 2060
【**yakata**】
○ **mansions**
邸 STATELY RESIDENCE → 1131
荘 VILLA → 2262

8-8 舎

舘 1749

▶**PUBLIC BUILDING**
nonstandard for 館 1748

8-8 卓

翰 1750

KAN

CH 翰 hàn

Radical	Strokes
羽 124	16-6-10
Grade	**Freq**
Reference	
1-8-8	

COMPOUNDS

❶ [now also 簡 2721] letter, note
書翰 *shokan* letter, correspondence
手翰 *shukan* letter
宸翰 *shinkan* Imperial letter
❷ the pen, literary work

輸林院 *kanrin'in* academy

隷 隷 隷 隷 ⒸⒽ 隶 lì

1751 REI

Radical	Strokes
隶 171	16-8-8
Grade	**Freq**
Jōyō	1930
◧ 1-8-8	

8-8 隶

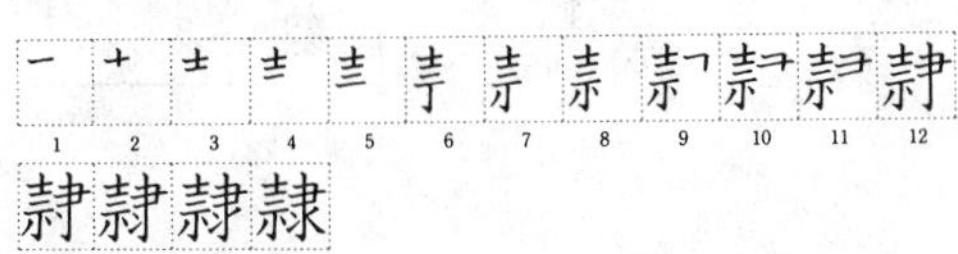

▶**UNDERLING**

COMPOUNDS

❶ (lowly person in servitude) **underling, subordinate, servant, lackey**

隷下 *reika* followers, subordinates

奴隷 *dorei* slave, servant

❷ [original meaning] **be subordinate** [**subject**] **to, be under, be attached to**

隷従 *reijū* slavery, servitude; servile obedience

隷属 *reizoku* subordination

❸ *reisho*, ancient square style of Chinese characters

隷書 *reisho reisho*, ancient square style of Chinese characters

篆隷 *tenrei* seal style and ancient square style

INDEPENDENT

【**rei** 隷】 *reisho* (⇨ ❸)

SYNONYMS

❶ **servants**

奴 SLAVE → 187

僕 MANSERVANT → 164

臣 RETAINER → 3068

従 follower → 415

供 attendant → 88

❷ **obey**

従 FOLLOW → 415

遵 OBEY → 3167

順 OBEY → 18

守 observe → 2173

鍋 鍋 鍋 ⒸⒽ 锅 guō

1752 KA nabe

Radical	Strokes
金 167	17-8-9
Grade	**Freq**
Non-Jōyō	1758
◧ 1-8-9	

8-9 金

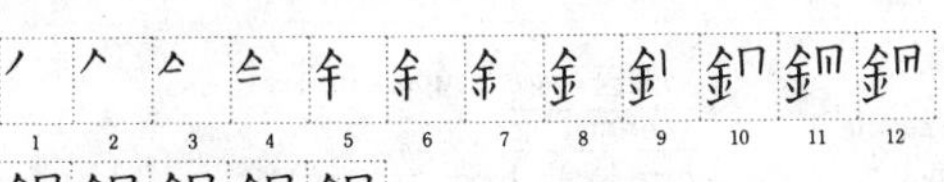

▶**POT**

COMPOUNDS

● [original meaning] **pot, pan**

KUN

【**nabe** 鍋】

ⓐ [also suffix] pot, pan

ⓑ food served in pots

鍋蓋 *nabebuta* pot lid; *nabebuta*, 'lid' radical (亠)

鍋焼き *nabeyaki* scalloped; scalloped noodles

土鍋 *donabe* earthen pot

大鍋 *ōnabe* cauldron

片手鍋 *katatenabe* single-handled pot

シチュー鍋 *shichūnabe* stew pot [pan], skillet

鍋物 *nabemono* food served in a pot

寄せ鍋 *yosenabe* chowder

SYNONYMS

【**nabe**】

ⓐ **vessels and receptacles**

鉢 BOWL → 1708

杯 CUP → 857

盆 TRAY → 2079

皿 PLATE → 3474

盤 dish → 2851

8-9
金

鍵 鍵 鍵

1753 KEN kagi

CH 键 jiàn

Radical	Strokes
金 167	17-8-9
Grade	Freq
Non-Jōyō	1771
1 - 8 - 9	

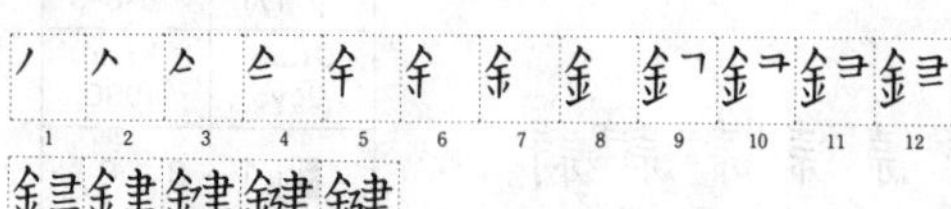

▶**KEY**

COMPOUNDS

❶ⓐ [original meaning] (implement for opening) **key**

ⓑ (control button or lever on musical instruments or machines) **key**

ⓒ counter for keys (of a piano)

関鍵 *kanken* [rare] lock and key; locking doors; vital point

鍵盤 *kenban* keyboard

黒鍵 *kokken* chromatic key

継電鍵 *keidenken* relay key

八十八鍵 *hachijūhachiken* 88 keys

❷ key to secret knowledge

秘鍵 *hiken* secret principle, hidden mysteries

INDEPENDENT

【ken 鍵】 key (of a piano or typewriter)

KUN

【kagi 鍵】 key; lock; (vital information) key, solution

鍵穴 *kagiana* keyhole

勝敗の鍵を握る *shōhai no kagi o nigiru* hold the key to victory, have the game in one's hands

SYNONYMS

❶ⓐ & 【kagi】 locks and keys

錠 LOCK → 1737

8-9
金

鍼

1754 SHIN hari

CH 针 zhēn

Radical	Strokes
金 167	17-8-9
Grade	Freq
Reference	
1 - 8 - 9	

COMPOUNDS

ⓐ [original meaning] acupuncture needle

ⓑ [now also 針 *shin* 1666] acupuncture

鍼 *hari* acupuncture needle; acupuncture

鍼術 *shinjutsu* acupuncture

鍼灸 *shinkyū* acupuncture and moxibustion

鍼医 *harii* acupuncturist

HOMOPHONES

hari ⇨ 針 1666

NOTE

⇨ see USAGE note at 針 1666

8-9
金

鍛 鍛 鍛

1755 TAN kita(eru)

CH 锻 duàn

Radical	Strokes
金 167	17-8-9
Grade	Freq
Jōyō	1675
1 - 8 - 9	

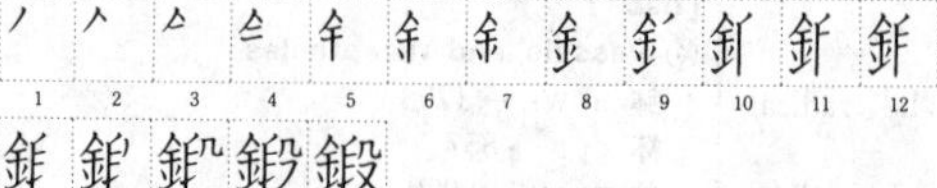

▶**FORGE**

COMPOUNDS

❶ [original meaning] **forge, work metal, temper**

鍛練(=鍛錬)する *tanren suru* temper, forge; train, discipline

鍛造 *tanzō* forging

鍛接 *tansetsu* forge welding

鍛鋼 *tankō* forged steel

鍛工 *tankō* metalworker

鍛鉄 *tantetsu* tempering iron, wrought iron

鍛冶 *tan'ya* (=*kaji*) forging; smith

❷ train, cultivate one's physical and mental skills, attain proficiency
鍛成 *tansei* training, cultivation

KUN

【kita(eru) 鍛える】 forge, temper; train, drill, discipline, attain proficiency
鍛え上げた腕 *kitaeageta ude* highly-trained skill

SYNONYMS

❶ **work metals**
鍊 REFINE (crude metals) → 1741
鋳 CAST → 1729
焼き annealing → 997
❷ **cultivate**
錬 REFINE → 1741
練 TRAIN → 1375
修 CULTIVATE → 123
養 FOSTER (one's intellect) → 2365
磨 POLISH → 3181
琢 POLISH → 971

鍊
1756

▶REFINE
nonstandard for 錬 1741

8-9 金

韓
1757 KAN kara

CH 韩 hán

Radical	Strokes
韋 178	17-9-8
Grade	**Freq**
Non-Jōyō	596
1-8-9	

8-9 卓

▶SOUTH KOREA

COMPOUNDS

❶ⓐ **South Korea, Republic of Korea**
ⓑ name of state in late Zhou Dynasty
ⓒ southern part of Korean Peninsula in ancient times
韓国 *kankoku* South Korea
大韓民国 *daikanminkoku* Republic of Korea
日韓 *nikkan* Japan and Korea
訪韓 *hōkan* visit to Korea
三韓 *sankan* the Three Han States; the Three Countries of Korea
❷ Chinese family name
韓非子 *kanpishi* Han Feizi, famous legalist in the Period of Warring Kingdoms; title of 20-volume work by Han Feizi

INDEPENDENT

【kan 韓】 South Korea

KUN

【kara 韓】
ⓐ elegant term for Korea
ⓑ [also 唐] foreign countries
韓人 *karabito* Korean

SYNONYMS

❶ **Korea**
鮮 Korea → 1877
朝 North Korea → 1695

HOMOPHONES

kara ⇨ 唐 3115

NOTE

⇨ see USAGE note at 唐 3115

頻
1758 HIN shiki(rini)[▲]

CH 频 pín

Radical	Strokes
頁 181	17-9-8
Grade	**Freq**
Jōyō	1939
1-8-9	

8-9 歩

▶FREQUENTLY

COMPOUNDS

❶ **frequently, repeatedly, often; frequent**
頻発する *hinpatsu suru* occur frequently
頻度 *hindo* frequency
頻繁に *hinpan ni* frequently, very often
頻出 *hinshutsu* frequent appearance
頻数 *hinsū* frequency

頻尿 *hinnyō* pollakiuria
❷ [now always 瀕 805] on the verge of
頻死 *hinshi* on the verge of death

KUN
【shiki(rini) 頻りに】 frequently, repeatedly, often; incessantly; earnestly

---

8-10
金

鎮 鎮 鎮 鎮

1759 CHIN shizu(meru) shizu(maru)

CH 镇 zhèn

Radical	Strokes
金 167	18-8-10
Grade	**Freq**
Jōyō	1555
1-8-10	

▶QUELL

COMPOUNDS

❶ⓐ (put down by force) **quell, pacify, suppress, subdue, put down**
ⓑ (make calm) **quell, pacify, appease, soothe**
鎮圧する *chin'atsu suru* quell, suppress
鎮定 *chintei* suppression, subdual
鎮火する *chinka suru* be extinguished
鎮守の神 *chinju no kami* guardian god, local deity
鎮痛剤 *chintsūzai* anodyne, painkiller
鎮静する *chinsei suru* calm down, be tranquilized, subside; calm, tranquilize
鎮魂曲 *chinkonkyoku* requiem
❷ⓐ [original meaning] weight (for pressing down)
ⓑ weighty, important, central
文鎮 *bunchin* paperweight
重鎮 *jūchin* man of influence, prominent figure
❸ be enshrined
鎮座する *chinza suru* be enshrined
❹ peace-keeping centers in ancient China, peace keeping force
鎮台 *chindai* garrison (in Meiji era)
❺ Chinese town or township (with a population of over 50,000)
景徳鎮 *keitokuchin* Jingdezhen

INDEPENDENT
【chin 鎮】 Chinese town or township

KUN
【shizu(meru) 鎮める】
① quell, suppress, put down, subdue, pacify
反乱を鎮める *hanran o shizumeru* quell a rebellion
② alleviate (pain), relieve, allay, soothe
痛みを鎮める *itami o shizumeru* alleviate pain
【shizu(maru) 鎮まる】
① be quelled, be suppressed, subside, be put down
暴動が鎮まった *Bōdō ga shizumatta* The riot was put down
② be alleviated, be relieved, be soothed
③ be enshrined

SYNONYMS
❶ **conquer and suppress**
靖 PACIFY → 1208
征 CONQUER → 293
討 SUPPRESS BY ARMED FORCE → 1456
伐 CUT DOWN → 42
❷ⓐ **weight**
錘 weight → 1744

HOMOPHONES
shizumeru ⇨ 静 1728 沈 261
shizumaru ⇨ 静 1728

NOTE
⇨ see USAGE note at 静 1728

鎌 鎌 鎌 鎌 (CH) 镰 lián

1760 REN kama NAMES KEN kata kane

Radical	Strokes
金 167	18-8-10
Grade	**Freq**
Names	1986
1-8-10	

8-10 金

▶**SICKLE**

COMPOUNDS

❶ [original meaning] **sickle, scythe**

❷ [archaic] abbrev. of 鎌倉 *kamakura*: Kamakura

鎌府 *renpu* Kamakura

KUN

【**kama 鎌**】sickle, scythe; trick, artifice

鎌入れ *kamaire* harvesting

鎌形の *kamagata no* sickle-shaped, falciform

鎌鼬 *kamaitachi* "weasel-cut" (cut in the skin from exposure to a vacuum formed by a cyclone)

大鎌 *ōgama* scythe

鎌を掛ける *kama o kakeru* ask a leading question

NAMES

鎌治 *kenji* male name

鎌倉 *kamakura* place name

鎌太郎 *kamatarō* male name

鎌本 *kamamoto* surname

重鎌 *shigekane* male name

SYNONYMS

❶ **cutting instruments**

刃 BLADE → 2929

刀 SWORD (single-edged) → 2926

剣 SWORD (double-edged) → 1672

矛 HALBERD → 2008

鎖 鎖 鎖 鎖 (CH) 锁 suǒ

1761 SA kusari

Radical	Strokes
金 167	18-8-10
Grade	**Freq**
Jōyō	1503
1-8-10	

8-10 金

▶**CHAIN**

COMPOUNDS

❶ⓐ [original meaning] **chain**

ⓑ **linked as if with a chain**

鎖状 *sajō* chainlike

測鎖 *sokusa* measuring chain

側鎖 *sokusa chem* side chain

鎖骨 *sakotsu* collar bone, clavicle

連鎖 *rensa* chain (as of reasoning), link, series; connection

❷ⓐ (from the idea of binding with a chain) **lock up, shut, confine**

ⓑ [archaic] lock, latch

鎖国 *sakoku* national isolation, exclusion of foreigners

閉鎖する *heisa suru* lock, close, shut

封鎖 *fūsa* blockade

KUN

【**kusari 鎖**】chain; tether; connection; passage (of a story), snatch (of a song)

金鎖 *kingusari* gold chain

鎖伝動 *kusaridendō* chain drive

鎖編み *kusariami* chain stitch

一鎖 *hitokusari* one passage

SYNONYMS

❶ⓐ **ropes and lines**

索 cable → 2455

線 LINE → 1392

弦 STRING → 287

綱 ROPE (esp. of fiber) → 1372

縄 ROPE (esp. of straw) → 1388

緒 cord → 1378

組 braid → 1337

❷ⓐ **close**

閉 CLOSE → 3319

封 SEAL → 1287

8-10 金

鎔
1762 YŌ to(keru) to(kasu)

CH 熔 róng

Radical	Strokes
金 167	18-8-10
Grade	Freq
Reference	
1-8-10	

COMPOUNDS

ⓐ [now replaced by 溶 yō 664] [original meaning] melt (up) metals, fuse, smelt

ⓑ [now usu. 溶ける *tokeru*] *vi* (of metals) melt (up), fuse, melt

ⓒ [now usu. 溶かす *tokasu*] *vt* melt (up) (metals), fuse, smelt

鎔解する *yōkai suru* melt, fuse
鎔接する *yōsetsu suru* weld
鎔鉱炉 *yōkōro* smelting [blast] furnace
鎔銑 *yōsen* molten iron
鉄を鎔かす *tetsu o tokasu* melt [fuse] iron

HOMOPHONES

tokeru ⇨ 解 1517 融 1831 溶 664 熔 1058
tokasu ⇨ 解 1517 融 1831 溶 664 熔 1058 梳 964

NOTE

⇨ see USAGE note at 解 1517

8-10 金

鎮
1763

▶**QUELL**
nonstandard for 鎮 1759

8-10 金

鎌
1764

▶**SICKLE**
nonstandard for 鎌 1760

8-10 金

鎖
1765

▶**CHAIN**
nonstandard for 鎖 1761

8-11 金

鏡 鏡 鏡 鏡
1766 KYŌ kagami

CH 镜 jìng

Radical	Strokes
金 167	19-8-11
Grade	Freq
Jōyō-4	1484
1-8-11	

▶**MIRROR** ▶**OPTICAL INSTRUMENT**

COMPOUNDS

❶ [also suffix] [original meaning] **mirror**

鏡台 *kyōdai* dressing table
鏡高 *kyōkō* height of a mirror stand
鏡面 *kyōmen* surface of a mirror
鏡鑑 *kyōkan* mirror; paragon, mirror
反射鏡 *hanshakyō* reflex mirror, reflector
三面鏡 *sanmenkyō* vanity [dresser] with three mirrors

❷ [also suffix] **optical instrument, viewing instrument, -scope, lens**

検鏡 *kenkyō* microscopic examination, microscopy
望遠鏡 *bōenkyō* telescope
顕微鏡 *kenbikyō* microscope
潜望鏡 *senbōkyō* periscope
老眼鏡 *rōgankyō* spectacles for the aged, far-sighted glasses

KUN

【kagami 鏡】

① mirror
鏡板 *kagamiita* panel, scene-panel
手鏡 *tekagami* hand glass

② round mirror-shaped rice cake
鏡開き *kagamibiraki* cutting of New Year's rice cakes

③ barrelhead
鏡を抜く *kagami o nuku* open a barrel, uncask

SPECIAL READINGS

眼鏡 *megane* (=*gankyō*) glasses, spectacles; judgment, insight

SYNONYMS

❷ **machines and tools**

儀 measuring instrument → 169
器 INSTRUMENT → 2713
具 IMPLEMENT → 2552
械 MECHANICAL CONTRIVANCE → 961
機 MACHINE → 1076

USAGE

kagami

鏡
① mirror
② round mirror-shaped rice cake
③ barrelhead

鑑
(something worthy of being copied) mirror, model, paragon

HOMOPHONES

kagami ⇨ 鑑 1773

鏡 1767

▶**MIRROR** ▶**OPTICAL INSTRUMENT** 8-11 金

nonstandard for 鏡 1766

鶏 鷄 雞 1768

KEI niwatori tori▲

Ⓒⓗ 鸡 jī 8-11 奚

Radical 鳥 196	Strokes 19-11-8
Grade Jōyō	Freq 1671
◧ 1-8-11	

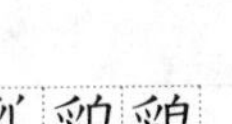

▶**CHICKEN**

COMPOUNDS

● [original meaning] **chicken, hen, cock; poultry**

鶏肉 *keiniku* chicken (meat)
鶏卵 *keiran* (hen's) egg
鶏舎 *keisha* henhouse
養鶏 *yōkei* chicken raising
闘鶏 *tōkei* cockfight, fighting cock
若鶏 *wakadori* spring chicken

KUN

【**niwatori** 鶏】chicken, hen, cock
【**tori** 鶏】[also 鳥] chicken; fowl, poultry

SPECIAL READINGS

鶏冠▲ *tosaka* cockscomb, crest
軍鶏▲ *shamo* game fowl, gamecock
矮鶏▲ *chabo* (Japanese) bantam

SYNONYMS

● **domesticated birds**

鳩 PIGEON → 163

HOMOPHONES

tori ⇨ 鳥 3312 酉 3544

NOTE

⇨ see USAGE note at 鳥 3312

鐘 1769

SHŌ kane

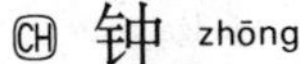

Ⓒⓗ 钟 zhōng 8-12 金

Radical 金 167	Strokes 20-8-12
Grade Jōyō	Freq 1356
◧ 1-8-12	

▶**BELL**

COMPOUNDS

ⓐ [original meaning] **bell (that tolls)**
ⓑ **bell or sound of a bell (as for announcing), alarm**

鐘楼 *shōrō* bell tower, belfry
梵鐘 *bonshō* temple bell
警鐘 *keishō* alarm bell, warning
時鐘 *jishō* time bell
半鐘 *hanshō* fire bell [alarm]

KUN

【**kane** 鐘】bell (that tolls), gong

釣鐘 *tsurigane* hanging bell

SYNONYMS

● **bells**

鈴 BELL (that jingles or rings) → 1710

8-12 金

鐘
1770

▶BELL

nonstandard for 鐘 1769

8-13 金

鐵
1771

▶IRON

nonstandard for 鉄 1711

8-14 金

鑄
1772

▶CAST

nonstandard for 鋳 1729

8-14 金

鑑

incorrect stroke count ⇨ see 1773

8-14 金

鑛

incorrect stroke count ⇨ see 1774
(nonstandard for 鉱 1709)

8-15 金

鑑 鑑 鑑
1773 KAN kanga(miru)▲ kagami▲

CH 鉴 jiàn

Radical	Strokes
金 167	23-8-15
Grade	**Freq**
Jōyō	1341
1-8-15	

▶APPRAISE ▶REFERENCE VOLUME

COMPOUNDS

❶ **appraise, judge, appreciate, discern, identify**

鑑賞 *kanshō* appreciation

鑑定する *kantei suru* appraise, judge, estimate, identify

鑑識する *kanshiki suru* identify, judge; discern

鑑別 *kanbetsu* discrimination, judgment

無鑑査の *mukansa no* not submitted to the selecting committee

❷ **reference volume, directory, handbook, book**

図鑑 *zukan* picture [illustrated] book

年鑑 *nenkan* yearbook

名鑑 *meikan* list, directory

宝鑑 *hōkan* handbook, thesaurus

❸ mark of identification, sign

鑑札 *kansatsu* license, certificate

印鑑 *inkan* personal seal

❹ⓐ [original meaning, now archaic] ancient bronze mirror

ⓑ (something worthy of being copied) mirror, paragon, model

亀鑑 *kikan* pattern, paragon, mirror

KUN

【kanga(miru) 鑑みる】 take into consideration, take warning by

...に鑑みて *...ni kangamite* in view of...

【kagami 鑑】 (something worthy of being copied) mirror, model, paragon

武士の鑑 *bushi no kagami* paragon of knighthood

SYNONYMS

❶ **judge**

判 JUDGE → 1122

裁 JUDGE → 3299

評 evaluate → 1501

審 TRY → 2360

決 DECIDE → 263

視 REGARD → 972

❷ **books**

編 volume → 1387

巻 VOLUME → 2645
典 STANDARD WORK → 2627
経 religious classic → 1331
本 BOOK → 3502
書 BOOK → 2658
冊 bound book → 3483
籍 books → 2731
著 literary work → 2300

HOMOPHONES

kagami ⇨ 鏡 1766

NOTE

⇨ see USAGE note at 鏡 1766

鑛

1774

▶ORE ▶MINE

nonstandard for 鉱 1709

8-15 金

飢

1775

▶STARVE

nonstandard for 飢 1668

9-2 食

副

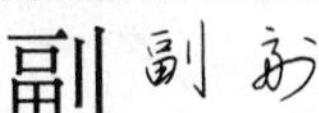

1776 FUKU

Ⓒⓗ 副 fù

Radical	Strokes
刂 18	11-2-9
Grade	**Freq**
Jōyō-4	592
◧ 1 - 9 - 2	

9-2 畐

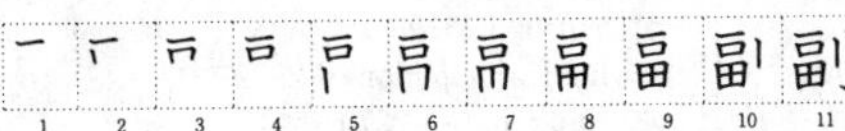

1 2 3 4 5 6 7 8 9 10 11

▶**SECONDARY**

COMPOUNDS

❶ [also prefix]

ⓐ **secondary, sub-, subordinate, vice-, deputy, assistant**

ⓑ (in addition to the main thing) **accessory, side-, extra, supplementary, additional**

副作用 *fukusayō* secondary effect, reaction
副次的な *fukujiteki na* secondary
副大統領 *fukudaitōryō* vice-president
副総理 *fukusōri* deputy prime minister
正副 *seifuku* principal and vice [assistant]; original and copy
副詞 *fukushi* adverb
副神経 *fukushinkei* accessory nerves
副賞 *fukushō* supplementary [extra] prize
副業 *fukugyō* subsidiary business
副収入 *fukushūnyū* additional income
副産物 *fukusanbutsu* by-product, side line

❷ duplicate, copy

副本 *fukuhon* duplicate, copy

INDEPENDENT

【**fuku** 副】 secondary, assistant; duplicate, copy

副二名 *fuku nimei* two assistants

SYNONYMS

❶ⓐ **subordinate**

次 secondary → 54
従 subordinate → 415
亜 SUB- → 3540
準 QUASI- → 2856
半 semi- → 3501
准 JUNIOR → 127
助 assistant → 1121

ⓑ **additional**

追 additional → 3096
補 supplementary → 1194

勘

1777 KAN

Ⓒⓗ 勘 kān

Radical	Strokes
力 19	11-2-9
Grade	**Freq**
Jōyō	1268
◧ 1 - 9 - 2	

9-2 甚

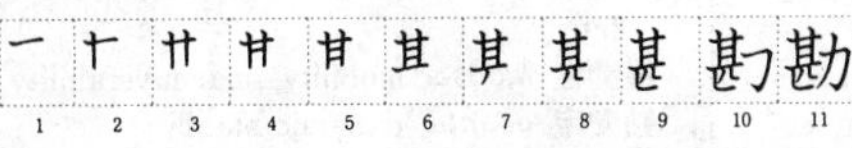

1 2 3 4 5 6 7 8 9 10 11

▶**CHECK** ▶**INTUITIVE PERCEPTION**

COMPOUNDS

❶ⓐ **check, examine, collate, compare**

ⓑ **take into consideration, give consideration to, think about**

勘定 *kanjō* calculation; account, settlement of accounts
勘校する *kankō suru* examine and correct, collate

勘合 *kangō* [rare] checking and verifying
勘考 *kankō* consideration, deliberation
勘案する *kan'an suru* take into consideration, give consideration (to)
勘弁する *kanben suru* pardon, forgive; tolerate

❷ check into a crime, examine officially (and pass judgment), interrogate, find fault with
勘当 *kandō* disinheritance
勘気 *kanki* disfavor, disgrace
勅勘 *chokkan* Imperial imputation

❸ abbrev. of 勘定 *kanjō*: check, bill, account
割り勘 *warikan* equal split, Dutch treat

❹ intuitive perception: **sense, perception; horse sense, intuition, sixth sense**
勘違い *kanchigai* wrong guess [impression]
勘付く *kanzuku* sense (a danger)
山勘で *yamakan de* by guesswork

❺ vital point
勘所 *kandokoro* vital point

❻ endure
勘忍(＝堪忍) *kannin* patience, forbearance; forgiveness, pardon

INDEPENDENT

【kan 勘】 sense, perception; horse sense, intuition
勘の良い人 *kan no ii hito* person of quick perception
音楽に対する勘 *ongaku ni taisuru kan* musical sense
勘を働かせる *kan o hatarakaseru* use one's head, think quickly

SYNONYMS

❶ⓐ investigate and examine
調 INVESTIGATE → 1567
查 LOOK INTO → 2437
審 EXAMINE CAREFULLY → 2360
験 TEST → 1833
診 EXAMINE A PATIENT → 1504
検 EXAMINE → 986
探 PROBE → 505
討 STUDY → 1456
察 INSPECT → 2347
究 STUDY EXHAUSTIVELY → 2203
閲 REVIEW → 3330
糾 INQUIRE INTO → 1278

ⓑ think and consider
慮 CONSIDER → 3266
量 weigh → 2471
惟 MEDITATE → 481
省 INTROSPECT → 2449
思 THINK → 2564
考 THINK → 3196
存 hold an opinion → 2982
案 think out → 2270
想 CONCEIVE → 2828

❹ sense
感 SENSE → 2835
覚 sense → 2604

NOTE

⇨ see COMPOUND FORMATION for
勘当 *kandō* ⇨ 当 2177
勘弁 *kanben* ⇨ 弁 2004
★do not confuse with 堪 559

9-2
者

都

incorrect stroke count ⇨ see 1780
(nonstandard for 都 1686)

9-2
重

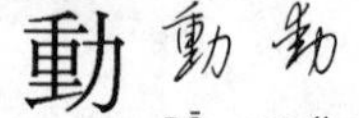

1778 DŌ ugo(ku) ugo(kasu)

Ⓒⓗ 动 dòng

Radical	Strokes
力 19	11-2-9
Grade	**Freq**
Jōyō-3	88
1 - 9 - 2	

▶MOVE

COMPOUNDS

❶ⓐ [original meaning] **move, be in action, vibrate, pulsate**
ⓑ [also prefix] dynamic, moving, kinetic
ⓒ [also suffix] *phys* motion, vibration, action
動物 *dōbutsu* animal
動揺する *dōyō suru* shake, tremble; be disturbed, waver
運動 *undō* motion, movement; exercise; campaign
自動 *jidō* automatic operation; automatic
移動する *idō suru* move, shift, transfer
不動産 *fudōsan* immovable property, real estate
機動性 *kidōsei* mobility, maneuverability
動安定 *dōantei* dynamic stability
動摩擦 *dōmasatsu* kinetic friction
波動 *hadō* wave motion, undulation
反動 *handō* backlash, recoil, reaction
上下動 *jōgedō* vertical motion [shock]

❷ⓐ (set in motion, esp. machines) **move, drive, operate**

ⓑ **move (personnel) to another position; make a motion**
ⓒ (be active) **move, change, vary**
動力 *dōryoku* power
駆動 *kudō* drive (of a machine)
始動 *shidō* starting (machines)
原動力 *gendōryoku* motive force
伝動 *dendō* transmission, drive, gearing
電動の *dendō no* electric powered
動議 *dōgi* a motion
人事異動 *jinji idō* personnel changes, reshuffle
動向 *dōkō* trend, tendency, movement
活動 *katsudō* activity, action; function
変動 *hendō* change, fluctuation
❸ⓐ **move to action, arouse, stir**
ⓑ **be moved with emotion, be excited, be startled**
動員する *dōin suru* mobilize (an army)
動機 *dōki* motive, incentive
出動する *shutsudō suru* take the field, be dispatched, turn out
扇動する *sendō suru* instigate, agitate
発動する *hatsudō suru* exercise, invoke; move, put in motion
動転する *dōten suru* be frightened, be stunned
感動する *kandō suru* be moved, be impressed
❹ⓐ **behave, act**
ⓑ **behavior, conduct**
動作 *dōsa* action, movement; bearing, behavior
行動 *kōdō* action, conduct, behavior
挙動 *kyodō* deportment, conduct, behavior, action
言動 *gendō* speech and behavior [conduct]
❺ fall into disorder, be disturbed
動乱 *dōran* upheaval, disturbance, agitation
騒動 *sōdō* disturbance, uproar; strife; confusion
暴動 *bōdō* riot, disturbance, uprising
❻ abbrev. of 動物 *dōbutsu*: animal
動植物 *dōshokubutsu* animals and plants
❼ abbrev. of 動詞 *dōshi*: verb
動名詞 *dōmeishi* gerund
他動 *tadō* transitive verb
❽ abbrev. of 動力車 *dōryokusha*: railway motive power
動労 *dōrō* National Railway Motive Power Union

INDEPENDENT

【dō 動】 motion, vibration; *phys* action
動と反動 *dō to handō* action and reaction
【dōjiru (=dōzuru) 動じる(=動ずる)】 be moved with emotion

KUN

【ugo(ku) 動く】 *vi* move, shift, stir, shake; work, run, operate; change, vary; (take action) move, act, be active; be moved, be touched
動き *ugoki* movement, motion, activity; trend, development
動き回る *ugokimawaru* move about; get about; be busily engaged
身動きする *miugoki suru* move (about), stir
電気で動く *denki de ugoku* run by electricity
値動き *neugoki* fluctuation [movement] in prices
陰で動く *kage de ugoku* act behind the scenes
心が動く *kokoro ga ugoku* feel inclined to
【ugo(kasu) 動かす】 *vt* move, shift, remove; set in motion, drive, operate; change, alter; (exert influence) move, affect, touch
机を動かす *tsukue o ugokasu* move [shift] a desk
揺り動かす *yuriugokasu* shake, swing; shock
動かし難い *ugokashigatai* immovable; unshakable, undeniable
心を動かされる *kokoro o ugokasareru* be moved

SYNONYMS

❶ⓐ **move**
運 MOVE → 3140
移 SHIFT → 1177
滑 SLIDE → 658
転 remove → 1480
遷 TRANSFER → 3170
繰る SHIFT ONWARD → 1427
ⓑ **active**
活 ACTIVE → 385
ⓒ **motion**
惰 inertia → 579
❷ⓐ **set in motion**
駆 DRIVE → 1823
掛ける set going → 493
❸ⓐ **incite**
振 arouse to action → 430
起 rise to action → 3307
奮 ROUSE UP → 2367
激 excite → 776
扇 FAN → 1950
挑 PROVOKE → 372
唆 INSTIGATE → 402
ⓑ **feel deeply**
感 feel deeply → 2835
嘆 sigh in admiration → 630
❹ⓑ **behavior**
行 conduct → 212
挙 deportment → 2456

NOTE

⇨ see COMPOUND FORMATION for 機動性 *kidōsei* ⇨ 機 1076

9-2
乗

剰 剰 剰 剰

1779 JŌ

CH 剩 shèng

Radical	Strokes
刂 18	11-2-9
Grade	**Freq**
Jōyō	1451
1 - 9 - 2	

1 2 3 4 5 6 7 8 9 10 11

▶**SURPLUS**

COMPOUNDS

● [original meaning] **surplus, excessive, redundant**

剰余 *jōyo* surplus, remainder, balance
剰員 *jōin* superfluous member
過剰 *kajō* surplus, excess
余剰 *yojō* surplus, remainder, residue

SYNONYMS

● **exceeding and excess**

冗 REDUNDANT → 1976
余 EXCESS → 2042
濫 EXCESSIVE → 801
過 EXCEED → 3137
超 SURPASS → 3313
越 GO BEYOND → 3314

9-3
者

都

1780

▶**METROPOLIS** ▶**METROPOLIS OF TOKYO**

nonstandard for 都 1686

9-4
革

靴 靴 靴

1781 KA kutsu

CH 靴 xuē

Radical	Strokes
革 177	13-9-4
Grade	**Freq**
Jōyō	1687
1 - 9 - 4	

1 2 3 4 5 6 7 8 9 10 11 12 13

▶**SHOES**

COMPOUNDS

● [original meaning] **shoes, boots**

製靴 *seika* shoemaking
軍靴 *gunka* military shoes, combat boots
隔靴搔痒 *kakkasōyō* having an itch that one cannot scratch
運動靴 *undōgutsu* sneakers
紳士靴 *shinshigutsu* men's shoes
スケート靴 *sukētogutsu* skates

KUN

【kutsu 靴】[also suffix] shoes, boots

靴下 *kutsushita* socks, stockings
靴墨 *kutsuzumi* shoe polish
靴音 *kutsuoto* sound of a person's footsteps
靴直し *kutsunaoshi* shoe mending
靴ブラシ *kutsuburashi* shoe brush
皮靴 *kawagutsu* leather shoes
長靴 *nagagutsu* boots, top boots

SYNONYMS

● **footwear**

駄 clogs → 1821
履 footwear → 3171
足 counter for footwear → 2188

USAGE

kutsu

靴
[also suffix] shoes, boots
沓
footwear, sandals, clogs

HOMOPHONES

kutsu ⇨ 沓 2419

9-4
食

飯

1782

▶**COOKED RICE** ▶**MEAL**

nonstandard for 飯 1691

飲 1783

▶DRINK
nonstandard for 飲 1692

新 新 新 1784

ⒸⒽ 新 xīn

SHIN atara(shii) ara(ta) ara- nii-

Radical	Strokes
斤 69	13-4-9
Grade	**Freq**
Jōyō-2	53
◧ 1 - 9 - 4	

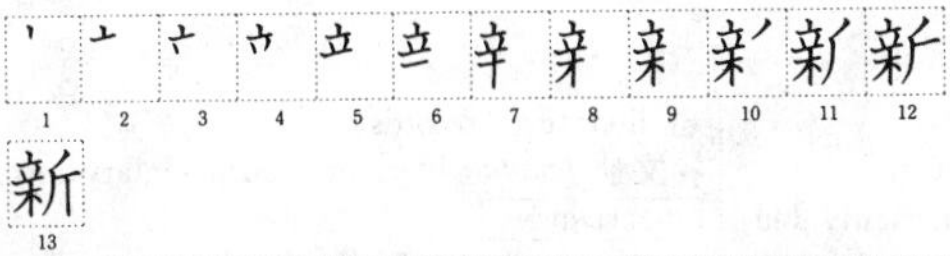

▶NEW

COMPOUNDS

❶ⓐ [also prefix] **new, novel, fresh**
ⓑ (close in time) new, recent; newly
新旧 *shinkyū* old and new
新聞 *shinbun* newspaper
新鮮な *shinsen na* fresh
新年 *shinnen* New Year
新製品 *shinseihin* new products
新発明 *shinhatsumei* new invention [discovery]
新世界 *shinsekai* new world, the New World
新設する *shinsetsu suru* establish newly, create
最新の *saishin no* newest, latest
新興の *shinkō no* rising, newly-established
新入生 *shinnyūsei* new student [pupil], freshman

❷ **make new, renew, renovate**
一新する *isshin suru* renovate, change completely; be renovated
革新 *kakushin* innovation, reform, renovation
更新する *kōshin suru* renew, renovate, innovate
維新 *ishin* renovation, restoration; Imperial Restoration of 1868

❸ abbrev. of 新暦 *shinreki*: new [Gregorian] calendar
新正月 *shinshōgatsu* January (according to the new calendar)

❹ abbrev. of 新記録 *shinkiroku*: new record
世界新 *sekaishin* new world record

INDEPENDENT

【shin 新】 newness, novelty; New [Gregorian] Calendar
新の七月七日 *shin no shichigatsu nanoka* 7th of July, New Style

KUN

【atara(shii) 新しい】 new, novel, fresh; recent, latest; modern
新しく *atarashiku* new, newly, anew
真新しい *maatarashii* brand-new
目新しい *meatarashii* novel, new, original

【ara(ta) 新た】
arata na 新たな new, fresh
新たに *arata ni* newly, afresh; again

【ara- 新-】 new, fresh
新手 *arate* fresh supply of troops; newcomer; new method

【nii- 新-】 new; first
新妻 *niizuma* new wife
新枕 *niimakura* bridal bed

SYNONYMS

❶ⓐ **new**
鮮 FRESH → 1877
生 raw → 3497
ⓑ **recent**
近 RECENT → 3061
❷ **reform**
更 RENEW → 3541
改 REFORM → 243
革 REFORM → 2448
❸ **calendars**
旧 old calendar → 14
暦 CALENDAR → 3018

NOTE

⇨ see COMPOUND FORMATION for 維新 *ishin* ⇨ 維 1370

9-4
南

献 獻 献 猷

1785 KEN KON

Ⓒⓗ 献 xiàn

Radical	Strokes
犬 94	13-4-9
Grade	**Freq**
Jōyō	1053
1 - 9 - 4	

▶**OFFER**

COMPOUNDS

❶ⓐ **offer (esp. to a superior), present, dedicate**

ⓑ **donate, contribute**

献納する *kennō suru* offer, present, donate

献上する *kenjō suru* present (a gift to a superior)

献身 *kenshin* self-sacrifice, devotion

献呈 *kentei* presentation

献木 *kenboku* donating lumber to a shrine

献金する *kenkin suru* donate [contribute] money

献血 *kenketsu* blood donation

貢献 *kōken* contribution, services

❷ⓐ offer wine to a guest

ⓑ counter for offerings [drinks] of wine

献酬 *kenshū* exchange of sake cups

献酌 *kenshaku* offering a drink

献立 *kondate* menu, preparations

一献 *ikkon* a cup of sake

❸ literature, records

文献 *bunken* literature, documentary records

INDEPENDENT

【**kenzuru 献ずる**】present, dedicate, offer

SYNONYMS

❶ⓐ **offer**

供 OFFER (to a person or god) → 88

納 offer (as to a god) → 1300

提 PRESENT → 591

貢 offer tribute → 2281

奉 DEDICATE → 2559

ⓑ **donate**

寄 CONTRIBUTE → 2291

恵む give charity → 2659

施 give alms → 891

❷ⓐ **offer wine**

酌 POUR WINE → 1461

酬 reciprocate wineglasses → 1539

NOTE

⇨ see COMPOUND FORMATION for 献立 *kondate* ⇨ 立 1992

9-4
壴

鼓 鼔 皷

1786 KO tsuzumi

Ⓒⓗ 鼓 gǔ

Radical	Strokes
鼓 207	13-13-0
Grade	**Freq**
Jōyō	1717
1 - 9 - 4	

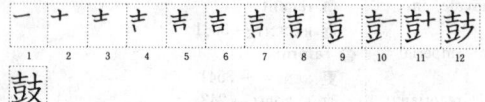

RADICAL 207

Standard form: 鼓 *tsuzumi* 'drum' (鼕)

Description: used in characters related to drums or their sound

▶**DRUM**

COMPOUNDS

❶ⓐ **drum**

ⓑ drum, beat, tap

鼓笛隊 *kotekitai* drum and fife band

鼓手 *koshu* drummer

鼓膜 *komaku* eardrum

太鼓 *taiko* (big) drum; professional jester; flatterer; big obi bow

鼓動 *kodō* beat, palpitation

鼓腹する *kofuku suru* drum the belly; be happy and contented

❷ rouse, stir up, encourage

鼓舞 *kobu* encouragement, stimulation

鼓吹 *kosui* inspiration, inculcation, advocacy

INDEPENDENT

【**kosuru 鼓する**】beat; rouse up

勇を鼓する *yū o kosuru* summon up one's courage

KUN

【tsuzumi 鼓】 hand drum, tabor
大鼓 *ōtsuzumi* large hand drum
腹鼓を打つ *haratsuzumi o utsu* drum the belly; eat to one's heart's content
舌鼓を打つ *shitatsuzumi o utsu* smack at, eat with relish

SYNONYMS

❶ⓐ musical instruments
琴 KOTO → 2781
笛 FLUTE → 2664

NOTE

⇨ see COMPOUND FORMATION for 鼓吹 *kosui* ⇨ 吹 231

戦 戰 戦 𢧐

1787 SEN ikusa tataka(u)

(CH) 战 zhàn

Radical	Strokes
戈 62	13-4-9
Grade	**Freq**
Jōyō-4	74
1-9-4	

9-4 単

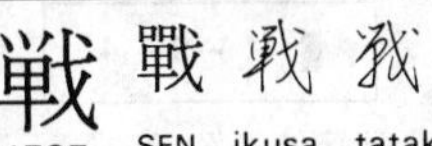

▶WAR

COMPOUNDS

❶ⓐ [original meaning] **war, wage war, fight**
ⓑ [also suffix] **war, battle, combat, warfare**
ⓒ [also suffix] (active hostility) **war, battle**
戦争 *sensō* war, battle
戦闘 *sentō* battle, fight, combat
戦場 *senjō* battlefield, front
戦前 *senzen* prewar period, period before Second World War
戦後 *sengo* postwar period, period after Second World War
戦線 *sensen* (war) front, battle line
作戦 *sakusen* tactics, strategy; (military) operations, maneuvers
敗戦 *haisen* lost battle, defeat
挑戦 *chōsen* challenge, defiance
空中戦 *kūchūsen* air battle, dogfight
生物戦 *seibutsusen* biological warfare
論戦 *ronsen* verbal battle, controversy
経済戦 *keizaisen* economic war

❷ [also suffix] **match, game, contest**
観戦する *kansen suru* watch (a ball game); observe (military operations)
早明戦 *sōmeisen* Waseda-Meiji (baseball) game
決勝戦 *kesshōsen* final round match, finals

❸ tremble, shudder
戦慄 *senritsu* shuddering, shivering
戦戦兢兢(＝戦戦恐恐)として *sensenkyōkyō to shite* with fear and trembling

KUN

【ikusa 戦】 war, fight, battle
【tataka(u) 戦う】
① wage war, fight
戦い *tatakai* war, fight, battle; match, game, contest
戦い抜く *tatakainuku* fight to a finish
敵と戦う *teki to tatakau* fight one's enemy
議論を戦わす *giron o tatakawasu* have a discussion
② contest, contend, play a match [game]
正正堂堂と戦おう *Seiseidōdō to tatakaō* Let's play the game fairly

SYNONYMS

❶ⓐ fight and war
闘 FIGHT → 3334
征 go on a military expedition → 293
ⓑ warfare and rebellions
軍 war → 2080
役 war → 244
陣 battle → 455
乱 rebellion → 1260
変 uprising → 2069
闘 FIGHT → 3334
❷ game
技 game → 248
【tatakau】
② compete
闘 FIGHT → 3334
争 CONTEND → 2030
競 COMPETE → 1847

USAGE

❶ tatakau
戦う
① wage war, fight
② contest, contend, play a match [game]
闘う
(struggle with) fight (against), contend with, strive against
❷ tatakai
戦い
① war, fight, battle
② match, game, contest
闘い
struggle, conflict

HOMOPHONES
tatakau ⇨ 闘 3334
tatakai ⇨ 闘 3334

9-4 曷

歇
1788 KETSU

CH 歇 xiē

Radical	Strokes
欠 76	13-4-9
Grade	Freq
Reference	
1 - 9 - 4	

COMPOUNDS
● [now replaced by 欠 1987] [original meaning] take a rest
間歇 *kanketsu* intermittence

9-4 苟

敬
1789

▶**RESPECT**
nonstandard for 敬 1701

9-4 娄

数 數 数 数
1790 SŪ SU kazu kazo(eru)

CH 数 shù shǔ shuò

Radical	Strokes
攵 66	13-4-9
Grade	Freq
Jōyō-2	185
1 - 9 - 4	

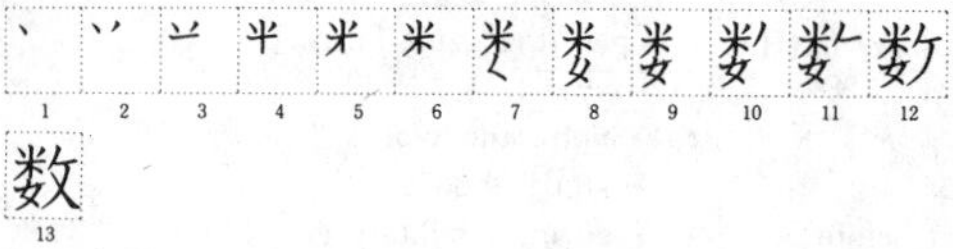

▶**NUMBER**
COMPOUNDS
❶ⓐ [also suffix] (amount) **number, quantity**
ⓑ *gram* number
数量 *sūryō* quantity, volume
総数 *sōsū* total (number)
多数の *tasū no* a number of, many
手数 *tesū* (=*tekazu*) trouble, bother, pains
トン数 *tonsū* tonnage
人数 *ninzū* (=*ninzu*) number of people
回数 *kaisū* frequency, number of times
生徒数 *seitosū* number of pupils
複数形 *fukusūkei* plural form
❷ [prefix] (a small number, esp. between three and five) **several**
数回 *sūkai* several times
数年間 *sūnenkan* several years
十数頁 *jūsūpēji* ten odd pages
❸ [also suffix] (abstract mathematical unit) **number, numbers**
数字 *sūji* figure, numeral
対数 *taisū* logarithm
指数 *shisū* index (number); exponent
関数(=函数) *kansū math* function
自然数 *shizensū* natural number
無理数 *murisū* irrational number
❹ count, enumerate, reckon
数詞 *sūshi gram* numeral
算数 *sansū* arithmetic; calculation
❺ mathematics
数学 *sūgaku* mathematics
英数 *eisū* English and mathematics
❻ fate, destiny
数奇な *sūki na* unlucky
❼ scheme, plot
権謀術数 *kenbō jussū* trickery, wiles, finesse
❽ used phonetically for *su*
数寄屋(=数奇屋) *sukiya* tea-ceremony arbor
手数入り *dezuiri* display of a sumo champion in the ring

INDEPENDENT
【sū 数】 number; fate, destiny
勝敗の数 *shōhai no sū* issue of the battle

KUN
【kazu 数】 number
数多く *kazuōku* in large numbers
数数の *kazukazu no* numerous, many
頭数 *atamakazu* number of persons, head count
【kazo(eru) 数える】 count, reckon, calculate, number, enumerate
数えで二十 *kazoe de hatachi* 20 years old by Japanese count
大作曲家の一人に数えられる *daisakkyokuka no hitori ni kazoerareru* be reckoned among the greatest composers

SPECIAL READINGS

数珠 *juzu* (Buddhist) rosary

SYNONYMS

❶ⓐ **quantity and number**

量 QUANTITY → 2471
嵩 BULK → 2331
積 size → 1236
額 AMOUNT → 1805
分 content → 1972
勢 strength → 2857

❷ **some**

何- several → 65
幾- SOME → 3582

❸ **kinds of numbers**

員 fixed number → 2269
号 NUMBER (numerical designation) → 2153
番 No. → 2748
第 ORDINAL NUMBER PREFIX → 2660
-目 ordinal number suffix → 3043
次 numerical order suffix → 54

❹ **calculate and count**

算 CALCULATE → 2702
計 COMPUTE → 1441

COMPOUND FORMATION

手数 *tesū* (=*tekazu*)
手数 'trouble, bother, pains' refers to a great deal (数 ❶ⓐ) of trouble (手).

毀

1791 KI kobo(tsu)

CH 毀 huǐ

Radical	Strokes
殳 79	13-4-9
Grade	**Freq**
Reference	
◧ 1 - 9 - 4	

9-4

COMPOUNDS

❶ [now also 棄 *ki* 2137] [original meaning] destroy, ruin, damage

毀棄する *kiki suru* destroy, demolish, damage
毀傷 *kishō* injury, damage
名誉毀損 *meiyo kison* libel, defamation, slander
破毀する *haki suru* reverse (the original judgment)
毀つ *kobotsu elegant* break, destroy, damage

❷ defame, slander

毀誉褒貶 *kiyohōhen* praise and censure, criticisms

殿 殿 殿

1792 DEN TEN tono -dono

CH 殿 diàn

Radical	Strokes
殳 79	13-4-9
Grade	**Freq**
Jōyō	1139
◧ 1 - 9 - 4	

9-4

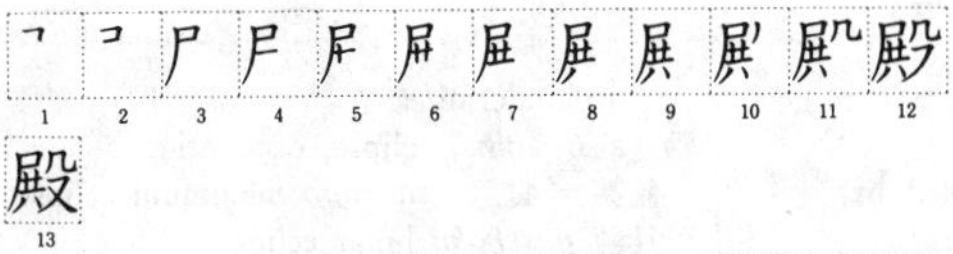

▶**PALACE**
▶**FORMAL HONORIFIC TITLE**

COMPOUNDS

❶ⓐ (large stately building) **palace, hall, mansion**

ⓑ (residence of nobility) **palace, shrine, temple**

ⓒ suffix after names of large buildings, esp. within the court or shrine grounds

殿堂 *dendō* hall, palace, shrine; sanctuary
寝殿 *shinden* main house
殿中で *denchū de* in the palace
宮殿 *kyūden* palace (of a royal person)
御殿 *goten* palace
神殿 *shinden* shrine, sanctuary
紫宸殿 *shishinden* Hall for State Ceremonies

❷ [also suffix] **formal honorific title**

殿下 *denka* His Imperial Highness
貴殿 *kiden* you
保善院殿 *hozen'inden* His Lordship Hozen of Blessed Memory

❸ [formerly 澱 *den* 775] settle, precipitate

沈殿 *chinden* precipitation, settlement

❹ the rear, the rear guard

殿軍 *dengun* rear guard

KUN

【**tono 殿**】

①ⓐ lord; my lord, his lordship
ⓑ gentleman

殿様 *tonosama* feudal lord

若殿 *wakatono* young lord
殿方 *tonogata* men, gentlemen
② part of a building, stately building
高殿 *takadono* stately mansion; two-[three-] storied house
湯殿 *yudono* bathroom
【-dono -殿】 formal honorific title: Esquire, Esq., Mister
山田太郎殿 *yamada tarō-dono* Taro Yamada, Esq.
議長殿 *gichōdono* Mr. Chairman

SYNONYMS

❶ⓐ buildings
宇 large building → 2175
閣 TALL MAGNIFICENT BUILDING → 3327
堂 HALL → 2589
館 PUBLIC BUILDING → 1748
舎 BUILDING → 2060
棟 BLOCK → 991
ⓑ palace
宮 ROYAL PALACE → 2274
❷ &【-dono】 titles of address
様 FORMAL TITLE → 1052
師 honorific title (clergymen) → 1326
公 honorific title (noblemen) → 1974
氏 COURTESY TITLE → 2951
兄 familiar title (seniors) → 2154
君 FAMILIAR TITLE (peers) → 3206
嬢 Miss → 758

9-5 飠
飽
1793
▶SATIATED
nonstandard for 飽 1715

9-5 飠
飼
1794
▶RAISE ANIMALS
nonstandard for 飼 1716

9-5 飠
飾
1795
▶DECORATE
nonstandard for 飾 1717

9-6 飠
蝕
1796 SHOKU mushiba(mu)

CH 蚀 shí

Radical	Strokes
虫 142	15-6-9
Grade	Freq
Reference	
1-9-6	

COMPOUNDS

[now replaced by 食 *shoku* 2075]
❶ [original meaning] (be eaten as if by worms) erode, corrode
浸蝕 *shinshoku* erosion, corrosion
腐蝕 *fushoku* corrosion
侵蝕 *shinshoku* infringement, violation
蝕む(＝虫食む) *mushibamu* (of worms) eat in; undermine
❷ [also suffix] eclipse, occultation
蝕甚(＝食尽) *shokujin* maximum eclipse
月蝕 *gesshoku* lunar eclipse
日蝕 *nisshoku* solar eclipse
皆既蝕 *kaikishoku* total solar [lunar] eclipse
金環蝕 *kinkanshoku* annular eclipse

9-7 飠
餓
1797
▶STARVED
nonstandard for 餓 1734

9-7 飠
餘
1798
▶REMAINING ▶EXCESS
nonstandard for 余 2042

親 1799

親 親 親

1799 SHIN oya oya- shita(shii) shita(shimu)

CH 亲 qīn qìng

Radical	Strokes
見 147	16-7-9
Grade	**Freq**
Jōyō-2	337
◧ 1 - 9 - 7	

9-7 辛

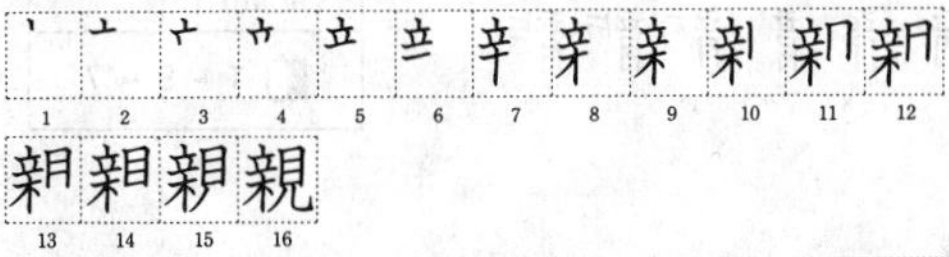

▶**PARENT** ▶**RELATIVES** ▶**INTIMATE**

COMPOUNDS

❶ **parent**
親権 *shinken* parental authority
親子 *shinshi* (=*oyako*) parent and child
両親 *ryōshin* parents

❷ **relatives, kin, relations** (**by marriage**)
親族 *shinzoku* relative
親類 *shinrui* relatives, relations
親戚 *shinseki* relative
三親等 *sanshintō* kinsman of the third degree (of consanguinity)
肉親 *nikushin* blood relation

❸ **intimate, familiar, close, friendly**
親友 *shin'yū* close [intimate] friend
親密な *shinmitsu na* intimate, close
親愛 *shin'ai* love, affection
親切な *shinsetsu na* kind, friendly, obliging
日イ親善 *nichii-shinzen* friendly relations between Japan and Israel

❹ [prefix] pro- (some country)
親日 *shinnichi* pro-Japan
親米 *shinbei* pro-American

❺ oneself, in person—said esp. of actions performed by the emperor
親展書 *shintensho* confidential letter
親政 *shinsei* direct Imperial rule

INDEPENDENT

【shin 親】 relatives
親は泣き寄る *Shin wa nakiyoru* Relatives come and mourn together

KUN

【oya 親】 parent, father, mother; card dealer; (gambling) banker
親指 *oyayubi* thumb
親分 *oyabun* boss, big shot
父親 *chichioya* father

【oya- 親-】 [also prefix] parent, mother; master
親船 *oyabune* mother ship
親会社 *oyagaisha* parent company

【shita(shii) 親しい】 intimate, familiar, close, friendly
親しさ *shitashisa* intimacy
親しい友達 *shitashii tomodachi* close [intimate] friend
親しく *shitashiku* intimately; personally, in person

【shita(shimu) 親しむ】 be intimate with, commune with; form a liking for, take to
親しみ *shitashimi* intimacy, familiarity

SYNONYMS

❶ **parents**
父 FATHER → 1973
母 MOTHER → 3475

❷ **family and relations**
縁 RELATION → 1386
姻 relative by marriage → 353
族 FAMILY → 958
家 FAMILY → 2273
門 family → 888
氏 clan → 2951

❸ **familiar and friendly**
密 CLOSE → 2292
近 NEAR → 3061
睦 FRIENDLY → 1199
懇 FAMILIAR → 2899
和 HARMONIOUS → 1130

【oya-】
○ **main**
主 MAIN → 1938
正 chief → 3484
本 head → 3502
首 leading → 2265

NOTE

⇨ see COMPOUND FORMATION for 親展書 *shintensho* ⇨ 展 3111

龍 1800

▶**DRAGON**
nonstandard for 竜 2099

9-7 音

9-7 音

龍 1801

▶DRAGON
nonstandard for 竜 2099

Radical	Strokes
龍 212	16-16-0
Grade	**Freq**
Variant	
1 - 9 - 7	

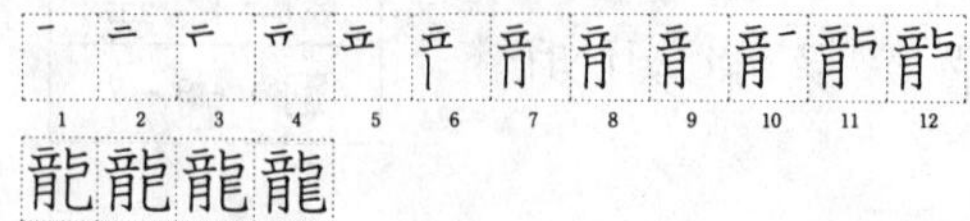

RADICAL 212
Standard form: 龍 *tatsu* 'dragon' (龕)
Description: used in characters related to dragons

9-7 県

縣 1802

▶PREFECTURE
nonstandard for 県 2641

9-8 食

館 1803

▶PUBLIC BUILDING
nonstandard for 館 1748

9-8 柰

隷 1804

▶UNDERLING
nonstandard for 隷 1751

9-9 客

額 1805

額 額 GAKU hitai

CH 额 é

Radical	Strokes
頁 181	18-9-9
Grade	**Freq**
Jōyō-5	525
1 - 9 - 9	

▶AMOUNT

COMPOUNDS

❶ [also suffix] **amount (of money), sum, volume, quantity**
額面 *gakumen* face value; denomination
金額 *kingaku* amount of money, sum
多額 *tagaku* large amount [sum]
総額 *sōgaku* total amount, sum total
全額 *zengaku* sum total, total amount
月額 *getsugaku* monthly amount [sum]
生産額 *seisangaku* amount of production

❷ **picture frame, frame, framed picture**
額縁 *gakubuchi* (picture) frame
扁額 *hengaku* tablet, framed picture

❸ [original meaning] **forehead, brow**
前額部 *zengakubu* forehead; frontlet

INDEPENDENT

【gaku 額】 amount (of money), sum, volume; picture frame, framed picture, tablet
巨大な額 *kyodai na gaku* colossal amount
額にする *gaku ni suru* set in a frame

KUN

【hitai 額】 forehead, brow
広い額 *hiroi hitai* broad forehead, high brow

SYNONYMS

❶ **quantity and number**
量 QUANTITY → 2471
嵩 BULK → 2331
積 size → 1236
分 content → 1972
数 NUMBER → 1790
勢 strength → 2857

❷ **frames**
枠 FRAME → 866
格 framework → 926

❸ **front parts of head**
顔 FACE → 1808
面 FACE → 2087

顯 顕 顕 显

1806 KEN

Ⓒⓗ 显 xiǎn

Radical	Strokes
頁 181	18-9-9
Grade	**Freq**
Jōyō	1600
◧ 1 - 9 - 9	

9-9 显

1 2 3 4 5 6 7 8 9 10 11 12

13 14 15 16 17 18

▶MANIFEST

COMPOUNDS

❶ⓐ (readily perceived) **manifest, apparent, noticeable, obvious**

ⓑ [original meaning] (show plainly) **manifest, reveal, expose**

顕著な *kencho na* notable, conspicuous; clear, obvious

顕示する *kenji suru* reveal

顕在化する *kenzaika suru* be actualized

顕現 *kengen* manifestation

露顕(＝露見) *roken* discovery, detection, exposure

顕微鏡 *kenbikyō* microscope

❷ⓐ make (a person's virtues) known

ⓑ well-known, prominent, high ranking

顕彰する *kenshō suru* give recognition, exalt, honor

顕揚する *ken'yō suru* extol, exalt

顕職 *kenshoku* prominent post

貴顕 *kiken* distinguished person

❸ *Buddhism* exoteric

顕教 *kenkyō* Exoteric Buddhism

SYNONYMS

❶ⓐ **conspicuous**

著 CONSPICUOUS → 2300

卓 PROMINENT → 2064

傑 outstanding → 155

ⓐ **evident**

亮 LUCID → 2071

鮮 VIVID → 1877

明 CLEAR → 855

ⓑ **appear**

現 APPEAR → 968

出 come out → 3498

ⓑ **reveal**

現 cause to appear → 968

発 reveal → 2565

露 EXPOSE → 2818

暴 disclose → 2515

披 OPEN OUT → 305

類 類 類 类

1807 RUI tagu(i)▲

Ⓒⓗ 类 lèi

Radical	Strokes
頁 181	18-9-9
Grade	**Freq**
Jōyō-4	682
◧ 1 - 9 - 9	

9-9 类

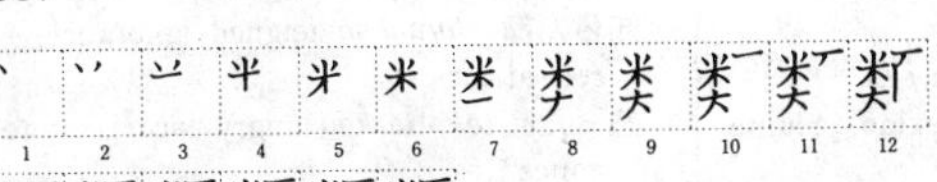

1 2 3 4 5 6 7 8 9 10 11 12

13 14 15 16 17 18

▶KIND

COMPOUNDS

❶ⓐ **kind, class, sort, category, genus, species**

ⓑ [suffix] **things of the same kind, group**

ⓒ **separate by kind, classify**

ⓓ [also suffix] **idiomatic term for biological class or order**

種類 *shurui* kind, sort, species, type

人類 *jinrui* mankind, humankind

同類 *dōrui* same kind, same class

衣類 *irui* clothes, garments

下着類 *shitagirui* underclothes

辞書類 *jishorui* dictionaries (and similar books)

分類 *bunrui* classification

哺乳類 *honyūrui* Mammalia

食肉類 *shokunikurui* carnivorous animals, Carnivora

❷ of the same kind:

ⓐ **similar, resembling, synonymous**

ⓑ **be similar, resemble, be alike**

ⓒ similar example, parallel, precedent

類書 *ruisho* books of the same kind, similar books

類型 *ruikei* similar type, prototype, pattern

類語 *ruigo* synonym, correlated word

類似 *ruiji* resemblance, similarity
類例 *ruirei* similar example, parallel
比類 *hirui* parallel, equal, match
❸ be affected by someone else's disaster (spreading flames)
類焼 *ruishō* catching fire from next door
❹ blood relation, kin
類縁 *ruien* affinity, family relationship
親類 *shinrui* relatives, relations

INDEPENDENT

【**rui 類**】kind, sort, class, genus, species; similar example, parallel; *logic* genus
この類の *kono rui no* this kind
同じ類に属する *onaji rui ni zokusuru* belong to the same class
類の無い *rui no nai* unparalleled, unprecedented

【**ruisuru 類する**】be similar, be like

KUN

【**tagu(i) 類い**】kind, sort, class; peer, equal
同じ類いの物 *onaji tagui no mono* things of the same kind
類い希な *taguimare na* unique, rare

SYNONYMS

❶ⓐ kinds and types
色 kind → 2029
種 VARIETY → 1218
様 variety → 1052
型 TYPE → 2638
般 SORT → 1317
属 genus → 3145
品 category → 2248
❷ⓐ similar
様 like → 1052
如 AS → 207
-通り as → 3109
云 SUCH → 1931
ⓑ resemble
似 RESEMBLE → 63

9-9
彦

顔 顔 顔 顔
1808 GAN kao

Ⓒ 颜 yán

Radical	Strokes
頁 181	18-9-9
Grade	**Freq**
Jōyō-2	517
1-9-9	

▶**FACE**

COMPOUNDS

❶ⓐ face, countenance
ⓑ (facial expression) **face, looks, features**
顔面 *ganmen* face
洗顔 *sengan* washing one's face
紅顔 *kōgan* rosy face, peachy cheeks
顔色 *ganshoku* (=*kaoiro*) complexion, countenance, expression
童顔の *dōgan no* boyish looking, baby-faced
厚顔な *kōgan na* impudent, shameless, brazen
破顔 *hagan* broad smile
❷ color, coloring
顔料 *ganryō* cosmetics; color, pigment
❸ [original meaning, now archaic] forehead
竜顔 *ryūgan* (=*ryōgan*) emperor's face

KUN

【**kao 顔**】
①ⓐ face
ⓑ [also suffix] (facial expression) face, looks, expression
顔付き *kaotsuki* face, countenance; expression, look
顔触れ *kaobure* personnel
顔合わせ *kaoawase* meeting, introduction; being matched against each other
素顔 *sugao* face without makeup
笑顔 *egao* smiling face, smile
知らん顔 *shirankao* feigned ignorance, unconcerned air
怒った顔 *okotta kao* angry face [countenance]
② face, prestige, honor
顔を潰される *kao o tsubusareru* be put out of countenance, lose face
顔が立つ *kao ga tatsu* save one's face
③ reputation, influence
顔の広い人 *kao no hiroi hito* person with many contacts

SYNONYMS

❶ⓐ front parts of head
面 FACE → 2087
額 forehead → 1805
ⓑ expression
色 COLOR → 2029

顏 1809

▶FACE
nonstandard for 顔 1808

9-9 彦

韻 1810

▶RHYME
nonstandard for 韻 1811

9-10 音

韻 1811 IN

韻 韻 韻 韵

CH 韵 yùn

Radical	Strokes
音 180	19-9-10
Grade	**Freq**
Jōyō	1832

1-9-10

9-10 音

Stroke order: 1–19

▶RHYME

COMPOUNDS

❶ⓐ [original meaning] **rhyme, rhyming**
ⓑ rhymed poetry, verse
韻律 *inritsu* rhythm, meter, measure
押韻 *ōin* rhyme, rhyming
頭韻 *tōin* alliteration, head rhyme
脚韻 *kyakuin* rhyme, end rhyme
韻文 *inbun* poetry, verse
❷ **melodious tone, agreeable sound, resonance**
余韻 *yoin* lingering tone, resonance, reverberation; aftertaste, impregnated elegance
松韻 *shōin* music of the pines
❸ simple or compound vowel, final (of a Chinese syllable or character)
韻母 *inbo* final
韻書 *insho* Chinese dictionary arranged by finals
音韻組織 *on'in soshiki* sound system
❹ charm, grace, elegance
風韻 *fūin* taste, grace

INDEPENDENT

【in 韻】rhyme
韻を踏む *in o fumu* rhyme (with)

SYNONYMS

❶ⓐ **musical elements**
律 RHYTHM → 363
拍 BEAT → 304
調 TONE → 1567
呂 ancient musical note → 2187
❷ **kinds of sound**
玲 TINKLING OF JADES → 910
響 reverberation → 2878
声 VOICE → 2198
音 SOUND → 2070

闗

incorrect classification ⇨ see 3335
(nonstandard for 関 3328)

9-10 門

饒 1812 JŌ

CH 饶 ráo

Radical	Strokes
食 184	21-9-12
Grade	**Freq**
Reference	

1-9-12

9-12 食

COMPOUNDS

● [now also 冗 1976] [original meaning] abundant, plentiful, rich
饒舌 *jōzetsu* garrulity, loquacity
豊饒 *hōjō* fertility, fruitfulness

9-12 食

饑 1813 KI

CH 饥 jī

Radical	Strokes
食 184	21-9-12
Grade	Freq
Reference	
1-9-12	

COMPOUNDS

[now replaced by 飢 1668]

ⓐ [original meaning] starve, be hungry, famish

ⓑ famine, hunger

饑餓 *kiga* starvation, hunger, famine

饑渇 *kikatsu* hunger and thirst

饑饉 *kikin* famine, failure of crops; shortage

10-2 馬

馭 1814 GYO

CH 驭 御 yù

Radical	Strokes
馬 187	12-10-2
Grade	Freq
Reference	
1-10-2	

COMPOUNDS

[now replaced by 御 577]

ⓐ handle, control, manage

ⓑ [original meaning] handle a horse well, train a horse

制馭する *seigyo suru* control, govern, suppress

馭者 *gyosha* coachman, driver

馭する *gyosuru* handle a horse well, train a horse

NOTE

⇨ see USAGE note at 御 577

10-2 倉

創 1815 SŌ tsuku(ru)▲

CH 创 chuàng chuāng

Radical	Strokes
刂 18	12-2-10
Grade	Freq
Jōyō-6	986
1-10-2	

▶CREATE

COMPOUNDS

❶ⓐ **create, bring into being, invent**

ⓑ **initiate, originate, start**

創造 *sōzō* creation

創作する *sōsaku suru* create, produce; write a story

創意 *sōi* original idea, ingenuity

創世記 *sōseiki* Genesis

独創的 *dokusōteki* original, creative

創立する *sōritsu suru* establish, organize, start

創始 *sōshi* initiating, creation, foundation

創刊 *sōkan* launching a magazine; first issue

創業 *sōgyō* inauguration of an enterprise

創設 *sōsetsu* establishment, founding

❷ [original meaning] wound, cut, laceration

創傷 *sōshō* wound

銃創 *jūsō* gunshot wound

絆創膏 *bansōkō* adhesive plaster [tape]

KUN

【tsuku(ru) 創る】[usu. 作る] create, bring into being

天地を創る *tenchi o tsukuru* create the heavens and the earth

SYNONYMS

❶ⓐ **create**

作 compose → 68

生 produce → 3497

発 START → 2565

起 generate → 3307

ⓑ **begin**

肇 ORIGINATE → 2799

始 BEGIN → 281

-出す begin to do → 3498

-掛ける start doing → 493

発 START → 2565

起 start → 3307

就 SET ABOUT → 1694
開 OPEN → 3321
❷ **injury**
傷 WOUND → 158
-擦れ sore → 790

HOMOPHONES
tsukuru ⇨ 作 68 造 3110

NOTE
⇨ see USAGE note at 作 68

割 割 割 割 ⒸⒽ 割 gē

1816 KATSU wa(ru) wari wa(ri) wa(reru) sa(ku)

丶 丷 宀 宀 中 宇 宝 害 害 害 割 割
1 2 3 4 5 6 7 8 9 10 11 12

Radical	Strokes
刂 18	12-2-10
Grade	**Freq**
Jōyō-6	375
◧ 1-10-2	

10-2
害

▶**DIVIDE**

COMPOUNDS

❶ (separate into parts) **divide (up), split; cede**
割賦 *kappu* (=*wappu*) payment by installments
割拠する *kakkyo suru* hold one's own ground
割愛する *katsuai suru* part with (something), give up; omit (reluctantly)
割譲 *katsujō* cession of territory
分割する *bunkatsu suru* divide up, partition, split

❷ [original meaning] **cut with a knife, cut in two**
割腹 *kappuku* disembowelment, hara-kiri
割礼 *katsurei* circumcision
割線 *kassen* secant

KUN

【wa(ru) 割る】
vi
①ⓐ divide (up), cut (in half), allot
ⓑ *math* divide
割り当て *wariate* assignment, allotment
割り勘 *warikan* equal split, Dutch treat
割り前 *warimae* share, one's lot, quota
割り算 *warizan* division
割り切る *warikiru* divide; give a clear-cut solution
②ⓐ crack, break
ⓑ split, chop (wood)
コップを割る *koppu o waru* crack [break] a glass
割り印 *wariin* tally impression
二つ割り *futatsuwari* cutting in two; one half
③ push open, separate, part
割り込む *warikomu* wedge (oneself) in, squeeze oneself into
④ open up, disclose
割り出す *waridasu* deduce, infer; calculate, compute
口を割る *kuchi o waru* speak out, confess
腹を割って *hara o watte* frankly
⑤ drop below (a price level)
原価を割って *genka o watte* below cost
⑥ *sumo* step out (of the ring)
⑦ dilute
炭酸で割る *tansan de waru* dilute with soda

【wari 割】
①ⓐ rate, proportion, ratio
ⓑ counter for units of 10%
ⓒ abbrev. of 割引 *waribiki*: discount
割に *wari ni* comparatively, rather
割引 *waribiki* discount, reduction
割合 *wariai* rate, proportion, ratio; comparatively
一日百円の割で *ichinichi hyakuen no wari de* at the rate of 100 yen a day
一割 *ichiwari* 10%
三割五分 *sanwari gobu* 35%
割興 *warikō* discount industrial bank bond
学割 *gakuwari* student discount
② profit, gain
割の良い *wari no ii* remunerative, paying, profitable, advantageous

【wa(ri) 割り】 dilution; equal split, Dutch treat; [in compounds] allotment, assignment
水割り *mizuwari* whisky and water
割りで払う *wari de harau* split the account
役割り *yakuwari* assigning [allotment of] parts; part, role, duty
時間割り *jikanwari* hour assignment, timetable

【wa(reru) 割れる】 *vi* crack, break, be smashed; be divided [forked], be separated; (lose unity) split (into); *math* be divisible; drop below (a price level); *colloq* be disclosed
割れた卵 *wareta tamago* broken egg
ひび割れ *hibiware* crack, fissure
前割れの *maeware no* open in front
仲間割れ *nakamaware* split among friends, division in the camp
二で割れる *ni de wareru* be divisible by two
コスト割れ *kosutoware* cutting into cost
身元が割れる *mimoto ga wareru* be identified

【sa(ku) 割く】
① spare (time), set [put] aside

時間を割く *jikan o saku* spare time (for)
② cede, alienate
領土を割く *ryōdo o saku* cede a territory

SYNONYMS

❶ **separate**
分 DIVIDE → 1972
解 TAKE APART → 1517
析 ANALYZE → 862
別 SEPARATE → 1117
離 SEPARATE → 1836
隔 partition → 671

❷ **cut**
剖 DISSECT → 1670
切 CUT → 27
断 CUT OFF → 1492
裁 CUT OUT → 3299
刈る CLIP → 28
伐 CUT DOWN → 42
削 CUT BY CHIPPING → 1448

【waru】
①ⓑ **divide**
除 divide → 456
② **break**
裂 SPLIT → 2687
破 BREAK → 1150
壊 BREAK DOWN → 756
折 BREAK OFF → 253
砕 CRUSH UP → 1134
崩 CRUMBLE → 2296

【wari】
①ⓐ **rate**
率 RATE → 2118
比 ratio → 26
歩 percentage → 2416

HOMOPHONES

saku ⇨ 裂 2687

NOTE

⇨ see USAGE note at 裂 2687

10-2
害

割 1817

▶DIVIDE
nonstandard for 割 1816

10-2
菫

勤 勤 勤 勤 1818

KIN GON tsuto(meru) -zuto(me) tsuto(maru) iso(shimu)▲

CH 勤 qín

Radical	Strokes
力 19	12-2-10
Grade	**Freq**
Jōyō-6	713
1-10-2	

▶SERVICE

COMPOUNDS

❶ (employment in general) **service, duty, work, employment**
勤続 *kinzoku* continuous service, continuance in service
通勤する *tsūkin suru* commute, go to one's office
転勤する *tenkin suru* be transferred (to another office)
欠勤 *kekkin* absence (from work)
夜勤 *yakin* night duty

❷ **work diligently [hard], labor, strive; work faithfully**
勤勉 *kinben* diligence, assiduity, industry
勤務する *kinmu suru* do duty, serve, be on duty, work
勤労 *kinrō* labor, work, service
勤倹 *kinken* diligence and thrift
勤行 *gongyō* Buddhistic service, sutra chanting
忠勤 *chūkin* loyal [faithful] service

KUN

【tsuto(meru) 勤める】 serve (in an office), hold a job, be in the service of
勤め *tsutome* service, employment, duties; Buddhistic service, sutra chanting; prostitute service
勤め先 *tsutomesaki* (one's place of) employment
勤め上げる *tsutomeageru* serve out one's time, perform one's service

【-zuto(me) -勤め】 [suffix] serving in, being in the service of
会社勤め *kaishazutome* serving in a company

【tsuto(maru) 勤まる】 be fit for, be equal to (the task)
勤まらない *tsutomaranai* be unfit [incompetent] for

【iso(shimu) 勤しむ】 work diligently, strive, make efforts
仕事に勤しむ *shigoto ni isoshimu* be assiduous in one's business

SYNONYMS

❶ **work and employment**
役 SERVICE (esp. public) → 244
職 EMPLOYMENT → 1425
労 LABOR → 2548

業 WORK → 2612
務 DUTY → 1173
任 OFFICE → 53
❷ **exert oneself**
励 make efforts → 1119
努 EXERT → 2547
勉 ENDEAVOR → 3318
尽 use all one's strength → 3050
精 put one's heart into → 1366
【tsutomeru】
○ **work**
仕 SERVE → 34
働 WORK → 153
稼 WORK (for a living) → 1230
労 LABOR → 2548

USAGE

❶ **tsutomeru**
勤める
serve (in an office), hold a job, be in the service of
務める
ⓐ discharge [perform] one's duties
ⓑ play [act, perform] (a part or role)
努める
[sometimes also 勉める] endeavor, make efforts, try hard, work diligently
勉める
[usu. 努める] same as 努める
❷ **tsutome**
勤め
① service, employment, duties
② Buddhistic service, sutra chanting
③ prostitute service
務め
duty, task, responsibility

HOMOPHONES

tsutomeru ⇨ 務 1173 努 2547 勉 3318
tsutome ⇨ 務 1173

剰
1819

▶**SURPLUS**
nonstandard for 剩 1779

10-2 乘

馴
1820 JUN na(reru) na(rasu)

Ⓒⓗ 驯 xún

Radical	Strokes
馬 187	13-10-3
Grade Reference	Freq
◧ 1-10-3	

10-3 馬

COMPOUNDS

❶ⓐ [original meaning] become tame [domesticated]
ⓑ [now also 順 *jun* 18] tame, domesticate
馴れた *nareta* tame, domesticated
馴染む *najimu* become familiar; grow accustomed; get (clothing) to fit
馴致する *junchi suru* tame, habituate; lead to
馴化 *junka* acclimation
馴らす *narasu* tame, domesticate
馴らし手 *narashite* tamer
馴鹿 *tonakai* reindeer
❷ [in compounds] become overfamiliar with
馴れ合う *nareau* collude, conspire; establish clandestine liaisons
馴れ馴れしい *narenareshii* overfamiliar, unceremonial

HOMOPHONES

nareru ⇨ 慣 685
narasu ⇨ 慣 685 均 235

NOTE

⇨ see USAGE note at 慣 685

10-4 馬

駄

1821 DA TA▲

CH 驮 tuó duò

Radical	Strokes
馬 187	14-10-4
Grade	**Freq**
Jōyō	1576
1-10-4	

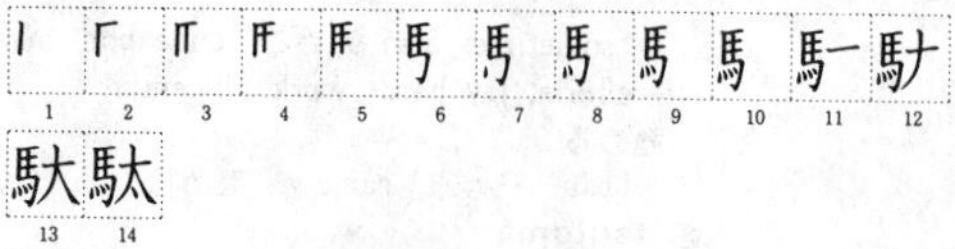

▶**GOOD FOR NOTHING**

COMPOUNDS

❶ [also prefix] **good for nothing, no good, poor, shabby, useless, worthless**

駄目 *dame go* cross that does not constitute a territory; no good, useless; No!

駄作 *dasaku* poor piece of writing

駄菓子 *dagashi* cheap sweets

駄洒落 *dajare* poor joke, pun

駄駄を捏ねる *dada o koneru* be unreasonable

無駄な *muda na* no good, fruitless, wasteful

❷ **clogs, sandals**

下駄 *geta* geta, wooden clogs

足駄 *ashida* high clogs, rain clogs

雪駄 *setta* leather-soled sandals

❸ⓐ carry by packhorse

ⓑ horse load, pack

ⓒ counter for horse loads

駄賃 *dachin* packhorse charge; tip

駄馬 *daba* packhorse, workhorse, hack

荷駄 *nida* horse load, pack

薪二駄 *takigi nida* two horse loads of firewood

SYNONYMS

❶ **bad**

廃 WASTE → 3146

下 of low grade → 3378

弊 shabby → 2884

粗 COARSE → 1329

悪 BAD → 2745

劣 INFERIOR → 2395

❷ **footwear**

靴 SHOES → 1781

履 footwear → 3171

足 counter for footwear → 2188

10-4 馬

駅 驛

1822 EKI

CH 驿 yì

Radical	Strokes
馬 187	14-10-4
Grade	**Freq**
Jōyō-3	584
1-10-4	

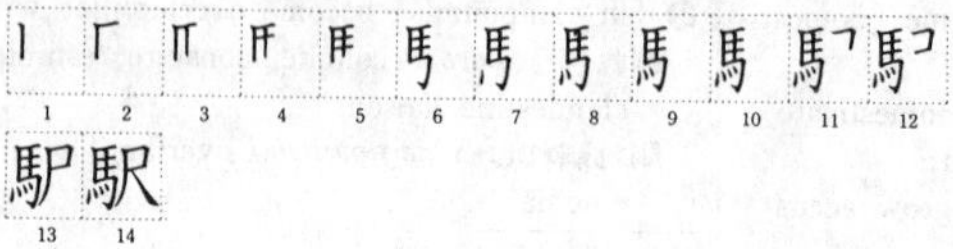

▶**STATION**

COMPOUNDS

❶ⓐ [also prefix and suffix] **station, railway station, railroad depot**

ⓑ **suffix after names of stations**

駅前の *ekimae no* in front of the station

駅長 *ekichō* stationmaster

駅員 *ekiin* station employee

駅ビル *ekibiru* station building

駅弁 *ekiben* station lunch

各駅 *kakueki* every station; local train

貨物駅 *kamotsueki* freight depot

神戸駅 *kōbeeki* Kobe Station

❷ⓐ [original meaning] relay station, post station, stage

ⓑ relay, transmit by stages

宿駅 *shukueki* post town, relay station

駅伝 *ekiden* post-horse, stagecoach; long-distance relay race

駅逓 *ekitei* transportation from post to post; postal service in Meiji era

INDEPENDENT

【**eki** 駅】railway station; relay station

駅迄歩く *eki made aruku* walk to the station

立派な駅 *rippa na eki* beautiful station

SYNONYMS

❶ **places for landing or stopping**

停 stopping place → 139

港 PORT → 605

津 HARBOR (*elegant*) → 390

❷ⓐ **post station**

逓 RELAY → 3106

宿 post station → 2293

駆 驅 駈° 駆 𢇛

1823 KU ka(keru) ka(ru)

CH 驱 qū

Radical	Strokes
馬 187	14-10-4
Grade	**Freq**
Jōyō	1486
1-10-4	

10-4 馬

丨 ┌ 𠂆 𠂇 𠂈 馬 馬 馬 馬 馬 馬 駆 駆 駆
1 2 3 4 5 6 7 8 9 10 11 12 13 14

▶DRIVE

COMPOUNDS

❶ⓐ drive (a machine), set in motion, handle
ⓑ [original meaning] drive a horse
駆動 *kudō* drive (of a machine)
駆使する *kushi suru* use freely, have good command of
馳駆する *chiku suru* dash around on a horse, run around; exert oneself (for another)

❷ drive away, drive out, expel
駆除する *kujo suru* exterminate, destroy, drive away
駆逐する *kuchiku suru* drive away, drive out, expel
駆虫剤 *kuchūzai* insecticide, vermicide

❸ gallop, run quickly
疾駆する *shikku suru* ride fast, drive a horse fast
長駆 *chōku* long march, expedition to a distant region
先駆者 *senkusha* pioneer, forerunner
前駆する *zenku suru* ride in advance, lead the way

KUN

【ka(keru) 駆ける】 gallop, run quickly, dash
駆けっこ *kakekko* race, foot race, running match
駆け回る *kakemawaru* bustle about, run about
駆け落ち *kakeochi* elopement
駆け引き *kakehiki* bargaining; tactics
先駆け *sakigake* the first to charge; lead, pioneer

【ka(ru) 駆る】
① drive (a car), urge (a horse) on, spur on
駆り立てる *karitateru* drive, spur on; stir up
駆り集める *kariatsumeru* mobilize, round up
② prompt, inspire
駆られる *karareru* be driven by (one's feelings), succumb to

SYNONYMS

❶ⓐ force to move
推 propel → 504
押す PUSH → 314

ⓐ set in motion
動 MOVE → 1778
掛ける set going → 493

❷ drive out
逐 DRIVE OUT → 3102
退 cause to retreat → 3094
追 chase away → 3096
斥 EXPEL → 2972
排 EXCLUDE → 490
払う clear out → 194

❸ run
走 RUN → 2194
奔 RUSH → 2218

HOMOPHONES

kakeru ⇨ 掛 493 懸 2915 架 2569 賭 1605 翔 1357
karu ⇨ 狩 397 刈 28

COMPOUND FORMATION

駆け引き *kakehiki*
駆け引き 'bargaining; tactics' originally referred to advance (駆ける) and retreat (引く) in battle.

NOTE

⇨ see USAGE notes at 掛 493 and 刈 28

駐

incorrect stroke count ⇨ see 1828 (nonstandard for 駐 1826)

10-4 馬

10-4
穀 穀 穀 穀

1824 KOKU

CH 谷 穀 gǔ

Radical	Strokes
禾 115	14-5-9
Grade	**Freq**
Jōyō-6	1465
1-10-4	

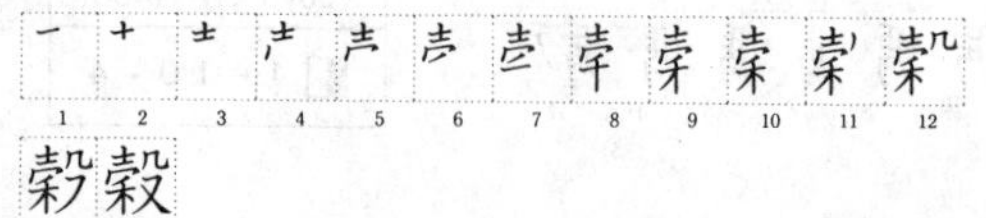

▶**CEREAL**

COMPOUNDS

❶ **cereal, grain, corn**

穀物 *kokumotsu* grain, cereals
穀類 *kokurui* grains
穀粒 *kokuryū* grain
穀倉 *kokusō* granary, grain elevator
穀粉 *kokufun* grain [rice] flour
穀食 *kokushoku* cereal diet, grain-eating
五穀 *gokoku* the five cereals, (staple) grains

❷ [original meaning] husk, hull

脱穀する *dakkoku suru* thresh

SYNONYMS

❶ **cereal**

粉 flour → 1291

NOTE

★do not confuse with 殻 1490

10-4
歌 歌 歌

1825 KA uta uta(u)

CH 歌 gē

Radical	Strokes
欠 76	14-4-10
Grade	**Freq**
Jōyō-2	495
1-10-4	

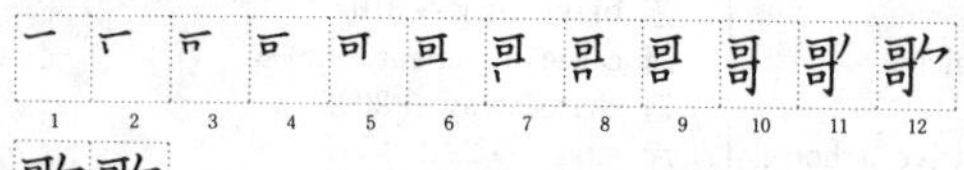

▶**SONG**

COMPOUNDS

❶ [also suffix] **song**

歌謡 *kayō* song, ballad
歌曲 *kakyoku* song (in the classical style)
歌詞 *kashi* words [lyrics] of a song
国歌 *kokka* national anthem
校歌 *kōka* school song, alma mater song
流行歌 *ryūkōka* popular song

❷ [original meaning] **sing**

歌手 *kashu* singer
歌劇 *kageki* opera
歌舞伎 *kabuki* kabuki

❸ Japanese poetry, waka, tanka, poem

詩歌 *shiika* (=*shika*) Chinese and Japanese poetry; poems
短歌 *tanka* tanka, Japanese verse
和歌 *waka* Japanese poem, tanka
連歌 *renga* verse linking, poetic dialogue

KUN

【uta 歌】

[also suffix]

① [sometimes also 唄] song, ballad

歌声 *utagoe* singing (voice)
歌合戦 *utagassen* singing matches
替え歌 *kaeuta* parody on a song
子守歌 *komoriuta* lullaby

② Japanese poem, waka, tanka, ode, verse

歌詠み *utayomi* tanka composer
召し歌 *meshiuta* tanka dedicated to the Emperor in response to His Majesty's public invitation

【uta(u) 歌う】

① [sometimes also 唄う] sing, recite

歌い手 *utaite* singer
歌い上げる *utaiageru* sing at the top of one's voice; express one's feelings fully in a poem

② express in a poem

神の徳を歌った歌 *kami no toku o utatta uta* poem in praise of God

SYNONYMS

❶ **music and songs**

謡 POPULAR SONG → 1597
曲 MUSICAL COMPOSITION → 3527
節 tune → 2691
調べ melody → 1567
楽 MUSIC → 2826
音 sound of music → 2070

❷ **sing**

唱 SING → 462

❸ **poetry**

詩 POETRY → 1524
俳 HAIKU → 112
句 HAIKU → 2967

USAGE

❶ **uta**

歌
[also suffix]
① [sometimes also 唄] song, ballad
② Japanese poem, waka, tanka, ode, verse

唄
[usu. 歌] [also suffix] song, ballad—used esp. in reference to traditional Japanese songs

❷ **utau**

歌う
① [sometimes also 唄う] sing, recite
② express in a poem

謡う
recite, chant (esp. from a noh drama text)

唄う
[usu. 歌う] recite, sing—used esp. in reference to traditional Japanese songs

謳う
ⓐ sing the joys of, extol, eulogize
ⓑ declare, state, express

HOMOPHONES

uta ⇨ 唄 400
utau ⇨ 謡 1597 唄 400 謳 1632

歎 incorrect stroke count ⇨ see 1869

10-4 歎

駐 駐

1826 CHŪ

CH 驻 zhù

Radical	Strokes
馬 187	15-10-5
Grade	**Freq**
Jōyō	872
1-10-5	

10-5 馬

1 2 3 4 5 6 7 8 9 10 11 12 13 14 15

▶**STATIONED**

COMPOUNDS

❶ [also prefix] **stationed (at, in), resident in**
駐留する *chūryū suru* be stationed at, stay
駐在 *chūzai* residence, stay
駐屯する *chūton suru* be stationed, occupy
駐日大使 *chūnichi taishi* ambassador to Japan
駐英 *chūei* stationed in England
駐独 *chūdoku* stationed in Germany

❷ **park**
駐車場 *chūshajō* parking area
駐輪場 *chūrinjō* bicycle parking lot
駐停車する *chūteisha suru* park or stop a vehicle

SYNONYMS

❶ **stay**
屯 STATION TROOPS → 3457
留 STAY → 2580
滞 STAY → 663
在 reside temporarily → 2984
泊 STAY OVERNIGHT → 331
宿 LODGE → 2293

❷ **stop**
停 HALT → 139
止 STOP → 2941

駒 駒

1827 KU koma

CH 驹 jū

Radical	Strokes
馬 187	15-10-5
Grade	**Freq**
Names	1980
1-10-5	

10-5 馬

1 2 3 4 5 6 7 8 9 10 11 12 13 14 15

▶**HORSE** ▶**CHESSMAN**

KUN

【**koma 駒**】

①ⓐ *elegant* horse, colt
ⓑ [original meaning] pony, small horse
駒座 *komaza* Equuleus

駒鳥 *komadori* robin
当歳駒 *tōsaigoma* one year-old colt, yearling
② chessman, shogi piece, piece used in various board games
駒損 *komason* (=*komazon*) loss of material (in shogi)
将棋の駒 *shōgi no koma* shogi pieces, chessmen
持ち駒 *mochi goma* captured piece
③ bridge (of musical instruments)
三味線の駒 *shamisen no koma* bridge of shamisen
④ wood piece

NAMES

駒沢 *komazawa* place name
駒吉 *komakichi* male name

SYNONYMS

【koma】
① **horse**
馬 HORSE → 3296
駿 FLEET STEED → 1832
午 the Horse → 1984

10-5 馬

駐

1828

▶STATIONED
nonstandard for 駐 1826

10-5 馬

駈

1829

▶DRIVE
nonstandard for 駆 1823

10-6 骨

骼

1830 KAKU

CH 骼 gé 胳 gē

Radical	Strokes
骨 188	16-10-6
Grade	**Freq**
Reference	
1-10-6	

COMPOUNDS

● [now replaced by 格 926] frame, skeleton, build
骨骼 *kokkaku* frame, physique; framework, skeletal structure

10-6 鬲

融

1831 YŪ to(keru)▲ to(kasu)▲

CH 融 róng

Radical	Strokes
虫 142	16-6-10
Grade	**Freq**
Jōyō	661
1-10-6	

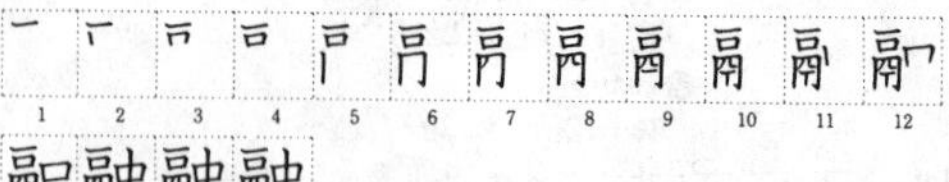

▶FUSE

COMPOUNDS

❶ (become liquefied by heat, esp. in the joining of metals) **fuse**
融解 *yūkai* fusion, melting
融点 *yūten* fusion point
融熱 *yūnetsu* heat of fusion
融接 *yūsetsu* fusion welding
溶融 *yōyū* melting, fusion
核融合 *kakuyūgō* nuclear fusion
❷ (be united as if by melting) fuse, blend, melt together
融合 *yūgō* fusion, merger; harmony
融和 *yūwa* harmony, reconciliation
❸ (from the idea of passing smoothly) **finance, accommodate with a loan**
融資 *yūshi* financing, advance of funds, loan
融通 *yūzū* financing, accommodation; flexibility
金融 *kin'yū* circulation of money, money market, finance
特融 *tokuyū* special loan [finance]
❹ [archaic] bright, glowing
融朗 *yūrō* clearness, brightness

KUN

【to(keru) 融ける】 [now usu. 解ける, some-

times also 溶ける] *vi* (esp. of snow or ice) melt, thaw
　雪融け *yukidoke* thawing of snow
【to(kasu) 融かす】 [now usu. 解かす] *vt* melt (snow or ice), thaw (out)
　氷を融かす *kōri o tokasu* melt ice

SYNONYMS

❶ **liquefy**
　溶 DISSOLVE, MELT → 664
　解 DISSOLVE → 1517

❸ **lend and borrow**
　貸 LEND → 2600
　借 BORROW → 122
　債 DEBT → 156

HOMOPHONES

tokeru ⇨ 解 1517　溶 664　熔 1058　鎔 1762
tokasu ⇨ 解 1517　溶 664　熔 1058　鎔 1762 梳 964

NOTE

⇨ see USAGE note at 解 1517

駿 駿 駿

1832　SHUN　SUN　NAMES　suru　toshi　hayashi

(CH) 骏 jùn

Radical	Strokes
馬 187	17-10-7
Grade	**Freq**
Names	2018
◧ 1-10-7	

10-7 馬

▶FLEET STEED

COMPOUNDS

❶ⓐ [original meaning] **fleet steed, swift horse, fine horse**
　ⓑ [also 俊 *shun* 102] **swift-footed, fleet-footed**
　駿馬 *shunba* (=*shunme*) fleet steed, fine horse
　駿足 *shunsoku* swift horse, fleet steed; fleet speed; fast runner; brilliant person
❷ [now usu. 俊 *shun* 102] brilliant, talented, bright
　駿才 *shunsai* genius, person of exceptional talent
❸ abbrev. of 駿河 *suruga*, old name for eastern Shizuoka Prefecture
　駿府 *sunpu* old name for Shizuoka City
❹ [now always 峻 412]
　ⓐ stern, strict
　ⓑ high and steep, precipitous
　⇨ see 峻 412 for compounds

INDEPENDENT

【shun 駿】 talent; talented person, genius
　関東の駿 *kantō no shun* genius of Kanto

NAMES

　駿太郎 *shuntarō* male name
　駿河台 *surugadai* place name
　駿男 *toshio* male name

SYNONYMS

❶ⓐ **horse**
　馬 HORSE → 3296
　駒 HORSE (*elegant*) → 1827
　午 the Horse → 1984

騖

incorrect classification ⇨ see 2874

10-7 騖

験 驗 験 験

1833　KEN　GEN

(CH) 验 yàn

Radical	Strokes
馬 187	18-10-8
Grade	**Freq**
Jōyō-4	402
◧ 1-10-8	

10-8 馬

▶TEST

COMPOUNDS

❶ [original meaning] **test, try, attempt, examine, verify**
　験算(=検算) *kenzan* verification of accounts, checking figures

試験する *shiken suru* test, examine
実験 *jikken* experiment
体験する *taiken suru* experience, go through, (actually) feel
受験する *juken suru* take an examination
❷ⓐ efficacy (as of medicine), effectiveness
ⓑ efficacy of a Buddhist prayer or ascetic practices
効験 *kōken* effect, efficacy, virtue
修験者 *shugenja* ascetic (living in the mountains)
霊験 *reigen* (=*reiken*) miracle, miraculous virtue

INDEPENDENT

【kensuru 験する】 test, examine
【gen 験】 omen
験が良い *Gen ga ii* The omen is good

SYNONYMS

❶ **try**
試 TRY → 1525
❶ **investigate and examine**
調 INVESTIGATE → 1567
査 LOOK INTO → 2437
審 EXAMINE CAREFULLY → 2360
診 EXAMINE A PATIENT → 1504
検 EXAMINE → 986
探 PROBE → 505
討 STUDY → 1456
察 INSPECT → 2347
究 STUDY EXHAUSTIVELY → 2203
閲 REVIEW → 3330
勘 CHECK → 1777
糾 INQUIRE INTO → 1278
❷ⓐ **potency**
効 EFFECT → 1265
能 action → 1323
機 function → 1076

10-8
馬

騎 騎 騎

1834 KI

Ⓒⓗ 骑 qí

Radical	Strokes
馬 187	18-10-8
Grade	**Freq**
Jōyō	1642
1-10-8	

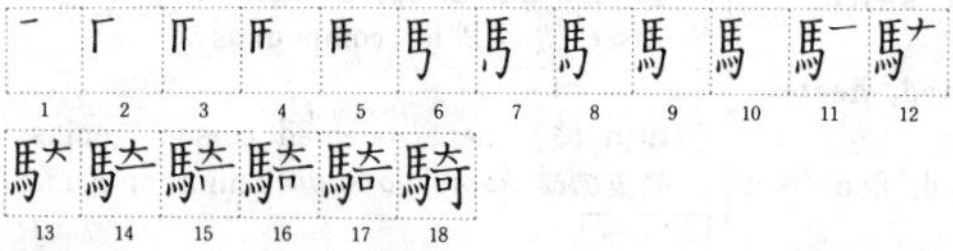

▶RIDE ON HORSEBACK

COMPOUNDS

❶ [original meaning] **ride on horseback**
騎馬 *kiba* horse riding
騎手 *kishu* rider, horseman, jockey
騎乗の *kijō no* mounted, on horseback
騎兵 *kihei* cavalry soldier, cavalry
騎士 *kishi* knight
❷ⓐ horseman, knight
ⓑ counter for horsemen
単騎 *tanki* single horseman, lone rider
一騎打ち *ikkiuchi* single combat; straight fight
侍八騎 *samurai hakki* eight samurai on horseback, eight mounted warriors

SYNONYMS

❶ **travel by vehicle**
乗 RIDE → 3576
走 travel by vehicle → 2194
航 NAVIGATE → 1318

10-8
馬

騒 騷 騷 騷

1835 SŌ sawa(gu)

Ⓒⓗ 骚 sāo

Radical	Strokes
馬 187	18-10-8
Grade	**Freq**
Jōyō	905
1-10-8	

▶CLAMOR

COMPOUNDS

❶ⓐ [original meaning] **clamor, raise a clamor, be uproarious, make a noise, bustle**
ⓑ **clamorous, uproarious, noisy**
騒音 *sōon* noise
騒騒しい *sōzōshii* clamorous, uproarious, noisy, boisterous
騒動 *sōdō* disturbance, uproar; strife; confu-

sion
騒然たる *sōzentaru* noisy, confused
騒乱 *sōran* commotion, riot
喧騒 *kensō* clamor, din, noise
物騒な *bussō na* dangerous, insecure, disturbed
❷ sentimental, poetic
騒人 *sōjin* poet, literary man

KUN

【sawa(gu) 騒ぐ】 clamor, raise a clamor, be uproarious, make a noise, bustle; make merry, have a spree; clamor against, kick up a row; get agitated, make a fuss; noise about
騒ぎ *sawagi* clamor, uproar; tumult, agitation; [in negative constructions] matter (of)
騒がしい *sawagashii* noisy, boisterous; troubled
騒ぎ立てる *sawagitateru* make a great fuss
大騒ぎ *ōsawagi* uproar, racket, row

SYNONYMS

❶ⓐ make sound or noise
鳴 SOUND → 674
響 REVERBERATE → 2878
ⓑ loud
高い loud → 2097
朗 CLEAR (voice) → 1325

髄 incorrect stroke count ⇨ see 1842 10-8 骨

離 离• 離 離 ㊥ 离 lí 10-8 离

1836 RI hana(reru) hana(su)

Radical	Strokes
隹 172	18-8-10
Grade	**Freq**
Jōyō	578
1 - 10 - 8	

▶SEPARATE

COMPOUNDS

❶ⓐ (be or become disconnected) **separate (from), be separated, be detached, disjoin, scatter**
ⓑ (be apart) **separated, distant**
離散する *risan suru* scatter, disperse, be broken up
分離する *bunri suru* separate, split; be separated
電離 *denri* electrolytic dissociation, ionization
剝離 *hakuri* exfoliation, peeling off
支離滅裂な *shirimetsuretsu na* incoherent, inconsistent, disconnected
隔離 *kakuri* isolation, segregation
離島 *ritō* outlying island
離心率 *rishinritsu* eccentricity
距離 *kyori* distance, range; interval
❷ (sever relations) **separate from, withdraw, be estranged, be alienated**
離婚 *rikon* divorce
離縁する *rien suru* divorce; cancel adoption
離反 *rihan* estrangement, alienation, desertion
背離する *hairi suru* be estranged, be alienated
乖離 *kairi* estrangement, alienation; detachment
❸ⓐ (part company) separate, part from, be separated
ⓑ **leave, depart, go away, quit, secede**
離別する *ribetsu suru* part from, be separated from; divorce
会者定離 *eshajōri* Those who meet must part
離合 *rigō* meeting and parting
離脱する *ridatsu suru* break away, leave, secede
離陸 *ririku* takeoff
離日 *rinichi* departure from Japan
離村する *rison suru* desert one's village
離党 *ritō* secession from a party
離農 *rinō* giving up farming
❹ third of the eight trigrams in the Book of Changes: south, the fire

KUN

【hana(reru) 離れる】
vi
①ⓐ separate, be separated, become disjointed
ⓑ be (a long time or distance) away
離れ離れになる *hanarebanare ni naru* get separated, be dispersed
遠く離れて *tōku hanarete* at a long distance
現実離れする *genjitsubanare suru* become disconnected from reality
② be estranged from, cut oneself off
③ leave, quit, go away
都会を離れる *tokai o hanareru* leave town

【hana(su) 離す】

vt

①ⓐ separate, part, divide

ⓑ detach, keep apart, isolate

切り離す *kirihanasu* cut [chop] off, sever, detach

引き離す *hikihanasu* draw apart, separate; get a lead on

② estrange

SYNONYMS

❶ⓐ separate

別 SEPARATE → 1117

隔 partition → 671

割 DIVIDE → 1816

分 DIVIDE → 1972

解 TAKE APART → 1517

析 ANALYZE → 862

ⓑ distant

隔 APART → 671

遠 DISTANT → 3150

遥 FAR → 3141

悠 far-off → 2741

遼 FARAWAY → 3168

❷ estrange

遠 DISTANT → 3150

疎 ESTRANGE → 1178

❸ⓐ part company

別 SEPARATE → 1117

ⓑ leave and set forth

去 GO AWAY → 2156

発 START → 2565

出 GO OUT → 3498

退 RETREAT → 3094

撤 WITHDRAW → 738

USAGE

❶ hanareru

離れる

①ⓐ separate, be separated, become disjointed

ⓑ be (a long time or distance) away

② be estranged from, cut oneself off

③ leave, quit, go away

放れる

free oneself of, get free

❷ hanasu

離す

①ⓐ separate, part, divide

ⓑ detach, keep apart, isolate

② estrange

放す

ⓐ (set free) let go, release, free, turn loose

ⓑ (release one's hold) let go (one's hold of), leave go

HOMOPHONES

hanareru ⇨ 放 853

hanasu ⇨ 放 853

10-8 卒

雜 1837

▶MISCELLANEOUS ▶MIXED

nonstandard for 雑 1385

10-8 莫

難 1838

難 難 難

CH 难 nán nàn

NAN kata(i) -gata(i) muzuka(shii) -niku(i)▲

Radical	Strokes
隹 172	18-8-10
Grade	**Freq**
Jōyō-6	368
1-10-8	

▶DIFFICULT ▶DISASTER

COMPOUNDS

❶ⓐ [also prefix] **difficult, hard, troublesome**

ⓑ [also suffix] **difficulty, trouble, hardship, distress**

難航 *nankō* hard passage, rough going

難問 *nanmon* difficult problem [question]

難解な *nankai na* difficult, hard to understand

難易 *nan'i* (relative) difficulty, hardness (or ease)

難事業 *nanjigyō* difficult undertaking [project], uphill task

難儀 *nangi* hardship, trouble

至難の *shinan no* most difficult

困難 *konnan* difficulty, trouble, distress, hardship

万難 *bannan* thousand and one difficulties, innumerable difficulties

生活難 *seikatsunan* living difficulties, economic distress

就職難 *shūshokunan* difficulty of finding employment, job shortage

❷ disaster, calamity, accident, misfortune

遭難する *sōnan suru* meet with disaster
避難 *hinan* refuge, shelter, evacuation
海難 *kainan* disaster at sea, shipwreck
災難 *sainan* calamity, disaster, accident, misfortune

❸ⓐ fault, defect, blemish
ⓑ **find fault with, criticize, blame, reproach**
難点 *nanten* weakness, fault, flaw; difficult point
無難 *bunan* safety, security; faultlessness
難色 *nanshoku* disapproval, reluctance
難詰する *nankitsu suru* blame, censure, reproach
非難(＝批難) *hinan* criticism, blame

INDEPENDENT

【nan 難】 disaster, accident, danger; fault, flaw; difficulty, trouble
難に遭う *nan ni au* meet with disaster
難を言えば… *Nan o ieba…* To be critical…
難中の難 *nanchū no nan* hardest of all

【nanjiru (＝nanzuru) 難じる(＝難ずる)】 criticize unfavorably, blame, reproach

KUN

【kata(i) 難い】 difficult, hard
言うは易く行うは難し *Iu wa yasuku okonau wa katashi* Easier said than done

【-gata(i) -難い】 [verbal suffix] difficult to do
し難い *shigatai* difficult to do, impossible
有り難う *arigatō* thank you

【muzuka(shii) 難しい】 difficult, hard, troublesome; doubtful, unpromising; sullen, glum, hard to please
難しさ *muzukashisa* difficulty, complexity
難しい病気 *muzukashii byōki* serious disease
気難しい *kimuzukashii* moody, hard to please

【-niku(i) -難い】 [verbal suffix] difficult, hard, troublesome, awkward
扱い難い *atsukainikui* hard to handle
答え難い質問 *kotaenikui shitsumon* awkward [difficult] question

SYNONYMS

❶ **trouble and suffering**
煩 VEXED → 1022
辛 HARD → 2038
痛 PAIN → 3285
苦 SUFFERING → 2243
悩 SUFFER → 421
窮 BE IN EXTREMITY → 2358
困 BE IN TROUBLE → 3070

❷ **misfortune and disaster**
災 NATURAL CALAMITY → 2206
禍 CALAMITY → 1030
厄 MISFORTUNE → 2947
凶 BAD LUCK → 2961

❸ⓐ **faults and flaws**
短 shortcoming → 1182
陥 defect → 457
欠 incompleteness → 1987

ⓑ **blame and accuse**
批 CRITICIZE → 250
責 BLAME → 2467
叱 SCOLD → 182
詰 REPRIMAND → 1521
劾 EXPOSE CRIMES → 1266
弾 impeach → 572

HOMOPHONES

katai ⇨ 硬 1183　堅 2823　固 3086

NOTE

⇨ see USAGE note at 固 3086
⇨ see COMPOUND FORMATION for 有り難う *arigatō* ⇨ 有 2983

雞
1839

▶**CHICKEN**
nonstandard for 鶏 1768

10-8 奚

歸
1840

▶**RETURN**
nonstandard for 帰 130

10-8 𠂤

騙
1841　HEN　kata(ru)　dama(su)

CH 骗 piàn

Radical	Strokes
馬 187	19-10-9
Grade	Freq
Reference	
◧ 1-10-9	

10-9 馬

COMPOUNDS

❶ deceive, cheat, swindle, defraud
騙り *katari* fraud, swindle
騙し討ち *damashiuchi* sneak attack, foul play
騙し絵 *damashie* trompe l'oeil
子供騙し *kodomodamashi* mere child's play,

kid stuff

❷ assume (another's) name

他人の名を騙って *tanin no na o katatte* under a false name

HOMOPHONES

kataru ⇨ 語 1543

katari ⇨ 語 1543

NOTE

⇨ see USAGE note at 語 1543

10-9 骨

髄 髄 髄 髄

1842 ZUI

CH 髓 suǐ

Radical	Strokes
骨 188	19-10-9
Grade	**Freq**
Jōyō	1789
1-10-9	

▶**MARROW**

COMPOUNDS

❶ [original meaning] **marrow, pith**

髄液 *zuieki* spinal fluid

髄虫 *zuimushi* rice borer, pearl moth

骨髄 *kotsuzui* bone marrow

脊髄 *sekizui* spinal cord

❷ (vital part) **essence, core, heart**

真髄(＝神髄) *shinzui* essence, quintessence, soul

精髄 *seizui* essence, soul, spirit, pith

INDEPENDENT

【**zui** 髄】 marrow, pith

葦の髄 *ashi no zui* pith of a ditch reed

SYNONYMS

❶ **bone**

骨 BONE → 2654

❷ **essential part**

精 ESSENCE (essential part) → 1366

粋 essence (best part) → 1293

枢 PIVOT → 865

幹 TRUNK → 1718

綱 ESSENTIAL POINTS → 1372

旨 PURPORT → 2024

要 summary → 2635

10-9 眞

1843 TEN

CH 颠 diān

Radical	Strokes
頁 181	19-9-10
Grade	**Freq**
Reference	
1-10-9	

COMPOUNDS

❶ [now usu. 転 1480] [original meaning] turn over, roll over, tumble down, fall over

顚倒する *tentō suru* tumble, fall down; invert, reverse; upset

顚落 *tenraku* fall, spill; degradation

顚覆する *tenpuku suru* overturn, turn over, upset; overthrow

七顚八倒する *shichitenhattō* (＝*shichitenbattō, shittenbattō*) *suru* toss oneself about in great pain

❷ⓐ top, summit

ⓑ top, beginning

山顚 *santen* top of a mountain

顚末 *tenmatsu* circumstances, details, course of events

10-9 米

類

1844

▶**KIND**

nonstandard for 類 1807

願 1845

GAN nega(u) -negai▲

CH 愿 yuàn

Radical	Strokes
頁 181	19-9-10
Grade	**Freq**
Jōyō-4	842
1-10-9	

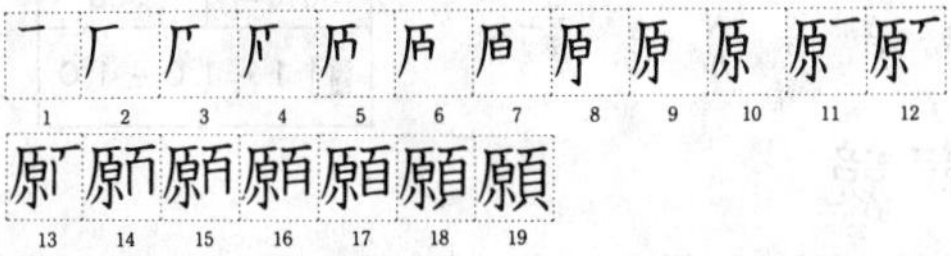

10-9 原

▶WISH ▶ASK A FAVOR

COMPOUNDS

❶ⓐ **wish, desire, hope for**
ⓑ **one's wish, one's desire**
願望 *ganbō* wish, desire, aspiration
念願する *nengan suru* desire, wish (for), pray (for)
宿願 *shukugan* long-cherished desire
悲願 *higan* one's pathetic wish; vows resulting from the compassion of the Buddhas

❷ⓐ pray, prayer
ⓑ vow
願文 *ganmon* written petition read before a god
祈願する *kigan suru* pray, implore
満願 *mangan* completion [fulfillment] of a vow
結願 *kechigan* expiration of one's vow term

❸ **ask a favor, petition, apply for, request, beg**
願書 *gansho* written application
出願 *shutsugan* application
志願する *shigan suru* volunteer, apply for
請願 *seigan* petition
懇願する *kongan suru* beg earnestly, implore, entreat
依願退職 *igan-taishoku* retirement at one's own request

INDEPENDENT

【**gan** 願】vow to some particular end
願を掛ける *gan o kakeru* make a wish (to a god)

KUN

【**nega(u)** 願う】wish, desire, hope for; pray; ask a favor, petition, apply for, request, beg
願い *negai* wish, desire; prayer; request, petition; application
願わくは *negawaku wa* I pray / I wish
宜しくお願いします *Yoroshiku onegai shimasu* Please be so kind as to... / I am glad to make your acquaintance
願い出る *negaideru* make an application

【**-negai -願**】[suffix] written application
辞職願 *jishokunegai* (written) resignation

SYNONYMS

❶ **wish and desire**
望 HOPE → 2742
希 ASPIRE → 2049
懐 LONG FOR → 763
慕 yearn for → 2353
渇 thirst for → 515
欲 DESIRE → 1475
求 SEEK → 3550

❷ⓐ **pray and worship**
祈 PRAY → 875
拝 WORSHIP → 303
崇 REVERENCE → 2297
斎 OBSERVE RELIGIOUS ABSTINENCE → 2115

❸ **request**
請 REQUEST → 1576
訴 APPEAL TO → 1507
頼 ASK → 1615
嘱 CHARGE WITH → 718
要 REQUIRE → 2635
求 SEEK → 3550

騷 1846

10-10 馬

▶CLAMOR

nonstandard for 騒 1835

10-10 竟

競 竞• 競 𥪰

1847 KYŌ KEI kiso(u) se(ru)

CH 竞 jìng

Radical	Strokes
立 117	20-5-15
Grade	**Freq**
Jōyō-4	553
1-10-10	

▶COMPETE

COMPOUNDS

❶ [original meaning] **compete, contend, vie**

競争する *kyōsō suru* compete, contend, vie
競技 *kyōgi* match, contest, game; sporting event
競泳 *kyōei* swimming race
競演 *kyōen* recital contest
競走 *kyōsō* race, sprint
競輪 *keirin* bicycle race
競馬 *keiba* horse racing

❷ bid, bid for

競売 *kyōbai* auction

KUN

【kiso(u) 競う】 compete with, contend, rival, vie

競い合う *kisoiau* compete with, vie for

【se(ru) 競る】 bid, make a bid for; compete, vie

競り市 *seriichi* auction sale

SYNONYMS

❶ **compete**

争 CONTEND → 2030
戦う contest → 1787
闘 FIGHT → 3334

10-11 馬

驅

1848

▶DRIVE

nonstandard for 駆 1823

10-11 奚

鷄

1849

▶CHICKEN

nonstandard for 鶏 1768

10-11 隺

鶴 鹤 𪀚

1850 KAKU tsuru NAMES tazu zu

CH 鹤 hè

Radical	Strokes
鳥 196	21-11-10
Grade	**Freq**
Names	1976
1-10-11	

▶CRANE

COMPOUNDS

❶ [original meaning] **crane, stork**

❷ await with a craned neck, await expectantly

鶴首して待つ *kakushu shite matsu* wait with a craned [an outstretched] neck, wait expectantly

KUN

【tsuru 鶴】 [also suffix] crane, stork

鶴科 *tsuruka* Gruidae
鶴嘴 *tsuruhashi* pickax, hack; mandrel
丹頂鶴 *tanchōzuru* Japanese crane
千羽鶴 *senbazuru* string of a thousand folded-paper cranes

NAMES

鶴見 *tsurumi* surname also place name
鶴岡 *tsuruoka* surname also place name
千鶴 *chizuru* female name

SYNONYMS

❶ **wild birds**

雀 SPARROW → 2469
隼 FALCON → 2756
鷹 HAWK → 3189

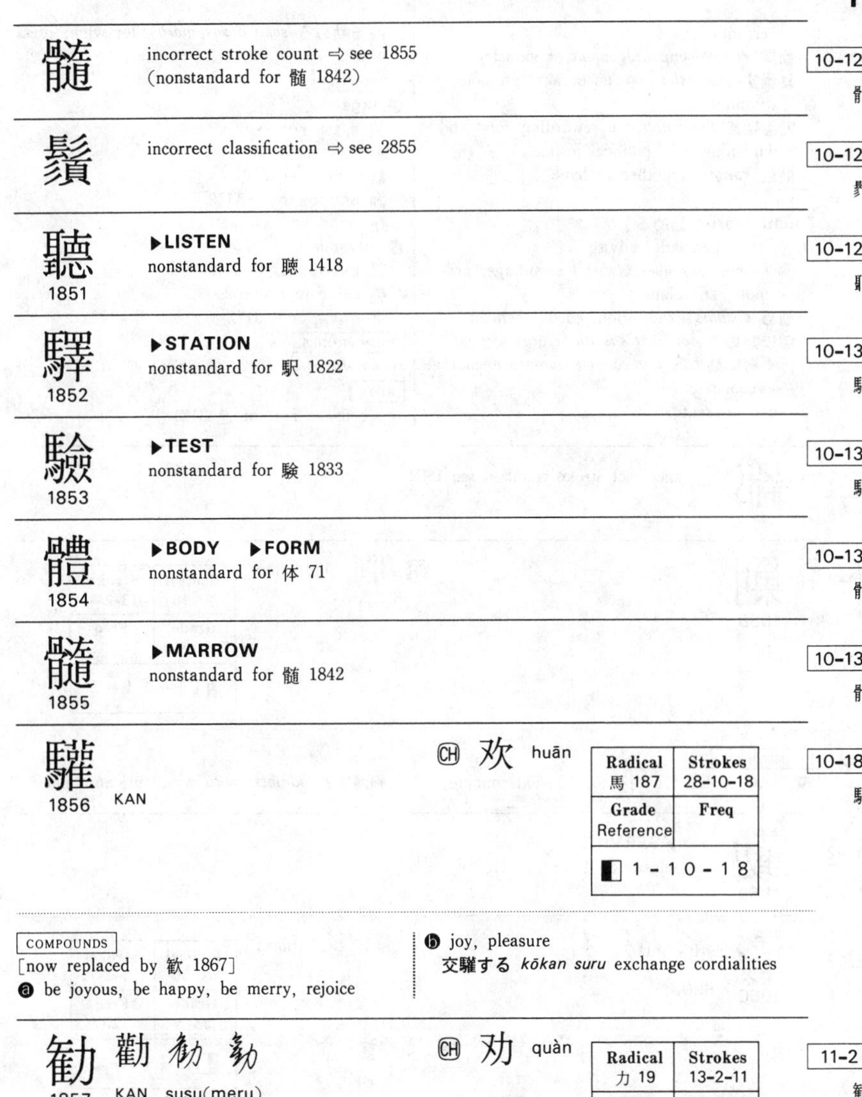

髄 incorrect stroke count ⇨ see 1855 (nonstandard for 髄 1842) 10-12 骨

鬢 incorrect classification ⇨ see 2855 10-12 髟

聽 ▶LISTEN
nonstandard for 聴 1418
1851 10-12 耳

驛 ▶STATION
nonstandard for 駅 1822
1852 10-13 馬

驗 ▶TEST
nonstandard for 験 1833
1853 10-13 馬

體 ▶BODY ▶FORM
nonstandard for 体 71
1854 10-13 骨

髓 ▶MARROW
nonstandard for 髄 1842
1855 10-13 骨

驩
1856 KAN

CH 欢 huān

Radical	Strokes
馬 187	28-10-18
Grade	**Freq**
Reference	
1-10-18	

10-18 馬

COMPOUNDS
[now replaced by 歓 1867]
ⓐ be joyous, be happy, be merry, rejoice

ⓑ joy, pleasure
交驩する *kōkan suru* exchange cordialities

勧 勸 勧 勧
1857 KAN susu(meru)

CH 劝 quàn

Radical	Strokes
力 19	13-2-11
Grade	**Freq**
Jōyō	1058
1-11-2	

11-2 隹

Stroke order: 1 2 3 4 5 6 7 8 9 10 11 12 13

▶URGE
COMPOUNDS
ⓐ [original meaning] (persuade to act) **urge, persuade, advise**

ⓑ **encourage, promote**
勧告 *kankoku* advice, counsel, recommendation
勧誘する *kan'yū suru* induce, invite, canvass,

persuade
勧業 *kangyō* encouragement of industry
勧奨する *kanshō suru* encourage, promote, stimulate
勧善懲悪 *kanzenchōaku* rewarding good and punishing evil, political justice
勧銀 *kangin* hypothecary bank

KUN

【susu(meru) 勧める】
①ⓐ urge, persuade, advise
ⓑ [sometimes also 奨める] encourage, promote, stimulate
勧め *susume* exhortation, encouragement
切に勧める *setsu ni susumeru* urge strongly
行く様に勧める *iku yō ni susumeru* encourage someone to go
② offer, present
酒を勧める *sake o susumeru* offer wine; press wine on

SYNONYMS

ⓐ **urge**
催 PRESS FOR → 157
促 HASTEN → 103
誘 INDUCE → 1550
励 ENCOURAGE → 1119
侑 URGE TO EAT → 91
ⓑ **advance**
奨 ENCOURAGE → 2842
興 cause to rise → 2909
進 ADVANCE → 3121

HOMOPHONES

susumeru ⇨ 奨 2842 薦 2373 進 3121

NOTE

⇨ see USAGE note at 進 3121

11-2

啚

incorrect stroke count ⇨ see 1862

11-2
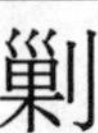
巣
1858 SŌ SHŌ

CH  jiǎo chāo

Radical	Strokes
刂 18	13-2-11
Grade Reference	Freq
1-11-2	

COMPOUNDS

● [now replaced by 掃 *sō* 503] exterminate, wipe out
剿滅する *sōmetsu suru* wipe out, annihilate

11-2
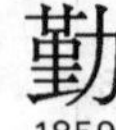
堇
1859

▶SERVICE
nonstandard for 勤 1818

11-3
彰 彰 彰 彰
章
1860 SHŌ

CH 彰 zhāng

Radical	Strokes
彡 59	14-3-11
Grade	Freq
Jōyō	1237
1-11-3	

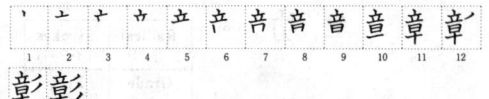

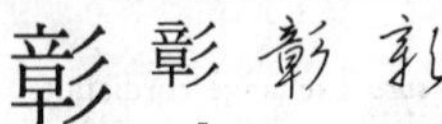

▶PROCLAIM MERITS

COMPOUNDS

❶ [sometimes also 章 2117] **proclaim the merits of a person (to the public), make (a person's virtues) well known, give public recognition**
彰徳する *shōtoku suru* [rare] praise publicly, make another's virtues well known
顕彰する *kenshō suru* give recognition, exalt, honor
表彰する *hyōshō suru* commend (officially), give public recognition
❷ [archaic]
ⓐ manifest, show clearly, reveal
ⓑ manifest, clear, obvious
彰明する *shōmei suru* manifest, exhibit clearly

SYNONYMS

❶ **praise**
称 acclaim → 1160
賞 express admiration → 2618
揚 EXALT → 593
頌 EULOGIZE → 1045
賛 PRAISE → 2809
美 regard as beautiful → 2264
褒 COMMEND → 2144
嘉 commend (esp. an inferior) → 2340

彰 ▶**PROCLAIM MERITS**
1861 nonstandard for 彰 1860

11-3 章

1862 HI hina hina(biru)

Ⓒⓗ 鄙 bǐ

Radical	Strokes
⻏ 163	14-3-11
Grade	Freq
Reference	
◧ 1 - 1 1 - 3	

11-3 啚

COMPOUNDS

❶ [now replaced by 卑 *hi* 2642] (lacking in elevating human qualities) mean, vulgar, despicable
鄙劣な *hiretsu na* mean, base, cowardly
鄙猥な *hiwai na* indecent, obscene
野鄙な *yahi na* vulgar, base, mean
❷ [now replaced by 卑 *hi* 2642] [humble] my humble
鄙見 *hiken* my humble opinion
❸ [original meaning] countryside, out-of-the-way place
都鄙 *tohi* town and country
辺鄙な *henpi na* out-of-the-way, unfrequented, remote
鄙 *hina* the country
鄙びる *hinabiru* be countryfied

對 ▶**OPPOSITE** ▶**OPPOSE**
1863 nonstandard for 対 831

11-3 丵

敵 敵 敵 敵
1864 TEKI kataki kana(u)▲

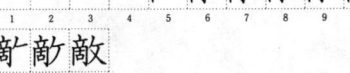

Ⓒⓗ 敌 dí

Radical	Strokes
攵 66	15-4-11
Grade	Freq
Jōyō-5	975
◧ 1 - 1 1 - 4	

11-4 商

▶**ENEMY**

COMPOUNDS

❶ⓐ [also prefix] **enemy, foe**
ⓑ **opponent, rival**
敵国 *tekkoku* enemy country
敵意 *tekii* hostility, enmity
強敵 *kyōteki* powerful enemy [rival]
敵王 *tekiō* opponent's king (in shogi)
敵艦隊 *tekikantai* enemy fleet
❷ⓐ confront the enemy, oppose, resist
ⓑ match, equal
敵対する *tekitai suru* oppose, fight against
不敵な *futeki na* daring, dauntless
無敵の *muteki no* matchless, invincible
❸ unclassified compounds
素敵な *suteki na* grand, cute, fine

INDEPENDENT

【**teki** 敵】enemy, foe; opponent, rival
【**tekisuru** 敵する】oppose, fight against, match, equal

KUN

【**kataki** 敵】enemy, foe; opponent, rival; revenge, retaliation
商売敵 *shōbaigataki* business rival
敵討ち *katakiuchi* vendetta, revenge
【**kana(u)** 敵う】
① be a match for, compare with

君には敵わない *Kimi ni wa kanawanai* I am no match for you
② stand, bear
こう暑くては敵わない *Kō atsukute wa kanawanai* I can't stand the heat

HOMOPHONES
kanau ⇨ 適 3160
NOTE
⇨ see USAGE note at 適 3160

11-4 啇

1865

▶ENEMY
nonstandard for 敵 1864

11-4 豙

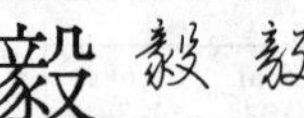
1866 KI NAMES tsuyoshi kowashi takeshi take hatasu

Ⓒⓗ 毅 yì

Radical	Strokes
殳 79	15-4-11
Grade	**Freq**
Names	2033
1 - 11 - 4	

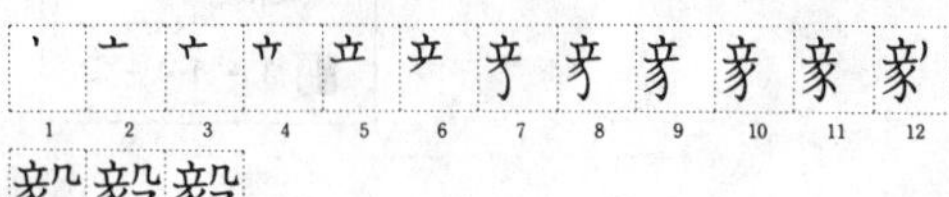
1 2 3 4 5 6 7 8 9 10 11 12
13 14 15

▶RESOLUTE
COMPOUNDS
● **resolute, determined, firm, dauntless**
毅然として *kizen to shite* resolutely, firmly, bravely
剛毅な *gōki na* hardy, sturdy
NAMES
弘毅 *kōki* male name
毅 *tsuyoshi* (=*takeshi*) male name
毅雄 *takeo* male name

SYNONYMS
● **firm and obstinate**
剛 TOUGH → 1673
頑 STUBBORN → 1040
硬 hard-line → 1183
堅 FIRM → 2823
固 FIRM, stiff → 3086
確 firm → 1228

11-4 雈

歓 歡 欵 𣃉
1867 KAN

Ⓒⓗ 欢 huān

Radical	Strokes
欠 76	15-4-11
Grade	**Freq**
Jōyō	973
1 - 11 - 4	

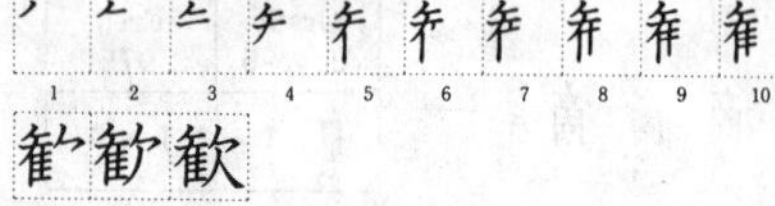
1 2 3 4 5 6 7 8 9 10 11 12
13 14 15

▶JOYOUS
COMPOUNDS
[formerly also 驩 1856]
ⓐ [original meaning] **be joyous, be happy, be merry, rejoice**
ⓑ joy, pleasure
ⓒ [sometimes also 款 1700] treat cordially, have friendly relations with
歓喜 *kanki* joy, delight
歓楽 *kanraku* pleasure, merriment
歓談 *kandan* pleasant chat [talk]
歓迎 *kangei* welcome
歓送 *kansō* sending off
歓声 *kansei* cheers, shout of joy
哀歓 *aikan* joys and sorrows
歓待 *kantai* cordial [warm] reception, hospitality
交歓 *kōkan* exchange of cordialities

INDEPENDENT
【**kan** 歓】joy, delight, pleasure
歓を尽くす *kan o tsukusu* enjoy oneself to one's heart's content

SYNONYMS
ⓐ **pleased and pleasant**
欣 JOYFUL → 852
喜 HAPPY → 2308
嬉しい GLAD → 722
悦 DELIGHTED → 418
愉 PLEASED → 582
楽 pleasurable → 2826

朗 CHEERFUL → 1325 | 快 PLEASANT → 245

穀 **▶CEREAL**
1868
nonstandard for 穀 1824

11-4 㝅

歎
1869 TAN nage(ku)

CH 叹 tàn

Radical	Strokes
欠 76	15-4-11
Grade	**Freq**
Reference	
1-11-4	

11-4 歎

COMPOUNDS

❶ [now usu. 嘆 *tan* 630 or 嘆く *nageku*] [original meaning] sigh (in grief or despair), grieve, lament; deplore
歎声 *tansei* sigh, lamentation; sigh of admiration
歎息する *tansoku suru* sigh; sigh in grief
歎願する *tangan suru* entreat, petition, appeal
悲歎 *hitan* grief, sorrow, lamentation
嗟歎 *satan* lamentation, deploration; admiration
慨歎する *gaitan suru* deplore, lament, regret
歎 *tan* sigh, grief, lamentation
歎じる(＝歎ずる) *tanjiru* (＝*tanzuru*) grieve, lament; sigh in admiration
歎き *nageki* grief, lamentation
❷ [now usu. 嘆く *nageku* 630] sigh in admiration, exclaim, admire, praise
驚歎する *kyōtan suru* admire, wonder, be struck with admiration
感歎符 *kantanfu* exclamation mark
詠歎 *eitan* exclamation, admiration

HOMOPHONES
nageku ⇨ 嘆 630
nageki ⇨ 嘆 630

NOTE
⇨ see USAGE note at 嘆 630

敷 敷 敷 敷
1870 FU shi(ku) -shi(ki)

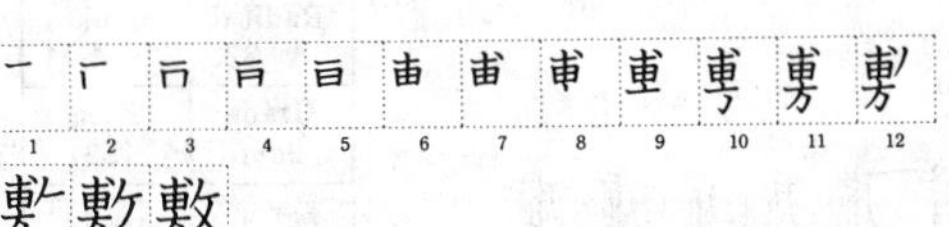

CH 敷 fū

Radical	Strokes
攵 66	15-4-11
Grade	**Freq**
Jōyō	1044
1-11-4	

11-4 尃

▶LAY

COMPOUNDS

● [also 布] [original meaning] (dispose over a surface) **lay (as a railroad track), spread**
敷設 *fusetsu* construction, laying
敷衍 *fuen* expatiation, amplification, elaboration

KUN

【shi(ku) 敷く】
①ⓐ (spread over a surface) lay, spread, lay under
ⓑ (dispose over a surface) lay (as a railroad track), construct, pave
ⓒ lay out, arrange
敷き詰める *shikitsumeru* spread all over
敷物 *shikimono* carpet, rug
敷布 *shikifu* sheet
布団を敷く *futon o shiku* make a bed
敷石 *shikiishi* paving stone, pavement
敷地 *shikichi* (building) site, (plot of) ground, lot
屋敷 *yashiki* [sometimes also 邸] mansion, residence; residential lot
陣を敷く *jin o shiku* take up a position, encamp
② promulgate
法令を敷く *hōrei o shiku* promulgate a law
③ [in compounds] make a deposit
敷金 *shikikin* deposit money

【-shi(ki) -敷き】
① [also suffix] underlay, mat
下敷き *shitajiki* underlay; being buried; model

土瓶敷き *dobinshiki* teapot mat [rest], tea cloth
② bed, foundation
板敷き *itajiki* wooden floor

SPECIAL READINGS

桟敷 *sajiki* reviewing stand, box, gallery

SYNONYMS

● **equip and install**
架 LAY ACROSS → 2569
据える INSTALL → 497
装 FIT OUT → 2685
設 SET UP → 1471
備 PROVIDE → 146

【shiku】
①ⓐ **spread**
布 SPREAD → 2973
舗 PAVE → 1735
塗 APPLY ON A SURFACE → 2841
抹 wipe over → 313
散 SCATTER → 1702

【-shiki】
① **mats**
薦 straw mat → 2373
畳 TATAMI → 2592

HOMOPHONES

yashiki ⇨ 邸 1131 屋敷 3098, 1870

NOTE

⇨ see USAGE note at 邸 1131

11-4 専 敷 1871
▶LAY
nonstandard for 敷 1870

11-4 婁 數 1872
▶NUMBER
nonstandard for 数 1790

11-4 區 毆 1873
▶BEAT
nonstandard for 殴 886

11-4 區  歐 1874
▶EUROPE
nonstandard for 欧 887

11-4 虚 戲 戲 戯 戏 1875
GI GE▲ tawamu(reru)

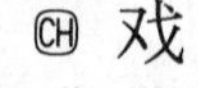
CH 戏 xì

Radical	Strokes
戈 62	15-4-11
Grade	**Freq**
Jōyō	1531
1-11-4	

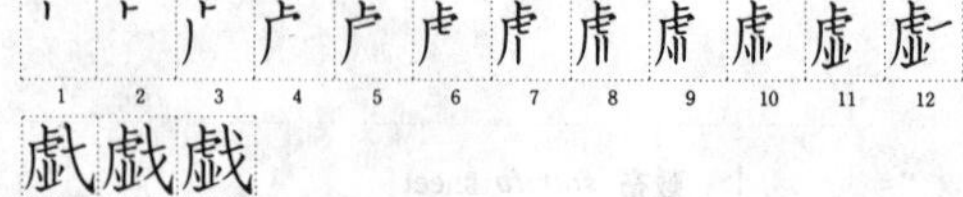

▶SPORT

COMPOUNDS

❶ⓐ **sport, frolic, play**
ⓑ sport, fun, play, jest, joke
ⓒ play with (a woman), dally, flirt
遊戯 *yūgi* game, pastime, amusement
嬉戯する *kigi suru* frisk, frolic
児戯 *jigi* child's play, kid stuff
球戯 *kyūgi* ball game
前戯 *zengi* foreplay
❷ sportive, frolicsome, humorous
戯評 *gihyō* humorous [sarcastic] comments, cartoon, caricature
戯画 *giga* cartoon, comics
戯文 *gibun* nonsense literature, burlesque, literary parody
戯作者 *gesakusha* fiction writer, author of popular stories
❸ theatrical play, performance, drama
戯曲 *gikyoku* drama, play

KUN

【tawamu(reru) 戯れる】 sport, play, frolic; joke, jest; dally, flirt
戯れ *tawamure* play, sport, fun, caprice; joke, jest; flirtation
子猫がボールに戯れている *Koneko ga bōru ni tawamurete iru* The kitten is playing with a ball

女と戯れる *onna to tawamureru* flirt with a woman

SPECIAL READINGS

悪戯▲ *itazura* mischief, prank, practical joke

SYNONYMS

❶ⓐ & ❶ⓒ **play**

遊 PLAY → 3142

❷ **comic**

漫 COMIC → 700

USAGE

itazura

悪戯

mischief, prank, practical joke

徒

uselessness, idleness

HOMOPHONES

itazura ⇨ 悪戯 2745, 1875 徒 416

鮎 鮎 鮎

1876 DEN NEN ayu

CH 鮎 nián

Radical	Strokes
魚 195	16-11-5
Grade	**Freq**
Names	2085
◧ 1 - 1 1 - 5	

11-5 魚

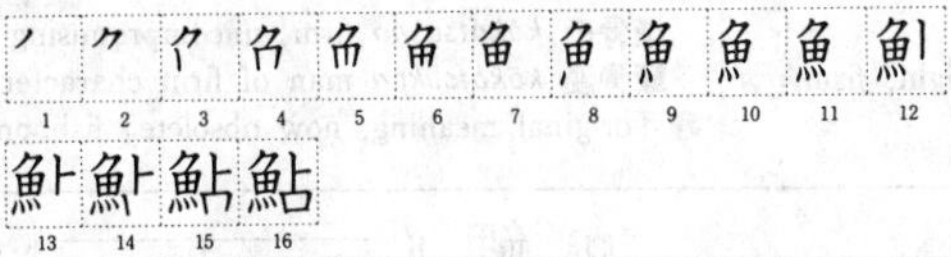

Stroke order: 1 2 3 4 5 6 7 8 9 10 11 12 13 14 15 16

▶**AYU**

KUN

【**ayu 鮎**】 ayu, sweetfish

鮎並 *ainame* rock trout

稚鮎 *chiayu* young ayu

NAMES

鮎川 *ayukawa* surname

SYNONYMS

【**ayu**】

○ **fishes**

鯉 CARP → 1879

鯛 TAI → 1881

鮮 鮮 鮮

1877 SEN aza(yaka)

CH 鮮 xiān xiǎn

Radical	Strokes
魚 195	17-11-6
Grade	**Freq**
Jōyō	801
◧ 1 - 1 1 - 6	

11-6 魚

Stroke order: 1 2 3 4 5 6 7 8 9 10 11 12 13 14 15 16 17

▶**FRESH** ▶**VIVID**

COMPOUNDS

❶ **fresh**

鮮魚 *sengyo* fresh fish

鮮度 *sendo* (degree of) freshness

新鮮な *shinsen na* fresh

生鮮な *seisen na* fresh

❷ⓐ **vivid, brilliant, clean**

ⓑ (of colors) **vivid, brightly-colored**

鮮麗な *senrei na* vivid, gorgeous

鮮烈な *senretsu na* glaringly vivid, striking

鮮明な *senmei na* vivid, clear

鮮紅 *senkō* scarlet, bright red

❸ **Korea**

朝鮮 *chōsen* (North) Korea

南鮮 *nansen* South Korea

北鮮 *hokusen* North Korea

❹ little, few

鮮少な *senshō na* very little

KUN

【**aza(yaka) 鮮やか**】

azayaka na 鮮やかな vivid, clear; (of colors) vivid, bright; neat, graceful

鮮やかさ *azayakasa* vividness, brightness

鮮やかな飛行振り *azayaka na hikōburi* skillful piloting

SYNONYMS

❶ **new**

生 raw → 3497

新 NEW → 1784

❷ⓐ **evident**

明 CLEAR → 855

亮 LUCID → 2071

顕 MANIFEST → 1806

ⓑ **vivid**

明 BRIGHT → 855

❸ **Korea**
朝 North Korea → 1695
韓 SOUTH KOREA → 1757
❸ **Asian countries**
日 JAPAN → 3027
華 CHINA → 2283
泰 Thailand → 2583
越 Vietnam → 3314
印 India → 828
比 Philippines → 26

11-7 魚

鯁
1878 KŌ

CH 鯁 gěng

Radical	Strokes
魚 195	18-11-7
Grade	Freq
Reference	
1-11-7	

COMPOUNDS
❶ [now replaced by 硬 1183] upright, firm, staunch, unyielding
鯁骨の *kōkotsu no* firm, uncompromising
鯁骨漢 *kōkotsukan* man of firm character
❷ [original meaning, now obsolete] fishbone

11-7 魚

鯉 鯉 鯉
1879 RI koi

CH 鲤 lǐ

Radical	Strokes
魚 195	18-11-7
Grade	Freq
Names	2045
1-11-7	

▶**CARP**
COMPOUNDS
● [original meaning] **carp**
養鯉 *yōri* [rare] carp breeding
KUN
【koi 鯉】carp
鯉幟 *koinobori* carp streamer
錦鯉 *nishikigoi* colored carp
NAMES
鯉三郎 *koisaburō* male name
鯉沼 *koinuma* surname
SYNONYMS
● **fishes**
鮎 AYU → 1876
鯛 TAI → 1881

11-7 隹

観 觀 観 観
1880 KAN mi(ru)▲

CH 观 guān guàn

Radical	Strokes
見 147	18-7-11
Grade	Freq
Jōyō-4	450
1-11-7	

▶**VIEW**
COMPOUNDS
❶ [original meaning] **view, behold, look; observe, inspect**
観光 *kankō* sightseeing
観客 *kankyaku* audience, spectators
観劇 *kangeki* theatergoing
観察 *kansatsu* observation, supervision
観賞 *kanshō* admiration, enjoyment
傍観する *bōkan suru* look on, sit as a spectator
楽観 *rakkan* optimism, hopeful view
❷ⓐ **view, spectacle, sight**
ⓑ appearance, look, condition
景観 *keikan* scene, spectacle, view, sight
美観 *bikan* fine view, beautiful sight
壮観 *sōkan* grand sight, magnificent view

外観 *gaikan* external appearance, outward show

❸ [also suffix] **view, conception, outlook, theory**

観点 *kanten* point of view

観念 *kannen* idea, conception, notion

主観 *shukan* subjectivity; subject

先入観 *sennyūkan* preconception, bias, prejudice

人生観 *jinseikan* one's view [theory] of life, outlook on life

世界観 *sekaikan* world view, outlook on the world

❹ Taoist temple

道観 *dōkan* Taoist temple

❺ [rare] watchtower, turret

楼観 *rōkan* watchtower

❻ unclassified compounds

観音 *kannon Avalokiteśvara*, Buddhist Goddess of Mercy

INDEPENDENT

【**kan 観**】appearance, look, condition; Taoist temple

...の観が有る *...no kan ga aru* appear, look like

【**kanjiru** (=**kanzuru**) **観じる(=観ずる)**】grasp the truth after thinking it over

KUN

【**mi(ru) 観る**】[usu. 見る] view (flowers), watch (a movie), see, observe, appreciate

花を観る *hana o miru* view (cherry) blossoms

SYNONYMS

❶ **see and look**

見 SEE → 2544

視 REGARD → 972

覧 LOOK OVER → 2854

看 WATCH → 3220

察 INSPECT → 2347

目 look → 3043

眺 LOOK OUT OVER → 1171

望 LOOK AFAR → 2742

仰 LOOK UP → 48

顧 LOOK BACK → 1900

❷ⓐ **view**

景 SCENE → 2470

風 (beautiful) scenery → 3007

光 scenery → 2391

❸ **opinion**

見 view (personal opinion) → 2544

説 opinion → 1547

論 opinion → 1574

HOMOPHONES

miru ⇨ 見 2544 看 3220 診 1504

NOTE

⇨ see USAGE note at 見 2544

闘 incorrect classification ⇨ see 3334 11-7 門

鯛 鯛 鯛 鯛 11-8 魚

1881 CHŌ tai

CH 鯛 diāo

Radical	Strokes
魚 195	19-11-8
Grade	**Freq**
Names	2048
◧ 1-11-8	

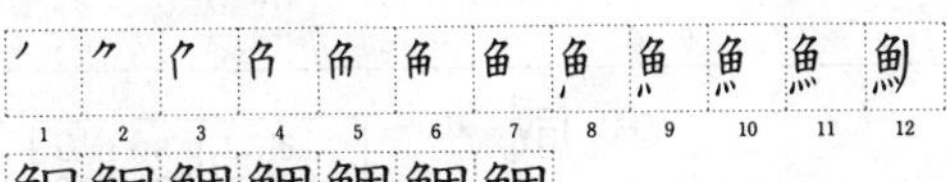

▶**TAI**

KUN

【**tai 鯛**】tai, sea bream, porgy

鯛飯 *taimeshi* rice and minced tai

鯛焼き *taiyaki* fish-shaped pancake filled with bean jam

真鯛 *madai* red tai, red sea bream

NAMES

鯛ノ浦 *tainoura* place name

鯛二 *taiji* male name

SYNONYMS

【**tai**】

○ **fishes**

鯉 CARP → 1879

鮎 AYU → 1876

11-8 魚

鯨

1882 GEI kujira

CH 鲸 jīng

Radical	Strokes
魚 195	19-11-8
Grade	Freq
Jōyō	1694
1-11-8	

▶**WHALE**

COMPOUNDS

ⓐ [original meaning] **whale**

ⓑ huge like a whale

鯨肉 *geiniku* whale meat

鯨油 *geiyu* whale oil

鯨骨 *geikotsu* whale bone

巨鯨 *kyogei* huge whale

捕鯨 *hogei* whaling

鯨飲馬食する *geiin-bashoku suru* drink like a fish and eat like a horse, eat mountains of food and drink oceans of liquor

鯨波 *geiha* huge waves; battle cry

KUN

【**kujira** 鯨】 whale

鯨幕 *kujiramaku* black and white curtain (spread at a funeral service)

鯨座 *kujiraza* the Whale, Cetus

鯨尺 *kujirajaku* long foot

抹香鯨 *makkōkujira* sperm whale

白長須鯨 *shironagasukujira* blue whale

SYNONYMS

ⓐ **undomesticated mammals**

猿 MONKEY → 669

鹿 DEER → 3126

猪 WILD BOAR → 536

象 ELEPHANT → 2134

熊 BEAR → 2848

虎 TIGER → 3212

11-8 魚

鯛

1883

▶**TAI**

nonstandard for 鯛 1881

11-8 离

離

incorrect stroke count ⇨ see 1836

11-8 莫

難

1884

▶**DIFFICULT** ▶**DISASTER**

nonstandard for 難 1838

11-9 鹵

鹹

1885 KAN kara(i)

CH 咸 xián

Radical	Strokes
鹵 197	20-11-9
Grade	Freq
Reference	
1-11-9	

COMPOUNDS

● [now usu. 辛い *karai*] [original meaning] salty, briny, saline

鹹水湖 *kansuiko* saltwater lake

海の水は鹹い *Umi no mizu wa karai* Sea water tastes salty

HOMOPHONES

karai ⇨ 辛 2038

NOTE

⇨ see USAGE note at 辛 2038

亂 1886 **▶DISORDERED**
nonstandard for 乱 1260 — 12-1 亂

鄭 incorrect stroke count ⇨ see 1888 — 12-2 奠

粼 incorrect stroke count ⇨ see 1890 (nonstandard for 隣 781) — 12-2 粦

劃 1887 KAKU

Ⓒ 划 huà huá huai

Radical	Strokes
刂 18	14-2-12
Grade	**Freq**
Reference	
1-12-2	

12-2 畫

COMPOUNDS

[now replaced by 画 3000]

❶ [original meaning] mark off, draw a line, demarcate, partition
劃期的 *kakkiteki* epoch-making, epochal
劃一化 *kakuitsuka* standardization
劃定する *kakutei suru* demarcate
劃然と *kakuzen to* distinctly, clearly
区劃 *kukaku* division, section; boundary
劃する *kakusuru* mark off; plan

❷ draw up a plan, plan, design
劃策する *kakusaku suru* plan, scheme
企劃 *kikaku* plan, project

鄭 1888 TEI JŌ

Ⓒ 郑 zhèng

Radical	Strokes
阝 163	15-3-12
Grade	**Freq**
Reference	
1-12-3	

12-3 奠

COMPOUNDS

❶ [now replaced by 丁 *tei* 3348] courteous
鄭重な *teichō na* polite, courteous

❷ [rare]
ⓐ Chinese family name: Zheng
ⓑ name of a state in ancient China: Zheng
鄭箋 *teisen* commentary on the Book of Odes by Zheng Xuan
鄭声 *teisei* (decadent) music of the state of Zheng

影 1889 EI kage

Ⓒ 影 yǐng

Radical	Strokes
彡 59	15-3-12
Grade	**Freq**
Jōyō	594
1-12-3	

12-3 景

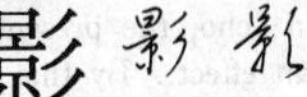

1 2 3 4 5 6 7 8 9 10 11 12 13 14 15

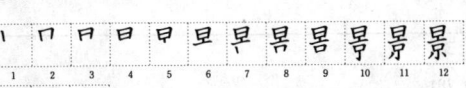

▶SHADOW

COMPOUNDS

❶ⓐ [formerly also 翳 2874] [original meaning] (partial darkness) **shadow, silhouette**

ⓑ (reflected image) **shadow, image, reflec-**

tion
影響 *eikyō* influence, effect
暗影 *an'ei* shadow, gloom
陰影 *in'ei* shadow
影像 *eizō* image; shadow, phantom
人影 *jin'ei* human figure; shadow of a person
投影 *tōei* cast shadow; projection
倒影 *tōei* inverted image
撮影 *satsuei* photographing, shooting (of a movie)
❷ⓐ (faint indication) shadow (of), traces (of), signs (of)
ⓑ (apparition) shadow, phantom, vision
機影 *kiei* sight [signs] of an airplane
船影 *sen'ei* signs of a ship
幻影 *gen'ei* vision, phantom, illusion
❸ light
月影 *getsuei* (=*tsukikage*) moonlight; moon
灯影 *tōei* (=*hokage*) firelight in the dark; shadows by the firelight
❹ picture, portrait
近影 *kin'ei* one's recent photograph

KUN

【kage 影】
①ⓐ (partial darkness) shadow, silhouette
ⓑ (reflected image) shadow, image, reflection
淡い影 *awai kage* light shadow
影武者 *kagemusha* dummy general, general's double
影を映す *kage o utsusu* mirror the image (of)
②ⓐ (faint indication) shadow (of), traces (of), signs (of)
ⓑ [in compounds] figure, appearance
影も形も無い *kage mo katachi mo nai* nowhere to be seen
面影 *omokage* face; traces
人影 *hitokage* human figure; shadow of a person
③ [in compounds] light
日影 *hikage* sunshine; shadow
火影(=灯影) *hokage* shadows from firelight
月影 *tsukikage* moonlight; moonshine

SYNONYMS

❶ⓐ shadow
陰 SHADE → 541
ⓑ image
像 IMAGE → 166

USAGE

❶ kage
影
①ⓐ (partial darkness) shadow, silhouette
ⓑ (reflected image) shadow, image, reflection
②ⓐ (faint indication) shadow (of), traces (of), signs (of)
ⓑ [in compounds] figure, appearance
③ [in compounds] light
陰
① [formerly also 蔭] shade
② [formerly also 蔭]
ⓐ back side, reverse side
ⓑ behind the scenes
③ [also 蔭] [in the form of お陰 *okage*] grace, favor
蔭
① [also 陰] [in the form of お蔭 *okage*] grace, favor
② [now usu. 陰] shade
③ [now usu. 陰]
ⓐ back side, reverse side
ⓑ behind the scenes

★Though 影 has the basic meaning of shadow, in compounds it is used in the more or less the opposite sense, i.e., light. 陰 specifically refers to shade; it also signifies the reverse side of something, or, figuratively, behind the scenes.

❷ hikage
日影
① sunshine
② shadow
日陰
the shade

HOMOPHONES

kage ⇨ 陰 541　蔭 2517

COMPOUND FORMATION

影響 *eikyō*
影響 'influence, effect' consists of 影 ❶ⓐ 'shadow' and 響 'echo'. "Just as the presence of a shape casts a shadow and the presence of a sound produces an echo, the presence of a cause must lead to an effect." By this strange logic, 影響 came to mean influence.

12-3
粦

1890

▶NEIGHBOR
nonstandard for 隣 781

12-4
黒

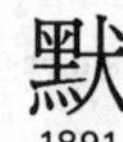
1891

▶SILENT
nonstandard for 黙 2865

獸 獸 獸 獸 ㊥ 兽 shòu

1892 JŪ kemono kedamono▲

Radical	Strokes
犬 94	16-4-12
Grade	**Freq**
Jōyō	1542
1-12-4	

12-4 兽

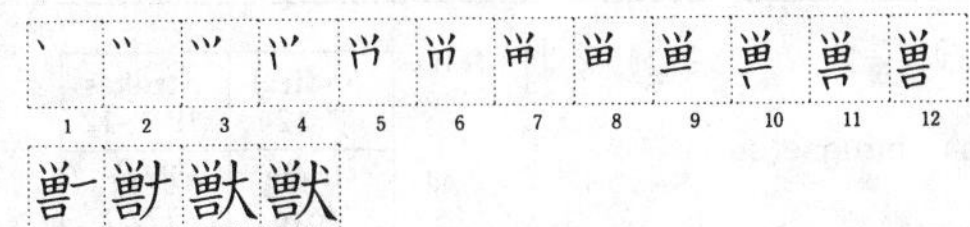

1 2 3 4 5 6 7 8 9 10 11 12 13 14 15 16

▶BEAST

COMPOUNDS

ⓐ [original meaning] **beast, animal**

ⓑ bestial, brutal

獸医 *jūi* veterinarian
野獸 *yajū* wild animal, wild game
猛獸 *mōjū* fierce [savage] animal [beast]
怪獸 *kaijū* monster; beast
珍獸 *chinjū* rare animal
獸心 *jūshin* brutal heart

INDEPENDENT

【**jū 獸**】beast; brute

KUN

【**kemono 獸**】beast; brute
獸道 *kemonomichi* animal trail
獸偏 *kemonohen* *kemonohen*, 'dog' radical (犭)

【**kedamono 獸**】beast; brute

SYNONYMS

ⓐ **animal**
畜 LIVESTOCK → 2096
生 LIFE → 3497
物 living thing → 874

戰

1893

▶WAR

nonstandard for 戦 1787

12-4 單

點

1894

▶POINT

nonstandard for 点 2084

12-5 黑

齡 齡 齢◇ 令◇ 令◇ 齡 齡 ㊥ 龄 líng

1895 REI yowai▲ toshi▲

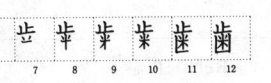

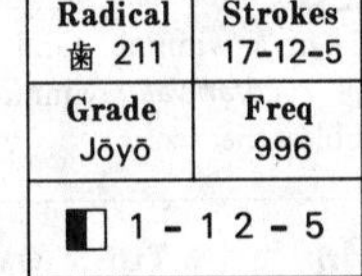

Radical	Strokes
歯 211	17-12-5
Grade	**Freq**
Jōyō	996
1-12-5	

12-5 歯

1 2 3 4 5 6 7 8 9 10 11 12 13 14 15 16 17

▶AGE

COMPOUNDS

● [also 令 1995] **age, years**

年齡 *nenrei* age, years
樹齡 *jurei* age of a tree
高齡 *kōrei* advanced age
老齡 *rōrei* old age
学齡 *gakurei* school age
月齡 *getsurei* moon's age

KUN

【**yowai 齡**】age
七十の齡を重ねる *nanajū no yowai o kasaneru* live to be 70 years old

【**toshi 齡**】[usu. 年] one's years, age

SYNONYMS

● **age**
令 age → 1995
年 years → 2035
才 AGE SUFFIX → 3410
歳 AGE SUFFIX → 2490
寿 life span → 3557

HOMOPHONES

toshi ⇨ 年 2035 歳 2490

NOTE

⇨ see USAGE note at 年 2035

★Though 齡 and 令 are distinct characters, the latter is also used as an abbreviated form of the former.

12-5 齒

齡 1896

▶**AGE**
nonstandard for 齢 1895

12-6 番

翻 翻 飜◇ 翻 翻 1897

Ⓒ 翻 fān

HON FAN▲ hirugae(ru) hirugae(su)

Radical	Strokes
羽 124	18-6-12
Grade	**Freq**
Jōyō	1720
1-12-6	

▶**TURN OVER** ▶**RENDER**

COMPOUNDS

❶ⓐ **turn over, reverse**
ⓑ turn (a person) round one's little finger, make sport of
翻倒する *hontō suru* [rare] turn upside-down
翻意する *hon'i suru* change one's mind
翻然と *honzen to* suddenly
翻弄する *honrō suru* toss (a ship) about; trifle with, make fun of

❷ⓐ **render (written texts) in another form, translate, adapt, transcribe**
ⓑ remake, reproduce
翻訳する *hon'yaku suru* translate, render
翻字 *honji* transliteration
翻案 *hon'an* adaptation
翻刻 *honkoku* reprint

❸ [original meaning] flutter, wave, fly
翩翻たる *henpontaru* fluttering, waving

❹ grade of a winning hand in mahjong
二翻役 *ryanfan'yaku* winning hand which redoubles the score

KUN

【**hirugae(ru)** 翻る】*vi* turn over; wave, flutter
翻って考えると *hirugaette kangaeru to* on (further) reflection, on second thought
風に翻る *kaze ni hirugaeru* flutter [wave] in the wind

【**hirugae(su)** 翻す】*vt* change (one's mind), reverse (a decision); wave, flutter; dodge
前説を翻す *zensetsu o hirugaesu* change one's former opinion
身を翻す *mi o hirugaesu* dodge, turn aside adroitly

SYNONYMS

❶ⓐ **overturn**
覆 OVERTURN → 2726
反 turn over → 2945
転 turn [roll] over → 1480
倒 TOPPLE → 124

❷ⓐ **translate**
訳 TRANSLATE → 1473

12-6 番

飜 1898

▶**TURN OVER** ▶**RENDER**
nonstandard for 翻 1897

12-7 辛

辭 1899

▶**WORD** ▶**RESIGN**
nonstandard for 辞 1364

顧 顧 顧 顧 Ⓒ 顾 gù

1900 KO kaeri(miru)

Radical	Strokes
頁 181	21-9-12
Grade	**Freq**
Jōyō	1328
◧ 1-12-9	

12-9 雇

一 ㇇ ⺕ 戸 戸 戸 戸 戸 戸 屏 雇 雇 雇 雇 雇 雇 顧 顧 顧 顧 顧

1 2 3 4 5 6 7 8 9 10 11 12 13 14 15 16 17 18 19 20 21

▶LOOK BACK

COMPOUNDS

❶ⓐ [original meaning] **look back, turn around**

ⓑ **look back upon (the past), retrospect**

顧問 *komon* adviser, consultant

一顧もしない *ikko mo shinai* take no notice of, not give a damn

右顧左眄する *ukosaben suru* look to the right and left, hesitate

後顧 *kōko* looking back, worry

回顧する *kaiko suru* look back on, retrospect

❷ have regard for, be concerned about

顧慮する *koryo suru* have regard, take into consideration

❸ **show favor to, patronize, take care of**

顧客 *kokyaku* customer, patron, client

恩顧 *onko* favors, patronage

愛顧 *aiko* patronage, favor

KUN

【kaeri(miru) 顧みる】

①ⓐ look back, turn around

ⓑ look back upon the past, review, retrospect

顧みて他を言う *kaerimite ta o iu* give an evasive answer

昔を顧みる *mukashi o kaerimiru* look back upon the past

② have regard for, consider

家庭を顧みない *katei o kaeriminai* think little of one's family

SYNONYMS

❶ⓐ **see and look**

仰 LOOK UP → 48

望 LOOK AFAR → 2742

眺 LOOK OUT OVER → 1171

覧 LOOK OVER → 2854

視 REGARD → 972

看 WATCH → 3220

察 INSPECT → 2347

観 VIEW → 1880

見 SEE → 2544

目 look → 3043

ⓑ **remember**

追 reminisce → 3096

憶 REMEMBER → 765

覚える COMMIT TO MEMORY → 2604

記 commit to memory → 1453

USAGE

kaerimiru

顧みる

①ⓐ look back, turn around

ⓑ look back upon the past, review, retrospect

② have regard for, consider

省みる

introspect, examine oneself, reflect upon oneself

HOMOPHONES

kaerimiru ⇨ 省 2449

COMPOUND FORMATION

顧問 *komon*

顧問 'adviser, consultant' originally referred to the emperor turning to (顧 ❶ⓐ) his subjects to ask (問) for advice.

1901

▶LOOK BACK

nonstandard for 顧 1900

12-9 雇

1902

▶TURN OVER ▶RENDER

nonstandard for 翻 1897

12-9 番

13-2 劍

劍 1903

▶**SWORD**
nonstandard for 剣 1672

13-2 豦

劇 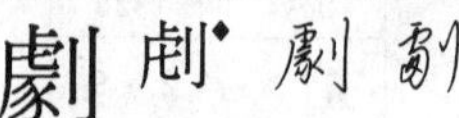 Ⓒⓗ 剧 jù

1904 GEKI

Radical	Strokes
刂 18	15-2-13
Grade	**Freq**
Jōyō-6	581
1-13-2	

▶**DRAMA**

COMPOUNDS

❶ⓐ [also suffix] **drama, play, theatrical performance**
ⓑ abbrev. of 劇場 *gekijō*: theater
劇場 *gekijō* theater
劇団 *gekidan* dramatic company, theatrical troupe
劇映画 *gekieiga* film drama
劇的な *gekiteki na* dramatic
演劇 *engeki* drama, play
歌劇 *kageki* opera
喜劇 *kigeki* comedy
悲劇 *higeki* tragedy, tragic drama
時代劇 *jidaigeki* period adventure drama, period film
帝劇 *teigeki* The Imperial Theater

❷ [usu. 激 776] [original meaning] intense, severe
劇薬 *gekiyaku* powerful medicine
劇痛(＝激痛) *gekitsū* violent [intense] pain
劇変(＝激変) *gekihen* sudden change, upheaval

❸ busy
劇務(＝激務) *gekimu* busy [hard] work, severe duty

INDEPENDENT

【**geki 劇**】drama, play, theatrical performance
劇を演じる *geki o enjiru* perform a play

SYNONYMS

❶ⓐ **performance**
演 performance → 697
芸 entertainment → 2209

13-3 僉

劒 1905

▶**SWORD**
nonstandard for 剣 1672

13-3 僉

劔 1906

▶**SWORD**
nonstandard for 剣 1672

13-4 虚

戱 1907

▶**SPORT**
nonstandard for 戯 1875

艶 艷 豔 豓 1908

EN tsuya nama(mekashii) ade(yaka) NAMES moro yoshi

Ⓒ 艳 yàn

Radical	Strokes
色 139	19-6-13
Grade	Freq
Names	2050
1-13-6	

13-6 豊

1 2 3 4 5 6 7 8 9 10 11 12 13 14 15 16 17 18 19

▶CHARMING ▶ROMANCE

COMPOUNDS

❶ [original meaning] **charming, beautiful, fascinating, voluptuous**

艶容 *en'yō* fascinating figure, charming look
艶美 *enbi* beauty, charm
濃艶な *nōen na* charming, bewitching, enchanting
妖艶な *yōen na* fascinating, voluptuous

❷ **romance, love, love affair**

艶聞 *enbun* love affair, romance, one's love story
艶書 *ensho* love letter
艶福 *enpuku* good fortune in love

INDEPENDENT

【en 艶】 charming beauty
艶な *en na* charming, fascinating, voluptuous

KUN

【tsuya 艶】

① gloss, luster, glaze
艶艶した *tsuyatsuya shita* glossy, bright
艶消し *tsuyakeshi* grinding, frosting; disillusionment

② charm, color
艶の有る声 *tsuya no aru koe* charming voice

③ [in compounds] love, romance
艶っぽい *tsuyappoi* romantic, spicy, coquettish
艶事 *tsuyagoto* love affair, romance

【nama(mekashii) 艶めかしい】 charming, fascinating; coquettish, voluptuous
艶めかしい姿 *namamekashii sugata* bewitching figure
艶めかしい目付きで *namamekashii metsuki de* with coquettish eyes

【ade(yaka) 艶やか】

adeyaka na 艶やかな charming, fascinating, fair
艶姿 *adesugata* charming figure

NAMES

艶子 *tsuyako* female name

SYNONYMS

❶ **beautiful**

麗 OF GRACEFUL BEAUTY → 2151
美 BEAUTIFUL → 2264
佳 FINE → 86
瑶 EXQUISITE → 1026
妙 of marvelous beauty → 239
華 MAGNIFICENT → 2283
絢 GORGEOUS → 1347
斐 florid → 2776

❷ **love**

恋 LOVE (for the opposite sex) → 2098
情 love → 482
愛 LOVE → 2492

【tsuya】

① **luster**

沢 luster → 267

劑 1909

▶PREPARATION

nonstandard for 剤 1669

14-2 齊

叡 1910

EI

Ⓒ 叡 ruì

Radical	Strokes
又 29	16-2-14
Grade	Freq
Reference	
1-14-2	

14-2 睿

COMPOUNDS

❶ [now usu. 英 2238] [original meaning] far-sighted, wise

叡智 *eichi* sagacity, wisdom

❷ Emperor, Imperial

叡覧 *eiran* [archaic] Emperor's personal in-

spection
叡慮 *eiryo* [archaic] Emperor's mind

叡聞に達する *eibun ni tassuru* reach the Emperor's ears

14-2 熏

勳
1911

▶**MERITORIOUS SERVICE**
nonstandard for 勲 2869

14-4 㡭

斷
1912

▶**CUT OFF** ▶**RESOLVE**
nonstandard for 断 1492

14-9 㬎

顯
1913

▶**MANIFEST**
nonstandard for 顕 1806

15-2 厲

勵
1914

▶**ENCOURAGE**
nonstandard for 励 1119

15-4 嘼

獸
1915

▶**BEAST**
nonstandard for 獣 1892

15-5 齒

齡
1916

▶**AGE**
nonstandard for 齢 1895

16-4 鬳

獻
1917

▶**OFFER**
nonstandard for 献 1785

18-2 雚

勸
1918

▶**URGE**
nonstandard for 勧 1857

18-4 雚

歡
1919

▶**JOYOUS**
nonstandard for 歓 1867

18-6 豐

艷
1920

▶**CHARMING** ▶**ROMANCE**
nonstandard for 艶 1908

18-7 雚

觀
1921

▶**VIEW**
nonstandard for 観 1880

UP–DOWN

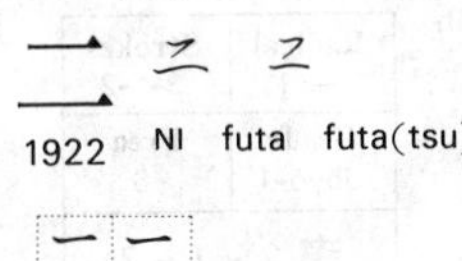

1922 NI futa futa(tsu)

Ⓒⓗ 二 èr

Radical	Strokes
二 7	2-2-0
Grade	Freq
Jōyō-1	4
▀ 2 - 1 - 1	

1-1 一

RADICAL 7

Standard form: 二 *ni* 'two' (五 互 井)

Description: used for character classification

▶**TWO**

COMPOUNDS

❶ⓐ [original meaning] **two, second**

ⓑ two times, twice

ⓒ divide in two

二百 *nihyaku* 200

二月 *nigatsu* February

二次 *niji* second, secondary

二塁 *nirui* second base

二番目 *nibanme* second

二度 *nido* two times [degrees]

二分する *nibun suru* halve, bisect

❷ *baseball* second base, second baseman

二遊間 *niyūkan* between second baseman and shortstop

❸ rank with, equal

無二の *muni no* peerless

INDEPENDENT

【ni 二】 two, second

KUN

【futa 二】 [in compounds] two

二言 *futakoto* two words; repetition

二人 *futari* two persons

二心 *futagokoro* (=*nishin*) duplicity, double dealing; divided loyalty

【futa(tsu) 二つ】 two; two years old

二つ目 *futatsume* second

SPECIAL READINGS

十重二十重 *toehatae* manyfold, multitude

二十歳(=二十) *hatachi* 20 years old

二十日 *hatsuka* 20 days; 20th of the month

二日 *futsuka* two days; 2nd of the month

SYNONYMS

❶ⓐ **two**

弐 TWO (in legal documents) → 3195

双 SET OF TWO → 25

対 pair → 831

偶 COUPLE → 132

両 BOTH → 3518

ⓐ **small numbers**

一 ONE → 3341

三 THREE → 1924

四 FOUR → 3044

五 FIVE → 3436

六 SIX → 1965

七 SEVEN → 3362

八 EIGHT → 3

九 NINE → 3369

十 TEN → 3365

USAGE

futa

二

[in compounds] two

双

[in compounds] set of two, pair

HOMOPHONES

futa ⇨ 双 25

1-1 ⺀

冫 1923

Radical	Strokes
冫 15	2-2-0
Grade	**Freq**
Radical	
2 - 1 - 1	

RADICAL 15
Standard form: 冫 *nisui* 'ice' (冷 冴 凍)
Description: used in characters related to freezing or cold

1-1 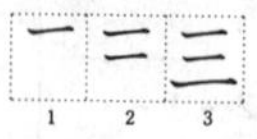 incorrect stroke count ⇨ see 1926

1-2 一 三 ⺄ ⺄

1924 SAN mi mi(tsu) mit(tsu)

Ⓒⓗ 三 sān

Radical	Strokes
一 1	3-1-2
Grade	**Freq**
Jōyō-1	6
2 - 1 - 2	

▶**THREE**

COMPOUNDS

❶ⓐ [original meaning] **three, third**
ⓑ three times
三千 *sanzen* 3000
三角 *sankaku* triangle
三人称 *sanninshō gram* third person
三塁 *sanrui* third base
三分する *sanbun suru* trisect
三脚 *sankyaku* tripod
七五三 *shichigosan* the lucky numbers; gala day for children of three, five and seven
第三 *daisan* third
三回 *sankai* three times

❷ *baseball* third base, third baseman
三本間 *sanponkan* between third and home base

❸ many, several
三拝九拝 *sanpai-kyūhai* kowtowing, bowing repeatedly

INDEPENDENT

【san 三】 three, third

KUN

【mi 三】 [in compounds] three
三日月 *mikazuki* new moon
【mi(tsu) 三つ】 three; three years old
三つ折 *mitsuori* threefold, folded in three
三日 *mikka* three days; 3rd of the month
【mit(tsu) 三つ】 three; three years old

SPECIAL READINGS

三味線 *shamisen* shamisen (Japanese three-stringed musical instrument)

SYNONYMS

❶ⓐ **three**
参 three (in legal documents) → 2066
ⓐ **small numbers**
一 ONE → 3341
二 TWO → 1922
四 FOUR → 3044
五 FIVE → 3436
六 SIX → 1965
七 SEVEN → 3362
八 EIGHT → 3
九 NINE → 3369
十 TEN → 3365

1925

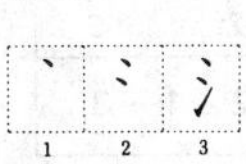

Radical 氵 85	Strokes 3-3-0
Grade Radical	Freq
2 - 1 - 2	

1-2
丶

RADICAL 85
sanzui, variant of 水 *mizu* ‘water’
⇨ see 水 10 for radical description

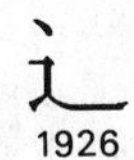
1926

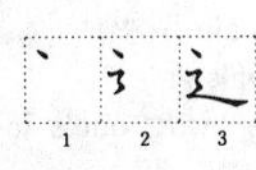

Radical 辶 162	Strokes 3-3-0
Grade Radical	Freq
2 - 1 - 2	

1-2
丶

RADICAL 162
variant of 辵 *shinnyō* or *shinnyū* ‘advance’
⇨ see 辵 1945 for radical description

1927

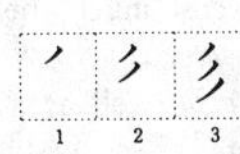

Radical 彡 59	Strokes 3-3-0
Grade Radical	Freq
2 - 1 - 2	

1-2
丿

RADICAL 59
Standard form: 彡 *sanzukuri* ‘decoration’ (形 影 彦)
Description: used in characters related to decorating or brilliance

1928

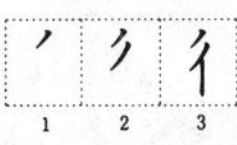

Radical 彳 60	Strokes 3-3-0
Grade Radical	Freq
2 - 1 - 2	

1-2
丿

RADICAL 60
Standard form: 彳 *gyōninben* ‘locomotion’ (後 得 彼)
Description: used in characters related to locomotion or roads

incorrect stroke count ⇨ see 1933

1-2
丿

1-3 元ええ 一

1929 GEN GAN moto

一 二 テ 元
1 2 3 4

Ⓒ 元 yuán

Radical	Strokes
儿 10	4-2-2
Grade	**Freq**
Jōyō-2	356
2 - 1 - 3	

▶ORIGIN

COMPOUNDS

❶ⓐ origin, beginning, original state
ⓑ original, first, basic
ⓒ beginning of a new period, first year of a new era
根元 *kongen* root; base
還元 *kangen* restoration; reduction, deoxidization
元来 *ganrai* originally, primarily, essentially
元祖 *ganso* originator, pioneer
元価(＝原価) *genka* cost price
紀元二千年 *kigen nisennen* year 2000 of the Christian era
中元 *chūgen* midyear gift; July 15th (lunar calendar)
❷ primordial energy of the universe
元気 *genki* vigor, energy; spirits; health
❸ (original amount) principal, capital
元利 *ganri* principal and interest
元金 *gankin* principal, capital
❹ⓐ element, unit, basic element, essence, entity
ⓑ *math* **element, dimension**
元素 *genso* element, chemical element
二元論 *nigenron* dualism
単元制度 *tangen seido* unit credit system
単位元 *tan'igen* unit element
三次元 *sanjigen* three dimensions
❺ *math* unknown quantity
多元方程式 *tagen hōteishiki* plural equation
❻ (Chinese monetary unit) yuan
百元 *hyakugen* 100 yuan
❼ Yuan Dynasty (1271-1368 A.D.) (Chinese dynasty ruled by the Mongols)
元寇 *genkō* the Mongolian Invasions
❽ⓐ [original meaning] head
ⓑ (leading figure) head, leader, chief, eldest
元服 *genpuku* ceremony of attaining manhood
元首 *genshu* ruler, sovereign
元老 *genrō* elder [senior] statesman; senior member

INDEPENDENT

【gen 元】 yuan; Yuan Dynasty; *math* element

KUN

【moto 元】
①ⓐ origin, beginning, genesis
ⓑ [also suffix] place of origin, source
ⓒ one's origin, one's antecedents, one's past
ⓓ (something that brings about a result) origin, cause
元は *moto wa* originally
火の元 *hi no moto* origin of a fire
製造元 *seizōmoto* manufacturer
ガスの元栓を切る *gasu no motosen o kiru* turn the gas off at the main
地元民 *jimotomin* local people
身元(＝身許) *mimoto* one's birth, one's identity, one's background
元を糾す *moto o tadasu* inquire into the origin, go to the bottom of an affair
② [also prefix] former, ex-, one-time, past
元首相 *motoshushō* ex-Prime Minister
元の通り *moto no tōri* as it was before
③ capital, principal; prime cost
元手 *motode* capital, fund
元が掛かる *moto ga kakaru* cost much, be expensive
元を切って売る *moto o kitte uru* sell at a loss, sell under prime cost
④ [formerly also 許] in the vicinity of, near (a person), with (someone), under (someone's roof)
⇨ see 許 1470 for compounds
⑤ [formerly also 素] raw material, base
⇨ see 素 2458 for compounds

SYNONYMS

❶ⓐ beginnings
本 origin → 3502
根 ROOT → 930
源 SOURCE → 656
緒 OUTSET → 1378
序 INTRODUCTORY PART → 3065
端 start → 1221
始 beginning → 281
初 beginning → 1116
❹ element
素 ELEMENT → 2458
単 unit → 2256
❼ later Chinese dynasties
唐 TANG DYNASTY → 3115
明 Ming Dynasty → 855
清 Qing Dynasty → 523
【moto】
② former
旧 FORMER → 14
故 OLD (earlier time) → 1141

前 previous → 2266
先 former → 2394
既 ALREADY → 1166

USAGE

moto

元

①ⓐ origin, beginning, genesis
ⓑ [also suffix] place of origin, source
ⓒ one's origin, one's antecedents, one's past
ⓓ (something that brings about a result) origin, cause
② [also prefix] former, ex-, one-time, past
③ capital, principal; prime cost
④ [formerly also 許] in the vicinity of, near (a person), with (someone), under (someone's roof)
⑤ [formerly also 素] raw material, base

本

① (the most important thing) basis, essential thing, principle
②ⓐ root (of a tree)
ⓑ counter for plants with roots
③ first half of a tanka poem

基

(underlying support) basis, foundation, grounds, authority

下

① lower part, bottom
② [in the form of 下に *moto ni*] (subject to the influence of) under (the supervision of)

許

[now usu. 元] in the vicinity of, near (a person), with (someone), under (someone's roof)

素

[now usu. 元] raw material, base

HOMOPHONES

moto ⇨ 本 3502 基 2673 下 3378 許 1470 素 2458

COMPOUND FORMATION

❶ 元気 *genki*

元気 'vigor, energy; spirits; health' originally referred to the primordial energy (気) of the universe (元 ❷).

❷ 元服 *genpuku*

元服 'ceremony of attaining manhood' originally referred to the ceremonial hat that was donned (服) on the head (元 ❽ⓐ).

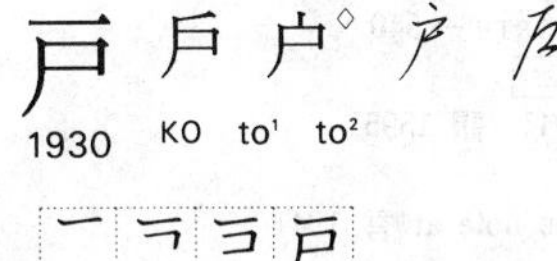

1930 KO to[1] to[2]

Ⓒⓗ 户 hù

Radical	Strokes
戸 63	4-4-0
Grade	**Freq**
Jōyō-2	381
2 - 1 - 3	

1-3

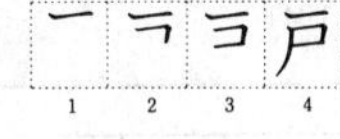

RADICAL 63

variant of 戶 *tobiranoto* 'door'

⇨ see 戶 2950 for radical description

▶**DOOR** ▶**HOUSEHOLD**

COMPOUNDS

❶ [original meaning] **door**

戸外 *kogai* open-air, outdoors
門戸 *monko* door, entrance; school

❷ⓐ (house as a social unit) **household, house, family**

ⓑ **counter for households or houses**

戸別に *kobetsu ni* from house to house
戸戸 *koko* every [each] house
戸籍 *koseki* family register
戸主 *koshu* head of a family, master of a house
戸数 *kosū* number of households [houses]
五戸 *goko* five houses

❸ one's capacity for alcohol

下戸 *geko* nondrinker, poor drinker
泣き上戸 *nakijōgo* maudlin drinker

KUN

[to[1] 戸] door, sliding door; shutter

戸口 *toguchi* door, doorway
雨戸 *amado* shutter
戸袋 *tobukuro* built-in box for shutters
戸締まり *tojimari* fastening the doors

[to[2] 戸] [in compounds] used phonetically for *to*

戸惑う *tomadou* be puzzled, be perplexed
井戸 *ido* (water) well
瀬戸際 *setogiwa* critical moment

SYNONYMS

❶ **doors**

扉 HINGED DOOR → 1955
門 GATE → 888
口 entrance (or exit) → 3382

❷ⓐ **houses**

家 HOUSE → 2273
屋 HOUSE → 3098

軒 house → 1459
宅 DWELLING HOUSE → 2174
居 residence → 3080
邸 STATELY RESIDENCE → 1131
住 housing → 64
ⓑ **counters for houses**
軒 COUNTER FOR HOUSES → 1459
棟 counter for buildings → 991

1-3 一

云 云 云

1931 UN i(u)

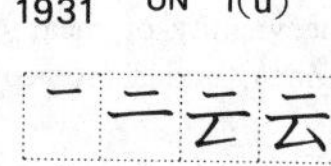

Ⓒ 云 yún

Radical	Strokes
二 7	4-2-2
Grade	**Freq**
Non-Jōyō	1722
2 - 1 - 3	

▶SUCH

COMPOUNDS

❶ **such, so**

云云 *unnun* so and so, such and such, and so forth, etcetera

云云する *unnun suru* say something or other, comment, criticize

云爾 *unji* (=*shika iu*) [archaic] such as

❷ say, speak

云為 *un'i* words and deeds, sayings and doings

KUN

【i(u) 云う】 such, such as, like, of this kind

そう云う物 *sō iu mono* thing such as this

こう云った話 *kō itta hanashi* this kind of story

SYNONYMS

❶ **similar**

如 AS → 207
-通り as → 3109
様 like → 1052
類 similar → 1807

❷ **speak and say**

言 SAY → 1941
話 SPEAK → 1527
口 give mouth to → 3382
申す SPEAK HUMBLY → 3507
弁 SPEAK ELOQUENTLY → 2004
語る TELL → 1543
談 TALK → 1569
述 STATE → 3075
陳 SET FORTH → 540

HOMOPHONES

iu ⇨ 言 1941 謂 1595

NOTE

⇨ see USAGE note at 言 1941

1-3 、

辶

1932

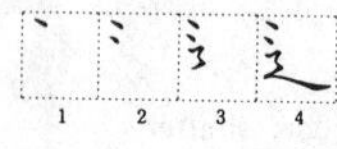

Radical	Strokes
辶 162	4-4-0
Grade	**Freq**
Radical	
2 - 1 - 3	

RADICAL 162

variant of 辵 *shinnyō* or *shinnyū* 'advance'

⇨ see 辵 1945 for radical description

1-3 ノ

乏 乏 乏

1933 BŌ tobo(shii)

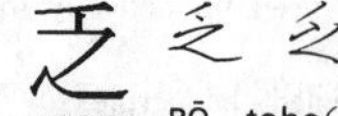

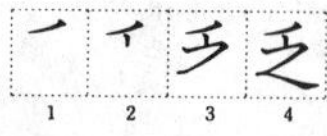

Ⓒ 乏 fá

Radical	Strokes
ノ 4	4-1-3
Grade	**Freq**
Jōyō	1432
2 - 1 - 3	

▶SCANTY

COMPOUNDS

ⓐ (insufficient) **scanty, scarce, lacking, deficient**

ⓑ (lacking in resources) **poor, destitute**

欠乏 *ketsubō* lack, shortage, scarcity
窮乏 *kyūbō* destitution, poverty
貧乏な *binbō na* poor, destitute
耐乏 *taibō* austerity, voluntary privation

KUN

【tobo(shii) 乏しい】 scanty, scarce, meager, short of; poor, destitute

乏しさ *toboshisa* scarcity

乏しくなる *toboshiku naru* run short, get scarce

金が乏しい *kane ga toboshii* be short of money

乏しきを分かつ *toboshiki o wakatsu* share poverty

SYNONYMS

ⓐ **few**

寡 FEW → 2344

少 LITTLE → 3467

薄 meager → 2370

微 SLIGHT → 639

寸 A BIT OF → 2935

ⓑ **poor**

貧 POOR → 2123

窮 destitute → 2358

⺤

1934

Radical ⺤ 87	Strokes 4-4-0
Grade Radical	Freq
2 - 1 - 3	

1-3

RADICAL 87

notsu, variant of 爪 *tsume* 'claw'

⇨ see 爪 3024 for radical description

⺥

1935

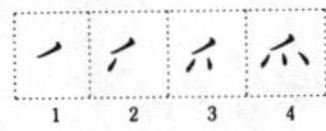

Radical ⺤ 87	Strokes 4-4-0
Grade Radical	Freq
2 - 1 - 3	

1-3

RADICAL 87

tsumekanmuri, variant of 爪 *tsume* 'claw'

⇨ see 爪 3024 for radical description

incorrect classification ⇨ see 3453

1-3

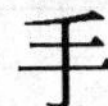

incorrect classification ⇨ see 3456

1-3

1-4
一

示

1936 JI SHI shime(su)

一 二 亍 亓 示
1 2 3 4 5

ⒸⒽ 示 shì

Radical	Strokes
示 113	5-5-0
Grade	**Freq**
Jōyō-5	372
2 - 1 - 4	

RADICAL 113
Standard form: 示 *shimesu* 'deity' (禁 票 祭)
Left variant: 礻 *nehen* or *shimesuhen* (福 神)
Left variant: 示 *shimesuhen* (祀)
Description: used in characters related to deities, worship or religion

▶SHOW

COMPOUNDS

❶ (cause to be seen) **show, display, present**
示圧計 *shiatsukei* pressure gauge
展示 *tenji* display, exhibition
表示する *hyōji suru* indicate, show, express, manifest
標示する *hyōji suru* post up, declare, demonstrate
掲示 *keiji* notice, bulletin
提示する *teiji suru* present, exhibit
告示 *kokuji* notification, bulletin

❷ (point out) **show, indicate, suggest, instruct**
示唆 *shisa* suggestion, hint
示談 *jidan* out-of-court [private] settlement
示威 *jii* show of force
示達 *jitatsu* (=*shitatsu*) instructions, directions
指示 *shiji* instruction; indication
暗示 *anji* hint, suggestion
誇示する *koji suru* make a display of, show off
啓示 *keiji* revelation
訓示 *kunji* instruction
教示 *kyōji* instruction, teaching

KUN

【shime(su) 示す】 (cause to be seen) show, display, present; (point out) show, indicate, suggest, instruct
示し *shimeshi* discipline; revelation
指し示す *sashishimesu* indicate, show, point to
示し合わす *shimeshiawasu* prearrange, conspire (with)

SYNONYMS

❶ **show**
見せる show → 2544
呈 PRESENT → 2189

❷ **indicate**
指 POINT → 378
標 MARK → 1064
宛てる ADDRESS → 2222

NOTE

⇨ see USAGE note at 表 2429

1-4

永

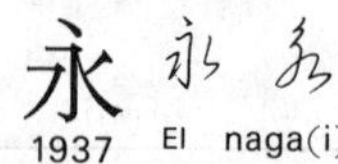

1937 EI naga(i)

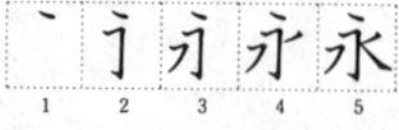

ⒸⒽ 永 yǒng

Radical	Strokes
水 85	5-4-1
Grade	**Freq**
Jōyō-5	770
2 - 1 - 4	

▶ETERNAL

COMPOUNDS

● **eternal, everlasting, permanent, long, perpetual**
永遠 *eien* eternity
永久 *eikyū* permanence, eternity
永住 *eijū* permanent residence
永続する *eizoku suru* last long, remain permanently
永眠 *eimin* eternal sleep, death
永寿 *eiju* long life
永小作 *eikosaku* perpetual land lease

KUN

【naga(i) 永い】 (lasting forever) eternal, everlasting, long
永年 *naganen* many years
末永く *suenagaku* forever
日永 *hinaga* a long day

SYNONYMS

● **of long duration**
久 OF LONG DURATION → 3384

長 LONG → 2556
恒 permanent → 367

HOMOPHONES

nagai ⇨ 長 2556

NOTE

⇨ see USAGE note at 長 2556
★do not confuse with 氷 39

主 主 主 主

1938 SHU SU SHŪ▲ nushi omo aruji▲

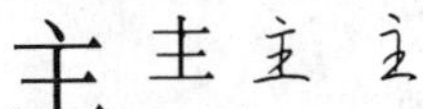

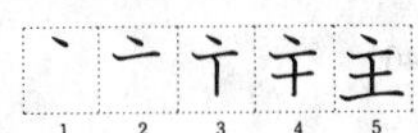

1 2 3 4 5

Ⓒ 主 zhǔ

Radical	Strokes
丶 3	5-1-4
Grade	**Freq**
Jōyō-3	87
2 - 1 - 4	

1-4

▶MAIN ▶MASTER

COMPOUNDS

❶ [also prefix] **main, principal, head, leading, chief**
主要な *shuyō na* main, principal, essential
主義 *shugi* principle, -ism
主力 *shuryoku* main force, main body
主流 *shuryū* main current, mainstream
主演する *shuen suru* play the leading part
主役 *shuyaku* leading part, starring role
主翼 *shuyoku* wing (of an aircraft)
主成分 *shuseibun* principal ingredient, main component

❷ⓐ **be the main performer of a function, preside over, sponsor, officiate**
ⓑ regard as main or central, hold in high regard
主催する *shusai suru* sponsor, promote
主導権 *shudōken* leadership, initiative
主宰する *shusai suru* preside (over), superintend, supervise
主知主義 *shuchishugi* intellectualism
主張する *shuchō suru* insist on, assert, maintain

❸ⓐ [also suffix] **master, lord, chief, host, head, owner, proprietor, employer**
ⓑ **master of the house, head of a family, husband**
ⓒ **master of a religious rite, chief priest; presiding officer, superintendent, manager**
ⓓ **master of a state, ruler**
主人 *shujin* master, head, host, proprietor; husband
主将 *shushō* captain
主従 *shujū* (=*shūjū*) master and servant, lord and vassal
喪主 *moshu* chief mourner
船主 *senshu* shipowner
商店主 *shōtenshu* proprietor of a shop, storekeeper
主客 *shukyaku* host and guest; principal and auxiliary; main guest
主婦 *shufu* housewife
戸主 *koshu* head of a family, master of a house
亭主 *teishu* husband; master, host
主事 *shuji* manager, director, superintendent
主任 *shunin* person in charge, head, chief
坊主 *bōzu* Buddhist priest [monk], bonze; shaven head; sonny, sonny boy, boy
法主 *hossu* (=*hōshu, hosshu*) high priest (of a Buddhist sect)
祭主 *saishu* master of a religious rite
毛沢東主席 *mō takutō-shuseki* Chairman Mao Zedong
自主 *jishu* independence, autonomy
民主主義 *minshushugi* democracy
君主 *kunshu* monarch, sovereign

❹ [also suffix] Lord, our Lord, Jesus Christ
天主 *tenshu* Lord of Heaven, God
救世主 *kyūseishu* the Savior, the Messiah
造物主 *zōbutsushu* Creator, Maker

❺ⓐ subject (opposite of object)
ⓑ *gram* subject
主体 *shutai* main part; subject
主観 *shukan* subjectivity; subject
主題 *shudai* subject, theme
主語 *shugo* subject (word)

INDEPENDENT

【shu 主】
① master, lord, chief; one's lord, ruler
主が主なら家来も家来 *Shu ga shu nara kerai mo kerai* Like master, like man
② Lord, our Lord
万軍の主 *bangun no shu* Lord of hosts
主の祈り *shu no inori* the Lord's Prayer
③ main thing, primary object, first consideration
主たる *shutaru* main, chief, principal
主として *shu to shite* mainly, chiefly
④ subject (opposite of object)

【shū 主】 one's master, one's lord

KUN

【nushi 主】
① [also suffix]
ⓐ owner, proprietor
ⓑ master, chief, head

主の無い傘 *nushi no nai kasa* ownerless umbrella
家主 *yanushi* house owner, landlord, landlady
株主 *kabunushi* stockholder
持ち主 *mochinushi* owner, proprietor
雇い主 *yatoinushi* employer, master
飼い主 *kainushi* pet owner
所帯主 *shotainushi* head of a family, householder

② [also suffix] performer of an action
落とし主 *otoshinushi* owner of a lost article, loser
買い主 *kainushi* buyer, purchaser

③ guardian spirit; great old-timer
会社の主 *kaisha no nushi* great old-timer of the firm

④ *slang* you
御主 *onushi* you

【omo 主】
omo na 主な [sometimes also 重な] chief, principal, main, foremost
主に *omo ni* mainly, chiefly; mostly
主立った *omodatta* principal, leading, chief, main

【aruji 主】 master, landlord; husband, mistress
一家の主 *ikka no aruji* master of the household

SYNONYMS

❶ main
正 chief → 3484
本 head → 3502
親- PARENT → 1799
首 leading → 2265

❸ⓐ leaders
王 KING → 3439
長 CHIEF → 2556
頭 HEAD → 1604
首 LEADER → 2265
領 leader → 1224

ⓑ husband
夫 HUSBAND → 3460

❹ god
神 GOD → 912
帝 the Supreme Being → 2073
天 HEAVEN → 3442

USAGE

omo na
主な
[sometimes also 重な] chief, principal, main, foremost
重な
[usu. 主な] chief, principal, main, foremost

HOMOPHONES

omo ⇨ 重 3573

COMPOUND FORMATION

主張 *shuchō*
主張する 'insist on, assert, maintain' is to have a high regard (主 ❷ⓑ) for one's own opinion and persist (張) in it.

1-4 禾 incorrect classification ⇨ see 3503

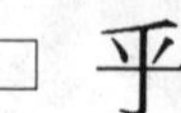
1-4 乎 incorrect classification ⇨ see 3504

1-5 亘 亙 亘 亘 Ⓒⓗ 亘 gèn

1939 KŌ wata(ru) NAMES SEN nobu tōru wataru hisashi

Radical 二 7	Strokes 6-2-4
Grade Names	Freq 2063
2-1-5	

1 2 3 4 5 6

▶EXTEND OVER

COMPOUNDS

● extend over, extend across, extend for, range
亘古 *kōko* [archaic] from ancient times, for ever
連亘 *renkō* [archaic] extending in a row

KUN

【wata(ru) 亘る】 extend over, extend for, range, span, last
幾年にも亘る *ikunen ni mo wataru* extend over so many years
数キロに亘る *sūkiro ni wataru* extend over several kilometers

NAMES

亘 *sen* (=*wataru*) male name
亘行 *nobuyuki* male name

SYNONYMS

● extend over
及 REACH TO → 3385

HOMOPHONES
wataru ⇨ 渡 611

NOTE
⇨ see USAGE note at 渡 611

亥 1940

▶THE BOAR
nonstandard for 亥 2012

舌

incorrect classification ⇨ see 2186

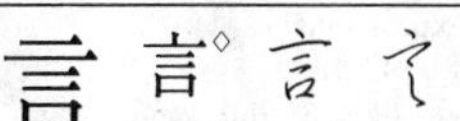

1941 GEN GON i(u) koto

Ⓒ言 yán

Radical	Strokes
言 149	7-7-0
Grade	**Freq**
Jōyō-2	249
2-1-6	

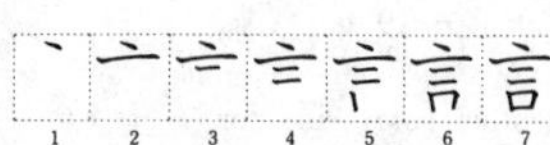

RADICAL 149
Standard form: 言 *kotoba* 'speech' (誉 誓 謄)
Left variant: 訁 *gonben* (訓 詠 調)
Description: used in characters related to speech, words or expressions

▶SAY ▶SPEECH

COMPOUNDS

❶ [original meaning] **say, speak, talk**
言明 *genmei* declaration, announcement
言及する *genkyū suru* refer to, mention, touch upon
発言する *hatsugen suru* speak, utter
宣言 *sengen* declaration, proclamation
予言する *yogen suru* predict, forecast
断言する *dangen suru* assert, declare
提言 *teigen* proposal, suggestion
過言 *kagon* saying too much, exaggeration
他言する *tagon suru* tell to others, divulge

❷ⓐ **speech, words, saying**
ⓑ counter for words or letters
言語 *gengo* language, speech, words
言論 *genron* speech, discussion
言語道断な *gongodōdan na* inexcusable, outrageous, absurd
証言 *shōgen* testimony, verbal evidence
格言 *kakugen* maxim, proverb
方言 *hōgen* dialect
狂言 *kyōgen* noh farce, comic interlude in a noh drama; kabuki play; sham, put-up job
無言 *mugon* silence, muteness
五言絶句 *gogonzekku* Chinese quatrain with five letters in each line

INDEPENDENT

【gen 言】 word, speech, remark, statement
言を左右にする *gen o sayū ni suru* equivocate, be noncommittal
言を守る *gen o mamoru* keep one's word

KUN

【i(u) 言う】
①ⓐ say, speak, talk (about)
ⓑ tell, relate
言い回し *iimawashi* expression, manner [turn] of expression
物言い *monoii* manner of speaking; objection
② state, declare, affirm
言い分 *iibun* one's say [claim]; objection, complaint
言い渡す *iiwatasu* announce, tell; sentence; order
意見を言う *iken o iu* state one's opinion
③ⓐ call, name; express (in a foreign language)
ⓑ [sometimes also 謂う] refer to, call—used chiefly in certain set expressions
典子と言う人 *noriko to iu hito* person called Noriko
これを音素と言う *Kore o onso to iu* To this is given the term "phoneme"
言うに言われぬ *iu ni iwarenu* inexpressible, indescribable
④ sound, be heard
ガタガタ言う音 *gatagata iu oto* rattling sound

【koto 言】 [in compounds] word
言の葉 *kotonoha literary* word
言葉 *kotoba* word, term; wording; language
一言も言わず *hitokoto mo iwazu* without saying a word
独り言 *hitorigoto* soliloquy, monologue
寝言 *negoto* sleep-talking

SYNONYMS

❶ **speak and say**

云 say → 1931
話 SPEAK → 1527
口 give mouth to → 3382
申す SPEAK HUMBLY → 3507
弁 SPEAK ELOQUENTLY → 2004
語る TELL → 1543
談 TALK → 1569
述 STATE → 3075
陳 SET FORTH → 540

❷ⓐ **speech**

談 TALK → 1569
舌 TONGUE → 2186
口 MOUTH → 3382

【iu】

③ⓐ **name**

呼 CALL → 273
称 name → 1160

USAGE

iu

言う

①ⓐ say, speak, talk (about)
ⓑ tell, relate
② state, declare, affirm
③ⓐ call, name; express (in a foreign language)
ⓑ [sometimes also 謂う] refer to, call—used chiefly in certain set expressions
④ sound, be heard

謂う

[usu. 言う] refer to, call—used chiefly in certain set expressions

云う

such, such as, like, of this kind

HOMOPHONES

iu ⇨ 謂 1595 云 1931

NOTE

⇨ see COMPOUND FORMATION for
格言 *kakugen* ⇨ 格 926
言葉 *kotoba* ⇨ 葉 2321

1-6

一

戻 戻 戻 戻

1942 REI modo(su) modo(ru)

Ⓒⓗ 戾 lì

Radical	Strokes
戸 63	7-4-3
Grade	**Freq**
Jōyō	840
2-1-6	

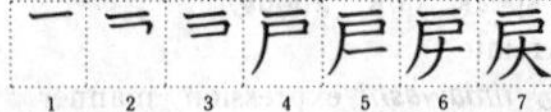

▶**RETURN**

COMPOUNDS

❶ **return, give back**

返戻する *henrei suru* return, give back

❷ [original meaning] go against, disobey

背戻する *hairei suru* disobey, infringe, run counter to
暴戻 *bōrei* tyranny, atrocity

KUN

【modo(su) 戻す】 return, give back, send back; throw up, vomit

戻し *modoshi* returning, giving back
払い戻し *haraimodoshi* refundment, repayment
取り戻す *torimodosu* take back, regain, restore
買い戻し *kaimodoshi* redemption, repurchase

【modo(ru) 戻る】 return, come [go] back; turn back; return to, revert to, unwind itself

戻り *modori* return; reaction, recovery
立ち戻る *tachimodoru* return, come back
戻り道 *modorimichi* the way back

SYNONYMS

❶ & **【modosu】 return and restore**

返 RETURN → 3060
還 RETURN → 3180
復 RETURN TO → 575

【modoru】

○ **return**

帰 RETURN → 130
還 RETURN → 3180
回 turn back → 3055
復 RETURN TO → 575

豆

1943 TŌ ZU mame mame-

Ⓒⓗ 豆 dòu

Radical	Strokes
豆 151	7-7-0
Grade	Freq
Jōyō-3	938
2 - 1 - 6	

1-6

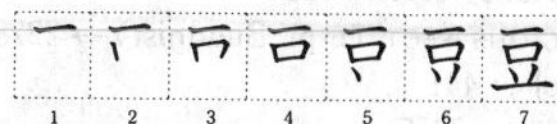

RADICAL 151

Standard form: 豆 *mame* 'ritual vessel' (豊 豎 豈)

Left variant: 豆 *mamehen* (豌)

Description: used in characters related to sacrificial vessels or pedestals

▶BEAN

COMPOUNDS

❶ⓐ bean, pea

ⓑ soybean

豆腐 *tōfu* tofu (Japanese bean curd)

大豆 *daizu* soybean

豆乳 *tōnyū* soybean milk

納豆 *nattō* fermented soybeans

❷ [original meaning, now archaic] ancient sacrificial vessel

俎豆 *sotō* ancient altar of sacrifice

KUN

【mame 豆】

①ⓐ [also suffix] bean, pea

ⓑ soybean

豌豆豆 *endōmame* peas

黒豆 *kuromame* black soybean

② blister, corn

血豆 *chimame* blood blister

【mame- 豆-】 [prefix] miniature, midget, mini-, small

豆電球 *mamedenkyū* miniature light bulb

豆台風 *mametaifū* small typhoon

SPECIAL READINGS

小豆 *azuki* adzuki bean

SYNONYMS

❶ vegetables

菜 greens → 2305

芋 POTATO → 2181

蕗 BUTTERBUR → 2372

❶ cereals

米 RICE → 3529

麦 WHEAT → 2408

【mame-】

○ small and tiny

小 SMALL → 7

微 SLIGHT → 639

細 MINUTE → 1333

寸 A BIT OF → 2935

NOTE

⇨ see COMPOUND FORMATION for 納豆 *nattō* ⇨ 納 1300

系

1944 KEI

Ⓒⓗ 系 xì jì

Radical	Strokes
糸 120	7-6-1
Grade	Freq
Jōyō-6	793
2 - 1 - 6	

1-6

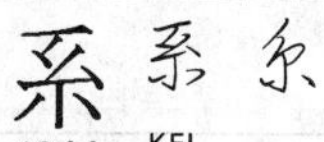

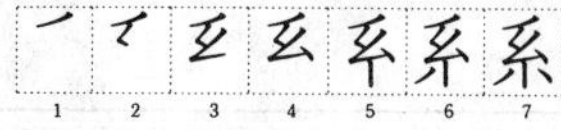

▶SYSTEM ▶LINEAGE

COMPOUNDS

❶ⓐ [also suffix] (group of interrelated elements) **system, interrelated group**

ⓑ *chem*, *phys*, *biol* system

ⓒ *geol* system

系統 *keitō* system; geological formation; lineage, ancestry

系列 *keiretsu* order, succession; series

体系 *taikei* system, organization

太陽系 *taiyōkei* solar system

結晶系 *kesshōkei* system of crystallization

二成文系 *niseibunkei* binary system

神経系 *shinkeikei* nervous system

消化系 *shōkakei* digestive system

デボン系 *debonkei* Devonian system

❷ [also suffix] **lineage, family line, descent, ancestry**

系図 *keizu* genealogy, pedigree

直系 *chokkei* direct descent line

家系 *kakei* family line, lineage, ancestry

日系米人 *nikkei-beijin* American of Japanese descent, Japanese-American

❸ [suffix] faction, clique, group

左派系 *sahakei* left faction

田中系の政治家 *tanakakei no seijika* politician

of the Tanaka faction [clique]

INDEPENDENT

【kei 系】 system; *math* corollary

SYNONYMS

❶ⓐ system

制 SYSTEM → 1274
統 INTERCONNECTED SYSTEM → 1352
網 network → 1374

❷ lineage

血 BLOOD → 3526

❸ parties and sects

派 SECT → 381
翼 WING → 2720
門 (religious) sect → 888
宗 RELIGIOUS SECT (esp. Buddhist) → 2228
流 school → 441
閥 CLIQUE → 3325
党 PARTY → 2581

1-6 ノ

1945

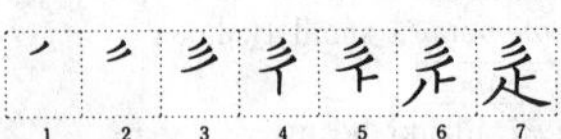

Radical	Strokes
辵 162	7-7-0
Grade	**Freq**
Radical	
2 - 1 - 6	

RADICAL 162

Standard form: 辵 *shinnyō* or *shinnyū* 'advance'

Enclosures: 辶 辶 *shinnyō* or *shinnyū* (込 辺 迄)

Description: used in characters related to advancing or going

---

1-6 ノ

incorrect classification ⇨ see 2400

1-6 ノ

呑 incorrect classification ⇨ see 2410

1-6 ノ

incorrect classification ⇨ see 2545

1-6 ノ

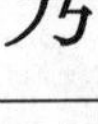

incorrect classification ⇨ see 2401

1-6 ノ

incorrect classification ⇨ see 3555

1-7 一

房 房 房 房

1946

BŌ fusa

Ⓒⓗ 房 fáng

Radical	Strokes
戶 63	8-4-4
Grade	**Freq**
Jōyō	804
2 - 1 - 7	

▶CHAMBER

COMPOUNDS

❶ⓐ [original meaning] **chamber, (small) room, cell**

ⓑ chamber for sleeping, bedroom

ⓒ enclosed space resembling a chamber

暖房 *danbō* heating
冷房 *reibō* air conditioning
監房 *kanbō* cell, ward
官房 *kanbō* secretariat
書房 *shobō* bookstore, publishing company
文房具 *bunbōgu* stationery, writing materials

房事 *bōji* sex, lovemaking
女房 *nyōbō* wife; court lady
心房 *shinbō* atrium, chamber of the heart
子房 *shibō* ovary (of plants)

❷ house, residence; living quarters of a priest
僧房(＝僧坊) *sōbō* priest's living quarters in a Buddhist temple

❸ suffix after names of publishing companies or bookstores
富山房 *fuzanbō* name of a publisher

❹ tuft, tassel
乳房 *nyūbō* (＝*chibusa*) breast, nipple

❺ abbrev. of 安房 *awa*, old name for south Chiba Prefecture
房総半島 *bōsō hantō* Boso Peninsula

INDEPENDENT

【bō 房】 chamber, room, cell; priest's lodge; cell
房の内 *bō no uchi* inside of a chamber

KUN

【fusa 房】 tuft, tassel, fringe; cluster, bunch
房房した *fusafusa shita* tufty, fringy
一房の髪 *hitofusa no kami* a tuft of hair
バナナ一房 *banana hitofusa* a bunch [cluster] of bananas

SYNONYMS

❶ **rooms**
室 ROOM → 2254
間 room → 3323
斎 study → 2115
堂 HALL → 2589

❹ **bundles and clusters**
束 BUNDLE → 3554

COMPOUND FORMATION

❶ **暖房** *danbō*
暖房 'heating' is to warm (暖) a room (房 ❶ⓐ).

❷ **官房** *kanbō*
官房 'secretariat' originally referred to a secretary's (官) chamber (房 ❶ⓐ).

❸ **文房具** *bunbōgu*
文房具 'stationery, writing materials' is an implement or implements (具) used in a chamber (房 ❶ⓐ) for writing (文).

❹ **房事** *bōji*
房事 'sex, lovemaking' refers to the affairs (事) of the bedroom (房 ❶ⓑ).

❺ **女房** *nyōbō*
女房 'wife; court lady' originally denoted the chamber (房 ❶ⓑ) of a court lady (女). It is now used in referring to one's wife.

肩 肩 肩 肩

1947 KEN kata

Ⓒⓗ 肩 jiān

Radical	Strokes
月 130	8-4-4
Grade	**Freq**
Jōyō	1080
2 - 1 - 7	

1-7 一

▶SHOULDER

COMPOUNDS

ⓐ [original meaning] **shoulder**
ⓑ something resembling a shoulder
肩甲骨 *kenkōkotsu* shoulder blade, scapula
肩章 *kenshō* shoulder strap
双肩 *sōken* both shoulders
比肩する *hiken suru* equal, rank with, compare favorably
強肩 *kyōken* *baseball* strong arm
路肩 *roken* (＝*rokata*) shoulder of a road

KUN

【kata 肩】 shoulder; upper right
肩に担ぐ *kata ni katsugu* shoulder, bear
肩凝り *katakori* stiff shoulders
肩書き *katagaki* title, degree

SYNONYMS

ⓐ **trunk parts**
背 BACK → 2573
胸 CHEST → 951
腹 BELLY → 1034
胴 TRUNK → 950
腰 WAIST → 1036

受 incorrect classification ⇨ see 2421 　1-7 ノ

秀 incorrect classification／stroke count ⇨ see 2545 　1-7 ノ

1-7 ノ **垂** incorrect classification ⇨ see 3565

1-7 ノ **爭** incorrect classification ⇨ see 2422 (nonstandard for 争 2030)

1-7 ノ **委 季** incorrect classification ⇨ see 5-3

1-8 一 **音** 1948

▶**SOUND**
nonstandard for 音 2070

Radical	Strokes
音 180	9-9-0
Grade Variant	Freq
2-1-8	

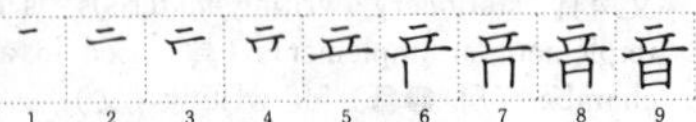

RADICAL 180
Standard form: 音 *oto* 'sound' (韶)
Variant: 音 *oto* (韻 響)
Description: used in characters related to sound or music

1-8 一 **帝** 1949

▶**EMPEROR**
nonstandard for 帝 2073

1-8 ノ **重** incorrect classification ⇨ see 3573

1-8 ノ **香** incorrect classification ⇨ see 2568

1-9 一 **扇** 1950 扇 扇 扇 SEN ōgi

 扇 shàn shān

Radical	Strokes
戸 63	10-4-6
Grade	Freq
Jōyō	1467
2-1-9	

一 ヨ ヨ 戸 戸 肩 扇 扇 扇 扇 (1–10)

▶**FAN**

COMPOUNDS

❶ⓐ (implement for creating a current) **fan, folding fan**
ⓑ (machine for creating a current) fan
扇子 *sensu* folding fan
扇状地 *senjōchi* alluvial delta
白扇 *hakusen* white fan
換気扇 *kankisen* ventilation fan
❷ⓐ (create a current) **fan, blow**
ⓑ [formerly also 煽 1056] (move to action) fan, stir up, instigate
扇風機 *senpūki* electric fan
扇動する *sendō suru* instigate, agitate
扇情的な *senjōteki na* inflammatory, lascivious

KUN

【ōgi 扇】 fan, folding fan
舞扇 *maiōgi* dancer's fan

SYNONYMS

❷ⓑ **incite**
挑 PROVOKE → 372
唆 INSTIGATE → 402
激 excite → 776

奮 ROUSE UP → 2367
振 arouse to action → 430

動 MOVE → 1778
起 rise to action → 3307

鬲 1951

一 丆 丙 丙 鬲 鬲 鬲 鬲 鬲 鬲 (1–10)

Radical	Strokes
鬲 193	10-10-0
Grade	**Freq**
Radical	
2 - 1 - 9	

1-9 一

RADICAL 193

Standard form: 鬲 *kaku* 'ritual tripod' (鬶)
Variant: 鬲 *kaku* (融)
Description: used in characters related to ritual tripod vessels or their use

---

晉 1952

▶**JIN DYNASTY**
nonstandard for 晋 2656

1-9 一

啇 1953

▶**TRADE**
nonstandard for 商 2116

1-10 一

章 1954

▶**CHAPTER** ▶**BADGE**
nonstandard for 章 2117

1-10 一

扉 1955

扉 扉 扉
HI tobira

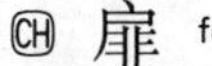

Radical	Strokes
戸 63	12-4-8
Grade	**Freq**
Jōyō	1790
2 - 1 - 11	

1-11 一

一 ㇇ 彐 戸 戸 戸 戸 戸 扉 扉 扉 扉 (1–12)

▶**HINGED DOOR**

COMPOUNDS

● [also suffix] [original meaning] **hinged door, door, door leaf**
開扉する *kaihi suru* open the door
門扉 *monpi* leaves [doors] of a gate
鉄扉 *teppi* iron door
防水扉 *bōsuihi* watertight door

KUN

【**tobira** 扉】
① [also suffix] hinged door, door; door leaf
扉を排する *tobira o haisuru* push open the door
扉は開かれた *Tobira wa hirakareta* The door is open (to the public)
自動扉 *jidōtobira* automatic door
防火扉 *bōkatobira* fire door
② title page [leaf], front page
扉絵 *tobirae* frontispiece
裏扉 *uratobira* back leaf

SYNONYMS

● **doors**
戸 DOOR → 1930
門 GATE → 888
口 entrance (or exit) → 3382

1-11
一

雇 雇 雇 雇

1956 KO yato(u)

Ⓒⓗ 雇 gù

Radical	Strokes
隹 172	12-8-4
Grade	**Freq**
Jōyō	1298
2-1-11	

一 コ ヨ 戸 戸 戸 戸 戸 戸 屏 屏 雇
1 2 3 4 5 6 7 8 9 10 11 12

▶EMPLOY

COMPOUNDS

● **employ, engage**

雇用(＝雇傭)する *koyō suru* employ, hire
雇主 *koshu* employer
雇員 *koin* employee
解雇 *kaiko* discharge, dismissal

KUN

【yato(u) 雇う】
[formerly also 傭う]
ⓐ employ, engage
ⓑ hire (as a boat), charter
雇い *yatoi* employee; employment
雇(＝傭) *yatoi* government employee
雇い入れる *yatoiireru* employ, engage
雇い口 *yatoiguchi* employment, job
日雇い *hiyatoi* daily employment; day laborer
船を雇う *fune o yatou* hire a boat

SYNONYMS

● **employ**
用 EMPLOY → 2976
使う employ → 90
役 press into service → 244

USAGE

❶ **yatou**
雇う
[formerly also 傭う]
ⓐ employ, engage
ⓑ hire (as a boat), charter
傭う
[now usu. 雇う]
ⓐ hire, employ
ⓑ hire (as a boat), charter

❷ **yatoi**
雇
[also 傭] government employee
傭
[also 雇] government employee

HOMOPHONES

yatou ⇨ 傭 160
yatoi ⇨ 傭 160

1-11
一

雇

1957

▶CHILD
nonstandard for 童 2130

1-11
ノ

番

incorrect classification ⇨ see 2748

1-11
ノ

黍

incorrect classification ⇨ see 2597

1-11
ノ

爲

incorrect classification ⇨ see 2477
(nonstandard for 為 3577)

1-12
一

意

1958

▶MIND ▶MEANING
nonstandard for 意 2136

1-12
ノ

愛

incorrect classification ⇨ see 2492

爵 incorrect classification ⇨ see 2524 | 1-16 ノ

亡 incorrect classification ⇨ see 3402 | 2-1 亠

个
1959
▶**COUNTER FOR ITEMS**
nonstandard for 箇 2700 | 2-1 人

个
1960
▶**INDIVIDUAL** ▶**GENERAL COUNTER**
nonstandard for 個 117 | 2-1 人

乞
1961 KOTSU KITSU KI ko(u)

CH 乞 qǐ | 2-1 𠂉

Radical	Strokes
乙 5	3-1-2
Grade	**Freq**
Reference	
2-2-1	

COMPOUNDS
ⓐ [also 請う *kou*] [original meaning] beg
ⓑ [in compounds] solicit, pray for
物乞い *monogoi* beggar; begging
命乞い *inochigoi* begging for one's life
乞食 *kojiki* beggar
雨乞い *amagoi* ritual prayer for rain
暇乞い *itomagoi* leave-taking, farewell visit

HOMOPHONES
kou ⇨ 請 1576

NOTE
⇨ see USAGE note at 請 1576

ケ incorrect classification ⇨ see 3430
(nonstandard for 箇 2700) | 2-1 𠂉

之 incorrect classification／stroke count ⇨ see 1933 | 2-1 丁

文 文 文 夂
1962 BUN MON fumi aya▲

CH 文 wén | 2-2 亠

Radical	Strokes
文 67	4-4-0
Grade	**Freq**
Jōyō-1	164
2-2-2	

Stroke order: 1 2 3 4

RADICAL 67
variant of 文 *bun* or *bunnyō* 'pattern'
⇨ see 文 1966 for radical description

▶**LETTER** ▶**WRITINGS**

COMPOUNDS
❶ⓐ (written symbol) **letter, character, script, inscription**
ⓑ style of writing, calligraphic style
文字 *moji* character, letter
文字 *monji* character, letter; writings
文盲 *monmō* illiteracy
金石文 *kinsekibun* ancient inscriptions on monuments

古文 *kobun* classics, ancient writings, paleography

❷ⓐ [also suffix] **writings, composition, text, document**

ⓑ **written or spoken language**

ⓒ written work, book

ⓓ letter, note

文章 *bunshō* writing, composition, essay; prose

文書 *bunsho* (=*monjo*) document, letter, note

文献 *bunken* literature, documentary records

文体 *buntai* (literary) style

文房具 *bunbōgu* stationery, writing materials

論文 *ronbun* thesis, paper, treatise, dissertation

作文 *sakubun* composition, essay; writing

原文 *genbun* text, original text

全文 *zenbun* whole text

不文律 *fubunritsu* unwritten law [rule]

注文 *chūmon* order, ordering; request

判決文 *hanketsubun* judgment paper

起請文 *kishōmon* written pledge

文法 *bunpō* grammar

文句 *monku* phrase, expression; complaint

和文 *wabun* Japanese text

文庫 *bunko* library; collection of literary works; box for stationery

文通 *buntsū* correspondence, exchange of letters

文面 *bunmen* contents of a letter

❸ [also suffix]

ⓐ sentence

ⓑ *computer science* statement

文脈 *bunmyaku* context

単文 *tanbun* simple sentence

疑問文 *gimonbun* interrogative sentence

条件文 *jōkenbun* conditional statement

❹ⓐ **letters, literature, the pen**

ⓑ abbrev. of 文学 *bungaku*: literature

文学 *bungaku* literature, letters

文芸 *bungei* literature, literary art, art and literature

文豪 *bungō* great man of letters, literary master

文語 *bungo* literary [written] language

文博 *bunhaku* doctor of literature

英文科 *eibunka* department of English literature

❺ⓐ **culture, learning, the arts**

ⓑ abbrev. of 文化 *bunka*: culture

ⓒ abbrev. of 文部省 *monbushō*: Ministry of Education, Science and Culture

文化 *bunka* culture

文明 *bunmei* civilization, culture

文教 *bunkyō* education, culture

文部省 *monbushō* Ministry of Education, Science and Culture

人文科学 *jinbun-kagaku* cultural sciences, humanities

文革 *bunkaku* cultural revolution

重文 *jūbun* important cultural property; compound sentence

文相 *bunshō* Minister of Education, Science and Culture

❻ civil, civil affairs

文民 *bunmin* civilian

文官 *bunkan* civil official

❼ [also suffix] [original meaning] decorative pattern, figure, design

文様 *mon'yō* pattern, design

縄文 *jōmon* straw-rope pattern

渦状文 *kajōmon* spiral pattern

❽ phenomenon, feature

天文学 *tenmongaku* astronomy

地文 *chimon* physiographical features

❾ *mon*:

ⓐ former monetary unit equiv. to 1/1000 of a *kan* (貫)

ⓑ unit of footwear size equiv. to 2.4 cm

文無しの *monnashi no* penniless

十文の足袋 *tomon no tabi* size 10 *tabi*, digitated socks of about 24 cm sole

❿ unclassified compounds

文楽 *bunraku* Japanese puppet show, *bunraku*

INDEPENDENT

[bun 文]

① writings, composition; (literary) style

文を練る *bun o neru* polish one's style

文は人なり *Bun wa hito nari* The style is the man

②ⓐ sentence

ⓑ *computer science* statement

文を組み立てる *bun o kumitateru* construct a sentence

③ literary culture or learning, literary attainments, culture

文は武に優る *Bun wa bu ni masaru* The pen is mightier than the sword

④ abbrev. of 文学部 *bungakubu*: faculty [department] of letters [literature]

東大文 *tōdai bun* Faculty of Letters, Tokyo University

[mon 文] *mon* (⇨ ❾)

文 symbol used in maps and signboards: school—in this sense 文 has no reading and usu. appears in the form ㊫ or 文 (boxed)

KUN

[fumi 文] letter, love letter; book

恋文 *koibumi* love letter

文読む月日 *fumi yomu tsukihi* days of reading

[aya 文]

[also 綾]

① figure, design, pattern (as of cloth)

美しい文 *utsukushii aya* beautiful design
②ⓐ figure of speech, rhetorical flourish
ⓑ intricate and subtle details, intricacies
文の無い文体 *aya no nai buntai* plain style

SYNONYMS

❶ characters
字 CHARACTER → 2172
漢 kanji → 657

❷ⓐ & ❷ⓑ writing
筆 WRITING → 2677
書 writing(s) → 2658
銘 INSCRIPTION → 1724

ⓓ written communications
状 LETTER → 272
書 letter → 2658
信 written communication → 100
電 telegram → 2790

❸ sentence and sentence parts
節 clause → 2691
句 PHRASE → 2967

❺ⓐ learning and knowledge
学 learning → 2555
業 studies → 2612
識 KNOWLEDGE → 1639
知 knowledge → 1127

❼ pattern
模 PATTERN (decorative design) → 1050
柄 pattern (on cloth) → 897
様 pattern → 1052
紋 figure → 1299

❾ⓐ Japanese money denominations
両 *ryo* → 3518
厘 *RIN* → 3004
銭 sen → 1725
円 YEN → 2955

USAGE

mon'yō
文様
pattern, design
紋様
crest pattern

HOMOPHONES

aya ⇨ 綾 1376

COMPOUND FORMATION

注文 *chūmon*
注文 'order, etc.' consists of 文 ❷ⓐ 'document' and 注 'write down'. It can be explained as a document or record (文書 *bunsho*) for submitting information (注進 *chūshin*). Now it usu. refers to a document or a request specifying one's wishes, i.e., an order.

NOTE

⇨ see also USAGE note at 綾 1376
⇨ see COMPOUND FORMATION for
文房具 *bunbōgu* ⇨ 房 1946
文化 *bunka* ⇨ 化 21
文明 *bunmei* ⇨ 明 855
文楽 *bunraku* ⇨ 楽 2826

方 方 方

1963 HŌ kata -kata -gata

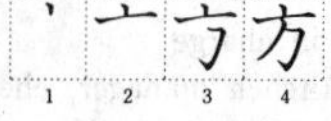

Ⓒ 方 fāng

Radical	Strokes
方 70	4-4-0
Grade	**Freq**
Jōyō-2	29
2 - 2 - 2	

2-2

RADICAL 70

Standard form: 方 *kata* 'square' (旁 施 族)
Description: used for character classification

▶DIRECTION ▶WAY ▶SQUARE

COMPOUNDS

❶ [original meaning] **direction, bearing, orientation**
方向 *hōkō* direction, bearing; course
方位 *hōi* direction, bearing
四方 *shihō* all directions, cardinal points
前方 *zenpō* front
左方に *sahō ni* to the left, on the left side
北方 *hoppō* north, northward; northern district
快方に向かう *kaihō ni mukau* get better, improve, convalesce
途方に暮れる *tohō ni kureru* be at a loss, be puzzled

❷ **locality, place, district, region, area, countryside**
方面 *hōmen* direction, district; field, sphere
方言 *hōgen* dialect
遠方 *enpō* great distance; distant place
地方 *chihō* locality, district, region

❸ⓐ (one part of) **side, one side**
ⓑ (one of concerned persons) **side, party, part**
一方 *ippō* one side, one hand; a party, the other party; in the mean time; only
片方 *katahō* one side, the other side
両方 *ryōhō* both
他方 *tahō* other side [hand]

双方 *sōhō* both sides [parties]
当方 *tōhō* I, we, our part
先方 *senpō* the other party, they; one's destination

❹ⓐ **way of doing, method, means, procedure**
ⓑ prescription, recipe
方法 *hōhō* method, way; system; scheme, means; process, procedure; plan
方針 *hōshin* course, policy, plan
方策 *hōsaku* plan, policy, scheme
方式 *hōshiki* formula, mode; method
方程式 *hōteishiki* equation
処方 *shohō* prescription; recipe
漢方 *kanpō* Chinese medicine
秘方 *hihō* secret method, secret recipe

❺ⓐ (equal-sided rectangle) **square**
ⓑ (second power) square
方円 *hōen* squares and circles
方眼紙 *hōganshi* graph paper
正方形 *seihōkei* square
方丈 *hōjō* 10 sq. feet; abbot's chamber; chief priest
平方 *heihō* square (measure); square (of a number)
立方 *rippō* cube

❻ upright, honest
品行方正な人 *hinkō hōsei na hito* person of good conduct

❼ just, just now
方今 *hōkon* present time

❽ occultism
方術 *hōjutsu* method; art; magic

INDEPENDENT

【hō 方】
① direction, side, way
. . . の方に *...no hō ni* in the direction of, towards
右の方に *migi no hō ni* on the right side, to the right
どちらの方へ? *Dochira no hō e*: Which way?
② (one of concerned persons) side, part
私の方では *watakushi no hō de wa* on [for] my part [side]
③ square
方二十マイル *hō nijū mairu* 20 sq. miles
④ function word used for comparison
彼は働くよりも遊ぶ方だ *Kare wa hataraku yori mo asobu hō da* He is more given to idling than to work
彼は怠ける方だ *Kare wa namakeru hō da* He is rather idle
君は帰った方が良い *Kimi wa kaetta hō ga yoi* You had better go home
侮辱を受けて生きるより死んだ方がましだ *Bujoku o ukete ikiru yori shinda hō ga mashi da* I would rather die than live in dishonor

KUN

【kata 方】
①ⓐ direction
ⓑ place, area
東の方に *higashi no kata ni* in an easterly direction
上方 *kamigata* Kyoto and its neighborhood
②ⓐ [honorific] person, gentleman, lady
ⓑ [archaic] honorific title
方方 *katagata* all gentlemen, all people
あの方 *ano kata* that gentlemen [lady], he, she
お万の方 *oman no kata* Lady Oman
③ time
来し方 *kishikata* (=*koshikata*) past, days gone by
久方振りに *hisakataburi ni* after a long time
今し方 *imashigata* just now, a moment ago

【-kata -方】
① [verbal suffix]
ⓐ way of doing, manner, style, method; how to (do)
ⓑ suffix of nominalization
仕方 *shikata* way, method, means
話し方 *hanashikata* one's way of speaking
教え方 *oshiekata* method of teaching
綴り方 *tsuzurikata* composition; spelling
出方 *dekata* one's attitude, move; theater attendant, usher
撃ち方止め *Uchikata yame* Cease fire!
② [also suffix] side, party
味方 *mikata* friend, ally, one's side
相手方 *aitekata* other [opposite] party
父方の *chichikata no* on the paternal side
売り方 *urikata* seller, selling side; art of selling
③ [also suffix] person in charge
賄い方 *makanaikata* kitchen manager, chef
裏方 *urakata* property man, sceneshifter
親方 *oyakata* boss, chief, master
土方 *dokata* construction laborer, navvy
④ [honorific] counter for persons
お二方 *ofutakata* two persons
⑤ [suffix] care of, c/o
足立様方高木様 *adachisama-kata takagisama* Mr. Takagi, c/o Mr. Adachi
⑥ about, approximately, roughly
大方 *ōkata* almost, nearly; probably
粗方 *arakata* mostly, roughly, almost, on the whole
一方ならず *hitokata narazu* unusually, exceedingly, not a little
目方 *mekata* weight

【-gata -方】
① [also suffix]
ⓐ about; by
ⓑ (of time) toward

二割方減 *niwarigata-gen* decrease of about 20 percent
利子を二分方引き下げる *rishi o nibugata hikisageru* lower the rate of interest by 2 percent
夕方 *yūgata* evening
明け方 *akegata* toward daylight
② polite plural suffix
お偉方 *oeragata* dignitary, exalted personalities
奥方 *okugata* wife of a nobleman
殿方 *tonogata* men, gentlemen
貴方方 *anatagata* you (plural)
先生方 *senseigata* teachers; doctors
③ [also suffix] the side of
敵方 *tekigata* hostile party
徳川方 *tokugawagata* Tokugawa's side

SPECIAL READINGS
行方 *yukue* one's whereabouts
貴方▲ *anata* you

SYNONYMS
❶ **direction**
向 direction → 3052
❷ **areas and localities**
地 PLACE → 204
辺 VICINITY → 3029
域 BOUNDED AREA → 465
区 DISTRICT → 2963
領 TERRITORY → 1224
帯 BELT → 2582
圏 SPHERE → 3148
❸ **side**
側 SIDE → 137
辺 -side → 3029
面 side → 2087
傍 BESIDE → 147
横 SIDEWAYS → 1066
❹ⓐ & **[-kata]** ①ⓐ **way and style**
途 WAY → 3107
法 METHOD → 333
式 STYLE → 3049
流 STYLE → 441
調 TONE → 1567
様 MODE → 1052
風 MANNER → 3007
❺ⓐ **square**
角 square → 2047
ⓑ **mathematical power**
平 square (measure) → 3478
乗 power → 3576
[kata]
②ⓐ **person**
者 PERSON → 3211
氏 person (*polite*) → 2951
人 HUMAN BEING → 3368
[-kata]
③ **person in charge**
係 PERSON IN CHARGE → 97
員 MEMBER (of a staff) → 2269
[-gata]
①ⓐ **approximately**
位 about → 61
-頃 ABOUT → 144
-程 ...or thereabouts → 1190
辺り thereabouts → 3029
約 APPROXIMATELY → 1280
概 GENERAL → 1048
大 in substance → 3416
② **plural suffixes**
-達 plural suffix → 3139
-等 plural suffix → 2682
衆 somewhat polite plural suffix → 2683
-共 belittling plural suffix → 2393

2-2

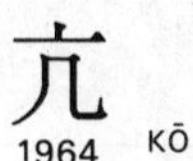

1964 KŌ

Ⓒⓗ 亢 kàng

Radical	Strokes
亠 8	4-2-2
Grade	**Freq**
Reference	
2-2-2	

COMPOUNDS
❶ [now replaced by 興 2909 or 高 2097] high-spirited, excited, elated
亢奮(=興奮)する *kōfun suru* get excited, be agitated, be aroused
亢進(=高進, 昂進)する *kōshin suru* rise, exasperate, accelerate
❷ [archaic] ascend
亢竜 *kōryō* (=*kōryū*) dragon which has already ascended to the heavens

2-2 亠

六 六 六

1965 ROKU RIKU▲ mu mu(tsu) mut(tsu) mui

Ⓒⓗ 六 liù lù

Radical	Strokes
八 12	4-2-2
Grade	**Freq**
Jōyō-1	27
2-2-2	

▶**SIX**

COMPOUNDS

● **six, sixth**

六百 *roppyaku* 600
六時 *rokuji* six o'clock
六月 *rokugatsu* June
六角 *rokkaku* hexagon
六法 *roppō* the six codes (of law), statute book
六書 *rikusho* the six classes of Chinese characters; Hexateuch
第六感 *dairokkan* the sixth sense, intuition

INDEPENDENT

【roku 六】 six

KUN

【mu 六】 [in compounds] six
六月目 *mutsukime* the sixth month

【mu(tsu) 六つ】 six; six years old, 6 o'clock (in former time system)
明け六つ *akemutsu* the sixth hour of the morning

【mut(tsu) 六つ】 six; six years old
六つ目 *muttsume* sixth

【mui 六】 [in compounds] six
六日 *muika* six days; 6th of the month

SYNONYMS

● **six**

陸 six (in legal documents) → 543

● **small numbers**

一 ONE → 3341
二 TWO → 1922
三 THREE → 1924
四 FOUR → 3044
五 FIVE → 3436
七 SEVEN → 3362
八 EIGHT → 3
九 NINE → 3369
十 TEN → 3365

2-2 亠

文

1966

▶**LETTER** ▶**WRITINGS**

nonstandard for 文 1962

Radical	Strokes
文 67	4-4-0
Grade	**Freq**
Variant	
2-2-2	

RADICAL 67

Standard form: 文 *bun* or *bunnyō* 'pattern' (斐)
Variant: 文 *bun* or *bunnyō* (斑)
Description: used in characters related to patterns or designs

2-2 人

介 介 介

1967 KAI

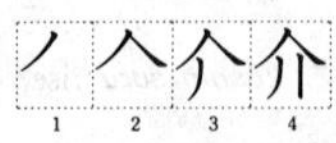

Ⓒⓗ 介 jiè

Radical	Strokes
人 9	4-2-2
Grade	**Freq**
Jōyō	695
2-2-2	

▶**MEDIATE**

COMPOUNDS

❶ **mediate, intervene, go between; lie between**

介入 *kainyū* intervention
介在する *kaizai suru* lie between
媒介 *baikai* mediation, intervention, intermediation
紹介 *shōkai* introduction, presentation
仲介 *chūkai* mediation

❷ give a helping hand, lend support to, protect

介抱する *kaihō suru* nurse, care for
介錯する *kaishaku suru* assist a person in committing hara-kiri
厄介 *yakkai* trouble, annoyance

❸ [usu. 貝 2543] shellfish
魚介 *gyokai* marine products
❹ take to heart, mind
介意する *kaii suru* care about
❺ little, trifling
一介の学生 *ikkai no gakusei* a mere student

INDEPENDENT

【**kaisuru** 介する】mediate; take to heart, mind
意に介する *i ni kaisuru* mind, take (something) to heart
仲人を介して *nakōdo o kaishite* through a matchmaker

SYNONYMS

❶ **mediating and mediators**
紹 INTRODUCE → 1335
媒 INTERMEDIATE → 564
仲 INTERMEDIARY → 43

COMPOUND FORMATION

厄介 *yakkai*
厄介 'trouble, annoyance' formerly meant to help (介 ❷) someone who is in trouble (厄).

今 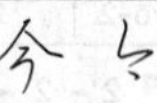

1968 KON KIN ima

Ⓒⓗ 今 jīn

Radical	Strokes
人 9	4-2-2
Grade	Freq
Jōyō-2	135
2 - 2 - 2	

2-2 人

▶PRESENT ▶THIS

COMPOUNDS

❶ⓐ **present, now**
ⓑ of the present, current
今後 *kongo* after this, from now on
今日 *konnichi* today, these days
今昔 *konjaku* past and present, yesterday and today
昨今 *sakkon* these days
今上陛下 *kinjōheika* the reigning emperor
❷ⓐ [also prefix] **this (week, etc.), the present (term)**
ⓑ **today, today's**
今回 *konkai* this time; lately
今月 *kongetsu* this month
今週 *konshū* this week
今期 *konki* present term
今夜 *kon'ya* tonight, this evening
❸ next, following
今度 *kondo* this time; next time, another time; recently

KUN

【**ima** 今】now, this moment; [also prefix] present day, modern; just now, a moment ago; soon, at once; further, another
今頃 *imagoro* about this time
只今 *tadaima* at present, now; just now; soon; Hello (used by person returning home)
今時 *imadoki* recently, these days
今風 *imafū* modern style
今浦島 *ima-urashima* Urashima [Rip Van Winkle] of today
今言った事 *ima itta koto* what you said just now
今行きます *Ima ikimasu* I'll come at once
今一度 *imaichido* once more
今少し *imasukoshi* a little more

SPECIAL READINGS

今日 *kyō* today
今朝 *kesa* this morning
今年 *kotoshi* this year
今宵▲ *koyoi* this evening, tonight

SYNONYMS

❶ⓐ **present**
当 THE PRESENT → 2177
現 ACTUAL → 968
❷ⓐ **this and that**
本 THIS → 3502
当 THE PRESENT → 2177
該 the said → 1519
同 the same → 2987
之 this → 3420
是 this → 2436
爾 THAT → 3587
彼 that → 290
ⓑ **yesterday and today**
昨 YESTERDAY → 893

1969

▶UMBRELLA
handwritten abbreviation for 傘 2131

2-2 人

2-2
八

分 1970

▶DIVIDE ▶PART ▶MINUTE
nonstandard for 分 1972

2-2
八

公 1971

▶PUBLIC
nonstandard for 公 1974

2-2
八

分 分 分 分 Ⓒⓗ 分 fēn fèn

1972 BUN FUN BU wa(keru) wa(ke) wa(kareru) wa(karu) wa(katsu)

Radical	Strokes
刀 18	4-2-2
Grade	**Freq**
Jōyō-2	30
2-2-2	

ノ 八 分 分
1 2 3 4

▶DIVIDE ▶PART ▶MINUTE

COMPOUNDS

❶ⓐ [original meaning] **divide into parts, part, separate, sever**
ⓑ (become separated into parts) **divide, be divided, come apart**
ⓒ (group according to kind) **divide, separate, sort, classify**
分割する *bunkatsu suru* divide up, partition, split
分譲 *bunjō* sale (of land) in lots, lotting-out
分析 *bunseki* analysis
分離 *bunri* separation, split
分担 *buntan* partial charge, allotment
分解 *bunkai* disintegration, disassembly; analysis, decomposition
処分する *shobun suru* dispose of, deal [do] with; punish
区分する *kubun suru* divide, section, subdivide
分野 *bun'ya* field, sphere, area
分裂する *bunretsu suru* be divided, split, break up, be disrupted
分科会 *bunkakai* sectional subcommittee
分散 *bunsan* dispersion, breakup, divergence; variance
分泌 *bunpitsu* (=*bunpi*) secretion
分布 *bunpu* distribution
分類する *bunrui suru* classify, divide into classes
分別する *bunbetsu suru* classify, distinguish; divide, separate
❷ (parcel out) **divide (up), distribute, apportion, share**
分配する *bunpai suru* divide, distribute, allot
配分 *haibun* distribution, division, allocation
按分(=案分)する *anbun suru* divide [distribute] proportionally
❸ⓐ **branch off, branch out, diverge**
ⓑ [also prefix] **branch, offshoot**
分岐する *bunki suru* diverge, branch off
分身 *bunshin* the other self, one's alter ego; branch, offshoot
分家 *bunke* branch family, offshoot; setting up a branch family
分派 *bunpa* branch, sect, denomination
分工場 *bunkōjō* branch factory
❹ tell apart, distinguish
分別 *funbetsu* discretion, prudence, judgment, good sense
不分明な *fubunmei na* obscure, vague
検分する *kenbun suru* inspect, examine, survey
❺ⓐ (segment of a whole) **part, division, section, piece**
ⓑ [also suffix] (equal portion of a whole) **part, fraction**
ⓒ (constituent element) **part, component**
ⓓ [also suffix] (allotted portion) **part, share, portion, ration, helping**
分量 *bunryō* quantity
部分 *bubun* part, section, portion
半分 *hanbun* half
積分 *sekibun* integral calculus, integration
自分 *jibun* self, oneself
三分の一 *sanbun no ichi* one third, a third part
分子 *bunshi* molecule; numerator
成分 *seibun* ingredient, component, constituent
言い分 *iibun* one's say [claim]; objection, complaint
余分 *yobun* excess, extra, surplus
取り分 *toribun* one's share, portion
四人分 *yoninbun* four helpings [servings]
一年分 *ichinenbun* a year's supply
❻ [also suffix] **content, percentage; quantity, amount**
水分 *suibun* water, moisture, humidity
糖分 *tōbun* sugar content

アルコール分 *arukōrubun* percentage of alcohol
栄養分 *eiyōbun* nutritious substance, nourishment
増加分 *zōkabun* increment
❼ⓐ **relative degree, extent, rate**
ⓑ **condition, state**
十分(＝充分)な *jūbun na* full, enough, sufficient; plentiful
多分 *tabun* probably, perhaps, maybe
幾分 *ikubun* partially, somewhat, in a way
随分 *zuibun* extremely, considerably ("as much as one pleases")
存分に *zonbun ni* to one's heart's content, freely
何分 *nanibun* anyway, anyhow; please
気分 *kibun* feeling, mood; atmosphere
❽ⓐ (one's share in something) one's part, one's duty
ⓑ **one's lot, one's place, one's station in life, social position**
ⓒ [also suffix] assumed relation between one person and another
本分 *honbun* one's duty, one's part
職分 *shokubun* duty, vocation
名分 *meibun* justification, just cause
身分 *mibun* social position [standing]; circumstances; rank, identity
性分 *shōbun* nature, temperament
天分 *tenbun* one's natural gift [endowment]
応分の *ōbun no* appropriate, reasonable (in view of one's position), within one's power [means]
親分 *oyabun* boss, big shot
兄弟分 *kyōdaibun* sworn brother, pal
❾ⓐ (unit of time) **minute**
ⓑ (unit of angular measure) minute
ⓒ **counter for minutes**
分速 *funsoku* speed per minute
毎分 *maifun* every minute
二十分 *nijippun* 20 minutes
北緯五度十分 *hokui godo jippun* 5°10′ north latitude
❿ time, short period of time
当分 *tōbun* for some time, for a while, for the present, temporarily
時分 *jibun* time, hour; season, time of the year
夜分 *yabun* nighttime, night, evening
⓫ equinox
分点 *bunten* equinox
春分 *shunbun* vernal equinox
⓬ⓐ **tenth part of an equally divided whole**
ⓑ 1/10 of 10%: **0.01**
四分六 *shiburoku* ratio of four to six
砂糖三分に水七分 *satō sanbu ni mizu shichibu* three parts of sugar to seven of water
三割五分 *sanwari gobu* 35%
百分率 *hyakubunritsu* percentage
⓭ *bu*: unit equiv. to one-tenth of other units:
ⓐ 1/10 of a degree of temperature
ⓑ former unit of length equiv. to approx. 3 mm or 1/10 of a *sun* (寸)
ⓒ unit of footwear size equiv. to 2.4 mm or 1/10 of a *mon* (文)
三十七度五分 *sanjūnanado gobu* 37.5°C (said of bodily temperature)
一寸五分 *issun gobu* 1 *sun* 5 *bu*
五分刈り *gobugari* short cropping, closely cropped hair
九文三分の足袋 *kumonsanbu no tabi tabi* (digitated socks) of 9 *mon* 3 *bu* (in size)
⓮ *fun*: former unit of weight equiv. to 0.375 g or 1/10 of a momme (匁)
八匁五分 *hachimonme gofun* 8 momme 5 *fun*
⓯ *bu*: former monetary unit equiv. to 1/4 of a *ryo* (両)
一分銀 *ichibugin* silver coin worth 1 *bu*
⓰ thickness
分厚い *buatsui* bulky, massive

INDEPENDENT

【**bun** 分】
① amount, quantity
残った分 *nokotta bun* amount left over
② (allotted portion) part, share, portion, ration, helping
自分の分 *jibun no bun* one's share [own]
③ⓐ (one's share in something) one's part, one's duty
ⓑ one's lot, one's place, one's station in life, social position
己の分を尽くす *onore no bun o tsukusu* do one's part [duty]
分に過ぎた *bun ni sugita* undue, above one's means [station]
④ⓐ relative degree, extent, rate
ⓑ condition, state
この分で行けば *kono bun de ikeba* if things go on at this rate
この分では *kono bun de wa* as things are
⑤ kind, lot
前に買った分 *mae ni katta bun* the lot I bought earlier

【**fun** 分】 minute (⇒ ❾ⓐ & ❾ⓑ); *fun* (⇒ ⓮)
分に直す *fun ni naosu* convert into minutes

【**bu** 分】
①ⓐ degree of advantage
ⓑ [usu. 歩 *bu* 2416] degree of profit
分が悪い *bu ga warui* be at a disadvantage, have no edge
分の良い仕事 *bu no ii shigoto* profitable job
② 0.01 (⇒ ⓬ⓑ)
③ *bu* (⇒ ⓭)
分迄読む *bu made yomu* read to the order of

1/10
④ thickness
分が薄い *bu ga usui* be thin
⑤ *bu* (⇒ ⓯)

KUN

【wa(keru) 分ける】
①ⓐ divide into parts, part, separate, sever
ⓑ (group according to kind) divide, separate, sort, classify
ⓒ [sometimes also 別ける] (cause to separate) part, separate, set aside
二つに分ける *futatsu ni wakeru* divide into two
切り分ける *kiriwakeru* cut and divide
項目別に分ける *kōmokubetsu ni wakeru* classify by subject
見分ける *miwakeru* discriminate, distinguish
喧嘩を分ける *kenka o wakeru* separate quarreling persons
② (parcel out) divide (up), distribute, apportion, share
分け前 *wakemae* share, portion
分け合う *wakeau* share (with a person)
③ draw (with), end in a tie
引き分け *hikiwake* draw; drawn game [match]

【wa(ke) 分け】 [also suffix] draw, drawn game
一勝二敗一分け *isshō nihai ichiwake* one victory, two defeats, one draw

【wa(kareru) 分かれる】
ⓐ (become separated into parts) divide, be divided, come apart; disperse
ⓑ branch off, branch out, diverge
分かれ *wakare* branch, offshoot, fork
左右に分かれる *sayū ni wakareru* part right and left
分かれ道 *wakaremichi* branch road, fork

【wa(karu) 分かる】
[sometimes also 判る or 解る]
①ⓐ (grasp the meaning of) understand, comprehend, see
ⓑ (be sympathetic toward) understand, show understanding for (another's feelings)
分かり *wakari* understanding
分かり難い *wakarinikui* hard to understand, incomprehensible, unintelligible
分からず屋 *wakarazuya* obstinate person, hardhead
物分かりの良い *monowakari no yoi* understanding, sensible
②ⓐ know, tell, recognize
ⓑ be made known, be brought to light
先の事は分からない *saki no koto wa wakaranai* cannot tell what will happen in the future
身元が分かる *mimoto ga wakaru* be identified
③ appreciate
音楽が分かる *ongaku ga wakaru* have appreciation of music

【wa(katsu) 分かつ】
① divide, separate
分かち難い *wakachigatai* inseparable
② distinguish, discriminate
昼夜を分かたず *chūya o wakatazu* day and night, by day and night
③ [sometimes also 頒つ] distribute (things among people)
分かち合う *wakachiau* share (with others)

SYNONYMS

❶ **separate**
割 DIVIDE → 1816
解 TAKE APART → 1517
析 ANALYZE → 862
別 SEPARATE → 1117
離 SEPARATE → 1836
隔 partition → 671

❷ **distribute**
配 DISTRIBUTE → 1460
頒 DISTRIBUTE WIDELY → 1043

❸ⓐ **diverge**
岐 DIVERGE → 241
ⓑ **branch**
支 BRANCH → 1979

❹ **discriminate**
識 DISCRIMINATE → 1639
弁 distinguish → 2004

❺ **part**
部 SECTION → 1676
局 LIMITED PART → 3063
片 FRAGMENT → 3461

❻ **quantity and number**
量 QUANTITY → 2471
嵩 BULK → 2331
積 size → 1236
額 AMOUNT → 1805
数 NUMBER → 1790
勢 strength → 2857

❼ⓐ **degree**
度 DEGREE → 3100
程 EXTENT → 1190

❽ⓐ **responsibility**
務 DUTY → 1173
任 duty → 53
責 RESPONSIBILITY → 2467

❾ⓐ **short time periods**
時 hour → 924
秒 SECOND → 1137
瞬 INSTANT → 1247
頃 moment → 144
暫 SHORT WHILE → 2864

【wakaru】
① **know and understand**

解 understand → 1517
諒 UNDERSTAND → 1575
了 COMPREHEND → 3350
知 KNOW → 1127
通 know thoroughly → 3109
得 gain understanding of → 477
悟 AWAKE TO → 419

USAGE

❶ **wakeru**
分ける
①ⓐ divide into parts, part, separate, sever
ⓑ (group according to kind) divide, separate, sort, classify
ⓒ [sometimes also 別ける] (cause to separate) part, separate, set aside
② (parcel out) divide (up), distribute, apportion, share
③ draw (with), end in a tie
別ける
[usu. 分ける] (cause to separate) part, separate, set aside

❷ **wakareru**
分かれる
ⓐ (become separated into parts) divide, be divided, come apart; disperse
ⓑ branch off, branch out, diverge
別れる
ⓐ separate, part from, bid farewell
ⓑ separate (from one's spouse), divorce

❸ **wakare**
分かれ
branch, offshoot, fork
別れ
separation, parting, leave-taking, farewell

❹ **wakaru**
分かる
[sometimes also 判る or 解る]
①ⓐ (grasp the meaning of) understand, comprehend, see
ⓑ (be sympathetic toward) understand, show understanding for (another's feelings)
②ⓐ know, tell, recognize
ⓑ be made known, be brought to light
③ appreciate
判る
[usu. 分かる, sometimes also 解る] same as 分かる
解る
[usu. 分かる, sometimes also 判る] same as 分かる

❺ **wakatsu**
分かつ
① divide, separate
② distinguish, discriminate
③ [sometimes also 頒つ] distribute (things among people)
頒つ
[usu. 分かつ] distribute (things among people)

❻ **bu**
分
①ⓐ degree of advantage
ⓑ [usu. 歩] degree of profit
② 1/10 of 10%: 0.01
③ *bu*: unit equiv. to one-tenth of other units:
ⓐ 1/10 of a degree of temperature
ⓑ former unit of length equiv. to approx. 3 mm or 1/10 of a *sun* (寸)
ⓒ unit of footwear size equiv. to 2.4 mm or 1/10 of a *mon* (文)
④ thickness
⑤ *bu*: former monetary unit equiv. to 1/4 of a *ryo* (両)
歩
① [sometimes also 分] percentage, commission
② *bu*: unit of sq. measure equiv. to approx. 3.3 sq.m or 36 sq. *shaku* (尺), used esp. for measuring fields or farms

HOMOPHONES

wakeru ⇨ 別 1117
wakareru ⇨ 別 1117
wakare ⇨ 別 1117
wakaru ⇨ 判 1122 解 1517
wakatsu ⇨ 頒 1043

NOTE

⇨ see COMPOUND FORMATION for 案分 *anbun* ⇨ 案 2270

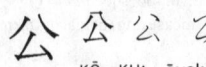

2-2
八

父 父 父 父

1973 FU chichi

丿 八 㐅 父
1 2 3 4

CH 父 fù fǔ

Radical	Strokes
父 88	4-4-0
Grade	**Freq**
Jōyō-2	662
2 - 2 - 2	

RADICAL 88
simplified form not used as radical
⇨ see 父 1975 for radical description

▶FATHER

COMPOUNDS

❶ⓐ (male parent) **father**
ⓑ father-in-law
ⓒ (term of respect for old man) father, elder
父母 *fubo* father and mother, parents
父兄 *fukei* one's father and older brothers; guardians
父子 *fushi* father and child
祖父 *sofu* grandfather
義父 *gifu* father-in-law; foster father, stepfather
岳父 *gakufu* one's wife's father
父老 *furō* elder
❷ (title of respect for priests) Father
神父 *shinpu* priest, Father
教父 *kyōfu* Father (of the Church); godfather

KUN

【chichi 父】 (male parent) father; founder, originator; *Christianity* Father, Lord
父親 *chichioya* father
原子物理学の父 *genshi-butsurigaku no chichi* father of atomic physics
在天の父 *zaiten no chichi* our Father in heaven

SPECIAL READINGS

お父さん *otōsan* daddy, papa
伯父 *oji* uncle (older than one's parent)
叔父 *oji* uncle (younger than one's parent)
お祖父さん▲ *ojiisan* grandfather

SYNONYMS

❶ⓐ **parents**
母 MOTHER → 3475
親 PARENT → 1799
❷ **clergymen**
僧 BONZE → 159
坊 Buddhist priest → 233
尼 BUDDHIST NUN → 3033

2-2
八

公 公 公 公

1974 KŌ KU▲ ōyake

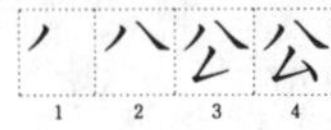

CH 公 gōng

Radical	Strokes
八 12	4-2-2
Grade	**Freq**
Jōyō-2	116
2 - 2 - 2	

▶PUBLIC

COMPOUNDS

❶ⓐ [original meaning] (relating to the public) **public, open**
ⓑ **the public, society, community**
公演 *kōen* public performance
公園 *kōen* park, public garden
公開 *kōkai* opening to the public
公害 *kōgai* environmental pollution
公表 *kōhyō* public [official] announcement, proclamation
公判 *kōhan* (public) trial [hearing]
公聴会 *kōchōkai* public [open] hearing
公選 *kōsen* public election, election by popular vote
公募 *kōbo* appeal for public subscription
公論 *kōron* public opinion, consensus
公共 *kōkyō* public society, community
公会堂 *kōkaidō* town [public] hall
公衆 *kōshū* the public
❷ⓐ [also prefix] (relating to the government) **public, formal, official, governmental, state-managed**
ⓑ **public office, government office**
公務員 *kōmuin* public service personnel, government worker
公社 *kōsha* public corporation
公団 *kōdan* public corporation
公式の *kōshiki no* formal, official

公認 *kōnin* official recognition [approval], authorization, certification
公営 *kōei* public management
公立の *kōritsu no* public (institution)
公約 *kōyaku* public pledge [promise]
公邸 *kōtei* official residence
公文書 *kōbunsho* official document
公報 *kōhō* public [official] report [bulletin]
奉公 *hōkō* public duty [service]; domestic service, apprenticeship

❸ [also prefix] *math* **common, general**
公式 *kōshiki* formula; formality
公算 *kōsan* probability
公約数 *kōyakusū* common divisor
公倍数 *kōbaisū* common multiple

❹ **impartial, fair, unbiased, just**
公明 *kōmei* fairness, justice
公正 *kōsei* justice, fairness, impartiality
公平 *kōhei* impartiality, fairness

❺ⓐ nobleman, lord, prince
ⓑ honorific title after names of noblemen
公子 *kōshi* young nobleman
公家(＝公卿) *kuge* court noble
公方 *kubō* Imperial Court; shogun, tycoon
徳川公 *tokugawakō* Prince Tokugawa

❻ⓐ duke
ⓑ title after names of dukes
公爵 *kōshaku* duke, prince
ヨーク公 *yōkukō* Duke of York

❼ⓐ term of respect used in addressing one's elders or peers
ⓑ suffix expressing intimacy or derision
貴公 *kikō* you
尊公 *sonkō* you
主人公 *shujinkō* head, master; hero, heroine
熊公八公 *kumakō hachikō* Tom, Dick and Harry

❽ abbrev. of 公明党 *kōmeitō*: Komeito (Clean Government Party)
社公連合 *shakōrengō* coalition of the Socialist Party and the Komeito

INDEPENDENT

【kō 公】 state, government; public, society; you (used on very formal occasions)

KUN

【ōyake 公】 the public, the government; Imperial Court; public affairs
公の *ōyake no* public, formal, official, governmental
公にする *ōyake ni suru* publish, announce officially

SYNONYMS

❶ⓐ public
俗 POPULAR → 104
ⓑ society
社 SOCIETY → 840
世 WORLD → 3496
ⓑ the people
民 PEOPLE → 3036
衆 the multitude(s) → 2683
庶 the masses → 3127
❷ⓑ public offices
府 government office → 3082
庁 GOVERNMENT AGENCY → 3034
省 MINISTRY → 2449
署 PUBLIC-SERVICE STATION → 2609
局 public service office → 3063
所 office → 851
❸ widespread
通 common → 3109
遍 ALL OVER → 3136
普 WIDESPREAD → 2323
❹ impartial
平 equal → 3478
❺ⓐ nobility
爵 RANK OF NOBILITY → 2524
侯 FEUDAL LORD → 98
ⓑ titles of address
師 honorific title (clergymen) → 1326
殿 FORMAL HONORIFIC TITLE → 1792
様 FORMAL TITLE → 1052
氏 COURTESY TITLE → 2951
兄 familiar title (seniors) → 2154
君 FAMILIAR TITLE (peers) → 3206
嬢 Miss → 758
❻ noblemen
侯 marquis → 98
伯 COUNT → 59
子 viscount → 3390
男 baron → 2542

NOTE

⇨ see USAGE note at 広 3035

2-2 八

父 ▶FATHER

nonstandard for 父 1973

1975

Radical	Strokes
父 88	4-4-0
Grade	**Freq**
Variant	
2 - 2 - 2	

1 2 3 4

RADICAL 88

Standard form: 父 *chichi* 'father' (爺)

Description: used in characters related to fathers or someone like a father

---

2-2 冖

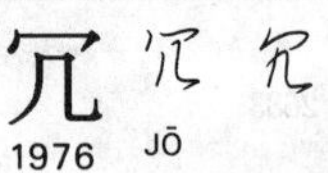

1976 JŌ

CH 冗 rǒng

Radical	Strokes
冖 14	4-2-2
Grade	**Freq**
Jōyō	1608
2 - 2 - 2	

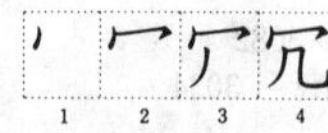

1 2 3 4

▶REDUNDANT

COMPOUNDS

❶ⓐ (exceeding what is necessary) **redundant, superfluous, useless, unnecessary**

ⓑ (needlessly repetitive) redundant, verbose, diffuse, tedious

冗長な *jōchō na* verbose, redundant, prolix

冗費 *jōhi* unnecessary expenses

冗員 *jōin* useless member of the staff

冗談 *jōdan* joke

冗漫な *jōman na* diffuse, verbose, prolix

冗語 *jōgo* redundant word, verbiage, superfluity

冗舌 *jōzetsu* garrulity, loquacity

❷ [also 饒 1812] abundant, plentiful, rich

SYNONYMS

❶ⓐ **exceeding and excess**

剰 SURPLUS → 1779

余 EXCESS → 2042

濫 EXCESSIVE → 801

過 EXCEED → 3137

超 SURPASS → 3313

越 GO BEYOND → 3314

COMPOUND FORMATION

冗談 *jōdan*

冗談 'joke' refers to useless or redundant (冗 ❶ⓐ) talk (談).

2-2 冖

罒

1977

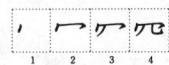

Radical	Strokes
网 122	4-4-0
Grade	**Freq**
Radical	
2 - 2 - 2	

1 2 3 4

RADICAL 122

yonkashira, variant of 网 *amigashira* 'net'

⇨ see 网 2988 for radical description

2-2 几

殳

1978

Radical	Strokes
殳 79	4-4-0
Grade	**Freq**
Radical	
2 - 2 - 2	

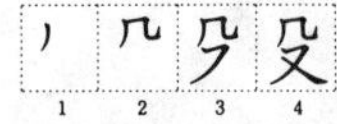

1 2 3 4

RADICAL 79

Standard form: 殳 *rumata* or *hokozukuri* 'club' (段 殺 殿)

Description: used in characters related to beating or killing

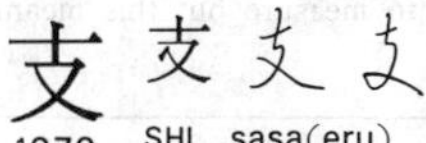

1979 SHI sasa(eru)

㊥ 支 zhī

Radical	Strokes
支 65	4-4-0
Grade	Freq
Jōyō-5	307
2-2-2	

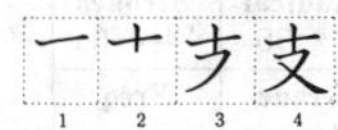

1 2 3 4

RADICAL 65

variant of 支 *shinyō* or *jūmata* 'branch'
⇨ see 支 1980 for radical description

▶**BRANCH** ▶**SUPPORT**

COMPOUNDS

❶ⓐ [sometimes also 枝 863] (something structurally analogous to a branch) **branch, offshoot**

ⓑ branch off, diverge

ⓒ [original meaning, now archaic] branch, twig

支店 *shiten* branch (office), branch (store)
支局 *shikyoku* branch office
支部 *shibu* branch office
支社 *shisha* branch office
支流 *shiryū* tributary, branch
支線 *shisen* branch line; spur
支離滅裂 *shirimetsuretsu* incoherence, inconsistency, disruption

❷ⓐ (bear the weight of) **support, prop up, hold up**

ⓑ (provide with aid) **support, maintain**

支柱 *shichū* prop, stay, support
支点 *shiten* fulcrum, point of support
支索 *shisaku* stay
支持 *shiji* support, maintenance, backing
支援 *shien* support, backing, aid

❸ⓐ **pay out, disburse, defray**

ⓑ **allocate, distribute, provide**

支出 *shishutsu* expenditure, disbursement, outgo
支払う *shiharau* pay
収支 *shūshi* incomings and outgoings, earnings and expenses
支給 *shikyū* provision, supply; allowance, grant; payment
支度する *shitaku suru* arrange, prepare; [original meaning, now archaic] measure, estimate

❹ control, regulate

支配する *shihai suru* control, manage, govern

❺ China

支那 *shina* China
南支 *nanshi* South China
駐支の *chūshi no* resident in China

❻ used phonetically for *shi*, esp. in the transliteration of foreign words

切支丹 *kirishitan* early Christianity in Japan; Jesuitism

❼ sign of the Oriental zodiac

十二支 *jūnishi* the twelve signs of the Oriental zodiac
干支 *kanshi* sexagenary cycle

❽ obstruction, hindrance

支障 *shishō* hindrance, obstacle, difficulty

KUN

【**sasa(eru) 支える**】(bear the weight of) support, prop up, hold up; (provide with aid) support, maintain; check

支え *sasae* prop, fulcrum, stay, support
屋根を支える *yane o sasaeru* hold up the roof
一家を支える *ikka o sasaeru* support one's family

SPECIAL READINGS

差し支える *sashitsukaeru* be hindered [impeded]

SYNONYMS

❶ⓐ **branch**

分 branch → 1972

❷ⓐ **bear**

担 BEAR ON SHOULDER → 318
負 BEAR (on the back) → 2091
荷 carry on shoulder → 2282

ⓑ **support**

擁 SUPPORT → 770
扶 LEND SUPPORT TO → 247
賛 back up → 2809

❸ⓐ **pay**

払う PAY → 194
納 PAY (to the authorities) → 1300
済 settle accounts → 522
賦 INSTALLMENT → 1583
償 RECOMPENSE → 176

❺ **China**

華 CHINA → 2283
漢 CHINESE → 657
中 People's Republic of China → 3451
台 Taiwan → 2005
唐 Cathay → 3115
呉 KINGDOM OF WU → 2549

COMPOUND FORMATION

支度 *shitaku*

支度する 'arrange, prepare, etc.', which consists of 支 ❸ⓑ 'allocate' and 度 'measure', originally meant to measure but this meaning is now archaic.

2-2 十

支 1980

▶BRANCH ▶SUPPORT
nonstandard for 支 1979

Radical	Strokes
支 65	4-4-0
Grade	**Freq**
Variant	
2 - 2 - 2	

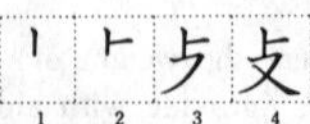

RADICAL 65
Standard form: 支 *shinyō* or *jūmata* 'branch'
Right variant: 支 *shinyō* or *jūmata*
Description: used in characters related to branching out or holding between

---

2-2 ト

攴 1981

Radical	Strokes
攴 66	4-4-0
Grade	**Freq**
Radical	
2 - 2 - 2	

RADICAL 66
Standard form: 攴 *bokuzukuri* or *tomata* 'strike' (敲)
Right variant: 攵 *nobun* (政 放 整)
Description: used in characters related to striking, forcing or other actions

---

2-2 ム

允 1982

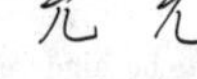

CH 允 yǔn

IN NAMES makoto nobu masa mitsu suke yoshi

Radical	Strokes
儿 10	4-2-2
Grade	**Freq**
Names	2096
2 - 2 - 2	

▶**GIVE CONSENT**

COMPOUNDS

❶ **give consent, comply, accede to, permit**
允可 *inka* compliance, permission, assent
允許 *inkyo* compliance, permission, assent

❷ [archaic] truly, greatly
允文允武 *inbun'inbu* be versed in the literary and military arts

❸ [archaic] sincerity
允恭 *inkyō* sincerity, courtesy

NAMES
允 *makoto* male name
允子 *nobuko* female name
允文 *masafumi* male name

SYNONYMS
❶ **permit**
許 PERMIT → 1470
免 license → 2067
准 grant permission → 127

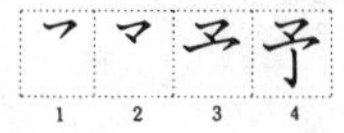

予 豫 予 豫

1983 YO arakaji(me)▲

CH 予 yú yǔ

Radical	Strokes
亅 6△	4-1-3
Grade	Freq
Jōyō-3	149
2-2-2	

2-2 マ

▶IN ADVANCE

COMPOUNDS

❶ [sometimes also 預 1042] **in advance, pre-, fore-, beforehand, previously, prior to, preliminary**

予言 *yogen* prediction, forecast
予知 *yochi* premonition, foreknowledge
予報 *yohō* forecast, prediction
予測 *yosoku* estimate, forecast, prediction
予算 *yosan* budget; estimate, calculation
予期 *yoki* expectation, anticipation, hope
予価 *yoka* probable [predetermined] price
予約 *yoyaku* reservation, preengagement; subscription
予定 *yotei* schedule, plan, prearrangement; expectation; estimate
予備 *yobi* reserve, spare; preparation, preliminaries
予科 *yoka* preparatory course
予防 *yobō* prevention, protection, precaution

❷ waver, vacillate; delay, dally
猶予する *yūyo suru* postpone, delay, extend; hesitate

❸ abbrev. of 伊予 *iyo*, old name for Ehime Prefecture
予讃本線 *yosanhonsen* Yosan Main Line (Ehime-Kagawa Railway)

INDEPENDENT

【yo 予】

① [also 余 2042] I, myself, the present writer—historically used as a formal first person pronoun but now only used pompously
予の辞書に不可能の文字は無い *Yo no jisho ni fukanō no moji wa nai* In my dictionary, there's no such word as impossible

② abbrev. of 予価 *yoka*: probable [predetermined] price
予五百円 *yo gohyakuen* probable price 500 yen

KUN

【arakaji(me) 予め】 in advance, beforehand, previously, ahead of time
予め計画を立てる *arakajime keikaku o tateru* plan ahead

SYNONYMS

❶ **before**
前 BEFORE → 2266
先 AHEAD → 2394

【yo】

① **first person pronouns**
余 I (*pompous*) → 2042
麿 I (*archaic*) → 3184
朕 IMPERIAL WE → 949
吾 I (*elegant*) → 2407
私 I (*polite*) → 1115
僕 I (*familiar*) → 164
俺 I (*intimate*) → 110
自 SELF → 3525
我 SELF → 3548
己 ONESELF → 3380
身 ONE'S PERSON → 3553

USAGE

yogen
予言
prediction, forecast
預言
prophecy (in Christianity)

NOTE

⇨ see NOTE at 余 2042

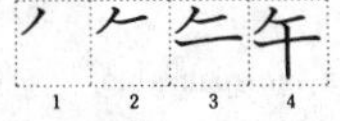

午 午 午

1984 GO uma▲

CH 午 wǔ

Radical	Strokes
十 24	4-2-2
Grade	Freq
Jōyō-2	83
2-2-2	

2-2 𠂉

▶NOON

COMPOUNDS

❶ **noon, noontime**
午睡 *gosui* nap, afternoon sleep
午前 *gozen* morning, forenoon
午後 *gogo* afternoon
正午 *shōgo* noon, noontime

❷ seventh sign of the Oriental zodiac: the

Horse—(time) 11 a.m.–1 p.m., (direction) south, (season) May (of the lunar calendar) (⇨ see APPENDIX 7)
子午線 *shigosen* meridian
端午 *tango* festival on the 5th of May (of the lunar calendar)

KUN

【uma 午】 seventh sign of the Oriental zodiac: the Horse (⇨ ❷)

SYNONYMS

❶ noon

昼 midday → 3097

❷ horse

馬 HORSE → 3296
駒 HORSE (*elegant*) → 1827
駿 FLEET STEED → 1832

HOMOPHONES

uma ⇨ 馬 3296

NOTE

⇨ see USAGE note at 馬 3296
⇨ see COMPOUND FORMATION for 子午線 *shigosen* ⇨ 子 3390

2-2

攵

1985

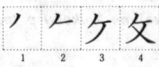

ノ 𠂉 ケ 攵
1 2 3 4

Radical	Strokes
攵 66	4-4-0
Grade	**Freq**
Radical	
2 - 2 - 2	

RADICAL 66

nobun, variant of 攴 *bokuzukuri* or *tomata* 'strike'
⇨ see 攴 1981 for radical description

2-2

1986

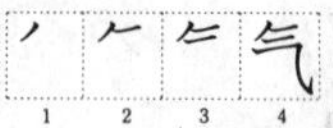

Radical	Strokes
气 84	4-4-0
Grade	**Freq**
Radical	
2 - 2 - 2	

RADICAL 84

Standard form: 气 *kigamae* 'vapor' (気 氣 氛)
Description: used in characters related to vapor or gas

2-2

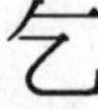

incorrect stroke count ⇨ see 1961

2-2

欠 缺 欠 㱁

Ⓒⓗ 缺 quē 欠 qiàn

1987 KETSU KEN▲ ka(keru) ka(ku)

ノ 𠂉 ケ 欠
1 2 3 4

Radical	Strokes
欠 76	4-4-0
Grade	**Freq**
Jōyō-4	875
2 - 2 - 2	

RADICAL 76

Standard form: 欠 *akubi* 'yawn' (次 欧 歌)
Description: used in characters related to opening or closing of the mouth

▶LACK

COMPOUNDS

❶ⓐ lack, be short of, be deficient
ⓑ lack, shortage, deficiency
欠乏 *ketsubō* lack, shortage, scarcity
欠如 *ketsujo* lack, shortage
欠員 *ketsuin* vacant position
不可欠な *fukaketsu na* indispensable
欠損 *kesson* deficit, deficiency; loss
ガス欠 *gasuketsu* running out of gas

❷ⓐ incompleteness, imperfection, defect
ⓑ incomplete, imperfect, defective
欠点 *ketten* weak point, defect
完全無欠 *kanzen-muketsu* absolute perfection

欠陥 *kekkan* defect, fault, deficiency
❸ⓐ **be absent from**
ⓑ missing, omitted
欠席 *kesseki* absence, nonattendance
欠勤 *kekkin* absence (from work)
欠字 *ketsuji* omitted word, blank type
❹ vacancy, vacant post, absence
補欠 *hoketsu* filling a vacancy; substitute, alternate
出欠 *shukketsu* attendance
❺ neglect, fail in
欠礼 *ketsurei* failure to pay one's compliments
❻ [formerly also 歇 1788] take a rest
間欠 *kanketsu* intermittence
❼ [archaic] yawn
欠伸 *kenshin* yawning and stretching

INDEPENDENT

【**ketsu 欠**】 lack, shortage, deficiency; absence; vacancy, vacant post
欠を補う *ketsu o oginau* supply a lack, bridge a gap

KUN

【**ka(keru) 欠ける**】 lack, be short of, be deficient; be vacant [missing]; wane; be broken off
常識に欠ける *jōshiki ni kakeru* lack in common sense
一人欠けている *hitori kakete iru* one person missing
欠けてゆく月 *kakete yuku tsuki* waning moon
欠けたコップ *kaketa koppu* chipped cup

【**ka(ku) 欠く**】 lack, want, be short of; neglect, omit; break off, chip
事欠く *kotokaku* lack, be in need of
義理を欠く *giri o kaku* fail in one's social duties
コップの縁を欠く *koppu no fuchi o kaku* chip the rim of a glass

SPECIAL READINGS

欠伸▲ *akubi* yawn

SYNONYMS

❶ⓐ **terms of negation**
没 lacking in → 260
無 WITHOUT (nonexistence) → 2135
非 IS NOT (contrariety) → 889
不 NOT (negation) → 3434
否 OR NOT → 2406
未 NOT YET → 3506
❷ⓐ **faults and flaws**
陥 defect → 457
難 fault → 1838
短 shortcoming → 1182
❸ⓑ **omit**
抜く leave out → 246
脱 leave out by mistake → 973
漏 omit → 701

NOTE

⇨ see USAGE note at 不 3434
★欠 *ken* 'yawn' was originally a different character from 缺 *ketsu* 'lack, etc.'. 欠 now replaces 缺, the latter which is considered a variant form of 欠.

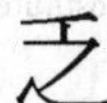

incorrect classification ⇨ see 1933

2-2 ⺄

1988

Radical	Strokes
爻 89	4-4-0
Grade	**Freq**
Radical	
2-2-2	

2-2 㐅

RADICAL 89

Standard form: 爻 *meme* 'crisscross'
Variant: 㸚 *meme* (爼 爽 爾)
Description: used for character classification

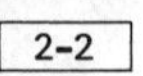

メ

交

1989

Radical	Strokes
交 89	4-4-0
Grade	**Freq**
Radical	
2-2-2	

RADICAL 89

variant of 交 *meme* 'crisscross'

⇨ see 交 1988 for radical description

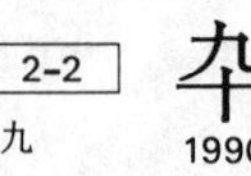

1990

▶**GRADUATE**

handwritten abbreviation for 卒 2055

2-3

亠

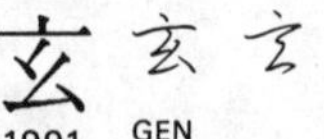

1991 GEN

Ⓒⓗ 玄 xuán

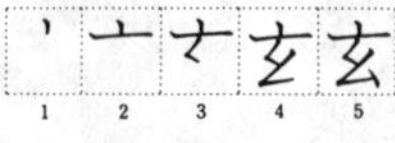

Radical	Strokes
玄 95	5-5-0
Grade	**Freq**
Jōyō	1473
2-2-3	

RADICAL 95

Standard form: 玄 *gen* 'dark' (率)

Description: used in characters related to darkness

▶**PROFOUND**

COMPOUNDS

❶ **profound, abstruse, mystic, occult, mysterious, esoteric**

玄妙な *genmyō na* abstruse, occult, mysterious

玄関 *genkan* entrance, (front) door

幽玄な *yūgen na* subtle and profound, quiet and beautiful, occult

❷ **unpolished**

玄米 *genmai* unpolished rice

玄麦 *genbaku* unpolished barley

❸ black tinged with red or yellow

玄武岩 *genbugan* basalt, whin(stone)

玄黄 *genkō* [rare] heaven and earth; black and yellow silk (offered to gods)

❹ great-great-grandchild

玄孫 *genson* great-great-grandchild

INDEPENDENT

【gen 玄】 profundity, occultness

SPECIAL READINGS

玄人 *kurōto* expert, master hand; prostitute

SYNONYMS

❶ **profound**

幽 deep hidden → 3008

奥 inmost → 2824

深 DEEP → 524

COMPOUND FORMATION

玄関 *genkan*

玄関 'entrance, (front) door' originally referred to the gateway (関) to the esoteric (玄 ❶) teachings of Buddhism.

立 立 立 ⒸⒽ 立 lì

Radical	Strokes
立 117	5-5-0
Grade	**Freq**
Jōyō-1	57
2-2-3	

1992 RITSU RYŪ RITTORU▲ ta(tsu) -ta(tsu) ta(chi)- ta(teru) -ta(teru) ta(te)- tate- -ta(te) -da(te) -da(teru)

丶 亠 亡 亣 立
1 2 3 4 5

RADICAL 117
Standard form: 立 *tatsu* 'stand' (競 章 竪)
Left variant: 𥫗 *tatsuhen* (端 竦 竭)
Description: used in characters related to standing

▶STAND ▶ESTABLISH

COMPOUNDS

❶ⓐ [original meaning] **stand, stand up, stand erect**
ⓑ **stand on one's own legs, be independent**
立像 *ritsuzō* standing image, statue
立腹する *rippuku suru* get angry, lose one's temper
立身する *risshin suru* establish oneself in life
起立 *kiritsu* standing up, rising
直立する *chokuritsu suru* stand erect [upright], rise perpendicularly
自立する *jiritsu suru* become independent, establish oneself
独立する *dokuritsu suru* become independent, stand on one's own legs [feet]
❷ standpoint, stand, position
対立 *tairitsu* opposition, antagonism
中立 *chūritsu* neutrality; neutralization
孤立する *koritsu suru* be isolated, stand alone
❸ⓐ **establish, set up, erect, found, institute**
ⓑ **established by (the nation, municipality, etc.)**
設立 *setsuritsu* establishment, foundation, setting up
樹立する *juritsu suru* establish, found
創立する *sōritsu suru* establish, organize, start
確立 *kakuritsu* establishment
建立 *konryū* erection, building (as a temple)
市立の *shiritsu* (=*ichiritsu*) *no* municipal, city
私立の *shiritsu* (=*watakushiritsu*) *no* private, nongovernmental
会社立の *kaisharitsu no* established by the company
❹ establish regulations, enact, lay down
立証 *risshō* proof, demonstration, substantiation
立法 *rippō* legislation, lawmaking
立案する *ritsuan suru* make a plan, devise, draft
立志 *risshi* fixing one's aim in life
❺ exist, come into existence
成立 *seiritsu* coming into existence, materialization; formation, organization; conclusion
両立 *ryōritsu* coexistence, compatibility
存立 *sonritsu* existence, subsistence
❻ begin
立春 *risshun* first day of spring
立冬 *rittō* first day of winter
❼ cubic, three-dimensional
立体 *rittai* solid (body), cube
立方体 *rippōtai* cube
立米 *ryūbei* cubic meter
❽ (help someone) ascend the throne
立太子 *rittaishi* official investiture of the Crown Prince
擁立する *yōritsu suru* give backing to, support, help (to the throne)
❾ abbrev. of 立教大学 *rikkyō daigaku*: Rikkyo University
立明戦 *ritsumeisen* Rikkyo-Meiji (baseball) game
❿ liter
五十立 *gojūrittoru* 50 liters
⓫ unclassified compounds
立派な *rippa na* fine, excellent, admirable

KUN

【ta(tsu) 立つ】
①ⓐ stand, stand up, rise
ⓑ stand out, be conspicuous
ⓒ (stand on one's own legs) establish oneself, begin life
ⓓ stand up to (criticism)
立場 *tachiba* standpoint
立ち上がる *tachiagaru* stand up, rise to one's feet; take action
立ち直る *tachinaoru* regain one's footing, recover; (of the market) improve
目立つ *medatsu* stand out, be conspicuous
引き立つ *hikitatsu* be set off, improve in appearance, contrast well
文を以て立つ *bun o motte tatsu* live by the

pen
面目が立つ *menmoku* (=*menboku*) *ga tatsu* save one's face
② [formerly 起つ] rise (to action), rouse oneself
祖国の為に立つ *sokoku no tame ni tatsu* rise to the rescue of one's country
③ begin an action:
ⓐ [formerly also 発つ] start (on a journey), leave, depart
ⓑ (of seasons) begin, come
ⓒ (of the market) open
先立つ *sakidatsu* precede, go before; die before
旅立ち *tabidachi* departure
秋立つ日 *akitatsuhi* first day [beginning] of autumn
市が立つ日 *ichi ga tatsu hi* market day
④ (of birds) take wing, rise in the air
飛び立つ *tobitatsu* rise in the air, take flight
⑤ evaporate, rise (in vapor), (of smoke) go up
立ち上る *tachinoboru* go up, rise, ascend
⑥ (of waves) run high
波立つ海 *namidatsu umi* choppy sea
⑦ (of plans or policies) be formed, be established; be decided; make sense, hold water
言い訳が立たない *iiwake ga tatanai* admit no excuse
⑧ be proficient in
筆が立つ *fude ga tatsu* wield a facile pen
⑨ stand in good stead, be useful
役立つ *yakudatsu* be of use, serve a purpose
⑩ (of rumors) spread
噂が立っている *Uwasa ga tatte iru* A rumor is about
⑪ get excited
苛立つ *iradatsu* be irritated, be nettled, be impatient
浮き立つ *ukitatsu* be enlivened, be exhilarated
腹が立つ *hara ga tatsu* get angry, take offense
⑫ *math* give, make (an integral quotient)
十六を五で割ると三が立って一が余る *Jūroku o go de waru to san ga tatte ichi ga amaru* Sixteen divided by five gives three with a remainder of one
⑬ (of arrows or thorns) stick into, run into
喉に骨が立った *Nodo ni hone ga tatta* A bone got caught in the throat

【-ta(tsu) -立つ】
① verbal suffix indicating intensity of action or beginning
煮立つ *nitatsu* boil up, begin to boil
② take form, be formed
成り立つ *naritatsu* consist of; be realized, be concluded, materialize

生い立ち *oitachi* one's upbringing, one's childhood
③ unclassified compounds
夕立ち *yūdachi* sudden evening shower
顔立ち *kaodachi* looks, features

【ta(chi)- 立ち-】
① [also prefix] standing
立ち読みする *tachiyomi suru* browse (in a bookstore)
立ち小便 *tachishōben* urinating outdoors (while standing)
② emphatic verbal prefix
立ち戻る *tachimodoru* return, come back
立ち入る *tachiiru* enter, trespass
立ち会う *tachiau* attend, take part in, witness

【ta(teru) 立てる】
① stand, make stand, erect, raise, set
立て掛ける *tatekakeru* lean against, set against
旗を立てる *hata o tateru* hoist a flag
候補者を立てる *kōhosha o tateru* put up a candidate
②ⓐ establish, set up, form
ⓑ establish (laws), enact, lay (plans), develop (a theory)
計画を立てる *keikaku o tateru* make plans
立て直す *tatenaosu* rally, make over; reorganize
献立 *kondate* menu, preparations
仮説を立てる *kasetsu o tateru* build up a hypothesis
③ establish oneself, support oneself
身を立てる *mi o tateru* make a success in life
生計を立てる *seikei o tateru* make a living
④ look up to, respect
夫を立てる *otto o tateru* treat one's husband with due respect
引き立てる *hikitateru* favor; set off; march (a prisoner) off
⑤ⓐ do one's duty, be loyal
ⓑ save face
義理を立てる *giri o tateru* do one's duty, be faithful
顔を立てる *kao o tateru* save (a person's) face
⑥ raise (one's voice)
音を立てるな *Oto o tateru na* Don't make a noise
⑦ set (a rumor) afloat
噂を立てられる *uwasa o taterareru* be gossiped about
⑧ make an oath
誓いを立てている *chikai o tatete iru* be under a vow
⑨ render (distinguished services)
手柄を立てる *tegara o tateru* do a meritori-

ous deed

⑩ sharpen (a saw)

目立をする *metate o suru* set the teeth of a saw

⑪ [usu. 閉てる] shut (as a paper sliding-door)

戸を立てる *to o tateru* shut a door

⑫ [formerly also 点てる] make tea

野立て *nodate* open-air tea ceremony

⑬ make use of

役立てる *yakudateru* put to use, make use of, turn to account

⑭ become angry

腹を立てる *hara o tateru* get angry, take offense

【-ta(teru) -立てる】

① emphatic verbal suffix:

ⓐ repeatedly, incessantly; intensely

ⓑ up, about (as in *stir up* and *noise about*)

攻め立てる *semetateru* make an incessant onslaught

見立てる *mitateru* diagnose, judge; select

騒ぎ立てる *sawagitateru* make a great fuss

書き立てる *kakitateru* write up

② assemble, make

組み立てる *kumitateru* assemble, construct, erect

仕立てる *shitateru* tailor; prepare

【ta(te)- 立て-, tate- 立-】

①ⓐ standing

ⓑ [formerly also 竪] vertical, upright

立て看板 *tatekanban* standing signboard

立て型ピアノ *tategata piano* upright piano

② leading

立て役者 *tateyakusha* leading actor; leader

③ unclassified compounds

立て替える *tatekaeru* pay for another; pay in advance

【-ta(te) -立て】

① [also suffix] stand, standing object

傘立て *kasatate* umbrella stand

衝立て *tsuitate* single-leaf screen

② [verbal suffix] fresh from, hot from, wet from

外国から帰り立ての人 *gaikoku kara kaeritate no hito* a man just returned from overseas

焼き立ての魚 *yakitate no sakana* fish hot from the oven

③ counter for successive victories [defeats]

三立てを食う *santate o kuu* lose three games straight

【-da(te) -立て】

① counter for:

ⓐ number of carriage horses or boat oars

ⓑ number of films in a multifeature movie

四頭立ての馬車 *yontōdate no basha* carriage and four

二本立ての映画 *nihondate no eiga* double feature movie

② doing on purpose, doing something uncalled for

隠し立て *kakushidate* keeping secret, concealment

【-da(teru) -立てる】 suffix for forming verbs from nouns

荒立てる *aradateru* aggravate, make serious

証拠立てる *shōkodateru* prove, substantiate

SYNONYMS

❶ **assume upright position**

起 RISE → 3307

❷ **standpoint**

地 one's ground → 204

❸ **found**

設 SET UP → 1471

置 found → 2608

❿ **capacity units**

勺 *SHAKU* (0.018 liters) → 2933

合 *go* (0.18 liters) → 2019

升 *SHO* (1.8 liters) → 3455

斗 *TO* (18 liters) → 2953

石 *koku* (180 liters) → 2971

【tateru】

① **raise**

起 raise up → 3307

上 raise → 3404

揚 RAISE HIGH → 593

掲 PUT UP → 494

挙 RAISE → 2456

拾う PICK UP → 379

【tate-】

① **vertical**

縦 VERTICAL → 1408

垂 perpendicular → 3565

直 STRAIGHT → 2932

USAGE

❶ **tatsu**

立つ

①ⓐ stand, stand up, rise

ⓑ stand out, be conspicuous

ⓒ (stand on one's own legs) establish oneself, begin life

ⓓ stand up to (criticism)

② [formerly 起つ] rise (to action), rouse oneself

③ begin an action:

ⓐ [formerly also 発つ] start (on a journey), leave, depart

ⓑ (of seasons) begin, come

ⓒ (of the market) open

④ (of birds) take wing, rise in the air

⑤ evaporate, rise (in vapor), (of smoke) go up

⑥ (of waves) run high

⑦ (of plans or policies) be formed, be established; be decided; make sense, hold

water
⑧ be proficient in
⑨ stand in good stead, be useful
⑩ (of rumors) spread
⑪ get excited
⑫ *math* give, make (an integral quotient)
⑬ (of arrows or thorns) stick into, run into

建つ
be built, be erected, be established

起つ
[now usu. 立つ] rise (to action), rouse oneself

発つ
[now usu. 立つ] start (on a journey), leave, depart

経つ
pass, elapse, go by

❷ tateru

立てる
① stand, make stand, erect, raise, set
②ⓐ establish, set up, form
ⓑ establish (laws), enact, lay (plans), develop (a theory)
③ establish oneself, support oneself
④ look up to, respect
⑤ⓐ do one's duty, be loyal
ⓑ save face
⑥ raise (one's voice)
⑦ set (a rumor) afloat
⑧ make an oath
⑨ render (distinguished services)
⑩ sharpen (a saw)
⑪ [usu. 閉てる] shut (as a paper sliding-door)
⑫ [formerly also 点てる] make tea
⑬ make use of
⑭ become angry

建てる
ⓐ build, construct, erect, put up
ⓑ establish (a nation)

点てる
[now usu. 立てる] make tea

閉てる
[sometimes also 立てる] shut (as a paper sliding-door)

❸ tate

立て-
①ⓐ standing
ⓑ [formerly also 竪] vertical, upright
② leading
③ unclassified compounds

縦
① [formerly also 竪] length, height
② warp

竪
① [now usu. 立て-] vertical, upright
② [now usu. 縦] length, height

建て
[in compounds] business commitment, sales contract

❹ -date

-立て
① counter for:
ⓐ number of carriage horses or boat oars
ⓑ number of films in a multifeature movie
② doing on purpose, doing something uncalled for

-建て
[also suffix]
① way of building, method of construction
② currency of exchange
③ average number of pages (of a newspaper or magazine)

HOMOPHONES

tatsu ⇨ 建 3090 起 3307 発 2565 経 1331
tateru ⇨ 建 3090 点 2084 閉 3319
tate- ⇨ 縦 1408 竪 2837 建 3090
-date ⇨ 建 3090

COMPOUND FORMATION

❶ 立腹 *rippuku*
立腹する 'get angry, etc.', literally to have one's bowels (腹) stand up (立 ❶ⓐ), derives from 腹が立つ *hara ga tatsu* 'get angry'.

❷ 献立 *kondate*
献立 'menu, preparations' originally referred to making plans (立てる ②ⓑ) for offering wine (献) to guests.

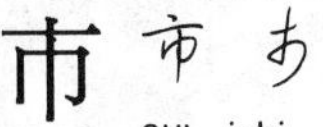

1993 SHI ichi

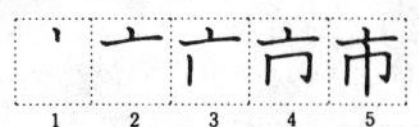

1 2 3 4 5

CH 市 shì

Radical	Strokes
巾 50	5-3-2
Grade	Freq
Jōyō-2	75
2-2-3	

2-3 亠

▶CITY ▶MARKET

COMPOUNDS

❶ⓐ **city, town**

ⓑ [also prefix] (unit of local administration) **city, municipality**

ⓒ **suffix after names of cities**

市井の出来事 *shisei no dekigoto* events on the street

市内 *shinai* city

市民 *shimin* citizens, townsmen

都市 *toshi* cities, urban communities

同市 *dōshi* same city

市長 *shichō* mayor

市営 *shiei* municipal management

市役所 *shiyakusho* municipal office, city hall

大阪市 *ōsakashi* Osaka city

高松市 *takamatsushi* Takamatsu city

❷ⓐ [original meaning] **market, fair**

ⓑ *economics* **market**

市場 *shijō* market, mart

市販 *shihan* marketing

市況 *shikyō* market conditions, tone of the market

市価 *shika* market price

INDEPENDENT

【shi 市】city (⇨ ❶ⓐ & ❶ⓑ)

KUN

【ichi 市】market, fair; crowded quarters

市場 *ichiba* market, marketplace

競り市 *seriichi* auction sale

闇市 *yamiichi* black market

我楽多市 *garakutaichi* rummage sale

市を成す *ichi o nasu* have a crowd of people

SYNONYMS

❶ **cities and towns**

町 TOWN → 1113

都 METROPOLIS → 1686

京 CAPITAL → 2052

❷ **market**

場 market → 558

1994

▶MAIN ▶MASTER

nonstandard for 主 1938

2-3 亠

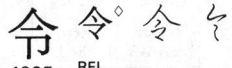

令 令 令 令

1995 REI

ノ 𠆢 亼 今 令

1 2 3 4 5

CH 令 lìng lǐng

Radical	Strokes
人 9	5-2-3
Grade	Freq
Jōyō-4	632
2-2-3	

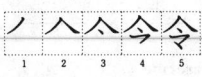

2-3 𠆢

▶COMMAND

COMPOUNDS

❶ [also suffix] [original meaning] **command, order, decree**

命令 *meirei* command, orders; edict, decree

司令 *shirei* commanding; commander, commandant

軍令 *gunrei* military command

辞令 *jirei* written appointment; wording, phraseology

指令 *shirei* order, instruction

訓令 *kunrei* instructions, (official) orders, directive

号令する *gōrei suru* give an order, command

動員令 *dōinrei* mobilization order(s)

❷ [also suffix] **ordinance, law, act**

政令 *seirei* government ordinance, cabinet order

法令 *hōrei* laws and ordinances, statute

戒厳令 *kaigenrei* martial law

❸ⓐ [also prefix] [honorific] your honorable

ⓑ good, fair

令嬢 *reijō* daughter; young lady

令夫人 *reifujin* Mrs., madam, your wife

令名 *reimei* fair name, good repute

巧言令色 *kōgen reishoku* flattery, honeyed words

❹ *hist* administrator, governor, chief

県令 *kenrei* (former) prefectural governor

❺ [also 齢 1895] age, years
年令 *nenrei* age, years
⇨ see 齢 1895 for other compounds

INDEPENDENT

【rei 令】 command, order
【reisuru 令する】 command, order, dictate

SYNONYMS

❶ **command**
命 ORDER → 2058
❷ **laws and rules**
法 LAW → 333
律 LAW → 363
典 CANON → 2627
憲 CONSTITUTION → 2368
則 RULE → 1444
矩 RULE → 1148
規 REGULATION → 978
紀 discipline → 1276
❸ⓐ **honorific prefixes**
貴 YOUR HONORABLE → 2606
尊 your honorable → 2324
御 GENERAL HONORIFIC TERM → 577
❺ **age**
齢 AGE → 1895
年 years → 2035
歳 AGE SUFFIX → 2490
才 AGE SUFFIX → 3410
寿 life span → 3557

2-3 人
仝 1996
▶**SAME**
nonstandard for 同 2987

2-3 人

1997
▶**COMMAND**
nonstandard for 令 1995

2-3 人
令 1998
▶**AGE**
nonstandard for 齢 1895

2-3 人
令 1999
▶**AGE**
nonstandard for 齢 1895

2-3 冖
写 寫 写 写
2000 SHA utsu(su) utsu(ru)

Ⓒⓗ 写 xiě

Radical	Strokes
冖 14△	5-2-3
Grade	**Freq**
Jōyō-3	542
2-2-3	

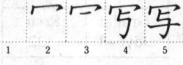

▶**COPY**

COMPOUNDS

❶ (reproduce an original, esp. by writing) **copy, make a copy, transcribe, reproduce, imitate**
写経 *shakyō* copying of a sutra, copied sutra
写生 *shasei* sketching [drawing] from nature; portrayal
写本 *shahon* manuscript, written copy
謄写 *tōsha* copy, reproduction, mimeograph
複写 *fukusha* copy, duplication
書写 *shosha* transcription, copying, handwriting
模写(=摸写) *mosha* copying, tracing, reproduction
❷ (depict in pictures or words) **portray, picture, depict, describe**
写真 *shashin* photograph
写実 *shajitsu* objective description; realism
描写 *byōsha* depiction, description; portrayal; drawing
❸ⓐ **shoot, photograph, take pictures**
ⓑ project (an image), show (a film), screen
写植 *shashoku* phototypesetting
特写 *tokusha* exclusive shooting [photographing] (for a magazine)
接写 *sessha* close-up photograph
映写 *eisha* projection
試写 *shisha* preview, private showing

KUN

【utsu(su) 写す】
vt

① copy, make a copy, transcribe, reproduce, imitate
写し *utsushi* copy, transcript, duplicate, imitation
生き写し *ikiutsushi* close resemblance
② portray, picture, depict, describe, express
山水を写した絵 *sansui o utsushita e* picture representing a landscape
③ take a picture, photograph, shoot
写真を写す *shashin o utsusu* take a picture, photograph

【utsu(ru) 写る】
vi
① (of pictures) be taken, come out
写り *utsuri* print, impression
この写真に写っている人 *kono shashin ni utsutte iru hito* the man in this photograph
② be seen through
透けて写る *sukete utsuru* be seen through
③ appear upon, be impressed upon (a surface in the original form)
紙の裏に写った字 *kami no ura ni utsutta ji* letter imprinted from the next page (by chance)

SYNONYMS

❶ copy
謄 TRANSCRIBE → 1093
複 duplicate → 1222
拓 copy by rubbing → 317

❶ write
記 WRITE DOWN → 1453
紀 record in writing → 1276
控える note down → 495
録 RECORD → 1742
登 register → 2595
書 WRITE → 2658
筆 write → 2677

❷ describe
叙 DESCRIBE → 1446
描 DEPICT → 488

❸ⓐ photograph
撮 PHOTOGRAPH → 737

ⓑ project
映 PROJECT → 892

USAGE

❶ utsusu

写す
vt
① copy, make a copy, transcribe, reproduce, imitate
② portray, picture, depict, describe, express
③ take a picture, photograph, shoot

映す
① reflect, mirror
② project (a motion picture)

移す
vt
①ⓐ shift, move, transfer
ⓑ transfuse (liquids or colors)
ⓒ divert, turn, direct
② transmit (a disease)

❷ utsuru

写る
vi
① (of pictures) be taken, come out
② be seen through
③ appear upon, be impressed upon (a surface in the original form)

映る
①ⓐ be reflected, be imaged, be mirrored
ⓑ be projected, be on (TV)
② match, suit, be becoming

移る
vi
① move (to a new house)
② shift, change, pass
③ be infected with; be contagious
④ (of odors) soak in

HOMOPHONES

utsusu ⇨ 映 892 移 1177
utsuru ⇨ 映 892 移 1177
utsuri ⇨ 映 892 移 1177

NOTE

⇨ see also USAGE note at 映 892

召 召 召

2001 SHŌ me(su)

ⒸⒽ 召 zhào shào

Radical	Strokes
口 30	5-3-2
Grade	**Freq**
Jōyō	1469
2 - 2 - 3	

2-3
刀

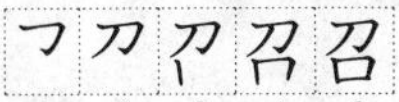

1 2 3 4 5

▶SUMMON

COMPOUNDS

● [original meaning] **summon (esp. one's inferior), call together, convene**
召集する *shōshū suru* call together
召還する *shōkan suru* recall, call back
召喚 *shōkan* summons, citation
応召者 *ōshōsha* draftee

KUN

【me(su) 召す】 [honorific] summon, call, send

for; wear, put on; take (as a bath, vehicle or food); be pleased with
召使 *meshitsukai* servant
お召し物 *omeshimono* dress, clothes
召し上がる *meshiagaru* eat, drink
思し召し *oboshimeshi* your (honorable) wishes
お気に召しましたか *Oki ni meshimashita ka* Is it pleasing to you, sir [madam]?

SYNONYMS

● **call and invite**
招 INVITE → 316
呼ぶ CALL → 273
喚 CALL → 550

2-3
十

古

2002 KO furu(i) furu- -furu(su)

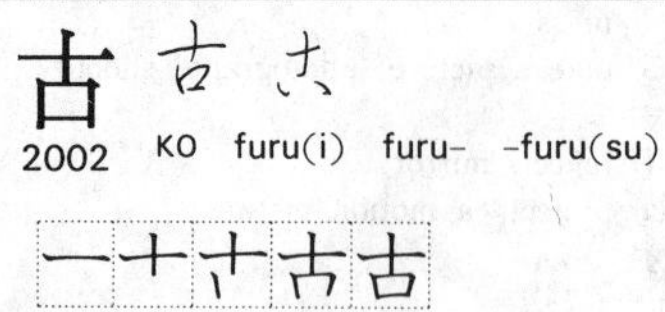

CH 古 gǔ

Radical	Strokes
口 30	5-3-2
Grade	**Freq**
Jōyō-2	384
2-2-3	

▶**OLD**

COMPOUNDS

ⓐ [original meaning] (not new) **old**
ⓑ [also prefix] (of the remote past) **old, ancient, obsolete**
ⓒ old times, ancient times
古書 *kosho* old book, rare book
古風 *kofū* old style; old customs
古典 *koten* classics; old book
古跡 *koseki* historic remains, ruins
古代 *kodai* ancient times, antiquity, remote ages
古語 *kogo* obsolete word; old proverb
古文書 *komonjo* ancient documents; paleography
古今 *kokon* ancient and modern times
古希 *koki* three score and ten, seventy years of age
考古学 *kōkogaku* archaeology
復古 *fukko* revival (of the ancient regime), restoration
中古 *chūko* Middle Ages; secondhand [used] goods

KUN

【**furu(i) 古い**】 old, antiquated, outdated, ancient
古 *furu* old thing, used article
古さ *furusa* oldness, antiqueness
古びる *furubiru* grow old; look old
古臭い *furukusai* antiquated, old-fashioned; obsolete
古本 *furuhon* old book, secondhand book
中古 *chūburu* (=*chūko*) secondhand [used] goods
【**furu- 古-**】 [prefix] old, secondhand
古新聞 *furushinbun* old newspapers
【**-furu(su) -古す**】 [verbal suffix] become or cause to become old
使い古す *tsukaifurusu* wear out (a thing) by use
言い古した言葉 *iifurushita kotoba* hackneyed saying

SYNONYMS

● **old**
老 OLD (not young) → 3197
故 OLD (of the past) → 1141
旧 old → 14

NOTE

⇨ see COMPOUND FORMATION for 古希 *koki* ⇨ 希 2049

2-3
十

卋

incorrect stroke count ⇨ see 2025
(nonstandard for 世 3496)

占 占 占 2003

CH 占 zhān zhàn

SEN shi(meru) urana(u)

Radical	Strokes
ト 25	5-2-3
Grade	Freq
Jōyō	808
2-2-3	

2-3 ト

1 2 3 4 5

▶OCCUPY ▶DIVINE

COMPOUNDS

❶ **occupy, hold, seize, take (up)**

占拠 *senkyo* occupation, exclusive possession
占有する *sen'yū suru* occupy, take possession of
占領地 *senryōchi* occupied area
独占 *dokusen* exclusive possession, monopoly

❷ [original meaning] **divine, tell fortune, augur**

占星術 *senseijutsu* astrology

KUN

【shi(meru) 占める】 occupy, hold, take (up); account for, amount to

独り占め *hitorijime* monopoly, exclusive possession
買い占める *kaishimeru* buy up
三割を占める *sanwari o shimeru* account for [amount to] 30%

【urana(u) 占う】 [formerly also トう] divine, tell (a person's) fortune, augur

占い *uranai* divination, fortunetelling
占い師 *uranaishi* diviner, fortuneteller
星占い *hoshiuranai* astrology, horoscopy

SYNONYMS

❶ **occupy**

拠 occupy → 312
領 take possession of → 1224
専 take exclusive possession of → 2644

❷ **divine**

易 divination → 2411

USAGE

❶ **uranau**

占う
[formerly also トう] divine, tell (a person's) fortune, augur

トう
[now usu. 占う] divine, tell (a person's) fortune, augur

❷ **uranai**

占い
[formerly also ト] divination, fortunetelling

ト
[now usu. 占い] divination, fortunetelling

HOMOPHONES

uranau ⇨ ト 3367
uranai ⇨ ト 3367

弁 辯 瓣 辨 弁 2004

CH 辨 辩 辫 弁 biàn 瓣 办 bàn

BEN wakima(eru)▲

Radical	Strokes
廾 55	5-3-2
Grade	Freq
Jōyō-5	722
2-2-3	

2-3 ム

1 2 3 4 5

▶SPEAK ELOQUENTLY ▶VALVE

COMPOUNDS

❶ [formerly 辯 1660]

ⓐ **speak eloquently, orate, talk**
ⓑ **speech, talk**

弁士 *benshi* speaker, talker; film interpreter
雄弁 *yūben* eloquence, fluency
熱弁 *netsuben* fervent speech, passionate eloquence
能弁家 *nōbenka* eloquent speaker, orator
答弁する *tōben suru* reply, answer; defend oneself
弁舌 *benzetsu* speech
多弁な *taben na* talkative
訥弁 *totsuben* slowness of speech

❷ [suffix] (regional speech) **dialect, accent**

東北弁 *tōhokuben* Tohoku dialect [accent]
関西弁 *kansaiben* Kansai dialect [accent]

❸ [formerly 辯 1660]

ⓐ **argue, debate, dispute**
ⓑ **argue for [in favor of], speak (up) for, defend, explain, justify**

弁論 *benron* discussion, argument; oral proceedings
弁護士 *bengoshi* lawyer, attorney
詭弁 *kiben* sophism, sophistry
代弁する *daiben suru* speak [act] for another; pay by proxy

弁明 *benmei* vindication, explanation, defense
弁解 *benkai* explanation, vindication, justification, excuse
抗弁する *kōben suru* make a plea, demur, defend oneself
❹ [formerly 瓣 1644] [also suffix]
ⓐ (machine part) **valve**
ⓑ *anat* valve
安全弁 *anzenben* safety valve
排気弁 *haikiben* exhaust valve
弁膜 *benmaku* valve (in internal organs)
半月弁 *hangetsuben* semilunar valve
❺ [formerly 辨 1610 or 辦 1609] **distinguish, discriminate, differentiate, discern**
弁別する *benbetsu suru* discriminate, distinguish
弁証法 *benshōhō* dialectic
思弁 *shiben* speculation
勘弁する *kanben suru* pardon, forgive; tolerate
❻ [formerly 辨 1610 or 辦 1609]
ⓐ [formerly 辦 1609] **dispose of, manage, attend to**
ⓑ **pay, defray**
弁務官 *benmukan* commissioner
弁理士 *benrishi* patent attorney
弁当 *bentō* box lunch, lunch, picnic lunch
合弁 *gōben* joint management [venture]
弁済 *bensai* repayment, payment, settlement
弁償する *benshō suru* compensate, indemnify
自弁する *jiben suru* pay one's own expenses
支弁する *shiben suru* pay, defray, disburse
❼ [formerly also 辨 1610 or 辦 1609] abbrev. of 弁当 *bentō*: box lunch, lunch
駅弁 *ekiben* station lunch
腰弁で *koshiben de* carrying lunch with one
❽ [formerly 辮 1653] pigtail, queue
弁髪 *benpatsu* pigtail, queue
❾ [formerly 瓣 1644] petal (of a flower)
花弁 *kaben* petal
離弁花 *ribenka* schizopetalous flower
❿ⓐ [original meaning, now archaic] conical cap worn by military officers in ancient times
ⓑ [archaic] military officer of low rank
武弁 *buben* soldier

INDEPENDENT

【ben 弁】 speech, tongue; valve (⇨ ❹); *bot* petal, valve
【benjiru (=benzuru) 弁じる(=弁ずる)】 speak, make a speech; argue for [in favor of]
弁じ立てる *benjitateru* speak eloquently, talk volubly

KUN

【wakima(eru) 弁える】 discern, discriminate; know, bear in mind
弁えの無い *wakimae no nai* undiscerning, indiscreet

SYNONYMS

❶ⓐ speak and say
語る TELL → 1543
談 TALK → 1569
申す SPEAK HUMBLY → 3507
口 give mouth to → 3382
話 SPEAK → 1527
言 SAY → 1941
云 say → 1931
述 STATE → 3075
陳 SET FORTH → 540
❷ language
語 LANGUAGE → 1543
❸ argue and discuss
論 ARGUE → 1574
議 DISCUSS → 1647
争 CONTEND → 2030
❹ⓐ stoppers
栓 STOPPER → 934
❺ discriminate
識 DISCRIMINATE → 1639
分 tell apart → 1972

COMPOUND FORMATION

勘弁 *kanben*
勘弁する 'pardon, forgive; tolerate' originally meant to give careful thought to a matter (勘) and distinguish (弁 ❺) between good and bad. How this is related to the current meaning 'pardon, etc.' is not clear.

NOTE

⇨ see COMPOUND FORMATION for 弁当 *bentō* ⇨ 当 2177

台 臺 台 臺

2005 DAI TAI

ム ム 台 台 台

1 2 3 4 5

(CH) 台 tái tāi

Radical	Strokes
口 30△	5-3-2
Grade	**Freq**
Jōyō-2	228
2-2-3	

2-3 ム

▶STAND ▶COUNTER FOR VEHICLES

COMPOUNDS

❶ [also suffix]

ⓐ (structure for placing on) **stand, pedestal, rack, table, support, mount**

ⓑ (elevated structure) **stand, platform**

台座 *daiza* pedestal, base, stand
燭台 *shokudai* candlestick, candlestand
楽譜台 *gakufudai* music stand
鏡台 *kyōdai* dressing table
荷台 *nidai* carrier, bed (of a truck)
寝台 *shindai* bed, sleeping berth
流し台 *nagashidai* sink, washstand
実験台 *jikkendai* testing bench; subject of an experiment
閲兵台 *eppeidai* reviewing stand
証人台 *shōnindai* witness stand
滑り台 *suberidai* (playground) slide; launching platform

❷ [also suffix] [original meaning] (elevated structure commanding a wide view) **observatory, lookout, tower, tall building**

天文台 *tenmondai* astronomical observatory
気象台 *kishōdai* meteorological observatory
灯台 *tōdai* lighthouse; oil-lamp stand
露台 *rodai* balcony
見張り台 *miharidai* lookout

❸ⓐ (elevated land structure) **heights, hill, terrace, tableland**

ⓑ suffix after names of elevated places such as heights or hills

台地 *daichi* plateau, tableland
高台 *takadai* high ground, hill, height
駿河台 *surugadai* Surugadai Hill

❹ⓐ **counter for vehicles (as automobiles or bicycles)**

ⓑ **counter for machines or mechanical devices (as sewing machines, televisions, telephones, etc.)**

台数 *daisū* number of vehicles [machines]
自動車十台 *jidōsha jūdai* ten cars
ミシン六台 *mishin rokudai* six sewing machines

❺ suffix indicating numerical range: level, mark

千円台 *sen'endai* the 1000 yen level (between 1000 and 2000 yen)
五十点台の成績 *gojuttendai no seiseki* school mark in the 50's (between 50 and 60)
大台 *ōdai* (stock) 100-yen unit, high level (of stock prices)

❻ⓐ (physical) base, framework, base material

ⓑ (nonphysical) basis, foundation

台紙 *daishi* paste board, ground paper
車台 *shadai* car body, chassis
土台 *dodai* foundation, base, basis; utterly
台帳 *daichō* ledger, register
台無しになる *dainashi ni naru* be spoiled, come to nothing

❼ stage; the stand, the theater

台本 *daihon* playbook, script, scenario
台辞 *daiji* one's lines, words
舞台 *butai* stage, the boards

❽ **Taiwan, Formosa**

台湾 *taiwan* Taiwan
台中関係 *taichū kankei* relations between Taiwan and China
台北 *taihoku* Taipei

❾ [formerly 颱 *tai* 3336] typhoon

台風 *taifū* typhoon

❿ kitchen

台所 *daidokoro* kitchen
御台 *midai* wife of a shogun or a highest-ranking nobleman

⓫ⓐ [honorific] you, your

ⓑ honorific term referring to the Emperor or the gods

台顔 *daigan* your face
尊台 *sondai* you
台覧 *tairan* inspection by the Emperor or extremely noble persons

⓬ trapezoid

台形 *daikei* trapezoid
円錐台 *ensuidai* circular truncated cone

⓭ office or official of the central government

台閣 *taikaku* (=*daikaku*) Cabinet; tall building
鎮台 *chindai* garrison (in Meiji era)

⓮ [also 擡 *tai* 791] raise (one's head), lift

台頭する *taitō suru* raise one's head; come to the fore

⓯ counter for 16-page units in printing

二台 *nidai* 2 16-page units

INDEPENDENT

【dai 台】 stand, pedestal, rack, table, mount; platform

台に載せる *dai ni noseru* set on a stand

【tai 台】 Taiwan; abbrev. of 台風 *taifū*: typhoon

SPECIAL READINGS

台詞▲ *serifu* one's lines, words

SYNONYMS

❶ **flat supports**

座 SEAT → 3116
壇 PLATFORM → 754
架 rack → 2569
棚 SHELF → 984
床 BED → 3067

❶ **tables and stands**

卓 TABLE → 2064
机 DESK → 820

❷ **tall buildings**

閣 TALL MAGNIFICENT BUILDING → 3327
楼 TALL BUILDING → 1019
塔 TOWER → 561

❸ⓐ **hills**

丘 HILL → 3495
岡 HILL → 2997
坂 SLOPE → 234
阪 slope → 271
塚 MOUND → 556
陵 high mound → 544

❹ⓐ **vehicle**

車 VEHICLE → 3552
乗 vehicle → 3576
輪 wheeled vehicle → 1589

❽ **China**

華 CHINA → 2283
漢 CHINESE → 657
支 China → 1979
中 People's Republic of China → 3451
唐 Cathay → 3115
呉 KINGDOM OF WU → 2549

❾ **wind**

嵐 STORM → 2314
風 WIND → 3007

USAGE

-dai

-台

suffix indicating numerical range: level, mark

千円台 *sen'endai* the 1000 yen level (between 1000 and 2000 yen)

五十点台の成績 *gojuttendai no seiseki* school mark in the 50's (between 50 and 60)

-代

ⓐ suffix for range of a person's age in ten-year periods: -ies

ⓑ suffix indicating years spanning a specific period: -ies, the...-hundreds

二十代の男 *nijūdai no otoko* a man in his twenties

千九百年代 *senkyūhyakunendai* the 1900's

★The above two suffixes are very similar in meaning and are easily confused. Study the equivalents and examples carefully.

2-3 又 — 圣 2006

▶PASS THROUGH ▶MANAGE

nonstandard for 経 1331

2-3 又 — 圣 2007

▶PATH ▶DIAMETER

nonstandard for 径 291

2-3 亠 — 主

incorrect classification ⇨ see 1938

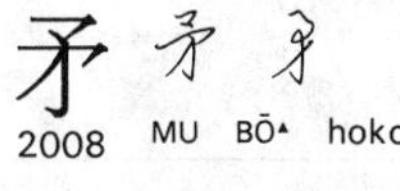

2008 MU BŌ▲ hoko

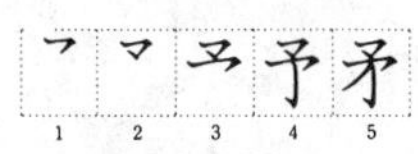

CH 矛 máo

Radical	Strokes
矛 110	5-5-0
Grade	**Freq**
Jōyō	1550
2-2-3	

2-3
マ

RADICAL 110
Standard form: 矛 *hoko* 'lance' (矜)
Description: used in characters related to lances, halberds or spears

▶**HALBERD**

COMPOUNDS

● [original meaning] **ancient Chinese weapon resembling a halberd or spear**
矛盾 *mujun* contradiction

KUN

【hoko 矛】
ⓐ ancient halberd or spear consisting of a long shaft and a double-edged blade
ⓑ [formerly 戈] arms
矛先 *hokosaki* spearhead; the aim (of an attack); the brunt (of an argument)

SYNONYMS

● & **【hoko】** ⓐ **cutting instruments**
剣 SWORD (double-edged) → 1672
刀 SWORD (single-edged) → 2926
刃 BLADE → 2929
鎌 SICKLE → 1760

USAGE

hoko
矛
ⓐ ancient halberd or spear consisting of a long shaft and a double-edged blade
ⓑ [formerly 戈] arms
鉾
decorative halberd
戈
ⓐ ancient Chinese weapon (similar to a spear or dagger-ax) consisting of a long shaft with a double-edged blade attached crosswise to its end
ⓑ [now usu. 矛] arms

HOMOPHONES

hoko ⇨ 鉾 1720 戈 3462

COMPOUND FORMATION

矛盾 *mujun*
矛盾 'contradiction' derives from an ancient Chinese legend. Once upon a time there was a proud merchant who claimed that his halberd (矛) was so powerful that it could pierce any shield, and that his shield (盾) was so strong that it could repel any halberd in the world. Then came along a wise man and queried: "What happens if your irresistible halberd strikes against your impenetrable shield?" The merchant considered this dilemma at great length. At last he exclaimed: "Golly! That must be a contradiction!" In this way, 矛盾 came to mean contradiction for all ages to come.

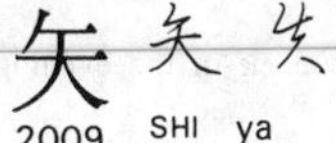

2009 SHI ya

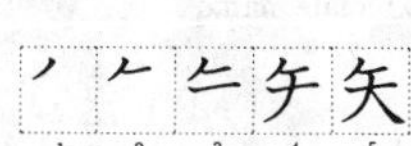

CH 矢 shǐ

Radical	Strokes
矢 111	5-5-0
Grade	**Freq**
Jōyō-2	1124
2-2-3	

2-3
𠂉

RADICAL 111
Standard form: 矢 *ya* 'arrow' (矣)
Left variant: 𥎦 *yahen* (知 短 矯)
Description: used in characters related to arrows or handling of arrows

▶**ARROW**

COMPOUNDS

● [original meaning] **arrow**
弓矢 *kyūshi* (= *yumiya*) bow and arrow
一矢を報いる *isshi o mukuiru* return a blow, retaliate

KUN

【ya 矢】 arrow, dart; wedge
矢印 *yajirushi* arrow (mark)
矢先 *yasaki* arrowhead
毒矢 *dokuya* poisoned arrow [dart]

SYNONYMS

● **projectiles and bombs**

弾 PROJECTILE → 572

丸 round projectile → 3417

爆 bomb → 1101

雷 explosive device → 2791

2-3 ⼇

尔

2010

▶**THAT**

nonstandard for 爾 3587

2-4 ⼇

亦 亦 亦

2011 EKI mata

Ⓒⓗ 亦 yì

Radical	Strokes
⼇ 8	6-2-4
Grade	Freq
Names	2074
2-2-4	

Stroke order: 1 2 3 4 5 6

▶**ALSO**

KUN

【**mata** 亦】[now usu. 又] [often preceded by も *mo*] also, too, as well

彼も亦良い人だ *Kare mo mata ii hito da* He is a nice man, too

私も亦 *watashi mo mata* I also, me too

NAMES

亦雄 *matao* male name

亦野 *matano* surname

SYNONYMS

【**mata**】

○ **additionally**

又 also, and → 3351

及び and → 3385

並びに and also → 2246

傍ら besides → 147

尚 STILL → 2233

更に furthermore → 3541

且つ AS WELL → 3485

兼 CONCURRENTLY → 2286

HOMOPHONES

mata ⇨ 又 3351 復 575

NOTE

⇨ see USAGE note at 又 3351

2-4 ⼇

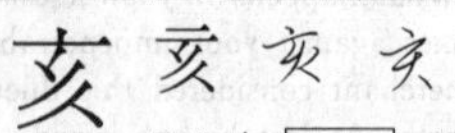

亥 亥 亥 亥

2012 GAI i NAMES ri

Ⓒⓗ 亥 hài

Radical	Strokes
⼇ 8	6-2-4
Grade	Freq
Names	2072
2-2-4	

Stroke order: 1 2 3 4 5 6

▶**THE BOAR**

COMPOUNDS

● twelfth sign of the Oriental zodiac: the Boar—(time) 9-11 p.m., (direction) NNW, (season) October (of the lunar calendar) (⇨ see APPENDIX 7)

亥月 *gaigetsu* October (of the lunar calendar)

KUN

【**i** 亥】twelfth sign of the Oriental zodiac: the Boar (⇨ ●)

亥の刻 *i no koku* 10 o'clock in the evening

NAMES

亥三 *izō* (=*isamu*) male name

SYNONYMS

● **swine**

猪 WILD BOAR → 536

豚 PIG → 976

HOMOPHONES

i ⇨ 猪 536

NOTE

⇨ see USAGE note at 猪 536

衣 *衣* *衣*

2013 I E▲ koromo kinu▲ -gi▲

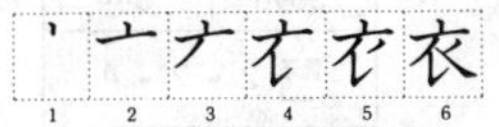

Ⓒ 衣 yī yì

Radical	Strokes
衣 145	6-6-0
Grade	**Freq**
Jōyō-4	1231
2-2-4	

2-4

RADICAL 145

Standard form: 衣 *koromo* 'clothes' (裁 袋 製)
Left variant: 衤 *koromohen* (補 被 袖)
Variant: 衣 *koromo* (裏 褒 衷)
Description: used in characters related to clothes or their qualities

▶**GARMENT**

COMPOUNDS

❶ⓐ **garment, garments, clothing, clothes** ⓑ **outer garment, gown, (priestly) robe, surplice**

衣装(=衣裳) *ishō* clothes, garment, dress, costume
衣類 *irui* clothes, garments
衣服 *ifuku* clothes, dress, clothing
衣食住 *ishokujū* food, clothing and shelter, the necessities of life
着衣 *chakui* one's clothes [clothing]
衣鉢 *ihatsu* (=*ehatsu*) mysteries (of Buddhism or an art)
白衣 *hakui* (=*byakue*) white robe [dress]; white coat
法衣 *hōi* (=*hōe*) sacerdotal robe
僧衣 *sōi* priestly robe
天衣無縫 *ten'imuhō* perfect beauty with no trace of artifice
胴衣 *dōi* jacket, vest
外衣 *gaii* outer garment

❷ outer coating

糖衣 *tōi* sugar coating
地衣 *chii* lichen

INDEPENDENT

【i 衣】 clothing, clothes
衣・食・住 *i-shoku-jū* food, clothing and shelter, the necessities of life

KUN

【koromo 衣】 outer garment, gown, (priestly) robe; garments, clothing, clothes: (outer covering) garment, coating (as of tempura), frosting

羽衣 *hagoromo* robe of feathers
墨染めの衣 *sumizome no koromo* black robe (of a priest)
衣替え *koromogae* seasonal change of clothes
緑の衣で覆われた山 *midori no koromo de ōwareta yama* mountain covered with a garment of green
砂糖の衣 *satō no koromo* icing

【kinu 衣】 *elegant* garment

衣擦れ *kinuzure* rustling (of clothes)
濡れ衣 *nureginu* false charge, unfounded suspicion
歯に衣を着せない *ha ni kinu o kisenai* not mince matters

【-gi -衣】 [usu. -着] outer garment, clothes, wear

上衣 *uwagi* outer garment, coat, jacket

SPECIAL READINGS

浴衣 *yukata* (=*yokui*) informal summer kimono, *yukata*

SYNONYMS

❶ **clothing**

服 CLOTHES → 878
-着 wear → 3316
装 DRESS → 2685

HOMOPHONES

kinu ⇨ 絹 1361
-gi ⇨ 着 3316

NOTE

⇨ see USAGE notes at 絹 1361 and 着 3316
⇨ see COMPOUND FORMATION for
衣鉢 *ihatsu* ⇨ 鉢 1708
天衣無縫 *ten'imuhō* ⇨ 縫 1406

2-4 ⼇

充 充 充 充

2014 JŪ a(teru) mi(tasu)▲

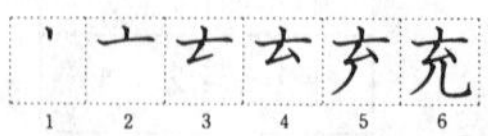

CH 充 chōng

Radical	Strokes
儿 10	6-2-4
Grade	Freq
Jōyō	944
2 - 2 - 4	

▶**FILL**

COMPOUNDS

❶ⓐ **fill, become full**

ⓑ **fill, fill up, stop up**

充填する *jūten suru* fill, fill up, plug

充満する *jūman suru* be full, be filled with, overflow

充分(＝十分)な *jūbun na* full, enough, sufficient; plentiful

拡充 *kakujū* expansion, amplification

充足 *jūsoku* sufficiency

充実した *jūjitsu shita* full, complete, rich

❷ **fill up (a vacancy), make up for (a deficiency)**

充員 *jūin* reserves

補充する *hojū suru* supplement, replenish, recruit

❸ allot, assign, appropriate

充当する *jūtō suru* allot, appropriate, earmark

充用する *jūyō suru* appropriate, earmark

KUN

【a(teru) 充てる】[sometimes also 当てる, but in compounds always 当てる] allot, assign, appropriate

金を借金の返済に充てる *kane o shakkin no hensai ni ateru* allot money to the payment of debts

【mi(tasu) 充たす】

[usu. 満たす]

① fill (up), pack

コップを充たす *koppu o mitasu* fill a glass

② fill, fulfill, satisfy, meet (the demand)

条件を充たす *jōken o mitasu* answer the requirement

SYNONYMS

❶ **fill**

満 fill → 607

詰める STUFF → 1521

❷ **supplement**

補 SUPPLEMENT → 1194

足 supplement → 2188

給 SUPPLY → 1350

❸ **allot**

当 assign → 2177

HOMOPHONES

ateru ⇨ 当 2177 宛 2222

mitasu ⇨ 満 607

NOTE

⇨ see USAGE notes at 当 2177 and 満 607

2-4 ⼇

交 交 交 交

2015 KŌ maji(waru) maji(eru) ma(jiru) ma(zaru) ma(zeru) -ka(u) ka(wasu) komogomo▲

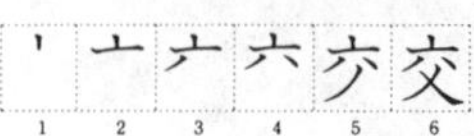

CH 交 jiāo

Radical	Strokes
⼇ 8	6-2-4
Grade	Freq
Jōyō-2	178
2 - 2 - 4	

▶**INTERCOURSE** ▶**INTERCHANGE**

COMPOUNDS

❶ⓐ **intercourse, friendly relations, association, friendship**

ⓑ **have friendly relations with, associate**

交際 *kōsai* association, friendship, intercourse

国交 *kokkō* diplomatic relations, national friendship

外交 *gaikō* diplomacy, foreign relations

断交 *dankō* severing [breaking off] relations

❷ unite in sexual intercourse

性交 *seikō* sexual intercourse

情交 *jōkō* sexual intercourse, illicit intercourse

❸ⓐ (give and receive mutually) **interchange, exchange**

ⓑ (succeed each other) **interchange, alternate, go back and forth**

交換する *kōkan suru* exchange, interchange, barter, substitute

交易 *kōeki* trade, commerce

文化交流 *bunka kōryū* cultural exchange

交代(＝交替)する *kōtai suru* relieve (a person), take turns, alternate

交番 *kōban* police box

交互に *kōgo ni* mutually, reciprocally, alternately

交流 *kōryū* alternating current; interchange

交通 *kōtsū* traffic, transport; communications
交渉 *kōshō* negotiation, bargaining, discussion

❹ [original meaning] **intercross, intersect, cross**
交差する *kōsa suru* cross, intersect (each other)
交戦 *kōsen* war, battle

❺ [formerly also 淆 518] **intermingle, mix, blend**
交織 *kōshoku* mixed weave
交錯 *kōsaku* mixture, blending, complication
混交する *konkō suru* mix up, jumble together

❻ hand over, deliver
交付する *kōfu suru* deliver, grant, hand (a ticket) to (a person)
手交する *shukō suru* hand, deliver

❼ abbrev. of 交通 *kōtsū*: traffic
道交法(=道路交通法) *dōkōhō* (=*dōrokōtsūhō*) Road Traffic Act

❽ abbrev. of 交渉 *kōshō*: negotiation, bargaining
団交 *dankō* collective bargaining

INDEPENDENT

【kō 交】 change (of season), turn
春夏の交 *shunka no kō* change from spring to summer

KUN

【maji(waru) 交わる】 *vi* cross, intersect; associate with, keep company with, mingle with, mix with; have friendly relations with, associate; have sexual relations with
二線の交わる点 *nisen no majiwaru ten* junction of two lines
交わり *majiwari* acquaintance, relations; sexual intercourse
女と交わる *onna to majiwaru* sleep with a woman

【maji(eru) 交える】 *vt* mix; cross; exchange
ユーモアを交える *yūmoa o majieru* intersperse with humor
膝を交えて *hiza o majiete* sitting knee to knee; intimately
言葉を交える *kotoba o majieru* exchange words

【ma(jiru) 交じる】 *vi* be mingled, be mixed, intermingle (with the constituents remaining distinct)
白髪交じりの髪 *shiragamajiri no kami* grizzly hair
子供に交じって遊ぶ *kodomo ni majitte asobu* join children at play

【ma(zaru) 交ざる】 same as **majiru 交じる**
英語が交ざった文 *eigo ga mazatta bun* writing interspersed with English

【ma(zeru) 交ぜる】 *vt* (combine together, with the constituents remaining distinct) mix, shuffle
交ぜ織り *mazeori* mixed weave
ない交ぜ *naimaze* intertwinement, blend

【-ka(u) -交う】 [verbal suffix] act reciprocally
飛び交う *tobikau* fly about
行き交う *ikikau* come and go, go back and forth

【ka(wasu) 交わす】 exchange; lay across
取り交わす *torikawasu* exchange, interchange
見交わす *mikawasu* exchange glances
枝を交わして *eda o kawashite* with branches crossing each other

【komogomo 交(=交交)】 alternately; in succession
悲喜交交 *hiki-komogomo* joy and sorrow in succession

SYNONYMS

❶ **personal relations**
好 friendship → 208
仲 PERSONAL RELATIONS → 43
縁 RELATION → 1386

❸ⓐ **change and replace**
換 EXCHANGE → 587
替 REPLACE → 2783
代 SUBSTITUTE → 30
迭 ALTERNATE → 3077
転 turn into → 1480
遷 undergo transition → 3170
化 CHANGE INTO, -ize → 21
変 CHANGE → 2069
更 change → 3541
改 change → 243
易 change → 2411

ⓑ **alternate**
迭 ALTERNATE → 3077
輪 take turns → 1589

❹ **intercross**
差 cross → 3311

❺ **mix**
混 MIX → 519
雑 MIXED → 1385
錯 MIXED UP → 1743

HOMOPHONES

majiru ⇨ 混 519
mazaru ⇨ 混 519
mazeru ⇨ 混 519

NOTE

⇨ see USAGE note at 混 519

2-4 亠

妄 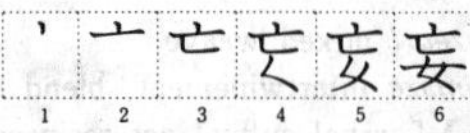

2016 MŌ BŌ mida(rini)▲

Ⓒⓗ 妄 wàng

Radical	Strokes
女 38	6-3-3
Grade	Freq
Jōyō	1950
2 - 2 - 4	

▶**RASH**

COMPOUNDS

❶ [sometimes also 盲 2053] [original meaning] **rash, reckless, wild, outrageous, thoughtless, indiscriminate**
妄言 *bōgen* (=*mōgen*) rash remark, thoughtless words
妄想 *mōsō* wild idea [fancy], paranoiac delusion
妄信 *mōshin* blind belief, credulity
妄評 *bōhyō* (=*mōhyō*) unjust [unfair] criticism
軽挙妄動する *keikyo-mōdō suru* act rashly
❷ false, untrue, absurd, preposterous
妄語 *mōgo* lie, falsehood
迷妄 *meimō* illusion, fallacy
虚妄 *kyomō* falsehood, untruth

KUN

【mida(rini) 妄りに】 without permission; without cause, unreasonably; indiscriminately, at random
妄りに入るべからず *Midarini hairubekarazu* No entry without permission

SYNONYMS

❶ **rash**
盲 BLIND → 2053
濫 unreasonable → 660
暴 unrestrained → 2515
荒 WILD → 2260
濫 EXCESSIVE → 801
乱 excessive → 1260

2-4 亠

2017

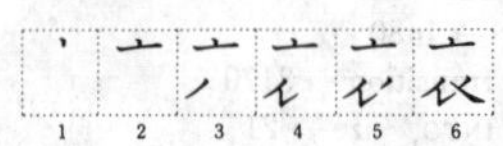

Radical	Strokes
衣 145	6-6-0
Grade	Freq
Radical	
2 - 2 - 4	

RADICAL 145

variant of 衣 *koromo* 'clothes'
⇨ see 衣 2013 for radical description

2-4 亠

交

2018

▶**INTERCOURSE** ▶**INTERCHANGE**

nonstandard for 交 2015

2-4 亠

亨

incorrect stroke count ⇨ see 2037

2-4 亠

incorrect stroke count ⇨ see 2039 (nonstandard for 学 2555)

合 合 𠆢

2019 GŌ GAT- KAT- a(u) -a(u) a(i) ai- -a(i) -ai a(wasu) a(waseru) -a(waseru)

ノ 𠆢 亼 亼 合 合
1 2 3 4 5 6

CH 合 hé gě

Radical	Strokes
口 30	6-3-3
Grade	**Freq**
Jōyō-2	39
2-2-4	

2-4 𠆢

▶**COMBINE** ▶**FIT**

COMPOUNDS

❶ [original meaning] **combine, unite, join together, meet**
合同の *gōdō no* combined, united, joint; congruent
合計する *gōkei suru* add up, total
合成 *gōsei* composition, synthesis
合弁 *gōben* joint management [venture]
合併する *gappei suru* combine, unite, merge
合衆国 *gasshūkoku* the United States (of America)
合唱 *gasshō* chorus
合宿する *gasshuku suru* lodge together, stay in a camp for training
合戦 *kassen* battle, encounter
集合する *shūgō suru* gather, meet, assemble; summon, call together
都合 *tsugō* convenience, circumstances; in all, altogether, totally
総合 *sōgō* synthesis, integration
結合する *ketsugō suru* unite, combine, join together
連合 *rengō* combination, union, alliance; association
統合する *tōgō suru* integrate, combine, unify
化合物 *kagōbutsu* (chemical) compound
混合する *kongō suru* mix, mingle

❷ juxtapose, put side by side
照合する *shōgō suru* verify, compare, collate
校合する *kyōgō* (=*kōgō*) *suru* collate, examine and compare

❸ **fit, suit, agree, accord, coincide**
合格 *gōkaku* passing an examination, eligibility
合理 *gōri* rationality
合法 *gōhō* legality, legitimacy
合意 *gōi* mutual agreement [consent]
合致 *gatchi* agreement, concurrence
適合する *tekigō suru* suit, be fit, conform (to)

❹ *go*:
ⓐ unit of capacity equiv. to approx. 0.18 liters or 1/10 of a *sho* (升)
ⓑ former unit of sq. measure equiv. to approx. 0.33 sq. m or 1/10 of a *tsubo* (坪)
五合升 *gogōmasu* 5-*go* measure

❺ 1/10 of the height of a given mountain
八合目 *hachigōme* eighth station (of Mt. Fuji)

❻ counter for engagements, esp. in fencing matches
合戦数合で *kassen sūgō de* after crossing swords several times

❼ counter for lidded utensils or receptacles

❽ *astron* conjunction
内合 *naigō* inferior conjunction

❾ abbrev. of 合成 *gōsei*: synthetic
合繊 *gōsen* synthetic fiber

INDEPENDENT

【gō 合】 *go* (⇨❹); *astron* conjunction; sum, total

KUN

【a(u) 合う】
vi
①ⓐ fit, suit
ⓑ harmonize, agree with, coincide
体に良く合う *karada ni yoku au* fit (a person) well
似合う *niau* befit, suit; match well
② come together, meet
噛み合う *kamiau* gear [engage] with, be in gear [mesh]; bite each other
③ⓐ be right [correct]
ⓑ (of a clock) indicate the right time
合わない答え *awanai kotae* incorrect answer
④ pay, be profitable
引き合う *hikiau* pay (off), be profitable; pull against each other

【-a(u) -合う】 [verbal suffix] act upon each other, act reciprocally
知り合う *shiriau* get acquainted with each other
折れ合う *oreau* make concessions, come to an agreement
殴り合う *naguriau* fight, exchange blows

【a(i) 合い, ai- 合-】
① [in compounds]
ⓐ fitting
ⓑ prearranged, agreed upon
合い鍵 *aikagi* duplicate key, passkey
合図 *aizu* signal, sign
合い言葉 *aikotoba* password
② [also 間] (space between) interval, space, opening
合いの戸 *ai no to* door between the rooms
③ [also 間]

ⓐ (time between) interval, intermission
ⓑ between seasons
合の手 *ainote* interlude
合間 *aima* interval
合い服 *aifuku* between-season wear
④ [also 間] [in compounds] mixed (blood)
合いの子 *ainoko derogatory* person of mixed parentage; crossbreed
合い挽き *aibiki* beef and pork ground together

【-a(i) -合い, -ai -合】
① element after verbs:
ⓐ for forming nouns
ⓑ indicating reciprocality
組合 *kumiai* union, guild, association
試合 *shiai* match, game
話し合い *hanashiai* talk, discussion, negotiation, consultation
見合い *miai* meeting with a view to marriage; looking at each other
②ⓐ appearance, general impression
ⓑ situation, condition, occasion
色合い *iroai* tone [shade] of color, coloring, tint
具合(＝工合) *guai* condition, state; health; manner, way
場合 *baai* occasion, situation, circumstances, case
③ degree, extent
度合 *doai* degree, extent, rate
歩合 *buai* rate, percentage; commission
割合 *wariai* rate, proportion, ratio; comparatively
④ suffix used to indicate general concepts
意味合い *imiai* meaning
筋合い *sujiai* reason

【a(wasu) 合わす】 same as **awaseru 合わせる**
合わせ鏡 *awasekagami* mirrors set against each other
混ぜ合わす *mazeawasu* mix together; blend, compound
仕合わせ *shiawase* [also 幸せ, formerly also 倖せ] happiness, blessing; good fortune

【a(waseru) 合わせる】
vt
①ⓐ (make into one) combine, unite, join
ⓑ [usu. 併せる] (bring two or more things together) join together, combine, merge
組み合わせる *kumiawaseru* combine, assort, join together, match
合わせ技 *awasewaza judo* combined trick
②ⓐ juxtapose, put side by side [on top]
ⓑ make (persons) confront each other
背中合わせに *senakaawase ni* back to back
詰め合わせ *tsumeawase* combination, assortment
顔合わせ *kaoawase* meeting, introduction; being matched against each other
③ mix, compound
薬を合わせる *kusuri o awaseru* compound a medicine
④ⓐ make fit, adjust, tune
ⓑ harmonize, match
ラジオを合わせる *rajio o awaseru* tune in the radio
音楽に合わせて踊る *ongaku ni awasete odoru* dance to the music
⑤ sum [add] up
合わせて百個 *awasete hyakko* a hundred in total
⑥ collate, tally with
照らし合わせる *terashiawaseru* test by comparison, collate, verify
問い合わせ *toiawase* reference, request for information
打ち合わせ *uchiawase* preliminary [previous] arrangement, preliminaries
申し合わせる *mōshiawaseru* make arrangement, mutually agree

【-a(waseru) -合わせる】
[verbal suffix]
① act upon each other, act reciprocally
見合わせる *miawaseru* look at each other; put off, give up
待ち合わせる *machiawaseru* wait, meet by appointment
② happen to
居合わせる *iawaseru* happen to be present
有り合わせの *ariawase no* ready, on hand

SYNONYMS

❶ **combine**
結 TIE → 1348
統 UNITE → 1352
括 LUMP TOGETHER → 376
総 integrate → 1379
併 join together → 83

❸ **fit**
適 suit → 3160
揃える MAKE UNIFORM → 590

❹ⓐ **capacity units**
勺 *SHAKU* (0.018 liters) → 2933
立 liter → 1992
升 *SHO* (1.8 liters) → 3455
斗 *TO* (18 liters) → 2953
石 *koku* (180 liters) → 2971

USAGE

awaseru
合わせる
①ⓐ (make into one) combine, unite, join
ⓑ [usu. 併せる] (bring two or more things together) join together, combine, merge
②ⓐ juxtapose, put side by side [on top]
ⓑ make (persons) confront each other
③ mix, compound

④ⓐ make fit, adjust, tune
ⓑ harmonize, match
⑤ sum [add] up
⑥ collate, tally with

併せる
[sometimes also 合わせる] (bring two or more things together) join together, combine, merge

会わせる
have (a person) meet (another), allow (a person) to see (someone)

遭わせる
subject to (an unfavorable experience), expose to

HOMOPHONES

au ⇨ 会 2020 遭 3159 遇 3135
ai ⇨ 間 3323 相 900
awaseru ⇨ 併 83 会 2020 遭 3159
shiawase ⇨ 幸せ 2216 倖せ 118
仕合わせ 34, 2019

COMPOUND FORMATION

仕合わせ *shiawase*
仕合わせ 'happiness, blessing; good fortune' consists of 仕 'do' and 合わす. It is a variant of 幸せ and derives from the verb 仕合わす *shiawasu* 'make shift'.

NOTE

⇨ see also USAGE notes at 会 2020 and 相 900 and 幸 2216
⇨ see COMPOUND FORMATION for
試合 *shiai* ⇨ 試 1525
合図 *aizu* ⇨ 図 3071
都合 *tsugō* ⇨ 都 1686

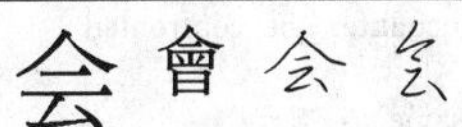

2020 KAI E a(u) a(waseru)

CH 会 huì kuài

Radical	Strokes
人 9△	6-2-4
Grade	**Freq**
Jōyō-2	8
2 - 2 - 4	

2-4 人

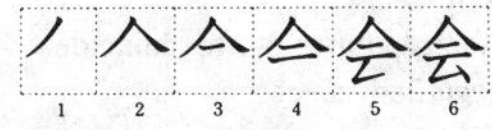

1 2 3 4 5 6

▶MEET ▶SOCIETY

COMPOUNDS

❶ [original meaning] (encounter by chance or arrangement) **meet, see, encounter, interview**
会話 *kaiwa* conversation
会談 *kaidan* conversation, talk, conference
会見 *kaiken* interview, audience
再会する *saikai suru* meet again
密会する *mikkai suru* meet secretly
面会 *menkai* seeing, interview

❷ⓐ [also suffix] **meeting, gathering; assembly, conference**
ⓑ [also suffix] **party**
ⓒ **session (of a legislative body, esp. the Japanese Diet)**
会合 *kaigō* meeting, gathering
会館 *kaikan* hall, assembly hall
会場 *kaijō* place of meeting, site
会議 *kaigi* conference, meeting, council
集会 *shūkai* gathering, meeting, assembly
総会 *sōkai* general meeting
開会 *kaikai* opening a meeting
大会 *taikai* mass meeting, rally; meet, tournament
座談会 *zadankai* round-table talk
忘年会 *bōnenkai* year-end party ("forget the year party")
晩餐会 *bansankai* dinner party
会期 *kaiki* session (of the Diet)
休会 *kyūkai* adjournment, recess (of the Diet)

❸ **(legislative) assembly, council**
議会 *gikai* assembly, national assembly
国会 *kokkai* National Diet; national assembly, congress
県会 *kenkai* prefectural assembly

❹ⓐ [also suffix] **society, association, club, circle, guild**
ⓑ **suffix after names of societies or clubs**
会社 *kaisha* company, corporation, firm
協会 *kyōkai* association, society
社会 *shakai* society, the world
同好会 *dōkōkai* association of like-minded persons; club
イエズス会 *iezusukai* Society of Jesus

❺ comprehend, understand, realize
会得 *etoku* understanding, comprehension, perception
会釈 *eshaku* salutation, greeting, bow

❻ opportunity, occasion
機会 *kikai* opportunity, occasion

❼ accounting
会計 *kaikei* account, finance; bill

❽ Buddhist ceremony
法会 *hōe* Buddhist mass
放生会 *hōjōe* ceremony of releasing captive animals

❾ chief city, capital
都会 *tokai* city, town

❿ verify
照会する *shōkai suru* inquire, apply for infor-

mation

INDEPENDENT

【**kai** 会】meeting, gathering, party; society, association

会に出席する *kai ni shusseki suru* attend a meeting

会の創立者 *kai no sōritsusha* founder of a society

【**kaisuru** 会する】meet, assemble; join

【**e** 会】Buddhist ceremony

KUN

【**a(u)** 会う】(encounter by chance or arrangement) meet, see, encounter, interview

人に会う *hito ni au* meet [see] a person

立ち会う *tachiau* attend, take part in, witness

出会い *deai* meeting, encounter

【**a(waseru)** 会わせる】have (a person) meet (another), allow (a person) to see (someone)

社長に会わせる *shachō ni awaseru* arrange a meeting with the company president

SYNONYMS

❶ **meet**

遭 MEET WITH → 3159
遇 ENCOUNTER → 3135
見 SEE → 2544
謁 BE GRANTED AN AUDIENCE → 1570

❷ⓐ **assembly**

集 gathering → 2771

ⓑ **social gatherings**

宴 BANQUET → 2271

❸ **legislature**

議 LEGISLATIVE BODY → 1647
院 House → 454

❹ **organized bodies**

協 association → 93
団 BODY → 3053
体 BODY → 71
組 union → 1337
労 workers' union → 2548
連 federation → 3103
講 fraternity → 1619
院 INSTITUTION → 454

❽ **ceremonies and festivities**

斎 religious ritual → 2115
礼 RITE → 818
祭 FESTIVAL → 2672
典 formal ceremony → 2627
儀 CEREMONY → 169
式 CEREMONY → 3049

USAGE

au

会う
(encounter by chance or arrangement) meet, see, encounter, interview

遭う
[also 遇う] (come upon, esp. by accident) meet with, encounter, be confronted

遇う
[also 遭う] same as 遭う

合う
①ⓐ fit, suit
ⓑ harmonize, agree with, coincide
② come together, meet
③ⓐ be right [correct]
ⓑ (of a clock) indicate the right time
④ pay, be profitable

HOMOPHONES

au ⇨ 遭 3159 遇 3135 合 2019
awaseru ⇨ 合 2019 併 83 遭 3159

COMPOUND FORMATION

会釈 *eshaku*

会釈 'salutation, greeting, bow' originally meant to comprehend (会 ❺) and interpret (釈) the precepts of Buddhism. What this has to do with bowing is not clear.

NOTE

⇨ see also USAGE note at 合 2019

2-4
人

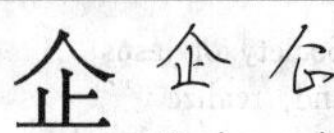

2021 KI kuwada(teru)

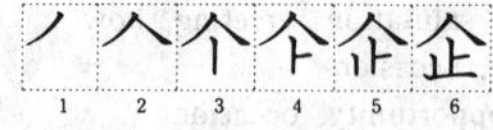

Ⓒ 企 qǐ

Radical	Strokes
人 9	6-2-4
Grade	**Freq**
Jōyō	447
2 - 2 - 4	

▶**PROJECT**

COMPOUNDS

❶ⓐ (form a plan or intention for) **project, draw up [organize] a project, lay plans, undertake a project**

ⓑ **project, plan, program**

企図 *kito* plan, scheme, intention

企業 *kigyō* undertaking, enterprise; business enterprise, company

企及する *kikyū suru* try to attain (something)

企画 *kikaku* plan, project

❷ⓐ [original meaning, now obsolete] stand on tiptoe

ⓑ [rare] expect anxiously (as if standing on tiptoe)

企望する *kibō suru* look forward to, hope for

KUN

【kuwada(teru) 企てる】 plan, contrive, design, plot, scheme, project; attempt, try, undertake

企て *kuwadate* plan, scheme, project, enterprise; attempt

陰謀を企てる *inbō o kuwadateru* plot against

殺害を企てる *satsugai o kuwadateru* make an attempt on a person's life

SYNONYMS

❶ plans and planning

画 DRAW UP A PLAN → 3000

図 systematic plan → 3071

計 PLAN → 1441

案 PROPOSAL → 2270

謀 SCHEME → 1593

策 SCHEME → 2679

略 STRATEGY → 1169

全 全 全 全

2022 ZEN matta(ku) sube(te)▲

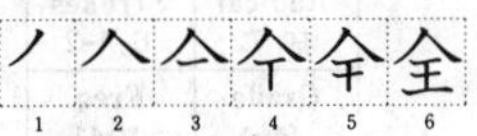

Ⓒ 全 quán

Radical	Strokes
人 9△	6-2-4
Grade	**Freq**
Jōyō-3	67
▀ 2 - 2 - 4	

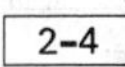

▶WHOLE

COMPOUNDS

❶ⓐ [also prefix] (including everything) **whole, all, complete, total, entire**

ⓑ wholly, completely; at the height of

ⓒ in all, a total of

全部 *zenbu* all, the whole; wholly, entirely

全体の *zentai no* whole, entire; general

全力 *zenryoku* all one's might, full capacity

全焼 *zenshō* total destruction by fire

全般の *zenpan no* whole, general, overall

全集 *zenshū* complete works

全員 *zen'in* all members, entire staff

全額 *zengaku* sum total, total amount

全勝する *zenshō suru* win all the games, make a clean sweep

全廃する *zenpai suru* abolish wholly, do away with

全国民 *zenkokumin* the whole nation

全然 *zenzen* wholly, totally, completely; (not) at all

全六巻 *zenrokkan* complete in six volumes, six volumes in all

❷ (extending over the full range) **whole, all, pan-**

全国 *zenkoku* the whole country

全校 *zenkō* the whole school

全米 *zenbei* all America, pan-America

全世界 *zensekai* the whole world

全アジア会議 *zen'ajia kaigi* Pan-Asiatic Conference

❸ⓐ (free from flaws or damage) **whole, complete, perfect, intact**

ⓑ (free from impurities) whole, pure

完全な *kanzen na* perfect, complete, whole

万全の *banzen no* perfect, infallible, absolutely secure

安全 *anzen* safety, security

健全な *kenzen na* healthy, sound

全乳 *zennyū* whole milk, pure milk

全麦の *zenbaku no* whole-wheat

❹ keep whole, keep intact

保全する *hozen suru* preserve the integrity of, keep intact

INDEPENDENT

【zen 全】 wholeness

KUN

【matta(ku) 全く】 entirely, completely, wholly, utterly; truly, indeed

全くの浪費 *mattaku no rōhi* sheer waste

全うする *mattō suru* accomplish, fulfill, carry out

【sube(te) 全て】

[also 凡て or 総べて]

①ⓐ all, everything, the whole

ⓑ entirely, wholly

全ての *subete no* all, entire, whole

② generally, as a rule

SYNONYMS

❶ & ❷ & ❸ all

一 all in one → 3341

皆 ALL → 2445

都 all → 1686

万 all → 2936

満 FULL → 607

丸 complete(ly) → 3417

完 COMPLETE → 2201

総 TOTAL → 1379

諸 VARIOUS → 1577

毎 EVERY → 2034

各 EACH → 2168

HOMOPHONES

subete ⇨ 凡 2938 総 1379

NOTE

⇨ see USAGE note at 凡 2938

2-4 入

仝
2023

▶WHOLE
nonstandard for 全 2022

2-4 丷

羊 䍧

incorrect classification ⇨ see 3–3

2-4 冖

写

incorrect stroke count ⇨ see 2000

2-4 匕

旨 旨 旨
2024 SHI mune uma(i)▲

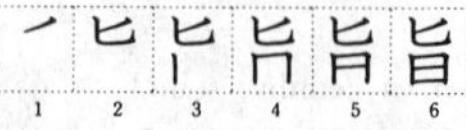

Ⓒⓗ 旨 zhǐ

Radical	Strokes
日 72	6-4-2
Grade	**Freq**
Jōyō	1041
2-2-4	

▶PURPORT

COMPOUNDS

❶ⓐ (main idea) **purport, meaning, tenet, substance, gist, point**
ⓑ (reason for an action) **purport, purpose, aim**
要旨 *yōshi* gist, point, essentials, summary; purport
主旨 *shushi* gist, main point, substance
論旨 *ronshi* point of an argument
趣旨 *shushi* purpose, aim; purport, meaning
宗旨 *shūshi* tenets of a religious sect; (religious) sect
本旨 *honshi* main object, true aim
❷ Imperial decree, orders, instructions; Imperial wish
聖旨 *seishi* Imperial will [wish]
❸ [original meaning] tasty, excellent
旨酒 *shishu* [archaic] good wine

KUN

【mune 旨】
① effect, purport
その旨を書き送る *sono mune o kakiokuru* write to (a person) to that effect
② order
③ [formerly also 宗] principle, aim
正確を旨とする *seikaku o mune to suru* aim at accuracy

【uma(i) 旨い】
① [also 甘い] delicious, tasty; sweet
旨い料理 *umai ryōri* tasty dish
② successful, satisfactory; profitable
旨い仕事 *umai shigoto* profitable business
③ [also 巧い or 上手い] skillful, clever; splendid, excellent
旨く *umaku* skillfully, cleverly; successfully; luckily
旨い絵 *umai e* excellent picture [painting]
英語が旨い *eigo ga umai* speak English well

SYNONYMS

❶ⓐ **essential part**
要 summary → 2635
綱 ESSENTIAL POINTS → 1372
精 ESSENCE (essential part) → 1366
粋 essence (best part) → 1293
髄 essence (vital part) → 1842
枢 PIVOT → 865
幹 TRUNK → 1718
ⓑ **meaning**
趣 PURPOSE → 3317
意 MEANING → 2136
義 MEANING → 2338
訳 SENSE → 1473

USAGE

❶ **mune**
旨
① effect, purport
② order
③ [formerly also 宗] principle, aim
宗
[now usu. 旨] principle, aim

❷ **umai**
旨い
① [also 甘い] delicious, tasty; sweet
② successful, satisfactory; profitable
③ [also 巧い or 上手い] skillful, clever; splendid, excellent
甘い
[also 旨い] delicious, tasty; sweet
巧い
[also 上手い or 旨い] skillful, clever; splendid, excellent

上手い
[also 巧い or 旨い] skillful, clever; splendid, excellent
❸ **shushi**
趣旨
purpose, aim; purport, meaning; opinion

主旨
gist, main point, substance

HOMOPHONES
mune ⇨ 宗 2228
umai ⇨ 甘い 3494 巧い 188 上手い 3404, 3456

卋 2025

▶**WORLD** ▶**AGE**
nonstandard for 世 3496

2-4 十

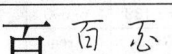

百 2026

HYAKU momo▲

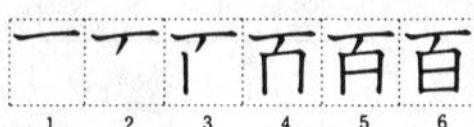

CH 百 bǎi bó

Radical	Strokes
白 106	6-5-1
Grade	**Freq**
Jōyō-1	63
2-2-4	

2-4 一

▶**HUNDRED**

COMPOUNDS
❶ **hundred**
百円 *hyakuen* 100 yen
百分率 *hyakubunritsu* percentage
百倍 *hyakubai* hundredfold, hundred times
五百七十 *gohyaku nanajū* 570
❷ **numerous, various**
百姓 *hyakushō* farmer, peasant
百貨店 *hyakkaten* department store
百科事典 *hyakka-jiten* encyclopedia
百計 *hyakkei* all means

INDEPENDENT
【**hyaku** 百】 hundred

KUN
【**momo** 百】 *elegant* hundred; many
百夜 *momoyo* a hundred nights
百千鳥 *momochidori* hundreds (and thousands) of birds, all sorts of birds

SPECIAL READINGS
八百長 *yaochō* rigged affair, fixed game
八百屋 *yaoya* greengrocer's; jack-of-all-trades
百舌▲ *mozu* shrike

SYNONYMS
❶ **large numbers**
千 THOUSAND → 3411
万 TEN THOUSAND → 2936
億 HUNDRED MILLION → 170
兆 TRILLION → 225
京 ten quadrillion → 2052
❷ **many**
万 myriad → 2936
多 MANY → 2170
豊 PLENTIFUL → 2697
沢 plentiful → 267
穣 YIELDING ABUNDANTLY → 1250
裕 ABUNDANT → 1195
富 RICH → 2310

NOTE
⇨ see COMPOUND FORMATION for 百姓 *hyakushō* ⇨ 姓 279

而 2027

JI shiko(oshite) shika(shite) shika(mo)

CH 而 ér

Radical	Strokes
而 126	6-6-0
Grade	**Freq**
Reference	
2-2-4	

2-4 一

RADICAL 126
Standard form: 而 *shikashite* 'beard' (耐)
Description: used for character classification

COMPOUNDS
❶ⓐ and
ⓑ [now usu. 然も *shikamo*] moreover, furthermore
ⓒ [now usu. 然も *shikamo*] and yet, nevertheless
然り而うして *Shikari shikōshite* Aye, and...
道の常は無為にして而も為さざるは無し *Michi no tsune wa mui ni shite shikamo nasazaru wa nashi* Tao abides in nonaction, yet nothing is left undone (Laozi)
❷ indicates direction in space or time

形而上学 *keijijōgaku* metaphysics
❸ [original meaning, now obsolete] beard

HOMOPHONES

shikamo ⇨ 然 2782

NOTE

⇨ see USAGE note at 然 2782

2-4
七

七 七七
2028

▶**HAPPY**
handwritten abbreviation for 喜 2308

2-4
⺈

色 色 色
2029 SHOKU SHIKI iro

CH 色 sè shǎi

Radical	Strokes
色 139	6-6-0
Grade	**Freq**
Jōyō-2	464
2 - 2 - 4	

Stroke order: 1 2 3 4 5 6

RADICAL 139
Standard form: 色 *iro* 'color'
Right variant: ⻏ *irozukuri* (艶 艷)
Description: used in characters related to facial expressions or colors

▶**COLOR**

COMPOUNDS

❶ⓐ [also suffix] **color, coloring**
ⓑ counter for colors
色彩 *shikisai* color, coloring, hue, tinge
色素 *shikiso* pigment, coloring matter
青色 *seishoku* (=*aoiro*) blue
原色 *genshoku* primary color
天然色 *tennenshoku* natural color; technicolor
三色写真 *sanshoku-shashin* three color photography
❷ⓐ (facial expression) **color, complexion, countenance, look**
ⓑ good looks (of a woman), beauty
顔色 *ganshoku* (=*kaoiro*) complexion, countenance, expression
血色 *kesshoku* complexion
気色 *kishoku* (=*keshiki*) mood, feeling; looks, countenance
容色 *yōshoku* looks, features
才色 *saishoku* wit and beauty
❸ [also suffix]
ⓐ (characteristic feature) **color, character, feature**
ⓑ (political tendency) coloring
特色 *tokushoku* characteristic
地方色 *chihōshoku* local color
異色の *ishoku no* novel, unique
物色する *busshoku suru* look for, pick out
政治色 *seijishoku* political coloring
❹ scenery, scene
景色 *keshiki* scenery, landscape
春色 *shunshoku* spring scenery
❺ⓐ **lust, sensual pleasure, sexual passion, love**
ⓑ [original meaning] sexual intercourse, sexual love
色情 *shikijō* lust
色欲 *shikiyoku* lust, carnal desire, sexual passion
色魔 *shikima* woman hunter, sex fiend
女色 *joshoku* woman's charms, lust
好色家 *kōshokuka* lecher, Don Juan
酒色 *shushoku* wine and women, sensual pleasures
男色 *danshoku* sodomy, unnatural act
❻ *Buddhism* things of this world directly perceptible by the senses; matter
色即是空 *Shikisokuzekū* Matter is void / Form [Matter] is nonsubstantial

KUN

[iro 色]
①ⓐ [also suffix] color, hue, tint, shade
ⓑ counter for colors
ⓒ (substance that imparts color) color, dye, pigment
色取る(=彩る) *irodoru* color, paint, dye; make up
黄色 *kiiro* yellow
小麦色 *komugiiro* light brown, suntan
三色 *miiro* three colors
色を塗る *iro o nuru* paint, daub
②ⓐ (skin tone) color, complexion
ⓑ (facial expression) color, look, expression; indication, tone
色を失う *iro o ushinau* lose color, turn pale
色香 *iroka* beauty, loveliness, feminine charms; color and scent
秋の色 *aki no iro* autumnal tints
③ⓐ sensuality, lust, sexual passion; love affair

ⓑ lover, mistress
色気 *iroke* sex appeal, sensuality; fancifulness; inclination, interest; shade of color
色男 *irootoko* beau, dandy, gallant
④ something extra, action to gratify another person
色を付ける *iro o tsukeru* add something extra; shade an account
⑤ⓐ kind, sort
ⓑ counter for kinds
色色な *iroiro na* various kinds of
十人十色 *Jūnin toiro* So many men, so many minds
二色 *futairo* two kinds

SYNONYMS

❶ **color**
彩 BEAUTIFUL COLORING → 1681
❷ⓐ **expression**
顔 FACE → 1808
❸ⓐ **appearance**
風 air → 3007
容 APPEARANCE → 2277
姿 FIGURE → 2636
相 PHASE → 900
体 FORM (outer appearance) → 71
❺ⓐ **sex**
情 (illicit) love → 482
春 love → 2576
性 SEX → 299
【iro】
⑤ **kinds and types**
類 KIND → 1807
種 VARIETY → 1218
様 variety → 1052
般 SORT → 1317
属 genus → 3145
品 category → 2248
型 TYPE → 2638

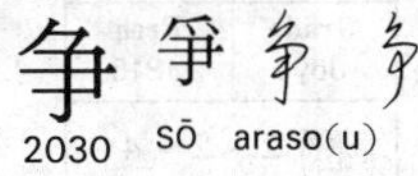

2030 SŌ araso(u)

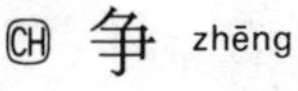

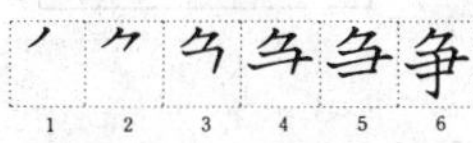

Radical	Strokes
亅 6△	6-1-5
Grade	**Freq**
Jōyō-4	229
2 - 2 - 4	

2-4

▶CONTEND

COMPOUNDS

ⓐ [original meaning] (struggle in opposition) **contend, contest, compete, struggle for**
ⓑ (strive in debate) contend, dispute, argue
争奪 *sōdatsu* scramble, contest, struggle
戦争 *sensō* war, battle
競争する *kyōsō suru* compete, contend, vie
紛争 *funsō* conflict, strife
闘争 *tōsō* fight, conflict
争議 *sōgi* dispute, strike
争点 *sōten* point of contention, issue
論争 *ronsō* dispute, argument

KUN

【araso(u) 争う】 (struggle in opposition) contend, contest, compete, struggle for; (strive in debate) contend, dispute, argue
争い *arasoi* dissension, feud, discord, quarrel; competition; dispute
優勝を争う *yūshō o arasou* contend for victory
一刻を争う *ikkoku o arasou* race against time
政権争い *seiken arasoi* struggle for political power
争われない *arasowarenai* indisputable
言い争い *iiarasoi* dispute, quarrel

SYNONYMS

ⓐ **compete**
闘 FIGHT → 3334
戦う contest → 1787
競 COMPETE → 1847
ⓑ **argue and discuss**
議 DISCUSS → 1647
論 ARGUE → 1574
弁 argue (for) → 2004

危 incorrect classification ⇨ see 3199

2-4

2031

▶DANGEROUS
nonstandard for 危 3199

2-4

2-4

缶

2032 FU hotogi

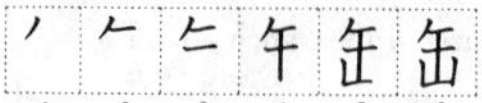

CH 缶 fǒu

Radical	Strokes
缶 121	6-6-0
Grade	Freq
Reference	
2-2-4	

RADICAL 121

Standard form: 缶 *hotogi* 'earthenware' (罐 罈 罍)

Description: used in characters related to earthenware or pottery

COMPOUNDS

● [original meaning, now rare] earthenware jar

撃缶 *gekifu* beating the vase for marking time

NOTE

★ do not confuse with 缶 2033

2-4

缶 罐

2033 KAN kama▲

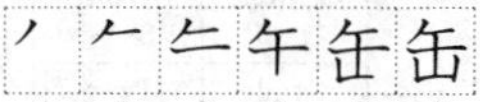

CH 缶 guàn

Radical	Strokes
缶 121	6-6-0
Grade	Freq
Jōyō	1815
2-2-4	

▶CAN

COMPOUNDS

❶ⓐ **can, tin**

ⓑ [suffix] **canned [tinned] food**

缶切り *kankiri* can opener

缶詰め *kanzume* canned goods, canning; cooping-up, confining

ビスケット缶 *bisukettokan* can of biscuits

蟹缶 *kanikan* canned crab

❷ⓐ [usu. 罐] **steam boiler**

ⓑ kettle

汽缶室 *kikanshitsu* boiler room; stokehold, fire room

薬缶 *yakan* kettle

INDEPENDENT

【kan 缶】can, tin

KUN

【kama 罐】boiler

罐焚き *kamataki* fireman, stoker

SYNONYMS

❶ⓐ **containers**

瓶 BOTTLE → 1344

器 VESSEL → 2713

袋 BAG → 2588

籠 BASKET → 2734

箱 BOX → 2711

槽 TANK → 1067

棺 COFFIN → 985

❷ⓐ **heating devices**

窯 KILN → 2361

炉 FURNACE → 869

HOMOPHONES

kama ⇨ 窯 2361 釜 2107

NOTE

⇨ see USAGE note at 窯 2361

★do not confuse with 缶 2032

★The word *kama* is written 罐, and is not abbreviated to 缶.

2-4

毎 毎

2034 MAI goto▲ -goto(ni)▲

CH 每 měi

Radical	Strokes
毋 80	6-4-2
Grade	Freq
Jōyō-2	508
2-2-4	

▶EVERY

COMPOUNDS

❶ [also prefix] **every, each**

毎日 *mainichi* every day

毎朝 *maiasa* every morning

毎回 *maikai* every time

毎年 *mainen* (=*maitoshi*) every year
毎号 *maigō* each [every] issue
毎度 *maido* every [each] time, always
毎土曜日 *maidoyōbi* every Saturday
❷ abbrev. of 毎日 *mainichi*—used in proper names
東毎 *tōmai* abbrev. of 東京毎日新聞社 *tōkyō mainichi shinbunsha* (name of a newspaper publisher)

KUN

【goto 毎】 every, each
夜毎 *yogoto* every night
【-gotoni -毎に】 every, each, at an interval of
二日目毎に *futsukame-gotoni* every other day

SYNONYMS

❶ **all**
各 EACH → 2168
諸 VARIOUS → 1577
総 TOTAL → 1379
完 COMPLETE → 2201
丸 complete(ly) → 3417
皆 ALL → 2445
都 all → 1686
万 all → 2936
全 WHOLE → 2022
一 all in one → 3341
満 FULL → 607

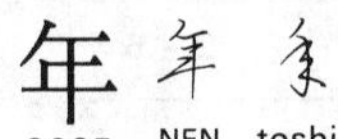

2035 NEN toshi

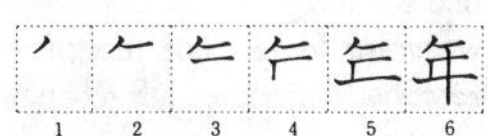

1 2 3 4 5 6

CH 年 nián

Radical	Strokes
干 51	6-3-3
Grade	**Freq**
Jōyō-1	10
2 - 2 - 4	

2-4

▶YEAR

COMPOUNDS

❶ⓐ [also suffix] (period of revolution around the sun) **year, solar year**
ⓑ [also suffix] (period from January 1 to December 31 or equiv.) **year, calendar year**
ⓒ **yearly, annual**
ⓓ **counter for years**
ⓔ **suffix indicating the chronological order of years in a given era**
太陽年 *taiyōnen* solar year
火星年 *kaseinen* Martian year
年度 *nendo* year, fiscal year; school year; term
年間 *nenkan* period of one year
毎年 *mainen* every year
去年 *kyonen* last year
新年 *shinnen* New Year
一昨年 *issakunen* the year before last
年金 *nenkin* annuity, pension
年産 *nensan* yearly output, annual production
五十年 *gojūnen* 50 years
千九百五十八年 *senkyūhyaku-gojūhachinen* 1958
昭和六十年 *shōwa rokujūnen* sixtieth year of the Showa era (1985)
❷ **years, one's age**
年齢(=年令) *nenrei* age, years
少年 *shōnen* boy
定年 *teinen* mandatory retirement age
中年 *chūnen* middle age
晩年 *bannen* late in life
❸ age, era, epoch
年代 *nendai* age, era, period; date
年号 *nengō* name of era, reign title
❹ term of service
年季(=年期) *nenki* one's term of service
❺ [original meaning, now rare] period of crop bearing, harvest
祈年祭 *kinensai* (=*toshigoimatsuri*) prayer service for a good crop

INDEPENDENT

【nen 年】 year; term of service
年に一度 *nen ni ichido* once a year
年が明けた *Nen ga aketa* My term of service is up

KUN

【toshi 年】
① [formerly also 歳] year
今年 *kotoshi* this year
毎年 *maitoshi* every year
半年 *hantoshi* half a year
② [sometimes also 齢] one's years, age
年寄り *toshiyori* old [aged] person, the aged; older councilor
年上の *toshiue no* older, senior

SYNONYMS

❶ **year**
歳 YEAR → 2490
❷ **age**
歳 AGE SUFFIX → 2490
齢 AGE → 1895
令 age → 1995
才 AGE SUFFIX → 3410
寿 life span → 3557

USAGE

toshi

年
① [formerly also 歳] year
② [sometimes also 齢] one's years, age
歳
[now usu. 年] year

齢
[usu. 年] one's years, age

HOMOPHONES
toshi ⇨ 歳 2490 齢 1895

2-4 𠂉

気

incorrect classification ⇨ see 3194

2-5 亠

忘

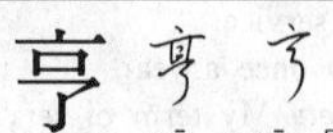

2036 BŌ wasu(reru)

Ⓒⓗ 忘 wàng

Radical	Strokes
心 61	7-4-3
Grade	Freq
Jōyō-6	1062
2 - 2 - 5	

▶**FORGET**

COMPOUNDS
● [original meaning] **forget**
忘却する *bōkyaku suru* forget
忘恩 *bōon* ingratitude
忘年会 *bōnenkai* year-end party ("forget the year party")
健忘 *kenbō* forgetfulness, short memory
備忘 *bibō* reminder

INDEPENDENT
【**bōzuru 忘ずる**】forget

KUN
【**wasu(reru) 忘れる**】forget; leave behind; dismiss from one's mind
見忘れる *miwasureru* forget, not recognize
忘れ物 *wasuremono* something left (behind), lost item
忘れっぽい *wasureppoi* forgetful, have a bad memory
忘れられる *wasurerareru* be forgotten, slip into obscurity

SYNONYMS
● **forget**
遺 LEAVE BEHIND → 3166

2-5 亠

亨

2037 KŌ KYŌ NAMES tōru michi yuki akira naga

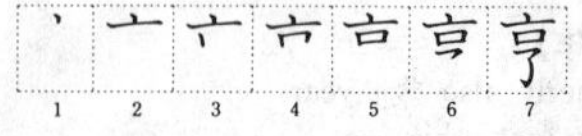

Ⓒⓗ 亨 hēng

Radical	Strokes
亠 8	7-2-5
Grade	Freq
Names	2064
2 - 2 - 5	

▶**GO SMOOTHLY**

COMPOUNDS
● [archaic] go smoothly, proceed well
亨通 *kōtsū* prosperous, doing well
亨運 *kōun* prosperity

NAMES
亨介 *kyōsuke* male name
亨子 *michiko* female name
亨 *tōru* male name

SYNONYMS
● **make progress**
進 ADVANCE → 3121

NOTE
★do not confuse with 享 2051

辛 辛 辛

2038 SHIN kara(i) tsura(i)▲ -zura(i)▲ kanoto▲

CH 辛 xīn

Radical	Strokes
辛 160	7-7-0
Grade	Freq
Jōyō	1567
2 - 2 - 5	

2-5

RADICAL 160

Standard form: 辛 *karai* 'acrid' (辜 辟 辞)

Left variant: 𧾷 *karai* (辦 辣)

Description: used for character classification

▶PUNGENT ▶HARD

COMPOUNDS

❶ **pungent, hot, spicy**

辛辣な *shinratsu na* bitter, pungent, acrid, poignant, severe

香辛料 *kōshinryō* spices, seasoning

❷ (difficult to bear) **hard, trying, bitter, painful, toilsome**

辛苦 *shinku* hardships, trials; labor, trouble

辛酸 *shinsan* hardships, privations

辛抱 *shinbō* patience, endurance, forbearance

辛労 *shinrō* toil, trouble

❸ barely, narrowly

辛勝 *shinshō* narrow victory

❹ eighth calendar sign (⇨ see APPENDIX 7)

辛亥 *shingai* 48th of the sexagenary cycle

KUN

【kara(i) 辛い】

①ⓐ pungent, hot

ⓑ [formerly also 鹹い] salty, briny, saline

ⓒ dry (wine)

辛い味 *karai aji* pungent taste

唐辛子 *tōgarashi* red pepper

塩辛い *shiokarai* salty

辛口の酒 *karakuchi no sake* dry sake

② strict, severe

点が辛い *ten ga karai* be severe in marking

世知辛い *sechigarai* hard to live, exigent

③ [in compounds] bare, narrow

辛うじて *karōjite* barely, narrowly

辛くも *karakumo* barely, narrowly, with difficulty

【tsura(i) 辛い】

ⓐ (difficult to bear) hard, trying, bitter

ⓑ (harsh in treatment) hard, harsh, heart-breaking

辛い目に会う *tsurai me ni au* have a hard time of it

辛く当たる *tsuraku ataru* treat badly

【-zura(i) -辛い】[verbal suffix] hard, difficult (to do something)

読み辛い *yomizurai* hard to read

【kanoto 辛】 eighth calendar sign

SYNONYMS

❶ **unsavory tastes**

苦 BITTER → 2243

酸 sour → 1563

渋い ASTRINGENT → 513

❷ **trouble and suffering**

痛 PAIN → 3285

煩 VEXED → 1022

難 DIFFICULT → 1838

苦 SUFFERING → 2243

悩 SUFFER → 421

窮 BE IN EXTREMITY → 2358

困 BE IN TROUBLE → 3070

【karai】

③ **barely**

甫めて BARELY → 3549

USAGE

karai

辛い

①ⓐ pungent, hot

ⓑ [formerly also 鹹い] salty, briny, saline

ⓒ dry (wine)

② strict, severe

③ [in compounds] bare, narrow

鹹い

[now usu. 辛い] salty, briny, saline

HOMOPHONES

karai ⇨ 鹹 1885

孶

2039 ▶STUDY ▶EDUCATIONAL INSTITUTION

nonstandard for 学 2555

2-5

2-5 亠

言 ▶SAY ▶SPEECH

2040

nonstandard for 言 1941

2-5 亠

享

incorrect stroke count ⇨ see 2051

2-5 人

含 含 含

2041 GAN fuku(mu) fuku(meru)

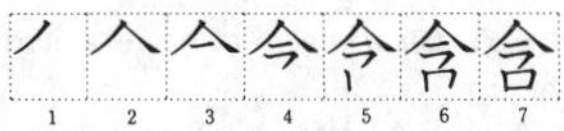

Ⓒ 含 hán

Radical	Strokes
口 30	7-3-4
Grade	**Freq**
Jōyō	612
2-2-5	

▶CONTAIN

COMPOUNDS

❶ (have as a part) **contain, include, comprise**

含有する *gan'yū suru* contain, have, hold

含糖量 *gantōryō* sugar content

含水炭素 *gansui-tanso* carbohydrate

包含する *hōgan suru* include, encompass, cover; imply

❷ [original meaning] hold [keep] in one's mouth

含味する *ganmi suru* taste, relish; appreciate

❸ imply, involve, contain, be pregnant with

含蓄の有る *ganchiku no aru* significant, pregnant, suggestive

KUN

【fuku(mu) 含む】 contain, include, comprise; hold [keep] in one's mouth; bear in mind, cherish; imply, involve

含み *fukumi* implication, hidden meaning; atmosphere, tone (of the market)

含まれる *fukumareru* be included [comprised] in

含ませる *fukumaseru* soak (in water), saturate

含み笑い *fukumiwarai* suppressed laugh [smile]

...と云う事を含んで *...to iu koto o fukunde* with the understanding that...

強含み *tsuyofukumi* strengthening, strong tone

【fuku(meru) 含める】 include; give instructions

...を含めて *...o fukumete* including, inclusive of

言い含める *iifukumeru* instruct carefully

含め煮 *fukumeni* food boiled in sugar syrup

SYNONYMS

❶ **contain and include**

容 CONTAIN (have within) → 2277

包 ENCOMPASS → 2966

挟 HOLD BETWEEN → 377

2-5 人

余 餘 余 餘

2042 YO ama(ru) ama(ri) ama(su)

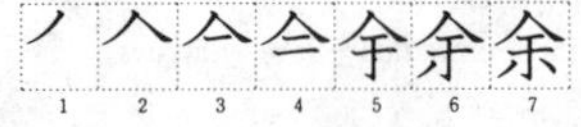

Ⓒ 余 yú

Radical	Strokes
人 9	7-2-5
Grade	**Freq**
Jōyō-5	708
2-2-5	

▶REMAINING ▶EXCESS

COMPOUNDS

❶ⓐ **remaining, lingering, secondary**

ⓑ **after**

余地 *yochi* room, space, margin

余暇 *yoka* leisure, spare time

余生 *yosei* one's remaining years

余波 *yoha* secondary effect, aftereffect

余韻 *yoin* lingering tone, resonance, reverberation; aftertaste, impregnated elegance

刑余の人 *keiyo no hito* ex-convict

余震 *yoshin* aftershock

❷ⓐ **excess, surplus, remainder, overplus**

ⓑ [suffix] **in excess of, over, more than**

余剰 *yojō* surplus, remainder, residue

余裕 *yoyū* surplus, margin, room; composure

余分 *yobun* excess, extra, surplus

余計な *yokei na* excess, surplus; needless

残余 *zan'yo* remainder, residue, remnant

千円余 *sen'en'yo* over 1000 yen

❸ other, another, additional
余所 *yoso* another place, strange parts
余罪 *yozai* other crimes [charges]
余儀無い *yoginai* unavoidable, inevitable
余録 *yoroku* additional gain
❹ complementary, co-
余角 *yokaku* complementary angle
余弦 *yogen* cosine
余色 *yoshoku* complementary color
❺ [also 予 1983] I, myself, the present writer
余輩 *yohai* we

INDEPENDENT

【yo 余】
① excess, surplus, remainder
二月の余も *futatsuki no yo mo* even longer than two months
② [also 予 1983] I, myself, the present writer—historically used as a formal first person pronoun but now only used pompously
余の辞書に不可能の文字は無い *Yo no jisho ni fukanō no moji wa nai* In my dictionary, there's no such word as impossible

KUN

【ama(ru) 余る】 remain over, be in excess, be more than enough; exceed (one's powers), be beyond one
思い余る *omoiamaru* be at a loss
有り余っている *ariamatte iru* be in excess
余った金 *amatta kane* surplus money
手に余る課題 *te ni amaru kadai* task beyond one's powers

【ama(ri) 余り】
① remainder, residual; surplus, excess
余りの *amari no* remaining, residual; excessive, too much
② [colloquially also *anmari*] excessively, too, too much; (not) very, (not) much
余りに(も) *amari ni (mo)* too, excessively
余り面白くない *amari omoshiroku nai* not very interesting
それは余りだ *Sore wa anmari da* That's too much
③ [suffix] over, more than
一月余り *hitotsukiamari* over a month

【ama(su) 余す】 leave over, let remain; save
持て余す *moteamasu* do not know what to do with, find unmanageable
余す所無く *amasu tokoro naku* exhaustively, thoroughly

SYNONYMS

❶ⓐ remain
残 REMAIN → 943
留 STAY → 2580
滞 STAY → 663
ⓑ after
後 AFTER → 361
❷ⓐ exceeding and excess
濫 EXCESSIVE → 801
剰 SURPLUS → 1779
冗 REDUNDANT → 1976
過 EXCEED → 3137
超 SURPASS → 3313
越 GO BEYOND → 3314
❸ other
他 OTHER → 35
別 ANOTHER → 1117
【yo】
② first person pronouns
予 I (*pompous*) → 1983
麿 I (*archaic*) → 3184
朕 IMPERIAL WE → 949
吾 I (*elegant*) → 2407
私 I (*polite*) → 1115
僕 I (*familiar*) → 164
俺 I (*intimate*) → 110
自 SELF → 3525
我 SELF → 3548
己 ONESELF → 3380
身 ONE'S PERSON → 3553

NOTE

⇨ see COMPOUND FORMATION for 余弦 *yogen* ⇨ 正 3484
★The old form of 余 in senses ❶ to ❹ is 餘. In sense ❺, 余 itself is the original form, which is interchangeable with 予.

2-5
八

谷 谷 そ

2043 KOKU tani kiwa(maru)▲

ⒸⒽ 谷 gǔ

Radical	Strokes
谷 150	7-7-0
Grade	**Freq**
Jōyō-2	290
2 - 2 - 5	

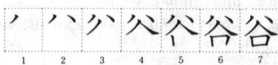

丿 八 㕣 𠔁 谷 谷 谷
1 2 3 4 5 6 7

RADICAL 150
Standard form: 谷 *tani* 'valley' (豁 谿)
Left variant: ⻒ *tanihen* (谺)
Description: used in characters related to valleys

▶VALLEY

COMPOUNDS

● [original meaning] **valley, gorge, ravine**
渓谷 *keikoku* ravine, valley, canyon
峡谷 *kyōkoku* gorge, ravine, canyon, valley
幽谷 *yūkoku* deep ravine, secluded valley

KUN

【tani 谷】 valley, ravine, gorge; trough
谷川 *tanigawa* valley stream, mountain stream
谷水 *tanimizu* valley water, rill
谷底 *tanisoko* bottom of a ravine, valley bottom
谷間 *tanima* valley, gorge

【kiwa(maru) 谷まる】
[usu. 窮まる]
ⓐ come to an end, terminate
ⓑ come to the end of one's tether, be at a loss
⇨ see 窮 2358 for compounds

SYNONYMS

● **valley**
渓 RAVINE → 516
峡 GORGE → 357

HOMOPHONES

kiwamaru ⇨ 極 1017 窮 2358

NOTE

⇨ see USAGE note at 極 1017

2-5
丷

弟 弟 矛

2044 TEI DAI DE otōto

ⒸⒽ 弟 dì

Radical	Strokes
弓 57	7-3-4
Grade	**Freq**
Jōyō-2	1016
2 - 2 - 5	

▶YOUNGER BROTHER

COMPOUNDS

❶ⓐ **younger brother**
ⓑ child
弟妹 *teimai* younger brothers and sisters
兄弟 *kyōdai* (=*keitei*) brother
義弟 *gitei* brother-in-law
愚弟 *gutei* my foolish younger brother
子弟 *shitei* son, child
❷ (someone who follows a master) disciple, pupil, apprentice
弟子 *deshi* disciple, pupil, apprentice
徒弟 *totei* apprentice
門弟 *montei* pupil, disciple
師弟 *shitei* master and pupil
❸ follower
孝弟(=孝悌) *kōtei* filial piety and brotherly love
❹ [humble] I
小弟 *shōtei* my foolish brother; I

INDEPENDENT

【tei 弟】 younger brother
兄たり難く弟たり難し *Kei tarigataku tei tarigatashi* There is little to choose between the two

KUN

【otōto 弟】 younger brother

SYNONYMS

❶ⓐ **siblings**
兄 OLDER BROTHER → 2154
姉 OLDER SISTER → 280
妹 YOUNGER SISTER → 278
❷ **students and followers**
門 pupil → 888
徒 FOLLOWER → 416
生 STUDENT → 3497
卒 graduate student → 2055
学 scholar → 2555

免
2045

2-5 刀

▶**EXEMPT**
nonstandard for 免 2067

克
2046 KOKU ka(tsu)▲

2-5 十

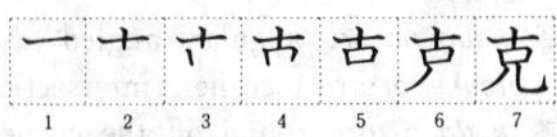

Ⓒⓗ 克 kè

Radical	Strokes
儿 10	7-2-5
Grade	**Freq**
Jōyō	1234
2-2-5	

▶**OVERCOME**

COMPOUNDS

❶ [formerly also 剋 3305] **overcome, conquer, win**
克服 *kokufuku* conquest, subjugation
克復 *kokufuku* restoration
克己 *kokki* self-denial, self-control
超克する *chōkoku suru* overcome, conquer, surmount, get over
相克する *sōkoku suru* struggle with each other, conflict
下克上 *gekokujō* the lower dominating the upper
❷ be able to do something well
克明 *kokumei* scrupulousness, diligence

KUN

【ka(tsu) 克つ】 [now usu. 勝つ] control (oneself), overcome
己に克つ *onore ni katsu* control oneself

SYNONYMS

❶ **win**
勝 WIN → 1005
征 CONQUER → 293
破 BREAK → 1150

HOMOPHONES

katsu ⇨ 勝 1005

NOTE

⇨ see USAGE note at 勝 1005

孟

2-5 子

incorrect stroke count ⇨ see 2220

角
2047 KAKU kado tsuno

2-5 ⺈

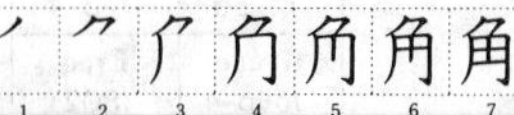

Ⓒⓗ 角 jiǎo jué

Radical	Strokes
角 148	7-7-0
Grade	**Freq**
Jōyō-2	741
2-2-5	

RADICAL 148

Standard form: 角 *tsuno* 'horn' (觜)
Left variant: 角 *tsunohen* (解 触 觝)
Description: used in characters related to horns or horn products

▶**ANGLE** ▶**HORN**

COMPOUNDS

❶ⓐ [also suffix] **angle**
ⓑ [prefix] *phys* **angular**
角度 *kakudo* angle, angular measure, degree
多角的な *takakuteki na* multilateral, many-sided, diversified
三角 *sankaku* triangle
直角 *chokkaku* right angle
方角 *hōgaku* direction
迎え角 *mukaekaku* angle of attack
前進角 *zenshinkaku* angle of advance
角速度 *kakusokudo* angular velocity
角分散 *kakubunsan* angular dispersion
❷ⓐ **corner, angle, edge**
ⓑ *baseball* **corner**
天の一角 *ten no ikkaku* corner of the sky, point of heaven
折角 *sekkaku* with much trouble; specially
内角 *naikaku* inside corner; inner angle
❸ⓐ [original meaning] **horn, antler, antenna**
ⓑ horny, keratinous
牛角 *gyūkaku* horns

触角 *shokkaku* feeler, antenna
角膜 *kakumaku* cornea
角質 *kakushitsu* horny substance, keratin
❹ⓐ [also prefix and suffix] **square; squared**
ⓑ cube, block
角瓶 *kakubin* square [shoulder] bottle
角材 *kakuzai* squared timber
角行灯 *kakuandon* square paper lantern
五センチ角 *gosenchikaku* 5 cm sq.
角砂糖 *kakuzatō* cube sugar
❺ name of chess piece in shogi (Japanese chess): *kaku*, bishop
角取り *kakutori* capturing a bishop
成り角 *narikaku narikaku*, promoted bishop
❻ compete, vie, fight, wrestle
角逐する *kakuchiku suru* compete with, vie with
角牛 *kakugyū* bullfight
❼ sumo wrestling
角界 *kakukai* sumo circles
好角家 *kōkakuka* sumo fan, wrestling enthusiast
❽ [sometimes also 格 926] unit of type size equiv. to one em quad
半角 *hankaku* en quad
❾ [rare] third note of the pentatonic scale (⇨ see APPENDIX 7)

INDEPENDENT

【kaku 角】 square; squared timber; angle; *kaku* (⇨ ❺); [rare] third note of the pentatonic scale
角に切る *kaku ni kiru* cut into squares [cubes]
二つの角 *futatsu no kaku* two angles
角を捨てる *kaku o suteru* sacrifice a bishop

KUN

【kado 角】 corner, edge; angle; stiffness, angularity, harshness
角の有る *kado no aru* angular, angled
四つ角 *yotsukado* street corner, intersection
角を取る *kado o toru* round off the corners

【tsuno 角】 horn, antler; tentacle, antenna; wing (of a building)
鹿の角 *shika no tsuno* antler
角笛 *tsunobue* bugle, horn

SYNONYMS

❶ **angle and angular measure**
度 DEGREE → 3100
❷ **corners**
圭 SHARP CORNER → 2165
隅 NOOK → 623
❸ⓐ **body projections**
尾 TAIL → 3062
❹ⓐ **square**
方 SQUARE → 1963

NOTE

⇨ see COMPOUND FORMATION for 折角 *sekkaku* ⇨ 折 253

2-5 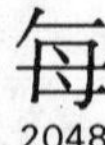
2048

▶EVERY
nonstandard for 毎 2034

2-5  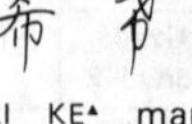
2049 KI KE▲ mare▲

Radical	Strokes
巾 50	7-3-4
Grade	**Freq**
Jōyō-4	802
2 - 2 - 5	

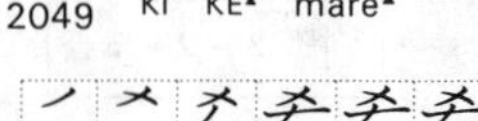
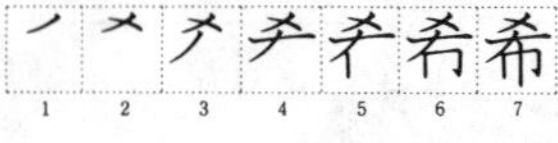

▶RARE ▶ASPIRE

COMPOUNDS

❶ [formerly also 稀 *ki, ke* 1189] (not frequent) **rare, uncommon, unusual, scarce**
希書 *kisho* rare book
希元素 *kigenso* rare element
希少な *kishō na* scarce, rare
希有な *keu* (=*kiyū*) *na* rare, unusual, uncommon
古希 *koki* three score and ten, seventy years of age
❷ [formerly also 稀 *ki* 1189]
ⓐ (thin in density) **rare, rarefied, dilute, thin**
ⓑ [also prefix] *chem* dilute
希薄な *kihaku na* dilute, thin, rare, sparse
希釈 *kishaku* dilution
希硫酸 *kiryūsan* dilute sulfuric acid
❸ **aspire, hope, desire, long for**
希望 *kibō* hope, wish, aspiration
希求する *kikyū suru* aspire to, seek, demand
❹ Greece, Greek
希臘 *girisha* Greece

KUN

【mare 希】
mare na 希な [formerly also 稀な] rare, uncommon, scarce, unique

SYNONYMS

❶ **rare**

珍 RARE → 909

❷ **rare and sparse**

薄い THIN → 2370
疎 SPARSE → 1178
粗 COARSE → 1329

❸ **wish and desire**

望 HOPE → 2742
懐 LONG FOR → 763
慕 yearn for → 2353
渇 thirst for → 515
欲 DESIRE → 1475
求 SEEK → 3550
願 WISH → 1845

USAGE

mare na

希な
[formerly also 稀な] rare, uncommon, scarce, unique

稀な
[now replaced by 希な] same as 希な

HOMOPHONES

mare ⇨ 稀 1189

COMPOUND FORMATION

古希 *koki*

古希 'three score and ten, etc.' derives from the passage 人生七十古来希なり *Jinsei shichijū korai mare nari* meaning that since ancient times (古) a life of seventy years has been a rare (希 ❶) phenomenon.

育 育 育 育

2050 IKU soda(tsu) soda(chi) soda(teru) hagu(kumu)▲

Ⓒ 育 yù

Radical	Strokes
月 130	8-4-4
Grade	**Freq**
Jōyō-3	232
2-2-6	

2-6

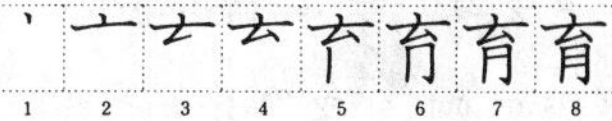

▶RAISE

COMPOUNDS

❶ (care for the growth of children, animals or plants) **raise, bring up, rear, breed, cultivate**

育成する *ikusei suru* bring up, rear
育児 *ikuji* infant rearing, nursing of children
育種 *ikushu* plant breeding
保育 *hoiku* nurture, upbringing; lactation, nursing
養育 *yōiku* fostering, bringing up, education
飼育する *shiiku suru* raise animals, breed, rear

❷ [original meaning] **grow, grow up, be brought up**

発育する *hatsuiku suru* grow, develop
成育する *seiiku suru* grow (up), be brought up

❸ **educate, teach, train**

育英 *ikuei* education of the gifted or promising
教育 *kyōiku* education, teaching
体育 *taiiku* physical training [education]

KUN

【soda(tsu) 育つ】 be brought up, grow up; grow, be bred

育ち過ぎる *sodachisugiru* be overgrown

【soda(chi) 育ち】

① breeding, upbringing

育ちが良い *sodachi ga yoi* be well-bred

② [suffix] raised in

神戸育ち *kōbesodachi* raised in Kobe

【soda(teru) 育てる】 bring up, rear, raise; breed, cultivate; educate, train

育て上げる *sodateageru* bring up, rear, educate
育ての親 *sodate no oya* foster parent

【hagu(kumu) 育くむ】 bring up, nurse; foster, cultivate; cover, sit over

自由の育くまれた所 *jiyū no hagukumareta tokoro* cradle of liberty

SYNONYMS

❶ **raise and nourish**

養 FOSTER → 2365
飼 RAISE ANIMALS → 1716
牧 PASTURE → 873
滋 NOURISH → 602

❷ **grow**

生 grow → 3497
長 grow (up) → 2556
成 grow up → 3537
発 develop → 2565
伸 expand → 70
展 UNFOLD → 3111

❸ **teach**

教 TEACH → 1493
授 teach → 492
練 TRAIN → 1375
訓 INSTRUCT → 1454
諭 ADMONISH → 1598
導 GUIDE → 2888
迪 EDIFY → 3076
啓 ENLIGHTEN → 2763

2-6 亠

享 享 享

2051 KYŌ u(keru)▲

CH 享 xiǎng

Radical	Strokes
亠 8	8-2-6
Grade	Freq
Jōyō	1888
2-2-6	

▶**ENJOY**

COMPOUNDS

● (benefit from something given) **enjoy, receive, be given, possess**

享受する *kyōju suru* enjoy, receive, be given

享有する *kyōyū suru* enjoy, possess, participate in

享楽 *kyōraku* enjoyment

享年 *kyōnen* age at death

KUN

【**u(keru) 享ける**】[usu. 受ける] enjoy, be granted

生を享ける *sei o ukeru* be born, live

恩寵を享ける *onchō o ukeru* enjoy (a person's) favor

SYNONYMS

● **receive**

受 RECEIVE → 2421

領 receive → 1224

収 TAKE IN → 198

納 ACCEPT → 1300

戴 RECEIVE HUMBLY → 3302

頂 RECEIVE HUMBLY → 145

拝 have the honor to receive → 303

● **possess**

有 HAVE → 2983

蔵 own → 2364

持 HOLD → 374

属 BELONG TO → 3145

具 possess → 2552

HOMOPHONES

ukeru ⇨ 受 2421 承 16 請 1576

NOTE

⇨ see USAGE note at 受 2421

★do not confuse with 亨 2037

2-6 亠

京 京 京

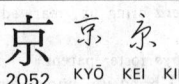

2052 KYŌ KEI KIN▲

CH 京 jīng

Radical	Strokes
亠 8	8-2-6
Grade	Freq
Jōyō-2	46
2-2-6	

▶**CAPITAL** ▶**TOKYO** ▶**KYOTO**

COMPOUNDS

❶ **capital, metropolis**

京洛 *keiraku* (=*kyōraku*) capital; Kyoto

京都 *kyōto* Kyoto

英京 *eikyō* capital of England, London

東京 *tōkyō* Tokyo

南京 *nankin* Nanjing (city in China)

❷ **Tokyo**

京浜 *keihin* Tokyo and Yokohama

上京する *jōkyō suru* go to Tokyo

帰京する *kikyō suru* return to Tokyo

滞京する *taikyō suru* stay in Tokyo [the capital]

在京中 *zaikyōchū* during one's stay in Tokyo

❸ **Kyoto**

京女 *kyōonna* Kyoto woman

京人形 *kyōningyō* Kyoto doll

京阪神 *keihanshin* Kyoto-Osaka-Kobe

京大 *kyōdai* University of Kyoto

❹ ten quadrillion (10^{16})

二京 *nikei* 20 quadrillion

INDEPENDENT

【**kyō 京**】capital, metropolis; Kyoto; ten quadrillion (10^{16})

京の都 *kyō no miyako* Kyoto

【**kei 京**】capital, metropolis; ten quadrillion (10^{16})

SYNONYMS

❶ **cities and towns**

都 METROPOLIS → 1686

市 CITY → 1993

町 TOWN → 1113

❷ **Kanto cities**

東 Tokyo → 3568

都 METROPOLIS OF TOKYO → 1686

浜 Yokohama → 436

❸ **Kansai cities**

阪 OSAKA → 271

神 Kobe → 912

❹ **large numbers**

兆 TRILLION → 225

億 HUNDRED MILLION → 170
万 TEN THOUSAND → 2936

千 THOUSAND → 3411
百 HUNDRED → 2026

盲 盲 盲 盲
2053 MŌ mekura▲

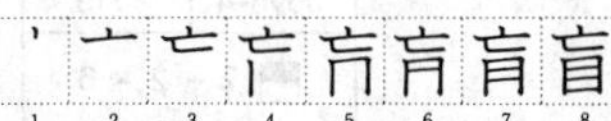

CH 盲 máng

Radical	Strokes
目 109	8-5-3
Grade	**Freq**
Jōyō	1425
2-2-6	

2-6
亠

▶ **BLIND**

COMPOUNDS

❶ⓐ [original meaning] **blind, blindness**
ⓑ [also prefix] **blind person**
ⓒ (closed at one end) blind
盲人 *mōjin* blind person
盲目 *mōmoku* blindness
色盲 *shikimō* color blindness
盲導犬 *mōdōken* guide dog, Seeing Eye dog
盲学校 *mōgakkō* school for the blind
盲管 *mōkan* cul-de-sac
盲腸 *mōchō* cecum, appendix
❷ [sometimes also 妄 2016] (not based on reason) **blind, reckless, aimless**
盲従 *mōjū* blind obedience
盲動 *mōdō* acting blindly
盲信 *mōshin* blind belief
盲想 *mōsō* wild idea [fancy], paranoiac illusion
盲爆 *mōbaku* blind [unscrupulous] bombing
❸ ignorant, illiterate
文盲 *monmō* illiteracy

KUN

【mekura 盲】 blindness, blind person; ignorance, illiteracy
明き盲 *akimekura* person blind to the outer world (due to carelessness or ignorance); illiterate person; amaurosis
盲穴 *mekuraana* blind hole
盲判 *mekuraban* undeliberated endorsement

SYNONYMS

❷ **rash**
妄 RASH → 2016
滅 unreasonable → 660
暴 unrestrained → 2515
荒 WILD → 2260
濫 EXCESSIVE → 801
乱 excessive → 1260

斉 齊 斉 斉
2054 SEI SAI▲

CH  qí

Radical	Strokes
斉 210	8-8-0
Grade	**Freq**
Jōyō	1439
2-2-6	

2-6
亠

RADICAL 210
variant of 齊 *sei* 'uniform'
⇨ see 齊 2142 for radical description

▶ **UNIFORM**

COMPOUNDS

❶ⓐ **uniform, equal, even, symmetrical**
ⓑ put in order, arrange
斉一 *seiitsu* uniformity, good order
均斉(＝均整) *kinsei* symmetry
整斉の *seisei no* symmetrical
不斉地用タイヤ *fuseichiyō-taiya* off the road tire
斉家 *seika* governing one's family
❷ **in unison, simultaneously**
斉唱する *seishō suru* sing in unison
斉射 *seisha* volley, fusillade
一斉に *issei ni* all together, all at once, simultaneously
❸ⓐ name of an ancient Chinese kingdom now in Shandong Province
ⓑ Southern Qi Dynasty (479–502 A.D.)
❹ [now always 斎 *sai* 2115] observe religious abstinence, abstain, purify oneself, fast
斉戒 *saikai* religious purification

INDEPENDENT

【sai 斉】 Southern Qi Dynasty

SYNONYMS

❶ⓐ **same and uniform**
均 EVEN → 235
等 EQUAL → 2682
平 equal → 3478

同 SAME → 2987
一 same → 3341

NOTE
★do not confuse with 斎 2115

2-6 亠

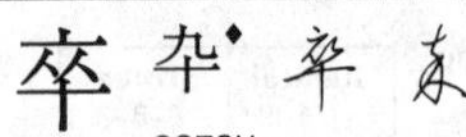

2055 SOTSU

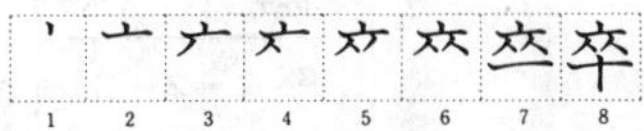

CH 卒 zú cù

Radical	Strokes
十 24	8-2-6
Grade	**Freq**
Jōyō-4	719
2-2-6	

▶**GRADUATE**

COMPOUNDS

❶ⓐ **graduate, complete one's studies**
ⓑ [also suffix] **graduate student, graduate**
卒業 *sotsugyō* graduation
卒論 *sotsuron* graduation thesis, dissertation
学卒 *gakusotsu* (university or school) graduate
中卒 *chūsotsu* junior high graduate
東大卒 *tōdaisotsu* graduate from Tokyo University
❷ⓐ [original meaning] **private, common soldier; pawn (in Chinese chess)**
ⓑ underling
兵卒 *heisotsu* private, common soldier
従卒 *jūsotsu* underling
❸ [also 率 2118] suddenly, unexpectedly
卒然(=率然) *sotsuzen* suddenly, unexpectedly
卒中 *sotchū* apoplexy
❹ die, pass away
卒去 *sokkyo* death

INDEPENDENT

【**sotsu** 卒】graduate(d); private
昨年度の卒 *sakunendo no sotsu* graduated last year
千九百七十九年卒 *senkyūhyaku-nanajūku-nen sotsu* graduated in 1979
【**sossuru** 卒する】die, pass away

SYNONYMS

❶ⓑ **students and followers**
生 STUDENT → 3497
学 scholar → 2555
門 pupil → 888
弟 disciple → 2044
徒 FOLLOWER → 416
❷ⓐ **soldiers and warriors**
兵 SOLDIER → 2551
士 MILITARY MAN → 3405
武 warrior → 3210
侍 SAMURAI → 85

2-6 亠

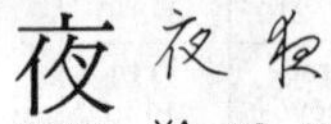

2056 YA yo yoru

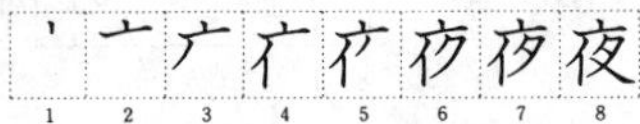

CH 夜 yè

Radical	Strokes
夕 36	8-3-5
Grade	**Freq**
Jōyō-2	255
2-2-6	

▶**NIGHT**

COMPOUNDS

❶ [original meaning] **night, evening**
夜間 *yakan* night, nighttime
夜分 *yabun* nighttime, night, evening
夜半 *yahan* midnight
昼夜 *chūya* day and night
今夜 *kon'ya* tonight, this evening
徹夜 *tetsuya* all night vigil [sitting]
深夜 *shin'ya* dead of night, midnight
前夜 *zen'ya* previous night; eve
❷ used phonetically for *ya* in the transliteration of Buddhist Sanscrit terms
夜叉 *yasha yakṣa*, demon

KUN

【**yo** 夜】night, evening
夜中 *yonaka* midnight, dead of night
夜明け *yoake* dawn, daybreak
夜空 *yozora* night sky
月夜 *tsukiyo* moonlit night
【**yoru** 夜】night, evening
夜昼 *yoruhiru* day and night

SYNONYMS

❶ **evening and night**
晩 EVENING → 979
夕 EVENING → 3387
宵 EARLY EVENING → 2276
暮 DUSK → 2354

(CH) 金 jīn

2057 KIN KON GON▲ kane kana- -gane

Radical	Strokes
金 167	8-8-0
Grade	Freq
Jōyō-1	71

2-2-6

1 2 3 4 5 6 7 8

RADICAL 167

Standard form: 金 *kane* 'metal' (釜 鑿)

Left variant: 金 *kanehen* (鉄 録 針)

Description: used in characters related to metals or metal products

▶METAL ▶GOLD ▶MONEY

COMPOUNDS

❶ⓐ [original meaning] **metal**

ⓑ the fourth of the five elements: metal (⇨ see APPENDIX 7)

金属 *kinzoku* metal

金鉄 *kintetsu* metal; firmness

合金 *gōkin* alloy, compound metal

冶金 *yakin* metallurgy

白金 *hakkin* platinum, platina

❷ⓐ [also prefix] **gold**

ⓑ [suffix] carats (of gold)

金貨 *kinka* gold coin

金鉱 *kinkō* gold ore; gold mine

金時計 *kindokei* gold watch

純金 *junkin* pure gold, solid gold

黄金 *ōgon* gold; money

十八金 *jūhachikin* 18-carat gold

❸ⓐ **golden, yellow**

ⓑ as precious as gold, excellent

金色 *kin'iro* (= *konjiki*) golden color

金髪 *kinpatsu* blonde, golden hair

金婚式 *kinkonshiki* golden wedding

金言 *kingen* golden rule, golden saying, maxim

金剛力 *kongōriki* Herculean strength

金堂 *kondō* main temple structure

❹ **money, cash, coin**

金額 *kingaku* amount of money, sum

金融 *kin'yū* circulation of money, money market, finance

現金 *genkin* cash

預金 *yokin* deposit, bank account

資金 *shikin* funds, capital

料金 *ryōkin* charge, rate, fee, fare

退職金 *taishokukin* retirement allowance [pay]

❺ **Friday**

金曜日 *kin'yōbi* Friday

月金 *getsukin* (= *gekkin*) Mondays and Fridays

❻ Venus

金星 *kinsei* Venus

❼ name of chess piece in shogi (Japanese chess): *kin*, the Gold

金将 *kinshō kin*

金取り *kintori* capturing a *kin*

❽ abbrev. of 金庫 *kinko*: depository, cash office

信金 *shinkin* credit union [guild]

INDEPENDENT

【**kin** 金】gold; sum of money; Friday; abbrev. of 金メダル *kinmedaru*: gold medal; *kin* (⇨ ❼)

金の指輪 *kin no yubiwa* gold ring

金千円 *kin sen'en* one thousand yen

水泳で金を取る *suiei de kin o toru* win the gold medal in a swimming race

【**gon** 金】the fourth of the five elements: metal

KUN

【**kane** 金】money, cash, coin; metal, iron

お金 *okane* money

金持ち *kanemochi* wealthy [rich] person

金貸し *kanekashi* moneylender, moneylending

金を払う *kane o harau* pay money

有り金 *arigane* money on hand, ready cash

金鋸 *kanenoko* hacksaw

【**kana-** 金-】metal

金物 *kanamono* hardware

金網 *kanaami* wire netting, screen

金具 *kanagu* metal fittings or fixtures

【**-gane** -金】something made of metal

引き金 *hikigane* trigger

口金 *kuchigane* metal clasp, snap; metal cap

針金 *harigane* wire

白金 *shirogane* [usu. 銀] silver; silver coin

赤金(=銅) *akagane* copper

SYNONYMS

❶ⓐ **metal**

鉱 ORE → 1709

❷ⓐ **metals**

銀 SILVER → 1722

銅 COPPER → 1721

鉄 IRON → 1711

鉛 LEAD → 1707

❸ⓐ **yellow colors**

黄 YELLOW → 2468

❹ **money**
銭 MONEY → 1725
貨 MONEY (legal tender), coin → 2465
幣 CURRENCY → 2885
銀 SILVER → 1722
財 finance → 1457
資 RESOURCES → 2695
-玉 coin suffix → 3477
札 bill → 817
❺ **days of the week**
木 Thursday → 3450
土 Saturday → 3403
日 Sunday → 3027
月 Monday → 2956
火 Tuesday → 3463
水 Wednesday → 10

USAGE
shirogane
白金
[usu. 銀]
ⓐ silver
ⓑ silver coin
銀
[sometimes also 白金]
ⓐ silver
ⓑ silver coin

HOMOPHONES
shirogane ⇨ 銀 1722 白金 3493, 2057
akagane ⇨ 銅 1721 赤金 2193, 2057

NOTE
⇨ see also USAGE note at 銅 1721

2-6
人

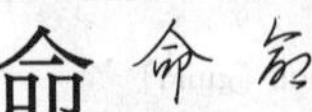
2058 MEI MYŌ inochi

Ⓒ 命 mìng

Radical	Strokes
口 30	8-3-5
Grade	**Freq**
Jōyō-3	393
2-2-6	

▶ORDER ▶LIFE

COMPOUNDS
❶ [original meaning] **order, command, instruction**
命令 *meirei* command, orders; edict, decree
使命 *shimei* mission, appointed task
勅命 *chokumei* Imperial order [command]
❷ **life**
生命 *seimei* life
一生懸命(=一所懸命)に *isshōkenmei* (=*isshokenmei*) *ni* for life, with all one's might
寿命 *jumyō* life span
長命 *chōmei* long life
人命 *jinmei* (human) life
亡命 *bōmei* exile
致命傷 *chimeishō* fatal wound
❸ **fate, god's will, destiny, luck**
命運 *meiun* one's fate [doom]
革命 *kakumei* revolution
運命 *unmei* fate, fortune, destiny
宿命 *shukumei* fate, destiny
本命 *honmei* probable [prospective] winner, most likely candidate
❹ⓐ assign a name [title], name
ⓑ appoint to a post
命題 *meidai* proposition, thesis
命中 *meichū* hit, on-target impact
命名 *meimei* naming, christening
任命する *ninmei suru* appoint, nominate

INDEPENDENT
【mei 命】 order, command, instruction; life; fate, destiny

命に依り *mei ni yori* by order [command], under the orders of
命旦夕に迫る *mei tanseki ni semaru* be on the brink of death
死生命有り *Shisei mei ari* Life and death are providential
【meizuru (=meijiru) 命ずる(=命じる)】 order, command; appoint, nominate

KUN
【inochi 命】 life
命懸けで *inochigake de* at the risk of one's life
命取りの *inochitori no* fatal, deadly

SYNONYMS
❶ **command**
令 COMMAND → 1995
❷ **life**
生 LIFE → 3497
寿 LONGEVITY → 3557
❸ **fate and fortune**
運 FORTUNE → 3140
業 karma → 2612
縁 karma relation → 1386

COMPOUND FORMATION
革命 *kakumei*
革命 'revolution' is a change (革) in God's will or fate (命 ❸).

NOTE
⇨ see COMPOUND FORMATION for
使命 *shimei* ⇨ 使 90
一生懸命(=一所懸命) *isshōkenmei* (=*isshokenmei*) ⇨ 生 3497

2059 NEN

ノ 𠆢 𠆢 今 今 念 念 念
1 2 3 4 5 6 7 8

CH 念 niàn

Radical	Strokes
心 61	8-4-4
Grade	**Freq**
Jōyō-4	473
2-2-6	

2-6 へ

▶**THOUGHTS**

COMPOUNDS

❶ⓐ **thoughts, inner thoughts, mind, idea, conception**
ⓑ **thought of doing something, intention, desire, wish**
念頭に置く *nentō ni oku* give thought to, bear in mind
観念 *kannen* idea, conception, notion
概念 *gainen* general idea, concept
残念 *zannen* regret, disappointment, chagrin
信念 *shinnen* belief, faith
懸念する *kenen suru* be anxious, feel concern, fear
断念する *dannen suru* give up (an idea), abandon, relinquish
専念する *sennen suru* give undivided attention to, concentrate (on), devote oneself to
邪念 *janen* vicious mind, evil thoughts
念願 *nengan* one's heart's desire, one's heartiest wish
執念 *shūnen* tenacity of purpose, vindictiveness, spite
一念 *ichinen* wholehearted wish, determined soul

❷ **attention, care, precaution**
念入りな *nen'iri na* careful, elaborate
入念に *nyūnen ni* carefully, scrupulously
丹念 *tannen* application, assiduity, diligence

❸ **keep one's thoughts on, bear in mind, remember**
記念 *kinen* commemoration, memory
失念 *shitsunen* lapse of memory, oblivion

❹ chant, intone, invoke
念仏 *nenbutsu* Buddhist invocation, prayer to Amitabha
念珠 *nenju* rosary
祈念する *kinen suru* pray, offer a prayer

❺ [usu. 廿 *nijū* 3449] twenty
念五日 *nengonichi* 25 days; 25th of the month

❻ *Buddhism* extremely short interval, moment, instant
一念 *ichinen* brief instant

INDEPENDENT

【nen 念】
① thoughts, feeling, sense
感謝の念 *kansha no nen* feelings of gratitude
② desire, wish, concern
復讐の念 *fukushū no nen* desire for vengeance
③ attention, care, precaution
念の為 *nen no tame* by way of precaution, to make sure
念を入れる *nen o ireru* pay attention to
念を押す *nen o osu* call attention to, make sure of, emphasize

【nenjiru (=nenzuru) 念じる(=念ずる)】
pray, invoke, chant (a sutra); have (something) at heart, wish
必勝を念じる *hisshō o nenjiru* pray for one's victory
経を念じる *kyō o nenjiru* chant a sutra
良かれと念じる *yokare to nenjiru* wish a person well

SYNONYMS

❶ⓐ **thought**
考え thought → 3196
意 MIND → 2136
想 conception → 2828
ⓑ **will and intention**
気 mind to do something → 3194
図 intention → 3071
意 MIND → 2136
志 AMBITION → 2199
趣 PURPOSE → 3317
欲 DESIRE → 1475
❷ **attention**
気 care → 3194

COMPOUND FORMATION

残念 *zannen*
残念 'regret, disappointment, chagrin' literally refers to one's lingering (残) thoughts (念 ❶ⓐ), i.e., the misgivings one feels when certain events fail to transpire.

2-6
人

舍 舍 舍

2060 SHA

Ⓒⓗ 舍 shè

Radical	Strokes
人 9△	8-2-6
Grade	**Freq**
Jōyō-5	1009
2-2-6	

1 2 3 4 5 6 7 8

▶**BUILDING**

COMPOUNDS

❶ **building, house, quarter, hut**

駅舎 *ekisha* station building
校舎 *kōsha* school building
庁舎 *chōsha* government building
鶏舎 *keisha* henhouse

❷ **temporary quarters, dormitory, lodging house, inn**

舎監 *shakan* dormitory inspector [superintendent]
兵舎 *heisha* barracks
宿舎 *shukusha* lodgings, quarters
客舎 *kyakusha* hotel, inn
寄宿舎 *kishukusha* dormitory, boarding house; hostel

❸ [humble] my

舎弟 *shatei* my younger brother

❹ unit of distance in ancient China equiv. to 30 *ri* (里)

三舎を避ける *sansha o sakeru* be put to shame, be outshone

❺ used phonetically for *sha* or *sei*

舎利 *shari* Buddha's bones, *sarira*; remains, ashes

INDEPENDENT

【**sha 舎**】 dormitory, boarding house

SPECIAL READINGS

田舎 *inaka* country, rural district

SYNONYMS

❶ **buildings**

棟 BLOCK → 991
館 PUBLIC BUILDING → 1748
堂 HALL → 2589
閣 TALL MAGNIFICENT BUILDING → 3327
宇 large building → 2175
殿 PALACE → 1792

❷ **temporary quarters**

寮 DORMITORY → 2359
宿 lodging → 2293
館 inn → 1748
亭 INN → 2072

2-6
人

2061

Radical	Strokes
飠 184	8-8-0
Grade	**Freq**
Radical	
2-2-6	

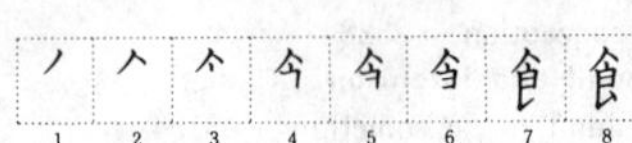

1 2 3 4 5 6 7 8

RADICAL 184

shokuhen, variant of 食 *shoku* 'food'
⇨ see 食 2077 for radical description

2-6
人

舎

2062

▶**BUILDING**

nonstandard for 舎 2060

2-6
八

劵 卷

incorrect classification ⇨ see 6-2

2-6
丷

並

incorrect classification ⇨ see 2246

尭 堯 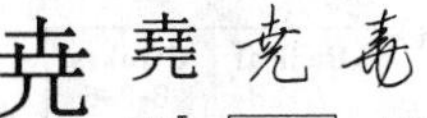

Ⓒ 尧 yáo

2063 GYŌ NAMES takashi taka nori aki

一 十 土 圡 垚 垚 尭 尭
1 2 3 4 5 6 7 8

Radical	Strokes
土 32	8-3-5
Grade	**Freq**
Names	2126
2-2-6	

2-6 十

▶YAO

COMPOUNDS

❶ name of a legendary sage king in ancient China: **Yao**

尭舜 *gyōshun* Yao and Shun (two of the most celebrated kings in ancient China)

❷ [archaic] high, noble

尭尭たる *gyōgyōtaru* high (as of a mountain)

INDEPENDENT

【gyō 尭】Yao (⇨ ❶)

NAMES

尭 *takashi* male name

尭文 *takafumi* male name

尭一 *akikazu* male name

直

incorrect classification ⇨ see 2932

2-6 十

卓 

Ⓒ 卓 桌 zhuō

2064 TAKU

Radical	Strokes
十 24	8-2-6
Grade	**Freq**
Jōyō	1466
2-2-6	

2-6 ト

▶TABLE ▶PROMINENT

COMPOUNDS

❶ **table, desk**

卓球 *takkyū* table tennis, ping-pong

卓上電話 *takujō-denwa* desk phone

食卓 *shokutaku* dining table

円卓 *entaku* round table

電卓 *dentaku* pocket calculator

❷ [original meaning] **prominent, eminent, outstanding, unexcelled, superior**

卓効 *takkō* remarkable efficacy

卓見 *takken* farsightedness, penetration, excellent views

卓越 *takuetsu* excellence, superiority

卓説 *takusetsu* excellent opinion

卓立する *takuritsu suru* be prominent, stand out

卓抜 *takubatsu* prominence, excellence, superiority

INDEPENDENT

【taku 卓】table, desk

卓を囲む *taku o kakomu* sit at table, have a meal together

SYNONYMS

❶ **tables and stands**

机 DESK → 820

台 STAND → 2005

❷ **excellent and superior**

優 SUPERIOR → 177

秀 EXCELLENT → 2545

英 DISTINGUISHED → 2238

傑 outstanding → 155

逸 exceptional → 3120

名 first-rate → 2169

上 of upper grade → 3404

絶 without match → 1353

快 splendid → 245

妙 MARVELOUS → 239

❷ **conspicuous**

傑 outstanding → 155

著 CONSPICUOUS → 2300

顕 MANIFEST → 1806

桌

2065

▶POINT

nonstandard for 点 2084

2-6 ト

2-6 ム

2066 SAN SHIN▲ mai(ru)

CH 参 cān shēn cēn

Radical	Strokes
ム 28	8-2-6
Grade	**Freq**
Jōyō-4	346
2-2-6	

▶**PARTICIPATE**
▶**VISIT A HOLY PLACE**

COMPOUNDS

❶ **participate, take part in, join in**
参加する *sanka suru* participate, join, take part in
参謀 *sanbō* staff officer, the staff; adviser, counselor
参事 *sanji* councilor, secretary
参議院 *sangiin* House of Councilors, Upper House
参戦 *sansen* participation in a war
参与 *san'yo* participation (in public affairs); counselor, consultant

❷ abbrev. of 参議院 *sangiin*: House of Councilors, Upper House
衆参両院 *shūsan-ryōin* both Houses (of the Diet)

❸ **visit a holy place (as a temple, shrine or the Imperial Palace), make a pilgrimage; visit (a superior) in order to pay one's respects**
参拝 *sanpai* worship, visit to a shrine [temple]
参詣 *sankei* visit to a temple [shrine], worship, pilgrimage
参上する *sanjō suru* go to see, call on, pay one's respects
参内 *sandai* attendance at the Imperial Court
墓参 *bosan* visit to a grave
日参 *nissan* daily visit (of worship); frequent visit

❹ **go somewhere, go (to), come**
参観 *sankan* visit, inspection
参集する *sanshū suru* gather, meet, congregate
持参する *jisan suru* bring [take] with one, carry
古参 *kosan* senior, old-timer, veteran; seniority
新参 *shinzan* newcomer, greenhorn

❺ **refer, consult, collate**
参考 *sankō* reference, consultation
参照 *sanshō* reference, comparison

❻ **be stumped, be beaten**
降参する *kōsan suru* surrender, submit, yield

❼ three—used in legal documents and checks
金参千円也 *kin sanzen'en nari* three thousand yen

❽ unclassified compounds
人参 *ninjin* carrot

INDEPENDENT

【san 参】 three (⇨ ❼)
【sanzuru (=sanjiru) 参ずる(=参じる)】
[humble] go, come

KUN

【mai(ru) 参る】
①ⓐ [humble] go, come
ⓑ [humble verb following the TE-form of other verbs] go and do, perform an action and return to the point of departure
今参ります *Ima mairimasu* I'm coming
そちらへは参りません *Sochira e wa mairimasen* I won't go there
取って参ります *Totte mairimasu* I'll fetch it
車を呼んで参りましょうか *Kuruma o yonde mairimashō ka* Shall I send for a cab?
② visit a holy place (as a temple, shrine or grave), make a pilgrimage
寺参り *teramairi* visit to a temple
お礼参り *oreimairi* visiting a shrine or temple to offer thanks; calling on a person to settle old scores
③ be stumped, be beaten; die
参った *Maitta* That licks me! / I'm done for! / You got me there
④ be captivated by (a woman's beauty), be infatuated
彼女にすっかり参っている *kanojo ni sukkari maitte iru* be dead gone on her

SYNONYMS

❶ **participate and join**
与 take part in → 3421
加 join → 38
入 ENTER → 3370

❸ **visit**
訪 VISIT → 1468
伺 call on → 69
寄 call at → 2291

❹ **go and come**
出 go to → 3498
来 COME → 3551
通 go to and from → 3109
向 head toward → 3052
赴 PROCEED TO → 3303
行 GO → 212
往 GO ON → 292

❺ compare
対 OPPOSE (contrast) → 831
照 check against → 2827
校 COLLATE → 929
比 COMPARE → 26
較 COMPARE → 1536
❼ three
三 THREE → 1924

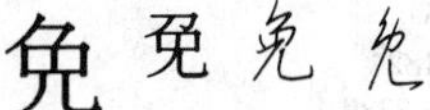

2067 MEN manuka(reru) manuga(reru)

CH 免 miǎn

Radical	Strokes
儿 10	8-2-6
Grade	Freq
Jōyō	1032
2-2-6	

2-6

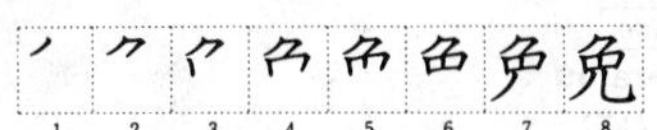

▶ EXEMPT

COMPOUNDS

❶ⓐ **exempt from, free from, release, excuse, forgive**
ⓑ **be exempted, be immune**
ⓒ exemption, remission
免除 *menjo* exemption, exoneration, dismissal
免税 *menzei* tax exemption
赦免 *shamen* pardon, amnesty, clemency
御免なさい *Gomen nasai* I'm sorry / Excuse me
免疫 *men'eki* immunity (from a disease)
減免 *genmen* reduction and exemption
❷ⓐ **license, permit, grant a request**
ⓑ abbrev. of 免許 *menkyo*: **license**
免許 *menkyo* license, permit
免状 *menjō* license, diploma
特免 *tokumen* special exemption; special license
❸ discharge, dismiss, remove from office
免職 *menshoku* dismissal, discharge
懲戒免職 *chōkaimenshoku* disciplinary discharge
罷免 *himen* dismissal, discharge
任免 *ninmen* appointment and dismissal [removal]

INDEPENDENT

【**menjiru 免じる**】exempt, release; dismiss, discharge
...に免じて *...ni menjite* out of respect for...

KUN

【**manuka(reru), manuga(reru) 免れる**】be exempted from, be released from; escape, be saved from, avoid
焼失を免れる *shōshitsu o manukareru* be saved from the fire

SYNONYMS

❶ **forgive**
赦 AMNESTY → 1478
許す forgive → 1470
❷ⓐ **permit**
許 PERMIT → 1470
准 grant permission → 127
允 GIVE CONSENT → 1982
ⓑ **certificates**
状 official document → 272
券 CERTIFICATE → 2630
証 CERTIFICATE → 1506
❸ **dismiss**
罷 DISMISS → 2617
解 release from office → 1517

哀 哀 哀

2068 AI awa(re) awa(remu) kana(shii)▲

CH 哀 āi

Radical	Strokes
口 30	9-3-6
Grade	Freq
Jōyō	1652
2-2-7	

2-7

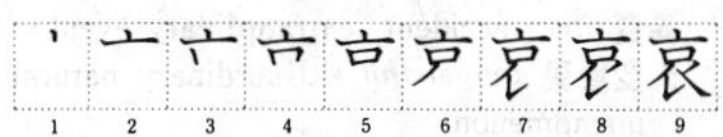

▶ SORROW ▶ PITY

COMPOUNDS

❶ⓐ **sorrow, grief, sadness, pathos**
ⓑ **sorrowful, sad, pathetic**
ⓒ feel sorrow for, grieve, mourn
哀歓 *aikan* joys and sorrows
喜怒哀楽 *kidoairaku* joy and anger; emotion
悲哀 *hiai* sorrow, sadness
哀感 *aikan* pathos
哀愁 *aishū* sadness, sorrow, pensiveness
哀話 *aiwa* sad story, tragic tale
哀切な *aisetsu na* pathetic, plaintive
哀悼 *aitō* condolence, mourning, grieving
哀哭する *aikoku suru* mourn, lament, wail
❷ⓐ **pity, sympathy**
ⓑ **feel pity for, pity**

ⓒ pitifully
哀憐 *airen* pity, compassion, affection
可哀相な *kawaisō na* poor, pitiable, pathetic
哀願 *aigan* entreaty, supplication

KUN

【awa(re) 哀れ】 pity, sympathy; pathos; Alas! (in aesthetic sense)
哀れな *aware na* pitiable; miserable

【awa(remu) 哀れむ】
① [formerly also 憐れむ] pity, sympathize, feel compassion
哀れみ *awaremi* pity, compassion
② feel the pathos of things, appreciate the beauties (of nature)
月を哀れむ *tsuki o awaremu* enjoy the beauty of the moon

【kana(shii) 哀しい】 [now usu. 悲しい] (causing sorrow) sad, sorrowful, pathetic
哀しい歌 *kanashii uta* sad song, doleful song
哀しい出来事 *kanashii dekigoto* sad event

SYNONYMS

❶ⓐ sorrow
憂 grief → 2145
ⓑ sad and depressed
悲 SAD → 2775
愁 MELANCHOLY → 2829
陰 gloomy → 541
沈 depressed → 261
寂 LONESOME → 2290
惨 MISERABLE → 483
❷ⓐ tender feelings for others
悲 mercy → 2775
情 sympathy → 482
慈 compassion → 2339
仁 BENEVOLENCE → 20

USAGE

awaremu
哀れむ
① [formerly also 憐れむ] pity, sympathize, feel compassion
② feel the pathos of things, appreciate the beauties (of nature)
憐れむ
[now usu. 哀れむ] pity, sympathize, feel compassion

HOMOPHONES

awaremu ⇨ 憐 731
kanashii ⇨ 悲 2775

NOTE

⇨ see also USAGE note at 悲 2775
★do not confuse with 衷 2575

2-7 亠

変 變 变 変

2069 HEN ka(waru) ka(wari) ka(eru)

CH 变 biàn

Radical	Strokes
夊 34△	9-3-6
Grade Jōyō-4	Freq 303
2-2-7	

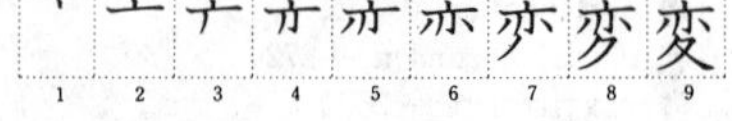

▶CHANGE ▶ABNORMAL

COMPOUNDS

❶ⓐ [original meaning] **change, alter, transform, vary, shift**
ⓑ **change, variation, mutation**
変化 *henka* change, transformation, variety; declension
変質 *henshitsu* change in quality, degeneration
変更 *henkō* alteration, change, modification
変動 *hendō* change, fluctuation
変形 *henkei* transformation
変電所 *hendensho* transformer substation
変革 *henkaku* change, reform, revolution
一変する *ippen suru* change completely
激変(=劇変) *gekihen* sudden change, upheaval

❷ **abnormal, extraordinary, unusual, irregular, eccentric, odd**
変則の *hensoku no* irregular, abnormal
変態性欲 *hentai seiyoku* abnormal sexuality, perversion
変人 *henjin* eccentric person, crank
変化 *henge* goblin, ghost

❸ extraordinary event:
ⓐ **unexpected event [incident], extraordinary phenomenon, accident, disaster, emergency**
ⓑ **uprising, upheaval, disturbance**
変事 *henji* accident, emergency
変死 *henshi* accidental [unnatural] death
異変 *ihen* accident, extraordinary event
天変地異 *tenpenchii* extraordinary natural phenomenon
大変な *taihen na* awful, terrible; serious, grave
事変 *jihen* incident, upheaval; accident
政変 *seihen* coup d'état

❹ *music* flat
変ホ長調 *henhochōchō* E flat major
重変 *jūhen* double flat

❺ *Buddhism* picture of paradise or hell
地獄変 *jigokuhen* Picture of Hell

INDEPENDENT

【hen 変】 uprising, disturbance, incident; emergency, accident
  承久の変 *jōkyū no hen* Jokyu Uprising
【hen na 変な】 strange, extraordinary, odd, weird, eccentric, funny-looking; suspicious-looking
  変な外人 *hen na gaijin* weird foreigner
【henjiru (=henzuru) 変じる(=変ずる)】 change, turn into, transmute

KUN

【ka(waru) 変わる】
①ⓐ change, undergo change, be altered, be transformed
ⓑ change addresses, move, be transferred
  変わり目 *kawarime* turning point
  移り変わる *utsurikawaru* change, shift
  生まれ変わる *umarekawaru* be born again; start one's life afresh
  天気が変わった *Tenki ga kawatta* The weather changed
  相変わらず *aikawarazu* as usual, as before
  新しい家に変わる *atarashii ie ni kawaru* move to a new house
② be different, differ; be extraordinary, be odd
  変わり者 *kawarimono* eccentric person, queer fish
  変わった *kawatta* different; unusual, extraordinary, odd
【ka(wari) 変わり】
① change
  変わり無く *kawarinaku* without change, uniformly; peacefully, well
② difference
  どっちでも変わりは無い *Dotchi demo kawari wa nai* Whichever you choose, it makes no difference
③ something wrong, accident
④ eccentricity
  風変わり *fūgawari* eccentricity, extraordinariness
【ka(eru) 変える】
ⓐ change, alter, convert, transform, turn into
ⓑ change to a different time or place
ⓒ reform, revise, amend
  変え *kae* change, changing
  形と色を変える *katachi to iro o kaeru* change the shape and color of
  鉛を金に変える *namari o kin ni kaeru* convert lead into gold
  観点を変える *kanten o kaeru* change one's point of view
  予定を変える *yotei o kaeru* change the schedule
  位置を変える *ichi o kaeru* change the position of
  法律を変える *hōritsu o kaeru* revise [amend] the law

SYNONYMS

❶ change and replace
更 change → 3541
改 change → 243
易 change → 2411
化 CHANGE INTO, -ize → 21
遷 undergo transition → 3170
転 turn into → 1480
換 EXCHANGE → 587
交 INTERCHANGE → 2015
替 REPLACE → 2783
代 SUBSTITUTE → 30
迭 ALTERNATE → 3077
❷ abnormal
奇 UNUSUAL → 2217
妙 strange → 239
異 not ordinary → 2584
怪 MYSTERIOUS → 297
珍 curious → 909
❸ⓐ incident
故 incident → 1141
事 AFFAIR → 3567
ⓑ warfare and rebellions
乱 rebellion → 1260
陣 battle → 455
戦 WAR → 1787
軍 war → 2080
役 war → 244
闘 FIGHT → 3334

USAGE

❶ kawaru
変わる
①ⓐ change, undergo change, be altered, be transformed
ⓑ change addresses, move, be transferred
② be different, differ; be extraordinary, be odd
  機械の機構が変わった *Kikai no kikō ga kawatta* The mechanism of the machine has been changed [altered]
代わる
substitute, be substituted for (a person), take the place of
  機械が人に代わる *Kikai ga hito ni kawaru* Machines take the place of human labor
換わる
be exchanged, become interchanged, be converted, change
  この機械は金に換わる *Kono kikai wa kane ni kawaru* This machine can be exchanged for money
替わる
be replaced, change places with, replace, take turns, relieve, change

機械が替わった *Kikai ga kawatta* The (old) machine was replaced (by a new one)

❷ **kawari**

変わり

① change
② difference
③ something wrong, accident
④ eccentricity

代わり

①ⓐ substitution, substitute
ⓑ substitute, deputy, proxy
② compensation, exchange
③ though...on the other hand

換わり

exchange

替わり

① turn, shift
② replacement (for a maid)
③ substitute program (of a kabuki play)

❸ **kaeru**

変える

ⓐ change, alter, convert, transform, turn into
ⓑ change to a different time or place
ⓒ reform, revise, amend

馬を牛に変える *Uma o ushi ni kaeru* Change a horse into a cow (by magic)

代える

substitute, use in place of, replace (something) with (another)

馬を牛に代える *Uma o ushi ni kaeru* Substitute a horse for a cow / Use a horse in place of a cow

換える

[sometimes also 替える] exchange, interchange, trade, barter, change (money), convert

馬を牛と換える *Uma o ushi to kaeru* Exchange a horse for a cow

替える

①ⓐ replace (one thing or person by another), renew, change
ⓑ change to something new (as a job or set of clothes), change over to

馬を替える *Uma o kaeru* Replace an old horse with a new one

② [usu. 換える] exchange, interchange, trade, barter, change (money), convert

❹ **kae**

変え

change, changing

代え

substitute, proxy

換え

rate of exchange

替え-

substitute, spare, extra

★The above words are easily confused. Study the examples above in addition to the examples under each entry. Note that the distinction between these words as independent *kun* words does not necessarily apply to their meanings in the formation of compounds. For example, though 両替え *ryōgae* 'changing money, exchange of money' is written with 替, *kaeru* in the sense of changing money is written 換える.

HOMOPHONES

kawaru ⇨ 代 30 換 587 替 2783
kawari ⇨ 代 30 換 587 替 2783
kaeru ⇨ 代 30 換 587 替 2783
kae ⇨ 代 30 換 587 替 2783

COMPOUND FORMATION

大変 *taihen*

大変な 'awful, terrible, etc.' formerly referred to a great (大) calamity (変 ❸ⓐ).

2-7

音 音 音 音

2070 ON -NON IN oto ne

CH 音 yīn

Radical	Strokes
音 180	9-9-0
Grade	**Freq**
Jōyō-1	459
2-2-7	

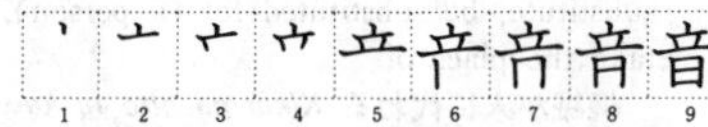

RADICAL 180

variant of 音 *oto* 'sound'

⇨ see 音 1948 for radical description

▶**SOUND**

COMPOUNDS

❶ [also suffix]

ⓐ (vibratory disturbance) **sound, noise, roar**

ⓑ (auditory sensation) **sound**

ⓒ [original meaning] **speech sound, voice, pronunciation**

音響 *onkyō* sound
騒音 *sōon* noise
録音 *rokuon* sound recording
音質 *onshitsu* sound [tone] quality

音声 *onsei* voice, sound
音韻論 *on'inron* phonology
音節 *onsetsu* syllable
発音 *hatsuon* pronunciation
英音 *eion* English pronunciation
子音 *shiin* (=*shion*) consonant ("child sound")
母音 *boin* vowel ("mother sound")
五十音 *gojūon* Japanese syllabary
破裂音 *haretsuon* plosive, stop

❷ⓐ **sound of music, music, note, tune, melody**
ⓑ abbrev. of 音楽 *ongaku*: music
音楽 *ongaku* music
音痴 *onchi* tone deafness
音符 *onpu* note; phonetic element of kanji
低音 *teion* low-pitched sound, bass
不協和音 *fukyōwaon* discord, dissonance
音大 *ondai* music college
労音 *rōon* Workers' Music Council

❸ **Chinese-derived pronunciation of kanji, *on* reading**
音読み *on'yomi* Chinese-derived pronunciation of kanji, *on* reading
音訓 *onkun* *on* and *kun* readings
漢音 *kan'on* Han reading of Chinese characters

❹ news, report, information
音信 *onshin* (=*inshin*) correspondence, communication
福音 *fukuin* gospel, good news

❺ unclassified compounds
観音 *kannon* *Avalokiteśvara*, Buddhist Goddess of Mercy

INDEPENDENT

【on 音】 sound; speech sound; *on* reading; abbrev. of 音楽 *ongaku*: music
Sの音 *esu no on* *s* sound
音で読む *on de yomu* read kanji in the *on* reading

KUN

【oto 音】 sound, noise, roar; fame
音を出す *oto o dasu* produce a sound
足音 *ashioto* sound of footsteps
物音 *monooto* noise, sound
波の音 *nami no oto* roar of waves
音に聞く *oto ni kiku* famous, widely known

【ne 音】 sound, note, tone
音色 *neiro* tone, quality of a sound
鐘の音 *kane no ne* toll of a bell, chimes
本音 *honne* one's real intentions

SYNONYMS

❶ **kinds of sound**
声 VOICE → 2198
響 reverberation → 2878
韻 melodious tone → 1811
玲 TINKLING OF JADES → 910

❷ **music and songs**
楽 MUSIC → 2826
節 tune → 2691
調べ melody → 1567
曲 MUSICAL COMPOSITION → 3527
歌 SONG → 1825
謡 POPULAR SONG → 1597

亮 亮 亮

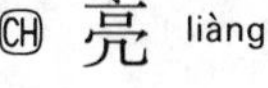

2071 RYŌ NAMES aki suke makoto akira yoshi

Radical	Strokes
亠 8	9-2-7
Grade	**Freq**
Names	2025
2-2-7	

2-7 亠

▶LUCID

COMPOUNDS

❶ⓐ [now always 瞭 1238] (easily understood) lucid, clear
ⓑ [now always 諒 1575] **show lucid understanding**
亮然たる *ryōzentaru* obvious, clear
明亮な *meiryō na* lucid, clear, plain
亮察する *ryōsatsu suru* consider, take into account, sympathize with

❷ [archaic] (suffused with light) bright, lucid, brilliant
亮月 *ryōgetsu* bright moonlight
亮直 *ryōchoku* rightfulness

NAMES

亮一 *ryōichi* male name
誠亮 *seisuke* male name

SYNONYMS

❶ⓐ **evident**
明 CLEAR → 855
鮮 VIVID → 1877
顕 MANIFEST → 1806

NOTE

★do not confuse with 亭 2072

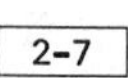

亭 2072 TEI CHIN▲

Ⓒⓗ 亭 tíng

Radical	Strokes
亠 8	9-2-7
Grade	**Freq**
Jōyō	1471
2-2-7	

▶INN ▶PSEUDONYM SUFFIX

COMPOUNDS

❶ⓐ inn, hostelry
ⓑ suffix after names of inns
亭主 *teishu* husband; master, host
旅亭 *ryotei* inn, hotel
石亭 *sekitei* The Sekitei (name of an inn)
❷ⓐ restaurant, Japanese restaurant
ⓑ suffix after names of quality restaurants
料亭 *ryōtei* high-class restaurant, Japanese restaurant
夕月亭 *yūzukitei* The Yuzukitei (name of a Japanese restaurant)
❸ [original meaning] arbor, bower, pavilion
池亭 *chitei* arbor [bower] by a lake
❹ suffix after names of vaudeville houses or variety theaters
若竹亭 *wakataketei* The Wakatake Variety Theater
❺ suffix for forming pseudonyms or stage names
二葉亭 *futabatei* Futabatei (name of a writer)
三遊亭円歌 *san'yūtei enka* Enka Sanyutei (name of a comic story teller)
❻ lofty
亭亭たる大木 *teiteitaru taiboku* lofty tree

INDEPENDENT

【tei 亭】 arbor, bower
【chin 亭】 arbor, bower

SYNONYMS

❶ temporary quarters
館 inn → 1748
宿 lodging → 2293
寮 DORMITORY → 2359
舎 temporary quarters → 2060
❷ⓑ restaurant suffixes
閣 high-class restaurant suffix → 3327
園 restaurant suffix → 3156
苑 restaurant suffix → 2239
❺ pseudonym suffixes
屋 stage name suffix → 3098

NOTE

★do not confuse with 亮 2071

2-7

帝 2073 TEI mikado▲

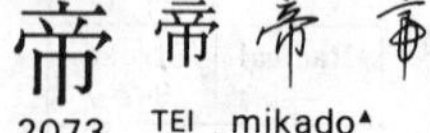

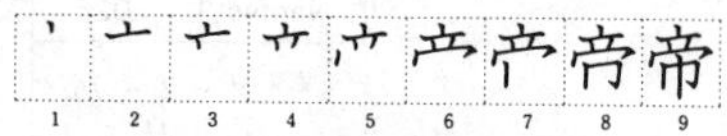

Ⓒⓗ 帝 dì

Radical	Strokes
巾 50	9-3-6
Grade	**Freq**
Jōyō	1000
2-2-7	

▶EMPEROR

COMPOUNDS

❶ⓐ emperor, empress
ⓑ imperial
帝王 *teiō* monarch, emperor
皇帝 *kōtei* emperor
女帝 *jotei* empress, queen
露帝 *rotei* Czar, Russian emperor
帝国 *teikoku* empire, imperial
帝政 *teisei* imperial government
帝劇 *teigeki* The Imperial Theater
❷ abbrev. of 帝国主義 *teikokushugi*: imperialism
反帝 *hantei* anti-imperialism
米帝 *beitei* U.S. imperialism
❸ [original meaning] the Supreme Being, Lord of Heaven
天帝 *tentei* Lord of Heaven, the Creator
上帝 *jōtei* God, the Lord

INDEPENDENT

【tei 帝】 emperor, empress

KUN

【mikado 帝】 *literary* emperor of Japan
時の帝 *toki no mikado* emperor of the time

SYNONYMS

❶ rulers
天 Heaven's messenger on earth → 3442
皇 EMPEROR → 2566
王 KING → 3439
君 RULER → 3206
❸ god
神 GOD → 912

天 HEAVEN → 3442 ┊ 主 Lord → 1938

2074

▶MALE NAME ELEMENT
nonstandard for 彦 3295

2-7 亠

彦

incorrect classification ⇨ see 3295

2-7 亠

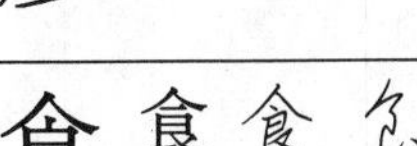

2-7 人

食 食 食 食 (CH) 食 shí sì
2075 SHOKU JIKI ku(u) ku(rau) ta(beru)

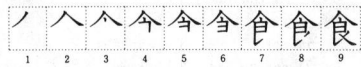

Radical	Strokes
食 184	9-9-0
Grade	Freq
Jōyō-2	289
2-2-7	

ノ 人 亼 今 今 今 食 食 食
1 2 3 4 5 6 7 8 9

RADICAL 184
variant of 食 *shoku* 'food'
⇨ see 食 2077 for radical description

▶EAT ▶FOOD

COMPOUNDS

❶ⓐ [original meaning] **eat**
ⓑ feed
食事 *shokuji* meal, dinner, board
食欲 *shokuyoku* appetite (for food)
食卓 *shokutaku* dining table
食堂 *shokudō* dining hall [room]; restaurant
飲食 *inshoku* eating and drinking
寝食 *shinshoku* eating and sleeping
断食 *danjiki* fasting
蚕食する *sanshoku suru* encroach on, make an inroad into
菜食主義者 *saishokushugisha* vegetarian
食客 *shokkaku* hanger-on, parasite

❷ [also prefix and suffix] **food, dish**
食糧 *shokuryō* provisions, food, foodstuffs
食中毒 *shokuchūdoku* food poisoning
主食 *shushoku* staple food
和食 *washoku* Japanese-style food
乞食 *kojiki* beggar
流動食 *ryūdōshoku* liquid food [diet]

❸ⓐ **meal**
ⓑ counter for meals
食後に *shokugo ni* after meals
朝食 *chōshoku* breakfast
給食 *kyūshoku* (provision of) meals.
三食賄い付きの *sanshoku-makanaitsuki no* with three meals served

❹ [formerly also 蝕 *shoku* 1796] [also suffix] eclipse, occultation
食連星 *shokurensei* eclipsing variable
日食 *nisshoku* solar eclipse
星食 *seishoku* occultation
皆既食 *kaikishoku* total solar [lunar] eclipse
金環食 *kinkanshoku* annular eclipse

❺ [formerly also 蝕 *shoku* 1796] erode, corrode
腐食 *fushoku* corrosion; erosion
浸食 *shinshoku* erosion, corrosion

INDEPENDENT

【shoku 食】
ⓐ eating; appetite; food
ⓑ eclipse
食を断つ *shoku o tatsu* fast
食が進む *shoku ga susumu* have a good appetite

KUN

【ku(u) 食う】
colloq
①ⓐ eat, have a meal
ⓑ live on, subsist on, feed on
食い物 *kuimono* food; victim
食い違う *kuichigau* cross; be in discord (with)
飯を食う *meshi o kuu* have a meal
食い詰める *kuitsumeru* go broke
翻訳で食って行く *hon'yaku de kutte iku* live on translation
② consume, spend
食い止める *kuitomeru* check, hold back
ガソリンを食う車 *gasorin o kuu kuruma* gas-guzzling car
③ beat, excel
横綱を食う *yokozuna o kuu* beat a grand champion
④ [formerly also 喰う] get (as a slap in the face)

【ku(rau) 食らう】
vulgar

① eat, drink
大食らい *ōgurai* glutton
② [formerly also 喰らう] get (as a slap in the face)
食らい込む *kuraikomu* be sent up, be imprisoned

【ta(beru) 食べる】 eat, have a meal; live on, subsist on, feed on
食べ過ぎ *tabesugi* overeating
食べ物 *tabemono* food
食べ頃の *tabegoro no* good for eating, ripe enough for eating

SYNONYMS

❶ⓐ ingest
飲 DRINK → 1692
喫 INGEST → 551
服 take → 878

❷ & ❸ⓐ food
飯 MEAL → 1691
糧 FOOD PROVISIONS → 1421

USAGE

❶ kuu
食う
colloq
①ⓐ eat, have a meal
ⓑ live on, subsist on, feed on
② consume, spend
③ beat, excel
④ [formerly also 喰う] get (as a slap in the face)
喰う
colloq
① eat (greedily), devour
② [now usu. 食う] get (as a slap in the face)

❷ kurau
食らう
vulgar
① eat, drink
② [formerly also 喰らう] get (as a slap in the face)
喰らう
vulgar
① eat (greedily), devour
② [now usu. 食らう] get (as a slap in the face)

HOMOPHONES

kuu ⇨ 喰 552
kurau ⇨ 喰 552

NOTE

⇨ see COMPOUND FORMATION for 蚕食 *sanshoku* ⇨ 蚕 2457

2-7

亻

2076

Radical	Strokes
食 184	9-9-0
Grade	Freq
Radical	
2-2-7	

RADICAL 184
shokuhen, variant of 食 *shoku* 'food'
⇨ see 食 2077 for radical description

2-7

亻

2077

▶EAT ▶FOOD
nonstandard for 食 2075

Radical	Strokes
食 184	9-9-0
Grade	Freq
Variant	
2-2-7	

RADICAL 184
Standard form: 食 *shoku* 'food' (饗 餐)
Left variants: 飠 亻 *shokuhen* (館 飲 饑)
Variant: 食 *shoku* (養)
Description: used in characters related to food or eating

2-7

八

盆 2078

▶TRAY ▶BON FESTIVAL
nonstandard for 盆 2079

盆 盆 盆 (calligraphic forms)

2079 BON

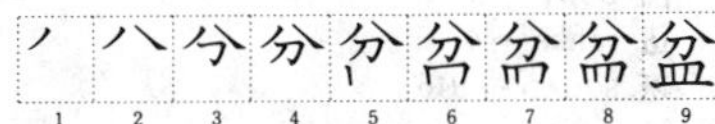

CH 盆 pén

Radical	Strokes
皿 108	9-5-4
Grade	**Freq**
Jōyō	1752
2-2-7	

2-7 八

▶TRAY ▶BON FESTIVAL

COMPOUNDS

❶ⓐ **tray, dish**

ⓑ [original meaning] basin, pot

茶盆 *chabon* tea tray

菓子盆 *kashibon* cake tray [dish]

盆景 *bonkei* tray landscape, miniature garden

盆栽 *bonsai* bonsai (potted dwarf tree)

盆地 *bonchi* basin, valley

❷ **Bon Festival, Feast of Lanterns** (Japanese festival held in July)

盆祭り *bonmatsuri* Bon Festival

盆踊り *bon'odori* Bon Festival dance

旧盆 *kyūbon* Bon Festival by the lunar calendar

INDEPENDENT

【**bon 盆**】tray; Bon Festival

お盆 *obon* Bon Festival

SYNONYMS

❶ **vessels and receptacles**

皿 PLATE → 3474

盤 dish → 2851

杯 CUP → 857

鉢 BOWL → 1708

鍋 POT → 1752

前 首 etc. incorrect classification ⇨ see 3-6

2-7 丷

軍 軍 軍 (calligraphic forms)

2080 GUN

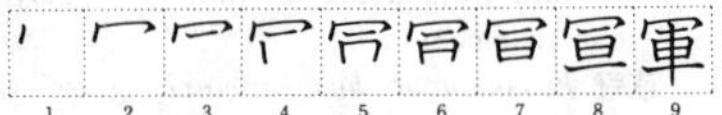

CH 军 jūn

Radical	Strokes
車 159	9-7-2
Grade	**Freq**
Jōyō-4	154
2-2-7	

2-7 冖

▶ARMY

COMPOUNDS

❶ⓐ [also prefix and suffix] **army, the military, armed forces, troops**

ⓑ suffix after names of armies

ⓒ military

ⓓ organization resembling an army

軍隊 *guntai* army, troops

軍人 *gunjin* soldier, military man

軍事力 *gunjiryoku* military force

軍縮 *gunshuku* reduction of armaments

軍部 *gunbu* military authorities, the military

軍当局 *guntōkyoku* military authorities

空軍 *kūgun* air force

敵軍 *tekigun* hostile army force, enemy troops

連合軍 *rengōgun* allied forces, the Allies

アメリカ軍 *amerikagun* U.S. Army

軍服 *gunpuku* military uniform

軍医 *gun'i* military doctor

軍政 *gunsei* military administration

救世軍 *kyūseigun* Salvation Army

❷ war, battle

軍陣 *gunjin* camp, battlefield

軍船 *gunsen* warship

軍歌 *gunka* war song

軍記 *gunki* war chronicle

❸ [also suffix] **team**

巨人軍 *kyojingun* Giants (Japanese baseball team)

一軍 *ichigun* major league team

女性軍 *joseigun* women's team

INDEPENDENT

【**gun 軍**】army, troops; war, battle

軍を駐屯させる *gun o chūton saseru* post military forces in

SYNONYMS

❶ **armed forces**

兵 the military → 2551

勢 forces → 2857

隊 PARTY → 625

❷ **warfare and rebellions**

戦 WAR → 1787

役 war → 244

陣 battle → 455
乱 rebellion → 1260
変 uprising → 2069
闘 FIGHT → 3334
❸ **groups**
群 GROUP (of any kind) → 1540
組 group (of people) → 1337
陣 lineup → 455
連 set → 3103
族 common-interest group (*slang*) → 958
党 PARTY → 2581
隊 PARTY (organized group) → 625
団 BODY → 3053
伍 ranks → 47
班 SQUAD → 946

2-7
冖

2081 KAN kanmuri

Ⓒⓗ 冠 guān guàn

Radical	Strokes
冖 14	9-2-7
Grade	**Freq**
Jōyō	1519
2-2-7	

▶CROWN

COMPOUNDS

❶ⓐ [original meaning] **crown, coronet; cap, headgear**
ⓑ wear a crown as a symbol of coming of age
王冠 *ōkan* crown, diadem, cap
戴冠式 *taikanshiki* coronation (ceremony)
冠婚葬祭 *kankonsōsai* ceremonial occasions (coming of age, marriage, funeral and ancestral worship)
冠者 *kanja* young man (come of age)
❷ⓐ something resembling a crown, top part
ⓑ (be at the highest part) crown, be on top
冠動脈 *kandōmyaku* coronary artery
極冠 *kyokkan* polar cap
金冠 *kinkan* (gold) crown (for a tooth); gold coronet
冠水 *kansui* submersion under water
冠詞 *kanshi gram* article
❸ (honorary distinction) crown, honor
冠絶する *kanzetsu suru* be unique, be unsurpassed, rank foremost
栄冠 *eikan* honor, glory; garland, laurels
三冠王 *sankan'ō* winner of a triple crown
❹ top radical of a Chinese character, crown radical
偏旁冠脚 *henbōkankyaku* the radicals

INDEPENDENT

【kan 冠】 crown, coronet, diadem; the first, the best
冠たる *kantaru* the first, the best
【kansuru 冠する】 invest (with), crown; name, designate, entitle

KUN

【kanmuri 冠】 crown, coronet, diadem; top radical (⇨ ❹); (bad) temper
冠を付ける *kanmuri o tsukeru* put on a crown
李下に冠を正さず *Rika ni kanmuri o tadasazu* Refrain from doing anything that may incur suspicion
草冠 *kusakanmuri kusakanmuri*, 'grass' radical (艹)
お冠だ *okanmuri da* be sulky
冠を曲げる *kanmuri o mageru* take offense

SPECIAL READINGS

鶏冠▲ *tosaka* cockscomb, crest

SYNONYMS

❶ⓐ **headgear**
帽 HEADGEAR → 568

NOTE

⇨ see COMPOUND FORMATION for 李下に冠を正さず *Rika ni kanmuri o tadasazu* ⇨ 李 2398

2-7
十

2082 NAN NA minami

Ⓒⓗ 南 nán

Radical	Strokes
十 24	9-2-7
Grade	**Freq**
Jōyō-2	194
2-2-7	

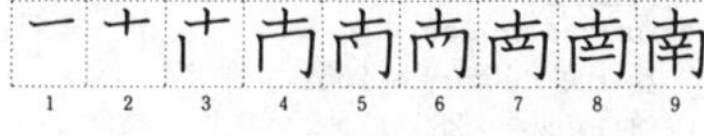

▶SOUTH

COMPOUNDS

❶ **south, southern**
南北 *nanboku* north and south
南阿 *nan'a* Republic of South Africa
南海 *nankai* southern sea; South Seas

南下する *nanka suru* go down south
南蛮人 *nanbanjin* early Europeans (in Japan); southern barbarians
東南 *tōnan* southeast
❷ used phonetically for *na*, esp. in the transliteration of Sanscrit Buddhist terms or foreign place names
南無 *namu* Amen, hail (in Buddhist prayers)
南無阿弥陀仏 *namu amidabutsu* Hail Amitabha! / I devote myself entirely to Amitabha
越南 *etsunan* Vietnam

KUN
【minami 南】[also prefix] south
南アメリカ *minamiamerika* South America
南風 *minamikaze* south wind
南口 *minamiguchi* south exit

SYNONYMS
❶ **cardinal points**
北 NORTH → 197
西 WEST → 3520
東 EAST → 3568

貞

2083 TEI

CH 贞 zhēn

Radical	Strokes
貝 154	9-7-2
Grade	**Freq**
Jōyō	1263
2-2-7	

2-7 ト

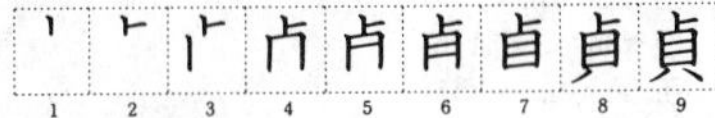

1 2 3 4 5 6 7 8 9

▶CHASTE

COMPOUNDS
❶ **chaste, faithful**
貞女 *teijo* chaste woman, faithful wife
貞操 *teisō* chastity, virginity
貞節 *teisetsu* chastity, virtue; constancy, principle
貞淑 *teishuku* chastity, female virtue
貞潔な *teiketsu na* chaste and pure
不貞な *futei na* unchaste
童貞 *dōtei* male virgin, virginity
❷ [original meaning, now archaic] divination in ancient China

SYNONYMS
❶ **chastity**
操 chastity → 769

点 點 奌°

2084 TEN tsu(keru)▲ tsu(ku)▲ ta(teru)▲ tomo(su)▲

CH 点 diǎn

Radical	Strokes
灬 86△	9-4-5
Grade	**Freq**
Jōyō-2	129
2-2-7	

2-7 ト

丨 ⺊ ⺊ 占 占 占 点 点 点

1 2 3 4 5 6 7 8 9

▶POINT

COMPOUNDS
❶ⓐ (small spot) **point, dot, spot**
ⓑ *math* **point**
ⓒ mark with a point [dot], punctuate
点在する *tenzai suru* be dotted [studded] with
点線 *tensen* dotted [perforated] line
交点 *kōten* intersecting point
画竜点睛 *garyō-tensei* "completing the eyes of a painted dragon," giving a finishing touch
❷ⓐ (any dotlike mark or symbol) **point, decimal point, dot, period**
ⓑ dot (as opposed to a stroke) of Chinese characters
点字 *tenji* Braille
小数点 *shōsūten* decimal point
句読点 *kutōten* punctuation marks
点画 *tenkaku* dots and strokes of Chinese characters
❸ [also suffix]
ⓐ (definite place) **point**
ⓑ (definite position) **point**
地点 *chiten* spot, point, point
焦点 *shōten* focus, focal point; (photographic) focus
拠点 *kyoten* strongpoint, base
終点 *shūten* last stop, terminus
出発点 *shuppatsuten* starting point
沸点 *futten* boiling point
死点 *shiten* dead point
凝固点 *gyōkoten* freezing point
❹ [also suffix] (unit of scoring) **point, mark**
点数 *tensū* points, score
得点 *tokuten* the marks obtained, the points made, score
同点 *dōten* tie, draw

採点 *saiten* marking, grading, rating
❺ⓐ [also suffix] (specific matter) **point, detail, particular**
ⓑ point of view
重点 *jūten* important point; importance, emphasis, stress; priority
欠点 *ketten* weak point, defect
争点 *sōten* point of contention, issue
問題点 *mondaiten* controversial point
観点 *kanten* point of view
❻ **counter for various articles**
三点セット *santen setto* set of three pieces (of furniture)
❼ kindle, light, ignite
点滅する *tenmetsu suru* (of light) go [come] on and off; turn [switch] on and off
❽ⓐ drop (of liquid)
ⓑ drip, pour (tea)
点点と *tenten to* in drops; here and there
点滴 *tenteki* falling drops of water; intravenous infusion
点眼器 *tenganki* eye dropper
点茶 *tencha* making tea (in a tea ceremony)

INDEPENDENT

【ten 点】
①ⓐ (small spot) point, dot, spot
ⓑ *math* point
点と線 *ten to sen* points and lines
②ⓐ (any dotlike mark or symbol) point, decimal point, dot, period
ⓑ dot (as opposed to a stroke) of Chinese characters
点を打つ *ten o utsu* mark with a dot [point]
③ (definite place) point
どの点迄 *dono ten made* to what extent
④ (unit of scoring) point, mark
点が良い *ten ga yoi* have good marks
⑤ (specific matter) point, detail, particular
問題の点 *mondai no ten* point in dispute
その点に於て *sono ten ni oite* on that point, in that respect
⑥ fault, defect
点の打ち所が無い *ten no uchidokoro ga nai* be above reproach
【tenjiru (=tenzuru) 点じる(=点ずる)】
drop, drip; kindle, light; make tea

KUN

【tsu(keru) 点ける】 light, turn [switch] on
電灯を点ける *dentō o tsukeru* turn [switch] on an electric lamp
【tsu(ku) 点く】 be lighted, be switched on, go on
ガスが点いている *Gasu ga tsuite iru* The gas is on
【ta(teru) 点てる】 [now usu. 立てる] make tea
野点て *nodate* open-air tea ceremony
【tomo(su) 点す】 [sometimes also 灯す] light (a lamp), set alight, turn on (a light)
松明を点す *taimatsu o tomosu* kindle a torch

SYNONYMS

❸ **places and positions**
位 POSITION → 61
座 place → 3116
所 PLACE → 851
処 place → 3031
場 PLACE (for specific activity) → 558
地 PLACE (particular location) → 204
席 meeting place → 3113
❻ **general counters**
個 GENERAL COUNTER → 117
箇 COUNTER FOR ITEMS → 2700
件 counter for cases → 51
丁 MISCELLANEOUS COUNTER → 3348

USAGE

tomosu
点す
[sometimes also 灯す] light (a lamp), set alight, turn on (a light)
灯す
[usu. 点す] same as 点す

HOMOPHONES

tsukeru ⇨ 付 31 附 347 着 3316 就 1694 即 1120 漬 702
tsuku ⇨ 付 31 附 347 着 3316 就 1694 即 1120
tateru ⇨ 立 1992 建 3090 閉 3319
tomosu ⇨ 灯 825

NOTE

⇨ see also USAGE notes at 付 31 and 立 1992
⇨ see COMPOUND FORMATION for 焦点 *shōten* ⇨ 焦 2770

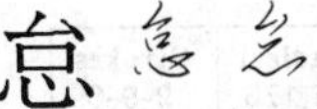

2085 TAI okota(ru) nama(keru)

Ⓒⓗ 怠 dài

Radical	Strokes
心 61	9-4-5
Grade	Freq
Jōyō	1577
2-2-7	

2-7
ム

1 2 3 4 5 6 7 8 9

▶**REMISS**

COMPOUNDS

ⓐ [original meaning] (inclined to idleness) **remiss, idle, lazy, sluggish**

ⓑ (neglectful) **remiss, negligent, careless**

怠惰な *taida na* lazy, idle
倦怠 *kentai* fatigue, languor, weariness
怠慢な *taiman na* negligent, inattentive, remiss
怠業 *taigyō* slowdown strike, deliberate idleness

KUN

【okota(ru) 怠る】 be remiss, neglect; be off one's guard; get better

怠り *okotari* negligence, carelessness
注意を怠る *chūi o okotaru* be off one's guard
病が怠る *Yamai ga okotaru* The patient has gotten better

【nama(keru) 怠ける】 be lazy, be idle; neglect

怠け者 *namakemono* idle [lazy] fellow
勉強を怠ける *benkyō o namakeru* neglect one's studies

SYNONYMS

● **lazy**

惰 LAZY → 579
慢 SLUGGISH → 686

頁 頁 頁

2086 KETSU pēji

Ⓒⓗ 页 yè

Radical	Strokes
頁 181	9-9-0
Grade	Freq
Non-Jōyō	1965
2-2-7	

2-7
一

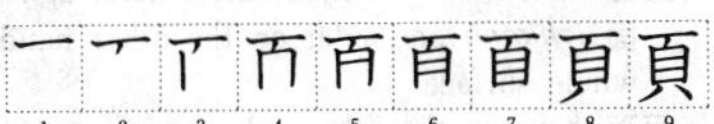

1 2 3 4 5 6 7 8 9

RADICAL 181

Standard form: 頁 *ōgai* 'head' (題 領 順)
Description: used in characters related to the head

▶**PAGE**

COMPOUNDS

❶ **page**

頁岩 *ketsugan* shale

❷ [original meaning, now obsolete] head

KUN

【pēji 頁】

ⓐ [also suffix] page, leaf
ⓑ counter for pages; page No.

頁数 *pējisū* number of pages
頁付け *pējizuke* pagination
余白頁 *yohakupēji* blank page
九十頁 *kyūjuppēji* page 90
五百頁の本 *gohyakupēji no hon* book of 500 pages

SYNONYMS

【pēji】

ⓐ **paper**

丁 sheet → 3348
面 page (of a newspaper) → 2087
紙 PAPER → 1302
葉 LEAF → 2321

ⓑ **counters for flat things**

丁 counter for sheets → 3348
葉 counter for leaves → 2321
通 counter for letters → 3109
枚 COUNTER FOR FLAT THINGS → 859

2-7 一

面 面 面

2087 MEN omo omote tsura

Ⓒ 面 miàn

Radical	Strokes
面 176	9-9-0
Grade	Freq
Jōyō-3	155
2-2-7	

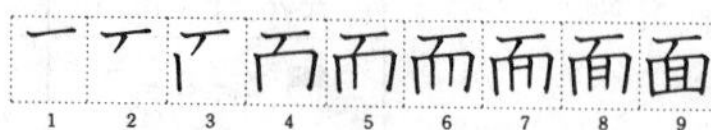

RADICAL 176

Standard form: 面 *men* 'face' (靨 靤 靦)

Description: used in characters related to the face or its qualities

▶**FACE**

COMPOUNDS

❶ⓐ [original meaning] (front of head) **face, countenance**

ⓑ (value in the eyes of others) face, dignity, honor

面相 *mensō* countenance, features, looks

面通し *mentōshi* identification parade

面食い *menkui* person who puts much store by good looks (in choosing his [her] lover)

面面 *menmen* everyone, all

顔面 *ganmen* face

洗面 *senmen* washing one's face

七面鳥 *shichimenchō* turkey

面目 *menboku* (=*menmoku*) face, honor, prestige

面子 *mentsu* face, honor

体面 *taimen* honor, dignity, reputation

❷ⓐ (front or significant surface) **face, front**

ⓑ (outer surface) **face, surface, side**

ⓒ counter for flat surfaces such as tennis courts, mirrors or go boards

表面 *hyōmen* surface, face, outside; appearance

全面 *zenmen* front, facade

正面衝突 *shōmen shōtotsu* head-on collision, front crash

画面 *gamen* picture; television field; screen

印面 *inmen* face of a seal

額面 *gakumen* face value; denomination

書面 *shomen* letter, document

図面 *zumen* drawing, plan, map, sketch

地面 *jimen* surface, ground, land

月面 *getsumen* lunar surface

斜面 *shamen* slope, slanting surface

テニスコート三面 *tenisu kōto sanmen* three tennis courts

❸ [also suffix] *math* face, surface, plane

面積 *menseki* area, square measure

曲面 *kyokumen* curved surface

七面体 *shichimentai* heptahedron

線織面 *senshikimen* ruled surface

❹ⓐ (have the front toward) **face, front on, look toward**

ⓑ **meet face to face, confront in person**

面壁 *menpeki* meditation facing the wall

直面する *chokumen suru* face, confront

当面の *tōmen no* present, immediate; urgent, pressing

面会する *menkai suru* see, have an interview

面接 *mensetsu* interview

面罵 *menba* abusing someone to his [her] face

面識 *menshiki* acquaintance

❺ⓐ **side, quarter, direction**

ⓑ [also suffix] (distinct aspect) **side, aspect, phase, plane**

側面 *sokumen* side, flank

両面 *ryōmen* both sides

方面 *hōmen* direction, district; field, sphere

一面 *ichimen* one side; on the other hand; whole surface

反面 *hanmen* the other side

全面的 *zenmenteki* all-out, overall, general

局面 *kyokumen* situation, aspect of an affair; position (in a chess game)

場面 *bamen* scene; situation

技術面 *gijutsumen* technical side

軍事面 *gunjimen* military plane

❻ⓐ [also suffix] **mask**

ⓑ (protective covering for the face) mask, face guard, protector, headgear

仮面 *kamen* mask, disguise

舞楽面 *bugakumen* mask worn by a *bugaku* dancer

面頬 *menpō* (=*menbō*) visor, face guard

防毒面 *bōdokumen* gas mask

❼ [also suffix] page (of a newspaper)

紙面 *shimen* space (on a printed page)

社会面 *shakaimen* local news page, city news page

二面 *nimen* second page (of a newspaper)

❽ counter for kotos (Japanese harps)

琴二面 *koto nimen* two kotos

❾ corner

面取り *mentori* chamfering, beveling

❿ unclassified compounds

面倒な *mendō na* troublesome, worrisome; difficult

面妖な *men'yō na* strange, mysterious, weird
面食らう *menkurau* be confused, be bewildered
工面する *kumen suru* contrive, manage, make shift; raise (money)

INDEPENDENT

【men 面】
① face
面と向かって *men to mukatte* face to face
②ⓐ mask
ⓑ face guard, headgear
狐の面 *kitsune no men* mask of the fox
③ⓐ surface, face, side
ⓑ *math* face
滑らかな面 *nameraka na men* smooth surface
立方体は六つの面を持つ *Rippōtai wa muttsu no men o motsu* A cube has six faces
④ (distinct aspect) side, aspect, phase
財政の面 *zaisei no men* the financial aspect
⑤ corner
面を取る *men o toru* plane off the corners
【mensuru 面する】 face, front on

KUN

【omo 面】
①ⓐ [in compounds] (front of head) face
ⓑ *elegant* surface of the water
面影 *omokage* face; traces
面持ち *omomochi* look, countenance, face
面白い *omoshiroi* interesting, amusing, pleasant
水の面 *mizu no omo* surface of the water
② unclassified compounds
面舵 *omokaji* starboarding the helm
【omote 面】
①ⓐ (front of head) face
ⓑ (outer surface) face, surface (as of water)
細面 *hosoomote* slender face
水の面 *mizu no omote* face of the water
② mask
【tsura 面】 *colloq* (front of head) face, surface; [suffix] (facial expression) face, look
痘痕面 *abatazura* pockmarked face
仏頂面 *butchōzura* sulky look, sour face
横っ面 *yokottsura* side face

字面 *jizura* appearance of written words, face
川面 *kawazura* (=*kawamo*) surface of a river

SPECIAL READINGS

真面目な▲ *majime na* serious, sober, earnest, steady
面皰▲ *nikibi* pimple, acne

SYNONYMS

❶ⓐ front parts of head
顔 FACE → 1808
額 forehead → 1805
❷ⓐ front
前 front → 2266
首 HEAD → 2265
ⓑ outside
表 SURFACE → 2429
外 OUTSIDE → 186
❹ face
向 TURN TOWARD → 3052
対 face (each other) → 831
❺ⓐ side
側 SIDE → 137
方 side → 1963
辺 -side → 3029
傍 BESIDE → 147
横 SIDEWAYS → 1066
ⓑ aspect
上 from the viewpoint of → 3404
柄 considering the character of → 897
❻ⓑ protective coverings
盾 SHIELD → 3006
甲 armor → 3481
❼ parts of periodicals
欄 COLUMN → 1103
❼ paper
頁 PAGE → 2086
丁 sheet → 3348
葉 LEAF → 2321
紙 PAPER → 1302

HOMOPHONES

omote ⇨ 表 2429

NOTE

⇨ see USAGE note at 表 2429
⇨ see COMPOUND FORMATION for 面白い *omoshiroi* ⇨ 白 3493

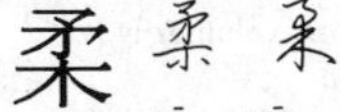

2-7

Radical	Strokes
木 75	9-4-5
Grade	**Freq**
Jōyō	1250
2-2-7	

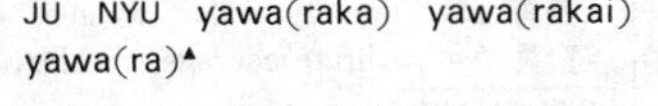

2088 JŪ NYŪ yawa(raka) yawa(rakai) yawa▲ yawa(ra)▲

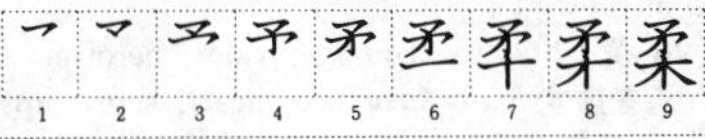

▶**SOFT**

COMPOUNDS

❶ⓐ [original meaning] (supple and yielding) **soft, tender, pliant**
ⓑ soften, appease, conciliate
柔毛 *jūmō* soft hair

柔軟な *jūnan na* soft, pliable, flexible
懐柔する *kaijū suru* appease, win over
❷ⓐ (of gentle disposition) **soft, softhearted, gentle, mild**
ⓑ (weakly) soft, weak-looking, frail
柔順な *jūjun na* obedient, gentle
柔和 *nyūwa* gentleness, mildness, tenderness, meekness
柔弱な *nyūjaku na* weak, effeminate
優柔不断の *yūjūfudan no* indecisive, vacillating
❸ **judo**
柔道 *jūdō* judo
柔術 *jūjutsu* jujitsu, jujutsu

INDEPENDENT

【jū 柔】 softness, gentleness
柔能く剛を制す *Jū yoku gō o seisu* Softness overcomes hardness / Soft words win hard hearts
剛と柔 *gō to jū* hardness and softness

KUN

【yawa(raka) 柔らか】
yawaraka na 柔らかな [also 軟らかな]
① soft, tender
柔らかみ *yawarakami* (touch of) softness
② soft, subdued (color or light)
柔らかな光 *yawaraka na hikari* soft light
③ gentle, meek, mild
柔らかな風 *yawaraka na kaze* gentle breeze
お手柔らかに *oteyawaraka ni* gently, mildly; Don't be hard on me!

【yawa(rakai) 柔らかい】
[also 軟らかい]
① soft, tender
柔らかい毛布 *yawarakai mōfu* soft blanket
② gentle, meek
物腰の柔らかい *monogoshi no yawarakai* gentle-mannered
③ informal
柔らかい文章 *yawarakai bunshō* informal style

【yawa 柔】
yawa na 柔な frail, fragile
柔肌 *yawahada* soft fair skin

【yawa(ra) 柔ら】 old term for judo or jujutsu

SYNONYMS

❶ⓐ **soft**
軟 SOFT (not hard) → 1479
塑 plastic → 2843
❷ⓐ **gentle**
穏 MILD → 1235
優しい gentle → 177
ⓑ **weak**
弱 WEAK → 1167

USAGE

❶ **yawaraka na**
柔らかな
[also 軟らかな]
① soft, tender
② soft, subdued (color or light)
③ gentle, meek, mild
軟らかな
[also 柔らかな] same as 柔らかな
❷ **yawarakai**
柔らかい
[also 軟らかい]
① soft, tender
② gentle, meek
③ informal
軟らかい
[also 柔らかい] same as 柔らかい

HOMOPHONES

yawaraka ⇨ 軟 1479
yawarakai ⇨ 軟 1479

2-7

勇 勇 勇 勇

2089 YŪ isa(mu)

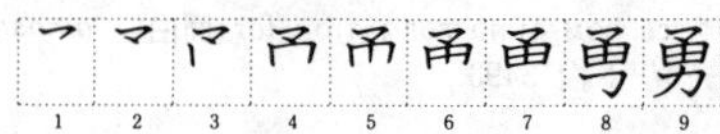

CH 勇 yǒng

Radical	Strokes
力 19	9-2-7
Grade	**Freq**
Jōyō-4	1126
2-2-7	

▶BRAVE

COMPOUNDS

ⓐ [original meaning] **brave, courageous, bold, valiant**
ⓑ **bravery, courage, valor, heroism**
勇敢な *yūkan na* brave, courageous, daring, heroic
勇気 *yūki* courage, valor, bravery, nerve
勇将 *yūshō* brave general
勇猛 *yūmō* daring, bravery, valor
勇士 *yūshi* brave warrior
勇退する *yūtai suru* retire voluntarily
武勇 *buyū* bravery, valor
豪勇 *gōyū* bravery, valor, daring
蛮勇 *ban'yū* brute courage, reckless valor

INDEPENDENT

【yū 勇】 bravery, courage, valor, heroism
勇を鼓す *yū o kosu* take heart, screw up one's courage

KUN

【isa(mu) 勇む】 be encouraged, be in high spirits; prance

勇ましい *isamashii* brave, courageous, bold, valiant

SYNONYMS

ⓐ **brave**

敢 bold → 1706

赳 VALIANT → 3308

豪 bold and unrestrained → 2140

雄 HEROIC → 1008

壮 heroic → 224

義 chivalrous → 2338

ⓑ **courage**

胆 pluck → 919

勇 ▶**BRAVE**

2090 nonstandard for 勇 2089

負 負 負 負

2091 FU ma(keru) ma(kasu) o(u)

CH 负 fù

Radical	Strokes
貝 154	9-7-2
Grade	**Freq**
Jōyō-3	412
2-2-7	

Stroke order: ノ ⺈ 𠂊 ⺈ 𠂊 各 各 負 負 (1–9)

▶**BEAR** ▶**LOSE**

COMPOUNDS

❶ [original meaning] **bear [carry] on the back**

負荷 *fuka* load, burden

❷ⓐ **bear (responsibility), take upon oneself, sustain**

ⓑ bear a debt, owe

負担 *futan* burden, charge, responsibility

負託する *futaku suru* charge (someone) with responsibility

負傷する *fushō suru* be injured [wounded], get hurt

負債 *fusai* debt, liabilities

❸ be proud

抱負 *hōfu* aspiration, ambition

自負する *jifu suru* be conceited, be self-confident

❹ **lose, be defeated**

勝負 *shōbu* victory or defeat; match, game

❺ⓐ *math* negative

ⓑ *elec* negative

負数 *fusū* negative number

正負 *seifu* positive and negative, plus and minus

負極 *fukyoku* cathode, negative pole; south magnetic pole

INDEPENDENT

【fu 負】*math*, *elec* negativeness

負の *fu no* negative

負の電荷 *fu no denka* negative charge

KUN

【ma(keru) 負ける】lose (a game), be defeated [beaten]; yield to, be overcome; reduce (the price); be poisoned (with lacquer)

負け *make* defeat, loss, losing (a game)

負け惜しみ *makeoshimi* unwillingness to admit oneself beaten

誘惑に負ける *yūwaku ni makeru* yield [succumb] to temptation

百円負ける *hyakuen makeru* take off 100 yen

漆に負ける *urushi ni makeru* be poisoned with lacquer

【ma(kasu) 負かす】defeat, beat, vanquish, outdo, outplay

相手を負かす *aite o makasu* defeat the opponent

言い負かす *iimakasu* talk (a person) down, confute

【o(u) 負う】bear [carry] on the back; bear (responsibility), take upon oneself; sustain; be proud; bear a debt, owe

背負う *seou* carry on one's back, shoulder, bear

請け負い *ukeoi* contract (for work), contracted work

傷を負う *kizu o ou* sustain a wound, be injured

気負う *kiou* be eager [enthusiastic]

負い目 *oime* debt, unfulfilled promise

SYNONYMS

❶ **bear**

荷 carry on shoulder → 2282

担 BEAR ON SHOULDER → 318

支 SUPPORT → 1979

❷ **undertake**

担 UNDERTAKE → 318

❹ **lose**

敗 BE DEFEATED → 1476

❺ **negative**

陰 negative → 541

2-7 ㇰ

急 急 急 㤂

2092 KYŪ iso(gu) iso(gi)

CH 急 jí

Radical	Strokes
心 61	9-4-5
Grade	Freq
Jōyō-3	263
2-2-7	

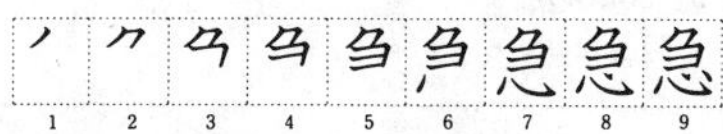

1 2 3 4 5 6 7 8 9

▶URGENT ▶HURRY ▶SUDDEN

COMPOUNDS

❶ⓐ **urgent, imminent, pressing**
ⓑ emergency, exigency, crisis
急務 *kyūmu* urgent business, pressing need
急迫 *kyūhaku* urgency, imminence
急用 *kyūyō* urgent business
緊急な *kinkyū na* urgent, pressing, emergent
早急な *sakkyū* (=*sōkyū*) *na* urgent, pressing
至急に *shikyū ni* urgently, with all haste, at once
急場 *kyūba* emergency, exigency, crisis
救急 *kyūkyū* first aid
応急 *ōkyū* emergency, makeshift

❷ⓐ **hurry, hasten**
ⓑ **rapid, fast, swift, speedy, express**
急造 *kyūzō* hurried construction
急派する *kyūha suru* dispatch, expedite, rush
急行 *kyūkō* express train [bus]; going in a hurry
急速な *kyūsoku na* rapid, swift, prompt
急ピッチ *kyūpitchi* quick [fast] pace
急性の *kyūsei no* acute
急進する *kyūshin suru* advance rapidly, make rapid progress
急流 *kyūryū* rapid stream, swift current; swift-running river; rapids
緩急 *kankyū* fast and slow motion, high and low speed; emergency

❸ abbrev. of 急行 *kyūkō*: express train [bus]
特急 *tokkyū* super-express
準急 *junkyū* local express, semi-express (train)
東急 *tōkyū* Tokyu Corporation

❹ [also prefix] **sudden, unexpected**
急激な *kyūgeki na* sudden, abrupt
急増 *kyūzō* sudden [rapid] increase
急落 *kyūraku* sudden drop [fall], steep decline
急変 *kyūhen* sudden change [turn]; accident
急死 *kyūshi* sudden death
急カーブ *kyūkābu* sharp curve [turn]
急停車 *kyūteisha* sudden stop

❺ [also prefix] (sharply inclined) **steep**
急坂 *kyūhan* steep hill [slope]
急傾斜 *kyūkeisha* steep slope [incline]

❻ vital
急所 *kyūsho* vital part; vital point, tender spot

❼ climax in a traditional Japanese performance (as court music)
序破急 *johakyū* artistic modulations in traditional Japanese performances; opening, middle and climax [end]

INDEPENDENT

【kyū 急】
① urgency
焦眉の急 *shōbi no kyū* urgent need
② emergency, crisis
急を救う *kyū o sukuu* help (a person) out of danger
急な *kyū na* urgent; hasty; rapid, sudden; steep, sharp
③ rapidity, swiftness
④ suddenness
⑤ steepness, sharpness
⑥ climax

KUN

【iso(gu) 急ぐ】 *vi* [also verbal suffix] hurry (up), hasten
道を急ぐ *michi o isogu* hurry on one's way
売り急ぐ *uriisogu* sell in haste, be eager to sell

【iso(gi) 急ぎ】 hurry, haste
急ぎの *isogi no* hurried, hasty; pressing, urgent
急ぎ足 *isogiashi* quick pace
大急ぎで *ōisogi de* in a great [urgent] hurry, against time

SYNONYMS

❶ⓐ **urgent**
緊 EXIGENT → 2838
迫 pressing → 3074

❷ⓐ **hurry**
促 HASTEN → 103
ⓑ **fast**
迅 SWIFT → 3046
快 fast → 245
疾 fast → 3279
速 QUICK → 3105
早 QUICK → 2390
敏 NIMBLE → 1322
即 IMMEDIATE → 1120

❹ **sudden**
激 sudden → 776
暴 sudden → 2515
突 abruptly → 2230

❺ **steep**
険 STEEP → 542

峻 high and steep → 412

急 2093 ▶**URGENT** ▶**HURRY** ▶**SUDDEN** 2-7

nonstandard for 急 2092

負 2094 ▶**BEAR** ▶**LOSE** 2-7

nonstandard for 負 2091

旁 2095 BŌ tsukuri katagata 2-8

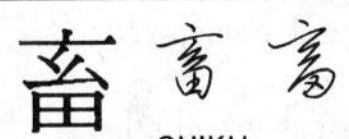

CH 旁 páng

Radical	Strokes
方 70	10-4-6
Grade	**Freq**
Reference	
2-2-8	

COMPOUNDS

❶ right side of Chinese characters, right radical
偏旁 *henbō* left and right radicals
筆旁 *fudezukuri fudezukuri*, 'brush' radical

(聿)

❷ [now usu. 傍 *bō* 147] beside, side
旁註(=傍注) *bōchū* side notes, gloss

❸ by way of, at the same time
散歩旁 *sanpo katagata* while taking a walk

畜 2096 CHIKU 2-8

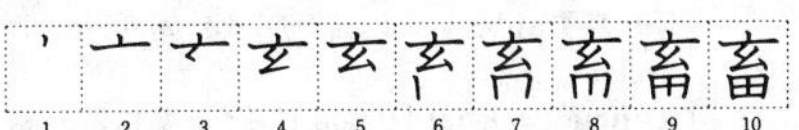

CH 畜 chù xù

Radical	Strokes
田 102	10-5-5
Grade	**Freq**
Jōyō	1627
2-2-8	

▶**LIVESTOCK**

COMPOUNDS

❶ⓐ **livestock, domestic animals or fowls**
ⓑ beast, animal
畜類 *chikurui* livestock, domestic animals
畜産業 *chikusangyō* stockraising
畜舎 *chikusha* barns and poultry sheds
家畜 *kachiku* domestic animal, livestock
有畜農業 *yūchiku-nōgyō* agriculture with livestock raising as a major side line
畜力 *chikuryoku* animal power
畜生 *chikushō* beast; Damn it!
人畜無害な *jinchiku mugai na* harmless to man and beast

❷ raise livestock, rear, domesticate
畜犬税 *chikukenzei* dog tax
牧畜 *bokuchiku* livestock farming, cattle breeding

SYNONYMS

❶ **animal**
獣 BEAST → 1892
生 LIFE → 3497
物 living thing → 874

NOTE

★do not confuse with 蓄 2333

2-8 ⼇

高 髙° 髙 㐬

2097 KŌ taka(i) taka -daka taka(maru) taka(meru)

Ⓒⓗ 高 gāo

Radical	Strokes
高 189	10-10-0
Grade	**Freq**
Jōyō-2	55
2-2-8	

RADICAL 189
Standard form: 高 *takai* 'high'
Description: used for character classification

▶HIGH

COMPOUNDS

❶ⓐ (extending upward) **high, tall, lofty**
ⓑ height; high place
高度 *kōdo* altitude, height; high degree
高山 *kōzan* high mountain, lofty peak
高地 *kōchi* high ground, plateau, heights
高原 *kōgen* plateau, tableland, heights
高架線 *kōkasen* elevated railway; overhead wires
最高峰 *saikōhō* highest peak; highest authority
標高 *hyōkō* elevation, (height) above the sea
座高 *zakō* one's sitting height
登高 *tōkō* climbing a height
❷ⓐ [also prefix] (of great degree or quantity) **high**
ⓑ high-priced, expensive
高速 *kōsoku* high speed, high gear
高熱 *kōnetsu* intense heat; high fever
高級 *kōkyū* high rank, high class [grade]
高等な *kōtō na* higher, high-grade, advanced
高校 *kōkō* senior high school
高裁 *kōsai* high court
高齢 *kōrei* advanced age
高給 *kōkyū* high salary
高血圧 *kōketsuatsu* high blood pressure
高炭素鋼 *kōtansokō* high-carbon steel
最高の *saikō no* maximum, supreme, highest
高価な *kōka na* expensive, high-priced
高騰(=昂騰) *kōtō* steep rise (in prices), jump
❸ (elevated in rank or character) **high, noble, eminent, lofty**
高位 *kōi* high rank, honors
高官 *kōkan* high office, high official, dignitary
高貴な *kōki na* high and noble
高名 *kōmei* fame, high reputation; your name
高尚な *kōshō na* high, noble, elegant
高潔な *kōketsu na* noble, high-minded, upright
❹ⓐ [formerly also 昂 2412] (showing pride or arrogance) high, high-hatted, proud, haughty
ⓑ [formerly also 昂 2412 or 亢 1964] high-spirited, excited, elated
高慢な *kōman na* haughty, arrogant, proud
高揚(=昂揚)する *kōyō suru* exalt, enhance, uplift; surge up
意気軒高(=意気軒昂)として *ikikenkō to shite* in high spirits
❺ⓐ abbrev. of 高等学校 *kōtōgakkō*: high school
ⓑ suffix after names of high schools
高卒 *kōsotsu* high school graduate
城北高 *jōhokukō* Johoku High School
❻ [honorific] your, your honorable
高評 *kōhyō* your esteemed opinion
高堂 *kōdō* your beautiful home; you
❼ great, great-grand
高祖父 *kōsofu* great-great-grandfather

INDEPENDENT

【kō 高】 abbrev. of 高気圧 *kōkiatsu*: anticyclone
【kōjiru (=kōzuru) 高じる(=昂じる, 高ずる, 昂ずる)】 grow worse, grow in intensity

KUN

【taka(i) 高い】
① (extending upward) high, tall, lofty
高さ *takasa* height, altitude; pitch
高み *takami* height, elevated place
高跳び *takatobi* high jump
高台 *takadai* high ground, hill, height
高波 *takanami* high waves
小高い *kodakai* slightly elevated
②ⓐ (of great degree) high, elevated, superior
ⓑ high-priced, expensive
ⓒ loud (voice)
高高 *takadaka* at most, at the highest
高い濃度 *takai nōdo* high concentration
甲高い *kandakai* high-pitched, shrill
名高い *nadakai* famous, well-known
高値 *takane* high price
高らかな *takaraka na* loud, sonorous, ringing
高笑い *takawarai* loud laughter
③ (elevated in rank or character) high, lofty, noble
気高い *kedakai* noble, lofty, high-minded
身分の高い人 *mibun no takai hito* man of

high position
④ high, proud, haughty
高ぶる *takaburu* be highly strung, get excited; be proud, be haughty
お高く留まる *otakaku tomaru* assume an air of importance, put on airs
【taka 高】 quantity, amount, sum
高が *taka ga* at most, at best, only
高を括る *taka o kukuru* make light of, underrate
高が知れている *taka ga shirete iru* not amount to much
【-daka -高】
[suffix]
①ⓐ amount of money, total (proceeds)
ⓑ amount, quantity, yield
売上高 *uriagedaka* sales, proceeds
生産高 *seisandaka* output, yield
② indicates a rise in prices
物価高 *bukkadaka* high prices of commodities
五円高 *goendaka* (be quoted) 5 yen higher
【taka(maru) 高まる】 rise (in degree or rank), be raised; increase; build
高まり *takamari* rise, swell, elevation
関心が高まる *kanshin ga takamaru* take a growing interest in
【taka(meru) 高める】 raise, elevate, enhance, improve
婦人の地位を高める *fujin no chii o takameru* raise the position of women

SYNONYMS
❶ⓐ high
喬 TALL → 2488
峻 high and steep → 412
ⓐ high
上 upper → 3404
ⓑ height
丈 STATURE → 3419
背 stature → 2573
❷ⓐ extreme in degree
重 HEAVY → 3573
深 DEEP → 524
大 BIG → 3416
強 STRONG → 475
超 super- → 3313
甚 EXTREMELY → 2643
切 keen → 27
痛 bitter(ly) → 3285
極 EXTREME → 1017
激 intense → 776
厳 SEVERE → 3289
酷 SEVERE → 1562
ⓑ expensive
貴 precious → 2606
❸ high-ranking
貴 NOBLE → 2606
上 upper → 3404
総 GENERAL → 1379
太 of highest rank → 2152
❹ⓑ elated
昂 high-spirited → 2412
揚 exalted → 593
奮 roused up → 2367
❺ schools
校 SCHOOL → 929
学 EDUCATIONAL INSTITUTION → 2555
塾 PRIVATE SCHOOL → 2860
院 INSTITUTION → 454
大 UNIVERSITY → 3416
中 junior high school → 3451
小 elementary school → 7
園 kindergarten → 3156
【takai】
②ⓒ loud
朗 CLEAR (voice) → 1325
騒 clamorous → 1835

恋 戀 恋 恋

Ⓒⓗ 恋 liàn

2098 REN ko(u) koi koi(shii)

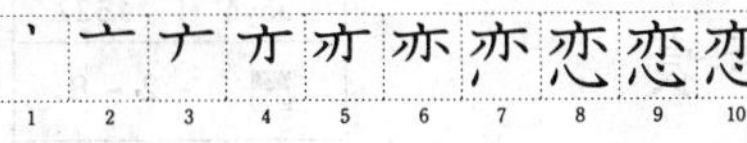

Radical	Strokes
心 61	10-4-6
Grade	**Freq**
Jōyō	1247
2-2-8	

2-8

▶LOVE

COMPOUNDS
❶ⓐ [original meaning] **love (the opposite sex)**
ⓑ love (for the opposite sex)
恋愛 *ren'ai* love (for the opposite sex)
恋情 *renjō* love, attachment
恋慕する *renbo suru* love, fall in love with
失恋 *shitsuren* unrequited love
悲恋 *hiren* blighted love
❷ beloved, dearest
恋恋とする *renren to suru* be ardently attached to (a girl)

KUN
【ko(u) 恋う】 love
恋い慕う *koishitau* miss, yearn for
【koi 恋】 love (for the opposite sex), tender passion
恋する *koisuru* love, fall in love with
恋人 *koibito* lover, sweetheart

恋文 *koibumi* love letter
初恋 *hatsukoi* first love
【**koi(shii) 恋しい**】beloved, dear, darling

SYNONYMS

❶ⓐ **love and like**
愛 LOVE → 2492
好 LIKE → 208

ⓑ **love**
艶 ROMANCE → 1908
愛 LOVE → 2492
情 love → 482

NOTE

⇨ see USAGE note at 愛 2492

2-8 亠

竜 龍 龍◇ 竜 龍

2099 RYŪ RYŌ▲ tatsu

CH 龙 lóng

Radical	Strokes
龍 212	10-10-0
Grade	**Freq**
Jōyō	1087
2 - 2 - 8	

RADICAL 212
simplified form not used as radical
⇨ see 龍 1801 for radical description

▶DRAGON

COMPOUNDS

❶ⓐ **dragon**
ⓑ suffix for forming names of extinct animals
竜神 *ryūjin* dragon god, dragon king
竜宮 *ryūgū* Palace of the Dragon King
竜虎 *ryūko* (=*ryōko*) dragon and tiger; hero
恐竜 *kyōryū* dinosaur, titanosaur
魚竜 *gyoryū* ichthyosaur
❷ imperial
竜顔 *ryūgan* (=*ryōgan*) emperor's face
❸ name of chess piece in shogi (Japanese chess): *naribisha*, promoted rook
竜王 *ryūō naribisha*; dragon king [god]

INDEPENDENT

【**ryū 竜**】dragon; fossil reptile; *naribisha* (⇨ ❸)

KUN

【**tatsu 竜**】dragon

SYNONYMS

❶ⓐ **dragon**
辰 THE DRAGON → 2992
ⓐ **reptiles**
蛇 SNAKE → 1343
亀 TURTLE → 2128

USAGE

tatsu
竜
dragon
辰
fifth sign of the Oriental zodiac: the Dragon

HOMOPHONES

tatsu ⇨ 辰 2992

2-8 亠

衰 衰 衰 衰

2100 SUI otoro(eru)

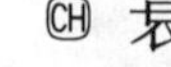
shuāi cuī

Radical	Strokes
衣 145	10-6-4
Grade	**Freq**
Jōyō	1527
2 - 2 - 8	

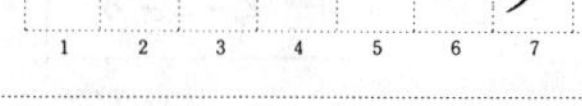

▶DECLINE

COMPOUNDS

ⓐ **decline, fall into decay, degenerate, weaken, emaciate**
ⓑ decline, downfall
衰退 *suitai* decline, decay, degeneration
衰弱する *suijaku suru* weaken, lose vigor
減衰する *gensui suru* damp, be attenuated
老衰 *rōsui* senility
盛衰 *seisui* ups and downs, rise and fall, prosperity and decline
衰運 *suiun* declining fortune
衰亡 *suibō* ruin, fall, collapse

KUN

【**otoro(eru) 衰える**】weaken, lose vigor, become emaciated; wither, fade; decline, decay, go downhill
衰え *otoroe* weakening, emaciation, decline
痩せ衰える *yaseotoroeru* become emaciated, grow thin and worn out

SYNONYMS

ⓐ weaken

弱 weaken → 1167

ⓐ degenerate

落 FALL → 2318

堕 DEGENERATE → 2822

破 break down → 1150

竞 2101 **▶COMPETE** 2-8 亠

handwritten abbreviation for 競 1847

离 2102 **▶SEPARATE** 2-8 亠

handwritten abbreviation for 離 1836

衰 2103 **▶DECLINE** 2-8 亠

nonstandard for 衰 2100

衷 2-8 亠

incorrect classification／stroke count ⇨ see 2575

倉 2104 2-8 人

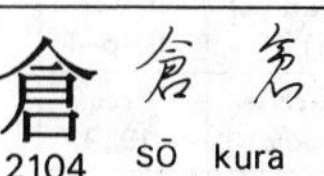

sō kura

Ⓒⓗ 仓 cāng

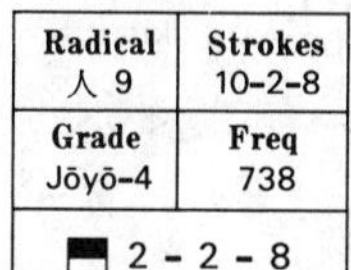

Radical	Strokes
人 9	10-2-8
Grade	**Freq**
Jōyō-4	738
2 - 2 - 8	

丿 𠆢 亼 今 今 今 今 倉 倉 倉

1 2 3 4 5 6 7 8 9 10

▶STOREHOUSE

COMPOUNDS

❶ⓐ storehouse, warehouse, granary

ⓑ [formerly 艙 1410] ship's hold, cabin

倉庫 *sōko* warehouse, storehouse

穀倉 *kokusō* granary, grain elevator

弾倉 *dansō* magazine (of a rifle)

船倉 *sensō* hold (of a ship), hatch

❷ [formerly also 蒼 *sō*] hurried, flurried

倉卒な *sōsotsu na* hurried, sudden

倉皇(＝蒼惶)として *sōkō to shite* in great haste

KUN

【**kura 倉**】[also 蔵, sometimes also 庫] storehouse (esp. for grains or goods), warehouse, granary

倉荷 *kurani* warehouse goods

倉渡し *kurawatashi* ex warehouse

SYNONYMS

❶ⓐ storehouse

蔵 storehouse → 2364

庫 STORAGE CHAMBER → 3112

USAGE

kura

倉

[also 蔵, sometimes also 庫] storehouse (esp. for grains or goods), warehouse, granary

蔵

[also 倉, sometimes also 庫] storehouse (for temporary preservation), storeroom, godown

庫

[usu. 倉, sometimes also 蔵] warehouse (for merchandise), storeroom

HOMOPHONES

kura ⇨ 蔵 2364 庫 3112

2105 **▶BENEFIT ▶PROFIT** 2-8 八

nonstandard for 益 2285

2-8 八

翁 2106

▶**OLD MAN**
nonstandard for 翁 2108

2-8 八

釜 2107

FU kama

Ⓒⓗ 釜 fǔ

Radical	Strokes
金 167	10-8-2
Grade	**Freq**
Reference	
2-2-8	

COMPOUNDS

❶ [original meaning] iron pot, kettle, cauldron
釜茹で *kamayude* boiling in a cauldron
電気釜 *denkigama* electric rice-cooker
後釜 *atogama* successor, replacement
❷ *slang* buttocks
お釜 *okama* (male) homosexual

HOMOPHONES

kama ⇨ 窯 2361 罐 1437

NOTE

⇨ see USAGE note at 窯 2361

2-8 八

翁 翁 翁 翁 2108

Ō okina▲

Ⓒⓗ 翁 wēng

Radical	Strokes
羽 124	10-6-4
Grade	**Freq**
Jōyō	1919
2-2-8	

丿 八 公 公 爷 爷 爷 翁 翁 翁
1 2 3 4 5 6 7 8 9 10

▶**OLD MAN**

COMPOUNDS

ⓐ **old man, aged man, elder**
ⓑ honorific suffix after names of venerable old men
老翁 *rōō* old man
村翁 *son'ō* village elder
白頭翁 *hakutōō* white-haired old man; windflower
吉田翁 *yoshidaō* the venerable Mr. Yoshida, old Mr. Yoshida
翁の面 *okina no men* old man's mask
翁貝 *okinagai* lantern shell

SYNONYMS

ⓐ **old persons**
老 old person → 3197
婆 OLD WOMAN → 2762
ⓐ **man**
男 MAN → 2542
郎 YOUNG MAN → 1289
夫 male adult → 3460
雄 MALE → 1008
ⓑ **honorific suffixes**
老 honorific suffix → 3197

INDEPENDENT

【ō 翁】 old man, aged man

KUN

【okina 翁】 old man, aged man

2-8 丷

差

incorrect classification ⇨ see 3311

2-8 丷

益 兼

incorrect classification ⇨ see 3-7

脅 2109

KYŌ obiya(kasu) odo(su) odo(kasu)

CH 胁 xié

Radical	Strokes
月 130	10-4-6
Grade	**Freq**
Jōyō	1308
2-2-8	

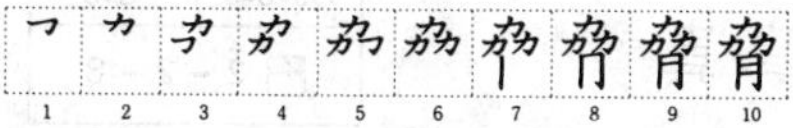

2-8 力

▶THREATEN

COMPOUNDS

❶ **threaten (with force), intimidate, menace, coerce**

脅迫する *kyōhaku suru* threaten, intimidate, menace

脅威 *kyōi* threat, menace

脅迫状 *kyōhakujō* intimidating letter

❷ [original meaning, now archaic] ribs, sides, flanks

KUN

【obiya(kasu) 脅かす】 threaten, menace, endanger; intimidate, scare; coerce

平和が脅かされている *Heiwa ga obiyakasarete iru* Peace is at stake

【odo(su) 脅す】 [formerly also 威す] threaten, menace, intimidate

脅し *odoshi* threat, menace, intimidation

脅し文句 *odoshimonku* threatening language, bluff

【odo(kasu) 脅かす】

[formerly also 威かす or 嚇かす]

ⓐ threaten, menace, intimidate

ⓑ startle

脅かして金を取る *odokashite kane o toru* scare money out of (a person)

脅かすなよ *Odokasu na yo* What a start you gave me!

SYNONYMS

❶ **threaten**

威 THREATEN BY FORCE → 3578

嚇 INTIMIDATE → 784

喝 shout threats at → 461

USAGE

❶ **odosu**

脅す

[formerly also 威す] threaten, menace, intimidate

威す

[now usu. 脅す] same as 脅す

❷ **odoshi**

脅し

[formerly also 威し] threat, menace, intimidation

威し

①ⓐ [now usu. 脅し] threat, menace, intimidation

ⓑ [in compounds] something that scares or startles

② [usu. 縅し] braid or thread of Japanese armor

縅し

[sometimes also 威し] braid or thread of Japanese armor

❸ **odokasu**

脅かす

[formerly also 威かす or 嚇かす]

ⓐ threaten, menace, intimidate

ⓑ startle

威かす

[now usu. 脅かす] same as 脅かす

嚇かす

[now usu. 脅かす] same as 脅かす

HOMOPHONES

odosu ⇨ 威 3578

odoshi ⇨ 威 3578 縅 1391

odokasu ⇨ 威 3578 嚇 784

眞 2110

▶TRUE

nonstandard for 真 2111

2-8 ヒ

2-8
十

真 眞 真 𥅭

2111 SHIN ma ma- makoto▲

Ⓒ 真 zhēn

Radical	Strokes
目 109	10-5-5
Grade	**Freq**
Jōyō-3	310
2-2-8	

一 十 𠂇 古 古 肯 直 直 真 真
1 2 3 4 5 6 7 8 9 10

▶**TRUE**

COMPOUNDS

❶ⓐ [also prefix] **true, real, actual, genuine**
ⓑ **truth, reality, genuineness**
ⓒ true nature, essence
真価 *shinka* true value
真意 *shin'i* true meaning [signification]; real intention
真剣 *shinken* real sword; seriousness
真相 *shinsō* truth, facts, real situation
真犯人 *shinhannin* the real criminal
真実 *shinjitsu* truth, reality
真偽 *shingi* truth or falsehood; authenticity
写真 *shashin* photograph
真如 *shinnyo* the absolute, absolute reality
❷ natural, inborn, pure
純真な *junshin na* naive, pure, genuine, sincere
天真 *tenshin* naïveté, simplicity, innocence
❸ square style of Chinese characters
真書 *shinsho* square style

INDEPENDENT

【shin 真】 truth, reality, genuineness; square style of Chinese characters; star performer
真の *shin no* true, real, genuine; utter
真に *shin ni* truly, indeed, really
真の友 *shin no tomo* true friend
真に迫る *shin ni semaru* be true to nature [life], be lifelike
真で書く *shin de kaku* write in the square style

KUN

【ma 真】 truth
真に受ける *ma ni ukeru* take seriously, believe

【ma- 真-】
[also prefix]
① true, genuine, pure
真心 *magokoro* sincerity, true heart
真ん中 *mannaka* center, middle
真似をする *mane o suru* imitate, mimic, mock
② right, just, exactly, due (north)
真上 *maue* right above
真北 *makita* due north
真正面 *mashōmen* right in front
③ complete, full
真帆 *maho* full sail
真四角 *mashikaku* regular square
真っ裸の *mappadaka no* stark naked
④ honest, serious
真顔 *magao* serious face
真人間 *maningen* honest man
⑤ in the midst of
真夏 *manatsu* midsummer
真っ最中 *massaichū* midst, height

【makoto 真】 [usu. 誠, sometimes also 実] truth, reality
真に *makoto ni* truly, really; very, extremely
嘘か真か *uso ka makoto ka* true or false

SYNONYMS

❶ⓐ & ❶ⓑ true
洵 TRULY → 383
実 REAL → 2225
本 real → 3502
正 genuine → 3484
現 ACTUAL → 968

【ma-】
② **exact**
正 RIGHT → 3484
確 CERTAIN → 1228

HOMOPHONES

makoto ⇨ 誠 1523 実 2225

NOTE

⇨ see USAGE note at 誠 1523

2-8
十

incorrect classification ⇨ see 2455

桑 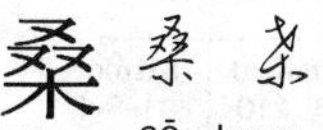

2112 SŌ kuwa

(CH) 桑 sāng

Radical	Strokes
木 75	10-4-6
Grade	Freq
Jōyō	1433
2-2-8	

2-8 又

▶MULBERRY

COMPOUNDS

❶ **mulberry; mulberry tree**

桑園 *sōen* mulberry farm [plantation]

桑田 *sōden* mulberry plantation

❷ used phonetically for *sō*

桑門 *sōmon* priesthood, Buddhism

KUN

【kuwa 桑】 mulberry; mulberry tree

桑畑 *kuwabatake* mulberry field

桑摘み *kuwatsumi* picking mulberry leaves

桑原桑原 *kuwabara kuwabara* Heaven forbid that thunder strike us!

SYNONYMS

❶ **trees**

漆 Japanese lacquer tree → 704

梓 CATALPA → 962

桂 AROMATIC TREE, katsura tree → 928

桐 PAULOWNIA → 937

楠 CAMPHOR TREE → 1018

槙 PODOCARPUS → 1051

杉 CRYPTOMERIA → 832

松 PINE → 864

楓 MAPLE → 1015

柳 WILLOW → 899

桜 CHERRY → 931

夏 夏 夏

2113 KA GE natsu

(CH) 夏 xià

Radical	Strokes
夊 35	10-3-7
Grade	Freq
Jōyō-2	658
2-2-8	

2-8 一

▶SUMMER

COMPOUNDS

❶ **summer**

夏季 *kaki* summer, summer season

夏至 *geshi* summer solstice

春夏秋冬 *shunkashūtō* four seasons, all (the) year round

初夏 *shoka* early summer

盛夏 *seika* midsummer

❷ Xia Dynasty (?2205-?1782 B.C.) (the first Chinese dynasty)

夏朝 *kachō* Xia Dynasty

INDEPENDENT

【ka 夏】 Xia Dynasty

KUN

【natsu 夏】 summer

夏休み *natsuyasumi* summer vacation

真夏 *manatsu* midsummer

常夏 *tokonatsu* everlasting summer

SYNONYMS

❶ **warm seasons**

春 SPRING → 2576

暑 SUMMER HEAT → 2473

❷ **earlier Chinese dynasties**

商 Shang Dynasty → 2116

周 Zhou Dynasty → 2998

漢 Han Dynasty → 657

晋 JIN DYNASTY → 2656

臭

2114

▶FISH

nonstandard for 魚 2127

2-8 ⺈

氣

incorrect classification ⇨ see 3228

(nonstandard for 気 3194)

2-8 𠂉

2-9

斎 齋 斎 斎

2115 SAI toki▲

㊥ 斎 zhāi

Radical	Strokes
斉 210	11-8-3
Grade	**Freq**
Jōyō	1258
2-2-9	

▶OBSERVE RELIGIOUS ABSTINENCE

COMPOUNDS

❶ⓐ [rarely also 斉 2054] **observe religious abstinence, abstain, purify oneself, fast**
ⓑ religious abstinence, purification
斎戒 *saikai* religious purification
潔斎 *kessai* religious abstinence, purification
斎日 *saijitsu* [rare] days of abstinence, fast day
小斎 *shōsai* abstinence (in Catholicism)
❷ⓐ religious ritual [service], Shinto ritual (esp. at Ise Shrine)
ⓑ Buddhist ritual [service]
斎主 *saishu* Chief Priest of the Great Shrine of Ise
斎場 *saijō* funeral hall; site of a religious service
❸ⓐ **study, room for study**
ⓑ suffix after names of studies
書斎 *shosai* study, library
❹ suffix after pen names or pseudonyms
北斎 *hokusai* Hokusai (name of a famous artist)

KUN

【toki 斎】 meal served to a Buddhist priest; meal served after a Buddhist service

SYNONYMS

❶ⓐ **pray and worship**
崇 REVERENCE → 2297
拝 WORSHIP → 303
祈 PRAY → 875
願 pray → 1845
❷ **ceremonies and festivities**
会 Buddhist ceremony → 2020
祭 FESTIVAL → 2672
礼 RITE → 818
典 formal ceremony → 2627
儀 CEREMONY → 169
式 CEREMONY → 3049
❸ **rooms**
室 ROOM → 2254
間 room → 3323
房 CHAMBER → 1946
堂 HALL → 2589

NOTE

★do not confuse with 斉 2054

2-9

商 商 商 商

2116 SHŌ akina(u)

㊥ 商 shāng

Radical	Strokes
口 30	11-3-8
Grade	**Freq**
Jōyō-3	342
2-2-9	

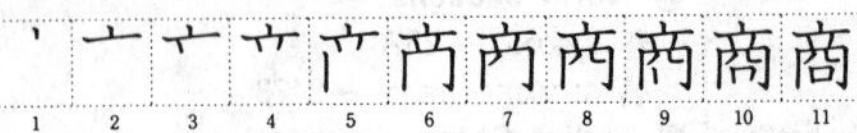

▶TRADE

COMPOUNDS

❶ⓐ **trade, trade in, deal in**
ⓑ **trade, commerce, business; sales**
商品 *shōhin* goods, commodities
商店 *shōten* shop, store
商業 *shōgyō* commerce, trade, business
商社 *shōsha* company, firm
商売 *shōbai* trade, business, commerce
商法 *shōhō* trade, business, commerce; commercial law
商人 *shōnin* merchant, trader, tradesman
商船 *shōsen* merchant ship, trading vessel
商標 *shōhyō* trademark
通商 *tsūshō* commerce, trade, commercial relation [intercourse]
行商 *gyōshō* itinerant trade, peddling
月商 *gesshō* monthly sales
❷ [also suffix] **merchant, trader, dealer, businessman, shopkeeper**
画商 *gashō* picture dealer
豪商 *gōshō* wealthy merchant
貿易商 *bōekishō* trading merchant, importer, exporter
士農工商 *shinōkōshō* warriors, farmers, artisans and tradesmen (the four classes of Tokugawa Japan)
❸ abbrev. of 商業高校 *shōgyō kōkō* and 商学部 *shōgakubu*: commercial high school, faculty of commerce

徳商 *tokushō* Tokushima Commercial High School
❹ confer, discuss
商量 *shōryō* consideration, deliberation
協商 *kyōshō* entente, agreement
❺ *math* quotient
微分商 *bibunshō* differential quotient
❻ Shang [Yin] Dynasty (16th-11th centuries B.C.)
商王朝 *shōōchō* Shang Dynasty
❼ [rare] second note of the pentatonic scale (⇨ see APPENDIX 7)

INDEPENDENT

【shō 商】 abbrev. of 商業 *shōgyō*: trade; *math* quotient; Shang [Yin] Dynasty; [rare] second note of the pentatonic scale

KUN

【akina(u) 商う】 sell, trade in, deal in, handle
商い *akinai* trade, business
大商い *ōakinai* heavy turnover [trading]
茶を商う *cha o akinau* sell [handle] tea, deal in tea

SYNONYMS

❶ⓐ sell and trade
貿 TRADE → 2601
売 SELL → 2196
販 ENGAGE IN SALES → 1477
卸す WHOLESALE → 1447
易 EXCHANGE → 2411
ⓑ industry and business
業 BUSINESS, INDUSTRY → 2612
産 industry → 3298
工 manufacturing industry → 3381
❷ merchant
屋 shopkeeper → 3098
❻ earlier Chinese dynasties
夏 Xia Dynasty → 2113
周 Zhou Dynasty → 2998
漢 Han Dynasty → 657
晋 JIN DYNASTY → 2656

章 章 章 𢀶

2117 SHŌ

CH 章 zhāng

Radical	Strokes
立 117	11-5-6
Grade	**Freq**
Jōyō-3	960
2-2-9	

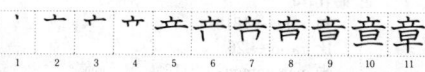

2-9

Stroke order: 1 2 3 4 5 6 7 8 9 10 11

▶CHAPTER ▶BADGE

COMPOUNDS

❶ⓐ [also suffix] (division of text) **chapter**
ⓑ [original meaning] (section of musical composition) movement
章句 *shōku* passage, chapter and verse
章節 *shōsetsu* chapter and verse
第一章 *daiisshō* Chapter 1
楽章 *gakushō* (music) movement
❷ **writing, letter**
文章 *bunshō* writing, composition, essay; prose
玉章 *gyokushō* excellent composition; your letter
❸ⓐ [also suffix] (device serving as insignia) **badge, emblem, medal, insignia**
ⓑ (distinctive mark) **badge, emblem**
帽章 *bōshō* badge on a cap
腕章 *wanshō* armband, arm badge
会員章 *kaiinshō* membership badge
紋章 *monshō* crest, family insignia, coat of arms
校章 *kōshō* school emblem
印章 *inshō* seal, stamp
❹ [also suffix] **decoration, medal, order**
勲章 *kunshō* decoration, order, medal
褒章 *hōshō* medal of merit
瑞宝章 *zuihōshō* Order of the Sacred Treasure
❺ regulations, constitution
憲章 *kenshō* constitution, charter
❻ be confused, be scared
周章狼狽する *shūshōrōbai suru* be disconcerted, be confused
❼ [usu. 彰 1860] [archaic] make known (someone's virtues to the public)
表章する *hyōshō suru* express, make clear (someone's virtues)

INDEPENDENT

【shō 章】 chapter
章を改める *shō o aratameru* begin a new chapter

SPECIAL READINGS

章魚▲ *tako* octopus

SYNONYMS

❶ⓐ parts of writing
段 passage → 1144
節 paragraph → 2691
款 ARTICLE → 1700
条 ARTICLE → 2200
項 CLAUSE → 567
目 ITEM → 3043
箇 item → 2700
❸ insignia
紋 CREST → 1299
❹ prizes

賞 PRIZE → 2618 | 杯 prize cup → 857

2-9 亠

率 2118

率 率 率 (calligraphic forms)

SOTSU RITSU hiki(iru)

CH 率 shuài lǜ

Radical	Strokes
玄 95	11-5-6
Grade	**Freq**
Jōyō-5	512
2-2-9	

Stroke order: 1 2 3 4 5 6 7 8 9 10 11

▶RATE ▶LEAD

COMPOUNDS

❶ [also suffix] **rate, proportion; index, coefficient; modulus**

比率 *hiritsu* ratio, percentage
効率 *kōritsu* efficiency
百分率 *hyakubunritsu* percentage
能率 *nōritsu* efficiency
伸び率 *nobiritsu* growth rate; coefficient of extension
利率 *riritsu* interest rate, interest
打率 *daritsu* batting average
確率 *kakuritsu* probability
保険料率 *hokenryōritsu* premium rate
弾性率 *danseiritsu* modulus of elasticity

❷ **lead, head, command (troops)**

率先 *sossen* taking the lead [initiative]
統率する *tōsotsu suru* lead, command
引率者 *insotsusha* leader, commander

❸ frank, straightforward

率直な *sotchoku na* frank, openhearted

❹ rash, hasty

軽率な *keisotsu na* rash, light-headed, careless

❺ [also 卒 *sotsu* 2055] suddenly, unexpectedly

率然 *sotsuzen* suddenly, unexpectedly

INDEPENDENT

【ritsu 率】 rate, proportion, percentage; index, coefficient; modulus

率を定める *ritsu o sadameru* fix the rate

KUN

【hiki(iru) 率いる】 lead, head, command (troops)

一軍を率いて *ichigun o hikiite* at the head of an army

SYNONYMS

❶ **rate**

割 rate → 1816
比 ratio → 26
歩 percentage → 2416

❷ **lead and escort**

引 lead → 181
導 GUIDE → 2888
連 take along → 3103

2-9 亠

髙 2119

▶HIGH

nonstandard for 高 2097

2-9 亠

產 2120

▶GIVE BIRTH ▶PRODUCE

nonstandard for 産 3298

2-9 亠

䢦 2121

▶RATE ▶LEAD

nonstandard for 率 2118

2-9 亠

産

incorrect classification ⇨ see 3298

2-9 八

貧 2122

▶POOR

nonstandard for 貧 2123

貧 貧 貧 貧 2123 HIN BIN mazu(shii)

CH 贫 pín

Radical	Strokes
貝 154	11-7-4
Grade	**Freq**
Jōyō-5	1209
2-2-9	

2-9 八

丿 八 分 分 分 贫 贫 貧 貧 貧 貧
1 2 3 4 5 6 7 8 9 10 11

▶POOR

COMPOUNDS

❶ [original meaning] (lacking in wealth) **poor, destitute**

貧乏 *binbō* poverty, destitution
貧困 *hinkon* poverty, indigence, destitution; lack, shortage
貧富 *hinpu* rich and poor
貧窮 *hinkyū* poverty
貧農 *hinnō* needy peasant
素寒貧 *sukanpin* dire poverty; pauper

❷ (lacking in) poor (in), scanty

貧弱な *hinjaku na* poor, meager, scanty
貧血 *hinketsu* anemia

INDEPENDENT

【hin 貧】 *literary* poverty

【hinsuru 貧する】 become poor, live in poverty

貧すれば鈍する *Hinsureba donsuru* Poverty dulls the wit

KUN

【mazu(shii) 貧しい】 poor, needy, destitute; (lacking in) poor (in), meager, scanty

貧しさ *mazushisa* poverty
貧しく暮らす *mazushiku kurasu* live in poverty
才能が貧しい *sainō ga mazushii* poor in ability

SYNONYMS

❶ **poor**

乏 poor → 1933
窮 destitute → 2358

冨 2124

▶RICH

nonstandard for 富 2310

2-9 冖

鹵 2125 RO

CH 卤 lǔ

Radical	Strokes
鹵 197	11-11-0
Grade	**Freq**
Reference	
2-2-9	

2-9 卜

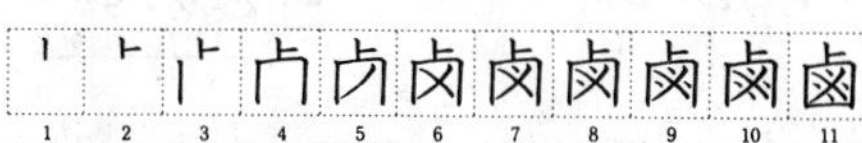

RADICAL 197

Standard form: 鹵 *ro* 'salt' (鹹 鹸)

Description: used in characters related to salt

COMPOUNDS

❶ capture, plunder, rob

鹵獲する *rokaku suru* capture, seize, plunder

❷ big shield

鹵簿 *robo* Imperial cortege [procession]

❸ [archaic] salt, rock salt

參 2126

▶PARTICIPATE ▶VISIT A HOLY PLACE

nonstandard for 参 2066

2-9 厶

2-9 ク

魚 奥◇

CH 鱼 yú

2127 GYO uo sakana -zakana

Radical	Strokes
魚 195	11-11-0
Grade	**Freq**
Jōyō-2	961
2-2-9	

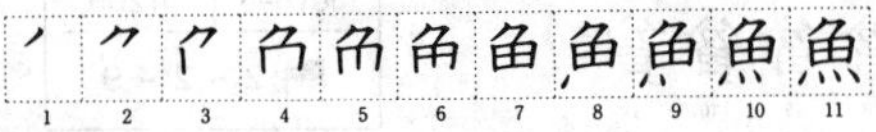

RADICAL 195
Standard form: 魚 *uo* 'fish' (魯 鯊)
Left variant: 魚 *uohen* (鮮 鯛 鯨)
Description: used in characters related to fish names or marine animals

▶**FISH**

COMPOUNDS

ⓐ [also suffix] [original meaning] **fish**
ⓑ something shaped like a fish

魚類 *gyorui* fishes
魚介類 *gyokairui* marine products
金魚 *kingyo* goldfish
鮮魚 *sengyo* fresh fish
人魚 *ningyo* mermaid, merman
深海魚 *shinkaigyo* deep-sea fish
熱帯魚 *nettaigyo* tropical fish
魚雷 *gyorai* torpedo

KUN

【uo 魚】 fish
魚市場 *uoichiba* fish market
川魚 *kawauo* (=*kawazakana*) river fish, freshwater fish
飛び魚 *tobiuo* flying fish

【sakana 魚, -zakana -魚】 [also suffix] fish
魚屋 *sakanaya* fish shop; fish dealer
小魚 *kozakana* small fish, fry
干し魚 *hoshizakana* dried fish, stockfish
焼き魚 *yakizakana* broiled fish

SPECIAL READINGS

雑魚 *zako* small fish, small fry; lesser fry

SYNONYMS

ⓐ **fish**
貝 SHELLFISH → 2543

2-9 ク

亀 龜 龜◇

CH 龟 guī jūn qiū

2128 KI kame NAMES hisa hisashi

Radical	Strokes
龜 213	11-11-0
Grade	**Freq**
Names	1989
2-2-9	

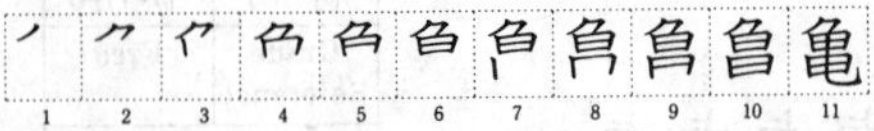

RADICAL 213
simplified form not used as radical
⇨ see 龜 2147 for radical description

▶**TURTLE**

COMPOUNDS

ⓐ [original meaning] **turtle, tortoise**
ⓑ shaped like a turtle

亀甲 *kikkō* carapace of a turtle, tortoiseshell
亀卜 *kiboku* divination by tortoiseshells
亀裂 *kiretsu* crack, fissure
亀頭 *kitō* glans

KUN

【kame 亀】 turtle, tortoise
海亀 *umigame* (sea) turtle

NAMES

亀井 *kamei* surname
亀吉 *kamekichi* male name
亀夫 *kameo* male name

SYNONYMS

ⓐ **reptiles**
蛇 SNAKE → 1343
竜 DRAGON → 2099

蛮 蠻 𫝀 𢆯 ⒸⒽ 蛮 mán

2129 BAN

Radical	Strokes
虫 142	12-6-6
Grade	**Freq**
Jōyō	1777
2-2-10	

2-10

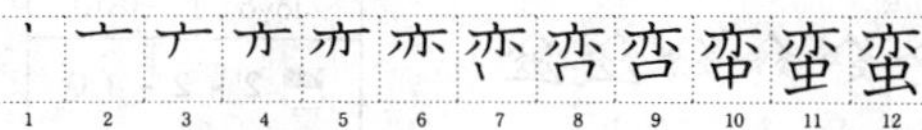

▶**BARBARIAN**

COMPOUNDS

❶ⓐ [formerly also 蕃 2522] **barbarian, savage, uncivilized tribe**
ⓑ foreigner, foreign country
ⓒ [original meaning] ancient name for tribes south of China

蛮人 *banjin* savage, barbarian; aboriginal
蛮語 *bango* language of the barbarians
蛮族 *banzoku* savage tribe
野蛮な *yaban na* savage, barbarous, uncivilized
南蛮 *nanban* southern barbarians, Europeans from the South (from 16th to 18th centuries); meat cooked with onions; red pepper

❷ barbaric, barbarous, coarse, wild
蛮声 *bansei* rough voice
蛮カラ *bankara* rough and uncouth vigor
蛮勇 *ban'yū* brute courage, reckless valor

SYNONYMS

❷ **vulgar and unrefined**
粗 COARSE → 1329
野 rustic → 1485
里 rural → 3542
卑 MEAN → 2642
俗 vulgar → 104

童 童 童 𥫗 ⒸⒽ 童 tóng

2130 DŌ warabe

Radical	Strokes
立 117	12-5-7
Grade	**Freq**
Jōyō-3	1067
2-2-10	

2-10

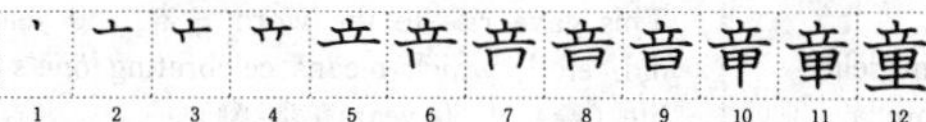

▶**CHILD**

COMPOUNDS

● (young person) **child, youngster**
童心 *dōshin* child's mind [heart]
童顔 *dōgan* boyish face, baby face
童謡 *dōyō* children's song, nursery rhyme
童話 *dōwa* nursery tale, fairy tale
児童 *jidō* child, juvenile
学童 *gakudō* schoolchild

KUN

【**warabe** 童】 child

童歌 *warabeuta* children's folk songs

SPECIAL READINGS

河童▲ *kappa* water sprite, *kappa*; excellent swimmer

SYNONYMS

● **child**
子 CHILD → 3390
児 CHILD (of any age) → 2546
坊 SONNY → 233
幼 young child → 191

棄

incorrect stroke count ⇨ see 2137

2-10

2-10 人

傘 仐 ✽ 傘 ✽ 傘 ✽ (CH) 伞 sǎn

2131 SAN kasa

Radical	Strokes
人 9	12-2-10
Grade	**Freq**
Jōyō	1810
2 - 2 - 10	

1 2 3 4 5 6 7 8 9 10 11 12

▶UMBRELLA

COMPOUNDS

❶ⓐ **something shaped like an umbrella**
ⓑ **something that protects like an umbrella**

傘形器官 *sankei-kikan bot* umbraculum
鉄傘 *tessan* iron dome
傘伐林 *sanbatsurin* shelterwood forest
傘下の *sanka no* under the influence or jurisdiction of, subsidiary
落下傘 *rakkasan* parachute

❷ abbrev. of 落下傘 *rakkasan*: parachute
主傘 *shusan* main parachute
開傘 *kaisan* opening of a parachute

❸ unclassified compounds
傘寿 *sanju* 80 years old, one's 80th birthday

KUN

【kasa 傘】
ⓐ umbrella, parasol
ⓑ something that protects like an umbrella
傘を差す *kasa o sasu* hold an umbrella
雨傘 *amagasa* umbrella
日傘 *higasa* parasol
洋傘 *yōgasa* umbrella, parasol
核の傘 *kaku no kasa* nuclear umbrella

USAGE

kasa
傘
ⓐ umbrella, parasol
ⓑ something that protects like an umbrella
笠
①ⓐ bamboo hat, sedge hat
ⓑ something that protects like a hat
② (lamp) shade, hood

HOMOPHONES

kasa ⇨ 笠 2662

COMPOUND FORMATION

傘寿 *sanju*
傘 is sometimes abbreviated to 仐, which consists of 八 'eight' and 十 'ten', i.e., 80. This gave rise to the word 傘寿, '80 years old, etc.', which means celebrating one's long life (寿) of 80 years (傘 ❸).

2-10 八

2132 TEN DEN (CH) 奠 diàn

Radical	Strokes
大 37	12-3-9
Grade	**Freq**
Reference	
2 - 2 - 10	

COMPOUNDS

❶ [now replaced by 典 *den* 2627] offering
香奠 *kōden* obituary [condolence] gift, incense money

❷ establish, settle
奠都 *tento* transfer of the capital

2-10 八

2133

▶HONOR
nonstandard for 尊 2324

2-10 丷

incorrect classification ⇨ see 3316

2-10 丷

善 普 etc. incorrect classification ⇨ see 3-9

象 2134 SHŌ ZŌ katado(ru)▲

CH 象 xiàng

Radical	Strokes
豕 152	12-7-5
Grade	Freq
Jōyō-4	503
2-2-10	

2-10

▶PHENOMENON ▶ELEPHANT

COMPOUNDS

❶ (outward manifestation of things) **phenomenon, outer appearance, material form; things, object**

現象 *genshō* phenomenon

気象 *kishō* atmospheric phenomena, weather conditions

天象 *tenshō* astronomical phenomena

万象 *banshō* all things [manifestations] in the universe

対象 *taishō* object (of study), subject, target

抽象 *chūshō* abstraction

❷ **represent, symbolize**

象徴する *shōchō suru* symbolize

象形文字 *shōkei-moji* hieroglyph, pictograph

❸ (mental representation) **image, mental image**

印象 *inshō* impression

心象 *shinshō* image, mental picture

表象 *hyōshō* representation, image, idea

❹ [original meaning] **elephant**

象さん *zōsan* elephant

象牙 *zōge* ivory

巨象 *kyozō* gigantic elephant

アフリカ象 *afurikazō* African elephant

INDEPENDENT

【zō 象】 elephant

象の鼻 *zō no hana* trunk of an elephant

KUN

【katado(ru) 象る】 [sometimes also 形どる] model after, represent

手を象った字 *te o katadotta ji* character representing a hand

SYNONYMS

❶ **phenomenon**

気 natural phenomenon → 3194

物 physical phenomena → 874

❷ **imitate**

模 pattern after → 1050

肖 MODEL → 2205

倣 COPY AFTER → 113

擬 IMITATE → 788

❹ **undomesticated mammals**

猪 WILD BOAR → 536

熊 BEAR → 2848

虎 TIGER → 3212

鹿 DEER → 3126

猿 MONKEY → 669

鯨 WHALE → 1882

USAGE

katadoru

象る

[sometimes also 形どる] model after, represent

形どる

[usu. 象る] model after, represent

HOMOPHONES

katadoru ⇨ 形 846

COMPOUND FORMATION

❶ 対象 *taishō*

対象 'object, etc.' (German *Gegenstand*) is the object or phenomenon (象 ❶) that stands in contradistinction (対) to oneself.

❷ 抽象 *chūshō*

抽象 'abstraction' is the process of separating or extracting (抽) the inherent properties of a physical phenomenon or object (象 ❶).

NOTE

⇨ see also USAGE note at 像 166

無 2135 MU BU na(i)

CH 无 wú

Radical	Strokes
灬 86	12-4-8
Grade	Freq
Jōyō-4	231
2-2-10	

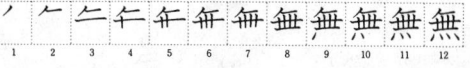

2-10

▶WITHOUT ▶NOTHING

COMPOUNDS

❶ [also prefix] **without, -less, non-, un-, in-, no**—element indicating nonexistence or lack

無給で *mukyū de* without pay [salary]

無用の *muyō no* useless; unnecessary; forbidden
無限の *mugen no* infinite, endless, unfathomable
無断で *mudan de* without permission; without notice [warning]
無料 *muryō* no charge, free
無理な *muri na* unreasonable, unjustifiable; impossible; forced; excessive; irrational (equation)
無死 *mushi baseball* with no outs
無礼 *burei* discourtesy, rudeness
無能 *munō* inefficiency, incompetence
無毒の *mudoku no* nonpoisonous
無休で *mukyū de* without leave [holiday]
無関係の *mukankei no* irrelevant, unrelated
無責任 *musekinin* irresponsibility
無事故 *mujiko* no accident, no trouble
無職の *mushoku no* without occupation, unemployed
無用心 *buyōjin* insecurity, carelessness

❷ **nothing, nothingness, nonexistence**
皆無 *kaimu* nothing
有無 *umu* existence, presence; yes or no
絶無 *zetsumu* nothing, nil, naught

❸ set at naught, disregard
無視する *mushi suru* ignore, disregard

❹ abbrev. of 無所属 *mushozoku*: independent, affiliated with no party
無現(=無所属現 *mushozoku gen*) incumbent candidate unaffiliated with a party

INDEPENDENT

【mu 無】 nothing, naught
無から有は生じない *Mu kara yū wa shōjinai* Nothing comes from nothing
無にする *mu ni suru* bring to naught
無に帰する *mu ni kisuru* come to naught [nothing]

KUN

【na(i) 無い】
①ⓐ there is no, do not exist, have not
ⓑ be missing, lack
金が無い *kane ga nai* have no money
資本無しで *shihon nashi de* without capital
子が無い *ko ga nai* have no children
無くす *nakusu* lose, be deprived of; get rid of, remove, do away with
無くなる *nakunaru* disappear, be gone; run short; get lost, be missing
財布が無い *Saifu ga nai* My purse is missing
② not, do not
行きたく無い *ikitaku nai* do not want to go
寒くも無いし暑くも無い *Samuku mo nai shi atsuku mo nai* It is neither hot nor cold

SYNONYMS

❶ **terms of negation**
非 IS NOT (contrariety) → 889
不 NOT (negation) → 3434
未 NOT YET → 3506
没 lacking in → 260
欠 LACK → 1987
否 OR NOT → 2406

❷ **emptiness and nothing**
虚 VOID → 3237
空 EMPTY → 2227
白 WHITE (blank) → 3493
零 ZERO → 2792

USAGE

❶ **nai**
無い
①ⓐ there is no, do not exist, have not
ⓑ be missing, lack
② not, do not
亡い
not in this world, dead

❷ **nakusu**
無くす
ⓐ lose, be deprived of
ⓑ get rid of, remove, do away with
亡くす
lose (a parent), be bereft of

❸ **nakunaru**
無くなる
ⓐ disappear, be gone; run short
ⓑ get lost, be missing
亡くなる
die, be dead

HOMOPHONES

nai ⇨ 亡 3402
nakusu ⇨ 亡 3402
nakunaru ⇨ 亡 3402

NOTE

⇨ see also USAGE note at 不 3434

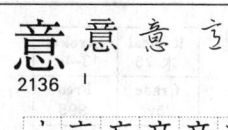

意 意 意

2136

(CH) 意 yì

Radical	Strokes
心 61	13-4-9
Grade	Freq
Jōyō-3	98

2 - 2 - 1 1

▶MIND ▶MEANING

COMPOUNDS

❶ **mind, heart, thoughts, feelings; opinion**

意識 *ishiki* consciousness, awareness
意見 *iken* opinion, view; admonition
意気 *iki* heart, mind, (high) spirits
意外な *igai na* unexpected, unforeseen, surprising
意地 *iji* nature, disposition; will power, backbone
注意 *chūi* attention, care, advice
用意する *yōi suru* prepare, ready oneself, make arrangements
好意 *kōi* goodwill, favor, kindness
誠意 *seii* sincerity, good faith
合意 *gōi* mutual agreement [consent]

❷ **mind (to do something), intention, will, inclination, desire**

意向 *ikō* intention, inclination
意志 *ishi* will, volition
意欲 *iyoku* volition, will, desire
意図 *ito* intention, aim
決意する *ketsui suru* make up one's mind, resolve, determine
得意 *tokui* one's forte; pride; customer
善意 *zen'i* good intention; favorable sense
任意の *nin'i no* optional, voluntary, discretionary

❸ **meaning, sense, intent**

意味 *imi* meaning, intention, significance, purport
意義 *igi* meaning, sense, signification, significance
意訳 *iyaku* free translation
真意 *shin'i* true meaning [signification]; real intention
文意 *bun'i* meaning (of a passage), purport
表意文字 *hyōi-moji* ideograph, ideographic character

INDEPENDENT

【i 意】

① mind, heart, thoughts, feelings; opinion
意に介する *i ni kaisuru* mind, take something to heart
意を強くする *i o tsuyoku suru* be reassured, feel encouraged

② mind (to do something), intention, will, inclination, desire
意を決する *i o kessuru* make up one's mind
人の意を受ける *hito no i o ukeru* comply with a person's wishes

③ meaning, sense, intent
意を得ない *i o enai* fail to make sense (of)

SYNONYMS

❶ **thought**

考え thought → 3196
念 THOUGHTS → 2059
想 conception → 2828

❷ **will and intention**

図 intention → 3071
志 AMBITION → 2199
気 mind to do something → 3194
念 thought of doing something → 2059
趣 PURPOSE → 3317
欲 DESIRE → 1475

❸ **meaning**

義 MEANING → 2338
訳 SENSE → 1473
旨 PURPORT → 2024
趣 PURPOSE → 3317

NOTE

⇨ see COMPOUND FORMATION for
得意 *tokui* ⇨ 得 477
表意文字 *hyōi-moji* ⇨ 表 2429

2-11
亠

棄 棄 棄 弃

2137 KI su(teru)▲

CH 弃 qì

Radical	Strokes
木 75	13-4-9
Grade	**Freq**
Jōyō	998
2-2-11	

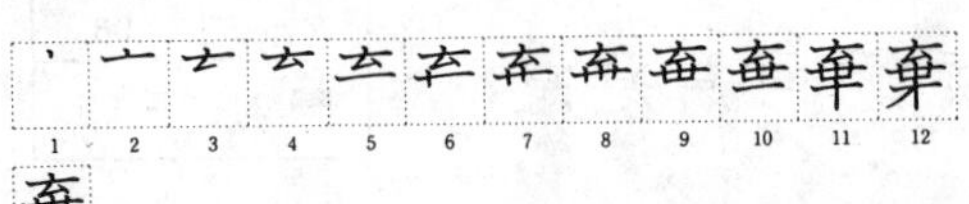

▶**ABANDON**

COMPOUNDS

❶ⓐ **abandon, forsake, desert, discard**

ⓑ [original meaning] **throw away; give up, abandon**

棄権する *kiken suru* abstain from voting, abandon one's right

棄却する *kikyaku suru* turn down, reject, renounce

放棄する *hōki suru* abandon, resign

破棄する *haki suru* break (a treaty), annul

廃棄 *haiki* discarding, abolition, annulment

投棄する *tōki suru* abandon, give up, throw away

❷ [formerly 毀 1791] destroy, ruin, damage

破棄する *haki suru* reverse (the original judgment)

KUN

[su(teru) 棄てる]

[usu. 捨てる]

ⓐ discard, throw away, cast aside

ⓑ abandon, desert, discard, forsake, give up

棄て売り *suteuri* sacrifice sale

権利を棄てる *kenri o suteru* abandon one's rights

SYNONYMS

❶ **discard and abandon**

捨 DISCARD → 501

HOMOPHONES

suteru ⇨ 捨 501

NOTE

⇨ see USAGE note at 捨 501

2-11
亠

裏 裡° 裏 裏

2138 RI ura

CH 里 lǐ

Radical	Strokes
衣 145	13-6-7
Grade	**Freq**
Jōyō-6	709
2-2-11	

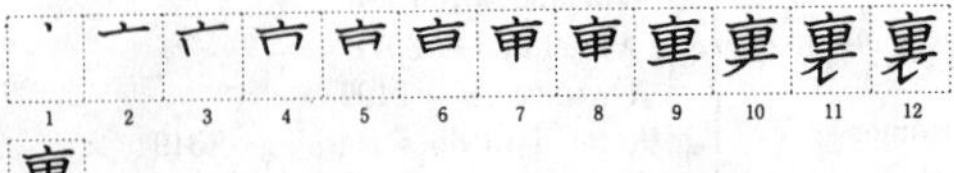

▶**REAR**

COMPOUNDS

❶ **rear, back, reverse, other side**

裏面 *rimen* back, reverse, other side, inside; background

表裏 *hyōri* front and rear, both sides (of a thing or matter); duplicity

庫裏 *kuri* temple's kitchen; priest's living quarters

❷ **inside, within, in**

脳裏 *nōri* brain, mind, memory

胸裏 *kyōri* one's bosom, one's heart, one's feelings

手裏剣 *shuriken* throwing knife

禁裏 *kinri* the Imperial Palace

❸ [suffix] in a state of, -ly

成功裏に *seikōri ni* in success

暗暗裏に *an'anri ni* tacitly, implicitly

KUN

[ura 裏] [also prefix and suffix] rear, back; reverse, other side; lining (of clothes); inside, hidden part; support, backing, proof; *baseball* second half (of an inning), bottom

裏を返す *ura o kaesu* turn the other way, turn inside out

裏庭 *uraniwa* rear garden

頁の裏に *pēji no ura ni* overleaf

裏側 *uragawa* back [reverse, other] side, wrong side

裏表 *uraomote* both sides; two faces; reverse, opposite; the reverse; double-dealing

裏打ち *urauchi* lining, backing

裏付け *urazuke* guarantee, endorsement; support, backing; substantiation, proof

裏切る *uragiru* betray, turn traitor, double-cross

裏を掻く *ura o kaku* counterplot, outwit, de-

feat
三回の裏 *sankai no ura* bottom [second half] of the third inning

SYNONYMS

❶ **rear**
背 BACK → 2573
後 after- → 361

尻 tail end → 3032
尾 TAIL → 3062

❷ **inside**
内 INSIDE → 3466
奥 INNER PART → 2824
中 IN → 3451

喪 incorrect classification / stroke count ⇨ see 2825 — 2-11 亠

會 ▶**MEET** ▶**SOCIETY**
2139
nonstandard for 会 2020 — 2-11 人

義 慈 incorrect classification ⇨ see 3-10 — 2-11 丷

豪 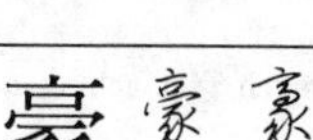 Ⓒ 豪 háo — 2-12 亠
2140 GŌ era(i)▲

Radical	Strokes
豕 152	14-7-7
Grade	**Freq**
Jōyō	1055
2-2-12	

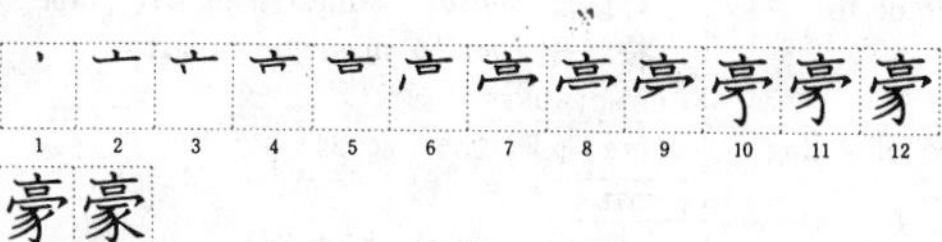

▶**GREAT MAN** ▶**MAGNIFICENT**

COMPOUNDS

❶ **great man, person of extraordinary powers, champion, hero**
豪傑 *gōketsu* hero, great [extraordinary] man
文豪 *bungō* great man of letters, literary master
酒豪 *shugō* great [heavy] drinker
剣豪 *kengō* great swordsman, master fencer
強豪(＝強剛) *kyōgō* veteran, champion
富豪 *fugō* wealthy man, millionaire

❷ⓐ **magnificent, grand, grandiose, great, splendid**
ⓑ bold and unrestrained, heroic, chivalrous
豪華な *gōka na* gorgeous, splendid, pompous
豪壮な *gōsō na* grand, magnificent, splendid
豪勢な *gōsei na* great, grand, magnificent
豪快な *gōkai na* exciting, heroic, largehearted
豪放な *gōhō na* largehearted, openhearted
豪語する *gōgo suru* talk big, boast, brag
豪遊 *gōyū* wild merrymaking

❸ wealthy
豪農 *gōnō* wealthy farmer
豪族 *gōzoku* wealthy and powerful family [clan]
豪商 *gōshō* wealthy merchant

❹ **powerful, heavy**
豪雨 *gōu* heavy rain, downpour
豪雪 *gōsetsu* tremendous snowfall

❺ [formerly also 濠 792] Australia
豪州 *gōshū* Australia
日豪の *nichigō no* Japanese-Australian

INDEPENDENT

【**gō 豪**】 Australia

KUN

【**era(i) 豪い**】
[usu. 偉い]
① remarkable, extraordinary
豪さ *erasa* remarkableness
豪物 *erabutsu* extraordinary [able] character
② awful, serious
ど豪い *doerai* terrible, very serious

SYNONYMS

❶ **great persons**
傑 OUTSTANDING PERSON → 155
雄 hero → 1008
匠 CRAFTSMAN → 2990
聖 great master → 2830

❷ⓐ **great**
壮 GRAND (having grandeur) → 224
宏 GRAND (large in scale) → 2202

雄 HEROIC → 1008
偉 GREAT (of superior character) → 148
大 BIG → 3416
ⓑ **brave**
勇 BRAVE → 2089
赳 VALIANT → 3308
敢 bold → 1706
雄 HEROIC → 1008
壮 heroic → 224
義 chivalrous → 2338
❸ **rich**
富 RICH → 2310
❺ **continents**
米 AMERICA → 3529
欧 EUROPE → 887
阿 Africa → 346
亜 Asia → 3540

HOMOPHONES
erai ⇨ 偉 148

NOTE
⇨ see USAGE note at 偉 148

2-12

膏
2141 KŌ abura

CH 膏 gāo gào

Radical	Strokes
月 130	14-4-10
Grade	**Freq**
Reference	
2-2-12	

COMPOUNDS
❶ [now usu. 脂 *abura*] [original meaning] fat, grease; greasy substance
膏肓 *kōkō* (=*kōmō*) inmost part (of the body)
膏血 *kōketsu* sweat and blood
豚の膏 *buta no abura* lard, grease of a hog
❷ [also suffix]
ⓐ ointment, cream
ⓑ plaster, medicated patch (for aching muscles)
軟膏 *nankō* ointment, salve
絆創膏 *bansōkō* adhesive plaster [tape]
按摩膏 *anmakō* massaging plaster

HOMOPHONES
abura ⇨ 脂 954 油 341

NOTE
⇨ see USAGE note at 油 341

2-12

齊
2142 ▶**UNIFORM**
nonstandard for 斉 2054

Radical	Strokes
齊 210	14-14-0
Grade	**Freq**
Variant	
2-2-12	

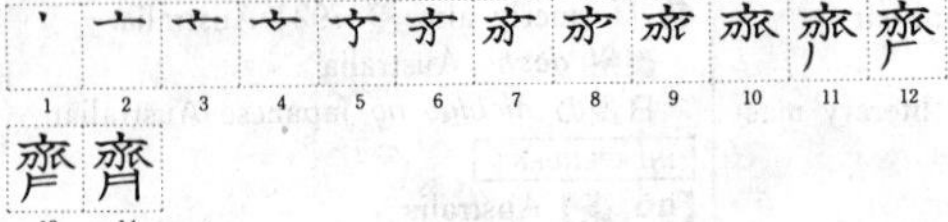

RADICAL 210
Standard form: 齊 *sei* 'uniform' (齋 齎)
Variant: 斉 *sei* (斎)
Description: used in characters related to uniformity or evenness

---

2-12

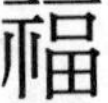

福
incorrect classification ⇨ see 1215
(nonstandard for 福 1029)

2-12

舞
2143 ▶**DANCE**
nonstandard for 舞 2146

褒 褒 褒

2144 HŌ ho(meru)

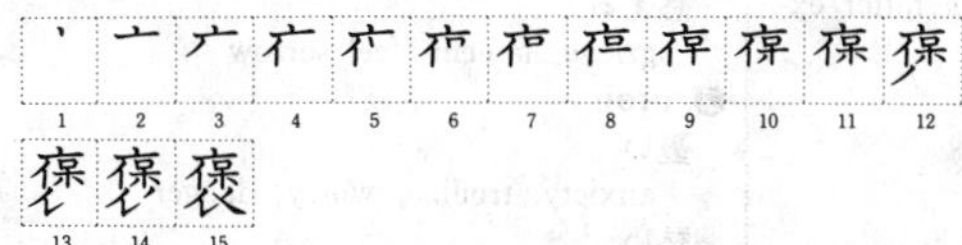

ⒸⒽ 褒 bāo

Radical	Strokes
衣 145	15-6-9
Grade	**Freq**
Jōyō	1740
▀ 2-2-13	

2-13

▶COMMEND

COMPOUNDS

● **commend, praise, laud, award, give recognition to**

褒章 *hōshō* medal of merit
褒美 *hōbi* reward, prize
褒賞 *hōshō* prize, reward
過褒 *kahō* overpraise, excessive compliment
毀誉褒貶 *kiyohōhen* praise and censure, criticisms

KUN

【ho(meru) 褒める】[sometimes also 誉める or 賞める] praise, commend, admire, compliment, eulogize
褒め称える *hometataeru* admire, applaud, praise

SYNONYMS

● **praise**

賛 PRAISE → 2809
美 regard as beautiful → 2264
嘉 commend (esp. an inferior) → 2340
彰 PROCLAIM MERITS → 1860
称 acclaim → 1160
賞 express admiration → 2618
揚 EXALT → 593
頌 EULOGIZE → 1045

USAGE

homeru

褒める
[sometimes also 誉める or 賞める] praise, commend, admire, compliment, eulogize

誉める
[usu. 褒める, sometimes also 賞める] same as 褒める

賞める
[usu. 褒める, sometimes also 誉める] same as 褒める

HOMOPHONES

homeru ⇨ 誉 2502 賞 2618

養

incorrect classification ⇨ see 2365

2-13

憂 憂 憂

2145 YŪ ure(eru) ure(i) u(i) u(ki)

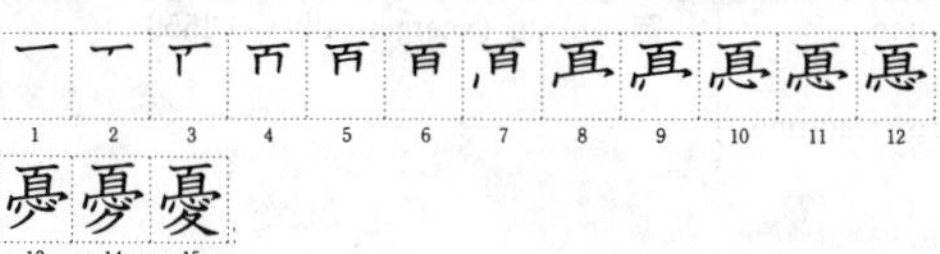

ⒸⒽ 忧 yōu

Radical	Strokes
心 61	15-4-11
Grade	**Freq**
Jōyō	1530
▀ 2-2-13	

2-13

▶BE ANXIOUS

COMPOUNDS

❶ⓐ **be [feel] anxious, fear, worry, be concerned**

ⓑ anxiety, fears, apprehension
憂慮 *yūryo* anxiety, concern, worry
憂国 *yūkoku* patriotism, concern for one's country
一喜一憂 *ikkiichiyū* alternation of joy and sorrow
杞憂 *kiyū* imaginary fears

❷ **grief, sorrow**

憂鬱 *yūutsu* melancholy, gloom
憂愁 *yūshū* melancholy, gloom, grief

KUN

【ure(eru) 憂える】 be anxious, fear, be apprehensive
国の将来を憂える *kuni no shōrai o ureeru* be anxious about the future of one's country

【ure(i) 憂い】 anxiety, trouble, worry; danger
後顧の憂い *kōko no urei* anxiety about the future

【u(i) 憂い】melancholy, sad
憂さ *usa* gloom, melancholy
物憂い *monoui* languid, melancholy
【u(ki) 憂き】*literary* grief, sorrow
憂き目を見る *ukime o miru* have a bitter experience, have a hard time of it

SYNONYMS

❶ **worry**
配 concern oneself → 1460
構う MIND → 1049
虞 FEARS (of undesirable event) → 3254

❷ **sorrow**
哀 SORROW → 2068

USAGE

❶ **ureeru**
憂える
be anxious, fear, be apprehensive
愁える
grieve, lament, feel sorrow

❷ **urei**
憂い
anxiety, trouble, worry; danger
愁い
melancholy, grief, sorrow, sadness

HOMOPHONES

ureeru ⇨ 愁 2829
urei ⇨ 愁 2829

2-13

舞 舞 舞 舞

2146 BU ma(u) -ma(u) mai

CH 舞 wǔ

Radical	Strokes
舛 136	15-7-8
Grade	**Freq**
Jōyō	701
2-2-13	

1 2 3 4 5 6 7 8 9 10 11 12 13 14 15

▶**DANCE**

COMPOUNDS

❶ [original meaning]
ⓐ **dance, dancing**
ⓑ **to dance**
舞曲 *bukyoku* dance music, music and dancing
剣舞 *kenbu* sword dance
日舞 *nichibu* Japanese dancing
歌舞伎 *kabuki* kabuki
舞踏 *butō* dancing
舞台 *butai* stage, the boards
舞踏会 *butōkai* ball, dance

❷ encourage, urge
鼓舞 *kobu* encouragement, stimulation

KUN

【ma(u) 舞う】dance (gracefully, esp. traditional dances); flutter, fly, circle (in the sky)
舞を舞う *mai o mau* perform a dance, dance
舞い上がる *maiagaru* soar, fly high
【-ma(u) -舞う】verbal suffix
振る舞う *furumau* behave oneself; entertain, treat
見舞う *mimau* ask for, visit (a sick person)
仕舞う *shimau* close, finish; put away, lay away
【mai 舞】dancing, dance
舞扇 *maiōgi* dancer's fan
舞姫 *maihime* dancing girl, dancer

SYNONYMS

❶ & 【mau】 **dance**
踊 DANCE (energetically) → 1558

▶TURTLE
nonstandard for 亀 2128

2147

Radical	Strokes
龜 213	16-16-0
Grade	**Freq**
Variant	
2 - 2 - 1 4	

2-14 ⺈

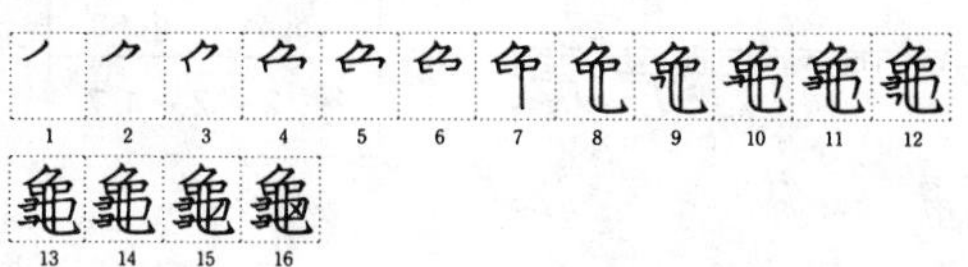

RADICAL 213

Standard form: 龜 *kame* 'tortoise'

Variant: 龜 *kame*

Description: used in characters related to tortoises or tortoiseshells

---

齋 **▶OBSERVE RELIGIOUS ABSTINENCE**
nonstandard for 斎 2115

2148

2-15 亠

龠

2149

Radical	Strokes
龠 214	17-17-0
Grade	**Freq**
Radical	
2 - 2 - 1 5	

2-15 人

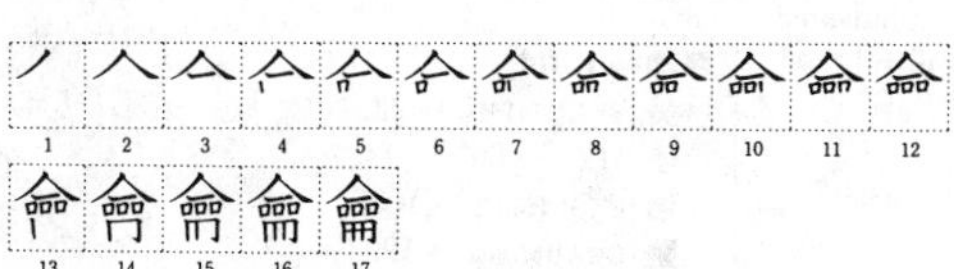

RADICAL 214

Standard form: 龠 *yaku* 'flute'

Description: used in characters related to music or musical instruments

---

▶TURTLE
nonstandard for 亀 2128

2150

Radical	Strokes
龜 213	18-18-0
Grade	**Freq**
Variant	
2 - 2 - 1 6	

2-16 ⺈

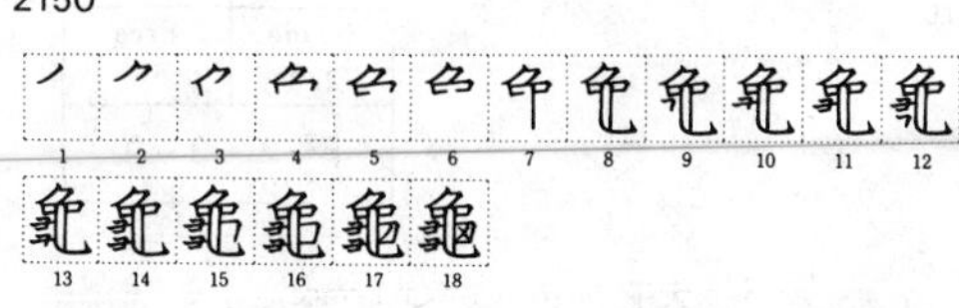

RADICAL 213

variant of 龜 *kame* 'tortoise'

⇨ see 龜 2147 for radical description

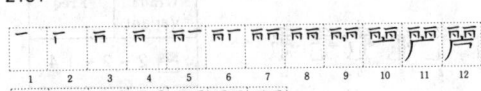

2-17
一

麗 麗 君

2151 REI uruwa(shii) ura(raka)▲

CH 丽 lì lí

Radical	Strokes
鹿 198	19-11-8
Grade	**Freq**
Jōyō	1668
2-2-17	

▶**OF GRACEFUL BEAUTY**

COMPOUNDS

● [original meaning] **of graceful beauty, lovely, beautiful and neat [refreshing], resplendent**

麗人 *reijin* beauty, belle
麗質 *reishitsu* beauty, charm
奇麗(=綺麗)な *kirei na* beautiful, pretty; clean; fair
美麗な *birei na* beautiful, gorgeous
華麗な *karei na* splendid, magnificent, resplendent, gorgeous
端麗な *tanrei na* graceful, elegant, handsome
豊麗な *hōrei na* rich (design), beautiful, splendid
鮮麗 *senrei* resplendent beauty
美辞麗句 *bijireiku* flowery words

KUN

【uruwa(shii) 麗しい】 beautiful and graceful, lovely, pretty; heartwarming, tenderly moving; (of humor or health) good

見目麗しい *mime-uruwashii* good-looking, fair
麗しい情景 *uruwashii jōkei* heartwarming scene
御機嫌麗しい *gokigen-uruwashii* be in good humor

【ura(raka) 麗らか】

uraraka na 麗らかな beautiful, lovely, bright (weather); bright (mood)

麗らかな春の日 *uraraka na haru no hi* beautiful [lovely] spring day
麗らかな気分 *uraraka na kibun* feeling bright

SYNONYMS

● **beautiful**

美 BEAUTIFUL → 2264
佳 FINE → 86
瑶 EXQUISITE → 1026
艶 CHARMING → 1908
妙 of marvelous beauty → 239
華 MAGNIFICENT → 2283
絢 GORGEOUS → 1347
斐 florid → 2776

3-1
大

太 太 た

2152 TAI TA futo(i) futo(ru)

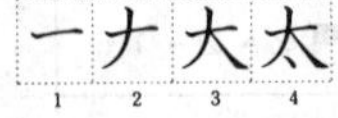

CH 太 tài

Radical	Strokes
大 37	4-3-1
Grade	**Freq**
Jōyō-2	395
2-3-1	

▶**GREAT** ▶**THICK**

COMPOUNDS

❶ⓐ (extremely large in size or scale) **great, large, big, enormous**

ⓑ [also 泰 *tai* 2583] greatest (in degree), most extreme

太陽 *taiyō* sun
太鼓 *taiko* (big) drum; professional jester; flatterer; big obi bow
太陰 *taiin* moon
太白 *taihaku* Venus; thick silk thread; kind of sweet potato
太古 *taiko* ancient times, remote ages
太平洋 *taiheiyō* Pacific Ocean

❷ **of highest rank, grand, great**

太子 *taishi* Crown Prince
太閤 *taikō* father of the Imperial adviser; Toyotomi Hideyoshi
太守 *taishu* governor general, viceroy
太夫 *tayū* chief actor in a noh play; entertainer, courtesan
太祖 *taiso* founder; first Emperor (of a Chinese dynasty)

❸ (great in diameter) **thick**

丸太 *maruta* log

❹ ultimate source

太初 *taisho* beginning of the world

KUN

【futo(i) 太い】

①ⓐ (of great diameter or width) thick, big;

fat; broad, wide
ⓑ thick (voice), deep
太さ *futosa* thickness; depth (of voice)
太糸 *futoito* thick thread, low count yarn
太字 *futoji* thick character, bold-faced type
太い線 *futoi sen* thick line
太っちょ *futotcho* fat person
太い腕 *futoi ude* big arm
太い鉛筆 *futoi enpitsu* broad pencil
② shameless, audacious, insolent
太っ腹な *futoppara na* generous, large-minded, big-hearted
図太い *zubutoi* audacious, brazen
【futo(ru) 太る】[sometimes also 肥る] grow fat, fatten, gain weight
太った *futotta* fat, stout, plump

SPECIAL READINGS

太刀 *tachi* long sword

SYNONYMS

❶ⓐ big and huge
大 BIG → 3416
浩 VAST → 438
巨 HUGE → 3039
❷ high-ranking
貴 NOBLE → 2606
上 upper → 3404
高 HIGH → 2097
総 GENERAL → 1379
❸ &【futoi】❶ⓐ thick
厚 THICK (great in depth) → 3003
【futoru】
○ fatten
肥 FATTEN → 879

USAGE

futoru
太る
[sometimes also 肥る] grow fat, fatten, gain weight
肥る
[usu. 太る] grow fat, fatten, gain weight

HOMOPHONES

futoru ⇨ 肥 879

incorrect classification ⇨ see 1983 3-1 予

今 incorrect classification ⇨ see 1968 3-1 今

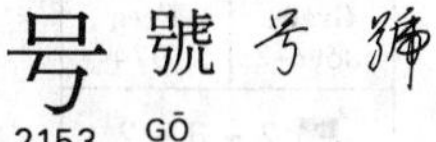

2153 GŌ

ⒸⒽ 号 hào háo

Radical	Strokes
口 30△	5-3-2
Grade	**Freq**
Jōyō-3	458
2-3-2	

3-2 口

▶NUMBER ▶DESIGNATION ▶SIGN

COMPOUNDS

❶ [also suffix]
ⓐ (numerical designation or label) **number, as: room No., house No., type size No., railroad car No., route No., item [subsection] No., etc.**
ⓑ (single copy of a periodical) **number, issue**
号数 *gōsū* number or size of periodicals or pictures, type size
番号 *bangō* number, serial number
百号室 *hyakugōshitsu* room No. 100
一丁目二番地九号 *itchōme nibanchi kyūgō* 2-9, 1-chome (part of an address)
五号活字 *gogō katsuji* No. 5 type, small pica
十五号車 *jūgogōsha* (railway) car No. 15
二号線 *nigōsen* Route No. 2
第二項第四号 *dainikō daiyongō* Subsection 2, Paragraph 4
号外 *gōgai* newspaper extra
第二号 *dainigō* second issue; number two
創刊号 *sōkangō* inaugural number, first issue
❷ⓐ designation, title, name, pen name, pseudonym
ⓑ suffix after names of ships, trains, aircraft, horses or dogs
称号 *shōgō* title, degree
雅号 *gagō* pen name, pseudonym
屋号 *yagō* name of a store; stage title
年号 *nengō* name of era, reign title
クイーンメリー号 *kuīnmerīgō* S.S. *Queen Mary*
ひかり号 *hikarigō Hikari* (name of a bullet train)
❸ (arbitrary sign, esp. in mathematics) **sign, symbol, mark**
等号 *tōgō* equal sign [mark]

負号 *fugō* negative sign
符号 *fugō* sign, mark, symbol
記号 *kigō* symbol, mark, sign
暗号 *angō* code, password
❹ signal
号砲 *gōhō* signal gun
信号 *shingō* signal; traffic light
❺ⓐ [original meaning] holler, call out, shout, cry, wail
ⓑ holler a command, order
号泣 *gōkyū* wailing, lamentation
怒号 *dogō* (angry) roar, outcry, bellow
号令 *gōrei* order, command
呼号する *kogō suru* cry out, proclaim

INDEPENDENT

【gō 号】
① (single copy of a periodical) number, issue
次の号 *tsugi no gō* next number [issue]
② designation, title, name, pen name, pseudonym
...と云う号を名乗る *...to iu gō o nanoru* assume the pseudonym of...

【gōsuru 号する】 name; call, declare

SYNONYMS

❶ **kinds of numbers**
番 No. → 2748
員 fixed number → 2269
数 NUMBER (mathematical unit) → 1790
第 ORDINAL NUMBER PREFIX → 2660
-目 ordinal number suffix → 3043
次 numerical order suffix → 54
❷ **name**
題 TITLE → 3337
称 APPELLATION → 1160
名 NAME → 2169
銘 name (inscribed by maker) → 1724
姓 SURNAME → 279
氏 FAMILY NAME → 2951
❸ **marks and signs**
符 SYMBOL → 2661
標 MARK (identifying sign) → 1064
印 MARK (visible sign) → 828
跡 TRACE → 1534
紋 print → 1299
❹ **signal**
報 signal → 1698
❺ⓐ **shout**
叫 SHOUT → 201
喝 SHOUT AT → 461
喚 call out → 550
呼 CALL → 273
鳴 CRY → 674

3-2 口

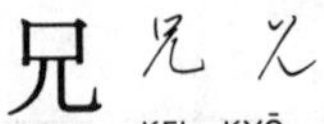

2154 KEI KYŌ ani

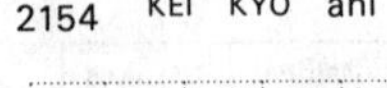

CH 兄 xiōng

Radical	Strokes
儿 10	5-2-3
Grade	**Freq**
Jōyō-2	974
2 - 3 - 2	

▶OLDER BROTHER

COMPOUNDS

❶ **older brother**
兄弟 *kyōdai* (=*keitei*) brother
長兄 *chōkei* eldest brother
実兄 *jikkei* one's own older brother
義兄 *gikei* brother-in-law
父兄 *fukei* one's father and older brothers; guardians
❷ familiar title used in addressing seniors or close friends
山田兄 *yamadakei* Mr. Yamada
❸ (fellow man) brother, friend
諸兄 *shokei* dear friends
学兄 *gakkei* my learned friend
貴兄 *kikei* you

INDEPENDENT

【kei 兄】 older brother; *literary* you
兄たり難く弟たり難し *Kei tarigataku tei tarigatashi* There is little to choose between the two

KUN

【ani 兄】 older brother, big brother
兄貴 *aniki* older brother; one's senior
兄弟子 *anideshi* senior schoolmate, senior apprentice

SPECIAL READINGS

兄さん *niisan* older brother

SYNONYMS

❶ **siblings**
弟 YOUNGER BROTHER → 2044
姉 OLDER SISTER → 280
妹 YOUNGER SISTER → 278
❷ **titles of address**
君 FAMILIAR TITLE (peers) → 3206
氏 COURTESY TITLE → 2951
嬢 Miss → 758
様 FORMAL TITLE → 1052
殿 FORMAL HONORIFIC TITLE → 1792
師 honorific title (clergymen) → 1326
公 honorific title (noblemen) → 1974

只

2155 SHI tada tada-

CH 只 zhǐ

Radical	Strokes
口 30	5-3-2
Grade	**Freq**
Names	2049
2-3-2	

3-2 口

▶**FREE OF CHARGE** ▶**ORDINARY**

COMPOUNDS

● [original meaning] only, just

只今 *shikon* [archaic] just now

KUN

【tada 只】

① no charge

只の *tada no* free of charge, cost-free, for nothing; ordinary, common, plain

② ordinariness, plainness

只の人 *tada no hito* common [ordinary] person, man in the street

只ならぬ *tadanaranu* unusual, alarming, serious

③ doing nothing, being idle

只では置かないぞ *Tada de wa okanai zo* You shall pay dear for that

【tada- 只-】

① free of charge, cost-free, for nothing

只働き *tadabataraki* working for nothing

只乗り *tadanori* free ride

② ordinary, common, plain

只者 *tadamono* ordinary person, common mortal

只事ではない *Tadagoto de wa nai* It is no common case

③ [also 唯] only, just, merely, solely

只今 *tadaima* at present, now; just now; soon; Hello (used by person returning home)

SYNONYMS

【tada-】

② **ordinary**

並 ordinary → 2246

常 NORMAL → 2590

平 common → 3478

普 common → 2323

庸 MEDIOCRE → 3128

凡 COMMONPLACE → 2938

NAMES

只野 *tadano* surname

只八 *tadahachi* male name

HOMOPHONES

tada ⇨ 唯 463

NOTE

⇨ see USAGE note at 唯 463

去

2156 KYO KO sa(ru) -sa(ru)

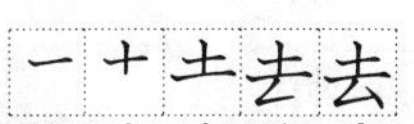

CH 去 qù

Radical	Strokes
ム 28	5-2-3
Grade	**Freq**
Jōyō-3	567
2-3-2	

3-2 土

▶**GO AWAY**

COMPOUNDS

❶ⓐ **go away, leave, retire, depart from**

ⓑ (go away from this world) pass away, die

去来 *kyorai* coming and going; recurrence

辞去する *jikyo suru* leave, quit, retire

退去する *taikyo suru* retreat, withdraw, evacuate

逝去 *seikyo* death

死去する *shikyo suru* die, pass away

❷ⓐ **pass away, elapse, go by**

ⓑ **last (year, etc.)**

過去 *kako* the past, bygone days

去年 *kyonen* last year

去月 *kyogetsu* last month

❸ take away, remove, get rid of, eliminate

去勢 *kyosei* castration; enervation

除去する *jokyo suru* rid of, remove, eliminate

撤去する *tekkyo suru* remove, dismantle (a building); evacuate (an army)

❹ falling tone in Chinese phonetics

去声 *kyoshō* falling tone

KUN

【sa(ru) 去る】 go away, leave, depart, resign; be distant [away] from; pass, elapse, go by; remove, take of, get rid of; divorce; last (November)

遠くに去る *tōku ni saru* go far away

置き去りにする *okizari ni suru* leave (a person) behind

過ぎ去る *sugisaru* pass (away), elapse

取り去る *torisaru* take away, remove, leave out
去る十一月 *saru jūichigatsu* last November
【-sa(ru) -去る】[verbal suffix] completely
忘れ去る *wasuresaru* forget completely

SYNONYMS

❶ⓐ leave and set forth
離 leave → 1836
発 START → 2565
出 GO OUT → 3498
退 RETREAT → 3094
撤 WITHDRAW → 738
ⓑ die
逝 DEPART THIS LIFE → 3104
亡 DECEASE → 3402
死 DIE → 3521
没 die → 260
殉 DIE A MARTYR → 941
枯 WITHER → 898
❷ⓐ elapse
過 PASS BY → 3137
経 pass → 1331
歴 pass → 3019
ⓑ most recent
昨 LAST → 893
先 last → 2394
❸ eliminate
脱 REMOVE → 973
外す take off → 186
除 RID OF → 456
省 leave out → 2449
却 ELIMINATE → 1118
削 cross out → 1448
抹 wipe off → 313
撤 WITHDRAW → 738
排 EXCLUDE → 490
払う CLEAR AWAY → 194

3-2
夂

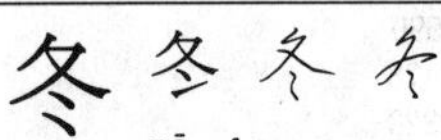

2157 TŌ fuyu

Ⓒⓗ 冬 dōng

Radical	Strokes
冫 15	5-2-3
Grade	**Freq**
Jōyō-2	913
2 - 3 - 2	

▶WINTER

COMPOUNDS

● [original meaning] **winter**
冬季 *tōki* winter season
冬期 *tōki* winter, wintertime
冬至 *tōji* winter solstice
冬眠 *tōmin* hibernation ("winter sleep")
越冬 *ettō* passing the winter, wintering
初冬 *shotō* early winter
立冬 *rittō* first day of winter
春夏秋冬 *shunkashūtō* four seasons, all (the) year round

KUN

【fuyu 冬】winter
冬めく *fuyumeku* become wintry
冬休み *fuyuyasumi* winter vacation
冬山 *fuyuyama* mountain in winter
冬物 *fuyumono* winter clothing, winter goods
冬将軍 *fuyushōgun* hard winter, Jack Frost
真冬 *mafuyu* depth of winter, midwinter

SYNONYMS

● cold seasons
寒 coldest season → 2311
秋 AUTUMN → 1139

3-2
夂

2158

▶WINTER
nonstandard for 冬 2157

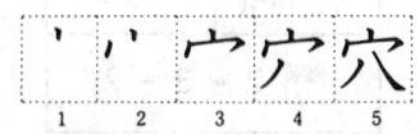

2159 KETSU ana

Ⓒ 穴 xué

Radical	Strokes
穴 116	5-5-0
Grade	**Freq**
Jōyō-6	1129
2 - 3 - 2	

3-2 宀

RADICAL 116

simplified form not used as radical

⇨ see 穴 2161 for radical description

▶HOLE

COMPOUNDS

❶ⓐ hole, cavity

ⓑ counter for holes

ⓒ [original meaning] cave, den

穴隙 *ketsugeki* aperture, crevice

墓穴 *boketsu* grave

二穴 *niketsu* two holes

穴居 *kekkyo* cave dwelling, troglodytism

虎穴 *koketsu* tiger's den; dangerous place

❷ [also suffix] points in the human body where acupuncture or moxibustion can be applied

経穴 *keiketsu* points in the human body where acupuncture or moxibustion can be applied

INDEPENDENT

【ketsu 穴】 *vulgar* ass, fanny; tail end

KUN

【ana 穴】

①ⓐ hole, opening, gap; hollow, cavity

ⓑ [sometimes also 孔] open or bottomless hole, opening, aperture, perforation

ⓒ cave, lair; pit

ボタンの穴 *botan no ana* buttonhole

落とし穴 *otoshiana* pit, trap

洞穴 *horaana* cave, cavern, den

②ⓐ fault, flaw, defect

ⓑ deficit, loss

穴だらけだ *anadarake da* be full of holes; hold no water

穴を開ける *ana o akeru* cause a loss

③ good place known to few

穴場 *anaba* good place known to few people

④ long shot, dark horse

大穴 *ōana* big hole; *horse racing* dark horse

SYNONYMS

❶ holes and cavities

孔 OPEN HOLE → 179

口 MOUTH → 3382

坑 PIT → 236

堀 DITCH → 467

溝 CHANNEL → 659

凹 concavity → 3482

洞 CAVE → 380

USAGE

ana

穴

①ⓐ hole, opening, gap; hollow, cavity

ⓑ [sometimes also 孔] open or bottomless hole, opening, aperture, perforation

ⓒ cave, lair; pit

②ⓐ fault, flaw, defect

ⓑ deficit, loss

③ good place known to few

④ long shot, dark horse

孔

[usu. 穴] open or bottomless hole, opening, aperture, perforation

HOMOPHONES

ana ⇨ 孔 179

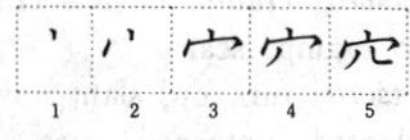

2160

Radical	Strokes
穴 116	5-5-0
Grade	**Freq**
Radical	
2 - 3 - 2	

3-2 宀

RADICAL 116

anakanmuri, variant of 穴 *ana* 'hole'

⇨ see 穴 2161 for radical description

3-2 宀

穴 ▶HOLE

nonstandard for 穴 2159

2161

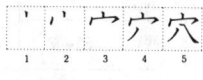

Radical	Strokes
穴 116	5-5-0
Grade	Freq
Variant	
2 - 3 - 2	

RADICAL 116

Standard form: 穴 *ana* 'hole'

Top variant: 宀 *anakanmuri* (空 究 突)

Description: used in characters related to holes or their qualities

---

3-2 宀

字

incorrect stroke count ⇨ see 2172

3-2 艹

芝

incorrect stroke count ⇨ see 2180

3-2 マ

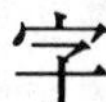

incorrect classification ⇨ see 2008

3-2 亼

令

incorrect classification ⇨ see 1995

3-2 亼

incorrect classification ⇨ see 1998
(nonstandard for 齢 1895)

3-2 亠

▶FILL

nonstandard for 充 2014

2162

3-3 口

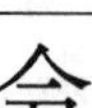

吊

2163 CHŌ tsu(ru) tsu(ri) tsu(rusu)

CH 吊 diào

Radical	Strokes
口 30	6-3-3
Grade	Freq
Reference	
2 - 3 - 3	

COMPOUNDS

❶ [original meaning] hang, suspend, swing, sling

吊り *tsuri* suspension, hanging; [also 釣り-] suspended, hanging; lifting by the loins (in sumo wrestling)

吊り上げる *tsuriageru* hang up, suspend; raise, lift

吊り棚 *tsuridana* hanging shelf

吊り革 *tsurikawa* (hand) strap

吊り輪 *tsuriwa* flying rings

ズボン吊り *zubontsuri* suspenders

❷ lift by the loins (in sumo wrestling)

吊り出す *tsuridasu* hold (the opponent) in the arms and carry him out of the ring

❸ [formerly 攣る *tsuru*] cramp, have a cramp

引き吊り *hikitsuri* cramp; scar

❹ [formerly 攣る *tsuru*] turn up, slant upward

吊り目 *tsurime* slanted [upturned] eyes

HOMOPHONES

tsuru ⇨ 釣 1674 攣 2919

tsuri ⇨ 釣 1674

NOTE

⇨ see USAGE note at 釣 1674

号 incorrect stroke count ⇨ see 2153

3-3 口

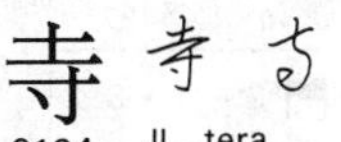

2164 JI tera

🄲🄷 寺 sì

Radical	Strokes
寸 41	6-3-3
Grade	**Freq**
Jōyō-2	744
2 - 3 - 3	

3-3 土

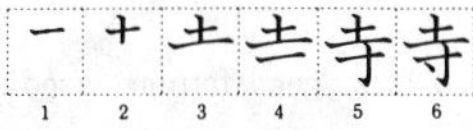

▶BUDDHIST TEMPLE

COMPOUNDS

❶ⓐ **Buddhist temple, temple**

ⓑ **suffix after names of Buddhist temples**

ⓒ counter for Buddhist temples

寺院 *jiin* temple

社寺 *shaji* shrines and temples

古寺 *koji* old temple

国分寺 *kokubunji* state-established provincial temple

東大寺 *tōdaiji* Todaiji Temple

金閣寺 *kinkakuji* Temple of the Golden Pavilion

一箇寺 *ikkaji* one temple

❷ [original meaning, now archaic] public office

KUN

【tera 寺】Buddhist temple, temple; (rent of a) gambling house

寺参り *teramairi* visit to a temple

尼寺 *amadera* nunnery, convent

山寺 *yamadera* mountain temple

寺銭 *terasen* rent of a gambling house

SYNONYMS

❶ **places of worship**

堂 temple building → 2589

塔 pagoda → 561

社 Shinto shrine → 840

宮 SHINTO SHRINE → 2274

院 monastery → 454

教 church → 1493

2165 KEI KE NAMES ka kiyo tama yoshi kado kiyoshi

🄲🄷 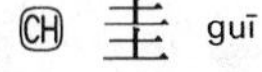 guī

Radical	Strokes
土 32	6-3-3
Grade	**Freq**
Names	2031
2 - 3 - 3	

3-3 土

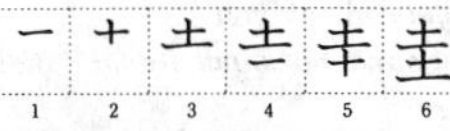

▶SHARP CORNER

COMPOUNDS

❶ **sharp corner (of ancient ceremonial jade tablet), point**

圭角の有る *keikaku no aru* angular, harsh-mannered, rough

尖圭コンジローム *senkei-konjirōmu* pointed condyloma

❷ [original meaning] ceremonial jade tablet with a rectangular base and pointed end used by the emperor in ancient China in appointing feudal lords

圭璧 *keiheki* [archaic] ritual jades worn by feudal lords in ancient China

刀圭 *tōkei* medicine, art of healing

NAMES

圭子 *keiko* female name

圭世子 *kayoko* female name

圭弘 *yoshihiro* male name

SYNONYMS

❶ **corners**

角 corner → 2047

隅 NOOK → 623

吉 **▶LUCKY**

2166 nonstandard for 吉 2167

3-3 土

3-3
士

吉 吉 吉 𠮷

2167 KICHI KITSU

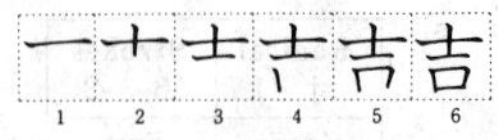

Ⓒ 吉 jí

Radical	Strokes
口 30	6-3-3
Grade	Freq
Jōyō	497
2-3-3	

▶LUCKY

COMPOUNDS

❶ [original meaning] **lucky, propitious, auspicious, favorable, good**

吉兆 *kitchō* good omen, lucky sign
吉日 *kichijitsu* (= *kitsujitsu*) lucky day
吉凶 *kikkyō* good or ill luck, fortune
吉事 *kichiji* auspicious event
大吉 *daikichi* excellent [good] luck
不吉 *fukitsu* ill omen, inauspiciousness

❷ good, excellent

吉報 *kippō* good news

INDEPENDENT

【kichi 吉】 good luck, good fortune, good omen

君の運勢は吉だ *Kimi no unsei wa kichi da*
You were born under a lucky star

SYNONYMS

❶ **good fortune**

嘉 HAPPY → 2340
祥 AUSPICIOUS → 948
瑞 AUSPICIOUS OMEN → 1027
禎 PROPITIOUS OMEN → 1031
幸 GOOD FORTUNE → 2216
福 FORTUNE → 1029

3-3
夂

各 各 各

2168 KAKU onoono

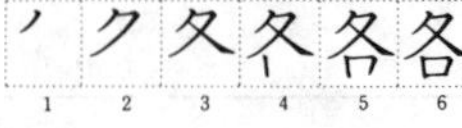

Ⓒ 各 gè gě

Radical	Strokes
口 30	6-3-3
Grade	Freq
Jōyō-4	213
2-3-3	

▶EACH

COMPOUNDS

● [also prefix] **each, every, every one, all, various**

各社 *kakusha* each company
各自 *kakuji* each one, every individual
各国 *kakkoku* every country, each nation, various states
各般 *kakuhan* every, various
各地 *kakuchi* every place, various parts [areas] (of the country)
各種の *kakushu no* each [every] kind, various
各位 *kakui* gentlemen, sirs
各団体 *kakudantai* each group
各大学 *kakudaigaku* each university, all universities
各一部 *kaku ichibu* one copy each

INDEPENDENT

【kaku 各】 each

KUN

【onoono 各】 each, every, respectively

各方 *onoonogata* all of you
各の考えで *onoono no kangae de* at individual discretion

SYNONYMS

● **all**

毎 EVERY → 2034
諸 VARIOUS → 1577
総 TOTAL → 1379
完 COMPLETE → 2201
丸 complete(ly) → 3417
皆 ALL → 2445
都 all → 1686
万 all → 2936
全 WHOLE → 2022
一 all in one → 3341
満 FULL → 607

名 名 名

2169 MEI MYŌ na -na

丿 ク タ タ 名 名
1 2 3 4 5 6

CH 名 míng

Radical	Strokes
口 30	6-3-3
Grade	**Freq**
Jōyō-1	147
2-3-3	

3-3 タ

▶NAME

COMPOUNDS

❶ⓐ [also suffix] **name, first name**
ⓑ (mere designation) name
名簿 *meibo* register [list] of names
名刺 *meishi* calling [business] card
名称 *meishō* appellation, name, title
名字(＝苗字) *myōji* surname, family name
氏名 *shimei* (full) name
署名 *shomei* signature, autograph
指名 *shimei* nomination, designation
匿名の *tokumei no* anonymous, incognito, pseudonymous
題名 *daimei* title
本名 *honmyō* one's real name
戒名 *kaimyō* posthumous Buddhist name
商品名 *shōhinmei* trade [brand] name
名目 *meimoku* name, title; pretext
名義 *meigi* name, title
名実 *meijitsu* name and reality
❷ (reputation, esp. good reputation) **name, fame, reputation**
名誉 *meiyo* honor, glory; dignity
名声 *meisei* fame, reputation
有名な *yūmei na* famous, noted, celebrated; notorious
著名 *chomei* prominence, eminence, distinction
汚名 *omei* bad name, ill fame, disgrace
功名 *kōmyō* great exploit; distinction, fame
❸ [also prefix]
ⓐ (of well known name) **famous, noted, celebrated**
ⓑ first-rate, master, excellent, fine, great
名物 *meibutsu* specialty, noted product
名所 *meisho* noted place, sights, scenic place
名勝 *meishō* place of scenic beauty
名門 *meimon* distinguished [noted] family; prestigeous establishment
名場面 *meibamen* famous [impressive] scene
名人 *meijin* (past) master, master hand, expert
名作 *meisaku* masterpiece, fine work
名画 *meiga* famous picture, masterpiece; noted film
名曲 *meikyoku* excellent [exquisite] piece of music, famous tune
名投手 *meitōshu* star pitcher
名探偵 *meitantei* great detective
❹ counter for persons
会員五名 *kaiin gomei* five members
❺ abbrev. of 名古屋 *nagoya*: Nagoya
名大 *meidai* Nagoya University
❻ persons or land of a feudal manor subject to taxation in medieval Japan
大名 *daimyō* daimyo, feudal lord
小名 *shōmyō* minor feudal lord

KUN

【na 名】 name, first name; (mere designation) name; (reputation, esp. good reputation) name, fame, reputation; pretext, plea, justification
名前 *namae* name, given name
本の名 *hon no na* name of a book
名高い *nadakai* famous, well-known
名ばかりの王 *na bakari no ō* a king in name only
名も無い人 *na mo nai hito* nameless [insignificant] person, nobody
正義の名に於て *seigi no na ni oite* in the name of justice

【-na -名】 [sometimes also -字] character, letter
仮名 *kana* kana, Japanese syllabary

SYNONYMS

❶ⓐ name
銘 name (inscribed by maker) → 1724
姓 SURNAME → 279
氏 FAMILY NAME → 2951
称 APPELLATION → 1160
号 DESIGNATION → 2153
題 TITLE → 3337
❷ repute
望 popularity → 2742
誉 HONOR → 2502
声 reputation → 2198
❸ⓑ excellent and superior
逸 exceptional → 3120
傑 outstanding → 155
英 DISTINGUISHED → 2238
秀 EXCELLENT → 2545
優 SUPERIOR → 177
上 of upper grade → 3404
絶 without match → 1353
卓 PROMINENT → 2064
快 splendid → 245

妙 MARVELOUS → 239
❹ **counters for persons**
人 counter for people → 3368

USAGE

-na
-名
[sometimes also -字] character, letter

-字
[usu. -名] character, letter

HOMOPHONES

-na ⇨ 字 2172

NOTE

⇨ see COMPOUND FORMATION for 苗字(=名字) *myōji* ⇨ 苗 2237

3-3
夕

多

2170 TA ō(i)

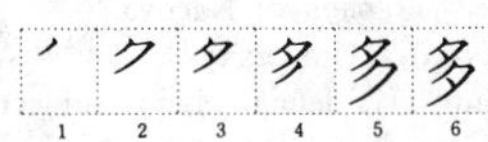

CH 多 duō

Radical	Strokes
夕 36	6-3-3
Grade	**Freq**
Jōyō-2	150
2 - 3 - 3	

▶MANY

COMPOUNDS

❶ⓐ [original meaning] **many, much, numerous**
ⓑ [prefix] **many-, multi-, poly-**
多角 *takaku* many-sided, versatile; polygonal
多数 *tasū* large number, multitude
多量 *taryō* large quantity, great deal
多面 *tamen* many sides, many phases
多分 *tabun* probably, perhaps, maybe
多少 *tashō* a little, somewhat
多目的 *tamokuteki* multipurpose
多神教 *tashinkyō* polytheism
多音節 *taonsetsu* polysyllable
❷ used phonetically for *ta*
滅多に *metta ni* rarely

INDEPENDENT

【ta 多】much, a great deal
多とする *ta to suru* appreciate, be thankful

KUN

【ō(i) 多い】much, lots of, many, numerous; frequent
多く *ōku* much, many, abundantly; largely, mostly
多目に *ōme ni* plenty, lots

SYNONYMS

❶ **many**
百 numerous → 2026
万 myriad → 2936
豊 PLENTIFUL → 2697
沢 plentiful → 267
穣 YIELDING ABUNDANTLY → 1250
裕 ABUNDANT → 1195
富 RICH → 2310

NOTE

⇨ see USAGE note at 大 3416

3-3
宀

安

2171 AN yasu(i) yasu(maru) yasu yasu(raka)

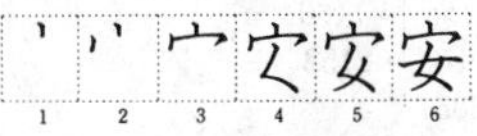

CH 安 ān

Radical	Strokes
宀 40	6-3-3
Grade	**Freq**
Jōyō-3	130
2 - 3 - 3	

▶PEACEFUL ▶INEXPENSIVE

COMPOUNDS

❶ⓐ **peaceful, tranquil, calm, quiet, gentle**
ⓑ **have peace of mind, feel contented, be at ease; give peace of mind, pacify**
ⓒ **public peace, order**
安住する *anjū suru* live peacefully
安泰 *antai* peace, security, tranquility
安眠 *anmin* quiet sleep, peaceful slumber
安定 *antei* stability; composure
安心 *anshin* peace of mind, relief
不安 *fuan* uneasiness, anxiety
治安 *chian* public peace and order
保安 *hoan* preservation of public peace
公安 *kōan* public peace
❷ **safe, secure**
安全 *anzen* safety, security
安否 *anpi* safety, welfare
安打 *anda* safe hit, base hit
安保条約 *anpo jōyaku* (Japan-U.S.) security treaty
❸ (without effort) **easy, comfortable**
安易な *an'i na* easy, easygoing
安産 *anzan* easy [smooth] delivery (of a baby)
安楽な *anraku na* comfortable, carefree, cozy

❹ **inexpensive, cheap**
安価 *anka* low price
安直な *anchoku na* cheap, inexpensive; easy, simple
❺ ammonia
硫安 *ryūan* ammonium sulfate
液安 *ekian* liquid ammonia

KUN

【yasu(i) 安い】
① inexpensive, cheap, low-priced
安く *yasuku* inexpensively
安値 *yasune* low price
安物 *yasumono* cheap article, bargain
安っぽい *yasuppoi* cheapish, flashy
じり安 *jiriyasu* gradual decline of stock prices
② peaceful, quiet, tranquil
安んじる *yasunjiru* feel at ease, ease a person's mind
安らぎ *yasuragi* peace of mind
気安い *kiyasui* friendly

【yasu(maru) 安まる】［usu. 休まる］feel rested; be set at ease
心の安まる時が無い *kokoro no yasumaru toki ga nai* have no moment of ease

【yasu 安】
① ［prefix］ cheap, inexpensive, low (cost)
安月給 *yasugekkyū* low salary
② ［suffix］ low price, cheap
十円安 *jūen'yasu* down 10 yen (stock market)
③ ［prefix］ lightheartedly, without due consideration
安請け合いする *yasuukeai suru* promise without due consideration

【yasu(raka) 安らか】
yasuraka na 安らかな peaceful, tranquil
安らかな眠り *yasuraka na nemuri* peaceful sleep

SYNONYMS

❶ⓐ **calm and peaceful**
康 peaceful → 3124
寧 peaceful → 2345
泰 TRANQUIL → 2583
静 QUIET → 1728
平 CALM → 3478
穏 CALM → 1235
ⓒ **peace**
和 PEACE → 1130
治 public order → 335
❸ **comfortable**
楽 COMFORTABLE → 2826
❸ **easy**
易 EASY (without difficulty) → 2411
簡 SIMPLE → 2721
軽 LIGHT → 1515
❹ **inexpensive**
廉 CHEAP → 3153
低 low-priced → 73

USAGE

yasui
安い
① inexpensive, cheap, low-priced
② peaceful, quiet, tranquil
易い
ⓐ easy, simple
ⓑ ［verbal suffix］ easy (to do)

HOMOPHONES

yasui ⇨ 易 2411
yasumaru ⇨ 休 52

NOTE

⇨ see also USAGE note at 休 52

字 字 字

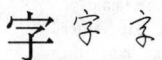

2172 JI aza azana▲ -na▲

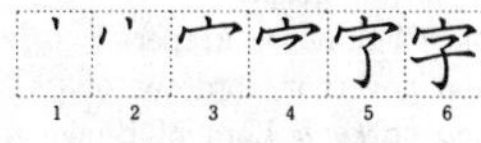

Ⓒⓗ 字 zì

Radical	Strokes
子 39	6-3-3
Grade	**Freq**
Jōyō-1	617
2-3-3	

3-3

▶**CHARACTER**

COMPOUNDS

❶ⓐ **character, letter; type; word**
ⓑ Chinese character, kanji, ideograph, logograph
ⓒ counter for (Chinese) characters
字体 *jitai* form of a character, type
字義 *jigi* character definition, meaning of a word ［term］
字引 *jibiki* dictionary
文字 *moji* character, letter
文字 *monji* character, letter; writings
ローマ字 *rōmaji* Roman letters
漢字 *kanji* Chinese characters, kanji
活字 *katsuji* movable type, printing type
数字 *sūji* figure, numeral
習字 *shūji* penmanship
赤字 *akaji* deficit, red figures
大文字 *ōmoji* capital letter
字音 *jion* Chinese-derived pronunciation of kanji, *on* reading
五百字 *gohyakuji* 500 (Chinese) characters
❷ nickname, pseudonym
字号 *jigō* nickname

名字(＝苗字) *myōji* surname, family name

INDEPENDENT

【ji 字】character, letter; word; Chinese character, ideograph; handwriting

細い字 *hosoi ji* slender character

字が上手である *ji ga jōzu de aru* have a good handwriting

KUN

【aza 字】village or town section in the Japanese addressing system

大字片山 *ōaza katayama* name of a town section

【azana 字】pseudonym, alias; nickname

【-na -字】[usu. -名] character, letter

仮字 *kana* kana, Japanese syllabary

SYNONYMS

❶ **characters**

文 LETTER → 1962

漢 kanji → 657

【aza】

○ **parts of towns**

丁 TOWN SUBSECTION (*chome*) → 3348

町 town section (*cho*) → 1113

街 CITY QUARTER → 576

区 WARD → 2963

HOMOPHONES

-na ⇨ 名 2169

NOTE

⇨ see USAGE note at 名 2169

⇨ see COMPOUND FORMATION for 苗字(＝名字) *myōji* ⇨ 苗 2237

3-3
宀

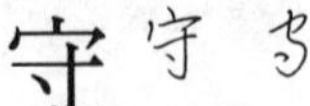

2173 SHU SU mamo(ru) mamo(ri) mori -mori kami▲

CH 守 shǒu

Radical	Strokes
宀 40	6-3-3
Grade	**Freq**
Jōyō-3	505
2-3-3	

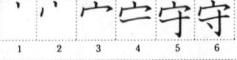

Stroke order: 1 2 3 4 5 6

▶PROTECT

COMPOUNDS

❶ⓐ **protect (from, against), defend, guard, watch over**

ⓑ guard, keeper

守備 *shubi* defense; fielding

守護 *shugo* protection, guard, defense, safeguard

守衛 *shuei* guard, doorkeeper

守株 *shushu* stupidity, lack of innovation

留守 *rusu* absence (from home); caretaking; defending when the lord is absent

攻守 *kōshu* offense and defense; batting and fielding

死守する *shishu suru* defend to the last, defend desperately

看守 *kanshu* jailer, prison guard

❷ **observe, obey, keep, adhere, abide by**

順守(＝遵守)する *junshu suru* observe, obey, follow, conform to

厳守 *genshu* strict observance

保守 *hoshu* conservatism; maintenance

❸ feudal governor, feudal lord

太守 *taishu* governor general, viceroy

国守 *kokushu* governor of a province, feudal lord

INDEPENDENT

【shu 守】*baseball* fielding

KUN

【mamo(ru) 守る】

① [formerly also 護る] protect, defend, guard, watch over

身を守る *mi o mamoru* defend oneself

見守る *mimamoru* watch, keep watch over

②ⓐ observe, obey, keep to, abide by

ⓑ adhere to

ⓒ keep (a promise), fulfill

規則を守る *kisoku o mamoru* keep to the regulations

【mamo(ri) 守り】protection, defense; good-luck charm

守り神 *mamorigami* guardian deity

お守り *omamori* good-luck charm

【mori 守】baby-sitting; nursemaid

お守 *omori* baby-sitting; baby-sitter

子守 *komori* baby-sitting; baby-sitter

【-mori -守】[also suffix] keeper

関守 *sekimori* barrier keeper

灯台守 *tōdaimori* lighthouse keeper

【kami 守】feudal governor, lord, baron

豊後の守 *bungo no kami* Lord of Bungo

SYNONYMS

❶ⓐ **protect**

護 PROTECT → 1648

衛 GUARD → 760

警 GUARD AGAINST → 2893

防 defend → 270

番 WATCH → 2748

保 PRESERVE → 96

看 CARE FOR → 3220

❷ **obey**

遵 OBEY → 3167

順 OBEY → 18

従 FOLLOW → 415

隷 be subordinate to → 1751

USAGE

mamoru

守る

① [formerly also 護る] protect, defend, guard, watch over

②ⓐ observe, obey, keep to, abide by

ⓑ adhere to

ⓒ keep (a promise), fulfill

護る [now usu. 守る] protect, defend, guard, watch over

HOMOPHONES

mamoru ⇨ 護 1648

kami ⇨ 上 3404

NOTE

⇨ see also USAGE note at 上 3404

⇨ see COMPOUND FORMATION for

留守 *rusu* ⇨ 留 2580

守株 *shushu* ⇨ 株 935

宅 宅 宅

2174 TAKU

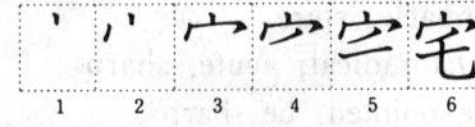

1 2 3 4 5 6

CH 宅 zhái

Radical	Strokes
宀 40	6-3-3
Grade	**Freq**
Jōyō-6	421
2 - 3 - 3	

3-3 宀

▶DWELLING HOUSE

COMPOUNDS

● [also suffix] (house where one lives) **dwelling house, home, abode, house, residence**

宅地 *takuchi* land for housing, residential land

お宅 *otaku* your home, your house; you

帰宅 *kitaku* homecoming

自宅 *jitaku* one's house, one's home

拙宅 *settaku* my home, my humble abode

住宅 *jūtaku* housing, dwelling house, residence

社宅 *shataku* company house

邸宅 *teitaku* residence, mansion

横江氏宅 *yokoeshi-taku* residence of Mr. Yokoe

INDEPENDENT

【taku 宅】 home, house; my home; my husband

宅の子供 *taku no kodomo* my [our] child

宅も参ります *Taku mo mairimasu* My husband is going too

SYNONYMS

● **houses**

家 HOUSE → 2273

屋 HOUSE → 3098

軒 house → 1459

戸 HOUSEHOLD → 1930

居 residence → 3080

邸 STATELY RESIDENCE → 1131

住 housing → 64

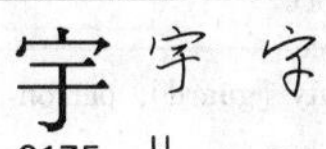

2175 U

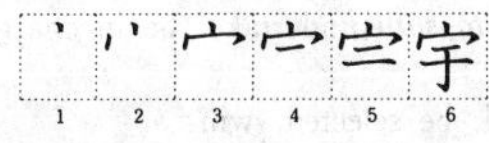

1 2 3 4 5 6

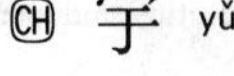

CH 宇 yǔ

Radical	Strokes
宀 40	6-3-3
Grade	**Freq**
Jōyō-6	716
2 - 3 - 3	

3-3 宀

▶UNIVERSE

COMPOUNDS

❶ **universe, infinite space, world**

宇宙 *uchū* universe, cosmos; (outer) space

宇内 *udai* the whole universe, the whole world

❷ⓐ large building, building with large roof

ⓑ counter for temple buildings

ⓒ [original meaning] roof, eaves

堂宇 *dōu* edifice, temple, hall

一宇の堂 *ichiu no dō* one temple building

八紘一宇 *hakkō-ichiu* the whole world under one roof

❸ the whole country, realm, land

御宇 *gyou* Imperial reign

❹ heart, soul

気宇広大な *kiukōdai na* large-minded, magnanimous

SYNONYMS

❶ **universe and space**

宙 SPACE → 2221

❷ⓐ **buildings**

殿 PALACE → 1792

閣 TALL MAGNIFICENT BUILDING → 3327

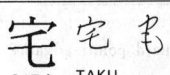

堂 HALL → 2589
館 PUBLIC BUILDING → 1748
舎 BUILDING → 2060
棟 BLOCK → 991
Ⓒ **roof**
屋 roof → 3098

3-3 小

尖 2176 SEN toga(ru)

ⒸⒽ 尖 jiān

Radical	Strokes
小 42	6-3-3
Grade	**Freq**
Reference	
2-3-3	

COMPOUNDS

[now also 先 *sen* 2394]
ⓐ (pointed end) point, end, tip
ⓑ [original meaning] pointed, acute
尖端 *sentan* pointed end, tip; spearhead; vanguard
尖兵 *senpei* advance-guard point; advance detachment
肺尖 *haisen* apex of a lung
尖塔 *sentō* pinnacle, spire
尖鋭な *sen'ei na* radical; acute, sharp
尖る *togaru* be pointed, be sharp

3-3 ⺌

当 當 2177 TŌ a(taru) a(tari)[1] a(tari)[2] a(teru) a(te) masa(ni)▲

ⒸⒽ 当 dāng dàng

Radical	Strokes
⺌ 42△	6-3-3
Grade	**Freq**
Jōyō-2	91
2-3-3	

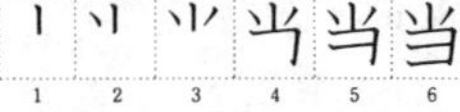

▶THE PRESENT ▶HIT

COMPOUNDS

❶ⓐ [also prefix] **the present, this, that, the said, the very**
ⓑ (occurring presently) **the present, present, current**
当局 *tōkyoku* the authorities concerned
当時 *tōji* at that time, in those days; at the present time
当人 *tōnin* the one concerned, the said person
当店 *tōten* this shop, we
当駅 *tōeki* this station
当該 *tōgai* the said, the concerned
当日 *tōjitsu* the appointed day, that day
当社 *tōsha* this firm; this shrine
当営業所 *tōeigyōsho* our [the present] business office
当分 *tōbun* for some time, for a while, for the present, temporarily
当面の *tōmen no* present, immediate; urgent, pressing
❷ **proper, appropriate, fitting, applicable**
当然 *tōzen* naturally, as a matter of course
当否 *tōhi* right or wrong, justice; propriety
正当な *seitō na* just, right, due; legal
適当な *tekitō na* suitable, fit; irresponsible
妥当な *datō na* proper, appropriate
該当する *gaitō suru* come under, be applicable to
不当な *futō na* unfair, unreasonable, unjust
本当の *hontō no* true, real, genuine
❸ⓐ **assign, allot, appropriate**
ⓑ **be assigned, undertake, take charge of**
配当 *haitō* apportionment, allotment
充当する *jūtō suru* allot, appropriate, earmark
日当 *nittō* daily allowance
勘当 *kandō* disinheritance
当番 *tōban* being on duty [guard]; person on duty
当直員 *tōchokuin* person on duty
担当する *tantō suru* undertake, be in charge of
❹ⓐ be elected, be selected, win
ⓑ abbrev. of 当選 *tōsen*: being elected, winning an election
当選 *tōsen* election to office; winning (a lottery)
当確 *tōkaku* be sure of being elected
❺ [original meaning] **be equivalent, correspond to, equal**
相当する *sōtō suru* correspond to, be proportionate; be suitable for, become
グラム当量 *guramutōryō* gram equivalent
❻ confront, come across, face
当面する *tōmen suru* face, confront
当惑する *tōwaku suru* be perplexed, be con-

fused [puzzled], be embarrassed
一騎当千の武者 *ikki-tōsen no musha* matchless warrior, match for a thousand
❼ pawn, mortgage
抵当 *teitō* mortgage, security
❽ guess, conjecture
見当 *kentō* estimate, guess; aim
❾ **unclassified compounds**
弁当 *bentō* box lunch, lunch, picnic lunch
芸当 *geitō* feat, trick, stunt

INDEPENDENT

【tō 当】 right, justice, propriety
当を得る *tō o uru* be right, be in order
【tō no 当の】 this, the present, that, the one in question
当の本人 *tō no honnin* the person himself

KUN

【a(taru) 当たる】
vi
①ⓐ hit, strike
ⓑ hit the mark
ⓒ strike against, touch, be touched, be exposed
ⓓ (be struck by light or heat) shine upon, strike; warm oneself, bask
突き当たる *tsukiataru* hit against, run into; come to the end of (a street)
体当たりする *taiatari suru* hurl oneself (at), dash oneself (against)
行き当たる *ikiataru* strike into, light on; come against
紛れ当たり *magureatari* chance hit, fluke
当たり障りの無い *atarisawari no nai* harmless and inoffensive
口当たり *kuchiatari* taste
手当たり次第 *teatari shidai* at random
風に当たる *kaze ni ataru* be exposed to wind
日当たり *hiatari* exposure to the sun
火に当たる *hi ni ataru* warm oneself at the fire
②ⓐ hit on, guess rightly; come true
ⓑ make a hit, come off, succeed; win in a lottery
思い当たる *omoiataru* occur to, strike
見当たらない *miataranai* not be found
心当たり *kokoroatari* knowledge, idea, clue
当たり屋 *atariya* lucky person, lucky batter; automobile accident faker
当たり役 *atariyaku* successful role
大当たり *ōatari* big hit, great success, bonanza; bumper crop
籤が当たった *Kuji ga atatta* I drew a prize
③ⓐ be equivalent to, be equal, correspond to
ⓑ be in relation to
一ドルは約百五十円に当たる *Ichidoru wa yaku hyakugojūen ni ataru* One dollar is roughly equivalent to 150 yen
彼は私の叔父に当たる *Kare wa watashi no oji ni ataru* He is my uncle
④ be applicable to, apply
この解釈は当たっていない *Kono kaishaku wa attatte inai* This interpretation does not apply
⑤ face, confront, attack
総当たり戦 *sōatarisen* round robin event
⑥ [in the form of 当たり *atari* or 当たって *atatte*] on the occasion of, at, in
この時に当たって *kono toki ni atatte* at this time [juncture]
⑦ undertake, take charge of
任に当たる *nin ni ataru* undertake a duty
⑧ [often in the form of 当たって見る *atatte miru*] try, have a look, take a chance, feel out, sound
人の意向を当たって見る *hito no ikō o atatte miru* sound out a person's thoughts
別の辞書に当たって見る *betsu no jisho ni atatte miru* try another dictionary
⑨ treat (unkindly)
当たり散らす *atarichirasu* find fault with everybody, make oneself disagreeable
八つ当たりする *yatsuatari suru* snarl (at the wrong person), take it out on (someone)
⑩ be assigned, be allotted; be selected
英語の時間に当たった *Eigo no jikan ni atatta* I was called on (to read aloud) in English class
⑪ lie, be located (in the direction of)
京都は東京の西に当たる *Kyōto wa tōkyō no nishi ni ataru* Kyoto lies to the west of Tokyo
⑫ [formerly also 中る] be poisoned, disagree with; suffer from
河豚に当たる *fugu ni ataru* get poisoned by swellfish
⑬ *theater jargon* next, coming
当たる日曜日 *ataru nichiyōbi* next Sunday
【a(tari)[1] 当たり】 hit, on-target impact; hit, success; clue, guess; manners; batting average; a bite (in fishing)
当たりを取る *atari o toru* make a hit
当たりを付ける *atari o tsukeru* give it a try
人当たりが良い *hitoatari ga yoi* have sociable manners
【a(tari)[2] 当たり】
① [suffix] per
一日当たり千円 *ichinichiatari sen'en* 1000 yen a day
② [in compounds] [often in the form of 当たって *atatte*] at present
差し当たり(＝差し当たって) *sashiatari* (＝*sashiatatte*) for the time being, for the present, at present
③ [in compounds] proper, appropriate
当たり前 *atarimae* proper, right, just; of

course

【a(teru) 当てる】

vt

①ⓐ hit, strike; touch
ⓑ hit the mark
ⓒ (cause to be struck) expose
当て逃げ *atenige* hit-and-run accident (causing property damage)
鞘当て *sayaate* rivalry ("touching of sheaths")
的を当てる *mato o ateru* hit the mark
日に当てる *hi ni ateru* expose to the sun
②ⓐ hit on, guess
ⓑ make a hit, succeed
言い当てる *iiateru* guess right
掘り当てる *horiateru* strike, find, dig up
③ apply (to), put (to), lay, place
当て嵌める *atehameru* apply, fit, adapt
手当て *teate* provision; medical care, treatment
手当 *teate* allowance, compensation, benefits
双眼鏡に目を当てる *sōgankyō ni me o ateru* put binoculars to one's eyes
座布団を当てる *zabuton o ateru* sit on a cushion
④ [usu. 充てる, but in compounds always 当てる] allot, assign, appropriate
割り当てる *wariateru* assign, allot
⑤ [usu. 宛てる, but in compounds also 当てる] assign Chinese characters to a word (as phonetic substitutes)
当前は当て字だ *tōzen wa ateji da* 当前 is written in phonetic substitute characters
⑥ call on (a pupil to answer a question)
問題を三人に当てる *mondai o sannin ni ateru* ask three pupils to solve a problem
⑦ [in the form of 当てられる *aterareru*]
ⓐ be poisoned by, agree badly with, be affected by
ⓑ be annoyed by (flirtation)
暑さに当てられる *atsusa ni aterareru* be affected by heat

【a(te) 当て】

① aim, end, goal
当ても無く *ate mo naku* aimlessly, at random
目当て *meate* guide, aiming; aim
② hopes, expectation
当て事 *ategoto* expectations, hopes; guessing
当てが外れる *ate ga hazureru* be disappointed
③ reliance, confidence, trust
当てにする *ate ni suru* rely upon, have trust in
④ [suffix] pad
肩当て *kataate* shoulder-pad

【masa(ni) 当に】 [always followed by 可し *beshi*] properly, naturally; it is proper to, ought to
当に人類を救う可き時だ *Masani jinrui o sukubeki toki da* Now is the time to save the human race

SYNONYMS

❶ⓐ this and that
本 THIS → 3502
今 THIS (week, etc.) → 1968
該 the said → 1519
同 the same → 2987
之 this → 3420
是 this → 2436
爾 THAT → 3587
彼 that → 290
ⓑ present
今 PRESENT → 1968
現 ACTUAL → 968
❷ suitable
適 SUITABLE → 3160
宜 RIGHT → 2223
便 CONVENIENT → 95
❸ⓐ allot
充 allot → 2014
❺ correspond to
該 CORRESPOND TO → 1519
準 apply correspondingly → 2856
❼ pawn
質 pawn → 2808

【ataru】

①ⓐ **collide**
突 DASH → 2230
衝 COLLIDE → 725

【ateru】

①ⓐ **strike**
打 STRIKE → 193
撃 STRIKE → 2863
拍 BEAT (strike repeatedly) → 304
撲 DEAL A BLOW → 733
殴 BEAT (strike a person) → 886
③ **touch**
触 TOUCH → 1518
接 CONTACT → 500

USAGE

❶ ataru
当たる
vi
①ⓐ hit, strike
ⓑ hit the mark
ⓒ strike against, touch, be touched, be exposed
ⓓ (be struck by light or heat) shine upon, strike; warm oneself, bask
②ⓐ hit on, guess rightly; come true
ⓑ make a hit, come off, succeed; win in a lottery
③ⓐ be equivalent to, be equal, correspond to
ⓑ be in relation to
④ be applicable to, apply
⑤ face, confront, attack

⑥ [in the form of 当たり *atari* or 当たって *atatte*] on the occasion of, at, in
⑦ undertake, take charge of
⑧ [often in the form of 当たって見る *atatte miru*] try, have a look, take a chance, feel out, sound
⑨ treat (unkindly)
⑩ be assigned, be allotted; be selected
⑪ lie, be located (in the direction of)
⑫ [formerly also 中る] be poisoned, disagree with; suffer from
⑬ *theater jargon* next, coming

中る
[now usu. 当たる] be poisoned, disagree with; suffer from

❷ atari
当たり
① [suffix] per
② [in compounds] [often in the form of 当たって *atatte*] at present
③ [in compounds] proper, appropriate

辺り
①ⓐ vicinity, neighborhood, surroundings
ⓑ [also suffix] (near that place or time) thereabouts, about
② for instance

❸ ateru
当てる
vt
①ⓐ hit, strike; touch
ⓑ hit the mark
ⓒ (cause to be struck) expose
②ⓐ hit on, guess
ⓑ make a hit, succeed
③ apply (to), put (to), lay, place
④ [usu. 充てる, but in compounds always 当てる] allot, assign, appropriate
⑤ [usu. 宛てる, but in compounds also 当てる] assign Chinese characters to a word (as phonetic substitutes)
⑥ call on (a pupil to answer a question)
⑦ [in the form of 当てられる *aterareru*]
ⓐ be poisoned by, agree badly with, be affected by
ⓑ be annoyed by (flirtation)

充てる
[sometimes also 当てる, but in compounds always 当てる] allot, assign, appropriate

宛てる
① address (a letter), direct
② [sometimes also 当てる] assign Chinese characters to a word (as phonetic substitutes)

★Both 当てる and 宛てる are used in the sense 'assigning Chinese characters', but the latter is preferred. However, in the compound *ateji* 'phonetic substitute, etc.', 当て字 is the preferred form.

❹ ate
当て
① aim, end, goal
② hopes, expectation
③ reliance, confidence, trust
④ [suffix] pad

-宛て
[suffix]
① addressed to
② per, apiece

HOMOPHONES

ataru ⇨ 中 3451
atari[2] ⇨ 辺 3029
ateru ⇨ 充 2014　宛 2222
ate ⇨ 宛 2222
masani ⇨ 正 3484　将 460

COMPOUND FORMATION

❶ 勘当 *kandō*
勘当 'disinheritance' originally meant to interrogate a criminal (勘) and assign (当 ❸ⓐ) the case to the authorities. This gave rise to the idea of finding disfavor with someone, as with one's children, which is how 勘当 acquired its current meaning.

❷ 当惑 *tōwaku*
当惑する 'be perplexed, etc.' is to confront (当 ❻) a perplexing (惑) situation.

❸ 弁当 *bentō*
The origin of 弁当 'box lunch, etc.' is not clear, but it appears that 当 ❾ is used phonetically without relation to its meaning.

❹ 当たり前 *atarimae*　当然 *tōzen*
当たり前 'proper, right, just; of course' consists of 当たり *atari*[2] ③ 'proper, appropriate' and 前. It derives from 当然 *tōzen* 'naturally, as a matter of course', which is a combination of 当 ❷ 'proper' and 然 'so, be definitely so'. Since 然 and 前 both have the *on* reading *zen*, the latter was mistakenly substituted for the former, and the resulting combination is pronounced in the *kun* reading, i.e., *atarimae*.

NOTE

⇨ see also USAGE note at 正 3484
⇨ see COMPOUND FORMATION for 相当 *sōtō* ⇨ 相 900

光　incorrect classification ⇨ see 2391　3-3

3-3 干

舌

2178

▶TONGUE

nonstandard for 舌 2186

3-3 幺

糸 絲 糸 𢆯

2179 SHI ito

Ⓒⓗ 丝 sī

Radical	Strokes
糸 120	6-6-0
Grade	**Freq**
Jōyō-1	626
2-3-3	

RADICAL 120

Standard form: 糸 *ito* 'thread' (素 繭 辮)

Left variant: 糸 *itohen* (終 経 約)

Description: used in characters related to threads, ropes or their qualities

▶THREAD

COMPOUNDS

❶ⓐ [original meaning] **thread, yarn, filament**

ⓑ silk thread, silk

ⓒ something as thin as thread

綿糸 *menshi* cotton yarn [thread]

絹糸 *kenshi* (=*kinuito*) silk thread

抜糸 *basshi* removal [extraction] of stitches

一糸も纏わずに *isshi mo matowazu ni* without a stitch of clothing on, stark-naked

製糸 *seishi* silk reeling, filature

蚕糸 *sanshi* silk-raising and reeling, sericulture

糸状虫 *shijōchū* heartworm, filaria

菌糸 *kinshi* hypha, mycelium

❷ [rare] stringed instruments

糸竹 *shichiku* musical instruments

❸ 1/100,000

一厘二毛三糸 *ichirin-nimō-sanshi* 0.00123

INDEPENDENT

【**shi** 糸】1/100,000

KUN

【**ito** 糸】[also suffix] thread, yarn, filament; (fish) line; string, chord (of musical instruments)

糸巻き *itomaki* spool, bobbin

毛糸 *keito* woolen yarn, wool

生糸 *kiito* raw silk (thread)

横糸 *yokoito* [also 緯糸 or 緯] woof

縦糸 *tateito* [also 経糸 or 経] warp

糸口 *itoguchi* [formerly also 緒] beginning, first step; clue

刺繡糸 *shishūito* embroidery thread

SYNONYMS

❶ⓐ **threads and fibers**

緯 woof → 1407

経 warp → 1331

繊 FIBER → 1413

維 FIBER → 1370

HOMOPHONES

itoguchi ⇨ 緒 1378 糸口 2179, 3382

yokoito ⇨ 緯 1407 横糸 1066, 2179
緯糸 1407, 2179

tateito ⇨ 経 1331 縦糸 1408, 2179
経糸 1331, 2179

NOTE

⇨ see USAGE notes at 緒 1378 and 緯 1407 and 経 1331

3-3 艹

芝 芝 之 芝

2180 SHI▲ shiba

Ⓒⓗ 芝 zhī

Radical	Strokes
艹 140	6-3-3
Grade	**Freq**
Jōyō	850
2-3-3	

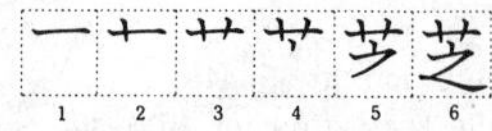

▶LAWN GRASS

COMPOUNDS

● [rare] purplish mushroom (traditionally considered good omen of long life)

霊芝 *reishi* *Fomes japonicus*

KUN

【**shiba** 芝】

ⓐ lawn grass, zoysia

ⓑ lawn, turf, sod
芝草 *shibakusa* lawn
芝地 *shibachi* grass plot
高麗芝 *kōraishiba* Korean lawn grass
芝生 *shibafu* lawn, turf
芝刈り機 *shibakariki* lawn mower
芝居 *shibai* play, drama

SYNONYMS

【shiba】

○ **kinds of grasses**
草 GRASS → 2263
笹 BAMBOO GRASS → 2663

USAGE

shiba

芝
ⓐ lawn grass, zoysia
ⓑ lawn, turf, sod
柴
brushwood, firewood

HOMOPHONES

shiba ⇨ 柴 2653

COMPOUND FORMATION

芝居 *shibai*
芝居 'play, drama' originated from the idea of sitting (居) on the lawn (芝 *shiba* ⓑ) to watch a play.

芋 芋 芋 芋

2181 U^ imo

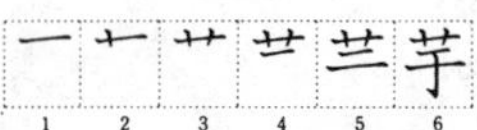

Ⓒⓗ 芋 yù

Radical	Strokes
艹 140	6-3-3
Grade	Freq
Jōyō	1869
2 - 3 - 3	

3-3 艹

▶POTATO

KUN

【imo 芋】

① potato; sweet potato; tuber
芋蔓 *imozuru* sweet potato vines
芋虫 *imomushi* green caterpillar
ジャガ芋 *jagaimo* potato, white potato
里芋 *satoimo* taro
焼き芋 *yakiimo* baked sweet potato

② [also prefix] unrefined, rustic
芋侍 *imozamurai* rustic (boorish) samurai

SYNONYMS

【imo】

① **vegetables**
菜 greens → 2305
豆 BEAN → 1943
蕗 BUTTERBUR → 2372

共

incorrect classification ⇨ see 2393

3-3 艹

至 至 至

2182 SHI ita(ru)

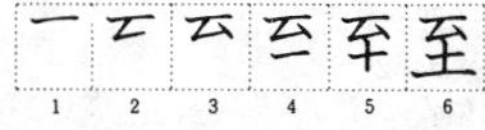

Ⓒⓗ 至 zhì

Radical	Strokes
至 133	6-6-0
Grade	Freq
Jōyō-6	1033
2 - 3 - 3	

3-3 至

RADICAL 133

Standard form: 至 *itaru* 'arrive' (致 臻)
Description: used in characters related to arriving or reaching

▶COME TO

COMPOUNDS

❶ [original meaning] **come to, arrive at, reach**
必至だ *hisshi da* be inevitable

❷ **to, as far as**
至徳島 *shitokushima* to Tokushima
乃至 *naishi* from...to..., between...and...; or

❸ **utmost, most, extreme**
至急の *shikyū no* urgent, pressing
至難の *shinan no* most difficult
至上 *shijō* supremacy
至極 *shigoku* very, most, exceedingly, extremely
至孝 *shikō* supreme filial piety

❹ solstice

夏至 *geshi* summer solstice
冬至 *tōji* winter solstice

KUN

【ita(ru) 至る】
① [sometimes also 到る] come to, arrive at, reach; lead (to)
至り *itari* extremity, utmost limit; result
至る処 *itaru tokoro* everywhere, all over
箱根に至る道 *hakone ni itaru michi* road leading to Hakone
② come to (do something), get to, result in
信じるに至る *shinjiru ni itaru* come to believe
大事に至る *daiji ni itaru* develop into a serious affair

SYNONYMS

❶ **arrive**
及 REACH TO → 3385
届く REACH → 3078
到 ARRIVE → 1264
着 ARRIVE → 3316
達 ATTAIN → 3139

❷ **direction indicators**
-行き bound for → 212
-向け (bound) for → 3052
迄 UP TO → 3201
以 TO THE...OF → 41
自 from → 3525
来 since → 3551

❸ **most**
最 MOST → 2472
極 EXTREME → 1017

USAGE

itaru
至る
① [sometimes also 到る] come to, arrive at, reach; lead (to)
② come to (do something), get to, result in
到る
[usu. 至る] arrive at, reach, come to

HOMOPHONES

itaru ⇨ 到 1264

3-3 羊 羊 羊
2183 YŌ hitsuji

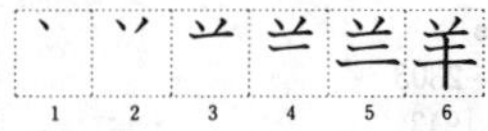

CH 羊 yáng

Radical	Strokes
羊 123	6-6-0
Grade	**Freq**
Jōyō-3	1688
2 - 3 - 3	

RADICAL 123
Standard form: 羊 *hitsuji* 'sheep' (群 羣 羸)
Top variant: ⺷ *hitsujikanmuri* (義 着 美)
Left variant: ⺶ *hitsujihen* (羝 羯 羚)
Description: used in characters related to sheep

▶SHEEP

COMPOUNDS

❶ [original meaning] **sheep, ram, ewe**
羊肉 *yōniku* mutton
羊毛 *yōmō* wool
羊頭狗肉 *yōtōkuniku* using a better name to sell inferior goods, crying wine and selling vinegar
羊羹 *yōkan* sweet jelly of beans
牧羊 *bokuyō* sheep farming
❷ something that envelops the fetus
羊水 *yōsui* amniotic fluid

KUN

【hitsuji 羊】 sheep, ram, ewe
羊飼い *hitsujikai* shepherd
羊雲 *hitsujigumo* floccus
子羊 *kohitsuji* lamb

SPECIAL READINGS

山羊▲ *yagi* goat
羊歯▲ *shida* fern

SYNONYMS

❶ **sheep**
未 the Ram → 3506
❶ **domesticated mammals**
豚 PIG → 976
馬 HORSE → 3296
牛 CATTLE → 3452
犬 DOG → 3464
猫 CAT → 535

USAGE

hitsuji
羊
sheep, ram, ewe
未
eighth sign of the Oriental zodiac: the Ram

HOMOPHONES

hitsuji ⇨ 未 3506

COMPOUND FORMATION

❶ 羊頭狗肉 *yōtōkuniku*

羊頭狗肉 'using a better name to sell inferior goods, etc.' is to sell dog (狗) meat (肉) under the pretense that it is sheep's (羊 ❶) head (頭).

❷ 羊羹 *yōkan*

羊羹 'sweet jelly of beans' originally referred to a broth (羹) of Chinese lamb (羊 ❶), but now refers to Japanese bean jelly, which resembles the former dish in shape (long and slender).

羊 2184

Radical	Strokes
羊 123	6-6-0
Grade	**Freq**
Radical	
2 - 3 - 3	

3-3 丷

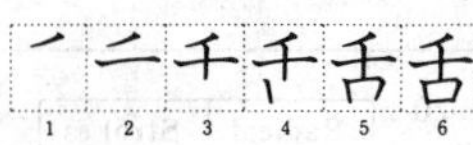

RADICAL 123

hitsujikanmuri, variant of 羊 *hitsuji* 'sheep'

⇨ see 羊 2183 for radical description

妄 2185

▶**RASH**

nonstandard for 妄 2016

3-3 亡

舌 2186

舌 舌 舌 ZETSU shita

CH 舌 shé

Radical	Strokes
舌 135	6-6-0
Grade	**Freq**
Jōyō-5	1673
2 - 3 - 3	

3-3 千

一 二 千 千 舌 舌 (1 2 3 4 5 6)

RADICAL 135

Standard form: 舌 *shita* 'tongue'(舒)

Left variant: 舌 *shitahen* (舐)

Description: used in characters related to actions performed by the tongue

▶**TONGUE**

COMPOUNDS

❶ [original meaning] **tongue**

舌端 *zettan* tip of the tongue; speech, way of talking

舌頭 *zettō* tip of the tongue; speech, way of talking

舌音 *zetsuon* lingual sound

舌癌 *zetsugan* cancer of the tongue

❷ (manner of speech) **tongue, speech, language, words**

舌戦 *zessen* war of words

舌鋒 *zeppō* (sharp) tongue

弁舌 *benzetsu* speech

毒舌 *dokuzetsu* wicked tongue, abusive language, blistering remarks

饒舌 *jōzetsu* garrulity, loquacity

筆舌に尽くし難い *hitsuzetsu ni tsukushigatai* be beyond description

KUN

【**shita** 舌】tongue; tongue-shaped objects as a clapper or reed

舌打ち *shitauchi* tongue clicking

猫舌だ *nekojita da* have a tongue too sensitive to heat

舌触りが良い *shitazawari ga yoi* be soft and pleasant on the tongue

舌足らずな *shitatarazu na* lisping; lame (expression)

二枚舌 *nimaijita* double-dealing

SYNONYMS

❶ **mouth parts**

歯 TOOTH → 2476

唇 LIP → 2737

❷ **speech**

口 MOUTH → 3382

言 SPEECH → 1941

談 TALK → 1569

3-3 亼

会 合

incorrect classification ⇨ see 2–4

3-4 口

呂

2187 RO RYO NAMES tomo naga

CH 吕 lǚ

Radical	Strokes
口 30	7-3-4
Grade	Freq
Names	2020
2-3-4	

▶**PHONETIC** [ro]

COMPOUNDS

❶ **used phonetically for *ro***
風呂 *furo* bath
語呂 *goro* sound harmony
伊呂波 *iroha iroha*, the Japanese syllabary [alphabet]

❷ ancient musical note in traditional Chinese and Japanese music
呂律 *roretsu* articulation
律呂 *ritsuryo* Chinese system of musical sounds, standard tones

❸ [original meaning, now archaic] backbone

NAMES
人麻呂 *hitomaro* male name
登呂 *toro* place name
呂久 *tomohisa* male name

SYNONYMS
❶ **phonetic** [r]
路 phonetic [ru] → 1533
羅 PHONETIC [ra] → 2622
❷ **musical elements**
調 TONE → 1567
韻 RHYME → 1811
律 RHYTHM → 363
拍 BEAT → 304

3-4 口

足

2188 SOKU ashi ta(riru) ta(ru) ta(su)

CH 足 zú

Radical	Strokes
足 157	7-7-0
Grade	Freq
Jōyō-1	277
2-3-4	

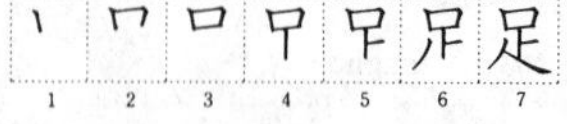

RADICAL 157
Standard form: 足 *ashi* 'foot' (趸 躄 蹇)
Left variant: 𧾷 *ashihen* (路 跡 踊)
Description: used in characters related to the foot or actions using feet

▶**FOOT** ▶**SUFFICE**

COMPOUNDS

❶ⓐ [original meaning] **foot, leg**
ⓑ **travel on foot, walk, run**
足跡 *sokuseki* footprint, footmark; the course of one's life, one's achievements
義足 *gisoku* artificial leg
蛇足 *dasoku* superfluity, redundancy
足労 *sokurō* trouble of going somewhere
遠足 *ensoku* excursion, hike, long walk
発足 *hossoku* (= *hassoku*) starting, inauguration
長足の進歩 *chōsoku no shinpo* rapid progress [strides]

❷ counter for steps
一足飛び *issokutobi* at a leap, at a jump

❸ **counter for pairs of footwear, as shoes, slippers or socks**
靴一足 *kutsu issoku* a pair of shoes

❹ **suffice, be enough, be adequate**
満足 *manzoku* satisfaction, contentment
不足 *fusoku* insufficiency, shortage, deficit; want; dissatisfaction
自足 *jisoku* self-sufficiency

❺ supplement
補足 *hosoku* supplement, replenishment
充足 *jūsoku* sufficiency

KUN

【ashi 足】
①ⓐ leg, limb; foot, paw
ⓑ [also 脚] (leg-shaped support) leg
ⓒ foot (of something standing), base
足腰 *ashikoshi* legs and loins
足場 *ashiba* scaffold, footing, foothold
手足 *teashi* hands and feet, limbs
机の足 *tsukue no ashi* legs of a table

垂線の足 *suisen no ashi* foot of a perpendicular line

②ⓐ [also suffix] walking, traveling
ⓑ step, stride
ⓒ means of transportation
足取り *ashidori* one's manner of walking; trace (of a culprit's movement); (price) movement
足並み *ashinami* pace, step
千鳥足 *chidoriashi* tottering gait
一足 *hitoashi* a step
通勤の足 *tsūkin no ashi* facilities for commutation

③ [also 脚] movement, pace
出足 *deashi* start
雨足 *amaashi* density of the falling rain; pace (of the approaching shower)

④ trace
足が付く *ashi ga tsuku* be traced [tracked]

⑤ deficit
足が出る *ashi ga deru* exceed the budget, do not cover the expense

⑥ relation
足を洗う *ashi o arau* wash one's hands of, quit (the shady business); wash one's feet
足入れ *ashiire* tentative marriage

【ta(riru) 足りる】 suffice, be sufficient [enough]; serve, answer, do; be satisfied [content]; be worth (doing); [in negative constructions] (not) intelligent
千円で足りる *Sen'en de tariru* A thousand yen will suffice
事足りる *kototariru* answer the purpose, be sufficient
満ち足りる *michitariru* be content, have enough, be happy
物足りない *monotarinai* be somehow unsatisfied, feel something wanting; be unsatisfactory
一見するに足りる *ikken suru ni tariru* be worth seeing
少少足りない *shōshō tarinai* somewhat weak in the head; somewhat lacking

【ta(ru) 足る】 literary or dialect form of **tariru** 足りる
舌足らずな *shitatarazu na* lisping; lame (expression)

【ta(su) 足す】 add; supplement, make up for; do (one's business)
足し算 *tashizan* addition
接ぎ足す *tsugitasu* add, extend
用を足す *yō o tasu* do one's business; relieve oneself, go to stool

SPECIAL READINGS

足袋 *tabi* Japanese [digitated] socks, *tabi*
百足▲ *mukade* centipede

SYNONYMS

❶ⓐ foot
脚 LEG → 974
ⓑ walk
脚 move on foot → 974
徒 go on foot → 416
歩 WALK → 2416
踏 TREAD → 1587
❸ footwear
履 footwear → 3171
靴 SHOES → 1781
駄 clogs → 1821
❹ suffice
満 satisfied → 607
❺ supplement
補 SUPPLEMENT → 1194
給 SUPPLY → 1350
充 fill up (a vacancy) → 2014

【tasu】
○ add
加 ADD → 38

USAGE

ashi
足
①ⓐ leg, limb; foot, paw
ⓑ [also 脚] (leg-shaped support) leg
ⓒ foot (of something standing), base
②ⓐ [also suffix] walking, traveling
ⓑ step, stride
ⓒ means of transportation
③ [also 脚] movement, pace
④ trace
⑤ deficit
⑥ relation
脚
① [also 足] (leg-shaped support) leg
② [also 足] movement, pace
③ bottom radical of Chinese characters, leg radical

HOMOPHONES

ashi ⇨ 脚 974

NOTE

⇨ see COMPOUND FORMATION for 蛇足 *dasoku* ⇨ 蛇 1343

3-4 口

呈 呈 呈 呈

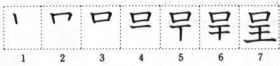

2189 TEI

Ⓒⓗ 呈 chéng

Radical	Strokes
口 30	7-3-4
Grade	**Freq**
Jōyō	1666
2-3-4	

丶 冖 口 旦 早 呈 呈 (1 2 3 4 5 6 7)

▶PRESENT

COMPOUNDS

❶ [also suffix] **present (a gift), give**
呈上 *teijō* presentation
進呈する *shintei suru* proffer, present
謹呈する *kintei suru* present, make a present
贈呈 *zōtei* presentation
案内書呈 *annaishotei* presentation of a guidebook

❷ (offer to view) **present, show, display, exhibit**
呈示する *teiji suru* exhibit, present
呈色 *teishiki* color, coloring
露呈 *rotei* exposure, disclosure

INDEPENDENT

【teisuru 呈する】present, offer; present (an appearance), display, assume (a color)
苦言を呈する *kugen o teisuru* give bitter-pill advice
青色を呈する *aoiro o teisuru* assume a blue color, turn blue

SYNONYMS

❶ **give**
進 present to a superior → 3121
贈 PRESENT A GIFT → 1634
賄 BRIBE → 1529
賜 DEIGN TO GIVE → 1585
授 CONFER → 492
与 GIVE → 3421
上 give (to superior or others) → 3404
下 give (to inferior or speaker) → 3378
呉れる give (to speaker) → 2549

❷ **show**
示 SHOW → 1936
見せる show → 2544

3-4 口

邑

2190 YŪ

Ⓒⓗ 邑 yì

Radical	Strokes
邑 163	7-7-0
Grade	**Freq**
Reference	
2-3-4	

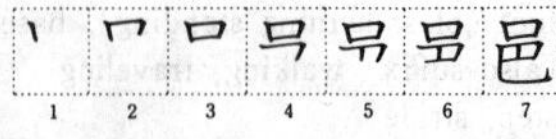

RADICAL 163
Standard form: 邑 *mura* 'city'
Right variant: 阝 *ōzato* (部 都 郎)
Description: used in characters related to place names or towns

COMPOUNDS

ⓐ city, town
ⓑ [archaic] village
都邑 *toyū* city, town
邑落 *yūraku* hamlet

3-4 口

𧾷

2191

Radical	Strokes
足 157	7-7-0
Grade	**Freq**
Radical	
2-3-4	

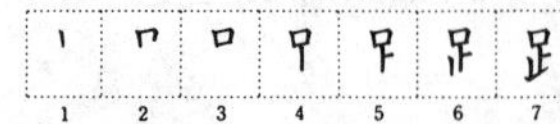

RADICAL 157
ashihen, variant of 足 *ashi* 'foot'
⇨ see 足 2188 for radical description

3-4 口

呈 2192

▶PRESENT
nonstandard for 呈 2189

3-4 土

赤 2193

赤 赤 𧺆 (CH) 赤 chì

SEKI SHAKU aka aka- aka(i) aka(ramu) aka(rameru)

Radical	Strokes
赤 155	7-7-0
Grade	**Freq**
Jōyō-1	510
2-3-4	

一 十 土 キ 赤 赤 赤 (1 2 3 4 5 6 7)

RADICAL 155
Standard form: 赤 *aka* 'red'
Left variant: 𧺆 *akahen* (赦 赫 赭)
Description: used in characters related to the color red

▶RED

COMPOUNDS

❶ⓐ **red, crimson, scarlet**
ⓑ **Red, Communist**
赤銅 *shakudō* gold-copper alloy
赤外線 *sekigaisen* infrared rays
赤痢 *sekiri* dysentery
赤十字 *sekijūji* Red Cross
赤色 *sekishoku* red; Communism
赤化する *sekka* (=*sekika*) *suru* turn red; go Communist
赤軍 *sekigun* Red Army

❷ utter, bare
赤貧 *sekihin* extreme poverty
赤裸裸な *sekirara na* naked, frank

❸ sincere, loyal
赤心 *sekishin* one's true heart, sincerity

❹ equator
赤道 *sekidō* equator
赤経 *sekkei* right ascension

KUN

【aka 赤】 red, crimson, scarlet; Red, Communist
赤紫 *akamurasaki* purplish red
赤線 *akasen* red-light district
赤字 *akaji* deficit, red figures
赤ん坊 *akanbō* baby
赤金(=銅) *akagane* copper
赤旗 *akahata* Red Flag

【aka- 赤-】
① [prefix] red
赤電話 *akadenwa* red public phone
② utter, total
赤裸 *akahadaka* stark naked

【aka(i) 赤い】 [sometimes also 紅い] red, crimson, scarlet

【aka(ramu) 赤らむ】 become red
赤らんだ *akaranda* ruddy, florid

【aka(rameru) 赤らめる】 blush, redden
顔を赤らめる *kao o akarameru* blush, change color

SPECIAL READINGS

真っ赤 *makka* deep red

SYNONYMS

❶ⓐ **red colors**
紅 CRIMSON → 1277
朱 VERMILION → 3531
丹 CINNABAR → 3441
緋 SCARLET → 1369
茜 MADDER → 2261
ⓑ **Communism**
左 the Left → 2974
共 Communism → 2393

USAGE

❶ **akai**
赤い
[sometimes also 紅い] red, crimson, scarlet
紅い
[usu. 赤い] crimson, deep red

❷ **akaramu**
赤らむ
become red
明らむ
brighten

HOMOPHONES

akagane ⇨ 銅 1721 赤金 2193, 2057
akai ⇨ 紅 1277
akaramu ⇨ 明 855

COMPOUND FORMATION

赤ん坊 *akanbō*
赤ん坊 'baby' derives from the red (赤 *aka*) state in which an infant is born. 坊 is a suffix of endearment.

NOTE

⇨ see also USAGE note at 銅 1721

3-4
土

走 走 走 2194

sō hashi(ru)

㊥ 走 zǒu

Radical	Strokes
走 156	7-7-0
Grade	**Freq**
Jōyō-2	660
2 - 3 - 4	

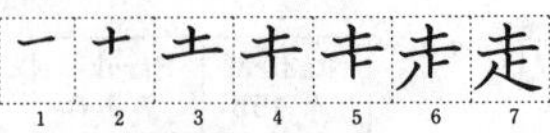

RADICAL 156

Standard form: 走 *hashiru* 'run'
Enclosure: 走 *sōnyō* (起 越 超)
Description: used in characters related to running or advancing quickly

▶RUN

COMPOUNDS

❶ⓐ [original meaning] **run, dash, rush**
ⓑ [suffix] run, dash
走者 *sōsha* runner
御馳走 *gochisō* feast, treat
奔走する *honsō suru* bustle about, exert oneself for, devote oneself to
競走 *kyōsō* race, sprint
独走 *dokusō* running alone; easy victory, walkover
五十メートル走 *gojūmētorusō* 50 meter dash

❷ run away, flee
逃走 *tōsō* flight, escape
脱走する *dassō suru* desert, escape

❸ travel by vehicle or craft, drive, sail
走行 *sōkō* traveling, driving
暴走 *bōsō* reckless driving; running wild
滑走路 *kassōro* runway
帆走 *hansō* sailing by boat

INDEPENDENT

【sō 走】 *baseball* base running

KUN

【hashi(ru) 走る】 run, dash, rush; drive, ride; turn to, become; go to excess; flow
走り *hashiri* season's first supply (of tomatoes); running; *dialect* sink
走り書き *hashirigaki* running script, cursive writing
四十キロで突っ走る *yonjukkiro de tsuppashiru* fly along at 40 kph
左翼に走る *sayoku ni hashiru* turn leftist
口走る *kuchibashiru* (run off at the mouth) blurt out
ペンが走る *pen ga hashiru* one's pen flows

SPECIAL READINGS

師走 *shiwasu* December

SYNONYMS

❶ run
奔 RUSH → 2218
駆 gallop → 1823

❷ escape
逃 ESCAPE → 3095
亡 flee → 3402
脱 ESCAPE FROM → 973

❸ travel by vehicle
乗 RIDE → 3576
航 NAVIGATE → 1318
騎 RIDE ON HORSEBACK → 1834

COMPOUND FORMATION

御馳走 *gochisō*
御馳走 'feast, treat' is a combination of the honorific prefix 御, 馳 'run' and 走 ❶ⓐ 'run'. The idea is that a person who prepares a feast must run around to gather ingredients.

NOTE

⇨ see COMPOUND FORMATION for 師走 *shiwasu* ⇨ 師 1326

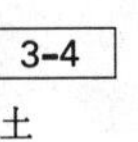

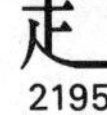

2195

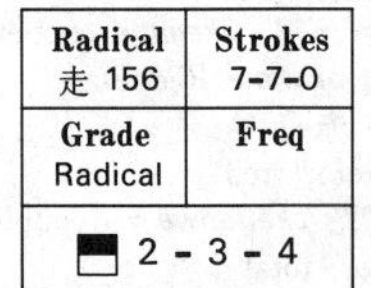

Radical	Strokes
走 156	7-7-0
Grade	**Freq**
Radical	
2 - 3 - 4	

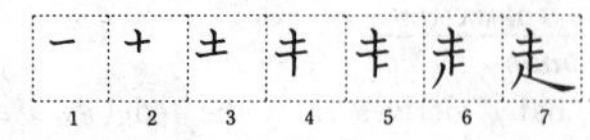

RADICAL 156

sōnyō, variant of 走 *hashiru* 'run'
⇨ see 走 2194 for radical description

売 賣 売 𡚁

2196 BAI u(ru) u(reru)

CH 卖 mài

Radical	Strokes
士 33△	7-3-4
Grade	Freq
Jōyō-2	207
2 - 3 - 4	

3-4 士

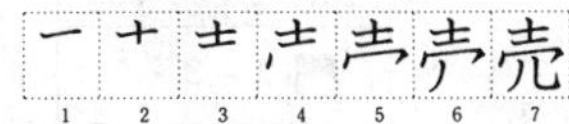

1 2 3 4 5 6 7

▶SELL

COMPOUNDS

❶ⓐ [original meaning] **sell**

ⓑ **sale**

売買 *baibai* buying and selling, trade
売店 *baiten* booth, stand; store
売却 *baikyaku* sale
売春 *baishun* prostitution
商売 *shōbai* trade, business, commerce
販売 *hanbai* sale, selling, marketing
発売する *hatsubai suru* sell, put on the market
即売 *sokubai* sale on the spot, spot sale
特売 *tokubai* special sale, bargain sale

❷ⓐ sell (oneself to the public), make known

ⓑ sell out (one's country)

売名 *baimei* self-advertisement, publicity stunt
売国 *baikoku* selling out [betrayal] of one's own country

KUN

【u(ru) 売る】 sell; sell out, betray; sell (oneself to the public), make known

売り *uri* sale, selling
売り上げ *uriage* sales, proceeds
売り出す *uridasu* put on sale; rise in fame
小売り *kouri* retail, sale in small quantities
卸売り *oroshiuri* wholesale
国を売る *kuni o uru* betray one's country (to an enemy)
名を売る *na o uru* make oneself famous, gain a reputation

【u(reru) 売れる】 sell, be in demand, enjoy a large sale; be well known, become popular

売れ行き *ureyuki* sales, demand
売れっ子 *urekko* person of great popularity

SYNONYMS

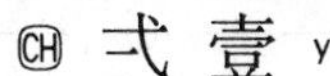
❶ⓐ & ❶ⓑ **sell and trade**

販 ENGAGE IN SALES → 1477
商 TRADE → 2116
卸す WHOLESALE → 1447
貿 TRADE → 2601
易 EXCHANGE → 2411

COMPOUND FORMATION

売春 *baishun*

売春 'prostitution' is, literally, to sell (売 ❶ⓐ) spring (春). In this instance 春 refers to lovemaking—what a picturesque way to depict prostitution!

壱 壹 壱 𡔜

2197 ICHI

CH 弌 壹 yī

Radical	Strokes
士 33	7-3-4
Grade	Freq
Jōyō	1820
2 - 3 - 4	

3-4 士

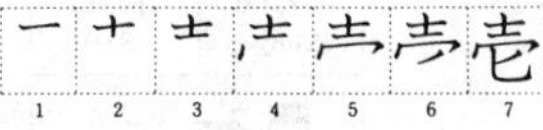

1 2 3 4 5 6 7

▶ONE

COMPOUNDS

● **one**—used in legal documents and checks

金壱阡参百円也 *kin issen sanbyaku-en nari* one thousand three hundred yen

INDEPENDENT

【ichi 壱】 one (⇒●)

SYNONYMS

● **one**

一 ONE → 3341
片- ONE OF TWO → 3461
隻 ONE OF A PAIR → 2755
単 SINGLE → 2256
個 INDIVIDUAL → 117

3-4
土

声 聲

2198 SEI SHŌ koe kowa-

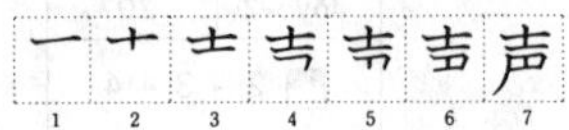

Ⓒ 声 shēng

Radical	Strokes
土 33△	7-3-4
Grade	Freq
Jōyō-2	405
2-3-4	

▶**VOICE**

COMPOUNDS

❶ⓐ [original meaning] **voice, sound**

ⓑ (tone produced in singing) voice

ⓒ *phonetics* voice

声調 *seichō* tone of voice, style; tone (in Chinese phonetics)

声帯 *seitai* vocal cords

音声 *onsei* voice, sound

発声 *hassei* vocalization, utterance

銃声 *jūsei* sound of gunfire

擬声語 *giseigo* onomatopoeic word

大音声 *daionjō* very loud voice

声楽 *seigaku* vocal music

混声合唱 *konsei-gasshō* mixed chorus

有声音 *yūseion* voiced sound

❷ tone in Chinese phonetics

四声 *shisei* the four tones (of Chinese)

第一声 *daiissei* first tone

❸ speak out, announce, declare

声明 *seimei* declaration

声援 *seien* shout of encouragement, cheering; support

声優 *seiyū* radio actor; dialogue speaker (in dubbing)

❹ reputation

声価 *seika* reputation, fame

名声 *meisei* fame, reputation

KUN

【koe 声, kowa- 声-】 [also suffix] voice, sound, cry; word; opinion

読者の声 *dokusha no koe* reader's voice

声色 *kowairo* tone of voice; vocal mimicry

歌声 *utagoe* singing (voice)

大声 *ōgoe* loud voice

掛け声 *kakegoe* shout to mark time, shout of encouragement

叫び声 *sakebigoe* shout, outcry

金切り声 *kanakirigoe* shrill voice, scream

SYNONYMS

❶ **kinds of sound**

音 SOUND → 2070

響 reverberation → 2878

韻 melodious tone → 1811

玲 TINKLING OF JADES → 910

❹ **repute**

誉 HONOR → 2502

名 NAME → 2169

望 popularity → 2742

NOTE

⇨ see COMPOUND FORMATION for 擬声語 *giseigo* ⇨ 擬 788

3-4
土

志

2199 SHI SHIRINGU△ kokoroza(su) kokorozashi

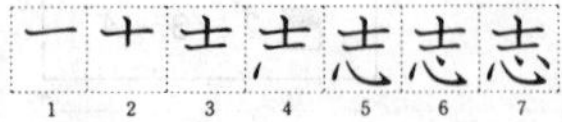

Ⓒ 志 zhì

Radical	Strokes
心 61	7-4-3
Grade	Freq
Jōyō-5	819
2-3-4	

▶**AMBITION**

COMPOUNDS

❶ⓐ **ambition, aim, intention, purpose, aspiration, desire, wishes**

ⓑ [original meaning] **have ambition to, intend, aim, aspire to**

志願する *shigan suru* volunteer, apply for

立志 *risshi* fixing one's aim in life

大志 *taishi* lofty ambition, aspiration

初志 *shoshi* original aim [intention]

有志の *yūshi no* voluntary, interested

志向 *shikō* intention, aim

志士 *shishi* noble minded patriot

❷ **will, mind, purpose, determination**

闘志 *tōshi* fighting spirit, will to fight

意志 *ishi* will, volition

同志 *dōshi* like-minded person, comrade

遺志 *ishi* wishes of a deceased person

❸ goodwill, kindness, benevolence

厚志 *kōshi* kindness, kind thought [intention]

寸志 *sunshi* little token of one's gratitude, small present

篤志家 *tokushika* benevolent person; volunteer, supporter

❹ *hist*

ⓐ historical record, annals; story

ⓑ record, write down
三国志 *sangokushi* Annals of the Three Kingdoms
聊斎志異 *ryōsai shii* *Liao Zhai Zhi I* (Strange Stories from a Chinese Studio)
❺ shilling
百志 *hyakushiringu* 100 shillings

KUN

【kokoroza(su) 志す】 aim, have an ambition for, intend, aspire
学問に志す *gakumon ni kokorozasu* set one's heart on learning

【kokorozashi 志】 ambition, aspiration, intention, desire, wish; will, mind; goodwill, kindness, gift
青雲の志 *seiun no kokorozashi* high [lofty] ambition
本の志ですが *Hon no kokorozashi desu ga* Please accept this as a small token of my appreciation

SYNONYMS

❶ⓐ & ❷ will and intention
意 MIND → 2136
図 intention → 3071
気 mind to do something → 3194
念 thought of doing something → 2059
趣 PURPOSE → 3317
欲 DESIRE → 1475

NOTE

⇨ see USAGE note at 士 3405

条 條 条 條

2200 JŌ

Ⓒⓗ 条 tiáo

Radical	Strokes
木 75	7-4-3
Grade	**Freq**
Jōyō-5	357
2-3-4	

3-4 夂

▶ARTICLE

COMPOUNDS

❶ⓐ article, item, section, clause
ⓑ (written regulations) **articles (of law), provision, stipulation, rule, law**
ⓒ **counter for articles or sections**
条項 *jōkō* articles (and clauses), terms
条目 *jōmoku* article, stipulation
条件 *jōken* condition; item, proviso
箇条書きする *kajōgaki suru* itemize
信条 *shinjō* principle, creed, article of a religion
教条 *kyōjō* tenet, dogma
条文 *jōbun* text (of a regulation), provision
条約 *jōyaku* treaty
条例 *jōrei* regulations, rules, law
前条 *zenjō* preceding article
憲法第九条 *kenpō daikyūjō* Article 9 of the constitution
百三条 *hyakusanjō* 103 articles (of a constitution)

❷ⓐ strip, stripe, streak, vein, line, groove, thread
ⓑ **strip of material (esp. metal), rod, rail**
ⓒ counter for striplike slender objects
ⓓ strips of land serving as units of subdivision; avenue (esp. in Kyoto)
条痕 *jōkon* streak
条虫 *jōchū* tapeworm
星条旗 *seijōki* the Stars and Stripes
多条カム *tajōkamu* multigrooved cam
鉄条網 *tetsujōmō* barbed wire entanglements
軌条 *kijō* rails
一条の煙 *ichijō no kemuri* a wisp of smoke
条里制 *jōrisei* system of land subdivision in ancient Japan
三条 *sanjō* name of a street in Kyoto

❸ thread of presentation, line of reasoning
条理 *jōri* reason, logic

❹ state of affairs
別条 *betsujō* something wrong, accident
蕭条たる *shōjōtaru* bleak, dreary, lonely

❺ [original meaning, now archaic] branch, twig
柳条 *ryūjō* willow twig

INDEPENDENT

【jō 条】
① article
この条の規定に従い *kono jō no kitei ni shitagai* in accordance with the provisions of this article
②ⓐ although, though
ⓑ [archaic] since, as; that
愚鈍とは言い条 *gudon to wa ii jō* fool as he is
係る次第に候条 *kakaru shidai ni sōrō jō* such being the case

SYNONYMS

❶ parts of writing
款 ARTICLE → 1700
項 CLAUSE → 567
目 ITEM → 3043
箇 item → 2700
節 paragraph → 2691
段 passage → 1144

章 CHAPTER → 2117
❷ⓐ **line**
脈 VEIN → 953
筋 THREADLIKE STRUCTURE → 2678

線 LINE → 1392
棒 straight line → 983
軸 AXIS → 1514

3-4
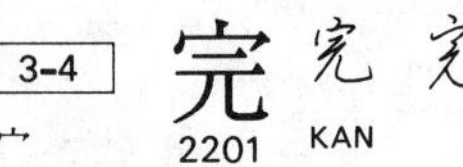
2201 KAN

CH 完 wán

Radical	Strokes
宀 40	7-3-4
Grade	**Freq**
Jōyō-4	547
2 - 3 - 4	

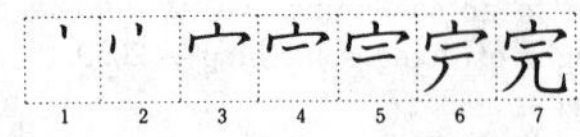
1 2 3 4 5 6 7

▶**COMPLETE**

COMPOUNDS

❶ (having all its parts intact) **complete, perfect, whole, full, intact**
完全な *kanzen na* perfect, complete, whole
完璧な *kanpeki na* perfect, flawless
完備した *kanbi shita* fully-equipped, perfect, complete
完投する *kantō suru* pitch a whole game
完封 *kanpū* complete blockade [seal]; baseball shutout

❷ⓐ (bring to a final stage) **complete, conclude, finish, end**
ⓑ **be completed, come to an end**
完成する *kansei suru* complete, finish; be completed, be finished
完結 *kanketsu* completion, conclusion, finish
完遂する *kansui suru* execute successfully, accomplish, bring to completion
完了する *kanryō suru* complete, finish; be completed, be finished
未完の *mikan no* incomplete, unfinished

INDEPENDENT

【**kan** 完】 completion, end

SYNONYMS

❶ **all**
万 all → 2936
全 WHOLE → 2022
一 all in one → 3341
満 FULL → 607
丸 complete(ly) → 3417
皆 ALL → 2445
都 all → 1686
総 TOTAL → 1379
諸 VARIOUS → 1577
毎 EVERY → 2034
各 EACH → 2168

❷ **end**
結 CONCLUDE → 1348
了 FINISH → 3350
済 SETTLE → 522
-上げる completion suffix → 3404
終 END → 1336
絶 COME TO AN END → 1353
閉 CLOSE → 3319

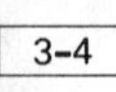
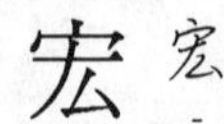
2202 KŌ NAMES hiro hiroshi

CH 宏 hóng

Radical	Strokes
宀 40	7-3-4
Grade	**Freq**
Names	1999
2 - 3 - 4	

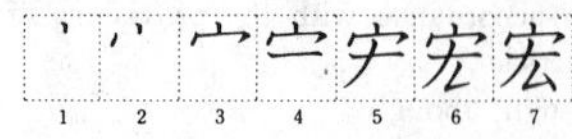
1 2 3 4 5 6 7

▶**GRAND**

COMPOUNDS

[now usu. 広 3035]

ⓐ (large in scale) **grand, great, magnificent**
ⓑ [original meaning] extensive, vast
宏壮な *kōsō na* grand, magnificent, imposing
宏弁 *kōben* [rare] eloquence, fluency
宏遠な *kōen na* vast and far-reaching
宏大な *kōdai na* vast, extensive, grand

NAMES

宏一 *kōichi* male name
宏 *hiroshi* male name
宏子 *hiroko* female name

SYNONYMS

ⓐ **great**
壮 GRAND (having grandeur) → 224
偉 GREAT (of superior character) → 148
大 BIG → 3416
豪 MAGNIFICENT → 2140
雄 HEROIC → 1008

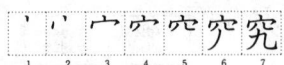

究 2203

KYŪ KU▲ kiwa(meru)

1 2 3 4 5 6 7

CH 究 jiū

Radical	Strokes
穴 116	7-5-2
Grade	**Freq**
Jōyō-3	428
2-3-4	

3-4 穴

▶STUDY EXHAUSTIVELY

COMPOUNDS

❶ **study exhaustively, investigate thoroughly, delve into, go to the bottom of**

究明する *kyūmei suru* investigate, study
究理 *kyūri* study of natural laws
研究 *kenkyū* research, study
追究する *tsuikyū suru* investigate thoroughly, inquire into
学究 *gakkyū* scholar, student
探究 *tankyū* investigation, search, inquiry

❷ reach the extreme, reach the very end

究極の *kyūkyoku no* ultimate, final
究竟の *kukkyō* (=*kyūkyō*) *no* excellent, superb, handy, appropriate, ideal

KUN

【kiwa(meru) 究める】[sometimes also 窮める] investigate thoroughly, study exhaustively, master

奥義を究める *ōgi o kiwameru* master the secrets of an art

SYNONYMS

❶ **investigate and examine**

閲 REVIEW → 3330
察 INSPECT → 2347
討 STUDY → 1456
探 PROBE → 505
検 EXAMINE → 986
診 EXAMINE A PATIENT → 1504
調 INVESTIGATE → 1567
査 LOOK INTO → 2437
審 EXAMINE CAREFULLY → 2360
験 TEST → 1833
勘 CHECK → 1777
糾 INQUIRE INTO → 1278

❶ **learn and study**

研 RESEARCH → 1132
学 STUDY → 2555
考 study → 3196
習 LEARN → 2667
攻 specialize → 242

HOMOPHONES

kiwameru ⇨ 極 1017 窮 2358

NOTE

⇨ see USAGE note at 極 1017

肖 2204

▶MODEL

nonstandard for 肖 2205

3-4 小

肖 2205

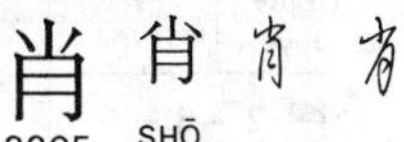
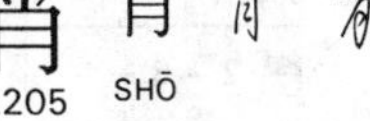

SHŌ

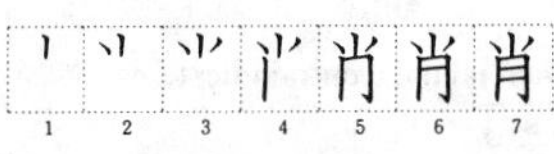

1 2 3 4 5 6 7

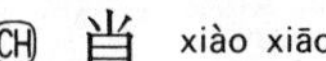

CH 肖 xiào xiāo

Radical	Strokes
月 130	7-4-3
Grade	**Freq**
Jōyō	1770
2-3-4	

3-4 ⺌

▶MODEL

COMPOUNDS

❶ [original meaning] (make a model of) **model, imitate**

肖像 *shōzō* portrait, likeness

❷ be like, resemble

不肖 *fushō* being unlike one's father; my humble self

SYNONYMS

❶ **imitate**

象 represent → 2134
模 pattern after → 1050
倣 COPY AFTER → 113
擬 IMITATE → 788

学

incorrect classification / stroke count ⇨ see 2555

3-4 ⺍

3-4 ⺍

労 incorrect classification ⇨ see 2548

3-4 巛

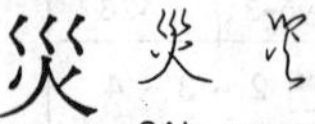

2206 SAI wazawa(i)

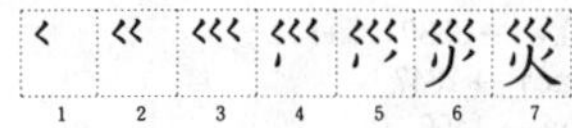

Ⓒⓗ 灾 zāi

Radical	Strokes
火 86	7-4-3
Grade	**Freq**
Jōyō-5	1003
2 - 3 - 4	

▶**NATURAL CALAMITY**

COMPOUNDS

● [original meaning] **natural calamity, disaster, misfortune, serious trouble**

災難 *sainan* calamity, disaster, accident, misfortune
災禍 *saika* accident, natural calamity, disaster, misfortune
災害 *saigai* calamity, disaster, accident
災厄 *saiyaku* calamity, disaster, accident
火災 *kasai* fire, conflagration
天災 *tensai* natural calamity [disaster]
人災 *jinsai* man-made calamity
戦災 *sensai* war damage
被災地 *hisaichi* disaster stricken area

KUN

【**wazawa(i)** 災い】[formerly also 禍] calamity, misfortune, disaster, evil, serious trouble
災いする *wazawai suru* be the ruin of (a person)
災い転じて福となる *Wazawai tenjite fuku to naru* Good comes out of evil
不測の災い *fusoku no wazawai* unexpected disaster

SYNONYMS

● **misfortune and disaster**
難 DISASTER → 1838
禍 CALAMITY → 1030
厄 MISFORTUNE → 2947
凶 BAD LUCK → 2961

USAGE

wazawai
災い
[formerly also 禍] calamity, misfortune, disaster, evil, serious trouble
禍
[now usu. 災い] calamity, misfortune, disaster, evil, serious trouble

HOMOPHONES

wazawai ⇨ 禍 1030

3-4 己

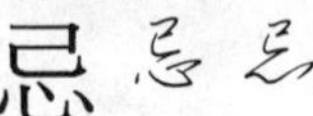

2207 KI i(mu) i(mi) i(mawashii)

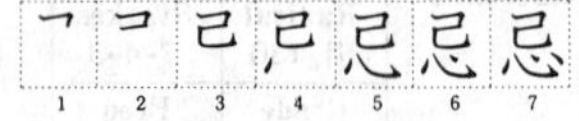

Ⓒⓗ 忌 jì

Radical	Strokes
心 61	7-4-3
Grade	**Freq**
Jōyō	1704
2 - 3 - 4	

▶**MOURNING** ▶**ABHOR**

COMPOUNDS

❶ **mourning, mourning period**
忌中 *kichū* in mourning
忌引き *kibiki* absence from work [school] due to mourning
忌服 *kifuku* mourning

❷ [also suffix] **death anniversary**
忌日 *kinichi* death anniversary
一周忌 *isshūki* first anniversary of death
桜桃忌 *ōtōki* Death Anniversary of Dazai Osamu

❸ shun, avoid, abstain from
忌避 *kihi* evasion, shirking
忌憚 *kitan* reserve, scruple
禁忌 *kinki* taboo; contraindication

INDEPENDENT

【**ki** 忌】mourning
忌が明ける *ki ga akeru* come out of mourning

KUN

【**i(mu)** 忌む】
ⓐ (regard with horror) abhor, loathe, detest, hate
ⓑ (reject vehemently) abhor, shun, avoid
忌み嫌う *imikirau* abhor, detest
忌むべき *imubeki* detestable, abominable
忌ま忌ましい *imaimashii* annoying
【**i(mi)** 忌み】mourning; abstinence, taboo
忌み日 *imibi* death anniversary; unlucky day

物忌み *monoimi* abstinence; confinement to one's house on an unlucky day

【i(mawashii) 忌まわしい】 disgusting, detestable

忌まわしい事件 *imawashii jiken* abominable incident

SYNONYMS

❶ **mourn and mourning**

喪 MOURNING → 2825

弔 CONDOLE → 3432

悼 MOURN → 485

❷ **date**

日 date → 3027

❸ **avoid and abstain**

避 AVOID → 3179

禁 abstain from → 2795

逃 ESCAPE → 3095

【imu】

ⓐ **hate and dislike**

憎 HATE → 687

悪 hate → 2745

嫌 DISLIKE → 636

恨 HOLD A GRUDGE → 369

芙 芙 芙 芙

2208 FU NAMES hasu

CH 芙 fú

Radical	Strokes
艹 140	7-3-4
Grade	**Freq**
Names	2091
2 - 3 - 4	

3-4 艹

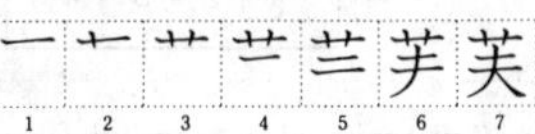

1 2 3 4 5 6 7

▶LOTUS

COMPOUNDS

● **lotus**

芙蓉 *fuyō* cotton rose; lotus

芙蓉峰 *fuyōhō* Mt. Fuji ("lotus-shaped mountain")

NAMES

芙美子 *fumiko* female name

SYNONYMS

● **flowering plants**

蓉 COTTON ROSE → 2337

葵 MALLOW → 2317

菊 CHRYSANTHEMUM → 2303

蘭 ORCHID → 2383

萩 *HAGI* → 2319

藤 WISTERIA → 2382

桜 cherry blossom → 931

梅 *ume* blossom → 925

芸 藝 芸 藝

2209 GEI

CH 艺 yì

Radical	Strokes
艹 140	7-3-4
Grade	**Freq**
Jōyō-4	631
2 - 3 - 4	

3-4 艹

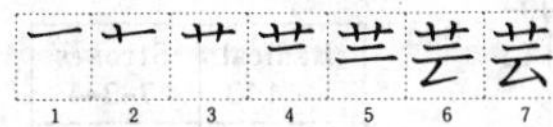

1 2 3 4 5 6 7

▶ART

COMPOUNDS

❶ **art, craft, skill**

芸術 *geijutsu* art, the arts

芸事 *geigoto* artistic accomplishments

工芸 *kōgei* technical art, technology

民芸 *mingei* folkcraft

手芸 *shugei* handicrafts, manual arts

技芸 *gigei* arts, crafts, accomplishments

文芸 *bungei* literature, literary art, art and literature

学芸 *gakugei* arts and sciences: culture

多芸は無芸 *Tagei wa mugei* Jack-of-all-trades and master of none

❷ [also suffix] **entertainment, performance, show business, acting**

芸能 *geinō* public entertainment

芸者 *geisha* geisha girl

芸名 *geimei* stage name

芸人 *geinin* artiste, entertainer

芸風 *geifū* style (of one's performance)

演芸 *engei* performance, entertainments

名人芸 *meijingei* masterly performance, virtuosity

大道芸 *daidōgei* street performing

❸ trick, feat, stunt

芸当 *geitō* feat, trick, stunt

曲芸 *kyokugei* acrobatics, trick, stunt

隠し芸 *kakushigei* hidden talent; parlor trick

❹ [original meaning] plant, cultivate

園芸 *engei* gardening, horticulture

❺ abbrev. of 安芸 *aki*, old name for west Hi-

roshima Prefecture
芸備線 *geibisen* Geibi Line (Hiroshima-North Okayama Railway)

INDEPENDENT

【**gei 芸**】art, craft, artistic accomplishment; trick, feat, stunt
芸は身を助く *Gei wa mi o tasuku* Accomplishments are a lifelong benefit to their possessor
芸をする犬 *gei o suru inu* dog that knows [does] tricks

SYNONYMS

❶ **art**
術 PRACTICAL ART → 476
技 SKILL → 248
道 the way of an art → 3134
❷ **performance**
演 performance → 697
劇 DRAMA → 1904

3-4
艹

芳 芳 芳 芳

2210 HŌ kanba(shii)

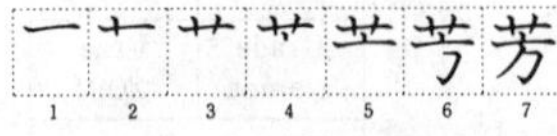

Ⓒ 芳 fāng

Radical	Strokes
艹 140	7-3-4
Grade	**Freq**
Jōyō	1301
2 - 3 - 4	

▶FRAGRANT

COMPOUNDS

❶ **fragrant, aromatic, balmy**
芳香 *hōkō* perfume, fragrance, aroma
芳気 *hōki* fragrant scent
芳草 *hōsō* fragrant herb
芳醇な *hōjun na* well-mellowed
❷ honorific prefix
芳名 *hōmei* your (honored) name
芳志 *hōshi* your good wishes, your kind intentions
芳情 *hōjō* your good wishes, your kind intentions
❸ bloom of youth, esp. of a beautiful young lady
芳気 *hōki* age (of a young lady)
芳眉 *hōbi* eyebrows of a beautiful woman
❹ honor, reputation
遺芳 *ihō* honor of the deceased

KUN

【**kanba(shii) 芳しい**】fragrant, aromatic; favorable, fair
芳しくない *kanbashiku nai* poor, unfavorable; disgraceful

SYNONYMS

❶ **smell and fragrance**
薫 BALMY → 2371
郁 AROMATIC → 1288
馨 PERFUME → 2879
気 smell → 3194
臭 BAD SMELL → 2633
香 SWEET SMELL → 2568

3-4
艹

花 花 花 花

2211 KA KE▲ hana

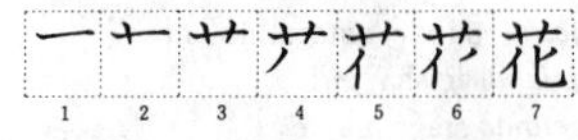

Ⓒ 花 huā

Radical	Strokes
艹 140	7-3-4
Grade	**Freq**
Jōyō-1	574
2 - 3 - 4	

▶FLOWER

COMPOUNDS

❶ [original meaning] **flower, blossom**
花壇 *kadan* flower bed
花弁 *kaben* petal
花瓶 *kabin* flower vase
花粉 *kafun* pollen
国花 *kokka* national flower
造花 *zōka* artificial flower; artificial flower making
開花する *kaika suru* flower, blossom, come into bloom
沈丁花 *jinchōge* (=*chinchōge*) (sweet-smelling) daphne
❷ as beautiful as a flower
名花 *meika* beautiful flower; celebrated beauty
❸ red-light district
花柳 *karyū* geisha girls, courtesans; red-light district
花柳界 *karyūkai* red-light district

KUN

【**hana 花**】
①ⓐ [also prefix] flower, blossom; cherry blos-

som

ⓑ flower arrangement

花見 *hanami* flower [cherry blossom] viewing

花嫁 *hanayome* bride

花火 *hanabi* fireworks, firecrackers

花形 *hanagata* floral pattern; star, lion; leading, popular, favorite

花時計 *hanadokei* flower clock

草花 *kusabana* flowering plant

お花 *ohana* flower arrangement

②ⓐ [also 華] (figuratively) flower (of life), essence, cream

ⓑ honor, success, glory

若い内が花だ *Wakai uchi ga hana da* Youth is a treasure

花を持たせる *hana o motaseru* let (a person) have the credit for (the success)

③ Japanese playing cards with floral patterns

花を引く *hana o hiku* play *hana* cards

④ [in compounds] geisha, prostitute

花代 *hanadai* tip to a geisha girl

花街 *hanamachi* red-light district

SPECIAL READINGS

浪花▲ *naniwa* old name for Osaka

SYNONYMS

❶ **flower**

華 flower → 2283

USAGE

hana

花

①ⓐ [also prefix] flower, blossom; cherry blossom

ⓑ flower arrangement

②ⓐ [also 華] (figuratively) flower (of life), essence, cream

ⓑ honor, success, glory

③ Japanese playing cards with floral patterns

④ [in compounds] geisha, prostitute

華

①ⓐ [also 花] (figuratively) flower (of life), essence, cream

ⓑ flower of youth, prime of life

② [in compounds] flowery, beautiful, gallant

HOMOPHONES

hana ⇨ 華 2283

NOTE

⇨ see COMPOUND FORMATION for 花柳 *karyū* ⇨ 柳 899

芯 incorrect stroke count ⇨ see 2423 3-4 艹

豸 incorrect classification ⇨ see 2401 3-4 ⺂

 3-4 刃

2212 NIN shino(bu) shino(baseru)

Ⓒⓗ 忍 rěn

Radical	Strokes
心 61	7-4-3
Grade	**Freq**
Jōyō	1344
2-3-4	

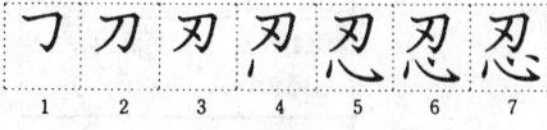

▶**BEAR**

COMPOUNDS

❶ⓐ **bear, endure, tolerate, suffer patiently**

ⓑ forbear, restrain, repress, hold back

忍耐する *nintai suru* persevere, be patient, endure

忍従 *ninjū* submission, resignation

忍苦 *ninku* endurance, stoicism

堪忍(＝勘忍) *kannin* patience, forbearance; forgiveness, pardon

隠忍 *innin* patience, endurance

❷ **perform by stealth, practice the art of making oneself invisible**

忍術 *ninjutsu* art of making oneself invisible

忍法 *ninpō* art of making oneself invisible

忍者 *ninja* ancient spy who mastered *ninjutsu*

❸ merciless, atrocious, truculent, cruel

残忍 *zannin* cruelty, atrocity, brutality

INDEPENDENT

[nin 忍] endurance, forbearance, patience

...は忍の一字に尽きる *...wa nin no ichiji ni tsukiru* Endurance is the only word to describe...

KUN

[shino(bu) 忍ぶ]

① bear, endure, suffer, stand, put up with

忍び難い *shinobigatai* unbearable, intolerable

恥を忍ぶ *haji o shinobu* abide one's shame
②ⓐ conceal oneself, hide
ⓑ perform by stealth, steal one's way to (a lover)
忍び *shinobi* stealing (into); art of mystification; incognito, traveling incognito
忍び泣く *shinobinaku* shed silent tears
忍び足 *shinobiashi* tiptoeing, stealthy steps
忍び込む *shinobikomu* steal in, sneak in
忍びやかな *shinobiyaka na* stealthy, secret
【shino(baseru) 忍ばせる】 *vt* conceal, secrete; suppress, subdue
ポケットにナイフを忍ばせる *poketto ni naifu o shinobaseru* conceal a knife in one's pocket
声を忍ばせて *koe o shinobasete* in a subdued voice

SYNONYMS

❶ⓐ bear and endure
耐 WITHSTAND → 1282
堪 ENDURE → 559
❷ hide
隠 HIDE → 713
伏 lie in concealment → 45
潜 LURK → 746
匿 CONCEAL → 3011

USAGE

shinobu
忍ぶ
① bear, endure, suffer, stand, put up with
②ⓐ conceal oneself, hide
ⓑ perform by stealth, steal one's way to (a lover)
偲ぶ
recall, recollect, remember, reminisce

HOMOPHONES

shinobu ⇨ 偲 135

3-4 刃

忍 2213

▶BEAR
nonstandard for 忍 2212

3-4 亡

忘 2214

▶FORGET
nonstandard for 忘 2036

3-4 亼

incorrect classification ⇨ see 2041

3-4 亠

育 2215

▶RAISE
nonstandard for 育 2050

3-5 土

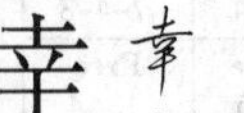

2216 KŌ saiwa(i) sachi shiawa(se)

Ⓒⓗ 幸 xìng

Radical	Strokes
干 51	8-3-5
Grade	**Freq**
Jōyō-3	740
2 - 3 - 5	

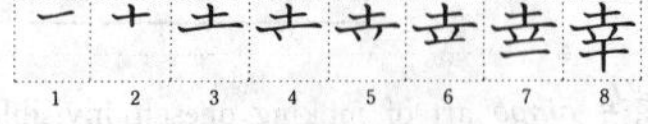

▶GOOD FORTUNE ▶HAPPINESS

COMPOUNDS

❶ [formerly also 倖 118]
ⓐ [original meaning] **good fortune, good luck**
ⓑ **happiness, well-being, felicity**
幸運 *kōun* good fortune, good luck
射幸心 *shakōshin* speculative spirit
幸福 *kōfuku* happiness; good fortune
薄幸 *hakkō* unhappiness; sad fate, misfortune
不幸 *fukō* unhappiness; misfortune; bereavement
多幸 *takō* great happiness; great fortune
❷ imperial tour
行幸 *gyōkō* Imperial visit
巡幸 *junkō* Imperial tour, royal progress
❸ [formerly also 倖 118] [rare] be in the good graces of (one's ruler); bestow favor upon
寵幸 *chōkō* grace, favor

INDEPENDENT

【kō 幸】 happiness, fortune
幸か不幸か *kō ka fukō ka* for good or for evil, luckily or unluckily

KUN

【saiwa(i) 幸い】 happiness, blessing; good fortune
幸いな *saiwai na* happy, blessed
幸いに *saiwai ni* fortunately, luckily
【sachi 幸】 happiness; good fortune; catch, game
幸有る *sachiaru* happy, fortunate, lucky
【shiawa(se) 幸せ】 [also 仕合わせ, formerly also 倖せ] happiness, blessing; good fortune
幸せな *shiawase na* happy, fortunate
不幸せ *fushiawase* unhappiness, misfortune, ill luck

SYNONYMS

❶ⓐ **good fortune**
福 FORTUNE → 1029
吉 LUCKY → 2167
嘉 HAPPY → 2340
祥 AUSPICIOUS → 948
瑞 AUSPICIOUS OMEN → 1027
禎 PROPITIOUS OMEN → 1031
ⓑ **happiness**
祉 BLESSEDNESS → 876
福 FORTUNE → 1029

USAGE

shiawase
幸せ
[also 仕合わせ, formerly also 倖せ] happiness, blessing; good fortune
倖せ
[now usu. 幸せ or 仕合わせ] same as 幸せ
仕合わせ
[also 幸せ, formerly also 倖せ] same as 幸せ

HOMOPHONES

shiawase ⇨ 倖せ 118 仕合わせ 34, 2019

NOTE

⇨ see COMPOUND FORMATION for 仕合わせ *shiawase* ⇨ 合 2019

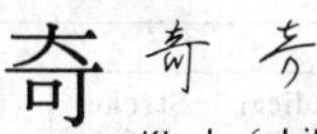

2217 KI ku(shiki)▲

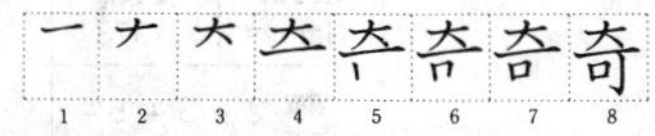

Ⓒ 奇 qí jī

Radical	Strokes
大 37	8-3-5
Grade	**Freq**
Jōyō	1225
2-3-5	

3-5 大

▶**UNUSUAL**

COMPOUNDS

❶ [formerly also 畸 1198]
ⓐ **unusual, strange, odd, extraordinary, queer, eccentric**
ⓑ deformity, malformation
奇異な *kii na* unusual, strange
奇人 *kijin* eccentric (person), queer [odd] fellow
奇妙な *kimyō na* strange, queer, odd
奇跡(＝奇蹟) *kiseki* miracle, wonder
奇談 *kidan* strange story
珍奇な *chinki na* novel, curious; rare; strange
怪奇 *kaiki* mystery, wonder
好奇心 *kōkishin* curiosity
偏奇 *henki* eccentricity
奇形 *kikei* deformity, malformation
❷ of unusual excellence
奇勝 *kishō* place of scenic beauty
❸ surprising, unexpected
奇襲 *kishū* surprise attack
奇遇 *kigū* unexpected meeting, chance encounter
❹ [formerly 綺 1371] beautiful, gorgeous, elegant
奇麗な *kirei na* beautiful, pretty; clean; fair
❺ *math* odd, odd number
奇数 *kisū* odd number
奇偶 *kigū* odd and even numbers
❻ [also 詭 1520] cheat, deceive, defraud
奇弁 *kiben* sophism, sophistry

INDEPENDENT

【ki 奇】 strangeness, oddity, eccentricity
奇を衒う *ki o terau* make a display of one's originality [eccentricity]
奇なる *kinaru* strange, odd, eccentric

KUN

【ku(shiki) 奇しき】 strange, mysterious
奇しくも *kushiku mo* mysteriously, strangely enough

SPECIAL READINGS

数奇屋(＝数寄屋) *sukiya* tea-ceremony arbor

SYNONYMS

❶ⓐ **abnormal**
変 ABNORMAL → 2069
妙 strange → 239
異 not ordinary → 2584
怪 MYSTERIOUS → 297
珍 curious → 909

3-5 大

奔 奔 奔 𡘜

2218 HON

CH 奔 bēn bèn

Radical	Strokes
大 37	8-3-5
Grade	Freq
Jōyō	1783
2 - 3 - 5	

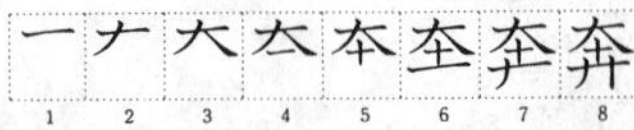

▶**RUSH**

COMPOUNDS

❶ⓐ [original meaning] **rush, rush about, run fast, gallop, hurry**

ⓑ run away, run off

奔走する *honsō suru* bustle about, exert oneself for, devote oneself to

奔流 *honryū* torrent, rapids

奔騰 *hontō* price jump, boom

奔馬 *honba* galloping horse

狂奔する *kyōhon suru* rush around, run madly about, run wild; make frantic efforts, be very busy (in)

東奔西走する *tōhon-seisō suru* be on the run, bustle about, bestir oneself

出奔 *shuppon* abscondence, flight

❷ let one's ego run wild, do as one pleases

奔放な *honpō na* wild, extravagant; free-spirited

淫奔 *inpon* wantonness, lustfulness, lewdness

SYNONYMS

❶ⓐ **run**

走 RUN → 2194

駆 gallop → 1823

3-5 大

奈 奈 奈

2219 NA NAI

CH 奈 nài

Radical	Strokes
大 37	8-3-5
Grade	Freq
Names	1973
2 - 3 - 5	

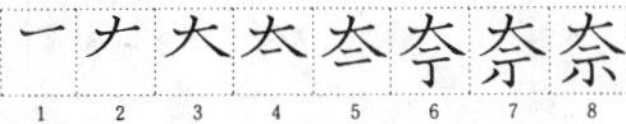

▶**PHONETIC** [na]

COMPOUNDS

❶ **used phonetically for *na*, esp. in the transliteration of foreign words**

奈落 *naraku* Hell; trap cellar

奈翁 *naō* Napoleon

加奈陀 *kanada* Canada

❷ [also 那 843] element for forming interrogative words

奈辺 *nahen* where?

❸ [original meaning, now obsolete] crab apple tree

SPECIAL READINGS

奈何▲(=如何▲) *ikan* what; how

NAMES

神奈川 *kanagawa* place name

奈良 *nara* place name

奈良岡 *naraoka* surname

美奈子 *minako* female name

SYNONYMS

❶ **phonetic** [na]

那 PHONETIC [na] → 843

❷ **interrogatives**

那 interrogative forming element → 843

何 WHAT → 65

誰 WHO → 1578

3-5 子

孟 孟 孟

2220 MŌ NAMES takeshi take haru hajime tsutomu osa

CH 孟 mèng

Radical	Strokes
子 39	8-3-5
Grade	Freq
Names	2042
2 - 3 - 5	

一 了 子 孑 孟 孟 孟 孟
1 2 3 4 5 6 7 8

▶**MENCIUS**

COMPOUNDS

❶ **Mencius**

孟子 *mōshi* Mencius; the works of Mencius

孔孟の教え *kōmō no oshie* the teachings of Confucius and Mencius

❷ⓐ first month of a season

ⓑ [archaic] firstborn [eldest] brother or sister

孟春 *mōshun* January (of the old calendar)

孟夏 *mōka* April (of the lunar calendar)

孟女 *mōjo* eldest daughter

NAMES

孟 *takeshi* male name

孟雄 *haruo* male name

SYNONYMS

❶ Confucius and Confucianists

孔 Confucius → 179

子 the Master (Confucius) → 3390

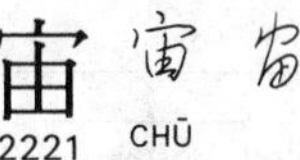

2221 CHŪ

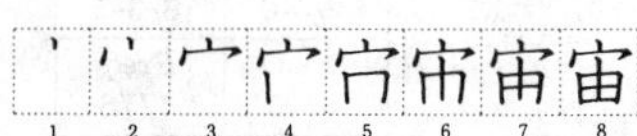

Ⓒⓗ 宙 zhòu

Radical	Strokes
宀 40	8-3-5
Grade	**Freq**
Jōyō-6	916
2 - 3 - 5	

3-5 宀

▶SPACE ▶MIDAIR

COMPOUNDS

❶ⓐ (expanse of the universe) **space, outer space, heavens**

ⓑ (point above the ground) **midair, air, space**

宇宙 *uchū* universe, cosmos; (outer) space

航宙 *kōchū* space flight

宙乗り *chūnori* aerial stunts

宙吊り *chūzuri* hanging in midair

宙返り *chūgaeri* somersault

❷ [original meaning, now archaic] infinite time, all ages

INDEPENDENT

【chū 宙】 midair, air, space; memory

宙に浮く *chū ni uku* float in the air

宙で読む *chū de yomu* recite from memory

SYNONYMS

❶ⓐ universe and space

宇 UNIVERSE → 2175

ⓑ sky

空 SKY → 2227

天 HEAVEN → 3442

宛 宛 宛

2222 EN a(teru) -a(te) -ate -zutsu ataka(mo)

丶 丷 宀 宂 夗 夗 宛 宛

1 2 3 4 5 6 7 8

Ⓒⓗ 宛 wǎn

Radical	Strokes
宀 40	8-3-5
Grade	**Freq**
Non-Jōyō	1817
2 - 3 - 5	

3-5 宀

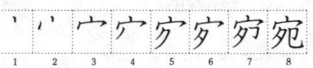

▶ADDRESS

COMPOUNDS

❶ as if, just as, just like

宛然 *enzen* as if

❷ [original meaning, now archaic] long and winding, lithe

宛転たる *ententaru* (of eyebrows) shapely; moving smoothly

KUN

【a(teru) 宛てる】

① address (a letter), direct

宛先 *atesaki* address

宛名 *atena* address

手紙を宛てる *tegami o ateru* address [direct] a letter to a person

② [sometimes also 当てる] assign Chinese characters to a word (as phonetic substitutes)

宛て字 *ateji* phonetic substitute, false substitute character

外来語に字を宛てる *gairaigo ni ji o ateru* assign Chinese characters to a foreign word

【-a(te) -宛て, -ate -宛】

[suffix]

① addressed to

A氏宛ての手紙 *ēshiate no tegami* letter addressed to Mr. A

② per, apiece

オレンジを一人宛て三個 *orenji o hitoriate sanko* three oranges apiece [per head]

【-zutsu -宛】 at a time, each, apiece

少し宛 *sukoshizutsu* a little for each; little by little, gradually

【ataka(mo) 宛も】 [now usu. 恰も] as if, just as, just like

宛も月明の如し *Atakamo getsumei no gotoshi* It is as bright as the moon

SYNONYMS

【ateru】

① **indicate**
指 POINT → 378
示 SHOW → 1936
標 MARK → 1064

USAGE

atakamo
宛も
[now usu. 恰も] as if, just as, just like
恰も
[formerly also 宛も] as if, just as, just like

HOMOPHONES

ateru ⇨ 当 2177 充 2014
-ate ⇨ 当 2177
atakamo ⇨ 恰 368

NOTE

⇨ see also USAGE note at 当 2177

3-5 宀

2223 GI yoro(shii)▲ yoro(shiku)▲

Ⓒⓗ 宜 yí

Radical	Strokes
宀 40	8-3-5
Grade	**Freq**
Jōyō	1776
2-3-5	

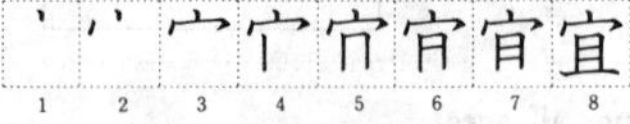

▶RIGHT

COMPOUNDS

❶ **right, just right, appropriate, suitable, opportune, good**
機宜 *kigi* opportunity, occasion
便宜 *bengi* convenience, facility
適宜 *tekigi* suitableness, appropriateness; suitably
時宜 *jigi* right time [occasion], proper time

❷ [also 誼 1571 or 義 2338] friendship; favor, kindness
友宜 *yūgi* friendship, fellowship
高宜 *kōgi* your kindness [favor]

KUN

【yoro(shii) 宜しい】 all right, well; all right, OK (in answer to a request)
宜しかったら *yoroshikattara* if you like; if you don't mind
しても宜しい *shite mo yoroshii* may (do), may as well (do), have a right (to do)

【yoro(shiku) 宜しく】 properly, suitably, as one thinks fit; one's regards, one's best wishes; [followed by べし *beshi*] *literary* by all means
宜しくやる *yoroshiku yaru* do at one's own discretion; make cozy with
宜しくお伝え下さい *Yoroshiku otsutae kudasai* Please send my best regards
宜しく反省すべし *Yoroshiku hansei subeshi* You are to reflect on your own deed

SYNONYMS

❶ **suitable**
適 SUITABLE → 3160
当 proper → 2177
便 CONVENIENT → 95

NOTE

★do not confuse with 宣 2252

3-5 宀

宝 寶

2224 HŌ takara

Ⓒⓗ 宝 bǎo

Radical	Strokes
宀 40	8-3-5
Grade	**Freq**
Jōyō-6	1010
2-3-5	

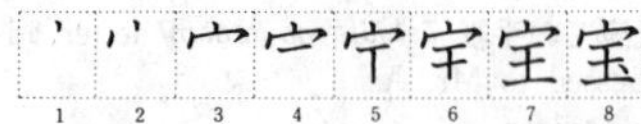

▶TREASURE

COMPOUNDS

❶ⓐ **treasure, treasured object**
ⓑ (something very valuable) **treasure, heirloom**
ⓒ treasured, precious
宝庫 *hōko* treasure house, treasury
宝石 *hōseki* gem, jewel
財宝 *zaihō* treasure, valuables; riches, wealth
重宝 *jūhō* (= *chōhō*) priceless treasure
国宝 *kokuhō* national treasure
家宝 *kahō* family treasure, heirloom
宝典 *hōten* thesaurus, treasury of words; precious book
重宝な *chōhō na* convenient, useful, handy

❷ honorific term used in reference to the Emperor or Buddha
宝算 *hōsan* the Emperor's age
宝塔 *hōtō* two-storied Buddhist tower

KUN

【takara 宝】 treasure, precious thing; riches, wealth, money; (something very valuable) treasure, jewel

宝物 *takaramono* treasure
宝船 *takarabune* treasure ship; picture of a treasure ship
宝捜し *takarasagashi* treasure hunt
宝島 *takarajima* treasure island
子宝 *kodakara* the treasure that is children; children

SYNONYMS

❶ⓐ & ❶ⓑ **wealth**
富 riches → 2310
財 WEALTH → 1457
産 property → 3298

実 實 実 實

2225 JITSU mi mino(ru) makoto▲

Ⓒⓗ 实 shí

Radical	Strokes
宀 40	8-3-5
Grade	**Freq**
Jōyō-3	86
2 - 3 - 5	

3-5 宀

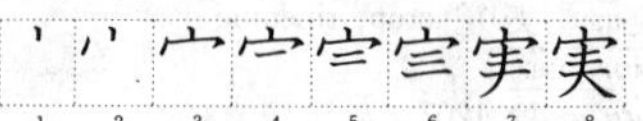

▶**REAL**

COMPOUNDS

❶ⓐ [also prefix] **real, actual, true**
ⓑ **reality, fact, truth**
ⓒ *math* real
実施する *jisshi suru* carry out, enforce, execute
実現する *jitsugen suru* realize, materialize
実験 *jikken* experiment
実力 *jitsuryoku* real ability [power], capability, competence
実績 *jisseki* (actual) result, positive achievements
実社会 *jisshakai* actual world
実際 *jissai* truth, reality; actual state; practice
事実 *jijitsu* fact, reality; as a matter of fact
現実 *genjitsu* actuality, reality
確実な *kakujitsu na* certain, sure, reliable; sound, solid
真実 *shinjitsu* truth, reality
実関数 *jitsukansū* real variable function

❷ practical
実用 *jitsuyō* practical use, utility
実務 *jitsumu* practical business
実技 *jitsugi* practical technique [skill]

❸ⓐ **substance, contents**
ⓑ substantial, solid, full
充実した *jūjitsu shita* full, complete, rich
情実 *jōjitsu* private circumstances, personal consideration; favoritism
口実 *kōjitsu* excuse, pretext, pretense
実車 *jissha* full-scale car (vs. model); occupied taxi
実名詞 *jitsumeishi* noun substantive

❹ faithfulness, sincerity, fidelity
実直な *jitchoku na* upright, honest, steady
切実な *setsujitsu na* acute, keen, earnest; urgent
誠実な *seijitsu na* sincere, honest, faithful
忠実な *chūjitsu na* faithful, devoted, honest

❺ **fruit**
果実 *kajitsu* fruit, berry
結実する *ketsujitsu suru* bear fruit; be successful, achieve success
綿実 *menjitsu* cottonseed

INDEPENDENT

【jitsu 実】
① reality, fact, truth
実に *jitsu ni* truly, surely
② substance, contents
虚を捨てて実を取る *kyo o sutete jitsu o toru* discard the shadow for the substance
③ faithfulness, sincerity, fidelity
実の有る *jitsu no aru* sincere, faithful
④ fruit, outcome
憲政の実を上げる *kensei no jitsu o ageru* realize constitutionalism
⑤ *math* dividend, multiplicand
法と実 *hō to jitsu* divisor and dividend

KUN

【mi 実】 fruit, nut, berry, seed; substance; ingredients
木の実 *ki no mi* nut, berry
実の有る *mi no aru* substantial, solid
実入り *miiri* crop, harvest; income, profits

【mino(ru) 実る】 [sometimes also 稔る] bear fruit, ripen
実り *minori* crop, ripening
実っている *minotte iru* be in bearing
実らなかった努力 *minoranakatta doryoku* fruitless [resultless] efforts

【makoto 実】 [usu. 誠, sometimes also 真] truth, reality
実の心 *makoto no kokoro* one's real intention
実しやかに *makotoshiyaka ni* plausibly, as if it were true

SYNONYMS

❶ⓐ & ❶ⓑ **true**
本 real → 3502

真 TRUE → 2111
洵 TRULY → 383
正 genuine → 3484
現 ACTUAL → 968
❸ⓐ **essential content**
体 substance → 71
味 contents → 274
❹ **fidelity**
信 fidelity → 100
誠 SINCERITY → 1523
忠 LOYALTY → 2433
義 faith → 2338
孝 FILIAL PIETY → 3205
悌 BROTHERLY LOVE → 424
操 constancy → 769
節 moral integrity → 2691
❺ **fruit**
果 FRUIT → 3560
【minoru】
○ **mature**
稔 RIPEN → 1207
熟 MATURE → 2868
成 grow up → 3537

USAGE

❶ **minoru**
実る
[sometimes also 稔る] bear fruit, ripen
稔る
[usu. 実る] bear fruit, ripen
❷ **minori**
実り
[sometimes also 稔り] crop, ripening
稔り
[usu. 実り] crop, ripening

HOMOPHONES

minoru ⇨ 稔 1207
minori ⇨ 稔 1207
makoto ⇨ 誠 1523 真 2111

NOTE

⇨ see also USAGE note at 誠 1523

3-5
宀

2226 KAN

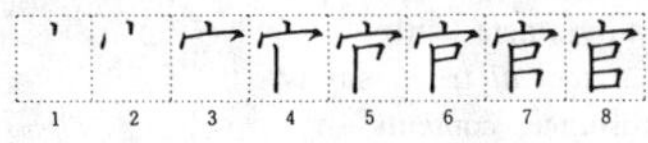

CH 官 guān

Radical	Strokes
宀 40	8-3-5
Grade	**Freq**
Jōyō-4	195
2-3-5	

▶**GOVERNMENT**
▶**GOVERNMENT OFFICIAL**

COMPOUNDS

❶ [original meaning] **government, court**
官房 *kanbō* secretariat
官邸 *kantei* official residence
官庁 *kanchō* government office [agency]
官僚 *kanryō* government official(s); bureaucracy, officialdom
官製の *kansei no* government manufactured
官吏 *kanri* government official
官女 *kanjo* court lady
❷ⓐ [also suffix] **government official, officer**
ⓑ government service [post]
長官 *chōkan* director, administrator, chief
警官 *keikan* police officer, policeman
次官 *jikan* vice-minister, undersecretary
裁判官 *saibankan* judge
行政官 *gyōseikan* executive [administrative] official
任官 *ninkan* appointment to an office, commission
退官 *taikan* retirement from office
❸ organ (of the body)
官能 *kannō* bodily function; fleshly sense, carnal desire
器官 *kikan* (body) organ
五官 *gokan* the five organs (of sense)

INDEPENDENT

【kan 官】 government, authorities; government service [post]
官に就く *kan ni tsuku* enter the government service

SYNONYMS

❶ **governments**
幕 SHOGUNATE → 2335
廷 COURT → 3058
朝 court → 1695
宮 Imperial Court → 2274
❷ⓐ **officials**
吏 OFFICIAL → 3536
僚 official → 165
司 officiator → 2931
役 executive → 244
事 officer → 3567
❸ **organ**
器 organ → 2713
臓 INTERNAL ORGAN → 1102

NOTE

⇨ see COMPOUND FORMATION for 官房 *kanbō* ⇨ 房 1946

空 空 空 空

2227 KŪ sora a(ku) a(ki) a(keru) kara su(ku)▲ su(kasu)▲ muna(shii)▲

CH 空 kōng kòng

Radical	Strokes
穴 116	8-5-3
Grade	**Freq**
Jōyō-1	224
2 - 3 - 5	

▶SKY ▶AIR ▶EMPTY

COMPOUNDS

❶ⓐ **sky, heavens, the air, space**
ⓑ (space where aircraft operate) **air, air-space**
空中で *kūchū de* in the air [sky]
空間 *kūkan* space, room
天空 *tenkū* sky, air, firmament, heavens
虚空 *kokū* empty space, sky
東京上空 *tōkyō jōkū* the skies of Tokyo
航空 *kōkū* aviation, aerial navigation
制空権 *seikūken* command of the air

❷ⓐ **aircraft, airplane**
ⓑ abbrev. of 空軍 *kūgun*: air force
空港 *kūkō* airport
空軍 *kūgun* air force
空輸 *kūyu* air transportation
空路 *kūro* air route, airway
空曹 *kūsō* noncommissioned officer of the Japanese Air Self Defense Forces
空陸 *kūriku* air force and army

❸ **air**
空気 *kūki* air; atmosphere
空調 *kūchō* air conditioning
空圧 *kūatsu* air [pneumatic] pressure

❹ [original meaning] **empty, vacant, unoccupied, blank**
空車 *kūsha* vacant taxi, empty car
空砲 *kūhō* blank shot [cartridge]
空白 *kūhaku* blank, empty space; void, vacuum
空席 *kūseki* vacant seat; vacancy
真空 *shinkū* vacuum

❺ⓐ (insubstantial) empty, void, vain, idle, futile, meaningless
ⓑ *Sunyata* (Sanskrit for emptiness or void): the nonexistence of matter and self, the transcendental void (in Buddhism)
空虚 *kūkyo* emptiness, voidness; inanity
空想 *kūsō* fancy, fantasy; imagination
空論 *kūron* abstract [impractical] theory
空費 *kūhi* waste
空性 *kūshō* *Sunyata*
色即是空 *Shikisokuzekū* Matter is void / Form [Matter] is nonsubstantial

INDEPENDENT

【kū 空】 air, airspace; air force; idleness, vanity; *Sunyata* (⇒ ❺ⓑ)
空を掴む *kū o tsukamu* grasp at the air
空対空ミサイル *kū tai kū misairu* air-to-air missile
空に帰する *kū ni kisuru* come to naught

KUN

【sora 空】
① sky, heavens; the skies, the air
空色 *sorairo* sky blue
空を飛ぶ *sora o tobu* fly in the air
曇り空 *kumorizora* cloudy sky [weather]
② weather
空模様 *soramoyō* weather
女心と秋の空 *onnagokoro to aki no sora* woman's heart and autumn weather (are both fickle)
③ memory
空で *sora de* from memory, by heart
④ pretense, feigning
空言 *soragoto* falsehood, lie
空空しい *sorazorashii* false, feigned, hypocritical, transparent
⑤ absentmindedness
上の空 *uwa no sora* absentminded, have a vacant air
⑥ vain, vague, strange
空頼み *soradanomi* vain hopes
空恐ろしい *soraosoroshii* have a vague fear

【a(ku) 空く】
① become vacant, become vacated [empty]
空いている部屋 *aite iru heya* vacant room
② become available for use
辞書が空いたら貸して下さい *Jisho ga aitara kashite kudasai* Let me use the dictionary when available
③ become free [unoccupied]
私は時間が空いている *Watashi wa jikan ga aite iru* I have time to spare
④ have (a hole or aperture) in, (a gap) is open
穴が空いている *ana ga aite iru* have [be pierced with] a hole

【a(ki) 空き】
① gap, aperture, space; vacancy; free time
空きを埋める *aki o umeru* fill a gap
② [prefix] vacant, empty
空き家 *akiya* vacant house
空き缶 *akikan* empty can

【a(keru) 空ける】
① empty, clear, vacate, clear out

部屋を空ける *heya o akeru* clear a room
② leave space, make room
一字空ける *ichiji akeru* leave a space (between words)
③ bore, make a hole
穴を空ける *ana o akeru* make a hole
④ free oneself (to do), make spare time
時間を空ける *jikan o akeru* make oneself available [free]

【kara 空】
① emptiness, vacancy, hollow
空の *kara no* empty, vacant, hollow
空っぽ *karappo* empty, hollow
空手 *karate* karate; empty hand
② [prefix]
ⓐ (void of content) empty
ⓑ (lacking substance) empty, vain, bogus, false
空瓶 *karabin* empty bottle
空梅雨 *karatsuyu* dry rainy season, rainless *tsuyu*
空約束 *karayakusoku* empty promise
空手形 *karategata* bad [fictitious] bill; empty promise

【su(ku) 空く】 become empty, become less crowded
空き *suki* vacancy, interval
空きっ腹 *sukippara* hunger
空いた電車 *suita densha* uncrowded train
手空きの *tesuki no* not busy, unengaged

【su(kasu) 空かす】
① feel hungry
腹を空かす *hara o sukasu* be hungry
② make available, make free
手を空かす *te o sukasu* make oneself available

【muna(shii) 空しい】
[sometimes also 虚しい]
①ⓐ empty, void
ⓑ vain, futile
空しさ *munashisa* emptiness, futility
空しい名声 *munashii meisei* empty name
努力も空しく *doryoku mo munashiku* after efforts in vain
② dead, lifeless
空しくなる *munashiku naru* die, expire

SYNONYMS

❶ sky
天 HEAVEN → 3442
宙 MIDAIR → 2221

❷ⓐ aircraft and spacecraft
機 AIRCRAFT → 1076
船 spaceship → 1341

❸ gas and vapor
気 GAS → 3194
汽 STEAM → 264

❹ emptiness and nothing
白 WHITE (blank) → 3493
虚 VOID → 3237
無 NOTHING → 2135
零 ZERO → 2792

❺ⓐ vain
虚 without substance → 3237
徒 vain → 416

USAGE

❶ kara

空
① emptiness, vacancy, hollow
② [prefix]
ⓐ (void of content) empty
ⓑ (lacking substance) empty, vain, bogus, false

殻
①ⓐ shell, crust
ⓑ husk, hull
② castoff skin, refuse

❷ munashii

空しい
[sometimes also 虚しい]
①ⓐ empty, void
ⓑ vain, futile
② dead, lifeless

虚しい
[usu. 空しい] same as 空しい

HOMOPHONES

aku ⇨ 明 855 開 3321
akeru ⇨ 明 855 開 3321
kara ⇨ 殻 1490
suku ⇨ 透 3108 隙 670
sukasu ⇨ 透 3108 隙 670
munashii ⇨ 虚 3237

NOTE

⇨ see also USAGE notes at 明 855 and 透 3108

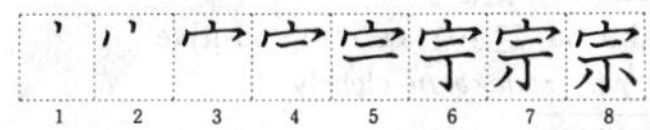

宗 宗 宗
2228 SHŪ SŌ mune▲

㊥ 宗 zōng

Radical	Strokes
宀 40	8-3-5
Grade	Freq
Jōyō-6	1008
2 - 3 - 5	

3-5 宀

▶**RELIGIOUS SECT**

COMPOUNDS

❶ⓐ **religious sect (esp. Buddhist), denomination**
ⓑ **suffix after names of religious sects**
ⓒ **religion**
宗派 *shūha* religious sect, denomination
宗旨 *shūshi* tenets of a religious sect; (religious) sect
浄土宗 *jōdoshū Jodo* sect (of Buddhism)
天台宗 *tendaishū Tendai* sect (of Buddhism)
宗教 *shūkyō* religion, faith, creed
改宗 *kaishū* conversion; proselytism
❷ ancestor, originator, patriarch
宗家 *sōke* head family, originator
宗主 *sōshu* suzerain
祖宗 *sosō* ancestors
❸ leader, great master
宗匠 *sōshō* master (of an art)
詩宗 *shisō* master poet
❹ [original meaning] ancestral shrine
宗廟 *sōbyō* ancestral shrine [temple]

INDEPENDENT

【**shū** 宗】 religious sect, denomination
我宗の徒 *waga shū no to* believer of my denomination

KUN

【**mune** 宗】 [now usu. 旨] principle, aim

SYNONYMS

❶ⓐ & ❶ⓑ **parties and sects**
門 (religious) sect → 888
系 faction → 1944
翼 WING → 2720
派 SECT → 381
流 school → 441
閥 CLIQUE → 3325
党 PARTY → 2581
ⓒ **religion**
教 RELIGION → 1493
道 the Way → 3134

HOMOPHONES

mune ⇨ 旨 2024

NOTE

⇨ see USAGE note at 旨 2024

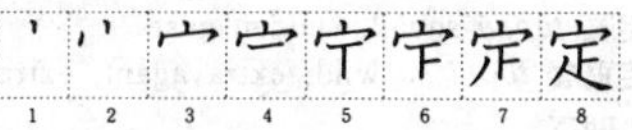

定 定 定
2229 TEI JŌ sada(meru) sada(maru) sada(ka)

㊥ 定 dìng

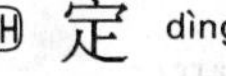

Radical	Strokes
宀 40	8-3-5
Grade	Freq
Jōyō-3	62
2 - 3 - 5	

3-5 宀

▶**FIX**

COMPOUNDS

❶ⓐ **fix, determine, decide, set, settle**
ⓑ **lay down, prescribe, establish**
決定 *kettei* decision, settlement, conclusion
断定 *dantei* decision, conclusion
一定する *ittei suru* fix, define, unify
確定する *kakutei suru* make a definite decision, decide upon; be decided
予定 *yotei* schedule, plan, prearrangement; expectation; estimate
否定 *hitei* denial, negation
指定 *shitei* designation, appointment
勘定 *kanjō* calculation; account, settlement of accounts
制定する *seitei suru* establish, enact
規定 *kitei* regulations, rules; provisions
協定 *kyōtei* agreement, pact
❷ⓐ (firmly in position) **fixed, stationary**
ⓑ [also prefix] [original meaning] (unchanging) **fixed, definite, regular, constant**
定着 *teichaku* fixing, fastening, fixation
定滑車 *teikassha* fixed pulley
固定する *kotei suru* fix, settle, be fixed
措定する *sotei suru* suppose, assume
定価 *teika* fixed [set] price
定員 *teiin* fixed number of regular personnel; capacity
定期の *teiki no* fixed, regular, periodic
定休 *teikyū* regular holiday
定数 *teisū* fixed number, constant
定則 *teisoku* established rule
定刻 *teikoku* regular [appointed] time
安定した *antei shita* stable, steady, firm;

calm

❸ pacify (a country), suppress
鎮定 *chintei* suppression, subdual
平定する *heitei suru* suppress, subjugate, subdue

❹ certainly, definitely
必定 *hitsujō* as certain as death

❺ *Buddhism* state of complete cessation of thought, meditation
入定 *nyūjō* calm contemplation
禅定 *zenjō* Samadhi, meditative concentration

❻ as it is; without fail
案の定 *annojō* as feared, sure enough

KUN

【sada(meru) 定める】 fix, determine, decide, set; lay down, prescribe, establish; pacify
定め *sadame* law; decision; destiny, karma; certainty
定めし *sademeshi* surely
見定める *misadameru* make sure of, ascertain

【sada(maru) 定まる】 be decided, be settled; quiet down
定まり *sadamari* custom, rule; tranquility
定まった場所 *sadamatta basho* specified place
定まらない天気 *sadamaranai tenki* changeable weather

【sada(ka) 定か】
sadaka na 定かな certain, positive
定かに *sadaka ni* clearly

SYNONYMS

❶ⓐ decide
決 DECIDE → 263
断 RESOLVE → 1492

❷ⓐ not moving
固 FIRM → 3086
静 still → 1728
止 still → 2941

ⓑ constant
恒 CONSTANT → 367
常 REGULAR → 2590
例 regular → 89

NOTE

⇨ see COMPOUND FORMATION for 措定 *sotei* ⇨ 措 502

3-5
宀

突 突 突 突

2230 TOTSU tsu(ku)

Ⓒⓗ 突 tū

Radical	Strokes
穴 116	8-5-3
Grade	**Freq**
Jōyō	518
2 - 3 - 5	

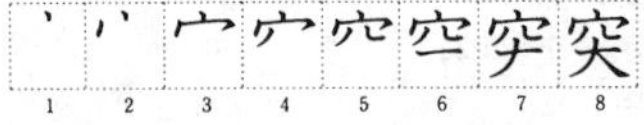

▶DASH ▶THRUST

COMPOUNDS

❶ dash forward, thrust, charge
突進する *tosshin suru* dash [rush] forward, push ahead
突貫する *tokkan suru* charge at, make a dash at (the enemy's position)
突入する *totsunyū suru* dash into, thrust into, rush into
突撃する *totsugeki suru* charge at, make a dash at (the enemy's position)
突破する *toppa suru* break [smash] through; surmount; exceed

❷ (strike with violence) **dash against, collide, crash against**
衝突する *shōtotsu suru* collide (with), crash (into); conflict [clash] (with)
追突する *tsuitotsu suru* collide with from behind
激突 *gekitotsu* crash, collision

❸ protruding, projecting, sticking out
突角 *tokkaku* convex angle
突出する *tosshutsu suru* project, protrude, stick out, jut out
突起 *tokki* projection, protuberance
突端 *tottan* tip, point
突堤 *tottei* pier, breakwater

❹ abruptly, suddenly, unexpectedly
突然 *totsuzen* abruptly, suddenly, unexpectedly
突如 *totsujo* suddenly, unexpectedly
突風 *toppū* squall, sudden gust
突飛な *toppi na* wild, extravagant, extraordinary
唐突に *tōtotsu ni* abruptly

❺ chimney
煙突 *entotsu* chimney, smokestack

KUN

【tsu(ku) 突く】
① (penetrate with a pointed end) thrust, pierce, stab, prick
突き刺す *tsukisasu* stab, pierce, thrust
突き殺す *tsukikorosu* stab to death
突き抜く *tsukinuku* pierce through
突き破る *tsukiyaburu* break [smash] through, pierce

② (strike forcibly with a pointed end) thrust, push, give a push [thrust]; poke, strike (a bell)
突き *tsuki* thrust, push; lunge
突き出す *tsukidasu* thrust out, push out; push out of a sumo ring

突き当たる *tsukiataru* hit against, run into; come to the end of (a street)
突っ込む *tsukkomu* thrust in, ram into, stuff into; dash [run] into
鐘を突く *kane o tsuku* strike a bell

③ [sometimes also 衝く] attack, strike at
中堅を突く *chūken o tsuku* strike [attack] at the center [heart]

④ [sometimes also 衝く] brave, face courageously
嵐を突いて進む *arashi o tsuite susumu* proceed in the face of a storm

⑤ [sometimes also 衝く] stimulate (the senses), be pungent
鼻を突く *hana o tsuku* assail the nostrils

SYNONYMS

❶ **move forward**
進 ADVANCE → 3121

❷ **collide**
衝 COLLIDE → 725
当たる HIT → 2177

❸ **protrude and protruding**
凸 CONVEX → 3486
隆 protuberant → 545
起 RISE → 3307
出る stick out → 3498

❹ **sudden**
急 SUDDEN → 2092
激 sudden → 776
暴 sudden → 2515

【tsuku】

① **stab**
刺 STAB → 1275

② **push**
押 PUSH → 314
圧 apply pressure → 2970

USAGE

tsuku

突く
① (penetrate with a pointed end) thrust, pierce, stab, prick
② (strike forcibly with a pointed end) thrust, push, give a push [thrust]; poke, strike (a bell)
③ [sometimes also 衝く] attack, strike at
④ [sometimes also 衝く] brave, face courageously
⑤ [sometimes also 衝く] stimulate (the senses), be pungent

衝く
① [usu. 突く] attack, strike at
② [usu. 突く] brave, face courageously
③ [usu. 突く] stimulate (the senses), be pungent
④ unclassified compounds

HOMOPHONES

tsuku ⇨ 衝 725

2231 ▶**SKY** ▶**AIR** ▶**EMPTY**
nonstandard for 空 2227

3-5 宀

2232 ▶**STILL** ▶**VALUE HIGHLY**
nonstandard for 尚 2233

3-5 小

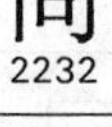

尚 尚 尚 ゟ
2233 SHŌ nao▲

CH 尚 shàng

Radical	Strokes
⺌ 42	8-3-5
Grade	**Freq**
Jōyō	1536
2-3-5	

3-5 ⺌

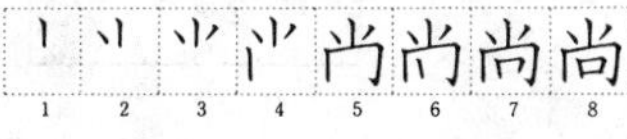

▶**STILL** ▶**VALUE HIGHLY**

COMPOUNDS

❶ **still, yet**
尚早の *shōsō no* premature

❷ **value highly, esteem, be enthusiastically devoted**
尚古 *shōko* worship of ancient things
尚武 *shōbu* militarism, warlike spirit
好尚 *kōshō* taste, fancy, fashion

❸ high, lofty, refined
高尚な *kōshō na* high, noble, elegant

❹ used phonetically for *shō*
和尚 *oshō* Buddhist priest [abbot] in charge of a temple

KUN

【nao 尚】
[sometimes also 猶]
①ⓐ (in increasing degree) still (more), all the more
ⓑ further, in addition, by the way

尚の事 *nao no koto* all the more, still more
尚一層悪い事は *nao issō warui koto wa* what is worse still
この方が尚良い *Kono hō ga nao yoi* This is still better
尚更 *naosara* still more, all the more
尚又 *naomata* further, besides
尚且つ *naokatsu* and yet
②ⓐ still, yet
ⓑ even, still
春尚浅し *Haru nao asashi* Spring is not yet far advanced
昼尚暗い *hiru nao kurai* be dark even in the daytime
③ *literary* as, just like, no more...than
鯨の魚にあらざるは尚馬の魚にあらざるが如し *Kujira no sakana ni arazaru wa nao uma no sakana ni arazaru ga gotoshi* A whale is no more a fish than a horse is

SYNONYMS

❶ **still**
未 NOT YET → 3506
❷ **respect**
重 set value on → 3573
崇 REVERENCE → 2297
欽 REVERE → 1690
仰 look up to → 48
敬 RESPECT → 1701

拝 WORSHIP → 303
慕 ADORE → 2353
尊 HONOR → 2324
【nao】
①ⓐ **additionally**
更に furthermore → 3541
且つ AS WELL → 3485
兼 CONCURRENTLY → 2286
亦 ALSO → 2011
又 also, and → 3351
及び and → 3385
並びに and also → 2246
傍ら besides → 147

USAGE

nao
尚
[sometimes also 猶]
①ⓐ (in increasing degree) still (more), all the more
ⓑ further, in addition, by the way
②ⓐ still, yet
ⓑ even, still
③ *literary* as, just like, no more...than
猶
[usu. 尚] same as 尚

HOMOPHONES

nao ⇨ 猶 619

3-5

2234

▶**KEEP** ▶**STAY**
handwritten abbreviation for 留 2580

3-5

incorrect classification ⇨ see 2555

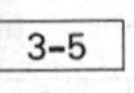

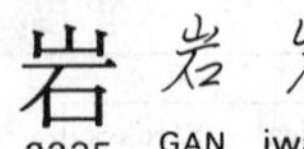
2235 GAN iwa

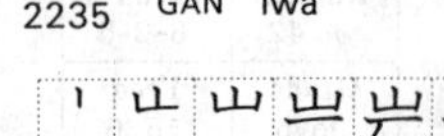

Ⓒⓗ 岩 yán

Radical	Strokes
山 46	8-3-5
Grade	**Freq**
Jōyō-2	746
2 - 3 - 5	

▶**ROCK**

COMPOUNDS

● [sometimes also 巌 2386] [also suffix] [original meaning] **rock**
岩石 *ganseki* rock
岩層 *gansō* rock formation
岩床 *ganshō* bedrock
岩礁 *ganshō* reef
岩塩 *gan'en* rock salt
火山岩 *kazangan* volcanic rock, lava
花崗岩 *kakōgan* granite

KUN

【iwa 岩】 [formerly also 磐] rock, crag
岩山 *iwayama* rocky mountain

SYNONYMS

● **rock and stone**
巌 CRAG → 2386
石 STONE → 2971

USAGE

iwa
岩
[formerly also 磐] rock, crag

磐
[now usu. 岩] rock, crag

HOMOPHONES
iwa ⇨ 磐 2850

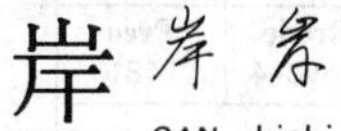

2236 GAN kishi

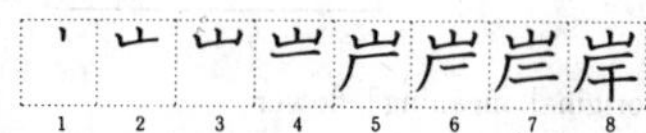

CH 岸 àn

Radical	Strokes
山 46	8-3-5
Grade	**Freq**
Jōyō-3	783
2 - 3 - 5	

3-5 山

▶SHORE

COMPOUNDS

❶ [original meaning] **shore, bank, coast, beach**
岸壁 *ganpeki* quay (wall), wharf
沿岸 *engan* coast, shore
海岸 *kaigan* seashore, (sea) coast, beach
左岸 *sagan* left bank (of a river)
対岸 *taigan* opposite bank [shore]

❷ proud, dignified
傲岸な *gōgan na* arrogant, haughty

KUN

【kishi 岸】 shore, bank, coast, beach

岸辺に *kishibe ni* ashore, on the shore
向こう岸 *mukōgishi* opposite bank, farther shore

SPECIAL READINGS
河岸 *kashi* riverside; fish market

SYNONYMS

❶ **shores and watersides**
浜 BEACH → 436
-辺 -side → 3029
畔 WATERSIDE → 1145
浦 SEASIDE → 437
渚 STRAND → 525
磯 ROCKY BEACH → 1242

苗 苗 苗 苗

2237 BYŌ MYŌ▲ nae nawa-

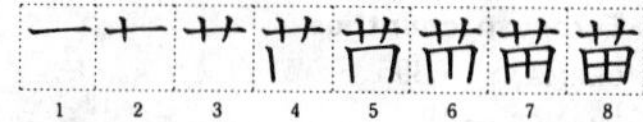

CH 苗 miáo

Radical	Strokes
艹 140	8-3-5
Grade	**Freq**
Jōyō	1631
2 - 3 - 5	

3-5 艹

▶SEEDLING

COMPOUNDS

❶ [original meaning] **seedling, sapling, young plant**
苗圃 *byōho* seedbed
苗字(=名字) *myōji* surname, family name
種苗 *shubyō* seedlings, seeds and saplings
育苗 *ikubyō* seedling culture

❷ offspring, descendants
苗裔 *byōei* offspring
痘苗 *tōbyō* vaccine, vaccine virus; smallpox vaccine

KUN

【nae 苗】 seedling, sapling
苗木 *naegi* sapling, young tree
苗床 *naedoko* seedbed
早苗 *sanae* rice sprouts

【nawa- 苗-】 seedling, rice seedling
苗代 *nawashiro* bed for rice seedlings, rice nursery
苗水 *nawamizu* water for a rice nursery

SYNONYMS

❶ **early states of plant life**
芽 BUD → 2240
種 SEED → 1218

COMPOUND FORMATION

❶ 苗字(=名字) *myōji*
According to one theory, 苗字 'surname, family name' refers to the name (字) of one's ancestors, who are likened to a seedling (苗 ❶).

❷ 痘苗 *tōbyō*
痘苗 'vaccine, etc.' is the offspring (苗 ❷), i.e., the virus or lymph, of a vaccine (痘).

3-5

艹

英 英 英 英

2238 EI hanabusa▲

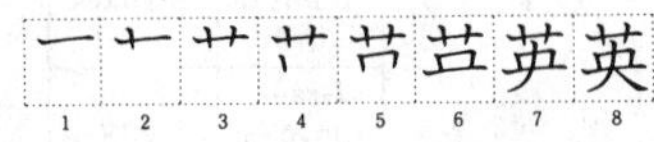

Ⓒ 英 yīng

Radical 艹 140	Strokes 8-3-5
Grade Jōyō-4	Freq 481
2-3-5	

▶DISTINGUISHED ▶ENGLAND

COMPOUNDS

❶ⓐ **distinguished, outstanding, excellent, talented; wise**

ⓑ person of distinguished talent, outstanding person

英雄 *eiyū* hero

英武 *eibu* distinguished [surpassing] valor

英才 *eisai* [formerly also 穎才] talent, genius; gifted person, talented person

英断 *eidan* prompt decision; resolute step

英知 *eichi* [sometimes also 叡智] sagacity, wisdom

英姿 *eishi* gallant figure, majestic appearance

俊英 *shun'ei* talent, genius; gifted person

育英 *ikuei* education of the gifted or promising

❷ⓐ **England, United Kingdom; English, British**

ⓑ Englishman

ⓒ **English (language)**

英国 *eikoku* England, Great Britain, the U.K.

英米 *eibei* England and America, Anglo-American

英領 *eiryō* British territory [possession]

英文学 *eibungaku* English literature

英数 *eisū* English and mathematics

英会話 *eikaiwa* English conversation

❸ [original meaning] flower

石英 *sekiei* quartz

INDEPENDENT

【ei 英】England, United Kingdom; English (language)

KUN

【hanabusa 英】corolla

SPECIAL READINGS

蒲公英▲ *tanpopo* dandelion

SYNONYMS

❶ⓐ **excellent and superior**

傑 outstanding → 155

逸 exceptional → 3120

優 SUPERIOR → 177

秀 EXCELLENT → 2545

名 first-rate → 2169

上 of upper grade → 3404

絶 without match → 1353

卓 PROMINENT → 2064

快 splendid → 245

妙 MARVELOUS → 239

❷ⓐ **European countries**

独 GERMANY → 395

仏 FRANCE → 19

伊 ITALY → 49

西 Spain → 3520

蘭 Holland → 2383

露 Russia → 2818

3-5

艹

苑 苑 苑 苑

2239 EN ON NAMES sono

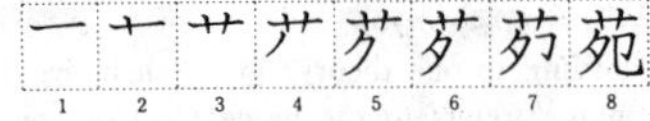

Ⓒ 苑 yuàn

Radical 艹 140	Strokes 8-3-5
Grade Names	Freq 2021
2-3-5	

▶IMPERIAL GARDEN

COMPOUNDS

❶ [sometimes also 園 *en* 3156] **Imperial garden, garden, park**

内苑 *naien* inner garden of the Imperial Palace

神宮外苑 *jingūgaien* Outer Gardens of Meiji Shrine

御苑 *gyoen* Imperial garden

鹿野苑 *rokuyaon* The Deer Park, *Mṛgadāva* (where Buddha delivered his first sermon)

❷ⓐ collection of artists or men of letters

ⓑ collection of artistic or literary works

文苑 *bun'en* literary world; anthology; collection of literary masterpieces

芸苑 *geien* world of artists and men of letters

広辞苑 *kōjien* name of a well-known Japanese-Japanese dictionary

❸ [usu. 園 *en* 3156] suffix after names of

business establishments such as restaurants and tea shops, esp. where there are gardens
珈琲苑 *kōhīen* name of a coffee shop

NAMES

苑五 *engo* male name
千苑 *chisono* female name

SYNONYMS

❶ **gardens**

園 GARDEN → 3156
庭 GARDEN → 3114

❸ **restaurant suffixes**

園 restaurant suffix → 3156
閣 high-class restaurant suffix → 3327
亭 quality restaurant suffix → 2072

NOTE

⇨ see USAGE note at 園 3156

芽 芽 芽 芽

2240 GA me

Ⓒⓗ 芽 yá

Radical	Strokes
艹 140	8-3-5
Grade	**Freq**
Jōyō-4	1560
2-3-5	

3-5 艹

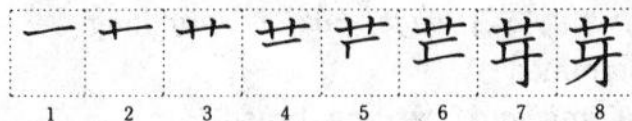

1 2 3 4 5 6 7 8

▶**BUD**

COMPOUNDS

● [original meaning] **bud, sprout**
芽胞 *gahō* spore
発芽する *hatsuga suru* bud, sprout, germinate
麦芽 *bakuga* wheat germ, malt
萌芽 *hōga* germination, beginning; sprout
胚芽 *haiga* embryo bud, germ

KUN

【me 芽】 bud, sprout, germ
芽生える *mebaeru* bud, sprout; begin
新芽 *shinme* sprout, bud, shoot, ratoon
若芽 *wakame* young bud

SYNONYMS

● **early states of plant life**

苗 SEEDLING → 2237
種 SEED → 1218

HOMOPHONES

me ⇨ 目 3043 眼 1172

NOTE

⇨ see USAGE note at 目 3043

若 若 若 若

2241 JAKU NYAKU NYA▲ waka(i) waka- mo(shikuwa) mo(shi)▲

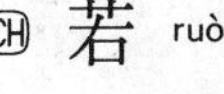

Ⓒⓗ 若 ruò

Radical	Strokes
艹 140	8-3-5
Grade	**Freq**
Jōyō-6	408
2-3-5	

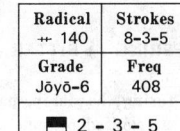

3-5 艹

1 2 3 4 5 6 7 8

▶**YOUNG**

COMPOUNDS

❶ [also 弱 *jaku* 1167] **young**
若年 *jakunen* youth, early age
若輩 *jakuhai* young people; greenhorn
老若男女 *rōjakudanjo* (=*rōnyakunannyo*) people of all ages and both sexes

❷ **somewhat, a certain amount, a little**
若干 *jakkan* a number of, some, a little

❸ function word for forming adjectives
泰然自若たる *taizenjijakutaru* imperturbable, self-possessed
瞠若たらしめる *dōjakutarashimeru* strike someone dumb with astonishment

❹ used phonetically for *nya*, esp. in the transliteration of Sanscrit Buddhist terms
般若 *hannya* wisdom, prajna

❺ like, similar to
傍若無人な *bōjakubujin na* overbearing, arrogant, audacious

KUN

【waka(i) 若い】 young, youthful, younger, junior; immature; low (number)
若さ *wakasa* youth, youthfulness
若若しい *wakawakashii* youthful, young-looking

【waka- 若-】 [also prefix] young
若手 *wakate* young man; young official
若者 *wakamono* young person [fellow], youth
若夫婦 *wakafūfu* young couple

【mo(shikuwa) 若しくは】 or, either...or; otherwise

【mo(shi) 若し】 if, in case of

SYNONYMS

❶ **young**

弱 young → 1167
少 young → 3467
青 youthful → 2430

幼 VERY YOUNG → 191 | 稚 CHILDISH → 1206

3-5 艹

茎 莖 茎 茎

2242 KEI kuki

Ⓒⓗ 茎 jīng

Radical	Strokes
艹 140	8-3-5
Grade	**Freq**
Jōyō	1861
2-3-5	

一 十 艹 艹 艾 芏 荃 茎 (1–8)

▶**STEM**

COMPOUNDS

❶ [also suffix] [original meaning] **stem, stalk**
茎葉 *keiyō* stems and leaves
球茎 *kyūkei* corn, bulb
地下茎 *chikakei* subterranean shoot, rootstock
❷ⓐ stem-shaped object, esp. the male genital organ
ⓑ [rare] counter for long and narrow objects
陰茎 *inkei* penis
一茎 *ikkei* a stem

KUN

【**kuki 茎**】 stem, stalk; long and narrow object; supportive structure
長い茎の有る *nagai kuki no aru* long-stemmed
水茎 *mizuguki* writing brush
歯茎 *haguki* gums

SYNONYMS

❶ **supporting parts of plants**
幹 TRUNK → 1718
株 stump → 935
根 ROOT → 930

3-5 艹

苦 苦 苦 苦

2243 KU kuru(shii) -guru(shii) kuru(shimu) kuru(shimeru) niga(i) niga(ru)

Ⓒⓗ 苦 kǔ

Radical	Strokes
艹 140	8-3-5
Grade	**Freq**
Jōyō-3	548
2-3-5	

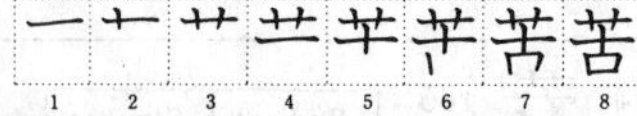

▶**SUFFERING** ▶**BITTER**

COMPOUNDS

❶ⓐ **suffering, hardship, pain, distress**
ⓑ (characterized by suffering) **hard, painful, distressing**
ⓒ hardship, trouble, difficulty
苦痛 *kutsū* pain, agony, anguish
苦悶 *kumon* agony, anguish
苦悩 *kunō* suffering, distress, anguish
苦難 *kunan* suffering, hardship
苦渋 *kujū* distress, affliction
苦境 *kukyō* distressing circumstances, straits
苦界 *kugai* bitter [hard] world; life of prostitution
苦労 *kurō* difficulties, trouble, hardships, labor
苦楽 *kuraku* pleasure and pain, joys and sorrows
辛苦 *shinku* hardships, trials; labor, trouble
貧苦 *hinku* hardship of poverty
❷ **hard, energetically**
苦戦 *kusen* hard fight, desperate battle
苦心 *kushin* pains, efforts, hard work
苦学する *kugaku suru* study under adversity, work one's way (through school)

❸ⓐ [original meaning] **bitter**
ⓑ (disagreeable) bitter, unpleasant
苦味 *kumi* bitter taste
苦土 *kudo* magnesia
苦情 *kujō* complaint, grievance
苦杯 *kuhai* bitter ordeal
苦笑 *kushō* forced [strained] smile
苦言 *kugen* frank advice; exhortation

INDEPENDENT

【**ku 苦**】 suffering, hardship, pain, distress; hardships, trouble, difficulty
苦にする *ku ni suru* take it seriously, distress oneself
苦も無く *ku mo naku* easily, without effort
苦は楽の種 *Ku wa raku no tane* No pain, no gain

KUN

【**kuru(shii) 苦しい**】 hard, painful, distressing; straitened, needy; strained, forced, awkward
苦しさ *kurushisa* pain, agony; suffering, hardship
苦しがる *kurushigaru* complain of a pain, suffer
胸が苦しい *mune ga kurushii* have a pain in one's chest

苦しい懐 *kurushii futokoro* tight budget
苦しい言い訳 *kurushii iiwake* lame [poor] excuse

【-guru(shii) -苦しい】 [also suffix] difficult to bear, disagreeable, unpleasant
見苦しい *migurushii* dishonorable, unsightly, ugly
聞き苦しい *kikigurushii* disagreeable to hear, offensive to the ear
息苦しい *ikigurushii* breathe with difficulty; suffocating, choking

【kuru(shimu) 苦しむ】 suffer (from), groan; be troubled, be distressed; be worried; be perplexed, try hard, make efforts
苦しみ *kurushimi* pain, anguish; distress, suffering, hardship
借金で苦しむ *shakkin de kurushimu* be distressed with debts

【kuru(shimeru) 苦しめる】 torment, distress, harass; trouble, worry; inflict pain
親を苦しめる *oya o kurushimeru* cause one's parents distress

【niga(i) 苦い】 bitter; (disagreeable) bitter, sour, trying, hard
苦さ *nigasa* bitterness, bitter taste
苦い薬 *nigai kusuri* bitter medicine
苦汁(＝苦塩) *nigari* bittern, brine
苦い経験 *nigai keiken* bitter experience
苦苦しい *niganigashii* unpleasant; shameful

【niga(ru) 苦る】 feel bitter, scowl
苦り顔 *nigarigao* sour [wry] face
苦り切る *nigarikiru* look sour [disgusted]

SYNONYMS

❶ trouble and suffering
悩 SUFFER → 421
窮 BE IN EXTREMITY → 2358
困 BE IN TROUBLE → 3070
痛 PAIN → 3285
辛 HARD → 2038
煩 VEXED → 1022
難 DIFFICULT → 1838

❸ⓐ unsavory tastes
辛 PUNGENT → 2038
酸 SOUR → 1563
渋い ASTRINGENT → 513

茉 茉 茉 茉

2244 MATSU NAMES ma

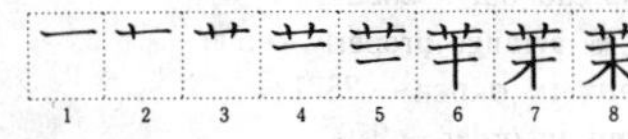

CH 茉 mò

Radical	Strokes
⺾ 140	8-3-5
Grade	**Freq**
Names	2124
2-3-5	

3-5 ⺾

▶JASMINE

COMPOUNDS

● jasmine, white jasmine
茉莉 *matsuri* jasmine, *Jasminum sambac*
茉莉花 *matsurika* jasmine, *Jasminum sambac*

NAMES
茉莉子 *mariko* female name

SYNONYMS

● shrubs
莉 JASMINE → 2284
藤 WISTERIA → 2382
蔦 JAPANESE IVY → 2355
萩 *HAGI* → 2319

茂 茂 茂 茂

2245 MO shige(ru)

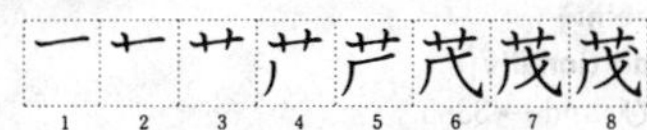

CH 茂 mào

Radical	Strokes
⺾ 140	8-3-5
Grade	**Freq**
Jōyō	1195
2-3-5	

3-5 ⺾

▶GROW THICK

COMPOUNDS

● grow thick, grow luxuriantly, be overgrown
茂林 *morin* [rare] luxuriant [dense] forest
繁茂する *hanmo suru* grow thick, luxuriate

KUN

【shige(ru) 茂る】 [formerly also 繁る] grow thick, be luxuriant, be overgrown
茂み *shigemi* thicket, bush
生い茂る *oishigeru* grow luxuriantly [thickly]

SYNONYMS

● flourish
繁 THRIVE → 2853

USAGE

shigeru

茂る
[formerly also 繁る] grow thick, be luxuriant, be overgrown

繁る
[now usu. 茂る] same as 茂る

HOMOPHONES

shigeru ⇨ 繁 2853

3-5

並 竝 竝 並 (CH) 并 bìng bīng

2246 HEI nami na(mi) nara(beru) nara(bu) nara(bini)

Radical	Strokes
一 1^Δ	8-1-7
Grade	**Freq**
Jōyō-6	649
2 - 3 - 5	

▶LINE UP

COMPOUNDS

ⓐ **line up, place in a row, place side by side, stand in a row**

ⓑ [also 併 83] [original meaning] **side by side, in line, together**

並立 *heiritsu* standing abreast

並列 *heiretsu* arrangement; row, parallel

並行(=平行) *heikō* going side by side; occurring together

並置 *heichi* juxtaposition, placing side by side

並用する *heiyō suru* use together [jointly]

KUN

[nami 並, na(mi) 並み]

①ⓐ medium quality, common run, average

ⓑ [in compounds] ordinary, common, average

並の *nami no* ordinary, average, mediocre

並肉 *naminiku* meat of medium quality

並製品 *namiseihin* common article, article of average quality

並外れて *namihazurete* extraordinary, uncommonly

② row, line

並木 *namiki* row of trees, roadside trees

軒並み *nokinami* row of houses; all round, across the board

③ [also suffix] equal, match, peer

人並の *hito nami no* common, ordinary, average; decent

欧米並みに *ōbei nami ni* as in Europe and America

[nara(beru) 並べる] *vt* line up, arrange, put side by side, juxtapose, place in order; display (goods); set up (chess pieces); enumerate, itemize; compare with

品物を並べる *shinamono o naraberu* arrange goods

五目並べ *gomokunarabe* gobang

並べ立てる *narabetateru* enumerate

並べて見ると *narabete miru to* in comparison

[nara(bu) 並ぶ] *vi* line up, form a line, stand in a row, be parallel; rank with, rival, equal

並び *narabi* line, row; side

立ち並ぶ *tachinarabu* stand in a row; be equal to

並び無い *narabinai* unrivaled, unequaled

[nara(bini) 並びに] and also, besides, and, in addition

性別並びに国籍 *seibetsu narabini kokuseki* sex and nationality

SYNONYMS

ⓐ **arrange**

比 rank → 26

列 arrange in a row → 824

陳 lay out (for exhibit) → 540

羅 spread out → 2622

揃える arrange properly → 590

整 PUT IN ORDER → 2871

理 put in order → 970

ⓑ **together**

併 TOGETHER → 83

同 together → 2987

共 JOINT → 2393

兼 CONCURRENTLY → 2286

[nami]

①ⓑ **ordinary**

只- ORDINARY → 2155

常 NORMAL → 2590

平 common → 3478

普 common → 2323

庸 MEDIOCRE → 3128

凡 COMMONPLACE → 2938

[narabini]

○ **additionally**

及び and → 3385

傍ら besides → 147

亦 ALSO → 2011

又 also, and → 3351

尚 STILL → 2233

更に furthermore → 3541

且つ AS WELL → 3485

兼 CONCURRENTLY → 2286

NOTE

⇨ see USAGE note at 平 3478

3-5 亡

2247

▶**BLIND**
nonstandard for 盲 2053

3-5 亼

命 念 incorrect classification ⇨ see 2-6

3-5 廾

革 incorrect stroke count ⇨ see 2448

3-6 口

品 2248 HIN HON▲ shina

Ⓒ 品 pǐn

Radical	Strokes
口 30	9-3-6
Grade	**Freq**
Jōyō-3	206
2-3-6	

▶**ARTICLE**

COMPOUNDS

❶ [also suffix]
ⓐ [original meaning] **article, thing**
ⓑ **article of merchandise, goods, commodity, product**
作品 *sakuhin* (piece of) work, performance, product
食品 *shokuhin* food, foodstuff
用品 *yōhin* article, supplies
薬品 *yakuhin* medicine, drug; chemicals
貴重品 *kichōhin* article of value
商品 *shōhin* goods, commodities
製品 *seihin* manufactured goods [articles], product; refined petroleum products
納品 *nōhin* delivery of goods; delivered goods
返品 *henpin* returning goods; returned goods, article sent back
舶来品 *hakuraihin* imported goods
❷ counter for courses of a meal
一品料理 *ippin-ryōri* one-dish meal
五品の定食 *gohin no teishoku* five-course meal
❸ⓐ **grade of excellence, quality, character**
ⓑ **refinement, grace, elegance, good character**
品質 *hinshitsu* quality
品性 *hinsei* character
品位 *hin'i* dignity, grace, nobility; grade, quality
品格 *hinkaku* dignity, grace
上品 *jōhin* elegance, refinement
気品 *kihin* dignity, grace, nobility
❹ **category, classification, type**
品目 *hinmoku* list of articles [items]
品種 *hinshu* kind, variety, description, brand
品詞 *hinshi* part of speech
❺ criticize, judge, grade
品評 *hinpyō* criticism, comment
❻ *Buddhism* chapter of a sutra
普門品 *fumonbon* Fumon (name of a chapter)
❼ [archaic] rank of a prince

INDEPENDENT

【hin 品】 refinement, grace, elegance, good character; grade of excellence, quality, character
品の良い人 *hin no yoi hito* person of refined manners

KUN

【shina 品】 article, thing; article of merchandise, goods, commodity, product, stock; quality, grade of excellence; type, kind
品物 *shinamono* article, thing, goods
品切れ *shinagire* absence [exhaustion] of stock
品が良い *shina ga ii* be of good quality
手を変え品を変え *te o kae shina o kae* by all possible means, by hook or by crook

SYNONYMS

❶ⓐ **object**
物 THING → 874
体 BODY → 71
ⓑ **merchandise**
産 product → 3298
貨 GOODS → 2465
物 commodity → 874
❸ⓐ **nature and character**
質 QUALITY → 2808
気 temperament → 3194
性 NATURE → 299
柄 CHARACTER → 897
格 (good) character → 926

ⓑ **flavor and elegance**
風 elegance → 3007
味 TASTE → 274
趣 FLAVOR → 3317
❹ **kinds and types**
属 genus → 3145
類 KIND → 1807
色 kind → 2029
般 SORT → 1317
型 TYPE → 2638
種 VARIETY → 1218
様 variety → 1052

3-6 大

奔 2249

▶**RUSH**
nonstandard for 奔 2218

3-6 宀

客 客 客 2250 KYAKU KAKU

Ⓒⓗ 客 kè

Radical	Strokes
宀 40	9-3-6
Grade	**Freq**
Jōyō-3	528
2-3-6	

Stroke order: 1–9

▶**VISITOR** ▶**CUSTOMER**

COMPOUNDS

❶ⓐ [original meaning] **visitor, caller, guest**
ⓑ (someone or something in a visiting capacity) guest, associate
客人 *kyakujin* caller, visitor, company
客室 *kyakushitsu* guest room, stateroom
来客 *raikyaku* visitor, guest
珍客 *chinkyaku* unexpected (but welcome) visitor
客員 *kyakuin* guest [associate] member
客演 *kyakuen* guest appearance
客土 *kyakudo* earth brought from another place to mix with the soil
❷ [also suffix] (one who pays for a product or service) **customer, client; spectator; passenger**
客席 *kyakuseki* seat (in the theater); passenger seat
客船 *kyakusen* passenger boat
客商売 *kyakushōbai* hotel, restaurant or entertainment business
乗客 *jōkyaku* passenger, fare
観客 *kankyaku* audience, spectators
観光客 *kankōkyaku* sightseer, tourist, visitor
❸ object
客観的な *kyakkanteki na* objective
客体 *kyakutai* (=*kakutai*) object
主客 *shukaku* host and guest; principal and auxiliary
❹ **skilled person, -er, -ian**
剣客 *kenkyaku* swordsman, fencer
侠客 *kyōkaku* chivalrous person, self-styled humanitarian
刺客 *shikaku* assassin
❺ traveler; travel
客死 *kakushi* dying abroad
❻ last (year)
客年 *kakunen* last year
❼ counter for utensils, tableware, etc. used for receiving guests
吸い物椀五客 *suimonowan gokyaku* five soup bowls

INDEPENDENT

【**kyaku 客**】visitor, caller, guest; customer, client; spectator, passenger; traveler
お客さん *okyakusan* visitor, caller, guest; customer, client; spectator; passenger; outsider
不帰の客 *fuki no kyaku* traveler on one's last journey, deceased person

SYNONYMS

❶ **visitor**
賓 GUEST → 2357
❹ **workers and professionals**
家 professional → 2273
士 PROFESSION SUFFIX → 3405
師 profession suffix → 1326
者 person who → 3211
人 person of certain category → 3368
員 MEMBER (of a staff) → 2269
屋 colloquial occupation suffix → 3098
手 OCCUPATION SUFFIX → 3456
婦 woman worker → 469
嬢 (unmarried) female worker → 758
夫 MAN LABORER → 3460
匠 CRAFTSMAN → 2990
工 workman → 3381

穿

2251 SEN uga(tsu) ha(ku)

Ⓒⓗ 穿 chuān

Radical	Strokes
穴 116	9-5-4
Grade	**Freq**
Reference	
2 - 3 - 6	

3-6 宀

COMPOUNDS

❶ [original meaning] drill, bore, pierce
穿孔 *senkō* perforation, punching; rupture
穿鑿する *sensaku suru* scrutinize, dig into
穿つ *ugatsu* drill, bore, pierce; put on, wear; be true to (nature), hit (the mark)

❷ put on (trousers or socks), wear (a skirt)
スカートを穿く *sukāto o haku* put on a skirt

HOMOPHONES

haku ⇨ 履 3171

NOTE

⇨ see USAGE note at 履 3171

宣 宣 宣

2252 SEN notama(u)▲ notama(waku)▲

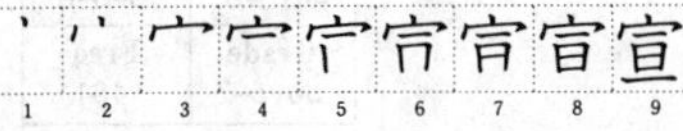

Ⓒⓗ 宣 xuān

Radical	Strokes
宀 40	9-3-6
Grade	**Freq**
Jōyō-6	966
2 - 3 - 6	

3-6 宀

▶PROCLAIM

COMPOUNDS

❶ⓐ (make widely known) **proclaim, declare, announce, publicize**
ⓑ (declare in public) **proclaim, pronounce, declare**
宣伝 *senden* publicity, propaganda; advertisement
宣教 *senkyō* missionary work
宣言 *sengen* declaration, proclamation
宣戦 *sensen* proclamation [declaration] of war
宣布 *senpu* proclamation, promulgation
宣告 *senkoku* sentence, verdict, pronouncement
宣誓 *sensei* oath, swearing, vowing

❷ imperial proclamation, imperial edict
宣下 *senge* imperial proclamation
院宣 *insen* imperial command [decree]

INDEPENDENT

【sensuru 宣する】 proclaim, announce

KUN

【notama(u) 宣う】 *literary* [honorific] say, be pleased to say
【notama(waku) 宣わく】 [formerly 曰わく] *literary* [honorific] say that...
子宣わく *Shi notamawaku* Confucius says...

SYNONYMS

❶ **inform and communicate**
申 REPORT → 3507
知 let know → 1127
告 NOTIFY → 2409
届ける give notice → 3078
達 issue a notice → 3139
報 INFORM → 1698
通 COMMUNICATE → 3109

❷ **imperial decree**
勅 IMPERIAL DECREE → 1451
詔 IMPERIAL EDICT → 1505

USAGE

notamawaku
宣わく
[formerly 曰わく] *literary* [honorific] say that...
曰わく
[now also 宣わく] same as 宣わく

HOMOPHONES

notamawaku ⇨ 曰 3025

NOTE

★do not confuse with 宜 2223

3-6 宀

窃 竊 窃 竊

2253 SETSU

ⒸⒽ 窃 qiè

Radical	Strokes
穴 116	9-5-4
Grade	**Freq**
Jōyō	1872
2 - 3 - 6	

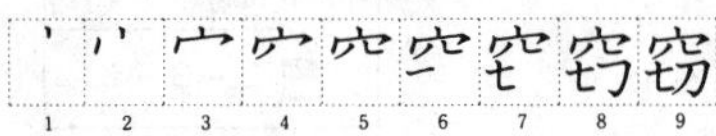

▶**STEAL**

COMPOUNDS

ⓐ **steal, pilfer**

ⓑ [rare] by stealth, secretly

窃盗 *settō* theft, larceny

窃取 *sesshu* theft, larceny

剽窃する *hyōsetsu suru* plagiarize

窃用する *setsuyō suru* [rare] use secretly, embezzle

SYNONYMS

ⓐ **steal and rob**

盗 STEAL → 2670

取 TAKE → 1262

奪 ROB → 2343

略 plunder → 1169

3-6 宀

室 室 室

2254 SHITSU muro

ⒸⒽ 室 shì

Radical	Strokes
宀 40	9-3-6
Grade	**Freq**
Jōyō-2	461
2 - 3 - 6	

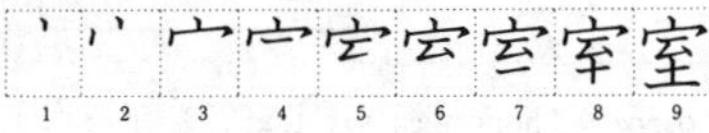

▶**ROOM**

COMPOUNDS

❶ⓐ [also suffix] [original meaning] **room, chamber, compartment**

ⓑ cave, house

室内 *shitsunai* indoors

教室 *kyōshitsu* classroom, class

個室 *koshitsu* private room, single room

寝室 *shinshitsu* bedroom

和室 *washitsu* Japanese style room

一等室 *ittōshitsu* first-class compartment

更衣室 *kōishitsu* changing room

氷室 *hyōshitsu* icehouse

温室 *onshitsu* greenhouse

❷ kinsmen, relatives, family

皇室 *kōshitsu* Imperial Family

❸ wife, esp. of persons of rank or noblemen

正室 *seishitsu* legal wife

後室 *kōshitsu* widow

INDEPENDENT

【**shitsu 室**】 room; wife (esp. of high ranking persons)

室を出る *shitsu o deru* leave the room

KUN

【**muro 室**】 cellar

室咲き *murozaki* blooming under glass

SYNONYMS

❶ⓐ **rooms**

間 room → 3323

房 CHAMBER → 1946

斎 study → 2115

堂 HALL → 2589

❸ **wives**

妻 WIFE → 2558

奥 wife → 2824

内 wife → 3466

嫡 legitimate wife → 680

婦 married woman → 469

嫁 BRIDE → 635

寡 widow → 2344

❸ **wives of rulers**

后 EMPRESS → 2981

妃 PRINCESS → 206

3-6 宀

窔

2255

▶**DASH** ▶**THRUST**

nonstandard for 突 2230

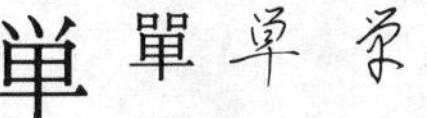

単 2256 TAN — CH 単 dān shàn chán

Radical	Strokes
⺌ 42△	9-3-6
Grade	**Freq**
Jōyō-4	562
2 - 3 - 6	

3-6

丶 丷 丷丶 𭕄 㓁 𫩏 𠮛 𠂉 単 (1–9)

▶SINGLE

COMPOUNDS

❶ⓐ [also prefix] **single, one, lone, uni-, mono-**
ⓑ singles (as in tennis)
単一な *tan'itsu na* single, simple, sole, individual
単車 *tansha* motorcycle, motorbike
単独の *tandoku no* single, independent, sole, lone
単色 *tanshoku* single color, monochrome
単数 *tansū gram* singular number
単眼 *tangan* one eye, ocellus
単弁 *tanben* univalve
単細胞 *tansaibō* single cell, one cell
単糖類 *tantōrui* monosaccharide
単勝式 *tanshōshiki* winning system (as in horse racing)
❷ **simple, uncomplicated, plain**
単純な *tanjun na* simple, uncomplicated, plain
単利 *tanri* simple interest
単調な *tanchō na* monotonous, dull
簡単な *kantan na* simple, easy, light
❸ⓐ **unit**
ⓑ term for designating size of dry cells
単位 *tan'i* unit
単価 *tanka* unit cost, unit price
単語 *tango* word
単元 *tangen* unit
単一の電池 *tan'ichi no denchi* D size battery
❹ slip of paper, card
伝単 *dentan* leaflet, handbill (in China)

INDEPENDENT

【tan 単】 singles (as in tennis); abbrev. of 単勝式 *tanshōshiki*: winning system (as in horse racing)
【tan ni 単に】 merely, simply
【tannaru 単なる】 mere, simple, sheer

SYNONYMS

❶ⓐ **one**
個 INDIVIDUAL → 117
一 ONE → 3341
壱 ONE (in legal documents) → 2197
片- ONE OF TWO → 3461
隻 ONE OF A PAIR → 2755
❷ **plain and simple**
朴 SIMPLE (unadorned) → 819
素 PLAIN → 2458
❸ⓐ **element**
素 ELEMENT → 2458
元 element → 1929

COMPOUND FORMATION

単車 *tansha*
単車 'motorcycle, motorbike' is a vehicle (車) for a single (単 ❶ⓐ) rider.

栄 incorrect classification ⇨ see 2574

3-6

炭 2257 TAN sumi — CH 炭 tàn

Radical	Strokes
火 86	9-4-5
Grade	**Freq**
Jōyō-3	924
2 - 3 - 6	

3-6

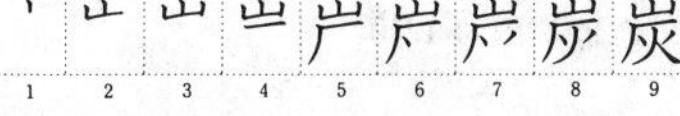

▶COAL ▶CHARCOAL

COMPOUNDS

❶ⓐ [also suffix] [original meaning] **coal**
ⓑ abbrev. of 炭鉱 *tankō*: coal mine
炭抗 *tankō* coal mine, coal pit
炭鉱 *tankō* coal mine
石炭 *sekitan* coal
無煙炭 *muentan* anthracite, smokeless coal
炭労 *tanrō* Japan Coal Miners' Union
❷ **charcoal**
木炭 *mokutan* charcoal
薪炭 *shintan* firewood and charcoal
塗炭 *totan* misery, distress
❸ **carbon**

炭素 *tanso* carbon
炭水化物 *tansuikabutsu* carbohydrates
炭酸 *tansan* carbonic acid; seltzer
炭化 *tanka* carbonization

KUN

【**sumi** 炭】 charcoal
炭火 *sumibi* charcoal fire
炭焼き *sumiyaki* charcoal making
消し炭 *keshizumi* cinders

SYNONYMS

❶ⓐ & ❷ kinds of fuel
薪 FIREWOOD → 2374
油 OIL → 341
❷ products of combustion
灰 ASH → 2979
殻 cinders → 1490
煙 SMOKE → 1021
❸ lighter elements
硫 SULFUR → 1184
水 hydrogen → 10
酸 OXYGEN → 1563
窒 NITROGEN → 2288
塩 chlorine → 631
臭 bromine → 2633

HOMOPHONES

sumi ⇨ 墨 2753

NOTE

⇨ see USAGE note at 墨 2753
⇨ see COMPOUND FORMATION for 塗炭 *totan* ⇨ 塗 2841

3-6 | 山

炭 2258

▶COAL ▶CHARCOAL
nonstandard for 炭 2257

3-6 | 艹

茶 茶 茶 茶 2259

CHA SA

Ⓒⓗ 茶 chá

Radical	Strokes
艹 140	9-3-6
Grade	**Freq**
Jōyō-2	871
2 - 3 - 6	

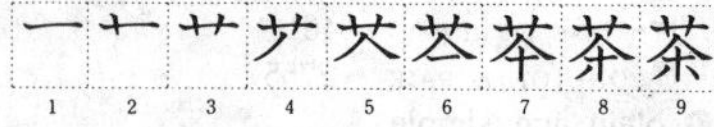

▶TEA

COMPOUNDS

❶ⓐ tea (the beverage), tea leaves
ⓑ [original meaning] tea plant, tea shrub [bush]
ⓒ tea ceremony
茶菓 *saka* (=*chaka*) tea and cakes, refreshments
茶話会 *sawakai* tea party
茶碗 *chawan* tea cup; rice bowl
茶の間 *chanoma* living room
茶の湯 *chanoyu* tea ceremony
新茶 *shincha* new season's tea
紅茶 *kōcha* black tea
番茶 *bancha* coarse tea
喫茶店 *kissaten* coffee shop, tea house
茶園 *chaen* tea plantation, tea shop
茶摘み *chatsumi* tea-picking
茶室 *chashitsu* tea arbor, tea ceremony room
茶道 *sadō* (=*chadō*) tea ceremony
❷ light brown
茶色 *chairo* light brown
焦げ茶 *kogecha* dark brown
❸ comicality, joke
茶番劇 *chabangeki* burlesque, low comedy
❹ used phonetically for *cha*
滅茶苦茶な *mechakucha na* confused, incoherent

INDEPENDENT

【**cha** 茶】 tea, green tea, tea leaves; tea ceremony; light brown
お茶 *ocha* tea, green tea; tea ceremony

SYNONYMS

❶ⓐ drinks
酒 ALCOHOLIC DRINK → 444
乳 MILK → 1438
汁 JUICE, SOUP → 195
❷ brown colors
褐 BROWN → 1210

荒 荒 荒 𦍒

2260 KŌ ara(i) ara- a(reru) a(rasu) -a(rashi) susa(mu)▲

一 十 艹 艹 茾 芒 芒 芹 荒
1 2 3 4 5 6 7 8 9

Ⓒ 荒 huāng

Radical	Strokes
艹 140	9-3-6
Grade	**Freq**
Jōyō	867
2-3-6	

3-6 艹

▶WILD

COMPOUNDS

❶ⓐ (in a primitive or uninhabited state) **wild, barren, desolate, bleak, deserted; devastated, ruined**

ⓑ the wild, frontier land, remote region

荒野 *kōya* wilderness, the wilds, wasteland
荒無地 *kōbuchi* wild [waste] land, wilderness
荒廃 *kōhai* desolation, waste, ruin
荒涼たる *kōryōtaru* desolate, dreary
荒城 *kōjō* ruined castle
八荒 *hakkō* national boundaries

❷ (of natural phenomena) **wild, stormy, fierce**

荒天 *kōten* stormy weather

❸ (unrestrained by reason) wild, absurd, ridiculous

荒唐無稽な *kōtōmukei na* absurd, nonsensical
破天荒の *hatenkō no* record-breaking, unprecedented

❹ indulge in pleasure

荒淫 *kōin* sexual indulgence

❺ famine, crop failure

備荒 *bikō* provision against famine

KUN

【ara(i) 荒い】

①ⓐ (of natural phenomena) wild, violent, rough

ⓑ (of behavior) wild, rough, rude, savage

荒さ *arasa* wildness, roughness; extravagance
荒い波 *arai nami* wild [raging] waves, stormy seas
荒荒しい *araarashii* wild, violent; rough, rude, gruff
手荒な *teara na* violent, rough

② unrestrained, lavish

金遣いの荒い *kanezukai no arai* wasteful of money, extravagant

【ara- 荒-】

① (in a natural state) wild, barren, desolate

荒野(=曠野) *arano* (=*areno*) wilderness, deserted land

②ⓐ (of natural phenomena) wild, violent, rough

ⓑ [prefix] (of behavior) wild, rough, rude, savage

荒海 *araumi* rough sea, stormy sea
荒武者 *aramusha* daredevil, rowdy

③ [also 粗-] (not elaborate) coarse, rough, crude, gross

荒削りの *arakezuri no* roughhewn; unrefined

④ unrestrained, extravagant

荒稼ぎ *arakasegi* making easy money; robbery

【a(reru) 荒れる】 (of natural phenomena) be wild, become rough, rage; (of people) run wild, rage, go berserk; run waste, be devastated; (of skin) become rough, get chapped

荒れ *are* tempest, stormy weather; chaps (of skin)
荒れ狂う *arekuruu* get stormy, rage; get angry
荒れ地 *arechi* wilderness
荒れた手 *areta te* rough [chapped] hands

【a(rasu) 荒らす】 devastate, lay waste, damage; break into

荒らし回る *arashimawaru* rampage; break into (houses here and there)
踏み荒らす *fumiarasu* trample down, devastate

【-a(rashi) -荒らし】

[suffix]

ⓐ robbery, burglary; intrusion
ⓑ robber, burglar; intruder

アパート荒らし *apātoarashi* apartment house robbery [robber]

【susa(mu) 荒む】 grow wild, roughen; come to live dissolutely, be degenerated

吹き荒む *fukisusamu* blow violently
荒んだ心 *susanda kokoro* hardened heart, dissolute mind

SYNONYMS

❷ & 【arai】①ⓐ **extreme in power**

激 VIOLENT → 776
狂 raging → 269
烈 VEHEMENT → 2652
猛 FIERCE → 537

❸ **rash**

暴 unrestrained → 2515
濫 EXCESSIVE → 801
乱 excessive → 1260
妄 RASH → 2016
盲 BLIND → 2053
滅 unreasonable → 660

【arai】

①ⓑ **violent**

暴 VIOLENT → 2515

猛 FIERCE → 537

USAGE

❶ **arai**

荒い

①ⓐ (of natural phenomena) wild, violent, rough

ⓑ (of behavior) wild, rough, rude, savage

② unrestrained, lavish

粗い

①ⓐ (not fine) coarse, rough, gross

ⓑ (not smooth) coarse, rough, rugged

ⓒ (not elaborate) coarse, rough, crude, gross

② sparse, scattered

❷ **ara-**

荒-

① (in a natural state) wild, barren, desolate

②ⓐ (of natural phenomena) wild, violent, rough

ⓑ [prefix](of behavior) wild, rough, rude, savage

③ [also 粗-] (not elaborate) coarse, rough, crude, gross

④ unrestrained, extravagant

粗-

①ⓐ [also 荒-] (not elaborate) coarse, rough, crude, gross

ⓑ (in the natural state) crude, raw, unrefined, unprocessed

② sparse, scattered

HOMOPHONES

arai ⇨ 粗 1329

ara- ⇨ 粗 1329

NOTE

★do not confuse with 慌 580

3-6 艹

茜 茜 茜 茜

2261 SEN akane

CH 茜 qiàn xī

Radical	Strokes
艹 140	9-3-6
Grade	**Freq**
Names	2082
2 - 3 - 6	

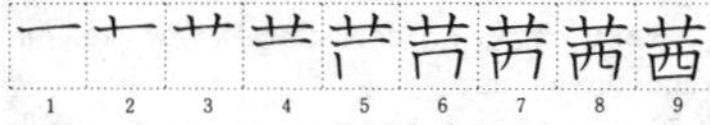

▶**MADDER**

KUN

【**akane 茜**】

ⓐ madder, *Rubia cordifolia*

ⓑ madder red, crimson

茜の根 *akane no ne* madder root

茜色 *akaneiro* madder, crimson

茜差す空 *akane sasu sora* glowing sky

NAMES

茜 *akane* female name

SYNONYMS

【**akane**】

ⓑ **red colors**

赤 RED → 2193

紅 CRIMSON → 1277

朱 VERMILION → 3531

丹 CINNABAR → 3441

緋 SCARLET → 1369

3-6 艹

莊 莊 莊 莊

2262 SŌ SHŌ▴ CHAN▴

CH 庄 zhuāng

Radical	Strokes
艹 140	9-3-6
Grade	**Freq**
Jōyō	1214
2 - 3 - 6	

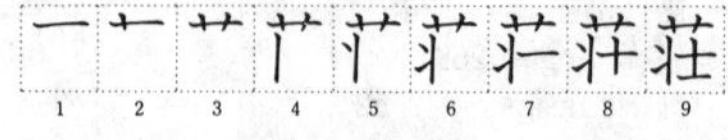

▶**VILLA** ▶**DIGNIFIED**

COMPOUNDS

❶ⓐ **villa, cottage**

ⓑ **suffix after names of villas, inns or apartment houses**

別荘 *bessō* villa, country cottage

山荘 *sansō* mountain villa

山水荘 *sansuisō* The Sansui Inn

❷ⓐ [sometimes also 庄 *shō* 3051] manor (in feudal Japan), village

ⓑ used in the formation of the names of former feudal villages (farm villages that were formerly manors) ⇨ see also 庄 3051 ❶

荘園 *shōen* manor

荘司 *shōji* administrator of a manor

五家荘 *gokanoshō* Gokanosho (place name)

❸ **dignified, solemn, grave, sublime**

荘厳な *sōgon na* solemn, sublime
荘重な *sōchō na* solemn, grave, impressive
❹ Zhuangzi (contemporary of Mencius)
老荘 *rōsō* Laozi and Zhuangzi
❺ adorn
荘厳する *shōgon suru* adorn (a Buddhist statue)
❻ⓐ mahjong
ⓑ counter for mahjong games
連荘 *renchan* extended game
一荘 *īchan* a game of mahjong

SYNONYMS

❶ mansions
邸 STATELY RESIDENCE → 1131
館 stately mansion → 1748
❷ feudal territorial divisions
封 daimiate → 1287
領 fief → 1224
国 province (in former Japan) → 3087
藩 FEUDAL DOMAIN → 2379
❸ dignified
威 dignified → 3578
厳 solemn → 3289
粛 solemnly → 3581

草 草 草 (variant forms)

2263 sō kusa kusa- -gusa

ⒸⒽ 草 cǎo

Radical	Strokes
艹 140	9-3-6
Grade	**Freq**
Jōyō-1	774
2 - 3 - 6	

3-6 艹

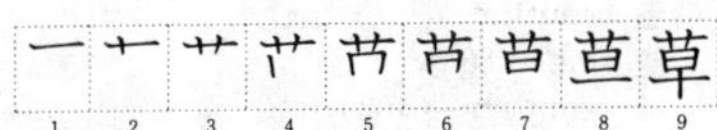

▶GRASS

COMPOUNDS

❶ [also suffix] **grass, weed**
草原 *sōgen* grassland, prairie, savannah, pampas, steppe
草木 *sōmoku* trees and plants, vegetation
野草 *yasō* wild grass
雑草 *zassō* weed
海草 *kaisō* seaweed
除草剤 *josōzai* herbicide
一年草 *ichinensō* annual plant, therophyte
❷ **draft, manuscript, outline**
草稿 *sōkō* outline, draft
草案 *sōan* (rough) draft
起草する *kisō suru* draft (a bill), draw up
❸ hurried, flurried, hasty
草草 *sōsō* closing words of a letter; hurried, flurried
❹ *sosho*, cursive style of Chinese characters
草書 *sōsho* *sosho*, cursive writing
❺ crude, shabby
草堂 *sōdō* monk's cell; (my) humble abode
❻ beginning
草創 *sōsō* inauguration, beginning

INDEPENDENT

【sō 草】 *sosho* (⇨ ❹); draft, manuscript
【sōsuru 草する】 draft, write

KUN

【kusa 草】 [also suffix] grass, weed
草花 *kusabana* flowering plant
草分け *kusawake* pioneer, pathfinder, originator
干し草 *hoshikusa* hay, dry grass
待宵草 *matsuyoigusa* evening primrose

【kusa- 草-】
[prefix]
① amateur, crude
草野球 *kusayakyū* sandlot baseball
② sham, similar
草雲雀 *kusahibari* grass cricket

【-gusa -草】
① [sometimes also -種] material, stuff
質草 *shichigusa* article for pawning
笑い草 *waraigusa* laughingstock
② [suffix] writing
徒然草 *tsurezuregusa* Random Thoughts from My Leisure Hours

SPECIAL READINGS

草履 *zōri* Japanese sandals, *zori*
煙草▲ *tabako* tobacco, cigarette

SYNONYMS

❶ kinds of grasses
芝 LAWN GRASS → 2180
笹 BAMBOO GRASS → 2663
❷ manuscript
案 draft → 2270
稿 MANUSCRIPT → 1231

USAGE

-gusa
-草
① [sometimes also -種] material, stuff
② [suffix] writing
-種
[usu. -草] material, stuff

HOMOPHONES

-gusa ⇨ 種 1218

NOTE

⇨ see also USAGE note at 早 2390

3-6 革 incorrect classification ⇨ see 2448

3-6 美 2264 BI MI▲ utsuku(shii)

CH 美 měi

Radical	Strokes
羊 123	9-6-3
Grade	**Freq**
Jōyō-3	407
2 - 3 - 6	

1 2 3 4 5 6 7 8 9

▶BEAUTIFUL

COMPOUNDS

❶ⓐ [sometimes also 媚 *bi* 565] [original meaning] **beautiful, pretty, lovely**

ⓑ [also suffix] beauty

美人 *bijin* beautiful woman

美少年 *bishōnen* handsome youth

美容院 *biyōin* beauty shop [parlor]

美術 *bijutsu* art, fine arts

美観 *bikan* fine view, beautiful sight

優美 *yūbi* grace, elegance

明美な *meibi na* picturesque, beautiful

肉体美 *nikutaibi* physical beauty

❷ abbrev. of 美術 *bijutsu*: art

美大 *bidai* school of fine arts

❸ (very satisfactory) **beautiful, good, superior**

美風 *bifū* beautiful [laudable] custom

美点 *biten* point of beauty, good point

美味 *bimi* good flavor, delicacy

美名 *bimei* good name, high reputation

美徳 *bitoku* virtue, good deed

❹ regard as beautiful, praise, extol

賛美する *sanbi suru* praise, admire

嘆美する *tanbi suru* admire, adore, extol

❺ used phonetically for *mi*

美事(=見事)な *migoto na* splendid, admirable, beautiful

INDEPENDENT

【bi 美】beauty, grace, charm

精神の美 *seishin no bi* moral beauty, mental charm

KUN

【utsuku(shii) 美しい】beautiful, pretty, lovely; fine, splendid; noble-minded

美しさ *utsukushisa* beauty, grace, charm

SYNONYMS

❶ⓐ **beautiful**

佳 FINE → 86

瑶 EXQUISITE → 1026

麗 OF GRACEFUL BEAUTY → 2151

艶 CHARMING → 1908

妙 of marvelous beauty → 239

華 MAGNIFICENT → 2283

絢 GORGEOUS → 1347

斐 florid → 2776

❸ **good**

佳 FINE → 86

好 FAVORABLE → 208

順 favorable → 18

良 GOOD → 3558

善 GOOD → 2325

❹ **praise**

賛 PRAISE → 2809

褒 COMMEND → 2144

嘉 commend (esp. an inferior) → 2340

彰 PROCLAIM MERITS → 1860

称 acclaim → 1160

賞 express admiration → 2618

揚 EXALT → 593

頌 EULOGIZE → 1045

NOTE

⇨ see COMPOUND FORMATION for 見事(=美事) *migoto* ⇨ 事 3567

首 2265

首 SHU kubi

ⒸⒽ 首 shǒu

Radical	Strokes
首 185	9-9-0
Grade	Freq
Jōyō-2	175
2-3-6	

3-6

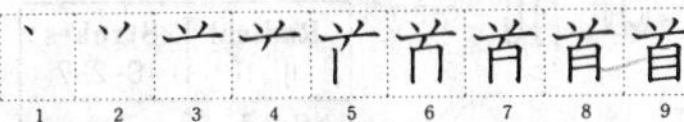

1 2 3 4 5 6 7 8 9

RADICAL 185

Standard form: 首 *kubi* 'neck' (馘 馗)

Description: used in characters related to the head or neck

▶HEAD ▶NECK ▶LEADER

COMPOUNDS

❶ⓐ [original meaning] **head**

ⓑ (forepart of a vessel) **head**

首肯する *shukō suru* assent, nod one's assent, consent

首級 *shukyū* decapitated head

斬首 *zanshu* decapitation

機首 *kishu* nose (of an airplane)

艦首 *kanshu* bow (of a war vessel)

❷ **neck**

絞首刑 *kōshukei* death [execution] by hanging

❸ (person occupying a head position) **leader, head, chief**

首長 *shuchō* leader, chief, head

首脳 *shunō* head, leader

首相 *shushō* prime minister

首謀者 *shubōsha* ringleader, mastermind

党首 *tōshu* party chief [leader]

元首 *genshu* ruler, sovereign

❹ⓐ (occupying a head position) **leading, top, first**

ⓑ (most important) **leading, main, principal**

首席 *shuseki* top seat [place]; chief, head

首都 *shuto* capital (city)

首位 *shui* first place, leading position

首班 *shuhan* head (of state or of a cabinet), prime minister

❺ beginning

首尾 *shubi* beginning and end; result, issue

首章 *shushō* beginning of a book

部首 *bushu* radical (of Chinese characters)

❻ⓐ poem

ⓑ counter for poems

落首 *rakushu* lampoon, satirical verse

和歌二首 *waka nishu* two tanka poems

百人一首 *hyakunin'isshu* the Hundred Poems by One Hundred Poets; (playing) cards of one hundred famous poems

❼ confess

自首 *jishu* self-surrender

KUN

【kubi 首】

① [formerly also 頸]

ⓐ neck

ⓑ narrow part, neck (of a bottle)

首飾り *kubikazari* necklace

手首 *tekubi* wrist

バイオリンの首 *baiorin no kubi* neck of a violin

② head

首を傾げる *kubi o kashigeru* put one's head on one side

③ firing, discharge

首切り *kubikiri* firing, dismissal; decapitation

首になる *kubi ni naru* be fired, be dismissed

SYNONYMS

❶ⓐ **head**

頭 HEAD → 1604

脳 BRAIN → 975

ⓑ **front**

面 FACE → 2087

前 front → 2266

❷ **neck**

項 nape → 567

❸ **leaders**

領 leader → 1224

頭 HEAD → 1604

長 CHIEF → 2556

王 KING → 3439

主 MASTER → 1938

❹ⓐ **main**

主 MAIN → 1938

正 chief → 3484

本 head → 3502

親- PARENT → 1799

USAGE

kubi

首

① [formerly also 頸]

ⓐ neck

ⓑ narrow part, neck (of a bottle)

② head

③ firing, discharge

頸

[now usu. 首]

ⓐ neck

ⓑ narrow part, neck (of a bottle)

HOMOPHONES

kubi ⇨ 頸 1611

NOTE

⇨ see COMPOUND FORMATION for 首班 *shuhan* ⇨ 班 946

3-6

前 前 前 前

2266 ZEN mae -mae

CH 前 qián

Radical	Strokes
刂 18	9-2-7
Grade	**Freq**
Jōyō-2	31
2 - 3 - 6	

▶BEFORE

COMPOUNDS

❶ [also prefix] (in front) **before, ahead, front, fore**

前後 *zengo* before and after; order, sequence
前方 *zenpō* front
前進 *zenshin* advance, going ahead
前面 *zenmen* front, frontage, facade
前線 *zensen* front line, fighting front; *meteorology* front
前途 *zento* one's future, prospects; distance yet to cover
前車輪 *zensharin* front wheel

❷ⓐ [also suffix] (preceding in time) **before, ago, previous, past**

ⓑ [also prefix] (immediately preceding in order of time) **previous, former, ex-, one-time**

前日 *zenjitsu* the day before
前年度 *zennendo* preceding (fiscal) year
午前 *gozen* morning, forenoon
以前 *izen* before, ago, since
寸前に *sunzen ni* immediately before
三年前 *sannenzen* three years ago
前夫 *zenpu* former husband, ex-husband
前大統領 *zendaitōryō* former president
前住所 *zenjūsho* one's former address

❸ⓐ (preceding in order) **former, preceding, first (of two)**

ⓑ (in an earlier part of a text) preceding, above

前者 *zensha* the former
前半 *zenhan* (=*zenpan*) first half
前編 *zenpen* first volume; first part
前場 *zenba* morning session (of stock market)
前記の *zenki no* the above-mentioned
前条 *zenjō* preceding article

❹ in the presence of (a superior)

面前で *menzen de* before, in the presence of
目前で *mokuzen de* in the face of, in the presence of
御前 *gozen* Your Excellency; the (Imperial) presence
神前に誓う *shinzen ni chikau* pledge before God

INDEPENDENT

【zen 前】 in the past, previously; abbrev. of 紀元前 *kigenzen*: B.C. (before Christ); abbrev. of 午前 *gozen*: morning, forenoon

前三百九年 *zen sanbyakukyūnen* 309 B.C.
前九時 *zen kuji* 9 a.m.

KUN

【mae 前】

①ⓐ front, fore part
ⓑ presence

前に *mae ni* ahead, before
前足 *maeashi* forelegs
人前で *hitomae de* before others

②ⓐ before, ago, since
ⓑ beforehand, in advance

前の *mae no* former, previous, old
前に *mae ni* previously, formerly
前以て *maemotte* in advance
前払い *maebarai* advance payment

③ private parts

前を隠す *mae o kakusu* cover one's private parts

④ unclassified compounds

名前 *namae* name, given name
当たり前 *atarimae* proper, right, just; of course

【-mae -前】

[also suffix]

①ⓐ ago, before, since
ⓑ (10 minutes) to (seven), before (seven)

二日前 *futsukamae* two days ago
十時五分前 *jūji gofunmae* five to ten

② in front of, before

駅前の *ekimae no* in front of the station

③ function word for forming pronouns

お前 *omae* you; darling, my child
手前 *temae* [humble] I; [belittling] you

④ portion, helping, serving

分け前 *wakemae* share, portion
一人前 *ichininmae* one helping, one portion

⑤ worthy of, becoming of

一人前 *ichininmae* full-fledged man
男前 *otokomae* man's looks
腕前 *udemae* skill, ability, capacity

気前 *kimae* generosity
⑥ honorific title after names of court ladies
玉藻の前 *tamamo-no-mae* Lady Tamamo

SYNONYMS
❶ **in front**
先 AHEAD → 2394
❷ⓐ **before**
先 AHEAD → 2394
予 IN ADVANCE → 1983
ⓑ **former**
先 former → 2394
旧 FORMER → 14
元 former → 1929
故 OLD (earlier time) → 1141
既 ALREADY → 1166
【mae】
①ⓐ **front**
面 FACE → 2087
首 HEAD → 2265

COMPOUND FORMATION
❶ **男前** ***otokomae***
男前 'man's looks' is looks becoming of (-前 ⑤) a man (男).
❷ **腕前** ***udemae***
腕前 'skill, etc.' is something worthy of (-前 ⑤) one's ability (腕).
❸ **気前** ***kimae***
気前 'generosity' is something worthy of (-前 ⑤) one's feelings (気).

NOTE
⇨ see COMPOUND FORMATION for 当たり前 *atari-mae* ⇨ 当 2177

3-6 丷

前 2267

▶BEFORE
nonstandard for 前 2266

3-6 韋

韋 2268

Ⓒⓗ 韦 wéi

Radical	Strokes
韋 178	9-9-0
Grade	**Freq**
Reference	
2-3-6	

RADICAL 178
Standard form: 韋 *nameshigawa* 'leather' (韜)
Variant: 韋 *nameshigawa* (韓)
Description: used in characters related to tanned leather products

COMPOUNDS
❶ leather, tanned [dressed] skin
韋編 *ihen* leather cord
❷ used phonetically for *i*
韋駄天 *idaten* swift-running heavenly warrior; great runner

3-6 𠆢

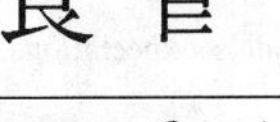

incorrect classification ⇨ see 2-7

3-7 口

員 2269 IN

Ⓒⓗ 员 yuán yún yùn

Radical	Strokes
口 30	10-3-7
Grade	**Freq**
Jōyō-3	44
2-3-7	

▶MEMBER
COMPOUNDS
❶ [also suffix]
ⓐ **member of a staff [profession], personnel, person in charge**
ⓑ **member of an organization**
社員 *shain* staff member, employee
職員 *shokuin* staff, employee, personnel
全員 *zen'in* all members, entire staff
係員 *kakariin* clerk in charge
検査員 *kensain* inspector
会社員 *kaishain* company employee, office worker

公務員 *kōmuin* public service personnel, government worker
事務員 *jimuin* clerk, clerical staff
警備員 *keibiin* guard
委員 *iin* committeeman; delegate
議員 *giin* member of an assembly, assemblyman
党員 *tōin* party member
❷ fixed number, capacity
員数 *inzū* (=*insū*) number, total
定員 *teiin* fixed number of regular personnel; capacity
満員 *man'in* full to capacity
❸ girth
幅員 *fukuin* width [extent] of roads or ships

INDEPENDENT

【in 員】 member of a staff
員に備わるのみ *in ni sonawaru nomi* be a member of staff but useless as a worker

SYNONYMS

❶ⓐ person in charge
係 PERSON IN CHARGE → 97
-方 person in charge → 1963
ⓐ workers and professionals
屋 colloquial occupation suffix → 3098
手 OCCUPATION SUFFIX → 3456
師 profession suffix → 1326
士 PROFESSION SUFFIX → 3405
客 skilled person → 2250
家 professional → 2273
者 person who → 3211
人 person of certain category → 3368
婦 woman worker → 469
嬢 (unmarried) female worker → 758
夫 MAN LABORER → 3460
匠 CRAFTSMAN → 2990
工 workman → 3381
❷ kinds of numbers
数 NUMBER (mathematical unit) → 1790
号 NUMBER (numerical designation) → 2153
番 No. → 2748
第 ORDINAL NUMBER PREFIX → 2660
-目 ordinal number suffix → 3043
次 numerical order suffix → 54
❸ width
幅 WIDTH → 569
径 DIAMETER → 291

3-7 宀

案 2270 AN

ⒸⒽ 案 àn

Radical	Strokes
木 75	10-4-6
Grade	**Freq**
Jōyō-4	199
2-3-7	

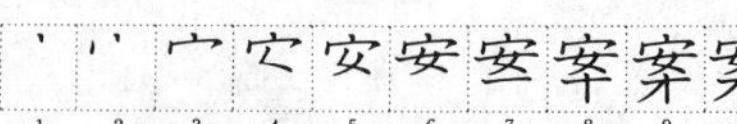

▶PROPOSAL

COMPOUNDS

❶ⓐ [also suffix] **proposal, plan, scheme**
ⓑ draft
案件 *anken* matter, case, item
提案 *teian* proposition, proposal, suggestion
法案 *hōan* bill, legislative proposal
議案 *gian* bill, measure
原案 *gen'an* original bill [plan]
試案 *shian* tentative plan, draft
対案 *taian* counterproposal
立案する *ritsuan suru* make a plan, devise, draft
増税案 *zōzeian* tax increase proposal
具体案 *gutaian* concrete proposal
案内する *annai suru* guide, show; inform, notify
草案 *sōan* (rough) draft
❷ⓐ think out, devise
ⓑ thought, idea, design
案出する *anshutsu suru* think out, contrive, devise, invent
思案 *shian* thought, consideration, reflection
考案 *kōan* idea, plan; project
懸案 *ken'an* pending question [problem]
名案 *meian* splendid idea
新案特許 *shin'an tokkyo* patent on a new device
❸ official documents, records
答案 *tōan* examination paper; answer
❹ expectations
案外 *angai* contrary to one's expectations, unexpectedly
案の定 *annojō* as feared, sure enough
❺ [formerly 按 371] according to
案分する *anbun suru* divide [distribute] proportionally
❻ [original meaning] desk, table
案下 *anka* beneath the desk

INDEPENDENT

【an 案】 plan, scheme; draft
案を立てる *an o tateru* draft a proposal
案に相違して *an ni sōi shite* contrary to one's expectations
【anjiru 案じる】 be anxious, be concerned about; think out, devise
【anzuru 案ずる】 ponder; worry over

SYNONYMS

❶ⓐ **plans and planning**
計 PLAN → 1441
画 DRAW UP A PLAN → 3000
企 PROJECT → 2021
図 systematic plan → 3071
謀 SCHEME → 1593
策 SCHEME → 2679
略 STRATEGY → 1169
ⓑ **manuscript**
草 draft → 2263
稿 MANUSCRIPT → 1231
❷ⓐ **think and consider**
思 THINK → 2564
考 THINK → 3196
存 hold an opinion → 2982
想 CONCEIVE → 2828
慮 CONSIDER → 3266
勘 take into consideration → 1777
量 weigh → 2471
惟 MEDITATE → 481
省 INTROSPECT → 2449

USAGE

anzuru
案ずる
plan, scheme: draft
按ずる
investigate, consider

COMPOUND FORMATION

❶ 案内 *annai*
案内 consists of 案 ❶ⓑ 'draft' and 内 'inside'. It derives from 文案の内容 *bun'an no naiyō*, which literally means the contents of a draft. By extension, 案内する 'guide, etc.' means to know or let know the contents of, that is, to guide, show or inform.
❷ 案外 *angai*
案外 'contrary to one's expectations, etc.' is to be beyond (外) one's thoughts or expectation (案 ❹).
❸ 案分 *anbun*
案分する 'divide [distribute] proportionally', formerly written 按分する, is to divide (分) something in accordance with (案 ❺) or in proportion to needs.

宴 宴 宴

2271 EN utage▲

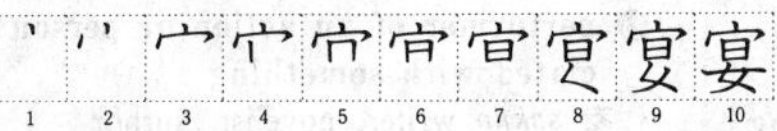

CH 宴 yàn

Radical	Strokes
宀 40	10-3-7
Grade	**Freq**
Jōyō	1541
2 - 3 - 7	

3-7 宀

▶BANQUET

COMPOUNDS

● [also suffix] **banquet, feast, dinner party, dinner; entertainment**
宴会 *enkai* dinner party, banquet, feast
宴席 *enseki* banquet hall, dinner party
招宴 *shōen* invitation to a party; party
披露宴 *hirōen* wedding reception
歓迎宴 *kangeien* welcome party
饗宴 *kyōen* banquet, feast, dinner

INDEPENDENT

【en 宴】banquet, feast, dinner party
宴を張る *en o haru* hold a banquet, give a dinner party

KUN

【utage 宴】banquet, feast, party, dinner
花見の宴 *hanami no utage* cherry-blossom viewing party

SYNONYMS

● **social gatherings**
会 party → 2020

害 害 害 害

2272 GAI

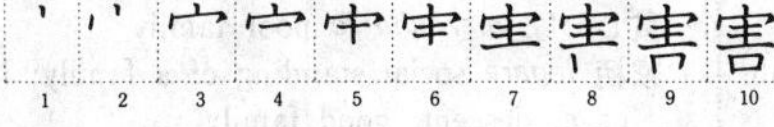

CH 害 hài

Radical	Strokes
宀 40	10-3-7
Grade	**Freq**
Jōyō-4	376
2 - 3 - 7	

3-7 宀

▶HARM

COMPOUNDS

❶ⓐ **harm, evil, ill effect**
ⓑ **harm, injure, damage**
害毒 *gaidoku* harm, evil, evil influence
被害 *higai* damage, harm
弊害 *heigai* evil, abuse, vice
有害な *yūgai na* harmful, pernicious, noxious

害虫 *gaichū* harmful insect
傷害 *shōgai* injury, bodily harm
侵害 *shingai* infringement, violation
❷ **damage; pollution**
公害 *kōgai* environmental pollution
災害 *saigai* calamity, disaster, accident
損害 *songai* damage, harm
冷害 *reigai* damage from cold weather
水害 *suigai* flood damage
❸ [formerly also 碍 1201] [original meaning] stand in the way, hinder, obstruct, interfere with
障害 *shōgai* obstacle, hindrance; (physical) disorder
妨害する *bōgai suru* disturb, hinder, obstruct, hamper, impede, interfere
阻害する *sogai suru* obstruct, check, impede, hinder
❹ kill
殺害する *satsugai* (=*setsugai*) *suru* murder, kill, assassinate
自害 *jigai* suicide
❺ vital point
要害 *yōgai* stronghold, strategic position

INDEPENDENT

【gai 害】 harm, evil, ill effect; damage
飲酒の害 *inshu no gai* ill effects of drinking
【gaisuru 害する】 harm, injure, damage

SYNONYMS

❶ & ❷ **harm and damage**
損 damage → 651
傷 WOUND → 158
❸ **obstruct and hinder**
妨 HINDER → 238
障 hinder → 715
阻 OBSTRUCT → 348
遮 INTERRUPT → 3158

3-7
宀

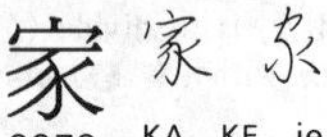

2273 KA KE ie ya uchi▲

CH 家 jiā jie

Radical	Strokes
宀 40	10-3-7
Grade	**Freq**
Jōyō-2	94
2 - 3 - 7	

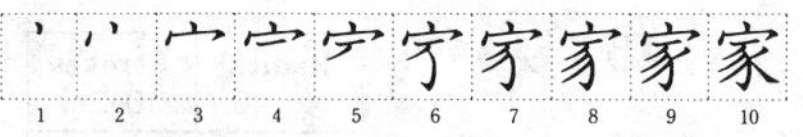

▶**HOUSE** ▶**FAMILY**

COMPOUNDS

❶ [original meaning] **house, home, dwelling**
家屋 *kaoku* house, building
家具 *kagu* furniture
人家 *jinka* dwelling (house), human habitation
民家 *minka* private house
❷ⓐ **family, house, household**
ⓑ [suffix] **family, House**
家族 *kazoku* family, household
家庭 *katei* home, family, household
家計 *kakei* household economy, family finances
家内 *kanai* family, household; wife
家事 *kaji* household affairs, housework
家裁 *kasai* family court
実家 *jikka* family in which one was born; one's parents' home
良家 *ryōke* good family
一家 *ikka* family, household; one's family; style (of established reputation)
将軍家 *shōgunke* family to inherit the shogunate
徳川家 *tokugawake* the Tokugawas, the House of Tokugawa
宮田家 *miyatake* the Miyata family
❸ [also suffix]
ⓐ **professional, member of a profession**
ⓑ **performer of an action or person associated with something**
作家 *sakka* writer, novelist, author
画家 *gaka* artist, painter
政治家 *seijika* politician
専門家 *senmonka* specialist, expert
勉強家 *benkyōka* diligent student, studious person
財産家 *zaisanka* person of wealth
儒家 *juka* Confucian, Confucianist
道家 *dōka* Taoist scholar
❹ territory, country
国家 *kokka* state, country, nation
邦家 *hōka* one's country, the state

KUN

【ie 家】 house, home, dwelling; family, household; family name
家家 *ieie* houses
家を興す *ie o okosu* found a house; raise the reputation of one's family
家出 *iede* running away from home
貧しい家 *mazushii ie* poor family
家柄 *iegara* social standing of a family; lineage, descent; good family
家元 *iemoto* head [master] of a school (of noh drama players)
【ya 家】
① [also suffix] house, home
家主 *yanushi* house owner, landlord, landlady

家賃 *yachin* (house) rent
我が家 *wagaya* one's home [house]
借家 *shakuya* house for rent, rented house
一軒家 *ikken'ya* solitary house; private home
② [usu. 屋] suffix after stage family names
林家正蔵 *hayashiya shōzō* Shozo Hayashiya (name of a comic story teller)

[uchi 家]
[also 内]
ⓐ house, one's home
ⓑ one's family, household
家を建てる *uchi o tateru* build one's house
家の人 *uchi no hito* my husband; one's family

SYNONYMS

❶ **houses**
屋 HOUSE → 3098
軒 house → 1459
戸 HOUSEHOLD → 1930
宅 DWELLING HOUSE → 2174
居 residence → 3080
邸 STATELY RESIDENCE → 1131
住 housing → 64
❷ **family and relations**
族 FAMILY → 958
門 family → 888
氏 clan → 2951
縁 RELATION → 1386
親 RELATIVES → 1799
姻 relative by marriage → 353
❸ **workers and professionals**
客 skilled person → 2250
士 PROFESSION SUFFIX → 3405
師 profession suffix → 1326
者 person who → 3211
人 person of certain category → 3368
員 MEMBER (of a staff) → 2269
屋 colloquial occupation suffix → 3098
手 OCCUPATION SUFFIX → 3456
婦 woman worker → 469
嬢 (unmarried) female worker → 758
夫 MAN LABORER → 3460
匠 CRAFTSMAN → 2990
工 workman → 3381

USAGE

家 **ka** 者 **sha**
★家 and 者 both refer to the performer of an action or holder of an occupation. The former often stresses that the action is performed by a professional engaged in that work, as in 作家 *sakka* 'writer, novelist, author', while the latter more often denotes the performer of the action, whether by profession or not, as in 読者 *dokusha* 'reader, subscriber'. The two are sometimes used interchangeably, as in 翻訳者[家] *hon'yakusha*[*ka*], the latter implying that the person is a professional translator.

HOMOPHONES

ya ⇨ 屋 3098
uchi ⇨ 内 3466 中 3451

NOTE

⇨ see also USAGE notes at 屋 3098 and 内 3466

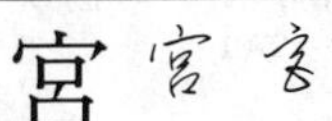
2274 KYŪ GŪ KU KŪ▲ miya

CH 宮 gōng

Radical	Strokes
宀 40	10-3-7
Grade	**Freq**
Jōyō-3	400
2-3-7	

3-7

1 2 3 4 5 6 7 8 9 10

▶**ROYAL PALACE** ▶**SHINTO SHRINE**

COMPOUNDS

❶ⓐ **royal palace, imperial palace, magnificent dwelling**
ⓑ **suffix after names of palaces**
宮殿 *kyūden* palace (of a royal person)
王宮 *ōkyū* King's palace, royal palace
離宮 *rikyū* detached palace, Imperial villa
迷宮 *meikyū* labyrinth, maze; mystery
竜宮 *ryūgū* Palace of the Dragon King
エリゼ宮 *erizekyū* Élysée
❷ Imperial Court, court
宮廷 *kyūtei* the Court, the Palace
宮中 *kyūchū* Imperial Court
宮内庁 *kunaichō* Imperial Household Agency
皇宮警察 *kōgū keisatsu* Imperial Guard
❸ⓐ **Shinto shrine, imperial Shinto shrine**
ⓑ suffix after names of Shinto shrines
宮司 *gūji* chief priest of a Shinto shrine
神宮 *jingū* Shinto shrine; Grand Shrine at Ise
遷宮 *sengū* transfer of a shrine
外宮 *gekū* Outer Shrine of Ise
東照宮 *tōshōgū* Toshogu Shrine
❹ (Imperial) prince or princess
中宮 *chūgū* Empress or second consort in Heian period
東宮 *tōgū* Crown Prince
❺ⓐ sex organ, womb
ⓑ castration as a punishment in ancient China
子宮 *shikyū* womb, uterus
宮刑 *kyūkei* castration
❻ section of the zodiac

十二宮 *jūnikyū* the twelve signs of the zodiac
獅子宮 *shishikyū* Leo, the Lion
❼ [rare] first note of the pentatonic scale (⇨ see APPENDIX 7)

INDEPENDENT

【kyū 宮】[rare] first note of the pentatonic scale

KUN

【miya 宮】
① Shinto shrine
宮参り *miyamairi* shrine visit
宮居 *miyai* shrine compound; Imperial Palace
② Imperial Court
宮仕え *miyazukae* court service
③ⓐ member of Imperial family
ⓑ title after names of Imperial princes or princesses
宮様 *miyasama* prince, princess
高松の宮 *takamatsu-no-miya* Prince Takamatsu

SYNONYMS

❶ **palace**
殿 PALACE → 1792
❷ **governments**
朝 court → 1695
廷 COURT → 3058
幕 SHOGUNATE → 2335
官 GOVERNMENT → 2226
❸ **places of worship**
社 Shinto shrine → 840
寺 BUDDHIST TEMPLE → 2164
堂 temple building → 2589
塔 pagoda → 561
院 monastery → 454
教 church → 1493

3-7
宀

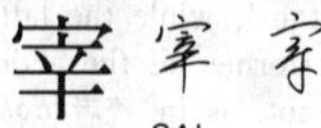

2275 SAI

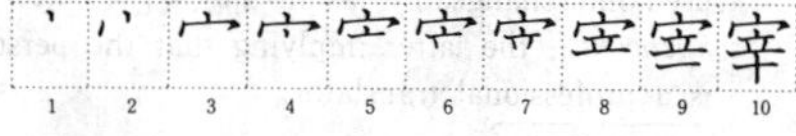

ⒸⒽ 宰 zǎi

Radical	Strokes
宀 40	10-3-7
Grade	Freq
Jōyō	1762
2 - 3 - 7	

▶**PRESIDE**

COMPOUNDS

❶ **preside (over), superintend, supervise, manage**
宰領 *sairyō* supervision, management; supervisor, superintendent
主宰する *shusai suru* preside (over), superintend, supervise
❷ chief minister
宰相 *saishō* prime minister, chancellor

SYNONYMS

❶ **direct and supervise**
司 OFFICIATE → 2931
督 SUPERVISE → 2796
監 OVERSEE → 2852
掌 TAKE CHARGE OF → 2602
轄 EXERCISE JURISDICTION OVER → 1627
管 EXERCISE CONTROL → 2701
制 CONTROL → 1274
営 MANAGE → 2603
理 manage → 970
経 MANAGE → 1331
❷ **high officials**
相 MINISTER → 900

3-7
宀

宵 宵 宵 宵
2276 SHŌ yoi

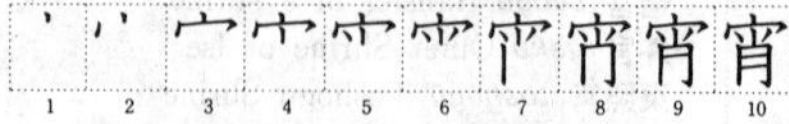

ⒸⒽ 宵 xiāo

Radical	Strokes
宀 40	10-3-7
Grade	Freq
Jōyō	1900
2 - 3 - 7	

▶**EARLY EVENING**

COMPOUNDS

ⓐ [original meaning] **early evening, evening, nightfall**
ⓑ night
春宵 *shunshō* spring evening
徹宵 *tesshō* all night long, throughout the night

KUN

【yoi 宵】early evening, early hours of the night; night
宵の口 *yoinokuchi* early evening
宵の明星 *yoi no myōjō* evening star, Venus
今宵 *koyoi* this evening, tonight
宵越しの *yoigoshi no* kept overnight

SYNONYMS

● **evening and night**

暮 DUSK → 2354

夕 EVENING → 3387

晩 EVENING → 979

夜 NIGHT → 2056

容 容 𠕇

2277 YŌ i(reru)▲

Ⓒⓗ 容 róng

Radical	Strokes
宀 40	10-3-7
Grade	**Freq**
Jōyō-5	419
2 - 3 - 7	

3-7 宀

1 2 3 4 5 6 7 8 9 10

▶**APPEARANCE** ▶**CONTAIN**

COMPOUNDS

❶ⓐ **appearance, looks, view, figure, countenance**

ⓑ shape, form, formation

容姿 *yōshi* face and figure, appearance

容貌 *yōbō* looks, personal appearance

美容 *biyō* beauty

威容 *iyō* dignified [majestic] appearance

変容 *hen'yō* transfiguration, transformation

陣容 *jin'yō* battle formation; members of a group

❷ⓐ (have within) **contain, hold, accommodate**

ⓑ contents, substance

容器 *yōki* receptacle, container, vessel

容量 *yōryō* capacity, volume

収容する *shūyō suru* accommodate, receive (guests)

包容する *hōyō suru* encompass, comprehend; imply; tolerate

内容 *naiyō* contents, import, substance

❸ **tolerate, permit, allow**

容赦する *yōsha suru* pardon, forgive, have mercy on

容疑者 *yōgisha* suspected person

容共 *yōkyō* procommunist

容認する *yōnin suru* admit, approve, accept

受容する *juyō suru* receive, accept

許容する *kyoyō suru* tolerate, allow, permit

❹ easy, simple

容易な *yōi na* easy, simple

INDEPENDENT

【yō 容】appearance, looks; shape, form

容を改む *yō o aratamu* change one's appearance

KUN

【i(reru) 容れる】[usu. 入れる] accept, tolerate, be compatible

相容れない *aiirenai* incompatible

SYNONYMS

❶ⓐ **appearance**

姿 FIGURE → 2636

相 PHASE → 900

体 FORM (outer appearance) → 71

色 COLOR → 2029

風 air → 3007

❷ⓐ **contain and include**

含 CONTAIN (have as a part) → 2041

包 ENCOMPASS → 2966

挟 HOLD BETWEEN → 377

❸ **agree and approve**

肯 ASSENT → 2417

承 AGREE TO → 16

諾 CONSENT → 1568

認 RECOGNIZE → 1546

可 APPROVE → 2969

賛 APPROVE OF → 2809

HOMOPHONES

ireru ⇨ 入 3370

NOTE

⇨ see USAGE note at 入 3370

害

2278 ▶**HARM**

nonstandard for 害 2272

3-7 宀

宵

2279 ▶**EARLY EVENING**

nonstandard for 宵 2276

3-7 宀

党

incorrect classification ⇨ see 2581

3-7 ⺌

3-7 ⺍

挙

incorrect classification ⇨ see 2456

3-7 山

峯
2280

▶**PEAK**
nonstandard for 峰 411

3-7 工

貢 貢 贡
2281 KŌ KU mitsu(gu)

Ⓒ 贡 gòng

Radical	Strokes
貝 154	10-7-3
Grade	**Freq**
Jōyō	1446
2-3-7	

1 2 3 4 5 6 7 8 9 10

▶**TRIBUTE**

COMPOUNDS

❶ⓐ [original meaning] **tribute**
ⓑ offer tribute, pay tribute
貢租 *kōso* tribute, annual tax
年貢 *nengu* land tax
入貢する *nyūkō suru* pay tribute
朝貢する *chōkō suru* bring tribute
❷ **render services to, contribute**
貢献する *kōken suru* contribute to, serve

KUN

【**mitsu(gu)** 貢ぐ】 support, finance, contribute
貢ぎ *mitsugi* tribute
貢ぎ物 *mitsugimono* tribute

SYNONYMS

❶ⓐ **offering**
幣 offering → 2885
ⓐ **tax**
税 TAX → 1191
租 LAND TAX → 1161
賦 levy → 1583
ⓑ **offer**
献 OFFER (esp. to a superior) → 1785
供 OFFER (to a person or god) → 88
納 offer (as to a god) → 1300
提 PRESENT → 591
奉 DEDICATE → 2559

3-7 艹

荷 荷 荷 荷
2282 KA ni

Ⓒ 荷 hé hè

Radical	Strokes
艹 140	10-3-7
Grade	**Freq**
Jōyō-3	946
2-3-7	

1 2 3 4 5 6 7 8 9 10

▶**LOAD**

COMPOUNDS

❶ⓐ **load, burden; cargo, goods**
ⓑ counter for loads or burdens
ⓒ *elec* load
荷重 *kajū* load
出荷する *shukka suru* forward, ship, consign
入荷 *nyūka* arrival of goods (at a shop), receipt of goods
集荷 *shūka* collection of cargo, cargo booking
在荷 *zaika* stock, goods on hand
一荷 *ikka* one load
電荷 *denka* electric charge
装荷 *sōka* loading
❷ **carry on shoulder, bear a burden**
荷担(=加担) *katan* assistance, support, participation
負荷 *fuka* load, burden
❸ [original meaning, now archaic] lotus, water lily
荷葉 *kayō* lotus leaves

KUN

【**ni** 荷】 load, burden; cargo, goods; (figuratively) load, burden
荷を下ろす *ni o orosu* take a load off
荷物 *nimotsu* baggage, load
荷台 *nidai* carrier, bed (of a truck)
荷造り *nizukuri* packing
荷役 *nieki* loading, handling cargo
初荷 *hatsuni* first cargo of the New Year
積み荷 *tsumini* load, freight, cargo
荷が勝つ *ni ga katsu* be unequal to the burden [job]
重荷 *omoni* heavy load; burden, encum-

brance

SPECIAL READINGS

稲荷▲ *inari* god of harvests; fox deity; flavored boiled rice wrapped up with fried bean curd

SYNONYMS

❶ **burden**

貨 freight → 2465

❷ **bear**

負 BEAR (on the back) → 2091

担 BEAR ON SHOULDER → 318

支 SUPPORT → 1979

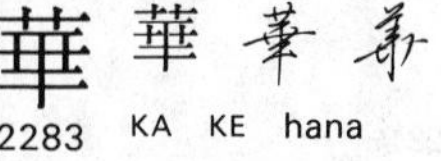

2283 KA KE hana

CH 华 huá huà huā

Radical	Strokes
艹 140	10-3-7
Grade	**Freq**
Jōyō	993
2-3-7	

3-7 艹

一 十 艹 艹 芏 芏 芏 萓 萓 華
1 2 3 4 5 6 7 8 9 10

▶**MAGNIFICENT** ▶**CHINA**

COMPOUNDS

❶ **magnificent, gorgeous, splendid, brilliant, flowery**

華麗な *karei na* splendid, magnificent, resplendent, gorgeous

華言 *kagen* [rare] flowery words, rhetorical flourishes

豪華な *gōka na* gorgeous, splendid, pompous

❷ⓐ [original meaning] **flower, blossom**

ⓑ *chem* flowers; *mining* bloom

華道 *kadō* flower arrangement

法華経 *hokekyō* the Lotus Sutra

香華 *kōge* incense and flowers

散華する *sange suru* fall as flowers do, die a glorious death

亜鉛華 *aenka* zinc flowers, zinc oxide

❸ (best part) flower, essence, cream

華実 *kajitsu* flowers and fruit; appearance and content

精華 *seika* flower, essence, glory

詞華集 *shikashū* anthology, florilegium

❹ prosperous, flourishing

繁華 *hanka* prosperity, bustle

栄華 *eiga* prosperity, splendor, glory

❺ China

華僑 *kakyō* Chinese merchant living abroad

華北 *kahoku* North China

中華料理 *chūka-ryōri* Chinese food

日華 *nikka* Japan and China

INDEPENDENT

【**ka** 華】 floweriness

華を去り実に就く *ka o sari jitsu ni tsuku* discard the flower for the fruit

KUN

【**hana** 華】

①ⓐ [also 花] (figuratively) flower (of life), essence, cream

ⓑ flower of youth, prime of life

武士道の華 *bushidō no hana* flower of chivalry [Bushido]

若い内が華 *Wakai uchi ga hana* Youth is a treasure

② [in compounds] flowery, beautiful, gallant

華やかな *hanayaka na* flowery, gay, bright, brilliant, gorgeous

華華しい *hanabanashii* brilliant, magnificent, spectacular

SYNONYMS

❶ **beautiful**

絢 GORGEOUS → 1347

斐 florid → 2776

美 BEAUTIFUL → 2264

佳 FINE → 86

瑶 EXQUISITE → 1026

麗 OF GRACEFUL BEAUTY → 2151

艶 CHARMING → 1908

妙 of marvelous beauty → 239

❷ⓐ **flower**

花 FLOWER → 2211

❺ **China**

漢 CHINESE → 657

支 China → 1979

中 People's Republic of China → 3451

台 Taiwan → 2005

唐 Cathay → 3115

呉 KINGDOM OF WU → 2549

❺ **Asian countries**

日 JAPAN → 3027

鮮 Korea → 1877

泰 Thailand → 2583

越 Vietnam → 3314

印 India → 828

比 Philippines → 26

HOMOPHONES

hana ⇨ 花 2211

NOTE

⇨ see USAGE note at 花 2211

3-7 艹

莉 莉 莉 莉
2284 RI

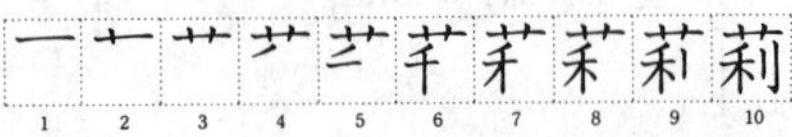

Ⓒ 莉 lì

Radical	Strokes
艹 140	10-3-7
Grade	Freq
Names	2125
2-3-7	

▶**JASMINE**

COMPOUNDS

● **jasmine, white jasmine**
茉莉 *matsuri* jasmine, *Jasminum sambac*
茉莉花 *matsurika* jasmine, *Jasminum sambac*

NAMES

茉莉子 *mariko* female name

SYNONYMS

● **shrubs**
茉 JASMINE → 2244
藤 WISTERIA → 2382
蔦 JAPANESE IVY → 2355
萩 *HAGI* → 2319

3-7 艹

恭
incorrect classification ⇨ see 2459

3-7 䒑

益 益 益 益
2285 EKI YAKU ma(su)▲

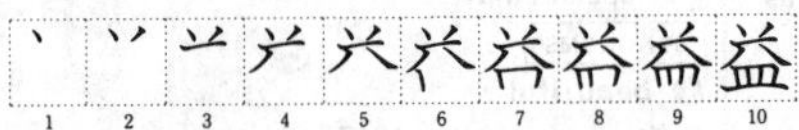

Ⓒ 益 yì

Radical	Strokes
皿 108	10-5-5
Grade	Freq
Jōyō-5	756
2-3-7	

▶**BENEFIT** ▶**PROFIT**

COMPOUNDS

❶ⓐ **benefit, good, advantage**
ⓑ **beneficial, useful**
有益な *yūeki na* beneficial; profitable
公益 *kōeki* public benefit
実益 *jitsueki* practical use, benefit, actual profit
御利益 *goriyaku* grace of God
益友 *ekiyū* useful friend
益虫 *ekichū* beneficial insect

❷ [also suffix] **profit, gain**
益金 *ekikin* profit, gain
差益 *saeki* marginal profits
利益 *rieki* profit, gains; benefit
収益 *shūeki* profit, earnings, proceeds, returns
損益 *son'eki* profit and loss; advantage and disadvantage
売却益 *baikyakueki* profit on sales

❸ increase, gain
増益 *zōeki* increase in profit; increase

INDEPENDENT

【**eki 益**】profit, benefit, advantage, use
益を与える人 *eki o ataeru hito* benefactor
【**ekisuru 益する**】be beneficial

KUN

【**ma(su) 益す**】[usu. 増す] *vi* & *vt* increase, augment, multiply
益益 *masumasu* increasingly

SYNONYMS

❶ **benefit**
利 ADVANTAGE → 1114
為 SAKE → 3577
用 use(ful) → 2976
役 SERVICE → 244

❷ **profit**
利 PROFIT → 1114
得 GAIN → 477

HOMOPHONES

masu ⇨ 増 677

NOTE

⇨ see USAGE note at 増 677

兼 兼 兼 兼 Ⓒ 兼 jiān

2286 KEN ka(neru) -ka(neru)

Radical ⺍ 12	Strokes 10-2-8
Grade Jōyō	Freq 995
2 - 3 - 7	

3-7 ⺍

Stroke order: 1–10

▶CONCURRENTLY

COMPOUNDS

❶ⓐ (serving two functions) **concurrently, simultaneously, together**

ⓑ **serve two functions or hold two jobs concurrently**

兼用 *ken'yō* combined use; serving two purposes

兼備する *kenbi suru* combine (one thing with another)

兼行 *kenkō* doing simultaneously

兼任 *kennin* holding two or more posts

兼務 *kenmu* holding another post; additional post

兼業 *kengyō* side business

❷ prepared, assigned

兼題 *kendai* prepared theme for a poem

INDEPENDENT

【ken 兼】 concurrently, simultaneously, and, cum, in addition

総理大臣兼外務大臣 *sōri-daijin ken gaimu-daijin* Prime Minister and (concurrently) Foreign Minister

居間兼食堂 *ima ken shokudō* living room-cum-dining room

KUN

【ka(neru) 兼ねる】 serve two functions, combine [unite] (one thing with another), serve as well; hold (another office) concurrently [in addition]

兼ね合い *kaneai* equilibrium, even balance

用事と遊びを兼ねて *yōji to asobi o kanete* on business combined with pleasure

両職を兼ねる *ryōshoku o kaneru* hold two offices concurrently

【-ka(neru) -兼ねる】 verbal suffix indicating hesitation, difficulty, or impatience in performing some action

申し兼ねますが *Mōshikanemasu ga* Excuse me, but...

やり兼ねない *yarikanenai* would stop at nothing, be capable of doing

見兼ねる *mikaneru* be unable to let pass unnoticed

お待ち兼ねの *omachikane no* long-waited-for

SYNONYMS

❶ⓐ **together**

並 side by side → 2246

併 TOGETHER → 83

同 together → 2987

共 JOINT → 2393

【ken】

○ **additionally**

且つ AS WELL → 3485

更に furthermore → 3541

尚 STILL → 2233

亦 ALSO → 2011

又 also, and → 3351

及び and → 3385

並びに and also → 2246

傍ら besides → 147

差

incorrect classification ⇨ see 3311

3-7 ⺍

韋

2287

Radical 韋 178	Strokes 10-10-0
Grade Radical	Freq
2 - 3 - 7	

3-7 韋

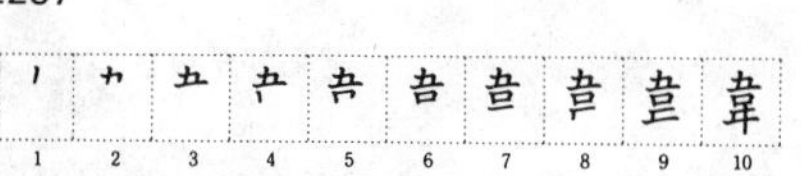

RADICAL 178

variant of 韋 *nameshigawa* 'leather'

⇨ see 韋 2268 for radical description

3-7 亼

倉

incorrect classification ⇨ see 2104

3-8 宀

窒 窒 窒

2288 CHITSU

1 2 3 4 5 6 7 8 9 10 11

Ⓒⓗ 窒 zhì

Radical	Strokes
穴 116	11-5-6
Grade	**Freq**
Jōyō	1831
2 - 3 - 8	

▶**CHOKE** ▶**NITROGEN**

COMPOUNDS

❶ⓐ choke, suffocate

ⓑ [original meaning, now rare] choke up, stuff up, block

窒息 ***chissoku*** suffocation, asphyxia

窒死 ***chisshi*** [rare] death from suffocation

窒塞する ***chissoku suru*** be blocked

❷ nitrogen

窒素 ***chisso*** nitrogen

窒化物 ***chikkabutsu*** nitride

SYNONYMS

❶ⓐ kill

絞 STRANGLE → 1349

殺 KILL → 1324

刺 stab to death → 1275

❷ nitrogen

硝 NITER → 1185

❷ lighter elements

水 hydrogen → 10

酸 OXYGEN → 1563

塩 chlorine → 631

臭 bromine → 2633

硫 SULFUR → 1184

炭 carbon → 2257

3-8 宀

寅 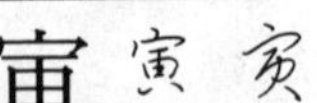

2289 IN tora NAMES tomo nobu

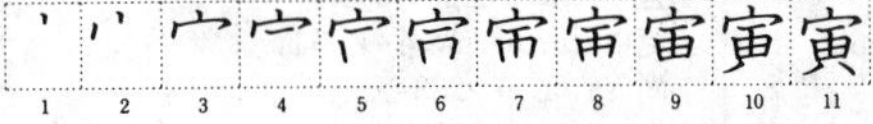

Ⓒⓗ 寅 yín

Radical	Strokes
宀 40	11-3-8
Grade	**Freq**
Names	2041
2 - 3 - 8	

▶**THE TIGER**

COMPOUNDS

● third sign of the Oriental zodiac: the Tiger—(time) 3-5 a.m., (direction) ENE, (season) January (of the lunar calendar) (⇨ see APPENDIX 7)

KUN

【**tora 寅**】third sign of the Oriental zodiac: the Tiger (⇨ ●)

寅の刻 ***tora no koku*** around four o'clock in the morning

NAMES

寅次 ***toraji*** male name

寅吉 ***torakichi*** male name

SYNONYMS

● tiger

虎 TIGER → 3212

HOMOPHONES

tora ⇨ 虎 3212

NOTE

⇨ see USAGE note at 虎 3212

寂 2290

JAKU SEKI sabi sabi(shii) sabi(reru) sami(shii)▲

Ⓒⓗ 寂 jì

Radical	Strokes
宀 40	11-3-8
Grade	**Freq**
Jōyō	1751
2 - 3 - 8	

3-8 宀

1 2 3 4 5 6 7 8 9 10 11

▶**LONESOME**

COMPOUNDS

❶ⓐ **lonesome, lonely, desolate, deserted**
ⓑ [original meaning] **quiet, still, serene**
寂寥たる *sekiryōtaru* lonely, desolate
寂然たる *sekizentaru* (=*jakunentaru*) lonely, desolate
静寂 *seijaku* silence, quietness, stillness
閑寂 *kanjaku* quietness, tranquility
❷ death of a Buddhist monk or nun
寂滅 *jakumetsu* Nirvana, death
入寂 *nyūjaku* death of saint, entering Nirvana

INDEPENDENT

【jaku 寂】 indicates date of death of a Buddhist monk or nun; hush, stillness
明治四年寂 *meiji yonen jaku* died 1871
寂とした *jaku to shita* hushed, still
【seki 寂】 hush, stillness
寂とした *seki to shita* hushed, still

KUN

【sabi 寂】 patina, elegant simplicity, *sabi*
侘と寂 *wabi to sabi wabi* and *sabi*, taste for the simple and quiet
【sabi(shii) 寂しい】
[sometimes also 淋しい]
ⓐ lonesome, lonely, desolate, deserted
ⓑ scarce, scanty
寂しさ *sabishisa* loneliness
寂しがる *sabishigaru* feel lonely, miss someone
懐が寂しい *futokoro ga sabishii* have a scanty supply of money
【sabi(reru) 寂れる】 decline in prosperity, become desolate
寂れた季節 *sabireta kisetsu* dead season
【sami(shii) 寂しい】 same as **sabishii 寂しい**

SYNONYMS

❶ⓐ **sad and depressed**
沈 depressed → 261
陰 gloomy → 541
愁 MELANCHOLY → 2829
哀 sorrowful → 2068
悲 SAD → 2775
惨 MISERABLE → 483
ⓑ **quiet**
静 QUIET → 1728
閑 QUIET → 3322
幽 QUIET AND SECLUDED → 3008
粛 still → 3581
黙 SILENT → 2865

USAGE

❶ **sabishii**
寂しい
[sometimes also 淋しい]
ⓐ lonesome, lonely, desolate, deserted
ⓑ scarce, scanty
淋しい
[usu. 寂しい] same as 寂しい *sabishii*
❷ **samishii**
寂しい
[sometimes also 淋しい] same as 寂しい *sabishii*
淋しい
[usu. 寂しい] same as 寂しい *samishii*

HOMOPHONES

sabishii ⇨ 淋 520
samishii ⇨ 淋 520

寄 2291

KI yo(ru) -yo(ri) yo(seru)

Ⓒⓗ 寄 jì

Radical	Strokes
宀 40	11-3-8
Grade	**Freq**
Jōyō-5	506
2 - 3 - 8	

3-8 宀

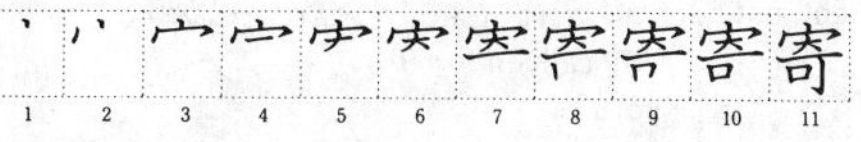

1 2 3 4 5 6 7 8 9 10 11

▶**CONTRIBUTE** ▶**DRAW NEAR**

COMPOUNDS

❶ⓐ (give money or goods) **contribute, donate**
ⓑ (submit for publication) **contribute**
寄付 *kifu* contribution, donation
寄金 *kikin* contribution, donation
寄贈する *kizō* (=*kisō*) *suru* donate, present as a gift
寄与 *kiyo* contribution, services

寄稿する *kikō suru* contribute (to a newspaper)
寄書 *kisho* contributed article
❷ lodge at, reside temporarily, be dependent on (someone for food)
寄宿 *kishuku* lodging, boarding
寄留 *kiryū* temporary residence, sojourn
寄生 *kisei* parasitism
寄食 *kishoku* parasitism, dependency
❸ call at, call on, make a short visit
寄港する *kikō suru* call at a port
寄航する *kikō suru* call at a(n) (air)port
❹ entrust to, consign, deposit
寄託する *kitaku suru* deposit, entrust
❺ send, deliver
寄語する *kigo suru* send word by
寄信 *kishin* sending a letter

KUN

【yo(ru) 寄る】
①ⓐ draw near, draw up, come near, approach
ⓑ draw aside, step aside
近寄る *chikayoru* go near, approach
歩み寄る *ayumiyoru* step up; compromise, meet halfway
最寄りの *moyori no* nearest, nearby
身寄り *miyori* relative, relation, kinsfolk
思いも寄らない *omoi mo yoranai* unexpected, unforeseen, inconceivable
脇に寄る *waki ni yoru* draw aside
片寄る *katayoru* concentrate on one side [place], go aside
② draw together, come together, gather, meet
寄り合い *yoriai* meeting, assembly, gathering
③ drop in, call on
寄り道する *yorimichi suru* drop in on the way, go out of the way
立ち寄る *tachiyoru* drop in for a short visit, call at
④ increase, gain
年寄り *toshiyori* old [aged] person, the aged; older councilor
皺が寄る *shiwa ga yoru* wrinkle, crumple
⑤ lean on, rest against
壁に寄り掛かる *kabe ni yorikakaru* rest against the wall
⑥ *sumo* push one's opponent while holding his belt
寄り切り *yorikiri* pushing one's opponent out of the ring while holding his belt
⑦ (of the stock market) open
寄り付き *yoritsuki* opening of a session
【-yo(ri) -寄り】 [also suffix] toward, leaning toward
北寄りの風 *kitayori no kaze* northerly wind
アメリカ寄りの外交 *amerikayori no gaikō* pro-American diplomacy

【yo(seru) 寄せる】
①ⓐ draw (a thing) near, allow to approach; come near
ⓑ draw up, bring together, gather, collect; add up
寄せ付けない *yosetsukenai* keep off, keep away
車寄せ *kurumayose* carriage porch
皺寄せ *shiwayose* shifting (the loss) to someone else
又寄せて頂きます *Mata yosete itadakimasu* I shall call on you again
打ち寄せる *uchiyoseru* break upon, beat upon (the shore)
引き寄せる *hikiyoseru* draw near, pull nearer
寄せ鍋 *yosenabe* chowder
寄せ算 *yosezan* addition, adding up
呼び寄せる *yobiyoseru* call, summon, send for, call together
② send (a letter), contribute, write
原稿を寄せる *genkō o yoseru* contribute an article
③ take to a person, let one's heart go out to someone
心を寄せる *kokoro o yoseru* let one's heart go out to, take to
④ be dependent on, under (a person's) roof
身を寄せる *mi o yoseru* become a dependent on, live under another's roof
⑤ⓐ attack, storm, surge
ⓑ bring (a game of shogi) to a victorious end
攻め寄せる *semeyoseru* make an onslaught on
寄せ *yose* last moves, end game
⑥ liken, make a pretext of
病気に事寄せて *byōki ni kotoyosete* under the pretext of being ill

SPECIAL READINGS

数寄屋(＝数奇屋) *sukiya* tea-ceremony arbor
寄席 *yose* storyteller's hall, variety hall

SYNONYMS

❶ⓐ donate
献 donate → 1785
施 give alms → 891
恵む give charity → 2659
❸ visit
訪 VISIT → 1468
参 VISIT A HOLY PLACE → 2066
伺 call on → 69
【yoru】
①ⓐ approach
近 NEAR → 3061
接 come close to → 500
迫 PRESS → 3074
【yoseru】
①ⓐ pull

引 DRAW → 181
抽 DRAW OUT → 302
抜 PULL OUT → 246
控える HOLD BACK → 495

HOMOPHONES

yoru ⇨ 因 3054 依 84 拠 312 由 3499
katayoru ⇨ 偏る 133 片寄る 3461, 2291

COMPOUND FORMATION

❶ 身寄り *miyori*
身寄り 'relative, etc.' refers to persons near (寄る ①ⓐ) one's person (身) or self.

❷ 寄席 *yose*
寄席 'storyteller's hall, variety hall' refers to the gathering of (寄せる *yoseru* ①ⓑ) people at an entertainment hall (席).

NOTE

⇨ see USAGE notes at 因 3054 and 偏 133

密 密 密
2292 MITSU

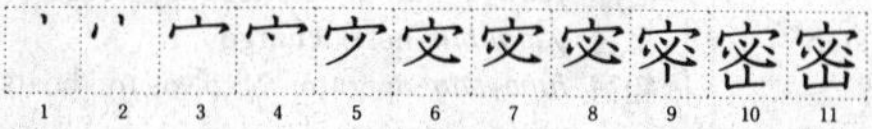

CH 密 mì

Radical	Strokes
宀 40	11-3-8
Grade	**Freq**
Jōyō-6	854
2-3-8	

3-8 宀

▶**CLOSE** ▶**SECRET**

COMPOUNDS

❶ⓐ (closely crowded) **close, dense, thick, compact, tight**
ⓑ (very near in relationship) **close, intimate**
密集する *misshū suru* crowd, swarm, aggregate densely
密林 *mitsurin* close thicket, dense forest, jungle
密度 *mitsudo* density
密室 *misshitsu* secret room [chamber]; locked room
過密な *kamitsu na* overcrowded
密接な *missetsu na* close, intimate
緊密な *kinmitsu na* close, tight
親密な *shinmitsu na* intimate, close

❷ (characterized by exacting minuteness) **close, minute, elaborate, careful**
精密 *seimitsu* precision, accuracy, minuteness
厳密な *genmitsu na* strict, precise, rigid, exact
綿密な *menmitsu na* close, minute, detailed
緻密な *chimitsu na* minute, close, elaborate, exact

❸ [also suffix] **secret, private, clandestine, illegal, stealthy**
密使 *misshi* secret messenger
密告 *mikkoku* secret information
密輸 *mitsuyu* smuggling, contraband trade
密売 *mitsubai* smuggling
秘密 *himitsu* secret, mystery; privacy
内密の *naimitsu no* secret, confidential, private

❹ abbrev. of 密教 *mikkyō*: esoteric Buddhism
密教 *mikkyō* esoteric Buddhism, secret religion
台密 *taimitsu* esoteric Buddhism of the Japanese *Tendai* Sect.

INDEPENDENT

【**mitsu na 密な**】close, dense, thick, crowded; close, intimate; close, minute, elaborate

SYNONYMS

❶ⓐ **dense**
濃 THICK (concentrated) → 777
ⓑ **familiar and friendly**
親 INTIMATE → 1799
近 NEAR → 3061
睦 FRIENDLY → 1199
懇 FAMILIAR → 2899
和 HARMONIOUS → 1130

❷ **detailed**
細 MINUTE → 1333
詳 DETAILED → 1526
精 meticulous → 1366

❸ **secret and private**
秘 SECRET → 1159
隠 hidden from view → 713
暗 in the dark → 1010
私 PRIVATE → 1115
内 not public → 3466

3-8 宀

宿 宿 宿 ⒸⒽ 宿 sù xiǔ xiù

2293 SHUKU yado yado(ru) yado(su)

Radical	Strokes
宀 40	11-3-8
Grade	**Freq**
Jōyō-3	556
2-3-8	

丶 丷 宀 宀 宀 宀 宀 宿 宿 宿 宿
1 2 3 4 5 6 7 8 9 10 11

▶LODGE

COMPOUNDS

❶ⓐ [original meaning] **lodge, board, stay overnight**
ⓑ be contained within the body
宿泊する *shukuhaku suru* lodge, stay
宿直 *shukuchoku* night duty, night watch
寄宿 *kishuku* lodging, boarding
合宿する *gasshuku suru* lodge together, stay in a camp for training
下宿 *geshuku* lodging, boarding house
宿便 *shukuben* feces contained long in the intestines, fecal stasis

❷ **lodging, inn, hotel, lodging house**
宿舎 *shukusha* lodgings, quarters
宿所 *shukusho* address, lodgings
宿営 *shukuei* billeting, camp
宿題 *shukudai* homework
民宿 *minshuku* tourist home

❸ from a previous time, remaining, old
宿根草 *shukkonsō* perennial plant
宿酔 *shukusui* hangover
宿敵 *shukuteki* old enemy
宿願 *shukugan* long-cherished desire

❹ from a previous life [incarnation]
宿命 *shukumei* fate, destiny
宿縁 *shukuen* karma, destiny, fate

❺ post station, relay station, stage, stopping place
宿場 *shukuba* post station, relay station

❻ stage along the zodiac, mansion; constellation
星宿 *seishuku* constellation
二十八宿 *nijūhasshuku* the twenty-eight stages along the zodiac

❼ experienced
宿老 *shukurō* old men, elders, seniors
宿将 *shukushō* veteran general

INDEPENDENT

【shuku 宿】 post town, relay station, stage
合いの宿 *ai no shuku* town situated between two post towns

【shukusu 宿す】 literary form of **yadoru 宿る**

KUN

【yado 宿】 lodging, inn, hotel; house, dwelling; *slang* my hubby, my good man
宿屋 *yadoya* inn, hotel, lodging house
宿賃 *yadochin* hotel charge
船宿 *funayado* operator of pleasure boats; shipping agent
宿無し *yadonashi* vagabond
宿六 *yadoroku* my old man, my hubby

【yado(ru) 宿る】 lodge, board, stay overnight; dwell [reside] in; (of a bird) roost
宿り *yadori* lodging abode; shelter
雨宿りする *amayadori suru* take shelter from the rain

【yado(su) 宿す】 conceive, be pregnant with; carry, let stay
子を宿す *ko o yadosu* be pregnant with a child
露を宿した葉 *tsuyu o yadoshita ha* leaf heavy with dew

SYNONYMS

❶ⓐ **stay**
泊 STAY OVERNIGHT → 331
在 reside temporarily → 2984
屯 STATION TROOPS → 3457
駐 STATIONED → 1826
留 STAY → 2580
滞 STAY → 663

❷ **temporary quarters**
舎 temporary quarters → 2060
寮 DORMITORY → 2359
館 inn → 1748
亭 INN → 2072

❺ **post station**
駅 relay station → 1822
逓 RELAY → 3106

NOTE

⇨ see COMPOUND FORMATION for 下宿 *geshuku* ⇨ 下 3378

窓 窓 窓

2294 sō mado

CH 窗 chuāng

Radical	Strokes
穴 116	11-5-6
Grade	**Freq**
Jōyō-6	935
2-3-8	

3-8 宀

丶 丷 宀 宀 穴 空 空 空 窓 窓 窓
1 2 3 4 5 6 7 8 9 10 11

▶WINDOW

COMPOUNDS

❶ [original meaning] **window**
窓外 *sōgai* outside the window
車窓 *shasō* car window
舷窓 *gensō* porthole

❷ windowed structure:
ⓐ chamber
ⓑ school
深窓に育つ *shinsō ni sodatsu* be brought up with tenderest care in a good family
学窓 *gakusō* school
同窓生 *dōsōsei* fellow student, alumnus, alumna

KUN

【mado 窓】 window, porthole; windowpane
窓ガラス *madogarasu* windowpane
窓口 *madoguchi* window, wicket; clerk at a window
飾り窓 *kazarimado* show window, display window
窓枠 *madowaku* window frame, sash
出窓 *demado* bow window, bay window

常 堂

incorrect classification ⇨ see 5-6

3-8 ⺌

巣 巣 巣 巣

2295 sō su su(kuu)▲

CH 巢 cháo

Radical	Strokes
⺌ 42△	11-3-8
Grade	**Freq**
Jōyō-4	1206
2-3-8	

3-8 ⺌

1 2 3 4 5 6 7 8 9 10 11

▶NEST

COMPOUNDS

❶ⓐ [original meaning] (structure for birds or insects) **nest**
ⓑ (place favoring the growth of something dangerous) nest (of robbers), hangout
営巣 *eisō* nest building
蜂巣 *hōsō* beehive, hive
巣窟 *sōkutsu* den, haunt, nest
病巣 *byōsō medicine* focus, lesion

❷ place where sperm or eggs accumulate
卵巣 *ransō* ovary
精巣 *seisō* spermary, testis

KUN

【su 巣】
ⓐ (structure for birds, insects or animals) nest, beehive; web; lair, den
ⓑ (place favoring the growth of something dangerous) nest, den, hangout (for bandits)
巣箱 *subako* bird box, bird house
巣立つ *sudatsu* leave one's nest; become independent
古巣 *furusu* old nest, one's former haunt
空き巣 *akisu* sneak thief

【su(kuu) 巣くう】 build a nest, nest; haunt, hang out

incorrect classification ⇨ see 2591

3-8 ⺌

3-8 山

崩 崩 崩 崩 ㊥ 崩 bēng

2296 HŌ kuzu(reru) -kuzu(re) kuzu(su)

Radical	Strokes
山 46	11-3-8
Grade	Freq
Jōyō	1582
2-3-8	

▶**CRUMBLE**

COMPOUNDS

❶ **crumble, collapse**

崩壊する *hōkai suru* collapse, crumble, break down, cave in

崩落 *hōraku* collapse, cave-in; crash; (of the market) decline

❷ (of an emperor) die

崩御 *hōgyo* demise [death] of an emperor

INDEPENDENT

【**hōjiru** (=**hōzuru**) **崩じる(=崩ずる)**】(of an emperor) demise, pass away

KUN

【**kuzu(reru) 崩れる**】*vi* crumble, collapse, break, cave in; get out of shape; slump; (of money) be changeable

崩れ *kuzure* crumbling, collapse

崩れ去る *kuzuresaru* collapse, crumble away

山崩れ *yamakuzure* landslide, landslip

型崩れ *katakuzure* getting out of shape

天気の崩れ *tenki no kuzure* break [change for the worse] in the weather

十円玉に崩れる *jūendama ni kuzureru* can be changed into ten-yen coins

【**-kuzu(re) -崩れ**】[suffix] delinquent, degenerate

学生崩れ *gakuseikuzure* degenerate ex-student

俳優崩れ *haiyūkuzure* down-and-out ex-film star

【**kuzu(su) 崩す**】*vt* destroy, pull down, level; cause to be relaxed or informal; write (a Chinese character) in running [simplified] style; change (money); cut (prices)

切り崩す *kirikuzusu* level (a hill); break (a strike)

持ち崩す *mochikuzusu* ruin [degrade] oneself

膝を崩す *hiza o kuzusu* sit at ease

崩し字 *kuzushiji* Chinese character written in running [simplified] style

SPECIAL READINGS

雪崩 *nadare* snowslide

SYNONYMS

❶ **break**

壊 BREAK DOWN → 756
破 BREAK → 1150
折 BREAK OFF → 253
割る crack → 1816
裂 SPLIT → 2687
砕 CRUSH UP → 1134

❶ **collapse**

陥 FALL IN → 457
落 FALL → 2318
没 SINK → 260

3-8 山

崇 崇 崇 ㊥ 崇 chóng

2297 SŪ aga(meru)▲

Radical	Strokes
山 46	11-3-8
Grade	Freq
Jōyō	1736
2-3-8	

▶**REVERENCE**

COMPOUNDS

❶ **reverence, revere, worship, venerate, adore, esteem**

崇敬 *sūkei* reverence, admiration

崇拝 *sūhai* worship, adoration

崇高な *sūkō na* lofty, sublime, noble

尊崇 *sonsū* reverence, veneration

❷ [usu. 嵩 2331] [original meaning, now archaic] lofty (mountain)

KUN

【**aga(meru) 崇める**】reverence, revere, worship, venerate, esteem

神と崇める *kami to agameru* deify

SYNONYMS

❶ **respect**

敬 RESPECT → 1701
欽 REVERE → 1690
仰 look up to → 48
尚 VALUE HIGHLY → 2233
重 set value on → 3573
拝 WORSHIP → 303
慕 ADORE → 2353
尊 HONOR → 2324

❶ pray and worship
拝 WORSHIP → 303
願 pray → 1845
祈 PRAY → 875
斎 OBSERVE RELIGIOUS ABSTINENCE → 2115

崩 2298 ▶CRUMBLE
nonstandard for 崩 2296
3-8

嵌 incorrect stroke count ⇨ see 2313
3-8

巣 2299 ▶NEST
nonstandard for 巢 2295
3-8

著 著 著 著 2300 CHO CHAKU▲ arawa(su) ichijiru(shii)

Ⓒℍ 著 zhù

Radical ++ 140	Strokes 11-3-8
Grade Jōyō-6	Freq 918
2-3-8	

3-8

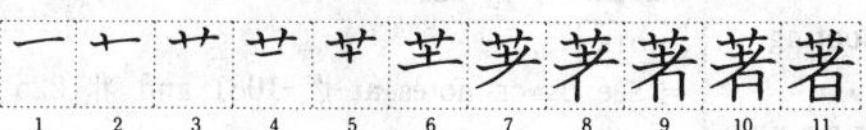

▶AUTHOR ▶CONSPICUOUS

COMPOUNDS

❶ⓐ **author, write, publish**
ⓑ [suffix] **authored by, by**
著作する *chosaku suru* write, author
著述家 *chojutsuka* writer, author
著者 *chosha* author, writer
著作権 *chosakuken* copyright
共著 *kyōcho* joint authorship, coauthorship
三島由紀夫著 *mishima yukio-cho* authored by Mishima Yukio
❷ literary work, book, writing
著書 *chosho* literary work, book
新著 *shincho* new book
拙著 *setcho* my humble work
名著 *meicho* famous book, masterpiece
❸ (since writing makes things clearly visible) (attracting attention) **conspicuous, remarkable, prominent, well-known**
著大な *chodai na* exceptionally large
著名 *chomei* prominence, eminence, distinction
顕著な *kencho na* notable, conspicuous; clear, obvious
❹ [now always 着 *chaku* 3316] same as 着 3316 ⇨ see 着 3316 for compounds

INDEPENDENT

【cho 著】literary work, book
...の著 *...no cho* book written by...

KUN

【arawa(su) 著す】author, write, publish
書き著す *kakiarawasu* publish (a book)

【ichijiru(shii) 著しい】remarkable, conspicuous, marked
著しく *ichijirushiku* remarkably, considerably, strikingly

SYNONYMS

❶ **compose**
作 compose → 68
書く WRITE → 2658
筆 write → 2677
❶ **compile**
編 COMPILE → 1387
集 edit → 2771
❷ **books**
本 BOOK → 3502
書 BOOK → 2658
冊 bound book → 3483
籍 books → 2731
巻 VOLUME → 2645
編 volume → 1387
鑑 REFERENCE VOLUME → 1773
典 STANDARD WORK → 2627
経 religious classic → 1331
❸ **conspicuous**
顕 MANIFEST → 1806
卓 PROMINENT → 2064
傑 outstanding → 155

HOMOPHONES

arawasu ⇨ 表 2429 現 968

NOTE

⇨ see USAGE note at 表 2429 and NOTE at 着 3316

3-8 艹

萌 萌 萠 萌 萌

Ⓒ 萌 méng

2301 HŌ BŌ mo(eru) kiza(su) NAMES moe kizashi

Radical	Strokes
艹 140	11-3-8
Grade	**Freq**
Names	2098
2-3-8	

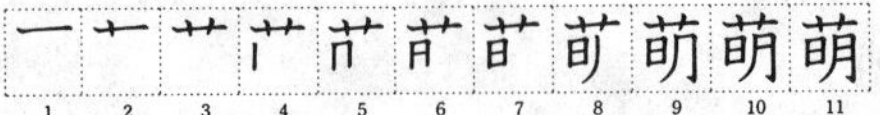

▶**GERMINATE**

COMPOUNDS

❶ⓐ **germinate, sprout, bud**

ⓑ **germination, beginning, sign, indication**

萌芽 *hōga* germination, beginning; sprout

❷ [archaic] the people, the masses

萌黎 *hōrei* common people, the masses

KUN

【mo(eru) 萌える】sprout, bud, burst into bud

萌え立つ *moetatsu* sprout, burst into leaf

萌黄色 *moegiiro* yellowish green

下萌え *shitamoe* sprout of a plant shooting from under the soil

【kiza(su) 萌す】germinate, sprout; spring up, dawn

萌し *kizashi* germination, sprouting; dawning

NAMES

萌子 *moeko* female name

萌 *kizashi* male name

SYNONYMS

❶ⓐ **sprout and bloom**

咲く BLOOM → 349

HOMOPHONES

moeru ⇨ 燃 1081

kizasu ⇨ 兆 225

kizashi ⇨ 兆 225

NOTE

⇨ see USAGE notes at 燃 1081 and 兆 225

3-8 艹

菓 菓 菓 菓

Ⓒ 果 guǒ

2302 KA

Radical	Strokes
艹 140	11-3-8
Grade	**Freq**
Jōyō	1546
2-3-8	

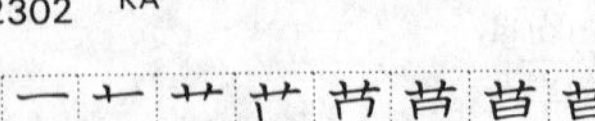

▶**CONFECTIONERY**

COMPOUNDS

❶ **confectionery, confection, cake, sweets, candy**

菓子 *kashi* confectionery, cake, sweets

和菓子 *wagashi* Japanese-style confection

糖菓 *tōka* sweetmeats, sweets, confection

氷菓 *hyōka* ice cream, sherbet

製菓 *seika* confectionary (making of confections)

茶菓 *saka* (=*chaka*) tea and cakes, refreshments

銘菓 *meika* excellent cake, cake of an established name

冷菓 *reika* ices, ice cream

❷ [original meaning] fruit

水菓子 *mizugashi* fruit

3-8 艹

菊 菊 菊 菊

Ⓒ 菊 jú

2303 KIKU

Radical	Strokes
艹 140	11-3-8
Grade	**Freq**
Jōyō	1158
2-3-8	

一 十 卄 艹 芍 芍 芍 芍 菊 菊 菊

▶**CHRYSANTHEMUM**

COMPOUNDS

❶ [also suffix] [original meaning] **chrysanthemum**

菊花 *kikka* chrysanthemum

菊人形 *kikuningyō* chrysanthemum figure [doll]

野菊 *nogiku* wild chrysanthemum; aster

白菊 *shiragiku* white chrysanthemum

除虫菊 *jochūgiku* pyrethrum

❷ kind of book size
菊判 *kikuban* small octavo, medium octavo
❸ abbrev. of 菊五郎 *kikugorō*, name of a kabuki actor
団菊祭 *dangikusai* kabuki performance in commemoration of Danjuro and Kikugoro

INDEPENDENT

【**kiku** 菊】chrysanthemum
菊の御紋 *kiku no gomon* Imperial crest of the chrysanthemum

SYNONYMS

❶ **flowering plants**
葵 MALLOW → 2317
蓉 COTTON ROSE → 2337
芙 LOTUS → 2208
蘭 ORCHID → 2383
萩 *HAGI* → 2319
藤 WISTERIA → 2382
桜 cherry blossom → 931
梅 *ume* blossom → 925

菌 菌 菌 菌 Ⓒⓗ 菌 jùn jūn

2304 KIN

Radical	Strokes
艹 140	11-3-8
Grade	Freq
Jōyō	1106
2 - 3 - 8	

3-8

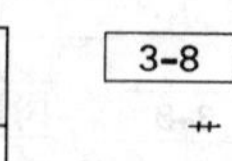

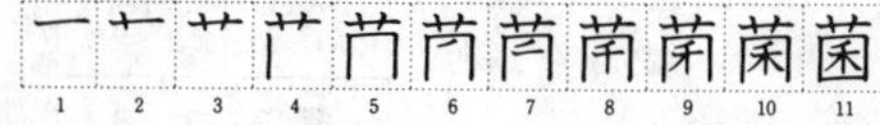

▶**BACTERIA**

COMPOUNDS

❶ [also suffix] **bacteria, bacillus, germ, microorganism**
細菌 *saikin* bacteria, germ, microbe
黴菌 *baikin* bacterium, germ
殺菌する *sakkin suru* sterilize, pasteurize
病菌 *byōkin* disease germ, virus
保菌者 *hokinsha* germ carrier
チフス菌 *chifusukin* typhoid bacillus
赤痢菌 *sekirikin* dysentery bacillus
❷ fungus, mushroom
菌類 *kinrui* fungi
菌毒 *kindoku* mushroom poison
菌糸 *kinshi* hypha, mycelium

INDEPENDENT

【**kin** 菌】bacteria, germ; fungus, mushroom
菌を培養する *kin o baiyō suru* culture [cultivate] bacteria

菜 菜 菜 菜 Ⓒⓗ 菜 cài

2305 SAI na

Radical	Strokes
艹 140	11-3-8
Grade	Freq
Jōyō-4	1075
2 - 3 - 8	

3-8

艹

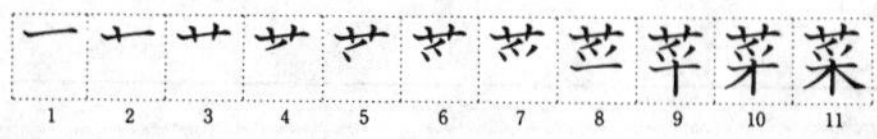

▶**VEGETABLE**

COMPOUNDS

❶ **vegetable, greens**
菜食主義 *saishokushugi* vegetarianism
菜園 *saien* vegetable garden
野菜 *yasai* vegetables, greens
白菜 *hakusai* Chinese cabbage, white rape
山菜 *sansai* edible wild plant
❷ⓐ **dish accompanying the rice in Japanese meals, side dish**
ⓑ counter for dishes
前菜 *zensai hors d'oeuvre*
惣菜(＝総菜) *sōzai* daily [household] dish, side dish
一汁一菜 *ichijū-issai* simple meal

INDEPENDENT

【**sai** 菜】side dish (⇨ ❷ⓐ)
粗末なお菜 *somatsu na osai* poor side dish

KUN

【**na** 菜】greens, vegetables; rape
青菜 *aona* greens
菜っ葉 *nappa* greens
菜種 *natane* rapeseed, coleseed

SYNONYMS

❶ **plants**
植 PLANT → 990
栽 garden plant → 3297
【**na**】
○ **vegetables**
芋 POTATO → 2181
豆 BEAN → 1943
蕗 BUTTERBUR → 2372

NOTE

⇨ see COMPOUND FORMATION for 惣菜 *sōzai* ⇨ 惣 2780

3-8 艹 **黄** incorrect classification ⇨ see 2468

3-8 艹 **葉** incorrect stroke count ⇨ see 2321

3-8 艹 **萃 萎** incorrect stroke count ⇨ see 4-8

3-8 䒑 **剪**
2306 SEN ki(ru) tsu(mu)

CH 剪 jiǎn

Radical	Strokes
刀 18	11-2-9
Grade	**Freq**
Reference	
2-3-8	

COMPOUNDS

ⓐ [now usu. 切る *kiru*] [original meaning] prune, trim, shear

ⓑ [also 摘む *tsumu*] cut (one's hair), trim
剪定する *sentei suru* prune, trim
剪断 *sendan* shearing, shear
枝を剪る *eda o kiru* prune a tree
髪を剪む *kami o tsumu* have one's hair cut [trimmed]

HOMOPHONES

kiru ⇨ 切 27 伐 42 截 3301 斬 1482
tsumu ⇨ 摘 694

NOTE

⇨ see USAGE notes at 切 27 and 摘 694

3-8 亠 **棄** incorrect stroke count ⇨ see 2326
(nonstandard for 棄 2137)

3-8 廿 **黃** incorrect stroke count ⇨ see 2487
(nonstandard for 黄 2468)

3-9 土 **堯**
2307
▶YAO
nonstandard for 尭 2063

3-9 土 **喜** 𠤎 喜 𢻱
2308 KI yoroko(bu) yoroko(basu)

CH 喜 xǐ

Radical	Strokes
口 30	12-3-9
Grade	**Freq**
Jōyō-4	787
2-3-9	

一 十 士 吉 吉 吉 吉 吉 壴 壴 喜 喜 (1 2 3 4 5 6 7 8 9 10 11 12)

▶**HAPPY**

COMPOUNDS

❶ⓐ [original meaning] **be happy [glad], rejoice**

ⓑ joy, pleasure
喜悦 *kietsu* delight, rapture, joy
喜色 *kishoku* glad countenance
歓喜する *kanki suru* rejoice, be greatly delighted
悲喜 *hiki* joy and sorrow
一喜一憂 *ikkiichiyū* alternation of joy and sorrow

❷ amusing, funny
喜劇 *kigeki* comedy

KUN

【**yoroko(bu) 喜ぶ**】[formerly also 悦ぶ] *vi*

be happy [glad], be delighted
喜び *yorokobi* [formerly also 悦び] joy, delight; [sometimes also 慶び] felicitation, congratulation; matter for congratulation
喜ばしい *yorokobashii* joyful, delightful, gratifying
喜んで *yorokonde* willingly, with pleasure
大喜び *ōyorokobi* great joy, delight

【**yoroko(basu) 喜ばす**】[formerly also 悦ばす] *vt* please, gladden, make happy
親を喜ばす *oya o yorokobasu* make one's parents happy
目を喜ばす *me o yorokobasu* feast one's eyes (on)

SYNONYMS

❶ **pleased and pleasant**
嬉しい GLAD → 722
歓 JOYOUS → 1867
欣 JOYFUL → 852
悦 DELIGHTED → 418
愉 PLEASED → 582
朗 CHEERFUL → 1325
快 PLEASANT → 245
楽 pleasurable → 2826

USAGE

❶ **yorokobu**
喜ぶ
[formerly also 悦ぶ] *vi* be happy [glad], be delighted
悦ぶ
[now usu. 喜ぶ] *vi* be happy [glad], be delighted

❷ **yorokobi**
喜び
ⓐ [formerly also 悦び] joy, delight
ⓑ [sometimes also 慶び] felicitation, congratulation; matter for congratulation
悦び
[now usu. 喜び] joy, delight
慶び
[usu. 喜び] felicitation, congratulation; matter for congratulation

❸ **yorokobasu**
喜ばす
[formerly also 悦ばす] *vt* please, gladden, make happy
悦ばす
[now usu. 喜ばす] *vt* please, gladden, make happy

HOMOPHONES

yorokobu ⇨ 悦 418
yorokobi ⇨ 悦 418 慶 3173
yorokobasu ⇨ 悦 418

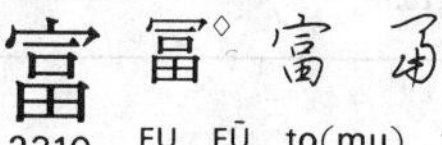

壹 2309

▶ONE
nonstandard for 壱 2197

3-9 士

富 2310

冨◇

FU FŪ to(mu) tomi

Ⓒ 富 fù

Radical	Strokes
宀 40	12-3-9
Grade	**Freq**
Jōyō-5	625
2 - 3 - 9	

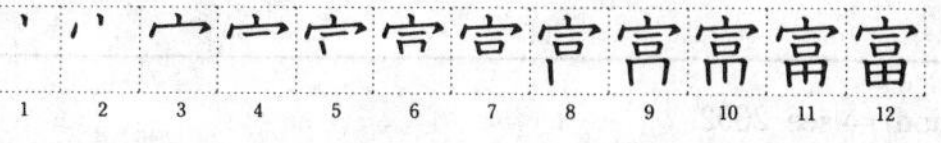

3-9 宀

▶RICH

COMPOUNDS

❶ⓐ [original meaning] **rich, wealthy, affluent**
ⓑ **riches, wealth**
ⓒ make rich, enrich
富裕 *fuyū* wealth, richness
富豪 *fugō* wealthy man, millionaire
富農 *funō* rich farmer
富力 *furyoku* wealth, riches
富貴な *fūki na* wealthy and noble
富国強兵策 *fukoku-kyōheisaku* measure to enrich and strengthen a country

❷ (abounding in) **rich, abundant, plentiful**
富鉱 *fukō* rich ore
豊富な *hōfu na* abundant, plentiful, rich

❸ Mt. Fuji
富士山 *fujisan* Mt. Fuji
富岳 *fugaku* Mt. Fuji

KUN

【**to(mu) 富む**】be rich; abound in, teem with
富ます *tomasu* enrich, make wealthy
資源に富む *shigen ni tomu* abound in natural resources

【**tomi 富**】wealth, riches; resources; lottery, lottery ticket
富の分配 *tomi no bunpai* distribution of wealth
富札 *tomifuda* lottery ticket
富籤 *tomikuji* lottery, lottery ticket

SYNONYMS

❶ⓐ **rich**

豪 wealthy → 2140
ⓑ **wealth**
財 WEALTH → 1457
産 property → 3298
宝 TREASURE → 2224
❷ **many**
裕 ABUNDANT → 1195
穣 YIELDING ABUNDANTLY → 1250
沢 plentiful → 267
多 MANY → 2170
豊 PLENTIFUL → 2697
万 myriad → 2936
百 numerous → 2026

3-9 宀

寒 寒 寒 寒

2311 KAN samu(i)

CH 寒 hán

Radical	Strokes
宀 40	12-3-9
Grade	Freq
Jōyō-3	1161
2-3-9	

1 2 3 4 5 6 7 8 9 10 11 12

▶**COLD**

COMPOUNDS

❶ (of weather) **cold, chilly**
寒気 *kanki* cold, cold weather
寒暑 *kansho* hot and cold
寒流 *kanryū* cold current
寒冷 *kanrei* cold, coldness, chilliness
寒波 *kanpa* cold wave
❷ coldest season, cold season, midwinter
寒鮒 *kanbuna* crucian caught in midwinter
大寒 *daikan* coldest season, midwinter
❸ poor, deserted
寒村 *kanson* deserted [poor] village
素寒貧 *sukanpin* dire poverty; pauper
❹ tremble, shudder
寒心すべき *kanshin subeki* alarming, deplorable

INDEPENDENT

【**kan 寒**】coldest season, midwinter
寒の入り *kan no iri* beginning of midwinter

KUN

【**samu(i) 寒い**】(of weather) cold, chilly
寒さ *samusa* coldness, cold
寒空 *samuzora* wintry sky, cold weather
肌寒い *hadazamui* chill, chilly

SYNONYMS

❶ **cold**
冷 COLD → 80
涼 COOL → 521
❷ **cold seasons**
冬 WINTER → 2157
秋 AUTUMN → 1139

3-9 宀

寒

2312

▶**COLD**
nonstandard for 寒 2311

3-9 ⺌

掌

incorrect classification ⇨ see 2602

3-9 ⺍

営 覚

incorrect classification ⇨ see 5-7

3-9 山

嵌

2313 KAN GAN ha(meru) ha(maru)

CH 嵌 qiàn

Radical	Strokes
山 46	12-3-9
Grade	Freq
Reference	
2-3-9	

COMPOUNDS

❶ [now also 眼 *gan* 1172] inlay, set in
嵌入する *kannyū suru* set in, inlay, dovetail
象嵌 *zōgan* inlaid work, inlaying
❷ⓐ put in, slip on; insert; slip in, be trapped
ⓑ entrap, ensnare

嵌め込み *hamekomi* insertion, inlaying
穴に嵌まる *ana ni hamaru* fall in a pit
旨く嵌められた *Umaku hamerareta* I was cleverly taken in

嵐 2314 RAN arashi

CH 岚 lán

Radical	Strokes
山 46	12-3-9
Grade	**Freq**
Non-Jōyō	1596
2 - 3 - 9	

3-9 山

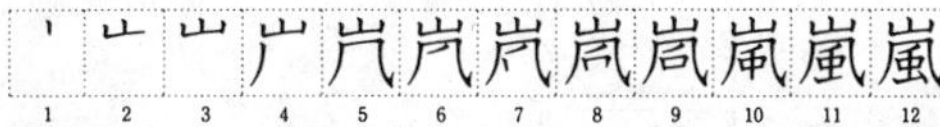

▶STORM

COMPOUNDS

❶ **storm, tempest**
春嵐 *shunran* spring storm
❷ [original meaning] mountain air, mountain vapor, mist
嵐気 *ranki* mountain air, mountain mist
晴嵐 *seiran* mountain vapor

KUN

【**arashi** 嵐】storm, tempest; stormy wind
嵐の前の静けさ *arashi no mae no shizukesa* the lull [calm] before a storm
政界の嵐 *seikai no arashi* political storm
砂嵐 *sunaarashi* sandstorm
青嵐 *aoarashi* wind blowing through verdure, mountain air

SYNONYMS

❶ **wind**
台 typhoon → 2005
風 WIND → 3007

尋 2315 **▶INQUIRE**
nonstandard for 尋 2322

3-9 ヨ

募 2316 BO tsuno(ru)

CH 募 mù

Radical	Strokes
力 19	12-2-10
Grade	**Freq**
Jōyō	925
2 - 3 - 9	

3-9 艹

▶RAISE

COMPOUNDS

● [original meaning] (gather persons or money by appealing to the public) **raise (troops or funds), collect, recruit, enlist**
募集する *boshū suru* recruit, enlist; raise, collect
募金 *bokin* fund-raising, collection of subscriptions
募債 *bosai* raising of a loan, loan floatation
応募する *ōbo suru* apply for, subscribe for [to], enlist for
公募 *kōbo* appeal for public subscription
徴募 *chōbo* recruitment

KUN

【**tsuno(ru)** 募る】*vt* recruit, enlist, levy; raise (subscriptions or funds); *vi* grow violent, increase severity
寄付金を募る *kifukin o tsunoru* make an appeal for contributions
募って来る食欲 *tsunotte kuru shokuyoku* rising appetite

SYNONYMS

● **enlist**
徴 LEVY → 683

3-9

艹

葵 葵 葵 葵

2317 KI aoi NAMES mamoru

Ⓒⓗ 葵 kuí

Radical	Strokes
艹 140	12-3-9
Grade	**Freq**
Names	2087
2 - 3 - 9	

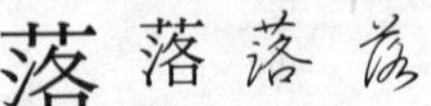

▶**MALLOW**

COMPOUNDS

❶ **mallow, hollyhock**

戎葵 *jūki* [archaic] hollyhock

❷ [archaic] sunflower

葵花 *kika* sunflower

KUN

【**aoi 葵**】 mallow, hollyhock; asarabacca; asarabacca crest (esp. of Shogunate government)

銭葵 *zeniaoi* common mallow

SPECIAL READINGS

向日葵▲ *himawari* sunflower

NAMES

葵 *aoi* surname also female name

葵 *mamoru* male name

SYNONYMS

❶ **flowering plants**

菊 CHRYSANTHEMUM → 2303

蓉 COTTON ROSE → 2337

芙 LOTUS → 2208

蘭 ORCHID → 2383

萩 *HAGI* → 2319

藤 WISTERIA → 2382

桜 cherry blossom → 931

梅 *ume* blossom → 925

3-9

艹

落 落 落 落

2318 RAKU o(chiru) o(chi) o(tosu)

Ⓒⓗ 落 luò lào là

Radical	Strokes
艹 140	12-3-9
Grade	**Freq**
Jōyō-3	347
2 - 3 - 9	

▶**FALL**

COMPOUNDS

❶ⓐ [original meaning] **fall, fall off, drop, sink**

ⓑ **let fall, drop**

ⓒ fall in, collapse, crumble

ⓓ fall into (one's hands), receive

落下 *rakka* fall, drop, descent

落馬する *rakuba suru* fall from a horse

落日 *rakujitsu* setting sun

墜落する *tsuiraku suru* fall, drop; crash

落球する *rakkyū suru* fail to catch a ball

落涙する *rakurui suru* shed tears

落盤 *rakuban* cave-in

陥落する *kanraku suru* fall in, cave in; surrender

落札する *rakusatsu suru* make a successful bid

❷ (esp. of stock prices)

ⓐ (become less) **fall, drop, decline**

ⓑ (reduction in value) fall, drop

低落する *teiraku suru* fall, depreciate, go down

下落 *geraku* fall, drop, decline; deterioration

急落 *kyūraku* sudden drop [fall], steep decline

暴落 *bōraku* slump, crash, heavy decline (in prices)

❸ⓐ (decline in status) **fall, decline, decay**

ⓑ (be defeated) fall, be defeated, surrender

ⓒ **fall through, fail (an examination)**

ⓓ fall off, drop out, become omitted, be missing

落魄 *rakuhaku* straitened [reduced] circumstances

堕落 *daraku* degeneration, corruption, decadence

没落 *botsuraku* ruin, fall, collapse

落城 *rakujō* fall of a castle

落選 *rakusen* election defeat; rejection

落第 *rakudai* failure in an examination

落伍者 *rakugosha* straggler

落丁 *rakuchō* missing page [leaf]

脱落する *datsuraku suru* be omitted; fall away [behind], drop out

❹ **be concluded, be settled, be completed**

落着する *rakuchaku suru* be settled, come to a conclusion

落成 *rakusei* completion

一段落付ける *ichidanraku tsukeru* settle for the time being, complete the first stage of

❺ village, town, settlement

村落 *sonraku* village, hamlet
部落 *buraku* community, village, hamlet

❻ **humor, jest, witticism**
落語 *rakugo rakugo*, Japanese-style comic story
落書き *rakugaki* scribbling, scrawling, graffiti

❼ perish, die
落命 *rakumei* death

❽ shave one's head to enter the Buddhist priesthood, take the tonsure
落髪 *rakuhatsu* tonsure

❾ lonesome, desolate
落莫たる *rakubakutaru* dreary, desolate, lonesome

KUN

【o(chiru) 落ちる】

①ⓐ fall, drop, go down; drip; sink
ⓑ fall in, collapse, crumble
ⓒ (of water) fall in, flow down, flow into
ⓓ fall into (one's hands), receive
ⓔ come off, be omitted, be missing
落ち込む *ochikomu* fall [cave] in; fall into depression
落ち葉 *ochiba* fallen leaves
崩れ落ちる *kuzureochiru* crumble down, tumble down
落ち合う *ochiau* gather, meet, join; flow together
人の手に落ちる *hito no te ni ochiru* fall into another's hands
訳が落ちている *Yaku ga ochite iru* The translation is missing

②ⓐ fall (in one's estimation); go down, be inferior, fall short of
ⓑ fail (in an examination); be defeated, surrender
信用がガタ落ちだ *shin'yō ga gataochi da* have a sudden fall in public estimation
気落ちする *kiochi suru* be discouraged, be dispirited
パリが落ちた *Pari ga ochita* Paris has fallen

③ⓐ go down (from the capital), leave; escape
ⓑ go downstream
都落ち *miyakoochi* rustication
駆け落ち *kakeochi* elopement
落ち鮎 *ochiayu* ayu coming down the river for spawning

④ [in compounds] be settled
落ち着く *ochitsuku* calm down, settle down, be steady; settle in, take up one's residence; harmonize with, match

⑤ (of wind) drop, abate, go down
風が落ちる *Kaze ga ochiru* The wind dies away

⑥ fall unconscious; die
落ち魚 *ochiuo* dead fish

【o(chi) 落ち】

① omission, slip, error, fault
落ち度 *ochido* fault, slip, error
片手落ち *katateochi* partiality, one-sidedness, favoritism

② end, upshot; punch line [point] of a joke
馬鹿を見るのが落ちだよ *Baka o miru no ga ochi da yo* The upshot of the matter will be that you'll make a fool of yourself

③ [suffix] (stock) ex, off, less, minus
配当落ち *haitōochi* ex dividend, dividend off

④ [suffix] handicap in a game of shogi
角落ち *kakuochi* shogi game with the superior player playing without the *kaku*

【o(tosu) 落とす】

① drop, let fall, throw down, dump
撃ち落とす *uchiotosu* shoot down

②ⓐ remove, take away, clean
ⓑ omit, miss
ⓒ fail to obtain
洗い落とす *araiotosu* wash off, wash out
見落とし *miotoshi* oversight, thing left unnoticed
単位を落とす *tan'i o otosu* fail to earn a credit

③ⓐ debase, abase, depreciate
ⓑ lessen, decrease
品質を落とす *hinshitsu o otosu* lower the quality
速力を落とす *sokuryoku o otosu* slow down

④ take, capture; win (a person) over
砦を落とす *toride o otosu* capture a fort
口説き落とす *kudokiotosu* persuade, prevail upon; win a woman's heart

⑤ bid in, knock (an article) down
競り落とす *seriotosu* knock down, make a successful bid

⑥ scatter, spend (money)
日本人観光客が落とす金 *nihonjin kankōkyaku ga otosu kane* money scattered by Japanese tourists

⑦ let escape
士を奥州へ落としてやる *shi o ōshū e otoshite yaru* help a samurai get away to Oshu

⑧ drive away, exorcise
狐を落とす *kitsune o otosu* exorcise a fox spirit (from a person)

SPECIAL READINGS

洒落▲ *share* witticism, joke; pun, wordplay

SYNONYMS

❶ⓐ & ❶ⓑ descend and fall
墜 DROP DOWN → 2881
降 DESCEND → 458
下 go down → 3378
倒 TOPPLE → 124

ⓒ collapse
陥 FALL IN → 457
崩 CRUMBLE → 2296

没 SINK → 260
❷ **decrease**
減 DECREASE → 601
耗 WEAR AWAY → 1309
削 cut down → 1448
縮 SHRINK → 1414
❸ⓐ **degenerate**
衰 DECLINE → 2100
堕 DEGENERATE → 2822
破 break down → 1150
ⓒ **fail**
敗 fail → 1476
-損なう fail to (do) → 651
❹ **settle**
着 settle (down) → 3316
帰 settle in place → 130

3-9
艹

萩 萩 萩 萩
2319 SHŪ hagi

CH 萩 qiū

Radical	Strokes
艹 140	12-3-9
Grade	**Freq**
Names	2016
2-3-9	

1 2 3 4 5 6 7 8 9 10 11 12

▶***HAGI***

COMPOUNDS

● [archaic] kind of rush

KUN

【hagi 萩】 *hagi*, Japanese bush clover, *Lespedeza bicolor*
萩属 *hagizoku Lespedeza*

NAMES

萩原 *hagiwara* surname
萩 *hagi* surname also female name also place name

SYNONYMS

【hagi】
○ **shrubs**
藤 WISTERIA → 2382
蔦 JAPANESE IVY → 2355
茉 JASMINE → 2244
莉 JASMINE → 2284
○ **flowering plants**
藤 WISTERIA → 2382
蘭 ORCHID → 2383
芙 LOTUS → 2208
蓉 COTTON ROSE → 2337
葵 MALLOW → 2317
菊 CHRYSANTHEMUM → 2303
桜 cherry blossom → 931
梅 *ume* blossom → 925

3-9
艹

葬 葬 葬 葬
2320 SŌ hōmu(ru)

CH 葬 zàng

Radical	Strokes
艹 140	12-3-9
Grade	**Freq**
Jōyō	1370
2-3-9	

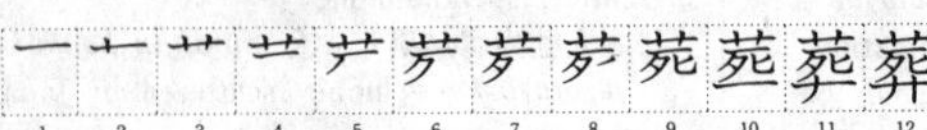

1 2 3 4 5 6 7 8 9 10 11 12

▶**FUNERAL**

COMPOUNDS

❶ [also suffix] **funeral**
葬式 *sōshiki* funeral ceremony
葬儀 *sōgi* funeral service [rites]
冠婚葬祭 *kankonsōsai* ceremonial occasions (coming of age, marriage, funeral and ancestral worship)
国葬 *kokusō* national funeral
会社葬 *kaishasō* company funeral
❷ [original meaning] **bury (a corpse), entomb, inter**
埋葬する *maisō suru* bury, inter
火葬 *kasō* cremation
水葬 *suisō* burial at sea

INDEPENDENT

【sō 葬】 funeral
葬の列 *sō no retsu* funeral procession

KUN

【hōmu(ru) 葬る】 bury (a corpse), entomb, inter; consign to oblivion, shelve
葬り去る *hōmurisaru* consign to oblivion

SYNONYMS

❷ **bury**
埋 BURY → 403

3-9 艹

葉 葉 葉

2321 YŌ ha¹ ha²

Ⓒ叶 yè xié

Radical	Strokes
艹 140	12-3-9
Grade	**Freq**
Jōyō-3	451
2 - 3 - 9	

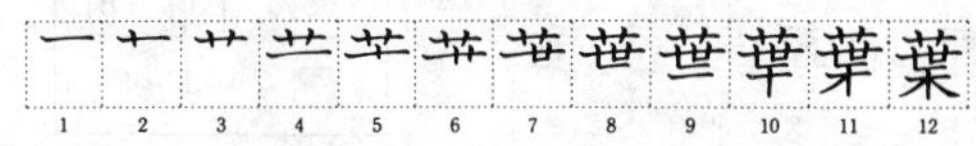

▶LEAF

COMPOUNDS

❶ [original meaning] **leaf, foliage**
葉脈 *yōmyaku* veins of a leaf
葉緑素 *yōryokuso* chlorophyll
紅葉 *kōyō* (=*momiji*) red leaves, crimson foliage, autumn tints
落葉 *rakuyō* fall of leaves; fallen leaves
子葉 *shiyō* seed leaf, cotyledon
針葉樹 *shin'yōju* conifer
枝葉末節 *shiyōmassetsu* unimportant details

❷ various leaflike objects, as:
ⓐ (sheet of paper) **leaf, sheet, page, paper**
ⓑ counter for leaves or sheets
ⓒ *anat* lobe, lobule
ⓓ plane (of an aircraft)
薄葉 *usuyō* Japanese tissue
前葉 *zen'yō* preceding page [leaf]
紙二葉 *kami niyō* two sheets of paper
三葉虫 *san'yōchū* trilobite
肝葉 *kan'yō* lobe of the liver
前頭葉 *zentōyō* frontal lobe
単葉飛行機 *tan'yō-hikōki* monoplane
複葉機 *fukuyōki* biplane

❸ part of a historical period divided into three
初葉 *shoyō* initial period, beginning of an epoch

INDEPENDENT

【yō 葉】 *anat* lobe, lobule

KUN

【ha¹ 葉】 leaf, foliage; needle; blade, spear
草の葉 *kusa no ha* blade of grass
松葉 *matsuba* pine needle
落ち葉 *ochiba* fallen leaves

【ha² 葉】 [in compounds] fragment, piece—historically sometimes interchangeable with 端, as in the word *hagaki*, which is now always written 葉書
葉書 *hagaki* postcard
言葉 *kotoba* word, term; wording; language

SPECIAL READINGS

紅葉 *momiji* red leaves, crimson foliage, autumn tints; Japanese maple

SYNONYMS

❷ⓐ **paper**
紙 PAPER → 1302
丁 sheet → 3348
頁 PAGE → 2086
面 page (of a newspaper) → 2087

ⓑ **counters for flat things**
枚 COUNTER FOR FLAT THINGS → 859
丁 counter for sheets → 3348
頁 counter for pages → 2086
通 counter for letters → 3109

ⓓ **wings**
翼 WING (of birds or aircraft) → 2720
羽 WING (of birds or insects) → 226

HOMOPHONES

ha² ⇨ 端 1221

COMPOUND FORMATION

言葉 *kotoba*

言葉 'word, etc.' consists of 言 *koto* 'word' and 葉 *ha²* 'fragment, piece'. In ancient times, 言 *koto* referred to both a word and its meaning. Later, 葉 was attached to 言 to show that it is used in the sense of 'word'. Now, however, 言 is used only in the latter sense.

NOTE

⇨ see USAGE note at 端 1221

蒸

incorrect stroke count ⇨ see 2334

3-9 艹

惹

incorrect stroke count ⇨ see 2493

3-9 艹

3-9 彐

尋 尋 尋 尋

2322 JIN tazu(neru) hiro▲

CH 寻 xún

Radical	Strokes
寸 41	12-3-9
Grade	Freq
Jōyō	1788
2-3-9	

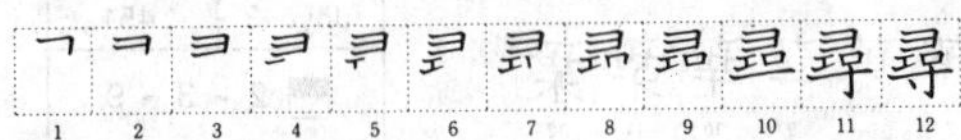

1 2 3 4 5 6 7 8 9 10 11 12

▶**INQUIRE**

COMPOUNDS

❶ inquire into, investigate

尋尋 *tōjin* [rare] thorough inquiry, minute investigation

❷ [formerly also 訊 1452] **interrogate, question**

尋問 *jinmon* questioning, examination, interrogation

❸ ordinary, usual, common, normal

尋常の *jinjō no* common, ordinary, normal

尋常に *jinjō ni* tamely; squarely; commonly, ordinarily, normally

❹ *hiro*, fathom: unit of length equiv. to approx. 1.8 m or 6 *shaku* (尺), used esp. for measuring the depth of water

千尋の谷 *senjin no tani* abysmal valley

INDEPENDENT

【jin 尋】fathom (⇨❹)

KUN

【tazu(neru) 尋ねる】

①ⓐ inquire (about, after), ask, question

ⓑ inquire into, investigate into

理由を尋ねる *riyū o tazuneru* ask the reason

由来を尋ねる *yurai o tazuneru* inquire into the origin

② search for, look for

尋ね人 *tazunebito* missing person

尋ね求める *tazunemotomeru* seek for

お尋ね者 *otazunemono* wanted person, person wanted by the police

【hiro 尋】*hiro*, fathom: unit of length equiv. to approx. 1.8 m or 6 *shaku* (尺), used esp. for measuring the depth of water

SYNONYMS

❹ **length units**

間 *ken* (1.8 m) → 3323

丈 *jo* (3.03 m) → 3419

町 *cho* (109 m) → 1113

里 LEAGUE, *ri* (3.4 km) → 3542

米 meter → 3529

尺 *SHAKU* (30.3 cm) → 3440

寸 *sun* (3.03 cm) → 2935

【tazuneru】

①ⓐ **inquire**

質 query → 2808

伺う INQUIRE (*humble*) → 69

諮 CONSULT → 1596

問 QUESTION → 3320

詰 question closely → 1521

聞く ask → 3326

USAGE

tazuneru

尋ねる

①ⓐ inquire (about, after), ask, question

ⓑ inquire into, investigate into

② search for, look for

訪ねる

visit, call on, pay a visit

HOMOPHONES

tazuneru ⇨ 訪 1468

3-9 ⺷

普 普 普

2323 FU amane(ku)▲

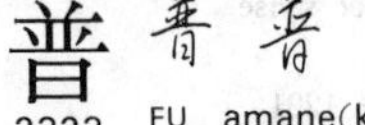

CH 普 pǔ

Radical	Strokes
日 72	12-4-8
Grade	Freq
Jōyō	937
2-3-9	

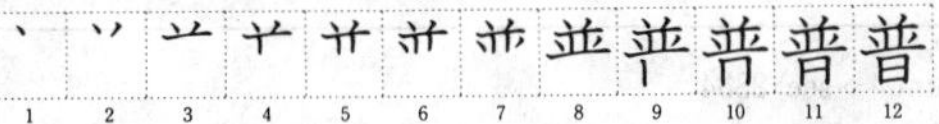

1 2 3 4 5 6 7 8 9 10 11 12

▶**WIDESPREAD**

COMPOUNDS

❶ⓐ **widespread, general, universal, common**

ⓑ **common, ordinary**

普及 *fukyū* diffusion, spread, propagation

普遍的な *fuhenteki na* universal, omnipresent, ubiquitous

普請 *fushin* building, construction

普通の *futsū no* normal, regular, ordinary

普選 *fusen* universal suffrage

普段(=不断)の *fudan no* usual, ordinary, everyday, habitual

❷ Prussia

普仏戦争 *fufutsu sensō* Franco-Prussian War

KUN

【amane(ku) 普く】[also 遍く] *literary* all over, everywhere, widely, universally
普く捜す *amaneku sagasu* make a wide search
普く世界に知られる *amaneku sekai ni shirareru* be known all over the world

SYNONYMS

❶ⓐ **widespread**
遍 ALL OVER → 3136
通 common → 3109
公 common (math) → 1974
ⓑ **ordinary**
平 common → 3478
只- ORDINARY → 2155
並 ordinary → 2246
常 NORMAL → 2590
庸 MEDIOCRE → 3128
凡 COMMONPLACE → 2938

USAGE

amaneku
普く
[also 遍く] *literary* all over, everywhere, widely, universally
遍く
[also 普く] same as 普く

HOMOPHONES

amaneku ⇨ 遍 3136

NOTE

⇨ see COMPOUND FORMATION for 普請 *fushin* ⇨ 請 1576
★do not confuse with 晋 2656

尊 2324

SON tatto(i) tōto(i) tatto(bu) tōto(bu)

CH 尊 zūn

Radical	Strokes
寸 41	12-3-9
Grade	**Freq**
Jōyō-6	1147
2-3-9	

3-9

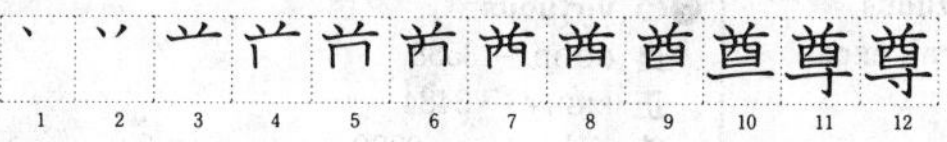

▶HONOR

COMPOUNDS

❶ⓐ **honor, respect, venerate, esteem**
ⓑ honorary, noble, exalted
尊重する *sonchō suru* respect, esteem, value
尊敬する *sonkei suru* respect, esteem, honor, revere
自尊心 *jisonshin* (spirit of) self-respect, pride
尊厳 *songen* dignity, majesty, prestige
尊王 *sonnō* reverence for the Emperor
尊称 *sonshō* honorary title
❷ [honorific] **your honorable, your**
尊顔 *songan* your countenance
尊父 *sonpu* your father
尊宅 *sontaku* your house
❸ [also suffix] honorific title after names of Buddhist deities or statues
釈尊 *shakuson* Sakyamuni, Buddha
本尊 *honzon* principal image of Buddha
地蔵尊 *jizōson* (image of) *Kṣitigarbha-bodhisattva*, *Jizo* (guardian deity of children)
❹ haughty, arrogant
尊大な *sondai na* haughty, arrogant, self-important
唯我独尊 *yuigadokuson* self-conceit; vainglory
❺ [original meaning, now archaic] kind of wine vessel used in ancient China

KUN

【tatto(i) 尊い】exalted, august, awe-inspiring, sacred
尊い高齢 *tattoi kōrei* sacred old age
【tōto(i) 尊い】same as **tattoi 尊い**
【tatto(bu) 尊ぶ】honor, respect, revere
神を尊ぶ *kami o tattobu* revere God
【tōto(bu) 尊ぶ】same as **tattobu 尊ぶ**

SYNONYMS

❶ⓐ **respect**
敬 RESPECT → 1701
欽 REVERE → 1690
仰 look up to → 48
崇 REVERENCE → 2297
尚 VALUE HIGHLY → 2233
重 set value on → 3573
拝 WORSHIP → 303
慕 ADORE → 2353
❷ **honorific prefixes**
貴 YOUR HONORABLE → 2606
令 your honorable → 1995
御 GENERAL HONORIFIC TERM → 577

HOMOPHONES

tattoi ⇨ 貴 2606
tōtoi ⇨ 貴 2606
tattobu ⇨ 貴 2606
tōtobu ⇨ 貴 2606

NOTE

⇨ see USAGE note at 貴 2606

3-9

善 善 善

2325 ZEN yo(i)

CH 善 shàn

Radical	Strokes
口 30	12-3-9
Grade	Freq
Jōyō-6	589
2 - 3 - 9	

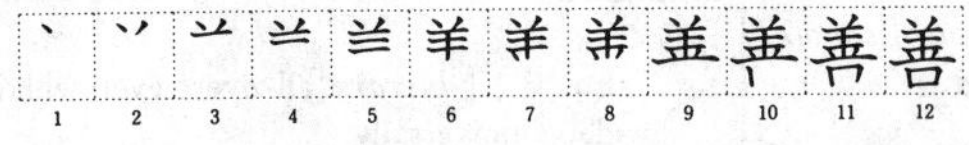

▶**GOOD**

COMPOUNDS

❶ⓐ (having positive qualities) **good**
ⓑ (satisfactory) good, well
善意 *zen'i* good intention; favorable sense
善良な *zenryō na* good, virtuous
善政 *zensei* good government [administration]
改善 *kaizen* improvement, amelioration
最善 *saizen* best
善処する *zensho suru* make the best of
善戦する *zensen suru* fight well
❷ⓐ (morally excellent) **good, virtuous**
ⓑ **good, goodness, virtue, moral excellence**
善人 *zennin* good people
善行 *zenkō* good deed, benevolence
善悪 *zen'aku* good and evil
偽善 *gizen* hypocrisy
❸ (on good terms) good, intimate
善隣関係 *zenrin kankei* good neighborly relations
親善 *shinzen* goodwill, friendly relations

INDEPENDENT

[zen 善] good, goodness, virtue
善と悪 *zen to aku* good and evil

KUN

[yo(i) 善い] (morally excellent) good, good-natured, virtuous, upright
善い行い *yoi okonai* good deed

SYNONYMS

❶ⓐ **good**
良 GOOD → 3558
好 FAVORABLE → 208
順 favorable → 18
佳 FINE → 86
美 BEAUTIFUL → 2264
❷ⓐ **virtuous**
良 GOOD → 3558
正 RIGHT → 3484
義 righteous → 2338
ⓑ **moral goodness**
義 RIGHTEOUSNESS → 2338
徳 VIRTUE → 684
道 the way of moral conduct → 3134

HOMOPHONES

yoi ⇨ 良 3558 好 208

NOTE

⇨ see USAGE note at 良 3558

3-9

着

incorrect classification ⇨ see 3316

3-9

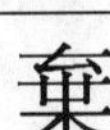

棄

2326

▶**ABANDON**
nonstandard for 棄 2137

3-10

寛 寛 寛 寛

2327 KAN kutsuro(gu)▲

CH 宽 kuān

Radical	Strokes
宀 40	13-3-10
Grade	Freq
Jōyō	1470
2 - 3 - 10	

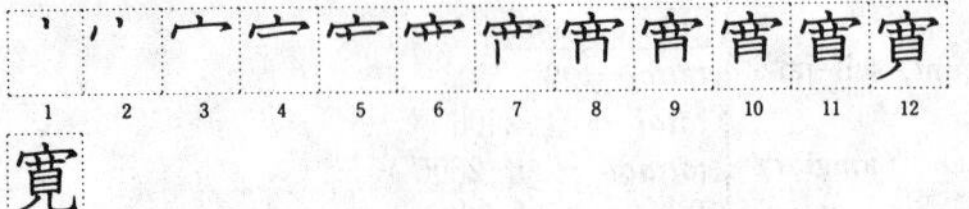

▶**LENIENT**

COMPOUNDS

● **lenient, tolerant, largehearted, generous, magnanimous, broad-minded**
寛大な *kandai na* generous, magnanimous, lenient
寛容な *kan'yō na* tolerant, liberal, generous

寛厳 *kangen* lenity and severity
寛闊な *kankatsu na* generous, largehearted
寛厚 *kankō* kindness and largeheartedness

INDEPENDENT

【kan 寛】 leniency, generosity
人には寛 *hito ni wa kan* leniency to others

KUN

【kutsuro(gu) 寛ぐ】 make oneself comfortable, be at ease, relax
寛ぎ *kutsurogi* ease, relaxation

SYNONYMS

● **tolerant**
甘い indulgent → 3494

窟

2328 KUTSU iwaya

Ⓒⓗ 窟 kū

Radical	Strokes
穴 116	13-5-8
Grade	**Freq**
Reference	
2-3-10	

3-10 宀

COMPOUNDS

❶ [now also 屈 *kutsu* 3079] [original meaning] cave, cavern, hole
洞窟 *dōkutsu* cavern, cave
岩窟王 *gankutsuō* The Count of Monte Cristo
理窟 *rikutsu* reason, logic; argument; pretext; theory
窟の中 *iwaya no naka* inside of a cave

❷ [also suffix] den
巣窟 *sōkutsu* den, haunt, nest
魔窟 *makutsu* haunts of the demon, den of iniquity; brothel, red-light district
阿片窟 *ahenkutsu* opium den
貧民窟 *hinminkutsu* slum
私娼窟 *shishōkutsu* house of ill fame, brothel

NOTE

⇨ see COMPOUND FORMATION for 理屈 *rikutsu* ⇨ 屈 3079

寝 寝 寝 寝

2329 SHIN ne(ru) ne(kasu)

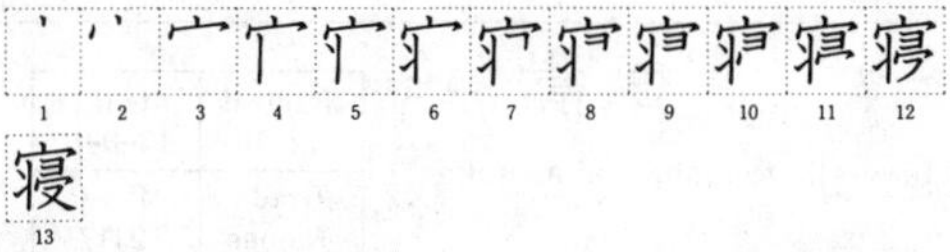

Ⓒⓗ 寝 qǐn

Radical	Strokes
宀 40	13-3-10
Grade	**Freq**
Jōyō	1089
2-3-10	

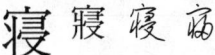

3-10 宀

▶**GO TO SLEEP**

COMPOUNDS

❶ [original meaning]
ⓐ **go to sleep [bed], sleep**
ⓑ **going to bed, sleeping, sleep**
寝台 *shindai* bed, sleeping berth
寝室 *shinshitsu* bedroom
寝具 *shingu* bedclothes, bedding
不寝番 *fushinban* night watch
寝食 *shinshoku* eating and sleeping
就寝する *shūshin suru* go to bed

❷ inner room, back room, recesses
寝殿造り *shindenzukuri* Heian residential architecture

INDEPENDENT

【shin 寝】 going to bed, sleeping, sleep
寝に就く *shin ni tsuku* go to bed

KUN

【ne(ru) 寝る】
①ⓐ go to sleep [bed], retire (to bed)
ⓑ sleep, fall asleep
ⓒ be confined to one's bed, be laid up
寝る時間 *neru jikan* bedtime
寝 *ne* sleep
寝床 *nedoko* bed
寝袋 *nebukuro* sleeping bag
寝坊 *nebō* late riser, sleepyhead; oversleeping
昼寝 *hirune* siesta, nap
② lie down
寝転ぶ *nekorobu* lie down
③ sleep with, share the bed with
人妻と寝る *hitozuma to neru* sleep with another person's wife
④ lie idle
寝ている資本 *nete iru shihon* dead capital

【ne(kasu) 寝かす】 put to sleep; bed down; lay down; let (goods) lie idle; ferment (rice malt)
寝かし付ける *nekashitsukeru* lull (a child) to sleep

筆を寝かせて書く *fude o nekasete kaku* write with one's brush slanted

SYNONYMS

❶ **sleep**

眠 SLEEP → 1147

睡 SLEEP → 1200

【neru】

② **lie down**

伏 PROSTRATE → 45

3-10 宀

塞

2330 SOKU SAI fusa(gu) toride

CH 塞 sāi sè sài

Radical	Strokes
土 32	13-3-10
Grade	Freq
Reference	
2-3-10	

COMPOUNDS

❶ [original meaning] stop up, fill in

閉塞 *heisoku* blockade, stoppage

梗塞 *kōsoku* stoppage; tightness; infraction

穴を塞ぐ *ana o fusagu* fill a hole with earth

耳を塞ぐ *mimi o fusagu* stop [plug] one's ears

❷ [now usu. 砦 *toride*] fort, fortress, stronghold

城塞(＝城砦) *jōsai* fortress, stronghold, citadel

要塞 *yōsai* fortress, stronghold

HOMOPHONES

toride ⇨ 塁 2593 砦 2671

NOTE

⇨ see USAGE note at 塁 2593

3-10 ⺌

當

incorrect classification ⇨ see 2611 (nonstandard for 当 2177)

3-10 ⺍

誉

incorrect classification ⇨ see 2502

3-10 山

嵩

2331 SŪ kasa kasa(mu) NAMES takashi taka take

CH 嵩 sōng

Radical	Strokes
山 46	13-3-10
Grade	Freq
Names	2117
2-3-10	

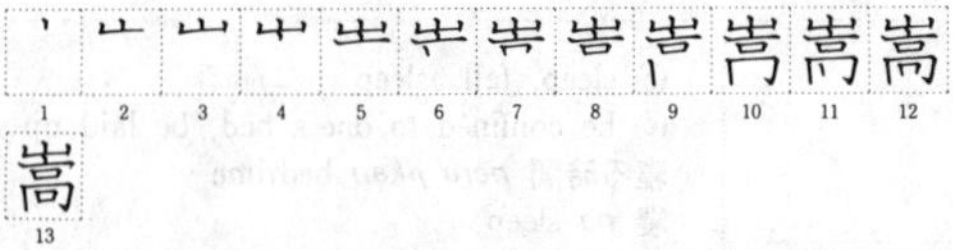

▶**BULK**

COMPOUNDS

ⓐ Songshan: the highest and central peak of the Five Sacred Mountains in Henan Province

ⓑ [sometimes also 崇 2297] [archaic] as lofty as Songshan

嵩山 *sūzan* Songshan

嵩高 *sūkō* Songshan; lofty

嵩呼 *sūko* shouting "Long live the Emperor"

KUN

【kasa 嵩】 bulk, volume, size, quantity

嵩に掛かって *kasa ni kakatte* arrogantly, high-handedly, overbearingly

嵩張る *kasabaru* be bulky [voluminous], bulk large

年嵩の *toshikasa no* older, aged, elderly, senior

水嵩 *mizukasa* volume of water

値嵩株 *negasakabu* high-priced stocks, blue-chip shares

【kasa(mu) 嵩む】 increase in volume [bulk], accumulate; run up to a large sum

借金が嵩む *shakkin ga kasamu* get deeper in debt

荷嵩み *nigasami* overstock, glut

NAMES

嵩 *takashi* male name

SYNONYMS

【kasa】

○ **quantity and number**
量 QUANTITY → 2471
積 size → 1236
額 AMOUNT → 1805
分 content → 1972
数 NUMBER → 1790
勢 strength → 2857

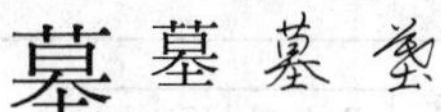

2332 BO haka

㊥ 墓 mù

Radical	Strokes
土 32	13-3-10
Grade	**Freq**
Jōyō-5	1302
2-3-10	

3-10

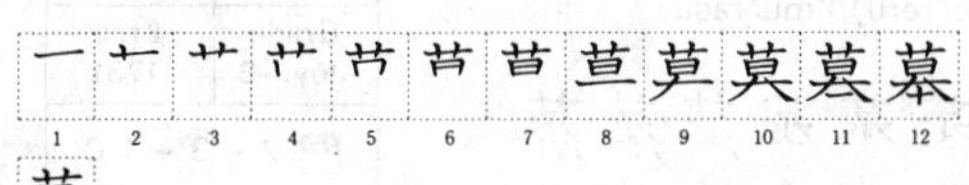

▶GRAVE

COMPOUNDS

● [original meaning] **grave, tomb**
墓碑 *bohi* tombstone, gravestone
墓地 *bochi* graveyard, cemetery, burial grounds
墓標 *bohyō* grave post, grave marker, gravestone
墓参 *bosan* visit to a grave

KUN

【**haka** 墓】grave, tomb, sepulcher; gravestone
墓石 *hakaishi* tombstone
墓参り *hakamairi* visit to a grave

SYNONYMS

● **graves**
墳 TUMULUS → 719
陵 IMPERIAL MAUSOLEUM → 544
塚 grave mound → 556

蓄 蓄 蓄 蓄
2333 CHIKU takuwa(eru)

㊥ 蓄 xù

Radical	Strokes
艹 140	13-3-10
Grade	**Freq**
Jōyō	1620
2-3-10	

3-10

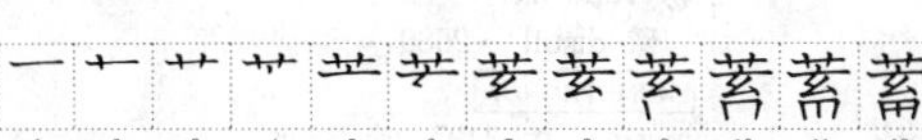

▶STORE UP

COMPOUNDS

❶ **store up, accumulate, amass, lay aside**
蓄積 *chikuseki* accumulation, stockpiling
蓄電池 *chikudenchi* storage battery, accumulator
蓄音機 *chikuonki* phonograph, gramophone
蓄財 *chikuzai* accumulation of wealth
貯蓄する *chochiku suru* save (money), lay aside
備蓄 *bichiku* saving for [against] emergency, storing
含蓄 *ganchiku* implication, significance, suggestiveness

❷ keep (a mistress)
蓄妾 *chikushō* keeping a mistress [concubine]

KUN

【**takuwa(eru)** 蓄える】
① [sometimes also 貯える] store up, lay in stock, save, lay aside
蓄え *takuwae* store, reserve, stock; savings
燃料を蓄える *nenryō o takuwaeru* store up fuel
知識を蓄える *chishiki o takuwaeru* store one's mind with knowledge
② have, wear (a mustache)

SYNONYMS

❶ **store**
蔵 STORE → 2364
貯 LAY UP → 1509
納 PUT AWAY → 1300

USAGE

❶ **takuwaeru**
蓄える
① [sometimes also 貯える] store up, lay in stock, save, lay aside
② have, wear (a mustache)
貯える
[usu. 蓄える] store up, lay in stock, save, lay aside

❷ **takuwae**
蓄え

[sometimes also 貯え] store, reserve, stock; savings

貯え

[usu. 蓄え] store, reserve, stock; savings

HOMOPHONES

takuwaeru ⇨ 貯 1509

takuwae ⇨ 貯 1509

NOTE

★do not confuse with 畜 2096

3-10 艹

蒸 蒸 蒸 蒸

2334 JŌ SEI▲ mu(su) mu(reru) mu(rasu)

CH 蒸 zhēng

Radical	Strokes
艹 140	13-3-10
Grade	**Freq**
Jōyō-6	1731
2-3-10	

一 十 艹 艹 艼 芓 芛 苂 茟 菉 荥 蒸 蒸
1 2 3 4 5 6 7 8 9 10 11 12 13

▶STEAM ▶EVAPORATE

COMPOUNDS

❶ **steam, heat with steam**

蒸籠 *seirō* steaming basket

薫蒸する *kunjō suru* fumigate, smoke

❷ **evaporate**

蒸発 *jōhatsu* evaporation, volatilization; mysterious disappearance

蒸散 *jōsan* transpiration

蒸留 *jōryū* distillation

蒸気 *jōki* steam, vapor

❸ [archaic] numerous, crowded

蒸民 *jōmin* the people, the masses

KUN

【mu(su) 蒸す】

① *vt* steam, heat with steam; foment

蒸し *mushi* steaming

蒸し菓子 *mushigashi* steamed cake

② *vi* be sultry, be stuffy

蒸し暑い *mushiatsui* sultry, sweltering

【mu(reru) 蒸れる】 *vi* be steamed (to the proper degree); be stuffy; molder

【mu(rasu) 蒸らす】 *vt* steam, cook by steam

飯を蒸らす *meshi o murasu* steam boiled rice

SYNONYMS

❶ **cook**

焼く cook by fire → 997

揚げる fry in deep fat → 593

炊 COOK → 870

煮 BOIL (cook by boiling) → 2785

沸 BOIL (undergo boiling) → 329

❷ **vaporize**

留 distill → 2580

HOMOPHONES

musu ⇨ 生 3497 産 3298

NOTE

⇨ see USAGE note at 生 3497

3-10 艹

幕 幕 幕 幕

2335 MAKU BAKU

CH 幕 mù

Radical	Strokes
巾 50	13-3-10
Grade	**Freq**
Jōyō-6	797
2-3-10	

▶CURTAIN ▶SHOGUNATE

COMPOUNDS

❶ⓐ [original meaning] **curtain, screen**

ⓑ curtainfall, end

幕屋 *makuya* tent, tabernacle; Makuya (Original Gospel Movement of Japan)

天幕 *tenmaku* tent

垂れ幕 *taremaku* hanging screen, curtain

内幕 *uchimaku* inside facts, inner workings; [original meaning] inner curtain

除幕式 *jomakushiki* unveiling ceremony

煙幕 *enmaku* smoke screen

幕切れ *makugire* curtainfall, end

❷ *theater*

ⓐ act, scene

ⓑ counter for acts

開幕 *kaimaku* rising of the curtain; opening scene of a play

序幕 *jomaku* opening act, curtain raiser

終幕 *shūmaku* end, close, curtainfall

第三幕 *daisanmaku* Act 3
❸ (since banquets in honor of champion wrestlers were held in a curtained enclosure) first grade in sumo wrestling
幕内 *makuuchi* first-class sumo wrestler
幕下 *makushita* junior class sumo wrestler
入幕する *nyūmaku suru* become a first grade sumo wrestler
❹ⓐ shogun's headquarters, camp
ⓑ **shogunate, feudal government of Japan**
幕営 *bakuei* camp, camping
幕僚 *bakuryō* staff, staff officer
幕府 *bakufu* shogunate
幕末 *bakumatsu* closing days of the Tokugawa shogunate
佐幕 *sabaku* adherence to the shogunate
❺ abbrev. of 幕僚 *bakuryō*: staff, staff officer

統幕 *tōbaku* general staff headquarters

INDEPENDENT

【maku 幕】 curtain; *theater* act; one's turn, place; first grade in sumo wrestling
幕を引く *maku o hiku* draw a curtain
愈君の出る幕が来た *Iyoiyo kimi no deru maku ga kita* This is where you come in / It's your turn now

SYNONYMS

❶ⓐ **curtain**
帳 drapery → 473
❷ **parts of plays**
場 scene → 558
❹ⓑ **governments**
廷 COURT → 3058
朝 court → 1695
宮 Imperial Court → 2274
官 GOVERNMENT → 2226

夢 夢 夢 夢 ㊥ 梦 mèng

2336 MU yume

Radical	Strokes
夕 36	13-3-10
Grade	Freq
Jōyō-5	1014
2-3-10	

3-10 艹

一 十 艹 艹 芇 芇 苗 苗 苗 苗 萝 夢 夢
1 2 3 4 5 6 7 8 9 10 11 12 13

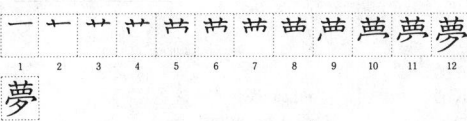

▶**DREAM**

COMPOUNDS

● [original meaning] **dream**
夢想家 *musōka* dreamer
夢幻 *mugen* dream; vision; fantasy
夢中で *muchū de* like one in a dream; like one dazed; frantically
悪夢 *akumu* nightmare, bad dream
白昼夢 *hakuchūmu* waking dream
迷夢 *meimu* illusion, delusion, fallacy

KUN

【yume 夢】 dream; vision, fancy, illusion, delusion

夢見る *yumemiru* dream, fancy
夢占い *yumeuranai* divination by means of dreams
夢枕に *yumemakura ni* in a dream
初夢 *hatsuyume* first dream of the New Year
正夢 *masayume* dream which comes true, prophetic dream
夢心地 *yumegokochi* ecstasy, trance
夢物語 *yumemonogatari* empty dream; fantastic story

SYNONYMS

● **illusory mental images**
幻 PHANTOM → 180

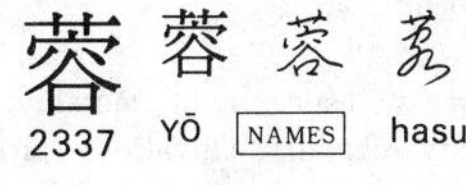

蓉 蓉 蓉 蓉 ㊥ 蓉 róng

2337 YŌ NAMES hasu

Radical	Strokes
艹 140	13-3-10
Grade	Freq
Names	2119
2-3-10	

3-10 艹

一 十 艹 艹 艹 芢 芢 芢 芙 荥 萗 蓉 蓉
1 2 3 4 5 6 7 8 9 10 11 12 13

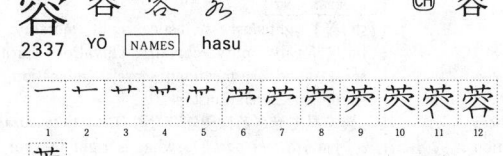

▶**COTTON ROSE**

COMPOUNDS

❶ **cotton rose, hibiscus**

芙蓉 *fuyō* cotton rose; lotus
❷ lotus

NAMES

蓉子 *yōko* female name
蓉美 *hasumi* female name

SYNONYMS

❶ **flowering plants**
芙 LOTUS → 2208
菊 CHRYSANTHEMUM → 2303
葵 MALLOW → 2317
蘭 ORCHID → 2383
萩 *HAGI* → 2319
藤 WISTERIA → 2382
桜 cherry blossom → 931
梅 *ume* blossom → 925

3-10 艹

incorrect stroke count ⇨ see 2517

3-10 艹

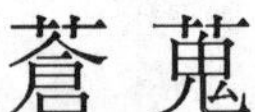

incorrect stroke count ⇨ see 4-10

3-10 ⺷

2338 GI

Ⓒ 义 yì

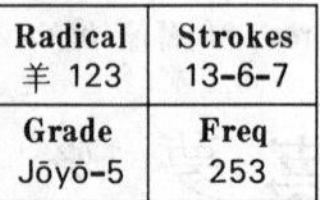

Radical	Strokes
羊 123	13-6-7
Grade Jōyō-5	**Freq** 253
2-3-10	

▶**RIGHTEOUSNESS** ▶**MEANING**

COMPOUNDS

❶ⓐ **righteousness, justice, right, morality**
ⓑ **righteous, just, upright**
正義 *seigi* justice, righteousness
道義 *dōgi* morality, moral principles
仁義 *jingi* humanity and justice; moral code; formal greeting among gamblers
情義 *jōgi* justice and humanity
義人 *gijin* righteous man
義憤 *gifun* righteous indignation
❷ chivalrous, heroic, self-sacrificing, public-spirited
義侠 *gikyō* chivalry, generosity
義気 *giki* chivalry, heroism
義兵 *gihei* army in the cause of justice, volunteer corps
義捐金(=義援金) *gienkin* donation, contribution
❸ⓐ **faith, loyalty, duty**
ⓑ faithful, loyal
義務 *gimu* duty, obligation
義理 *giri* sense of duty [honor], obligation, debt of gratitude; justice; courtesy
忠義 *chūgi* loyalty, fidelity, devotion
信義 *shingi* fidelity, faith, loyalty
恩義 *ongi* obligation, debt of gratitude
義臣 *gishin* loyal retainer
❹ **meaning, sense, signification, significance**
意義 *igi* meaning, sense, signification, significance
講義 *kōgi* lecture
定義 *teigi* definition
字義 *jigi* character definition, meaning of a word [term]
疑義 *gigi* doubt, doubtful points
❺ moral principle
主義 *shugi* principle, -ism
❻ -in-law; step-, foster
義父 *gifu* father-in-law; foster father, stepfather
義兄 *gikei* brother-in-law
❼ artificial
義足 *gisoku* artificial leg
義眼 *gigan* artificial eye
❽ [also 宜 2223 or 誼 1571] friendship; favor, kindness
情義 *jōgi* friendship

INDEPENDENT

【**gi** 義】 righteousness, justice, right, morality; faith, loyalty, duty; chivalry, chivalrous spirit, sense of honor; meaning, sense, signification, significance; relationship
義を見てせざるは勇無きなり *Gi o mite sezaru wa yū naki nari* Do what is right in your sight / Knowing what is right without practicing it betrays one's cowardice
義を破る *gi o yaburu* break faith with
義を重んじる *gi o omonjiru* value honor
経文の義を説く *kyōmon no gi o toku* explain the meaning of a sutra

兄弟の義を結ぶ *kyōdai no gi o musubu* become sworn brothers

SYNONYMS

❶ⓐ **moral goodness**

善 GOOD → 2325
道 the way of moral conduct → 3134
徳 VIRTUE → 684

ⓑ **virtuous**

正 RIGHT → 3484
善 GOOD → 2325
良 GOOD → 3558

❷ **brave**

壮 heroic → 224
雄 HEROIC → 1008
豪 bold and unrestrained → 2140
敢 bold → 1706
赳 VALIANT → 3308
勇 BRAVE → 2089

❸ⓐ **fidelity**

忠 LOYALTY → 2433
孝 FILIAL PIETY → 3205
悌 BROTHERLY LOVE → 424
誠 SINCERITY → 1523
実 faithfulness → 2225
信 fidelity → 100
操 constancy → 769
節 moral integrity → 2691

❹ **meaning**

意 MEANING → 2136
訳 SENSE → 1473
旨 PURPORT → 2024
趣 PURPOSE → 3317

❻ **related by marriage**

継 step- → 1360

❼ **false**

虚 FALSE → 3237
仮 fake → 50
偽 sham → 131
擬 imitation → 788

慈 慈 慈 慈

2339 JI itsuku(shimu)▲

ⒸⒽ 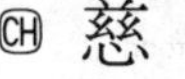 cí

Radical	Strokes
心 61	13-4-9
Grade	**Freq**
Jōyō	1705
2 - 3 - 10	

3-10

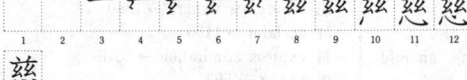

Stroke order: 1–12,  13

▶**AFFECTIONATE**

COMPOUNDS

❶ [original meaning] **affectionate (towards one's child), tender, gentle and loving, kind**

慈愛 *jiai* affection, love, benevolence
慈母 *jibo* affectionate [loving] mother

❷ⓐ *Buddhism* **compassion, active benevolence, universal love, loving kindness**

ⓑ compassionate, charitable, merciful

慈悲 *jihi* mercy, compassion
慈善 *jizen* charity
慈雨 *jiu* beneficial [welcome] rain
仁慈 *jinji* benevolence

KUN

【**itsuku(shimu) 慈しむ**】 be affectionate to, treat tenderly, love

慈しみ *itsukushimi* affection, love
親が子を慈しむ *Oya ga ko o itsukushimu* Parents care tenderly for their children

SYNONYMS

❶ **kind**

温 warmhearted → 608
渥 GRACIOUS → 600
優 kindly → 177
篤 cordial → 2716
懇 cordial → 2899
厚 KIND → 3003

❷ⓐ **tender feelings for others**

仁 BENEVOLENCE → 20
情 sympathy → 482
悲 mercy → 2775
哀 PITY → 2068

incorrect classification ⇨ see 2139
(nonstandard for 会 2020)

3-10 

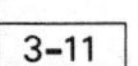

3-11 士

嘉 2340

KA yomi(suru) NAMES hiro yoshi yoshimi

CH 嘉 jiā

Radical	Strokes
口 30	14-3-11
Grade	**Freq**
Names	2001

2-3-11

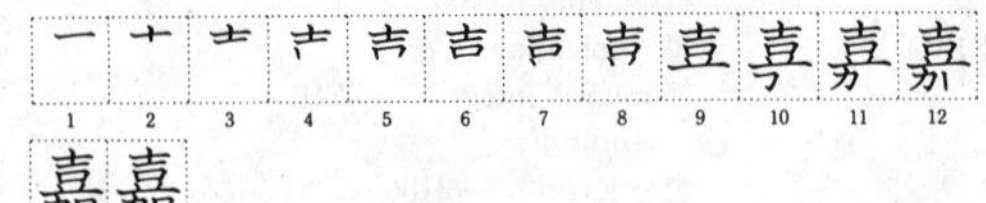

▶**HAPPY**

COMPOUNDS

❶ [also 佳 86] **happy, auspicious, lucky, good**

嘉節 *kasetsu* happy [auspicious] occasion
嘉例 *karei* happy precedent, festive annual custom
嘉日 *kajitsu* auspicious day, good day

❷ [original meaning] good, fine, delicious

嘉言善行 *kagen-zenkō* good words and good deeds
嘉肴(=佳肴) *kakō* delicious food

❸ commend (esp. an inferior), praise, approve of, applaud

嘉納する *kanō suru* accept with pleasure
嘉賞 *kashō* commendation, approval

KUN

【yomi(suru) 嘉する】 commend (esp. an inferior), praise, approve of, applaud

家臣の功績を嘉する *kashin no kōseki o yomi-suru* approve one's retainer's achievement

NAMES

嘉次郎 *kajirō* male name
嘉子 *yoshiko* female name

SYNONYMS

❶ **good fortune**

吉 LUCKY → 2167
祥 AUSPICIOUS → 948
瑞 AUSPICIOUS OMEN → 1027
禎 PROPITIOUS OMEN → 1031
幸 GOOD FORTUNE → 2216
福 FORTUNE → 1029

❸ **praise**

褒 COMMEND → 2144
賛 PRAISE → 2809
美 regard as beautiful → 2264
彰 PROCLAIM MERITS → 1860
称 acclaim → 1160
賞 express admiration → 2618
揚 EXALT → 593
頌 EULOGIZE → 1045

3-11 士

臺 2341

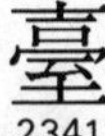

▶**STAND** ▶**COUNTER FOR VEHICLES**

nonstandard for 台 2005

3-11 士

壽 2342

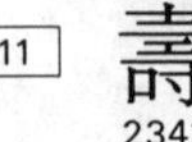

▶**LONGEVITY** ▶**CONGRATULATIONS**

nonstandard for 寿 3557

3-11 大

奪 2343

DATSU uba(u)

CH 夺 duó

Radical	Strokes
大 37	14-3-11
Grade	**Freq**
Jōyō	977

2-3-11

▶**ROB**

COMPOUNDS

ⓐ **rob, take by force, seize, deprive**

ⓑ *baseball* rob

奪還 *dakkan* recapture, recovery
奪取 *dasshu* capture, seizure
略奪 *ryakudatsu* pillage, plunder, looting
強奪する *gōdatsu suru* rob, seize, plunder; hijack
争奪 *sōdatsu* scramble, contest, struggle

剝奪する *hakudatsu suru* deprive, divest
奪三振 *datsusanshin* striking a batter out

KUN

【uba(u) 奪う】 rob, take by force, deprive; absorb, engross, fascinate
奪い取る *ubaitoru* plunder
奪い返す *ubaikaesu* take back, recapture
女に心を奪われる *onna ni kokoro o ubawareru* be fascinated [captivated] by a woman

SYNONYMS

ⓐ take forcibly

拐 KIDNAP → 308
収 take possession by force → 198

ⓐ steal and rob

略 plunder → 1169
取 TAKE → 1262
盗 STEAL → 2670
窃 STEAL → 2253

NOTE

★do not confuse with 奮 2367

寡

2344 KA

CH 寡 guǎ

Radical	Strokes
宀 40	14-3-11
Grade	Freq
Jōyō	1912
2 - 3 - 1 1	

3-11 宀

▶FEW

COMPOUNDS

❶ few, little
寡少の *kashō no* few, little, scanty
寡占 *kasen* oligopoly
寡黙な *kamoku na* silent, taciturn, reticent
寡聞 *kabun* having little knowledge (of), being ill-informed
多寡 *taka* quantity, number, amount

❷ widow, widower, widowed spouse; widowed
寡婦 *kafu* (= *yamome*) widow
寡居 *kakyo* widowhood

❸ [archaic] [humble] my unbenevolent, my humble
寡人 *kajin* my humble self

INDEPENDENT

【ka 寡】 *literary* small number of people, minority
寡は衆に敵せず *Ka wa shū ni tekisezu* There is no contending against numbers

SYNONYMS

❶ few

乏 SCANTY → 1933
少 LITTLE → 3467
薄 meager → 2370
微 SLIGHT → 639
寸 A BIT OF → 2935

❷ wives

嫁 BRIDE → 635
婦 married woman → 469
妻 WIFE → 2558
奥 wife → 2824
内 wife → 3466
室 wife (esp. of persons of rank) → 2254
嫡 legitimate wife → 680

寧

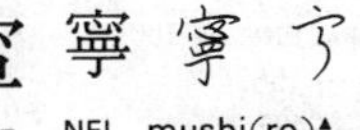

2345 NEI mushi(ro)▲

CH 宁 níng nìng

Radical	Strokes
宀 40	14-3-11
Grade	Freq
Jōyō	1836
2 - 3 - 1 1	

3-11 宀

▶COURTEOUS

COMPOUNDS

❶ [formerly 嚀 785] **courteous, polite**
丁寧(＝叮嚀)な *teinei na* polite, courteous

❷ peaceful, quiet, tranquil
寧日 *neijitsu* peaceful day
安寧 *annei* public peace, tranquility
康寧 *kōnei* [rare] peacefulness, tranquility

KUN

【mushi(ro) 寧ろ】 rather, better

彼は学者と言うより寧ろ詩人だ *Kare wa gakusha to iu yori mushiro shijin da* He is not so much a scholar as a poet

SYNONYMS

❶ **courteous**

丁 courteous → 3348

❷ **calm and peaceful**

安 PEACEFUL → 2171
康 peaceful → 3124
泰 TRANQUIL → 2583
静 QUIET → 1728
平 CALM → 3478
穏 CALM → 1235

3-11 宀

2346 RYŌ

CH 寥 liáo

Radical	Strokes
宀 40	14-3-11
Grade	Freq
Reference	
2-3-11	

COMPOUNDS

❶ [now also 涼 521] desolate, deserted, empty

荒寥たる *kōryōtaru* desolate, dreary

寂寥たる *sekiryōtaru* lonely, desolate

❷ [original meaning] few, scarce

寥寥たる *ryōryōtaru* few, rare; lonesome

3-11 宀

察 察 察

2347 SATSU

CH 察 chá

Radical	Strokes
宀 40	14-3-11
Grade	Freq
Jōyō-4	616
2-3-11	

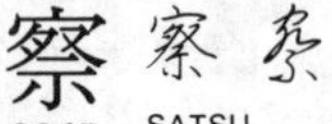

▶**INSPECT** ▶**GUESS**

COMPOUNDS

❶ⓐ (examine officially) **inspect, investigate, examine**

ⓑ (examine carefully) **inspect, observe, scrutinize, examine**

警察 *keisatsu* police, police station
視察 *shisatsu* inspection, observation
巡察 *junsatsu* round of inspection, patrol
検察 *kensatsu* criminal investigation; prosecution
査察 *sasatsu* inspection, investigation
診察 *shinsatsu* medical examination
観察 *kansatsu* observation, supervision
洞察する *dōsatsu suru* see through, penetrate

❷ **guess, conjecture, infer, surmise, gather, judge**

察知する *satchi suru* infer, gather
推察する *suisatsu suru* guess, conjecture, infer, imagine
予察する *yosatsu suru* [rare] guess beforehand, conjecture in advance
考察する *kōsatsu suru* consider, contemplate, study

INDEPENDENT

【satsu 察】 abbrev. of 警察 *keisatsu*: *underworld slang* cop, dick

【sassuru 察する】 guess, conjecture, infer, gather, judge, imagine; sympathize with

察し *sasshi* guess, conjecture, judgment

SYNONYMS

❶ⓐ **investigate and examine**

閲 REVIEW → 3330
究 STUDY EXHAUSTIVELY → 2203
討 STUDY → 1456
探 PROBE → 505
検 EXAMINE → 986
診 EXAMINE A PATIENT → 1504
調 INVESTIGATE → 1567
査 LOOK INTO → 2437
審 EXAMINE CAREFULLY → 2360
験 TEST → 1833
勘 CHECK → 1777
糾 INQUIRE INTO → 1278

ⓑ **see and look**

観 VIEW → 1880
看 WATCH → 3220
覧 LOOK OVER → 2854
仰 LOOK UP → 48
顧 LOOK BACK → 1900
視 REGARD → 972
見 SEE → 2544

目 look → 3043
眺 LOOK OUT OVER → 1171
望 LOOK AFAR → 2742
❷ **conjecture**

推 INFER → 504
憶 SPECULATE → 765
測 CONJECTURE → 610

窪
2348 WA kubo(mu) kubo(maru) kubo

Ⓒⓗ 洼 wā

Radical	Strokes
穴 116	14-5-9
Grade	**Freq**
Reference	
2 - 3 - 1 1	

3-11 穴

COMPOUNDS

● [original meaning] (of the ground) become hollow, become depressed, cave in
窪地 *kubochi* depressed ground, hollow

HOMOPHONES

kubomu ⇨ 凹 3482

NOTE

⇨ see USAGE note at 凹 3482

賓
2349
▶GUEST
nonstandard for 賓 2357

3-11 穴

實
2350
▶REAL
nonstandard for 実 2225

3-11 穴

寧
2351
▶COURTEOUS
nonstandard for 寧 2345

3-11 穴

寢
2352
▶GO TO SLEEP
nonstandard for 寝 2329

3-11 穴

寫
incorrect stroke count ⇨ see 2363
(nonstandard for 写 2000)

3-11 穴

裳
incorrect classification ⇨ see 2615

3-11 小

慕 慕 慕 慕
2353 BO shita(u)

Ⓒⓗ 慕 mù

Radical	Strokes
小 61	14-4-10
Grade	**Freq**
Jōyō	1785
2 - 3 - 1 1	

3-11 艹

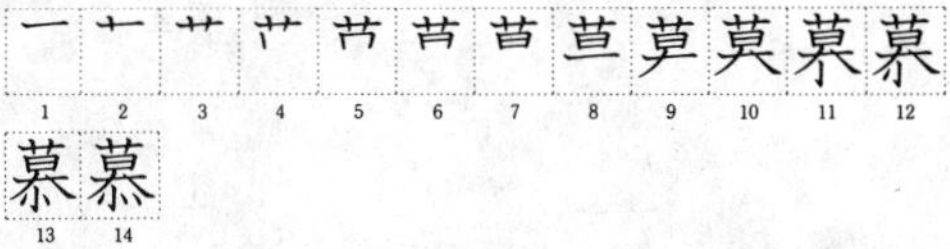

▶ADORE

COMPOUNDS

ⓐ **adore, love deeply, be attached to**

ⓑ yearn for, long for
敬慕する *keibo suru* adore, love and respect, admire

恋慕 *renbo* love, attachment
慕情 *bojō* longing; love, affection
思慕する *shibo suru* love dearly, yearn for
追慕する *tsuibo suru* cherish one's memory, yearn after, sigh for

KUN

【shita(u) 慕う】 adore, love deeply, be attached to; yearn for, long for; follow
慕わしい *shitawashii* dear, beloved
慕い寄る *shitaiyoru* approach in adoration
故郷を慕う *kokyō o shitau* pine for home
後を慕って *ato o shitatte* following (a person to a place)

SYNONYMS

ⓐ respect
拝 WORSHIP → 303
重 set value on → 3573
尚 VALUE HIGHLY → 2233
崇 REVERENCE → 2297
仰 look up to → 48
欽 REVERE → 1690
敬 RESPECT → 1701
尊 HONOR → 2324

ⓑ wish and desire
懐 LONG FOR → 763
渇 thirst for → 515
欲 DESIRE → 1475
求 SEEK → 3550
希 ASPIRE → 2049
望 HOPE → 2742
願 WISH → 1845

3-11 艹

暮 暮 暮 暮

2354 BO ku(reru) ku(rasu)

ⒸⒽ 暮 mù

Radical	Strokes
日 72	14-4-10
Grade	**Freq**
Jōyō-6	926
2-3-11	

一 1 十 2 艹 3 艹 4 苎 5 苎 6 昔 7 荁 8 莫 9 莫 10 莫 11 暮 12 暮 13 暮 14

▶DUSK ▶LIVE

COMPOUNDS

❶ [original meaning] **dusk, nightfall**
暮色 *boshoku* dusk, twilight scene
暮夜 *boya* night
薄暮 *hakubo* nightfall, dusk, twilight

❷ towards the end (of the year), late
暮春 *boshun* late spring
歳暮 *seibo* end of the year; year-end present

KUN

【ku(reru) 暮れる】 grow dark; come to an end, close; be at a loss
暮れ *kure* dusk, twilight, nightfall
日暮れ *higure* nightfall, dusk, evening
今年も暮れた *Kotoshi mo kureta* The year has come to an end
思案に暮れる *shian ni kureru* be lost in thought
途方に暮れる *tohō ni kureru* be at a loss, be puzzled

【ku(rasu) 暮らす】 (pass one's life) live, lead one's life, spend one's day; (make a living) live, earn one's livelihood
暮らし *kurashi* living, livelihood, subsistence; circumstances
一人暮らしをする *hitorigurashi o suru* live alone
暮らし向き *kurashimuki* circumstances
その日暮らし *sonohigurashi* hand-to-mouth life

SYNONYMS

❶ evening and night
宵 EARLY EVENING → 2276
夕 EVENING → 3387
晩 EVENING → 979
夜 NIGHT → 2056

【kurasu】

○ live
活 LIVE → 385
生 live (be alive) → 3497

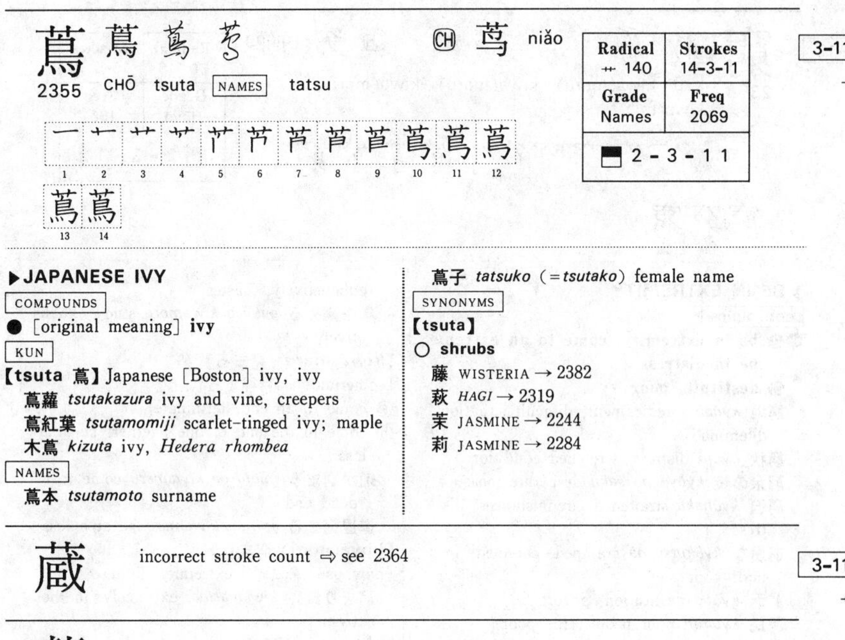

蔦 蔦 蔦 蔦 ⒸⒽ 茑 niǎo

2355 CHŌ tsuta NAMES tatsu

Radical	Strokes
艹 140	14-3-11
Grade	**Freq**
Names	2069

2-3-11

3-11 艹

▶JAPANESE IVY

COMPOUNDS

● [original meaning] **ivy**

KUN

【tsuta 蔦】 Japanese [Boston] ivy, ivy
蔦蘿 *tsutakazura* ivy and vine, creepers
蔦紅葉 *tsutamomiji* scarlet-tinged ivy; maple
木蔦 *kizuta* ivy, *Hedera rhombea*

NAMES

蔦本 *tsutamoto* surname
蔦子 *tatsuko* (= *tsutako*) female name

SYNONYMS

【tsuta】
○ **shrubs**
藤 WISTERIA → 2382
萩 *HAGI* → 2319
茉 JASMINE → 2244
莉 JASMINE → 2284

蔵 incorrect stroke count ⇨ see 2364 — 3-11 艹

蔭 incorrect stroke count ⇨ see 2517 — 3-11 艹

賣 **▶SELL** — 3-12 士
2356 nonstandard for 売 2196

賓 賓 賓 賓 ⒸⒽ 宾 bīn

2357 HIN

Radical	Strokes
貝 154	15-7-8
Grade	**Freq**
Jōyō	1619

2-3-12

3-12 宀

▶GUEST

COMPOUNDS

❶ [original meaning] **guest, visitor**
賓客 *hinkyaku* (= *hinkaku*) guest, guest of honor
国賓 *kokuhin* state guest
来賓 *raihin* guest, visitor
迎賓館 *geihinkan* guest house [palace]

❷ⓐ object of a verb
ⓑ *logic* predicate
賓辞 *hinji* object of a verb
賓位語 *hin'igo logic* predicate

SYNONYMS

❶ **visitor**
客 VISITOR → 2250

3-12

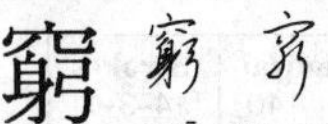

2358 KYŪ kiwa(meru) kiwa(maru) kiwa(mari) kiwa(mi)

Ⓒⓗ 穷 qióng

Radical	Strokes
穴 116	15-5-10
Grade	Freq
Jōyō	1661
2-3-12	

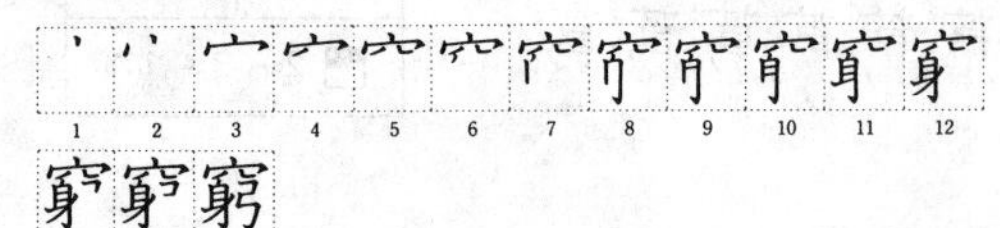

▶**BE IN EXTREMITY**

COMPOUNDS

❶ⓐ **be in extremity, come to an extreme, be in distress**
ⓑ **destitute, poor**
窮地 *kyūchi* predicament, difficult situation, dilemma
窮状 *kyūjō* distress, wretched condition
窮余の策 *kyūyo no saku* desperate measure
窮迫 *kyūhaku* straitened circumstances, distress
窮屈な *kyūkutsu na* cramped, confined; formal; poor
窮乏 *kyūbō* destitution, poverty
窮民 *kyūmin* poor people, the poor
窮措大 *kyūsodai* poor student [scholar]
困窮 *konkyū* destitution, poverty, distress
貧窮 *hinkyū* poverty

❷ⓐ **go to the extremity [extreme], go to the limit, reach the end**
ⓑ extremity, limit, end
窮極の *kyūkyoku no* ultimate, extreme
無窮 *mukyū* eternity, infinitude, immortality

INDEPENDENT

【**kyūsuru** 窮する】be in extremity, come to an extreme, be in distress, be in want [need]
窮すれば通ず *Kyūsureba tsūzu* Necessity is the mother of invention
返答に窮する *hentō ni kyūsuru* be at a loss for an answer

KUN

【**kiwa(meru)** 窮める】
① [also 極める]
ⓐ carry to extremity, go to extremes, be extremely (cruel)
ⓑ go to the extreme [end], reach an extreme, go to the highest point
口を窮めて誉める *kuchi o kiwamete homeru* be lavish in another's praise
貧困を窮める *hinkon o kiwameru* be reduced to extreme poverty, be extremely poor
② [usu. 究める] investigate thoroughly, study exhaustively, master
学を窮める *gaku o kiwameru* study exhaustively

【**kiwa(maru)** 窮まる】
[sometimes also 谷まる]
ⓐ come to an end, terminate
ⓑ come to the end of one's tether, be at a loss
道が窮まる *michi ga kiwamaru* come to a dead end
進退窮まる *shintai kiwamaru* be at a loss

【**kiwa(mari)** 窮まり】
[now usu. 極まり] extremity, limit
窮まり無い *kiwamarinai* extremely, in the extreme

【**kiwa(mi)** 窮み】extremity, end, limit
窮み無き *kiwaminaki* endless, without limit

SYNONYMS

❶ⓐ **trouble and suffering**
困 BE IN TROUBLE → 3070
悩 SUFFER → 421
苦 SUFFERING → 2243
痛 PAIN → 3285
辛 HARD → 2038
煩 VEXED → 1022
難 DIFFICULT → 1838
ⓑ **poor**
貧 POOR → 2123
乏 poor → 1933
❷ⓑ **extreme**
極 EXTREME → 1017
限 LIMIT → 398
涯 OUTER LIMITS → 512
果て end → 3560

HOMOPHONES

kiwameru ⇨ 極 1017 究 2203
kiwamaru ⇨ 極 1017 谷 2043
kiwamari ⇨ 極 1017
kiwami ⇨ 極 1017

NOTE

⇨ see USAGE note at 極 1017

寮 2359 RYŌ

CH 寮 liáo

Radical	Strokes
宀 40	15-3-12
Grade	**Freq**
Jōyō	1515
2 - 3 - 1 2	

3-12 宀

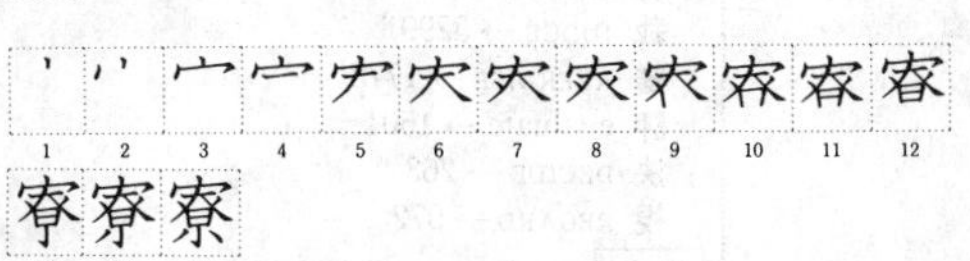

▶**DORMITORY**

COMPOUNDS

❶ lodging accommodations or similar facilities for use by students, company employees or members of an organization:

ⓐ **student dormitory, hostel**

ⓑ [also suffix] **company dormitory, lodging house, villa**

ⓒ suffix after names of dormitories

寮長 *ryōchō* dormitory leader

寮母 *ryōbo* matron of a dormitory

寮歌 *ryōka* dormitory song

寮生 *ryōsei* boarder

学寮 *gakuryō* dormitory, hostel; seminary

工員寮 *kōinryō* dormitory for factory workers

独身寮 *dokushinryō* company dormitory for unmarried employees

若葉寮 *wakabaryō* Wakaba Dormitory

❷ fanciful building, pavilion

茶寮 *saryō* (=*charyō*) tea cottage, tea house

御寮人 *goryōnin* madam, mistress

❸ former government bureau

大学寮 *daigakuryō* Bureau of Education

INDEPENDENT

【ryō 寮】dormitory, lodging house, villa; former government bureau

寮に住む *ryō ni sumu* live in a dormitory

SYNONYMS

❶ **temporary quarters**

舎 temporary quarters → 2060

宿 lodging → 2293

館 inn → 1748

亭 INN → 2072

審 2360 SHIN

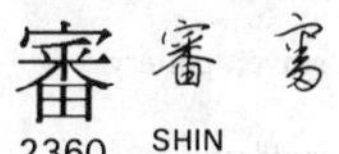

CH 审 shěn

Radical	Strokes
宀 40	15-3-12
Grade	**Freq**
Jōyō	323
2 - 3 - 1 2	

3-12 宀

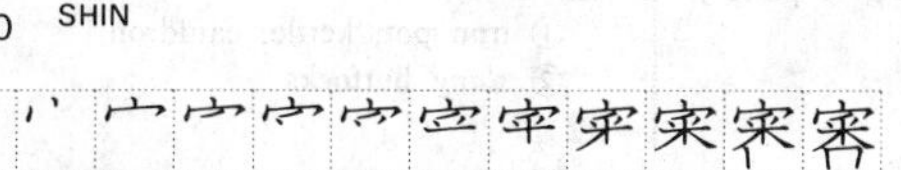

▶**EXAMINE CAREFULLY** ▶**TRY**

COMPOUNDS

❶ⓐ **examine carefully, investigate**

ⓑ abbrev. of 審議会 *shingikai*: (deliberative) council

ⓒ appraise, appreciate

審議 *shingi* deliberation, consideration, careful discussion

審査する *shinsa suru* examine, investigate, judge

審判 *shinpan* (=*shinban*) refereeing, judgment; referee, umpire

米審(=米価審議会) *beishin* (=*beika shingikai*) Rice Price Deliberative Council

審美 *shinbi* appreciation of the beautiful

❷ⓐ **try, hold a court trial, hear, judge**

ⓑ [also suffix] trial, hearing, examination, judgment

審理する *shinri suru* try, examine, inquire into

審問 *shinmon* trial, hearing, formal interrogation

結審 *kesshin* conclusion of a hearing

陪審 *baishin* jury

予審 *yoshin* preliminary examination

再審 *saishin* retrial, new trial, review of

第二審 *dainishin* second hearing

控訴審 *kōsoshin* hearing of an intermediate appeal

❸ umpire, referee

球審 *kyūshin baseball* chief umpire

主審 *shushin* chief umpire

塁審 *ruishin* base umpire

❹ detailed, clear

不審 *fushin* doubt, question

SYNONYMS

❶ⓐ **investigate and examine**

査 LOOK INTO → 2437
調 INVESTIGATE → 1567
診 EXAMINE A PATIENT → 1504
検 EXAMINE → 986
探 PROBE → 505
討 STUDY → 1456
察 INSPECT → 2347
究 STUDY EXHAUSTIVELY → 2203
閲 REVIEW → 3330
験 TEST → 1833
勘 CHECK → 1777
糾 INQUIRE INTO → 1278

❷ⓐ **judge**

判 JUDGE → 1122
裁 JUDGE → 3299
鑑 APPRAISE → 1773
評 evaluate → 1501
決 DECIDE → 263
視 REGARD → 972

NOTE

⇨ see COMPOUND FORMATION for 陪審 *baishin* ⇨ 陪 539

3-12
宀

窯

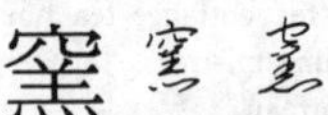

2361 YŌ kama

CH 窑 yáo

Radical	Strokes
穴 116	15-5-10
Grade	**Freq**
Jōyō	1878
2 - 3 - 12	

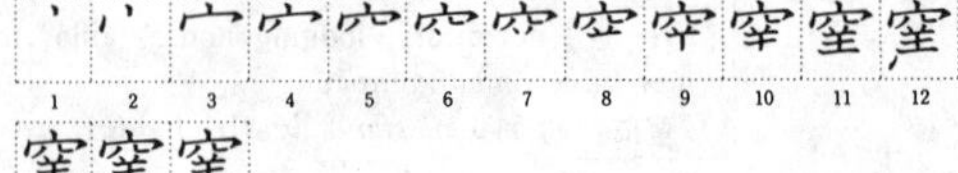

▶KILN

COMPOUNDS

ⓐ **kiln, furnace**

ⓑ ceramics

官窯 *kan'yō* governmental porcelain furnace
窯業 *yōgyō* ceramics, ceramic industry

KUN

【kama 窯】kiln, oven, furnace, stove; pottery

窯元 *kamamoto* pottery
窯印 *kamajirushi* potter's mark

SYNONYMS

ⓐ **heating devices**

炉 FURNACE → 869
缶 steam boiler → 2033

ⓑ **ceramics ware**

陶 POTTERY → 546
磁 porcelain → 1214

USAGE

kama

窯
kiln, oven, furnace, stove; pottery

釜
① iron pot, kettle, cauldron
② *slang* buttocks

罐
boiler

HOMOPHONES

kama ⇨ 釜 2107 罐 1437

3-12
宀

寛

2362

▶LENIENT

nonstandard for 寛 2327

3-12
宀

寫

2363

▶COPY

nonstandard for 写 2000

3-12
⺌

賞

incorrect classification ⇨ see 2618

蔵 藏 蔵 𦾔

2364 zō kura

Ⓒⓗ 藏 cáng zàng

Radical	Strokes
艹 140	15-3-12
Grade	**Freq**
Jōyō-6	413
2-3-12	

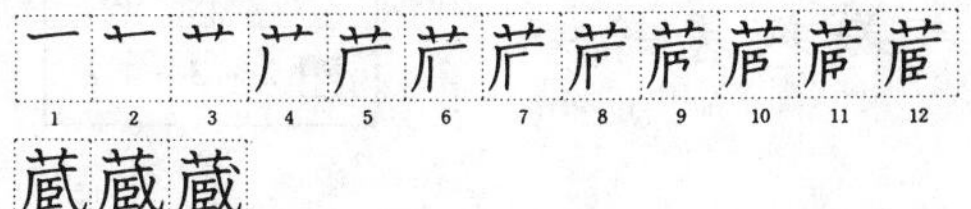

蔵 蔵 蔵
13 14 15

▶**STORE**

COMPOUNDS

❶ⓐ **store, put away, lay by**
ⓑ hide, conceal
貯蔵 *chozō* storage, preservation
収蔵 *shūzō* garnering, storage
死蔵する *shizō suru* hoard (up), keep (something) idle
秘蔵 *hizō* treasuring
冷蔵庫 *reizōko* refrigerator
内蔵する *naizō suru* have (a thing) within, have (something) built in
蔵匿する *zōtoku suru* [rare] conceal, shelter, harbor
埋蔵する *maizō suru* bury in the ground, have (oil) deposits underground

❷ **own, possess, keep (a collection of books)**
蔵書 *zōsho* one's library, book collection
蔵本 *zōhon* one's library
所蔵 *shozō* possession

❸ storehouse, storing place, treasury
土蔵 *dozō* storehouse, godown
宝蔵 *hōzō* treasury
経蔵 *kyōzō* scripture house

❹ abbrev. of 大蔵省 *ōkurashō*: **Ministry of Finance**
蔵相 *zōshō* Minister of Finance

❺ Tibet
漢蔵語 *kanzōgo* Sino-Tibetan (languages)

❻ *Buddhism* encompassing the whole universe
地蔵 *jizō* (image of) *Kṣitigarbha-bodhisattva*, *Jizo* (guardian deity of children)

❼ collection of Buddhist sutras
三蔵 *sanzō tripitaka* (three branches of Buddhist sutras)

INDEPENDENT

【**zō 蔵**】possession
中村家蔵 *nakamurake zō* property of the Nakamura family

【**zōsuru 蔵する**】own, cherish

KUN

【**kura 蔵**】[also 倉, sometimes also 庫] storehouse (for temporary preservation), storeroom, godown
蔵出し *kuradashi* delivery of goods from a storehouse
米蔵 *komegura* rice granary
大蔵省 *ōkurashō* Ministry of Finance

SYNONYMS

❶ⓐ **store**
蓄 STORE UP → 2333
貯 LAY UP → 1509
納 PUT AWAY → 1300

❷ **possess**
具 possess → 2552
有 HAVE → 2983
持 HOLD → 374
属 BELONG TO → 3145
享 ENJOY → 2051

❸ **storehouse**
倉 STOREHOUSE → 2104
庫 STORAGE CHAMBER → 3112

HOMOPHONES

kura ⇨ 倉 2104 庫 3112

NOTE

⇨ see USAGE note at 倉 2104

蕃 蔽

incorrect stroke count ⇨ see 4-12

3-12

養 養 養 (CH) 养 yǎng

2365 YŌ yashina(u)

Radical	Strokes
食 184	15-9-6
Grade	**Freq**
Jōyō-4	731
2-3-12	

▶FOSTER

COMPOUNDS

❶ⓐ **foster, bring up, raise to maturity, rear, support, care for**

ⓑ (affording parental care) foster (parent), adopted

ⓒ **breed, raise (animals or plants), keep**

養育する *yōiku suru* foster, bring up, educate
養護 *yōgo* protective care
扶養 *fuyō* support, maintenance
養子 *yōshi* foster [adopted] child
養父 *yōfu* foster father
養殖 *yōshoku* culture, cultivation, raising
養鶏 *yōkei* chicken raising
養毛剤 *yōmōzai* hair tonic
培養する *baiyō suru* cultivate, culture, incubate

❷ⓐ **foster one's intellect, cultivate one's mind, train**

ⓑ foster one's physical strength, nurse, cure

養成する *yōsei suru* train, educate, bring up
教養 *kyōyō* culture, education, cultivation
修養 *shūyō* mental culture, cultivation of the mind, character-building
養生 *yōjō* care of health, recuperation
休養 *kyūyō* rest, recuperation, relaxation
療養する *ryōyō suru* recruit one's health, recuperate, receive medical care

❸ nourishment

養分 *yōbun* nourishment, nutrient
栄養 *eiyō* nutrition, nourishment
滋養 *jiyō* nourishment, nutrition

KUN

【yashina(u) 養う】 foster, bring up, raise to maturity, rear, support, care for; breed, raise animals, keep; foster (one's character), cultivate, develop; foster one's physical strength, nurse, cure

養い *yashinai* bringing up, nurture; nutrition, nourishment, sustenance
養い子 *yashinaigo* foster child
養い育てる *yashinaisodateru* foster, bring up, rear

SYNONYMS

❶ **raise and nourish**

育 RAISE → 2050
飼 RAISE ANIMALS → 1716
牧 PASTURE → 873
滋 NOURISH → 602

❷ⓐ **cultivate**

修 CULTIVATE → 123
練 TRAIN → 1375
錬 REFINE → 1741
鍛 train → 1755
磨 POLISH → 3181
琢 POLISH → 971

3-12

養

2366

▶FOSTER

nonstandard for 養 2365

奮 2367

FUN furu(u)

CH 奋 fèn

Radical	Strokes
大 37	16-3-13
Grade	Freq
Jōyō-6	1456
2-3-13	

3-13

▶ROUSE UP

COMPOUNDS

❶ⓐ rouse up, rouse oneself (to action), be stirred up, be stimulated, be enlivened
ⓑ be roused up, get excited, be angered
ⓒ energetically, strenuously, vigorously, courageously

奮起する *funki suru* rouse [bestir] oneself, rise (to the occasion)
発奮(＝発憤)する *happun suru* be stimulated, be inspired, be roused
感奮する *kanpun suru* be inspired, be moved to action
興奮(＝昂奮) *kōfun* excitement, agitation, stimulation
奮戦する *funsen suru* fight desperately, fight hard
奮撃 *fungeki* fierce attack
奮迅 *funjin* dashing forward impetuously
奮励 *funrei* strenuous efforts [exertions]
奮然と *funzen to* resolutely, courageously, vigorously
奮発する *funpatsu suru* exert oneself, make strenuous efforts; come down handsomely
❷ [original meaning, now archaic] (of birds) rouse (in the sense of take wing), spring up, fly away
奮飛する *funpi suru* spring up, fly away

KUN

【furu(u) 奮う】rouse up, rouse oneself, arouse
奮って *furutte* with energy, strenuously; heartily, willingly
勇気を奮い起こす *yūki o furuiokosu* muster up one's courage

SYNONYMS

❶ⓐ incite
振 arouse to action → 430
起 rise to action → 3307
動 MOVE → 1778
激 excite → 776
扇 FAN → 1950
挑 PROVOKE → 372
唆 INSTIGATE → 402
ⓑ elated
高 high-spirited → 2097
昂 high-spirited → 2412
揚 exalted → 593

HOMOPHONES

furuu ⇨ 振 430 震 2806 揮 589

NOTE

⇨ see USAGE note at 振 430
★do not confuse with 奪 2343

憲 2368

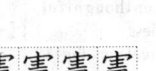

KEN

CH  xiàn

Radical	Strokes
心 61	16-4-12
Grade	Freq
Jōyō-6	869
2-3-13	

3-13

▶CONSTITUTION

COMPOUNDS

❶ⓐ constitution, code of laws
ⓑ rules, regulations
憲法 *kenpō* constitution, constitutional law
憲政 *kensei* constitutional government
憲章 *kenshō* constitution, charter
制憲する *seiken suru* establish a constitution
合憲的 *gōkenteki* constitutional
立憲 *rikken* constitutionalism
家憲 *kaken* family constitution [rules]
❷ official, authorities
憲兵 *kenpei* military policeman [police]
官憲 *kanken* authorities, officials; police

SYNONYMS

❶ⓐ laws and rules
典 CANON → 2627
令 ordinance → 1995

法 LAW → 333	矩 RULE → 1148
律 LAW → 363	規 REGULATION → 978
則 RULE → 1444	紀 discipline → 1276

3-13 宀

憲 2369

▶CONSTITUTION
nonstandard for 憲 2368

3-13 艹

薄 2370

薄 薄 薄 ㉄ 薄 báo bó bò

HAKU usu(i) usu- -usu usu(meru) usu(maru) usu(ragu) usu(ra)- usu(reru) susuki▲

Radical	Strokes
艹 140	16-3-13
Grade	**Freq**
Jōyō	894

2-3-13

1 2 3 4 5 6 7 8 9 10 11 12 13 14 15 16

▶THIN

COMPOUNDS

❶ⓐ (not thick) **thin, flimsy**
ⓑ (lacking intensity) **thin, weak**
薄片 *hakuhen* thin leaf; slice
薄氷 *hakuhyō* thin ice; danger
厚薄 *kōhaku* (relative) thickness
薄光 *hakkō* pale light, faint light
薄力粉 *hakurikiko* wheat flour of low viscosity
希薄な *kihaku na* dilute, thin, rare, sparse
❷ⓐ **meager, scanty, little, small (amount)**
ⓑ thin (luck), ill (fate)
薄給 *hakkyū* meager [scanty, small] salary
薄利 *hakuri* small profits, low interest
薄謝 *hakusha* small remuneration, small token of gratitude
薄弱な *hakujaku na* weak, feeble, frail
薄幸(=薄倖) *hakkō* unhappiness; sad fate, misfortune
薄命 *hakumei* evil fate, misfortune
❸ⓐ **frivolous, flippant, light, unthoughtful**
ⓑ lacking warmth, cold, heartless
軽薄な *keihaku na* insincere, frivolous, flippant, fickle
浮薄な *fuhaku na* frivolous, fickle, insincere
浅薄な *senpaku na* shallow, superficial, flimsy
薄情な *hakujō na* unfeeling, heartless, cruel
酷薄(=刻薄)な *kokuhaku na* cruel, inhumane
❹ close in on, press near
薄暮 *hakubo* nightfall, dusk, twilight
肉薄(=肉迫)する *nikuhaku suru* close in upon, press (the enemy) hard

KUN

【usu(i) 薄い】
① (not thick) thin, flimsy
薄い板 *usui ita* thin plate, sheet
②ⓐ (not dense) thin, weak, watery
ⓑ (of colors) pale, thin, light
ⓒ (of taste) light, slightly salted
髪が薄い *kami ga usui* have thin hair
薄い色 *usui iro* light color
味が薄い *aji ga usui* lightly seasoned
③ meager, scanty, little
興味が薄い *kyōmi ga usui* uninteresting
情が薄い *jō ga usui* be coldhearted [hardhearted]
【usu- 薄-】
① (not thick) thin
薄紙 *usugami* thin paper
② (low in intensity or degree)
ⓐ slightly
ⓑ [also prefix] pale, light (color)
薄曇りの *usugumori no* slightly cloudy
薄紫色 *usumurasakiiro* light purple, orchid
③ [also prefix] somehow, vaguely
薄薄 *usuusu* dimly, vaguely
薄気味悪い *usukimiwarui* weird, uncanny, eerie
薄汚い *usugitanai* filthy, dirty, bedraggled
【-usu -薄】 [also suffix] scarcity (of), shortage (of)
品薄 *shinausu* scarcity of goods, shortage of stock
手薄な *teusu na* short of hands
期待薄だ *kitaiusu da* be of little hope, not to be depended on
【usu(meru) 薄める】 *vt* thin, lighten, weaken, dilute
水で薄める *mizu de usumeru* dilute with water, water down
【usu(maru) 薄まる】 *vi* thin out [down], be diluted
【usu(ragu) 薄らぐ】 *vi* fade, become dim; abate, decline, lessen
光が薄らいだ *Hikari ga usuraida* The light

has faded
時と共に悲しみも薄らぐ *Toki to tomoni kanashimi mo usuragu* Time wears away grief
【usu(ra)- 薄ら-】 [also prefix] (low in intensity or degree) slightly, somewhat, rather; slight, a little, faint
薄ら寒い *usurasamui* chilly, rather cold, somewhat cold
薄ら馬鹿 *usurabaka* dimwit, simpleton, sluggard
【usu(reru) 薄れる】 same as **usuragu 薄らぐ**
【susuki 薄】 eulalia

SYNONYMS

❶ⓐ thin
細 SLENDER → 1333
繊 FINE → 1413
ⓑ less in degree
弱 WEAK → 1167
軽 LIGHT → 1515
微 SLIGHT → 639
低 LOW → 73
浅 SHALLOW → 389
❷ⓐ few
乏 SCANTY → 1933
微 SLIGHT → 639
寸 A BIT OF → 2935
寡 FEW → 2344
少 LITTLE → 3467
【usui】
②ⓐ rare and sparse
希 RARE → 2049
疎 SPARSE → 1178
粗 COARSE → 1329
ⓑ light-colored
淡 LIGHT → 528
浅 light → 389
鈍- DULL → 1689

NOTE

★do not confuse with 簿 2727

薫 薫 薫 薫

Ⓒⓗ 薰 xūn

2371 KUN kao(ru)

Radical	Strokes
艹 140	16-3-13
Grade	**Freq**
Jōyō	1710
2-3-13	

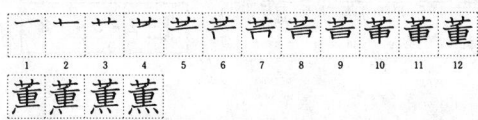

3-13 艹

1 2 3 4 5 6 7 8 9 10 11 12 13 14 15 16

▶BALMY

COMPOUNDS

❶ⓐ [original meaning] **balmy, sweet-smelling, fragrant**
ⓑ fragrance, sweet smell
薫風 *kunpū* balmy breeze
薫煙 *kun'en* fragrant smoke
余薫 *yokun* lingering fragrance
❷ influence, educate
薫化 *kunka* influencing people by one's virtue
薫育 *kun'iku* moral education
薫陶 *kuntō* education, discipline
❸ [formerly also 燻 1098] smoke, fumigate, fume
薫香 *kunkō* incense; fragrance
薫製 *kunsei* smoking (fish or meat)

INDEPENDENT

【kunzuru 薫ずる】 be fragrant; perfume

KUN

【kao(ru) 薫る】 look sweet-smelling [balmy], look fragrant
薫り *kaori* fragrance, aroma
若葉が薫る *Wakaba ga kaoru* The fresh verdure looks sweet-smelling

SYNONYMS

❶ smell and fragrance
郁 AROMATIC → 1288
芳 FRAGRANT → 2210
馨 PERFUME → 2879
気 smell → 3194
臭 BAD SMELL → 2633
香 SWEET SMELL → 2568
❸ preservatize
漬ける PICKLE → 702

HOMOPHONES

kaoru ⇨ 香 2568
kaori ⇨ 香 2568

NOTE

⇨ see USAGE note at 香 2568

3-13 ⺾

蕗 蕗 蕗 蕗

2372 RO fuki NAMES RU

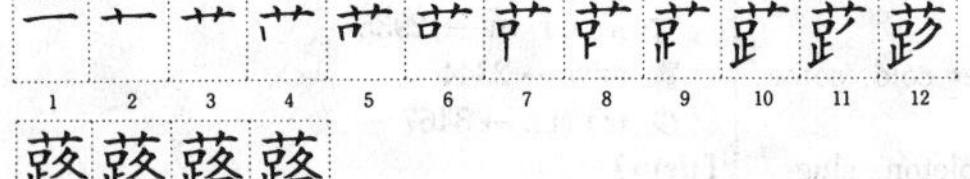

CH 蕗 lù

Radical	Strokes
⺾ 140	16-3-13
Grade	Freq
Names	2121
2-3-13	

▶**BUTTERBUR**

COMPOUNDS

● [archaic] licorice

蕗草 *rosō* licorice

KUN

【fuki 蕗】 butterbur

NAMES

蕗津子 *rutsuko* female name

蕗子 *fukiko* female name

SYNONYMS

【fuki】

○ **vegetables**

菜 greens → 2305

芋 POTATO → 2181

豆 BEAN → 1943

3-13 ⺾

薦 薦 薦 薦

2373 SEN susu(meru)

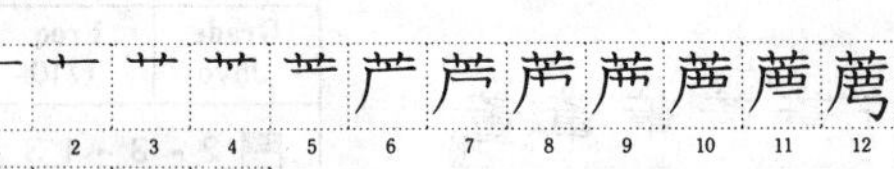

CH 荐 jiàn

Radical	Strokes
⺾ 140	16-3-13
Grade	Freq
Jōyō	1485
2-3-13	

▶**RECOMMEND**

COMPOUNDS

❶ **recommend (a person to a post or a product)**

薦挙 *senkyo* recommendation

推薦する *suisen suru* recommend, nominate

自薦 *jisen* self-recommendation

❷ [rare] straw mat

蒲薦 *hosen* bulrush mat

KUN

【susu(meru) 薦める】 recommend (a person to a post or a product to a person)

...に薦められて ...*ni susumerarete* on the recommendation of...

SYNONYMS

❶ **recommend**

推 recommend → 504

❷ **mats**

畳 TATAMI → 2592

-敷き underlay → 1870

HOMOPHONES

susumeru ⇨ 勧 1857 奨 2842 進 3121

NOTE

⇨ see USAGE note at 進 3121

3-13 ⺾

薪 薪 薪 薪

2374 SHIN takigi maki▲

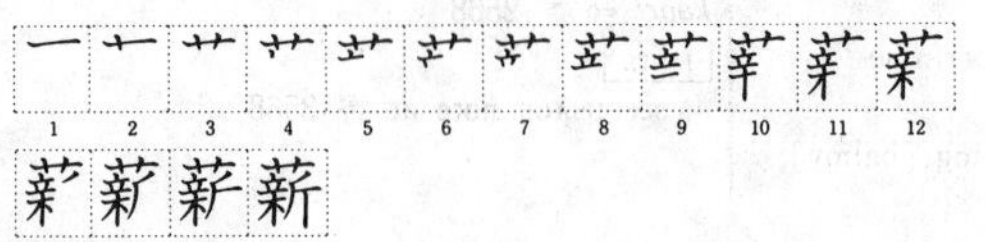

CH 薪 xīn

Radical	Strokes
⺾ 140	16-3-13
Grade	Freq
Jōyō	1924
2-3-13	

▶**FIREWOOD**

COMPOUNDS

● **firewood, wood for fuel**

薪炭 *shintan* firewood and charcoal

薪水 *shinsui* cooking

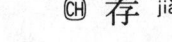

KUN

【takigi 薪】 firewood
薪拾い *takigihiroi* firewood gathering
【maki 薪】 firewood
薪割り *makiwari* wood-chopping[-splitting]; hatchet, axe

SYNONYMS

● **kinds of wood**
木 WOOD → 3450
材 TIMBER → 836
● **kinds of fuel**
炭 COAL, CHARCOAL → 2257
油 OIL → 341

薬 藥 薬

2375 YAKU kusuri

CH 药 yào

Radical	Strokes
艹 140	16-3-13
Grade	**Freq**
Jōyō-3	911
2-3-13	

3-13 艹

▶**DRUG**

COMPOUNDS

❶ [also suffix] [original meaning] **drug, medicine, remedy, pharmaceutical**
薬剤 *yakuzai* medicine, drugs
薬品 *yakuhin* medicine, drug; chemicals
薬局 *yakkyoku* drugstore, pharmacy
薬効 *yakkō* effect of a medicine
麻薬 *mayaku* narcotic, drug
医薬 *iyaku* medicine, drug; medical practice and dispensary
製薬 *seiyaku* pharmaceutical manufacture
妙薬 *myōyaku* miracle drug, golden remedy
胃腸薬 *ichōyaku* medicine for the stomach and bowels
❷ chemical, compound
農薬 *nōyaku* agricultural chemicals
試薬 *shiyaku* (chemical) reagent
火薬 *kayaku* gunpowder
爆薬 *bakuyaku* explosive compound, blasting powder

INDEPENDENT

【yaku 薬】 *slang* dope, narcotics
薬を打つ *yaku o utsu* inject a unit of dope

KUN

【kusuri 薬】 drug, medicine, remedy; powdered medicine, pill; chemical; enamel, glaze; benefit
薬屋 *kusuriya* drugstore
飲み薬 *nomigusuri* medicine, internal medicine
風邪薬 *kazegusuri* remedy for a cold
上薬 *uwagusuri* glaze, enamel
薬になる *kusuri ni naru* be beneficial (to), do (a person) good

SYNONYMS

❶ **medicines**
剤 PREPARATION → 1669
錠 PILL → 1737
丸 pill suffix → 3417

嶺 嶺° 嶺

2376 REI RYŌ NAMES mine ne

CH 岭 lǐng

Radical	Strokes
山 46	17-3-14
Grade	**Freq**
Names	2102
2-3-14	

3-14 山

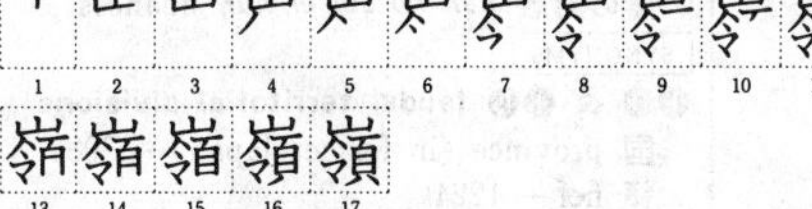

▶**RIDGE**

COMPOUNDS

ⓐ **ridge, ridge of a mountain, summit, peak**
ⓑ high mountain, lofty peak, mountain range
分水嶺 *bunsuirei* ridge, watershed
海嶺 *kairei* (submarine) ridge
雪嶺 *setsurei* snow-capped peak
峻嶺 *shunrei* steep peak, high rugged mountain
鷲尾嶺 *washioryō* Washio Mountains

NAMES

嶺村 *minemura* surname
嶺子 *mineko* female name

SYNONYMS
ⓐ **high parts of mountains**
峰 PEAK → 411
頂 SUMMIT → 145
峠 MOUNTAIN PASS → 358

3-14 山
嶽
2377
▶HIGH MOUNTAIN
nonstandard for 岳 2557

3-14 山
嶺
2378
▶RIDGE
nonstandard for 嶺 2376

3-14 艹
藍
incorrect stroke count ⇨ see 2381

3-14 艹
薦
incorrect stroke count ⇨ see 2373

3-14 艹
藉
incorrect stroke count ⇨ see 2529

3-14 人
龠
incorrect classification ⇨ see 2149

3-15 艹
藩 藩 藩 藩
2379 HAN

CH 藩 fān

Radical	Strokes
艹 140	18-3-15
Grade	**Freq**
Jōyō	1414
2-3-15	

▶FEUDAL DOMAIN

COMPOUNDS
❶ⓐ ***han*: feudal domain (governed by a daimyo in Edo Japan), fief; feudal clan**
ⓑ **suffix after names of feudal domains**
ⓒ feudal lord, daimyo
藩校 *hankō* *han* school
藩内 *hannai* within the *han*
藩閥 *hanbatsu* clan favoritism, clanship
廃藩 *haihan* abolition of the *han* system
薩摩藩 *satsumahan* Satsuma Han
藩主 *hanshu* feudal lord, daimyo
藩邸 *hantei* daimyo's estate in Edo
藩儒 *hanju* daimyo's scholar
❷ [original meaning, now archaic] hedge, fence

INDEPENDENT
【han 藩】 *han* (⇨ ❶ⓐ)
藩の財政 *han no zaisei* *han* finances

SYNONYMS
❶ⓐ & ❶ⓑ **feudal territorial divisions**
国 province (in former Japan) → 3087
領 fief → 1224
封 daimiate → 1287
荘 manor (in feudal Japan) → 2262

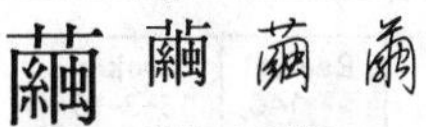

2380 KEN mayu

CH 茧 jiǎn

Radical	Strokes
糸 120	18-6-12
Grade	Freq
Jōyō	1897
2-3-15	

3-15 艹

▶**COCOON**

COMPOUNDS

● [original meaning] **cocoon**

繭糸 *kenshi* cocoon and silk-thread, silk-thread

繭価 *kenka* price of cocoons

KUN

【**mayu** 繭】 cocoon

繭玉 *mayudama* festive cocoons

繭を掛ける *mayu o kakeru* spin a cocoon

春繭 *harumayu* spring cocoon crop

SYNONYMS

● **insect**

虫 INSECT → 3530

昆 INSECT → 2413

藍

2381 RAN ai

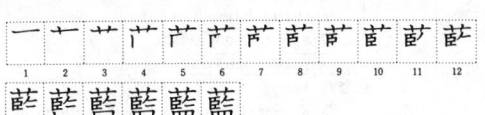

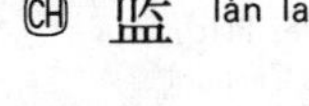

Radical	Strokes
艹 140	18-3-15
Grade	Freq
Names	2077
2-3-15	

3-15 艹

▶**INDIGO**

COMPOUNDS

❶ⓐ [also prefix] **indigo blue, deep blue, blue**

ⓑ **indigo plant, indigo dye**

藍綬褒章 *ranju-hōshō* Blue Ribbon Medal

藍晶石 *ranshōseki* cyanite

青藍 *seiran* indigo blue

出藍の誉れ *shutsuran no homare* surpassing one's master

❷ [now always 襤 1257] rags, tattered clothes

藍褸 *ranru* rags, tattered clothes

KUN

【**ai** 藍】 Japanese indigo plant, indigo plant; indigo blue

藍に染める *ai ni someru* dye deep blue

藍色 *airo* indigo blue

人造藍 *jinzōai* synthetic indigo

NAMES

藍子 *aiko* female name

SYNONYMS

❶ⓐ **blue and purple colors**

紫 PURPLE → 2688

紺 DARK BLUE → 1332

瑠 LAPIS LAZULI (bright blue) → 1060

碧 DEEP BLUE → 2836

青 BLUE → 2430

ⓑ **pigments**

墨 INDIA INK → 2753

漆 LACQUER → 704

3-15 艹

藤 藤 藤 藤

2382 TŌ fuji

CH 藤 téng

Radical	Strokes
艹 140	18-3-15
Grade	Freq
Names	1970
2 - 3 - 15	

1 2 3 4 5 6 7 8 9 10 11 12

13 14 15 16 17 18

▶WISTERIA

COMPOUNDS

❶ⓐ **wisteria**

ⓑ [original meaning] climbing plants, vines, liana

葛藤 *kattō* complication, troubles, discord

藤本 *tōhon* liana, climbing trees

❷ Fujiwara family

藤氏 *tōshi* Fujiwara family

KUN

【**fuji 藤**】 wisteria; light purple, lilac

藤棚 *fujidana* wisteria trellis [arbor]

上り藤 *noborifuji* lupine

藤色 *fujiiro* light purple, lilac

NAMES

藤堂 *tōdō* surname

伊藤 *itō* surname

佐藤 *satō* surname

藤沢 *fujisawa* surname also place name

藤本 *fujimoto* surname also place name

SYNONYMS

❶ⓐ **shrubs**

蔦 JAPANESE IVY → 2355

萩 *HAGI* → 2319

茉 JASMINE → 2244

莉 JASMINE → 2284

ⓐ **flowering plants**

萩 *HAGI* → 2319

蘭 ORCHID → 2383

芙 LOTUS → 2208

蓉 COTTON ROSE → 2337

葵 MALLOW → 2317

菊 CHRYSANTHEMUM → 2303

桜 cherry blossom → 931

梅 *ume* blossom → 925

COMPOUND FORMATION

葛藤 *kattō*

葛藤 'complication, etc.' is something as complicated or entangled as kudzu vines (葛) and wisterias (藤 ❶ⓐ).

3-16 艹

蘭 蘭 蘭 蘭

2383 RAN NAMES ka

CH 兰 lán

Radical	Strokes
艹 140	19-3-16
Grade	Freq
Names	2011
2 - 3 - 16	

1 2 3 4 5 6 7 8 9 10 11 12

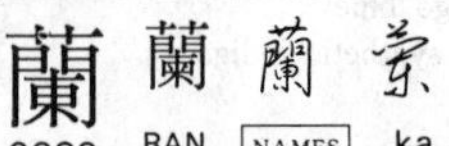

13 14 15 16 17 18 19

▶ORCHID

COMPOUNDS

❶ **orchid**

蘭栽培法 *ransaibaihō* orchidology

❷ⓐ Holland, the Netherlands

ⓑ Dutch (language)

蘭人 *ranjin* Dutch people

蘭学 *rangaku* study of Western science (in the Edo period) by means of the Dutch language

INDEPENDENT

【**ran 蘭**】 orchid; Holland, the Netherlands

NAMES

蘭子 *ranko* female name

室蘭 *muroran* place name

SYNONYMS

❶ **flowering plants**

芙 LOTUS → 2208

蓉 COTTON ROSE → 2337

葵 MALLOW → 2317

菊 CHRYSANTHEMUM → 2303

萩 *HAGI* → 2319

藤 WISTERIA → 2382

桜 cherry blossom → 931

梅 *ume* blossom → 925

❷ⓐ **European countries**

英 ENGLAND → 2238

独 GERMANY → 395

仏 FRANCE → 19

伊 ITALY → 49
西 Spain → 3520
露 Russia → 2818

藻

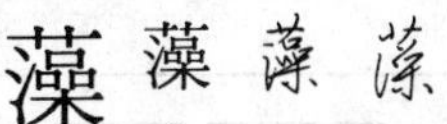

2384 SŌ mo

Ⓒ𝐇 藻 zǎo

Radical	Strokes
艹 140	19-3-16
Grade	**Freq**
Jōyō	1959
2-3-16	

3-16 艹

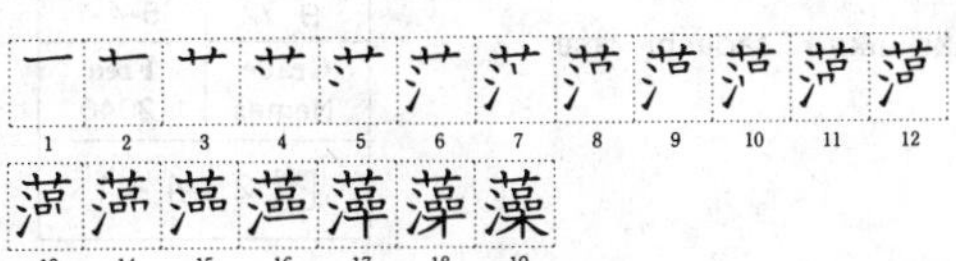

▶**ALGAE**

COMPOUNDS

❶ [original meaning] **algae, seaweed**
藻類 *sōrui* algae, seaweed
海藻 *kaisō* marine algae, seaweed, kelp
緑藻 *ryokusō* green algae
❷ elegant expression, rhetorical flourish
詩藻(＝詞藻) *shisō* florid expression, poetical talent
文藻 *bunsō* literary talent

KUN

【**mo** 藻】algae, duckweed, seaweed
藻屑 *mokuzu* seaweed

寶

2385

▶**TREASURE**
nonstandard for 宝 2224

3-17 宀

黨

incorrect classification ⇨ see 2623
(nonstandard for 党 2581)

3-17 ⺌

巖

2386 GAN iwao NAMES iwa yoshi

巖 巗 巌

Ⓒ𝐇 岩 yán

Radical	Strokes
山 46	20-3-17
Grade	**Freq**
Names	2036
2-3-17	

3-17 山

▶**CRAG**

COMPOUNDS

❶ [usu. 岩 2235] [original meaning] **crag, (massive) rock**
巖頭 *gantō* top of a massive rock
巖窟 *gankutsu* cave, rocky cavern
奇巖 *kigan* massive rock of unusual shape
❷ [rare] craggy, precipitous, steep
巖巖とした *gangan to shita* steep (as of a mountain), craggy

KUN

【**iwao** 巖】massive rock, crag

NAMES

巖川 *iwakawa* surname
巖 *iwao* male name
季巖 *sueyoshi* male name

SYNONYMS

❶ **rock and stone**
岩 ROCK → 2235
石 STONE → 2971

竊

2387

▶**STEAL**
nonstandard for 窃 2253

3-19 宀

3-20 山

巖 2388

▶CRAG

nonstandard for 巌 2386

4-1 日

旦 2389

CH 旦 dàn

TAN DAN NAMES aki akira tadashi asa

Radical 日 72	Strokes 5-4-1
Grade Names	Freq 2040
2-4-1	

▶DAYBREAK

COMPOUNDS

❶ⓐ [original meaning] **daybreak, dawn, morn, morning**

ⓑ **first day, day**

旦暮 *tanbo* morn and eve, dawn and dusk

旦夕 *tanseki* morning and evening, day and night

一旦 *ittan* once; for a while; [archaic] one morning, one day

元旦 *gantan* New Year's Day

月旦 *gettan* criticism, comment; [rare] first day of the month

❷ master, gentleman; husband

旦那 *danna* master, husband, patron, protector; sir; [original meaning] donor

震旦 *shintan* ancient Indian name for China

NAMES

旦 *akira* (=*tadashi*) male name

SYNONYMS

❶ⓐ **morning and dawn**

暁 DAWN → 980

朝 MORNING → 1695

ⓑ **days**

日 DAY → 3027

曜 DAY OF THE WEEK → 1096

昼 DAYTIME → 3097

4-1 氶

丞

incorrect stroke count ⇨ see 2541

4-2 文

斈

incorrect classification/stroke count ⇨ see 2039 (nonstandard for 学 2555)

4-2 日

早 2390

CH 早 zǎo

SŌ SAT- haya(i) haya haya- haya(maru) haya(meru) sa-*

Radical 日 72	Strokes 6-4-2
Grade Jōyō-1	Freq 246
2-4-2	

▶EARLY ▶QUICK

COMPOUNDS

❶ⓐ [original meaning] (near the beginning of a time period) **early**

ⓑ (occurring before the usual time) **early, premature**

早朝 *sōchō* early morning

早期 *sōki* early stage

早春 *sōshun* early spring

早晩 *sōban* sooner or later

早熟な *sōjuku na* precocious, forward

早世 *sōsei* early death

早産 *sōzan* premature birth

尚早の *shōsō no* premature

❷ⓐ **quick, fast**

ⓑ hasty, rash

早早 *sōsō* quickly, without delay, immediately; early

早速 *sassoku* immediately

早急に *sakkyū* (=*sōkyū*) *ni* urgently, pressingly, in a hurry

早計 *sōkei* rashness

❸ abbrev. of 早稲田大学 *waseda daigaku*: Waseda University

早明戦 *sōmeisen* Waseda-Meiji (baseball) game

KUN

【haya(i) 早い】

① early, premature

日暮れが早い *Higure ga hayai* Dusk falls early

親に早く死なれる *oya ni hayaku shinareru* be orphaned while still young

② [sometimes also 速い] (requiring little time) quick, prompt

早い話が *hayai hanashi ga* in short

早い事 *hayai koto* quickly

耳が早い *mimi ga hayai* be quick-eared

手っ取り早く *tettoribayaku* expeditiously, with dispatch

【haya 早】 already, now

五月も早半ばだ *Gogatsu mo haya nakaba da* It's already the middle of May

【haya- 早-】

① early

早起き *hayaoki* early rising

早立ち(=早発ち) *hayadachi* early morning departure

早引き *hayabiki* early leaving

②ⓐ [also prefix] [sometimes also 速-] quick, fast, rapid

ⓑ [prefix] hasty, rash

早見表 *hayamihyō* list, chart

早業 *hayawaza* quick work, (clever) feat

早口 *hayakuchi* fast [rapid] talking

早合点 *hayagaten* hasty conclusion

早呑み込み *hayanomikomi* hasty conclusion

【haya(maru) 早まる】

① take place ahead of time

梅雨明けは早まるだろう *Tsuyuake wa hayamaru darō* The rainy season will end early

② be rash, be too hasty, act rashly

早まって *hayamatte* in one's hurry

【haya(meru) 早める】 perform an action early, do ahead of time

期日を早める *kijitsu o hayameru* advance the date (of)

【sa- 早-】 young, supple

早乙女 *saotome* rice-planting girl; girl

早苗 *sanae* rice sprouts

SPECIAL READINGS

早生▲ *wase* early ripening; precocious

早稲▲ *wase* early ripening rice

SYNONYMS

❷ **fast**

速 QUICK → 3105

疾 fast → 3279

快 fast → 245

急 rapid → 2092

迅 SWIFT → 3046

敏 NIMBLE → 1322

即 IMMEDIATE → 1120

USAGE

❶ **hayai**

早い

① early, premature

② [sometimes also 速い] (requiring little time) quick, prompt

速い

ⓐ (acting or moving quickly) quick, speedy, fast, rapid, swift

ⓑ [usu. 早い] (requiring little time) quick, prompt

❷ **haya-**

早-

① early

②ⓐ [also prefix] [sometimes also 速-] quick, fast, rapid

ⓑ [prefix] hasty, rash

速-

[usu. 早-] quick, fast, rapid

★Though 早い and 速い as independent *kun* words can be discriminated as shown above, they are often interchangeable in the formation of compounds related to speed.

❸ **hayameru**

早める

perform an action early, do ahead of time

速める

quicken, accelerate, speed up, hasten

❹ **sōsō**

早早

① quickly, without delay, immediately

② early

草草

① closing words of a letter

② hurried, flurried

HOMOPHONES

hayai ⇨ 速 3105

haya- ⇨ 速 3105

hayameru ⇨ 速 3105

sa- ⇨ 小 7

NOTE

⇨ see also USAGE note at 小 7

李 incorrect stroke count ⇨ see 2398

4-2 木

4-2 耂 **孝** incorrect classification／stroke count ⇨ see 3205

4-2 耂 **考 老** incorrect classification ⇨ see 4-2

4-2 艹 **芝** incorrect stroke count ⇨ see 2404 (nonstandard for 芝 2180)

4-2 六 **交** incorrect classification ⇨ see 2015

4-2 亠 **充** incorrect classification ⇨ see 2014

4-2 ⺌ **光 光 光**

2391 KŌ hika(ru) hikari

Stroke order: 1 2 3 4 5 6

CH 光 guāng

Radical	Strokes
儿 10	6-2-4
Grade	**Freq**
Jōyō-2	439
2-4-2	

▶LIGHT

COMPOUNDS

❶ⓐ [also suffix] **light, glow**

ⓑ brightness, luster

光線 *kōsen* ray (of light), beam
光熱 *kōnetsu* light and heat
光化学 *kōkagaku* photochemistry
日光 *nikkō* sunshine, sunlight
月光 *gekkō* moonlight, moonshine
発光する *hakkō suru* radiate, emit light
太陽光 *taiyōkō* sunlight
光沢 *kōtaku* luster, gloss, polish

❷ [original meaning] **shine, glow, glitter**

光照 *kōshō* shining
光輝有る *kōkiaru* shining, brilliant, glorious, splendid

❸ honor, glory

光明 *kōmyō* glory, hope, right future
光栄 *kōei* honor, glory; privilege
栄光 *eikō* glory

❹ scenery, sight

光景 *kōkei* spectacle, sight, scene
風光 *fūkō* (beautiful) scenery, natural beauty
観光 *kankō* sightseeing

❺ time

光陰矢の如し *Kōin ya no gotoshi* Time flies like an arrow
消光する *shōkō suru* pass one's time

❻ term of respect

光来 *kōrai* your visit [presence]

KUN

【**hika(ru) 光る**】shine, emit light, glitter, sparkle

光り輝く *hikarikagayaku* shine brilliantly
光り物 *hikarimono* luminous body like a shooting star; any bright metal

【**hikari 光**】light, flash, sparkle, beam; glory, honor

稲光 *inabikari* lightning
親の光は七光 *Oya no hikari wa nanahikari* It is a great help to have a famous parent

SYNONYMS

❶ⓐ **light**

明 light → 855
灯 LAMP → 825
照 sunlight → 2827
虹 RAINBOW → 1285

❷ **shine and reflect**

輝 SHINE BRILLIANTLY → 1402
照 ILLUMINATE → 2827
映 REFLECT → 892

❸ **great respect**

誉 HONOR → 2502
栄 GLORY → 2574

❹ **view**

風 (beautiful) scenery → 3007
景 SCENE → 2470
観 VIEW → 1880

兇 2392 KYŌ

Ⓒ 凶 xiōng

Radical	Strokes
儿 10	6-2-4
Grade	Freq
Reference	
2-4-2	

4-2 凶

COMPOUNDS

❶ [now replaced by 凶 2961]

ⓐ atrocious, ferocious, wicked, brutal, cruel

ⓑ atrocious [lethal] crime, murder, wicked deed

ⓒ wicked person, villain

兇悪な *kyōaku na* atrocious, villainous, fiendish

兇暴な *kyōbō na* atrocious, ferocious, brutal

兇漢 *kyōkan* villain, ruffian, assailant

兇行 *kyōkō* violence, murder, crime

兇器 *kyōki* murder [dangerous] weapon

兇刃 *kyōjin* assassin's dagger [knife]

元兇 *genkyō* ringleader, chief instigator

❷ [usu. 凶 2961] unlucky, bad, disastrous

兇変 *kyōhen* calamity, disaster; tragic accident

共 2393 KYŌ tomo tomo(ni) -domo

Ⓒ 共 gòng

Radical	Strokes
八 12	6-2-4
Grade	Freq
Jōyō-4	140
2-4-2	

4-2 共

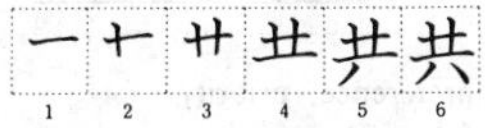

▶JOINT

COMPOUNDS

❶ [original meaning] **joint, united, together, co-**

共同の *kyōdō no* joint; common, concerted, united; public

共通の *kyōtsū no* common

共和制 *kyōwasei* republicanism

共催 *kyōsai* joint auspices, cosponsorship

共感 *kyōkan* sympathy

共演 *kyōen* coacting, costarring

共産党 *kyōsantō* Communist Party

共存 *kyōzon* coexistence

共闘 *kyōtō* joint struggle, common [united] front

共著 *kyōcho* joint authorship, coauthorship

公共の *kōkyō no* public, common

❷ abbrev. of 共産主義 *kyōsanshugi* or 共産党 *kyōsantō*: Communism, Communist Party

反共 *hankyō* anticommunist

容共 *yōkyō* procommunist

INDEPENDENT

【kyō 共】Communist Party

社・共 *sha-kyō* Social and Communist Parties

KUN

【tomo 共】

① [in compounds]

ⓐ joint, together, simultaneous

ⓑ of the same quality [kind]

ⓒ both, neither; including

共稼ぎ *tomokasegi* working together (for a living), working in double harness

共倒れ *tomodaore* falling together, joint bankruptcy

共布 *tomonuno* same cloth

両方共 *ryōhōtomo* both, the two

送料共 *sōryōtomo* including postage

② same cloth

共のハンカチ *tomo no hankachi* handkerchief of the same cloth

【tomo(ni) 共に】

① [formerly also 倶に] together

共に天を戴かず *tomoni ten o itadakazu* cannot live together under the canopy of heaven

② both, alike

母子共に *boshi tomoni* both mother and child

【-domo -共】belittling or humble plural suffix

私共 *watakushidomo* we

大人共 *otonadomo* adults

餓鬼共 *gakidomo* those damn kids

SYNONYMS

❶ **together**

同 together → 2987

併 TOGETHER → 83

並 side by side → 2246

兼 CONCURRENTLY → 2286

❷ & 【kyō】 **Communism**

左 the Left → 2974
赤 RED → 2193

【-domo】

○ **plural suffixes**

衆 somewhat polite plural suffix → 2683
-等 plural suffix → 2682
-達 plural suffix → 3139
-方 polite plural suffix → 1963

USAGE

❶ **tomoni**

共に
① [formerly also 倶に] together
② both, alike

倶に
[now usu. 共に] together

❷ **-domo**

-共
belittling or humble plural suffix

-供
plural suffix—now used only in 子供 *kodomo* without implying plurality

★Note that *kodomo* is correctly written 子供, *not* 子共.

HOMOPHONES

tomo ⇨ 供 88 友 2952
tomoni ⇨ 倶 111
-domo ⇨ 供 88

NOTE

⇨ see also USAGE note at 友 2952

4-2

儿

先 先 先

2394 SEN saki ma(zu)▲

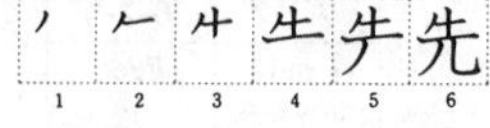

Ⓒⓗ 先 xiān

Radical	Strokes
儿 10	6-2-4
Grade	**Freq**
Jōyō-1	192
2 - 4 - 2	

▶**AHEAD**

COMPOUNDS

❶ⓐ [original meaning] (at the head or front) **ahead, fore, before, forward**
ⓑ **go ahead, precede**

先頭 *sentō* forefront, head, top
先駆者 *senkusha* pioneer, forerunner
先陣 *senjin* advance guard, vanguard
先遣する *senken suru* send ahead [in advance]
率先する *sossen suru* take the lead [initiative]
先行する *senkō suru* precede, go ahead of
先進国 *senshinkoku* advanced [developed] nation [country]

❷ⓐ (antecedent in time or order) **ahead of, in advance, first, previous, preceding, prior, beforehand**
ⓑ former, previous
ⓒ late, deceased

先発する *senpatsu suru* start in advance, go ahead, precede
先着 *senchaku* first arrival
先取する *senshu suru* take first, score first
先見 *senken* foresight, anticipation
先決 *senketsu* previous decision, prior settlement
先入観 *sennyūkan* preconception, bias, prejudice
先番 *senban* one's turn to make the first move
先輩 *senpai* senior, superior, elder
先生 *sensei* teacher; doctor
優先 *yūsen* preference, priority
先夫 *senpu* former husband
先主 *senshu* former master
先君 *senkun* previous ruler
先父 *senpu* deceased father

❸ⓐ **last (week, etc.)**
ⓑ the other (day), recently

先月 *sengetsu* last month
先先週 *sensenshū* week before last
先日 *senjitsu* the other day, a few days ago
先達て *sendatte* the other day, some time ago; lately

❹ ancient, past

先古 *senko* ancient times
先哲 *sentetsu* ancient sage [wise man]

❺ [formerly also 尖 2176]
ⓐ (pointed end) **point, end, tip**
ⓑ pointed, acute

先端 *sentan* pointed end, tip; spearhead; vanguard
先兵 *senpei* advance-guard point; advance detachment
先鋭な *sen'ei na* radical; acute, sharp

❻ the other party

先方 *senpō* the other party, they; one's destination

INDEPENDENT

【**sen** 先】 priority, precedence; former time; the first move (in a game of go)

先を越す *sen o kosu* forestall, take the initiative
先の *sen no* former, previous, old, late

KUN

【saki 先】

①ⓐ (at the front) ahead, away, off

ⓑ the head, the lead; the first; precedence

三キロ先に *sankiro saki ni* three kilometers ahead

目先 *mesaki* before one's eyes; near future; foresight; appearance

店先 *misesaki* storefront

水先案内 *mizusaki annai* pilotage; pilot

真っ先 *massaki* head, beginning

春先 *harusaki* early spring

先にする *saki ni suru* give priority (to)

② [usu. followed by particle]

ⓐ ahead of, in advance, prior to, previously, beforehand

ⓑ previous, former, ex-; recent

先に *saki ni* previously, beforehand, formerly

先んじる *sakinjiru* go ahead, precede; forestall, get the start of

先立つ *sakidatsu* precede, go before; die before

先払い *sakibarai* payment in advance, payment on delivery

先の総理大臣 *saki no sōri daijin* former prime minister

③ the future

先行き *sakiyuki* future, future prospects

先物 *sakimono* (market) futures

老い先 *oisaki* remaining years (of one's life)

④ point, tip, end

先細の *sakiboso no* tapering

爪先 *tsumasaki* tip of a toe, tiptoe, toe

ペン先 *pensaki* pen point, nib

手先 *tesaki* fingers; tool, implement

⑤ [also suffix] destination, place

行き先 *ikisaki* (=*yukisaki*) one's destination

宛て先 *atesaki* destination, address

勤務先 *kinmusaki* one's place of employment

連絡先 *renrakusaki* where to make contact

⑥ the other party

先様 *sakisama* the other party

⑦ sequel

話の先 *hanashi no saki* sequel of a story

【ma(zu) 先ず】 first, to begin with; nearly, hardly, on the whole; anyway; well, now

SYNONYMS

❶ⓐ in front

前 BEFORE → 2266

❷ⓐ before

前 BEFORE → 2266

予 IN ADVANCE → 1983

ⓑ former

前 previous → 2266

旧 FORMER → 14

元 former → 1929

故 OLD (earlier time) → 1141

既 ALREADY → 1166

❸ⓐ most recent

昨 LAST → 893

去 last → 2156

❺ⓐ extremity

端 END → 1221

末 end → 3505

梢 tip → 963

ⓑ sharp

鋭 SHARP → 1730

NOTE

⇨ see COMPOUND FORMATION for 先生 *sensei* ⇨ 生 3497

虫 incorrect classification ⇨ see 3530

劣

劣 劣 2395 RETSU oto(ru)

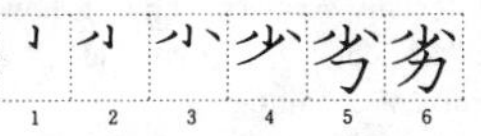

Ⓒⓗ 劣 liè

Radical	Strokes
力 19	6-2-4
Grade	**Freq**
Jōyō	1431
2 - 4 - 2	

▶INFERIOR

COMPOUNDS

❶ⓐ (lower in quality or status) **inferior, poor, subgrade, low-grade; weak**

ⓑ [original meaning] (of little strength) inferior, weak

劣等感 *rettōkan* inferiority complex

劣悪な *retsuaku na* inferior, coarse

優劣 *yūretsu* superiority or inferiority, quality

卑劣な *hiretsu na* mean, base, cowardly

劣情 *retsujō* animal passion, carnal desire

劣勢 *ressei* numerical inferiority

劣性 *ressei* inferiority; recessiveness

❷ *math* minor

劣角 *rekkaku* minor angle

劣弧 *rekko* minor arc

INDEPENDENT

【retsu 劣】 inferiority

KUN

【oto(ru) 劣る】 be inferior to, be worse than, be second to

見劣りがする *miotori ga suru* compare unfavorably [poorly] with, be not so good as

優るとも劣らぬ *masaru to mo otoranu* not at all inferior to

SYNONYMS

❶ⓐ **bad**

悪 BAD → 2745

下 of low grade → 3378

弊 shabby → 2884

粗 COARSE → 1329

駄 GOOD FOR NOTHING → 1821

廃 WASTE → 3146

4-3 文

斈

incorrect classification ⇨ see 2039 (nonstandard for 学 2555)

4-3 日

旱

2396 KAN

Ⓒⓗ 旱 hàn

Radical	Strokes
日 72	7-4-3
Grade	**Freq**
Reference	
2-4-3	

COMPOUNDS

● [now replaced by 干 3379] drought, dry weather

旱害 *kangai* drought damage

旱天 *kanten* drought, dry weather

4-3 木

杏 杏 杏

2397 KYŌ AN anzu

一 十 才 木 木 杏 杏

1 2 3 4 5 6 7

Ⓒⓗ 杏 xìng

Radical	Strokes
木 75	7-4-3
Grade	**Freq**
Names	2081
2-4-3	

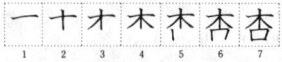

▶**APRICOT**

COMPOUNDS

● [original meaning] **apricot tree; apricot**

杏子 *anzu* apricot; apricot tree

杏仁 *kyōnin* apricot stone

杏林 *kyōrin* doctor

銀杏 *ginnan* (=*ichō*) ginkgo nut, ginkgo tree

KUN

【anzu 杏】 apricot; apricot tree

杏ジャム *anzu jamu* apricot jam

NAMES

杏子 *kyōko* female name

SYNONYMS

● **fruits and fruit trees**

梅 JAPANESE APRICOT → 925

桃 PEACH → 936

李 PLUM → 2398

橘 MANDARIN → 1077

栗 CHESTNUT → 2649

梨 PEAR → 2744

COMPOUND FORMATION

杏林 *kyōrin*

杏林 'doctor' originally referred to a Chinese doctor who had an apricot tree (杏) planted as payment for his services. This is how 杏林, literally "apricot (杏) grove (林)," acquired its current meaning.

李

2398 RI sumomo NAMES momo

CH 李 lǐ

Radical	Strokes
木 75	7-4-3
Grade	Freq
Names	2002
2-4-3	

4-3 木

▶PLUM

COMPOUNDS

❶ **plum tree; plum**

李花 *rika* plum blossoms

李下に冠を正さず *Rika ni kanmuri o tadasazu* Refrain from doing anything that may incur suspicion

❷ common Chinese family name: Li

李白 *rihaku* Li Bo (one of China's greatest poets in the Tang Dynasty)

❸ Li Dynasty of Korea

李朝 *richō* Li Dynasty

❹ portmanteau

行李 *kōri* portmanteau, wicker trunk; luggage

KUN

【sumomo 李】 plum, Japanese plum, prune; plum tree

干し李 *hoshisumomo* prune

NAMES

李上 *rinoue* surname

李子 *momoko* female name

SYNONYMS

❶ **fruits and fruit trees**

桃 PEACH → 936

杏 APRICOT → 2397

梅 JAPANESE APRICOT → 925

橘 MANDARIN → 1077

栗 CHESTNUT → 2649

梨 PEAR → 2744

COMPOUND FORMATION

李下に冠を正さず ***Rika ni kanmuri o tadasazu***

李下に冠を正さず 'Refrain from doing anything that may incur suspicion' is a proverb that literally means to avoid adjusting (正) one's hat (冠) under (下) a plum tree (李 ❶); that is, to avoid incurring the suspicion of being a plum thief.

NOTE

★do not confuse with 季 2554

歩

2399

▶WALK

nonstandard for 歩 2416

4-3 止

妥

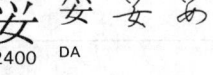

2400 DA

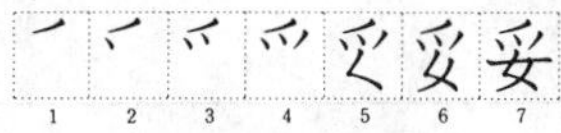

CH 妥 tuǒ

Radical	Strokes
女 38	7-3-4
Grade	Freq
Jōyō	1221
2-4-3	

4-3 爫

▶COME TO TERMS

COMPOUNDS

❶ **come to terms, compromise, arrive at an understanding, agree**

妥協 *dakyō* compromise, agreement, understanding

妥結 *daketsu* compromise, agreement, understanding

❷ appropriate, proper, satisfactory

妥当な *datō na* proper, appropriate

SYNONYMS

❶ **compromise**

譲 concede → 1649

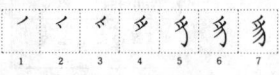

4-3 彡

豸
2401

Stroke order: 1 2 3 4 5 6 7

Radical	Strokes
豸 153	7-7-0
Grade	**Freq**
Radical	
2 - 4 - 3	

RADICAL 153
Standard form: 豸 *mujina* 'wild animal' (貌 豹 貂)
Description: used in characters related to wild animals

4-3 爫

妥
2402

▶**COME TO TERMS**
nonstandard for 妥 2400

4-3 牛

告
2403

▶**NOTIFY**
nonstandard for 告 2409

4-3 耂

孝

incorrect classification ⇨ see 3205

4-3 耂

考

incorrect classification/stroke count ⇨ see 3196

4-3 艹

芝
2404

▶**LAWN GRASS**
nonstandard for 芝 2180

4-3 艹

芋
2405

▶**POTATO**
nonstandard for 芋 2181

4-3 玄

系

incorrect classification ⇨ see 1944

4-3 今

含

incorrect classification ⇨ see 2041

4-3 不

否
2406 HI ina iya▲

Ⓒⓗ 否 fǒu pǐ

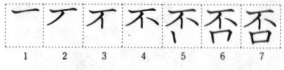

Stroke order: 1 2 3 4 5 6 7

Radical	Strokes
口 30	7-3-4
Grade	**Freq**
Jōyō-6	734
2 - 4 - 3	

▶**SAY NO** ▶**OR NOT**

COMPOUNDS

❶ **say no, negate, deny**
否定する *hitei suru* deny, negate
否決 *hiketsu* rejection, voting down, negation
否認 *hinin* denial, negation
拒否 *kyohi* denial, rejection

❷ⓐ **or not**—used as the second element of

a compound to negate the meaning of the first
ⓑ no, nay
良否 *ryōhi* good or bad, quality
当否 *tōhi* right or wrong, justice; propriety
賛否 *sanpi* approval or disapproval; yes or no
❸ bad, evil
否運(＝非運) *hiun* bad luck, misfortune

INDEPENDENT

【hi 否】 no
否か応か *hi ka ō ka* yes or no

KUN

【ina 否】 *literary* no, nay
否む *inamu* refuse, decline
否めない *inamenai* undeniable, incontrovertible
否や *inaya* (whether...) or not; objection; as soon as, no sooner than

【iya 否】
ⓐ no
ⓑ being unwilling, wanting to say no
否でも応でも *iya demo ō demo* whether one likes it or not, willy-nilly
否応無しに *iyaō nashi ni* whether one likes it or not, willy-nilly
否否 *iyaiya* definitely [absolutely] not

SYNONYMS

❶ refuse and reject
拒 REFUSE → 311
断る refuse → 1492
却 reject → 1118
❷ terms of negation
不 NOT (negation) → 3434
非 IS NOT (contrariety) → 889
無 WITHOUT (nonexistence) → 2135
未 NOT YET → 3506
没 lacking in → 260
欠 LACK → 1987

HOMOPHONES

iya ⇨ 嫌 636 厭 3017

NOTE

⇨ see USAGE notes at 嫌 636 and 不 3434

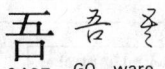

吾 吾 吾

2407 GO ware waga- a- NAMES a

Ⓒⓗ 吾 wú

Radical	Strokes
口 30	7-3-4
Grade	**Freq**
Names	1992
2-4-3	

4-3 五

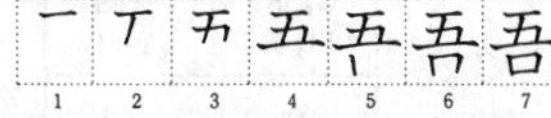

1 2 3 4 5 6 7

▶I

COMPOUNDS

❶ [original meaning] I
ⓑ [archaic] my
吾人 *gojin literary* we

KUN

【ware 吾】
[usu. 我]
ⓐ *elegant* I; we
ⓑ *slang* you
吾等 *warera* we, I; you

【waga- 吾-】 [usu. 我が-] *literary* my; our
吾輩 *wagahai* I

【a- 吾-】 *elegant* my
吾子 *ako* my child

NAMES

正吾 *shōgo* male name
吾妻 *azuma* surname also place name
吾郎 *gorō* male name

SYNONYMS

【ware】
ⓐ **first person pronouns**
私 I (*polite*) → 1115
僕 I (*familiar*) → 164
俺 I (*intimate*) → 110
予 I (*pompous*) → 1983
余 I (*pompous*) → 2042
麿 I (*archaic*) → 3184
朕 IMPERIAL WE → 949
自 SELF → 3525
我 SELF → 3548
己 ONESELF → 3380
身 ONE'S PERSON → 3553

HOMOPHONES

ware ⇨ 我 3548
waga- ⇨ 我 3548

NOTE

⇨ see USAGE note at 我 3548

4-3 龶

麦 麥 麦 麦

2408 BAKU mugi

一 十 キ 主 丰 麦 麦

1 2 3 4 5 6 7

RADICAL 199

simplified form not used as radical

⇨ see 麥 2767 for radical description

Ⓒⓗ 麦 mài

Radical	Strokes
麥 199	7-7-0
Grade	**Freq**
Jōyō-2	1306
2 - 4 - 3	

▶WHEAT

COMPOUNDS

● **wheat, barley, oats, rye**

麦秋 ***bakushū*** wheat harvest [season]; early summer

麦価 ***bakuka*** price of wheat

麦芽 ***bakuga*** wheat germ, malt

麦酒 ***bakushu*** (=*bīru*) beer

米麦 ***beibaku*** rice and barley; corn

精麦 ***seibaku*** cleaning barley or wheat; polished barley or wheat

KUN

【mugi 麦】 wheat, barley, oats, rye

麦畑 ***mugibatake*** wheat field

小麦 ***komugi*** wheat

大麦 ***ōmugi*** barley

ライ麦 ***raimugi*** rye

SYNONYMS

● **cereals**

米 RICE → 3529

豆 BEAN → 1943

4-3 生

告 告 告 告

2409 KOKU tsu(geru)

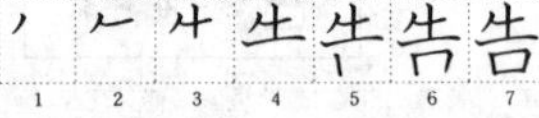

1 2 3 4 5 6 7

Ⓒⓗ 告 gào

Radical	Strokes
口 30	7-3-4
Grade	**Freq**
Jōyō-4	287
2 - 4 - 3	

▶NOTIFY

COMPOUNDS

❶ⓐ (let know, esp. in writing) **notify, inform, announce, advise, tell, report**

ⓑ (make widely known) **notify, announce, proclaim**

ⓒ notice, announcement, information

告知する ***kokuchi suru*** notify, announce

通告する ***tsūkoku suru*** notify, announce

報告 ***hōkoku*** report, information

申告 ***shinkoku*** report, statement, notification

予告 ***yokoku*** advance notice, preliminary announcement

公告 ***kōkoku*** public notice

広告 ***kōkoku*** public notice; advertisement

告示 ***kokuji*** notification, bulletin

布告 ***fukoku*** proclamation, declaration

❷ **advise, instruct, warn, admonish**

忠告 ***chūkoku*** advice; counsel, warning; admonition

警告 ***keikoku*** warning, admonition

勧告 ***kankoku*** advice, counsel, recommendation

❸ **accuse of (an offense), sue, accuse, appeal to the law**

告訴する ***kokuso suru*** sue, complain, accuse

告発 ***kokuhatsu*** prosecution, indictment, accusation

上告 ***jōkoku*** final appeal

被告 ***hikoku*** defendant, the accused

宣告 ***senkoku*** sentence, verdict, pronouncement

誣告 ***bukoku*** false accusation

❹ bid farewell to

告別 ***kokubetsu*** leave taking, farewell

告辞 ***kokuji*** farewell address

KUN

【tsu(geru) 告げる】 tell, inform, let know; notify, announce; bid, tell, order

お告げ ***otsuge*** oracle, revelation

告げ口 ***tsugeguchi*** taletelling

SYNONYMS

❶ⓐ & ❶ⓑ **inform and communicate**

報 INFORM → 1698

通 COMMUNICATE → 3109

届ける give notice → 3078

達 issue a notice → 3139

知 let know → 1127

申 REPORT → 3507

宣 PROCLAIM → 2252
❷ **warn**
警 WARN → 2893
戒 CAUTION → 3204
諭 ADMONISH → 1598
❸ **sue**
控 accuse in court → 495
訴 SUE → 1507
訟 LITIGATE → 1472

呑

2410 DON no(mu)

Ⓒⓗ 呑 tūn

Radical	Strokes
口 30	7-3-4
Grade	Freq
Reference	
2-4-3	

4-3 夭

COMPOUNDS

❶ⓐ [original meaning] swallow, gulp
ⓑ swallow (one's feelings), hold back
呑舟の魚 *donshū no uo* great fish; great man; notorious man
併呑 *heidon* annexation, merger
蛇が卵を呑んだ *Hebi ga tamago o nonda* The snake swallowed an egg
涙を呑む *namida o nomu* choke back one's tears, pocket an insult
❷ accept
条件を呑む *jōken o nomu* accept the conditions
❸ despise
呑んで掛かる *nonde kakaru* hold lightly, make light of
❹ conceal
どすを呑む *dosu o nomu* wear a dagger in one's bosom

HOMOPHONES

nomu ⇨ 飲 1692

NOTE

⇨ see USAGE note at 飲 1692

斉

incorrect classification ⇨ see 2054

4-4 文

易 𠃓 ㇌

2411 EKI I yasa(shii) yasu(i)▲

Ⓒⓗ 易 yì

Radical	Strokes
日 72	8-4-4
Grade	Freq
Jōyō-5	752
2-4-4	

4-4 日

▶**EASY** ▶**EXCHANGE**

COMPOUNDS

❶ [also prefix] (without difficulty) **easy, simple**
易損品 *isonhin* fragile article
容易な *yōi na* easy, simple
安易な *an'i na* easy, easygoing
簡易な *kan'i na* simple, simplified; easy
平易な *heii na* plain, simple, easy
❷ⓐ **exchange, trade**
ⓑ change, be transformed; be reformed
貿易 *bōeki* trade, commerce
交易 *kōeki* trade, commerce
不易の *fueki no* immutable, unchangeable
改易 *kaieki* change of rank
❸ⓐ **divination, fortunetelling**
ⓑ Book of Changes, *Yi Jing*
易者 *ekisha* fortuneteller, diviner
易学 *ekigaku* science of divination
易経 *ekikyō* Book of Changes, *Yi Jing*

INDEPENDENT

【**eki** 易】divination, fortunetelling; Book of Changes, *Yi Jing*
易を見る *eki o miru* divine
易の六十四卦 *eki no rokujūshike* the 64 hexagrams of the Book of Changes
【**i** 易】ease, simplicity
易より難へ進む *i yori nan e susumu* proceed from the easy to the difficult

KUN

【**yasa(shii)** 易しい】easy, simple
易しさ *yasashisa* easiness
易しい文章 *yasashii bunshō* easy [simple] writing

【yasu(i) 易い】
ⓐ easy, simple
ⓑ [verbal suffix] easy (to do)
易易と *yasuyasu to* easily, without difficulty
お易い御用 *oyasui goyō* easy request
壊れ易い *kowareyasui* break easily, fragile
分かり易い *wakariyasui* easy to understand

SYNONYMS

❶ **easy**
安 easy (without effort) → 2171
簡 SIMPLE → 2721
軽 LIGHT → 1515

❷ⓐ **sell and trade**
貿 TRADE → 2601
商 TRADE → 2116
売 SELL → 2196
卸す WHOLESALE → 1447
販 ENGAGE IN SALES → 1477

ⓑ **change and replace**
変 CHANGE → 2069
更 change → 3541
改 change → 243
化 CHANGE INTO, -ize → 21
遷 undergo transition → 3170
転 turn into → 1480
換 EXCHANGE → 587
交 INTERCHANGE → 2015
替 REPLACE → 2783
代 SUBSTITUTE → 30
迭 ALTERNATE → 3077

❸ⓐ **divine**
占 DIVINE → 2003

HOMOPHONES

yasashii ⇨ 優 177
yasui ⇨ 安 2171

NOTE

⇨ see USAGE notes at 安 2171 and 優 177

4-4
日

2412 KŌ NAMES aki akira taka takashi noboru

Ⓒⓗ 昂 áng

Radical	Strokes
日 72	8-4-4
Grade	**Freq**
Names	2105
2-4-4	

1 2 3 4 5 6 7 8

▶**HIGH**

COMPOUNDS

❶ⓐ [now replaced by 高 2097 or 興 2909] **high-spirited, excited, elated**
ⓑ [now replaced by 高 2097] (showing pride) high, proud, haughty
昂奮(=興奮) *kōfun* excitement, agitation, stimulation
昂進(=高進, 亢進)する *kōshin suru* rise, exasperate, accelerate
昂揚(=高揚)する *kōyō suru* exalt, enhance, uplift; surge up
激昂(=激高)する *gekkō* (=*gekikō*) *suru* get excited, be exasperated, become indignant
意気軒昂(=意気軒高)として *ikikenkō to shite* in high spirits
昂然(=高然)たる *kōzentaru* elated, triumphant, proud

❷ⓐ [now replaced by 高 2097] high
ⓑ [original meaning, now archaic] hold one's head high
昂騰(=高騰) *kōtō* steep rise (in prices), jump

INDEPENDENT

【kōjiru (=kōzuru) 昂じる(=高じる, 昂ずる, 高ずる)】 grow worse, grow in intensity

NAMES

昂一 *kōichi* male name
昂 *akira* male name
重昂 *shigetaka* male name

SYNONYMS

❶ⓐ **elated**
高 high-spirited → 2097
揚 exalted → 593
奮 roused up → 2367

昆 2413 KON

CH 昆 kūn

Radical	Strokes
日 72	8-4-4
Grade	**Freq**
Jōyō	1782
2-4-4	

4-4 日

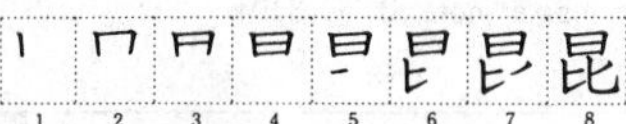

▶INSECT

COMPOUNDS

❶ **insect; swarm of insects**

昆虫 *konchū* insect

昆布 *konbu* (=*kobu*) sea tangle, kelp

❷ [rare] progeny, posterity, descendants

後昆 *kōkon* posterity, grandchildren

❸ [archaic] brethren, older brother

SYNONYMS

❶ **insect**

虫 INSECT → 3530

繭 COCOON → 2380

昌 2414 SHŌ

NAMES masa masashi yoshi aki akira sakae

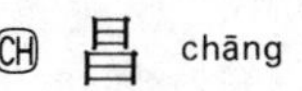

CH 昌 chāng

Radical	Strokes
日 72	8-4-4
Grade	**Freq**
Names	1991
2-4-4	

4-4 日

1 2 3 4 5 6 7 8

▶PROSPERING

COMPOUNDS

● **prospering, flourishing, prosperous, glorious**

繁昌(=繁盛) *hanjō* prosperity

NAMES

昌次 *shōji* male name

昌子 *masako* female name

SYNONYMS

● **prospering and prosperity**

盛 PROSPEROUS → 2675

栄 FLOURISH → 2574

繁 THRIVE → 2853

隆 PROSPER → 545

振 rise → 430

興 RISE TO PROSPERITY → 2909

NOTE

★do not confuse with 冒 2434

昇 2415 SHŌ nobo(ru)

CH 升 shēng

Radical	Strokes
日 72	8-4-4
Grade	**Freq**
Jōyō	813
2-4-4	

4-4 日

▶ASCEND

COMPOUNDS

ⓐ [original meaning] **ascend, rise, go up**

ⓑ [formerly also 陞 459] **ascend to a higher rank, rise in rank, be promoted**

昇天 *shōten* the Ascension; death

昇降口 *shōkōguchi* entrance, hatchway

上昇する *jōshō suru* ascend, rise

昇順 *shōjun* ascending order

昇格する *shōkaku suru* be promoted [raised] to a higher status

昇進する *shōshin suru* be promoted, rise in rank

昇給 *shōkyū* salary raise

昇叙 *shōjo* promotion, advancement

KUN

【nobo(ru) 昇る】

ⓐ (rise up to the sky) ascend, rise

ⓑ ascend to a higher rank, rise in rank, be promoted

太陽は東から昇る *Taiyō wa higashi kara noboru* The sun rises in the east

煙が昇って行く *Kemuri ga nobotte iku* Smoke is going up

位が昇る *kurai ga noboru* rise in rank

SYNONYMS

ⓐ **ascend**
上 go up → 3404
騰 RISE (esp. in price) → 1106
登 CLIMB → 2595
ⓑ **rise in rank**
進 advance in rank → 3121

HOMOPHONES

noboru ⇨ 上 3404 登 2595

NOTE

⇨ see USAGE note at 上 3404

4-4
止

歩 歩 歩 歩

2416 HO BU FU aru(ku) ayu(mu)

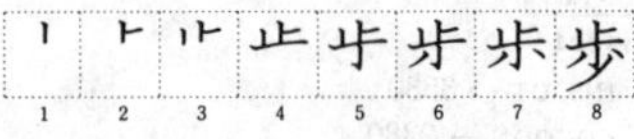

Ⓒ 歩 bù

Radical	Strokes
止 77	8-4-4
Grade	Freq
Jōyō-2	299
2 - 4 - 4	

▶WALK

COMPOUNDS

❶ [original meaning] **walk, go on foot**
歩行する *hokō suru* walk
歩道 *hodō* sidewalk, footpath
歩兵 *hohei* foot soldier, infantry
散歩する *sanpo suru* go for a walk [stroll]
徒歩 *toho* walking, going on foot
❷ⓐ **step, pace**
ⓑ **steps, progress, course, path**
ⓒ **counter for steps**
歩調 *hochō* pace, step, cadence
歩数 *hosū* number of steps
進歩 *shinpo* progress, advancement, improvement
初歩 *shoho* first steps, rudiments, the ABCs (of)
譲歩 *jōho* concession, compromise
退歩 *taiho* retrogression, backward step; deterioration
二歩 *niho* two steps
❸ name of chess piece in shogi (Japanese chess): *fu*, pawn
敵歩 *tekifu* opponent's pawn
❹ percentage, rate
歩合 *buai* rate, percentage, commission
歩留まり *budomari* yield, yield rate
❺ *bu*: unit of sq. measure equiv. to approx. 3.3 sq.m or 36 sq. *shaku* (尺), used esp. for measuring fields or farms
三十歩 *sanjūbu* 30 *bu*

INDEPENDENT

【ho 歩】 step, pace; foot soldier; walk
歩を進める *ho o susumeru* step forward, make progress
歩五分 *ho gofun* five-minutes' walk
【bu 歩】
① [sometimes also 分 *bu* 1972] percentage; commission
歩が悪い *Bu ga warui* The percentage is unfavorable
三割の歩 *sanwari no bu* commission of 30%
② *bu* (⇨ ❺)
【fu 歩】 *fu*, pawn (⇨ ❸)
歩を突く *fu o tsuku* advance a pawn

KUN

【aru(ku) 歩く】 walk, go on foot, step
歩き回る *arukimawaru* walk about, walk to and fro, pace around
持ち歩く *mochiaruku* carry about
【ayu(mu) 歩む】 *elegant* walk, step
歩み *ayumi* walking; step, pace
時代と共に歩む *jidai to tomoni ayumu* move along with the times

SYNONYMS

❶ **walk**
徒 go on foot → 416
脚 move on foot → 974
足 travel on foot → 2188
踏 TREAD → 1587
❹ **rate**
率 RATE → 2118
割 rate → 1816
比 ratio → 26
❺ **area units**
坪 *TSUBO* (3.3 sq.m) → 275
畝 *SE* (0.99 ares) → 1465
反 *tan* (9.9 ares) → 2945
町 *cho* (99.2 ares) → 1113

NOTE

⇨ see USAGE note at 分 1972
⇨ see COMPOUND FORMATION for 歩留まり *budomari* ⇨ 留 2580

肯 肯 肯
2417 KŌ

Stroke order: 1 2 3 4 5 6 7 8

CH 肯 kěn

Radical	Strokes
月 130	8-4-4
Grade	Freq
Jōyō	1868
2 - 4 - 4	

4-4 止

▶**ASSENT**

COMPOUNDS

❶ **assent, nod agreement, consent, permit**

肯定 *kōtei* affirmation, affirmative

首肯する *shukō suru* assent, nod one's assent, consent

❷ [original meaning] meat sticking to a bone

肯綮 *kōkei* important point, gist

SYNONYMS

❶ **agree and approve**

承 AGREE TO → 16

容 tolerate → 2277

諾 CONSENT → 1568

認 RECOGNIZE → 1546

可 APPROVE → 2969

賛 APPROVE OF → 2809

昏
2418 KON

CH 昏 hūn

Radical	Strokes
日 72	8-4-4
Grade	Freq
Reference	
2 - 4 - 4	

4-4 氏

COMPOUNDS

❶ lose consciousness, faint

昏迷 *konmei* [now usu. 混迷] stupor, unconsciousness

昏倒 *kontō* swoon, faint

昏睡 *konsui* coma, lethargy; dead sleep

昏昏と眠っている *konkon to nemutte iru* be sound asleep; be in coma

❷ⓐ [original meaning] dark

ⓑ dusk, twilight

黄昏 *kōkon* (=*tasogare*) dusk, twilight

沓
2419 TŌ kutsu

CH 沓 tà dá

Radical	Strokes
水 85	8-4-4
Grade	Freq
Reference	
2 - 4 - 4	

4-4 水

COMPOUNDS

❶ [now replaced by 踏 *tō* 1587] crowded, confused

雑沓 *zattō* hustle and bustle, traffic jam

❷ footwear, sandals, clogs

沓脱ぎ *kutsunugi* stepstone, doorstone

HOMOPHONES

kutsu ⇨ 靴 1781

NOTE

⇨ see USAGE note at 靴 1781

4-4
火

炎

2420 EN honō

CH 炎 yán

Radical	Strokes
火 86	8-4-4
Grade	**Freq**
Jōyō	1216
2-4-4	

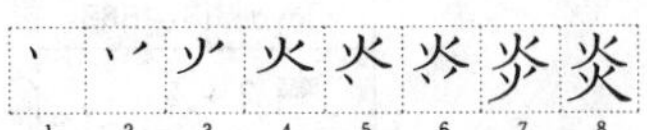

▶FLAME ▶INFLAMMATION

COMPOUNDS

❶ [formerly also 焰 996]
ⓐ [original meaning] **flame, blaze**
ⓑ (figuratively) **flames (as of passion)**
火炎 *kaen* flames, blaze
紅炎 *kōen* red blazes of flame
気炎を吐く *kien o haku* talk big, talk a lot of hot air
情炎 *jōen* flaming desires, burning passions
妖炎 *yōen* The Fires of Enchantment (movie title)

❷ⓐ go up in flames, burn up
ⓑ (hot like a flame) scorching, sweltering, burning hot
炎上する *enjō suru* go up in flames
炎暑 *ensho* scorching heat of summer
炎天下で *entenka de* under the blazing sun
炎熱 *ennetsu* scorching weather, extreme heat

❸ [also suffix] **inflammation, -itis**
炎症 *enshō* inflammation
脳炎 *nōen* brain inflammation, encephalitis
肺炎 *haien* pneumonia, inflammation of the lungs
虫垂炎 *chūsuien* appendicitis

KUN

【honō 炎】
[formerly also 焰]
ⓐ flame, blaze
ⓑ (figuratively) flames (as of passion)
炎を上げて燃える *honō o agete moeru* flame up
嫉妬の炎 *shitto no honō* flames of jealousy

SYNONYMS

❶ⓐ fire
火 FIRE → 3463
❷ⓑ hot
熱 HOT → 2866
暑い HOT (weather) → 2473
温 WARM → 608
暖 WARM (esp. weather) → 1011
❸ diseases and disease symptoms
熱 fever → 2866
痘 SMALLPOX → 3284
痢 DIARRHEA → 3283
下 diarrhea → 3378

USAGE

honō
炎
[formerly also 焰]
ⓐ flame, blaze
ⓑ (figuratively) flames (as of passion)
焰
ⓐ [now replaced by 炎] flame, blaze
ⓑ [now usu. 炎] (figuratively) flames (as of passion)

HOMOPHONES

honō ⇨ 焰 996

4-4
又

受

2421 JU u(keru) -u(ke) u(karu)

CH 受 shòu

Radical	Strokes
又 29	8-2-6
Grade	**Freq**
Jōyō-3	223
2-4-4	

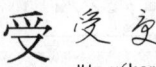

▶RECEIVE

COMPOUNDS

❶ [original meaning] **receive, accept, take, get**
受信 *jushin* reception (of radio waves); receipt of a message
受講 *jukō* attending lectures
受領 *juryō* receipt
受注する *juchū suru* receive an order
受納する *junō suru* accept, receive
受賞する *jushō suru* win a prize
受諾する *judaku suru* receive, accept
受験する *juken suru* take an examination
受動的な *judōteki na* passive
感受性 *kanjusei* sensibility

❷ be subjected to, undergo, suffer
受難 *junan* ordeal, crucifixion
受刑者 *jukeisha* prisoner, convict

❸ *Buddhism* one of the five aggregates; perception

受蘊 *juun* perception

KUN

【u(keru) 受ける】

①ⓐ receive, accept, get, take, catch
ⓑ accept (an offer)
ⓒ receive (an insult), suffer, be subjected to
ⓓ [sometimes also 享ける] enjoy, be granted

受け取る *uketoru* receive, accept; understand
受付 *uketsuke* receipt, reception, acceptance; receptionist, information clerk; information office [desk]
お受けしましょう *Ouke shimashō* I will accept it
受け入れる *ukeireru* accept, consent to; receive, accommodate
引き受ける *hikiukeru* undertake; answer for, guarantee
被害を受ける *higai o ukeru* be damaged
恩寵を受ける *onchō o ukeru* enjoy (a person's) favor

② [sometimes also 承ける] inherit, get
受け継ぐ *uketsugu* inherit, succeed to

③ parry (a blow), defend (in chess, etc.)
受けを誤る *uke o ayamaru* make a faulty defense
受け流す *ukenagasu* ward off, elude; turn aside (a joke)

④ take, interpret
真に受ける *ma ni ukeru* take seriously, believe

⑤ appeal to the public, be popular
受けが良い *uke ga yoi* be popular (with)
馬鹿受け *bakauke* great hit

⑥ face, front on
南を受ける *minami o ukeru* face the south

⑦ be modified

【-u(ke) -受け】

ⓐ receptacle
ⓑ support
郵便受け *yūbin'uke* mailbox
軸受け *jikuuke* bearing

【u(karu) 受かる】 pass an examination
大学に受かる *daigaku ni ukaru* pass the entrance examination to a university

SYNONYMS

❶ receive
享 ENJOY → 2051
領 receive → 1224
収 TAKE IN → 198
納 ACCEPT → 1300
戴 RECEIVE HUMBLY → 3302
頂 RECEIVE HUMBLY → 145
拝 have the honor to receive → 303

❷ be subjected to
被 BE SUBJECTED TO → 1163

USAGE

ukeru

受ける
①ⓐ receive, accept, get, take, catch
ⓑ accept (an offer)
ⓒ receive (an insult), suffer, be subjected to
ⓓ [sometimes also 享ける] enjoy, be granted
② [sometimes also 承ける] inherit, get
③ parry (a blow), defend (in chess, etc.)
④ take, interpret
⑤ appeal to the public, be popular
⑥ face, front on
⑦ be modified

享ける
[usu. 受ける] enjoy, be granted

承ける
[usu. 受ける] inherit, get

請ける
① undertake, take upon oneself
② redeem (pawned goods), ransom

HOMOPHONES

ukeru ⇨ 享 2051 承 16 請 1576

2422

▶CONTEND
nonstandard for 争 2030

4-4 爫

incorrect classification ⇨ see 3211

4-4 耂

4-4 ⺾

芯 2423 SHIN

Ⓒ 芯 xīn xìn

Radical	Strokes
⺾ 140	8-4-4
Grade	Freq
Reference	
2-4-4	

COMPOUNDS

● [sometimes also 心 11] core (of fruit); wick; lead (of a pencil); padding

替え芯 *kaeshin* spare lead

花芯 *kashin* center of a flower

芯 *shin* core; wick; lead (of a pencil); padding

芯を切る *shin o kiru* trim a wick

芯が腐っている *shin ga kusatte iru* be rotten to the core

NOTE

⇨ see USAGE note at 心 11

4-4 ⺾

芙 2424

▶**LOTUS**

nonstandard for 芙 2208

4-4 ⺾

芽 2425

▶**BUD**

nonstandard for 芽 2240

4-4 ⺾

芳 2426

▶**FRAGRANT**

nonstandard for 芳 2210

4-4 ⺾

花 2427

▶**FLOWER**

nonstandard for 花 2211

4-4 今

念

incorrect classification ⇨ see 2059

4-4 𠫓

育

incorrect classification ⇨ see 2050

4-4 龶

毒 毒 毒 2428 DOKU

Stroke order: 一 十 キ 主 ... 毒 (1–8)

Ⓒ 毒 dú

Radical	Strokes
毋 80	8-4-4
Grade	Freq
Jōyō-4	1127
2-4-4	

▶**POISON**

COMPOUNDS

❶ [original meaning] **poison, toxin**

毒殺 *dokusatsu* poisoning, killing by poison

毒ガス *dokugasu* poison gas

毒薬 *dokuyaku* poisonous drug

毒物 *dokubutsu* poisonous substance, toxin

有毒な *yūdoku na* poisonous

中毒 *chūdoku* poisoning, toxication; addiction

消毒 *shōdoku* disinfection, sterilization

猛毒 *mōdoku* deadly poison

❷ malice, harm

毒舌 *dokuzetsu* wicked tongue, abusive language, blistering remarks

毒突く *dokuzuku* spit, curse, abuse

INDEPENDENT

【**doku** 毒】poison, venom, toxicant; harm, injury; malice, spite
毒の有る *doku no aru* poisonous; harmful, malicious
気の毒な *kinodoku na* pitiable, miserable; regrettable, too bad
【**dokusuru** 毒する】poison; do harm, injure; spoil, contaminate

---

表 表 表

2429 HYŌ omote -omote arawa(su) arawa(reru)

一 十 キ 主 声 表 表 表

1 2 3 4 5 6 7 8

CH 表 biǎo

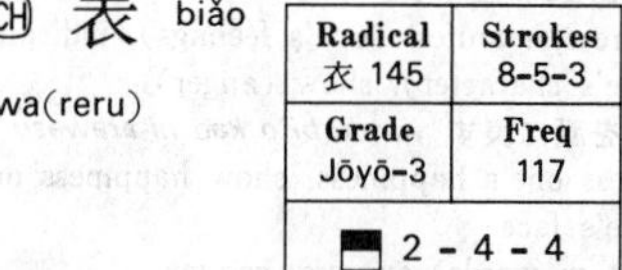

Radical	Strokes
衣 145	8-5-3
Grade	**Freq**
Jōyō-3	117

2 - 4 - 4

4-4 主

▶**EXPRESS** ▶**SURFACE** ▶**TABLE**

COMPOUNDS

❶ⓐ express, manifest, show
ⓑ appear (on the surface)
ⓒ be made public, become open
表明する *hyōmei suru* express, state, show, demonstrate
表現する *hyōgen suru* express, represent, manifest; give expression to
表示する *hyōji suru* indicate, show, express, manifest
表彰 *hyōshō* commendation, awarding
表決 *hyōketsu* decision, resolution
表意文字 *hyōi-moji* ideograph, ideographic character
発表する *happyō suru* announce, make public, publish
公表する *kōhyō suru* announce officially [in public], proclaim
表象 *hyōshō* representation, image, idea
表情 *hyōjō* expression, look
代表する *daihyō suru* represent, stand for; typify
❷ surface, face, exterior, outside
表面 *hyōmen* surface, face, outside; appearance
表紙 *hyōshi* cover, binding
表皮 *hyōhi* epidermis; bark, rind
表裏 *hyōri* front and rear, both sides (of a thing or matter); duplicity
表記する *hyōki suru* write on a surface; write, express in writing
地表 *chihyō* surface of the earth, ground surface
意表 *ihyō* limits of one's expectation
❸ [also suffix]
ⓐ table, chart, diagram, schedule, tabular form
ⓑ list
図表 *zuhyō* chart, diagram
年表 *nenpyō* chronological table
時刻表 *jikokuhyō* timetable, schedule
予定表 *yoteihyō* schedule
一覧表 *ichiranhyō* list, table, schedule, catalog
❹ memorial to the throne, written appeal, letter
上表 *jōhyō* one's opinion presented to the throne; the table above
辞表 *jihyō* (letter of) resignation
賀表 *gahyō* congratulatory address
❺ [also 標 1064] inscription, mark
表札 *hyōsatsu* nameplate, doorplate
❻ model, paragon
師表 *shihyō* model, paragon

INDEPENDENT

【**hyō** 表】table, chart, diagram, schedule, tabular form; list
表にする *hyō ni suru* tabulate; make a list of
【**hyōsuru** 表する】express, manifest; pay (one's respects)

KUN

【**omote** 表】
①ⓐ [also prefix] (front or outer side) front side, face, outside, right side; the obverse, the head
ⓑ the front (of a house)
ⓒ superficial [outward] appearance, outside
表門 *omotemon* front gate
表日本 *omotenihon* Pacific side of Japan
葉書の表 *hagaki no omote* front of a post card
裏表に着る *uraomote ni kiru* wear (a coat) wrong side out
表の戸 *omote no to* street [front] door
表向きの理由 *omotemuki no riyū* ostensible [surface] reason
② outdoors, outside
表で遊ぶ *omote de asobu* play outside [out of doors]
③ matting
表替え *omotegae* refacing mats
④ *baseball* first half of an inning, top
五回の表 *gokai no omote* top of the fifth inning
⑤ formal, official, public

表立つ *omotedatsu* become public [open]

[-omote -表] [also suffix] quarters, place, direction

国表 *kuniomote* one's native province, one's home

江戸表 *edoomote* Edo

[arawa(su) 表す]

① express, manifest (one's feelings), indicate (one's character), show (anger)

喜びを顔に表す *yorokobi o kao ni arawasu* express one's happiness, show happiness on one's face

② (put in words) express, convey

言葉に表せない *kotoba ni arawasenai* inexpressible, ineffable

③ express in symbols, represent, stand for, symbolize

記号で表す *kigō de arawasu* represent by signs

[arawa(reru) 表れる] be expressed, find expression in, show, become manifest

表れ *araware* expression, manifestation, indication

地方色の表れた小説 *chihōshoku no arawareta shōsetsu* novel with local color

SYNONYMS

❶ⓐ express

揮 WIELD → 589

❷ outside

面 FACE → 2087

外 OUTSIDE → 186

❸ⓐ diagram

図 DRAWING → 3071

USAGE

❶ omote

表

①ⓐ [also prefix] (front or outer side) front side, face, outside, right side; the obverse, the head

ⓑ the front (of a house)

ⓒ superficial [outward] appearance, outside

② outdoors, outside

③ matting

④ *baseball* first half of an inning, top

⑤ formal, official, public

面

①ⓐ (front of head) face

ⓑ (outer surface) face, surface (as of water)

② mask

❷ arawasu

表す

① express, manifest (one's feelings), indicate (one's character), show (anger)

② (put in words) express, convey

③ express in symbols, represent, stand for, symbolize

現す

① cause to appear, show, display, reveal

② attain distinction, become famous

著す

author, write, publish

❸ arawareru

表れる

be expressed, find expression in, show, become manifest

現れる

① appear, emerge, come out, become visible, materialize

② become known, attain distinction; be exposed [found out]

❹ araware

表れ

expression, manifestation, indication

現れ

embodiment, materialization

❺ hyōji suru

表示する

indicate, show, express, manifest

標示する

post up, declare, demonstrate

❻ hyōki suru

表記する

write on a surface; write, express in writing

標記する

mark; write a title

HOMOPHONES

omote ⇨ 面 2087

arawasu ⇨ 現 968 著 2300

arawareru ⇨ 現 968

araware ⇨ 現 968

COMPOUND FORMATION

表意文字 *hyōi-moji*

表意文字 'ideograph, ideographic character' refers to characters (文字) that express (表❶ⓐ) meaning (意).

青 青 青 青

2430 SEI SHŌ ao ao- ao(i)

CH 青 qīng

Radical	Strokes
青 174	8-8-0
Grade	Freq
Jōyō-1	394
2 - 4 - 4	

4-4

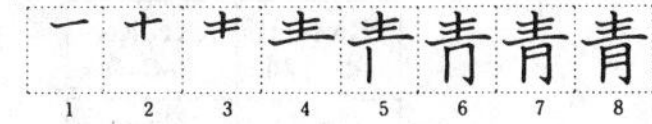

RADICAL 174
variant of 青 *ao* 'blue'
⇨ see 青 2431 for radical description

▶BLUE ▶GREEN

COMPOUNDS

❶ⓐ blue
ⓑ green, greenish
青色 *seishoku* blue
青天 *seiten* blue sky
青色症 *seishokushō* cyanosis
紺青 *konjō* Prussian blue, deep blue
緑青 *rokushō* verdigris, copper [green] rust
丹青 *tansei* red and blue; painting
青松 *seishō* green pine
❷ greens, vegetables
青果 *seika* vegetables and fruits
❸ⓐ youthful, young
ⓑ abbrev. of 青年 *seinen*: youth
青春 *seishun* bloom of youth
青年 *seinen* youth, young man
青少年 *seishōnen* youth, young people
民青 *minsei* Democratic Youth League of Japan
❹ *chem* cyanide
青化物 *seikabutsu* cyanide
青酸 *seisan* prussic acid (Blausäure)
❺ strips of bamboo formerly used for writing
青史 *seishi* history, history book

KUN

【ao 青】 blue; green; green light; bluish-gray horse
光沢の有る青 *kōtaku no aru ao* peacock blue
【ao- 青-】
① [also prefix]
ⓐ blue
ⓑ green
青色 *aoiro* blue
青空 *aozora* blue sky
青信号 *aoshingō* green light, green (traffic) signal
青草 *aokusa* green grass
青物 *aomono* greens, vegetables
青菜 *aona* greens
② (not mature) green, unripe
青二才 *aonisai* green [immature] youth, novice, greenhorn
青臭い *aokusai* inexperienced, immature; grassy-smelling
③ (pale in appearance) green, pale
青白い *aojiroi* pale, pallid
青ざめる *aozameru* become pale
【ao(i) 青い】
①ⓐ blue
ⓑ green
青い旗 *aoi hata* blue flag
② [sometimes also 蒼い] (pale in appearance) green, pale
顔が青い *kao ga aoi* look pale [green]
③ (not mature) green, unripe
青い果実 *aoi kajitsu* unripe [green] fruit

SPECIAL READINGS

真っ青 *massao* deep blue; paleness, ghastliness

SYNONYMS

❶ⓐ blue and purple colors
碧 DEEP BLUE → 2836
瑠 LAPIS LAZULI (bright blue) → 1060
紺 DARK BLUE → 1332
藍 INDIGO → 2381
紫 PURPLE → 2688
ⓑ green colors
緑 GREEN → 1377
翠 JADE GREEN → 2705
❸ⓐ young
若 YOUNG → 2241
弱 young → 1167
少 young → 3467
幼 VERY YOUNG → 191
稚 CHILDISH → 1206

USAGE

aoi
青い
①ⓐ blue
ⓑ green
② [sometimes also 蒼い] (pale in appearance) green, pale
③ (not mature) green, unripe
蒼い
[usu. 青い] (pale in appearance) green, pale

HOMOPHONES

aoi ⇨ 蒼 2507

COMPOUND FORMATION

青史 *seishi*
青史 'history, history book' originally referred to history (史) written on bamboo strips (青 ❺).

4-4 龶

靑 ▶BLUE ▶GREEN

2431

nonstandard for 青 2430

Radical	Strokes
靑 174	8-8-0
Grade	**Freq**
Variant	
2-4-4	

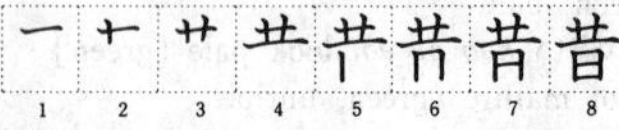

RADICAL 174

Standard form: 青 *ao* 'blue' (靜)
Variant: 靑 *ao* (靖 静)
Description: used for character classification

4-4 龷

昔

2432 SEKI SHAKU mukashi

CH 昔 xī

Radical	Strokes
日 72	8-4-4
Grade	**Freq**
Jōyō-3	1146
2-4-4	

▶FORMER TIMES

COMPOUNDS

● [original meaning] **former times, ancient times, past, antiquity**
昔時 *sekiji* former times, old times
昔日 *sekijitsu* ancient times, former days, bygone days
昔年 *sekinen* antiquity, former years
今昔 *konjaku* past and present, yesterday and today

KUN

【**mukashi 昔**】 former times, old times, antiquity, bygone years
昔話 *mukashibanashi* legend, old tale
昔風 *mukashifū* old-fashioned

SYNONYMS

● **old times**
往 bygone days → 292

4-4 龷

芽

incorrect classification ⇨ see 2240

4-4 中

忠

2433 CHŪ

CH 忠 zhōng

Radical	Strokes
心 61	8-4-4
Grade	**Freq**
Jōyō-6	1107
2-4-4	

▶LOYALTY

COMPOUNDS

❶ⓐ **loyalty, devotion, faithfulness, fidelity**
ⓑ loyal, devoted, faithful
忠実 *chūjitsu* faithfulness, devotion, honesty
忠孝 *chūkō* loyalty and filial piety
忠義 *chūgi* loyalty, fidelity, devotion
忠臣 *chūshin* loyal retainer, loyal subject
忠犬 *chūken* faithful dog
❷ [original meaning] sincerity, honesty
忠告する *chūkoku suru* advise; counsel, give warning; admonish

INDEPENDENT

【**chū 忠**】 loyalty, devotion; faithfulness, fidelity
忠なる *chūnaru* loyal, devoted, faithful, true
君に忠である *kimi ni chū de aru* be loyal to one's sovereign

SYNONYMS

❶ⓐ **fidelity**
義 faith → 2338

孝 FILIAL PIETY → 3205
悌 BROTHERLY LOVE → 424
誠 SINCERITY → 1523
実 faithfulness → 2225
信 fidelity → 100
操 constancy → 769
節 moral integrity → 2691

奈

incorrect classification ⇨ see 2219 4-4 大

彥

incorrect classification ⇨ see 2074
(nonstandard for 彦 3295) 4-5 文

冒 冒 冒 冒

2434 BŌ oka(su)

CH 冒 mào

Radical	Strokes
目 109△	9-5-4
Grade	**Freq**
Jōyō	1455
2 - 4 - 5	

4-5 日

▶**RISK**

COMPOUNDS

❶ **risk, brave, defy**
冒険 *bōken* adventure, risk
冒瀆する *bōtoku suru* desecrate, profane
❷ affect, attack, afflict
感冒 *kanbō* cold, catarrh
❸ beginning
冒頭 *bōtō* beginning, opening

KUN

【oka(su) 冒す】
①ⓐ risk, brave, defy
ⓑ (risk the danger of using a great person's name) assume (another's name); bear
危険を冒す *kiken o okasu* brave [defy] a danger
源の姓を冒す *minamoto no sei o okasu* assume the clan name of Minamoto
② affect, attack, afflict
病に冒される *yamai ni okasareru* be attacked by a disease

SYNONYMS

❶ **risk**
懸 stake → 2915

HOMOPHONES

okasu ⇨ 犯 196 侵 101

NOTE

⇨ see USAGE note at 侵 101
★do not confuse with 昌 2414

星 星 星

2435 SEI SHŌ hoshi -boshi

CH 星 xīng

Radical	Strokes
日 72	9-4-5
Grade	**Freq**
Jōyō-2	847
2 - 4 - 5	

4-5 日

▶**STAR**

COMPOUNDS

❶ⓐ [also suffix] **star**
ⓑ **suffix after names of stars**
恒星 *kōsei* fixed star
星座 *seiza* constellation
超巨星 *chōkyosei* supergiant star
一等星 *ittōsei* first magnitude star
北極星 *hokkyokusei* Polaris
織女星 *shokujosei* Vega
❷ **celestial body, planet, satellite**
惑星 *wakusei* planet
衛星 *eisei* satellite; moon
流星 *ryūsei* shooting star, falling star
火星 *kasei* Mars
冥王星 *meiōsei* Pluto
明星 *myōjō* Venus
❸ (prominent personage) star, great man
巨星 *kyosei* giant star; great man [star], big shot
将星 *shōsei* general
❹ time, years

星霜 *seisō* years, time

KUN

【**hoshi 星**】star, heavenly body, planet; spot, dot; bull's eye; point, score; criminal

星占い *hoshiuranai* astrology, horoscopy

図星 *zuboshi* bull's eye, mark

【**-boshi -星**】[also suffix] star, heavenly body, planet

帚星 *hōkiboshi* comet

綺羅星 *kiraboshi* glittering stars

SYNONYMS

❶ⓐ & ❶ⓑ stars

座 constellation → 3116

NOTE

⇨ see COMPOUND FORMATION for 織女星 *shokujo-sei* ⇨ 織 1422

4-5 日

是

2436 ZE kore▲

CH 是 shì

Radical	Strokes
日 72	9-4-5
Grade	**Freq**
Jōyō	1317
2-4-5	

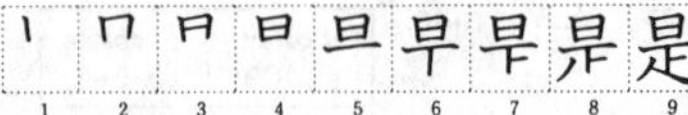

▶RIGHT

COMPOUNDS

❶ⓐ right

ⓑ (set right) right, correct

是非 *zehi* right and/or wrong; by all means, at any cost

是是非非主義 *zezehihishugi* fair and unbiased policy, principle of being fair and just

是認 *zenin* approval

是正 *zesei* correction

❷ policy, guideline

国是 *kokuze* national policy

社是 *shaze* company policy

店是 *tenze* shop policy

❸ this

如是我聞 *nyozegamon* these ears have heard; thus I hear (quote from the sutras)

INDEPENDENT

【**ze 是**】right, righteousness

是を是とし非を非とする *Ze o ze to shi hi o hi to suru* Call what is right right, and wrong wrong

KUN

【**kore 是**】[also 之] *pronoun* this

SYNONYMS

❶ⓐ right

正 RIGHT → 3484

端 correct → 1221

❷ policy

策 policy → 2679

綱 guiding principle → 1372

【**kore**】

○ this and that

之 this → 3420

爾 THAT → 3587

彼 that → 290

本 THIS → 3502

今 THIS (week, etc.) → 1968

当 THE PRESENT → 2177

該 the said → 1519

同 the same → 2987

USAGE

kore

是

[also 之] *pronoun* this

之

[also 是] *pronoun* this

此れ

pronoun this

惟

[archaic] emphatic adverb

HOMOPHONES

kore ⇨ 之 3420 此 823 惟 481

4-5 木

査

2437 SA

CH 査 chá zhā

Radical	Strokes
木 75	9-4-5
Grade	**Freq**
Jōyō-5	242
2-4-5	

一 十 才 木 木 杏 杳 杳 査 (stroke order 1–9)

▶LOOK INTO

COMPOUNDS

❶ look into, investigate, examine, check, inspect, find out, inquire into

査察 *sasatsu* inspection, investigation

査閲 *saetsu* inspection, examination

査問 *samon* inquiry, hearing
調査 *chōsa* investigation, examination, inquiry, survey
捜査 *sōsa* criminal investigation, search
検査 *kensa* inspection, examination, test
審査する *shinsa suru* examine, investigate, judge
鑑査 *kansa* inspection, audit
❷ investigator, examiner
主査 *shusa* chairman of an investigation
巡査 *junsa* police, patrolman

SYNONYMS

❶ **investigate and examine**

調 INVESTIGATE → 1567
審 EXAMINE CAREFULLY → 2360
診 EXAMINE A PATIENT → 1504
検 EXAMINE → 986
探 PROBE → 505
討 STUDY → 1456
察 INSPECT → 2347
究 STUDY EXHAUSTIVELY → 2203
閲 REVIEW → 3330
験 TEST → 1833
勘 CHECK → 1777
糾 INQUIRE INTO → 1278

者

incorrect classification ⇨ see 3217
(nonstandard for 者 3211)

4-5 耂

2438 苗

▶**SEEDLING**
nonstandard for 苗 2237

4-5 艹

2439 英

▶**DISTINGUISHED** ▶**ENGLAND**
nonstandard for 英 2238

4-5 艹

2440 苑

▶**IMPERIAL GARDEN**
nonstandard for 苑 2239

4-5 艹

2441 若

▶**YOUNG**
nonstandard for 若 2241

4-5 艹

2442 苦

▶**SUFFERING** ▶**BITTER**
nonstandard for 苦 2243

4-5 艹

2443 茉

▶**JASMINE**
nonstandard for 茉 2244

4-5 艹

2444 茂

▶**GROW THICK**
nonstandard for 茂 2245

4-5 艹

盆

incorrect classification ⇨ see 2079

4-5 分

4-5 比

皆 皆 𠔉

2445 KAI mina minna▲

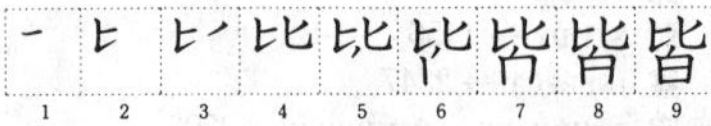

Ⓒⓗ 皆 jiē

Radical	Strokes
白 106	9-5-4
Grade	**Freq**
Jōyō	1423
2 - 4 - 5	

▶ALL

COMPOUNDS

● [original meaning] **all, whole, everything; everybody, everyone**

皆目 *kaimoku* altogether, wholly; (not) at all
皆無 *kaimu* nothing
皆勤 *kaikin* perfect attendance
皆既食 *kaikishoku* total solar [lunar] eclipse
免許皆伝 *menkyo-kaiden* initiation into all the mysteries of an art
国民皆兵 *kokumin-kaihei* universal conscription
国民皆保険 *kokumin-kaihoken* medical insurance for the whole nation

KUN

【mina 皆】 all, everything; everybody, everyone

皆様 *minasama* all of you, all the people
皆殺し *minagoroshi* massacre, annihilation

【minna 皆】 colloquial form of **mina** 皆

SYNONYMS

● **all**

都 all → 1686
万 all → 2936
全 WHOLE → 2022
一 all in one → 3341
満 FULL → 607
丸 complete(ly) → 3417
完 COMPLETE → 2201
総 TOTAL → 1379
諸 VARIOUS → 1577
毎 EVERY → 2034
各 EACH → 2168

4-5 亠

彦

incorrect classification ⇨ see 3295

4-5 冂

冐

2446

▶RISK

nonstandard for 冒 2434

4-5 不

盃

2447

▶CUP

nonstandard for 杯 857

4-5 廾

革 革 革

2448 KAKU kawa

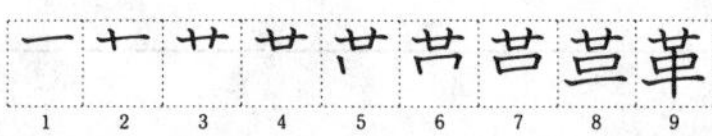

Ⓒⓗ 革 gé jí

Radical	Strokes
革 177	9-9-0
Grade	**Freq**
Jōyō-6	656
2 - 4 - 5	

RADICAL 177

Standard form: 革 *kawa* 'rawhide' (鞏)
Left variant: 革 *kawahen* (靴 鞄 鞭)
Description: used in characters related to hide or leather products

▶LEATHER ▶REFORM

COMPOUNDS

❶ **leather, tanned skin**

革質の *kakushitsu no* coriaceous, leathery
皮革 *hikaku* leather, hides

❷ⓐ **reform, transform, change**

ⓑ abbrev. of 改革 *kaikaku*: **reform, reformation**

革新 *kakushin* innovation, reform, renovation
革命 *kakumei* revolution
改革 *kaikaku* reform, reformation
変革 *henkaku* change, reform, revolution

沿革 *enkaku* history, annals
保革 *hokaku* conservatives and reformists
行革(=行政改革) *gyōkaku* (=*gyōsei kaikaku*) administrative reform
❸ abbrev. of 革命 *kakumei*: revolution
マル革 *marukaku* Marxist revolution

KUN

【kawa 革】 [also prefix and suffix] leather
革靴 *kawagutsu* leather shoes
革手袋 *kawatebukuro* leather gloves
牛革 *gyūkawa* cowhide, oxhide
エナメル革 *enamerugawa* enameled [patent] leather

SYNONYMS

❶ kinds of skin
皮 SKIN (of any kind) → 3037
膚 SKIN (of the human body) → 3265
肌 SKIN (of the human body) → 827
❷ reform
改 REFORM → 243
更 RENEW → 3541
新 make new → 1784

HOMOPHONES

kawa ⇨ 皮 3037

NOTE

⇨ see USAGE note at 皮 3037
⇨ see COMPOUND FORMATION for
沿革 *enkaku* ⇨ 沿 328
革命 *kakumei* ⇨ 命 2058

省

CH 省 shěng xǐng

2449 SEI SHŌ kaeri(miru) habu(ku)

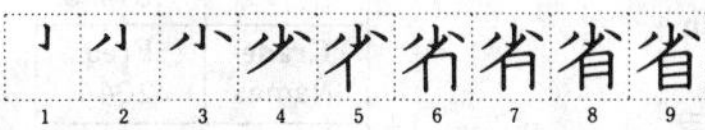

Radical	Strokes
目 109	9-5-4
Grade	**Freq**
Jōyō-4	204
2 - 4 - 5	

4-5 少

▶MINISTRY ▶SAVE ▶INTROSPECT

COMPOUNDS

❶ [also suffix] **ministry, government department [office]**
省庁 *shōchō* Ministries and Agencies
省令 *shōrei* Ministerial ordinance
同省 *dōshō* the said Ministry
文部省 *monbushō* Ministry of Education, Science and Culture
大蔵省 *ōkurashō* Ministry of Finance
❷ **save, conserve**
省力 *shōryoku* labor saving
省エネルギー *shōenerugī* energy conservation
省資源 *shōshigen* saving resources
❸ leave out, omit
省略 *shōryaku* omission, abbreviation, abridgment
❹ⓐ (examine oneself critically) **introspect, reflect upon oneself**
ⓑ [original meaning] examine carefully, scrutinize
反省 *hansei* reflection, introspection
三省する *sansei suru* reflect upon oneself (three times a day), examine oneself over and over again
自省 *jisei* self-examination [reflection], introspection
省察 *seisatsu* reflection; self-reflection, introspection
人事不省 *jinji-fusei* unconsciousness
❺ pay a visit
帰省 *kisei* homecoming
❻ [suffix] province in China
山東省 *santōshō* Shandong Province

INDEPENDENT

【shō 省】 ministry, government department [office]; province in China

KUN

【kaeri(miru) 省みる】 introspect, examine oneself, reflect upon oneself
自分の行いを省みる *jibun no okonai o kaerimiru* reflect upon one's deeds
【habu(ku) 省く】 leave out, omit, exclude; save, curtail, cut down, reduce
無駄を省く *muda o habuku* exclude wastefulness
労力を省く *rōryoku o habuku* save labor

SYNONYMS

❶ parts of governments
閣 CABINET → 3327
❶ public offices
庁 GOVERNMENT AGENCY → 3034
府 government office → 3082
公 public office → 1974
署 PUBLIC-SERVICE STATION → 2609
局 public service office → 3063
所 office → 851
❷ economizing and economy
節 economize → 2691
倹 FRUGAL → 116
❸ eliminate
却 ELIMINATE → 1118
抹 wipe off → 313
削 cross out → 1448
脱 REMOVE → 973
去 take away → 2156

外す take off → 186
除 RID OF → 456
撤 WITHDRAW → 738
排 EXCLUDE → 490
払う CLEAR AWAY → 194
4a think and consider
惟 MEDITATE → 481
量 weigh → 2471
勘 take into consideration → 1777
慮 CONSIDER → 3266
想 CONCEIVE → 2828
思 THINK → 2564
考 THINK → 3196
存 hold an opinion → 2982
案 think out → 2270
6 territorial divisions
州 STATE → 57
県 PREFECTURE → 2641
府 URBAN PREFECTURE → 3082
道 district of Hokkaido → 3134
都 METROPOLIS OF TOKYO → 1686
郡 COUNTY → 1466

HOMOPHONES

kaerimiru ⇨ 顧 1900

NOTE

⇨ see USAGE note at 顧 1900

4-5 帯 incorrect stroke count ⇨ see 2582
世

4-6 晃 2450 KŌ NAMES aki akira teru hikaru
日

CH 晃 huǎng huàng

Radical	Strokes
日 72	10-4-6
Grade	**Freq**
Names	2044
2 - 4 - 6	

▶DAZZLING

COMPOUNDS

● [archaic] dazzling, brilliant
晃晃たる *kōkōtaru* dazzling, brilliant
晃朗たる *kōrōtaru* bright and brilliant
晃曜 *kōyō* dazzling brightness

NAMES

晃一 *kōichi* male name
晃子 *akiko* female name
正晃 *masaaki* male name

SYNONYMS

● **bright**
明 BRIGHT → 855
昭 LUMINOUS → 894
蛍 fluorescent → 2591

4-6 釜 incorrect classification ⇨ see 2107
父

4-6 茶 2451 **▶TEA**
艹
nonstandard for 茶 2259

4-6 荒 2452 **▶WILD**
艹
nonstandard for 荒 2260

4-6 茜 2453 **▶MADDER**
艹
nonstandard for 茜 2261

4-6 草 2454 **▶GRASS**
艹
nonstandard for 草 2263

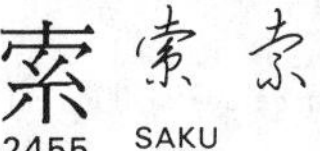

incorrect classification ⇨ see 2108

4-6 公

索 索 索

2455 SAKU

CH 索 suǒ

Radical	Strokes
糸 120	10-6-4
Grade	**Freq**
Jōyō	1084
2 - 4 - 6	

4-6 十

一 十 † 卉 卉 玄 玄 索 索 索

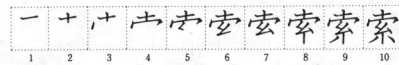

1 2 3 4 5 6 7 8 9 10

▶**SEARCH FOR**

COMPOUNDS

❶ **search for (a word in a dictionary), look up, retrieve, locate**

索引 *sakuin* index
搜索する *sōsaku suru* search for, investigate
探索する *tansaku suru* search for; inquire into, investigate
模索(=摸索)する *mosaku suru* grope for
検索する *kensaku suru* look up (a word in a dictionary), search for, refer to
思索する *shisaku suru* think, speculate

❷ [original meaning] **cable, thick rope, cord**

索条 *sakujō* cable, rope
索道 *sakudō* cableway, ropeway
鋼索 *kōsaku* cable, steel wire rope
鉄索 *tessaku* cable, cableway
軸索 *jikusaku* axon, axis cylinder

❸ alone, solitary

索莫たる *sakubakutaru* desolate, bleak

INDEPENDENT

【saku 索】 rope, steel cable

SYNONYMS

❶ **seek**

探 SEARCH → 505
捜 LOOK FOR → 432
求 SEEK → 3550
猟 hunt for → 538

❷ **ropes and lines**

線 LINE → 1392
弦 STRING → 287
鎖 CHAIN → 1761
綱 ROPE (esp. of fiber) → 1372
縄 ROPE (esp. of straw) → 1388
緒 cord → 1378
組 braid → 1337

COMPOUND FORMATION

思索 *shisaku*

思索する 'think, speculate' is to search for (索 ❶) by thinking about (思).

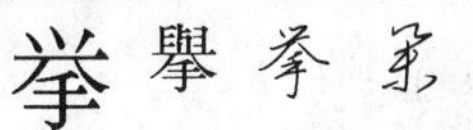

2456 KYO a(geru) a(garu)

Radical	Strokes
手 64	10-4-6
Grade	**Freq**
Jōyō-4	361
2 - 4 - 6	

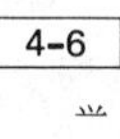

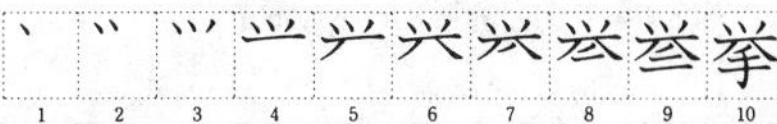

▶**NOMINATE** ▶**NOTEWORTHY ACT**
▶**RAISE**

COMPOUNDS

❶ **nominate, appoint, recommend**

挙用する *kyoyō suru* appoint, promote
選挙 *senkyo* election
推挙する *suikyo suru* recommend, nominate

❷ **noteworthy act, deed, scheme, attempt, undertaking**

暴挙 *bōkyo* rash act, reckless attempt
壮挙 *sōkyo* grand scheme, heroic [daring] attempt
快挙 *kaikyo* brilliant achievement, heroic deed [feat]

❸ **deportment, behavior, action, conduct, bearing**

挙動 *kyodō* deportment, conduct, behavior, action
挙措 *kyoso* behavior, manner
挙止 *kyoshi* bearing, deportment

❹❺ [original meaning] **raise (one's hand), hold up, lift**

❺ raise (an army), recruit

挙手 *kyoshu* raising [holding up] one's hand; salute
挙兵 *kyohei* raising an army

❺ hold a function, perform (a ceremony)

挙式 *kyoshiki* holding a ceremony
挙行する *kyokō suru* hold, perform, celebrate

❻ cite, give (an example), mention

挙証 *kyoshō* presentation of proof
列挙する *rekkyo suru* enumerate, list
枚挙する *maikyo suru* list, enumerate
❼ arrest, round up, nab
検挙する *kenkyo suru* arrest, round up
❽ whole, entire, all
挙国 *kyokoku* whole nation
挙党 *kyotō* whole party
一挙に *ikkyo ni* at a stroke, with a single swoop

INDEPENDENT

【kyo 挙】 noteworthy act, deed, scheme, attempt, undertaking
軽率な挙 *keisotsu na kyo* rash act

KUN

【a(geru) 挙げる】
①ⓐ (raise something and hold it up for display) hold up, raise (one's hand or a wineglass)
ⓑ (gather together) raise (an army), recruit
ⓒ (elevate in dignity) raise oneself, raise one's reputation
手を挙げろ *Te o agero* Hold up! / Stick 'em up!
兵を挙げる *hei o ageru* raise an army
名を挙げる *na o ageru* make one's name, gain fame
② cite, give (an example), mention
例を挙げる *rei o ageru* cite an example
③ hold (a function), perform (a ceremony)
式を挙げる *shiki o ageru* hold a ceremony
④ arrest, round up, nab
挙げられる *agerareru* be arrested, be caught
⑤ give birth to, have children
三人の子を挙げる *sannin no ko o ageru* have three children
⑥ use fully
挙げて *agete* all, whole, en masse
⑦ gain (points), score
先取点を挙げる *senshuten o ageru* score the first point

【a(garu) 挙がる】
① be cited, be mentioned, be listed
良い例が挙がっている *Yoi rei ga agatte iru* A good example is given
② be arrested, be caught, be nabbed
犯人が挙がった *Hannin ga agatta* The culprit was arrested
③ become famous
名が挙がる *na ga agaru* become famous
④ come into possession, be recovered
証拠が挙がった *Shōko ga agatta* Evidence turned up

SYNONYMS

❶ appoint
任 appoint → 53
補 appoint → 1194
❷ acts
行 ACT → 212
業 deed → 2612
❸ behavior
行 conduct → 212
動 behavior → 1778
❹ⓐ raise
揚 RAISE HIGH → 593
掲 PUT UP → 494
上 raise → 3404
起 raise up → 3307
立てる STAND → 1992
拾う PICK UP → 379
❺ hold an event
催 HOLD AN EVENT → 157
❻ quote
引 quote → 181

HOMOPHONES

ageru ⇨ 上 3404 揚 593
agaru ⇨ 上 3404 揚 593

NOTE

⇨ see USAGE note at 上 3404

4-6
天

蚕 蠶 蚕 𧎥

2457 SAN kaiko ko▲

Ⓒⓗ 蚕 cán

Radical	Strokes
虫 142	10-6-4
Grade	**Freq**
Jōyō-6	1819

2-4-6

Stroke order: 一 二 チ 天 天 吞 吞 奞 蚕 蚕 (1–10)

▶SILKWORM

COMPOUNDS

● [original meaning] **silkworm**
蚕糸 *sanshi* silk-raising and reeling, sericulture
蚕室 *sanshitsu* silkworm-raising room
蚕食する *sanshoku suru* encroach on, make an inroad into
養蚕 *yōsan* sericulture, silkworm culture

KUN

【kaiko 蚕】 silkworm
三眠蚕 *sanminkaiko* three-molt silkworm
【ko 蚕】 silkworm
春蚕 *harugo* spring breed of silkworm

SYNONYMS

● **insects**

蝶 BUTTERFLY → 1401
蛍 FIREFLY → 2591
蚊 MOSQUITO → 1319

COMPOUND FORMATION

蚕食 *sanshoku*

蚕食する 'encroach on, etc.' is to encroach on another's territory like a silkworm (蚕) nibbling (食) at the edge of a mulberry leaf.

素

2458 SO SU moto▲

一 十 キ 丰 主 𡗗 妻 素 素 素
1 2 3 4 5 6 7 8 9 10

CH 素 sù

Radical	Strokes
糸 120	10-6-4
Grade	**Freq**
Jōyō-5	786
2-4-6	

4-6
圭

▶ELEMENT ▶PLAIN

COMPOUNDS

❶ [also suffix]

ⓐ **element, basic constituent, component**

ⓑ **chemical element**

ⓒ (structural element of language) -eme

ⓓ (pertaining to an element) elementary, elemental

素子 *soshi elec* element

要素 *yōso* (essential) element, constituent, factor

酵素 *kōso* ferment; enzyme

色素 *shikiso* pigment, coloring matter

栄養素 *eiyōso* nutritive elements [substance]

葉緑素 *yōryokuso* chlorophyll

元素 *genso* element, chemical element

酸素 *sanso* oxygen

炭素 *tanso* carbon

音素 *onso* phoneme

形態素 *keitaiso* morpheme

素反応 *sohannō* elementary reaction

❷ⓐ [also prefix] **primary, elemental, fundamental, original, primordial**

ⓑ *math* prime

素質 *soshitsu* character, nature, makings, constitution

素因 *soin* basic factor, predisposition

素粒子 *soryūshi* elementary particle

素数 *sosū* prime (number)

素体 *sotai* prime field

素因数 *soinsū* prime factor

❸ⓐ [also prefix] (lacking ornament) **plain, simple, unpretentious, natural, unadorned, unrefined, raw, crude**

ⓑ (lacking distinction) plain, ordinary, common

素材 *sozai* material; subject matter

素描 *sobyō* (rough) sketch

素朴な *soboku na* simple, naive, artless

素顔 *sugao* face without makeup

素直な *sunao na* docile, obedient; honest, frank

簡素な *kanso na* plain, simple

質素な *shisso na* simple, modest, frugal

素通りする *sudōri suru* pass through without stopping, pass by

素泊り *sudomari* staying overnight without meals

❹ **bare, naked**

素肌 *suhada* bare skin

素手 *sude* bare hands

素足 *suashi* bare [naked] feet

❺ usually, formerly

素行 *sokō* usual behavior

素志 *soshi* long-cherished [long-fostered] desire

平素は *heiso wa* ordinarily, usually; in the past

❻ *chem* principle

苦味素 *kumiso* bitter principle

❼ emphatic prefix

素敵な *suteki na* grand, cute, fine

素晴らしい *subarashii* splendid, magnificent, wonderful, excellent

素っ頓狂 *suttonkyō* harum-scarum, hysteric

❽ [original meaning] plain white cloth; white

素絹 *soken* coarse silk

緇素 *shiso* old term for Buddhist priesthood and the common people (since they used to wear black and white clothing, respectively)

INDEPENDENT

【**so** 素】 *math* prime(ness); mutual indivisibility

素の *so no* prime

KUN

【**moto** 素】 [now usu. 元] raw material, base

味の素 *ajinomoto* AJI-NO-MOTO (registered trademark)

スープの素 *sūpu no moto* soup stock

SPECIAL READINGS

素人 *shirōto* amateur, novice, outsider; decent woman

SYNONYMS

❶ **element**

元 element → 1929

単 unit → 2256

ⓐ **basis**
基 BASE → 2673
本 BASIS → 3502
礎 foundation → 1248
底 BOTTOM → 3084
根 ROOT → 930
拠 GROUNDS → 312
❷ **original**
原 ORIGINAL → 3009
本 original → 3502
初 FIRST → 1116

❸ **plain and simple**
朴 SIMPLE (unadorned) → 819
単 simple (uncomplicated) → 2256
❹ **naked**
裸 NAKED → 1211

HOMOPHONES

moto ⇨ 本 3502 元 1929 基 2673 下 3378 許 1470

NOTE

⇨ see USAGE note at 元 1929

4-6 艹

恭 2459

KYŌ uyauya(shii)

Ⓒⓗ 恭 gōng

Radical	Strokes
小 61	10-4-6
Grade	**Freq**
Jōyō	1628
2 - 4 - 6	

Stroke order: 1 2 3 4 5 6 7 8 9 10

▶RESPECTFUL

COMPOUNDS

● [original meaning] **respectful, reverent**
恭敬 *kyōkei* respect, reverence
恭順 *kyōjun* obedience, submission
恭賀 *kyōga* respectful congratulations
恭謙 *kyōken* modesty, humility
恭検 *kyōken* humility, respect

KUN

【uyauya(shii) 恭しい】 respectful, reverent
恭しく *uyauyashiku* respectfully, reverentially

SYNONYMS

● **respectful**
謹 RESPECTFULLY → 1618
奉 reverentially → 2559
拝 HUMBLY → 303

4-6 艹

華

incorrect classification ⇨ see 2283

4-7 文

斎

incorrect classification ⇨ see 2115

4-7 文

產

incorrect classification ⇨ see 2120
(nonstandard for 産 3298)

4-7 毌

貫 2460

KAN tsuranu(ku) nuki▲

Ⓒⓗ 贯 guàn

Radical	Strokes
貝 154	11-7-4
Grade	**Freq**
Jōyō	1036
2 - 4 - 7	

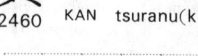

Stroke order: 1 2 3 4 5 6 7 8 9 10 11

▶PENETRATE

COMPOUNDS

❶ **penetrate, pierce through, pass through**
貫通する *kantsū suru* penetrate, pierce, pass through
貫流する *kanryū suru* flow through
貫入 *kannyū* penetration
縦貫する *jūkan suru* run through, traverse
突貫 *tokkan* (bayonet) charge, rush
❷ **carry through, attain, carry out**
貫徹する *kantetsu suru* carry through, go through with, accomplish, attain
一貫して *ikkan shite* consistently
❸ *kan*:

ⓐ unit of weight equiv. to 3.75 kg or 1000 momme (匁)
ⓑ former monetary unit equiv. to 1000 *mon* (文)
尺貫法 *shakkanhō* Japanese system of weights and measures
八貫目 *hakkanme* 8 *kan*
貫禄 *kanroku* dignity; [original meaning] retainer's stipend
一貫五十文 *ikkan gojūmon* 1 *kan* 50 *mon*
❹ place of one's ancestral home (in ancient times)
貫主(＝貫首) *kanju* chief abbot (of a Buddhist temple)

INDEPENDENT

【kan 貫】 *kan* (⇨ ❸)

KUN

【tsuranu(ku) 貫く】 penetrate, pierce, perforate, go through; carry through [out], attain
壁を貫く *kabe o tsuranuku* penetrate the wall
目的を貫く *mokuteki o tsuranuku* accomplish [attain] one's object
【nuki 貫】 brace; thin and narrow board

SYNONYMS

❶ **penetrate**
破 break through → 1150
透 PASS THROUGH → 3108
❸ⓐ **weight units**
斤 CATTY (600 g) → 2949
匁 MOMME (3.75 g) → 3465
屯 ton → 3457

荷 2461 4-7 艹

▶**LOAD**
nonstandard for 荷 2282

莖 2462 4-7 艹

▶**STEM**
nonstandard for 茎 2242

莉 2463 4-7 艹

▶**JASMINE**
nonstandard for 莉 2284

莊 2464 4-7 艹

▶**VILLA** ▶**DIGNIFIED**
nonstandard for 荘 2262

貨 貨 貨 貨 2465 KA 4-7 化

CH 货 huò

Radical	Strokes
貝 154	11-7-4
Grade	**Freq**
Jōyō-4	958
2 - 4 - 7	

ノ イ イ一 化 化 貨 貨 貨 貨 貨 貨
1 2 3 4 5 6 7 8 9 10 11

▶**MONEY** ▶**GOODS**

COMPOUNDS

❶ⓐ [original meaning] (legal tender) **money, currency**
ⓑ **coin**
ⓒ (assets) money, property
貨幣 *kahei* money, currency, coinage
外貨 *gaika* foreign currency [money]; foreign [imported] goods
通貨 *tsūka* currency, current money
米貨 *beika* American currency, U.S. dollar
硬貨 *kōka* coin, metallic currency
白銅貨 *hakudōka* nickel coin
鋳貨 *chūka* coinage, mintage
貨殖 *kashoku* moneymaking
❷ **goods, commodity**
百貨店 *hyakkaten* department store
雑貨 *zakka* sundries, general cargo; miscellaneous goods
奇貨 *kika* curiosity, rarity; good opportunity
❸ **freight, cargo**
貨物 *kamotsu* freight, cargo, goods
貨車 *kasha* freight car
貨客 *kakyaku* freight and passengers

SYNONYMS

❶ⓐ & ❶ⓑ **money**
銭 MONEY → 1725
金 MONEY → 2057
銀 SILVER → 1722
幣 CURRENCY → 2885

一玉 coin suffix → 3477
札 bill → 817
財 finance → 1457
資 RESOURCES → 2695
❷ **merchandise**
物 commodity → 874
品 ARTICLE (of merchandise) → 2248
産 product → 3298
❸ **burden**
荷 LOAD → 2282

4-7 化

貨 2466

▶MONEY ▶GOODS
nonstandard for 貨 2465

4-7 分

貧

incorrect classification ⇨ see 2123

4-7 亠

incorrect classification ⇨ see 3298

4-7 亠

incorrect classification ⇨ see 2116

4-7 龶

2467 SEKI se(meru)

Ⓒⓗ 责 zé

Radical	Strokes
貝 154	11-7-4
Grade	**Freq**
Jōyō-5	683
2-4-7	

1 2 3 4 5 6 7 8 9 10 11

▶RESPONSIBILITY ▶BLAME

COMPOUNDS

❶ **responsibility, liability**
責任 *sekinin* responsibility, liability
責務 *sekimu* responsibility and obligation, responsibility to do one's duty
重責 *jūseki* heavy responsibility, important duty
職責 *shokuseki* responsibilities pertaining to one's work
引責する *inseki suru* take responsibility upon oneself

❷ **blame, condemn, censure**
叱責する *shisseki suru* reproach, scold, reprove
問責 *monseki* censure, reproof
自責 *jiseki* self-accusation

❸ [original meaning] torture, torment

INDEPENDENT

【seki 責】 responsibility
責を果たす *seki o hatasu* fulfill one's responsibility

KUN

【se(meru) 責める】
① blame, condemn, censure, accuse, criticize, reproach
責め *seme* responsibility; blame; [also suffix] torture, persecution
人の怠慢を責める *hito no taiman o semeru* blame [denounce] a person for his [her] negligence
② torture, persecute
責め道具 *semedōgu* instruments of torture
責め立てる *semetateru* torture severely; urge
水責め *mizuzeme* water torture
③ urge, press; tease
金を払えと責める *kane o harae to semeru* press for payment

SYNONYMS

❶ **responsibility**
務 DUTY → 1173
任 duty → 53
分 one's part → 1972
❷ **blame and accuse**
叱 SCOLD → 182
詰 REPRIMAND → 1521
難 find fault with → 1838
批 CRITICIZE → 250
劾 EXPOSE CRIMES → 1266
弾 impeach → 572
【semeru】
② **torture and oppress**
拷 TORTURE → 373

虐 treat cruelly → 3218
迫 oppress → 3074

HOMOPHONES

semeru ⇨ 攻 242

seme ⇨ 攻 242

NOTE

⇨ see USAGE note at 攻 242

黄 黄 黄 黄

2468 KŌ Ō ki ko-

CH 黄 huáng

Radical	Strokes
黄 201	11-11-0
Grade	**Freq**
Jōyō-2	1101
2 - 4 - 7	

4-7 艹

RADICAL 201

simplified form not used as radical
⇨ see 黃 2487 for radical description

▶YELLOW

COMPOUNDS

❶ⓐ [original meaning] **yellow**
ⓑ yellow-skinned, yellow
ⓒ turn yellow
黄色 *kōshoku* (=*ōshoku*) yellow
黄海 *kōkai* the Yellow Sea
黄金 *ōgon* gold; money
黄鉄鉱 *ōtekkō* iron pyrite, fool's gold
黄熱病 *ōnetsubyō* yellow fever
卵黄 *ran'ō* yolk
硫黄 *iō* sulfur
黄禍 *kōka* Yellow Peril
黄人 *ōjin* yellow race
黄葉する *kōyō suru* turn yellow, put on autumnal leaves
❷ *astron* ecliptic
黄緯 *kōi* ecliptic latitude
黄道 *kōdō* ecliptic

KUN

【**ki** 黄】[also prefix] yellow
黄ばむ *kibamu* grow yellowish
黄色 *kiiro* yellow
黄八丈 *kihachijō* yellow silk cloth
【**ko-** 黄-】yellow
黄金 *kogane* gold; money

SYNONYMS

❶ⓐ **yellow colors**
金 golden → 2057

雀 雀 雀

2469 JAKU JAN suzume

CH 雀 què qiāo qiǎo

Radical	Strokes
隹 172	11-8-3
Grade	**Freq**
Non-Jōyō	1801
2 - 4 - 7	

4-7 少

▶SPARROW ▶MAHJONG

COMPOUNDS

❶ⓐ **sparrow**
ⓑ happy like a sparrow, delighted
燕雀 *enjaku* small birds
孔雀 *kujaku* peacock
欣喜雀躍する *kinkijakuyaku suru* dance [jump] for joy
❷ **unclassified compounds**
麻雀 *mājan* mahjong
❸ abbrev. of 麻雀 *mājan*: **mahjong**
雀荘 *jansō* mahjong club
雀球 *jankyū jankyu* (combination of Japanese pinball and mahjong)
雀卓 *jantaku* mahjong board

KUN

【**suzume** 雀】sparrow, Japanese sparrow

SYNONYMS

❶ⓐ **wild birds**
鶴 CRANE → 1850
隼 FALCON → 2756
鷹 HAWK → 3189
❸ **board games**
棋 SHOGI → 987
碁 GO → 2699
局 board game → 3063

4-8
日

景 景 京

2470 KEI

CH 景 jǐng

Radical	Strokes
日 72	12-4-8
Grade	**Freq**
Jōyō-4	621
2 - 4 - 8	

▶SCENE

COMPOUNDS

❶ⓐ **scene, scenery, view, -scape**
ⓑ *theater* scene
景勝 *keishō* picturesque scenery
背景 *haikei* background; (stage) scenery, setting, scene; backing
夜景 *yakei* night view [scene]
風景 *fūkei* scenery, landscape, view
光景 *kōkei* spectacle, sight, scene
絶景 *zekkei* superb view, picturesque scenery
情景 *jōkei* scene, sight; nature and sentiment
海景 *kaikei* seascape
全景 *zenkei* complete view
雲景 *unkei* cloudscape
第一景 *daiikkei* first scene

❷ **business conditions, market situation, conditions, circumstances**
景気 *keiki* things, times; business conditions
景況 *keikyō* situation, outlook
不景気 *fukeiki* business depression, slump, dull market

❸ premium, present
景品 *keihin* premium, gift
景物 *keibutsu* seasonal scenery; present, premium

❹ respect, admire
景仰する *keikō* (=*keigyō*) *suru* adore, admire, revere

❺ [rare] auspicious, great
景雲 *keiun* auspicious cloud

INDEPENDENT

【kei 景】 scene, view
天下の景 *tenka no kei* superlative view

SPECIAL READINGS

景色 *keshiki* scenery, landscape

SYNONYMS

❶ⓐ **view**
風 (beautiful) scenery → 3007
光 scenery → 2391
観 VIEW → 1880

❷ **states and situations**
況 CONDITIONS → 337
状 CONDITION → 272
態 STATE → 2847
勢 course of events → 2857
境 SITUATION → 676
局 current situation → 3063
情 ACTUAL CONDITIONS → 482
訳 circumstances → 1473
調 TONE → 1567
様 MODE → 1052
相 PHASE → 900

4-8
日

量 量 量

2471 RYŌ haka(ru)

CH 量 liáng liàng

Radical	Strokes
里 166	12-7-5
Grade	**Freq**
Jōyō-4	536
2 - 4 - 8	

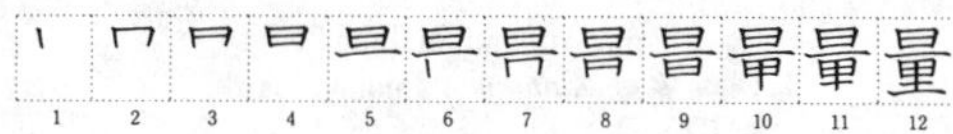

▶QUANTITY

COMPOUNDS

❶ [also suffix] **quantity, amount, volume, capacity, magnitude; weight**
量産 *ryōsan* mass production
量感 *ryōkan* massiveness
量子論 *ryōshiron* quantum theory
数量 *sūryō* quantity, volume
大量 *tairyō* large quantity, great volume, mass
容量 *yōryō* capacity, volume
重量 *jūryō* weight
交通量 *kōtsūryō* traffic volume
消費量 *shōhiryō* amount of consumption

❷ⓐ [original meaning] (determine the volume, area or weight of) **measure, gauge, weigh**
ⓑ weighing instrument, balance, scale
測量する *sokuryō suru* measure, survey
計量する *keiryō suru* measure, weigh
度量衡 *doryōkō* weights and measures

❸ weigh, consider, estimate, assess
量刑 *ryōkei* assessment of a case
推量する *suiryō suru* guess, conjecture, infer

裁量 *sairyō* discretion

❹ [formerly also 倆 121] capacity, ability, skill

器量 *kiryō* ability, capacity; personal appearance; dignity

力量 *rikiryō* ability, capacity; physical strength

技量 *giryō* skill, ability, capacity

❺ magnanimity

度量 *doryō* magnanimity, generosity

INDEPENDENT

【ryō 量】 quantity, amount, volume, capacity, magnitude

量より質 *ryō yori shitsu* quality before quantity

KUN

【haka(ru) 量る】

① (determine the weight or volume of) measure, weigh

量り *hakari* measurements; weighing

量り売り *hakariuri* sale by measure; sale by weight

肉の目方を量る *niku no mekata o hakaru* weigh the meat

② [in compounds] guess, surmise, fathom

推し量る *oshihakaru* conjecture, surmise, guess

SYNONYMS

❶ quantity and number

嵩 BULK → 2331
積 size → 1236
額 AMOUNT → 1805
分 content → 1972
数 NUMBER → 1790
勢 strength → 2857

❷ⓐ measure

測 MEASURE → 610

❸ think and consider

勘 take into consideration → 1777
慮 CONSIDER → 3266
惟 MEDITATE → 481
省 INTROSPECT → 2449
想 CONCEIVE → 2828
思 THINK → 2564
考 THINK → 3196
存 hold an opinion → 2982
案 think out → 2270

HOMOPHONES

hakaru ⇨ 計 1441 測 610 図 3071 謀 1593 諮 1596

NOTE

⇨ see USAGE note at 計 1441

最 最 冣

2472 SAI motto(mo)

Ⓒⓗ 最 zuì

Radical	Strokes
日 73	12-4-8
Grade	**Freq**
Jōyō-4	118
2-4-8	

4-8 日

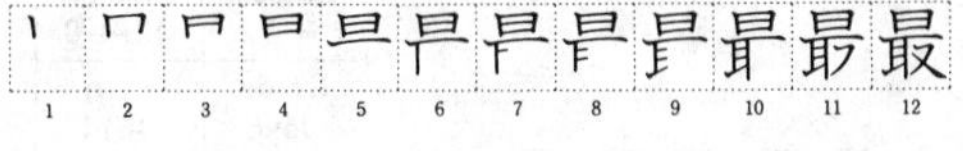

▶MOST

COMPOUNDS

● [also prefix] **most, the most, -est, -most, ultra-, extreme**—used to indicate the superlative degree

最高の *saikō no* maximum, supreme, highest
最少 *saishō* smallest, minimum, least
最大の *saidai no* biggest, largest, greatest
最新の *saishin no* newest, latest
最終 *saishū* last, the end; final
最低の *saitei no* lowest
最南の *sainan no* southernmost
最高級 *saikōkyū* highest grade, top class

INDEPENDENT

【sai 最】 the best, the greatest

最たる物 *saitaru mono* the most extreme

KUN

【motto(mo) 最も】 the most

最も重要な事 *mottomo jūyō na koto* the most important thing

SPECIAL READINGS

最寄りの *moyori no* nearest, nearby

SYNONYMS

● most

至 utmost → 2182
極 EXTREME → 1017

USAGE

mottomo

最も
the most

尤も
① right, reasonable, natural
② indeed, it is true; but

HOMOPHONES

mottomo ⇨ 尤 3023

4-8
日

暑 暑 署 [calligraphic forms]

2473 SHO atsu(i)

Ⓒⓗ 暑 shǔ

Radical	Strokes
日 72	12-4-8
Grade	**Freq**
Jōyō-3	1201
2 - 4 - 8	

▶**SUMMER HEAT** ▶**HOT**

COMPOUNDS

● [original meaning] **summer heat, hot weather, hottest day of summer, summer**

暑気 *shoki* hot weather
暑中 *shochū* midsummer
暑熱 *shonetsu* heat of summer
避暑 *hisho* summering
炎暑 *ensho* scorching heat of summer
残暑 *zansho* lingering summer
猛暑 *mōsho* fierce heat
酷暑 *kokusho* severe heat
大暑 *taisho* Japanese midsummer day

INDEPENDENT

【**sho** 暑】 summer heat
暑を避ける *sho o sakeru* go away for the summer, summer

KUN

【**atsu(i)** 暑い】 hot (weather), warm, sultry
暑さ *atsusa* heat, summer heat, hot weather
真夏の暑さ *manatsu no atsusa* heat of high summer
蒸し暑い *mushiatsui* sultry, sweltering

SYNONYMS

● **heat**
熱 HEAT → 2866
● **warm seasons**
夏 SUMMER → 2113
春 SPRING → 2576
【**atsui**】
○ **hot**
熱 HOT → 2866
炎 scorching → 2420
暖 WARM (esp. weather) → 1011
温 WARM → 608

HOMOPHONES

atsui ⇨ 熱 2866

NOTE

⇨ see USAGE note at 熱 2866

4-8
日

晶

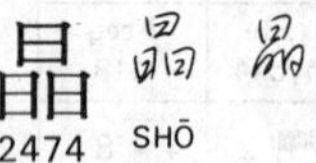

2474 SHŌ

Ⓒⓗ 晶 jīng

Radical	Strokes
日 72	12-4-8
Grade	**Freq**
Jōyō	1614
2 - 4 - 8	

▶**CRYSTAL**

COMPOUNDS

❶ⓐ (body of crystalline structure) **crystal**
ⓑ (transparent mineral) crystal
晶化 *shōka* crystallization
晶子 *shōshi* crystallite
結晶 *kesshō* crystallization, crystal; grain; fruit(s)
氷晶 *hyōshō* ice crystal
液晶 *ekishō* crystalline liquid
水晶 *suishō* rock crystal

❷ [original meaning] crystal-clear, brilliant
晶光 *shōkō* brilliant light

SYNONYMS

❶ⓑ **precious stones**
璃 GLASSY SUBSTANCE → 1059
瑠 LAPIS LAZULI → 1060
玉 GEM → 3477
珠 PEARL → 947
瑛 TRANSPARENT GEM → 999

森 森 森
2475 SHIN mori

CH 森 sēn

Radical	Strokes
木 75	12-4-8
Grade	Freq
Jōyō-1	568
2 - 4 - 8	

4-8 木

▶THICK WOODS

COMPOUNDS

❶ⓐ [original meaning] **thick woods, forest**
ⓑ in close rows as trees in a forest, thickly wooded
森林 *shinrin* forest, woodland
森森 *shinshin* deeply forested
森羅万象 *shinrabanshō* all creation, Nature
❷ⓐ solemn
ⓑ hushed, quiet
森厳な *shingen na* solemn, grave
森閑とした *shinkan to shita* quiet, still, silent as a graveyard

KUN

【mori 森】 [sometimes also 杜] thick woods, forest
森の都 *mori no miyako* tree-clad town
鎮守の森 *chinju no mori* grove of the village shrine

SYNONYMS

❶ⓐ **forest**
林 FOREST, small woods → 861

USAGE

mori
森
[sometimes also 杜] thick woods, forest
杜
[usu. 森] thick woods, forest

HOMOPHONES

mori ⇨ 杜 835

NOTE

⇨ see also USAGE note at 林 861

歯 齒 歯 歯
2476 SHI ha

CH 齿 chǐ

Radical	Strokes
歯 211	12-12-0
Grade	Freq
Jōyō-3	1157
2 - 4 - 8	

4-8 止

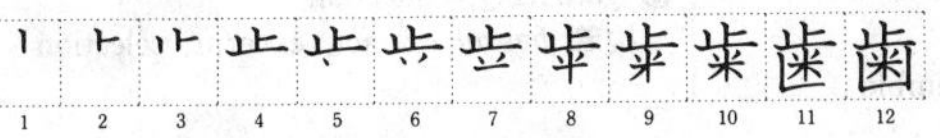

RADICAL 211
variant of 齒 *ha* 'tooth'
⇨ see 齒 2516 for radical description

▶TOOTH

COMPOUNDS

❶ⓐ [original meaning] **tooth**
ⓑ something resembling a tooth
歯科 *shika* dentistry
歯石 *shiseki* tartar (on teeth), dental calculus
抜歯 *basshi* tooth extraction
永久歯 *eikyūshi* permanent tooth
義歯 *gishi* false tooth
鋸歯 *kyoshi* saw tooth
❷ age
年歯 *nenshi* age

INDEPENDENT

【shisuru 歯する】 join, become a member; fall in the same line

KUN

【ha 歯】 [also prefix] tooth; (machine or tool element) tooth, cog, dent
歯磨(=歯磨き) *hamigaki* toothpaste; brushing one's teeth
歯切れの良い *hagire no yoi* crisp; clear and crisp (in speaking); piquant (manner)
歯医者 *haisha* dentist
入れ歯 *ireba* dentures
虫歯 *mushiba* decayed tooth
歯車 *haguruma* cog, toothed wheel
歯付ベルト *hatsukiberuto* toothed belt
歯止め *hadome* drag, pallet; brake

SYNONYMS

❶ⓐ **mouth parts**
舌 TONGUE → 2186
唇 LIP → 2737

4-8 ⺤

爲
2477

▶DO ▶SAKE
nonstandard for 為 3577

4-8 ⺾

萎
2478

Ⓒⓗ 萎 wēi wěi

I shio(reru) shina(biru) shibo(mu) na(eru)

Radical	Strokes
⺾ 140	12-4-8
Grade	Freq
Reference	
2 - 4 - 8	

COMPOUNDS

● [now also 委 *i* 2553] [original meaning] wither, weaken, decline

萎縮 *ishuku* withering, atrophy; being crest-fallen

萎黄病 *iōbyō* greensickness, chlorosis

陰萎 *in'i* impotence

萎れる *shioreru* droop, wither; have the blues, be downcast

萎びる *shinabiru* wither, shrivel, wilt

萎む *shibomu* fade (away), wither, wilt, shrivel

萎える *naeru* wither, droop; weaken, lose strength

4-8 ⺾

萃
2479

Ⓒⓗ 萃 cuì

SUI

Radical	Strokes
⺾ 140	12-4-8
Grade	Freq
Reference	
2 - 4 - 8	

COMPOUNDS

[now replaced by 粋 1293]

ⓐ [original meaning] gather, assemble

ⓑ gathering, collection

抜萃 *bassui* extract, excerpt, selection

4-8 ⺾

萠
2480

▶GERMINATE
nonstandard for 萌 2301

4-8 ⺾

萠
2481

▶GERMINATE
nonstandard for 萌 2301

4-8 ⺾

菓
2482

▶CONFECTIONERY
nonstandard for 菓 2302

4-8 ⺾

華
2483

▶MAGNIFICENT ▶CHINA
nonstandard for 華 2283

4-8 ⺾

菊
2484

▶CHRYSANTHEMUM
nonstandard for 菊 2303

菌 2485

▶**BACTERIA**
nonstandard for 菌 2304

4-8 艹

菜 2486

▶**VEGETABLE**
nonstandard for 菜 2305

4-8 艹

葉

incorrect stroke count ⇨ see 2501
(nonstandard for 葉 2321)

4-8 艹

棄

incorrect classification／stroke count ⇨ see 2137

4-8 去

葬

incorrect classification ⇨ see 2320

4-8 廾

黃 2487

▶**YELLOW**
nonstandard for 黄 2468

Radical	Strokes
黃 201	12-12-0
Grade	**Freq**
Variant	
2 - 4 - 8	

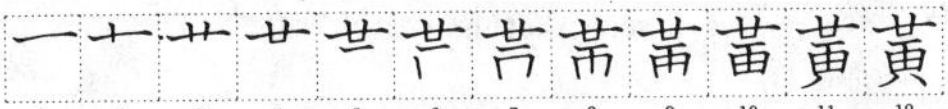

4-8 廿

1 2 3 4 5 6 7 8 9 10 11 12

RADICAL 201
Standard form: 黃 *kiiro* 'yellow' (黌)
Description: used in characters related to the color yellow

貴

incorrect classification ⇨ see 2606

4-8 中

喬 2488

KYŌ NAMES takashi taka

CH 乔 qiáo

Radical	Strokes
口 30	12-3-9
Grade	**Freq**
Names	2032
2 - 4 - 8	

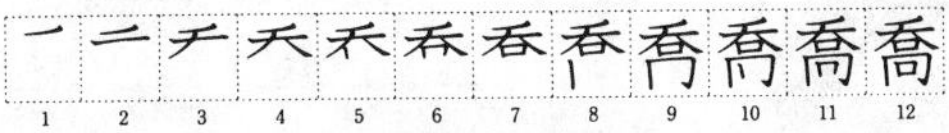

4-8 夭

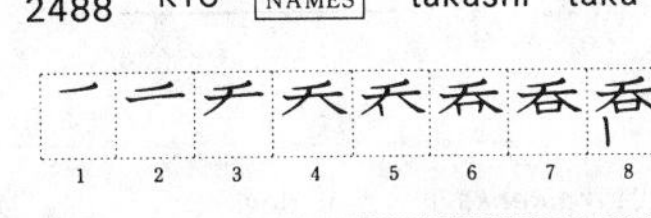

▶**TALL**

COMPOUNDS
❶ **tall**—said esp. of trees
喬木 *kyōboku* tall tree, forest tree
❷ [archaic] boast
喬志 *kyōshi* self-conceit, pride

NAMES
喬 *takashi* male name
義喬 *yoshitaka* male name

SYNONYMS
❶ **high**
高 HIGH → 2097
峻 high and steep → 412

暑 2489

▶**SUMMER HEAT** ▶**HOT**
nonstandard for 暑 2473

4-9 日

4-9 止

歳 2490

歳 歳 歳

SAI SEI toshi▲

(CH) 岁 suì

Radical	Strokes
止 77	13-4-9
Grade	**Freq**
Jōyō	521

2 - 4 - 9

歳 13

▶YEAR ▶AGE SUFFIX

COMPOUNDS

❶ **year**
歳末 *saimatsu* year end
歳費 *saihi* annual expenditure
歳月 *saigetsu* time
歳入 *sainyū* revenue, annual income
歳暮 *seibo* end of the year; year-end present
❷ [also 才 *sai* 3410] **age suffix**
一歳 *issai* one year old
何歳 *nansai* how old, what age
万歳 *banzai* Banzai! / Hurrah! / Long live...!
❸ [rare] literary expression for Jupiter
歳星 *saisei* Jupiter

KUN

【**toshi 歳**】[now usu. 年] year

SPECIAL READINGS

二十歳(=二十) *hatachi* 20 years old

SYNONYMS

❶ **year**
年 YEAR → 2035
❷ **age**
才 AGE SUFFIX → 3410
齢 AGE → 1895
令 age → 1995
年 years → 2035
寿 life span → 3557

HOMOPHONES

toshi ⇨ 年 2035 齢 1895

NOTE

⇨ see USAGE note at 年 2035

4-9 止

歳 2491

▶YEAR ▶AGE SUFFIX
nonstandard for 歳 2490

4-9 ⺍

愛 2492

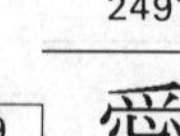

愛 愛 愛

AI ito(shii)▲

(CH) 爱 ài

Radical	Strokes
心 61	13-4-9
Grade	**Freq**
Jōyō-4	524

2 - 4 - 9

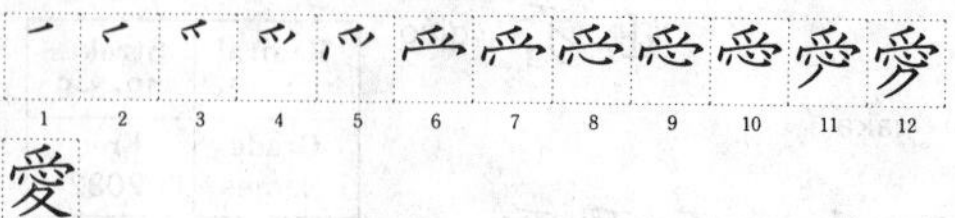

愛 13

▶LOVE

COMPOUNDS

❶ⓐ [also suffix] **love, affection**
ⓑ *Buddhism* love
愛情 *aijō* love, affection
愛憎 *aizō* love and hate
博愛 *hakuai* philanthropy
母性愛 *boseiai* maternal love
同性愛 *dōseiai* homosexual love, lesbianism
慈愛 *jiai* affection, love, benevolence
❷ⓐ **love, have affection for**
ⓑ **love (a person of the opposite sex), care deeply for**
愛児 *aiji* one's beloved [favorite] child
愛犬家 *aikenka* lover of dogs
愛国心 *aikokushin* patriotism, nationalism
愛車 *aisha* one's own car [bicycle]
愛妻 *aisai* one's beloved wife
愛人 *aijin* lover
愛欲 *aiyoku* love and lust, sexual passion
恋愛 *ren'ai* love (for the opposite sex)
❸ (have a strong liking for) **love, like, be fond of**
愛好する *aikō suru* love, be fond of
愛用する *aiyō suru* use habitually
愛読する *aidoku suru* read with pleasure
愛唱する *aishō suru* love to sing
❹ⓐ be reluctant to part with

ⓑ cherish, treasure, hold dear
愛惜する *aiseki suru* be reluctant (to part)
割愛する *katsuai suru* part with (something), give up; omit (reluctantly)
愛護 *aigo* protection
自愛する *jiai suru* take care of oneself
❺ used phonetically for *ai* in the transliteration of foreign words
愛蘭 *airurando* Ireland

INDEPENDENT

【ai 愛】 love, tender passion; charity
神の愛 *kami no ai* divine love
【aisuru 愛する】 love, care for, be fond of

KUN

【ito(shii) 愛しい】 darling, beloved, dear

SYNONYMS

❶ **love**
情 love → 482
恋 LOVE (for the opposite sex) → 2098
艶 ROMANCE → 1908
❷ & ❸ **love and like**
恋 LOVE (the opposite sex) → 2098
好 LIKE → 208

USAGE

愛 ai 恋 ren
★Though both 恋 and 愛 mean love, the former is mostly restricted to love between man and woman while the latter is a general term roughly equivalent to the English word *love*.

惹
2493 JAKU hi(ku)

Ⓒⓗ 惹 rě

Radical	Strokes
心 61	13-4-9
Grade	Freq
Reference	
2-4-9	

4-9

COMPOUNDS

❶ [now usu. 引く *hiku*]
ⓐ draw (attention or sympathy), attract, catch
ⓑ catch (a cold)
惹き付ける *hikitsukeru* attract, charm
注意を惹く *chūi o hiku* draw attention
風邪を惹いている *kaze o hiite iru* have a cold
❷ cause, induce
惹起する *jakki suru* bring about, cause, provoke

HOMOPHONES

hiku ⇨ 引 181 弾 572 退 3094 挽 427 轢 1662

NOTE

⇨ see USAGE note at 引 181

慕
2494

▶**RAISE**
nonstandard for 募 2316

4-9

著
2495

▶**AUTHOR** ▶**CONSPICUOUS**
nonstandard for 著 2300

4-9

葵
2496

▶**MALLOW**
nonstandard for 葵 2317

4-9

萬
2497

▶**TEN THOUSAND**
nonstandard for 万 2936

4-9

落
2498

▶**FALL**
nonstandard for 落 2318

4-9

4-9 艹

萩
2499

▶ ***HAGI***
nonstandard for 萩 2319

4-9 艹

葬
2500

▶ **FUNERAL**
nonstandard for 葬 2320

4-9 艹

葉
2501

▶ **LEAF**
nonstandard for 葉 2321

4-9 艹

蒸

incorrect stroke count ⇨ see 2511
(nonstandard for 蒸 2334)

4-9 去

棄

incorrect classification ⇨ see 2137

4-9 ⺍

誉 譽

2502 YO homa(re) ho(meru)▲

CH 誉 yù

Radical	Strokes
言 149	13-7-6
Grade	**Freq**
Jōyō	1278
2-4-9	

Stroke order: 1 2 3 4 5 6 7 8 9 10 11 12 13

▶ **HONOR**

COMPOUNDS

❶ **honor, good reputation, fame, glory**
名誉 *meiyo* honor, glory; dignity
栄誉 *eiyo* honor, glory, distinction
声誉 *seiyo* fame, reputation, honor and distinction, credit

❷ praise
毀誉褒貶 *kiyohōhen* praise or censure, criticisms

KUN

【homa(re) 誉れ】 honor, glory, fame
国の誉れ *kuni no homare* national glory

【ho(meru) 誉める】 [usu. 褒める, sometimes also 賞める] praise, commend, admire, compliment, eulogize
誉め称える *hometataeru* admire, applaud, praise

SYNONYMS

❶ **repute**
声 reputation → 2198
名 NAME → 2169
望 popularity → 2742

❶ **great respect**
栄 GLORY → 2574
光 honor → 2391

HOMOPHONES

homeru ⇨ 賞 2618 褒 2144

NOTE

⇨ see USAGE note at 褒 2144

蓋
2503 GAI futa ō(u) keda(shi)

CH 盖 gài gě

Radical	Strokes
艹 140	14-4-10
Grade	Freq
Reference	
2-4-10	

4-10 艹

COMPOUNDS

❶ⓐ cover, lid
ⓑ counter for lid-shaped objects such as bamboo hats
頭蓋骨 *zugaikotsu* cranium
無蓋車 *mugaisha* open freight car
蓋 *futa* cover, lid
鍋蓋 *nabebuta* pot lid; *nabebuta*, 'lid' radical (亠)
笠三蓋 *kasa sangai* three bamboo hats
❷ [usu. 覆う *ōu*]
ⓐ [original meaning] cover, veil
ⓑ hide, conceal, screen
ⓒ enfold, envelop
空を蓋う *sora o ōu* cover up the sky
❸ probable
蓋然性 *gaizensei* probability
蓋し *kedashi* probably

HOMOPHONES

ōu ⇨ 覆 2726 被 1163 蔽 2523 掩 489

NOTE

⇨ see USAGE note at 覆 2726

蒲
2504 HO FU gama kaba kama

CH 蒲 pú

Radical	Strokes
艹 140	14-4-10
Grade	Freq
Reference	
2-4-10	

4-10 艹

COMPOUNDS

ⓐ cattail, reed mace
ⓑ resembling a cattail
蒲団 *futon* [now usu. 布団] *futon*, bedquilt
蒲柳の質 *horyū no shitsu* delicate [fragile] health
蒲 *gama* (=*kama*) cattail, reed mace
蒲焼き *kabayaki* eels split and broiled in soy
蒲鉾 *kamaboko* steamed fish paste
蒲公英 *tanpopo* dandelion

蒙
2505 MŌ kōmu(ru)

CH 蒙 méng mēng měng

Radical	Strokes
艹 140	14-4-10
Grade	Freq
Reference	
2-4-10	

4-10 艹

COMPOUNDS

❶ ignorance
蒙昧 *mōmai* ignorance
啓蒙 *keimō* enlightenment, instruction
蒙 *mō* ignorance
❷ Mongolia, Mongolian
蒙古 *mōko* Mongolia
❸ [also 被る *kōmuru*] be subjected to, undergo, receive, sustain
損害を蒙る *songai o kōmuru* suffer a loss

HOMOPHONES

kōmuru ⇨ 被 1163

NOTE

⇨ see USAGE note at 被 1163

4-10 艹

蒐
2506 SHŪ

CH 搜 sōu

Radical	Strokes
艹 140	14-4-10
Grade Reference	Freq
2-4-10	

COMPOUNDS

● [now replaced by 収 198 or 集 2771] collect, gather
蒐集(＝収集)する *shūshū suru* collect, gather, accumulate
蒐荷(＝集荷) *shūka* collection of cargo, cargo booking

4-10 艹

蒼
2507 SŌ ao(i)

CH 苍 cāng

Radical	Strokes
艹 140	14-4-10
Grade Reference	Freq
2-4-10	

COMPOUNDS

❶ [original meaning] deep blue; green; gray
蒼天 *sōten* blue [azure] sky
蒼生 *sōsei* people, the masses
暮色蒼然として迫る *Boshoku sōzen to shite semaru* Evening dusk is fast gathering
古色蒼然たる *koshoku-sōzentaru* antique-looking
❷ [usu. 青い] (pale in appearance) green, pale
蒼白な *sōhaku na* pale, pallid
顔が蒼い *kao ga aoi* look pale [green]
❸ old, hoary
❹ [now replaced by 倉 *sō* 2104] hurried, flurried
蒼惶(＝倉皇)として *sōkō to shite* in great haste

HOMOPHONES

aoi ⇨ 青 2430

NOTE

⇨ see USAGE note at 青 2430

4-10 艹

墓
2508

▶GRAVE
nonstandard for 墓 2332

4-10 艹

蓄
2509

▶STORE UP
nonstandard for 蓄 2333

4-10 艹

慈
2510

▶AFFECTIONATE
nonstandard for 慈 2339

4-10 艹

蒸
2511

▶STEAM ▶EVAPORATE
nonstandard for 蒸 2334

4-10 艹

幕
2512

▶CURTAIN ▶SHOGUNATE
nonstandard for 幕 2335

蓉 2513 **▶COTTON ROSE** nonstandard for 蓉 2337 4-10 艹

蔭 incorrect stroke count ⇨ see 2517 4-10 艹

夢 2514 **▶DREAM** nonstandard for 夢 2336 4-10 艹

態 熊 incorrect classification ⇨ see 10-4 4-10 能

暴 2515 BŌ BAKU aba(ku) aba(reru) Ⓒⓗ 暴 bào 4-11 日

Radical	Strokes
日 72	15-4-11
Grade	**Freq**
Jōyō-5	757
2-4-11	

▶VIOLENT

COMPOUNDS

❶ⓐ (acting with destructive force) **violent, rough, wild, cruel, harsh, tyrannical**

ⓑ act violently, rage about

暴力 *bōryoku* violence, force
暴行 *bōkō* act of violence, assault
暴走 *bōsō* reckless driving; running wild
暴言 *bōgen* offensive [abusive] language
暴君 *bōkun* tyrant, despot
暴風 *bōfū* storm, violent wind
乱暴 *ranbō* violence, roughness; rape
横暴な *ōbō na* arbitrary, tyrannical, despotic
暴動 *bōdō* riot, disturbance, uprising
暴徒 *bōto* rioters, mobsters, insurgents

❷ **sudden, abrupt**

暴落 *bōraku* slump, crash, heavy decline (in prices)
暴発 *bōhatsu* spontaneous discharge, accidental gun discharge
暴騰 *bōtō* sudden (price) rise

❸ **unrestrained, inordinate, wild, excessive, irrational**

暴飲 *bōin* heavy drinking
暴利 *bōri* excessive profits, usury

❹ⓐ [formerly also 曝 *baku* 1099] disclose, divulge, expose

ⓑ [original meaning, now archaic] expose to the sun

暴露 *bakuro* exposure, disclosure

❺ strike with one's bare hands

暴虎馮河 *bōkohyōga* foolhardy courage

INDEPENDENT

【bō 暴】 violence

KUN

【aba(ku) 暴く】 [sometimes also 発く] disclose (a secret), expose (a crime), lay bare, divulge

秘密を暴く *himitsu o abaku* disclose a secret

【aba(reru) 暴れる】 act violently, rage about

暴れ回る *abaremawaru* rampage, run riot
暴れ出す *abaredasu* grow restive, begin to act violently
暴れ者 *abaremono* rowdy, roughneck
暴れ馬 *abareuma* restive horse, runaway

SYNONYMS

❶ⓐ **violent**

猛 FIERCE → 537
荒い WILD → 2260

❷ **sudden**

急 SUDDEN → 2092
激 sudden → 776
突 abruptly → 2230

❸ **rash**

荒 WILD → 2260
濫 EXCESSIVE → 801
乱 excessive → 1260
妄 RASH → 2016
盲 BLIND → 2053
滅 unreasonable → 660

❹ⓐ **reveal**
露 EXPOSE → 2818
発 reveal → 2565
披 OPEN OUT → 305
顕 MANIFEST → 1806
現 cause to appear → 968

USAGE

abaku
暴く
[sometimes also 発く] disclose (a secret), expose (a crime), lay bare, divulge
発く
[usu. 暴く] same as 暴く

HOMOPHONES

abaku ⇨ 発 2565

COMPOUND FORMATION

暴虎馮河 *bōkohyōga*
暴虎馮河 'foolhardy courage' refers to killing a tiger (虎) with one's bare hands (暴 ❺) and wading across (馮) the river (河).

4-11
止

齒 ▶TOOTH

2516

nonstandard for 歯 2476

Radical	Strokes
齒 211	15-15-0
Grade	**Freq**
Variant	
2-4-11	

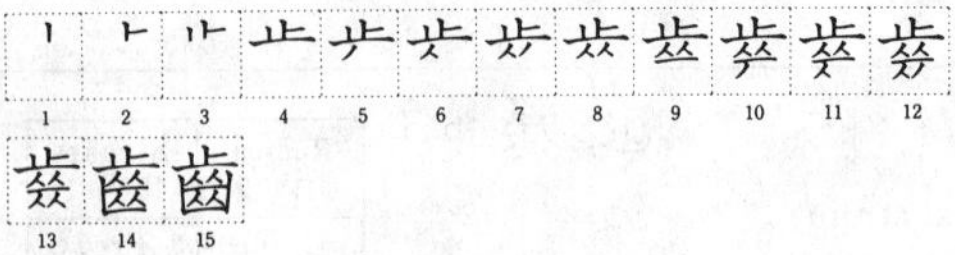

RADICAL 211

Standard form: 齒 *ha* 'tooth' (齧)
Left variants: 𧾷 𧾷 *hahen* (齢 齠 齶)
Variant: 歯 *ha*
Description: used in characters related to teeth or actions using teeth

---

4-11
艹

蔭

2517 IN kage

CH 荫 yīn yìn

Radical	Strokes
艹 140	15-4-11
Grade	**Freq**
Reference	
2-4-11	

COMPOUNDS

❶ [also 陰 *kage*] [in the form of お蔭 *okage*] grace, favor
お蔭で *okage de* thanks to; due to
お蔭様で皆元気です *Okagesama de mina genki desu* We are all well and fine, thank you

❷ [now usu. 陰 *kage*] [original meaning] shade
木蔭 *kokage* shade of a tree, bower

❸ [now usu. 陰 *kage*]
ⓐ back side, reverse side
ⓑ behind the scenes
カーテンの蔭に隠れる *kāten no kage ni kakureru* hide behind a curtain
蔭口 *kageguchi* backbiting

HOMOPHONES

kage ⇨ 陰 541 影 1889

NOTE

⇨ see USAGE note at 影 1889

4-11
艹

慕 ▶ADORE

2518

nonstandard for 慕 2353

4-11
艹

暮 ▶DUSK ▶LIVE

2519

nonstandard for 暮 2354

蔦 2520

▶JAPANESE IVY
nonstandard for 蔦 2355

4-11 艹

曇 2521

DON kumo(ru)

Ⓒ㫰 tán

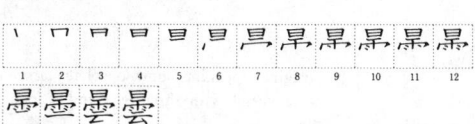

Radical	Strokes
日 72	16-4-12
Grade	Freq
Jōyō	865
2-4-12	

4-12 日

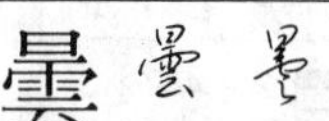

▶CLOUDY

COMPOUNDS

● [original meaning] **cloudy**
曇天 *donten* cloudy weather
晴曇 *seidon* fine and cloudy weather

KUN

【**kumo(ru)** 曇る】 become cloudy, cloud up; become dim, fog up, be blurred; be gloomy

曇り(=曇) *kumori* cloudiness, cloudy weather
曇り空 *kumorizora* cloudy sky [weather]
曇り勝ち *kumorigachi* cloudy
薄曇り *usugumori* slightly cloudy weather
花曇り *hanagumori* cloudy weather in springtime
曇りガラス *kumorigarasu* frosted glass, stained glass

蕃 2522

BAN HAN

Ⓒ蕃 fán fān

Radical	Strokes
艹 140	16-4-12
Grade	Freq
Reference	
2-4-12	

4-12 艹

COMPOUNDS

❶ⓐ [now also 蛮 *ban* 2129] barbarian, savage
ⓑ barbarian, aboriginal; foreign
蕃夷 *ban'i* savages, barbarians
蕃族 *banzoku* savage tribe
蕃人 *banjin* savage, barbarian; aboriginal
蕃社 *bansha* aborigines' village
蕃椒 *banshō* [rare] Guinea pepper

❷ [now replaced by 繁 *han* 2853] thrive, luxuriate, grow thick
蕃殖する *hanshoku suru* breed, propagate, increase, multiply

蔽 2523

HEI ō(u)

Ⓒ蔽 bì

Radical	Strokes
艹 140	16-4-12
Grade	Freq
Reference	
2-4-12	

4-12 艹

COMPOUNDS

❶ cover
遮蔽 *shahei* shield, cover, screen; *elec* shielding
隠蔽する *inpei suru* conceal, cover up, hide
掩蔽 *enpei* cover, obscuration

❷ [now usu. 覆う *ōu*] [original meaning] screen, shield, hide
事実を蔽う *jijitsu o ōu* disguise a fact

HOMOPHONES

ōu ⇨ 覆 2726 被 1163 蓋 2503 掩 489

NOTE

⇨ see USAGE note at 覆 2726

4-13 ⺫

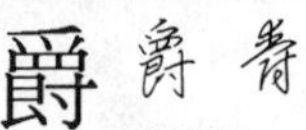
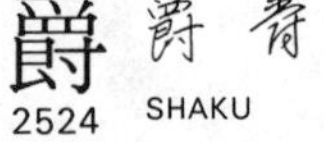

爵 2524 SHAKU

CH 爵 jué

Radical	Strokes
⺤ 87	17-4-13
Grade	**Freq**
Jōyō	1929
2-4-13	

▶**RANK OF NOBILITY**

COMPOUNDS

❶ **rank of nobility, peerage, court rank**
爵位 *shakui* rank of nobility
伯爵 *hakushaku* count, earl
男爵 *danshaku* baron
授爵 *jushaku* ennoblement

❷ [original meaning, now obsolete] ancient wine vessel with three legs and a loop handle

SYNONYMS

❶ **nobility**
公 nobleman → 1974
侯 FEUDAL LORD → 98

4-13 ⺾

薄 2525 ▶**THIN**
nonstandard for 薄 2370

4-13 ⺾

蕗 2526 ▶**BUTTERBUR**
nonstandard for 蕗 2372

4-13 ⺾

薦 2527 ▶**RECOMMEND**
nonstandard for 薦 2373

4-13 ⺾

薪 2528 ▶**FIREWOOD**
nonstandard for 薪 2374

4-13 ⺾

舊 incorrect stroke count ⇨ see 2531
(nonstandard for 旧 14)

4-14 ⺾

藉 2529 SHA SEKI

CH 藉 jí jiè

Radical	Strokes
⺾ 140	18-4-14
Grade	**Freq**
Reference	
2-4-14	

COMPOUNDS

❶ [now replaced by 謝 *sha* 1620] console, solace
慰藉料 *isharyō* consolation money

❷ borrow, use (as a pretext)
...に藉口して *...ni shakō shite* under the pretext of...

❸ disorder, confusion
狼藉 *rōzeki* disorder; violence

薰 2530

▶**BALMY**
nonstandard for 薫 2371

4-14 艹

藍

incorrect stroke count ⇨ see 2534
(nonstandard for 藍 2381)

4-14 艹

薦

incorrect stroke count ⇨ see 2527
(nonstandard for 薦 2373)

4-14 艹

藏

incorrect stroke count ⇨ see 2537
(nonstandard for 蔵 2364)

4-14 艹

舊 2531

▶**FORMER**
nonstandard for 旧 14

4-14 艹

藝 2532

▶**ART**
nonstandard for 芸 2209

4-15 艹

藩 2533

▶**FEUDAL DOMAIN**
nonstandard for 藩 2379

4-15 艹

藍 2534

▶**INDIGO**
nonstandard for 藍 2381

4-15 艹

藤 2535

▶**WISTERIA**
nonstandard for 藤 2382

4-15 艹

藥 2536

▶**DRUG**
nonstandard for 薬 2375

4-15 艹

藏 2537

▶**STORE**
nonstandard for 蔵 2364

4-15 艹

繭 2538

▶**COCOON**
nonstandard for 繭 2380

4-15 艹

藻 2539

▶**ALGAE**
nonstandard for 藻 2384

4-16 艹

4-17 艹

蘭 2540

▶**ORCHID**

nonstandard for 蘭 2383

5-1 丞

丞 2541

JŌ NAMES suke

1 2 3 4 5 6

㊥ 丞 chéng

Radical	Strokes
一 1	6-1-5
Grade	**Freq**
Names	2068
2-5-1	

▶**AIDE**

COMPOUNDS

ⓐ aide, assistant officer (in ancient China)

ⓑ [original meaning, now archaic] aid, assist, help

丞相 *jōshō* prime minister (in ancient China)

NAMES

雪之丞 *yukinojō* male name

兵丞 *hyōsuke* male name

SYNONYMS

ⓐ **assistant**

補 assistant → 1194

5-2 田

男 2542

DAN NAN otoko o▲

1 2 3 4 5 6 7

㊥ 男 nán

Radical	Strokes
田 102	7-5-2
Grade	**Freq**
Jōyō-1	237
2-5-2	

▶**MAN**

COMPOUNDS

❶ [original meaning] **man, male**

男子 *danshi* boy, young man, man

男性 *dansei* male, man

男女 *danjo* men and women, both sexes

男尊女卑 *dansonjohi* predominance of men over women, sexism

男児 *danji* boy, son; man

美男子 *bidanshi* (=*binanshi*) handsome man

下男 *genan* male servant, manservant

❷ **son**—used esp. to indicate order of birth

一男二女 *ichinan-nijo* one son and two daughters

長男 *chōnan* eldest son

三男 *sannan* third son

❸ⓐ baron

ⓑ title after names of barons

男爵 *danshaku* baron

吉川男 *yoshikawadan* Baron Yoshikawa

INDEPENDENT

【**dan** 男】*literary* man; son

KUN

【**otoko** 男】man, male; adult male; lover, paramour; manservant, fellow, guy; manliness, honor

男らしい *otokorashii* manly, masculine

男の子 *otoko no ko* boy, baby boy

男前 *otokomae* man's looks

男盛り *otokozakari* prime of manhood

雪男 *yukiotoko* abominable snowman

【**o** 男】

① *elegant* man, male

男の子 *o no ko* man

② [in compounds] the larger or stronger of two

男滝(=雄滝) *odaki* the greater waterfall (of the two)

益荒男(=丈夫) *masurao* manly [brave] man

SYNONYMS

❶ **man**

郎 YOUNG MAN → 1289

雄 MALE → 1008

夫 male adult → 3460

翁 OLD MAN → 2108

❷ **offspring**

息 son → 2647

惣 eldest son → 2780

子 CHILD → 3390

孤 orphan → 356

嫡 LEGITIMATE CHILD → 680

娘 DAUGHTER → 406

女 daughter → 3418

姫 DAUGHTER OF NOBLE BIRTH → 407

❸ **noblemen**

子 viscount → 3390

伯 COUNT → 59

侯 marquis → 98
公 duke → 1974

HOMOPHONES

o ⇨ 雄 1008 牡 839

NOTE

⇨ see USAGE note at 雄 1008
⇨ see COMPOUND FORMATION for 男前 *otokomae* ⇨ 前 2266

貝 2543 BAI▲ kai

Ⓒ𝐇 贝 bèi

Radical	Strokes
貝 154	7-7-0
Grade	**Freq**
Jōyō-1	1520
2 - 5 - 2	

5-2 目

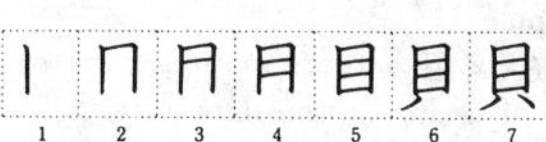

RADICAL 154
Standard form: 貝 *kai* 'cowry' (買 貨 貴)
Variant: 貝 *kaihen* (財 貯 贈)
Description: used in characters related to valuables or money

▶SHELLFISH

COMPOUNDS

❶ **shellfish**
魚貝 *gyobai* fish and shellfish
❷ **seashell, shell**
貝独楽 *baigoma* shell top
❸ [original meaning, now archaic] cowries used as currency in ancient China
貝貨 *baika* (ancient) shell money

INDEPENDENT

【bai 貝】 kind of shellfish

KUN

【kai 貝】
① [sometimes also 介 1967] shellfish
貝類 *kairui* shellfish
貝柱 *kaibashira* adductor muscle
赤貝 *akagai* arc shell
巻き貝 *makigai* roll-shell; snail
魚貝類(＝魚介類) *gyokairui* marine products
②ⓐ seashell, shell
ⓑ trumpet shell
貝殻 *kaigara* shell
貝細工 *kaizaiku* shellwork

SYNONYMS

❶ &【kai】① **fish**
魚 FISH → 2127
❷ &【kai】②ⓐ **shells**
殻 SHELL (of any kind) → 1490
甲 SHELL (of animals) → 3481

見 2544 KEN mi(ru) mi(eru) mi(seru)

Ⓒ𝐇 见 jiàn xiàn

Radical	Strokes
見 147	7-7-0
Grade	**Freq**
Jōyō-1	45
2 - 5 - 2	

5-2 目

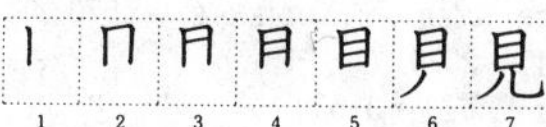

RADICAL 147
Standard form: 見 *miru* 'see' (視 覚 覧)
Description: used in characters related to seeing

▶SEE

COMPOUNDS

❶ⓐ [original meaning] **see, look at, observe**
ⓑ become seen, come into view, appear
見物 *kenbutsu* sightseeing, visit
見学 *kengaku* tour [field trip] for study and observation
見聞する *kenbun suru* experience, observe
拝見する *haiken suru* have the honor of seeing, see, look at, inspect
一見 *ikken* a look, a glance; apparently
外見 *gaiken* outward appearance
見当 *kentō* estimate, guess; aim
発見 *hakken* discovery, revelation, detection
露見 *roken* discovery, detection, exposure
❷ (grant or be granted an audience) see (someone), interview, give [be given] an audience
会見 *kaiken* interview, audience
接見する *sekken suru* receive, give an interview
朝見 *chōken* audience with the Emperor
❸ **view, personal opinion**
見解 *kenkai* opinion, view

見地 *kenchi* standpoint, viewpoint
意見 *iken* opinion, view; admonition
偏見 *henken* prejudice, biased view, narrow view

INDEPENDENT

【ken 見】 view, opinion
皮相の見 *hisō no ken* shallow view

KUN

【mi(ru) 見る】
①ⓐ see, look (at), have a look
ⓑ [sometimes also 観る] view (flowers), watch (a movie), see, observe, appreciate
ⓒ read (casually), skim through
見つける *mitsukeru* find (out), locate, spot, turn up
見本 *mihon* sample, specimen
見通し *mitōshi* perspective, vista; prospect, outlook
見合い *miai* meeting with a view to marriage; looking at each other
見当たる *miataru* be found
見事(＝美事)な *migoto na* splendid, admirable, beautiful
花見 *hanami* flower [cherry blossom] viewing
② look over, examine; look up, refer to
見積もり *mitsumori* estimate, assessment
見極める *mikiwameru* see through, discern; ascertain, grasp
下見 *shitami* preliminary inspection; preview
書類を見る *shorui o miru* examine papers
③ take (for), regard (as), judge, estimate
見なす *minasu* regard as, presume
見込み *mikomi* hope, promise; prospect, possibility
④ⓐ attend (to), manage
ⓑ [sometimes also 看る] take care of, look after
事務を見る *jimu o miru* attend to business
面倒見が良い *mendōmi ga yoi* take good care of, be very helpful
⑤ experience, undergo
憂き目を見る *ukime o miru* have a bitter experience, have a hard time of it
血を見る争い *chi o miru arasoi* struggle with bloodshed
⑥ [following the TE-form of verbs]
ⓐ try (doing something), do and see
ⓑ [usu. in the form of 見ると *miru to*] upon doing, when (the action is achieved), once
やって見る *yatte miru* try (to do)
聞いて見ましょう *Kiite mimashō* Let's ask (him)
知って見ると詰まらない *Shitte miru to tsumaranai* When you know it, its charm is gone

【mi(eru) 見える】 be visible, be seen; look like, seem, appear; [honorific] come; be able to see
見え *mie* appearance; [usu. 見栄] show, ostentation, vanity; [usu. 見得] pose, posture
今夜は星が見える *Kon'ya wa hoshi ga mieru* Stars can be seen tonight
若く見える *wakaku mieru* look [seem] young
病気だと見える *byōki da to mieru* seem to be sick
先生が見えた *Sensei ga mieta* The teacher has come
夜でも見える目 *yoru de mo mieru me* eyes capable of seeing in the dark

【mi(seru) 見せる】 show, let see, disclose, exhibit; make (a thing) look like, give an air of, pretend; make (a person) experience [understand]; [following the TE-form of verbs] be determined to
見せ物 *misemono* show, exhibition
古く見せる *furuku miseru* impart an ancient appearance
見せ掛ける *misekakeru* make (a thing) look like, pretend
見せしめ *miseshime* lesson, warning
彼を負かして見せる *Kare o makashite miseru* I'll win him over

SYNONYMS

❶ⓐ see and look
観 VIEW → 1880
目 look → 3043
覧 LOOK OVER → 2854
眺 LOOK OUT OVER → 1171
望 LOOK AFAR → 2742
仰 LOOK UP → 48
顧 LOOK BACK → 1900
視 REGARD → 972
看 WATCH → 3220
察 INSPECT → 2347

❷ meet
謁 BE GRANTED AN AUDIENCE → 1570
会 MEET → 2020
遭 MEET WITH → 3159
遇 ENCOUNTER → 3135

❸ opinion
観 VIEW (conception) → 1880
説 opinion → 1547
論 opinion → 1574

【miseru】
○ show
示 SHOW → 1936
呈 PRESENT → 2189

USAGE

❶ miru
見る
①ⓐ see, look (at), have a look
ⓑ [sometimes also 観る] view (flowers), watch (a movie), see, observe, appreciate

ⓒ read (casually), skim through
② look over, examine; look up, refer to
③ take (for), regard (as), judge, estimate
④ⓐ attend (to), manage
ⓑ [sometimes also 看る] take care of, look after
⑤ experience, undergo
⑥ [following the TE-form of verbs]
ⓐ try (doing something), do and see
ⓑ [usu. in the form of 見ると *miru to*] upon doing, when (the action is achieved), once

観る
[usu. 見る] view (flowers), watch (a movie), see, observe, appreciate

看る
[usu. 見る] take care of, look after

診る
examine (a patient)

❷ **mie**

見え
① appearance
② [usu. 見栄] show, ostentation, vanity
③ [usu. 見得] pose, posture

見栄
[sometimes also 見え] show, ostentation, vanity

見得
[sometimes also 見え] pose, posture

HOMOPHONES

miru ⇨ 観 1880 看 3220 診 1504
mie ⇨ 見栄 2544, 2574 見得 2544, 477

NOTE

⇨ see COMPOUND FORMATION for 見事(＝美事) *migoto* ⇨ 事 3567

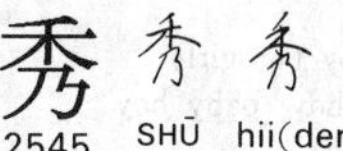

2545 SHŪ hii(deru)

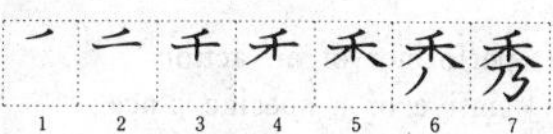

Radical	Strokes
禾 115	7-5-2
Grade	**Freq**
Jōyō	952
2 - 5 - 2	

5-2 禾

▶**EXCELLENT**

COMPOUNDS

❶ **excellent, supreme**
秀逸 *shūitsu* supreme excellence
秀歌 *shūka* excellent [superb] tanka, gem of tankas
秀麗な *shūrei na* graceful, beautiful, handsome
優秀な *yūshū na* excellent, superior, best

❷ **genius, prodigy**
秀才 *shūsai* (person of) genius
俊秀 *shunshū* genius, prodigy
閨秀 *keishū* accomplished lady

INDEPENDENT

【shū 秀】 Excellent (school mark), A

KUN

【hii(deru) 秀でる】 excel, surpass
英語に秀でる *eigo ni hiideru* excel in English

SYNONYMS

❶ **excellent and superior**
優 SUPERIOR → 177
英 DISTINGUISHED → 2238
傑 outstanding → 155
逸 exceptional → 3120
名 first-rate → 2169
上 of upper grade → 3404
絶 without match → 1353
卓 PROMINENT → 2064
快 splendid → 245
妙 MARVELOUS → 239

❷ **wise and talented persons**
俊 BRILLIANT PERSON → 102
才 person of talent → 3410
通 well-informed person → 3109
博 DOCTOR → 151
賢 wise man → 2839
哲 sage → 2738

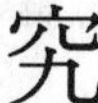
incorrect stroke count ⇨ see 2554

5-2 禾

究 incorrect classification ⇨ see 2203

5-2 穴

5-2 立

辛

incorrect classification ⇨ see 2038

5-2 臼

兒

incorrect stroke count ⇨ see 2625
(nonstandard for 児 2546)

5-2 旧

児 兒 児 児

2546 JI NI ko▲ -ko▲ -(k)ko▲

CH 儿 ér

Radical	Strokes
儿 10	7-2-5
Grade	**Freq**
Jōyō-4	561
2-5-2	

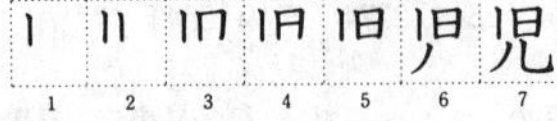

▶CHILD

COMPOUNDS

❶ⓐ [also suffix] **child (of any age), youngster, youth**
ⓑ [original meaning] **small child, infant**
ⓒ (offspring of man) child, son, daughter
児童 *jidō* child, juvenile
園児 *enji* kindergarten child
小児科 *shōnika* (department of) pediatrics
健康児 *kenkōji* healthy child
幼児 *yōji* young child, infant
男児 *danji* boy, son; man
二歳児 *nisaiji* two-year old child
乳児 *nyūji* infant, baby, suckling
育児 *ikuji* infant rearing, nursing of children
胎児 *taiji* embryo, fetus
児孫 *jison* children and grandchildren; descendants
愛児 *aiji* one's beloved [favorite] child
❷ [suffix] person
革命児 *kakumeiji* man of revolutionary temperament
熱血児 *nekketsuji* hot-blooded man

KUN

【ko 児】[now usu. 子] (boy or girl) child, kid, youngster
良い児 *ii ko* good boy (or girl)
男の児 *otoko no ko* boy, baby boy
【-ko -児, -(k)ko -っ児】
[usu. 子]
ⓐ person, performer of an action
ⓑ [suffix] native of a specific place
売り児 *uriko* shopgirl, sales clerk

SPECIAL READINGS

稚児 *chigo* infant, child

SYNONYMS

❶ⓐ & ❶ⓑ child
子 CHILD → 3390
童 CHILD (young person) → 2130
幼 young child → 191
坊 SONNY → 233

HOMOPHONES

ko ⇨ 子 3390 娘 406 仔 33 小 7
-ko ⇨ 子 3390

NOTE

⇨ see USAGE note at 子 3390

5-2 奴

努 努 努

2547 DO tsuto(meru)

CH 努 nǔ

Radical	Strokes
力 19	7-2-5
Grade	**Freq**
Jōyō-4	694
2-5-2	

く	久	女	女フ	奴	努	努
1	2	3	4	5	6	7

▶EXERT

COMPOUNDS

● [original meaning] **exert (oneself), make efforts, endeavor**
努力 *doryoku* endeavor, effort, exertion
努力家 *doryokuka* hard worker
努力賞 *doryokushō* prize awarded for a person's effort

KUN

【tsuto(meru) 努める】[sometimes also 勉める] endeavor, make efforts, try hard, work diligently
努めて *tsutomete* with effort, as much as possible
極力努める *kyokuryoku tsutomeru* do one's best

SYNONYMS

● **exert oneself**

勉 ENDEAVOR → 3318
励 make efforts → 1119
勤 work diligently → 1818
尽 use all one's strength → 3050
精 put one's heart into → 1366

HOMOPHONES

tsutomeru ⇨ 勉 3318 勤 1818 務 1173

NOTE

⇨ see USAGE note at 勤 1818

克 incorrect classification ⇨ see 2046

5-2 古

労 労 労 労
2548 RŌ

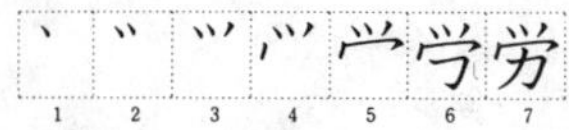

CH 劳 láo

Radical	Strokes
力 19	7-2-5
Grade	**Freq**
Jōyō-4	285
2 - 5 - 2	

5-2 ⺍

▶LABOR

COMPOUNDS

❶ⓐ (work hard) **labor, toil, do manual work**

ⓑ (hard work) **labor, toil, work, trouble, pains**

労働 *rōdō* (manual) labor, toil
労働者 *rōdōsha* laborer, worker
労務 *rōmu* labor, work, service
労力 *rōryoku* trouble, labors, efforts
勤労 *kinrō* labor, work, service
苦労 *kurō* difficulties, trouble, hardships, labor

❷ abbrev. of 労働組合 *rōdō kumiai* or 労働者 *rōdōsha*: **workers' union, labor union, labor, laborer**

労資 *rōshi* capital and labor
労相 *rōshō* Labor Minister
国労 *kokurō* National Railway Workers' Union

❸ **fatigue, become fatigued**

疲労 *hirō* fatigue
心労 *shinrō* cares, worries, anxiety

❹ meritorious deed, service

功労 *kōrō* meritorious deed, (distinguished) services

❺ express one's appreciation, reward, bring comfort to

慰労する *irō suru* acknowledge a person's services

❻ [formerly 撈 735] drag for, dredge up, fish for

漁労 *gyorō* fishing, fishery

INDEPENDENT

【rō 労】labor, trouble, service

労を謝する *rō o shasuru* thank a person for his [her] trouble

【rōsuru 労する】labor, exert oneself, toil

SYNONYMS

❶ⓐ **work**

働 WORK → 153
稼 WORK (for a living) → 1230
勤める serve (in an office) → 1818
仕 SERVE → 34

ⓑ **work and employment**

務 DUTY → 1173
任 OFFICE → 53
役 SERVICE (esp. public) → 244
勤 SERVICE (employment) → 1818
業 WORK → 2612
職 EMPLOYMENT → 1425

❷ **organized bodies**

組 union → 1337
連 federation → 3103
講 fraternity → 1619
院 INSTITUTION → 454
体 BODY → 71
団 BODY → 3053
協 association → 93
会 SOCIETY → 2020

❸ **tire**

疲 TIRED → 3278

学 incorrect stroke count ⇨ see 2555

5-2 ⺍

5-2 呉

呉 呉 呉 呉

2549 GO ku(reru)▲

ⒸⒽ 呉 wú

Radical	Strokes
口 30	7-3-4
Grade	**Freq**
Jōyō	1424
2-5-2	

▶**KINGDOM OF WU**

COMPOUNDS

❶ **Kingdom of Wu, name of an ancient Chinese state in the Three Kingdom period** (220-280 A.D.)

呉国 *gokoku* Kingdom of Wu
呉音 *goon* Wu reading of Chinese characters
呉越 *goetsu* Wu and Yue, two rival states in ancient China
呉越同舟 *goetsu-dōshū* bitter enemies in the same boat

❷ **originating from China or the Chinese mainland**

呉服 *gofuku* dry goods; drapery
呉須 *gosu* asbolite; *gosu* porcelain

INDEPENDENT

【**go** 呉】Kingdom of Wu

KUN

【**ku(reru)** 呉れる】give (to the speaker); give (to an inferior, animal or plant); [following the TE-form of verbs] do something for (the benefit of the speaker)

それを呉れ *Sore o kure* Give it to me
乞食に金を呉れてやる *kojiki ni kane o kurete yaru* give money to a beggar
彼が仕事をして呉れた *Kare ga shigoto o shite kureta* He did the work for me
呉れ呉れも宜しく *Kuregure mo yoroshiku* Give my best regards to (her)

SYNONYMS

❶ **China**

唐 Cathay → 3115
華 CHINA → 2283
漢 CHINESE → 657
支 China → 1979
中 People's Republic of China → 3451
台 Taiwan → 2005

【**kureru**】

○ **give**

下 give (to inferior or speaker) → 3378
上 give (to superior or others) → 3404
与 GIVE → 3421
授 CONFER → 492
賜 DEIGN TO GIVE → 1585
贈 PRESENT A GIFT → 1634
賄 BRIBE → 1529
呈 PRESENT → 2189
進 present to a superior → 3121

5-2 镸

镸

2550 ▶**LONG** ▶**CHIEF**

nonstandard for 長 2556

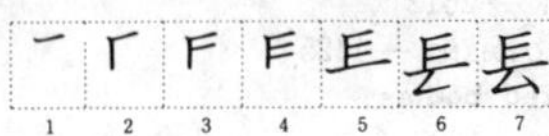

Radical	Strokes
镸 168	7-7-0
Grade	**Freq**
Variant	
2-5-2	

RADICAL 168

variant of 長 *nagai* 'long'

⇨ see 長 2556 for radical description

5-2 丘

兵 兵 兵

2551 HEI HYŌ

ⒸⒽ 兵 bīng

Radical	Strokes
八 12	7-2-5
Grade	**Freq**
Jōyō-4	386
2-5-2	

▶**SOLDIER**

COMPOUNDS

❶ⓐ [also suffix] **soldier, private, rank and file**

ⓑ [suffix] (rank of) private

兵士 *heishi* soldier

兵卒 *heisotsu* private, common soldier
兵隊 *heitai* soldier; troops
兵舎 *heisha* barracks
カナダ兵 *kanadahei* Canadian soldier
騎兵 *kihei* cavalry soldier, cavalry
上等兵 *jōtōhei* private first class
❷ⓐ **the military, army, soldiery**
ⓑ military, military science
兵事 *heiji* military affairs
兵役 *heieki* military service
兵糧 *hyōrō* army provisions, food
徴兵 *chōhei* conscription, enlistment, draft
兵学 *heigaku* military science, strategy, tactics
兵法 *hyōhō* (=*heihō*) art of war, strategy
❸ weapons, arms; sword
兵器 *heiki* arms, weapon, ordnance
造兵 *zōhei* manufacture of arms
白兵 *hakuhei* unsheathed sword
❹ war, battle
兵備 *heibi* war preparations
兵禍 *heika* ravages of war

INDEPENDENT

【hei 兵】 soldier; troops, army
兵を向ける *hei o mukeru* send an army

SYNONYMS

❶ **soldiers and warriors**
卒 private → 2055
士 MILITARY MAN → 3405
武 warrior → 3210
侍 SAMURAI → 85
❷ⓐ **armed forces**
軍 ARMY → 2080
勢 forces → 2857
隊 PARTY → 625
ⓑ **military**
武 MILITARY → 3210

具 具 具 具

2552 GU

Ⓒⓗ 具 jù

Radical	Strokes
八 12	8-2-6
Grade	**Freq**
Jōyō-3	564
2-5-3	

5-3 目

▶IMPLEMENT

COMPOUNDS

❶ [also suffix]
ⓐ (utensil for work) **implement, tool, utensil**
ⓑ (article serving to equip) **implement, equipment, gear, fittings, fixtures, outfit**
道具 *dōgu* tool, utensil, implement; furniture; theatrical appurtenances; tool, means; ingredient
器具 *kigu* utensil, implement, appliance
用具 *yōgu* tool, instrument, appliance; outfit
工具 *kōgu* tool, implement
治具 *jigu* jig
絵の具 *enogu* coloring materials, colors, oils, paint
文房具 *bunbōgu* stationery, writing materials
家具 *kagu* furniture
寝具 *shingu* bedclothes, bedding
仏具 *butsugu* Buddhist altar fittings
筆記具 *hikkigu* writing materials
装身具 *sōshingu* personal ornaments [outfit]
❷ [original meaning] **possess, be possessed of, be endowed with**
具備する *gubi suru* be endowed [equipped] with, possess
具象する *gushō suru* embody, express concretely
具体的な *gutaiteki na* concrete, definite, specific
具足 *gusoku* completeness; armor, coat of mail
❸ in detail, fully
具申書 *gushinsho* full [detailed] report
具陳 *guchin* formal statement
具現 *gugen* incarnation, embodiment
❹ counter for sets of articles, as suits of armor
鎧一具 *yoroi ichigu* a suit of armor
❺ unclassified compounds
具合(=工合) *guai* condition, state; health; manner, way

INDEPENDENT

【gu 具】 tool, means; ingredient
政争の具とする *seisō no gu to suru* make a political issue of (something)
具の無いスープ *gu no nai sūpu* soup with no ingredients
寿司の具 *sushi no gu* ingredients for sushi
【gusuru 具する(=倶する)】 possess; take (retainers) with (one), be followed by

SYNONYMS

❶ **machines and tools**
器 INSTRUMENT → 2713
械 MECHANICAL CONTRIVANCE → 961
機 MACHINE → 1076
儀 measuring instrument → 169
鏡 OPTICAL INSTRUMENT → 1766

❷ **possess**
有 HAVE → 2983
蔵 own → 2364
持 HOLD → 374
属 BELONG TO → 3145
享 ENJOY → 2051

NOTE
⇨ see COMPOUND FORMATION for
道具 *dōgu* ⇨ 道 3134
治具 *jigu* ⇨ 治 335
文房具 *bunbōgu* ⇨ 房 1946

5-3
禾

委 委 委
2553 I yuda(neru)▲

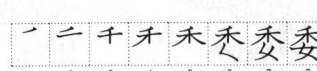

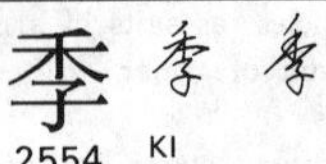

CH 委 wěi wēi

Radical	Strokes
女 38	8-3-5
Grade	**Freq**
Jōyō-3	138
2-5-3	

▶COMMIT

COMPOUNDS

❶ [original meaning] **commit, entrust, leave to, delegate**
委員会 *iinkai* committee
委託する *itaku suru* entrust with, charge with, consign
委任する *inin suru* entrust, delegate, commit
委嘱する *ishoku suru* charge, commission [entrust] with
❷ abbrev. of 委員 *iin* or 委員会 *iinkai*: committeeperson, committee
教委 *kyōi* Board of Education
中労委(=中央労働委員会) *chūrōi* (=*chūō rōdō iinkai*) Central Labor Relations Committee
❸ details
委細 *isai* details, particulars
委曲 *ikyoku* details, circumstances
❹ [also 萎 2478] wither, weaken, decline
委縮 *ishuku* withering, atrophy; being crestfallen
❺ abandon
委棄 *iki* waiver

INDEPENDENT
【**isuru 委する**】commit, entrust, delegate

KUN
【**yuda(neru) 委ねる**】commit, entrust, leave to, delegate; give [yield] oneself to
全権を委ねる *zenken o yudaneru* entrust (a person) with power of attorney (to do something for one)
激情に身を委ねる *gekijō ni mi o yudaneru* yield oneself to passion

SYNONYMS
❶ **commit**
託 ENTRUST → 1455
預 DEPOSIT → 1042
任 LEAVE TO → 53
嘱 CHARGE WITH → 718

5-3
禾

季 季 季
2554 KI

CH 季 jì

Radical	Strokes
子 39	8-3-5
Grade	**Freq**
Jōyō-4	920
2-5-3	

▶SEASON

COMPOUNDS

❶ⓐ (division of the year) **season, quarter**
ⓑ (period of time) season
季節 *kisetsu* season
季候 *kikō* season
季刊 *kikan* quarterly publication
夏季 *kaki* summer, summer season
四季 *shiki* the four seasons
ボーナス季 *bōnasuki* bonus season
年季 *nenki* one's term of service
雨季(=雨期) *uki* rainy season
❷ feature of a season term in haiku poetry, season word
季語 *kigo* season word (in haiku)
❸ [archaic] youngest or fourth born child
季子 *kishi* last child
❹ end of a period
季春 *kishun* late spring

INDEPENDENT
【**ki 季**】season

SYNONYMS
❶ **time periods**
節 SEASON OF THE YEAR → 2691

候 SEASON (time of year) → 119
期 TERM → 1704
間 INTERVAL → 3323
刻 POINT OF TIME → 1267
般 period of time → 1317
暇 FREE TIME → 1012
頃 TIME → 144
時 TIME → 924

NOTE
★do not confuse with 李 2398

秀 incorrect stroke count ⇨ see 2545

空 突 incorrect classification ⇨ see 3–5

要 incorrect stroke count ⇨ see 2634
(nonstandard for 要 2635)

点 incorrect classification ⇨ see 2065
(nonstandard for 点 2084)

学 學 學◊ 斈◊ 学 斈 Ⓒⓗ 学 xué

2555 GAKU mana(bu)

Radical	Strokes
子 39	8-3-5
Grade	**Freq**
Jōyō-1	23
2-5-3	

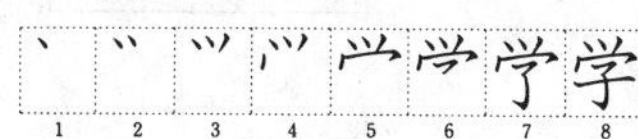

▶**STUDY**
▶**EDUCATIONAL INSTITUTION**

COMPOUNDS

❶ **study, learn**
学習する *gakushū suru* study, learn
学力 *gakuryoku* scholarship, scholastic ability
独学 *dokugaku* self-study, self-teaching
留学 *ryūgaku* studying abroad
見学 *kengaku* tour [field trip] for study and observation

❷ⓐ [also suffix] **branch of study, -ology**
ⓑ **learning, study, education, scholarship, knowledge, science**
文学 *bungaku* literature, letters
医学 *igaku* medical science, medicine
数学 *sūgaku* mathematics
化学 *kagaku* chemistry
物理学 *butsurigaku* physics, physical science
学問 *gakumon* learning, study
学会 *gakkai* institute, academy, learned society; meeting of a research organization
学識 *gakushiki* learning, scholarship
学芸 *gakugei* arts and sciences: culture
学術 *gakujutsu* science, learning; arts and sciences

❸ [original meaning] **educational institution, school, university, academy**
学園 *gakuen* educational institution, school
学校 *gakkō* school, college
学院 *gakuin* institute, academy
学長 *gakuchō* college president, rector; dean
小学校 *shōgakkō* elementary [primary] school
中学 *chūgaku* junior high school
大学 *daigaku* university, college
私学 *shigaku* private [nongovernmental] school [college, university]
通学する *tsūgaku suru* attend [go to] school
入学する *nyūgaku suru* enter a school, matriculate

❹ **scholar, student**
学究 *gakkyū* scholar, student
学生 *gakusei* student
学者 *gakusha* scholar, learned man
学割 *gakuwari* student discount
学界 *gakkai* academic circles [world]
先学 *sengaku* scholars of the past, senior scholar
宿学 *shukugaku* renowned scholar
後学 *kōgaku* junior scholar; future reference
篤学 *tokugaku* love of learning, devotion to one's studies

INDEPENDENT

【gaku 学】 studies, learning
学が有る *gaku ga aru* have learning, be edu-

cated
学の独立 *gaku no dokuritsu* freedom of learning

KUN

【mana(bu) 学ぶ】learn, study, take lessons
学び *manabi* learning, study

SYNONYMS

❶ **learn and study**
考 study → 3196
習 LEARN → 2667
研 RESEARCH → 1132
究 STUDY EXHAUSTIVELY → 2203
攻 specialize → 242
❷ⓐ **branch of study**
門 field → 888
科 SUBJECT OF STUDY → 1138
ⓑ **learning and knowledge**
業 studies → 2612
識 KNOWLEDGE → 1639
知 knowledge → 1127
文 culture → 1962
❸ **schools**
校 SCHOOL → 929
塾 PRIVATE SCHOOL → 2860
院 INSTITUTION → 454
大 UNIVERSITY → 3416
高 high school → 2097
中 junior high school → 3451
小 elementary school → 7
園 kindergarten → 3156
❹ **students and followers**
生 STUDENT → 3497
卒 graduate student → 2055
門 pupil → 888
弟 disciple → 2044
徒 FOLLOWER → 416

5-3 長

長 镸 長 長 ㊥ 长 cháng zhǎng

2556 CHŌ naga(i)

Radical	Strokes
長 168	8-8-0
Grade	**Freq**
Jōyō-2	19
2 - 5 - 3	

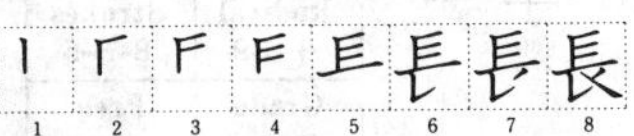

RADICAL 168

Standard form: 長 *nagai* 'long'
Left variant: 镸 *nagai*
Description: used in characters related to longness

▶**LONG** ▶**CHIEF**

COMPOUNDS

❶ⓐ [also prefix] (of considerable extent) **long**
ⓑ length
ⓒ tall
長編 *chōhen* long section (as of a novel or a film)
長打 *chōda* long hit
長距離 *chōkyori* long distance
身長 *shinchō* stature, height
測長機 *sokuchōki* length measuring machine
長身 *chōshin* tall figure, high stature
❷ [also prefix] (of considerable duration) **long**
長期 *chōki* long period
長寿 *chōju* long life, longevity
長時間 *chōjikan* long time
❸ grow (up), develop, prolong
成長 *seichō* growth
延長 *enchō* extension, prolongation, continuation
❹ [also suffix] **chief, head, president, director, chairman**
長官 *chōkan* director, administrator, chief
課長 *kachō* section chief [head]
市長 *shichō* mayor
船長 *senchō* (ship) captain
社長 *shachō* president (of a company)
会長 *kaichō* president (of a society)
議長 *gichō* chairman, president (of the senate)
酋長 *shūchō* chieftain
裁判長 *saibanchō* presiding [chief] judge
❺ strong point, merit, advantage, superiority
長所 *chōsho* strong point, merit
特長 *tokuchō* strong point, forte
一長一短 *itchō ittan* merits and demerits, strong and weak points
❻ eldest, older; old, senior
長男 *chōnan* eldest son
長女 *chōjo* eldest daughter
年長 *nenchō* seniority
❼ useless, wasteful
長物 *chōbutsu* useless thing, white elephant
❽ *music* major
長調 *chōchō* major key
長音階 *chōonkai* major scale
❾ abbrev. of 長門 *nagato*, old name for western Yamaguchi Prefecture

長州 *chōshū* Choshu, Nagato
薩長 *satchō* Satsuma and Choshu

INDEPENDENT

【chō 長】 chief, head, leader; strong point, merit; superiority
一家の長 *ikka no chō* head of a family
...より一日の長が有る *...yori ichijitsu no chō ga aru* be ahead of (someone)

【chōzuru (＝chōjiru) 長ずる(＝長じる)】 grow; be older; excel

KUN

【naga(i) 長い】
ⓐ (of considerable extent) long, lengthy, prolonged
ⓑ (of considerable duration) long
長さ *nagasa* length
長引く *nagabiku* be prolonged, drag on
長持ちする *nagamochi suru* last [keep] long, endure

SYNONYMS

❷ of long duration
永 ETERNAL → 1937
久 OF LONG DURATION → 3384
恒 permanent → 367

❸ grow
成 grow up → 3537
生 grow → 3497
育 grow → 2050
発 develop → 2565
伸 expand → 70
展 UNFOLD → 3111

❹ leaders
主 MASTER → 1938
王 KING → 3439
頭 HEAD → 1604
首 LEADER → 2265
領 leader → 1224

USAGE

nagai
長い
ⓐ (of considerable extent) long, lengthy, prolonged
ⓑ (of considerable duration) long
永い
(lasting forever) eternal, everlasting, long

HOMOPHONES

nagai ⇨ 永 1937

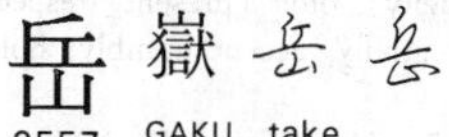

2557 GAKU take

CH 岳 yuè

Radical	Strokes
山 46	8-3-5
Grade	Freq
Jōyō	1034
2-5-3	

5-3 丘

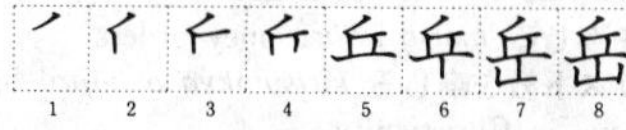

▶**HIGH MOUNTAIN**

COMPOUNDS

❶ high mountain, mountain, peak
岳友会 *gakuyūkai* mountaineering club
山岳 *sangaku* mountains
❷ Mt. Fuji
岳麓 *gakuroku* foot of Mt. Fuji
富岳 *fugaku* Mt. Fuji
❸ wife's father, father-in-law
岳父 *gakufu* one's wife's father

KUN

【take 岳】 high mountain, mountain, peak; suffix after names of mountains
浅間の岳 *asama no take* Mt. Asama
朝日岳 *asahidake* Mt. Asahi

SYNONYMS

❶ mountains
峰 PEAK → 411
山 MOUNTAIN → 2940

妻 妻 妻

2558 SAI tsuma

CH 妻 qī

Radical	Strokes
女 38	8-3-5
Grade	Freq
Jōyō-5	732
2-5-3	

5-3 妻

▶**WIFE**

COMPOUNDS

● [original meaning] **wife**
妻子 *saishi* one's wife and children, one's family
夫妻 *fusai* husband and wife, Mr. and Mrs., married couple
恐妻家 *kyōsaika* henpecked husband, man

bossed by his wife
正妻 *seisai* lawful [legal] wife

INDEPENDENT

【sai 妻】 wife, my wife

KUN

【tsuma 妻】 wife, one's wife; gable
人妻 *hitozuma* married woman, another's wife
稲妻 *inazuma* lightning
切妻 *kirizuma* gable

SYNONYMS

● **wives**
奥 wife → 2824
内 wife → 3466
室 wife (esp. of persons of rank) → 2254
嫡 legitimate wife → 680
婦 married woman → 469
嫁 BRIDE → 635
寡 widow → 2344

NOTE

⇨ see COMPOUND FORMATION for 稲妻 *inazuma* ⇨ 稲 1219

5-3 夫

奉

2559 HŌ BU tatematsu(ru)

Ⓒⓗ 奉 fèng

Radical	Strokes
大 37	8-3-5
Grade	**Freq**
Jōyō	1280
2 - 5 - 3	

▶DEDICATE

COMPOUNDS

❶ [original meaning] **dedicate (esp. to a deity), offer, present, proffer**
奉納する *hōnō suru* dedicate (to a deity), offer
奉呈する *hōtei suru* dedicate, present, offer (to a high personage)
奉献する *hōken suru* offer (to a shrine)
奉加 *hōga* donation
奉幣 *hōhei* offering a wand with hemp and paper streamers to a Shinto god
奉灯 *hōtō* dedicated lantern

❷ⓐ **reverentially, respectfully, humbly**—honorific term expressing respect toward the person addressed, esp. the Emperor of Japan
ⓑ **serve reverentially, serve under (a master)**
奉読する *hōdoku suru* read reverentially
奉還 *hōkan* restoration to the Emperor
奉答 *hōtō* reply to the Throne
奉賀 *hōga* respectful congratulation
奉仕する *hōshi suru* attend, serve
奉公 *hōkō* public duty [service]; domestic service, apprenticeship
奉職する *hōshoku suru* be in the service of

❸ obey reverentially, accept humbly
奉行 *bugyō* magistrate, chief of an administrative department
信奉する *shinpō suru* believe in, have faith
遵奉(=順奉)する *junpō suru* observe, obey, follow
供奉 *gubu* attendance (on the Emperor in his travels); attendant

❹ [formerly 捧 *hō* 491] hold in both hands
奉持する *hōji suru* hold up, bear

INDEPENDENT

【hōjiru (=hōzuru) 奉じる(=奉ずる)】 dedicate (esp. to a deity), offer [present] respectfully; obey reverentially, accept humbly; hold in both hands
神前に舞を奉じる *shinzen ni mai o hōjiru* dedicate a dance to a god
命を奉じる *mei o hōjiru* obey orders
キリスト教を奉じる *kirisutokyō o hōjiru* believe in Christianity
国旗を奉じる *kokki o hōjiru* hold up the national flag

KUN

【tatematsu(ru) 奉る】
① [honorific] dedicate, offer [present] respectfully
国王に書を奉る *kokuō ni sho o tatematsuru* address a memorial to the King
② revere at a distance
長老として奉る *chōrō to shite tatematsuru* revere (a person) as one's leader; kick (a person) upstairs
③ [in compounds] do respectfully
無事の御帰国を謹んで賀し奉ります *Buji no gokikoku o tsutsushinde gashitatematsurimasu* We respectfully tender our congratulations on your safe return home

SYNONYMS

❶ **offer**
献 OFFER (esp. to a superior) → 1785
納 offer (as to a god) → 1300
供 OFFER (to a person or god) → 88
提 PRESENT → 591
貢 offer tribute → 2281

❷ **respectful**
謹 RESPECTFULLY → 1618
恭 RESPECTFUL → 2459
拝 HUMBLY → 303

某 2560

BŌ nanigashi▲

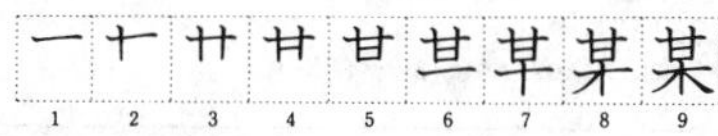

Ⓒ 某 mǒu

Radical	Strokes
木 75	9-4-5
Grade	**Freq**
Jōyō	1649
2 - 5 - 4	

5-4 甘

▶A CERTAIN

COMPOUNDS

ⓐ [also prefix] **a certain, one**
ⓑ [suffix] a certain person

某日 *bōjitsu* a certain day
某氏 *bōshi* a certain person
某国 *bōkoku* a certain country
某女 *bōjo* Ms. So-and-so
某某 *bōbō* so-and-so
某所 *bōsho* a certain place
某高校 *bōkōkō* a certain high school
某博士 *bōhakase* Dr. X
山田某 *yamadabō* a certain Mr. Yamada

INDEPENDENT

【bō 某】 a certain person
某の仕業 *bō no shiwaza* the work [doings] of so-and-so

KUN

【nanigashi 某】 a certain person; some (amount)
山田某 *yamada nanigashi* a certain Mr. Yamada
某かの金 *nanigashi ka no kane* some money, a certain sum of money

SYNONYMS

ⓐ **a certain**
一 ONE → 3341

胃 2561

I

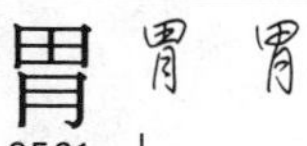

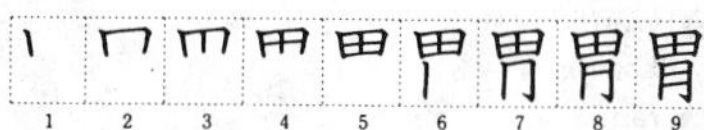

Ⓒ 胃 wèi

Radical	Strokes
月 130	9-4-5
Grade	**Freq**
Jōyō-4	1563
2 - 5 - 4	

5-4 田

▶STOMACH

COMPOUNDS

ⓐ [original meaning] **stomach**
ⓑ [prefix] gastric

胃腸 *ichō* stomach and intestines [bowels]
胃腸病学 *ichōbyōgaku* gastroenterology
胃弱 *ijaku* dyspepsia, indigestion
胃袋 *ibukuro* stomach
胃下垂 *ikasui* gastric ptosis
胃炎 *ien* gastritis
胃潰瘍 *ikaiyō* stomach ulcer
胃癌 *igan* gastric cancer
胃カタル *ikataru* gastric catarrh

INDEPENDENT

【i 胃】 stomach; paunch

SYNONYMS

● **internal organs**
腸 INTESTINES → 1033
心 HEART → 11
肺 LUNG → 916
肝 LIVER → 841
胆 GALLBLADDER → 919

畏 2562

I oso(reru) kashiko(maru)

Ⓒ 畏 wèi

Radical	Strokes
田 102	9-5-4
Grade	**Freq**
Reference	
2 - 5 - 4	

5-4 田

COMPOUNDS

❶ⓐ [now usu. 恐れる *osoreru*] [original meaning] be overawed, stand in awe, fear
ⓑ be awed, humble oneself, listen respectful-

ly
畏怖 *ifu* awe, fear, dread, fright
畏縮する *ishuku suru* shrink, flinch, wince
畏れ多くも *osoreōku mo* graciously
神を畏れる *kami o osoreru* fear God
畏まる *kashikomaru* be awed, humble oneself, listen respectfully; sit straight [respectfully]
畏まりました *Kashikomarimashita* Certainly, Sir
畏くも *kashikoku mo* graciously
❷ respect, revere
畏友 *iyū* one's respected friend
畏敬 *ikei* awe and respect, reverence

HOMOPHONES
osoreru ⇨ 恐 2650

NOTE
⇨ see USAGE note at 恐 2650

5-4
田

界 堺◇

2563 KAI

Ⓒⓗ 界 jiè

Radical	Strokes
田 102	9-5-4
Grade	**Freq**
Jōyō-3	187
2-5-4	

▶**WORLD** ▶**BOUNDS**

COMPOUNDS

❶ [also suffix] (segment of society engaged in same activity) **world, circles**
業界 *gyōkai* industry, business world
政界 *seikai* political world
各界 *kakkai* every sphere of life, various circles
学界 *gakkai* academic circles [world]
経済界 *keizaikai* economic world, financial circles
芸能界 *geinōkai* entertainment world, world of show business
❷ⓐ (physical world) **world**
ⓑ [also suffix] (sphere or realm) world, kingdom, realm
世界 *sekai* world, universe
他界する *takai suru* die, pass away
外界 *gaikai* external world
界隈 *kaiwai* neighborhood, vicinity
自然界 *shizenkai* realm of nature
動物界 *dōbutsukai* animal kingdom
❸ *phys* field
界磁極 *kaijikyoku* field pole
視界 *shikai* field of vision, visibility
電界 *denkai* electric field
❹ⓐ [original meaning] **bounds, boundary, border**
ⓑ *math* bound
界面 *kaimen* interface
限界 *genkai* boundary, limit, bounds
境界 *kyōkai* boundary, border
臨界点 *rinkaiten* critical point [temperature]
下界 *kakai* lower bound
❺ *geol* group
古生界 *koseikai* Paleozoic group

INDEPENDENT
【kai 界】 *math* bound

SYNONYMS
❶ **circles**
壇 circles → 754
❷ **world**
世 WORLD → 3496
❸ **range**
野 FIELD → 1485
場 field (*phys*, *psychol*) → 558
圏 SPHERE → 3148
域 area → 465
範 range → 2709
程 EXTENT → 1190
❹ⓐ **edges and boundaries**
境 BOUNDARY → 676
辺 border → 3029
端 edge → 1221
縁 EDGE → 1386
際 VERGE → 714
涯 OUTER LIMITS → 512

思

2564 SHI omo(u)

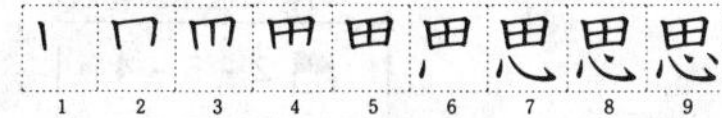

Ⓒ思 sī

Radical	Strokes
心 61	9-4-5
Grade	**Freq**
Jōyō-2	121
2 - 5 - 4	

5-4 田

▶**THINK**

COMPOUNDS

❶ⓐ [original meaning] **think, consider, regard, believe, feel**
ⓑ thought, idea
思考 *shikō* thinking, thought, consideration
思惟 *shii* thinking, speculation
思案する *shian suru* think, consider, reflect
思索する *shisaku suru* think, speculate
思慮 *shiryo* consideration, thought, discretion
思想 *shisō* thought, conception, idea
意思 *ishi* intention, purpose
不思議な *fushigi na* strange, mysterious, wonderful
思潮 *shichō* trend of thought
❷ think of someone, care for, love
思慕する *shibo suru* love dearly, yearn for
相思 *sōshi* mutual love

KUN

【omo(u) 思う】
①ⓐ think, consider; regard
ⓑ (believe) think, believe, hold
ⓒ (consider likely) think, expect, hope; guess
思い *omoi* thought, idea; feelings; desire, wish; heart
思い付く *omoitsuku* think of, hit upon
私は彼が間違っていると思います *Watashi wa kare ga machigatte iru to omoimasu* I believe that he is wrong
思わず *omowazu* unintentionally; unconsciously; unexpectedly
② wish, desire, want
思惑 *omowaku* thought, intention, purpose
思い切る *omoikiru* resign oneself to, give up; resolve, determine
したいと思う *shitai to omou* want to do something
③ [sometimes also 想う] (recall a thought) think, recollect, recall, remember
思い出 *omoide* recollections, memory, reminiscences
思い出す *omoidasu* recollect, recall, remember
④ think of, care for, love
⑤ wonder

SYNONYMS

❶ⓐ & 【omou】①ⓐ think and consider
考 THINK → 3196
存 hold an opinion → 2982
案 think out → 2270
想 CONCEIVE → 2828
慮 CONSIDER → 3266
勘 take into consideration → 1777
量 weigh → 2471
惟 MEDITATE → 481
省 INTROSPECT → 2449

USAGE

omou
思う
①ⓐ think, consider; regard
ⓑ (believe) think, believe, hold
ⓒ (consider likely) think, expect, hope; guess
② wish, desire, want
③ [sometimes also 想う] (recall a thought) think, recollect, recall, remember
④ think of, care for, love
⑤ wonder
想う
[usu. 思う] (recall a thought) think, recollect, recall, remember

HOMOPHONES

omou ⇨ 想 2828

NOTE

⇨ see COMPOUND FORMATION for 思索 *shisaku* ⇨ 索 2455

5-4
癶

発 發 癸 𤼵

2565 HATSU HOTSU ta(tsu)▲ aba(ku)▲

CH 发 fā

Radical	Strokes
癶 105	9-5-4
Grade	Freq
Jōyō-3	38
2-5-4	

▶START ▶EMIT

COMPOUNDS

❶ (bring into being) **start, originate, initiate, give rise to, generate, produce**
発端 *hottan* origin, beginning, outset
発会 *hakkai* opening of a meeting; first meeting
発足する *hossoku* (=*hassoku*) *suru* start, be inaugurated
発刊する *hakkan suru* publish, issue
発動する *hatsudō suru* exercise, invoke; move, put in motion
発電 *hatsuden* generation of electricity; telegraphing
発熱 *hatsunetsu* generation of heat; attack of fever
発癌 *hatsugan* carcinogenesis, production of cancer
発想 *hassō* conception; *music* expression
発明 *hatsumei* invention, contrivance

❷ (come into being) **start up, arise, become, occur**
発生する *hassei suru* occur, happen; grow, breed
発効する *hakkō suru* become effective, take effect, come into force
発狂する *hakkyō suru* go mad, become insane [crazy]
発奮(=発憤)する *happun suru* be stimulated, be inspired, be roused
発作 *hossa* fit, attack, seizure
自発性 *jihatsusei* spontaneity, spontaneousness

❸ⓐ (begin forward movement) **start, depart, set out, leave**
ⓑ departure
ⓒ **suffix indicating time or point of departure**
発着 *hatchaku* departure and arrival
発車する *hassha suru* start, leave, depart
出発 *shuppatsu* departure, starting
先発する *senpatsu suru* start in advance, go ahead, precede
始発 *shihatsu* first departure; starting station
八時発の列車 *hachijihatsu no ressha* train leaving at eight
ニューヨーク発の便 *nyūyōkuhatsu no bin* flight from New York

❹ⓐ (give off) **emit, send out, issue, discharge, dispatch, transmit**
ⓑ (put forth or distribute officially) **issue, promulgate, publish**
ⓒ suffix indicating point [time] of origin or transmission (of cables)
発光 *hakkō* radiation, luminescence
発汗 *hakkan* perspiring, sweating
発音 *hatsuon* pronunciation
蒸発 *jōhatsu* evaporation, volatilization; mysterious disappearance
発信 *hasshin* sending a letter [telegram]
発送 *hassō* sending, forwarding, shipping
発言する *hatsugen suru* speak, utter
発行 *hakkō* publication, issue; (of bank notes) issue
発布 *happu* proclamation, promulgation
発令する *hatsurei suru* announce officially, issue
発売する *hatsubai suru* sell, put on the market
発注 *hatchū* ordering
発禁(=発売禁止) *hakkin* (=*hatsubai kinshi*) prohibition of sale, suppression (of a book)
濫発(=乱発) *ranpatsu* excessive issue
ロンドン発の報道 *rondonhatsu no hōdō* news under a London dateline

❺ⓐ [original meaning] (emit a projectile) **discharge, fire, shoot**
ⓑ (be discharged) **discharge, explode**
ⓒ counter for shots or rounds
発射する *hassha suru* discharge, shoot, launch
発砲 *happō* firing, discharge of a gun
連発 *renpatsu* running fire, volley
暴発 *bōhatsu* spontaneous discharge, accidental gun discharge
不発 *fuhatsu* misfire
爆発する *bakuhatsu suru* explode, burst; erupt
一触即発 *isshokusokuhatsu* touch-and-go situation, hair-trigger crisis
三発撃つ *sanpatsu utsu* fire three shots

❻ **reveal, open up, disclose, make public, announce**
発表する *happyō suru* announce, make public, publish
発見 *hakken* discovery, revelation, detection
発掘する *hakkutsu suru* dig, excavate
発揮する *hakki suru* display, exhibit, demonstrate

発露 *hatsuro* expression, manifestation
摘発する *tekihatsu suru* expose, lay bare, disclose
❼ **develop, grow**
発達 *hattatsu* development, growth, progress
発育する *hatsuiku suru* grow, develop
発展する *hatten suru* expand, grow, develop; prosper
開発する *kaihatsu suru* develop, open out; enlighten
❽ counter for engines
双発機 *sōhatsuki* twin-engined plane
❾ counter for blows
一発食らわす *ippatsu kurawasu* give a blow
❿ abbrev. of 発電所 *hatsudensho*: power generation plant
原発 *genpatsu* nuclear power plant
⓫ [formerly also 撥 *hatsu* 734] rebound, repel, repulse
発条 *hatsujō* (=*bane*) spring
反発 *hanpatsu* repulsion, repelling; rally (of the market); opposition
⓬ [formerly 撥 *hatsu* 734] stir, stir up
挑発 *chōhatsu* provocation, incitement, excitement, stimulation
⓭ [formerly 醱 *hatsu* 1645] brew, ferment
発酵 *hakkō* fermentation, zymosis
⓮ [formerly 潑 *hatsu* 741] lively, energetic
活発な *kappatsu na* lively, active
⓯ collect, conscript
徴発する *chōhatsu suru* commandeer, requisition

INDEPENDENT

【hassuru 発する】 emit, radiate, send forth; issue (orders), promulgate; originate in; utter
放射線を発する *hōshasen o hassuru* emit radioactive rays
喪を発する *mo o hassuru* put (the court) into mourning
源を湖水に発する *minamoto o kosui ni hassuru* rise [flow] from a lake
奇声を発する *kisei o hassuru* raise a queer voice, squeak

KUN

【ta(tsu) 発つ】 [now usu. 立つ] start (on a journey), leave, depart
東京を発つ *tōkyō o tatsu* leave Tokyo
【aba(ku) 発く】 [usu. 暴く] disclose (a secret), expose (a crime), lay bare, divulge
秘密を発く *himitsu o abaku* disclose a secret

SYNONYMS

❶ **create**
起 generate → 3307
生 produce → 3497
創 CREATE → 1815
作 compose → 68
❶ **begin**
就 SET ABOUT → 1694
始 BEGIN → 281
-出す begin to do → 3498
-掛ける start doing → 493
起 start → 3307
開 OPEN → 3321
創 initiate → 1815
肇 ORIGINATE → 2799
❸ⓐ **leave and set forth**
出 GO OUT → 3498
去 GO AWAY → 2156
離 leave → 1836
退 RETREAT → 3094
撤 WITHDRAW → 738
❹ⓐ **emit**
出 PUT OUT → 3498
放 radiate → 853
排 DISCHARGE → 490
射 SHOOT → 1458
噴 SPOUT → 717
吐 SPEW → 203
❺ⓐ **shoot**
射 SHOOT → 1458
撃 fire → 2863
ⓑ **explode**
爆 EXPLODE → 1101
❻ **reveal**
露 EXPOSE → 2818
暴 disclose → 2515
披 OPEN OUT → 305
顕 MANIFEST → 1806
現 cause to appear → 968
❼ **grow**
伸 expand → 70
展 UNFOLD → 3111
成 grow up → 3537
長 grow (up) → 2556
生 grow → 3497
育 grow → 2050

HOMOPHONES

tatsu ⇨ 立 1992 建 3090 起 3307 経 1331
abaku ⇨ 暴 2515

NOTE

⇨ see USAGE notes at 立 1992 and 暴 2515
⇨ see COMPOUND FORMATION for 発達 *hattatsu* ⇨ 達 3139

5-4
白

皇 皇 皇

2566 KŌ Ō

CH 皇 huáng

Radical	Strokes
白 106	9-5-4
Grade	Freq
Jōyō-6	879
2-5-4	

▶**EMPEROR**

COMPOUNDS

❶ⓐ **emperor, sovereign**

ⓑ **related to the emperor, imperial**

皇帝 *kōtei* emperor
皇后 *kōgō* empress, queen
皇妃 *kōhi* empress, queen
皇太子 *kōtaishi* crown prince
天皇 *tennō* Emperor of Japan
皇居 *kōkyo* Imperial Palace
皇室 *kōshitsu* Imperial Family
皇子 *ōji* imperial prince

❷ Japan under imperial rule

皇典 *kōten* Japanese classics
皇国 *kōkoku* the Japanese Empire

❸ Lord of Heaven, God

皇天 *kōten* Heaven, Providence

❹ [formerly 惶 *kō* 581] be afraid, be anxious; be flurried

倉皇として *sōkō to shite* in great haste

SYNONYMS

❶ⓐ **rulers**

帝 EMPEROR → 2073
天 Heaven's messenger on earth → 3442
王 KING → 3439
君 RULER → 3206

5-4
白

泉 泉 泉

2567 SEN izumi

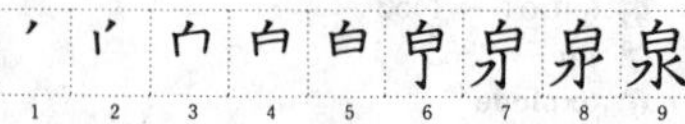

CH 泉 quán

Radical	Strokes
水 85	9-4-5
Grade	Freq
Jōyō-6	1005
2-5-4	

▶**SPRING**

COMPOUNDS

❶ⓐ (source or issue of water) **spring, fountain**

ⓑ [also suffix] **hot spring**

泉水 *sensui* fountain, garden pond
温泉 *onsen* hot spring
冷泉 *reisen* cold water spring
鉱泉 *kōsen* mineral spring
源泉 *gensen* fountainhead, source
硫黄泉 *iōsen* sulfur spring
アルカリ泉 *arukarisen* alkali spring

❷ [archaic] waterfall

飛泉 *hisen* waterfall

❸ Hades, the underworld

黄泉 *kōsen* (＝*yomi*) Hades, nether world

❹ money

泉貨紙(＝仙花紙) *senkashi* reclaimed paper

❺ abbrev. of 和泉 *izumi*, old name for southeast Osaka Prefecture

泉南 *sennan* southern Izumi district; Sennan City

KUN

【izumi 泉】 spring, fountain; fountainhead, source

知識の泉 *chishiki no izumi* source of knowledge

SYNONYMS

❶ⓐ **water sources**

井 WELL → 3454
源 SOURCE → 656

ⓑ **baths**

湯 hot bath → 612
浴 bath → 445

5-4
目

県

incorrect classification ⇨ see 2641

香

5-4 禾

Ⓒ 香 xiāng

2568 KŌ KYŌ ka kao(ri) kao(ru)

Radical	Strokes
香 186	9-9-0
Grade	Freq
Jōyō	919
2 - 5 - 4	

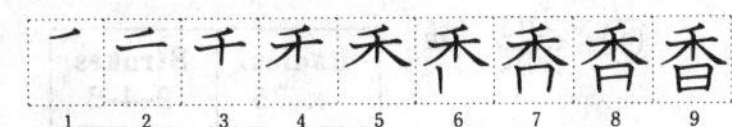

RADICAL 186

Standard form: 香 *nioikō* 'fragrance' (馨 馥)

Description: used in characters related to fragrance or sweet smell

▶SWEET SMELL

COMPOUNDS

❶ⓐ [original meaning] **sweet smell, pleasant odor, perfume, fragrance, aroma, scent**

ⓑ **sweet-smelling, fragrant**

香ばしい *kōbashii* nice-smelling, fragrant

芳香 *hōkō* perfume, fragrance, aroma

新香 *shinkō* pickles

香水 *kōsui* perfume

香気 *kōki* fragrance, perfume, scent

香油 *kōyu* pomade, balm, perfumed oil

❷ sweet-smelling substance:

ⓐ [also suffix] incense, joss stick

ⓑ spices

香典(=香奠) *kōden* obituary [condolence] gift, incense money

焼香する *shōkō suru* burn [offer] incense

線香 *senkō* stick of incense, joss stick

安息香 *ansokukō* benzoin

香辛料 *kōshinryō* spices, seasoning

香料 *kōryō* spices; perfumes

❸ incense smelling game

香道 *kōdō* art of incense smelling

❹ name of chess piece in shogi (Japanese chess): *yari*, spear

香車 *kyōsha* chess piece in shogi (Japanese chess), *yari*, spear

❺ unclassified compounds

香港 *honkon* Hong Kong

INDEPENDENT

【kō 香】 incense; incense smelling game

香を焚く *kō o taku* burn incense, cense

香を聞く *kō o kiku* smell incense

【kyō 香】 *kyo*, *yari* (⇨ ❹)

KUN

【ka 香】 sweet smell, fragrance, perfume, aroma

花の香 *hana no ka* fragrance of flowers

移り香 *utsuriga* lingering [absorbed] scent

色香 *iroka* beauty, loveliness, feminine charms; color and scent

【kao(ri) 香り】 sweet smell, perfume, fragrance, scent

桃の花の香り *momo no hana no kaori* fragrance of peach blossom

【kao(ru) 香る】 smell sweet, be fragrant

SYNONYMS

❶ **smell and fragrance**

気 smell → 3194

臭 BAD SMELL → 2633

馨 PERFUME → 2879

芳 FRAGRANT → 2210

薫 BALMY → 2371

郁 AROMATIC → 1288

USAGE

❶ **kaori**

香り

sweet smell, perfume, fragrance, scent

薫り

fragrance, aroma

❷ **kaoru**

香る

smell sweet, be fragrant

薫る

look sweet-smelling [balmy], look fragrant

★香 and 薫 are practically indistinguishable. Strictly speaking, 香 refers to physical perception by the olfactory organ, while 薫 is used figuratively or poetically.

HOMOPHONES

kaori ⇨ 薫 2371

kaoru ⇨ 薫 2371

窃 穿 etc.

incorrect classification ⇨ see 3 – 6

5-4 穴

5-4 立

音

incorrect classification ⇨ see 2070

5-4 加

架 架 架

2569 KA ka(keru) ka(karu)

Ⓒⓗ 架 jià

Radical	Strokes
木 75	9-4-5
Grade	**Freq**
Jōyō	1539
2-5-4	

Stroke order: 1 つ 2 カ 3 か 4 加 5 加 6 加 7 架 8 架 9 架

▶LAY ACROSS

COMPOUNDS

❶ **lay (a bridge or wire) across, build across, span (a river) with (a bridge), bridge**

架設する *kasetsu suru* construct, erect, build, install

架線 *kasen* aerial wiring

架橋 *kakyō* bridge building

架空の *kakū no* overhead, aerial; fanciful, fictitious

高架橋 *kōkakyō* elevated bridge

❷ **rack, shelf, stand, mount, support, frame**

銃架 *jūka* arm rack, rifle stand

画架 *gaka* easel

担架 *tanka* stretcher

十字架 *jūjika* cross, crucifix

書架 *shoka* bookshelf, bookstack

開架 *kaika* open access, open shelves

INDEPENDENT

【kasuru 架する】 construct, erect, build, install

KUN

【ka(keru) 架ける】 lay (a bridge or wire) across, build across, span (a river) with (a bridge), bridge

電線を架ける *densen o kakeru* lay a wire

【ka(karu) 架かる】 span, (of cables) be laid across, be built across

川に架かる橋 *kawa ni kakaru hashi* bridge spanning a river

SYNONYMS

❶ **equip and install**

敷 LAY → 1870

据える INSTALL → 497

装 FIT OUT → 2685

設 SET UP → 1471

備 PROVIDE → 146

❷ **flat supports**

棚 SHELF → 984

壇 PLATFORM → 754

座 SEAT → 3116

台 STAND → 2005

床 BED → 3067

HOMOPHONES

kakeru ⇨ 掛 493 懸 2915 賭 1605 駆 1823 翔 1357

kakaru ⇨ 掛 493 懸 2915 係 97 繫 2902 罹 2619

NOTE

⇨ see USAGE note at 掛 493

5-4 夗

怨

2570 EN ON ura(mu) ura(mi) ura(meshii)

Ⓒⓗ 怨 yuàn

Radical	Strokes
心 61	9-4-5
Grade	**Freq**
Reference	
2-5-4	

COMPOUNDS

ⓐ [now usu. 恨む *uramu*] [original meaning] hold a grudge, feel resentment, feel bitter against

ⓑ [now usu. 恨み *urami*] grudge, hatred, malice

ⓒ [now usu. 恨めしい *urameshii*] resentful, reproachful, indignant

怨恨 *enkon* grudge, enmity

怨霊 *onryō* revengeful ghost [specter]

怨み言 *uramigoto* grudge, reproach

怨めしや *Urameshi ya* You shall feel my wrath!

HOMOPHONES

uramu ⇨ 恨 369 憾 764

urami ⇨ 恨 369 憾 764

urameshii ⇨ 恨 369

NOTE

⇨ see USAGE note at 恨 369

怒 2571 DO NU▲ ika(ru) oko(ru)

CH 怒 nù

Radical	Strokes
心 61	9-4-5
Grade	Freq
Jōyō	1331
2-5-4	

5-4 奴

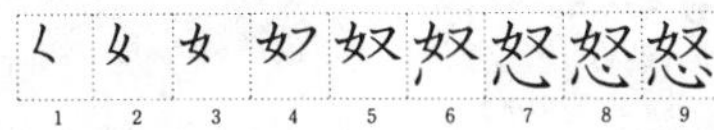

▶**GET ANGRY**

COMPOUNDS

❶ⓐ [original meaning] **get angry, be enraged**

ⓑ **anger, rage**

憤怒 *fundo* (=*funnu*) anger, rage, resentment
怒気 *doki* anger, indignation
怒声 *dosei* angry voice, harsh words
怒濤 *dotō* raging billows [waves]
怒号 *dogō* (angry) roar, outcry, bellow
激怒 *gekido* wild rage, fury
喜怒哀楽 *kidoairaku* joy and anger; emotion

❷ excessive, extreme

怒張 *dochō* overswelling (of a blood vessel)

KUN

【ika(ru) 怒る】 get angry, be enraged, get excited

怒らす *ikarasu* offend, make angry
怒り *ikari* anger, rage
怒り狂う *ikarikuruu* rage, be in a fit (of anger)

【oko(ru) 怒る】 get angry, be enraged, get excited; scold, rebuke

かんかんに怒る *kankan ni okoru* blow one's top

SYNONYMS

❶ **anger**

憤 INDIGNATION → 730
慨 resent → 641

染 2572 SEN so(meru) -zo(me) -zome so(maru) shi(miru) -ji(miru) shi(mi) -shi(meru)▲

CH 染 rǎn

Radical	Strokes
木 75	9-4-5
Grade	Freq
Jōyō-6	1151
2-5-4	

5-4 氿

▶**DYE**

COMPOUNDS

❶ **dye, color**

染色 *senshoku* dyeing
染髪 *senpatsu* hair dyeing
染織 *senshoku* dyeing and weaving
染料 *senryō* dyes, dyestuffs
媒染剤 *baisenzai* mordant

❷ⓐ **be infected, contract** (**a disease**)

ⓑ **contaminate**

感染 *kansen* infection
伝染病 *densenbyō* infectious disease
汚染 *osen* pollution, contamination

KUN

【so(meru) 染める】

①ⓐ dye

ⓑ color, stain, tinge

染め *some* dyeing, printing
染物屋 *somemonoya* dyer
染め直す *somenaosu* redye
頰を染める *hō o someru* blush
血染めの *chizome no* bloodstained

② have a hand in, dabble in

手を染める *te o someru* have a hand (in)
見染める *misomeru* fall in love at first glance

【-zo(me) -染め, -zome -染】

[also suffix]

ⓐ dyeing process

ⓑ dyed fabric

先染め *sakizome* yarn dyeing
友禅染め *yūzenzome* silk printed by the *yuzen* process

【so(maru) 染まる】 be dyed, take color; be imbued [stained]

染まり工合(=染まり具合) *somariguai* effect of dyeing
黒く染まる *kuroku somaru* be dyed black
悪に染まる *aku ni somaru* steeped in vice

【shi(miru) 染みる】

[also 滲みる]

① soak into, permeate

染み *shimi* stain, blot, spot

染み込む *shimikomu* soak into, permeate
染み付く *shimitsuku* be dyed in deeply, be stained
② penetrate (to the bone), come home to one's heart
身に染みる風 *mi ni shimiru kaze* piercing wind
馴染み *najimi* familiarity, intimacy; old acquaintance, crony
③ smart from irritation
煙が目に染みた *Kemuri ga me ni shimita* My eyes smarted from the smoke

【-ji(miru) -染みる】
[verbal suffix]
① be imbued with, be stained with
油染みる(＝脂染みる) *aburajimiru* become greasy, be oil-stained
② have a touch of, look like
気違い染みている *kichigaijimite iru* have a touch of insanity, be slightly crazy

【shi(mi) 染み】 stain, blot, spot
インキの染み *inki no shimi* ink stain

【-shi(meru) -染める】 permeate with fluid or smoke
煮染める *nishimeru* boil thoroughly with seasoning
焚き染める *takishimeru* perfume clothes by burning incense

SYNONYMS

❶ **color**
彩 color → 1681

❷ⓑ **dirty**
汚 DIRTY → 222

USAGE

❶ **someru**
染める
①ⓐ dye
ⓑ color, stain, tinge
② have a hand in, dabble in

-初める
[verbal suffix] begin to (occur); for the first time

❷ **-zome**
-染め
[also suffix]
ⓐ dyeing process
ⓑ dyed fabric

-初め
[verbal suffix] performing an action for the first time (of the year)

❸ **shimiru**
染みる
[also 滲みる]
① soak into, permeate
② penetrate (to the bone), come home to one's heart
③ smart from irritation

滲みる
[also 染みる] same as 染みる

凍みる
freeze, congeal

HOMOPHONES

someru ⇨ 初 1116
-zome ⇨ 初 1116
shimiru ⇨ 滲 703 凍 129
-shimeru ⇨ 湿 609

NOTE

⇨ see also USAGE note at 湿 609

5-4
北

背 背 背

2573 HAI se sei somu(ku) somu(keru)

CH 背 bèi bēi

Radical	Strokes
月 130	9-4-5
Grade	**Freq**
Jōyō-6	776

2-5-4

Stroke order: 1 2 3 4 5 6 7 8 9

▶**BACK**

COMPOUNDS

❶ⓐ **back** (of the body)
ⓑ (backside) **back, reverse side, rear**
ⓒ abbrev. of 背泳 *haiei*: backstroke
背部 *haibu* back
背泳 *haiei* backstroke
背後 *haigo* back, rear
背面 *haimen* rear, back, reverse
背景 *haikei* background; (stage) scenery, setting, scene; backing
腹背 *fukuhai* back and front; opposition in the heart
百背 *hyakuhai* 100 meter backstroke

❷ [formerly also 悖 420] (turn one's back on) go against, disobey, rebel, betray
背反 *haihan* revolt, rebellion; going against, violation
背信 *haishin* breach of faith [trust], betrayal
背徳 *haitoku* immorality, corruption, lapse from virtue

INDEPENDENT

【hai 背】 backstroke

KUN

【se 背】
① back; backside

背中 *senaka* back
背骨 *sebone* backbone, spine
背負う *seou* carry on one's back, shoulder, bear
背を向ける *se o mukeru* turn one's back on, pretend not to see
② stature, height
背の順 *se no jun* order of height
③ ridge
山の背 *yama no se* ridge (of a mountain)
④ unclassified compounds
背広 *sebiro* business suit

【sei 背】 stature, height
背比べ *seikurabe* comparison of statures
上背 *uwazei* height, stature

【somu(ku) 背く】
① [sometimes also 叛く] go against, disobey, rebel against, violate
約束に背く *yakusoku ni somuku* break one's promise
② turn one's back on

【somu(keru) 背ける】 turn (one's face) away
顔を背ける *kao o somukeru* turn one's face away

SYNONYMS

❶ⓐ trunk parts
肩 SHOULDER → 1947
胸 CHEST → 951
腹 BELLY → 1034
胴 TRUNK → 950
腰 WAIST → 1036

ⓑ rear
裏 REAR → 2138
後 after- → 361
尻 tail end → 3032
尾 TAIL → 3062

❷ violate
反 act contrary to → 2945
犯 offend against → 196
破 BREAK → 1150
違 VIOLATE → 3151

【se】
② height
丈 STATURE → 3419
高 height → 2097

USAGE

somuku
背く
① [sometimes also 叛く] go against, disobey, rebel against, violate
② turn one's back on
叛く
[usu. 背く] go against, disobey, rebel against, violate

HOMOPHONES

somuku ⇨ 叛 1143

NOTE

⇨ see COMPOUND FORMATION for 背広 *sebiro* ⇨ 広 3035

incorrect classification ⇨ see 2084 — 5-4 占

急 incorrect classification ⇨ see 2092 — 5-4 刍

incorrect classification ⇨ see 2088 — 5-4 矛

 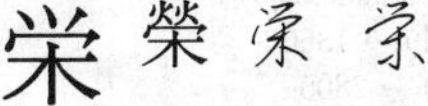

2574 EI saka(eru) ha(e) -ba(e) ha(eru) e▲

Ⓒⓗ 荣 róng

Radical	Strokes
木 75	9-4-5
Grade	**Freq**
Jōyō-4	832
2 - 5 - 4	

5-4 ⺍

▶FLOURISH ▶GLORY

COMPOUNDS

❶ⓐ flourish, prosper, thrive, be prosperous
ⓑ [original meaning, now archaic] (grow thick) flourish, grow luxuriantly
栄落 *eiraku* flourishing and declining
栄枯盛衰 *eikoseisui* prosperity and decline, rise and fall
繁栄する *han'ei suru* prosper, thrive, flourish

❷ glory, honor, splendor, fame, distinction
栄誉 *eiyo* honor, glory, distinction
栄光 *eikō* glory

栄華 *eiga* prosperity, splendor, glory
栄達 *eitatsu* success in life, rise in the world
栄冠 *eikan* honor, glory; garland, laurels
栄転 *eiten* promotion

❸ [sometimes also 営 2603] tonic, blood (in Chinese medicine)
栄養 *eiyō* nutrition, nourishment

INDEPENDENT

【ei 栄】 *literary* glory, honor
身に余る栄を被る *mi ni amaru ei o kōmuru* receive undeserved honor

KUN

【saka(eru) 栄える】 flourish, prosper, thrive, be prosperous
栄えた時代 *sakaeta jidai* prosperous age
国の栄え *kuni no sakae* prosperity of a country

【ha(e) 栄え】 glory, splendor
栄え有る *haearu* glorious, splendid

【-ba(e) -栄え】
① [also -映え] looking better
見栄え *mibae* improvement in appearance, good show
② [sometimes also -映え] result, effect
出来栄え *dekibae* result, effect, workmanship

【ha(eru) 栄える】 [also 映える] look better [to advantage], go well with
栄えない色 *haenai iro* dull color
その木のお蔭で庭が栄える *Sono ki no okage de niwa ga haeru* The tree sets off the garden

【e 栄】 [in compounds] glory, splendor
見栄 *mie* [sometimes also 見え] show, ostentation, vanity

SYNONYMS

❶ⓐ prospering and prosperity
繁 THRIVE → 2853
盛 PROSPEROUS → 2675
昌 PROSPERING → 2414
隆 PROSPER → 545
振 rise → 430
興 RISE TO PROSPERITY → 2909

❷ great respect
誉 HONOR → 2502
光 honor → 2391

HOMOPHONES

-bae ⇨ 映 892
haeru ⇨ 映 892
mie ⇨ 見え 2544 見得 2544, 477
見栄 2544, 2574

NOTE

⇨ see USAGE notes at 映 892 and 見 2544
⇨ see COMPOUND FORMATION for 栄達 *eitatsu* ⇨ 達 3139

5-4
吉

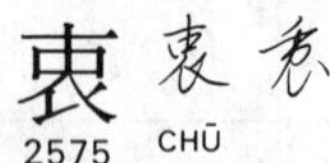

2575 CHŪ

Ⓒⓗ 衷 zhōng

Radical	Strokes
衣 145	9-5-4
Grade	**Freq**
Jōyō	1894
2-5-4	

▶INNER HEART

COMPOUNDS

❶ inner heart, true heart, inner feelings; sincerity
衷心 *chūshin* inner heart, inmost feelings
衷情 *chūjō* inmost feeling, true heart
苦衷 *kuchū* mental suffering, dilemma
微衷 *bichū* one's innermost thoughts [feelings]

❷ happy mean, moderation, propriety
折衷 *setchū* compromise, eclecticism

SYNONYMS

❶ psyche
襟 inner mind → 1252
心 HEART → 11
腹 heart → 1034
胸 breast → 951
懐 BOSOM → 763
神 MIND → 912
気 SPIRIT (consciousness) → 3194
精 SPIRIT (mind) → 1366
霊 SPIRIT (soul) → 2805
魂 SOUL, spirit → 1063

NOTE

★do not confuse with 哀 2068

春 2576 SHUN haru

CH 春 chūn

Radical	Strokes
日 72	9-4-5
Grade	Freq
Jōyō-2	498
2-5-4	

5-4 夫

1 2 3 4 5 6 7 8 9

▶**SPRING**

COMPOUNDS

❶ⓐ [original meaning] **spring**

ⓑ the spring of life, youth

春季 *shunki* spring

春闘 *shuntō* spring labor offensive

春分 *shunbun* vernal equinox

春眠 *shunmin* morning sleep in spring

春夏秋冬 *shunkashūtō* four seasons, all (the) year round

立春 *risshun* first day of spring

来春 *raishun* next spring

今春 *konshun* this spring

春秋に富む *shunjū ni tomu* be young

青春 *seishun* bloom of youth

❷ beginning of the year

新春 *shinshun* the New Year

❸ love, sex, sexual desire, eros

春情 *shunjō* sexual passion

春画 *shunga* pornography, obscene picture

売春 *baishun* prostitution

思春期 *shishunki* puberty, adolescence

KUN

【haru 春】 spring; the New Year; spring of life, youth; love, sexual desire, eros

春雨 *harusame* spring rain; sticks of bean jelly

春風 *harukaze* spring breeze

春先 *harusaki* early spring

春めく *harumeku* become springlike

春一番 *haruichiban* first storm in the spring

人生の春 *jinsei no haru* the spring of life, the flower [prime] of youth

初春 *hatsuharu* early spring; the New Year

春の目覚め *haru no mezame* awakening of the spring, puberty

春を売る *haru o uru* become a prostitute

SYNONYMS

❶ⓐ **warm seasons**

夏 SUMMER → 2113

暑 SUMMER HEAT → 2473

❸ **sex**

色 lust → 2029

情 (illicit) love → 482

性 SEX → 299

NOTE

⇨ see COMPOUND FORMATION for 売春 *baishun* ⇨ 売 2196

奏 2577 SŌ kana(deru)

CH 奏 zòu

Radical	Strokes
大 37	9-3-6
Grade	Freq
Jōyō-6	816
2-5-4	

5-4 夫

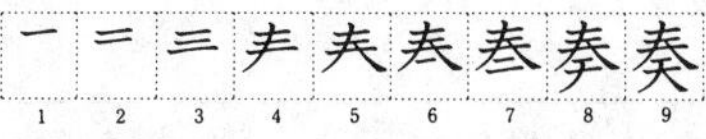

1 2 3 4 5 6 7 8 9

▶**PLAY MUSIC**

COMPOUNDS

❶ **play music, perform (on a musical instrument)**

演奏する *ensō suru* perform, play

吹奏楽 *suisōgaku* wind instrument music

重奏 *jūsō* duet

合奏 *gassō* ensemble, concert

伴奏 *bansō* accompaniment

協奏曲 *kyōsōkyoku* concerto

❷ speak (to a ruler), report (to the throne or emperor)

奏上 *sōjō* report to the emperor

奏請 *sōsei* petitioning the emperor

❸ achieve, accomplish

奏功 *sōkō* success, fruition

奏効 *sōkō* efficacy

INDEPENDENT

【sōsuru 奏する】 play, perform; report to the emperor; be successful, work well

効を奏する *kō o sōsuru* take effect, work well

KUN

【kana(deru) 奏でる】 play on (a musical instrument), perform

ピアノを奏でる *piano o kanaderu* play the piano

SYNONYMS

❶ **play music**

弾 play on (stringed instruments) → 572

吹 BLOW → 231

NOTE
★do not confuse with 泰 2583

5-4 此 **柴** incorrect stroke count ⇨ see 2653

5-5 玄 **畜** incorrect classification ⇨ see 2096

5-5 白 **畠** 2578 hatake hata

CH none (国字)

Radical	Strokes
田 102	10-5-5
Grade	**Freq**
Reference	
2-5-5	

COMPOUNDS

❶ [now usu. 畑 *hatake, hata*] [original meaning] (plowed or cultivated) field, farm, vegetable garden, plantation

段段畠 *dandanbatake* terraced fields, terraced farm

❷ [now usu. 畑 *hatake*] one's field, one's specialty

畠違いだ *hatakechigai da* be out of one's field

HOMOPHONES

hatake ⇨ 畑 905

hata ⇨ 畑 905

NOTE

⇨ see USAGE note at 畑 905

5-5 立 **竜** incorrect classification ⇨ see 2099

5-5 立 **竞** incorrect classification ⇨ see 2101
(nonstandard for 競 1847)

5-5 **监** 2579

▶**OVERSEE**

handwritten abbreviation for 監 2852

5-5 **留** 畄◆ 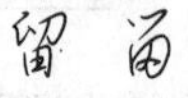 2580

RYŪ RU RŪBURU▲ to(meru) -to(meru) -do(me) to(maru) todo(meru)▲ todo(maru)▲

CH 畄 liú

Radical	Strokes
田 102	10-5-5
Grade	**Freq**
Jōyō-5	773
2-5-5	

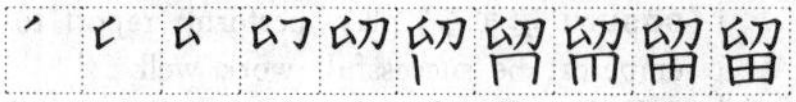

▶**KEEP** ▶**STAY**

COMPOUNDS

❶ cause to remain in a given place or condition:

ⓐ [original meaning] **keep in place, keep from moving, keep in position**

ⓑ **keep in custody, detain**

ⓒ **keep for future use, leave behind**

ⓓ keep in mind, pay attention to

係留する *keiryū suru* moor, anchor

慰留する *iryū suru* dissuade from resigning

留置 *ryūchi* detention, custody, retention

抑留する *yokuryū suru* detain, intern, seize, arrest

留保する *ryūho suru* reserve, withhold, keep back

保留 *horyū* reservation
遺留品 *iryūhin* article left behind, lost property
留意 *ryūi* attention, heed, regard

❷ⓐ (remain in a given condition) **stay, remain, continue**
ⓑ (remain in a given place) **stay, sojourn, reside**
留任する *ryūnin suru* remain [stay] in office
留年する *ryūnen suru* stay more than two years in the same class
残留する *zanryū suru* stay behind
停留所 *teiryūjo* (bus) stop, station
留学生 *ryūgakusei* student studying abroad
留守 *rusu* absence (from home); caretaking; defending when the lord is absent
駐留する *chūryū suru* be stationed at, stay
逗留する *tōryū suru* stay, sojourn
在留邦人 *zairyū-hōjin* Japanese residents

❸ [formerly 溜 *ryū* 662] distill
蒸留 *jōryū* distillation
分留 *bunryū* fraction, fractional distillation
乾留 *kanryū* dry distillation

❹ ruble
一留 *ichirūburu* one ruble

INDEPENDENT

【ryū 留】 *astron* stationary (point)

KUN

【to(meru) 留める】
①ⓐ keep in place, retain, fix, fasten
ⓑ keep (a parcel) until called for
ⓒ keep in custody, detain
ⓓ (keep a vehicle from moving) park
留め金 *tomegane* clasp, latch, fastening
取り留めの無い *toritome no nai* wandering, rambling, incoherent
局留め *kyokudome* poste restante
引き留める *hikitomeru* detain
足留めする *ashidome suru* keep indoors, induce to stay
車を留める *kuruma o tomeru* park a car
② keep in mind
気に留める *ki ni tomeru* mind, give heed to, pay attention to
③ keep (a quarrel) from intensifying, stop
留め男 *tomeotoko* man who stops a quarrel

【-to(meru) -留める】
[also -止める]
① kill
仕留める *shitomeru* kill, shoot dead
② write down, register
書留 *kakitome* registered mail

【-do(me) -留め】 clip, fastener, retainer
帯留め *obidome* sash clip [fastener]
土留め *dodome* sheathing, retaining (wall)

【to(maru) 留まる】
① be held in position, be fastened
釘で留まっている *kugi de tomatte iru* be fastened with a nail
②ⓐ remain in one's perception, strike one's senses
ⓑ [in compounds] remain, be left over
目に留まる *me ni tomaru* attract one's attention, strike the eye
歩留まり *budomari* yield, yield rate
③ perch on
木に留まる *ki ni tomaru* sit in a tree
お高く留まる *otakaku tomaru* assume an air of importance, put on airs

【todo(meru) 留める】
① leave (behind)
書き留める *kakitodomeru* leave a note behind
② make stay, detain
原級に留める *genkyū ni todomeru* keep (a student) back (to repeat a grade)

【todo(maru) 留まる】 stay behind, remain
家に留まる *ie ni todomaru* stay home

SYNONYMS

❶ⓐ preserve
保 PRESERVE → 96
持 uphold → 374
ⓑ imprison and confine
拘 ARREST → 310
置 place in custody → 2608
禁 confine → 2795
❷ⓐ remain
残 REMAIN → 943
余 REMAINING → 2042
滞 STAY → 663
ⓑ stay
滞 STAY → 663
駐 STATIONED → 1826
屯 STATION TROOPS → 3457
在 reside temporarily → 2984
泊 STAY OVERNIGHT → 331
宿 LODGE → 2293
❸ refine
錬 REFINE (crude metals) → 1741
精 REFINE (crude materials) → 1366
❸ vaporize
蒸 EVAPORATE → 2334

HOMOPHONES

tomeru ⇨ 止 2941 泊 331 停 139
-tomeru ⇨ 止 2941
-dome ⇨ 止 2941
tomaru ⇨ 止 2941 泊 331 停 139
todomeru ⇨ 止 2941
todomaru ⇨ 止 2941

COMPOUND FORMATION

❶ 留守 *rusu*
留守 'absence, etc.' originally meant to stay behind (留 ❷ⓑ) and defend (守) the castle during the absence of one's lord, but was extended to mean absence from the castle or

home. Thus although 留 normally means to stay or remain, in this case it is used in a word related to the opposite idea of *not* to stay.

❷ 歩留まり *budomari*

歩留まり 'yield, yield rate' is the percentage (歩) of what is left over (留まる *tomaru* ② ⓑ).

NOTE

⇨ see USAGE note at 止 2941

5-5 晉 incorrect classification ⇨ see 1952 (nonstandard for 晋 2656)

5-5 益 incorrect classification ⇨ see 2285

5-5 党 黨 党 㓙

2581 TŌ

ⒸⒽ 党 dǎng

Radical	Strokes
儿 10△	10-2-8
Grade	**Freq**
Jōyō-6	90
2 - 5 - 5	

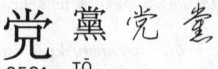

1 2 3 4 5 6 7 8 9 10

▶**PARTY**

COMPOUNDS

❶ⓐ (political group) **party, political party, faction**

ⓑ **suffix after names of political parties**

党員 *tōin* party member
党首 *tōshu* party chief [leader]
党大会 *tōtaikai* party convention
党派 *tōha* party, faction, clique
政党 *seitō* political party
野党 *yatō* opposition party
粛党 *shukutō* purging disloyal elements from a party
共和党 *kyōwatō* Republican Party
社会党 *shakaitō* Socialist Party

❷ (group of persons) party, companions, clique, fellows, fellow

一党 *ittō* party, league, clique; a political party
徒党 *totō* clique, faction, conspirators
残党 *zantō* remnants (of a defeated party), refugees
悪党 *akutō* scoundrel, rogue

❸ person who likes a particular food or beverage, fan

辛党 *karatō* drinker
巨人党 *kyojintō* Giants fan

INDEPENDENT

【tō 党】political party, faction
党を脱退する *tō o dattai suru* leave the party

SYNONYMS

❶ **parties and sects**

閥 CLIQUE → 3325
流 school → 441
派 SECT → 381
翼 WING → 2720
系 faction → 1944
門 (religious) sect → 888
宗 RELIGIOUS SECT (esp. Buddhist) → 2228

❷ **groups**

隊 PARTY (organized group) → 625
団 BODY → 3053
伍 ranks → 47
班 SQUAD → 946
軍 team → 2080
群 GROUP (of any kind) → 1540
組 group (of people) → 1337
陣 lineup → 455
連 set → 3103
族 common-interest group (*slang*) → 958

帯 帯 帯 帯

2582 TAI o(biru) obi

Ⓒⓗ 帯 dài

Radical	Strokes
巾 50	10-3-7
Grade	Freq
Jōyō-4	700
2 - 5 - 5	

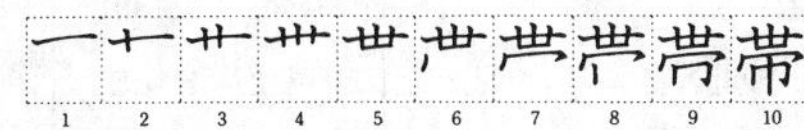

1 2 3 4 5 6 7 8 9 10

▶BELT ▶WEAR

COMPOUNDS

❶ⓐ [also suffix] [original meaning] **belt, sash, girdle, band, obi**
ⓑ *engineering* band
ⓒ [suffix] *anat* girdle
包帯 *hōtai* bandage, dressing
腹帯 *fukutai* bellyband
着帯する *chakutai suru* wear a maternity belt
止血帯 *shiketsutai* tourniquet
帯域幅 *taiikihaba* band width
声帯 *seitai* vocal cords
肩甲帯 *kenkōtai* shoulder girdle

❷ [also suffix] (geographical area) **belt, zone, region**
帯状の *obijō* (=*taijō*) *no* belt-shaped
地帯 *chitai* zone, area
一帯 *ittai* belt, zone, tract (of land), area
熱帯 *nettai* tropics, torrid zone
緑地帯 *ryokuchitai* green belt
時間帯 *jikantai* time belt
バンアレン帯 *ban'arentai* Van Allen Belt

❸ **wear (esp. at [on] the belt), bear, carry on one's person, be armed with**
帯刀 *taitō* wearing a sword
帯剣する *taiken suru* wear a sword, be armed with a sword
携帯する *keitai suru* carry, bring with one, equip oneself with

❹ⓐ **have, possess**
ⓑ be tinged with (a color), be charged with (electricity)
所帯(=世帯) *shotai* household, home
妻帯者 *saitaisha* married man
拐帯 *kaitai* abscondence with money
付帯的な *futaiteki na* incidental, secondary, accessory
帯黄色 *taiōshoku* yellowish color
帯緑の *tairyoku no* greenish
帯電体 *taidentai* charged body

❺ work together, cooperate
帯同する *taidō suru* be accompanied by, take (a person) along
連帯 *rentai* solidarity

INDEPENDENT

【tai 帯】 *anat* girdle

【taisuru 帯する】 wear (esp. at [on] the belt), bear, carry on one's person be armed with
剣を帯する *ken o taisuru* wear a sword

KUN

【o(biru) 帯びる】 wear (esp. at [on] the belt), bear, carry on one's person be armed with; wear (a sad look), assume, have; be tinged with (a color), be charged with (electricity); be entrusted with, be charged with (a mission)
剣を帯びる *ken o obiru* wear a sword at one's side
赤味を帯びた *akami o obita* reddish, tinged with red
憂いを帯びた顔 *urei o obita kao* sorrowful look
電気を帯びる *denki o obiru* be charged with electricity
使命を帯びる *shimei o obiru* be charged with a mission

【obi 帯】 belt, sash, girdle, band; belting
帯を締める *obi o shimeru* do up a sash
帯止め(=帯留め) *obidome* sash clip [fastener]
帯革(=帯皮) *obikawa* leather belt
袋帯 *fukuroobi* double-woven obi
帯封 *obifū* half wrapper, strip of paper

SYNONYMS

❷ **areas and localities**
圏 SPHERE → 3148
域 BOUNDED AREA → 465
区 DISTRICT → 2963
領 TERRITORY → 1224
辺 VICINITY → 3029
方 locality → 1963
地 PLACE → 204

❸ **wear and put on**
着 PUT ON → 3316
装 DRESS → 2685
履く put on footwear → 3171
被る put on headgear → 1163

5-5 夫

泰 泰 泰

2583 TAI

Ⓒⓗ 泰 tài

Radical	Strokes
水 85	10-5-5
Grade	Freq
Jōyō	1391
2 - 5 - 5	

一 二 三 夫 夫 夫 泰 泰 泰 泰

1 2 3 4 5 6 7 8 9 10

▶**TRANQUIL**

COMPOUNDS

❶ **tranquil, peaceful, composed, calm**

泰平 *taihei* tranquility, perfect peace

泰然たる *taizentaru* calm, composed; firm

安泰 *antai* peace, security, tranquility

❷ [also 太 2152] extreme, great

泰西 *taisei* the Occident

❸ Thailand, Siam

泰国 *taikoku* Thailand, Siam

泰語 *taigo* Thai, Siamese

対泰関係 *taitai-kankei* relations with Thailand

❹ Mt. Taishan (sacred Chinese mountain associated with Confucius)

泰山 *taizan* Mt. Taishan

泰斗 *taito* leading authority

INDEPENDENT

【tai 泰】 Thailand

SYNONYMS

❶ **calm and peaceful**

安 PEACEFUL → 2171

康 peaceful → 3124

寧 peaceful → 2345

静 QUIET → 1728

平 CALM → 3478

穏 CALM → 1235

❸ **Asian countries**

越 Vietnam → 3314

印 India → 828

比 Philippines → 26

鮮 Korea → 1877

華 CHINA → 2283

日 JAPAN → 3027

NOTE

⇨ see COMPOUND FORMATION for 泰斗 *taito* ⇨斗 2953

★do not confuse with 奏 2577

5-5 此

砦

incorrect stroke count ⇨ see 2671

5-5 帯

帶

incorrect stroke count ⇨ see 2676 (nonstandard for 帯 2582)

5-6 田

異 異 異 異

2584 I koto koto(naru)

Ⓒⓗ 异 yì

Radical	Strokes
田 102	11-5-6
Grade	Freq
Jōyō-6	697
2 - 5 - 6	

丨 口 日 田 田 田 田 畀 畀 異 異

1 2 3 4 5 6 7 8 9 10 11

▶**DIFFERENT**

COMPOUNDS

❶ [also prefix]

ⓐ [original meaning] (not alike) **different, unlike; opposite**

ⓑ (of a different place) **foreign**

ⓒ (different or distinct from) another, other

異議 *igi* objection, complaint

異性 *isei* opposite sex

異動 *idō* shifting, reshuffle

差異 *sai* difference, disparity

異文化 *ibunka* different cultures

異境 *ikyō* foreign country, strange land

異邦人 *ihōjin* foreigner, alien

異名 *imyō* another name, alias

❷ **not ordinary: strange, unusual, abnormal, unorthodox, extraordinary, exceptional, peculiar**

異常な *ijō na* abnormal, unusual, extraordinary

異端 *itan* heresy, paganism, heterodoxy

異心 *ishin* treasonous intention, betrayal; eccentricity

異例 *irei* singular case, exception

異色の *ishoku no* novel, unique
異才 *isai* genius, prodigy
奇異な *kii na* unusual, strange
❸ calamity
天変地異 *tenpenchii* extraordinary natural phenomenon
❹ marvel, be surprised
驚異 *kyōi* wonder, marvel, miracle

INDEPENDENT

【i 異】 different opinion; difference; uncommonness
異を立てる *i o tateru* raise an objection
異な気分 *i na kibun* queer feeling

KUN

【koto 異】 difference
異にする *koto ni suru* differ, be different
【koto(naru) 異なる】 different, be different from
二つの異なる点 *futatsu no kotonaru ten* two different points

SYNONYMS

❶ⓐ differing and difference
違 DIFFER → 3151
差 DIFFERENCE → 3311
ⓑ foreign
外 foreign → 186
❷ abnormal
変 ABNORMAL → 2069
奇 UNUSUAL → 2217
妙 strange → 239
怪 MYSTERIOUS → 297
珍 curious → 909

USAGE

i 異 違
★異 is sometimes used interchangeably with 違 in sense ❶ⓐ above in such words as 差異 *sai* 'difference' and 相違 *sōi* 'difference', which are preferably written as shown.

HOMOPHONES

koto ⇨ 殊 942

NOTE

⇨ see also USAGE note at 殊 942

累 累 𥿻

2585 RUI

Ⓒ 累 lěi lèi léi

Radical	Strokes
糸 120	11-6-5
Grade	**Freq**
Jōyō	1685
▀ 2-5-6	

Stroke order: 1–11

5-6 田

▶CUMULATE

COMPOUNDS

❶ⓐ cumulate, accumulate, pile up
ⓑ successive, repeated, gradual
累積 *ruiseki* accumulation
累加 *ruika* cumulation, cumulative rise
累計 *ruikei* total
累増 *ruizō* cumulative increase, progressive increase
累乗 *ruijō math* involution, power
累算温度 *ruisan ondo* cumulative temperature
累累と *ruirui to* heaps on heaps, one upon another
累進する *ruishin suru* successive promotions, graduated increase
累次に *ruiji ni* successively, repeatedly
❷ involvement, implication
係累 *keirui* family ties, dependents
連累 *renrui* implication, involvement

INDEPENDENT

【rui 累】 involvement, implication, trouble
他に累を及ぼす *ta ni rui o oyobosu* involve others in trouble

SYNONYMS

❶ⓐ accumulate
積 ACCUMULATE → 1236
重 pile up → 3573
盛る heap up → 2675

畧

2586

▶ABRIDGED ▶STRATEGY
nonstandard for 略 1169

5-6 田

窓 窒

incorrect classification ⇨ see ▀ 3–8

5-6 穴

5-6 立

章

incorrect classification ⇨ see 2117

5-6 罒

眾
2587

▶**MULTITUDE**
nonstandard for 衆 2683

5-6 代

袋 2588 TAI fukuro

Ⓒ袋 dài

Radical	Strokes
衣 145	11-6-5
Grade	**Freq**
Jōyō	992
2-5-6	

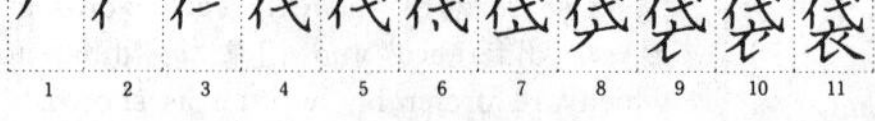

▶**BAG**

COMPOUNDS

ⓐ [original meaning] **bag, sack**
ⓑ counter for bags or bagfuls
郵袋 *yūtai* mailbag
製袋 *seitai* bag manufacturing
風袋 *fūtai* tare
二袋 *nitai* two sacks

KUN

【**fukuro** 袋】
①ⓐ [also suffix] bag, sack, pouch
ⓑ counter for bags or bagfuls
お袋 *ofukuro* one's mother
袋入り *fukuroiri* pouched, sacked
袋帯 *fukuroobi* double-woven obi
紙袋 *kamibukuro* paper bag
手袋 *tebukuro* gloves
浮き袋 *ukibukuro* air bladder
給料袋 *kyūryōbukuro* pay envelope
一袋 *hitofukuro* one bag
② [also prefix] cul-de-sac
袋小路 *fukurokōji* blind alley

SPECIAL READINGS

足袋 *tabi* Japanese [digitated] socks, *tabi*

SYNONYMS

ⓐ **bags**
俵 STRAW SACK → 115
包 wrapper → 2966
胞 MEMBRANOUS SAC → 917
ⓐ **containers**
籠 BASKET → 2734
箱 BOX → 2711
器 VESSEL → 2713
瓶 BOTTLE → 1344
缶 CAN → 2033
槽 TANK → 1067
棺 COFFIN → 985

COMPOUND FORMATION

お袋 *ofukuro*
お袋 'one's mother', literally "honorable bag," is an expression indicating intimacy or respect for one's mother. The origin of this word is not clear. According to one theory, it is related to the fact that the placenta enveloping the fetus is similar in shape to a bag.

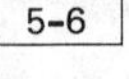

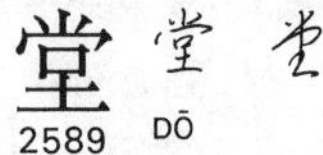

堂 2589 DŌ

Ⓒ堂 táng

Radical	Strokes
土 32	11-3-8
Grade	**Freq**
Jōyō-4	768
2-5-6	

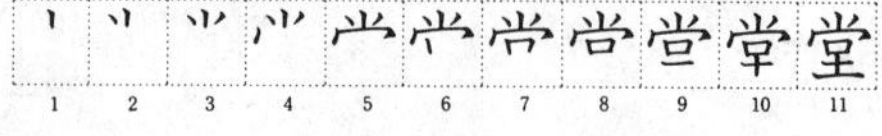

▶**HALL**

COMPOUNDS

❶ [also suffix] (building for public gatherings) **hall, public building**
公会堂 *kōkaidō* town [public] hall
議事堂 *gijidō* assembly hall; Diet Building

❷ⓐ (large room for public gatherings) **hall, meeting place**
ⓑ [original meaning] large reception room
講堂 *kōdō* lecture hall, auditorium
食堂 *shokudō* dining hall [room]; restaurant
音楽堂 *ongakudō* concert hall
殿堂 *dendō* hall, palace, shrine; sanctuary

❸ⓐ (building or hall for worship) **temple building, temple, shrine, church**
ⓑ suffix after names of temple buildings
堂塔 *dōtō* temple buildings, temple
堂宇 *dōu* edifice, temple, hall
聖堂 *seidō* shrine [temple] of Confucius; sanctuary, church
本堂 *hondō* main temple, main building (of a temple)
金色堂 *konjikidō* Konjikido (name of a temple building)
❹ house, abode
草堂 *sōdō* monk's cell; (my) humble abode
❺ suffix for forming names of business establishments or pen names
三省堂 *sanseidō* Sanseido (name of a publisher)
❻ the Court
廟堂 *byōdō* the Court
❼ dignified, majestic
堂堂たる *dōdōtaru* dignified, magnificent, imposing, majestic, stately
❽ honorific title for another's mother
母堂 *bodō* your [his] mother
❾ secret knowledge
堂奥 *dōō* secret knowledge; interior of a temple

INDEPENDENT

【dō 堂】 temple or shrine building; hall, public building; secret knowledge
堂に入る *dō ni iru* become expert, be master at

SYNONYMS

❶ **buildings**
館 PUBLIC BUILDING → 1748
舎 BUILDING → 2060
棟 BLOCK → 991
閣 TALL MAGNIFICENT BUILDING → 3327
宇 large building → 2175
殿 PALACE → 1792
❷ **rooms**
房 CHAMBER → 1946
間 room → 3323
室 ROOM → 2254
斎 study → 2115
❸ **places of worship**
塔 pagoda → 561
寺 BUDDHIST TEMPLE → 2164
社 Shinto shrine → 840
宮 SHINTO SHRINE → 2274
院 monastery → 454
教 church → 1493

常 常 (cursive forms)

2590 JŌ tsune toko-

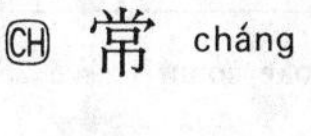

CH 常 cháng

Radical	Strokes
巾 50	11-3-8
Grade	**Freq**
Jōyō-5	344
2-5-6	

5-6

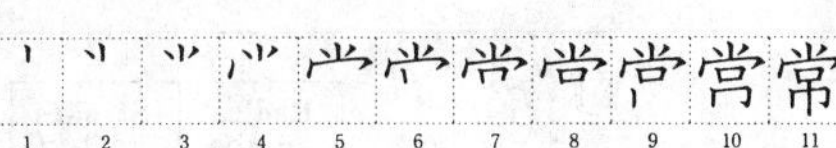

▶**NORMAL** ▶**REGULAR**

COMPOUNDS

❶ **normal, ordinary, usual, common, regular**
常識 *jōshiki* common sense, common knowledge
常態 *jōtai* normal state [condition]
非常 *hijō* emergency, calamity
異常な *ijō na* abnormal, unusual, extraordinary
正常 *seijō* normality, normalcy
通常の *tsūjō no* common, ordinary, usual
平常の *heijō no* ordinary, normal, usual
❷ **regular, habitual, standing**
常務 *jōmu* managing [executive] director
常連 *jōren* regular visitors [customers], frequenters
常緑樹 *jōryokuju* evergreen tree
常食 *jōshoku* daily food, staple food
常用 *jōyō* common use, daily use
常時の *jōji no* regular, standing
常任委員 *jōnin iin* standing committee
日常の *nichijō no* daily, everyday
❸ code of morals
五常 *gojō* the five cardinal virtues (of Confucianism)
綱常 *kōjō* moral principles, code of morals
❹ abbrev. of 常陸 *hitachi*, old name for Ibaraki Prefecture
常磐炭田 *jōban tanden* Joban coalfield

KUN

【tsune 常】 ordinary course of events, normal condition
常に *tsune ni* always, at all times
世の常 *yo no tsune* the way of the world
【toko- 常-】 everlasting, unending
常夏の国 *tokonatsu no kuni* land of everlasting summer

SYNONYMS

❶ **ordinary**
只- ORDINARY → 2155
並 ordinary → 2246
平 common → 3478
普 common → 2323

庸 MEDIOCRE → 3128
凡 COMMONPLACE → 2938
❷ **constant**
例 regular → 89
恒 CONSTANT → 367
定 fixed → 2229

5-6 ⺍

蛍 螢 蛍 蛍

2591 KEI hotaru

Ⓒⓗ 萤 yíng

Radical	Strokes
虫 142	11-6-5
Grade	**Freq**
Jōyō	1938
2 - 5 - 6	

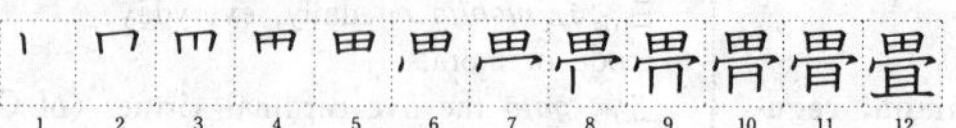

▶**FIREFLY**

COMPOUNDS

❶ [original meaning] **firefly, glowfly**
蛍火 *keika* light of a firefly
蛍雪 *keisetsu* diligent study
❷ (luminous as a firefly) **fluorescent**
蛍光 *keikō* fluorescence
蛍光灯 *keikōtō* fluorescent lamp [light]
蛍石 *keiseki* fluorite

KUN

【**hotaru** 蛍】firefly, glowfly
蛍の光 *hotaru no hikari* firefly glow; *Auld Lang Syne*
蛍烏賊 *hotaruika* firefly squid
土蛍 *tsuchibotaru* glowworm

SYNONYMS

❶ **insects**
蚊 MOSQUITO → 1319
蝶 BUTTERFLY → 1401
蚕 SILKWORM → 2457
❷ **bright**
昭 LUMINOUS → 894
明 BRIGHT → 855
晃 DAZZLING → 2450

COMPOUND FORMATION

蛍雪 *keisetsu*
蛍雪 'diligent study' refers to studying by the light of fireflies (蛍 ❶) and snow (雪).

5-6 此

紫

incorrect stroke count ⇨ see 2688

5-7 田

畳 疊 畳 畳

2592 JŌ tata(mu) tata(mi)- tatami

Ⓒⓗ 叠 dié

Radical	Strokes
田 102	12-5-7
Grade	**Freq**
Jōyō	1483
2 - 5 - 7	

1 2 3 4 5 6 7 8 9 10 11 12

▶**TATAMI** ▶**FOLD UP**

COMPOUNDS

❶ [sometimes also 帖 286] **counter for tatami or (straw) mats**
畳数 *jōsū* number of tatami [mats]
四畳半の部屋 *yojōhan no heya* four-and-a-half-mat room
❷ⓐ reduplicate (a word), repeat, reiterate
ⓑ [original meaning] pile up, place one upon another
畳成語 *jōseigo* reiterative
畳語 *jōgo* syllable repetition to indicate plurals (as 人人 *hitobito*)
畳韻 *jōin* repeated [recurring] rhymes (in Chinese poetry)
重畳たる *chōjōtaru* piled up, placed one upon another; excellent, splendid

KUN

【**tata(mu)** 畳む】fold up, fold; shut; bear in mind; do away with
畳まる *tatamaru* be folded (up)
折り畳みの *oritatami no* collapsible
家を畳む *ie o tatamu* shut up one's house
胸に畳む *mune ni tatamu* bear in mind
畳んでしまえ *Tatande shimae* Down with him!
【**tata(mi)-** 畳み-】[prefix] folding, collapsible
畳み椅子 *tatamiisu* folding [collapsible] chair
畳み地図 *tatamichizu* folding map
【**tatami** 畳】tatami, mat, straw mat
畳表 *tatamiomote* mat facing
畳替え *tatamigae* refacing [renewing] mats
畳敷きの部屋 *tatamijiki no heya* straw-matted room

青畳 *aodatami* new mat

SYNONYMS

❶ &【tatami】 **mats**

薦 straw mat → 2373

-敷き underlay → 1870

❷ⓐ **repeating and repetition**

重 DUPLICATE → 3573

復 repeat → 575

又 AGAIN → 3351

再 ANOTHER TIME → 3519

改 redo → 243

-換える redo → 587

-直す repetition suffix → 2932

-返す do over → 3060

【tatamu】

○ **fold**

折 FOLD → 253

塁 壘 塁 塁

2593 RUI toride▲

CH 垒 lěi

Radical	Strokes
土 32	12-3-9
Grade	**Freq**
Jōyō	534
2 - 5 - 7	

5-7 田

Stroke order: 1–12

▶BASE ▶SMALL FORT

COMPOUNDS

❶ *baseball* **base**

塁審 *ruishin* base umpire

満塁 *manrui* full bases

三塁 *sanrui* third base

本塁打 *honruida* home run

盗塁 *tōrui* base stealing, steal

❷ [original meaning] (small military fortification consisting of raised earthwork) **small fort, rampart, parapet, fortress, redoubt**

塁壁 *ruiheki* rampart

敵塁 *tekirui* enemy fortress, enemy position

堅塁 *kenrui* strong fort(ress)

堡塁 *hōrui* (= *horui*) fort, fortress, stronghold

土塁 *dorui* earthwork, fieldwork

INDEPENDENT

【rui 塁】 *baseball* base; fort, rampart, parapet

塁に出る *rui ni deru* go to first

塁を守る *rui o mamoru* defend a fort

塁を摩する *rui o masuru* rival, run close to

KUN

【toride 塁】 [now usu. 砦] fort, fortress, stronghold

SYNONYMS

❷ **strongholds**

城 CASTLE → 352

USAGE

toride

塁

[now usu. 砦] fort, fortress, stronghold

砦

[formerly also 塁] fort, fortress, stronghold

塞

[now usu. 砦] fort, fortress, stronghold

HOMOPHONES

toride ⇨ 砦 2671 塞 2330

異

2594

▶DIFFERENT

nonstandard for 異 2584

5-7 田

登 登 登

2595 TŌ TO nobo(ru)

CH 登 dēng

Radical	Strokes
癶 105	12-5-7
Grade	**Freq**
Jōyō-3	566
2 - 5 - 7	

5-7 癶

Stroke order: 1–12

▶CLIMB

COMPOUNDS

❶ⓐ **climb, ascend, mount, go up**

ⓑ climb or promote to a higher rank or position

登山 *tozan* mountain climbing, mountaineering

登頂 *tōchō* climbing to the summit

登楼する *tōrō suru* go into a tall building; visit a brothel

登高する *tōkō suru* climb up

登用する *tōyō suru* appoint, designate; pro-

mote, advance
登竜門 *tōryūmon* gateway to success, opening to honors
❷ **attend, go to, appear**
登校 *tōkō* attending school
登庁する *tōchō suru* attend a government office
登院 *tōin* attendance at the House
登城 *tojō* attendance at a castle
登場する *tōjō suru* come on stage; appear
❸ **register, enter, record**
登録 *tōroku* registration
登記 *tōki* registration, registry
登載 *tōsai* registration, record
❹ [rare] pass (an examination)
登科 *tōka* passing the civil service examination
登第 *tōdai* passing the examination

KUN

【nobo(ru) 登る】 (move up, esp. by using the hands and feet) climb, mount, ascend, scale
登り *nobori* climbing, ascent
登り口 *noboriguchi* starting point (for the ascent of a mountain)
山登り *yamanobori* mountain climbing
演壇に登る *endan ni noboru* mount the platform

SYNONYMS

❶ⓐ ascend
昇 ASCEND → 2415
上 go up → 3404
騰 RISE (esp. in price) → 1106
❷ attend
出 appear → 3498
臨 BE PRESENT AT → 1630
❸ write
録 RECORD → 1742
控える note down → 495
紀 record in writing → 1276
記 WRITE DOWN → 1453
写 COPY → 2000
書 WRITE → 2658
筆 write → 2677

HOMOPHONES

noboru ⇨ 上 3404 昇 2415
nobori ⇨ 上 3404

NOTE

⇨ see USAGE note at 上 3404

5-7
癶

2596

▶START ▶EMIT
nonstandard for 発 2565

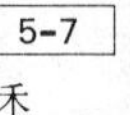

黍
2597 SHO kibi

Ⓒⓗ 黍 shǔ

Radical	Strokes
黍 202	12-12-0
Grade	**Freq**
Reference	
2 - 5 - 7	

RADICAL 202
Standard form: 黍 *kibi* 'millet' (黎 黐)
Description: used in characters related to millet or its qualities

COMPOUNDS

● [original meaning] millet
黍団子 *kibidango* millet dumpling
唐黍 *tōkibi* (=*morokoshi*) African [Indian] millet, sorghum
砂糖黍 *satōkibi* sugarcane

5-7
立

incorrect classification ⇨ see 2130

買  Ⓒⓗ 买 mǎi

2598 BAI ka(u)

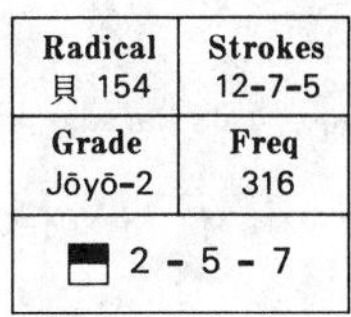

Radical	Strokes
貝 154	12-7-5
Grade	**Freq**
Jōyō-2	316
2 - 5 - 7	

5-7 罒

1 2 3 4 5 6 7 8 9 10 11 12

▶BUY

COMPOUNDS

● [original meaning] **buy, purchase**

買収 *baishū* buying up, purchasing; bribing
購買 *kōbai* purchase, buying
売買 *baibai* buying and selling, trade

KUN

【ka(u) 買う】

① buy, purchase

買い *kai* buying
買い手 *kaite* buyer, customer
買物 *kaimono* shopping, purchase, buying
買い上げる *kaiageru* buy, buy up; bid up
買い入れ *kaiire* purchase, buying
買い気 *kaiki* bullish [buying] sentiment [feeling]
買い戻し *kaimodoshi* redemption, repurchase

② incur, invite

人の恨みを買う *hito no urami o kau* incur a person's enmity

③ appreciate

苦心を買われる *kushin o kawareru* have one's labor appreciated

SYNONYMS

● **buy**

購 PURCHASE → 1624

鼠 incorrect stroke count ⇨ see 2693

5-7 臼

賀 賀 賀 Ⓒⓗ 贺 hè

2599 GA

Radical	Strokes
貝 154	12-7-5
Grade	**Freq**
Jōyō-5	748
2 - 5 - 7	

5-7 加

1 2 3 4 5 6 7 8 9 10 11 12

▶CONGRATULATE

COMPOUNDS

ⓐ **congratulate, greet**
ⓑ **celebrate**

賀状 *gajō* greeting card
賀詞 *gashi* greetings, congratulations
賀正 *gashō* New Year's congratulations, Happy New Year
慶賀 *keiga* congratulation, felicitation
年賀 *nenga* New Year's greetings; New Year's card
祝賀会 *shukugakai* celebration, party of congratulation

INDEPENDENT

【ga 賀】 celebration; congratulation, felicitations

七十の賀 *shichijū no ga* celebration of one's 70th birthday

【gasuru 賀する】 congratulate, greet

SYNONYMS

● **celebrating and congratulating**

寿 CONGRATULATIONS → 3557
慶 FELICITATION → 3173
祝 CELEBRATE → 913

5-7 代

貸 貸 貸

2600 TAI ka(su) ka(shi)- kashi-

CH 贷 dài

Radical	Strokes
貝 154	12-7-5
Grade	Freq
Jōyō-5	900
2 - 5 - 7	

▶LEND

COMPOUNDS

● [original meaning] **lend, loan; rent, hire out**

貸借 *taishaku* lending and borrowing, debt and credit, loan

貸与 *taiyo* loan, lending

賃貸 *chintai* lease, hiring out, charter

KUN

【ka(su) 貸す】 lend, loan; rent, hire out; give credit

貸し *kashi* loan, lending; renting

貸し倒れ *kashidaore* irrecoverable debt

貸金 *kashikin* loan

貸し出し *kashidashi* loan; lending service

高利貸し *kōrigashi* (=*kōrikashi*) loansharking, usury

【ka(shi)- 貸し-, kashi- 貸-】 [also prefix] for rent, for hire

貸し本屋 *kashihon'ya* rental library

貸し室 *kashishitsu* room for rent

貸家 *kashiya* house for rent

貸店舗 *kashitenpo* store for rent

SYNONYMS

● **lend and borrow**

借 BORROW → 122

債 DEBT → 156

融 finance → 1831

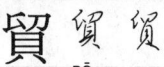

5-7 卯

貿 貿 貿

2601 BŌ

CH 贸 mào

Radical	Strokes
貝 154	12-7-5
Grade	Freq
Jōyō-5	950
2 - 5 - 7	

▶TRADE

COMPOUNDS

● [original meaning] **trade, buy and sell, exchange**

貿易 *bōeki* trade, commerce

貿易会社 *bōekigaisha* trading firm

貿易風 *bōekifū* trade wind

貿易品 *bōekihin* articles of commerce

貿易業 *bōekigyō* trading business

SYNONYMS

● **sell and trade**

商 TRADE → 2116

易 EXCHANGE → 2411

売 SELL → 2196

販 ENGAGE IN SALES → 1477

卸す WHOLESALE → 1447

5-7 ⺌

掌 掌 掌

2602 SHŌ tenohira▲ tanagokoro▲

CH 掌 zhǎng

Radical	Strokes
手 64	12-4-8
Grade	Freq
Jōyō	1478
2 - 5 - 7	

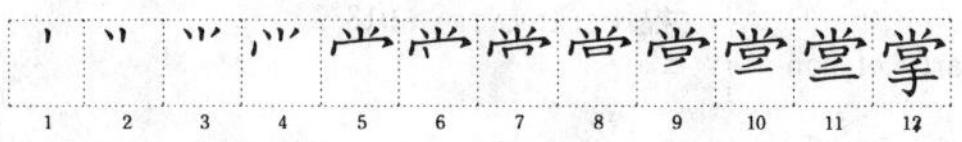

▶PALM ▶TAKE CHARGE OF

COMPOUNDS

❶ [original meaning] **palm of the hand**

掌中本 *shōchūbon* pocket edition

掌握する *shōaku suru* hold, seize, grasp, command

合掌する *gasshō suru* join one's hands (in prayer)

指掌紋 *shishōmon* hand print

❷ⓐ **take charge of, be in charge of, supervise**

ⓑ charge, duties

掌理する *shōri suru* take charge of, preside over, manage

職掌 *shokushō* office, function
車掌 *shashō* conductor
分掌 *bunshō* division of duties
管掌 *kanshō* taking charge, management

INDEPENDENT

【shō 掌】 palm of the hand

KUN

【tenohira 掌】 [also 手の平] palm of the hand
【tanagokoro 掌】 palm of the hand
掌を指す様に知っている *tanagokoro o sasu yō ni shitte iru* know (something) like the palm of one's hand

SYNONYMS

❶ **hand and arm**
指 FINGER → 378
手 HAND → 3456
腕 ARM → 1006

❷ **direct and supervise**
監 OVERSEE → 2852
督 SUPERVISE → 2796
轄 EXERCISE JURISDICTION OVER → 1627
管 EXERCISE CONTROL → 2701
制 CONTROL → 1274
司 OFFICIATE → 2931
宰 PRESIDE → 2275
営 MANAGE → 2603
理 manage → 970
経 MANAGE → 1331

USAGE

tenohira
掌
[also 手の平] palm of the hand
手の平
[also 掌] palm of the hand

HOMOPHONES

tenohira ⇨ 手の平 3456, 3478

営 營 営 営

2603 EI itona(mu)

Ⓒⓗ 营 yíng

Radical	Strokes
⺍ 42△	12-3-9
Grade	**Freq**
Jōyō-5	406
2-5-7	

5-7 ⺍

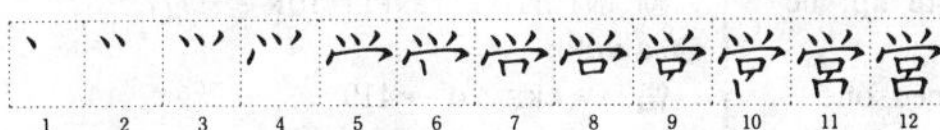

▶**MANAGE** ▶**BARRACKS**

COMPOUNDS

❶ⓐ **manage (the affairs of an organization), conduct, administer, operate, run, engage in**
ⓑ [also suffix] **managed by, operated by**
営業する *eigyō suru* conduct [do] business, trade in
営林 *eirin* forest management
経営する *keiei suru* manage (a firm), conduct (a business)
運営する *un'ei suru* operate, manage
公営 *kōei* public management
名古屋市営 *nagoyashiei* managed by the Nagoya Municipality

❷ **barracks, camp, encampment; fort**
兵営 *heiei* barracks
陣営 *jin'ei* camp, quarters
野営 *yaei* camping, campground

❸ construct, build, erect
営繕 *eizen* building and repairs, maintenance
造営 *zōei* building, construction

❹ plan, realize (profits)
営利 *eiri* profit, gain

❺ [usu. 栄] vitality obtained from nutriments (in Chinese medicine)
営養 *eiyō* nutrition, nourishment

KUN

【itona(mu) 営む】 manage, operate, conduct; build; perform (a religious service)
営み *itonami* business, occupation, operation

SYNONYMS

❶ **direct and supervise**
経 MANAGE → 1331
理 manage → 970
宰 PRESIDE → 2275
司 OFFICIATE → 2931
督 SUPERVISE → 2796
監 OVERSEE → 2852
掌 TAKE CHARGE OF → 2602
轄 EXERCISE JURISDICTION OVER → 1627
管 EXERCISE CONTROL → 2701
制 CONTROL → 1274

❷ **camps**
陣 CAMP → 455

5-7 覚 覺 覚 覚 ⒸⒽ 觉 jué jiào

⺍

2604 KAKU obo(eru) sa(masu) sa(meru) sato(ru)▲

Radical	Strokes
見 147	12-7-5
Grade	Freq
Jōyō-4	858
2 - 5 - 7	

▶PERCEIVE ▶COMMIT TO MEMORY

COMPOUNDS

❶ⓐ perceive, sense, discern, feel, be conscious; realize, know, comprehend

ⓑ sense, sensation

覚悟 *kakugo* readiness, preparedness; resignation; resolution

知覚 *chikaku* perception, sensation

自覚する *jikaku suru* be conscious of, realize

感覚 *kankaku* sense, sensation, feeling

視覚 *shikaku* sense of sight

痛覚 *tsūkaku* sense of pain

❷ⓐ awake, wake up; be disillusioned

ⓑ awake to the Truth, become enlightened

覚醒する *kakusei suru* awake, wake up; be awakened, be disillusioned

覚者 *kakusha* Buddha, the awakened one

❸ be detected, be disclosed, be discovered

発覚する *hakkaku suru* be detected, be disclosed, be discovered

KUN

【obo(eru) 覚える】

① commit to memory, remember, memorize

覚え *oboe* recollection, memory; learning; favor; feeling

覚え書き *oboegaki* memorandum, memo, note

見覚え *mioboe* recognition, remembrance

物覚え *monooboe* memory

② learn, know, acquire

覚え易い *oboeyasui* be easy to learn

③ feel, experience

痛みを覚える *itami o oboeru* feel a pain

【sa(masu) 覚ます】

vt

① awake, wake up

目を覚ます *me o samasu* awake, wake up, awaken

目覚まし *mezamashi* alarm clock

② disillusion

③ make sober

【sa(meru) 覚める】

vi

① awake, wake up

眠りから覚める *nemuri kara sameru* awake from one's sleep

② be disillusioned

③ become sober

酔い覚め *yoizame* recovering from intoxication, sobering up

【sato(ru) 覚る】[now usu. 悟る] awake to, be aware of, perceive, discern, realize

覚り *satori* comprehension, understanding

覚りが早い *satori ga hayai* be quick to understand

SYNONYMS

❶ⓐ perceive

知 KNOW → 1127

感 FEEL → 2835

認 RECOGNIZE → 1546

ⓑ sense

感 SENSE → 2835

勘 INTUITIVE PERCEPTION → 1777

❷ awake

悟 AWAKE TO → 419

【oboeru】

① remember

記 commit to memory → 1453

憶 REMEMBER → 765

追 reminisce → 3096

顧 LOOK BACK → 1900

USAGE

❶ samasu

覚ます

vt

① awake, wake up

② disillusion

③ make sober

冷ます

vt

① cool, let cool

② dampen, spoil

❷ sameru

覚める

vi

① awake, wake up

② be disillusioned

③ become sober

冷める

vi

ⓐ cool off, get cold

ⓑ cool down, subside, flag, be dampened

HOMOPHONES

samasu ⇨ 冷 80

sameru ⇨ 冷 80

satoru ⇨ 悟 419

satori ⇨ 悟 419

NOTE
⇨ see also USAGE note at 悟 419

2605

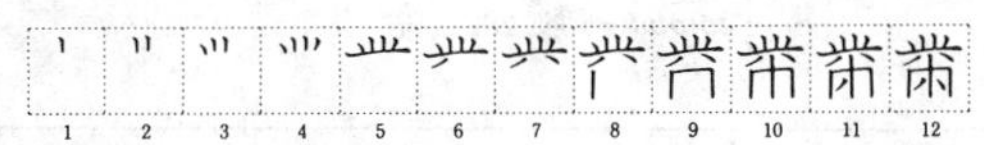

Radical	Strokes
黹 204	12-12-0
Grade	**Freq**
Radical	
2 - 5 - 7	

5-7

RADICAL 204
Standard form: 黹 *futsu* 'embroidery' (黻)
Description: used in characters related to embroidery or designs on clothing

貴 貴 𢀳 Ⓒⓗ 贵 guì
2606 KI tatto(i) tōto(i) tatto(bu) tōto(bu)

Radical	Strokes
貝 154	12-7-5
Grade	**Freq**
Jōyō-6	1116
2 - 5 - 7	

5-7

▶NOBLE ▶YOUR HONORABLE

COMPOUNDS

❶ⓐ (of noble rank) **noble, high-ranking**
ⓑ (lofty in character) **noble, exalted, honorable, dignified**
ⓒ (chemically inactive) noble, inert
貴族 *kizoku* nobility, noble
貴婦人 *kifujin* lady of rank, gentlewoman
富貴な *fūki na* wealthy and noble
高貴な *kōki na* high and noble
貴金属 *kikinzoku* noble metals
貴ガス *kigasu* noble gas, inert gas

❷ⓐ [also prefix] [honorific] **your honorable, your, your esteemed**
ⓑ [honorific] you
貴社 *kisha* your company
貴翰 *kikan* your letter
貴下 *kika* you
貴殿 *kiden* you
貴様 *kisama* [belittling] you; [original meaning] sir, madam

❸ **precious, valuable, costly**
貴重な *kichō na* precious, valuable
物価騰貴 *bukka tōki* rise in prices

❹ colloquial suffix expressing intimacy
兄貴 *aniki* older brother; one's senior
伯父貴 *ojiki* uncle

KUN

【tatto(i) 貴い】
① precious, valuable, priceless
貴い命 *tattoi inochi* precious life
② (of noble rank) noble, high-ranking
貴い家柄である *tattoi iegara de aru* be of noble birth

【tōto(i) 貴い】 same as **tattoi 貴い**

【tatto(bu) 貴ぶ】 value, set a high value on, have a high regard for
命より名を貴ぶ *inochi yori na o tattobu* value honor above life

【tōto(bu) 貴ぶ】 same as **tattobu 貴ぶ**

SPECIAL READINGS

貴方▲ *anata* you
貴女▲ *anata* you (feminine pronoun)

SYNONYMS

❶ⓐ & ❶ⓑ high-ranking
高 HIGH → 2097
上 upper → 3404
総 GENERAL → 1379
太 of highest rank → 2152

❷ⓐ honorific prefixes
尊 your honorable → 2324
令 your honorable → 1995
御 GENERAL HONORIFIC TERM → 577

ⓑ second person pronouns
君 YOU (*familiar*) → 3206
爾 thou → 3587

❸ expensive
高 high-priced → 2097

USAGE

❶ tattoi
貴い
① precious, valuable, priceless
② (of noble rank) noble, high-ranking
尊い
exalted, august, awe-inspiring, sacred

❷ tōtoi
貴い
same as 貴い *tattoi*
尊い

same as 尊い *tattoi*
❸ **tattobu**
貴ぶ
value, set a high value on, have a high regard for
尊ぶ
honor, respect, revere
❹ **tōtobu**
貴ぶ
same as 貴ぶ *tattobu*
尊ぶ
same as 尊ぶ *tattobu*

HOMOPHONES
tattoi ⇨ 尊 2324
tōtoi ⇨ 尊 2324
tattobu ⇨ 尊 2324
tōtobu ⇨ 尊 2324

5-7
弗

費 2607

HI tsui(yasu) tsui(eru)

CH 费 fèi

Radical	Strokes
貝 154	12-7-5
Grade	**Freq**
Jōyō-4	304
2-5-7	

1 2 3 4 5 6 7 8 9 10 11 12

▶**EXPENSE**

COMPOUNDS

❶ [also suffix] **expense, expenses, expenditure, cost**
費用 *hiyō* expenses, outlay
費目 *himoku* item of expenditure
会費 *kaihi* fee, membership fee
学費 *gakuhi* school [educational] expenses
食費 *shokuhi* food expenses; (charge for) board
出費 *shuppi* expenses, expenditure, outlay
経費 *keihi* expense(s), cost(s), expenditure, upkeep
生活費 *seikatsuhi* living expenses, cost of living

❷ [original meaning] **expend, spend, consume, use up**
消費 *shōhi* consumption, spending
浪費 *rōhi* waste, extravagance
空費 *kūhi* waste

KUN

【tsui(yasu) 費やす】 expend, spend, consume, use up; waste, squander
多くの金を費やす *ōku no kane o tsuiyasu* spend [expend] a lot of money
空しく費やされた時 *munashiku tsuiyasareta toki* time passed in vain, wasted time

【tsui(eru) 費える】 be wasted
費え *tsuie* wasteful expenses
無為に費えた年月 *mui ni tsuieta toshitsuki* years spent idly

SYNONYMS

❶ **fee and price**
料 FEE → 1292
代 CHARGE → 30
賃 CHARGES → 2694
銭 money paid → 1725
価 PRICE → 87
値 price → 109

❷ **consume**
消 SPEND → 443
尽 EXHAUST → 3050
耗 WEAR AWAY → 1309

USAGE

tsuieru
費える
be wasted
潰える
① be routed, be utterly defeated
② collapse

HOMOPHONES
tsuieru ⇨ 潰 743

5-8
穴

窟 incorrect classification ⇨ see 2328

5-8
立

incorrect classification ⇨ see 2136

置 逼 𡈽 Ⓒ 置 zhì

2608 CHI o(ku) -o(ki)

Radical	Strokes
罒 122	13-5-8
Grade	Freq
Jōyō-4	279
2-5-8	

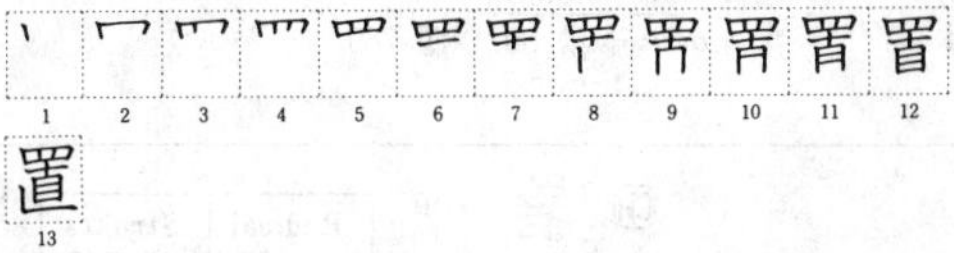

5-8 罒

▶**PLACE**

COMPOUNDS

❶ⓐ **place, put, install, set**
ⓑ place in custody, detain
ⓒ place, position
置換 *chikan* substitution, replacement, displacement
倒置 *tōchi* turning upside down; *gram* inversion
配置する *haichi suru* arrange; post (troops)
布置 *fuchi* arrangement, grouping
前置詞 *zenchishi* preposition
安置する *anchi suru* install, lay in state
対置する *taichi suru* oppose (a thing) to (another)
装置 *sōchi* equipment, device, installation
留置 *ryūchi* detention, custody, retention
拘置する *kōchi suru* detain, confine, arrest
位置 *ichi* position, place
❷ **found, establish, set up**
設置する *setchi suru* establish, found, set up
増置する *zōchi suru* establish more (offices)
常置の *jōchi no* permanent; standing
❸ **take proper steps, adopt measures, deal with**
処置する *shochi suru* dispose of, deal with
措置 *sochi* measure, step, action
❹ leave, let (alone)
放置する *hōchi suru* leave alone, neglect, leave as it is

KUN

【o(ku) 置く】
①ⓐ put, place, set
ⓑ assign; post, station
置き場 *okiba* storehouse, place to put something in [on]
置き時計 *okidokei* table clock
置き換える *okikaeru* replace, rearrange, interchange
歩哨を置く *hoshō o oku* post a sentinel
②ⓐ leave, leave behind, leave with
ⓑ leave (undone), let (alone)
ⓒ leave (a day or space) open
書き置き *kakioki* note [letter] left behind
置き忘れる *okiwasureru* leave behind, forget
据え置く *sueoku* leave as it is; defer (payment)
一軒置いて隣 *ikken oite tonari* next door but one
③ [following the TE-form of verbs] (perform an action and leave it in the state of having been done) do beforehand, do anyhow
調べて置く *shirabete oku* examine beforehand
一応聞いて置く *ichiō kiite oku* hear someone out anyway
④ establish, set up, organize
委員会を置く *iinkai o oku* form a committee
⑤ engage, employ; lodge, keep
下宿人を置く *geshukunin o oku* keep boarders
⑥ (of frost or dew) be formed
霜を置いた *shimo o oita* frosted; gray, hoary
【-o(ki) -置き】[suffix] every other, alternate
一日置きに *ichinichioki ni* every other [second] day
十分置きに運転する *juppun'oki ni unten suru* operate on a ten-minute schedule

SYNONYMS

❶ⓐ **put**
措 DISPOSE → 502
掛ける SET → 493
据える INSTALL → 497
ⓑ **imprison and confine**
拘 ARREST → 310
禁 confine → 2795
留 keep in custody → 2580
❷ **found**
立 ESTABLISH → 1992
設 SET UP → 1471
❸ **deal with**
措 dispose of → 502
処 DEAL WITH → 3031
扱う HANDLE → 217

USAGE

oku
置く
①ⓐ put, place, set
ⓑ assign; post, station
②ⓐ leave, leave behind, leave with
ⓑ leave (undone), let (alone)
ⓒ leave (a day or space) open
③ [following the TE-form of verbs] (per-

form an action and leave it in the state of having been done) do beforehand, do anyhow
④ establish, set up, organize
⑤ engage, employ; lodge, keep
⑥ (of frost or dew) be formed

措く
① desist from, discontinue
② except, set apart, lay aside

擱く
lay down (one's pen)

HOMOPHONES

oku ⇨ 措 502 擱 789

5-8 罒

署 署 署 署

2609 SHO

CH 署 shǔ

Radical	Strokes
罒 122	13-5-8
Grade	**Freq**
Jōyō-6	453
2-5-8	

▶PUBLIC-SERVICE STATION

COMPOUNDS

❶ [also suffix] **public-service station or office, as a police station, fire station or tax office**

署長 *shochō* chief of police, office head
署員 *shoin* member of an office, staff
警察署 *keisatsusho* police station
消防署 *shōbōsho* fire station
税務署 *zeimusho* tax office
本署 *honsho* chief police station, principal office
公署 *kōsho* government office

❷ **sign one's name**

署名 *shomei* signature, autograph
連署 *rensho* joint signature
代署する *daisho suru* sign for another

❸ assign duties to, post

部署 *busho* one's post, one's place of duty

INDEPENDENT

【sho 署】 public-service station [office] (⇨ ❶)
【shosuru 署する】 sign one's name

SYNONYMS

❶ **public offices**

局 public service office → 3063
所 office → 851
公 public office → 1974
府 government office → 3082
庁 GOVERNMENT AGENCY → 3034
省 MINISTRY → 2449

5-8 罒

罪 罪 罪

2610 ZAI tsumi

CH 罪 zuì

Radical	Strokes
罒 122	13-5-8
Grade	**Freq**
Jōyō-5	856
2-5-8	

▶CRIME

COMPOUNDS

❶ⓐ [also suffix] **crime, offense**
ⓑ **guilt**

罪状 *zaijō* offense, charges
罪人 *zainin* criminal, offender; sinner
犯罪 *hanzai* offense, crime
余罪 *yozai* other crimes [charges]
微罪 *bizai* minor offense, misdemeanor
破廉恥罪 *harenchizai* infamous offense
有罪 *yūzai* guiltiness, guilt
無罪の *muzai no* not guilty, innocent

❷ **sin**

罪悪 *zaiaku* crime, sin, vice
罪業 *zaigō* sin, iniquity
罪障 *zaishō* sins
原罪 *genzai* original sin

❸ fault, demerit

功罪 *kōzai* merits and demerits
謝罪 *shazai* apology

❹ [also suffix] punishment, penalty

斬罪 *zanzai* decapitation
流罪 *ruzai* banishment, exile
死罪 *shizai* capital punishment; capital

offense

KUN

【tsumi 罪】crime, offense; sin; sinful act; vice; punishment
罪する *tsumisuru* charge, sentence, punish
罪人 *tsumibito* sinner
罪な事 *tsumi na koto* sinful act, trick, cruel thing
罪の無い *tsumi no nai* innocent, guiltless
罪に服する *tsumi ni fukusuru* submit to a sentence, admit an offense

SYNONYMS

❶ **crimes and offenses**
犯 OFFENSE → 196
凶 atrocious crime → 2961
❷ **wrongdoing and evil**
非 wrong(doing) → 889
邪 wrong → 1124
悪 evil (something bad) → 2745
弊 evil(s) (something undesirable) → 2884

嵩 incorrect classification ⇨ see 2331

5-8

當 ▶THE PRESENT ▶HIT
2611
nonstandard for 当 2177

5-8

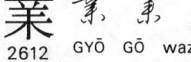

業 2612 GYŌ GŌ waza

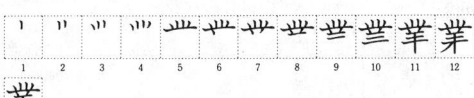

CH 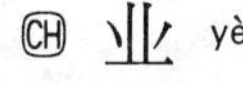 yè

Radical	Strokes
木 75	13-4-9
Grade	**Freq**
Jōyō-3	50
2 - 5 - 8	

5-8

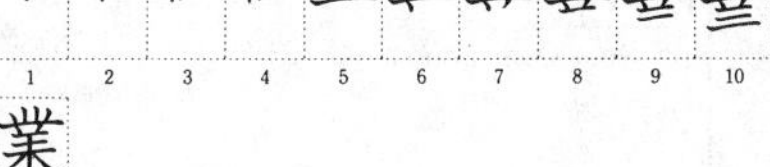

▶WORK ▶BUSINESS ▶INDUSTRY

COMPOUNDS

❶ⓐ (work as a means of livelihood) **work, occupation, business, employment, trade, profession**
ⓑ (operative activity or task) **work, operation**
職業 *shokugyō* occupation, vocation, profession
失業する *shitsugyō suru* be out of work, lose one's job
生業 *seigyō* occupation, calling
生業 *seigyō* (=*nariwai*) livelihood; calling, occupation
従業員 *jūgyōin* employee, workers
業績 *gyōseki* achievements; business results
操業する *sōgyō suru* operate, work, run
分業 *bungyō* division of labor [work]
作業 *sagyō* work, operation
❷ [also suffix] **business, trade, enterprise**
業務 *gyōmu* business, affairs, work, service
業者 *gyōsha* the trade, businessman
開業する *kaigyō suru* start a business, open a practice
商業 *shōgyō* commerce, trade, business
営業 *eigyō* business, trade
兼業 *kengyō* side business
事業 *jigyō* undertaking, enterprise, business; achievement
企業 *kigyō* undertaking, enterprise; business enterprise, company
印刷業 *insatsugyō* printing business
❸ [also suffix] **industry**
業界 *gyōkai* industry, business world
業種 *gyōshu* type of industry, category of business
産業 *sangyō* industry
工業 *kōgyō* industry, manufacturing industry
農業 *nōgyō* agriculture
鉱業 *kōgyō* mining (industry)
興業 *kōgyō* promotion of industry
製造業 *seizōgyō* manufacturing industry
❹ studies, course of study, schoolwork
学業 *gakugyō* studies; scholastic attainments
授業 *jugyō* teaching, instruction; lesson
卒業 *sotsugyō* graduation
修業する *shūgyō* (=*shugyō*) *suru* pursue one's studies, study, complete a course
❺ⓐ deed, work, achievement
ⓑ (one's deeds as a determinant factor in one's future life) karma
所業 *shogyō* deed, one's doings
偉業 *igyō* great work [achievement]
業報 *gōhō* karmic effects, fate, inevitable ret-

ribution
悪業 *akugō* evil doings in one's former existence, evil karma
自業自得 *jigō-jitoku* natural consequence of one's own deeds
罪業 *zaigō* sin, iniquity
非業の死 *higō no shi* unnatural death
❻ resentment, vexation
業腹 *gōhara* resentment, vexation, spite

INDEPENDENT

【gyō 業】 occupation, work; business; studies, arts
医を業とする *i o gyō to suru* practice medicine, be a physician by profession

【gō 業】 karma, karmic effect; resentment, vexation
業が深い *gō ga fukai* be sinful, be past redemption
業を煮やす *gō o niyasu* be exasperated, lose one's temper

KUN

【waza 業】 work, act, deed
業師 *wazashi* tricky wrestler, shrewd fellow
仕業 *shiwaza* act, action, deed, work
人間業 *ningenwaza* work of man
軽業 *karuwaza* acrobatics

SYNONYMS

❶ⓐ work and employment
職 EMPLOYMENT → 1425
労 LABOR → 2548
務 DUTY → 1173
任 OFFICE → 53
役 SERVICE (esp. public) → 244
勤 SERVICE (employment) → 1818
❷ & ❸ industry and business
商 TRADE → 2116
産 industry → 3298
工 manufacturing industry → 3381
❹ learning and knowledge
学 learning → 2555
文 culture → 1962
識 KNOWLEDGE → 1639
知 knowledge → 1127
❺ⓐ acts
挙 NOTEWORTHY ACT → 2456
行 ACT → 212
ⓑ fate and fortune
縁 karma relation → 1386
命 fate → 2058
運 FORTUNE → 3140

HOMOPHONES

waza ⇨ 技 248

NOTE

⇨ see USAGE note at 技 248

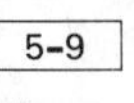
5-9

窪 incorrect classification ⇨ see 2348

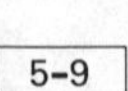
5-9
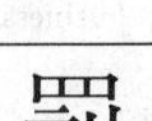

罰 罰 罰 2613 BATSU BACHI

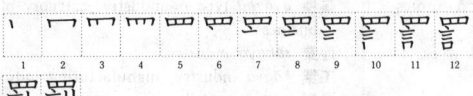

Ⓒ 罚 fá

Radical	Strokes
罒 122	14-5-9
Grade	**Freq**
Jōyō	1272
2-5-9	

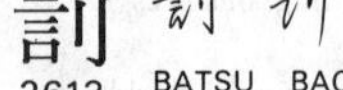
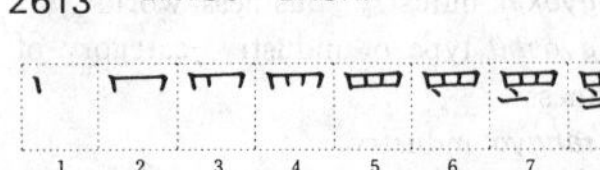

▶PUNISHMENT

COMPOUNDS

ⓐ punishment, penalty
ⓑ divine punishment, Heaven's vengeance
ⓒ [original meaning] punish, penalize
罰金 *bakkin* fine, penalty
罰則 *bassoku* penal regulations, punitive provisions
刑罰 *keibatsu* penalty, punishment
天罰 *tenbatsu* divine punishment
懲罰 *chōbatsu* discipline, punishment
処罰 *shobatsu* punishment, penalty

INDEPENDENT

【batsu 罰】 punishment, penalty
罰を科する *batsu o kasuru* inflict a punishment

【bassuru 罰する】 punish

【bachi 罰】 divine punishment, retribution, Heaven's vengeance
罰当たり *bachiatari* the damned, the cursed

SYNONYMS

● punishment
刑 PENALTY → 830
懲 CHASTISE → 2910
処 DEAL WITH (lawbreakers) → 3031

罯 2614

▶**PUBLIC-SERVICE STATION**

nonstandard for 署 2609

5-9 罒

裳 2615

SHŌ mo

Ⓒⓗ 裳 cháng shang

Radical	Strokes
衣 145	14-6-8
Grade	**Freq**
Reference	
2-5-9	

5-9 ⺌

COMPOUNDS

ⓐ [now replaced by 装 *shō* 2685] dress, clothing

ⓑ [original meaning] long skirt worn in ancient China

衣裳 *ishō* clothes, garment, dress, costume

裳 *mo* ancient skirt

盡 2616

▶**EXHAUST**

nonstandard for 尽 3050

5-9 聿

窮 窯

incorrect classification ⇨ see 3-12

5-10 穴

罷 2617

HI maka(ri)-▲ ya(meru)▲

Ⓒⓗ 罢 bà ba

Radical	Strokes
罒 122	15-5-10
Grade	**Freq**
Jōyō	1907
2-5-10	

5-10 罒

1 2 3 4 5 6 7 8 9 10 11 12 13 14 15

▶**DISMISS**

COMPOUNDS

❶ **dismiss, remove from office**

罷免 *himen* dismissal, discharge

罷官 *hikan* [archaic] removal from office

❷ stop working, go on strike

罷業 *higyō* strike, walkout

KUN

【**maka(ri)- 罷り-**】 emphatic verbal prefix

罷り通る *makaritōru* push one's way through; be unchallenged

罷り成らぬ *makarinaranu* must not, not be allowed

罷り間違えば *makarimachigaeba* if the worst happens, if things go wrong

【**ya(meru) 罷める**】 [in the form of 罷めさせる *yamesaseru*] fire, discharge

罷めさせる *yamesaseru* fire, discharge

SYNONYMS

❶ **dismiss**

免 discharge → 2067

解 release from office → 1517

HOMOPHONES

yameru ⇨ 辞 1364 止 2941

NOTE

⇨ see USAGE note at 辞 1364

5-10
⺌

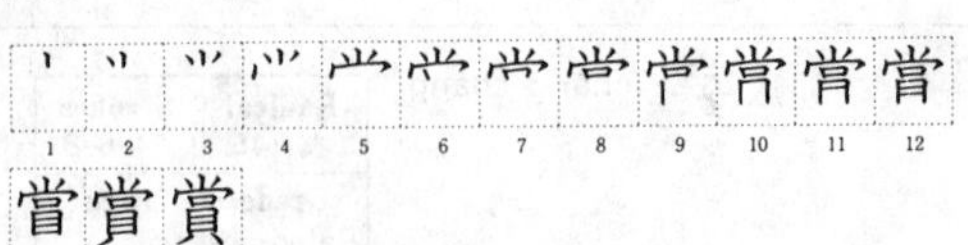

賞 賞 赏
2618 SHŌ ho(meru)▲

CH 赏 shǎng

Radical	Strokes
貝 154	15-7-8
Grade	Freq
Jōyō-4	607
2-5-10	

▶**PRIZE**

COMPOUNDS

❶ⓐ [also suffix] **prize, award, reward**
ⓑ award a prize
賞金 *shōkin* prize, award, reward
賞状 *shōjō* certificate of merit
賞品 *shōhin* prize, trophy
懸賞 *kenshō* prize competition; prize, reward
受賞する *jushō suru* win a prize
ノーベル医学・生理学賞 *nōberu igaku-seirigakushō* Nobel Prize for physiology and medicine
アカデミー賞 *akademīshō* Academy Award
褒賞 *hōshō* prize, reward
❷ⓐ **express admiration, praise, commend**
ⓑ admire, appreciate, enjoy
賞賛(=称賛)する *shōsan suru* laud, praise, admire, commend
激賞 *gekishō* high praise, unbounded admiration
賞美する *shōbi suru* admire, praise; prize; appreciate
賞味する *shōmi suru* relish, appreciate
鑑賞する *kanshō suru* appreciate
観賞する *kanshō suru* admire, enjoy

INDEPENDENT

【**shō** 賞】prize
賞を受ける *shō o ukeru* receive a prize
【**shōsuru** 賞する】commend, praise, award

KUN

【**ho(meru)** 賞める】[usu. 褒める, sometimes also 誉める] praise, commend, admire, compliment, eulogize
人の勤勉さを賞める *hito no kinbensa o homeru* praise a person for his [her] diligence

SYNONYMS

❶ⓐ **prizes**
章 decoration → 2117
杯 prize cup → 857
❷ⓐ **praise**
賛 PRAISE → 2809
美 regard as beautiful → 2264
褒 COMMEND → 2144
嘉 commend (esp. an inferior) → 2340
彰 PROCLAIM MERITS → 1860
称 acclaim → 1160
揚 EXALT → 593
頌 EULOGIZE → 1045

HOMOPHONES

homeru ⇨ 誉 2502 褒 2144

NOTE

⇨ see USAGE note at 褒 2144

5-11
罒

罹
2619 RI kaka(ru)

CH 罹 lí

Radical	Strokes
罒 122	16-5-11
Grade	Freq
Reference	
2-5-11	

COMPOUNDS

ⓐ fall ill, contract (a disease)
ⓑ suffer (from a calamity)
病気に罹る *byōki ni kakaru* contract a disease
罹災者 *risaisha* sufferers, victims

HOMOPHONES

kakaru ⇨ 掛 493 懸 2915 架 2569 係 97 繫 2902

NOTE

⇨ see USAGE note at 掛 493

5-12
襾

覆

incorrect stroke count ⇨ see 2725
(nonstandard for 覆 2726)

聲 incorrect classification ⇨ see 2872
(nonstandard for 声 2198) 5-12

壘 ▶BASE ▶SMALL FORT
nonstandard for 塁 2593 5-13 田
2620

叢 ⒸⒽ 丛 cóng 5-13
2621 SŌ kusamura mura mura(garu)

Radical	Strokes
又 29	18-2-16
Grade	**Freq**
Reference	
2-5-13	

COMPOUNDS

❶ grassy place, thicket, bush
叢林 *sōrin* Buddhist monastery
叢 *kusamura* grass, grassy place
竹叢(＝篁) *takamura* bamboo grove
稲叢 *inamura* rick, stack (of rice straw)
❷ⓐ [also 双 *sō* 25] crowd together, meet in large numbers
ⓑ [usu. 群がる *muragaru*] crowd together, throng, flock together, swarm
叢生する *sōsei suru* grow in clusters
叢書(＝双書) *sōsho* series, library
叢談 *sōdan* collection of stories
叢氷 *sōhyō* ice pack
論叢 *ronsō* collection of treatises
蜂が叢がる *hachi ga muragaru* be swarmed with bees
❸ [usu. 群 *mura*]
ⓐ [in compounds] group, crowd, flock
ⓑ counter for groups or flocks
❹ [also suffix] plexus
太陽神経叢 *taiyō-shinkeisō* solar plexus

HOMOPHONES

mura ⇨ 群 1540
muragaru ⇨ 群 1540

NOTE

⇨ see USAGE note at 群 1540

羅 ⒸⒽ 罗 luó luo luō 5-14 罒
2622 RA

Radical	Strokes
罒 122	19-5-14
Grade	**Freq**
Jōyō	1692
2-5-14	

▶**PHONETIC** [ra]

COMPOUNDS

❶ **used phonetically for *ra* or similar sounds, esp. in the transliteration of proper names or Sanscrit Buddhist terms**
羅紗 *rasha* woolen cloth
羅馬 *rōma* Rome
天麩羅 *tenpura* tempura, Japanese deep-fat fried food
阿羅漢 *arakan* Arhat, Buddhist monk who has attained Nirvana
金毘羅 *konpira* guardian deity of seafaring
❷ **spread out, arrange, line up; lie in a row**
羅列する *raretsu suru* arrange, itemize
羅針盤 *rashinban* compass
森羅万象 *shinrabanshō* all creation, Nature
❸ⓐ [original meaning] bird net, net
ⓑ **catch (birds) with a net**
雀羅 *jakura* sparrow net
網羅する *mōra suru* encompass, comprehend
❹ (netlike silk) silk gauze, thin silk
綺羅 *kira* fine clothes, gorgeous dress
一張羅 *itchōra* one's Sunday best; only suit one has
❺ abbrev. of 羅典 *raten*: Latin
羅葡日辞典 *raponichi jiten* Latin-Portuguese-Japanese dictionary
❻ abbrev. of 羅針盤 *rashinban*: compass

羅方位 *rahōi* compass bearing
羅北 *rahoku* compass north

INDEPENDENT

【ra 羅】 silk gauze, thin silk

SYNONYMS

❶ **phonetic** [r]
呂 PHONETIC [ro] → 2187
路 phonetic [ru] → 1533

❷ **arrange**
陳 lay out (for exhibit) → 540
列 arrange in a row → 824
揃える arrange properly → 590
整 PUT IN ORDER → 2871
理 put in order → 970
並 LINE UP → 2246
比 rank → 26

❸ⓐ **net**
網 NET → 1374

COMPOUND FORMATION

羅針盤 *rashinban*
羅針盤 'compass' is a disk (盤) with a pointer (針) that lines up with (羅 ❷), or points to, the north.

5-15 馨 incorrect classification ⇨ see 2879

5-15 黨 2623 **▶PARTY**
nonstandard for 党 2581

5-17 疊 2624 **▶TATAMI ▶FOLD UP**
nonstandard for 畳 2592

5-17 竊 incorrect classification ⇨ see 2387
(nonstandard for 窃 2253)

6-2 兒 2625 **▶CHILD**
nonstandard for 児 2546

6-2 呉 incorrect stroke count ⇨ see 2549

6-2 卓 incorrect classification ⇨ see 2064

6-2 免 incorrect classification ⇨ see 2067

6-2 尭 incorrect classification ⇨ see 2063

6-2 卒 incorrect classification ⇨ see 2055

6-2 受 incorrect classification ⇨ see 2421

2626

▶**IMPLEMENT**
nonstandard for 具 2552

2627 TEN DEN▲

Ⓒ 典 diǎn

Radical	Strokes
八 12	8-2-6
Grade	**Freq**
Jōyō-4	1105
2-6-2	

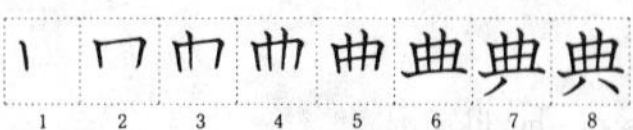

▶**STANDARD WORK** ▶**CANON**

COMPOUNDS

❶ [original meaning] standard work of reference or scholarship:
ⓐ **reference book, dictionary, encyclopedia**
ⓑ **classics, scriptures**
辞典 *jiten* dictionary
事典 *jiten* cyclopedia
字典 *jiten* Chinese character dictionary
原典 *genten* original text
古典 *koten* classics; old book
聖典 *seiten* sacred book, scriptures
❷ⓐ (standard code of laws) **canon, code, law, rule, principle**
ⓑ (standard of authority or evaluation) **canon, model, standard, authority**
典則 *tensoku* regulations
法典 *hōten* code of laws, statute
刑典 *keiten* penal code
典範 *tenpan* model, standard; law, code
典型 *tenkei* type, pattern, model, exemplar
典拠 *tenkyo* authority
❸ **formal ceremony, celebration**
典礼 *tenrei* formal ceremony
式典 *shikiten* ceremony
祭典 *saiten* festival
祝典 *shukuten* celebration, festival
❹ decent, decorous, seemly, classic
典雅な *tenga na* refine, graceful, elegant, classic
典麗な *tenrei na* graceful, elegant
❺ [formerly 奠 *den* 2132] offering
香典 *kōden* obituary [condolence] gift, incense money
❻ be in charge of, supervise
典獄 *tengoku* prison warden
❼ used phonetically for *ten* or *den*
羅典 *raten* Latin
瑞典 *suēden* Sweden

INDEPENDENT

【ten 典】 formal ceremony, celebration
華燭の典 *kashoku no ten* wedding ceremony

SYNONYMS

❶ **books**
経 religious classic → 1331
鑑 REFERENCE VOLUME → 1773
編 volume → 1387
巻 VOLUME → 2645
本 BOOK → 3502
書 BOOK → 2658
冊 bound book → 3483
籍 books → 2731
著 literary work → 2300
❷ⓐ **laws and rules**
法 LAW → 333
律 LAW → 363
憲 CONSTITUTION → 2368
令 ordinance → 1995
則 RULE → 1444
矩 RULE → 1148
規 REGULATION → 978
紀 discipline → 1276
ⓑ **model**
範 MODEL → 2709
模 PATTERN → 1050
程 ESTABLISHED FORM → 1190
式 form → 3049
準 STANDARD → 2856
格 NORM → 926
❸ **ceremonies and festivities**
式 CEREMONY → 3049
儀 CEREMONY → 169
礼 RITE → 818
斎 religious ritual → 2115
会 Buddhist ceremony → 2020
祭 FESTIVAL → 2672

6-2
自

阜

2628 FU FŪ

CH 阜 fù

Radical	Strokes
阜 170	8-8-0
Grade	Freq
Reference	
2 - 6 - 2	

RADICAL 170
Standard form: 阜 *gifunofu* 'mound'
Left variant: 阝 *kozatohen* (院 防 阪)
Description: used in characters related to mounds, hills or the like

COMPOUNDS
● [original meaning] mound
陰阜 *infu* mons pubis, mons veneris
岐阜 *gifu* Gifu (place name)

6-2
甘

其

2629 KI so(re) so(no)

CH 其 qí

Radical	Strokes
八 12	8-2-6
Grade	Freq
Reference	
2 - 6 - 2	

COMPOUNDS
❶ [also 夫れ *sore*] *pronoun* it, that
其れ其れ *sorezore* respectively, each
❷ⓐ *demonstrative* that, the
ⓑ *possessive pronoun* its; [archaic] his
其の後 *sono go* after that, thereafter
其処 *soko* that place, there
其の国に入りては其の俗に従う *Sono kuni ni irite wa sono zoku ni shitagō* When in Rome do as the Romans do

HOMOPHONES
sore ⇨ 夫 3460

NOTE
⇨ see USAGE note at 夫 3460

6-2
龹

券 券 券 券

2630 KEN

CH 券 quàn xuàn

Radical	Strokes
刀 18	8-2-6
Grade	Freq
Jōyō-5	593
2 - 6 - 2	

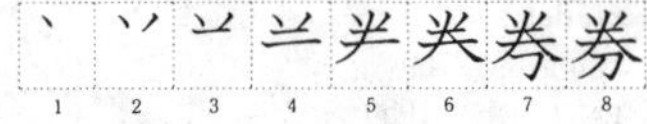

▶TICKET ▶CERTIFICATE

COMPOUNDS
❶ [also suffix] **ticket, coupon**
食券 *shokken* food ticket
乗車券 *jōshaken* railway [passenger] ticket
入場券 *nyūjōken* entrance [admission] ticket
定期券 *teikiken* commuter's pass [ticket]
❷ [also suffix] **certificate, voucher, bond**
旅券 *ryoken* passport
証券 *shōken* bill, bond, securities
債券 *saiken* bond, debenture
株券 *kabuken* share [stock] certificate
日銀券 *nichiginken* Bank of Japan bond

INDEPENDENT
【ken 券】 certificate, voucher; ticket, coupon

SYNONYMS
❶ **labels and slips**
札 TAG → 817
票 SLIP → 2669
符 tally → 2661
節 token → 2691
❷ **certificates**
証 CERTIFICATE → 1506
状 official document → 272
免 license → 2067

卷 2631

▶**ROLL UP** ▶**VOLUME**

nonstandard for 巻 2645

6-2 关

 2632

▶**TICKET** ▶**CERTIFICATE**

nonstandard for 券 2630

6-2 关

incorrect classification ⇨ see 2264

6-3 羊

臭 2633

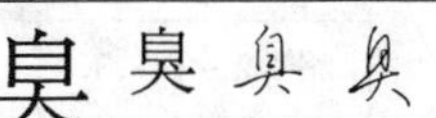

CH 臭 chòu xiù

SHŪ kusa(i) -kusa(i) nio(u)▲ nio(i)▲

Stroke order: 1 丿 2 丿 3 白 4 白 5 自 6 自 7 自 8 臭 9 臭

Radical	Strokes
自 132	9-6-3
Grade	**Freq**
Jōyō	1534
2 - 6 - 3	

6-3 自

▶**BAD SMELL**

COMPOUNDS

❶ⓐ **bad smell, stink**

ⓑ [also suffix] smell, odor

ⓒ **smelly, stinking**

臭味 *shūmi* bad smell, offensive odor; a smack of
体臭 *taishū* body smell
悪臭 *akushū* offensive [foul] odor, stench
防臭 *bōshū* deodorization
異臭 *ishū* offensive smell, stink
臭覚 *shūkaku* sense of smell
刺激臭 *shigekishū* irritating smell [odor], irritant odor
臭気 *shūki* offensive [odious] smell, bad [foul] odor, stench

❷ smack, taste

俗臭 *zokushū* low taste, vulgarity
官僚臭 *kanryōshū* smack of the bureaucrat

❸ bromine

臭素 *shūso* bromine

KUN

【kusa(i) 臭い】 ill-smelling, stinking, smelly; suspicious-looking, fishy

臭み *kusami* bad smell; fulsomeness
酒臭い *sakekusai* reek of liquor
水臭い *mizukusai* not frank, reserved; watery
生臭い *namagusai* smelling of fish [blood]
臭い奴 *kusai yatsu* dubious fellow

【-kusa(i) -臭い】 [suffix] smack of, look like

人間臭い *ningenkusai* quite human, full of human traits
素人臭い *shirōtokusai* amateurish

【nio(u) 臭う】 stink, reek

ガスが臭う *Gasu ga niou* There is a smell of gas

【nio(i) 臭い】

ⓐ stench, stink
ⓑ smack, inkling (of something disagreeable)

臭い消し *nioikeshi* deodorant
不正の臭い *fusei no nioi* smack of evil

SYNONYMS

❶ **smell and fragrance**

気 smell → 3194
香 SWEET SMELL → 2568
馨 PERFUME → 2879
芳 FRAGRANT → 2210
薫 BALMY → 2371
郁 AROMATIC → 1288

❸ **lighter elements**

塩 chlorine → 631
水 hydrogen → 10
酸 OXYGEN → 1563
窒 NITROGEN → 2288
硫 SULFUR → 1184
炭 carbon → 2257

USAGE

❶ **niou**

臭う
stink, reek

匂う
① smell (sweet), give out a smell [fragrance]
② (of blossoms) glow, be shiningly beautiful

❷ **nioi**

臭い
ⓐ stench, stink
ⓑ smack, inkling (of something disagreeable)

匂い
ⓐ smell, scent, fragrance, aroma

ⓑ flavor, touch (of something agreeable)

HOMOPHONES

niou ⇨ 匂 2944

nioi ⇨ 匂 2944

6-3 襾

要 ▶**IMPORTANT** ▶**SUMMARIZE** ▶**REQUIRE**

2634 nonstandard for 要 2635

6-3 襾

要 要 要 要 🄲🄷 要 yào yāo

2635 YŌ i(ru)

Radical	Strokes
襾 146	9-6-3
Grade	**Freq**
Jōyō-4	102
2-6-3	

一 1 冂 2 冖 3 襾 4 襾 5 襾 6 要 7 要 8 要 9

▶**IMPORTANT** ▶**SUMMARIZE** ▶**REQUIRE**

COMPOUNDS

❶ **important, essential, principal, leading**

要素 *yōso* (essential) element, constituent, factor
要因 *yōin* primary factor, main cause
要件 *yōken* important matter; necessary condition
要談 *yōdan* important talk
重要な *jūyō na* important, essential, principal
主要な *shuyō na* main, principal, essential
枢要な *sūyō na* pivotal, cardinal
肝要な *kan'yō na* important, vital, essential, necessary

❷ⓐ **summarize (the important points), outline**
ⓑ [also suffix] **summary (of important points), gist, essence**

要旨 *yōshi* gist, point, essentials, summary; purport
要綱 *yōkō* outline, gist; general plan
要領 *yōryō* gist, essentials; outline; procedure
概要 *gaiyō* outline, summary, synopsis
紀要 *kiyō* bulletin, proceedings
提要 *teiyō* summary, outline
哲学史要 *tetsugakushiyō* Concise History of Philosophy

❸ⓐ **require, demand, request**
ⓑ [also prefix] **required, necessary, essential**

要求 *yōkyū* requirement, demand, request
要請 *yōsei* request, demand
要望 *yōbō* demand, request
強要 *kyōyō* coercion, extortion
必要な *hitsuyō na* needed, necessary
需要 *juyō* demand
所要の *shoyō no* required, needed
要注意 *yōchūi* attention [care] required
要確認 *yōkakunin* confirmation required

❹ secret

要諦 *yōtei* secret, cardinal point

❺ ambush, waylay

要撃 *yōgeki* ambush attack

❻ [original meaning, now archaic] waist, hips

INDEPENDENT

【**yō 要**】main [essential] point, secret; summary, gist; necessity, need; required, necessary
要は *yō wa* the point is...; in short
要を得ている *yō o ete iru* be to the point
保証人要 *hoshōnin yō* guarantor required

【**yōsuru 要する**】require, need; ambush, waylay
修理を要する *shūri o yōsuru* want [need] mending
要するに *yōsuru ni* in a word, in short

KUN

【**i(ru) 要る**】
[sometimes also 入る]
ⓐ need, want, require
ⓑ be necessary [required]; cost, take
金が要る *Kane ga iru* I need [want] money / It takes money
要り *iri* expense(s)

SYNONYMS

❶ **important**
重 HEAVY → 3573

❷ⓐ **abridge**
抄 EXCERPT → 254
約 CONTRACT → 1280
略 omit → 1169

ⓑ **essential part**
旨 PURPORT → 2024
綱 ESSENTIAL POINTS → 1372
精 ESSENCE (essential part) → 1366
粋 essence (best part) → 1293
髄 essence (vital part) → 1842
枢 PIVOT → 865
幹 TRUNK → 1718

❸ⓐ **request**
願 ASK A FAVOR → 1845

求 SEEK → 3550
請 REQUEST → 1576
訴 APPEAL TO → 1507
頼 ASK → 1615
嘱 CHARGE WITH → 718
ⓑ need and necessity
必 must → 15
須 MUST → 574
需 DEMAND → 2797
入 necessary → 3370
用 needed for (a specific use) → 2976

USAGE

❶ iru
要る
[sometimes also 入る]
ⓐ need, want, require
ⓑ be necessary [required]; cost, take

入る
①ⓐ enter, go in, come in
ⓑ (of the sun) set
② attain
③ [usu. 要る]
ⓐ need, want, require
ⓑ be necessary [required]; cost, take

❷ iri
要り
[also 入り] expense(s)
入り
[also 要り] expense(s)

HOMOPHONES

iru ⇨ 入 3370
iri ⇨ 入 3370

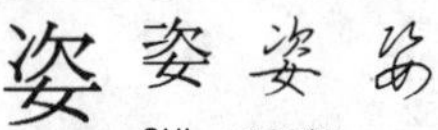

2636 SHI sugata

Ⓒ 姿 zī

Radical	Strokes
女 38	9-3-6
Grade	**Freq**
Jōyō-6	533
2-6-3	

6-3
次

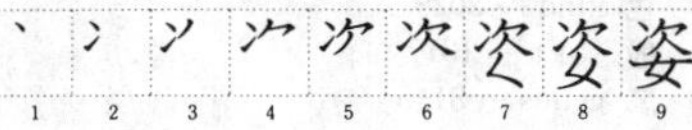

▶FIGURE

COMPOUNDS

ⓐ [original meaning] (outer shape, esp. of the body) **figure, form, shape, appearance, looks, aspect**
ⓑ posture, bearing, pose
容姿 *yōshi* face and figure, appearance
英姿 *eishi* gallant figure, majestic appearance
雄姿 *yūshi* brave [imposing] figure
姿勢 *shisei* posture, position, poise, attitude
姿態 *shitai* figure, person; pose

KUN

【sugata 姿】 figure, form, shape, appearance; portrait; posture; condition, state
姿を消す *sugata o kesu* disappear
女の姿になる *onna no sugata ni naru* disguise oneself as a woman
パジャマ姿で *pajamasugata de* in pajamas
姿見 *sugatami* full-length mirror
姿絵 *sugatae* portrait
孤立の姿 *koritsu no sugata* state of isolation

SYNONYMS

ⓐ appearance
容 APPEARANCE → 2277
相 PHASE → 900
体 FORM (outer appearance) → 71
色 COLOR → 2029
風 air → 3007
ⓐ form
形 SHAPE → 846
状 FORM (external) → 272
体 FORM (characteristic) → 71
ⓑ posture
態 attitude → 2847

2637

▶FIGURE
nonstandard for 姿 2636

6-3
次

6-3 刑

型

2638 KEI kata -gata

Ⓒℍ 型 xíng

Radical	Strokes
土 32	9-3-6
Grade	**Freq**
Jōyō-4	462
2 - 6 - 3	

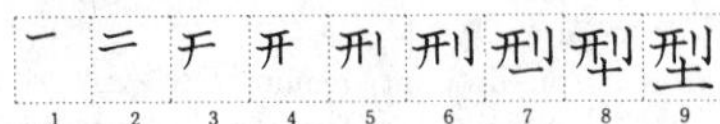

▶**TYPE**

COMPOUNDS

❶ⓐ (pattern from which something is made) **type, mold, model**

ⓑ (representative specimen) type, model

原型 *genkei* archetype, prototype, model
模型 *mokei* model, pattern, mold
紙型 *shikei* papier-mâché mold, paper mold
造型(＝造形) *zōkei* molding, modeling
典型 *tenkei* type, pattern, model, exemplar

❷ (general form characterizing a class) **type, kind, pattern, form**

型式 *keishiki* model
類型 *ruikei* similar type, prototype, pattern
同型 *dōkei* same type [pattern]
定型 *teikei* type, definite form
体型 *taikei* form, figure

KUN

【kata 型】

① (general form characterizing a class) type, kind, pattern, form

型に嵌める *kata ni hameru* squeeze into a pattern, regiment
大型 *ōgata* large size; large pattern
新型 *shingata* new style, new model
痩せ型 *yasegata* slender figure

② (pattern from which something is made) type, mold, model

型紙 *katagami* paper pattern (for a dress)
鋳型 *igata* mold, cast, matrix, die
歯型 *hagata* impression of the teeth, tooth-mark

③ set [traditional] form, *kata* (in martial arts and plays)

空手の型 *karate no kata kata* (in karate)

【-gata -型】 [also suffix] type, model

O型 *ōgata* model O; blood type O
血液型 *ketsuekigata* blood type
千九百五十四年型 *sen kyūhyaku gojūyo-nen-gata* 1954 model

SYNONYMS

❶ⓐ **prototype**

儀 model → 169

ⓑ **example**

例 EXAMPLE → 89

❷ **kinds and types**

種 VARIETY → 1218
様 variety → 1052
類 KIND → 1807
色 kind → 2029
般 SORT → 1317
属 genus → 3145
品 category → 2248

USAGE

❶ **kata**

型

① (general form characterizing a class) type, kind, pattern, form
② (pattern from which something is made) type, mold, model
③ set [traditional] form, *kata* (in martial arts and plays)

形

①ⓐ shape, form; pattern, design
ⓑ marks, traces
② security, pledge

❷ **-gata**

-型

[also suffix] type, model

-形

[also suffix] -shaped

HOMOPHONES

kata ⇨ 形 846
-gata ⇨ 形 846

契 契 契 契

2639 KEI chigi(ru)

CH 契 qì xiè

Radical	Strokes
大 37	9-3-6
Grade	Freq
Jōyō	1083
2 - 6 - 3	

6-3 㓞

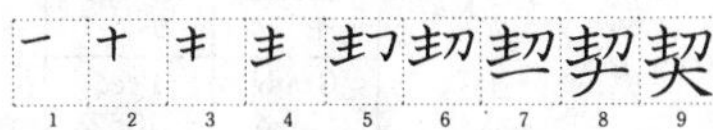

▶**MAKE AN AGREEMENT**

COMPOUNDS

❶ⓐ **make an agreement, agree on, pledge, promise**

ⓑ agreement, contract

契約 *keiyaku* contract, agreement

黙契 *mokkei* implicit agreement, tacit understanding

❷ⓐ (coincide exactly) agree with, match, coincide

ⓑ tally impression

契合する *keigō suru* coincide, agree

契印 *keiin* impression of a seal over the joint of two papers, tally

❸ chance, opportunity

契機 *keiki* opportunity, chance; *philosophy* moment

INDEPENDENT

【**kei** 契】tally impression

KUN

【**chigi(ru)** 契る】pledge, vow, swear, promise

契り *chigiri* pledge, vow, promise

固く契った恋人 *kataku chigitta koibito* plighted lovers

SYNONYMS

❶ **promise**

協 reach an agreement → 93

締 CONCLUDE (a treaty) → 1393

盟 ALLIANCE → 2794

誓 VOW → 2754

約 PROMISE → 1280

契

2640

▶**MAKE AN AGREEMENT**

nonstandard for 契 2639

6-3 㓞

変

incorrect classification ⇨ see 2069

6-3 亦

帝

incorrect classification ⇨ see 2073

6-3 产

県 縣 県 県

2641 KEN

CH 县 xiàn

Radical	Strokes
目 109ᴬ	9-5-4
Grade	Freq
Jōyō-3	182
2 - 6 - 3	

6-3 𥃭

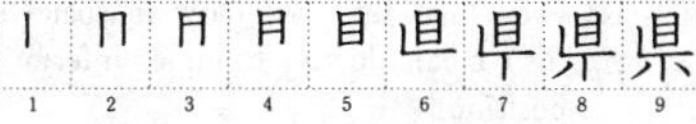

▶**PREFECTURE**

COMPOUNDS

❶ⓐ [also prefix and suffix] (largest administrative subdivision of Japan) **prefecture**

ⓑ **suffix after names of prefectures**

県庁 *kenchō* prefectural office

県警 *kenkei* prefectural police

県税 *kenzei* prefectural tax

県立病院 *kenritsu byōin* prefectural hospital

県民 *kenmin* citizens of a prefecture

県知事 *kenchiji* prefectural governor

府県 *fuken* prefectures

隣接県 *rinsetsuken* neighboring prefecture

香川県 *kagawaken* Kagawa Prefecture

❷ (administrative subdivision of China smaller than a province) county

INDEPENDENT

【**ken** 県】prefecture (⇨ ❶ⓐ)

SYNONYMS

❶ **territorial divisions**

府 URBAN PREFECTURE → 3082

道 district of Hokkaido → 3134

都 METROPOLIS OF TOKYO → 1686
省 province in China → 2449
州 STATE → 57
郡 COUNTY → 1466

6-3
由

卑 卑 卑 卑

Ⓒ 卑 bēi

2642 HI iya(shii) iya(shimu) iya(shimeru)

Radical	Strokes
十 24	9-2-7
Grade	Freq
Jōyō	1852
2-6-3	

▶**MEAN**

COMPOUNDS

❶ⓐ (low in social status) **mean, lowly, humble**
ⓑ [formerly also 鄙 1862] [humble] my humble
卑賤 *hisen* lowly position, humble condition
尊卑 *sonpi* upper and lower classes, high and low
卑見 *hiken* my humble opinion
❷ [formerly also 鄙 1862] (lacking in elevating human qualities) **mean, vulgar, despicable**
卑屈な *hikutsu na* mean, meanspirited; servile
卑劣な *hiretsu na* mean, base, cowardly
卑怯 *hikyō* cowardice, meanness, unfairness
卑語 *higo* vulgarism, vulgar word
野卑 *yahi* vulgarity, meanness
❸ⓐ humble oneself
ⓑ despise, look down on
卑下 *hige* humility, self-depreciation
男尊女卑 *dansonjohi* predominance of men over women, sexism
❹ familiar, common
卑近 *hikin* familiar, common; plain
卑金属 *hikinzoku* base metals
❺ (of land) low
卑湿な *hishitsu na* low and damp (land)

KUN

【iya(shii) 卑しい】
① [formerly also 賤しい] (low in social status) mean, lowly, humble, inferior in position
卑しさ *iyashisa* meanness, vulgarity
卑しい生まれの *iyashii umare no* lowborn
② [formerly also 賤しい]
ⓐ (of poor appearance) mean, shabby, seedy
ⓑ (lacking elevating human qualities) mean, base, vulgar, despicable
卑しい身形 *iyashii minari* shabby appearance
卑しからぬ *iyashikaranu* decent, respectable
卑しい根性 *iyashii konjō* mean spirit
卑しい笑い *iyashii warai* mean smirk
③ greedy, gluttonous
卑しん坊 *iyashinbō* greedy person, glutton

【iya(shimu) 卑しむ】 [formerly also 賤しむ] despise, disdain, look down on, regard with contempt
卑しみ *iyashimi* contempt
卑しむべき *iyashimubeki* despicable
労働を卑しむ *rōdō o iyashimu* despise labor

【iya(shimeru) 卑しめる】 [formerly also 賤しめる] same as **iyashimu 卑しむ**

SYNONYMS

❶ⓐ **lowly**
下 of low rank → 3378
低 LOW → 73
❷ **vulgar and unrefined**
俗 vulgar → 104
里 rural → 3542
粗 COARSE → 1329
野 rustic → 1485
蛮 barbaric → 2129

USAGE

❶ **iyashii**
卑しい
① [formerly also 賤しい] (low in social status) mean, lowly, humble, inferior in position
② [formerly also 賤しい]
ⓐ (of poor appearance) mean, shabby, seedy
ⓑ (lacking elevating human qualities) mean, base, vulgar, despicable
③ greedy, gluttonous
賤しい
① [now usu. 卑しい] (low in social status) mean, lowly, humble, inferior in position
② [now usu. 卑しい]
ⓐ (of poor appearance) mean, shabby, seedy
ⓑ (lacking elevating human qualities) mean, base, vulgar, despicable
❷ **iyashimu**
卑しむ
[formerly also 賤しむ] despise, disdain, look down on, regard with contempt
賤しむ
[now usu. 卑しむ] same as 卑しむ *iyashimu*

❸ iyashimeru
卑しめる
same as 卑しむ *iyashimu*
賤しめる
same as 卑しめる *iyashimeru*

HOMOPHONES
iyashii ⇨賤 1584
iyashimu ⇨賤 1584
iyashimeru ⇨賤 1584

甚

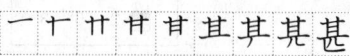

2643 JIN hanaha(da) hanaha(dashii)

CH 甚 shèn shén

Radical 甘 99	Strokes 9-5-4
Grade Jōyō	Freq 1935
2-6-3	

一 十 卄 廾 甘 甘 其 其 甚
1 2 3 4 5 6 7 8 9

▶**EXTREMELY**

COMPOUNDS

ⓐ **extremely, very, exceedingly**
ⓑ **extreme, excessive**
甚大な *jindai na* extremely big, very great; serious; heavy
幸甚である *kōjin de aru* be very glad, deem a favor
深甚な *shinjin na* profound; careful, mature
蝕甚(=食尽) *shokujin* maximum eclipse

KUN

【hanaha(da) 甚だ】 extremely, very, excessively, greatly
甚だ不親切である *hanahada fushinsetsu de aru* be extremely unkind
【hanaha(dashii) 甚だしい】 extreme, excessive, intense, tremendous
甚だしい誤解 *hanahadashii gokai* serious misunderstanding

SYNONYMS

● **extreme in degree**
極 EXTREME → 1017
酷 SEVERE → 1562
厳 SEVERE → 3289
激 intense → 776
痛 bitter(ly) → 3285
切 keen → 27
超 super- → 3313
強 STRONG → 475
重 HEAVY → 3573
高 HIGH → 2097
深 DEEP → 524
大 BIG → 3416

専

2644 SEN moppa(ra)

CH 专 zhuān

Radical 寸 41	Strokes 9-3-6
Grade Jōyō-6	Freq 559
2-6-3	

一 冂 冃 冃 日 由 亩 専 専
1 2 3 4 5 6 7 8 9

▶**EXCLUSIVE**

COMPOUNDS

❶ⓐ [original meaning] **exclusive, special, specialized**
ⓑ **take exclusive possession of, monopolize**
専用 *sen'yō* exclusive use, private use
専攻する *senkō suru* major in, specialize in
専門 *senmon* specialty, profession
専念 *sennen* close attention, concentration
専売 *senbai* monopoly
専有 *sen'yū* exclusive possession, monopoly
❷ [formerly also 擅] arrogate to oneself, claim arbitrarily, do something on one's own authority
専横 *sen'ō* arbitrariness, despotism
専行 *senkō* arbitrary action
専断 *sendan* arbitrary decision, arbitrariness
❸ abbrev. of 専門学校 *senmon gakkō*: professional school
高専 *kōsen* technical college
❹ abbrev. of 専攻 *senkō*: specialty, major
国文専 *kokubunsen* major in Japanese literature

KUN

【moppa(ra) 専ら】 entirely, exclusively, wholly, solely
専ら...を研究する *moppara...o kenkyū suru* devote oneself to the study of...

SYNONYMS

❶ⓐ **special**
特 SPECIAL (distinct) → 945
別 special (distinct) → 1117
殊 SPECIAL (exceptional) → 942

❶ occupy	❷ acting arbitrarily
領 take possession of → 1224	横 arbitrary → 1066
拠 occupy → 312	独 act arbitrarily → 395
占 OCCUPY → 2003	

6-3 关

巻 巻 巻 巻

2645 KAN KEN▲ ma(ku) maki ma(ki)

CH 卷 juàn juǎn

Radical	Strokes
己 49△	9-3-6
Grade	**Freq**
Jōyō-6	940
2-6-3	

丶 丷 䒑 丷 龹 龹 巻 巻 巻
1 2 3 4 5 6 7 8 9

▶**ROLL UP** ▶**VOLUME**

COMPOUNDS

❶ⓐ [original meaning] **roll up, roll, scroll**

ⓑ counter for film reels

巻子本 *kanshihon* scroll, roll, rolled book

巻雲(＝絹雲) *ken'un* cirrus cloud

五巻物 *gokanmono* five-reel film

❷ⓐ **volume, book**

ⓑ counter for volumes

巻末 *kanmatsu* end of a book

全巻 *zenkan* the whole volume [reel]

上中下巻 *jōchūgekan* set of three volumes

別巻 *bekkan* separate volume, extra issue

全六巻の著作 *zenrokkan no chosaku* work in six volumes

第一巻 *daiikkan* first volume, Vol. 1

INDEPENDENT

【kan 巻】 scroll, hanging scroll; volume, book

KUN

【ma(ku) 巻く】 roll up, roll; wind, reel; wrap

巻き上げる *makiageru* roll up; hoist, heave up; take away; blow up (dust)

巻き起こす *makiokosu* create (a sensation); give rise to

巻き付ける *makitsukeru* wind or tie around, coil

巻き返し作戦 *makikaeshi sakusen* rollback operation

渦巻き *uzumaki* eddy, whirlpool; coil

【maki 巻, ma(ki) 巻き】

①ⓐ roll, winding

ⓑ counter for rolls, scrolls or windings

巻き紙 *makigami* rolled letter paper

巻き物 *makimono* scroll

葉巻 *hamaki* cigar

絹布一巻 *kenpu hitomaki* one roll of silk

② book, volume

一の巻 *ichi no maki* Vol. 1

虎の巻 *tora no maki* key, crib, pony; secret (of a trade)

SYNONYMS

❶ⓐ **wind and twine**

繰る REEL → 1427

絡 ENTWINE → 1351

❷ⓐ **books**

編 volume → 1387

鑑 REFERENCE VOLUME → 1773

典 STANDARD WORK → 2627

経 religious classic → 1331

本 BOOK → 3502

書 BOOK → 2658

冊 bound book → 3483

籍 books → 2731

著 literary work → 2300

ⓑ **counters for books**

冊 COUNTER FOR BOOKS → 3483

部 counter for copies → 1676

6-4 ⺮

笑 笑 笑

2646 SHŌ wara(u) e(mu)

CH 笑 xiào

Radical	Strokes
⺮ 118	10-6-4
Grade	**Freq**
Jōyō-4	860
2-6-4	

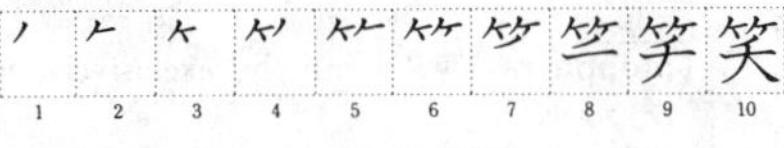

▶**LAUGH**

COMPOUNDS

❶ⓐ **laugh, smile**

ⓑ **laughter, smile**

ⓒ laugh at, ridicule, deride

一笑する *isshō suru* laugh a laugh, smile a smile

爆笑する *bakushō suru* roar with laughter, burst into laughter

微笑 *bishō* smile

苦笑 *kushō* forced [strained] smile
冷笑 *reishō* derisive smile, sneer
嘲笑する *chōshō suru* laugh at, deride
❷ indicates humility when presenting someone with something
笑覧 *shōran* your inspection

KUN

【wara(u) 笑う】 laugh, smile; laugh at, ridicule, deride; bloom beautifully
笑い *warai* laughter, smile; sneer
笑い声 *waraigoe* laughter
笑い話 *waraibanashi* funny [humorous] story
笑い物 *waraimono* object of ridicule, subject of derision
笑い草(＝笑い種) *waraigusa* laughingstock

【e(mu) 笑む】 smile, beam; bloom, come out
笑み *emi* smile

SPECIAL READINGS

笑顔 *egao* smiling face, smile

笹 incorrect stroke count ⇨ see 2663 6-4 ⺮

差 incorrect classification ⇨ see 3311 6-4 ⺶

息 6-4 自

2647 SOKU iki

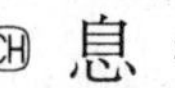

CH 息 xī

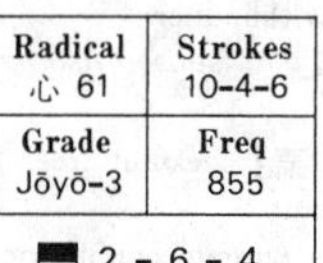

Radical	Strokes
心 61	10-4-6
Grade	**Freq**
Jōyō-3	855
2 - 6 - 4	

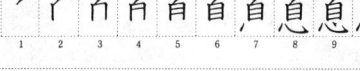

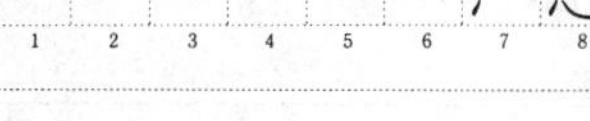

1 2 3 4 5 6 7 8 9 10

▶BREATH

COMPOUNDS

❶ [original meaning] **breath, respiration**
嘆息 *tansoku* sigh
喘息 *zensoku* asthma
窒息 *chissoku* suffocation, asphyxia

❷ live, breathe, be alive
生息(＝棲息)する *seisoku suru* inhabit, live
消息 *shōsoku* (personal) news, movements; letter

❸ **rest, repose**
休息 *kyūsoku* rest, repose
安息日 *ansokubi* Sabbath

❹ **son, child**
息女 *sokujo* daughter
子息 *shisoku* son

❺ interest
利息 *risoku* interest

❻ [formerly 熄 1057] go out, die out
終息する *shūsoku suru* cease, come to an end

INDEPENDENT

【soku 息】 son
山本氏の息 *yamamotoshi no soku* Mr. Yamamoto's son

KUN

【iki 息】 breath; tone
息切れ *ikigire* breathlessness
溜め息 *tameiki* sigh
一息 *hitoiki* breath; pause, rest; a little bit of effort
息抜き *ikinuki* rest, relaxation
息の合った *iki no atta* in good coordination

SPECIAL READINGS

息子 *musuko* son
息吹 *ibuki* breath

SYNONYMS

❶ **breathe and blow**
気 breath → 3194
吸 BREATHE IN → 202
呼 breathe out → 273
吹 BLOW → 231

❸ **rest**
休 REST → 52
憩 TAKE A REST → 2890

❹ **offspring**
男 son → 2542
惣 eldest son → 2780
子 CHILD → 3390
孤 orphan → 356
嫡 LEGITIMATE CHILD → 680
娘 DAUGHTER → 406
女 daughter → 3418
姫 DAUGHTER OF NOBLE BIRTH → 407

COMPOUND FORMATION

消息 *shōsoku*
消息 '(personal) news, movements; letter' originally referred to life (息 ❷) or death (消). This was extended to mean news about a person's state of being or movements.

6-4 自

臭 2648

▶BAD SMELL
nonstandard for 臭 2633

6-4 西

栗 2649

RITSU RI kuri NAMES kuru

CH 栗 lì

Radical	Strokes
木 75	10-4-6
Grade	Freq
Names	1994

2 - 6 - 4

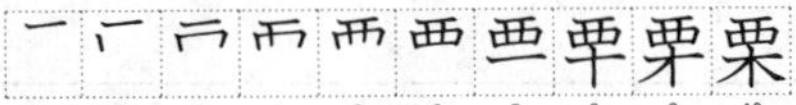

▶CHESTNUT

COMPOUNDS

❶ [original meaning] **chestnut tree, Japanese chestnut tree; chestnut**

栗鼠 *risu* squirrel

❷ [now always 慄 *ritsu* 642] tremble with fear, shudder

戦戦栗栗 *sensenritsuritsu* trembling with fear

KUN

【**kuri** 栗】chestnut tree, Japanese chestnut tree; chestnut

栗石 *kuriishi* cobblestone
栗毛 *kurige* chestnut (horse)
勝ち栗 *kachiguri* dried chestnut

NAMES

栗原 *kurihara* surname
栗栖 *kurusu* surname

SYNONYMS

❶ & 【**kuri**】 **fruits and fruit trees**

桃 PEACH → 936
李 PLUM → 2398
杏 APRICOT → 2397
梅 JAPANESE APRICOT → 925
橘 MANDARIN → 1077
梨 PEAR → 2744

6-4 巩

恐 2650

KYŌ oso(reru) oso(ru) oso(roshii) kowa(i)▲ kowa(garu)▲

CH 恐 kǒng

Radical	Strokes
心 61	10-4-6
Grade	Freq
Jōyō	891

2 - 6 - 4

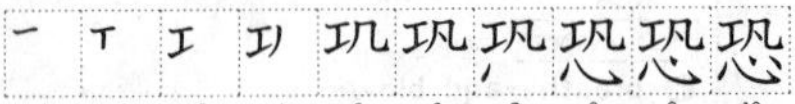

▶FEAR

COMPOUNDS

❶ⓐ [formerly also 兢 1566] [original meaning] **fear, be afraid of, dread**
ⓑ **fearful, frightening**

恐怖 *kyōfu* fear
恐慌 *kyōkō* panic, scare, alarm
恐懼 *kyōku* dread, fear, awe
恐妻家 *kyōsaika* henpecked husband, man bossed by his wife
恐水病 *kyōsuibyō* hydrophobia
閉所恐怖症 *heisho-kyōfushō* claustrophobia
戦戦恐恐として *sensenkyōkyō to shite* with fear and trembling
恐竜 *kyōryū* dinosaur, titanosaur

❷ **be overwhelmed** (**as with gratitude or astonishment**)

恐縮する *kyōshuku suru* feel much obliged, deeply appreciate; regret; feel embarrassed
恐悦がる *kyōetsugaru* congratulate oneself, chuckle with delight

❸ threaten

恐喝する *kyōkatsu suru* threaten, menace

KUN

【**oso(reru)** 恐れる】

ⓐ fear, dread, be afraid of
ⓑ apprehend, be anxious about
ⓒ [formerly also 畏れる] be overawed, stand in awe, fear

恐れ *osore* fear, dread, terror; [also 虞] fears (of undesirable event), danger, risk, signs, adverse chance, possibility
恐れていた通り *osorete ita tōri* as apprehended
恐れ多い *osoreōi* gracious, august
恐れ入る *osoreiru* be overwhelmed [dumfounded] (as with gratitude, shame, regret or astonishment)

【**oso(ru)** 恐る】 *literary* fear

恐るべき *osorubeki* fearful, formidable
恐らく *osoraku* probably

【**oso(roshii)** 恐ろしい】 terrible, fearful, fierce; awful, tremendous, marvelous

恐ろしさ *osoroshisa* fear, terror

恐ろしく *osoroshiku* fearfully, terribly, awfully

【kowa(i) 恐い】 [also 怖い] fearful, scary, uncanny; be afraid

恐さ *kowasa* fear, dreadfulness

犬が恐い *inu ga kowai* be afraid of dogs

【kowa(garu) 恐がる】 [also 怖がる] be afraid of, be frightened

恐がり *kowagari* timidity; coward

SYNONYMS

❶ **fear**

怖 FEARFUL → 296

USAGE

❶ **osoreru**

恐れる

ⓐ fear, dread, be afraid of

ⓑ apprehend, be anxious about

ⓒ [formerly also 畏れる] be overawed, stand in awe, fear

畏れる

[now usu. 恐れる] be overawed, stand in awe, fear

❷ **osore**

恐れ

① fear, dread, terror

② [also 虞] fears (of undesirable event), danger, risk, signs, adverse chance, possibility

虞

[also 恐れ] fears (of undesirable event), danger, risk, signs, adverse chance, possibility

HOMOPHONES

osoreru ⇨ 畏 2562

osore ⇨ 虞 3254

kowai ⇨ 怖 296 強 475

kowagaru ⇨ 怖 296

NOTE

⇨ see also USAGE note at 怖 296

恐 2651

▶**FEAR**

nonstandard for 恐 2650

6-4 巩

烈 2652 RETSU hage(shii)▲

CH 烈 liè

Radical	Strokes
灬 86	10-4-6
Grade	**Freq**
Jōyō	1381
2-6-4	

6-4 列

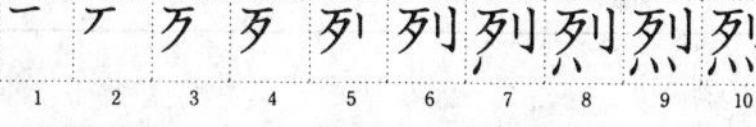

▶**VEHEMENT**

COMPOUNDS

❶ⓐ **vehement, violent, strong, furious, fierce, intense**

ⓑ [original meaning] (of fire) vehement (flames), raging, fiery

烈風 *reppū* violent [strong] wind

烈震 *resshin* violent [disastrous] earthquake

強烈な *kyōretsu na* intense, severe

痛烈な *tsūretsu na* sharp, biting, scathing, cutting

猛烈な *mōretsu na* violent, vehement, fierce

激烈な *gekiretsu na* vehement, furious, violent, severe

熱烈な *netsuretsu na* ardent, fervent, vehement

烈火 *rekka* raging fire, vehement flames

烈日 *retsujitsu* hot day, scorching sun

❷ staunch, virtuous, gallant, heroic

烈士 *resshi* patriot, hero

烈婦 *reppu* virtuous woman, heroine

壮烈な *sōretsu na* heroic, brave

KUN

【hage(shii) 烈しい】

[usu. 激しい]

① (acting with extreme force) violent, fierce, vehement

烈しさ *hageshisa* intensity, severity

烈しい風 *hageshii kaze* strong wind

② (of great intensity) intense, violent, severe

烈しい競争 *hageshii kyōsō* hot competition

SYNONYMS

❶ⓐ **extreme in power**

激 VIOLENT → 776

荒 WILD → 2260

狂 raging → 269

猛 FIERCE → 537

HOMOPHONES

hageshii ⇨ 激 776

NOTE

⇨ see USAGE note at 激 776

6-4 此

柴

2653 SAI shiba

 柴 chái

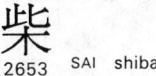

Radical	Strokes
木 75	10-4-6
Grade	Freq
Reference	
2-6-4	

COMPOUNDS

● [original meaning] brushwood, firewood
柴刈り *shibakari* firewood gathering
柴垣 *shibagaki* brushwood fence
柴犬 *shibainu* (Japanese) midget *Shiba* (kind of dog)

HOMOPHONES

shiba ⇨ 芝 2180

NOTE

⇨ see USAGE note at 芝 2180

6-4 亦

恋

incorrect classification ⇨ see 2098

6-4 劦

脅

incorrect classification ⇨ see 2109

6-4 叒

桑

incorrect classification ⇨ see 2112

6-4 立

旁

incorrect classification ⇨ see 2095

6-4 禸

离

incorrect classification ⇨ see 2102
(nonstandard for 離 1836)

6-4 兴

挙

incorrect classification ⇨ see 2456

6-4 安

案

incorrect classification ⇨ see 2270

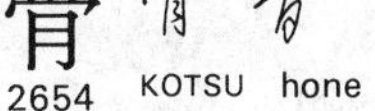

2654 KOTSU hone

CH 骨 gǔ gú gū

Radical	Strokes
骨 188	10-10-0
Grade	Freq
Jōyō-6	1021
2 - 6 - 4	

6-4

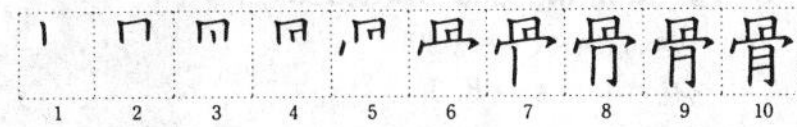

RADICAL 188

Standard form: 骨 *hone* 'bone'

Left variant: 骨 *honehen* (髄 骼 骸)

Description: used in characters related to bones or bone products

▶**BONE**

COMPOUNDS

❶ⓐ [also suffix] [original meaning] **bone**

ⓑ bones, body

骨折 *kossetsu* bone fracture

骨格 *kokkaku* frame, physique; framework, skeletal structure

人骨 *jinkotsu* human bone

肋骨 *rokkotsu* rib, costa

遺骨 *ikotsu* (skeletal) remains; ashes

白骨 *hakkotsu* bleached bone, skeleton

大腿骨 *daitaikotsu* thighbone, femur

老骨 *rōkotsu* old bones, old man

❷ (strength of character) backbone, spirit, grit

気骨 *kikotsu* (moral) backbone, spirit, soul, grit

反骨の精神 *hankotsu no seishin* spirit of defiance, backbone

❸ remains (of a body), ashes

納骨する *nōkotsu suru* lay (a person's) ashes to rest

❹ essence, gist

骨子 *kosshi* essence, gist

❺ knack, the ropes

骨法 *koppō* knack, the ropes

INDEPENDENT

【kotsu 骨】 remains (of a body), ashes; knack, trick, the ropes

お骨 *okotsu* ashes, remains

骨を覚える *kotsu o oboeru* get the knack, learn the ropes

KUN

【hone 骨】 bone, skeleton; frame, rib; backbone, spirit, grit; essence

骨組み *honegumi* skeleton; framework

骨休め *honeyasume* relaxation, recreation

骨っぽい *honeppoi* bony; spirited; hard to deal with

骨の有る男 *hone no aru otoko* man of spirit

骨を折る *hone o oru* take pains, make efforts; break one's bone

骨が折れる *hone ga oreru* require much effort, be hard to do; have one's bone broken

SYNONYMS

❶ⓐ **bone**

髄 MARROW → 1842

恩 恩 恩

2655 ON

CH 恩 ēn

Radical	Strokes
心 61	10-4-6
Grade	Freq
Jōyō-5	1352
2 - 6 - 4	

6-4 因

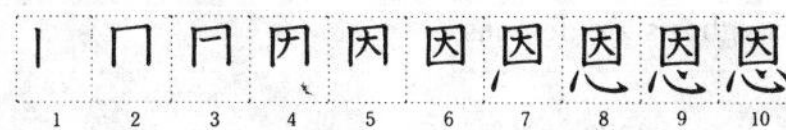

▶**GRACE** ▶**DEBT OF GRATITUDE**

COMPOUNDS

❶ⓐ [original meaning] **grace, favor, kindness, benevolence, blessing**

ⓑ gracious, compassionate, benevolent

ⓒ by grace of the Emperor

恩恵 *onkei* benefit, grace, favor, blessing

恩返し *ongaeshi* repaying another's kindness

恩人 *onjin* benefactor, patron

恩寵 *onchō* grace (of God), favor

恩情 *onjō* compassion, affection

恩命 *onmei* gracious command [words]

恩賜 *onshi* Imperial gift

❷ **debt of gratitude, gratitude, obligation, indebtedness**

恩義 *ongi* obligation, debt of gratitude

恩師 *onshi* one's respected teacher, one's former teacher

恩給 *onkyū* pension

恩知らず *onshirazu* ingratitude, ingrate

謝恩 *shaon* expression of gratitude

忘恩 *bōon* ingratitude

❸ love (esp. between family members)
恩讐 *onshū* love and hate

INDEPENDENT

【**on** 恩】debt of gratitude, gratitude, obligation, indebtedness; kindness, favor; love
恩が有る *on ga aru* owe a debt of gratitude
恩に着せる *on ni kiseru* demand gratitude
恩を忘れる *on o wasureru* be ungrateful

SYNONYMS

❶ⓐ **favor**
恵 FAVOR → 2659
徳 act of kindness → 684
❷ **thanking and gratitude**
謝 THANK → 1620
礼 thanks → 818

6-4 亚

晋

2656 SHIN NAMES susumu yuki

CH 晋 jìn

Radical	Strokes
日 72	10-4-6
Grade	**Freq**
Names	2059
2-6-4	

Stroke order: 一 丅 丌 亚 亚 亚 亚 晋 晋 晋 (1–10)

▶**JIN DYNASTY**

COMPOUNDS

❶ⓐ **Jin Dynasty (265–420 A.D.)**
ⓑ name of an ancient Chinese state
ⓒ another name for Shanxi Province (山西省)
晋書 *shinjo* History of the Jin Dynasty
❷ [original meaning, now rare] advance, proceed to
晋山 *shinzan* taking up a new position as chief priest of a Buddhist temple

INDEPENDENT

【**shin** 晋】Jin Dynasty

NAMES

晋次郎 *shinjirō* male name
晋 *susumu* male name

SYNONYMS

❶ⓐ **earlier Chinese dynasties**
漢 Han Dynasty → 657
周 Zhou Dynasty → 2998
商 Shang Dynasty → 2116
夏 Xia Dynasty → 2113

NOTE

★do not confuse with 普 2323

6-4 由

鬼

2657 KI oni oni-

CH 鬼 guǐ

Radical	Strokes
鬼 194	10-10-0
Grade	**Freq**
Jōyō	1181
2-6-4	

Stroke order: ノ 丿 白 白 白 由 甶 鬼 鬼 鬼 (1–10)

RADICAL 194

Standard form: 鬼 *oni* 'ghost' (魔 魂 魄)
Enclosure: 鬼 *kinyō* (魅 魍 魎)
Description: used in characters related to spirits, ghosts or demons

▶**DEVIL**

COMPOUNDS

❶ⓐ (harmful evil spirit) **devil, demon**
ⓑ (imaginary evil monster with horns) **devil, ogre**
鬼神 *kishin* terrible god; departed spirit, ghost
鬼畜 *kichiku* devil
鬼気迫る *kikisemaru* ghastly, bloodcurdling
鬼女 *kijo* demoness, witch
悪鬼 *akki* devil, demon, evil spirit, goblin
疑心暗鬼 *gishin'anki* suspicion and fear
鬼面 *kimen* mask of a devil, startling appearance
❷ [original meaning] **ghost, departed spirit**
鬼籍に入る *kiseki ni iru* join the majority, pass away
餓鬼 *gaki* hungry ghost; *slang* kid
❸ clever, artful, extremely competent
鬼才 *kisai* genius, wizard, prodigy
神出鬼没の *shinshutsukibotsu no* appearing and disappearing unexpectedly, elusive
❹ [also suffix] devilish or wicked person
債鬼 *saiki* creditor
剣鬼 *kenki* devilish swordsman
殺人鬼 *satsujinki* devilish homicide, cutthroat

KUN

【oni 鬼】 (imaginary evil monster with horns) devil, demon, ogre; (person with a demonical passion for something) demon, fiend; tagger, "it"

鬼婆 *onibaba* hag, witch

仕事の鬼 *shigoto no oni* devil for work, work fiend

鬼ごっこ *onigokko* tag game

【oni- 鬼-】

① [prefix] daredevil, extremely competent, inhumanly sharp

鬼武者 *onimusha* daredevil warrior

鬼刑事 *onikeiji* crack detective

② unbecomingly large

鬼蓮 *onibasu* prickly water lily

鬼歯 *oniba* protruding tooth

SYNONYMS

❶ & ❷ supernatural and evil beings

魔 DEMON → 3187

怪 monster → 297

霊 SPIRIT → 2805

精 SPIRIT → 1366

書 書 𠀋

2658 SHO ka(ku) -ga(ki) -gaki

1 2 3 4 5 6 7 8 9 10

ⒸⒽ 书 shū

Radical	Strokes
日 73	10-4-6
Grade	**Freq**
Jōyō-2	161
2 - 6 - 4	

6-4 書

▶WRITE ▶BOOK

COMPOUNDS

❶ write

書写 *shosha* transcription, copying, handwriting

書記 *shoki* clerk, secretary

清書する *seisho suru* write out fair, make a fair [clean] copy

代書する *daisho suru* write for another

❷ⓐ writing, art of writing, calligraphy, penmanship

ⓑ style of writing, calligraphic style

ⓒ written symbols, writings, characters

書法 *shohō* penmanship, calligraphy

書道 *shodō* calligraphy, penmanship

書家 *shoka* calligrapher

書体 *shotai* penmanship style, calligraphic style

楷書 *kaisho* printed [square] style of Chinese characters

行書 *gyōsho* semicursive style of Chinese characters

草書 *sōsho sosho*, cursive writing

書画 *shoga* pictures and writings

❸ written materials:

ⓐ [also suffix] **writings, document, papers, certificate**

ⓑ (written message) **letter, note, message**

書類 *shorui* documents, papers

書面 *shomen* letter, document

文書 *bunsho* (=*monjo*) document, letter, note

秘書 *hisho* secretary; treasured book

証明書 *shōmeisho* certificate, diploma

書簡 *shokan* letter, correspondence

書状 *shojō* letter, note

投書 *tōsho* contribution, letter (from a reader)

遺書 *isho* testamentary letter, will

私書箱 *shishobako* post office box (P.O.B.)

親展書 *shintensho* confidential letter

一般教書 *ippan kyōsho* State of the Union message

❹ⓐ [also suffix] **book, literary work**

ⓑ history book, chronicles, Chinese classics

ⓒ abbrev. of 書経 *shokyō*: Book of Documents [History] (name of a Chinese classic)

書物 *shomotsu* book, volume

書店 *shoten* bookstore

書籍 *shoseki* books, publications

辞書 *jisho* dictionary

図書 *tosho* books

図書館 *toshokan* library

読書 *dokusho* reading a book, reading

良書 *ryōsho* good book, valuable work

教科書 *kyōkasho* textbook, schoolbook

漢書 *kanjo* Chronicles of the Han Dynasty; Chinese classics

四書 *shisho* the Four Chinese Classics

INDEPENDENT

【sho 書】 calligraphy, penmanship, handwriting; book; letter

書の旨い人 *sho no umai hito* excellent calligrapher

座右の書 *zayū no sho* one's desk-side book

書を呈する *sho o teisuru* write a letter

KUN

【ka(ku) 書く】

ⓐ write, pen

ⓑ (compose written texts) write, compose

書き換える *kakikaeru* rewrite, renew (a bill),

transfer
書き順 *kakijun* stroke order (in writing Chinese characters)
書留 *kakitome* registered mail
読み書き *yomikaki* reading and writing
小説を書く *shōsetsu o kaku* write a novel

【-ga(ki) -書き, -gaki -書】 writing, written document, written statement, note
横書きする *yokogaki suru* write laterally, write from left to right
覚え書き *oboegaki* memorandum, memo, note
肩書き *katagaki* title, degree
葉書 *hagaki* postcard

SYNONYMS

❶ write
筆 write → 2677
写 COPY → 2000
記 WRITE DOWN → 1453
紀 record in writing → 1276
控える note down → 495
録 RECORD → 1742
登 register → 2595

❷ⓐ & ❸ⓐ writing
筆 WRITING → 2677
文 WRITINGS → 1962
銘 INSCRIPTION → 1724

❸ⓑ written communications
状 LETTER → 272
文 LETTER → 1962
信 written communication → 100
電 telegram → 2790

❹ⓐ books
本 BOOK → 3502
冊 bound book → 3483
籍 books → 2731
典 STANDARD WORK → 2627
鑑 REFERENCE VOLUME → 1773
著 literary work → 2300
巻 VOLUME → 2645
編 volume → 1387
経 religious classic → 1331

【kaku】
ⓑ compose
筆 write → 2677
著 AUTHOR → 2300
作 compose → 68

USAGE

kaku
書く
ⓐ write, pen
ⓑ (compose written texts) write, compose
描く
draw, paint

HOMOPHONES

kaku ⇨ 描 488

COMPOUND FORMATION

秘書 *hisho*
秘書 'secretary; treasured book' originally referred to secret (秘) documents (書 ❸ⓐ) and was extended to mean a person who handles such documents.

NOTE

⇨ see COMPOUND FORMATION for
図書 *tosho* ⇨ 図 3071
親展書 *shintensho* ⇨ 展 3111

6-4
恵

恵 恵 恵 恵

2659 KEI E megu(mu)

Ⓒⓗ 恵 huì

Radical	Strokes
心 61	10-4-6
Grade	**Freq**
Jōyō	942
2 - 6 - 4	

▶FAVOR

COMPOUNDS

❶ⓐ favor, grace, kindness
ⓑ [original meaning] **favor, bestow with a favor, show kindness to**
恵沢 *keitaku* blessing, pity, favor, benefit
恩恵 *onkei* benefit, grace, favor, blessing
互恵 *gokei* reciprocity, mutual benefits
特恵 *tokkei* special favor [benefit], preference, preferentialism
恵方 *ehō* lucky direction

❷ give, bestow, present
恵与する *keiyo suru* present, give, bestow
恵贈 *keizō* presentation

❸ [formerly 慧 *e* 2810] intelligence, wisdom
知恵 *chie* wisdom, intelligence, sagacity

KUN

【megu(mu) 恵む】
① bestow with a favor, show kindness to; have mercy on, render benevolence
恵み *megumi* favor, benefaction; blessing, grace, mercy
恵まれた人人 *megumareta hitobito* favored [privileged] people; blessed people
② give charity [alms]
乞食に金を恵む *kojiki ni kane o megumu* give money to a beggar

SYNONYMS

❶ favor

恩 GRACE → 2655
徳 act of kindness → 684
【megumu】
② **donate**
施 give alms → 891
寄 CONTRIBUTE → 2291
献 donate → 1785

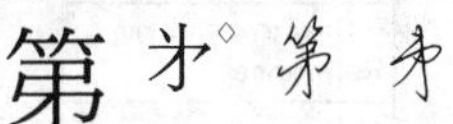
2660 DAI TEI▲

Ⓒⓗ 第 dì

Radical	Strokes
⺮ 118	11-6-5
Grade	**Freq**
Jōyō-3	85
2 - 6 - 5	

6-5 ⺮

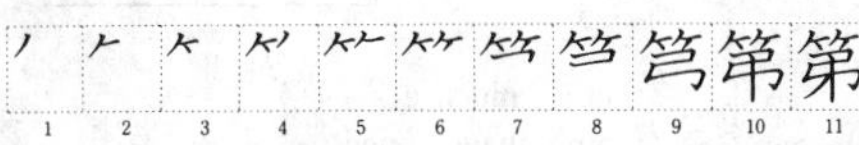

▶ORDINAL NUMBER PREFIX

COMPOUNDS

❶ **prefix for forming ordinal numbers**
第五 *daigo* the fifth, No. 5
第一印象 *daiichi-inshō* first impression
第一 *daiichi* the first, number one; the best; to begin with, above everything else
第三者 *daisansha* third party
第六感 *dairokkan* the sixth sense, intuition
❷ [original meaning] **order, sequence**
次第 *shidai* order; circumstances, reasons; as soon as
❸ examination (originally referred to grades into which successful candidates in the imperial examinations in China were placed)
及第する *kyūdai suru* pass an examination
落第 *rakudai* failure in an examination
❹ *hist* mansion or residence of a high official
聚楽第 *jurakudai* (= *jurakutei*) mansion of Toyotomi Hideyoshi (16th century)

INDEPENDENT

【dai 第】 examination in ancient China; mansion or residence of a high official

SYNONYMS

❶ **kinds of numbers**
-目 ordinal number suffix → 3043
次 numerical order suffix → 54
番 No. → 2748
号 NUMBER (numerical designation) → 2153
員 fixed number → 2269
数 NUMBER (mathematical unit) → 1790

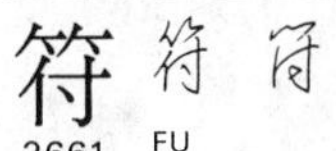
2661 FU

Ⓒⓗ 符 fú

Radical	Strokes
⺮ 118	11-6-5
Grade	**Freq**
Jōyō	1537
2 - 6 - 5	

6-5 ⺮

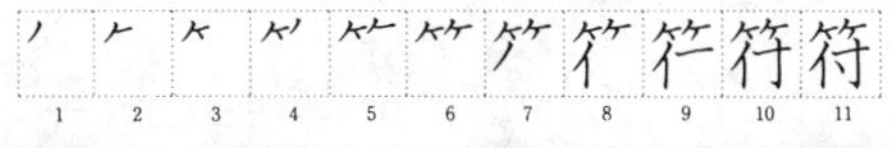

▶SYMBOL

COMPOUNDS

❶ [also suffix]
ⓐ (arbitrary sign other than a letter representing meaning) **symbol, sign, mark**
ⓑ *music* note
符号 *fugō* sign, mark, symbol
符牒 *fuchō* sign; secret price tag; password
疑問符 *gimonfu* question mark
終止符 *shūshifu* period
音符 *onpu* note; phonetic element of kanji
二分音符 *nibuonpu* half note
❷ⓐ [original meaning] **tally (of wood or bamboo) split in half used for identification (esp. in ancient China); tag**
ⓑ tally with, accord with
符節 *fusetsu* tally, check
割符 *warifu* tally, check
切符 *kippu* ticket
符合する *fugō suru* coincide [agree] with, conform with
❸ charm, amulet
護符 *gofu* charm, amulet
神符 *shinpu* charm, talisman, amulet

INDEPENDENT

【fu 符】 paper charm

SYNONYMS

❶ⓐ **marks and signs**
号 SIGN → 2153
標 MARK (identifying sign) → 1064
印 MARK (visible sign) → 828
跡 TRACE → 1534
紋 print → 1299
❷ⓐ **labels and slips**
節 token → 2691
札 TAG → 817

券 TICKET → 2630 | 票 SLIP → 2669

6-5

笠

2662 RYŪ kasa

CH 笠 lì

Radical	Strokes
⺮ 118	11-6-5
Grade	Freq
Reference	
2-6-5	

COMPOUNDS

❶ⓐ [original meaning] bamboo hat, sedge hat
ⓑ something that protects like a hat
笠の台が飛ぶ *kasa no dai ga tobu* be decapitated; be fired
編み笠 *amigasa* braided hat
父親の威光を笠に着る *chichioya no ikō o kasa ni kiru* shelter oneself under his father's influence

❷ (lamp) shade, hood
煙突の笠 *entotsu no kasa* chimney cap

HOMOPHONES

kasa ⇨ 傘 2131

NOTE

⇨ see USAGE note at 傘 2131

6-5

笹 笹 笹

2663 sasa

CH none (国字)

Radical	Strokes
⺮ 118	11-6-5
Grade	Freq
Names	2006
2-6-5	

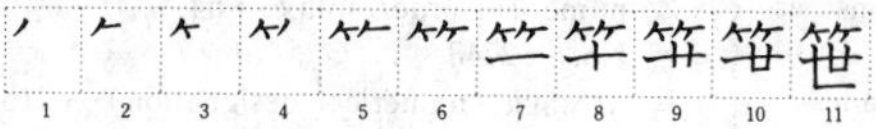

▶**BAMBOO GRASS**

KUN

【**sasa** 笹】 bamboo grass
笹原 *sasahara* field of bamboo grass
笹舟 *sasabune* toy bamboo-leaf boat
熊笹 *kumazasa Sasa albo-marginata*, low and striped bamboo

NAMES

笹川 *sasagawa* surname

SYNONYMS

【**sasa**】
○ **bamboo**
竹 BAMBOO → 228
○ **kinds of grasses**
草 GRASS → 2263
芝 LAWN GRASS → 2180

6-5

笛 笛 笛

2664 TEKI fue

CH 笛 dí

Radical	Strokes
⺮ 118	11-6-5
Grade	Freq
Jōyō-3	1624
2-6-5	

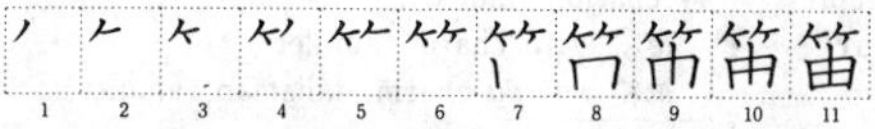

▶**FLUTE**

COMPOUNDS

❶ [original meaning] **flute, pipe, recorder**
鼓笛隊 *kotekitai* drum and fife band
牧笛 *bokuteki* shepherd's pipe
銀笛 *ginteki* flageolet
魔笛 *mateki* magic flute; The Magic Flute (by Mozart)

❷ **whistle, horn**
汽笛 *kiteki* steam whistle
霧笛 *muteki* foghorn
警笛 *keiteki* alarm-whistle, horn

KUN

【**fue** 笛】 flute, pipe, clarinet, oboe; whistle
笛吹き *fuefuki* flute player
横笛 *yokobue* flute, fife
草笛 *kusabue* reed
麦笛 *mugibue* oaten pipe
喉笛 *nodobue* windpipe
口笛を吹く *kuchibue o fuku* whistle

SYNONYMS

❶ **musical instruments**

琴 KOTO → 2781 | 鼓 DRUM → 1786

習 2665 ▶LEARN ▶CUSTOM
nonstandard for 習 2667 — 6-5 羽

翌 2666 ▶THE FOLLOWING
nonstandard for 翌 2668 — 6-5 羽

習 2667

習 習 習 — CH 习 xí — 6-5 羽

SHŪ JU▲ nara(u) nara(i)

Radical	Strokes
羽 124	11-6-5
Grade	Freq
Jōyō-3	637
2-6-5	

Stroke order: 1–11

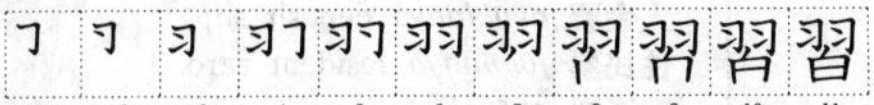

▶LEARN ▶CUSTOM

COMPOUNDS

❶ **learn, acquire, be taught, study**

習得 *shūtoku* learning, acquirement
学習 *gakushū* study, learning
練習 *renshū* practice, training
講習 *kōshū* short training course
独習 *dokushū* self-study, self-teaching
実習 *jisshū* practice, training
演習 *enshū* exercise, practice; military maneuvers; seminar
補習 *hoshū* supplementary lessons

❷ **custom, habit, practice, tradition**

習慣 *shūkan* custom, habit
慣習 *kanshū* custom, usage, tradition
風習 *fūshū* manners and customs
悪習 *akushū* bad habit
奇習 *kishū* strange custom

❸ be familiar with, become attached to

近習 *kinju* attendant

KUN

[nara(u) 習う] learn, be taught, study; practice

見習い *minarai* apprenticeship, apprentice
習い事 *naraigoto* practice

[nara(i) 習い] habit, custom, practice

習わし *narawashi* custom, practice

SYNONYMS

❶ **learn and study**

学 STUDY → 2555
考 study → 3196
研 RESEARCH → 1132
究 STUDY EXHAUSTIVELY → 2203
攻 specialize → 242

❷ **custom**

慣 HABITUAL PRACTICE → 685
例 established practice → 89
風 manners → 3007
俗 popular custom → 104
癖 HABIT → 3290
弊 EVIL PRACTICE → 2884

USAGE

narau

習う
learn, be taught, study; practice

倣う
copy after, copy from, imitate, follow an example

HOMOPHONES

narau ⇨ 倣 113

翌 2668

翌 翌 翌 — CH 翌 yì — 6-5 羽

YOKU

Radical	Strokes
羽 124	11-6-5
Grade	Freq
Jōyō-6	1218
2-6-5	

Stroke order: 1–11

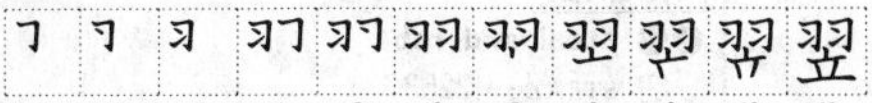

▶THE FOLLOWING

COMPOUNDS

● **the following, the next (month or year)**

翌日 *yokujitsu* the following [next] day
翌年 *yokunen* the next [following] year
翌春 *yokushun* next spring
翌翌日 *yokuyokujitsu* two days after
翌朝 *yokuasa* the following morning

INDEPENDENT

【yoku 翌】next, the following (month or year)

翌二十日 *yoku hatsuka* the following day, the 20th

SYNONYMS

● **next**

来 the coming → 3551

次 NEXT → 54

明 next → 855

6-5
襾

票 2669 HYŌ

ⒸⒽ 票 piào

Radical	Strokes
示 113	11-5-6
Grade	**Freq**
Jōyō-4	790
2-6-5	

▶VOTE ▶SLIP

COMPOUNDS

❶ⓐ [also suffix] **vote, ballot**

ⓑ counter for votes

票田 *hyōden* favorable voting constituency

投票 *tōhyō* vote, ballot

白票 *hakuhyō* blank ballot

得票 *tokuhyō* number of votes obtained

開票 *kaihyō* official counting of votes

賛否同票 *sanpi dōhyō* tie vote

二千票 *nisenbyō* 2000 votes

❷ [also suffix] **slip, chit, voucher, card**

伝票 *denpyō* slip, chit, ticket

証票 *shōhyō* voucher, chit

軍票 *gunpyō* military scrip, army note

入金票 *nyūkinhyō* deposit slip

住民票 *jūminhyō* resident card

調査票 *chōsahyō* questionnaire

INDEPENDENT

【hyō 票】vote, ballot

票を読む *hyō o yomu* count the votes

SYNONYMS

❶ⓐ **vote and election**

選 election → 3169

❷ **labels and slips**

札 TAG → 817

券 TICKET → 2630

符 tally → 2661

節 token → 2691

6-5
次

盗 2670 TŌ nusu(mu)

ⒸⒽ 盗 dào

Radical	Strokes
皿 108	11-5-6
Grade	**Freq**
Jōyō	866
2-6-5	

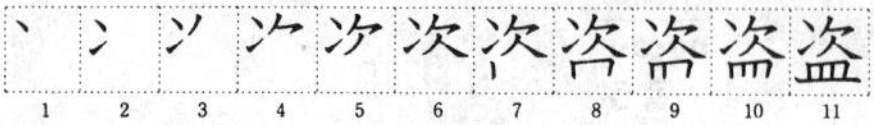

▶STEAL

COMPOUNDS

❶ⓐ **steal, burglarize**

ⓑ perform by stealth, steal

盗品 *tōhin* stolen article [goods]

盗癖 *tōheki* kleptomania

盗難 *tōnan* robbery, burglary, theft

窃盗 *settō* theft, larceny

盗作 *tōsaku* plagiarism

盗聴 *tōchō* wire tapping, unlicensed radio listening

❷ thief, burglar, robber

盗賊 *tōzoku* thief, robber, bandit

怪盗 *kaitō* mysterious thief

群盗 *guntō* group [gang] of robbers

夜盗 *yatō* night thief

❸ *baseball* steal

盗塁 *tōrui* base stealing, steal

重盗 *jūtō* double steal

KUN

【nusu(mu) 盗む】steal, rob; plagiarize; *baseball* steal

盗み *nusumi* theft

盗人 *nusubito* (=*nusutto*) thief

盗み聞き *nusumigiki* eavesdropping, tapping

盗み出す *nusumidasu* steal (from a person)

SYNONYMS

❶ⓐ **steal and rob**

窃 STEAL → 2253

取 TAKE → 1262

奪 ROB → 2343

略 plunder → 1169

❷ **thieves**

泥 petty thief → 326

賊 BANDIT → 1530

砦

2671 SAI toride

Ⓒ 砦 zhài

Radical	Strokes
石 112	11-5-6
Grade	Freq
Reference	
2-6-5	

6-5 此

COMPOUNDS

● [formerly also 塁 *toride* or 塞 *toride*] fort, fortress, stronghold

城砦(=城塞) *jōsai* fortress, stronghold, citadel

砦を築く *toride o kizuku* construct a fort

HOMOPHONES

toride ⇨ 塁 2593 塞 2330

NOTE

⇨ see USAGE note at 塁 2593

祭 祭 祭

2672 SAI matsu(ru) matsu(ri) matsuri

Ⓒ 祭 jì

Radical	Strokes
示 113	11-5-6
Grade	Freq
Jōyō-3	934
2-6-5	

6-5 癶

Stroke order: 1–11

▶**FESTIVAL**

COMPOUNDS

❶ⓐ [also suffix] **festival, feast, celebration, holiday**

ⓑ religious festival, rite

祭日 *saijitsu* national holiday, festival [feast] day

祝祭日 *shukusaijitsu* national holiday, festival [feast] day

文化祭 *bunkasai* cultural festival

芸術祭 *geijutsusai* art festival

前夜祭 *zen'yasai* eve

祭礼 *sairei* festival, feast, rituals

祭祀 *saishi* religious service; festival

❷ [original meaning] offer a sacrifice, worship a god

祭壇 *saidan* altar

祭神 *saijin* the enshrined deity

祭司 *saishi* priest

KUN

【matsu(ru) 祭る】

[formerly also 祀る]

ⓐ worship as god, deify

ⓑ enshrine

先祖を祭る *senzo o matsuru* worship one's ancestors

【matsu(ri) 祭り, matsuri 祭】 [also suffix] festival, celebration, feast day

夏祭り *natsumatsuri* summer festival

雛祭り *hinamatsuri* Doll Festival (March 3)

SYNONYMS

❶ **ceremonies and festivities**

会 Buddhist ceremony → 2020

斎 religious ritual → 2115

礼 RITE → 818

典 formal ceremony → 2627

儀 CEREMONY → 169

式 CEREMONY → 3049

USAGE

matsuru

祭る

[formerly also 祀る]

ⓐ worship as god, deify

ⓑ enshrine

祀る

[now usu. 祭る] same as 祭る

HOMOPHONES

matsuru ⇨ 祀 1128

參

incorrect classification ⇨ see 2126
(nonstandard for 参 2066)

6-5 厶

6-5 崇 incorrect classification ⇨ see 2297

6-5 甘

基 2673 KI moto motoi

CH 基 jī

Radical	Strokes
土 32	11-3-8
Grade	Freq
Jōyō-5	345
2-6-5	

一 十 廾 廿 甘 甘 其 其 基 基 基
1 2 3 4 5 6 7 8 9 10 11

▶**BASE**

COMPOUNDS

❶ⓐ (physical support) **base, basis, foundation**
ⓑ [also suffix] *chem* base; radical, group
ⓒ *math* base, radix
ⓓ [suffix] base material
基礎 *kiso* basis, foundation
基盤 *kiban* bedrock, base, foundation
基底 *kitei* base, basis, foundation; *math* base
基石 *kiseki* foundation stone
基地 *kichi* base
開基 *kaiki* foundation of a temple
塩基 *enki* base
水酸基 *suisanki* hydroxyl group [radical]
遊離基 *yūriki* free radical
根基 *konki* radical
培養基 *baiyōki* (culture) medium

❷ⓐ (nonphysical support) **base, basis, foundation, ground**
ⓑ basic, fundamental, cardinal
ⓒ be based on, be founded on
基本 *kihon* basis, foundation
基準 *kijun* standard, criterion, basis
基幹 *kikan* mainstay, nucleus
基金 *kikin* fund, foundation, endowment
基調 *kichō* keynote, underlying tone, basis
基音 *kion* fundamental tone
基点 *kiten* cardinal point, reference point
基因する *kiin suru* cause

❸ counter for mounted objects, esp. lanterns, gravestones, heavy machinery, torii (shrine archways) or large wreaths of flowers
石塔二基 *sekitō niki* two tombstones
エレベーター三基 *erebētā sanki* three elevators

❹ Christianity
基教 *kikyō* Christianity

❺ origin
基源 *kigen* origin

INDEPENDENT

【**ki** 基】*math* radix; base; *chem* radical; (nonphysical) basis, base

KUN

【**moto** 基】(underlying support) basis, foundation, grounds, authority
基づく *motozuku* be based on, be grounded on; originate, be due to
資料を基にする *shiryō o moto ni suru* on the basis [grounds] of the data

【**motoi** 基】(nonphysical) basis, foundation, essence
信仰を基とする *shinkō o motoi to suru* be based on faith

SPECIAL READINGS

基督▲ *kirisuto* Jesus Christ

SYNONYMS

❶ⓐ **bottoms and bases**
下 lower part → 3378
底 BOTTOM → 3084
礎 FOUNDATION STONE → 1248
盤 bedrock → 2851
床 BED → 3067

❷ⓐ **basis**
本 BASIS → 3502
礎 foundation → 1248
素 ELEMENT → 2458
底 BOTTOM → 3084
根 ROOT → 930
拠 GROUNDS → 312

HOMOPHONES

moto ⇨ 本 3502 元 1929 下 3378 素 2458 許 1470

NOTE

⇨ see USAGE note at 元 1929

6-5 晝

晝 2674

▶**DAYTIME**
nonstandard for 昼 3097

盛 盛 𢦑 𢦏 ㊥ 盛 shèng chéng

Radical	Strokes
皿 108	11-5-6
Grade	**Freq**
Jōyō-6	692
2 - 6 - 5	

6-5 成

2675 SEI JŌ mo(ru) saka(ru) saka(n)

丿 厂 厅 成 成 成 成 成 成 成 盛
1 2 3 4 5 6 7 8 9 10 11

▶**PROSPEROUS**

COMPOUNDS

❶ⓐ **prosperous, flourishing, successful, booming**
ⓑ at the height of, in the midst of
盛衰 *seisui* ups and downs, rise and fall, prosperity and decline
盛況 *seikyō* prosperity, boom, success
繁盛(=繁昌)する *hanjō suru* prosper, flourish, thrive
隆盛 *ryūsei* prosperity
最盛期 *saiseiki* height of prosperity
盛夏 *seika* midsummer
❷ grand, splendid, great, excellent
盛大な *seidai na* grand, magnificent, prosperous
盛儀 *seigi* grand ceremony
盛装 *seisō* gala dress, beautiful attire

KUN

【mo(ru) 盛る】
①ⓐ heap up (sand), pile (up)
ⓑ fill (a bowl with rice), serve food
盛り上がり *moriagari* climax (of a story), upsurge
盛り上げる *moriageru* pile up, heap up; stir up, bring to a climax
盆に胡桃を盛る *bon ni kurumi o moru* heap a tray with walnuts
盛り *mori* helping, serving; quantity
盛り付ける *moritsukeru* dish up
山盛り *yamamori* a heap, a full measure
酒盛り *sakamori* drinking bout, merrymaking
② administer (medicine), prescribe
毒を盛る *doku o moru* kill with poison
③ put into
盛り込む *morikomu* incorporate, include
④ mark out (in degrees), graduate
目盛 *memori* division, scale, graduations

【saka(ru) 盛る】prosper, thrive, flourish; (of animals) copulate
盛り *sakari* height, peak, prime; heat, rut
盛り場 *sakariba* public resort, bustling place
働き盛り *hatarakizakari* prime of life
盛りが付く *sakari ga tsuku* rut, get on heat

【saka(n) 盛ん】
sakan na 盛んな prosperous, flourishing; vigorous, energetic, active; hearty, cordial, enthusiastic, furious; keen; extensive, large; popular
盛んに *sakan ni* vigorously, energetically, actively; heartily, enthusiastically
盛んな商売 *sakan na shōbai* thriving business
盛んになる *sakan ni naru* prosper, grow prosperous, thrive
盛んな歓迎 *sakan na kangei* cordial reception

SYNONYMS

❶ⓐ **prospering and prosperity**
昌 PROSPERING → 2414
栄 FLOURISH → 2574
繁 THRIVE → 2853
隆 PROSPER → 545
振 rise → 430
興 RISE TO PROSPERITY → 2909

【moru】
①ⓐ **accumulate**
重 pile up → 3573
積 ACCUMULATE → 1236
累 CUMULATE → 2585

帯 ▶**BELT** ▶**WEAR**
2676 nonstandard for 帯 2582

6-5 帯

6-6 ⺮

筆 筆 筆 (CH) 笔 bǐ

2677 HITSU fude

Radical	Strokes
⺮ 118	12-6-6
Grade	**Freq**
Jōyō-3	956
2-6-6	

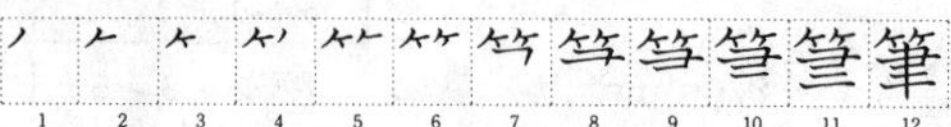

1 2 3 4 5 6 7 8 9 10 11 12

▶BRUSH ▶WRITING

COMPOUNDS

❶ [original meaning] **brush, writing brush, paintbrush**
毛筆 *mōhitsu* (writing or painting) brush
画筆 *gahitsu* paintbrush

❷ **writing instrument, pen, pencil**
鉛筆 *enpitsu* pencil
万年筆 *mannenhitsu* fountain pen
鉄筆 *teppitsu* steel pen, stencil pen
潤筆料 *junpitsuryō* fee for writing or painting

❸ⓐ **writing, literary profession**
ⓑ art of writing, calligraphy, penmanship
ⓒ (something written) writings, handwriting, writing, composition
文筆業 *bunpitsugyō* literary profession, writing
筆力 *hitsuryoku* power of the pen; ability to write
筆才 *hissai* literary talent
筆法 *hippō* style of penmanship
筆跡 *hisseki* handwriting, holograph
自筆 *jihitsu* one's own handwriting
随筆 *zuihitsu* essay; stray notes

❹ⓐ **write**
ⓑ writer
筆者 *hissha* writer
筆記する *hikki suru* take notes of, write down
執筆 *shippitsu* writing
特筆する *tokuhitsu suru* mention specially
主筆 *shuhitsu* chief editor

❺ subdivision of land
分筆 *bunpitsu* subdivision of a lot

INDEPENDENT

【hitsu 筆】 writing; written by
これは弘法大師の筆だそうです *Kore wa kōbō daishi no hitsu da sō desu* This writing is ascribed to Saint Kobo

KUN

【fude 筆】 writing brush, paintbrush; writing, painting; handwriting, penmanship; literary work, painting
筆先 *fudesaki* brush tip
絵筆 *efude* paintbrush, drawing pen
弘法筆を選ばず *Kōbō fude o erabazu* The cunning workman does not quarrel with his tools
一筆 *hitofude* a stroke (of the pen or brush)
筆不精 *fudebushō* poor correspondent
筆を置く *fude o oku* put down one's pen, stop writing, close (a letter)
雪舟の筆 *sesshū no fude* work of Sesshu

SYNONYMS

❸ **writing**
書 writing(s) → 2658
文 WRITINGS → 1962
銘 INSCRIPTION → 1724

❹ⓐ **write**
書 WRITE → 2658
写 COPY → 2000
記 WRITE DOWN → 1453
紀 record in writing → 1276
控える note down → 495
録 RECORD → 1742
登 register → 2595

ⓐ **compose**
書く WRITE → 2658
著 AUTHOR → 2300
作 compose → 68

NOTE

⇨ see COMPOUND FORMATION for
随筆 *zuihitsu* ⇨ 随 627
潤筆料 *junpitsuryō* ⇨ 潤 742

筋 筋 筋

2678 KIN suji

Ⓒ 筋 jīn

Radical	Strokes
⺮ 118	12-6-6
Grade	Freq
Jōyō-6	674
2 - 6 - 6	

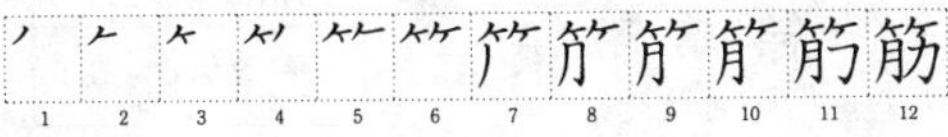

1 2 3 4 5 6 7 8 9 10 11 12

▶**MUSCLE**
▶**THREADLIKE STRUCTURE**

COMPOUNDS

❶ [also suffix] [original meaning] **muscle**
筋肉 *kinniku* muscle, sinews
筋骨 *kinkotsu* sinews and bones
筋炎 *kin'en* myositis, inflammation of a muscle
心筋 *shinkin* myocardium, heart muscle
腹筋 *fukkin* abdominal muscle
上腕筋 *jōwankin* brachial muscle

❷ reinforcement
鉄筋コンクリート *tekkin-konkurīto* reinforced concrete, ferroconcrete
補強筋 *hokyōkin* reinforcement bar

INDEPENDENT

【kin 筋】 muscle

KUN

【suji 筋】

① muscle; tendon, sinew
筋張った *sujibatta* sinewy, brawny; stringy
筋違い *sujichigai* cramp, sprain; misplacement, irrelevance

② threadlike structure, as:
ⓐ line, stripe, strip, streak
ⓑ vein
ⓒ fiber (of a plant), string; grain
ⓓ counter for long, slender objects
背筋 *sesuji* spinal column, spine; seam in the back
金筋 *kinsuji* gold stripes
青筋 *aosuji* veins bulging along the temples
豆の筋を取る *mame no suji o toru* string peas
一筋の涙 *hitosuji no namida* a trickle of tears

③ lineage, descent
血筋 *chisuji* blood relationship, lineage
長生きの筋 *nagaiki no suji* long-lived family

④ thread, coherence, reason, logic
筋合い *sujiai* reason
筋道 *sujimichi* reason, thread (of an argument), coherence; systematic method, due formality
筋の通った *suji no tōtta* logical, rational, coherent
本筋 *honsuji* right course (of action); main thread
大筋 *ōsuji* outline

⑤ plot
筋書き *sujigaki* plot (of a play), synopsis, outline; plan, scheme
芝居の筋 *shibai no suji* plot of a play

⑥ [also suffix] quarters, circles, source, channel
その筋 *sonosuji* authorities concerned
政府筋 *seifu-suji* official quarters
消息筋 *shōsoku-suji* informed circles

⑦ aptitude, nature
手筋 *tesuji* aptitude; handwriting; apt move (in a go or shogi game)

⑧ [in compounds] wayside, roadside, route, way
道筋 *michisuji* route, course, way
東海道筋の町 *tōkaidō-suji no machi* towns on the Tokaido
川筋 *kawasuji* course of a river; land along a river

SYNONYMS

❶ **flesh**
肉 FLESH → 3200

【suji】

②ⓐ **line**
条 strip → 2200
脈 VEIN → 953
線 LINE → 1392
棒 straight line → 983
軸 AXIS → 1514

ⓓ **counters for long objects**
本 counter for cylindrical objects → 3502

④ **reasoning**
理 REASON → 970
脈 VEIN → 953

⑧ **ways and routes**
路 ROAD → 1533
途 WAY (route) → 3107
道 WAY (path) → 3134
通り street → 3109
街 city street → 576
辻 CROSSROADS → 3192
岐 forked road → 241
径 PATH → 291
軌 TRACK → 1445
線 LINE → 1392

6-6

策 策 策
2679 SAKU

㊥ 策 cè

Radical	Strokes
⺮ 118	12-6-6
Grade	**Freq**
Jōyō-6	214
2-6-6	

1 2 3 4 5 6 7 8 9 10 11 12

▶SCHEME ▶MEASURE

COMPOUNDS

❶ⓐ (clever plan of action) **scheme, device, plan, stratagem**
ⓑ [also suffix] **policy**
策謀 *sakubō* artifice, stratagem
策士 *sakushi* tactician; schemer, machinator
政策 *seisaku* policy, political measures
方策 *hōsaku* plan, policy, scheme
国策 *kokusaku* national policy
強硬策 *kyōkōsaku* hard-line policy, drastic measures

❷ [also suffix] **measure, means, step, resource**
対策 *taisaku* countermeasure, counterplan
施策 *shisaku* enforcement of a policy
万策 *bansaku* all means [measures]
失策 *shissaku* blunder, slip, error
善後策 *zengosaku* remedial [relief] measure, countermeasure

❸ⓐ [original meaning, now rare] whip
ⓑ walking stick
策励 *sakurei* whipping (up), urging
散策する *sansaku suru* go for a walk

INDEPENDENT

【saku 策】 scheme, device, plan, stratagem; policy; measure, means, step, resource
最善の策 *saizen no saku* the best policy [measure]
策を講ずる *saku o kōzuru* take [adopt] measures

【sakusuru 策する】 plan

SYNONYMS

❶ⓐ **plans and planning**
謀 SCHEME → 1593
略 STRATEGY → 1169
図 systematic plan → 3071
企 PROJECT → 2021
計 PLAN → 1441
画 DRAW UP A PLAN → 3000
案 PROPOSAL → 2270
ⓑ **policy**
是 policy → 2436
綱 guiding principle → 1372
❷ **means**
段 STEP → 1144
手 means → 3456

6-6

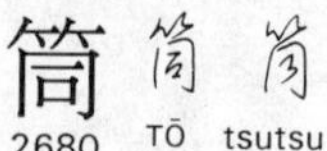
2680 TŌ tsutsu

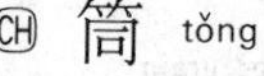

Radical	Strokes
⺮ 118	12-6-6
Grade	**Freq**
Jōyō	1622
2-6-6	

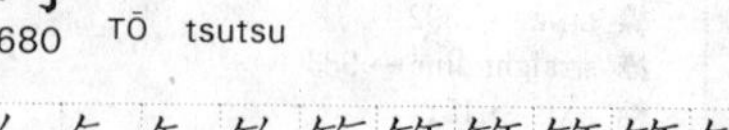

▶TUBE

COMPOUNDS

ⓐ [also suffix] [original meaning] **tube, cylinder, pipe**
ⓑ **tube-shaped encasement**
円筒 *entō* cylinder
発煙筒 *hatsuentō* smoke ball [bomb]
水筒 *suitō* canteen
封筒 *fūtō* envelope
筒形 *tsutsugata* cylindrical, tube-shaped
筒袖 *tsutsusode* tight-sleeved kimono
筒抜け *tsutsunuke* passing directly through (to)
茶筒 *chazutsu* tea caddy
短筒 *tanzutsu* revolver, pistol
井筒 *izutsu* well curb

KUN

【tsutsu 筒】 tube, cylinder, pipe; tube-shaped encasement; gun barrel; gun; well curb

SYNONYMS

● **tubular passages**
管 PIPE → 2701
道 passage → 3134
脈 VEIN → 953

答

2681 TŌ kota(eru) kota(e)

CH 答 dá dā

Radical	Strokes
⺮ 118	12-6-6
Grade	**Freq**
Jōyō-2	391
2-6-6	

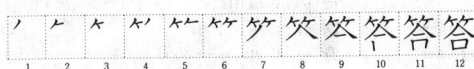

6-6 ⺮

▶ANSWER

COMPOUNDS

ⓐ [original meaning] **answer (a question), reply, respond**

ⓑ [also suffix] **answer (to a question), reply**

ⓒ answer, solve

ⓓ answer (to a problem), solution

答礼 *tōrei* return salute

答申 *tōshin* report, reply (to the jury)

答弁 *tōben* reply, answer; defending oneself

応答 *ōtō* answer, response, reply

回答 *kaitō* reply, answer

確答 *kakutō* definite answer [reply]

返答 *hentō* reply, answer

問答 *mondō* questions and answers, catechism

答案 *tōan* examination paper; answer

解答 *kaitō* solution, answer

KUN

【kota(eru) 答える】

ⓐ answer (a question), reply, respond

ⓑ answer (a problem), solve

質問に答える *shitsumon ni kotaeru* answer a question

【kota(e) 答え】 answer (to a question), reply; answer (to a problem), solution

受け答え *ukekotae* reply, response

SYNONYMS

● **answer**

解 solve → 1517

返 reply → 3060

応 RESPOND → 3066

USAGE

kotaeru

答える

ⓐ answer (a question), reply, respond

ⓑ answer (a problem), solve

応える

① come home to (one), strike home, have effect on; be a great strain

② repay, reward

HOMOPHONES

kotaeru ⇨ 応 3066

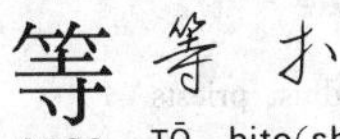

2682 TŌ hito(shii) nado▲ -ra▲

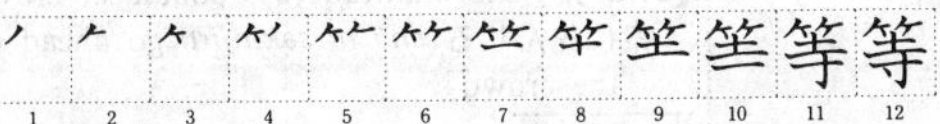

CH 等 děng

Radical	Strokes
⺮ 118	12-6-6
Grade	**Freq**
Jōyō-3	652
2-6-6	

6-6 ⺮

▶EQUAL ▶CLASS

COMPOUNDS

❶ [also prefix] [original meaning] **equal, same, alike**

等号 *tōgō* equal sign [mark]

等分する *tōbun suru* divide equally

平等 *byōdō* equality, impartiality

均等 *kintō* equality, uniformity

二等辺三角形 *nitōhen-sankakkei* equilateral [isosceles] triangle

❷ [also suffix] **class, grade, rank, degree, place, magnitude (of a star)**

等級 *tōkyū* class, grade, rank, magnitude

高等な *kōtō na* higher, high-grade, advanced

上等の *jōtō no* first-class, superior

劣等 *rettō* inferiority

中等 *chūtō* middle-class, secondary grade

一等 *ittō* first class; first place

三等星 *santōsei* third magnitude star

❸ **etcetera, and the like, and so forth**

等等 *tōtō* etcetera, and so forth

INDEPENDENT

【tō 等】 class, grade; etcetera, and the like, and so forth

等を分ける *tō o wakeru* classify, grade

家具等 *kagu-tō* furniture and the like

KUN

【hito(shii) 等しい】 equal, same, alike

Xは2Yに等しい *Ekkusu wa niwai ni hitoshii* X equals 2Y

【nado 等】 and the like, and what not, etcetera

等等 *nado nado* etcetera, etcetera

飛行機等 *hikōki nado* airplanes and the like

私等には *watakushi nado ni wa* for the likes of me

【-ra -等】

[suffix]

① and others, and the like, et al.

山田等 *yamadara* Yamada and the others

② plural suffix with deprecatory overtones

奴等 *yatsura* those guys, they

SYNONYMS

❶ **same and uniform**

平 equal → 3478

均 EVEN → 235

斉 UNIFORM → 2054

同 SAME → 2987

一 same → 3341

❷ **class**

流 class → 441

級 GRADE → 1279

段 grade → 1144

位 RANK → 61

階 RANK → 624

身 social status → 3553

格 STATUS → 926

層 STRATUM → 3161

【-ra】

② **plural suffixes**

-達 plural suffix → 3139

-共 belittling plural suffix → 2393

衆 somewhat polite plural suffix → 2683

-方 polite plural suffix → 1963

6-6 羊

着

incorrect classification ⇨ see 3316

6-6 血

衆 2683

眾 SHŪ 眾 SHU 衆 衆

CH 众 zhòng

Radical	Strokes
血 143	12-6-6
Grade	**Freq**
Jōyō-6	493
2-6-6	

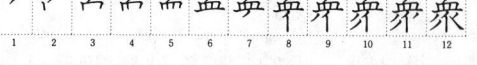

Stroke order: 1 2 3 4 5 6 7 8 9 10 11 12

▶MULTITUDE

COMPOUNDS

❶ⓐ **the multitude(s), populace, the masses, the public**

ⓑ (large crowd) **multitude, crowd**

ⓒ (great number) multitude, numerous, many

民衆 *minshū* populace, the people, the masses

大衆 *taishū* the masses, populace

公衆 *kōshū* the public

群衆 *gunshū* crowd of people, multitude

観衆 *kanshū* audience

アメリカ合衆国 *amerikagasshūkoku* United States of America

衆多 *shūta* great numbers, multitude

❷ abbrev. of 衆議院 *shūgiin*: **Lower House, House of Representatives**

衆参両院 *shūsan-ryōin* both Houses (of the Diet)

衆院 *shūin* Lower House, House of Representatives

❸ all kinds, various

衆説 *shūsetsu* various theories

❹ somewhat polite plural suffix

旦那衆 *dannashū* (=*dannashu*) gentlemen, gents

❺ Buddhist priest

衆徒 *shuto* many Buddhist priests

INDEPENDENT

【shū 衆】 the multitude(s), populace; crowd

衆に先んじる *shū ni sakinjiru* go ahead of the crowd

SYNONYMS

❶ⓐ **the people**

庶 the masses → 3127

民 PEOPLE → 3036

公 PUBLIC → 1974

ⓑ **crowd**

群 GROUP → 1540

❹ **plural suffixes**

-達 plural suffix → 3139

-等 plural suffix → 2682

-共 belittling plural suffix → 2393

-方 polite plural suffix → 1963

6-6 血

衆 2684

▶MULTITUDE

nonstandard for 衆 2683

装 装 装 装

2685 SŌ SHŌ yosoo(u)

㊥ 装 zhuāng

Radical	Strokes
衣 145	12-6-6
Grade	**Freq**
Jōyō-6	684
2 - 6 - 6	

6-6 壮

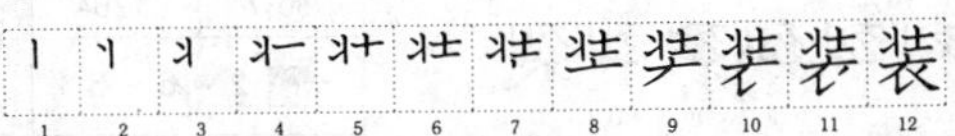

▶DRESS ▶FIT OUT

COMPOUNDS

❶ⓐ **dress, put on clothes**
ⓑ **dress up, disguise, play the part**
ⓒ **dress, outfit, attire, ornaments**
正装する *seisō suru* dress up
装身具 *sōshingu* personal ornaments [outfit]
男装する *dansō suru* disguise oneself as a man, wear men's clothes
変装する *hensō suru* disguise oneself
仮装する *kasō suru* disguise oneself, dress up (as)
装束 *shōzoku* costume, attire
服装 *fukusō* dress, garments, attire
旅装 *ryosō* traveling outfit
和装 *wasō* Japanese dress, kimono
衣装(＝衣裳) *ishō* clothes, garment, dress, costume
❷ **fit out, equip, outfit, furnish, install**
装備する *sōbi suru* equip, fit out, furnish
装置 *sōchi* equipment, device, installation
艤装する *gisō suru* fit out (a ship), equip
武装 *busō* armament, equipment
❸ⓐ (decorate) **dress (up), ornament, trim**
ⓑ coat, lay on
装飾する *sōshoku suru* ornament, adorn, decorate
新装 *shinsō* refurbishment, redecoration
改装 *kaisō* remodeling, refurbishing
塗装 *tosō* painting, coating
舗装 *hosō* paving
❹ⓐ load (a gun), charge; pack
ⓑ load (as of gunpowder), charge
装塡する *sōten suru* load, charge
包装 *hōsō* wrapping, packing
口装 *kōsō* muzzle loading gun
二連装 *nirensō* double load
❺ [also suffix] binding
装丁(＝装幀) *sōtei* binding, format
革装 *kawasō* leather binding

INDEPENDENT

【sō 装】 dress, outfit, attire; appearance
装を新たにする *sō o arata ni suru* renew one's dress; refurbish

KUN

【yosoo(u) 装う】 dress [attire] oneself, wear; make up; pretend
装い *yosooi* dress, outfit; equipment

SYNONYMS

❶ⓐ **wear and put on**
着 PUT ON → 3316
帯 WEAR (esp. at the belt) → 2582
履く put on footwear → 3171
被る put on headgear → 1163
ⓑ **disguise**
化 change oneself into → 21
ⓒ **clothing**
衣 GARMENT → 2013
服 CLOTHES → 878
-着 wear → 3316
❷ **equip and install**
据える INSTALL → 497
敷 LAY → 1870
架 LAY ACROSS → 2569
設 SET UP → 1471
備 PROVIDE → 146
❸ⓐ **decorate**
飾 DECORATE → 1717
粧 APPLY MAKEUP → 1345
粉 apply face powder → 1291

單

2686

▶**SINGLE**
nonstandard for 単 2256

6-6 口口

6-6 列

裂

2687 RETSU sa(ku) sa(keru) -gi(re)▲

CH 裂 liè liě

Radical	Strokes
衣 145	12-6-6
Grade	Freq
Jōyō	1264
2-6-6	

▶**SPLIT**

COMPOUNDS

❶ⓐ [original meaning] (separate or become separated into pieces) **split, tear, crack**

ⓑ crack, fissure

破裂 *haretsu* explosion, bursting

核分裂 *kakubunretsu* nuclear fission

裂傷 *resshō* lacerated wound

亀裂 *kiretsu* crack, fissure

❷ (sever relations) split up, separate, break off

分裂する *bunretsu suru* be divided, split, break up, be disrupted

決裂 *ketsuretsu* breakdown, rupture

四分五裂 *shibun-goretsu* disruption

KUN

【**sa(ku)** 裂く】

vt

① split, tear, rend, rip

引き裂く *hikisaku* tear off, tear to pieces, split; separate, estrange, sever

八つ裂きにする *yatsuzaki ni suru* tear (a person) limb from limb, tear to pieces

② (sever relations) split up, separate, break off

夫婦の仲を裂く *fūfu no naka o saku* bring about marital separation

【**sa(keru)** 裂ける】 *vi* split, tear, crack, burst

裂け目 *sakeme* rent, tear, crack, split, cleft, rip

張り裂ける *harisakeru* burst (open), break, split

【**-gi(re)** -裂れ】 [also suffix] fragment (of old textile), strip

縁裂れ *fuchigire* border strip

古代裂れ *kodaigire* ancient cloth fragment

SYNONYMS

❶ **break**

砕 CRUSH UP → 1134

割る crack → 1816

破 BREAK → 1150

壊 BREAK DOWN → 756

折 BREAK OFF → 253

崩 CRUMBLE → 2296

USAGE

saku

裂く

① split, tear, rend, rip

② (sever relations) split up, separate, break off

割く

① spare (time), set [put] aside

② cede, alienate

HOMOPHONES

saku ⇨ 割 1816

-gire ⇨ 切 27

NOTE

⇨ see also USAGE note at 切 27

6-6 此

紫

2688 SHI murasaki

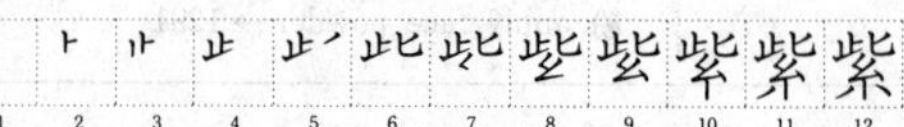

CH 紫 zǐ

Radical	Strokes
糸 120	12-6-6
Grade	Freq
Jōyō	1525
2-6-6	

▶**PURPLE**

COMPOUNDS

❶ [original meaning] **purple, violet**

紫紺 *shikon* purplish blue

紫外線 *shigaisen* ultraviolet rays

紫斑病 *shihanbyō* purpura

❷ related to a monarch or supernatural being

紫宸殿 *shishinden* Hall for State Ceremonies

KUN

【**murasaki** 紫】 purple, amethyst; gromwell; soy

紫色 *murasakiiro* purple color, purple

赤紫 *akamurasaki* purplish red

SYNONYMS

❶ **blue and purple colors**

藍 INDIGO → 2381

紺 DARK BLUE → 1332

瑠 LAPIS LAZULI (bright blue) → 1060

碧 DEEP BLUE → 2836

青 BLUE → 2430

蛋 incorrect classification ⇨ see 2129

象 incorrect classification ⇨ see 2134

景 incorrect classification ⇨ see 2470

碁 2689

▶**SHOGI**

nonstandard for 棋 987

畫 2690

▶**PICTURE** ▶**DRAW UP A PLAN**

nonstandard for 画 3000

登 incorrect classification ⇨ see 2595

節 節 節 𠮟 2691

SETSU SECHI fushi -bushi notto▲

CH 节 jié·jiē

Radical	Strokes
⺮ 118	13-6-7
Grade	**Freq**
Jōyō-4	763
2-6-7	

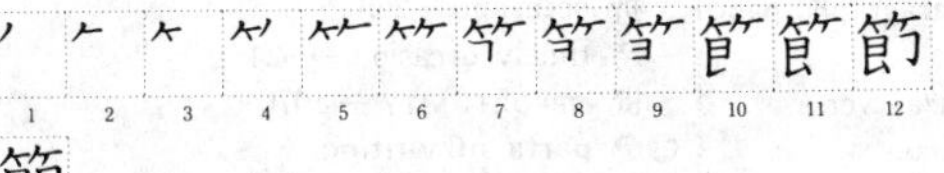

▶**JOINT** ▶**SEASON OF THE YEAR**

COMPOUNDS

❶ⓐ [also suffix] *anat* **joint, knuckle, node**

ⓑ [original meaning] *bot* **joint (as in a bamboo), node, knot**

ⓒ link (for transmitting motion in a machine)

節足動物 *sessokudōbutsu* arthropod
関節 *kansetsu* joint
結節 *kessetsu* node, knotting, knot
リンパ節 *rinpasetsu* lymph node
神経節 *shinkeisetsu* ganglion
末節 *massetsu* minor details, nonessentials
単節 *tansetsu* simple link

❷ⓐ **season [division] of the year, season, turning of the seasons**

ⓑ **time, occasion**

節分 *setsubun* eve of the beginning of spring, close of winter
節季 *sekki* end of year, year end
季節 *kisetsu* season
時節 *jisetsu* season, times; occasion
当節 *tōsetsu* these days

❸ [also suffix] festival, annual festival

節句 *sekku* seasonal festival
節会 *sechie* [rare] seasonal court banquet
佳節 *kasetsu* happy [auspicious] occasion
紀元節 *kigensetsu* Empire Day

❹ⓐ [also suffix] (subdivision, as of a text) **paragraph, passage, section, part**

ⓑ (subdivision of a poem) stanza, verse

ⓒ [also suffix] (subdivision of a sentence) clause

章節 *shōsetsu* chapter and verse
第二節 *dainisetsu* Paragraph 2
小節 *shōsetsu* bar, measure
音節 *onsetsu* syllable
主節 *shusetsu* principal clause
従属節 *jūzokusetsu* subordinate clause

❺ **tune, air, melody**

節奏 *sessō* rhythm
曲節 *kyokusetsu* tune, air

❻ⓐ **economize, save, be frugal**

ⓑ **be moderate, be temperate**

節約する *setsuyaku suru* economize, save
節減 *setsugen* curtailment, economy
節水 *sessui* water economy
節電 *setsuden* economy of electric power
節炭器 *settanki* coal [fuel] economizer
節制 *sessei* temperance, moderation, self-restraint
節度 *setsudo* standard; moderation
節煙 *setsuen* moderation in smoking
節食 *sesshoku* moderation in eating, spare diet
調節 *chōsetsu* regulation, adjustment; modulation, tuning

❼ **moral integrity, principle, fidelity, loyalty**
節操 *sessō* constancy, fidelity, integrity, honor
貞節 *teisetsu* chastity, virtue; constancy, principle
忠節 *chūsetsu* loyalty, allegiance, fidelity

❽ token or bamboo tally used in ancient times as credentials
使節 *shisetsu* envoy, ambassador
符節 *fusetsu* tally, check

INDEPENDENT

【setsu 節】
① time, occasion
この節 *kono setsu* now, at present, in these days
②ⓐ (subdivision, as of a text) paragraph, passage, section, part
ⓑ (subdivision of a poem) stanza, verse
ⓒ (subdivision of a sentence) clause
前の節で *mae no setsu de* in the former section [stanza]
③ moral integrity, principle, fidelity, loyalty
節を曲げない *setsu o magenai* stick by one's principles, remain firm

【sessuru 節する】 be moderate [temperate], control; save, curtail
酒を節する *sake o sessuru* be temperate in drinking
時間を節する *jikan o sessuru* save time

【osechi お節】 dishes for the New Year

KUN

【fushi 節】
①ⓐ joint, knuckle
ⓑ joint (as of a bamboo), node, knot
ⓒ knot (of a thread), burl
節節 *fushibushi* joints
指の節 *yubi no fushi* knuckle
竹の節 *take no fushi* node [joint] of a bamboo
節糸 *fushiito* knotted silk
② (subdivision of a poem) stanza, verse
一節歌う *hitofushi utau* sing a tune
③ point
疑わしい節 *utagawashii fushi* dubious points
④ tune, air, melody
節回し *fushimawashi* melody, intonation
節付け *fushizuke* setting to music, composition
⑤ time, occasion
折節 *orifushi* occasionally, at times

【-bushi -節】 suffix after names of (traditional) Japanese folk songs
ソーラン節 *sōranbushi Soran-bushi* (Hokkaido folk song)

【notto 節】 knot, nautical mile
時速二十節 *jisoku nijū notto* speed of 20 knots per hour

SYNONYMS

❶ⓐ & ❶ⓑ **joint**
関 connection → 3328

❷ⓐ **time periods**
季 SEASON (quarter) → 2554
候 SEASON (time of year) → 119
期 TERM → 1704
間 INTERVAL → 3323
刻 POINT OF TIME → 1267
般 period of time → 1317
暇 FREE TIME → 1012
頃 TIME → 144
時 TIME → 924

ⓑ **occasions**
際 OCCASION → 714
折 occasion → 253
時 timely occasion → 924
機 OPPORTUNITY → 1076

❹ⓐ **parts of writing**
段 passage → 1144
章 CHAPTER → 2117
款 ARTICLE → 1700
条 ARTICLE → 2200
項 CLAUSE → 567
目 ITEM → 3043
箇 item → 2700

ⓒ **sentence and sentence parts**
文 sentence → 1962
句 PHRASE → 2967

❺ **music and songs**
調べ melody → 1567
曲 MUSICAL COMPOSITION → 3527
楽 MUSIC → 2826
音 sound of music → 2070
歌 SONG → 1825
謡 POPULAR SONG → 1597

❻ **economizing and economy**
省 SAVE → 2449
倹 FRUGAL → 116

❼ **fidelity**
操 constancy → 769
信 fidelity → 100
実 faithfulness → 2225
誠 SINCERITY → 1523

悌 BROTHERLY LOVE → 424
孝 FILIAL PIETY → 3205
義 faith → 2338
忠 LOYALTY → 2433
❽ **labels and slips**
符 tally → 2661
票 SLIP → 2669
券 TICKET → 2630
札 TAG → 817

COMPOUND FORMATION

使節 *shisetsu*
使節 'envoy, ambassador' is a messenger (使) bearing a tally (節 ❽) of identification when going abroad.

笵

2692

6-7 ⺮

▶RECORD BOOK
handwritten abbreviation for 簿 2727

義

6-7 ⺶

incorrect classification ⇨ see 2338

鼠

2693 SO nezumi nezu

6-7 臼

Ⓒ 鼠 shǔ

Radical	Strokes
鼠 208	13-13-0
Grade	**Freq**
Reference	
2 - 6 - 7	

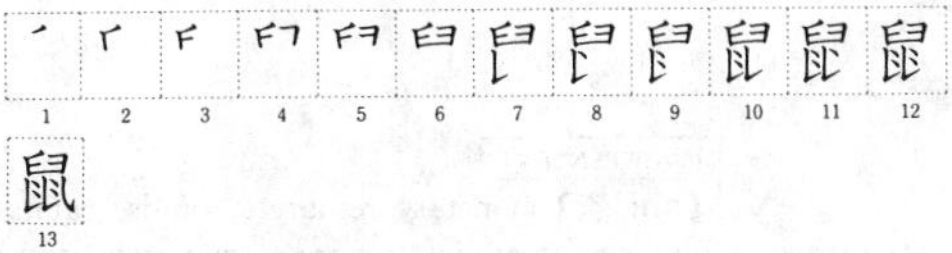

RADICAL 208
Standard form: 鼠 *nezumi* 'rat'
Enclosure: 鼠 *nezuminyō* (鼬)
Description: used in characters related to rats, mice or similar animals

COMPOUNDS

❶ [original meaning] rat, mouse
鼠蹊部 *sokeibu* inguinal region
窮鼠 *kyūso* cornered mouse
殺鼠剤 *sassozai* rat poison
鼠 *nezumi* rat, mouse; dark gray, slate color
鼠入らず *nezumiirazu* meat safe
鼠算 *nezumizan* geometrical progression
二十日鼠 *hatsukanezumi* mouse
鼠 *nezu* rat, mouse; dark gray, slate color
栗鼠 *risu* squirrel
❷ injurious person
鼠賊 *sozoku* sneak thief
鼠輩 *sohai* insignificant fellow, small fry
❸ dark gray, slate color
鼠色 *nezumiiro* dark gray, slate color
銀鼠 *ginnezu* silver gray

賃 賃 赁

2694 CHIN

6-7 任

Ⓒ 赁 lìn

Radical	Strokes
貝 154	13-7-6
Grade	**Freq**
Jōyō-6	673
2 - 6 - 7	

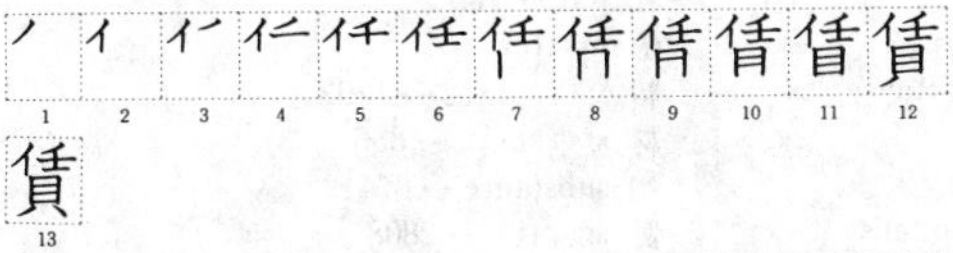

▶WAGE ▶CHARGES

COMPOUNDS

❶ⓐ **wage, wages, salary, pay**
ⓑ [original meaning] hire for wages, employ
賃上げ *chin'age* wage increase
労賃 *rōchin* wages, pay
工賃 *kōchin* wage, wages, pay
手間賃 *temachin* wages [charge] for labor
最賃法 *saichinhō* Minimum Wages Act
賃金(＝賃銀) *chingin* wages, pay

❷ [also suffix] **charges (for rental or transportation), fare, rent, hire, fee**
賃貸し *chingashi* lease, hire
家賃 *yachin* (house) rent
運賃 *unchin* freight [shipping] expense, passenger fare
船賃 *funachin* boat fare, passage; shipping charges
無賃の *muchin no* charge-free
借り賃 *karichin* rent, hire

SYNONYMS
❶ⓐ pay and earnings
給 PAY → 1350
料 FEE → 1292
俸 SALARY → 114
禄 RETAINER'S STIPEND → 1002
収 income → 198
❷ fee and price
代 CHARGE → 30
料 FEE → 1292
銭 money paid → 1725
費 EXPENSE → 2607
価 PRICE → 87
値 price → 109

6-7
次

資 資 資 资
2695 SHI

CH 资 zi

Radical	Strokes
貝 154	13-7-6
Grade	**Freq**
Jōyō-5	217
2 - 6 - 7	

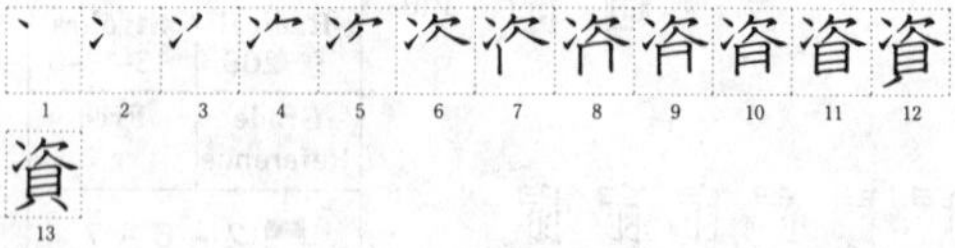

(Stroke order: 1–13)

▶RESOURCES

COMPOUNDS
❶ⓐ [original meaning] **monetary resources, funds, capital, money**
ⓑ **material resources, materials, means**
ⓒ supply with monetary or material resources, provide
資金 *shikin* funds, capital
資本 *shihon* funds, capital
資産 *shisan* property, assets, fortune
投資 *tōshi* investment
融資 *yūshi* financing, advance of funds, loan
増資 *zōshi* increase of capital, capital increase
出資 *shusshi* investment, financing
外資 *gaishi* foreign capital
学資 *gakushi* school expenses, education fund
資料 *shiryō* materials, data
資源 *shigen* resources
資材 *shizai* materials
物資 *busshi* commodities, goods, resources
師資 *shishi* relying on someone as one's teacher
❷ natural ability, qualification
資格 *shikaku* qualifications, competence, capacity
資質 *shishitsu* nature, disposition
❸ abbrev. of 資本家 *shihonka*: capitalist
労資 *rōshi* capital and labor

INDEPENDENT
【shi 資】 monetary resources, funds, capital, money; material resources, materials, means; natural ability
資を投ずる *shi o tōzuru* invest in, lay out (one's money) in
生活の資 *seikatsu no shi* means of living
天与の資 *ten'yo no shi* natural endowment [ability]
【shisuru 資する】 contribute to, be conductive to, be helpful
問題の解決に資する *mondai no kaiketsu ni shisuru* contribute to solving a problem

SYNONYMS
❶ⓐ money
財 finance → 1457
金 MONEY → 2057
銭 MONEY → 1725
貨 MONEY (legal tender), coin → 2465
幣 CURRENCY → 2885
銀 SILVER → 1722
-玉 coin suffix → 3477
札 bill → 817
ⓑ matter
料 MATERIALS → 1292
材 MATERIAL → 836
物 substance → 874
質 MATTER → 2808

6-7
次

2696

▶RESOURCES
nonstandard for 資 2695

誉 incorrect classification ⇨ see 2502

蓉 incorrect classification ⇨ see 2337

愛 incorrect classification ⇨ see 2492

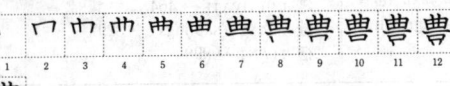

豊 豐 豊

2697 HŌ BU▴ yuta(ka)

CH 丰 fēng

Radical	Strokes
豆 151	13-7-6
Grade	**Freq**
Jōyō-5	765
2 - 6 - 7	

丶 冂 巾 巾 曲 曲 曲 典 豊 豊 豊 豊 豊
1 2 3 4 5 6 7 8 9 10 11 12 13

▶**PLENTIFUL**

COMPOUNDS

❶ **plentiful, abundant, ample, rich**
豊富な *hōfu na* abundant, plentiful, rich
豊水 *hōsui* abundance of water
豊潤な *hōjun na* rich and prosperous, luxurious
豊麗な *hōrei na* rich (design), beautiful, splendid
豊満な *hōman na* plump, corpulent

❷ abundant harvest, good crop
豊作 *hōsaku* good [abundant] harvest
豊年 *hōnen* fruitful year
豊凶 *hōkyō* rich or poor harvest
豊穣 *hōjō* abundant crop, rich harvest

❸ old name for northeast Kyushu
豊前 *buzen* Buzen
築豊炭田 *chikuhō tanden* Chikuho Coalfield

KUN

【yuta(ka) 豊か】
yutaka na 豊かな abundant, plentiful, ample, rich
資源の豊かな国 *shigen no yutaka na kuni* country rich in natural resources

SYNONYMS

❶ **many**
沢 plentiful → 267
穣 YIELDING ABUNDANTLY → 1250
裕 ABUNDANT → 1195
富 RICH → 2310
多 MANY → 2170
万 myriad → 2936
百 numerous → 2026

農 農 農

2698 NŌ

CH 农 nóng

Radical	Strokes
辰 161	13-7-6
Grade	**Freq**
Jōyō-3	309
2 - 6 - 7	

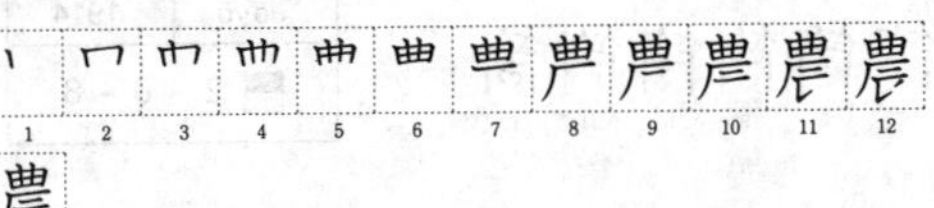

農
13

▶**FARMING**

COMPOUNDS

❶ⓐ **farming, agriculture**
ⓑ [original meaning] farm, till
農業 *nōgyō* agriculture
農家 *nōka* farmhouse, farmer
農村 *nōson* farm village, agricultural community
農地 *nōchi* farmland, farming land
農協 *nōkyō* agricultural cooperative
農政 *nōsei* agricultural administration
農閑期 *nōkanki* leisure season for farmers

農具 *nōgu* farming implements
離農 *rinō* giving up farming
酪農 *rakunō* dairy farming
農作 *nōsaku* land cultivation
農婦 *nōfu* farmerette
農民 *nōmin* peasants, farmers
❷ⓐ abbrev. of 農学 *nōgaku*: (science of) agriculture
ⓑ abbrev. of 農学部 *nōgakubu*, 農業高校 *nōgyō kōkō* or 農業大学 *nōgyō daigaku*: department of agriculture, agricultural high school, agricultural college
農博 *nōhaku* doctor of agriculture
東大農卒 *tōdainōsotsu* graduated from the department of agriculture of Tokyo University
瀬田農入学資格 *setanō nyūgaku shikaku* requirements for admission to Seta Agricultural High School

❸ **farmer**
豪農 *gōnō* wealthy farmer
貧農 *hinnō* needy peasant
自作農 *jisakunō* owner farmer
篤農家 *tokunōka* exemplary good farmer
士農工商 *shinōkōshō* warriors, farmers, artisans and tradesmen (the four classes of Tokugawa Japan)

INDEPENDENT

【**nō 農**】 agriculture
農を業とする *nō o gyō to suru* be occupied with agriculture

SYNONYMS

❶ **farm and plant**
作 raise crops → 68
耕 TILL → 1308
培 CULTIVATE → 464
栽 PLANT (saplings) → 3297
植 PLANT → 990

6-7
甘

碁 2699 GO

CH 棋 qí

Radical	Strokes
石 112	13-5-8
Grade	**Freq**
Jōyō	1428
2-6-7	

一 十 廾 廾 甘 甘 其 其 其 其 其 碁
1 2 3 4 5 6 7 8 9 10 11 12

13

▶**GO**

COMPOUNDS

● [original meaning] **go, Japanese checkers**
碁石 *goishi* go stone
碁盤 *goban* go board, checkerboard
碁会所 *gokaisho* commercial go playing parlor
囲碁 *igo* (the game of) go
西洋碁 *seiyōgo* checkers

INDEPENDENT

【**go 碁**】 go
碁を打つ *go o utsu* play (a game of) go

SYNONYMS

● **board games**
棋 SHOGI → 987
雀 MAHJONG → 2469
局 board game → 3063

6-8
⺮

箇 2700 KA KO▲

CH 个 gè

Radical	Strokes
⺮ 118	14-6-8
Grade	**Freq**
Jōyō	1914
2-6-8	

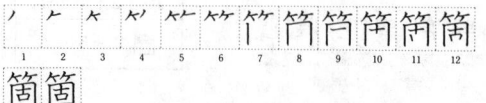

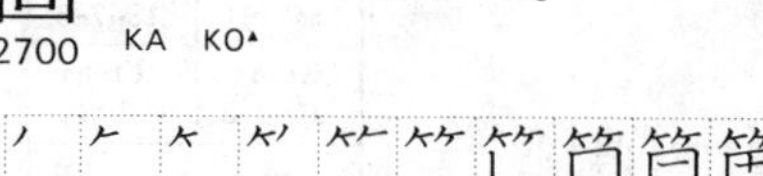
1 2 3 4 5 6 7 8 9 10 11 12

箇 箇
13 14

▶**COUNTER FOR ITEMS**

COMPOUNDS

❶ⓐ **counter for items, places or units of time**
ⓑ [sometimes also 個 *ka* 117] **item, place**
二箇所 *nikasho* two places
一箇月 *ikkagetsu* one month
箇条 *kajō* items, articles
箇条書き *kajōgaki* itemization
不通箇所 *futsūkasho* tied-up places [spots]
❷ [usu. 個 *ko* 117] individual, single unit, person or thing

箇箇に *koko ni* individually, separately

SYNONYMS

❶ⓐ **general counters**

個 GENERAL COUNTER → 117
点 counter for articles → 2084
件 counter for cases → 51
丁 MISCELLANEOUS COUNTER → 3348

ⓑ **parts of writing**

目 ITEM → 3043
項 CLAUSE → 567
条 ARTICLE → 2200
款 ARTICLE → 1700
節 paragraph → 2691
段 passage → 1144
章 CHAPTER → 2117

USAGE

ka, ko

箇

①ⓐ counter for items, places or units of time
ⓑ [sometimes also 個 *ka*] item, place
② [usu. 個 *ko*] individual, single unit, person or thing

個

① [sometimes also 箇 *ko*] individual, single unit, person or thing
② general counter for things or articles
③ [usu. 箇 *ka*] item, place

★箇 is easily confused with 個, to which it is similar in shape, sound and meaning. 箇, often simplified to ヶ, is restricted to counting items, places or units of time (mostly months), while 個 is a counter for things or articles in general. Strictly speaking, 箇 should be read *ka* and 個 should be read *ko*, but in practice both have both readings and are sometimes used interchangeably.

2701 KAN kuda

Ⓒ 管 guǎn

Radical	Strokes
⺮ 118	14-6-8
Grade	**Freq**
Jōyō-4	526
2-6-8	

6-8 ⺮

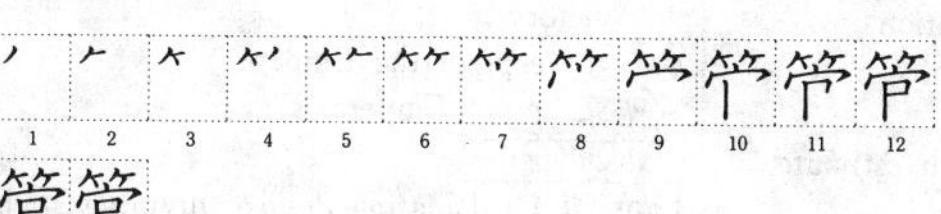

▶**PIPE** ▶**EXERCISE CONTROL**

COMPOUNDS

❶ [also suffix]

ⓐ (tubular conveyance) **pipe, tube, duct**
ⓑ *anat* (tubular part or organ) **tube, pipe, duct**

管状の *kanjō no* tubular
鋼管 *kōkan* steel pipe [tubing]
配管 *haikan* piping
真空管 *shinkūkan* vacuum tube
試験管 *shikenkan* test tube
血管 *kekkan* blood vessel
気管 *kikan* trachea, windpipe

❷ⓐ wind instrument, pipe
ⓑ counter for wind instruments

管弦 *kangen* wind and string instruments
管楽器 *kangakki* wind instruments
木管 *mokkan* woodwind (instrument); wood pipe
二管の笛 *nikan no fue* two flutes

❸ⓐ **exercise control [jurisdiction] over, control, manage, administer, take charge of**
ⓑ control, jurisdiction

管理する *kanri suru* administer, supervise, manage, exercise control [jurisdiction] over
管轄 *kankatsu* jurisdiction, control
管制 *kansei* control
保管する *hokan suru* take custody [charge] of, keep
移管 *ikan* transfer of control [jurisdiction]
選管 *senkan* Election Administration Commission
管内 *kannai* within (the area of) the jurisdiction
八管 *hachikan* 8th District

INDEPENDENT

【**kan** 管】 pipe, tube, duct

KUN

【**kuda** 管】 tube, pipe; drunken talk

ゴムの管 *gomu no kuda* rubber tube
管を巻く *kuda o maku* grumble over one's wine cups

SYNONYMS

❶ **tubular passages**

筒 TUBE → 2680
道 passage → 3134
脈 VEIN → 953

❷ⓐ **musical instrument**

弦 string instrument → 287

❸ⓐ **direct and supervise**

制 CONTROL → 1274
轄 EXERCISE JURISDICTION OVER → 1627
掌 TAKE CHARGE OF → 2602

監 OVERSEE → 2852
督 SUPERVISE → 2796
司 OFFICIATE → 2931
宰 PRESIDE → 2275
営 MANAGE → 2603
理 manage → 970
経 MANAGE → 1331

6-8

算

2702 SAN soro▲

CH 算 suàn

Radical	Strokes
⺮ 118	14-6-8
Grade Jōyō-2	Freq 300
2-6-8	

1 2 3 4 5 6 7 8 9 10 11 12 13 14

▶CALCULATE

COMPOUNDS

❶ⓐ calculate, compute reckon, count
ⓑ [also suffix] **calculation, arithmetical operation**

算出する *sanshutsu suru* compute, calculate
算数 *sansū* arithmetic; calculation
算術 *sanjutsu* arithmetic
計算 *keisan* computation, calculation
換算表 *kansanhyō* conversion table
採算 *saisan* (commercial) profit
概算 *gaisan* approximation, rough estimate [calculation]
清算 *seisan* settlement, liquidation; clearing (off)
暗算 *anzan* mental arithmetic [calculation]
予算 *yosan* budget; estimate, calculation
電算機 *densanki* electronic computer
足し算 *tashizan* addition
読み上げ算 *yomiagezan* calculation by abacus, having the figures read aloud by another person

❷ calculating device, divining stick
算木 *sangi* calculating device, divining stick
珠算 *shuzan* calculation on the abacus

❸ calculate (one's chances), take into account, foretell; scheme, infer
算段する *sandan suru* contrive, manage
打算 *dasan* calculation, self-interest, selfishness

❹ probability, chance
公算 *kōsan* probability
勝算 *shōsan* chance of success, prospects of victory

❺ age (esp. of the Emperor)
聖算 *seisan* Emperor's age

INDEPENDENT

【san 算】 calculating device, divining stick; calculation, counting
算を置く *san o oku* divine; calculate

KUN

【soro 算】 [in compounds] Japanese abacus, *soroban*
算盤 *soroban* Japanese abacus, *soroban*
電算 *densoro* electronic calculator combined with a *soroban*

SYNONYMS

❶ calculate and count
計 COMPUTE → 1441
数 count → 1790

6-8

箏

2703 SŌ koto

CH 箏 zhēng

Radical	Strokes
⺮ 118	14-6-8
Grade Reference	Freq
2-6-8	

COMPOUNDS

● [usu. 琴 *koto*] [original meaning] koto, (Japanese) harp, lyre
箏曲 *sōkyoku* koto music

HOMOPHONES

koto ⇨ 琴 2781

NOTE

⇨ see USAGE note at 琴 2781

2704

▶JADE GREEN
nonstandard for 翠 2705

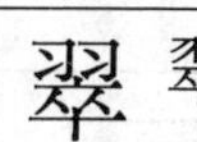
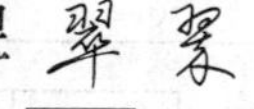
2705 SUI NAMES midori akira

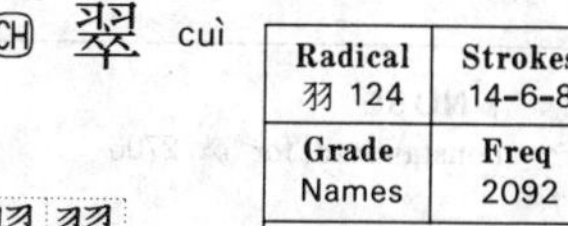
CH 翠 cuì

Radical	Strokes
羽 124	14-6-8
Grade	**Freq**
Names	2092
2 - 6 - 8	

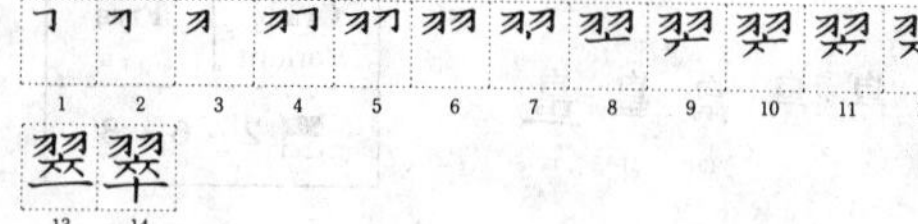

▶JADE GREEN

COMPOUNDS

❶ **jade green, emerald green, verdure, yellowish green**
翠色 *suishoku* verdure, emerald green
翠玉 *suigyoku* emerald, jade
翡翠色 *hisuiiro* jade green
❷ [original meaning] kingfisher
翡翠 *hisui* green jadeite, jade; kingfisher

NAMES

翠扇 *suisen* female name
翠 *midori* male name also female name

SYNONYMS

❶ **green colors**
緑 GREEN → 1377
青 GREEN → 2430

2706 BI hana

CH 鼻 bí

Radical	Strokes
鼻 209	14-14-0
Grade	**Freq**
Jōyō-3	1403
2 - 6 - 8	

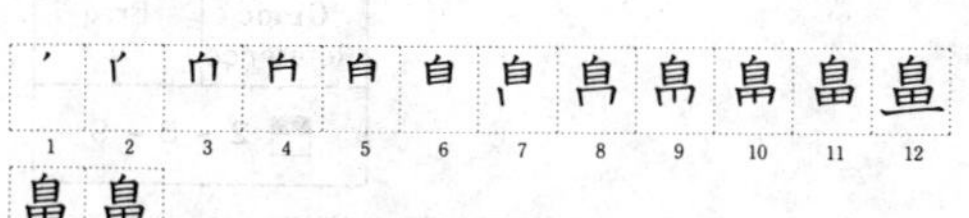

RADICAL 209
simplified form not used as radical
⇨ see 鼻 2707 for radical description

▶NOSE

COMPOUNDS

❶ **nose**
鼻音 *bion* nasal sound
鼻孔 *bikō* nostrils
鼻炎 *bien* nasal inflammation
鼻下長 *bikachō* amorous man, spoony
耳鼻 *jibi* nose and ears
❷ beginning
鼻祖 *biso* founder, originator

KUN

【hana 鼻】
①ⓐ nose, snout, trunk
ⓑ [also 端] end, protruded point
鼻血 *hanaji* nosebleed
鼻水 *hanamizu* nasal discharge
鼻柱 *hanabashira* bridge of the nose; self-assertion
鼻息 *hanaiki* snorting; temper; vigor
鼻摘まみ *hanatsumami* disgusting fellow
鼻が高い *hana ga takai* be proud (have one's nose up)
鼻持ちならない *hanamochinaranai* be intolerable; stink
目鼻が付く *mehana ga tsuku* take a concrete shape, materialize
② [also 端] beginning
出鼻 *debana* outset, start; point of going out

SYNONYMS

❶ **face orifices**
口 MOUTH → 3382
耳 EAR → 3516
目 EYE → 3043

USAGE

hana
鼻

①ⓐ nose, snout, trunk
ⓑ [also 端] end, protruded point
② [also 端] beginning
端
[also 鼻]

① beginning
② end, protruded point

HOMOPHONES
hana ⇨ 端 1221

6-8 自

鼻 ▶NOSE

nonstandard for 鼻 2706

2707

Radical	Strokes
鼻 209	14-14-0
Grade	**Freq**
Variant	
2 - 6 - 8	

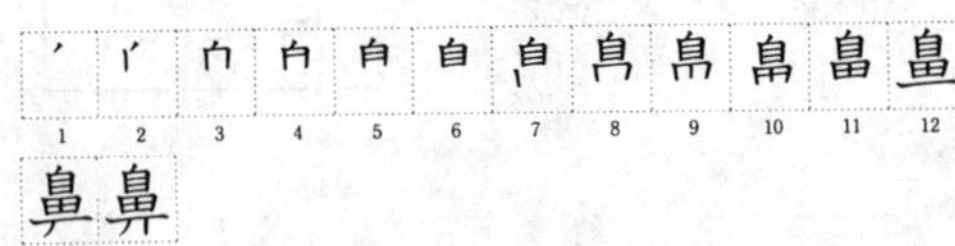

RADICAL 209
Standard form: 鼻 *hana* 'nose'
Left variant: 鼻 *hanahen* (鼾)
Description: used in characters related to the nose

6-8

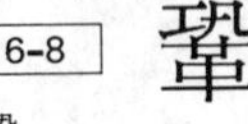

輩

incorrect stroke count ⇨ see 2714

6-9 ⺮

箸

2708 CHO hashi

Ⓒⓗ 箸 zhù

Radical	Strokes
⺮ 118	15-6-9
Grade	**Freq**
Reference	
2 - 6 - 9	

COMPOUNDS
● [original meaning] chopsticks
割り箸 *waribashi* splittable chopsticks
火箸 *hibashi* tongs

HOMOPHONES
hashi ⇨ 橋 1078 端 1221

NOTE
⇨ see USAGE note at 橋 1078

6-9 ⺮

範 範 範

2709 HAN

Ⓒⓗ 范 fàn

Radical	Strokes
⺮ 118	15-6-9
Grade	**Freq**
Jōyō	1096
2 - 6 - 9	

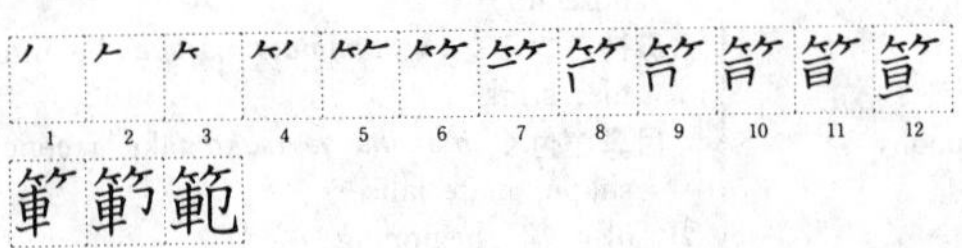

▶**MODEL**

COMPOUNDS
❶ (something to be followed) **model, example, pattern, standard**
模範 *mohan* model, pattern, example
軌範 *kihan* standard, norm
師範 *shihan* teacher, master, coach
典範 *tenpan* model, standard; law, code

❷ⓐ **range, limits, scope, sphere**
ⓑ [formerly 汎 219] extensive, wide-ranging
範囲 *han'i* range, scope
範疇 *hanchū* category
広範な *kōhan na* extensive, wide-ranging, comprehensive

INDEPENDENT
【**han** 範】model, example, pattern

範を垂れる *han o tareru* give an example

SYNONYMS

❶ **model**

典 CANON → 2627
模 PATTERN → 1050
程 ESTABLISHED FORM → 1190
式 form → 3049
準 STANDARD → 2856
格 NORM → 926

❷ⓐ **range**

程 EXTENT → 1190
域 area → 465
圏 SPHERE → 3148
野 FIELD → 1485
界 field (*phys*) → 2563
場 field (*phys, psychol*) → 558

篇

2710 HEN

CH 篇 piān

Radical	Strokes
⺮ 118	15-6-9
Grade Reference	Freq
2-6-9	

6-9 ⺮

COMPOUNDS

[now replaced by 編 1387]

❶ⓐ [also suffix] volume, book, literary work; film
ⓑ chapter, section, part, canto
ⓒ counter for chapters or parts

巨篇 *kyohen* great literary work
短篇 *tanpen* short piece
予告篇 *yokokuhen* preview
前篇 *zenpen* first volume; first part
続篇 *zokuhen* sequel, supplementary volume
第二篇 *dainihen* Chapter 2, Canto 2

❷ⓐ one poem
ⓑ counter for poems

詩篇 *shihen* Psalms
一篇の詩 *ippen no shi* one poem

箱

2711 SŌ▲ hako

CH 箱 xiāng

Radical	Strokes
⺮ 118	15-6-9
Grade Jōyō-3	Freq 1078
2-6-9	

6-9 ⺮

1 2 3 4 5 6 7 8 9 10 11 12 13 14 15

▶**BOX**

KUN

【**hako** 箱】

①ⓐ [sometimes also 函] [also suffix] box, case, chest, bin
ⓑ counter for boxes

箱入りの *hakoiri no* cased, boxed
箱入り娘 *hakoirimusume* innocent [naive] girl of a good family
小箱 *kobako* small box; casket
郵便箱 *yūbinbako* mailbox
巣箱 *subako* bird box, bird house
本箱 *honbako* bookcase
救急箱 *kyūkyūbako* first-aid kit
二箱 *futahako* two boxes

② *slang* railway car

箱師 *hakoshi* train pickpocket

③ *slang* shamisen

SYNONYMS

【**hako**】

① **containers**

籠 BASKET → 2734
袋 BAG → 2588
器 VESSEL → 2713
瓶 BOTTLE → 1344
缶 CAN → 2033
槽 TANK → 1067
棺 COFFIN → 985

USAGE

hako

箱

①ⓐ [sometimes also 函] [also suffix] box, case, chest, bin
ⓑ counter for boxes
② *slang* railway car
③ *slang* shamisen

函

[now usu. 箱] box, case, mailbox

HOMOPHONES

hako ⇨ 函 3001

6-9 ⺮

節

2712

▶JOINT ▶SEASON OF THE YEAR

nonstandard for 節 2691

6-9 ⺷

養

incorrect classification ⇨ see 2365

6-9 口口

器 器 器 ⺍

2713 KI utsuwa

Ⓒ 器 qì

Radical	Strokes
口 30	15-3-12
Grade	**Freq**
Jōyō-4	543
2-6-9	

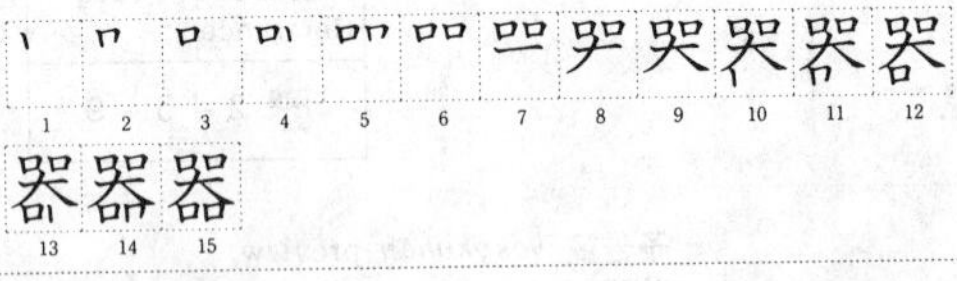

▶VESSEL ▶INSTRUMENT

COMPOUNDS

❶ [original meaning] **vessel, receptacle, container**

容器 *yōki* receptacle, container, vessel
陶器 *tōki* pottery, porcelain, chinaware
便器 *benki* toilet bowl, urinal
食器 *shokki* tableware, dinner set
花器 *kaki* flower vase [bowl]

❷ [also suffix] **instrument, device, appliance, implement, utensil**

器具 *kigu* utensil, implement, appliance
器械 *kikai* instrument, apparatus, appliance
楽器 *gakki* musical instrument
機器 *kiki* machinery and tools, apparatus
計器 *keiki* meter, gauge; instrument
兵器 *heiki* arms, weapon, ordnance
注射器 *chūshaki* syringe
消火器 *shōkaki* fire extinguisher
電熱器 *dennetsuki* electric heater, electric cooker

❸ [also suffix] organ (of the body)

器官 *kikan* (body) organ
臓器 *zōki* internal organs, viscera
呼吸器 *kokyūki* respiratory organs
消化器 *shōkaki* digestive organs

❹ capacity, ability, talent

器量 *kiryō* ability, capacity; personal appearance; dignity
器用な *kiyō na* skillful, clever, ingenious
大器 *taiki* person of great talent

INDEPENDENT

【ki 器】 capacity, ability; person of capability
宰相の器 *saishō no ki* person qualified for prime minister

KUN

【utsuwa 器】 vessel, receptacle; capacity, ability
奇麗な器 *kirei na utsuwa* beautiful bowl
その器ではない *sono utsuwa de wa nai* not be fit for, not be equal to

SYNONYMS

❶ **containers**

箱 BOX → 2711
籠 BASKET → 2734
袋 BAG → 2588
瓶 BOTTLE → 1344
缶 CAN → 2033
槽 TANK → 1067
棺 COFFIN → 985

❷ **machines and tools**

具 IMPLEMENT → 2552
儀 measuring instrument → 169
鏡 OPTICAL INSTRUMENT → 1766
械 MECHANICAL CONTRIVANCE → 961
機 MACHINE → 1076

❸ **organ**

官 organ → 2226
臓 INTERNAL ORGAN → 1102

鞏
2714 KYŌ

Ⓒ 巩 gǒng

Radical	Strokes
革 177	15-9-6
Grade	**Freq**
Reference	

2 - 6 - 9

6-9 巩

COMPOUNDS

● [now also 強 475] [original meaning] solid, strong, hard, tough

鞏固な *kyōko na* firm, stable, solid, strong
鞏膜 *kyōmaku* sclera

築 築 築 築
2715 CHIKU kizu(ku)

Ⓒ 筑 zhù zhú

Radical	Strokes
⺮ 118	16-6-10
Grade	**Freq**
Jōyō-5	861

2 - 6 - 10

6-10 ⺮

1 2 3 4 5 6 7 8 9 10 11 12 13 14 15 16

▶CONSTRUCT

COMPOUNDS

● [original meaning] **construct, erect, build**

築港 *chikkō* harbor construction
築城 *chikujō* castle construction
建築 *kenchiku* construction, building, architecture
建築家 *kenchikuka* architect
構築 *kōchiku* construction, building
新築 *shinchiku* new building [construction]
増築 *zōchiku* enlargement of a building

KUN

【**kizu(ku)** 築く】 build, construct, erect, throw up

築き上げる *kizukiageru* build up, establish (one's reputation)
堤防を築く *teibō o kizuku* construct an embankment

SPECIAL READINGS

築山 *tsukiyama* artificial hill

SYNONYMS

● **build**

建 BUILD (a building) → 3090
造 build (various structures) → 3110
設 SET UP → 1471

篤 篤 篤
2716 TOKU atsu(i)▲

Ⓒ 笃 dǔ

Radical	Strokes
⺮ 118	16-6-10
Grade	**Freq**
Jōyō	1656

2 - 6 - 10

6-10 ⺮

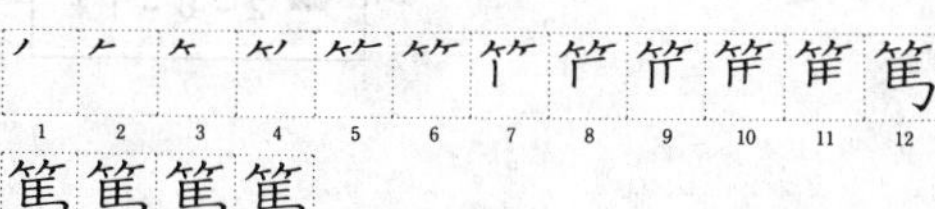

1 2 3 4 5 6 7 8 9 10 11 12 13 14 15 16

▶DEVOTED

COMPOUNDS

❶ⓐ **devoted, fervent, sincere**
ⓑ **cordial, warmhearted, affectionate**

篤信 *tokushin* devoutness
篤学 *tokugaku* love of learning, devotion to one's studies
篤農家 *tokunōka* exemplary good farmer
篤実 *tokujitsu* sincerity, faithfulness
篤志家 *tokushika* benevolent person; volunteer, supporter
篤行 *tokkō* good deed
懇篤な *kontoku na* cordial, kind

❷ (of an illness) critical, serious, dangerous

危篤である *kitoku de aru* be dangerously ill, be in critical condition

KUN

【**atsu(i)** 篤い】

① [now usu. 厚い] cordial, kind, hearty, warm, deep
篤い持てなし *atsui motenashi* cordial reception
篤い友情 *atsui yūjō* warm friendship
篤い信仰 *atsui shinkō* deep faith
② (of an illness) critical, serious, dangerous
病が篤い *yamai ga atsui* be seriously ill

SYNONYMS

❶ⓐ **eager**
懇 EARNEST → 2899
切 eager → 27
熱 HOT → 2866
ⓑ **kind**
懇 cordial → 2899
厚 KIND → 3003
慈 AFFECTIONATE → 2339
温 warmhearted → 608
渥 GRACIOUS → 600
優 kindly → 177

HOMOPHONES

atsui ⇨ 厚 3003

NOTE

⇨ see USAGE note at 厚 3003

6-10
⺮
築
2717

▶**CONSTRUCT**
nonstandard for 築 2715

6-10
口口
器
2718

▶**VESSEL** ▶**INSTRUMENT**
nonstandard for 器 2713

6-11
⺮
簇
2719 ZOKU SŌ

Ⓒⓗ 簇 cù

Radical	Strokes
⺮ 118	17-6-11
Grade	Freq
Reference	
2 - 6 - 1 1	

COMPOUNDS

● [now also 族 *zoku* 958] [original meaning] form a cluster
簇生する *zokusei* (=*sōsei*) *suru* (of plants) grow in clusters
簇出する *zokushutsu* (=*sōshutsu*) *suru* spring up in clusters

6-11
羽
翼 翼 翼 翼
2720 YOKU tsubasa

Ⓒⓗ 翼 yì

Radical	Strokes
羽 124	17-6-11
Grade	Freq
Jōyō	930
2 - 6 - 1 1	

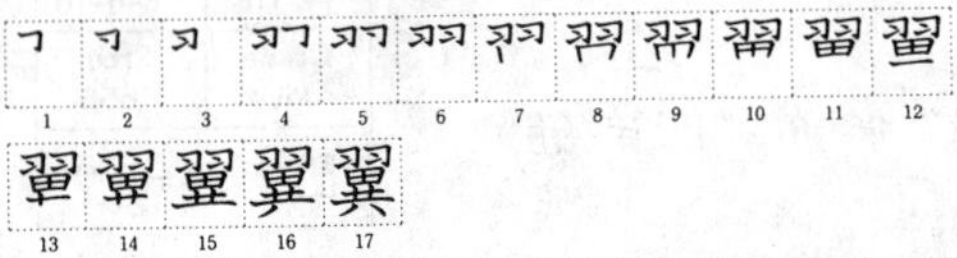

▶**WING**

COMPOUNDS

❶ⓐ [original meaning] **wing of a bird, wings**
ⓑ [also suffix] **wing of an aircraft, airfoil**
翼状 *yokujō* wing shape
羽翼 *uyoku* wings; assistance
主翼 *shuyoku* wing (of an aircraft)
水平翼 *suiheiyoku* horizontal plane
補助翼 *hojoyoku* aileron
❷ⓐ something resembling a wing in structure, function or appearance
ⓑ **(political) wing, faction; (army) wing, flank**
翼棟 *yokutō* wing (of a building)
左翼 *sayoku* left wing [flank]; left wing [faction]; left field
両翼 *ryōyoku* both flanks; two wings
❸ assist, help (as if taking someone under one's wings)
翼賛する *yokusan suru* support, countenance, assist

輔翼する *hoyoku suru* aid, assist

❹ respectful, reverent

小心翼翼と *shōshin-yokuyoku to* timidly, nervously

INDEPENDENT

【**yoku** 翼】wing; aircraft wing, airfoil

KUN

【**tsubasa** 翼】wing; airfoil

翼を広げる *tsubasa o hirogeru* spread the wings

SYNONYMS

❶ **wings**

羽 WING (of birds or insects) → 226

葉 plane → 2321

❷ⓑ **parties and sects**

派 SECT → 381

系 faction → 1944

流 school → 441

閥 CLIQUE → 3325

党 PARTY → 2581

門 (religious) sect → 888

宗 RELIGIOUS SECT (esp. Buddhist) → 2228

簡 簡 簡 简

2721 KAN

(CH) 简 jiǎn

Radical	Strokes
⺮ 118	18-6-12
Grade	**Freq**
Jōyō-6	846
2 - 6 - 1 2	

6-12 ⺮

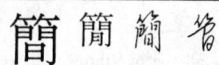

1 2 3 4 5 6 7 8 9 10 11 12 13 14 15 16 17 18

▶**SIMPLE**

COMPOUNDS

❶ⓐ **simple, easy, light**

ⓑ **simplified, brief, concise**

簡単な *kantan na* simple, easy, light

簡素な *kanso na* plain, simple

簡易な *kan'i na* simple, simplified; easy

簡明な *kanmei na* terse, concise

簡略 *kanryaku* simplicity, brevity, conciseness; informality

簡潔な *kanketsu na* brief, concise

簡裁 *kansai* summary court

❷ [formerly also 翰 1750] letter, note

書簡 *shokan* letter, correspondence

手簡 *shukan* letter

❸ [original meaning] bamboo strips used for writing in ancient China

簡札 *kansatsu* wooden tag

竹簡 *chikukan* bamboo writing strip

❹ [archaic] select

簡抜 *kanbatsu* selection

INDEPENDENT

【**kan** 簡】simplicity, brevity

簡にして要を得た *kan ni shite yō o eta* brief, succinct

SYNONYMS

❶ⓐ **easy**

易 EASY (without difficulty) → 2411

安 easy (without effort) → 2171

軽 LIGHT → 1515

ⓑ **short and shortened**

略 ABRIDGED → 1169

短 SHORT → 1182

❸ **writing strips**

竹 bamboo writing tablets → 228

簡

2722

▶**SIMPLE**

nonstandard for 簡 2721

6-12 ⺮

翼

2723

▶**WING**

nonstandard for 翼 2720

6-12 羽

蟲

2724

▶**INSECT**

nonstandard for 虫 3530

6-12 虫

6-12
西

覆
2725

▶COVER ▶OVERTURN
nonstandard for 覆 2726

6-12
西

覆 覆 覆 覆
2726 FUKU ō(u) kutsugae(su) kutsugae(ru)

CH 覆 fù

Radical	Strokes
西 146	18-6-12
Grade	**Freq**
Jōyō	1505

2-6-12

1 2 3 4 5 6 7 8 9 10 11 12 13 14 15 16 17 18

▶COVER ▶OVERTURN

COMPOUNDS

❶ [original meaning] **cover**
覆面 *fukumen* mask, veil
覆土 *fukudo* covering up seeds with soil
被覆 *hifuku* covering, coating

❷ **overturn, upset, turn over**
覆没する *fukubotsu suru* capsize and sink
覆水盆に返らず *Fukusui bon ni kaerazu* It is no use crying over spilt milk
転覆する *tenpuku suru* overturn, turn over, upset; overthrow

❸ [usu. 復 575] reproduce, repeat
覆刻する *fukkoku suru* republish, reissue
反覆する *hanpuku suru* repeat, do over again

KUN

【ō(u) 覆う】
[sometimes also 被う or 蓋う, formerly also 蔽う or 掩う]
ⓐ cover, veil
ⓑ hide, conceal, screen
ⓒ enfold, envelop
覆い *ōi* cover, mantle
顔を覆う *kao o ōu* cover one's face
事実を覆う *jijitsu o ōu* disguise a fact
日覆い *hiōi* sunscreen
霧に覆われる *kiri ni ōwareru* be enveloped in mist

【kutsugae(su) 覆す】 *vt* overturn, upset, turn over, capsize; overthrow, undermine; overrule, reverse
現体制を覆す *gentaisei o kutsugaesu* overthrow the present regime
判決を覆す *hanketsu o kutsugaesu* overrule a decision

【kutsugae(ru) 覆る】 *vi* overturn, upset, topple over, capsize; fall, be overthrown; be reversed, be overruled
大きな船も覆る程の波 *ōkina fune mo kutsugaeru hodo no nami* wave so high as to capsize a big ship
覆った説 *kutsugaetta setsu* overthrown theory

SYNONYMS

❶ **cover and wrap**
被 cover → 1163
包 WRAP → 2966

❷ **overturn**
翻 TURN OVER → 1897
反 turn over → 2945
転 turn [roll] over → 1480
倒 TOPPLE → 124

USAGE

ōu
覆う
[sometimes also 被う or 蓋う, formerly also 蔽う or 掩う]
ⓐ cover, veil
ⓑ hide, conceal, screen
ⓒ enfold, envelop
被う
[usu. 覆う] cover, veil
蓋う
[usu. 覆う] same as 覆う
蔽う
[now usu. 覆う] screen, shield, hide
掩う
[now usu. 覆う]
ⓐ cover, veil
ⓑ hide, conceal, screen

HOMOPHONES

ōu ⇨ 被 1163 蓋 2503 蔽 2523 掩 489

6-12
西

覇

incorrect stroke count ⇨ see 2730

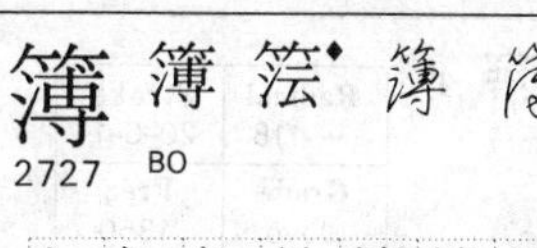

2727 BO

CH 簿 bù

Radical	Strokes
⺮ 118	19-6-13
Grade	Freq
Jōyō	1336
2 - 6 - 1 3	

6-13 ⺮

▶**RECORD BOOK**

COMPOUNDS

❶ [also suffix] **record book, book(s), account book, register**

簿記 *boki* bookkeeping
帳簿 *chōbo* account book, ledger, register
名簿 *meibo* register [list] of names
計算簿 *keisanbo* account book
登記簿 *tōkibo* register
家計簿 *kakeibo* housekeeping account book
通知簿 *tsūchibo* report card [book]

❷ Imperial procession, cortege

鹵簿 *robo* Imperial cortege [procession]

SYNONYMS

❶ **notebook**

帳 NOTEBOOK → 473
籍 REGISTER → 2731

NOTE

★ do not confuse with 薄 2370

簿 2728

▶**RECORD BOOK**

nonstandard for 簿 2727

6-13 ⺮

覇 2729

▶**SUPREMACY**

nonstandard for 覇 2730

6-13 襾

覇 覇 覇 覇 2730 HA

CH 霸 bà

Radical	Strokes
襾 146	19-6-13
Grade	Freq
Jōyō	1513
2 - 6 - 1 3	

6-13 襾

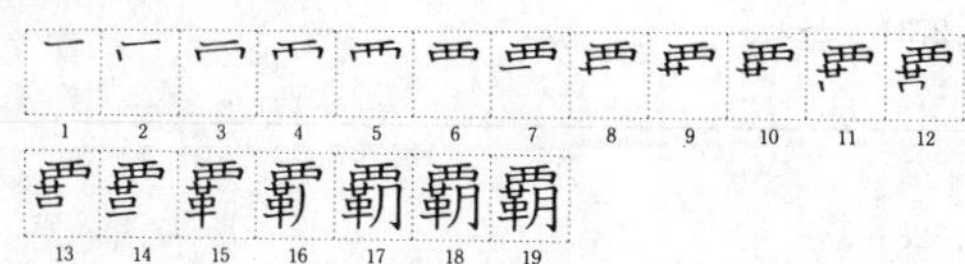

▶**SUPREMACY**

COMPOUNDS

❶ⓐ **supremacy, mastery, hegemony, domination, leadership**

ⓑ supremacy in a contest, victory, championship

覇権 *haken* supremacy, mastery, hegemony, supreme power
覇道 *hadō* military government [rule]
制覇する *seiha suru* conquer, dominate, gain supremacy; win the championship
覇気 *haki* ambitious spirit, aspiration
争覇 *sōha* contending for victory, struggling for supremacy
連覇 *renpa* successive victories

❷ [original meaning] supreme ruler, chief of the feudal lords

覇者 *hasha* supreme ruler; champion

INDEPENDENT

【**ha** 覇】 supremacy, leadership, domination, hegemony; victory, championship

覇を唱える *ha o tonaeru* assume the leadership [hegemony], reign supreme, dominate

SYNONYMS

❶ⓐ **power and authority**

権 POWER (to control) → 1065
勢 POWER (to influence) → 2857
威 MIGHT → 3578
力 POWER → 3371

6-14

籍 籍 籍 籍

2731 SEKI

CH 籍 jí

Radical	Strokes
⺮ 118	20-6-14
Grade	Freq
Jōyō	1350
2-6-14	

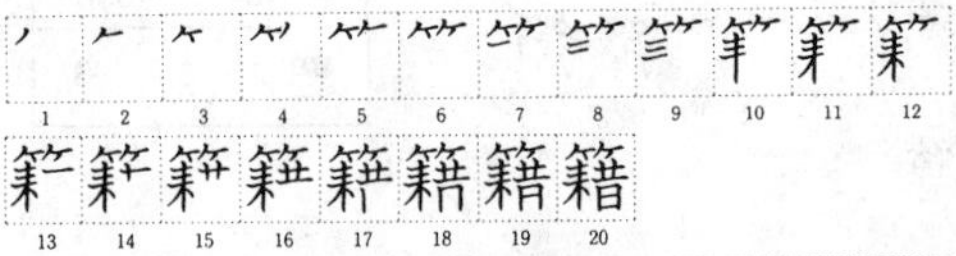

▶**REGISTER**

COMPOUNDS

❶ⓐ **register, family [domiciliary] register; record**

ⓑ one's domicile, nationality

ⓒ membership

戸籍 *koseki* family register

軍籍 *gunseki* army register

移籍 *iseki* transfer of one's name in the register

入籍 *nyūseki* entry in the family register

国籍 *kokuseki* nationality, citizenship

本籍 *honseki* one's legal domicile, one's permanent residence

在籍する *zaiseki suru* be on the register, be a member of

党籍 *tōseki* party membership

❷ **books, written works, records**

書籍 *shoseki* books, publications

史籍 *shiseki* history books

漢籍 *kanseki* Chinese books, Chinese classics

典籍 *tenseki* classical books, books

INDEPENDENT

【seki 籍】 domiciliary register, one's domicile; membership

籍を入れる *seki o ireru* have a name entered in the family register

SYNONYMS

❶ⓐ **notebook**

簿 RECORD BOOK → 2727

帳 NOTEBOOK → 473

❷ **books**

本 BOOK → 3502

書 BOOK → 2658

冊 bound book → 3483

著 literary work → 2300

巻 VOLUME → 2645

編 volume → 1387

鑑 REFERENCE VOLUME → 1773

典 STANDARD WORK → 2627

経 religious classic → 1331

6-14

籍

2732

▶**REGISTER**

nonstandard for 籍 2731

6-14

嚴

2733

▶**SEVERE**

nonstandard for 厳 3289

6-16

籠 籠 籠

2734 RŌ kago ko(meru) ko(moru)

CH 笼 lóng lǒng

Radical	Strokes
⺮ 118	22-6-16
Grade	Freq
Non-Jōyō	1734
2-6-16	

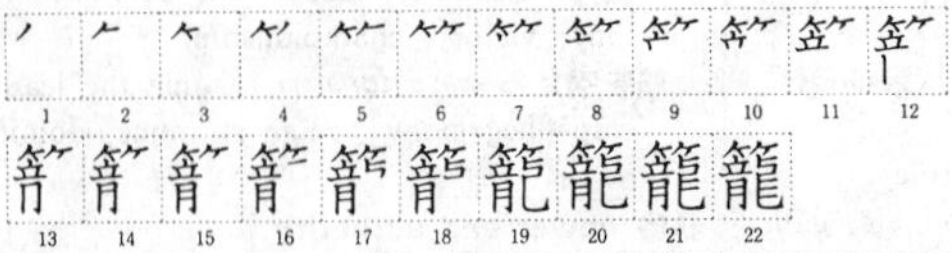

▶**BASKET**

COMPOUNDS

❶ [original meaning] **basket, cage, coop, case**

籠球 *rōkyū* basketball

灯籠 *tōrō* garden lantern; hanging lantern

薬籠 *yakurō* medicine chest [container]

❷ **be confined in, shut oneself, seclude oneself**

籠城 *rōjō* confinement, keeping inside; hold-

ing a castle, sustaining a siege
籠居 *rōkyo* living in seclusion, retirement
参籠 *sanrō* confinement in a temple [shrine] to pray

❸ cajole, entice
籠絡する *rōraku suru* inveigle, ensnare, entice

KUN

【kago 籠】[also suffix] basket, hamper, crate, cage, case
屑籠 *kuzukago* wastebasket
鳥籠 *torikago* bird cage
果物籠 *kudamonokago* fruit basket

【ko(meru) 籠める】
[now usu. 込める]
① concentrate on, devote oneself to
心を籠めて *kokoro o komete* with all one's heart, wholeheartedly
② impregnate with, imply
警告の意味を籠めて *keikoku no imi o komete* with an implication of warning
③ hang over, envelop, shroud
霧が立ち籠めた港 *kiri ga tachikometa minato* harbor wrapped in a mist

【ko(moru) 籠もる】 be confined in, shut oneself up, seclude oneself; be pregnant [filled] with, be fraught with; (be prevented from free outflow) be heavy [thick], be stuffy [close]
書斎に籠もる *shosai ni komoru* shut oneself up in one's study
憎悪の籠もった目 *zōo no komotta me* eyes fraught with hatred
煙草の煙が籠もっている *tabako no kemuri ga komotte iru* be heavy with tobacco smoke
籠もった声 *komotta koe* thick voice

SYNONYMS

❶ & **【kago】 containers**
袋 BAG → 2588
箱 BOX → 2711
器 VESSEL → 2713
瓶 BOTTLE → 1344
缶 CAN → 2033
槽 TANK → 1067
棺 COFFIN → 985

HOMOPHONES

komeru ⇨ 込 3030

NOTE

⇨ see USAGE note at 込 3030

籤

2735 SEN kuji

Ⓒⓗ 签 qiān

Radical	Strokes
⺮ 118	23-6-17
Grade	**Freq**
Reference	
2 - 6 - 1 7	

6-17 ⺮

COMPOUNDS

● [now also 選 *sen* 3169] lot, lottery
抽籤 *chūsen* drawing of lots
当籤する *tōsen suru* win a prize, draw a lucky number
籤引き *kujibiki* drawing of lots

貞

incorrect classification ⇨ see 2083

7-2 貞

頁

incorrect classification ⇨ see 2086

7-2 頁

負

incorrect classification ⇨ see 2091

7-2 負

勇

incorrect classification ⇨ see 2089

7-2 勇

7-3
辰

辱 辱 辱

2736 JOKU hazukashi(meru)

Ⓒⓗ 辱 rǔ

Radical	Strokes
辰 161	10-7-3
Grade	**Freq**
Jōyō	1838
2 - 7 - 3	

▶HUMILIATE

COMPOUNDS

❶ **humiliate, disgrace, dishonor, insult**

侮辱する *bujoku suru* insult, treat with contempt
屈辱 *kutsujoku* humiliation, disgrace, insult
恥辱 *chijoku* disgrace, dishonor, shame
雪辱する *setsujoku suru* vindicate one's honor, get revenge for one's defeat
凌辱する *ryōjoku suru* insult, disgrace; rape

❷ grateful, thankful

辱知 *jokuchi* friend (that one is grateful to have)

KUN

【hazukashi(meru) 辱める】 humiliate, put to shame; disgrace, insult, dishonor; rape, violate

辱め *hazukashime* shame, disgrace; being raped
家名を辱める *kamei o hazukashimeru* bring disgrace upon one's family name

SYNONYMS

❶ **disgrace**

侮 INSULT → 82
恥 SHAME → 1313
汚 defile → 222

7-3
辰

唇 脣◇ 唇 唇

2737 SHIN kuchibiru

Ⓒⓗ 唇 chún

Radical	Strokes
口 30	10-3-7
Grade	**Freq**
Jōyō	1940
2 - 7 - 3	

▶LIP

COMPOUNDS

● [original meaning] **lip, lips, labium, labia**

唇音 *shin'on* labial sound
陰唇 *inshin* labium
口唇 *kōshin* lips, labia

INDEPENDENT

【shin 唇】 lip, labium

KUN

【kuchibiru 唇】 lip, lips

上唇 *uwakuchibiru* upper lip

SYNONYMS

● **mouth parts**

歯 TOOTH → 2476
舌 TONGUE → 2186

7-3
折

哲 哲 哲

2738 TETSU

Ⓒⓗ 哲 zhé

Radical	Strokes
口 30	10-3-7
Grade	**Freq**
Jōyō	1323
2 - 7 - 3	

▶SAGACIOUS ▶PHILOSOPHY

COMPOUNDS

❶ⓐ [original meaning] **sagacious, wise, intelligent**

ⓑ sage, philosopher, wise man

明哲 *meitetsu* wisdom, sagacity; wise man
賢哲 *kentetsu* sage, wise man
哲人 *tetsujin* philosopher, sage
西哲 *seitetsu* Western philosopher
先哲 *sentetsu* ancient sage [wise man]
十哲 *jittetsu* ten sages

❷ **philosophy**

哲学 *tetsugaku* philosophy
哲理 *tetsuri* philosophy (of something)
中哲 *chūtetsu* Chinese philosophy
印哲 *intetsu* Indian philosophy

❸ used phonetically for *tetsu*
何の変哲も無い *nan no hentetsu mo nai* plain, commonplace

SYNONYMS

❶ⓐ **intelligent and wise**
賢 WISE → 2839
智 wise → 2784
慧 INTELLIGENT → 2810
伶 CLEVER → 298
明 clear-sighted → 855
聡 SHARP-WITTED → 1384
俊 brilliant → 102
鋭 SHARP → 1730
敏 NIMBLE → 1322
ⓑ **wise and talented persons**
賢 wise man → 2839
博 DOCTOR → 151
秀 genius → 2545
俊 BRILLIANT PERSON → 102
才 person of talent → 3410
通 well-informed person → 3109
❷ **wisdom**
智 WISDOM → 2784
慧 prajna (transcendental wisdom) → 2810
知 knowledge → 1127
識 KNOWLEDGE → 1639

真

incorrect classification ⇨ see 2111

夏

incorrect classification ⇨ see 2113

奐

incorrect classification ⇨ see 2114
(nonstandard for 魚 2127)

脣

2739

▶**LIP**

nonstandard for 唇 2737

黒 黑

2740 KOKU kuro kuro(i)

Ⓒⓗ 黑 hēi

Radical	Strokes
黒 203	11-11-0
Grade	**Freq**
Jōyō-2	302

2 - 7 - 4

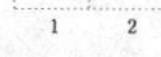

RADICAL 203
variant of 黑 *kuroi* 'black'
⇨ see 黑 2787 for radical description

▶**BLACK**

COMPOUNDS

❶ⓐ [also suffix] [original meaning] **black, blackish**
ⓑ (lacking light) black, dark
黒海 *kokkai* Black Sea
黒板 *kokuban* blackboard
黒点 *kokuten* black [dark] spot, sunspot
黒人 *kokujin* Black, Negro
黒褐色 *kokkasshoku* blackish brown
漆黒 *shikkoku* pitch black
暗黒 *ankoku* darkness
❷ black, evil, wicked
黒白 *kokubyaku* right and wrong; black and white

KUN

【kuro 黒】 black
黒豆 *kuromame* black soybean
黒髪 *kurokami* black hair
黒字 *kuroji* the black, surplus
黒ずむ *kurozumu* blacken, darken
白黒 *shirokuro* black and white; right or wrong
真っ黒な *makkuro na* deep-black, jet-black
【kuro(i) 黒い】 black; dark(-colored)
腹黒い *haraguroi* blackhearted, malicious
浅黒い *asaguroi* dark-complexioned, tanned, swarthy

SYNONYMS

❶ⓐ **black colors**

7-3 直 7-3 百 7-3 魚 7-4 辰 7-4 里

漆 pitch-black → 704
ⓑ **dark**

暗 DARK → 1010
陰 shaded → 541

7-4 攸

悠 悠 悠

2741 YŪ

CH 悠 yōu

Radical	Strokes
心 61	11-4-7
Grade	**Freq**
Jōyō	1804
2 - 7 - 4	

Stroke order: ノ 亻 仆 攸 … 悠 (1–11)

▶LEISURELY

COMPOUNDS

❶ **leisurely, at ease, relaxed, composed, serene**

悠悠と *yūyū to* calmly, leisurely; easily, without difficulty; boundlessly
悠長な *yūchō na* leisurely, easygoing; tedious
悠然として *yūzen to shite* with an air of perfect composure

❷ [original meaning] (remote in space or time) far-off, faraway, remote, distant

悠遠 *yūen* remoteness
悠久な *yūkyū na* eternal, everlasting, permanent

SYNONYMS

❶ **leisurely**
閑 idle → 3322

❷ **distant**
遥 FAR → 3141
遼 FARAWAY → 3168
遠 DISTANT → 3150
隔 APART → 671
離 separated → 1836

7-4 㫗

望 望 望 望

2742 BŌ MŌ nozo(mu) mochi▲

CH 望 wàng

Radical	Strokes
月 74	11-4-7
Grade	**Freq**
Jōyō-4	340
2 - 7 - 4	

Stroke order: 丶 亠 亡 … 望 (1–11)

▶HOPE ▶LOOK AFAR

COMPOUNDS

❶ **hope, expect, wish, aspire to, desire**

望外の *bōgai no* unexpected, unanticipated
希望する *kibō suru* hope, wish, aspire to
要望 *yōbō* demand, request
絶望 *zetsubō* despair, hopelessness
失望する *shitsubō suru* be disappointed, lose hope
欲望 *yokubō* desire, craving
志望する *shibō suru* desire, wish, aspire to
待望の *taibō no* hoped-for, long-awaited
有望な *yūbō na* promising, hopeful
本望 *honmō* one's long cherished desire; satisfaction
懇望する *konmō suru* entreat, solicit, beg earnestly

❷ **look afar, gaze into the distance, command a view of**

望見する *bōken suru* watch from afar
望郷 *bōkyō* homesickness, nostalgia
望遠鏡 *bōenkyō* telescope
展望する *tenbō suru* have a view of
眺望 *chōbō* view, prospect, outlook

❸ popularity, reputation

信望 *shinbō* prestige, popularity
人望 *jinbō* popularity, popular favor
声望 *seibō* popularity, reputation

❹ [original meaning] full moon

既望 *kibō* [archaic] moon sixteen days old; sixteenth night (of the lunar month)

KUN

【nozo(mu) 望む】

①ⓐ desire, wish, crave for
ⓑ hope (for), expect, look forward to
望み *nozomi* desire, wish; hope, expectation, prospect; preference
望ましい *nozomashii* desirable, welcome
平和を望む *heiwa o nozomu* crave for peace
成功を望む *seikō o nozomu* hope to succeed
待ち望む *machinozomu* expect, look forward to

② expect (a person) to do, ask for
自重を望む *jichō o nozomu* ask for prudence

③ look afar, gaze into the distance, command a view of
富士を望む家 *fuji o nozomu ie* house commanding a view of Mt. Fuji

【mochi 望】 *elegant* full moon
望月 *mochizuki* full moon

SYNONYMS

❶ **wish and desire**
希 ASPIRE → 2049
願 WISH → 1845
懐 LONG FOR → 763
慕 yearn for → 2353
渇 thirst for → 515
欲 DESIRE → 1475
求 SEEK → 3550

❷ **see and look**
眺 LOOK OUT OVER → 1171
仰 LOOK UP → 48
顧 LOOK BACK → 1900
覧 LOOK OVER → 2854
観 VIEW → 1880
目 look → 3043
見 SEE → 2544
視 REGARD → 972
看 WATCH → 3220
察 INSPECT → 2347

❸ **repute**
名 NAME → 2169
誉 HONOR → 2502
声 reputation → 2198

USAGE

nozomu

望む
①ⓐ desire, wish, crave for
ⓑ hope (for), expect, look forward to
② expect (a person) to do, ask for
③ look afar, gaze into the distance, command a view of

臨む
① be present at, be on the spot, attend, come to, visit
② come face to face, meet, be confronted with
③ overlook, face, border on

HOMOPHONES

nozomu ⇨ 臨 1630

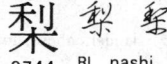

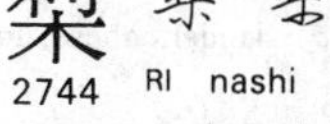
2743

▶HOPE ▶LOOK AFAR
nonstandard for 望 2742

7-4 亡月

梨 梨 梨
2744 RI nashi

Ⓒⓗ 梨 lí

Radical	Strokes
木 75	11-4-7
Grade	**Freq**
Names	1996
2-7-4	

7-4 利

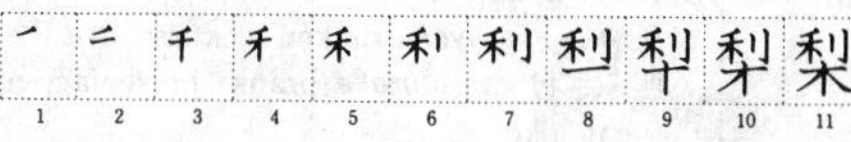

▶PEAR

COMPOUNDS

❶ **pear tree; pear**
梨花 *rika* pear blossoms
梨果 *rika* pome

❷ theatrical world
梨園 *rien* theatrical world; pear orchard

KUN

【nashi 梨】 pear; pear tree
梨の実 *nashi no mi* pear
梨の礫 *nashi no tsubute* no communication

NAMES

梨花 *rika* female name
梨本 *nashimoto* surname

SYNONYMS

❶ **fruits and fruit trees**
桃 PEACH → 936
李 PLUM → 2398
杏 APRICOT → 2397
梅 JAPANESE APRICOT → 925
橘 MANDARIN → 1077
栗 CHESTNUT → 2649

魚
incorrect classification ⇨ see 2127

7-4 魚

7-4 亜

悪 惡 悪 𢙣 ㊥ 恶 è wù ě wū

2745 AKU O waru(i) waru- a(shi)▲

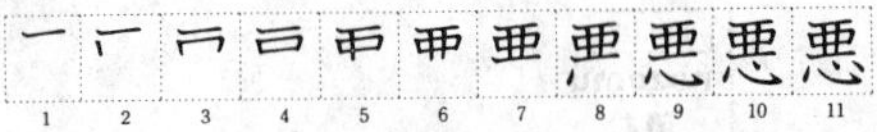

Radical 心 61	Strokes 11-4-7
Grade Jōyō-3	Freq 469
2-7-4	

▶**BAD**

COMPOUNDS

❶ [also prefix]

ⓐ (morally evil) **bad, evil, wicked, immoral**

ⓑ (inferior in quality) **bad, inferior, poor, unsatisfactory**

ⓒ (disagreeable) bad, unpleasant

悪魔 *akuma* devil, demon, satan
悪徳 *akutoku* vice, corruption, immorality
悪化する *akka suru* worsen, aggravate, deteriorate
悪質な *akushitsu na* bad, malicious; malignant
悪筆 *akuhitsu* poor handwriting
悪日 *akunichi* (=*akubi*) unlucky day
悪条件 *akujōken* bad terms
最悪 *saiaku* the worst
悪臭 *akushū* offensive [foul] odor, stench
悪寒 *okan* chill
悪天候 *akutenkō* bad weather

❷ [also suffix] (something bad) **evil, badness, vice**

善悪 *zen'aku* good and evil
諸悪 *shoaku* various evils
社会悪 *shakaiaku* social ills
必要悪 *hitsuyōaku* necessary evil

❸ hate, bear ill will, despise

悪意 *akui* malicious intent
憎悪 *zōo* abhorrence, hatred
嫌悪 *ken'o* hatred, dislike, repugnance

❹ intense, hard

悪戦苦闘する *akusenkutō suru* fight desperately, fight against heavy odds

INDEPENDENT

【**aku** 悪】evil, badness, vice; villain's part (in a play)

悪に染まる *aku ni somaru* steeped in vice
彼は悪だ *Kare wa aku da* He is the villain

KUN

【**waru(i)** 悪い】

①ⓐ bad, evil, wicked, immoral

ⓑ (inferior in quality) bad, inferior, poor, unsatisfactory

ⓒ (disagreeable) bad, unpleasant

悪 *waru* bad fellow, knave
悪い行い *warui okonai* bad [evil] deed
頭が悪い *atama ga warui* weak-headed, slow
悪い評判 *warui hyōban* unsavory rumor

②ⓐ (causing harm) bad, injurious, harmful

ⓑ bad (luck), ill (omen)

悪い風邪 *warui kaze* bad cold
目に悪い *me ni warui* bad for the eyes
悪い知らせ *warui shirase* bad news

③ (of the body) bad (eyesight), sick, ill

目が悪い *me ga warui* have bad eyesight

④ blamable, in fault

悪かった *Warukatta* I'm sorry / It's my fault
私が悪い *Watakushi ga warui* I am to blame / It is my fault

【**waru-** 悪-】

① bad, evil

悪気 *warugi* malice
悪賢い *warugashikoi* cunning, artful, sly, crafty
悪知恵 *warujie* cunning, craft, serpentine wisdom
悪口 *warukuchi* (=*akkō*) slander, abuse, foul language

② disagreeably excessive

悪酔い *waruyoi* drunken sickness
悪ふざけ *warufuzake* prank, horseplay, practical joke
悪乗りする *warunori suru* overdo, do (something) to death, run (something) into the ground

【**a(shi)** 悪し】*elegant* bad, evil, wrong

悪しからず御了承願います *Ashikarazu goryōshō negaimasu* I beg you to understand my position
善し悪し *yoshiashi* good or bad [evil], right or wrong

SPECIAL READINGS

悪戯▲ *itazura* mischief, prank, practical joke
悪阻▲ *tsuwari* (=*oso*) morning sickness

SYNONYMS

❶ⓐ **evil**

邪 EVIL → 1124
凶 ATROCIOUS → 2961

ⓑ **bad**

劣 INFERIOR → 2395
下 of low grade → 3378
弊 shabby → 2884
粗 COARSE → 1329
駄 GOOD FOR NOTHING → 1821
廃 WASTE → 3146

❷ **wrongdoing and evil**
弊 evil(s) (something undesirable) → 2884
邪 wrong → 1124
非 wrong(doing) → 889
罪 sin → 2610
❸ **hate and dislike**
憎 HATE → 687

忌む ABHOR → 2207
嫌 DISLIKE → 636
恨 HOLD A GRUDGE → 369

HOMOPHONES
itazura ⇨ 徒 416 悪戯 2745, 1875

NOTE
⇨ see USAGE note at 戯 1875

曹

2746 SŌ ZŌ▲

Ⓒ曹 cáo

Radical	Strokes
日 73	11-4-7
Grade	Freq
Jōyō	1585
2 - 7 - 4	

7-4 曲

▶SERGEANT

COMPOUNDS
❶ **sergeant, petty officer**
曹長 *sōchō* sergeant officer, sergeant major
軍曹 *gunsō* sergeant
海曹 *kaisō* petty officer (navy)
陸曹 *rikusō* noncommissioned officer
❷ soda
曹達 *sōda* soda
重曹 *jūsō* bicarbonate of soda
❸ officials, government office
法曹 *hōsō* legal profession, judicial officer, lawyer
❹ chamber in the Imperial court
御曹司 *onzōshi* son of a noble family
❺ [original meaning] friends, companions

INDEPENDENT
【**sō 曹**】friends, companions

SYNONYMS
❶ **military officers and ranks**
尉 COMPANY OFFICER → 1685
佐 FIELD OFFICER → 67
将 GENERAL OFFICER → 460
督 COMMANDER → 2796
帥 COMMANDER IN CHIEF → 1290

患

2747 KAN wazura(u)

Ⓒ患 huàn

Radical	Strokes
心 61	11-4-7
Grade	Freq
Jōyō	1047
2 - 7 - 4	

7-4 串

▶AFFECTED BY DISEASE

COMPOUNDS
❶ⓐ **affected by disease, diseased, sick**
ⓑ affection, disease
患者 *kanja* patient
患部 *kanbu* diseased part, affected area
罹患 *rikan* contraction of a disease
疾患 *shikkan* disease, ailment, trouble, disorder
❷ abbrev. of 患者 *kanja*: patient
急患 *kyūkan* emergency case, acutely sick patient
新患 *shinkan* new patient
❸ [original meaning] trouble, worry, anxiety
内憂外患 *naiyū gaikan* troubles from within and without
後患 *kōkan* future trouble
憂患 *yūkan* sorrow, grief, distress

KUN
【**wazura(u) 患う**】fall ill, be afflicted with
患い *wazurai* illness, sickness
長患い *nagawazurai* lingering sickness
胸を患う *mune o wazurau* have trouble in one's lungs, suffer from pulmonary tuberculosis

SYNONYMS
❶ **disease**
病 ILLNESS → 3277
疾 DISEASE → 3279
風 (infectious) disease → 3007
症 PATHOLOGICAL CONDITION → 3280
疫 EPIDEMIC → 3276

USAGE
❶ **wazurau**
患う
fall ill, be afflicted with

煩う
worry about, feel anxious, be vexed

❷ **wazurai**

患い
illness, sickness

煩い
worry, agony, vexation

HOMOPHONES

wazurau ⇨ 煩 1022
wazurai ⇨ 煩 1022

7-4 ⺠

祭

incorrect classification ⇨ see 2672

7-5 釆

番 番 番

2748 BAN tsuga(i)▲

Ⓒⓗ 番 fān pān

Radical	Strokes
田 102	12-5-7
Grade	**Freq**
Jōyō-2	328
2 - 7 - 5	

Stroke order: 1 2 3 4 5 6 7 8 9 10 11 12

▶NUMERICAL ORDER ▶WATCH

COMPOUNDS

❶ⓐ suffix for expressing numerical order or forming ordinal numbers: **No., number**

ⓑ **numerical order, order, ranking, place**

一番 *ichiban* first, first place; first verse; most, best; a game, a round, a bout; a number, a piece
三番線 *sanbansen* Track No.3
番号 *bangō* number, serial number
番地 *banchi* lot [house] number, address
番組 *bangumi* (TV) program
番付 *banzuke* ranking list
番頭 *bantō* (head) clerk
番狂わせ *bankuruwase* upsetting of arrangements, upset, surprise
先番 *senban* one's turn to make the first move
本番 *honban* acting for the audience, take, going on the air
順番 *junban* order, turn

❷ⓐ [also suffix] **watch, vigil, guard, lookout**

ⓑ watchman, guard, keeper

番人 *bannin* watchman, guard, caretaker
番犬 *banken* watchdog
留守番 *rusuban* caretaking (during a person's absence); caretaker
門番 *monban* gatekeeper, janitor
下足番 *gesokuban* caretaker of footwear

❸ (**one's**) **turn, duty, shift**

交番 *kōban* police box
出番 *deban* one's turn, one's time
当番 *tōban* being on duty [guard]; person on duty
非番 *hiban* off duty
輪番 *rinban* turn, rotation

❹ coarse

番茶 *bancha* coarse tea
番傘 *bangasa* coarse oilpaper umbrella

❺ counter for number of games, dances or kabuki plays

三番勝負 *sanban shōbu* three-game match
十八番 *jūhachiban* repertoire comprising eighteen classical kabuki pieces; one's specialty

INDEPENDENT

【ban 番】 one's turn, duty, shift; watch, vigil, guard, lookout
番に当たる *ban ni ataru* be on duty, have one's inning

【bansuru 番する】 keep watch, guard

KUN

【tsuga(i) 番い】 couple, brace, pair
一番いの鴨 *hitotsugai no kamo* a brace of ducks
蝶番い *chōtsugai* hinge

SYNONYMS

❶ⓐ **kinds of numbers**

号 NUMBER (numerical designation) → 2153
数 NUMBER (mathematical unit) → 1790
員 fixed number → 2269
第 ORDINAL NUMBER PREFIX → 2660
-目 ordinal number suffix → 3043
次 numerical order suffix → 54

ⓑ **order**

次 order (sequence) → 54
順 ORDER (sequence) → 18
序 ORDER (sequence/arrangement) → 3065
秩 ORDER (methodical arrangement) → 1158

❷ⓐ **protect**

衛 GUARD → 760
警 GUARD AGAINST → 2893
守 PROTECT → 2173
護 PROTECT → 1648
防 defend → 270
保 PRESERVE → 96
看 CARE FOR → 3220

COMPOUND FORMATION

番組 *bangumi*
番組 '(TV) program' is a scheduled or planned out (組) order (番 ❶ⓑ) of events of some public presentation, such as a TV or radio program.

盜
2749

▶**STEAL**
nonstandard for 盗 2670

7-5
次

募

incorrect classification ⇨ see 2316

7-5
莫

喬

incorrect classification ⇨ see 2488

7-5
呑

黍

incorrect classification ⇨ see 2597

7-5
禾

盛
2750

▶**PROSPEROUS**
nonstandard for 盛 2675

7-5
成

裝
2751

▶**DRESS** ▶**FIT OUT**
nonstandard for 装 2685

7-6
壯

幕 墓 incorrect classification ⇨ see 3-10

7-6
莫

羣
2752

▶**GROUP**
nonstandard for 群 1540

7-6
君

墨 
2753 BOKU sumi

CH 墨 mò

Radical	Strokes
土 32	14-3-11
Grade	**Freq**
Jōyō	1357
2-7-7	

7-7
里

▶**INDIA INK**

COMPOUNDS

❶ **India ink, Chinese ink, ink stick**
墨汁 *bokujū* India ink, black writing fluid
水墨画 *suibokuga* India ink drawing, painting in India ink

❷ⓐ something written in India ink
ⓑ something used like or resembling India ink

墨痕 *bokkon* handwriting; ink marks
遺墨 *iboku* autographs of a departed person
石墨 *sekiboku* graphite, black lead
白墨 *hakuboku* chalk
筆墨 *hitsuboku* pen and ink; writing materials, stationery

❸ [rare] tattooing, ancient Chinese punishment by tattooing
墨刑 *bokkei* punishment by tattooing

❹ Mexico
日墨 *nichiboku* Japan and Mexico
❺ Mozi (name of a Chinese philosopher)
墨子 *bokushi* Mozi
墨守 *bokushu* strict adherence ("defending like Mozi")

KUN

【sumi 墨】
ⓐ India ink, Chinese ink, ink stick
ⓑ (black substance) ink, soot, black dye
墨色 *sumiiro* India ink color
墨絵 *sumie* India ink drawing, painting in India ink
お墨付き *osumitsuki* handwriting; certificate, authorization; paper bearing the signature of the shogun or feudal lord
墨染め *sumizome* dyeing black; (Buddhist priest's) black robe
眉墨 *mayuzumi* eyebrow pencil
入れ墨 *irezumi* tattooing, tattoo, tattoo marks

SYNONYMS

❶ pigments
漆 LACQUER → 704
藍 INDIGO → 2381

USAGE

sumi
墨
ⓐ India ink, Chinese ink, ink stick
ⓑ (black substance) ink, soot, black dye
炭
charcoal

HOMOPHONES

sumi ⇨ 炭 2257

7-7 折

誓

2754 SEI chika(u)

CH 誓 shì

Radical	Strokes
言 149	14-7-7
Grade	**Freq**
Jōyō	1606
2-7-7	

1 2 3 4 5 6 7 8 9 10 11 12 13 14

▶VOW

COMPOUNDS

● [original meaning] **vow, swear, pledge, make [take] an oath**
誓約する *seiyaku suru* vow, pledge, make [take] an oath, swear
誓願 *seigan* oath, vow, pledge
宣誓する *sensei suru* make [take] an oath, swear, vow

KUN

【chika(u) 誓う】 vow, swear, pledge, make [take] an oath
誓い *chikai* vow, oath, pledge
誓って *chikatte* upon my word, by Jove
誓い交わす *chikaikawasu* vow to each other

SYNONYMS

● promise
約 PROMISE → 1280
締 CONCLUDE (a treaty) → 1393
協 reach an agreement → 93
契 MAKE AN AGREEMENT → 2639
盟 ALLIANCE → 2794

7-7 莫

暮 慕 incorrect classification ⇨ see 3-11

7-7 艹

蓉 incorrect classification ⇨ see 2513 (nonstandard for 蓉 2337)

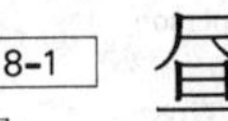

8-1 昼

昼 incorrect classification ⇨ see 3097

隻 隻 隻 隻

2755 SEKI

CH 只 zhī

Radical	Strokes
隹 172	10-8-2
Grade	Freq
Jōyō	1279
2-8-2	

8-2 隹

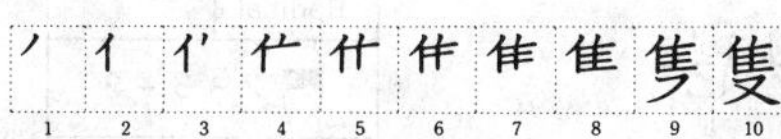

▶ONE OF A PAIR
▶COUNTER FOR SHIPS

COMPOUNDS

❶ⓐ [original meaning] **one of a pair, esp. when the second member is absent**
ⓑ one only, single, lone
隻手 *sekishu* one arm, one hand
隻眼 *sekigan* one eye
隻影 *sekiei* a single shadow; a speck (of cloud)
❷ just a little, a bit
隻語 *sekigo* just a few words
隻句 *sekku* a few words
❸ **counter for ships**
一隻 *isseki* one ship
数隻 *sūseki* several ships

SYNONYMS

❶ **one**
片- ONE OF TWO → 3461
一 ONE → 3341
壱 ONE (in legal documents) → 2197
単 SINGLE → 2256
個 INDIVIDUAL → 117
❸ **boats and ships**
船 SHIP → 1341
舶 OCEANGOING SHIP → 1340
艦 WARSHIP → 1435
潜 submarine → 746
舟 SMALL BOAT → 3538
艇 BOAT → 1365

隼 隼 隼

2756 SHUN hayabusa NAMES haya

CH 隼 sǔn

Radical	Strokes
隹 172	10-8-2
Grade	Freq
Names	2086
2-8-2	

8-2 隹

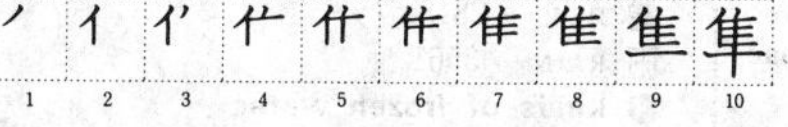

▶FALCON

COMPOUNDS

● [original meaning] **falcon**
鷹隼 *yōshun* [archaic] hawk and falcon

KUN

【hayabusa 隼】
ⓐ falcon, peregrine falcon, duck hawk
ⓑ as fast and brave as a falcon
隼科 *hayabusaka Falconidae*
大隼 *ōhayabusa* gerfalcon

NAMES

隼人 *hayato* male name
隼町 *hayabusachō* place name

SYNONYMS

● **wild birds**
鷹 HAWK → 3189
鶴 CRANE → 1850
雀 SPARROW → 2469

隻

2757

▶ONE OF A PAIR ▶COUNTER FOR SHIPS
nonstandard for 隻 2755

8-2 隹

8-2 鬯

鬯
2758

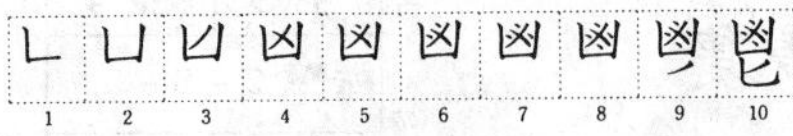

Radical	Strokes
鬯 192	10-10-0
Grade	Freq
Radical	
2 - 8 - 2	

RADICAL 192

Standard form: 鬯 *chō* 'fragrant wine'

Description: used in characters related to fragrant wine or fragrance

---

8-3 雨

雪 雪 雪 雪
2759 SETSU yuki

CH 雪 xuě

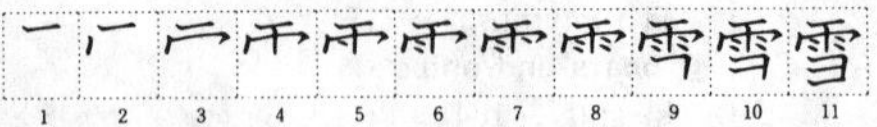

Radical	Strokes
雨 173	11-8-3
Grade	Freq
Jōyō-2	883
2 - 8 - 3	

▶**SNOW**

COMPOUNDS

❶ⓐ **snow, snowfall**

ⓑ as white (and pure) as snow

雪上車 *setsujōsha* snowmobile

豪雪 *gōsetsu* tremendous snowfall

降雪 *kōsetsu* snowfall, snow

積雪 *sekisetsu* (fallen) snow

新雪 *shinsetsu* fresh snow

蛍雪 *keisetsu* diligent study

雪白の *seppaku no* snow-white; pure, immaculate

❷ wipe out (disgrace), vindicate

雪辱 *setsujoku* vindication of honor, revenge

KUN

【**yuki** 雪】 snow, snowfall

雪合戦 *yukigassen* snowball fight

雪焼け *yukiyake* snow-tan

雪祭り *yukimatsuri* Snow Festival

初雪 *hatsuyuki* first snow of the season

SPECIAL READINGS

雪崩 *nadare* snowslide

吹雪 *fubuki* snowstorm

SYNONYMS

ⓐ **kinds of precipitation**

霜 FROST → 2815

露 DEW → 2818

雨 RAIN → 3561

ⓐ **kinds of frozen water**

氷 ICE → 39

NOTE

⇨ see COMPOUND FORMATION for 蛍雪 *keisetsu* ⇨ 蛍 2591

8-3 雨

雫
2760 shizuku

CH none (国字)

Radical	Strokes
雨 173	11-8-3
Grade	Freq
Reference	
2 - 8 - 3	

COMPOUNDS

[also 滴 *shizuku*]

ⓐ [original meaning] (liquid globule) drop

ⓑ counter for drops

露の雫 *tsuyu no shizuku* dewdrop

一雫 *hitoshizuku* a drop

HOMOPHONES

shizuku ⇨ 滴 705

NOTE

⇨ see USAGE note at 滴 705

8-3 雨

雪
2761

▶**SNOW**

nonstandard for 雪 2759

婆 婆 婆 (CH) 婆 pó

2762 BA baba▲ bā▲

Radical	Strokes
女 38	11-3-8
Grade	**Freq**
Jōyō	1920
2-8-3	

8-3 波

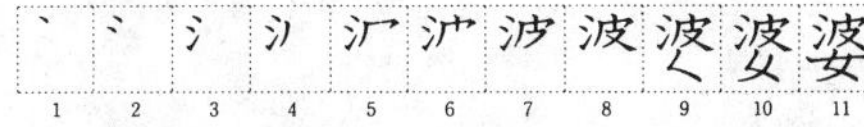

▶**OLD WOMAN**

COMPOUNDS

❶ **old woman, old maid, old mother; woman**

老婆 *rōba* old woman
妖婆 *yōba* witch, hag
老婆心 *rōbashin* grandmotherly solicitude
産婆 *sanba* midwife

❷ used phonetically for *ba*, esp. in the transliteration of Sanscrit Buddhist terms

婆羅門 *baramon* Brahman
娑婆 *shaba* this world, outside world (as viewed from prison)
卒塔婆 *sotoba* wooden grave tablet; stupa, dagoba

KUN

【baba 婆】 old woman; joker (in playing cards); something detestable

婆あ *babā slang* old woman, hag
婆抜き *babanuki* Old Maid; living without one's mother-in-law
鬼婆 *onibaba* hag, witch

【bā 婆】 [in compounds] old woman, old wife
婆や *bāya* old housekeeper; wet nurse
お婆さん *obāsan* old woman, old wife, grandma

SYNONYMS

❶ **old persons**
老 old person → 3197
翁 OLD MAN → 2108

❶ **woman**
婦 ADULT WOMAN → 469
女 WOMAN → 3418
嬢 YOUNG LADY → 758
娘 GIRL → 406
雌 FEMALE → 1055

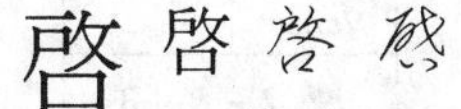

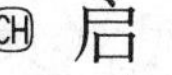

啓 啓 啓 啓 (CH) 启 qǐ

2763 KEI hira(ku)▲

Radical	Strokes
口 30	11-3-8
Grade	**Freq**
Jōyō	1441
2-8-3	

8-3 敀

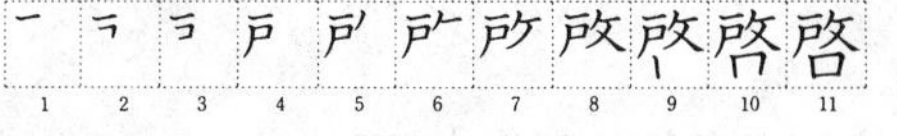

▶**ENLIGHTEN**

COMPOUNDS

❶ⓐ **enlighten, edify, awaken, educate**
ⓑ reveal

啓蒙 *keimō* enlightenment, instruction
啓発する *keihatsu suru* enlighten, develop, edify
啓示 *keiji* revelation
天啓 *tenkei* divine revelation

❷ **address respectfully**—used esp. in polite salutations

啓上する *keijō suru* speak respectfully
拝啓 *haikei* Dear Sir, Dear Madam
謹啓 *kinkei* Dear Sirs, Gentlemen

❸ [original meaning] open (a door)

中啓 *chūkei* ceremonial folding fan

❹ favor with one's presence, deign to come

行啓 *gyōkei* attendance (of the Empress)

KUN

【hira(ku) 啓く】 [usu. 開く] enlighten, edify

蒙を啓く *mō o hiraku* enlighten (a person's mind)

SYNONYMS

❶ **teach**
迪 EDIFY → 3076
教 TEACH → 1493
授 teach → 492
育 educate → 2050
練 TRAIN → 1375
訓 INSTRUCT → 1454
諭 ADMONISH → 1598
導 GUIDE → 2888

❷ **speak humbly**
申す SPEAK HUMBLY → 3507

HOMOPHONES

hiraku ⇨ 開 3321 拓 317

NOTE

⇨ see USAGE note at 開 3321

8-3 攴

啓 2764

▶**ENLIGHTEN**
nonstandard for 啓 2763

8-3 林

埜 2765

▶**FIELD**
nonstandard for 野 1485

8-3 其

基

incorrect classification ⇨ see 2673

8-3 來

麦 2766

Radical	Strokes
麥 199	11-11-0
Grade	**Freq**
Radical	
2-8-3	

一 十 才 才 办 本 夾 夾 夾 麦 麦
1 2 3 4 5 6 7 8 9 10 11

RADICAL 199
bakunyō, variant of 麥 *baku* 'wheat'
⇨ see 麥 2767 for radical description

8-3 來

麥 2767

▶**WHEAT**
nonstandard for 麦 2408

Radical	Strokes
麥 199	11-11-0
Grade	**Freq**
Variant	
2-8-3	

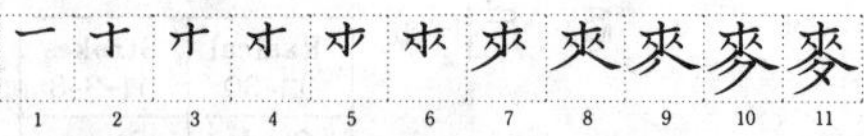
1 2 3 4 5 6 7 8 9 10 11

RADICAL 199
Standard form: 麥 *baku* 'wheat' (麫)
Enclosure: 麦 *bakunyō* (麴 麵)
Description: used in characters related to wheat or foods made of wheat

8-3 亞

堊 2768

AKU A

Ⓒⓗ 垩 è

Radical	Strokes
土 32	11-3-8
Grade	**Freq**
Reference	
2-8-3	

COMPOUNDS
● [now also 亜 *a* 3540] whitewash

白堊 *hakua* chalk; white wall

8-3 叀

專 2769

▶**EXCLUSIVE**
nonstandard for 専 2644

8-3 陏

隋

incorrect stroke count ⇨ see 2822

8-3 臤

堅 incorrect stroke count ⇨ see 2823

8-4 隹

焦

2770 SHŌ ko(geru) ko(gasu) ko(gareru) ase(ru)

CH 焦 jiāo

Radical	Strokes
灬 86	12-4-8
Grade	**Freq**
Jōyō	1134
2 - 8 - 4	

▶SCORCH ▶BE IMPATIENT

COMPOUNDS

❶ⓐ [original meaning] **scorch, burn**

ⓑ [also prefix] pyro-

焦点 *shōten* focus, focal point; (photographic) focus

焦土 *shōdo* scorched earth

焦熱 *shōnetsu* scorching heat

焦眉 *shōbi* emergency, urgency, imminence

焦性硫酸 *shōsei-ryūsan* pyrosulfuric acid

焦電気 *shōdenki* pyroelectricity

❷ **be impatient, be too eager, burn to do something**

焦燥 *shōsō* fretfulness, impatience

焦慮 *shōryo* impatience; worry

焦心 *shōshin* impatience

KUN

【ko(geru) 焦げる】*vi* scorch, burn, singe

焦げ臭い *kogekusai* smell burnt

焦げ茶色 *kogechairo* dark brown, olive brown

【ko(gasu) 焦がす】*vt* scorch, burn, char

【ko(gareru) 焦がれる】pine for, yearn for; be deeply in love with

恋い焦がれる *koikogareru* pine for, burn with passion

【ase(ru) 焦る】be impatient, be hasty, be in a hurry, be too eager

焦り *aseri* impatience

焦るなよ *Aseru na yo* Don't be in such a hurry / Take your time

SYNONYMS

❶ **burn**

焼 BURN → 997

燃 BURN (undergo combustion) → 1081

❷ **impatient**

燥 restless → 1087

COMPOUND FORMATION

焦点 *shōten*

焦点 'focus, etc.' is the point (点) of burning (焦 ❶ⓐ), i.e., a point of great significance or focal point.

8-4 隹

集

2771 SHŪ atsu(maru) atsu(meru) tsudo(u)

CH 集 jí

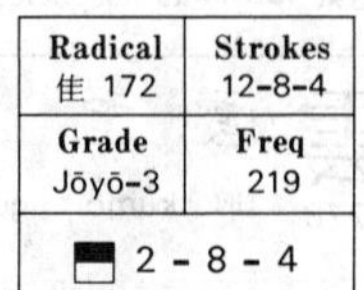

Radical	Strokes
隹 172	12-8-4
Grade	**Freq**
Jōyō-3	219
2 - 8 - 4	

▶COLLECT

COMPOUNDS

❶ [formerly also 聚 2804 or 蒐 2506]

ⓐ (bring together) **collect, gather, concentrate, assemble, recruit**

ⓑ [original meaning] (come together) **collect, gather, congregate**

ⓒ gathering, meeting, assembly; collection

集金 *shūkin* collecting money

集配 *shūhai* collection and delivery

集貨 *shūka* collection of freight

採集する *saishū suru* collect, gather

収集(＝蒐集)する *shūshū suru* collect, gather, accumulate

招集する *shōshū suru* call, summon, convene

募集する *boshū suru* recruit, enlist; raise, collect

徴集する *chōshū suru* levy, recruit

集中する *shūchū suru* concentrate, focus; converge

集合する *shūgō suru* gather, meet, assemble; summon, call together

結集する *kesshū suru* concentrate, marshal

集会 *shūkai* gathering, meeting, assembly

集団 *shūdan* group, body, mass, crowd

群集 *gunshū* crowd, mob; forming a large group (of people)

❷ [also suffix] **collection of literary works,**

anthology, series
詩集 *shishū* anthology of poems
川端全集 *kawabata-zenshū* the complete works of Kawabata
万葉集 *man'yōshū* (=*mannyōshū*) Japan's oldest anthology of poems
書簡集 *shokanshū* collection of letters
❸ [formerly also 輯 1606]
ⓐ (collect written materials) **edit, compile**
ⓑ edition, series
集録 *shūroku* compilation, editing
編集する *henshū suru* edit, compile
特集 *tokushū* special edition
第一集 *daiisshū* first series

INDEPENDENT

【shū 集】 collection of literary works, anthology

KUN

【atsu(maru) 集まる】 *vi* gather, collect, meet, crowd, flock; (of money) be collected; center, converge, focus
集まり *atsumari* gathering, meeting, assembly; collection
寄り集まる *yoriatsumaru* gather, assemble

【atsu(meru) 集める】 *vt* collect, gather, assemble, recruit; raise (funds); focus, concentrate
搔き集める *kakiatsumeru* gather up, scrape up together
切手集め *kitteatsume* stamp collecting

【tsudo(u) 集う】 *vi* gather, collect, meet
集い *tsudoi* meeting, gathering, get-together

SYNONYMS

❶ⓐ & ❶ⓑ gather
収 collect → 198
採 GATHER → 499
ⓒ assembly
会 meeting → 2020
❷ collected works
選 selection → 3169
❸ⓐ compile
編 COMPILE → 1387
著 AUTHOR → 2300

NOTE

⇨ see USAGE note at 徴 683

8-4

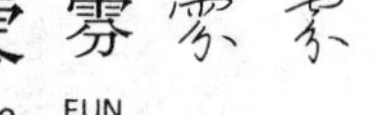
2772 FUN

CH  fēn

Radical	Strokes
雨 173	12-8-4
Grade	**Freq**
Jōyō	1963
2-8-4	

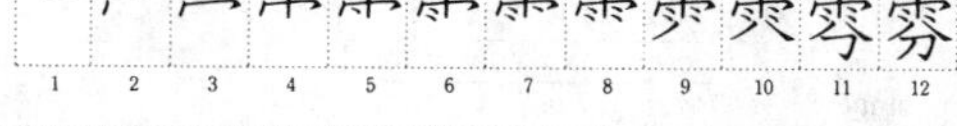

▶ATMOSPHERE

COMPOUNDS

❶ atmosphere
雰囲気 *fun'iki* atmosphere, mood
❷ [original meaning, now archaic] mist, fog

SYNONYMS

❶ atmosphere
気 atmosphere → 3194

8-4

雲
2773 UN kumo -gumo

CH 云 yún

Radical	Strokes
雨 173	12-8-4
Grade	**Freq**
Jōyō-2	1119
2-8-4	

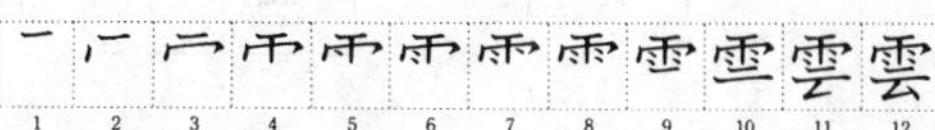

▶CLOUD

COMPOUNDS

❶ⓐ [original meaning] **cloud**
ⓑ something resembling a cloud
雲海 *unkai* sea of clouds
雲霧 *unmu* clouds and fog
雲泥の差 *undei no sa* great difference (as between clouds and mud)
積乱雲 *sekiran'un* cumulonimbus
風雲 *fūun* state of affairs, situation
星雲 *seiun* nebula
❷ (figuratively) as high as the clouds
青雲の志 *seiun no kokorozashi* high [lofty] ambition

KUN

【kumo 雲】 cloud
雲隠れする *kumogakure suru* vanish behind clouds; disappear, run away
雲間 *kumoma* rift between clouds
浮き雲 *ukigumo* cloud drift

【-gumo -雲】 [suffix] cloud
入道雲 *nyūdōgumo* gigantic columns of clouds (in summer), cumulonimbus
キノコ雲 *kinokogumo* mushroom cloud (from

a nuclear blast)

SYNONYMS

❶ **kinds of atmospheric vapor**

霧 FOG → 2817
霞 MIST → 2814

雰 ▶ATMOSPHERE
2774

nonstandard for 雰 2772

悲 悲 悲
2775 HI kana(shii) kana(shimu)

(CH) 悲 bēi

Radical	Strokes
心 61	12-4-8
Grade	**Freq**
Jōyō-3	1025

2 - 8 - 4

▶**SAD**

COMPOUNDS

❶ⓐ **sad, sorrowful, pathetic**
ⓑ [original meaning] feel sad, feel sorrow
ⓒ sorrow, grief
悲痛な *hitsū na* sad, grievous
悲惨な *hisan na* miserable, wretched, tragic, pitiable
悲壮な *hisō na* pathetic, tragic
悲劇 *higeki* tragedy, tragic drama
悲鳴 *himei* shriek, scream
悲観する *hikan suru* be pessimistic, lose heart
悲嘆 *hitan* grief, sorrow, lamentation
悲哀 *hiai* sorrow, sadness
悲喜 *hiki* joy and sorrow

❷ⓐ *Buddhism* mercy, compassion
ⓑ merciful, compassionate
慈悲 *jihi* mercy, compassion
大慈大悲 *daijidaihi* great mercy and compassion
悲願 *higan* one's pathetic wish; vows resulting from the compassion of the Buddhas

INDEPENDENT

【hi 悲】 *Buddhism* mercy, compassion

KUN

【kana(shii) 悲しい】
ⓐ (low in spirit) sad, unhappy, sorrowful
ⓑ [formerly also 哀しい] (causing sorrow) sad, sorrowful, pathetic
悲しさ *kanashisa* sadness, sorrow, grief
悲しげに *kanashige ni* sadly, with a sad look
悲しがる *kanashigaru* be sad, feel sorrow

【kana(shimu) 悲しむ】 feel [be] sad, grieve, feel sorrow; lament, regret
悲しみ *kanashimi* grief, sadness
悲しむべき境遇 *kanashimubeki kyōgū* pitiable condition

SYNONYMS

❶ⓐ & ❶ⓒ **sad and depressed**
哀 sorrowful → 2068
愁 MELANCHOLY → 2829
陰 gloomy → 541
沈 depressed → 261
寂 LONESOME → 2290
惨 MISERABLE → 483

ⓑ **grieve**
傷 grieve → 158
嘆 SIGH → 630
慨 DEPLORE → 641
悼 MOURN → 485

❷ⓐ **tender feelings for others**
哀 PITY → 2068
情 sympathy → 482
慈 compassion → 2339
仁 BENEVOLENCE → 20

USAGE

kanashii

悲しい
ⓐ (low in spirit) sad, unhappy, sorrowful
ⓑ [formerly also 哀しい] (causing sorrow) sad, sorrowful, pathetic

哀しい
[now usu. 悲しい] (causing sorrow) sad, sorrowful, pathetic

HOMOPHONES

kanashii ⇨ 哀 2068

8-4 非

斐 斐 斐 斐

2776 HI I NAMES aya

CH 斐 fěi

Radical	Strokes
文 67	12-4-8
Grade	Freq
Names	2029
2-8-4	

1 2 3 4 5 6 7 8 9 10 11 12

▶**PHONETIC** [i]

COMPOUNDS

❶ **used phonetically for** ***i***

甲斐が有る *kai ga aru* fruitful, effective, worth, worthwhile

❷ [archaic] florid, embellished, beautiful

斐然たる *hizentaru* florid, beautiful

NAMES

甲斐 *kai* surname also place name

斐子 *ayako* female name

SYNONYMS

❶ **phonetic** [i]

伊 PHONETIC [i] → 49

❷ **beautiful**

絢 GORGEOUS → 1347

華 MAGNIFICENT → 2283

美 BEAUTIFUL → 2264

佳 FINE → 86

瑶 EXQUISITE → 1026

麗 OF GRACEFUL BEAUTY → 2151

艶 CHARMING → 1908

妙 of marvelous beauty → 239

8-4 非

斐

2777

▶**PHONETIC** [i]

nonstandard for 斐 2776

8-4 林

焚

2778 FUN ta(ku)

CH 焚 fén

Radical	Strokes
火 86	12-4-8
Grade	Freq
Reference	
2-8-4	

COMPOUNDS

● [original meaning] burn, kindle, build a fire

焚書 *funsho* book burning

焚き火 *takibi* bonfire

焚き付け *takitsuke* kindling, fire lighter

焚き付ける *takitsukeru* kindle, build a fire; instigate, stir up

空焚き *karadaki* heating a pan or bath tub without water in it

HOMOPHONES

taku ⇨ 炊 870

NOTE

⇨ see USAGE note at 炊 870

8-4 炏

勞

2779

▶**LABOR**

nonstandard for 労 2548

惣 2780 SŌ NAMES fusa

CH none（国字）

Radical	Strokes
心 61	12-4-8
Grade	Freq
Names	2073

2-8-4

8-4 物

▶GENERAL

COMPOUNDS

[now usu. 総 1379]

❶ (applicable to the whole or the usual) **general, overall; ordinary**

惣菜 *sōzai* daily [household] dish, side dish
惣社 *sōja* shrine enshrining several gods
惣嫁 *sōka* streetwalker (in the Edo period)

❷ⓐ (of supreme rank) general, supreme, chief
ⓑ [archaic] exercise general control, administer, govern

惣管領 *sōkanryō hist* governor-general
惣領する *sōryō suru* govern, administer (a fief)

❸ eldest son, eldest child—used esp. in names

惣領 *sōryō* eldest son, eldest child

NAMES

惣太郎 *sōtarō* male name
惣一 *sōichi* male name

SYNONYMS

❶ **general**

総 GENERAL → 1379

❸ **offspring**

息 son → 2647
男 son → 2542
子 CHILD → 3390
孤 orphan → 356
嫡 LEGITIMATE CHILD → 680
娘 DAUGHTER → 406
女 daughter → 3418
姫 DAUGHTER OF NOBLE BIRTH → 407

USAGE

sō 惣 総

★The function of 惣 in Japanese is vague and does not lend itself to logical analysis. Originally it was a corrupt form of 総 (core meanings GENERAL and TOTAL), but is now restricted mostly to personal names, esp. of an eldest son. It can be said that 惣 is actually a *variant* of 総, *not* a different character with the same meanings.

COMPOUND FORMATION

惣菜 *sōzai* 惣社 *sōja* 惣嫁 *sōka*

惣菜 and 惣社, the only compounds one is likely to encounter, are now normally written 総菜 and 総社. 惣菜 'daily [household] dish, side dish' can be interpreted as an ordinary (惣 ❶) side dish (菜), and 惣社 'shrine enshrining several gods' as a general (惣 ❶) shrine (社), i.e., a shrine not limited in scope to one deity, while 惣嫁, a colorful word to describe a streetwalker, is a general (惣 ❶) bride (嫁), i.e., "a bride to be shared by everyone."

琴 2781 KIN koto

CH 琴 qín

Radical	Strokes
王 96	12-4-8
Grade	Freq
Jōyō	1436

2-8-4

8-4 王

▶KOTO

COMPOUNDS

ⓐ [original meaning] **koto, (Japanese) harp, lyre**
ⓑ musical instrument resembling a koto

琴曲 *kinkyoku* koto music
弾琴 *dankin* playing on the koto
琴線 *kinsen* heartstrings
木琴 *mokkin* xylophone
風琴 *fūkin* organ, accordion
提琴 *teikin* violin

INDEPENDENT

【**kin 琴**】Chinese harp

KUN

【**koto 琴**】[sometimes also 箏] [also suffix]
koto, (Japanese) harp, lyre

琴爪 *kotozume* artificial fingernail [plectrum] of ivory used in playing the koto
竪琴 *tategoto* harp
大正琴 *taishōgoto* Japanese harp with three to five strings

SYNONYMS

ⓐ **musical instruments**

鼓 DRUM → 1786
笛 FLUTE → 2664

USAGE

koto
琴
[sometimes also 箏] [also suffix] koto, (Japanese) harp, lyre
箏
[usu. 琴] koto, (Japanese) harp, lyre

HOMOPHONES

koto ⇨ 箏 2703

8-4 肰

然

2782 ZEN NEN shika▲ shika(ri)▲ shika(shi)▲ sa▲

CH 然 rán

Radical	Strokes
灬 86	12-4-8
Grade	**Freq**
Jōyō-4	409
2 - 8 - 4	

▶MODIFIER FORMING SUFFIX ▶SO

COMPOUNDS

❶ⓐ **suffix for forming modifiers (noun adjectives and adverbs); suffix attached to a one-character base to express a state of being or quality**
ⓑ suffix after nouns to express likeness: -like, smack of
突然 *totsuzen* abruptly, suddenly, unexpectedly
公然の *kōzen no* open, public
平然と *heizen to* calmly, quietly, with composure
純然たる *junzentaru* pure, sheer; absolute
憤然として *funzen to shite* indignantly, wrathfully, in a rage
全然 *zenzen* wholly, totally, completely; (not) at all
断然 *danzen* resolutely, decisively
学者然としている *gakushazen to shite iru* be quite like a scholar

❷ⓐ **so, be definitely so, be as it is**
ⓑ just so, just as you say, yes
天然の *tennen no* natural
自然 *shizen* nature
偶然 *gūzen* chance, accident, coincidence
当然 *tōzen* naturally, as a matter of course
依然 *izen* still, as yet
然諾する *zendaku suru* consent, say yes

KUN

【shika 然】 so, thus; yes, aye
然も *shikamo* [formerly also 而も] moreover, furthermore; and yet, nevertheless
【shika(ri) 然り】 just so, just as you say, yes
然るに *shikaru ni* however, still, but
然るべき *shikarubeki* due, proper, appropriate
【shika(shi) 然し】 however, but, nevertheless
然しながら *shikashinagara* however, nevertheless
【sa 然】 so
然る *saru* a certain; so
然り気ない *sarigenai* unconcerned, nonchalant

SYNONYMS

❶ **modifier suffixes**
如 modifier suffix → 207
爾 adjective suffix → 3587
的 ADJECTIVAL SUFFIX → 1125
❷ **terms of assent**
諾 yes → 1568
【shikashi】
○ **conditional conjunctions**
但し PROVIDED THAT → 72

USAGE

shikamo
然も
[formerly also 而も]
ⓐ moreover, furthermore
ⓑ and yet, nevertheless
而も
[now usu. 然も] same as 然も

HOMOPHONES

shikamo ⇨ 而 2027

COMPOUND FORMATION

自然 *shizen*
自然 'nature' is to be (然 ❷ⓐ) in a spontaneous or natural (自) state.

NOTE

⇨ see COMPOUND FORMATION for 当然 *tōzen* ⇨ 当 2177

替 2783

替 替 替 (CH) 替 tì

2783 TAI ka(eru) ka(e)- ka(waru)

Radical	Strokes
日 73	12-4-8
Grade	Freq
Jōyō	1136
2-8-4	

8-4 䒹

一 二 ≠ 夫 夫一 夫二 夫扌 夫夫 夫夫 替 替 替
1 2 3 4 5 6 7 8 9 10 11 12

▶REPLACE

COMPOUNDS

❶ [original meaning] **replace (one thing or person by another), change places, substitute, change**
代替 *daitai* substitution
交替(＝交代) *kōtai* alternation, shift, change

❷ decline, decay
隆替 *ryūtai* rise and decline

KUN

【ka(eru) 替える】
①ⓐ replace (one thing or person by another), renew, change
ⓑ change to something new (as a job or set of clothes), change over to
替え *kae* replacement, spare
畳の表を替える *tatami no omote o kaeru* replace the covers of old mats with new ones
塗り替える *nurikaeru* repaint
取り替える *torikaeru* change, renew, replace, substitute
両替 *ryōgae* money changing, exchange of money
商売を替える *shōbai o kaeru* change to a new business
着替える *kigaeru* change clothes
② [usu. 換える] exchange, interchange, trade, barter, change (money), convert
引き替える *hikikaeru* exchange, change, convert

【ka(e)- 替え-】 substitute, spare, extra
替え玉 *kaedama* substitute, double
替え刃 *kaeba* extra blades
替え着 *kaegi* spare (change of) clothes

【ka(waru) 替わる】 be replaced, change places with, replace, take turns, relieve, change
替わり *kawari* turn, shift; replacement (for a maid); substitute program (of a kabuki play)
替わってくれないか *Kawatte kurenai ka* Could you take over, please?
立ち替わる *tachikawaru* take turns, alternate
入れ替わり *irekawari* replacement, substitution, change, shifting
校長が替わった *Kōchō ga kawatta* A new school principal took over the job

SPECIAL READINGS

為替 *kawase* money order, exchange

SYNONYMS

❶ **change and replace**
代 SUBSTITUTE → 30
迭 ALTERNATE → 3077
交 INTERCHANGE → 2015
換 EXCHANGE → 587
転 turn into → 1480
遷 undergo transition → 3170
化 CHANGE INTO, -ize → 21
変 CHANGE → 2069
更 change → 3541
改 change → 243
易 change → 2411

HOMOPHONES

kaeru ⇨ 変 2069 換 587 代 30
kae- ⇨ 変 2069 換 587 代 30
kawaru ⇨ 変 2069 換 587 代 30
kawari ⇨ 変 2069 換 587 代 30

NOTE

⇨ see USAGE note at 変 2069
⇨ see COMPOUND FORMATION for 為替 *kawase* ⇨ 為 3577

智 2784

智 智 智 (CH) 智 zhì

2784 CHI NAMES sato satoshi satoru tomo nori toshi

Radical	Strokes
日 72	12-4-8
Grade	Freq
Names	1998
2-8-4	

8-4 知

丿 𠂉 𠂉 矢 矢 矢丨 知 知 知 智 智 智
1 2 3 4 5 6 7 8 9 10 11 12

▶WISDOM

COMPOUNDS

❶ [now replaced by 知 1127]
ⓐ **wisdom, intelligence**
ⓑ [original meaning] **wise, clever, resourceful**

智能 *chinō* intelligence, mental capacity
智慧(＝知恵) *chie* wisdom, intelligence, sagacity
智識 *chishiki* wisdom; Buddhist priest of renown
智謀 *chibō* resources, artifice
無智 *muchi* ignorance, stupidity
智慮 *chiryo* foresight
智者 *chisha* wise man; learned priest
智将 *chishō* resourceful general

❷ Chile
智日 *chinichi* Chile and Japan

INDEPENDENT

【chi 智(＝知)】 wisdom, intellect, intelligence, sense; stratagem
智を磨く *chi o migaku* cultivate wisdom

NAMES

智恵子 *chieko* female name
美智子 *michiko* female name
那智 *nachi* place name
智子 *tomoko* female name

SYNONYMS

❶ⓐ wisdom
識 KNOWLEDGE → 1639
知 knowledge → 1127
哲 PHILOSOPHY → 2738
慧 prajna (transcendental wisdom) → 2810

ⓑ intelligent and wise
賢 WISE → 2839
慧 INTELLIGENT → 2810
怜 CLEVER → 298
哲 SAGACIOUS → 2738
明 clear-sighted → 855
聡 SHARP-WITTED → 1384
俊 brilliant → 102
鋭 SHARP → 1730
敏 NIMBLE → 1322

8-4 無

無

incorrect classification ⇨ see 2135

8-4 並

普

incorrect classification ⇨ see 2323

8-4 其

棊

incorrect classification ⇨ see 2689
(nonstandard for 棋 987)

8-4 者

煮 煮 者 煮

2785 SHA ni(ru) -ni ni(eru) ni(yasu)

Ⓒⓗ 煮 zhǔ

Radical	Strokes
灬 86	12-4-8
Grade	**Freq**
Jōyō	1229
2-8-4	

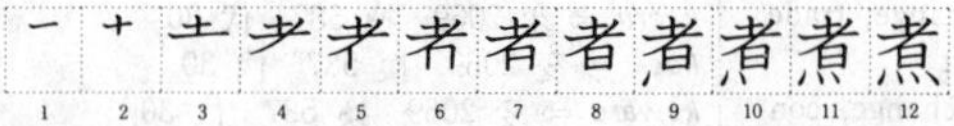

▶BOIL

COMPOUNDS

● [original meaning] (cook by boiling) **boil, cook**
煮沸 *shafutsu* boiling

KUN

【ni(ru) 煮る】 *vt* boil, cook, do
煮込む *nikomu* boil well; stew, cook together
煮立つ *nitatsu* boil up, begin to boil
煮豆 *nimame* boiled (cooked) beans

【-ni -煮】 [suffix] boiled food, boiling
甘露煮 *kanroni* sweet boiled food

【ni(eru) 煮える】 *vi* boil, be boiled, be cooked
煮え切らない *niekiranai* half-cooked; vague, halfhearted
煮え湯 *nieyu* boiling water
煮え湯を飲まされる *nieyu o nomasareru* be betrayed

【ni(yasu) 煮やす】 *vt* boil down, wear out
業を煮やす *gō o niyasu* be exasperated, lose one's temper

SYNONYMS

● cook
沸 BOIL (undergo boiling) → 329
炊 COOK → 870
蒸 STEAM → 2334
焼く cook by fire → 997
揚げる fry in deep fat → 593

【-ni】
○ cooked dishes
-揚げ fried food → 593
-焼き roasted, baked or fried food → 997

惑 惑 惑
2786 WAKU mado(u)

Ⓒⓗ 惑 huò

Radical	Strokes
心 61	12-4-8
Grade	Freq
Jōyō	1099
2 - 8 - 4	

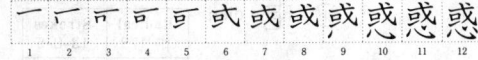

一 ｰ 〒 亓 亖 式 或 或 或 或 惑 惑
1 2 3 4 5 6 7 8 9 10 11 12

▶BEWILDERED

COMPOUNDS

❶ⓐ [original meaning] **bewildered, perplexed, puzzled, confused**
ⓑ **mislead, lead astray, entice**
惑乱 *wakuran* bewilderment, confusion
迷惑 *meiwaku* trouble, annoyance
当惑 *tōwaku* perplexity, confusion, embarrassment
困惑 *konwaku* embarrassment, perplexity, confusion
魅惑 *miwaku* fascination, enchantment, charm
誘惑 *yūwaku* temptation, seduction
眩惑 *genwaku* dazzle, daze, bewilderment
❷ wander
惑星 *wakusei* planet
❸ doubt, suspect
疑惑 *giwaku* doubt, suspicion
❹ *Buddhism* illusion
三惑 *sanwaku* three kinds of illusion
❺ used phonetically for *waku*
思惑 *omowaku* thought, intention, purpose

KUN

【**mado(u) 惑う**】 be bewildered, be puzzled; [in compounds] do something in confusion, be at a loss
惑い *madoi* delusion, illusion, infatuation; bewilderment, perplexity
戸惑い *tomadoi* loss of orientation, bewilderment
逃げ惑う *nigemadou* run about trying to escape
惑わす *madowasu* mislead, lead astray, entice; fascinate; bewilder, perplex, puzzle

SYNONYMS

❶ⓐ **bewildered**
迷 PERPLEXED → 3092
ⓑ **deceive**
偽 FALSIFY → 131
拐 defraud → 308
欺 DECEIVE → 1703
詐 SWINDLE → 1502

NOTE

⇨ see COMPOUND FORMATION for 当惑 *tōwaku* ⇨ 当 2177

黑
2787

▶BLACK
nonstandard for 黒 2740

Radical	Strokes
黑 203	12-12-0
Grade	Freq
Variant	
2 - 8 - 4	

1 2 3 4 5 6 7 8 9 10 11 12

RADICAL 203
Standard form: 黒 *kuroi* 'black' (黴)
Variant: 黑 *kuroi* (黙)
Description: used in characters related to blackness

惡
2788

▶BAD
nonstandard for 悪 2745

惠
2789

▶FAVOR
nonstandard for 恵 2659

腎

incorrect stroke count ⇨ see 2832

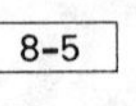

愚 incorrect stroke count ⇨ see 2834

8-5 雨

電 電 電

2790 DEN

CH 电 diàn

Radical	Strokes
雨 173	13-8-5
Grade	**Freq**
Jōyō-2	205
2 - 8 - 5	

一 1, 𠂉 2, 𠂉 3, 币 4, 币 5, 币 6, 雨 7, 雨 8, 雨 9, 雨 10, 雨 11, 雷 12, 電 13

▶ELECTRICITY

COMPOUNDS

❶ **electricity**

電気 *denki* electricity; electric light
電子 *denshi* electron
電力 *denryoku* electric power, electricity
電車 *densha* train, electric train, trolley
電波 *denpa* electromagnetic waves, radio waves
電話 *denwa* telephone; phone call
電報 *denpō* telegram
電算機 *densanki* electronic computer
発電する *hatsuden suru* generate electricity; telegraph
停電 *teiden* stoppage of electric power, power failure

❷ various devices operated by electricity, as:
ⓐ abbrev. of 電車 *densha*: **electric railway, train**
ⓑ abbrev. of 電話 *denwa*: **telephone**
ⓒ abbrev. of 電報 *denpō*: [also suffix] **telegram**

終電 *shūden* last train
国電 *kokuden* National Railway
電電公社 *denden kōsha* Nippon Telegraph and Telephone Public Corporation (defunct)
外電 *gaiden* foreign telegram, cablegram
打電する *daden suru* send a telegram, telegraph
ロイター電 *roitāden* Reuter dispatch

❸ [original meaning] lightning

電光 *denkō* lightning; electric light
雷電 *raiden* thunder and lightning, thunderbolt

SYNONYMS

❶ **electricity and magnetism**

流 electric current → 441
磁 MAGNETISM → 1214

❷ⓐ **kinds of railway**

鉄 railway → 1711
車 railway car → 3552
両 counter for railway cars → 3518

ⓒ **written communications**

信 written communication → 100
状 LETTER → 272
文 LETTER → 1962
書 letter → 2658

❸ **atmospheric discharges**

雷 THUNDER → 2791

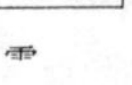

8-5 雨

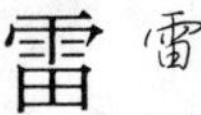
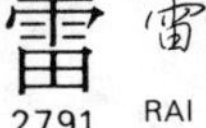

雷 雷 雷

2791 RAI kaminari

CH 雷 léi

Radical	Strokes
雨 173	13-8-5
Grade	**Freq**
Jōyō	1457
2 - 8 - 5	

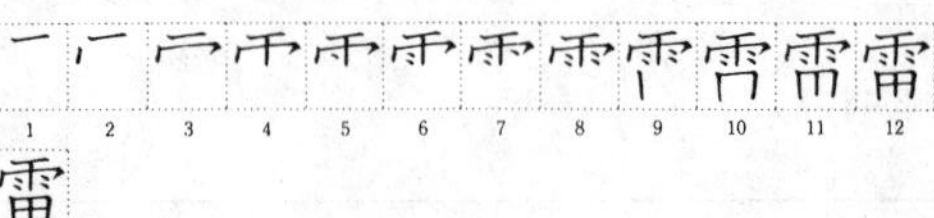

1, 2, 3, 4, 5, 6, 7, 8, 9, 10, 11, 12, 13

▶THUNDER

COMPOUNDS

❶ⓐ [original meaning] **thunder**
ⓑ lightning

雷電 *raiden* thunder and lightning, thunderbolt
雷雲 *raiun* thunder cloud
雷神 *raijin* god of thunder
落雷 *rakurai* strike of a thunderbolt
避雷針 *hiraishin* lightning rod

❷ explosive device, mine, torpedo

雷撃 *raigeki* torpedo attack

機雷 *kirai* mine
地雷 *jirai* land mine
水雷 *suirai* torpedo, mine
❸ fame, renown
雷名 *raimei* renown, fame, great name

INDEPENDENT

【**rai 雷**】 thunder

KUN

【**kaminari 雷**】 thunder, thunderbolt; lightning; thunderous rebuke, thundering at (a person); roaring sound

雷親父 *kaminarioyaji* irascible old man
雷族 *kaminarizoku* Thunder Herd, hot-rodders

SYNONYMS

❶ **atmospheric discharges**
電 lightning → 2790
❷ **projectiles and bombs**
爆 bomb → 1101
弾 PROJECTILE → 572
丸 round projectile → 3417
矢 ARROW → 2009

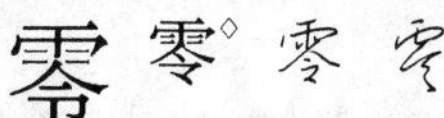

2792 REI zero▲

Ⓒ 零 líng

Radical	Strokes
雨 173	13-8-5
Grade	**Freq**
Jōyō	1092
2 - 8 - 5	

8-5

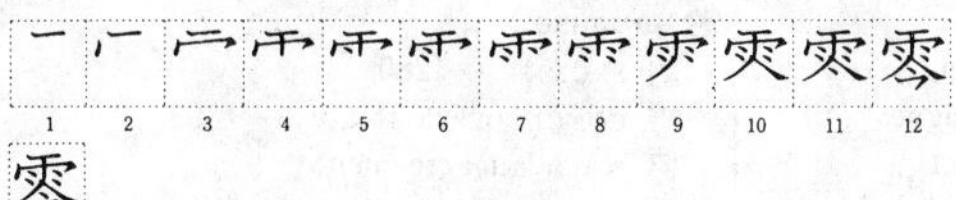

▶ZERO

COMPOUNDS

❶ **zero, naught**
零度 *reido* zero, freezing point
零下 *reika* below zero, sub-zero
零時 *reiji* twelve o'clock
零敗 *reihai* whitewash, being shut out
零点 *reiten* zero, no marks
❷ few, scanty, infinitesimal
零細な *reisai na* small, trifling, petty
零砕 *reisai* [rare] a tiny bit
❸ⓐ [original meaning, now rare] fall, drip (as of rain)
ⓑ fall low, go to ruin
零露 *reiro* dripping dew
零落 *reiraku* downfall, ruin

INDEPENDENT

【**rei 零**】 zero, naught

KUN

【**zero 零**】 zero (the number)
零戦 *zerosen* Zero fighter

SYNONYMS

❶ **emptiness and nothing**
無 NOTHING → 2135
虚 VOID → 3237
白 WHITE (blank) → 3493
空 EMPTY → 2227

USAGE

zero
零
zero (the number)
○
zero (the numeral)

HOMOPHONES

zero ⇨ ○ 3342

NOTE

⇨ see NOTE at ○ 3342

零

2793

▶ZERO
nonstandard for 零 2792

8-5

8-5
明

盟 盟 盟

2794 MEI

CH 盟 méng míng

Radical	Strokes
皿 108	13-5-8
Grade	**Freq**
Jōyō-6	664
2-8-5	

丨 冂 日 日 日丿 明 明 明 明 明 明 明 盟
1 2 3 4 5 6 7 8 9 10 11 12 13

▶**ALLIANCE**

COMPOUNDS

❶ **alliance, league, pledge, pact**
盟約 *meiyaku* pledge, pact, alliance, league
盟邦 *meihō* ally, allied powers
盟友 *meiyū* sworn friend
同盟 *dōmei* alliance, league, union
連盟 *renmei* union, federation, league
加盟 *kamei* participation, affiliation
❷ [original meaning] make a blood pledge by drinking sacrificial blood from a plate
血盟 *ketsumei* blood pledge

INDEPENDENT

【**mei** 盟】 alliance
盟を結ぶ *mei o musubu* form an alliance

SYNONYMS

❶ **promise**
約 PROMISE → 1280
締 CONCLUDE (a treaty) → 1393
協 reach an agreement → 93
誓 VOW → 2754
契 MAKE AN AGREEMENT → 2639

8-5
林

禁 禁 禁

2795 KIN

CH 禁 jìn jīn

Radical	Strokes
示 113	13-5-8
Grade	**Freq**
Jōyō-5	784
2-8-5	

一 十 才 木 木一 村 林 林 林 埜 埜 禁 禁
1 2 3 4 5 6 7 8 9 10 11 12 13

▶**PROHIBIT**

COMPOUNDS

❶ⓐ **prohibit, forbid, ban**
ⓑ prohibition, ban, embargo
禁止する *kinshi suru* prohibit, forbid, ban
禁煙 *kin'en* NO SMOKING; giving up smoking
禁句 *kinku* tabooed word
厳禁する *genkin suru* prohibit strictly, taboo
発禁 *hakkin* prohibition of sale, suppression (of a book)
禁令 *kinrei* prohibition, ban, embargo
解禁 *kaikin* removal of a ban; opening of the fishing [hunting] season
❷ abstain from, refrain from, give up
禁酒する *kinshu suru* abstain from [give up] drinking
禁欲 *kin'yoku* abstinence, self-denial
❸ (prohibited place) Imperial Palace, the Court
禁中 *kinchū* the court, the Imperial Palace
禁裏 *kinri* the Imperial Palace
❹ **confine, imprison**
禁固 *kinko* imprisonment
監禁する *kankin suru* imprison, confine
拘禁 *kōkin* detention, confinement, imprisonment

INDEPENDENT

【**kin** 禁】 prohibition, ban, embargo
禁を犯す *kin o okasu* violate the ban, break the prohibition (law)
【**kinjiru** (=**kinzuru**) 禁じる(=禁ずる)】 prohibit, forbid; suppress, restrain

SYNONYMS

❶ⓐ **restrain**
制 CONTROL (restrain) → 1274
限 LIMIT → 398
抑 SUPPRESS → 257
束 TIE UP → 3554
縛 BIND → 1405
控える HOLD BACK → 495
渋る hang [hold] back → 513
❷ **avoid and abstain**
忌 shun → 2207
避 AVOID → 3179
逃 ESCAPE → 3095
❹ **imprison and confine**
拘 ARREST → 310

留 keep in custody → 2580 | 置 place in custody → 2608

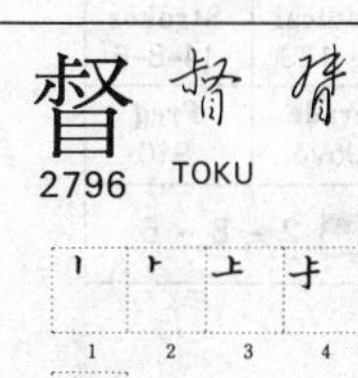

2796 TOKU

Ⓒⓗ 督 dū

Radical	Strokes
目 109	13-5-8
Grade	Freq
Jōyō	758
2-8-5	

Stroke order: 1 2 3 4 5 6 7 8 9 10 11 12 13

▶ SUPERVISE ▶ COMMANDER

COMPOUNDS

❶ [original meaning] **supervise, oversee, superintend**

督学官 *tokugakukan* school inspector

監督 *kantoku* supervision, superintendence; supervisor; film director

❷ⓐ **commander, governor-general, viceroy**

ⓑ command (troops), lead

総督 *sōtoku* governor-general, viceroy

都督 *totoku* governor general

提督 *teitoku* admiral

❸ urge, press, demand

督促する *tokusoku suru* urge, press, demand

督戦する *tokusen suru* urge soldiers to fight more vigorously

❹ inheritor of an estate

家督 *katoku* headship of a family, family estate

SYNONYMS

❶ **direct and supervise**

監 OVERSEE → 2852

制 CONTROL → 1274

管 EXERCISE CONTROL → 2701

轄 EXERCISE JURISDICTION OVER → 1627

掌 TAKE CHARGE OF → 2602

司 OFFICIATE → 2931

宰 PRESIDE → 2275

営 MANAGE → 2603

理 manage → 970

経 MANAGE → 1331

❷ⓐ **military officers and ranks**

帥 COMMANDER IN CHIEF → 1290

将 GENERAL OFFICER → 460

佐 FIELD OFFICER → 67

尉 COMPANY OFFICER → 1685

曹 SERGEANT → 2746

夢 incorrect classification ⇨ see 2336 — 8-5 艹

蓄 incorrect classification ⇨ see 2333 — 8-5 艹

募 incorrect classification ⇨ see 2494 (nonstandard for 募 2316) — 8-5 艹

碁 incorrect classification ⇨ see 2699 — 8-5 其

豎 incorrect stroke count ⇨ see 2837 — 8-5 臤

8-6
雨

需 2797 JU

CH 需 xū

Radical	Strokes
雨 173	14-8-6
Grade	Freq
Jōyō	910
2-8-6	

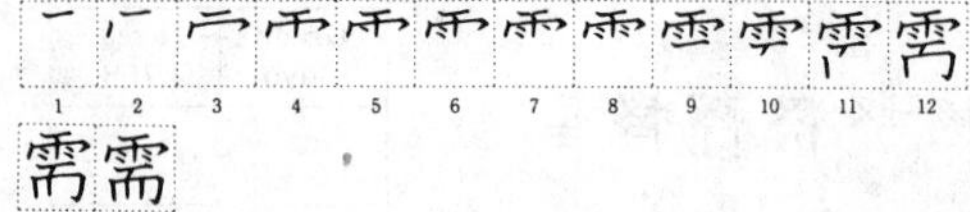

▶**DEMAND**

COMPOUNDS

ⓐ **demand, needs, requirements**
ⓑ **need, require**
需給 *jukyū* supply and demand
特需 *tokuju* emergency demand, special procurements
軍需品 *gunjuhin* war supplies
実需 *jitsuju* actual demand
民需 *minju* private demands, civilian requirements
外需 *gaiju* foreign demand
需要 *juyō* demand
必需品 *hitsujuhin* necessaries, necessities

SYNONYMS

● **need and necessity**
要 required → 2635
必 must → 15
須 MUST → 574
入 necessary → 3370
用 needed for (a specific use) → 2976

8-6
非

蜚 2798 HI

CH 蜚 fēi fěi

Radical	Strokes
虫 142	14-6-8
Grade	Freq
Reference	
2-8-6	

COMPOUNDS

❶ [now replaced by 飛 3572]
ⓐ fly
ⓑ (baseless) flying (rumor), wild, unfounded
蜚鳥 *hichō* flying bird
蜚語 *higo* false report, flying rumor
❷ [archaic] cockroach

8-6
攵

肇 2799 CHŌ

NAMES toshi hajime tadashi hatsu

CH 肇 zhào

Radical	Strokes
聿 129	14-6-8
Grade	Freq
Names	2037
2-8-6	

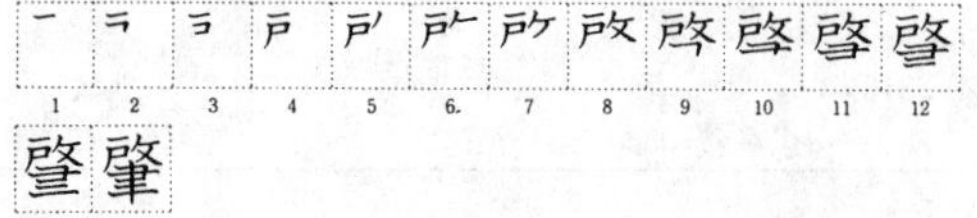

▶**ORIGINATE**

COMPOUNDS

❶ⓐ [rare] originate, found, create, begin
ⓑ [archaic] beginning
肇国 *chōkoku* founding of a state
肇歳 *chōsai* beginning of the year
❷ [archaic] make right, adjust

NAMES

肇 *hajime* (= *tadashi*) male name
肇子 *hatsuko* female name

SYNONYMS

❶ⓐ **begin**
創 initiate → 1815
開 OPEN → 3321
就 SET ABOUT → 1694
発 START → 2565
起 start → 3307
-掛ける start doing → 493
始 BEGIN → 281
-出す begin to do → 3498

肇 2800 ▶**ORIGINATE**
nonstandard for 肇 2799
8-6 攵

榮 2801 ▶**FLOURISH** ▶**GLORY**
nonstandard for 栄 2574
8-6 炏

聟 2802 ▶**SON-IN-LAW**
nonstandard for 婿 566
8-6 知

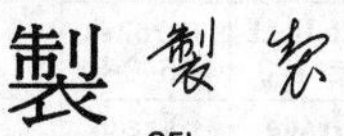

製 2803 SEI
CH 制 zhì
8-6 制

Radical	Strokes
衣 145	14-6-8
Grade	**Freq**
Jōyō-5	463
2 - 8 - 6	

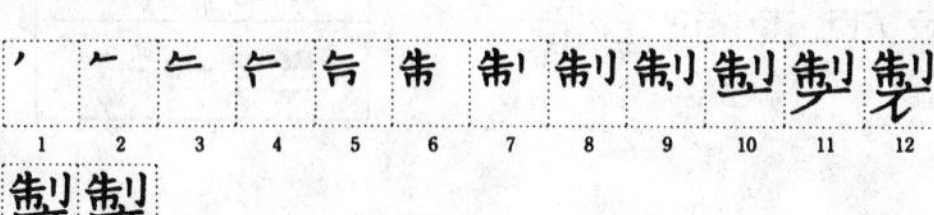

1 2 3 4 5 6 7 8 9 10 11 12 13 14

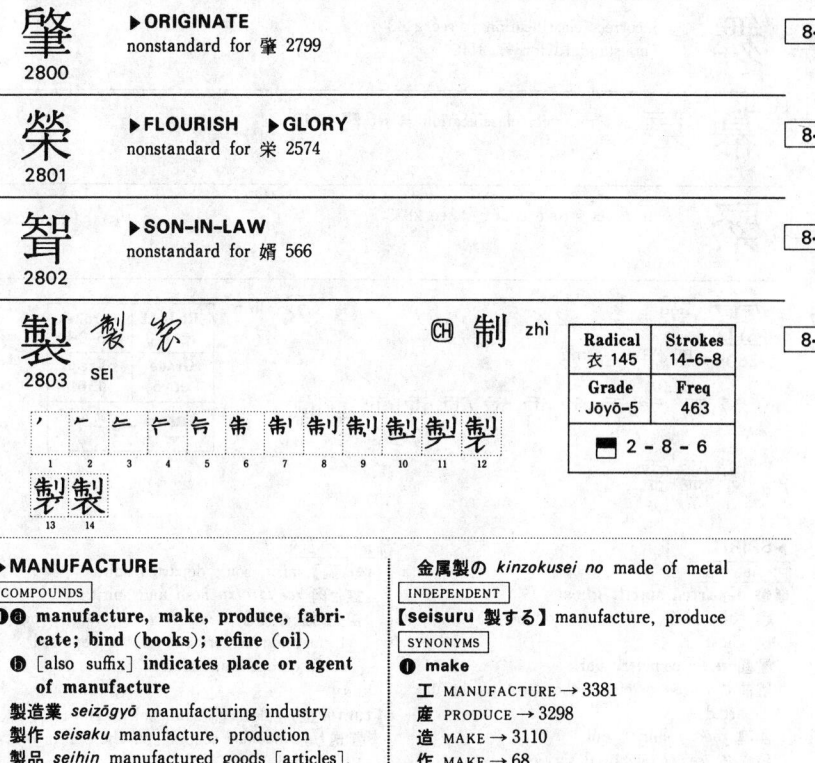

▶**MANUFACTURE**

COMPOUNDS

❶ⓐ **manufacture, make, produce, fabricate; bind (books); refine (oil)**
ⓑ [also suffix] **indicates place or agent of manufacture**
製造業 *seizōgyō* manufacturing industry
製作 *seisaku* manufacture, production
製品 *seihin* manufactured goods [articles], product; refined petroleum products
製薬 *seiyaku* pharmaceutical manufacture
製本 *seihon* bookbinding
精製 *seisei* refining; careful manufacture
特製の *tokusei no* specially made [manufactured]
手製の *tesei no* handmade
官製の *kansei no* government manufactured
日本製の *nihonsei no* made in Japan
❷ [also suffix] indicates material composition
木製の *mokusei no* wooden, made of wood
金属製の *kinzokusei no* made of metal

INDEPENDENT

【seisuru 製する】 manufacture, produce

SYNONYMS

❶ **make**
工 MANUFACTURE → 3381
産 PRODUCE → 3298
造 MAKE → 3110
作 MAKE → 68
成 FORM → 3537
調 PREPARE → 1567
組む ASSEMBLE → 1337
構 CONSTRUCT → 1049

USAGE

seisaku
製作
manufacture, production
制作
production (of a film), (literary) work

聚 2804 SHŪ
CH 聚 jù
8-6 取

Radical	Strokes
耳 128	14-6-8
Grade	**Freq**
Reference	
2 - 8 - 6	

COMPOUNDS

● [now replaced by 集 2771] collect, gather
聚落 *shūraku* colony, community, village
聚散 *shūsan* collection and distribution

8-6 無

舞 incorrect classification ⇨ see 2143
(nonstandard for 舞 2146)

8-6 苜

幕 墓 incorrect classification ⇨ see 4-10

8-6 臤

緊 incorrect stroke count ⇨ see 2838

8-7 雨

霊 靈 霊 霊 CH 灵 líng

2805 REI RYŌ tama

Radical	Strokes
雨 173	15-8-7
Grade	**Freq**
Jōyō	1361
2-8-7	

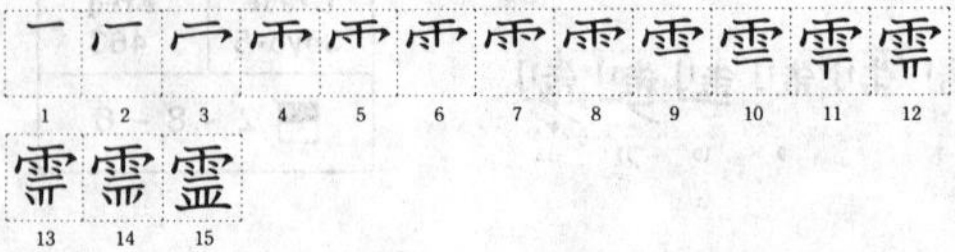

▶**SPIRIT**

COMPOUNDS

❶ⓐ **departed spirit, ghost**
ⓑ [also suffix] (supernatural being) spirit, ghost
霊園 *reien* cemetery park
霊前に *reizen ni* before the spirit of the departed
霊魂 *reikon* spirit, soul
慰霊祭 *ireisai* memorial service
幽霊 *yūrei* ghost, apparition
亡霊 *bōrei* departed spirit, ghost
英霊 *eirei* spirit of the war dead
精霊 *shōryō* spirit of a dead person
神霊 *shinrei* divine spirit
悪霊 *akuryō* evil spirit
聖霊 *seirei* Holy Ghost, Holy Spirit
守護霊 *shugorei* guardian spirit
❷ (incorporeal part of man) **spirit, soul**
霊長類 *reichōrui* Primates
霊的な *reiteki na* spiritual, incorporeal
心霊 *shinrei* spirit
全身全霊 *zenshin-zenrei* body and soul; one's best
❸ **miraculous, sacred, divine**
霊場 *reijō* holy ground, sacred place
霊峰 *reihō* sacred mountain
霊験 *reigen* (=*reiken*) miracle, miraculous virtue
霊感 *reikan* inspiration, extrasensory perception
霊水 *reisui* miracle-working water
霊妙な *reimyō na* miraculous, wonderful

INDEPENDENT

【**rei** 霊】 spirit, soul; departed spirit
霊と肉 *rei to niku* flesh and spirit
祖先の霊を祭る *sosen no rei o matsuru* perform religious services for the departed souls of one's ancestors

KUN

【**tama** 霊】 [also 魂] soul, spirit, ghost
霊送り *tamaokuri* sending off the spirits of the dead
御霊屋 *mitamaya* mausoleum

SYNONYMS

❶ **supernatural and evil beings**
精 SPIRIT → 1366
怪 monster → 297
魔 DEMON → 3187
鬼 DEVIL → 2657
❷ **psyche**
精 SPIRIT (mind) → 1366
気 SPIRIT (consciousness) → 3194
魂 SOUL, spirit → 1063
神 MIND → 912
心 HEART → 11
腹 heart → 1034
衷 INNER HEART → 2575
襟 inner mind → 1252
胸 breast → 951
懐 BOSOM → 763
❸ **holy**
聖 HOLY → 2830
神 divine → 912

HOMOPHONES

tama ⇨ 魂 1063

NOTE
⇨ see USAGE note at 魂 1063

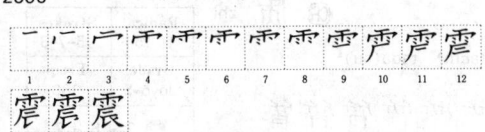

震
2806 SHIN furu(u) furu(eru)

Ⓒⓗ 震 zhèn

Radical	Strokes
雨 173	15-8-7
Grade	**Freq**
Jōyō	710
2 - 8 - 7	

8-7
雨

1 2 3 4 5 6 7 8 9 10 11 12
13 14 15

▶QUAKE

COMPOUNDS

❶ⓐ **quake, shake, vibrate**
ⓑ **quake, earthquake, shock, tremor**
震動 *shindō* shock, tremor, vibration
地震 *jishin* earthquake
震源 *shingen* earthquake [seismic] center
震度 *shindo* seismic intensity
震災 *shinsai* earthquake disaster
弱震 *jakushin* weak earthquake, minor tremor

❷ quake with (fear), tremble, shudder
震撼させる *shinkan saseru* shake, shock
震駭させる *shingai saseru* terrify, frighten, shock

❸ 4th of the eight trigrams in the Book of Changes: east, thunder
震旦 *shintan* ancient Indian name for China

KUN

【**furu(u) 震う**】tremble, quiver, shudder
震い *furui* trembling, shaking, shivering
身震い *miburui* shivering

【**furu(eru) 震える**】tremble, quiver, shake, vibrate, shudder
震え *furue* trembling, shaking, shivering
震え声 *furuegoe* trembling voice
震え上がる *furueagaru* tremble violently, shudder up

SYNONYMS

❶ⓐ **shake**
揺 SHAKE → 594
振 SWING → 430

HOMOPHONES

furuu ⇨ 振 430 奮 2367 揮 589

NOTE

⇨ see USAGE note at 振 430

輩
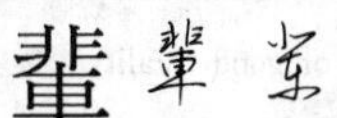
2807 HAI -bara▲ yakara▲

Ⓒⓗ 輩 bèi

Radical	Strokes
車 159	15-7-8
Grade	**Freq**
Jōyō	1445
2 - 8 - 7	

8-7
非

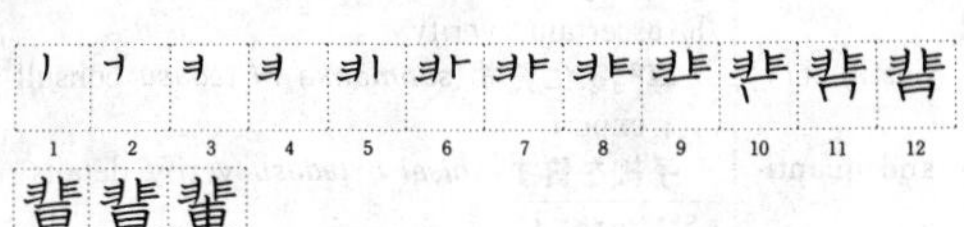
1 2 3 4 5 6 7 8 9 10 11 12
13 14 15

▶FELLOW

COMPOUNDS

❶ⓐ **fellow(s), companion, comrade**
ⓑ [also suffix] [belittling] **fellow, guy**
先輩 *senpai* senior, superior, elder
後輩 *kōhai* one's junior, younger generation
同輩 *dōhai* fellow, comrade, colleague, peer
朋輩 *hōbai* comrade, friend, associate
若輩 *jakuhai* young people; greenhorn
鼠輩 *sohai* insignificant fellow, small fry
徒輩 *tohai* set, company, fellows
我が輩(＝吾輩) *wagahai* I
中野輩 *nakanohai* the likes of Nakano

❷ plural suffix
青年輩 *seinenhai* young people

❸ [original meaning] successively
輩出する *haishutsu suru* appear successively

INDEPENDENT

【**hai 輩**】*literary* fellow, people

KUN

【**-bara -輩**】[belittling] plural suffix
奴輩 *yatsubara* fellows, guys

【**yakara 輩**】[belittling] fellows, guys; family; kinsmen

SYNONYMS

❶ⓐ **friends and associates**
僚 COLLEAGUE → 165
朋 COMRADE → 880

友 FRIEND → 2952
ⓑ **fellow**
漢 FELLOW → 657
徒 fellows → 416
奴 GUY → 187
棒 tough guy → 983
坊 COLLOQUIAL PERSON SUFFIX → 233
屋 colloquial person suffix → 3098
物 character → 874

8-7

質 貭◆ 質 贅

2808 SHITSU SHICHI CHI tachi▲ tada(su)▲

CH 质 zhì

Radical	Strokes
貝 154	15-7-8
Grade	**Freq**
Jōyō-5	380
2-8-7	

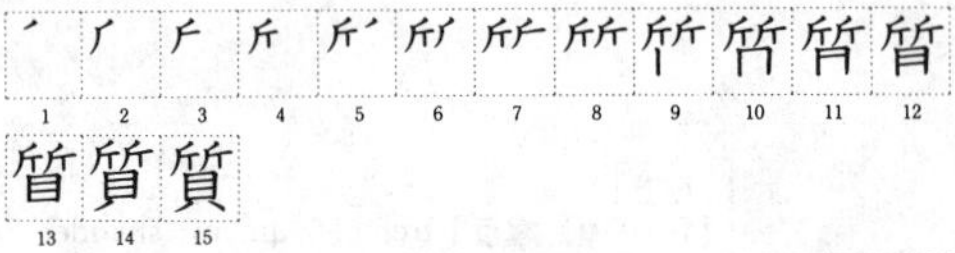

▶**QUALITY** ▶**MATTER**

COMPOUNDS

❶ⓐ [also suffix] (natural attribute) **quality, nature, character, property, temperament, disposition**
ⓑ (degree of excellence) **quality, grade**
本質 *honshitsu* essence, reality
性質 *seishitsu* nature, temperament, character; (characteristic) property, quality
体質 *taishitsu* physical constitution
素質 *soshitsu* character, nature, makings, constitution
実質 *jisshitsu* substance, essence
特質 *tokushitsu* characteristic, property, quality
神経質 *shinkeishitsu* nervous temperament
品質 *hinshitsu* quality
悪質な *akushitsu na* bad, malicious; malignant
音質 *onshitsu* sound [tone] quality
❷ⓐ **matter, substance, material**
ⓑ [suffix] (specific substance or constituent) **matter**
質量 *shitsuryō phys* mass; quality and quantity
物質 *busshitsu* matter, substance
植物質 *shokubutsushitsu* vegetable matter
蛋白質 *tanpakushitsu* protein, albuminous substance
❸ **query, question, verify, confront**
質問 *shitsumon* question
質疑 *shitsugi* question, interrogation
対質する *taishitsu suru* confront, cross-examine
❹ⓐ (thing serving as security) pawn, pledge
ⓑ (person serving as security) pawn, hostage
質屋 *shichiya* pawnshop
質草 *shichigusa* article for pawning
質入れ *shichiire* pawning
言質 *genchi* pledge, promise
人質 *hitojichi* hostage, prisoner
❺ simple, unadorned
質素 *shisso* simplicity, modesty, frugality
質実 *shitsujitsu* plainness, simplicity

INDEPENDENT

【**shitsu** 質】quality; nature, disposition; *logic* (positive or negative character of a proposition) quality
質を良くする *shitsu o yoku suru* improve the quality
量より質だ *Ryō yori shitsu da* Quality matters more than quantity
【**shichi** 質】pawn, pledge
質に入れる *shichi ni ireru* pawn, pledge

KUN

【**tachi** 質】quality, nature, character, disposition, inclination
質の良い *tachi no yoi* of good quality
【**tada(su)** 質す】
ⓐ query, question, consult, inquire
ⓑ ascertain, verify
専門家に質す *senmonka ni tadasu* consult an expert
子細を質す *shisai o tadasu* verify details

SYNONYMS

❶ **nature and character**
性 NATURE → 299
気 temperament → 3194
柄 CHARACTER → 897
格 (good) character → 926
品 grade of excellence → 2248
❷ **matter**
物 substance → 874
材 MATERIAL → 836
料 MATERIALS → 1292
資 material resources → 2695
❸ **inquire**
尋ねる INQUIRE → 2322
伺う INQUIRE (*humble*) → 69
諮 CONSULT → 1596
問 QUESTION → 3320

詰 question closely → 1521
聞く ask → 3326
❹ⓐ **pawn**
当 pawn → 2177

HOMOPHONES
tadasu ⇨ 正 3484 糾 1278

NOTE
⇨ see USAGE note at 正 3484

賛 賛 賛 賛

2809 SAN

Ⓒ 赞 zàn

Radical	Strokes
貝 154	15-7-8
Grade	**Freq**
Jōyō-5	943
2 - 8 - 7	

8–7

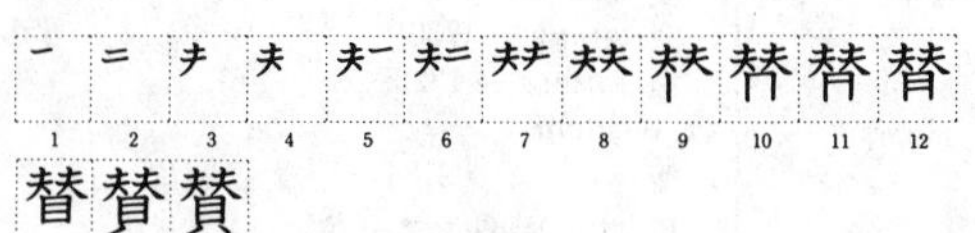

▶**APPROVE OF** ▶**PRAISE**

COMPOUNDS

❶ⓐ **approve of, agree with**
ⓑ **back up, give support, assist, help**
賛成 *sansei* approval, agreement, support
賛否 *sanpi* approval or disapproval; yes or no
賛意 *san'i* approval
賛同 *sandō* approval, endorsement
賛助 *sanjo* backing, support, approval
協賛 *kyōsan* support, cooperation
翼賛 *yokusan* support, countenance, assistance
❷ [formerly also 讃 1665] **praise, laud, admire, commend**
賛辞 *sanji* eulogy, praise, compliment
賛美 *sanbi* praise, admiration
賛嘆 *santan* praise, admiration
賞賛(＝称賛)する *shōsan suru* laud, praise, admire, commend
絶賛 *zessan* great admiration
礼賛 *raisan* worship, adoration, glorification
❸ [formerly also 讃 1665] legend or inscription on a picture
画賛 *gasan* legend [writing] on a picture
自画自賛 *jigajisan* painting with the eulogy written in by the artist himself; self-praise

INDEPENDENT

【**san** 賛(＝讃)】 legend or inscription on a picture; a style of Chinese poetry
画に賛をする *e ni san o suru* write a legend on a picture

SYNONYMS

❶ⓐ **agree and approve**
可 APPROVE → 2969
認 RECOGNIZE → 1546
諾 CONSENT → 1568
承 AGREE TO → 16
肯 ASSENT → 2417
容 tolerate → 2277
ⓑ **support**
支 SUPPORT → 1979
擁 SUPPORT → 770
扶 LEND SUPPORT TO → 247
❷ **praise**
美 regard as beautiful → 2264
褒 COMMEND → 2144
嘉 commend (esp. an inferior) → 2340
彰 PROCLAIM MERITS → 1860
称 acclaim → 1160
賞 express admiration → 2618
揚 EXALT → 593
頌 EULOGIZE → 1045

慧 慧 慧 慧

2810 KEI E NAMES sato satoshi satoru akira

Ⓒ 慧 huì

Radical	Strokes
心 61	15-4-11
Grade	**Freq**
Names	2114
2 - 8 - 7	

8–7

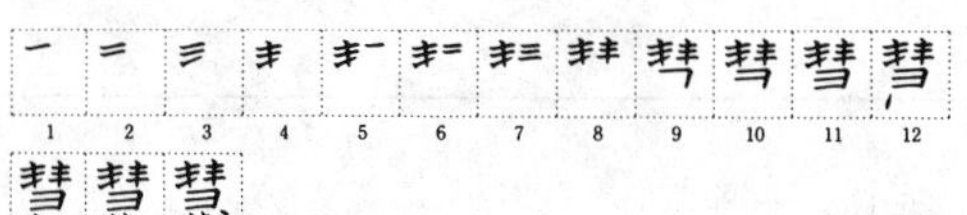

▶**INTELLIGENT**

COMPOUNDS

❶ⓐ [original meaning] **intelligent, wise, bright, clever, cunning**
ⓑ [now replaced by 恵 *e* 2659] **intelligence, wisdom**

慧眼 *keigan* discerning [quick] eye, keen insight
慧敏な *keibin na* [rare] clever, of quick intellect
智慧(＝知恵) *chie* wisdom, intelligence, sagacity

❷ *Buddhism* prajna, transcendental wisdom—often used in the names of Buddhist priests
慧遠 *eon* Hui-yuan (Chinese priest of the Jin Dynasty)

INDEPENDENT

【e 慧】 *Buddhism* transcendental wisdom, prajna

NAMES

慧子 *keiko* female name
慧 *satoshi* male name

SYNONYMS

❶ⓐ intelligent and wise
賢 WISE → 2839
智 wise → 2784
怜 CLEVER → 298
哲 SAGACIOUS → 2738
明 clear-sighted → 855
聡 SHARP-WITTED → 1384
俊 brilliant → 102
鋭 SHARP → 1730
敏 NIMBLE → 1322

❷ wisdom
智 WISDOM → 2784
哲 PHILOSOPHY → 2738
識 KNOWLEDGE → 1639
知 knowledge → 1127

8-7 彗

慧 2811

▶INTELLIGENT
nonstandard for 慧 2810

8-7 直

憂 incorrect classification ⇨ see 2145

8-7 無

舞 incorrect classification ⇨ see 2146

8-7 关

養 incorrect classification ⇨ see 2365

8-7 星

暴 incorrect classification ⇨ see 2515

8-7 昔

暮 慕 incorrect classification ⇨ see 4-11

8-7 里

墨 2812

▶INDIA INK
nonstandard for 墨 2753

8-7 臤

賢 incorrect stroke count ⇨ see 2839

8-8 炏

螢 2813

▶FIREFLY
nonstandard for 蛍 2591

霞 霞 (variants)

2814 KA kasumi kasu(mu)

Ⓒⓗ 霞 xiá

Radical	Strokes
雨 173	17-8-9
Grade	Freq
Names	2000
2-8-9	

8-9

▶MIST

COMPOUNDS

❶ **mist, haze**

煙霞 *enka* mist [haze] and smoke; beauties of nature

雲霞の如く *unka no gotoku* in swarms

朝霞 *chōka* morning mist [haze]; [archaic] morning glow

❷ [original meaning, now archaic] morning or evening glow

KUN

【**kasumi** 霞】 mist, haze; dimness of sight, mist; Japanese mist net

霞を食う *kasumi o kuu* live on air

霞ヶ関 *kasumigaseki* Japanese Foreign Ministry

春霞 *harugasumi* spring haze

【**kasu(mu)** 霞む】 haze, be hazy, mist; have dim sight

遠くに霞む *tōku ni kasumu* loom in the distance

年で霞んだ目 *toshi de kasunda me* eyes dimmed with age

NAMES

霞ヶ浦 *kasumigaura* place name

霞 *kasumi* male name also female name

SYNONYMS

❶ **kinds of atmospheric vapor**

霧 FOG → 2817

雲 CLOUD → 2773

COMPOUND FORMATION

霞ヶ関 *kasumigaseki*

霞ヶ関 'Japanese Foreign Ministry' is so called because it is located in Kasumigaseki, Tokyo.

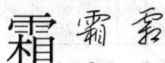

霜 霜 (variants)

2815 SŌ shimo

Ⓒⓗ 霜 shuāng

Radical	Strokes
雨 173	17-8-9
Grade	Freq
Jōyō	1623
2-8-9	

8-9

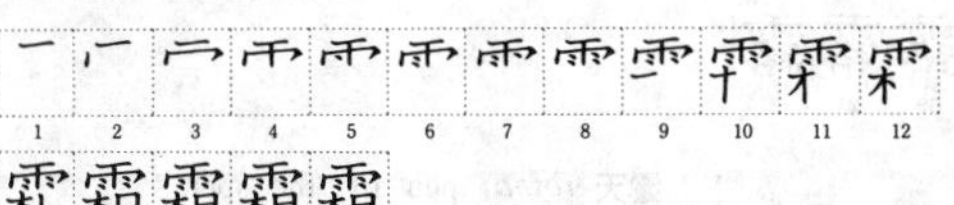

▶FROST

COMPOUNDS

❶ [original meaning] **frost, hoarfrost**

霜害 *sōgai* frost damage

霜雪 *sōsetsu* frost and snow

降霜 *kōsō* (fall of) frost

❷ years, time

星霜 *seisō* years, time

KUN

【**shimo** 霜】 frost, hoarfrost

霜柱 *shimobashira* frost columns

霜焼け *shimoyake* frostbite, chilblains

霜降り *shimofuri* pepper-and-salt; marbled meat

遅霜 *osojimo* late frosting

SYNONYMS

❶ **kinds of precipitation**

雪 SNOW → 2759

雨 RAIN → 3561

露 DEW → 2818

營

2816

▶MANAGE ▶BARRACKS

nonstandard for 営 2603

8-9

8-11 雨

霧 霧 霧

2817 MU kiri

CH 雾 wù

Radical	Strokes
雨 173	19-8-11
Grade	**Freq**
Jōyō	1046
2 - 8 - 1 1	

1 2 3 4 5 6 7 8 9 10 11 12

13 14 15 16 17 18 19

▶FOG

COMPOUNDS

❶ [original meaning] **fog, mist**

霧笛 *muteki* foghorn

霧氷 *muhyō* rime, hoarfrost, silver frost

濃霧 *nōmu* dense [thick] fog

煙霧 *enmu* smog

雲散霧消する *unsan-mushō suru* scatter and vanish, vanish like mist

❷ spray

噴霧器 *funmuki* sprayer, vaporizer, atomizer

KUN

【**kiri 霧**】 fog, mist; spray

夜霧 *yogiri* night fog [mist]

霧雨 *kirisame* (=*kiriame*) drizzle, misting rain

霧吹き *kirifuki* sprayer, atomizer

SYNONYMS

❶ **kinds of atmospheric vapor**

霞 MIST → 2814

雲 CLOUD → 2773

8-11 罒

罷

incorrect classification ⇨ see 2151

8-13 雨

露 露 露

2818 RO RŌ tsuyu

CH 露 lù lòu

Radical	Strokes
雨 173	21-8-13
Grade	**Freq**
Jōyō	1176
2 - 8 - 1 3	

▶DEW ▶EXPOSE

COMPOUNDS

❶ⓐ [original meaning] **dew, dewdrop**

ⓑ as evanescent as the dew, transient

露滴 *roteki* dewdrop

露点 *roten* dew point

雨露 *uro* rain and dew

露命 *romei* transient life

❷ⓐ **expose, bare to view, disclose**

ⓑ exposed, uncovered, open

露出 *roshutsu* exposure, disclosure; (photographic) exposure

露呈 *rotei* exposure, disclosure

露顕(=露見) *roken* discovery, detection, exposure

露骨な *rokotsu na* candid, plainspoken; indecent

披露 *hirō* announcement, introduction

お披露目(=お広め) *ohirome* début

暴露 *bakuro* exposure, disclosure

露天 *roten* open air, the open

露店 *roten* roadside stand

❸ⓐ Russia

ⓑ Russian (language)

日露戦争 *nichiro sensō* Russo-Japanese war (of 1904-05)

露帝 *rotei* Czar, Russian emperor

露語 *rogo* Russian (language)

INDEPENDENT

【**ro 露**】 Russia

KUN

【**tsuyu 露**】 dew, dewdrop; tears; evanescence, frailty; [in negative constructions] (not) in the least, (not) at all

露に濡れた *tsuyu ni nureta* dewy, wet with dew

露払い *tsuyuharai* herald; heralding, ushering

夜露 *yotsuyu* evening dew

袖の露 *sode no tsuyu* tears falling onto the sleeve

露の命 *tsuyu no inochi* life as evanescent as the dew
露知らず *tsuyushirazu* not knowing at all

SYNONYMS

❶ⓐ **kinds of precipitation**
雨 RAIN → 3561
霜 FROST → 2815
雪 SNOW → 2759
❷ⓐ **reveal**
発 reveal → 2565
暴 disclose → 2515
披 OPEN OUT → 305
顕 MANIFEST → 1806
現 cause to appear → 968
❸ⓐ **European countries**
英 ENGLAND → 2238
独 GERMANY → 395
仏 FRANCE → 19
伊 ITALY → 49
西 Spain → 3520
蘭 Holland → 2383

靈
2819

▶**SPIRIT**
nonstandard for 霊 2805

8-16 雨

蠶
2820

▶**SILKWORM**
nonstandard for 蚕 2457

8-16 䖵

率

incorrect classification ⇨ see 2118

9-2 亠

黄

incorrect classification ⇨ see 2468

9-2 艹

異

incorrect classification ⇨ see 2584

9-2 田

堡
2821

HO HŌ

Ⓒℍ 堡 bǎo bǔ pù

Radical	Strokes
土 32	12-3-9
Grade Reference	Freq
2 - 9 - 3	

9-3 保

COMPOUNDS

● [now also 保 *ho* 96] fort
堡塁 *hōrui* (= *horui*) fort, fortress, stronghold
海堡 *kaihō* coast battery; breakwater
橋頭堡 *kyōtōho* bridgehead, beachhead

喫

incorrect classification ⇨ see 551

9-3 口

9-3 陏

堕 墮 堕 堕

2822 DA

ⒸⒽ 堕 duò

Radical	Strokes
土 32	12-3-9
Grade	**Freq**
Jōyō	1826
2-9-3	

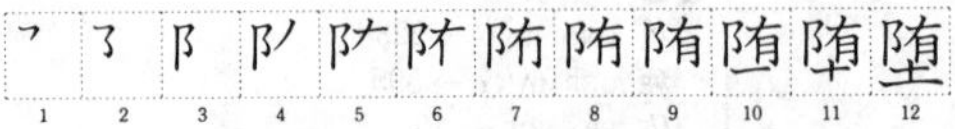

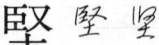

1 2 3 4 5 6 7 8 9 10 11 12

▶DEGENERATE

COMPOUNDS

❶ **degenerate, become degraded into, sink into evil ways, descend to**

堕落 *daraku* degeneration, corruption, decadence

堕罪 *dazai* sinking into sin

❷ cause to fall, drop, abort

堕胎 *datai* abortion

INDEPENDENT

【dasuru 堕する】 descend to, lapse into, become degraded into

SYNONYMS

❶ **degenerate**

衰 DECLINE → 2100

落 FALL → 2318

破 break down → 1150

9-3 臤

堅 堅 堅

2823 KEN kata(i) -gata(i)

ⒸⒽ 坚 jiān

Radical	Strokes
土 32	12-3-9
Grade	**Freq**
Jōyō	848
2-9-3	

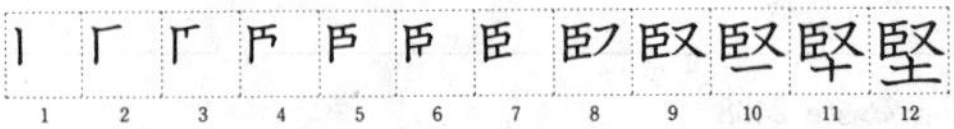

1 2 3 4 5 6 7 8 9 10 11 12

▶FIRM

COMPOUNDS

❶ [original meaning] (resisting deformation) **firm, hard, solid, sturdy**

堅材 *kenzai* hard wood

堅牢な *kenrō na* solid, durable, fast

堅果 *kenka* nut (hard fruit)

❷ⓐ (of a person's character) **firm, steadfast, trustworthy**

ⓑ (unfluctuating) **firm, steady, stable**

ⓒ firmly, resolutely

堅固な *kengo na* strong, secure, firm, steadfast

堅実な *kenjitsu na* steady, sound, reliable

堅志 *kenshi* iron purpose

中堅 *chūken* the mainstay, nucleus (of a company)

堅調 *kenchō* bullish, firm (market)

堅持する *kenji suru* maintain firmly, hold fast to

❸ strong (defenses), secure, firm

堅守 *kenshu* strong defense

堅陣 *kenjin* stronghold

INDEPENDENT

【ken 堅】 firmness, hardness

敵の堅を破る *teki no ken o yaburu* break the strong defenses of the enemy

KUN

【kata(i) 堅い, -gata(i) -堅い】

① (resisting deformation) firm, hard (lumber)

堅さ *katasa* firmness, hardness; steadiness, honesty

堅い材木 *katai zaimoku* hard lumber

堅パン *katapan* hardtack, hard biscuits

② steady (market or business), sound (investment)

堅い商売 *katai shōbai* sound business

底堅い *sokogatai* steady undertone (of the market)

手堅い *tegatai* steady (market); safe; trustworthy

③ⓐ steadfast, reliable, trustworthy

ⓑ honest, honorable, upright, serious, chaste

堅気な *katagi na* honest, respectable

堅人 *katajin* trustworthy person

堅い女 *katai onna* chaste woman

④ stiff, formal, bookish

堅苦しい *katakurushii* formal, stiff-mannered

堅物 *katabutsu* straight-laced person

堅い言葉 *katai kotoba* stiff speech

SYNONYMS

❶ **hard**

硬 HARD → 1183

固 SOLID → 3086

剛 TOUGH → 1673

強 STRONG → 475

❷ **firm and obstinate**

固 FIRM, stiff → 3086

確 firm → 1228

毅 RESOLUTE → 1866

剛 TOUGH → 1673
頑 STUBBORN → 1040
硬 hard-line → 1183

HOMOPHONES
katai ⇨ 固 3086 硬 1183 難 1838

NOTE
⇨ see USAGE note at 固 3086

善 incorrect classification ⇨ see 2325

9-3 䒑

尊 incorrect classification ⇨ see 2324

9-3 酋

葬 incorrect classification ⇨ see 2320

9-3 茻

堯 incorrect classification ⇨ see 2307
(nonstandard for 尭 2063)

9-3 垚

9-3 奥

奧 奧 奥 𡘙

2824 Ō OKU▴ oku

CH 奥 ào

Radical	Strokes
大 37	12-3-9
Grade	**Freq**
Jōyō	895
2 - 9 - 3	

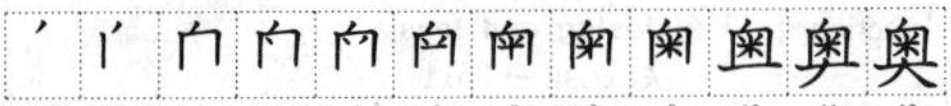

1 2 3 4 5 6 7 8 9 10 11 12

▶**INNER PART**

COMPOUNDS

❶ⓐ inmost, mysterious, deep, profound
ⓑ inmost part, innermost, mystery, inner depths

奥義 *ōgi* (= *okugi*) secret principles, secrets, hidden mysteries
胸奥 *kyōō* one's heart of hearts, the depths of one's mind
深奥 *shin'ō* esoteric doctrines, mysteries, depth
内奥 *naiō* inner part, depths, recesses

❷ old name for Tohoku district
奥州 *ōshū* old name for Tohoku district

KUN

【oku 奥】

①ⓐ inner part, interior, the back, the heart, the depths, the recesses
ⓑ [also prefix] the interior (of a country), inland, back country
ⓒ interior room, inner chamber, parlor
ⓓ [in compounds] inner, interior
奥まる *okumaru* extend far back, lie deep in
奥行き *okuyuki* depth, length
山奥 *yamaoku* deep in the mountains, in the recesses of a mountain
森の奥 *mori no oku* deep in the forest
奥地 *okuchi* interior, hinterland, backwoods
奥の間 *oku no ma* back room
大奥 *ōoku* inner palace; place where shogun's wife resided
奥庭 *okuniwa* inner garden, backyard
奥歯 *okuba* molars, back teeth
奥日光 *okunikkō* the secluded spots [recesses] of Nikko
奥座敷 *okuzashiki* inner room [chamber]

② innermost part, mystery, inner depths
奥床しい *okuyukashii* refined, graceful, modest
奥の手 *oku no te* last resort; secrets
心の奥 *kokoro no oku* inner heart

③ (from the idea that the wife of a nobleman lives in the inner chambers) wife
奥さん *okusan* married lady, Mrs.; your wife
奥様 *okusama* married lady, Mrs.; your wife
奥方 *okugata* wife of a nobleman

SYNONYMS

❶ profound
深 DEEP → 524
幽 deep hidden → 3008
玄 PROFOUND → 1991

【oku】

①ⓐ inside
内 INSIDE → 3466
裏 inside → 2138
中 IN → 3451

ⓓ **inner**
深 DEEP → 524
幽 QUIET AND SECLUDED → 3008
③ **wives**
妻 WIFE → 2558
内 wife → 3466
室 wife (esp. of persons of rank) → 2254
嫡 legitimate wife → 680
婦 married woman → 469
嫁 BRIDE → 635
寡 widow → 2344

NOTE
★The reading *oku* is both the *on* and *kun* reading of 奥, but as an *on* reading it is not in the Jōyō Kanji list. When read *oku*, 奥 forms compounds in the *kun* reading.

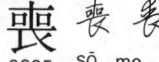

9-3
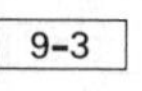

喪
2825 SŌ mo

CH 丧 sāng sàng

Radical	Strokes
口 30	12-3-9
Grade	**Freq**
Jōyō	1494
2-9-3	

▶**MOURNING**

COMPOUNDS
❶ [original meaning] **mourning**
喪家 *sōka* [rare] family in mourning
大喪 *taisō* [rare] Imperial mourning
❷ **lose, be deprived of**
喪失 *sōshitsu* loss, forfeit
喪神する *sōshin suru* lose consciousness
阻喪(=沮喪) *sosō* loss of spirit, dejection

KUN
【mo 喪】mourning
喪服 *mofuku* mourning dress
喪主 *moshu* chief mourner
喪中 *mochū* in mourning
服喪 *fukumo* mourning

SYNONYMS
❶ **mourn and mourning**
忌 MOURNING → 2207
弔 CONDOLE → 3432
悼 MOURN → 485
❷ **losing and loss**
失 LOSE → 3511
損 LOSS, lose → 651
逸 LET SLIP → 3120

9-4

2826 GAKU RAKU tano(shii) tano(shimu)

CH 乐 lè yuè

Radical	Strokes
木 75	13-4-9
Grade	**Freq**
Jōyō-2	266
2-9-4	

▶**PLEASURE** ▶**COMFORTABLE**
▶**MUSIC**

COMPOUNDS
❶ⓐ **pleasure, joy**
ⓑ **pleasurable, pleasant, merry**
享楽 *kyōraku* enjoyment
快楽 *kairaku* pleasure, enjoyment
娯楽 *goraku* amusement, pastime
行楽 *kōraku* excursion, outing, holidaymaking
楽園 *rakuen* paradise
❷ **comfortable, easy**
楽観する *rakkan suru* be optimistic, take a hopeful view
楽隠居 *rakuinkyo* comfortable life in retirement
楽楽と *rakuraku to* comfortably; very easily
楽勝 *rakushō* easy victory, walkaway
安楽な *anraku na* comfortable, carefree, cozy
❸ⓐ [also suffix] **music, musical composition**
ⓑ suffix after names of Japanese court music compositions
ⓒ play music compositions
楽譜 *gakufu* (sheet of) music, musical score
楽器 *gakki* musical instrument
音楽 *ongaku* music
邦楽 *hōgaku* Japanese music
越天楽 *etenraku* Etenraku (name of a Japanese court music composition)
吹奏楽 *suisōgaku* wind instrument music
❹ end of public performance
千秋楽の日 *senshūraku no hi* closing day of a show

❺ hand-molded earthenware
楽焼き *rakuyaki* hand-molded pottery
❻ unclassified compounds
文楽 *bunraku* Japanese puppet show, *bunraku*

INDEPENDENT

【raku 楽】 comfort, ease; relief; closing day (of a public performance); hand-molded pottery
楽な *raku na* easy, light; comfortable
楽に暮らす *raku ni kurasu* live in comfort

【gaku 楽】 music
楽を奏する *gaku o sōsuru* play music

KUN

【tano(shii) 楽しい】 [sometimes also 愉しい] pleasurable, pleasant, enjoyable, merry
楽しさ *tanoshisa* pleasure, joy; pleasantness
楽しい思い出 *tanoshii omoide* happy [sweet] memory

【tano(shimu) 楽しむ】 [sometimes also 愉しむ] take pleasure in, enjoy (oneself)
楽しみ *tanoshimi* pleasure, enjoyment; amusement, diversion, hobby; expectation
映画を楽しむ *eiga o tanoshimu* enjoy a movie

SPECIAL READINGS

神楽 *kagura* sacred (Shinto) music and dancing
独楽▲ *koma* top

SYNONYMS

❶ⓐ pleasure
娯 ENJOYMENT → 405
興 AMUSEMENT → 2909
ⓑ pleased and pleasant
快 PLEASANT → 245
朗 CHEERFUL → 1325
愉 PLEASED → 582
悦 DELIGHTED → 418
嬉しい GLAD → 722
喜 HAPPY → 2308
歓 JOYOUS → 1867
欣 JOYFUL → 852

❷ comfortable
安 easy (without effort) → 2171
❸ⓐ & ❸ⓑ music and songs
音 sound of music → 2070
節 tune → 2691
調べ melody → 1567
曲 MUSICAL COMPOSITION → 3527
歌 SONG → 1825
謡 POPULAR SONG → 1597

USAGE

❶ tanoshii
楽しい
[sometimes also 愉しい] pleasurable, pleasant, enjoyable, merry
愉しい
[usu. 楽しい] same as 楽しい
❷ tanoshimu
楽しむ
[sometimes also 愉しむ] take pleasure in, enjoy (oneself)
愉しむ
[usu. 楽しむ] same as 楽しむ
❸ tanoshimi
楽しみ
① [sometimes also 愉しみ]
ⓐ pleasure, enjoyment
ⓑ amusement, diversion, hobby
② expectation
愉しみ
[usu. 楽しみ]
ⓐ pleasure, enjoyment
ⓑ amusement, diversion, hobby

HOMOPHONES

tanoshii ⇨ 愉 582
tanoshimu ⇨ 愉 582
tanoshimi ⇨ 愉 582

COMPOUND FORMATION

文楽 *bunraku*
The word 文楽 'Japanese puppet show, *bunraku*' originates from the name of its founder, 植村文楽軒 *uemura bunrakuken*.

照 2827

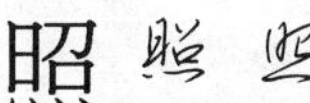

SHŌ te(ru) te(rasu) te(reru)

(CH) 照 zhào

Radical	Strokes
灬 86	13-4-9
Grade	**Freq**
Jōyō-4	1066
2-9-4	

9-4 照

照 13

▶ILLUMINATE

COMPOUNDS

❶ [original meaning] **illuminate, shine, reflect**
照明 *shōmei* illumination, lighting
照射 *shōsha* irradiation
照度 *shōdo* intensity of illumination
日照権 *nisshōken* right to sunshine
❷ sunlight, light

返照 *henshō* reflection of light [sunlight]
晩照 *banshō* sunset, setting sun

❸ **check (one thing) against (another), collate, examine by comparison, refer**
照査する *shōsa suru* check against [up], examine by reference, verify
照合する *shōgō suru* verify, compare, collate
照会する *shōkai suru* inquire, apply for information
対照 *taishō* contrast, comparison; control

❹ picture
照映 *shōei* portrait

KUN

【te(ru) 照る】 *vi* shine; be fine
照り *teri* sunshine; dry weather; luster
降っても照っても *futte mo tette mo* rain or shine

【te(rasu) 照らす】 illuminate, shine on, shed light; check (one thing) against another, collate, examine by comparison, refer
事実に照らして *jijitsu ni terashite* in view of the facts
照らし合わせる *terashiawaseru* check by comparison, collate, verify

【te(reru) 照れる】 feel shy, be abashed; feel awkward, become self-conscious, be ill at ease
照れ臭い *terekusai* embarrassed

SYNONYMS

❶ **shine and reflect**
輝 SHINE BRILLIANTLY → 1402
光 shine → 2391
映 REFLECT → 892

❷ **light**
光 LIGHT → 2391
明 light → 855
灯 LAMP → 825
虹 RAINBOW → 1285

❸ **compare**
対 OPPOSE (contrast) → 831
参 refer → 2066
校 COLLATE → 929
比 COMPARE → 26
較 COMPARE → 1536

9-4
相

想

2828 SŌ SO omo(u)▲

CH 想 xiǎng

Radical	Strokes
心 61	13-4-9
Grade	**Freq**
Jōyō-3	350
2 - 9 - 4	

Stroke order: 一 十 才 木 札 机 相 相 相 相 想 想 想 (1–13)

▶CONCEIVE

COMPOUNDS

❶ⓐ **conceive, think of, think, contemplate, imagine**
ⓑ think of the past, recollect, reminisce
想像 *sōzō* imagination
予想 *yosō* prospect, expectation, conjecture
感想 *kansō* thoughts, impressions
連想 *rensō* association (of ideas)
想起する *sōki suru* remember, recollect
回想 *kaisō* recollection, reminiscence

❷ **conception, idea, thought, image, concept**
思想 *shisō* thought, conception, idea
構想 *kōsō* conception, idea; plot, plan
理想 *risō* ideal
幻想 *gensō* fantasy, illusion
愛想 *aiso* (=*aisō*) civility, hospitality
発想 *hassō* conception; *music* expression

INDEPENDENT

【sō 想】 conception, idea, thought
想を練る *sō o neru* think deeply, turn (a matter) over in one's mind

KUN

【omo(u) 想う】 [usu. 思う] (recall a thought) think, recollect, recall, remember
昔を想う *mukashi o omou* recall the old days

SYNONYMS

❶ⓐ **think and consider**
思 THINK → 2564
考 THINK → 3196
存 hold an opinion → 2982
案 think out → 2270
慮 CONSIDER → 3266
勘 take into consideration → 1777
量 weigh → 2471
惟 MEDITATE → 481
省 INTROSPECT → 2449

❷ **thought**
考え thought → 3196
念 THOUGHTS → 2059
意 MIND → 2136

HOMOPHONES

omou ⇨ 思 2564

NOTE

⇨ see USAGE note at 思 2564

愁 愁 愁

2829 SHŪ ure(eru) ure(i)

CH 愁 chóu

Radical	Strokes
心 61	13-4-9
Grade	Freq
Jōyō	1709
2 - 9 - 4	

9-4 秋

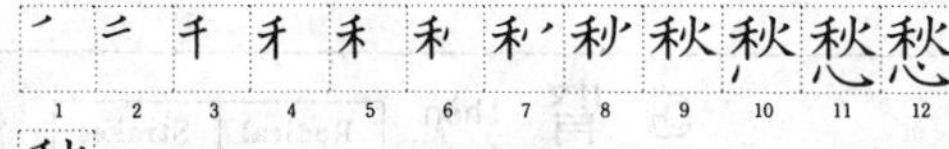

▶**MELANCHOLY**

COMPOUNDS

ⓐ **melancholy, sad, gloomy, worried**
ⓑ **melancholy, sadness, grief, sorrow, loneliness**
愁眉 *shūbi* worried look, melancholy air
憂愁 *yūshū* melancholy, gloom, grief
哀愁 *aishū* sadness, sorrow, pensiveness
郷愁 *kyōshū* homesickness, nostalgia
旅愁 *ryoshū* loneliness on a journey

KUN

【**ure(eru) 愁える**】 grieve, lament, feel sorrow
友の死を愁える *tomo no shi o ureeru* grieve for the death of a friend
【**ure(i) 愁い**】 melancholy, grief, sorrow, sadness
愁い顔 *ureigao* sad face

SYNONYMS

● **sad and depressed**
哀 sorrowful → 2068
悲 SAD → 2775
陰 gloomy → 541
沈 depressed → 261
寂 LONESOME → 2290
惨 MISERABLE → 483

HOMOPHONES

ureeru ⇨ 憂 2145
urei ⇨ 憂 2145

NOTE

⇨ see USAGE note at 憂 2145

聖 聖 聖 聖

2830 SEI hijiri▲

CH 圣 shèng

Radical	Strokes
耳 128	13-6-7
Grade	Freq
Jōyō-6	1299
2 - 9 - 4	

9-4 耶

▶**HOLY** ▶**SAINT**

COMPOUNDS

❶ **holy, sacred, divine**
聖書 *seisho* Bible
聖霊 *seirei* Holy Ghost, Holy Spirit
聖歌 *seika* sacred song, hymn
聖域 *seiiki* holy [sacred] precincts, sanctuary
聖火 *seika* sacred fire [torch]
神聖な *shinsei na* holy, sacred, divine
❷ⓐ **saint**
ⓑ title before names of saints: **St.**
ⓒ (Confucian) sage
聖賢 *seiken* saints and sages
聖ペテロ *seipetero* St. Peter
聖路加病院 *seiroka byōin* St. Luke Hospital
四聖 *shisei* the four greatest sages of the world
❸ great master
楽聖ベートーベン *gakusei bētōben* Beethoven, the great musician
棋聖 *kisei* great master of go [shogi]
❹ [honorific] imperial, emperor's
聖断 *seidan* emperor's decision
聖恩 *seion* imperial favor

INDEPENDENT

【**seinaru 聖なる**】 holy

KUN

【**hijiri 聖**】 saint; master; emperor
高野聖 *kōyahijiri* saint living at Koyasan
聖の御代 *hijiri no miyo* emperor's reign

SYNONYMS

❶ **holy**
神 divine → 912
霊 miraculous → 2805
❷ⓐ & ❷ⓑ **religious persons**
仙 IMMORTAL MOUNTAIN FAIRY → 32
❸ **great persons**
匠 CRAFTSMAN → 2990
雄 hero → 1008

傑 OUTSTANDING PERSON → 155 | 豪 GREAT MAN → 2140

9-4 耶

聖 ▶HOLY ▶SAINT
2831
nonstandard for 聖 2830

9-4 臤

腎 2832 JIN

Ⓒⓗ 肾 shèn

Radical	Strokes
月 130	13-4-9
Grade	**Freq**
Reference	
2 - 9 - 4	

COMPOUNDS

❶ [original meaning] kidney
腎臓 *jinzō* kidneys

❷ [now replaced by 心 *shin* 11] heart of a matter, vital point
肝腎な *kanjin na* vital, essential, main

9-4 玆

慈 incorrect classification ⇨ see 2339

9-4 者

煮 ▶BOIL
2833
nonstandard for 煮 2785

9-4 禺

愚 2834 GU oro(ka)

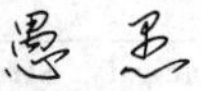

Ⓒⓗ 愚 yú

Radical	Strokes
心 61	13-4-9
Grade	**Freq**
Jōyō	1766
2 - 9 - 4	

▶FOOLISH

COMPOUNDS

❶ [original meaning] **foolish, stupid, ignorant**
愚劣な *guretsu na* stupid, silly, foolish
愚痴 *guchi* idle complaint, grumble; querulousness
愚人 *gujin* fool
愚鈍な *gudon na* stupid, silly
愚問 *gumon* silly question

❷ [humble] my foolish, my humble
愚息 *gusoku* my (foolish) son
愚妻 *gusai* my (foolish) wife
愚案 *guan* my humble opinion, my (foolish) plan

INDEPENDENT

【gu 愚】foolishness, folly, stupidity
愚な *gu na* foolish, silly, stupid

KUN

【oro(ka) 愚か】
oroka na 愚かな foolish, stupid, dull, silly
愚かさ *orokasa* foolishness, stupidity
愚かしい *orokashii* foolish, stupid, dull, silly
愚か者 *orokamono* fool, dunce

SYNONYMS

❶ **foolish**
暗 DARK → 1010
痴 STUPID → 3286
鈍 DULL → 1689

❷ **humble prefixes**
弊 our [my] humble → 2884
拙 my humble → 315
小 my little (*humble*) → 7

2835 KAN

ⒸⒽ 感 gǎn

Radical 心 61	Strokes 13-4-9
Grade Jōyō-3	Freq 267
2-9-4	

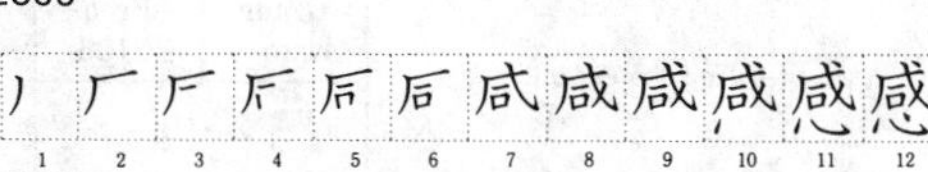

▶SENSE ▶FEEL

COMPOUNDS

❶ⓐ [also suffix] **sense, feeling, sensation, sentiment, emotion**
ⓑ (faculty of perception) **sense**
ⓒ (detect) sense, be sensitive to
感情 *kanjō* feelings, emotion, sentiment
感想 *kansō* thoughts, impressions
同感 *dōkan* same sentiment, sympathy
劣等感 *rettōkan* inferiority complex
責任感 *sekininkan* sense of responsibility
親近感 *shinkinkan* feeling of intimacy
五感 *gokan* the five senses
第六感 *dairokkan* the sixth sense, intuition
敏感な *binkan na* sensitive
感光板 *kankōban* sensitive plate
感熱剤 *kannetsuzai* heat sensitizer

❷ⓐ **feel, perceive**
ⓑ [original meaning] **feel deeply, feel admiration, be moved, be affected, be impressed**
感覚 *kankaku* sense, sensation, feeling
感知する *kanchi suru* perceive, become aware of
感応作用 *kannō sayō* induction
共感する *kyōkan suru* sympathize with, feel sympathy (for)
実感する *jikkan suru* feel actually; realize, experience personally
感動する *kandō suru* be moved, be impressed
感銘 *kanmei* deep impression
感激 *kangeki* deep emotion
感心 *kanshin* admiration

❸ be affected, be influenced, be struck by, contract
感電 *kanden* electric shock
感染 *kansen* infection
流感(=流行性感冒) *ryūkan* (=*ryūkōsei kanbō*) cold, influenza

❹ feel gratitude, thank
感謝 *kansha* gratitude, thanks

INDEPENDENT

【kan 感】 feeling, sensation, sentiment, sense, emotion; impression
隔世の感が有る *kakusei no kan ga aru* be poles apart

【kanjiru (=kanzuru) 感じる(=感ずる)】 be conscious of, suffer, be sensible to, have a feeling that; be impressed, be struck
感じ *kanji* feeling, sense, sensation, touch, feel; impression, sentiment

SYNONYMS

❶ⓐ **feeling**
情 EMOTION → 482
心 HEART → 11
気 spirits → 3194
ⓑ **sense**
覚 sense → 2604
勘 INTUITIVE PERCEPTION → 1777
ⓒ **detect**
検 detect → 986

❷ⓐ **perceive**
覚 PERCEIVE → 2604
知 KNOW → 1127
認 RECOGNIZE → 1546
ⓑ **feel deeply**
動 be moved → 1778
嘆 sigh in admiration → 630

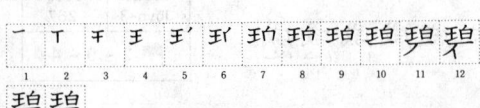

9-5 碧

碧 碧 𥓌

2836 HEKI NAMES midori ao tama

CH 碧 bì

Radical	Strokes
石 112	14-5-9
Grade	Freq
Names	2106
2 - 9 - 5	

▶**DEEP BLUE**

COMPOUNDS

❶ [original meaning] **deep blue, azure, blue**
碧水 *hekisui* blue water
碧空 *hekikū* blue sky
金髪碧眼の外人 *kinpatsu-hekigan no gaijin* foreigner with golden hair and blue eyes
紺碧 *konpeki* deep blue, azure
❷ green, verdant, emerald green
碧山 *hekizan* green mountains
碧玉 *hekigyoku* jasper

NAMES

一碧湖 *ippekiko* place name
碧 *midori* female name

SYNONYMS

❶ **blue and purple colors**
青 BLUE → 2430
瑠 LAPIS LAZULI (bright blue) → 1060
紺 DARK BLUE → 1332
藍 INDIGO → 2381
紫 PURPLE → 2688

9-5 豎

豎

2837 JU tate

CH 竖 shù

Radical	Strokes
立 117	14-5-9
Grade	Freq
Reference	
2 - 9 - 5	

COMPOUNDS

❶ [now usu. 立て- *tate*-] vertical, upright
豎琴 *tategoto* harp
❷ [now usu. 縦 *tate*] length, height
豎縞 *tatejima* vertical stripes
❸ [archaic] boy, child

豎子 *jushi* stripling, greenhorn

HOMOPHONES

tate ⇨ 立 1992 縦 1408 建 3090

NOTE

⇨ see USAGE note at 立 1992

9-5 蓄

蓄

incorrect classification ⇨ see 2509
(nonstandard for 蓄 2333)

9-5 夢

夢

incorrect classification ⇨ see 2514
(nonstandard for 夢 2336)

9-5 管

管

incorrect classification ⇨ see 2701

9-5 監

監

incorrect stroke count ⇨ see 2852

緊 2838 KIN

CH 紧 jǐn

Radical	Strokes
糸 120	15-6-9
Grade	**Freq**
Jōyō	834
2 - 9 - 6	

9-6 臤

▶TIGHTEN ▶EXIGENT

COMPOUNDS

❶ⓐ [original meaning] **tighten, make tight [tense], become tight [tense]**

ⓑ tight, close, tense

緊縛する *kinbaku suru* bind tightly

緊張する *kinchō suru* become tense, be strained, be keyed up

緊縮 *kinshuku* contraction, shrinkage; strict economy

緊密な *kinmitsu na* close, tight

❷ **exigent, urgent, pressing, imminent**

緊急な *kinkyū na* urgent, pressing, emergent

緊要な *kin'yō na* important, momentous; exigent, urgent

緊迫した *kinpaku shita* tense, strained

緊切な *kinsetsu na* urgent, pressing

喫緊事 *kikkinji* urgent [pressing] matter

SYNONYMS

❶ⓐ **tighten**

締める TIGHTEN → 1393

張 STRAIN → 474

❷ **urgent**

急 URGENT → 2092

迫 pressing → 3074

賢 2839 KEN kashiko(i)

CH 贤 xián

Radical	Strokes
貝 154	16-7-9
Grade	**Freq**
Jōyō	1498
2 - 9 - 7	

9-7 臤

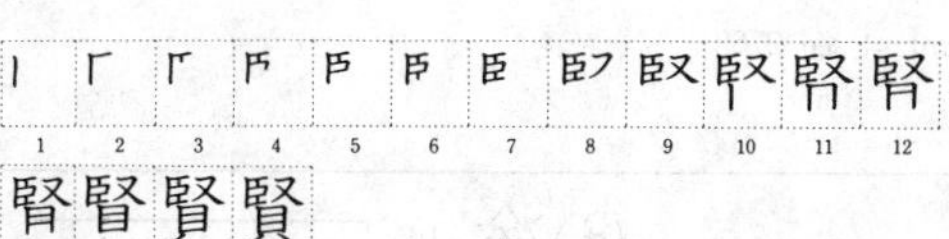

▶WISE

COMPOUNDS

❶ⓐ **wise, intelligent, sagacious, bright**

ⓑ **wise man, sage**

賢明な *kenmei na* wise, intelligent; sensible

賢者 *kenja* wise man

賢母 *kenbo* wise mother

賢哲 *kentetsu* sage, wise man

❷ capable, talented

賢才 *kensai* man of ability

❸ [honorific] your

賢察 *kensatsu* your discernment

諸賢 *shoken* gentlemen

KUN

【kashiko(i) 賢い】 wise, intelligent, sagacious, bright

賢さ *kashikosa* wisdom, intelligence, sagacity

悪賢い *warugashikoi* cunning, artful, sly, crafty

SYNONYMS

❶ⓐ **intelligent and wise**

智 wise → 2784

慧 INTELLIGENT → 2810

怜 CLEVER → 298

哲 SAGACIOUS → 2738

明 clear-sighted → 855

聡 SHARP-WITTED → 1384

俊 brilliant → 102

鋭 SHARP → 1730

敏 NIMBLE → 1322

ⓑ **wise and talented persons**

哲 sage → 2738

博 DOCTOR → 151

秀 genius → 2545

俊 BRILLIANT PERSON → 102

才 person of talent → 3410

通 well-informed person → 3109

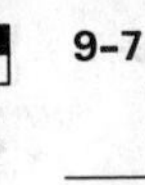

9-7 臣

覽 incorrect stroke count ⇨ see 2854

9-8 爫

爵 incorrect classification ⇨ see 2524

10-2 准

準 ▶**STANDARD** ▶**QUASI-**

2840

nonstandard for 準 2856

10-2 莫

募 incorrect classification ⇨ see 2316

10-2 里

異 incorrect classification ⇨ see 2594
(nonstandard for 異 2584)

10-2 炏

勞 incorrect classification ⇨ see 2779
(nonstandard for 労 2548)

10-2 奧

奧 incorrect classification ⇨ see 2824

10-3 亞

堊 incorrect stroke count ⇨ see 2768

10-3 涂

塗 塗 塗 CH 涂 tú

2841 TO nu(ru) nu(ri) mami(reru)▲

Radical	Strokes
土 32	13-3-10
Grade	**Freq**
Jōyō	1367
2-10-3	

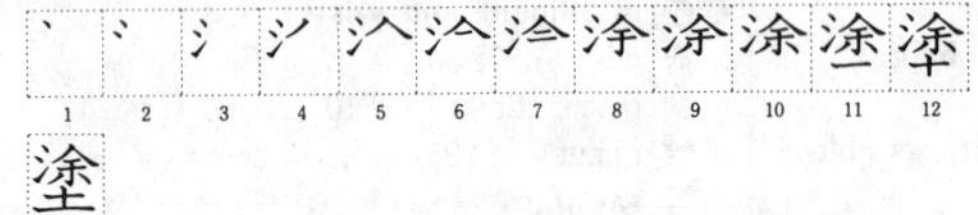

▶**APPLY ON A SURFACE**

COMPOUNDS

❶ [original meaning] **apply on a surface, lay on, spread on, coat, paint**
塗装 *tosō* painting, coating
塗料 *toryō* paint
塗布する *tofu suru* apply (an ointment)
塗工 *tokō* painter

❷ mud
塗炭 *totan* misery, distress

KUN

【**nu(ru) 塗る**】 lay on, spread on, paint, coat; blame someone, pin a crime on
塗り付ける *nuritsukeru* daub, smear
塗り絵 *nurie* picture for coloring

【**nu(ri) 塗り**】 [also suffix] coating, painting; painted or lacquered product
上塗り *uwanuri* final coating of paint
一塗り *hitonuri* one coat of paint
輪島塗り *wajimanuri* Wajima lacquer

【**mami(reru) 塗れる**】 be covered, be smeared, be stained
泥に塗れる *doro ni mamireru* be covered with mud

SYNONYMS

❶ **spread**
抹 wipe over → 313
舗 PAVE → 1735

敷く LAY → 1870
布 SPREAD → 2973
散 SCATTER → 1702

COMPOUND FORMATION

塗炭 *totan*

塗炭 'misery, distress' is, literally, to be smeared with mud (塗 ❷) and burned with charcoal (炭); that is, to be in a totally miserable state.

奨 獎 奨 奨

2842 SHŌ susu(meru)▲

CH 奖 jiǎng

Radical	Strokes
大 37	13-3-10
Grade	**Freq**
Jōyō	1475
2-10-3	

10-3 将

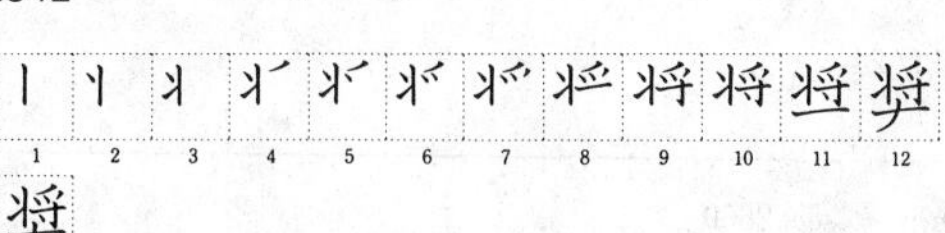

▶ENCOURAGE

COMPOUNDS

❶ (stimulate by assistance) **encourage, promote, stimulate**

奨励 *shōrei* encouragement, promotion, stimulation, incitement

奨学金 *shōgakukin* scholarship (grant)

報奨 *hōshō* reward, compensation

❷ praise, commend, reward

推奨する *suishō suru* recommend, commend, praise

選奨 *senshō* recommendation

KUN

【susu(meru) 奨める】[usu. 勧める] encourage, promote, stimulate

学問の奨め *gakumon no susume* encouragement of learning

SYNONYMS

❶ **advance**

勧 encourage → 1857
興 cause to rise → 2909
進 ADVANCE → 3121

HOMOPHONES

susumeru ⇨ 勧 1857 薦 2373 進 3121

NOTE

⇨ see USAGE note at 進 3121

塑 塑 塑 塑

2843 SO

CH 塑 sù

Radical	Strokes
土 32	13-3-10
Grade	**Freq**
Jōyō	1882
2-10-3	

10-3 朔

▶MODEL

COMPOUNDS

❶ⓐ [original meaning] (make by shaping a plastic material, esp. clay) **model, mold, sculpt**

ⓑ figure modeled of clay or plaster, plastic figure

塑造 *sozō* modeling, molding

彫塑 *chōso* carving and modeling, plastic arts; clay model

塑像 *sozō* plastic image, clay figure

❷ *phys* plastic

塑性変形 *sosei henkei* plastic deformation

塑弾性 *sodansei* plasto-elasticity

可塑材 *kasozai* plastic material

SYNONYMS

❶ⓐ **form and carve**

彫 CARVE → 1683
刻 ENGRAVE → 1267
鋳 CAST → 1729

❷ **soft**

柔 SOFT (supple and yielding) → 2088
軟 SOFT (not hard) → 1479

10-3 朔

塑 2844 ▶**MODEL**
nonstandard for 塑 2843

10-3 莫

幕 墓 incorrect classification ⇨ see 3－10

10-3 奧

奧 2845 ▶**INNER PART**
nonstandard for 奥 2824

10-3 孰

塾 incorrect stroke count ⇨ see 2860

10-4 髟

髮 髪 髮 2846 HATSU kami

CH 发 fà

Radical	Strokes
髟 190	14-10-4
Grade	**Freq**
Jōyō	1386
2－10－4	

Stroke order: 1–14

▶**HAIR**

COMPOUNDS

ⓐ **hair (on the head)**
ⓑ hairsbreadth
頭髪 *tōhatsu* hair, head hair
毛髪 *mōhatsu* hair
散髪 *sanpatsu* haircut
白髪 *hakuhatsu* white [gray] hair
一髪 *ippatsu* a hairsbreadth; a hair
危機一髪の脱出 *kiki-ippatsu no dasshutsu* escape by a hairsbreadth

INDEPENDENT

【hatsu 髪】 *literary* hairsbreadth
間、髪を入れず *kan, hatsu o irezu* in a flash, in no time

KUN

【kami 髪】 hair (of the head); [also suffix] hairstyle, coiffeur
髪の毛 *kaminoke* hair
髪結い *kamiyui* hairdresser; hairdressing
日本髪 *nihongami* Japanese coiffeur

SPECIAL READINGS

白髪 *shiraga* white [gray] hair

SYNONYMS

ⓐ **hair**
毛 HAIR (of any kind) → 3453
羽 FEATHER → 226

10-4 亞

惡 incorrect stroke count ⇨ see 2788
(nonstandard for 悪 2745)

態 2847 TAI waza(to)▲

CH 态 tài

Radical	Strokes
心 61	14-4-10
Grade	**Freq**
Jōyō-5	308
2-10-4	

10-4 能

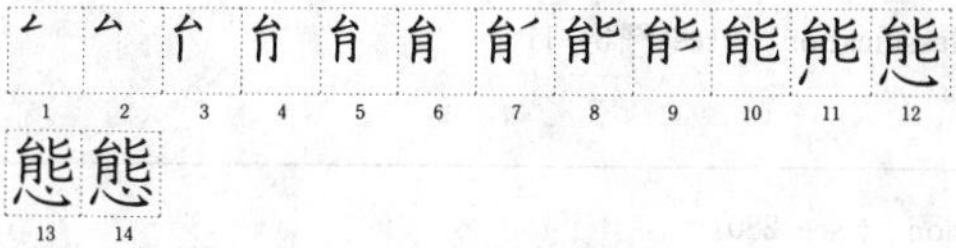

▶STATE

COMPOUNDS

❶ [also suffix] **state, condition, situation; form, appearance**
状態 *jōtai* state, condition, appearance, situation, aspect
生態 *seitai* ecology; mode of life
実態 *jittai* actual conditions, state
重態(=重体) *jūtai* serious condition, critical state
事態 *jitai* situation, state of affairs
形態(=形体) *keitai* shape, form, structure, morphology
姿態 *shitai* figure, person; pose

❷ [original meaning] **attitude, posture**
態度 *taido* attitude, manner
態勢 *taisei* attitude, preparedness, condition

❸ [suffix] *gram* voice
受動態 *judōtai* passive voice
能動態 *nōdōtai* active voice

KUN

【**waza(to)** 態と】 on purpose, intentionally
態態 *wazawaza* on purpose, purposely; expressly

SYNONYMS

❶ **states and situations**
状 CONDITION → 272
況 CONDITIONS → 337
景 business conditions → 2470
勢 course of events → 2857
境 SITUATION → 676
局 current situation → 3063
情 ACTUAL CONDITIONS → 482
訳 circumstances → 1473
調 TONE → 1567
様 MODE → 1052
相 PHASE → 900

❷ **posture**
姿 posture → 2636

熊 2848 YŪ kuma

CH 熊 xióng

Radical	Strokes
灬 86	14-4-10
Grade	**Freq**
Names	1975
2-10-4	

10-4 能

▶BEAR

COMPOUNDS

● **bear**
熊掌 *yūshō* [rare] bear's paw (as a rare Chinese delicacy)

KUN

【**kuma** 熊】 bear; [in compounds] as fierce or big as a bear
熊の胆 *kuma-no-i* bear's gall (used as medicine for the stomach)
白熊 *shirokuma* sea bear, polar bear
熊手 *kumade* rake, fork, bamboo rake
熊蜂 *kumabachi* hornet
熊笹 *kumazasa* *Sasa albo-marginata*, low and striped bamboo

NAMES

熊本 *kumamoto* place name
熊井 *kumai* surname
熊雄 *kumao* male name

SYNONYMS

● **undomesticated mammals**
虎 TIGER → 3212
象 ELEPHANT → 2134
猪 WILD BOAR → 536
鹿 DEER → 3126
猿 MONKEY → 669
鯨 WHALE → 1882

10-4 亝

齊

incorrect classification ⇨ see 2142
(nonstandard for 斉 2054)

10-4 莫

暮 慕

incorrect classification ⇨ see 3-11

10-4 𤇾

榮

incorrect classification ⇨ see 2801
(nonstandard for 栄 2574)

10-4 孰

熟

incorrect stroke count ⇨ see 2868

10-5 髟

髪

2849

▶**HAIR**
nonstandard for 髮 2846

10-5 般

磐

2850 BAN iwa

CH 磐 pán

Radical	**Strokes**
石 112	15-5-10
Grade	**Freq**
Reference	
2-10-5	

COMPOUNDS

❶ [now usu. 盤 *ban* 2851] bedrock, base rock, base, foundation
磐石 *banjaku* huge rock; firmness
落磐 *rakuban* cave-in
大磐石である *daibanjaku de aru* be as firm as rock
磐 *iwa* [now usu. 岩] rock, crag

❷ abbrev. of 磐城 *iwaki*, old name for eastern Fukushima Prefecture
常磐炭田 *jōban tanden* Joban coalfield

HOMOPHONES

iwa ⇨ 岩 2235

NOTE

⇨ see USAGE note at 岩 2235

10-5 般

盤 盤 𥁞

2851 BAN

丿 丿 𠃌 月 舟 舟 舟 舟 般 般 般 盤 盤 盤 盤
1 2 3 4 5 6 7 8 9 10 11 12 13 14 15

CH 盘 pán

Radical	**Strokes**
皿 108	15-5-10
Grade	**Freq**
Jōyō	877
2-10-5	

▶**DISK** ▶**BOARD**

COMPOUNDS

❶ⓐ **disk, round plate**
ⓑ [also suffix] **phonograph disk, record**
円盤 *enban* disk; flying saucer
吸盤 *kyūban* sucker, sucking disk
羅針盤 *rashinban* compass
胎盤 *taiban* placenta
音盤 *onban* disk, record
輸入盤 *yunyūban* foreign [imported] record

❷ⓐ [also suffix] (flat surface for specific purpose) **board (as for shogi or chess), panel, plate**
ⓑ board game, esp. shogi or go
将棋盤 *shōgiban* chessboard
鍵盤 *kenban* keyboard
算盤 *soroban* Japanese abacus, *soroban*
制御盤 *seigyoban* control panel

配電盤 *haidenban* distributing board [panel], switchboard
序盤 *joban* opening (in the game of go)
❸ⓐ dish, plate, tray, platter
ⓑ [original meaning] basin, pan, tub, bowl
杯盤 *haiban* glasses and plates
銀盤 *ginban* silver plate; surface of ice, skating rink
水盤 *suiban* basin; flower bowl
銅盤 *dōban* bronze bowl
骨盤 *kotsuban* pelvis
❹ [formerly also 磐 2850] **bedrock, base rock, base, foundation**
盤石 *banjaku* huge rock; firmness
基盤 *kiban* bedrock, base, foundation
岩盤 *ganban* bedrock, base rock
地盤 *jiban* ground, foundation, base
落盤 *rakuban* cave-in
❺ [also suffix] machine tool
旋盤 *senban* lathe
フライス盤 *furaisuban* milling machine
研削盤 *kensakuban* grinding machine
❻ entwine, twist about
盤根 *bankon* entwined roots

INDEPENDENT

【ban 盤】 go board, shogi board, chessboard; phonograph disk, record
将棋の盤 *shōgi no ban* shogi board, Japanese chessboard

SYNONYMS

❶ⓐ **circular objects**
環 RING → 1090
輪 WHEEL, RING → 1589
車 WHEEL → 3552
❷ⓐ **boards and plates**
板 BOARD, PLATE → 858
❸ **vessels and receptacles**
皿 PLATE → 3474
盆 TRAY → 2079
杯 CUP → 857
鉢 BOWL → 1708
鍋 POT → 1752
❹ **bottoms and bases**
床 BED → 3067
礎 FOUNDATION STONE → 1248
底 BOTTOM → 3084
下 lower part → 3378
基 BASE → 2673

NOTE

⇨ see COMPOUND FORMATION for 羅針盤 *rashinban* ⇨ 羅 2622

監 監◆ 監 監

2852 KAN

CH 监 jiān jiàn

Radical	Strokes
皿 108	15-5-10
Grade	**Freq**
Jōyō	598
2-10-5	

10-5

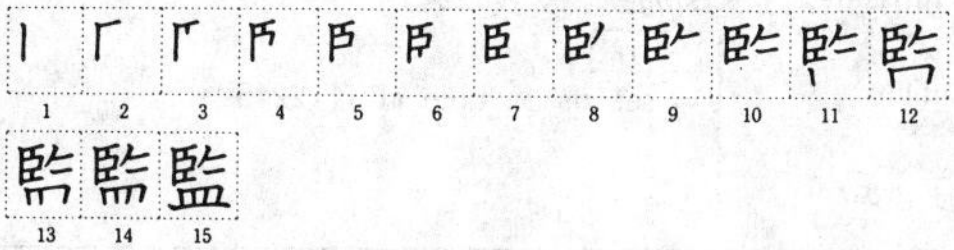

▶OVERSEE

COMPOUNDS

❶ⓐ **oversee, supervise, overlook, watch over, superintend, inspect**
ⓑ overseer, supervisor, inspector
監督する *kantoku suru* supervise, superintend; direct (a film)
監視する *kanshi suru* watch, keep under observation, exercise surveillance
監査 *kansa* inspection; inspector, supervisor
監修 *kanshū* (editorial) supervision
総監 *sōkan* governor-general, inspector general
舎監 *shakan* dormitory inspector [superintendent]
学監 *gakkan* school superintendent [overseer]; dean
❷ prison
監獄 *kangoku* prison, jail
監禁 *kankin* imprisonment, confinement
監房 *kanbō* cell, ward

SYNONYMS

❶ⓐ **direct and supervise**
督 SUPERVISE → 2796
制 CONTROL → 1274
管 EXERCISE CONTROL → 2701
轄 EXERCISE JURISDICTION OVER → 1627
掌 TAKE CHARGE OF → 2602
司 OFFICIATE → 2931
宰 PRESIDE → 2275
営 MANAGE → 2603
理 manage → 970
経 MANAGE → 1331
❷ **prison**
獄 PRISON → 712

10-6 敏

繁 繁 繁
2853 HAN shige(ru)▲ shige(ku)▲

Ⓒ 繁 fán pó

Radical	Strokes
糸 120	16-6-10
Grade	**Freq**
Jōyō	1111

2-10-6

▶**THRIVE**

COMPOUNDS

❶ [formerly also 蕃 2522] (grow vigorously) **thrive, luxuriate, grow thick**

繁殖する *hanshoku suru* breed, propagate, increase, multiply

繁茂 *hanmo* luxuriant growth

❷ⓐ (enjoy prosperity) **thrive, prosper, flourish**

ⓑ **bustling, busy**

繁栄する *han'ei suru* prosper, thrive, flourish

繁華 *hanka* prosperity, bustle

繁盛(＝繁昌)する *hanjō suru* prosper, flourish, thrive

繁忙 *hanbō* pressure of business, business

繁閑 *hankan* press and slack of business

農繁期 *nōhanki* busy farming season

❸ numerous, frequent

頻繁に *hinpan ni* frequently, very often

❹ complicated, complex, intricate

繁雑な *hanzatsu na* complicated, intricate, confused

繁簡 *hankan* complexity and simplicity

KUN

【shige(ru) 繁る】[now usu. 茂る] grow thick, be luxuriant, be overgrown

【shige(ku) 繁く】 frequently, often

繁繁 *shigeshige* very frequently; (look) steadily

SYNONYMS

❶ **flourish**

茂 GROW THICK → 2245

❷ⓐ **prospering and prosperity**

栄 FLOURISH → 2574

盛 PROSPEROUS → 2675

昌 PROSPERING → 2414

隆 PROSPER → 545

振 rise → 430

興 RISE TO PROSPERITY → 2909

ⓑ **busy**

忙 BUSY → 214

慌てる FLURRIED → 580

❹ **complex**

煩 vexatious → 1022

HOMOPHONES

shigeru ⇨ 茂 2245

NOTE

⇨ see USAGE note at 茂 2245

10-6 𤇾

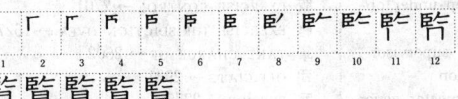

螢

incorrect classification ⇨ see 2813
(nonstandard for 蛍 2591)

10-7 臣

覽 覽 覧
2854 RAN

Ⓒ 览 lǎn

Radical	Strokes
見 147	17-7-10
Grade	**Freq**
Jōyō-6	1309

2-10-7

▶**LOOK OVER**

COMPOUNDS

ⓐ [original meaning] **look over (a wide area), look at, glance at, view, see**

ⓑ (make an overall inspection of) **look over, inspect, read**

一覧 *ichiran* a look, a glance, a reading; summary, synopsis

一覧する *ichiran suru* look, glance through, inspect

御覧 *goran* [honorific] look, see; try

観覧車 *kanransha* Ferris wheel

展覧する *tenran suru* exhibit, show
博覧会 *hakurankai* exhibition, fair, exposition
閲覧室 *etsuranshitsu* reading room
便覧 *benran* (=*binran*) handbook, manual
要覧 *yōran* survey, outline, handbook

SYNONYMS

● **see and look**
観 VIEW → 1880
見 SEE → 2544
目 look → 3043
眺 LOOK OUT OVER → 1171
望 LOOK AFAR → 2742
仰 LOOK UP → 48
顧 LOOK BACK → 1900
視 REGARD → 972
看 WATCH → 3220
察 INSPECT → 2347

齋

incorrect classification ⇨ see 2148
(nonstandard for 斎 2115)

10-7 齊

營

incorrect classification ⇨ see 2816
(nonstandard for 営 2603)

10-7 𤇾

響

incorrect stroke count ⇨ see 2878

10-9 鄉

競

incorrect classification ⇨ see 1847

10-10 竝

鬚

2855 SHU hige

CH 须 xū

Radical	Strokes
髟 190	22-10-12
Grade	Freq
Reference	
2-10-12	

10-12 髟

COMPOUNDS

● [rarely also 須 *shu* 574] [original meaning] beard
鬚髯 *shuzen* beard

準 準◇ 凖 㴨

2856 JUN

CH 准 zhǔn

Radical	Strokes
氵 85	13-3-10
Grade	Freq
Jōyō-5	520
2-11-2	

11-2 淮

Stroke order: 1–13

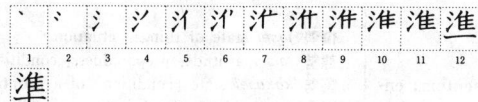

▶**STANDARD** ▶**QUASI-**

COMPOUNDS

❶ **standard, norm, criterion**
準則 *junsoku* regulations, standard
水準 *suijun* level, standard; water level
基準 *kijun* standard, criterion, basis
標準 *hyōjun* standard, norm, criterion
平準 *heijun* level; equality

❷ [original meaning] water level (the instrument)
準縄 *junjō* level and inked string; rule, standard

❸ [also prefix] **quasi-, semi-, associate**
準急 *junkyū* local express, semi-express (train)
準星 *junsei* quasar
準決勝 *junkesshō* semifinal
準会員 *junkaiin* associate member

❹ apply correspondingly, conform to, be proportionate

準拠 *junkyo* conformity

準用する *jun'yō suru* apply correspondingly

❺ prepare, provide for

準備する *junbi suru* provide for [against], prepare for [against]

INDEPENDENT

【junjiru (=junzuru) 準じる(=準ずる)】 be treated [regarded] correspondingly; apply correspondingly, be proportionate to

SYNONYMS

❶ **model**

格 NORM → 926

式 form → 3049

程 ESTABLISHED FORM → 1190

模 PATTERN → 1050

典 CANON → 2627

範 MODEL → 2709

❸ **subordinate**

亜 SUB- → 3540

半 semi- → 3501

副 SECONDARY → 1776

次 secondary → 54

従 subordinate → 415

准 JUNIOR → 127

助 assistant → 1121

❹ **correspond to**

該 CORRESPOND TO → 1519

当 be equivalent → 2177

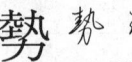

11-2 埶

勢 勢 勢

2857 SEI ZEI▲ ikio(i)

CH 势 shì

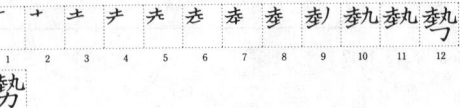

Radical	Strokes
力 19	13-2-11
Grade	**Freq**
Jōyō-5	330
2-11-2	

一 十 土 夫 夫 坴 坴 坴 坴 埶 埶 埶 勢
1 2 3 4 5 6 7 8 9 10 11 12 13

▶**POWER**

COMPOUNDS

❶ⓐ (ability to influence) **power to influence, influence, strength, authority**

ⓑ spiritual energy or power, vigor, spirit, dash

勢力 *seiryoku* influence, power, might; force (of a typhoon)

勢門 *seimon* influential family

権勢 *kensei* power, influence, authority

党勢 *tōsei* strength of a party

優勢な *yūsei na* superior, leading, predominant

豪勢な *gōsei na* great, grand, magnificent

虚勢 *kyosei* bluff, bluster, false show of power

気勢 *kisei* spirit, ardor

威勢 *isei* spirits, dash; power

❷ⓐ **physical power, force; momentum; energy**

ⓑ procreative power, male genitals

火勢 *kasei* force of the fire, flames

強勢 *kyōsei* emphasis, stress, accent

筆勢 *hissei* stroke [dash] of the pen

余勢 *yosei* surplus power, reserve energy

去勢する *kyosei suru* castrate; enervate

❸ⓐ (numerical force) **strength, number (of soldiers or people), large numbers**

ⓑ [also suffix] forces, army

ⓒ [also suffix] party, group

多勢 *tazei* great numbers, superiority in number

大勢の *ōzei no* great number of, multitude of

勢揃いする *seizoroi suru* assemble in full force, muster

加勢する *kasei suru* held, aid, assist

軍勢 *gunzei* army, force; number of soldiers

総勢 *sōzei* the whole army

徳川勢 *tokugawazei* Tokugawa forces

同勢 *dōzei* company, party

外国勢 *gaikokuzei* (group of) foreigners

埼玉勢 *saitamazei* the Saitama group

❹ⓐ **course of events, state of affairs, situation, condition, circumstances**

ⓑ trend of events, drift, tendency

形勢 *keisei* situation, state of affairs; prospects

情勢 *jōsei* state of things, situation

態勢 *taisei* attitude, preparedness, condition

国勢 *kokusei* state [condition] of a country

勝勢である *shōsei de aru* stand a good chance of winning the game

大勢 *taisei* general trend [tendency]

時勢 *jisei* trend of the times, spirit of the age

運勢 *unsei* one's star, fortune, luck

❺ outward appearance

地勢 *chisei* geographical features, topography

姿勢 *shisei* posture, position, poise, attitude

体勢 *taisei* posture, stance

❻ abbrev. of 伊勢 *ise*, old name for Mie Prefecture

紀勢本線 *kisei honsen* Kisei Main Line (Wakayama-Mie Railway)

INDEPENDENT

【**sei** 勢】army, force; strength, number of soldiers

【**zei** 勢】same as **sei** 勢

敵の勢 *teki no zei* enemy's strength [forces]

KUN

【**ikio(i)** 勢い】force, vigor, power, energy, spirit; momentum, impetus; influence, power; course of events, trend, tendency; naturally, necessarily

勢い良く *ikioiyoku* forcibly, with vigor

勢い込む *ikioikomu* brace oneself up

勢い付く *ikioizuku* gain strength, take heart

勢いを振るう *ikioi o furuu* exercise authority, wield power

自然の勢いで *shizen no ikioi de* by force of circumstances

SYNONYMS

❶ⓐ power and authority

権 POWER (to control) → 1065

力 POWER → 3371

威 MIGHT → 3578

覇 SUPREMACY → 2730

❷ⓐ energy and force

力 POWER, force → 3371

気 energy → 3194

圧 PRESSURE → 2970

❸ⓐ quantity and number

数 NUMBER → 1790

量 QUANTITY → 2471

嵩 BULK → 2331

積 size → 1236

額 AMOUNT → 1805

分 content → 1972

ⓑ armed forces

軍 ARMY → 2080

兵 the military → 2551

隊 PARTY → 625

❹ⓐ states and situations

状 CONDITION → 272

況 CONDITIONS → 337

景 business conditions → 2470

態 STATE → 2847

境 SITUATION → 676

局 current situation → 3063

情 ACTUAL CONDITIONS → 482

訳 circumstances → 1473

調 TONE → 1567

様 MODE → 1052

相 PHASE → 900

ⓑ tendency

向 tendency → 3052

性 NATURE → 299

傾 inclination → 154

潮 TIDE → 739

流 CURRENT → 441

募 incorrect classification ⇨ see 2494 (nonstandard for 募 2316) — 11-2 莫

零 incorrect classification ⇨ see 2792 — 11-2 雨

與 2858

▶GIVE

nonstandard for 与 3421 — 11-2 臼

奬 2859

▶ENCOURAGE

nonstandard for 奨 2842 — 11-3 將

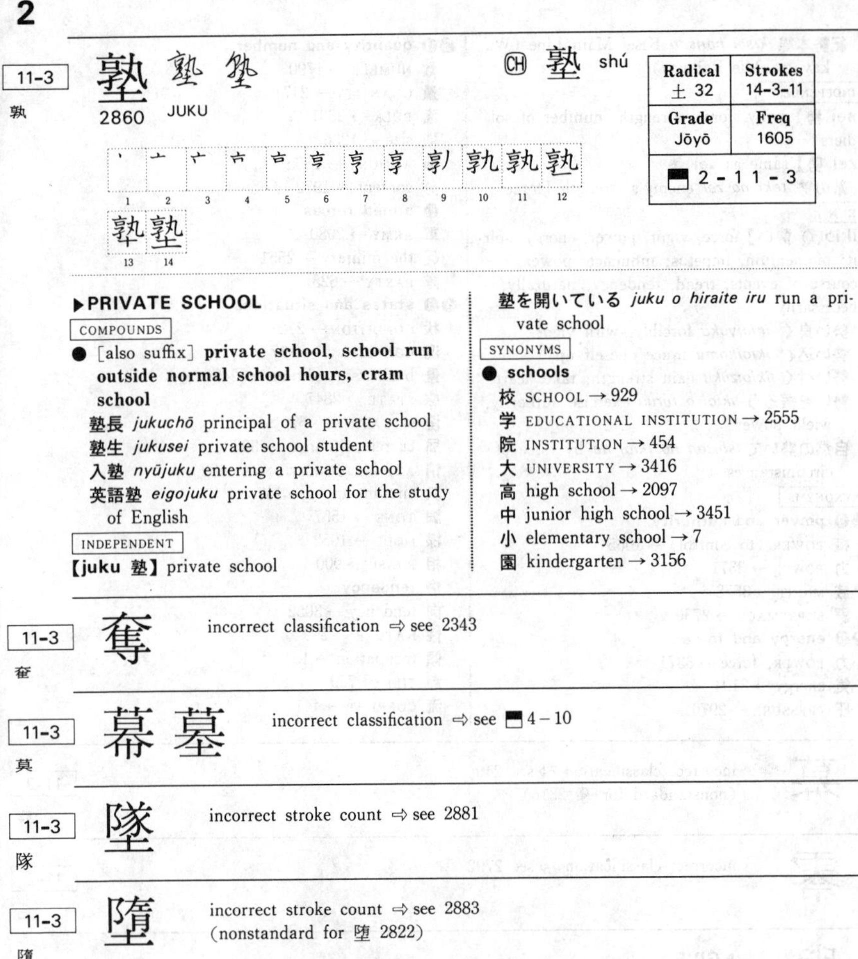

11-3 孰

塾 塾 塾

2860 JUKU

(CH) 塾 shú

Radical	Strokes
土 32	14-3-11
Grade	**Freq**
Jōyō	1605
2-11-3	

Stroke order: 1 2 3 4 5 6 7 8 9 10 11 12 13 14

▶**PRIVATE SCHOOL**

COMPOUNDS

● [also suffix] **private school, school run outside normal school hours, cram school**

塾長 *jukuchō* principal of a private school
塾生 *jukusei* private school student
入塾 *nyūjuku* entering a private school
英語塾 *eigojuku* private school for the study of English

INDEPENDENT

【**juku 塾**】 private school

塾を開いている *juku o hiraite iru* run a private school

SYNONYMS

● **schools**

校 SCHOOL → 929
学 EDUCATIONAL INSTITUTION → 2555
院 INSTITUTION → 454
大 UNIVERSITY → 3416
高 high school → 2097
中 junior high school → 3451
小 elementary school → 7
園 kindergarten → 3156

11-3 奞

奪 incorrect classification ⇨ see 2343

11-3 莫

幕 墓 incorrect classification ⇨ see 4-10

11-3 隊

墜 incorrect stroke count ⇨ see 2881

11-3 隋

墮 incorrect stroke count ⇨ see 2883
(nonstandard for 堕 2822)

11-3 道

導 incorrect stroke count ⇨ see 2888

11-4 幺幺

樂 2861

▶**PLEASURE** ▶**COMFORTABLE** ▶**MUSIC**

nonstandard for 楽 2826

慾 2862 YOKU

CH 欲 yù

Radical	Strokes
心 61	15-4-11
Grade	**Freq**
Reference	
2-11-4	

11-4 欲

COMPOUNDS

● [now replaced by 欲 1475] [also suffix] [original meaning] desire, craving; avarice, greed
性慾 *seiyoku* sexual desire, lust
愛慾 *aiyoku* love and lust, sexual passion
物慾 *butsuyoku* worldly desires
無慾 *muyoku* freedom from avarice
色慾 *shikiyoku* sexual appetite
食慾 *shokuyoku* appetite (for food)
名誉慾 *meiyoyoku* love of fame
慾 *yoku* desire, craving; avarice, greed

擊 撃 車• 2863 GEKI u(tsu)

CH 击 jī

Radical	Strokes
手 64	15-4-11
Grade	**Freq**
Jōyō	366
2-11-4	

11-4 毄

▶**STRIKE**

COMPOUNDS

❶ **strike, make a military attack, destroy**
撃破する *gekiha suru* defeat, rout; destroy
攻撃 *kōgeki* attack, assault; criticism; *baseball* batting
爆撃 *bakugeki* bombing, bombardment
反撃する *hangeki suru* counterattack, strike [fight] back
襲撃する *shūgeki suru* raid, attack, assault

❷ **fire, shoot, discharge**
撃墜する *gekitsui suru* shoot down
撃沈する *gekichin suru* attack and sink a ship
射撃する *shageki suru* shoot, fire at
銃撃 *jūgeki* shooting, gunning (down)

❸ⓐ [original meaning] **strike, beat**
ⓑ come in contact with
打撃 *dageki* blow, strike; batting, hitting
直撃 *chokugeki* direct hit
衝撃 *shōgeki* impact, shock, impulse
目撃者 *mokugekisha* eyewitness
電撃 *dengeki* electric shock; lightning attack, blitz

KUN

【u(tsu) 撃つ】
① fire, shoot, discharge
撃ち落とす *uchiotosu* shoot down
早撃ち *hayauchi* quick [snap] shooting; quick [snap] shot [draw]
② [sometimes also 打つ or 討つ] attack, strike, assault
撃ち破る *uchiyaburu* defeat, crush
迎え撃つ *mukaeutsu* fight the attack of an enemy

SYNONYMS

❶ **attack**
襲 RAID → 2917
攻 ATTACK → 242
侵 INVADE → 101
爆 bomb → 1101

❷ **shoot**
射 SHOOT → 1458
発 discharge → 2565

❸ⓐ **strike**
打 STRIKE → 193
当てる HIT → 2177
拍 BEAT (strike repeatedly) → 304
撲 DEAL A BLOW → 733
殴 BEAT (strike a person) → 886

HOMOPHONES

utsu ⇨ 討 1456 打 193

NOTE

⇨ see USAGE note at 打 193

11-4
斬

暫 𣈆 𣈇

2864 ZAN shibara(ku)▲

CH 暂 zàn

Radical	Strokes
日 72	15-4-11
Grade	**Freq**
Jōyō	1586
2-11-4	

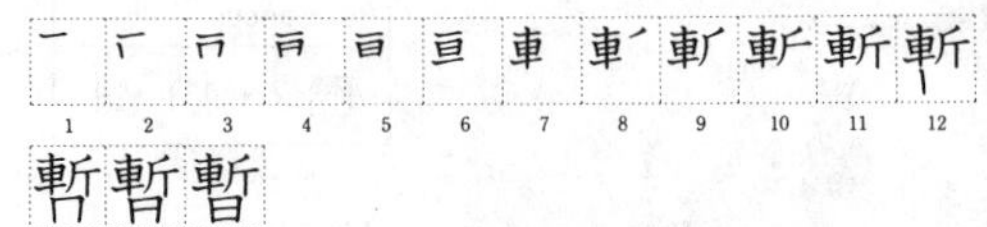

暫暫暫
13 14 15

▶**SHORT WHILE**

COMPOUNDS

ⓐ [original meaning] **short while, a while**

ⓑ **for the time being, temporary, provisional**

暫時 *zanji* short while, a moment

暫定の *zantei no* provisional, tentative

暫定案 *zanteian* provisional plan

KUN

【**shibara(ku)** 暫く】awhile, a moment; good while, long time; for the time being

暫くですね *Shibaraku desu ne* It's been a while

SYNONYMS

ⓐ **short time periods**

頃 moment → 144

瞬 INSTANT → 1247

秒 SECOND → 1137

分 MINUTE → 1972

時 hour → 924

ⓑ **temporary**

仮 TEMPORARY → 50

NOTE

★do not confuse with 漸 706

11-4
默

黙 默 𪐴 𪐴

2865 MOKU dama(ru) moda(su)▲

CH 默 mò

Radical	Strokes
黑 203	15-11-4
Grade	**Freq**
Jōyō	1337
2-11-4	

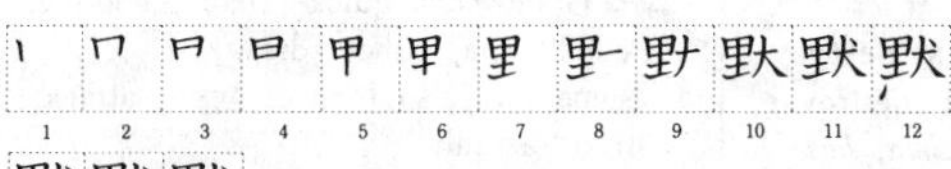

默黙黙
13 14 15

▶**SILENT**

COMPOUNDS

ⓐ **silent, taciturn**

ⓑ (unexpressed) silent, tacit

黙秘する *mokuhi suru* keep silent, keep secret

黙禱 *mokutō* silent prayer

黙読する *mokudoku suru* read silently

沈黙 *chinmoku* silence, reticence, taciturnity

寡黙な *kamoku na* silent, taciturn, reticent

黙認 *mokunin* tacit [silent] approval, toleration

黙許 *mokkyo* tacit permission

暗黙の *anmoku no* tacit

INDEPENDENT

【**mokusuru** 黙する】keep silent

KUN

【**dama(ru)** 黙る】become silent, shut one's mouth

黙り *danmari* silence; taciturnity; refusing explanation; pantomime

黙り込む *damarikomu* sink into silence

【**moda(su)** 黙す】be silent; leave something unattended

黙し難い *modashigatai* be unable to decline

SYNONYMS

ⓐ **quiet**

静 QUIET → 1728

閑 QUIET → 3322

寂 quiet → 2290

幽 QUIET AND SECLUDED → 3008

粛 still → 3581

熱 熱 𤍠

2866 NETSU atsu(i)

Ⓒⓗ 热 rè

Radical	Strokes
灬 86	15-4-11
Grade	Freq
Jōyō-4	644
2 - 1 1 - 4	

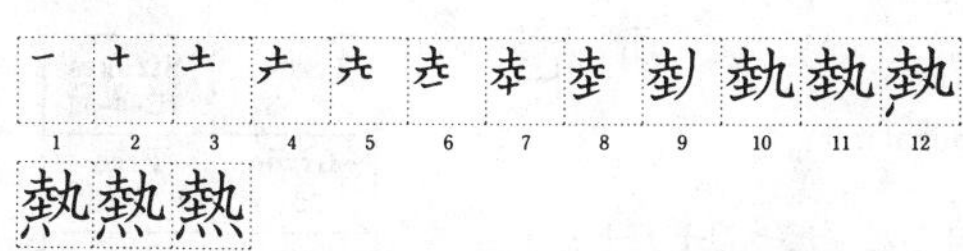

▶HEAT ▶HOT

COMPOUNDS

❶ⓐ (source of warmth) **heat**
ⓑ [also prefix] heat energy, thermo-
ⓒ heat, make hot
高熱 *kōnetsu* intense heat; high fever
加熱 *kanetsu* heating
光熱費 *kōnetsuhi* fuel and electricity expenses
地熱 *jinetsu* (=*chinetsu*) terrestrial heat
耐熱性 *tainetsusei* heat-resisting property
熱機関 *netsukikan* heat engine, thermomotor
熱原子核 *netsugenshikaku* thermal nucleus
過熱する *kanetsu suru* overheat, superheat

❷ [also suffix] (abnormal bodily heat) fever, temperature
熱病 *netsubyō* fever
発熱 *hatsunetsu* generation of heat; attack of fever
微熱 *binetsu* slight fever
産褥熱 *sanjokunetsu* puerperal fever

❸ [original meaning] **hot, boiling**
熱湯 *nettō* boiling water
熱帯 *nettai* tropics, torrid zone
熱気 *nekki* hot air, heat; fevered air, enthusiasm
灼熱 *shakunetsu* heat

❹ (showing intense feeling) **hot (with excitement), fervent, passionate, ardent, enthusiastic, earnest**
熱意 *netsui* zeal, ardor, enthusiasm
熱心に *nesshin ni* enthusiastically, zealously, fervently, earnestly
熱戦 *nessen* hot contest, hard fight
熱中する *netchū suru* be absorbed in, become enthusiastic
熱望 *netsubō* fervent hope, earnest desire
熱烈な *netsuretsu na* ardent, fervent, vehement
熱血漢 *nekketsukan* hot-blooded man
情熱 *jōnetsu* passion, enthusiasm

❺ [suffix] fever, craze, enthusiasm, mania
野球熱 *yakyūnetsu* baseball fever, enthusiasm for baseball
海外留学熱 *kaigai-ryūgakunetsu* craze for studying abroad
投機熱 *tōkinetsu* speculation fever

INDEPENDENT

【netsu 熱】 heat; fever; enthusiasm, passion
勉強に熱が入る *benkyō ni netsu ga hairu* become very keen on one's studies
熱を上げる *netsu o ageru* become enthusiastic

【nessuru 熱する】 heat, make hot; become hot, get excited
熱し易い *nesshiyasui* excitable

KUN

【atsu(i) 熱い】
① hot (to the touch), heated
熱さ *atsusa* heat
熱いコーヒー *atsui kōhī* hot coffee
②ⓐ hot (with excitement), passionate
ⓑ be madly in love
熱い仲だ *atsui naka da* be sweet on each other

SYNONYMS

❶ⓐ heat
暑 SUMMER HEAT → 2473
ⓒ raise the temperature
温める WARM (a thing) → 608
暖 WARM (the air) → 1011

❷ diseases and disease symptoms
炎 INFLAMMATION → 2420
痘 SMALLPOX → 3284
痢 DIARRHEA → 3283
下 diarrhea → 3378

❸ hot
暑い HOT (weather) → 2473
炎 scorching → 2420
温 WARM → 608
暖 WARM (esp. weather) → 1011

❹ eager
篤 DEVOTED → 2716
切 eager → 27
懇 EARNEST → 2899

❺ mania and maniacs
狂 maniac → 269
魔 maniac → 3187
痴 infatuated → 3286

USAGE

atsui
熱い
① hot (to the touch), heated
②ⓐ hot (with excitement), passionate

ⓑ be madly in love

暑い
hot (weather), warm, sultry

HOMOPHONES

atsui ⇨ 暑 2473

11-4
尉

慰 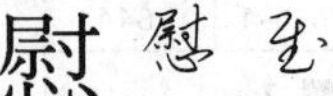

2867 I nagusa(meru) nagusa(mu)

CH 慰 wèi

Radical	Strokes
心 61	15-4-11
Grade	**Freq**
Jōyō	1375
2-11-4	

1 2 3 4 5 6 7 8 9 10 11 12 13 14 15

▶CONSOLE

COMPOUNDS

ⓐ [original meaning] **console, comfort; show sympathy to**

ⓑ divert, amuse; amuse oneself sexually

慰問 *imon* inquiring after a person's health; consolation

慰霊 *irei* comforting the spirits of the dead

慰謝料 *isharyō* consolation money

慰労 *irō* recognition of services

慰安 *ian* solace, consolation; recreation

弔慰 *chōi* condolence, sympathy

自慰 *jii* self-consolation; masturbation

INDEPENDENT

【isuru 慰する】 console, comfort

KUN

【nagusa(meru) 慰める】 console, comfort, cheer up

慰め *nagusame* consolation, comfort

慰め顔 *nagusamegao* comforting look

酒は心を慰める *Sake wa kokoro o nagusameru* Drink comforts the soul

【nagusa(mu) 慰む】 be diverted (by); make fun of; make a plaything of, play around with (an innocent girl)

慰み *nagusami* amusement, pastime, pleasure; fooling around

何の慰みも無い毎日 *nan no nagusami mo nai mainichi* a pleasureless life

慰み半分 *nagusamihanbun* half for fun

慰んだ挙句に捨てる *nagusanda ageku ni suteru* throw a girl away after making her one's plaything

SYNONYMS

ⓐ **console**

弔 CONDOLE → 3432

11-4
孰

熟 熟 熟

2868 JUKU u(reru)

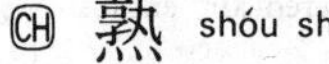

Radical	Strokes
灬 86	15-4-11
Grade	**Freq**
Jōyō-6	1488
2-11-4	

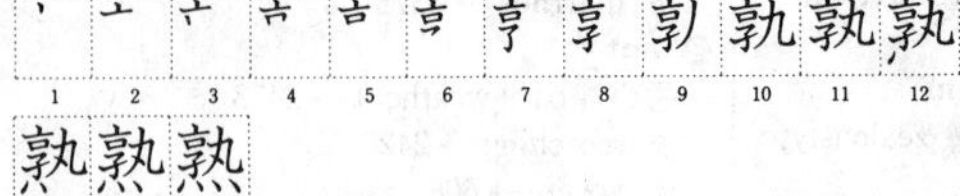

1 2 3 4 5 6 7 8 9 10 11 12 13 14 15

▶MATURE

COMPOUNDS

❶ (become ripe, as of fruit) **mature, ripen**

熟柿 *jukushi* ripe persimmon

未熟な *mijuku na* unripe, immature; unskilled, poor

❷ⓐ (become fully developed) **mature, ripen, attain full growth**

ⓑ **become skilled, attain proficiency**

熟成 *jukusei* aging, ripening, maturation

成熟する *seijuku suru* mature, ripen, attain full growth

早熟な *sōjuku na* precocious, forward

熟練 *jukuren* skill, dexterity

熟達する *jukutatsu suru* attain proficiency, become expert

円熟した *enjuku shita* mature, mellow, ripe, fully developed

習熟する *shūjuku suru* get skilled (in), become practiced (in)

❸ [original meaning] boiled, cooked

熟食 *jukushoku* [rare] well-cooked[-boiled] food

半熟卵 *hanjukutamago* soft boiled egg

❹ thoroughly, carefully, completely

熟読 *jukudoku* careful reading

熟睡 *jukusui* sound sleep
熟知 *jukuchi* thorough knowledge
熟考 *jukkō* due consideration, mature reflection

❺ (of words) get into popular use, come to sound natural
熟語 *jukugo* compound word (esp. in Japanese); phrase, idiom

INDEPENDENT

【jukusu 熟す】 (become ripe, as of fruit) mature, ripen, be ripe for; get into popular use
機が熟すのを待つ *ki ga jukusu no o matsu* wait for a ripe moment

KUN

【u(reru) 熟れる】 ripen, become ripe, mellow, mature
熟れ *ure* ripeness, maturity
熟れ過ぎ *uresugi* overripeness
熟れた果実 *ureta kajitsu* mellow [ripe] fruit

SYNONYMS

❶ & ❷ⓐ mature
成 grow up → 3537
稔 RIPEN → 1207
実る bear fruit → 2225

❷ⓑ attain proficiency
達 attain proficiency → 3139

勳 勳 勳 勳

2869 KUN isao▲

CH 勋 xūn

Radical	Strokes
力 19	15-2-13
Grade	**Freq**
Jōyō	1227
2 - 11 - 4	

11-4 勳

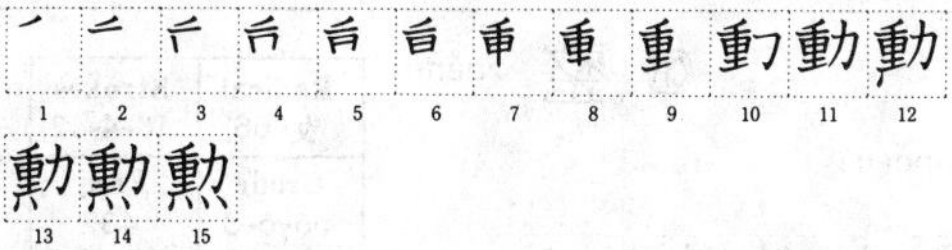

▶MERITORIOUS SERVICE

COMPOUNDS

ⓐ **meritorious [distinguished] service, merit, meritorious deed, exploits**

ⓑ order of merit, decoration
勳功 *kunkō* distinguished services, merit
勳章 *kunshō* decoration, order, medal
殊勳 *shukun* meritorious deeds, distinguished service
武勳 *bukun* deeds of arms, distinguished military service
勳記 *kunki* decoration diploma, diploma
叙勳 *jokun* decoration, bestowal of an order

INDEPENDENT

【kun 勳】 order of merit
勳一等 *kun ittō* First Order of Merit

KUN

【isao 勳】 [also 功] *elegant* meritorious service, merit

SYNONYMS

ⓐ accomplishment
功 MERIT → 189
績 ACHIEVEMENTS → 1412

USAGE

isao
勳
[also 功] *elegant* meritorious service, merit
功
[also 勳] *elegant* meritorious service, merit

HOMOPHONES

isao ⇨ 功 189

窯

incorrect classification ⇨ see 2361

11-4 窯

暮 慕

incorrect classification ⇨ see 4-11

11-4 莫

11-5 御

禦

2870 GYO fuse(gu)

Ⓒ 御 yù

Radical	Strokes
示 113	16-5-11
Grade	Freq
Reference	
2-11-5	

COMPOUNDS

❶ⓐ [now replaced by 御 *gyo* 577] [original meaning] resist, keep out, ward off

ⓑ [now usu. 防ぐ *fusegu*] prevent, keep off, ward off; defend, protect, resist

防禦する *bōgyo suru* defend, protect, safeguard

侵略を禦ぐ *shinryaku o fusegu* defend against an invasion

❷ [now replaced by 御 *gyo* 577] handle, control

制禦する *seigyo suru* control, govern, suppress

HOMOPHONES

fusegu ⇨ 防 270

NOTE

⇨ see USAGE note at 防 270

11-5 敕

整

2871 SEI totono(eru) totono(u)

Ⓒ 整 zhěng

Radical	Strokes
攵 66	16-4-12
Grade	Freq
Jōyō-3	432
2-11-5	

Stroke order: 1–16

▶**PUT IN ORDER**

COMPOUNDS

ⓐ [original meaning] **put in order, arrange, adjust properly, make straight**

ⓑ in good order, well-arranged, proper, intact

整理する *seiri suru* put in order, arrange; liquidate, disorganize; retrench; cut, dispose of

整備 *seibi* maintenance, servicing, preparation

整風 *seifū* rectification

整形外科 *seikei geka* orthopedic surgery, orthopedics

整列する *seiretsu suru* stand in a row, line up

整地 *seichi* leveling of ground, soil preparation

整頓 *seiton* proper arrangement

調整 *chōsei* regulation, adjustment

整然たる *seizentaru* orderly, systematic

整数 *seisū* integer

均整(=均斉) *kinsei* symmetry

KUN

【totono(eru) 整える】 (put in order) arrange, tidy up, adjust (clothes), regulate

髪を整える *kami o totonoeru* arrange [tidy up] one's hair

調子を整える *chōshi o totonoeru* put in tune

【totono(u) 整う】 be in order, be adjusted [regulated], be made up properly

整った *totonotta* in good order, well-ordered, well-regulated; well-featured

服装が整っている *fukusō ga totonotte iru* be properly dressed

SYNONYMS

ⓐ **arrange**

理 put in order → 970

揃える arrange properly → 590

列 arrange in a row → 824

陳 lay out (for exhibit) → 540

羅 spread out → 2622

並 LINE UP → 2246

比 rank → 26

HOMOPHONES

totonoeru ⇨ 調 1567

totonou ⇨ 調 1567

NOTE

⇨ see USAGE note at 調 1567

奮 incorrect classification ⇨ see 2367 11-5 奞

聲 2872 ▶**VOICE** nonstandard for 声 2198 11-6 殸

繁 2873 ▶**THRIVE** nonstandard for 繁 2853 11-6 敏

翳 2874 EI kage(ri) 11-6 殹

CH 翳 yì

Radical	Strokes
羽 124	17-6-11
Grade	Freq
Reference	
2-11-6	

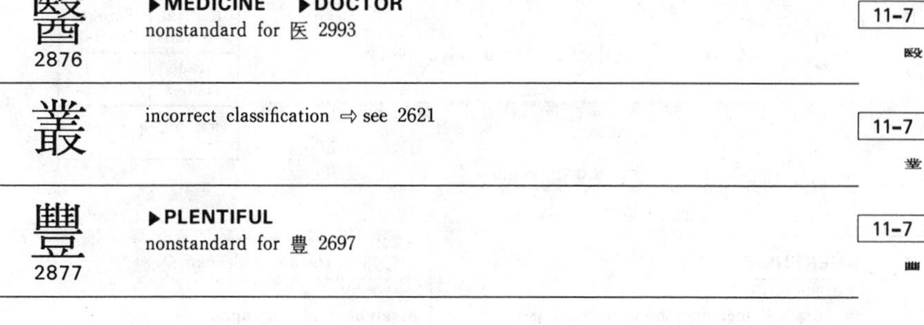

COMPOUNDS

ⓐ [now replaced by 影 *ei* 1889] shadow, shade

ⓑ [now usu. 陰り *kageri*] shade; gloom

暗翳 *an'ei* shadow, gloom

陰翳 *in'ei* shadow

翳りの有る顔 *kageri no aru kao* face shaded with pensiveness

HOMOPHONES

kageri ⇨ 陰 541

NOTE

⇨ see USAGE note at 陰 541

擧 2875 ▶**NOMINATE** ▶**NOTEWORTHY ACT** ▶**RAISE** nonstandard for 挙 2456 11-6 𦥑

醫 2876 ▶**MEDICINE** ▶**DOCTOR** nonstandard for 医 2993 11-7 殹

叢 incorrect classification ⇨ see 2621 11-7 丵

豐 2877 ▶**PLENTIFUL** nonstandard for 豊 2697 11-7 丰

11-9 郷

響 響 響 響

ⒸⒽ 响 xiǎng

2878 KYŌ hibi(ku)

Radical	Strokes
音 180	20-9-11
Grade	**Freq**
Jōyō	603
2-11-9	

▶REVERBERATE

COMPOUNDS

❶ⓐ [original meaning] **reverberate, resound, echo, ring**
ⓑ **reverberation, echo, sound**
反響する *hankyō suru* echo, reverberate
反響 *hankyō* echo, reverberation; response, repercussions
影響 *eikyō* influence, effect
音響 *onkyō* sound
交響 *kōkyō* reverberation
無響室 *mukyōshitsu* anechoic room
交響曲 *kōkyōkyoku* symphony
❷ abbrev. of 交響楽団 *kōkyō gakudan*: symphony orchestra
N響 *enukyō* NHK Symphony Orchestra
ボストン響 *bosutonkyō* Boston Symphony Orchestra

KUN

【hibi(ku) 響く】 reverberate, resound; ring, sound; vibrate; affect, have an unfavorable influence; get known
響き *hibiki* sound, echo; vibration; influence
鳴り響く *narihibiku* reverberate, echo, resound
地響き *jihibiki* earth tremor
暮らしに響く *kurashi ni hibiku* affect the cost of living
名が響いている *na ga hibiite iru* be famous

SYNONYMS

❶ⓐ **make sound or noise**
鳴 SOUND → 674
騒 CLAMOR → 1835
ⓑ **kinds of sound**
音 SOUND → 2070
声 VOICE → 2198
韻 melodious tone → 1811
玲 TINKLING OF JADES → 910

NOTE

⇨ see COMPOUND FORMATION for 影響 *eikyō* ⇨ 影 1889

11-9 殸

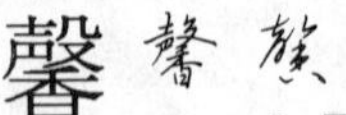

ⒸⒽ 馨 xīn

2879 KEI KYŌ NAMES ka kaoru kiyo yoshi

Radical	Strokes
香 186	20-9-11
Grade	**Freq**
Names	2065
2-11-9	

▶PERFUME

COMPOUNDS

● [original meaning, now archaic] perfume, fragrance, aroma
馨香 *keikō* (=*keikyō*) perfume, fragrance, aroma; honor, fame

NAMES

馨一 *keiichi* male name
馨 *kaoru* female name
馨邦 *yoshikuni* male name

SYNONYMS

● **smell and fragrance**
香 SWEET SMELL → 2568
気 smell → 3194
臭 BAD SMELL → 2633
芳 FRAGRANT → 2210
薫 BALMY → 2371
郁 AROMATIC → 1288

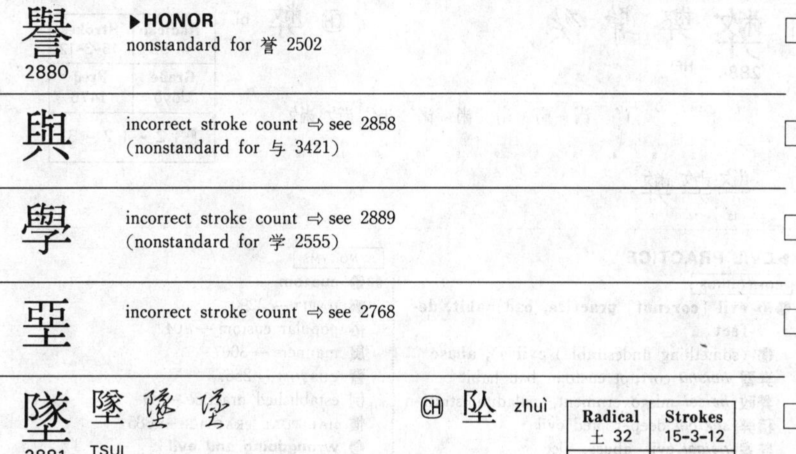

礜 2880 ▶**HONOR**
nonstandard for 誉 2502 — 11-9 䑕

與 incorrect stroke count ⇨ see 2858
(nonstandard for 与 3421) — 12-2 䑕

學 incorrect stroke count ⇨ see 2889
(nonstandard for 学 2555) — 12-2 䑕

堊 incorrect stroke count ⇨ see 2768 — 12-3 亞

墜 墜 墜 墜 2881 TSUI — 12-3 隊

Ⓒⓗ 坠 zhuì

Radical	Strokes
土 32	15-3-12
Grade	**Freq**
Jōyō	1198
2-12-3	

▶**DROP DOWN**

COMPOUNDS

❶ⓐ [original meaning] (fall suddenly from a great height) **drop down, drop, fall down, crash down**

ⓑ **cause to drop down, drop**

墜落 *tsuiraku* fall, crash

墜死する *tsuishi suru* fall to one's death (as from a cliff)

撃墜する *gekitsui suru* shoot down

❷ fall to ruin, decline, lose

失墜 *shittsui* loss, fall

SYNONYMS

❶ **descend and fall**

落 FALL → 2318
降 DESCEND → 458
下 go down → 3378
倒 TOPPLE → 124

2882 ▶**DROP DOWN**
nonstandard for 墜 2881 — 12-3 隊

2883 ▶**DEGENERATE**
nonstandard for 堕 2822 — 12-3 隋

12-3

弊 弊 弊 𢁉

2884 HEI

Ⓒ 弊 bì

Radical	Strokes
廾 55	15-3-12
Grade	**Freq**
Jōyō	1476
2-12-3	

▶EVIL PRACTICE

COMPOUNDS

❶ⓐ **evil [corrupt] practice, bad habit, defect**

ⓑ (something undesirable) **evil(s), abuse**

弊習 *heishū* corrupt custom, bad habit
弊政 *heisei* misgovernment, maladministration
積弊 *sekihei* deep-rooted evil
弊害 *heigai* evil, abuse, vice
悪弊 *akuhei* evil, vice, abuse
語弊 *gohei* defects in expression, improper word
党弊 *tōhei* party evils

❷ shabby, worn-out, ragged, poor, impoverished

弊衣破帽 *heiihabō* shabby clothes and an old hat
弊履 *heiri* worn-out sandals [shoes]

❸ [humble] **our [my] humble**

弊社 *heisha* our firm
弊店 *heiten* our shop

INDEPENDENT

[hei 弊] evil [corrupt] practice, bad habit, defect; (something undesirable) evil(s), abuse
飲酒の弊 *inshu no hei* bad habit of drinking
時代の弊 *jidai no hei* abuses of the times

SYNONYMS

❶ⓐ **custom**
癖 HABIT → 3290
俗 popular custom → 104
風 manners → 3007
習 CUSTOM → 2667
例 established practice → 89
慣 HABITUAL PRACTICE → 685

ⓑ **wrongdoing and evil**
悪 evil (something bad) → 2745
邪 wrong → 1124
非 wrong(doing) → 889
罪 sin → 2610

❷ **bad**
粗 COARSE → 1329
駄 GOOD FOR NOTHING → 1821
廃 WASTE → 3146
下 of low grade → 3378
劣 INFERIOR → 2395
悪 BAD → 2745

❸ **humble prefixes**
拙 my humble → 315
小 my little (*humble*) → 7
愚 my foolish → 2834

NOTE

★do not confuse with 幣 2885

12-3

幣 幣 幣 幣

2885 HEI nusa▲

Ⓒ 币 bì

Radical	Strokes
巾 50	15-3-12
Grade	**Freq**
Jōyō	1827
2-12-3	

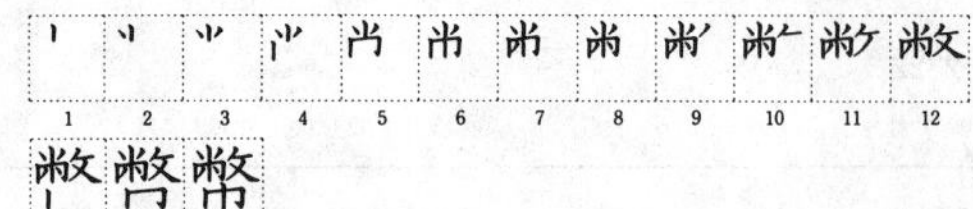

▶CURRENCY

COMPOUNDS

❶ **currency, money, coins, legal tender**

幣制 *heisei* currency [monetary] system
貨幣 *kahei* money, currency, coinage
造幣 *zōhei* coinage, mintage
紙幣 *shihei* paper currency, bank note, bill

❷ⓐ **offering of cloth or paper to the gods, esp. in Shinto rituals**

ⓑ offering (to a ruler or guest), tribute, present

幣帛 *heihaku* Shinto offering of cloth (or paper)
御幣 *gohei* pendant paper strips in a Shinto shrine, sacred staff with cut paper
奉幣 *hōhei* offering a wand with hemp and paper streamers to a Shinto god
幣物 *heimotsu* (= *heibutsu*) Shinto offerings;

present to a guest
幣貢 *heikō* tribute, offering

INDEPENDENT

【hei 幣】 Shinto offering of cloth or paper; tribute, present

KUN

【nusa 幣】 offering of cloth or paper to the gods, esp. in Shinto rituals
幣を奉る *nusa o tatematsuru* offer a wand with hemp and paper streamers to a Shinto god

SYNONYMS

❶ **money**
貨 MONEY (legal tender), coin → 2465
銭 MONEY → 1725
金 MONEY → 2057
銀 SILVER → 1722
財 finance → 1457
資 RESOURCES → 2695
-玉 coin suffix → 3477
札 bill → 817
❷ **offering**
貢 TRIBUTE → 2281

NOTE

★do not confuse with 弊 2884

弊
2886

▶EVIL PRACTICE
nonstandard for 弊 2884

12-3 敝

幣
2887

▶CURRENCY
nonstandard for 幣 2885

12-3 敝

導 導 導 导
2888 DŌ michibi(ku)

Ⓒⓗ 导 dǎo

Radical	Strokes
寸 41	15-3-12
Grade	**Freq**
Jōyō-5	488
2 - 1 2 - 3	

12-3 道

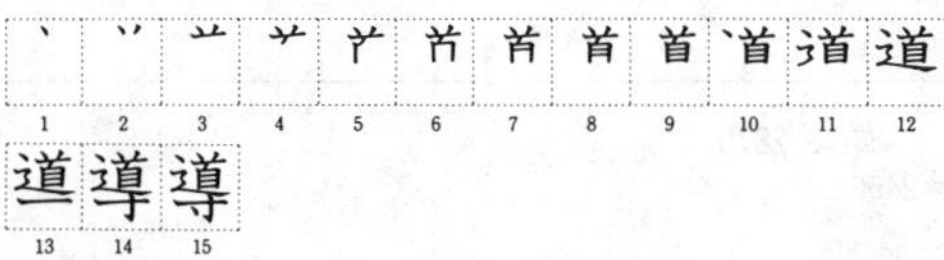

▶GUIDE

COMPOUNDS

❶ⓐ (show the way) **guide, lead, conduct**
ⓑ (give guidance to) **guide, teach, instruct, direct**
導入する *dōnyū suru* lead into, bring into
導因 *dōin* inducement, incentive
主導権 *shudōken* leadership, initiative
誘導する *yūdō suru* induce, incite; guide, lead
盲導犬 *mōdōken* guide dog, Seeing Eye dog
指導する *shidō suru* guide, lead, instruct
教導する *kyōdō suru* instruct, teach, train
❷ (serve as a medium) conduct, transmit
導火線 *dōkasen* fuse; cause, incentive
伝導 *dendō* conduction, transmission
半導体 *handōtai* semiconductor

KUN

【michibi(ku) 導く】 guide, lead, conduct, usher
導き *michibiki* guidance
導き出す *michibikidasu* draw (a conclusion), deduce
導き手 *michibikite* guide

SYNONYMS

❶ⓐ **lead and escort**
率 LEAD → 2118
引 lead → 181
連 take along → 3103
ⓑ **teach**
諭 ADMONISH → 1598
訓 INSTRUCT → 1454
迪 EDIFY → 3076
啓 ENLIGHTEN → 2763
教 TEACH → 1493
授 teach → 492
育 educate → 2050
練 TRAIN → 1375

學
2889

▶STUDY ▶EDUCATIONAL INSTITUTION
nonstandard for 学 2555

12-3 𦥯

12-4 亞

惡

incorrect stroke count ⇨ see 2788
(nonstandard for 悪 2745)

12-4 舌

憩

2890 KEI iko(i) iko(u)

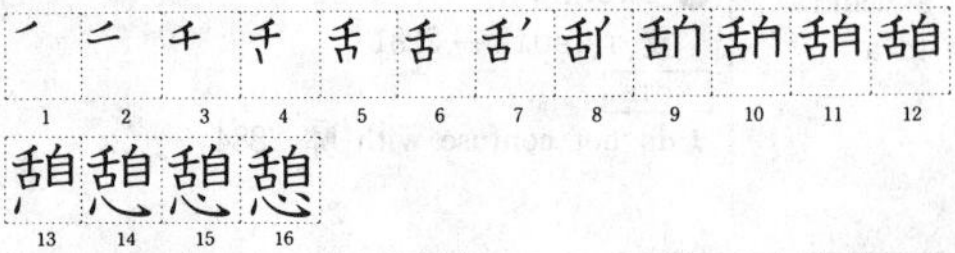

CH 憩 qì

Radical	Strokes
心 61	16-4-12
Grade	**Freq**
Jōyō	1427
2-12-4	

▶**TAKE A REST**

COMPOUNDS

● **take a rest, repose, relax, rest**

憩室 *keishitsu* diverticulum

休憩する *kyūkei suru* rest, repose

小憩 *shōkei* short rest, brief recess

KUN

【**iko(i) 憩い**】rest, repose, relaxation, vacation

憩いの場 *ikoi no ba* place for relaxation and refreshment

【**iko(u) 憩う**】take a rest, repose, relax, rest

木陰に憩う *kokage ni ikou* take a rest under a tree

SYNONYMS

● **rest**

休 REST → 52

息 rest → 2647

12-5 御

禦

incorrect stroke count ⇨ see 2870

12-6 與

擧

incorrect stroke count ⇨ see 2875
(nonstandard for 挙 2456)

12-6 敝

斃

2891 HEI tao(reru) tao(su)

CH 毙 bì

Radical	Strokes
攵 66	18-4-14
Grade	**Freq**
Reference	
2-12-6	

COMPOUNDS

❶ [now usu. 倒れる *taoreru*] [original meaning] fall down dead, perish, die

斃死する *heishi suru* fall dead, perish

凶弾に斃れる *kyōdan ni taoreru* be shot to death by an assassin

❷ [now usu. 倒す *taosu*] kill

敵を斃す *teki o taosu* kill one's enemy [opponent]

HOMOPHONES

taoreru ⇨ 倒 124

taosu ⇨ 倒 124

NOTE

⇨ see USAGE note at 倒 124

12-6 鄕

嚮

incorrect stroke count ⇨ see 2901

12-7 先先

贊

2892

▶**APPROVE OF** ▶**PRAISE**

nonstandard for 賛 2809

警 警 警 警

2893 KEI imashi(meru)▲

CH 警 jǐng

Radical	Strokes
言 149	19-7-12
Grade	Freq
Jōyō-6	335
2-12-7	

12-7 敬

一 1 十 2 艹 3 芦 4 芍 5 芍 6 苟 7 苟 8 苟 9 苟 10 荀 11 敬 12 敬 13 敬 14 敬 15 敬 16 警 17 警 18 警 19

▶**GUARD AGAINST** ▶**WARN**

COMPOUNDS

❶ⓐ **guard against, protect, police, watch**
ⓑ **guard, watchman, police officer**
警察 *keisatsu* police, police station
警官 *keikan* police officer, policeman
警視庁 *keishichō* Metropolitan Police Office
警戒 *keikai* caution, precaution, warning; watch, guard, vigilance
警備 *keibi* guard, defense
警手 *keishu* guard, attendant
夜警 *yakei* night watch; night watchman
婦警 *fukei* policewoman

❷ abbrev. of 警察 *keisatsu*: **police (force)**
警部 *keibu* police inspector
警務 *keimu* police affairs
県警 *kenkei* prefectural police
京都府警 *kyōtofukei* Kyoto Prefectural Police

❸ [original meaning] **warn, admonish**
警告 *keikoku* warning, admonition
警報 *keihō* warning signal, alarm
警鐘 *keishō* alarm bell, warning

❹ witty, smart, original, extraordinary
警句 *keiku* witticism
警抜な *keibatsu na* scintillating, extraordinarily excellent

KUN

【imashi(meru) 警める】
[usu. 戒める]
ⓐ caution against, admonish, warn
ⓑ take caution (against), take precautions, guard against
警め *imashime* caution, admonition, warning; caution, guard; commandment, precept
自ら警める *mizukara imashimeru* take precautions, guard against

SYNONYMS

❶ⓐ **protect**
衛 GUARD → 760
護 PROTECT → 1648
守 PROTECT → 2173
防 defend → 270
番 WATCH → 2748
保 PRESERVE → 96
看 CARE FOR → 3220
ⓐ **take precautions**
戒 take caution → 3204
❸ **warn**
戒 CAUTION → 3204
諭 ADMONISH → 1598
告 advise → 2409

HOMOPHONES

imashimeru ⇨ 戒 3204
imashime ⇨ 戒 3204

NOTE

⇨ see USAGE note at 戒 3204
★do not confuse with 驚 2894

譽

incorrect stroke count ⇨ see 2880
(nonstandard for 誉 2502)

12-9 且

饗 嚮

incorrect stroke count ⇨ see 13-9

12-9 郷

12-10 敬

驚 驚 驚 驚

2894 KYŌ odoro(ku) odoro(kasu)

CH 惊 jīng

Radical	Strokes
馬 187	22-10-12
Grade	**Freq**
Jōyō	1108
2-12-10	

▶**SURPRISE**

COMPOUNDS

ⓐ **surprise, startle, astonish, frighten**

ⓑ [original meaning] **be surprised, be startled, be astonished**

驚愕 *kyōgaku* astonishment, surprise, fright, shock

驚天動地 *kyōten-dōchi* world-shaking, astounding

驚嘆する *kyōtan suru* admire, wonder, be struck with admiration

驚異 *kyōi* wonder, marvel, miracle

驚喜 *kyōki* pleasant surprise

KUN

【odoro(ku) 驚く】 be surprised, be astonished, be startled; be frightened

驚き *odoroki* surprise, astonishment, amazement; fright

驚くべき *odorokubeki* astonishing, amazing, surprising, wonderful

【odoro(kasu) 驚かす】 surprise, astonish, amaze; frighten

驚かされる *odorokasareru* be surprised

世人を驚かす *sejin o odorokasu* strike terror in people's hearts

NOTE

★do not confuse with 警 2893

13-2 晢

質

incorrect classification ⇨ see 2808

13-2 替

賛

incorrect classification ⇨ see 2809

13-2 與

學

incorrect stroke count ⇨ see 2898
(nonstandard for 学 2555)

13-3 辟

壁 壁 壁

2895 HEKI kabe

CH 壁 bì

Radical	Strokes
土 32	16-3-13
Grade	**Freq**
Jōyō	1031
2-13-3	

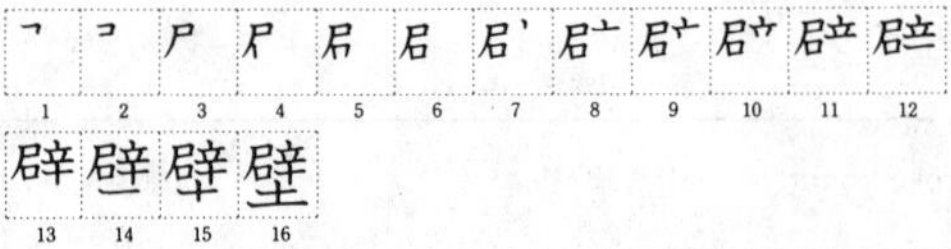

▶**WALL**

COMPOUNDS

[also suffix]

❶ [original meaning] **wall, partition, fence, barrier**

壁画 *hekiga* wall painting, fresco

障壁 *shōheki* [formerly also 牆壁] fence, wall; barrier

防火壁 *bōkaheki* fire wall

❷ **any wall-like structure such as a cliff or precipice**

絶壁 *zeppeki* precipice, cliff

岸壁 *ganpeki* quay (wall), wharf

胃壁 *iheki* walls of the stomach

北壁 *hokuheki* northern cliff

氷壁 *hyōheki* ice ridge

城壁 *jōheki* castle wall, rampart

火口壁 *kakōheki* crater wall

KUN

【kabe 壁】wall, partition, barrier
壁紙 *kabegami* wallpaper
壁塗り *kabenuri* plastering
壁新聞 *kabeshinbun* wall newspaper; wall poster
言葉の壁 *kotoba no kabe* language barrier

SYNONYMS

❶ **fences and walls**
塀 FENCE (for screening) → 557
垣 FENCE (for partitioning) → 351
囲い enclosure → 3069
欄 railing → 1103

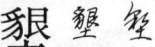

墾

2896 KON

CH 垦 kěn

Radical	Strokes
土 32	16-3-13
Grade	**Freq**
Jōyō	1876
2-13-3	

13-3 豤

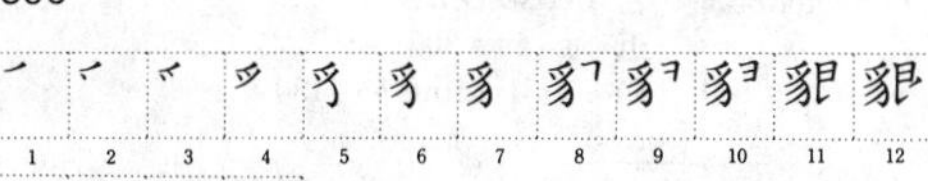

▶RECLAIM

COMPOUNDS

● [original meaning] **reclaim (wasteland), open up new land for farming, clear land, cultivate**
墾田 *konden* new rice field
開墾 *kaikon* clearing, reclamation
未墾の *mikon no* uncultivated, wild

SYNONYMS

● **reclaim**
拓 OPEN UP → 317
開 OPEN → 3321

NOTE

★do not confuse with 懇 2899

導

2897

▶GUIDE

nonstandard for 導 2888

13-3 道

學

2898

▶STUDY ▶EDUCATIONAL INSTITUTION

nonstandard for 学 2555

13-3 𦥯

懇

2899 KON nengo(ro)

CH 恳 kěn

Radical	Strokes
心 61	17-4-13
Grade	**Freq**
Jōyō	1115
2-13-4	

13-4 豤

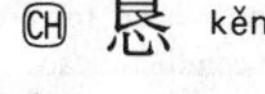

▶EARNEST ▶FAMILIAR

COMPOUNDS

❶ⓐ **earnest, fervent, sincere**
ⓑ cordial, kindly, kind
懇願する *kongan suru* beg earnestly, implore, entreat
懇望 *konmō* entreaty, solicitation, earnest request
懇請する *konsei suru* request earnestly, solicit, entreat
懇懇と *konkon to* earnestly, repeatedly
懇切な *konsetsu na* kind, cordial; exhaustive
懇篤 *kontoku* cordiality, kindness
懇書 *konsho* your kind letter
懇情 *konjō* kindliness

❷ **familiar, friendly, intimate**
懇談 *kondan* familiar talk [chat]
懇談会 *kondankai* social gathering; round table conference
懇意 *kon'i* intimacy, friendship; kindness
懇親 *konshin* friendship, intimacy
懇話 *konwa* friendly [familiar] chat [talk]

別懇 *bekkon* intimacy
❸ abbrev. of 懇談会 *kondankai*: round table conference, consultation
米懇 *beikon* Round Table Conference on Rice Price

KUN

【nengo(ro) 懇ろ】
nengoro na 懇ろな cordial, kind, hearty; polite, courteous; familiar, intimate
懇ろに葬る *nengoro ni hōmuru* bury with due ceremony
懇ろになる *nengoro ni naru* become acquainted; become intimate

SYNONYMS

❶ⓐ eager
切 eager → 27
篤 DEVOTED → 2716
熱 HOT → 2866
ⓑ kind
篤 cordial → 2716
厚 KIND → 3003
慈 AFFECTIONATE → 2339
温 warmhearted → 608
渥 GRACIOUS → 600
優 kindly → 177
❷ familiar and friendly
睦 FRIENDLY → 1199
親 INTIMATE → 1799
密 CLOSE → 2292
近 NEAR → 3061
和 HARMONIOUS → 1130

NOTE

★do not confuse with 墾 2896

13-4
殿

2900

▶STRIKE
nonstandard for 擊 2863

13-4
與

incorrect classification ⇨ see 2875
(nonstandard for 挙 2456)

13-6
郷

2901 KŌ KYŌ

Ⓒⓗ  xiàng 响 xiǎng

Radical	Strokes
口 30	19-3-16
Grade	Freq
Reference	
2-13-6	

COMPOUNDS

❶ [original meaning] go toward, head toward
嚮導する *kyōdō suru* guide, conduct, lead
❷ [now replaced by 向 *kō* 3052] turn toward, be inclined toward, lean toward
意嚮 *ikō* intention, inclination

13-6
殿

2902 KEI tsuna(gu) kaka(ru)

Ⓒⓗ 系 jì xì

Radical	Strokes
糸 120	19-6-13
Grade	Freq
Reference	
2-13-6	

COMPOUNDS

❶ [now replaced by 係 *kei* 97]
ⓐ [original meaning] connect, link, bind, fasten, anchor, moor
ⓑ be connected with, relate to
繫船 *keisen* mooring a ship
繫留 *keiryū* mooring, anchorage
手を繫ぐ *te o tsunagu* join hands (with)
繫属 *keizoku* pendency (of a legal case); relationship
繫争 *keisō* dispute, contention (of a legal case); lawsuit
連繫 *renkei* connection, linking, contact
❷ [now usu. 掛かる] anchor, moor
沖に繫る船 *oki ni kakaru fune* ship mooring off the coast

HOMOPHONES

kakaru ⇨ 掛 493 懸 2915 架 2569 係 97 罹 2619

NOTE
⇨ see USAGE note at 掛 493

2903 HI tato(eru)

Ⓒⓗ 譬 pì

Radical	Strokes
言 149	20-7-13
Grade	Freq
Reference	
2-13-7	

13-7 辟

COMPOUNDS
ⓐ [now also 比 *hi* 26] compare to, liken
ⓑ [also 喩える *tatoeru*] compare to, liken, speak figuratively
譬喩 *hiyu* simile, metaphor, allegory
譬え *tatoe* simile, metaphor, allegory
譬え話 *tatoebanashi* fable, allegory

死を眠りに譬える *shi o nemuri ni tatoeru* compare death to sleep

HOMOPHONES
tatoeru ⇨ 例 89 喩 553

NOTE
⇨ see USAGE note at 例 89

警
2904
▶**GUARD AGAINST** ▶**WARN**
nonstandard for 警 2893

13-7 敬

譽
incorrect classification ⇨ see 2880
(nonstandard for 誉 2502)

13-7 與

覺
2905
▶**PERCEIVE** ▶**COMMIT TO MEMORY**
nonstandard for 覚 2604

13-7 𦥯

饗
2906 KYŌ

Ⓒⓗ 飨 xiǎng

Radical	Strokes
食 184	22-9-13
Grade	Freq
Reference	
2-13-9	

13-9 鄉

COMPOUNDS
● [now replaced by 供 88] [original meaning] treat, provide dinner for, entertain, banquet

饗応 *kyōō* treat, feast, banquet
饗宴 *kyōen* banquet, feast, dinner
饗する *kyōsuru* treat, provide dinner for

響
2907
▶**REVERBERATE**
nonstandard for 響 2878

13-9 鄉

驚
2908
▶**SURPRISE**
nonstandard for 驚 2894

13-10 敬

14-2
臼

興 ⓒⒽ 兴 xīng xìng

2909 KŌ KYŌ oko(ru) oko(su)

Radical	Strokes
臼 134	16-7-9
Grade	**Freq**
Jōyō-5	696
2-14-2	

▶**RISE TO PROSPERITY**
▶**AMUSEMENT**

COMPOUNDS

❶ **rise to prosperity, rise, prosper, flourish**
興隆 *kōryū* prosperity, rise
興亡 *kōbō* rise and fall, ups and downs
興起する *kōki suru* rise, be in the ascendant; rouse, stir
新興の *shinkō no* rising, newly-established
勃興 *bokkō* sudden rise, sudden increase in power

❷ⓐ **cause to rise (to prosperity), promote, further, advance, develop**
ⓑ [formerly also 昂 *kō* 2412 or 亢 *kō* 1964] rouse up, be stirred, be excited
興業 *kōgyō* promotion of industry
興国 *kōkoku* making a country prosperous
興信所 *kōshinjo* private inquiry agency, credit bureau
振興 *shinkō* promotion, furtherance, rousing
復興する *fukkō suru* revive, restore to the original state, reconstruct
再興する *saikō suru* revive, restore
作興する *sakkō suru* promote; awaken, arouse, enhance
興奮する *kōfun suru* get excited, be agitated, be aroused

❸ **amusement, entertainment, fun, interest, desire to enjoy**
興味 *kyōmi* interest
興行 *kōgyō* public entertainment, show business
余興 *yokyō* entertainment, side show
遊興 *yūkyō* merrymaking, spree
感興 *kankyō* interest, fun, inspiration
一興 *ikkyō* amusement, fun

INDEPENDENT

【**kyō 興**】 interest, fun, amusement
興が有る *kyō ga aru* be interesting, be fun

【**kyōjiru (=kyōzuru) 興じる(=興ずる)**】 amuse oneself, have fun, make merry

KUN

【**oko(ru) 興る**】
① rise to prosperity, prosper, thrive, flourish
国が興る *Kuni ga okoru* The country prospers
② [also 起こる] (come into existence) rise, spring up, be established
新しい産業が興った *Atarashii sangyō ga okotta* A new industry has sprung up

【**oko(su) 興す**】 cause to rise (to prosperity), promote, further, advance, develop
工業を興す *kōgyō o okosu* promote industry
廃れた家を興す *sutareta ie o okosu* restore a family to its former prosperity

SYNONYMS

❶ **prospering and prosperity**
振 rise → 430
隆 PROSPER → 545
栄 FLOURISH → 2574
繁 THRIVE → 2853
盛 PROSPEROUS → 2675
昌 PROSPERING → 2414

❷ⓐ **advance**
進 ADVANCE → 3121
奨 ENCOURAGE → 2842
勧 encourage → 1857

❸ **pleasure**
娯 ENJOYMENT → 405
楽 PLEASURE → 2826

HOMOPHONES

okoru ⇨ 起 3307
okosu ⇨ 起 3307

NOTE

⇨ see USAGE note at 起 3307

14-4
與

擧

incorrect classification/stroke count ⇨ see 2875
(nonstandard for 挙 2456)

懲 懲 懲 懲 (CH) 惩 chéng

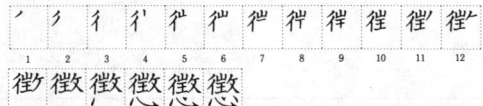

2910 CHŌ ko(riru) ko(rasu) ko(rashimeru)

Radical	Strokes
心 61	18-4-14
Grade	**Freq**
Jōyō	1479
2-1 4-4	

14-4 徴

▶**CHASTISE**

COMPOUNDS

● [original meaning] **chastise, punish, discipline**

懲悪 *chōaku* chastisement, punishment
懲罰 *chōbatsu* discipline, punishment
懲戒 *chōkai* official reprimand, discipline
懲役 *chōeki* penal servitude, imprisonment with hard labor

KUN

【ko(riru) 懲りる】 learn by experience, learn a lesson; have had enough of, be sick of
懲り懲りする *korigori suru* learn to one's sorrow
性懲りも無く *shōkori mo naku* incorrigibly

【ko(rasu) 懲らす】 chastise, punish, discipline
悪を懲らす *aku o korasu* punish the wicked

【ko(rashimeru) 懲らしめる】 same as **korasu** 懲らす
懲らしめ *korashime* chastisement

SYNONYMS

● **punishment**

罰 PUNISHMENT → 2613
刑 PENALTY → 830
処 DEAL WITH (lawbreakers) → 3031

璽 璽 璽 (CH) 玺 xǐ

2911 JI

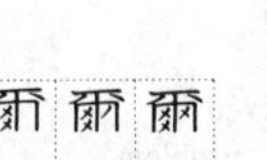

Radical	Strokes
玉 96	19-5-14
Grade	**Freq**
Jōyō	1918
2-1 4-5	

14-5 爾

▶**IMPERIAL SEAL**

COMPOUNDS

❶ⓐ **Imperial seal**
ⓑ [original meaning] seal
御璽 *gyoji* Imperial seal
国璽 *kokuji* seal of state

❷ sacred comma-shaped bead signifying Imperial sovereignty
神璽 *shinji* Yasakani no Magatama (one of the three insignia of the Imperial throne); Imperial seal

INDEPENDENT

【ji 璽】 seal (of state)

SYNONYMS

❶ **seals**

印 SEAL → 828
判 personal seal → 1122

譽 incorrect classification / stroke count ⇨ see 2880 (nonstandard for 誉 2502)

14-7 輿

覽 incorrect stroke count ⇨ see 2913 (nonstandard for 覧 2854)

14-7 臨

懲 **2912**

▶**CHASTISE**

nonstandard for 懲 2910

15-4 徴

15-7

覽 ▶LOOK OVER

2913

nonstandard for 覧 2854

16-2

雙 ▶SET OF TWO

2914

nonstandard for 双 25

16-4

懸 懸

2915 KEN KE ka(keru) ka(karu)

CH 悬 xuán

Radical	Strokes
心 61	20-4-16
Grade	**Freq**
Jōyō	1226
2-16-4	

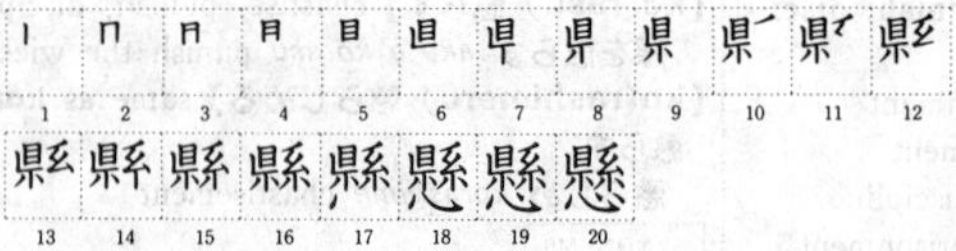

▶SUSPEND

COMPOUNDS

❶ **suspend, be suspended (in midair), hang (over), overhang**

懸垂 *kensui* suspension, pendency; chinning exercises

懸架 *kenga* suspension (of an automobile)

懸吊 *kenchō* suspension

懸濁 *kendaku chem* suspension

懸崖 *kengai* overhanging cliff

❷ **pending, unsettled, unresolved**

懸案 *ken'an* pending question [problem]

❸ occupy the mind, be anxious

懸念 *kenen* anxiety, concern, fear

懸想 *kesō* falling in love, attachment

❹ **stake, risk**

一生懸命(＝一所懸命)に *isshōkenmei* (＝*isshokenmei*) *ni* for life, with all one's might

❺ offer [set] a prize

懸賞 *kenshō* prize competition; prize, reward

❻ be (greatly) different from, be far apart

懸隔 *kenkaku* difference, discrepancy

懸絶 *kenzetsu* great difference

懸軍 *kengun* expeditionary army

KUN

【ka(keru) 懸ける】

① [sometimes also 賭ける] stake (one's life), risk

命懸けで *inochigake de* at the risk of one's life

② offer [set] a prize

賞金を懸ける *shōkin o kakeru* offer a prize

③ [in compounds] be (greatly) different from, be far apart

懸け離れる *kakehanareru* be far apart; be greatly different from

【ka(karu) 懸かる】

① be suspended in midair (as of the moon), hang

月が空に懸かる *Tsuki ga sora ni kakaru* The moon hangs in the sky

② have a prize offered, have a reward (set on one's head)

犯人の首に賞金が懸かっている *Hannin no kubi ni shōkin ga kakatte iru* There is a reward on the criminal's head

SYNONYMS

❶ **hang**

釣り- suspended → 1674

垂 HANG DOWN → 3565

掛ける HANG → 493

❹ **risk**

冒 RISK → 2434

HOMOPHONES

kakeru ⇨ 掛 493 架 2569 駆 1823 賭 1605 翔 1357

kakaru ⇨ 掛 493 架 2569 係 97 繋 2902 罹 2619

NOTE

⇨ see USAGE note at 掛 493

⇨ see COMPOUND FORMATION for 一生懸命(＝一所懸命) *isshōkenmei* (＝*isshokenmei*) ⇨ 生 3497

16-6

襲 ▶RAID

2916

nonstandard for 襲 2917

襲 襲 襲 襲

ⒸⒽ 袭 xí

2917 SHŪ oso(u)

Radical 衣 145	Strokes 22-6-16
Grade Jōyō	Freq 1184
2-16-6	

16-6 龍

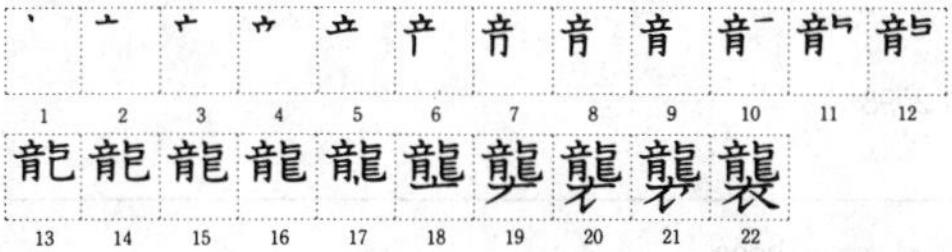

▶**RAID**

COMPOUNDS

❶ⓐ **raid, make a surprise attack on, assault, invade**

ⓑ **raid, surprise attack**

襲撃 *shūgeki* raid, attack, assault
来襲 *raishū* attack, invasion, raid
急襲 *kyūshū* raid, surprise attack
空襲 *kūshū* air raid
奇襲 *kishū* surprise attack
逆襲 *gyakushū* counterattack

❷ⓐ inherit old customs, carry on without change

ⓑ succeed, take over

踏襲 *tōshū* following (former policies)
因襲(=因習) *inshū* conventions
襲名 *shūmei* succession to another's professional name
世襲 *seshū* heredity, descent

❸ [original meaning, now archaic] wear one garment over another

襲衣する *shūi suru* wear one garment over another

KUN

【**oso(u)** 襲う】 raid, attack, invade; inherit, succeed

襲い掛かる *osoikakaru* assault, pounce upon, sweep down on (a person)
城を襲う *shiro o osou* raid a fort
大統領の後を襲う *daitōryō no ato o osou* succeed to the presidency

SYNONYMS

❶ **attack**

撃 STRIKE → 2863
攻 ATTACK → 242
侵 INVADE → 101
爆 bomb → 1101

彎

ⒸⒽ 弯 wān

2918 WAN

Radical 弓 57	Strokes 22-3-19
Grade Reference	Freq
2-19-3	

19-3 䜌

COMPOUNDS

● [now replaced by 湾 613] [original meaning] curve

彎曲 *wankyoku* curve, crook, bend
彎入する *wannyū suru* curve in

攣

ⒸⒽ 挛 luán

2919 REN tsu(ru)

Radical 手 64	Strokes 23-4-19
Grade Reference	Freq
2-19-4	

19-4 䜌

COMPOUNDS

[now usu. 吊る *tsuru*]

❶ [original meaning] cramp, have a cramp

痙攣 *keiren* convulsions, cramp

❷ turn up, slant upward

攣り目 *tsurime* slanted [upturned] eyes

HOMOPHONES

tsuru ⇨ 釣 1674 吊 2163

NOTE

⇨ see USAGE note at 釣 1674

19-4 變 2920

▶**CHANGE** ▶**ABNORMAL**
nonstandard for 変 2069

19-4 戀 2921

▶**LOVE**
nonstandard for 恋 2098

19-5 鹽

incorrect stroke count ⇨ see 2923
(nonstandard for 塩 631)

19-6 蠻 2922

▶**BARBARIAN**
nonstandard for 蛮 2129

20-5 鹽 2923

▶**SALT**
nonstandard for 塩 631

20-8 鑿 2924

SAKU nomi

CH 凿 záo zuò

Radical	Strokes
金 167	28-8-20
Grade	**Freq**
Reference	
2-20-8	

COMPOUNDS

❶ [now also 削 *saku* 1448] excavate, drill, bore, dig
鑿岩機 *sakuganki* rock drill
鑿井 *sakusei* well drilling
開鑿 *kaisaku* excavation, cutting, digging
掘鑿する *kussaku suru* dig out, excavate
穿鑿する *sensaku suru* scrutinize, dig into

❷ [original meaning] chisel
平鑿 *heisaku* flat chisel
斧鑿 *fusaku* [archaic] elaboration; lucubration; chisel and ax
鑿 *nomi* chisel

ENCLOSURE

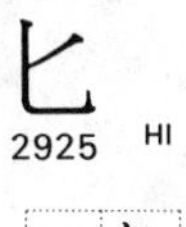

匕
2925 HI

ⒸⒽ 匕 bǐ

Radical	Strokes
匕 21	2-2-0
Grade	Freq
Reference	
□ 3-1-1	

1-1 乚

RADICAL 21
Standard form: 匕 *sajinohi* 'spoon' (北 化 匙)
Description: used in characters related to spoons or people

COMPOUNDS
❶ [original meaning, now archaic] spoon
匕箸 *hicho* spoon and chopsticks

❷ dagger
匕首 *hishu* (=*aikuchi*) dagger, dirk

刀 刀 刀
2926 TŌ katana

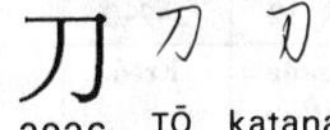

ⒸⒽ 刀 dāo

Radical	Strokes
刀 18	2-2-0
Grade	Freq
Jōyō-2	1417
□ 3-1-1	

1-1 ㇆

RADICAL 18
Standard form: 刀 *katana* 'sword' (分 切 剪)
Right variant: 刂 *rittō* (利 判 別)
Description: used in characters related to swords, cutting tools or cutting

▶**SWORD**

COMPOUNDS
● [also suffix] [original meaning] (**single-edged**) **sword, blade, cutting tool**
刀剣 *tōken* sword
刀身 *tōshin* sword blade
名刀 *meitō* excellent blade, famous sword
短刀 *tantō* dagger
彫刻刀 *chōkokutō* graver, chisel
日本刀 *nihontō* Japanese sword

INDEPENDENT
【**tō** 刀】sword, saber; burin

刀を帯びる *tō o obiru* wear a sword

KUN
【**katana** 刀】sword, blade
刀鍛冶 *katanakaji* sword smith
小刀 *kogatana* pocketknife
守り刀 *mamorigatana* sword for self-defense
懐刀 *futokorogatana* dagger; one's right-hand man, henchman
手刀 *tegatana* hand used like a sword in striking

SPECIAL READINGS
太刀 *tachi* long sword

竹刀 *shinai* bamboo sword

SYNONYMS

● **cutting instruments**

剣 SWORD (double-edged) → 1672
矛 HALBERD → 2008
鎌 SICKLE → 1760
刃 BLADE → 2929

1-1
乃

乃 乃 乃

2927 NAI DAI no sunawa(chi) NAMES osamu

CH 乃 nǎi

Radical	Strokes
丿 4	2-1-1
Grade	**Freq**
Names	1985
□ 3 - 1 - 1	

丿 乃
1 2

▶POSSESSIVE PARTICLE

COMPOUNDS

❶ **otherwise**

乃至 *naishi* from...to..., between...and...; or

❷ thou, you; your—also functions as a reflexive pronoun

乃父 *daifu* [rare] your father, father

乃公 *daikō* I

KUN

【no 乃】 possessive particle

日乃丸 *hinomaru* Rising Sun flag

波乃花 *nami no hana* crest of a wave; salt

【sunawa(chi) 乃ち】

ⓐ thereupon, whereupon, accordingly

ⓑ and then

戦えば乃ち勝つ *tatakaeba sunawachi katsu* win every battle (that is fought)

NAMES

乃木 *nogi* surname

乃木坂 *nogizaka* place name

乃武 *nobu* female name

清乃 *kiyono* female name

SYNONYMS

【no】

○ **possessive particles**

之 POSSESSIVE PARTICLE → 3420

HOMOPHONES

no ⇨ 之 3420

sunawachi ⇨ 即 1120

NOTE

⇨ see USAGE notes at 之 3420 and 即 1120

1-1
乀

八

2928

▶EIGHT

nonstandard for 八 3

Radical	Strokes
八 12	2-2-0
Grade	**Freq**
Variant	
□ 3 - 1 - 1	

丿 八
1 2

RADICAL 12

Standard form: 八 *hachigashira* 'eight' (兮)

Variant: 八 *hachi* (六 共 具)

Top variant: ﾍ *hachigashira* (兼)

Description: used for character classification

1-1
乀

incorrect classification ⇨ see 3370

1-2
乚

incorrect classification ⇨ see 3388

刃 刃 双 刃 刃 　㊥ 刃 rèn

2929 JIN NIN▲ ha yaiba▲

Radical	Strokes
刀 18	3-2-1
Grade	**Freq**
Jōyō	1587
口 3 - 1 - 2	

1-2 𠃍

ㇷ 刀 刃
1 2 3

▶BLADE

COMPOUNDS

❶ⓐ [original meaning] (part for cutting) **blade, edge**

ⓑ (weapon for cutting) **blade, sword, dagger, knife**

白刃 *hakujin* drawn sword
凶刃 *kyōjin* assassin's dagger [knife]
利刃 *rijin* sharp sword
兵刃 *heijin* sword

❷ cut

刃傷 *ninjō* bloodshed
自刃 *jijin* suicide by sword

INDEPENDENT

【jin 刃】 blade

KUN

【ha 刃】 blade, edge; [in compounds] sword

刃物 *hamono* edged tool, cutlery; sword
刃先 *hasaki* edge of a blade
両刃の *ryōba no* double-edged
刃渡り *hawatari* length of a sword; walking on the edge of a sword

【yaiba 刃】 blade; sword

刃を交える *yaiba o majieru* cross swords (with)
氷の刃 *kōri no yaiba* gleaming sword

SYNONYMS

❶ **cutting instruments**

刀 SWORD (single-edged) → 2926
剣 SWORD (double-edged) → 1672
矛 HALBERD → 2008
鎌 SICKLE → 1760

刄

2930

▶BLADE

nonstandard for 刃 2929

1-2 𠃍

巳 incorrect classification ⇨ see 3438

1-3 乚

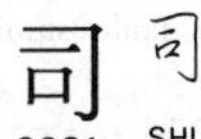

司 司 司 　㊥ 司 sī

2931 SHI tsukasado(ru)▲

Radical	Strokes
口 30	5-3-2
Grade	**Freq**
Jōyō-4	680
口 3 - 1 - 4	

1-4 𠃍

▶OFFICIATE

COMPOUNDS

❶ [original meaning] **officiate, administer, take charge of, manage**

司法 *shihō* administration of justice
司書 *shisho* librarian
司祭 *shisai* Catholic priest, rabbi
司直 *shichoku* administration of justice; judicial authorities
司令官 *shireikan* commander
司会する *shikai suru* preside at, take the chair, officiate; emcee (a show)

❷ [also suffix] officiator, officer, official, administrator

上司 *jōshi* superior officer; superior
行司 *gyōji* sumo umpire
保護司 *hogoshi* probation officer

❸ used phonetically for *shi*

寿司 *sushi* sushi (raw fish and vinegared rice)

KUN

【tsukasado(ru) 司る】 administer, officiate, take charge of, manage, preside over

国政を司る *kokusei o tsukasadoru* administer the affairs of state

SYNONYMS

❶ **direct and supervise**

宰 PRESIDE → 2275
営 MANAGE → 2603
理 manage → 970
経 MANAGE → 1331
督 SUPERVISE → 2796
監 OVERSEE → 2852
掌 TAKE CHARGE OF → 2602
轄 EXERCISE JURISDICTION OVER → 1627
管 EXERCISE CONTROL → 2701
制 CONTROL → 1274
❷ **officials**
僚 official → 165
吏 OFFICIAL → 3536
官 GOVERNMENT OFFICIAL → 2226
役 executive → 244
事 officer → 3567

1-5 迅 incorrect classification ⇨ see 3046

1-6 迅 incorrect classification ⇨ see 3202
(nonstandard for 迅 3046)

1-7 直 直 直 Ⓒⓗ 直 zhí

2932 CHOKU JIKI JIKA▲ tada(chini) nao(su) -nao(su) nao(ru) nao(ki) su(gu)▲

Radical	Strokes
目 109	8-5-3
Grade	**Freq**
Jōyō-2	314
口 3-1-7	

一 十 十 古 古 育 直 直
1 2 3 4 5 6 7 8

▶**STRAIGHT** ▶**FIX**

COMPOUNDS

❶ⓐ [original meaning] (unbent) **straight**
ⓑ (upright) **straight, vertical, perpendicular, right**
直線 *chokusen* straight line
直球 *chokkyū* straight ball [pitch]
直進する *chokushin suru* go straight on
直滑降 *chokkakkō* straight descent, schuss
直径 *chokkei* diameter
直視する *chokushi suru* look in the face, look straight at
硬直 *kōchoku* stiffness, rigidity
直立する *chokuritsu suru* stand erect [upright], rise perpendicularly
直角 *chokkaku* right angle
直円柱 *chokuenchū* right cylinder
垂直の *suichoku no* vertical, perpendicular
❷ⓐ **straight away, immediately**
ⓑ [also prefix] **direct, personal**
直後 *chokugo* immediately after
直答 *chokutō* prompt answer; direct answer
直答 *jikitō* direct answer
直流 *chokuryū* direct current
直通 *chokutsū* direct communication [service]; through service [traffic]
直感 *chokkan* intuition
直結する *chokketsu suru* connect directly with
直面する *chokumen suru* face, confront
直訳 *chokuyaku* literal translation
直喩 *chokuyu* simile
直筆 *jikihitsu* autograph, one's own handwriting
直輸入 *chokuyunyū* direct import [importation]
直談判 *jikadanpan* personal negotiations, direct bargaining
❸ **straightforward, straight, upright, honest**
正直な *shōjiki na* honest, upright, frank
実直な *jitchoku na* upright, honest, steady
愚直な *guchoku na* honest to a fault, stupidly honest
曲直 *kyokuchoku* right and wrong
司直 *shichoku* administration of justice; judicial authorities
❹ duty, watch
当直する *tōchoku suru* be on duty
宿直 *shukuchoku* night duty, night watch
❺ price, cost
安直な *anchoku na* cheap, inexpensive; easy, simple
高直な *kōjiki na* expensive
❻ *baseball* liner, line drive
左直 *sachoku* left liner

INDEPENDENT

【**jiki** 直】 at once, soon
直に *jiki ni* at once, soon, on the spot; easily
【**jika ni** 直に】 directly, at first hand; personally
【**choku na** 直な】 openhearted; free and easy; cheap

KUN

【tada(chini) 直ちに】 at once, immediately; directly

直ちに返事する *tadachini henji suru* replay immediately

【nao(su) 直す】

①ⓐ fix, repair, mend, set right

ⓑ fix up, adjust, put in order

直し物 *naoshimono* mending, thing to be mended

パンクを直す *panku o naosu* fix a flat tire

化粧直し *keshōnaoshi* adjusting one's makeup

② correct, rectify, remedy, reform, cure (a bad habit)

誤りを直す *ayamari o naosu* correct an error

行儀を直す *gyōgi o naosu* mend one's manners

③ⓐ alter, change

ⓑ convert

ⓒ render, translate

時間割りを直す *jikanwari o naosu* alter the schedule

キロをポンドに直す *kiro o pondo ni naosu* convert kilograms to pounds

日本語に直す *nihongo ni naosu* render into Japanese

【-nao(su) -直す】 verbal suffix indicating repetition: do over again

やり直す *yarinaosu* do over again

書き直す *kakinaosu* rewrite

思い直す *omoinaosu* reconsider, think better of

焼き直し *yakinaoshi* rebaking; adaptation (from)

【nao(ru) 直る】

① be fixed, be mended, be repaired

直らない *naoranai* irreparable, beyond repair

② be corrected, be reformed, be cured (of a bad habit)

悪癖が直る *akuheki ga naoru* get over a bad habit

③ⓐ be restored, return to normal

ⓑ improve in status, change for the better

仲直り *nakanaori* reconciliation

立ち直る *tachinaoru* regain one's footing, recover; (of the market) improve

開き直る *hirakinaoru* switch to a defiant attitude

【nao(ki) 直き】 *elegant* straight, upright, honest

素直な *sunao na* docile, obedient; honest, frank

【su(gu) 直ぐ】 at once, immediately, directly; soon; easily, readily; just, right

真っ直ぐに *massugu ni* dead straight; honestly

SYNONYMS

❶ⓐ straight

棒 straight → 983

ⓑ vertical

縦 VERTICAL → 1408

垂 perpendicular → 3565

立て- standing → 1992

❷ⓐ immediate

即 IMMEDIATE → 1120

❸ purehearted

惇 SINCERE → 486

敦 HONEST → 1693

廉 INCORRUPT → 3153

潔 IMMACULATE → 744

清 clean → 523

淳 PUREHEARTED → 514

純 PURE → 1297

【naosu】

①ⓐ **repair**

修 REPAIR → 123

繕 MEND → 1423

② **correct**

正 RIGHT → 3484

訂 REVISE → 1442

矯 RECTIFY → 1241

匡 RECTIFY → 2989

改 REFORM → 243

【-naosu】

○ **repeating and repetition**

-返す do over → 3060

-換える redo → 587

改 redo → 243

再 ANOTHER TIME → 3519

又 AGAIN → 3351

復 repeat → 575

重 DUPLICATE → 3573

畳 reduplicate → 2592

USAGE

❶ naosu

直す

①ⓐ fix, repair, mend, set right

ⓑ fix up, adjust, put in order

② correct, rectify, remedy, reform, cure (a bad habit)

③ⓐ alter, change

ⓑ convert

ⓒ render, translate

治す

cure, heal

❷ naoru

直る

① be fixed, be mended, be repaired

② be corrected, be reformed, be cured (of a bad habit)

③ⓐ be restored, return to normal

ⓑ improve in status, change for the better

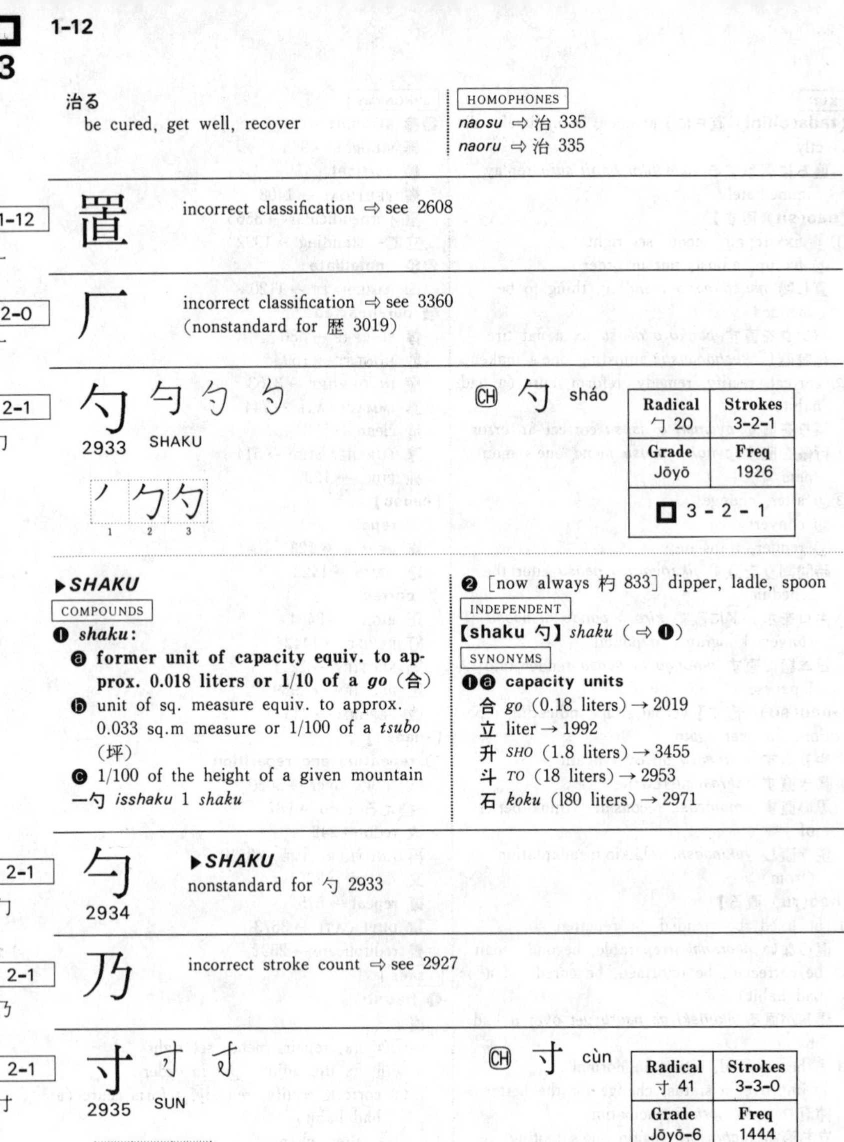

治る
be cured, get well, recover

HOMOPHONES
naosu ⇨ 治 335
naoru ⇨ 治 335

1-12 乚 置 incorrect classification ⇨ see 2608

2-0 厂 厂 incorrect classification ⇨ see 3360
(nonstandard for 歴 3019)

2-1 勹 勺 勺 勺 勺
2933 SHAKU

CH 勺 sháo

Radical	Strokes
勹 20	3-2-1
Grade	Freq
Jōyō	1926
□ 3 - 2 - 1	

▶SHAKU

COMPOUNDS

❶ ***shaku*:**
ⓐ **former unit of capacity equiv. to approx. 0.018 liters or 1/10 of a *go* (合)**
ⓑ unit of sq. measure equiv. to approx. 0.033 sq.m measure or 1/100 of a *tsubo* (坪)
ⓒ 1/100 of the height of a given mountain
一勺 *isshaku* 1 *shaku*

❷ [now always 杓 833] dipper, ladle, spoon

INDEPENDENT
【shaku 勺】 *shaku* (⇨ ❶)

SYNONYMS
❶ⓐ **capacity units**
合 *go* (0.18 liters) → 2019
立 liter → 1992
升 *SHO* (1.8 liters) → 3455
斗 *TO* (18 liters) → 2953
石 *koku* (180 liters) → 2971

2-1 勹 勺
2934

▶SHAKU
nonstandard for 勺 2933

2-1 ㇋ 乃 incorrect stroke count ⇨ see 2927

2-1 寸 寸 寸 寸
2935 SUN

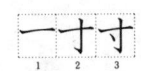

CH 寸 cùn

Radical	Strokes
寸 41	3-3-0
Grade	Freq
Jōyō-6	1444
□ 3 - 2 - 1	

RADICAL 41
Standard form: 寸 *sun* 'inch' (対 寺 将)
Description: used for character classification

▶A BIT OF

COMPOUNDS

❶ⓐ (of small amount) **a bit of, very little, small, brief**
ⓑ (of small size) **a bit of, very little,**

small
寸前に *sunzen ni* immediately before
寸時 *sunji* a moment, a minute
寸劇 *sungeki* skit, short play
寸描 *sunbyō* thumbnail [brief] sketch
寸断する *sundan suru* cut into pieces

[shreds]
❷ ***sun***, **(Japanese) inch: unit of length equiv. to approx. 3.03 cm or 1/10 of a *shaku* (尺)**
二寸 *nisun* 2 *sun*
❸ **measurement, measure, dimensions, length, size**
寸法 *sunpō* measurements, size; plan
原寸 *gensun* full [actual] size
採寸 *saisun* taking measurements
❹ [rare] rule, law

INDEPENDENT

【sun 寸】 measure, length; *sun* (⇨ ❷)
寸が足りない *sun ga tarinai* be too short

SPECIAL READINGS

一寸▲ *chotto* just a moment; just a little, a bit; [in negative constructions] easily, readily

SYNONYMS

❶ⓐ few
微 SLIGHT → 639
薄 meager → 2370
乏 SCANTY → 1933
寡 FEW → 2344
少 LITTLE → 3467
ⓑ small and tiny
微 SLIGHT → 639
細 MINUTE → 1333
小 SMALL → 7
豆- miniature → 1943
❷ length units
尺 *SHAKU* (30.3 cm) → 3440
米 meter → 3529
尋 fathom (1.8 m) → 2322
間 *ken* (1.8 m) → 3323
丈 *jo* (3.03 m) → 3419
町 *cho* (109 m) → 1113
里 LEAGUE, *ri* (3.4 km) → 3542
❸ size
大 size → 3416

万 萬 万 𠀋

2936 MAN BAN yorozu▲

CH 万 wàn mò

Radical	Strokes
一 1△	3-1-2
Grade	**Freq**
Jōyō-2	115
口 3-2-1	

2-1 丆

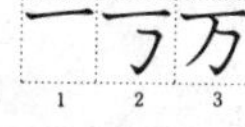

▶TEN THOUSAND

COMPOUNDS

❶ ten thousand
万年 *mannen* 10,000 years, eternity
万一 *man'ichi* (=*man'itsu*) if by any chance
一万 *ichiman* 10,000
❷ⓐ myriad, multitude, many
ⓑ all
万緑 *banryoku* myriad green leaves
万歳 *banzai* Banzai! / Hurrah! / Long live...!
巨万 *kyoman* myriads, millions, vast fortune
万国 *bankoku* all nations
万病 *manbyō* all kinds of diseases
万全の *banzen no* perfect, infallible, absolutely secure
万能 *bannō* omnipotence
万事 *banji* all things, everything
❸ used phonetically for *man*
万引 *manbiki* shoplifting
❹ [original meaning, now obsolete] scorpion

INDEPENDENT

【man 万】 ten thousand
【ban 万】 by any chance
万已むを得なければ *ban yamu o enakereba* if necessary

KUN

【yorozu 万】 ten thousand, myriad; all things, everything
万屋 *yorozuya* general dealer; Jack-of-all-trades

SYNONYMS

❶ large numbers
千 THOUSAND → 3411
億 HUNDRED MILLION → 170
百 HUNDRED → 2026
兆 TRILLION → 225
京 ten quadrillion → 2052
❷ⓐ many
百 numerous → 2026
多 MANY → 2170
豊 PLENTIFUL → 2697
沢 plentiful → 267
穣 YIELDING ABUNDANTLY → 1250
裕 ABUNDANT → 1195
富 RICH → 2310
ⓑ all
皆 ALL → 2445
都 all → 1686
全 WHOLE → 2022
一 all in one → 3341
満 FULL → 607
丸 complete(ly) → 3417
完 COMPLETE → 2201
総 TOTAL → 1379
諸 VARIOUS → 1577

毎 EVERY → 2034 | 各 EACH → 2168

2-1
ナ

尢
2937

一 ナ 尢
1 2 3

Radical	Strokes
尢 43	3-3-0
Grade	Freq
Radical	
□ 3 - 2 - 1	

RADICAL 43
Standard form: 尢 *mageashi* 'lame' (就 尤 尨)
Description: used in characters related to lameness or physical disability

2-1
几

凡 凡 凡 凡 ㊥ 凡 fán
2938 BON HAN oyo(so)▲ ōyo(so)▲ sube(te)▲

ノ 几 凡
1 2 3

Radical	Strokes
几 16	3-2-1
Grade	Freq
Jōyō	1517
□ 3 - 2 - 1	

▶**COMMONPLACE**

COMPOUNDS

❶ [also prefix] **commonplace, mediocre, ordinary, common**
凡庸な *bon'yō na* commonplace, mediocre, banal
凡才 *bonsai* mediocrity, ordinary ability; (man of) mediocrity, man of no genius
凡夫 *bonpu* (=*bonbu*) ordinary man; *Buddhism* common mortal
凡人 *bonjin* (man of) mediocrity, ordinary person
凡俗 *bonzoku* mediocrity, commonplaceness; (man of) mediocrity, ordinary person
凡フライ *bonfurai* easy fly (in baseball)
凡試合 *bonshiai* dull game (of baseball)
平凡な *heibon na* common, ordinary, commonplace, mediocre
非凡な *hibon na* rare, unique, extraordinary

❷ every, all
凡百の *bonpyaku no* many, many kinds of
凡例 *hanrei* introductory remarks, explanatory notes, legend

INDEPENDENT

【**bon 凡**】mediocrity
凡ならざる人物 *bonnarazaru jinbutsu* remarkable man, man of unusual ability

KUN

【**oyo(so), ōyo(so) 凡そ**】generally, on the whole; approximately, almost; quite, entirely
凡そ正しい *oyoso tadashii* be right on the whole
凡その見当 *oyoso no kentō* rough estimation
凡そ百人 *oyoso hyakunin* about 100 people
凡そ無意味だ *oyoso muimi da* be quite meaningless

【**sube(te) 凡て**】
[also 全て or 総べて]
①ⓐ all, everything, the whole
ⓑ entirely, wholly
凡ての *subete no* all, entire, whole
② generally, as a rule

SYNONYMS

❶ **ordinary**
庸 MEDIOCRE → 3128
普 common → 2323
平 common → 3478
只- ORDINARY → 2155
並 ordinary → 2246
常 NORMAL → 2590

USAGE

subete
凡て
[also 全て or 総べて]
①ⓐ all, everything, the whole
ⓑ entirely, wholly
② generally, as a rule
全て
[also 凡て or 総べて] same as 凡て
総べて
[also 凡て or 全て] same as 凡て

HOMOPHONES

subete ⇨ 全 2022 総 1379

凡 **▶COMMONPLACE**
2939 nonstandard for 凡 2938

2-1 凡

山 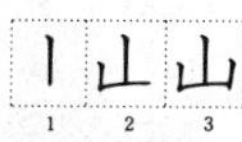 Ⓒⓗ 山 shān
2940 SAN SEN▲ yama

Radical	Strokes
山 46	3-3-0
Grade	**Freq**
Jōyō-1	70
□ 3-2-1	

2-1 山

RADICAL 46
Standard form: 山 *yama* 'mountain' (島 岡 岳)
Left variant: 山 *yamahen* (崎 峰 岬)
Top variant: 山 *yamakanmuri* (岩 岸 崩)
Description: used in characters related to mountains

▶MOUNTAIN

COMPOUNDS

❶ⓐ [original meaning] **mountain**
ⓑ **suffix after names of mountains**
山岳 *sangaku* mountains
山脈 *sanmyaku* mountain range
登山 *tozan* mountain climbing, mountaineering
火山 *kazan* volcano
富士山 *fujisan* Mt. Fuji
須弥山 *shumisen* Mt. Sumeru (in Buddhism, said to be the highest mountain rising in the center of the world)

❷ mine
鉱山 *kōzan* mine
閉山 *heizan* closing a mine; closing of the climbing season

❸ⓐ Buddhist temple
ⓑ suffix after names of Buddhist temples
山門 *sanmon* main temple gate
本山 *honzan* head temple; this temple
高野山 *kōyasan* name of a Buddhist temple

KUN

【yama 山】 mountain, peak; heap, pile; crown (of a hat); speculation; climax; forest; mine
山山 *yamayama* mountains; very much
岩山 *iwayama* rocky mountain
トマト一山 *tomato hitoyama* a pile of tomatoes
山場 *yamaba* climax, turning point
硫黄山 *iōyama* sulfur mine

SPECIAL READINGS

山車 *dashi* festival car, float
山羊▲ *yagi* goat

SYNONYMS

❶ **mountains**
岳 HIGH MOUNTAIN → 2557
峰 PEAK → 411

❷ **mine**
鉱 MINE → 1709
坑 PIT → 236

NOTE

⇨ see COMPOUND FORMATION for 梁山泊 *ryōzanpaku* ⇨ 泊 331

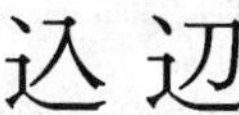

込 辺 incorrect stroke count ⇨ see □ 3-2

2-2 辶

2-2 ⊥

止 止 ㄴ

Ⓒ 止 zhǐ

2941 SHI to(maru) -do(mari) to(meru) -to(meru) -do(me) todo(meru)▲ todo(me)▲ todo(maru)▲ ya(meru)▲ ya(mu)▲ -ya(mu)▲ yo(su)▲ -sa(su)▲ -sa(shi)▲

Radical	Strokes
止 77	4-4-0
Grade	**Freq**
Jōyō-2	331
口 3-2-2	

丨 1 ⺊ 2 ⺊ 3 止 4

RADICAL 77

Standard form: 止 *tomeru* 'stop' (正 歩 武)
Left variant: 止 *tomehen* (此)
Description: used in characters related to feet or actions using feet

▶STOP

COMPOUNDS

❶ⓐ (cease moving) **stop, come to a standstill, halt; stop over**
ⓑ (motionless) **still, quiet**
止宿 *shishuku* lodging
停止する *teishi suru* stop, stand still; suspend, put to an end
静止する *seishi suru* stand still, come to a standstill
止水 *shisui* still water
黙止する *mokushi suru* keep quiet; take no measures

❷ⓐ (cease acting) **stop, cease, discontinue**
ⓑ **cause to stop, arrest, discontinue, suspend**
終止 *shūshi* termination, cessation
休止 *kyūshi* pause, standstill, dormancy; rest
止血する *shiketsu suru* stop [arrest] bleeding
中止する *chūshi suru* suspend, stop, discontinue
廃止する *haishi suru* abolish, abandon, discontinue

❸ **stop an action from occurring, check, deter, dissuade**
止音器 *shionki* (piano) damper
抑止する *yokushi suru* deter, check, hold back
阻止する *soshi suru* obstruct, check, hinder
制止する *seishi suru* control, check, stop (a person) from (doing)
禁止 *kinshi* prohibition, forbiddance, ban
防止 *bōshi* prevention, check
諌止する *kanshi suru* dissuade

❹ behavior, manner
挙止 *kyoshi* bearing, deportment

❺ *śamatha*: concentrating the mind, calming oneself (in Buddhism)
止観 *shikan* giving up illusions and attaining enlightenment

❻ unclassified compounds
笑止千万 *shōshisenban* be highly ridiculous, quite absurd

INDEPENDENT

【shi 止】 *śamatha* (⇨❺); OFF (marking on taps or valves)

KUN

【to(maru) 止まる】
①ⓐ come to a stop, stop, halt
ⓑ [formerly also 停まる] (of vehicles) roll to a stop, stop (at a station)
ⓒ be stopped up
止まり *tomari* stop, stoppage; end
止まり木 *tomarigi* perch, roost; footrail
立ち止まる *tachidomaru* stop, halt, stand still
駅に止まる *eki ni tomaru* stop at a station
② (cease acting) stop, cease; be suspended, be interrupted
行き止まり *ikidomari* dead end, blind alley, *cul-de-sac*
血が止まる *chi ga tomaru* stop bleeding

【-do(mari) -止まり】
[suffix]
① stop, stopping, last stop
品川止まり *shinagawadomari* train whose last stop is Shinagawa Station
② limit, extreme
高いと言っても一万円止まりだ *Takai to itte mo ichiman'endomari da* Ten thousand yen is as high as the price will go
あいつは課長止まりだ *Aitsu wa kachōdomari da* The likes of him will never be promoted beyond section chief

【to(meru) 止める】
①ⓐ (arrest motion) stop, bring to a standstill, arrest
ⓑ [formerly also 停める] (bring a vehicle to a temporary halt) stop (a bus or train), bring to a halt, brake
呼び止める *yobitomeru* stop, call to stop
受け止める *uketomeru* stop, catch; receive
塞き止める *sekitomeru* dam up
車を止める *kuruma o tomeru* bring a car to a halt

② (cause an action to cease) stop (an engine), turn off; arrest, stop, hold
止め処無く *tomedo naku* endlessly, ceaselessly
ガスを止める *gasu o tomeru* turn off the gas
通行止め *tsūkōdome* suspension of traffic
消し止める *keshitomeru* put out, extinguish
客止め *kyakudome* full house
打ち止め *uchidome* close, end
③ⓐ stop an action from occurring, check, arrest
ⓑ stop a person from doing, dissuade
食い止める *kuitomeru* check, hold back
差し止める *sashitomeru* prohibit, forbid; suspend (a paper)
口止めする *kuchidome suru* forbid to mention, hush up
【-to(meru) -止める】[also -留める] kill
射止める *itomeru* shoot to death; win, acquire
突き止める *tsukitomeru* ascertain, run to the ground; [archaic] stab [thrust] to death
【-do(me) -止め】
① device for stopping, stopper
車止め *kurumadome* bumping post, bumper
歯止め *hadome* drag, pallet; brake
滑り止め *suberidome* tire chains; creepers; taking the entrance examination to a university as a safety measure in case one fails at other universities
② something that prevents, preventive
咳止め *sekidome* cough medicine
錆止め *sabidome* anticorrosive, rust preventive
【todo(meru) 止める】
① (arrest motion) stop, arrest
押し止める *oshitodomeru* stop, check, keep back
② confine (oneself) to, be restricted to
...と言うだけに止めよう *...to iu dake ni todomeyō* Suffice it to say that...
【todo(me) 止め】 finishing blow, *coup de grâce*
止めを刺す *todome o sasu* finish by a stab in the neck; put an end to
花は桜に止めを刺す *Hana wa sakura ni todome o sasu* Of all flowers cherry blossom is the best
【todo(maru) 止まる】
① come to a stop, stop, halt
思い止まる *omoitodomaru* give up (a plan), desist from (doing)
② be limited [confined] to
単に希望を述べたに止まる *Tan ni kibō o nobeta ni todomaru* I simply expressed my desire
【ya(meru) 止める】
①ⓐ stop (performing an action), cease, discontinue
ⓑ give up, abandon, quit
仕事を止める *shigoto o yameru* stop [leave off] work
止めになる *yame ni naru* be discontinued, be given up
取り止める *toriyameru* cancel, call off
煙草を止める *tabako o yameru* give up smoking
② abolish, do away with
【ya(mu) 止む】
ⓐ [sometimes also 已む] stop, cease, come to an end
ⓑ abate, die away
嵐が止んだ *Arashi ga yanda* The storm has calmed down
【-ya(mu) -止む】[verbal suffix] stop, come to an end
泣き止む *nakiyamu* stop crying, cry oneself out
雨が降り止んだ *Ame ga furiyanda* It stopped raining
【yo(su) 止す】 stop, drop, give up
止せ *Yose* Cut it out!
【-sa(su) -止す】[verbal suffix] leave something unfinished, stop in the middle
言い止す *iisasu* break off, stop (in the middle of a sentence)
【-sa(shi) -止し】[verbal suffix] leaving something unfinished
読み止しの本 *yomisashi no hon* unfinished book

SPECIAL READINGS
波止場 *hatoba* wharf, quay

SYNONYMS
❶ⓐ stop
停 HALT → 139
駐 park → 1826
ⓑ not moving
静 still → 1728
定 fixed → 2229
固 FIRM → 3086
❷ discontinue
絶 BREAK OFF → 1353
断 CUT OFF → 1492
廃 ABOLISH → 3146
休 suspend → 52
停 suspend → 139
❸ prevent
防 PREVENT → 270

USAGE
❶ tomaru
止まる
①ⓐ come to a stop, stop, halt
ⓑ [formerly also 停まる] (of vehicles) roll to a stop, stop (at a station)
ⓒ be stopped up
② (cease acting) stop, cease; be suspend-

ed, be interrupted

留まる

① be held in position, be fastened

②ⓐ remain in one's perception, strike one's senses

ⓑ [in compounds] remain, be left over

③ perch on

泊まる

① stay overnight, lodge, stay at

② stay at anchor

③ be on night duty

停まる

[now usu. 止まる] (of vehicles) roll to a stop, stop (at a station)

❷ tomari

止まり

ⓐ stop, stoppage

ⓑ end

泊まり

①ⓐ stopover, stay

ⓑ night duty

② anchorage

❸ tomeru

止める

①ⓐ (arrest motion) stop, bring to a standstill, arrest

ⓑ [formerly also 停める] (bring a vehicle to a temporary halt) stop (a bus or train), bring to a halt, brake

② (cause an action to cease) stop (an engine), turn off; arrest, stop, hold

③ⓐ stop an action from occurring, check, arrest

ⓑ stop a person from doing, dissuade

留める

①ⓐ keep in place, retain, fix, fasten

ⓑ keep (a parcel) until called for

ⓒ keep in custody, detain

ⓓ (keep a vehicle from moving) park

② keep in mind

③ keep (a quarrel) from intensifying, stop

泊める

① lodge, give shelter, accommodate

② anchor a ship

停める

[now usu. 止める] (bring a vehicle to a temporary halt) stop (a bus or train), bring to a halt, brake

❹ -tomeru

-止める

[also -留める] kill

-留める

[also -止める]

① kill

② write down, register

★Both forms are used in compounds in the sense of kill, but -留める is preferred in the word 仕留める *shitomeru* 'kill, shoot dead'. *Tomeru* is not used independently in this sense.

❺ -dome

-止め

① device for stopping, stopper

② something that prevents, preventive

-留め

clip, fastener, retainer

❻ todomeru

止める

① (arrest motion) stop, arrest

② confine (oneself) to, be restricted to

留める

① leave (behind)

② make stay, detain

❼ todomaru

止まる

① come to a stop, stop, halt

② be limited [confined] to

留まる

stay behind, remain

❽ yamu

止む

ⓐ [sometimes also 已む] stop, cease, come to an end

ⓑ abate, die away

已む

ⓐ (cannot) help

ⓑ [usu. 止む] come to an end

HOMOPHONES

tomaru ⇨ 留 2580 泊 331 停 139

tomari ⇨ 泊 331

tomeru ⇨ 留 2580 泊 331 停 139

-tomeru ⇨ 留 2580

-dome ⇨ 留 2580

todomeru ⇨ 留 2580

todomaru ⇨ 留 2580

yameru ⇨ 辞 1364 罷 2617

yamu ⇨ 已 3377

-sasu ⇨ 差 3311 指 378 刺 1275 挿 431 注 325 射 1458

-sashi ⇨ 差 3311 刺 1275 指 378

NOTE

⇨ see also USAGE notes at 辞 1364 and 差 3311

勾

2942 KŌ

CH 勾 gōu gòu

Radical	Strokes
勹 20	4-2-2
Grade	Freq
Reference	
□ 3 - 2 - 2	

2-2 勹

COMPOUNDS

❶ [now also 拘 310] arrest, detain, confine
勾引 *kōin* arrest, custody
勾留 *kōryū* detention for investigation

❷ hook, curve, bend
勾配 *kōbai* slope, incline
勾玉(＝曲玉) *magatama* comma-shaped bead

勿

2943 MOCHI MOT- naka(re)

CH 勿 wù

Radical	Strokes
勹 20	4-2-2
Grade	Freq
Reference	
□ 3 - 2 - 2	

2-2 勹

COMPOUNDS

❶ do not, not, never
勿論 *mochiron* of course, no doubt, naturally
勿忘草 *wasurenagusa* forget-me-not
勿れ主義の道徳 *nakareshugi no dōtoku* negative virtues
恐るる勿れ *Osoruru nakare* Be not afraid!

❷ [sometimes also 物 *motsu* 874] used phonetically for *mot-*
勿体 *mottai* air of importance, superior airs
勿体無い *mottainai* wasteful; be more than one deserves
勿怪の幸い *mokke no saiwai* piece of good luck, windfall

NOTE

⇨ see COMPOUND FORMATION for 勿論 *mochiron* ⇨ 論 1574

匂

2944 nio(u) nio(i) nio(waseru)

CH none (国字)

Radical	Strokes
勹 20	4-2-2
Grade	Freq
Reference	
□ 3 - 2 - 2	

2-2 勹

COMPOUNDS

❶ smell (sweet), give out a smell [fragrance]
香水が髪から匂った *Kōsui ga kami kara niotta* Her hair emitted a fragrance

❷ (of blossoms) glow, be shiningly beautiful
桜が咲き匂う *Sakura ga sakiniou* Cherry trees are in beautiful bloom

❸ⓐ [original meaning] smell, scent, fragrance, aroma
ⓑ flavor, touch (of something agreeable)
文学的な匂い *bungakuteki na nioi* literary flavor

❹ⓐ give out an odor [scent]
ⓑ drop a hint, give an inkling (of)
介入を匂わせる *kainyū o niowaseru* hint at one's intervention

HOMOPHONES

niou ⇨ 臭 2633
nioi ⇨ 臭 2633

NOTE

⇨ see USAGE note at 臭 2633

2-2
厂

反 2945

HAN HON TAN HO▲ so(ru) so(rasu) kae(su)▲ kae(ru)▲ -kae(ru)▲

CH 反 fǎn

Radical	Strokes
又 29	4-2-2
Grade	**Freq**
Jōyō-3	156
口 3-2-2	

1 2 3 4

▶**COUNTER**

COMPOUNDS

❶ⓐ **counter, oppose, go against**
ⓑ **act contrary to (the rule), act against, violate, infringe**
ⓒ [formerly also 叛 *han, hon* 1143] rebel, revolt
反対する *hantai suru* oppose, object (to)
反抗 *hankō* resistance, opposition, defiance
反目 *hanmoku* antagonism, hostility, feud
反則 *hansoku* violation of rules, infringement, foul
違反(=違犯)する *ihan suru* violate (the law), infringe; act contrary to
背反する *haihan suru* revolt, rebel; go against, violate
反乱 *hanran* rebellion, revolt
反逆 *hangyaku* revolt, rebellion, mutiny
離反 *rihan* estrangement, alienation, desertion
謀反 *muhon* rebellion, revolt, treason

❷ [also prefix] **counter, counter-, anti-, opposite, reverse, inverse**
反発する *hanpatsu suru* repulse, repel; rally; oppose
反論 *hanron* counterargument, refutation
反撃 *hangeki* counterattack
反動 *handō* backlash, recoil, reaction
反戦 *hansen* antiwar
反米 *hanbei* anti-America
反落 *hanraku* reactionary fall (in stock prices)
反比例 *hanpirei* inverse proportion
反政府 *hanseifu* anti-government

❸ⓐ [original meaning] turn over, reverse
ⓑ **return in the original direction, reflect, be reflected; react**
反転する *hanten suru* turn around, reverse, roll over
反側する *hansoku suru* turn over in bed
反応 *hannō* reaction, response
反響 *hankyō* echo, reverberation; response, repercussions
反射 *hansha* reflection
反省 *hansei* reflection, introspection

❹ repeat
反復 *hanpuku* repetition, reiteration
反芻 *hansū* chewing the cud, rumination

❺ *tan*:
ⓐ unit for measuring rolls of cloth equiv. to approx. 10.6 m in length and 34 cm in width
ⓑ [formerly also 段 *tan* 1144] unit of sq. measure equiv. to approx. 9.9 ares or 300 *bu* (歩)
ⓒ former unit of length equiv. to approx. 10.9 m or 6 *ken* (間)
反物 *tanmono* cloth, textiles, dry goods
木綿三反 *momen santan* three rolls of cotton cloth
土地四反 *tochi yontan* a lot of 4 *tan* (approx. 1 acre)

❻ unclassified compounds
反古(=反故) *hogo* (=*hogu*) wastepaper, scrap of paper

INDEPENDENT

【**han** 反】 antithesis
正と反 *sei to han* thesis and antithesis
【**hansuru** 反する】 oppose, be opposed to, go against; act contrary to (the rule), act against, violate, infringe
【**tan** 反】 *tan* (⇨ ❺)

KUN

【**so(ru)** 反る】 *vi* bend, curve, warp, lean backwards
反り *sori* curve, bend, warp; disposition, natural inclination
反った板 *sotta ita* warped board
反り返る *sorikaeru* warp, bend backwards; throw back one's head
【**so(rasu)** 反らす】 *vt* bend (backward), curve, warp
体を反らす *karada o sorasu* bend oneself backward
胸を反らす *mune o sorasu* throw out one's chest, be puffed up with pride
【**kae(su)** 反す】 *vt* turn over, overturn, upset, reverse
干し草を反す *hoshikusa o kaesu* turn over hay
【**kae(ru)** 反る】 *vi* turn over, become overturned
スカートの裾が反る *Sukāto no suso ga kaeru* The hem of the skirt turns over
【**-kae(ru)** -反る】 [also -返る] [emphatic verbal suffix] utterly, completely
呆れ反る *akirekaeru* be utterly amazed

SYNONYMS

❶ⓐ **resist**
対 OPPOSE → 831
逆 rebel → 3091
抵 RESIST → 319
抗 RESIST → 252
耐 WITHSTAND → 1282
ⓑ **violate**
背 go against → 2573
犯 offend against → 196
破 BREAK → 1150
違 VIOLATE → 3151
❷ **opposite**
対 OPPOSITE → 831
逆 REVERSE → 3091
倒 upside-down → 124
❸ⓐ **overturn**
覆 OVERTURN → 2726
翻 TURN OVER → 1897
転 turn [roll] over → 1480
倒 TOPPLE → 124
ⓑ **spring back**
弾 SPRING BACK → 572
❺ⓑ **area units**
畝 *SE* (0.99 ares) → 1465
町 *cho* (99.2 ares) → 1113
歩 *bu* (3.3 sq.m) → 2416
坪 *TSUBO* (3.3 sq.m) → 275

USAGE

sorasu
反らす
vt bend (backward), curve, warp
逸らす
① let slip, miss, lose, let go, let pass
② (cause to deviate) divert, avert, dodge, evade

HOMOPHONES

sorasu ⇨ 逸 3120
kaesu ⇨ 返 3060 帰 130
kaeru ⇨ 返 3060 帰 130 還 3180
-kaeru ⇨ 返 3060

NOTE

⇨ see also USAGE notes at 返 3060 and 帰 130

仄

2946 SOKU hono(ka) hono- hono(mekasu) hono(meku)

Ⓒⓗ 仄 zè

Radical	Strokes
人 9	4-2-2
Grade	**Freq**
Reference	
□ 3 - 2 - 2	

2-2 厂

COMPOUNDS

❶ [now also 側 *soku* 137] from the side
仄聞する *sokubun suru* learn by hearsay
❷ faint, vague, indistinct
仄かな *honoka na* faint, vague, indistinct
仄仄と *honobono to* dimly, faintly; heart-warming
仄白い *honojiroi* dimly white
仄めかす *honomekasu* hint, allude, show faintly
仄めく *honomeku* appear faintly, be seen dimly
❸ oblique (tone)
平仄 *hyōsoku* different tones in which characters are pronounced in Chinese; consistency

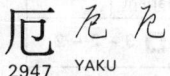

厄 厄 厄

2947 YAKU

一 厂 㔾 厄
1 2 3 4

Ⓒⓗ 厄 è

Radical	Strokes
厂 27	4-2-2
Grade	**Freq**
Jōyō	1902
□ 3 - 2 - 2	

2-2 厂

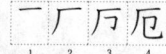

▶**MISFORTUNE**

COMPOUNDS

❶ **misfortune, trouble, evil, ill luck**
厄除け *yakuyoke* warding off evil fortune; talisman against evils
厄日 *yakubi* unlucky day, critical day
厄年 *yakudoshi* climacteric [critical] age, unlucky year
厄介 *yakkai* trouble, annoyance
大厄 *taiyaku* great misfortune [calamity]; grand climacteric
災厄 *saiyaku* calamity, disaster, accident
❷ abbrev. of 厄年 *yakudoshi*: climacteric [critical] age, unlucky year
前厄 *maeyaku* the year preceding a critical age, the year before one's grand climacteric

INDEPENDENT
【yaku 厄】misfortune, ill luck, evil
厄を落とす *yaku o otosu* escape evil; exorcise

SYNONYMS
❶ **misfortune and disaster**
禍 CALAMITY → 1030
凶 BAD LUCK → 2961
災 NATURAL CALAMITY → 2206
難 DISASTER → 1838

NOTE
⇨ see COMPOUND FORMATION for 厄介 *yakkai* ⇨ 介 1967

2-2 厂

incorrect classification ⇨ see 3434

2-2 ア

2948

▶REACH TO
nonstandard for 及 3385

2-2 厂

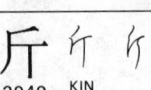

斤 2949 KIN

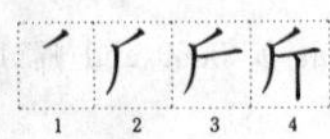

Ⓒⓗ 斤 jīn

Radical	Strokes
斤 69	4-4-0
Grade	**Freq**
Jōyō	1899
口 3 - 2 - 2	

RADICAL 69
Standard form: 斤 *ono* 'ax' (斥 新 断)
Description: used in characters related to cutting or chopping

▶CATTY

COMPOUNDS
❶ **catty, *kin*: unit of weight equiv. to 600 g or 160 momme (匁)**
斤目 *kinme* weight (in catties)
斤量 *kinryō* weight
パン三斤 *pan sangin* three catties of bread
❷ [original meaning, now archaic] axe
斧斤 *fukin* axe

INDEPENDENT
【kin 斤】catty, *kin* (⇨ ❶)

SYNONYMS
❶ **weight units**
匁 MOMME (3.75 g) → 3465
貫 *kan* (3.75 kg) → 2460
屯 ton → 3457

2-2 厂

2950

▶DOOR **▶HOUSEHOLD**
nonstandard for 戸 1930

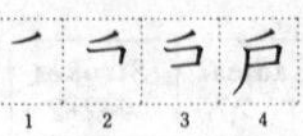

Radical	Strokes
戶 63	4-4-0
Grade	**Freq**
Variant	
口 3 - 2 - 2	

RADICAL 63
Standard form: 戶 *tobiranoto* 'door' (扁 扈)
Enclosure: 戸 *tobiranoto* (戻 房 扇)
Description: used in characters related to doors or houses

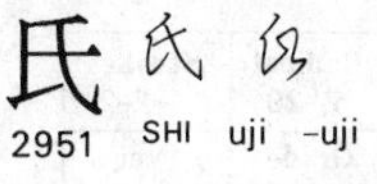

2951 SHI uji -uji

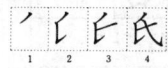

Ⓒ 氏 shì zhī

Radical	Strokes
氏 83	4-4-0
Grade	**Freq**
Jōyō-4	163
□ 3 - 2 - 2	

2-2

RADICAL 83

Standard form: 氏 *uji* 'family name' (民 氏)

Description: used for character classification

▶**COURTESY TITLE** ▶**FAMILY NAME**

COMPOUNDS

❶ⓐ courtesy title after family names: **Mr., Mister**

ⓑ [polite] **person**

田中氏 *tanakashi* Mr. Tanaka

某氏 *bōshi* a certain person

同氏 *dōshi* the said person, he

無名氏 *mumeishi* anonymous person, a nobody

❷ⓐ **family name, surname**

ⓑ [archaic] suffix after a married woman's maiden name: née

氏名 *shimei* (full) name

氏姓制度 *shisei seido* former naming system

夫人李氏 *fujin ri-shi* his wife née Li

❸ⓐ **clan, family**

ⓑ **suffix after names of clans or families**

氏族 *shizoku* clan, family

源氏 *genji* the Genji family, the Minamotos

平氏 *heishi* the Heike [Taira] clan [family], the Heikes

❹ suffix for temperature scales

摂氏 *sesshi* centigrade

華氏 *kashi* Fahrenheit

❺ **he**

彼氏 *kareshi* he; lover, beau

INDEPENDENT

【**shi** 氏】[polite] third person pronoun, he; family name

氏の意見 *shi no iken* his opinion

KUN

【**uji** 氏】family name, surname; lineage, stock, birth

氏素性 *ujisujō* (a person's) family background

氏神 *ujigami* tutelary god

氏より育ち *Uji yori sodachi* Birth is much, but breeding is more

【**-uji** -氏】honorific courtesy title: Mr.

加藤氏 *Katōuji* Mr. Kato

SYNONYMS

❶ⓐ **titles of address**

兄 familiar title (seniors) → 2154

君 FAMILIAR TITLE (peers) → 3206

嬢 Miss → 758

様 FORMAL TITLE → 1052

殿 FORMAL HONORIFIC TITLE → 1792

師 honorific title (clergymen) → 1326

公 honorific title (noblemen) → 1974

ⓑ **person**

方 person (*honorific*) → 1963

者 PERSON → 3211

人 HUMAN BEING → 3368

❷ⓐ **name**

姓 SURNAME → 279

名 NAME → 2169

称 APPELLATION → 1160

題 TITLE → 3337

号 DESIGNATION → 2153

銘 name (inscribed by maker) → 1724

❸ **family and relations**

族 FAMILY → 958

家 FAMILY → 2273

門 family → 888

縁 RELATION → 1386

姻 relative by marriage → 353

親 RELATIVES → 1799

【**shi**】

○ **third person pronouns**

彼 THIRD PERSON PRONOUN (*neutral*) → 290

奴 third person pronoun (*slang*) → 187

2-2
ナ

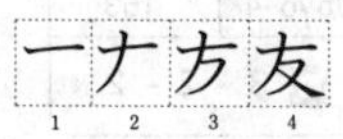

友 友 友
2952 YŪ tomo

Ⓒ𝐇 友 yǒu

Radical	Strokes
又 29	4-2-2
Grade	Freq
Jōyō-2	560
口 3-2-2	

▶**FRIEND**

COMPOUNDS

ⓐ **friend, comrade**
ⓑ friendly
ⓒ be friends with
友人 *yūjin* friend
友情 *yūjō* friendship, fellowship
親友 *shin'yū* close [intimate] friend
朋友 *hōyū* friend, companion
僚友 *ryōyū* comrade, colleague, fellow worker
戦友 *sen'yū* comrade-in-arms
友軍 *yūgun* allied army, friendly troops
友好 *yūkō* friendship, amity

KUN

【**tomo** 友】friend, companion, pal
友達 *tomodachi* friend, companion
竹馬の友 *chikuba no tomo* childhood friend, old playmate

SYNONYMS

ⓐ **friends and associates**
朋 COMRADE → 880
輩 FELLOW → 2807
僚 COLLEAGUE → 165

USAGE

tomo
友
friend, companion, pal
供
attendant, retinue
共
① [in compounds]
ⓐ joint, together, simultaneous
ⓑ of the same quality [kind]
ⓒ both, neither; including
② same cloth

HOMOPHONES

tomo ⇨ 供 88 共 2393

NOTE

⇨ see COMPOUND FORMATION for 竹馬の友 *chikuba no tomo* ⇨ 竹 228

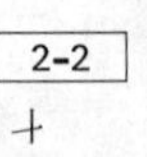

2-2
十

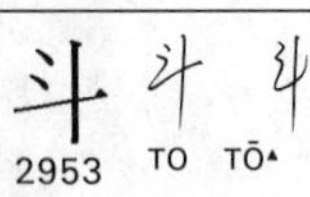

斗 斗 斗
2953 TO TŌ▲

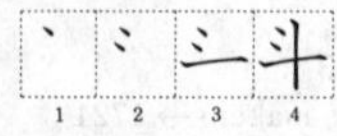

Ⓒ𝐇 斗 dǒu

Radical	Strokes
斗 68	4-4-0
Grade	Freq
Jōyō	1799
口 3-2-2	

RADICAL 68

Standard form: 斗 *tomasu* 'measure' (料 斜 斡)
Description: used in characters related to measures, measuring or scooping

▶**DIPPER** ▶***TO***

COMPOUNDS

❶ⓐ [original meaning] **dipper, ladle**
ⓑ **the Big Dipper**
漏斗 *rōto* funnel ("dipper for leaking")
斗南 *tonan* [archaic] south of the Big Dipper; the whole world
北斗七星 *hokuto shichisei* the Big Dipper
泰斗 *taito* leading authority
南斗 *nanto* [rare] constellation in Sagittarius
❷ ***to*: unit of capacity equiv. to approx. 18 liters or 10 *sho* (升), used esp. for sake or rice**
斗酒 *toshu* a *to* of sake, big supply of sake
二斗 *nito* 2 *to*
❸ [usu. 闘 *tō* 3334] fight (with)
⇨ see 闘 3334 for compounds

INDEPENDENT

【**to** 斗】*to* (⇨ ❷); one-*to* measure
胆、斗の如し *tan to no gotoshi* be as bold as a lion

SYNONYMS

❷ **capacity units**
石 *koku* (180 liters) → 2971
升 *SHO* (1.8 liters) → 3455
立 liter → 1992
合 *go* (0.18 liters) → 2019
勺 *SHAKU* (0.018 liters) → 2933

COMPOUND FORMATION

泰斗 *taito*

泰斗 'leading authority' is someone as great as Mt. Taishan (泰), one of the Five Sacred Mountains in China, and as eminent as the Big Dipper (斗 ❶ⓑ).

NOTE
⇨ see NOTE at 闘 3334

2954

▶FIGHT
nonstandard for 闘 3334

2-2 十

円 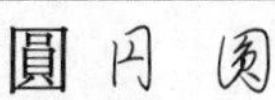
2955 EN maru(i) maru

CH 圆 yuán

Radical	Strokes
冂 13ᐞ	4-2-2
Grade	**Freq**
Jōyō-1	68
□ 3-2-2	

2-2 冂

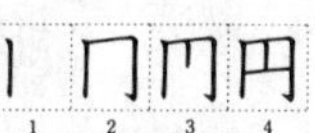

▶CIRCLE ▶YEN

COMPOUNDS

❶ⓐ **circle**
ⓑ [also prefix] **circular, round**
円周 *enshū* circumference
楕円 *daen* ellipse, oval
同心円 *dōshin'en* concentric circles
円卓 *entaku* round table
円盤 *enban* disk; flying saucer
円軌道 *enkidō* circular orbit
❷ rounded out, whole, complete; smooth
円満な *enman na* perfect, harmonious, well-rounded
円滑な *enkatsu na* smooth, harmonious
円熟 *enjuku* maturity, perfection
❸ vicinity, whole district
関東一円 *kantō ichien* whole district of Kanto
❹ [also prefix and suffix] **yen, ¥**
円貨 *enka* yen currency
円高 *endaka* appreciation of the yen
円相場 *ensōba* yen exchange rate
五百円 *gohyakuen* 500 yen

INDEPENDENT

【en 円】 circle; yen
円を描く *en o egaku* draw a circle
円の騰貴 *en no tōki* rise of the yen

KUN

【maru(i) 円い】 [also 丸い] (shaped like a circle) circular, round
円さ *marusa* roundness
円く輪になって踊る *maruku wa ni natte odoru* dance in a circle

【maru 円】
① [usu. 丸] circle
円で囲む *maru de kakomu* enclose (a word) with a circle
② *slang* money, dough—used in telegrams

SYNONYMS

❶ⓐ **circle**
圏 circle → 3148
丸 round or spherical shape → 3417
ⓑ **round**
丸い ROUND → 3417
❹ **Japanese money denominations**
銭 sen → 1725
厘 *RIN* → 3004
両 *ryo* → 3518
文 *mon* → 1962

HOMOPHONES

marui ⇨ 丸 3417
maru ⇨ 丸 3417 ○ 3342

NOTE
⇨ see USAGE note at 丸 3417

2-2 冂

月 月 月 月

2956 GETSU GATSU tsuki

Ⓒ 月 yuè

Radical	Strokes
月 74	4-4-0
Grade	**Freq**
Jōyō-1	25
▢ 3-2-2	

1 2 3 4

RADICAL 74

variant of 月 *tsuki* 'moon'

⇨ see 月 2959 for radical description

▶MOON ▶MONTH

COMPOUNDS

❶ [original meaning] **moon**

月光 *gekkō* moonlight, moonshine

月面 *getsumen* lunar surface

月齢 *getsurei* moon's age

満月 *mangetsu* full moon

❷ⓐ **month**

ⓑ **suffix after names of the months**

ⓒ monthly

今月 *kongetsu* this month

来月 *raigetsu* next month

二箇月 *nikagetsu* two months

正月 *shōgatsu* New Year, New Year's day; January

生年月日 *seinengappi* date of birth

二月 *nigatsu* February

月賦 *geppu* monthly installments

月給 *gekkyū* monthly pay [salary]

❸ **Monday**

月曜日 *getsuyōbi* Monday

月水金 *gessuikin* Mondays, Wednesdays and Fridays

INDEPENDENT

【getsu 月】 Monday

KUN

【tsuki 月】

① moon

月夜 *tsukiyo* moonlit night

三日月 *mikazuki* new moon

② month

毎月 *maitsuki* every month

年月 *toshitsuki* time, years

SPECIAL READINGS

五月雨 *samidare* early summer rain

SYNONYMS

❶ **moon**

陰 moon → 541

❷ **weeks and months**

週 WEEK → 3122

旬 TEN-DAY PERIOD → 2978

❸ **days of the week**

日 Sunday → 3027

火 Tuesday → 3463

水 Wednesday → 10

木 Thursday → 3450

金 Friday → 2057

土 Saturday → 3403

2-2 冂

2957

Radical	Strokes
月 74	4-4-0
Grade	**Freq**
Radical	
▢ 3-2-2	

1 2 3 4

RADICAL 74

variant of 月 *tsuki* 'moon'

⇨ see 月 2959 for radical description

月
2958

Radical	Strokes
月 130	4-4-0
Grade	**Freq**
Radical	
□ 3 - 2 - 2	

2-2 冂

RADICAL 130
nikuzuki, variant of 肉 *niku* 'flesh'
⇨ see 肉 3200 for radical description

月
2959

▶**MOON** ▶**MONTH**
nonstandard for 月 2956

Radical	Strokes
月 74	4-4-0
Grade	**Freq**
Variant	
□ 3 - 2 - 2	

2-2 冂

RADICAL 74
Standard form: 月 *tsuki* 'moon' (望)
Variants: 月 月 *tsuki* (服 朝 朋)
Description: used in characters related to the moon or time

几
2960

▶**WIND** ▶**MANNER**
handwritten abbreviation for 風 3007

2-2 几

凶 凶 凶
2961 KYŌ

CH 凶 xiōng

Radical	Strokes
凵 17	4-2-2
Grade	**Freq**
Jōyō	1603
□ 3 - 2 - 2	

2-2 凵

▶**BAD LUCK** ▶**ATROCIOUS**

COMPOUNDS

❶ⓐ **bad luck, misfortune, calamity**
ⓑ **unlucky, bad, disastrous**
吉凶 *kikkyō* good or ill luck, fortune
凶事 *kyōji* calamity, misfortune
凶報 *kyōhō* bad news
凶日 *kyōjitsu* unlucky day
凶変(=兇変) *kyōhen* calamity, disaster; tragic accident
❷ [original meaning] bad harvest
凶作 *kyōsaku* bad harvest
凶年 *kyōnen* bad year, bad harvest
❸ [formerly also 兇 2392]
ⓐ **atrocious, ferocious, wicked, brutal, cruel**
ⓑ **atrocious [lethal] crime, murder, wicked deed**
ⓒ wicked person, villain
凶悪な *kyōaku na* atrocious, villainous, fiendish
凶暴な *kyōbō na* atrocious, ferocious, brutal
凶漢 *kyōkan* villain, ruffian, assailant
凶行 *kyōkō* violence, murder, crime
凶器 *kyōki* murder [dangerous] weapon
凶刃 *kyōjin* assassin's dagger [knife]
元凶 *genkyō* ringleader, chief instigator

INDEPENDENT

【**kyō 凶**】bad luck
お神籤は凶と出た *Omikuji wa kyō to deta*
The written oracle read "unlucky"

SYNONYMS

❶ **misfortune and disaster**
厄 MISFORTUNE → 2947
禍 CALAMITY → 1030
災 NATURAL CALAMITY → 2206
難 DISASTER → 1838
❸ⓐ **evil**
邪 EVIL → 1124
悪 BAD → 2745
ⓐ **cruel**
虐 CRUEL → 3218

惨 CRUEL → 483
酷 SEVERE → 1562
残 RUTHLESS → 943

ⓑ **crimes and offenses**
罪 CRIME → 2610
犯 OFFENSE → 196

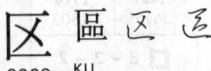

2-2 匸

匹 匹 匹 匹

2962 HITSU hiki

1 2 3 4

Ⓒⓗ 匹 pǐ

Radical	Strokes
匸 23	4-2-2
Grade	**Freq**
Jōyō	1543
□ 3-2-2	

▶COUNTER FOR ANIMALS

COMPOUNDS

❶ match, be a match for
匹敵する *hitteki suru* match, rival
❷ coarse, plain
匹夫 *hippu* coarse man, man of low rank
❸ shaped like the buttocks of a horse
馬匹 *bahitsu* horses

KUN

【hiki 匹】
① [formerly also 疋] counter for animals
犬五匹 *inu gohiki* five dogs
数匹 *sūhiki* several animals
② [also 疋] *hiki*: unit of measure for rolls of cloth equiv. to 2 *tan* (反)
絹一匹 *kinu ippiki* one *hiki* of silk

SYNONYMS

【hiki】
① **counters for animals**
頭 counter for large animals → 1604
羽 counter for birds → 226

USAGE

hiki
匹
① [formerly also 疋] counter for animals
② [also 疋] *hiki*: unit of measure for rolls of cloth equiv. to 2 *tan* (反)
疋
① *hiki*:
ⓐ [also 匹] unit of measure for rolls of cloth equiv. to 2 *tan* (反)
ⓑ former monetary unit equiv. to 10 (later 25) *mon* (文)
② [now usu. 匹] counter for animals

HOMOPHONES

hiki ⇨ 疋 3480

2-2 匸

区 區 区 区

2963 KU

Ⓒⓗ 区 qū ōu

Radical	Strokes
匸 23	4-2-2
Grade	**Freq**
Jōyō-3	99
□ 3-2-2	

▶DISTRICT ▶WARD

COMPOUNDS

❶ⓐ [also suffix] **district, zone, region, area, section**
ⓑ *biogeography* region
区域 *kuiki* zone, area; limits
区間 *kukan* section, territory
地区 *chiku* district, area, region, lot
管区 *kanku* district (under jurisdiction); parish
学区 *gakku* school district [area]
選挙区 *senkyoku* electoral district, precinct
禁漁区 *kinryōku* game preserve, wildlife sanctuary
新熱帯区 *shinnettaiku* neotropical region
❷ⓐ (major subdivision of a city, esp. in Japan) **ward, municipal [urban] district, borough**
ⓑ **suffix after names of wards or municipal districts**
ⓒ counter for wards
区役所 *kuyakusho* ward office
区長 *kuchō* ward headman, borough mayor
区立の *kuritsu no* established by the ward
区会 *kukai* ward assembly
新宿区 *shinjukuku* Shinjuku Ward
クィーンズ区 *kuīnzuku* Queens Borough
東京二十三区 *tōkyō nijūsanku* the 23 wards of Tokyo
❸ⓐ [original meaning] divide into sections, partition
ⓑ divided, in little pieces
区分する *kubun suru* divide, section, subdivide

区別する *kubetsu suru* distinguish; classify, divide
区区たる *kukutaru* various, diverse; irregular
区切る(＝句切る) *kugiru* punctuate, mark off by a comma

INDEPENDENT

【ku 区】 ward (⇨ ❷ⓐ)
区の財政 *ku no zaisei* ward finances

SYNONYMS

❶ⓐ **areas and localities**
域 BOUNDED AREA → 465
領 TERRITORY → 1224
帯 BELT → 2582
圏 SPHERE → 3148
辺 VICINITY → 3029
方 locality → 1963
地 PLACE → 204
❷ **parts of towns**
街 CITY QUARTER → 576
町 town section (*cho*) → 1113
丁 TOWN SUBSECTION (*chome*) → 3348
字 village or town section → 2172

巨 incorrect stroke count ⇨ see 3039

2-2 匚

匹 **▶COUNTER FOR ANIMALS**
nonstandard for 匹 2962

2964

2-2 匚

丑 **▶THE OX**
nonstandard for 丑 3433

2965

2-2 ⺕

巡 迅 incorrect stroke count ⇨ see 口 3–3

2-3 辶

包 包 包 包 Ⓒⓗ 包 bāo

2966 HŌ tsutsu(mu)

ノ 勹 勺 匀 包
1 2 3 4 5

Radical	Strokes
勹 20	5-2-3
Grade	**Freq**
Jōyō-4	1094
口 3-2-3	

2-3 勹

▶WRAP ▶ENCOMPASS

COMPOUNDS

❶ⓐ [formerly also 緥 1411] **wrap, pack, envelop, cover**
ⓑ **wrap(per), package, parcel**
ⓒ counter for packets of powder medicine
包装 *hōsō* wrapping, packing
梱包 *konpō* packing, crating, package
包帯 *hōtai* bandage, dressing
二包 *nihō* two packets (of medicine)
❷ cartridge
薬包 *yakuhō* cartridge; chartula
空包 *kūhō* blank cartridge
❸ⓐ (hold within) **encompass, include, envelop, contain; include hidden meanings, imply**
ⓑ [original meaning] (surround with) **encompass, surround, encircle**
包含する *hōgan suru* include, encompass, cover; imply
包容する *hōyō suru* encompass, comprehend; imply; tolerate
包蔵する *hōzō suru* contain, comprehend; imply; cherish
内包 *naihō* connotation, intention, comprehension
包括的 *hōkatsuteki* inclusive, comprehensive
包囲する *hōi suru* surround, encircle, envelop
❹ [formerly 庖 3083] kitchen
包丁 *hōchō* kitchen knife, carving knife

KUN

【tsutsu(mu) 包む】 wrap, pack; cover, envelop, enshroud; conceal
包み *tsutsumi* bundle, wrapper, package, parcel
包み込む *tsutsumikomu* wrap up
小包 *kozutsumi* parcel, package
霧に包まれる *kiri ni tsutsumareru* be shrouded in mist
包み隠す *tsutsumikakusu* conceal, keep secret

SYNONYMS

❶ⓐ **cover and wrap**
覆 COVER → 2726
被 cover → 1163
ⓑ **bags**
袋 BAG → 2588
俵 STRAW SACK → 115
胞 MEMBRANOUS SAC → 917
❸ⓐ **contain and include**
含 CONTAIN (have as a part) → 2041
容 CONTAIN (have within) → 2277
挟 HOLD BETWEEN → 377
ⓑ **surround**
囲む ENCLOSE → 3069
環 SURROUND → 1090

NOTE

⇨ see COMPOUND FORMATION for 庖丁(=包丁) *hōchō* ⇨ 丁 3348

2-3 勹

句 句 句

2967 KU

ノ 勹 勹 句 句 (1 2 3 4 5)

CH 句 jù gōu

Radical	Strokes
口 30	5-3-2
Grade	**Freq**
Jōyō-5	1166
口 3-2-3	

▶**PHRASE** ▶**HAIKU**

COMPOUNDS

❶ [also suffix]
ⓐ **phrase, expression, set phrase**
ⓑ *gram* (sentence subdivision) phrase, clause
語句 *goku* words and phrases
文句 *monku* phrase, expression; complaint
慣用句 *kan'yōku* idiom, common phrase
句読点 *kutōten* punctuation marks
句法 *kuhō* phraseology, diction
名詞句 *meishiku* noun phrase
❷ line of poetry, verse, poem, stanza
起句 *kiku* opening line of a Chinese quatrain
❸ⓐ **haiku, 17-syllable poem**
ⓑ counter for haiku poems
句会 *kukai* gathering of haiku
句集 *kushū* collection of haiku poems
俳句 *haiku* haiku
発句 *hokku* haiku, hokku
三句 *sanku* three haiku poems

INDEPENDENT

【**ku 句**】 phrase, set phrase; clause; verse; haiku
句を切る *ku o kiru* punctuate a sentence
上の句 *kami no ku* first half of a tanka poem
句を作る *ku o tsukuru* compose a haiku poem

SYNONYMS

❶ⓐ **words and expressions**
詞 WORDS → 1503
辞 WORD → 1364
語 WORD → 1543
ⓑ **sentence and sentence parts**
文 sentence → 1962
節 clause → 2691
❸ⓐ **poetry**
俳 HAIKU → 112
歌 Japanese poetry → 1825
詩 POETRY → 1524

2-3 勹

2968

▶**WRAP** ▶**ENCOMPASS**
nonstandard for 包 2966

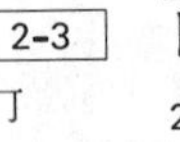

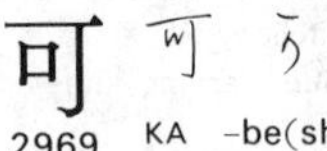

2969 KA -be(shi)▲

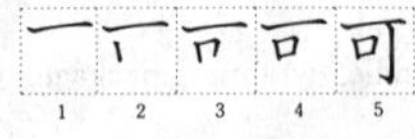

CH 可 kě kè

Radical	Strokes
口 30	5-3-2
Grade	**Freq**
Jōyō-5	487
口 3-2-3	

▶**-ABLE** ▶**APPROVE**

COMPOUNDS

❶ [also prefix] **-able, -ible, possible, can**
可能な *kanō na* possible, potential, practical
可動の *kadō no* movable
可溶性 *kayōsei* solubility
可視光線 *kashi kōsen* visible ray
可処分の *kashobun no* disposable

不可解な *fukakai na* incomprehensible, inexplicable, baffling

❷ [original meaning] **approve, be in favor of, permit**

可決 *kaketsu* approval [adoption] of a bill

可否 *kahi* right or wrong, propriety

許可する *kyoka suru* permit, approve, authorize

認可 *ninka* approval, authorization, permission

❸ be worthy of

可憐な *karen na* cute, sweet, pretty; tiny

可愛い *kawaii* dear, darling, charming, lovely, sweet

可哀相な *kawaisō na* poor, pitiable, pathetic

INDEPENDENT

【ka 可】 fair, passable, grade C; approval

可の評点 *ka no hyōten* Passable, grade C

可とする *ka to suru* approve (of), be in favor of

KUN

【-be(shi) -可し】 [auxiliary] *literary* can; should, must, ought to; expected to; perhaps, maybe

見る可き成果 *mirubeki seika* noticeable [remarkable] result

行く可し *Yukubeshi* Go!

風雨強かる可し *Fūu tsuyokarubeshi* It will be stormy

SYNONYMS

❶ **possible**

能 possible → 1323

❷ **agree and approve**

賛 APPROVE OF → 2809

認 RECOGNIZE → 1546

諾 CONSENT → 1568

承 AGREE TO → 16

肯 ASSENT → 2417

容 tolerate → 2277

圧 壓 圧 壓

2970 ATSU o(su)▲

Ⓒⓗ 压 yā

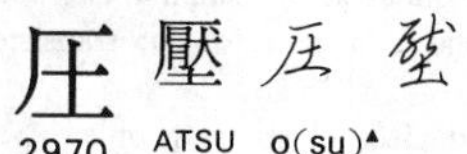

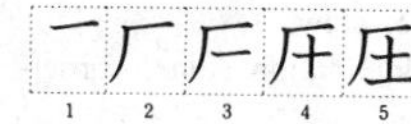

Radical	Strokes
土 32	5-3-2
Grade	**Freq**
Jōyō-5	572
口 3-2-3	

2-3 厂

▶**PRESSURE**

COMPOUNDS

❶ⓐ **pressure**

ⓑ [original meaning] **apply pressure, press down**

水圧 *suiatsu* water pressure

気圧 *kiatsu* atmospheric [air] pressure

血圧 *ketsuatsu* blood pressure

電圧 *den'atsu* voltage, electric pressure

圧力 *atsuryoku* pressure

圧縮する *asshuku suru* compress, constrict

圧搾する *assaku suru* press, compress

圧砕 *assai* crushing

❷ **pressure, bring pressure to bear on, press, suppress**

圧迫する *appaku suru* press, oppress, pressure

圧制 *assei* oppression, coercion

抑圧する *yokuatsu suru* oppress, repress, suppress

弾圧する *dan'atsu suru* oppress, suppress

❸ overwhelming

圧倒する *attō suru* overwhelm, overpower, crush

圧勝 *asshō* overwhelming victory

圧巻 *akkan* the best part, masterpiece

INDEPENDENT

【atsu 圧】 pressure

【assuru 圧する】 press (down), oppress; overpower, overwhelm

KUN

【o(su) 圧す】 [now usu. 押す] press down, press; compress, squash

圧し *oshi* pressing down; weight; authority, commanding presence

SYNONYMS

❶ⓐ **energy and force**

力 POWER, force → 3371

勢 physical power → 2857

気 energy → 3194

ⓑ **push**

押 PUSH → 314

突く THRUST → 2230

ⓑ **squeeze**

絞る WRING → 1349

搾 SQUEEZE → 649

❷ **compel and press**

迫 PRESS → 3074

強 force → 475

押す PUSH → 314

HOMOPHONES

osu ⇨ 押 314 推 504

oshi ⇨ 押 314

NOTE

⇨ see USAGE note at 押 314

★do not confuse with 庄 3051

2-3 丆

石 2971 SEKI SHAKU KOKU ishi

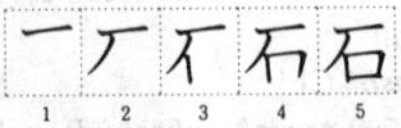

CH 石 shí dàn

Radical	Strokes
石 112	5-5-0
Grade	**Freq**
Jōyō-1	281
口 3 - 2 - 3	

RADICAL 112

Standard form: 石 *ishi* 'stone' (碧 磐 磨)

Left variant: 石 *ishihen* (研 破 確)

Description: used in characters related to stones, minerals or their qualities

▶**STONE**

COMPOUNDS

❶ⓐ [also suffix] [original meaning] **stone, rock**

ⓑ playing stone in a game of go

石像 *sekizō* stone statue

石炭 *sekitan* coal

石鹸 *sekken* soap

石油 *sekiyu* petroleum, oil

岩石 *ganseki* rock

宝石 *hōseki* gem, jewel

磁石 *jishaku* magnet; compass

大理石 *dairiseki* marble

定石 *jōseki* set [standard] moves in the game of go

❷ counter for jewels of a watch, transistors or diodes

二十一石の時計 *nijūisseki no tokei* 21-jewel watch

五石ラジオ *goseki-rajio* five-transistor radio

❸ *koku*:

ⓐ former unit of capacity equiv. to approx. 180 liters or 10 *to* (斗), used esp. as unit of rice stipends in feudal Japan

ⓑ former unit of capacity equiv. to approx. 278 liters or 10 cubic *shaku* (尺), used esp. for measuring lumber

石高 *kokudaka* yield, fief, stipend

二千石 *nisengoku* stipend of 2000 *koku* in rice

一石 *ikkoku* 1 *koku*

INDEPENDENT

【**koku** 石】*koku* (⇨ ❸)

KUN

【**ishi** 石】[also suffix] stone, small rock, pebble; playing stone in a game of go; transistor; silicon chip

石ころ *ishikoro* piece of stone, pebble

石頭 *ishiatama* hard head, obstinate person

小石 *koishi* pebble, stone

土台石 *dodaiishi* foundation stone, cornerstone

碁石 *goishi* go stone

SYNONYMS

❶ⓐ **rock and stone**

岩 ROCK → 2235

巌 CRAG → 2386

❸ⓐ **capacity units**

斗 *TO* (18 liters) → 2953

升 *SHO* (1.8 liters) → 3455

立 liter → 1992

合 *go* (0.18 liters) → 2019

勺 *SHAKU* (0.018 liters) → 2933

2-3 厂

斥 2972 SEKI shirizo(keru)▲

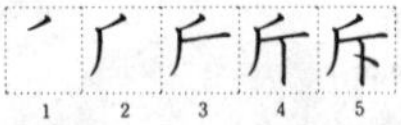

CH 斥 chì

Radical	Strokes
斤 69	5-4-1
Grade	**Freq**
Jōyō	1886
口 3 - 2 - 3	

▶**EXPEL**

COMPOUNDS

❶ **expel, repel, reject, exclude**

斥力 *sekiryoku* repulsion, repulsive force

排斥する *haiseki suru* expel, reject, exclude, ostracize

擯斥 *hinseki* rejection, ostracism

❷ survey, scout, patrol

斥候 *sekkō* scout, patrol, reconnoitering soldier

KUN

【**shirizo(keru)** 斥ける】[usu. 退ける] reject, refuse, turn down

提案を斥ける *teian o shirizokeru* turn down a proposal

SYNONYMS

❶ **drive out**

追 chase away → 3096
退 cause to retreat → 3094
駆 drive away → 1823
逐 DRIVE OUT → 3102
排 EXCLUDE → 490
払う clear out → 194

HOMOPHONES

shirizokeru ⇨ 退 3094

NOTE

⇨ see USAGE note at 退 3094

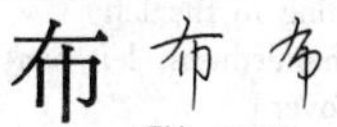

2973 FU nuno

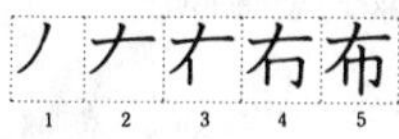

Ⓒⓗ 布 bù

Radical	Strokes
巾 50	5-3-2
Grade	**Freq**
Jōyō-5	759
⼝ 3 - 2 - 3	

2-3 ナ

▶**CLOTH** ▶**SPREAD**

COMPOUNDS

❶ [original meaning] **cloth, textile**

布巾 *fukin* dishcloth, napkin
毛布 *mōfu* blanket
綿布 *menpu* cotton cloth
財布 *saifu* purse, wallet

❷ distribute over a surface:

ⓐ [also 敷 1870] **spread, lay out, apply**
ⓑ spread out, arrange, line up

塗布する *tofu suru* apply (an ointment)
散布する *sanpu* (=*sappu*) *suru* scatter, sprinkle, spray
配布 *haifu* wide distribution
頒布 *hanpu* distribution, circulation
布陣 *fujin* lineup
布石 *fuseki* arrangement of go stones; preparation

❸ (become or cause to become widely known) **spread, disseminate, distribute**

布告する *fukoku suru* proclaim, declare
布教 *fukyō* propagation, missionary work
布令 *furei* official notice, proclamation, announcement
公布する *kōfu suru* promulgate, proclaim
流布する *rufu suru* circulate, disseminate, spread

❹ [formerly 蒲 2504] cattail, reed mace

布団 *futon futon*, bedquilt

INDEPENDENT

【**fu** 布】cloth; coin used in ancient China

KUN

【**nuno** 布】cloth

布地 *nunoji* cloth
麻布 *asanuno* hemp cloth, linen

SYNONYMS

❶ **fabric**

地 fabric → 204

❷ⓐ **spread**

敷く LAY → 1870
舗 PAVE → 1735
散 SCATTER → 1702
塗 APPLY ON A SURFACE → 2841
抹 wipe over → 313

❸ **make widely known**

流 spread → 441
伝 spread → 44
広 spread → 3035
弘 DISSEMINATE (esp. Buddhism) → 192
及 REACH TO → 3385

NOTE

⇨ see COMPOUND FORMATION for 布団 *futon* ⇨ 団 3053

左 左 ㄜ

2974 SA SHA▴ hidari

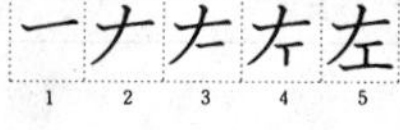

Ⓒⓗ 左 zuǒ

Radical	Strokes
工 48	5-3-2
Grade	**Freq**
Jōyō-1	452
⼝ 3 - 2 - 3	

2-3 ナ

▶**LEFT**

COMPOUNDS

❶ⓐ [original meaning] **left**
ⓑ abbrev. of 左翼手 *sayokushu*: left fielder

左方 *sahō* left side
左折する *sasetsu suru* turn to the left
左記 *saki* undermentioned (statement), following
左表 *sahyō* chart at the left
左右 *sayū* right and left

左右する *sayū suru* command, dominate, control
左中間 *sachūkan* between left and center fielders
左直 *sachoku* left liner
❷ **the Left, leftist**
左派 *saha* left wing, left faction
左翼 *sayoku* left wing [flank]; left wing [faction]; left field
❸ low rank
左遷 *sasen* relegation, demotion
❹ drunkard, drinker
左党 *satō* drinker, wine lover; left (wing), leftist
❺ supporting evidence
証左 *shōsa* evidence, proof
❻ used phonetically for *sa* or *sha*
左様 *sayō* such; yes; let me see
左官 *sakan* (=*shakan*) plasterer

INDEPENDENT
【sa 左】 left; the following
左の通り *sa no tōri* as following

KUN
【hidari 左】 left; left hand; leftist; drinking
左側 *hidarigawa* left side
左手 *hidarite* left hand
左向き *hidarimuki* turning to the left
左利き *hidarikiki* left-handedness; left-hander; drinker, wine lover
左寄り *hidariyori* tending to the left
左党 *hidaritō* drinker, wine lover

SYNONYMS
❶ⓐ **left and right**
右 RIGHT → 2975
❷ **Communism**
共 Communism → 2393
赤 RED → 2193

2-3
ナ

2975 U YŪ migi

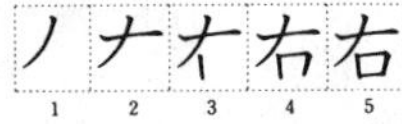

Ⓒⓗ 右 yòu

Radical	Strokes
口 30	5-3-2
Grade	**Freq**
Jōyō-1	474
口 3 - 2 - 3	

▶**RIGHT**

COMPOUNDS
❶ⓐ [original meaning] **right**
ⓑ abbrev. of 右翼手 *uyokushu*: right fielder
右折 *usetsu* right turn
右往左往する *uōsaō suru* go this way and that
右岸 *ugan* right bank
左右 *sayū* right and left
座右に *zayū ni* at one's (right) hand; by one's side
右中間 *uchūkan* between right and center fielders
❷ **the Right, right wing**
右派 *uha* right wing
右翼 *uyoku* right wing; right field
極右 *kyokuu* extreme right
❸ [also 祐 *yū* 915] help, assist
右筆 *yūhitsu* amanuensis, private secretary
❹ regard highly
右文 *yūbun* respect for literary culture

KUN
【migi 右】 [also prefix] right; the above mentioned; superiority
右側 *migigawa* (=*usoku*) right side
右手 *migite* right hand
右の通り *migi no tōri* as above mentioned
右寄り *migiyori* tending to the Right
右に出る *migi ni deru* be superior to

SYNONYMS
❶ⓐ **left and right**
左 LEFT → 2974

2-3
ナ

incorrect stroke count ⇨ see 2982

2976 YŌ mochi(iru)

ノ 冂 月 月 用

CH 用 yòng

Radical	Strokes
用 101	5-5-0
Grade	**Freq**
Jōyō-2	128
口 3-2-3	

2-3 冂

RADICAL 101

Standard form: 用 *mochiiru* 'use' (甫 甬)

Description: used for character classification

▶EMPLOY ▶THINGS TO DO

COMPOUNDS

❶ⓐ employ, use, make use of, utilize, apply

ⓑ [also suffix] **used for, for**

用意する *yōi suru* prepare, ready oneself, make arrangements

用語 *yōgo* terminology; diction, wording; vocabulary

用途 *yōto* use, service, application

用法 *yōhō* usage, directions for use, use

利用する *riyō suru* utilize, make use of, avail oneself of

使用する *shiyō suru* use, employ, apply

採用 *saiyō* adoption, acceptance; employment, appointment

適用 *tekiyō* application

運用する *un'yō suru* make use of; invest in; apply to

乗用車 *jōyōsha* passenger car, automobile

家庭用 *kateiyō* for domestic use

返信用 *henshin'yō* for reply

❷ [sometimes also 傭 160 or 庸 3128] employ (a person), engage

用人 *yōnin* steward, manager

雇用(=雇傭) *koyō* employment, hire

❸ⓐ be useful, be effective, work

ⓑ **use, usefulness, utility**

作用 *sayō* action, operation, function; effect

信用 *shin'yō* trust, credit, confidence

効用 *kōyō* use, usefulness, effect

無用の *muyō no* useless; unnecessary; forbidden

有用な *yūyō na* useful, serviceable

❹ things to do, business, task, errand

用事 *yōji* things to do, errand, business, engagement

用件 *yōken* matter (of business), things to be done

用談 *yōdan* business talk

所用 *shoyō* things to do, errand, business, engagement

公用 *kōyō* official business [duty], official mission; public use

私用 *shiyō* private business; private use

❺ needed for (a specific use), required

用紙 *yōshi* blank form, stationery

用地 *yōchi* land, lot, site

用具 *yōgu* tool, instrument, appliance; outfit

不用な *fuyō na* unnecessary, useless; disused, waste

入用 *nyūyō* need, demand, necessity

学校用品 *gakkō yōhin* school requisites [supplies]

❻ expenses, expenditures

用度 *yōdo* expenditure, office expenses; supplies

費用 *hiyō* expenses, outlay

❼ answering nature's call

用便 *yōben* defecation, urination

INDEPENDENT

【yō 用】

① things to do, business, task, errand

用が有る *yō ga aru* have things to do

② use, usefulness, utility

用に立つ *yō ni tatsu* be of use [service]

用に足りない *yō ni tarinai* be useless, be of no use

③ [archaic] expenses, expenditures

用を節する *yō o sessuru* save expenses

④ answering nature's call

用を足す *yō o tasu* do one's business; relieve oneself, go to stool

KUN

【mochi(iru) 用いる】 employ, use, make use of, utilize, apply; employ, engage

広く用いる *hiroku mochiiru* be in wide use

重く用いる *omoku mochiiru* give an important position

SYNONYMS

❶ⓐ use

使 USE → 90

❷ employ

雇 EMPLOY → 1956

使う employ → 90

役 press into service → 244

❸ benefit

為 SAKE → 3577

益 BENEFIT → 2285

利 ADVANTAGE → 1114

役 SERVICE → 244
❹ **affairs**
事 affairs → 3567
務 affairs → 1173
❺ **need and necessity**
要 required → 2635
必 must → 15
須 MUST → 574
需 DEMAND → 2797
入 necessary → 3370
NOTE
⇨ see COMPOUND FORMATION for 用途 *yōto* ⇨ 途 3107

2-4 廴 **廷** incorrect stroke count ⇨ see 3058

2-4 辶 **近 返 etc.** incorrect stroke count ⇨ see □ 3-4

2-4 九

旭

2977 KYOKU asahi NAMES akira aki teru

CH 旭 xù

Radical	Strokes
日 72	6-4-2
Grade	**Freq**
Names	1979
□ 3-2-4	

▶RISING SUN

COMPOUNDS
● [original meaning] **rising sun, morning sun**
旭日 *kyokujitsu* rising sun
旭日章 *kyokujitsushō* Order of the Rising Sun
旭光 *kyokkō* rays of the morning [rising] sun

INDEPENDENT
【kyoku 旭】 abbrev. of 旭日章: Order of the Rising Sun

KUN
【asahi 旭】 [usu. 朝日] rising sun, morning sun; rays of the morning sun

NAMES
旭 *akira* male name
旭川 *asahikawa* place name

SYNONYMS
● **sun**
日 SUN → 3027
陽 SUN → 626

USAGE
asahi
旭
[usu. 朝日] rising sun, morning sun; rays of the morning sun
朝日
[sometimes also 旭] rising sun, morning sun; rays of the morning sun

HOMOPHONES
asahi ⇨ 朝日 1695, 3027

2-4 勹

旬

2978 JUN SHUN▲

CH 旬 xún

Radical	Strokes
日 72	6-4-2
Grade	**Freq**
Jōyō	896
□ 3-2-4	

▶TEN-DAY PERIOD

COMPOUNDS
ⓐ [original meaning] **ten-day period**
ⓑ [rare] ten years (in counting age)
旬日 *junjitsu* ten-day period
旬刊 *junkan* published every ten days
旬報 *junpō* ten-day report
上旬 *jōjun* first ten days of a month
中旬 *chūjun* middle [second] ten days of a month
齢七旬 *yowai shichijun* three score and ten

INDEPENDENT

【shun 旬】season (for specific products), the best season (for sports)

旬の魚 *shun no sakana* fish in season

SYNONYMS

ⓐ **weeks and months**

月 MONTH → 2956

週 WEEK → 3122

灰 灰 灰 𠂆

2979 KAI hai

Ⓒⓗ 灰 huī

Radical	Strokes
火 86	6-4-2
Grade	**Freq**
Jōyō-6	1659
口 3-2-4	

2-4 厂

一 厂 𠂇 𠂇 𠂇 灰 (1 2 3 4 5 6)

▶ASH

COMPOUNDS

❶ⓐ [original meaning] **ash, ashes**

ⓑ **ashen, gray, grayish**

灰燼 *kaijin* ashes, ashes and cinder

灰分 *kaibun* ash content

重灰 *jūkai* dense ash

灰白色 *kaihakushoku* ash color, light gray

灰緑色 *kairyokushoku* greenish gray

❷ lime

石灰 *sekkai* lime

苦灰石 *kukaiseki* dolomite

❸ lifeless, spiritless

死灰 *shikai* as lifeless as cold ashes

KUN

【hai 灰】ashes

灰皿 *haizara* ashtray

灰色の *haiiro no* ashen, gray

死の灰 *shi no hai* lethal radioactive fallout, atomic dust

ソーダ灰 *sōdabai* soda ash

火山灰 *kazanbai* volcano ashes

SPECIAL READINGS

灰汁▲ *aku* lye, ash; harshness, harsh taste

SYNONYMS

❶ⓐ **products of combustion**

殼 cinders → 1490

炭 CHARCOAL → 2257

煙 SMOKE → 1021

圧

2980

▶PERSONAL HISTORY

handwritten abbreviation for 歴 3019

2-4 厂

后 后 后

2981 KŌ GO▲ kisaki▲

Ⓒⓗ 后 hòu

Radical	Strokes
口 30	6-3-3
Grade	**Freq**
Jōyō-6	1676
口 3-2-4	

2-4 厂

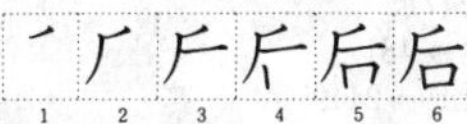

▶EMPRESS

COMPOUNDS

❶ (wife of an emperor) **empress, queen**

后妃 *kōhi* queen consort, empress, queen

皇后 *kōgō* empress, queen

皇太后 *kōtaikō* empress dowager, queen mother

❷ [usu. 後 *go* 361] after, later

午后 *gogo* afternoon

KUN

【kisaki 后】empress, queen; consort

SYNONYMS

❶ **wives of rulers**

妃 PRINCESS → 206

室 wife (esp. of persons of rank) → 2254

2-4
ナ

存 存 存

2982 SON ZON

1 2 3 4 5 6

CH 存 cún

Radical	Strokes
子 39	6-3-3
Grade	**Freq**
Jōyō-6	677
口 3 - 2 - 4	

▶EXIST

COMPOUNDS

❶ⓐ (have actuality) **exist, be**

ⓑ (have life) exist, live, remain alive

存在 *sonzai* existence, being
存否 *sonpi* existence; life or death
存続 *sonzoku* continuation, maintenance
存亡 *sonbō* destiny; life or death
共存 *kyōzon* coexistence
依存 *izon* (=*ison*) dependence, reliance
既存の *kison no* existing
現存の *genzon* (=*genson*) *no* existing, living
残存する *zanson* (=*zanzon*) *suru* survive, subsist, be extant
実存 *jitsuzon* existence
存命中 *zonmeichū* (while) in life, in one's lifetime
生存する *seizon suru* exist, live, survive

❷ keep, preserve, maintain

保存する *hozon suru* preserve, conserve, maintain, store, keep
温存する *onzon suru* preserve, retain

❸ⓐ **hold an opinion, believe, think**

ⓑ know

存外 *zongai* contrary to one's expectations; beyond expectation
存分に *zonbun ni* to one's heart's content, freely
所存 *shozon* one's opinion [view], intention
異存 *izon* objection
存知 *zonchi* having knowledge of

INDEPENDENT

【sonsuru 存する】 (have actuality) exist, be; (have life) exist, live, remain alive; consist in, rest with

猶疑問が存する *Nao gimon ga sonsuru* A doubt still remains
幸福は満足に存する *Kōfuku wa manzoku ni sonsuru* Happiness consists in contentment

【zonjiru (=zonzuru) 存じる(=存ずる)】 [humble] think, believe; know, be aware of, be acquainted with

お元気の事と存じます *Ogenki no koto to zonjimasu* I trust you are in good health
御存じ(=御存知)の通り *gozonji no tōri* as you know

SYNONYMS

❶ⓐ **exist and be**

在 BE → 2984
有 exist → 2983
居 be present → 3080
臨 BE PRESENT AT → 1630
也 CLASSICAL COPULA → 3406

❸ⓐ **think and consider**

考 THINK → 3196
思 THINK → 2564
案 think out → 2270
想 CONCEIVE → 2828
慮 CONSIDER → 3266
勘 take into consideration → 1777
量 weigh → 2471
惟 MEDITATE → 481
省 INTROSPECT → 2449

2-4
ナ

有 有 有 有

2983 YŪ U a(ru)

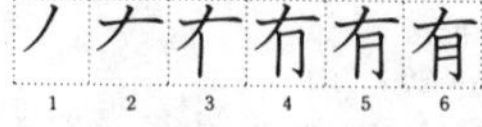

1 2 3 4 5 6

CH 有 yǒu yòu

Radical	Strokes
月 74	6-4-2
Grade	**Freq**
Jōyō-3	283
口 3 - 2 - 4	

▶HAVE

COMPOUNDS

❶ⓐ [also prefix] **have, possess, own, retain**

ⓑ **having the characteristic [property] of**

有産階級 *yūsan-kaikyū* propertied [proprietary] classes, bourgeoisie
有意義な *yūigi na* significant, useful, worthwhile
有資格者 *yūshikakusha* eligible person, qualified person
所有する *shoyū suru* have, own, possess
保有 *hoyū* possession, maintenance
有望な *yūbō na* promising, hopeful

有害な *yūgai na* harmful, pernicious, noxious
有利な *yūri na* advantageous, favorable; profitable
有名な *yūmei na* famous, noted, celebrated; notorious
有効な *yūkō na* effective, valid

❷ⓐ **exist, be, be present**
ⓑ existence; *bhava*, existence (in Buddhism)
有無 *umu* existence, presence; yes or no
現有の *gen'yū no* present, existing
仮有 *keu* temporary existence

❸ again; in addition to
十有五年 *jūyūgonen* 15 years

❹ [archaic] used before one-character names of countries or groups of people
有衆 *yūshū* the people, the multitudes
有夏 *yūka* Mainland China

INDEPENDENT

【yū 有】 existence; possession
...の有に帰する *...no yū ni kisuru* come into possession of...
【yūsuru 有する】 have, possess, own
【u 有】 existence (⇨ ❷ⓑ)

KUN

【a(ru) 有る】
① be, exist, be present, there is
有り様 *arisama* condition, state of affairs; sight
有り難う *arigatō* thank you
月にはクレーターが有る *Tsuki ni wa kurētā ga aru* There are craters on the moon
② have, possess, own
有り金 *arigane* money on hand, ready cash
彼女には子供が二人有る *Kanojo ni wa kodomo ga futari aru* She has two children
③ have the experience of doing something
フランスに行った事が有るか *Furansu ni itta koto ga aru ka* Have you ever been to France?
④ (have a magnitude of) number, cover, weigh, measure
あの農場は二百平方メートル有る *Ano nōjō wa nihyaku heihōmētoru aru* That farm covers 200 sq. meters
⑤ happen, occur, take place
事故が有った *Jiko ga atta* There was an accident
昨日会議が有った *Kinō kaigi ga atta* The conference was held yesterday
⑥ consist [lie] in, depend on
幸福は満足に有る *Kōfuku wa manzoku ni aru* Happiness consists in contentment
⑦ [in the form of transitive verb followed by て有る *te aru*] describes a state resulting from an action
部屋が暖めて有る *Heya ga atatamete aru* The room is kept [has been made] warm

SYNONYMS

❶ **possess**
持 HOLD → 374
蔵 own → 2364
属 BELONG TO → 3145
享 ENJOY → 2051
具 possess → 2552

❷ⓐ **exist and be**
存 EXIST → 2982
在 BE → 2984
居 be present → 3080
臨 BE PRESENT AT → 1630
也 CLASSICAL COPULA → 3406

USAGE

aru
有る
① be, exist, be present, there is
② have, possess, own
③ have the experience of doing something
④ (have a magnitude of) number, cover, weigh, measure
⑤ happen, occur, take place
⑥ consist [lie] in, depend on
⑦ [in the form of transitive verb followed by て有る *te aru*] describes a state resulting from an action

在る
① (exist in a specified place) be at [in], be situated in, be sited
② be alive, live

HOMOPHONES

aru ⇨ 在 2984

COMPOUND FORMATION

有り難う *arigatō*
有り難う 'thank you' literally means "I find it difficult (難) to exist (有る ①)"; that is, "I could never be content until I have shown you my gratitude." Another interpretation is "the kindness you have shown me is so rare as to seldom exist."

2-4 ナ

在 在 在

2984 ZAI a(ru)

一 ナ ナ 𠂇 𠂇 在

1 2 3 4 5 6

Ⓒⓗ 在 zài

Radical	Strokes
土 32	6-3-3
Grade	**Freq**
Jōyō-5	209
口 3 - 2 - 4	

▶**BE**

COMPOUNDS

❶ [also prefix] [original meaning] (exist in a specified place) **be at [in], be situated in, be sited**

在庫 *zaiko* stock, stockpile
在学する *zaigaku suru* be in school
在校する *zaikō suru* be in school
在宅する *zaitaku suru* be in, be at home
在東京 *zaitōkyō* situated in Tokyo
不在 *fuzai* absence
所在 *shozai* whereabouts, position, situation

❷ⓐ **reside [live] temporarily, stay**

ⓑ [prefix] **resident in**

在日の *zainichi no* (staying) in Japan
在外の *zaigai no* overseas
在住する *zaijū suru* live, reside, dwell
在米中 *zaibeichū* while resident in America
駐在 *chūzai* residence, stay
滞在 *taizai* stay, sojourn
在西ベルリン邦人 *zainishiberurin hōjin* Japanese (resident) in West Berlin

❸ⓐ (exist in actuality) **be, exist**

ⓑ be alive, live

現在の *genzai no* present time, now; present tense; actually
存在する *sonzai suru* exist, be
自在に *jizai ni* freely, unrestrictedly, at will
実在 *jitsuzai* real [actual] existence, entity
在世中 *zaiseichū* during one's lifetime
健在だ *kenzai da* be well, be in good health

❹ the country; outskirts, suburbs

在郷 *zaigō* rural districts
在所 *zaisho* the country; one's residence
近在 *kinzai* neighboring villages, suburban districts

INDEPENDENT

【zai 在】 the country; outskirts, suburbs

練馬の在 *nerima no zai* the Nerima countryside

KUN

【a(ru) 在る】

① (exist in a specified place) be at [in], be situated in, be sited

机の上に本が在る *Tsukue no ue ni hon ga aru* There is a book on the desk

② be alive, live

在りし日 *arishi hi* the days when one was alive; bygone days

SYNONYMS

❶ & ❸ⓐ **exist and be**

存 EXIST → 2982
有 exist → 2983
居 be present → 3080
臨 BE PRESENT AT → 1630
也 CLASSICAL COPULA → 3406

❷ **stay**

滞 STAY → 663
留 STAY → 2580
駐 STATIONED → 1826
屯 STATION TROOPS → 3457
泊 STAY OVERNIGHT → 331
宿 LODGE → 2293

HOMOPHONES

aru ⇨ 有 2983

NOTE

⇨ see USAGE note at 有 2983

2-4 ナ

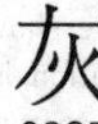

2985

▶**ASH**

nonstandard for 灰 2979

2-4 ナ

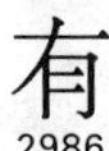

2986

▶**HAVE**

nonstandard for 有 2983

同 仝 同 冋

2987 DŌ ona(ji)

Ⓒ 同 tóng tòng

Radical	Strokes
口 30	6-3-3
Grade	**Freq**
Jōyō-2	18
口 3-2-4	

2-4 冂

▶SAME

COMPOUNDS

❶ [also prefix]

ⓐ **same, similar, equal**

ⓑ (the one previously mentioned) **the same (as above), the said, the aforementioned**

同一 *dōitsu* sameness, identity
同様の *dōyō no* similar
同好 *dōkō* similar tastes
同盟 *dōmei* alliance, league, union
同胞 *dōhō* brothers; brethren, fellow countrymen
同窓会 *dōsōkai* alumni association
同意 *dōi* consent, approval
同音語 *dōongo* homophone, homonym
同日 *dōjitsu* the same day, the said day
同氏 *dōshi* the said person, he
同国 *dōkoku* the same country, the said country
同委員会 *dōiinkai* the same committee

❷ⓐ **together, in common**

ⓑ come together, gather

同居する *dōkyo suru* live together
同情 *dōjō* sympathy, compassion
同封する *dōfū suru* enclose (in a letter)
共同する *kyōdō suru* work together, cooperate
一同 *ichidō* all (of us), all persons concerned
合同 *gōdō* combination, union, joint, merger; congruence

❸ abbrev. of 同志社大学 *dōshisha daigaku*: Doshisha University

同大 *dōdai* Doshisha University; the said university

INDEPENDENT

【**dōzuru** 同ずる】agree
和して同ぜず *washite dōzezu* harmonize but not agree

KUN

【**ona(ji)** 同じ】same, identical, similar; common
同じく *onajiku* in the same way, similarly
同い年 *onaidoshi* same age
同じ様に *onaji yō ni* in the same way

SYNONYMS

❶ⓐ **same and uniform**
一 same → 3341
等 EQUAL → 2682
平 equal → 3478
均 EVEN → 235
斉 UNIFORM → 2054

ⓑ **this and that**
該 the said → 1519
当 THE PRESENT → 2177
本 THIS → 3502
今 THIS (week, etc.) → 1968
之 this → 3420
是 this → 2436
爾 THAT → 3587
彼 that → 290

❷ⓐ **together**
併 TOGETHER → 83
並 side by side → 2246
共 JOINT → 2393
兼 CONCURRENTLY → 2286

NOTE

⇨ see COMPOUND FORMATION for 同胞 *dōhō* ⇨ 胞 917

2988

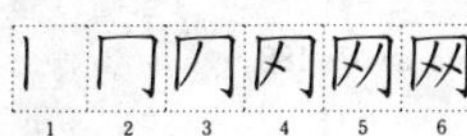

Radical	Strokes
网 122	6-6-0
Grade	**Freq**
Radical	
口 3-2-4	

2-4 冂

RADICAL 122

Standard form: 网 *amigashira* 'net'

Top variants: 罒 ⺳ *yonkashira* (置 署 罕)

Description: used in characters related to nets or their qualities

2-4 冂

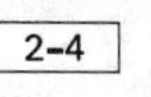

肉 incorrect classification ⇨ see 3200

2-4 匚

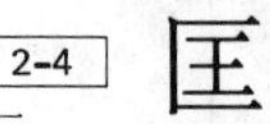

匡

2989 KYŌ NAMES tada tadashi tadasu masa masashi

CH 匡 kuāng

Radical	Strokes
匚 22	6-2-4
Grade	**Freq**
Names	2062
口 3-2-4	

一 二 𠄟 干 王 匡 (1 2 3 4 5 6)

▶RECTIFY

COMPOUNDS

❶ **rectify, correct, reform**

匡正する *kyōsei suru* reform (bad customs)

❷ [rare] save, deliver

匡救する *kyōkyū suru* deliver from sin; succor

NAMES

匡子 *masako* female name

匡四郎 *kyōshirō* male name

SYNONYMS

❶ **correct**

矯 RECTIFY → 1241
訂 REVISE → 1442
改 REFORM → 243
正 RIGHT → 3484
直す correct → 2932

2-4 匚

匠

2990 SHŌ takumi▲

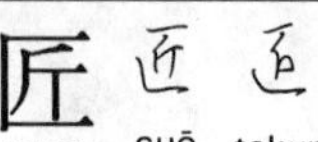

CH 匠 jiàng

Radical	Strokes
匚 22	6-2-4
Grade	**Freq**
Jōyō	1634
口 3-2-4	

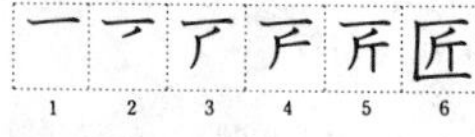

(1 2 3 4 5 6)

▶CRAFTSMAN

COMPOUNDS

❶ⓐ (skilled workman) **craftsman, artisan, workman**

ⓑ (master of an art) **craftsman, master, artist**

工匠 *kōshō* artisan, mechanic
名匠 *meishō* skilled craftsman
師匠 *shishō* master, teacher
巨匠 *kyoshō* great master, maestro

❷ idea, design, ingenuity

匠気 *shōki* affectation, showmanship
意匠 *ishō* design, idea

KUN

【takumi 匠】 artisan; woodworker, carpenter

SYNONYMS

❶ⓐ **workers and professionals**

工 workman → 3381
夫 MAN LABORER → 3460
嬢 (unmarried) female worker → 758
婦 woman worker → 469
手 OCCUPATION SUFFIX → 3456
屋 colloquial occupation suffix → 3098
員 MEMBER (of a staff) → 2269
人 person of certain category → 3368
者 person who → 3211
師 profession suffix → 1326
士 PROFESSION SUFFIX → 3405
客 skilled person → 2250
家 professional → 2273

ⓑ **great persons**

聖 great master → 2830
雄 hero → 1008
傑 OUTSTANDING PERSON → 155
豪 GREAT MAN → 2140

HOMOPHONES

takumi ⇨ 巧 188

NOTE

⇨ see USAGE note at 巧 188

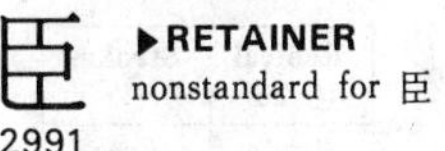

臣 ▶**RETAINER**
nonstandard for 臣 3068

2991

Radical	Strokes
臣 131	6-6-0
Grade	**Freq**
Variant	
□ 3 - 2 - 4	

2-4 匚

RADICAL 131
Standard form: 臣 *shin* 'retainer'
Left variant: 臣 *shin* (臨 臥)
Description: used for character classification

延 incorrect stroke count ⇨ see 3073

2-5 廴

述 迫 etc. incorrect stroke count ⇨ see □ 3–5

2-5 辶

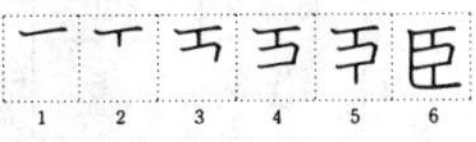

辰 辰 辰 (CH) 辰 chén

2992 SHIN tatsu NAMES toki nobu noburu

Radical	Strokes
辰 161	7-7-0
Grade	**Freq**
Names	1988
□ 3 - 2 - 5	

2-5 厂

RADICAL 161
Standard form: 辰 *shinnotatsu* 'the Dragon' (農 辱)
Description: used in characters related to agriculture

▶**THE DRAGON**

COMPOUNDS

❶ fifth sign of the Oriental zodiac: the Dragon —(time) 7–9 a.m., (direction) ESE, (season) March (of the lunar calendar) (⇨ see APPENDIX 7)

戊辰 *boshin* fifth of the sexagenary cycle

❷ time, day

誕辰 *tanshin* birthday

❸ celestial body

星辰 *seishin* stars, celestial bodies

KUN

【**tatsu** 辰】 fifth sign of the Oriental zodiac: the Dragon (⇨ ❶)

辰の年 *tatsu no toshi* the year of the Dragon

辰の刻 *tatsu no koku* the fifth hour, 8 a.m.; the Hour of the Dragon

NAMES

辰之助 *tatsunosuke* male name

辰巳 *tatsumi* surname also place name

辰夫 *tatsuo* (=*tokio*) male name

SYNONYMS

❶ **dragon**

竜 DRAGON → 2099

HOMOPHONES

tatsu ⇨ 竜 2099

NOTE

⇨ see USAGE note at 竜 2099

2-5 匚

医 醫 医 𠤏

2993

一 ㄏ 𠂇 𠂉 𠂊 矢 医

Ⓒ 医 yī

Radical	Strokes
匚 23	7-2-5
Grade	**Freq**
Jōyō-3	539
3-2-5	

▶MEDICINE ▶DOCTOR

COMPOUNDS

❶ **medicine, medical science, art of healing**

医道 *idō* art of medicine
医大 *idai* medical college
医化学 *ikagaku* medical chemistry
法医学 *hōigaku* legal medicine

❷ [also suffix] **doctor, physician**

医師 *ishi* doctor, physician, surgeon
医局 *ikyoku* medical staff room, medical office
獣医 *jūi* veterinarian
女医 *joi* woman doctor
歯科医 *shikai* dentist

❸ **cure**

医学 *igaku* medical science, medicine
医療 *iryō* medical treatment [care]
医者 *isha* doctor
医薬 *iyaku* medicine, drug; medical practice and dispensary
医院 *iin* clinic

INDEPENDENT

【i 医】 medicine, art of medicine, medical practice
医は仁術 *I wa jinjutsu* Medicine is a benevolent art

【isuru 医する】 treat, heal, cure

SYNONYMS

❸ **cure and recover**

治 CURE → 335
療 TREAT → 3288
癒 HEAL → 3291
快 recover → 245

2-6 廴

建 廻 incorrect stroke count ⇨ see 3-6

2-6 辶

送 追 etc. incorrect stroke count ⇨ see 3-6

2-6 厂

厚 incorrect stroke count ⇨ see 3003

2-6 厂

房 2994

▶CHAMBER
nonstandard for 房 1946

2-6 厂

肩 2995

▶SHOULDER
nonstandard for 肩 1947

2-6 厂

戻 2996

▶RETURN
nonstandard for 戻 1942

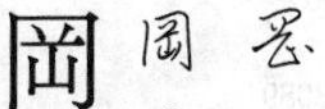

2997 KŌ oka

CH 冈 gāng

Radical	Strokes
山 46	8-3-5
Grade	**Freq**
Non-Jōyō	420
囗 3-2-6	

2-6 冂

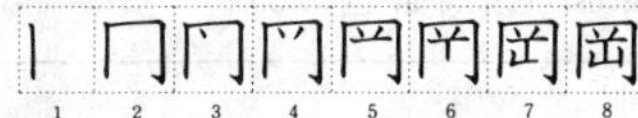

▶**HILL**

COMPOUNDS

❶ **hill**

岡陵 *kōryō* [archaic] hill

❷ [original meaning, now archaic] ridge (of a mountain)

KUN

【oka 岡】

① [usu. 丘] hill, hillock, mound—used chiefly in proper names

岡山県 *okayamaken* Okayama Prefecture

岡野 *okano* surname

② [sometimes also 傍-] [in compounds] outsider, third party, bystander

岡っ引き *okappiki* detective, secret policeman (in Edo Japan)

岡惚れ *okabore* illicit love

SYNONYMS

❶ **hills**

丘 HILL → 3495

台 heights → 2005

坂 SLOPE → 234

阪 slope → 271

塚 MOUND → 556

陵 high mound → 544

HOMOPHONES

oka ⇨ 丘 3495 陸 543 傍 147

NOTE

⇨ see USAGE note at 丘 3495

周 周 周 周

2998 SHŪ mawa(ri)

CH 周 zhōu

Radical	Strokes
口 30	8-3-5
Grade	**Freq**
Jōyō-4	678
囗 3-2-6	

2-6 冂

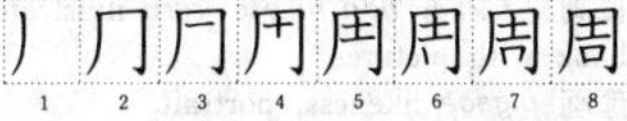

▶**PERIPHERY**

COMPOUNDS

❶ **periphery, circumference, perimeter**

周囲 *shūi* circumference, periphery; surroundings

周辺 *shūhen* environs, outskirts; circumference

周回 *shūkai* circumference, girth, surroundings

円周 *enshū* circumference

四周 *shishū* circumference, periphery

❷ⓐ **circuit, cycle, circle**

ⓑ **counter for circuits or laps**

ⓒ [rarely also 週 3122] **circuit, circle, go round**

周波 *shūha* cycle

半周 *hanshū* semicircle, hemicycle

三周 *sanshū* three rounds [laps]

一周する *isshū suru* make a round, circuit; sail round, revolve

周期 *shūki* period, cycle

周遊 *shūyū* (circular) tour, pleasure [round] trip

❸ anniversary

周年 *shūnen* anniversary; whole year

三周忌 *sanshūki* second anniversary of death

❹ throughout, everywhere

周知 *shūchi* common knowledge

周到な *shūtō na* scrupulous, cautious, circumspect

❺ Zhou Dynasty (approx. 1100–256 B.C.)

周王朝 *shūōchō* Zhou Dynasty

INDEPENDENT

【shū 周】 periphery; Zhou Dynasty

周五百メートル *shū gohyaku mētoru* periphery of 500 meters

KUN

【mawa(ri) 周り】

ⓐ periphery, surroundings, circumference

ⓑ border, fringe

周りの人 *mawari no hito* surrounding people

地球の周り *chikyū no mawari* circumference of the earth; space around the earth

池の周りを一回りする *ike no mawari o hitomawari suru* go round a pond

SYNONYMS

❶ **periphery**

囲 circumference → 3069

郭 OUTER ENCLOSURE → 1678
❺ **earlier Chinese dynasties**
商 Shang Dynasty → 2116
夏 Xia Dynasty → 2113
漢 Han Dynasty → 657
晋 JIN DYNASTY → 2656

HOMOPHONES

mawari ⇨ 回 3055 廻 3089

NOTE

⇨ see USAGE note at 回 3055

2-6 冂

周

2999

▶**PERIPHERY**

nonstandard for 周 2998

2-6 凵

画 畫

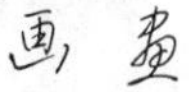

3000 GA KAKU e▲ ega(ku)▲

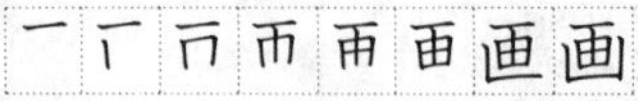

Ⓒⓗ 画 huà

Radical	Strokes
田 102	8-5-3
Grade	**Freq**
Jōyō-2	176
口 3 - 2 - 6	

▶**PICTURE** ▶**DRAW UP A PLAN**

COMPOUNDS

❶ⓐ [also suffix] **picture, drawing, painting**
ⓑ **draw, paint**
ⓒ abbrev. of 映画 *eiga*: **film, movie, motion picture**
ⓓ (television) field
画廊 *garō* picture gallery
絵画 *kaiga* pictures, paintings, drawings
漫画 *manga* cartoon, comic strip
名画 *meiga* famous picture, masterpiece; noted film
映画 *eiga* cinema, film, movie
日本画 *nihonga* picture in the Japanese style
画家 *gaka* artist, painter
洋画 *yōga* foreign film; Western painting
邦画 *hōga* Japanese film [movie]; Japanese painting
画面 *gamen* picture; television field; screen
❷ [formerly also 劃 *kaku* 1887] [original meaning] **mark off, draw a line, demarcate, partition**
画期的な *kakkiteki na* epoch-making, epochal
画一的な *kakuitsuteki na* uniform, standardized
画定 *kakutei* demarcation
区画する *kukaku suru* divide, draw a line, mark off
❸ [formerly also 劃 *kaku* 1887]
ⓐ **draw up a plan, plan, design**
ⓑ **plan**
画策する *kakusaku suru* plan, scheme
計画 *keikaku* plan, project
企画 *kikaku* plan, project
参画 *sankaku* participation in planning
❹ⓐ stroke of a Chinese character
ⓑ counter for strokes
画数 *kakusū* stroke-count
四画の字 *yonkaku no ji* four-stroke character

INDEPENDENT

【kakusuru 画する(=劃する)】 mark off; plan

KUN

【e 画】
ⓐ [usu. 絵] [also suffix] picture, painting, drawing, sketch, illustration, cut, (woodcut) print
ⓑ [sometimes also 絵] television field
本に画を入れる *hon ni e o ireru* illustrate a book with pictures
似顔画 *nigaoe* likeness, portrait

【ega(ku) 画く】 [usu. 描く] draw, paint
油絵を画く *aburae o egaku* paint in oil

SYNONYMS

❶ⓐ **picture**
図 DRAWING → 3071
絵 PICTURE → 1346
ⓑ **draw**
描 DEPICT → 488
ⓒ **motion picture**
映 motion picture → 892
❷ **mark**
印 imprint → 828
押 seal → 314
❸ **plans and planning**
計 PLAN → 1441
企 PROJECT → 2021
案 PROPOSAL → 2270
図 systematic plan → 3071
謀 SCHEME → 1593
策 SCHEME → 2679
略 STRATEGY → 1169

HOMOPHONES

e ⇨ 絵 1346
egaku ⇨ 描 488

NOTE

⇨ see USAGE notes at 絵 1346 and 描 488

函

3001 KAN hako

CH 函 hán

Radical	Strokes
凵 17	8-2-6
Grade Reference	Freq
口 3 - 2 - 6	

2-6 凵

COMPOUNDS

❶ [now usu. 箱 *hako*] [original meaning] box, case, mailbox

投函する *tōkan suru* mail (a letter), put in the post

潜函病 *senkanbyō* caisson disease

私書函 *shishobako* post office box (P.O.B.)

❷ [now also 関 *kan* 3328] used phonetically for *han* (in Chinese)

函数 *kansū math* function

❸ abbrev. of 函館 *hakodate*, name of a city in Hokkaido

青函トンネル *seikan tonneru* Seikan Tunnel

HOMOPHONES

hako ⇨ 箱 2711

NOTE

⇨ see USAGE note at 箱 2711

通 連 etc.

incorrect stroke count ⇨ see 口 3 – 7

2-7 辶

厖

3002 BŌ

CH 庞 páng máng

Radical	Strokes
厂 27	9-2-7
Grade Reference	Freq
口 3 - 2 - 7	

2-7 厂

COMPOUNDS

● [now replaced by 膨 1084] bulky, extensive

厖大な *bōdai na* bulky, massive, extensive

厚 厚 厚

3003 KŌ atsu(i)

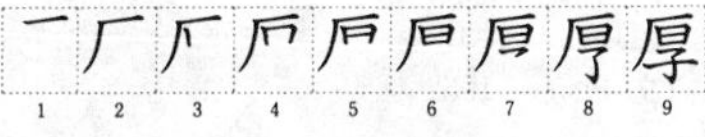

CH 厚 hòu

Radical	Strokes
厂 27	9-2-7
Grade	Freq
Jōyō-5	721
口 3 - 2 - 7	

2-7 厂

▶**THICK** ▶**KIND**

COMPOUNDS

❶ⓐ (great in depth) **thick, deep**

ⓑ thick, rich, plentiful

厚薄 *kōhaku* (relative) thickness

濃厚な *nōkō na* thick, dense, heavy, rich

重厚 *jūkō* profoundness, depth, seriousness

❷ **kind, cordial, hearty, heartfelt, kind-hearted, warm**

厚意 *kōi* kindness, favor

厚情 *kōjō* kindness, favor, hospitality

厚志 *kōshi* kindness, kind thought [intention]

厚遇 *kōgū* cordial welcome, kind treatment

温厚な *onkō na* gentle, courteous

❸ make plentiful, enrich

厚生 *kōsei* public welfare, health promotion

厚生省 *kōseishō* Ministry of Health and Welfare

❹ abbrev. of 厚生省 *kōseishō*: Ministry of Health and Welfare

厚相 *kōshō* Minister of Health and Welfare

❺ great, excessive

厚恩 *kōon* great favor [kindness]

厚顔な *kōgan na* impudent, shameless, brazen

KUN

【atsu(i) 厚い】

① (great in depth) thick, bulky, deep
厚さ *atsusa* thickness
厚板 *atsuita* thick board, plank
厚かましい *atsukamashii* unabashed, brazen
分厚い *buatsui* bulky, massive

② [formerly also 篤い] cordial, kind, hearty, warm, deep
厚い持てなし *atsui motenashi* cordial reception
厚く礼を述べる *atsuku rei o noberu* thank (a person) heartily
手厚い *teatsui* warm, hearty, cordial
下に厚く *shita ni atsuku* more generously for the lower-paid

SYNONYMS

❶ⓐ thick
太 THICK (great in diameter) → 2152

❷ kind
篤 cordial → 2716
懇 cordial → 2899
慈 AFFECTIONATE → 2339
温 warmhearted → 608
渥 GRACIOUS → 600
優 kindly → 177

USAGE

atsui

厚い
① (great in depth) thick, bulky, deep
② [formerly also 篤い] cordial, kind, hearty, warm, deep

篤い
① [now usu. 厚い] cordial, kind, hearty, warm, deep
② (of an illness) critical, serious, dangerous

HOMOPHONES

atsui ⇨ 篤 2716

2-7 厂

厘

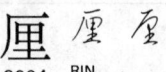

3004 RIN

(CH) 厘 lí

Radical	Strokes
厂 27	9-2-7
Grade	**Freq**
Jōyō	1514
口 3-2-7	

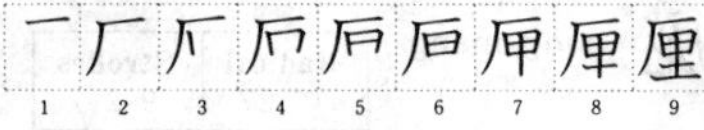

▶*RIN*

COMPOUNDS

rin:

❶ former monetary unit equiv. to 1/1000 of a yen (円)
一厘 *ichirin* 1 *rin*

❷ⓐ former unit of length equiv. to approx. 0.3 mm or 1/100 of a *sun* (寸)

ⓑ former unit of weight equiv. to 37.5 mg or 1/100 of a momme (匁)
一分一厘も違わず *ichibu ichirin mo tagawazu* be exactly alike
厘毛の軽重無し *rinmō no keichō nashi* be equal in weight [significance]

❸ⓐ 1/100

ⓑ 1/100 of 10%: 0.001
九分九厘 *kubu kurin* ten to one, in all probability
年利六分五厘 *nenri rokubu gorin* annual interest of 6.5%

INDEPENDENT

【rin 厘】*rin* (⇨ ❶ & ❷); 1/100 ; 0.001 (⇨ ❸ ⓑ)

SYNONYMS

❶ Japanese money denominations
銭 sen → 1725
円 YEN → 2955
両 *ryo* → 3518
文 *mon* → 1962

2-7 厂

扁

3005 HEN

(CH) 扁 biǎn piān

Radical	Strokes
戶 63	9-4-5
Grade	**Freq**
Reference	
口 3-2-7	

COMPOUNDS

❶ flat
扁平な *henpei na* flat
扁桃 *hentō* almond; tonsils

❷ small, little
扁舟 *henshū* little boat

❸ [now usu. 偏 133] left-side radical of Chinese characters, left radical

扁旁 *henbō* left and right radicals

盾 𥄉 𥅊

3006 JUN tate

一 厂 𠂆 𠂇 𠂈 𠂉 盾 盾 盾
1 2 3 4 5 6 7 8 9

Ⓒⓗ 盾 dùn

Radical	Strokes
目 109	9-5-4
Grade	**Freq**
Jōyō	1538
☐ 3 - 2 - 7	

2-7 厂

▶**SHIELD**

COMPOUNDS

● [original meaning] **shield**

矛盾 *mujun* contradiction

矛盾する *mujun suru* be contradictory, be at variance

KUN

【**tate 盾**】[sometimes also 楯] shield, escutcheon

盾突く *tatetsuku* oppose, defy, rebel

盾座 *tateza* the Shield, Scutum

法律を盾に取って *hōritsu o tate ni totte* on the authority of law

SYNONYMS

● **protective coverings**

甲 armor → 3481

面 mask → 2087

USAGE

tate

盾

[sometimes also 楯] shield, escutcheon

楯

[usu. 盾] shield, escutcheon

HOMOPHONES

tate ⇨ 楯 1016

NOTE

⇨ see COMPOUND FORMATION for 矛盾 *mujun* ⇨ 矛 2008

風 𠘨 風 𠙖

3007 FŪ FU kaze kaza- -kaze

Ⓒⓗ 风 fēng

Radical	Strokes
風 182	9-9-0
Grade	**Freq**
Jōyō-2	240
☐ 3 - 2 - 7	

2-7 几

RADICAL 182

Standard form: 風 *kaze* 'wind' (颯 飄 颪)

Left variant: 風 *kaze* (颱 颶)

Description: used in characters related to wind or its qualities

▶**WIND** ▶**MANNER**

COMPOUNDS

❶ [also suffix] **wind, breeze**

風速 *fūsoku* wind velocity

風波 *fūha* wind and waves, rough seas, storm

台風(＝颱風) *taifū* typhoon

強風 *kyōfū* strong [high] wind

扇風機 *senpūki* electric fan

季節風 *kisetsufū* seasonal wind, periodic wind

❷ (trend of events) wind, trend, movement, tendency

風潮 *fūchō* tide, trend, tendency

風雲 *fūun* state of affairs, situation

❸ (prevailing customs) **manners, customs, tradition**

風俗 *fūzoku* manners, customs; popular [public] morals

風習 *fūshū* manners and customs

家風 *kafū* family traditions [customs]

❹ [also suffix] (characteristic style) **manner, style, school**

整風 *seifū* rectification

洋風 *yōfū* Western [foreign] style

歌風 *kafū* style of poetry

日本風 *nihonfū* Japanese style

鷗外風に *ōgaifū ni* in [after] the manner of Ogai

❺ [also suffix] **air, airs, appearance, manner, bearing, atmosphere**

風格 *fūkaku* (distinctive) character, (admirable) appearance; style, race

風采 *fūsai* appearance, air, mien, getup

風体 *fūtei* (=*fūtai*) appearance, looks; posture
軍人風の *gunjinfū no* of military bearing
❻ elegance, charm, taste
風味 *fūmi* flavor, taste
風雅 *fūga* elegance, refinement, daintiness
風流 *fūryū* refined elegance, taste
風情 *fuzei* appearance, air, taste, elegance
❼ **(beautiful) scenery**
風景 *fūkei* scenery, landscape, view
風物 *fūbutsu* natural objects [features], scenery; scenes and manners
風光 *fūkō* (beautiful) scenery, natural beauty
風土記 *fudoki* topography
❽ spread a rumor
風説 *fūsetsu* rumor, hearsay
風評 *fūhyō* rumor, report
風聞 *fūbun* rumor, hearsay
❾ (infectious) disease, serious disease
風疹 *fūshin* German measles, rubella
中風 *chūbu* (=*chūbū, chūfū*) palsy, paralysis
破傷風 *hashōfū* tetanus
❿ [formerly also 諷 *fū* 1594] insinuate, hint, satirize
風刺 *fūshi* satire, sarcasm
風喩 *fūyu* hint, insinuation, allegory
⓫ influence, educate
風靡する *fūbi suru* overwhelm, dominate, sweep

INDEPENDENT

【fū 風】
① (prevailing customs) manners, customs, tradition
勤倹の風 *kinken no fū* custom [habit] of diligence and thrift
② tendency, inclination
小成に安んじる風 *shōsei ni yasunjiru fū* tendency to be content with small successes
③ (characteristic style) manner, style, school
こんな風に *konna fū ni* in this way
④ air, airs, appearance, manner, mien, bearing, atmosphere
偉そうな風 *erasō na fū* air of importance
⑤ type, kind
こんな風な物 *konna fū na mono* things of this kind

KUN

【kaze 風, kaza- 風-】 wind, breeze, draft, current; turn of events
風車 *kazaguruma* (=*fūsha*) windmill; pinwheel
風向き *kazamuki* wind direction
風当りが強い *kazeatari ga tsuyoi* be windswept; receive harsh treatment
北風 *kitakaze* north wind
神風 *kamikaze* providential [divine] wind; suicide plane, kamikaze
風の吹き回しで *kaze no fukimawashi de* by a (curious) turn of events

【-kaze -風】 [suffix] air, airs; touch of
先輩風を吹かす *senpaikaze o fukasu* put on a patronizing air
臆病風 *okubyōkaze* panic, funk

SPECIAL READINGS

風邪 *kaze* (=*fūja*) (common) cold

SYNONYMS

❶ **wind**
嵐 STORM → 2314
台 typhoon → 2005
❸ **custom**
習 CUSTOM → 2667
俗 popular custom → 104
慣 HABITUAL PRACTICE → 685
例 established practice → 89
癖 HABIT → 3290
弊 EVIL PRACTICE → 2884
❹ **way and style**
様 MODE → 1052
方 WAY → 1963
途 WAY → 3107
法 METHOD → 333
流 STYLE → 441
式 STYLE → 3049
調 TONE → 1567
❺ **appearance**
色 COLOR → 2029
容 APPEARANCE → 2277
姿 FIGURE → 2636
相 PHASE → 900
体 FORM (outer appearance) → 71
❻ **flavor and elegance**
品 refinement → 2248
味 TASTE → 274
趣 FLAVOR → 3317
❼ **view**
景 SCENE → 2470
光 scenery → 2391
観 VIEW → 1880
❾ **disease**
病 ILLNESS → 3277
疾 DISEASE → 3279
症 PATHOLOGICAL CONDITION → 3280
患 AFFECTED BY DISEASE → 2747
疫 EPIDEMIC → 3276

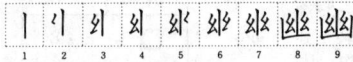

幽 幽 幽 3008 YŪ

CH 幽 yōu

Radical	Strokes
幺 52	9-3-6
Grade	**Freq**
Jōyō	1747
□ 3-2-7	

2-7 凵

▶QUIET AND SECLUDED

COMPOUNDS

❶ⓐ quiet and secluded, deep and remote
ⓑ seclude, confine, imprison
幽棲(＝幽栖)する *yūsei suru* live a quiet life in seclusion away from the masses
幽谷 *yūkoku* deep ravine, secluded valley
幽寂な *yūjaku na* quiet, sequestered
幽居 *yūkyo* hermitage, retirement, seclusion
幽閉 *yūhei* house arrest, confinement
幽囚 *yūshū* imprisonment

❷ deep hidden, profound
幽玄な *yūgen na* subtle and profound, quiet and beautiful, occult
幽愁 *yūshū* deep contemplation

❸ world of the dead, the other world, Hades
幽霊 *yūrei* ghost, apparition
幽冥 *yūmei* this and the other world
幽界 *yūkai* Hades, realm of the dead
幽鬼 *yūki* departed soul, spirit of the dead

❹ [original meaning] dim, indistinct
幽暗 *yūan* gloom, darkness

INDEPENDENT

【yū 幽】 quietness and seclusion; invisible world
【yūsuru 幽する】 confine (to a house), imprison

SYNONYMS

❶ⓐ inner
深 DEEP → 524
奥 inner → 2824

ⓐ quiet
粛 still → 3581
寂 quiet → 2290
閑 QUIET → 3322
静 QUIET → 1728
黙 SILENT → 2865

❷ profound
玄 PROFOUND → 1991
奥 inmost → 2824
深 DEEP → 524

❸ posthumous worlds
天 HEAVEN → 3442
獄 hell → 712

函 incorrect stroke count ⇨ see 3001 — 2-7 凵

遇 incorrect stroke count ⇨ see 3135 — 2-8 辶

遊 incorrect stroke count ⇨ see 3142 — 2-8 辶

進 週 etc. incorrect stroke count ⇨ see □ 3-8 — 2-8 辶

2-8 厂

原 原 原

3009 GEN hara

CH 原 yuán

Radical	Strokes
厂 27	10-2-8
Grade	Freq
Jōyō-2	141
□ 3-2-8	

一 厂 厂 厂 历 戸 盾 厚 原 原
1 2 3 4 5 6 7 8 9 10

▶PLAIN ▶ORIGINAL

COMPOUNDS

❶ [also suffix] **plain, field, plateau**

原野 *gen'ya* vast plain, wilderness, field
高原 *kōgen* plateau, tableland, heights
草原 *sōgen* grassland, prairie, savannah, pampas, steppe
平原 *heigen* plain, prairie
氷原 *hyōgen* ice field
火口原 *kakōgen* crater basin

❷ⓐ [also prefix] **original, primary, primitive**

ⓑ [original meaning] origin, source, root

ⓒ in the original state, raw, crude

原因 *gen'in* cause, origin
原則 *gensoku* principle, general rule
原作 *gensaku* original (work)
原子 *genshi* atom
原案 *gen'an* original bill [plan]
原始的な *genshiteki na* primitive, primeval
原色 *genshoku* primary color
原判決 *genhanketsu* original decision [judgment]
病原体 *byōgentai* pathogen
抗原 *kōgen* antigen
原料 *genryō* raw material
原油 *gen'yu* crude oil

❸ abbrev. of 原子力 *genshiryoku*: atomic energy

原爆 *genbaku* atomic bomb
原発 *genpatsu* nuclear power plant

KUN

【hara 原】 plain, field, plateau

野原 *nohara* field, plain
海原 *unabara* sea, ocean

SPECIAL READINGS

河原(＝川原) *kawara* dry riverbed, river beach

SYNONYMS

❶ **uncultivated expanses of land**

野 FIELD → 1485
漠 DESERT → 655

❷ⓐ **original**

本 original → 3502
素 primary → 2458
初 FIRST → 1116

ⓒ **natural**

粗 crude → 1329
野 wild → 1485
地 natural → 204

2-8 厂

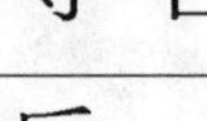

辱 唇 incorrect classification ⇨ see 7-3

2-8

扇

3010

▶FAN

nonstandard for 扇 1950

2-8 匚

匿 匿 匿 匿

3011 TOKU kakuma(u)▲

CH 匿 nì

Radical	Strokes
匚 23	10-2-8
Grade	Freq
Jōyō	1572
□ 3-2-8	

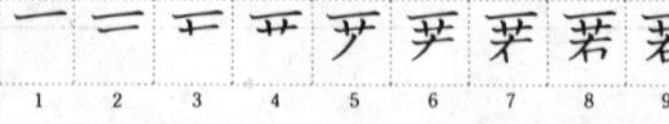

一 二 亠 艹 芋 芋 若 若 若 匿
1 2 3 4 5 6 7 8 9 10

▶CONCEAL

COMPOUNDS

● [original meaning] **conceal, hide**

匿名 *tokumei* anonymity, incognito, pseudonym
隠匿 *intoku* concealment; misprision
秘匿する *hitoku suru* hide, conceal
蔵匿する *zōtoku suru* [rare] conceal, shelter, harbor

KUN

【kakuma(u) 匿う】 shelter (a prisoner), harbor, give refuge

犯人を匿う *hannin o kakumau* shelter a criminal

SYNONYMS

● hide

隠 HIDE → 713
伏 lie in concealment → 45
潜 LURK → 746
忍 perform by stealth → 2212

道 運 etc. incorrect stroke count ⇨ see □3-9 | 2-9 辶

厝 incorrect classification ⇨ see 2739 (nonstandard for 唇 2737) | 2-9 厂

盾
3012
▶QUALITY ▶MATTER
handwritten abbreviation for 質 2808 | 2-9 厂

區
3013
▶DISTRICT ▶WARD
nonstandard for 区 2963 | 2-9 匚

匿
3014
▶CONCEAL
nonstandard for 匿 3011 | 2-9 匚

違 遠 etc. incorrect stroke count ⇨ see □3-10 | 2-10 辶

扉
3015
▶HINGED DOOR
nonstandard for 扉 1955 | 2-10 厂

雇
3016
▶EMPLOY
nonstandard for 雇 1956 | 2-10 厂

適 遭 etc. incorrect stroke count ⇨ see □3-11 | 2-11 辶

選 遺 etc. incorrect stroke count ⇨ see □3-12 | 2-12 辶

厭
3017
EN ON iya a(kiru) ito(u)

CH 厌 yàn

Radical	Strokes
厂 27	14-2-12
Grade Reference	Freq
□ 3-2-12	

2-12 厂

COMPOUNDS

❶ [now usu. 嫌な *iya na*] disagreeable, repulsive

厭な気持ち *iya na kimochi* unpleasant feeling

厭厭 *iyaiya* grudgingly, unwillingly; (of children) shaking of the head in refusal
厭がらせ *iyagarase* harassment
❷ⓐ [usu. 飽きる *akiru*] grow tired of, lose interest in
ⓑ be disgusted with, detest, dislike
厭世観 *enseikan* pessimism
厭戦 *ensen* war-weariness
厭き厭きする *akiaki suru* be sick (of), be bored (with)
厭離 *onri Buddhism* depart from (in disdain)

厭う *itou* dislike; be disgusted with; take (good) care of
危険を厭わない *kiken o itowanai* do not mind running a risk
❸ take (good) care of
身を厭う *mi o itou* take good care of oneself

HOMOPHONES
iya ⇨ 嫌 636 否 2406
akiru ⇨ 飽 1715

NOTE
⇨ see USAGE notes at 嫌 636 and 飽 1715

2-12 厂

暦 暦 暦 暦 — CH 历 lì

3018 REKI koyomi

Radical	Strokes
日 72	14-4-10
Grade	**Freq**
Jōyō	1681
□ 3-2-12	

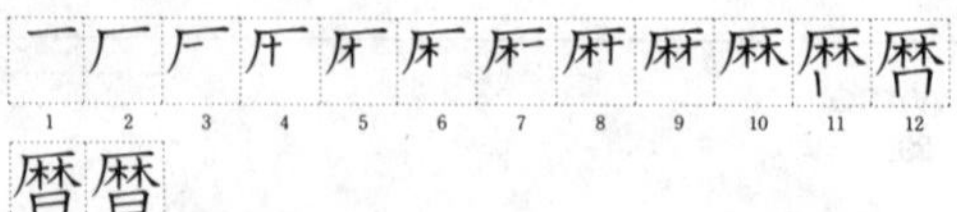

▶**CALENDAR**

COMPOUNDS
❶ [also suffix] **calendar**
暦年 *rekinen* calendar year
太陽暦 *taiyōreki* solar calendar
旧暦 *kyūreki* old [lunar] calendar
西暦 *seireki* Christian Era, A.D.
陰暦 *inreki* lunar calendar
❷ years, time
還暦 *kanreki* sixtieth anniversary of one's birthday

INDEPENDENT
【**reki** 暦】calendar, almanac

KUN
【**koyomi** 暦】calendar, almanac
花暦 *hanagoyomi* floral calendar

SYNONYMS
❶ **calendars**
新 new calendar → 1784
旧 old calendar → 14

NOTE
★do not confuse with 歴 3019

2-12 厂

歴 歴 歴 厂 歴 歴 — CH 历 lì

3019 REKI REKKI▲

Radical	Strokes
止 77	14-4-10
Grade	**Freq**
Jōyō-4	753
□ 3-2-12	

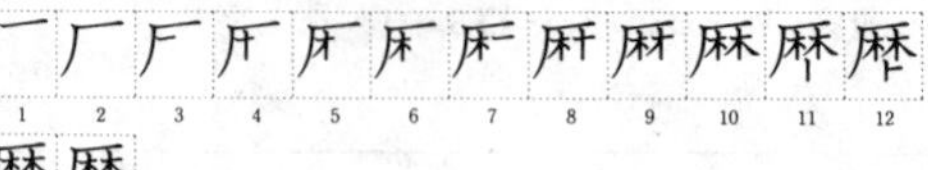

▶**PERSONAL HISTORY**

COMPOUNDS
❶ [also suffix] **personal history, one's career, experience, personal record**
履歴 *rireki* personal history, career
学歴 *gakureki* academic career
経歴 *keireki* personal history
病歴 *byōreki* case history
逮捕歴 *taihoreki* criminal record
一輪車歴 *ichirinshareki* one's experience as a unicyclist
❷ **pass, elapse, pass through, experience**
歴史 *rekishi* history
歴戦 *rekisen* long record of active service
遍歴 *henreki* travels, pilgrimage
❸ successive, successively, one by one
歴任 *rekinin* successive service in various posts
歴訪する *rekihō suru* make a round of calls
歴代 *rekidai* successive reigns
❹ clear, plain, obvious
歴然たる *rekizentaru* clear, obvious, plain
お歴歴 *orekireki* notables, distinguished persons

❺ [also 瀝 *reki* 807]
ⓐ drip, trickle
ⓑ pour
歴青炭 *rekiseitan* bituminous coal
披歴する *hireki suru* express (one's opinion), reveal (one's thoughts)

INDEPENDENT

【rekki to shita 歴とした】 clear, plain; respectable, decent

SYNONYMS

❶ **history**
伝 biography → 44
史 HISTORY → 3510

❷ **elapse**
経 pass → 1331
去 pass away → 2156
過 PASS BY → 3137

❸ **in succession**
連 IN SUCCESSION → 3103
逐 ONE BY ONE → 3102
逓 progressively → 3106
漸 GRADUALLY → 706

NOTE

⇨ see COMPOUND FORMATION for 履歴 *rireki* ⇨ 履 3171
★do not confuse with 暦 3018

避 還 incorrect stroke count ⇨ see 口 3-13 — 2-13 辶

暦 3020 **▶CALENDAR** — 2-14 厂
nonstandard for 暦 3018

歷 3021 **▶PERSONAL HISTORY** — 2-14 厂
nonstandard for 歴 3019

壓 3022 **▶PRESSURE** — 2-15 厂
nonstandard for 圧 2970

门 incorrect classification ⇨ see 3431 (nonstandard for 門 888) — 3-0 门

口 incorrect classification ⇨ see 3382 — 3-0 口

囗 incorrect classification ⇨ see 3391 — 3-0 囗

辶 incorrect stroke count ⇨ see 3191 — 3-1 辶

牙 incorrect classification ⇨ see 3435 — 3-1 牙

尺 incorrect classification ⇨ see 3440 — 3-1 尸

3-1 不 incorrect classification ⇨ see 3434

3-1 斤 incorrect classification ⇨ see 2949

3-1

尤

3023 YŪ motto(mo)

CH 尤 yóu

Radical	Strokes
尢 43	4-3-1
Grade	Freq
Reference	
口 3-3-1	

COMPOUNDS

❶ outstanding, excellent
尤物 *yūbutsu* superfine thing; beauty, belle
尤なる *yūnaru* best, most excellent
❷ right, reasonable, natural
尤もらしい *mottomorashii* plausible, specious
御尤も *Gomottomo* You are quite right
❸ indeed, it is true; but
尤も例外は有る *Mottomo reigai wa aru* There are, indeed, some exceptions

HOMOPHONES

mottomo ⇨ 最 2472

NOTE

⇨ see USAGE note at 最 2472

3-1 方 incorrect classification ⇨ see 1963

3-1 片 incorrect classification ⇨ see 3461

3-1

爪

3024 SŌ tsume tsuma-

CH 爪 zhǎo zhuǎ

Radical	Strokes
爪 87	4-4-0
Grade	Freq
Reference	
口 3-3-1	

1 2 3 4

RADICAL 87
Standard form: 爪 *tsume* 'claw' (爬)
Top variant: ⺥ *notsu* (爵)
Top variant: ⺤ *tsumekanmuri* (争)
Description: used in characters related to grasping or pulling

COMPOUNDS

❶ [original meaning] nail, claw, talon, hoof
爪切り *tsumekiri* nail clipper [nipper]
爪跡 *tsumeato* scratch, nail mark
蹴爪 *kezume* cockspur
❷ plectrum, pick
爪音 *tsumaoto* sound of a koto; clang of hoofs
琴爪 *kotozume* artificial fingernail [plectrum] of ivory used in playing the koto
❸ pawl, catch, hook
爪クラッチ *tsumekuratchi* claw clutch
❹ [in compounds]
ⓐ fingertip
ⓑ tiptoe
爪印 *tsumein* thumbprint, thumb impression
爪弾く *tsumabiku* pluck the strings (of a guitar)
爪弾き *tsumahajiki* fillip; ostracism; black sheep (of a family)
爪楊枝 *tsumayōji* toothpick
爪先 *tsumasaki* tip of a toe, tiptoe, toe

爪立つ *tsumadatsu* stand on tiptoe

曰

3025 ETSU iwa(ku) notama(waku)

Ⓒⓗ 曰 yuē

Radical 曰 73	Strokes 4-4-0
Grade Reference	Freq
口 3 - 3 - 1	

3-1 口

RADICAL 73

Standard form: 曰 *hirabi* 'say'
Variant: 曰 *hirabi* (書 最 曲)
Description: used for character classification

COMPOUNDS

❶ *literary*

ⓐ [original meaning] say (that…)

ⓑ [now also 宣わく *notamawaku*] [honorific] say that…

曰く言い難し *Iwaku iigatashi* It is hard to say

子曰わく *Shi notamawaku* Confucius says…

❷ reason, pretext; history

曰く付きの *iwakutsuki no* with a history [story]

HOMOPHONES

notamawaku ⇨ 宣 2252

NOTE

⇨ see USAGE note at 宣 2252
★ do not confuse with 日 3027

曰

3026

Radical 曰 73	Strokes 4-4-0
Grade Radical	Freq
口 3 - 3 - 1	

3-1 口

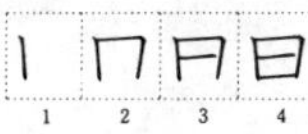

RADICAL 73

variant of 曰 *hirabi* 'say'
⇨ see 曰 3025 for radical description

日 日 㘝 㫡

3027 NICHI JITSU hi -bi -ka

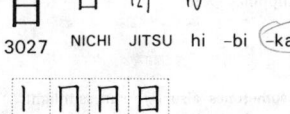

Ⓒⓗ 日 rì

Radical 日 72	Strokes 4-4-0
Grade Jōyō-1	Freq 1
口 3 - 3 - 1	

3-1 口

RADICAL 72

variant of 日 *hi* 'sun'
⇨ see 日 3028 for radical description

▶DAY ▶SUN ▶JAPAN

COMPOUNDS

❶ⓐ (period of light) **day**

ⓑ [also suffix] (24-hour period) **day, daily**

ⓒ **counter for days**

ⓓ **suffix for days of the month**

日夜 *nichiya* day and night
日中 *nitchū* during the day
日給 *nikkyū* daily wage
日運動 *nichiundō* daily motion
毎日 *mainichi* every day
今日 *konnichi* today, these days
一日 *ichinichi* a day; all day
本日 *honjitsu* today
平日 *heijitsu* weekday
太陽日 *taiyōjitsu* solar day
五十日 *gojūnichi* 50 days
十一月三十日 *jūichigatsu sanjūnichi* November 30

❷ (day on which something occurs) date, day, anniversary

日時 *nichiji* date, time
期日 *kijitsu* (fixed) date, due date
生年月日 *seinengappi* date of birth
命日 *meinichi* anniversary of death

❸ [original meaning] **sun, sunlight**

日光 *nikkō* sunshine, sunlight
日没 *nichibotsu* sunset
日食 *nisshoku* solar eclipse
日月 *jitsugetsu* sun and moon; time, days, years
落日 *rakujitsu* setting sun

❹ **Sunday**
日曜日 *nichiyōbi* Sunday
土日 *donichi* Saturday and Sunday, weekend

❺ⓐ **Japan**
ⓑ Japanese (language)
日本 *nihon* (=*nippon*) Japan
日銀 *nichigin* Bank of Japan
日米 *nichibei* Japan and U.S.
来日する *rainichi suru* come to Japan
日英通訳 *nichiei tsūyaku* Japanese-English interpreting

❻ abbrev. of 日向 *hyūga*, old name for Miyazaki Prefecture
日豊本線 *nippō honsen* Nippo Main Line (Kagoshima-Miyazaki-Fukuoka Railway)
日南海岸 *nichinan kaigan* Nichinan coastline

INDEPENDENT

【nichi 日】 Japan; Sunday

KUN

【hi 日】
① [sometimes also 陽] sun, sunlight
日の丸 *hinomaru* Rising Sun Flag
日時計 *hidokei* sundial
日の出 *hi no de* sunrise
日陰 *hikage* the shade
日影 *hikage* sunshine; shadow
朝日 *asahi* [sometimes also 旭] rising sun, morning sun; rays of the morning sun
② day, date, time
日日 *hibi* daily; days
日付 *hizuke* date, dating
日頃 *higoro* usually, always
曜日 *yōbi* day of the week

【-bi -日】 [suffix] day
誕生日 *tanjōbi* birthday
記念日 *kinenbi* memorial day, anniversary
最終日 *saishūbi* the last day

【-ka -日】
ⓐ counter for days
ⓑ suffix for days of the month
三日前 *mikkamae* three days ago
十月十日 *jūgatsu tōka* October 10

SPECIAL READINGS

今日 *kyō* today
一日 *tsuitachi* 1st of the month
明日 *asu* tomorrow
明日▲ *ashita* tomorrow
昨日 *kinō* yesterday

SYNONYMS

❶ **days**
曜 DAY OF THE WEEK → 1096
昼 DAYTIME → 3097
旦 first day → 2389

❷ **date**
忌 death anniversary → 2207

❸ **sun**
陽 SUN → 626
旭 RISING SUN → 2977

❹ **days of the week**
土 Saturday → 3403
月 Monday → 2956
火 Tuesday → 3463
水 Wednesday → 10
木 Thursday → 3450
金 Friday → 2057

❺ⓐ **Japan**
和 JAPAN → 1130
邦 JAPAN → 847
国 Japanese → 3087
ⓐ **Asian countries**
華 CHINA → 2283
鮮 Korea → 1877
泰 Thailand → 2583
越 Vietnam → 3314
印 India → 828
比 Philippines → 26

USAGE

hi
日
① [sometimes also 陽] sun, sunlight
② day, date, time
陽
[usu. 日] sun, sunlight

HOMOPHONES

hi ⇨ 陽 626
asahi ⇨ 旭 2977 朝日 1695, 3027

NOTE

⇨ see also USAGE note at 旭 2977
⇨ see COMPOUND FORMATION for 日本 *nihon* (=*nippon*) ⇨ 本 3502
★ do not confuse with 曰 3025

日 ▶DAY ▶SUN ▶JAPAN

nonstandard for 日 3027

3028

Radical	Strokes
日 72	4-4-0
Grade	Freq
Variant	
口 3-3-1	

RADICAL 72

Standard form: 日 *hi* 'sun'

Variant: 日 *hi* (明 春 星)

Description: used in characters related to the sun, sunlight or time

辺 邊 辺 ⻌

3029 HEN ata(ri) -be

Ⓒⓗ 边 biān

Radical	Strokes
⻌ 162	5-3-2
Grade	Freq
Jōyō-4	640
口 3-3-2	

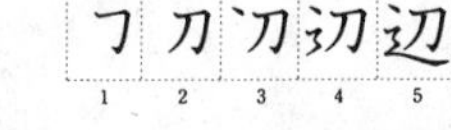

▶VICINITY ▶BORDERLAND

COMPOUNDS

❶ⓐ [also suffix] (nearby area) **vicinity, surroundings, neighborhood, environs, outskirts**

ⓑ (space next to something, as a body of water) **-side**

周辺 *shūhen* environs, outskirts; circumference

身辺 *shinpen* one's person, one's immediate surroundings

近辺 *kinpen* vicinity, neighborhood

官辺 *kanpen* government [official] circles, official quarters

東京辺で *tōkyōhen de* in the vicinity of Tokyo

水辺 *suihen* waterside, shore

❷ *math*

ⓐ **side**

ⓑ member

一辺 *ippen* a side (of a triangle)

二等辺三角形 *nitōhen-sankakkei* equilateral [isosceles] triangle

右辺 *uhen* right member

❸ⓐ [original meaning] border, edge, periphery, fringe

ⓑ **borderland, frontier, remote region, outer regions, deep rural areas**

広大無辺な *kōdai-muhen na* boundless, infinite

縁辺 *enpen* border, edge; relations

辺地 *henchi* remote place

辺境 *henkyō* frontier (district), remote region, border(land)

辺鄙な *henpi na* out-of-the-way, unfrequented, remote

INDEPENDENT

[hen 辺]

①ⓐ vicinity, neighborhood, part, locality, quarters

ⓑ vicinity (of a figure), approximate level

この辺に *kono hen ni* in this neighborhood

五百円の辺で *gohyakuen no hen de* in the vicinity of 500 yen

② *math* side

多角形の辺 *takakkei no hen* side of a polygon

KUN

[ata(ri) 辺り]

①ⓐ vicinity, neighborhood, surroundings

ⓑ [also suffix] (near that place or time) thereabouts, about

家の辺りに *ie no atari ni* around the house

一昨年辺り *issakunen'atari* the year before last or thereabouts

② for instance

ロンドン辺りなら *rondon atari nara* in the case of London, for instance

[-be -辺]

①ⓐ (space next to something) -side, vicinity, surroundings

ⓑ (space next to a body of water) -side, waterside, bank

窓辺で *madobe de* near the window

道辺 *michibe* roadside

海辺 *umibe* seaside, beach, seashore

川辺 *kawabe* riverside, edge of a river

岸辺に *kishibe ni* ashore, on the shore

② indefinite term referring to a person or thing

知る辺 *shirube* acquaintance, friend

寄る辺 *yorube* person to depend on, one's resort

SYNONYMS

❶ⓐ areas and localities
域 BOUNDED AREA → 465
地 PLACE → 204
方 locality → 1963
区 DISTRICT → 2963
領 TERRITORY → 1224
帯 BELT → 2582
圏 SPHERE → 3148
ⓑ side
側 SIDE → 137
方 side → 1963
面 side → 2087
傍 BESIDE → 147
横 SIDEWAYS → 1066
❷ⓐ lines and line segments
径 DIAMETER → 291
弦 chord → 287
弧 ARC → 360
線 LINE → 1392
❸ⓐ edges and boundaries
境 BOUNDARY → 676
界 BOUNDS → 2563
縁 EDGE → 1386
端 edge → 1221
際 VERGE → 714
涯 OUTER LIMITS → 512
ⓑ the country
郷 the country → 549
里 COUNTRYSIDE → 3542
郊 SUBURB → 1286
【atari】
①ⓑ approximately
-程 ...or thereabouts → 1190
-方 about → 1963
位 about → 61
-頃 ABOUT → 144
約 APPROXIMATELY → 1280
概 GENERAL → 1048
大 in substance → 3416
【-be】
①ⓑ shores and watersides
畔 WATERSIDE → 1145
浜 BEACH → 436
岸 SHORE → 2236
浦 SEASIDE → 437
渚 STRAND → 525
磯 ROCKY BEACH → 1242

HOMOPHONES

atari ⇨ 当 2177

NOTE

⇨ see USAGE note at 当 2177

3-2 ⻌

込 込 込 込

3030 -ko(mu) ko(mu) ko(mi) -ko(mi) ko(meru)

Ⓒⓗ none (国字)

Radical	Strokes
⻌ 162	5-3-2
Grade Jōyō	Freq 271
口 3-3-2	

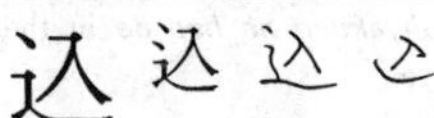

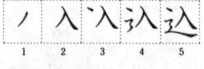

▶MOVE INWARD
▶EMPHATIC VERBAL SUFFIX

KUN

【-ko(mu) -込む】

①ⓐ [original meaning] move inward, get in, come in

ⓑ cause to move inward, put in, bring in—used as a verbal suffix to indicate action directed inward

乗り込む *norikomu* board, go on board; march into
迷い込む *mayoikomu* stray [wander] into
割り込み *warikomi* breaking into a queue, wedging oneself in
払い込む *haraikomu* pay in, pay up
吸い込む *suikomu* inhale, breathe in; suck in
持ち込む *mochikomu* carry [bring] in; propose, refer to; bring (a matter) to

②ⓐ emphatic verbal suffix indicating intense involvement in an activity (similar to *up* in *polish up*)

ⓑ verbal suffix indicating continuation of present state

眠り込む *nemurikomu* fall asleep
黙り込む *damarikomu* sink into silence
住み込みの *sumikomi no* live-in
泊まり込み *tomarikomi* staying in (to do one's job)

【ko(mu) 込む】

① [sometimes also 混む] be crowded, be congested, be packed

込み合う *komiau* be crowded, be packed, be jammed
込み上げる *komiageru* fill (one's heart); feel nausea

② be intricate

込み入った *komiitta* complicated, intricate

【ko(mi) 込み】 inclusiveness; handicap (in the game of go)

込みで買う *komi de kau* buy in bulk, buy the whole lot

【-ko(mi) -込み】 [also suffix] including

税込み四万円 *zeikomi yonman'en* 40,000 yen, tax included

運賃込みで *unchinkomi de* freight included [prepaid]

【ko(meru) 込める】

① [also verbal suffix] put in, coop in, shut up

閉じ込める *tojikomeru* shut in [up], lock in [up]

引っ込める *hikkomeru* put [pull, move] back

② load (a gun), charge

元込め銃 *motogomejū* breechloading rifle, breechloader

③ⓐ include, count in

ⓑ [formerly also 籠める] impregnate with, imply

一切を込めた宿泊料 *issai o kometa shukuhakuryō* all-inclusive hotel charges

警告の意味を込めて *keikoku no imi o komete* with an implication of warning

④ [formerly also 籠める] concentrate on, devote oneself to

心を込めて *kokoro o komete* with all one's heart, wholeheartedly

⑤ [formerly also 籠める] hang over, envelop, shroud

霧が立ち込めた港 *kiri ga tachikometa minato* harbor wrapped in a mist

SYNONYMS

【-komu】

①ⓐ **enter**

入 ENTER → 3370

ⓑ **put in**

入 PUT IN → 3370

挿 INSERT → 431

USAGE

❶ **komu**

込む

① [sometimes also 混む] be crowded, be congested, be packed

② be intricate

混む

[usu. 込む] be crowded, be congested, be packed

❷ **komeru**

込める

① [also verbal suffix] put in, coop in, shut up

② load (a gun), charge

③ⓐ include, count in

ⓑ [formerly also 籠める] impregnate with, imply

④ [formerly also 籠める] concentrate on, devote oneself to

⑤ [formerly also 籠める] hang over, envelop, shroud

籠める

[now usu. 込める]

① concentrate on, devote oneself to

② impregnate with, imply

③ hang over, envelop, shroud

HOMOPHONES

komu ⇨ 混 519

komeru ⇨ 籠 2734

辻 incorrect stroke count ⇨ see 3192 3-2 辶

処 處 3031 SHO tokoro▲ -ko▲

CH 处 chù chǔ

Radical	Strokes
几 16△	5-2-3
Grade	Freq
Jōyō-6	645
□ 3-3-2	

3-2 夂

▶DEAL WITH

COMPOUNDS

❶ⓐ **deal with, dispose of, manage, cope with, treat**

ⓑ **deal with (lawbreakers), punish**

処理する *shori suru* manage, deal with, dispose of; process, treat

処置 *shochi* disposal, measure, treatment

処方箋 *shohōsen* prescription

処分 *shobun* disposal, measure; punishment

対処する *taisho suru* cope [deal] with, meet

善処する *zensho suru* make the best of

処刑 *shokei* execution, punishment

処罰 *shobatsu* punishment, penalty

❷ [usu. 所 851] place, proper place, location

処処 *shosho* several places

❸ [original meaning] stay in one's place, stay home, as:

ⓐ stay home and not get married

ⓑ stay home and not take on a government post, remain civilian

処女 *shojo* virgin, maiden

出処進退 *shussho shintai* one's move, course of action (whether one gets a government job or not)

❹ act, behave, conduct

處世術 *shoseijutsu* how to get on in the world

INDEPENDENT

【**shosuru** 処する】deal with, dispose of, manage; sentence, condemn; act, behave

KUN

【**tokoro** 処】place (for a specific purpose, as eating or resting)

御食事処 *oshokujidokoro* (Japanese) restaurant

【**-ko** -処】suffix for forming demonstratives

何処 *doko* where?

此処 *koko* here, this place

SYNONYMS

❶ⓐ deal with

扱う HANDLE → 217

措 dispose of → 502

置 take proper steps → 2608

ⓑ punishment

刑 PENALTY → 830

罰 PUNISHMENT → 2613

懲 CHASTISE → 2910

❷ places and positions

所 PLACE → 851

場 PLACE (for specific activity) → 558

地 PLACE (particular location) → 204

席 meeting place → 3113

位 POSITION → 61

点 POINT → 2084

座 place → 3116

HOMOPHONES

tokoro ⇨ 所 851

NOTE

⇨ see USAGE note at 所 851

3-2
尸

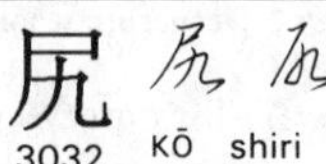

3032 KŌ shiri

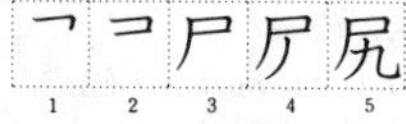

Ⓒⓗ 尻 kāo

Radical	Strokes
尸 44	5-3-2
Grade	**Freq**
Non-Jōyō	1615
口 3-3-2	

▶BUTTOCKS

COMPOUNDS

● [original meaning] **buttocks**

尻座 *kōza* [archaic] crouching

KUN

【**shiri** 尻】

①ⓐ buttocks, hips, the rear, ass

ⓑ bottom, base

お尻 *oshiri* buttocks; backside (of a kettle)

尻に帆掛けて逃げる *shiri ni ho kakete nigeru* take to one's heels ("stick a sail in one's ass and take off like the devil")

尻の軽い女 *shiri no karui onna* wanton girl

尻尾 *shippo* tail; one's true colors

鍋尻 *nabejiri* bottom of a pan

② tail end, end, back part, rear

尻取り *shiritori* capping (verses)

尻切れ蜻蛉 *shirikire-tonbo* unfinished ending

尻上がり *shiriagari* rising intonation; head over heels; rising market

尻込みする *shirigomi suru* flinch, shrink back

尻窄み *shiritsubomi* tapering, weak ending

尻目に懸ける *shirime ni kakeru* look askance (contemptuously)

台尻 *daijiri* butt end (of a gun)

縄尻 *nawajiri* end of a rope

どん尻 *donjiri* tail end; tailender

言葉尻を捉える *kotobajiri o toraeru* cavil at a person's words

③ aftermath, consequence

尻拭い *shirinugui* bearing the consequences of someone else's error [failure]

喧嘩の尻 *kenka no shiri* aftermath of a quarrel

SYNONYMS

【**shiri**】

①ⓐ **buttocks**

肛 ANUS → 842

② **rear**

尾 TAIL → 3062

裏 REAR → 2138

背 BACK → 2573

後 after- → 361

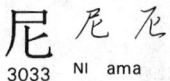

尼 尼 尼

3033 NI ama

㊥ 尼 ní

Radical	Strokes
尸 44	5-3-2
Grade	**Freq**
Jōyō	1570
□ 3-3-2	

3-2 尸

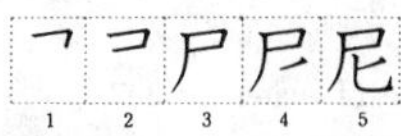

▶**BUDDHIST NUN**

COMPOUNDS

❶ⓐ **Buddhist nun [priestess], sister**

ⓑ title after names of Buddhist nuns

尼僧 *nisō* nun, sister; (Buddhist) priestess

僧尼 *sōni* monks and nuns

禅尼 *zenni* Zen nun

修道尼 *shūdōni* nun

蓮月尼 *rengetsuni* name of a famous Buddhist nun

❷ used phonetically for *ni*, esp. in the transliteration of Sanscrit Buddhist terms

陀羅尼 *darani dhārāṇi*, mystic Buddhist incantation

KUN

【ama 尼】 Buddhist nun, sister

尼寺 *amadera* nunnery, convent

SYNONYMS

❶ⓐ **clergymen**

坊 Buddhist priest → 233

僧 BONZE → 159

父 FATHER → 1973

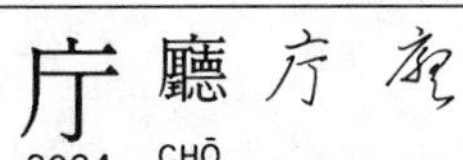

3034 CHŌ

㊥ 厅 tīng

Radical	Strokes
广 53	5-3-2
Grade	**Freq**
Jōyō-6	388
□ 3-3-2	

3-2 广

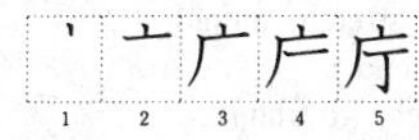

▶**GOVERNMENT AGENCY**

COMPOUNDS

● [also suffix] [original meaning] **government agency, government [public] office**

庁舎 *chōsha* government building

官庁 *kanchō* government office [agency]

都庁 *tochō* Tokyo Metropolitan Government Office

県庁 *kenchō* prefectural office

警視庁 *keishichō* Metropolitan Police Office

環境庁 *kankyōchō* Environment Agency

INDEPENDENT

【chō 庁】 *literary* public office

閻魔の庁 *enma no chō* judgment seat of Yama

SYNONYMS

● **public offices**

府 government office → 3082

省 MINISTRY → 2449

公 public office → 1974

署 PUBLIC-SERVICE STATION → 2609

局 public service office → 3063

所 office → 851

広 廣

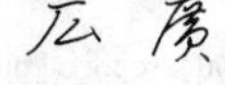

3035 KŌ hiro(i) hiro(maru) hiro(meru) hiro(garu) hiro(geru)

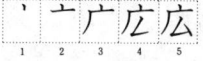

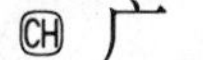 guǎng

Radical	Strokes
广 53	5-3-2
Grade	**Freq**
Jōyō-2	324
□ 3-3-2	

3-2 广

' 亠 广 広 広 (1 2 3 4 5)

▶**WIDE**

COMPOUNDS

❶ⓐ [original meaning] (extending over a large area) **wide, broad, vast, extensive, large, spacious**

ⓑ [also prefix] (having great scope) **wide, wide-ranging**

広大な *kōdai na* vast, extensive, grand

広域 *kōiki* wide area

広野 *kōya* [formerly also 曠野] vast plain, prairie

広角 *kōkaku* wide angle

広義 *kōgi* broad sense, broader application
広範囲 *kōhan'i* wide scope, vast range
❷ spread, disseminate
広告 *kōkoku* public notice; advertisement
広報(＝弘報) *kōhō* (public) information, public relations
❸ [formerly also 宏 2202] grand, great, magnificent
広壮な *kōsō na* grand, magnificent, imposing

KUN

【hiro(i) 広い】 wide, broad, vast, extensive, large, spacious; wide-ranging; generous
広さ *hirosa* area, extent
広広とした *hirobiro to shita* spacious, open, extensive
手広く *tebiroku* extensively, widely, on an extensive scale
幅広い *habahiroi* wide, broad
心の広い *kokoro no hiroi* broad-minded, generous
背広 *sebiro* business suit

【hiro(maru) 広まる】 spread, be diffused, be in general circulation, become popular
広まり *hiromari* spread
噂が広まった *Uwasa ga hiromatta* A rumor went about [spread]

【hiro(meru) 広める】 spread, disseminate; extend, broaden, widen
お広め(＝お披露目) *ohirome* début
仏教を広める *bukkyō o hiromeru* propagate Buddhism
知識を広める *chishiki o hiromeru* extend one's knowledge

【hiro(garu) 広がる】
[sometimes also 拡がる] *vi*
ⓐ spread out, stretch, unfold
ⓑ expand, extend
ⓒ spread, reach, go about
広がった枝 *hirogatta eda* spreading branches
広がり *hirogari* extent, expanse, stretch, spread
火が燃え広がった *Hi ga moehirogatta* The fire spread

【hiro(geru) 広げる】
[sometimes also 拡げる] *vt*
①ⓐ spread (out), outstretch
ⓑ unfold, unroll, open
地図を広げる *chizu o hirogeru* spread a map
広げた腕 *hirogeta ude* outstretched arms
本を広げる *hon o hirogeru* open a book
繰り広げる *kurihirogeru* roll out, unfold, spread out; develop
② widen, enlarge, expand, extend
運動場を広げる *undōjō o hirogeru* enlarge the playground

SYNONYMS

❶ **wide and extensive**
紘 WIDE-RANGING → 1298
博 EXTENSIVE → 151
浩 VAST → 438
洸 VAST (expanse of water) → 387
❷ **make widely known**
布 SPREAD → 2973
流 spread → 441
伝 spread → 44
弘 DISSEMINATE (esp. Buddhism) → 192
及 REACH TO → 3385
【hirogeru】
①ⓐ **expand**
張 SPREAD → 474
拡 ENLARGE → 309
膨 EXPAND → 1084
脹 SWELL → 1003
伸 STRETCH → 70
延 EXTEND → 3073

USAGE

❶ **hirogaru**
広がる
[sometimes also 拡がる] *vi*
ⓐ spread out, stretch, unfold
ⓑ expand, extend
ⓒ spread, reach, go about
拡がる
[usu. 広がる] same as 広がる
❷ **hirogeru**
広げる
[sometimes also 拡げる] *vt*
①ⓐ spread (out), outstretch
ⓑ unfold, unroll, open
② widen, enlarge, expand, extend
拡げる
[usu. 広げる] same as 広げる
❸ **kōhō**
広報
(public) information, public relations
弘報
(public) information, public relations
公報
public [official] report [bulletin]

HOMOPHONES

hirogaru ⇨ 拡 309
hirogeru ⇨ 拡 309

COMPOUND FORMATION

背広 *sebiro*
背広 'business suit' is a corruption either of "civil clothes" or of "Savile Row," the name of a famous street of tailors in London.

斥 incorrect classification ⇨ see 2972

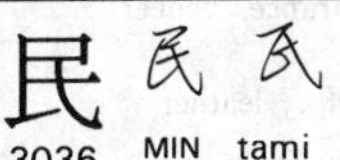

3036 MIN tami

一 ㇕ 尸 民 民

1 2 3 4 5

Ⓒⓗ 民 mín

Radical	Strokes
氏 83	5-4-1
Grade	**Freq**
Jōyō-4	77
口 3-3-2	

▶PEOPLE

COMPOUNDS

❶ [also suffix]

ⓐ people, nation, race

ⓑ the people, populace, folk, civilians, citizens, inhabitants

民族 *minzoku* race, people, nation

民衆 *minshū* populace, the people, the masses

国民 *kokumin* people, nation; the people

選民 *senmin* chosen people

民主主義 *minshushugi* democracy

民謡 *min'yō* folk song [ballad]

民間 *minkan* private citizens, civilians

民営 *min'ei* private management

人民 *jinmin* the people, populace, subjects

住民 *jūmin* residents, dwellers

庶民 *shomin* common people, the masses

県民 *kenmin* citizens of a prefecture

農漁民 *nōgyomin* the fishing and agrarian populace

❷ subjects

臣民 *shinmin* subjects

INDEPENDENT

【min 民】 civilians, private citizens

官と民の協力 *kan to min no kyōryoku* cooperation between the private and public sectors

KUN

【tami 民】 people, nation, race; subjects

流浪の民 *rurō no tami* wandering people, the Jews

民草 *tamigusa* (=*tamikusa*) subjects

SYNONYMS

❶ⓐ people

族 race → 958

ⓑ the people

衆 the multitude(s) → 2683

庶 the masses → 3127

公 PUBLIC → 1974

皮 皮 皮

3037 HI kawa

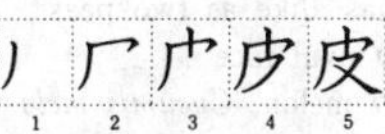

1 2 3 4 5

Ⓒⓗ 皮 pí

Radical	Strokes
皮 107	5-5-0
Grade	**Freq**
Jōyō-3	989
口 3-3-2	

RADICAL 107

Standard form: 皮 *kegawa* 'skin' (皺 皰 皸)

Description: used in characters related to the skin

▶SKIN

COMPOUNDS

❶ⓐ [original meaning] **skin (of human beings or animals), hide, pelt; fur; leather**

ⓑ skin (of plants), bark, peel, husk, shell

皮膚 *hifu* skin

皮革 *hikaku* leather, hides

皮下注射 *hika-chūsha* hypodermic injection

皮肉 *hiniku* cynicism, sarcasm; irony

脱皮 *dappi* ecdysis; self-renewal

樹皮 *juhi* bark

❷ appearance

皮相 *hisō* outward look; superficiality

KUN

【kawa 皮】

①ⓐ skin, hide, pelt; fur; leather

ⓑ skin, bark, peel, husk, shell

皮財布 *kawazaifu* leather wallet

牛皮 *gyūkawa* cowhide, oxhide

毛皮 *kegawa* fur

鰐皮 *wanigawa* crocodile skin [hide]
バナナの皮 *banana no kawa* banana peel

②ⓐ outer covering of articles
ⓑ outward appearance, veneer
薄皮 *usukawa* thin skin film
布団皮(=蒲団皮) *futongawa* ticking, quilting
皮切り *kawakiri* beginning, start
化けの皮を現わす *bake no kawa o arawasu* expose one's true colors [character]

SYNONYMS

❶ **kinds of skin**
膚 SKIN (of the human body) → 3265
肌 SKIN (of the human body) → 827
革 LEATHER → 2448

USAGE

kawa

皮
①ⓐ skin, hide, pelt; fur; leather
ⓑ skin, bark, peel, husk, shell
②ⓐ outer covering of articles
ⓑ outward appearance, veneer

革
[also prefix and suffix] leather

HOMOPHONES

kawa ⇨ 革 2448

COMPOUND FORMATION

皮肉 *hiniku*
皮肉 'cynicism, etc.' originally referred to the skin (皮 ❶ⓐ) and flesh (肉), i.e., the human body. It is not clear how it acquired its current meaning.

3-2 亻

存 incorrect classification / stroke count ⇨ see 2982

3-2 片

片 incorrect classification ⇨ see 3514 (nonstandard for 片 3461)

3-2 爪

瓜
3038 KA uri

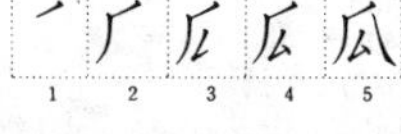

Ⓒⓗ 瓜 guā

Radical	Strokes
瓜 97	5-5-0
Grade	**Freq**
Reference	
口 3-3-2	

RADICAL 97

Standard form: 瓜 *uri* 'gourd' (瓠 瓢)
Description: used in characters related to gourds, melons or cucumbers

COMPOUNDS

● [original meaning] gourd, melon
瓜田に履を納れず *Kaden ni kutsu o irezu* Refrain from doing anything that may incur suspicion
瓜科 *urika* gourd family, *Cucurbitaceae*
瓜二つ *urifutatsu* as alike as two peas
瓜実顔 *urizanegao* oval face
真桑瓜 *makuwauri* melon, *Cucumis melo var. Makuwa*
南瓜 *kabocha* pumpkin

3-2 匚

巨 巨 巨 𢀴
3039 KYO

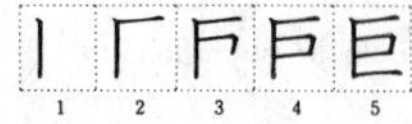

Ⓒⓗ 巨 jù

Radical	Strokes
二 7^Δ	5-2-3
Grade	**Freq**
Jōyō	726
口 3-3-2	

▶**HUGE**

COMPOUNDS

❶ⓐ (of extraordinary size) **huge, enormous, giant, big, large, great**
ⓑ (of extraordinary quantity) huge, enormous, great
巨大な *kyodai na* huge, gigantic, enormous
巨人 *kyojin* giant; great person
巨星 *kyosei* giant star; great person [star], big shot

巨象 *kyozō* gigantic elephant
巨岩 *kyogan* huge rock, crag
巨額 *kyogaku* enormous sum
巨費 *kyohi* great expenditure
❷ great, grand
巨匠 *kyoshō* great master, maestro

SYNONYMS
❶ **big and huge**
大 BIG → 3416
太 GREAT → 2152
浩 VAST → 438

巨
3040

▶**HUGE**
nonstandard for 巨 3039

田
3041 DEN ta

CH 田 tián

Radical	Strokes
田 102	5-5-0
Grade	**Freq**
Jōyō-1	43
口 3-3-2	

RADICAL 102
Standard form: 田 *ta* 'field' (町 男 畑)
Description: used in characters related to fields, rice fields or surfaces

▶**RICE FIELD**

COMPOUNDS
❶ⓐ **rice field, paddy field**
ⓑ [original meaning] field, farmland
田畑 *denpata* (= *tahata*) fields and rice paddies
田地 *denchi* land, farm, rice fields
田作 *densaku* rice-field tilling
乾田 *kanden* dry rice field
水田 *suiden* paddy field, rice field
田園 *den'en* fields and gardens, rural districts
❷ (land area yielding or worked for a natural resource) field
油田 *yuden* oil field
塩田 *enden* salt field
炭田 *tanden* coal field
❸ country, rural district
田家 *denka* rural cottage
田夫野人 *denpu-yajin* rustic, boor, hick

KUN
【**ta** 田】 rice field, paddy field
田植え *taue* rice planting
田圃 *tanbo* rice field
稲田 *inada* rice field

SPECIAL READINGS
田舎 *inaka* country, rural district

SYNONYMS
❶ **cultivated fields**
畑 FIELD → 905
牧 PASTURE → 873
園 GARDEN → 3156
甫 vegetable garden → 3549

囚
3042 SHŪ tora(wareru)▲

CH 囚 qiú

Radical	Strokes
口 31	5-3-2
Grade	**Freq**
Jōyō	1746
口 3-3-2	

▶**PRISONER**

COMPOUNDS
❶ [also suffix] **prisoner, convict, criminal**
囚人 *shūjin* prisoner, convict
囚衣 *shūi* prison uniform
女囚 *joshū* female convict
虜囚 *ryoshū* captive, prisoner
死刑囚 *shikeishū* criminal condemned to death
脱獄囚 *datsugokushū* jailbreaker, escaped prisoner
❷ [original meaning] arrest, imprison
幽囚 *yūshū* imprisonment

INDEPENDENT
【**shū** 囚】 imprisonment, captivity
囚を解く *shū o toku* be relieved from captivi-

ty

KUN

【tora(wareru) 囚われる】

[also 捕らわれる]

① be imprisoned, be taken captive

囚われ *toraware* captive, imprisonment

② adhere to (tradition), be swayed by

囚われた考え *torawareta kangae* conventional ideas, prejudiced opinion

SYNONYMS

❶ **prisoner**

虜 CAPTIVE → 3255

HOMOPHONES

torawareru ⇨ 捕 429

NOTE

⇨ see USAGE note at 捕 429

3-2 口

皿 incorrect classification ⇨ see 3474

3-2 口

目

3043 MOKU BOKU me –me ma–

CH 目 mù

Radical	Strokes
目 109	5-5-0
Grade	Freq
Jōyō-1	64
口 3 - 3 - 2	

1 2 3 4 5

RADICAL 109

Standard form: 目 *me* 'eye' (直 相 眠)

Description: used in characters related to the eye, seeing or perceiving

▶EYE ▶ITEM

COMPOUNDS

❶ⓐ [original meaning] **eye**

ⓑ (perform an action with the eyes) **look, eye, gaze, glance, keep an eye on**

ⓒ before one's eyes, right now

目前の *mokuzen no* before one's eyes, imminent

盲目 *mōmoku* blindness

耳目 *jimoku* eyes and ears; one's attention

目撃する *mokugeki suru* observe, witness, see

目測 *mokusoku* eye measurement

目礼する *mokurei suru* nod, greet

目送する *mokusō suru* follow with one's eyes, gaze after

注目 *chūmoku* attention, notice

一目瞭然の *ichimokuryōzen no* quite obvious, as clear as day

目下 *mokka* now, at present

❷ⓐ point, pivot

ⓑ **aim, object, objective**

眼目 *ganmoku* main object [point], gist, essence

目標 *mokuhyō* mark, target, goal, object

目的 *mokuteki* object, purpose

❸ⓐ [also suffix] **item, subdivision, subitem, category**

ⓑ **counter for items**

ⓒ **list of items, list, catalog**

ⓓ **item heading, title, name**

項目 *kōmoku* clause, item, provision

種目 *shumoku* item; event (as a race)

細目 *saimoku* details, specified items

科目 *kamoku* school subject; subdivision, items

第一目 *daiichimoku* item one

目録 *mokuroku* catalog

目次 *mokuji* table of contents

品目 *hinmoku* list of articles [items]

曲目 *kyokumoku* number; program, selection (for a concert)

名目 *meimoku* name, title; pretext

題目 *daimoku* title, heading; theme; prayer of the Nichiren sect

❹ *biol* order

食肉目 *shokunikumoku* Carnivora

半翅目 *hanshimoku* Hemiptera

❺ⓐ cross of a go board, go piece

ⓑ counter for crosses of a go board or go pieces

小目 *komoku* cross next to the star

一目置く *ichimoku oku* put a stone, give a piece; acknowledge another's superiority

五目の勝ち *gomoku no kachi* win by five crosses

❻ bearing, attitude

面目 *menboku* (=*menmoku*) face, honor, prestige

❼ head, chief

頭目 *tōmoku* chief, head, boss

❽ forecast, estimate, planning for the future

目算 *mokusan* expectations, anticipation, calculation

目論見 *mokuromi* plan, scheme; intention

INDEPENDENT

【moku 目】 item, subdivision; *biol* order
同じ目に属する *onaji moku ni zokusuru* coordinal (animals)

【mokusuru 目する】 look upon, regard as

KUN

【me 目】
①ⓐ [sometimes also 眼] eye; eyesight
ⓑ looking, seeing, watching
ⓒ look, stare, expression
ⓓ point of view
目玉 *medama* eyeball; loss leader (of merchandise)
目先 *mesaki* before one's eyes; near future; foresight; appearance
目印 *mejirushi* mark, sign, landmark
一目 *hitome* a look, a glimpse
お目に掛かりたい *Ome ni kakaritai* I want to see you
目指す(＝目差す) *mezasu* aim for, have an eye on
非難の目を向ける *hinan no me o mukeru* turn a look of reproach
外人の目から見ると *gaijin no me kara miru to* from a foreigner's point of view
②ⓐ watchful eye, attention, notice
ⓑ discerning eye, judgment, an eye for
目に触れる *me ni fureru* catch the eye, attract attention
目をくらます *me o kuramasu* blind the eyes of; deceive
目立つ *medatsu* stand out, be conspicuous
目が効く *me ga kiku* have an eye for
大目に見る *ōme ni miru* overlook
素人目 *shirōtome* untrained eye
③ experience, treatment
憂き目を見る *ukime o miru* have a bitter experience, have a hard time of it
酷い目に遇う *hidoi me ni au* have a bad time
④ (linear pattern) texture, weave; grain (of wood); mesh (of a net)
目の粗い *me no arai* coarse (texture or grain)
編み目 *amime* stitch
網目 *amime* meshes (of a net)
⑤ cross of a go board; territory (in a go game)
相手の目 *aite no me* the opponent's territory
駄目 *dame go* cross that does not constitute a territory; no good, useless; No!
⑥ pip, spot (of dice); [in compounds] chances (of winning in dice or the like)
裏目 *urame* the reverse side of a dice; disappointment
勝ち目 *kachime* good chance of winning
⑦ tooth (of a saw)
目立て *metate* setting of a saw
⑧ graduations (of a scale)
目盛り *memori* graduations
⑨ eye (of a typhoon)
台風の目 *taifū no me* eye of a typhoon
⑩ weight
目減り *meberi* loss of weight
目方 *mekata* weight

【-me -目】
① suffix indicating ordinal numbers or order
五十年目 *gojūnenme* 50th year
二番目 *nibanme* second
② adjectival suffix indicating that the quality in question is slightly greater than normal: rather, -ish, on the (large) side
軽目 *karume* rather light, lighter
控え目な *hikaeme na* modest, temperate, reserved
③ dividing point, border line
変わり目 *kawarime* turning point
切れ目 *kireme* rift, gap, break; end, pause, interval
④ momme: unit of weight equiv. to 3.75 g or 1 momme (匁)
百目蠟燭 *hyakumerōsoku* big candle (weighing 100 momme)
⑤ degree, extent
効き目 *kikime* effect, efficacy
⑥ things (to do), role
役目 *yakume* duty, function; role

【ma- 目-】 eye
目の当たりに *manoatari ni* before one's eyes; personally; actually
目蓋 *mabuta* eyelid

SYNONYMS

❶ⓐ eye
眼 EYE → 1172
眸 EYE → 1170
瞳 PUPIL → 1237
ⓐ face orifices
耳 EAR → 3516
鼻 NOSE → 2706
口 MOUTH → 3382
ⓑ see and look
見 SEE → 2544
観 VIEW → 1880
覧 LOOK OVER → 2854
眺 LOOK OUT OVER → 1171
望 LOOK AFAR → 2742
仰 LOOK UP → 48
顧 LOOK BACK → 1900
視 REGARD → 972
看 WATCH → 3220
察 INSPECT → 2347
❷ⓑ target
標 MARK → 1064
的 TARGET → 1125

❸ⓐ **parts of writing**
箇 item → 2700
項 CLAUSE → 567
条 ARTICLE → 2200
款 ARTICLE → 1700
節 paragraph → 2691
段 passage → 1144
章 CHAPTER → 2117
【-me】
① **kinds of numbers**
第 ORDINAL NUMBER PREFIX → 2660
次 numerical order suffix → 54
番 No. → 2748
号 NUMBER (numerical designation) → 2153
員 fixed number → 2269
数 NUMBER (mathematical unit) → 1790

USAGE

me
目
①ⓐ [sometimes also 眼] eye; eyesight
ⓑ looking, seeing, watching
ⓒ look, stare, expression
ⓓ point of view
②ⓐ watchful eye, attention, notice
ⓑ discerning eye, judgment, an eye for
③ experience, treatment
④ (linear pattern) texture, weave; grain (of wood); mesh (of a net)
⑤ cross of a go board; territory (in a go game)
⑥ pip, spot (of dice); [in compounds] chances (of winning in dice or the like)
⑦ tooth (of a saw)
⑧ graduations (of a scale)
⑨ eye (of a typhoon)
⑩ weight
眼
[usu. 目] eye
芽
bud, sprout, germ

HOMOPHONES

me ⇨ 眼 1172 芽 2240

3-2 皿

且

incorrect classification ⇨ see 3485

3-2 口

四

3044 SHI yo yo(tsu) yot(tsu) yon

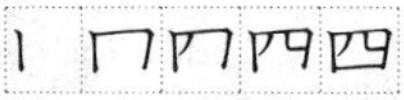

CH 四 sì

Radical	Strokes
口 31	5-3-2
Grade	**Freq**
Jōyō-1	14
口 3-3-2	

▶**FOUR**

COMPOUNDS

❶ⓐ **four**
ⓑ four times
四角 *shikaku* square, quadrilateral
四月 *shigatsu* April
四球 *shikyū* base on balls
四季 *shiki* the four seasons
十四 *jūshi* 14
再三再四 *saisan-saishi* again and again
❷ in all directions
四方八方 *shihōhappō* in all directions
四海 *shikai* the whole world; the seven seas

INDEPENDENT

【shi 四】 four; base on balls

KUN

【yo 四】 [in compounds] four
四人 *yonin* four people
四時 *yoji* four o'clock
【yo(tsu) 四つ】 four; 10 o'clock (in former time system); *sumo* cross grips
四つ角 *yotsukado* street corner, intersection
四日 *yokka* four days; 4th of the month
【yot(tsu) 四つ】 four; four years old
四つ目 *yottsume* fourth
【yon 四】 four
四回 *yonkai* four times
四階 *yonkai* 4th floor

SYNONYMS

❶ⓐ **small numbers**
一 ONE → 3341
二 TWO → 1922
三 THREE → 1924
五 FIVE → 3436
六 SIX → 1965
七 SEVEN → 3362
八 EIGHT → 3
九 NINE → 3369
十 TEN → 3365

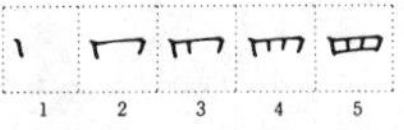

3045

Radical	Strokes
罒 122	5-5-0
Grade	**Freq**
Radical	
口 3 - 3 - 2	

3-2 口

RADICAL 122

yonkashira, variant of 网 *amigashira* 'net'

⇨ see 网 2988 for radical description

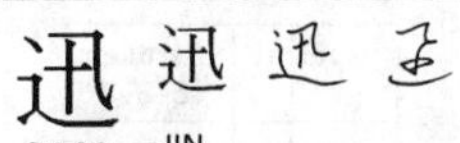

3046 JIN

CH 迅 xùn

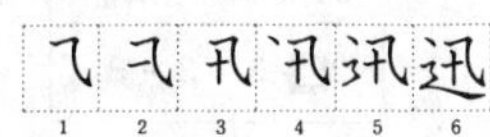

Radical	Strokes
辶 162	6-3-3
Grade	**Freq**
Jōyō	1915
口 3 - 3 - 3	

3-3 辶

▶SWIFT

COMPOUNDS

ⓐ [original meaning] **swift, fast, rapid**

ⓑ sudden, violent

迅速な *jinsoku na* swift, rapid

迅雷 *jinrai* sudden peal of thunder, thunderclap

疾風迅雷 *shippūjinrai* swiftly, as quick as the wind and as swift as thunder

獅子奮迅の勢いで *shishi funjin no ikioi de* with irresistable force

SYNONYMS

ⓐ **fast**

急 rapid → 2092

快 fast → 245

疾 fast → 3279

速 QUICK → 3105

早 QUICK → 2390

敏 NIMBLE → 1322

即 IMMEDIATE → 1120

巡 巡 巡 巡

3047 JUN megu(ru) megu(ri)

CH 巡 xún

Radical	Strokes
巛 47	6-3-3
Grade	**Freq**
Jōyō	971
口 3 - 3 - 3	

3-3 辶

▶MAKE THE ROUNDS

COMPOUNDS

❶ **make the rounds, patrol, make a round of inspection, go round**

巡査 *junsa* police, patrolman

巡視 *junshi* inspection tour

巡回 *junkai* round, patrol

巡洋艦 *jun'yōkan* cruiser

巡察する *junsatsu suru* make a round of inspection, patrol

巡航 *junkō* cruise, cruising

一巡する *ichijun suru* make a round

❷ **tour around, visit, make a pilgrimage**

巡業 *jungyō* provincial tour

巡歴 *junreki* tour, trip

巡礼 *junrei* pilgrimage; pilgrim

巡行 *junkō* round, patrol, tour

巡拝 *junpai* circuit pilgrimage

KUN

【megu(ru) 巡る】 go round, turn round, revolve; circulate; tour, visit, make a pilgrimage

巡らす *megurasu* enclose (with), surround (with), encircle

巡り歩く *meguriaruku* travel around; walk around

巡り合う *meguriau* come across, meet by chance

【megu(ri) 巡り】 going round, circulation; tour; circumference; turn of the fortune wheel, fate

堂堂巡り *dōdōmeguri* roll-call vote; going round and round, vicious circle

血の巡り *chi no meguri* circulation of blood

お寺巡り *oterameguri* pilgrimage to famous temples

SPECIAL READINGS

お巡りさん *omawarisan* policeman

SYNONYMS

❶ **turn**

回 TURN ROUND → 3055
転 TURN → 1480
循 CIRCULATE → 578
旋 GYRATE → 957

❷ **journey**

遊 tour → 3142
行 trip → 212
旅 TRAVEL → 922

3-3 辶

迄 3048

▶UP TO

nonstandard for 迄 3201

3-3 弋

式 3049 SHIKI

一 二 ㇀ 三 式 式 (1 2 3 4 5 6)

Ⓒⓗ 式 shì

Radical	Strokes
弋 56	6-3-3
Grade	**Freq**
Jōyō-3	254
口 3 - 3 - 3	

▶STYLE ▶CEREMONY

COMPOUNDS

❶ [also suffix]

ⓐ **style, type, form, sort, manner**

ⓑ (way of doing) **style, method, system, way**

様式 *yōshiki* mode, manner; style, order
旧式 *kyūshiki* old style, old type
株式 *kabushiki* stocks, shares
ドリス式 *dorisushiki* Doric style (architecture)
和式 *washiki* Japanese style
方式 *hōshiki* formula, mode; method
電動式 *dendōshiki* electric, electrically operated
ヘボン式ローマ字 *hebonshiki rōmaji* Hepburn romanization system
山本式 *yamamotoshiki* Yamamoto's way (of doing things)

❷ [also suffix] **ceremony, rite, rituals, celebration, exercises**

式典 *shikiten* ceremony
儀式 *gishiki* ceremony, rite, ritual
挙式 *kyoshiki* holding a ceremony
葬式 *sōshiki* funeral ceremony
結婚式 *kekkonshiki* wedding ceremony
卒業式 *sotsugyōshiki* graduation ceremony

❸ⓐ **form, prescribed regulation, model, law, standard**

ⓑ [also suffix] detailed regulations, code of laws

形式 *keishiki* form, model, formality
正式に *seishiki ni* formally, regularly
略式の *ryakushiki no* informal, summary
律令格式 *ritsuryō-kyakushiki* codes of laws and ethics

❹ [also suffix] **formula, expression**

公式 *kōshiki* formula; formality
方程式 *hōteishiki* equation
無理式 *murishiki* irrational expression
化学式 *kagakushiki* chemical formula

INDEPENDENT

【shiki 式】

①ⓐ style, type, form, sort, manner
ⓑ (way of doing) style, method, system, way

. . .の式に *...no shiki ni* after the fashion [manner] of
他の式の銃 *ta no shiki no jū* another type of gun
. . .と云った式のやり方 *...to itta shiki no yarikata* a method in the style of...

② ceremony, rite, ritual, celebration, exercises

式を挙げる *shiki o ageru* hold a ceremony

③ⓐ formula, expression, equation
ⓑ *logic* form

式を立てる *shiki o tateru* formularize (a theory)

SYNONYMS

❶ **way and style**

流 STYLE → 441
法 METHOD → 333
途 WAY → 3107
方 WAY → 1963
調 TONE → 1567
風 MANNER → 3007
様 MODE → 1052

❷ **ceremonies and festivities**

儀 CEREMONY → 169
典 formal ceremony → 2627
礼 RITE → 818
斎 religious ritual → 2115
会 Buddhist ceremony → 2020
祭 FESTIVAL → 2672

❸ⓐ **model**
程 ESTABLISHED FORM → 1190
準 STANDARD → 2856
格 NORM → 926
範 MODEL → 2709
典 CANON → 2627

模 PATTERN → 1050

COMPOUND FORMATION

株式 *kabushiki*
株式 'stocks, shares' signifies the mode (式 ❶ⓐ) of capital investiture, i.e., by stock (株) issuance.

incorrect classification ⇨ see 2169

3-3 タ

多 incorrect classification ⇨ see 2170

3-3 タ

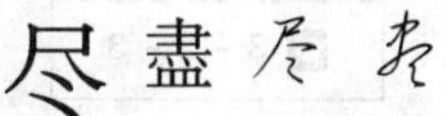

ⒸⒽ 尽 jìn jǐn

3050 JIN tsu(kusu) -tsu(kusu) -zu(kushi) tsu(kiru) tsu(kasu)

3-3 戸

Radical	Strokes
戸 44△	6-3-3
Grade	**Freq**
Jōyō	1452
□ 3-3-3	

(stroke order: 1 2 3 4 5 6)

▶EXHAUST

COMPOUNDS

❶ⓐ **exhaust, use up completely, finish**
ⓑ **be exhausted, come to an end**
ⓒ exhaust one's days, end one's life, die
蕩尽する *tōjin suru* squander, dissipate
理不尽な *rifujin na* unreasonable, unjust, absurd
大尽 *daijin* millionaire, magnate; seeker of riotous pleasures; last day of 31-day month
無尽 *mujin* inexhaustibility; mutual financing association
無尽蔵 *mujinzō* inexhaustible supply
自尽 *jijin* suicide

❷ **use [exhaust] all one's strength (in the performance of one's duties), make utmost efforts, exert oneself**
尽力 *jinryoku* efforts, assistance
尽忠報国 *jinchū hōkoku* loyalty and patriotism
不尽 *fujin* Yours sincerely

❸ wholly, completely, all
尽日 *jinjitsu* whole day; last day of a month [year]
食尽(=蝕甚) *shokujin* maximum eclipse
一網打尽にする *ichimō dajin ni suru* catch the whole group with one throw

❹ [suffix] last day of a month
十月尽 *jūgatsujin* last day of October

KUN

【tsu(kusu) 尽くす】 use [exhaust] all one's strength (in the performance of one's duties), make utmost efforts, exert oneself
心尽くし *kokorozukushi* kindness, consideration, solicitude
最善を尽くす *saizen o tsukusu* do something to the best of one's ability, do one's best
手段を尽くす *shudan o tsukusu* leave no stone unturned, try everything
人類の為に尽くす *jinrui no tame ni tsukusu* render a service to humanity

【-tsu(kusu) -尽くす】
[verbal suffix]
ⓐ exhaust, use up completely
ⓑ do to the utmost
食べ尽くす *tabetsukusu* eat up
言い尽くす *iitsukusu* tell all, exhaust a subject
し尽くす *shitsukusu* do everything possible, exhaust

【-zu(kushi) -尽くし】 [also suffix] full enumeration of
国尽くし *kunizukushi* enumeration of the names of countries

【tsu(kiru) 尽きる】 be exhausted, be used up, be consumed; come to an end, terminate
尽き果てる *tsukihateru* be exhausted
食料が尽きた *Shokuryō ga tsukita* The provisions have run out
尽きない *tsukinai* inexhaustible, everlasting

【tsu(kasu) 尽かす】 run out of, use up
愛想を尽かす *aiso o tsukasu* run out of patience, be disgusted with, fall out of love

SYNONYMS

❶ⓐ **consume**
費 expend → 2607
消 SPEND → 443
耗 WEAR AWAY → 1309

ⓑ **come to an end**
絶 COME TO AN END → 1353
❷ & 【tsukusu】 **exert oneself**
精 put one's heart into → 1366
努 EXERT → 2547
勉 ENDEAVOR → 3318
励 make efforts → 1119
勤 work diligently → 1818

COMPOUND FORMATION
❶ **理不尽** *rifujin*
理不尽な 'unreasonable, unjust, absurd' is not (不) fully using (尽 ❶ⓐ) one's reason (理).
❷ **不尽** *fujin*
不尽 'Yours sincerely' is a sort of apology for not (不) having made sufficient efforts (尽 ❷) in expressing one's intentions.

3-3 广

庄 庄 庄

3051 SHŌ SŌ NAMES masa

CH 庄 zhuāng

Radical	Strokes
广 53	6-3-3
Grade	Freq
Names	2010
口 3-3-3	

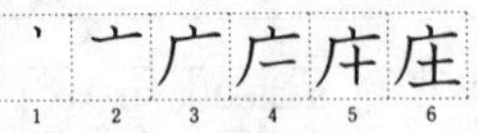

▶**FEUDAL VILLAGE**

COMPOUNDS
❶ⓐ **feudal farm village, hamlet or district in Edo period that used to be a manor until the end of Muromachi period**
ⓑ used chiefly in the formation of names of former feudal villages ⇨ see also 荘 2262 ❷
庄屋 *shōya* village headman
院庄 *innoshō* Innosho (place name)
❷ [usu. 荘 2262] manor (in feudal Japan)
庄園 *shōen* manor
❸ [archaic] farmhouse
村庄 *sonshō* countryside, village; country house

NAMES
庄野 *shōno* surname
庄之助 *shōnosuke* male name

SYNONYMS
❶ⓐ **villages and towns**
里 hamlet → 3542
村 VILLAGE → 834
郷 HOMETOWN → 549
町 TOWN → 1113

NOTE
★do not confuse with 圧 2970

3-3 𠂆

后

incorrect classification ⇨ see 2981

3-3 𠂇

衣

incorrect classification ⇨ see 2013

3-3 𠂇

在 存

incorrect classification ⇨ see 口 2-4

3-3 冂

向 向 向

3052 KŌ mu(ku) mu(ki) -mu(ki) mu(keru) -mu(ke) mu(kau) mu(kō) mu(kō)-

CH 向 xiàng

Radical	Strokes
口 30	6-3-3
Grade	Freq
Jōyō-3	190
口 3-3-3	

丿 亻 门 向 向 向
1 2 3 4 5 6

▶**TURN TOWARD**

COMPOUNDS
❶ⓐ **turn toward, face, look toward**
ⓑ **turn (one's heart or mind) to**
ⓒ (meet face to face) **face, confront**
向日性 *kōjitsusei* disposition (in flowers) to turn toward the sun, heliotropism
向上心 *kōjōshin* ambition, aspiration

向学心 *kōgakushin* desire for learning, intellectual appetite
向寒 *kōkan* facing the winter
対向車 *taikōsha* car (running) on the opposite lane

❷ **head toward, go toward, proceed to**
向心力 *kōshinryoku* central force, centripetal force
出向する *shukkō suru* proceed to, leave for, be temporarily transferred to
下向する *gekō suru* go away from the capital, go down (to a province)

❸ **direction, orientation**
方向 *hōkō* direction, bearing; course
転向 *tenkō* turn, conversion, about-face
指向する *shikō suru* point to
風向 *fūkō* direction of the wind
偏向 *henkō* deviation, deflection

❹ [formerly also 嚮 2901] **tendency, inclination, turn**
傾向 *keikō* tendency, trend; disposition
意向 *ikō* intention, inclination
動向 *dōkō* trend, tendency, movement
性向 *seikō* inclination, disposition
趣向 *shukō* idea, contrivance, plan

❺ pro-
向米的な *kōbeiteki na* pro-American

❻ in the future
向後 *kōgo* hence(forth), hereafter

KUN

【mu(ku) 向く】 *vi* face, front, look upon; turn toward, look toward; tend toward, be inclined to; suit, be fit, be geared for
北に向いた窓 *kita ni muita mado* window to the north
上向く *uwamuku* look upward; turn upward, rise
運が向く *un ga muku* be in luck's way
気が向かない *ki ga mukanai* be not inclined (to do)
教師に向いている *kyōshi ni muite iru* be cut out for a teacher

【mu(ki) 向き】
①ⓐ direction, turn
ⓑ (manner of facing) aspect, exposure, situation
風の向き *kaze no muki* direction of the wind
家の向き *ie no muki* aspect of a house
② suitability
向き不向きが有る *muki fumuki ga aru* have one's own field of work
③ purport, intention, inclination
その向きを伝える *sono muki o tsutaeru* tell (a person) the purport as such
④ those (who), some people
御希望の向きは *gokibō no muki wa* those who want it
⑤ [followed by に成る *ni naru*] become serious, get hot
向きに成って怒る *muki ni natte okoru* flare up

【-mu(ki) -向き】
① facing toward
前向きに *maemuki ni* facing forward; positively, constructively
② [suffix] suitable for, fit for
万人向きである *banninmuki de aru* suit all tastes

【mu(keru) 向ける】 *vt* turn toward, look toward; point at, aim at, direct; send (a messenger) to; apply, appropriate
背を向ける *se o mukeru* turn one's back on, pretend not to see
仰向ける *aomukeru* turn up (one's face)
我我に向けられた非難 *wareware ni mukerareta hinan* criticism leveled against us
差し向ける *sashimukeru* send, dispatch
振り向ける *furimukeru* apply [appropriate] (money) toward

【-mu(ke) -向け】 [suffix] (bound) for, meant for
国内向けの *kokunaimuke no* for domestic use

【mu(kau) 向かう】 *vi* face, front, look upon; confront, oppose; head toward, go toward, proceed to; near, approach
向かい *mukai* opposite side
向かって左に *mukatte hidari ni* on the left as one faces (it)
向かい風 *mukaikaze* head wind, adverse wind
立ち向かう *tachimukau* stand against; head for
...に向かっている *...ni mukatte iru* be going (toward), be headed (for)
寒さに向かうと *samusa ni mukau to* as winter approaches

【mu(kō) 向こう】 the other side, the opposite direction; the other party; opponent; abroad, overseas; beyond, across; destination
向こうから来る *mukō kara kuru* come from the opposite direction
向こうが悪い *Mukō ga warui* He is in the wrong
向こうに回して *mukō ni mawashite* in opposition to
向こうで暮らす *mukō de kurasu* live overseas
向こうに着いたら *mukō ni tsuitara* when you get to the destination

【mu(kō)- 向こう-】
[prefix]
① (days) to come, coming, next
向こう十日間 *mukō-tōkakan* for the next ten days
② facing, opposite
向こう三軒 *mukō-sangen* three houses on the opposite side

SYNONYMS

❶ **face**

面 FACE → 2087
対 face (each other) → 831

❷ **go and come**

赴 PROCEED TO → 3303
通 go to and from → 3109
来 COME → 3551
参 go somewhere → 2066
出 go to → 3498
行 GO → 212
往 GO ON → 292

❸ **direction**

方 DIRECTION → 1963

❹ **tendency**

傾 inclination → 154
性 NATURE → 299
勢 trend → 2857
潮 TIDE → 739
流 CURRENT → 441

【-muke】

○ **direction indicators**

至 to → 2182
-行き bound for → 212
迄 UP TO → 3201
以 TO THE...OF → 41
自 from → 3525
来 since → 3551

3-3
口

3053 DAN TON

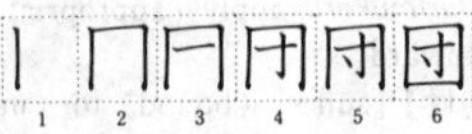
1 2 3 4 5 6

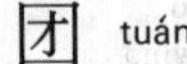 tuán

Radical	Strokes
口 31	6-3-3
Grade	**Freq**
Jōyō-5	165

口 3-3-3

▶**BODY**

COMPOUNDS

❶ⓐ [also suffix] (collective group) **body, corps, group, party**
ⓑ gather in one body, form a group
団体 *dantai* group, party, body, corps; corporation, organization
団長 *danchō* leader [head] of a body [party]
団交 *dankō* collective bargaining
集団 *shūdan* group, body, mass, crowd
一団 *ichidan* body, group, party, troupe
星団 *seidan* star cluster
観光団 *kankōdan* sightseeing party
外交団 *gaikōdan* diplomatic corps [body]
顧問団 *komondan* advisory body
団地 *danchi* (public) housing development
団結 *danketsu* unity, union, solidarity

❷ (organized entity) **body, corporation, organization, association**
公団 *kōdan* public corporation
劇団 *gekidan* dramatic company, theatrical troupe
師団 *shidan* army division
社団 *shadan* corporation, association
財団 *zaidan* foundation, consortium, endowment; syndicate
軍団 *gundan* army corps, corps
経団連(＝経済団体連合会) *keidanren* (＝*keizai dantai rengōkai*) Federation of Economic Organizations

❸ⓐ [original meaning] round
ⓑ perfect; harmonious
団子 *dango* dumpling
布団 *futon* [sometimes also 蒲団] *futon*, bedquilt
大団円 *daidan'en* (grand) finale, dénouement, conclusion
団欒 *danran* family circle; harmony

INDEPENDENT

【dan 団】 (collective group) body, corps, group, party
団の精神 *dan no seishin* spirit of the corps, esprit de corps

SYNONYMS

❶ⓐ **groups**

群 GROUP (of any kind) → 1540
組 group (of people) → 1337
陣 lineup → 455
連 set → 3103
族 common-interest group (*slang*) → 958
党 PARTY → 2581
隊 PARTY (organized group) → 625
伍 ranks → 47
班 SQUAD → 946
軍 team → 2080

❷ **organized bodies**

会 SOCIETY → 2020
協 association → 93
体 BODY → 71
組 union → 1337
労 workers' union → 2548
連 federation → 3103
講 fraternity → 1619
院 INSTITUTION → 454

COMPOUND FORMATION

布団 *futon*

布団 '*futon*, bedquilt' originally referred to a round (団 ❸ⓐ) mat made of cattail (布).

布 is a phonetic substitute for 蒲 'cattail'.

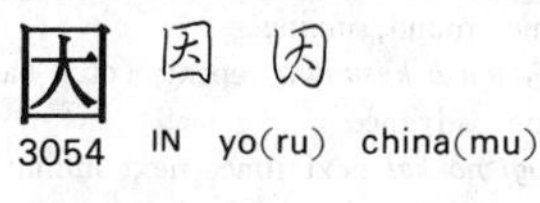

3054 IN yo(ru) china(mu)▲

ⒸⒽ 因 yīn

Radical	Strokes
口 31	6-3-3
Grade	**Freq**
Jōyō-5	586
口 3-3-3	

3-3 口

1 2 3 4 5 6

▶CAUSE

COMPOUNDS

❶ⓐ **cause, reason, origin, factor**
ⓑ *Buddhism* direct cause, connection, relation, affinity
因果 *inga* cause and effect; karma
因子 *inshi math* factor
因数 *insū math* factor
死因 *shiin* cause of death
原因 *gen'in* cause, origin
要因 *yōin* primary factor, main cause
因縁 *innen* karma, fate; direct and indirect causes; connection, affinity; pretext; origin
❷ follow (customs), be based on
因習(＝因襲) *inshū* conventions
❸ abbrev. of 因幡 *inaba*, old name for east Tottori Prefecture
因美線 *inbisen* Inbi Line (East Okayama Railway)

INDEPENDENT

【in 因】 cause, origin, factor
因をなす *in o nasu* cause, give rise to

KUN

【yo(ru) 因る】 [formerly also 由る] be caused by, be due to
風邪に因る発熱 *kaze ni yoru hatsunetsu* fever caused by a cold
【china(mu) 因む】 be related, be connected
因みに *chinami ni* in this connection, by the way
それは仏教に因んでいる *Sore wa bukkyō ni chinande iru* It comes from Buddhism

SYNONYMS

❶ⓐ **cause and reason**
由 REASON → 3499
為 because → 3577
故 reason → 1141
訳 reason → 1473

USAGE

yoru
因る
[formerly also 由る] be caused by, be due to
由る
[now usu. 因る] be caused by, be due to
依る
① depend on, rely on, hang on
② do by (means of), resort to, have recourse to
拠る
① be based on, be grounded on
② occupy (a fortress), hold
寄る
①ⓐ draw near, draw up, come near, approach
ⓑ draw aside, step aside
② draw together, come together, gather, meet
③ drop in, call on
④ increase, gain
⑤ lean on, rest against
⑥ *sumo* push one's opponent while holding his belt
⑦ (of the stock market) open

HOMOPHONES

yoru ⇨ 由 3499 依 84 拠 312 寄 2291

NOTE

★do not confuse with 困 3070

回 囬◇ 回 回

3055 KAI E mawa(ru) -mawa(ru) -mawa(ri) mawa(su) -mawa(su) mawa(shi)- -mawa(shi)

ⒸⒽ 回 huí

Radical	Strokes
口 31	6-3-3
Grade	**Freq**
Jōyō-2	60
口 3-3-3	

3-3 口

1 2 3 4 5 6

▶TURN ROUND ▶TIME

COMPOUNDS

❶ [formerly 廻 *kai* 3089]
ⓐ [original meaning] **turn round, revolve, rotate, circulate**
ⓑ **go round, make the rounds; circulate,**

make a circular tour
回転する *kaiten suru* revolve, rotate, turn
転回 *tenkai* turning over; revolution, rotation
旋回 *senkai* revolution, rotation, circling, swiveling
回診 *kaishin* make a round of visits (to one's patients)
回路 *kairo* (electric) circuit
回覧する *kairan suru* circulate, send round
巡回する *junkai suru* go round, make the rounds, patrol
徘回(＝徘徊)する *haikai suru* loiter, wander about

❷ [formerly also 廻 *kai, e* 3089]
ⓐ **turn back, return, come round**
ⓑ **turn (something) back, return, reply, bring back**
回復 *kaifuku* [formerly also 恢復] recovery, restoration; rehabilitation
回帰 *kaiki* revolution, recurrence, regression
回忌 *kaiki* death anniversary
回向 *ekō* Buddhist memorial service
輪回 *rinne Buddhism* transmigration of souls, *saṃsāra*
回答 *kaitō* reply, answer
回収する *kaishū suru* collect, recover; withdraw
回心 *kaishin* (＝*eshin*) conversion
撤回する *tekkai suru* withdraw, retract

❸ [formerly 廻 *kai* 3089] send round, forward, transport
回送 *kaisō* forwarding
回漕業 *kaisōgyō* shipping business
回船 *kaisen* lighter, cargo vessel

❹ turn one's thoughts back to, look back, retrospect
回想 *kaisō* recollection, reminiscence
回顧する *kaiko suru* look back on, retrospect

❺ turn away, avert, avoid
回避する *kaihi suru* evade, dodge, avoid
迂回する *ukai suru* take a long way around, make a detour

❻ⓐ [also suffix] **time; round, game; inning**
ⓑ **counter for number of times, rounds or innings**
回数 *kaisū* frequency, number of times
今回 *konkai* this time; lately
最終回 *saishūkai* last time; last inning
百回 *hyakkai* 100 times
八回裏 *hachikaiura* second half of the eighth inning

❼ Mohammedanism, Islam
回教 *kaikyō* Mohammedanism, Islam

❽ *anat* gyrus, convolution
海馬回 *kaibakai* hippocampal gyrus

❾ *music* volta
二回 *nikai due volte*

❿ [formerly 蛔 *kai* 1359] roundworm, ascarid
回虫 *kaichū* roundworm, ascarid

INDEPENDENT

【kai 回】 time, round; inning
回を重ねる *kai o kasaneru* repeat; (of a baseball game) advance
次の回 *tsugi no kai* next time; next inning

KUN

【mawa(ru) 回る】
[formerly 廻る]
①ⓐ turn round, revolve, rotate
ⓑ go round, circulate, make a round
ⓒ detour, go round (to)
回り *mawari* rotation; detour; close surroundings; spreading (of flames); efficacy
回り舞台 *mawaributai* rotative stage
見回る *mimawaru* make one's rounds
回りくどい *mawarikudoi* roundabout, circuitous, indirect
② swing over to, come round to, be transferred
反対に回る *hantai ni mawaru* go into opposition
③ be past (a certain hour)
もう十一時を回った *Mō jūichiji o mawatta* It is already past eleven
④ pass (from hand to hand), circulate, spread; take effect
火が回る *Hi ga mawaru* Fire spreads
酔いが回る *yoi ga mawaru* get drunk, become tipsy
⑤ yield interest
利回り *rimawari* (investment) yield, interest, profits

【-mawa(ru) -回る】
[verbal suffix]
① about, around, to and fro
歩き回る *arukimawaru* walk about, walk to and fro, pace around
飛び回る *tobimawaru* fly about, jump about, rush around
出回る *demawaru* appear on the market, be moving
② reach, attain
上回る *uwamawaru* exceed, be more than
下回る *shitamawaru* be less than, fall below

【-mawa(ri) -回り】
[also suffix]
①ⓐ indicates direction of turning
ⓑ counter for rounds
時計回りの *tokeimawari no* clockwise
西回り *nishimawari* west circuit
三回り *mimawari* three rounds
② a size (larger or smaller)
一回り小さな *hitomawari chiisa na* a size smaller
③ via, by way of
欧州回りで合衆国へ行く *ōshūmawari de gasshūkoku e iku* go to the U.S. via Europe

④ cycle of 12 years
彼は私より一回り若い *Kare wa watakushi yori hitomawari wakai* He is my junior by twelve years
⑤ girth, circumference
胴回り *dōmawari* girth

【mawa(su) 回す】
[formerly 廻す]
① turn (round), rotate
独楽を回す *koma o mawasu* spin a top
②ⓐ send round, pass around, circulate
ⓑ send round, forward, transfer
回し *mawashi* sumo wrestler's loincloth; gang rape
塩を回して下さい *Shio o mawashite kudasai* Pass me the salt, please
③ lend money at interest
金を上手く回す *kane o umaku mawasu* invest one's money profitably
④ arrange, prepare
手回し *temawashi* preparations
⑤ perform gang rape

【-mawa(su) -回す】 [emphatic verbal suffix]
about, around
追い回す *oimawasu* chase about, follow about
乗り回す *norimawasu* drive about, ride around
言い回し *iimawashi* expression, manner [turn] of expression

【mawa(shi)- 回し-】
① by turns, alternately
回し飲み *mawashinomi* drinking in turn from one cup
回し読み *mawashiyomi* reading a book in turn
② turning, swivel
回し金 *mawashigane* lathe dog

【-mawa(shi) -回し】 turning, rotating
ねじ回し *nejimawashi* screwdriver
盥回し *taraimawashi* passing the buck; balancing a spinning washtub

SYNONYMS

❶ turn
転 TURN → 1480
巡 MAKE THE ROUNDS → 3047
循 CIRCULATE → 578
旋 GYRATE → 957

❷❸ return
還 RETURN → 3180
帰 RETURN → 130
戻る RETURN → 1942
復 RETURN TO → 575

❸ send
送 SEND → 3093
投 SEND IN → 256
遣 DISPATCH → 3152
派 DISPATCH → 381

❻ time and time counters
度 TIME → 3100
遍 counter for number of times → 3136
返 counter for number of times → 3060

USAGE

❶ mawaru
回る
[formerly 廻る]
①ⓐ turn round, revolve, rotate
ⓑ go round, circulate, make a round
ⓒ detour, go round (to)
② swing over to, come round to, be transferred
③ be past (a certain hour)
④ pass (from hand to hand), circulate, spread; take effect
⑤ yield interest
廻る
[now usu. 回る] same as 回る

❷ mawari
回り
[formerly 廻り]
①ⓐ rotation
ⓑ detour
② close surroundings
③ spreading (of flames)
④ efficacy
廻り
[now usu. 回り] same as 回り
周り
ⓐ periphery, surroundings, circumference
ⓑ border, fringe

❸ mawasu
回す
[formerly 廻す]
① turn (round), rotate
②ⓐ send round, pass around, circulate
ⓑ send round, forward, transfer
③ lend money at interest
④ arrange, prepare
⑤ perform gang rape
廻す
[now usu. 回す] same as 回す

HOMOPHONES

mawaru ⇨ 廻 3089
mawari ⇨ 廻 3089 周 2998
mawasu ⇨ 廻 3089

延 3056 **▶EXTEND ▶POSTPONE**
nonstandard for 延 3073
3-4 廴

3-4
廴

廷 3057

▶COURT

nonstandard for 廷 3058

3-4
廴

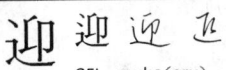

廷 廷 廷 廷 3058 TEI

Ⓒⓗ 廷 tíng

Radical	Strokes
廴 54	7-3-4
Grade	**Freq**
Jōyō	1390
3-3-4	

▶COURT

COMPOUNDS

❶ [also suffix] **court of law**

廷内で *teinai de* in the court
法廷 *hōtei* law court
開廷 *kaitei* opening of a court, trial
出廷 *shuttei* appearance in court
公判廷 *kōhantei* court, public trial court

❷ [rarely also 庭 3114] **court, Imperial Court**

廷臣 *teishin* court official
朝廷 *chōtei* Imperial Court
宮廷 *kyūtei* the Court, the Palace

SYNONYMS

❶ **court**

裁 court → 3299

❷ **governments**

朝 court → 1695
宮 Imperial Court → 2274
幕 SHOGUNATE → 2335
官 GOVERNMENT → 2226

NOTE

★do not confuse with 延 3073

3-4
辶

迎 迎 迎 迎 3059 GEI muka(eru)

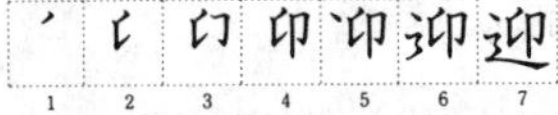

Ⓒⓗ 迎 yíng

Radical	Strokes
辶 162	7-3-4
Grade	**Freq**
Jōyō	653
3-3-4	

▶WELCOME

COMPOUNDS

❶ⓐ **welcome, greet, receive**

ⓑ [original meaning] **go (out) to meet, meet face to face**

迎賓 *geihin* welcoming guests
歓迎する *kangei suru* welcome
送迎する *sōgei suru* welcome and send off
迎撃 *geigeki* interception, counter

❷ flatter, curry favor with

迎合する *geigō suru* flatter, curry favor with, ingratiate oneself with

KUN

【muka(eru) 迎える】 welcome, greet, receive, play host; meet, go out to meet; invite, call, send for; meet (an occasion); cater to, ingratiate

迎え *mukae* meeting; person sent to pick up an arrival
迎え酒 *mukaezake* another drink in the morning
迎え入れる *mukaeireru* receive (a person), usher
迎え撃つ *mukaeutsu* fight the attack of an enemy
意を迎える *i o mukaeru* cater to another's wish

SYNONYMS

❶ⓐ **treat and welcome**

遇 TREAT → 3135
待 treat → 364
扱う HANDLE → 217
款 treat cordially → 1700
接 receive → 500

返 返 返 返

3060 HEN kae(su) -kae(su) kae(ru) -kae(ru)

CH 返 fǎn

Radical	Strokes
辶 162	7-3-4
Grade	**Freq**
Jōyō-3	529
□ 3 - 3 - 4	

一 厂 万 反 ˋ反 汳 返
1 2 3 4 5 6 7

▶RETURN

COMPOUNDS

❶ⓐ return, give back, send back, repay
ⓑ [original meaning] return, go back
返還 *henkan* return, restoration, repayment
返上する *henjō suru* return, send back
返戻する *henrei suru* return, give back
返品 *henpin* returning goods; returned goods, article sent back
返送する *hensō suru* send back, return
返却 *henkyaku* return
返金 *henkin* repayment
返報 *henpō* requital, retaliation, revenge

❷ reply, answer
返信 *henshin* reply, answer
返事 *henji* answer, reply
返電 *henden* reply telegram
返答 *hentō* reply, answer

❸ [usu. 遍 3136] counter for number of times
二返 *nihen* two times

INDEPENDENT

【hen 返】 abbrev. of 返事 *henji*: reply (in telegrams)

KUN

【kae(su) 返す】
①ⓐ return, send back, put back, give back, repay
ⓑ return (a kindness), repay
お返し *okaeshi* return present; answer, reply; revenge; change (for money)
恩返し *ongaeshi* repaying another's kindness
② dismiss, discharge, divorce

【-kae(su) -返す】
[verbal suffix]
① do over, redo, re-
繰り返す *kurikaesu* repeat, do over again
読み返す *yomikaesu* reread, read again
②ⓐ do back, do in return
ⓑ take back, recover
仕返し *shikaeshi* doing over, tit for tat, revenge
言い返す *iikaesu* talk back, retort
取り返す *torikaesu* take back, regain
引き返す *hikikaesu* turn back, retrace one's steps
③ turn over, overturn, reverse
ひっくり返す *hikkurikaesu* turn over, upset
裏返す *uragaesu* turn over, turn inside out

【kae(ru) 返る】
① be restored to, return to (the original state)
返り咲き *kaerizaki* second bloom; a comeback (in business)
振り返る *furikaeru* turn one's head, turn round
生き返る *ikikaeru* revive, come to oneself; be restored to life
② be given back

【-kae(ru) -返る】 [also -反る] [emphatic verbal suffix] utterly, completely
静まり返る *shizumarikaeru* become still as death
呆れ返る *akirekaeru* be utterly amazed

SYNONYMS

❶ⓐ return and restore
戻 RETURN → 1942
還 RETURN → 3180
復 RETURN TO → 575

❷ answer
答 ANSWER → 2681
応 RESPOND → 3066
解 solve → 1517

❸ time and time counters
遍 counter for number of times → 3136
回 TIME → 3055
度 TIME → 3100

【-kaesu】
① **repeating and repetition**
-直す repetition suffix → 2932
-換える redo → 587
改 redo → 243
再 ANOTHER TIME → 3519
又 AGAIN → 3351
復 repeat → 575
重 DUPLICATE → 3573
畳 reduplicate → 2592

USAGE

❶ kaesu
返す
①ⓐ return, send back, put back, give back, repay
ⓑ return (a kindness), repay
② dismiss, discharge, divorce
-返す
[verbal suffix]
① do over, redo, re-
②ⓐ do back, do in return

ⓑ take back, recover
③ turn over, overturn, reverse

帰す
let (someone) return, see out, send (someone) home, dismiss

反す
vt turn over, overturn, upset, reverse

★In the sense of overturn, *kaesu* should be written 反す, though this reading is not approved. However, as a verbal suffix meaning to overturn, *kaesu* is written 返す, as in 裏返す *uragaesu* 'turn over, turn inside out'.

❷ **-kaeru**
-返る
[also -反る] [emphatic verbal suffix] utterly, completely
-反る
[also -返る] same as -返る

HOMOPHONES

kaesu ⇨ 帰 130 反 2945
kaeru ⇨ 帰 130 反 2945 還 3180
-kaeru ⇨ 反 2945

NOTE

⇨ see also USAGE note at 帰 130

3-4 辶

近 近 近 [calligraphic form]

3061 KIN KON▲ chika(i)

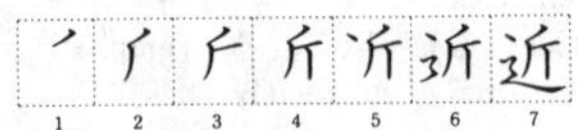

ⒸⒽ 近 jìn

Radical	Strokes
辶 162	7-3-4
Grade	**Freq**
Jōyō-2	119
□ 3-3-4	

▶**NEAR** ▶**RECENT**

COMPOUNDS

❶ⓐ (close in space) **near, close, nearby, neighboring**
ⓑ [original meaning] (come close) near, approach
近視 *kinshi* nearsightedness, shortsightedness
近郊 *kinkō* suburbs, outskirts
近所 *kinjo* neighborhood
近隣 *kinrin* neighborhood
近県 *kinken* neighboring prefectures
付近 *fukin* neighborhood, environs, vicinity
接近する *sekkin suru* approach, draw near, come close

❷ (close in time) **recent, near, modern**
近況 *kinkyō* recent condition [situation]
近影 *kin'ei* one's recent photograph
近年 *kinnen* recent years, late years
近世 *kinsei* modern ages
近代的な *kindaiteki na* modern
最近の *saikin no* late, recent

❸ (close in relationship) near, close, personal; intimate
近親 *kinshin* near relative
近衛 *konoe* Imperial Guards
親近感 *shinkinkan* feeling of intimacy
側近 *sokkin* close associate, aide

❹ abbrev. of 近畿 *kinki*: Kinki district
近鉄 *kintetsu* Kinki Nippon Railway

KUN

【chika(i) 近い】 near (in space), close, not far; near (in time), early, soon; near (in relationship), close; akin to, close to
近さ *chikasa* nearness
近くの *chikaku no* nearby, neighboring
近付く *chikazuku* approach, near, get near; get acquainted
近道 *chikamichi* shortcut
近頃 *chikagoro* recently, nowadays
身近な *mijika na* near oneself, close to one, familiar

SYNONYMS

❶ⓐ **near**
隣 neighboring → 781
傍 BESIDE → 147
沿 ALONG → 328
ⓑ **approach**
寄る DRAW NEAR → 2291
接 come close to → 500
迫 PRESS → 3074
❷ **recent**
新 NEW → 1784
❸ **familiar and friendly**
親 INTIMATE → 1799
密 CLOSE → 2292
睦 FRIENDLY → 1199
懇 FAMILIAR → 2899
和 HARMONIOUS → 1130

3-4 辶

迄

incorrect stroke count ⇨ see 3048
(nonstandard for 迄 3201)

尾 尾 尾

3062 BI o

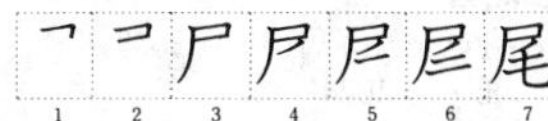

CH 尾 wěi yǐ

Radical	Strokes
尸 44	7-3-4
Grade	**Freq**
Jōyō	650
□ 3 - 3 - 4	

3-4 尸

▶**TAIL**

COMPOUNDS

❶ⓐ [original meaning] **tail**
ⓑ buttocks
有尾類 *yūbirui* tailed amphibians
尾骶骨 *biteikotsu* coccyx
❷ⓐ (rear part) **tail, rear**
ⓑ **end**
尾部 *bibu* tail, tail section
尾翼 *biyoku* tail, tail plane
尾灯 *bitō* taillight
尾行 *bikō* following, shadowing
船尾 *senbi* stern, poop
首尾 *shubi* beginning and end; result, issue
竜頭蛇尾 *ryūtōdabi* bright start, dull finish
巻尾 *kanbi* end of a book
末尾 *matsubi* end, close
語尾 *gobi* ending of a word
❸ counter for fish
鮪二十尾 *maguro nijūbi* 20 tunnies
❹ copulate, mate
交尾 *kōbi* copulation, coupling
❺ abbrev. of 尾張 *owari*, old name for West Aichi Prefecture
濃尾平野 *nōbi heiya* Nobi Plain

KUN

【o 尾】tail, scut, caudal fin; trail (as of a meteor); ridge
尾長猿 *onagazaru* long-tailed monkey
尾頭付き *okashiratsuki* fish served whole [complete with head and tail]
尾鰭 *ohire* (=*obire*) tail and fin
尾を引く *o o hiku* leave a trail; leave a lasting effect
尾根 *one* mountain ridge

SYNONYMS

❶ⓐ **body projections**
角 HORN → 2047
❷ⓐ **rear**
尻 tail end → 3032
裏 REAR → 2138
背 BACK → 2573
後 after- → 361
ⓑ **ends**
終 END → 1336
局 close → 3063
末 LAST PART → 3505

局 局 局

3063 KYOKU tsubone▲

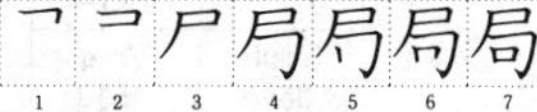

CH 局 jú

Radical	Strokes
尸 44	7-3-4
Grade	**Freq**
Jōyō-3	188
□ 3 - 3 - 4	

3-4 尸

▶**BUREAU** ▶**LIMITED PART**

COMPOUNDS

❶ [also suffix] **bureau, department (esp. of a government office)**
局長 *kyokuchō* bureau chief, director, postmaster
部局 *bukyoku* department, bureau
水道局 *suidōkyoku* Water Works Bureau
法制局 *hōseikyoku* Legislative Bureau
総務局 *sōmukyoku* General Affairs Bureau
薬局 *yakkyoku* drugstore, pharmacy
事務局 *jimukyoku* secretariat
当局 *tōkyoku* the authorities concerned
❷ [also suffix] **public service office or station, as a post office, telegraph office, telephone exchange office or broadcasting station**
郵便局 *yūbinkyoku* post office
電報局 *denpōkyoku* telegraph office
放送局 *hōsōkyoku* radio broadcasting station
支局 *shikyoku* branch office
テレビ局 *terebikyoku* TV station
電話局 *denwakyoku* telephone exchange office
❸ [suffix] telephone office number, exchange number
42局2012番 *yonjūnikyoku nisenjūniban* 42-2012 (phone number)
❹ **limited part, portion (of space), locality**
局限する *kyokugen suru* localize, limit, set limits to

局部 *kyokubu* limited part, section; affected part
局所 *kyokusho* (limited) part, section
局地的 *kyokuchiteki* local

❺ **current situation, state of affairs**
局面 *kyokumen* situation, aspect of an affair; position (in a chess game)
時局 *jikyoku* situation, circumstances
戦局 *senkyoku* state of the war, war situation
難局 *nankyoku* difficult [delicate] situation, deadlock
政局 *seikyoku* political situation

❻ **close, end, conclusion**
終局 *shūkyoku* end, conclusion, termination; end of a game
結局 *kekkyoku* after all, finally, in conclusion

❼ⓐ board game (as chess or shogi)
ⓑ counter for board games
対局 *taikyoku* game of go [shogi]
一局 *ikkyoku* a game (of go or shogi)
チェス十二局 *chesu jūnikyoku* 12 chess games

INDEPENDENT

【kyoku 局】 bureau, department; public service office (⇨ ❷); affair, situation; close, end, conclusion
同じ局 *onaji kyoku* same (radio) station
局に当たる *kyoku ni ataru* take charge of an affair, deal with a situation
局を結ぶ *kyoku o musubu* come to a close [an end], be settled

KUN

【tsubone 局】 apartment of a court lady; court lady, lady in waiting

SYNONYMS

❶ **divisions of organizations**
課 SECTION → 1573
部 department → 1676

❷ **public offices**
署 PUBLIC-SERVICE STATION → 2609
公 public office → 1974
所 office → 851
府 government office → 3082
庁 GOVERNMENT AGENCY → 3034
省 MINISTRY → 2449

❹ **part**
部 SECTION → 1676
分 PART → 1972
片 FRAGMENT → 3461

❺ **states and situations**
境 SITUATION → 676
勢 course of events → 2857
状 CONDITION → 272
況 CONDITIONS → 337
景 business conditions → 2470
態 STATE → 2847
情 ACTUAL CONDITIONS → 482
訳 circumstances → 1473
調 TONE → 1567
様 MODE → 1052
相 PHASE → 900

❻ **ends**
尾 end → 3062
終 END → 1336
末 LAST PART → 3505

❼ **board games**
棋 SHOGI → 987
碁 GO → 2699
雀 MAHJONG → 2469

3-4
尸

尿 尿 尿

3064 NYŌ

Ⓒⓗ 尿 niào suī

Radical	Strokes
尸 44	7-3-4
Grade	**Freq**
Jōyō	1518
3 - 3 - 4	

Stroke order: 1 2 3 4 5 6 7

▶URINE

COMPOUNDS

● [original meaning] **urine**
尿素 *nyōso* urea
尿酸 *nyōsan* uric acid
排尿 *hainyō* urination
検尿 *kennyō* urinalysis
糖尿病 *tōnyōbyō* diabetes
夜尿症 *yanyōshō* bed wetting, nocturia

INDEPENDENT

【nyō 尿】 urine
尿の検査 *nyō no kensa* urinalysis

SYNONYMS

● **excreta**
便 EXCRETA → 95
汗 SWEAT → 220

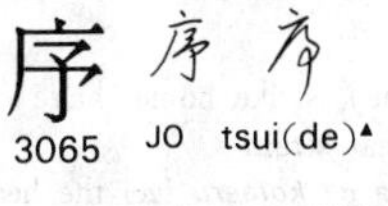

3065 JO tsui(de)▲

(CH) 序 xù

Radical	Strokes
广 53	7-3-4
Grade	**Freq**
Jōyō-5	1245
□ 3-3-4	

3-4 广

▶**INTRODUCTORY PART** ▶**ORDER**

COMPOUNDS

❶ⓐ introductory part of something: **opening, beginning, inception, first stage**

ⓑ introductory part of a book: **preface, introduction, foreword**

ⓒ introductory [first] part of a traditional Japanese performance

序盤 *joban* opening (in the game of go)
序曲 *jokyoku* prelude, overture
序説 *josetsu* introduction
序幕 *jomaku* opening act, curtain raiser
自序 *jijo* author's preface
序破急 *johakyū* artistic modulations in traditional Japanese performances; opening, middle and climax [end]

❷ⓐ **order, precedence, sequence**

ⓑ **order(liness), methodical arrangement**

ⓒ [archaic] order, arrange in order

序列 *joretsu* rank, grade, order
序次 *joji* order, sequence
順序 *junjo* order, sequence; system, procedure
秩序 *chitsujo* order, discipline; method, system
花序 *kajo* inflorescence
序歯 *joshi* [archaic] arranging seats by seniority

INDEPENDENT

【**jo** 序】introductory part, opening, beginning, the first stage; order, precedence; preface; first part of a play
序の口 *jo no kuchi* start, the first stage
長幼序有り *Chōyō jo ari* Seniores priores, Elders first

KUN

【**tsui(de)** 序で】occasion, opportunity
序でが有る *tsuide ga aru* have occasion to do
序でに *tsuide ni* while, on the occasion

SYNONYMS

❶ **beginnings**
緒 OUTSET → 1378
端 start → 1221
始 beginning → 281
初 beginning → 1116
元 ORIGIN → 1929
本 origin → 3502
根 ROOT → 930
源 SOURCE → 656

❷ **order**
順 ORDER (sequence) → 18
次 order (sequence) → 54
番 NUMERICAL ORDER → 2748
秩 ORDER (methodical arrangement) → 1158

応 應

3066 Ō -NŌ kota(eru)▲

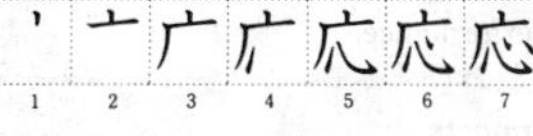

(CH) 应 yīng yìng

Radical	Strokes
心 61	7-4-3
Grade	**Freq**
Jōyō-5	443
□ 3-3-4	

3-4 广

▶**RESPOND**

COMPOUNDS

❶ (act in return) **respond to (a situation), react, act in accordance with, cope with**

応募 *ōbo* application, subscription, enlistment
応援する *ōen suru* aid, reinforce; support; cheer
応酬する *ōshū suru* respond, reply; counter
応接 *ōsetsu* reception
応力 *ōryoku phys* stress
反応する *hannō suru* react, respond
対応する *taiō suru* correspond to, answer to; be equivalent; deal [cope] with
適応する *tekiō suru* adapt (oneself) to, adjust (things) to
順応 *junnō* adaptation, accommodation, adjustment

❷ (make a reply) **respond, answer, reply**

応答 *ōtō* answer, response, reply
呼応して *koō shite* in concert, in response

❸ [original meaning] comply with, accede to, consent

応諾する *ōdaku suru* consent, assent

❹ suitable, appropriate

応用 *ōyō* practical application
応分の *ōbun no* appropriate, reasonable (in view of one's position), within one's power [means]
相応する *sōō suru* be suitable, befit, correspond

❺ **used phonetically for *ō***
一応(＝一往) *ichiō* once; in outline; tentatively; for the time being

INDEPENDENT

【**ō** 応】yes, all right
応と答える *ō to kotaeru* say yes

【**ōjiru** (＝**ōzuru**) 応じる(＝応ずる)】(act in return) respond to (a situation), act in accordance with; (make a reply) respond, answer; comply with, accede to, consent; be suitable [appropriate]
力に力で応じる *chikara ni chikara de ōjiru* meet force with force
求めに応じる *motome ni ōjiru* answer a request
場合に応じて *baai ni ōjite* in accordance with the situation

KUN

【**kota(eru)** 応える】
① come home to (one), strike home, have effect on; be a great strain
暑さが応える *atsusa ga kotaeru* feel the heat very much
② repay, reward
親切に応える *shinsetsu ni kotaeru* repay a kindness

SYNONYMS

❷ **answer**
答 ANSWER → 2681
返 reply → 3060
解 solve → 1517

HOMOPHONES

kotaeru ⇨ 答 2681

COMPOUND FORMATION

一応 (＝一往) *ichiō*
一応 'once, etc.', formerly written 一往, originally meant to proceed (往) one time (一). Later, 応 ❺ was phonetically substituted for 往.

NOTE

⇨ see USAGE note at 答 2681

3-4
广

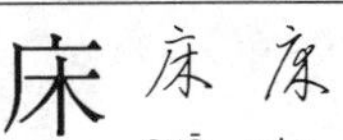

3067 SHŌ toko yuka

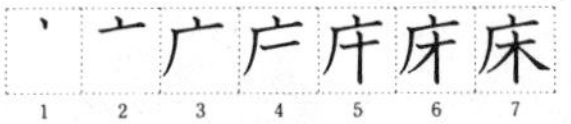

1 2 3 4 5 6 7

Ⓒ 床 chuáng

Radical	Strokes
广 53	7-3-4
Grade	**Freq**
Jōyō	1192
口 3-3-4	

▶**BED** ▶**FLOOR**

COMPOUNDS

❶ⓐ **bed, sickbed**
ⓑ counter for beds
起床する *kishō suru* get up, rise
臨床医 *rinshōi* clinician
百床病院 *hyakushō byōin* hospital with 100 beds

❷ (bed-shaped support or underlying part) **bed, foundation or ore deposit**
温床 *onshō* hotbed
岩床 *ganshō* bedrock
視床 *shishō* thalamus
銃床 *jūshō* gunstock
鉱床 *kōshō* ore deposit

❸ [original meaning] campstool
床几 *shōgi* campstool, folding stool

KUN

【**toko** 床】bed, sickbed; bed (as of flowers); alcove; barber
床に就く *toko ni tsuku* go to bed; be sick in bed, be laid up
寝床 *nedoko* bed
川床 *kawadoko* riverbed
床の間 *toko no ma* alcove
床屋 *tokoya* barber; barbershop

【**yuka** 床】floor; platform for *joruri* music players; floor exercises
床下 *yukashita* under the floor
床で金メダルを取る *yuka de kinmedaru o toru* win a gold medal for one's floor exercise performance

SYNONYMS

❶ **flat supports**
架 rack → 2569
棚 SHELF → 984
壇 PLATFORM → 754
座 SEAT → 3116
台 STAND → 2005

❷ **bottoms and bases**
盤 bedrock → 2851
礎 FOUNDATION STONE → 1248
底 BOTTOM → 3084
下 lower part → 3378
基 BASE → 2673

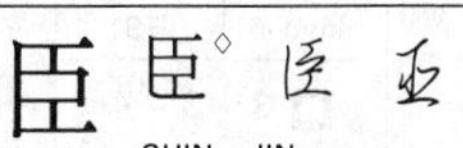

伺 incorrect classification ⇨ see 69

臣 臣 3068 SHIN JIN

㊥ 臣 chén

Radical	Strokes
臣 131	7-7-0
Grade	**Freq**
Jōyō-4	901
口 3-3-4	

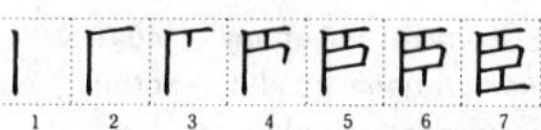

RADICAL 131

variant of 臣 *shin* 'retainer'

⇨ see 臣 2991 for radical description

▶RETAINER

COMPOUNDS

ⓐ **retainer, subject, vassal**

ⓑ first person pronoun used by retainers

臣下 *shinka* retainer, subject, vassal

臣民 *shinmin* subjects

家臣 *kashin* retainer, vassal

君臣 *kunshin* sovereign and subject, lord and vassal

忠臣 *chūshin* loyal retainer, loyal subject

大臣 *daijin* minister (of state)

INDEPENDENT

【shin 臣】 retainer, subject

SYNONYMS

ⓐ **servants**

従 follower → 415

供 attendant → 88

隷 UNDERLING → 1751

僕 MANSERVANT → 164

奴 SLAVE → 187

囲 3069 I kako(mu) kako(u) kako(i)

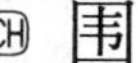

㊥ 围 wéi

Radical	Strokes
口 31	7-3-4
Grade	**Freq**
Jōyō-4	886
口 3-3-4	

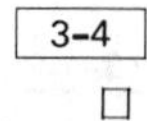

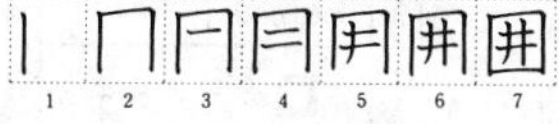

▶ENCLOSE

COMPOUNDS

ⓐ [original meaning] **enclose, encircle, surround**

ⓑ circumference, surroundings

囲碁 *igo* (the game of) go

包囲する *hōi suru* surround, encircle, envelop

範囲 *han'i* range, scope

雰囲気 *fun'iki* atmosphere, mood

周囲 *shūi* circumference, periphery; surroundings

胸囲 *kyōi* chest measurement

外囲 *gaii* surroundings, periphery

KUN

【kako(mu) 囲む】 enclose, encircle, surround; enclose with a fence, fence in; besiege

囲み *kakomi* enclosure; siege

取り囲む *torikakomu* enclose, encircle

【kako(u) 囲う】 enclose, fence; preserve (food), keep (a mistress)

庭を垣で囲う *niwa o kaki de kakou* enclose a garden with a fence

【kako(i) 囲い】 enclosure, fence

囲いに入れる *kakoi ni ireru* place in an enclosure

SYNONYMS

ⓐ & **【kakomu】 surround**

環 SURROUND → 1090

包 ENCOMPASS → 2966

ⓑ **periphery**

周 PERIPHERY → 2998

郭 OUTER ENCLOSURE → 1678

【kakoi】

○ **fences and walls**

垣 FENCE (for partitioning) → 351

塀 FENCE (for screening) → 557

壁 WALL → 2895

欄 railing → 1103

3-4 □

 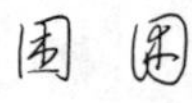

3070 KON koma(ru)

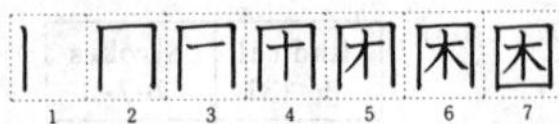

CH 困 kùn

Radical	Strokes
囗 31	7-3-4
Grade	**Freq**
Jōyō-6	791
囗 3 - 3 - 4	

▶BE IN TROUBLE

COMPOUNDS

❶ [original meaning] **be in trouble, be hard-pressed, be distressed, suffer**

困難 *konnan* difficulty, trouble, distress, hardship

困惑 *konwaku* embarrassment, perplexity, confusion

困窮 *konkyū* destitution, poverty, distress

困苦 *konku* hardships, privation

貧困 *hinkon* poverty, indigence, destitution; lack, shortage

❷ tired, exhausted

困憊 *konpai* exhaustion, fatigue

KUN

【**koma(ru)** 困る】 be in trouble, be distressed, be annoyed, be embarrassed, be perplexed; be destitute

困らせる *komaraseru* annoy, embarrass

困り者 *komarimono* good-for-nothing, scapegrace, nuisance, trouble

困り果てる *komarihateru* be hard up, be at one's wit's end, be in a bad fix

生活に困る *seikatsu ni komaru* live in want

SYNONYMS

❶ **trouble and suffering**

窮 BE IN EXTREMITY → 2358

悩 SUFFER → 421

苦 SUFFERING → 2243

痛 PAIN → 3285

辛 HARD → 2038

煩 VEXED → 1022

難 DIFFICULT → 1838

NOTE

★do not confuse with 因 3054

3-4 □

3071 ZU TO haka(ru)

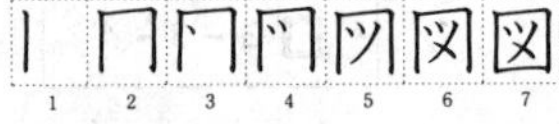

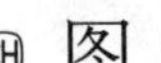 tú

Radical	Strokes
囗 31	7-3-4
Grade	**Freq**
Jōyō-2	642
囗 3 - 3 - 4	

▶DRAWING

COMPOUNDS

❶ [also suffix]

ⓐ **drawing, plan, diagram, figure, illustration, picture**

ⓑ [original meaning] **map, chart**

図面 *zumen* drawing, plan, map, sketch

図形 *zukei* figure, diagram

図表 *zuhyō* chart, diagram

図鑑 *zukan* picture [illustrated] book

図書 *tosho* books

設計図 *sekkeizu* plan, blueprint

地図 *chizu* map, atlas

版図 *hanto* territory

天気図 *tenkizu* weather chart

市街図 *shigaizu* city map

❷ⓐ **systematic plan, scheme, attempt**

ⓑ **intention**

壮図 *sōto* grand scheme

企図する *kito suru* plan, scheme, intend

雄図 *yūto* ambitious enterprise, grand project

意図 *ito* intention, aim

合図 *aizu* signal, sign

❸ [emphatic prefix] extraordinary, outrageous, audacious

図太い *zubutoi* audacious, brazen

図抜けている *zunukete iru* be outstanding

図図しい *zūzūshii* cheeky, impudent

図体 *zūtai* body, frame

❹ limits, bounds (of common sense)

野放図な *nohōzu na* unrestrained, unruly

❺ expectation

図星 *zuboshi* bull's eye, mark

INDEPENDENT

【**zu** 図】

① drawing, plan, figure, illustration, diagram; map, chart

図を描く *zu o kaku* draw a diagram

② *slang* sight; situation

滅多に見られない図 *metta ni mirarenai zu* seldom seen sight

③ *slang* expectation, intention

図に当たる *zu ni ataru* hit the bull's eye, go as expected
図に乗る *zu ni noru* push a good thing too far

KUN

【haka(ru) 図る】
① strive for, work for, promote, look to, provide for, seek
相互理解を図る *sōgo rikai o hakaru* strive for mutual understanding
公益を図る *kōeki o hakaru* labor for the public good
安全を図る *anzen o hakaru* provide for safety
② bring about, attempt
便宜を図る *bengi o hakaru* accommodate, suit the convenience of
自殺を図る *jisatsu o hakaru* attempt suicide
③ [in negative constructions] expect, look forward to
図らずも *hakarazumo* unexpectedly

SYNONYMS

❶ⓐ picture
絵 PICTURE → 1346
画 PICTURE → 3000
ⓐ diagram
表 TABLE → 2429
❷ⓐ plans and planning
企 PROJECT → 2021
計 PLAN → 1441
画 DRAW UP A PLAN → 3000
案 PROPOSAL → 2270
謀 SCHEME → 1593
策 SCHEME → 2679
略 STRATEGY → 1169
ⓑ will and intention
意 MIND → 2136
志 AMBITION → 2199
気 mind to do something → 3194
念 thought of doing something → 2059
趣 PURPOSE → 3317
欲 DESIRE → 1475

HOMOPHONES

hakaru ⇨ 計 1441 謀 1593 量 2471 測 610 諮 1596

COMPOUND FORMATION

❶ 図書 *tosho*
図書 'books' formerly meant drawings (図 ❶ⓐ) and books (書).
❷ 合図 *aizu*
合図 'signal, sign' is the transmission of an agreed upon (合) intention (図 ❷ⓑ).

NOTE

⇨ see USAGE note at 計 1441

囬
3072

▶TURN ROUND ▶TIME
nonstandard for 回 3055

3-4 口

延 延 延

3073 EN no(biru) no(beru) no(be) no(basu)

Ⓒⓗ 延 yán

Radical	Strokes
廴 54	8-3-5
Grade	**Freq**
Jōyō-6	663
口 3-3-5	

3-5 廴

▶EXTEND ▶POSTPONE

COMPOUNDS

❶ⓐ [original meaning] **extend (in space or time), prolong, spread**
ⓑ *metallurgy* (cause to extend) flatten out, roll
延長 *enchō* extension, prolongation, continuation
延焼 *enshō* spread of a fire
延延たる *en'entaru* lengthy
延髄 *enzui* medulla oblongata
熱延 *netsuen* hot rolling
圧延鋼 *atsuenkō* rolled steel
❷ postpone, delay, defer
延期 *enki* postponement, deferment
延納 *ennō* delayed [deferred] payment
延着 *enchaku* delayed arrival
延発 *enpatsu* postponement of departure, delayed departure
延会 *enkai* adjournment [postponement] of a meeting
延滞 *entai* arrear, arrearage
遅延 *chien* delay, retardation

KUN

【no(biru) 延びる】
vi
① extend (in space or time), be extended, be prolonged
延び *nobi* extension; postponement
延び率 *nobiritsu* growth rate
この鉄道は国境迄延びている *Kono tetsudō wa kokkyō made nobite iru* This railway

extends as far as the frontier
② be postponed, be delayed
延び延び *nobinobi* repeated delays, dragging on and on
出発が延びた *Shuppatsu ga nobita* The departure was postponed

【no(beru) 延べる】
① [also 伸べる]
ⓐ extend, stretch out (one's arm)
ⓑ spread out (bedding)
手を延べる *te o noberu* stretch one's arm
② postpone, delay
日延べ *hinobe* postponement, adjournment

【no(be) 延べ】
① [also prefix] total, aggregate
延べ時間 *nobejikan* total man hours
② deferment
延べ払い *nobebarai* deferred payment

【no(basu) 延ばす】
vt
① extend (in space or time), prolong, spread
引き延ばす *hikinobasu* extend, draw out; enlarge; prolong, filibuster
寿命を延ばす *jumyō o nobasu* prolong one's life
期限を延ばす *kigen o nobasu* extend the term
② postpone, delay, defer
返事を延ばす *henji o nobasu* delay one's answer

SYNONYMS
❶ **expand**
伸 STRETCH → 70
拡 ENLARGE → 309
広げる spread (out) → 3035
張 SPREAD → 474
膨 EXPAND → 1084
脹 SWELL → 1003
❷ **be late and delay**
猶 DELAY → 619
遅 be late → 3133
後 fall behind → 361
滞 fall into arrears → 663

HOMOPHONES
nobiru ⇨ 伸 70
nobi ⇨ 伸 70
noberu ⇨ 伸 70
nobasu ⇨ 伸 70

NOTE
⇨ see USAGE note at 伸 70
★do not confuse with 廷 3058

3-5

辶

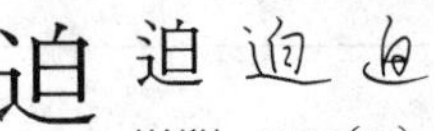

3074 HAKU sema(ru)

CH 迫 pò pǎi

Radical	Strokes
辶 162	8-3-5
Grade	**Freq**
Jōyō	809
□ 3 - 3 - 5	

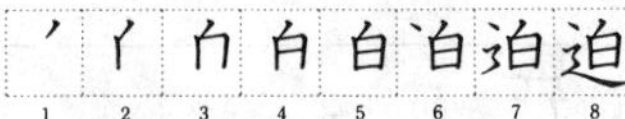

▶PRESS

COMPOUNDS
❶ⓐ [original meaning] (close in on) **press on, close in, draw near**
ⓑ **pressing, urgent, imminent, impending, close**
迫撃 *hakugeki* close attack
迫真の *hakushin no* true to life, realistic
切迫する *seppaku suru* draw near, press; become acute, grow tense
急迫した *kyūhaku shita* pressing, urgent, imminent
緊迫する *kinpaku suru* become tense, grow strained
❷ⓐ (force to action) **press upon, press for, urge, force, compel**
ⓑ (cause distress) **oppress, press hard, persecute**
ⓒ hard-pressed, in distress
迫力 *hakuryoku* power, force, punch, appeal
脅迫する *kyōhaku suru* threaten, intimidate, menace
強迫 *kyōhaku* coercion, compulsion
圧迫する *appaku suru* press, oppress, pressure
迫害 *hakugai* persecution, oppression
窮迫 *kyūhaku* straitened circumstances, distress
逼迫する *hippaku suru* be tight, get stringent
❸ [also 魄 1227] spirit, soul
気迫 *kihaku* spirit, soul, vigor

KUN
【sema(ru) 迫る】 press (a person), urge, compel; close in on, press, draw near; be imminent
辞職を迫る *jishoku o semaru* urge to resign
真に迫る *shin ni semaru* be true to nature [life], be lifelike
差し迫る *sashisemaru* be imminent, be impending

SYNONYMS
❶ⓐ **approach**
寄る DRAW NEAR → 2291
近 NEAR → 3061
接 come close to → 500

ⓑ **urgent**
急 URGENT → 2092
緊 EXIGENT → 2838
❷ⓐ **compel and press**
圧 PRESSURE → 2970
強 force → 475
押す PUSH → 314
ⓑ **torture and oppress**
虐 treat cruelly → 3218
拷 TORTURE → 373
責める torture → 2467

COMPOUND FORMATION

迫力 *hakuryoku*
迫力 'power, etc.' is the power (力) to compel (迫 ❷ⓐ) or influence a person.

述 述 述 述

3075 JUTSU no(beru)

一 十 才 木 朮 朮 述 述
1 2 3 4 5 6 7 8

CH 述 shù

Radical	Strokes
辶 162	8-3-5
Grade	**Freq**
Jōyō-5	634
口 3 - 3 - 5	

3-5 辶

▶**STATE**

COMPOUNDS

❶ⓐ **state orally, expound, mention, declare**
ⓑ state [express] in writing
述懐 *jukkai* effusion of one's thoughts (and feelings), reminiscence
述語 *jutsugo* predicate
供述 *kyōjutsu* testimony, statement; confession
口述する *kōjutsu suru* state orally, dictate
陳述 *chinjutsu* statement, declaration
叙述 *jojutsu* description, depiction
詳述 *shōjutsu* (detailed) expatiation, full account
前述の通り *zenjutsu no tōri* as stated [mentioned] above
述作 *jussaku* writing a book; literary work
記述する *kijutsu suru* describe, give an account, write
著述 *chojutsu* writing (of books); book, literary work
❷ *gram* abbrev. of 述語 *jutsugo*: predicate
主述 *shujutsu* subject and predicate
❸ hand down, transmit
祖述 *sojutsu* exposition [propagation] of one's master's doctrines

INDEPENDENT

【**jutsu 述**】 statement
先生の述 *sensei no jutsu* teacher's statement [expounding]

KUN

【**no(beru) 述べる**】 state orally (or in writing), expound, mention, declare; relate, tell
詳しく述べる *kuwashiku noberu* expound
述べ立てる *nobetateru* dwell eloquently (on), relate at great length
申し述べる *mōshinoberu* state, mention, tell

SYNONYMS

❶ⓐ **speak and say**
陳 SET FORTH → 540
弁 SPEAK ELOQUENTLY → 2004
申す SPEAK HUMBLY → 3507
語る TELL → 1543
談 TALK → 1569
口 give mouth to → 3382
話 SPEAK → 1527
言 SAY → 1941
云 say → 1931

迪 迪 迪 迪

3076 TEKI NAMES susumu michi

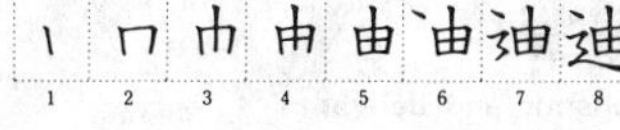

CH 迪 dí

Radical	Strokes
辶 162	8-3-5
Grade	**Freq**
Names	2135
口 3 - 3 - 5	

3-5 辶

▶**EDIFY**

COMPOUNDS

❶ [rare] edify, enlighten, guide, teach
啓迪する *keiteki suru* edify, enlighten, guide
訓迪 *kunteki* guide, teach; master
❷ [archaic] advance, proceed
❸ [original meaning, now obsolete] way, path

NAMES

迪子 *michiko* female name

SYNONYMS

❶ **teach**
啓 ENLIGHTEN → 2763

導 GUIDE → 2888
諭 ADMONISH → 1598
訓 INSTRUCT → 1454
教 TEACH → 1493
授 teach → 492
育 educate → 2050
練 TRAIN → 1375

3-5 辶

迭 迭 迭 迭

3077 TETSU

Ⓒⓗ 迭 dié

Radical	Strokes
辶 162	8-3-5
Grade	**Freq**
Jōyō	1738
口 3 - 3 - 5	

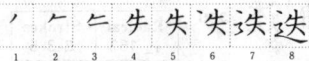

1 2 3 4 5 6 7 8

▶**ALTERNATE**

COMPOUNDS

● [original meaning] **alternate, change, take turns**

更迭する *kōtetsu suru* reshuffle, change (as of government officials), exchange places

SYNONYMS

● **alternate**
交 INTERCHANGE → 2015
輪 take turns → 1589

● **change and replace**
代 SUBSTITUTE → 30
替 REPLACE → 2783
交 INTERCHANGE → 2015
換 EXCHANGE → 587
転 turn into → 1480
遷 undergo transition → 3170
化 CHANGE INTO, -ize → 21
変 CHANGE → 2069
更 change → 3541
改 change → 243
易 change → 2411

NOTE

★do not confuse with 送 3093

3-5 尸

届 届 届 届

3078 KAI▲ todo(keru) -todo(ke) todo(ku)

Ⓒⓗ 届 jiè

Radical	Strokes
尸 44	8-3-5
Grade	**Freq**
Jōyō-6	908
口 3 - 3 - 5	

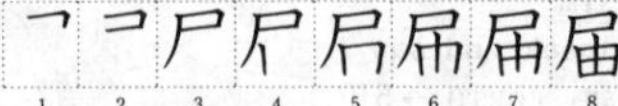

1 2 3 4 5 6 7 8

▶**DELIVER** ▶**REACH**

KUN

[todo(keru) 届ける]

① deliver (a letter or goods), send, forward
届け先 *todokesaki* destination, address
送り届ける *okuritodokeru* send to, deliver; escort (a person) home
付け届け *tsuketodoke* present, tip; bribe

② give notice (to the authorities), report, notify, file notice
届け *todoke* report, notice; delivery, forwarding
届け出る *todokederu* report, notify
無届けの *mutodoke no* without notice

[-todo(ke) -届け] [suffix] report, notice; notification
被害届け *higaitodoke* report of damage
出生届け *shusshōtodoke* register of birth

[todo(ku) 届く]

①ⓐ (succeed in touching) reach, get at
ⓑ (be delivered) reach (a destination), arrive, be received
手の届く所 *te no todoku tokoro* within one's reach
目の届く限り *me no todoku kagiri* as far as the eye can reach
届かない手紙 *todokanai tegami* letter that fails to reach its destination

② be attained, be fulfilled, be realized
届かぬ願い *todokanu negai* unfulfilled wish

③ be attentive, be careful
行き届く *yukitodoku* be scrupulous, be attentive, be prudent; be complete, be thorough
不届きな *futodoki na* insolent, outrageous

SYNONYMS

[todokeru]

① **transmit and deliver**
達 deliver → 3139
伝 TRANSMIT → 44
逓 RELAY → 3106

② **inform and communicate**
達 issue a notice → 3139
告 NOTIFY → 2409
通 COMMUNICATE → 3109

報 INFORM → 1698
知 let know → 1127
申 REPORT → 3507
宣 PROCLAIM → 2252
【todoku】
① **arrive**
及 REACH TO → 3385
至 COME TO → 2182
到 ARRIVE → 1264
着 ARRIVE → 3316
達 ATTAIN → 3139

屈

3079 KUTSU kaga(mu)▲ kaga(meru)▲

Ⓒⓗ 屈 qū

Radical	Strokes
尸 44	8-3-5
Grade	**Freq**
Jōyō	1448
口 3 - 3 - 5	

3-5 尸

▶BEND

COMPOUNDS

❶ⓐ [original meaning] **bend, flex, crouch**
ⓑ crooked
屈伸 *kusshin* bending and stretching, extension and contraction
屈折 *kussetsu* bending, turn; refraction
屈曲する *kukkyoku suru* bend, wind
屈指の *kusshi no* leading, foremost
前屈 *zenkutsu* bending forward, anteflexion
偏屈な *henkutsu na* eccentric, narrow-minded, obstinate

❷ **bend in submission, bow, submit to, yield**
屈伏(=屈服)する *kuppuku suru* bend in submission, submit to, surrender, yield to
屈従 *kutsujū* servile submission, subservience
屈辱 *kutsujoku* humiliation, disgrace, insult
不屈の *fukutsu no* indomitable, unyielding
卑屈な *hikutsu na* mean, meanspirited; servile

❸ be in an uncomfortable position, be cramped, reach the limit
屈託 *kuttaku* worry, vexation
退屈な *taikutsu na* tedious, boring
窮屈な *kyūkutsu na* cramped, confined; formal; poor

❹ strong, robust
屈強な *kukkyō na* strong, sturdy, robust

❺ [formerly 窟 2328] cave, cavern
理屈 *rikutsu* reason, logic; argument; pretext; theory

INDEPENDENT

【kussuru 屈する】 bend, flex; bend in submission, bow, submit to, yield

KUN

【kaga(mu) 屈む】 *vi* stoop, lean over; crouch
屈み込む *kagamikomu* lean in, lean over
前屈み *maekagami* slouch

【kaga(meru) 屈める】 *vt* bend (one's legs), bow (one's knee), incline (one's head)
腰を屈めて歩く *koshi o kagamete aruku* walk with a stoop

SYNONYMS

❶ⓐ **bend**
曲 CURVE → 3527
折 bend → 253

❷ **submit and surrender**
服 SUBMIT → 878
伏 submit → 45
降 surrender → 458

COMPOUND FORMATION

理屈 *rikutsu*
According to one theory, 理屈 'reason, etc.' originally referred to a cave (屈 ❺) for amassing truth or reason (理).

居

3080 KYO i(ru) -i o(ru)▲

Ⓒⓗ 居 jū

Radical	Strokes
尸 44	8-3-5
Grade	**Freq**
Jōyō-5	736
口 3 - 3 - 5	

3-5 尸

▶RESIDE

COMPOUNDS

❶ⓐ **reside, live, dwell**
ⓑ **residence, dwelling, address**
居住する *kyojū suru* live, dwell, reside
居留地 *kyoryūchi* settlement, concession
同居する *dōkyo suru* live together
別居 *bekkyo* separation, limited divorce

群居する *gunkyo suru* live gregariously
住居 *jūkyo* house, dwelling, residence
皇居 *kōkyo* Imperial Palace
入居する *nyūkyo suru* move into (a flat)
転居する *tenkyo suru* move, change one's residence

❷ⓐ (of living beings) **be present, be, be found, stay**
ⓑ be still, do nothing
家居する *kakyo suru* stay at home
居然たる *kyozentaru* still, doing nothing

❸ [original meaning] **sit**
起居 *kikyo* one's daily life

❹ [rare] ordinary, usual
居常 *kyojō* daily life

INDEPENDENT

【kyo 居】 residence, dwelling
居を構える *kyo o kamaeru* take up one's residence

KUN

【i(ru) 居る】
① be present, exist, be found—said esp. of living things
居合わせる *iawaseru* happen to be present
居候 *isōrō* hanger-on, parasite
②ⓐ reside, live, dwell, inhabit
ⓑ (of animals) inhabit, live
居所 *idokoro* one's address [residence], one's whereabouts
③ sit
居眠り *inemuri* doze, nap
居並ぶ *inarabu* sit in a row, be arrayed
居間 *ima* living [sitting] room
④ [following the TE-form of verbs] be-ing, be engaged in
笑って居る *waratte iru* be smiling [laughing]

【-i -居】
① presence; someone present
長居 *nagai* long visit [stay]
仲居 *nakai* parlormaid, waitress
留守居 *rusui* caretaker, janitor; caretaking (during a person's absence)
② sitting; seat
芝居 *shibai* play, drama

【o(ru) 居る】 variant of 居る *iru*
父は居りません *Chichi wa orimasen* Father is not home

SPECIAL READINGS

一言居士 *ichigenkoji* ready critic, one ready to comment on any and every subject

SYNONYMS

❶ⓐ **reside**
住 LIVE → 64
生 inhabit → 3497
植 colonize → 990
ⓑ **houses**
住 housing → 64
邸 STATELY RESIDENCE → 1131
宅 DWELLING HOUSE → 2174
戸 HOUSEHOLD → 1930
家 HOUSE → 2273
屋 HOUSE → 3098
軒 house → 1459
❷ⓐ **exist and be**
臨 BE PRESENT AT → 1630
在 BE → 2984
存 EXIST → 2982
有 exist → 2983
也 CLASSICAL COPULA → 3406
❸ **sit**
座 SIT → 3116

NOTE

⇨ see COMPOUND FORMATION for
芝居 *shibai* ⇨ 芝 2180
居候 *isōrō* ⇨ 候 119
仲居 *nakai* ⇨ 仲 43

3-5 戸

屆 3081

▶DELIVER ▶REACH
nonstandard for 届 3078

3-5 广

府 3082 FU

CH 府 fǔ

Radical	Strokes
广 53	8-3-5
Grade	**Freq**
Jōyō-4	125
口 3-3-5	

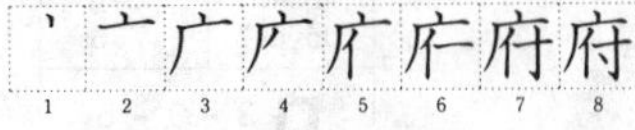

▶URBAN PREFECTURE

COMPOUNDS

❶ **urban [metropolitan] prefecture (limited to Kyoto and Osaka prefectures)**
府庁 *fuchō* urban prefectural office
府警 *fukei* prefectural police
府税 *fuzei* urban prefectural tax
京都府 *kyōtofu* Kyoto Prefecture
❷ⓐ **capital, metropolis**
ⓑ Edo in feudal Japan

府下 *fuka* suburban districts (of a metropolis)
首府 *shufu* capital, metropolis
御府内 *gofunai* within the town limits of Edo
❸ **government office, seat of government**
政府 *seifu* government, administration
総理府 *sōrifu* Prime Minister's Office
国府 *kokufu* National Government (of China); provincial capital
幕府 *bakufu* shogunate
❹ center, focus (as of learning)
学府 *gakufu* academic center
❺ [original meaning, now rare] storehouse, treasury, archives
府庫 *fuko* treasury

INDEPENDENT

【fu 府】 urban prefecture (⇨ ❶); center, focus
禍の府 *wazawai no fu* sink of iniquity
文教の府 *bunkyō no fu* fountainhead of culture; Ministry of Education

SYNONYMS

❶ **territorial divisions**
県 PREFECTURE → 2641
道 district of Hokkaido → 3134
都 METROPOLIS OF TOKYO → 1686
州 STATE → 57
省 province in China → 2449
郡 COUNTY → 1466
❸ **public offices**
庁 GOVERNMENT AGENCY → 3034
省 MINISTRY → 2449
公 public office → 1974
署 PUBLIC-SERVICE STATION → 2609
局 public service office → 3063
所 office → 851

3083 HŌ

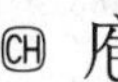
páo

Radical	Strokes
广 53	8-3-5
Grade	**Freq**
Reference	
口 3-3-5	

3-5 广

COMPOUNDS

● [now also 包 2966] [original meaning] kitchen
庖丁 *hōchō* kitchen knife, carving knife
庖厨 *hōchū* kitchen

NOTE

⇨ see COMPOUND FORMATION for 庖丁(=包丁) *hōchō* ⇨ 丁 3348

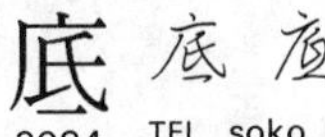
3084 TEI soko

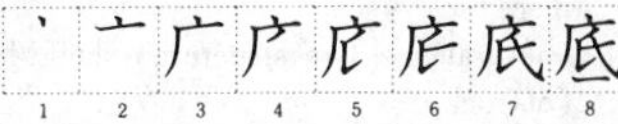

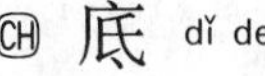
dǐ de

Radical	Strokes
广 53	8-3-5
Grade	**Freq**
Jōyō-4	739
口 3-3-5	

3-5 广

▶BOTTOM

COMPOUNDS

❶ⓐ **bottom, base**
ⓑ *math* base, radix
底流 *teiryū* bottom current, undercurrent
海底 *kaitei* sea bottom
心底 *shintei* bottom of one's heart, inmost thoughts
底数 *teisū* base, radix
底角 *teikaku* base angle
底辺 *teihen* base (in geometry)
❷ [formerly also 柢 901] (fundamental part) **bottom, basis, origin**
底本 *teihon* original text
根底 *kontei* root, basis, foundation
基底 *kitei* base, basis, foundation; *math* base
徹底 *tettei* thoroughness, completeness

INDEPENDENT

【tei 底】 bottom, base; base, radix; kind, sort
この底の本 *kono tei no hon* this sort of book

KUN

【soko 底】 bottom, sole, bed; bottom (as of one's heart), depths; bowels (of the earth)
底革 *sokogawa* sole, sole leather
箱の底 *hako no soko* bottom of a box
川底 *kawazoko* riverbed
底値 *sokone* bottom price
どん底 *donzoko* rock bottom, depths
心の奥底 *kokoro no okusoko* innermost depths of one's heart
地の底深く *chi no soko fukaku* deep in the bowels of the earth

SYNONYMS

❶ⓐ bottoms and bases
下 lower part → 3378
基 BASE → 2673
礎 FOUNDATION STONE → 1248
盤 bedrock → 2851
床 BED → 3067

❷ basis
基 BASE → 2673
本 BASIS → 3502
根 ROOT → 930
礎 foundation → 1248
拠 GROUNDS → 312
素 ELEMENT → 2458

3-5 广

店 店 店

3085 TEN mise tana▲

CH 店 diàn

Radical	Strokes
广 53	8-3-5
Grade	**Freq**
Jōyō-2	418
口 3-3-5	

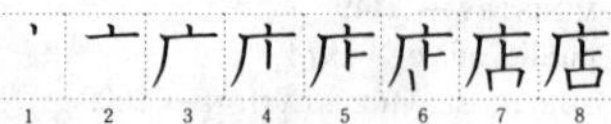

▶SHOP

COMPOUNDS

ⓐ [also suffix] [original meaning] **shop, store; stall**
ⓑ [also suffix] (**small**) **business establishment, as a bank or restaurant**
ⓒ counter for shops or firms
店員 *ten'in* clerk
店舗 *tenpo* shop, store
店頭 *tentō* shop [store] front
商店 *shōten* shop, store
書店 *shoten* bookstore
売店 *baiten* booth, stand; store
百貨店 *hyakkaten* department store
支店 *shiten* branch (office), branch (store)
本店 *honten* head [main] office [store]
店屋物 *ten'yamono* dishes from a caterer
代理店 *dairiten* agency, agent
特約店 *tokuyakuten* special [sole] agency [agent]
喫茶店 *kissaten* coffee shop, tea house
五十店 *gojutten* 50 shops [branch offices]

KUN

【mise 店】 shop, store
店屋 *miseya* shop, store
店先 *misesaki* storefront
茶店 *chamise* tea stall, rest house
出店 *demise* branch (store)

【tana 店】
① shop, store
店卸し(＝棚卸し) *tanaoroshi* inventory
大店 *ōdana* large store
② house for rent
店子 *tanako* tenant

SYNONYMS

● places of business
舗 SHOP (esp. traditional) → 1735
屋 SMALL SHOP → 3098
社 COMPANY → 840

USAGE

tana
店
① shop, store
② house for rent
棚
ⓐ [also suffix] shelf, rack, ledge, mantelpiece
ⓑ (natural shelflike structure) shelf, ledge (of rock)
ⓒ continental shelf

HOMOPHONES

tana ⇨ 棚 984

3-5 广

度

incorrect stroke count ⇨ see 3100

3-5 广

夜

incorrect classification ⇨ see 2056

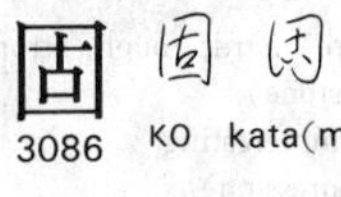

Ⓒⓗ 固 gù

Radical	Strokes
口 31	8-3-5
Grade	**Freq**
Jōyō-4	767
口 3-3-5	

3-5 口

3086 KO kata(meru) kata(maru) kata(mari) kata(i)

▶SOLID ▶FIRM

COMPOUNDS

❶ⓐ **solid**

ⓑ **solidify, harden**

固体 *kotai* solid, solid matter
固溶体 *koyōtai* solid solution
固化 *koka* solidification
凝固 *gyōko* solidification, coagulation, congelation

❷ⓐ [original meaning] (fixed in place) **firm, fixed, immovable, stable**

ⓑ (having determination) **firm, resolute, determined**

ⓒ defend firmly, hold firm

固定された *kotei sareta* fixed, stationary, permanent
固着する *kochaku suru* adhere to, stick fast
固辞する *koji suru* decline positively, decline firmly
堅固な *kengo na* strong, secure, firm, steadfast
強固な *kyōko na* firm, stable, solid, strong
固守する *koshu suru* defend stubbornly [firmly], keep to old customs

❸ firmly persistent, stiff, unyielding, stubborn

固執する *koshitsu* (=*koshū*) *suru* adhere to, persist in
頑固な *ganko na* stubborn, obstinate, bigoted

❹ intrinsically, originally

固有の *koyū no* peculiar to, characteristic, inborn

❺ [also 乎] suffix for forming modifiers

断固たる *dankotaru* firm, conclusive, determined
確固たる *kakkotaru* firm, sure, resolute

❻ [formerly 錮 1739] imprison, hold in custody

禁固 *kinko* imprisonment

KUN

【kata(meru) 固める】 *vt* harden, solidify; tamp; strengthen, make secure, establish oneself; fortify, defend

固め *katame* hardening; defense, fortifying; pledge
土を固める *tsuchi o katameru* harden earth into a mass
国境を固める *kokkyō o katameru* fortify the frontier
決心を固める *kesshin o katameru* make a firm resolution

【kata(maru) 固まる】 *vi* harden, solidify, congeal; become firm, become stiff; gather, huddle; be devoted to; become certain

固く固まる *kataku katamaru* form a hard mass
思想が固まっていない *shisō ga katamatte inai* have no fixed ideas
隅っこに固まる *sumikko ni katamaru* huddle in a corner
凝り固まる *korikatamaru* be fanatical; coagulate, clot

【kata(mari) 固まり】

① [sometimes also 塊] lump, mass, clod; ingot

鉄の固まり *tetsu no katamari* iron ingot

② [usu. 塊] group, crowd, cluster

③ [sometimes also 塊] devotee, worshiper; incarnation (of selfishness), personification

欲の固まり *yoku no katamari* incarnation of selfishness
拝金主義の固まり *haikinshugi no katamari* money worshiper

【kata(i) 固い】

①ⓐ (glutinous or not flexible) stiff, firm, thick

ⓑ (not easily moved) stiff, tight, fast

固さ *katasa* stiffness
固練りコンクリート *kataneri konkurīto* stiff-consistency concrete
固いカラー *katai karā* stiff collar
ドアが固い *Doa ga katai* The door sticks [has stiff hinges]
固い結び目 *katai musubime* tight knot
固い握り *katai nigiri* tight grip

②ⓐ (unshakable) stiff, firm, resolute, strong

ⓑ (unyielding) stiff (stand), obstinate, stubborn, inflexible

固い約束 *katai yakusoku* solemn promise
決意が固い *ketsui ga katai* be firmly determined
団結が固い *danketsu ga katai* be strongly united
頭が固い *atama ga katai* obstinate, thickheaded, inflexible

③ rigid, strict, stern

固く戒める *kataku imashimeru* admonish sternly

④ certain, sure

合格は固い *Gōkaku wa katai* He is certain to pass the exam

SYNONYMS

❶ⓐ hard
硬 HARD → 1183
堅 FIRM → 2823
剛 TOUGH → 1673
強 STRONG → 475
ⓑ solidify and coagulate
凝 CONGEAL → 175
結 form into a mass → 1348
凍 FREEZE → 129
❷ⓐ not moving
定 fixed → 2229
静 still → 1728
止 still → 2941
❷ⓑ & ❸ firm and obstinate
堅 FIRM → 2823
確 firm → 1228
毅 RESOLUTE → 1866
剛 TOUGH → 1673
頑 STUBBORN → 1040
硬 hard-line → 1183

USAGE

❶ katamari
固まり
① [sometimes also 塊] lump, mass, clod; ingot
② [usu. 塊] group, crowd, cluster
③ [sometimes also 塊] devotee, worshiper; incarnation (of selfishness), personification
塊
① [usu. 固まり] lump, mass, clod; ingot
② [sometimes also 固まり] group, crowd, cluster
③ [usu. 固まり] devotee, worshiper; incarnation (of selfishness), personification

❷ katai
固い
①ⓐ (glutinous or not flexible) stiff, firm, thick
ⓑ (not easily moved) stiff, tight, fast
②ⓐ (unshakable) stiff, firm, resolute, strong
ⓑ (unyielding) stiff (stand), obstinate, stubborn, inflexible
③ rigid, strict, stern
④ certain, sure
硬い
① (resisting pressure) hard, tough, strong (esp. metals or stone)
②ⓐ stiff (style), uninteresting
ⓑ stiff (facial expression)
堅い
① (resisting deformation) firm, hard (lumber)
② steady (market or business), sound (investment)
③ⓐ steadfast, reliable, trustworthy
ⓑ honest, honorable, upright, serious, chaste
④ stiff, formal, bookish
難い
difficult, hard

★ *katai* is a source of confusion to all users of Japanese, with many dictionaries disagreeing with each other. Though the information here is lexically "correct," it is not always reliable for determining meaning in actual occurrences, esp. in reference to physical hardness. Study the equivalents and examples under each entry. In the ordinary sense of hard, 硬い is used, esp. in reference to metals or stone. In reference to wood, 堅い is the correct choice, though the two are often used interchangeably. 固い implies stickiness, as in pasty substances, resistance to motion (stiff hinges) or tightness (tight knot or grip). It does *not* mean solid, despite the fact that it has this meaning in *on* compounds. In figurative uses, 堅い is basically positive (steadfast, trustworthy, upright, chaste), while 固い has negative overtones (stiff, obstinate). However, 固い is also used positively (solemn promise, firm determination). In reference to speech or writing, 硬い means uninteresting or unpolished, while 堅い means formal (style) or bookish. The verbs *katameru* and *katamaru* are always written 固める and 固まる. 難い is a literary expression for difficult or a verbal suffix meaning hard to do. It is never interchangeable with the above three.

HOMOPHONES

katamari ⇨ 塊 632
katai ⇨ 硬 1183 堅 2823 難 1838

国 國 圀° 囗° 囯 囻 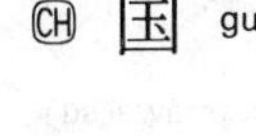

3087 KOKU kuni

Radical	Strokes
囗 31	8-3-5
Grade	**Freq**
Jōyō-2	9
口 3 - 3 - 5	

1 2 3 4 5 6 7 8

3-5 口

▶COUNTRY

COMPOUNDS

❶ⓐ [also suffix] **country, nation, state**

ⓑ **national, government-operated**

国家 *kokka* state, country, nation
国会 *kokkai* National Diet; national assembly, congress
国際的な *kokusaiteki na* international
国旗 *kokki* national flag
国防 *kokubō* national defense
国民 *kokumin* people, nation; the people
国境 *kokkyō* (national) boundary [border]
全国 *zenkoku* the whole country
外国 *gaikoku* foreign country
傾国 *keikoku* beautiful woman; courtesan
先進国 *senshinkoku* advanced [developed] nation [country]
国債 *kokusai* national bonds; national debt [loan]
国立 *kokuritsu* national (park, etc.)
国鉄 *kokutetsu* Japanese National Railways (defunct)

❷ native country, homeland

郷国 *kyōkoku* one's native country [land]

❸ (unit of administration in former Japan equiv. to modern prefecture) province

国司 *kokushi* provincial governor
国府 *kokufu* National Government (of China); provincial capital

❹ⓐ abbrev. of 国鉄 *kokutetsu*: Japanese National Railways

ⓑ abbrev. of 国会 *kokkai*: National Diet

国労 *kokurō* National Railway Workers' Union
国対(=国会対策委員会) *kokutai* (=*kokkai taisaku iinkai*) Committee of the National Diet

❺ⓐ (of Japan) Japanese

ⓑ abbrev. of 国語 *kokugo*: Japanese language

国語 *kokugo* national language; Japanese
国文学 *kokubungaku* Japanese literature
国史 *kokushi* Japanese history
国漢 *kokkan* Japanese and Chinese
英数国 *eisūkoku* English, Mathematics and Japanese

❻ distinguished in one's country

国手 *kokushu* noted doctor; master
国士 *kokushi* distinguished citizen; patriot

KUN

【kuni 国】 country, state, nation, land, territory, realm; one's native country, homeland, home town; province (⇨ ❸)

国境 *kunizakai* (national, state or provincial) boundary [border]
国国 *kuniguni* nations
島国 *shimaguni* island country
国自慢 *kunijiman* provincial pride
国侍 *kunizamurai* provincial samurai
大和の国 *yamato no kuni* Japan, Yamato

SYNONYMS

❶ⓐ **country**

邦 STATE → 847
土 land → 3403

ⓑ **national**

内 internal → 3466

❸ **feudal territorial divisions**

藩 FEUDAL DOMAIN → 2379
領 fief → 1224
封 daimiate → 1287
荘 manor (in feudal Japan) → 2262

❺ⓐ **Japan**

日 JAPAN → 3027
和 JAPAN → 1130
邦 JAPAN → 847

NOTE

⇨ see COMPOUND FORMATION for 傾国 *keikoku* ⇨ 傾 154

建

3088

▶BUILD

nonstandard for 建 3090

3-6 廴

3-6 ⻍

廻

3089 KAI E mawa(ru) mawa(su)

CH 回 huí

Radical	Strokes
⻍ 54	9-3-6
Grade Reference	Freq
3-3-6	

COMPOUNDS

❶ [now replaced by 回 *kai* 3055]
ⓐ turn round, revolve, rotate, circulate
ⓑ go round, make the rounds; circulate, make a circular tour
廻転する *kaiten suru* revolve, rotate, turn
旋廻 *senkai* revolution, rotation, circling, swiveling
廻覧する *kairan suru* circulate, send round
廻状 *kaijō* circular (letter)
廻文 *kaibun* palindrome; circular
廻廊 *kairō* corridor, gallery
❷ [now replaced by 回 *kai, e* 3055]
ⓐ turn back, return, come back
ⓑ turn (something) back, return, reply, bring back
廻向 *kaikō* Buddhist memorial service
輪廻 *rinne Buddhism* transmigration of souls, *saṃsāra*
廻心 *kaishin* (=*eshin*) conversion
❸ [now replaced by 回 *kai* 3055] send round, forward, transmit
廻送 *kaisō* forwarding
廻漕業 *kaisōgyō* shipping business
廻船 *kaisen* lighter, cargo vessel
❹ [now usu. 回る *mawaru*] same as **mawaru 回る**
⇨ see 回 3055 for compounds
❺ [now usu. 回す *mawasu*] same as **mawasu 回す**
⇨ see 回 3055 for compounds

HOMOPHONES

mawaru ⇨ 回 3055
mawari ⇨ 回 3055 周 2998
mawasu ⇨ 回 3055

NOTE

⇨ see USAGE note at 回 3055

3-6 ⻍

建 建 建 建

3090 KEN KON ta(teru) ta(te) -da(te) ta(tsu)

CH 建 jiàn

Radical	Strokes
⻍ 54	9-3-6
Grade	Freq
Jōyō-4	235
3-3-6	

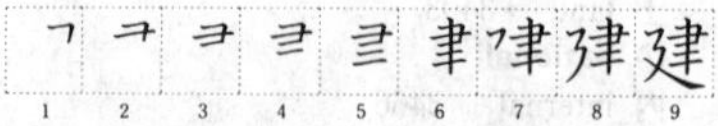

▶**BUILD**

COMPOUNDS

❶ⓐ **build (a building), construct, erect, put up**
ⓑ establish (a nation)
建築 *kenchiku* construction, building, architecture
建設する *kensetsu suru* construct, build, erect
建造 *kenzō* building, construction
建碑 *kenpi* erection of a monument
建立 *konryū* erection, building (as a temple)
再建 *saiken* reconstruction, rehabilitation
建国 *kenkoku* establishing a nation
❷ propose, suggest, petition
建議 *kengi* proposal, suggestion
建白 *kenpaku* petition, memorial
建策 *kensaku* recommendation, suggestion

KUN

【ta(teru) 建てる】
ⓐ build, construct, erect, put up
ⓑ establish (a nation)
建物 *tatemono* building, structure
建て直し *tatenaoshi* rebuilding, re-erection

【ta(te) 建て】 [in compounds] business commitment, sales contract
建て値 *tatene* official quotations, rates of exchange, market

【-da(te) -建て】
[also suffix]
① way of building, method of construction
二階建ての家 *nikaidate no ie* two-storied house
② currency of exchange
ドル建て *dorudate* quotation in dollars
③ average number of pages (of a newspaper or magazine)
十六頁建ての新聞 *jūrokupējidate no shinbun* 16-page newspaper

【ta(tsu) 建つ】 be built, be erected, be established

銅像が建った *Dōzō ga tatta* A bronze statue was erected

SYNONYMS

❶ⓐ **build**

造 build (various structures) → 3110

築 CONSTRUCT → 2715

設 SET UP → 1471

HOMOPHONES

tateru ⇨ 立 1992 点 2084 閉 3319

tate ⇨ 立 1992 縦 1408 竪 2837

-date ⇨ 立 1992

tatsu ⇨ 立 1992 起 3307 発 2565 経 1331

NOTE

⇨ see USAGE note at 立 1992

逆 逆 逆 ⿱

3091 GYAKU GEKI▲ saka saka(sa) saka(rau)

Ⓒⓗ 逆 nì

Radical	Strokes
⻍ 162	9-3-6
Grade	**Freq**
Jōyō-5	779
□ 3-3-6	

3-6 ⻍

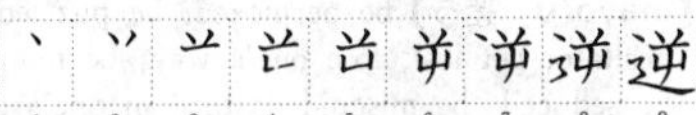

▶**REVERSE**

COMPOUNDS

❶ [also prefix] **reverse, inverse, backward, contrary, counter**

逆転 *gyakuten* reversal, turnabout, inversion; reverse rotation

逆流 *gyakuryū* countercurrent, adverse tide; regurgitation (of blood)

逆戻り *gyakumodori* retrogression, reversal, going back

逆数 *gyakusū* reciprocal number

逆説 *gyakusetsu* paradox

逆効果 *gyakukōka* counter result, reverse effect

逆比例 *gyakuhirei* inverse proportion

❷ contrary, adverse, unfavorable

逆境 *gyakkyō* adversity, adverse [unfavorable] circumstances

逆風 *gyakufū* adverse [contrary] wind

❸ **rebel, defy, disobey**

逆徒 *gyakuto* rebel, traitor

反逆する *hangyaku suru* revolt [rebel] against, rise in mutiny

❹ receive, welcome

逆旅 *gekiryo* inn

INDEPENDENT

【**gyaku 逆**】reverse, inverse, contrariness; *math* converse

逆な *gyaku na* contrary, adverse; reverse, inverse

KUN

【**saka 逆**】

ⓐ [in compounds] reverse, inverse

ⓑ upside-down

逆立ち *sakadachi* handstand

逆立つ *sakadatsu* stand on end, stand up, bristle up

逆上る *sakanoboru* [usu. 遡る] go upstream; go back (to the past); retroact

逆子 *sakago* foot presentation, agrippa

逆様の *sakasama no* upside-down, reverse

逆になる *saka ni naru* turn upside down

【**saka(sa) 逆さ**】reverse, inversion

逆さの *sakasa no* inverted, upside-down, reverse

逆さに *sakasa ni* bottom up, upside-down

【**saka(rau) 逆らう**】act contrary to, go against, oppose, disobey, defy

親に逆らう *oya ni sakarau* disobey one's parents

SPECIAL READINGS

逆上せる▲ *noboseru* have a rush of blood to the head, feel dizzy; get excited; run mad after; become conceited

SYNONYMS

❶ **opposite**

反 COUNTER → 2945

倒 upside-down → 124

対 OPPOSITE → 831

❸ **resist**

反 COUNTER → 2945

対 OPPOSE → 831

抗 RESIST → 252

抵 RESIST → 319

耐 WITHSTAND → 1282

USAGE

sakanoboru

逆上る

[usu. 遡る]

ⓐ go upstream

ⓑ go back (to the past); retroact

遡る

[sometimes also 逆上る] same as 逆上る

HOMOPHONES

sakanoboru ⇨ 遡る 3257 逆上る 3091, 3404

noboseru ⇨ 上せる 3404 逆上せる 3091, 3404

NOTE

⇨ see also USAGE note at 上 3404

3-6 辶

迷 迷 迷 迷

3092 MEI mayo(u)

CH 迷 mí

Radical	Strokes
辶 162	9-3-6
Grade	**Freq**
Jōyō-5	1183
口 3-3-6	

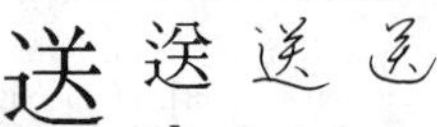

▶**PERPLEXED**

COMPOUNDS

❶ (be at a loss at what to do) **be perplexed, be puzzled, be bewildered; hesitate**

迷惑 *meiwaku* trouble, annoyance
迷信 *meishin* superstition
混迷 *konmei* confusion, bewilderment
混迷 *konmei* [formerly 昏迷] stupor, unconsciousness
低迷する *teimei suru* hang low; (of the market) be sluggish

❷ [original meaning] **lose one's way, get lost, go astray**

迷路 *meiro* maze, labyrinth
迷宮 *meikyū* labyrinth, maze; mystery
迷鳥 *meichō* stray bird

❸ absurd, ridiculous, bizarre, fantastic

迷論 *meiron* fallacy, absurd opinion
迷答 *meitō* ridiculous answer, boner

KUN

【mayo(u) 迷う】 be perplexed, be puzzled; hesitate; get lost, lose one's way; be tempted, be seduced, be misguided; turn in one's grave

迷い *mayoi* bewilderment, doubt, indecision; infatuation; *Buddhism* maya
迷わす *mayowasu* perplex, puzzle; fascinate, infatuate; lead astray
血迷う *chimayou* lose control of oneself
迷い込む *mayoikomu* stray [wander] into

SPECIAL READINGS

迷子 *maigo* lost child

SYNONYMS

❶ **bewildered**

惑 BEWILDERED → 2786

3-6 辶

送 送 送 送

3093 SŌ oku(ru)

CH 送 sòng

Radical	Strokes
辶 162	9-3-6
Grade	**Freq**
Jōyō-3	236
口 3-3-6	

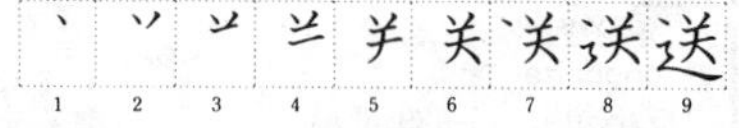

▶**SEND**

COMPOUNDS

❶ⓐ [original meaning] **send, dispatch, deliver, mail**

ⓑ **transmit**

送金 *sōkin* remittance
送付 *sōfu* sending, remittance
送検する *sōken suru* commit for trial, send to the prosecutors office
送料 *sōryō* postage, carriage
郵送する *yūsō suru* mail, send by mail
輸送 *yusō* transport, conveyance
発送する *hassō suru* send out, dispatch, ship
送電 *sōden* electrical transmission
放送 *hōsō* broadcasting

❷ send off, see off, escort

送迎する *sōgei suru* welcome and send off
送別 *sōbetsu* farewell, send-off
護送 *gosō* safeguard, convoy, escort

❸ give as a present

送呈する *sōtei suru* send a book as a present

INDEPENDENT

【sō 送】 postage

送五百円 *sō gohyakuen* postage 500 yen

KUN

【oku(ru) 送る】

① send, ship, dispatch, mail; transmit

送り先 *okurisaki* destination; receiver, consignee
送り込む *okurikomu* send into
申し送る *mōshiokuru* send word to, hand over (one's business to another)

②ⓐ see off, send off

ⓑ escort, take a person (home)

送り *okuri* seeing off; funeral; sending
見送る *miokuru* see off
送り届ける *okuritodokeru* send to, deliver; escort (a person) home

③ spend (time), lead (one's life)

空しく日を送る *munashiku hi o okuru* spend days in vain

④ add kana affixes to Chinese characters

送り仮名 *okurigana okurigana*, kana affixes

(⇨ see APPENDIX 5)

SYNONYMS

❶ **send**

投 SEND IN → 256
回 send round → 3055
遣 DISPATCH → 3152
派 DISPATCH → 381

USAGE

okuru

送る
① send, ship, dispatch, mail; transmit
②ⓐ see off, send off
ⓑ escort, take a person (home)
③ spend (time), lead (one's life)
④ add kana affixes to Chinese characters

贈る
① present (a gift), give (a present)
② bestow on, confer upon

HOMOPHONES

okuru ⇨ 贈 1634

NOTE

★do not confuse with 迭 3077

退 退 退 退

Ⓒ 退 tuì

3094 TAI shirizo(ku) shirizo(keru) hi(ku)▲

Radical	Strokes
⻌ 162	9-3-6
Grade	**Freq**
Jōyō-5	575
□ 3-3-6	

3-6 ⻌

▶**RETREAT**

COMPOUNDS

❶ⓐ [original meaning] **retreat, move back, withdraw, leave**
ⓑ **cause to retreat, drive back, repulse**
退場する *taijō suru* leave, exit
退去 *taikyo* retreat, withdrawal, evacuation
退出 *taishutsu* leaving, withdrawal
退院 *taiin* discharge from a hospital
撤退する *tettai suru* withdraw, evacuate, pull out
後退する *kōtai suru* retreat, recede
脱退 *dattai* withdrawal, secession
退学 *taigaku* leave school; be expelled from school
撃退する *gekitai suru* repulse, drive back; reject, repulse

❷ (retreat from public life) **retire, resign, leave**
退職 *taishoku* retirement, resignation
引退する *intai suru* retire, go into retirement
隠退 *intai* retirement, seclusion from the world

❸ keep one's distance, hesitate
辞退する *jitai suru* decline, refuse

❹ [formerly also 頹 1614] decline, decay
退廃 *taihai* degeneration, decadence, deterioration
退勢 *taisei* one's declining fortunes, decay
衰退 *suitai* decline, decay, degeneration

❺ become spiritless, be languid
退屈 *taikutsu* tedium, boredom

❻ [formerly also 褪 1234] fade, discolor
退色 *taishoku* fading, faded color

KUN

【shirizo(ku) 退く】 retreat, recede, back; withdraw, leave; retire, resign
一歩退く *ippo shirizoku* take a step backward
御前を退く *gozen* (=*omae*) *o shirizoku* withdraw from the presence (of the Emperor)
職を退く *shoku o shirizoku* resign from one's post

【shirizo(keru) 退ける】
① (cause to retreat) drive away, repel, expel, keep away
要職から退ける *yōshoku kara shirizokeru* expel (a person) from an important position
人を退ける *hito o shirizokeru* keep others away
② defeat, beat
敵の攻撃を退ける *teki no kōgeki o shirizokeru* beat off an attack by the enemy
③ [sometimes also 斥ける] reject, refuse, turn down
提案を退ける *teian o shirizokeru* turn down a proposal

【hi(ku) 退く】
[also 引く]
①ⓐ retreat, withdraw
ⓑ retire, resign
後へ退く *ato e hiku* retreat, recede
役所を退く *yakusho o hiku* leave office, resign one's post in an office
② subside, abate, go down
熱が退く *Netsu ga hiku* The fever abates

SPECIAL READINGS

立ち退く *tachinoku* leave, depart, evacuate; take refuge; vacate, leave, quit

SYNONYMS

❶ⓐ **leave and set forth**
撤 WITHDRAW → 738
離 leave → 1836
去 GO AWAY → 2156

発 START → 2565
出 GO OUT → 3498
ⓑ **drive out**
追 chase away → 3096
駆 drive away → 1823
逐 DRIVE OUT → 3102
斥 EXPEL → 2972
排 EXCLUDE → 490
払う clear out → 194
❷ **resign**
辞 RESIGN → 1364

USAGE

shirizokeru
退ける
① (cause to retreat) drive away, repel, expel, keep away
② defeat, beat
③ [sometimes also 斥ける] reject, refuse, turn down

斥ける
[usu. 退ける] reject, refuse, turn down

HOMOPHONES

shirizokeru ⇨ 斥 2972
hiku ⇨ 引 181 弾 572 惹 2493 挽 427 轢 1662

NOTE

⇨ see also USAGE note at 引 181

3-6 辶

逃 逃 逃 逃

3095 TŌ ni(geru) ni(gasu) noga(su) noga(reru)

CH 逃 táo

Radical	Strokes
辶 162	9-3-6
Grade	**Freq**
Jōyō	798
口 3-3-6	

▶**ESCAPE**

COMPOUNDS

❶ [original meaning] **escape, run away, flee**
逃亡する *tōbō suru* escape, abscond, desert
逃走 *tōsō* flight, escape
❷ (succeed in avoiding) escape, evade, shirk
逃避 *tōhi* escape, evasion, flight

KUN

【ni(geru) 逃げる】 escape, run away, flee; escape, evade, shirk
逃げ *nige* escape, evasion
逃げ出す *nigedasu* make a break, run off, make off
逃げ道 *nigemichi* way of escape
轢き逃げする *hikinige suru* hit and run

【ni(gasu) 逃がす】 let go, set free; let escape; let slip, miss
取り逃がす *torinigasu* fail to catch, let slip

【noga(su) 逃す】 same as **nigasu 逃がす**
見逃す *minogasu* overlook, miss
好機を逃す *kōki o nogasu* let an opportunity slip

【noga(reru) 逃れる】 escape, get away; get clear of; escape, evade, shirk
責任を逃れる *sekinin o nogareru* shirk one's responsibility
言い逃れ *iinogare* evasion, subterfuge, excuse

SYNONYMS

❶ **escape**
亡 flee → 3402
走 run away → 2194
脱 ESCAPE FROM → 973
❷ **avoid and abstain**
避 AVOID → 3179
忌 shun → 2207
禁 abstain from → 2795

3-6 辶

追 追 追 追

3096 TSUI o(u)

CH 追 zhuī

Radical	Strokes
辶 162	9-3-6
Grade	**Freq**
Jōyō-3	398
口 3-3-6	

▶**CHASE**

COMPOUNDS

❶ⓐ **chase, pursue, follow, seek**
ⓑ chase away, drive out, expel
追跡する *tsuiseki suru* pursue, chase, follow up
追突 *tsuitotsu* rear-end collision
追求する *tsuikyū suru* pursue
追及する *tsuikyū suru* pursue, seek after, follow, press (a person) hard
追究 *tsuikyū* thorough investigation, close inquiry

追随する *tsuizui suru* follow (in the wake of)
追従 *tsuishō* flattery, sycophancy
猛追 *mōtsui* hot chase [pursuit]
追放する *tsuihō suru* banish, purge, exile
追儺 *tsuina* ceremony of driving out the devils

❷ⓐ **add, perform in addition to**
ⓑ [also prefix] **additional, supplementary**
追加 *tsuika* addition, appendix, supplement
追刊 *tsuikan* additional publication
追徴金 *tsuichōkin* additional imposition
追試験 *tsuishiken* supplementary exam

❸ⓐ post-, subsequent(ly), afterwards
ⓑ posthumous
追記 *tsuiki* postscript
追体験する *tsuitaiken suru* experience for oneself what another person has gone through
追認 *tsuinin* ratification, confirmation
追贈する *tsuizō suru* confer court rank posthumously

❹ⓐ reminisce, recollect, recall the past
ⓑ remember the dead, mourn
追想 *tsuisō* recollection, reminiscence
追悼 *tsuitō* mourning
追善 *tsuizen* mass for the dead

KUN

【o(u) 追う】chase, pursue, follow; drive away
追って *otte* later, afterwards, by and by
追い掛ける(=追っ掛ける) *oikakeru* (=*okkakeru*) chase, run after
追い詰める *oitsumeru* corner, drive to the wall, run down
追い付く *oitsuku* overtake, catch up with
追い越す *oikosu* outrun, pass; overtake
追い込み *oikomi* last spurt, final lap
追い払う(=追っ払う) *oiharau* (=*opparau*) drive away, expel, exorcise

SYNONYMS

❶ⓐ **follow and pursue**
従 FOLLOW → 415
随 FOLLOW → 627
ⓑ **drive out**
退 cause to retreat → 3094
逐 DRIVE OUT → 3102
駆 drive away → 1823
斥 EXPEL → 2972
排 EXCLUDE → 490
払う clear out → 194

❷ⓐ **add to**
加 ADD → 38
添 ADD TO → 529
付 ATTACH → 31
附 ATTACH → 347
ⓑ **additional**
補 supplementary → 1194
副 accessory → 1776

❹ⓐ **remember**
顧 LOOK BACK → 1900
憶 REMEMBER → 765
覚える COMMIT TO MEMORY → 2604
記 commit to memory → 1453

飛 incorrect classification ⇨ see 3572

3-6 乁

3-6 尸

昼 晝 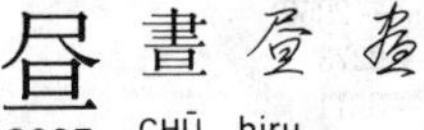

3097 CHŪ hiru

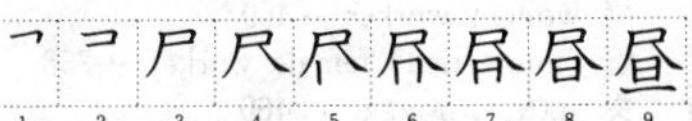

Ⓒⓗ 昼 zhòu

Radical	Strokes
日 72	9-4-5
Grade	**Freq**
Jōyō-2	890
□ 3 - 3 - 6	

▶**DAYTIME**

COMPOUNDS

❶ [original meaning] **daytime**
昼間 *chūkan* daytime, day
昼夜 *chūya* day and night

❷ **midday, noon**
昼食 *chūshoku* lunch
白昼 *hakuchū* daytime, broad daylight
真昼 *mahiru* noon
昼寝 *hirune* siesta, nap
昼時 *hirudoki* noon, lunch time
昼休み *hiruyasumi* noon recess, lunch break

KUN

【hiru 昼】daytime; midday, noon; lunch
昼間 *hiruma* daytime, day

SYNONYMS

❶ **days**
日 DAY → 3027
曜 DAY OF THE WEEK → 1096
旦 first day → 2389

❷ **noon**
午 NOON → 1984

3-6 戸

屋 屋 屋

3098 OKU ya

1 2 3 4 5 6 7 8 9

CH 屋 wū

Radical	Strokes
戸 44	9-3-6
Grade	Freq
Jōyō-3	318
口 3-3-6	

▶HOUSE ▶SMALL SHOP

COMPOUNDS

❶ **house, building**

屋外 *okugai* outdoors, open air, exterior of a house

家屋 *kaoku* house, building

社屋 *shaoku* office building

廃屋 *haioku* deserted house

❷ [original meaning] **roof**

屋上 *okujō* housetop, roof

INDEPENDENT

【**oku 屋**】roof; house

屋上屋を架す *okujō oku o kasu* gild refined gold, paint the lily

KUN

【**ya 屋**】

①[in compounds] house, dwelling house

屋敷 *yashiki* [sometimes also 邸] mansion, residence; residential lot

小屋 *koya* cottage, hut, cabin; playhouse

部屋 *heya* room, chamber

母屋(＝母家) *omoya* main house [wing]

② [in compounds] roof

屋根 *yane* roof

③ⓐ [also suffix] small shop or place of business, store

ⓑ [suffix] shopkeeper, dealer

ⓒ suffix for forming names of business establishments

屋台 *yatai* stall, stand; float, festival car

店屋 *miseya* shop, store

料理屋 *ryōriya* restaurant

魚屋 *sakanaya* fish shop; fish dealer

花屋 *hanaya* flower shop; florist

本屋 *hon'ya* bookstore; bookseller

不動産屋 *fudōsan'ya* real estate agent, Realtor

松坂屋 *matsuzakaya* Matsuzakaya Department Store

④ colloquial occupation suffix—sometimes indicates slight contempt or humility

事務屋 *jimuya* clerk, office worker

何でも屋 *nandemoya* jack-of-all-trades

⑤ colloquial suffix indicating the peculiarity or idiosyncrasy of a person

気取り屋 *kidoriya* affected person, snob

分からず屋 *wakarazuya* obstinate person, hardhead

恥ずかしがり屋 *hazukashigariya* shy person

⑥ [sometimes also 家] suffix after stage family names

音羽屋 *otowaya* Otowaya (stage name of a kabuki family)

SYNONYMS

❶ **houses**

家 HOUSE → 2273

軒 house → 1459

戸 HOUSEHOLD → 1930

宅 DWELLING HOUSE → 2174

居 residence → 3080

邸 STATELY RESIDENCE → 1131

住 housing → 64

❷ **roof**

宇 roof → 2175

【**ya**】

③ⓐ **places of business**

店 SHOP (of any kind) → 3085

舗 SHOP (esp. traditional) → 1735

社 COMPANY → 840

ⓑ **merchant**

商 merchant → 2116

④ **workers and professionals**

手 OCCUPATION SUFFIX → 3456

員 MEMBER (of a staff) → 2269

師 profession suffix → 1326

士 PROFESSION SUFFIX → 3405

客 skilled person → 2250

家 professional → 2273

者 person who → 3211

人 person of certain category → 3368

婦 woman worker → 469

嬢 (unmarried) female worker → 758

夫 MAN LABORER → 3460

匠 CRAFTSMAN → 2990

工 workman → 3381

⑤ **fellow**

坊 COLLOQUIAL PERSON SUFFIX → 233

物 character → 874

奴 GUY → 187

漢 FELLOW → 657

輩 FELLOW (*belittling*) → 2807

徒 fellows → 416

棒 tough guy → 983

⑥ **pseudonym suffixes**

亭 PSEUDONYM SUFFIX → 2072

USAGE

ya

屋
① [in compounds] house, dwelling house
② [in compounds] roof
③ⓐ [also suffix] small shop or place of business, store
ⓑ [suffix] shopkeeper, dealer
ⓒ suffix for forming names of business establishments
④ colloquial occupation suffix—sometimes indicates slight contempt or humility
⑤ colloquial suffix indicating the peculiarity or idiosyncrasy of a person
⑥ [sometimes also 家] suffix after stage family names

家
① [also suffix] house, home
② [usu. 屋] suffix after stage family names

★Both 屋 and 家 refer to a house or dwelling, but they are not used interchangeably in the same compounds.

HOMOPHONES

ya ⇨ 家 2273
yashiki ⇨ 邸 1131 屋敷 3098, 1870

NOTE

⇨ see also USAGE note at 邸 1131

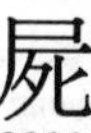
3099 SHI shikabane

CH 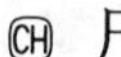 shī

Radical	Strokes
尸 44	9-3-6
Grade	**Freq**
Reference	
□ 3 - 3 - 6	

3-6 尸

COMPOUNDS

ⓐ [now also 死 *shi* 3521] [original meaning] dead body, corpse
ⓑ [sometimes also 尸 *shikabane*] corpse
屍体 *shitai* corpse
屍蠟 *shirō* adipocere
屍 *shikabane* corpse

HOMOPHONES

shikabane ⇨ 尸 3389

度 度 度
3100 DO TO TAKU tabi -ta(i)▲

CH 度 dù duó

Radical	Strokes
广 53	9-3-6
Grade	**Freq**
Jōyō-3	59
□ 3 - 3 - 6	

3-6 广

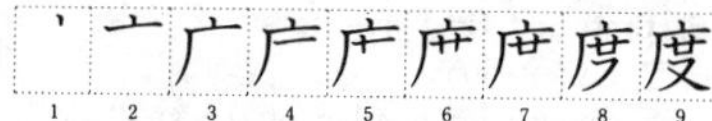

▶DEGREE ▶TIME

COMPOUNDS

❶ [also suffix] **degree, extent**
度合 *doai* degree, extent, rate
程度 *teido* degree, extent, standard
高度 *kōdo* altitude, height; high degree
震度 *shindo* seismic intensity
限度 *gendo* limit, bounds
速度 *sokudo* speed, velocity
精度 *seido* precision, accuracy
透明度 *tōmeido* transparency, degree of clearness
知名度 *chimeido* publicity

❷ⓐ (unit of angular measure, latitude, longitude, etc.) **degree**
ⓑ (unit of temperature or humidity) **degree**
ⓒ *optics* degree (of refraction), diopter unit
ⓓ *music* degree
ⓔ (strength of a liquor) proof
度数 *dosū* degree
角度 *kakudo* angle, angular measure, degree
緯度 *ido* latitude
経度 *keido* longitude
二度三十分 *nido sanjuppun* 2°30′
温度 *ondo* temperature
湿度 *shitsudo* humidity
体温三十八度 *taion sanjūhachido* 38° (of fever)
十八度 *jūhachido* 18 diopter units
三度の和音 *sando no waon* triad, common chord
四十度のウイスキー *yonjūdo no uisukī* 80-proof whisky

❸ⓐ **time, occasion**
ⓑ **counter for number of times**
度数 *dosū* number of times
今度 *kondo* this time; next time, another time; recently
何度 *nando* how many degrees; how many times

每度 *maido* every [each] time, always
二度 *nido* two times [degrees]
❹ **standard of propriety, limit**
度外視する *dogaishi suru* leave out of account, neglect
制度 *seido* system, organization, institution
節度 *setsudo* standard; moderation
落度 *ochido* fault, error; guilt
過度の *kado no* excessive
法度 *hatto* law, ordinance, prohibition
❺ period, term
年度 *nendo* year, fiscal year; school year; term
❻ generosity, liberality
度量 *doryō* magnanimity, generosity
度胸 *dokyō* courage, pluck, heart
襟度 *kindo* magnanimity, generosity
❼ manner, bearing, attitude
態度 *taido* attitude, manner
❽ⓐ conjecture, guess
ⓑ [original meaning] measure
忖度 *sontaku* conjecture, surmise
支度する *shitaku suru* arrange, prepare; [original meaning, now archaic] measure, estimate
❾ measuring instrument, ruler
度量衡 *doryōkō* weights and measures
❿ provisions, necessary supplies
調度 *chōdo* personal effects, furnishings, supplies
用度 *yōdo* expenditure, office expenses; supplies
⓫ save, redeem
済度 *saido Buddhism* salvation
⓬ become a bonze
得度 *tokudo* entering of Buddhist priesthood
⓭ unclassified compounds
丁度 *chōdo* [sometimes also 恰度] just, exactly; as if

INDEPENDENT

【**do** 度】
① degree, extent
緊張の度 *kinchō no do* degree of tenseness
② *optics* degree (of refraction), diopter unit
度の強い眼鏡 *do no tsuyoi megane* powerful spectacles
③ times, frequency
度を重ねる *do o kasaneru* repeat
④ standard of propriety, limit
度が過ぎる *do ga sugiru* go to excess, carry too far
度を失う *do o ushinau* lose one's presence of mind

【**dosuru** 度する】 save, redeem

KUN

【**tabi** 度】 time, occasion; counter for number of times
見る度に *miru tabi ni* whenever [each time] one sees (it)
度度 *tabitabi* often
一度 *hitotabi* one time

【**-ta(i)** -度い】 [desiderative verbal suffix] want [wish] to do
行き度い *ikitai* want to go
し度くない *shitaku nai* do not want to do (it)

SYNONYMS

❶ **degree**
分 relative degree → 1972
程 EXTENT → 1190
❷ⓐ **angle and angular measure**
角 ANGLE → 2047
❸ **time and time counters**
回 TIME → 3055
遍 counter for number of times → 3136
返 counter for number of times → 3060

NOTE

⇨ see COMPOUND FORMATION for 支度 *shitaku* ⇨ 支 1979

3-6 广 **席** incorrect stroke count ⇨ see 3113

3-6 广 **庭** incorrect stroke count ⇨ see 3114

3-6 口 **囝** 3101

▶**COUNTRY**
nonstandard for 国 3087

逐 逐 逐 逐 3102 CHIKU

Ⓒ逐 zhú

Radical	Strokes
辶 162	10-3-7
Grade	Freq
Jōyō	1843
□ 3 - 3 - 7	

▶ONE BY ONE ▶DRIVE OUT

COMPOUNDS

❶ **one by one, successively, one after another**

逐一 *chikuichi* one by one, in detail
逐次 *chikuji* one by one, successively
逐条審議 *chikujō shingi* article-by-article discussion
逐語訳 *chikugoyaku* word for word translation
逐日 *chikujitsu* day after day, every day
逐年 *chikunen* annually, year by year

❷ⓐ **drive out, expel**

ⓑ [original meaning] pursue, chase after
放逐する *hōchiku suru* expel, banish, expatriate
駆逐する *kuchiku suru* drive away, drive out, expel

❸ compete, contend
角逐する *kakuchiku suru* compete with, vie with

SYNONYMS

❶ **in succession**
歴 successive → 3019
連 IN SUCCESSION → 3103
逓 progressively → 3106
漸 GRADUALLY → 706

❷ **drive out**
追 chase away → 3096
退 cause to retreat → 3094
駆 drive away → 1823
斥 EXPEL → 2972
排 EXCLUDE → 490
払う clear out → 194

NOTE

★do not confuse with 遂 3138

連 連 連 连 3103 REN tsura(naru) tsura(neru) tsu(reru) -zu(re)

Ⓒ连 lián

Radical	Strokes
辶 162	10-3-7
Grade	Freq
Jōyō-4	79
□ 3 - 3 - 7	

一 𠄌 冂 百 亘 亘 車 車 連 連
1 2 3 4 5 6 7 8 9 10

▶LINK ▶IN SUCCESSION

COMPOUNDS

❶ [formerly also 聯 1419]

ⓐ (join together) **link, join**

ⓑ (connect as if by linking) **link, connect, join, unite**

連結 *renketsu* connection, coupling, linking
連辞 *renji* copula
連鎖 *rensa* chain (as of reasoning), link, series; connection
連星 *rensei* binary star
連絡 *renraku* connection, contact; communication
連立 *renritsu* alliance, coalition
連係 *renkei* connection, linking, contact
連帯 *rentai* solidarity
連合 *rengō* combination, union, alliance; association
連盟 *renmei* union, federation, league
関連 *kanren* connection, relation, association

❷ **federation, union, alliance, league**

ソ連 *soren* Soviet Union
国連 *kokuren* United Nations
全学連 *zengakuren* All-Japan Federation of Student Self-Government Associations

❸ⓐ **in succession, in series, continually, repeatedly**

ⓑ [also prefix] **successive, in a row, consecutive, continued**

連発する *renpatsu suru* fire in rapid succession, fire in volleys
連載する *rensai suru* serialize, publish serially
連続する *renzoku suru* continue, occur in succession
連戦 *rensen* series of battles [games], every battle [game]
五連敗 *gorenpai* five-game losing streak
連休 *renkyū* consecutive holidays
連日 *renjitsu* day after day, everyday
連山 *renzan* mountain range
連分数 *renbunsū* continued fraction

❹ [also suffix] set, party, company, gang,

clique

連中 *renchū* (=*renjū*) party, company, clique; those fellows [guys]

常連 *jōren* regular visitors [customers], frequenters

愚連隊 *gurentai* hooligans, hoodlums

文士連 *bunshiren* the literary set

ハイカラ連 *haikararen* the smart set

❺ take along, bring along, accompany

連行する *renkō suru* take a suspect to the police

❻ counter for:

ⓐ reams (of paper)

ⓑ miscellaneous linked objects or sets of objects such as chains, necklaces, etc.

一連 *ichiren* one ream

数珠一連 *juzu ichiren* a string of beads, a rosary

KUN

【tsura(naru) 連なる】 range, stand in a row; attend

山は南北に連なっている *Yama wa nanboku ni tsuranatte iru* The mountains range north and south

【tsura(neru) 連ねる】 put in a row, join, put together

名を連ねる *na o tsuraneru* have one's name entered (in a list)

【tsu(reru) 連れる】 take along, bring along, accompany

連れ *tsure* companion

連れ合い *tsureai* spouse, mate

連れ立つ *tsuredatsu* accompany

引き連れる *hikitsureru* take [bring, have] along (with one)

【-zu(re) -連れ】 [suffix] with, accompanied by

二人連れ *futarizure* party of two

子供連れ *kodomozure* accompanied by children

SYNONYMS

❶ⓐ join

結 TIE → 1348

係 CONNECT → 97

接 join → 500

縛 BIND → 1405

束 TIE UP → 3554

ⓑ relate

絡 INTERLINK → 1351

渉 HAVE RELATIONS WITH → 526

関 CONCERN → 3328

係 CONNECT → 97

❷ organized bodies

労 workers' union → 2548

組 union → 1337

体 BODY → 71

団 BODY → 3053

協 association → 93

会 SOCIETY → 2020

講 fraternity → 1619

院 INSTITUTION → 454

❸ in succession

歴 successive → 3019

逓 progressively → 3106

漸 GRADUALLY → 706

逐 ONE BY ONE → 3102

❸ continue

継 SUCCEED → 1360

続 CONTINUE → 1362

持 HOLD → 374

❹ groups

族 common-interest group (*slang*) → 958

党 PARTY → 2581

隊 PARTY (organized group) → 625

団 BODY → 3053

伍 ranks → 47

班 SQUAD → 946

軍 team → 2080

群 GROUP (of any kind) → 1540

組 group (of people) → 1337

陣 lineup → 455

❺ lead and escort

率 LEAD → 2118

引 lead → 181

導 GUIDE → 2888

3-7
辶

逝 逝 逝 逝

3104 SEI yu(ku)

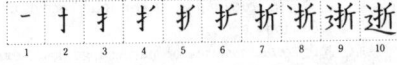

Ⓒⓗ 逝 shì

Radical	Strokes
辶 162	10-3-7
Grade	**Freq**
Jōyō	1960
口 3-3-7	

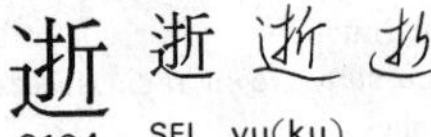

▶DEPART THIS LIFE

COMPOUNDS

ⓐ depart this life, pass away, die suddenly

ⓑ [original meaning, now archaic] depart, be gone, leave

逝去する *seikyo suru* pass away, die

急逝する *kyūsei suru* die suddenly

長逝 *chōsei* death, passing

KUN

【yu(ku) 逝く】 depart this life, pass away, die

SYNONYMS

ⓐ die

去 pass away → 2156
死 DIE → 3521
没 die → 260
亡 DECEASE → 3402
殉 DIE A MARTYR → 941

枯 WITHER → 898

HOMOPHONES

yuku ⇨ 行 212

NOTE

⇨ see USAGE note at 行 212

速 速 速 速 ㊥ 速 sù

3105 SOKU haya(i) haya- haya(meru) sumi(yaka)

Radical	Strokes
辶 162	10-3-7
Grade	**Freq**
Jōyō-3	681
□ 3 - 3 - 7	

一 厂 冂 可 由 申 束 涑 涑 速

1 2 3 4 5 6 7 8 9 10

▶QUICK

COMPOUNDS

❶ⓐ [original meaning] **quick, speedy, fast, rapid, swift, prompt, hasty**
ⓑ **quickly, swiftly**
速球 *sokkyū* fast ball
速射 *sokusha* quick firing
速達 *sokutatsu* special delivery, express mail
速報 *sokuhō* prompt report, news flash
快速 *kaisoku* high speed; fast (local) train
急速な *kyūsoku na* rapid, swift, prompt
迅速な *jinsoku na* swift, rapid
速記 *sokki* shorthand, stenography
速断 *sokudan* hasty conclusion; prompt decision
早速 *sassoku* immediately

❷ speed, velocity
速度 *sokudo* speed, velocity
時速 *jisoku* speed per hour
風速 *fūsoku* wind velocity
変速機 *hensokuki* speed change gear

KUN

【haya(i) 速い】
ⓐ (acting or moving quickly) quick, speedy, fast, rapid, swift
ⓑ [usu. 早い] (requiring little time) quick, prompt
速さ *hayasa* speed
足速い *ashibayai* swift-footed, light-footed
素速い *subayai* quick, nimble, agile
耳が速い *mimi ga hayai* be quick-eared

【haya- 速-】 [usu. 早-] quick, fast, rapid
速口 *hayakuchi* fast [rapid] talking
速業 *hayawaza* quick work, (clever) feat
速分かり *hayawakari* quick understanding; guide, handbook

【haya(meru) 速める】 quicken, accelerate, speed up, hasten
足を速める *ashi o hayameru* quicken one's pace [steps]

【sumi(yaka) 速やか】
速やかな *sumiyaka na* swift, quick, prompt
速やかに *sumiyaka ni* swiftly, quickly, promptly, immediately
速やかさ *sumiyakasa* swiftness, promptness

SYNONYMS

❶ **fast**
早 QUICK → 2390
疾 fast → 3279
快 fast → 245
急 rapid → 2092
迅 SWIFT → 3046
敏 NIMBLE → 1322
即 IMMEDIATE → 1120

USAGE

soku

速
quick, speedy, fast, rapid, swift, prompt, hasty

即
immediate, prompt, instant, on the spot

HOMOPHONES

hayai ⇨ 早 2390
haya- ⇨ 早 2390
hayameru ⇨ 早 2390

NOTE

⇨ see also USAGE note at 早 2390

3-7 ⻌

逓 遞 逓 逓

3106 TEI

1 2 3 4 5 6 7 8 9 10

CH 递 dì

Radical	Strokes
⻌ 162	10-3-7
Grade	**Freq**
Jōyō	1737
□ 3 - 3 - 7	

▶RELAY

COMPOUNDS

❶ⓐ (transmit by stages) **relay, forward**

ⓑ (place where fresh horses are posted) relay, post station

逓伝する *teiden suru* relay (a message)
逓信 *teishin* communications
逓送 *teisō* forwarding
駅逓 *ekitei* transportation from post to post; postal service in Meiji era

❷ **progressively, successively, gradually, in order**

逓増する *teizō suru* increase progressively [gradually]
逓減する *teigen suru* diminish successively, decrease in order
逓次 *teiji* in order, successively
逓降変圧器 *teikō-hen'atsuki* step-down transformer

SYNONYMS

❶ⓐ **transmit and deliver**

伝 TRANSMIT → 44
届ける DELIVER → 3078
達 deliver → 3139

ⓑ **post station**

駅 relay station → 1822
宿 post station → 2293

❷ **in succession**

漸 GRADUALLY → 706
連 IN SUCCESSION → 3103
歴 successive → 3019
逐 ONE BY ONE → 3102

3-7 ⻌

途 途 途 途

3107 TO

CH 途 tú

Radical	Strokes
⻌ 162	10-3-7
Grade	**Freq**
Jōyō	745
□ 3 - 3 - 7	

▶WAY

COMPOUNDS

❶ [original meaning] **way, route, course, road, path**

途中で *tochū de* on the way
中途で *chūto de* halfway, in the middle
発展途上国 *hatten-tojōkoku* developing countries
前途 *zento* one's future, prospects; distance yet to cover
帰途 *kito* one's way home, return trip

❷ (method of doing) **way, means**

方途 *hōto* means, way, measure
用途 *yōto* use, service, application
金の使途 *kane no shito* how money is used

❸ [formerly also 杜 835] shut out, stop, prevent

途絶 *tozetsu* stoppage, interruption, cessation

INDEPENDENT

【to 途】 way

帰国の途に就く *kikoku no to ni tsuku* leave for home

SYNONYMS

❶ **ways and routes**

道 WAY (path) → 3134
路 ROAD → 1533
筋 wayside → 2678
通り street → 3109
街 city street → 576
辻 CROSSROADS → 3192
岐 forked road → 241
径 PATH → 291
軌 TRACK → 1445
線 LINE → 1392

❷ **way and style**

方 WAY → 1963
法 METHOD → 333
流 STYLE → 441
式 STYLE → 3049
調 TONE → 1567
風 MANNER → 3007
様 MODE → 1052

COMPOUND FORMATION

用途 *yōto*

用途 'use, service, application' is the way

(途 ❷) of using (用) something.

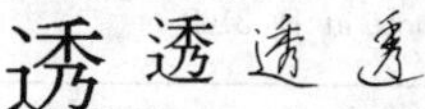

3108 TŌ su(ku) su(kasu) su(keru) tō(ru)▲ tō(su)▲

Ⓒ 透 tòu

Radical	Strokes
辶 162	10-3-7
Grade	**Freq**
Jōyō	1502
□ 3-3-7	

3-7 辶

一 二 千 禾 禾 乔 秀 秀 透 透 (1 2 3 4 5 6 7 8 9 10)

▶PASS THROUGH ▶TRANSPARENT

COMPOUNDS

❶ (move through something) **pass through, let through, permeate, penetrate**

透過 *tōka* penetration, transmission
透析 *tōseki chem* dialysis
透磁性 *tōjisei* magnetic permeability
浸透 *shintō* permeation, penetration

❷ⓐ (allow light to pass through) **be transparent, be seen through**

ⓑ see through
透明な *tōmei na* transparent
透視図 *tōshizu* perspective drawing, transparent view
透徹した *tōtetsu shita* lucid, clear, penetrating
透視 *tōshi* seeing through; clairvoyance
透察 *tōsatsu* insight

KUN

【su(ku) 透く】
① be transparent, be seen through
見え透く *miesuku* be easily seen, be obvious
②ⓐ become sparse
ⓑ [formerly also 隙く] leave a gap
透いた枝 *suita eda* thinned branches
透き(=隙) *suki* gap, interval
透き間(=隙間) *sukima* gap, opening; crack, crevice

【su(kasu) 透かす】
①ⓐ make transparent
ⓑ look through, peer into
透かし *sukashi* watermark; openwork
闇を透かす *yami o sukasu* peer into the darkness
② [formerly also 隙かす] leave a space [opening], thin (out)
透かさず *sukasazu* without a moment's delay
木を透かす *ki o sukasu* thin trees
③ *slang* break wind noiselessly

【su(keru) 透ける】 be [grow] transparent
透けるブラウス *sukeru burausu* sheer blouse

【tō(ru) 透る】
[also 通る]
ⓐ be transparent, be pervious to (light)
ⓑ penetrate, pierce, permeate
透り *tōri* penetration (as of light)
光が透るカーテン *hikari ga tōru kāten* curtain pervious to light
透る声 *tōru koe* carrying voice

【tō(su) 透す】 [also 通す] be transparent, be pervious to (light)
光を透す *hikari o tōsu* be pervious to light

SYNONYMS

❶ **penetrate**
貫 PENETRATE → 2460
破 break through → 1150

❷ **clear**
澄 LIMPID → 740
清 CLEAR (liquid) → 523
明 CLEAR (unclouded) → 855
朗 CLEAR (sky) → 1325
冴える CRISP AND CLEAR → 79

USAGE

❶ **suku**
透く
① be transparent, be seen through
②ⓐ become sparse
ⓑ [formerly also 隙く] leave a gap
空く
become empty, become less crowded
隙く
[now usu. 透く] leave a gap

❷ **suki**
透き
[also 隙] gap, interval
隙
① [also 透き] gap, interval
② chance; unguarded moment

❸ **sukasu**
透かす
①ⓐ make transparent
ⓑ look through, peer into
② [formerly also 隙かす] leave a space [opening], thin (out)
③ *slang* break wind noiselessly
空かす
① feel hungry
② make available, make free
隙かす
[now usu. 透かす] leave a space [opening], thin (out)

HOMOPHONES

suku ⇨ 空 2227 隙 670
suki ⇨ 隙 670

sukasu ⇨ 空 2227 隙 670
tōru ⇨ 通 3109
tōri ⇨ 通 3109

tōsu ⇨ 通 3109

NOTE
⇨ see also USAGE note at 通 3109

3-7
⻌

通 通 通 通 (CH) 通 tōng tòng

3109 TSŪ TSU tō(ru) tō(ri) -tō(ri) -dō(ri) tō(su) tō(shi) -dō(shi) kayo(u)

Radical	Strokes
⻌ 162	10-3-7
Grade	**Freq**
Jōyō-2	72
口 3-3-7	

Stroke order: 1–10

▶PASS ▶COMMUNICATE

COMPOUNDS

❶ⓐ [original meaning] **pass (by), pass through**
ⓑ **pass current, pass for**
通過 *tsūka* passing, passage
通行 *tsūkō* passing, passage, transit, traffic
通路 *tsūro* passage, pathway, alley, aisle
開通する *kaitsū suru* be opened to [for] traffic
不通 *futsū* impassability, interruption, stoppage, tie-up
通用する *tsūyō suru* pass, circulate, pass [go] current, hold good
通貨 *tsūka* currency, current money
流通 *ryūtsū* circulation of money or goods; flow of water; ventilation

❷ **go to and from, go back and forth, commute**
通勤 *tsūkin* commuting, commutation, attending office
通学 *tsūgaku* attending school, going to school
通商 *tsūshō* commerce, trade, commercial relation [intercourse]

❸ⓐ (transmit or interchange information) **communicate, exchange information, let know**
ⓑ **interpret (from a foreign language)**
ⓒ (form a connecting passage) **communicate (with), lead to**
通信 *tsūshin* correspondence, communication, information
通達する *tsūtatsu suru* communicate, notify; attain proficiency
通告 *tsūkoku* notice, notification, announcement
文通 *buntsū* correspondence, exchange of letters
通訳 *tsūyaku* interpreting; interpreter
通弁 *tsūben* interpreter (in Edo period)
直通 *chokutsū* direct communication [service]; through service [traffic]

❹ **through, from beginning to end**
通算 *tsūsan* sum total, aggregate
通読する *tsūdoku suru* read through
通巻 *tsūkan* consecutive number of volumes
通夜 *tsuya* vigil, deathwatch

❺ **common, general, universal, popular**
通常の *tsūjō no* common, ordinary, usual
通称 *tsūshō* popular [common] name
通念 *tsūnen* common idea, generally accepted idea
通説 *tsūsetsu* common opinion, popular view
普通の *futsū no* normal, regular, ordinary
共通の *kyōtsū no* common

❻ⓐ **know [understand] thoroughly, be thoroughly familiar with, master**
ⓑ [also suffix] well-informed person, authority, expert
通人 *tsūjin* man of the world, man about town; dilettante
精通する *seitsū suru* be well versed in, have thorough knowledge of
食通 *shokutsū* gourmet
消息通 *shōsokutsū* well-informed person, insider

❼ have sexual intercourse
密通 *mittsū* illicit intercourse, misconduct
姦通 *kantsū* adultery, illicit intercourse

❽ counter for letters or documents
手紙二通 *tegami nitsū* two letters

❾ occult [magic] powers
神通力 *jintsūriki* occult [supernatural] power, divine power

INDEPENDENT

【tsū 通】 man of the world, man about town, dilettante; thorough knowledge; occult powers
通を気取る *tsū o kidoru* set up for a man about town

【tsūjiru (=tsūzuru) 通じる(=通ずる)】
①ⓐ pass, run, be opened to, communicate with
ⓑ pass electric current, transmit
通じ *tsūji* passage, evacuation; movement of the bowels
通じて *tsūjite* through; through(out)
② put through (a call)
③ be understood [comprehensible]
④ be versed in, know thoroughly

⑤ communicate secretly with; have sexual intercourse

KUN

【tō(ru) 通る】

①ⓐ pass (by), go along [past], get through

ⓑ pass for [as], be known as, pass current

通り掛かる *tōrikakaru* happen to pass by

通り道 *tōrimichi* path

町を通る *machi o tōru* pass through town

本物で通る *honmono de tōru* pass for [as] genuine

② [also 透る]

ⓐ penetrate, pierce, permeate

ⓑ be transparent, be pervious to (light)

通る声 *tōru koe* carrying voice

透き通る *sukitōru* be transparent

③ⓐ pass (an examination)

ⓑ pass, be admissible

議案が通った *Gian ga tōtta* The bill passed (the House)

そんな言い訳は通らない *Sonna iiwake wa tōranai* Such excuses will not do

④ come in, be ushered into

客間に通る *kyakuma ni tōru* enter the parlor

⑤ be understood [comprehensible]

意味が通らない *imi ga tōranai* not make sense, be incomprehensible

【tō(ri) 通り】

①ⓐ passage; drainage

ⓑ street traffic, coming and going

通りが良い *tōri ga yoi* pass [run] well

人通り *hitodōri* traffic

② street, avenue, road

大通り *ōdōri* main street

③ reputation; favor

世間の通り *seken no tōri* reputation

④ accordance, agreement, conformity

約束の通り *yakusoku no tōri* true to one's promise, as promised

【-tō(ri) -通り】

ⓐ counter for kinds

ⓑ counter for ways (of doing)

三通り *mitōri* (=*santōri*) three kinds; three ways

【-dō(ri) -通り】

① suffix after names of streets [avenues]

青山通り *aoyamadōri* Aoyama Street

② [also suffix] as, according to, in accordance with

型通り *katadōri* formally, in due form

注文通り *chūmondōri* as ordered

③ degree, proportion

九分通り *kubudōri* nine parts, almost

【tō(su) 通す】

①ⓐ let pass, let go by; run (a thread) through

ⓑ let in, admit, usher

ⓒ pass through, penetrate, pierce

通せん坊 *tōsenbō* barring (a person's) way

先に通す *saki ni tōsu* let (a person) pass first

客を通す *kyaku o tōsu* show a guest in

千枚通し *senmaidōshi* eyeleteer

水を通さない *mizu o tōsanai* be impervious to water

② [also 透す] be transparent, be pervious to (light)

光を通す *hikari o tōsu* be pervious to light

③ pass [carry] (a bill)

議案を通す *gian o tōsu* pass [see] a bill (through the House)

④ [also verbal suffix] carry through, stick to

押し通す *oshitōsu* push through, carry it through, hold out to the end

⑤ [also verbal suffix] continue, keep doing, remain

三日通して *mikka tōshite* for three days on end

泣き通す *nakitōsu* keep crying

⑥ do (something) through an intermediary

仲人を通して *nakōdo o tōshite* through a go-between

【tō(shi) 通し】

① letting pass; showing in

風通し *kazetōshi* ventilation

お通ししなさい *Otōshi shinasai* Ask [Show] him in

② through, consecutive, straight

通しで *tōshi de* right through, direct, straight

通し切符 *tōshikippu* through ticket

見通し *mitōshi* perspective, vista; prospect, outlook

切り通し *kiridōshi* sunken road, excavation; opencut

【-dō(shi) -通し】 continuing

夜通し *yodōshi* all through the night

立ち通しである *tachidōshi de aru* keep standing (all the way)

【kayo(u) 通う】 go to and from, go back and forth, commute; frequent a place, visit often; circulate, ventilate; resemble closely

通い *kayoi* going back and forth, commuting; living out; passbook

学校へ通う *gakkō e kayou* attend school

血の通った *chi no kayotta* blood-circulating; warm, compassionate

心が通う *kokoro ga kayou* call forth response in another's heart

似通う *nikayou* resemble closely

SYNONYMS

❶ **pass**

過 PASS BY → 3137

経 PASS THROUGH → 1331

❷ **go and come**

出 go to → 3498

参 go somewhere → 2066

来 COME → 3551
向 head toward → 3052
赴 PROCEED TO → 3303
行 GO → 212
往 GO ON → 292

❸ⓐ **inform and communicate**
報 INFORM → 1698
告 NOTIFY → 2409
届ける give notice → 3078
達 issue a notice → 3139
知 let know → 1127
申 REPORT → 3507
宣 PROCLAIM → 2252

❹ **throughout**
徹 all through → 726
終 from beginning to end → 1336
中 throughout → 3451

❺ **widespread**
公 common (math) → 1974
普 WIDESPREAD → 2323
遍 ALL OVER → 3136

❻ⓐ **know and understand**
知 KNOW → 1127
得 gain understanding of → 477
分かる understand → 1972
解 understand → 1517
諒 UNDERSTAND → 1575
了 COMPREHEND → 3350
悟 AWAKE TO → 419

ⓑ **wise and talented persons**
才 person of talent → 3410
俊 BRILLIANT PERSON → 102
秀 genius → 2545
博 DOCTOR → 151
賢 wise man → 2839
哲 sage → 2738

❽ **counters for flat things**
枚 COUNTER FOR FLAT THINGS → 859
葉 counter for leaves → 2321
丁 counter for sheets → 3348
頁 counter for pages → 2086

【tōri】

② & **【-dōri】** ① **ways and routes**
街 city street → 576
道 WAY (path) → 3134
途 WAY (route) → 3107
路 ROAD → 1533
筋 wayside → 2678
辻 CROSSROADS → 3192
岐 forked road → 241
径 PATH → 291
軌 TRACK → 1445
線 LINE → 1392

【-dōri】

② **similar**
如 AS → 207
様 like → 1052
云 SUCH → 1931
類 similar → 1807

USAGE

❶ **tōru**

通る
①ⓐ pass (by), go along [past], get through
ⓑ pass for [as], be known as, pass current
② [also 透る]
ⓐ penetrate, pierce, permeate
ⓑ be transparent, be pervious to (light)
③ⓐ pass (an examination)
ⓑ pass, be admissible
④ come in, be ushered into
⑤ be understood [comprehensible]

透る
[also 通る]
ⓐ be transparent, be pervious to (light)
ⓑ penetrate, pierce, permeate

❷ **tōri**

通り
①ⓐ passage; drainage
ⓑ street traffic, coming and going
② street, avenue, road
③ reputation; favor
④ accordance, agreement, conformity

透り
penetration (as of light)

❸ **tōsu**

通す
①ⓐ let pass, let go by; run (a thread) through
ⓑ let in, admit, usher
ⓒ pass through, penetrate, pierce
② [also 透す] be transparent, be pervious to (light)
③ pass [carry] (a bill)
④ [also verbal suffix] carry through, stick to
⑤ [also verbal suffix] continue, keep doing, remain
⑥ do (something) through an intermediary

透す
[also 通す] be transparent, be pervious to (light)

HOMOPHONES

tōru ⇨ 透 3108
tōri ⇨ 透 3108
tōsu ⇨ 透 3108

造 造 造 造

3110 ZŌ tsuku(ru) tsuku(ri) -zuku(ri)

CH 造 zào

Radical	Strokes
辶 162	10-3-7
Grade	**Freq**
Jōyō-5	478
口 3-3-7	

Stroke order: 丿 𠂉 牛 生 牛 告 告 浩 浩 造 (1–10)

▶**MAKE**

COMPOUNDS

❶ⓐ **make, produce, manufacture, shape, coin**

ⓑ **build (various structures as building or ships), construct**

造血 *zōketsu* blood making, hematosis
造花 *zōka* artificial flower; artificial flower making
造形(=造型) *zōkei* molding, modeling
造幣 *zōhei* coinage, mintage
製造 *seizō* production, manufacture
改造 *kaizō* remodeling; reorganization
構造 *kōzō* structure, construction, framework
創造 *sōzō* creation
酒造 *shuzō* sake brewing; distilling
造船 *zōsen* shipbuilding
造成する *zōsei suru* create, clear, reclaim
築造 *chikuzō* building, construction

❷ suffix indicating material composition

木造の *mokuzō no* wooden
石造の *sekizō no* stone-built

❸ reach, attain

造詣 *zōkei* attainments, scholarship

❹ fleeting

造次 *zōji* moment, very short time

KUN

【**tsuku(ru)** 造る】

①ⓐ make (as an object that requires time and skill), manufacture, fabricate, fashion
ⓑ build (ships or buildings), construct
船を造る *fune o tsukuru* build a ship

② make (wine), brew
酒造り *sakezukuri* sake brewing

③ coin, mint
新語を造る *shingo o tsukuru* coin a new word

【**tsuku(ri)** 造り】

ⓐ making, building, constructing (as buildings or ships)

ⓑ make, structure, construction
造り付けの *tsukuritsuke no* built-in
造りの頑丈な家 *tsukuri no ganjō na ie* house of solid structure

【**-zuku(ri)** -造り】

[also suffix]

ⓐ make, structure; style of building

ⓑ building, constructing, developing
防火造り *bōkazukuri* fireproof construction
数寄屋造り(=数奇屋造り) *sukiyazukuri sukiya* style of building, style of a tea-ceremony arbor
別荘地造り *bessōchizukuri* developing a villa site

SYNONYMS

❶ⓐ **make**

作 MAKE → 68
成 FORM → 3537
工 MANUFACTURE → 3381
製 MANUFACTURE → 2803
産 PRODUCE → 3298
調 PREPARE → 1567
組む ASSEMBLE → 1337
構 CONSTRUCT → 1049

ⓑ **build**

建 BUILD (a building) → 3090
築 CONSTRUCT → 2715
設 SET UP → 1471

【**tsukuri**】

ⓑ **structure**

構 structure → 1049

HOMOPHONES

tsukuru ⇨ 作 68 創 1815
tsukuri ⇨ 作 68
-zukuri ⇨ 作 68

NOTE

⇨ see USAGE note at 作 68

眞

incorrect classification ⇨ see 2110
(nonstandard for 真 2111)

3-7 戸

展 展 展

3111 TEN

CH 展 zhǎn

Radical	Strokes
戸 44	10-3-7
Grade	**Freq**
Jōyō-6	429
□ 3 - 3 - 7	

▶UNFOLD ▶DISPLAY

COMPOUNDS

❶ **unfold, develop, expand, evolve**

展開 *tenkai* unfolding, development, evolution; deployment

発展 *hatten* expansion, growth, development; prosperity

進展 *shinten* development, progress

伸展する *shinten suru* expand, extend

❷ⓐ (open) unfold, spread out, open (a letter)

ⓑ [original meaning] extend, flatten

親展書 *shintensho* confidential letter

展性 *tensei* malleability

❸ⓐ (spread out before the view of the public) **display, exhibit, put on display**

ⓑ [also suffix] abbrev. of 展覧会 *tenrankai*: **exhibition, exhibit**

展示する *tenji suru* put on display, exhibit

展覧会 *tenrankai* exhibition

展観する *tenkan suru* exhibit

個展 *koten* personal exhibition

デザイン展 *dezainten* design exhibition

ダリ展 *dariten* exhibition of Dali's paintings

❹ take an extensive view of

展望 *tenbō* view, outlook, prospect

❺ visit

展墓 *tenbo* visiting a grave

SYNONYMS

❶ **grow**

発 develop → 2565

伸 expand → 70

成 grow up → 3537

長 grow (up) → 2556

生 grow → 3497

育 grow → 2050

❷ⓐ **open**

開 OPEN → 3321

披 open and read → 305

❸ⓐ **display**

陳 lay out (for exhibit) → 540

掲 PUT UP → 494

ⓑ **public display**

博 exposition → 151

COMPOUND FORMATION

親展書 *shintensho*

親展書 'confidential letter' is a letter (書) to be opened (展 ❷ⓐ) only by the person himself (親).

3-7 广

庫 庫 庫

3112 KO KU kura▲

CH 库 kù

Radical	Strokes
广 53	10-3-7
Grade	**Freq**
Jōyō-3	705
□ 3 - 3 - 7	

▶STORAGE CHAMBER

COMPOUNDS

❶ [also suffix] [original meaning] **storage chamber, esp. a large structure for storing vehicles; storehouse, warehouse**

倉庫 *sōko* warehouse, storehouse

金庫 *kinko* strong box, cashbox

車庫 *shako* car shed, garage

艇庫 *teiko* boathouse

宝庫 *hōko* treasure house, treasury

文庫 *bunko* library; collection of literary works; box for stationery

在庫 *zaiko* stock, stockpile

国庫 *kokko* (National) Treasury

公庫 *kōko* municipal [state] treasury

格納庫 *kakunōko* hangar, airplane shed

❷ temple's kitchen; priest's living quarters

庫裏 *kuri* temple's kitchen; priest's living quarters

KUN

【kura 庫】 [usu. 倉, sometimes also 蔵] warehouse (for merchandise), storeroom

庫入れ *kuraire* warehousing

SYNONYMS

❶ **storehouse**

倉 STOREHOUSE → 2104

蔵 storehouse → 2364

HOMOPHONES

kura ⇨ 蔵 2364 倉 2104

NOTE
⇨ see USAGE note at 倉 2104

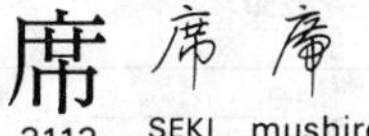

席

3113 SEKI mushiro▲

CH 席 xí

Radical	Strokes
巾 50	10-3-7
Grade	**Freq**
Jōyō-4	338
□ 3 - 3 - 7	

3-7 广

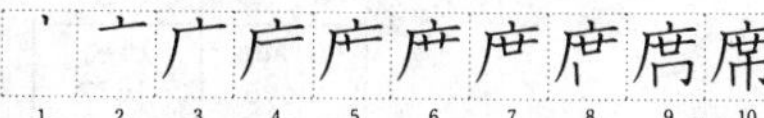

1 2 3 4 5 6 7 8 9 10

▶SEAT

COMPOUNDS

❶ⓐ [also suffix] **seat, one's place**

ⓑ [original meaning] reed mat, rush mat

席次 *sekiji* order of seats, seating precedence; class standing
座席 *zaseki* seat
議席 *giseki* seat (in an assembly house)
即席の *sokuseki no* impromptu, offhand
打席 *daseki* batter's box; one's turn at bat
主席 *shuseki* top seat; the Chairman
指定席 *shiteiseki* reserved seat
一般席 *ippanseki* general admission seat
席巻する *sekken suru* sweep over (the whole land); make a conquest

❷ meeting place, hall; meeting

席上で *sekijō de* at the meeting; on the occasion
出席 *shusseki* attendance, presence
欠席 *kesseki* absence, nonattendance
会席 *kaiseki* meeting place
宴席 *enseki* banquet hall, dinner party

❸ entertainment hall, variety hall, club

定席 *jōseki* regular hall; entertainment hall
碁席 *goseki* go club

INDEPENDENT

【seki 席】 seat, one's place; meeting place, room; occasion; vaudeville theater
席に着く *seki ni tsuku* take a seat
公開の席で *kōkai no seki de* in public

KUN

【mushiro 席】 (straw) mat

SPECIAL READINGS

寄席 *yose* storyteller's hall, variety hall

SYNONYMS

❶ⓐ seat
座 SEAT → 3116

❷ places and positions
所 PLACE → 851
処 place → 3031
場 PLACE (for specific activity) → 558
地 PLACE (particular location) → 204
位 POSITION → 61
点 POINT → 2084
座 place → 3116

NOTE

⇨ see COMPOUND FORMATION for 寄席 *yose* ⇨ 寄 2291

庭 庭 庭 庭

3114 TEI niwa

CH 庭 tíng

Radical	Strokes
广 53	10-3-7
Grade	**Freq**
Jōyō-3	571
□ 3 - 3 - 7	

3-7 广

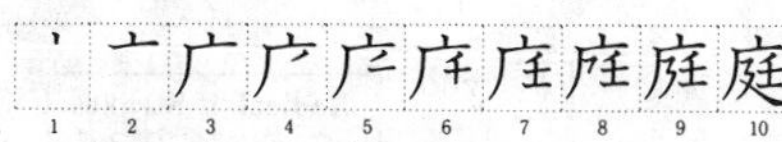

1 2 3 4 5 6 7 8 9 10

▶COURT ▶GARDEN

COMPOUNDS

❶ⓐ [original meaning] **court, courtyard, yard**

ⓑ (sports) court, tennis court

校庭 *kōtei* schoolyard, campus
庭球 *teikyū* tennis

❷ garden, ornamental garden

庭園 *teien* garden, park
庭前 *teizen* garden
石庭 *sekitei* rock garden

❸ [now always 廷 3058] the Court, Imperial Court

宮庭 *kyūtei* the Court, the Palace

❹ home, family

庭訓 *teikin* [archaic] home education
家庭 *katei* home, family, household

KUN

【niwa 庭】 garden; court, courtyard; *elegant* place
庭木 *niwaki* garden tree, shrub
庭師 *niwashi* gardener
中庭 *nakaniwa* courtyard
学びの庭 *manabi no niwa* school

戦いの庭 *tatakai no niwa* battlefield

SYNONYMS

❶ⓑ **sports fields**

場 ground(s) → 558

野 baseball field → 1485

❷ **gardens**

園 GARDEN → 3156

苑 IMPERIAL GARDEN → 2239

3-7
广

唐 唐 唐 唐

3115 TŌ kara

' 亠 广 户 户 声 声 庚 唐 唐 唐
1 2 3 4 5 6 7 8 9 10

CH 唐 táng

Radical	Strokes
口 30	10-3-7
Grade	**Freq**
Jōyō	1672
口 3 - 3 - 7	

▶TANG DYNASTY

COMPOUNDS

❶ **Tang Dynasty (618–907 A.D.)**

唐朝 *tōchō* Tang Dynasty

唐詩 *tōshi* Tang poetry

❷ **Cathay, China; foreign countries in general**

唐人 *tōjin* Chinese; foreigner

唐音 *tōon* Tang reading of Chinese characters

唐辛子 *tōgarashi* red pepper

毛唐 *ketō slang* foreigner, Westerner

❸ abrupt

唐突に *tōtotsu ni* abruptly

❹ wild talk, nonsense

荒唐無稽 *kōtōmukei* absurdity, nonsense

INDEPENDENT

【tō 唐】 Tang Dynasty

KUN

【kara 唐】

ⓐ elegant term for China, Cathay

ⓑ [also 韓] foreign countries

唐様 *karayō* Chinese style [design]

唐草模様 *karakusa-moyō* arabesque design

唐獅子 *karajishi* imaginary animal similar to a lion

SYNONYMS

❶ **later Chinese dynasties**

元 Yuan Dynasty → 1929

明 Ming Dynasty → 855

清 Qing Dynasty → 523

❷ **China**

呉 KINGDOM OF WU → 2549

華 CHINA → 2283

漢 CHINESE → 657

支 China → 1979

中 People's Republic of China → 3451

台 Taiwan → 2005

USAGE

kara

唐

ⓐ elegant term for China, Cathay

ⓑ [also 韓] foreign countries

韓

ⓐ elegant term for Korea

ⓑ [also 唐] foreign countries

HOMOPHONES

kara ⇨ 韓 1757

COMPOUND FORMATION

毛唐 *ketō*

毛唐 'foreigner, Westerner', literally a "hairy (毛) Chinaman (唐 ❷)," is a derogatory term referring to foreigners of Western origin.

3-7
广

座 座 座

3116 ZA suwa(ru)

' 亠 广 广 广 広 広 座 座 座
1 2 3 4 5 6 7 8 9 10

CH 座 zuò

Radical	Strokes
广 53	10-3-7
Grade	**Freq**
Jōyō-6	611
口 3 - 3 - 7	

▶SEAT ▶SIT

COMPOUNDS

❶ⓐ [original meaning] (place for sitting) **seat**

ⓑ (part on which one sits) seat, bottom

座席 *zaseki* seat

座右の書 *zayū no sho* one's desk-side book

座敷 *zashiki* drawing room, parlor; Japanese-style room

王座 *ōza* throne

上座 *kamiza* (=*jōza*) top seat, seat of honor

便座 *benza* toilet seat

❷ (supporting base) seat, mount, base, platform, stand

座金 *zagane* (metal) washer

台座 *daiza* pedestal, base, stand
弁座 *benza* valve seat
機関座 *kikanza* seat of an engine
❸ⓐ (one's position) **seat, status, (social) position**
ⓑ **place, position**
司教権座 *shikyōkenza* the episcopal seat
講座 *kōza* lectureship, (professor's) chair; course of study
座標 *zahyō* coordinates
即座に *sokuza ni* immediately, promptly, at once
口座 *kōza* (bank) account
当座 *tōza* the present, the time being; current account
❹ [formerly also 坐 3547]
ⓐ **sit, take a seat, sit down**
ⓑ sit still without doing anything, not stir
座臥 *zaga* sitting and lying down
座禅 *zazen* Zen meditation
座礁する *zashō suru* run aground, be stranded
正座する *seiza suru* sit upright [straight]
座視する *zashi suru* remain an idle spectator, look on idly [doing nothing]
❺ company, gathering, party
座談会 *zadankai* round table talk, symposium
座興 *zakyō* amusement of the company
❻ⓐ theater, theatrical company [troupe]
ⓑ **suffix after names of theaters**
座長 *zachō* leader of a troupe; chairman, president
同座 *dōza* same theater
明治座 *meijiza* the Meijiza Theater
文学座 *bungakuza* the Bungaku Company
❼ religious organization, temple, shrine
座主 *zasu* head priest of a temple, abbot
遷座 *senza* transfer of an object of worship
❽ⓐ constellation
ⓑ suffix after names of constellations
星座 *seiza* constellation
大熊座 *ōkumaza* the Big Bear
❾ *hist* guild in medieval times
鉄砲座 *teppōza* gunmakers guild
❿ mint (during the Edo period)
銀座 *ginza* the Ginza; mint (during Edo period)
⓫ counter for:
ⓐ Shinto deities or sedentary statues (seated figures)
ⓑ high mountains or forests
仏像二座 *butsuzō niza* two images of Buddha
高峰八座 *kōhō hachiza* eight lofty peaks
⓬ [formerly also 坐 3547] be accused of a crime
連座する *renza suru* be implicated [involved] in (a crime)
⓭ [formerly also 坐 3547] travel (by ship)
座乗する *zajō suru* go on board (a ship)
⓮ used phonetically for *za*
御座る *gozaru* go, come; be in love; rot
御座います *gozaimasu* [polite] be, exist

INDEPENDENT

【za 座】 seat, seat (of a chair), bottom; seat (of power), status, position; company, gathering, party
天子の座 *tenshi no za* throne
権力の座 *kenryoku no za* position of power
妻の座 *tsuma no za* status of wifehood
座が白けた *Za ga shiraketa* A chill was cast over the party
【zasuru 座する(=坐する)】 sit down, take a seat; be implicated [involved] in (a crime)

KUN

【suwa(ru) 座る】 [formerly also 坐る] sit down, take a seat
座り *suwari* stability
座り込み *suwarikomi* sit-in, sit-down (strike)
居座る *isuwaru* settle down, stay on; remain in the same position unwantedly

SYNONYMS

❶ **seat**
席 SEAT → 3113
❷ **flat supports**
台 STAND → 2005
壇 PLATFORM → 754
棚 SHELF → 984
架 rack → 2569
床 BED → 3067
❸ⓑ **places and positions**
点 POINT → 2084
位 POSITION → 61
席 meeting place → 3113
地 PLACE (particular location) → 204
場 PLACE (for specific activity) → 558
処 place → 3031
所 PLACE → 851
❹ⓐ **sit**
居 sit → 3080
❽ **stars**
星 STAR → 2435

USAGE

❶ **suwaru**
座る
[formerly also 坐る] sit down, take a seat
坐る
[now usu. 座る] sit down, take a seat
据わる
be set
❷ **suwari**
座り
[formerly also 坐り] stability
坐り
[now usu. 座り] stability

HOMOPHONES
suwaru ⇨ 坐 3547 据 497
suwari ⇨ 坐 3547

COMPOUND FORMATION

❶ 即座 *sokuza*
即座に 'immediately, etc,' refers to performing an action right on (即) the spot (座 ❸ ⓑ).

❷ 口座 *kōza*
口座 '(bank) account' refers to the place (座 ❸ⓑ) where account items (口) are recorded.

❸ 銀座 *ginza*
銀座 'the Ginza; mint (during Edo period)' refers to a former mint (座 ❿) where silver coins (銀) were made. The famous Ginza district in Tokyo is so named since it was formerly the location of such a mint.

3-7 广

庭 3117

▶COURT ▶GARDEN
nonstandard for 庭 3114

3-7 广

唐 3118

▶TANG DYNASTY
nonstandard for 唐 3115

3-7 广

庶

incorrect stroke count ⇨ see 3127

3-7 囗

圃 3119

HO

CH 圃 pǔ

Radical	Strokes
囗 31	10-3-7
Grade	Freq
Reference	
口 3 - 3 - 7	

COMPOUNDS

● [sometimes also 甫 3549] [original meaning] vegetable garden; rice nursery
田圃 *denpo* fields, farm
田圃 *tanbo* rice field

3-8 辶

逸 3120

ITSU so(reru)▲ so(rasu)▲

CH 逸 yì

Radical	Strokes
辶 162	11-3-8
Grade	Freq
Jōyō	1564
口 3 - 3 - 8	

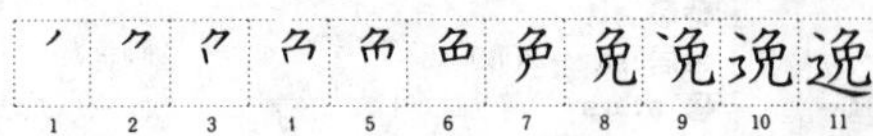

▶LET SLIP

COMPOUNDS

❶ⓐ let slip, miss, lose, let go, let pass
ⓑ [formerly also 佚 62] lost, missing
逸球 *ikkyū* muffed ball, missed ball
逸機する *ikki suru* miss a chance, lose an opportunity
後逸する *kōitsu suru* let (a ball) pass, miss (a grounder)
逸書 *issho* lost book
散逸する *san'itsu suru* be lost and scattered

❷ⓐ [original meaning] slip away, run (away), escape
ⓑ escape from the world, seclude oneself, be secluded
逸走する *issō suru* escape, scamper away
逸話 *itsuwa* uncommon tale, anecdote
隠逸 *in'itsu* seclusion

❸ deviate from the norm, swerve from a course
逸脱 *itsudatsu* deviation, departure from the norm
放逸 *hōitsu* self-indulgence, looseness, dissoluteness

❹ exceptional, superb, outstanding, excellent
逸品 *ippin* superb article
逸材 *itsuzai* person of (exceptional) talent

秀逸 *shūitsu* supreme excellence
❺ [formerly also 佚 62] indulge in idle pleasure
逸楽 *itsuraku* idle pursuit of pleasure
安逸 *an'itsu* (idle) ease, idleness, indolence

INDEPENDENT

【itsu 逸】 ease
逸を以て労を待つ *itsu o motte rō o matsu* wait for the enemy to tire at ease

【issuru 逸する】 let slip, miss, lose, let go, let pass; deviate from the norm, swerve from a course
好機を逸する *kōki o issuru* miss a chance
常軌を逸した *jōki o isshita* aberrant

KUN

【so(reru) 逸れる】 deviate from, swerve from (a course), miss
針路を逸れる *shinro o soreru* swerve from the course
的を逸れる *mato o soreru* miss the target

【so(rasu) 逸らす】
① let slip, miss, lose, let go, let pass
ボールを逸らす *bōru o sorasu* miss a ball, let a ball pass
注意を逸らす *chūi o sorasu* distract a person's attention
② (cause to deviate) divert, avert, dodge, evade
目を逸らす *me o sorasu* avert one's eyes, look away

SYNONYMS

❶ⓐ losing and loss
失 LOSE → 3511
損 LOSS, lose → 651
喪 lose → 2825
❸ deviate
外れる miss → 186
❹ excellent and superior
傑 outstanding → 155
英 DISTINGUISHED → 2238
優 SUPERIOR → 177
秀 EXCELLENT → 2545
名 first-rate → 2169
上 of upper grade → 3404
絶 without match → 1353
卓 PROMINENT → 2064
快 splendid → 245
妙 MARVELOUS → 239

HOMOPHONES

sorasu ⇨ 反 2945

NOTE

⇨ see USAGE note at 反 2945

進 進 進 进

3121 SHIN susu(mu) susu(meru)

Ⓒ 进 jìn

Radical	Strokes
⻌ 162	11-3-8
Grade	**Freq**
Jōyō-3	169
口 3 - 3 - 8	

3-8 ⻌

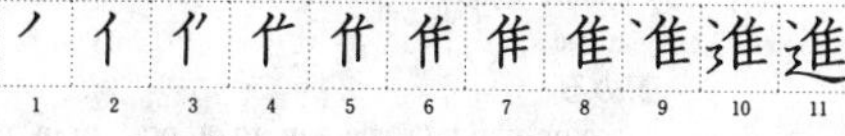

▶ADVANCE

COMPOUNDS

❶ⓐ [original meaning] (move forward in position) **advance, go forward, proceed**
ⓑ (move forward in rank) **advance in rank, become promoted**
進行する *shinkō suru* advance, make progress, go forward
進路 *shinro* course, route
進出 *shinshutsu* advance, march; debouchment
前進する *zenshin suru* advance, go ahead
行進する *kōshin suru* march, parade
突進する *tosshin suru* dash [rush] forward, push ahead
二進する *nishin suru* advance to second (base)
進学 *shingaku* entering a school of higher grade
進級 *shinkyū* promotion (to a higher grade)
昇進 *shōshin* promotion, advancement
❷ⓐ (make progress) **advance, make progress, improve**
ⓑ (aid the progress of) **advance, promote, further**
進歩 *shinpo* progress, advancement, improvement
進展 *shinten* development, progress
進化 *shinka* evolution, progress
先進国 *senshinkoku* advanced [developed] nation [country]
躍進 *yakushin* rapid advance [progress]
推進する *suishin suru* propel, drive; promote
促進する *sokushin suru* promote, spur on, facilitate
増進する *zōshin suru* promote, improve, advance
❸ⓐ present to a superior, proffer, offer
ⓑ do something for someone, esp. a superior
進呈する *shintei suru* proffer, present
進物 *shinmotsu* gift
寄進 *kishin* contribution, donation
進言 *shingen* counsel, advice (to a superior)
進講 *shinkō* lecturing to the emperor

注進 *chūshin* information, report (to a superior)

KUN

【susu(mu) 進む】

①ⓐ (move forward in position) advance, go forward

ⓑ (of clocks) go too fast

進み出る *susumideru* step forward

② (make progress) advance, make progress, be promoted

進み *susumi* progress

文明が進むに連れて *bunmei ga susumu ni tsurete* with the advance of civilization

大学へ進む *daigaku e susumu* enter a university

③ feel inclined to

食が進む *shoku ga susumu* have a good appetite

【susu(meru) 進める】

①ⓐ (cause to move forward in position) advance, move forward

ⓑ (raise in rank) advance, raise, promote

ⓒ set (a clock) ahead

軍を進める *gun o susumeru* move troops forward

②ⓐ (aid the progress of) advance, promote, further

ⓑ stimulate, hasten

計画を進める *keikaku o susumeru* carry a plan forward

工事を進める *kōji o susumeru* hasten [speed up] the works

SYNONYMS

❶ⓐ move forward

突 DASH → 2230

ⓑ rise in rank

昇 ascend to a higher rank → 2415

❷ⓐ make progress

亨 GO SMOOTHLY → 2037

ⓑ advance

興 cause to rise → 2909

奨 ENCOURAGE → 2842

勧 encourage → 1857

❸ⓐ give

呈 PRESENT → 2189

賄 BRIBE → 1529

贈 PRESENT A GIFT → 1634

賜 DEIGN TO GIVE → 1585

授 CONFER → 492

与 GIVE → 3421

上 give (to superior or others) → 3404

下 give (to inferior or speaker) → 3378

呉れる give (to speaker) → 2549

USAGE

susumeru

進める

①ⓐ (cause to move forward in position) advance, move forward

ⓑ (raise in rank) advance, raise, promote

ⓒ set (a clock) ahead

②ⓐ (aid the progress of) advance, promote, further

ⓑ stimulate, hasten

勧める

①ⓐ urge, persuade, advise

ⓑ [sometimes also 奨める] encourage, promote, stimulate

② offer, present

奨める

[usu. 勧める] encourage, promote, stimulate

薦める

recommend (a person to a post or a product to a person)

HOMOPHONES

susumeru ⇨ 勧 1857　奨 2842　薦 2373

3-8
⻌

週 週 週 週

3122　SHŪ

CH 周 zhōu

Radical	Strokes
⻌ 162	11-3-8
Grade	**Freq**
Jōyō-2	454
口 3-3-8	

丿 冂 月 円 用 周 周 周 周 凋 週
1 2 3 4 5 6 7 8 9 10 11

▶WEEK

COMPOUNDS

❶ⓐ week, weekly

ⓑ counter for order of weeks within a month

週間 *shūkan* week

週刊 *shūkan* weekly publication, weekly

今週 *konshū* this week

二週間 *nishūkan* two weeks

五月の第二週 *gogatsu no dainishū* second week of May

❷ [now always 周 2998] [original meaning] go round

週期 *shūki* period, cycle

INDEPENDENT

【shū 週】 week

週に三回 *shū ni sankai* three times a week

SYNONYMS

❶ⓐ **weeks and months**

旬 TEN-DAY PERIOD → 2978
月 MONTH → 2956

3123 TAI

Ⓒⓗ 逮 dài dǎi

Radical	Strokes
辶 162	11-3-8
Grade	**Freq**
Jōyō	799
□ 3 - 3 - 8	

3-8 辶

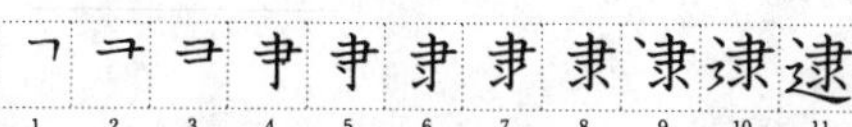

▶**CATCH A CRIMINAL**

COMPOUNDS

❶ [original meaning] (chase after and reach out to capture) **catch a criminal, capture**
逮捕 *taiho* arrest, capture
逮捕状 *taihojō* warrant of arrest

❷ reach
逮夜 *taiya* eve of death anniversary

SYNONYMS

❶ **catch a criminal**
捕 CATCH → 429
拘 ARREST → 310

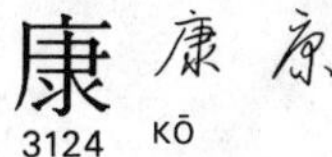

incorrect stroke count ⇨ see 3135

3-8 辶

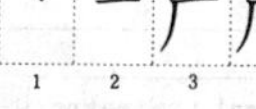

incorrect stroke count ⇨ see 3108

3-8 辶

遊

incorrect stroke count ⇨ see 3142

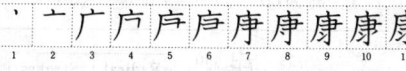

3-8 辶

康

3124 KŌ

Ⓒⓗ 康 kāng

Radical	Strokes
广 53	11-3-8
Grade	**Freq**
Jōyō-4	880
□ 3 - 3 - 8	

3-8 广

▶**HEALTHY**

COMPOUNDS

❶ **healthy, robust**
健康 *kenkō* health
健康な *kenkō na* healthy, sound, well

❷ (free from danger or hardship) **peaceful, secure, safe**
康寧 *kōnei* [rare] peacefulness, tranquility
小康 *shōkō* lull, respite, breathing spell (of peace)

SYNONYMS

❶ **healthy**
生 health → 3497
健 ROBUST → 134

❶ **strong**
健 ROBUST → 134
丈 STOUT → 3419
壮 VIGOROUS → 224
強 STRONG → 475

❷ **calm and peaceful**
安 PEACEFUL → 2171
寧 peaceful → 2345
泰 TRANQUIL → 2583
静 QUIET → 1728
平 CALM → 3478
穏 CALM → 1235

3-8 广

麻 痲 麻 麻

3125 MA MĀ▲ asa

CH 麻 má

Radical	Strokes
痲 200	11-11-0
Grade	**Freq**
Jōyō	1145
口 3-3-8	

RADICAL 200
simplified form not used as radical
⇨ see 痲 3130 for radical description

▶HEMP ▶BECOME NUMB

COMPOUNDS

❶ⓐ [original meaning] **hemp, flax or other similar plants**
ⓑ **hemp fiber, flax fiber**
亜麻 *ama* flax
黄麻 *kōma* (=*ōma*) jute
製麻 *seima* hemp dressing, flax [hemp] spinning
大麻 *taima* hemp; paper amulet used in Shinto rites

❷ sesame
胡麻 *goma* sesame

❸ **become numb, become palsied**
麻酔 *masui* anesthesia
麻薬 *mayaku* narcotic, drug
麻痺 *mahi* paralysis, palsy, numbness, anesthesia

❹ pockmarks
蕁麻疹 *jinmashin* hives, urticaria

❺ unclassified compounds
麻雀 *mājan* mahjong

INDEPENDENT
[ma 麻] hemp

KUN
[asa 麻] hemp, flax, jute; hemp fiber, flax fiber
麻布 *asanuno* hemp cloth, linen
麻袋 *asabukuro* jute bag
マニラ麻 *maniraasa* Manila hemp

SPECIAL READINGS
麻疹▲ *hashika* measles

SYNONYMS
❶ⓐ fiber-producing plants
綿 COTTON → 1373
❶ⓑ & [asa] fabrics
綿 COTTON → 1373
毛 wool → 3453
綾 TWILL → 1376
絹 SILK → 1361
紗 GAUZE → 1301
織 woven fabric → 1422
錦 BROCADE → 1738
❸ become stupefied
酔 BECOME INTOXICATED → 1483

3-8 广

鹿 鹿 鹿

3126 ROKU shika ka

CH 鹿 lù

Radical	Strokes
鹿 198	11-11-0
Grade	**Freq**
Names	1977
口 3-3-8	

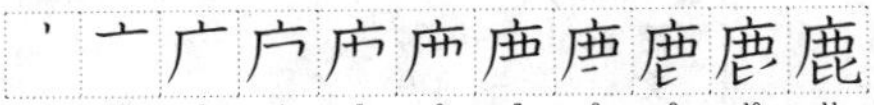

RADICAL 198
Standard form: 鹿 *shika* 'deer' (麗 麟)
Description: used in characters related to deers or similar animals

▶DEER

COMPOUNDS

● [original meaning] **deer**
鹿砦 *rokusai* [rare] abatis

KUN
[shika 鹿] deer, stag, hind
鹿皮 *shikagawa* deerskin
[ka 鹿]
① [in compounds] deer
鹿の子 *kanoko* dapples, pattern of white spots; fawn
② used phonetically for *ka*
馬鹿 *baka* fool, blockhead; nonsense

NAMES
鹿児島 *kagoshima* place name
鈴鹿 *suzuka* place name
鹿島 *kashima* surname also place name

SYNONYMS

【shika】

○ **undomesticated mammals**

猪 WILD BOAR → 536
象 ELEPHANT → 2134
熊 BEAR → 2848
虎 TIGER → 3212
猿 MONKEY → 669
鯨 WHALE → 1882

NOTE

⇨ see COMPOUND FORMATION for 馬鹿 *baka* ⇨ 馬 3296

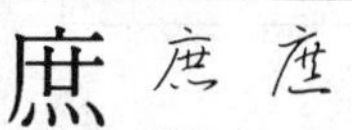

3127 SHO

CH 庶 shù

Radical	Strokes
广 53	11-3-8
Grade	**Freq**
Jōyō	1613
□ 3 - 3 - 8	

3-8 广

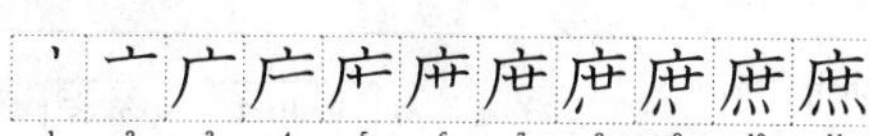

1 2 3 4 5 6 7 8 9 10 11

▶MANIFOLD

COMPOUNDS

❶ **manifold, many, numerous, various, general**
庶務 *shomu* general affairs
庶事(＝諸事) *shoji* various matters
庶政(＝諸政) *shosei* all phases of government
❷ **the masses, common people, populace**
庶民 *shomin* common people, the masses
衆庶 *shūsho* common people, the masses
❸ illegitimate (child), born of a concubine
庶子 *shoshi* illegitimate child
庶出 *shoshutsu* illegitimate birth
❹ desire, hope for
庶機する *shoki suru* desire, hope

SYNONYMS

❶ **various**
諸 VARIOUS → 1577
雑 MISCELLANEOUS → 1385
❷ **the people**
民 PEOPLE → 3036
衆 the multitude(s) → 2683
公 PUBLIC → 1974

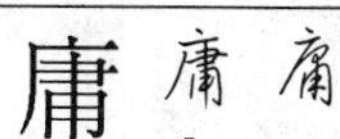

3128 YŌ

 yōng

Radical	Strokes
广 53	11-3-8
Grade	**Freq**
Jōyō	1892
□ 3 - 3 - 8	

3-8 广

1 2 3 4 5 6 7 8 9 10 11

▶MEDIOCRE

COMPOUNDS

❶ **mediocre, commonplace, common, ordinary, banal; stupid**
庸才 *yōsai* mediocre talent
庸愚 *yōgu* mediocrity, imbecility
庸君 *yōkun* stupid ruler
凡庸な *bon'yō na* commonplace, mediocre, banal
中庸 *chūyō* the (golden) mean, the middle path
❷ [now usu. 用 2976] employ (a person), engage
登庸 *tōyō* appointment, promotion
❸ tax paid in labor during the Asuka period
租庸調 *soyōchō* taxes in kind or service (former tax system), corvée

SYNONYMS

❶ **ordinary**
凡 COMMONPLACE → 2938
普 common → 2323
平 common → 3478
只- ORDINARY → 2155
並 ordinary → 2246
常 NORMAL → 2590

NOTE

★do not confuse with 傭 160

3-8 广

麻 3129

Radical	Strokes
麻 200	11-11-0
Grade	**Freq**
Radical	
□ 3-3-8	

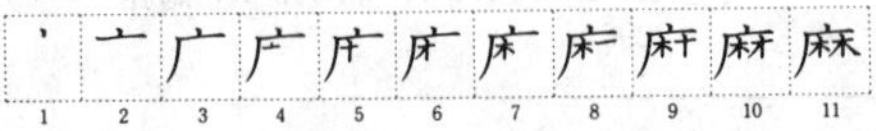

RADICAL 200

asakanmuri, variant of 麻 *asa* 'hemp'

⇨ see 麻 3130 for radical description

3-8 广

麻 3130

▶**HEMP** ▶**BECOME NUMB**

nonstandard for 麻 3125

Radical	Strokes
麻 200	11-11-0
Grade	**Freq**
Variant	
□ 3-3-8	

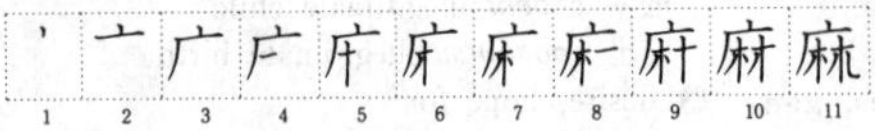

RADICAL 200

Standard form: 麻 *asa* 'hemp' (黀)

Enclosures: 麻 麻 *asakanmuri* (磨 魔)

Description: used in characters related to hemp or flax

3-8 广

廊

incorrect stroke count ⇨ see 3147

3-8 囗

圏 3131

▶**SPHERE**

nonstandard for 圏 3148

3-8 囗

國 3132

▶**COUNTRY**

nonstandard for 国 3087

3-9 辶

遅 3133

遅 遅 遅 — CH 迟 chí

CHI oku(reru) oku(rasu) oso(i)

Radical	Strokes
辶 162	12-3-9
Grade	**Freq**
Jōyō	814
□ 3-3-9	

▶**SLOW** ▶**LATE**

COMPOUNDS

❶ⓐ [original meaning] (not fast) **slow, tardy**

ⓑ (mentally dull) slow, dull

遅遅たる *chichitaru* slow, lagging, tardy

遅脈 *chimyaku* slow pulse

遅鈍 *chidon* dull, stupid

❷ⓐ (delayed) **late, tardy**

ⓑ **be late, be tardy, be delayed**

遅延 *chien* delay, retardation

遅配 *chihai* delay in rationing

遅刻 *chikoku* tardiness, lateness

遅参 *chisan* lateness, tardiness

KUN

【oku(reru) 遅れる】

ⓐ be late, be tardy, be delayed

ⓑ (of clocks) go slow, lose

遅れ *okure* being late; (of clocks) going slow

遅れ馳せの *okurebase no* belated, eleventh-hour

知恵遅れ *chieokure* mental retardation

乗り遅れる *noriokureru* miss [fail to catch] (a train)

【oku(rasu) 遅らす】 delay, put off, retard

返事を遅らす *henji o okurasu* defer one's reply

時計を一時間遅らせる *tokei o ichijikan okuraseru* turn back a watch one hour

【oso(i) 遅い】 (not fast) slow, tardy; (delayed) late, tardy

足が遅い *ashi ga osoi* be slow-footed

遅生まれの *osoumare no* born after April 1 (school entrance date)

遅咲き *osozaki* late blooming, late flower

SYNONYMS

❶ⓐ slow

徐 SLOWLY → 414

緩 SLACK → 1389

慢 SLUGGISH → 686

❷ⓐ late

晩 late (advanced) → 979

ⓑ be late and delay

後 fall behind → 361

滞 fall into arrears → 663

延 POSTPONE → 3073

猶 DELAY → 619

HOMOPHONES

okureru ⇨ 後 361

okure ⇨ 後 361

NOTE

⇨ see USAGE note at 後 361

道

3134 DŌ TŌ michi

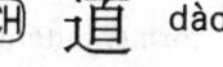

dào

Radical	Strokes
⻌ 162	12-3-9
Grade	**Freq**
Jōyō-2	124
口 3-3-9	

Stroke order: 1 2 3 4 5 6 7 8 9 10 11 12

3-9 ⻌

▶WAY

COMPOUNDS

❶ [also suffix]

ⓐ [original meaning] **way, path, road, track**

ⓑ passage, duct

道路 *dōro* road, street, way

道程 *dōtei* distance, journey, itinerary; process

鉄道 *tetsudō* railway

街道 *kaidō* thoroughfare, highway

軌道 *kidō* track, railway; planetary orbit; beaten track

歩道 *hodō* sidewalk, footpath

地下道 *chikadō* underpass, underground passage

水道 *suidō* water service [supply]; channel

気道 *kidō* air passage

食道 *shokudō* esophagus

外耳道 *gaijidō* external auditory meatus

❷ **the way of moral conduct, moral principles, morality, right way of life** (esp. **according to Confucian precepts), truth**

道徳 *dōtoku* morality, morals

道理 *dōri* reason, right, justice, truth

道義 *dōgi* morality, moral principles

正道 *seidō* path of righteousness, right track

人道的な *jindōteki na* humane, humanitarian

❸ **the Way, Tao, *Do***—a basic concept in Oriental religion and philosophy:

ⓐ *Taoism* **unitary first principle of existence, Taoism**

ⓑ *Confucianism* ultimate principle of cosmic reason

ⓒ *Buddhism* **the way of the Buddha, the teachings of Buddha**

神道 *shintō* Shinto, the Way of the Gods

伝道 *dendō* gospel preaching, missionary work, evangelism

道教 *dōkyō* Taoism

道家 *dōka* Taoist scholar

道学 *dōgaku* Confucian philosophy; Taoism

道具 *dōgu* tool, utensil, implement; furniture; theatrical appurtenances; tool, means; ingredient

道心 *dōshin* faith (in Buddha), piety; bonze, priest; sense of morality

入道する *nyūdō suru* become a bonze, renounce the world

❹ [also suffix] **the way of an art, esp. the principles of training and mental discipline of an art (as a martial art); art, way of life**

道場 *dōjō* *dojo*, gymnasium

柔道 *jūdō* judo

武道 *budō* martial arts

書道 *shodō* calligraphy, penmanship

茶道 *sadō* (=*chadō*) tea ceremony

武士道 *bushidō* Bushido (samurai code of behavior)

陰陽道 *onmyōdō* (=*on'yōdō*) art of divining

❺ⓐ [also prefix] **District of Hokkaido** (northern island of Japan)

ⓑ [also suffix] former administrative division of Japan

道民 *dōmin* people of Hokkaido

道議会 *dōgikai* Hokkaido Prefectural Assembly

北海道 *hokkaidō* Hokkaido
都道府県 *todōfuken* urban and rural prefectures
七道 *shichidō* the seven districts of ancient Japan
東海道 *tōkaidō* Tokaido district; Tokaido highway

❻ say, convey
道破 *dōha* declaration
報道 *hōdō* news, report, information
言語道断な *gongodōdan na* inexcusable, outrageous, absurd

❼ [also suffix] *Buddhism* posthumous world
六道 *rokudō* six posthumous worlds
餓鬼道 *gakidō* world of hungry spirits

INDEPENDENT

【dō 道】 District of Hokkaido; former administrative division of Japan
道の将来 *dō no shōrai* future of Hokkaido

KUN

【michi 道】
①ⓐ [formerly also 路] [also prefix and suffix] way, road, path, street; highway, track
ⓑ (distance in general) way, distance, journey
ⓒ halfway
道端 *michibata* roadside, wayside
道順 *michijun* route, itinerary
道案内 *michiannai* guiding, guide; guidepost
坂道 *sakamichi* slope
筋道 *sujimichi* reason, thread (of an argument), coherence; systematic method, due formality
散歩道 *sanpomichi* walk, promenade, esplanade
五キロの道 *gokiro no michi* distance of five kilometers
帰り道で *kaerimichi de* on one's way home

② way of doing, means, course of action
自活の道 *jikatsu no michi* independent living
地道な *jimichi na* steady, straight, fair
使い道 *tsukaimichi* use, application

③ the way of moral conduct, path of righteousness, moral principles, morality, right way of life
道ならぬ *michinaranu* improper, illicit
人たる道に背く *hitotaru michi ni somuku* stray from the path of righteousness

④ art, line (of work), career
剣の道 *ken no michi* swordsmanship
歌の道 *uta no michi* art of tanka poetry
その道 *sono-michi* the line (of business), the profession, the art, the field

SPECIAL READINGS

非道い▲(=酷い) *hidoi* cruel, harsh, rough; severe, intense, heavy

SYNONYMS

❶ⓐ ways and routes
途 WAY (route) → 3107
路 ROAD → 1533
筋 wayside → 2678
通り street → 3109
街 city street → 576
辻 CROSSROADS → 3192
岐 forked road → 241
径 PATH → 291
軌 TRACK → 1445
線 LINE → 1392

ⓑ tubular passages
管 PIPE → 2701
筒 TUBE → 2680
脈 VEIN → 953

❷ moral principles
倫 MORALS → 120

❷ moral goodness
徳 VIRTUE → 684
善 GOOD → 2325
義 RIGHTEOUSNESS → 2338

❸ religion
教 RELIGION → 1493
宗 religion → 2228

ⓐ religions and sects
儒 CONFUCIANISM → 174
禅 ZEN → 1032
仏 Buddhism → 19
法 Buddha's teachings → 333

❹ art
技 SKILL → 248
術 PRACTICAL ART → 476
芸 ART → 2209

❺ⓐ territorial divisions
県 PREFECTURE → 2641
府 URBAN PREFECTURE → 3082
都 METROPOLIS OF TOKYO → 1686
州 STATE → 57
省 province of China → 2449
郡 COUNTY → 1466

USAGE

michi

道
①ⓐ [formerly also 路] [also prefix and suffix] way, road, path, street; highway, track
ⓑ (distance in general) way, distance, journey
ⓒ halfway
② way of doing, means, course of action
③ the way of moral conduct, path of righteousness, moral principles, morality, right way of life
④ art, line (of work), career

路
[now usu. 道] road, avenue, boulevard

HOMOPHONES
michi ⇨ 路 1533
hidoi ⇨ 酷い 1562 非道い 889, 3134

COMPOUND FORMATION
道具 *dōgu*

道具 'tool, etc.' originally referred to the implements (具) used in performing Buddhist (道 ❸Ⓒ) ceremonies.

NOTE
⇨ see also USAGE note at 酷 1562

遇

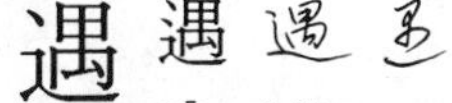

3135 GŪ a(u)▲

Ⓒⓗ 遇 yù

Radical	Strokes
⻌ 162	12-3-9
Grade	**Freq**
Jōyō	1379
□ 3 - 3 - 9	

3-9 ⻌

1 2 3 4 5 6 7 8 9 10 11 12

▶TREAT ▶ENCOUNTER

COMPOUNDS

❶ **treat, entertain, receive, deal with**
待遇する *taigū suru* treat, receive, entertain
処遇する *shogū suru* treat, deal with
冷遇 *reigū* cold treatment, frigid reception
知遇 *chigū* favor, warm friendship
優遇する *yūgū suru* treat favorably, receive warmly

❷ (meet by chance) **encounter, happen to meet, come across, meet with**
遭遇する *sōgū suru* encounter, come across
奇遇 *kigū* unexpected meeting, chance encounter
千載一遇の *senzai-ichigū no* experienced once in a thousand years, very rare

❸ fate, luck, one's lot
遇不遇 *gūfugū* happiness and sorrows
不遇 *fugū* misfortune, ill luck
境遇 *kyōgū* one's lot, circumstances, situation in life

INDEPENDENT
【gūsuru 遇する】 treat, entertain

KUN
【a(u) 遇う】 [also 遭う] (come upon, esp. by accident) meet with, encounter, be confronted
酷い目に遇う *hidoi me ni au* have a bad time

SYNONYMS
❶ **treat and welcome**
待 treat → 364
扱う HANDLE → 217
款 treat cordially → 1700
接 receive → 500
迎 WELCOME → 3059

❷ **meet**
遭 MEET WITH → 3159
会 MEET → 2020
見 SEE → 2544
謁 BE GRANTED AN AUDIENCE → 1570

HOMOPHONES
au ⇨ 遭 3159 会 2020 合 2019

NOTE
⇨ see USAGE note at 会 2020

遍

3136 HEN amane(ku)▲

Ⓒⓗ 遍 biàn

Radical	Strokes
⻌ 162	12-3-9
Grade	**Freq**
Jōyō	1774
□ 3 - 3 - 9	

3-9 ⻌

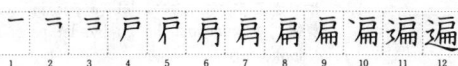

1 2 3 4 5 6 7 8 9 10 11 12

▶ALL OVER

COMPOUNDS

❶ **all over, everywhere, universal, ubiquitous, widespread**
遍在 *henzai* omnipresence, ubiquity
遍歴 *henreki* travels, pilgrimage
遍路 *henro* pilgrim
普遍的な *fuhenteki na* universal, omnipresent, ubiquitous
満遍無く(＝万遍無く) *manben naku* evenly, equally; without exception; all over

❷ [sometimes also 返 3060] **counter for number of times**
五遍 *gohen* five times
何遍も *nanben mo* several [many] times, very often

KUN
【amane(ku) 遍く】 [also 普く] *literary* all over, everywhere, widely, universally
遍く捜す *amaneku sagasu* make a wide

search
遍く世界に知られる *amaneku sekai ni shirareru* be known all over the world

SYNONYMS

❶ **widespread**
普 WIDESPREAD → 2323
通 common → 3109
公 common (math) → 1974

❷ **time and time counters**
度 TIME → 3100
回 TIME → 3055
返 counter for number of times → 3060

HOMOPHONES

amaneku ⇨ 普 2323

NOTE

⇨ see USAGE note at 普 2323

3-9 辶

過 過 過 過 ㊥ 过 guò guō

3137 KA su(giru) -su(giru) -su(gi) su(gosu) ayama(tsu) ayama(chi)

Radical	Strokes
辶 162	12-3-9
Grade	**Freq**
Jōyō-5	377

□ 3-3-9

Stroke order: 1 丨 2 冂 3 冂 4 冋 5 冎 6 冎 7 咼 8 咼 9 咼 10 咼 11 過 12 過

▶**PASS BY** ▶**EXCEED**

COMPOUNDS

❶ [original meaning] **pass by, go past, pass through**
過程 *katei* process, course
過渡期 *katoki* transitional period [stage]
通過する *tsūka suru* pass through, carry (a resolution)
経過 *keika* progress, course, development; lapse, passage
一過性の *ikkasei no* temporary, transitory

❷ (of time) **pass by [away], elapse**
過去 *kako* the past, bygone days
過日 *kajitsu* the other day, some days ago

❸ⓐ **exceed, be above, be over**
ⓑ [prefix] **excessive, over-, too much, super-**
過剰 *kajō* surplus, excess
過密 *kamitsu* overcrowding
過当な *katō na* excessive, undue, unreasonable
過熱する *kanetsu suru* overheat, superheat
超過する *chōka suru* exceed, be in excess, be above
過半数 *kahansū* majority, more than half
過保護 *kahogo* overprotectiveness

❹ⓐ **error, fault, mistake, slip**
ⓑ err, make a mistake
過失 *kashitsu* error, fault, mistake; negligence
大過 *taika* serious error, gross mistake
罪過 *zaika* fault
過誤 *kago* mistake, error, fault

❺ *chem* per-
過酸化水素 *kasanka suiso* hydrogen peroxide
過硫酸 *karyūsan* persulfuric acid

❻ *Buddhism* past
過現未 *kagenmi* past, present and future, three temporal states of existence

KUN

【su(giru) 過ぎる】 pass by, go past, pass through; (of time) pass by [away], elapse, expire; exceed, be above, go too far
過ぎ去る *sugisaru* pass (away), elapse
通り過ぎる *tōrisugiru* go past, pass
過ぎた事 *sugita koto* the past, bygones, past event
五十を過ぎる *gojū o sugiru* be above 50
冗談が過ぎる *jōdan ga sugiru* carry a joke too far

【-su(giru) -過ぎる】 [verbal suffix] over-, too, to excess, to a fault
食べ過ぎる *tabesugiru* overeat oneself
利口過ぎる *rikōsugiru* be too clever

【-su(gi) -過ぎ】
① [suffix] past, after
二時過ぎに *niji sugi ni* after two o'clock
② [verbal suffix] over-, too much, excessive
飲み過ぎ *nomisugi* overdrinking

【su(gosu) 過ごす】
① pass [spend] (time), tide over, get through
一日を過ごす *ichinichi o sugosu* pass a day
冬を過ごす *fuyu o sugosu* go through the winter
②ⓐ [verbal suffix] let pass, leave alone
ⓑ [also verbal suffix] go too far, overdo
やり過ごす *yarisugosu* let (a person) go past
見過ごす *misugosu* let go by, let pass; overlook, miss
寝過ごす *nesugosu* oversleep

【ayama(tsu) 過つ】 err, make a mistake
過って *ayamatte* be mistaken, in error; by accident

【ayama(chi) 過ち】 fault; error, mistake
過ちを改める *ayamachi o aratameru* correct a fault

SYNONYMS

❶ **pass**
通 PASS → 3109
経 PASS THROUGH → 1331

❷ **elapse**

経 pass → 1331
歴 pass → 3019
去 pass away → 2156
❸ **exceeding and excess**
超 SURPASS → 3313
越 GO BEYOND → 3314
濫 EXCESSIVE → 801
余 EXCESS → 2042

剰 SURPLUS → 1779
冗 REDUNDANT → 1976
❹ⓐ **mistakes and mistaking**
失 SLIP → 3511
誤 MISTAKE → 1542
錯 mistaken → 1743
-違える mis- → 3151

遂 3138

SUI to(geru) tsui(ni)▲

Ⓒⓗ 遂 suì suí

Radical	Strokes
⻌ 162	12-3-9
Grade	**Freq**
Jōyō	1388
口 3-3-9	

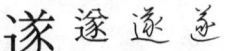

3-9 ⻌

▶ACCOMPLISH

COMPOUNDS

● (complete successfully) **accomplish, achieve, attain, complete, carry out, execute, commit, perform**
遂行する *suikō suru* accomplish, execute, perform, carry out
完遂する *kansui suru* execute successfully, accomplish, bring to completion
未遂の *misui no* attempted (suicide, etc.)

KUN

【to(geru) 遂げる】 accomplish, achieve, attain, fulfill, realize, carry out
成し遂げる *nashitogeru* complete, carry out, accomplish
【tsui(ni) 遂に】 [sometimes also 終に] at last, at length, in the end, finally

SYNONYMS

● **accomplish**
達 ATTAIN → 3139
成 ACHIEVE → 3537
徹 GO THROUGH → 726
破 carry through with → 1150
● **execute**
果たす effect → 3560
執 EXECUTE → 1680
行 ACT → 212
履 FULFILL → 3171
施 CARRY OUT → 891
践 IMPLEMENT → 1535

USAGE

tsuini
遂に
[sometimes also 終に] at last, at length, in the end, finally
終に
[usu. 遂に] same as 遂に

HOMOPHONES

tsuini ⇨ 終 1336

NOTE

★do not confuse with 逐 3102

達 3139

TATSU DA▲ -tachi▲

Ⓒⓗ 达 dá

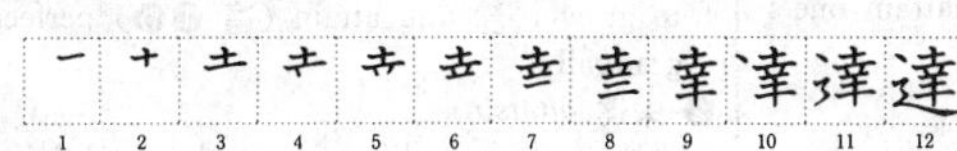

Radical	Strokes
⻌ 162	12-3-9
Grade	**Freq**
Jōyō-4	502
口 3-3-9	

3-9 ⻌

▶ATTAIN

COMPOUNDS

❶ⓐ (arrive at) **attain, reach, arrive, come up to, gain**
ⓑ (succeed in reaching a goal) **attain, achieve, reach, realize**
到達 *tōtatsu* arrival; attainment
先達 *sendatsu* guide, precursor, pioneer, leader
発達する *hattatsu suru* develop, grow, make progress
達成する *tassei suru* attain, achieve, accomplish
調達 *chōtatsu* supply, procurement; execution (of an order); raising (money)
栄達 *eitatsu* success in life, rise in the world
❷ **attain proficiency or maturity, understand thoroughly, be versed in, be skill-**

ful
達観 *takkan* philosophic view [ripeness]; far-sighted view
達人 *tatsujin* expert, master
達筆 *tappitsu* good handwriting
達者な *tassha na* expert, proficient, clever; healthy, well, strong, robust
上達する *jōtatsu suru* make progress, attain proficiency
熟達する *jukutatsu suru* attain proficiency, become expert

❸ **deliver, convey**
達意 *tatsui* intelligibility, perspicuity
配達 *haitatsu* delivery
速達 *sokutatsu* special delivery, express mail
伝達 *dentatsu* transmission, conveyance, communication; propagation
送達 *sōtatsu* conveyance, delivery, dispatch

❹ issue a notice, issue [deliver] orders, notify
通達 *tsūtatsu* communication, notification; proficiency
示達 *jitatsu* (=*shitatsu*) instructions, directions
上意下達する *jōikatatsu suru* convey the will of the governing to the governed
執達吏 *shittatsuri* bailiff

❺ [original meaning] extend to, reach to
四通八達 *shitsūhattatsu* traffic network extending in all directions
闊達な *kattatsu na* openhearted, frank, broad-minded

❻ used phonetically for *da* or similar sounds
達磨 *daruma* Bodhidharma; tumbler
曹達 *sōda* soda

INDEPENDENT

【tassuru 達する】 (arrive at) attain, reach, arrive, come up to, amount to; (succeed in reaching a goal) attain, achieve, reach, realize; issue a notice, issue [deliver] orders, notify
頂上に達する *chōjō ni tassuru* attain the summit
成年に達する *seinen ni tassuru* come of age
目的を達する *mokuteki o tassuru* attain one's aim, achieve one's purpose

【tasshi 達し】 government notice

KUN

【-tachi -達】
[suffix]
① suffix, often polite, for forming the plural of pronouns, people or animals
私達 *watakushitachi* we
動物達 *dōbutsutachi* animals
② ...and the others
山田さん達 *yamadasantachi* Mr. Yamada and the others

SPECIAL READINGS

友達 *tomodachi* friend, companion

SYNONYMS

❶ⓐ **arrive**
届く REACH → 3078
及 REACH TO → 3385
至 COME TO → 2182
到 ARRIVE → 1264
着 ARRIVE → 3316

ⓑ **accomplish**
遂 ACCOMPLISH → 3138
成 ACHIEVE → 3537
徹 GO THROUGH → 726
破 carry through with → 1150

❷ **attain proficiency**
熟 become skilled → 2868

❸ **transmit and deliver**
届ける DELIVER → 3078
伝 TRANSMIT → 44
逓 RELAY → 3106

❹ **inform and communicate**
告 NOTIFY → 2409
届ける give notice → 3078
通 COMMUNICATE → 3109
報 INFORM → 1698
知 let know → 1127
申 REPORT → 3507
宣 PROCLAIM → 2252

[-tachi]

ⓐ **plural suffixes**
-等 plural suffix → 2682
衆 somewhat polite plural suffix → 2683
-共 belittling plural suffix → 2393
-方 polite plural suffix → 1963

COMPOUND FORMATION

❶ 発達 *hattatsu*
発達する 'develop, grow, make progress' is to grow (発) and attain (達 ❶ⓑ) perfection gradually.

❷ 栄達 *eitatsu*
栄達 'success in life, rise in the world' is the attainment (達 ❶ⓑ) of glory (栄) or worldly fame.

運 運 運 ⻌

3140 UN hako(bu)

CH 运 yùn

Radical	Strokes
⻌ 162	12-3-9
Grade	Freq
Jōyō-3	158
□ 3-3-9	

3-9 ⻌

▶CARRY ▶MOVE ▶FORTUNE

COMPOUNDS

❶ⓐ (move something from one place to another in one's hands or in a vehicle) **carry, transport, ship**

ⓑ **carriage, transport, transportation**

運輸 *un'yu* transport(ation), conveyance
運送 *unsō* shipping, transportation
運搬する *unpan suru* carry, transport, convey, deliver
海運 *kaiun* marine transportation, merchant shipping
陸運 *rikuun* land transportation [carriage]
舟運 *shūun* transportation by water
運賃 *unchin* freight [shipping] expense, passenger fare
運河 *unga* canal

❷ⓐ [original meaning] **move, revolve**

ⓑ **control movement skillfully, handle, set in motion**

運動 *undō* motion, movement; exercise; campaign
運航 *unkō* navigation; (airline or shipping) service
運行する *unkō suru* revolve, orbit; operate
運休 *unkyū* suspension of (bus) service
運転する *unten suru* operate, drive, run
運営する *un'ei suru* operate, manage
運用する *un'yō suru* make use of; invest in; apply to
運筆 *unpitsu* handling the brush

❸ **fortune, luck, fate, destiny, chance**

運命 *unmei* fate, fortune, destiny
好運 *kōun* good luck
不運 *fuun* misfortune, bad luck
社運 *shaun* fortune of the company

❹ [formerly 耘 1310] weed, remove weeds

耕運機 *kōunki* cultivator, tiller

INDEPENDENT

【un 運】 fortune, luck, fate, destiny, chance

運が悪い *un ga warui* out of luck
運に任せる *un ni makaseru* trust to luck

KUN

【hako(bu) 運ぶ】 carry, transport; progress, advance, go on (well)

運び *hakobi* carriage; step, pace; progress, development; stage
運び出す *hakobidasu* bring out, carry out
すらすらと運ぶ *surasura to hakobu* go smoothly

SYNONYMS

❶ **carry**

搬 CARRY → 647
輸 TRANSPORT → 1607

❷ⓐ **move**

動 MOVE → 1778
転 remove → 1480
滑 SLIDE → 658
遷 TRANSFER → 3170
移 SHIFT → 1177
繰る SHIFT ONWARD → 1427

ⓑ **handle**

扱う HANDLE → 217
操 MANIPULATE → 769
揮 WIELD → 589

❸ **fate and fortune**

命 fate → 2058
業 karma → 2612
縁 karma relation → 1386

NOTE

⇨ see COMPOUND FORMATION for 運転 *unten* ⇨ 転 1480

遥 遥 遥 ⻌

3141 YŌ haru(ka) NAMES haruka

CH 遥 yáo

Radical	Strokes
⻌ 162	12-3-9
Grade	Freq
Names	2101
□ 3-3-9	

3-9 ⻌

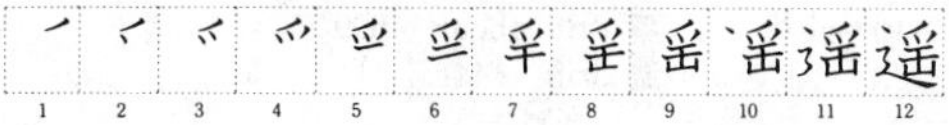

▶FAR

COMPOUNDS

❶ **far, faraway, far-off, distant, remote**

遥拝 *yōhai* worshiping from afar
遥遠な *yōen na* [rare] very far-off, remote

❷ walk about, wander about

逍遥学派 *shōyō gakuha* Peripatetic school (of philosophy)

KUN

【haru(ka) 遥か】 far, faraway, far-off, distant, remote

遥か彼方の *haruka kanata no* faraway, far-off
遥か昔 *haruka mukashi* long ago
遥かに *haruka ni* far, far off, in the distance; a long time ago; by far
遥遥 *harubaru* from afar, all the way; at a great distance

NAMES

遥子 *yōko* female name
遥 *haruka* male name also female name

SYNONYMS

❶ distant
悠 far-off → 2741
遼 FARAWAY → 3168
隔 APART → 671
離 separated → 1836
遠 DISTANT → 3150

3-9
辶

遊 遊 遊 遊
3142 YŪ YU aso(bu) aso(basu)

CH 遊 yóu

Radical	Strokes
辶 162	12-3-9
Grade	**Freq**
Jōyō-3	665
□ 3-3-9	

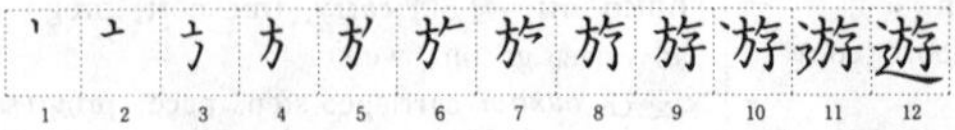

▶PLAY

COMPOUNDS

❶ⓐ play, amuse oneself
ⓑ play around with (the opposite sex), flirt
ⓒ associate intimately with
遊戯 *yūgi* game, pastime, amusement
遊興 *yūkyō* merrymaking, spree
遊園地 *yūenchi* amusement park
遊女 *yūjo* harlot, prostitute
遊里 *yūri* licensed quarters, red-light district
交遊 *kōyū* companionship, friendship

❷ be idle, be unemployed
遊民 *yūmin* idle people, the unemployed
遊休施設 *yūkyū-shisetsu* idle facilities
遊食する *yūshoku suru* live in idleness
遊資 *yūshi* idle capital

❸ tour, take a pleasure trip or excursion, make a study tour
遊学 *yūgaku* traveling to study
遊山 *yusan* excursion, outing, picnic
遊説 *yūzei* electioneering tour; campaign speech
外遊 *gaiyū* foreign tour, trip abroad
歴遊 *rekiyū* traveling, tour, pleasure trip

❹ⓐ move about freely, wander, roam
ⓑ mobile, free moving
遊星 *yūsei* wandering star, planet
遊牧 *yūboku* nomadism
遊離する *yūri suru* isolate, separate
遊撃 *yūgeki* attack by a mobile unit
浮遊物 *fuyūbutsu* floating matter, suspended particles

❺ [sometimes also 游 *yū* 614] swim
遊泳する *yūei suru* swim
回遊 *kaiyū* excursion, circular tour; migration (of fish)

❻ *baseball* abbrev. of 遊撃手 *yūgekishu*: shortstop
遊失 *yūshitsu* shortstop error

KUN

【aso(bu) 遊ぶ】 play, amuse oneself; play around with, flirt; be idle, loaf; be not in use; be unemployed; make an excursion, take a trip; visit

遊び *asobi* play, sport; amusement, fun; diversion; visit; outing; dissipation; play (of a wheel)
遊び場 *asobiba* playground
遊び人 *asobinin* gambler; playboy

【aso(basu) 遊ばす】 [honorific] be pleased to, deign, condescend

遊ばせ言葉 *asobasekotoba* polite language used by women

SYNONYMS

❶ⓐ & ❶ⓑ play
戯 SPORT → 1875
❸ journey
巡 tour around → 3047
行 trip → 212
旅 TRAVEL → 922
❹ⓐ wander
浪 WANDER → 439
漂 drift about → 699
流 drift → 441

3-9
辶

遅
3143

▶CHOOSE
handwritten abbreviation for 選 3169

貮 ▶TWO
3144
nonstandard for 弐 3195

3-9 弋

属 屬 属 属 ㊥ 属 shǔ zhǔ
3145 ZOKU SHOKU▴

Radical 尸 44	Strokes 12-3-9
Grade Jōyō-5	Freq 750
口 3-3-9	

3-9 尸

▶BELONG TO

COMPOUNDS

❶ⓐ **belong to, pertain to, be one of**
ⓑ **be subordinate to, depend upon**
付属する *fuzoku suru* be attached to, belong to
所属する *shozoku suru* belong to, be attached to
専属する *senzoku suru* belong exclusively to
軍属 *gunzoku* army civilian employee
属領 *zokuryō* possession, dependency, dominion
属国 *zokkoku* vassal state, dependency
従属 *jūzoku* subordination, dependency
❷ [also suffix] subordinate official
属官 *zokkan* subordinate, government clerk
配属する *haizoku suru* assign, attach
部属 *buzoku* section, division
文部属山本氏 *monbuzoku yamamotoshi* Mr. Yamamoto, clerk of the Ministry of Education, Science and Culture
❸ⓐ **genus, kind, sort, family; category**
ⓑ *biol* **genus**
金属 *kinzoku* metal
尊属 *sonzoku* ascendant
属名 *zokumei* generic name
属差 *zokusa* generic difference
猫属 *nekozoku* the cat genus
❹ [usu. 嘱 *shoku* 718] charge, entrust
属託する *shokutaku suru* entrust with
❺ [usu. 嘱 *shoku* 718] fasten one's attention upon
属目する *shokumoku suru* pay attention to

INDEPENDENT

【**zoku** 属】genus, kind, sort, family; *biol* genus
【**zokusuru** 属する】belong to, pertain to, be one of, be associated with
政党に属する *seitō ni zokusuru* belong to a political party

SYNONYMS

❶ⓐ **possess**
有 HAVE → 2983
持 HOLD → 374
蔵 own → 2364
享 ENJOY → 2051
具 possess → 2552
❸ⓐ **kinds and types**
品 category → 2248
類 KIND → 1807
色 kind → 2029
般 SORT → 1317
型 TYPE → 2638
種 VARIETY → 1218
様 variety → 1052

廃 廢 廃 廃 ㊥ 废 fèi
3146 HAI suta(reru) suta(ru)

Radical 广 53	Strokes 12-3-9
Grade Jōyō	Freq 907
口 3-3-9	

3-9 广

▶ABOLISH ▶WASTE

COMPOUNDS

❶ **abolish, abandon, discontinue, give up**
廃止する *haishi suru* abolish, abandon, discontinue
廃案 *haian* rejected bill [project]
廃刊 *haikan* discontinuance of publication
廃棄 *haiki* discarding, abolition, annulment
廃藩 *haihan* abolition of the *han* system
全廃 *zenpai* (total) abolition
撤廃 *teppai* abolition, removal
❷ⓐ **waste, useless, discarded, abandoned, obsolete**
ⓑ [formerly also 癈 3287] disabled, crippled

廃品 *haihin* waste articles, junk
廃ガス *haigasu* waste gas
廃熱 *hainetsu* waste heat
廃坑 *haikō* abandoned mine
廃語 *haigo* obsolete word
荒廃 *kōhai* desolation, waste, ruin
廃疾 *haishitsu* disablement
廃人 *haijin* invalid, crippled person

INDEPENDENT

【haisuru 廃する】 abolish, abandon; annul, repeal; dethrone, depose

KUN

【suta(reru) 廃れる】 go out of use, fall into disuse, be outmoded
廃れた *sutareta* disused, out of date, obsolete

【suta(ru) 廃る】 same as **sutareru 廃れる**

廃り *sutari* waste, wastage, waster

SYNONYMS

❶ **discontinue**
絶 BREAK OFF → 1353
断 CUT OFF → 1492
止 STOP → 2941
休 suspend → 52
停 suspend → 139

❷ⓐ **bad**
悪 BAD → 2745
劣 INFERIOR → 2395
下 of low grade → 3378
弊 shabby → 2884
粗 COARSE → 1329
駄 GOOD FOR NOTHING → 1821

3-9
广

廊 廊 廊 

3147 RŌ

CH 廊 láng

Radical	Strokes
广 53	12-3-9
Grade	**Freq**
Jōyō	1251
口 3-3-9	

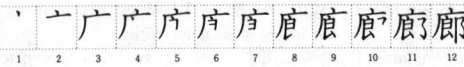

(stroke order 1–12)

▶CORRIDOR

COMPOUNDS

● [original meaning] **corridor, gallery, passageway, hall**

廊下 *rōka* corridor, gallery, passage
画廊 *garō* picture gallery
回廊 *kairō* corridor, gallery
歩廊 *horō* corridor, gallery; platform

3-9
广

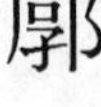

incorrect stroke count ⇨ see 3163

3-9
口

  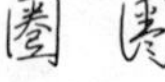 圏

3148 KEN

CH 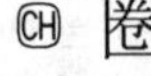 quān juàn juān

Radical	Strokes
口 31	12-3-9
Grade	**Freq**
Jōyō	1318
口 3-3-9	

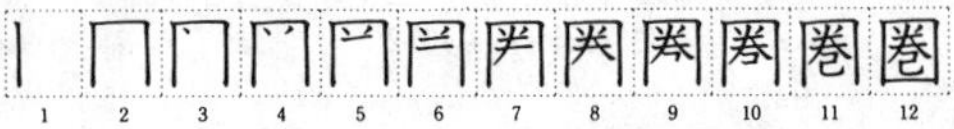

(stroke order 1–12)

▶SPHERE

COMPOUNDS

❶ [also suffix]
ⓐ (spherical domain of action) **sphere, realm, circle, domain, zone, radius, range**
ⓑ circle
対流圏 *tairyūken* troposphere
生物圏 *seibutsuken* biosphere
暴風圏 *bōfūken* storm zone
通信圏外 *tsūshinkengai* out of the range of communication
ポンド圏 *pondoken* sterling zone
北極圏 *hokkyokuken* arctic zone; Arctic Circle
圏点 *kenten* circle (for emphasis)
大圏コース *taiken kōsu* great circle route

❷ [also suffix] (domain of influence) **sphere, circle, domain**
影響圏 *eikyōken* sphere of influence
共産圏 *kyōsanken* the Communist bloc

SYNONYMS

❶ⓐ **areas and localities**
帯 BELT → 2582
領 TERRITORY → 1224
区 DISTRICT → 2963
域 BOUNDED AREA → 465
辺 VICINITY → 3029

方 locality → 1963
地 PLACE → 204
❶ⓐ & ❷ **range**
域 area → 465
範 range → 2709
程 EXTENT → 1190
野 FIELD → 1485
界 field (*phys*) → 2563
場 field (*phys*, *psychol*) → 558
ⓑ **circle**
円 CIRCLE → 2955
丸 round or spherical shape → 3417

圍
3149

▶**ENCLOSE**
nonstandard for 囲 3069

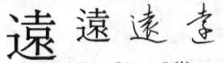

遠 遠 遠 [calligraphic forms]
3150 EN ON tō(i)

CH 远 yuǎn

Radical	Strokes
⻍ 162	13-3-10
Grade	**Freq**
Jōyō-2	777
囗 3-3-10	

Stroke order: 一 + 土 ± 吉 吉 声 专 袁 袁 遠 遠 (1–12), 遠 (13)

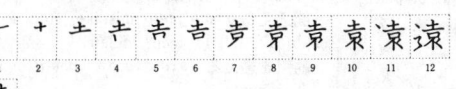

▶**DISTANT**

COMPOUNDS

❶ⓐ **distant (in space), far, remote**
ⓑ **distant (in time), far-off, remote**
ⓒ **become distant**
遠隔の *enkaku no* distant, remote, far
遠景 *enkei* distant view, perspective
遠方 *enpō* great distance; distant place
遠足 *ensoku* excursion, hike, long walk
遠征 *ensei* (punitive) expedition, invasion; tour
遠視 *enshi* farsightedness
望遠鏡 *bōenkyō* telescope
永遠 *eien* eternity
久遠 *kuon* eternity
遠心力 *enshinryoku* centrifugal force
❷ distant (in relationship), estranged
遠慮 *enryo* reserve; hesitation; forethought, prudence
敬遠する *keien suru* keep at a respectful distance; avoid
疎遠 *soen* estrangement, alienation, neglect
❸ profound, deep
深遠な *shin'en na* profound, deep

KUN

【tō(i) 遠い】 far(-off), distant, remote (in time or space); distant (in relationship); hard of hearing
遠ざかる *tōzakaru* become distant; keep away
遠くから *tōku kara* from a distance
遠回り *tōmawari* roundabout way
遠い昔 *tōi mukashi* remote past
遠からず *tōkarazu* in the offing
遠縁 *tōen* distant relation
耳が遠い *mimi ga tōi* hard of hearing

SYNONYMS

❶ **distant**
遥 FAR → 3141
悠 far-off → 2741
遼 FARAWAY → 3168
隔 APART → 671
離 separated → 1836
❷ **estrange**
離 separate from → 1836
疎 ESTRANGE → 1178

3-10
⻌

違 違 違 违　CH 违 wéi

3151　I chiga(u)　chiga(i)　chiga(eru)　-chiga(eru)
taga(u)▲　taga(eru)▲

Radical	Strokes
⻌ 162	13-3-10
Grade	Freq
Jōyō	438
3-3-10	

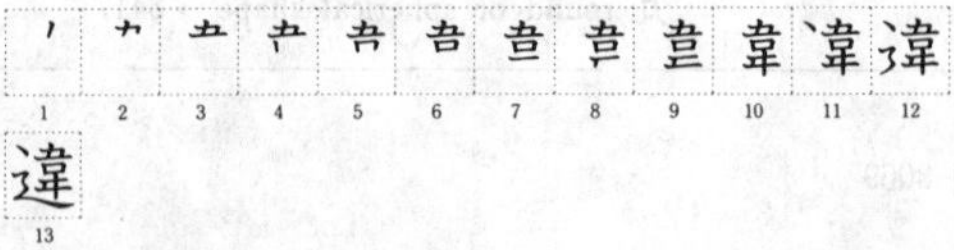

▶DIFFER ▶VIOLATE

COMPOUNDS

❶ **differ, be different**
違和感 *iwakan* feeling of being out of place, incongruity
相違 *sōi* difference, disparity

❷ **violate, break, disobey**
違反(=違犯) *ihan* violation (of the law), infringement; breach
違法 *ihō* illegality, unlawfulness
違憲 *iken* unconstitutionality, violation of the constitution
違約 *iyaku* breach of promise

❸ mistake, error
違算 *isan* miscalculation, misjudgment

KUN

【chiga(u) 違う】
① differ, be different; differ in opinion, disagree
違う! *Chigau!* No (that's not true)!
話が違う *Hanashi ga chigau* That's a different story
② be mistaken, be wrong
間違う *machigau* be mistaken, be incorrect
③ cross, go by
擦れ違う *surechigau* pass by each other, brush past

【chiga(i) 違い】
① difference
食い違い *kuichigai* difference (in opinion), cross-purposes; cross
② [also suffix] mistake
違い無い *chigainai* no mistaking it, for certain
勘違いする *kanchigai suru* be under the wrong impression
計算違い *keisanchigai* miscalculation

【chiga(eru) 違える】
① change, alter
話し方を違える *hanashikata o chigaeru* disguise one's speech
② mistake, make a mistake
間違える *machigaeru* mistake, confuse
③ break, fail to keep, violate
約束を違える *yakusoku o chigaeru* break a promise
④ sprain, wrench
首筋を違える *kubisuji o chigaeru* wrench one's neck

【-chiga(eru) -違える】 [verbal suffix] mis-, make a mistake in performing an action
言い違える *iichigaeru* mistake, make a slip
見違える *michigaeru* mistake, fail to recognize
薬を飲み違える *kusuri o nomichigaeru* take the wrong medicine

【taga(u) 違う】 same as **chigau** 違う

【taga(eru) 違える】 same as **chigaeru** 違える

SYNONYMS

❶ **differing and difference**
異 DIFFERENT → 2584
差 DIFFERENCE → 3311

❷ **violate**
破 BREAK → 1150
犯 offend against → 196
反 act contrary to → 2945
背 go against → 2573

【-chigaeru】
○ **mistakes and mistaking**
誤 MISTAKE → 1542
錯 mistaken → 1743
過 error → 3137
失 SLIP → 3511

NOTE

⇨ see USAGE note at 異 2584

3-10 ⻌

遣 遣 遣 ⻌ ㊥ 遣 qiǎn

3152 KEN tsuka(u) -tsuka(i) -zuka(i) tsuka(wasu) ya(ru)▲

Radical	Strokes
⻌ 162	13-3-10
Grade	**Freq**
Jōyō	1072
口 3-3-10	

1 2 3 4 5 6 7 8 9 10 11 12 13

▶**DISPATCH**

COMPOUNDS

❶ **dispatch, send**

遣外の *kengai no* dispatched abroad
遣唐使 *kentōshi* Japanese envoy to Tang China
遣米 *kenbei* sending to America
派遣する *haken suru* dispatch, send
分遣 *bunken* detachment, detail
先遣する *senken suru* send ahead [in advance]

❷ [rare] banish, drive away

遣悶する *kenmon suru* drive away melancholy

KUN

【tsuka(u) 遣う】

① [sometimes also 使う] spend, use (time or money)
金を遣う *kane o tsukau* spend money
② be anxious, worry
気遣う *kizukau* feel anxious about, worry about, have apprehensions of
③ use (language properly), spell
正しい言葉を遣う *tadashii kotoba o tsukau* use the correct word
④ manipulate
人形を遣う *ningyō o tsukau* manipulate puppets

【-tsuka(i), -zuka(i) -遣い】

① spending, spending money
無駄遣い *mudazukai* wasting money
小遣い *kozukai* pocket money, spending money
② worrying, being anxious
心遣い *kokorozukai* consideration, anxiety
③ use (of language), spelling
仮名遣い *kanazukai* kana orthography, use of kana
④ manipulating
人形遣い *ningyōtsukai* puppet manipulator

【tsuka(wasu) 遣わす】 dispatch, send; present, bestow; [following the TE-form of verbs] do something for someone
使者を遣わす *shisha o tsukawasu* dispatch a messenger
誉めて遣わす *Homete tsukawasu* You have my praise

【ya(ru) 遣る】 give (to an inferior); send (a person); do, perform; perform, act, play; perform an action for the benefit of an inferior; drink alcohol
使いに遣る *tsukai ni yaru* send a person on an errand
おもちゃを買って遣る *omocha o katte yaru* buy a toy (for a child)

SYNONYMS

❶ **send**
派 DISPATCH → 381
回 send round → 3055
送 SEND → 3093
投 SEND IN → 256

HOMOPHONES

tsukau ⇨ 使 90
-tsukai ⇨ 使 90

NOTE

⇨ see USAGE note at 使 90
★do not confuse with 遺 3166

遮 incorrect stroke count ⇨ see 3158 — 3-10 ⻌

遡 incorrect stroke count ⇨ see 3257 — 3-10 ⻌

3-10 广

廉 廉 廉 廉

3153 REN

CH 廉 lián

Radical	Strokes
广 53	13-3-10
Grade	**Freq**
Jōyō	1805
□ 3-3-10	

Stroke order: 1 2 3 4 5 6 7 8 9 10 11 12 13

▶**INCORRUPT** ▶**CHEAP**

COMPOUNDS

❶ **incorrupt, honest and clean, upright, cleanhanded**

廉直 *renchoku* integrity, uprightness
廉潔な *renketsu na* honest, incorruptible
清廉な *seiren na* incorruptible, honest, upright
破廉恥な *harenchi na* shameless, infamous, impudent

❷ **cheap, low-priced, bargain-priced, inexpensive**

廉価な *renka na* cheap, low-priced
廉売 *renbai* bargain sale
低廉な *teiren na* cheap, inexpensive

SYNONYMS

❶ **purehearted**

潔 IMMACULATE → 744
清 clean → 523
淳 PUREHEARTED → 514
純 PURE → 1297
敦 HONEST → 1693
惇 SINCERE → 486
直 straightforward → 2932

❷ **inexpensive**

安 INEXPENSIVE → 2171
低 low-priced → 73

3-10 广

亷

3154

▶**INCORRUPT** ▶**CHEAP**

nonstandard for 廉 3153

3-10 广

廊

3155

▶**CORRIDOR**

nonstandard for 廊 3147

3-10 广

廓

incorrect stroke count ⇨ see 3163

3-10 囗

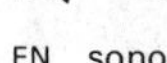

3156 EN sono

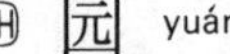

CH 园 yuán

Radical	Strokes
囗 31	13-3-10
Grade	**Freq**
Jōyō-2	424
□ 3-3-10	

Stroke order: 1 2 3 4 5 6 7 8 9 10 11 12 13

▶**GARDEN**

COMPOUNDS

❶ [sometimes also 苑 2239] [also suffix] [original meaning] **garden, park, plantation, farm**

園芸 *engei* gardening, horticulture
田園 *den'en* fields and gardens, rural districts
庭園 *teien* garden, park
公園 *kōen* park, public garden
楽園 *rakuen* paradise
果樹園 *kajuen* fruit garden, orchard

❷ **public premises, institution**

学園 *gakuen* educational institution, school
動物園 *dōbutsuen* zoo
遊園地 *yūenchi* amusement park
幼稚園 *yōchien* kindergarten

❸ⓐ abbrev. of 幼稚園 *yōchien*: **kindergarten**
ⓑ counter for kindergartens
園児 *enji* kindergarten children
入園 *nyūen* entering kindergarten
四百園 *yonhyakuen* 400 kindergartens
❹ [sometimes also 苑 2239] **suffix after names of business establishments such as restaurants and tea shops, esp. where there are gardens**
永谷園 *nagatanien* Nagatanien (name of a tea shop)

INDEPENDENT

【en 園】 (our) kindergarten; park; zoo
園の方針 *en no hōshin* policy of our kindergarten

KUN

【sono 園】 *literary* garden; institution
花園 *hanazono* flower garden
学びの園 *manabi no sono* educational institution

SYNONYMS

❶ **gardens**
庭 GARDEN → 3114
苑 IMPERIAL GARDEN → 2239
❶ **cultivated fields**
甫 vegetable garden → 3549
畑 FIELD → 905
牧 PASTURE → 873
田 RICE FIELD → 3041
❸ **schools**
校 SCHOOL → 929
学 EDUCATIONAL INSTITUTION → 2555
小 elementary school → 7
中 junior high school → 3451
高 high school → 2097
大 UNIVERSITY → 3416
院 INSTITUTION → 454
塾 PRIVATE SCHOOL → 2860
❹ **restaurant suffixes**
苑 restaurant suffix → 2239
閣 high-class restaurant suffix → 3327
亭 quality restaurant suffix → 2072

USAGE

en
園
[sometimes also 苑] [also suffix] garden, park, plantation, farm
苑
[sometimes also 園] Imperial garden, garden, park
★苑, now mostly replaced by 園, was formerly used in the sense of garden or farm, but is now more or less limited to the Imperial garden and proper names, such as 神宮外苑 *jingūgaien*.

圓
3157

▶CIRCLE ▶YEN
nonstandard for 円 2955

3-10 口

遮 遮 遮 遮
3158 SHA saegi(ru)

ⒸⒽ 遮 zhē

Radical	Strokes
⻌ 162	14-3-11
Grade	**Freq**
Jōyō	1942
口 3-3-11	

3-11 ⻌

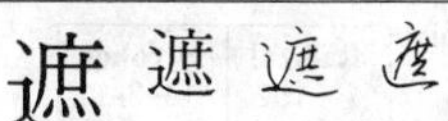

▶INTERRUPT

COMPOUNDS

❶ⓐ **interrupt, block (off), intercept, obstruct**
ⓑ shield, screen, cover
遮断する *shadan suru* intercept, interrupt, block, blockade, isolate
遮蔽 *shahei* shield, cover, screen; *elec* shielding
遮光する *shakō suru* shield [shade] light
❷ used phonetically for *sha*, esp. in the transliteration of Sanscrit Buddhist terms
遮二無二 *shanimuni* recklessly, madly
毘盧遮那仏 *birushanabutsu* Vairocana-buddha

INDEPENDENT

【sha 遮】 name of chess piece in shogi (Japanese chess): *hisha*, rook

KUN

【saegi(ru) 遮る】 interrupt, block (off), intercept, obstruct; shield, screen, cover
道を遮る *michi o saegiru* block the way
光線を遮る *kōsen o saegiru* intercept the light
話を遮る *hanashi o saegiru* interrupt (a person)

SYNONYMS

❶ⓐ **obstruct and hinder**

阻 OBSTRUCT → 348
妨 HINDER → 238
障 hinder → 715
害 stand in the way → 2272

❷ **phonetic [s]/[sh]**

沙 phonetic [sha] → 266
世 phonetic [se] → 3496
須 phonetic [shu] → 574
修 phonetic [shu] → 123
西 phonetic [su] → 3520
相 phonetic [sō] → 900

3-11 ⻌

遭 遭 遭 遭

3159 SŌ a(u) a(waseru)

CH 遭 zāo

Radical	Strokes
⻌ 162	14-3-11
Grade	**Freq**
Jōyō	1059
□ 3-3-11	

1 2 3 4 5 6 7 8 9 10 11 12 13 14

▶MEET WITH

COMPOUNDS

● [original meaning] (come upon, esp. by accident) **meet with (disaster)**

遭難する *sōnan suru* meet with disaster
遭遇する *sōgū suru* encounter, come across

KUN

【a(u) 遭う】[also 遇う] (come upon, esp. by accident) meet with, encounter, be confronted

酷い目に遭う *hidoi me ni au* have a bad time

【a(waseru) 遭わせる】 subject to (an unfavorable experience), expose to

痛い目に遭わせる *itai me ni awaseru* make (a person) pay for (something)

SYNONYMS

● **meet**

遇 ENCOUNTER → 3135
会 MEET → 2020
見 SEE → 2544
謁 BE GRANTED AN AUDIENCE → 1570

HOMOPHONES

au ⇨ 遇 3135 会 2020 合 2019
awaseru ⇨ 会 2020 合 2019 併 83

NOTE

⇨ see USAGE notes at 会 2020 and 合 2019

3-11 ⻌

適 適 適 適

3160 TEKI kana(u)▲

CH 适 shì

Radical	Strokes
⻌ 162	14-3-11
Grade	**Freq**
Jōyō-5	671
□ 3-3-11	

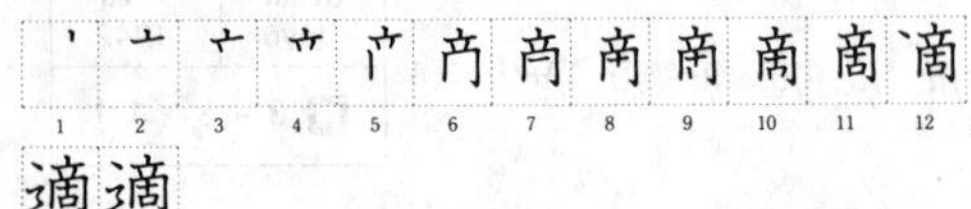

1 2 3 4 5 6 7 8 9 10 11 12 13 14

▶SUITABLE

COMPOUNDS

❶ⓐ **suitable, fit, proper, appropriate, right**
ⓑ suit, fit

適当な *tekitō na* suitable, fit; irresponsible
適正な *tekisei na* proper, appropriate, reasonable, right
適切な *tekisetsu na* appropriate, adequate, proper
適時の *tekiji no* timely, opportune
適宜 *tekigi* suitableness, appropriateness; suitably
適量 *tekiryō* proper quantity
適者 *tekisha* suitable person
最適な *saiteki na* optimum
適用する *tekiyō suru* apply
適法 *tekihō* legality, lawfulness
適応 *tekiō* adaptation, adjustment
適合する *tekigō suru* suit, be fit, conform (to)

❷ agreeable

快適な *kaiteki na* comfortable, pleasant, agreeable
悠悠自適の生活 *yūyūjiteki no seikatsu* life free from worldly cares

INDEPENDENT

【tekisuru 適する】 suit, fit; be suitable [appropriate]; be qualified [competent]

KUN

【kana(u) 適う】
①ⓐ suit, serve (the purpose)
ⓑ agree with, be consistent with
道理に適う *dōri ni kanau* stand to reason
② (of a wish) be fulfilled, be realized, be granted
望みが適う *nozomi ga kanau* have one's wish realized
③ be able to, can (do)
適わない *kanawanai* be unable, be beyond one's power

SYNONYMS

❶ⓐ **suitable**
当 proper → 2177
宜 RIGHT → 2223
便 CONVENIENT → 95
ⓑ **fit**
合 FIT → 2019
揃える MAKE UNIFORM → 590

USAGE

kanau
適う
①ⓐ suit, serve (the purpose)
ⓑ agree with, be consistent with
② (of a wish) be fulfilled, be realized, be granted
③ be able to, can (do)
敵う
① be a match for, compare with
② stand, bear

HOMOPHONES

kanau ⇨ 敵 1864

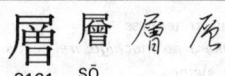

層 層 層 层

3161 sō

CH 层 céng

Radical	Strokes
戸 44	14-3-11
Grade	**Freq**
Jōyō-6	829
口 3 - 3 - 1	

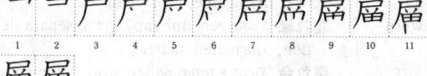

3-11 戸

1 2 3 4 5 6 7 8 9 10 11 12 13 14

▶STRATUM

COMPOUNDS

❶ [also suffix]
ⓐ **stratum, layer**
ⓑ *geol* stratum, measures; seam, bed
ⓒ *biol* stratum
ⓓ counter for layers
層状 *sōjō* stratiform, stratified
成層圏 *seisōken* stratosphere
電離層 *denrisō* ionosphere
地層 *chisō* layer, stratum
鉱層 *kōsō* ore bed
断層 *dansō* dislocation, fault
高木層 *kōbokusō* tree stratum
一層目 *issōme* first layer
❷ [also suffix] **social stratum, class, bracket**
階層 *kaisō* social stratum, class; tier
下層 *kasō* lower classes
社会層 *shakaisō* stratum of society
知識層 *chishikisō* the intellectual class
読者層 *dokushasō* class of readers [subscribers]
❸ⓐ story (of a building)
ⓑ counter for stories
高層ビル *kōsōbiru* skyscraper
三層楼 *sansōrō* three-storied house [building]

INDEPENDENT

【sō 層】stratum, layer; seam, bed; stratum, class
石炭の層 *sekitan no sō* coal bed, coal seam

SYNONYMS

❷ **class**
等 CLASS → 2682
流 class → 441
級 GRADE → 1279
段 grade → 1144
位 RANK → 61
階 RANK → 624
身 social status → 3553
格 STATUS → 926
❸ **floor**
階 FLOOR → 624

3-11 广

腐 3162

CH 腐 fǔ

FU kusa(ru) -kusa(ru) kusa(reru) kusa(re) kusa(rasu) kusa(su)▲

Radical	Strokes
肉 130	14-6-8
Grade	Freq
Jōyō	1319
口 3-3-11	

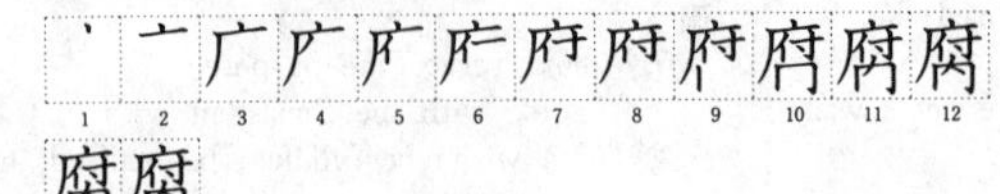

▶**ROT**

COMPOUNDS

❶ [original meaning] **rot, decay, decompose; corrode**
腐敗する *fuhai suru* rot, decay; become corrupt
腐朽 *fukyū* deterioration, decay
腐食 *fushoku* corrosion; erosion
防腐 *bōfu* preservation from decay
豆腐 *tōfu* tofu (Japanese bean curd)

❷ worn-out, worthless, useless, old
腐儒 *fuju* pedant, worthless scholar
陳腐な *chinpu na* old-fashioned, trite, worn-out

❸ worry, be anxious
腐心する *fushin suru* rack one's brains

❹ [rare] castration (as a punishment in ancient China)
腐刑 *fukei* castration

KUN

【kusa(ru) 腐る】 rot, decay, decompose; corrode; feel blue; be corrupted
腐り *kusari* rottenness, decay; corruption
腐るな *Kusaru na* Cheer up!
腐り果てる *kusarihateru* be completely rotten; be corrupted to the bottom

【-kusa(ru) -腐る】 suffix indicating speaker's spite
威張り腐る *ibarikusaru* be puffed up, throw one's weight around

【kusa(reru) 腐れる】 go rotten; become worthless
不貞腐れる *futekusareru* have a fit of the sulks; become desperate

【kusa(re) 腐れ】
[in compounds]
① becoming rotten, rottenness
宝の持ち腐れ *takara no mochigusare* pearls thrown before swine
不貞腐れ *futekusare* sulkiness
② base, despicable, worthless
腐れ縁 *kusareen* unhappy yet inseparable relation; mismated marriage
腐れ金 *kusaregane* paltry sum (of money)

【kusa(rasu) 腐らす】 rot, spoil, decay; corrode; be depressed
野菜を腐らす *yasai o kusarasu* spoil the vegetables
気を腐らす *ki o kusarasu* be depressed, be in the blues

【kusa(su) 腐す】 speak ill of, disparage, slander
作品を腐す *sakuhin o kusasu* speak ill of a person's work

SYNONYMS

❶ **decay**
朽 DECAY → 821
枯 WITHER → 898

3-11 广

廓 3163

CH 廓 kuò

KAKU kuruwa

Radical	Strokes
广 53	14-3-11
Grade	Freq
Reference	
口 3-3-11	

COMPOUNDS

[now usu. 郭 *kaku* 1678]

❶ outer enclosure [walls], outline, contour
外廓 *gaikaku* outer block [enclosure]; outline, contour
輪廓 *rinkaku* contour, outline, profile
城廓 *jōkaku* castle, fortress; castle walls, enclosure

❷ district; red-light district
一廓 *ikkaku* a block
遊廓 *yūkaku* licensed quarters, red-light district
廓 *kuruwa* red-light district; area enclosed by earthwork

❸ open, wide, empty
廓清する *kakusei suru* purify, clean up, purge

HOMOPHONES
kuruwa ⇨ 郭 1678

NOTE
⇨ see USAGE note at 郭 1678

incorrect stroke count ⇨ see 3177
(nonstandard for 広 3035)

3-11 广

團
3164

▶**BODY**
nonstandard for 団 3053

3-11 囗

圖
3165

▶**DRAWING**
nonstandard for 図 3071

3-11 囗

遺 遺 遺 遗
3166 I YUI

CH 遗 yí wèi

Radical	Strokes
辶 162	15-3-12
Grade	**Freq**
Jōyō-6	699
□ 3 - 3 - 1 2	

3-12 辶

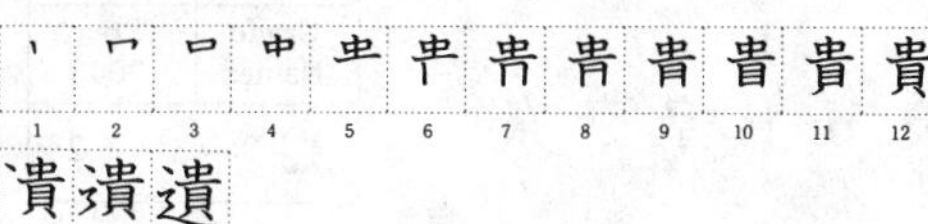

▶**LEAVE BEHIND**

COMPOUNDS

❶ⓐ **leave behind (at one's death), bequeath, bestow; be left behind, remain**
ⓑ [original meaning] **leave (a thing) behind, forget**

遺産 *isan* inheritance, bequest
遺族 *izoku* bereaved family
遺骨 *ikotsu* (skeletal) remains; ashes
遺憾な *ikan na* regrettable
遺伝 *iden* hereditary transmission
遺体 *itai* remains, body, corpse
遺品 *ihin* article left by the deceased, article left behind
遺賢 *iken* able men left out of office
遺言 *yuigon* will, testament
後遺症 *kōishō* sequela, aftereffect (of a disease)
遺失物 *ishitsubutsu* lost article

❷ omit, be negligent
遺漏 *irō* omission, oversight, neglect

❸ discharge involuntarily from the penis, urinate
遺尿 *inyō* bed wetting
遺精 *isei* involuntary emission of semen

SYNONYMS

❶ⓐ **leave**
残す leave → 943

ⓑ **forget**
忘 FORGET → 2036

COMPOUND FORMATION

遺伝 *iden*
遺伝 'hereditary transmission' means to leave behind (遺 ❶ⓐ) and transmit (伝) one's characteristics to posterity.

NOTE
★do not confuse with 遣 3152

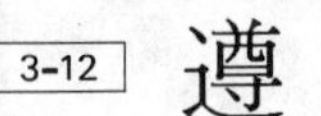

遵 遵 遵 遵

3167 JUN

zūn

Radical	Strokes
辶 162	15-3-12
Grade	**Freq**
Jōyō	1913
口 3-3-12	

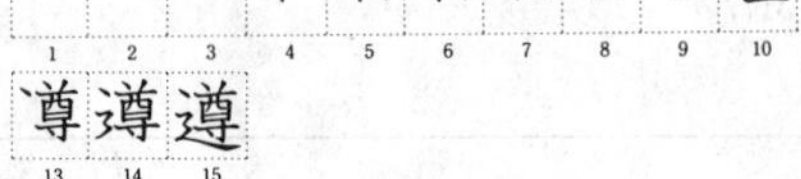

1 2 3 4 5 6 7 8 9 10 11 12 13 14 15

▶OBEY

COMPOUNDS

● [also 順 18] [original meaning] **obey, observe, abide by, follow**

遵守する *junshu suru* observe, obey, follow, conform to

遵法 *junpō* law observance

遵奉する *junpō suru* observe, obey, follow

SYNONYMS

● **obey**

順 OBEY → 18

守 observe → 2173

従 FOLLOW → 415

隷 be subordinate to → 1751

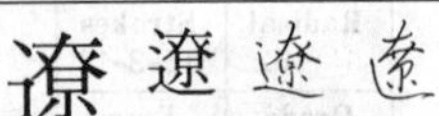

遼 遼 遼 遼

3168 RYŌ NAMES haruka

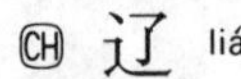

liáo

Radical	Strokes
辶 162	15-3-12
Grade	**Freq**
Names	2043
口 3-3-12	

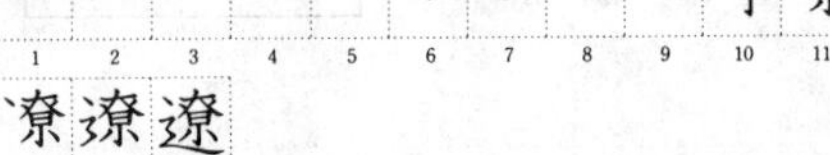

1 2 3 4 5 6 7 8 9 10 11 12 13 14 15

▶FARAWAY

COMPOUNDS

❶ **faraway, remote, distant, stretching a great distance**

遼遠な *ryōen na* remote, far-off

❷ⓐ Liao River in Manchuria

ⓑ Liao Dynasty (916-1125 A.D.)

遼東半島 *ryōtō hantō* Liaotung Peninsula

遼東の豕 *ryōtō no inoko* being self-complacent

西遼 *seiryō* Western Liao Dynasty

NAMES

遼太郎 *ryōtarō* male name

遼 *haruka* male name

SYNONYMS

❶ **distant**

悠 far-off → 2741

遥 FAR → 3141

遠 DISTANT → 3150

隔 APART → 671

離 separated → 1836

COMPOUND FORMATION

遼東の豕 ***ryōtō no inoko***

遼東の豕 'being self-complacent' refers literally to the pigs (豕) of Liaotung province (遼東 ❷ⓐ). An ancient tradition says that the residents of Liaotung province in ancient China thought that the white-headed pigs born in their district must be extremely rare, yet in the neighboring province white-headed pigs were commonplace. The saying 遼東の豕 came to denote self-complacence because of the false confidence they had in their mistaken belief.

選 選 迭 選 選

3169 SEN era(bu)

CH 选 xuǎn

Radical	Strokes
辶 162	15-3-12
Grade	**Freq**
Jōyō-4	113
□ 3-3-12	

3-12 辶

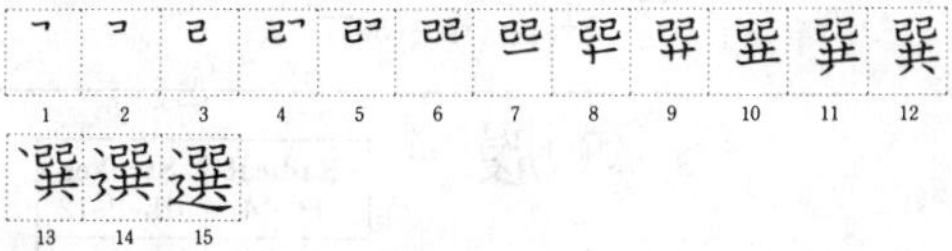

▶CHOOSE

COMPOUNDS

❶ⓐ [original meaning] **choose, select, elect**
ⓑ [also suffix] selection, anthology
選択する *sentaku suru* select, choose
選抜 *senbatsu* selection, choice
選民 *senmin* chosen people
選者 *senja* judge, selector
選考(=銓衡)する *senkō suru* select, screen
選挙 *senkyo* election
選出する *senshutsu suru* elect
選手 *senshu* representative athlete [player]
選任 *sennin* assignment, nomination
予選 *yosen* preliminary match; primary election
名作選 *meisakusen* selection of masterpieces
❷ [also suffix] **election**
当選 *tōsen* election to office; winning (a lottery)
公選 *kōsen* public election, election by popular vote
再選 *saisen* reelection
市長選 *shichōsen* mayoral election
❸ [also 籤 2735] lot, lottery
抽選 *chūsen* drawing of lots

INDEPENDENT

【sen 選】 selection, choice
選に入る *sen ni hairu* be chosen, be selected

KUN

【era(bu) 選ぶ】 choose, prefer, select; elect
上手に選ぶ *jōzu ni erabu* make a good choice
選ばれる *erabareru* be elected
選び出す *erabidasu* select, pick out

SYNONYMS

❶ⓐ **choose**
択 SELECT → 255
採 PICK → 499
摘 pick out → 694
抜 single out → 246
ⓑ **collected works**
集 collection → 2771
❷ **vote and election**
票 VOTE → 2669

遷 遷 遷 遷

3170 SEN

CH 迁 qiān

Radical	Strokes
辶 162	15-3-12
Grade	**Freq**
Jōyō	1824
□ 3-3-12	

3-12 辶

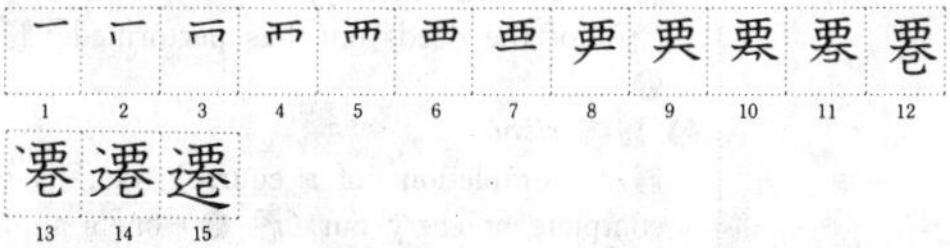

▶TRANSFER

COMPOUNDS

❶ⓐ **transfer, relocate, move**
ⓑ transfer (an official) to
遷座 *senza* transfer of an object of worship
遷宮 *sengū* transfer of a shrine
遷都 *sento* transfer of the capital
左遷 *sasen* relegation, demotion
❷ **undergo transition, change, elapse, pass by**
遷移 *sen'i* transition, change
遷延 *sen'en* delay, procrastination
変遷 *hensen* changes, vicissitudes
❸ [archaic] drive away, exile
遷客 *senkaku* exiled person
❹ [original meaning, now archaic] rise (up to heaven)
升遷 *shōsen* rising up

SYNONYMS

❶ⓐ **move**
動 MOVE → 1778
運 MOVE → 3140
滑 SLIDE → 658
移 SHIFT → 1177
繰る SHIFT ONWARD → 1427
転 remove → 1480

❷ **change and replace**
化 CHANGE INTO, -ize → 21
変 CHANGE → 2069
更 change → 3541
改 change → 243
易 change → 2411
転 turn into → 1480
換 EXCHANGE → 587
交 INTERCHANGE → 2015
替 REPLACE → 2783
代 SUBSTITUTE → 30
迭 ALTERNATE → 3077

3-12
尸

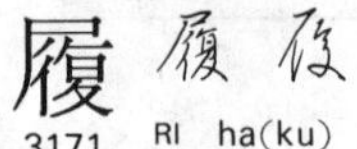
3171 RI ha(ku)

Ⓒⓗ 履 lǚ

Radical	Strokes
尸 44	15-3-12
Grade	**Freq**
Jōyō	1795
口 3-3-12	

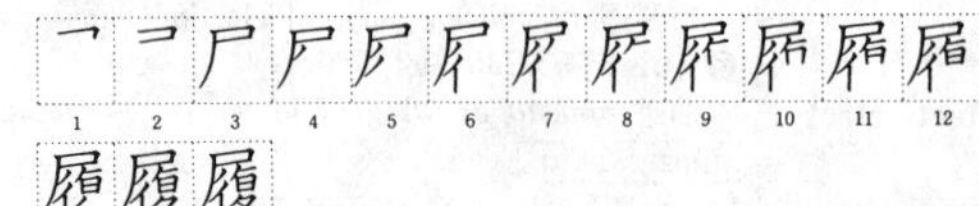

▶FULFILL

COMPOUNDS

❶ (carry out an obligation) **fulfill, carry out, execute, perform, complete**
履行する *rikō suru* fulfill, perform, carry out
履歴 *rireki* personal history, career
履歴書 *rirekisho* résumé, personal history
履修 *rishū* completion (of a course), taking (a course)

❷ **footwear, footgear; sandals, shoes, clogs**
草履 *zōri* Japanese sandals, *zori*
弊履 *heiri* worn-out sandals [shoes]

❸ [original meaning, now archaic] tread, step, trample

KUN

【ha(ku) 履く】 put on footwear, wear (shoes)
履物 *hakimono* footwear, footgear; clogs, sandals
履き違える *hakichigaeru* put on another's shoes; be mistaken

SYNONYMS

❶ **execute**
施 CARRY OUT → 891
執 EXECUTE → 1680
行 ACT → 212
践 IMPLEMENT → 1535
果たす effect → 3560
遂 ACCOMPLISH → 3138

❷ **footwear**
靴 SHOES → 1781
駄 clogs → 1821
足 counter for footwear → 2188

【haku】
○ **wear and put on**
着 PUT ON → 3316
装 DRESS → 2685
帯 WEAR (esp. at the belt) → 2582
被る put on headgear → 1163

USAGE

haku
履く
put on footwear, wear (shoes)
穿く
put on (trousers or socks), wear (a skirt)

HOMOPHONES

haku ⇨ 穿 2251

COMPOUND FORMATION

❶ 履歴 *rireki*
履歴 'personal history, career' is the history (歴) of the deeds one has performed (履 ❶).

❷ 履修 *rishū*
履修 'completion (of a course), etc.' is to complete or carry out (履 ❶) one's studies (修).

3-12
尸

3172

▶STRATUM
nonstandard for 層 3161

3173 KEI yoroko(bi)▲

CH 庆 qìng

Radical	Strokes
心 61	15-4-11
Grade	**Freq**
Jōyō	881
□ 3 - 3 - 1 2	

3-12 广

▶**FELICITATION**

COMPOUNDS

❶ **felicitation, congratulation; celebration, rejoicing**

慶祝 *keishuku* celebration, congratulation
慶弔 *keichō* congratulations and condolences
慶事 *keiji* happy [auspicious] event
同慶 *dōkei* (matter of) mutual congratulations
国慶 *kokkei* National day (of China)

❷ abbrev. of 慶応大学 *keiō daigaku*: Keio University

慶大 *keidai* Keio University
早慶戦 *sōkeisen* Waseda-Keio (baseball) game

INDEPENDENT

【**keisuru** 慶する】felicitate, congratulate

KUN

【**yoroko(bi)** 慶び】[usu. 喜び] felicitation, congratulation; matter for congratulation

SYNONYMS

❶ **celebrating and congratulating**

賀 CONGRATULATE → 2599
寿 CONGRATULATIONS → 3557
祝 CELEBRATE → 913

HOMOPHONES

yorokobi ⇨ 喜 2308 悦 418

NOTE

⇨ see USAGE note at 喜 2308

麾

3174 KI

CH 麾 huī

Radical	Strokes
麻 200	15-11-4
Grade	**Freq**
Reference	
□ 3 - 3 - 1 2	

3-12 广

COMPOUNDS

❶ [archaic] flag, banner, standard
❷ [now also 旗 1047] command

麾下の *kika no* under one's command, under the banner (of)

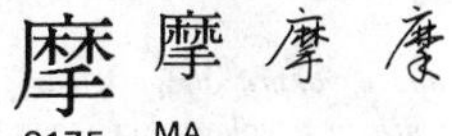

3175 MA

CH 摩 mó mā

Radical	Strokes
手 64	15-4-11
Grade	**Freq**
Jōyō	1085
□ 3 - 3 - 1 2	

3-12 广

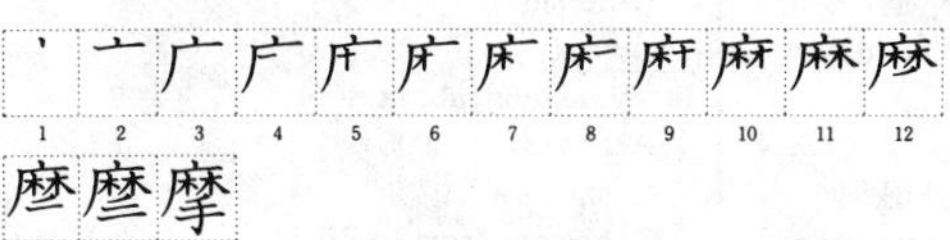

▶**RUB AGAINST**

COMPOUNDS

❶ [sometimes also 磨 3181] **rub against, rub, chafe, scrape, wear away**

摩擦 *masatsu* friction; rubbing, chafing
摩耗 *mamō* wear, abrasion
摩滅 *mametsu* wear, defacement
摩損 *mason* wear and tear, friction loss, abrasion

❷ graze, scrape, nearly touch

摩天楼 *matenrō* skyscraper

❸ [original meaning] stroke gently, pat

按摩 *anma* massage; massager, masseur, masseuse

❹ used phonetically for *ma* in the transliteration of Sanscrit Buddhist terms
摩利支天 *marishiten* Marīci, god of war
護摩 *goma* homa, Buddhist rite of cedar-stick burning

INDEPENDENT

【**masuru** 摩する】 graze, scrape, nearly touch
塁を摩する *rui o masuru* rival, run close to

SYNONYMS

❶ **polish and rub**
擦 RUB → 790
磨 POLISH → 3181
削 CUT BY CHIPPING → 1448
研 GRIND → 1132
❹ **phonetic** [m]
弥 PHONETIC [mi] → 288

NOTE

★do not confuse with 磨 3181

3-12 广

廢 3176

▶**ABOLISH** ▶**WASTE**
nonstandard for 廃 3146

3-12 广

廣 3177

▶**WIDE**
nonstandard for 広 3035

3-12 广

靡 3178

▶**RUB AGAINST**
nonstandard for 摩 3175

3-13 辶

避 3179

避 避 避

HI sa(keru) yo(keru)▲

Ⓒ 避 bì

Radical	Strokes
⻌ 162	16-3-13
Grade	**Freq**
Jōyō	817
口 3-3-13	

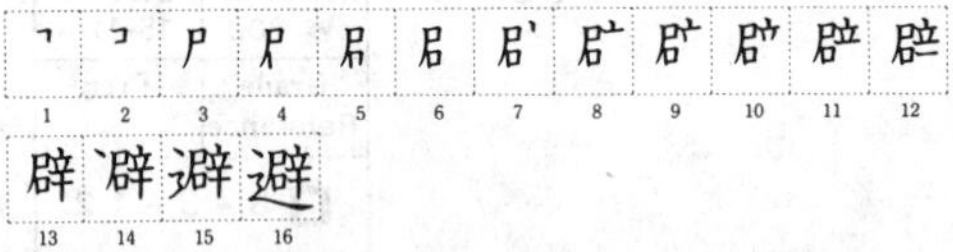

▶**AVOID**

COMPOUNDS

● [original meaning] **avoid, evade, shirk**
避暑 *hisho* summering
避妊 *hinin* contraception
避難 *hinan* refuge, shelter, evacuation
逃避 *tōhi* escape, evasion, flight
退避 *taihi* taking refuge, evacuation
回避する *kaihi suru* evade, dodge, avoid
不可避な *fukahi na* inevitable, unavoidable, unescapable

KUN

【**sa(keru)** 避ける】 avoid, evade, shirk
人の目を避ける *hito no me o sakeru* avert people's eyes
責任を避ける *sekinin o sakeru* shirk a responsibility
ラッシュ時を避ける *rasshuji o sakeru* avoid the rush hours

【**yo(keru)** 避ける】 avoid, shun, evade; avert, ward off
車を避ける *kuruma o yokeru* dodge a car
日射しを避ける *hizashi o yokeru* keep out of the sun

SYNONYMS

● **avoid and abstain**
逃 ESCAPE → 3095
忌 shun → 2207
禁 abstain from → 2795

還 還 還 还

3180 KAN kae(ru)▲

CH 还 huán hái

Radical	Strokes
辶 162	16-3-13
Grade	Freq
Jōyō	1070
□ 3-3-13	

3-13 辶

1 2 3 4 5 6 7 8 9 10 11 12 13 14 15 16

▶RETURN

COMPOUNDS

ⓐ [original meaning] **return, come back, come round**

ⓑ **return, give back, restore**

還流 *kanryū* return current; convection

帰還する *kikan suru* return, come home, be repatriated

償還 *shōkan* repayment, refunding, reimbursement

生還する *seikan suru* return alive; *baseball* reach the home plate

還付する *kanpu suru* return, restore, refund

還元 *kangen* restoration; reduction, deoxidization

返還 *henkan* return, restoration, repayment

送還 *sōkan* sending back, repatriation

奪還 *dakkan* recapture, recovery

KUN

【kae(ru) 還る】[usu. 帰る]

ⓐ return (to one's original position), come back, come home

ⓑ go back [home], take one's leave

家に還る *ie ni kaeru* go back home

SYNONYMS

ⓐ **return**

帰 RETURN → 130

回 turn back → 3055

戻る RETURN → 1942

復 RETURN TO → 575

ⓑ **return and restore**

戻 RETURN → 1942

返 RETURN → 3060

復 RETURN TO → 575

HOMOPHONES

kaeru ⇨ 帰 130 返 3060 反 2945

NOTE

⇨ see USAGE note at 帰 130

磨 磨 磨 磨

3181 MA miga(ku) su(ru)▲

CH 磨 mó mò

Radical	Strokes
石 112	16-5-11
Grade	Freq
Jōyō	1633
□ 3-3-13	

3-13 广

1 2 3 4 5 6 7 8 9 10 11 12 13 14 15 16

▶POLISH

COMPOUNDS

❶ⓐ [now usu. 摩 3175] [original meaning] **polish, grind**

ⓑ wear down, rub away, abrade

磨滅 *mametsu* wear, defacement

研磨する *kenma suru* grind, polish; study hard, brush up

消磨 *shōma* abrasion, wearing out

❷ polish [improve] (one's skill), cultivate, train

錬磨 *renma* training, practice, cultivation

❸ used phonetically for *ma* in the transliteration of Sanscrit Buddhist terms

達磨 *daruma* Bodhidharma; tumbler

KUN

【miga(ku) 磨く】 polish, grind, burnish, rub; polish [improve] (one's skill), cultivate, train

磨き *migaki* polish, burnishing

磨き上げる *migakiageru* polish up

歯磨き *hamigaki* toothpaste; brushing one's teeth

【su(ru) 磨る】 polish, file, rub down

磨りガラス *surigarasu* frosted glass

磨り減らす *suriherasu* wear away [out]; exhaust

SYNONYMS

❶ **polish and rub**

擦 RUB → 790

摩 RUB AGAINST → 3175

研 GRIND → 1132
削 CUT BY CHIPPING → 1448
❷ **cultivate**
琢 POLISH → 971
錬 REFINE → 1741
鍛 train → 1755
練 TRAIN → 1375
修 CULTIVATE → 123
養 FOSTER (one's intellect) → 2365

HOMOPHONES

suru ⇨ 擦 790 摺 693 刷 1273

NOTE

⇨ see USAGE note at 擦 790
★do not confuse with 摩 3175

3-13 广 **麿** 3182

▶**POLISH**
nonstandard for 磨 3181

3-14 广 **應** 3183

▶**RESPOND**
nonstandard for 応 3066

3-15 广 **麿** 麿 麿 麿 3184 maro

CH none (国字)

Radical	Strokes
麻 200	18-11-7
Grade	Freq
Names	2067
口 3-3-15	

▶**CLASSICAL MALE NAME SUFFIX**

KUN

【maro 麿】
① classical suffix for forming male names
坂上田村麿 *sakanoueno tamuramaro* Sakanoue Tamuramaro
② [archaic] I—used esp. by noblemen mainly in the Heian period

NAMES

人麿 *hitomaro* male name
秀麿 *hidemaro* male name

SYNONYMS

【maro】
① **name suffixes**
郎 MALE NAME SUFFIX → 1289
彦 MALE NAME ELEMENT → 3295
-子 female name element → 3390
② **first person pronouns**
予 I (*pompous*) → 1983
余 I (*pompous*) → 2042
朕 IMPERIAL WE → 949
吾 I (*elegant*) → 2407
私 I (*polite*) → 1115
僕 I (*familiar*) → 164
俺 I (*intimate*) → 110
自 SELF → 3525
我 SELF → 3548
己 ONESELF → 3380
身 ONE'S PERSON → 3553

3-15 广 **麿** 3185

▶**CLASSICAL MALE NAME SUFFIX**
nonstandard for 麿 3184

3-16 广 **頋**

incorrect classification ⇨ see 1845

3-18 尸 **屬** 3186

▶**BELONG TO**
nonstandard for 属 3145

魔 魔 魔 魔 ㊥ 魔 mó

3187 MA

Radical	Strokes
鬼 194	21-10-11
Grade	Freq
Jōyō	1316
☐ 3-3-18	

3-18 广

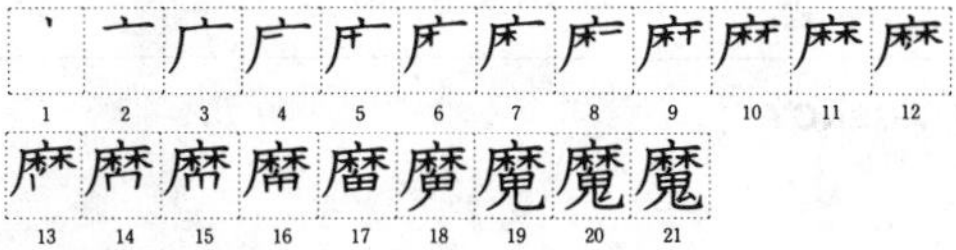

▶**DEMON**

COMPOUNDS

❶ **demon, devil, evil spirit**

魔神 *majin* evil spirit, devil
魔物 *mamono* goblin, apparition
悪魔 *akuma* devil, demon, satan
病魔 *byōma* demon of ill health; disease
邪魔 *jama* hindrance, obstruction, impediment

❷ (related to the powers of a demon) **magic(al), evil**

魔法 *mahō* magic, sorcery, witchcraft
魔法瓶 *mahōbin* thermos bottle
魔術 *majutsu* magic, sorcery, witchcraft
魔力 *maryoku* magical powers
魔女 *majo* witch, sorceress
魔笛 *mateki* magic flute; The Magic Flute (by Mozart)
魔手 *mashu* evil power

❸ [also suffix] (person with excessive passion for something) maniac

放火魔 *hōkama* pyromaniac
収集魔 *shūshūma* collecting maniac
通り魔 *tōrima* phantom killer [robber]

INDEPENDENT

【**ma** 魔】 demon, evil spirit, evil influence
魔が差す *ma ga sasu* be tempted by an evil spirit
魔の海峡 *ma no kaikyō* dangerous strait

SYNONYMS

❶ **supernatural and evil beings**

怪 monster → 297
鬼 DEVIL → 2657
霊 SPIRIT → 2805
精 SPIRIT → 1366

❷ **miraculous**

妙 MARVELOUS → 239

❸ **mania and maniacs**

狂 maniac → 269
熱 fever → 2866
痴 infatuated → 3286

COMPOUND FORMATION

❶ 邪魔 *jama*

邪魔 'hindrance, etc.' originally represented an evil (邪) demon (魔 ❶) that stood in the way of Buddhist righteousness.

❷ 魔法瓶 *mahōbin*

魔法瓶 'thermos bottle' is a bottle (瓶) that keeps water warm by "magical" (魔 ❷) means (法).

魔 ▶**DEMON**

3188 nonstandard for 魔 3187

3-18 广

鷹 鷹 鷹 ㊥ 鹰 yīng

3189 YŌ Ō taka

Radical	Strokes
鳥 196	24-11-13
Grade	Freq
Names	1995
☐ 3-3-21	

3-21 广

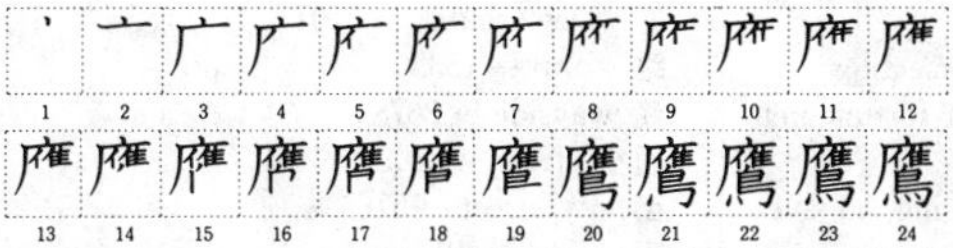

▶**HAWK**

COMPOUNDS

ⓐ [original meaning] **hawk, falcon**

ⓑ as unhurried and calm as the flight of a hawk

放鷹 *hōyō* hawking, falconry
鷹揚(=大様)な *ōyō na* largehearted, generous

KUN

【**taka** 鷹】 hawk, falcon
鷹匠 *takajō* falconer, hawker

夜鷹 *yotaka* Japanese goatsucker; nightwalker

NAMES

鷹取 *takatori* surname

三鷹 *mitaka* place name

SYNONYMS

ⓐ **wild birds**

隼 FALCON → 2756

鶴 CRANE → 1850

雀 SPARROW → 2469

3-22 广

廳 3190

▶**GOVERNMENT AGENCY**

nonstandard for 庁 3034

4-1 辶

辷 3191 sube(ru) sube(rasu)

CH none (国字)

Radical	Strokes
辶 162	5-4-1
Grade	**Freq**
Reference	
3-4-1	

COMPOUNDS

[now usu. 滑る *suberu*]

❶ [original meaning] slip

辷らす *suberasu* let slip, slide, glide

地辷り *jisuberi* landslide

口が辷る *kuchi ga suberu* make a slip of the tongue

❷ flunk an (entrance) examination

辷り止め *suberidome* tire chains; creepers; taking the entrance examination to a university as a safety measure in case one fails at other universities

HOMOPHONES

suberu ⇨ 滑 658

NOTE

⇨ see USAGE note at 滑 658

4-1 于

牙 incorrect classification ⇨ see 3488

4-2 辶

辻 辻 辻 3192 tsuji

CH none (国字)

Radical	Strokes
辶 162	6-4-2
Grade	**Freq**
Non-Jōyō	1435
3-4-2	

一 十 十 汁 汁 辻 (1 2 3 4 5 6)

▶**CROSSROADS**

KUN

[tsuji 辻]

ⓐ [original meaning] crossroads, crossing, intersection

ⓑ street, roadside, street corner

四つ辻 *yotsutsuji* crossroads, intersection

辻占 *tsujiura* slip of paper with a fortune-telling message

辻辻に *tsujitsuji ni* at every crossing, at every street corner

辻君 *tsujigimi* streetwalker, nightwalker

辻説法 *tsujiseppō* street preaching

辻店 *tsujimise* street stall

SYNONYMS

[tsuji]

○ **ways and routes**

岐 forked road → 241

道 WAY (path) → 3134

途 WAY (route) → 3107

路 ROAD → 1533

筋 wayside → 2678

通り street → 3109

街 city street → 576

径 PATH → 291

軌 TRACK → 1445

線 LINE → 1392

込 ▶MOVE INWARD ▶EMPHATIC VERBAL SUFFIX
nonstandard for 込 3030
3193

気 氣 気 气 ㊥ 气 qì
3194 KI KE

Radical	Strokes
气 84	6-4-2
Grade	**Freq**
Jōyō-1	69
☐ 3 - 4 - 2	

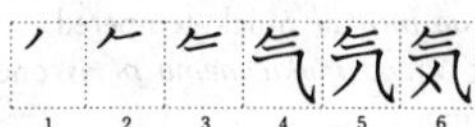

▶GAS ▶SPIRIT

COMPOUNDS

❶ⓐ [original meaning] **gas, vapor**
ⓑ **air**
気体 *kitai* gas, vapor, gaseous body
気化 *kika* gasification, evaporation
空気 *kūki* air; atmosphere
排気 *haiki* exhaust, used steam; exhaustion, evacuation
気流 *kiryū* air [atmospheric] current, air stream
気団 *kidan* air mass
冷気 *reiki* cold air; cold, chill
換気 *kanki* ventilation
❷ⓐ **atmosphere**
ⓑ (psychological environment) atmosphere, tone
気圧 *kiatsu* atmospheric [air] pressure
気温 *kion* (atmospheric) temperature
大気 *taiki* the atmosphere
気運 *kiun* luck, tendency, opportunity
景気 *keiki* things, times; business conditions
雰囲気 *fun'iki* atmosphere, mood
殺気 *sakki* menace of death, reek of murder
熱気 *nekki* hot air, heat; fevered air, enthusiasm
❸ breath
気管 *kikan* trachea, windpipe
気息 *kisoku* breathing; breath
一気に *ikki ni* at a breath, in one breath; on [at] a stretch [stroke]
❹ⓐ **vital energy, spirit, breath of life, vitality**
ⓑ vital energy in Chinese medicine: *ki, chi*
気力 *kiryoku* energy, spirit, vitality, pluck, guts
気勢 *kisei* spirit, ardor
病気 *byōki* illness, sickness, disease
元気 *genki* vigor, energy; spirits; health
意気盛んだ *ikisakan da* be in high spirits
勇気 *yūki* courage, valor, bravery, nerve
活気 *kakki* vigor, spirit, animation
精気 *seiki* spirit, energy, essence
❺ **energy, force**
電気 *denki* electricity; electric light
磁気 *jiki* magnetism
❻ **natural phenomenon**
気象 *kishō* atmospheric phenomena, weather conditions
気候 *kikō* climate, weather; season
天気 *tenki* weather, atmospheric conditions; fine weather
❼ⓐ **spirit, mind, consciousness**
ⓑ (emotional state) **spirits, one's feelings, mood, frame of mind**
気付く *kizuku* notice, become aware of, find out
気の毒な *kinodoku na* pitiable, miserable; regrettable, too bad
気構え *kigamae* readiness of mind, preparedness; expectation
気絶 *kizetsu* fainting
気違い *kichigai* insanity; insane person, lunatic
正気 *shōki* consciousness; sanity, reason
狂気 *kyōki* insanity, madness
気持 *kimochi* feeling, sensation, mood
気分 *kibun* feeling, mood; atmosphere
気前 *kimae* generosity
気軽な *kigaru na* lighthearted, cheerful; ready
人気 *ninki* popularity; temper of the people; business conditions
平気 *heiki* nonchalance, unconcern; composure
本気 *honki* seriousness, earnestness
❽ [also suffix] **temperament, temper, disposition, one's nature, character**
気質 *kishitsu* temperament, disposition
気性 *kishō* disposition, nature, temper
気難しい *kimuzukashii* moody, hard to please
強気の *tsuyoki no* strong, firm, bullish
短気な *tanki na* short-tempered, hot-tempered
負けん気 *makenki* unyielding [competitive] spirit
移り気 *utsurigi* caprice, fickleness, frivolity
❾ **mind to do something, intention, will**
気儘な *kimama na* willful, selfish

気乗りしない *kinori shinai* halfhearted, indisposed
買い気 *kaiki* bullish [buying] sentiment [feeling]
やる気 *yaruki* mind to do something, determination to do
眠気 *nemuke* sleepiness
吐き気 *hakike* nausea
何気無い *nanigenai* casually, unconcernedly

⑩ **care, attention, precaution**
気遣う *kizukau* feel anxious about, worry about, have apprehensions of
気付 *kizuke* c/o (care of)

⑪ [also suffix] sign, indication, symptom, trace, air
気配 *kehai* sign, indication
気品 *kihin* dignity, grace, nobility
気取る *kidoru* make an affected pose, assume airs
気高い *kedakai* noble, lofty, high-minded
人気が無い *hitoke ga nai* no sign of life
色気 *iroke* sex appeal, sensuality; fancifulness; inclination, interest; shade of color
飾り気 *kazarike* affectation, love of display
得意気に *tokuige ni* with an air of expertise
惜し気に *oshige ni* grudgingly

⑫ⓐ smell, odor
ⓑ flavor, a dash of
香気 *kōki* fragrance, perfume, scent
臭気 *shūki* offensive [odious] smell, bad [foul] odor, stench
気味 *kimi* feeling, sensation; a touch [tinge] (of)
味気無い *ajikenai* (=*ajikinai*) wearisome, insipid
塩気 *shioke* salty
湿気 *shikke* (=*shikki*) moisture, dampness, humidity

⑬ [prefix] somehow, in some way or other
気だるい *kedarui* listless, languid, languish
気圧される *keosareru* be overawed [overpowered]

⑭ period of fifteen days
節気 *sekki* seasonal turning point (that comes every fifteen days)

⑮ unclassified compounds
中気 *chūki* palsy, paralysis
脚気 *kakke* beriberi

INDEPENDENT

【ki 気】

①ⓐ spirit, mind, consciousness
ⓑ (emotional state) spirits, one's feelings, mood, frame of mind
気が狂う *ki ga kuruu* go mad [insane]
気に掛かる *ki ni kakaru* weigh on one's mind
気にする *ki ni suru* take to heart, be concerned
気に入る *ki ni iru* like, be pleased with
気が付く *ki ga tsuku* notice, become aware; be attentive
気が重い *ki ga omoi* be heavyhearted, be dispirited
気の詰まる *ki no tsumaru* stuffy
気がする *ki ga suru* have a feeling [hunch]

② temperament, temper, disposition, one's nature, character
気が強い *ki ga tsuyoi* strong of heart
気が短い *ki ga mijikai* quick-tempered
気の向く儘に *ki no muku mama ni* at one's fancy [whim]
気を悪くする *ki o waruku suru* take offense, feel hurt

③ mind to do something, intention, will
気が変わる *ki ga kawaru* change one's mind
何の気無しに *nan no ki nashi ni* unintentionally, casually
したい気がする *shitai ki ga suru* feel like doing

④ care, attention, precaution
気を付ける *ki o tsukeru* take care of, pay attention to
気を許す *ki o yurusu* be off one's guard
気が利く *ki ga kiku* be smart [tactful]

⑤ⓐ atmosphere, air
ⓑ (psychological environment) atmosphere, tone
山の気 *yama no ki* mountain air
清新の気 *seishin no ki* general mood of freshness

⑥ sign, indication, symptom, trace, air
復興の気 *fukkō no ki* signs of revival

⑦ flavor, savor, dash of
気が抜ける *ki ga nukeru* become stale, lose flavor

⑧ vital energy in Chinese medicine: *ki*, *chi*

【ke 気】

① sign, indication, symptom, trace, air
火の気 *hi no ke* trace of fire
風邪の気 *kaze no ke* signs of a cold

② flavor, savor, dash of
酒の気が有る *sake no ke ga aru* smack of wine

SPECIAL READINGS

意気地 *ikuji* (=*ikiji*) pride, (a sense of) honor, self-respect
気質▲ *katagi* spirit, character

SYNONYMS

❶ **gas and vapor**
空 AIR → 2227
汽 STEAM → 264

❷ **atmosphere**
雰 ATMOSPHERE → 2772

❸ **breathe and blow**
息 BREATH → 2647
吸 BREATHE IN → 202

呼 breathe out → 273
吹 BLOW → 231
❹ⓐ **life energy**
精 SPIRIT → 1366
❺ **energy and force**
力 POWER, force → 3371
勢 physical power → 2857
圧 PRESSURE → 2970
❻ **phenomenon**
物 physical phenomena → 874
象 PHENOMENON → 2134
❼ⓐ **psyche**
精 SPIRIT (mind) → 1366
霊 SPIRIT (soul) → 2805
魂 SOUL, spirit → 1063
神 MIND → 912
心 HEART → 11
腹 heart → 1034
衷 INNER HEART → 2575
襟 inner mind → 1252
胸 breast → 951
懐 BOSOM → 763
ⓑ **feeling**
心 HEART → 11
情 EMOTION → 482
感 SENSE (feeling) → 2835
❽ **nature and character**
性 NATURE → 299
質 QUALITY → 2808
品 grade of excellence → 2248
柄 CHARACTER → 897
格 (good) character → 926
❾ **will and intention**
念 thought of doing something → 2059
図 intention → 3071
意 MIND → 2136
志 AMBITION → 2199
趣 PURPOSE → 3317
欲 DESIRE → 1475
❿ **attention**
念 attention → 2059
⓫ **signs**
候 indication → 119
徴 SYMPTOM → 683
症 symptom (of a disease) → 3280
兆 OMEN → 225
⓬ⓐ **smell and fragrance**
臭 BAD SMELL → 2633
香 SWEET SMELL → 2568
馨 PERFUME → 2879
芳 FRAGRANT → 2210
薫 BALMY → 2371
郁 AROMATIC → 1288

NOTE
⇨ see COMPOUND FORMATION for
気前 *kimae* ⇨ 前 2266
元気 *genki* ⇨ 元 1929

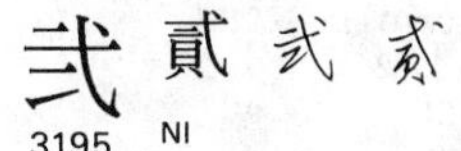
3195 NI

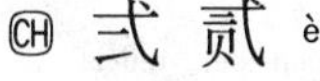
CH 弍 贰 èr

Radical	Strokes
弋 56△	6-3-3
Grade	**Freq**
Jōyō	1821
☐ 3-4-2	

4-2 弋

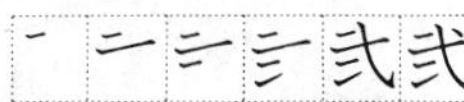
1 2 3 4 5 6

▶**TWO**

COMPOUNDS
● [original meaning] **two**—used in legal documents and checks
金弐阡円 *kin nisen'en* the sum of two thousand yen

INDEPENDENT
【ni 弐】 two (⇨ ●)

SYNONYMS
● **two**
二 TWO → 1922
双 SET OF TWO → 25
対 pair → 831
偶 COUPLE → 132
両 BOTH → 3518

4-2 耂

考 考 考

3196 KŌ kanga(eru) kanga(e)

一 十 土 耂 耂 考
1 2 3 4 5 6

Ⓒⓗ 考 kǎo

Radical	Strokes
耂 125	6-4-2
Grade	**Freq**
Jōyō-2	170
□ 3-4-2	

▶**THINK**

COMPOUNDS

❶ **think, give thought to, consider, reflect**
考慮 *kōryo* consideration, deliberation, careful thought
考察する *kōsatsu suru* consider, contemplate, study
考案 *kōan* idea, plan; project
思考 *shikō* thinking, thought, consideration
一考 *ikkō* consideration, thought

❷ⓐ **study, investigate, research**
ⓑ [also suffix] **study, treatise, monograph**
考査 *kōsa* consideration, test, quiz
考証 *kōshō* investigation, research
考古学 *kōkogaku* archaeology
参考 *sankō* reference, consultation
選考(=銓衡)する *senkō suru* select, screen
論考 *ronkō* study (on English literature)
万葉考 *man'yōkō* A Study of Manyoshu

❸ one's deceased father
先考 *senkō* one's deceased father

KUN

【**kanga(eru) 考える**】 think, consider, reflect, deliberate; imagine, suppose; invent, devise; expect, hope; intend, mean; be prepared for
考え深い *kangaebukai* deep-thinking, thoughtful
考えられない *kangaerarenai* unimaginable
考え出す *kangaedasu* think out, devise, invent; begin to think
万一を考える *man'ichi o kangaeru* be prepared for the worst

【**kanga(e) 考え**】 thought, thinking, consideration, reflection, deliberation; thought, view, opinion; idea, fancy, imagination; intention, resolution
考えを伝える *kangae o tsutaeru* convey one's thoughts

SYNONYMS

❶ **think and consider**
思 THINK → 2564
存 hold an opinion → 2982
案 think out → 2270
想 CONCEIVE → 2828
慮 CONSIDER → 3266
勘 take into consideration → 1777
量 weigh → 2471
惟 MEDITATE → 481
省 INTROSPECT → 2449

❷ⓐ **learn and study**
学 STUDY → 2555
究 STUDY EXHAUSTIVELY → 2203
研 RESEARCH → 1132
攻 specialize → 242
習 LEARN → 2667

【**kangae**】
○ **thought**
念 THOUGHTS → 2059
意 MIND → 2136
想 conception → 2828

4-2 耂

老 老 老

3197 RŌ o(iru) fu(keru)

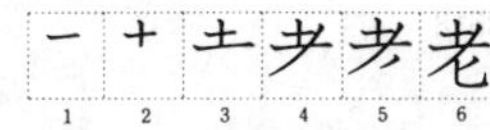

Ⓒⓗ 老 lǎo

Radical	Strokes
老 125	6-6-0
Grade	**Freq**
Jōyō-4	749
□ 3-4-2	

RADICAL 125
Standard form: 老 *oi* 'old person' (耆 耄 耋)
Top variant: 耂 *oikanmuri* or *oigashira* (者 考)
Description: used in characters related to old people

▶**OLD**

COMPOUNDS

❶ⓐ [also prefix] (not young) **old, aged**
ⓑ **grow old, degenerate**
老人 *rōjin* old person, old folks
老年 *rōnen* old age
老齢 *rōrei* old age
老木 *rōboku* old tree
老後 *rōgo* one's old age
老政治家 *rōseijika* venerable statesman

老化 *rōka* aging
老衰 *rōsui* senility
老朽化した *rōkyūka shita* outworn, deteriorated
❷ⓐ [original meaning] **old person**
ⓑ honorific suffix after names of old men
老若 *rōnyaku* the old and the young
敬老 *keirō* respect for the aged
古老(＝故老) *korō* elder, old man; old-timer
野村老 *nomurarō* old Mr. Nomura
❸ⓐ (of long experience) old, experienced, veteran
ⓑ elder, senior member, chief vassal
老練な *rōren na* experienced, veteran
老巧な *rōkō na* veteran, experienced
老成する *rōsei suru* mature, become precocious
長老 *chōrō* elder, senior; superior priest
元老 *genrō* elder [senior] statesman; senior member
❹ (not new) old
老舗 *rōho* (＝*shinise*) old [long-established] shop
老酒 *raochū* vintage wine (esp. rice wine made in Shaoxing)
❺ Laozi (legendary founder of Taoism)

老子 *rōshi* Laozi; the works of Laozi
老荘 *rōsō* Laozi and Zhuangzi

INDEPENDENT

【rō 老】 old age; old person
老と病 *rō to byō* old age and sickness
老を労わる *rō o itawaru* be kind to old people

KUN

【o(iru) 老いる】 grow old
老い *oi* old age; old person
老い先 *oisaki* remaining years (of one's life)
老い込む *oikomu* grow old, weaken with age
【fu(keru) 老ける】 grow old
老け役 *fukeyaku* role of an aged person

SPECIAL READINGS

海老▲ *ebi* lobster, shrimp

SYNONYMS

❶ⓐ **old**
古 OLD (not new) → 2002
故 OLD (of the past) → 1141
旧 old → 14
❷ⓐ **old persons**
翁 OLD MAN → 2108
婆 OLD WOMAN → 2762
ⓑ **honorific suffixes**
翁 honorific suffix → 2108

孝 incorrect stroke count ⇨ see 3205 — 4-2 耂

虍

3198

Radical	Strokes
虍 141	6-6-0
Grade	**Freq**
Radical	
口 3-4-2	

4-2 虍

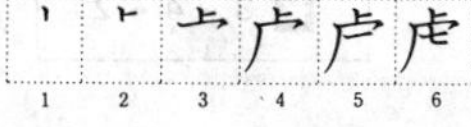

RADICAL 141

Standard form: 虍 *torakanmuri* 'tiger' (虚 虜 虐)
Description: used in characters related to tigers or their qualities

---

危 危 危 危

3199 KI abu(nai) aya(ui) aya(bumu)

CH 危 wēi

Radical	Strokes
㔾 26	6-2-4
Grade	**Freq**
Jōyō-6	703
口 3-4-2	

4-2 ⺈

1 2 3 4 5 6

▶**DANGEROUS**

COMPOUNDS

❶ [original meaning] **dangerous, precarious**
危険な *kiken na* dangerous
危機 *kiki* crisis, emergency
危害 *kigai* injury, harm; danger, risk
危難 *kinan* danger, distress, hazard
危篤 *kitoku* on the verge of death, critical condition
安危 *anki* safety or danger, fate, welfare
❷ fear, apprehend
危惧(＝危虞) *kigu* fear, misgivings

INDEPENDENT

危 symbol on fuel trucks and the like: DANGER!

KUN

【abu(nai) 危ない】 dangerous, perilous, risky; critical, serious, uncertain, insecure; limping; narrow, close; Watch out!

危ながる *abunagaru* be afraid, be apprehensive, doubt

彼の命が危ない *Kare no inochi ga abunai* His life is in danger

【aya(ui) 危うい】 same as **abunai 危ない**

危うく *ayauku* almost, nearly, in imminent danger of

【aya(bumu) 危ぶむ】 fear, apprehend

SYNONYMS

❶ **danger**

険 DANGER → 542

4-2 衤 **衣** incorrect classification ⇨ see 2013

4-2 尸 **艮** incorrect classification ⇨ see 3517

4-2 少 **劣** incorrect classification ⇨ see 2395

4-2 丙 **而** incorrect classification ⇨ see 2027

4-2 尺 **尽** incorrect classification ⇨ see 3050

4-2 内 **肉** 肉 肉

3200 NIKU

CH 肉 ròu

Radical	Strokes
肉 130	6-6-0
Grade	**Freq**
Jōyō-2	775
口 3 - 4 - 2	

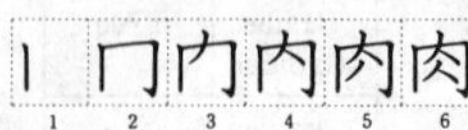

RADICAL 130

Standard form: 肉 *niku* 'flesh' (腐 臠)

Variant: 月 *nikuzuki* (育 能 腕)

Description: used in characters related to the flesh, body or body parts

▶FLESH

COMPOUNDS

❶ⓐ [original meaning] **flesh (of humans or animals)**

ⓑ flesh (of fruit), pulp

ⓒ (article of food) **flesh, meat**

肉腫 *nikushu* sarcoma

肉離れ *nikubanare* torn muscle

筋肉 *kinniku* muscle, sinews

皮肉 *hiniku* cynicism, sarcasm; irony

果肉 *kaniku* flesh, pulp

肉食 *nikushoku* meat diet

牛肉 *gyūniku* beef

食肉 *shokuniku* meat

羊頭狗肉 *yōtōkuniku* using a better name to sell inferior goods, crying wine and selling vinegar

❷ⓐ (degree of fatness) flesh, weight

ⓑ thickness

中肉中背の *chūniku-chūzei no* of medium build

肉付け *nikuzuke* modeling; giving body and substance

肉太 *nikubuto* boldface (type)

❸ **the flesh (versus the spirit)**

肉体 *nikutai* body, flesh

肉欲 *nikuyoku* lusts of the flesh, animal passions

❹ one's flesh and blood, one's kindred
肉親 *nikushin* blood relation
骨肉 *kotsuniku* one's own flesh and blood, kinsmen
❺ unaided by mechanical devices, in the natural state; in person
肉眼 *nikugan* naked eye
肉声 *nikusei* natural voice
肉筆 *nikuhitsu* one's own handwriting, autograph
❻ ink pad
印肉 *inniku* ink pad

INDEPENDENT

【niku 肉】
①ⓐ flesh (of humans or animals)
ⓑ flesh (of fruit), pulp
ⓒ (article of food) flesh, meat
人間の肉 *ningen no niku* human flesh
②ⓐ (degree of fatness) flesh, weight
ⓑ thickness
肉の厚い *niku no atsui* thick
③ the flesh (versus the spirit)
霊と肉 *rei to niku* flesh and spirit
④ ink pad

SYNONYMS

❶ⓐ flesh
筋 MUSCLE → 2678
ⓒ meat
身 meat → 3553
脩 DRIED MEAT → 136
❸ body
体 BODY → 71
身 BODY (esp. vs. mind) → 3553

NOTE

⇨ see COMPOUND FORMATION for
皮肉 *hiniku* ⇨ 皮 3037
羊頭狗肉 *yōtōkuniku* ⇨ 羊 2183

迄 迄 迄 迄

3201 KITSU made

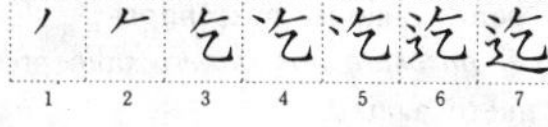

Ⓒⓗ 迄 qì

Radical	Strokes
辶 162	7-4-3
Grade	**Freq**
Non-Jōyō	1812
口 3-4-3	

4-3 辶

▶UP TO

KUN

【made 迄】
①ⓐ (as far as a designated place) up to, as far as
ⓑ (as far as a designated time) up to, till, until, to
京都迄の切符 *kyōto made no kippu* ticket to Kyoto
今迄 *ima made* till now, so far, up to the present
百歳迄生きる *hyakusai made ikiru* live to be a hundred
② (to the limit of) up to, to the extent [limit] of
五十迄数える *gojū made kazoeru* count up to fifty
盗み迄する *nusumi made suru* go to the extent of committing theft
親に迄見放される *oya ni made mihanasareru* be the despair of one's parents
③ [followed by に *ni*] by, by the time, before
次の日曜迄に *tsugi no nichiyō made ni* by next Sunday
年末迄に *nenmatsu made ni* before the end of this year
④ only, merely, just
当然の事をした迄だ *Tōzen no koto o shita made da* I simply have done what I ought to do
君が言うから来た迄だ *Kimi ga iu kara kita made da* I came just because you asked me to
⑤ [in negative constructions]
ⓐ (no) need (to)
ⓑ even (not) so
言う迄も無い *Iu made mo nai* There is no need to say so / but of course
全部ではない迄も *zenbu de wa nai made mo* though all of them may not be included

SYNONYMS

【made】
① direction indicators
至 to → 2182
-行き bound for → 212
-向け (bound) for → 3052
以 TO THE...OF → 41
自 from → 3525
来 since → 3551

4-3 辶

迅 3202

▶SWIFT
nonstandard for 迅 3046

4-3 辶

巡 3203

▶MAKE THE ROUNDS
nonstandard for 巡 3047

4-3 兵

呉

incorrect classification ⇨ see 2549

4-3 戈

戒 戒 戒 3204

KAI imashi(meru)

一 二 チ 开 戒 戒 戒 (1 2 3 4 5 6 7)

CH 戒 jiè

Radical	Strokes
戈 62	7-4-3
Grade	**Freq**
Jōyō	1091
口 3-4-3	

▶CAUTION

COMPOUNDS

❶ⓐ [formerly also 誡 1545] **caution against, admonish, warn, give warning**
ⓑ [original meaning] **take caution (against), guard against, be careful**
戒告 *kaikoku* caution, warning, reprimand
訓戒する *kunkai suru* admonish, warn
自戒する *jikai suru* admonish oneself
戒厳令 *kaigenrei* martial law
戒心 *kaishin* caution, precaution, care
戒慎する *kaishin suru* be cautious, be discreet
警戒 *keikai* caution, precaution, warning; watch, guard, vigilance

❷ commandment, Buddhist commandment, *śīla*, precept
戒律 *kairitsu* commandments, precepts
十戒 *jikkai* the ten precepts of Buddhism
破戒 *hakai* offense against the Buddhist commandments

❸ [formerly 誨 1544 or 誡 1545] instruct, teach
教戒 *kyōkai* exhortation, preaching

INDEPENDENT

【kai 戒】[formerly also 誡 1545] Buddhist commandment
戒を破る *kai o yaburu* break the Buddhist commandments

KUN

【imashi(meru) 戒める】
① [sometimes also 警める]
ⓐ caution against, admonish, warn
ⓑ take caution (against), take precautions, guard against
戒め *imashime* caution, admonition, warning; caution, guard; commandment, precept; binding, bondage
不心得を戒める *fukokoroe o imashimeru* caution a person against misconduct
自ら戒める *mizukara imashimeru* take precautions, guard against
② bind, restrict
後ろ手に戒める *ushirode ni imashimeru* bind a person's hands behind his back

SYNONYMS

❶ⓐ **warn**
警 WARN → 2893
諭 ADMONISH → 1598
告 advise → 2409
ⓑ **take precautions**
警 GUARD AGAINST → 2893
❷ **precept**
訓 precept → 1454

USAGE

❶ **imashimeru**
戒める
① [sometimes also 警める]
ⓐ caution against, admonish, warn
ⓑ take caution (against), take precautions, guard against
② bind, restrict
警める
[usu. 戒める]
ⓐ caution against, admonish, warn
ⓑ take caution (against), take precautions, guard against
❷ **imashime**
戒め
① [sometimes also 警め]
ⓐ caution, admonition, warning
ⓑ caution, guard

ⓒ commandment, precept
② binding, bondage
警め
［usu. 戒め］
ⓐ caution, admonition, warning
ⓑ caution, guard
ⓒ commandment, precept
❸ **jikkai**
十戒
the ten precepts of Buddhism
十誡
the Ten Commandments (of Moses)

HOMOPHONES

imashimeru ⇨ 警 2893
imashime ⇨ 警 2893

戻 incorrect classification ⇨ see 1942

孝 孝 孝

3205 KŌ KYŌ▲

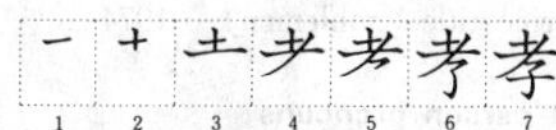

CH 孝 xiào

Radical	Strokes
子 39	7-3-4
Grade	**Freq**
Jōyō-6	1274
口 3 - 4 - 3	

▶FILIAL PIETY

COMPOUNDS

● **filial piety, filial devotion**
孝行 *kōkō* filial piety
孝心 *kōshin* filial devotion [affection]
孝養 *kōyō* discharge of filial duties
孝子 *kōshi* filial child, good son
忠孝 *chūkō* loyalty and filial piety
不孝 *fukō* (=*fukyō*) lack of filial piety, undutifulness

INDEPENDENT

【kō 孝】filial piety, filial devotion
孝は百行の本 *Kō wa hyakkō no moto* Filial devotion is the basis of human conduct

SYNONYMS

● **fidelity**
悌 BROTHERLY LOVE → 424
忠 LOYALTY → 2433
義 faith → 2338
誠 SINCERITY → 1523
実 faithfulness → 2225
信 fidelity → 100
操 constancy → 769
節 moral integrity → 2691

考 incorrect stroke count ⇨ see 3196

希 incorrect classification ⇨ see 2049

君 君 君

3206 KUN kimi -gimi

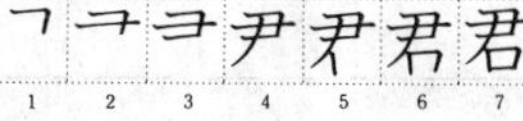

CH 君 jūn

Radical	Strokes
口 30	7-3-4
Grade	**Freq**
Jōyō-3	630
口 3 - 4 - 3	

▶RULER ▶FAMILIAR TITLE ▶YOU

COMPOUNDS

❶ [original meaning] **ruler, sovereign, monarch, king; lord**
君主 *kunshu* monarch, sovereign
君臨する *kunrin suru* reign, rule over, dominate
暴君 *bōkun* tyrant, despot
主君 *shukun* one's lord, one's master
名君 *meikun* wise ruler, enlightened monarch, benevolent lord
❷ **familiar title used in addressing peers,**

friends or inferiors (usu. restricted to men)
山田君 *yamadakun* Mr. Yamada
太郎君 *tarōkun* Taro
❸ term of respect used in addressing family members, peers or men of rank
君子 *kunshi* man of virtue, wise man
諸君 *shokun* Ladies and Gentlemen, my friends, you
父君 *fukun* (your) father

KUN

【kimi 君】
① ruler, sovereign, emperor, one's master [lord]
君が代 *kimigayo* Imperial reign; title of Japanese national anthem
我が君 *wagakimi* my lord
大君 *ōkimi* sovereign, Emperor
② you, old boy—familiar second person pronoun used in addressing friends, peers or inferiors
君達 *kimitachi* you (plural)
君の *kimi no* your

【-gimi -君】 former title of respect used in addressing parents, ancestors and men of rank
母君 *hahagimi* mother
姫君 *himegimi* princess, highborn young lady

SYNONYMS

❶ **rulers**
王 KING → 3439
皇 EMPEROR → 2566
帝 EMPEROR → 2073
天 Heaven's messenger on earth → 3442
❷ **titles of address**
兄 familiar title (seniors) → 2154
氏 COURTESY TITLE → 2951
嬢 Miss → 758
様 FORMAL TITLE → 1052
殿 FORMAL HONORIFIC TITLE → 1792
師 honorific title (clergymen) → 1326
公 honorific title (noblemen) → 1974
【kimi】
② **second person pronouns**
爾 thou → 3587
貴 you (*honorific*) → 2606

4-3 亻
何
incorrect classification ⇨ see 65

4-3 𠂊
角
incorrect classification ⇨ see 2047

4-3 月
局
incorrect classification ⇨ see 3063

4-4 辶
迎
3207
▶WELCOME
nonstandard for 迎 3059

4-4 辶
返
3208
▶RETURN
nonstandard for 返 3060

4-4 辶
近
3209
▶NEAR ▶RECENT
nonstandard for 近 3061

4-4 辶
迄
incorrect stroke count ⇨ see 3201

武 武 𢦏

3210 BU MU

ⒸⒽ 武 wǔ

Radical	Strokes
止 77	8-4-4
Grade	Freq
Jōyō-5	494
□ 3 - 4 - 4	

4-4 弋

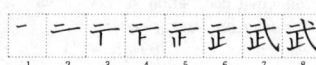

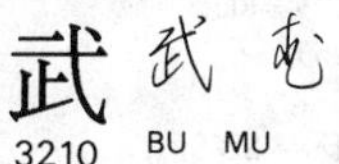

▶**MILITARY**

COMPOUNDS

❶ⓐ **military, martial; military affairs, military might**

ⓑ **military [martial] arts, science of war, Bushido**

武力 *buryoku* military power, armed might
武術 *bujutsu* military [martial] arts
武道 *budō* martial arts
文武 *bunbu* literary and military arts

❷ **warrior, samurai; military man, officer**

武士 *bushi* samurai, warrior
武者 *musha* warrior, soldier
武官 *bukan* military officer

❸ (military equipment) armaments, weapons

武装する *busō suru* arm, bear arms
武器 *buki* weapon, arms

❹ war

武運 *buun* fortunes of war

❺ brave, chivalrous, valiant

武勇 *buyū* bravery, valor

❻ abbrev. of 武蔵 *musashi*, old name for Tokyo-Saitama area

総武線 *sōbusen* Sobu Line (Chiba-Tokyo Railway)

INDEPENDENT

【**bu 武**】military [martial] arts, Bushido; military power, arms

武を練る *bu o neru* train oneself in military arts

SYNONYMS

❶ **military**

兵 military → 2551

❷ **soldiers and warriors**

士 MILITARY MAN → 3405
侍 SAMURAI → 85
兵 SOLDIER → 2551
卒 private → 2055

房 戻 etc.

incorrect classification ⇨ see □ 2－6

4-4 戶

房 肩

incorrect classification ⇨ see ▀ 1－7

4-4 戶

者 者 者 者

3211 SHA mono

ⒸⒽ 者 zhě

Radical	Strokes
耂 125	8-4-4
Grade	Freq
Jōyō-3	26
□ 3 - 4 - 4	

4-4 耂

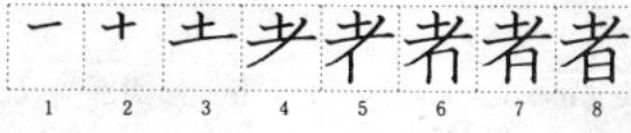

▶**PERSON**

COMPOUNDS

❶ⓐ **person**

ⓑ person concerned, party

弱者 *jakusha* weak person, the weak
死者 *shisha* dead person, the deceased
三者会談 *sansha-kaidan* tripartite conference
第三者 *daisansha* third party

❷ [also suffix] person [one] who performs an action or holds an occupation: **-er** (**as in *reader***)

読者 *dokusha* reader, subscriber
学者 *gakusha* scholar, learned man
記者 *kisha* journalist, reporter; editor
著者 *chosha* author, writer
医者 *isha* doctor
打者 *dasha* batter, hitter
賛成者 *sanseisha* approver, supporter
被爆者 *hibakusha* victim of atomic air raid
科学者 *kagakusha* scientist

❸ used to designate a thing or person

前者 *zensha* the former
後者 *kōsha* the latter
両者 *ryōsha* both

KUN

【mono 者】person, fellow, somebody
若者 *wakamono* young person [fellow], youth
怠け者 *namakemono* idle [lazy] fellow
悪者 *warumono* bad fellow, ruffian

SPECIAL READINGS

猛者 *mosa* stalwart; veteran

SYNONYMS

❶ⓐ person
方 person (*honorific*) → 1963
氏 person (*polite*) → 2951
人 HUMAN BEING → 3368

❷ workers and professionals
人 person of certain category → 3368
師 profession suffix → 1326
士 PROFESSION SUFFIX → 3405
客 skilled person → 2250
家 professional → 2273
員 MEMBER (of a staff) → 2269
屋 colloquial occupation suffix → 3098
手 OCCUPATION SUFFIX → 3456
婦 woman worker → 469
嬢 (unmarried) female worker → 758
夫 MAN LABORER → 3460
匠 CRAFTSMAN → 2990
工 workman → 3381

HOMOPHONES

mono ⇨ 物 874

NOTE

⇨ see USAGE notes at 物 874 and 家 2273

4-4 广

3212 KO tora NAMES take

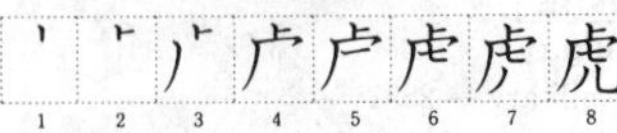

Ⓒⓗ 虎 hǔ

Radical	Strokes
虍 141	8-6-2
Grade	**Freq**
Names	2003
口 3 - 4 - 4	

▶TIGER

COMPOUNDS

● [original meaning] **tiger**
虎穴 *koketsu* tiger's den; dangerous place
虎口 *kokō* tiger's den; dangerous place
虎視眈眈 *koshitantan* on the alert, eye covetously
竜虎の争い *ryūko no arasoi* well matched contest ("serpent and tiger fight")
暴虎馮河 *bōkohyōga* foolhardy courage

KUN

【tora 虎】
① tiger
虎の巻 *tora no maki* key, crib, pony; secret (of a trade)
② drunkard

NAMES

虎ノ門 *toranomon* place name
虎雄 *torao* male name

SYNONYMS

● tiger
寅 THE TIGER → 2289

● undomesticated mammals
熊 BEAR → 2848
象 ELEPHANT → 2134
猪 WILD BOAR → 536
鹿 DEER → 3126
猿 MONKEY → 669
鯨 WHALE → 1882

USAGE

tora
虎
① tiger
② drunkard
寅
third sign of the Oriental zodiac: the Tiger

HOMOPHONES

tora ⇨ 寅 2289

NOTE

⇨ see COMPOUND FORMATION for 暴虎馮河 *bōkohyōga* ⇨ 暴 2515

4-4 广

incorrect classification ⇨ see 2056

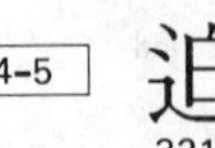

4-5 辶

迫 3213

▶PRESS

nonstandard for 迫 3074

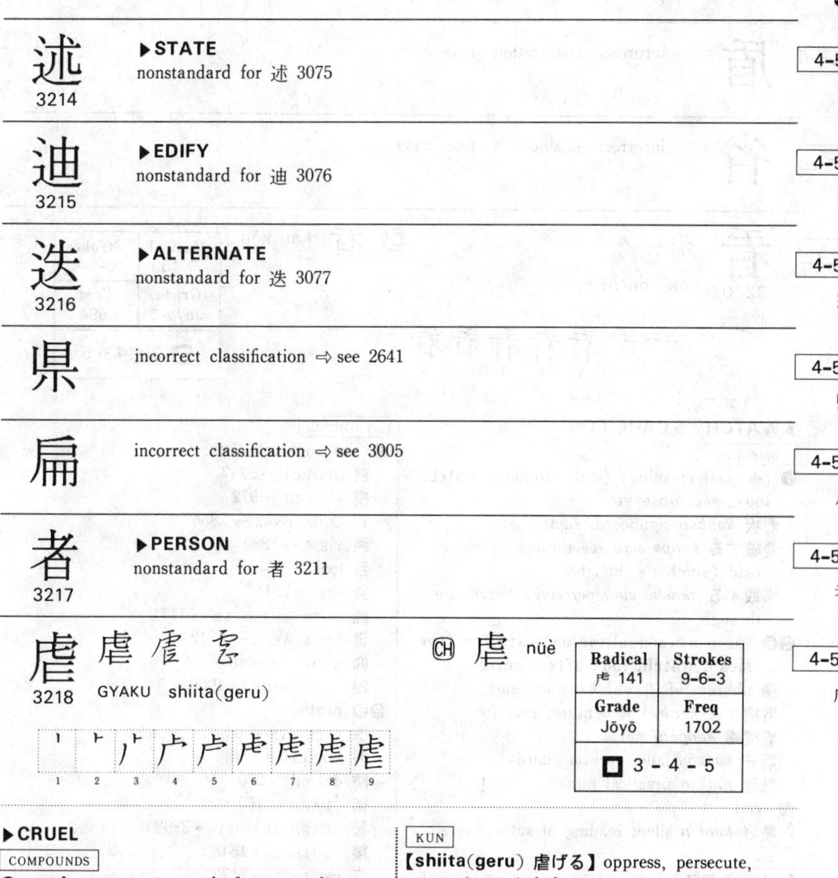

述 3214 ▶STATE
nonstandard for 述 3075 — 4-5 辶

油 3215 ▶EDIFY
nonstandard for 廸 3076 — 4-5 辶

迭 3216 ▶ALTERNATE
nonstandard for 迭 3077 — 4-5 辶

県 incorrect classification ⇨ see 2641 — 4-5 糸

扁 incorrect classification ⇨ see 3005 — 4-5 戸

者 3217 ▶PERSON
nonstandard for 者 3211 — 4-5 耂

虐 3218 虐 虐 虐 GYAKU shiita(geru) — 4-5 虍

CH 虐 nüè

Radical	Strokes
虍 141	9-6-3
Grade	**Freq**
Jōyō	1702
□ 3-4-5	

Stroke order: 1 2 3 4 5 6 7 8 9

▶CRUEL

COMPOUNDS

ⓐ **cruel, savage, tyrannical, oppressive**

ⓑ [original meaning] **treat cruelly, oppress, tyrannize**

虐待 *gyakutai* maltreatment, abuse, cruelty

残虐な *zangyaku na* cruel, atrocious, brutal, inhuman

悪虐無道の *akugyakumudō no* treacherous, heinous

暴虐な *bōgyaku na* tyrannical, cruel, atrocious

虐政 *gyakusei* oppressive [tyrannical] government

虐殺 *gyakusatsu* massacre, butchery, genocide

KUN

【shiita(geru) 虐げる】 oppress, persecute, tyrannize, grind down

虐げられた人人 *shiitagerareta hitobito* downtrodden people, the oppressed

SYNONYMS

ⓐ **cruel**

惨 CRUEL → 483

酷 SEVERE → 1562

残 RUTHLESS → 943

凶 ATROCIOUS → 2961

ⓑ **torture and oppress**

拷 TORTURE → 373

責める torture → 2467

迫 oppress → 3074

虐 3219 ▶CRUEL
nonstandard for 虐 3218 — 4-5 虍

4-5 厂 **盾** incorrect classification ⇨ see 3006

4-5 少 **省** incorrect classification ⇨ see 2449

4-5 手 **看** 看 㸔

3220 KAN mi(ru)▲

Ⓒℍ 看 kàn kān

Radical	Strokes
目 109	9-5-4
Grade	**Freq**
Jōyō-6	994
□ 3 - 4 - 5	

一 二 三 手 看 看 看 看 看 (1 2 3 4 5 6 7 8 9)

▶**WATCH** ▶**CARE FOR**

COMPOUNDS

❶ [original meaning] (look carefully) **watch, look, see, observe**

看板 *kanban* signboard, sign

看破する *kanpa suru* see through, penetrate, read (another's thoughts)

看取する *kanshu suru* perceive, detect; see through

❷ⓐ (keep a watchful eye on) **care for** (**the sick**), **watch, look after, nurse**

ⓑ abbrev. of 看護婦 *kangofu*: nurse

看病する *kanbyō suru* nurse, care for

看護婦 *kangofu* nurse

看守 *kanshu* jailer, prison guard

准看 *junkan* practical nurse

❸ read

看経 *kankin* silent reading of sutra

KUN

【**mi(ru) 看る**】[usu. 見る] take care of, look after

看取る *mitoru* nurse, tend [care for] (the sick)

SYNONYMS

❶ **see and look**

察 INSPECT → 2347

視 REGARD → 972

覧 LOOK OVER → 2854

観 VIEW → 1880

目 look → 3043

見 SEE → 2544

眺 LOOK OUT OVER → 1171

望 LOOK AFAR → 2742

仰 LOOK UP → 48

顧 LOOK BACK → 1900

❷ⓐ **protect**

保 PRESERVE → 96

番 WATCH → 2748

防 defend → 270

衛 GUARD → 760

警 GUARD AGAINST → 2893

護 PROTECT → 1648

守 PROTECT → 2173

HOMOPHONES

miru ⇨ 見 2544 診 1504 観 1880

NOTE

⇨ see USAGE note at 見 2544

4-5 冂 **南** incorrect classification ⇨ see 2082

4-5 尺 **昼** incorrect classification ⇨ see 3097

4-6 辶 **逆** 3221

▶**REVERSE**

nonstandard for 逆 3091

迷 3222 ▶PERPLEXED nonstandard for 迷 3092 4-6 辶

迹 3223 ▶TRACE nonstandard for 跡 1534 4-6 辶

送 3224 ▶SEND nonstandard for 送 3093 4-6 辶

退 3225 ▶RETREAT nonstandard for 退 3094 4-6 辶

逃 3226 ▶ESCAPE nonstandard for 逃 3095 4-6 辶

追 3227 ▶CHASE nonstandard for 追 3096 4-6 辶

氣 3228 ▶GAS ▶SPIRIT nonstandard for 気 3194 4-6 气

扇 incorrect classification ⇨ see 1950 4-6 戸

虐 incorrect stroke count ⇨ see 3218 4-6 广

逐 3229 ▶ONE BY ONE ▶DRIVE OUT nonstandard for 逐 3102 4-7 辶

連 3230 ▶LINK ▶IN SUCCESSION nonstandard for 連 3103 4-7 辶

逝 3231 ▶DEPART THIS LIFE nonstandard for 逝 3104 4-7 辶

速 3232 ▶QUICK nonstandard for 速 3105 4-7 辶

4-7 辶 **途** 3233

▶**WAY**
nonstandard for 途 3107

4-7 辶 **透** 3234

▶**PASS THROUGH** ▶**TRANSPARENT**
nonstandard for 透 3108

4-7 辶 **通** 3235

▶**PASS** ▶**COMMUNICATE**
nonstandard for 通 3109

4-7 辶 **造** 3236

▶**MAKE**
nonstandard for 造 3110

4-7 虍 **虛** 虛 虛 虛 Ⓒ 虚 xū
3237 KYO KO muna(shii)▲ utsu(ro)▲

Radical	Strokes
虍 141	11-6-5
Grade	**Freq**
Jōyō	1529
口 3-4-7	

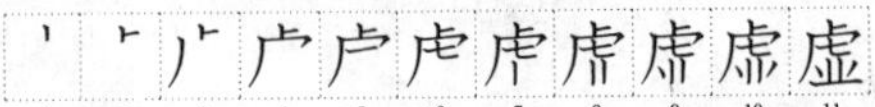
1 2 3 4 5 6 7 8 9 10 11

▶**VOID** ▶**FALSE**

COMPOUNDS

❶ (containing nothing) **void, empty, vacant, hollow**
虛無 *kyomu* nothingness; nihility
虛無僧 *komusō* flute-playing Zen mendicant priest
虛脱 *kyodatsu* (physical) collapse, prostration; absentmindedness
虛空 *kokū* empty space, sky
空虛な *kūkyo na* empty, void; inane

❷ **without substance, in name only, empty, vain, inane, hollow, void**
虛栄 *kyoei* vanity, vainglory
虛勢 *kyosei* bluff, bluster, false show of power
虛飾 *kyoshoku* ostentation, affectation, show
虛礼 *kyorei* empty [useless] formalities

❸ **false, sham, untrue, feigned**
虛偽 *kyogi* falsehood, lie, fallacy
虛言 *kyogen* falsehood
虛報 *kyohō* false alarm
虛構 *kyokō* fabrication, fiction
虛虛実実の戦い *kyokyojitsujitsu no tatakai* match between persons equal in shrewdness

❹ *math* imaginary
虛数 *kyosū* imaginary number
虛式 *kyoshiki* imaginary expression

❺ openhearted, humble
虛心 *kyoshin* disinterestedness, freedom from prejudice
謙虛な *kenkyo na* humble, modest

❻ weak, feeble
虛弱な *kyojaku na* weak, feeble, sickly

❼ [also 墟 *kyo*] ruins
廃虛 *haikyo* ruins, remains

INDEPENDENT

【**kyo** 虛】insubstantiality, emptiness, inanity, void; unguarded position, unpreparedness; *math* imaginary unit
虛を衝く *kyo o tsuku* attack the enemy in his unguarded moment

KUN

【**muna(shii)** 虛しい】
[usu. 空しい]
①ⓐ empty, void
ⓑ vain, futile
虛しさ *munashisa* emptiness, futility
虛しい名声 *munashii meisei* empty name
努力も虛しく *doryoku mo munashiku* after efforts in vain
② dead, lifeless
虛しくなる *munashiku naru* die, expire

【**utsu(ro)** 虛ろ】hollow, cavity, void, vacant
虛ろな目 *utsuro na me* vacant eyes
木の虛ろ *ki no utsuro* hollow in a tree

SYNONYMS

❶ **emptiness and nothing**
空 EMPTY → 2227
無 NOTHING → 2135
白 WHITE (blank) → 3493
零 ZERO → 2792

❷ **vain**
空 EMPTY → 2227
徒 vain → 416
❸ **false**
仮 fake → 50
偽 sham → 131

擬 imitation → 788
義 artificial → 2338

HOMOPHONES
munashii ⇨ 空 2227

NOTE
⇨ see USAGE note at 空 2227

處 3238 **▶DEAL WITH**
nonstandard for 処 3031 — 4-7 广

盾 incorrect classification ⇨ see 3012
(nonstandard for 質 2808) — 4-7 厂

雀 incorrect classification ⇨ see 2469 — 4-7 少

逸 3239 **▶LET SLIP**
nonstandard for 逸 3120 — 4-8 辶

進 3240 **▶ADVANCE**
nonstandard for 進 3121 — 4-8 辶

週 3241 **▶WEEK**
nonstandard for 週 3122 — 4-8 辶

逮 3242 **▶CATCH A CRIMINAL**
nonstandard for 逮 3123 — 4-8 辶

遇 incorrect stroke count ⇨ see 3246
(nonstandard for 遇 3135) — 4-8 辶

透 incorrect stroke count ⇨ see 3234
(nonstandard for 透 3108) — 4-8 辶

遊 incorrect stroke count ⇨ see 3253
(nonstandard for 遊 3142) — 4-8 辶

雇 扉 incorrect classification ⇨ see □ 2-10 — 4-8 戸

雇 扉 incorrect classification ⇨ see ▀ 1-11 — 4-8 戸

4-8 龵 煮 incorrect classification ⇨ see 2785

4-8 虍 虛 3243
▶VOID ▶FALSE
nonstandard for 虚 3237

4-8 虍 虜 3244
▶CAPTIVE
nonstandard for 虏 3255

4-9 辶 道 3245
▶WAY
nonstandard for 道 3134

4-9 辶 遇 3246
▶TREAT ▶ENCOUNTER
nonstandard for 遇 3135

4-9 辶 遍 3247
▶ALL OVER
nonstandard for 遍 3136

4-9 辶 違 3248
▶DIFFER ▶VIOLATE
nonstandard for 違 3151

4-9 辶 過 3249
▶PASS BY ▶EXCEED
nonstandard for 過 3137

4-9 辶 遂 3250
▶ACCOMPLISH
nonstandard for 遂 3138

4-9 辶 達 3251
▶ATTAIN
nonstandard for 達 3139

4-9 辶 運 3252
▶CARRY ▶MOVE ▶FORTUNE
nonstandard for 運 3140

4-9 辶 遊 3253
▶PLAY
nonstandard for 遊 3142

4-9 龵 煮 incorrect classification ⇨ see 2833
(nonstandard for 煮 2785)

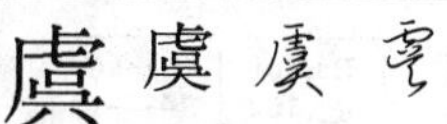

虞 3254

GU▲ osore

CH 虞 yú

Radical	Strokes
虍 141	13-6-7
Grade	**Freq**
Jōyō	1928
□ 3 - 4 - 9	

4-9 广

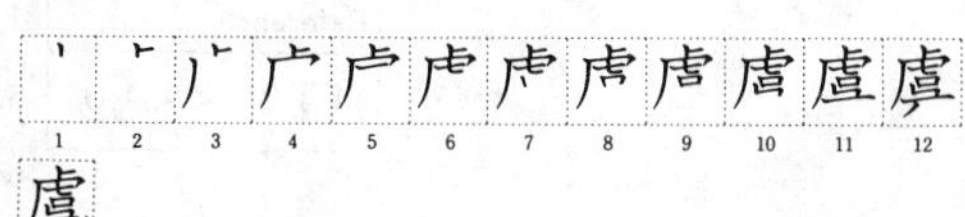

▶FEARS

COMPOUNDS

● [original meaning, now rare] be anxious, be apprehensive

危虞(＝危惧) *kigu* fear, misgivings

憂虞 *yūgu* fear, anxiety

KUN

【osore 虞】 [also 恐れ] fears (of undesirable event), danger, risk, signs, adverse chance, possibility

失敗の虞 *shippai no osore* risk of failure

雨の虞が有る *Ame no osore ga aru* There are some fears of raining

感染の虞を無くす *kansen no osore o nakusu* preclude the possibility of infection

SYNONYMS

【osore】

○ **worry**

憂 BE ANXIOUS → 2145

配 concern oneself → 1460

構う MIND → 1049

HOMOPHONES

osore ⇨ 恐 2650

NOTE

⇨ see USAGE note at 恐 2650

虜 3255

虜 RYO toriko▲

CH 虏 lǔ

Radical	Strokes
虍 141	13-6-7
Grade	**Freq**
Jōyō	1549
□ 3 - 4 - 9	

4-9 广

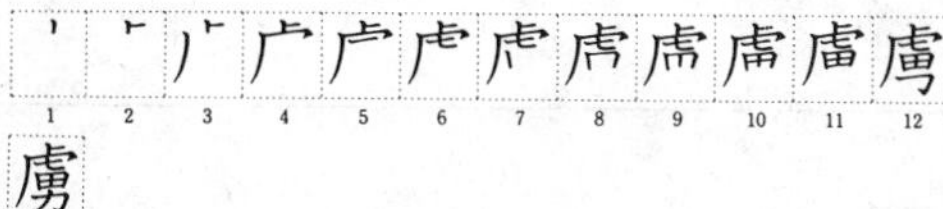

▶CAPTIVE

COMPOUNDS

● [original meaning] **captive, prisoner**

虜囚 *ryoshū* captive, prisoner

捕虜 *horyo* prisoner of war, captive

俘虜 *furyo* prisoner, POW, captive

KUN

【toriko 虜】 captive; victim, slave

美貌の虜になる *bibō no toriko ni naru* be enslaved by a woman's beauty

SYNONYMS

● **prisoner**

囚 PRISONER → 3042

虞 3256

▶FEARS

nonstandard for 虞 3254

4-9 广

4-10 ⻍

遡

3257 SO sakanobo(ru)

(CH) 遡 sù

Radical	Strokes
⻍ 162	14-4-10
Grade	**Freq**
Reference	
□ 3-4-10	

COMPOUNDS

[sometimes also 逆上る *sakanoboru*]

ⓐ [original meaning] go upstream

ⓑ go back (to the past); retroact

鮭は川を遡る *Sake wa kawa o sakanoboru* Salmon swim up the river

遡及する *sokyū suru* retroact

キリスト教の伝来は十六世紀に遡る *Kirisutokyō no denrai wa jūrokuseiki ni sakanoboru* The introduction of Christianity goes back to the sixteenth century

五月一日に遡って *gogatsu tsuitachi ni sakanobotte* retroactive to May 1

HOMOPHONES

sakanoboru ⇨ 逆上る 3091, 3404

NOTE

⇨ see USAGE note at 逆 3091

4-10 ⻍

逺

3258

▶**DISTANT**

nonstandard for 遠 3150

4-10 ⻍

遣

3259

▶**DISPATCH**

nonstandard for 遣 3152

4-10 ⻍

遞

3260

▶**RELAY**

nonstandard for 逓 3106

4-10 ⻍

遙

3261

▶**FAR**

nonstandard for 遥 3141

4-10 ⻍

遮

incorrect stroke count ⇨ see 3262

(nonstandard for 遮 3158)

4-10 广

虞

incorrect stroke count ⇨ see 3254

4-11 ⻍

遮

3262

▶**INTERRUPT**

nonstandard for 遮 3158

4-11 ⻍

遭

3263

▶**MEET WITH**

nonstandard for 遭 3159

4-11 ⻍

適

3264

▶**SUITABLE**

nonstandard for 適 3160

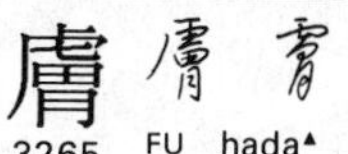

膚

3265 FU hada▲

㊥ 肤 fū

Radical	Strokes
月 130	15-4-11
Grade	**Freq**
Jōyō	1712
□ 3 - 4 - 1 1	

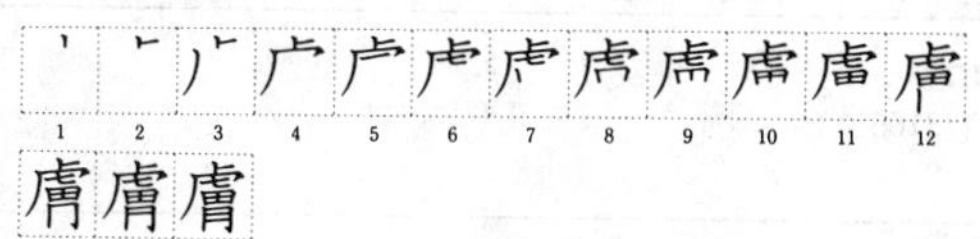

▶ **SKIN**

COMPOUNDS

● **skin (of the human body)**

皮膚 *hifu* skin

完膚無き迄 *kanpu-naki made* thoroughly, beyond recognition; scathingly

KUN

【hada 膚】

[now replaced by 肌]

①ⓐ skin, body

ⓑ surface; grain (of wood)

膚身 *hadami* body

赤膚 *akahada* abraded skin

山膚 *yamahada* surface of a mountain

膚の美しい材 *hada no utsukushii zai* wood of fine grain

②ⓐ disposition, temperament

ⓑ [suffix] turn of mind

学者膚 *gakushahada* scholarly bent of mind

SYNONYMS

● **kinds of skin**

肌 SKIN (of the human body) → 827

皮 SKIN (of any kind) → 3037

革 LEATHER → 2448

HOMOPHONES

hada ⇨ 肌 827

NOTE

⇨ see USAGE note at 肌 827

慮

3266 RYO omonpaka(ru)▲

㊥ 虑 lǜ

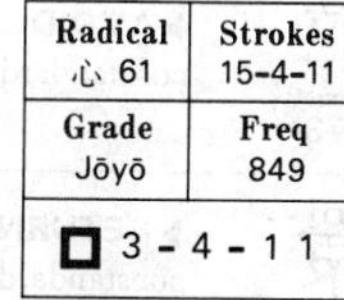

Radical	Strokes
心 61	15-4-11
Grade	**Freq**
Jōyō	849
□ 3 - 4 - 1 1	

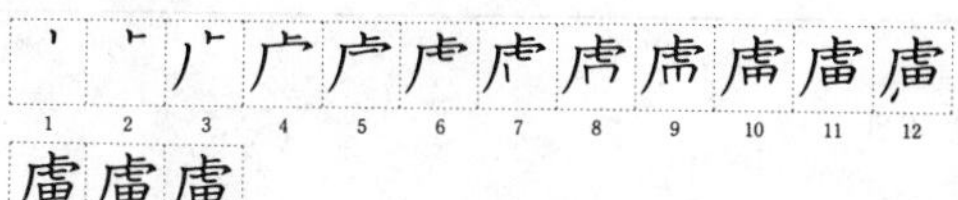

▶ **CONSIDER**

COMPOUNDS

ⓐ [original meaning] **consider, think over, deliberate**

ⓑ **show consideration, be prudent, be discreet**

ⓒ consideration, concern

考慮する *kōryo suru* consider, deliberate, give thought to

浅慮 *senryo* indiscretion, imprudence, thoughtlessness

思慮 *shiryo* consideration, thought, discretion

深慮 *shinryo* thoughtfulness, prudence

遠慮する *enryo suru* be reserved; hesitate; refrain

顧慮 *koryo* regard, consideration

配慮 *hairyo* consideration, care, concern

憂慮 *yūryo* anxiety, concern, worry

KUN

【omonpaka(ru) 慮る】 consider, take thought of; fear, apprehend

慮り *omonpakari* thought, consideration; fears

SYNONYMS

ⓐ **think and consider**

勘 take into consideration → 1777

量 weigh → 2471

惟 MEDITATE → 481

省 INTROSPECT → 2449

思 THINK → 2564

考 THINK → 3196

存 hold an opinion → 2982

案 think out → 2270

想 CONCEIVE → 2828

4-12 辶 遲 3267
▶**SLOW** ▶**LATE**
nonstandard for 遅 3133

4-12 辶 遺 3268
▶**LEAVE BEHIND**
nonstandard for 遺 3166

4-12 辶 遵 3269
▶**OBEY**
nonstandard for 遵 3167

4-12 辶 遼 3270
▶**FARAWAY**
nonstandard for 遼 3168

4-12 辶 選 3271
▶**CHOOSE**
nonstandard for 選 3169

4-12 辶 遷 3272
▶**TRANSFER**
nonstandard for 遷 3170

4-13 辶 避 3273
▶**AVOID**
nonstandard for 避 3179

4-13 辶 還 3274
▶**RETURN**
nonstandard for 還 3180

4-15 辶 邊 3275
▶**VICINITY** ▶**BORDERLAND**
nonstandard for 辺 3029

5-1 戊 戌
incorrect classification ⇨ see 3535

5-1 戊 成
incorrect classification ⇨ see 3537

5-2 㠯 良
incorrect classification ⇨ see 3558

5-2 肖 肖
incorrect classification ⇨ see 2205

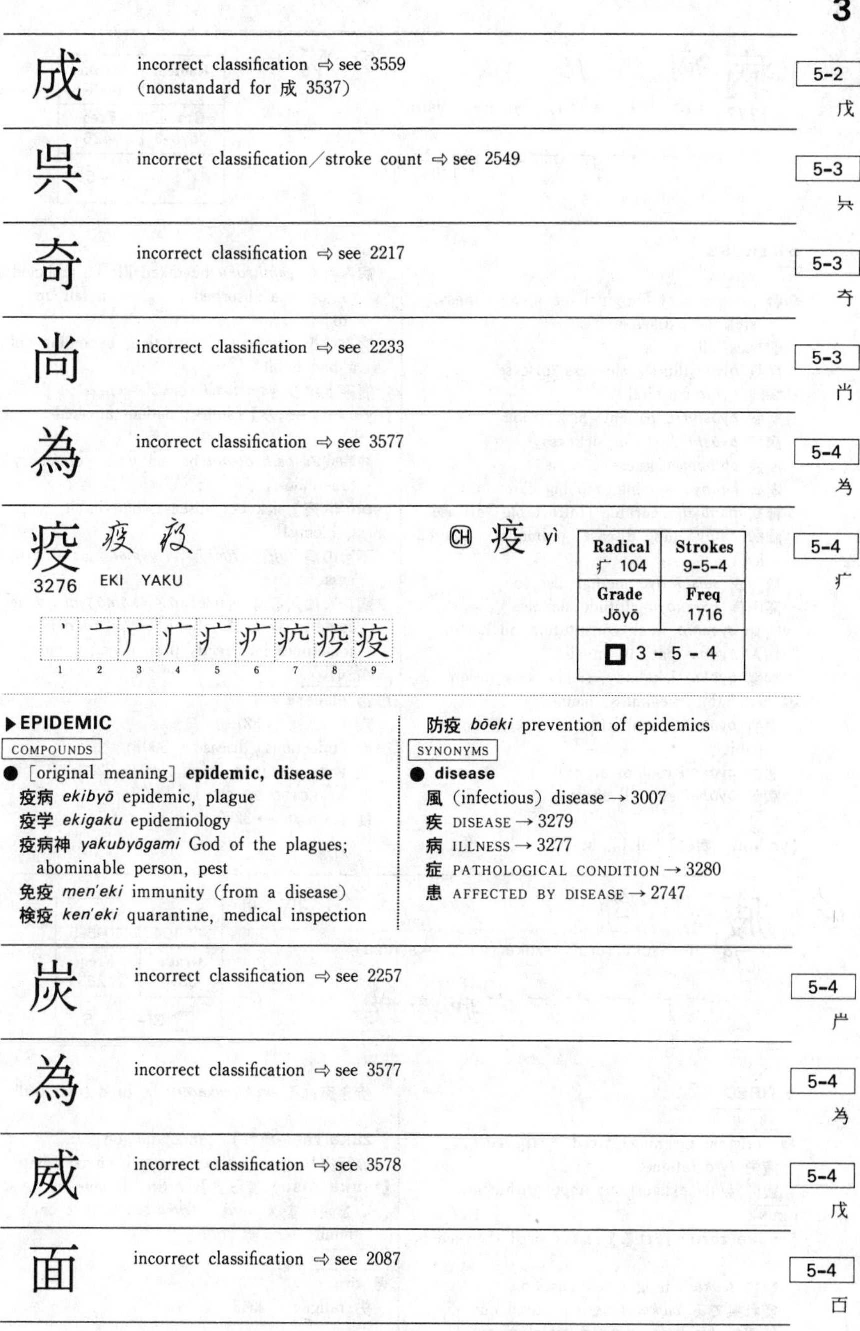

成 incorrect classification ⇨ see 3559 (nonstandard for 成 3537) — 5-2 戊

呉 incorrect classification／stroke count ⇨ see 2549 — 5-3 𠀍

奇 incorrect classification ⇨ see 2217 — 5-3 夸

尚 incorrect classification ⇨ see 2233 — 5-3 肖

為 incorrect classification ⇨ see 3577 — 5-4 为

疫 疫 疫

3276 EKI YAKU

Ⓒⓗ 疫 yì

Radical	Strokes
疒 104	9-5-4
Grade	**Freq**
Jōyō	1716
□ 3 - 5 - 4	

Stroke order: 1–9

5-4 疒

▶EPIDEMIC

COMPOUNDS

● [original meaning] **epidemic, disease**

疫病 *ekibyō* epidemic, plague
疫学 *ekigaku* epidemiology
疫病神 *yakubyōgami* God of the plagues; abominable person, pest
免疫 *men'eki* immunity (from a disease)
検疫 *ken'eki* quarantine, medical inspection
防疫 *bōeki* prevention of epidemics

SYNONYMS

● **disease**

風 (infectious) disease → 3007
疾 DISEASE → 3279
病 ILLNESS → 3277
症 PATHOLOGICAL CONDITION → 3280
患 AFFECTED BY DISEASE → 2747

炭 incorrect classification ⇨ see 2257 — 5-4 岸

為 incorrect classification ⇨ see 3577 — 5-4 为

威 incorrect classification ⇨ see 3578 — 5-4 戊

面 incorrect classification ⇨ see 2087 — 5-4 百

5-5 疒

病 病 病 病

3277 BYŌ HEI ya(mu) -ya(mi) yamai

CH 病 bìng

Radical	Strokes
疒 104	10-5-5
Grade	**Freq**
Jōyō-3	426
口 3-5-5	

▶ILLNESS

COMPOUNDS

❶ⓐ [also suffix] [original meaning] **illness, sickness, disease**
ⓑ sick, ill, weak
病気 *byōki* illness, sickness, disease
病院 *byōin* hospital
病室 *byōshitsu* patient [sick] room
病死 *byōshi* death of sickness
疾病 *shippei* sickness, disease
看病 *kanbyō* nursing, nursing care
難病 *nanbyō* incurable [intractable] disease
肺病 *haibyō* lung disease; pulmonary tuberculosis
精神病 *seishinbyō* mental disease
高山病 *kōzanbyō* altitude sickness
病身 *byōshin* weak constitution, ill health
病人 *byōnin* patient, invalid
病軀 *byōku* sick body, sickly constitution
❷ bad habit, weakness, blemish
病癖 *byōheki* peculiarity, weakness, morbid habit
病根 *byōkon* root of an evil
病弊 *byōhei* evil, ill effect

KUN

【ya(mu) 病む】 fall ill, be taken ill, suffer from
病み付く *yamitsuku* be taken ill; be addicted to, become absorbed in, give oneself up [to]
病み付き *yamitsuki* infatuation, beginning (of a bad habit)
病み上がり *yamiagari* convalescence
【-ya(mi) -病み】 [suffix] patient affected with...
肺病病み *haibyōyami* patient with pulmonary tuberculosis
【yamai 病】 sickness, disease; bad habit, weakness, blemish
不治の病 *fuji* (=*fuchi*) *no yamai* incurable illness
病膏肓に入る *yamai kōkō* (=*kōmō*) *ni iru* become a slave of a habit (膏肓 *kōkō* is sometimes incorrectly pronounced *kōmō*)

SYNONYMS

❶ⓐ **disease**
疾 DISEASE → 3279
風 (infectious) disease → 3007
症 PATHOLOGICAL CONDITION → 3280
患 AFFECTED BY DISEASE → 2747
疫 EPIDEMIC → 3276

5-5 疒

疲 疲 疲

3278 HI tsuka(reru) -zuka(re) tsuka(rasu)

CH 疲 pí

Radical	Strokes
疒 104	10-5-5
Grade	**Freq**
Jōyō	1265
口 3-5-5	

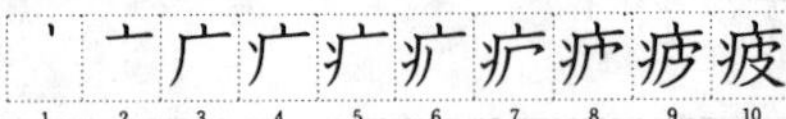

▶TIRED

COMPOUNDS

● [original meaning] **tired, fatigued**
疲労 *hirō* fatigue
疲弊 *hihei* exhaustion; impoverishment

KUN

【tsuka(reru) 疲れる】 *vi* get tired, become fatigued
疲れ *tsukare* fatigue, exhaustion
疲れ果てる *tsukarehateru* be tired out
気疲れ *kizukare* nervous strain, worry
歩き疲れる *arukitsukareru* be tired from walking
【-zuka(re) -疲れ】 [suffix] fatigue
旅行疲れ *ryokōzukare* fatigue from traveling
【tsuka(rasu) 疲らす】 *vt* tire, fatigue, exhaust
心を疲らす *kokoro o tsukarasu* fatigue one's mind

SYNONYMS

● **tire**
労 fatigue → 2548

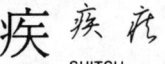

疾 疾 疾
3279 SHITSU

CH 疾 jí

Radical	Strokes
疒 104	10-5-5
Grade	**Freq**
Jōyō	1730
□ 3 - 5 - 5	

5-5 疒

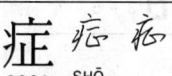

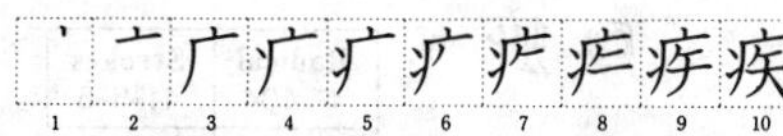

1 2 3 4 5 6 7 8 9 10

▶DISEASE

COMPOUNDS

❶ [original meaning] **disease, illness**
疾患 *shikkan* disease, ailment, trouble, disorder
疾病 *shippei* sickness, disease
悪疾 *akushitsu* malignant disease
痼疾 *koshitsu* chronic disease
廃疾 *haishitsu* disablement
❷ **fast, swift, at full speed**
疾走 *shissō* sprint, dash
疾駆する *shikku suru* ride fast, drive a horse fast
疾風 *shippū* gale, strong wind
❸ [rare] suffering, distress
疾苦 *shikku* suffering, affliction
❹ [rare] hate, detest
疾視 *shisshi* spiteful gaze

SYNONYMS

❶ **disease**
病 ILLNESS → 3277
風 (infectious) disease → 3007
症 PATHOLOGICAL CONDITION → 3280
患 AFFECTED BY DISEASE → 2747
疫 EPIDEMIC → 3276
❷ **fast**
快 fast → 245
速 QUICK → 3105
早 QUICK → 2390
急 rapid → 2092
迅 SWIFT → 3046
敏 NIMBLE → 1322
即 IMMEDIATE → 1120

症 症 症
3280 SHŌ

CH 症 zhèng zhēng

Radical	Strokes
疒 104	10-5-5
Grade	**Freq**
Jōyō	1121
□ 3 - 5 - 5	

5-5 疒

丶 亠 广 广 疒 疒 疔 疔 疔 症
1 2 3 4 5 6 7 8 9 10

▶PATHOLOGICAL CONDITION

COMPOUNDS

[also suffix]
❶ **pathological condition, illness, disease, -osis, -ia**
神経症 *shinkeishō* neurosis, nervous disease
既往症 *kiōshō* previous illness, medical history
不眠症 *fuminshō* insomnia
尿毒症 *nyōdokushō* uremia
重症 *jūshō* serious illness
❷ [original meaning] **symptom, nature of a disease, syndrome**
症状 *shōjō* symptom
症候 *shōkō* symptom
後遺症 *kōishō* sequela, aftereffect (of a disease)
ダウン症 *daunshō* Down's syndrome

SYNONYMS

❶ **disease**
病 ILLNESS → 3277
疾 DISEASE → 3279
風 (infectious) disease → 3007
患 AFFECTED BY DISEASE → 2747
疫 EPIDEMIC → 3276
❷ **signs**
徴 SYMPTOM → 683
兆 OMEN → 225
候 indication → 119
気 sign → 3194

痫
3281

▶ILLNESS
nonstandard for 病 3277

5-5 疒

5-5 疒

疪 incorrect stroke count ⇨ see 3282

5-6 疒

疵

3282 SHI kizu

Ⓒⓗ 疵 cī

Radical	Strokes
疒 104	11-5-6
Grade	**Freq**
Reference	
□ 3 - 5 - 6	

COMPOUNDS

● [now usu. 傷 *kizu*] defect, flaw, crack, fault, weak point

疵瑕 *shika* flaw, blemish, defect

疵物 *kizumono* defective article; deflowered girl

玉に疵(＝玉に瑕) *tama ni kizu* flaw in the crystal, fly in the ointment

脛に疵持つ *sune ni kizu motsu* have a guilty conscience

HOMOPHONES

kizu ⇨ 傷 158

NOTE

⇨ see USAGE note at 傷 158

5-7 疒

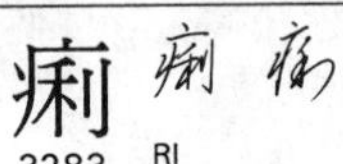

3283 RI

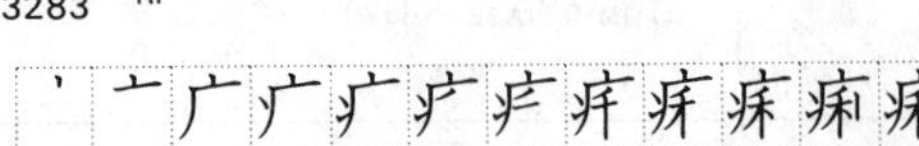

Ⓒⓗ 痢 lì

Radical	Strokes
疒 104	12-5-7
Grade	**Freq**
Jōyō	1383
□ 3 - 5 - 7	

▶DIARRHEA

COMPOUNDS

● **diarrhea**

下痢 *geri* diarrhea

赤痢 *sekiri* dysentery

疫痢 *ekiri* children's dysentery

INDEPENDENT

【ri 痢】 diarrhea

SYNONYMS

● **diseases and disease symptoms**

下 diarrhea → 3378

炎 INFLAMMATION → 2420

熱 fever → 2866

痘 SMALLPOX → 3284

5-7 疒

痘

3284 TŌ

` 亠 广 疒 疒 疒 疔 疔 疔 疖 疸 痘 (stroke order 1–12)

Ⓒⓗ 痘 dòu

Radical	Strokes
疒 104	12-5-7
Grade	**Freq**
Jōyō	1879
□ 3 - 5 - 7	

▶SMALLPOX

COMPOUNDS

❶ [original meaning] **smallpox**

痘瘡 *tōsō* smallpox

痘苗 *tōbyō* vaccine, vaccine virus; smallpox vaccine

天然痘 *tennentō* smallpox

種痘 *shutō* vaccination against smallpox

❷ pox

牛痘 *gyūtō* cow pox, vaccinia

水痘 *suitō* chicken pox, varicella

SYNONYMS

❶ & ❷ **diseases and disease symptoms**

熱 fever → 2866

炎 INFLAMMATION → 2420

痢 DIARRHEA → 3283

下 diarrhea → 3378

NOTE

⇨ see COMPOUND FORMATION for 痘苗 *tōbyō* ⇨ 苗 2237

痛 痛 痛

3285 TSŪ ita(i) ita(mu) ita(mashii) ita(meru)

CH 痛 tòng

Radical	Strokes
疒 104	12-5-7
Grade	**Freq**
Jōyō-6	941
□ 3 - 5 - 7	

5-7 疒

丶 亠 广 广 疒 疒 疒 疗 疗 病 痟 痛

1 2 3 4 5 6 7 8 9 10 11 12

▶**PAIN**

COMPOUNDS

❶ⓐ [also suffix] [original meaning] (physical suffering) **pain, ache**

ⓑ (mental suffering) pain, agony, grief, sadness

痛覚 *tsūkaku* sense of pain
苦痛 *kutsū* pain, agony, anguish
頭痛 *zutsū* headache
鎮痛剤 *chintsūzai* anodyne, painkiller
神経痛 *shinkeitsū* neuralgia
筋肉痛 *kinnikutsū* muscular pain
痛痒 *tsūyō* interest, concern; pain and tickling
心痛 *shintsū* mental agony, heartache
悲痛な *hitsū na* sad, grievous
沈痛な *chintsū na* grave, serious, sad

❷ **bitter(ly), severe(ly), vehement(ly), keen(ly)**

痛言 *tsūgen* bitter criticism, harsh words
痛烈な *tsūretsu na* sharp, biting, scathing, cutting
痛感する *tsūkan suru* feel strongly, take to heart
痛快 *tsūkai* thrill, keen pleasure
痛切に *tsūsetsu ni* keenly, acutely
痛打 *tsūda* hard blow, severe attack
痛恨 *tsūkon* deep regret, great sorrow

KUN

【ita(i) 痛い】 painful, sore; hard to bear, trying

痛さ *itasa* pain, ache
痛痛しい *itaitashii* pitiful, pathetic
歯痛 *haita* toothache
痛い目に遭わす *itai me ni awasu* make a person sweat for it
痛い損失 *itai sonshitsu* painful loss
手痛い *teitai* severe, hard, heavy

【ita(mu) 痛む】

① feel pain, hurt, ache

痛み *itami* (physical or mental suffering) pain, ache
痛み止め *itamidome* painkiller, analgesic

② be pained, be grieved at heart

痛み入る *itamiiru* be greatly obliged; be very sorry
懐が痛む *futokoro ga itamu* suffer in one's pocket [purse]
胸が痛む様な出来事 *mune ga itamu yō na dekigoto* painful incident

【ita(mashii) 痛ましい】 sad, piteous, miserable, heartbreaking, pathetic

痛ましさ *itamashisa* sadness, piteousness

【ita(meru) 痛める】

① inflict pain, hurt, injure

腹を痛める *hara o itameru* have a stomachache; give birth to
心を痛める *kokoro o itameru* be grieved at heart

② pain, bother, worry, afflict

痛め付ける *itametsukeru* rebuke, taunt; give a good shaking, knock about

SYNONYMS

❶ **trouble and suffering**

苦 SUFFERING → 2243
辛 HARD → 2038
悩 SUFFER → 421
窮 BE IN EXTREMITY → 2358
困 BE IN TROUBLE → 3070
煩 VEXED → 1022
難 DIFFICULT → 1838

❷ **extreme in degree**

切 keen → 27
酷 SEVERE → 1562
厳 SEVERE → 3289
激 intense → 776
極 EXTREME → 1017
甚 EXTREMELY → 2643
超 super- → 3313
強 STRONG → 475
重 HEAVY → 3573
高 HIGH → 2097
深 DEEP → 524
大 BIG → 3416

USAGE

❶ **itamu**

痛む
① feel pain, hurt, ache
② be pained, be grieved at heart

傷む
① be damaged, be spoiled, wear out
② rot, spoil

悼む
mourn, grieve over, be grieved at

❷ **itameru**

痛める

① inflict pain, hurt, injure
② pain, bother, worry, afflict

傷める
damage, spoil

HOMOPHONES
itamu ⇨ 傷 158　悼 485
itameru ⇨ 傷 158

5-8
疒

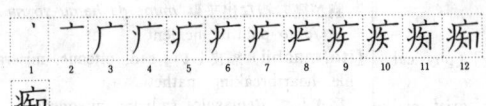

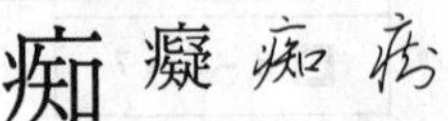

3286　CHI　shi(reru)▲

Ⓒ 痴 chī

Radical	Strokes
疒 104	13-5-8
Grade	**Freq**
Jōyō	1847
口 3 - 5 - 8	

▶**STUPID**

COMPOUNDS

❶ⓐ [original meaning] **stupid, foolish, silly**
ⓑ lacking ability, slow
痴呆 *chihō* imbecility, dementia
痴人 *chijin* fool, simpleton, idiot, dunce
白痴 *hakuchi* idiocy, idiot
愚痴 *guchi* idle complaint, grumble; querulousness
音痴 *onchi* tone deafness
運痴 *unchi colloq* slow in one's movements

❷ **infatuated, crazy about, blindly in love, amorous**
痴漢 *chikan* molester of women, masher
痴情 *chijō* blind love, infatuation, amorous passion; jealousy
痴話 *chiwa* lover's talk, sweet nothings
情痴 *jōchi* love foolery

KUN

【**shi(reru) 痴れる**】 *literary* be infatuated
痴れ者 *shiremono* fool, dunce, idiot
酔い痴れる *yoishireru* be fuddled [drunk] (with)

SYNONYMS

❶ **foolish**
愚 FOOLISH → 2834
暗 DARK → 1010
鈍 DULL → 1689

❷ **mania and maniacs**
狂 maniac → 269
魔 maniac → 3187
熱 fever → 2866

5-9
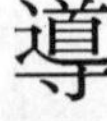

incorrect classification／stroke count ⇨ see 2888

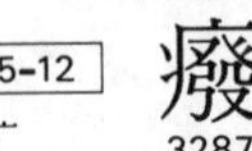
疒

3287　HAI

Ⓒ 废 fèi

Radical	Strokes
疒 104	17-5-12
Grade	**Freq**
Reference	
口 3 - 5 - 1 2	

COMPOUNDS

● [now also 廃 3146] [original meaning] disabled, crippled
癈疾 *haishitsu* disablement
癈人 *haijin* invalid, crippled person
癈兵 *haihei* disabled soldier, crippled soldier

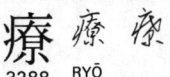

療 𤻲 𤺌

3288 RYŌ

Ⓒⓗ 疗 liáo

Radical	Strokes
疒 104	17-5-12
Grade	Freq
Jōyō	828
囗 3-5-12	

5-12 疒

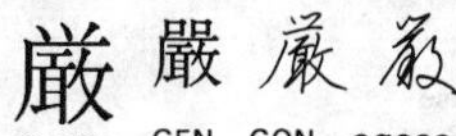

1 2 3 4 5 6 7 8 9 10 11 12 13 14 15 16 17

▶**TREAT**

COMPOUNDS

ⓐ [original meaning] **treat, care for**

ⓑ **medical treatment**

治療する *chiryō suru* treat, cure

診療 *shinryō* diagnosis and treatment

療法 *ryōhō* method of treatment, cure, remedy

療養中 *ryōyōchū* under medical care, in recuperation

医療 *iryō* medical treatment [care]

施療 *seryō* gratuitous treatment, free medical treatment

物療 *butsuryō* physiotherapy, physical treatment

SYNONYMS

● **cure and recover**

治 CURE → 335

医 cure → 2993

癒 HEAL → 3291

快 recover → 245

厳 嚴 𠪚 𠪛

3289 GEN GON ogoso(ka) kibi(shii) ika(meshii)▲

Ⓒⓗ 严 yán

Radical	Strokes
⺍ 42△	17-3-14
Grade	Freq
Jōyō-6	1030
囗 3-5-12	

5-12 厂

1 2 3 4 5 6 7 8 9 10 11 12 13 14 15 16 17

▶**SEVERE**

COMPOUNDS

❶ [original meaning] **strict, severe, stern, rigorous, harsh**

厳格な *genkaku na* strict, stern, severe, rigorous

厳密な *genmitsu na* strict, precise, rigid, exact

厳正 *gensei* exactness, strictness, rigor

厳重な *genjū na* strict, severe, close; secure, firm, strong

厳守 *genshu* strict observance

厳罰 *genbatsu* severe punishment

厳選 *gensen* careful selection

戒厳令 *kaigenrei* martial law

❷ (of great intensity) **severe, intense, extreme**

厳寒 *genkan* severe [intense] cold

厳冬 *gentō* severe winter

❸ [formerly also 儼 *gen* 178] **solemn, grave, awe-inspiring, dignified**

厳然たる *genzentaru* solemn, grave, majestic, stern

厳粛な *genshuku na* grave, solemn, austere

威厳 *igen* solemn dignity

謹厳な *kingen na* stern, grave, solemn

荘厳な *sōgon na* solemn, sublime

❹ [honorific] **father**

厳父 *genpu* your honored father

INDEPENDENT

【gen 厳】 severeness, strictness, rigor

警戒を厳にする *keikai o gen ni suru* take strict precautions

厳として *gen to shite* strictly

KUN

【ogoso(ka) 厳か】

ogosoka na 厳かな solemn, grave, awe-inspiring, dignified

厳かな儀式 *ogosoka na gishiki* solemn ceremony

【kibi(shii) 厳しい】 severe, strict, stern, rigorous, harsh; (of great intensity) severe, intense, extreme

厳しさ *kibishisa* severity, strictness; intensity

厳しい批評 *kibishii hihyō* severe criticism

厳しい暑さ *kibishii atsusa* intense heat

【ika(meshii) 厳めしい】 grave, stern, dignified, majestic

厳めしい顔付き *ikameshii kaotsuki* grave [stern] look

SYNONYMS

❶ **strict**
酷 SEVERE → 1562
峻 STERN → 412

❷ **extreme in degree**
酷 SEVERE → 1562
激 intense → 776
極 EXTREME → 1017
痛 bitter(ly) → 3285
切 keen → 27
甚 EXTREMELY → 2643
超 super- → 3313
強 STRONG → 475
重 HEAVY → 3573
高 HIGH → 2097
深 DEEP → 524
大 BIG → 3416

❸ **dignified**
粛 solemnly → 3581
荘 DIGNIFIED → 2262
威 dignified → 3578

NOTE

⇨ see COMPOUND FORMATION for 厳格 *genkaku* ⇨ 格 926

5-13
疒

癖 
3290 HEKI kuse kuse(ni)

Ⓒ 癖 pǐ

Radical	Strokes
疒 104	18-5-13
Grade	**Freq**
Jōyō	1823
口 3-5-13	

▶**HABIT**

COMPOUNDS

● [also suffix] **habit, habitual practice, propensity, peculiarity, weakness**
悪癖 *akuheki* bad habit, vice
性癖 *seiheki* one's natural disposition, propensity, mental habit
習癖 *shūheki* (bad) habit, habitual practice
病癖 *byōheki* peculiarity, weakness, morbid habit
潔癖 *keppeki* love of cleanliness, fastidiousness
飲酒癖 *inshuheki* inebriety, drinking habit
放浪癖 *hōrōheki* vagrant habits, vagabondism

INDEPENDENT

【**heki** 癖】habit
奇矯な癖 *kikyō na heki* eccentric habit

KUN

【**kuse** 癖】habit, habitual practice, propensity, peculiarity, weakness; mannerism, affectation; curl, kink
口癖 *kuchiguse* way [habit] of saying, one's favorite phrase
難癖 *nankuse* fault, blemish
無くて七癖 *Nakute nanakuse* Every man has his own peculiar habits
爪を噛む癖 *tsume o kamu kuse* habit of biting one's nails
癖の有る文章 *kuse no aru bunshō* mannered style
癖毛 *kusege* kinky hair

【**kuse(ni)** 癖に】though, in spite of
新米の癖に *shinmai no kuseni* though (one is) only a beginner
知ってる癖に *Shitteru kuseni* As if you didn't know!

SYNONYMS

● **custom**
弊 EVIL PRACTICE → 2884
俗 popular custom → 104
風 manners → 3007
習 CUSTOM → 2667
例 established practice → 89
慣 HABITUAL PRACTICE → 685

癒 3291

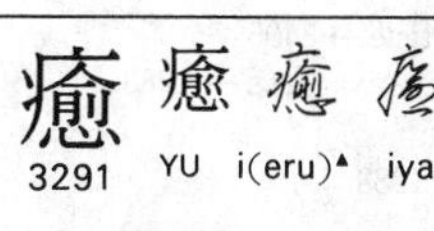

Ⓒⓗ 愈 yù

YU i(eru)▲ iya(su)▲

Radical	Strokes
疒 104	18-5-13
Grade	**Freq**
Jōyō	1961
口 3-5-13	

5-13 疒

▶**HEAL**

COMPOUNDS

ⓐ [original meaning] **heal, recover**

ⓑ heal (a wound), cure

治癒 *chiyu* healing, cure, recovery

平癒 *heiyu* recovery, restoration to health

癒着 *yuchaku* adhesion, conglutination; connection, collusion

癒傷組織 *yushō soshiki* wound-healing tissue

KUN

【i(eru) 癒える】 *poetic* be cured, recover

【iya(su) 癒す】 *poetic* heal, cure, restore

病を癒す *yamai o iyasu* cure an illness [a disease]

SYNONYMS

● **cure and recover**

快 recover → 245

治 CURE → 335

医 cure → 2993

療 TREAT → 3288

癒 3292

5-13 疒

▶**HEAL**

nonstandard for 癒 3291

繭

5-13 冂

incorrect classification ⇨ see 2380

癡 3293

5-14 疒

▶**STUPID**

nonstandard for 痴 3286

虎

6-2 虍

incorrect classification ⇨ see 3212

哉 3294

哉 哉

Ⓒⓗ 哉 zāi

SAI kana ya NAMES ka suke toshi chika hajime

Radical	Strokes
口 30	9-3-6
Grade	**Freq**
Names	2023
口 3-6-3	

6-3 戈

▶**EXCLAMATORY PARTICLE**

COMPOUNDS

● exclamatory particle

快哉を叫ぶ *kaisai o sakebu* shout for joy, shout with exultation

善哉 *zenzai* Well done! / That's it!; thick bean-meal soup (with sugar and rice cake)

KUN

【kana 哉】 *literary* exclamatory particle, used esp. in classical texts: Alas! Oh! How...! What...!

悲しい哉 *Kanashii kana!* Alas! / How sad!

天なる哉、命なる哉 *Ten naru kana, mei naru kana* All is decreed by Heaven

【ya 哉】 [also 也 or 耶] classical interrogative or rhetorical particle like modern か *ka*

君迷える哉 *Kimi mayoeru ya* Did you lose your way?

NAMES
哉女 *kaname* female name
廉哉 *yasuya* (=*yasutoshi*) male name
寛哉 *kansuke* male name

SYNONYMS
● **classical particles**
也 rhetorical particle → 3406
耶 INTERROGATIVE PARTICLE → 1283

HOMOPHONES
ya ⇨ 也 3406 耶 1283

NOTE
⇨ see USAGE note at 也 3406

6-3
虍

incorrect classification ⇨ see 3218

6-3
产

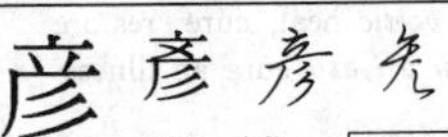

3295 GEN hiko NAMES yoshi

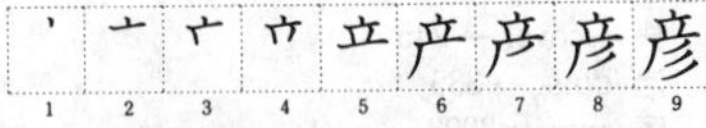

Ⓒⓗ 彦 yàn

Radical	Strokes
彡 59	9-3-6
Grade	**Freq**
Names	1981
□ 3 - 6 - 3	

▶**MALE NAME ELEMENT**

COMPOUNDS
● [rare] gifted and virtuous man, man of fine character; handsome man; possessing laudable masculine qualities
俊彦 *shungen* [rare] gifted [accomplished] man
諸彦 *shogen* [rare] many accomplished persons

KUN
【**hiko** 彦】 element for forming male names; [archaic] handsome man, prince

NAMES
輝彦 *teruhiko* male name
邦彦 *kunihiko* male name
彦根 *hikone* place name

SYNONYMS
【**hiko**】
○ **name suffixes**
麿 CLASSICAL MALE NAME SUFFIX → 3184
郎 MALE NAME SUFFIX → 1289
-子 female name element → 3390

6-4
馬

馬 馬 马

3296 BA MA▲ uma uma- ma

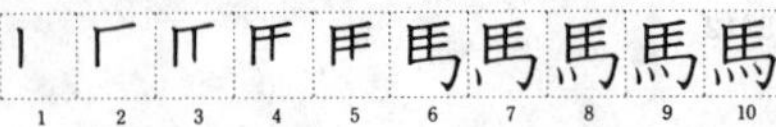

Ⓒⓗ 马 mǎ

Radical	Strokes
馬 187	10-10-0
Grade	**Freq**
Jōyō-2	531
□ 3 - 6 - 4	

RADICAL 187
Standard form: 馬 *uma* 'horse' (驚 騰 駕)
Left variant: 馬 *umahen* (験 駅 駐)
Description: used in characters related to horses or their qualities

▶**HORSE**

COMPOUNDS
❶ [also suffix] [original meaning] **horse**
馬車 *basha* horse-drawn carriage, coach, wagon
馬力 *bariki* horsepower; energy, effort; cart, wagon
馬身 *bashin* horse's length
馬肉 *baniku* horsemeat
乗馬 *jōba* horse riding
競馬 *keiba* horse racing
竹馬の友 *chikuba no tomo* childhood friend, old playmate
関西馬 *kansaiba* Kansai horse
❷ name of chess piece in shogi (Japanese chess): *keima*, knight; *narikaku*, promoted bishop
桂馬 *keima keima*, knight
竜馬 *ryūme narikaku*, promoted bishop
❸ **candidate (for an election)**
出馬する *shutsuba suru* come forward as a candidate; go in person
有力馬 *yūryokuba* hopeful [promising, strong] candidate
❹ used phonetically for *ba* or *ma*
馬鹿 *baka* fool, blockhead; nonsense

馬克 *maruku* (Deutsche) mark

KUN

【uma 馬】

①ⓐ horse, pony

ⓑ vaulting horse

馬が合う *uma ga au* get on well (with a person)

勝馬 *kachiuma* winning horse

竹馬 *takeuma* (=*chikuba*) stilts

② *keima*, *narikaku* (shogi chess pieces) (⇨ ❷)

③ stepping ladder

④ person who accompanies a reveler home to collect payment

付け馬 *tsukeuma* person who accompanies a reveler home to collect payment

【uma- 馬-】 the larger of a species of animals or plants

馬蠅 *umabae* horse botfly

【ma 馬】 [in compounds] horse

馬子 *mago* packhorse driver

絵馬 *ema* votive picture of a horse

SYNONYMS

❶ **horse**

駿 FLEET STEED → 1832

駒 HORSE (*elegant*) → 1827

午 the Horse → 1984

❶ **domesticated mammals**

牛 CATTLE → 3452

豚 PIG → 976

羊 SHEEP → 2183

犬 DOG → 3464

猫 CAT → 535

USAGE

uma

馬

①ⓐ horse, pony

ⓑ vaulting horse

② *keima*, *narikaku* (shogi chess pieces)

③ stepping ladder

④ person who accompanies a reveler home to collect payment

午

seventh sign of the Oriental zodiac: the Horse

HOMOPHONES

uma ⇨ 午 1984

COMPOUND FORMATION

馬鹿 *baka*

馬鹿 'fool, blockhead; nonsense' is unrelated to its constituent elements of 馬 ❹ 'horse' and 鹿 'deer', but is a transliteration of the Sanskrit word *moha* 'ignorance'.

NOTE

⇨ see COMPOUND FORMATION for

竹馬 *takeuma* (=*chikuba*) ⇨ 竹 228

竹馬の友 *chikuba no tomo* ⇨ see 竹 228

栽 栽 栽

3297 SAI

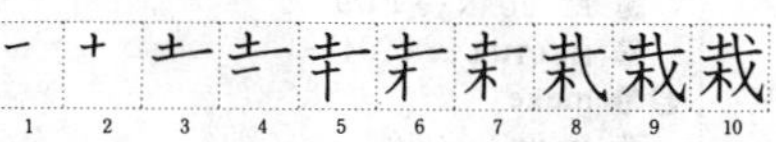

1 2 3 4 5 6 7 8 9 10

Ⓒⓗ 栽 zāi

Radical	Strokes
木 75	10-4-6
Grade	**Freq**
Jōyō	1592

⼝ 3 - 6 - 4

6-4 戈

▶PLANT

COMPOUNDS

❶ **plant (saplings), transplant, grow, raise**

栽培 *saibai* cultivation, raising, growing

植栽 *shokusai* raising trees and plants

輪栽 *rinsai* rotation of crops

果樹栽培 *kaju saibai* fruit culture, pomiculture

❷ **garden plant, potted plant**

盆栽 *bonsai* bonsai (potted dwarf tree)

前栽 *senzai elegant* trees and flowers in a garden; garden

SYNONYMS

❶ **farm and plant**

植 PLANT → 990

培 CULTIVATE → 464

耕 TILL → 1308

作 raise crops → 68

農 farm, FARMING → 2698

❷ **plants**

植 PLANT → 990

菜 VEGETABLE → 2305

虚 處

incorrect classification ⇨ see ⼝4－7

6-5 虍

6-5
产

産 産 産 産

Ⓒⓗ 产 chǎn

3298 SAN u(mu) u(mareru) ubu- mu(su)▲

Radical	Strokes
生 100	11-5-6
Grade	Freq
Jōyō-4	134
口 3 - 6 - 5	

▶**GIVE BIRTH** ▶**PRODUCE**

COMPOUNDS

❶ⓐ **give birth (to), deliver, bear, breed**
ⓑ **be born**
ⓒ **childbirth, delivery**
産婦 *sanpu* woman in childbirth
産卵 *sanran* egg-laying, spawning
出産する *shussan suru* give birth (to), deliver, bear (a child)
産制 *sansei* birth control
安産 *anzan* easy [smooth] delivery (of a baby)
死産 *shizan* stillbirth

❷ⓐ **produce, yield**
ⓑ [also suffix] **production**
産出する *sanshutsu suru* produce, yield
産業 *sangyō* industry
産地 *sanchi* place of production; place of birth
産物 *sanbutsu* product, produce
国産 *kokusan* home [domestic] production

❸ product, produce
水産 *suisan* marine products, fisheries
物産 *bussan* product, produce
名産 *meisan* noted product

❹ abbrev. of 産業 *sangyō*: industry
産別会議 *sanbetsu kaigi* Congress of Industrial Organizations (CIO)
通産省 *tsūsanshō* Ministry of International Trade and Industry

❺ **property, fortune, wealth**
財産 *zaisan* property, fortune, wealth
資産 *shisan* property, assets, fortune
倒産 *tōsan* insolvency, bankruptcy; breech birth
破産 *hasan* bankruptcy
共産主義 *kyōsanshugi* Communism
不動産 *fudōsan* immovable property, real estate

❻ suffix indicating place of origin or of birth
フロリダ産のオレンジ *furoridasan no orenji* oranges grown in Florida

INDEPENDENT

【san 産】 childbirth; native of...; product; property, fortune, wealth
お産 *osan* childbirth, delivery
京都の産 *kyōto no san* native of Kyoto
産を成す *san o nasu* amass a fortune

【sansuru 産する】 produce, grow

KUN

【u(mu) 産む】 (produce offspring) give birth to, bear offspring, beget, breed; spawn
産み *umi* (physical) birth
産み出す *umidasu* begin to give birth to
産み月 *umizuki* last month of pregnancy
彼女は五人子供を産んだ *Kanojo wa gonin kodomo o unda* She gave birth to five children

【u(mareru) 産まれる】 (undergo the physical act of birth) be born
赤ん坊が産まれた *Akanbō ga umareta* The baby was born

【ubu- 産-】 related to birth, as when born
産声 *ubugoe* baby's first cry
産毛 *ubuge* downy hair

【mu(su) 産す】 [also 生す] grow
苔産した *kokemushita* moss-grown, mossy

SPECIAL READINGS

土産 *miyage* souvenir

SYNONYMS

❶ **give birth**
生 BE BORN → 3497
誕 BE BORN → 1579
殖 MULTIPLY → 994

❷ⓐ **make**
造 MAKE → 3110
作 MAKE → 68
成 FORM → 3537
工 MANUFACTURE → 3381
製 MANUFACTURE → 2803
調 PREPARE → 1567
組む ASSEMBLE → 1337
構 CONSTRUCT → 1049

❸ **merchandise**
品 ARTICLE (of merchandise) → 2248
貨 GOODS → 2465
物 commodity → 874

❹ **industry and business**
業 BUSINESS, INDUSTRY → 2612
商 TRADE → 2116
工 manufacturing industry → 3381

❺ **wealth**
財 WEALTH → 1457
富 riches → 2310
宝 TREASURE → 2224

USAGE

❶ **umu**

産む

(produce offspring) give birth to, bear offspring, beget, breed; spawn

彼女は五人子供を産んだ *Kanojo wa gonin kodomo o unda* She gave birth to five children

生む

① have children

② produce, bring forth, give rise to, yield

彼女は五人子供を生んだ *Kanojo wa gonin kodomo o unda* She has five children

★These verbs share the meaning of giving birth. 産む, the more common form, refers to the physical act of bearing offspring, while 生む is used in the more abstract sense of having children. The principal use of 生む is in the sense of producing or giving rise to.

❷ **umi**

産み

(physical) birth

生み

production, bringing into the world

❸ **umareru**

産まれる

(undergo the physical act of birth) be born

男の子が産まれた *Otoko no ko ga umareta* A boy was born

生まれる

ⓐ (of persons) (come into being) be born, come into existence

ⓑ (of things in general) appear, see the light, be a result (of)

彼はアメリカで生まれた *Kare wa amerika de umareta* He was born in America

★産まれる is used in the narrow sense of being born, referring to the physical act of birth. 生まれる is used in the broader sense of a person coming into the world.

HOMOPHONES

umu ⇨ 生 3497

umi ⇨ 生 3497

umareru ⇨ 生 3497

musu ⇨ 生 3497 蒸 2334

NOTE

⇨ see also USAGE note at 生 3497

商

incorrect classification ⇨ see 2116

6-5 冂

裁 裁 裁

3299 SAI ta(tsu) saba(ku)

Ⓒⓗ 裁 cái

Radical	Strokes
衣 145	12-6-6
Grade	**Freq**
Jōyō-6	460
口 3-6-6	

6-6 戈

1 2 3 4 5 6 7 8 9 10 11 12

▶**CUT OUT** ▶**JUDGE**

COMPOUNDS

❶ⓐ [original meaning] **cut out (a garment)**

ⓑ abbrev. of 裁縫 *saihō*: sewing, dressmaking

裁縫 *saihō* sewing, needlework, dressmaking

裁断師 *saidanshi* (tailor's) cutter

洋裁 *yōsai* foreign-style dressmaking

和裁 *wasai* Japanese dressmaking

❷ (pass judgment) **judge, decide, try, arbitrate**

裁判 *saiban* trial, judgment, decision

裁定 *saitei* decision, ruling, arbitration

裁決 *saiketsu* decision, ruling

裁量 *sairyō* discretion

制裁 *seisai* sanction, punishment, discipline

仲裁 *chūsai* arbitration, mediation

❸ abbrev. of 裁判所 *saibansho*: court

最高裁 *saikōsai* Supreme Court

家裁 *kasai* family court

❹ rule, administer, manage

総裁 *sōsai* president, governor

独裁 *dokusai* dictatorship, autocracy

❺ form, style

体裁 *teisai* decency, form, style, appearance

KUN

【ta(tsu) 裁つ】 cut out (a garment), cut (paper)

裁ち出す *tachidasu* cut out (a dress) from cloth

裁ち縫い *tachinui* cutting and sewing

裁ち板 *tachiita* (tailor's) cutting board

【saba(ku) 裁く】 judge, pass judgment, decide

裁き *sabaki* judgment, decision, verdict

裁きの庭 *sabaki no niwa* law court

SYNONYMS

❶ⓐ **cut**

断 CUT OFF → 1492

切 CUT → 27
割 cut with a knife → 1816
剖 DISSECT → 1670
刈る CLIP → 28
伐 CUT DOWN → 42
削 CUT BY CHIPPING → 1448
❷ **judge**
判 JUDGE → 1122
鑑 APPRAISE → 1773
評 evaluate → 1501
審 TRY → 2360
決 DECIDE → 263
視 REGARD → 972
❸ **court**
廷 COURT → 3058

HOMOPHONES

tatsu ⇨ 断 1492 絶 1353

NOTE

⇨ see USAGE note at 断 1492

6-6 虍

虚 虜

incorrect classification ⇨ see 口 4－8

6-7 戈

載 載 戴

3300 SAI no(seru) no(ru)

CH 载 zài zǎi

Radical	Strokes
車 159	13-7-6
Grade	**Freq**
Jōyō	1123
口 3 - 6 - 7	

一 1 十 2 土 3 圭 4 去 5 吉 6 青 7 吉 8 壹 9 車 10 載 11 載 12 載 13

▶**LOAD** ▶**PUT IN PRINT**

COMPOUNDS

❶ [original meaning] **load (a vehicle or ship with cargo), lade, carry**
満載する *mansai suru* be loaded to capacity (with)
積載する *sekisai suru* load (a vehicle or ship with cargo), carry
搭載 *tōsai* loading, embarkation
混載 *konsai* mixed loading

❷ⓐ **put in print, publish, carry, put on record**
ⓑ **appear in print, be published**
載録する *sairoku suru* record
掲載 *keisai* publication, insertion, printing
記載する *kisai suru* record, state, mention
連載 *rensai* serialization, serial publication
転載する *tensai suru* reproduce, reprint
登載する *tōsai suru* register, record

❸ year
千載一遇 *senzai-ichigū* once in a thousand years

❹ [archaic] one hundred tredecillion (10^{44})

KUN

【no(seru) 載せる】
① load (a vehicle or ship with cargo), lade, carry
船に貨物を載せる *fune ni kamotsu o noseru* load a ship with cargo
② place on, put on
棚に本を載せる *tana ni hon o noseru* place a book on a shelf
③ put in print, publish, carry, put on record
記録に載せる *kiroku ni noseru* put on record

【no(ru) 載る】
① appear in print, be published, be recorded
新聞に載る *shinbun ni noru* appear in the newspaper
② be placed upon
棚の上に載っている *tana no ue ni notte iru* be [lie] on a shelf
③ be loaded (on a vehicle)

SYNONYMS

❶ **load**
積む load → 1236
搭 load on board → 592
❷ **print and publish**
掲 display in writing → 494
版 PUBLISHING → 872
刊 PUBLISH → 190
刷 PRINT → 1273
印 print → 828
植 typeset → 990

HOMOPHONES

noseru ⇨ 乗 3576
noru ⇨ 乗 3576

NOTE

⇨ see USAGE note at 乗 3576
★do not confuse with 戴 3302

虜 虞 incorrect classification ⇨ see □ 4-9 6-7 虍

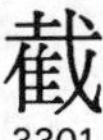 6-8 戈

3301 SETSU SAI ki(ru)

Ⓒⓗ 截 jié

Radical	Strokes
戈 62	14-4-10
Grade	**Freq**
Reference	
□ 3 - 6 - 8	

COMPOUNDS

ⓐ [now also 切 *setsu* 27] [original meaning] cut, sever

ⓑ [now usu. 切る *kiru*] cut (flat things such as cloth or paper)

截断 *setsudan* cutting

截然たる *setsuzentaru* distinct, clear-cut, sharp

直截な *chokusetsu* (=*chokusai*) *na* direct, plain, straightforward

布を截る *nuno o kiru* cut cloth

HOMOPHONES

kiru ⇨ 切 27 伐 42 剪 2306 斬 1482

NOTE

⇨ see USAGE note at 切 27

 incorrect classification ⇨ see 2888 6-9 辶

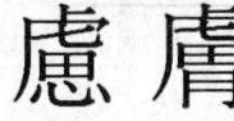 incorrect classification ⇨ see □ 4-11 6-9 虍

 incorrect classification ⇨ see 2373 6-10 艹

薦 incorrect classification/stroke count ⇨ see 2373 6-11 艹

戴 戴 戴 6-12 戈

3302 TAI itada(ku)

Stroke order: 1–18

Ⓒⓗ 戴 dài

Radical	Strokes
戈 62	18-4-14
Grade	**Freq**
Non-Jōyō	1768
□ 3 - 6 - 1 2	

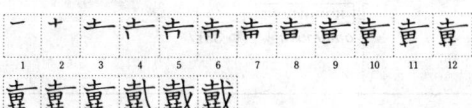

▶RECEIVE HUMBLY

COMPOUNDS

❶ **receive humbly, accept with thanks**

頂戴する *chōdai suru* [humble] receive, accept, take; eat, drink

❷ have over, be presided over by, live under (a ruler)

推戴する *suitai suru* have over, be presided over by

奉戴する *hōtai suru* have over, be presided over by, live under

不倶戴天 *fugutaiten* cannot live together under the canopy of heaven

❸ [original meaning] be crowned with, wear (a crown)

戴冠式 *taikanshiki* coronation (ceremony)

戴白 *taihaku* becoming gray haired; old people

KUN

【itada(ku) 戴く】
[usu. 頂く]
① [humble]
ⓐ receive humbly, accept with thanks, be given, be favored with
ⓑ eat, drink
ⓒ trouble someone to do something, have something done
② have over, be presided over by, live under (a ruler)
③ wear (a crown); be crowned (with snow)
⇨ see 頂 145 for compounds

SYNONYMS

❶ receive
頂 RECEIVE HUMBLY → 145
拝 have the honor to receive → 303
受 RECEIVE → 2421
享 ENJOY → 2051
領 receive → 1224
収 TAKE IN → 198
納 ACCEPT → 1300

HOMOPHONES

itadaku ⇨ 頂 145

NOTE

⇨ see USAGE note at 頂 145
★do not confuse with 截 3300

6-13
門

incorrect classification ⇨ see 2538
(nonstandard for 藺 2380)

7-2
走

赴 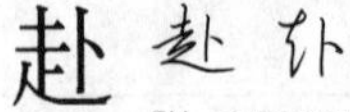
3303 FU omomu(ku)

Ⓒⓗ 赴 fù

Radical	Strokes
走 156	9-7-2
Grade	**Freq**
Jōyō	1750
口 3 - 7 - 2	

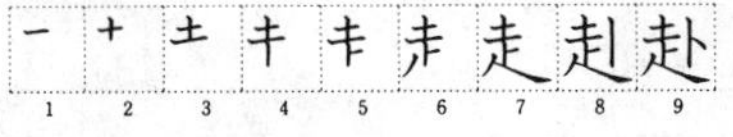

▶PROCEED TO

COMPOUNDS

● proceed to (as a new appointment), go to, head for, attend
赴任 *funin* proceeding to a new post

KUN

【omomu(ku) 赴く】
[sometimes also 趣く]
① proceed to, go to, head for
死地に赴く *shichi ni omomuku* ride into the jaws of death
② become, tend towards
快方に赴く *kaihō ni omomuku* get better, improve, convalesce

SYNONYMS

● go and come
向 head toward → 3052
通 go to and from → 3109
来 COME → 3551
参 go somewhere → 2066
出 go to → 3498
行 GO → 212
往 GO ON → 292

USAGE

omomuku
赴く
[sometimes also 趣く]
① proceed to, go to, head for
② become, tend towards
趣く
[usu. 赴く] same as 赴く

HOMOPHONES

omomuku ⇨ 趣 3317

7-2
走

3304

▶VALIANT
nonstandard for 赳 3308

剋 3305 KOKU

Ⓒ克 kè 尅 kēi

Radical	Strokes
刂 18	9-2-7
Grade	**Freq**
Reference	
口 3-7-2	

7-2 克

COMPOUNDS

● [now replaced by 克 2046] [original meaning] overcome, conquer, win

下剋上 *gekokujō* the lower dominating the upper

相剋する *sōkoku suru* struggle with each other, conflict

勉 3306

▶**ENDEAVOR**

nonstandard for 勉 3318

7-2 免

起 3307 起 起 起

KI o(kiru) o(koru) o(kosu) ta(tsu)▲

Ⓒ起 qǐ

Radical	Strokes
走 156	10-7-3
Grade	**Freq**
Jōyō-3	369
口 3-7-3	

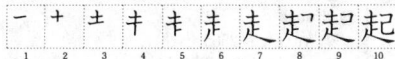

7-3 走

一	十	土	丰	丰	走	走	起	起	起
1	2	3	4	5	6	7	8	9	10

▶**RISE**

COMPOUNDS

❶ⓐ [original meaning] (assume a standing position) **rise** (**to one's feet**), **stand up**

ⓑ (get out of bed) **rise, get up**

起立する *kiritsu suru* stand up, rise

起居 *kikyo* one's daily life

起床 *kishō* getting up, rising

起座する *kiza suru* sit up in bed

❷ⓐ (project upward) **rise, protrude**

ⓑ **raise up, lift**

起伏 *kifuku* ups and downs, undulations

突起する *tokki suru* project, protrude

隆起 *ryūki* protuberance, elevation

起重機 *kijūki* crane, derrick

❸ used in forming verbal compounds—roughly equiv. to *up* in *bring up*

提起する *teiki suru* raise (a question), bring forward

喚起する *kanki suru* awaken, rouse, arouse

想起する *sōki suru* remember, recollect

❹ call into office

起用 *kiyō* appointment, employment

❺ **rise** [**rouse oneself**] **to action, spring up, be stirred up**

奮起する *funki suru* rouse [bestir] oneself, rise (to the occasion)

決起する *kekki suru* rise to action, spring up

再起 *saiki* comeback, recovery, restoration

❻ⓐ **start, begin, initiate, promote**

ⓑ starting point, beginning, origin

ⓒ first stanza in a Chinese quatrain; the opening line

起訴 *kiso* prosecution, indictment, litigation

起草する *kisō suru* draft (a bill), draw up

起工 *kikō* start of construction work

起爆 *kibaku* priming (in explosives)

起点 *kiten* starting point, terminus

起源 *kigen* origin, beginning

起因する *kiin suru* originate in, be attributable to

縁起 *engi* origin, history; omen, luck

起承転結 *kishōtenketsu* introduction, development, turn and conclusion (of a Chinese quatrain)

起句 *kiku* opening line of a Chinese quatrain

❼ generate, produce

起電 *kiden* generation of electricity

起磁力 *kijiryoku* magnetomotive force

励起 *reiki* excitation

KUN

【**o**(**kiru**) 起きる】

①ⓐ rise to one's feet, get up

ⓑ rise (from one's bed), get out of bed

起き上がる *okiagaru* get up, rise

早起き *hayaoki* early rising

② wake up, awake

遅く迄起きている *osoku made okite iru* stay up late

③ happen, take place, occur, break out

クーデターが起きた *Kūdetā ga okita* A coup d'état broke out

④ begin to burn, be kindled
良く起きた火 *yoku okita hi* blazing fire

【o(koru) 起こる】
① happen, occur, take place
沸き起こる *wakiokoru* arise
② [also 興る] (come into existence) rise, spring up, be established
新たに起こった国 *arata ni okotta kuni* newly established country
③ arise from, originate in, result from
起こり *okori* origin, source, beginning; cause, genesis
不眠から起こる疲労 *fumin kara okoru hirō* fatigue resulting from insomnia
④ (of heat or electricity) be generated, be produced
摩擦で起こった熱 *masatsu de okotta netsu* heat generated from friction
⑤ (of diseases) develop, have an attack of
喘息が起こる *zensoku ga okoru* have an attack of asthma
⑥ be kindled
赤赤と起こった火 *akaaka to okotta hi* blazing fire

【o(kosu) 起こす】
① raise up, set upright
抱き起こす *dakiokosu* lift (a person) in one's arms, help (a person) sit up
② wake up, awake, arouse
揺り起こす *yuriokosu* shake up, wake by shaking
③ give rise to, bring about, raise
引き起こす *hikiokosu* bring about, cause, provoke; pull up
④ⓐ start, begin, launch, inaugurate
ⓑ establish, set up
書き起こす *kakiokosu* begin [start] writing
会社を起こす *kaisha o okosu* set up a company
⑤ (of heat or electricity) produce, generate
水力で電気を起こす *suiryoku de denki o okosu* generate electricity by hydraulic power
⑥ plow
畑を起こす *hatake o okosu* plow a field

【ta(tsu) 起つ】 [now usu. 立つ] rise (to action), rouse oneself
起ち居 *tachii* one's movement
祖国の為に起つ *sokoku no tame ni tatsu* rise to the rescue of one's country

SYNONYMS

❶ assume upright position
立 STAND → 1992

❷ⓐ protrude and protruding
出る stick out → 3498
突 protruding → 2230
凸 CONVEX → 3486
隆 protuberant → 545

ⓑ raise
上 raise → 3404
立てる STAND → 1992
揚 RAISE HIGH → 593
掲 PUT UP → 494
挙 RAISE → 2456
拾う PICK UP → 379

❺ incite
動 MOVE → 1778
振 arouse to action → 430
奮 ROUSE UP → 2367
激 excite → 776
扇 FAN → 1950
挑 PROVOKE → 372
唆 INSTIGATE → 402

❻ⓐ begin
発 START → 2565
始 BEGIN → 281
-出す begin to do → 3498
-掛ける start doing → 493
就 SET ABOUT → 1694
開 OPEN → 3321
創 initiate → 1815
肇 ORIGINATE → 2799

❼ create
発 START → 2565
生 produce → 3497
創 CREATE → 1815
作 compose → 68

USAGE

❶ okoru
起こる
① happen, occur, take place
② [also 興る] (come into existence) rise, spring up, be established
③ arise from, originate in, result from
④ (of heat or electricity) be generated, be produced
⑤ (of diseases) develop, have an attack of
⑥ be kindled
興る
① rise to prosperity, prosper, thrive, flourish
② [also 起こる] (come into existence) rise, spring up, be established

❷ okosu
起こす
① raise up, set upright
② wake up, awake, arouse
③ give rise to, bring about, raise
④ⓐ start, begin, launch, inaugurate
ⓑ establish, set up
⑤ (of heat or electricity) produce, generate
⑥ plow
興す
cause to rise (to prosperity), promote, further, advance, develop

HOMOPHONES

okoru ⇨ 興 2909
okosu ⇨ 興 2909
tatsu ⇨ 立 1992 建 3090 発 2565 経 1331

NOTE

⇨ see also USAGE note at 立 1992

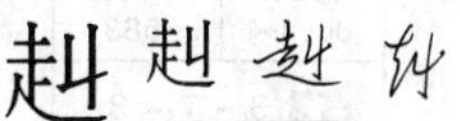

3308 KYŪ NAMES take takeshi

Ⓒ赳 jiū

Radical	Strokes
走 156	10-7-3
Grade	**Freq**
Names	2123
口 3-7-3	

7-3 走

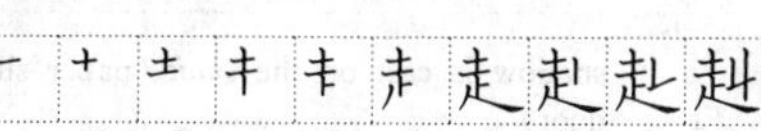

1 2 3 4 5 6 7 8 9 10

▶**VALIANT**

COMPOUNDS

● [rare] valiant, brave and strong, gallant
赳赳たる武夫 *kyūkyūtaru bufu* soldier of dauntless courage

NAMES

赳夫 *takeo* male name
赳 *takeshi* male name

SYNONYMS

● **brave**
勇 BRAVE → 2089
敢 bold → 1706
豪 bold and unrestrained → 2140
雄 HEROIC → 1008
壮 heroic → 224
義 chivalrous → 2338

趆

3309

▶**RISE**
nonstandard for 起 3307

7-3 走

島 嶋° 島 島

3310 TŌ shima

Ⓒ岛 dǎo

Radical	Strokes
山 46	10-3-7
Grade	**Freq**
Jōyō-3	179
口 3-7-3	

7-3 鳥

1 2 3 4 5 6 7 8 9 10

▶**ISLAND**

COMPOUNDS

ⓐ [also suffix] [original meaning] **island**
ⓑ suffix after names of islands
島嶼 *tōsho* islands
島民 *tōmin* islanders
諸島 *shotō* archipelago
半島 *hantō* peninsula
列島 *rettō* archipelago
無人島 *mujintō* uninhabited island
色丹島 *shikotantō* Shikotan Island

KUN

【shima 島】 [also suffix] island, isle, islet
島国 *shimaguni* island country
島巡り *shimameguri* tour of the islands, tour of an island
離れ島 *hanarejima* solitary island
宝島 *takarajima* treasure island
八丈島 *hachijōjima* Hachijo Island

SYNONYMS

● **elevations in water**
州 sandbar → 57
礁 REEF → 1243

7-3 羊

差 差 差

3311 SA sa(su) sa(shi)

CH 差 chà chā chāi cī

Radical	Strokes
工 48	10-3-7
Grade	**Freq**
Jōyō-4	583
口 3-7-3	

丶 丷 䒑 䒑 羊 羊 差 差 差 差 (1 2 3 4 5 6 7 8 9 10)

▶DIFFERENCE

COMPOUNDS

❶ [also suffix]

ⓐ [original meaning] **difference, discrepancy, inequality, differential**

ⓑ (**quantitative**) **difference;** *math* **remainder**

差異 *sai* difference, disparity
差別 *sabetsu* discrimination
大差 *taisa* big difference
格差 *kakusa* difference in quality [price]
個人差 *kojinsa* individual differences
差額 *sagaku* difference (in prices), balance
時差 *jisa* time difference

❷ [formerly 叉 3386] cross, intersect
交差 *kōsa* crossing, intersection
三差路 *sansaro* three-forked road

❸ dispatch, expedite
差遣する *saken suru* dispatch, send
差配人 *sahainin* real estate agent

INDEPENDENT

【**sa 差**】difference; *math* remainder
差を付ける *sa o tsukeru* discriminate; establish a lead
賃金の差 *chingin no sa* wage difference

KUN

【**sa(su) 差す**】

① offer, present, provide
杯を差す *sakazuki o sasu* offer a cup (of sake)

② hold up, spread (over one's hand)
傘を差す *kasa o sasu* hold an umbrella

③ wear in one's belt or hair
刀を差す *katana o sasu* wear a sword

④ become tinged with
赤味が差している *akami ga sashite iru* tinged red

⑤ (of water) rise, flow
潮が差す *Shio ga sasu* The tide comes in

⑥ be struck by
魔が差す *ma ga sasu* be tempted by an evil spirit

⑦ [sometimes also 注す] pour (into), fill up
器に水を差す *utsuwa ni mizu o sasu* fill a pitcher with water

⑧ [sometimes also 注す] color

⑨ [formerly also 射す] shine on
障子に影が差す *Shōji ni kage ga sasu* A shadow is cast on the *shoji* (paper sliding-door)

【**sa(shi) 差し**】

①ⓐ [emphatic or polite prefix] do, execute
ⓑ [verbal prefix] send, present
差し当たり(=差し当たって) *sashiatari* (=*sashiatatte*) for the time being, for the present, at present
差し上げる *sashiageru* give (to superior)
差し控える *sashihikaeru* be moderate in; withhold, desist from, refrain from
差し止める *sashitomeru* prohibit, forbid; suspend (a paper)
差し支え *sashitsukae* hindrance, complications; objections
差し回す *sashimawasu* send (a car) around
差し出し先 *sashidashisaki* address

② [in compounds] measure, measuring
物差し *monosashi* ruler

③ [in compounds] vessel for pouring
水差し *mizusashi* pitcher, jug

④ counter for dances

⑤ sumo move

⑥ tête-à-tête
差しで *sashi de* between two persons, face to face

SYNONYMS

❶ **differing and difference**
異 DIFFERENT → 2584
違 DIFFER → 3151

❷ **intercross**
交 intercross → 2015

USAGE

❶ **sasu**

差す
① offer, present, provide
② hold up, spread (over one's hand)
③ wear in one's belt or hair
④ become tinged with
⑤ (of water) rise, flow
⑥ be struck by
⑦ [sometimes also 注す] pour (into), fill up
⑧ [sometimes also 注す] color
⑨ [formerly also 射す] shine on

指す
①ⓐ point to, point at, indicate
ⓑ aim at, have in view

② appoint, nominate; finger, accuse
③ play board games (esp. shogi)

刺す
①ⓐ stab, pierce, prick, thrust
ⓑ sting, bite
② sew, stitch
③ *baseball* catch (a runner) out

挿す
ⓐ insert, put into, stick between
ⓑ insert seedlings, plant

注す
① [usu. 差す] pour (into), fill up
② [usu. 差す] color

射す
[now usu. 差す] shine on

-止す
[verbal suffix] leave something unfinished, stop in the middle

★The relationship between the above seven verbs is complicated, and lexicographers disagree as to their proper usage. Their recommended, but not necessarily universal, usage is as shown. Study the equivalents and examples under the respective entries. It is interesting to note that *sasu* can be written in a total of 91 different ways!

❷ **sashi**

差し
①ⓐ [emphatic or polite prefix] do, execute
ⓑ [verbal prefix] send, present
② [in compounds] measure, measuring
③ [in compounds] vessel for pouring
④ counter for dances
⑤ sumo move
⑥ tête-à-tête

刺し
① stabbing, piercing, pricking
② stitch
③ *sashimi*, sliced raw flesh (esp. of fish)

-指し
[suffix] player (of shogi)

-止し
[verbal suffix] leaving something unfinished

HOMOPHONES
sasu ⇨ 指 378 刺 1275 挿 431 注 325 射 1458 止 2941
sashi ⇨ 刺 1275 指 378 止 2941

荷 incorrect classification ⇨ see 2282 7-3 荇

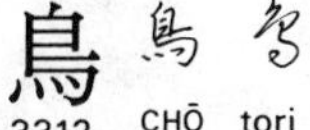

3312 CHŌ tori

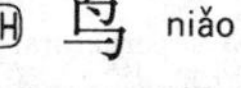

niǎo

Radical	Strokes
鳥 196	11-11-0
Grade	**Freq**
Jōyō-2	898
口 3 - 7 - 4	

7-4 鳥

RADICAL 196
Standard form: 鳥 *tori* 'bird' (鷹 鶯 鷲)
Right variant: 鳥 *tori* (鳴 鶏 鳩)
Description: used in characters related to bird names

▶**BIRD**

COMPOUNDS
● [also suffix] [original meaning] **bird, fowl**
鳥類 *chōrui* birds, fowls
野鳥 *yachō* wild fowl, wild bird
愛鳥週間 *aichō shūkan* Bird Week
保護鳥 *hogochō* protected bird
益鳥 *ekichō* beneficial bird
害鳥 *gaichō* injurious bird
白鳥 *hakuchō* swan
七面鳥 *shichimenchō* turkey
雷鳥 *raichō* snow grouse
一石二鳥 *isseki-nichō* killing two birds with one stone

KUN
【**tori 鳥**】
ⓐ bird, fowl
ⓑ [also 鶏] chicken; fowl, poultry
鳥居 *torii* torii, Shinto shrine archway (⛩)
海鳥 *umidori* seabird
小鳥 *kotori* small [little] bird
渡り鳥 *wataridori* migratory bird
水鳥 *mizutori* waterfowl
鳥肉 *toriniku* chicken
鳥屋 *toriya* bird dealer; poulterer
雌鳥 *mendori* hen

SYNONYMS
● **bird**
酉 THE BIRD → 3544

USAGE

tori

鳥
ⓐ bird, fowl
ⓑ [also 鶏] chicken; fowl, poultry

鶏
[also 鳥] chicken; fowl, poultry

酉
tenth sign of the Oriental zodiac: the Bird

HOMOPHONES

tori ⇨ 鶏 1768 酉 3544

7-4 著 incorrect classification ⇨ see 2300

7-5 超

3313 CHŌ ko(eru) ko(su)

Stroke order: 一 + 土 キ キ 走 走 起 超 超 超 超 (1–12)

Ⓒ 超 chāo

Radical	Strokes
走 156	12-7-5
Grade	**Freq**
Jōyō	1056
口 3-7-5	

▶SURPASS

COMPOUNDS

❶ⓐ (go beyond the limit) **surpass, transcend, excel**
ⓑ [also prefix] **super-, ultra-**
超越する *chōetsu suru* transcend, surpass
超絶 *chōzetsu* transcendence; excellence, superiority
超然たる *chōzentaru* transcendental, standing aloof
超人 *chōjin* superman
超自然的な *chōshizenteki na* supernatural
超国家的な *chōkokkateki na* ultranationalistic
超音速 *chōonsoku* supersonic speed
超大型 *chōōgata* extra-large

❷ⓐ (go beyond in quantity or degree) **surpass, exceed, be over**
ⓑ [suffix] excess, in excess of, over
超過 *chōka* excess
入超 *nyūchō* excess of imports over exports
五千円超 *gosen'enchō* 5000 yen in excess
払い超 *haraichō* deficit in long-term capital

❸ [original meaning, now archaic] jump over (an obstacle), cross over

KUN

【ko(eru) 超える】
ⓐ (go beyond in quantity or degree) exceed, surpass, be over
ⓑ (go beyond the limit) surpass, excel, be above, transcend
限度を超える *gendo o koeru* pass the limit, go beyond the limit
観客は百人を超えた *Kankyaku wa hyakunin o koeta* The audience exceeded 100
人知を超えた *jinchi o koeta* beyond human understanding

【ko(su) 超す】 (go beyond in quantity or degree) surpass, exceed, rise above, be over
一万人を超す人人 ***ichimannin o kosu hitobito*** more than 10,000 people

SYNONYMS

❶ⓐ **excel**
越 GO BEYOND → 3314
抜 STAND OUT → 246
勝 EXCEL → 1005

ⓑ **extreme in degree**
甚 EXTREMELY → 2643
強 STRONG → 475
重 HEAVY → 3573
高 HIGH → 2097
深 DEEP → 524
大 BIG → 3416
切 keen → 27
痛 bitter(ly) → 3285
極 EXTREME → 1017
激 intense → 776
厳 SEVERE → 3289
酷 SEVERE → 1562

❷ⓐ **exceeding and excess**
過 EXCEED → 3137
越 GO BEYOND → 3314
濫 EXCESSIVE → 801
余 EXCESS → 2042
剰 SURPLUS → 1779
冗 REDUNDANT → 1976

HOMOPHONES

koeru ⇨ 越 3314
kosu ⇨ 越 3314

NOTE

⇨ see USAGE note at 越 3314

越 越 𫟼

3314 ETSU OTSU▲ ko(su) -ko(su) -go(shi) ko(eru) -go(e)

ⒸⒽ 越 yuè

Radical	Strokes
走 156	12-7-5
Grade	**Freq**
Jōyō	522

口 3-7-5

一 十 土 キ キ 走 走 赴 赴 越 越 越
1 2 3 4 5 6 7 8 9 10 11 12

▶**GO BEYOND**

COMPOUNDS

❶ⓐ go beyond or over a physical or abstract boundary: **go over, skip over, jump over**

ⓑ go beyond the bounds of propriety or authority: **transgress, overstep, exceed**

飛越する *hietsu suru* jump over (a hurdle), clear (a fence)

越訴 *esso* (=*osso*) appeal made directly to a senior official without going through formalities

越境 *ekkyō* border transgression, violation of the border

越権 *ekken* going beyond one's authority

僭越な *sen'etsu na* presumptuous, arrogant

❷ⓐ go or be beyond in degree: **be more than, exceed, surpass**

ⓑ go beyond the bounds of the ordinary: **be better than, transcend, surpass, excel**

激越な *gekietsu na* violent, vehement

超越する *chōetsu suru* transcend, surpass

優越 *yūetsu* superiority, supremacy

卓越する *takuetsu suru* excel, surpass

❸ pass, spend (time)

越冬 *ettō* passing the winter, wintering

越年草本 *etsunen sōhon* biennial herb

❹ⓐ Yue, name of an ancient Chinese state

ⓑ abbrev. of 越南 *etsunan*: Vietnam

呉越 *goetsu* Wu and Yue, two rival states in ancient China

中越紛争 *chūetsu funsō* dispute between China and Vietnam

反越 *han'etsu* anti-Vietnam

❺ Esshu, old name for Niigata, Toyama and east Fukui prefectures

越後 *echigo* Echigo, old name for Niigata Prefecture

信越本線 *shin'etsu honsen* Shinetsu Main Line (Gunma-Nagano-Niigata Railway)

INDEPENDENT

【**etsu 越**】Yue (⇒❹ⓐ)

KUN

【**ko(su) 越す**】

①ⓐ go over, cross over, pass, go across

ⓑ surmount, pass through, overcome

通り越す *tōrikosu* go beyond, pass through

乗り越す *norikosu* ride past

山を越す *yama o kosu* go across a mountain; surmount a difficulty

②ⓐ be better than, surpass

ⓑ outstrip, outrun

それに越した事は無い *Sore ni koshita koto wa nai* Nothing could be better

勝ち越す *kachikosu* have more wins than losses; lead (someone) by (three) matches

追い越す *oikosu* outrun, pass; overtake

③ pass, spend (time)

年越し *toshikoshi* welcoming the new year

④ move, change quarters

引っ越す *hikkosu* move, change quarters

⑤ go, come

斎藤さんがお越しです *Saitōsan ga okoshi desu* Mr. Saito has come

【**-ko(su) -越す**】shift over, shift onward

持ち越す *mochikosu* carry forward, bring over, defer

繰り越す *kurikosu* transfer, bring forward, carry over

見越す *mikosu* anticipate, speculate (on), foresee

【**-go(shi) -越し**】

[also suffix]

ⓐ across, over, beyond

ⓑ after, over

垣根越しに見る *kakinegoshi ni miru* look over the fence

十年越しの付き合い *jūnengoshi no tsukiai* acquaintance of ten years' standing

【**ko(eru) 越える**】go over, go across, go beyond, jump over

乗り越える *norikoeru* get over, climb over; surmount, overcome

川を越える *kawa o koeru* cross a river

【**-go(e) -越え**】

ⓐ crossing over, going over

ⓑ [suffix] road across (a place or mountain)

バンカー越えの一打 *bankāgoe no ichida* a shot over the bunker

伊賀越え *igagoe* road across Iga

SYNONYMS

❶ⓐ **cross**

渡 CROSS → 611

渉 wade → 526

❷ⓐ **exceeding and excess**

超 SURPASS → 3313

過 EXCEED → 3137

濫 EXCESSIVE → 801
余 EXCESS → 2042
剰 SURPLUS → 1779
冗 REDUNDANT → 1976
ⓑ **excel**
超 SURPASS → 3313
抜 STAND OUT → 246
勝 EXCEL → 1005
❹ⓑ **Asian countries**
泰 Thailand → 2583
印 India → 828
比 Philippines → 26
鮮 Korea → 1877
華 CHINA → 2283
日 JAPAN → 3027

USAGE

❶ **kosu**

越す
①ⓐ go over, cross over, pass, go across
ⓑ surmount, pass through, overcome
②ⓐ be better than, surpass
ⓑ outstrip, outrun
③ pass, spend (time)
④ move, change quarters
⑤ go, come

超す
(go beyond in quantity or degree) surpass, exceed, rise above, be over

❷ **koeru**

越える
go over, go across, go beyond, jump over

超える
ⓐ (go beyond in quantity or degree) exceed, surpass, be over
ⓑ (go beyond the limit) surpass, excel, be above, transcend

★The differences between the above verbs are subtle, and they are easily confused. Make a careful study of the equivalents and examples under each entry. There is no consensus among lexicographers as to their correct usage.

HOMOPHONES

kosu ⇨ 超 3313
koeru ⇨ 超 3313

7-5 更

甦

3315 SO KŌ yomigae(ru)

Ⓒⓗ 苏 sū

Radical	Strokes
生 100	12-5-7
Grade	**Freq**
Reference	
□ 3 - 7 - 5	

COMPOUNDS

● [now replaced by 更 *kō* 3541] [original meaning] revive, come back to life

甦生する *sosei* (=*kōsei*) *suru* revive, resuscitate
甦る(=蘇る) *yomigaeru* revive, resuscitate

7-5 𦍌

着 着 着

3316 CHAKU JAKU ki(ru) -gi ki(seru) -ki(se) tsu(ku) tsu(keru)

Ⓒⓗ 着 zhuó zháo zhāo zhe

Radical	Strokes
羊 123	12-6-6
Grade	**Freq**
Jōyō-3	351
□ 3 - 7 - 5	

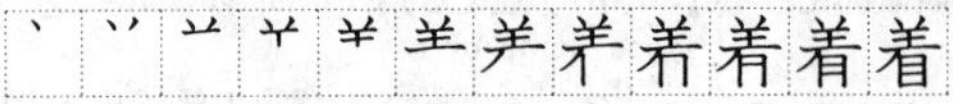

1 2 3 4 5 6 7 8 9 10 11 12

▶PUT ON ▶ARRIVE ▶STICK

COMPOUNDS

❶ⓐ **put on (clothes), don, dress, wear**
ⓑ counter for suits of clothes or garments
着用する *chakuyō suru* wear, have on
着衣 *chakui* one's clothes [clothing]
着帽 *chakubō* putting on one's hat
ズボン二着 *zubon nichaku* two pairs of trousers

❷ [rarely also 著 2300]
ⓐ **arrive at, reach, come to hand**
ⓑ **land**
ⓒ **suffix indicating time, place or order of arrival**
着駅 *chakueki* destination station
着信 *chakushin* arrival of mail
着米 *chakubei* arriving in America
到着 *tōchaku* arrival
先着順 *senchakujun* order of arrival
帰着する *kichaku suru* return, come back; arrive at, result in
発着 *hatchaku* departure and arrival
着陸 *chakuriku* landing, alighting
着地 *chakuchi* landing
着水 *chakusui* alighting [landing] on the water

五時着の列車 *gojichaku no ressha* train due at five o'clock
東京着の時間 *tōkyōchaku no jikan* time of arrival in Tokyo
第一着 *daiitchaku* first to arrive

❸ⓐ **stick, adhere, become attached**
ⓑ (figuratively) **stick to, adhere to, hold fast to**
付着 *fuchaku* adhesion, agglutination; cohesion
密着 *mitchaku* close adhesion
吸着 *kyūchaku* adsorption
接着 *setchaku* adhesion, gluing
癒着 *yuchaku* adhesion, conglutination; connection, collusion
粘着する *nenchaku suru* stick to, be glued to, adhere to
執着 *shūchaku* (=*shūjaku*) attachment; tenacity
愛着 *aichaku* (=*aijaku*) attachment, affection; love
無頓着な *mutonchaku na* indifferent, unmindful, careless

❹ apply, coat, cover, attach to
着色 *chakushoku* color, coloring
装着する *sōchaku suru* fit, install

❺ⓐ (come to rest in one place) **settle (down), settle [seat] oneself, become situated, settle down** (**in a place**)
ⓑ (reach a decision) **settle, come to a settlement**
ⓒ **settle down, become calm [composed], become steady**
着席する *chakuseki suru* take one's seat
着座 *chakuza* taking a seat
着氷 *chakuhyō* icing (on a plane); ice formed by icing
着床 *chakushō* implantation
土着の *dochaku no* native, indigenous, aboriginal
決着 *ketchaku* conclusion, decision
落着 *rakuchaku* settlement, conclusion
着着と *chakuchaku to* steadily, step by step
着実な *chakujitsu na* steady, solid, sound
横着な *ōchaku na* impudent, brazen; idle, lazy
沈着 *chinchaku* composure, self-possession

❻ set about, start, commence
着工 *chakkō* starting construction
着手 *chakushu* start, commencement

❼ bring one's attention to, come to one's attention, think of
着眼 *chakugan* viewpoint, observation
着想 *chakusō* idea, conception
着意 *chakui* idea, conception; caution

❽ be ignited
着火する *chakka suru* be ignited, be kindled, catch (fire)

❾ play board games (esp. go)
勝着 *shōchaku* winning move (in a go game)

❿ take upon oneself
着服 *chakufuku* embezzlement, misappropriation

⓫ auxiliary particle
瞞着 *manchaku* deception, cheating, trickery
悶着 *monchaku* trouble(s), difficulty, dispute

INDEPENDENT

【chaku 着】 arrival
早朝の着 *sōchō no chaku* early morning arrival

【chakusuru 着する】 put on clothes, dress, don, wear
法衣を着する *hōi* (=*hōe*) *o chakusuru* put on a priest's robe

KUN

【ki(ru) 着る】
vi
① put on clothes, dress, don, wear
着物 *kimono* clothes, kimono
着付け *kitsuke* dressing, fitting
着こなす *kikonasu* wear [dress (oneself)] stylishly
着飾る *kikazaru* dress up
コートを着る *kōto o kiru* put on [don] one's coat
② be charged with (a crime), take upon oneself
罪を着る *tsumi o kiru* be accused of, take (another's guilt) on oneself
恩に着る *on ni kiru* feel oneself indebted to

【-gi -着】 [sometimes also -衣] [also suffix] wear, clothes, dress, suit
晴れ着 *haregi* one's best (clothes), gala [holiday] dress
肌着 *hadagi* underwear
上着 *uwagi* outer garment, coat, jacket
水着 *mizugi* bathing [swimming] suit
不断着(=普段着) *fudangi* everyday wear [clothes], home wear
訪問着 *hōmongi* visiting [gala] dress

【ki(seru) 着せる】
vt
①ⓐ dress (a person), put on clothes, clothe
ⓑ coat, plate
手伝って着せる *tetsudatte kiseru* help (a person) dress
お仕着せ *oshikise* clothes provided by the employer; livery
金を着せた指輪 *kin o kiseta yubiwa* ring plated with gold
② charge, pin a crime on, fix
罪を着せる *tsumi o kiseru* pin a crime on

【-ki(se) -着せ】 coated with
銀着せの *ginkise no* silver-plated

【tsu(ku) 着く】

①ⓐ arrive at, reach, come to hand
ⓑ (succeed in touching) reach, come in contact with, touch
駅に着く *eki ni tsuku* arrive at the station
行き着く *ikitsuku* arrive at, get to
船着き場 *funatsukiba* harbor; landing place
追い着く *oitsuku* catch up with
② (come to rest in a position) settle, settle [seat] oneself, become situated, settle down (in a place)
席に着く *seki ni tsuku* take a seat
帰途に着く *kito ni tsuku* leave for home
落ち着く *ochitsuku* calm down, settle down, be steady; settle in, take up one's residence; harmonize with, match

【tsu(keru) 着ける】
① (cause to arrive) bring (a vehicle or boat) alongside, put ashore, berth
ボートを岸に着ける *bōto o kishi ni tsukeru* put a boat ashore
車を門に着ける *kuruma o mon ni tsukeru* pull a car up at the gate
② put on clothes, don, wear, be dressed
面を着ける *men o tsukeru* put a mask on
③ (place a person in a position) settle, settle [seat] a person, situate, steady
落ち着ける *ochitsukeru* calm (down); settle (down)
④ set about, start, commence
手を着ける *te o tsukeru* start; set one's hand to

SYNONYMS
❶ⓐ wear and put on
装 DRESS → 2685
帯 WEAR (esp. at the belt) → 2582
履く put on footwear → 3171
被る put on headgear → 1163
❷ arrive
到 ARRIVE → 1264
至 COME TO → 2182
及 REACH TO → 3385
届く REACH → 3078
達 ATTAIN → 3139
❸ⓐ stick
付 attach itself to → 31
附 attach itself to → 347
ⓑ adhere to
執 adhere to → 1680
❺ settle
帰 settle in place → 130
落 be concluded → 2318
【-gi】
○ clothing
服 CLOTHES → 878
衣 GARMENT → 2013
装 DRESS → 2685

USAGE
-gi
-着
[sometimes also -衣] [also suffix] wear, clothes, dress, suit
-衣
[usu. -着] outer garment, clothes, wear

HOMOPHONES
-gi ⇨ 衣 2013
tsuku ⇨ 付 31 附 347 就 1694 即 1120 点 2084
tsukeru ⇨ 付 31 附 347 就 1694 即 1120 点 2084 漬 702

NOTE
⇨ see also USAGE note at 付 31
★着 was originally a variant of 著 2300.

7-8
走

趣 趣 趣

3317 SHU omomuki omomu(ku)▲

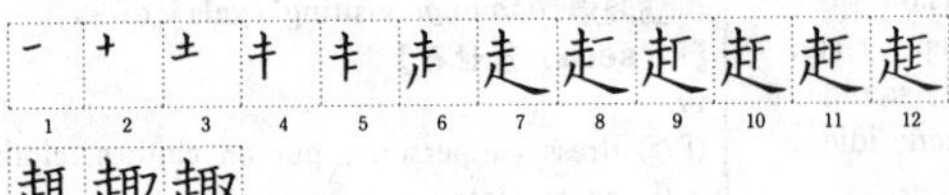

CH 趣 qù

Radical	Strokes
走 156	15-7-8
Grade	**Freq**
Jōyō	1140
□ 3 - 7 - 8	

▶FLAVOR ▶PURPOSE

COMPOUNDS
❶ⓐ flavor, distinctive charm, elegance, taste, beauty, sentiment
ⓑ interest, taste, hobby
情趣 *jōshu* mood, sentiment, artistic effects, charms
野趣 *yashu* charms of the countryside, rural beauty
興趣 *kyōshu* taste, elegance, flavor
趣味 *shumi* hobby, interest, taste
俗趣 *zokushu* vulgar taste
❷ purpose, aim, motive, object, meaning, purport
趣旨 *shushi* purpose, aim; purport, meaning
趣意 *shui* purpose, motive, aim; purport, meaning, point
趣向 *shukō* idea, contrivance, plan
意趣 *ishu* spite, grudge, enmity; [original meaning] purpose, meaning

❸ appearance, air, complexion
異趣 *ishu* extraordinary appearance
❹ *Buddhism* lower levels of the ten realms of living beings
三悪趣 *san'akushu* (=*sannakushu*) three evil worlds: hell, the world of hungry spirits and the world of animals

KUN

【omomuki 趣】 purport, effect, meaning, tenor, gist; flavor, distinctive charm, taste, elegance; appearance, air, aspect
お手紙の趣承知しました *Otegami no omomuki shōchi shimashita* I have duly noted the contents of your letter
趣の有る *omomuki no aru* tasteful, zestful, elegant
趣を異にする *omomuki o koto ni suru* differ in features, be unlike

【omomu(ku) 趣く】
[usu. 赴く]
① proceed to, go to, head for
死地に趣く *shichi ni omomuku* ride into the jaws of death
② become, tend towards
盛大に趣く *seidai ni omomuku* grow in prosperity

SYNONYMS

❶ **flavor and elegance**
品 refinement → 2248
風 elegance → 3007
味 TASTE → 274
❷ **meaning**
旨 PURPORT → 2024
意 MEANING → 2136
義 MEANING → 2338
訳 SENSE → 1473
❷ **will and intention**
志 AMBITION → 2199
意 MIND → 2136
図 intention → 3071
気 mind to do something → 3194
念 thought of doing something → 2059
欲 DESIRE → 1475

HOMOPHONES

omomuku ⇨ 赴 3303

NOTE

⇨ see USAGE notes at 旨 2024 and 赴 3303

7-9 导

導 incorrect classification ⇨ see 2897
(nonstandard for 導 2888)

7-10 产

薦 incorrect classification ⇨ see 2527
(nonstandard for 薦 2373)

7-11 产

薦 incorrect classification／stroke count ⇨ see 2527
(nonstandard for 薦 2373)

8-0 門

門 incorrect classification ⇨ see 888

8-2 免

勉 勉 勉 勉

3318 BEN tsuto(meru)▲

Ⓒⓗ 勉 miǎn

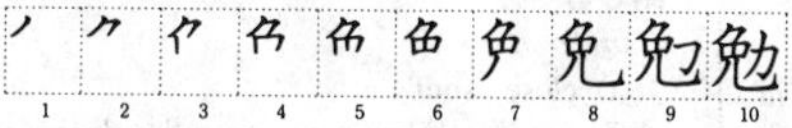

Radical	Strokes
力 19	10-2-8
Grade	**Freq**
Jōyō-3	957
口 3 - 8 - 2	

▶**ENDEAVOR**

COMPOUNDS

❶ [original meaning] **endeavor, make efforts, work diligently, exert oneself**
勉励 *benrei* diligence, industry
勉強 *benkyō* study; selling cheap; [rare] diligence
勉学 *bengaku* study
勤勉な *kinben na* diligent, assiduous, industrious, hardworking
❷ study
ガリ勉 *gariben* [belittling] studying hard, digging; diligent student, grind

KUN

【tsuto(meru) 勉める】 [usu. 努める] endeavor, make efforts, try hard, work diligently

勉めて *tsutomete* with effort, as much as possible
極力勉める *kyokuryoku tsutomeru* do one's best

SYNONYMS

❶ **exert oneself**
努 EXERT → 2547
励 make efforts → 1119
勤 work diligently → 1818
尽 use all one's strength → 3050
精 put one's heart into → 1366

HOMOPHONES

tsutomeru ⇨ 努 2547 勤 1818 務 1173

NOTE

⇨ see USAGE note at 勤 1818
⇨ see COMPOUND FORMATION for 勉強 *benkyō* ⇨ 強 475

8-3
門

閉 閉 𠂇

3319 HEI to(jiru) to(zasu) shi(meru) shi(maru) ta(teru)▲

CH 闭 bì

Radical	Strokes
門 169	11-8-3
Grade	**Freq**
Jōyō-6	1048
口 3-8-3	

▶**CLOSE**

COMPOUNDS

❶ⓐ [original meaning] (move into closed position) **close, shut, confine**
ⓑ (plug up) close, stop up
閉鎖 *heisa* closing, closure, shutdown
閉口する *heikō suru* be dumfounded [stumped], be silenced
開閉する *kaihei suru* open and shut [close]; make and break (circuits)
密閉する *mippei suru* close up tightly, seal hermetically
閉塞 *heisoku* blockade, stoppage
❷ (bring to an end) **close (a shop), adjourn, end**
閉会 *heikai* closing (of a meeting), adjournment
閉店 *heiten* closing the shop
閉幕となる *heimaku to naru* come to a close [end]
閉校 *heikō* closing a school

INDEPENDENT

【**hei** 閉】OFF, CLOSE (marking on switches or taps)

KUN

【**to(jiru)** 閉じる】
vi & vt
① close, shut
閉じ込める *tojikomeru* shut in [up], lock in [up]
② (come or bring to an end) close (a meeting)
幕を閉じる *maku o tojiru* close the curtain; come to an end
【**to(zasu)** 閉ざす】*vt* shut, close, fasten, lock; cause to be buried (in grief)
門戸を閉ざす *monko o tozasu* close the door to, exclude
悲しみに閉ざされる *kanashimi ni tozasareru* be buried in grief
【**shi(meru)** 閉める】*vt* (move into closed position) shut, close
蓋を閉める *futa o shimeru* shut the lid
【**shi(maru)** 閉まる】*vi* be shut, be closed, shut, close
閉まり *shimari* shutting, closing
戸が閉まった *To ga shimatta* The door shut [closed]
【**ta(teru)** 閉てる】[sometimes also 立てる] shut (as a paper sliding-door)
開け閉て *aketate* opening and shutting

SYNONYMS

❶ⓐ **close**
鎖 lock up → 1761
封 SEAL → 1287
❷ **end**
終 END → 1336
絶 COME TO AN END → 1353
了 FINISH → 3350
済 SETTLE → 522
-上げる completion suffix → 3404
完 COMPLETE → 2201
結 CONCLUDE → 1348

USAGE

tojiru
閉じる
vi & vt
① close, shut
② (come or bring to an end) close (a meeting)
綴じる
ⓐ bind, file
ⓑ sew up, stitch together; mend

HOMOPHONES

tojiru ⇨ 綴 1381
shimeru ⇨ 締 1393 〆 3372 絞 1349
shimaru ⇨ 締 1393 絞 1349
tateru ⇨ 立 1992 建 3090 点 2084

NOTE
⇨ see also USAGE notes at 締 1393 and 立 1992

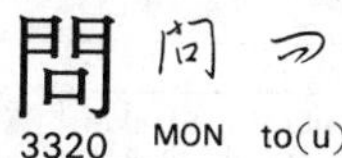

3320 MON to(u) to(i) ton

CH 问 wèn

Radical	Strokes
口 30	11-3-8
Grade	**Freq**
Jōyō-3	61
口 3-8-3	

8-3 門

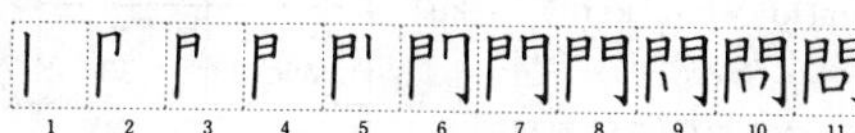

1 2 3 4 5 6 7 8 9 10 11

▶QUESTION

COMPOUNDS

❶ⓐ [original meaning] **question, ask, inquire**

ⓑ **question, inquiry, problem**

ⓒ counter for questions

質問 *shitsumon* question

尋問する *jinmon suru* question, examine, interrogate

詰問する *kitsumon suru* cross-examine, cross-question, question closely

顧問 *komon* adviser, consultant

問題 *mondai* problem, question, issue, matter

問答 *mondō* questions and answers, catechism

難問 *nanmon* difficult problem [question]

第一問 *daiichimon* first question [problem]

❷ call on, pay a visit

訪問 *hōmon* visit

慰問 *imon* inquiring after a person's health; consolation

❸ accuse, charge

問罪 *monzai* accusation, indictment

❹ care, mind

不問 *fumon* regardless, irrespective

KUN

【to(u) 問う】

① ask, question, inquire

問い合わせる *toiawaseru* inquire, make a reference, apply

問い質す *toitadasu* inquire, question

問い詰める *toitsumeru* press a question, cross-examine

② accuse, charge

殺人罪に問われて *satsujinzai ni towarete* on a charge of murder

③ care, mind

経験を問わず *keiken o towazu* no experience necessary

【to(i) 問い】 question, query, inquiry, interrogation

問いを掛ける *toi o kakeru* ask a question of (a person)

【ton 問】 [in compounds] unclassified compounds

問屋 *ton'ya* (=*toiya*) wholesale store, wholesaler, commission agent

SYNONYMS

❶ⓐ **inquire**

詰 question closely → 1521

聞く ask → 3326

質 query → 2808

尋ねる INQUIRE → 2322

伺う INQUIRE (*humble*) → 69

諮 CONSULT → 1596

ⓑ **question**

題 PROBLEM → 3337

論 question (issue) → 1574

USAGE

tou

問う

① ask, question, inquire

② accuse, charge

③ care, mind

訪う

call on, visit

HOMOPHONES

tou ⇨ 訪 1468

NOTE

⇨ see COMPOUND FORMATION for 顧問 *komon* ⇨ 顧 1900

incorrect classification ⇨ see 2116

8-3 冏

髙

incorrect classification ⇨ see 2119
(nonstandard for 高 2097)

8-3 冂

8-4 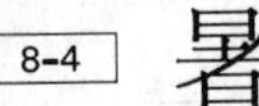 暑 incorrect classification ⇨ see 2473

8-4 門

開 (閉) (开)

3321 KAI hira(ku) hira(ki) -bira(ki) hira(keru) a(ku) a(keru)

Ⓒⓗ 开 kāi

Radical	Strokes
門 169	12-8-4
Grade	**Freq**
Jōyō-3	73
口 3 - 8 - 4	

Stroke order: 丨 1, 冂 2, 3, 4, 5, 6, 7, 8, 9, 10, 11, 開 12

▶ **OPEN**

COMPOUNDS

❶ⓐ [original meaning] **open, open up, become open, unfold, expand**

ⓑ open up land, develop, clear (land), reclaim

開閉する *kaihei suru* open and shut [close]; make and break (circuits)

開封する *kaifū suru* open (a letter), unseal

開通 *kaitsū* opening to [for] traffic

展開 *tenkai* unfolding, development, evolution; deployment

公開 *kōkai* opening to the public

開発する *kaihatsu suru* develop, open out; enlighten

開拓 *kaitaku* reclamation, opening up, clearing; exploitation

新開地 *shinkaichi* newly-opened land

❷ⓐ open to the benefits of civilization, become enlightened [civilized], be developed

ⓑ open oneself to eternal truths, become enlightened

開化 *kaika* civilization; enlightenment

開悟 *kaigo* enlightenment, wisdom

❸ **open, commence, establish**

開始する *kaishi suru* begin, commence, open

開会 *kaikai* opening a meeting

開祖 *kaiso* founder, originator

開運 *kaiun* beginning of good luck

開催する *kaisai suru* hold an event, open (an exhibition)

再開する *saikai suru* reopen, resume

❹ *math* root extraction

開方 *kaihō* extraction of roots

開平 *kaihei* square root extraction

❺ state, mention

開陳する *kaichin suru* state, express (one's opinion)

INDEPENDENT

【kai 開】 ON, OPEN (marking on switches or taps)

KUN

【hira(ku) 開く】

①ⓐ open, open up; unfold, flower

ⓑ open up, commence operations

ⓒ open (a conference), hold (a meeting)

開き直る *hirakinaoru* switch to a defiant attitude

店を開く *mise o hiraku* open a business

パーティーを開く *pātī o hiraku* give a party

② [sometimes also 拓く] open up (land), clear, reclaim, develop

道を切り開く *michi o kirihiraku* open a path

③ differ, widen the margin between

距離を開く *kyori o hiraku* open the distance

④ [sometimes also 啓く] enlighten, edify

蒙を開く *mō o hiraku* enlighten (a person's mind)

【hira(ki) 開き】 opening; aperture; hinged door; split and dried fish; adjournment, breakup (of a wedding); *navigation* tack

開き鯵 *hirakiaji* split and dried saurel

御開き *ohiraki* breakup of a wedding

【-bira(ki) -開き】

① opening

両開き *ryōbiraki* double door

② opening, commencement, first day of the season

スキー開き *sukībiraki* opening of the skiing season

【hira(keru) 開ける】 widen, become opened up; develop, become civilized; be up-to-date

街が開けている *Machi ga hirakete iru* The town is opened up

【a(ku) 開く】

ⓐ open, become open

ⓑ (of a shop) open, begin

ドアが開いている *Doa ga aite iru* The door is open

幕開き *makuaki* raising of the curtains; beginning

十時に開く *jūji ni aku* (the shop) opens ten o'clock

【a(keru) 開ける】 open, unlock

戸を開ける *to o akeru* open the door

SYNONYMS

❶ⓐ **open**

展 UNFOLD → 3111

披 open and read → 305

ⓑ **reclaim**
拓 OPEN UP → 317
墾 RECLAIM → 2896
❸ **begin**
始 BEGIN → 281
-出す begin to do → 3498
-掛ける start doing → 493
発 START → 2565
起 start → 3307
就 SET ABOUT → 1694
創 initiate → 1815
肇 ORIGINATE → 2799

USAGE

hiraku
開く
①ⓐ open, open up; unfold, flower
ⓑ open up, commence operations
ⓒ open (a conference), hold (a meeting)
② [sometimes also 拓く] open up (land), clear, reclaim, develop
③ differ, widen the margin between
④ [sometimes also 啓く] enlighten, edify
拓く
[usu. 開く] open up (land), clear, reclaim, develop
啓く
[usu. 開く] enlighten, edify

HOMOPHONES

hiraku ⇨ 拓 317 啓 2763
aku ⇨ 空 2227 明 855
akeru ⇨ 空 2227 明 855

NOTE

⇨ see also USAGE note at 明 855

閑 閑 𫝊

3322 KAN

Ⓒⓗ 闲 xián

Radical	Strokes
門 169	12-8-4
Grade	**Freq**
Jōyō	1532
□ 3 - 8 - 4	

8-4 門

丨 1 ｢ 2 ｢ 3 ｢ 4 ｢ 5 門 6 門 7 門 8 門 9 閂 10 閑 11 閑 12

▶LEISURE ▶QUIET

COMPOUNDS

❶ⓐ **leisure, idleness, spare time**
ⓑ **idle, leisurely, idly**
閑暇 *kanka* leisure
閑散 *kansan* leisure, inactivity
農閑期 *nōkanki* leisure season for farmers
閑居 *kankyo* [sometimes also 間居] idle life, quiet retreat
閑職 *kanshoku* leisurely post, do-nothing job
安閑と *ankan to* idly, in idleness
❷ idle, trifling, rambling
閑談 *kandan* idle talk
閑話休題 *kanwakyūdai* to return to the subject
❸ **quiet, tranquil**
閑静な *kansei na* quiet, tranquil
閑寂な *kanjaku na* quiet, tranquil
森閑とした *shinkan to shita* quiet, still, silent as a graveyard
❹ neglect, make slight of
閑却する *kankyaku suru* neglect, disregard
等閑 *tōkan* negligence, neglect, disregard

INDEPENDENT

【kan 閑】 leisure, idleness, spare time
忙中閑有り *bōchū kan ari* find odd moments of leisure in one's busy life

SYNONYMS

❶ⓐ **leisure**
暇 FREE TIME → 1012
ⓑ **leisurely**
悠 LEISURELY → 2741
❸ **quiet**
静 QUIET → 1728
寂 quiet → 2290
幽 QUIET AND SECLUDED → 3008
粛 still → 3581
黙 SILENT → 2865

COMPOUND FORMATION

閑話休題 *kanwakyūdai*
閑話休題 'to return to the subject' means "we have been engaging in idle (閑 ❷) talk (話) and have stopped (休) the main topic (題), so let's get back to the subject."

8-4 門

間 間 間 𨳢 ㊥ 间 jiān jiàn

3323 KAN KEN aida ma ai▲

Radical	Strokes
門 169	12-8-4
Grade	**Freq**
Jōyō-2	28
□ 3-8-4	

丨 冂 冂 冃 冃 門 門 門 閂 閅 間 間
1 2 3 4 5 6 7 8 9 10 11 12

▶**INTERVAL** ▶**BETWEEN**

COMPOUNDS

❶ [also suffix] (space between) **interval, space, opening, distance**
間隔 *kankaku* interval, space
間接的な *kansetsuteki na* indirect, roundabout
空間 *kūkan* space, room
区間 *kukan* section, territory
東京大阪間 *tōkyō-ōsaka-kan* between Tokyo and Osaka

❷ [also suffix]
ⓐ (time between) **interval, duration of time, period**
ⓑ **for an interval of, during**
時間 *jikan* time, period; hour
夜間に *yakan ni* at night
期間 *kikan* term, period
週間 *shūkan* week
十年間 *jūnenkan* for ten years

❸ [also suffix] **between, among, midway**
中間 *chūkan* middle, midway
民間の *minkan no* private, nongovernmental, civil
世間 *seken* world, society; the public, people
人間 *ningen* human being, man; people, mankind
三遊間 *san'yūkan baseball* between third and shortstop
友人間に *yūjinkan ni* among one's friends

❹ *ken*: unit of length equiv. to approx. 1.8 m or 6 *shaku* (尺)
間数 *kensū* length in *ken*
三間 *sangen* 3 *ken*

❺ spy on
間者 *kanja* spy

❻ [usu. 閑 3322] idleness, leisure, spare time
間居 *kankyo* idle life, quiet retreat

❼ separate, divide
離間 *rikan* alienation, estrangement

INDEPENDENT

【**kan** 間】(space between) interval, space, opening, distance; (time between) interval, duration of time, period
指呼の間 *shiko no kan* hailing distance
間、髪を入れず *kan, hatsu o irezu* in a flash, in no time
この間 *kono kan* during this period

【**ken** 間】*ken* (⇨ ❹)

KUN

【**aida** 間】
① (space between) interval, space, opening, distance
間を空ける *aida o akeru* leave space (between)
数キロの間 *sūkiro no aida* for several kilometers
② (time between) interval, duration of time, period
間を置いて *aida o oite* at intervals (of), intermittently
長い間 *nagai aida* long time
③ (something between) middle; between, among, midway; relationship, terms
間柄 *aidagara* relation, terms
間を取る *aida o toru* take the middle (between the two)
本の間に *hon no aida ni* between two books; between the pages
我我の間で *wareware no aida de* among ourselves

【**ma** 間】
① (space between) interval, space, opening
谷間 *tanima* valley, gorge
隙間 *sukima* gap, opening; crack, crevice
② (time between) interval, duration of time, period
間も無く *ma mo naku* soon, in a short time
昼間 *hiruma* daytime, day
手間 *tema* labor, trouble; time (required for a task)
③ between, among
仲間 *nakama* company, fellow, comrade, associate
④ timing, situation, occasion
間に合う *ma ni au* be in time; answer the purpose; can do without
間が良い *ma ga ii* be lucky
間違い *machigai* mistake, error
⑤ⓐ [also suffix] room, chamber
ⓑ counter for rooms
居間 *ima* living [sitting] room
茶の間 *chanoma* living room
応接間 *ōsetsuma* drawing room, guest room
孔雀の間 *kujaku no ma* the Peacock Room
二間 *futama* two rooms

【**ai** 間】
[also 合い or 合]

① (space between) interval, space, opening
間の戸 *ai no to* door between the rooms
②ⓐ [also prefix] (time between) interval, intermission
ⓑ between seasons
間の手 *ainote* interlude
間狂言 *aikyōgen* interlude (in a noh drama)
幕間 *makuai* intermission, interval
間服 *aifuku* between season wear
③ [in compounds] mixed (blood)
間の子 *ainoko derogatory* person of mixed parentage; crossbreed

SYNONYMS

❶ distance and interval
距 DISTANCE → 1511
程 EXTENT → 1190
❷ⓐ time periods
時 TIME → 924
頃 TIME → 144
暇 FREE TIME → 1012
般 period of time → 1317
刻 POINT OF TIME → 1267
期 TERM → 1704
節 SEASON OF THE YEAR → 2691
季 SEASON (quarter) → 2554
候 SEASON (time of year) → 119
ⓑ during
中 IN (the course of) → 3451
内 within (a given period) → 3466
❸ between
中 MIDDLE → 3451
仲 intermediate → 43
際 inter- → 714
❹ length units
尋 fathom (1.8 m) → 2322
丈 *jo* (3.03 m) → 3419
町 *cho* (109 m) → 1113
里 LEAGUE, *ri* (3.4 km) → 3542
米 meter → 3529
尺 *SHAKU* (30.3 cm) → 3440
寸 *sun* (3.03 cm) → 2935
【ma】
⑤ⓐ rooms
室 ROOM → 2254
房 CHAMBER → 1946
斎 study → 2115
堂 HALL → 2589

HOMOPHONES

ai ⇨ 相 900 合 2019

COMPOUND FORMATION

人間 *ningen* **世間** *seken*
人間 'human being, etc.' and 世間 'world, society, etc.' originally meant among (間 ❸) the people (人) and among (間 ❸) society (世).

NOTE

⇨ see USAGE note at 相 900

閒
3324

▶INTERVAL ▶BETWEEN
nonstandard for 間 3323

8-4 門

incorrect classification ⇨ see 2477
(nonstandard for 為 3577)

8-4 爲

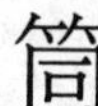

incorrect classification ⇨ see 2680

8-4 筒

暑

incorrect classification ⇨ see 2489
(nonstandard for 暑 2473)

8-5 暑

8-6
門

閥 閥 闷

3325 BATSU

CH 阀 fá

Radical	Strokes
門 169	14-8-6
Grade	**Freq**
Jōyō	1334
口 3 - 8 - 6	

1 2 3 4 5 6 7 8 9 10 11 12 13 14

▶CLIQUE

COMPOUNDS

❶ [also suffix] **clique, clan, power group**
派閥 *habatsu* clique, faction, coterie
財閥 *zaibatsu* financial clique [combine], *zaibatsu*
学閥 *gakubatsu* academic clique, academic cliquism
軍閥 *gunbatsu* military clique
藩閥 *hanbatsu* clan favoritism, clanship
薩摩閥 *satsumabatsu* Satsuma clan
❷ [original meaning] pedigree, lineage, descent
閥族 *batsuzoku* clan, clique
門閥 *monbatsu* (renowned) lineage, pedigree

INDEPENDENT

【**batsu 閥**】clique, faction
閥を作る *batsu o tsukuru* form a clique

SYNONYMS

❶ **parties and sects**
党 PARTY → 2581
流 school → 441
派 SECT → 381
翼 WING → 2720
系 faction → 1944
門 (religious) sect → 888
宗 RELIGIOUS SECT (esp. Buddhist) → 2228

8-6
門

聞 聞 す

3326 BUN MON ki(ku) ki(koeru)

CH 闻 wén

Radical	Strokes
耳 128	14-6-8
Grade	**Freq**
Jōyō-2	247
口 3 - 8 - 6	

1 2 3 4 5 6 7 8 9 10 11 12 13 14

▶HEAR

COMPOUNDS

❶ⓐ (perceive by ear) **hear**
ⓑ (learn by being told) **hear of, be told**
見聞 *kenbun* experience, observation, knowledge
上聞 *jōbun* imperial hearing
聴聞会 *chōmonkai* hearing
前代未聞の *zendaimimon no* unheard-of, unprecedented
❷ⓐ **hearsay, rumor, news**
ⓑ fame, reputation
伝聞 *denbun* hearsay, rumor, report
風聞 *fūbun* rumor, hearsay
新聞 *shinbun* newspaper
旧聞 *kyūbun* old news
醜聞 *shūbun* scandal, ill fame

KUN

【**ki(ku) 聞く**】
①ⓐ hear
ⓑ hear of, be informed
聞き苦しい *kikigurushii* disagreeable to hear, offensive to the ear
聞き手 *kikite* listener, audience
聞き取る *kikitoru* catch, follow, understand
盗み聞き *nusumigiki* eavesdropping, tapping
聞かせる(=聞かす) *kikaseru* (=*kikasu*) inform, tell; read to, play for, sing for
② obey, follow
親の言う事を聞く *oya no iu koto o kiku* obey one's parents
③ [formerly also 訊く] ask, inquire
聞き返す *kikikaesu* inquire again
道を聞く *michi o kiku* ask the way
【**ki(koeru) 聞こえる**】hear, be heard [audible]; sound, seem; be known [famed]
声が聞こえる *Koe ga kikoeru* I hear a voice

SYNONYMS

❶ **hear**
聴 LISTEN → 1418
【**kiku**】
③ **inquire**
問 QUESTION → 3320
詰 question closely → 1521

質 query → 2808
尋ねる INQUIRE → 2322
伺う INQUIRE (*humble*) → 69
諮 CONSULT → 1596

USAGE

kiku
聞く
①ⓐ hear
ⓑ hear of, be informed
② obey, follow
③ [formerly also 訊く] ask, inquire
聴く
listen (to), give an ear to
訊く
[now usu. 聞く] ask, inquire

HOMOPHONES

kiku ⇨ 聴 1418 訊 1452

閣 阁 𫔶

3327 KAKU

Ⓒⓗ 阁 gé

Radical	Strokes
門 169	14-8-6
Grade	**Freq**
Jōyō-6	416
口 3-8-6	

8-6 門

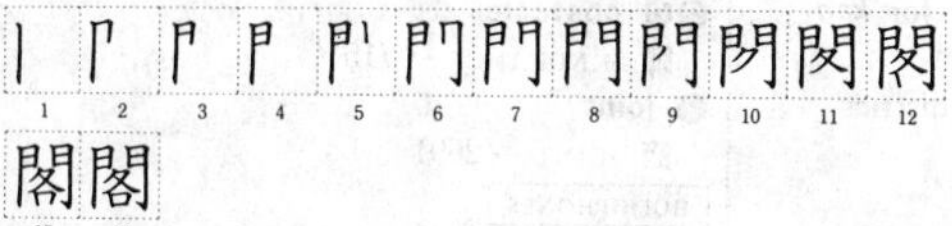

丨 1 ｢ 2 ｢ 3 ｢ 4 ｢ 5 門 6 門 7 門 8 門 9 閃 10 閃 11 閃 12 閣 13 閣 14

▶**TALL MAGNIFICENT BUILDING**
▶**CABINET**

COMPOUNDS

❶ⓐ **tall magnificent building, tower, pavilion, stately mansion, palace**
ⓑ suffix after names of magnificent buildings such as high-class restaurants
閣下 *kakka* Your [His] Excellency
楼閣 *rōkaku* multistoried building
天守閣 *tenshukaku* castle-tower; dungeon, keep
仏閣 *bukkaku* Buddhist temple
銀閣寺 *ginkakuji* Ginkaku Temple
山水閣 *sansuikaku* Sansuikaku (restaurant's name)
❷ **cabinet (of a government)**
閣僚 *kakuryō* cabinet members
閣議 *kakugi* cabinet conference
内閣 *naikaku* cabinet

SYNONYMS

❶ⓐ **tall buildings**
塔 TOWER → 561
楼 TALL BUILDING → 1019
台 observatory → 2005
ⓐ **buildings**
宇 large building → 2175
殿 PALACE → 1792
堂 HALL → 2589
館 PUBLIC BUILDING → 1748
舎 BUILDING → 2060
棟 BLOCK → 991
ⓑ **restaurant suffixes**
亭 quality restaurant suffix → 2072
園 restaurant suffix → 3156
苑 restaurant suffix → 2239
❷ **parts of governments**
省 MINISTRY → 2449

関 關 関 𫔭

3328 KAN seki -zeki kaka(waru)▲

Ⓒⓗ 关 guān

Radical	Strokes
門 169	14-8-6
Grade	**Freq**
Jōyō-4	93
口 3-8-6	

8-6 門

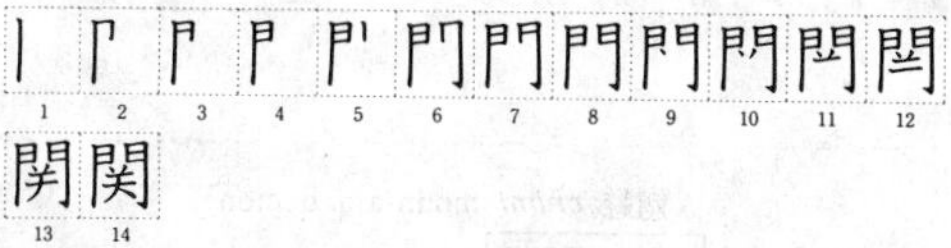

丨 1 ｢ 2 ｢ 3 ｢ 4 ｢ 5 門 6 門 7 門 8 門 9 門 10 閂 11 閂 12 関 13 関 14

▶**CONCERN** ▶**BARRIER**

COMPOUNDS

❶ **concern (oneself), be concerned (with), relate, involve, be connected with**
関係 *kankei* relation, relationship, connection
関連 *kanren* connection, relation, association
関心 *kanshin* concern, interest
関与する *kan'yo suru* take part in, participate in, be concerned in
関知する *kanchi suru* be concerned (with), have a concern (in)
相関 *sōkan* mutual relationship, correlation

❷ⓐ **barrier, customs barrier, checkpoint**
ⓑ entranceway, gateway
関税 *kanzei* customs, custom duty
関門 *kanmon* barrier, gateway
関東 *kantō* Kanto district
関西 *kansai* Kansai district
税関 *zeikan* customhouse
難関 *nankan* barrier, obstacle, difficulty
通関 *tsūkan* customs clearance, entry
玄関 *genkan* entrance, (front) door
❸ **connection, link; turning point**
関節 *kansetsu* joint
機関 *kikan* engine, machine; agency, facilities, institution
❹ [also 函 3001] used phonetically for *kan*
関数 *kansū math* function
❺ abbrev. of 関西 *kansai*: Kansai district
関大 *kandai* Kansai University

INDEPENDENT

【kansuru 関する】 concern, relate to, be connected with; affect, involve

KUN

【seki 関】 barrier, checkpoint; [in compounds] champion wrestler, sumo wrestler
関所 *sekisho* barrier, checkpoint
箱根の関 *hakone no seki* Barrier of Hakone
霞ヶ関 *kasumigaseki* Japanese Foreign Ministry
関取 *sekitori* ranking sumo wrestler
大関 *ōzeki* sumo wrestler of second highest rank

【-zeki -関】 suffix after names of sumo wrestlers
輪島関 *wajimazeki* Champion Wajima (sumo wrestler)

【kaka(waru) 関わる】
[also 係わる]
① be concerned in, be involved
関わり *kakawari* relation, connection
事件に関わる *jiken ni kakawaru* be involved in a case
② influence (adversely), affect
命に関わる *inochi ni kakawaru* be threatening to one's life, be a matter of life and death, fatal

SYNONYMS

❶ **relate**
係 CONNECT → 97
絡 INTERLINK → 1351
渉 HAVE RELATIONS WITH → 526
連 LINK → 3103
❷ⓐ **obstacle**
障 HINDRANCE → 715
❸ **joint**
節 JOINT → 2691

HOMOPHONES

kakawaru ⇨ 係 97 拘 310

COMPOUND FORMATION

❶ **関東** *kantō*
関東 'Kanto district', a major district centered around Tokyo, originally meant 'east (東) of the barrier (関 ❷ⓐ)'. The reference is to an ancient barrier located in the Hakone area.
❷ **関西** *kansai*
関西 'Kansai district' is similar in origin to 関東 above.

NOTE

⇨ see USAGE note at 係 97
⇨ see COMPOUND FORMATION for
関取 *sekitori* ⇨ 取 1262
玄関 *genkan* ⇨ 玄 1991
霞ヶ関 *kasumigaseki* ⇨ 霞 2814

8-7
鬼

魅 魅 魅

3329 MI

Ⓒⓗ 魅 mèi

Radical	Strokes
鬼 194	15-10-5
Grade	**Freq**
Jōyō	1290
口 3-8-7	

▶**CHARM**

COMPOUNDS

❶ **charm, bewitch, enchant, fascinate**
魅力 *miryoku* charm, glamour, appeal
魅惑 *miwaku* fascination, enchantment, charm
魅了する *miryō suru* charm, fascinate
❷ [original meaning] evil spirit, mischievous ghost
魑魅 *chimi* mountain demon

INDEPENDENT

【misuru 魅する】 charm, bewitch
魅せられる *miserareru* be charmed, be enchanted

SYNONYMS

❶ **charm**
幻 bewitch → 180

閱 閲 閱 𠒎

3330 ETSU kemi(suru)▲

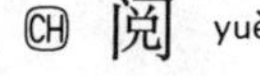

Ⓒ阅 yuè

Radical	Strokes
門 169	15-8-7
Grade	**Freq**
Jōyō	1662
口 3-8-7	

8-7 門

1 2 3 4 5 6 7 8 9 10 11 12 13 14 15

▶**REVIEW**

COMPOUNDS

❶ⓐ **review manuscripts, read carefully, look over, revise, edit**

ⓑ [suffix] reviewed by, revised by

ⓒ [original meaning] **review (troops), inspect, examine**

閲覧する *etsuran suru* read, pursue

検閲 *ken'etsu* censorship; inspection, review

校閲 *kōetsu* revision, reviewing, editing

部長閲 *buchōetsu* revised by section chief

閲兵 *eppei* inspection [review] of troops

観閲 *kan'etsu* inspection of troops

❷ elapse, pass

閲歴 *etsureki* one's career

INDEPENDENT

【**etsu 閲**】revision, inspection

閲を請う *etsu o kou* ask for a revision

【**essuru 閲する**】review, revise, look over

KUN

【**kemi(suru) 閲する**】examine, inspect; pass, elapse

SYNONYMS

❶ⓐ **revise**

訂 REVISE → 1442

校 COLLATE → 929

ⓒ **investigate and examine**

究 STUDY EXHAUSTIVELY → 2203

察 INSPECT → 2347

討 STUDY → 1456

探 PROBE → 505

検 EXAMINE → 986

診 EXAMINE A PATIENT → 1504

調 INVESTIGATE → 1567

査 LOOK INTO → 2437

審 EXAMINE CAREFULLY → 2360

験 TEST → 1833

勘 CHECK → 1777

糾 INQUIRE INTO → 1278

閲

3331

▶**REVIEW**

nonstandard for 閲 3330

8-7 門

闇

3332 AN yami

Ⓒ暗 àn

Radical	Strokes
門 169	17-8-9
Grade	**Freq**
Reference	
口 3-8-9	

8-9 門

COMPOUNDS

[now usu. 暗 *an* 1010]

❶ⓐ [original meaning] dark, dim

ⓑ darkness

闇夜 *an'ya* dark night

諒闇 *ryōan* court [national] mourning

真の闇 *shin no yami* pitch-darkness

❷ (lacking wisdom) dark, ignorant, foolish

闇愚 *angu* imbecility, feeblemindedness

NOTE

⇨ see COMPOUND FORMATION for 諒闇 *ryōan* ⇨ 諒 1575

8-9
門

闊
3333 KATSU

Ⓒ 阔 kuò

Radical	Strokes
門 169	17-8-9
Grade	Freq
Reference	
□ 3 - 8 - 9	

COMPOUNDS

❶ⓐ [original meaning] broad, wide
ⓑ [now also 活 385] broad-minded, generous
闊葉樹 *katsuyōju* broadleaf tree
闊歩する *kappo suru* stride, swagger
闊達な *kattatsu na* openhearted, frank, broad-minded
快闊な *kaikatsu na* cheerful, lively, lighthearted
迂闊な *ukatsu na* thoughtless, careless
❷ be separated, live apart
久闊 *kyūkatsu* silence, neglecting to write

8-10
門

闘 鬪 斗◇ 鬭 鬦
3334 TŌ tataka(u)

Ⓒ 斗 dòu

Radical	Strokes
門 169△	18-8-10
Grade	Freq
Jōyō	590
□ 3 - 8 - 10	

1 2 3 4 5 6 7 8 9 10 11 12 13 14 15 16 17 18

▶**FIGHT**

COMPOUNDS

[sometimes also 斗 2953]
❶ⓐ **fight (with)**
ⓑ **fight, fighting, struggle**
闘牛 *tōgyū* bullfight, fighting bull
奮闘 *funtō* hard fighting
乱闘 *rantō* free-for-all [confused] fight, melee
戦闘 *sentō* battle, fight, combat
決闘 *kettō* duel
❷ **(struggle with) fight (against), contend with, compete with**
闘争 *tōsō* fight, conflict
闘士 *tōshi* fighter, boxer
闘技 *tōgi* competition, contest
健闘 *kentō* good fight; strenuous efforts
春闘 *shuntō* spring labor offensive

KUN

【**tataka(u)** 闘う】(struggle with) fight (against), contend with, strive against
闘い *tatakai* struggle, conflict
困難と闘う *konnan to tatakau* contend with difficulties

SYNONYMS

❶ⓐ **fight and war**
戦 WAR → 1787
征 go on a military expedition → 293
ⓑ **warfare and rebellions**
戦 WAR → 1787
軍 war → 2080
役 war → 244
陣 battle → 455
乱 rebellion → 1260
変 uprising → 2069
❷ **compete**
戦う contest → 1787
争 CONTEND → 2030
競 COMPETE → 1847

HOMOPHONES

tatakau ⇨ 戦 1787
tatakai ⇨ 戦 1787

NOTE

⇨ see USAGE note at 戦 1787
★Though 闘 and 斗 are distinct characters, the latter is also used as an abbreviated form of the former.

8-11
門

關
3335

▶**CONCERN** ▶**BARRIER**
nonstandard for 関 3328

巌 incorrect classification ⇨ see 2386 | 8-12 严

巖 incorrect classification ⇨ see 2733 (nonstandard for 巌 3289) | 8-12 严

署 incorrect classification ⇨ see 2609 | 9-4 罒

颱 3336 TAI | CH 台 tái | 9-5 風

Radical	Strokes
風 182	14-9-5
Grade	Freq
Reference	
□ 3-9-5	

COMPOUNDS

● [now replaced by 台 2005] typhoon

颱風 *taifū* typhoon

署 incorrect classification ⇨ see 2614 (nonstandard for 署 2609) | 9-5 罒

題  3337 DAI | CH 题 tí | 9-9 是

Radical	Strokes
頁 181	18-9-9
Grade	Freq
Jōyō-3	96
□ 3-9-9	

▶TITLE ▶TOPIC ▶PROBLEM

COMPOUNDS

❶ **title, caption, heading, headline**

題目 *daimoku* title, heading; theme; prayer of the Nichiren sect
題名 *daimei* title
表題 *hyōdai* title, heading, caption
改題 *kaidai* change of title

❷ **topic, subject, theme**

題材 *daizai* subject matter, theme
主題 *shudai* subject, theme
話題 *wadai* topic [subject] of conversation
演題 *endai* subject of a speech, speech title
議題 *gidai* topic for discussion
閑話休題 *kanwakyūdai* to return to the subject

❸ⓐ **problem, question**

ⓑ counter for problems

問題 *mondai* problem, question, issue, matter
課題 *kadai* task, assignment; problem
難題 *nandai* difficult problem [question]
出題する *shutsudai suru* set a problem
宿題 *shukudai* homework
五題 *godai* five problems [questions]

❹ [original meaning, now archaic] forehead

INDEPENDENT

【dai 題】title, caption; topic, subject, theme
題を付ける *dai o tsukeru* entitle
作文の題 *sakubun no dai* subject of a composition

【daisuru 題する】entitle

SYNONYMS

❶ **name**

号 DESIGNATION → 2153
称 APPELLATION → 1160
名 NAME → 2169
銘 name (inscribed by maker) → 1724
姓 SURNAME → 279

氏 FAMILY NAME → 2951
❸ⓐ **question**
問 QUESTION (inquiry) → 3320
論 question (issue) → 1574

NOTE
⇨ see COMPOUND FORMATION for 閑話休題 *kanwa-kyūdai* ⇨ 閑 3322

10-5 鬼 魅 incorrect classification ⇨ see 3329

10-10 門 鬪 3338
▶FIGHT
nonstandard for 鬭 3334

11-4 麻 摩 incorrect classification ⇨ see 3175

11-4 麻 麾 摩 incorrect classification ⇨ see □ 3–12

11-5 麻 磨 incorrect classification ⇨ see 3181

11-7 麻 麿 incorrect classification ⇨ see 3184

11-8 門 蘭 incorrect classification ⇨ see 2383

11-10 麻 魔 incorrect classification ⇨ see 3187

11-12 严 巖 incorrect classification ⇨ see 2388
(nonstandard for 巌 2386)

12-9 門 蘭 incorrect classification ⇨ see 2540
(nonstandard for 蘭 2383)

14-4 門 簡 incorrect classification ⇨ see 2721

4
SOLID

乙 乙 乙 Ⓒⓗ 乙 yǐ

3339 OTSU ITSU▲ oto-▲ kinoto▲

乙
1

Radical	Strokes
乙 5	1-1-0
Grade	**Freq**
Jōyō	1708
■ 4 - 1 - 1	

1-1□

RADICAL 5

Standard form: 乙 *otsu* 'hook' (九 乞 乾)

Variant: ㇄ *re* (乱 乳 也)

Description: used for character classification

▶**SECOND**

COMPOUNDS

ⓐ **the second, B; second class, grade B; the latter**

ⓑ second calendar sign (⇨ see APPENDIX 7)

乙種 *otsushu* second grade

甲乙 *kōotsu* first and second, former and latter

乙卯 *itsubō* 52nd of the sexagenary cycle

INDEPENDENT

【otsu 乙】 the second, B; the latter; second calendar sign; bass (in traditional Japanese music)

【otsu na 乙な】 queer, strange, odd; smartish, chic; nice, fanciful, delicate; romantic

乙な味 *otsu na aji* delicate flavor

乙に澄ます *otsu ni sumasu* pose affectedly serene

KUN

【oto- 乙-】 (of girls) young, youngest

乙女 *otome* virgin, maiden

乙姫 *otohime* Princess of the Dragon Palace; younger princess

【kinoto 乙】 second calendar sign

SYNONYMS

ⓐ **second**

次 second → 54

中 MIDDLE → 3451

後 AFTER (latter) → 361

NOTE

⇨ see 甲 3481 FIRST, 丙 3479 THIRD and 丁 3348 fourth

了 incorrect stroke count ⇨ see 3350 1-1□

1-2☐ 乚
3340

乚
1

Radical	Strokes
乚 5	1-1-0
Grade	**Freq**
Radical	
■ 4 - 1 - 2	

RADICAL 5
re, variant of 乙 *otsu* 'hook'
⇨ see 乙 3339 for radical description

1-4☐ 一 一 一 Ⓒ 一 yī
3341 ICHI ITSU hito- hito(tsu)

一
1

Radical	Strokes
一 1	1-1-0
Grade	**Freq**
Jōyō-1	2
■ 4 - 1 - 4	

RADICAL 1
Standard form: 一 *ichi* 'one' (丁 七 上)
Description: used in characters related to numbers or horizontal things

▶ **ONE**

COMPOUNDS

❶ⓐ [also prefix] [original meaning] **one, unity, first**
ⓑ one time, once
ⓒ make one, unify, become one
一方 *ippō* one side, one hand; a party, the other party; in the mean time; only
一部 *ichibu* part, portion, section; a copy (of a book)
一緒に *issho ni* together; at the same time; in a lump
一番 *ichiban* first, first place; first verse; most, best; a game, a round, a bout; a number, a piece
一千 *issen* 1000
一体 *ittai* one body; a style, a form; (why, what) on earth, (what, why) in the world
一家 *ikka* family, household; one's family; style (of established reputation)
一応(=一往) *ichiō* once; in outline; tentatively; for the time being
一月 *ichigatsu* January
一瞬 *isshun* instant, moment
一生懸命(=一所懸命)に *isshōkenmei* (=*isshokenmei*) *ni* for life, with all one's might
一大事 *ichidaiji* matter of great importance
第一 *daiichi* the first, number one; the best; to begin with, above everything else
唯一の *yuiitsu no* the only, the sole
一敗 *ippai* one defeat
一括 *ikkatsu* one lump, summing up
統一する *tōitsu suru* unify, coordinate, standardize

❷ [also prefix] (a certain) one, a, an, another
一夜 *ichiya* (=*hitoyo*) one night, a night
一説 *issetsu* another view, another version [report]
一日本人 *ichinihonjin* one [a] Japanese
一要素 *ichiyōso* one factor, one element

❸ (one and the) **same, identical**
一致 *itchi* accord, agreement
一律 *ichiritsu* uniformity, equality
均一 *kin'itsu* uniformity, equality, evenness

❹ **all in one, everything, the whole**
一般の *ippan no* general, universal, widespread
一切の *issai no* all, entire, whole
一掃する *issō suru* clean out, wipe out, dispel, eradicate
一同 *ichidō* all (of us), all persons concerned
一座 *ichiza* the whole company, all present
一天 *itten* the whole sky

❺ one and only, sole, exclusive
一途に *ichizu ni* with all one's might; blindly
一意専心 *ichii-senshin* wholeheartedly, single-mindedly

❻ the best
一流の *ichiryū no* first-rate; peculiar
日本一 *nihon'ichi* (=*nippon'ichi*) best in Japan

❼ one little bit, slight amount
一見 *ikken* a look, a glance; apparently
一時 *ichiji* for a time, temporarily; once; one o'clock

❽ *baseball* first base, first baseman
一飛 *ichihi* first fly

INDEPENDENT

【ichi 一】one, unity
一、二、三、四… *ichi, ni, san, shi…* one, two, three, four…
七分の一 *nanabun no ichi* one seventh
【itsu 一】(one and the) same, identical
軌を一にする *ki o itsu ni suru* have the same way of doing
【itsu ni 一に】solely, wholly, entirely; in part, partially; besides; one

KUN

【hito- 一-】
① one, one time
一人 *hitori* one person; only (child, son or daughter)
一月目 *hitotsukime* first month
一勝負 *hitoshōbu* one round
② at one time, once
一頃 *hitokoro* at one time, once
一昔前に *hitomukashi mae ni* an age ago, a decade ago
③ just a little
一筆書く *hitofude* (=*ippitsu*) *kaku* drop a few lines
一息 *hitoiki* breath; pause, rest; a little bit of effort
【hito(tsu) 一つ】one; the same; just
一つ目の *hitotsume no* one-eyed; first
一つ頼む *Hitotsu tanomu* I want to ask you for a favor

SPECIAL READINGS

一日 *tsuitachi* 1st of the month

SYNONYMS

❶ⓐ one
壱 ONE (in legal documents) → 2197
片- ONE OF TWO → 3461
隻 ONE OF A PAIR → 2755
単 SINGLE → 2256
個 INDIVIDUAL → 117
ⓐ small numbers
二 TWO → 1922
三 THREE → 1924
四 FOUR → 3044
五 FIVE → 3436
六 SIX → 1965
七 SEVEN → 3362
八 EIGHT → 3
九 NINE → 3369
十 TEN → 3365
❷ a certain
某 A CERTAIN → 2560
❸ same and uniform
同 SAME → 2987
等 EQUAL → 2682
平 equal → 3478
均 EVEN → 235
斉 UNIFORM → 2054
❹ all
全 WHOLE → 2022
満 FULL → 607
丸 complete(ly) → 3417
皆 ALL → 2445
都 all → 1686
万 all → 2936
完 COMPLETE → 2201
総 TOTAL → 1379
諸 VARIOUS → 1577
毎 EVERY → 2034
各 EACH → 2168
❺ only
唯 ONLY → 463

HOMOPHONES

hitori ⇨ 独り 395　一人 3341, 3368

NOTE

⇨ see USAGE note at 独 395
⇨ see COMPOUND FORMATION for
一生懸命(=一所懸命) *isshōkenmei* (=*isshokenmei*) ⇨ 生 3497
一緒 *issho* ⇨ 緒 1378
一応(=一往) *ichiō* ⇨ 応 3066
一律 *ichiritsu* ⇨ 律 363

3342　REI　zero　maru

CH 〇 líng

Radical	Strokes
囗 31	1-1-0
Grade	Freq
Reference	
■ 4 - 1 - 4	

1-4□

COMPOUNDS

❶ zero (the numeral)
電話二三〇の九四一一 *denwa ni-san-rei no kyū-yon-ichi-ichi* Phone 230-9411
❷ [also 丸 *maru*] check mark for correct answers (similar to ✓)
〇×式の試験 *marubatsushiki no shiken* examination paper in which correct answers are to be marked with circles and the wrong ones with crosses
❸ indicates omitted or unprintable letters [characters]
〇〇氏 *marumarushi* Mr. X
お〇んこ *o—nko* c—t; f—king

HOMOPHONES
zero ⇨ 零 2792
maru ⇨ 丸 3417 円 2955

NOTE
⇨ see USAGE notes at 零 2792 and 丸 3417
★The character ○ is not recorded in any Japanese character dictionary, though it is used very frequently. Since ○ has *on* and *kun* readings, it is clear that it is a kanji, no matter how the latter term is defined. The editor has therefore decided to include it in this dictionary.

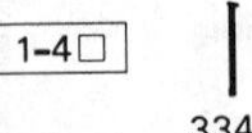
1-4□ 丨
3343

丨 1

Radical 丨 2	Strokes 1-1-0
Grade Radical	Freq
■ 4 - 1 - 4	

RADICAL 2
Standard form: 丨 *bō* 'downstroke' (中 个 串)
Description: used for character classification

1-4□ 丶
3344

丶 1

Radical 丶 3	Strokes 1-1-0
Grade Radical	Freq
■ 4 - 1 - 4	

RADICAL 3
Standard form: 丶 *ten* 'dot' (丸 丹 主)
Description: used for character classification

1-4□ 丿
3345

丿 1

Radical 丿 4	Strokes 1-1-0
Grade Radical	Freq
■ 4 - 1 - 4	

RADICAL 4
Standard form: 丿 *no* 'left stroke' (乃 及 久)
Top variant: ノ *no* (乏 乎 乗)
Description: used for character classification

1-4□ 
3346

Radical 丿 4	Strokes 1-1-0
Grade Radical	Freq
■ 4 - 1 - 4	

RADICAL 4
variant of 丿 *no* 'left stroke'
⇨ see 丿 3345 for radical description

丿
3347

丿

RADICAL 6

Radical	Strokes
亅 6	1-1-0
Grade	**Freq**
Radical	
■ 4-1-4	

1-4□

Standard form: 亅 *hanebō* 'hooked stroke' (事 予 了)
Description: used for character classification

丁 丁 丁 Ⓒⓗ 丁 dīng zhēng

3348 CHŌ TEI CHIN▲ hinoto▲

Radical	Strokes
一 1	2-1-1
Grade	**Freq**
Jōyō-3	863
■ 4-2-1	

2-1□

▶**TOWN SUBSECTION**
▶**MISCELLANEOUS COUNTER**

COMPOUNDS

❶ⓐ (minor subdivision in the Japanese addressing system) **town subsection, *chome*, subsection of a 町 *chō* (town section)**
ⓑ counter for town blocks
二丁目 *nichōme* 2-chome
国府町三丁目 *kokufuchō sanchōme* 3-chome, Kokufu-cho
二丁 *nichō* two blocks
❷ **counter for miscellaneous things, as:**
ⓐ **cakes (of bean curd)**
ⓑ **servings (as of cutlet, noodles, etc.)**
ⓒ **carpenter's tools**
ⓓ [also 挺 *chō* 428] **guns**
豆腐一丁 *tōfu itchō* one cake of bean curd
ラーメン三丁 *rāmen sanchō* three bowls of Chinese noodles
鋸二丁 *nokogiri nichō* two saws
ピストル五丁 *pisutoru gochō* five pistols
❸ⓐ full-fledged man, adult, young man
ⓑ worker, servant
丁年 *teinen* full age, conscription age
壮丁 *sōtei* young man of conscription age
馬丁 *batei* batman, footman
園丁 *entei* gardener
庖丁(=包丁) *hōchō* kitchen knife, carving knife
❹ [sometimes also 恰 *chō* 368] just, exactly
丁度 *chōdo* just, exactly; as if
❺ⓐ the fourth, D; fourth class, grade D
ⓑ fourth calendar sign (⇨ see APPENDIX 7)
甲乙丙丁 *kōotsuheitei* first, second, third and fourth, A, B, C and D
丁亥 *teigai* 24th of the sexagenary cycle
❻ [formerly 叮 *tei* 183 or 鄭 *tei* 1888] **courteous**
丁寧(=叮嚀)な *teinei na* polite, courteous
丁重(=鄭重)に *teichō ni* politely, courteously
❼ [formerly 釘 *tei* 1667 or 幀 *tei* 570] bookbinding
装丁する *sōtei suru* bind (a book)
❽ⓐ sheet or leaf, esp. of books bound in the Japanese style
ⓑ counter for such sheets (1 丁 = 2 pages)
丁数 *chōsū* number of pages; paging
丁付け *chōzuke* pagination, numbering
落丁 *rakuchō* missing page [leaf]
五丁 *gochō* five sheets
❾ T-shaped
丁字形の *teijikei no* T-shaped
丁定規 *teijōgi* T-square
❿ even number
丁半 *chōhan* odd and even (numbers); gambling
⓫ [formerly 牒 *chō* 1025] wooden placard, label, tag
符丁 *fuchō* sign; secret price tag; password
⓬ [usu. 町 *chō* 1113] *cho*: former unit of length equiv. to approx. 109 m or 60 *ken* (間)
⓭ [rare] used phonetically for *chin* in the transliteration of foreign words
沃度丁幾 *yōdo chinki* iodine tincture
⓮ [original meaning, now obsolete] nail

INDEPENDENT

【chō 丁】 even number; *cho* (⇨ ⓬)
丁か半か *chō ka han ka* even or odd
【tei 丁】 the fourth, D; fourth calendar sign

KUN

【hinoto 丁】 fourth calendar sign

SYNONYMS

❶ⓐ **parts of towns**

町 town section (*cho*) → 1113

字 village or town section → 2172

区 WARD → 2963

街 CITY QUARTER → 576

❷ **general counters**

個 GENERAL COUNTER → 117

箇 COUNTER FOR ITEMS → 2700

点 counter for articles → 2084

件 counter for cases → 51

❻ **courteous**

寧 COURTEOUS → 2345

❽ⓐ **paper**

頁 PAGE → 2086

面 page (of a newspaper) → 2087

紙 PAPER → 1302

葉 LEAF → 2321

ⓑ **counters for flat things**

頁 counter for pages → 2086

葉 counter for leaves → 2321

枚 COUNTER FOR FLAT THINGS → 859

通 counter for letters → 3109

COMPOUND FORMATION

庖丁（＝包丁）*hōchō*

庖丁 'kitchen knife, carving knife' originally meant a worker (丁 ❸ⓑ) of the kitchen (庖), i.e., a cook. It acquired its current meaning since a cook uses a kitchen knife in his work.

NOTE

⇨ see 甲 3481 FIRST, 乙 3339 SECOND and 丙 3479 THIRD

2-1□

几

3349 KI

CH 几 jī

Radical	Strokes
几 16	2-2-0
Grade	Freq
Reference	
■ 4 - 2 - 1	

RADICAL 16

Standard form: 几 *tsukue* 'table' (凡 処 凱)

Enclosure: 几 *kazagamae* (凧 凰 凪)

Description: used in characters related to laying on, leaning against or wind

COMPOUNDS

● [original meaning] desk, small table

几案 *kian* [rare] desk

几帳 *kichō* screen

几帳面な *kichōmen na* exact, precise, punctual

浄几(＝浄机) *jōki* clean [tidy] writing desk

床几(＝床机) *shōgi* [rare] campstool, folding stool

2-1□

了 了 了

3350 RYŌ

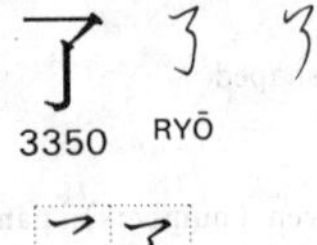

CH 了 liǎo le

Radical	Strokes
亅 6	2-1-1
Grade	Freq
Jōyō	843
■ 4 - 2 - 1	

▶FINISH ▶COMPREHEND

COMPOUNDS

❶ **finish, complete, conclude**

議了する *giryō suru* finish discussion, close a debate

未了 *miryō* unfinished, incomplete

完了する *kanryō suru* complete, finish; be completed, be finished

終了する *shūryō suru* end, conclude, complete; expire

修了 *shūryō* completion (of a course)

満了する *manryō suru* expire, become due

❷ [sometimes also 諒 1575 or 領 1224]

ⓐ **comprehend, know clearly, understand**

ⓑ show understanding, be sympathetic, acknowledge

了解 *ryōkai* understanding, comprehension; consent

了承する *ryōshō suru* acknowledge, understand, note

了知する *ryōchi suru* know, understand, appreciate

了察する *ryōsatsu suru* consider, take into account, sympathize with

INDEPENDENT

【ryō 了】 end (following the end of a novel or thesis); [usu. 諒 1575] understanding, comprehension

了とする(＝諒とする) *ryō to suru* understand, appreciate; excuse

SYNONYMS

❶ **end**

済 SETTLE → 522
終 END → 1336
絶 COME TO AN END → 1353
閉 CLOSE → 3319
-上げる completion suffix → 3404
完 COMPLETE → 2201
結 CONCLUDE → 1348

❷ **know and understand**

諒 UNDERSTAND → 1575
解 understand → 1517
分かる understand → 1972
得 gain understanding of → 477
知 KNOW → 1127
通 know thoroughly → 3109
悟 AWAKE TO → 419

又 又 又 又 Ⓒⓗ 又 yòu

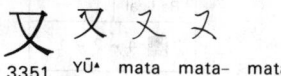

3351 YŪ▲ mata mata- mata(no)-

Radical	Strokes
又 29	2-2-0
Grade	Freq
Jōyō	1553
■ 4-2-1	

2-1□

RADICAL 29
variant of 又 *mata* 'right hand'
⇒ see 又 3361 for radical description

▶AGAIN

KUN

【mata 又】

① [formerly also 復] again, once more [again], repeatedly
又会う日迄 *mata au hi made* till we meet again
又しても *matashitemo* once again
② [formerly also 亦] [often preceded by も *mo*] also, too, as well
私も又 *watakushi mo mata* I also, me too
それも又結構だ *Sore mo mata kekkō da* That's also good
③ⓐ and, besides, further
ⓑ on the other hand
ⓒ [often followed by は *wa*] or, in other words
勝利又勝利 *shōri mata shōri* victory after victory
夫は病弱だが妻は又元気が良い *Otto wa byōjaku da ga, tsuma wa mata genki ga yoi* The husband is invalid, while the wife is robust
言っても良いし、又言わなくても良い *Itte mo yoi shi, mata iwanakute mo yoi* You can either say it or not say it
④ adverb expressing surprise or doubt
これは又何の騒ぎだ *Kore wa mata nan no sawagi da* Well, what's this row?
そりゃ又酷い話だ *Sorya mata hidoi hanashi da* What a shame!

【mata- 又-】 [also prefix] indirect, through an intermediary
又貸し *matagashi* underlease, sublease
又聞き *matagiki* hearsay, secondhand information
又従兄弟 *mataitoko* second cousin

【mata(no)- 又の-】 another, next
又の名 *matanona* another name, alias
又の日 *matanohi* the next day; another day, some other day

SYNONYMS

【mata】

① **repeating and repetition**
再 ANOTHER TIME → 3519
復 repeat → 575
重 DUPLICATE → 3573
畳 reduplicate → 2592
改 redo → 243
-換える redo → 587
-直す repetition suffix → 2932
-返す do over → 3060

② **&** ③ⓐ **additionally**
亦 ALSO → 2011
及び and → 3385
並びに and also → 2246
傍ら besides → 147
尚 STILL → 2233
更に furthermore → 3541
且つ AS WELL → 3485
兼 CONCURRENTLY → 2286

USAGE

mata

又
① [formerly also 復] again, once more [again], repeatedly
② [formerly also 亦] [often preceded by も *mo*] also, too, as well
③ⓐ and, besides, further
ⓑ on the other hand
ⓒ [often followed by は *wa*] or, in other words

④ adverb expressing surprise or doubt

亦

[now usu. 又] [often preceded by も *mo*] also, too, as well

復

[now usu. 又] again, once more [again], repeatedly

HOMOPHONES

mata ⇨ 亦 2011 復 575

2-1□

3352

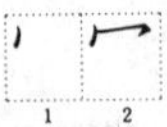

Radical 冂 13	Strokes 2-2-0
Grade Radical	Freq
■ 4 - 2 - 1	

RADICAL 13

Standard form: 冂 *keigamae* 'border' (内 円 再)

Description: used for character classification

2-1□

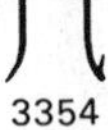

3353

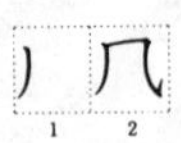

Radical 冖 14	Strokes 2-2-0
Grade Radical	Freq
■ 4 - 2 - 1	

RADICAL 14

Standard form: 冖 *wakanmuri* 'cover' (写 冠 冗)

Description: used in characters related to covering or covers

---

2-1□

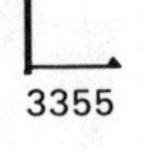

3354

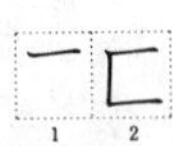

Radical 几 16	Strokes 2-2-0
Grade Radical	Freq
■ 4 - 2 - 1	

RADICAL 16

kazagamae, variant of 几 *tsukue* 'table'

⇨ see 几 3349 for radical description

2-1□

匚

3355

一 匚

1 2

Radical 匚 22	Strokes 2-2-0
Grade Radical	Freq
■ 4 - 2 - 1	

RADICAL 22

Standard form: 匚 *hakogamae* 'box' (匠 匡 匪)

Description: used in characters related to boxes or receptacles

匚
3356

一 匚
1 2

Radical 匚 23	Strokes 2-2-0
Grade Radical	Freq
■ 4-2-1	

2-1□

RADICAL 23
Standard form: 匚 *kakushigamae* 'enclose' (匿)
Enclosure: 匸 *kakushigamae* (区 匹)
Description: used in characters related to concealing or enclosing

---

卩
3357

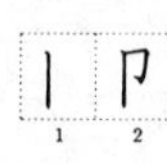

Radical 卩 26	Strokes 2-2-0
Grade Radical	Freq
■ 4-2-1	

2-1□

RADICAL 26
Standard form: 卩 *fushizukuri* 'seal' (印 卵 卸)
Variant: 㔾 *fushizukuri* (危 厄 巻)
Description: used in characters related to actions performed while kneeling

---

㔾
3358

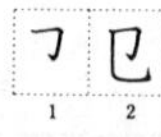

Radical 㔾 26	Strokes 2-2-0
Grade Radical	Freq
■ 4-2-1	

2-1□

RADICAL 26
variant of 卩 *fushizukuri* 'seal'
⇨ see 卩 3357 for radical description

厂
3359

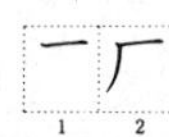

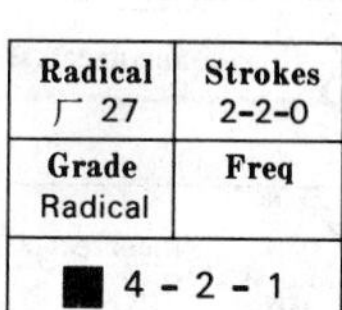

Radical 厂 27	Strokes 2-2-0
Grade Radical	Freq
■ 4-2-1	

2-1□

RADICAL 27
Standard form: 厂 *gandare* 'cliff' (原 厚 厘)
Description: used in characters related to cliffs, rocks or stones

---

厂
3360

▶PERSONAL HISTORY
handwritten abbreviation for 歴 3019

2-1□

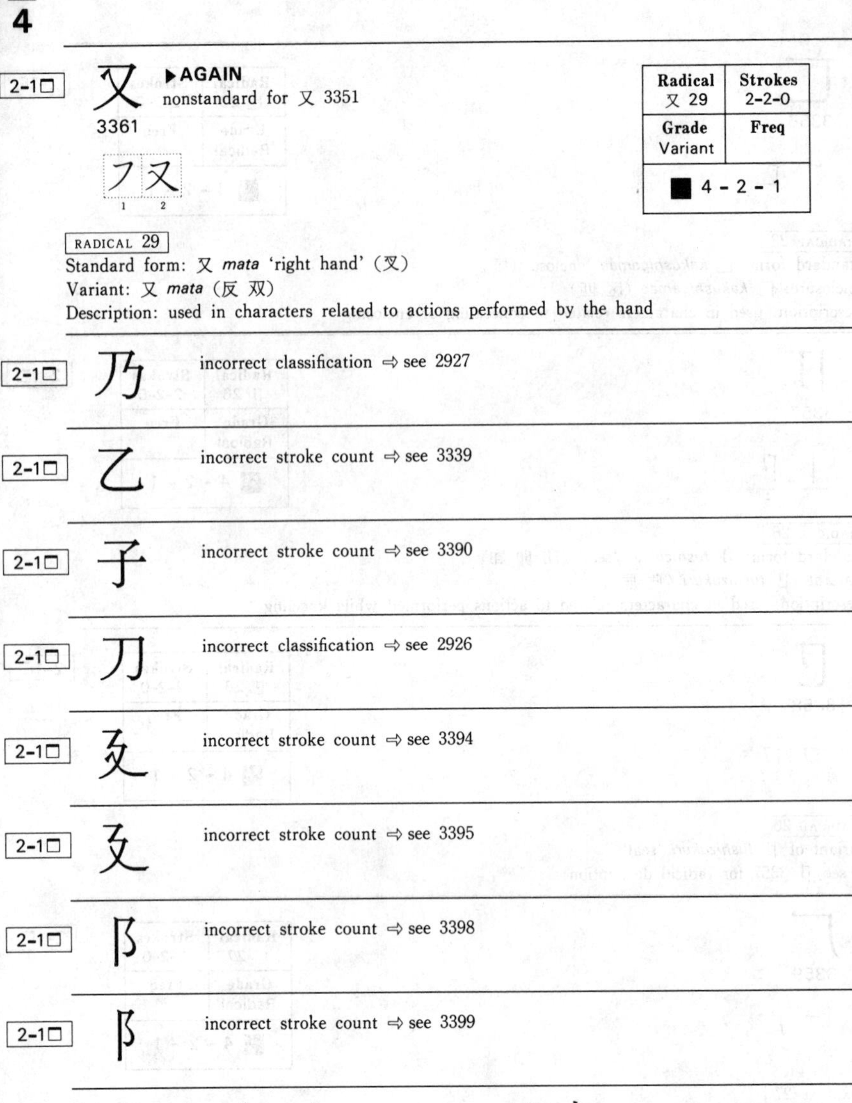

2-1□ 又 3361 ▶**AGAIN**
nonstandard for 又 3351

Radical	Strokes
又 29	2-2-0
Grade	**Freq**
Variant	
■ 4 - 2 - 1	

RADICAL 29
Standard form: 又 *mata* 'right hand' (叉)
Variant: 又 *mata* (反 双)
Description: used in characters related to actions performed by the hand

2-1□ 乃 incorrect classification ⇨ see 2927

2-1□ 乙 incorrect stroke count ⇨ see 3339

2-1□ 子 incorrect stroke count ⇨ see 3390

2-1□ 刀 incorrect classification ⇨ see 2926

2-1□ 攵 incorrect stroke count ⇨ see 3394

2-1□ 夊 incorrect stroke count ⇨ see 3395

2-1□ 阝 incorrect stroke count ⇨ see 3398

2-1□ 阝 incorrect stroke count ⇨ see 3399

2-2□ 七 七 七 3362
SHICHI nana nana(tsu) nano
CH 七 qī

Radical	Strokes
一 1	2-1-1
Grade	**Freq**
Jōyō-1	51
■ 4 - 2 - 2	

▶**SEVEN**

COMPOUNDS

● **seven, seventh**
七曜表 *shichiyōhyō* calendar
七月 *shichigatsu* July
十七日 *jūshichinichi* 17 days; 17th of the month

INDEPENDENT

【shichi 七】 seven

KUN

【nana 七】 seven

七週間 *nanashūkan* seven weeks

七草 *nanakusa* the seven spring herbs, the seven autumnal flowers

【nana(tsu) 七つ】 seven; seven years old; 4 o'clock (in former time system)

七つ目 *nanatsume* seventh

【nano 七】 [in compounds] seven

七日 *nanoka* (=*nanuka*) seven days; 7th of the month

SPECIAL READINGS

七夕 *tanabata* Festival of the Weaver [Star Vega]; the Star Festival

SYNONYMS

● **small numbers**

一 ONE → 3341
二 TWO → 1922
三 THREE → 1924
四 FOUR → 3044
五 FIVE → 3436
六 SIX → 1965
八 EIGHT → 3
九 NINE → 3369
十 TEN → 3365

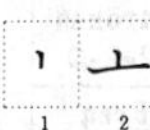

3363

2-2□

Radical ⼇ 8	Strokes 2-2-0
Grade Radical	Freq
■ 4 - 2 - 2	

RADICAL 8

Standard form: ⼇ *nabebuta* 'lid' (亡 亢 亦)

Description: used for character classification

凵

3364

2-2□

Radical 凵 17	Strokes 2-2-0
Grade Radical	Freq
■ 4 - 2 - 2	

RADICAL 17

Standard form: 凵 *kannyō* or *ukebako* 'receptacle' (出 凶 函)

Description: used for character classification

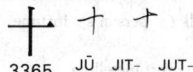

十 十 ⺘

3365 JŪ JIT- JUT-▲ tō to

CH 十 shí

2-3□

Radical 十 24	Strokes 2-2-0
Grade Jōyō-1	Freq 3
■ 4 - 2 - 3	

RADICAL 24

Standard form: 十 *jū* 'ten' (千 南 卓)

Left variant: ⺘ *jūhen* (協 博)

Description: used for character classification

▶TEN

COMPOUNDS

❶ⓐ ten, tenth

ⓑ ten times

十時 *jūji* ten o'clock

七十 *shichijū* 70

第十 *daijū* tenth

十回 *jikkai* (=*jukkai*) ten times

十進法 *jisshinhō* decimal system

❷ complete, completely, perfect

十分(=充分)な *jūbun na* full, enough, sufficient; plentiful

十全の *jūzen no* perfect, absolute

❸ many

十目 *jūmoku* all eyes
❹ cross
十字架 *jūjika* cross, crucifix
十文字 *jūmonji* cross

INDEPENDENT

【jū 十】 ten
一から十迄 *ichi kara jū made* without exception

KUN

【tō 十】 ten, tenth
十日 *tōka* ten days; 10th of the month
【to 十】 ten
十重 *toe* tenfold
十人十色 *Jūnin toiro* So many men, so many minds

SPECIAL READINGS

二十(＝二十歳) *hatachi* 20 years old
二十日 *hatsuka* 20 days; 20th of the month
十重二十重 *toehatae* manyfold, multitude

SYNONYMS

❶ⓐ **ten**
拾 ten (in legal documents) → 379
ⓐ **small numbers**
一 ONE → 3341
二 TWO → 1922
三 THREE → 1924
四 FOUR → 3044
五 FIVE → 3436
六 SIX → 1965
七 SEVEN → 3362
八 EIGHT → 3
九 NINE → 3369

2-3◫

十

3366

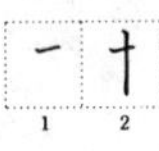

Radical	Strokes
十 24	2-2-0
Grade	**Freq**
Radical	
■ 4 - 2 - 3	

RADICAL 24

jūhen, variant of 十 *jū* 'ten'
⇨ see 十 3365 for radical description

2-4□

卜

3367 BOKU urana(u) uranai

CH 卜 bǔ bo

Radical	Strokes
卜 25	2-2-0
Grade	**Freq**
Reference	
■ 4 - 2 - 4	

RADICAL 25

Standard form: 卜 *bokunoto* 'divine' (占 卦)
Description: used in characters related to divination

COMPOUNDS

● [now usu. 占う *uranau*] [original meaning] divine, tell (a person's) fortune, augur
卜者 *bokusha* fortuneteller, diviner
卜占 *bokusen* augury
卜筮 *bokuzei* fortunetelling, divination
亀卜 *kiboku* divination by tortoiseshells
売卜 *baiboku* fortunetelling (as an occupation)
卜する *bokusuru* tell (a person's) fortune, divine; fix, choose
卜 *uranai* divination, fortunetelling

HOMOPHONES

uranau ⇨ 占 2003
uranai ⇨ 占 2003

NOTE

⇨ see USAGE note at 占 2003

人 人 人

3368 JIN NIN hito -ri* -to*

丿 人
1 2

CH 人 rén

Radical	Strokes
人 9	2-2-0
Grade	**Freq**
Jōyō-1	7
■ 4-2-4	

2-4□

RADICAL 9

Standard form: 人 *hito* 'person' (仄 以 來)
Left variant: 亻 *ninben* (仏 仁 代)
Top variant: 𠆢 *hitoyane* (今 令 会)
Description: used in characters related to human beings

▶HUMAN BEING

COMPOUNDS

❶ⓐ [also suffix] [original meaning] **human being, person, man; people, mankind**

ⓑ counter for people

人間 *ningen* human being, man; people, mankind
人類 *jinrui* mankind, humankind
人工の *jinkō no* artificial
人為 *jin'i* human work, artificiality
人民 *jinmin* the people, populace, subjects
人生 *jinsei* human life, life
人気 *ninki* popularity; temper of the people; business conditions
夫人 *fujin* wife, married lady, Mrs.
商人 *shōnin* merchant, trader, tradesman
他人 *tanin* another person, other people; stranger
個人 *kojin* individual
現代人 *gendaijin* modern person [people]
人数 *ninzū* number of people
二十人 *nijūnin* 20 people

❷ [suffix]

ⓐ person of specific geographical origin, nationality or race

ⓑ person of certain category, as the performer of an action or holder of an occupation: **-er** (as in ***manager***)

アメリカ人 *amerikajin* American
外国人 *gaikokujin* foreigner, alien
見物人 *kenbutsunin* spectator, sightseer
料理人 *ryōrinin* cook
支配人 *shihainin* manager, executive
芸能人 *geinōjin* performing artist

❸ [rare] other people, others

人我 *jinga* oneself and others

❹ personality, character, disposition

人格 *jinkaku* character, personality

INDEPENDENT

【nin 人】 *literary* person; character

KUN

【hito 人】

①ⓐ man, human being, person, mankind

ⓑ people, men

人殺し *hitogoroshi* murder; murderer
人質 *hitojichi* hostage, prisoner
人人 *hitobito* people
恋人 *koibito* lover, sweetheart
人出 *hitode* turnout, crowd

② other people, others

人事 *hitogoto* other people's affairs
人の金 *hito no kane* other people's money

③ man of talent, able man

人を得る *hito o eru* employ the right person

④ nature, character, personality

人柄 *hitogara* character, personality
人の良い *hito no yoi* good natured, kindhearted
お人好し *ohitoyoshi* good natured person; credulous person

【-ri -人】 counter for people

一人 *hitori* one person; only (child, son or daughter)
二人 *futari* two persons

【-to -人】 person

玄人 *kurōto* expert, master hand; prostitute
素人 *shirōto* amateur, novice, outsider; decent woman
仲人 *nakōdo* go-between, matchmaker
若人 *wakōdo* youth, young man

SPECIAL READINGS

大人 *otona* adult

SYNONYMS

❶ⓐ person

者 PERSON → 3211
方 person (*honorific*) → 1963
氏 person (*polite*) → 2951

ⓑ counters for persons

名 counter for persons → 2169

❷ⓑ workers and professionals

者 person who → 3211
員 MEMBER (of a staff) → 2269
師 profession suffix → 1326
士 PROFESSION SUFFIX → 3405
客 skilled person → 2250
家 professional → 2273

屋 colloquial occupation suffix → 3098
手 OCCUPATION SUFFIX → 3456
婦 woman worker → 469
嬢 (unmarried) female worker → 758
夫 MAN LABORER → 3460
匠 CRAFTSMAN → 2990
工 workman → 3381

HOMOPHONES
hitori ⇨ 独り 395　一人 3341, 3368

NOTE
⇨ see USAGE note at 独 395
⇨ see COMPOUND FORMATION for
人間 *ningen* ⇨ 間 3323
夫人 *fujin* ⇨ 夫 3460

2-4□

九 九 九

3369　KYŪ　KU　kokono　kokono(tsu)

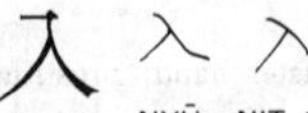

Ⓒⓗ 九 jiǔ

Radical	Strokes
乙 5	2-1-1
Grade	**Freq**
Jōyō-1	47
■ 4 - 2 - 4	

▶**NINE**

COMPOUNDS

❶ **nine**
九百 *kyūhyaku* 900
九回 *kyūkai* nine times
九星術 *kyūseijutsu* astrology
九月 *kugatsu* September
九人 *kyūnin* nine people

❷ many
九死に一生を得る *kyūshi ni isshō o uru* have a narrow escape from death
九拝 *kyūhai* bowing many times (in apology)

❸ abbrev. of 九州 *kyūshū*: Kyushu district
九大 *kyūdai* Kyushu University

INDEPENDENT
【kyū 九】 nine
【ku 九】 nine

KUN
【kokono 九】 [in compounds] nine
九日 *kokonoka* nine days; 9th of the month
九重 *kokonoe* ninefold; Imperial Palace
【kokono(tsu) 九つ】 nine; nine years old; 12 o'clock (in former time system)

SYNONYMS
❶ **small numbers**
一 ONE → 3341
二 TWO → 1922
三 THREE → 1924
四 FOUR → 3044
五 FIVE → 3436
六 SIX → 1965
七 SEVEN → 3362
八 EIGHT → 3
十 TEN → 3365

2-4□

入 入 入

3370　NYŪ　NIT-ᐞ　i(ru)　-i(ru)　-i(ri)　i(reru)　-i(re)　hai(ru)

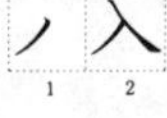

Ⓒⓗ 入 rù

Radical	Strokes
入 11	2-2-0
Grade	**Freq**
Jōyō-1	82
■ 4 - 2 - 4	

RADICAL 11
Standard form: 入 *iru* 'enter' (全 兪 兩)
Description: used for character classification

▶**ENTER**　▶**PUT IN**

COMPOUNDS

❶ [original meaning] **enter, come in, go in**
入場 *nyūjō* entrance, admission
入国 *nyūkoku* entry [entrance] into a country
収入 *shūnyū* income, earnings, receipts
侵入する *shinnyū suru* invade, raid, trespass, intrude
介入 *kainyū* intervention

❷ⓐ (become a member of) **enter, join, be admitted**

ⓑ abbrev. of 入学 *nyūgaku*: entering a school
入学する *nyūgaku suru* enter a school, matriculate
入門する *nyūmon suru* become a pupil of, enter a private school
入閣する *nyūkaku suru* join the Cabinet, become a Cabinet member
入賞 *nyūshō* winning a prize

加入する *kanyū suru* enter, join
入試 *nyūshi* entrance examination
❸ **put in, insert, enter, admit**
入札 *nyūsatsu* tender, bidding
入手する *nyūshu suru* obtain, get, come by, procure
記入する *kinyū suru* enter, write in, record
注入 *chūnyū* pouring into, injection
輸入 *yunyū* import, importation
導入 *dōnyū* introduction
❹ necessary
入用 *nyūyō* need, demand, necessity
入費 *nyūhi* expense(s)
❺ entering tone in Chinese phonetics
入声 *nisshō* (=*nissei*) entering tone

INDEPENDENT

【nyū 入】 ON (marking on switches)
切一入 *setsu-nyū* OFF-ON (marking on switches)

KUN

【i(ru) 入る】
①ⓐ enter, go in, come in
ⓑ (of the sun) set
入り *iri* setting (of the sun); attendance; beginning; income
入り口 *iriguchi* entrance
押し入る *oshiiru* enter by force, break into
入り日 *irihi* setting sun
② attain
老境に入る *rōkyō ni iru* be advanced in age
③ [usu. 要る]
ⓐ need, want, require
ⓑ be necessary [required]; cost, take
入り *iri* expense(s)
入り用 *iriyō* need, want

【-i(ru) -入る】 emphatic verbal suffix
恐れ入る *osoreiru* be overwhelmed [dumfounded] (as with gratitude, shame, regret or astonishment)
聞き入る *kikiiru* listen attentively to, be lost in

【-i(ri) -入り】
[also suffix]
①ⓐ entering
ⓑ be encased, be placed in
出入り *deiri* going in and out; frequentation, usual visit (as by a merchant); indentations; incomings and outgoings; trouble, fight
立ち入り *tachiiri* entering
箱入りの *hakoiri no* cased, boxed
② (be accepted as a member) enter, join, enroll
プロ入り *puroiri* turning professional
仲間入り *nakamairi* joining the ranks of
③ⓐ including, accompanied by
ⓑ containing, having a capacity of
蜂蜜入りの *hachimitsuiri no* containing honey
鳴り物入りで *narimonoiri de* with a flourish of trumpets
一リットル入りの瓶 *ichirittoruiri no bin* bottle holding a liter

【i(reru) 入れる】
①ⓐ put in, enter, insert, fit; add to
ⓑ let in, admit, show in
入れ替え *irekae* replacement, shifting; switching
ポケットに入れる *poketto ni ireru* put (a thing) in one's pocket
②ⓐ (cause to enter) send, deliver, extend
ⓑ (permit to enter or join) take in, admit; hire, employ
ⓒ (put into action or use) exercise (care), exert
申し入れる *mōshiireru* propose; make representations to
患者を入れる *kanja o ireru* admit a patient
手入れ *teire* care, repairs, trimming; (police) raid
③ accommodate, hold, contain
受け入れ *ukeire* reception; acceptance
乗り入れ *noriire* extension (of a railway line) into
取り入れる *toriireru* take in; harvest; accept, adopt, introduce
④ include, count in
数に入れる *kazu ni ireru* include in the number
⑤ make (tea), brew (coffee)
⑥ [sometimes also 容れる] accept, tolerate, be compatible
受け入れる *ukeireru* accept, consent to; receive, accommodate
相入れない *aiirenai* incompatible
聞き入れる *kikiireru* comply with, accept

【-i(re) -入れ】 [suffix] receptacle, container
小銭入れ *kozeniire* change purse

【hai(ru) 入る】 enter, come in, go in; break in; enter (a school), join, go into; contain, hold, accommodate; have, get, receive; begin, set in
入り込む *hairikomu* get in, come in, enter
クラブに入る *kurabu ni hairu* join a club
千人入る講堂 *sennin hairu kōdō* auditorium with a seating capacity of 1000
金が手に入る *kane ga te ni hairu* get hold of money
梅雨に入った *Tsuyu ni haitta* The rainy season has set in

SYNONYMS

❶ **enter**
-込む MOVE INWARD → 3030
❷ⓐ **participate and join**
加 join → 38
参 PARTICIPATE → 2066
与 take part in → 3421

❸ **put in**
挿 INSERT → 431
-込む cause to move inward → 3030
❹ **need and necessity**
要 required → 2635
必 must → 15
須 MUST → 574
需 DEMAND → 2797
用 needed for (a specific use) → 2976

USAGE

ireru
入れる
①ⓐ put in, enter, insert, fit; add to
ⓑ let in, admit, show in
②ⓐ (cause to enter) send, deliver, extend
ⓑ (permit to enter or join) take in, admit; hire, employ
ⓒ (put into action or use) exercise (care), exert
③ accommodate, hold, contain
④ include, count in
⑤ make (tea), brew (coffee)
⑥ [sometimes also 容れる] accept, tolerate, be compatible
容れる
[usu. 入れる] accept, tolerate, be compatible

HOMOPHONES

iru ⇨ 要 2635
iri ⇨ 要 2635
ireru ⇨ 容 2277

NOTE

⇨ see also USAGE note at 要 2635

2-4□ 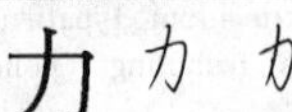
3371 RYOKU RIKI RĪ* chikara

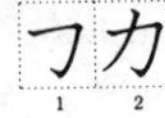

CH 力 lì

Radical	Strokes
力 19	2-2-0
Grade	**Freq**
Jōyō-1	66
■ 4 - 2 - 4	

RADICAL 19
Standard form: 力 *chikara* 'strength' (加 勢 功)
Description: used in characters related to strength, work or effort

▶**POWER**

COMPOUNDS

❶ⓐ [also suffix] [original meaning] **muscular power, physical strength, force, might**
ⓑ military power, armed force
ⓒ (power in general) **power to influence, strength, influence, authority**
人力 *jinryoku* human power [strength]
筋力 *kinryoku* muscular strength [power]
体力 *tairyoku* physical strength, strength of one's body
暴力 *bōryoku* violence, force
強力(=剛力) *gōriki* Herculean strength; mountain carrier [guide]
省力化 *shōryokuka* labor savings
全力で *zenryoku de* with all one's might, to the best of one's ability
苦力 *kūrī* coolie
五人力が有る *goninriki ga aru* have the strength of five men
兵力 *heiryoku* military force; strength of an army
主力 *shuryoku* main force, main body
武力 *buryoku* military power, armed might
権力 *kenryoku* power, authority, influence
勢力 *seiryoku* influence, power, might; force (of a typhoon)
威力 *iryoku* power, might, authority, influence
迫力 *hakuryoku* power, force, punch, appeal
有力者 *yūryokusha* influential person, man of importance
金力 *kinryoku* power of money
強力な *kyōryoku na* strong, powerful, mighty
❷ⓐ (source of energy) **power, energy; motive power**
ⓑ *phys* **force**
電力 *denryoku* electric power, electricity
原子力 *genshiryoku* atomic energy, nuclear power
馬力 *bariki* horsepower; energy, effort; cart, wagon
力織機 *rikishokki* power loom
動力源 *dōryokugen* power source
出力 *shutsuryoku* generating power, output
重力 *jūryoku* gravity, force of gravity
圧力 *atsuryoku* pressure
表面張力 *hyōmen chōryoku* surface tension
❸ⓐ [also suffix] (ability to do or act) **power, ability, faculty**
ⓑ mental power, vigor, vitality
能力 *nōryoku* ability, capacity, faculty
実力 *jitsuryoku* real ability [power], capability, competence
理解力 *rikairyoku* comprehensive faculty, power to understand

戦力 *senryoku* war potentials, fighting power
学力 *gakuryoku* scholarship, scholastic ability
魅力 *miryoku* charm, glamour, appeal
効力 *kōryoku* effect, efficacy; effect (as of a law), validity
弾力 *danryoku* elasticity, spring
極力 *kyokuryoku* to the utmost, to the best of one's power
気力 *kiryoku* energy, spirit, vitality, pluck, guts
念力 *nenriki* will power; psychokinesis
活力 *katsuryoku* vital power [force], vitality, energy

❹ powerful(ly), all-out, hard, strenuously
力泳 *rikiei* powerful swimming
力投 *rikitō* all-out pitching
力漕する *rikisō suru* row hard
力作 *rikisaku* labored work, masterpiece
力説する *rikisetsu suru* emphasize, lay stress on, insist upon

❺ⓐ efforts, endeavors
ⓑ assistance, help
努力 *doryoku* endeavor, effort, exertion
死力を尽くす *shiryoku o tsukusu* make frantic efforts
独力 *dokuryoku* one's own efforts
協力する *kyōryoku suru* cooperate, collaborate, work together
他力 *tariki* help from without
助力 *joryoku* help, aid, support, cooperation

INDEPENDENT

【riki 力】 physical strength
【rikimu 力む】 strain (oneself); swagger, brag
力んで見せる *rikinde miseru* show a bold front

KUN

【chikara 力】
①ⓐ muscular strength, power, force
ⓑ (physical) force; power, energy
ⓒ (power in general) power, authority, influence, force, emphasis
力持ち *chikaramochi* man of great strength, muscleman
力一杯 *chikara ippai* with full force, with all one's might
力ずくで *chikarazuku de* by force, by sheer strength
力強い *chikarazuyoi* powerful, vigorous, reassuring
力仕事 *chikarashigoto* heavy work
馬鹿力 *bakajikara* great physical power, animal strength
力の場 *chikara no ba* field of force
力関係 *chikara-kankei* power relationship
②ⓐ (ability to perform) power, ability, faculty; proficiency
ⓑ vigor, spirit, energy
力試し *chikaradameshi* test of one's ability [strength]
底力 *sokojikara* latent power
語学の力 *gogaku no chikara* one's linguistic ability
力付ける *chikarazukeru* encourage, cheer up, support
力落とし *chikaraotoshi* disappointment, sorrow, grief
③ⓐ efforts, endeavors
ⓑ assistance, aid, help
力を尽くす *chikara o tsukusu* make efforts, exert oneself
力添え *chikarazoe* aid, help, assistance
④ efficacy, effectiveness
薬の力 *kusuri no chikara* efficacy of a drug

SYNONYMS

❶ⓒ power and authority
威 MIGHT → 3578
勢 POWER (to influence) → 2857
権 POWER (to control) → 1065
覇 SUPREMACY → 2730

❷ energy and force
勢 physical power → 2857
気 energy → 3194
圧 PRESSURE → 2970

❸ⓐ skill
能 ABILITY → 1323
技 SKILL → 248
腕 skill → 1006
才 TALENT → 3410

NOTE

⇨ see COMPOUND FORMATION for 迫力 *hakuryoku* ⇨ 迫 3074

〆

3372 shi(meru)

Ⓒⓗ none (国字)

Radical	Strokes
ノ 4	2-1-1
Grade Reference	Freq
■ 4 - 2 - 4	

2-4□

COMPOUNDS

[also 締める *shimeru*]

❶ add up, sum up; close the account
〆 *shime* summing up; mark on envelope

seal
〆めて *shimete* in all, all told
〆切日 *shimekiribi* closing day, time limit
❷ [in compounds] fasten, lock (a door or window), shut
〆切(＝締め切り) *shimekiri* closing day, deadline; Closed, No Entrance

HOMOPHONES
shimeru ⇨ 締 1393 閉 3319 絞 1349

NOTE
⇨ see USAGE note at 締 1393

2-4□

3373

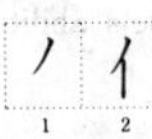

Radical	Strokes
亻 9	2-2-0
Grade	**Freq**
Radical	
■ 4 - 2 - 4	

RADICAL 9
ninben, variant of 人 *hito* ‘person’
⇨ see 人 3368 for radical description

2-4□

3374

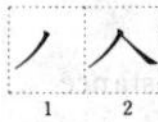

Radical	Strokes
人 9	2-2-0
Grade	**Freq**
Radical	
■ 4 - 2 - 4	

RADICAL 9
hitoyane, variant of 人 *hito* ‘person’
⇨ see 人 3368 for radical description

2-4□

勹

3375

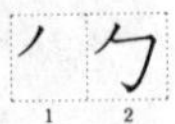

Radical	Strokes
勹 20	2-2-0
Grade	**Freq**
Radical	
■ 4 - 2 - 4	

RADICAL 20
Standard form: 勹 *tsutsumigamae* ‘wrap’ (勺 勿 包)
Description: used in characters related to enclosing

2-4□

3376

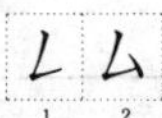

Radical	Strokes
厶 28	2-2-0
Grade	**Freq**
Radical	
■ 4 - 2 - 4	

RADICAL 28
Standard form: 厶 *mu* ‘oneself’ (参 去)
Description: used for character classification

2-4□

incorrect classification ⇨ see 2925

之 incorrect stroke count ⇨ see 3420 2-4□

七 incorrect classification ⇨ see 3362 2-4□

已
3377 I ya(mu) sude(ni)

Ⓒⓗ 已 yǐ 3-1□

Radical	Strokes
己 49	3-3-0
Grade	Freq
Reference	
■ 4 - 3 - 1	

COMPOUNDS

❶ⓐ (cannot) help
ⓑ [usu. 止む yamu] come to an end
已むを得ない yamu o enai unavoidable, cannot be helped
已む無く yamunaku unavoidably, out of necessity
已むに已まれぬ事情 yamu ni yamarenu jijō circumstances beyond one's control
已んぬる哉 Yannuru kana I give up!
死して後已む Shishite nochi yamu I am determined to do or die
❷ [now usu. 既に sudeni] already
時已に遅し Toki sudeni ososhi It is too late now

HOMOPHONES

yamu ⇨ 止 2941
sudeni ⇨ 既 1166

NOTE

⇨ see USAGE notes at 止 2941 and 既 1166
★do not confuse with 己 3380

下 下 ふ
3378 KA GE shita[1] shita[2] shimo moto sa(geru) sa(garu) kuda(ru) kuda(ri) kuda(su) -kuda(su) kuda(saru) o(rosu) o(riru)

一 丅 下
1 2 3

Ⓒⓗ 下 xià 3-1□

Radical	Strokes
一 1	3-1-2
Grade	Freq
Jōyō-1	92
■ 4 - 3 - 1	

▶**DOWN**

COMPOUNDS

❶ⓐ [also suffix] **down, under, below; lower part**
ⓑ [also prefix] (in a lower position) **lower, under-, sub-**
下線 kasen underline
下記の kaki no following, undermentioned
上下 jōge upper and lower parts [sides], high and low; going up and down, rise and fall; first and second volumes
地下 chika underground
投下する tōka suru throw down, drop, airdrop; invest
廊下 rōka corridor, gallery, passage
以下 ika or less than, not more than, under; and downward; the following
氷点下 hyōtenka below the freezing point
下流 karyū downstream, lower reaches of a stream
下部 kabu lower part
下段 gedan lowest step; lower berth
下駄 geta geta, wooden clogs
下半身 kahanshin lower half of one's body
下意識 kaishiki subconsciousness
❷ⓐ **of low rank, inferior**
ⓑ **of low grade, low-class, humble**
ⓒ persons of low rank, juniors, inferiors, the people
下位 kai lower rank [grade], subordinate position
下院 kain Lower House
下級 kakyū lower grade [class]
下等な katō na low, lower, inferior, mean
下宿 geshuku lodging, boarding house
下水 gesui sewerage, drainage; foul water
下男 genan male servant, manservant
下劣な geretsu na base, mean, vulgar

下情 *kajō* conditions of the common people
下克上 *gekokujō* the lower dominating the upper
部下 *buka* subordinate
❸ [also suffix] (subject to the influence of) **under (the rule of), in a state of**
眼下の *ganka no* under one's eyes
灯下で *tōka de* by lamplight
管下の *kanka no* under the jurisdiction of
治下の *chika no* under the rule of
城下 *jōka* castle town, capital of a daimyo's fief
県下 *kenka* throughout the prefecture
目下 *mokka* now, at present
戦時下 *senjika* in times of war
❹ⓐ (proceed to or as if to a lower place) **go down, descend, drop, sink**
ⓑ go down or away from a central place (as the capital), withdraw, leave
ⓒ **get down from (a horse or vehicle), dismount, alight**
ⓓ (cause to go down) **bring down, lower**
下降する *kakō suru* descend, go down; subside
下山する *gezan suru* descend a mountain; leave a temple
落下する *rakka suru* fall, drop, descend
低下する *teika suru* fall, sink, lower, go down
南下する *nanka suru* go down south
下阪する *gehan suru* go down to Osaka
下校する *gekō suru* leave school, come home from school
下車する *gesha suru* alight, get off
下馬 *geba* dismounting
却下する *kyakka suru* reject, dismiss, turn down
❺ⓐ **give to an inferior, grant**
ⓑ give a command, issue orders
下賜 *kashi* imperial grant
下付する *kafu suru* grant, issue
下命する *kamei suru* order, command
❻ honorific indicating respect without referring directly to a superior
閣下 *kakka* Your [His] Excellency
陛下 *heika* His [Her, Your] Majesty; [original meaning] at the palace steps
貴下 *kika* you
❼ last (in a series of two or three)
下旬 *gejun* last ten days of a month
下巻 *gekan* second [third] volume
❽ diarrhea
下痢 *geri* diarrhea
下剤 *gezai* purgative, laxative
下血 *geketsu* bloody bowel discharge

INDEPENDENT

【ge 下】 low class, inferiority; last volume
下の下 *ge no ge* the lowest of its kind

KUN

【shita[1] 下】
①ⓐ [in the form of 下 *shita* + particle] down, under, below, underneath
ⓑ lower part, bottom, foot
ⓒ downstairs
下の *shita no* under, lower
真下に *mashita ni* just under, directly below
靴下 *kutsushita* socks, stockings
机の下に *tsukue no shita ni* under the desk
坂の下に *saka no shita ni* at the foot of a slope
下の部屋 *shita no heya* downstairs room
② (of lower rank, grade or degree) lower, under, below, inferior, younger
下回る *shitamawaru* be less than, fall below
下火になる *shitabi ni naru* burn low; decline
手下 *teshita* subordinate, underling
年下の *toshishita no* younger, junior
③ part payment
下取りする *shitadori suru* take a trade-in

【shita[2] 下】
① [in compounds]
ⓐ lower, under-
ⓑ of lower rank or degree, inferior
下唇 *shitakuchibiru* lower lip
下着 *shitagi* underwear
下心 *shitagokoro* underlying motive, secret intention
下値 *shitane* lower price
下請け *shitauke* subcontract
② [also prefix] preliminary
下調べ *shitashirabe* preliminary examination [inquiry], preparation
下準備 *shitajunbi* prearrangement
版下 *hanshita* block copy

【shimo 下】
①ⓐ lower part, bottom, foot
ⓑ lower stream
ⓒ [also prefix] Lower—used before place names
下に *shimo ni* below, down, downward
風下 *kazashimo* leeward, lee side
川下 *kawashimo* lower part of a river
下エジプト *shimoejiputo* Lower Egypt
② [also prefix] last (in a series of two or three)
下の句 *shimo no ku* second half of a tanka poem
下半期 *shimohanki* second half of the year
下二桁 *shimofutaketa* last two figures of a number
③ persons of lower rank:
ⓐ inferiors, servants
ⓑ the governed, the ruled, the people, the lower classes

下座 *shimoza* seat for inferiors
下下 *shimojimo* lower classes, the masses
④ lower part of the body, the genitals
下掛かった話をする *shimogakatta hanashi o suru* talk about indecent things

【moto 下】
① lower part, bottom
木の下に *ki no moto ni* under a tree
② [in the form of 下に *moto ni*] (subject to the influence of) under (the supervision of)
ナポレオンの指揮の下に *naporeon no shiki no moto ni* under the command of Napoleon
一撃の下に *ichigeki no moto ni* by a single blow

【sa(geru) 下げる】
①ⓐ (move downward) lower, bring down, drop
ⓑ (lower the level of) lower (the price), bring down, cut
ⓒ reduce to lower rank, demote
頭を下げる *atama o sageru* bow one's head
掘り下げる *horisageru* dig down; investigate, probe, delve into
値下げ *nesage* reduction in price
引き下げる *hikisageru* lower, reduce, put back; pull down
格下げ *kakusage* degradation
② hang (down), suspend
お下げ *osage* hair hanging down the back, pigtail
ぶら下げる *burasageru* hang, suspend, dangle
③ⓐ move back [backwards]
ⓑ let (a person) go away, dismiss
お膳を下げる *ozen o sageru* clear the table
下げ渡す *sagewatasu* grant, release
取り下げる *torisageru* withdraw, dismiss
④ withdraw (one's deposit from the bank)
貯金を下げる *chokin o sageru* withdraw one's savings
⑤ (of tides) ebb
下げ潮 *sageshio* ebb tide

【sa(garu) 下がる】
①ⓐ come down, go down
ⓑ hang down, dangle, sag
彼女の靴下が下がる *Kanojo no kutsushita ga sagaru* Her socks slip down
垂れ下がる *taresagaru* hang, dangle
②ⓐ (decline in level or intensity) go down, fall, drop, decline
ⓑ (decline in rank, status or quality) sink down (to a lower level), drop, be degraded, decline, deteriorate
上がり下がり *agarisagari* rise and fall, ups and downs, fluctuations
値下がり *nesagari* fall in price, depreciation of price
成り下がる *narisagaru* degrade oneself, fall low, come down in the world
③ⓐ draw back, step back
ⓑ withdraw, leave
一歩下がる *ippo sagaru* take a step backward
引き下がる *hikisagaru* retire, withdraw; disclaim
お下がり *osagari* clothes handed down, hand-me-downs; withdrawn offering
④ elapse, pass
昼下がり *hirusagari* early afternoon

【kuda(ru) 下る】
①ⓐ go down, descend, step down from; go downstream
ⓑ go down or away from a central place (as the capital)
ⓒ (decline in level or grade) fall, drop, be inferior
丘を下る *oka o kudaru* go down a hill
川を下る *kawa o kudaru* descend a river
駆け下る *kakekudaru* run down
九州へ下る *kyūshū e kudaru* go down to Kyushu
野に下る *ya ni kudaru* leave the government service
下らない *kudaranai* be no less than; trifling, worthless; absurd
② be given (orders), be issued
判決が下る *Hanketsu ga kudaru* Sentence is passed
③ have loose bowels
腹が下る *hara ga kudaru* have loose bowels
④ elapse, pass
時代が更に下って *jidai ga sarani kudatte* later in the period

【kuda(ri) 下り】
①ⓐ [also prefix] downhill, descend, going down
ⓑ [also suffix] going downstream
下り坂 *kudarizaka* downward path; decline, ebb
球磨川下り *kumagawakudari* shooting down the Kuma Rapids
② going down (away from the capital, esp. Tokyo), outbound
下り線 *kudarisen* down line (away from Tokyo)
東下り *azumakudari* going down to the eastern provinces
③ diarrhea
下り腹 *kudaribara* loose bowels

【kuda(su) 下す】
① bring down, lower
位を下す *kurai o kudasu* lower in rank, degrade
見下す *mikudasu* look down upon, think lightly of
②ⓐ give to an inferior, grant, bestow
ⓑ give a command, issue orders

神の下し給うた物 *kami no kudashitamōta mono* heavenly gift, godsend
進軍の命令を下す *shingun no meirei o kudasu* give a marching order
③ pass (judgment), hand down (a decision)
結論を下す *ketsuron o kudasu* draw a conclusion
④ [sometimes also 降す] subjugate, subdue; defeat, beat
⑤ have loose bowels
腹下し *harakudashi* diarrhea, laxity; purgative (medicine), evacuant
【-kuda(su) -下す】 perform an action smoothly
書き下す *kakikudasu* write down; transliterate [read] classical Chinese (into Japanese)
読み下す *yomikudasu* transliterate classical Chinese into Japanese
【kuda(saru) 下さる】
ⓐ [honorific] give, confer (to the speaker or speaker's group)
ⓑ [following the TE-form of verbs] perform an action for the benefit of the speaker: favor with, oblige, do (a courtesy)
それを私に下さい *Sore o watashi ni kudasai* Give it to me
その人は親切に道を教えて下さった *Sono hito wa shinsetsu ni michi o oshiete kudasatta* The man kindly told me the way
お心安くして下さる方 *okokoroyasuku shite kudasaru kata* gentleman who favors me with friendship
【o(rosu) 下ろす】
① bring down, take down, let down, lower, pull down
振り下ろす *furiorosu* swing downward
雪下ろし *yukioroshi* removing snow from the roof of a house
ボートを下ろす *bōto o orosu* lower a boat
根を下ろす *ne o orosu* take root
② wear for the first time
仕立て下ろし *shitateoroshi* brand-new clothes
③ have an abortion performed
下ろし薬 *oroshigusuri* aborticide
④ withdraw (one's savings)
貯金を下ろす *chokin o orosu* withdraw one's savings
⑤ lock up
錠を下ろす *jō o orosu* fasten a lock, lock
⑥ grate (vegetables)
下ろし *oroshi* grated radish; vegetable grater
下ろし金 *oroshigane* vegetable grater
【o(riru) 下りる】
① (move downward) go down, come down(stairs), descend (from a mountain)
駆け下りる *kakeoriru* run down
坂を下りる *saka o oriru* go down a slope, go downhill

幕が下りる *Maku ga oriru* The curtain falls
② be discharged; abort
下り物 *orimono* discharge from the womb
③ be granted, be issued
免許が下りた *Menkyo ga orita* The license was granted
④ be locked
錠が下りている *jō ga orite iru* be locked

SPECIAL READINGS

下手な *heta na* unskillful, unskilled, poor, clumsy

SYNONYMS

❶ⓐ & 【shita[1]】 ①ⓑ bottoms and bases
底 BOTTOM → 3084
基 BASE → 2673
礎 FOUNDATION STONE → 1248
盤 bedrock → 2851
床 BED → 3067
ⓑ low
低 LOW → 73
❷ⓐ lowly
卑 MEAN → 2642
低 LOW → 73
ⓑ bad
劣 INFERIOR → 2395
悪 BAD → 2745
弊 shabby → 2884
粗 COARSE → 1329
駄 GOOD FOR NOTHING → 1821
廃 WASTE → 3146
❹ⓐ descend and fall
降 DESCEND → 458
落 FALL → 2318
墜 DROP DOWN → 2881
倒 TOPPLE → 124
ⓒ get off
降 alight → 458
ⓓ & 【sageru】 ①ⓐ lower
低 lower → 73
❺ⓐ & 【kudasaru】 ⓐ give
上 give (to superior or others) → 3404
呉れる give (to speaker) → 2549
与 GIVE → 3421
授 CONFER → 492
賜 DEIGN TO GIVE → 1585
贈 PRESENT A GIFT → 1634
賄 BRIBE → 1529
呈 PRESENT → 2189
進 present to a superior → 3121
❽ diseases and disease symptoms
痢 DIARRHEA → 3283
炎 INFLAMMATION → 2420
熱 fever → 2866
痘 SMALLPOX → 3284

USAGE

❶ sageru
下げる

①ⓐ (move downward) lower, bring down, drop
ⓑ (lower the level of) lower (the price), bring down, cut
ⓒ reduce to lower rank, demote
② hang (down), suspend
③ⓐ move back [backwards]
ⓑ let (a person) go away, dismiss
④ withdraw (one's deposit from the bank)
⑤ (of tides) ebb

提げる
carry in hand, take (a thing) with (a person)

❷ kudaru

下る
①ⓐ go down, descend, step down from; go downstream
ⓑ go down or away from a central place (as the capital)
ⓒ (decline in level or grade) fall, drop, be inferior
② be given (orders), be issued
③ have loose bowels
④ elapse, pass

降る
surrender, submit to

❸ kudasu

下す
① bring down, lower
②ⓐ give to an inferior, grant, bestow
ⓑ give a command, issue orders
③ pass (judgment), hand down (a decision)
④ [sometimes also 降す] subjugate, subdue; defeat, beat
⑤ have loose bowels

降す
[usu. 下す] subjugate, subdue; defeat, beat

❹ orosu

下ろす
① bring down, take down, let down, lower, pull down
② wear for the first time
③ have an abortion performed
④ withdraw (one's savings)
⑤ lock up
⑥ grate (vegetables)

降ろす
① set (a passenger) down, discharge, unload
② demote, deprive (someone) of (his) role

卸す
wholesale, sell wholesale

★In the sense of grating vegetables, *orosu* is sometimes mistakenly written 卸す.

❺ oriru

下りる
① (move downward) go down, come down(stairs), descend (from a mountain)
② be discharged; abort
③ be granted, be issued
④ be locked

降りる
①ⓐ (dismount) alight, get off, disembark
ⓑ (come down from a high place) alight, land, swoop
ⓒ (of frost or rain) fall, come down
② retire (from a position), withdraw, drop out (of a program), quit

HOMOPHONES

moto ⇨ 元 1929 本 3502 基 2673 許 1470 素 2458
sageru ⇨ 提 591
kudaru ⇨ 降 458
kudasu ⇨ 降 458
orosu ⇨ 降 458 卸 1447
oroshi ⇨ 卸 1447
oriru ⇨ 降 458

COMPOUND FORMATION

下宿 *geshuku*
下宿 'lodging, boarding house' originally referred to an inn or lodging (宿) of low class (下 ❷ⓑ).

NOTE

⇨ see also USAGE notes at 元 1929 and 卸 1447

3-1□ 干 𠦃 𠂊 Ⓒⓗ 干 gān

3379 KAN ho(su) ho(shi)- -bo(shi) hi(ru)

Radical 干 51	Strokes 3-3-0
Grade Jōyō-6	Freq 1132
■ 4 - 3 - 1	

一 二 干
1 2 3

RADICAL 51

Standard form: 干 *hosu* 'shield' (年 幹 幸)

Description: used for character classification

▶**DRY**

COMPOUNDS

❶ⓐ **dry, dry up, desiccate**

ⓑ (of tides) **ebb, recede**

ⓒ [formerly 旱 2396] **drought, dry weather**

干拓する *kantaku suru* reclaim by drainage

干魚(=乾魚) *kangyo* dried fish

干潮 *kanchō* ebb tide

干満 *kanman* ebb and flow, tide

干害 *kangai* drought damage

干天 *kanten* drought, dry weather

❷ **concern oneself in, interfere, intervene**

干渉する *kanshō suru* interfere, intervene

❸ offend against

干犯 *kanpan* infringement, violation

❹ sexagenary cycle, calendar signs (⇨ see APPENDIX 7)

干支 *kanshi* sexagenary cycle

十干 *jikkan* the ten calendar signs

❺ somewhat, a little

若干 *jakkan* a number of, some, a little

❻ defend

干城 *kanjō* bulwark, defender, safeguard

❼ rail, handrail

欄干 *rankan* railing, handrail, balustrade

❽ shield

干戈 *kanka* arms, weapons

KUN

【ho(su) 干す】

vt

① dry (up), desiccate, air (clothes)

物干し *monohoshi* clotheshorse, clothes-drier

日干しの *hiboshi no* sun-dried

② [formerly also 乾す]

ⓐ draw off (liquids), drain off

ⓑ drink up, drain dry

役を干される *yaku o hosareru* be deprived of one's role

飲み干す *nomihosu* drink up

【ho(shi)- 干し-】 [also prefix] dried

干し草 *hoshikusa* hay, dry grass

干し柿 *hoshigaki* dried persimmons

【-bo(shi) -干し】

[also suffix]

① sunning, drying, airing

甲羅干し *kōraboshi* basking in the sun

土用干し *doyōboshi* summer airing

② dried food

梅干し *umeboshi* pickled *ume*

白子干し *shirasuboshi* dried young sardines

【hi(ru) 干る】

vi

① [formerly also 乾る] get dry, parch

干魚 *hiuo* (=*hoshizakana*) dried fish

干涸びる *hikarabiru* dry up completely

干上がる *hiagaru* dry up, parch; ebb away

② (of tides) ebb, recede

潮干狩り *shiohigari* shell gathering (at low tide)

SYNONYMS

❶ⓐ **dry**

乾 DRY → 1679

燥 DRY UP → 1087

渇 RUN DRY → 515

【-boshi】

② **preserved foods**

-漬け pickles → 702

USAGE

❶ **hosu**

干す

vt

① dry (up), desiccate, air (clothes)

② [formerly also 乾す]

ⓐ draw off (liquids), drain off

ⓑ drink up, drain dry

乾す

[now usu. 干す] *vt*

ⓐ draw off (liquids), drain off

ⓑ drink up, drain dry

❷ **hiru**

干る

vi

① [formerly also 乾る] get dry, parch

② (of tides) ebb, recede

乾る

[now usu. 干る] *vi* get dry, parch

HOMOPHONES

hosu ⇨ 乾 1679

hiru ⇨ 乾 1679

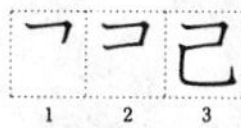

3380 KO KI onore tsuchinoto▲

(CH) 己 jǐ

Radical	Strokes
己 49	3-3-0
Grade	**Freq**
Jōyō-6	1275
■ 4-3-1	

3-1口

1 2 3

RADICAL 49
Standard form: 己 *onore* 'self' (巻)
Variant: 巳 *mi* (巴 巽 巷)
Description: used for character classification

▶**ONESELF**

COMPOUNDS

❶ **oneself, self**
自己 *jiko* oneself, self, ego
利己主義 *rikoshugi* egoism
克己 *kokki* self-denial, self-control
知己 *chiki* acquaintance; intimate friend
❷ sixth calendar sign (⇨ see APPENDIX 7)
己巳 *kishi* sixth of the sexagenary cycle

KUN

【**onore** 己】myself; *slang* you; You wretch!
己を捨てる *onore o suteru* rise above oneself
【**tsuchinoto** 己】sixth calendar sign

SYNONYMS

❶ **first person pronouns**

我 SELF → 3548
自 SELF → 3525
身 ONE'S PERSON → 3553
私 I (*polite*) → 1115
僕 I (*familiar*) → 164
俺 I (*intimate*) → 110
吾 I (*elegant*) → 2407
予 I (*pompous*) → 1983
余 I (*pompous*) → 2042
麿 I (*archaic*) → 3184
朕 IMPERIAL WE → 949

NOTE

★do not confuse with 巳 3377

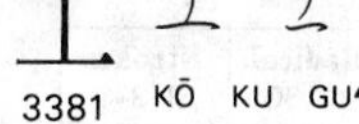

3381 KŌ KU GU▲

(CH) 工 gōng

Radical	Strokes
工 48	3-3-0
Grade	**Freq**
Jōyō-2	189
■ 4-3-1	

3-1口

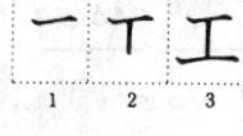

1 2 3

RADICAL 48
Standard form: 工 *takumi* 'work' (左 差 巫)
Left variant: 工 *takumihen* (巧)
Description: used in characters related to working or building

▶**MANUFACTURE** ▶**CONSTRUCTION**

COMPOUNDS

❶ (make by tools or machinery) **manufacture, process, fabricate, construct**
工作する *kōsaku suru* make; construct, build; maneuver, scheme
工場 *kōjō* factory, plant, workshop
工具 *kōgu* tool, implement
工芸 *kōgei* technical art, technology
工学 *kōgaku* engineering
工業 *kōgyō* industry, manufacturing industry
工員 *kōin* industrial worker
加工 *kakō* processing, manufacturing
❷ⓐ abbrev. of 工業 *kōgyō*: **manufacturing industry**
ⓑ abbrev. of 工学 *kōgaku*: engineering technology
ⓒ abbrev. of 工業高校 *kōgyō kōkō*: suffix after names of technical high schools
商工 *shōkō* commerce and industry
重工 *jūkō* heavy industry
工大 *kōdai* technical college
工科 *kōka* department of engineering
工博 *kōhaku* Doctor of Engineering
小倉工 *kokurakō* Kokura Technical High School
❸ **construction, building, engineering project**
工事 *kōji* construction
工務 *kōmu* engineering

工費 *kōhi* cost of construction
施工する *sekō* (=*shikō*) *suru* execute (a building contract), carry out
着工する *chakkō suru* start (construction) work
❹ⓐ [also suffix] **workman, worker, artisan, craftsman, mechanic**
ⓑ workmanship, craftsmanship, work
工人 *kōjin* workman, craftsman
職工 *shokkō* workman, mechanic, (factory) hand
大工 *daiku* carpenter
石工 *ishiku* (=*sekkō*) stonemason, mason
印刷工 *insatsukō* printer
熟練工 *jukurenkō* skilled workman, master mechanic
細工 *saiku* work, craftsmanship; artifice, tactics
❺ used phonetically for *ku* or *gu*
工夫 *kufū* device, contrivance; scheme, resources
工面する *kumen suru* contrive, manage, make shift; raise (money)
工合(=具合) *guai* condition, state; health; manner, way

INDEPENDENT

【kō 工】 construction, building; abbrev. of 工学部 *kōgakubu*: faculty of technology, department of engineering

SYNONYMS

❶ **make**
製 MANUFACTURE → 2803
産 PRODUCE → 3298
造 MAKE → 3110
作 MAKE → 68
成 FORM → 3537
調 PREPARE → 1567
組む ASSEMBLE → 1337
構 CONSTRUCT → 1049
❷ⓐ **industry and business**
業 BUSINESS, INDUSTRY → 2612
産 industry → 3298
商 TRADE → 2116
❹ⓐ **workers and professionals**
匠 CRAFTSMAN → 2990
夫 MAN LABORER → 3460
嬢 (unmarried) female worker → 758
婦 woman worker → 469
手 OCCUPATION SUFFIX → 3456
屋 colloquial occupation suffix → 3098
員 MEMBER (of a staff) → 2269
人 person of certain category → 3368
者 person who → 3211
師 profession suffix → 1326
士 PROFESSION SUFFIX → 3405
客 skilled person → 2250
家 professional → 2273

3-1口

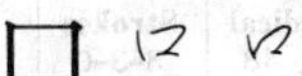

3382 KŌ KU kuchi

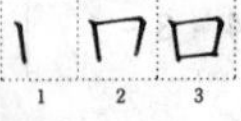

CH 口 kǒu

Radical	Strokes
口 30	3-3-0
Grade	**Freq**
Jōyō-1	244
■ 4 - 3 - 1	

RADICAL 30

Standard form: 口 *kuchi* 'mouth' (只 台 和)
Left variant: 口 *kuchihen* (叱 吸 吐)
Description: used in characters related to actions performed by the mouth

▶MOUTH

COMPOUNDS

❶ [original meaning] (oral cavity) **mouth**
口腔 *kōkō* mouth, oral cavity
口内 *kōnai* in the mouth
口角 *kōkaku* corners of one's mouth
経口の *keikō no* oral
閉口する *heikō suru* be dumfounded [stumped], be silenced
❷ [also suffix] (mouthlike opening) **mouth, opening, hole, aperture**
口径 *kōkei* caliber, bore; diameter
河口 *kakō* river mouth, estuary
火口 *kakō* crater
銃口 *jūkō* muzzle (of a rifle)
排気口 *haikikō* exhaust port
突破口 *toppakō* breach, breakthrough
❸ⓐ **give mouth to, mouth, speak, talk**
ⓑ (expression in words) **mouth, speech**
口論 *kōron* argument
口語 *kōgo* colloquial language
口外する *kōgai suru* tell, divulge
口実 *kōjitsu* excuse, pretext, pretense
口調 *kuchō* tone, expression
口説く *kudoku* persuade; seduce
口述 *kōjutsu* oral statement, dictation
悪口 *akkō* (=*warukuchi*) slander, abuse, foul language
異口同音に *ikudōon ni* with one voice, unanimously

利口(＝悧巧)な *rikō na* clever, bright, sharp, shrewd

❹ **number of persons** (mouths to feed)

人口 *jinkō* population

戸口 *kokō* houses and inhabitants, population

❺❸ subdivision of a whole, unit, item

❺ counter for swords

口座 *kōza* (bank) account

口銭 *kōsen* commission

一口の剣 *ikkō no ken* a sword

❻ unclassified compounds

口惜しい(＝悔しい) *kuyashii* vexing, mortifying, regrettable

KUN

【kuchi 口】

①ⓐ (oral cavity) mouth

ⓑ counter for mouthfuls

ⓒ (one's) taste, (one's) palate

口の小さい *kuchi no chiisai* small mouthed

口元(＝口許) *kuchimoto* mouth, shape of the mouth

口紅 *kuchibeni* lipstick, rouge

一口食べる *hitokuchi taberu* eat a mouthful

口に合う *kuchi ni au* suit one's taste, be palatable

口当たり *kuchiatari* taste

②ⓐ (mouthlike opening) mouth (as of a receptacle or river), opening, hole

ⓑ [also suffix] entrance, exit, entranceway, doorway, gateway, door

急須の口 *kyūsu no kuchi* spout of a teapot

口金 *kuchigane* metal clasp, snap; metal cap

窓口 *madoguchi* window, wicket; clerk at a window

間口 *maguchi* frontage, front; width

入り口 *iriguchi* entrance

西口 *nishiguchi* westside entrance [exit]

非常口 *hijōguchi* emergency exit

改札口 *kaisatsuguchi* ticket barrier [gate], wicket

③ (expression in words) mouth, tongue, speech, talk, words

口が巧い(＝口が上手い) *kuchi ga umai* honey-mouthed, fair-spoken

口を出す *kuchi o dasu* butt [chip] in

口口に *kuchiguchi ni* mutually; unanimously

口癖 *kuchiguse* way [habit] of saying, one's favorite phrase

無駄口 *mudaguchi* idle talk

無口 *mukuchi* taciturnity, reticence

④ⓐ (place from which an ascent to a mountain is made) route, ascent

ⓑ suffix after names of ascents

登山口 *tozanguchi* place where an ascent to a mountain is made

吉田口 *yoshidaguchi* Yoshida route [ascent]

⑤ mouths to feed, number of persons

口が多い *kuchi ga ōi* have a large family to support

口減らし *kuchiberashi* reducing the mouths to feed

⑥ⓐ employment, job, position; vacancy

ⓑ call, engagement

口が無い *kuchi ga nai* be unable to find a job

就職口 *shūshokuguchi* employment, work

口を掛ける *kuchi o kakeru* call for (a doctor); apply for (a job)

⑦ⓐ share, item, lot

ⓑ counter for shares, items or lots

ⓒ kind, sort

小口 *koguchi* small lot, small sum [amount]; end, edge

大口 *ōguchi* large amount; big mouth; tall talk

一口 *hitokuchi* an item, a share, a unit

品物が十口 *shinamono ga jukkuchi* goods of ten lots

手口 *teguchi* way of doing, method, trick

この口の品 *kono kuchi no shina* this kind of goods

⑧ beginning

糸口 *itoguchi* [formerly also 緒] beginning, first step; clue

SYNONYMS

❶ **face orifices**

鼻 NOSE → 2706

耳 EAR → 3516

目 EYE → 3043

❷ **holes and cavities**

穴 HOLE → 2159

孔 OPEN HOLE → 179

坑 PIT → 236

堀 DITCH → 467

溝 CHANNEL → 659

凹 concavity → 3482

洞 CAVE → 380

❸❸ **speak and say**

話 SPEAK → 1527

言 SAY → 1941

云 say → 1931

申す SPEAK HUMBLY → 3507

弁 SPEAK ELOQUENTLY → 2004

語る TELL → 1543

談 TALK → 1569

述 STATE → 3075

陳 SET FORTH → 540

❺ **speech**

舌 TONGUE → 2186

言 SPEECH → 1941

談 TALK → 1569

【kuchi】

②ⓑ **doors**

戸 DOOR → 1930

扉 HINGED DOOR → 1955

門 GATE → 888

HOMOPHONES

kuyashii ⇨ 悔しい 365　口惜しい 3382, 484
itoguchi ⇨ 緒 1378　糸口 2179, 3382

NOTE

⇨ see USAGE notes at 悔 365 and 緒 1378
⇨ see COMPOUND FORMATION for 口座 *kōza* ⇨ 座 3116

3-1□

弓 弓 弓

3383　KYŪ　yumi

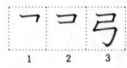

Ⓒⓗ 弓 gōng

Radical	Strokes
弓 57	3-3-0
Grade	Freq
Jōyō-2	1535
■ 4 - 3 - 1	

RADICAL 57

Standard form: 弓 *yumi* 'bow' (弟 弔 彎)
Left variant: 弓 *yumihen* (強 引 張)
Description: used in characters related to bows or actions performed with bows

▶**BOW**

COMPOUNDS

❶ⓐ [original meaning] **bow**
ⓑ violin bow
弓道 *kyūdō* archery
弓状の *kyūjō no* bow-shaped, arched
弓術 *kyūjutsu* archery
洋弓 *yōkyū* Western archery
胡弓 *kokyū* Chinese fiddle
❷ [suffix] *anat* arch
内臓弓 *naizōkyū* visceral arch

INDEPENDENT

【**kyū** 弓】 violin bow

KUN

【**yumi** 弓】 bow; archery; bow (of a violin)
弓矢 *yumiya* bow and arrow
弓弦 *yumizuru* (=*yuzuru*) bowstring
弓形 *yuminari* arch, curve
弓取り式 *yumitorishiki* conferment of the championship bow (in sumo)

SYNONYMS

❶ⓐ **weapons for shooting**
銃 GUN (portable firearm) → 1723
砲 HEAVY GUN → 1151
火 firearms → 3463

3-1□

久 久 久

3384　KYŪ　KU　hisa(shii)

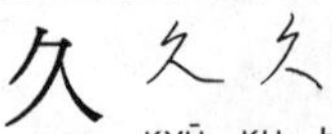

Ⓒⓗ 久 jiǔ

Radical	Strokes
ノ 4	3-1-2
Grade	Freq
Jōyō-5	635
■ 4 - 3 - 1	

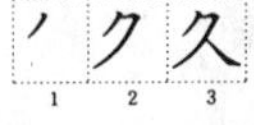

▶**OF LONG DURATION**

COMPOUNDS

● **of long duration, longstanding, lasting for a long time**
久遠 *kuon* eternity
永久の *eikyū no* permanent, eternal, lasting
恒久の *kōkyū no* lasting, everlasting, permanent, eternal
耐久性 *taikyūsei* durability, persistence, lasting quality
悠久な *yūkyū na* eternal, everlasting, permanent

KUN

【**hisa(shii)** 久しい】 (of long duration) long, longstanding
久しい昔 *hisashii mukashi* a long time ago
久久に *hisabisa ni* after a long time, for the first time in a long period
久し振りに *hisashiburi ni* after a long time [interval]

SYNONYMS

● **of long duration**
永 ETERNAL → 1937
恒 permanent → 367
長 LONG → 2556

及 及 及 及

3385 KYŪ oyo(bu) oyo(bi) oyobi oyo(bosu)

CH 及 jí

Radical	Strokes
ノ 4△	3-1-2
Grade	**Freq**
Jōyō	730
■ 4 - 3 - 1	

3-1□

ノ 乃 及
1 2 3

▶**REACH TO**

COMPOUNDS

❶ⓐ [original meaning] (go as far as or arrive at a goal) **reach to, come up to (a standard), attain (successful results)**

ⓑ (extend as far as) **reach to, extend over, range over**

及第する *kyūdai suru* pass an examination

及落 *kyūraku* passing or failing an examination

追及する *tsuikyū suru* pursue, seek after, follow, press (a person) hard

企及する *kikyū suru* try to attain (something)

普及 *fukyū* diffusion, spread, propagation

波及する *hakyū suru* be propagated; extend, spread; affect

遡及的な *sokyūteki* (=*sakkyūteki*) *na* retroactive

❷ refer to, mention

言及する *genkyū suru* refer to, mention, touch upon

論及する *ronkyū suru* mention, refer to

KUN

【**oyo(bu) 及ぶ**】(go as far as or arrive at a goal) reach to, come up to, amount to; come up with; equal to, match

及び腰で *oyobigoshi de* with one's back bent; unconfidently

数百万に及ぶ *sūhyakuman ni oyobu* reach [range] into the millions

聞き及ぶ *kikioyobu* hear of, learn of

遠く及ばない *tōku oyobanai* be no equal [match] for, fall far short of

及びも付かぬ *oyobi mo tsukanu* not at all equal, far beyond one's power

【**oyo(bi) 及び, oyobi 及**】and, as well as

太陽及び地球 *taiyō oyobi chikyū* the sun and the earth

【**oyo(bosu) 及ぼす**】exert (influence upon), cause (harm), extend (benefits)

害を及ぼす *gai o oyobosu* cause harm (to)

SYNONYMS

❶ⓐ **arrive**

至 COME TO → 2182
到 ARRIVE → 1264
着 ARRIVE → 3316
届く REACH → 3078
達 ATTAIN → 3139

ⓑ **make widely known**

布 SPREAD → 2973
流 spread → 441
伝 spread → 44
広 spread → 3035
弘 DISSEMINATE (esp. Buddhism) → 192

ⓑ **extend over**

亘 EXTEND OVER → 1939

【**oyobi**】

○ **additionally**

並びに and also → 2246
傍ら besides → 147
亦 ALSO → 2011
又 also, and → 3351
尚 STILL → 2233
更に furthermore → 3541
且つ AS WELL → 3485
兼 CONCURRENTLY → 2286

叉

3386 SA SHA mata

CH 叉 chā chá chǎ

Radical	Strokes
又 29	3-2-1
Grade	**Freq**
Reference	
■ 4 - 3 - 1	

3-1□

COMPOUNDS

❶ (place of furcation) crotch (of a tree), fork (of a road)

音叉 *onsa* tuning fork

蹄叉 *teisa* fourchette

轍叉 *tessa railway* frog

木の叉 *ki no mata* crotch of a tree

三つ叉 *mitsumata* three-pronged fork, trident, trifurcation

❷ [now replaced by 差 *sa* 3311] cross, inter-

sect
交叉 *kōsa* crossing, intersection
三叉路 *sansaro* three-forked road
❸ used phonetically for *sha*
夜叉 *yasha yakṣa*, demon

❹ [original meaning] hold between
叉手網 *sadeami* scoop net

HOMOPHONES
mata ⇨ 股 881

3-1□

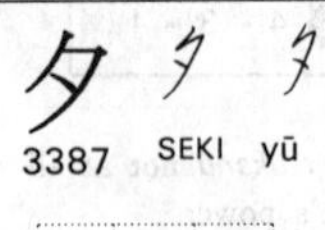

3387 SEKI yū

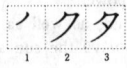

CH 夕 xī

Radical	Strokes
夕 36	3-3-0
Grade	**Freq**
Jōyō-1	751
■ 4 - 3 - 1	

ノ ク 夕
1 2 3

RADICAL 36
Standard form: 夕 *yūbe* 'evening' (外 多 夢)
Description: used in characters related to nighttime

▶EVENING

COMPOUNDS

● [original meaning] **evening, dusk, night**
今夕 *konseki* this evening, tonight
一朝一夕に *itchō-isseki ni* in one day, in a short time
旦夕 *tanseki* morning and evening, day and night

KUN
【yū 夕】evening, dusk
夕べ *yūbe* evening
夕方 *yūgata* evening
夕闇 *yūyami* dusk, twilight

夕陽 *yūhi* setting sun
夕食 *yūshoku* supper
夕刊 *yūkan* evening edition [paper]

SPECIAL READINGS
七夕 *tanabata* Festival of the Weaver [Star Vega]; the Star Festival

SYNONYMS
● **evening and night**
晩 EVENING → 979
夜 NIGHT → 2056
宵 EARLY EVENING → 2276
暮 DUSK → 2354

3-1□

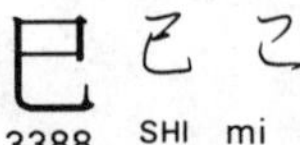

3388 SHI mi

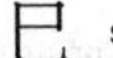

CH 巳 sì

Radical	Strokes
己 49	3-3-0
Grade	**Freq**
Names	2024
■ 4 - 3 - 1	

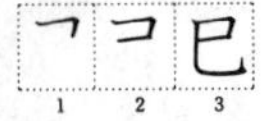

1 2 3

RADICAL 49
mi, variant of 己 *onore* 'self'
⇨ see 己 3380 for radical description

▶THE SERPENT

COMPOUNDS

● sixth sign of the Oriental zodiac: the Serpent—(time) 9-11 a.m., (direction) SSE, (season) April (of the lunar calendar) (⇨ see APPENDIX 7)
上巳 *jōshi* March 3rd of the lunar calendar (one of the five annual festivals)

KUN
【mi 巳】sixth sign of the Oriental zodiac: the Serpent (⇨ ●)
初巳 *hatsumi* first Serpent day of the year

NAMES
辰巳 *tatsumi* surname also place name
巳喜男 *mikio* male name

SYNONYMS
● **snake**
蛇 SNAKE → 1343

尸

3389 SHI shikabane

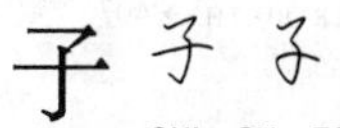

CH 尸 shī

Radical	Strokes
尸 44	3-3-0
Grade	Freq
Reference	
■ 4-3-1	

3-1□

RADICAL 44

Standard form: 尸 *shikabane* 'corpse' (尺 局 展)

Description: used in characters related to the human body or buttocks

COMPOUNDS

❶ⓐ [original meaning] corpse

ⓑ [usu. 屍 *shikabane*] corpse

尸諫(=屍諫)する *shikan suru* admonish (one's master) at the cost of one's life

尸 *shikabane* corpse

❷ [archaic] personator of the dead at sacrifices

尸位素餐 *shii-sosan* neglecting the duties of an office while taking pay

HOMOPHONES

shikabane ⇨ 屍 3099

子 子 子

3390 SHI SU TSU▲ ko -ko -(k)ko ne▲

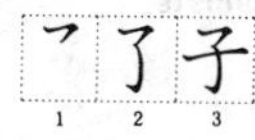

CH 子 zǐ zi

Radical	Strokes
子 39	3-3-0
Grade	Freq
Jōyō-1	52
■ 4-3-1	

3-1□

RADICAL 39

Standard form: 子 *ko* 'child' (字 孫 孟)

Description: used in characters related to children

▶**CHILD** ▶**NOUN SUFFIX**

COMPOUNDS

❶ⓐ [original meaning] (offspring of man) **child, son, daughter, offspring**

ⓑ boy, young man

子女 *shijo* children, sons and daughters

子息 *shisoku* son

子音 *shiin* (=*shion*) consonant ("child sound")

母子 *boshi* mother and child

養子 *yōshi* foster [adopted] child

太子 *taishi* Crown Prince

男子 *danshi* boy, young man, man

弟子 *deshi* disciple, pupil, apprentice

❷ (offspring of plants or animals) seed, egg, fruit

種子 *shushi* seed, pit, stone

卵子 *ranshi* ovum, ovule, egg

❸ term of respect for men:

ⓐ **gentleman, man of learning**—sometimes used as familiar second person pronoun

ⓑ (male) member of a group or profession

ⓒ honorific after names of Chinese sages or their works, esp. authors of the Chinese classics

ⓓ the Master, esp. Confucius

君子 *kunshi* man of virtue, wise man

遊子 *yūshi* wanderer, traveler

編集子 *henshūshi* member of editorial staff

老子 *rōshi* Laozi; the works of Laozi

孟子 *mōshi* Mencius; the works of Mencius

諸子 *shoshi* Chinese sages or their works (except for Confucius and Mencius); gentlemen, you

孔子 *kōshi* Confucius

❹ **suffix after nouns, esp. names of small objects:**

ⓐ **various articles and fixtures, esp. furniture**

ⓑ **small entities such as particles, esp. nuclear particles**

ⓒ **various abstract concepts**

障子 *shōji* paper sliding-door, *shoji*

椅子 *isu* chair

菓子 *kashi* confectionery, cake, sweets

帽子 *bōshi* cap, hat

粒子 *ryūshi* particle, grain

原子 *genshi* atom

電子 *denshi* electron

遺伝子 *idenshi* gene

晶子 *shōshi* crystallite

骨子 *kosshi* essence, gist

調子 *chōshi* tone, tune; key, note; condition, state (of health); manner, way
様子 *yōsu* situation, aspect, circumstances; appearance, looks; sign, indication
面子 *mentsu* face, honor
❺ ("offspring" of money) interest
利子 *rishi* interest
金子 *kinsu* money, funds
❻ first sign of the Oriental zodiac: the Rat—(time) midnight (11 p.m.-1 a.m.), (direction) north, (season) November (of the lunar calendar) (⇨see APPENDIX 7)
子午線 *shigosen* meridian
正子 *shōshi* midnight
❼ viscount
子爵 *shishaku* viscount
❽ⓐ counter for go pieces
ⓑ go pieces
三子 *sanshi* three go pieces
❾ [sometimes also 仔 *shi* 33] minute, fine, small
子細 *shisai* particulars; reasons, circumstances

INDEPENDENT

【shi 子】 viscount; Confucius, the Master
子曰く *shi iwaku* Confucius said

KUN

【ko 子】
① offspring of humans or animals:
ⓐ child, son, daughter
ⓑ [formerly also 仔] offspring, youngling; puppy; cub: roe
ⓒ [sometimes also 児] (boy or girl) child, kid, youngster
子供 *kodomo* child, kid; son, daughter
親子 *oyako* (=*shinshi*) parent and child
息子 *musuko* son
子犬 *koinu* puppy
男の子 *otoko no ko* boy, baby boy
迷子 *maigo* lost child
② [also 娘 or コ] girl, gal
あいつは行ける子だ *Aitsu wa ikeru ko da* She's a nice gal [good-looking broad]
③ interest

【-ko -子, -(k)ko -っ子】
① [also suffix] [also *-kko*] child, kid, boy, girl
継子 *mamako* stepchild
悪戯っ子 *itazurakko* mischievous kid
② [also *-kko*] [sometimes also 児]
ⓐ person, performer of an action
ⓑ [suffix] native of a specific place
売り子 *uriko* shopgirl, sales clerk
踊り子 *odoriko* dancer, dancing girl
売れっ子歌手 *urekko-kashu* popular singer
江戸っ子 *edokko* Edoite, Tokyoite
神戸っ子 *kōbekko* native of Kobe
③ [also *-kko*] noun forming suffix, esp. for small objects
振り子 *furiko* pendulum
玉子(=卵) *tamago* egg
根っ子 *nekko* root; stump, stub
④ element for forming female names
恵子 *keiko* Keiko
典子 *noriko* Noriko

【ne 子】 first sign of the Oriental zodiac: the Rat (⇨❻)
子の刻 *ne no koku* midnight

SYNONYMS

❶ⓐ offspring
孤 orphan → 356
嫡 LEGITIMATE CHILD → 680
息 son → 2647
男 son → 2542
惣 eldest son → 2780
娘 DAUGHTER → 406
女 daughter → 3418
姫 DAUGHTER OF NOBLE BIRTH → 407

❸ⓐ gentleman
紳 GENTLEMAN → 1334
士 man of learning and virtue → 3405

ⓓ Confucius and Confucianists
孔 Confucius → 179
孟 MENCIUS → 2220

❹ nominalizers
所 PARTICLE OF NOMINALIZATION → 851
事 nominalization word → 3567
性 -ITY → 299

ⓑ particle
粒 GRAIN → 1328
核 NUCLEUS → 927

❺ interest and dividend
利 interest → 1114
配 dividend → 1460

❼ noblemen
男 baron → 2542
伯 COUNT → 59
侯 marquis → 98
公 duke → 1974

【ko】
①ⓒ child
児 CHILD (of any age) → 2546
童 CHILD (young person) → 2130
幼 young child → 191
坊 SONNY → 233

【-ko】
④ name suffixes
彦 MALE NAME ELEMENT → 3295
郎 MALE NAME SUFFIX → 1289
麿 CLASSICAL MALE NAME SUFFIX → 3184

USAGE

❶ ko
子
① offspring of humans or animals:
ⓐ child, son, daughter

ⓑ [formerly also 仔] offspring, youngling; puppy; cub; roe
ⓒ [sometimes also 児] (boy or girl) child, kid, youngster
② [also 娘 or コ] girl, gal
③ interest

児
[now usu. 子] (boy or girl) child, kid, youngster

娘
[also 子 or コ] girl, gal

仔
[now usu. 子] offspring, youngling; puppy; cub; roe

小-
[also prefix]
①ⓐ (less in size or quantity) small, little, short
ⓑ (less in intensity) small, light, slight
②ⓐ (of secondary importance) secondary, sub-
ⓑ [belittling] small, petty, little
③ [emphatic preceding adjectives or verbs] a little, slightly, very
④ nearly, almost

❷ -ko

-子
① [also suffix] [also *-kko*] child, kid, boy, girl
② [also *-kko*] [sometimes also 児]
ⓐ person, performer of an action
ⓑ [suffix] native of a specific place
③ [also *-kko*] noun forming suffix, esp. for small objects
④ element for forming female names

-児
[usu. 子]
ⓐ person, performer of an action
ⓑ [suffix] native of a specific place

HOMOPHONES

ko ⇨ 児 2546　娘 406　仔 33　小 7
-ko ⇨ 児 2546
tamago ⇨ 卵 849　玉子 3477, 3390

COMPOUND FORMATION

子午線 ***shigosen***
子午線 'meridian' is a line (線) going from north (子 ❻) to south (午).

NOTE

⇨ see also USAGE note at 卵 849

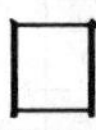
3391

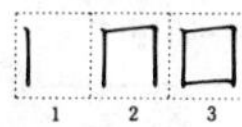

Radical 囗 31	Strokes 3-3-0
Grade Radical	Freq
■ 4 - 3 - 1	

3-1囗

RADICAL 31
Standard form: 囗 *kunigamae* 'enclosure' (回 四 国)
Description: used in characters related to enclosures, enclosing or encircling

---

3392

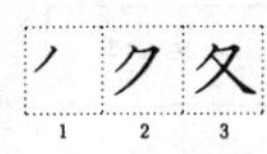

Radical 夂 34	Strokes 3-3-0
Grade Radical	Freq
■ 4 - 3 - 1	

3-1囗

RADICAL 34
Standard form: 夂 *fuyugashira* 'descend' (変)
Description: used in characters related to things descending or coming down

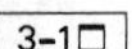

3393

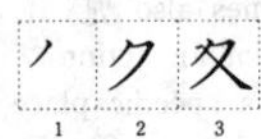

Radical	Strokes
夊 35	3-3-0
Grade	Freq
Radical	
■ 4 - 3 - 1	

RADICAL 35

Standard form: 夊 *suinyō* 'move slowly'

Bottom variant: 夂 *natsuashi* (夏)

Description: used for character classification

3-1□

3394

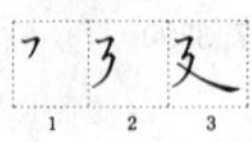

Radical	Strokes
廴 54	3-3-0
Grade	Freq
Radical	
■ 4 - 3 - 1	

RADICAL 54

Standard form: 廴 *ennyō* 'proceed' (建 延 廷)

Enclosure: 廴 *ennyō* (建 延 廷)

Description: used in characters related to advancing or going

---

3-1□

廴

3395

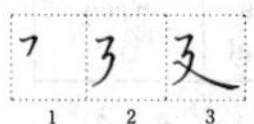

Radical	Strokes
廴 54	3-3-0
Grade	Freq
Radical	
■ 4 - 3 - 1	

RADICAL 54

variant of 廴 *ennyō* 'proceed'

⇨ see 廴 3394 for radical description

3-1□

彐

3396

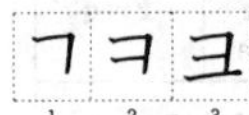

Radical	Strokes
彐 58	3-3-0
Grade	Freq
Radical	
■ 4 - 3 - 1	

RADICAL 58

Standard form: 彐 *keigashira* 'pig's head'

Variants: 彑 彑 *keigashira* (彗 彙 彖)

Description: used for character classification

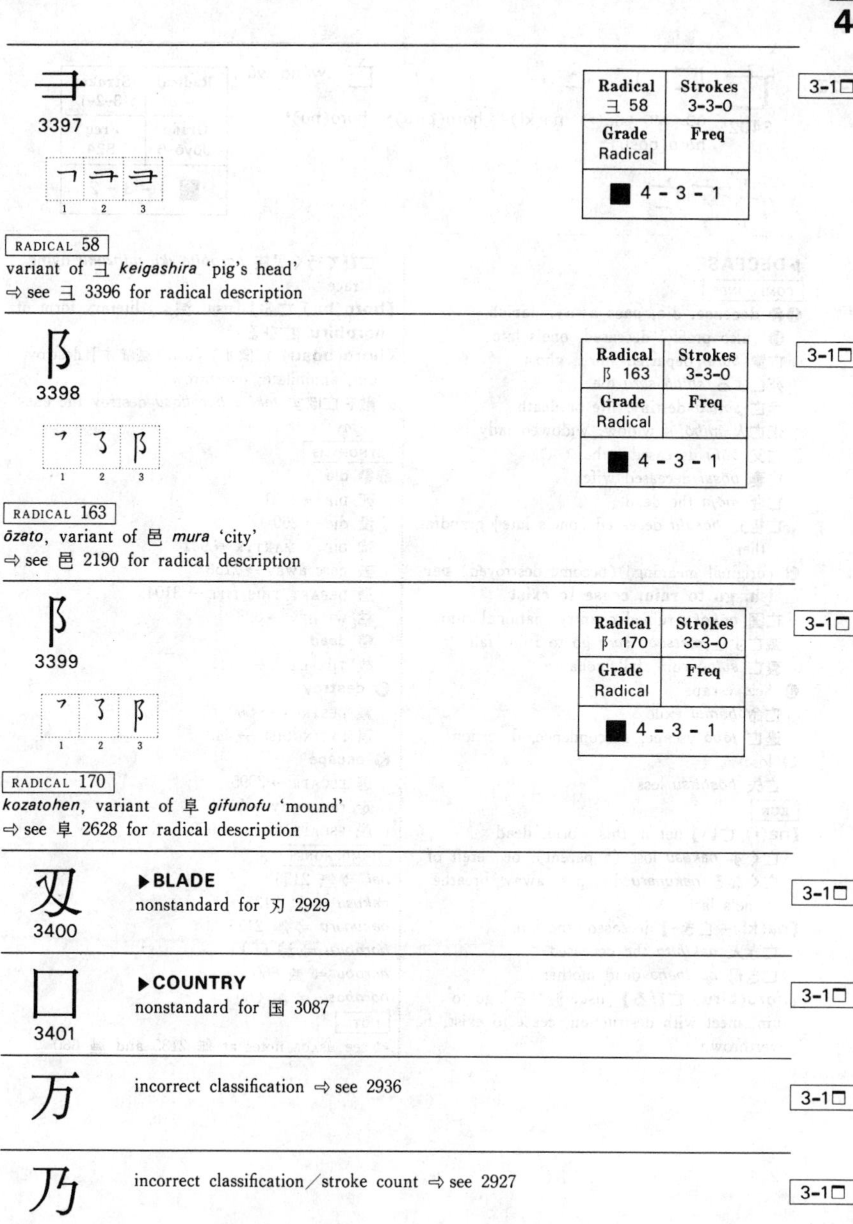

⺕
3397

Radical	Strokes
⺕ 58	3-3-0
Grade	**Freq**
Radical	
■ 4 - 3 - 1	

3-1□

RADICAL 58

variant of 彐 *keigashira* 'pig's head'

⇨ see 彐 3396 for radical description

阝
3398

Radical	Strokes
阝 163	3-3-0
Grade	**Freq**
Radical	
■ 4 - 3 - 1	

3-1□

RADICAL 163

ōzato, variant of 邑 *mura* 'city'

⇨ see 邑 2190 for radical description

阝
3399

Radical	Strokes
阝 170	3-3-0
Grade	**Freq**
Radical	
■ 4 - 3 - 1	

3-1□

RADICAL 170

kozatohen, variant of 阜 *gifunofu* 'mound'

⇨ see 阜 2628 for radical description

双
3400

▶BLADE

nonstandard for 刃 2929

3-1□

囗
3401

▶COUNTRY

nonstandard for 国 3087

3-1□

万

incorrect classification ⇨ see 2936

3-1□

乃

incorrect classification／stroke count ⇨ see 2927

3-1□

刃 刄

incorrect classification ⇨ see ■ 1－2

3-1□

3-2□

亡 亡 亡 亡

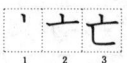

3402 BŌ MŌ na(i) na(ki)- horo(biru)▲ horo(bu)▲ horo(bosu)▲

CH 亡 wáng wú

Radical	Strokes
亠 8	3-2-1
Grade	**Freq**
Jōyō-6	824
■ 4-3-2	

1 2 3

▶**DECEASE**

COMPOUNDS

❶ⓐ **decease, die, pass away, perish**
ⓑ [also prefix] deceased, one's late
亡霊 *bōrei* departed spirit, ghost
死亡する *shibō suru* die
存亡 *sonbō* destiny; life or death
未亡人 *mibōjin* widow, widowed lady
亡父 *bōfu* deceased father
亡妻 *bōsai* deceased wife
亡者 *mōja* the dead
亡祖父 *bōsofu* deceased [one's late] grandfather

❷ [original meaning] (become destroyed) **perish, go to ruin, cease to exist**
亡国 *bōkoku* ruined country, national ruin
滅亡する *metsubō suru* go to ruin, fall
衰亡 *suibō* ruin, fall, collapse

❸ flee, escape
亡命 *bōmei* exile
逃亡 *tōbō* escape, abscondence, desertion

❹ lose
亡失 *bōshitsu* loss

KUN

【**na(i) 亡い**】 not in this world, dead
亡くす *nakusu* lose (a parent), be bereft of
亡くなる *nakunaru* die, pass away, breathe one's last

【**na(ki)- 亡き-**】 deceased, the late
亡き人 *nakihito* the deceased
亡き母 *nakihaha* dead mother

【**horo(biru) 亡びる**】 [usu. 滅びる] go to ruin, meet with destruction, cease to exist; be overthrown
亡びて行く民族 *horobite iku minzoku* dying race

【**horo(bu) 亡ぶ**】 [usu. 滅ぶ] literary form of **horobiru 亡びる**

【**horo(bosu) 亡ぼす**】 [usu. 滅ぼす] destroy, ruin, annihilate; overthrow
敵を亡ぼす *teki o horobosu* destroy the enemy

SYNONYMS

❶ⓐ **die**
死 DIE → 3521
没 die → 260
殉 DIE A MARTYR → 941
去 pass away → 2156
逝 DEPART THIS LIFE → 3104
枯 WITHER → 898
ⓑ **dead**
故 THE LATE → 1141
❷ **destroy**
滅 DESTROY → 660
消 EXTINGUISH → 443
❸ **escape**
逃 ESCAPE → 3095
走 run away → 2194
脱 ESCAPE FROM → 973

HOMOPHONES

nai ⇨ 無 2135
nakusu ⇨ 無 2135
nakunaru ⇨ 無 2135
horobiru ⇨ 滅 660
horobu ⇨ 滅 660
horobosu ⇨ 滅 660

NOTE

⇨ see USAGE notes at 無 2135 and 滅 660

土 土 土

3403 DO TO tsuchi

一 十 土
1 2 3

Ⓒⓗ 土 tǔ

Radical	Strokes
土 32	3-3-0
Grade	Freq
Jōyō-1	382
■ 4 - 3 - 2	

3-2□

RADICAL 32

Standard form: 土 *tsuchi* 'earth' (型 圧 坐)

Left variant: ± *tsuchihen* (地 場 坂)

Description: used in characters related to earth or things built on the ground

▶**SOIL**

COMPOUNDS

❶ⓐ [also suffix] [original meaning] **soil, earth, mud, sand, clay**

ⓑ **earthen**

ⓒ the third of the five elements: earth (⇨see APPENDIX 7)

土砂 *dosha* earth and sand

土壌 *dojō* soil, earth

土俵 *dohyō* sumo (wrestling) ring; sandbag

土台 *dodai* foundation, base, basis; utterly

土木 *doboku* engineering works

土砂降り *doshaburi* pouring rain, downpour

土壇場 *dotanba* the last moment

粘土 *nendo* clay

耕土 *kōdo* arable soil

珪藻土 *keisōdo* diatomite, silicious marl

アルカリ土類 *arukaridorui* alkaline earths

土器 *doki* earthenware

土瓶 *dobin* earthen teapot, pipkin

土用 *doyō* midsummer

❷ⓐ **land, ground, territory, country**

ⓑ **of the land, local, native**

土地 *tochi* land

国土 *kokudo* country, territory, realm

領土 *ryōdo* territory, domain

本土 *hondo* mainland; the country proper

風土 *fūdo* natural features (of a region), climate

郷土 *kyōdo* one's birthplace

土俗 *dozoku* local customs

土着民 *dochakumin* natives, aborigines

❸ **Saturday**

土曜日 *doyōbi* Saturday

土日 *donichi* Saturday and Sunday, weekend

❹ Saturn

土星 *dosei* Saturn

❺ abbrev. of 土佐 *tosa*, old name for Kochi Prefecture

土讃本線 *dosan honsen* Dosan Main Line (Kochi-Kagawa Railway)

❻ Turkey

土国 *dokoku* Turkey

❼ *colloq* emphatic prefix

土根性 *dokonjō* disposition

土真ん中 *domannaka* right in the center

土偉い *doerai* immense, great; hell of a lot

INDEPENDENT

【**do** 土】Saturday; land, country; the third of the five elements: earth

KUN

【**tsuchi** 土】

①ⓐ soil, earth, mud, clay; ground

ⓑ mother earth

土色 *tsuchiiro* earth color

土壁 *tsuchikabe* mud wall

肥えた土 *koeta tsuchi* rich [fertile] soil

盛り土 *moritsuchi* earth pile

土に帰る *tsuchi ni kaeru* return to mother earth, die

② *sumo* defeat

土付かず *tsuchitsukazu* clean record, no defeat

SPECIAL READINGS

土産 *miyage* souvenir

SYNONYMS

❶ⓐ & ❶ⓑ **land and soil**

壌 ARABLE SOIL → 755

地 GROUND → 204

陸 LAND → 543

泥 MUD → 326

❷ⓐ **country**

国 COUNTRY → 3087

邦 STATE → 847

❸ **days of the week**

金 Friday → 2057

日 Sunday → 3027

月 Monday → 2956

火 Tuesday → 3463

水 Wednesday → 10

木 Thursday → 3450

COMPOUND FORMATION

土壇場 *dotanba*

土壇場 'the last moment' originally referred to a place (場) of execution where there is a mound (壇) of earth (土 ❶ⓐ).

NOTE

★do not confuse with 士 3405

3-2□ 上 ⺊ 𠄌 CH 上 shàng shǎng

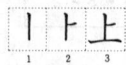

3404 JŌ SHŌ SHAN▲ ue -ue uwa- kami a(geru) -a(geru) a(garu) -a(garu) a(gari) -a(gari) nobo(ru) nobo(ri) nobo(seru) nobo(su)

Radical	Strokes
一 1	3-1-2
Grade	**Freq**
Jōyō-1	16
■ 4-3-2	

丨 1 ⺊ 2 上 3

▶**UP**

COMPOUNDS

❶ⓐ **upper part, top; up, above**
ⓑ [also prefix] **upper, higher, outer**
ⓒ [also suffix] **on top of, over; on, at; aboard**

上下 *jōge* upper and lower parts [sides], high and low; going up and down, rise and fall; first and second volumes
頂上 *chōjō* summit, peak, top; climax
屋上 *okujō* housetop, roof
上部 *jōbu* upper part [section], top; surface
上空 *jōkū* skies, upper air
上記の *jōki no* above-mentioned
上流 *jōryū* upper stream (of a river); upper class
上皮 *jōhi* outer skin, epidermis
上甲板 *jōkanpan* upper deck
上半身 *jōhanshin* upper part of the body
以上 *ijō* or more than, not less than; beyond; the above-mentioned; now that; that's all
陸上 *rikujō* land, ground; shore; track and field
海上の *kaijō no* maritime
紙上で *shijō de* on paper, in print; by letter
発展途上国 *hatten-tojōkoku* developing countries
席上で *sekijō de* at the meeting; on the occasion
地球上の *chikyūjō no* on the earth

❷ⓐ (of higher rank or position) **upper, higher, superior, advanced**
ⓑ [also prefix] **of upper grade, top-quality, first-class, excellent, best, good**

上位 *jōi* higher rank, precedence
上級 *jōkyū* higher grade, advanced class, high class
上官 *jōkan* higher officer, senior
上院 *jōin* Upper House
上人 *shōnin* Buddhist saint
上水 *jōsui* water supply; tap water
上手な *jōzu na* skilled, dexterous, good at
上等の *jōtō no* first-class, superior
上製 *jōsei* superior make; superior (book) binding
上白 *jōhaku* first-class rice; first-class sugar
上出来 *jōdeki* good performance, master stroke
上天気 *jōtenki* fine weather, splendid weather

❸ proceed upward:
ⓐ (proceed to or as if to a higher place) **go up, rise, ascend; board, get on**
ⓑ go up [proceed] to the capital
ⓒ **go up in value or quality, rise, advance, make progress**
ⓓ (cause to move upward) **raise**

上昇する *jōshō suru* ascend, rise
上陸する *jōriku suru* land, disembark
上船する *jōsen suru* embark
浮上する *fujō suru* surface, rise [float] to the surface
遡上する *sojō suru* go upstream; retroact, retrospect
北上する *hokujō suru* go up north
上京する *jōkyō suru* go to Tokyo
上進 *jōshin* advance, progress
上達する *jōtatsu suru* make progress, attain proficiency
向上 *kōjō* elevation, improvement, progress
上棟式 *jōtōshiki* ceremony of raising the ridgepole

❹ [also suffix] **from the viewpoint of, -ly, by reasons of**

史上 *shijō* historically, from the historical point of view
身上 *shinjō* one's history; one's merit
身上 *shinshō* fortune, property
事実上 *jijitsujō* actually, as a matter of fact
便宜上 *bengijō* for convenience' sake

❺ⓐ **present something before a superior or higher authority; perform an action for a superior**
ⓑ **present for consideration, introduce; take up, deal with**
ⓒ **present before the public, exhibit, make public**

上納 *jōnō* payment (to the authorities)
上奏する *jōsō suru* report to the Throne
献上する *kenjō suru* present (a gift to a superior)
参上する *sanjō suru* go to see, call on, pay one's respects
上告する *jōkoku suru* appeal to a higher court
上程する *jōtei suru* introduce on the agenda,

lay [introduce] a bill before the Diet
上場する *jōjō suru* list (stocks)
上演 *jōen* stage performance
上映する *jōei suru* screen, show, project
❻ first (in a series of two or three)
上巻 *jōkan* first book [volume]
上旬 *jōjun* first ten days of a month
❼ early, ancient
上代 *jōdai* ancient times, remote ages
上古の *jōko no* ancient, of remote ages
❽ have blood rush up to one's head, get dizzy
上気する *jōki suru* have a rush of blood to the head
逆上する *gyakujō suru* be driven to frenzy, explode
❾ emperor, shogun; imperial
上意 *jōi* command of the Emperor
上使 *jōshi* shogun's envoy
主上 *shujō* Emperor
❿ verbal intensifier expressing a state of completion (as *up* in *add up*)
炎上する *enjō suru* go up in flames
計上する *keijō suru* sum up, appropriate (a sum for some purpose)
⓫ abbrev. of 上野 *kōzuke*, old name for Gunma Prefecture
上越本線 *jōetsu honsen* Joetsu Main Line
⓬ rising tone in Chinese phonetics
上声 *jōshō* (=*jōsei*) rising tone

INDEPENDENT

【jō 上】 first class, the best; first book [volume]; (marking on gift wrapper) With one's compliments
上の *jō no* first, best, excellent
上の巻 *jō no maki* Volume I

KUN

【ue 上】
①ⓐ [in the form of 上 *ue* + particle] up, over, above, on
ⓑ upside, upper part, top, summit; the surface
上の *ue no* upward, upper, higher (than)
机の上の本 *tsukue no ue no hon* book on the desk
上を向く *ue o muku* look upward
②ⓐ (of higher rank, position or grade) upper, higher, above, better, greater, older
ⓑ (persons of) higher rank, superiors, nobility
上の地位 *ue no chii* higher position
上の子 *ue no ko* the older child
上からの命令 *ue kara no meirei* order from above
③ as far as...is concerned, concerning
身の上 *minoue* one's career, one's condition, one's fortune
理屈の上では正しい *Rikutsu no ue de wa tadashii* It's correct as far as the theory goes
④ besides, moreover, in addition
金が有る上に美男子だ *kane ga aru ue ni bidanshi da* be handsome as well as rich
⑤ after, on, upon
照合の上 *shōgō no ue* after checking up

【-ue -上】
① honorific title for addressing persons of superior rank, esp. family members
母上 *hahaue* my dear mother
② honorific title after names of court ladies
葵の上 *aoi-no-ue* Lady Aoi

【uwa- 上-】
①ⓐ upper, top, upward
ⓑ (of higher rank, grade or quantity) upper, higher, better, greater
上唇 *uwakuchibiru* upper lip
上手 *uwate* upper part; better hand, superior
上回る *uwamawaru* exceed, be more than
②ⓐ outer, external
ⓑ superficial, shallow; careless
上着 *uwagi* outer garment, coat, jacket
上辺 *uwabe* outward appearance; exterior, surface
上っ調子な *uwatchōshi na* flippant, shallow
上滑りな *uwasuberi na* superficial, shallow, careless

【kami 上】
①ⓐ upper part, top, head
ⓑ upper stream
ⓒ [also prefix before place names] Upper, Northern
上手 *kamite* upper part, upper reaches; left stage
川上 *kawakami* upstream, upriver
上カプアス山脈 *kami-kapuasu sanmyaku* Upper Kapuas Mountains
② first (in a series of two or three)
上の句 *kami no ku* first half of a tanka poem
上半期 *kamihanki* first half of the (fiscal) year
③ persons of superior rank:
ⓐ superiors, high rank
ⓑ government, authorities
ⓒ Emperor, sovereign
上下 *kamishimo* superiors and inferiors
御上 *okami* government, authorities; Emperor; wife, madam, landlady

【a(geru) 上げる】
①ⓐ (cause to move upward) raise, elevate, lift up
ⓑ (increase the level of) raise, increase, hike
ⓒ (elevate in rank) raise, promote, elevate
ⓓ raise one's voice, shout
ⓔ (raise the quality of) improve (one's skill), advance
顔を上げる *kao o ageru* raise one's face

引き上げる *hikiageru* draw [pull] up; promote; increase
棚上げする *tanaage suru* shelve (up), pigeonhole
上げ *age* rise in price; making a tuck
値上げする *neage suru* raise [increase] the price
賃上げ *chin'age* wage increase
格上げする *kakuage suru* raise the status, promote to a higher rank
声を上げる *koe o ageru* raise one's voice
腕を上げる *ude o ageru* improve one's skill
②ⓐ give, offer, present, hand (to a superior, equal or others, not the speaker)
ⓑ offer, make an offering (to a deity)
彼に本を上げた *Kare ni hon o ageta* I gave him a book
仏壇に花を上げる *Butsudan ni hana o ageru* offer flowers before the family Buddhist altar
③ [following the TE-form of verbs] perform an action for (the benefit of) someone, do for a person
本を読んで上げよう *Hon o yonde ageyō* I'll read a book for you
席を譲って上げる *seki o yuzutte ageru* offer a seat to someone
④ complete, finish
仕事を上げる *shigoto o ageru* finish the work
⑤ achieve (results), gain (profits)
良い成績を上げる *yoi seiseki o ageru* achieve satisfactory results
売り上げ *uriage* sales, proceeds
⑥ show in, usher in, admit
芸者を上げる *geisha o ageru* call in a geisha
⑦ send, enter (a child in school)
子供を学校に上げる *kodomo o gakkō ni ageru* send one's child to school
⑧ manage (to do something)
安く上げる *yasuku ageru* make it less expensive
⑨ praise
上げたり下げたり *agetari sagetari* praising and blaming; raising and lowering
⑩ dress up
髪を上げる *kami o ageru* put up one's hair
⑪ throw up, vomit
上げてしまった *Agete shimatta* I threw up
⑫ (of tides) rise
上げ潮 *ageshio* rising [flowing] tide

【-a(geru) -上げる】
① up, upward
持ち上げる *mochiageru* raise, lift up; flatter
積み上げる *tsumiageru* pile [heap] up, accumulate
打ち上げ *uchiage* letting off, launching; close (of a run of performances)
取り上げる *toriageru* take [pick] up; take away, confiscate; deliver a baby; accept, listen to; adopt (a proposal)
繰り上げる *kuriageru* advance, move up
②ⓐ emphatic verbal suffix (as *up* in *stir up*)
ⓑ verbal suffix indicating completion of an action
縛り上げる *shibariageru* bind [tie] up
磨き上げる *migakiageru* polish up
買い上げる *kaiageru* buy, buy up; bid up
作り上げる *tsukuriageru* make up, build up, complete
仕上げる *shiageru* finish, complete, perfect
書き上げる *kakiageru* finish writing
③ honorific verbal suffix
申し上げる *mōshiageru* tell, say, speak humbly; (have the honor to) do

【a(garu) 上がる】
①ⓐ go up, come up, rise, climb
ⓑ go up in price, rise, jump
ⓒ go up in rank or quality: rise, be promoted; make progress, advance
屋根に上がる *yane ni agaru* go up on the roof
風呂から上がる *furo kara agaru* step out of the bath
月給が上がる *gekkyū ga agaru* get a raise in salary
腕が上がる *ude ga agaru* gain in skill
②ⓐ be completed, be finished
ⓑ come to an end, stop (raining); die, die out
ⓒ (of games like Japanese parcheesi) come to the finish
原稿が上がった *Genkō ga agatta* The manuscript is completed
雨が上がった *Ame ga agatta* It stopped raining
商売が上がったりだ *Shōbai ga agattari da* My business is ruined
一番で上がる *ichiban de agaru* win the first place
③ issue, accrue, be derived
効果が上がる *kōka ga agaru* take effect, bear fruit
④ lose control of oneself, get excited, be nervous, get stage fright
試験で上がる *shiken de agaru* get nervous at an examination
⑤ [honorific] take, have; eat, drink
ワインを召し上がれ *Wain o meshiagare* Please help yourself to the wine
⑥ be sufficient
安く上がる *yasuku agaru* cost little
⑦ⓐ come in, enter (a house), be admitted to (a school)
ⓑ [honorific] call on, visit
上がり込む *agarikomu* enter, come in, step in
駅迄お迎えに上がります *Eki made omukae ni*

agarimasu I'll go to the station to meet you
⑧ land, go ashore
上がり場 *agariba* landing place
⑨ be offered
灯明が上がっている *Tōmyō ga agatte iru* Sacred candles are lighted (before a household shrine)
【-a(garu) -上がる】
① up, upward
立ち上がる *tachiagaru* stand up, rise to one's feet; take action
盛り上がる *moriagaru* swell, rise; upsurge; be brought to climax
浮かび上がる *ukabiagaru* rise to the surface
②ⓐ emphatic verbal suffix (as *up* in *stir up*)
ⓑ verbal suffix indicating completion of an action
縮み上がる *chijimiagaru* cringe, wince, flinch
煮上がる *niagaru* boil up, be thoroughly cooked
出来上がる *dekiagaru* be completed, be finished
【a(gari) 上がり】
① rise, advance; ascent
値上がり *neagari* rise in price
② finish, completion
仕上がり *shiagari* finish, completion; result
③ⓐ proceeds, income, return
ⓑ crop, yield
店の上がり *mise no agari* income from a shop
蚕の上がりが良い *Kaiko no agari ga yoi* Silkworms are spinning well
④ tea, green tea (esp. in sushi shops)
上がり一丁 *Agari itchō* One tea!
【-a(gari) -上がり】
[also suffix]
① just after the completion of an action
雨上がりの虹 *ameagari no niji* rainbow after the rain
風呂上がり *furoagari* just out of the bath
② ex-
軍人上がりの実業家 *gunjin'agari no jitsugyōka* businessman who was once a military man
【nobo(ru) 上る】
①ⓐ go up (stairs), walk up (a hill); go [swim] upstream
ⓑ go up to the capital
階段を上る *kaidan o noboru* go up the stairs
煙が立ち上る *Kemuri ga tachinoboru* Smoke ascends to the sky
逆上る *sakanoboru* [usu. 遡る] go upstream; go back (to the past); retroact
鮭が川を上る *Sake ga kawa o noboru* Salmon run up the rivers
京に上る *kyō ni noboru* go up to Kyoto
② reach, amount to, add up to
かなりの数に上る *kanari no kazu ni noboru* amount to a considerable number
③ come up, be brought up (for discussion)
噂に上る *uwasa ni noboru* be gossiped about
【nobo(ri) 上り】
ⓐ going up, going upstream
ⓑ ascent, uphill road
ⓒ upward-bound train, Tokyo-bound train
上り下り *noborikudari* going up and down
上り坂 *noborizaka* ascent, upward slope
上り勾配 *noborikōbai* upgrade, uphill grade
上り列車 *noboriressha* up train [line]
【nobo(seru) 上せる】
ⓐ bring up (a proposal for discussion)
ⓑ enter, put on record
梓に上せる *shi ni noboseru* publish, bring (a book) into the world
【nobo(su) 上す】 same as **noboseru 上せる**
議題に上す *gidai ni nobosu* bring up for discussion

SPECIAL READINGS

逆上せる▲ *noboseru* have a rush of blood to the head, feel dizzy; get excited; run mad after; become conceited
上手い▲(＝巧い, 旨い) *umai* skillful, clever; splendid, excellent

SYNONYMS

❶ⓐ & 【ue】①ⓑ tops
頂 SUMMIT → 145
頭 HEAD → 1604
ⓑ high
高 HIGH → 2097
❷ⓐ high-ranking
高 HIGH → 2097
貴 NOBLE → 2606
総 GENERAL → 1379
太 of highest rank → 2152
ⓑ excellent and superior
名 first-rate → 2169
逸 exceptional → 3120
傑 outstanding → 155
英 DISTINGUISHED → 2238
秀 EXCELLENT → 2545
優 SUPERIOR → 177
絶 without match → 1353
卓 PROMINENT → 2064
快 splendid → 245
妙 MARVELOUS → 239
❸ⓐ & 【agaru】①ⓐ ascend
昇 ASCEND → 2415
登 CLIMB → 2595
騰 RISE (esp. in price) → 1106
❸ⓓ & 【ageru】①ⓐ raise
揚 RAISE HIGH → 593
挙 RAISE → 2456
掲 PUT UP → 494
起 raise up → 3307

立てる STAND → 1992
拾う PICK UP → 379

❹ **aspect**
柄 considering the character of → 897
面 side → 2087

❺ⓐ & **【ageru】** ②ⓐ **give**
下 give (to inferior or speaker) → 3378
呉れる give (to speaker) → 2549
与 GIVE → 3421
授 CONFER → 492
賜 DEIGN TO GIVE → 1585
贈 PRESENT A GIFT → 1634
賄 BRIBE → 1529
呈 PRESENT → 2189
進 present to a superior → 3121

【-ageru】
②ⓑ **end**
終 END → 1336
絶 COME TO AN END → 1353
閉 CLOSE → 3319
了 FINISH → 3350
済 SETTLE → 522
完 COMPLETE → 2201
結 CONCLUDE → 1348

USAGE

❶ **kami**
上
①ⓐ upper part, top, head
ⓑ upper stream
ⓒ [also prefix before place names] Upper, Northern
② first (in a series of two or three)
③ persons of superior rank:
ⓐ superiors, high rank
ⓑ government, authorities
ⓒ Emperor, sovereign

守
feudal governor, lord, baron

❷ **ageru**
上げる
①ⓐ (cause to move upward) raise, elevate, lift up
ⓑ (increase the level of) raise, increase, hike
ⓒ (elevate in rank) raise, promote, elevate
ⓓ raise one's voice, shout
ⓔ (raise the quality of) improve (one's skill), advance
②ⓐ give, offer, present, hand (to a superior, equal or others, not the speaker)
ⓑ offer, make an offering (to a deity)
③ [following the TE-form of verbs] perform an action for (the benefit of) someone, do for a person
④ complete, finish
⑤ achieve (results), gain (profits)
⑥ show in, usher in, admit
⑦ send, enter (a child in school)
⑧ manage (to do something)
⑨ praise
⑩ dress up
⑪ throw up, vomit
⑫ (of tides) rise

挙げる
①ⓐ (raise something and hold it up for display) hold up, raise (one's hand or a wineglass)
ⓑ (gather together) raise (an army), recruit
ⓒ (elevate in dignity) raise oneself, raise one's reputation
② cite, give (an example), mention
③ hold (a function), perform (a ceremony)
④ arrest, round up, nab
⑤ give birth to, have children
⑥ use fully
⑦ gain (points), score

揚げる
① (cause to rise high or float in the air) raise (a flag), send up, hoist, lift, fly (a kite), shoot up (fireworks)
② fry in deep fat
③ land, unload, disembark

❸ **age**
上げ
① rise in price
② making a tuck

-揚げ
ⓐ [also suffix] fried food, fry
ⓑ fried bean curd

❹ **agaru**
上がる
①ⓐ go up, come up, rise, climb
ⓑ go up in price, rise, jump
ⓒ go up in rank or quality: rise, be promoted; make progress, advance
②ⓐ be completed, be finished
ⓑ come to an end, stop (raining); die, die out
ⓒ (of games like Japanese parcheesi) come to the finish
③ issue, accrue, be derived
④ lose control of oneself, get excited, be nervous, get stage fright
⑤ [honorific] take, have; eat, drink
⑥ be sufficient
⑦ⓐ come in, enter (a house), be admitted to (a school)
ⓑ [honorific] call on, visit
⑧ land, go ashore
⑨ be offered

挙がる
① be cited, be mentioned, be listed
② be arrested, be caught, be nabbed

③ become famous
④ come into possession, be recovered

揚がる
① (rise high or float in the air) (of kites or flags) be up, fly, be flying; (of fireworks) be shot up, be set off
② be fried, fry
③ (of appearance) stand out, improve
④ become elated, get into high spirits

❺ noboru

上る
①ⓐ go up (stairs), walk up (a hill); go [swim] upstream
ⓑ go up to the capital
② reach, amount to, add up to
③ come up, be brought up (for discussion)

登る
(move up, esp. by using the hands and feet) climb, mount, ascend, scale

昇る
ⓐ (rise up to the sky) ascend, rise
ⓑ ascend to a higher rank, rise in rank, be promoted

★In the sense of moving upwards, the above three verbs are easily confused. Whereas 上る refers only to the process of going up (as a hill or steps), 登る implies that an effort is made to reach the top, as when climbing a mountain. 昇る refers to something rising toward the sky, such as smoke or the rising sun, or a soul rising to heaven.

❻ nobori

上り
ⓐ going up, going upstream
ⓑ ascent, uphill road
ⓒ upward-bound train, Tokyo-bound train

登り
climbing, ascent

❼ noboseru

上せる
ⓐ bring up (a proposal for discussion)
ⓑ enter, put on record

逆上せる
① have a rush of blood to the head, feel dizzy
② get excited; run mad after; become conceited

❽ hikiageru

引き上げる
draw [pull] up; promote; increase

引き揚げる
withdraw, leave, return, repatriate

HOMOPHONES

kami ⇨ 守 2173
ageru ⇨ 挙 2456 揚 593
age ⇨ 揚 593
agaru ⇨ 挙 2456 揚 593
noboru ⇨ 登 2595 昇 2415
sakanoboru ⇨ 遡る 3257 逆上る 3091, 3404
nobori ⇨ 登 2595
noboseru ⇨ 上せる 3404 逆上せる 3091, 3404
umai ⇨ 巧い 188 甘い 3494 上手い 3404, 3456

NOTE

⇨ see also USAGE notes at 逆 3091 and 旨 2024

土 士 ち

3405 SHI

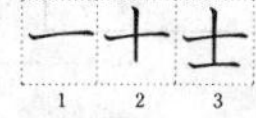

Ⓒⓗ 士 shì

Radical	Strokes
士 33	3-3-0
Grade	**Freq**
Jōyō-4	353
■ 4 - 3 - 2	

3-2□

RADICAL 33

Standard form: 士 *samurai* 'knight' (壬 声 壮)
Description: used for character classification

▶**MILITARY MAN**
▶**PROFESSION SUFFIX**

COMPOUNDS

❶ⓐ military man, warrior, soldier, knight; officer
ⓑ warrior class of feudal Japan: **samurai, retainer**
ⓒ private (military rank of Japanese Self Defense Forces)

士官 *shikan* officer
士気 *shiki* fighting spirit
兵士 *heishi* soldier
騎士 *kishi* knight
武士 *bushi* samurai, warrior
士族 *shizoku* descendant of samurai
士分 *shibun* status of samurai
士農工商 *shinōkōshō* warriors, farmers, artisans and tradesmen (the four classes of Tokugawa Japan)
四十七士 *shijūshichishi* Forty-Seven Loyal Retainers
一等陸士 *ittōrikushi* private first class

❷ⓐ **man of learning and virtue, gentleman, scholar, man of good breeding**
ⓑ [original meaning] man, man of full age
士君子 *shikunshi* man of learning and virtue, gentleman
博士 *hakushi* doctor, Ph.D.
紳士 *shinshi* gentleman
名士 *meishi* man of distinction, big name
国士 *kokushi* distinguished citizen; patriot
同士 *dōshi* fellow (as in 学生同士 *gakuseidōshi* 'fellow students')
士女 *shijo* men and women
❸ **suffix for members of a profession, esp. for a licensed profession**
弁護士 *bengoshi* lawyer, attorney
力士 *rikishi* sumo wrestler
棋士 *kishi* professional go [shogi] player
❹ suffix for academic degrees
文学士 *bungakushi* Bachelor of Arts
理学修士 *rigaku shūshi* Master of Science

INDEPENDENT

【**shi** 士】man of learning and virtue, gentleman; samurai
篤学の士 *tokugaku no shi* diligent student, devoted scholar

SPECIAL READINGS

博士 *hakase* expert, learned man; doctor, Ph.D.
一言居士 *ichigenkoji* ready critic, one ready to comment on any and every subject

SYNONYMS

❶ **soldiers and warriors**
武 warrior → 3210
侍 SAMURAI → 85
兵 SOLDIER → 2551
卒 private → 2055
❷ⓐ **gentleman**
紳 GENTLEMAN → 1334
子 gentleman → 3390
❸ **workers and professionals**
師 profession suffix → 1326
家 professional → 2273
客 skilled person → 2250
者 person who → 3211
人 person of certain category → 3368
員 MEMBER (of a staff) → 2269
屋 colloquial occupation suffix → 3098
手 OCCUPATION SUFFIX → 3456
婦 woman worker → 469
嬢 (unmarried) female worker → 758
夫 MAN LABORER → 3460
匠 CRAFTSMAN → 2990
工 workman → 3381

USAGE

dōshi
同士
fellow (as in 学生同士 *gakuseidōshi* 'fellow students')
同志
like-minded person, comrade

NOTE

★do not confuse with 土 3403

3-2□

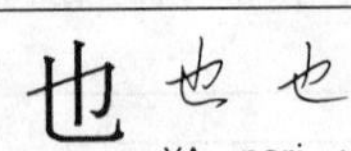

3406 YA nari ya

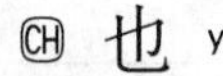

ⒸⒽ 也 yě

Radical	Strokes
乚 5	3-1-2
Grade	Freq
Names	1993
■ 4-3-2	

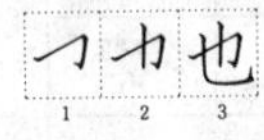

▶**CLASSICAL COPULA**

KUN

【**nari** 也】classical copula equiv. to である *de aru*: be
金十円也 *kin jūen nari* ten yen
【**ya** 也】[also 哉 or 耶] *classical particle* rhetorical or interrogative particle like modern か *ka*
これは何ぞ也 *Kore wa nanzo ya* What can this be?

NAMES

達也 *tatsuya* male name
也寸志 *yasushi* male name
道也 *michiya* male name

SYNONYMS

【**nari**】
○ **exist and be**
在 BE → 2984
存 EXIST → 2982
有 exist → 2983
居 be present → 3080
臨 BE PRESENT AT → 1630
【**ya**】
○ **classical particles**
耶 INTERROGATIVE PARTICLE → 1283
哉 EXCLAMATORY PARTICLE → 3294

USAGE

ya
也
[also 哉 or 耶] *classical particle* rhetorical

or interrogative particle like modern か *ka*
哉
[also 也 or 耶] classical interrogative or rhetorical particle like modern か *ka*
耶
[also 哉 or 也] classical rhetorical or exclamatory particle

HOMOPHONES
ya ⇨ 哉 3294 耶 1283

彑 3-2□

3407

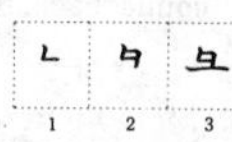

Radical	Strokes
彐 58	3-3-0
Grade	**Freq**
Radical	
■ 4 - 3 - 2	

RADICAL 58
variant of 彐 *keigashira* 'pig's head'
⇨ see 彐 3396 for radical description

亡 3-2□

3408

▶DECEASE
nonstandard for 亡 3402

廿 3-2□

incorrect stroke count ⇨ see 3449

山 3-2□

incorrect classification ⇨ see 2940

巾 3-3◫

3409 KIN

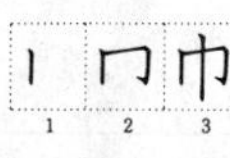

CH 巾 jīn

Radical	Strokes
巾 50	3-3-0
Grade	**Freq**
Reference	
■ 4 - 3 - 3	

RADICAL 50
Standard form: 巾 *haba* 'cloth' (布 帳 師)
Description: used in characters related to fabrics or their qualities

COMPOUNDS
❶ [original meaning] cloth, napkin
巾着 *kinchaku* purse
雑巾 *zōkin* rag; mop
布巾 *fukin* dishcloth, napkin
茶巾 *chakin* tea cloth [napkin]
三角巾 *sankakukin* triangle bandage
巾 *kin* cloth, napkin
❷ headgear
頭巾 *zukin* hood, kerchief
❸ [usu. 幅 569] width, breadth, range
⇨ see 幅 569 for compounds

NOTE
⇨ see NOTE at 幅 569

3-3 ◫

才 才 才

3410 SAI

一 十 才
1 2 3

Ⓒⓗ 才 cái

Radical	Strokes
扌 64	3-3-0
Grade	**Freq**
Jōyō-2	718
■ 4 - 3 - 3	

▶**TALENT** ▶**AGE SUFFIX**

COMPOUNDS

❶ⓐ **talent, natural ability, gift, genius**
ⓑ **person of talent, man of ability, capable person**
才能 *sainō* talent, ability
才気 *saiki* talent
才知 *saichi* wit and intelligence
英才 *eisai* [formerly also 頴才] talent, genius; gifted person, talented person
詩才 *shisai* poetic genius
商才 *shōsai* business ability [talent]
俊才 *shunsai* genius, person of exceptional talent
天才 *tensai* (person of) genius
秀才 *shūsai* (person of) genius

❷ [also 歳 2490] **age suffix**
十二才 *jūnisai* 12 years old
何才 *nansai* how old, what age

❸ *sai*:
ⓐ unit of volume equiv. to approx. 0.0278 cubic cm or 1 cubic *shaku* (尺), used esp. for measuring lumber or freight
ⓑ unit of capacity equiv. to approx. 1/10 of a *shaku* (勺)
ⓒ unit of sq. measure equiv. to approx. 1 sq. foot, used for measuring textiles

❹ used phonetically for *sai*
漫才 *manzai* comic dialogue, comic backchat, *manzai*

INDEPENDENT

【**sai** 才】talent, ability, gift; wit; *sai* (⇨ ❸)
語学の才 *gogaku no sai* talent for languages
外交の才 *gaikō no sai* diplomatic talent

SYNONYMS

❶ⓐ **skill**
能 ABILITY → 1323
技 SKILL → 248
腕 skill → 1006
力 POWER → 3371

ⓑ **wise and talented persons**
秀 genius → 2545
俊 BRILLIANT PERSON → 102
通 well-informed person → 3109
博 DOCTOR → 151
賢 wise man → 2839
哲 sage → 2738

❷ **age**
歳 AGE SUFFIX → 2490
年 years → 2035
齢 AGE → 1895
令 age → 1995
寿 life span → 3557

3-3 ◫

千 千 千

3411 SEN chi

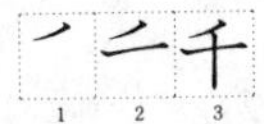

Ⓒⓗ 千 qiān

Radical	Strokes
十 24	3-2-1
Grade	**Freq**
Jōyō-1	78
■ 4 - 3 - 3	

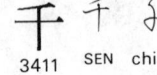

▶**THOUSAND**

COMPOUNDS

❶ **thousand**
千円 *sen'en* 1000 yen
五千 *gosen* 5000

❷ a large number
千差万別 *sensabanbetsu* infinite variety
千秋 *senshū* a thousand years, many years
千代 *chiyo* a thousand years, a very long period
千草 *chigusa* various flowering plants
千千に *chiji ni* in pieces
千鳥足 *chidoriashi* tottering gait

INDEPENDENT

【**sen** 千】thousand

KUN

【**chi** 千】[in compounds] thousand

SYNONYMS

❶ **large numbers**
百 HUNDRED → 2026
万 TEN THOUSAND → 2936
億 HUNDRED MILLION → 170
兆 TRILLION → 225
京 ten quadrillion → 2052

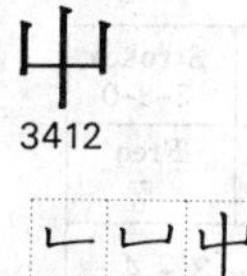

3412

Radical	Strokes
屮 45	3-3-0
Grade	**Freq**
Radical	
■ 4 - 3 - 3	

3-3◫

RADICAL 45

Standard form: 屮 *tetsu* ‘sprout’ (屯)

Description: used for character classification

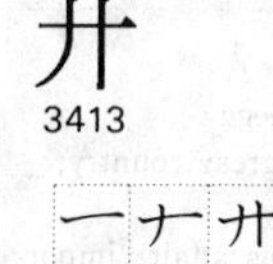

3413

Radical	Strokes
廾 55	3-3-0
Grade	**Freq**
Radical	
■ 4 - 3 - 3	

3-3◫

RADICAL 55

Standard form: 廾 *nijūashi* ‘clasp hands’ (弁 弊 弄)

Description: used in characters related to offering or presenting

3414

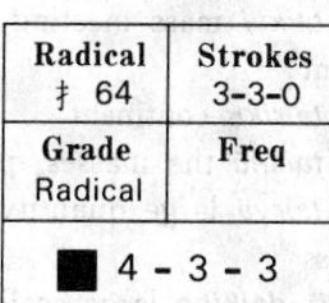

Radical	Strokes
扌 64	3-3-0
Grade	**Freq**
Radical	
■ 4 - 3 - 3	

3-3◫

RADICAL 64

tehen, variant of 手 *te* ‘hand’

⇨ see 手 3456 for radical description

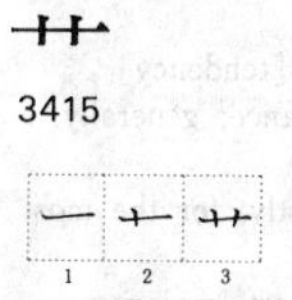

3415

Radical	Strokes
艹 140	3-3-0
Grade	**Freq**
Radical	
■ 4 - 3 - 3	

3-3◫

RADICAL 140

kusakanmuri, variant of 艸 *kusa* ‘plants’

⇨ see 艸 209 for radical description

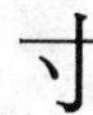

incorrect classification ⇨ see 2935

3-3◫

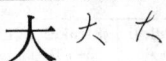

3-4□ 大 大 大 Ⓒⓗ 大 dà dài

3416 DAI TAI ō- ō(kii) ō(ini)

一 ナ 大
1 2 3

Radical	Strokes
大 37	3-3-0
Grade	**Freq**
Jōyō-1	5
■ 4 - 3 - 4	

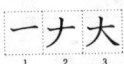

RADICAL 37
Standard form: 大 *ōkii* or *dai* 'big' (太 天 契)
Top variant: 大 *ōkii* or *dai* (奪 奮 奔)
Description: used in characters related to standing persons or largeness

▶BIG ▶UNIVERSITY

COMPOUNDS

❶ⓐ [also prefix] (great in size, extent or quantity) **big, large, great, major, grand, vast, numerous**
ⓑ [prefix] (before place names) Great, Greater
ⓒ [suffix] size
大小 *daishō* large and small; size; long and short swords
大会 *taikai* mass meeting, rally; meet, tournament
大陸 *tairiku* continent
大衆 *taishū* the masses, populace
大量 *tairyō* large quantity, great volume, mass
大規模 *daikibo* large scale
拡大する *kakudai suru* magnify, enlarge, expand
最大の *saidai no* biggest, largest, greatest
巨大な *kyodai na* huge, gigantic, enormous
大ニューヨーク *dai-nyūyōku* Greater New York
大ブリテン島 *dai-buritentō* Great Britain
卵大の *tamagodai no* egg-sized
20cm×20cm大 *nijussenchi kakeru nijussenchi-dai* 20 cm by 20 cm in size
❷ [also prefix] (of great intensity or degree) **big, great, extreme, intense, severe, loud**
大変な *taihen na* awful, terrible; serious, grave
大病 *taibyō* serious illness, dangerous disease
大切な *taisetsu na* important, weighty; valuable
大丈夫 *daijōbu* safe, sure, all right
大地震 *daijishin* big earthquake
大歓迎 *daikangei* warm welcome
❸ⓐ (characterized by greatness) **big, great, grand, important, chief, prominent, excellent**
ⓑ big-hearted, generous, kindly
大使 *taishi* ambassador
大統領 *daitōryō* president
大臣 *daijin* minister (of state)
大学 *daigaku* university, college
大国 *taikoku* world power, great country; large country
大事 *daiji* great thing, serious affair; importance
偉大な *idai na* great, mighty, grand
重大な *jūdai na* important, serious, grave
寛大な *kandai na* generous, magnanimous, lenient
❹ⓐ abbrev. of 大学 *daigaku*: **university, college**
ⓑ **suffix after names of universities**
大卒 *daisotsu* university graduate
女子大生 *joshidaisei* female university student
オックスフォード大 *okkusufōdodai* Oxford University
東大 *tōdai* Tokyo University
❺ **in substance, on the whole, in general, for the most part**
大意 *taii* substance, gist, general outline
大概 *taigai* generally, mostly; probably, maybe
大勢 *taisei* general trend [tendency]
大体 *daitai* outline, substance; generally, roughly, on the whole
大抵 *taitei* generally, mostly, for the most part
大半 *taihan* the greater part, majority
大部分 *daibubun* most, greater part; mostly, for the most part
❻ [honorific prefix]
ⓐ great, honorable
ⓑ Imperial
大西郷 *dai-saigō* the Great Saigo
大政奉還 *taiseihōkan* restoration of Imperial rule
❼ⓐ senior, older, eldest
ⓑ (one generation removed) great-, grand-
大兄 *taikei* older brother; honorific title for someone a little older
大祖父 *daisofu* great-grandfather

INDEPENDENT

【**dai** 大】bigness, largeness; large size, large;

adult; greatness; long month (of 31 days)
大は小を兼ねる *Dai wa shō o kaneru* The greater serves for the lesser
ビールの大 *bīru no dai* large beer
【dai no 大の】 passionate, confirmed; (of months) long; big, large
大の猫好き *dai no nekozuki* ardent cat lover [fancier]
【tai 大】 abbrev. of 大正 *taishō*: Taisho era
【taishita 大した】 enormous, great, grand; important, serious
【taishite 大して】 (not) very, greatly

KUN

【ō- 大-】
[also prefix]
①ⓐ (of considerable extent or intensity) big, large, great, extreme, severe
ⓑ grand, great, big, magnificent
ⓒ many, much
大形 *ōgata* large size
大目に *ōme ni* rather large
大手 *ōte* major companies
大急ぎで *ōisogi de* in a great [urgent] hurry, against time
大幅に *ōhaba ni* sharply, by a large margin
大蔵省 *ōkurashō* Ministry of Finance
大物 *ōmono* great man, big shot
大勢の *ōzei no* great number of, multitude of
大助かり *ōdasukari* big help
② main, chief, representative
大詰め *ōzume* finale, end
大晦日 *ōmisoka* last day of the year, December 31
③ (one generation removed) great-
大伯母 *ōoba* great-aunt
④ honorific prefix
大宮人 *ōmiyabito* courtier
大御代 *ōmiyo* glorious reign of the Emperor
⑤ more or less
大方 *ōkata* almost, nearly; probably
大まかな *ōmaka na* rough, general, broad
大筋 *ōsuji* outline
【ō(kii) 大きい】 big, large, extensive; massive, enormous; great, grand
大きな *ōki na* noun adjective form of 大きい *ōkii*
大きさ *ōkisa* size, dimensions
【ō(ini) 大いに】 very, greatly, highly, exceedingly
大いに喜ぶ *ōini yorokobu* be highly pleased

SPECIAL READINGS

大人 *otona* adult
大和 *yamato* Yamato (old name for Japan)

SYNONYMS

❶ⓐ big and huge
太 GREAT → 2152
浩 VAST → 438
巨 HUGE → 3039
ⓒ size
寸 measurement → 2935
❷ extreme in degree
深 DEEP → 524
高 HIGH → 2097
重 HEAVY → 3573
強 STRONG → 475
超 super- → 3313
甚 EXTREMELY → 2643
切 keen → 27
痛 bitter(ly) → 3285
極 EXTREME → 1017
激 intense → 776
厳 SEVERE → 3289
酷 SEVERE → 1562
❸ⓐ great
偉 GREAT (of superior character) → 148
宏 GRAND (large in scale) → 2202
壮 GRAND (having grandeur) → 224
豪 MAGNIFICENT → 2140
雄 HEROIC → 1008
❹ schools
校 SCHOOL → 929
学 EDUCATIONAL INSTITUTION → 2555
院 INSTITUTION → 454
塾 PRIVATE SCHOOL → 2860
高 high school → 2097
中 junior high school → 3451
小 elementary school → 7
園 kindergarten → 3156
❺ approximately
概 GENERAL → 1048
約 APPROXIMATELY → 1280
-頃 ABOUT → 144
位 about → 61
-方 about → 1963
-程 ...or thereabouts → 1190
辺り thereabouts → 3029

USAGE

ō- 大- 多-
★大 is a word-forming element meaning big or large, but in some compounds it is used in the sense of many, as in 大勢 *ōzei* 'crowd of people' and 大人数 *ōninzū* 'many people'. Though 多い *ōi* also means much or many, the prefix *ō-* in the sense of many is written 大-, not 多-. However, compare the following words:
大目に *ōme ni* rather large
多目に *ōme ni* plenty, lots

NOTE

⇨ see COMPOUND FORMATION for
大変 *taihen* ⇨ 変 2069
大切 *taisetsu* ⇨ 切 27
大丈夫 *daijōbu* ⇨ 夫 3460

3-4□

丸 丸 丸

3417 GAN maru[1] maru[2] maru(i) maru(meru)

ノ 九 丸
1 2 3

Ⓒⓗ 丸 wán

Radical	Strokes
3	3-1-2
Grade	**Freq**
Jōyō-2	651
■ 4-3-4	

▶**ROUND**

COMPOUNDS

❶ⓐ round body, pellet, ball
ⓑ round projectile, ball
丸薬 *gan'yaku* pill
一丸となって *ichigan to natte* in a body [lump]
砲丸 *hōgan* cannon ball
弾丸 *dangan* shot, bullet, shell
銃丸 *jūgan* bullet
❷ suffix after names of pills
救命丸 *kyūmeigan* Kyumeigan (pill's name)

KUN

【maru[1] 丸】
①ⓐ round or spherical shape
ⓑ [sometimes also 円] circle
日の丸 *hinomaru* Rising Sun Flag
② wholeness, completeness
丸の儘 *maru no mama* whole, in its entirety
丸で *maru de* just like; completely, perfectly
③ [also ○] check mark for correct answers (similar to ✓)
丸を付ける *maru o tsukeru* mark a correct answer with a circle
④ small circle corresponding to a period in a sentence
⑤ within the castle walls
二の丸 *ni no maru* outworks of a castle
本丸 *honmaru* keep of a castle, donjon

【maru[2] 丸】
① [in compounds] round, circular, spherical
丸顔 *marugao* round face, moon face
丸丸と太った *marumaru to futotta* plump, rotund, chubby
② [also prefix] complete(ly), total(ly), perfect(ly)
丸丸 *marumaru* completely, entirely
丸儲け *marumōke* clear profit
丸二日 *marufutsuka* for a full two days
丸焼けになった *maruyake ni natta* completely burned
魚を丸ごと食べる *sakana o marugoto taberu* eat a fish whole
③ suffix after names of ships—formerly also used after names of swords, children or dogs
南海丸 *nankaimaru* Nankaimaru (ship's name)
日吉丸 *hiyoshimaru* name of Toyotomi Hideyoshi during his youth

【maru(i) 丸い】
①ⓐ (shaped like a ball) round, spherical
ⓑ [also 円い] (shaped like a circle) round, circular
丸み *marumi* roundness
背が丸い *se ga marui* round-backed
丸くなって *maruku natte* in a circle [ring]
② rounded, amicable, harmonious
丸く治まる *maruku osamaru* become reconciled, settle peacefully

【maru(meru) 丸める】 round, make round, roll up; cajole, coax, wheedle
雪を丸める *yuki o marumeru* make a snowball
女を丸め込む *onna o marumekomu* twist a woman round one's little finger, cajole a woman

SYNONYMS

❶ⓐ spherical object
球 BALL → 969
玉 spherical object → 3477
ⓑ projectiles and bombs
弾 PROJECTILE → 572
矢 ARROW → 2009
爆 bomb → 1101
雷 explosive device → 2791
❷ medicines
錠 PILL → 1737
薬 DRUG → 2375
剤 PREPARATION → 1669
【maru[1]】
① **circle**
円 CIRCLE → 2955
圏 circle → 3148
【maru[2]】
② **all**
満 FULL → 607
一 all in one → 3341
全 WHOLE → 2022
万 all → 2936
皆 ALL → 2445
都 all → 1686
完 COMPLETE → 2201
総 TOTAL → 1379
諸 VARIOUS → 1577
毎 EVERY → 2034
各 EACH → 2168

【marui】
① **round**
円 circular → 2955

USAGE

❶ **maru**
丸
①ⓐ round or spherical shape
ⓑ [sometimes also 円] circle
② wholeness, completeness
③ [also ○] check mark for correct answers (similar to ✓)
④ small circle corresponding to a period in a sentence
⑤ within the castle walls

円
① [usu. 丸] circle
② *slang* money, dough—used in telegrams

○
① zero (the numeral)
② [also 丸] check mark for correct answers (similar to ✓)
③ indicates omitted or unprintable letters [characters]

❷ **marui**
丸い
①ⓐ (shaped like a ball) round, spherical
ⓑ [also 円い] (shaped like a circle) round, circular
② rounded, amicable, harmonious

円い
[also 丸い] (shaped like a circle) circular, round

HOMOPHONES

maru[1] ⇨ 円 2955 ○ 3342
marui ⇨ 円 2955

女 女 め

3418 JO NYO NYŌ onna me

Ⓒ 女 nǚ

Radical	Strokes
女 38	3-3-0
Grade	**Freq**
Jōyō-1	201
■ 4 - 3 - 4	

3-4□

く 女 女 (1 2 3)

RADICAL 38

Standard form: 女 *onna* 'woman' (姿 姦 威)
Left variant: 女 *onnahen* (好 妙 妹)
Description: used in characters related to women, marriage or sex

▶WOMAN

COMPOUNDS

❶ [also prefix and suffix]
ⓐ [original meaning] **woman, female**
ⓑ **girl, maiden**
女性 *josei* woman, female; feminine gender
女子 *joshi* woman, girl
女優 *joyū* actress
女王 *joō* (=*jōō*) queen; belle, mistress
女人 *nyonin* woman
女房 *nyōbō* wife; court lady
女中 *jochū* maidservant, maid
彼女 *kanojo* she; one's sweetheart
男女 *danjo* men and women, both sexes
修道女 *shūdōjo* nun, sister
女生徒 *joseito* schoolgirl, girl student
少女 *shōjo* girl
処女 *shojo* virgin, maiden
織女星 *shokujosei* Vega

❷ daughter—used esp. to indicate order of birth
長女 *chōjo* eldest daughter
養女 *yōjo* adopted daughter, stepdaughter
三女 *sanjo* third daughter

❸ suffix after names of women, esp. haiku poetesses
千代女 *chiyojo* name of a haiku poetess

INDEPENDENT

【jo 女】woman; girl; daughter

KUN

【onna 女】[also prefix] woman, lady, female; girl; mistress
女の子 *onna no ko* girl, daughter
女らしい *onnarashii* womanly, ladylike; feminine
女手 *onnade* hiragana, woman's handwriting; woman in a family
女歌舞伎 *onna-kabuki* girls' kabuki

【me 女】
① *elegant* the fair sex, woman, female
女神 *megami* goddess
賤の女 *shizu no me* woman of lowly birth
② [in compounds] the weaker or smaller of two
女女しい *memeshii* effeminate, unmanly
女波 *menami* the smaller waves
女滝 (=雌滝) *medaki* the smaller waterfall (of the two)

SPECIAL READINGS

海女 *ama* woman diver
巫女▲ *miko* maiden in the service of a

shrine; medium
女将▲ *okami* mistress, landlady, proprietress
貴女▲ *anata* you (feminine pronoun)

SYNONYMS

❶ **woman**
婦 ADULT WOMAN → 469
嬢 YOUNG LADY → 758
娘 GIRL → 406
婆 OLD WOMAN → 2762
雌 FEMALE → 1055

❷ **offspring**
娘 DAUGHTER → 406
姫 DAUGHTER OF NOBLE BIRTH → 407
子 CHILD → 3390
孤 orphan → 356
嫡 LEGITIMATE CHILD → 680
息 son → 2647
男 son → 2542
惣 eldest son → 2780

HOMOPHONES

me ⇨ 雌 1055 牝 826

NOTE

⇨ see USAGE note at 雌 1055
⇨ see COMPOUND FORMATION for
女中 *jochū* ⇨ 中 3451
織女星 *shokujosei* ⇨ 織 1422
女房 *nyōbō* ⇨ 房 1946

3-4□

丈 丈 丈 丈

3419 JŌ take dake▲

CH 丈 zhàng

Radical	Strokes
一 1	3-1-2
Grade	**Freq**
Jōyō	1385
■ 4-3-4	

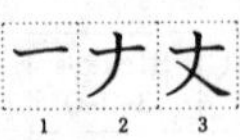

▶**STOUT** ▶**STATURE**

COMPOUNDS

❶ **stout, robust, strong, tough**
丈夫な *jōbu na* healthy, strong, robust; stout, solid
気丈な *kijō na* stouthearted, courageous
頑丈な *ganjō na* solid, firm; strong

❷ **stature, height**
偉丈夫 *ijōfu* towering [great] man; hero
大丈夫 *daijōbu* safe, sure, all right

❸ [original meaning] *jo*: unit of length equiv. to approx. 3.03 m or 10 *shaku* (尺)
一丈一尺 *ichijō isshaku* 1 *jo* 1 *shaku*
方丈 *hōjō* 10 sq. feet; abbot's chamber; chief priest
万丈 *banjō* unfathomable height

❹ title after names of artists
団十郎丈 *danjūrōjō* Mr. Danjuro (kabuki actor)

INDEPENDENT

【jō 丈】 *jo* (⇨ ❸)

KUN

【take 丈】 stature, height; length, measure; all (one has)
丈比べ *takekurabe* comparison of statures
背丈 *setake* stature, height
思いの丈 *omoi no take* one's inmost heart

【dake 丈】 only, merely; as much; the more...the more
一度丈 *ichido dake* only once

SYNONYMS

❶ **strong**
壮 VIGOROUS → 224
強 STRONG → 475
健 ROBUST → 134
康 HEALTHY → 3124

❷ **height**
背 stature → 2573
高 height → 2097

❸ **length units**
里 LEAGUE, *ri* (3.4 km) → 3542
町 *cho* (109 m) → 1113
間 *ken* (1.8 m) → 3323
尋 fathom (1.8 m) → 2322
米 meter → 3529
尺 *SHAKU* (30.3 cm) → 3440
寸 *sun* (3.03 cm) → 2935

NOTE

⇨ see COMPOUND FORMATION for 大丈夫 *daijōbu* ⇨ 夫 3460

之 之 辶

3420 SHI no kore NAMES yuki itaru

丶 ㇇ 之
1 2 3

CH 之 zhī

Radical	Strokes
丶 3	3-1-2
Grade	**Freq**
Names	1972
■ 4 - 3 - 4	

3-4□

▶POSSESSIVE PARTICLE

COMPOUNDS

❶ shaped like the character 辶

之繞 *shinnyō* (=*shinnyū*) *shinnyo*, 'advance' radical (辶)

❷ [original meaning, now archaic] go, proceed toward

KUN

【no 之】 possessive particle

鳥之巣 *tori no su* bird's nest

実業之日本 *jitsugyō no nihon* name of a publishing company

【kore 之】 [also 是] *pronoun* this

之は何ですか *Kore wa nan desu ka* What is this?

NAMES

丸之内 *marunouchi* place name

錦之介 *kinnosuke* male name

正之 *masayuki* male name

SYNONYMS

【no】

○ **possessive particles**

乃 POSSESSIVE PARTICLE → 2927

【kore】

○ **this and that**

是 this → 2436

爾 THAT → 3587

彼 that → 290

本 THIS → 3502

今 THIS (week, etc.) → 1968

当 THE PRESENT → 2177

該 the said → 1519

同 the same → 2987

USAGE

no

之

possessive particle

乃

possessive particle

HOMOPHONES

no ⇨ 乃 2927

kore ⇨ 是 2436 此 823 惟 481

NOTE

⇨ see also USAGE note at 是 2436

与 與 与 ち

3421 YO ata(eru) azuka(ru)▲

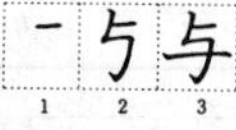

CH 与 yǔ yù yú

Radical	Strokes
一 1△	3-1-2
Grade	**Freq**
Jōyō	445
■ 4 - 3 - 4	

3-4□

▶GIVE

COMPOUNDS

❶ **give, present, grant**

与件 *yoken* postulate, given conditions

供与する *kyōyo suru* offer, present, submit

給与する *kyūyo suru* allow, grant; pay (a salary)

授与する *juyo suru* grant, give, confer

寄与する *kiyo suru* contribute, render services to

贈与する *zōyo suru* donate, present

❷ **take part in, participate in, side with**

与党 *yotō* party in power

与野党 *yoyatō* both parties, parties in and out of power

与国 *yokoku* ally

参与する *san'yo suru* participate in, take part in

関与する *kan'yo suru* take part in, participate in, be concerned in

INDEPENDENT

【yo 与】 [archaic] and, together with

KUN

【ata(eru) 与える】 give, present, grant, award; provide (with food); cause, inflict (damage)

分け与える *wakeataeru* distribute, hand out

【azuka(ru) 与る】

① participate in, take part in, share in

相談に与る *sōdan ni azukaru* be consulted

② enjoy, receive

招待に与る *shōtai ni azukaru* receive an invitation

SYNONYMS

❶ **give**
上 give (to superior or others) → 3404
下 give (to inferior or speaker) → 3378
呉れる give (to speaker) → 2549
授 CONFER → 492
賜 DEIGN TO GIVE → 1585
贈 PRESENT A GIFT → 1634
賄 BRIBE → 1529
呈 PRESENT → 2189
進 present to a superior → 3121

❷ **participate and join**
参 PARTICIPATE → 2066
加 join → 38
入 ENTER → 3370

HOMOPHONES

azukaru ⇨ 預 1042

NOTE

⇨ see USAGE note at 預 1042

3-4□

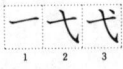

弋

3422 YOKU

㊥ 弋 yì

Radical	Strokes
弋 56	3-3-0
Grade	**Freq**
Reference	
■ 4 - 3 - 4	

RADICAL 56

Standard form: 弋 *shikigamae* 'spike' (式 弐 弑)
Description: used for character classification

COMPOUNDS

❶ catch, capture
遊弋する *yūyoku suru* cruise, patrol

❷ [original meaning, now archaic] arrow with a string for catching birds
弋人 *yokujin* archer, hunter

3-4□

大

3423

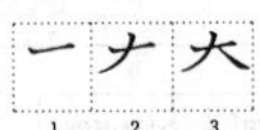

Radical	Strokes
大 37	3-3-0
Grade	**Freq**
Radical	
■ 4 - 3 - 4	

RADICAL 37

variant of 大 *ōkii* or *dai* 'big'
⇨ see 大 3416 for radical description

3-4□

女

3424

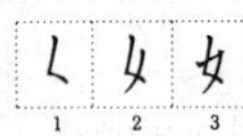

Radical	Strokes
女 38	3-3-0
Grade	**Freq**
Radical	
■ 4 - 3 - 4	

RADICAL 38

onnahen, variant of 女 *onna* 'woman'
⇨ see 女 3418 for radical description

宀
3425

Radical 宀 40	Strokes 3-3-0
Grade Radical	Freq
■ 4 - 3 - 4	

3-4□

RADICAL 40
Standard form: 宀 *ukanmuri* 'roof' (実 家 定)
Description: used in characters related to roofs or houses

幺
3426

Radical 幺 52	Strokes 3-3-0
Grade Radical	Freq
■ 4 - 3 - 4	

3-4□

RADICAL 52
Standard form: 幺 *itogashira* 'tiny' (幼 幾 幽)
Description: used in characters related to threads, dimness or slightness

---

广
3427

Radical 广 53	Strokes 3-3-0
Grade Radical	Freq
■ 4 - 3 - 4	

3-4□

RADICAL 53
Standard form: 广 *madare* 'roof' (府 広 庁)
Description: used in characters related to roofs or buildings

---

犭
3428

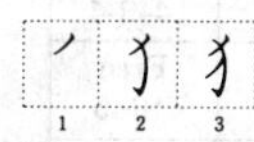

Radical 犭 94	Strokes 3-3-0
Grade Radical	Freq
■ 4 - 3 - 4	

3-4□

RADICAL 94
kemonohen, variant of 犬 *inu* 'dog'
⇨ see 犬 3464 for radical description

丈
3429

▶**STOUT** ▶**STATURE**
nonstandard for 丈 3419

3-4□

ケ
3430

▶**COUNTER FOR ITEMS**
nonstandard for 箇 2700

3-4□

3-4□ 门 3431

▶**GATE**
handwritten abbreviation for 門 888

3-4□ 乏

incorrect classification／stroke count ⇨ see 1933

3-4□ 亡

incorrect classification ⇨ see 3402

3-4□ 久

incorrect classification ⇨ see 3384

3-4□ 夕

incorrect classification ⇨ see 3387

3-4□ 也

incorrect classification ⇨ see 3406

3-4□ 夂

incorrect classification ⇨ see 3392

3-4□ 夊

incorrect classification ⇨ see 3393

3-4□ 尢

incorrect classification ⇨ see 2937

4-1□ 弔 弔 弔
3432 CHŌ tomura(u)

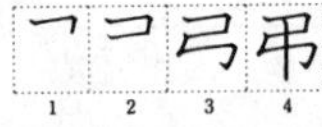

Ⓒ 吊 diào

Radical 弓 57	Strokes 4-3-1
Grade Jōyō	Freq 1865
■ 4 - 4 - 1	

▶**CONDOLE**

COMPOUNDS

ⓐ **condole, offer one's condolences to a bereaved person, console, mourn**

ⓑ condolence, condolences, funeral condolences

弔辞 *chōji* message of condolence
弔電 *chōden* telegram of condolence
弔問 *chōmon* condolence call
弔慰 *chōi* condolence, sympathy
慶弔 *keichō* congratulations and condolences

KUN

【**tomura(u)** 弔う】 mourn, condole (with a bereaved family); perform a memorial service, hold a Buddhist mass

弔い *tomurai* funeral service; mass for the dead; condolence

SYNONYMS

ⓐ **console**
慰 CONSOLE → 2867

ⓐ **mourn and mourning**
悼 MOURN → 485
喪 MOURNING → 2825
忌 MOURNING → 2207

丑 丑 丑 丑

3433 CHŪ ushi NAMES hiro

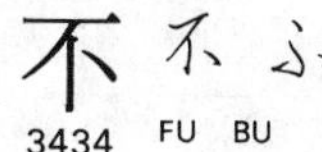

Ⓒⓗ 丑 chǒu

Radical	Strokes
一 1	4-1-3
Grade	Freq
Names	2075
■ 4-4-1	

4-1□

▶**THE OX**

COMPOUNDS

● second sign of the Oriental zodiac: the Ox—(time) 1-3 a.m., (direction) NNE, (season) December (of the lunar calendar) (⇨ see APPENDIX 7)

癸丑 *kichū* 50th of the sexagenary cycle

KUN

【ushi 丑】 second sign of the Oriental zodiac: the Ox (⇨ ●)

丑の刻 *ushi no koku* two o'clock in the morning

丑の年 *ushi no toshi* Year of the Ox

丑三つ時 *ushimitsudoki* midnight

NAMES

丑二 *ushiji* male name

丑次郎 *ushijirō* male name

丑徳 *hironori* male name

SYNONYMS

● **cattle**

牛 CATTLE → 3452

HOMOPHONES

ushi ⇨ 牛 3452

NOTE

⇨ see USAGE note at 牛 3452

不 不 ふ

3434 FU BU

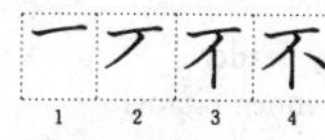

Ⓒⓗ 不 bù

Radical	Strokes
一 1	4-1-3
Grade	Freq
Jōyō-4	131
■ 4-4-1	

4-1□

▶**NOT**

COMPOUNDS

● [also prefix] **not, un-, in-, non-, dis-**—element of negation usu. placed before nouns or noun adjectives

不足 *fusoku* insufficiency, shortage, deficit; want; dissatisfaction

不安 *fuan* uneasiness, anxiety

不動の *fudō no* immobile

不況 *fukyō* depression, slump, recession

不運 *fuun* misfortune, bad luck

不満 *fuman* dissatisfaction, discontent

不思議 *fushigi* mystery, wonder

不尽 *fujin* Yours sincerely

不気味な *bukimi na* uncanny, weird, ghastly

不器用な *bukiyō na* clumsy, unskillful

不用心 *buyōjin* insecurity; carelessness

SYNONYMS

● **terms of negation**

非 IS NOT (contrariety) → 889

無 WITHOUT (nonexistence) → 2135

没 lacking in → 260

欠 LACK → 1987

未 NOT YET → 3506

否 OR NOT → 2406

USAGE

不 fu

[also prefix] not, un-, in-, non-, dis-—element of negation usu. placed before nouns or noun adjectives

非 hi

[also prefix] is not, not, non-, un-, in-—element of contrariety usu. placed before nouns

無 mu

[also prefix] without, -less, non-, un-, in-, no—element indicating nonexistence or lack

没 botsu

[prefix] lacking in, not, un-

欠 ketsu

lack, be short of, be deficient

未 mi

[also prefix] not yet, un- (as in *uncompleted*)

否 hi

or not—used as the second element of a compound to negate the meaning of the first

★不, 非 and 無 are comparable to English prefixes of negation such as *non-*, *un-*, *in-*, dis-, etc. 非 is best described as a prefix of contrariety with strong negative overtones. It is equivalent to the *in-* of *inhuman* (非人間的な *hiningenteki na*) and to the *un-* of *unscientific* (非科学的な *hikagakuteki na*). 不 is the general prefix of negation like the *un-* of *unhappy* (不幸な *fukō na*) or the *dis-* of *disagreement* (不一致 *fuitchi*). 不, the most frequently used, is usu. placed before nouns or noun adjectives, while 非 is rather restricted to nouns. 無 usu. stresses mere lack and implies nothing further, much like the English *non-* in *nonpoisonous* (無毒の *mudoku no*). 没, the less frequently used prefix, implies a complete lack of something, as in 没個性 *botsukosei* 'lack of individuality'. 未 is equivalent to *un-* in the sense of 'not yet', as 未完の *mikan no* 'uncompleted' and 未婚の *mikon no* 'unmarried'. The whole question is rather complicated and only idiom will tell which choice is correct in each case.

NOTE

⇨ see COMPOUND FORMATION for 不尽 *fujin* ⇨ 尽 3050

4-1□

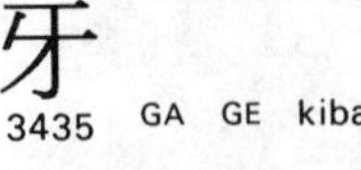

3435 GA GE kiba

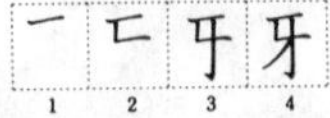

Ⓒⓗ 牙 yá

Radical	Strokes
牙 92	4-4-0
Grade	**Freq**
Reference	
■ 4 - 4 - 1	

RADICAL 92

Standard form: 牙 *kiba* 'sharp tooth'
Left variant: 牙 *kiba*
Description: used in characters related to teeth

COMPOUNDS

❶ fang, tusk
歯牙 *shiga* teeth
毒牙 *dokuga* poison fang
象牙 *zōge* ivory
牙 *kiba* fang, tusk

❷ standard of a military leader
牙城 *gajō* stronghold, inner citadel

4-1□

3436 GO itsu itsu(tsu)

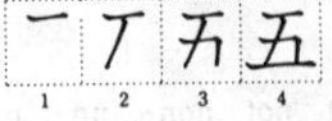

Ⓒⓗ 五 wǔ

Radical	Strokes
二 7	4-2-2
Grade	**Freq**
Jōyō-1	13
■ 4 - 4 - 1	

▶**FIVE**

COMPOUNDS

ⓐ [original meaning] **five, fifth**
ⓑ five times
五百 *gohyaku* 500
五十音 *gojūon* Japanese syllabary
五感 *gokan* the five senses
五指 *goshi* the five fingers
五分五分 *gobugobu* evenly matched; tie
五輪旗 *gorinki* five ringed Olympic flag
五目飯 *gomokumeshi* Japanese pilaf
五月 *gogatsu* May
五階 *gokai* fifth floor
五回 *gokai* five times

INDEPENDENT

【go 五】 five, fifth
ダイヤの五 *daiya no go* five of diamonds
五の組 *go no kumi* fifth group

KUN

【itsu 五】 [in compounds] five
五日 *itsuka* five days; 5th of the month
五月 *itsutsuki* five months

【itsu(tsu) 五つ】 five
五つ児 *itsutsugo* quintuplets

SPECIAL READINGS

五月晴れ *satsukibare* fine weather in early summer [during the rainy season]
五月雨 *samidare* early summer rain

SYNONYMS

ⓐ **five**
伍 five (in legal documents) → 47

ⓐ **small numbers**
一 ONE → 3341
二 TWO → 1922
三 THREE → 1924
四 FOUR → 3044

六 SIX → 1965
七 SEVEN → 3362
八 EIGHT → 3

九 NINE → 3369
十 TEN → 3365

互 互 互

3437 GO taga(i)

一 工 互 互
1 2 3 4

CH 互 hù

Radical	Strokes
二 7	4-2-2
Grade	**Freq**
Jōyō	874
■ 4 - 4 - 1	

4-1□

▶RECIPROCAL

COMPOUNDS

● [original meaning] **reciprocal, mutual, each other**

互恵 *gokei* reciprocity, mutual benefits
互助 *gojo* mutual aid, cooperation
互角 *gokaku* equality; good match
互選 *gosen* co-optation, mutual election
相互の *sōgo no* mutual, reciprocal
交互に *kōgo ni* mutually, reciprocally, alternately

KUN

【taga(i) 互い】 reciprocality
互いの *tagai no* mutual, reciprocal
互いに *tagai ni* mutually, reciprocally
互い違いに *tagaichigai ni* alternately

SYNONYMS

● **mutual**
相 MUTUAL → 900

3438 HA tomoe NAMES tomo

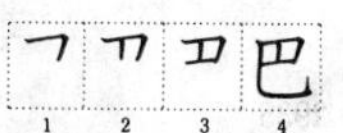

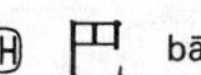 bā

Radical	Strokes
己 49	4-3-1
Grade	**Freq**
Names	2104
■ 4 - 4 - 1	

4-1□

▶CIRCULAR COMMA PATTERN

COMPOUNDS

❶ used phonetically for *ha* or *pa*
巴旦杏 *hatankyō* plum
巴里 *pari* Paris

❷ [archaic] ancient name for east Sichuan Province
巴人 *hajin* resident of ancient Sichuan; uneducated bumpkin

KUN

【tomoe 巴】 circular comma pattern, eddy, whirl (☯)
巴瓦 *tomoegawara* comma pattern tile
三つ巴 *mitsudomoe* circular pattern of three commas; three-sided fight
卍巴と *manjitomoe to* in whirls

NAMES

巴 *tomoe* male name also female name

SYNONYMS

❶ **phonetic** [**ha**]
波 phonetic [ha] → 330

王 王 王

3439 Ō -NŌ

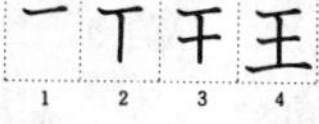

CH 王 wáng wàng

Radical	Strokes
玉 96	4-4-0
Grade	**Freq**
Jōyō-1	544
■ 4 - 4 - 1	

4-1□

▶KING

COMPOUNDS

❶ⓐ **king, monarch, ruler, emperor**
ⓑ [also suffix] (the most powerful of a group) **king, magnate, baron**

王様 *ōsama* king
王国 *ōkoku* kingdom, monarchy
王座 *ōza* throne
王子 *ōji* prince
国王 *kokuō* king, monarch

女王 *joō* (=*jōō*) queen; belle, mistress
帝王 *teiō* monarch, emperor
王者 *ōja* king, monarch, champion
法王 *hōō* Pope
海賊王 *kaizokuō* pirate king
石油王 *sekiyuō* oil magnate
❷ name of chess piece in shogi (Japanese chess) or chess: king
王将 *ōshō* king (in shogi)
王手 *ōte* check!
❸ Imperial prince
親王 *shinnō* Imperial prince

INDEPENDENT

【ō 王】 king, monarch; (the most powerful of a group) king, magnate; king (⇨ ❷)

王を立てる *ō o tateru* enthrone a king
百獣の王 *hyakujū no ō* king of beasts
王を詰める *ō o tsumeru* checkmate the king

SYNONYMS

❶ⓐ rulers
皇 EMPEROR → 2566
帝 EMPEROR → 2073
天 Heaven's messenger on earth → 3442
君 RULER → 3206
ⓑ leaders
主 MASTER → 1938
長 CHIEF → 2556
頭 HEAD → 1604
首 LEADER → 2265
領 leader → 1224

4-1☐

尺

3440 SHAKU

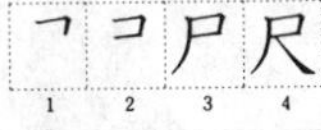

CH 尺 chǐ chě

Radical	Strokes
尸 44	4-3-1
Grade	**Freq**
Jōyō-6	1772
■ 4 - 4 - 1	

▶SHAKU

COMPOUNDS

❶ **shaku: unit of length equiv. to approx. 30.3 cm or 10 *sun* (寸)**
尺貫法 *shakkanhō* Japanese system of weights and measures
尺八 *shakuhachi* bamboo flute
一尺 *isshaku* 1 *shaku*
❷ⓐ [also suffix] **rule, measure, scale**
ⓑ length
尺度 *shakudo* linear measure; standard
巻き尺 *makijaku* measuring tape
計算尺 *keisanjaku* slide rule
尺取り虫 *shakutorimushi* measuring worm
間尺に合わない *mashaku ni awanai* do not pay, be not worth (one's) while
❸ slight amount
尺地 *shakuchi* small plot of land

INDEPENDENT

【shaku 尺】 *shaku* (⇨ ❶); rule, measure, scale; length

尺を当てる *shaku o ateru* measure with a rule
尺を取る *shaku o toru* measure (the length)

SYNONYMS

❶ length units
寸 *sun* (3.03 cm) → 2935
米 meter → 3529
尋 fathom (1.8 m) → 2322
間 *ken* (1.8 m) → 3323
丈 *jo* (3.03 m) → 3419
町 *cho* (109 m) → 1113
里 LEAGUE, *ri* (3.4 km) → 3542
❷ⓐ measuring devices
計 meter → 1441
衡 scales → 761

COMPOUND FORMATION

尺八 *shakuhachi*
尺八 'bamboo flute' is so called because it is 1 *shaku* (尺 ❶) and 8 (八) *sun* (寸) in length.

丹 丹 丹

3441 TAN ni▲

Ⓒⓗ 丹 dān

Radical	Strokes
丶 3	4-1-3
Grade	**Freq**
Jōyō	1399
■ 4 - 4 - 1	

4-1□

▶CINNABAR

COMPOUNDS

❶ **cinnabar red, vermilion, red**
丹朱 *tanshu* vermilion, red; cinnabar
丹青 *tansei* red and blue; painting
丹花 *tanka* red flower
牡丹 *botan* peony, *Paeonia suffruticosa*

❷ [original meaning] cinnabar, minium, red lead
丹砂 *tansha* cinnabar
鉛丹 *entan* red lead, minium

❸ **wholeheartedly, sincerely, devotedly**
丹精(=丹誠) *tansei* efforts, pains
丹念な *tannen na* painstaking, assiduous, diligent

❹ⓐ pill, medicine (esp. in Chinese medicine)
ⓑ suffix after names of pills
煉丹 *rentan* elixir of life (prepared from cinnabar in ancient China)

❺ old name for Kyoto Prefecture
丹後 *tango* old name for north Kyoto Prefecture

❻ used phonetically for *tan* in the transliteration of foreign words
切支丹 *kirishitan* early Christianity in Japan; Jesuitism

KUN

【ni 丹】 cinnabar red, vermilion
丹塗りの *ninuri no* red-painted, vermilion-lacquered

SYNONYMS

❶ **red colors**
朱 VERMILION → 3531
赤 RED → 2193
紅 CRIMSON → 1277
緋 SCARLET → 1369
茜 MADDER → 2261

天 天 天

3442 TEN ame ama-

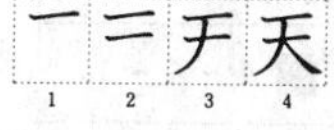

Ⓒⓗ 天 tiān

Radical	Strokes
大 37	4-3-1
Grade	**Freq**
Jōyō-1	422
■ 4 - 4 - 1	

4-1□

▶HEAVEN

COMPOUNDS

❶ⓐ **heaven(s), sky, celestial sphere**
ⓑ **(state of the) weather, look of the sky**
天地 *tenchi* heaven and earth; top and bottom
天空 *tenkū* sky, air, firmament, heavens
天体 *tentai* heavenly body
天文学 *tenmongaku* astronomy
天下 *tenka* the whole country [empire], the world
天衣無縫 *ten'imuhō* perfect beauty with no trace of artifice
衝天 *shōten* high spirits
天気 *tenki* weather, atmospheric conditions; fine weather
天候 *tenkō* weather
晴天 *seiten* fine [fair] weather, cloudless sky
雨天 *uten* rainy weather, rainy day

❷ (abode of God and blessed souls) Heaven, paradise
天国 *tengoku* Kingdom of Heaven, Paradise
天使 *tenshi* angel
昇天 *shōten* the Ascension; death

❸ⓐ **Heaven, the Creator, Ruler of the Universe, God**
ⓑ Heaven's will, fate, destiny
天帝 *tentei* Lord of Heaven, the Creator
天主 *tenshu* Lord of Heaven, God
天罰 *tenbatsu* divine punishment
天命 *tenmei* providence, fate, Heaven's will
天運 *ten'un* fate, destiny, fortune

❹ⓐ **Heaven's messenger on earth, the Emperor**
ⓑ imperial
天皇 *tennō* Emperor of Japan
天子 *tenshi* son of Heaven, Emperor
天顔 *tengan* Emperor's countenance
天覧 *tenran* imperial inspection

❺ⓐ **nature, laws of nature**
ⓑ by nature, innate
天然 *tennen* nature
天災 *tensai* natural calamity [disaster]
天才 *tensai* (person of) genius
天性 *tensei* nature, one's innate disposition
先天的な *sententeki na* native, inborn
❻ *Buddhism* deva, divine being
梵天 *bonten* Brahma-Deva
帝釈天 *taishakuten Śakra devānām Indra*
❼ [also 纏 1432] put on, be wrapped in
半天 *hanten* short coat, workman's livery coat
❽ [original meaning] top, head
脳天 *nōten* crown of the head
❾ abbrev. of 天麩羅 *tenpura*: tempura, Japanese deep-fat fried food
天つゆ *tentsuyu* sauce for tempura

INDEPENDENT

【ten 天】 heavens, sky; Heaven, God; Heaven's will, providence; fate, destiny
天から降りる *ten kara oriru* fall from heaven [the sky]
天に坐します我等の父 *ten ni mashimasu warera no chichi* our Father who art in Heaven...
天なり命なり *Ten nari mei nari* It is Heaven's will

KUN

【ame 天, ama- 天-】 *literary* heaven, sky
天が下 *amegashita* the world
天の川 *amanogawa* Milky Way

SYNONYMS

❶ⓐ **sky**
空 SKY → 2227
宙 MIDAIR → 2221
ⓑ **weather**
候 SEASONAL WEATHER → 119
晴 FINE WEATHER → 981
❷ **posthumous worlds**
幽 world of the dead → 3008
獄 hell → 712
❸ⓐ **god**
帝 the Supreme Being → 2073
神 GOD → 912
主 Lord → 1938
❹ **rulers**
帝 EMPEROR → 2073
王 KING → 3439
皇 EMPEROR → 2566
君 RULER → 3206

NOTE

⇨ see COMPOUND FORMATION for
衝天 *shōten* ⇨ 衝 725
天衣無縫 *ten'imuhō* ⇨ 縫 1406

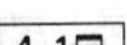

3443

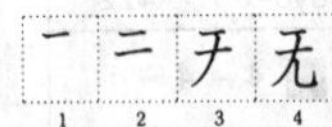

Radical	Strokes
无 71	4-4-0
Grade	**Freq**
Radical	
■ 4 - 4 - 1	

RADICAL 71

Standard form: 无 *munyō* 'without'
Right variants: 旡 旡 *sudenotsukuri* (既 既)
Description: used in characters related to surfeit or choking

---

4-1□

旡

3444

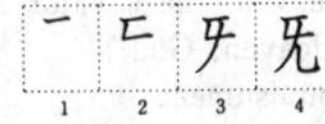

Radical	Strokes
无 71	4-4-0
Grade	**Freq**
Radical	
■ 4 - 4 - 1	

RADICAL 71

sudenotsukuri, variant of 无 *munyō* 'without'
⇨ see 无 3443 for radical description

歹
3445

Radical 歹 78	Strokes 4-4-0
Grade Radical	Freq
■ 4 - 4 - 1	

4-1□

RADICAL 78
Standard form: 歹 *gatsuhen* 'death' (死 残 殊)
Description: used in characters related to death or serious injury

---

毋
3446

Radical 毋 80	Strokes 4-4-0
Grade Radical	Freq
■ 4 - 4 - 1	

4-1□

RADICAL 80
Standard form: 毋 *haha* or *nakare* 'mother' (毎 毒)
Variant: 毌 *haha* or *nakare*
Description: used in characters related to mothers or for classification

---

毌
3447

Radical 毌 80	Strokes 4-4-0
Grade Radical	Freq
■ 4 - 4 - 1	

4-1□

RADICAL 80
variant of 毋 *haha* or *nakare* 'mother'
⇨ see 毋 3446 for radical description

王
3448

Radical 王 96	Strokes 4-4-0
Grade Radical	Freq
■ 4 - 4 - 1	

4-1□

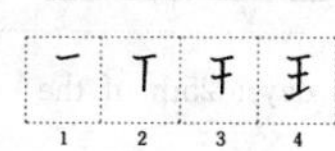

RADICAL 96
tamahen, variant of 玉 *tama* 'gem'
⇨ see 玉 3477 for radical description

反 incorrect classification ⇨ see 2945 4-1□

弓 incorrect stroke count ⇨ see 3383 4-1□

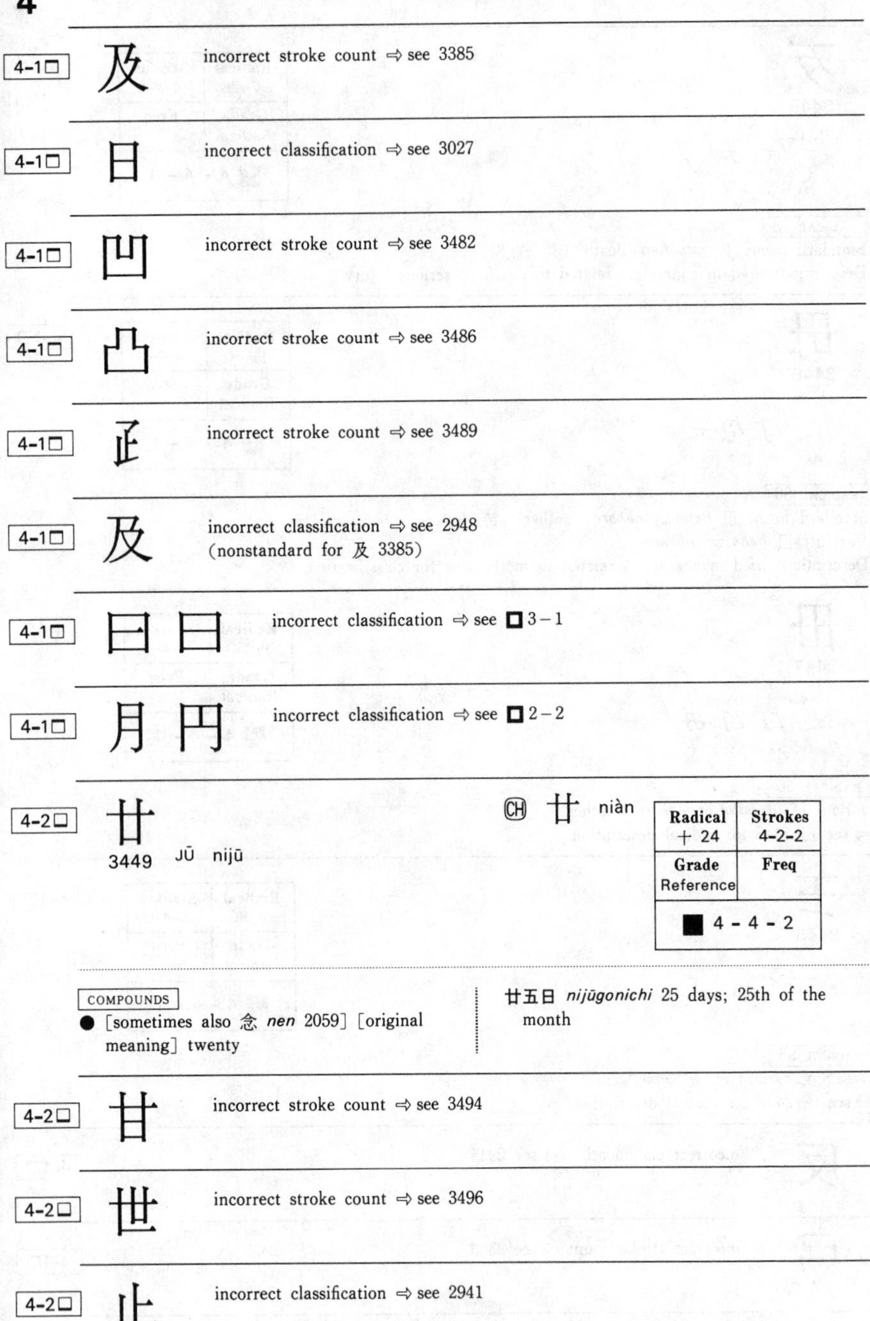

4-1□ 及 incorrect stroke count ⇨ see 3385

4-1□ 日 incorrect classification ⇨ see 3027

4-1□ 凹 incorrect stroke count ⇨ see 3482

4-1□ 凸 incorrect stroke count ⇨ see 3486

4-1□ 疋 incorrect stroke count ⇨ see 3489

4-1□ 及 incorrect classification ⇨ see 2948 (nonstandard for 及 3385)

4-1□ 日 日 incorrect classification ⇨ see □ 3 – 1

4-1□ 月 円 incorrect classification ⇨ see □ 2 – 2

4-2□ 廿 3449 JŪ nijū

Ⓒⓗ 廿 niàn

Radical	Strokes
十 24	4-2-2
Grade	Freq
Reference	
■ 4 - 4 - 2	

COMPOUNDS

● [sometimes also 念 *nen* 2059] [original meaning] twenty

廿五日 *nijūgonichi* 25 days; 25th of the month

4-2□ 甘 incorrect stroke count ⇨ see 3494

4-2□ 世 incorrect stroke count ⇨ see 3496

4-2□ 止 incorrect classification ⇨ see 2941

incorrect stroke count ⇨ see 3500
(nonstandard for 世 3496)
4-2□

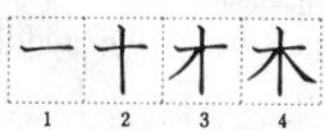
incorrect classification／stroke count ⇨ see 1994
(nonstandard for 主 1938)
4-2□

木 3450 BOKU MOKU ki ko-

Ⓒⓗ 木 mù

4-3◫

Radical	Strokes
木 75	4-4-0
Grade	**Freq**
Jōyō-1	157
■ 4 - 4 - 3	

一 十 才 木 (1 2 3 4)

RADICAL 75
Standard form: 木 *ki* 'tree' (本 査 某)
Left variant: 木 *kihen* (梅 校 株)
Description: used in characters related to trees, wood or wooden objects

▶TREE ▶WOOD

COMPOUNDS

❶ [also suffix] [original meaning] **tree**
木石 *bokuseki* trees and stones, inanimate objects
樹木 *jumoku* tree; trees and shrubs
草木 *sōmoku* trees and plants, vegetation
大木 *taiboku* gigantic tree
香木 *kōboku* fragrant wood; aromatic tree
❷ⓐ wood, timber
ⓑ wooden
ⓒ the first of the five elements: wood (⇨ see APPENDIX 7)
木材 *mokuzai* wood, timber, lumber
木目 *mokume* wood grain
木工 *mokkō* woodworking, woodworker
原木 *genboku* material wood; pulpwood
土木 *doboku* engineering works
木刀 *bokutō* wooden sword
木製の *mokusei no* wooden, made of wood
木造の *mokuzō no* wooden
❸ Thursday
木曜日 *mokuyōbi* Thursday
火木 *kamoku* Tuesdays and Thursdays
❹ Jupiter
木星 *mokusei* Jupiter

INDEPENDENT

【boku 木】 (old gnarled) tree, trunk
見事な木 *migoto na boku* magnificent tree
【moku 木】 Thursday; grain of wood; the first of the five elements: wood

KUN

【ki 木】
① [sometimes also 樹] tree
木登り *kinobori* tree climbing
植木 *ueki* garden plant, shrub, pot plant
苗木 *naegi* sapling, young tree
並木 *namiki* row of trees, roadside trees
② wood, timber, lumber
木切れ *kigire* piece of wood, splinter
木彫り *kibori* woodcarving
白木 *shiraki* plain wood
③ wooden clappers
【ko- 木-】 tree
木陰 *kokage* shade of a tree, bower
木立ち *kodachi* clump of trees, thicket
木の葉 *konoha* foliage of trees

SPECIAL READINGS

木綿 *momen* cotton, cotton cloth

SYNONYMS

❶ tree
樹 STANDING TREE → 1075
❷ⓐ & ❷ⓑ kinds of wood
材 TIMBER → 836
薪 FIREWOOD → 2374
❸ days of the week
水 Wednesday → 10
金 Friday → 2057
土 Saturday → 3403
日 Sunday → 3027
月 Monday → 2956
火 Tuesday → 3463

USAGE

ki
木
① [sometimes also 樹] tree
② wood, timber, lumber
③ wooden clappers
樹
[usu. 木] standing tree, tree

HOMOPHONES

ki ⇨ 樹 1075

4-3Ⅲ

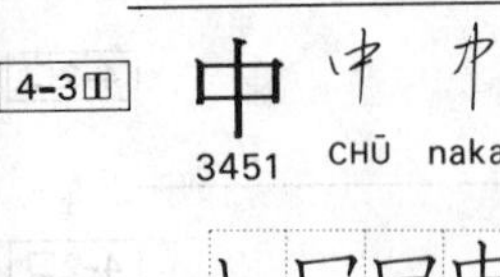

3451 CHŪ naka uchi▲ ata(ru)▲

Ⓒ中 zhōng zhòng

Radical	Strokes
丨 2	4-1-3
Grade	**Freq**
Jōyō-1	11

■ 4 - 4 - 3

丨 冂 口 中
1 2 3 4

▶MIDDLE ▶IN

COMPOUNDS

❶ lying between two extremes of space:
ⓐ [original meaning] **middle, center, midway**
ⓑ **middle, Middle, mid-, central, intermediate**
中間 *chūkan* middle, midway
中心 *chūshin* center, middle
中核 *chūkaku* core, nucleus; kernel
集中する *shūchū suru* concentrate, focus; converge
中点 *chūten* middle point
中部 *chūbu* central [middle] part
中衛 *chūei* middle guard
中耳 *chūji* middle ear, *auris media*
中欧 *chūō* Central Europe
中東 *chūtō* Middle East
中労委(＝中央労働委員会) *chūrōi* (＝*chūō rōdō iinkai*) Central Labor Relations Committee
中継する *chūkei suru* relay, rebroadcast
❷ⓐ (of time) **middle, medieval, Middle**
ⓑ **in the middle, halfway**
中年 *chūnen* middle age
中古の *chūko no* medieval
中世 *chūsei* Middle [Medieval] Ages
中石器時代 *chūsekki jidai* Mesolithic period
中期 *chūki* middle period; metaphase
中止する *chūshi suru* suspend, stop, discontinue
中断 *chūdan* interruption, discontinuance, suspension
途中で *tochū de* on the way
❸ⓐ [also prefix] (of intermediate size, quality or extent) **middle, medium, intermediate, average**
ⓑ (being at neither extreme) **middle (course), moderate, neutral, medial**
中型 *chūgata* medium size
中肉中背の *chūniku-chūzei no* of medium build
中ヒール *chūhīru* medium-high heel
中小企業 *chūshō kigyō* small-to-medium-sized enterprises
中細の *chūboso no* medium-fine
中古の *chūko* (＝*chūburu*) *no* secondhand, used
中波 *chūha* medium waves
中辞典 *chūjiten* medium-sized dictionary
中産階級 *chūsan kaikyū* middle class, bourgeoisie
中学 *chūgaku* junior high school
中庸 *chūyō* the (golden) mean, the middle path
中立 *chūritsu* neutrality; neutralization
中和する *chūwa suru* neutralize; counteract
❹ second in a series of three: middle, second
中編 *chūhen* second part [volume]; medium-length story
中旬 *chūjun* middle [second] ten days of a month
中元 *chūgen* midyear gift; July 15th (lunar calendar)
❺ [also suffix] within the confines of a given range:
ⓐ **in, within, inside, interior**
ⓑ (indicates one of many) **in, one of, among**
空中で *kūchū de* in the air [sky]
水中眼鏡 *suichū megane* swimming goggles
市中銀行 *shichū ginkō* city bank
暗中模索 *anchū-mosaku* groping in the dark
意中の人 *ichū no hito* person one is thinking of; man of one's heart
一酸化炭素中で *issankatansochū de* in an atmosphere of carbon monoxide
十中八九 *jitchū hakku* nine cases out of ten
連中 *renchū* (＝*renjū*) party, company, clique; those fellows [guys]
女中 *jochū* maidservant, maid
乗客中の一人 *jōkyakuchū no hitori* one of the passengers
❻ [also suffix] within the confines of a given period:
ⓐ **in, in the course of, during, while**
ⓑ **in the process of, in progress, under**
午前中 *gozenchū* in the morning
今週中に *konshūchū ni* in the course of the week, before the week is over
授業中 *jugyōchū* while in class
建築中 *kenchikuchū* under construction
修繕中 *shūzenchū* during repairs, in the process of being repaired
❼ [also suffix]
ⓐ (in every part) **throughout, all over, everywhere**
ⓑ (during the entire time) **throughout (the**

night), all through
国中で *kunijū de* all over the country
東京中 *tōkyōjū* all over Tokyo
年中 *nenjū* throughout the year, always
一日中 *ichinichijū* all day long
❽ⓐ **People's Republic of China, China**
ⓑ **Modern Chinese, Mandarin**
中華 *chūka* Middle Kingdom, China; Chinese food
中共 *chūkyō* Communist China
訪中 *hōchū* visit to China
日中友好協会 *nitchū yūkō kyōkai* Japan-China Amity Association
中日辞典 *chūnichi jiten* Chinese-Japanese dictionary
❾ⓐ abbrev. of 中学校 *chūgakkō*: junior high school, middle school
ⓑ suffix after names of junior high schools
中二 *chūni* second-year of junior high
中卒 *chūsotsu* junior high graduate
武蔵中 *musashichū* Musashi Junior High School
❿ hit the target [mark]
的中する *tekichū suru* hit the mark, hit (on) it
命中する *meichū suru* hit the mark [target]
⓫ be absorbed in, be immersed
熱中 *netchū* absorption, enthusiasm
夢中で *muchū de* like one in a dream; like one dazed; frantically
⓬ be subjected to the harmful effects of (poison); suffer from
中毒する *chūdoku suru* get poisoned; be addicted
中風 *chūbu* (=*chūbū, chūfū*) palsy, paralysis
中傷する *chūshō suru* slander, libel
⓭ abbrev. of 中堅手 *chūkenshu*: center fielder
中飛 *chūhi* center fly
左中間 *sachūkan* between left and center fielders

INDEPENDENT

【chū 中】 middle, medium; medium size, medium quality; mediocrity, average; second (volume of three); China
ビールの中 *bīru no chū* medium-sized beer
中の *chū no* medium, mediocre
中以上 *chū ijō* above average

KUN

【naka 中】
① inside, interior
中へ入る *naka e hairu* step into, go [come] inside, enter
中味 *nakami* interior, content, substance
中庭 *nakaniwa* courtyard
②ⓐ middle, the second
ⓑ middle course, mean
中の兄 *naka no ani* middle brother
中指 *nakayubi* middle finger
真ん中 *mannaka* center, middle
背中 *senaka* back
中を取る *naka o toru* take the middle course [mean]
③ⓐ within the confines of a given range
ⓑ amidst an undesirable event
中に *naka ni* in; in the middle of; between, among
中には *naka ni wa* some (of them), among (them)
町中で *machinaka de* in the streets
夜中 *yonaka* midnight, dead of night
世の中 *yo no naka* the world, society, life
多くの中から選ぶ *ōku no naka kara erabu* choose among many things
雨の中で *ame no naka de* in the rain

【uchi 中】
[usu. 内]
① inside, interior
心の中で *kokoro no uchi de* in one's mind
② within (a given period), in the course of, while, during
一週間の中に *isshūkan no uchi ni* within a week
③ among, between
両者の中 *ryōsha no uchi* between the two

【ata(ru) 中る】 [now usu. 当たる] be poisoned, disagree with; suffer from
河豚に中る *fugu ni ataru* get poisoned by swellfish

SYNONYMS

❶ⓐ **middle**
央 CENTER → 3509
心 HEART → 11
核 NUCLEUS → 927
❶ⓑ & ❷ & ❸ **between**
仲 intermediate → 43
間 BETWEEN → 3323
際 inter- → 714
❹ **second**
乙 SECOND → 3339
次 second → 54
後 AFTER (latter) → 361
❺ⓐ **inside**
内 INSIDE → 3466
裏 inside → 2138
奥 INNER PART → 2824
❻ **during**
間 for an interval of → 3323
内 within (a given period) → 3466
❼ⓑ **throughout**
終 from beginning to end → 1336
徹 all through → 726
通 through → 3109
❽ⓐ **China**
華 CHINA → 2283
漢 CHINESE → 657

支 China → 1979
台 Taiwan → 2005
唐 Cathay → 3115
呉 KINGDOM OF WU → 2549
ⓑ **Chinese**
漢 CHINESE (language) → 657
❾ **schools**
小 elementary school → 7
高 high school → 2097
校 SCHOOL → 929
学 EDUCATIONAL INSTITUTION → 2555
塾 PRIVATE SCHOOL → 2860
院 INSTITUTION → 454
大 UNIVERSITY → 3416
園 kindergarten → 3156

USAGE

naka

中
① inside, interior
②ⓐ middle, the second
ⓑ middle course, mean
③ⓐ within the confines of a given range
ⓑ amidst an undesirable event

仲
① personal relations, relationship, (familiar) terms, fellowship, friendship
② intermediary, go-between
③ [in compounds] inner, middle

HOMOPHONES

naka ⇨ 仲 43
uchi ⇨ 内 3466 家 2273
ataru ⇨ 当 2177

COMPOUND FORMATION

女中 *jochū*
女中 'maidservant, maid' originally meant one woman (女) among many (中 ❺ⓑ).

NOTE

⇨ see also USAGE notes at 当 2177 and 内 3466

4-3◫

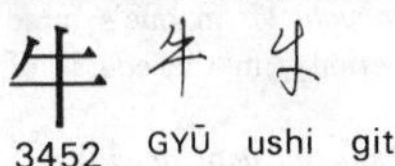

3452 GYŪ ushi git-▲

Ⓒⓗ 牛 niú

Radical	Strokes
牛 93	4-4-0
Grade	**Freq**
Jōyō-2	972
■ 4 - 4 - 3	

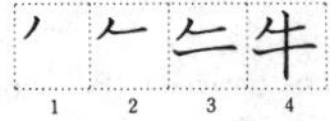

RADICAL 93

Standard form: 牛 *ushi* 'cattle' (牢 牽 犂)
Left variant: 牜 *ushihen* (物 特 牧)
Description: used in characters related to cattle or related animals

▶**CATTLE**

COMPOUNDS

ⓐ [original meaning] (any bovine animal) **cattle, cow, bull, ox**
ⓑ **beef**
牛乳 *gyūnyū* (cow's) milk
牛肉 *gyūniku* beef
牛皮(=牛革) *gyūkawa* cowhide, oxhide
牛飲馬食する *gyūin-bashoku suru* gorge and swill, drink like a cow and eat like a horse
牛歩戦術 *gyūho-senjutsu* cow's-pace tactics
乳牛 *nyūgyū* (=*chichiushi*) milch cow, dairy cattle
闘牛 *tōgyū* bullfight, fighting bull
牛脂 *gyūshi* beef tallow

INDEPENDENT

【**gyū** 牛】beef; cowhide
牛百グラム *gyū hyakuguramu* 100 g of beef
牛の鞄 *gyū no kaban* cowhide bag

KUN

【**ushi** 牛】[also suffix] cattle, cow, bull, ox
小牛 *koushi* calf
去勢牛 *kyoseiushi* bullock
【**git-** 牛-】ox, cow
牛車 *gissha* cow carriage (for noblemen in Heian period)

SYNONYMS

ⓐ **cattle**
丑 THE OX → 3433
ⓐ **domesticated mammals**
馬 HORSE → 3296
豚 PIG → 976
羊 SHEEP → 2183
犬 DOG → 3464
猫 CAT → 535

USAGE

ushi

牛
[also suffix] cattle, cow, bull, ox

丑
second sign of the Oriental zodiac: the Ox

HOMOPHONES

ushi ⇨ 丑 3433

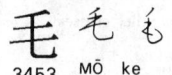

毛 毛 毛

3453 MŌ ke

4-3Ⅲ

🄲🄷 毛 máo

Radical	Strokes
毛 82	4-4-0
Grade	**Freq**
Jōyō-2	676
■ 4 - 4 - 3	

RADICAL 82

Standard form: 毛 *ke* 'hair' (毫 毬 氈)

Description: used in characters related to hair or fur

▶HAIR

COMPOUNDS

❶ⓐ [original meaning] **hair (of humans or animals), fur, feather**

ⓑ hair (of plants)

毛髪 *mōhatsu* hair

毛筆 *mōhitsu* (writing or painting) brush

羊毛 *yōmō* wool

羽毛 *umō* feathers, plumage, down

毛茸 *mōjō* trichome

❷ **wool**

毛製品 *mōseihin* woolen goods

毛布 *mōfu* blanket

純毛 *junmō* pure wool, all wool

原毛 *genmō* raw wool

❸ as thin as hair, slight

毛頭 *mōtō* (not) in the least, (not) a bit

毛管 *mōkan* capillary (tube)

❹ vegetation

不毛の地 *fumō no chi* barren land

二毛作 *nimōsaku* two crops a year, semiannual crop

❺ⓐ 1/1000

ⓑ 1/1000 of 10%: 0.0001

三分五厘二毛 *sanbu gorin nimō* 0.0352

❻ *mo*:

ⓐ former unit of length equiv. to approx. 0.03 mm or 1/1000 of a *sun* (寸)

ⓑ former unit of weight equiv. to 3.75 mg or 1/1000 of a momme (匁)

ⓒ former monetary unit equiv. to 1/10,000 of a yen (円)

三毛 *sanmō* 3 *mo*

INDEPENDENT

【**mō** 毛】 *mo* (⇨❻); 0.0001 (⇨❺ⓑ)

KUN

【**ke** 毛】 hair, fur; trichome; wool

毛深い *kebukai* hairy, thickly haired

毛糸 *keito* woolen yarn, wool

毛織 *keori* woolen fabric, woolen cloth

毛唐 *ketō* *slang* foreigner, Westerner

髪の毛 *kaminoke* hair

鼻毛 *hanage* hairs of the nostril

赤毛 *akage* red hair, carroty hair

SYNONYMS

❶ **hair**

髪 HAIR (on the head) → 2846

羽 FEATHER → 226

❷ **fabrics**

麻 HEMP → 3125

綿 COTTON → 1373

絹 SILK → 1361

綾 TWILL → 1376

紗 GAUZE → 1301

織 woven fabric → 1422

錦 BROCADE → 1738

NOTE

⇨ see COMPOUND FORMATION for 毛唐 *ketō* ⇨ 唐 3115

4-3Ⅲ

井 井 井

3454 SEI SHŌ i

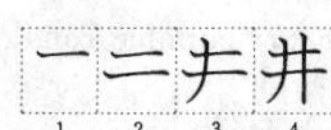

4-3Ⅲ

🄲🄷 井 jǐng

Radical	Strokes
二 7	4-2-2
Grade	**Freq**
Jōyō	268
■ 4 - 4 - 3	

▶WELL

COMPOUNDS

❶ [original meaning] **well**

油井 *yusei* oil well

鑿井 *sakusei* well drilling

ガス井 *gasusei* gas well

❷ something resembling a well crib

井目 *seimoku* the nine principal points in a game of go

天井 *tenjō* ceiling

❸ town, community

市井 *shisei* the streets

KUN

【i 井】well
井戸 *ido* (water) well
井の中の蛙大海を知らず *I no naka no kawazu taikai o shirazu* A frog in the well knows nothing of the great ocean / have limited views [opinions]
井桁 *igeta* well crib; parallel crosses

SYNONYMS

❶ **water sources**
泉 SPRING → 2567
源 SOURCE → 656

4-3Ⅱ

升 升 升

3455 SHŌ masu

Ⓒⓗ 升 shēng

Radical	Strokes
十 24	4-2-2
Grade	**Freq**
Jōyō	1421
■ 4 - 4 - 3	

丿 丿 千 升
1 2 3 4

▶***SHO***

COMPOUNDS

● ***sho*: unit of capacity equiv. to approx. 1.8 liters or 10 *go* (合), used esp. for sake or rice**
一升瓶 *isshōbin* 1-*sho* bottle

INDEPENDENT

【shō 升】*sho* (⇨ ●)

KUN

【masu 升】
[formerly also 枡]
①ⓐ measure, measuring box
ⓑ box (seat)
升目 *masume* measure; square (of graph paper)
五升升 *goshōmasu* 5-*sho* measure
② square (as of graph paper)
升形 *masugata* square (shape)

SYNONYMS

● **capacity units**
立 liter → 1992
合 *go* (0.18 liters) → 2019
勺 *SHAKU* (0.018 liters) → 2933
斗 *TO* (18 liters) → 2953
石 *koku* (180 liters) → 2971

USAGE

masu
升
[formerly also 枡]
①ⓐ measure, measuring box
ⓑ box (seat)
② square (as of graph paper)
枡
[now usu. 升] same as 升

HOMOPHONES

masu ⇨ 枡 860

4-3Ⅱ

手 手 手

3456 SHU ZU* te te- -te tə-

Ⓒⓗ 手 shǒu

Radical	Strokes
手 64	4-4-0
Grade	**Freq**
Jōyō-1	35
■ 4 - 4 - 3	

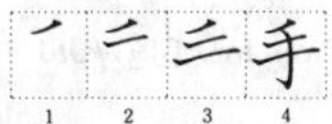
1 2 3 4

RADICAL 64
Standard form: 手 *te* 'hand' (挙 承 摩)
Left variant: 扌 *tehen* (打 投 招)
Description: used in characters related to hands or actions using hands

▶**HAND** ▶**OCCUPATION SUFFIX**

COMPOUNDS

❶ⓐ [original meaning] **hand, palm, arm**
ⓑ [rare] hold in the hands
手中に *shuchū ni* in the hands
握手 *akushu* handshake, handshaking
拍手 *hakushu* applause, clapping
義手 *gishu* artificial arm [hand]
入手する *nyūshu suru* obtain, get, come by, procure
手燭 *shushoku* (= *teshoku*) portable candlestick
❷ perform an action with one's hands
手術 *shujutsu* surgical operation
手芸 *shugei* handicrafts, manual arts
手記 *shuki* note, memorandum; memoirs
手話 *shuwa* talking with the hands; sign language
❸ⓐ [also suffix] holder of an occupation or performer of an action: **-er (as in *sing-***

er)
❻ skilled person
歌手 *kashu* singer
騎手 *kishu* rider, horseman, jockey
選手 *senshu* representative athlete [player]
投手 *tōshu* pitcher
助手 *joshu* assistant, helper
運転手 *untenshu* driver
名手 *meishu* master, expert
❹ⓐ means, method
❻ move (as in shogi)
手段 *shudan* means, way, step
手法 *shuhō* technique, mechanism, style
好手 *kōshu* good move
❺ skill, proficiency
手腕 *shuwan* ability, skill
手練 *shuren* skill, dexterity
上手な *jōzu na* skilled, dexterous, good at

KUN

【te 手】
① hand, palm, arm
手の平(=掌) *tenohira* palm of the hand
手足 *teashi* hands and feet, limbs
手首 *tekubi* wrist
手に入れる *te ni ireru* obtain
手形 *tegata* promissory note; hand print
② handle, knob
取っ手(=把っ手) *totte* handle, knob
③ⓐ hand, help
ⓑ subordinate
手が足りない *te ga tarinai* be short of hands
手の者 *te no mono* one's subordinate
④ labor, trouble, care, charge
手の込んだ *te no konda* elaborate, intricate
手間 *tema* labor, trouble; time (required for a task)
手数 *tesū* (=*tekazu*) trouble, bother, pains
手当 *teate* allowance, compensation, benefits
手当て *teate* provision; medical care, treatment
⑤ handwriting
女の手 *onna no te* feminine handwriting
⑥ achievement, skill
手が上がる *te ga agaru* improve one's skill
⑦ⓐ means, device, trick
ⓑ move (as in shogi); hand (of a game)
手を変える *te o kaeru* resort to other means
手続き *tetsuzuki* procedure, formalities
奥の手 *oku no te* last resort; secrets
決め手 *kimete* decisive factor, clincher; trump card, winning move
先手 *sente* moving first; forestalling
⑧ kind, type, line
薄手の *usude no* of thin make, light
大手 *ōte* major companies
⑨ injury, damage
痛手 *itade* severe wound; home thrust, heavy blow
⑩ direction, side, part
山の手 *yama no te* hilly section
⑪ connection
手切れ *tegire* severance of connections; solatium for severing connections

【te- 手-】
① [also prefix] performed with one's hands, manually handled
手製の *tesei no* handmade
手編み *teami* hand-knitting
手荷物 *tenimotsu* hand baggage, personal effects
手仕事 *teshigoto* handwork, manual labor
② emphatic before certain adjectives
手広く *tebiroku* extensively, widely, on an extensive scale
手厳しい *tekibishii* severe, unsparing, harsh

【-te -手】
① performer of an action, holder of an occupation
相手 *aite* partner; opponent
買い手 *kaite* buyer, customer
語り手 *katarite* narrator, storyteller
② counter for moves in shogi or go
次の一手 *tsugi no itte* next move

【ta- 手-】 performed with one's hands, manually handled
手綱 *tazuna* bridle, reins
手繰る *taguru* pull in hand over hand, draw in, reel in; retrace

SPECIAL READINGS

下手な *heta na* unskillful, unskilled, poor, clumsy
上手い▲(=巧い, 旨い) *umai* skillful, clever; splendid, excellent

SYNONYMS

❶ⓐ hand and arm
腕 ARM → 1006
掌 PALM → 2602
指 FINGER → 378
❸ workers and professionals
屋 colloquial occupation suffix → 3098
員 MEMBER (of a staff) → 2269
人 person of certain category → 3368
者 person who → 3211
師 profession suffix → 1326
士 PROFESSION SUFFIX → 3405
客 skilled person → 2250
家 professional → 2273
婦 woman worker → 469
嬢 (unmarried) female worker → 758
夫 MAN LABORER → 3460
匠 CRAFTSMAN → 2990
工 workman → 3381
❹ⓐ means
段 STEP → 1144
策 MEASURE → 2679

【te】
② **handles**
把 GRIP → 249
柄 HANDLE → 897

HOMOPHONES

tenohira ⇨ 掌 2602 手の平 3456, 3478
umai ⇨ 巧い 188 甘い 3494 上手い 3404, 3456

NOTE

⇨ see USAGE notes at 旨 2024 and 掌 2602
⇨ see COMPOUND FORMATION for 手数 *tesū* (= *tekazu*) ⇨ 数 1790

4-3Ⅱ 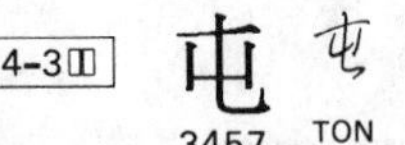

3457 TON

ⒸⒽ 屯 tún zhūn

Radical	Strokes
屮 45	4-3-1
Grade	Freq
Jōyō	1964
■ 4-4-3	

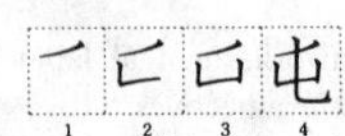

▶**STATION TROOPS**

COMPOUNDS

❶ⓐ **station troops, encamp, post**
ⓑ military station, post
駐屯する *chūton suru* be stationed, occupy
屯田 *tonden* stationing an army in the countryside to engage in farming (during the Meiji period)
屯営 *ton'ei* military camp station, barracks, camping
屯所 *tonsho* post, quarters, military station; police station
❷ [also 噸 752]
ⓐ ton, tonnage
ⓑ shipping ton
五屯 *goton* 5 tons
英屯 *eiton* British [long] ton

SYNONYMS

❶ⓐ **stay**
駐 STATIONED → 1826
留 STAY → 2580
滞 STAY → 663
在 reside temporarily → 2984
泊 STAY OVERNIGHT → 331
宿 LODGE → 2293
❷ **weight units**
貫 *kan* (3.75 kg) → 2460
斤 CATTY (600 g) → 2949
匁 MOMME (3.75 g) → 3465

4-3Ⅱ 

3458

Radical	Strokes
牛 93	4-4-0
Grade	Freq
Radical	
■ 4-4-3	

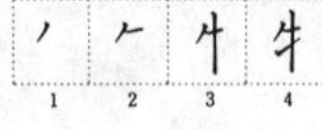

RADICAL 93

ushihen, variant of 牛 *ushi* 'cattle'
⇨ see 牛 3452 for radical description

4-3Ⅱ 

3459

▶**ORDINAL NUMBER PREFIX**
nonstandard for 第 2660

4-3Ⅱ 

incorrect classification ⇨ see 1984

4-3Ⅱ 市

incorrect classification/stroke count ⇨ see 1993

爪 incorrect classification ⇨ see 3024 4-3◫

水 incorrect classification ⇨ see 10 4-3◫

斗 incorrect classification ⇨ see 2953 4-3◫

斗 incorrect classification ⇨ see 2954 4-3◫
(nonstandard for 闘 3334)

夫 夫 夫 Ⓒⓗ 夫 fū fú 4-4□

3460 FU FŪ BU▲ otto so(re)▲

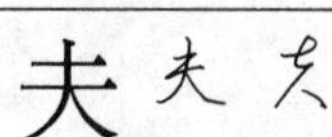

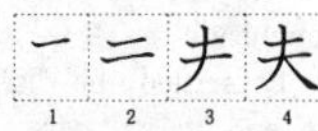

Radical	Strokes
大 37	4-3-1
Grade	**Freq**
Jōyō-3	296
■ 4 - 4 - 4	

▶**HUSBAND** ▶**MAN LABORER**

COMPOUNDS

❶ **husband**
夫婦 *fūfu* husband and wife, married couple
夫妻 *fusai* husband and wife, Mr. and Mrs., married couple
夫人 *fujin* wife, married lady, Mrs.
前夫 *zenpu* former husband, ex-husband

❷ [also suffix] **man laborer, male worker**
農夫 *nōfu* peasant, plowman
人夫 *ninpu* coolie, porter, laborer
煙突掃除夫 *entotsu sōjifu* chimney sweeper [cleaner]

❸ male adult, man
凡夫 *bonpu* (=*bonbu*) ordinary man; *Buddhism* common mortal
大丈夫 *daijōbu* safe, sure, all right

❹ unclassified compounds
工夫 *kufū* device, contrivance; scheme, resources
義太夫 *gidayū gidayu* (a form of ballad drama)

KUN

【otto 夫】 husband
夫の権利 *otto no kenri* marital rights
愛する夫 *aisuru otto* lord of one's bosom

【so(re) 夫れ】
① [archaic] emphatic adverb at the beginning of a sentence
夫れ、秦王虎狼之心有り *Sore, shinnō korō no kokoro ari* The King of Chin had the heart of tigers and wolves
② [also 其れ] *pronoun* it, that
夫れ夫れ *sorezore* respectively, each

SYNONYMS

❶ **husband**
主 master of the house → 1938

❷ **workers and professionals**
匠 CRAFTSMAN → 2990
工 workman → 3381
嬢 (unmarried) female worker → 758
婦 woman worker → 469
手 OCCUPATION SUFFIX → 3456
屋 colloquial occupation suffix → 3098
員 MEMBER (of a staff) → 2269
人 person of certain category → 3368
者 person who → 3211
師 profession suffix → 1326
士 PROFESSION SUFFIX → 3405
客 skilled person → 2250
家 professional → 2273

❸ **man**
男 MAN → 2542
郎 YOUNG MAN → 1289
雄 MALE → 1008
翁 OLD MAN → 2108

USAGE

sore
夫れ
① [archaic] emphatic adverb at the beginning of a sentence
② [also 其れ] *pronoun* it, that
其れ
[also 夫れ] *pronoun* it, that

HOMOPHONES

sore ⇨ 其 2629

COMPOUND FORMATION

❶ 夫人 *fujin*
夫人 'wife, etc.' was originally written 扶人, meaning a person (人) who helps or assists (扶). 扶 was later replaced by 夫 ❶.

❷ 大丈夫 *daijōbu*
大丈夫 'safe, sure, all right' is a man (夫 ❸) of great (大) height (丈). Since such a man symbolizes security and stability, 大丈夫 acquired its current meaning.

4-4□

片 片 片 片

3461 HEN kata- kata

丿 丿' 片' 片 (stroke order 1 2 3 4)

CH 片 piàn piān

Radical	Strokes
片 91	4-4-0
Grade	**Freq**
Jōyō-6	864
■ 4 - 4 - 4	

RADICAL 91

Standard form: 片 *kata* 'board' (版 牒 牌)
Description: used in characters related to boards or things made of boards

▶FRAGMENT ▶ONE OF TWO

COMPOUNDS

❶ⓐ [also suffix] **fragment, (flat thin) piece, slice, chip, flake**
ⓑ counter for fragments or flakes
片雲 *hen'un* scattered clouds
断片 *danpen* fragment, piece
破片 *hahen* fragment, broken piece, scrap
木片 *mokuhen* block, chip [piece] of wood
一片 *ippen* piece, bit, fragment, scrap
雪片 *seppen* snowflake
紙片 *shihen* piece [scrap, bit] of paper
金属片 *kinzokuhen* piece of metal
五片 *gohen* five fragments [pieces]
❷ a bit, a slight amount
片言 *hengen* a word, few words

KUN

【kata- 片-】
[also prefix]
ⓐ one of two, one, single
ⓑ one side, one part, one way
片一方 *kataippō* one side, the other one
片面 *katamen* one side, one face
片手 *katate* one hand
片道 *katamichi* one way
片言 *katakoto* imperfect speech, baby talk
片寄る *katayoru* concentrate on one side [place], go aside
片貿易 *kataboēki* one way [unbalanced] trade

【kata 片】 settlement, conclusion
片が付く *kata ga tsuku* be settled, be disposed of, come to an end
片付ける *katazukeru* put in order, tidy up, clear away; dispose of, deal with, bring to a conclusion; do away with, kill; give one's daughter in marriage

SYNONYMS

❶ⓐ **part**
分 PART → 1972
部 SECTION → 1676
局 LIMITED PART → 3063

[kata-]
ⓐ **one**
隻 ONE OF A PAIR → 2755
一 ONE → 3341
壱 ONE (in legal documents) → 2197
単 SINGLE → 2256
個 INDIVIDUAL → 117
ⓑ **one side**
偏 ONE-SIDED → 133

HOMOPHONES

katayoru ⇨ 偏る 133 片寄る 3461, 2291

NOTE

⇨ see USAGE note at 偏 133

戈 3462 KA hoko

㊥ 戈 gē

Radical	Strokes
戈 62	4-4-0
Grade	Freq
Reference	
■ 4-4-4	

4-4□

RADICAL 62

Standard form: 戈 *kanohoko* 'spear' (戦 成 戒)

Description: used in characters related to weapons or fighting

COMPOUNDS

ⓐ [original meaning] ancient Chinese weapon (similar to a spear or dagger-ax) consisting of a long shaft with a double-edged blade attached crosswise to its end

ⓑ [now usu. 矛 *hoko*] arms

戈 *ka* ancient Chinese weapon

干戈 *kanka* arms, weapons

戈を収める *hoko o osameru* lay down arms, sheathe one's sword

HOMOPHONES

hoko ⇨ 矛 2008 鉾 1720

NOTE

⇨ see USAGE note at 矛 2008

火 3463 KA hi -bi ho-

㊥ 火 huǒ

Radical	Strokes
火 86	4-4-0
Grade	Freq
Jōyō-1	414
■ 4-4-4	

4-4□

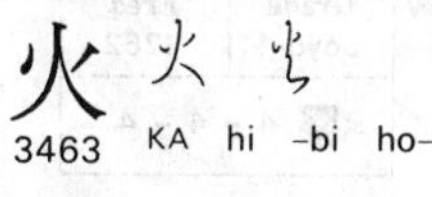

RADICAL 86

Standard form: 火 *hi* 'fire' (災 灯 灰)

Bottom variant: 灬 *rekka* (点 為 無)

Description: used in characters related to firelight, heat or fire qualities

▶FIRE

COMPOUNDS

❶ⓐ [original meaning] **fire**

ⓑ the second of the five elements: fire (⇨ see APPENDIX 7)

ⓒ (figuratively) fire, burning passion

火災 *kasai* fire, conflagration

火事 *kaji* fire

火炎 *kaen* flames, blaze

火力 *karyoku* caloric force; firepower

点火 *tenka* ignition, lighting

出火 *shukka* outbreak of fire

大火 *taika* great fire, conflagration

消火 *shōka* fire fighting

情火 *jōka* fire of passion, passion of love

❷ light

灯火 *tōka* light, lamplight

❸ⓐ firearms

ⓑ (discharge of firearms) fire, firing

火器 *kaki* firearms

地雷火 *jiraika* (land) mine

十字砲火 *jūji hōka* cross fire

❹ **Tuesday**

火曜日 *kayōbi* Tuesday

❺ Mars

火星 *kasei* Mars

❻ urgent, pressing

火急の *kakyū no* urgent, pressing

INDEPENDENT

【ka 火】 Tuesday; the second of the five elements: fire

KUN

【hi 火, -bi -火】

①ⓐ [also prefix and suffix] fire, flame

ⓑ firelight

火元 *himoto* origin [source] of a fire

火加減 *hikagen* condition of the fire

灯し火(=灯) *tomoshibi* light, lamp, flame

花火 *hanabi* fireworks, firecrackers

口火 *kuchibi* fuse; pilot burner; cause (of a war)

不審火 *fushinbi* suspected case of arson

② heat

火を通す *hi o tōsu* heat, cook

【ho- 火-】 [also 灯-] fire

火影(=灯影) *hokage* shadows from firelight

火照る *hoteru* feel hot, flush

SPECIAL READINGS

火傷▲ *yakedo* burn

SYNONYMS

❶ⓐ **fire**

炎 FLAME → 2420

❸ⓐ **weapons for shooting**

銃 GUN (portable firearm) → 1723

砲 HEAVY GUN → 1151
弓 BOW → 3383
❹ **days of the week**
月 Monday → 2956
水 Wednesday → 10
木 Thursday → 3450
金 Friday → 2057
土 Saturday → 3403
日 Sunday → 3027

USAGE

❶ **hi**
火
①ⓐ [also prefix and suffix] fire, flame
ⓑ firelight
② heat
灯
(source of illumination) light, lantern, lamp
❷ **ho-**
火-
[also 灯-] fire
灯-
[also 火-] fire

HOMOPHONES

hi ⇨ 灯 825
ho- ⇨ 灯 825

4-4□

3464 KEN inu inu-

一 ナ 大 犬
1 2 3 4

Ⓒⓗ 犬 quǎn

Radical	Strokes
犬 94	4-4-0
Grade	**Freq**
Jōyō-1	1262
■ 4 - 4 - 4	

RADICAL 94

Standard form: 犬 *inu* 'dog' (状 献 獣)
Left variant: 犭 *kemonohen* (独 猫 獲)
Description: used in characters related to dogs, related animals or qualities

▶**DOG**

COMPOUNDS

ⓐ [also suffix] [original meaning] **dog, hound**
ⓑ [humble] as worthless as a dog
忠犬 *chūken* faithful dog
番犬 *banken* watchdog
猟犬 *ryōken* hound, hunting dog
野犬 *yaken* stray dog
コリー犬 *korīken* collie
盲導犬 *mōdōken* guide dog, Seeing Eye dog
犬儒学派 *kenjugakuha* the Cynics
犬馬の労 *kenba no rō* rendering what little service one can

KUN

【inu 犬】
[formerly also 狗]
① dog, hound, puppy
飼い犬 *kaiinu* house dog
小犬 *koinu* little dog, puppy
② spy
警察の犬 *keisatsu no inu* police spy
【inu- 犬-】
① [prefix] pseudo
犬黄楊 *inutsuge* Japanese holly
② worthless, shameless
犬侍 *inuzamurai* shameless [depraved] samurai
犬死にする *inujini suru* die in vain

SYNONYMS

ⓐ **domesticated mammals**
猫 CAT → 535
牛 CATTLE → 3452
馬 HORSE → 3296
豚 PIG → 976
羊 SHEEP → 2183

USAGE

inu
犬
[formerly also 狗]
① dog, hound, puppy
② spy
狗
[now usu. 犬]
① dog (esp. of small variety)
② spy
戌
eleventh sign of the Oriental zodiac: the Dog

HOMOPHONES

inu ⇨ 狗 345 戌 3535

匁 匁 匁 ㊥ none (国字)

3465 monme

丿 勹 勺 匁
1 2 3 4

Radical	Strokes
勹 20	4-2-2
Grade	**Freq**
Jōyō	1925
■ 4 - 4 - 4	

4-4□

▶MOMME

KUN

【monme 匁】

ⓐ momme: unit of weight equiv. to 3.75 g or 1/1000 of a *kan* (貫), now used esp. for weighing pearls

ⓑ *monme*: former monetary unit equiv. to 1/60 of a *ryo* (両)

一匁 *ichimonme* 1 momme

SYNONYMS

【monme】

ⓐ **weight units**

斤 CATTY (600 g) → 2949

貫 *kan* (3.75 kg) → 2460

屯 ton → 3457

 内 内 内 ㊥ 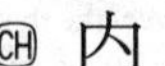 nèi

3466 NAI DAI uchi

Radical	Strokes
冂 13△	4-2-2
Grade	**Freq**
Jōyō-2	56
■ 4 - 4 - 4	

4-4□

▶INSIDE

COMPOUNDS

❶ⓐ [also prefix] [original meaning] (inner side or part) **inside, interior, within, internal, inner**

ⓑ [also suffix] (inside a given range) **within, within the scope of, in**

ⓒ place inside (the body), take in

内容 *naiyō* contents, import, substance

内部 *naibu* interior, inner parts

内外 *naigai* inside and outside; approximately

内科 *naika* (department of) internal medicine

内出血 *naishukketsu* internal hemorrhage

内分泌 *naibunpitsu* internal secretion

案内する *annai suru* guide, show; inform, notify

国内の *kokunai no* domestic, internal, inland

境内 *keidai* grounds [premises] (of a shrine or temple)

以内 *inai* within, less than

権限内に *kengennai ni* within the scope of authority

都内で *tonai de* in Tokyo Metropolis

内服する *naifuku suru* take (a medicine) internally

❷ (pertaining to the affairs of a country) **internal, domestic**

内政 *naisei* domestic administration, internal affairs

内戦 *naisen* civil war

内紛 *naifun* internal trouble [strife]; storm in a teacup

内務 *naimu* internal [domestic] affairs

内需 *naiju* domestic demand

❸ **not public, private, secret, unofficial, informal**

内内の *nainai no* private, informal; secret, confidential

内定 *naitei* informal decision

内申 *naishin* unofficial report

内規 *naiki* private rules [regulations], bylaws

内報 *naihō* secret report [information]

内密の *naimitsu no* secret, confidential, private

❹ (person inside the house) **wife**

内助 *naijo* wife's help

内儀 *naigi* other's wife

家内 *kanai* family, household; wife

❺ Imperial Palace, Imperial Court; center of politics

内裏 *dairi* Imperial Palace

内閣 *naikaku* cabinet

参内 *sandai* attendance at the Imperial Court

❻ pertaining to Buddhism

内典 *naiten* Buddhist literature [sutras]

KUN

【uchi 内】

① [sometimes also 中] [also prefix and suffix] inside, interior

内側 *uchigawa* inside, interior

内幕 *uchimaku* inside facts, inner workings; [original meaning] inner curtain

内訳 *uchiwake* items (of an account), details, breakdown
内ポケット *uchipoketto* inside pocket
仲間内の *nakamauchi no* private, informal, among one's people [group]
② [sometimes also 中] within (a given period), in the course of, while, during
一週間の内に *isshūkan no uchi ni* within a week
若い内 *wakai uchi* while young
③ [sometimes also 中] among, between
両者の内 *ryōsha no uchi* between the two
④ [also 家]
ⓐ house, one's home
ⓑ one's family, household
内を建てる *uchi o tateru* build one's house
内の人 *uchi no hito* my husband; one's family
内中 *uchijū* whole family; all over the house
内弟子 *uchideshi* pupil boarding in his master's home, apprentice
⑤ (group or organization one belongs to) we; ourselves; our group, our company
内の会社 *uchi no kaisha* our company
内内で *uchiuchi de* among ourselves
身内 *miuchi* relations, relative

SYNONYMS

❶ⓐ & ❶ⓑ inside
裏 inside → 2138
奥 INNER PART → 2824
中 IN → 3451

❷ national
国 national → 3087

❸ secret and private
私 PRIVATE → 1115
密 SECRET → 2292
秘 SECRET → 1159
暗 in the dark → 1010
隠 hidden from view → 713

❹ wives
妻 WIFE → 2558
奥 wife → 2824
室 wife (esp. of persons of rank) → 2254
嫡 legitimate wife → 680
婦 married woman → 469
嫁 BRIDE → 635
寡 widow → 2344

【uchi】
② during
中 IN (the course of) → 3451
間 for an interval of → 3323

USAGE

uchi
内
① [sometimes also 中] [also prefix and suffix] inside, interior
② [sometimes also 中] within (a given period), in the course of, while, during
③ [sometimes also 中] among, between
④ [also 家]
ⓐ house, one's home
ⓑ one's family, household
⑤ (group or organization one belongs to) we; ourselves; our group, our company

中
[usu. 内]
① inside, interior
② within (a given period), in the course of, while, during
③ among, between

家
[also 内]
ⓐ house, one's home
ⓑ one's family, household

HOMOPHONES

uchi ⇨ 中 3451 家 2273

NOTE

⇨ see COMPOUND FORMATION for 案内 *annai* ⇨ 案 2270

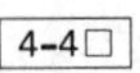
4-4□

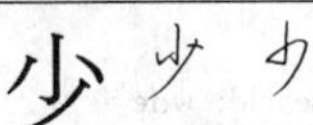
3467 SHŌ suku(nai) suko(shi)

Ⓒⓗ 少 shǎo shào

Radical	Strokes
小 42	4-3-1
Grade	**Freq**
Jōyō-2	200
■ 4-4-4	

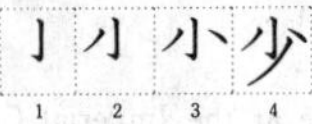

▶LITTLE

COMPOUNDS

❶ⓐ (of small quantity or number) **little, few, small**
ⓑ [original meaning] reduce in quantity
少少 *shōshō* a little, a few, slightly
少数 *shōsū* small number, minority
少量 *shōryō* small quantity [amount]
少額 *shōgaku* small sum
多少 *tashō* a little, somewhat
軽少の *keishō no* little, slight, trifling
僅少差 *kinshōsa* narrow [slim] margin
減少 *genshō* decrease, reduction, lessening

❷ⓐ young
ⓑ the young, youth
少年 *shōnen* boy

少女 *shōjo* girl
年少の *nenshō no* young, juvenile
幼少 *yōshō* infancy, childhood
❸ performing a secondary function
少尉 *shōi* second lieutenant

KUN

【suku(nai) 少ない】 (of small quantity or number) little, few, limited, insufficient
少なからぬ *sukunakaranu* not a little [few]
少なくとも *sukunakutomo* at least
少ない時間 *sukunai jikan* limited time

【suko(shi) 少し】 (of small quantity) a little, a few, some; a bit, somewhat; a little while; short distance
少しも *sukoshi mo* (not) at all
少しづつ *sukoshizutsu* little by little

SYNONYMS

❶ⓐ few
寡 FEW → 2344
乏 SCANTY → 1933
薄 meager → 2370
微 SLIGHT → 639
寸 A BIT OF → 2935

❷ⓐ young
若 YOUNG → 2241
弱 young → 1167
青 youthful → 2430
幼 VERY YOUNG → 191
稚 CHILDISH → 1206

爿

3468

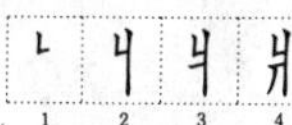

Radical	Strokes
爿 90	4-4-0
Grade	**Freq**
Radical	
■ 4 - 4 - 4	

4-4□

RADICAL 90

Standard form: 爿 *shōhen* 'stand' (牆 牀)
Description: used in characters related to stands, frames or enclosures

---

礻

3469

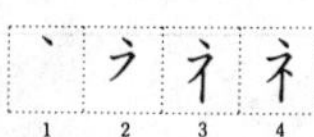

Radical	Strokes
礻 113	4-4-0
Grade	**Freq**
Radical	
■ 4 - 4 - 4	

4-4□

RADICAL 113

nehen or *shimesuhen*, variant of 示 *shimesu* 'deity'
⇨ see 示 1936 for radical description

内

3470

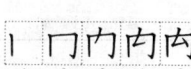

丨 冂 内 内 内
1 2 3 4 5

Radical	Strokes
内 114	5-5-0
Grade	**Freq**
Radical	
■ 4 - 4 - 4	

4-4□

RADICAL 114

Standard form: 内 *gūnoashi* 'track' (禹 禺 禽)
Description: used for character classification

NOTE

★内 has a traditional stroke-count of 5.

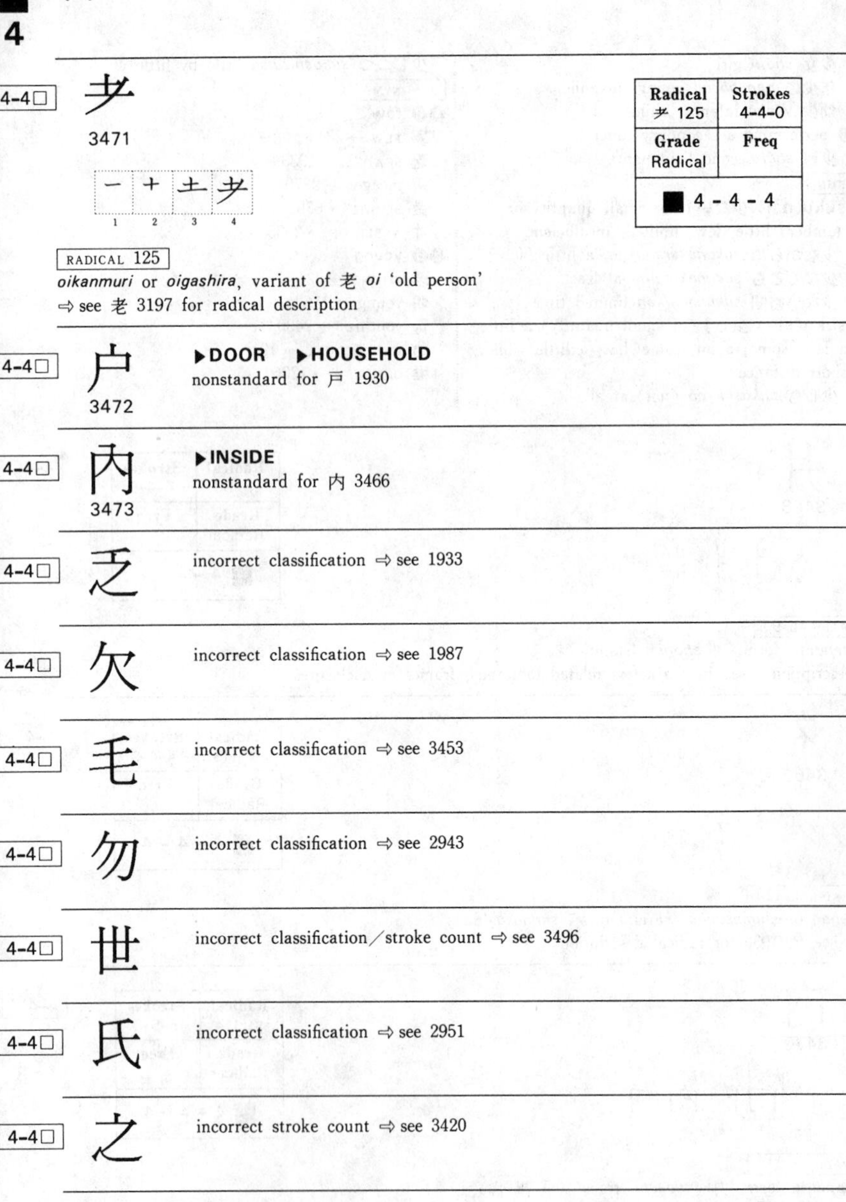

4-4□ 耂 3471

一	十	土	耂
1	2	3	4

Radical	Strokes
耂 125	4-4-0
Grade	**Freq**
Radical	

■ 4 - 4 - 4

RADICAL 125

oikanmuri or *oigashira*, variant of 老 *oi* 'old person'

⇨ see 老 3197 for radical description

4-4□ 户 3472

▶**DOOR** ▶**HOUSEHOLD**

nonstandard for 戸 1930

4-4□ 內 3473

▶**INSIDE**

nonstandard for 内 3466

4-4□ 乏 incorrect classification ⇨ see 1933

4-4□ 欠 incorrect classification ⇨ see 1987

4-4□ 毛 incorrect classification ⇨ see 3453

4-4□ 勿 incorrect classification ⇨ see 2943

4-4□ 世 incorrect classification／stroke count ⇨ see 3496

4-4□ 氏 incorrect classification ⇨ see 2951

4-4□ 之 incorrect stroke count ⇨ see 3420

4-4□ 心 incorrect classification ⇨ see 11

4-4□ 太 incorrect classification ⇨ see 2152

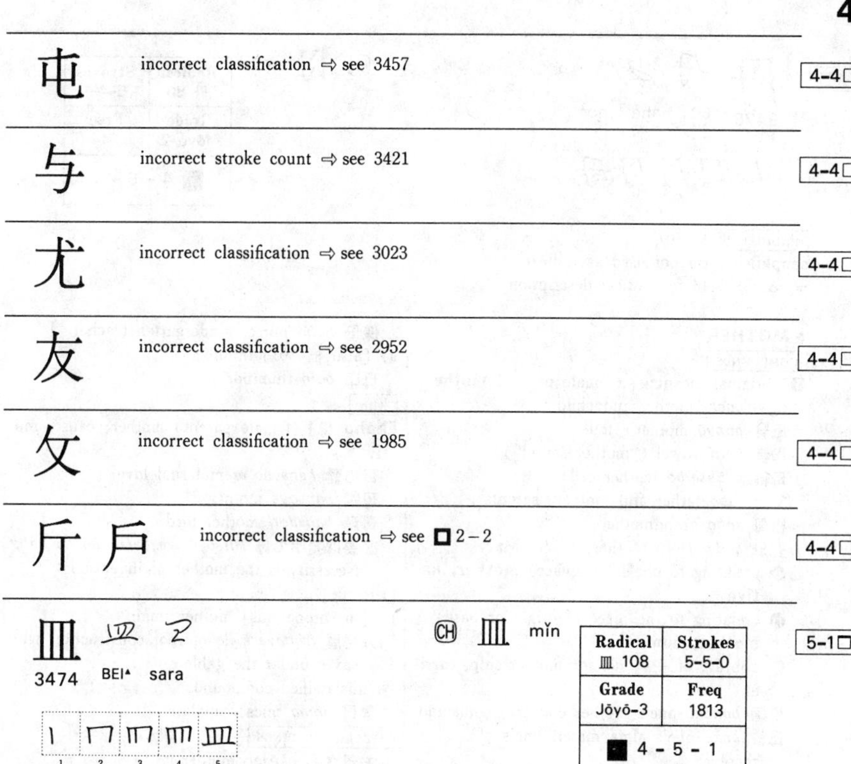

屯 incorrect classification ⇨ see 3457 4-4□

与 incorrect stroke count ⇨ see 3421 4-4□

尤 incorrect classification ⇨ see 3023 4-4□

友 incorrect classification ⇨ see 2952 4-4□

攵 incorrect classification ⇨ see 1985 4-4□

斤 戶 incorrect classification ⇨ see □ 2-2 4-4□

皿 5-1□

3474 BEI▲ sara

Ⓒⓗ 皿 mǐn

Radical	Strokes
皿 108	5-5-0
Grade	**Freq**
Jōyō-3	1813
■ 4-5-1	

RADICAL 108

Standard form: 皿 *sara* 'dish' (監 盟 盛)

Description: used in characters related to dishes, vessels or their uses

▶PLATE

KUN

【sara 皿】

① [also suffix] [original meaning] (shallow container for holding food) plate, dish

皿洗い *saraarai* dishwashing; dishwasher

皿回し *saramawashi* dish-spinning

スープ皿 *sūpuzara* soup plate

受け皿 *ukezara* saucer

蒸発皿 *jōhatsuzara* evaporating dish

製氷皿 *seihyōzara* ice-making pan

②ⓐ (food served in a plate) plate (of vegetables), dish, helping, course

ⓑ counter for plates or helpings

最初の皿 *saisho no sara* first course

野菜一皿 *yasai hitosara* a dish of vegetables

③ various platelike objects, as:

ⓐ scale, bowl (of scales)

ⓑ kneecap, patella

ⓒ *slang* record, disk

皿秤 *sarabakari* balance

膝の皿 *hiza no sara* kneecap

お皿 *osara* record, disk

SYNONYMS

【sara】

Ⓘ **vessels and receptacles**

盤 dish → 2851

盆 TRAY → 2079

杯 CUP → 857

鉢 BOWL → 1708

鍋 POT → 1752

5-1□ 母 母 め

3475 BO haha mo▲

1 2 3 4 5

CH 母 mǔ

Radical	Strokes
毋 80	5-4-1
Grade	Freq
Jōyō-2	514
■ 4 - 5 - 1	

RADICAL 80
simplified form not used as radical
⇨ see 毋 3446 for radical description

▶**MOTHER**

COMPOUNDS

❶ [original meaning] (female parent) **mother**
母子 *boshi* mother and child
母乳 *bonyū* mother's milk
母音 *boin* vowel ("mother sound")
母細胞 *bosaibō* mother cell
父母 *fubo* father and mother, parents
祖母 *sobo* grandmother
聖母 *seibo* Holy Mother, Virgin Mary

❷ⓐ (relating to one's birthplace) **mother, native**
ⓑ (relating to the place of origin or base) **mother, home**
ⓒ abbrev. of 母艦 *bokan*: mother ship, carrier
母国 *bokoku* one's mother country, homeland
母校 *bokō* one's alma mater, one's old school
母港 *bokō* home port
母船 *bosen* mother ship
空母 *kūbo* (airplane) carrier, flattop

❸ base material
母材 *bozai welding* base metal
母型 *bokei* matrix
酵母 *kōbo* yeast; ferment
分母 *bunbo* denominator

❹ [formerly 姆 277] wet nurse, amah
保母 *hobo* nurse, kindergarten teacher

❺ [also 拇 301] thumb
母印 *boin* thumbprint

KUN

【haha 母】 (female parent) mother; cause, motive
母の愛 *haha no ai* maternal love
母親 *hahaoya* mother
母鳥 *hahadori* mother bird
必要は発明の母 *Hitsuyō wa hatsumei no haha* Necessity is the mother of invention

【mo 母】
① [in compounds] mother, main
入母屋 *irimoya* style of roof construction with eaves under the gable
② unclassified compounds
雲母 *unmo* mica, isinglass

SPECIAL READINGS

お母さん *okāsan* mother
伯母 *oba* aunt (older than one's parent)
叔母 *oba* aunt (younger than one's parent)
お祖母さん▲ *obāsan* grandmother
乳母 *uba* wet nurse
母屋(=母家) *omoya* main house [wing]

SYNONYMS

❶ **parents**
父 FATHER → 1973
親 PARENT → 1799

5-1□ 瓦

3476 GA kawara guramu

1 2 3 4 5

CH 瓦 wǎ wà

Radical	Strokes
瓦 98	5-5-0
Grade	Freq
Reference	
■ 4 - 5 - 1	

RADICAL 98
Standard form: 瓦 *kawara* 'tile' (瓶 甓)
Description: used in characters related to earthenware, ceramics or tiles

COMPOUNDS

❶ⓐ [original meaning] tile, roof tile
ⓑ as fragile as a tile, easily broken
瓦礫 *gareki* tiles and pebbles; trash
煉瓦 *renga* brick
瓦版 *kawaraban* tile block print (newspaper in Tokugawa period)
瓦煎餅 *kawarasenbei* tile-shaped rice-cracker

鬼瓦 *onigawara* tile with the figure of a devil
瓦解する *gakai suru* collapse, break up, fall to pieces
❷ used phonetically for *ga*
瓦斯 *gasu* gas
❸ gram
五十瓦 *gojūguramu* 50 g

玉 玉 玉

3477 GYOKU tama tama- -dama

一 丅 干 王 玉
1 2 3 4 5

Ⓒ 玉 yù

Radical	Strokes
玉 96	5-5-0
Grade	**Freq**
Jōyō-1	618
■ 4 - 5 - 1	

5-1□

RADICAL 96
Standard form: 玉 *tama* 'gem' (璽 琴)
Left variant: 王 *tamahen* (現 理 球)
Description: used in characters related to gems, jewels or treasures

▶GEM

COMPOUNDS

❶ⓐ gem, jewel(ry), precious stone
ⓑ [original meaning] jade
玉石混淆(＝玉石混交) *gyokuseki-konkō* mixture of good and bad, jumble of wheat and tares
宝玉 *hōgyoku* jewel, gem, precious stone
珠玉 *shugyoku* jewel, gem
硬玉 *kōgyoku* jadeite
玉杯 *gyokuhai* jade cup
❷ as beautiful as a jewel, exquisite
玉露 *gyokuro* refined green tea
玉砕 *gyokusai* death for honor
❸ [honorific]
ⓐ imperial
ⓑ your
玉音 *gyokuon* Emperor's voice
玉顔 *gyokugan* imperial face
玉稿 *gyokkō* your manuscript
❹ engagements, stock bought or sold
玉整理 *gyokuseiri* liquidation of speculative accounts
売り玉 *urigyoku* short account, short interest
❺ geisha
玉代 *gyokudai* time charge for a geisha
❻ name of chess piece in shogi (Japanese chess): *gyoku*, white king
自玉 *jigyoku* one's own king

INDEPENDENT

【gyoku 玉】 jewel, gem; jade; geisha, time charge for a geisha; *gyoku* (⇨ ❻); egg, egg roll

KUN

【tama 玉】
①ⓐ [formerly also 珠] gem, jewel, precious stone, pearl; bead
ⓑ something as beautiful or precious as a jewel
玉に疵(＝玉に瑕) *tama ni kizu* flaw in the crystal, fly in the ointment
勾玉(＝曲玉) *magatama* comma-shaped bead
掌中の玉 *shōchū no tama* apple of one's eye
玉の輿 *tama no koshi* marriage to a man of wealth
② various spherical objects, as:
ⓐ ball, globe; lump of noodles; egg; lens
ⓑ *slang* testicles
玉突き *tamatsuki* billiards; serial collisions (of cars)
玉子(＝卵) *tamago* egg
目玉 *medama* eyeball; loss leader (of merchandise)
鉄砲玉(＝鉄砲弾) *teppōdama* gunshot, bullet; lost [truant] messenger; bull's-eye
金玉 *kintama* testicles, balls
③ *slang*
ⓐ guy, chap
ⓑ pretty girl, doll
親玉 *oyadama* big shot, kingpin
表六玉(＝兵六玉) *hyōrokudama* nincompoop, simpleton
大変な玉だ *Taihen na tama da* He's a caution!
上玉 *jōdama* pretty girl

【tama- 玉-】
[also prefix]
①ⓐ beautiful, exquisite
ⓑ sacred, precious
玉手箱 *tamatebako* Pandora's box; treasured casket
玉垣 *tamagaki* shrine fence
② round, spherical
玉葱 *tamanegi* onion
玉砂利 *tamajari* gravel

【-dama -玉】
① coin suffix
十円玉 *jūendama* 10-yen coin
五セント玉 *gosentodama* nickel

② [also suffix] round or spherical object
シャボン玉 *shabondama* soap bubble
癇癪玉 *kanshakudama* firecracker; temper, fit of rage

SYNONYMS

❶ⓐ precious stones
珠 PEARL → 947
瑛 TRANSPARENT GEM → 999
瑠 LAPIS LAZULI → 1060
璃 GLASSY SUBSTANCE → 1059
晶 CRYSTAL → 2474

【tama】
② spherical object
球 BALL → 969
丸 round body → 3417

【-dama】
① money
札 bill → 817
貨 MONEY (legal tender), coin → 2465
銭 MONEY → 1725
金 MONEY → 2057
幣 CURRENCY → 2885
銀 SILVER → 1722
財 finance → 1457
資 RESOURCES → 2695

USAGE

tama

玉
①ⓐ [formerly also 珠] gem, jewel, precious stone, pearl; bead
ⓑ something as beautiful or precious as a jewel
② various spherical objects, as:
ⓐ ball, globe; lump of noodles; egg; lens
ⓑ *slang* testicles
③ *slang*
ⓐ guy, chap
ⓑ pretty girl, doll

珠
[now usu. 玉] gem, jewel, precious stone, pearl; bead

球
ⓐ ball (in a sports game)
ⓑ light bulb

弾
bullet, shot, shell

HOMOPHONES

tama ⇨ 珠 947 球 969 弾 572
tamago ⇨ 卵 849 玉子 3477, 3390

NOTE

⇨ see also USAGE note at 卵 849

5-1□

平 平 平 ㄜ (CH) 平 píng

3478 HEI BYŌ HYŌ▲ tai(ra) -daira hira hira-

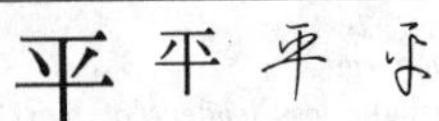

1 2 3 4 5

Radical	Strokes
干 51	5-3-2
Grade	**Freq**
Jōyō-3	160
■ 4 - 5 - 1	

▶FLAT ▶CALM

COMPOUNDS

❶ⓐ [original meaning] **flat, level, even**
ⓑ flat on the ground, low
平方 *heihō* square (measure); square (of a number)
平野 *heiya* plain(s), open field
平面 *heimen* level surface, plain
平坦な *heitan na* flat, level, even
水平の *suihei no* horizontal, level, even
平伏する *heifuku suru* prostrate oneself (before), kiss the ground

❷ equal, impartial, fair
平均 *heikin* average, (arithmetical) mean; equilibrium, balance
平行 *heikō* parallelism, parallel; going side by side; occurring together
平等 *byōdō* equality, impartiality
公平 *kōhei* impartiality, fairness

❸ common, ordinary, average
平日 *heijitsu* weekday
平凡な *heibon na* common, ordinary, commonplace, mediocre
平年 *heinen* normal [average] year, common year
平常の *heijō no* ordinary, normal, usual

❹ simple, plain
平易 *heii* plainness, simplicity, easiness
平明な *heimei na* clear, simple

❺ⓐ calm, peaceful, quiet
ⓑ bring peace to, pacify
平和 *heiwa* peace, harmony
平気 *heiki* nonchalance, unconcern; composure
平穏 *heion* calmness, quiet, tranquility
平静な *heisei na* calm, serene
平安 *heian* calmness, peace, quietness, tranquility; Heian period
和平 *wahei* peace
太平(=泰平) *taihei* tranquility, perfect peace
平定 *heitei* suppression, subjugation, subdual

❻ⓐ abbrev. of 平方 *heihō*: square (measure)

ⓑ abbrev. of 平方根 *heihōkon*: square root
平米 *heibei* sq. meter
開平 *kaihei* square root extraction
❼ abbrev. of 平家 *heike*: Taira Family
平語 *heigo* The Tale of the Taira Clan
源平 *genpei* Genji and Heike clans; two opposing sides
❽ first tone in old Chinese phonetics
平声 *hyōshō* first tone in old Chinese phonetics
平上去入 *hyōjōkyonyū* the four tones in old Chinese phonetics
❾ unclassified compounds
助平 *sukebei* lewd person; Peeping Tom

KUN

【tai(ra) 平ら】
taira na 平らな flat, even, level, smooth; calm, peaceful, tranquil
平らな道 *taira na michi* level road
心の平らな *kokoro no taira na* even-tempered
平らげる *tairageru* eat up, finish, consume; quell, subdue, put down

【-daira -平】 suffix after names of flats or plains
日本平 *nihondaira* Nihon Plain

【hira 平】 common [ordinary] member(ship) of an organization; the broad [flat] (of a hand); shallow bowl; breaststroke
平の社員 *hira no shain* mere clerk
手の平(=掌) *tenohira* palm of the hand
平泳ぎ *hiraoyogi* breast stroke

【hira- 平-】
[also prefix]
① flat, not elevated
平たい *hiratai* flat, even, level; simple, plain
平屋 *hiraya* one-story house
平地 *hirachi* flat [level] ground
平仮名 *hiragana* hiragana, cursive kana characters
平屋根 *hirayane* flat roof
② common, ordinary, plain
平教員 *hirakyōin* common teacher
平幕 *hiramaku* plain sumo wrestler of senior grade
平党員 *hiratōin* rank-and-file party member

SYNONYMS

❷ **impartial**
公 impartial → 1974
❷ **same and uniform**
等 EQUAL → 2682
均 EVEN → 235
斉 UNIFORM → 2054
同 SAME → 2987
一 same → 3341
❸ **ordinary**
普 common → 2323
只- ORDINARY → 2155
並 ordinary → 2246
常 NORMAL → 2590
庸 MEDIOCRE → 3128
凡 COMMONPLACE → 2938
❺ⓐ **calm and peaceful**
穏 CALM → 1235
静 QUIET → 1728
泰 TRANQUIL → 2583
安 PEACEFUL → 2171
康 peaceful → 3124
寧 peaceful → 2345
❻ⓐ **mathematical power**
方 SQUARE → 1963
乗 power → 3576

USAGE

heikō
平行
① parallelism, parallel
②ⓐ going side by side
ⓑ occurring together
並行
ⓐ going side by side
ⓑ occurring together

HOMOPHONES

tenohira ⇨ 掌 2602 手の平 3456, 3478

NOTE

⇨ see also USAGE note at 掌 2602

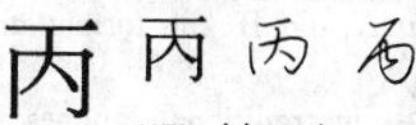
3479 HEI hinoe▲

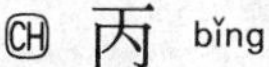

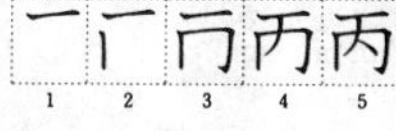

Radical	Strokes
一 1	5-1-4
Grade	**Freq**
Jōyō	1898
■ 4 - 5 - 1	

5-1□

▶**THIRD**

COMPOUNDS

❶ **the third, C; third class, grade C**
ⓑ third calendar sign (⇨ see APPENDIX 7)
丙種 *heishu* third class, class C
甲乙丙 *kōotsuhei* 1st, 2nd and 3rd; A, B and C
丙午 *heigo* 43rd of the sexagenary cycle

INDEPENDENT

【hei 丙】 the third, C; third calendar sign

KUN

【hinoe 丙】third calendar sign
丙午 *hinoeuma* 43rd of the sexagenary cycle

NOTE

⇨ see 甲 3481 FIRST, 乙 3339 SECOND and 丁 3348 fourth

5-1□

疋

3480 HIKI

(CH) 匹 pǐ

Radical	Strokes
疋 103	5-5-0
Grade	Freq
Reference	
■ 4 - 5 - 1	

RADICAL 103

Standard form: 疋 *hiki* 'animal counter' (疑)
Left variant: 𤴔 *hikihen* (疎 疏)
Description: used for character classification

COMPOUNDS

❶ *hiki*:
ⓐ [also 匹 2962] unit of measure for rolls of cloth equiv. to 2 *tan* (反)
ⓑ former monetary unit equiv. to 10 (later 25) *mon* (文)
疋 *hiki hiki* (⇨ ❶)

❷ [now usu. 匹 2962] counter for animals
猫三疋 *neko sanbiki* three cats

HOMOPHONES

hiki ⇨ 匹 2962

NOTE

⇨ see USAGE note at 匹 2962

5-1□

甲

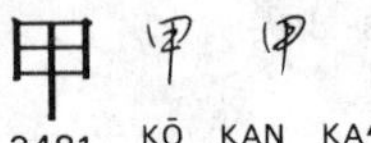

3481 KŌ KAN KA▲ kinoe▲

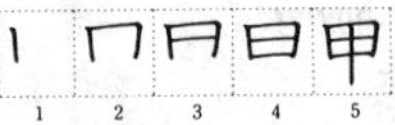

(CH) 甲 jiǎ

Radical	Strokes
田 102	5-5-0
Grade	Freq
Jōyō	1045
■ 4 - 5 - 1	

▶SHELL ▶FIRST

COMPOUNDS

❶ **shell (of animals); carapace, tortoise carapace**
甲殻 *kōkaku* carapace, shell, crust
甲羅 *kōra* shell, carapace
甲骨文 *kōkotsubun* ancient inscriptions of Chinese characters on oracle bones and carapaces
甲虫 *kōchū* beetle
甲板 *kanpan* (=*kōhan*) deck
亀甲 *kikkō* carapace of a turtle, tortoiseshell

❷ armor; helmet
甲鉄 *kōtetsu* armor plate
甲冑 *katchū* armor and helmet
装甲部隊 *sōkō-butai* armored corps

❸ⓐ **the first, A; first class, grade A; the former**
ⓑ first calendar sign (⇨ see APPENDIX 7)
甲乙 *kōotsu* first and second, former and latter
甲種 *kōshu* grade A, first grade
甲子 *kasshi* first of the sexagenary cycle

❹ high tone, treble
甲高い *kandakai* high-pitched, shrill

❺ back of the hand, instep
甲高な *kōdaka na* high-backed, high in the instep

❻ used phonetically for *ka*
甲斐が有る *kai ga aru* fruitful, effective, worth, worthwhile

❼ abbrev. of 甲斐 *kai*, old name for Yamanashi Prefecture
甲州 *kōshū* old name for Yamanashi Prefecture

INDEPENDENT

【kō 甲】shell, tortoiseshell; armor; back of the hand, instep; the first, A; the former; first calendar sign
手の甲 *te no kō* back of the hand
甲と乙 *kō to otsu* A and B, the former and the latter

【kan 甲】high tone (in traditional Japanese music)

KUN

【kinoe 甲】first calendar sign

SYNONYMS

❶ **shells**
殻 SHELL (of any kind) → 1490
貝 seashell → 2543

❷ **protective coverings**
盾 SHIELD → 3006
面 mask → 2087

❸ⓐ **first**

初 FIRST → 1116

NOTE
⇨ see 乙 3339 SECOND, 丙 3479 THIRD and 丁 3348 fourth

3482 Ō kubo(mu)▲ boko*

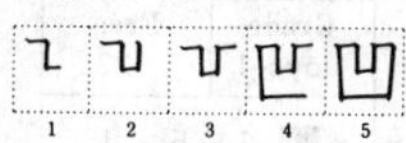

CH 凹 āo

Radical 凵 17	Strokes 5-2-3
Grade Jōyō	Freq 1954
■ 4 - 5 - 1	

5-1□

▶CONCAVE

COMPOUNDS

● [original meaning] **concave, hollow, indented**
凹面鏡 *ōmenkyō* concave mirror
凹地 *ōchi* hollow, pit
凹凸 *ōtotsu* unevenness, irregularities
凹レンズ *ōrenzu* concave lens
凹版印刷 *ōhan insatsu* intaglio printing
凸凹紙 *totsuōshi* embossed paper

KUN

【kubo(mu) 凹む】 [in compounds] (of things) become hollow, become depressed
凹目 *kubome* sunken [deep-set] eyes

【boko 凹】 [in compounds] concavity
凸凹 *dekoboko* unevenness, roughness; imbalance
穴凹 *anaboko* hole, hollow

SYNONYMS

● **bowed**
凸 CONVEX → 3486

【boko】
○ **holes and cavities**
溝 CHANNEL → 659
洞 CAVE → 380
堀 DITCH → 467
坑 PIT → 236
口 MOUTH → 3382
孔 OPEN HOLE → 179
穴 HOLE → 2159

USAGE

kubomu
凹む
[in compounds] (of things) become hollow, become depressed
窪む
(of the ground) become hollow, become depressed, cave in

HOMOPHONES

kubomu ⇨ 窪 2348

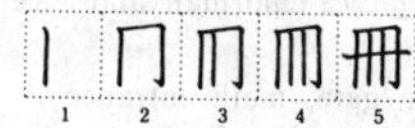

3483 SATSU SAKU

(stroke order 1 2 3 4 5)

CH 册 cè

Radical 冂 13	Strokes 5-2-3
Grade Jōyō-6	Freq 1481
■ 4 - 5 - 1	

5-1□

▶COUNTER FOR BOOKS

COMPOUNDS

❶ⓐ **counter for books, volumes or copies**
ⓑ **bound book, volume, copy**
冊数 *sassū* number of books
四冊 *yonsatsu* four volumes
小冊子 *shōsasshi* booklet, pamphlet
分冊 *bunsatsu* separate volume
大冊 *taisatsu* great volume, bulky book
各冊 *kakusatsu* each book [volume, copy]
別冊 *bessatsu* separate volume, extra issue

❷ ancient form of book consisting of bamboo strips strung together
短冊 *tanzaku* strip of fancy paper for writing tanka poetry

❸ formal writ conferring honors or stipends
冊立 *sakuritsu* installation, investiture (of the Crown Prince)

INDEPENDENT

【satsu 冊】 bound book, volume

SYNONYMS

❶ⓐ **counters for books**
巻 counter for volumes → 2645
部 counter for copies → 1676

ⓑ **books**
本 BOOK → 3502

書 BOOK → 2658
籍 books → 2731
著 literary work → 2300
巻 VOLUME → 2645
編 volume → 1387
鑑 REFERENCE VOLUME → 1773
典 STANDARD WORK → 2627
経 religious classic → 1331

5-1□ 正 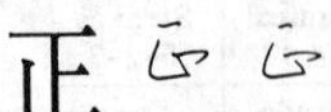 Ⓒⓗ 正 zhèng zhēng

3484 SEI SHŌ tada(shii) tada(su) masa masa(ni)

Radical	Strokes
止 77	5-4-1
Grade	**Freq**
Jōyō-1	122
■ 4 - 5 - 1	

一 丅 下 亚 正
1 2 3 4 5

▶**RIGHT**

COMPOUNDS

❶ⓐ (not mistaken) **right, correct, proper**
ⓑ (set right) **right, correct, rectify**
正解 *seikai* right answer, correct solution
正味の *shōmi no* net, full, clear
適正な *tekisei na* proper, appropriate, reasonable, right
改正する *kaisei suru* revise, amend
訂正する *teisei suru* correct, amend, revise
修正する *shūsei suru* amend, revise, correct; retouch
是正する *zesei suru* correct
校正 *kōsei* proofreading
綱紀粛正 *kōki shukusei* enforcing discipline (among government officials)

❷ⓐ [also prefix] (in a precise manner) **right, accurate, exact(ly), just, due (north)**
ⓑ net
正確な *seikaku na* accurate, precise, exact
正午 *shōgo* noon, noontime
正北 *seihoku* due north
正反対 *seihantai* exactly opposite
正六時に *shōrokuji ni* at six sharp
正札 *shōfuda* net price

❸ (morally correct) **right, righteous, just, upright**
正邪 *seija* right and wrong
正義 *seigi* justice, righteousness
正当な *seitō na* just, right, due; legal
正論 *seiron* sound argument
正直な *shōjiki na* honest, upright, frank
公正な *kōsei na* just, fair, impartial
不正 *fusei* injustice, wrong, illegality

❹ right side, front
正面 *shōmen* front, frontage, facade
正攻法 *seikōhō* regular tactics for attack
正視する *seishi suru* look in the face; confront

❺ⓐ [also prefix] **regular, full, normal, proper, formal, orthodox; legitimate, legal**
ⓑ genuine, authentic, pure
正規の *seiki no* regular, formal, legitimate
正式の *seishiki no* formal, regular
正統の *seitō no* legitimate, orthodox, traditional
正常な *seijō na* normal, regular
正座する *seiza suru* sit upright [straight]
正気 *shōki* consciousness; sanity, reason
正妻 *seisai* lawful [legal] wife
正会員 *seikaiin* regular member
正教授 *seikyōju* full professor
正真正銘の *shōshin-shōmei no* true, genuine, authentic
正史 *seishi* authentic history
正体 *shōtai* one's natural [true] shape; consciousness

❻ [also prefix]
ⓐ *math* (of equal sides or congruent faces) regular
ⓑ *chem* normal, ortho-
正方形 *seihōkei* square
正多面体 *seitamentai* regular polyhedron
正塩 *seien* normal salt
正安息香酸 *seiansokukōsan* orthobenzoic acid

❼ⓐ [also prefix] **chief, main, principal**
ⓑ (person of highest rank) chief
正使 *seishi* senior envoy, chief
正犯 *seihan* principal offender
正副議長 *seifuku gichō* chairman and vice-chairman
正門 *seimon* main gate, main entrance
正編 *seihen* main part of a book
正弦 *seigen* sine (of an angle)
正三位 *shōsanmi* senior grade of the third court rank
検事正 *kenjisei* chief public prosecutor
僧正 *sōjō* bishop

❽ original
正副二通 *seifuku nitsū* original and duplicate

❾ⓐ *math* positive
ⓑ *elec* positive
正数 *seisū* positive number
正号 *seigō* plus sign
正比例 *seihirei* direct proportion
正電気 *seidenki* positive electricity

❿ first month of the year, January

正月 *shōgatsu* New Year, New Year's day; January
賀正 *gashō* New Year's congratulations, Happy New Year

⓫ [archaic] ten duodecillion (10^{40})

INDEPENDENT

【sei 正】 right, righteousness, justice; first volume (as opposed to the sequel); *math*, *elec* positiveness
正の *sei no* *math*, *elec* positive

KUN

【tada(shii) 正しい】 correct, right, accurate, exact; right, righteous, just; lawful, legitimate
正しさ *tadashisa* rightness, righteousness, lawfulness; correctness, propriety
正しい答え *tadashii kotae* correct answer
規則正しい *kisoku-tadashii* regular, systematic
正しい行い *tadashii okonai* right conduct
礼儀正しい *reigi-tadashii* courteous, decorous, polite

【tada(su) 正す】
ⓐ correct, rectify
ⓑ set right, reform, redress
誤りが有れば正せ *Ayamari ga areba tadase* Correct mistakes, if any
姿勢を正す *shisei o tadasu* straighten oneself

【masa 正】 [in compounds] just, exact, definite
正夢 *masayume* dream which comes true, prophetic dream

【masa(ni) 正に】 just, exactly; surely, certainly; really
正に春だ *Masani haru da* Spring is really here

SYNONYMS

❶ⓐ right
是 RIGHT → 2436
端 correct → 1221
ⓑ correct
矯 RECTIFY → 1241
匡 RECTIFY → 2989
直す correct → 2932
訂 REVISE → 1442
改 REFORM → 243
❷ⓐ exact
確 CERTAIN → 1228
真 right → 2111
❸ virtuous
義 righteous → 2338
善 GOOD → 2325
良 GOOD → 3558
❺ⓐ regular
本 regular → 3502
ⓑ true
真 TRUE → 2111
洵 TRULY → 383
実 REAL → 2225
本 real → 3502
現 ACTUAL → 968
❼ⓐ main
主 MAIN → 1938
本 head → 3502
首 leading → 2265
親- PARENT → 1799
❾ positive
陽 positive → 626

USAGE

❶ tadasu
正す
ⓐ correct, rectify
ⓑ set right, reform, redress
質す
ⓐ query, question, consult, inquire
ⓑ ascertain, verify
糾す
inquire into, investigate into, examine

❷ masani
正に
just, exactly; surely, certainly; really
当に
[always followed by 可し *beshi*] properly, naturally; it is proper to, ought to
将に
be about to, on the verge of

HOMOPHONES

tadasu ⇨ 質 2808 糾 1278
masani ⇨ 当 2177 将 460

COMPOUND FORMATION

正弦 *seigen* 余弦 *yogen*
The trigonometric function 正弦 'sine' refers to the principal (正 ❼ⓐ) arc (弦), whereas 余弦 'cosine' refers to the complementary (余) arc (弦).

NOTE

⇨ see COMPOUND FORMATION for 正味 *shōmi* ⇨ 味 274

5-1□

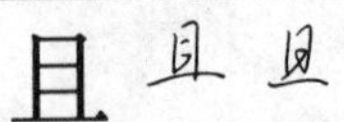
3485 SHO▲ SO▲ ka(tsu)

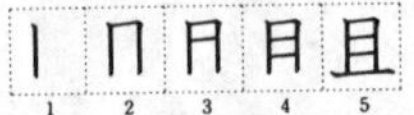

CH 且 qiě jū

Radical	Strokes
一 1	5-1-4
Grade	Freq
Jōyō	1934
■ 4 - 5 - 1	

▶**AS WELL**

KUN

【**ka(tsu) 且つ**】as well (as), at the same time, besides, moreover, both...and

且つ又 *katsumata* moreover

且つ飲み且つ歌う *katsu nomi katsu utau* drink as well as sing, drink and sing at the same time

彼は英語を話し且つ書く *Kare wa eigo o hanashi katsu kaku* He speaks English and writes it as well

SYNONYMS

【**katsu**】

○ **additionally**

兼 CONCURRENTLY → 2286
更に furthermore → 3541
尚 STILL → 2233
亦 ALSO → 2011
又 also, and → 3351
及び and → 3385
並びに and also → 2246
傍ら besides → 147

5-1□

3486 TOTSU deko*

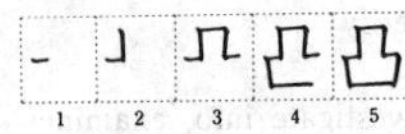

 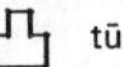 tū

Radical	Strokes
凵 17	5-2-3
Grade	Freq
Jōyō	1955
■ 4 - 5 - 1	

▶**CONVEX**

COMPOUNDS

● [original meaning] **convex, gibbous, protruding**

凸レンズ *totsurenzu* convex lens
凸面 *totsumen* convex surface
凸角 *tokkaku* convex angle
凸版 *toppan* letterpress, relief printing
凹凸 *ōtotsu* unevenness, irregularities

KUN

【**deko 凸**】[in compounds] convexity

お凸 *odeko* brow, forehead
凸凹 *dekoboko* unevenness, roughness; imbalance

SYNONYMS

● **protrude and protruding**

突 protruding → 2230
隆 protuberant → 545
起 RISE → 3307
出る stick out → 3498

● **bowed**

凹 CONCAVE → 3482

5-1□

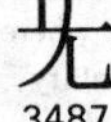
3487

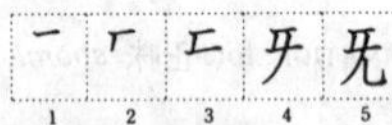

Radical	Strokes
旡 71	5-5-0
Grade	Freq
Radical	
■ 4 - 5 - 1	

RADICAL 71

sudenotsukuri, variant of 无 *munyō* 'without'
⇨ see 无 3443 for radical description

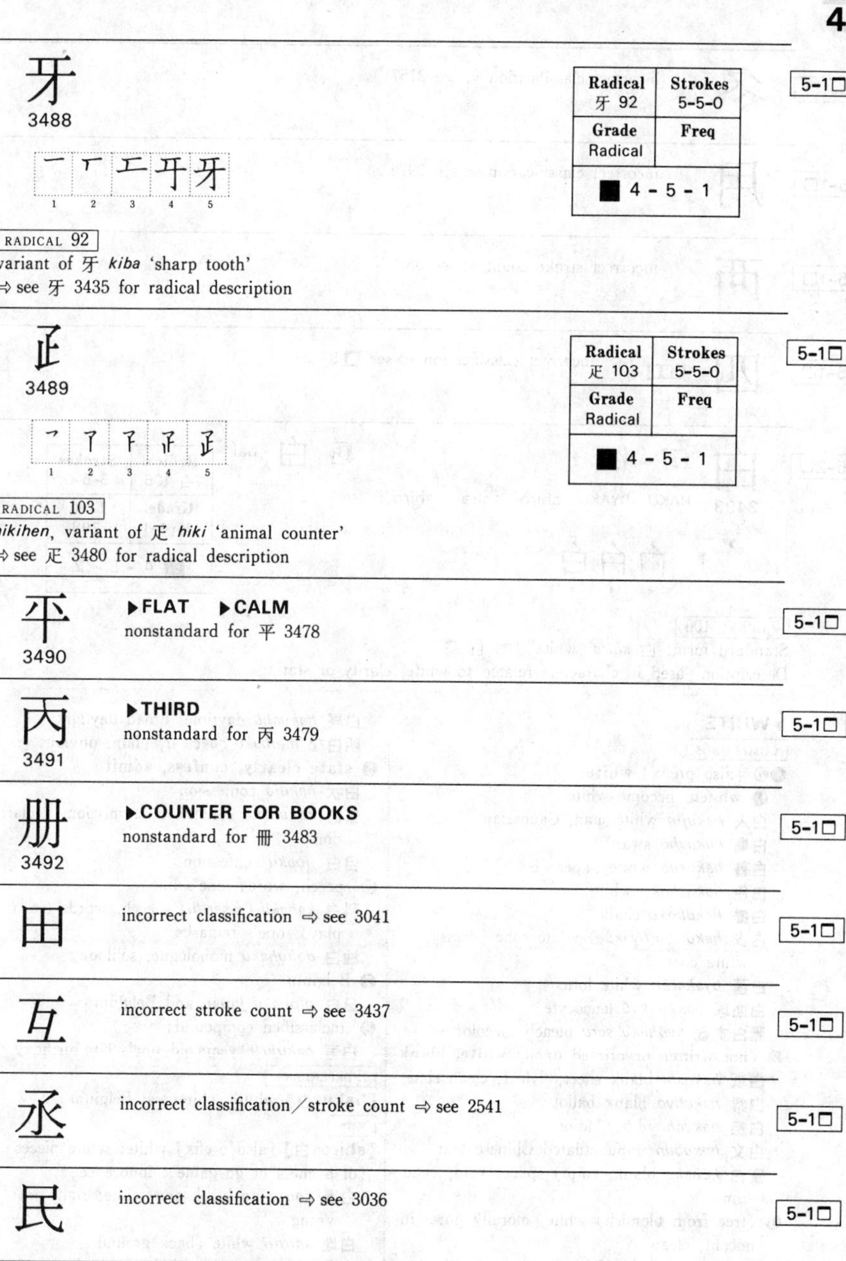

牙
3488

一 丆 工 牙 牙
1 2 3 4 5

Radical 牙 92	Strokes 5-5-0
Grade Radical	Freq
■ 4 - 5 - 1	

5-1□

RADICAL 92
variant of 牙 *kiba* 'sharp tooth'
⇨ see 牙 3435 for radical description

⻊
3489

1 2 3 4 5

Radical ⻊ 103	Strokes 5-5-0
Grade Radical	Freq
■ 4 - 5 - 1	

5-1□

RADICAL 103
hikihen, variant of 疋 *hiki* 'animal counter'
⇨ see 疋 3480 for radical description

平
3490
▶**FLAT** ▶**CALM**
nonstandard for 平 3478
5-1□

丙
3491
▶**THIRD**
nonstandard for 丙 3479
5-1□

册
3492
▶**COUNTER FOR BOOKS**
nonstandard for 冊 3483
5-1□

田 incorrect classification ⇨ see 3041
5-1□

互 incorrect stroke count ⇨ see 3437
5-1□

丞 incorrect classification／stroke count ⇨ see 2541
5-1□

民 incorrect classification ⇨ see 3036
5-1□

目 incorrect classification ⇨ see 3043
5-1□

5-1□ 冬 incorrect classification ⇨ see 2157

5-1□ 用 incorrect classification ⇨ see 2976

5-1□  incorrect stroke count ⇨ see 3522

5-1□ 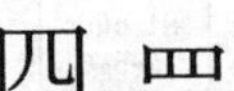 incorrect classification ⇨ see ■3-2

5-2□ 白 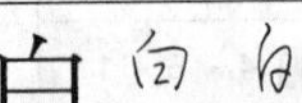 Ⓒⓗ 白 bái

3493 HAKU BYAKU shiro shira- shiro(i)

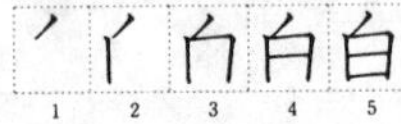

Radical	Strokes
白 106	5-5-0
Grade	**Freq**
Jōyō-1	298
■ 4 - 5 - 2	

RADICAL 106

Standard form: 白 *shiro* 'white' (的 百 皇)

Description: used in characters related to white, clarity or stating

▶WHITE

COMPOUNDS

❶ⓐ [also prefix] **white**

ⓑ whiten, become white

白人 *hakujin* white man, Caucasian

白鳥 *hakuchō* swan

白書 *hakusho* white paper [book]

白色 *hakushoku* white

白墨 *hakuboku* chalk

白衣 *hakui* (=*byakue*) white robe [dress]; white coat

白蓮 *byakuren* white lotus

白血球 *hakkekkyū* leucocyte

漂白する *hyōhaku suru* bleach, decolor

❷ (not written or printed upon) **white, blank**

白紙 *hakushi* blank sheet, flyleaf; clean slate

白票 *hakuhyō* blank ballot

白痴 *hakuchi* idiocy, idiot

白文 *hakubun* unpunctuated Chinese text

空白 *kūhaku* blank, empty space; void, vacuum

❸ (free from blemish) white, morally pure, innocent, clean

潔白な *keppaku na* innocent, pure, upright

黒白 *kokubyaku* right and wrong; black and white

❹ⓐ clear, bright

ⓑ clean, plain, distinct

白熱 *hakunetsu* white heat [glow]; climax

白昼 *hakuchū* daytime, broad daylight

明白な *meihaku na* clear, plain, obvious

❺ **state clearly, confess, admit**

白状 *hakujō* confession

告白 *kokuhaku* confession, admission, declaration

自白 *jihaku* confession

❻ speech, words, one's line

科白 *kahaku* (=*serifu*) speech, words (in a play); one's remarks

独白 *dokuhaku* monologue, soliloquy

❼ Belgium

日白 *nippaku* Japan and Belgium

❽ unclassified compounds

白寿 *hakuju* 99 years old, one's 99th birthday

INDEPENDENT

【haku 白】 white, whiteness; Belgium

KUN

【shiro 白】 [also prefix] white; white pieces (of a chess or go game); innocence

白黒 *shirokuro* black and white; right or wrong

白地 *shiroji* white (back)ground

白金 *shirogane* [usu. 銀] silver; silver coin

白鉢巻 *shirohachimaki* white hairband

白の帽子 *shiro no bōshi* white hat

真っ白 *masshiro* pure [immaculate] white

色白の *irojiro no* fair, light-complexioned

白だと判る *shiro da to wakaru* be found inno-

cent
【shira- 白-】 white
白む *shiramu* grow light, turn gray; (of the atmosphere) become chilled
白髪 *shiraga* white [gray] hair
【shiro(i) 白い】 white; gray (hair); blank, white
白い物 *shiroi mono* something white; snow; gray hair
白いままの紙 *shiroi mama no kami* blank [unwritten] paper
白さ *shirosa* whiteness
青白い *aojiroi* pale, pallid
面白い *omoshiroi* interesting, amusing, pleasant

SYNONYMS

❶ⓐ white colors
皓 BRIGHT WHITE → 1180
銀 SILVER → 1722
❷ emptiness and nothing
空 EMPTY → 2227
虚 VOID → 3237
無 NOTHING → 2135
零 ZERO → 2792

HOMOPHONES

shirogane ⇨ 銀 1722 白金 3493, 2057

COMPOUND FORMATION

❶ 白寿 *hakuju*
白寿 '99 years old, etc.' refers to the celebration (寿) of one's 99th (白 ❽) birthday. 白 denotes 99 since it consists of 百 'one hundred' minus 一 'one'.
❷ 面白い *omoshiroi*
面白い 'interesting, amusing, pleasant' is said to have originally expressed a state of brightness (白 ❹ⓐ) in front of one's face (面) or eyes. The idea is that when all is bright and rosy, things become interesting.

NOTE

⇨ see USAGE note at 金 2057

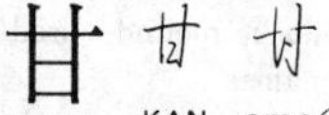

3494 KAN ama(i) ama(eru) ama(yakasu) uma(i)▲

Ⓒⓗ 甘 gān

Radical	Strokes
甘 99	5-5-0
Grade	**Freq**
Jōyō	1153
■ 4 - 5 - 2	

5-2☐

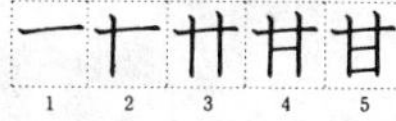

RADICAL 99

Standard form: 甘 *amai* 'sweet' (甚 甜)
Description: used in characters related to sweetness

▶SWEET

COMPOUNDS

❶ (of sugary taste) **sweet**
甘味料 *kanmiryō* sweetener
甘藷 *kansho* sweet potato
甘露 *kanro* nectar, honeydew
甘蔗 *kansho* sugar cane
甘酸 *kansan* sweet and bitter; pain and pleasure
❷ (pleasing to the feelings) sweet, pleasant, satisfying
甘言 *kangen* sweet words, flattery
甘美な *kanbi na* sweet (dream or music)
甘夢 *kanmu* sweet [pleasant] dreams
甘心 *kanshin* satisfaction
❸ be resigned to, submit tamely
甘受する *kanju suru* submit to, put up with

KUN

【ama(i) 甘い】
①ⓐ sweet, sugary
ⓑ sweet [honeyed] (words)
甘み *amami* sweetness, sugary taste
甘栗 *amaguri* broiled sweet chestnuts
甘口の *amakuchi no* sweet (wine), mild (tobacco)
②ⓐ indulgent, lenient, generous
ⓑ easygoing, too optimistic
ⓒ soft, mild, loose
甘んじる *amanjiru* be resigned to (one's fate), be contented [satisfied] with (one's lot)
子供に甘い *kodomo ni amai* be indulgent to (one's) children
③ sentimental
甘い小説 *amai shōsetsu* sentimental novel
【ama(eru) 甘える】 play the baby (to), be coquettish; fawn on (a person); presume upon (another's love); take advantage of
甘え *amae amae*, dependence
甘えた調子で *amaeta chōshi de* in a coquettish tone
甘えっ子 *amaekko* spoilt child
【ama(yakasu) 甘やかす】 be indulgent to, spoil, pamper
甘やかして育てる *amayakashite sodateru* bring up indulgently
【uma(i) 甘い】 [also 旨い] delicious, tasty; sweet

甘さ *umasa* deliciousness, relish
甘い料理 *umai ryōri* tasty dish

SYNONYMS

【amai】
②ⓐ **tolerant**
寛 LENIENT → 2327

HOMOPHONES

umai ⇨ 旨い 2024 巧い 188
上手い 3404, 3456

NOTE

⇨ see USAGE note at 旨 2024

5-2□

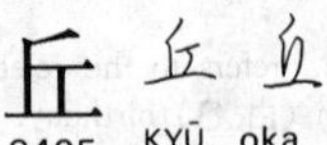

3495 KYŪ oka

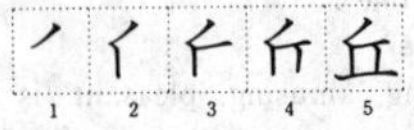

Ⓒⓗ 丘 qiū

Radical	Strokes
一 1	5-1-4
Grade	**Freq**
Jōyō	1291
■ 4 - 5 - 2	

▶HILL

COMPOUNDS

❶ [original meaning] **hill**
丘陵 *kyūryō* hill, hillock
砂丘 *sakyū* sand dune, sand hill
段丘 *dankyū* terrace, bench (in geography)
円丘 *enkyū* knoll
火口丘 *kakōkyū* volcanic cone
❷ [rare] grave mound
墳丘 *funkyū* grave mound, tumulus

KUN

【oka 丘】[sometimes also 岡] hill, hillock, mound
丘辺 *okabe* vicinity of a hill

SYNONYMS

❶ **hills**
岡 HILL → 2997
台 heights → 2005
坂 SLOPE → 234
阪 slope → 271
塚 MOUND → 556
陵 high mound → 544

USAGE

oka
丘
[sometimes also 岡] hill, hillock, mound
岡
① [usu. 丘] hill, hillock, mound—used chiefly in proper names
② [sometimes also 傍-] [in compounds] outsider, third party, bystander
陸
land, shore
傍-
[usu. 岡] outsider, third party, bystander
★丘 and 岡 have the same meaning. The former is used in both common nouns and place names, while the latter is used chiefly in the writing of proper names.

HOMOPHONES

oka ⇨ 岡 2997 陸 543 傍 147

5-2□

世 世° 卋° 丗 ㄝ

3496 SEI SE yo

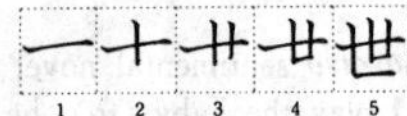

Ⓒⓗ 世 shì

Radical	Strokes
一 1	5-1-4
Grade	**Freq**
Jōyō-3	172
■ 4 - 5 - 2	

▶WORLD ▶AGE

COMPOUNDS

❶ⓐ (human society) **world, society, community, public**
ⓑ worldly, earthly, public, popular
世間 *seken* world, society; the public, people
世論 *seron* (=*yoron*) public opinion
出世 *shusse* success in life; promotion
世事 *seji* worldly affairs
世話 *sewa* help, aid, good offices; care; everyday affairs
世評 *sehyō* public opinion; reputation
世俗の *sezoku no* common, worldly
❷ⓐ (physical world) **world, universe**
ⓑ (spiritual world) this world, this life, living, existence
世界 *sekai* world, universe
創世記 *sōseiki* Genesis
世銀(=世界銀行) *segin* (=*sekai ginkō*) World Bank
現世 *gense* this world, this life
来世 *raise* future life, world to come

❸ⓐ **age, period, century, era, the times**
ⓑ geological epoch
世紀 *seiki* century
中世 *chūsei* Middle [Medieval] Ages
近世 *kinsei* modern ages
乱世 *ransei* turbulent times
洪積世 *kōsekisei* diluvial epoch
❹ⓐ **generation, family line**
ⓑ of previous generations, hereditary
ⓒ **counter for generations or reign periods**
世代 *sedai* generation
世襲 *seshū* heredity, descent
二世 *nisei* second-generation [American-born] Japanese, nisei
ナポレオン三世 *naporeon-sansei* Napoleon III
❺ used phonetically for *se*
世帯 *setai* household, home
仲見世通り *nakamisedōri* shopping street in the precincts of a shrine [temple]

KUN

【yo 世】
①ⓐ world, society, public
ⓑ this world, life, existence
世の中 *yo no naka* the world, society, life
あの世 *ano yo* the other world, world of the dead
② the times, age
世に遅れる *yo ni okureru* fall behind the times

SYNONYMS

❶ⓐ **society**
社 SOCIETY → 840
公 PUBLIC → 1974
ⓑ **worldly**
俗 worldly → 104
❷ⓐ **world**
界 WORLD → 2563
❸ⓐ **long time periods**
代 age → 30
紀 ERA → 1276
時 TIME → 924
期 period → 1704
朝 dynastic period → 1695
❹ **generation**
代 GENERATION → 30
❺ **phonetic** [s]/[sh]
須 phonetic [shu] → 574
修 phonetic [shu] → 123
西 phonetic [su] → 3520
相 phonetic [sō] → 900
沙 phonetic [sha] → 266
遮 phonetic [sha] → 3158

USAGE

yo
世
①ⓐ world, society, public
ⓑ this world, life, existence
② the times, age
代
① era of rule, age
② reign, rule
★The word *yo* has a somewhat poetic flavor. Whereas 世 refers to age or times in general, 代 is restricted to a specific era of rule, as under the reign of a particular emperor.

HOMOPHONES

yo ⇨ 代 30

NOTE

⇨ see COMPOUND FORMATION for
世話 *sewa* ⇨ 話 1527
世間 *seken* ⇨ 間 3323

生 生 生

3497 SEI SHŌ i(kiru) i(kasu) i(keru) u(mareru) u(mare) umare u(mu) o(u) ha(eru) ha(yasu) ki nama nama- na(ru)▲ na(su)▲ mu(su)▲ -u▲

ⒸⒽ 生 shēng

Radical	Strokes
生 100	5-5-0
Grade	**Freq**
Jōyō-1	24
■ 4 – 5 – 2	

5-2□

Stroke order: 丿 𠂉 牛 生 生 (1 2 3 4 5)

RADICAL 100

Standard form: 生 *umareru* 'birth' (産 甦 甥)
Description: used in characters related to birth

▶LIFE ▶BE BORN ▶STUDENT

COMPOUNDS

❶ⓐ (act of being alive) **life, existence**
ⓑ (interval between birth and death) **lifetime, life**
生命 *seimei* life
生保(＝生命保険) *seiho* (＝*seimei hoken*) life insurance
生死 *seishi* life and death
生涯 *shōgai* life, lifetime, career; for life
人生 *jinsei* human life, life
生前 *seizen* during one's lifetime

一生 *isshō* a lifetime
終生 *shūsei* all one's life
余生 *yosei* one's remaining years
平生は *heizei wa* in ordinary days
❷ⓐ (living organisms) **life, living things**
ⓑ bio-, -zoic
生物 *seibutsu* living thing, life, organism
生理学 *seirigaku* physiology
生態 *seitai* ecology; mode of life
原生動物 *gensei dōbutsu* protozoan
幼生 *yōsei* larva
抗生物質 *kōsei busshitsu* antibiotic
殺生 *sesshō* destruction of life; cruelty
畜生 *chikushō* beast; Damn it!
写生する *shasei suru* sketch [draw] from nature; portray
生化学 *seikagaku* biochemistry
新生代 *shinseidai* Cenozoic era
❸ⓐ livelihood, living
ⓑ health, welfare
生計 *seikei* livelihood, living
生活 *seikatsu* life, existence; livelihood
生協 *seikyō* cooperative association [society]
生業 *seigyō* occupation, calling
衛生 *eisei* hygiene, sanitation, preservation of health
摂生 *sessei* preservation of one's health
厚生 *kōsei* public welfare, health promotion
民生 *minsei* public welfare, people's livelihood
❹ⓐ (be alive) **live, exist**
ⓑ living, alive
ⓒ lively, vivid, fresh
生存する *seizon suru* exist, live, survive
生別 *seibetsu* separation, parting
寄生 *kisei* parasitism
蘇生 *sosei* revival, resuscitation
野生の *yasei no* wild, feral
生還する *seikan suru* return alive; *baseball* reach the home plate
生体 *seitai* living body, organism
生者 *shōja* living things, animate nature
生鮮な *seisen na* fresh
生彩 *seisai* life, vividness
生気 *seiki* animation, vitality, spirit
❺ [formerly 棲 *sei* or 栖 *sei*] (of animals) (occupy a habitat) inhabit, live
生息する *seisoku suru* inhabit, live
水生の *suisei no* aquatic, living in the water
両生類 *ryōseirui* Amphibia, amphibian
❻ⓐ **be born**
ⓑ **bear, give birth to**
ⓒ birth
生家 *seika* house where one was born
生年月日 *seinengappi* date of birth
誕生する *tanjō suru* be born, come into the world
更生する *kōsei suru* be born again, start one's life all over; recycle
再生 *saisei* reclamation; regeneration, resuscitation; playback
双生児 *sōseiji* twins
往生する *ōjō suru* pass away; be at a loss
生母 *seibo* one's (biological) mother
生殖 *seishoku* reproduction, procreation, generation
卵生の *ransei no* oviparous
生後二週間 *seigo nishūkan* two weeks after one's birth
生滅 *shōmetsu* birth and death
❼ (bring into existence) **produce, give rise to**
生産 *seisan* production
生成する *seisei suru* create, generate; be created
❽ inborn, natural, innate
生得の *shōtoku* (=*seitoku*) *no* natural, inborn, innate
生得権 *seitokuken* one's birthright
生来 *seirai* by nature [birth], congenitally
❾ⓐ **raw, uncooked, crude**
ⓑ immature
生乳 *seinyū* raw milk
生薬 *shōyaku* crude drug
生石灰 *seisekkai* quicklime, unslaked lime
生硬な *seikō na* crude, immature, unpolished
❿ⓐ [original meaning] (of plants) **grow**
ⓑ suffix indicating number of years of growth
生育する *seiiku suru* grow, vegetate
自生する *jisei suru* grow wild [naturally]
群生する *gunsei suru* grow gregariously [in crowds]
実生 *mishō* seedling, plant raised from the seed
晩生植物 *bansei shokubutsu* slow grower
対生葉 *taiseiyō* opposite leaves
多年生植物 *tanensei shokubutsu* perennial plant
⓫ occur, happen
生起する *seiki suru* occur, take place
発生する *hassei suru* occur, happen; grow, breed
⓬ⓐ [also suffix] **student, pupil; scholar**
ⓑ person, people
生徒 *seito* pupil, student
学生 *gakusei* student
高校生 *kōkōsei* high school student
同級生 *dōkyūsei* classmate
門下生 *monkasei* disciple, pupil
教生 *kyōsei* student teacher
先生 *sensei* teacher; doctor
儒生 *jusei* Confucianist, student of Confucianism
筆生 *hissei* copyist, amanuensis
衆生 *shujō* living things; the people

⓭ⓐ [humble] I
ⓑ suffix indicating humility on part of speaker
小生 *shōsei* I
山田生 *yamadasei* Your humble servant, Yamada
⓮ unclassified compounds
一生懸命(=一所懸命)に *isshōkenmei* (=*isshokenmei*) *ni* for life, with all one's might

INDEPENDENT

【sei 生】 life, living; [humble] I
生を享ける *sei o ukeru* be born, live
【shōjiru (=shōzuru) 生じる(=生ずる)】 happen, arise, be produced; produce, create, cause; grow
変化が生じた *Henka ga shōjita* Change took place
根を生じる *ne o shōjiru* put forth roots, take root

KUN

【i(kiru) 生きる】
①ⓐ (be alive) live, exist
ⓑ (make a living) live (on), subsist
生き *iki* freshness; stet
生き物 *ikimono* living creature
生ける屍 *ikeru shikabane* living corpse
生き字引き *ikijibiki* walking dictionary
長生き *nagaiki* long life, longevity
人はパンのみにて生くるに非ず *Hito wa pan nomi nite ikuru ni arazu* Man does not live by bread alone
② [formerly also 活きる] be enlivened
生き生きと *ikiiki to* lively, vividly
その一語で文章が生きる *Sono ichigo de bunshō ga ikiru* That single word gives life to the style
③ *baseball* be safe
一塁に生きる *ichirui ni ikiru* be safe on first base
【i(kasu) 生かす】
①ⓐ let live, keep alive
ⓑ revive; stet
あいつは生かして置けない *Aitsu wa ikashite okenai* I can't let him live
死者を生かす *shisha o ikasu* revive the dead
② [formerly also 活かす] make the most of
学問を生かす *gakumon o ikasu* put one's learning to practical use
③ [formerly also 活かす] put life [vividness] into, vivify
絵を生かす *e o ikasu* put life into a painting
【i(keru) 生ける】
① [mainly in compounds] keep alive
生け捕る *ikedoru* catch [capture] alive
生け贄 *ikenie* victims, sacrifice
② [formerly also 活ける] arrange (flowers)
生け花 *ikebana* flower arrangement
【u(mareru) 生まれる】
ⓐ (of persons) (come into being) be born, come into existence
ⓑ (of things in general) appear, see the light, be a result (of)
生まれ付き *umaretsuki* one's nature; by nature
生まれて初めて *umarete hajimete* for the first time in one's life
生まれ乍らの詩人 *umarenagara no shijin* born poet
彼はアメリカで生まれた *Kare wa amerika de umareta* He was born in America
貧乏に生まれる *binbō ni umareru* be born poor
持って生まれた *motte umareta* natural, inborn, innate
同情から愛が生まれた *Dōjō kara ai ga umareta* Sympathy engendered love
【u(mare) 生まれ, umare 生】 [also suffix] birth; origin, lineage
昭和三十二年三月五日生 *Shōwa sanjūninen sangatsu itsuka umare* born on March 5, 1957
どちらのお生まれですか *Dochira no oumare desu ka* Where do you come from?
生まれの良い *umare no yoi* wellborn, of noble birth
良家の生まれである *ryōke no umare de aru* be of good family
ドイツ生まれのユダヤ人 *doitsuumare no yudayajin* German Jew
【u(mu) 生む】
① have children
生み *umi* production, bringing into the world
生みの親 *umi no oya* one's real parent; creator
彼女は子供を五人生んだ *Kanojo wa kodomo o gonin unda* She has five children
② produce, bring forth, give rise to, yield
生み出す *umidasu* bring forth, produce, yield
【o(u) 生う】 [in compounds] grow
生い茂る *oishigeru* grow luxuriantly [thickly]
生い立ち *oitachi* one's upbringing, one's childhood
相生の松 *aioi no matsu* twin pines, double pine
【ha(eru) 生える】 grow, spring up; grow (hair or wings), cut (a tooth)
生え抜きの *haenuki no* native-born, trueborn
生え際 *haegiwa* borders of the hair, (receding) hairline
芽生える *mebaeru* bud, sprout; begin
【ha(yasu) 生やす】 grow (a beard), cultivate
髭を生やしている *hige o hayashite iru* have [wear] a beard
【ki 生】
[also prefix]
ⓐ pure, genuine

ⓑ raw
生で飲む *ki de nomu* drink (whisky) straight
生粋の *kissui no* trueborn, pure, genuine
生地 *kiji* one's true color [character]; (plain) cloth, texture; unglazed pottery
生醤油 *kijōyu* pure soy, raw soy
生一本な *kiippon na* straightforward, honest
生娘 *kimusume* virgin, innocent girl
生糸 *kiito* raw silk (thread)
生蠟 *kirō* crude Japan wax
生紙 *kigami* unsized paper

【nama 生】 raw, uncooked, green, fresh, live; impudence, cheek; hard cash; draft beer
生で食べる *nama de taberu* eat raw [fresh]
生生しい *namanamashii* green, fresh, vivid
生の情報 *nama no jōhō* firsthand information
生意気な *namaiki na* impudent, audacious, conceited, affected
生を言うんじゃない *Nama o iun ja nai* None of your cheek
現生 *gennama* real money

【nama- 生-】
①ⓐ raw, uncooked, green, fresh; crude
ⓑ [also prefix] live
生物 *namamono* uncooked food; perishables
生水 *namamizu* unboiled water
生身 *namami* living body; raw meat [fish]
生唾 *namatsuba* saliva (in one's mouth)
生ワク *namawaku* live vaccine
生演奏 *namaensō* live performance
② [also prefix] imperfect, half-, slight, little
生焼けの *namayake no* half-roasted[-baked], rare
生暖かい *namaatatakai* lukewarm, tepid
生易しい *namayasashii* simple, easy
生学問 *namagakumon* imperfect [superficial] knowledge
生返事 *namahenji* vague answer, reluctant answer
生欠伸 *namaakubi* slight yawn

【na(ru) 生る】 bear fruit, fruit
生り年 *naridoshi* year of large crop
生業 *nariwai* (=*seigyō*) livelihood; calling, occupation
末生り *uranari* fruit grown near the top end of the vine; pale-faced man
鈴生りに生る *suzunari ni naru* grow in clusters

【na(su) 生す】 give birth, bear
生さぬ仲の *nasanu-naka no* with no blood relation

【mu(su) 生す】 [also 産す] grow
苔生した *kokemushita* moss-grown, mossy

【-u -生】 place overgrown with vegetation
蓬生 *yomogiu* area overgrown with weeds, wasteland
浅茅生 *asajiu* [rare] broad field of sparsely growing cogon grass

SPECIAL READINGS
芝生 *shibafu* lawn, turf
生憎▲ *ainiku* unfortunately, unluckily; I am sorry, but...
弥生▲ *yayoi* third month (of the lunar calendar), March
生絹▲ *suzushi* raw silk goods

SYNONYMS
❶ **life**
命 LIFE → 2058
寿 LONGEVITY → 3557
❷ⓐ **animal**
獣 BEAST → 1892
畜 LIVESTOCK → 2096
物 living thing → 874
❸ⓑ **healthy**
康 HEALTHY → 3124
健 ROBUST → 134
❹ **live**
活 LIVE → 385
暮らす LIVE (pass one's life) → 2354
❺ **reside**
住 LIVE → 64
居 RESIDE → 3080
植 colonize → 990
❻ **give birth**
誕 BE BORN → 1579
産 GIVE BIRTH → 3298
殖 MULTIPLY → 994
❼ **create**
創 CREATE → 1815
作 compose → 68
発 START → 2565
起 generate → 3307
❾ⓐ **new**
鮮 FRESH → 1877
新 NEW → 1784
❿ⓐ **grow**
育 grow → 2050
成 grow up → 3537
長 grow (up) → 2556
発 develop → 2565
伸 expand → 70
展 UNFOLD → 3111
⓬ⓐ **students and followers**
卒 graduate student → 2055
学 scholar → 2555
門 pupil → 888
弟 disciple → 2044
徒 FOLLOWER → 416

USAGE
❶ **ikiru**
生きる
①ⓐ (be alive) live, exist
ⓑ (make a living) live (on), subsist
② [formerly also 活きる] be enlivened
③ *baseball* be safe

3497

活きる
［now usu. 生きる］ be enlivened

❷ **ikasu**

生かす
①ⓐ let live, keep alive
ⓑ revive; stet
② ［formerly also 活かす］ make the most of
③ ［formerly also 活かす］ put life ［vividness］ into, vivify

活かす
［now usu. 生かす］
① make the most of
② put life ［vividness］ into, vivify

❸ **ikeru**

生ける
① ［mainly in compounds］ keep alive
② ［formerly also 活ける］ arrange （flowers）

活ける
［now usu. 生ける］ arrange （flowers）

埋ける
bury; bury coals in ashes

❹ **musu**

生す
［also 産す］ grow

産す
［also 生す］ grow

蒸す
① *vt* steam, heat with steam; foment
② *vi* be sultry, be stuffy

HOMOPHONES

ikiru ⇨ 活 385
ikasu ⇨ 活 385
ikeru ⇨ 活 385 埋 403
umareru ⇨ 産 3298
umu ⇨ 産 3298
umi ⇨ 産 3298
naru ⇨ 成 3537 為 3577
nasu ⇨ 成 3537 為 3577
musu ⇨ 産 3298 蒸 2334

COMPOUND FORMATION

❶ **先生** *sensei*
先生 'teacher; doctor' is a scholar （生 ⓬ⓐ） who studied ahead （先） of others.

❷ **一生懸命（＝一所懸命）** *isshōkenmei* （＝ *isshokenmei*）
一生懸命に 'for life, with all one's might', originally written 一所懸命に, is to risk （懸） one's life （命） in protecting a single （一） place （所）, i.e., the territory of one's feudal lord. 所 was mistakenly replaced by 生 ⓮, which is more common today.

NOTE

⇨ see also USAGE notes at 産 3298 and 成 3537
⇨ see COMPOUND FORMATION for 生涯 *shōgai* ⇨ 涯 512
★生 is said to have a total of more than 200 readings, which is more than any other character.

出

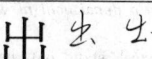

3498 SHUTSU SUI de(ru) -de da(su) -da(su) i(deru)▲ i(dasu)▲

ⒸⒽ 出 chū

Radical	Strokes
凵 17	5-2-3
Grade	**Freq**
Jōyō-1	15
■ 4 - 5 - 2	

5-2□

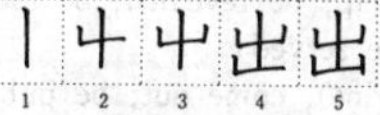

▶**GO OUT** ▶**PUT OUT**

COMPOUNDS

❶ⓐ ［original meaning］ （of persons） **go out, come out; depart, leave**
ⓑ cause to go out （on a military expedition）, dispatch （troops）
ⓒ （of things） **come out, issue, flow out**

出国する *shukkoku suru* go out of a country
出発 *shuppatsu* departure, starting
出港する *shukkō suru* leave port, set sail
出張する *shutchō suru* travel on official business
出動する *shutsudō suru* take the field, be dispatched, turn out
脱出する *dasshutsu suru* escape, extricate
外出する *gaishutsu suru* go out
出兵する *shuppei suru* dispatch troops
派出所 *hashutsujo* branch office; police box
出血する *shukketsu suru* bleed; hemorrhage
流出する *ryūshutsu suru* flow out, effuse

❷ⓐ （come into view or existence） **come out, appear, emerge, occur**
ⓑ **come from, originate**

出現 *shutsugen* appearance, emergence
出火 *shukka* outbreak of fire
神出鬼没の *shinshutsukibotsu no* appearing and disappearing unexpectedly, elusive
初出 *shoshutsu* first appearance
続出する *zokushutsu suru* appear in succession
露出 *roshutsu* exposure, disclosure; （photographic） exposure
出所 *shussho* origin, source; release from prison
出身地 *shusshinchi* one's native place
出典 *shutten* source, authority

❸ⓐ **go to, proceed to, come to**
ⓑ **appear, attend, be present at**
出漁する *shutsuryō suru* go (off) fishing
出馬する *shutsuba suru* come forward as a candidate; go in person
出世する *shusse suru* succeed in life; be promoted
進出する *shinshutsu suru* advance, go [march] into; debouch
出席 *shusseki* attendance, presence
出勤する *shukkin suru* attend one's office, go to work
出頭する *shuttō suru* attend, present oneself
出演する *shutsuen suru* appear on stage, perform, play
出場する *shutsujō suru* take part, participate
出願する *shutsugan suru* make an application
❹ cause to move toward or as if toward an outward direction:
ⓐ **put out, give out, discharge, send out, take out**
ⓑ put on display, exhibit
出荷する *shukka suru* forward, ship, consign
出超 *shutchō* excess of exports over imports
放出する *hōshutsu suru* release, discharge, emit
検出する *kenshutsu suru* detect, find
選出する *senshutsu suru* elect
救出する *kyūshutsu suru* rescue, relieve, deliver
輸出 *yushutsu* export
提出する *teishutsu suru* present, submit, turn in
出版する *shuppan suru* publish
出品する *shuppin suru* exhibit, show, display
❺ expend, spend, pay
出資する *shusshi suru* invest, finance
出納 *suitō* receipts and expenses, incomings and outgoings
支出 *shishutsu* expenditure, disbursement, outgo
歳出 *saishutsu* annual expenditure
❻ (bring into being) put out, produce, beget
出炭 *shuttan* coal production
出産 *shussan* birth, delivery
産出する *sanshutsu suru* produce, yield
演出する *enshutsu suru* produce (a play); represent
案出する *anshutsu suru* think out, contrive, devise, invent
❼ stand out, excel
出色の *shusshoku no* prominent, excellent, outstanding
傑出する *kesshutsu suru* excel, stand out
❽ (of the sun or moon) rise
日出 *nisshutsu* sunrise

INDEPENDENT

【shutsu 出】 origin, birth; abbrev. of 出席 *shusseki*: presence
藤原氏の出 *fujiwarashi no shutsu* of Fujiwara descent

KUN

【de(ru) 出る】
①ⓐ go out, come out; leave, go away
ⓑ depart, start
ⓒ (of things) come out, issue, flow out
出 *de* coming [going] out; outflow; rising (of the sun or moon); graduate (of); one's turn to appear on stage
出入り *deiri* going in and out; frequentation, usual visit (as by a merchant); indentations; incomings and outgoings; trouble, fight
出会う *deau* (happen to) meet; transact
出掛ける *dekakeru* go out, set off; be about to go out
良い出足 *yoi deashi* good start; good turnout of people
水の出が悪い *Mizu no de ga warui* The water does not come out well
② go beyond the limit:
ⓐ stick out, protrude, project
ⓑ intrude, interfere
ⓒ be more than, exceed
出っ張る *depparu* project, protrude
出っ歯 *deppa* projecting teeth
突き出る *tsukideru* project, stick out, stand out
出しゃばる *deshabaru* intrude, butt in
十年を出ない内に *jūnen o denai uchi ni* within ten years
抜きん出る *nukinderu* excel, stand out, be preeminent
③ⓐ (come into view) come out, appear, emerge, turn up; be revealed; be found; (of dishes) be served
ⓑ appear (in print), come out; be published
出揃う *desorou* appear all together, come out fully
出回る *demawaru* appear on the market, be moving
お化けが出る *Obake ga deru* A ghost haunts the place
無くした時計が出て来た *Nakushita tokei ga dete kita* The lost watch was found
思い出 *omoide* recollections, memory, reminiscences
ビフテキが出た *Bifuteki ga deta* Beefsteak was served
新聞に出ている *Shinbun ni dete iru* It is in the papers
④ⓐ attend, be present, appear; go to (work)
ⓑ take part in, join
出稼ぎする *dekasegi suru* work away from home
会社に出ている *kaisha ni dete iru* work for a

3498

company
レースに出る *rēsu ni deru* run in a race
⑤ⓐ go to, proceed to; lead to
ⓑ go forth into (the world), enter upon
東京へ出る *tōkyō e deru* go to Tokyo
この道は海に出る *Kono michi wa umi ni deru* This path leads to the sea
世に出る *yo ni deru* go out into the world, come to the front
選挙に出る *senkyo ni deru* run for election
⑥ⓐ come from, originate, arise; graduate
ⓑ break out, occur, originate
ⓒ (results) come out, work out
出来る *dekiru* be made, be completed, come into being; can; be good at (a subject)
彼女は京都の出だ *Kanojo wa kyōto no de da* She is from Kyoto
このモーターは百馬力出る *Kono mōtā wa hyakubariki deru* This motor has an output of 100 hp
大学を出る *daigaku o deru* graduate from a university
火が出た *Hi ga deta* A fire started
⑦ sell
この本は良く出る *Kono hon wa yoku deru* This book is a good seller
⑧ assume [take] (an attitude)
出方 *dekata* one's attitude, move; theater attendant, usher
⑨ draw, infuse (properly)
このティーバッグは良く出る *Kono tībaggu wa yoku deru* This tea bag draws well
⑩ unclassified compounds
出鱈目な *detarame na* random, haphazard
目出度い(＝芽出度い) *medetai* happy, propitious, joyous

【-de -出】
① [suffix] graduate (of)
大学出の人 *daigakude no hito* university graduate
② substance
使い出が有る *tsukaide ga aru* bear long use

【da(su) 出す】
①ⓐ put out, push [thrust] out, send out, hold out
ⓑ take out, bring out
舌を出す *shita o dasu* put out one's tongue
芽を出す *me o dasu* put forth buds, sprout
舟を出す *fune o dasu* put [take] out a boat
手を出す *te o dasu* reach out one's hand, turn one's hand to
旗を出す *hata o dasu* hang out a flag
手紙を出す *tegami o dasu* mail a letter
財布を出す *saifu o dasu* draw [take] out one's purse
②ⓐ (bring into being) put out, produce, yield
ⓑ (issue printed material) put out, publish; print, insert
生み出す *umidasu* bring forth, produce, yield
作り出す *tsukuridasu* make, turn out, create
五十キロを出す *gojikkiro o dasu* drive 50 kph
辞書を出す *jisho o dasu* publish a dictionary
③ pay, put up, invest
資金を出す *shikin o dasu* furnish with funds
④ⓐ put out (a dish), serve
ⓑ present, submit; tender
朝食を出す *chōshoku o dasu* serve breakfast
レポートを出す *repōto o dasu* turn in a report
⑤ⓐ expose, lay bare
ⓑ put on display, exhibit
背中を出す *senaka o dasu* bare one's back
展覧会に出す *tenrankai ni dasu* send to an exhibition
名前を出したくない *Namae o dashitaku nai* I want to remain anonymous
⑥ utter
大声を出す *ōgoe o dasu* shout, raise one's voice

【-da(su) -出す】
[verbal suffix]
① proceed or cause to proceed outward:
ⓐ go out, come out; put out, send out; jut out
ⓑ come out, appear
飛び出す *tobidasu* fly out, run out, jump out; project
乗り出す *noridasu* lean forward; start, set out; embark on, launch into
送り出す *okuridasu* send out, forward; show (a person) out
売り出す *uridasu* put on sale; rise in fame
取り出す *toridasu* take out, pick out, extract
持ち出す *mochidasu* take out, carry out; run away with; advance (one's opinion); begin to have
引き出し *hikidashi* drawer; withdrawal (of money)
思い出す *omoidasu* recollect, recall, remember
張り出す *haridasu* project, jut out
浮き出す *ukidasu* come up to the surface, loom
② begin to do, start doing
勉強し出す *benkyō shidasu* begin to study
雨が降り出した *Ame ga furidashita* It began to rain
逃げ出す *nigedasu* make a break, run off, make off
打ち出す *uchidasu* set out [forth], work out, hammer out; strike out, emboss; announce

【i(deru) 出でる】 literary form of **deru 出る**
出で立ち *idetachi* dress, outfit
出で湯 *ideyu* hot spring
日出ずる国 *hi izuru kuni* Land of the Rising Sun

届け出でる *todokeideru* submit notice, give notice
申し出で *mōshiide* offer, proposal, application
【i(dasu) 出だす】 literary form of **dasu 出す**
見出だす *miidasu* find out, discover

SYNONYMS

❶ & 【deru】① leave and set forth
発 START → 2565
去 GO AWAY → 2156
離 leave → 1836
退 RETREAT → 3094
撤 WITHDRAW → 738
❷ⓐ appear
現 APPEAR → 968
顕 MANIFEST → 1806
❸ⓐ go and come
参 go somewhere → 2066
来 COME → 3551
通 go to and from → 3109
向 head toward → 3052
赴 PROCEED TO → 3303
行 GO → 212
往 GO ON → 292
ⓑ attend
登 attend → 2595
臨 BE PRESENT AT → 1630
❹ⓐ emit
発 EMIT → 2565
排 DISCHARGE → 490
放 radiate → 853
射 SHOOT → 1458
噴 SPOUT → 717
吐 SPEW → 203
【deru】
②ⓐ protrude and protruding
起 RISE → 3307
突 protruding → 2230
凸 CONVEX → 3486
隆 protuberant → 545
【-dasu】
② begin
-掛ける start doing → 493
始 BEGIN → 281
発 START → 2565
起 start → 3307
就 SET ABOUT → 1694
開 OPEN → 3321
創 initiate → 1815
肇 ORIGINATE → 2799

NOTE

⇨ see COMPOUND FORMATION for 出張 *shutchō* ⇨ 張 474

5-2□

由

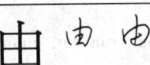

3499 YU YŪ YUI yoshi yo(ru)▲

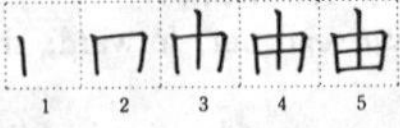

1 2 3 4 5

Ⓒ 由 yóu

Radical	Strokes
田 102	5-5-0
Grade	**Freq**
Jōyō-3	367
■ 4 - 5 - 2	

▶REASON

COMPOUNDS

❶ⓐ reason (for what has happened), cause, origin, derivation
ⓑ be caused by, originate in, derive from, be based on
由来 *yurai* origin, source, cause; history
由緒 *yuisho* history, lineage
理由 *riyū* reason, cause, ground
事由 *jiyū* reason, cause, ground
来由 *raiyu* (=*raiyū*) cause, origin
自由 *jiyū* freedom
❷ pass through
経由 *keiyu* via, through

KUN

【yoshi 由】 reason, ground, cause; means, way; effect, point, purport
由無き *yoshinaki* senseless, meaningless, absurd
...の由です *...no yoshi desu* hear that... / It is said that...
【yo(ru) 由る】［now usu. 因る］be caused by, be due to
不注意に由る *fuchūi ni yoru* be due to carelessness

SYNONYMS

❶ⓐ cause and reason
因 CAUSE → 3054
為 because → 3577
故 reason → 1141
訳 reason → 1473

HOMOPHONES

yoru ⇨ 因 3054 依 84 拠 312 寄 2291

COMPOUND FORMATION

自由 *jiyū*
自由 'freedom' is a state resulting from (由 ❶ⓑ) following one's own heart or free will (自).

NOTE

⇨ see USAGE note at 因 3054

世 3500 ▶WORLD ▶AGE
nonstandard for 世 3496 5-2◻

包 incorrect classification ⇨ see 2966 5-2◻

圭 incorrect classification／stroke count ⇨ see 2165 5-2◻

曰 incorrect stroke count ⇨ see 3528 5-2◻

立 incorrect classification ⇨ see 1992 5-2◻

主 incorrect classification ⇨ see 1938 5-2◻

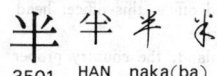

半 3501 HAN naka(ba) 5-3◫

CH 半 bàn

Radical	Strokes
十 24	5-2-3
Grade	**Freq**
Jōyō-2	212
■ 4-5-3	

▶HALF

COMPOUNDS

❶ⓐ [also suffix] **half, ...and a half**
ⓑ [also prefix] **half (of), semi-, hemi-, demi-, bi-**
ⓒ split in half, halve
半分 *hanbun* half
前半 *zenhan* (=*zenpan*) first half
夜半 *yahan* midnight
大半 *taihan* the greater part, majority
二年半 *ninenhan* two years and a half
半面 *hanmen* profile; one side
半額 *hangaku* half price, half amount
半球 *hankyū* hemisphere
半径 *hankei* radius, semidiameter
半世紀 *hanseiki* half a century
折半 *seppan* halving

❷ⓐ **halfway, half-done, uncompleted**
ⓑ [also prefix] (not fully) **semi-, quasi-, partly**
半端な *hanpa na* fragmentary, odd; half-done, incomplete; noncommittal
半途 *hanto* halfway, unfinished
半島 *hantō* peninsula
半熟の *hanjuku no* half-boiled; half ripe
半製品 *hanseihin* semimanufactured goods
半導体 *handōtai* semiconductor
半永久的 *han'eikyūteki* semipermanent

❸ odd number
丁半 *chōhan* odd and even (numbers); gambling

INDEPENDENT

【**han 半**】odd number

KUN

【**naka(ba) 半ば**】half; semi; middle, halfway; in part, partially
半ば眠っている *nakaba nemutte iru* half asleep
月半ばに *tsukinakaba ni* in the middle of the month
半ばまぐれで *nakaba magure de* partly due to luck

SYNONYMS

❷ⓑ **subordinate**
準 QUASI- → 2856
亜 SUB- → 3540
副 SECONDARY → 1776
次 secondary → 54

従 subordinate → 415
准 JUNIOR → 127

助 assistant → 1121

5-3⑪

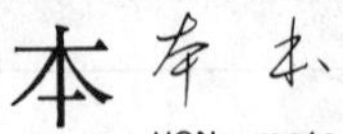

3502 HON moto

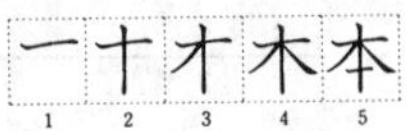

Ⓒⓗ 本 běn

Radical	Strokes
木 75	5-4-1
Grade	**Freq**
Jōyō-1	12
■ 4 - 5 - 3	

▶BASIS ▶BOOK ▶THIS

COMPOUNDS

❶ⓐ **basis, base, foundation**
ⓑ (basic funds) **principal, capital**
本拠 *honkyo* base, stronghold, headquarters
本位 *hon'i* (monetary) standard; standard, basis; original standing
基本 *kihon* basis, foundation
国本 *kokuhon* foundation of a country
抜本的な *bapponteki na* radical, drastic
根本 *konpon* basis, foundation; origin, source
農本主義 *nōhonshugi* "agriculture-first" principle
資本 *shihon* funds, capital
元本 *ganpon* capital, principal

❷ⓐ **origin, source, root, beginning**
ⓑ **original, inherent, inborn**
ⓒ **originally, from the start**
本源 *hongen* source, origin; principle
本初 *honsho* origin, beginning, start
日本 *nihon* (=*nippon*) Japan
本質 *honshitsu* essence, reality
本能 *honnō* instinct
本国 *hongoku* one's native country, fatherland
本場 *honba* home, habitat, center
本来 *honrai* originally, essentially, naturally

❸ the original, model, sample
見本 *mihon* sample, specimen
手本 *tehon* model, example, pattern
写本 *shahon* manuscript, written copy

❹ *baseball* home base, home plate
本盗 *hontō* home steal
三本間 *sanponkan* between third and home base

❺ⓐ [also suffix] (source of knowledge) **book, volume, work, magazine**
ⓑ **playbook, script**
本屋 *hon'ya* bookstore; bookseller
読本 *tokuhon* reader, reading book
絵本 *ehon* picture book
ビニ本 *binibon* vinyl-covered porno magazine
単行本 *tankōbon* separate volume, independent volume
脚本 *kyakuhon* script, playbook, drama, scenario
台本 *daihon* playbook, script, scenario

❻ [also prefix] **this, the same, the present, in question**
本日 *honjitsu* today
本書 *honsho* this book
本紙 *honshi* this newspaper
本人 *honnin* the person himself, the said person
本年度 *honnendo* the current fiscal year

❼ [also prefix] **head, main, principal**
本部 *honbu* head office, headquarters, administrative building
本店 *honten* head [main] office [store]
本社 *honsha* head office, this office; head shrine, this shrine
本土 *hondo* mainland; the country proper
本予算 *hon'yosan* main budget

❽ⓐ **real, true, genuine**
ⓑ [also prefix] regular, proper, formal, legal, full-fledged
本体 *hontai* substance, thing itself; object of worship; main part
本当の *hontō no* true, real, genuine
本物 *honmono* real thing [stuff], genuine article; expert performance
本名 *honmyō* one's real name
本格 *honkaku* fundamental rules, propriety
本番 *honban* acting for the audience, take, going on the air
本会議 *honkaigi* plenary session, regular session

❾ **counter for:**
ⓐ **cylindrical objects, as bottles, pencils, etc.**
ⓑ movies
ⓒ rounds or points of a match (as of karate)
ⓓ *baseball* safety hits
八本の鉛筆 *happon no enpitsu* eight pencils
ビール二本 *bīru nihon* two bottles of beer
二本立ての映画 *nihondate no eiga* double feature movie
一本取る *ippon toru* gain a point; beat, upset

❿ⓐ [original meaning] root
ⓑ plant

一年生草本 *ichinensei sōhon* annual herb

INDEPENDENT

【hon 本】 book, volume, work, reading magazine; playbook, script; abbrev. of 本塁打 *honruida*: home run

本を出す *hon o dasu* publish a book

【hon no 本の】 mere, slight; just, but, only

本の推測に過ぎない *Hon no suisoku ni sugi-nai* It's mere guesswork

本の少し *hon no sukoshi* just a little

本の五分 *hon no gofun* just five minutes

KUN

【moto 本】

① (the most important thing) basis, essential thing, principle

国の本 *kuni no moto* foundation of the country, national principles

②ⓐ root (of a tree)

ⓑ counter for plants with roots

木の本に *ki no moto ni* at the root of a tree

一本の草 *hitomoto no kusa* a blade of grass

③ first half of a tanka poem

SYNONYMS

❶ⓐ basis

基 BASE → 2673
礎 foundation → 1248
素 ELEMENT → 2458
底 BOTTOM → 3084
根 ROOT → 930
拠 GROUNDS → 312

❷ⓐ beginnings

元 ORIGIN → 1929
根 ROOT → 930
源 SOURCE → 656
緒 OUTSET → 1378
序 INTRODUCTORY PART → 3065
端 start → 1221
始 beginning → 281
初 beginning → 1116

ⓑ original

原 ORIGINAL → 3009
素 primary → 2458
初 FIRST → 1116

❺ⓐ books

書 BOOK → 2658
冊 bound book → 3483
籍 books → 2731
著 literary work → 2300
巻 VOLUME → 2645
編 volume → 1387
鑑 REFERENCE VOLUME → 1773
典 STANDARD WORK → 2627
経 religious classic → 1331

❻ this and that

今 THIS (week, etc.) → 1968
当 THE PRESENT → 2177
該 the said → 1519
同 the same → 2987
之 this → 3420
是 this → 2436
爾 THAT → 3587
彼 that → 290

❼ main

主 MAIN → 1938
正 chief → 3484
親- PARENT → 1799
首 leading → 2265

❽ⓐ true

実 REAL → 2225
真 TRUE → 2111
洵 TRULY → 383
正 genuine → 3484
現 ACTUAL → 968

ⓑ regular

正 regular → 3484

❾ⓐ counters for long objects

筋 counter for slender objects → 2678

HOMOPHONES

moto ⇨ 元 1929 基 2673 下 3378 素 2458 許 1470

COMPOUND FORMATION

日本 *nihon* (=*nippon*)

日本 'Japan' is the source (本 ❷ⓐ) of the sun (日)—often expressed in the form "Land of the Rising Sun."

NOTE

⇨ see USAGE note at 元 1929

5-3Ⅱ

禾

3503 KA

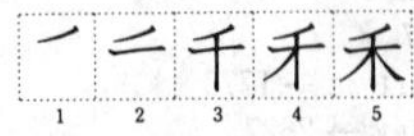

(CH) 禾 hé

Radical	Strokes
禾 115	5-5-0
Grade	Freq
Reference	
■ 4-5-3	

RADICAL 115

Standard form: 禾 *nogi* 'growing grain' (秀 穀 穎)
Left variant: 禾 *nogihen* (私 税 科)
Description: used in characters related to grains or rice plants

COMPOUNDS

ⓐ grain, cereals

ⓑ [archaic] rice; foxtail millet
禾本科 *kahonka* Gramineae

5-3Ⅱ

乎

3504 KO O ka

(CH) 乎 hū

Radical	Strokes
ノ 4	5-1-4
Grade	Freq
Reference	
■ 4-5-3	

COMPOUNDS

❶ [now also 固 *ko* 3086] suffix for forming modifiers
断乎たる *dankotaru* firm, conclusive, determined
確乎たる *kakkotaru* firm, sure, resolute
醇乎たる *junkotaru* sheer, pure

❷ [formerly also 耶 *ka*, now always か *ka*] interrogative particle
管仲は倹なる乎 *Kanchū wa kennaru ka* Is Guan Zhong thrifty?

❸ [now usu. を *o*] objective case particle
乎古止点 *okototen* aid marks for construing classical Chinese

HOMOPHONES

ka ⇒ 耶 1283

NOTE

⇒ see USAGE note at 耶 1283

5-3Ⅱ

末 末 末

3505 MATSU BATSU sue

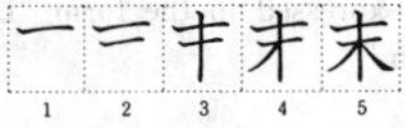

(CH) 末 mò

Radical	Strokes
木 75	5-4-1
Grade	Freq
Jōyō-4	485
■ 4-5-3	

▶**LAST PART**

COMPOUNDS

❶ **last part, last stage, termination, end**
末尾 *matsubi* end, close
年末 *nenmatsu* end of year
期末 *kimatsu* end of term
週末 *shūmatsu* weekend
結末 *ketsumatsu* termination, end, close, conclusion
始末 *shimatsu* management, dealing, disposal; circumstances; result, outcome

❷ⓐ **last in time, terminal, final**

ⓑ (relating to the terminal stage) last (days), closing (years)
末日 *matsujitsu* last day
末期 *makki* closing years, final stage
末葉 *matsuyō* end [close] of an epoch; descendant
末期 *matsugo* hour of death, one's last moments
末路 *matsuro* last days; fate
末世 *masse* these latter days, degenerate [corrupt] age

ⓒ last (child), youngest
末弟 *mattei* (=*battei*) youngest brother
末子 *masshi* (=*basshi*) youngest child

❸ posterity, descendants
末裔 *matsuei* descendant, offspring

末代 *matsudai* all generations, all ages to come

❹ⓐ last in importance, trivial, insignificant

ⓑ last in place, subordinate, secondary

末節 *massetsu* minor details, nonessentials

粗末な *somatsu na* coarse, crude, inferior, humble

本末 *honmatsu* root and branch, means and end

末席 *masseki* lowest seat

末寺 *matsuji* secondary temple

末輩 *mappai* underling, rank and file

❺ **end, tip**

末端 *mattan* end, tip, termination

末梢 *masshō* tip, end; tip of a twig; *anat* periphery

端末 *tanmatsu* terminal

❻ⓐ powder

ⓑ suffix after names of powders

粉末 *funmatsu* powder

硼酸末 *hōsanmatsu* borax powder

KUN

【**sue** 末】 last part, last stage, termination, end; last (child), youngest; descendant, offspring; trifles, trivialities; lower [outer] end, bounds; future

三月の末 *sangatsu no sue* end of March

議論の末に *giron no sue ni* after a heated discussion

末っ子 *suekko* youngest child

平家の末 *heike no sue* descendant of the Taira family

末の問題 *sue no mondai* a mere trifle

末広がりの *suehirogari no* widening toward the end

場末 *basue* squalid outskirts

末頼もしい *suetanomoshii* promising (future)

SYNONYMS

❶ **ends**

終 END → 1336

尾 end → 3062

局 close → 3063

❷ⓐ **last**

終 last → 1336

❸ **descendant**

孫 GRANDCHILD, descendant → 410

胤 PROGENY → 17

❹ⓐ **unimportant**

小 SMALL → 7

微 SLIGHT → 639

細 MINUTE → 1333

❺ **extremity**

先 point → 2394

端 END → 1221

梢 tip → 963

❻ **powder**

粉 POWDER → 1291

NOTE

⇨ see COMPOUND FORMATION for 始末 *shimatsu* ⇨ 始 281

★do not confuse with 未 3506

未 3506 MI BI▲ ima(da)▲ ma(da)▲ hitsuji▲

CH 未 wèi

5-3 Ⅱ

Radical	Strokes
木 75	5-4-1
Grade	**Freq**
Jōyō-4	771
■ 4 - 5 - 3	

Stroke order: 1 2 3 4 5

▶**NOT YET**

COMPOUNDS

❶ [also prefix] **not yet, un-** (**as in *unpublished***)

未満 *miman* less than

未来 *mirai* future

未練 *miren* lingering affection, reluctance to give up

未完成 *mikansei* incompletion

未知の *michi no* unknown

未刊の *mikan no* unpublished

未定の *mitei no* undecided, pending

未払いの *miharai no* unpaid

未婚の *mikon no* unmarried

前代未聞の *zendaimimon no* unheard-of, unprecedented

❷ *Buddhism* the world to come, future existence

過現未 *kagenmi* past, present and future, three temporal states of existence

❸ eighth sign of the Oriental zodiac: the Ram—(time) 1–3 p.m., (direction) SSW, (season) June (of the lunar calendar) (⇨ see APPENDIX 7)

癸未 *kibi* 20th of the sexagenary cycle

KUN

【**ima(da)** 未だ】 yet, as yet, never; up to now

未だ嘗て無い偉大な人 *imada katsute nai idai na hito* the greatest man that ever lived

【**ma(da)** 未だ】 (not) yet, still; more, besides

彼は未だ来ていない *Kare wa mada kite inai* He has not come yet

【**hitsuji** 未】 eighth sign of the Oriental zodiac: the Ram (⇨ ❸)

SYNONYMS

❶ **still**

尚 STILL → 2233

❶ **terms of negation**

不 NOT (negation) → 3434
無 WITHOUT (nonexistence) → 2135
非 IS NOT (contrariety) → 889
没 lacking in → 260
欠 LACK → 1987
否 OR NOT → 2406

❸ **sheep**

羊 SHEEP → 2183

HOMOPHONES

hitsuji ⇨ 羊 2183

NOTE

⇨ see USAGE notes at 不 3434 and 羊 2183
⇨ see COMPOUND FORMATION for 未練 *miren* ⇨ 練 1375
★do not confuse with 末 3505

5-3Ⅲ

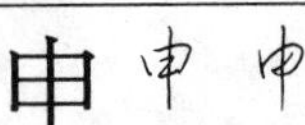

3507 SHIN mō(su) mō(shi)- saru▲

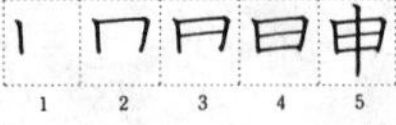

Ⓒⓗ 申 shēn

Radical	Strokes
田 102	5-5-0
Grade	**Freq**
Jōyō-3	378
■ 4 - 5 - 3	

▶**REPORT** ▶**SPEAK HUMBLY**

COMPOUNDS

❶ **report (to a superior), state, submit a report**

申告 *shinkoku* report, statement, notification
上申する *jōshin suru* report (to a superior official)
答申する *tōshin suru* submit a report [reply]
内申 *naishin* unofficial report
追申 *tsuishin* [usu. 追伸] postscript

❷ apply, appeal

申請 *shinsei* application, petition, request

❸ ninth sign of the Oriental zodiac: the Monkey—(time) 3-5 p.m., (direction) WSW, (season) July (of the lunar calendar) (⇨ see APPENDIX 7)

庚申 *kōshin* 57th of the sexagenary cycle

KUN

【mō(su) 申す】

[humble]

①ⓐ speak humbly, say, tell, speak of, talk about

ⓑ state humbly, declare, affirm, assert

主人もそう申しております *Shujin mo sō mōshite orimasu* My husband also says so
申し述べる *mōshinoberu* state, mention, tell
申し訳 *mōshiwake* excuse, apology, explanation
申し上げる *mōshiageru* tell, say, speak humbly; (have the honor to) do

② call, name; express (in a foreign language)

私は荒木一郎と申します *Watakushi wa araki ichirō to mōshimasu* My name is Ichiro Araki

③ (have the honor to) do

私が御案内申します *Watakushi ga goannai mōshimasu* I will show you the way

【mō(shi)- 申し-】 apply, appeal

申し込み *mōshikomi* application; proposal, request
申し出る *mōshideru* offer; propose; apply; report
申し子 *mōshigo* child born in answer to one's prayer

【saru 申】 ninth sign of the Oriental zodiac: the Monkey (⇨ ❸)

SYNONYMS

❶ **inform and communicate**

宣 PROCLAIM → 2252
知 let know → 1127
告 NOTIFY → 2409
届ける give notice → 3078
達 issue a notice → 3139
報 INFORM → 1698
通 COMMUNICATE → 3109

❸ **monkey**

猿 MONKEY → 669

【mōsu】

①ⓐ **speak humbly**

啓 address respectfully → 2763

ⓐ **speak and say**

言 SAY → 1941
云 say → 1931
話 SPEAK → 1527
口 give mouth to → 3382
弁 SPEAK ELOQUENTLY → 2004
語る TELL → 1543
談 TALK → 1569
述 STATE → 3075
陳 SET FORTH → 540

HOMOPHONES

saru ⇨ 猿 669

NOTE

⇨ see USAGE note at 猿 669

丬 ▶**HALF**
nonstandard for 半 3501
3508
5-3□

氷 incorrect classification ⇨ see 39
5-3□

氺 incorrect classification ⇨ see 37
5-3□

尔 incorrect classification ⇨ see 2010
(nonstandard for 爾 3587)
5-3□

册 incorrect classification ⇨ see 3492
(nonstandard for 冊 3483)
5-3□

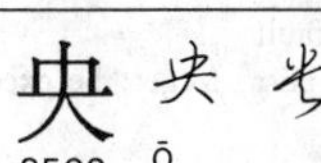
3509 Ō

Radical	Strokes
大 37	5-3-2
Grade	**Freq**
Jōyō-4	538
■ 4 - 5 - 4	

5-4□

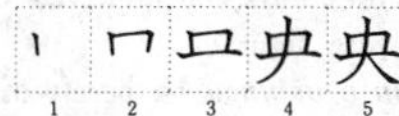

▶**CENTER**

COMPOUNDS

● [original meaning] **center, middle**
中央 *chūō* center
月央 *getsuō* middle of the month
震央 *shin'ō* epicenter (of an earthquake)
中央線 *chūōsen* Chuo Line (central railway line in Tokyo)
道央 *dōō* central Hokkaido

SYNONYMS

● **middle**
中 MIDDLE → 3451
心 HEART → 11
核 NUCLEUS → 927

史 史 史 史
3510 SHI

Ⓒⓗ 史 shǐ

Radical	Strokes
口 30	5-3-2
Grade	**Freq**
Jōyō-4	610
■ 4 - 5 - 4	

5-4□

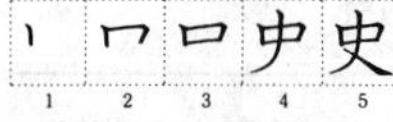

▶**HISTORY**

COMPOUNDS

ⓐ [also suffix] **history, chronicles; history book**
ⓑ [original meaning] historian
史料 *shiryō* historical materials [records]
史書 *shisho* history book
史跡 *shiseki* historic spot [remains]
史学者 *shigakusha* historian
史上に例を見ない *shijō ni rei o minai* be unparalleled in history
歴史 *rekishi* history
青史 *seishi* history, history book
世界史 *sekaishi* world history
日本史 *nihonshi* Japanese history
女史 *joshi* madame, Mrs.; Miss

INDEPENDENT

【**shi** 史】history; history book
史に名を留める *shi ni na o todomeru* inscribe one's name in history

SYNONYMS

ⓐ **history**
歴 PERSONAL HISTORY → 3019
伝 biography → 44

ⓐ **records**
伝 biography → 44
誌 records → 1548
譜 SYSTEMATIC RECORD → 1637
録 RECORD → 1742
記 written account → 1453

NOTE
⇨ see COMPOUND FORMATION for 青史 *seishi* ⇨ 青 2430

5-4□

失 失 失

3511 SHITSU ushina(u) u(seru)▲

丿 𠂉 𠂉 生 失
1 2 3 4 5

Ⓒ 失 shī

Radical	Strokes
大 37	5-3-2
Grade	**Freq**
Jōyō-4	479
■ 4 - 5 - 4	

▶**LOSE** ▶**SLIP**

COMPOUNDS

❶ⓐ **lose, miss**
ⓑ lose one's memory, forget
失業する *shitsugyō suru* be out of work, lose one's job
失礼 *shitsurei* impoliteness, rudeness; bad manners; I beg your pardon / Good-by
失望する *shitsubō suru* be disappointed, lose hope
紛失 *funshitsu* loss
喪失 *sōshitsu* loss, forfeit
遺失する *ishitsu suru* lose, leave behind
失念 *shitsunen* lapse of memory, oblivion

❷ abbrev. of 失業 *shitsugyō*: loss of employment, unemployment
失保 *shitsuho* unemployment insurance
失対 *shittai* measure against unemployment

❸ⓐ **slip (up), make a slip, make a mistake**
ⓑ **slip, oversight, mistake, error**
ⓒ *baseball* error
失言 *shitsugen* slip of the tongue
失笑する *shisshō suru* burst out laughing
失策 *shissaku* blunder, slip, error
失敗 *shippai* failure, mistake
過失 *kashitsu* error, fault, mistake; negligence
捕失 *hoshitsu* catcher's error

❹ improper, mis-
栄養失調 *eiyō shitchō* malnutrition

❺ disappear, vanish
消失する *shōshitsu suru* disappear, vanish; die away

INDEPENDENT

【**shitsu 失**】loss; error, fault
【**shissuru 失する**】lose, miss; forget; be excessive

KUN

【**ushina(u) 失う**】lose, miss, be deprived of
見失う *miushinau* lose sight of
両親を失う *ryōshin o ushinau* be bereft of one's parents
【**u(seru) 失せる**】disappear, vanish, be gone; be lost, be missing
失せろ! *Usero!* Get out of my sight! / Beat it!

SYNONYMS

❶ **losing and loss**
損 LOSS, lose → 651
喪 lose → 2825
逸 LET SLIP → 3120
❸ **mistakes and mistaking**
過 error → 3137
誤 MISTAKE → 1542
錯 mistaken → 1743
-違える mis- → 3151

5-4□

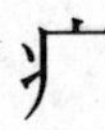

3512

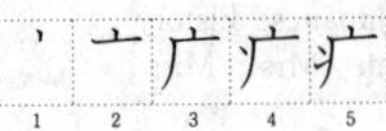
1 2 3 4 5

Radical	Strokes
疒 104	5-5-0
Grade	**Freq**
Radical	
■ 4 - 5 - 4	

RADICAL 104
Standard form: 疒 *yamaidare* 'illness' (病 痛 療)
Description: used in characters related to illness, diseases or injury

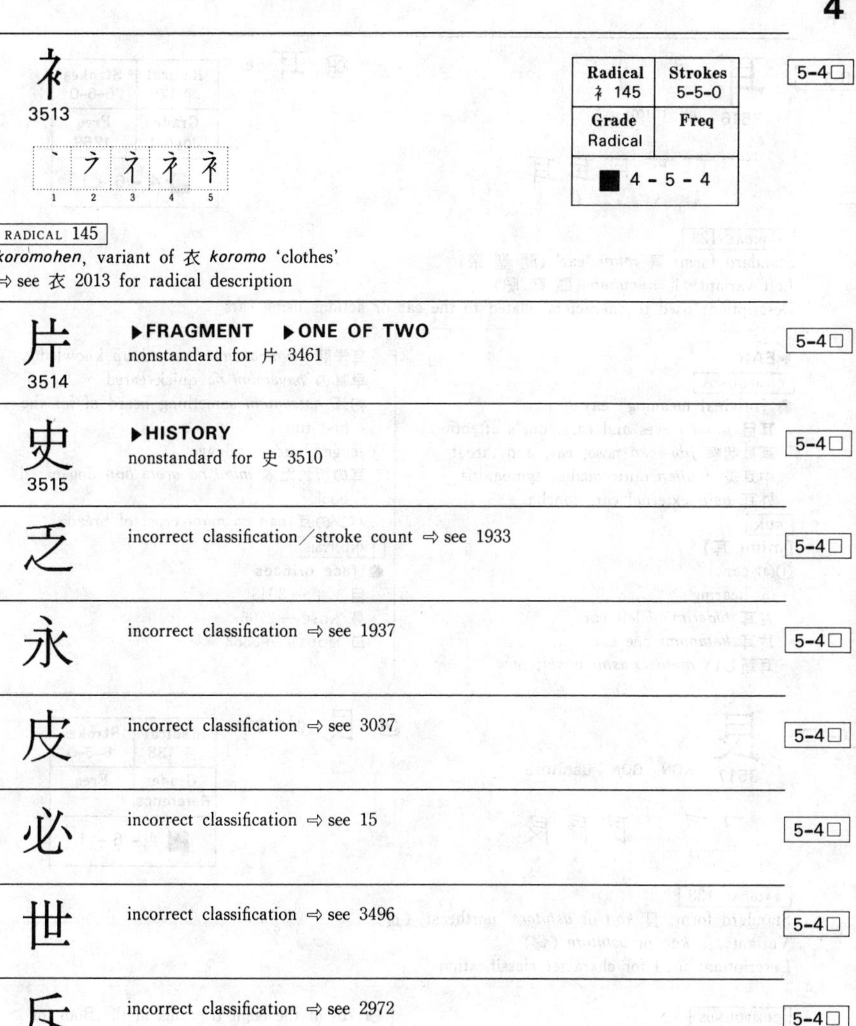

衤
3513

Radical	Strokes
衤 145	5-5-0
Grade	**Freq**
Radical	
■ 4 - 5 - 4	

5-4□

RADICAL 145
koromohen, variant of 衣 *koromo* 'clothes'
⇨ see 衣 2013 for radical description

片
3514

▶FRAGMENT ▶ONE OF TWO
nonstandard for 片 3461

5-4□

史
3515

▶HISTORY
nonstandard for 史 3510

5-4□

之 incorrect classification／stroke count ⇨ see 1933 5-4□

永 incorrect classification ⇨ see 1937 5-4□

皮 incorrect classification ⇨ see 3037 5-4□

必 incorrect classification ⇨ see 15 5-4□

世 incorrect classification ⇨ see 3496 5-4□

斥 incorrect classification ⇨ see 2972 5-4□

矢 incorrect classification ⇨ see 2009 5-4□

6-1□

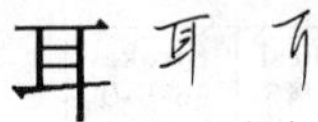

3516 JI mimi

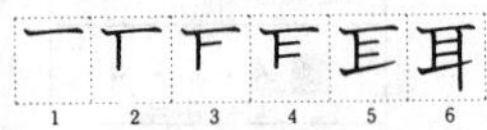

(CH) 耳 ěr

Radical	Strokes
耳 128	6-6-0
Grade	**Freq**
Jōyō-1	1269
■ 4 - 6 - 1	

RADICAL 128
Standard form: 耳 *mimi* 'ear' (聞 聖 聚)
Left variant: 耳 *mimihen* (職 聴 聡)
Description: used in characters related to the ear or actions using ears

▶EAR

COMPOUNDS

● [original meaning] **ear**
耳目 *jimoku* eyes and ears; one's attention
耳鼻咽喉 *jibi-inkō* nose, ear, and throat
中耳炎 *chūjien* otitis media; tympanitis
外耳 *gaiji* external ear, concha

KUN

【mimi 耳】
①ⓐ ear
ⓑ hearing
左耳 *hidarimimi* left ear
片耳 *katamimi* one ear
耳新しい *mimiatarashii* novel; new
耳学問 *mimigakumon* picked-up knowledge
早耳の *hayamimi no* quick-eared
初耳 *hatsumimi* something heard of for the first time
② edge, border; selvage
耳の折れた本 *mimi no oreta hon* dog-eared book
パンの耳 *pan no mimi* crust of bread

SYNONYMS

● **face orifices**
目 EYE → 3043
鼻 NOSE → 2706
口 MOUTH → 3382

6-1□

3517 KON GON ushitora

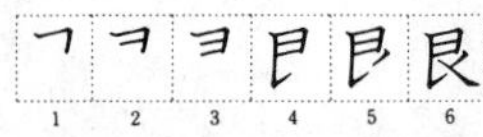

(CH) 艮 gèn gěn

Radical	Strokes
艮 138	6-6-0
Grade	**Freq**
Reference	
■ 4 - 6 - 1	

RADICAL 138
Standard form: 艮 *kon* or *ushitora* 'northeast' (良)
Variant: 艮 *kon* or *ushitora* (艱)
Description: used for character classification

COMPOUNDS

❶ one of the four supplementary signs of the Oriental zodiac: northeast
艮の方角に *ushitora no hōgaku ni* in the direction of northeast

❷ 7th of the eight trigrams in the Book of Changes
艮下艮上 *gonkagonshō* one of the 64 trigrams

両 兩 ~~ ~~

3518 RYŌ

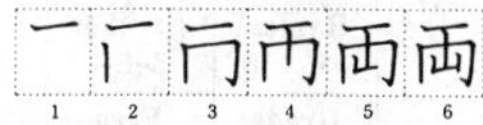

Ⓒ 两 liǎng

Radical	Strokes
一 1△	6-1-5
Grade	Freq
Jōyō-3	239
■ 4 - 6 - 1	

6-1□

▶**BOTH**

COMPOUNDS

❶ [also prefix] **both, two**

両方 *ryōhō* both
両側 *ryōgawa* both sides
両院 *ryōin* both Houses
両手 *ryōte* both hands
両用 *ryōyō* dual use
両親 *ryōshin* parents
両雄 *ryōyū* two great men
両性的 *ryōseiteki* bisexual
両義 *ryōgi* double meaning, two meanings

❷ [formerly also 輛 1590]

ⓐ vehicle, railway car
ⓑ counter for railway cars

車両 *sharyō* vehicle, car; rolling stock
三両 *sanryō* three cars, three coaches

❸ *ryo*:

ⓐ former monetary unit equiv. to 4 *kan* (貫)
ⓑ former unit of weight equiv. to 37.5 g or 1/16 of a *kin* (斤)

両替 *ryōgae* money changing, exchange of money
千両箱 *senryōbako* chest containing a thousand pieces of gold
銀五両 *gin goryō* 5 *ryo* of silver
十両 *jūryō* 10 *ryo*

❹ *slang* yen

二十両 *nijūryō* 20 yen

INDEPENDENT

【ryō 両】 *ryo* (⇨❸); *slang* yen; *literary* both
両の手 *ryō no te* both hands

SYNONYMS

❶ **two**

偶 COUPLE → 132
対 pair → 831
双 SET OF TWO → 25
二 TWO → 1922
弐 TWO (in legal documents) → 3195

❷ⓑ **kinds of railway**

車 railway car → 3552
鉄 railway → 1711
電 electric railway → 2790

❸ⓐ **Japanese money denominations**

文 *mon* → 1962
厘 RIN → 3004
銭 sen → 1725
円 YEN → 2955

再 ~~ ~~

3519 SAI SA futata(bi)

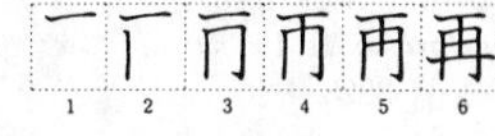

Ⓒ 再 zài

Radical	Strokes
冂 13	6-2-4
Grade	Freq
Jōyō-5	322
■ 4 - 6 - 1	

6-1□

▶**ANOTHER TIME**

COMPOUNDS

❶ [also prefix] **another time, re-, again, a second time, another**

再度 *saido* another time, a second time
再開 *saikai* reopening, resumption
再来 *sairai* return, second coming; Second Advent
再現する *saigen suru* reenact, reproduce
再三 *saisan* again and again, repeatedly
再興 *saikō* revival, restoration
再生 *saisei* reclamation; regeneration, resuscitation; playback
再訂版 *saiteiban* second revised edition
再婚 *saikon* remarriage, second marriage
再検討 *saikentō* reexamination, restudying

❷ [prefix] **after next**

再来週 *saraishū* the week after next
再来年 *sarainen* the year after next

KUN

【futata(bi) 再び】 again, twice, a second time, once more
再び読む *futatabi yomu* read again, reread

SYNONYMS

❶ **repeating and repetition**

又 AGAIN → 3351
復 repeat → 575
重 DUPLICATE → 3573

畳 reduplicate → 2592
改 redo → 243
-換える redo → 587
-直す repetition suffix → 2932
-返す do over → 3060

6-1☐

西 3520 SEI SAI SU▲ nishi

Ⓒ 西 xī

Radical	Strokes
襾 146	6-6-0
Grade	**Freq**
Jōyō-2	183
■ 4 - 6 - 1	

RADICAL 146
simplified form not used as radical
⇨ see 襾 3522 for radical description

▶**WEST**

COMPOUNDS

❶ⓐ **west, western**
ⓑ the West, the Occident; Western
西部 *seibu* western part; the West
西経 *seikei* west longitude
関西 *kansai* Kansai district
東西 *tōzai* east and west
北西 *hokusei* northwest
西欧 *seiō* West Europe, the Occident
西暦 *seireki* Christian Era, A.D.
泰西 *taisei* the Occident
❷ⓐ Spain
ⓑ Spanish (language)
米西戦争 *beisei-sensō* Spanish-American War
日西辞典 *nissei-jiten* Japanese-Spanish dictionary
❸ used phonetically for *su*, esp. in the transliteration of foreign place names
仏蘭西 *furansu* France

INDEPENDENT
【sei 西】Spain

KUN
【nishi 西】[also prefix] west, western
西側 *nishigawa* west side; west European countries and America
西半球 *nishihankyū* western hemisphere
西陣織 *nishijin'ori* *Nishijin* brocade

SYNONYMS

❶ⓐ **cardinal points**
東 EAST → 3568
北 NORTH → 197
南 SOUTH → 2082
ⓑ **west**
洋 WESTERN → 392
❷ⓐ **European countries**
伊 ITALY → 49
仏 FRANCE → 19
独 GERMANY → 395
英 ENGLAND → 2238
蘭 Holland → 2383
露 Russia → 2818
❸ **phonetic [s]/[sh]**
相 phonetic [sō] → 900
沙 phonetic [sha] → 266
遮 phonetic [sha] → 3158
世 phonetic [se] → 3496
須 phonetic [shu] → 574
修 phonetic [shu] → 123

NOTE
⇨ see COMPOUND FORMATION for
西陣織 *nishijin'ori* ⇨ 陣 455
関西 *kansai* ⇨ 関 3328

6-1☐

死 3521 SHI shi(nu) shi(ni)-

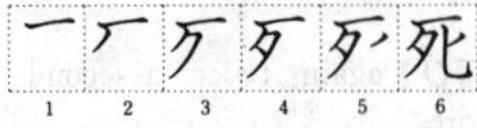

Ⓒ 死 sǐ

Radical	Strokes
歹 78	6-4-2
Grade	**Freq**
Jōyō-3	221
■ 4 - 6 - 1	

▶**DIE**

COMPOUNDS

❶ⓐ [original meaning] **die, perish, come to an end**
ⓑ [also suffix] **death, demise**
ⓒ [formerly also 屍 3099] [original meaning] dead body, corpse
ⓓ (no longer useful) dead, obsolete, useless
死亡 *shibō* death
死刑 *shikei* capital punishment, death penalty

死後 *shigo* after one's death
死去 *shikyo* death, passing away
戦死する *senshi suru* die in battle
即死 *sokushi* instant death, death on the spot
焼死 *shōshi* death by fire
中毒死 *chūdokushi* death from poisoning
死体 *shitai* corpse
死語 *shigo* dead language; obsolete word

❷ struggle to the death, desperation
死守する *shishu suru* defend to the last, defend desperately
必死になって *hisshi ni natte* for one's dear life, desperately

❸ *baseball* out; dead (ball)
死球 *shikyū* dead ball
無死満塁 *mushi manrui* bases are loaded with no outs

INDEPENDENT

【shi 死】 death; *baseball* out; dead ball
死を覚悟する *shi o kakugo suru* be ready to die

【shisuru 死する】 die

KUN

【shi(nu) 死ぬ】 die, pass away; commit suicide; *baseball* be put out; be captured (in go or chess)
死ぬ迄戦う *shinu made tatakau* fight to the last [death]

【shi(ni)- 死に-】 [also verbal prefix] dying, death
死に絶える *shinitaeru* die out, become extinct
死に金 *shinigane* wasted money, idle capital
死に物狂いで *shinimonogurui de* desperately, frantically

SYNONYMS

❶ⓐ & ❶ⓑ die
没 die → 260
亡 DECEASE → 3402
殉 DIE A MARTYR → 941
去 pass away → 2156
逝 DEPART THIS LIFE → 3104
枯 WITHER → 898

3522

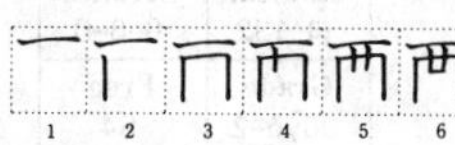

Radical	Strokes
襾 146	6-6-0
Grade Radical	Freq
■ 4 - 6 - 1	

6-1□

RADICAL 146

Standard form: 襾 *nishi* 'cover' (覃 覈 羈)
Top variant: 西 *nishi* (要 覆 覇)
Description: used in characters related to covering

西

3523

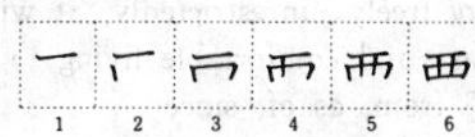

Radical	Strokes
西 146	6-6-0
Grade Radical	Freq
■ 4 - 6 - 1	

6-1□

RADICAL 146

variant of 襾 *nishi* 'cover'
⇨ see 襾 3522 for radical description

亙

3524

▶**EXTEND OVER**

nonstandard for 亘 1939

6-1□

百

incorrect classification ⇨ see 2026

6-1□

6-1□ 而 incorrect classification ⇨ see 2027

6-1□ 丞 incorrect classification ⇨ see 2541

6-1□ 各 incorrect classification ⇨ see 2168

6-1□ 名 incorrect classification ⇨ see 2169

6-1□ 凹 incorrect stroke count ⇨ see 3482

6-1□ 凸 incorrect stroke count ⇨ see 3486

6-2□ 自 自 自 Ⓒⓗ 自 zì

3525 JI SHI mizuka(ra) ono(zukara)▲ ono(zuto)▲

Radical	Strokes
自 132	6-6-0
Grade	**Freq**
Jōyō-2	54
■ 4 - 6 - 2	

Stroke order: 1 2 3 4 5 6

RADICAL 132
Standard form: 自 *mizukara* 'self' (臭)
Description: used in characters related to the nose

▶**SELF**

COMPOUNDS

❶ⓐ [also prefix] **self, oneself**
ⓑ **one's own, one's**
自分 *jibun* self, oneself
自己 *jiko* oneself, self, ego
自身 *jishin* self, oneself; itself
自信 *jishin* self-confidence
自殺 *jisatsu* suicide
自供 *jikyō* (voluntary) confession
自衛 *jiei* self-defense, self-protection
自慢 *jiman* pride, self-praise, vanity
独自の *dokuji no* original; personal, individual
自宅 *jitaku* one's house, one's home
自国 *jikoku* one's own country

❷ **by itself, naturally, spontaneously**
自然 *shizen* nature
自動車 *jidōsha* automobile
自転 *jiten* rotation (of the earth)
自発的 *jihatsuteki* spontaneous, voluntary

❸ **as one pleases**
自由 *jiyū* freedom
自在に *jizai ni* freely, unrestrictedly, at will
自適 *jiteki* easy and comfortable living

❹ [also prefix] from, as of, since
自今 *jikon* hereafter
自東京 *jitōkyō* from Tokyo

❺ abbrev. of 自由民主党 *jiyūminshutō*: Liberal Democratic Party
自公民 *jikōmin* Liberal Democratic Party, Komeito and Democratic Socialist Party

❻ abbrev. of 自動車 *jidōsha*: automobile
自販 *jihan* automobile sales
自工 *jikō* automobile industry

❼ intransitive verb
自他 *jita* oneself and others; transitive and intransitive

❽ [original meaning, now obsolete] nose

KUN

【**mizuka(ra)** 自ら】 oneself; in person, personally

自らの *mizukara no* one's own, personal

【ono(zukara) 自ずから】 naturally, by itself, spontaneously

自ずから明かな *onozukara akiraka na* self-evident

【ono(zuto) 自ずと】 naturally, by itself, spontaneously

SYNONYMS

❶ **first person pronouns**

我 SELF → 3548
己 ONESELF → 3380
身 ONE'S PERSON → 3553
私 I (*polite*) → 1115
僕 I (*familiar*) → 164
俺 I (*intimate*) → 110
吾 I (*elegant*) → 2407
予 I (*pompous*) → 1983
余 I (*pompous*) → 2042
麿 I (*archaic*) → 3184
朕 IMPERIAL WE → 949

❹ **direction indicators**

来 since → 3551
以 TO THE...OF → 41
迄 UP TO → 3201
-向け (bound) for → 3052
-行き bound for → 212
至 to → 2182

NOTE

⇨ see COMPOUND FORMATION for
自由 *jiyū* ⇨ 由 3499
自然 *shizen* ⇨ 然 2782

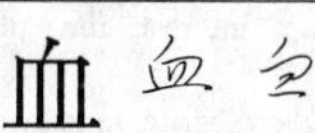

3526 KETSU chi

Ⓒⓗ 血 xuè xiě

Radical	Strokes
血 143	6-6-0
Grade	Freq
Jōyō-3	689
■ 4 - 6 - 2	

6-2□

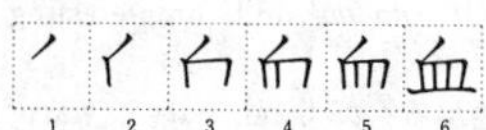

RADICAL 143

Standard form: 血 *chi* 'blood' (衆)
Left variant: 血 *chihen* (衄)
Description: used in characters related to blood

▶BLOOD

COMPOUNDS

❶ [also suffix] [original meaning] **blood**

血液 *ketsueki* blood
血管 *kekkan* blood vessel
血圧 *ketsuatsu* blood pressure
献血 *kenketsu* blood donation
貧血 *hinketsu* anemia
出血 *shukketsu* bleeding; hemorrhage; sacrifice

❷ hot-blooded, lively

血気 *kekki* hot blood of youth, youthful vigor
冷血な *reiketsu na* cold-blooded, coldhearted, heartless
熱血漢 *nekketsukan* hot-blooded man

❸ blood (relation), lineage

血族 *ketsuzoku* blood relative
血統 *kettō* lineage, blood, bloodline
混血 *konketsu* mixed-blood, racial mixture

KUN

【chi 血】 blood; blood (relation), lineage

血眼 *chimanako* bloodshot eye
血塗れの *chimamire no* bloodstained, bloody
鼻血 *hanaji* nosebleed
血筋 *chisuji* blood relationship, lineage
血の繋がり *chi no tsunagari* blood relationship

SYNONYMS

❸ **lineage**

系 LINEAGE → 1944

6-2☐

曲 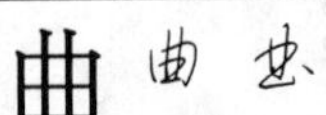

3527 KYOKU ma(garu) ma(geru)

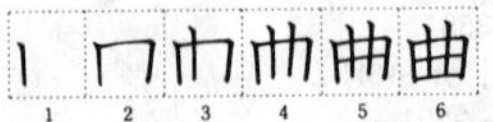

CH 曲 qū qǔ

Radical	Strokes
日 73	6-4-2
Grade	**Freq**
Jōyō-3	602
4-6-2	

▶**MUSICAL COMPOSITION** ▶**CURVE**

COMPOUNDS

❶ⓐ [also suffix] **musical composition, (piece of) music, melody, tune, song**

ⓑ counter for musical compositions

曲調 *kyokuchō* melody, tune

曲節 *kyokusetsu* tune, air

曲名 *kyokumei* title of a musical composition [song]

曲目 *kyokumoku* number; program, selection (for a concert)

楽曲 *gakkyoku* musical piece, composition, tune

作曲 *sakkyoku* composition

編曲 *henkyoku* arrangement (of a melody)

名曲 *meikyoku* excellent [exquisite] piece of music, famous tune

新曲 *shinkyoku* new musical composition, new tune [song]

舞曲 *bukyoku* dance music, music and dancing

戯曲 *gikyoku* drama, play

歌謡曲 *kayōkyoku* popular song

交響曲 *kōkyōkyoku* symphony

五曲 *gokyoku* five compositions

❷ⓐ **curve, bend**

ⓑ **curved, bent**

曲折する *kyokusetsu suru* bend, wind; zigzag

曲率 *kyokuritsu* curvature

曲度 *kyokudo* curvature

湾曲 *wankyoku* curve, crook, bend

屈曲 *kukkyoku* bending, winding

曲線 *kyokusen* curve, curved line

曲管 *kyokukan* curved pipe, siphon

❸ wrong, not right, perverse

曲事 *kyokuji* wickedness, injustice

曲解する *kyokkai* (=*kyokukai*) *suru* misinterpret, distort

曲直 *kyokuchoku* right and wrong

歪曲 *waikyoku* distortion; perversion

❹ acrobatics

曲芸 *kyokugei* acrobatics, trick, stunt

曲乗り *kyokunori* trick riding

❺ detailed

同工異曲である *dōkōikyoku de aru* be practically the same, be equally excellent in workmanship though difficult in style

INDEPENDENT

【**kyoku** 曲】musical composition, (piece of) music, melody, tune, song; interest, fun, pleasure; wrong; injustice

曲を付ける *kyoku o tsukeru* write music for a song

曲の無い *kyoku no nai* dull, uninteresting

KUN

【**ma(garu)** 曲がる】*vi* bend, curve; warp, get crooked; turn (to the left); be perverse

曲がり *magari* curvature, warp

曲がりくねる *magarikuneru* turn and twist, zigzag

曲がり角 *magarikado* street corner, turning

左に曲がる *hidari ni magaru* turn to the left

曲がりなりにも *magarinari ni mo* somehow, though imperfect

【**ma(geru)** 曲げる】*vt* bend, curve; pervert, depart from; pawn, hock

曲げ *mage* bending, flexure

曲げ物 *magemono* round chip [bent wood] box

事実を曲げる *jijitsu o mageru* falsify a fact

SYNONYMS

❶ⓐ **music and songs**

楽 MUSIC → 2826

音 sound of music → 2070

節 tune → 2691

調べ melody → 1567

歌 SONG → 1825

謡 POPULAR SONG → 1597

❷ **bend**

屈 BEND → 3079

折 bend → 253

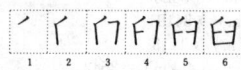

臼

3528 KYŪ usu

Radical	Strokes
臼 134	6-6-0
Grade	Freq
Reference	
■ 4-6-2	

Ⓒⓗ 臼 jiù

6-2□

RADICAL 134

Standard form: 臼 *usu* 'mortar' (舂 舅)

Variant: 𦥑 *usu* (與 興)

Description: used in characters related to mortars or lifting with both hands

COMPOUNDS

ⓐ [original meaning] mortar; hand mill

ⓑ something resembling a mortar

臼砲 *kyūhō* (trench) mortar

石臼 *ishiusu* stone mortar [mill]

碾き臼 *hikiusu* hand mill, quern

臼歯 *kyūshi* molar (tooth)

脱臼 *dakkyū* dislocation

羊

incorrect classification ⇨ see 2184

6-2□

缶 缶

incorrect classification ⇨ see ■2-4

6-2□

米 米 米

3529 BEI MAI MĒTORU▲ kome yone▲

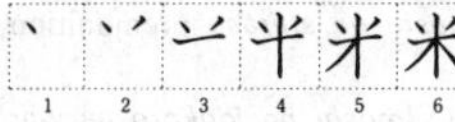

Radical	Strokes
米 119	6-6-0
Grade	Freq
Jōyō-2	76
■ 4-6-3	

Ⓒⓗ 米 mǐ

6-3Ⅱ

RADICAL 119

Standard form: 米 *kome* 'rice' (粟 粥 粤)

Left variant: 米 *komehen* (精 糖 粉)

Description: used in characters related to rice or rice products

▶RICE ▶AMERICA

COMPOUNDS

❶ [also suffix] **rice**

米穀 *beikoku* rice

米価 *beika* price of rice

米作 *beisaku* rice crop

米飯 *beihan* cooked rice

玄米 *genmai* unpolished rice

精米 *seimai* rice polishing; polished [white] rice

外米 *gaimai* foreign [imported] rice

配給米 *haikyūmai* rationed rice

新潟米 *niigatamai* Niigata rice

❷ⓐ **America, United States; American**

ⓑ **continent of America**

米国 *beikoku* U.S.A.

米軍 *beigun* American armed forces

米貨 *beika* American currency, U.S. dollar

日米 *nichibei* Japan and U.S.

渡米 *tobei* going to America

欧米 *ōbei* Europe and America

南米 *nanbei* South America

❸ meter

百米 *hyakumētoru* 100 m

❹ unclassified compounds

米寿 *beiju* 88 years old, one's 88th birthday

INDEPENDENT

【**bei** 米】America, United States

米の介入 *bei no kainyū* intervention of America

KUN

【**kome** 米】rice

米粒 *kometsubu* grain of rice

米俵 *komedawara* (straw) rice bag

米屋 *komeya* rice merchant

【**yone** 米】*elegant* rice

SYNONYMS

❶ rice
飯 COOKED RICE → 1691
稲 RICE PLANT → 1219

❶ cereals
麦 WHEAT → 2408
豆 BEAN → 1943

❷ⓐ North American countries
加 Canada → 38

ⓑ continents
欧 EUROPE → 887
豪 Australia → 2140
阿 Africa → 346
亜 Asia → 3540

❸ length units
寸 *sun* (3.03 cm) → 2935
尺 *SHAKU* (30.3 cm) → 3440
尋 fathom (1.8 m) → 2322
間 *ken* (1.8 m) → 3323
丈 *jo* (3.03 m) → 3419
町 *cho* (109 m) → 1113
里 LEAGUE, *ri* (3.4 km) → 3542

COMPOUND FORMATION

米寿 *beiju*
米寿 '88 years old, etc.' refers to one's 88th birthday since 米 can be split into ⺍ (variant of 八), 十 and 八, i.e., 八十八 or 88.

6-3Ⅱ

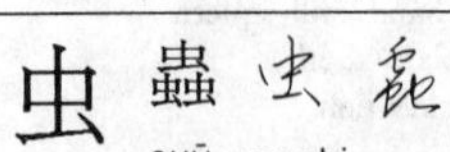

3530 CHŪ mushi

Ⓒⓗ 虫 chóng

Radical	Strokes
虫 142	6-6-0
Grade	**Freq**
Jōyō-1	1211
■ 4 - 6 - 3	

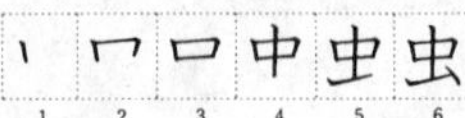

RADICAL 142
Standard form: 虫 *mushi* 'bug' (融 蛮 蛍)
Left variant: 虫 *mushihen* (虹 蚊 蛇)
Description: used in characters related to insects, reptiles or small animals

▶**INSECT**

COMPOUNDS

● [also suffix] **insect, worm, bug**
虫類 *chūrui* insects and worms
虫害 *chūgai* insect damage
虫垂 *chūsui* appendix
昆虫 *konchū* insect
防虫加工の *bōchūkakō no* mothproof
殺虫剤 *satchūzai* insecticide, vermicide
寄生虫 *kiseichū* parasite

KUN

【mushi 虫】
① [also suffix] insect, worm; bug; roundworm
虫下し *mushikudashi* vermifuge, anthelmintic
虫が付く *mushi ga tsuku* become verminous; begin to keep bad company; have an (unfavorable) lover
毛虫 *kemushi* hairy caterpillar
油虫 *aburamushi* cockroach
貝殻虫 *kaigaramushi* scale insect
② worm-eaten; in an unfavorable condition
虫歯 *mushiba* decayed tooth
水虫 *mizumushi* athlete's foot, dermatophytosis
③ feeling; temper; self-seeking
虫の知らせ *mushi no shirase* premonition, hunch
虫の居所が悪い *mushi no idokoro ga warui* be in a cross mood
虫が良い *mushi ga ii* selfish, asking too much
④ enthusiastic fan (as of books)
本の虫 *hon no mushi* bookworm
⑤ [also suffix] belittling term indicating a negative quality in a person
弱虫 *yowamushi* weakling
泣き虫 *nakimushi* blubberer, crybaby
点取り虫 *tentorimushi* grinder, dig
⑥ *elec* valve core
弁の虫 *ben no mushi* valve core

SYNONYMS

● **insect**
昆 INSECT → 2413
繭 COCOON → 2380

朱 朱 朱

3531 SHU ake▲

CH 朱 zhū

Radical	Strokes
木 75	6-4-2
Grade	Freq
Jōyō	1689
■ 4 - 6 - 3	

6-3

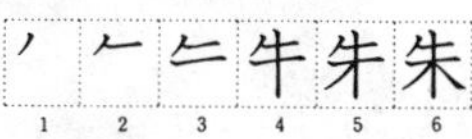

▶**VERMILION**

COMPOUNDS

❶ **vermilion, red**

朱顔 *shugan* flushed face
朱色 *shuiro* vermilion, Chinese red
朱肉 *shuniku* red ink pad
朱書する *shusho suru* write in red
丹朱 *tanshu* vermilion, red; cinnabar

❷ cinnabar

朱筆 *shuhitsu* cinnabar brush
朱墨 *shuzumi* cinnabar stick

❸ *shu*: former monetary unit equiv. to 1/16 of a *ryo* (両)

一朱銀 *isshugin* type of silver coin in Edo period

❹ Zhu Xi, great scholar of the Song Dynasty

朱子学 *shushigaku* doctrines of Zhu Xi; neo-Confucianism

INDEPENDENT

【**shu 朱**】vermilion, red; cinnabar stick; *shu* (⇨ ❸)
朱を入れる *shu o ireru* correct, retouch

KUN

【**ake 朱**】red, blood red
朱に染まる *ake ni somaru* welter in blood

SYNONYMS

❶ **red colors**

丹 CINNABAR → 3441
赤 RED → 2193
紅 CRIMSON → 1277
緋 SCARLET → 1369
茜 MADDER → 2261

3532

Radical	Strokes
耒 127	6-6-0
Grade	Freq
Radical	
■ 4 - 6 - 3	

6-3

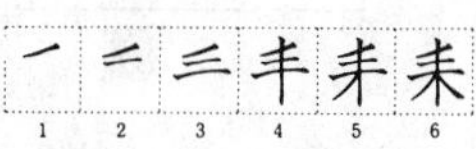

RADICAL 127

Standard form: 耒 *raisuki* 'plow'
Left variant: 耒 *raihen* (耕 耗)
Left variant: 耒 *sukihen* (耘 耡)
Description: used in characters related to farm implements or farming

3533

Radical	Strokes
聿 129	6-6-0
Grade	Freq
Radical	
■ 4 - 6 - 3	

6-3

RADICAL 129

Standard form: 聿 *fudezukuri* 'brush' (粛 肇 肆)
Description: used in characters related to writing with a brush

耒

3534

▶**COME**

nonstandard for 来 3551

6-3

6-3◫ 年 incorrect classification ⇨ see 2035

6-3◫ 羊 incorrect classification ⇨ see 2183

6-4□ 戌
3535 JUTSU inu

Ⓒ 戌 xū

Radical	Strokes
戈 62	6-4-2
Grade	Freq
Reference	
■ 4 - 6 - 4	

COMPOUNDS

● eleventh sign of the Oriental zodiac: the Dog—(time) 7-9 p.m., (direction) WNW, (season) September (of the lunar calendar) (⇨ see APPENDIX 7)

戊戌 *bojutsu* 35th of the sexagenary cycle

HOMOPHONES

inu ⇨ 犬 3464 狗 345

NOTE

⇨ see USAGE note at 犬 3464

6-4□ 吏 吏 吏 吏
3536 RI

一 𠂇 戸 ⼸ 吏 吏
1 2 3 4 5 6

Ⓒ 吏 lì

Radical	Strokes
口 30	6-3-3
Grade	Freq
Jōyō	1880
■ 4 - 6 - 4	

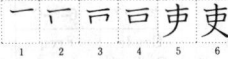

▶OFFICIAL

COMPOUNDS

● [also suffix] [original meaning] **official, officer**

吏人 *rijin* officials
吏員 *riin* official
吏臭 *rishū* officialdom, red tape
官吏 *kanri* government official
公吏 *kōri* public official
税関吏 *zeikanri* customs officer

INDEPENDENT

【ri 吏】 official, officer

SYNONYMS

● **officials**

官 GOVERNMENT OFFICIAL → 2226
僚 official → 165
司 officiator → 2931
役 executive → 244
事 officer → 3567

6-4□ 成 成 成 成
3537 SEI JŌ na(ru) na(su) -na(su)

丿 厂 万 成 成 成
1 2 3 4 5 6

Ⓒ 成 chéng

Radical	Strokes
戈 62	6-4-2
Grade	Freq
Jōyō-4	109
■ 4 - 6 - 4	

▶FORM ▶ACHIEVE

COMPOUNDS

❶ⓐ [original meaning] (become formed) **form, constitute, be completed, come into existence**

ⓑ (give form to) **form, make, create, bring to completion**

ⓒ **established, existing, completed**

成分 *seibun* ingredient, component, constituent

成立する *seiritsu suru* come into existence, materialize; be formed, be organized; be

concluded
形成する *keisei suru* form, make up, mold
生成文法 *seisei-bunpō* generative grammar
完成する *kansei suru* complete, finish; be completed, be finished
合成する *gōsei suru* compose, compound, synthesize
編成する *hensei suru* form, compose, compile
結成する *kessei suru* form, organize
構成 *kōsei* composition, construction, formation, organization
成句 *seiku* set phrase
既成の *kisei no* established, existing

❷ⓐ achieve, attain, accomplish, succeed
ⓑ achievement, success
成功する *seikō suru* succeed, be successful
成果 *seika* result, fruit, outcome
成績 *seiseki* results, record, achievement
成就する *jōju suru* accomplish, achieve, attain
成仏する *jōbutsu suru* enter Nirvana, attain Buddhahood; die
成否 *seihi* success or failure, result

❸ⓐ grow up, mature
ⓑ fully grown, adult
成長する *seichō suru* grow up
成熟 *seijuku* maturity, ripeness, full growth
成育する *seiiku suru* grow (up), be brought up
養成する *yōsei suru* train, educate, bring up
促成栽培の野菜 *sokusei-saibai no yasai* forced vegetables
成人 *seijin* adult, grownup
成虫 *seichū* imago, adult (insect)

❹ acceptable
賛成する *sansei suru* approve of, agree, support

❺ become, turn into
成空 *seikū* come to nothingness

KUN

【na(ru) 成る】
① be accomplished, succeed, be attained, materialize
成るべく *narubeku* as...as possible, if possible
成程 *naruhodo* I see, really, indeed
工事が成った *Kōji ga natta* The work was finished
丸で成ってない *maru de natte nai* not good at all
② form, constitute, consist of, be composed of
成り立つ *naritatsu* consist of; be realized, be concluded, materialize
成り行き *nariyuki* course [turn] of events, issue
委員会は五人から成る *Iinkai wa gonin kara naru* The committee consists of five members
③ honorific auxiliary verb
山田さんがお見えに成りました *Yamadasan ga omie ni narimashita* Mr. Yamada is here to see you
④ bear, put up with
そんな事をされて成る物か *Sonna koto o sarete naru mono ka* I can't put up with such a thing
⑤ (of chessmen) be promoted
成り駒 *narikoma* promoted chessman
成り上がる *nariagaru* suddenly rise to a higher position

【na(su) 成す】
① form, make, constitute
円を成す *en o nasu* form a circle
山成す *yamanasu* mountainlike, a mountain of
② achieve, accomplish, succeed
成し遂げる *nashitogeru* complete, carry out, accomplish
名を成す *na o nasu* make a name, become famous

【-na(su) -成す】 [verbal suffix] perform an action deliberately
取り成す *torinasu* mediate, intercede; recommend
持て成す *motenasu* entertain, show hospitality

SYNONYMS

❶ⓑ make
作 MAKE → 68
造 MAKE → 3110
工 MANUFACTURE → 3381
製 MANUFACTURE → 2803
産 PRODUCE → 3298
調 PREPARE → 1567
組む ASSEMBLE → 1337
構 CONSTRUCT → 1049

❷ⓐ accomplish
遂 ACCOMPLISH → 3138
達 ATTAIN → 3139
徹 GO THROUGH → 726
破 carry through with → 1150

❸ⓐ grow
長 grow (up) → 2556
生 grow → 3497
育 grow → 2050
発 develop → 2565
伸 expand → 70
展 UNFOLD → 3111

ⓐ mature
熟 MATURE → 2868
稔 RIPEN → 1207
実る bear fruit → 2225

USAGE

❶ naru
成る

① be accomplished, succeed, be attained, materialize
② form, constitute, consist of, be composed of
③ honorific auxiliary verb
④ bear, put up with
⑤ (of chessmen) be promoted

為る
①ⓐ become, turn into, grow, get
ⓑ begin to (do), come to (do)
②ⓐ result in, turn out
ⓑ amount [come] to
③ⓐ (of seasons) come, set in
ⓑ elapse, pass
④ serve [act] as

生る
bear fruit, fruit

❷ **nasu**

成す
① form, make, constitute
② achieve, accomplish, succeed

為す
do, perform, carry out

生す
give birth, bear

HOMOPHONES

naru ⇨ 為 3577 生 3497
nasu ⇨ 為 3577 生 3497

NOTE

⇨ see COMPOUND FORMATION for 成程 *naruhodo* ⇨ 程 1190

6-4□

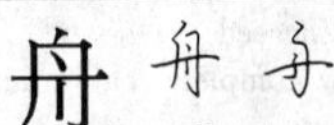

3538 SHŪ fune funa- -bune

Ⓒⓗ 舟 zhōu

Radical	Strokes
舟 137	6-6-0
Grade	**Freq**
Jōyō	1380
■ 4 - 6 - 4	

RADICAL 137

Standard form: 舟 *fune* 'ship'
Left variant: 舟 *funehen* (船 航 般)
Description: used in characters related to ships, boats or their parts

▶SMALL BOAT

COMPOUNDS

● [original meaning] (**small**) **boat, ship**
舟艇 *shūtei* boat, craft
舟行 *shūkō* navigation, going by ship
舟運 *shūun* transportation by water
呉越同舟 *goetsu-dōshū* bitter enemies in the same boat

KUN

【fune 舟】 small boat [craft], (row)boat
小舟 *kobune* small craft

【funa- 舟-】 [also 船-] [also prefix] small boat
舟着き場 *funatsukiba* wharf
舟人 *funabito* sailor
舟大工 *funadaiku* boatbuilder

【-bune -舟】 [also -船] [also suffix] small boat
釣り舟 *tsuribune* fishing boat
渡し舟 *watashibune* ferryboat

SYNONYMS

● & **【fune】 boats and ships**
船 SHIP → 1341
艇 BOAT → 1365
舶 OCEANGOING SHIP → 1340
艦 WARSHIP → 1435
潜 submarine → 746
隻 COUNTER FOR SHIPS → 2755

HOMOPHONES

fune ⇨ 船 1341 槽 1067
funa- ⇨ 船 1341
-bune ⇨ 船 1341

NOTE

⇨ see USAGE note at 船 1341

6-4□

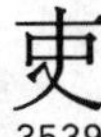

3539

▶OFFICIAL

nonstandard for 吏 3536

6-4□ 孝

incorrect classification/stroke count ⇨ see 3205

肉 incorrect classification ⇨ see 3200 6-4□

劣 incorrect classification ⇨ see 2395 6-4□

糸 incorrect classification ⇨ see 2179 6-4□

考 老 incorrect classification ⇨ see ■ 4 – 2 6-4□

亜 亞 亜 亜 ⒸⒽ 亚 yà 7-1□

3540 A

Radical 二 7	Strokes 7-2-5
Grade Jōyō	Freq 1244
■ 4 - 7 - 1	

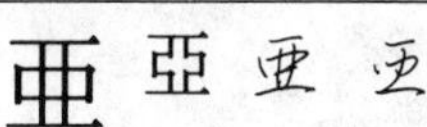

1 2 3 4 5 6 7

▶SUB- ▶PHONETIC [a]

COMPOUNDS

❶ [also prefix]

ⓐ **sub-, subordinate**

ⓑ *chem* sub-, -ite, -ous

亜熱帯 *anettai* subtropics

亜科 *aka* suborder

亜麻 *ama* flax

亜鉛 *aen* zinc

亜炭化物 *atankabutsu* subcarbide

亜硫酸ナトリウム *aryūsan natoriumu* sodium sulfite

亜硝酸 *ashōsan* nitrous acid

❷ⓐ **used phonetically for *a*, esp. in the transliteration of foreign place names**

ⓑ Argentina

亜米利加 *amerika* America

亜爾然丁 *aruzenchin* Argentina

亜国 *akoku* Argentina

❸ **Asia**

東亜 *tōa* East Asia

興亜 *kōa* development of Asia

❹ [also 堊 2768] whitewash

白亜 *hakua* chalk; white wall

INDEPENDENT

【a 亜】Asia

SYNONYMS

❶ⓐ **subordinate**

準 QUASI- → 2856

半 semi- → 3501

従 subordinate → 415

副 SECONDARY → 1776

次 secondary → 54

准 JUNIOR → 127

助 assistant → 1121

❷ⓐ **phonetic** [a]

阿 PHONETIC [a] → 346

❸ **continents**

阿 Africa → 346

欧 EUROPE → 887

米 AMERICA → 3529

豪 Australia → 2140

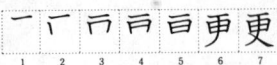

7-1□ 更 更 更 更 ㊥ 更 gēng gèng

3541 KŌ sara sara(ni) fu(keru) fu(kasu)

Radical	Strokes
日 73	7-4-3
Grade	**Freq**
Jōyō	922
■ 4 - 7 - 1	

一 丆 戸 百 亘 更 更
1 2 3 4 5 6 7

▶RENEW

COMPOUNDS

❶ⓐ renew, replace, change, alter
ⓑ change, exchange, alternate
更新する *kōshin suru* renew, renovate, innovate
更改 *kōkai* renewal, renovation
更正 *kōsei* correction, revision, rectification
更生 *kōsei* rebirth, rehabilitation; recycling
更衣する *kōi suru* change one's clothes
変更する *henkō suru* alter, change, modify, shift
更迭 *kōtetsu* reshuffle, change, exchanging places
❷ watches of the night, lateness of the night
深更 *shinkō* dead of night, midnight
初更 *shokō* first watch of the night
三更 *sankō* midnight, in the dead of night
❸ [formerly 甦 3315] revive, come back to life
更生する *kōsei suru* revive, resuscitate

INDEPENDENT

【kō 更】 watches of the night, lateness of the night

KUN

【sara 更】 *literary* of course, naturally; [in compounds] furthermore, moreover, still more
尚更 *naosara* still more, all the more
今更 *imasara* now, after so long a time
満更 *manzara* (not) wholly, (not) altogether
【sara(ni) 更に】 furthermore, moreover; still more; anew, afresh, again; (not) in the least
更に一歩を進める *sarani ippo o susumeru* go a step further
【fu(keru) 更ける】 *vi* grow late, advance, wear on
秋更けて *aki fukete* late in autumn
【fu(kasu) 更かす】 *vt* sit up till late (at night)
夜更かし *yofukashi* sitting up late at night, keeping late hours

SYNONYMS

❶ⓐ reform
改 REFORM → 243
革 REFORM → 2448
新 make new → 1784
ⓑ change and replace
変 CHANGE → 2069
改 change → 243
易 change → 2411
化 CHANGE INTO, -ize → 21
遷 undergo transition → 3170
転 turn into → 1480
換 EXCHANGE → 587
交 INTERCHANGE → 2015
替 REPLACE → 2783
代 SUBSTITUTE → 30
迭 ALTERNATE → 3077
【sarani】
○ additionally
尚 STILL → 2233
且つ AS WELL → 3485
兼 CONCURRENTLY → 2286
亦 ALSO → 2011
又 also, and → 3351
及び and → 3385
並びに and also → 2246
傍ら besides → 147

里 里 里

3542 RI sato

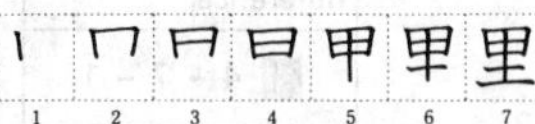

Ⓒⓗ 里 lǐ

Radical	Strokes
里 166	7-7-0
Grade	**Freq**
Jōyō-2	1074
■ 4 - 7 - 1	

7-1□

RADICAL 166

Standard form: 里 *sato* 'hamlet' (重 量 釐)
Left variant: 里 *satohen* (野)
Description: used for character classification

▶**COUNTRYSIDE** ▶**LEAGUE**

COMPOUNDS

❶ⓐ **countryside, country, rural district**
ⓑ [formerly also 俚 99] (of the countryside) **rural, rustic, vulgar**
郷里 *kyōri* one's old home, native place
里謡 *riyō* ballad, folk song
里言 *rigen* dialect
❷ⓐ **hamlet, village**
ⓑ *ri*: unit of administration in ancient Japan similar to a hamlet
里人 *rijin* villagers, countryfolk
遊里 *yūri* licensed quarters, red-light district
❸ⓐ (former unit of distance) **league, mile, *ri***
ⓑ *ri*, Japanese league: unit of length equiv. to approx. 3.9 km or 36 *cho* (町)
里程 *ritei* mileage
海里 *kairi* nautical mile
一里塚 *ichirizuka* milepost, milestone
千里の道も一歩から *Senri no michi mo ippo kara* A journey of a thousand miles starts with but a single step
万里の長城 *banri no chōjō* Great Wall of China
❹ used phonetically for *ri*, esp. in the transliteration of foreign words
巴里 *pari* Paris

INDEPENDENT

【**ri 里**】*ri*, Japanese league (⇨ ❸ⓑ)

KUN

【**sato 里**】
① hamlet, village
里芋 *satoimo* taro
村里 *murazato* village
古里(＝故郷) *furusato* hometown, birthplace
山里 *yamazato* mountain hamlet [village]
② countryside
③ⓐ one's parents' home
ⓑ [sometimes also 郷] hometown, one's birthplace
里心 *satogokoro* homesickness

SYNONYMS

❶ⓐ **the country**
郷 the country → 549
郊 SUBURB → 1286
辺 BORDERLAND → 3029
ⓑ **vulgar and unrefined**
野 rustic → 1485
粗 COARSE → 1329
俗 vulgar → 104
卑 MEAN → 2642
蛮 barbaric → 2129
❷ⓐ **villages and towns**
村 VILLAGE → 834
郷 HOMETOWN → 549
庄 FEUDAL VILLAGE → 3051
町 TOWN → 1113
❸ⓐ & ❸ⓑ **length units**
町 *cho* (109 m) → 1113
丈 *jo* (3.03 m) → 3419
間 *ken* (1.8 m) → 3323
尋 fathom (1.8 m) → 2322
米 meter → 3529
尺 *SHAKU* (30.3 cm) → 3440
寸 *sun* (3.03 cm) → 2935

USAGE

sato
里
① hamlet, village
② countryside
③ⓐ one's parents' home
ⓑ [sometimes also 郷] hometown, one's birthplace
郷
[usu. 里] hometown, one's birthplace

HOMOPHONES

sato ⇨ 郷 549

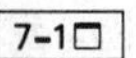

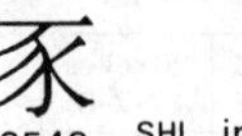

3543 SHI inoko

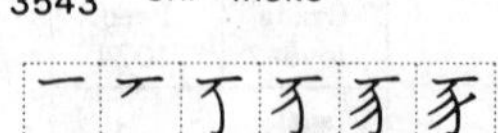

Ⓒⓗ 豕 shǐ

Radical	Strokes
豕 152	7-7-0
Grade	Freq
Reference	
■ 4 - 7 - 1	

RADICAL 152

Standard form: 豕 *inoko* 'pig' (象 豪 豢)

Variant: 豸 *inokohen* (豬)

Description: used in characters related to pigs, boars or similar animals

COMPOUNDS

● [original meaning] pig, hog

遼東の豕 *ryōtō no inoko* being self-complacent

NOTE

⇨ see COMPOUND FORMATION for 遼東の豕 *ryōtō no inoko* ⇨ 遼 3168

7-1□ 酉

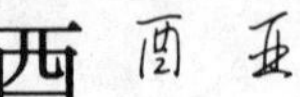

3544 YŪ tori NAMES naga minoru

一 丆 丙 丙 西 西 酉
1 2 3 4 5 6 7

Ⓒⓗ 酉 yǒu

Radical	Strokes
酉 164	7-7-0
Grade	Freq
Names	2070
■ 4 - 7 - 1	

RADICAL 164

Standard form: 酉 *hiyominotori* 'wine' (酒 醤)

Left variant: 酉 *torihen* (配 酔 酸)

Description: used in characters related to alcoholic beverages or the like

▶THE BIRD

COMPOUNDS

● tenth sign of the Oriental zodiac: the Bird—(time) 5–7 p.m., (direction) west, (season) August (of the lunar calendar)(⇨ see APPENDIX 7)

丁酉 *teiyū* 34th of the sexagenary cycle

KUN

【tori 酉】 tenth sign of the Oriental zodiac: the Bird (⇨ ●)

酉年 *toridoshi* Year of the Bird

酉の方角 *tori no hōgaku* west

酉の市 *tori no ichi* "Bird Day"

NAMES

酉三 *torizō* (=*yūzō*) male name

酉井 *torii* surname

SYNONYMS

● **bird**

鳥 BIRD → 3312

HOMOPHONES

tori ⇨ 鳥 3312 鶏 1768

NOTE

⇨ see USAGE note at 鳥 3312

7-1□ 呉 3545

▶KINGDOM OF WU

nonstandard for 呉 2549

7-1□ 更 3546

▶RENEW

nonstandard for 更 3541

7-1□ 条

incorrect classification ⇨ see 2200

君 incorrect classification ⇨ see 3206 7-1□

呂 incorrect classification ⇨ see 2187 7-1□

承 incorrect classification／stroke count ⇨ see 16 7-1□

镸 incorrect classification ⇨ see 2550 (nonstandard for 長 2556) 7-1□

坐

3547 ZA suwa(ru)

Ⓒ 坐 zuò 7-2□

Radical	Strokes
土 32	7-3-4
Grade	Freq
Reference	
■ 4 - 7 - 2	

COMPOUNDS

❶ⓐ [now usu. 座 *za* 3116 or 座る *suwaru*] [original meaning] sit down, take a seat
ⓑ [now usu. 座 *za* 3116] sit still without doing anything, not stir

坐像 *zazō* sedentary statue [image]
坐禅 *zazen* Zen meditation
坐礁する *zashō suru* run aground, be stranded
正坐する *seiza suru* sit upright [straight]
行住坐臥 *gyōjūzaga* the four cardinal behaviors (walking, stopping [standing], sitting and lying); daily life
坐する *zasuru* sit down, take a seat; be implicated [involved] in (a crime)
坐り *suwari* stability
坐視する *zashi suru* remain an idle spectator, look on idly [doing nothing]
坐食の徒 *zashoku no to* idler, drone

❷ [now usu. 座 3116] be accused of a crime

連坐する *renza suru* be implicated [involved] in (a crime)

❸ [now usu. 座 3116] travel (by ship)

坐乗する *zajō suru* go on board (a ship)

HOMOPHONES

suwaru ⇨ 座 3116 据 497
suwari ⇨ 座 3116

NOTE

⇨ see USAGE note at 座 3116

我 𢦏 㦱

3548 GA ware wa wa(ga)- waga-

丿 二 于 手 我 我 我 (1 2 3 4 5 6 7)

Ⓒ 我 wǒ 7-3□

Radical	Strokes
戈 62	7-4-3
Grade	Freq
Jōyō-6	1387
■ 4 - 7 - 3	

▶SELF

COMPOUNDS

❶ⓐ **self, one's own self**
ⓑ ego, self

我慢 *gaman* patience, endurance; self-restraint
我流 *garyū* self-taught method, one's own way
自我 *jiga* self, ego
無我 *muga* self-effacement; *Buddhism* non-self, nonego

❷ **selfishness, egotism**

我欲 *gayoku* selfishness
我利 *gari* one's own interests, self-interest
我執 *gashū* egoistic attachment, egotism

❸ **one's own, my**

我田引水 *gaden'insui* seeking one's own interests

❹ used phonetically for *ga*

怪我 *kega* injury, wound; accident

INDEPENDENT

【ga 我】 self, ego; selfishness, egotism, egoism

我が強い *ga ga tsuyoi* egoistic, selfish, self-willed

我を通す *ga o tōsu* persist in one's own way

KUN

【ware 我】

① oneself, self, ego

我知らず *wareshirazu* in spite of oneself, unconsciously

② [sometimes also 吾]

ⓐ I; we

ⓑ *slang* you

我我 *wareware* we

【wa 我】 [archaic] I

【wa(ga)- 我が-, waga- 我-】 [sometimes also 吾-] *literary* my; our

我が輩(=吾輩) *wagahai* I

我が儘 *wagamama* selfishness, willfulness

我が国 *wagakuni* our country, Japan

我が家 *wagaya* one's home [house]

SYNONYMS

❶ first person pronouns

自 SELF → 3525

己 ONESELF → 3380

身 ONE'S PERSON → 3553

私 I (*polite*) → 1115

僕 I (*familiar*) → 164

俺 I (*intimate*) → 110

吾 I (*elegant*) → 2407

予 I (*pompous*) → 1983

余 I (*pompous*) → 2042

麿 I (*archaic*) → 3184

朕 IMPERIAL WE → 949

USAGE

❶ ware

我

① oneself, self, ego

② [sometimes also 吾]

ⓐ I; we

ⓑ *slang* you

吾

[usu. 我]

ⓐ *elegant* I; we

ⓑ *slang* you

❷ waga-

我が-

[sometimes also 吾-] *literary* my; our

吾-

[usu. 我が-] *literary* my; our

HOMOPHONES

ware ⇨ 吾 2407

waga- ⇨ 吾 2407

NOTE

⇨ see COMPOUND FORMATION for 我慢 *gaman* ⇨ 慢 686

7-3 ◫

甫

3549 HO FU haji(mete) NAMES hajime toshi nami suke yoshi

(CH) 甫 fǔ

Radical	Strokes
用 101	7-5-2
Grade	**Freq**
Names	2039

■ 4 - 7 - 3

Stroke order: 1 2 3 4 5 6 7

▶BARELY

COMPOUNDS

❶ [usu. 圃 *ho* 3119] vegetable garden; rice nursery

田甫 *tanbo* rice field

❷ beginning

新甫 *shinpo* new futures on the first trading session of the month

❸ [archaic]

ⓐ courtesy title for elderly men

ⓑ man's courtesy name, pseudonym

尼甫 *jiho* Confucius

台甫 *taiho* your personal name

KUN

【haji(mete) 甫めて】 *literary* barely, just

我齢は甫めて九つなるに *Waga yowai wa hajimete kokonotsu naru ni* I was barely nine years old

NAMES

甫 *hajime* male name

杜甫 *to ho* Du Fu (famous Chinese poet)

甫子 *toshiko* female name

SYNONYMS

❶ cultivated fields

田 RICE FIELD → 3041

畑 FIELD → 905

牧 PASTURE → 873

園 GARDEN → 3156

【hajimete】

○ barely

辛い bare → 2038

HOMOPHONES

hajimete ⇨ 初 1116 始 281

NOTE

⇨ see USAGE note at 初 1116

求 求 求

3550 KYŪ GU▲ moto(meru)

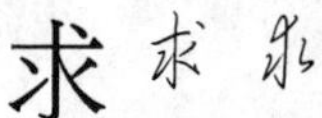

Ⓒⓗ 求 qiú

Radical	Strokes
水 85	7-5-2
Grade	Freq
Jōyō-4	358
■ 4-7-3	

7-3▢

▶SEEK

COMPOUNDS

❶ (go in search of) **seek (for), search, pursue; wish for, desire**

求人 *kyūjin* job offer
求職 *kyūshoku* seeking employment
求道 *kyūdō* (=*gudō*) seeking for truth; seeking for enlightenment
探求する *tankyū suru* investigate, search (for), pursue
追求 *tsuikyū* pursuit
欣求浄土 *gongujōdo* seeking rebirth in the Pure Land
欲求 *yokkyū* want(s), desire, wish

❷ (ask for) **seek, request, demand**

求婚 *kyūkon* proposal of marriage
求刑する *kyūkei suru* demand a sentence (for the accused)
要求する *yōkyū suru* require, demand, request
請求 *seikyū* demand, request, claim

KUN

【moto(meru) 求める】 (go in search of) seek (for), search, pursue; wish for, desire; (ask for) seek, request, demand; buy

求め *motome* request, appeal, claim, demand
追い求める *oimotomeru* seek after, pursue
幸福を求めて *kōfuku o motomete* in search [pursuit] of happiness
買い求める *kaimotomeru* buy

SYNONYMS

❶ **seek**

探 SEARCH → 505
索 SEARCH FOR → 2455
捜 LOOK FOR → 432
猟 hunt for → 538

❶ **wish and desire**

欲 DESIRE → 1475
渇 thirst for → 515
慕 yearn for → 2353
懐 LONG FOR → 763
希 ASPIRE → 2049
望 HOPE → 2742
願 WISH → 1845

❷ **request**

請 REQUEST → 1576
訴 APPEAL TO → 1507
頼 ASK → 1615
嘱 CHARGE WITH → 718
要 REQUIRE → 2635
願 ASK A FAVOR → 1845

来 來 耒° 来 来

3551 RAI TAI▲ ku(ru) kita(ru) kita(su)

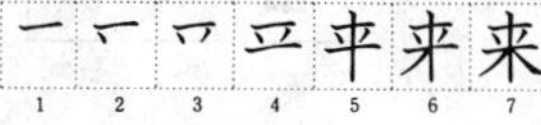

Ⓒⓗ 来 lái

Radical	Strokes
木 75△	7-4-3
Grade	Freq
Jōyō-2	105
■ 4-7-3	

7-3▢

▶COME

COMPOUNDS

❶ⓐ **come, come to**
ⓑ come from, derive

来訪 *raihō* visit, call
来日 *rainichi* coming to Japan
来客 *raikyaku* visitor, guest
到来する *tōrai suru* come, arrive
伝来する *denrai suru* be transmitted, be imported
舶来の *hakurai no* imported, foreign-made
在来の *zairai no* ordinary, common, usual
往来 *ōrai* come-and-go, traffic; road, street
由来 *yurai* origin, source, cause; history
生来 *seirai* by nature [birth], congenitally

❷ⓐ **the coming, the following, the next**
ⓑ **coming generations, the future**

来年 *rainen* next year
来週 *raishū* next week
来学期 *raigakki* next school term

未来 *mirai* future
将来 *shōrai* future; in the future
❸ [also suffix] **since, as of, from**
以来 *irai* as of, since then, from that time on
従来は *jūrai wa* hitherto, so far
本来 *honrai* originally, essentially, naturally
古来 *korai* from ancient times
昨年来 *sakunenrai* since last year
❹ bring about, cause
招来する *shōrai suru* bring about, give rise to, cause
出来する *shuttai suru* happen, occur, take place
❺ used phonetically for *rai*
家来 *kerai* retainer, vassal, follower
矢来 *yarai* palisade, stockade, barrier

KUN

【ku(ru) 来る】
①ⓐ come (over), come near, arrive
ⓑ come to see, call on, visit
ⓒ (seasons) come (round), set in
ⓓ come from, derive from, be due to
帰って来る *kaette kuru* come back, return
又遊びに来て下さい *Mata asobi ni kite kudasai* Come and see me again
春が来た *Haru ga kita* Spring has come
ギリシャ語から来た言葉 *girishago kara kita kotoba* word derived from Greek
②ⓐ [auxiliary following the TE-form] come to be, become, grow
ⓑ [in the form of て来た *te kita*] auxiliary indicating present perfect progressive
暖かくなって来た *Atatakaku natte kita* It's getting warmer
酷く質素な生活を送って来た *Hidoku shisso na seikatsu o okutte kita* We have been living in the simplest way
③ assume (an attitude), take (a move)
そう来なくっちゃ *Sō konakutcha* That's the idea

【kita(ru) 来る】
① come, arrive
レーガン大統領来る *Rēgan daitōryō kitaru* President Reagan Arrives
② the coming, next, to come
来る木曜日 *kitaru mokuyōbi* next Thursday

【kita(su) 来す】 bring about, cause, give rise to; result in
破綻を来す *hatan o kitasu* fail, be ruined; go bankrupt

SYNONYMS

❶ⓐ go and come
参 go somewhere → 2066
通 go to and from → 3109
向 head toward → 3052
赴 PROCEED TO → 3303
行 GO → 212
往 GO ON → 292
出 go to → 3498
❷ⓐ next
次 NEXT → 54
明 next → 855
翌 THE FOLLOWING → 2668
ⓑ future
後 afteryears → 361
❸ direction indicators
自 from → 3525
以 TO THE...OF → 41
迄 UP TO → 3201
-向け (bound) for → 3052
-行き bound for → 212
至 to → 2182

7-3Ⅱ

車 車 车

3552 SHA kuruma

Ⓒⓗ 车 chē jū

Radical	Strokes
車 159	7-7-0
Grade	**Freq**
Jōyō-1	181
■ 4 - 7 - 3	

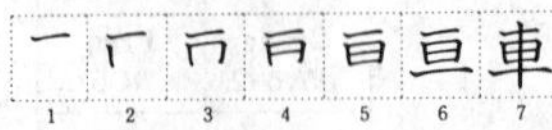

RADICAL 159
Standard form: 車 *kuruma* 'vehicle' (軍 輩 轟)
Left variant: 車 *kurumahen* (転 輪 軽)
Description: used in characters related to wheeled vehicles or their qualities

▶**VEHICLE** ▶**WHEEL**

COMPOUNDS

❶ [also suffix] any wheeled vehicle:
ⓐ [original meaning] **vehicle, cart, wagon**
ⓑ **motor vehicle, car, automobile**
ⓒ **railway car, train**
ⓓ suffix for wheeled vehicles, -cycle
馬車 *basha* horse-drawn carriage, coach, wagon
唇歯輔車 *shinshi-hosha* mutual dependence
人力車 *jinrikisha* rickshaw, man-pulled cart
単車 *tansha* motorcycle, motorbike
自動車 *jidōsha* automobile
駐車 *chūsha* parking
車両 *sharyō* vehicle, car; rolling stock

下車する *gesha suru* alight, get off
停車 *teisha* stoppage
救急車 *kyūkyūsha* ambulance car
電車 *densha* train, electric train, trolley
列車 *ressha* (railway) train
客車 *kyakusha* passenger car
機関車 *kikansha* locomotive
三輪車 *sanrinsha* tricycle, three-wheeler
❷ **wheel**
車輪 *sharin* wheel
水車 *suisha* water wheel
拍車 *hakusha* spur, rowel spur

KUN

【**kuruma 車**】wheel, caster; wheeled vehicle, esp. cars or taxis; rickshaw
風車 *kazaguruma* (=*fūsha*) windmill; pinwheel
車椅子 *kurumaisu* wheelchair
車酔い *kurumayoi* car sickness
荷車 *niguruma* cart, wagon
車屋 *kurumaya* rickshawman; rickshaw station

SPECIAL READINGS

山車 *dashi* festival car, float

SYNONYMS

❶ **vehicle**
乗 vehicle → 3576
輪 wheeled vehicle → 1589
台 COUNTER FOR VEHICLES → 2005
ⓒ **kinds of railway**
両 counter for railway cars → 3518
電 electric railway → 2790
鉄 railway → 1711
❷ **circular objects**
輪 WHEEL, RING → 1589
環 RING → 1090
盤 DISK → 2851

NOTE

⇨ see COMPOUND FORMATION for
単車 *tansha* ⇨ 単 2256
唇歯輔車 *shinshi-hosha* ⇨ 輔 1559

3553 SHIN mi

ⒸⒽ 身 shēn

Radical	Strokes
身 158	7-7-0
Grade	**Freq**
Jōyō-3	305
■ 4 - 7 - 3	

7-3⃞

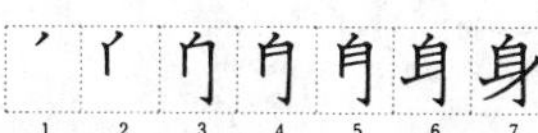

RADICAL 158

Standard form: 身 *mi* 'body'
Left variant: 身 *mihen* (躬 躾)
Description: used in characters related to the body

▶BODY ▶ONE'S PERSON

COMPOUNDS

❶ⓐ **(material) body, human body (esp. vs. mind), one's person, the flesh**
ⓑ body length, height
身体 *shintai* body
身長 *shinchō* stature, height
身障者 *shinshōsha* physically handicapped person, disabled person
全身 *zenshin* the whole body
心身 *shinshin* mind and body
焼身 *shōshin* burning oneself (to death), self-immolation
変身 *henshin* transformation, metamorphosis
馬身 *bashin* horse's length
艇身 *teishin* boat's length
長身 *chōshin* tall figure, high stature
❷ body or main part of a thing, esp. a sword or gun
刀身 *tōshin* sword blade
銃身 *jūshin* barrel of a gun, gun barrel
❸ **one's person, one's own person, oneself, self**
身辺 *shinpen* one's person, one's immediate surroundings
自身 *jishin* self, oneself; itself
出身地 *shusshinchi* one's native place
独身 *dokushin* single life; celibacy
単身 *tanshin* alone, by oneself, unaccompanied
前身 *zenshin* one's former self, one's past life; predecessor
保身 *hoshin* self-protection
献身 *kenshin* self-sacrifice, devotion
❹ **social status, social standing**
身代 *shindai* fortune, one's property
立身する *risshin suru* establish oneself in life
小身 *shōshin* humble position
❺ life
終身 *shūshin* all through life
捨身 *shashin* becoming a priest; risking one's life for others

KUN

【**mi 身**】
① body, one's person

身に着ける *mi ni tsukeru* put on, wear
身軽な *migaru na* light, agile, nimble
細身 *hosomi* slender figure; narrow blade
不死身 *fujimi* immortality, invulnerability
② body or main part of a thing
中身 *nakami* content, substance; interior
黄身 *kimi* yolk, vitellus
抜き身 *nukimi* naked sword
③ one's person, one's own person, oneself, self
身の上 *minoue* one's career, one's condition, one's fortune
身近な *mijika na* near oneself, close to one, familiar
身元(＝身許) *mimoto* one's birth, one's identity, one's background
身寄り *miyori* relative, relation, kinsfolk
身投げ *minage* suicide by drowning or jumping from a high place
身柄 *migara* one's person; social standing
身勝手 *migatte* selfishness, egoism, egotism
④ (one's) social status, one's station in life; one's position
身の程 *minohodo* one's social position, one's own place
身分 *mibun* social position [standing]; circumstances; rank, identity
⑤ heart, soul, mind
身を入れる *mi o ireru* devote oneself to, exert oneself
身に染みる *mi ni shimiru* go to one's heart, come home to
⑥ meat, flesh
脂身 *aburami* fat, fatty meat
刺身 *sashimi sashimi*, sliced raw flesh (esp. of fish)
⑦ life
身を捨てる *mi o suteru* throw away one's life

SYNONYMS

❶ⓐ body
体 BODY → 71
肉 FLESH → 3200
❸ &【mi】③ first person pronouns
己 ONESELF → 3380
我 SELF → 3548
自 SELF → 3525
私 I (*polite*) → 1115
僕 I (*familiar*) → 164
俺 I (*intimate*) → 110
吾 I (*elegant*) → 2407
予 I (*pompous*) → 1983
余 I (*pompous*) → 2042
麿 I (*archaic*) → 3184
朕 IMPERIAL WE → 949
❹ class
階 RANK → 624
位 RANK → 61
格 STATUS → 926
級 GRADE → 1279
段 grade → 1144
等 CLASS → 2682
流 class → 441
層 STRATUM → 3161
【mi】
⑥ meat
肉 FLESH → 3200
脩 DRIED MEAT → 136

NOTE

⇨ see COMPOUND FORMATION for 身寄り *miyori* ⇨ 寄 2291

7-3Ⅱ

束

3554 SOKU taba taba(neru) tsuka▲ tsuka(neru)▲

CH 束 shù

Radical	Strokes
木 75	7-4-3
Grade	**Freq**
Jōyō-4	906
■ 4-7-3	

Stroke order: 1 2 3 4 5 6 7

▶TIE UP ▶BUNDLE

COMPOUNDS

❶ⓐ [original meaning] **tie up (in a bundle), bundle, bind**
ⓑ (restrict the freedom of) **tie (a person) up, restrain, bind**
束髪 *sokuhatsu* bundled hair, hair done up in a bun
束帯 *sokutai* old ceremonial court dress
装束 *shōzoku* costume, attire
束縛する *sokubaku suru* restrain, restrict, bind, fetter
約束する *yakusoku suru* promise, vow, pledge
拘束 *kōsoku* restriction, restraint, binding
結束する *kessoku suru* band together, unite
❷ technical term for various bundlelike clusters:
ⓐ [also suffix] *anat*, *biol* **bundle**
ⓑ *chem*, *math* lattice
ⓒ [also suffix] *phys*, *biol* flux
繊維束 *sen'isoku* fiber bundle, fascicle
維管束 *ikansoku* vascular bundle
束群 *sokugun* lattice group
磁束 *jisoku* magnetic flux
中性子束 *chūseishisoku* neutron flux
❸ counter for various items in bundles or

batches, as: fagots, sheaves (of straw), reams (of 200 sheets of Japanese paper)
薪五束 *maki gosoku* five bundles of firewood
二束三文の *nisokusanmon no* dirt-cheap, dog-cheap
❹ⓐ unit of one hundred items (esp. fish)
ⓑ arrow length unit (measured in hand breadths)

INDEPENDENT

【soku 束】 *anat* bundle; *math* lattice; *phys* flux

KUN

【taba 束】 bundle, bunch, batch, sheaf; counter for bundles
束になって *taba ni natte* in a bunch; in a group
花束 *hanataba* bunch of flowers
札束 *satsutaba* bundle of (bank) notes, wad of bills
一束十円 *hitotaba jūen* 10 yen a bundle

【taba(neru) 束ねる】 tie up in a bundle, bundle; control, manage
束ね *tabane* bundle; management

【tsuka 束】
① hand breadth
束の間 *tsukanoma* brief space of time, moment
② short support
③ bulk (of a book)

【tsuka(neru) 束ねる】 bundle, tie up
手を束ねて *te o tsukanete* folding one's arms, doing nothing

SYNONYMS

❶ⓐ join
縛 BIND → 1405
結 TIE → 1348
連 LINK → 3103
係 CONNECT → 97
接 join → 500
ⓑ restrain
縛 BIND → 1405
抑 SUPPRESS → 257
限 LIMIT → 398
禁 PROHIBIT → 2795
制 CONTROL (restrain) → 1274
控える HOLD BACK → 495
渋る hang [hold] back → 513
❷ bundles and clusters
房 tuft → 1946

HOMOPHONES

tsuka ⇨ 柄 897

NOTE

⇨ see USAGE note at 柄 897

釆
3555

7-3Ⅱ

Radical	Strokes
釆 165	7-7-0
Grade Radical	**Freq**
■ 4 - 7 - 3	

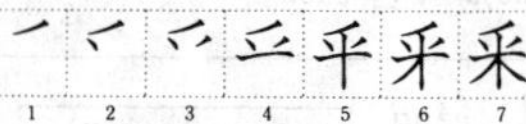

RADICAL 165

Standard form: 釆 *nogome* 'separate'
Left variant: 釆 *nogomehen* (釈 釉 釋)
Description: used in characters related to separating

事
3556

7-3Ⅱ

▶AFFAIR ▶ABSTRACT THING
handwritten abbreviation for 事 3567

弟

7-3Ⅱ

incorrect classification ⇨ see 2044

7-4□

寿 壽 寿 寿

3557 JU SU▲ kotobuki kotoho(gu)▲

CH 寿 shòu

Radical	Strokes
寸 41^A^	7-3-4
Grade	**Freq**
Jōyō	1150

■ 4 - 7 - 4

▶**LONGEVITY** ▶**CONGRATULATIONS**

COMPOUNDS

❶ⓐ [original meaning] **longevity, long life, old age**

ⓑ celebration of longevity, birthday in one's old age

寿老人 *jurōjin* God of Longevity

長寿 *chōju* long life, longevity

白寿 *hakuju* 99 years old, one's 99th birthday

❷ **life span, age, natural life**

寿命 *jumyō* life span

天寿 *tenju* one's natural life span

❸ used phonetically for *su*

寿司 *sushi* sushi (raw fish and vinegared rice)

INDEPENDENT

【**ju 寿**】 life span, age; longevity; celebration

百歳の寿 *hyakusai no ju* 100 years of age

KUN

【**kotobuki 寿**】 congratulations, felicitation, celebration, greetings; longevity

新年の寿 *shinnen no kotobuki* New Year's greetings

寿教室 *kotobuki kyōshitsu* culture courses for the aged

【**kotoho(gu) 寿ぐ**】 *elegant* congratulate, felicitate, extend one's best wishes

SYNONYMS

❶ⓐ **life**

生 LIFE → 3497

命 LIFE → 2058

❷ **age**

年 years → 2035

齢 AGE → 1895

令 age → 1995

歳 AGE SUFFIX → 2490

才 AGE SUFFIX → 3410

【**kotobuki**】

○ **celebrating and congratulating**

祝 CELEBRATE → 913

慶 FELICITATION → 3173

賀 CONGRATULATE → 2599

NOTE

⇨ see COMPOUND FORMATION for

傘寿 *sanju* ⇨ 傘 2131

米寿 *beiju* ⇨ 米 3529

白寿 *hakuju* ⇨ 白 3493

7-4□

良 良 良

3558 RYŌ yo(i) -yo(i) i(i)▲ -i(i)▲

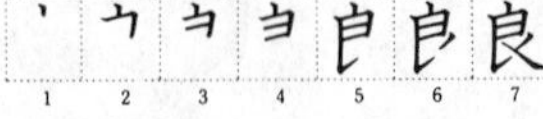

CH 良 liáng

Radical	Strokes
艮 138	7-6-1
Grade	**Freq**
Jōyō-4	558

■ 4 - 7 - 4

▶**GOOD**

COMPOUNDS

❶ⓐ (having positive qualities) **good, fine, favorable, excellent**

ⓑ (characterized by good luck) good, lucky, auspicious, happy

良好な *ryōkō na* good, fine, excellent, favorable

良質の *ryōshitsu no* of fine quality, superior

良否 *ryōhi* good or bad, quality

良導体 *ryōdōtai* good conductor

最良の *sairyō no* best, superfine, most excellent

優良な *yūryō na* superior, excellent

改良する *kairyō suru* improve, reform, make better

純良品 *junryōhin* genuine article

不良 *furyō* badness, inferiority; delinquency; juvenile delinquent

良日 *ryōjitsu* lucky [auspicious] day

❷ⓐ (having good character or moral excellence) **good, good-natured, virtuous**

ⓑ (well-behaved) good, obedient, law-abiding

良心 *ryōshin* conscience

良識 *ryōshiki* good sense

善良な *zenryō na* good, virtuous

良民 *ryōmin* good citizens, law-abiding people

順良な *junryō na* good and obedient, gentle,

meek
温良な *onryō na* obedient, meek
❸ innate, natural, inborn
良知 *ryōchi* innate intellect [intelligence]
良能 *ryōnō* natural ability
❹ [archaic] (considerable) good (while), fairly
良久 *ryōkyū* for a good while

INDEPENDENT

【ryō 良】(school mark) Good, B; good, fine
数学の成績は良だった *Sūgaku no seiseki wa ryō datta* I got a B in math

KUN

【yo(i) 良い】
[sometimes also 好い]
①ⓐ good, fine, nice, pleasant, excellent
ⓑ good-looking, handsome, beautiful, pretty
ⓒ good for (one's health), beneficial
ⓓ (of considerable amount) good (price)
良さ *yosa* merit, virtue, good quality, good point
良く *yoku* well, right(ly), thoroughly, skillfully, carefully, closely; much, usually, often
良い天気 *yoi tenki* fine [fair] weather
良かったら *yokattara* if you like
ああ良かった *Ā yokatta* Thank God!
気分が良い *kibun ga yoi* feel good [pleasant]
良い男 *yoi otoko* handsome man
健康に良い *kenkō ni yoi* be good for the health
良い値で *yoi ne de* at a good price
② suitable, proper, fitting; useful
丁度良い時に *chōdo yoi toki ni* just at the right moment
これで良いか *Kore de yoi ka* Will this do?
盗むのは良くない *Nusumu no wa yoku nai* It's wrong to steal
③ lucky, auspicious
良い日を選ぶ *yoi hi o erabu* choose a lucky [auspicious] day
④ intimate, friendly
仲良し *nakayoshi* intimacy, familiar terms; bosom friend
⑤ⓐ preferable, better
ⓑ I wish, I hope
君はここに居ない方が良い *Kimi wa koko ni inai hō ga yoi* You had better not stay here
助けてくれても良かったのに *Tasukete kurete mo yokatta no ni* You might have helped me
⑥ [following the TE-form of verbs]
ⓐ may, can, be allowed
ⓑ need not (do), do not have to
入っても良い *Haitte mo yoi* You may enter
君は行かなくて良い *Kimi wa ikanakute yoi* You need not go
⑦ do not mind (doing), have no objection
やって見ても良い *Yatte mite mo yoi* I wouldn't mind trying it

【-yo(i) -良い】[verbal suffix] easy
読み良い *yomiyoi* easy to read

【i(i) 良い】[sometimes also 好い] colloquial form of **yoi 良い**
良い資料 *ii shiryō* valuable material
良い気味だ *Ii kimi da* Serves you right!
良いですか *Ii desu ka* Is it all right? / You see?
天気が良くなってくれれば良いのだが *Tenki ga yoku natte kurereba ii no da ga* I wish the weather would improve
車をお借りして良いですか *Kuruma o okari shite ii desu ka* May I use your car?
行っても良い *Itte mo ii* I wouldn't mind going there

【-i(i) -良い】 same as **-yoi -良い**

SPECIAL READINGS

野良 *nora* the fields

SYNONYMS

❶ⓐ good
善 GOOD → 2325
好 FAVORABLE → 208
順 favorable → 18
佳 FINE → 86
美 BEAUTIFUL → 2264

❷ⓐ virtuous
善 GOOD → 2325
正 RIGHT → 3484
義 righteous → 2338

USAGE

❶ yoi
良い
[sometimes also 好い]
①ⓐ good, fine, nice, pleasant, excellent
ⓑ good-looking, handsome, beautiful, pretty
ⓒ good for (one's health), beneficial
ⓓ (of considerable amount) good (price)
② suitable, proper, fitting; useful
③ lucky, auspicious
④ intimate, friendly
⑤ⓐ preferable, better
ⓑ I wish, I hope
⑥ [following the TE-form of verbs]
ⓐ may, can, be allowed
ⓑ need not (do), do not have to
⑦ do not mind (doing), have no objection
善い
(morally excellent) good, good-natured, virtuous, upright
好い
[now usu. 良い] same as 良い

❷ ii
良い

[sometimes also 好い] colloquial form of 良い *yoi*
好い
[now usu. 良い] colloquial form of 好い

yoi

HOMOPHONES
yoi ⇨ 善 2325 好 208
ii ⇨ 好 208

7-4□ 成 3559
▶FORM ▶ACHIEVE
nonstandard for 成 3537

7-4□ 我
incorrect classification ⇨ see 3548

7-4□ 系
incorrect classification ⇨ see 1944

7-4□ 希
incorrect classification ⇨ see 2049

7-4□ 孝
incorrect classification ⇨ see 3205

7-4□ 考
incorrect classification／stroke count ⇨ see 3196

7-4□ 身
incorrect classification ⇨ see 3553

7-4□ 呉
incorrect classification ⇨ see 3545
(nonstandard for 呉 2549)

8-1□ 果 3560
KA ha(tasu) -ha(tasu) ha(teru) -ha(teru) ha(te)

Ⓒⓗ 果 guǒ

Radical	Strokes
木 75	8-4-4
Grade	**Freq**
Jōyō-4	262
■ 4-8-1	

Stroke order: 1 2 3 4 5 6 7 8

▶FRUIT

COMPOUNDS

❶ⓐ [original meaning] **fruit**
ⓑ counter for fruits, jewels or seals
果実 *kajitsu* fruit, berry
果汁 *kajū* fruit juice
青果 *seika* vegetables and fruits
摘果 *tekika* thinning out superfluous fruit
林檎一果 *ringo ikka* one apple
❷ **fruit, result, outcome; effect**
結果 *kekka* result, outcome, consequence
成果 *seika* result, fruit, outcome
効果 *kōka* effect, efficacy; result
因果 *inga* cause and effect; karma
戦果 *senka* fruit of battle, war results
❸ resolutely, decisively
果断な *kadan na* resolute, decisive
果敢な *kakan na* bold, daring; resolute
❹ really; as was expected
果然 *kazen* as was expected

INDEPENDENT
【ka 果】result; effect; satori

因となり果となる *in to nari ka to naru* constitute the cause and effect

KUN

【ha(tasu) 果たす】 *vt* effect, carry out, discharge, accomplish; realize (one's wishes); kill
 使命を果たす *shimei o hatasu* carry out one's mission
 果たして *hatashite* as was expected, sure enough; really
 果たし合い *hatashiai* duel, fight to death

【-ha(tasu) -果たす】 emphatic verbal suffix indicating completeness
 使い果たす *tsukaihatasu* use up, spend all

【ha(teru) 果てる】 *vi* end, be finished; be exhausted; die
 宴が果てる *Utage ga hateru* The party has ended
 異境に果てる *ikyō ni hateru* die in a strange land

【-ha(teru) -果てる】 emphatic verbal suffix indicating completeness
 朽ち果てる *kuchihateru* decay completely, rot away; rust away; rusticate oneself
 絶え果てる *taehateru* be extinguished, be exterminated; cease completely

【ha(te) 果て】 end, extremity, limit; result
 世界の果て *sekai no hate* end of the world
 果てしない *hateshinai* endless, boundless, everlasting
 挙げ句の果てに *ageku no hate ni* in the end, on top of all this

SPECIAL READINGS

果物 *kudamono* fruit

SYNONYMS

❶ fruit
 実 fruit → 2225

【hatasu】
○ execute
 遂 ACCOMPLISH → 3138
 施 CARRY OUT → 891
 践 IMPLEMENT → 1535
 履 FULFILL → 3171
 行 ACT → 212
 執 EXECUTE → 1680

【hate】
○ extreme
 極 EXTREME → 1017
 窮 extremity → 2358
 限 LIMIT → 398
 涯 OUTER LIMITS → 512

雨

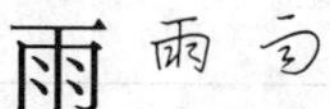

Ⓒ 雨 yǔ yù

3561 U ame ama- -same*

Radical	Strokes
雨 173	8-8-0
Grade	**Freq**
Jōyō-1	595
■ 4-8-1	

8-1□

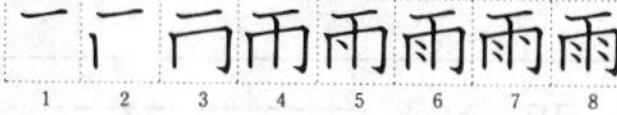

RADICAL 173

Standard form: 雨 *ame* 'rain'
Top variant: ⻗ *amekanmuri* (雪 霧 雫)
Description: used in characters related to precipitation

▶RAIN

COMPOUNDS

● [original meaning] **rain, rainfall**
 雨量 *uryō* rain, rainfall
 雨期(＝雨季) *uki* rainy season
 降雨 *kōu* rainfall, rain
 豪雨 *gōu* heavy rain, downpour
 梅雨(＝黴雨) *baiu* rainy season (of early summer)
 風雨 *fūu* wind and rain, storm

KUN

【ame 雨, ama- 雨-】 rain
 雨戸 *amado* shutter
 雨水 *amamizu* rainwater
 雨雲 *amagumo* rain cloud
 雨曇 *amagumori* overcast weather
 雨上がり *ameagari* just after a rainfall
 大雨 *ōame* heavy rain

【-same -雨】 rain
 春雨 *harusame* spring rain; sticks of bean jelly
 小雨 *kosame* drizzle

SPECIAL READINGS

五月雨 *samidare* early summer rain
時雨 *shigure* late fall or early winter rain
梅雨 *tsuyu* rainy season (of early summer)

SYNONYMS

● kinds of precipitation
 雪 SNOW → 2759
 露 DEW → 2818
 霜 FROST → 2815

8-1□ 𠕒
3562

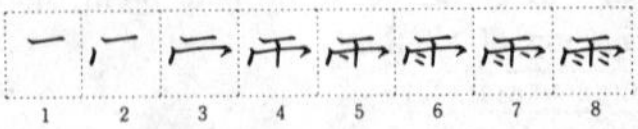

Radical	Strokes
雨 173	8-8-0
Grade	**Freq**
Radical	
■ 4 - 8 - 1	

RADICAL 173
amekanmuri, variant of 雨 *ame* 'rain'
⇨ see 雨 3561 for radical description

8-1□ 亞
3563
▶**SUB-** ▶**PHONETIC** [a]
nonstandard for 亜 3540

8-1□ 兩
3564
▶**BOTH**
nonstandard for 両 3518

8-1□ 長
incorrect classification ⇨ see 2556

8-1□ 承
incorrect classification ⇨ see 16

8-1□ 吳
incorrect stroke count ⇨ see 3545
(nonstandard for 呉 2549)

8-2□ 垂 垂 𠂹
3565
SUI ta(reru) ta(rasu) ta(re) -ta(re)
Ⓒⓗ 垂 chuí

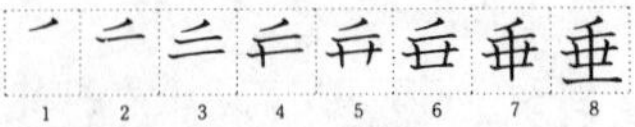

Radical	Strokes
土 32	8-3-5
Grade	**Freq**
Jōyō-6	1639
■ 4 - 8 - 2	

▶**HANG DOWN**

COMPOUNDS

❶ⓐ **hang down, hang, droop, dangle**
ⓑ drip, drop
懸垂 *kensui* suspension, pendency; chinning exercises
口蓋垂 *kōgaisui* uvula
垂涎する *suizen* (=*suien*) *suru* covet
❷ **perpendicular, vertical**
垂直の *suichoku no* vertical, perpendicular
垂線 *suisen* perpendicular line
❸ hand down, leave to posterity
垂迹 *suijaku* Shinto god who is the reincarnation of a Buddha or bodhisattva
❹ confer, bestow, grant
垂範する *suihan suru* set an example
山上の垂訓 *sanjō no suikun* the Sermon on the Mount
❺ [rare] nearly, almost, on the verge of
垂死 *suishi* on the verge of dying

KUN

【**ta(reru) 垂れる**】 hang down, hang, droop; drip, drop; leave to posterity; confer, bestow, grant; *slang* evacuate (as excreta or wind)
垂れ下がる *taresagaru* hang, dangle
雨垂れ *amadare* raindrops
教訓を垂れる *kyōkun o tareru* give a lesson, lecture
【**ta(rasu) 垂らす**】 hang down, suspend; drop, drip
髪を垂らす *kami o tarasu* let one's hair hang down

床に水を垂らす *yuka ni mizu o tarasu* spill water on the floor

【ta(re) 垂れ】 sauce, gravy; lappet, flap, tassel; hanging, straw curtain; hanging radical (of Chinese characters), enclosure radicals

胡麻垂れ *gomadare* sesame sauce

籠の垂れ *kago no tare* hanging of a palanquin

病垂れ *yamaidare yamaidare*, 'illness' radical (疒)

【-ta(re) -垂れ】 suffix for forming swearwords

糞っ垂れ *Kusottare* You swine!

しみっ垂れ *shimittare* stinginess; miser

阿呆垂れ *Ahotare* You ass!

SYNONYMS

❶ⓐ hang

掛ける HANG → 493

懸 SUSPEND → 2915

釣り- suspended → 1674

❷ vertical

縦 VERTICAL → 1408

直 STRAIGHT → 2932

立て- standing → 1992

隹

3566

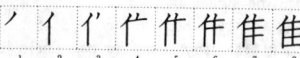

Radical	Strokes
隹 172	8-8-0
Grade	**Freq**
Radical	
■ 4 - 8 - 2	

8-2□

RADICAL 172

Standard form: 隹 *furutori* 'small bird' (集 雅 雀)

Description: used in characters related to small birds or their qualities

---

者

incorrect classification ⇨ see 3211

8-2□

卷

incorrect classification ⇨ see 2631

(nonstandard for 巻 2645)

8-2□

事 亊 事 孑

3567 JI ZU koto

Ⓒⓗ 事 shì

Radical	Strokes
亅 6	8-1-7
Grade	**Freq**
Jōyō-3	22
■ 4 - 8 - 3	

8-3□

▶AFFAIR ▶ABSTRACT THING

COMPOUNDS

❶ [also suffix]

ⓐ (something that is done) **affair, something, matter, thing, fact**

ⓑ (something that occurs) **affair, something, event, occurrence, incident, unexpected event, accident**

事物 *jibutsu* things, affairs

事実 *jijitsu* fact, reality; as a matter of fact

事項 *jikō* matters, facts; articles, items

返事 *henji* answer, reply

房事 *bōji* sex, lovemaking

記事 *kiji* news, article; account

食事 *shokuji* meal, dinner, board

事件 *jiken* affair, incident, case, event

事故 *jiko* accident, incident, trouble

事情 *jijō* circumstances, conditions, situation

事態 *jitai* situation, state of affairs

無事に *buji ni* safely, without accident, successfully; peacefully, amicably

火事 *kaji* fire

好事家 *kōzuka* dilettante, person of fantastic taste

関心事 *kanshinji* matter of concern and interest

❷ (business matters) **affairs, business, work**

事務 *jimu* business, clerical work, duties of an office

事業 *jigyō* undertaking, enterprise, business; achievement

用事 *yōji* things to do, errand, business, engagement

家事 *kaji* household affairs, housework

軍事 *gunji* naval and military affairs
工事 *kōji* construction
人事 *jinji* human affairs, personnel affairs
❸ serve, be in the service of
事大主義 *jidaishugi* worship of the powerful
師事する *shiji suru* study under, look up to (a person) as one's teacher
❹ **officer, official, public officer [servant]**
知事 *chiji* (prefectural) governor
刑事 *keiji* (police) detective
判事 *hanji* judge
幹事 *kanji* manager, secretary; organizer
領事 *ryōji* consul, consular representative
理事 *riji* director, trustee

KUN

【koto 事】

①ⓐ [also suffix] abstract thing, affair, matter, fact
ⓑ abstract thing or act—word used for the nominalization of verbs, adjectives or phrases
事柄 *kotogara* matter, affair, circumstances
明白な事 *meihaku na koto* obvious fact
学校の事を話す *gakkō no koto o hanasu* speak about the school, talk about school affairs
物事 *monogoto* things, matter; everything
勝負事 *shōbugoto* gambling, competition, game
考える事 *kangaeru koto* what one thinks
...する事にしている *...suru koto ni shite iru* make a point of (doing), be in the habit of (doing)
永い事 *nagai koto* for a long time
...との事である *...to no koto de aru* It is said that... / They say that... / I hear that...
② (event of special import) affair, something, incident, case, occurrence; trouble
事を起こす *koto o okosu* cause trouble [a disturbance]
事勿れ主義 *kotonakareshugi* peace-at-any-price principle
どんな事にも準備が出来ている *donna koto ni mo junbi ga dekite iru* be ready for any contingency
大変な事が起こった *Taihen na koto ga okotta* A terrible accident occurred
出来事 *dekigoto* occurrence, happening; affair, incident; accident
③ (business matters) affairs, business, work, duty
事を成し遂げる *koto o nashitogeru* achieve a task
事を運ぶ *koto o hakobu* proceed, go ahead, carry on
毎日の事 *mainichi no koto* daily affairs, daily routine
仕事 *shigoto* work, employment, business
④ⓐ things, occasions, circumstances, details, particulars
ⓑ cause, reason, account
事と次第で *koto to shidai de* under certain circumstances, if things permit
どんな事が有っても *donna koto ga atte mo* under any circumstances
彼は学校を遅刻する事が有る *Kare wa gakkō o chikoku suru koto ga aru* He is sometimes late for school
事を分ける *koto o wakeru* reason with (a person)
⑤ⓐ need, necessity
ⓑ worthwhileness
事が足りる *koto ga tariru* answer the purpose, be sufficient
事欠く *kotokaku* lack, be in need of
急ぐ事は無い *Isogu koto wa nai* There is no need for haste
漢字を勉強しただけの事は有る *Kanji o benkyō shita dake no koto wa aru* I didn't study kanji for nothing
見事(=美事)な *migoto na* splendid, admirable, beautiful
⑥ experience
京都に行った事が有りますか *Kyōto ni itta koto ga arimasu ka* Have you ever been to Kyoto?
行った事は行ったが会えなかった *Itta koto wa itta ga aenakatta* I did go, but I could not see him
⑦ⓐ exclamatory particle
ⓑ indicates imperative mood
まあ親切な事 *Mā shinsetsu na koto* How nice [kind] of you!
ごみを捨てない事 *Gomi o sutenai koto* No litter please
⑧ alias, viz
鷗外事森林太郎 *ōgai koto mori rintarō* Mori Rintaro alias Ogai

SYNONYMS

❶ⓐ affair
儀 affair → 169
件 MATTER → 51
❶ⓑ & 【koto】② incident
故 incident → 1141
変 unexpected event → 2069
❷ affairs
務 affairs → 1173
用 THINGS TO DO → 2976
❹ officials
役 executive → 244
司 officiator → 2931
僚 official → 165
吏 OFFICIAL → 3536

官 GOVERNMENT OFFICIAL → 2226
【koto】
①ⓐ **abstract thing**
物 THING → 874
ⓑ **nominalizers**
所 PARTICLE OF NOMINALIZATION → 851
子 NOUN SUFFIX → 3390
性 -ITY → 299

COMPOUND FORMATION
見事（＝美事）*migoto*
見事な 'splendid, admirable, beautiful' refers to something that is worthwhile（事 *koto* ⑤ⓑ）seeing（見）.

NOTE
⇨ see COMPOUND FORMATION for
房事 *bōji* ⇨ 房 1946
事柄 *kotogara* ⇨ 柄 897

東 東 东

3568 TŌ higashi

ⒸⒽ 东 dōng

Radical	Strokes
木 75	8-4-4
Grade	Freq
Jōyō-2	20
■ 4-8-3	

8-3Ⅱ

▶**EAST**

COMPOUNDS
❶ⓐ **east, eastern**
ⓑ go eastward
東方 *tōhō* east, eastward
東南 *tōnan* southeast
東亜 *tōa* East Asia
東洋 *tōyō* Orient
東西南北 *tōzainanboku* north, south, east and west
関東 *kantō* Kanto district
中東 *chūtō* Middle East
遼東の豕 *ryōtō no inoko* being self-complacent
東征 *tōsei* eastern expedition
❷ **Tokyo**
東京 *tōkyō* Tokyo
東上 *tōjō* going up to Tokyo
東名高速道路 *tōmei kōsokudōro* Tokyo-Nagoya Expressway
❸ abbrev. of 東京大学 *tōkyō daigaku*: University of Tokyo
早東戦 *sōtōsen* (baseball) game between Waseda and Tokyo universities

KUN
【**higashi 東**】[also prefix] east, eastern
東側 *higashigawa* eastern side
東口 *higashiguchi* east exit
東半球 *higashihankyū* Eastern Hemisphere

SYNONYMS
❶ⓐ **cardinal points**
西 WEST → 3520
北 NORTH → 197
南 SOUTH → 2082
❷ **Kanto cities**
京 TOKYO → 2052
都 METROPOLIS OF TOKYO → 1686
浜 Yokohama → 436

NOTE
⇨ see COMPOUND FORMATION for
関東 *kantō* ⇨ 関 3328
遼東の豕 *ryōtō no inoko* ⇨ 遼 3168

隶

3569

Radical	Strokes
隶 171	8-8-0
Grade	Freq
Radical	
■ 4-8-3	

8-3Ⅱ

RADICAL 171
Standard form: 隶 *reizukuri* 'capture'（隷）
Description: used in characters related to capturing

來

3570

▶**COME**
nonstandard for 来 3551

8-3Ⅱ

8-4□ 畀 3571

▶**MEAN**
nonstandard for 畁 2642

8-4□ 武 incorrect classification ⇨ see 3210

8-4□ 奉 incorrect classification ⇨ see 2559

8-4□ 奔 incorrect classification ⇨ see 2218

8-4□ 券 incorrect classification ⇨ see 2630

8-4□ 斉 incorrect classification ⇨ see 2054

8-4□ 呉 incorrect classification／stroke count ⇨ see 3545 (nonstandard for 呉 2549)

9-1□ 飛 飛 飞 3572 HI to(bu) to(basu) -to(basu)

CH 飞 fēi

(stroke order 1–9)

Radical	**Strokes**
飛 183	9-9-0
Grade	**Freq**
Jōyō-4	373
■ 4 - 9 - 1	

RADICAL 183
Standard form: 飛 *tobu* 'fly'
Description: used in characters related to flying

▶**FLY**

COMPOUNDS

❶ⓐ [formerly also 蜚 *hi*] **fly**
ⓑ fly about, scatter
ⓒ *baseball* **fly**
飛行 *hikō* flight, aviation
飛行機 *hikōki* airplane
飛来する *hirai suru* come flying, come by air
飛鳥 *hichō* flying bird
雄飛する *yūhi suru* launch out, embark upon (a career)
飛沫 *himatsu* splash, spray
飛散する *hisan suru* disperse, scatter, fly
飛球 *hikyū* fly ball
犠飛 *gihi* sacrifice fly
中飛 *chūhi* center fly
❷ⓐ flying, swift, quick, urgent
ⓑ [formerly 蜚 *hi*] (baseless) flying (rumor), wild, unfounded
飛脚 *hikyaku* express messenger; postman (in former times)
飛報 *hihō* urgent message
流言飛語 *ryūgen-higo* false report, flying rumor
❸ leap, spring up, jump
飛躍する *hiyaku suru* leap, jump
突飛な *toppi na* wild, extravagant, extraordinary
❹ name of chess piece in shogi (Japanese chess): *hisha*, rook
飛車 *hisha hisha*
敵飛 *tekihi* opponent's *hisha*
❺ [archaic] high
飛簷 *hien* high roof, upturned eaves

飛瀑 *hibaku* waterfall

INDEPENDENT

【hi 飛】 *hisha* (⇨ ❹)

KUN

【to(bu) 飛ぶ】

①ⓐ fly; travel by air

ⓑ rush [fly] (to the scene)

ⓒ fly about, be scattered

飛び上がる *tobiagaru* fly up, jump up

飛び魚 *tobiuo* flying fish

② skip (pages), skip over

二頁から四頁へ飛ぶ *nipēji kara yonpēji e tobu* skip from page two to page four

【to(basu) 飛ばす】 *vt* fly; shoot, send; drive fast; skip over (pages); issue; scatter, spatter

鳩を飛ばす *hato o tobasu* fly a pigeon

檄を飛ばす *geki o tobasu* issue a manifesto

水を飛ばす *mizu o tobasu* splash water

【-to(basu) -飛ばす】 [emphatic verbal suffix] off, away, recklessly

叱り飛ばす *shikaritobasu* scold away, rebuke strongly

書き飛ばす *kakitobasu* write [dash] off

SYNONYMS

❶ⓐ fly

翔 SOAR → 1357

航 NAVIGATE → 1318

USAGE

tobu

飛ぶ

①ⓐ fly; travel by air

ⓑ rush [fly] (to the scene)

ⓒ fly about, be scattered

② skip (pages), skip over

翔ぶ

soar, fly

跳ぶ

ⓐ jump, leap, spring

ⓑ jump [leap] over, vault

★Though when used independently 飛ぶ means to fly and 跳ぶ to leap or jump, both 飛 and 跳 can mean to jump when used as components of compounds, as for example 飛び掛かる *tobikakaru* 'spring [jump] upon'. 翔ぶ and 飛ぶ both mean to fly, but the former has a more poetic or elegant flavor.

HOMOPHONES

tobu ⇨ 翔 1357 跳 1532

重 重 重 Ⓒⓗ 重 zhòng chóng

9-2□

3573 JŪ CHŌ e omo(i) omo(ri) kasa(neru) kasa(naru) omo▲

Radical	Strokes
里 166	9-7-2
Grade	**Freq**
Jōyō-3	142
■ 4 - 9 - 2	

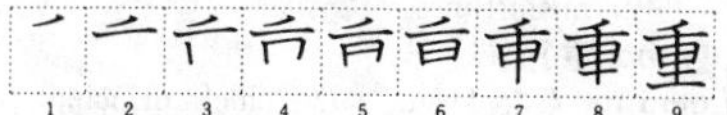

1 2 3 4 5 6 7 8 9

▶HEAVY ▶DUPLICATE

COMPOUNDS

❶ⓐ [also prefix] [original meaning] **heavy, weighty**

ⓑ *phys* (designating a heavier isotope) heavy

ⓒ [also prefix] *chem* heavy

ⓓ **weight, heaviness, load, gravity**

重油 *jūyu* fuel oil

重金属 *jūkinzoku* heavy metal

過重な *kajū na* too heavy

重水素 *jūsuiso* heavy hydrogen

重液分離 *jūeki-bunri* heavy media [liquid] separation

重量 *jūryō* weight

重力 *jūryoku* gravity, force of gravity

体重 *taijū* body weight

比重 *hijū* specific gravity, density; relative importance

荷重 *kajū* load

❷ [also prefix]

ⓐ (involving large-scale manufacture) **heavy**

ⓑ (great in degree) **heavy, serious, severe**

重爆 *jūbaku* heavy bomber

重工業 *jūkōgyō* heavy industry

重電機 *jūdenki* heavy electric apparatus

重騎兵 *jūkihei* heavy cavalry

重傷 *jūshō* heavy [serious] wound, severe injury

重態(=重体) *jūtai* serious condition, critical state

重税 *jūzei* heavy taxation

重労働 *jūrōdō* heavy labor

厳重に *genjū ni* strictly, severely, closely; securely, firmly

❸ⓐ (great in importance) **heavy, weighty, important, grave**

ⓑ **set value on, value, attach importance to, esteem**

重要な *jūyō na* important, essential, principal

重点 *jūten* important point; importance, emphasis, stress; priority

重大な *jūdai na* important, serious, grave

重視する *jūshi suru* attach importance to, think much of

重任 *jūnin* heavy responsibility, important

duty; reappointment
重宝 *chōhō* convenience, usefulness, handiness
重文(＝重要文化財) *jūbun* (＝*jūyō bunkazai*) important cultural property
貴重な *kichō na* precious, valuable
重商主義 *jūshōshugi* mercantilism
尊重する *sonchō suru* respect, esteem, value
偏重する *henchō suru* attach too much importance, overemphasize
珍重する *chinchō suru* value highly, treasure

❹ dignified, composed, solemn
重厚さ *jūkōsa* profoundness, depth, seriousness
慎重 *shinchō* prudence, discretion, circumspection
自重する *jichō suru* be prudent [circumspect]; take care of oneself
荘重な *sōchō na* solemn, grave, impressive

❺ⓐ pile up, heap up, stack
ⓑ -fold, layer, story (of a building)
重箱 *jūbako* nest [tier] of boxes
重奏 *jūsō* duet
重合 *jūgō* polymerization
重積する *jūseki suru* pile up
重層的 *jūsōteki* multilayered, stratified
重畳たる *chōjōtaru* piled up, placed one upon another; excellent, splendid
多重の *tajū no* multiple, multiplex
三重の *sanjū no* threefold, triple

❻ⓐ duplicate, repeat, redo
ⓑ duplicate, double, multiple
ⓒ [prefix] *chem* bi-
重重 *jūjū* repeatedly; extremely, very much
重複 *chōfuku* (＝*jūfuku*) duplication, overlapping; repetition
重盗 *jūtō* double steal
重訳 *jūyaku* retranslation
重版 *jūhan* second printing, reprint; second edition
重婚 *jūkon* bigamy
重炭酸ソーダ *jūtansansōda* sodium bicarbonate, baking soda

❼ cordial, hospitable, liberal
丁重(＝鄭重)な *teichō na* polite, courteous

❽ abbrev. of 重箱 *jūbako*: nest [tier] of boxes; box lunch
天重 *tenjū* box lunch with tempura

INDEPENDENT

【jū 重】 nest [tier] of boxes
お重 *ojū* nest [tier] of boxes

KUN

【e 重】 [in compounds] fold, layer, row
幾重 *ikue* (＝*ikujū*) many folds
二重の *futae* (＝*nijū*) *no* twofold
八重咲きの *yaezaki no* double-flowering

【omo(i) 重い】
①ⓐ heavy, weighty
ⓑ (difficult to move) heavy, slow to move
重さ *omosa* weight
重荷 *omoni* heavy load; burden, encumbrance
腰が重い *koshi ga omoi* be slow to act, be slow in starting work
② (weighed with concern) heavy, depressed
重苦しい *omokurushii* heavy, oppressed, gloomy
③ (great in degree) heavy, serious, severe
重い罪 *omoi tsumi* serious [grave] crime
④ (great in importance) heavy, weighty, important, grave
重い任務 *omoi ninmu* important task

【omo(ri) 重り】 [also 錘] weight, plumb, sinker, plummet
糸に重りを付ける *ito ni omori o tsukeru* weight a line

【kasa(neru) 重ねる】 *vt* pile up, heap up, stack in layers; repeat, add
重ね *kasane* pile, heap; lapping over; suit
積み重ねる *tsumikasaneru* pile up, heap up, stack in layers
重ねて *kasanete* repeatedly, again

【kasa(naru) 重なる】 *vi* be piled up, lie on top of one another; fall on, coincide with; come one after another, happen in succession
重なり *kasanari* pile, piling; overlapping
折り重なる *orikasanaru* lie on top of one another, be in a heap
不幸が重なる *fukō ga kasanaru* have a series of misfortunes

【omo 重】
omo na 重な [usu. 主な] chief, principal, main, foremost
重立った *omodatta* principal, leading, chief, main

SYNONYMS

❷ⓑ extreme in degree
強 STRONG → 475
高 HIGH → 2097
深 DEEP → 524
大 BIG → 3416
超 super- → 3313
甚 EXTREMELY → 2643
切 keen → 27
痛 bitter(ly) → 3285
極 EXTREME → 1017
激 intense → 776
厳 SEVERE → 3289
酷 SEVERE → 1562

❸ⓐ important
要 IMPORTANT → 2635
ⓑ respect
尚 VALUE HIGHLY → 2233
崇 REVERENCE → 2297
欽 REVERE → 1690

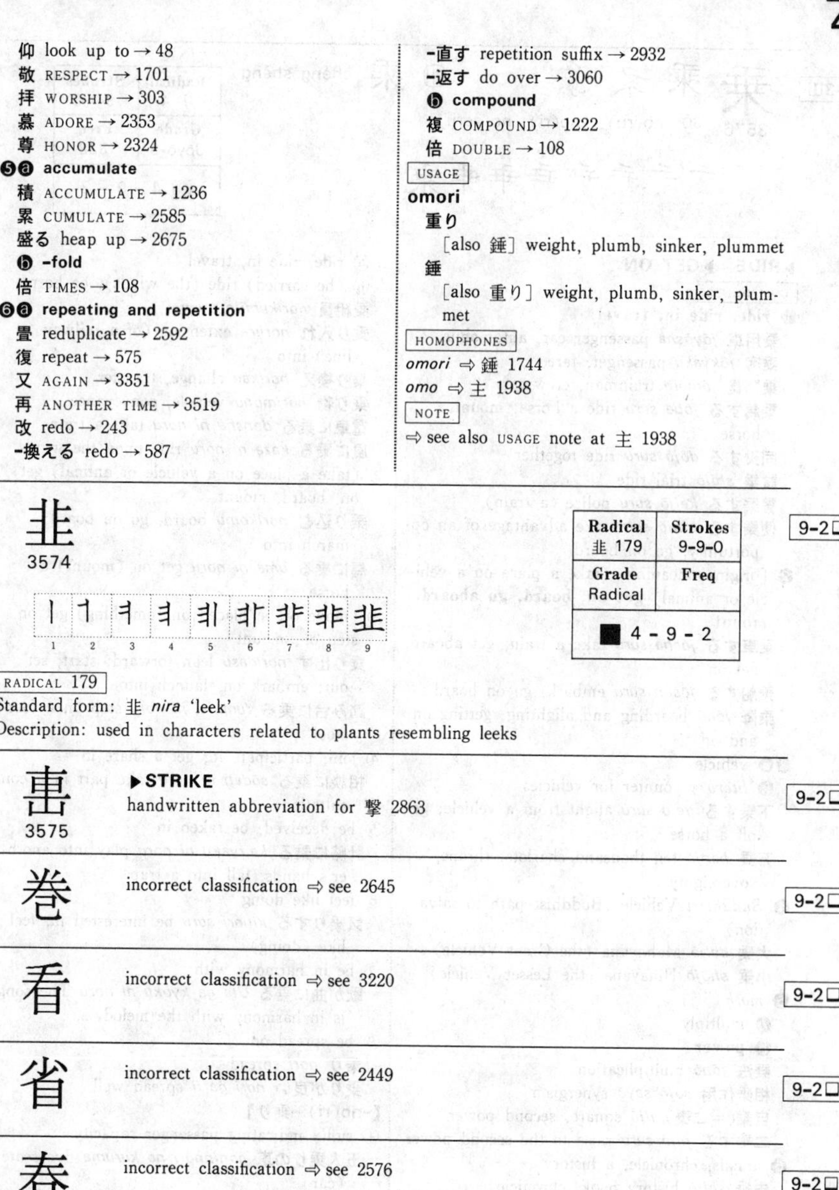

仰 look up to → 48
敬 RESPECT → 1701
拝 WORSHIP → 303
慕 ADORE → 2353
尊 HONOR → 2324

❺ⓐ accumulate

積 ACCUMULATE → 1236
累 CUMULATE → 2585
盛る heap up → 2675

ⓑ -fold

倍 TIMES → 108

❻ⓐ repeating and repetition

畳 reduplicate → 2592
復 repeat → 575
又 AGAIN → 3351
再 ANOTHER TIME → 3519
改 redo → 243
-換える redo → 587
-直す repetition suffix → 2932
-返す do over → 3060

ⓑ compound

複 COMPOUND → 1222
倍 DOUBLE → 108

USAGE

omori

重り

［also 錘］ weight, plumb, sinker, plummet

錘

［also 重り］ weight, plumb, sinker, plummet

HOMOPHONES

omori ⇨ 錘 1744
omo ⇨ 主 1938

NOTE

⇨ see also USAGE note at 主 1938

韭

3574

Radical	Strokes
韭 179	9-9-0
Grade	**Freq**
Radical	
■ 4 - 9 - 2	

9-2□

1 2 3 4 5 6 7 8 9

RADICAL 179

Standard form: 韭 *nira* 'leek'

Description: used in characters related to plants resembling leeks

---

𦍒

3575

9-2□

▶STRIKE

handwritten abbreviation for 撃 2863

巻

9-2□

incorrect classification ⇨ see 2645

看

9-2□

incorrect classification ⇨ see 3220

省

9-2□

incorrect classification ⇨ see 2449

春

9-2□

incorrect classification ⇨ see 2576

者

9-2□

incorrect classification ⇨ see 3217
(nonstandard for 者 3211)

9-3Ⅱ

乗 乘 𠂢 𠂢 ㊥ 乘 chéng shèng

3576 JŌ no(ru) -no(ri) no(seru)

Radical	Strokes
丿 4	9-1-8
Grade	**Freq**
Jōyō-3	333
■ 4-9-3	

1 2 3 4 5 6 7 8 9

▶RIDE ▶GET ON

COMPOUNDS

❶ **ride, ride in, travel**
乗用車 *jōyōsha* passenger car, automobile
乗客 *jōkyaku* passenger, fare
乗務員 *jōmuin* trainman, crewman
乗馬する *jōba suru* ride a horse; mount a horse
同乗する *dōjō suru* ride together
試乗 *shijō* trial ride
警乗する *keijō suru* police (a train)
便乗する *binjō suru* take advantage of an opportunity; go on board

❷ [original meaning] (take a place on a vehicle or animal) **get on, board, go aboard, mount**
乗車する *jōsha suru* take a train, get aboard, get on
乗船する *jōsen suru* embark, go on board
乗降 *jōkō* boarding and alighting, getting on and off

❸ⓐ vehicle
ⓑ *literary* counter for vehicles
下乗する *gejō suru* alight from a vehicle; get off a horse
万乗 *banjō* ten thousand chariots; throne, sovereignty

❹ *Buddhism* Vehicle (Buddhist path to salvation)
大乗 *daijō* Mahayana (the Great Vehicle)
小乗 *shōjō* Hinayana (the Lesser Vehicle)

❺ *math*
ⓐ multiply
ⓑ **power**
乗法 *jōhō* multiplication
相乗作用 *sōjō sayō* synergism
自乗(=二乗) *jijō* square, second power
二乗する *nijō suru* raise to the second power

❻ annals, chronicle, a history
史乗 *shijō* history book, chronicle

INDEPENDENT

【**jōjiru** (=**jōzuru**) 乗じる(=乗ずる)】 take advantage of, avail oneself of; multiply
人の無知に乗じる *hito no muchi ni jōjiru* abuse [take advantage of] another's ignorance

KUN

【**no(ru)** 乗る】
①ⓐ ride, ride in, travel
ⓑ (be carried) ride (the winds), be borne
乗組員 *norikumiin* crew
乗り入れ *noriire* extension (of a railway line) into
乗り換え *norikae* change, transfer
乗り物 *norimono* vehicle, conveyance
電車に乗る *densha ni noru* take a train
風に乗る *kaze ni noru* ride upon the winds
② (take a place on a vehicle or animal) get on, board, mount
乗り込む *norikomu* board, go on board; march into
馬に乗る *uma ni noru* get on (mount) a horse
③ (move or be placed on something) get on, step on, mount
乗り出す *noridasu* lean forward; start, set out; embark on, launch into
踏み台に乗る *fumidai ni noru* step on a footstool
④ join, participate in, get a share in
相談に乗る *sōdan ni noru* take part in a consultation
⑤ be deceived, be taken in
計略に乗る *keiryaku ni noru* play into another's hands, fall into a trap
⑥ feel like doing
気乗りする *kinori suru* be interested in, feel like (doing)
⑦ be in harmony with
歌が曲に乗る *Uta ga kyoku ni noru* The song is in harmony with the melody
⑧ be spread on
乗り *nori* spread
乗りが良い *nori ga ii* spread well

【**-no(ri)** -乗り】
① suffix indicating passenger capacity
五人乗りの車 *goninnori no kuruma* five-seater (car)
②ⓐ riding
ⓑ rider
只乗り *tadanori* free ride
波乗り *naminori* surfriding, surfing
ブランコ乗り *burankonori* trapeze performer

【**no(seru)** 乗せる】
① take (a person) on board, carry (passengers), pick up (passengers)
乗客を乗せる *jōkyaku o noseru* take passen-

gers on board
② let (a person) take part in (a scheme)
その仕事に私も一口乗せてくれないか *Sono shigoto ni watashi mo hitokuchi nosete kurenai ka* Let me in on that job, won't you?
③ take in, impose upon
そんな話に乗せられる物か *Sonna hanashi ni noserareru mono ka* You can't come round me with such yarns
④ bring into harmony

SYNONYMS

❶ **travel by vehicle**
走 travel by vehicle → 2194
航 NAVIGATE → 1318
騎 RIDE ON HORSEBACK → 1834
❷ **get on**
搭 BOARD → 592
❸ **vehicle**
車 VEHICLE → 3552
輪 wheeled vehicle → 1589
台 COUNTER FOR VEHICLES → 2005
❺ⓐ **multiply**
掛ける multiply → 493
ⓑ **mathematical power**
方 SQUARE → 1963
平 square (measure) → 3478

USAGE

❶ **noru**
乗る
①ⓐ ride, ride in, travel
ⓑ (be carried) ride (the winds), be borne
② (take a place on a vehicle or animal) get on, board, mount
③ (move or be placed on something) get on, step on, mount
④ join, participate in, get a share in
⑤ be deceived, be taken in
⑥ feel like doing
⑦ be in harmony with
⑧ be spread on
載る
① appear in print, be published, be recorded
② be placed upon
③ be loaded (on a vehicle)
❷ **noseru**
乗せる
① take (a person) on board, carry (passengers), pick up (passengers)
② let (a person) take part in (a scheme)
③ take in, impose upon
④ bring into harmony
載せる
① load (a vehicle or ship with cargo), lade, carry
② place on, put on
③ put in print, publish, carry, put on record

HOMOPHONES

noru ⇨ 載 3300
noseru ⇨ 載 3300

為 爲 為 為 ㊥ 为 wéi wèi

3577 I tame[1▲] tame[2▲] na(ru)[▲] na(su)[▲] su(ru)[▲]

Radical	Strokes
灬 86[△]	9-4-5
Grade	**Freq**
Jōyō	1049
■ 4-9-4	

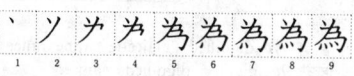

9-4□

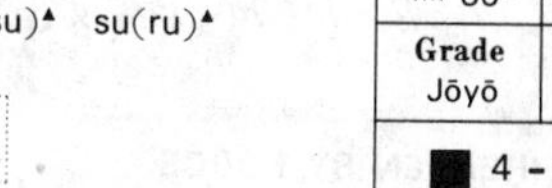

▶DO ▶SAKE

COMPOUNDS

❶ **do, make; act, behave**
為政家 *iseika* politician
行為 *kōi* act, deed, conduct, transaction
無為 *mui* inactivity; *Buddhism* that which is not created
作為 *sakui* artificiality, intention; commission (of a crime)
❷ that which is produced through causation
有為 *ui* vicissitudes of life; *Buddhism* perpetual change caused by karma; that which is made

KUN

【tame[1] 為】
①ⓐ sake, benefit, advantage, profit
ⓑ [often followed by に *ni*] for the sake [purpose] of, on behalf of, so that
人の為を思う *hito no tame o omou* wish someone well
自分の為に *jibun no tame ni* for one's own sake, for oneself
...しない為に *...shinai tame ni* so as not to
② [often followed by に *ni*] because (of), owing to, as a result of
雨の為に *ame no tame ni* because of the rain
【tame[2] 為】 [in compounds] exchange
為銀 *tamegin* exchange bank
外為 *gaitame* foreign exchange
【na(ru) 為る】
①ⓐ become, turn into, grow, get
ⓑ begin to (do), come to (do)

病気に為る *byōki ni naru* fall [be taken] ill
泳げる様に為る *oyogeru yō ni naru* learn how to swim
②ⓐ result in, turn out
ⓑ amount [come] to
幾らに為りますか *Ikura ni narimasu ka* How much will that be?
③ⓐ (of seasons) come, set in
ⓑ elapse, pass
④ serve [act] as

【na(su) 為す】do, perform, carry out
不善を為す *fuzen o nasu* do evil, commit vice

【su(ru) 為る】do, perform, carry out; make, convert; cost; elapse
馬鹿な事を為る *baka na koto o suru* do a silly thing
水を水蒸気に為る *mizu o suijōki ni suru* change water into steam
数時間為れば *sūjikan sureba* in a few hours

SPECIAL READINGS

為替 *kawase* money order, exchange

SYNONYMS

❶ **do and act**
仕 DO → 34
致す DO HUMBLY → 1316
行 ACT → 212
作 WORK → 68

【tame[1]】
①ⓐ **benefit**
益 BENEFIT → 2285
利 ADVANTAGE → 1114
用 use(ful) → 2976
役 SERVICE → 244
② **cause and reason**
故 reason → 1141
訳 reason → 1473
因 CAUSE → 3054
由 REASON → 3499

HOMOPHONES

naru ⇨ 成 3537 生 3497
nasu ⇨ 成 3537 生 3497

COMPOUND FORMATION

❶ 外為 *gaitame*
外為 'foreign exchange' is an abbreviation of 外国為替 *gaikoku-kawase* 'foreign exchange'.
❷ 為替 *kawase*
為替 'money order, exchange' consists of 為 (為る *suru*) 'let do, allow' and 替 'exchange'; that is, to allow someone to exchange money.

NOTE

⇨ see USAGE note at 成 3537
★This character has various old readings that form many compounds, including *naru*, *nasu*, *suru* 'become, do', all of which are now written in hiragana.

9-4□

威 威 戓

3578 I odo(su)▲ odo(shi)▲ odo(kasu)▲

Ⓒⓗ 威 wēi

Radical	Strokes
女 38	9-3-6
Grade	**Freq**
Jōyō	928
■ 4-9-4	

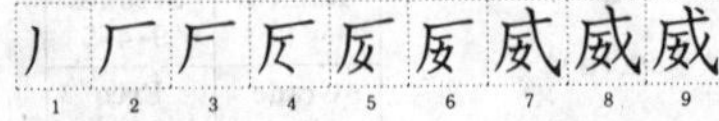
1 2 3 4 5 6 7 8 9

▶**MIGHT** ▶**THREATEN BY FORCE**

COMPOUNDS

❶ **might, impressive strength, power, authority, influence**
威力 *iryoku* power, might, authority, influence
威勢 *isei* spirits, dash; power
威張る *ibaru* put on airs, be haughty; boast, brag
権威 *ken'i* authority, power
示威 *jii* show of force
猛威 *mōi* fierceness, fury, vehemence
球威の有る投球 *kyūi no aru tōkyū baseball* powerful delivery
神威 *shin'i* might of Heaven
❷ⓐ **dignified, majestic, imposing**
ⓑ dignity, prestige
威厳 *igen* solemn dignity
威風 *ifū* majesty, dignity
威容 *iyō* dignified [majestic] appearance
威儀 *igi* dignity, dignified manner
威信 *ishin* prestige, dignity, authority
国威 *kokui* national prestige
❸ **threaten by force, dominate by power**
威圧 *iatsu* coercion, high-handedness
威嚇する *ikaku suru* intimidate, threaten, menace
脅威 *kyōi* threat, menace

INDEPENDENT

【i 威】dignity; power, authority, influence
威有って猛からず *i atte takekarazu* dignified without being overbearing
威を振るう *i o furuu* exercise authority

KUN

【odo(su) 威す】[now usu. 脅す] threaten, menace, intimidate
敵を威す *teki o odosu* threaten the enemy

【odo(shi) 威し】

①ⓐ [now usu. 脅し] threat, menace, intimidation
ⓑ [in compounds] something that scares or startles

鳥威し *toriodoshi* scarecrow

② [usu. 縅し] braid or thread of Japanese armor

【odo(kasu) 威かす】

ⓐ [now usu. 脅かす] threaten, menace, intimidate

ⓑ startle

威かして金を取る *odokashite kane o toru* scare money out of (a person)

SYNONYMS

❶ **power and authority**

力 POWER → 3371
勢 POWER (to influence) → 2857
権 POWER (to control) → 1065
覇 SUPREMACY → 2730

❷ⓐ **dignified**

荘 DIGNIFIED → 2262
厳 solemn → 3289
粛 solemnly → 3581

❸ **threaten**

脅 THREATEN → 2109
嚇 INTIMIDATE → 784
喝 shout threats at → 461

HOMOPHONES

odosu ⇨ 脅 2109
odoshi ⇨ 脅 2109 縅 1391
odokasu ⇨ 脅 2109 嚇 784

COMPOUND FORMATION

威張る *ibaru*

威張る 'put on airs, etc.' is to spread (張) authority or impressive strength (威 ❶); that is, to flaunt prestige.

NOTE

⇨ see USAGE note at 脅 2109

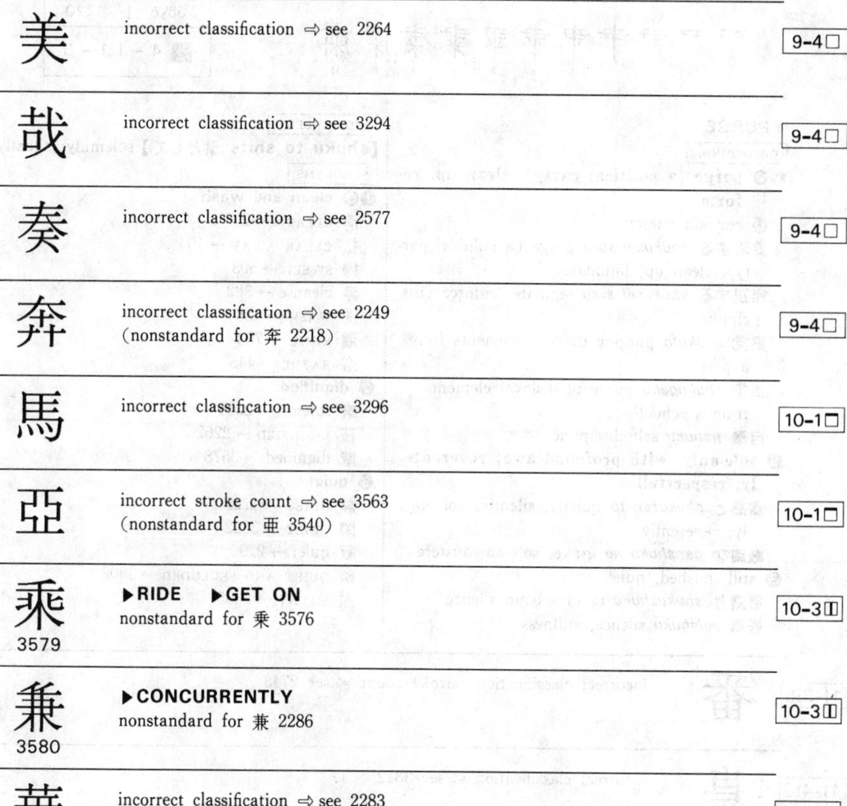

美 incorrect classification ⇨ see 2264 9-4□

哉 incorrect classification ⇨ see 3294 9-4□

奏 incorrect classification ⇨ see 2577 9-4□

奔 incorrect classification ⇨ see 2249 (nonstandard for 奔 2218) 9-4□

馬 incorrect classification ⇨ see 3296 10-1□

亞 incorrect stroke count ⇨ see 3563 (nonstandard for 亜 3540) 10-1□

乘 3579 ▶**RIDE** ▶**GET ON** nonstandard for 乗 3576 10-3◫

兼 3580 ▶**CONCURRENTLY** nonstandard for 兼 2286 10-3◫

華 incorrect classification ⇨ see 2283 10-4□

10-4□ **栽** incorrect classification ⇨ see 3297

10-4□ **泰** incorrect classification ⇨ see 2583

10-4□ **島** incorrect classification ⇨ see 3310

11-2□ **雀** incorrect classification ⇨ see 2469

11-3□ **粛** 肅 粛 粛 Ⓒ𝐇 肃 sù

3581 SHUKU

Radical	Strokes
聿 129	11-6-5
Grade	**Freq**
Jōyō	1220
■ 4 - 1 1 - 3	

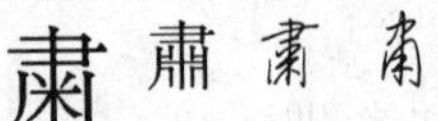

1 2 3 4 5 6 7 8 9 10 11

▶**PURGE**

COMPOUNDS

❶ⓐ **purge (a political party), clean up, reform**

ⓑ restrain oneself

粛清する *shukusei suru* purge (a political party), clean up, liquidate

粛正する *shukusei suru* regulate, enforce (discipline)

粛党 *shukutō* purging disloyal elements from a party

粛学 *shukugaku* purge of disloyal elements from a school

自粛 *jishuku* self-discipline

❷ **solemnly, with profound awe; reverently, respectfully**

粛然と *shukuzen to* quietly, silently; solemnly; reverently

厳粛な *genshuku na* grave, solemn, austere

❸ still, hushed, quiet

粛粛と *shukushuku to* in solemn silence

静粛 *seishuku* silence, stillness

INDEPENDENT

【shuku to shite 粛として】 solemnly; silently

SYNONYMS

❶ⓐ **clean and wash**

清 CLEAR → 523

払 CLEAR AWAY → 194

掃 SWEEP → 503

浄 cleanse → 382

洗 WASH → 388

濯 RINSE → 793

浴 BATHE → 445

❷ **dignified**

厳 solemn → 3289

荘 DIGNIFIED → 2262

威 dignified → 3578

❸ **quiet**

静 QUIET → 1728

閑 QUIET → 3322

寂 quiet → 2290

幽 QUIET AND SECLUDED → 3008

黙 SILENT → 2865

11-3□  incorrect classification／stroke count ⇨ see 2748

11-4□  incorrect classification ⇨ see 3312

亀 incorrect classification ⇨ see 2128 11-4□

斎 incorrect classification ⇨ see 2115 11-4□

麥 incorrect classification ⇨ see 2767 (nonstandard for 麦 2408) 11-4□

亞 incorrect stroke count ⇨ see 3563 (nonstandard for 亜 3540) 12-1□

幾 幾 幾 幾 ㊥ 几 jǐ jī 12-4□

3582 KI iku- iku(tsu) iku(ra)

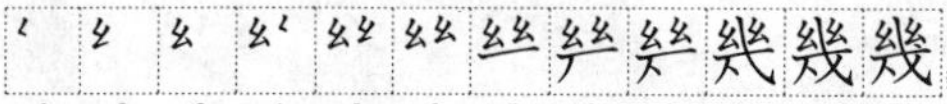

Radical	Strokes
幺 52	12-3-9
Grade	**Freq**
Jōyō	1599
■ 4-12-4	

▶HOW MANY ▶SOME

COMPOUNDS

❶ **how many, how much**

幾何学 *kikagaku* geometry

❷ desire, hope

庶幾 *shoki* desire, hope

KUN

【iku- 幾-】

[also prefix]

① how many, how much

幾時間 *ikujikan* how many hours

幾箱要りますか *Ikuhako irimasu ka* How many boxes do you want?

②ⓐ (being of indefinite number or quantity) some, several

ⓑ (being of considerable number) some, very many

幾夜も *ikuyo mo* for several nights

幾分 *ikubun* partially, somewhat, in a way

幾千と云う人 *ikusen to iu hito* thousands of people

幾日も *ikunichi mo* for some days, for many days

幾度も *ikudo* (=*ikutabi*) *mo* many times, frequently

【iku(tsu) 幾つ】 how many; how old

幾つ欲しいのか *Ikutsu hoshii no ka* How many do you want?

幾つになっても *ikutsu ni natte mo* however old one may be

お幾つですか *Oikutsu desu ka* How old are you?

【iku(ra) 幾ら】 how much, how many; no matter how much [many], however; even, with all (something)

数は幾らか *Kazu wa ikura ka* How many are there?

これは幾らですか *Kore wa ikura desu ka* How much does this cost?

幾らか *ikuraka* some, something; anything; somewhat, a little, in part

幾ら勉強しても *ikura benkyō shite mo* however hard one may work

幾らでも *ikura de mo* as many [much] as one likes

幾許(=幾何)も無く *ikubaku mo naku* not long after, before long

幾ら欠点が有っても *ikura ketten ga atte mo* with all one's faults

SYNONYMS

❶ **how many**

何- HOW MANY → 65

【iku-】

②ⓐ **some**

何- several → 65

数 several → 1790

NOTE

⇨ see COMPOUND FORMATION for 幾何学 *kikagaku* ⇨ 何 65

12-4

幾 3583

▶HOW MANY ▶SOME

nonstandard for 幾 3582

12-4

奥 incorrect classification ⇨ see 2824

12-4

裁 incorrect classification ⇨ see 3299

13-1

黽 3584 BŌ BIN BEN

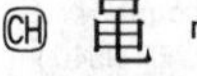

CH 黾 mǐn

Radical	Strokes
黽 205	13-13-0
Grade	Freq
Reference	
■ 4-13-1	

RADICAL 205

Standard form: 黽 *ben* 'frog' (鼈 鼈)

Description: used in characters related to frogs or toads

COMPOUNDS

❶ [original meaning] toad, frog

蛙黽 *abō* [archaic] tree frog [toad]

水黽 *amenbo* pond skater, water strider

❷ [archaic] make an effort, exert oneself

黽勉 *binben* working [trying] hard

13-1

鼎 3585 TEI kanae

CH 鼎 dǐng

Radical	Strokes
鼎 206	13-13-0
Grade	Freq
Reference	
■ 4-13-1	

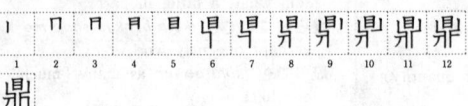

RADICAL 206

Standard form: 鼎 *kanae* 'ritual cauldron'

Description: used in characters related to ritual cauldrons or tripod vessels

COMPOUNDS

❶ [original meaning] tripod cauldron

鼎の軽重を問う *kanae no keichō o tou* weigh one's ability, call one's ability into question

❷ [archaic] symbol of dynasty [the throne]

鼎革 *teikaku* change of dynasty

❸ involving three parts or things, triangular

鼎立 *teiritsu* triangular position

鼎談 *teidan* three-man talk, tricornered conversation

鼎坐する *teiza suru* sit in a triangle

13-3

肅 3586

▶PURGE

nonstandard for 粛 3581

載 incorrect classification ⇨ see 3300 13-4□

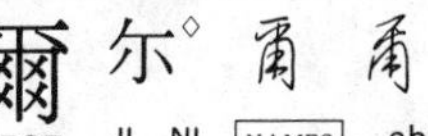

爾 尓° 3587 JI NI NAMES chika ㊥ 尔 ěr 14-1□

Radical	Strokes
爻 89	14-4-10
Grade	**Freq**
Names	2058
■ 4 - 14 - 1	

▶**THAT**

COMPOUNDS

❶ **that**

爾来 *jirai* from that time on, ever since
爾後 *jigo* from this [that] time onward, henceforth, thereafter

❷ thou, you

爾汝 *jijo* thou, you

❸ suffix after adjectives

徒爾 *toji* uselessness
莞爾として *kanji to shite* with a smile

❹ used phonetically for *ni*

天爾乎波 *tenioha* particles, postpositions (i.e., て, に, を and は)

NAMES

政爾 *seiji* male name
爾也 *chikaya* male name

SYNONYMS

❶ **this and that**

之 this → 3420
是 this → 2436
彼 that → 290
本 THIS → 3502
今 THIS (week, etc.) → 1968
当 THE PRESENT → 2177
該 the said → 1519
同 the same → 2987

❷ **second person pronouns**

君 YOU (*familiar*) → 3206
貴 you (*honorific*) → 2606

❸ **modifier suffixes**

然 MODIFIER FORMING SUFFIX → 2782
如 modifier suffix → 207
的 ADJECTIVAL SUFFIX → 1125

截 incorrect classification ⇨ see 3301 14-4□

器 incorrect classification ⇨ see 2713 15-1□

噐 incorrect classification ⇨ see 2718 (nonstandard for 器 2713) 16-1□

龜 incorrect classification ⇨ see 2147 (nonstandard for 亀 2128) 16-4□

齋 incorrect classification ⇨ see 2148 (nonstandard for 斎 2115) 17-4□

戴 incorrect classification ⇨ see 3302 18-4□

incorrect classification ⇨ see 2150
(nonstandard for 亀 2128)

APPENDIXES

付録

APPENDIX 1

SKIP RULES: THEORY AND PRACTICE

To locate a character according to SKIP (**System of Kanji Indexing by Patterns**) rules, you must identify the pattern to which your character belongs in order to determine the first part of the **SKIP number**, then divide or subclassify the character in order to determine the second and third parts of that number.

In actual practice, you normally identify the pattern of a character and divide it or subclassify it more or less simultaneously; that is, you identify the pattern as consisting of parts in a particular spatial arrangement, such as left-right or up-down. When you see a character like 相, for example, you identify it as a left-right pattern, and, at the same time, decide that it can be divided into 木 and 目. Nevertheless, for the sake of clarity and convenience of presentation, pattern identification and character division are treated here as separate topics.

This appendix presents a detailed description of the rules for identifying the pattern and dividing the character, and a full theoretical treatment of SKIP related concepts. Although it includes many interesting details on the structure of kanji patterns, it is not necessary to acquire a thorough knowledge of these in order to use the system. Since the system is essentially simple, the description in the front matter (SYSTEM OF KANJI INDEXING BY PATTERNS on p. 106a), which includes a summary of all the rules presented here, should normally be sufficient for understanding and using the system without referring to this appendix.

It is most important that you acquire a clear understanding of the various terms used in a technical sense, particularly the term **division point**. All technical terms are briefly defined in SYSTEM OF KANJI INDEXING BY PATTERNS **§ 7. Glossary,** while a detailed description of division points and related concepts appears below in **§ 1. Definitions of Pattern Terminology.** The definitions are printed in **century boldface,** and the technical terms are printed in **sanserif boldface** whenever it is necessary to draw attention to them, especially the first time they are used in a topic of discussion. To distinguish SKIP rules from ordinary text, the principal rules are set in sanserif boldface **CAPITAL LETTERS** and SMALL CAPITALS, while subrules are set in sanserif lowercase.

1. DEFINITIONS OF PATTERN TERMINOLOGY

The sections that follow define and describe the most important SKIP terms. The descriptions are very detailed, since they aim to present a full treatment of all the theoretical and practical aspects of the system. Do not be overly concerned with understanding the finer details. Since the SKIP classification scheme is easy to use even with only a superficial knowledge of these terms, you may skip this section altogether and refer to it only when necessary. All terms are briefly defined in **SYSTEM OF KANJI INDEXING BY PATTERNS §7. Glossary,** which should be sufficient for most purposes.

Although such terms as **conceptual space** and **tangential contact** are defined as rigorously as possible, it is impossible to make such definitions with absolute precision. The problem is caused by the large number of graphic variants and kanji typefaces. For example, the strokes of a character may be in physical contact in one typeface style, but not so in another. There may also be differences between the printed and written forms. For example, the character for *sora* 'sky' is 空 in one style but 空 in another. Notice how 儿 is either separated from or in contact with 宀 depending on the typeface style.

For these reasons, SKIP is based on the printed form of characters, particularly the Ming typeface, which is the most common typeface used in Japan. Once you gain minimal familiarity with kanji elements, you should have no trouble interpreting the definitions in the way they were intended.

1.1 Space

Space is defined as **a gap or breaking point between elements.** Spaces are of two kinds: (1) **clear space** and (2) **conceptual space.** There is no absolute way to distinguish between the two, nor is it normally necessary to do so. For division purposes, both are treated as a single type of division point. However, an understanding of these concepts will enable you to clearly distinguish between a space and actual physical contact (**tangential contact**).

1.1.1 Clear Space **Clear space** is defined as **a clearly visible gap, especially one formed by parallel strokes or elements.** 二 and 川, for example, are separated by a clear space between parallel strokes. A clear space may also be formed by inclined strokes, as in 八, 公, and 小, or by inclined elements, as in 多. A character can always be divided at the first clear space, except for the rare cases in which it violates the principle of **element integrity**. For example, although in 情 there is a clear space after 丶, divide into 忄 and 青, *not* 丶 and 情, since 忄 is an **indivisible unit** (see **§3.8 Element Integrity**).

1.1.2 Conceptual Space **Conceptual space** refers to **a natural breaking point where one would expect a gap; i.e., a gap that may not be visible because the elements are crowded closely together.** To rephrase: it is the "theoretical" space between one or more **independent elements** (**§1.4**) that may be in accidental contact, as the top 力 in 脅, マ and 丁 in 予, or 夫 and 日 in 春. Although such elements may appear to be in **tangential contact** (which is considered full physical contact), it is quite evident that the contact is accidental; that is, that the elements constitute distinct units.

Strokes separated by a conceptual space usually have little flips or hooks (serifs) at their ends, whereas strokes in tangential contact are in full physical contact with the relevant strokes merging into each other. For example, the strokes shown in red in 字, 応, and 前 cannot be separated from the horizontal strokes to which they are attached, since they are in tangential contact. On the other hand, diagonal elements are often separated by a conceptual space, as in 系, 主, and 乏, since they constitute independent elements. However, there is no conceptual space between ノ and 木 in 禾, which are in tangential contact.

Some complex characters, such as 墜 and 響, may consist of several independent elements, all of which appear to be in physical contact with each other. Such contacts should be ignored since they are considered to form a conceptual space.

When dividing by conceptual space, be sure not to violate the **element integrity** principle (§3.8). Common sense will be your best guide to avoid incorrect divisions. The rules for division by conceptual space are only a logical statement of the intuitive way in which kanji elements are normally perceived (except by the complete beginner).

1.2 Tangential Contact

Tangential contact refers to **full physical contact between strokes or stroke segments that join at one point without intersecting.** Tangential contact is a concept introduced to clarify the distinction between actual physical contact and the appearance of physical contact, such as the accidental contact between elements separated by a **conceptual space.**

Branch refers to **a stroke or stroke segment that abuts with other strokes or stroke segments at a point of tangential contact.** The number of branches meeting at a point of tangential contact may be two, three, four, or more. **Two-branch tangential contact** is defined as **tangential contact in which two branches join at one point; three-branch tangential contact** is defined as **tangential contact in which three branches join at one point;** and so on. The small circles in the diagram below represent points of tangential contact:

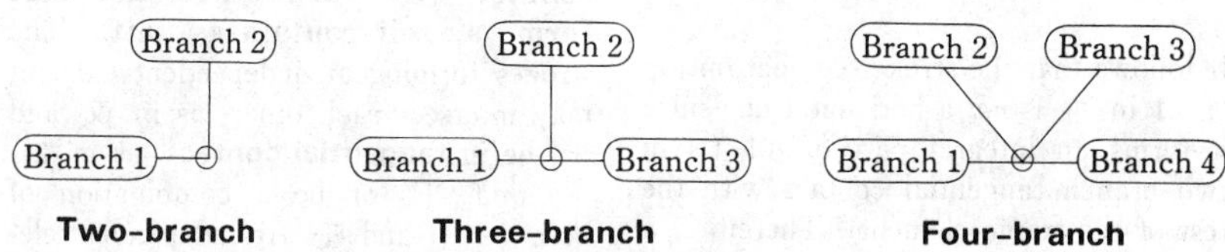

The following characters illustrate tangential contact:

2 branches	3 branches	4 branches	5 branches
吉	京	井	美

The branches may meet at right angles or at some other angle. Points of tangential contact may be formed by (*a*) verticals over horizontals, (*b*) horizontals over verticals, (*c*) diagonals over verticals, (*d*) verticals over diagonals, or by similar combinations:

上	下	亻	虫
(*a*)	(*b*)	(*c*)	(*d*)

Note that tangential contact requires actual physical contact; the strokes or elements must not be separated by little flips, hooks, or protrusions (serifs). For example, 丶 is not in tangential contact with 一 in 主, but 丨 *is* in tangential contact with 冖 in 字. Likewise, ノ is not considered to be in tangential contact with 糸 in 系.

Strokes or stroke segments in two-branch tangential contact can

never be separated from each other. It follows that **end attachments,** as in 軍, and the strokes or stroke segments forming most **frame elements,** as in 早, cannot be separated. See also footnote 3 in **§ 3.8 Element Integrity.**

1.3 Horizontal Line

Horizontal line is defined as **a horizontal, or almost horizontal, stroke not intersected by any other strokes.** Horizontal lines may have minor **attachments** appended to their sides or ends:

Right	Wrong
赤 忘 学 文 業 索 堂	古 百 南 支 車 兄 足

A horizontal line is a full stroke in its own right, not merely a line segment that forms part of another stroke. Therefore, if the end or ends of a horizontal stroke or stroke segment come in **two-branch tangential contact** with the sides of a **frame element** (which is usually of rectangular (as 口 in 古) or inverted **U** shape (as 冂 in 南), that horizontal stroke or stroke segment does not qualify as a horizontal line.

It follows that the stroke segment on top of 口 in 古 is *not* a horizontal line since it forms an integral part of 口 (is in two-branch tangential contact with the rest of the frame element). Therefore, a character like 古 cannot be split into 土 and 凵 (which in any case would be breaking through the stroke ㇆), since 一 in 古 does *not* qualify as a horizontal line. However, if a horizontal stroke sits on top of a frame element and protrudes from both sides, that is, if it comes in three-branch tangential contact with the frame element below it on both sides, as in 歯 and 赤, it *is* considered a horizontal line since neither one of its ends is in two-branch tangential contact with the sides of the frame element below it (see also **§ 1.6**).

To divide up-down characters correctly, it is important to understand the concept of horizontal line. When dividing up-down characters by horizontal line, **the horizontal line, along with its side, top, and end attachments, goes to the top.** Elements attached to the bottom of the horizontal line are separated from it and go to the bottom (see **§ 3.5.2** for details).

1.4 Independent Element

Independent element is defined as **a stroke or combination of strokes that intersect or come in tangential contact with each other and that form a self-contained unit.** The strokes forming an independent element may intersect each other, as in 又 and 十, be in **tangential contact,** as in 口, 卜, and 下, or be a combination of both, as 土 and 壬. An independent element is often a combination of strokes in tangential contact, but this does not include *accidental* contact between independent elements; i.e., 口 and 夕 are two separate independent elements in 名, not a single independent element consisting of two parts.

Normally, it is not necessary to be aware of independent elements. The concept is useful for understanding the division of up-down characters by **conceptual space** (see **§ 1.1.2**). For example, since the top 又 in 桑 is an independent element separated from the rest of the character by a conceptual space, 桑 is divided into 又 and 桒, not 叒 and 木. Similarly, 耒 and 日 are independent elements in 春, which is divided as an up-down character by conceptual space.

1.5 Attachment

Attachment is defined as **one or more usually short strokes, stroke segments, or elements in physical contact, or almost in physical contact, with the main body of an element.** It will normally be clear at a glance that it forms an integral part of the element to which it is attached.

An attachment may be physically attached to the main element, as 十 in 索, or slightly apart, as 冫 in 疒. Although 冫 is not in complete physical contact with 广, it is clear that they form an inseparable whole. However, elements separated by a **conceptual space,** as 炏 in 勞, are not considered attachments, since they do not form an integral part of each other. Attachments may be perpendicular, or inclined, to the main element, as 丨 in 字, or 丷 in 前, but parallel strokes, as 一 in 音, are not considered attachments since they are separated from each other by a **clear space.**

Attachments are of three kinds: top, side, and end. Strokes appended to the bottom of an element are *not* considered attachments. Therefore, in the character 亡, 丨 is an attachment in relation to 一, but 𠃊 is not.

1.5.1 Top Attachment

Top attachment is **one or more usually short strokes, stroke segments, or elements in physical contact, or almost in physical contact, with the top of the main body of an element.** Top attachments are nearly always dots or minor elements attached to horizontal strokes, as in:

字 京 学 美 賞 業 胄 危 度

Top attachments may also be found over diagonal elements, as in 豸 and 発. In rare cases, especially in nonstandard character forms, top attachments may be fairly large, as in 光, 學, and 譽. However, note that if the top element is separated from the bottom element by a conceptual space, as ⺮ in 筒, 敝 in 斃, and 炏 in 螢, it is not considered an attachment but an **independent element** in its own right.

Never separate top attachments from a main element except when dividing up-down characters by frame element. For example, in the character 索, 十 is a top attachment in relation to the main element 冖. 索 is thus divided by horizontal line into 𡿺 and 糸, where the element 十 goes to the top along with 冖. On the other hand, the same element 十 in the character 古 is separated from 口 since the latter is a frame element (see **§ 3.5.3**).

1.5.2 Side and End Attachments

Side attachment is defined as **one or more relatively short strokes or stroke segments in physical contact, or almost in physical contact, with the side of the main body of an element.** Similarly, **end attachment** is defined as **one or more relatively short strokes or stroke segments in physical contact, or almost in physical contact, with the end of the main body of an element.** Side attachments are thus in three-branch tangential contact with the main element, whereas end attachments are in two-branch tangential contact with the main element:

Side attachments 年 午 台 情 疒 旬
End attachments 軍 字 岩 民

If the stroke attached to the side or end is long in relation to the main element, as 丿 in 片 and 度, it is not considered a side or end attachment. Likewise, if a stroke forms part of a **frame element,** it is not considered an attachment. For example, 丨 on the left of 冂 and 早 is not considered an attachment since it is part of the frame elements 冂 and 口

respectively, but ′ and ′ are end attachments in 䒑, since they are short and do not constitute a frame element.

All this may sound extremely complicated, when in fact it is not. In the great majority of cases you can intuitively identify attachments by a mere glance. The important thing to remember is: **Never separate side or end attachments from the main element.**

1.6 Frame Element

Frame element is defined as **a combination of strokes or stroke segments forming a figure enclosed on two, three, or four sides.** Be sure not to confuse frame elements with **enclosure elements** (see **§ 1.7**). An enclosure element must enclose the rest of the character on two or more sides, but a frame element could be anywhere in the character. A frame element need not necessarily enclose other elements, though it often does. Enclosure elements are used for identifying the main pattern of a character, whereas frame elements are used for dividing the character into up and down parts.

Frame Elements and Enclosure Elements

Sides	Frame Elements		Enclosure Elements
	Right	Wrong	
4	古 器 真 百 克 早 景 夢		国 田 目 四
3	当 南 肖 忘	索 字 写 忘	問 向 凶 医
2	支 糸 弁	予 矛	進 処 可 麻

Most frame elements are four-sided. Four-sided frame elements may be located at the top (早), the middle (免), or the bottom (古) of a character, and may be square or rectangular. Three-sided frame elements are less common, while two-sided elements are quite rare. The sides of two-and three-sided frame elements must be relatively long so that they extend well into the character. For example, 冖 is not a frame element in 索, but 冂, which is similar to 冖 in shape, *is* a frame element in 南. Likewise, ′ and ′ in 冖 are merely side attachments so that 冖 is not a frame element. Similarly, ㇇ in 予 does not qualify as a frame element since the diagonal stroke segment of ㇇ is too short, but ㇇ *is* a frame element in 支 since it extends well into the character.

Although the contours of most frame elements are smooth, some frame elements include strokes or stroke segments that protrude beyond the frame wall, that is, that intersect the frame wall, as in 単, 曲, and 弟, or even cut right through it, as in 母. Such intersecting strokes do not disqualify an element from being a frame element.

The corners of almost all frame elements consist of strokes or stroke segments abutting in two-branch tangential contact; that is, the corners are smooth (without protrusions), as in 古, 争, and 南. Since strokes in two-branch tangential contact can never be separated from each other (**§ 1.2**), it follows that most frame elements cannot be broken up.

However, two-branch tangential contact between sides is not a necessary condition. The sides of some frame elements may intersect, as in 某, 尭, and 击, while in other cases the sides abut in a **T**, i.e., come in three-branch tangential contact, as in 色. All such elements qualify as frame elements regardless of the number of branches in tangential contact.

In rare cases, both ends of a horizontal stroke on top of a frame element protrude beyond the edges, that is, are in three-branch tangential contact, as in 歯 and 赤, so that such a stroke qualifies as a **horizontal line.** Thus, since the horizontal line in 歯 *precedes* the frame element in 歯, 歯 is divided by horizontal line into 止 and [illegible]. This means that if a horizontal stroke on top of a frame element also qualifies as a horizontal line, the sides of the frame element may be separated from each other. See also **§ 3.5.3 Division by Frame Element** and footnote 3 in **§ 3.8 Element Integrity.**

1.7 Enclosure Element

An **enclosure element** is defined as **a completely exterior element enclosing the rest of a character on two or more sides.** The characteristics of enclosure elements are described below. Each characteristic is explained in greater detail in the sections that follow.

1. An enclosure element must enclose the rest of the character on two, three, or four sides. It may occupy any position or face any direction along the exterior of the character.

2. An enclosure element must enclose the entire, or almost the entire, remaining part of the character. It must also be completely exterior; that is, it must not protrude into nor intersect the rest of the character.

3. The contour of an enclosure element must be identical with, or closely resemble, the contour of the corresponding **subpattern symbol.** The contour of a two-sided or three-sided enclosure element may be identical, or nearly identical, with the contour of the subpattern symbol, or it may have *minor* **attachments** or protrusions. The contour of a four-sided enclosure element must be nearly perfectly smooth: i.e., it must not have any protrusions or attachments.

4. An enclosure element must resemble the corresponding subpattern symbol in proportion. It must not consist of **independent elements** arranged so that the character is divisible into left-right or up-down parts.

Example					
反 2-2	向 3-3	園 3-10	送 3-6	司 1-4	
度 3-6	間 8-4	凶 2-2	区 2-2	斗 2-2	
還 3-13	直 1-7	疫 5-4	有 2-4	山 2-1	
画 2-6	可 2-3	后 2-4	者 4-4	闘 8-10	
匕 1-1	司 1-4	同 2-4	幽 2-7	日 3-1	
旬 2-4	向 3-3	右 2-3	考 4-2		
進 3-8	赴 7-2	勉 8-2	魅 8-7	司 1-4	馬 6-4
雇 2-10	危 4-2				

The enclosure element usually dominates the character's visual pattern and stands out as its most prominent feature. The above description and a study of the chart in the next section should enable you to instantly identify enclosure patterns in the absolute majority of cases. For the sake of completeness, the following sections present a full description that covers also unusual and difficult cases.

1.7.1 Enclosure Subpatterns **Enclosure subpattern** is defined as **one of the eleven groups into which the enclosure pattern is subdivided according to the number of sides of the enclosure element and its position along the exterior of the character.** The structure of each subpattern resembles that of the **subpattern symbols** shown in the chart below:

Enclosure Subpatterns

Sides	Subpattern Symbol	Right	Wrong
2	□	進迄赴延直止処勉魅題匕旭	呉県導
	□	句載刃式鳥気司乃可寸馬戒	牙為飛
	□	麻屋厚痴雇虎右考石産着	不尺方名衣艮省
	□	斗	
3	□	閉岡瓜凡風向闘肉	而南商角成肖
	□	凶山幽画	
	□	医臣匿	
	□	丑	
4	□	団囲田	皿面白
	□	目日	且自
	□	四罒	

An enclosure element must enclose the rest of the character on two (司), **three** (匠), **or four sides** (国). It may occupy any position or face any direction along the exterior of the character. Two-sided enclosure elements may be located at the bottom-left (延), the top-right (司), the top-left (麻) or, in rare cases, the bottom right (斗). Likewise, three-sided enclosure elements may face the bottom (風), the top 凶, the right (医) or, in rare cases, the left (丑). Four-sided enclosure elements must surround the entire character, as in 回 and 目. Thus, any element enclosing two or more sides is regarded as an enclosure element, regardless of its position or the direction it faces.

It is important to keep in mind that the enclosure pattern constitutes a single category, just like the left-right or up-down pattern. Therefore, you need not concern yourself with the details of enclosure subpatterns, nor is it necessary to be particularly aware of to which subpattern your character belongs. Any character that qualifies as an enclosure character is classified under the enclosure pattern and identified by the symbol □3, regardless of its subpattern. The subpattern symbols are merely visual aids. The main reason why enclosure subpatterns are introduced is to make it clear that *any* enclosure element qualifies, regardless of its number of sides or its position in the character, and to make it easier to explain their geometrical properties.

1.7.2 Mode of Enclosure

1. **An enclosure element must enclose the entire, or almost the entire, remaining part of the character.** It must not merely sit on the side, top, or bottom of the character. The element 厂 in 辰, for example, qualifies as an enclosure element since it encloses the remaining part, but the same element in 唇 or 農 does not qualify since it merely sits on the top and bottom respectively;

likewise, 寸 does not qualify as an enclosure element in 村 since it is located on the side of the character and does not enclose the left part, but it does qualify as an enclosure element in 寸 since it encloses the element 丶.

2. **An enclosure element must be completely exterior.** This means that it must actually *enclose* two or more sides of the character, as in 斤 and 同. It must not *protrude* into the rest of the character, as 戈 in 載, nor *intersect* any strokes, as in 耳 (載 is correctly classified under □ 3-6-7 and 耳 under ■ 4-6-1). Similarly, although 冊 closely resembles 用, which is a perfect example of an enclosure character, 冊 does *not* qualify as an enclosure character because 冂 is intersected by 一; that is, because 冂 is not completely exterior.

1.7.3 Contour Resemblance

1. **The contour of an enclosure element must be identical with, or closely resemble, the contour of the corresponding subpattern symbol.** This means that the outline of an enclosure element must be fairly smooth. The contour and shape of some enclosure elements, such as 厂 (□), 冂 (□), and 囗 (□) are identical or nearly identical with those of the corresponding subpattern symbols (shown in parentheses).

Two-sided and three-sided enclosure elements may have a variety of minor **attachments** or protrusions on the top, sides, or ends, as in 疒, 辶, and 耂. As long as these attachments are *minor* and the overall form and contours of the element closely resemble those of the subpattern symbol, such elements qualify as enclosure elements. However, if an element has *relatively large* attachments or protrusions along its exterior, like 十 in 冂 (南) or 亠 in 冂 (商), it does not qualify as an enclosure element since its shape and contour do not sufficiently resemble the subpattern symbol (in this case □). The difference between major and minor attachments cannot be precisely defined. Your intuition should be right most of the time. Borderline cases have been cross-referenced as necessary. A study of the charts below should make the concept of contour resemblance quite clear.

2. **The contour of a four-sided enclosure element must be nearly perfectly smooth; i.e., it must not have any protrusions or attachments.** 回 and 目 are examples of enclosure elements with smooth contours. Protrusions, as in 且, 皿, and 甘, or any kind of attachments, as in 白 and 面, are *not* allowed. However, disregard the tiny extensions at the edges, as at the bottom of 四, since these are merely stylistic serifs not intrinsic to the character's form.

Enclosure Elements with Identical or Nearly-Identical Contours

Sides	Subpattern	Examples
2	□ □ □	直 司 匣 届
3	□ □ □ □	用 山 凶 臣 丑
4	□ □ □	図 田 目 四

Enclosure Elements with Closely-Resembling Contours and Minor Attachments

Sides	Subpattern	Examples
2	□ □	進 止 勉 趣 旬 載 鳥 乃
2	□ □	広 病 者 氏 産 石 着 危 斗
3	□	間 風 向 肉
4	□	attachments not allowed

Elements Not Qualifying as Enclosure Elements

Char.	Wrong	Remarks	Right
呉	□3-4-3	Attachments too large. Divide into up-down parts at first horizontal line.	▀2-5-2
県	□3-4-5	Attachments too large. Divide into up-down parts at first horizontal line.	▀2-6-3
名	□3-3-3	Poor contour resemblance. Diagonal divisions are classified under ▀ 2.	▀2-3-3
為	□3-5-4	Poor contour resemblance.	■4-9-4
商	□3-6-5	Poor contour resemblance because of large top attachment.	▀2-2-9
南	□3-4-5	Poor contour resemblance because of large top attachment.	▀2-2-7
角	□3-4-3	Poor contour resemblance because of large top attachment.	▀2-2-5
白	□3-4-1	Attachments not allowed in four-sided enclosure elements.	■4-5-2
且	□3-3-2	Side protrusions not allowed in four-sided enclosure elements.	■4-5-1

1.7.4 Pattern Structure

1. **An enclosure element must resemble the corresponding subpattern symbol in proportion.** Since the subpattern symbols, such as □ and □, represent subgroups of enclosure characters in an abstract manner, the proportion of shaded area to blank area within each symbol is constant. When a character is actually written or printed as a visual sign, this proportion will of course vary with the character. For example, both 進 and 赴 are enclosure characters of type □, but the proportion of shaded area to blank area in 赴 is greater than in 進. Nevertheless, both are classified as enclosure characters. On the other hand, characters like 犬 and 式, whose shaded parts occupy nearly the entire character, could, with some stretch of the imagination, be classified under subpattern □ because the large element at the lower left actually encloses the dot at the upper right. Though it is highly unlikely that anyone would make such a division, a formal rule to exclude this possibility is necessary.

Certain categories of shade-to-blank proportions in two-sided enclosure characters are intuitively perceived as enclosure patterns, while others are not. The characteristics of the acceptable categories, the gist of which is explained below, are complex and purely theoretical; there is no need for the general user to understand all the details. For practical purposes, a study of the various example charts is adequate.

Two-sided enclosure characters can be classified into two subgroups. The first subgroup consists of characters of types ┏ and ┓, which are intuitively felt to have a vertical structure, and will be referred to as *vertical type*. The second subgroup consists of characters of types ┗ and ┛, which are intuitively felt to have a horizontal structure, and will be referred to as *horizontal type*. For explanatory purposes, the subpattern symbols of the horizontal type are divided into two equal halves by a *horizontal midline*, while the subpattern symbols of the vertical type are divided into two equal halves by a *vertical midline*. The imaginary line that divides the character itself (*not* the pattern symbol) into parts will be referred to as the *dividing line*.[1]

Vertical Type

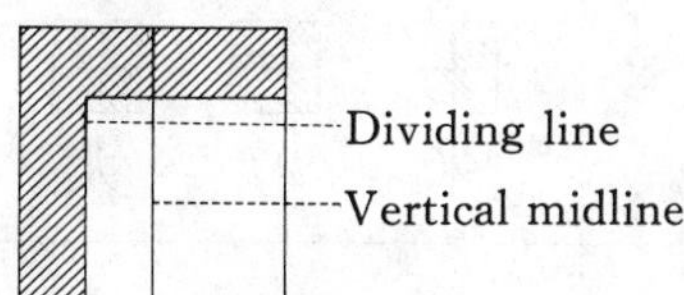

Horizontal Type

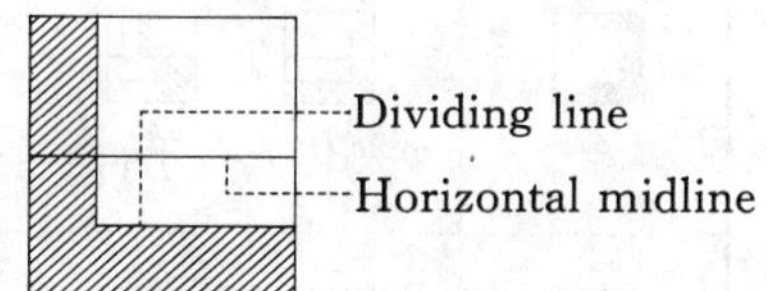

The patterns that are intuitively acceptable as enclosure patterns have the following characteristics. In horizontal type characters, the horizontal portion (or the end of the horizontal portion) of the dividing line must terminate *below* the horizontal midline; in vertical type characters, the vertical portion (or the end of the vertical portion) of the dividing line must terminate *to the left* (for ┏ characters) or *to the right* (for ┓ characters) of the vertical midline. If the vertical portion of the dividing line of a vertical type character, or the horizontal portion of the dividing line of a horizontal type character, *coincides* with its respective vertical or horizontal midline, that is, if it splits the character into two equal halves (as in 木 and 米), the character does not qualify as an enclosure element under that subpattern. Note in the chart below where the end of the dividing line is positioned in relation to the midline.

1. In the diagrams below, the slanted line patterns (▨) represent actual character parts, not abstract pattern symbols (┗).

Pattern Proportion in Two-Sided Enclosure Characters

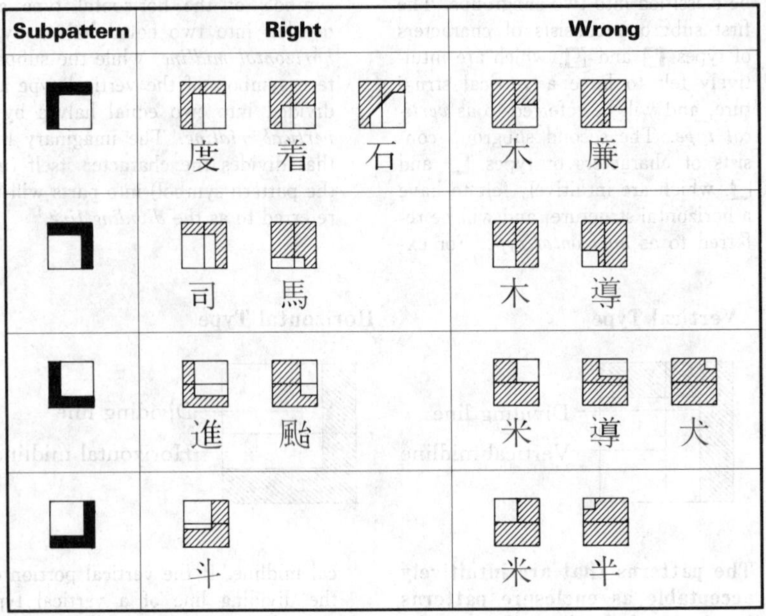

Subpattern	Right	Wrong
	度 着 石	木 廉
	司 馬	木 導
	進 颱	米 導 犬
	斗	米 半

2. **An enclosure element must not consist of independent elements arranged so that the character as a whole is divisible into left-right or up-down parts.** If an enclosure element consists of independent elements separated by a **space** (either clear or conceptual), arranged in a manner that allows the character to be divided vertically or horizontally, then that character is divided as a left-right or up-down character, not as an enclosure character. For example, 農 is classified under 2, although it includes the element 厂, which in other circumstances could be an enclosure element. However, note that the presence of a space within an element does not automatically disqualify it from being an enclosure element. For example, 門 and 風 contain a space, but they qualify as enclosure elements in the characters 間 and 颱.

The elements shown in red in the table below do not qualify as enclosure elements because they include a space at which the character can be split into up-down parts:

Enclosurelike Elements Not Qualifying as Enclosure Elements

Char.	Wrong	Right
雇	3-4-8	2-1-11
危	3-4-2	2-2-4
箇	3-14-4	2-6-12

1.8 Solid Subpatterns

The solid pattern is classified into four subpatterns on the basis of easy to identify lines located on the top, at the bottom, or in the middle of a character. **Solid subpattern** is defined as **one of the four groups into which the solid characters are subdivided according**

to the presence or absence of prominent lines. There are four solid subpatterns: **top line** (□1), **bottom line** (□2), **through line** (□3), and **others** (□4). Each subpattern is described in detail in the sections that follow.

Solid Subpatterns

No.	Subpattern Symbol	Subpattern Name	Right	Wrong
1	□	top line	下 耳 雨 子 久 凸 口 亜 爾	千 垂 丘
2	□	bottom line	七 上 亡 丘 由 自 血 垂 重	山 包 者
3	□	through line	中 十 手 本 米 車 求 乗 粛	寸 午 弟
4	□	others	人 九 女 火 犬 史 成 舟 為	久 友 劣

1.8.1 Top Line and Bottom Line

Top line is defined as **a horizontal, or almost horizontal, stroke or stroke segment**[2] **extending across the very top of a solid character.** It is identified by the subpattern symbol □1. Similarly, a **bottom line** is defined as **a horizontal, or almost horizontal, stroke or stroke segment extending across the very bottom of a solid character.** It is identified by the subpattern symbol □2. (Be sure not to confuse these subpattern symbols with ■2, the pattern symbol for up-down characters.) Since top and bottom lines have similar characteristics, they are treated here together.

Top and bottom lines must meet the following conditions:

1. **A top or bottom line must extend across the very top or the very bottom of the character.** That is, a top line must not have any strokes or elements protruding above it, and a bottom line must not have any lines protruding below it. Neither type of line must be intersected by any other strokes. For example, the horizontal stroke and stroke segment in 广 and 血 do not qualify as top lines since they have small attachments on top, while the horizontal strokes in 牛, 生, and 車 do not qualify as top or bottom lines since they are intersected by other strokes.

2. **A top or bottom line must be horizontal, or almost horizontal.** Thus the top or bottom strokes of such characters as 平, 久, and 也 qualify as top or bottom lines, but strongly inclined strokes, as in 垂 and 少, do not.

3. **A top or bottom line need not extend across the full width of the character.** Although a top or bottom line usually extends more or less across the full width of the character, as in 果, 飛, and 坐, this is not a necessary condition. Some top or bottom lines may be fairly short in relation to the character's width, as in 鼎, 子, 夊, and 七.

4. **A top or bottom line need not be an independent stroke.** A top or bottom line may be an independent stroke, as in 雨, 平, and 土, but it often forms part of a larger stroke or frame element, as in 疋, 里, 世, and 由. As long as the horizontal stroke

2. Be sure not to confuse the expression "horizontal stroke segment" and "horizontal stroke" with the technical term **horizontal line** used in reference to up-down characters.

or stroke segment is at the top or the bottom, it qualifies as a top or bottom line.

Remember that, according to the subclassification rules for solid characters, if a character contains any combination of top, bottom, and through lines, **the subpattern with the smallest number takes precedence.** For example, 工 is classified under ⊓1 (top line), although it includes a bottom line; 生 is classified under ⊔2 (bottom line), although it also includes a through line.

Top and bottom lines are very easy to identify. Just make sure that the character has a horizontal, or almost horizontal, stroke or stroke segment at the very top or the very bottom.

1.8.2 Through Line **Through line** is defined as **a perfectly vertical stroke or stroke segment intersecting another stroke of a solid character and extending over its entire, or almost its entire, length.** It is identified by the subpattern symbol ⎅3. (Be sure not to confuse this symbol with ◧1, the pattern symbol for left-right characters.) Through lines must meet the following conditions:

1. **A through line must be perfectly vertical.** Diagonal and sweeping strokes do not qualify. The vertical strokes in 中 and 本, for example, qualify as through lines, but those in 寿, 大, and 史 do not. Through lines may have little hooks (serifs) attached to the bottom, as in 才 and 求.

2. **A through line must intersect one or more strokes or elements.** The vertical stroke in 米, for instance, qualifies since it intersects the horizontal stroke, but the vertical stroke in 亻 does not since it does not intersect any other strokes. The angle of intersection is not important; it is nearly always a right angle, as in 中, but it may be slightly inclined.

   A through line must pass *through* the character, but not necessarily through its geometrical center. 井, 我, and 升, for example, include through lines that are off-center. However, a vertical stroke sitting on the *side* of a character does not qualify as a through line. The vertical strokes in 卜 and 内, for example, do not qualify.

3. **A through line must extend over the entire, or almost the entire, length of the character.** A through line normally passes right through the character and extends over its entire length, as in 東 and 車. In some characters, however, the vertical stroke may have a stroke or a relatively small element over it, as in 乘 and 身, or a stroke under it, as in 虫. Such vertical strokes also qualify as through lines since they extend over almost the entire length of the character.

4. **Solid characters may have more than one through line.** Almost all solid characters contain only one through line, as in 来 and 甫, but this is not a necessary condition. Some characters, like 升 and 井, may contain two (or even three) through lines. They are still classified under subpattern ⎅3.

Remember that if a character containing a through line also includes a top or bottom line, it is *not* classified under subpattern ⎅3 since **top and bottom lines take precedence over through lines.** For example, though 生 and 果 contain through lines, they are classified under subpatterns ⊔2 and ⊓1 respectively since they also contain bottom and top lines respectively.

You should have no trouble identifying

through lines since they are clearly visible elements that dominate the character's visual pattern.

1.8.3 Others The subpattern **others** includes **solid characters that cannot be classified under subpatterns □ 1, □ 2, or □ 3.** It is identified by the subpattern symbol □ 4. (Be sure not to confuse this symbol with ■, the pattern symbol for solid characters.) If a solid character does not include a top line, bottom line, or through line, then it is classified under subpattern □ 4. Many of these characters include sweeping vertical strokes that may appear to be through lines, as in 丸, 史, and 寿, but these do not qualify as such since they are not perfectly vertical.

Some characters may appear to belong to subpattern □ 4 at first sight, whereas in fact they should be classified under one of the divisible patterns (◧ 1, ⊟ 2, or ▣ 3). Some of these are cross-referenced at their incorrect locations. Study the table below.

Characters Mistakenly Classified Under Subpattern □ 4

Character	Wrong	Remarks	Right
奥	■4–12–4	Divide into up-down parts at first conceptual space.	⊟2–9–3
穴	■4–5–4	Divide into up-down parts at first horizontal line.	⊟2–3–2
武	■4–8–4	Divide at first enclosure element.	▣3–4–4
奉	■4–8–4	Divide into up-down parts at first conceptual space.	⊟2–5–3
島	■4–10–4	Divide at first enclosure element.	▣3–7–3
矢	■4–5–4	Divide into up-down parts at first horizontal line.	⊟2–2–3

Although the number of characters classified under subpattern □ 4 is not very large, it constitutes an important subgroup since it includes many common high-frequency characters, such as 人, 大, and 力.

2. HOW TO IDENTIFY THE PATTERN

2.1 Pattern Identification

To locate a character according to SKIP rules, the first task you face is to determine to which of the four patterns your character belongs. The **pattern number** will constitute the first part of the three-part **SKIP number** of your character. For example, 宙 is divisible into top and bottom parts, so it is classified under the up-down pattern ⊟ 2. Its SKIP number becomes ⊟ 2–3–5, where the first part stands for the pattern number, and the second and third parts stand for the stroke-counts of the top and bottom parts respectively (see **SYSTEM OF KANJI INDEXING BY PATTERNS §2.4 SKIP Number** for details).

To identify the pattern, just *look* at the character (or imagine it in your mind's eye) and decide to which pattern it belongs. Most of the time, your intuition will lead you to the correct classification at once. For example, 好, 充, and 尾 look like they belong to patterns ◧ 1, ⊟ 2, and ▣ 3 respectively, while 下

and 曲 look like they are indivisible and therefore belong to pattern ■4. If you have trouble classifying your character, a glance at the pattern chart inside the back covers should usually enable you to easily identify the pattern without referring to the detailed identification rules described herein.

In some unusual cases it may be possible to classify a character under more than one pattern. There is no priority of one pattern over another—the "**natural construction**" of the character is the determining factor. 児, for example, could conceivably be classified under ◧1 by dividing it into り and 已, but ⬒2 is the correct choice since it is in harmony with the natural construction of 児. This rule is described in detail in **§2.7 Pattern Priority.** Such characters, which are quite rare, are cross-referenced at all places where they might be mistakenly looked for.

A formal statement of the rules for identifying the pattern is given in **§2.2** below. Each rule is explained in greater detail in the sections that follow. Be sure to get a clear understanding of the various technical terms, which are defined in **SYSTEM OF KANJI INDEXING BY PATTERNS §7. Glossary.**

2.2 Pattern Identification Rules

❶ DETERMINE TO WHICH OF THE FOUR PATTERNS YOUR CHARACTER BELONGS	Right	Wrong
◧1 CHARACTERS THAT CAN BE DIVIDED INTO LEFT AND RIGHT PARTS		
(*a*) The resulting parts must be separated by a **space.**	相 4-5 八 1-1 順 1-11	片 1-3 用 1-4 隹 2-6
(*b*) The resulting division must be more or less vertical.	体 2-5 吹 3-4 扱 3-3	可 3-2 延 3-5 多 3-3
⬒2 CHARACTERS THAT CAN BE DIVIDED INTO TOP AND BOTTOM PARTS		
(*a*) The resulting parts must be separated by a **space, horizontal line,** or **frame element.**	二 1-1 寺 3-3 古 2-3	万 1-2 考 4-2
(*b*) The resulting division need not be horizontal.	会 2-4 字 3-3 春 5-4	間 8-4 坐 4-3 凶 2-2
◻3 CHARACTERS THAT CAN BE DIVIDED BY AN ENCLOSURE ELEMENT		
(*a*) The resulting parts may be separated by a **space** or be in full physical contact.	進 3-8 問 8-3 国 3-5	入 1-1 伺 3-4 呉 4-3

(*b*) The resulting division must be more or less rectangular.	可 2-3 広 3-2 凶 2-2	吹 4-3 名 3-3 為 5-4
■4 CHARACTERS THAT CANNOT BE CLASSIFIED UNDER **PATTERNS** ◧1, ⬒2, OR ◘3	雨 8-1 丘 5-2 中 4-3 与 3-4	刀 2-1 日 4-1 水 4-3
❷ IF A CHARACTER CAN BE CLASSIFIED UNDER MORE THAN ONE PATTERN, SELECT THE ONE THAT FOLLOWS THE NATURAL CONSTRUCTION OF THE CHARACTER	児 ⬒2-5-2 箱 ⬒2-6-9	児 ◧1-2-5 箱 ◧1-7-8
❸ DO NOT VIOLATE THE PRINCIPLE OF ELEMENT INTEGRITY 1. NEVER BREAK THROUGH STROKES 2. NEVER BREAK THROUGH **INDIVISIBLE UNITS** 3. NEVER MAKE **UNNATURAL DIVISIONS**	口 ■4-3-1 情 ◧1-3-8 箱 ⬒2-6-9	口 ⬒2-1-3 情 ◧1-1-10 箱 ◧1-7-8

2.3 Left-Right Pattern

Left-right pattern is defined as **a configuration of character elements placed side by side.** It is identified by the pattern symbol ◧1. The left-right pattern is very easy to identify. Left-right characters consists of two, sometimes three or more, parts arranged next to each other and separated by a **space.** Spaces are of two kinds: (1) **clear space** and (2) **conceptual space** (see **§1.1** for details).

The left-right pattern is basically of vertical construction. That is, the imaginary line that divides the character must be more or less vertical, as in 休, but it may bend slightly around protruding elements, as in 級. However, the imaginary dividing line must *not* form a right angle, as in 可. Characters of the latter type are classified under ◘3.

The formal rules for identifying the left-right pattern are given below:

CHARACTERS THAT CAN BE DIVIDED INTO LEFT AND RIGHT PARTS	Right	Wrong
(*a*) The resulting parts must be separated by a **space.**		
Characters that can be divided into left and right parts by a clear or conceptual space are classified under pattern ◧1. Characters in which the elements come in physical contact (**tangential contact**), as in 片, cannot be divided. In rare cases, a character that includes a space, as 病 and 鬪, cannot be divided into left and right parts because that would violate the principle of **element integrity.**	相 4-5 八 1-1 順 1-11 体 2-5 吹 3-4 伺 2-5	鬪 1-19 病 2-8 片 1-3 用 1-4 佳 2-6
(*b*) The resulting division must be more or less vertical.		

The imaginary line that divides the character may bend a little around elements, as in 吹, but must not form a right angle, as in 可, and must not be a diagonal, as in 多.	級 6-3 扱 3-3 雌 4-10	可 3-2 延 3-5 多 3-3

2.4 Up-Down Pattern

Up-down pattern is defined as **a configuration of character elements stacked more or less one on top of the other.** It is identified by the pattern symbol ▀ 2. The up-down pattern is not difficult to identify, but may pose some difficulties when deciding at which of several possible points the character should be divided. Up-down characters consist of two, three, or more parts stacked one over another. The parts may be separated from each other by three kinds of **division points**: a **space** (示 桑), a **horizontal line** (赤 義), or a **frame element** (古 早). Refer to **§1. Definitions of Pattern Terminology** for a detailed explanation of these terms.

Although the basic construction of up-down characters is more or less horizontal (二 真 吉), the imaginary line that divides the character may bend a little around protruding elements, as in 字, or may even bend sharply to form a triangular division, as in 合 and 春. Diagonal divisions, as in 多 and 省, are also permitted, though they are rather infrequent. However, the imaginary dividing line must *not* form a right angle, as in 間 and 進. Characters of the latter type are classified under ◘ 3.

The formal rules for identifying the up-down pattern are given below:

CHARACTERS THAT CAN BE DIVIDED INTO TOP AND BOTTOM PARTS	Right	Wrong
(*a*) The resulting parts must be separated by a **space, horizontal line,** or **frame element.**		
Characters that can be divided into top and bottom parts by a clear or conceptual space:	喜 3-9 会 2-4 示 1-4 合 2-4 桑 2-8 主 1-4	白 1-4 万 1-2 口 1-3 上 2-1
Characters that can be divided into top and bottom parts by a horizontal line:	寺 3-3 空 3-5 育 2-6	下 1-2 身 1-6
Characters that can be divided into top and bottom parts by a frame element:	古 2-3 早 4-2 南 2-7 支 2-2	自 1-5
Characters that contain a single horizontal stroke on top (as in 下) or characters that contain a frame element with one additional stroke on top (as in 白) do not qualify since division by horizontal line or by frame element requires each part to have at least two strokes (see **§3.5.4**).	下 ■4-3-1 白 ■4-5-2	下 ▀2-1-2 白 ▀2-1-4

	Right	Wrong
(*b*) The resulting division need not be horizontal.		
The imaginary line that divides the character may bend a little around elements, as in 宇, but must not form a right angle, as in 呉, or an inverted **U**, as in 問 and 早. Diagonal divisions, as in 多, and triangular divisions, as in 会, 春, and 券, are permitted.	安 3-3 軍 2-7 多 3-3 名 3-3 省 4-5 劣 4-2 公 2-2 个 2-1 会 2-4 父 2-2 春 5-4 券 6-2	間 8-4 早 3-3 直 7-1

2.5 Enclosure Pattern

Enclosure pattern is defined as **a configuration of character elements in which an exterior element encloses the rest of a character on two or more sides.** It is identified by the pattern symbol ◘ 3. An enclosure character must contain an **enclosure element** as its **shaded part**. An **enclosure element** is defined as **a completely exterior element that encloses the rest of the character on two or more sides.** It may be separated from the rest of the character by a **space**, as in 広 and 回, or the two parts may come in full physical contact, as in 氏 and 田. Refer to **§ 1.7 Enclosure Element** for a detailed description.

Although all four sides of the pattern symbol ◘ are shaded, the latter is actually an all-inclusive symbol that represents two-sided (度), three-sided (問), as well as four-sided (国) enclosure elements. The enclosure characters are further subdivided into **enclosure subpatterns** according to the number of sides and the position of the enclosure element along the exterior of the character (see **§ 1.7.1**).

The formal rules for identifying the enclosure pattern are given below:

CHARACTERS THAT CAN BE DIVIDED BY AN ENCLOSURE ELEMENT	**Right**	**Wrong**
(*a*) The resulting parts may be separated by a **space** or be in full physical contact.		
An enclosure element must enclose the rest of the character. It is not important if the enclosure element is separated from or is in physical contact with the rest of the character.	迎 3-4 馬 6-4 向 3-3 四 3-2	入 1-1 伺 3-4 飛 3-6
Characters that can be divided by a clear or conceptual space:	広 3-2 載 6-7 岡 2-6 団 3-3	商 6-5 角 4-3 衣 3-3
Characters in which the enclosure element is in full physical contact with the rest of the character:	止 2-2 臣 3-4 用 2-3 田 3-2	

(*b*) The resulting division must be more or less rectangular. The sides of the imaginary line that divides the character must be more or less at right angles to each other. This line may bend a little around elements, as in 者, but must not form a vertical, horizontal, or diagonal, which would make the character a left-right or up-down character.	可 2-3 広 3-2 凶 2-2 国 3-5	吹 4-3 名 3-3 為 5-4

2.6 Solid Pattern

Solid pattern is defined as **a character element or combination of elements that does not constitute a left-right, up-down, or enclosure pattern.** It is identified by the pattern symbol ■4. The **indivisible** or **solid characters** are defined as **characters that cannot be divided according to SKIP rules; i.e., characters that are classified under pattern ■4.** If a character can be divided, then it is not solid. Therefore, to identify the solid pattern, you must understand the rules of pattern division described in **§3.3 Pattern Division Rules.** The indivisible characters are subclassified according to a principle described in **§4.1 Subclassification of Solid Pattern.** Although the absolute number of solid characters is not very large, they constitute an important group since they include some of the most frequently-used characters.

Most solid characters cannot be physically divided without actually breaking through strokes or **indivisible units** (**§3.8**), which is why they are referred to as solid or indivisible. Since the **element integrity** principle does not allow breaking through strokes or indivisible units, it follows that a character like 口 cannot be divided. Dividing 口 into up and down parts (凵 and 一) involves breaking through the stroke ㇕, whereas dividing it into left and right parts (丨 and ⺆) involves breaking up the indivisible unit 口. 口 is thus an indivisible character.

Some solid characters could conceivably be divided, but such a division would violate the rules of pattern division. For example, 飛 cannot be divided as an up-down character into ⺄ and 飛 since the imaginary line that divides it forms a right angle; on the other hand, ⺄ cannot be considered an enclosure element since it does not properly enclose the rest of the character. Thus, since 飛 cannot be divided in conformity with the pattern division rules, it is classified as a solid character under pattern ■4.

Another good example is 亡. It would seem as if 亡 could be divided into 亠 and 𠃊 and thus be classified under ▀2-2-1. However, this would violate the **two-stroke rule** (**§3.5.4**), which states that when dividing by horizontal line or by frame element each part must have at least two strokes. 亡 is thus indivisible and is classified under ■4.

The formal rule for identifying the solid pattern is given below:

CHARACTERS THAT CANNOT BE CLASSIFIED UNDER PATTERNS ◧1, ⬒2, OR ◘3	Right	Wrong
The solid characters cannot be divided according to the rules for classifying characters under patterns ◧1, ⬒2, or ◘3. If a character cannot be divided without violating a SKIP rule (such as by breaking through strokes or making **unnatural divisions**), then it is a solid character.	雨 8-1 下 3-1 耳 6-1	刀 2-1 十 2-1 垂 8-1 丘 5-1
	上 3-2 丘 5-2 垂 8-2	山 3-2 包 5-2 者 8-2
	中 4-3 東 8-3 毛 4-3	水 4-3 寸 3-3 午 4-3 弟 7-3
	与 3-4 大 3-4 寿 7-4	糸 6-4 久 3-4 友 4-4 劣 6-4

2.7 Pattern Priority

In the great majority of cases it is obvious at first glance under which of the four patterns a character is to be classified. On rare occasions, it may be possible to classify a character under more than one pattern. For example, in some typefaces all the elements of 児 are separated by a space so that it is possible to classify it under ◧1 by dividing it into 丿 and 旧儿, or under ⬒2 by dividing it into 旧 and 儿.

In such cases, the **pattern priority rule** calls for dividing the character according to its **natural construction.** This term cannot be precisely defined. Basically, it refers to **an arrangement of character elements that is in harmony with the way a character is intuitively perceived as a combination of certain constituent parts.** It almost always coincides with the division of a character into etymologically meaningful parts such as radicals, but does not depend on etymological integrity. For example, 箱, which consists of four units, could be divided horizontally into ⺮ and 相, or vertically into ⺮木 and ⺮目. The natural construction of 箱, which coincides with its etymological integrity, calls for classifying it as an up-down character under ⬒2-6-9.

Dividing a character according to its natural construction is, in effect, the opposite of making **unnatural divisions,** described in **§3.8 Element Integrity.** The important point about the pattern priority rule is that no pattern has priority over any other—only the natural construction of the character, which in practice but not in theory is related to character etymology, is the determining factor.

You need not overly concern yourself with pattern priority. Only a complete beginner totally unfamiliar with kanji elements is ever likely to divide a character in a manner that conflicts with its natural construction.

A formal statement of the pattern priority rule is given below:

IF A CHARACTER CAN BE CLASSIFIED UNDER MORE THAN ONE PATTERN, SELECT THE ONE THAT FOLLOWS THE NATURAL CONSTRUCTION OF THE CHARACTER	Right	Wrong
The natural construction of a character is related to, but not dependent on, its etymological integrity; i.e., it nearly always coincides with the division of the character into etymologically meaningful parts.	児 ⬒2-5-2	児 ◧1-2-5
	漢 ◧1-3-10	漢 ⬒2-4-9
	箱 ⬒2-6-9	箱 ◧1-7-8
	闘 ◘3-10-10	闘 ◧1-1-19
	送 ◘3-3-6	送 ⬒2-3-6
	導 ⬒2-12-3	導 ◘3-6-9

3. HOW TO DIVIDE THE CHARACTER

3.1 Character Division

Once you have determined to which of the four patterns your character belongs, you must divide it or subclassify it in order to determine the second and third parts of the **SKIP number.** Characters that can be divided into two or more parts are classified under the first three patterns. The **divisible characters** are defined as **characters that can be divided according to SKIP rules; i.e., characters classified under patterns ◧1, ⬒2, and ◘3.** This section explains in detail how to divide the divisible characters. Characters that cannot be classified under the above patterns are classified under pattern ■4. These **indivisible characters** are subclassified according to a different principle described in **§ 4.1 Subclassification of Solid Pattern.**

The imaginary line that divides the character splits it into a pattern whose shape roughly resembles the pattern symbol. The divisible characters are divided into two parts: the **shaded part** and the **blank part.** The second part of the SKIP number indicates the stroke-count of the former, whereas the third part indicates that of the latter. For example, 相 is divided into 木 (4 strokes) and 目 (5 strokes), giving a SKIP number of ◧1-4-5. See SYSTEM OF KANJI INDEXING BY PATTERNS **§ 2.4 SKIP Number** for details.

In the great majority of cases, you should have no problem in identifying the pattern and, at the same time, deciding at which point to divide the character. Sometimes, however, you may identify a character as belonging to a particular pattern but not be sure at which point the division should be made. That is, some characters, like 川, 三, and 磨, may contain several points at which a division could conceivably be made.

To divide such characters correctly and without hesitation, it is important that you get a clear understanding of **division points.** A brief description of these is given in **§ 3.2** below, while a more thorough treatment can be found in **§ 1. Definitions of Pattern Terminology.** The most important thing to remember is: **if there is more than one way to divide a character, divide at the first division point.**

When dividing a character, be sure not to violate the principle of **element integrity.** This rule prohibits breaking through strokes or **indivisible units.** For example, you must not divide characters like 口 into 丨 and コ, or characters like 情 into ' and 情. It also prohibits making **unnatural divisions.** For example, 鬪 should be classified under ◘3, and not be divided into left and right parts, i.e., 丨 and 鬪. See **§ 3.8 Element Integrity** for details.

A formal statement of the rules for dividing the divisible characters, i.e., the characters classified under patterns ◧1, ⬒2, and ◘3, is given in **§ 3.3** below. Each rule is explained in greater detail in the sections that follow.

3.2 Division Points

The first rule for dividing the character is: DIVIDE THE CHARACTER INTO TWO PARTS AT THE FIRST **DIVISION POINT**. That is, if there are several ways in which a character can be divided, always divide at the *first* place possible. **Division point** is defined as a **space, horizontal line, frame element, or enclosure element at which it may be possible to divide a character.** A division point is not necessarily the point at which a character is actually divided according to SKIP rules. Whether a character can or cannot be divided at a given point depends on its structure and the particular SKIP rule applying to it. Each division point is defined below, followed by a reference to the section where it is described in detail.

	Examples
1. **Space** ⇨ § 1.1 Space **A gap or breaking point between elements.** Division by space applies to patterns ◧ 1, ⬒ 2, and ▣ 3.	川 1-2 州 2-4 傾 2-11 三 1-2 言 1-6 公 2-2 街 3-9 町 5-2 翻 12-6 桑 2-8 系 1-6 雀 4-7
2. **Horizontal Line** ⇨ § 1.3 Horizontal Line **A horizontal, or almost horizontal, stroke not intersected by any other strokes.** Division by horizontal line applies only to pattern ⬒ 2.	寺 3-3 空 3-5 文 2-2 亭 2-7 学 5-3 義 3-10
3. **Frame Element** ⇨ § 1.6 Frame Element **A combination of strokes or stroke segments forming a figure enclosed on two, three, or four sides.** Division by frame element applies only to pattern ⬒ 2.	古 2-3 免 2-6 早 4-2 当 3-3 南 2-7 支 2-2
4. **Enclosure Element** ⇨ § 1.7 Enclosure Element **A completely exterior element that encloses the rest of a character on two or more sides.** Division by enclosure element applies only to pattern ▣ 3.	進 3-8 旬 2-4 麻 3-8 間 8-4 医 2-5 回 3-3

3.3 Character Division Rules

MAIN RULES	Right	Wrong
❶ DIVIDE THE CHARACTER INTO TWO PARTS AT THE FIRST DIVISION POINT		
◧ GOING FROM LEFT TO RIGHT, DIVIDE AT THE FIRST **SPACE** Divide at the first **clear or conceptual space.**	明 4-4 小 1-2 扱 3-3	小 2-1 街 9-3
⬒ GOING FROM TOP TO BOTTOM, DIVIDE AT THE FIRST **SPACE, HORIZONTAL LINE,** OR **FRAME ELEMENT,** WHICHEVER COMES FIRST (*a*) Divide at the first **clear or conceptual space.**	三 1-2 会 2-4 脅 2-8	三 2-1 会 3-3 脅 6-4

(*b*) Divide after the first **horizontal line.** The horizontal line, along with its side, top, and end **attachments,** goes to the top.	赤 3-4 空 3-5 業 5-8 年 2-4	赤 2-5 空 5-3 業 8-5
(*c*) Divide at the first point where the first **frame element** is encountered.	古 2-3 当 3-3 南 2-7 早 4-2	呂 4-3 免 6-2
(*d*) When dividing by **horizontal line** or by **frame element,** each part must have at least two strokes.	京 2-6 方 2-2 午 2-2 予 2-2	下 1-2 亡 2-1 了 1-1 白 1-4
□ GOING FROM THE OUTSIDE TOWARD THE INSIDE, DIVIDE AFTER THE FIRST **ENCLOSURE ELEMENT** Separate the first **enclosure element** from the rest of the character, whether it is separated from it by a **clear** or **conceptual space,** or is in full physical contact with it.	度 3-6 進 3-8 閉 8-3 目 3-2	度 7-2 磨 11-5
❷ **DO NOT VIOLATE THE PRINCIPLE OF ELEMENT INTEGRITY** 1. NEVER BREAK THROUGH STROKES 2. NEVER BREAK THROUGH **INDIVISIBLE UNITS** 3. NEVER MAKE **UNNATURAL DIVISIONS**	凶 □3-2-2 情 ◧1-3-8 気 □3-4-2 漢 ◧1-3-10	凶 ◧1-1-4 情 ◧1-1-10 気 ⬒2-2-4 漢 ⬒2-4-9
COROLLARIES ❶ EACH PART MUST HAVE AT LEAST ONE STROKE ❷ THE **SHADED PART** MUST NOT BE FURTHER DIVISIBLE UNDER THE SAME **PATTERN**	門 ◧1-4-4 口 ■4-3-1 測 ◧1-3-9 順 ◧1-1-11	門 □3-8-0 口 □3-3-0 測 ◧1-10-2 順 ◧1-3-9

3.4 Left–Right Characters

Left–right characters are easy to divide. Your intuition will be your best guide most of the time. The rules below will always lead to the correct division. The important thing to remember is that you **divide at the first division point without breaking through strokes or indivisible units.** For example, 小 should be split at the first space into 丶 and 卜, but 灯 should not be split into 丶 and 灯 since 丶 is an integral part of the indivisible unit 火 (see **§ 3.8 Element Integrity**).

The formal rule for dividing the left–right pattern is given below:

GOING FROM LEFT TO RIGHT, DIVIDE AT THE FIRST SPACE	Right	Wrong
Divide at the first **clear** or **conceptual space.**		
Divide at the first clear space, as in 川 or 小, or conceptual space (the theoretical space between **independent elements**), as in 級 or 歓. Be sure to divide at the *first* space you encounter, even if the left part forms part of a larger element, as 川 in 順.	相 4-5 八 1-1 扱 3-3 川 1-2 修 2-8 順 1-11 雌 4-10	川 2-1 徹 11-4 潮 11-4 候 3-7 順 3-9 傾 4-9
Do not violate the principle of **element integrity.** Specifically, do not separate short one-stroke elements if they form an integral part of an **indivisible unit.**	情 3-8 灯 4-2 州 2-4	情 1-10 灯 1-5 州 1-5

3.5 Up-Down Characters

Although the up-down pattern is not too difficult to identify, it may pose some difficulties when deciding at which of several possible points the character should be divided. The manner in which up-down characters are psychologically perceived in terms of their parts is more complex than in the case of left-right characters. Although there is almost universal agreement on the division point for left-right characters, opinion on how to divide up-down characters may vary with the individual.

Up-down characters consist of two, three, or more parts stacked more or less one on top of the other. The parts may be separated from each other by a **space** (示 桑), a **horizontal line,** (赤 義) or a **frame element** (古 早). Refer to **§1. Definitions of Pattern Terminology** for a detailed explanation of these terms.

The character division rule calls for dividing at the *first* division point, whether this is a space, a horizontal line, or a frame element. In the majority of cases, dividing at the first point possible is in harmony with the way most people would intuitively divide up-down characters anyway. At any rate, following the rule faithfully will always lead to the correct division, although it may on occasion go against your intuition.

For example, to most people 忘 and 真 probably look like they should be divided at the space, but the rule calls for dividing at 亠 and 十 since we encounter a horizontal line and frame element respectively *before* we encounter the space further down. As long as you remember to follow this rule, such characters should not cause a problem. In any case, they are small in number and are cross-referenced at their incorrect locations.

Our research has shown that when a character that does not contain a space is divided into up and down parts, it is psychologically unpleasing for either of the parts to have only one stroke. Although it is possible to divide a character like 上 into ⊦ and 一, or 白 into ′ and 日, most people reject this as "not looking right." On the other hand, one-stroke parts separated by a clear or conceptual space, as in 言 and 主, are intuitively acceptable. For this reason, we have introduced the **two stroke rule,** which states that when dividing by horizontal line or by frame element, each part must have at least two strokes

(§ **3.5.4**). Since 上 and 白 cannot be divided into up and down parts without violating this rule, they are classified as indivisible characters under pattern ■4.

Although the up-down pattern is somewhat more difficult to divide than the other patterns, an understanding of the rules and a little practice will lead to satisfactory results. The formal rules for dividing the up-down pattern are given below:

GOING FROM TOP TO BOTTOM, DIVIDE AT THE FIRST SPACE, HORIZONTAL LINE, OR FRAME ELEMENT, WHICHEVER COMES FIRST	**Right**	**Wrong**
Divide at the first division point, whether it is a space, a horizontal line, or a frame element. For example, going from top to bottom, if you encounter a horizontal line, as in 忘, split into 亠 and 乚心, since the horizontal line *precedes* the space further down. Make the division even if the top element forms part of a larger element. For example, it might seem natural to divide 章 into 立 and 早, but since we must divide at the *first* division point (least number of strokes), the correct division is at the first horizontal line, i.e., into 亠 and 草.	喜 3-9 会 2-4 雇 1-11 真 2-8 忘 2-5 黄 4-7 景 4-8 夢 3-10 脅 2-8 柔 2-7 京 2-6 章 2-9 音 2-7 害 3-7	喜 9-3 会 3-3 真 7-3 忘 3-4 黄 9-2 景 6-6 夢 8-5 脅 6-4 柔 5-4 京 5-3 章 5-6 音 5-4 害 7-3
Be sure not to violate the principle of **element integrity**. For example, 受 is *not* divided into 丿 and 受, since ⺤ is an **indivisible unit.**	昌 4-4 受 4-4	昌 1-8 受 1-7 口 1-3

3.5.1 Division by Space

Divide at the first **clear** or **conceptual space.**	**Right**	**Wrong**
Divide at the first clear space or conceptual space (the theoretical space between **independent elements**). If there is more than one space, as in 三 or 喜, always divide at the *first* space.	示 1-4 公 2-2 三 1-2 谷 2-5	三 2-1 谷 4-3
Be sure not to confuse conceptual space with **tangential contact** (§ **1.2**). Strokes in tangential contact, as in 土, must *not* be separated from each other. However, elements separated by flips or hooks (serifs), as in 予, *are* separated by a conceptual space and thus may be divided.	合 2-4 桑 2-8 主 1-4 系 1-6 光 4-2 予 2-2	合 3-3 桑 6-4 主 2-3 系 4-3 光 3-3 予 3-1

3.5.2 Division by Horizontal Line

Divide after the first **horizontal line.** The horizontal line, along with its side, top, and end **attachments,** goes to the top.	Right	Wrong
All attachments, **except for elements attached to the bottom,** go to the top part along with the horizontal line itself. For example, 挙 is divided into 龸 and [illegible]. The element 龸 includes the horizontal line and its top attachments, so it goes the top. Since 八 is attached to the bottom of the horizontal line, it goes to the bottom.	寺 3-3 吉 3-3 学 5-3 索 4-6 年 2-4 美 3-6 義 3-10 光 4-2	寺 2-4 吉 2-4 学 3-5 索 2-8 美 6-3 義 6-7 光 3-3
Another example: 空 is divided into 宀 and [illegible]. Going from top to bottom, the first division point we encounter in 空 is the horizontal line shown in red. It goes to the top along with its top and end attachments, but 儿 stays in the bottom part.	空 3-5 育 2-6	空 5-3 育 4-4
In rare cases, a horizontal line may form part of a frame element immediately below it, as the frame elements shown in red in 歯 and 赤. Since the horizontal lines in 歯 and 赤 *precede* the frame elements, that is, since as we go from top to bottom the *first* division point we encounter is a horizontal line, we divide these characters by horizontal line, *not* by frame element. See **§ 1.6 Frame Element** for details.	歯 4-8 赤 3-4	歯 3-9 赤 2-5

3.5.3 Division by Frame Element

Divide at the first point where the first **frame element** is encountered.	Right	Wrong
For example, going from top to bottom in 免, the first point where a frame element is encountered is the point where ⺈ comes in contact with the frame element 口. 免 is thus divided into ⺈ and 兄. Frame elements on top (as in 早) go to the top, whereas frame elements in the middle (as in 免) or bottom (as in 古) go to the bottom. Anyway, **never separate the sides of frame elements in two-branch tangential contact** (**§ 1.2**).	呂 3-4 免 2-6 古 2-3 頁 2-7 南 2-7 支 2-2 早 4-2 界 5-4	呂 4-3 免 6-2 頁 7-2 早 3-3

When a frame element is separated from the rest of the character, it will include any elements inside it (as in 早) or attached to its sides (as in 楽). Frame elements are normally found in the bottom or middle part of a character. When a frame element goes to the bottom, it will of course take along with it all strokes below it, as in 点 and 頁. However, note that because of the **two stroke rule** (see next section), only a one-stroke attachment on top of a frame element, as in 卑, goes to the top along with a top frame element. If there is a two-stroke attachment on top, as in 免, the attachment is separated from the frame element and the frame element goes to the bottom, e.g., 免 is divided into ⺈ and 兄. All this should, on the whole, be quite self-evident.

Although most frame elements consist of a clean frame whose sides are in two-branch tangential contact, some frame elements, as in 単 and 弟, contain internal strokes that protrude beyond the frame or even cut right through it, as in 貫. In rare cases, the sides of a frame element may intersect, as in 𠀋. All these details should be ignored. These elements still qualify as frame elements and the character is divided into up and down parts at the first point where the frame element is encountered. (See also footnote 3 in **§ 3.8 Element Integrity.**)

Frame elements are usually four-sided, but they sometimes may consist of three or even two sides. For example, going from top to the bottom in 弟 we encounter the frame element ⺕. Since we divide at the first point where the frame element is encountered, 弟 is divided into ⺍ and 弔.

3.5.4 Two Stroke Rule

When dividing by **horizontal line** or by **frame element**, each part must have at least two strokes.	Right	Wrong
For example, though 下, 土, and 予 contain horizontal lines, they *cannot* be split at the horizontal line, since a part with only one stroke would remain. Likewise, though 白 contains the frame element 口, it cannot be split into ′ and 日 since only one stroke would remain.	京 2-6 方 2-2 年 2-4 予 2-2	下 1-2 土 2-1 予 3-1 亡 2-1
	白 ■4-5-2	白 ■2-1-4
The two stroke rule applies only to division by horizontal line or by frame element. It does *not* apply to division by clear or conceptual space; i.e., 三, 主, and 扉 *are* divided at the first stroke because they are followed by a space.	三 1-2 主 1-4 扉 1-11	三 2-1 主 2-3

3.6 Enclosure Characters

Once you have identified an enclosure pattern, dividing the character should not pose any difficulties. Simply separate the first **enclosure element** from the rest of the character; e.g., 度 (2-sided enclosure), 間 (3-sided enclosure), and 囲 (four-sided enclosure). Refer to **§ 1.7 Enclosure Element** and **§ 2.5 Enclosure Pattern** for a detailed explanation of terms related to enclosure characters.

In rare cases, a character may be divided under the same **enclosure subpattern** in more than one way. For example, 摩 forms a □ type enclosure pattern in two ways, 摩 and 摩. Since the rule calls for dividing at the *first* enclosure element, the former is correct. Since each part of the divided character must have at least one stroke, you should not be tempted to make divisions like 門 □ 3-8-0 or 口 □ 3-3-0. These characters are correctly classified under ◧ 1-4-4 and ■ 4-3-1 respectively.

The formal rule for identifying the enclosure pattern is given below:

GOING FROM THE OUTSIDE TOWARD THE INSIDE, DIVIDE AFTER THE FIRST ENCLOSURE ELEMENT	**Right**	**Wrong**
Separate the first **enclosure element** from the rest of the character, whether it is separated from it by a **clear or conceptual space,** or is in full physical contact with it.		
The enclosure element constitutes the shaded part. It may be separated from the rest of the character by a clear or conceptual space, as in 広 and 旬, or the two parts may be in full physical contact, as in 展 and 田. Ignore these contacts and divide immediately after the *first* enclosure element. Make the division at the first enclosure element even if it forms part of a larger enclosure element. For example, 磨 is divided into 广 and 替, even though it could conceivably be divided into 麻 and 石.	広 3-2 可 2-3 展 3-7 向 3-3 間 8-4 回 3-3 田 3-2 目 3-2 磨 3-13 度 3-6	門 8-0 商 6-5 面 5-4 申 3-2 口 3-0 磨 11-5 度 7-2
Be sure not to separate single strokes in tangential contact at an internal corner of an enclosure element, such as ㇏ in 尺. Such characters are classified under ■ 4. However, 局 and 昼 *are* divided by enclosure element since ㇆ and ㇏ do not contact 尸 at a corner.	尺 ■4-4-1 大 ■4-3-4 牙 ■4-5-1	尺 □3-3-1 大 □3-2-1 牙 □3-4-1

3.7 Corollaries to Division Rules

1. **EACH PART MUST HAVE AT LEAST ONE STROKE**

The first part of the character division rule states: DIVIDE THE CHARACTER INTO TWO PARTS. This implies that each part must have at least one stroke. It is self-evident that you cannot "divide" a character like 目 into left and right parts with the right part consisting of "zero" strokes, i.e., you cannot classify it under ◧ 1-5-0. Nevertheless, some people may be tempted to classify characters like 厂, 門, and 口 under ▣ 3, since they look like enclosure elements. To do so, however, would result in a blank part of zero strokes. Since EACH PART MUST HAVE AT LEAST ONE STROKE, such divisions are not allowed.

Right	Wrong
目 ▣3-3-2	目 ◧1-5-0
土 ■4-3-2	土 ⬒2-3-0
厂 ■4-2-1	厂 ▣3-2-0
辶 ⬒2-1-2	辶 ▣3-3-0
冂 ■4-2-1	冂 ▣3-2-0
門 ◧1-4-4	門 ▣3-8-0
口 ■4-3-1	口 ▣3-3-0

2. **THE SHADED PART MUST NOT BE FURTHER DIVISIBLE UNDER THE SAME PATTERN**

The second part of the character division rule states: AT THE FIRST **DIVISION POINT.** Dividing at the *first* division point implies that the shaded part cannot be further subdivided under the same pattern. In other words, as soon as you encounter a division point, you must divide at that point unless doing so violates a SKIP rule (such as the element integrity principle or the two stroke rule).

Say, for example, that you classified 測 under ◧ 1 and tentatively divided it into 浿 and 刂. Since 浿, the shaded part, can be further subdivided as a left-right pattern into 氵 and 貝, this division is not permissible. Dividing at the *first* division point (least number of strokes), in this case a space, means that 測 must be split into 氵 and 則.

Right			Wrong		
測 3-9	街 3-9	三 1-2	測 10-2	街 9-3	三 2-1
川 1-2	夢 3-10	業 5-8	川 2-1	夢 8-5	業 8-5

<table>
<tr>
<td>Make the division even if the shaded part forms part of a larger element. For example, it is tempting to divide 順 into 川 and 頁, or 真 into 直 and 六, but dividing at the first division point means that you split 順 at the first space into 丿 and 順, and 真 at the first frame element into 十 and 具. However, you should not make the division if it involves breaking through strokes or indivisible units.

Many of these "tempting" divisions are cross-referenced at their incorrect locations, but it is advisable to study the examples to get a proper understanding of division at the first division point.</td>
<td>雌 4-10 修 2-8 真 2-8 呂 3-4

音 2-7 点 2-7 度 3-6 磨 3-13</td>
<td>雌 6-8 修 3-7 真 7-3 呂 4-3

音 5-4 点 5-4 度 7-2 磨 11-5</td>
</tr>
</table>

3.8 Element Integrity

The rules for dividing characters by patterns are in harmony with what most people feel to be intuitively correct. Most people need not be told that to divide 漢 into 艹 and 湨 or 口 into 丨 and コ is incorrect. Just to be on the safe side, we introduce here the principle of **element integrity**, which is a formal statement of what common sense dictates. Before reading on, make sure that you understand the term **tangential contact** explained in **§ 1.2.**

The second rule for dividing the character is: DO NOT VIOLATE THE PRINCIPLE OF ELEMENT INTEGRITY. **Element Integrity** is defined as **a principle that consists of three parts: (1) Never break through strokes, (2) Never break through indivisible units, and (3) Never make unnatural divisions.** The principle of element integrity thus prohibits three kinds of division: division of strokes, division of indivisible units, and unnatural division. These terms are described in detail below.

1. **Stroke** is defined as **a character element such as a dot or line segment traditionally written with one sweep of the brush or pen.** Strokes may be straight (一丨), diagonal (丿丶) or bent (乛乚㇉). See **Appendix 2. How To Count Strokes** and **Appendix 3. How To Write Kanji** to get a better understanding of what a stroke is.

2. **Indivisible unit** is defined as **a combination of strokes regarded as an indivisible whole.** Indivisible units are of the following kinds:

   (*a*) A combination of strokes *intersecting* each other:

   十 中 艹 又 メ

   (*b*) A combination of strokes in **two-branch tangential contact**:

   口 弓 亡 冖 广 冂

   (*c*) A single stroke in tangential contact with an internal corner of an **enclosure element**:

   大 尺 牙 无

   (*d*) A few arbitrary elements, listed

below, which are considered indivisible units on intuitive/etymological grounds:

Indivisible Units

Pattern	Element	Right		Wrong	
1	忄	情	忙	情	忙
	火	灯	熔	灯	熔
	刂	帰	州	帰	州
2	⺤	受	愛	受	愛
3	气	気	氣	気	氣

Since the above elements contain a space within them, one might be tempted to divide the character as shown in the **Wrong** column. However, since these elements form an integrated whole, both intuitively and etymologically, they are considered indivisible units when they constitute a component part of a character. However, as independent characters in their own right they are classified according to normal SKIP rules, i.e.:

忄 1-1-2
刂 1-1-1
⺤ 2-1-3
气 2-2-2

3. **Unnatural division** basically refers to **division of a character in a manner that is in conflict with the way it is intuitively perceived as a combination of certain constituent parts.** Another way of putting it is that the division yields elements that are in conflict with the **natural construction** of the character. Making an unnatural division is, in effect, the opposite of dividing a character according to its natural construction (see **§2.7**).

All this may sound much more difficult than it actually is. The fact is that very few people would ever think of dividing a character in a manner referred to here as "unnatural," with the possible exception of the complete beginner totally unfamiliar with kanji elements. Since the likelihood of making such divisions is small, unnatural divisions are not usually cross-referenced. Study the examples below:

Unnatural Divisions

Right	Wrong
漢 1-3-10	漢 2-4-9
箱 2-6-9	箱 1-7-8
闘 3-10-10	闘 1-1-19
送 3-3-6	送 2-3-6
導 2-12-3	導 3-6-9

A formal statement of the element integrity rule is given below:

DO NOT VIOLATE THE PRINCIPLE OF ELEMENT INTEGRITY	Right	Wrong
1. NEVER BREAK THROUGH STROKES For example, 口 consists of the strokes 丨 (left), ㇕ (corner), and 一 (bottom). It should not be split as an up-down character into 一 and 凵, since doing so breaks through the stroke ㇕.	口 4-3-1 昌 2-4-4 古 2-2-3	口 2-1-3 昌 2-1-7 古 2-3-3

2. **NEVER BREAK THROUGH INDIVISIBLE UNITS**		
Do not split short one-stroke elements if they form an integral part of an indivisible unit. Specifically, characters containing the indivisible units 忄, 火, 刂, and ⺤ should *not* be split at the first stroke.	情 ◧1-3-8 灯 ◧1-4-2 帰 ◧1-2-8 受 ⬒2-4-4 気 □3-4-2	情 ◧1-1-10 灯 ◧1-1-5 帰 ◧1-1-9 受 ⬒2-1-7 気 ⬒2-2-4
Since strokes or elements in **two-branch tangential contact** are indivisible units, it follows that **end attachments,** such as in 冖 and 山, can never be separated from the element to which they are attached. It also follows that since the sides of nearly all **frame elements** abut, that is, are in two-branch tangential contact, they cannot be separated from each other.[3] For example, elements such as 口 in 古 and 冂 in 南 should never be broken up.	冖 ■4-2-1 山 □3-2-1 南 ⬒2-2-7	冖 ◧1-1-1 山 ◧1-1-3 南 ⬒2-3-7
Since a single stroke in tangential contact at an internal corner of an **enclosure element** is part of an indivisible unit, ㇏ in such characters as 尺 and 大 cannot be separated.	尺 ■4-4-1 大 ■4-3-4 牙 ■4-5-1	尺 □3-3-1 大 □3-2-1 牙 □3-4-1
3. **NEVER MAKE UNNATURAL DIVISIONS**		
For example, although there is a slight gap after the leftmost vertical in 鬪, this character should not be classified as a left-right character consisting of 丨 and 鬥, since 丨 forms an integral part of the enclosure element 鬥. 鬪 is correctly classified under □ 3-10-10.	児 ⬒2-5-2 箱 ⬒2-6-9 鬪 □3-10-10	児 ◧1-2-5 箱 ◧1-7-8 鬪 ◧1-1-19

4. HOW TO SUBCLASSIFY THE SOLID PATTERN

4.1 Subclassification of Solid Pattern

Characters that cannot be divided according to SKIP rules are referred to as **indivisible** or **solid characters** and are classified under pattern ■4. The second and third parts of the **SKIP number** of the divisible characters, i.e., the characters classified under patterns ◧1, ⬒2, or □3, are determined by dividing the character into two parts and counting the strokes of each part. Since the solid characters are, by definition, indivisible, a different principle is required for subclassifying them.

The indivisible characters are arranged in ascending order of their total stroke-counts and are subclassified into four **solid subpatterns** (see §**4.2** below). The second part of the SKIP number indicates

3. However, note that in some up-down characters, such as 歯 and 赤, neither end of the horizontal stroke on top of the frame element is in two-branch tangential contact. If such a stroke qualifies as a **horizontal line,** as it does in 歯 and 赤, the chracters are divided by horizontal line, i.e., 歯 and 赤, even though this involves breaking up the frame elements 口 and 亦.

the total stroke-count of the character, whereas the third part indicates one of the four solid subpatterns. 下, for example, is a three-stroke character containing a **top line** (subpattern □ 1), giving a SKIP number of ■ 4-3-1. See SYSTEM OF KANJI INDEXING BY PATTERNS § 2.4 **SKIP Number** for details.

4.2 Solid Subpatterns

The solid pattern is classified into four **solid subpatterns** on the basis of easy to identify lines located on the top, at the bottom, or in the middle of a character. **Solid subpattern** is defined as **one of the four groups into which the solid characters are subdivided according to the presence or absence of prominent lines.** There are four solid subpatterns: **top line** (□ 1), **bottom line** (□ 2), **through line** (□ 3), and **others** (□ 4). The **solid subpattern symbol** is **a symbol that identifies one of the four solid subpatterns.** The **solid subpattern number** is **a number that identifies one of the four solid subpatterns.**

A formal definition of each subpattern is given below. Refer to **§ 1.8 Solid Subpatterns** for a detailed description.

	Solid Subpattern	Examples
□ 1	**Top Line** A horizontal, or almost horizontal, stroke or stroke segment extending across the very top of a solid character.	下 3-1, 耳 6-1, 雨 8-1, 予 3-1, 久 3-1 凸 5-1, 口 3-1, 亜 7-1, 爾 14-1
□ 2	**Bottom Line** A horizontal, or almost horizontal, stroke or stroke segment extending across the very bottom of a solid character.	七 2-2, 上 3-2, 亡 3-2, 丘 5-2, 由 5-2 自 6-2, 血 6-2, 垂 8-2, 重 9-2
□ 3	**Through Line** A perfectly vertical stroke or stroke segment intersecting another stroke of a solid character and extending over its entire, or almost its entire, length.	中 4-3, 十 2-3, 手 4-3, 本 5-3, 米 6-3 車 7-3, 求 7-3, 乗 9-3, 粛 11-3
□ 4	**Others** Solid characters that cannot be classified under subpatterns □ 1, □ 2, or □ 3.	人 2-4, 九 2-4, 女 3-4, 火 4-4, 犬 4-4 史 5-4, 成 6-4, 舟 6-4, 為 9-4

4.3 Pattern Subclassification Rules

	Right	Wrong
❶ **DETERMINE TO WHICH OF THE FOUR SOLID SUBPATTERNS YOUR CHARACTER BELONGS**		
☐ 1 CHARACTERS THAT CONTAIN A **TOP LINE**	雨 8-1 下 3-1 耳 6-1 果 8-1	刀 2-1 千 3-1 垂 8-1 丘 5-1
☐ 2 CHARACTERS THAT CONTAIN A **BOTTOM LINE**	上 3-2 丘 5-2 垂 8-2	山 3-2 包 5-2 者 8-2
☐ 3 CHARACTERS THAT CONTAIN A **THROUGH LINE**	中 4-3 東 8-3 毛 4-3	水 4-3 寸 3-3 午 4-3 弟 7-3
☐ 4 CHARACTERS THAT DO NOT CONTAIN A **TOP LINE, BOTTOM LINE**, OR **THROUGH LINE**	与 3-4 大 3-4 寿 7-4	糸 6-4 久 3-4 友 4-4 劣 6-4
❷ **IF A CHARACTER CAN BE CLASSIFIED UNDER MORE THAN ONE SUBPATTERN, THE SUBPATTERN WITH THE SMALLEST NUMBER TAKES PRECEDENCE**		
A solid character may contain any combination of top, bottom, and through lines. 己 and 酉, for example, include both top and bottom lines. Since a top line takes precedence over a bottom line, these characters are classified under ☐ 1. 出 contains a through line and a bottom line, and is classified under ☐ 2; 王 contains a top, bottom, and through line and is classified under ☐ 1 since the top line has the highest priority.	王 4-1 己 3-1 酉 7-1 果 8-1 出 5-2 生 5-2 甲 5-1	王 4-2 己 3-2 酉 7-2 果 8-3 出 5-3 生 5-3 甲 5-3

APPENDIX 2

HOW TO COUNT STROKES

1. Introduction

Chinese characters consist of one or more interconnected line segments called **strokes.** Most character dictionaries, including this one, require the user to count strokes. This appendix briefly explains the principles of counting strokes, and includes several supplementary charts to help speed up the counting process.

The ability to count strokes quickly and accurately is useful in two ways: (1) it helps you use character dictionaries more efficiently, and (2) it helps you write the characters correctly by making you aware of where one stroke ends and the next one begins.

Stroke counting may be difficult for two reasons:

1. The standard typeface used in Japan often includes ornamental serifs that make a character appear to have a stroke-count different from its hand-written form. For example, 表 appears to have nine strokes in its printed form, but has only eight strokes in its written form (表).

2. For the beginner, it is sometimes difficult to tell where one stroke ends and the next one begins. An element such as 口, for example, may be viewed as consisting of four separate line segments, of two **L**-shaped components (㇄ + ㇕), of one continuous line, or of three segments (| + ㇕ + 一). Only the last division is considered correct according to the traditional method of counting strokes.

In this dictionary, we have made every effort to ease the task of locating difficult-to-count characters by cross-referencing them at incorrect stroke-count locations. For example, 子 is a three-stroke character cross-referenced under two strokes (see SYSTEM OF KANJI INDEXING BY PATTERNS **§ 2.6 Cross-References** for details). Nevertheless, to attain maximum lookup speed, it will be worth your while to master the stroke counting principles given below.

2. Stroke Counting Principles

To count strokes with complete accuracy, a knowledge of how to write the characters is necessary (see **Appendix 3. How to Write Kanji**). For practical purposes, however, the guidelines below will enable even the complete beginner to count strokes accurately with just a little practice.

1. **Learn to recognize the basic strokes.** A **stroke** is defined as a character element such as a dot or line segment traditionally written with one

sweep of the brush or pen. To rephrase: if a line or element is written continuously without lifting the pen or brush, it is considered a single stroke. To the beginner, however, it may not always be obvious what constitutes "one sweep" or when to lift the pen. It is thus necessary to learn to recognize the basic stroke types. Strokes may be straight (一 丨), diagonal (丿 丶) or bent (㇆ ㇄ ㇉). The chart below shows elements that must always be counted as single strokes:

Basic Strokes

	Strokes	Examples
1	一	一 in 五
2	㇇ ㇆ ㇇ ㇈ ㇉	㇉ in 弓
3	丨 ㇓ 丿 亅 ㇁	亅 in 予
4	㇙ ㇙ ㇜ ㇛	㇙ in 民
5	㇄ ㇗ ㇗	㇄ in 礼
6	㇈ 乙 ㇂	㇂ in 呉
7	丶 ㇏ ㇏ ㇂	㇂ in 恩
8	㇋ ㇋	㇋ in 辺

2. **Ignore serifs.** There are various flips, hooks, and protrusions sometimes found at the ends of strokes that must be ignored when counting strokes. Many of these are merely ornamental serifs (shown by small circles in the chart below) appearing in the printed form that are not considered strokes in their own right. It is the handwritten form (square style), not the printed form (Ming typeface), that forms the basis for stroke counting. The chart below lists typical characters of this kind.

Apparent and Actual Stroke-Counts

Ming typeface	Apparent stroke-count	Square style	Actual stroke-count
表	9	表	8
民	6	民	5
良	8	良	7
長	9	長	8
号	6	号	5
留	11	留	10
比	5	比	4
氏	5	氏	4

3. **Count element by element, rather than stroke by stroke.** Do not count all the strokes of a complex character one at the time. It is easier to break the character up into several components, count the strokes of each component, then add the subtotals to get the total stroke-count. For example, to determine the stroke-count of 筋, count as follows: ⺮ (6) + 月 (4) + 力 (2) = 12. This method is especially effective if you have memorized the stroke-counts of the important radicals (see next item).

4. **Memorize the stroke-counts of important radicals.** Since certain radicals occur very frequently as character components, memorizing the stroke-counts of high-frequency radicals will help you count strokes faster. The most frequently occurring radicals are listed below in increasing order of their stroke-counts. The numeral to the right of each radical is its **radical number,** which is followed by a typical character in which it occurs.

Important Radicals

Count	Radical	Example	Count	Radical	Example	Count	Radical	Example
1	一 1	下		忄 61	忙		穴 116	窓
2	亠 8	京		扌 64	指		罒 122	買
	亻 9	仙		艹 140	芽		衤 145	被
	儿 10	元		辶 162	達	6	⺮ 118	笛
	八 12	公		阝 163	邸		米 119	粒
	刂 18	刊		阝 170	防		糸 120	紡
	力 19	加	4	戈 62	戦		耳 128	聴
	十 24	博		攵 66	放		舟 137	船
	卩 26	即		日 72	旭		虫 142	蚊
	厂 27	原		月 74	朝	7	言 149	語
3	口 30	叱		木 75	机		貝 154	貯
	囗 31	囚		欠 76	次		貝 154	責
	土 32	地		氵 85	汗		足 157	跡
	大 37	奈		火 86	焼		車 159	転
	女 38	好		灬 86	煮		酉 164	酔
	子 39	存		牛 93	物	8	金 167	鉄
	宀 40	宗		犭 94	狐		門 169	閉
	寸 41	寺		王 96	現		隹 172	雀
	尸 44	尾		礻 113	祈		雨 173	電
	山 46	峰		月 130	肢		食 184	飯
	山 46	嵐	5	田 102	畑	9	頁 181	順
	巾 50	帆		疒 104	病	10	馬 187	駅
	广 53	店		目 109	盲	11	魚 195	鯉
	弓 57	弘		石 112	研			
	彳 60	役		禾 115	穂			

5. **Memorize the stroke-counts of difficult-to-count elements.** The stroke-counts of some elements are difficult to determine without some knowledge of how to write them. For example, 子 (Radical 39) is a three-stroke element that is often miscounted as a two-stroke element. The most common elements of this kind are listed below, accompanied by their correct and incorrect stroke-counts and typical character examples. Pay special attention to the elements marked by an asterisk. Memorizing their stroke-counts will help you count strokes with greater speed and accu-

racy. The **Variant** column gives a variant of the element (usually an old form) that slightly differs from it in form and consequently in stroke-count.

Incorrect Stroke-Counts

Element	Right	Wrong	Example	Variant
勹	1	2	与 3	
乙	1	2	乞 3	
了	2	1	了 2	
阝*	3	2	阪 7	
阝*	3	2	邦 7	
子*	3	2	孔 4	
丩	3	2	収 5	丩 2
辶*	3	2	込 5	辶 4
之	3	2 or 4	芝 6	
廴	3	2	廷 7	
夂	3	4	変 9	夂 4
及*	3	4	扱 6	
囗*	3	4	困 7	
弓*	3	4	引 4	
廿	4	3	革 9	
𠫓	4	3	育 8	𠫓 3
㐄*	4	3	降 10	㐄 3
艹	4	3	芯 8	
巨	5	4	距 12	
世	5	4	笹 11	
牙	5	4	芽 8	牙 4
疋	5	4	疎 12	
此	6	5	柴 10	
臼	6	5	舊 18	
臣*	7	6	臨 18	
禺	9	8	偶 11	

As a further aid to learning how to count strokes, you may wish to check the stroke-counts of individual characters. Refer to the **reference data box** for your character entry, which gives the stroke-count and **stroke structure** for the character (see GUIDE **§7.3 Strokes** for details).

APPENDIX 3
HOW TO WRITE KANJI

The serious student of Japanese will no doubt want to learn how to write the characters. A knowledge of stroke order is essential for learning how to write the characters correctly, and is a prerequisite for the study of calligraphy. It is also an effective way to master stroke counting.

The guidelines below will enable the student to write most characters in the correct stroke order without referring to the diagrams given for each main entry character. Although there are general principles for writing the characters in the proper stroke order, in some cases a character can be written in more than one way, while in others reference works disagree as to the correct sequence. The basic principle of stroke direction and stroke order is: from left to right and from top to bottom.

The only official guidelines were published by the Japanese Ministry of Education under the title 筆順指導の手びき *hitsujun shidō no tebiki* in March 1958. Given below is an unabridged translation of the above publication, reproduced here with the author's permission from *The Study of Kanji* (Hokuseido Press, Tokyo, revised edition 1984, pp. 277–286), by Michael Pye, which is an excellent introduction to the Japanese writing system. The characters are presented in the handwritten form of the 楷書 *kaisho* or square style. The object of the said publication is to explain the principles of stroke order; it is not meant to be an introduction to calligraphy, which is a separate study in itself.

The following terms and symbols appear in the text:

hen	left-side radical（亻 in 休）
tsukuri	right-side radical（阝 in 都）
nyō	bottom-left enclosure radical（辶 in 進）
*	indicates that the element is not used as an independent character

See also the **Radical Chart** on p. 1772 for more information on radicals and FEATURES OF THIS DICTIONARY **§ 4. Writing.**

PRINCIPLES OF STROKE ORDER IN THE PRESENT WORK

The stroke orders given in the present work have been classified under the Major Principles 1 and 2 and the more detailed Principles 1 to 8 shown below. Furthermore, we have also explained our attitude in cases where 2 or more different stroke orders are widely current.

MAJOR PRINCIPLE 1

FROM TOP TO BOTTOM

Write from top to bottom or from the top part to the bottom part.

a. Begin with the top stroke.

三(一 二 三)言

工(一 丅 工)

b. Begin with the upper part.

喜(士 吉 吉 壴 喜)

客(宀 安 客)

築(⺮ 筑 築)

MAJOR PRINCIPLE 2

FROM LEFT TO RIGHT

Write from left to right or from the left-hand part to the right-hand part.

a. Begin with the left-hand stroke.

川(丿 川 川)順州

学(丶 丷 ⺍)挙魚 1234

帯(一 卄 卌 卌)

脈(𠂆 𠂢 𠂢)

b. Begin with the left-hand part.

竹(𠂉 竹)羽

The *hen* comes first and the *tsukuri* afterwards. (Characters of this kind are very numerous.)

休(亻 休)林語

Write across from the left in cases with 3 parts.

例(亻 伢 例)

側湖術

PRINCIPLE 1

HORIZONTAL STROKES FIRST

When horizontal and vertical strokes cross, the horizontals are usually written first.

(For cases in which horizontals come afterwards, see Principle 2.)

a. Horizontal, vertical;

十(一十)
計古支草

土(一十土)
圧至舎周

士(一十士)
志吉喜

even if the vertical curves after crossing the horizontal;

七(一七)切

大(一ナ大)太

and when additional strokes precede or follow.

告(′ 𠂉 牛 生)
先任庭

木(一十木)述

寸(一十寸)寺

b. Horizontal, vertical, vertical; cases with only 2 following verticals;

共(一 卄 廾)散港

編(冂 月 冊)

花(一 艹)荷

算(一 廾)形鼻

and cases with 3 or more verticals.

帯(一 十 卅 卌)

無(𠂉 無 無)

c. Horizontal, horizontal, vertical; cases with only 2 horizontals;

用(冂 月 用)通

even when additional strokes precede or follow;

末未妹

cases with 3 or more horizontals; 耕(⺕ 丰 耒)

even if the vertical curves after crossing the horizontals. 夫(二 夫 夫)春実

d. Horizontal, horizontal, vertical, vertical; cases in which there are 2 of each. 耕(二井)囲

PRINCIPLE 2

HORIZONTAL STROKES AFTERWARDS

When horizontal and vertical strokes cross, the horizontals come afterwards in the following cases only.

a. 田 — 田(冂 冂 田 田) 男異町細

b. Elements based on 田. — 由(冂 巾 由 由) 油黄横画

曲(冂 巾 曲 曲 曲) 豊農

角(⺆ 冂 用 用)解

再(⺆ 冂 再 再)構

c. 王. — 王(二 丁 干 王)玉 主美差義

d. Elements based on 王; even if there are 2 horizontals in the middle; — 王*(一 丁 干 王 王)

進(亻 仁 仹 隹)

雑集確観

馬(厂 厂 冂 馬)駅

even if the vertical protrudes at the top; — 主*(一 十 丰 主)生

麦表清星

even if there are 2 verticals.

井*(一 十 廾 井 井)
寒構

PRINCIPLE 3

CENTER FIRST

When there is a center part flanked on left and right by 1 or 2 strokes, the center is written first.

小(亅 小 小)少京
示宗 糸細
当(丨 ⺌ ⺌)光常
水(亅 才 水)氷永
氺*(亅 氺 氺)緑暴
𠂉*(亻 𠂉 𠂉)衆

This holds good if the center consists of 2 strokes;

業(" " " 业)

赤(丿 丿 小)変

or is a little complicated.

楽(白 泊 楽)薬
承(手 手 承)率

Exceptions
There are 2 exceptions to Principle 3.

忄(丶 丶 忄)性
火(丷 火)火
秋炭 焼

PRINCIPLE 4

OUTSIDE FIRST

When there is an enclosing shape such as *kunigamae*, it is written first.

国(冂 国 国)因
同(冂 同) 円
内(冂 内)肉納
司(𠃌 司)詞羽

Cases such as 日, 月, etc. may be considered to fall under this principle.

日月目田

N.B. 区 is written as shown; similary 医.

区(一 ㄨ 区)

PRINCIPLE 5

STROKES WHICH CURVE AWAY TO THE LEFT COME FIRST

When slanting strokes cross, the one which curves away to the left comes first.

文(亠ナ文)父
故支収処

The same holds good when they abut.

人入欠金

PRINCIPLE 6

A THROUGH-GOING VERTICAL COMES LAST

A vertical which runs right through the character is to be written last;

中(口中)申神
車半事建

even if it is closed off at the bottom;

書(⺻聿)妻

or at the top.

平(亚平)評
羊洋達拝
手(三手)争

When the vertical protrudes neither at the top nor at the bottom, the order is: top part, vertical, bottom part.

里(日甲里)野黒
重(亩亩重)動
謹(艹茾菫)勤

N.B. the difference between 菫 and 莫.

漢(艹茣莫)難

PRINCIPLE 7

A THROUGH-GOING HORIZONTAL COMES LAST

A horizontal which runs right through the character is to be written last.

女(𡿨女)安努
子(了子)字存
母 毎海 慣
舟→舟船 与

N.B. The only exception is 世.

世(一廿世)

PRINCIPLE 8

HORIZONTALS AND STROKES WHICH CURVE AWAY TO THE LEFT

When the horizontal is long and the slanting stroke short, the slanting stroke is to be written first.

右(ノナ右)
有布希

When the horizontal is short and the slanting stroke long, the horizontal is to be written first.

左(一ナ左)
友在存抜

CASES TO BE SPECIALLY NOTED

A. Cases in which there are 2 or more widely current stroke orders.

1. The characters marked (a) have always had only the stroke order indicated.

(a) 止正足走武
(丨 ト)

Those marked (b) have 2 possibilities, (i) and (ii); we prefer (i) in conformity with (a) above.

(b) 上点店
(丨 ト)……(i)
(一 ト)……(ii)

N.B. (ii) is more frequently used in *gyōsho* however.

上点店

2. The character 耳 (a) is usually written as indicated.

(a) 耳 (⺕ 耳)

As a left radical (b) it has 2 possibilities, (i) and (ii); we prefer (i) in conformity with (a) above.

(b) 取最職厳
(⺕ 耳)……(i)
(⺁ 耳)……(ii)

3. 必 has several possibilities. We strongly reject (iii), and since (i) gives a good form more easily than (ii) we prefer (i).

必
(丶 ノ 义 义 必)…(i)
(ノ 乂 乂 义 必)…(ii)
(心 必)…………(iii)
and others

4. *Hatsugashira* has several possibilities. In (i) the right-hand part is symmetrical with the left and is also more natural; we therefore prefer (i).

発登
(ノ 癶 癶)……(i)
(八 癶 癶)……(ii)
(ノ ノ 癶)……(iii)

N.B. The top of 祭 is written as indicated, following Principle 5.

祭(夕 炙)

5. 感 has 2 possibilities, (i) and (ii). In conformity with the standardized form we prefer (i), following Major Principle 1.

感
(后 咸 感)……(i)
(后 㥯 感)……(ii)

N.B. 盛 is not in the Education Kanji list, but note that the same considerations apply.

盛
(𠂆 成 盛)……(i)
(𠂆 㿟 盛)……(ii)

6. 馬 has (i), (ii) and others; we prefer (i) in accordance with Major Principle 1.

馬
(厂 IT π 馬)……(i)
(厂 F 馬 馬)……(ii)

N.B. In this way it is also brought into line with 隹.

隹*(亻 什 隹 隹)

7. 無 has (i), (ii) and others; we prefer (i) in accordance with Major Principle 1.

無
(𠂉 無 無)……(i)
(𠂉 亖 無)……(ii)

8. 興 might be thought of as in (i) or as in (ii); we prefer (i) in accordance with Major Principle 2.

興
(𦥑 𦥑 𦥑)……(i)
(月 𦥑 𦥑)……(ii)

B. Characters which cannot be explained according to the above principles.

1. Some *nyō* are written first (a), and some afterwards (b).

(a) 夂走免是
処起勉題

(b) 辶廴𠃊
近建直

2. Some strokes which curve away to the left are written first (a) and some afterwards (b).

(a) 九及
(b) 力刀万方別

APPENDIX 4
KANA AND ROMANIZATION

The Japanese writing system uses two syllabic scripts, called 平仮名 **hiragana** and 片仮名 **katakana**. Collectively, they are referred to as 仮名 **kana.** The two scripts are used in conjunction with thousands of kanji to write the Japanese vocabulary. Hiragana is used primarily to write grammatical elements and certain native Japanese words; katakana, mostly to write Western loanwords.

Prewar kana orthography was highly complex. The sound こう *kō*, for example, was written by such combinations as かふ, こふ, and かう. Shortly after World War II, kana orthography underwent extensive reforms to reflect actual pronunciation. This appendix describes the two kana systems based on the official orthographic reforms, and explains the differences between the three principal romanization systems. The pronunciation of the kana symbols, a description of which can be found in most Japanese language primers, is only lightly touched upon. The history of the kana scripts is briefly discussed in **§ 2.** of **OUTLINE OF JAPANESE WRITING SYSTEM.**

1. Hiragana

1.1 Uses of Hiragana Hiragana is used primarily to write grammatical words and elements, such as inflectional endings, particles, conjunctions, and auxiliary verbs. Inflectional kana endings are called 送り仮名 *okurigana* (see **Appendix 5** for details).

書いた	*kaita*	wrote	kanji stem + kana suffix
を	*o*		object marker
この	*kono*	this	demonstrative adjective
そして	*soshite*	and	conjunction
する	*suru*	to do	auxiliary verb

Hiragana is also used to write some native Japanese words not normally written in kanji, such as adverbs and certain nouns and adjectives, as well as words whose kanji are difficult or obsolete:

はっきり	*hakkiri*	clearly	しゃべる	*shaberu*	talk
ほとんど	*hotondo*	almost	ふざけ	*fuzake*	frolic

Sometimes, small hiragana characters, called 振り仮名 *furigana* or ルビ *rubi*, are placed along the top or the side of kanji to indicate their pronunciations:

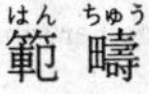

1.2 Kana Syllabary Each kana character represents one syllable. The basic syllables are arranged in a table called the 五十音図 *gojūonzu* 'table of 50 sounds'. Here we will refer to it as the **kana table**. The table, which consists of ten columns running from right to left arranged in five rows, can be written in either hiragana or katakana. In either script, the symbols represent exactly the same sounds. All the sounds in the table, except for ん *n*, end in a vowel.

Note that some syllables are missing from the original table, while others have become obsolete. Later, the nasal consonant ん *n* was added, so that the table now contains distinct symbols for 46 sounds.

Hiragana Syllabary

ん n	わ wa	ら ra	や ya	ま ma	は ha	な na	た ta	さ sa	か ka	あ a
	[ゐ] i	り ri		み mi	ひ hi	に ni	ち chi	し shi	き ki	い i
		る ru	ゆ yu	む mu	ふ fu	ぬ nu	つ tsu	す su	く ku	う u
	[ゑ] e	れ re		め me	へ he	ね ne	て te	せ se	け ke	え e
	を o	ろ ro	よ yo	も mo	ほ ho	の no	と to	そ so	こ ko	お o

[ ] indicates obsolete characters

REMARKS:
1. The syllables し *shi*, ち *chi*, つ *tsu*, ふ *fu*, and を *o* are not phonetically uniform with the other syllables in the same column.
2. Although へ and は are normally pronounced *he* and *ha*, they are pronounced *e* and *wa* when used as particles, e.g., 彼は海へ行く is pronounced *kare wa umi e iku*.

1.3 Voiced Sounds The voiceless consonants *k, s, t,* and *h* are turned into the **voiced sounds** *g, z, d,* and *b* (濁音 *dakuon*) by adding a diacritical mark called 濁点 *dakuten* or 濁り *nigori* (゛) to the right of the kana character. Another mark, called 半濁点 *handakuten* (°), is used to write the *p* sound.[1]

1. Phonetically, *p* is a voiceless consonant, but traditionally it is treated together with the *b* sounds.

Voiced Sounds

ぱ pa	ば ba	だ da	ざ za	が ga
ぴ pi	び bi	ぢ ji	じ ji	ぎ gi
ぷ pu	ぶ bu	づ zu	ず zu	ぐ gu
ぺ pe	べ be	で de	ぜ ze	げ ge
ぽ po	ぼ bo	ど do	ぞ zo	ご go

REMARKS: The sounds *ji* and *zu* are normally written じ and ず. ぢ and づ are used when (1) they are preceded by ち or つ respectively, as in つづく (続く) *tsuzuku,* and (2) when ち and つ are voiced in compound words; e.g., 鼻血 *hanaji* is written はなぢ, not はなじ, because *ji* derives from the voiceless 血 (ち) *chi.*

1.4 Palatalized Sounds Syllables ending in *i* can be followed by a small ゃ *ya,* ゅ *yu,* or ょ *yo* to form new combinations pronounced as a single syllable. For example, き is combined with ゃ to give きゃ *kya.* These contracted or **palatalized sounds** are called 拗音 *yōon* in Japanese.

Palatalized Sounds

りゃ rya	みゃ mya	ひゃ hya	にゃ nya	ちゃ cha	しゃ sha	きゃ kya
りゅ ryu	みゅ myu	ひゅ hyu	にゅ nyu	ちゅ chu	しゅ shu	きゅ kyu
りょ ryo	みょ myo	ひょ hyo	にょ nyo	ちょ cho	しょ sho	きょ kyo

Voiced sounds are also combined in a similar manner to form the syllables shown below:

Palatalized Voiced Sounds

ぴゃ pya	びゃ bya	ぢゃ ja	じゃ ja	ぎゃ gya
ぴゅ pyu	びゅ byu	ぢゅ ju	じゅ ju	ぎゅ gyu
ぴょ pyo	びょ byo	ぢょ jo	じょ jo	ぎょ gyo

REMARKS: ぢゃ, ぢゅ, and ぢょ are used only in voiced compounds derived from words written with the voiceless ちゃ, ちゅ, and ちょ; e.g., 茶飲み茶碗 *chanomi-jawan* is written ちゃのみぢゃわん because *ja* derives from the voiceless 茶碗 (ちゃわん) *chawan*.

1.5 Long Vowels Japanese vowels are of two kinds: **short vowels** (短音 *tan'on*) and **long vowels** (長音 *chōon*). All the basic sounds of the kana table, except for ん *n*, end in a short vowel. A long vowel is approximately double the length of a short vowel (*ā* sounds like *a* in *father*). A long vowel is written by repeating the vowel of sounds ending in *a*, *i*, or *u*:

か + あ → かあ *kā*　　く + う → くう *kū*
き + い → きい *kii*

Sounds ending in *o* are normally lengthened by adding the vowel う to a sound ending in *o*:

こ + う → こう *kō*　　と + う → とう *tō*

In a small number of exceptions, お is used instead of う for historical reasons:

おおきい	大きい	*ōkii*	big
おおい	多い	*ōi*	many
とおる	通る	*tōru*	pass

Sounds ending in *e* are sometimes lengthened by adding え, but more often by adding い:

ね + え → ねえ *nē*　　け + い → けい *kei*

The vowel of a palatalized sound is lengthened in the same way as an ordinary sound:

きょ + う → きょう *kyō*　　にゅ + う → にゅう *nyū*

1.6 Double Consonants The consonants *k, s, sh, t, ch,* and *p* can be doubled. These **double consonants** (促音 *sokuon*) are pronounced separately as if they were distinct syllables. They are indicated by a small っ placed before the consonant to be doubled. Note that both basic sounds such as か *ka,* as well as palatalized sounds such as しゃ *sha,* can be doubled:

けっか	結果	*kekka*	けっとう	決闘	*kettō*
かっさい	喝采	*kassai*	はっちゅう	発注	*hatchū*
はっしゃ	発射	*hassha*	けっぱく	潔白	*keppaku*

1.7 Ordering Scheme Most modern Japanese dictionaries and reference works order words according to a scheme based on the kana table called アイウエオ順 *aiueo-jun* or 五十音順 *gojūon-jun.* The table (see **§ 1.2** above) is read from top to bottom starting with the first column on the right, i.e.: *a, i, u, e, o, ka, ki, ku, ke, ko, sa, shi...* The details of the scheme, which are fairly complex, can be found in the introduction to most Japanese dictionaries.

Formerly, a scheme called いろは順 *iroha-jun,* based on a Buddhist poem, was in use. Presently, it is used mostly like ordinal numbers in lists and the like.

The I–RO–HA Arrangement

い i	ろ ro	は ha	に ni	ほ ho	へ he	と to
ち chi	り ri	ぬ nu	る ru	を o		
わ wa	か ka	よ yo	た ta	れ re	そ so	
つ tsu	ね ne	な na	ら ra	む mu		
う u	ゐ i	の no	お o	く ku	や ya	ま ma
け ke	ふ fu	こ ko	え e	て te		
あ a	さ sa	き ki	ゆ yu	め me	み mi	し shi
ゑ e	ひ hi	も mo	せ se	す su		

1.8 Origin of Hiragana The hiragana characters are derived from Chinese characters having the same or similar pronunciations. For example, あ *a* originates from the character 安 *an*. Hiragana is based on the cursive form of Chinese characters, so that the characters have rounded, smoothly flowing contours and an elegant appearance. The table below shows the original Chinese characters from which hiragana is derived.

Derivation of Hiragana

あ 安	い 以	う 宇	え 衣	お 於
か 加	き 幾	く 久	け 計	こ 己
さ 左	し 之	す 寸	せ 世	そ 曽
た 太	ち 知	つ 川	て 天	と 止
な 奈	に 仁	ぬ 奴	ね 袮	の 乃
は 波	ひ 比	ふ 不	へ 部	ほ 保
ま 末	み 美	む 武	め 女	も 毛
や 也		ゆ 由		よ 与
ら 良	り 利	る 留	れ 礼	ろ 呂
わ 和	ゐ 為		ゑ 恵	を 遠
ん 无				

2. Katakana

2.1 Uses of Katakana Katakana is used primarily to write Western loanwords, non-Japanese proper names (except for Chinese and Korean ones), and onomatopoeic words. It is also used to write the names of some plants and animals, for writing telegrams, and for emphasis (like italics in English).

コーヒー	*kōhī*	coffee
イギリス	*igirisu*	England
ガチャン	*gachan*	clanging
ネズミ	*nezumi*	mouse

2.2 Katakana Tables

Katakana Syllabary

ン n	ワ wa	ラ ra	ヤ ya	マ ma	ハ ha	ナ na	タ ta	サ sa	カ ka	ア a
	[ヰ] i	リ ri		ミ mi	ヒ hi	ニ ni	チ chi	シ shi	キ ki	イ i
		ル ru	ユ yu	ム mu	フ fu	ヌ nu	ツ tsu	ス su	ク ku	ウ u
	[ヱ] e	レ re		メ me	ヘ he	ネ ne	テ te	セ se	ケ ke	エ e
	ヲ o	ロ ro	ヨ yo	モ mo	ホ ho	ノ no	ト to	ソ so	コ ko	オ o

[ ] indicates obsolete characters

Voiced Sounds

パ pa	バ ba	ダ da	ザ za	ガ ga
ピ pi	ビ bi	ヂ ji	ジ ji	ギ gi
プ pu	ブ bu	ヅ zu	ズ zu	グ gu
ペ pe	ベ be	デ de	ゼ ze	ゲ ge
ポ po	ボ bo	ド do	ゾ zo	ゴ go

Palatalized Sounds

リャ rya	ミャ mya	ヒャ hya	ニャ nya	チャ cha	シャ sha	キャ kya
リュ ryu	ミュ myu	ヒュ hyu	ニュ nyu	チュ chu	シュ shu	キュ kyu
リョ ryo	ミョ myo	ヒョ hyo	ニョ nyo	チョ cho	ショ sho	キョ kyo

Palatalized Voiced Sounds

ピャ pya	ビャ bya	ヂャ ja	ジャ ja	ギャ gya
ピュ pyu	ビュ byu	ヂュ ju	ジュ ju	ギュ gyu
ピョ pyo	ビョ byo	ヂョ jo	ジョ jo	ギョ gyo

2.3 Katakana Orthography The katakana symbols represent exactly the same sounds as the corresponding hiragana symbols. In principle, everything that has been said about hiragana orthography applies in every detail to katakana orthography as well. For example, double consonants are indicated by a small ッ (バット *batto*) and palatalized sounds by a small ャ, ュ, and ョ (キョ *kyo*).

The main difference between the two scripts is that in writing katakana loanwords long vowels are indicated by adding to the previous character a dash-like symbol called 長音符 *chōonfu*:

カ + ー → カー	*kā*	ケ + ー → ケー	*kē*
キ + ー → キー	*kī*	コ + ー → コー	*kō*
ク + ー → クー	*kū*	ギャ + ー → ギャー	*gyā*

However, the vowels of words that are not Western loanwords are lengthened in the same manner as in hiragana:

空気　クウキ　*kūki*　　　　教徒　キョウト　*kyōto*

2.4 Katakana Loanwords Foreign loanwords in katakana attempt to imitate the pronunciation of the original language within the limitations of the Japanese phonetic system. This often results in pronunciations markedly different from the original language. For example, *roller* becomes ローラー *rōrā*, *general strike* becomes ゼネラルストライキ *zeneraru sutoraiki*, which is shortened to ゼネスト *zenesuto*, etc.

It is often not possible to write certain sounds with the traditional kana syllables. For example, there is no traditional combination for expressing the *je* sound in *jet*. A number of special kana combinations have evolved to write such words. However, the orthography of katakana loanwords is not completely standardized, so that some words may be written in more than one way.[2] For example, *gesture* is sometimes rendered as ゼスチャー *zesuchā* and sometimes as ジェスチャー *jesuchā*.

The most common nontraditional kana combinations used in writing katakana loanwords are shown in the table below, along with typical examples:

Kana Combinations in Loanwords

Combinations	Examples
スィ si　シェ she　ジェ je	シェード *shēdo* shade ジェスチャー *jesuchā* gesture
ティ ti　トゥ tu　ディ di　ドゥ du　チェ che	パーティ *pāti* party チェック *chekku* check
ファ fa　フィ fi　フェ fe　フォ fo	フォーク *fōku* fork ファイル *fairu* file
ヴァ va　ヴィ vi　ヴ vu　ヴェ ve　ヴォ vo	ヴァイオリン *vaiorin* violin ヴェール *vēru* veil
ウィ ui (wi)　ウェ ue (we)　ウォ uo (wo)	ウィンナ *uinna* sausage ウォール街 *uōrugai* Wall Street

In addition to these combinations, katakana loanwords sometimes include double consonants not used in hiragana, such as double *d* and *g* (e.g., ベッド *beddo*).

2.5 Origin of Katakana The katakana characters are derived from Chinese characters having the same or similar pronunciations. For example, ア *a* originates from the character 阿 *a*. Unlike hiragana, which is based on simplifications of whole Chinese characters, most katakana characters originate from single character components. Since katakana is based on the square style of Chinese characters, the characters have square, angular contours and a clean appearance. The table below shows the original Chinese characters from which katakana is derived.

2. Just before this dictionary went to press (March 1990), the National Language Council published a proposal for standardizing katakana orthography. There was not enough time to incorporate these changes into the above table.

Derivation of Katakana

ア 阿	イ 伊	ウ 宇	エ 江	オ 於
カ 加	キ 幾	ク 久	ケ 介	コ 己
サ 散	シ 之	ス 須	セ 世	ソ 曽
タ 多	チ 千	ツ 川	テ 天	ト 止
ナ 奈	ニ 仁	ヌ 奴	ネ 祢	ノ 乃
ハ 八	ヒ 比	フ 不	ヘ 部	ホ 保
マ 末	ミ 三	ム 牟	メ 女	モ 毛
ヤ 也		ユ 由		ヨ 與
ラ 良	リ 利	ル 流	レ 礼	ロ 呂
ワ 和	ヰ 井		ヱ 恵	ヲ 乎
ン ?				

3. Romanization

Below is a description of the main romanization systems used in Japanese. See also FEATURES OF THIS DICTIONARY **§3.4 Romanization** and GUIDE **§29.1 Romanization System.**

3.1 Principal Systems There are three important systems for romanizing Japanese: the Hepburn system (ヘボン式 *hebonshiki*), the Kunrei system (訓令式 *kunreishiki*), and the Nippon system (日本式 *nipponshiki*). The tables below show the differences between the three systems. Syllables not appearing in these tables are romanized in exactly the same way in all three systems. See the kana charts in **§2.2 Katakana Tables** above for a full listing of kana syllables.

Basic Sounds

Kana	Hepburn	Kunrei	Nippon
し	shi	si	si
じ	ji	zi	zi
ち	chi	ti	ti
ぢ	ji	zi	di
つ	tsu	tu	tu
づ	zu	zu	du
ふ	fu	hu	hu
を	o	o	wo
ん	n (m)	n	n

Palatalized Sounds

Kana	Hepburn	Kunrei	Nippon
しゃ	sha	sya	sya
しゅ	shu	syu	syu
しょ	sho	syo	syo
じゃ	ja	zya	zya
じゅ	ju	zyu	zyu
じょ	jo	zyo	zyo
ちゃ	cha	tya	tya
ちゅ	chu	tyu	tyu
ちょ	cho	tyo	tyo
ぢゃ	ja	zya	dya
ぢゅ	ju	zyu	dyu
ぢょ	jo	zyo	dyo

Long Vowels

Kana	Hepburn	Kunrei/ Nippon
ああ	ā	â
いい	ii	ii
うう	ū	û
ええ	ē	ê
えい	ei	ei
おう	ō	ô
アー	ā	â
イー	ī	î
ウー	ū	û
エー	ē	ê
オー	ō	ô

Note that in some works long vowels are written by doubling the vowel, e.g., *Tookyoo* instead of *Tōkyō* or *Tôkyô*. In Japanese wordprocessors, long vowels are inputted by doubling the vowel, except for *ō*, which is inputted by adding *u*, i.e., 東京 *tōkyō* is inputted as *toukyou*.

3.2 Hepburn System The most common romanization system today is the Hepburn system. It came into wide use with the publication of the 1886 edition of a Japanese-English dictionary compiled by the well-known American missionary, the Reverend James Curtis Hepburn. Although this system is not ideally suited for pedagogical purposes, it is relatively easy for English speakers to learn because it is based on English orthography. For example, し, pronounced approximately like English *she*, is written *shi*, rather than the *si* used in other systems.

The romanization system adopted in this dictionary is the Hepburn system with the slight modifications introduced in Kenkyusha's *New Japanese-English Dictionary*. The transliteration rules of the system are as follows:

1. In principle, long vowels, especially *a, u,* and *o,* are indicated by placing a macron (¯) over the vowel:

   かあ *kā*　　こう *kō*　　くう *kū*　　ちょう *chō*

   Long *i* is normally written by repeating the vowel, but in transcribing katakana loanwords it is indicated by a macron:

にいさん	兄さん	*niisan*	older brother
ビール		*bīru*	beer

   Long *e* is written *ē* if it is indicated by the kana え or エ. If it is indicated by the kana い or イ, then it is romanized as *ei*:

ケーブル		*kēburu*	cable
せいと	生徒	*seito*	pupil

   If two identical vowels are pronounced as distinct syllables, rather than as a single long vowel, a macron is not used and the vowel is repeated. For example, ばあい (場合) is written *baai,* not *bāi.*

2. The consonants *k, s, t,* and *p* are doubled by repetition; i.e., *kk, ss, tt,* and *pp.* This also applies to consonants used only in katakana loanwords, such as *d, g,* and *h.* The double consonants for *sh* and *ch* are represented by *ssh* and *tch*:

はっこう	発行	*hakkō*	ねっちゅう	熱中	*netchū*
はっそう	発想	*hassō*	かっしょく	褐色	*kasshoku*
はってん	発展	*hatten*	ベッド		*beddo*
あっぱく	圧迫	*appaku*	バッハ		*bahha*

3. The nasal consonant ん is always transcribed as *n,* although in the original Hepburn system it is represented by *m* if it occurs after *b, p,* or *m.* Thus しんぶん (新聞) is written *shinbun,* not *shimbun.*

4. An apostrophe (') is placed after *n* representing the syllable ん if it is followed by a vowel or by a *y.* This is done to show that the *n* is not part of the following syllable:

たんい	単位	*tan'i*	たに	谷	*tani*
きんゆう	金融	*kin'yū*	きにゅう	記入	*kinyū*

   In the example, the apostrophe of *tan'i* serves to distinguish between たんい and たに.

5. The conventions for capitalization and word division of romanized transcriptions in this dictionary are described in GUIDE **§ 29.1 Romanization System.**

6. The romanization of katakana loanwords is shown in the table in **§ 2.4 Katakana Loanwords** above.

7. A small number of words are romanized on the basis of their pronunciations, rather than their kana spellings. Specifically, the particles へ and は are romanized as *e* and *wa*, not *he* and *ha*.

3.3 Kunrei System The Kunrei system is the official romanization system used by the Japanese government and in various linguistic works such as language textbooks. It was promulgated in 1937 and underwent minor modifications in 1954.

A distinguishing feature of the Kunrei system is its uniform manner of transcribing consonants. For example, all the syllables of the *t* column are uniformly represented by a *t* followed by a vowel:

Kana	た	ち	つ	て	と
Kunrei	ta	ti	tu	te	to
Hepburn	ta	chi	tsu	te	to

The Hepburn system, on the other hand, is more inconsistent since it aims at approximating pronunciation on the basis of English orthography. The Kunrei system is thus often said to be more logical and better suited for linguistic analysis and pedagogic purposes. Nevertheless, it produces some strange spellings for English speakers, such as *Huzi* for the familiar Mount Fuji, which is probably the main reason that it has not gained wide acceptance.

The kana syllables in the Kunrei system are, for the most part, romanized in the same way as in the Hepburn system, except for the differences shown in the tables in **§ 3.1** above. Another difference is that long vowels are written by placing a circumflex (ˆ) over the vowel, not a macron as in the Hepburn system, i.e. *kô* versus *kō*. However, in the case of capital letters the vowel may be repeated. Thus おおいたけん (大分県) may be written *Ôitaken* or *Ooitaken*. Otherwise, everything that has been said about the Hepburn system basically applies to the Kunrei system.

3.4 Nippon System The Nippon system, the least used of the three systems, was introduced in 1881 by 田中館愛橘 *tanakadate aikitsu*. With a few minor exceptions, everything that has been said about the Kunrei system applies to the Nippon system.

In the Nippon system, the kana syllables are transcribed in almost the same manner as in the Kunrei system, except for the differences shown in the tables in **§ 3.1** above. The main difference is that all the syllables of the *d* column and their corresponding palatalized sounds always begin with *d*:

Kana	だ	ぢ	づ	で	ど	ぢゃ	ぢゅ	ぢょ
Nippon	da	di	du	de	do	dya	dyu	dyo
Kunrei	da	zi	zu	de	do	zya	zyu	zyo
Hepburn	da	ji	zu	de	do	ja	ju	jo

Long vowels are usually represented by a circumflex, just like in the Kunrei system. Thus, Hepburn *kō* is rendered as *kô* in the Nippon system. In all other respects, the Nippon system is the same as the Kunrei system.

APPENDIX 5

RULES FOR OKURIGANA

Inflected words of Japanese origin normally consist of a kanji base or stem to which kana inflections are added, or *affixed*. These kana affixes are called *okurigana* (送り仮名). For example, the verb kaku 書く *kaku* 'to write' consists of the kanji stem 書 and the *okurigana* ending く.

One difficulty faced by students learning how to write the language is that *okurigana* orthography is not completely standardized; that is, there are different ways to "spell" the same word. For example, *yuki-* 'bound for' is written either 行き or 行, depending on editorial policy or personal preference. To help the student, the *okurigana* of all *kun* readings is indicated in parentheses in the entry-head data, and the Japanese words in this dictionary conform to the standard *okurigana* orthography (except for special contexts).

As part of the postwar language reforms, the Japanese Ministry of Education issued guidelines aimed at standardizing kana orthography. The principles for the affixing of *okurigana* currently in effect were approved by the cabinet on June 18, 1973, and underwent some minor revisions as a result of the promulgation of the Jōyō Kanji list in 1981. This appendix presents a translation of the revised edition published on October 1, 1981 entitled 送り仮名の付け方 *okurigana no tsukekata,* "The Affixation of *Okurigana*." Except for some minor changes, it is a faithful translation of the official document.[1]

See also GUIDE **§ 4.4 *Kun* Reading** and FEATURES OF THIS DICTIONARY **§ 4.4 Kana Orthography.**

THE AFFIXATION OF OKURIGANA

1. Introduction

1. "**The Affixation of Okurigana**" describes the principles governing the affixation of *okurigana* in the writing of modern Japanese in accordance with the *on-kun* readings of the Jōyō Kanji list as it applies to the public at large in such areas as law, official documents, newspapers, magazines, and broadcasting.

---

1. To make the text more readable, it differs from the original in several minor points. First, only those examples deemed necessary for understanding the rules have been included, and the underlining of word parts was eliminated. Second, transcriptions of Japanese words have been added in italics, and word meanings are sometimes supplied in square brackets. Lastly, the layout was changed a little and a numbering system was introduced in the Main Text to make its complex structure easier to grasp.

2. This document does not apply to the orthography used in the various branches of learning, such as science, technology, the arts, and other fields, nor to personal writings.

3. This document does not apply to the use of kanji as symbols, to the use of kanji in charts, nor to the writing of proper nouns.

2. Guide to the Main Text

1. The structure of the Main Text of this document is as follows:

One-Character Words

(*a*) Inflected Words

General Rule 1: (Words affixed with inflectional endings)
General Rule 2: (Words that, in consideration of their derived and corresponding forms, are affixed at a point before their inflectional endings begin)

(*b*) Uninflected Words

General Rule 3: (Nouns that are not affixed with *okurigana*)
General Rule 4: (Nouns formed by nominalizing inflected words, and whose *okurigana* conforms to that of the original inflected word)
General Rule 5: (Adverbs, uninflected adjectives, and conjunctions)

Compound Words

General Rule 6: (Affixing *okurigana* on the basis of one-character words)
General Rule 7: (Omitting *okurigana* in conformity with popular usage)

Words in Appendix

1. (Words affixed with *okurigana*)
2. (Words not affixed with *okurigana*)

2. The term "General Rule" refers to a basic principle of affixing *okurigana* on the basis of distinctions between such categories as one-character words and compound words, inflected words and uninflected words, etc. When necessary, exceptional items and alternative forms have been included.

Consequently, for each General Rule, in addition to the Standard Orthography, both Exceptions and Alternatives are given when necessary. However, because of the the large number of exceptions to General Rule 6, a separate category, General Rule 7, was established to embrace those exceptions.

3. The meanings of the terms used in this document are as follows:

One-character words	Words written with a single kanji, using either the *on* or *kun* reading.
Compound words	Words written with two or more kanji, pronounced in various combinations of readings such as *kun*+*kun*, *on*+*kun*, etc.
Words in appendix	Of the words that appear in the appendix to the Jōyō Kanji list, those that present some problem in the affixing of *okurigana*.
Inflected words	Verbs, adjectives, and noun adjectives.
Uninflected words	Nouns, adverbs, uninflected adjectives, and conjunctions.
Standard Orthography	A rule that is considered to be a basic principle in the affixation of *okurigana*.
Exceptions	Words whose *okurigana* does not conform to the Standard Orthography but that conforms to popular usage. The popular orthography of such words is acceptable although it deviates from the Standard Orthography.
Alternatives	Words whose *okurigana* conforms to the Standard Orthography but that have an alternative form conforming to popular usage. The popular orthography of such words is acceptable in addition to the version conforming to the Standard Orthography.

4. Since *okurigana* is not required for the parts of one-character words or compound words that are read in the *on* reading, such words are not covered here unless necessary.

5. Under each General Rule, words that have alternative orthographies may be written according to the Standard Orthography or according to the Alternatives. If when applying the rules to individual cases it is difficult to judge whether the Alternatives apply, the Standard Orthography shall take precedence.

3. MAIN TEXT

3.1 One-Character Words

3.1.1 Inflected Words

GENERAL RULE 1

Standard Orthography: The *okurigana* of inflected words (except for words to which General Rule 2 applies) begins at their inflectional endings.

Examples:

書く	*kaku*	賢い	*kashikoi*
考える	*kangaeru*	主だ	*omo da*

Exceptions: 1. For adjectives whose stems end in し *shi*, the *okurigana* begins with し:

Examples:

著しい *ichijirushii* 珍しい *mezurashii*

2. For noun adjectives whose inflectional endings are preceded by か *ka*, やか *yaka*, or らか *raka*, the *okurigana* begins with those syllables.

Examples:

静かだ *shizuka da* 明らかだ *akiraka da*
和やかだ *nagoyaka da*

3. The *okurigana* of the following words is affixed as shown:

Examples:

明らむ *akaramu* 危うい *ayaui*
味わう *ajiwau* 大きい *ōkii*
哀れむ *awaremu* 少ない *sukunai*
慈しむ *itsukushimu* 小さい *chiisai*
教わる *osowaru* 冷たい *tsumetai*
脅かす *odokasu* 平たい *hiratai*
脅かす *obiyakasu* 新ただ *arata da*
食らう *kurau* 同じだ *onaji da*
異なる *kotonaru* 盛んだ *sakan da*
逆らう *sakarau* 平らだ *taira da*
捕まる *tsukamaru* 懇ろだ *nengoro da*
群がる *muragaru* 惨めだ *mijime da*
和らぐ *yawaragu* 哀れだ *aware da*
揺する *yusuru* 幸いだ *saiwai da*
明るい *akarui* 幸せだ *shiawase da*
危ない *abunai* 巧みだ *takumi da*

Alternatives: The *okurigana* of the following words can also begin at the syllable before their inflectional endings, as shown in parentheses:

表す(表わす) *arawasu* 行う(行なう) *okonau*
現れる(現われる) *arawareru* 断る(断わる) *kotowaru*

NOTE: The *okurigana* of verbs whose stems and inflectional endings cannot be separated, such as 着る *kiru*, 寝る *neru*, and 来る *kuru*, is affixed as indicated.

GENERAL RULE 2

Standard Orthography: The *okurigana* of words that embed another word in a part other than their inflectional endings conforms to the *okurigana* of the embedded word. (The embedded word is shown in square brackets.)

Examples:

1. The inflected forms of verbs, and other words based on those forms:

照らす *terasu* [照る *teru*]
生まれる *umareru* [生む *umu*]
聞こえる *kikoeru* [聞く *kiku*]
混ざる・混じる *mazaru, majiru* [混ぜる *mazeru*]

2. Words embedding the stems of adjectives or noun adjectives:

重んずる *omonzuru* [重い *omoi*]
確かめる *tashikameru* [確かだ *tashika da*]
清らかだ *kiyoraka da* [清い *kiyoi*]

3. Words that embed nouns:

春めく *harumeku* [春 *haru*]
男らしい *otokorashii* [男 *otoko*]
後ろめたい *ushirometai* [後ろ *ushiro*]

Alternatives: When there is no danger of misreading, the *okurigana* of parts of words other than the inflectional endings can be omitted, as shown by the forms in parentheses:

Examples:

生まれる(生れる) *umareru* 終わる(終る) *owaru*
当たる(当る) *ataru*

NOTE: The following words are not considered to embed the words shown in square brackets. Their *okurigana* conforms to General Rule 1.

明るい *akarui* [明ける *akeru*]
荒い *arai* [荒れる *areru*]
悔しい *kuyashii* [悔いる *kuiru*]
恋しい *koishii* [恋う *kou*]

3.1.2 Uninflected Words

GENERAL RULE 3

Standard Orthography: Nouns (except for those to which General Rule 4 applies) are not affixed with *okurigana*.

Examples:

山 *yama* 彼 *kare*

Exceptions: 1. The *okurigana* of the following words begins at their last syllables:

辺り	*atari*	便り	*tayori*
哀れ	*aware*	半ば	*nakaba*
勢い	*ikioi*	情け	*nasake*
幾ら	*ikura*	斜め	*naname*
後ろ	*ushiro*	独り	*hitori*
傍ら	*katawara*	誉れ	*homare*
幸い	*saiwai*	自ら	*mizukara*
幸せ	*shiawase*	災い	*wazawai*
互い	*tagai*		

2. The *okurigana* of nouns used for counting containing the syllable つ *tsu* begins at the つ:

Examples:

一つ	*hitotsu*	幾つ	*ikutsu*

GENERAL RULE 4

Standard Orthography: The *okurigana* of nouns derived from inflected words, and of nouns formed by adding suffixes such as さ *sa*, み *mi*, and げ *ge* to inflected words, conforms to the *okurigana* of the original words from which they are derived.

Examples:

1. Words derived from inflected words:

願い	*negai*	答え	*kotae*
当たり	*atari*	初め	*hajime*
向かい	*mukai*	遠く	*tōku*

2. Words suffixed with さ *sa*, み *mi*, げ *ge*, etc.:

正しさ	*tadashisa*	惜しげ	*oshige*
明るみ	*akarumi*		

Exceptions: *Okurigana* is not affixed to the following words:

印	*shirushi*	折	*ori*
恋	*koi*	係	*kakari*
次	*tsugi*	掛	*kakari*
話	*hanashi*	組	*kumi*
光	*hikari*		

NOTE: The word 組 *kumi* given above is the *kumi* used in such expressions as 花の組 *hana no kumi* ['bouquet of flowers'] and 赤の組 *aka no kumi* ['the red team']; it does not refer to cases like 活字の組みがゆるむ *katsuji no kumi ga yurumu* ['the setting of the type loosens']. This also applies to other similar words such as 光 *hikari*, 折 *ori*, and 係 *kakari*, for which this exception does not apply if the verbal sense is strong. Therefore, in such cases *okurigana* is affixed in accordance with the Standard Orthography.

Alternatives: When there is no danger of misreading, *okurigana* may be omitted, as shown by the forms in parentheses:

Examples:

届け(届)	*todoke*	問い(問)	*toi*
当たり(当り)	*atari*	祭り(祭)	*matsuri*
答え(答)	*kotae*		

GENERAL RULE 5

Standard Orthography: The *okurigana* of adverbs, uninflected adjectives, and conjunctions begins at their last syllables.

Examples:

少し	*sukoshi*	及び	*oyobi*
去る	*saru*	但し	*tadashi*

Exceptions: 1. The *okurigana* of the following words is affixed as shown:

明くる	*akuru*	並びに	*narabini*
大いに	*ōini*	若しくは	*moshikuwa*
直ちに	*tadachini*		

2. *Okurigana* is not affixed to the following word:

又 *mata*

3. The *okurigana* of words that are embedded in another word conforms to the *okurigana* of the embedded word. (The embedded word is shown in square brackets.)

Examples:

至って	*itatte* [至る *itaru*]
例えば	*tatoeba* [例える *tatoeru*]
少なくとも	*sukunakutomo* [少ない *sukunai*]
互いに	*tagai ni* [互い *tagai*]
必ずしも	*kanarazushimo* [必ず *kanarazu*]

3.2 Compound Words

GENERAL RULE 6

Standard Orthography: The *okurigana* of compound words (except for those to which General Rule 7 applies) is affixed to each kanji in conformity with the *okurigana* of the individual one-character words having the respective *on* and *kun* readings.

Examples:

1. Inflected words:

打ち合わせる	*uchiawaseru*	気軽だ	*kigaru da*
聞き苦しい	*kikigurushii*		

2. Uninflected words:

竹馬	*takeuma*	取り扱い	*toriatsukai*
後ろ姿	*ushirosugata*	申し込み	*mōshikomi*
落書き	*rakugaki*	長生き	*nagaiki*
落ち葉	*ochiba*	常常	*tsunezune*
売り上げ	*uriage*	休み休み	*yasumiyasumi*
呼び出し電話	*yobidashi-denwa*		

Alternatives: When there is no danger of misreading, *okurigana* may be omitted, as shown by the forms in parentheses:

Examples:

打ち合わせる(打ち合せる・打合せる)	*uchiawaseru*
聞き苦しい(聞苦しい)	*kikigurushii*
取り扱い(取扱い・取扱)	*toriatsukai*
申し込み(申込み・申込)	*mōshikomi*
呼び出し電話(呼出し電話・呼出電話)	*yobidashi-denwa*

NOTE: In words such as こけら落とし (こけら落し) *kokeraotoshi,* さび止め *sabidome,* 洗いざらし *araizarashi,* and 打ちひも *uchihimo,* whose first or second parts are written in kana, the *okurigana* of the remaining part conforms to that of the corresponding one-character word.

GENERAL RULE 7

Of the compound words, the following types of nouns are written without *okurigana* in conformity with popular usage.

Examples:

1. Words used in specific fields whose orthography is considered to be fixed by popular usage:

(*a*) Titles indicating rank, status, managerial position, etc.:

関取	*sekitori*	取締役	*torishimariyaku*

(*b*) Words used for names of craftworks, such as 織 *ori* ['woven fabric, brocade'], 染 *zome* ['dyed fabric'], and 塗 *nuri* ['lacquered product']:

((博多))織	*hakataori*	((鎌倉))彫	*kamakurabori*
((型絵))染	*kataezome*	((備前))焼	*bizen'yaki*
((春慶))塗	*shunkeinuri*		

(*c*) Others:

書留	*kakitome*	繰越(金)	*kurikoshikin*
両替	*ryōgae*	乗換(駅)	*norikaeeki*
組合	*kumiai*	乗組(員)	*norikumiin*
作付面積	*sakutsuke-menseki*	待合(室)	*machiaishitsu*
売上(高)	*uriagedaka*	申込(書)	*mōshikomisho*

2. In general, words whose orthography is considered to be fixed by popular usage:

字引	*jibiki*	建物	*tatemono*
日付	*hizuke*	受付	*uketsuke*
役割	*yakuwari*	受取	*uketori*
貸家	*kashiya*	絵巻物	*emakimono*

NOTE: 1. This General Rule applies to the words appearing above in the form ((博多))織 *hakataori,* ((売上))高 *uriagedaka,* etc., even if the part enclosed in double parentheses is replaced by other kanji.

2. The items above to which General Rule 7 applies are only examples, not an exhaustive list. Therefore, this rule shall apply by analogy to other words of a similar kind whose orthography is considered to be fixed by popular usage. When it is difficult to determine whether General Rule 7 applies, General Rule 6 takes precedence.

3.3 Words in Appendix

The *okurigana* of the following "problem words" appearing in the appendix to the Jōyō Kanji list is affixed as shown below:

1. The *okurigana* of the following words is affixed as shown:

浮つく	*uwatsuku*	立ち退く	*tachinoku*
お巡りさん	*omawarisan*	手伝う	*tetsudau*
差し支える	*sashitsukaeru*	最寄り	*moyori*
五月晴れ	*satsukibare*		

The *okurigana* of the following words may be omitted, as shown by the forms in parentheses:

差し支える(差支える)	*sashitsukaeru*
五月晴れ(五月晴)	*satsukibare*
立ち退く(立退く)	*tachinoku*

2. *Okurigana* is not affixed to the following words:

息吹	*ibuki*	築山	*tsukiyama*	吹雪	*fubuki*
桟敷	*sajiki*	名残	*nagori*	迷子	*maigo*
時雨	*shigure*	雪崩	*nadare*	行方	*yukue*

APPENDIX 6

THE RADICALS

1. History and Background

The traditional method of ordering entries in Chinese and Japanese character dictionaries is known as the **radical system**. This system is based on a table of 214 elements (plus about 150 variants) called **radicals**. A radical is a frequently recurring graphic component used for classifying characters into groups sharing a common element. The radicals are listed in increasing order of their stroke-counts. Characters sharing the same radical are further grouped in increasing order of the stroke-counts of their *nonradical* elements.

The radical broadly suggests the area of meaning of the character, and is often related to the character's etymology. For example, 木 'tree; wood' is found in many characters designating the names of trees or wooden objects, e.g., 梅 *bai* 'plum tree'. Often, however, the radical is merely an element used for classification purposes and is unrelated to the character's meaning, e.g., 寸 in the characters 対 and 将.

The radical system was first introduced some 1900 years ago in the well-known Chinese classic dictionary 説文解字 *setsumon kaiji* (Chinese: *shuowen jiezi*), in which the characters were classified under 540 categories. In 1716, a comprehensive character dictionary called 康熙字典 *kōki jiten* (Chinese: *kangxi zidian*) was published in China, reducing the number of radicals to 214. The latter has served as a model for all later character dictionaries, and the radical system it introduced is still in use as the most widespread scheme of lexicographic classification today.

The original forms of the 214 traditional radicals are referred to here as the **standard** or **parent form**. A radical may also have one or more **variant forms** of considerably different shape and/or stroke-count. For example, 氵 is a three-stroke variant of the four-stroke 'water' radical 水 (Radical 85). On the other hand, the difference between some variants is merely a slight difference in proportion. For example, the standard form 弓 of Radical 57 (as in 彎) has the left-side variant 弓 (as in 弾).

The position of many radicals is constant in relation to the other elements of the character. Traditionally, the radicals are classified into categories according to their position within the character, as shown in the table below:

Types of Radicals

偏	*hen*	left	亻 in 使
旁	*tsukuri*	right	欠 in 欧
冠	*kanmuri*	top	宀 in 定
脚	*ashi*	bottom	儿 in 兄
垂	*tare*	top-left	广 in 広
繞	*nyō*	left-bottom	廴 in 廷
構	*kamae*	enclosure	門 in 問

The radical system is complex and difficult to master. One problem is that the simplification of the characters that took place with the introduction of the Tōyō Kanji and Jōyō Kanji lists in the postwar period has resulted in the disappearance of the radical element from some characters. For example, 並 is traditionally classified under 立 (Radical 157) based on its old form 竝, but the element 立 has completely disappeared from the abbreviated form 並. (The traditional radical of these "lost-radical" characters can be determined by looking the character up in the **Radical Index.**)

Another problem is that some characters include several radical elements and one must choose between them. For example, 副 consists of four elements, all of which are radicals (see SYSTEM OF KANJI INDEXING BY PATTERNS **§1.1.1 The Radical System** for details). Because of these difficulties, determining which element of a character is the radical can be a laborious task. Some useful guidelines can be found in **§4. How to Determine the Radical** on p. 1931.

Despite these problems, the time-honored radical system, which is still in widespread use today, is important and should be learned by the serious student. A knowledge of radicals is useful for looking up characters in dictionaries and reference works based on the radical system, and helps the learner understand character etymology.

2. Radical Chart

The **Radical Chart** below gives a full list of radical forms, variants, names, and cross-references. It includes the following information:

1. **Radical** The **radicals** and their **variant forms** are listed in increasing order of the stroke-counts of their standard forms, and are numbered consecutively from 1 to 214 according to the traditional historical arrangement. The **radical number** is a serial number assigned to each radical that is widely used in character dictionaries and reference works for identification. The left part of the **Radical** column gives the radical number; the right part gives the radical. Note that the radical and radical number for each entry character appear in the main part of the dictionary (see GUIDE **§7.2 Radical**).

2. **Radical Name** When talking about the components of Chinese characters it is convenient to describe them by naming their constituent radicals. For example, we can say that 洋 consists of *sanzui* (the 'water' radical) on the left and *hitsuji* (the 'sheep' radical) on the right. Most radicals have well-established names in Japanese. The left part of the **Radical Name** column gives the romanized version of the most common name in Japanese; the right part gives the name in Japanese script.[1] If a radical has more than one name, the less common one appears after a comma.

The words "variant not used as radical" sometimes appear in this column. This indicates a variant used only as an independent character but not as a radical in its own right. For example, 竜 *ryū* is an independent character meaning 'dragon', but as a radical it always appears in its full form 龍.

3. **English Name** Some common radicals, such as 水 the 'water' radical, have well-established names in English, but many others are called by different names in different works. The names appearing in the **English Name** column are based primarily on tradition, where such tradition exists, and on the meaning and/or function of the radical as a character-building element.

4. **Standard and Variant Forms** The **Form** column indicates if the radical is a **standard form** or a **variant form.** If it is a variant form, it shows the position in which it normally appears within the character, as explained below:

Standard	parent radical in its full traditional form (心 in 必) (this form may appear in various positions)
Left	variant normally appearing on the left (忄 in 情)
Right	variant normally appearing on the right (刂 in 削)
Top	variant normally appearing at the top (山 in 岩)
Bottom	variant normally appearing at the bottom (⺗ in 慕)
Enclosure	variant normally enclosing the remainder of the character (戸 in 戻)
Variant	variant appearing in a position other than the above (羽 in 習)

For a given radical, the standard form appears first, followed by its variants. Although the original forms are called "standard," it should be noted that some variants are more common than their standard forms. For example, 辶 (Radical 162) is now the common form while the original 辵 is never used.

5. **Number** The **Number** column indicates the **entry number** where the radical appears as an entry character in the body of the dictionary. That entry includes the RADICAL section, which gives further information about the radical, such as a description of its meaning and function, and examples of characters in which the standard and variant forms appear as a radical. See **GUIDE §8. RADICAL Section** for details.

---

1. Japanese radical names are often written in hiragana. As far as we know, this is the first list of radical names in their full kana-kanji "spellings."

RADICAL CHART

Radical		Radical Name		English Name	Form	Number
1 STROKE						
1	一	ichi	一	one	standard	3341
2	丨	bō	棒	downstroke	standard	3343
3	丶	ten	点	dot	standard	3344
4	丿	no	ノ	left stroke	standard	3345
	ノ	no	ノ		top	3346
5	乙	otsu	乙	hook	standard	3339
	㇄	re	レ		variant	3340
6	亅	hanebō	撥棒	hooked stroke	standard	3347
2 STROKES						
7	二	ni	二	two	standard	1922
8	亠	nabebuta	鍋蓋	lid	standard	3363
9	人	hito	人	person	standard	3368
	亻	ninben	人偏		left	3373
	𠆢	hitoyane	人屋根		top	3374
10	儿	ninnyō, hitoashi	人繞，人足	legs	standard	4
11	入	iru	入	enter	standard	3370
12	八	hachigashira	八頭	eight	standard	2928
	八	hachi	八		variant	3
	丷	hachigashira	八頭		top	2
13	冂	keigamae	冂構	border	standard	3352
14	冖	wakanmuri	ワ冠	cover	standard	3353
15	冫	nisui	二水	ice	standard	1923
16	几	tsukue	机，几	table	standard	3349
	𠘨	kazagamae	風構		enclosure	3354
17	凵	kannyō, ukebako	凵繞，受け箱	receptacle	standard	3364
18	刀	katana	刀	sword	standard	2926
	刂	rittō	立刀		right	1
19	力	chikara	力	strength	standard	3371
20	勹	tsutsumigamae	包構	wrap	standard	3375
21	匕	sajinohi	ヒのヒ	spoon	standard	2925
22	匚	hakogamae	匚構	box	standard	3355
23	匸	kakushigamae	隠構，匸構	enclose	standard	3356
	匸	kakushigamae	隠構，匸構		enclosure	—
24	十	jū	十	ten	standard	3365
	十	jūhen	十偏		left	3366
25	卜	bokunoto	トのト	divine	standard	3367
26	卩	fushizukuri	節旁	seal	standard	3357
	㔾	fushizukuri	節旁		variant	3358
27	厂	gandare	雁垂	cliff	standard	3359

Radical		Radical Name		English Name	Form	Number
28	厶	mu	厶	oneself	standard	3376
29	又	mata	又	right hand	standard	3361
	又	mata	又		variant	3351
			3 STROKES			
30	口	kuchi	口	mouth	standard	3382
	口	kuchihen	口偏		left	—
31	囗	kunigamae	国構	enclosure	standard	3391
32	土	tsuchi	土	earth	standard	3403
	土	tsuchihen	土偏		left	—
33	士	samurai	士	knight	standard	3405
34	夂	fuyugashira	冬頭	descend	standard	3392
35	夊	suinyō	夊繞	move slowly	standard	3393
	夂	natsuashi	夏脚		bottom	—
36	夕	yūbe	夕	evening	standard	3387
37	大	ōkii, dai	大	big	standard	3416
	大	ōkii, dai	大		top	3423
38	女	onna	女	woman	standard	3418
	女	onnahen	女偏		left	3424
39	子	ko	子	child	standard	3390
40	宀	ukanmuri	ウ冠	roof	standard	3425
41	寸	sun	寸	inch	standard	2935
42	小	chiisai	小	small	standard	7
	⺌	naogashira	尚頭		top	5
	⺍	tsu	ツ		top	—
43	尢	mageashi	曲足	lame	standard	2937
44	尸	shikabane	尸	corpse	standard	3389
45	屮	tetsu	屮	sprout	standard	3412
46	山	yama	山	mountain	standard	2940
	山	yamahen	山偏		left	—
	山	yamakanmuri	山冠		top	—
47	巛	magarigawa	曲がり川	river	standard	9
	川	sanbongawa	三本川		variant	6
48	工	takumi	工	work	standard	3381
	工	takumihen	工偏		left	—
49	己	onore	己	self	standard	3380
	巳	mi	巳		variant	3388
50	巾	haba	幅	cloth	standard	3409
51	干	hosu	干	shield	standard	3379
52	幺	itogashira	糸頭	tiny	standard	3426
53	广	madare	麻垂	roof	standard	3427
54	廴	ennyō	延繞	proceed	standard	3394
	廴	ennyō	延繞		enclosure	3395
55	廾	nijūashi	廿脚	clasp hands	standard	3413
56	弋	shikigamae	式構	spike	standard	3422

Radical		Radical Name		English Name	Form	Number
57	弓	yumi	弓	bow	standard	3383
	弓	yumihen	弓偏		left	—
58	彐	keigashira	彐頭	pig's head	standard	3396
	ヨ	keigashira	彐頭		variant	3397
	彑	keigashira	彐頭		variant	3407
59	彡	sanzukuri	彡旁	decoration	standard	1927
60	彳	gyōninben	行人偏	locomotion	standard	1928
4 STROKES						
61	心	kokoro	心	heart	standard	11
	忄	risshinben	立心偏		left	8
	㣺	shitagokoro	下心		bottom	12
62	戈	kanohoko	戈	spear	standard	3462
63	戶	tobiranoto	扉の戸	door	standard	2950
	戸	tobiranoto	扉の戸		enclosure	1930
64	手	te	手	hand	standard	3456
	扌	tehen	手偏		left	3414
65	支	shinyō, jūmata	支繞，十又	branch	standard	1980
	支	shinyō, jūmata	支繞，十又		right	1979
66	攴	bokuzukuri, tomata	攴旁，攴	strike	standard	1981
	攵	nobun	ノ文		right	1985
67	文	bun, bunnyō	文，文繞	pattern	standard	1966
	文	bun, bunnyō	文，文繞		variant	1962
68	斗	tomasu	斗	measure	standard	2953
69	斤	ono	斧	ax	standard	2949
70	方	kata	方	square	standard	1963
71	无	munyō	无繞	without	standard	3443
	旡	sudenotsukuri	既の旁		right	3444
	旡	sudenotsukuri	既の旁		right	3487
72	日	hi	日	sun	standard	3028
	日	hi	日		variant	3027
73	曰	hirabi	平日	say	standard	3025
	曰	hirabi	平日		variant	3026
74	月	tsuki	月	moon	standard	2959
	月	tsuki	月		variant	2956
	月	tsuki	月		variant	2957
75	木	ki	木	tree	standard	3450
	木	kihen	木偏		left	—
76	欠	akubi	欠伸	yawn	standard	1987
77	止	tomeru	止	stop	standard	2941
	止	tomehen	止偏		left	—
78	歹	gatsuhen	歹偏	death	standard	3445
79	殳	rumata, hokozukuri	ル又，殳旁	club	standard	1978
80	毋	haha, nakare	母	mother	standard	3446
	毌	haha, nakare	母		variant	3447

Radical		Radical Name		English Name	Form	Number
	母	variant not used as radical				3475
81	比	kuraberu, hi	比	compare	standard	26
82	毛	ke	毛	hair	standard	3453
83	氏	uji	氏	family name	standard	2951
84	气	kigamae	気構	vapor	standard	1986
85	水	mizu	水	water	standard	10
	氵	sanzui	三水		left	1925
	氺	shitamizu	下水		bottom	37
86	火	hi	火	fire	standard	3463
	灬	rekka	烈火		bottom	13
87	爪	tsume	爪	claw	standard	3024
	爫	notsu	ノツ		top	1934
	爫	tsumekanmuri	爪冠		top	1935
88	父	chichi	父	father	standard	1975
	父	variant not used as radical				1973
89	爻	meme	メメ	crisscross	standard	1988
	爻	meme	メメ		variant	1989
90	爿	shōhen	爿偏	stand	standard	3468
91	片	kata	片	board	standard	3461
92	牙	kiba	牙	sharp tooth	standard	3435
	牙	kiba	牙		left	3488
93	牛	ushi	牛	cattle	standard	3452
	牜	ushihen	牛偏		left	3458
94	犬	inu	犬	dog	standard	3464
	犭	kemonohen	獣偏		left	3428
5 STROKES						
95	玄	gen	玄	dark	standard	1991
96	玉	tama	玉	gem	standard	3477
	王	tamahen	玉偏		left	3448
97	瓜	uri	瓜	gourd	standard	3038
98	瓦	kawara	瓦	tile	standard	3476
99	甘	amai	甘	sweet	standard	3494
100	生	umareru	生	birth	standard	3497
101	用	mochiiru	用	use	standard	2976
102	田	ta	田	field	standard	3041
103	疋	hiki	疋	animal counter	standard	3480
	⺪	hikihen	疋偏		left	3489
104	疒	yamaidare	病垂	illness	standard	3512
105	癶	hatsugashira	発頭	spread legs	standard	40
106	白	shiro	白	white	standard	3493
107	皮	kegawa	毛皮	skin	standard	3037
108	皿	sara	皿	dish	standard	3474
109	目	me	目	eye	standard	3043
110	矛	hoko	矛	lance	standard	2008

Radical		Radical Name		English Name	Form	Number
111	矢	ya	矢	arrow	standard	2009
	矢	yahen	矢偏		left	—
112	石	ishi	石	stone	standard	2971
	石	ishihen	石偏		left	—
113	示	shimesu	示	deity	standard	1936
	ネ	nehen, shimesuhen	ネ偏，示偏		left	3469
	示	shimesuhen	示偏		left	—
114	内	gūnoashi	禺脚	track	standard	3470
115	禾	nogi	ノ木	growing grain	standard	3503
	禾	nogihen	ノ木偏		left	—
116	穴	ana	穴	hole	standard	2161
	穴	anakanmuri	穴冠		top	2160
	穴	variant not used as radical				2159
117	立	tatsu	立	stand	standard	1992
	立	tatsuhen	立偏		left	—
6 STROKES						
118	竹	take	竹	bamboo	standard	228
	⺮	takekanmuri	竹冠		top	229
119	米	kome	米	rice	standard	3529
	米	komehen	米偏		left	—
120	糸	ito	糸	thread	standard	2179
	糸	itohen	糸偏		left	—
121	缶	hotogi	缶	earthenware	standard	2032
122	网	amigashira	網頭	net	standard	2988
	罒	yonkashira	四頭		top	3045
	罒	yonkashira	四頭		top	1977
123	羊	hitsuji	羊	sheep	standard	2183
	𦍌	hitsujikanmuri	羊冠		top	2184
	𦍌	hitsujihen	羊偏		left	—
124	羽	hane	羽	wing	standard	227
	羽	hane	羽		variant	226
125	老	oi	老	old person	standard	3197
	耂	oikanmuri, oigashira	老冠，老頭		top	3471
126	而	shikashite	而して	beard	standard	2027
127	耒	raisuki	耒	plow	standard	3532
	耒	raihen	来偏		left	—
	耒	sukihen	耒偏		left	—
128	耳	mimi	耳	ear	standard	3516
	耳	mimihen	耳偏		left	—
129	聿	fudezukuri	筆旁	brush	standard	3533
130	肉	niku	肉	flesh	standard	3200
	月	nikuzuki	肉月		variant	2958
131	臣	shin	臣	retainer	standard	2991
	臣	shin	臣		left	3068

Radical		Radical Name		English Name	Form	Number
132	自	mizukara	自	self	standard	3525
133	至	itaru	至	arrive	standard	2182
134	臼	usu	臼	mortar	standard	3528
	臼	usu	臼		variant	845
135	舌	shita	舌	tongue	standard	2186
	舌	shitahen	舌偏		left	—
136	舛	masu	舛	dancing	standard	205
	舛	maiashi	舞脚		bottom	237
137	舟	fune	舟	ship	standard	3538
	舟	funehen	舟偏		left	—
138	艮	kon, ushitora	艮	northeast	standard	3517
	艮	kon, ushitora	艮		variant	—
139	色	iro	色	color	standard	2029
	色	irozukuri	色旁		right	—
140	艸	kusa	草	plants	standard	209
	艹	kusakanmuri	草冠		top	3415
	艹	kusakanmuri	草冠		top	24
	艹	kusakanmuri	草冠		top	29
141	虍	torakanmuri	虎冠	tiger	standard	3198
142	虫	mushi	虫	bug	standard	3530
	虫	mushihen	虫偏		left	—
143	血	chi	血	blood	standard	3526
	血	chihen	血偏		left	—
144	行	gyō	行	road	standard	212
	行	gyōgamae	行構		enclosure	213
145	衣	koromo	衣	clothes	standard	2013
	衤	koromohen	衣偏		left	3513
	𧘇	koromo	衣		variant	2017
146	襾	nishi	西	cover	standard	3522
	覀	nishi	西		top	3523
	西	variant not used as radical				3520
7 STROKES						
147	見	miru	見	see	standard	2544
148	角	tsuno	角	horn	standard	2047
	角	tsunohen	角偏		left	—
149	言	kotoba	言葉	speech	standard	1941
	訁	gonben	言偏		left	—
150	谷	tani	谷	valley	standard	2043
	谷	tanihen	谷偏		left	—
151	豆	mame	豆	ritual vessel	standard	1943
	豆	mamehen	豆偏		left	—
152	豕	inoko	豕	pig	standard	3543
	豕	inokohen	豕偏		variant	—
153	豸	mujina	貉	wild animal	standard	2401

Radical		Radical Name		English Name	Form	Number
154	貝	kai	貝	cowry	standard	2543
	貝	kaihen	貝偏		variant	—
155	赤	aka	赤	red	standard	2193
	赤	akahen	赤偏		left	—
156	走	hashiru	走	run	standard	2194
	走	sōnyō	走繞		enclosure	2195
157	足	ashi	足	foot	standard	2188
	𧾷	ashihen	足偏		left	2191
158	身	mi	身	body	standard	3553
	身	mihen	身偏		left	—
159	車	kuruma	車	vehicle	standard	3552
	車	kurumahen	車偏		left	—
160	辛	karai	辛	acrid	standard	2038
	辛	karai	辛		left	—
161	辰	shinnotatsu	辰の辰	the Dragon	standard	2992
162	辵	shinnyō, shinnyū	之繞	advance	standard	1945
	辶	shinnyō, shinnyū	之繞		enclosure	1926
	辶	shinnyō, shinnyū	之繞		enclosure	1932
163	邑	mura	邑	city	standard	2190
	阝	ōzato	大里		right	3398
164	酉	hiyominotori	日読みの酉	wine	standard	3544
	酉	torihen	酉偏		left	—
165	釆	nogome	ノ米	separate	standard	3555
	釆	nogomehen	ノ米偏		left	—
166	里	sato	里	hamlet	standard	3542
	里	satohen	里偏		left	—
		8 STROKES				
167	金	kane	金	metal	standard	2057
	金	kanehen	金偏		left	—
168	長	nagai	長	long	standard	2556
	镸	nagai	長		left	2550
169	門	mon, mongamae	門，門構	gate	standard	888
170	阜	gifunofu	岐阜の阜	mound	standard	2628
	阝	kozatohen	阜偏		left	3399
171	隶	reizukuri	隷旁	capture	standard	3569
172	隹	furutori	隹	small bird	standard	3566
173	雨	ame	雨	rain	standard	3561
	⻗	amekanmuri	雨冠		top	3562
174	青	ao	青	blue	standard	2431
	青	ao	青		variant	2430
175	非	arazu	非	not	standard	889

Radical		Radical Name		English Name	Form	Number
9 STROKES						
176	面	men	面	face	standard	2087
177	革	kawa	革	rawhide	standard	2448
	革	kawahen	革偏		left	—
178	韋	nameshigawa	鞣革	leather	standard	2268
	韋	nameshigawa	鞣革		variant	2287
179	韭	nira	韭	leek	standard	3574
180	音	oto	音	sound	standard	1948
	音	oto	音		variant	2070
181	頁	ōgai	大貝	head	standard	2086
182	風	kaze	風	wind	standard	3007
	風	kaze	風		left	—
183	飛	tobu	飛	fly	standard	3572
184	食	shoku	食	food	standard	2077
	飠	shokuhen	食偏		left	2061
	食	shokuhen	食偏		left	2076
	食	shoku	食		variant	2075
185	首	kubi	首	neck	standard	2265
186	香	nioikō	匂い香	fragrance	standard	2568
10 STROKES						
187	馬	uma	馬	horse	standard	3296
	馬	umahen	馬偏		left	—
188	骨	hone	骨	bone	standard	2654
	骨	honehen	骨偏		left	—
189	高	takai	高	high	standard	2097
190	髟	kamikanmuri	髪冠	hair	standard	1464
191	鬥	tōgamae	闘構	fight	standard	1165
192	鬯	chō	鬯	fragrant wine	standard	2758
193	鬲	kaku	鬲	ritual tripod	standard	1951
	鬲	kaku	鬲		variant	—
194	鬼	oni	鬼	ghost	standard	2657
	鬼	kinyō	鬼繞		enclosure	—
11 STROKES						
195	魚	uo	魚	fish	standard	2127
	魚	uohen	魚偏		left	—
196	鳥	tori	鳥	bird	standard	3312
	鳥	tori	鳥		right	—
197	鹵	ro	鹵	salt	standard	2125
198	鹿	shika	鹿	deer	standard	3126
199	麥	baku	麦	wheat	standard	2767
	麦	bakunyō	麦繞		enclosure	2766
	麦	variant not used as radical				2408

Radical		Radical Name		English Name	Form	Number
200	麻	asa	麻	hemp	standard	3130
	麻	asakanmuri	麻冠		enclosure	3129
	麻	asakanmuri	麻冠		enclosure	—
	麻	variant not used as radical				3125
12 STROKES						
201	黃	kiiro	黄色	yellow	standard	2487
	黄	variant not used as radical				2468
202	黍	kibi	黍	millet	standard	2597
203	黑	kuroi	黒	black	standard	2787
	黒	kuroi	黒		variant	2740
204	黹	futsu	黹	embroidery	standard	2605
13 STROKES						
205	黽	ben	黽	frog	standard	3584
206	鼎	kanae	鼎	ritual cauldron	standard	3585
207	鼓	tsuzumi	鼓	drum	standard	1786
208	鼠	nezumi	鼠	rat	standard	2693
	鼠	nezuminyō	鼠繞		enclosure	—
14 STROKES						
209	鼻	hana	鼻	nose	standard	2707
	鼻	hanahen	鼻偏		left	—
	鼻	variant not used as radical				2706
210	齊	sei	斉	uniform	standard	2142
	斉	sei	斉		variant	2054
15 STROKES						
211	齒	ha	歯	tooth	standard	2516
	齒	hahen	歯偏		left	—
	歯	hahen	歯偏		left	—
	歯	ha	歯		variant	2476
16 STROKES						
212	龍	tatsu	竜	dragon	standard	1801
	竜	variant not used as radical				2099
	龍	variant not used as radical				1800
213	龜	kame	亀	tortoise	standard	2147
	龜	kame	亀		variant	2150
	亀	variant not used as radical				2128
17 STROKES						
214	龠	yaku	龠	flute	standard	2149

APPENDIX 7

HISTORICAL TABLES

This appendix presents various historical tables, such as the signs of the zodiac and the calendar signs, which are useful for reading historical texts and for general reference.

1. The Signs of the Oriental Zodiac

The 十二支 *jūnishi,* literally 'the twelve branches', is an ancient set of twelve symbols that were formerly used to indicate time and direction. Later, the symbols became associated with the names of animals and began to be used as a system of divination similar to the signs of the zodiac used in Western astrology. In this dictionary, the 十二支 is referred to as **the signs of the Oriental zodiac.**

The twelve signs were marked on a circle clockwise beginning with 子 *ne* 'the Rat', and were used to designate time in two-hour intervals. For example, 午の刻 *uma no koku* indicates "the hour of the Horse" (from 11 a.m. to 1 p.m.). Each sign was also associated with a direction and a month of the year, as shown in the charts below.

The Signs of the Oriental Zodiac

Sign	Entry No.	Reading		English	Time	Direction	Month
		On	*Kun*				
1 子	3390	*shi*	*ne*	the Rat	11 p.m.-1 a.m.	north	November
2 丑	3433	*chū*	*ushi*	the Ox	1-3 a.m.	NNE	December
3 寅	2289	*in*	*tora*	the Tiger	3-5 a.m.	ENE	January
4 卯	199	*bō*	*u*	the Hare	5-7 a.m.	east	February
5 辰	2992	*shin*	*tatsu*	the Dragon	7-9 a.m.	ESE	March
6 巳	3388	*shi*	*mi*	the Serpent	9-11 a.m.	SSE	April
7 午	1984	*go*	*uma*	the Horse	11 a.m.-1 p.m.	south	May
8 未	3506	*bi*	*hitsuji*	the Ram	1-3 p.m.	SSW	June
9 申	3507	*shin*	*saru*	the Monkey	3-5 p.m.	WSW	July
10 酉	3544	*yū*	*tori*	the Bird	5-7 p.m.	west	August
11 戌	3535	*jutsu*	*inu*	the Dog	7-9 p.m.	WNW	September
12 亥	2012	*gai*	*i*	the Boar	9-11 p.m.	NNW	October

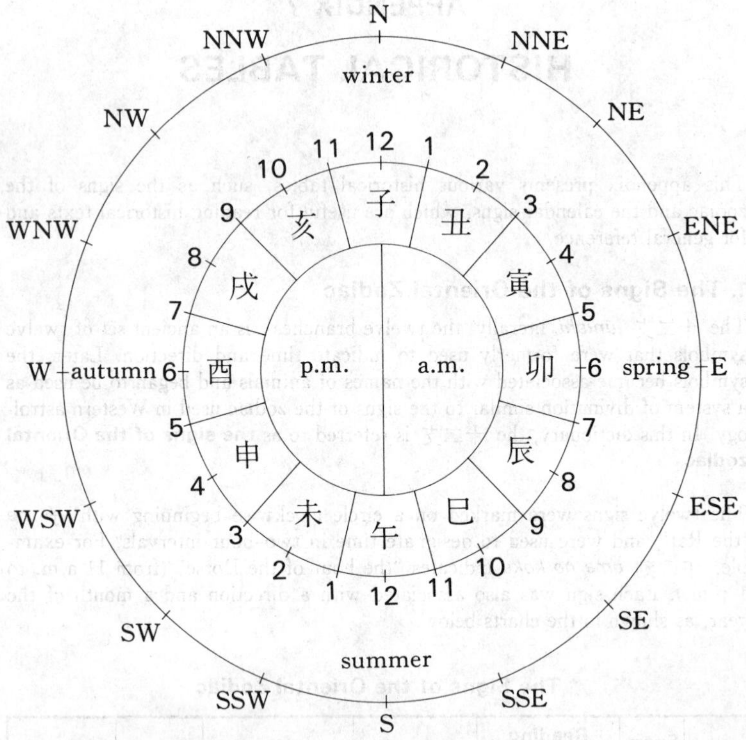

Formerly, the twelve signs were used as the basis of various methods of divination. They are still used today to designate the names of years. 1989, for example, is the Year of the Serpent, and the Serpent is believed to be the guardian angel of those born in that year. Another important use of the twelve signs is in conjunction with the ten calendar signs to form the sixty combinations of the sexagenary cycle (see below).

2. The Five Elements

The ancient Chinese believed that all the things in the universe are composed of five elements (wood, fire, earth, metal, and water), called 五行 *gogyō*, that interact with the two opposing forces, *yin* (陰) and *yang* (陽), the passive and active principles in Chinese dualistic philosophy. Each element is associated with a direction, time, planet, body organ, sound, etc.

The Five Elements

Element	Entry No.	Reading		English
		On	*Kun*	
木	3450	*moku*	*ki*	wood
火	3463	*ka*	*hi*	fire
土	3403	*do*	*tsuchi*	earth
金	2057	*gon*	*kane*	metal
水	10	*sui*	*mizu*	water

The five elements are used to designate the names of the planets, i.e., 木星 *mokusei* Jupiter, 火星 *kasei* Mars, 土星 *dosei* Saturn, 金星 *kinsei* Venus, and 水星 *suisei* Mercury. They are also used along with the names for the sun (日 *nichi*) and the moon (月 *getsu*) to form the names of the days of the week:

日曜日	*nichiyōbi*	Sunday
月曜日	*getsuyōbi*	Monday
火曜日	*kayōbi*	Tuesday
水曜日	*suiyōbi*	Wednesday
木曜日	*mokuyōbi*	Thursday
金曜日	*kin'yōbi*	Friday
土曜日	*doyōbi*	Saturday

Another important use of the five elements is to form the names of the ten calendar signs.

3. The Ten Calendar Signs

The 十干 *jikkan,* literally 'the ten stems', is an ancient Chinese set of ten symbols formerly used in conjunction with the twelve signs of the zodiac to form the sixty combinations of the sexagenary cycle (see below). Today, their chief use, especially of the first four, is as ordinal numbers to indicate grade or rank, as for example in the word 甲種 *kōshu* 'grade A, first grade'.

The ten calendar signs have two sets of names in Japanese. The first uses the *on* readings of the characters, as shown in the chart below. The second is formed by combining the five elements with the two forces, *yin* and *yang*, which are represented by 兄 *e* 'older brother' and 弟 *to* 'younger brother'. For example, 甲 *kinoe* 'wood-*yang*' derives from the first element 木 *ki* combined with *yang* represented by 兄 *e*.

The Ten Calendar Signs

Sign	Entry No.	Reading		Ranking
		On	*Kun*	
1 甲	3481	*kō*	*kinoe*	first
2 乙	3339	*otsu*	*kinoto*	second
3 丙	3479	*hei*	*hinoe*	third
4 丁	3348	*tei*	*hinoto*	fourth
5 戊	3535	*bo*	*tsuchinoe*	fifth
6 己	3380	*ki*	*tsuchinoto*	sixth
7 庚	—	*kō*	*kanoe*	seventh
8 辛	2038	*shin*	*kanoto*	eighth
9 壬	—	*jin*	*mizunoe*	ninth
10 癸	—	*ki*	*mizunoto*	tenth

4. The Sexagenary Cycle

The ancient Chinese had a calendar system based on the 十干 and 十二支 described above, which was used in both China and Japan to count days, months, and years in cycles of sixty. Called 干支 *kanshi* or *eto* in Japanese, the system is usually referred to as the sexagenary cycle in English. By combining the two sets of symbols a total of sixty two-character combinations is obtained. For example, the third calendar sign 丙 *hinoe* is combined with the eleventh zodiac sign 戌 *inu* to give 丙戌 *hinoe inu* 'fire-*yang* dog', the 23rd unit in the cycle. The combinations may also be read in their *on* readings, as for example 丙戌 *heijutsu*.

5. The Pentatonic Scale

Traditional Chinese and Japanese music is based on a scale consisting of five notes, called 五音 *goin* in Japanese or pentatonic scale in English. Each note corresponds to one of the five elements.

The Pentatonic Scale

Note	Entry No.	Reading	Musical Value	Element
宮	2274	*kyū*	C	土
商	2116	*shō*	D	金
角	2047	*kaku*	E	木
徵	683	*chi*	G	火
羽	226	*u*	A	水

APPENDIX 8

ABBREVIATIONS OF PLACE NAMES

This appendix lists one-character abbreviations of foreign place names, especially country names, in alphabetical order of their English equivalents. 独 *doku*, for example, is an abbreviation for "Germany" and is commonly used in such compound words as 日独 *nichidoku* 'Japan and Germany'. Abbreviations in common use are marked by an asterisk after the character. Others are less common or only rarely used. Each place name is followed by the **entry number** for the character or by a dash if that character is not listed in the dictionary. See also GUIDE **§ 20.11.4 Abbreviations.**

阿	*a*	Africa	346
米*	*bei*	America	3529
亜	*a*	Argentina	3540
亜*	*a*	Asia	3540
豪*	*gō*	Australia	2140
墺	*ō*	Austria	—
白	*haku*	Belgium	3493
伯	*haku*	Brazil	59
勃	*botsu*	Bulgaria	—
緬	*men*	Burma	1390
加*	*ka*	California	38
加	*ka*	Canada	38
智	*chi*	Chile	2784
中*	*chū*	China	3451
漢	*kan*	China	657
埃	*ai*	Egypt	—
英*	*ei*	England	2238
欧*	*ō*	Europe	887
仏*	*futsu*	France	19
独*	*doku*	Germany	395
希	*ki*	Greece	2049
蘭*	*ran*	Holland	2383
香	*kō*	Hong Kong	2568
洪	*kō*	Hungary	386
印*	*in*	India	828
伊*	*i*	Italy	49
日*	*nichi*	Japan	3027
邦	*hō*	Japan	847
和*	*wa*	Japan	1130
倭	*wa*	Japan	—
猶	*yū*	Judea	619
鮮	*sen*	Korea	1877
朝	*chō*	North Korea	1695
韓*	*kan*	South Korea	1757
満	*man*	Manchuria	607
墨	*boku*	Mexico	2753
蒙	*mō*	Mongolia	2505
諾	*daku*	Norway	1568
比*	*hi*	Philippines	26
波	*po*	Poland	330
葡	*po, ho*	Portugal	—
普	*fu*	Prussia	2323
露*	*ro*	Russia	2818
西*	*sei*	Spain	3520
瑞	*zui*	Sweden	1027
瑞	*zui*	Switzerland	1027
台*	*tai*	Taiwan	2005
泰	*tai*	Thailand	2583
蔵	*zō*	Tibet	2364
土	*to*	Turkey	3403
越	*etsu*	Vietnam	3314

APPENDIX 9

CORE MEANINGS ARRANGED BY FREQUENCY

This appendix lists all main entry characters in order of frequency of occurrence along with their core meanings for ready reference. The **core meaning** is a concise keyword that defines the most dominant character meaning. The **frequency** is a number that expresses the relative frequency of occurence of a character in Modern Japanese.[1]

This appendix could be highly useful to both student and teacher in at least three ways: (1) it enables the student of kanji to know the relative importance of each character, (2) it helps the developer of teaching materials compile graded lessons, and (3) it enables the student to review the core meanings of the most frequent characters in a convenient, easy-to-read format.

The characters are listed in increasing order of their frequency numbers. The numerals to the left of the character column indicate the frequency; the numerals to the right are the **entry numbers.**

For more information on core meanings and frequency, see **§ 2.2 Core Meaning** and **§ 6.3 Character Importance** in FEATURES OF THIS DICTIONARY and **§ 7.5 Frequency** in GUIDE TO THE DICTIONARY.

Frequency	Character	Core Meaning	Entry
1	日	DAY SUN JAPAN	3027
2	一	ONE	3341
3	十	TEN	3365
4	二	TWO	1922
5	大	BIG UNIVERSITY	3416
6	三	THREE	1924
7	人	HUMAN BEING	3368
8	会	MEET SOCIETY	2020
9	国	COUNTRY	3087
10	年	YEAR	2035
11	中	MIDDLE IN	3451
12	本	BASIS BOOK THIS	3502
13	五	FIVE	3436
14	四	FOUR	3044
15	出	GO OUT PUT OUT	3498
16	上	UP	3404
17	時	TIME	924
18	同	SAME	2987
19	長	LONG CHIEF	2556
20	東	EAST	3568
21	行	GO	212

1. The frequency data are based on statistics published by The National Language Research Institute, interpreted and adapted in a manner to make them particularly useful to the learner.

		ACT	
		LINE	
22	事	AFFAIR	3567
		ABSTRACT THING	
23	学	STUDY	2555
		EDUCATIONAL INSTITUTION	
24	生	LIFE	3497
		BE BORN	
		STUDENT	
25	月	MOON	2956
		MONTH	
26	者	PERSON	3211
27	六	SIX	1965
28	間	INTERVAL	3323
		BETWEEN	
29	方	DIRECTION	1963
		WAY	
		SQUARE	
30	分	DIVIDE	1972
		PART	
		MINUTE	
31	前	BEFORE	2266
32	後	AFTER	361
33	地	GROUND	204
		PLACE	
34	場	PLACE	558
35	手	HAND	3456
		OCCUPATION SUFFIX	
36	政	POLITICAL ADMINISTRATION	1142
37	的	TARGET	1125
		ADJECTIVAL SUFFIX	
38	発	START	2565
		EMIT	
39	合	COMBINE	2019
		FIT	
40	八	EIGHT	3
41	議	DISCUSS	1647
		LEGISLATIVE BODY	
42	部	SECTION	1676
43	田	RICE FIELD	3041
44	員	MEMBER	2269
45	見	SEE	2544
46	京	CAPITAL	2052
		TOKYO	
		KYOTO	
47	九	NINE	3369
48	社	COMPANY	840

		SOCIETY	
49	対	OPPOSITE	831
		OPPOSE	
50	業	WORK	2612
		BUSINESS	
		INDUSTRY	
51	七	SEVEN	3362
52	子	CHILD	3390
		NOUN SUFFIX	
53	新	NEW	1784
54	自	SELF	3525
55	高	HIGH	2097
56	内	INSIDE	3466
57	立	STAND	1992
		ESTABLISH	
58	相	PHASE	900
		MUTUAL	
		MINISTER	
59	度	DEGREE	3100
		TIME	
60	回	TURN ROUND	3055
		TIME	
61	問	QUESTION	3320
62	定	FIX	2229
63	百	HUNDRED	2026
64	目	EYE	3043
		ITEM	
65	小	SMALL	7
66	力	POWER	3371
67	全	WHOLE	2022
68	円	CIRCLE	2955
		YEN	
69	気	GAS	3194
		SPIRIT	
70	山	MOUNTAIN	2940
71	金	METAL	2057
		GOLD	
		MONEY	
72	通	PASS	3109
		COMMUNICATE	
73	開	OPEN	3321
74	戦	WAR	1787
75	市	CITY	1993
		MARKET	
76	米	RICE	3529
		AMERICA	
77	民	PEOPLE	3036

No.	Kanji	Meaning	Ref.
78	千	THOUSAND	3411
79	連	LINK IN SUCCESSION	3103
80	決	DECIDE	263
81	現	ACTUAL APPEAR	968
82	入	ENTER PUT IN	3370
83	午	NOON	1984
84	代	SUBSTITUTE GENERATION CHARGE	30
85	第	ORDINAL NUMBER PREFIX	2660
86	実	REAL	2225
87	主	MAIN MASTER	1938
88	動	MOVE	1778
89	明	BRIGHT CLEAR	855
90	党	PARTY	2581
91	当	THE PRESENT HIT	2177
92	下	DOWN	3378
93	関	CONCERN BARRIER	3328
94	家	HOUSE FAMILY	2273
95	調	TONE INVESTIGATE PREPARE	1567
96	題	TITLE TOPIC PROBLEM	3337
97	教	TEACH RELIGION	1493
98	意	MIND MEANING	2136
99	区	DISTRICT WARD	2963
100	北	NORTH	197
101	機	MACHINE AIRCRAFT OPPORTUNITY	1076
102	要	IMPORTANT SUMMARIZE REQUIRE	2635
103	化	CHANGE INTO	21
104	野	FIELD	1485
105	来	COME	3551
106	理	REASON BASIC PRINCIPLE	970
107	体	BODY FORM	71
108	強	STRONG	475
109	成	FORM ACHIEVE	3537
110	外	OUTSIDE	186
111	都	METROPOLIS METROPOLIS OF TOKYO	1686
112	作	MAKE WORK	68
113	選	CHOOSE	3169
114	所	PLACE PARTICLE OF NOMINALIZATION	851
115	万	TEN THOUSAND	2936
116	公	PUBLIC	1974
117	表	EXPRESS SURFACE TABLE	2429
118	最	MOST	2472
119	近	NEAR RECENT	3061
120	期	TERM EXPECT	1704
121	思	THINK	2564
122	正	RIGHT	3484
123	物	THING	874
124	道	WAY	3134
125	府	URBAN PREFECTURE	3082
126	法	LAW METHOD	333
127	約	PROMISE CONTRACT APPROXIMATELY	1280
128	用	EMPLOY THINGS TO DO	2976
129	点	POINT	2084
130	安	PEACEFUL INEXPENSIVE	2171
131	不	NOT	3434
132	務	DUTY	1173
133	心	HEART	11
134	産	GIVE BIRTH PRODUCE	3298

No.	Kanji	Meaning	Number
135	今	PRESENT	1968
		THIS	
136	川	RIVER	6
137	経	PASS THROUGH	1331
		MANAGE	
138	委	COMMIT	2553
139	以	TO THE...OF	41
		BY MEANS OF	
140	共	JOINT	2393
141	原	PLAIN	3009
		ORIGINAL	
142	重	HEAVY	3573
		DUPLICATE	
143	結	TIE	1348
		CONCLUDE	
144	海	SEA	384
145	水	WATER	10
146	打	STRIKE	193
147	名	NAME	2169
148	町	TOWN	1113
149	予	IN ADVANCE	1983
150	多	MANY	2170
151	話	SPEAK	1527
152	総	TOTAL	1379
		GENERAL	
153	設	SET UP	1471
154	軍	ARMY	2080
155	面	FACE	2087
156	反	COUNTER	2945
157	木	TREE	3450
		WOOD	
158	運	CARRY	3140
		MOVE	
		FORTUNE	
159	記	WRITE DOWN	1453
160	平	FLAT	3478
		CALM	
161	書	WRITE	2658
		BOOK	
162	持	HOLD	374
163	氏	COURTESY TITLE	2951
		FAMILY NAME	
164	文	LETTER	1962
		WRITINGS	
165	団	BODY	3053
166	和	HARMONIOUS	1130
		PEACE	
		JAPAN	
167	勝	WIN	1005
		EXCEL	
168	校	SCHOOL	929
		COLLATE	
169	進	ADVANCE	3121
170	考	THINK	3196
171	組	ORGANIZE	1337
		ASSEMBLE	
172	世	WORLD	3496
		AGE	
173	保	PRESERVE	96
174	制	SYSTEM	1274
		CONTROL	
175	首	HEAD	2265
		NECK	
		LEADER	
176	画	PICTURE	3000
		DRAW UP A PLAN	
177	加	ADD	38
178	交	INTERCOURSE	2015
		INTERCHANGE	
179	島	ISLAND	3310
180	治	GOVERN	335
		CURE	
181	車	VEHICLE	3552
		WHEEL	
182	県	PREFECTURE	2641
183	西	WEST	3520
184	取	TAKE	1262
185	数	NUMBER	1790
186	協	COOPERATE	93
187	界	WORLD	2563
		BOUNDS	
188	局	BUREAU	3063
		LIMITED PART	
189	工	MANUFACTURE	3381
		CONSTRUCTION	
190	向	TURN TOWARD	3052
191	解	TAKE APART	1517
		DISSOLVE	
		CLARIFY	
192	先	AHEAD	2394
193	計	PLAN	1441
		COMPUTE	
194	南	SOUTH	2082
195	官	GOVERNMENT	2226

		GOVERNMENT OFFICIAL	
196	続	CONTINUE	1362
197	切	CUT	27
198	側	SIDE	137
199	案	PROPOSAL	2270
200	少	LITTLE	3467
201	女	WOMAN	3418
202	統	UNITE	1352
		INTERCONNECTED SYSTEM	
203	私	PRIVATE	1115
		I	
204	省	MINISTRY	2449
		SAVE	
		INTROSPECT	
205	電	ELECTRICITY	2790
206	品	ARTICLE	2248
207	売	SELL	2196
208	知	KNOW	1127
209	在	BE	2984
210	引	DRAW	181
211	院	INSTITUTION	454
212	半	HALF	3501
213	各	EACH	2168
214	策	SCHEME	2679
		MEASURE	
215	特	SPECIAL	945
216	次	NEXT	54
217	資	RESOURCES	2695
218	村	VILLAGE	834
219	集	COLLECT	2771
220	演	PERFORM	697
221	死	DIE	3521
222	権	RIGHT	1065
		POWER	
223	受	RECEIVE	2421
224	空	SKY	2227
		AIR	
		EMPTY	
225	活	ACTIVE	385
		LIVE	
226	使	USE	90
		ENVOY	
227	投	THROW	256
		SEND IN	
228	台	STAND	2005
		COUNTER FOR VEHICLES	
229	争	CONTEND	2030
230	信	BELIEVE	100
		MESSAGE	
231	無	WITHOUT	2135
		NOTHING	
232	育	RAISE	2050
233	指	FINGER	378
		POINT	
234	性	NATURE	299
		SEX	
		-ITY	
235	建	BUILD	3090
236	送	SEND	3093
237	男	MAN	2542
238	線	LINE	1392
239	両	BOTH	3518
240	風	WIND	3007
		MANNER	
241	係	CONNECT	97
		PERSON IN CHARGE	
242	査	LOOK INTO	2437
243	料	FEE	1292
		MATERIALS	
244	口	MOUTH	3382
245	論	ARGUE	1574
		THEORY	
246	早	EARLY	2390
		QUICK	
247	聞	HEAR	3326
248	朝	MORNING	1695
		DYNASTY	
249	言	SAY	1941
		SPEECH	
250	放	LET GO	853
251	派	SECT	381
		DISPATCH	
252	利	ADVANTAGE	1114
		PROFIT	
253	義	RIGHTEOUSNESS	2338
		MEANING	
254	式	STYLE	3049
		CEREMONY	
255	夜	NIGHT	2056
256	件	MATTER	51
257	改	REFORM	243
258	佐	ASSIST	67
		FIELD OFFICER	
259	神	GOD	912

No.	Kanji	Meaning	Ref.
		MIND	
260	松	PINE	864
261	情	EMOTION	482
		ACTUAL CONDITIONS	
262	果	FRUIT	3560
263	急	URGENT	2092
		HURRY	
		SUDDEN	
264	必	WITHOUT FAIL	15
265	語	LANGUAGE	1543
		WORD	
		TELL	
266	楽	PLEASURE	2826
		COMFORTABLE	
		MUSIC	
267	感	SENSE	2835
		FEEL	
268	井	WELL	3454
269	価	PRICE	87
		VALUE	
270	任	OFFICE	53
		LEAVE TO	
271	込	MOVE INWARD	3030
		EMPHATIC VERBAL SUFFIX	
272	船	SHIP	1341
273	済	SETTLE	522
		RELIEVE	
274	報	INFORM	1698
		REQUITE	
275	初	FIRST	1116
276	判	JUDGE	1122
277	足	FOOT	2188
		SUFFICE	
278	別	SEPARATE	1117
		ANOTHER	
279	置	PLACE	2608
280	住	LIVE	64
281	石	STONE	2971
282	増	INCREASE	677
283	有	HAVE	2983
284	領	TERRITORY	1224
285	労	LABOR	2548
286	際	VERGE	714
		OCCASION	
287	告	NOTIFY	2409
288	昨	YESTERDAY	893
		LAST	

No.	Kanji	Meaning	Ref.
289	食	EAT	2075
		FOOD	
290	谷	VALLEY	2043
291	終	END	1336
292	防	PREVENT	270
293	郎	YOUNG MAN	1289
		MALE NAME SUFFIX	
294	役	SERVICE	244
295	鉄	IRON	1711
296	夫	HUSBAND	3460
		MAN LABORER	
297	検	EXAMINE	986
298	白	WHITE	3493
299	歩	WALK	2416
300	算	CALCULATE	2702
301	流	FLOW	441
		CURRENT	
		STYLE	
302	黒	BLACK	2740
303	変	CHANGE	2069
		ABNORMAL	
304	費	EXPENSE	2607
305	身	BODY	3553
		ONE'S PERSON	
306	認	RECOGNIZE	1546
307	支	BRANCH	1979
		SUPPORT	
308	態	STATE	2847
309	農	FARMING	2698
310	真	TRUE	2111
311	職	EMPLOYMENT	1425
312	転	TURN	1480
313	株	STOCK	935
314	直	STRAIGHT	2932
		FIX	
315	段	STEP	1144
316	買	BUY	2598
317	備	PROVIDE	146
318	屋	HOUSE	3098
		SMALL SHOP	
319	配	DISTRIBUTE	1460
320	値	VALUE	109
321	得	ACQUIRE	477
		GAIN	
322	再	ANOTHER TIME	3519
323	審	EXAMINE CAREFULLY	2360
		TRY	

No.	Kanji	Meaning	Number
324	広	WIDE	3035
325	球	BALL	969
326	付	ATTACH	31
327	談	TALK	1569
328	番	NUMERICAL ORDER	2748
		WATCH	
329	億	HUNDRED MILLION	170
330	勢	POWER	2857
331	止	STOP	2941
332	消	EXTINGUISH	443
		SPEND	
333	乗	RIDE	3576
		GET ON	
334	説	EXPLAIN	1547
		THEORY	
335	警	GUARD AGAINST	2893
		WARN	
336	衛	GUARD	760
337	親	PARENT	1799
		RELATIVES	
		INTIMATE	
338	席	SEAT	3113
339	橋	BRIDGE	1078
340	望	HOPE	2742
		LOOK AFAR	
341	味	TASTE	274
342	商	TRADE	2116
343	好	LIKE	208
		FAVORABLE	
344	常	NORMAL	2590
		REGULAR	
345	基	BASE	2673
346	参	PARTICIPATE	2066
		VISIT A HOLY PLACE	
347	落	FALL	2318
348	術	PRACTICAL ART	476
349	確	CERTAIN	1228
350	想	CONCEIVE	2828
351	着	PUT ON	3316
		ARRIVE	
		STICK	
352	館	PUBLIC BUILDING	1748
353	士	MILITARY MAN	3405
		PROFESSION SUFFIX	
354	格	NORM	926
		STATUS	
355	提	PRESENT	591

No.	Kanji	Meaning	Number
356	元	ORIGIN	1929
357	条	ARTICLE	2200
358	求	SEEK	3550
359	路	ROAD	1533
360	輸	TRANSPORT	1607
361	挙	NOMINATE	2456
		NOTEWORTHY ACT	
		RAISE	
362	映	REFLECT	892
		PROJECT	
363	銀	SILVER	1722
364	助	HELP	1121
365	状	FORM	272
		CONDITION	
		LETTER	
366	撃	STRIKE	2863
367	由	REASON	3499
368	難	DIFFICULT	1838
		DISASTER	
369	起	RISE	3307
370	待	WAIT	364
371	税	TAX	1191
372	示	SHOW	1936
373	飛	FLY	3572
374	横	SIDEWAYS	1066
375	割	DIVIDE	1816
376	害	HARM	2272
377	過	PASS BY	3137
		EXCEED	
378	申	REPORT	3507
		SPEAK HUMBLY	
379	階	FLOOR	624
		RANK	
380	質	QUALITY	2808
		MATTER	
381	戸	DOOR	1930
		HOUSEHOLD	
382	土	SOIL	3403
383	能	ABILITY	1323
384	古	OLD	2002
385	討	STUDY	1456
		SUPPRESS BY ARMED FORCE	
386	兵	SOLDIER	2551
387	収	TAKE IN	198
388	庁	GOVERNMENT AGENCY	3034
389	試	TRY	1525
390	頭	HEAD	1604

No.	Kanji	Meaning	Ref.
391	答	ANSWER	2681
392	注	POUR	325
		CONCENTRATE	
393	命	ORDER	2058
		LIFE	
394	青	BLUE	2430
		GREEN	
395	太	GREAT	2152
		THICK	
396	隊	PARTY	625
397	阪	OSAKA	271
398	追	CHASE	3096
399	帰	RETURN	130
400	宮	ROYAL PALACE	2274
		SHINTO SHRINE	
401	故	OLD	1141
		THE LATE	
402	験	TEST	1833
403	証	PROVE	1506
		CERTIFICATE	
404	形	SHAPE	846
405	声	VOICE	2198
406	営	MANAGE	2603
		BARRACKS	
407	美	BEAUTIFUL	2264
408	若	YOUNG	2241
409	然	MODIFIER FORMING SUFFIX	2782
		SO	
410	林	FOREST	861
411	構	CONSTRUCT	1049
		MIND	
412	負	BEAR	2091
		LOSE	
413	蔵	STORE	2364
414	火	FIRE	3463
415	施	CARRY OUT	891
416	閣	TALL MAGNIFICENT BUILDING	3327
		CABINET	
417	沢	MARSH	267
418	店	SHOP	3085
419	容	APPEARANCE	2277
		CONTAIN	
420	岡	HILL	2997
421	宅	DWELLING HOUSE	2174
422	天	HEAVEN	3442
423	働	WORK	153
424	園	GARDEN	3156
425	科	SUBJECT OF STUDY	1138
426	病	ILLNESS	3277
427	洋	OCEAN	392
		WESTERN	
428	究	STUDY EXHAUSTIVELY	2203
429	展	UNFOLD	3111
		DISPLAY	
430	爆	EXPLODE	1101
431	研	GRIND	1132
		RESEARCH	
432	整	PUT IN ORDER	2871
433	技	SKILL	248
434	規	REGULATION	978
435	門	GATE	888
436	張	SPREAD	474
		STRAIN	
437	始	BEGIN	281
438	違	DIFFER	3151
		VIOLATE	
439	光	LIGHT	2391
440	限	LIMIT	398
441	位	RANK	61
		POSITION	
442	非	IS NOT	889
443	応	RESPOND	3066
444	港	PORT	605
445	与	GIVE	3421
446	何	WHAT	65
		HOW MANY	
447	企	PROJECT	2021
448	断	CUT OFF	1492
		RESOLVE	
449	残	REMAIN	943
		RUTHLESS	
450	観	VIEW	1880
451	葉	LEAF	2321
452	左	LEFT	2974
453	署	PUBLIC-SERVICE STATION	2609
454	週	WEEK	3122
455	優	SUPERIOR	177
		ACTOR	
456	航	NAVIGATE	1318
457	視	REGARD	972
458	号	NUMBER	2153
		DESIGNATION	
		SIGN	
459	音	SOUND	2070

No.	Kanji	Meaning	Ref.
460	裁	CUT OUT JUDGE	3299
461	室	ROOM	2254
462	型	TYPE	2638
463	製	MANUFACTURE	2803
464	色	COLOR	2029
465	他	OTHER	35
466	福	FORTUNE	1029
467	供	OFFER	88
468	独	ALONE GERMANY	395
469	悪	BAD	2745
470	録	RECORD	1742
471	補	SUPPLEMENT	1194
472	仕	SERVE DO	34
473	念	THOUGHTS	2059
474	右	RIGHT	2975
475	師	MASTER	1326
476	程	EXTENT ESTABLISHED FORM	1190
477	低	LOW	73
478	造	MAKE	3110
479	失	LOSE SLIP	3511
480	彼	THIRD PERSON PRONOUN	290
481	英	DISTINGUISHED ENGLAND	2238
482	伝	TRANSMIT	44
483	減	DECREASE	601
484	評	COMMENT	1501
485	末	LAST PART	3505
486	種	VARIETY SEED	1218
487	可	-ABLE APPROVE	2969
488	導	GUIDE	2888
489	崎	PROMONTORY	472
490	例	EXAMPLE	89
491	敗	BE DEFEATED	1476
492	訪	VISIT	1468
493	衆	MULTITUDE	2683
494	武	MILITARY	3210
495	歌	SONG	1825
496	根	ROOT	930
497	吉	LUCKY	2167
498	春	SPRING	2576
499	比	COMPARE	26
500	将	GENERAL OFFICER	460
501	紙	PAPER	1302
502	達	ATTAIN	3139
503	象	PHENOMENON ELEPHANT	2134
504	針	NEEDLE	1666
505	守	PROTECT	2173
506	寄	CONTRIBUTE DRAW NEAR	2291
507	深	DEEP	524
508	毎	EVERY	2034
509	課	SECTION LESSON	1573
510	赤	RED	2193
511	婦	ADULT WOMAN	469
512	率	RATE LEAD	2118
513	読	READ	1541
514	母	MOTHER	3475
515	州	STATE	57
516	核	NUCLEUS	927
517	顔	FACE	1808
518	突	DASH THRUST	2230
519	援	AID	586
520	準	STANDARD QUASI-	2856
521	歳	YEAR AGE SUFFIX	2490
522	越	GO BEYOND	3314
523	押	PUSH	314
524	愛	LOVE	2492
525	額	AMOUNT	1805
526	管	PIPE EXERCISE CONTROL	2701
527	財	WEALTH	1457
528	客	VISITOR CUSTOMER	2250
529	返	RETURN	3060
530	攻	ATTACK	242
531	馬	HORSE	3296
532	授	CONFER	492
533	姿	FIGURE	2636
534	塁	BASE SMALL FORT	2593
535	疑	DOUBT	1565

No.	Kanji	Meaning	Freq.
536	量	QUANTITY	2471
537	積	ACCUMULATE	1236
538	央	CENTER	3509
539	医	MEDICINE	2993
		DOCTOR	
540	江	INLET	221
541	殺	KILL	1324
542	写	COPY	2000
543	器	VESSEL	2713
		INSTRUMENT	
544	王	KING	3439
545	浜	BEACH	436
546	給	SUPPLY	1350
		PAY	
547	完	COMPLETE	2201
548	苦	SUFFERING	2243
		BITTER	
549	散	SCATTER	1702
550	様	MODE	1052
		FORMAL TITLE	
551	般	SORT	1317
552	復	RETURN TO	575
553	競	COMPETE	1847
554	個	INDIVIDUAL	117
		GENERAL COUNTER	
555	接	CONTACT	500
556	宿	LODGE	2293
557	満	FULL	607
558	良	GOOD	3558
559	専	EXCLUSIVE	2644
560	友	FRIEND	2952
561	児	CHILD	2546
562	単	SINGLE	2256
563	諸	VARIOUS	1577
564	具	IMPLEMENT	2552
565	激	VIOLENT	776
566	登	CLIMB	2595
567	去	GO AWAY	2156
568	森	THICK WOODS	2475
569	昭	LUMINOUS	894
570	護	PROTECT	1648
571	庭	COURT	3114
		GARDEN	
572	圧	PRESSURE	2970
573	級	GRADE	1279
574	花	FLOWER	2211
575	退	RETREAT	3094
576	捕	CATCH	429
577	族	FAMILY	958
578	離	SEPARATE	1836
579	波	WAVE	330
580	呼	CALL	273
581	劇	DRAMA	1904
582	陸	LAND	543
583	差	DIFFERENCE	3311
584	駅	STATION	1822
585	秋	AUTUMN	1139
586	因	CAUSE	3054
587	雄	MALE	1008
		HEROIC	
588	渡	CROSS	611
589	善	GOOD	2325
590	闘	FIGHT	3334
591	識	DISCRIMINATE	1639
		KNOWLEDGE	
592	副	SECONDARY	1776
593	券	TICKET	2630
		CERTIFICATE	
594	影	SHADOW	1889
595	雨	RAIN	3561
596	韓	SOUTH KOREA	1757
597	極	EXTREME	1017
		POLE	
598	監	OVERSEE	2852
599	材	TIMBER	836
		MATERIAL	
600	破	BREAK	1150
601	況	CONDITIONS	337
602	曲	MUSICAL COMPOSITION	3527
		CURVE	
603	響	REVERBERATE	2878
604	仏	BUDDHA	19
		FRANCE	
605	捜	LOOK FOR	432
606	編	COMPILE	1387
		KNIT	
607	賞	PRIZE	2618
608	旅	TRAVEL	922
609	域	BOUNDED AREA	465
610	史	HISTORY	3510
611	座	SEAT	3116
		SIT	
612	含	CONTAIN	2041
613	担	BEAR ON SHOULDER	318

		UNDERTAKE	
614	健	ROBUST	134
615	険	DANGER	542
		STEEP	
616	察	INSPECT	2347
		GUESS	
617	字	CHARACTER	2172
618	玉	GEM	3477
619	犯	OFFENSE	196
620	請	REQUEST	1576
621	景	SCENE	2470
622	推	INFER	504
623	練	TRAIN	1375
624	清	CLEAR	523
625	富	RICH	2310
626	糸	THREAD	2179
627	修	CULTIVATE	123
		REPAIR	
628	幅	WIDTH	569
629	移	SHIFT	1177
630	君	RULER	3206
		FAMILIAR TITLE	
		YOU	
631	芸	ART	2209
632	令	COMMAND	1995
633	傷	WOUND	158
634	述	STATE	3075
635	久	OF LONG DURATION	3384
636	休	REST	52
637	習	LEARN	2667
		CUSTOM	
638	油	OIL	341
639	模	PATTERN	1050
640	辺	VICINITY	3029
		BORDERLAND	
641	乱	DISORDERED	1260
642	図	DRAWING	3071
643	除	RID OF	456
644	熱	HEAT	2866
		HOT	
645	処	DEAL WITH	3031
646	坂	SLOPE	234
647	障	HINDRANCE	715
648	従	FOLLOW	415
649	並	LINE UP	2246
650	尾	TAIL	3062
651	丸	ROUND	3417

652	等	EQUAL	2682
		CLASS	
653	迎	WELCOME	3059
654	抜	PULL OUT	246
		STAND OUT	
655	訴	APPEAL TO	1507
		SUE	
656	革	LEATHER	2448
		REFORM	
657	城	CASTLE	352
658	夏	SUMMER	2113
659	精	REFINE	1366
		ESSENCE	
		SPIRIT	
660	走	RUN	2194
661	融	FUSE	1831
662	父	FATHER	1973
663	延	EXTEND	3073
		POSTPONE	
664	盟	ALLIANCE	2794
665	遊	PLAY	3142
666	伸	STRETCH	70
667	批	CRITICIZE	250
668	幹	TRUNK	1718
669	効	EFFECT	1265
670	講	LECTURE	1619
671	適	SUITABLE	3160
672	焼	BURN	997
673	賃	WAGE	2694
		CHARGES	
674	筋	MUSCLE	2678
		THREADLIKE STRUCTURE	
675	締	CONCLUDE	1393
		TIGHTEN	
676	毛	HAIR	3453
677	存	EXIST	2982
678	周	PERIPHERY	2998
679	晴	FINE WEATHER	981
680	司	OFFICIATE	2931
681	速	QUICK	3105
682	類	KIND	1807
683	責	RESPONSIBILITY	2467
		BLAME	
684	装	DRESS	2685
		FIT OUT	
685	静	QUIET	1728
686	降	DESCEND	458

No.	Kanji	Meaning	Ref.
687	抗	RESIST	252
688	拡	ENLARGE	309
689	血	BLOOD	3526
690	軽	LIGHT	1515
691	津	HARBOR	390
692	盛	PROSPEROUS	2675
693	欧	EUROPE	887
694	努	EXERT	2547
695	介	MEDIATE	1967
696	興	RISE TO PROSPERITY AMUSEMENT	2909
697	異	DIFFERENT	2584
698	績	ACHIEVEMENTS	1412
699	遺	LEAVE BEHIND	3166
700	帯	BELT WEAR	2582
701	舞	DANCE	2146
702	功	MERIT	189
703	危	DANGEROUS	3199
704	池	POND	218
705	庫	STORAGE CHAMBER	3112
706	許	PERMIT	1470
707	債	DEBT BOND	156
708	余	REMAINING EXCESS	2042
709	裏	REAR	2138
710	震	QUAKE	2806
711	払	CLEAR AWAY PAY	194
712	板	BOARD PLATE	858
713	勤	SERVICE	1818
714	漁	FISH	698
715	招	INVITE	316
716	宇	UNIVERSE	2175
717	渉	HAVE RELATIONS WITH	526
718	才	TALENT AGE SUFFIX	3410
719	卒	GRADUATE	2055
720	停	HALT	139
721	厚	THICK KIND	3003
722	弁	SPEAK ELOQUENTLY VALVE	2004
723	河	RIVER	336
724	印	MARK SEAL	828
725	羽	FEATHER WING	226
726	巨	HUGE	3039
727	境	BOUNDARY SITUATION	676
728	振	SWING	430
729	細	SLENDER MINUTE	1333
730	及	REACH TO	3385
731	養	FOSTER	2365
732	妻	WIFE	2558
733	服	CLOTHES SUBMIT	878
734	否	SAY NO OR NOT	2406
735	織	WEAVE	1422
736	居	RESIDE	3080
737	候	SEASON SEASONAL WEATHER	119
738	倉	STOREHOUSE	2104
739	底	BOTTOM	3084
740	幸	GOOD FORTUNE HAPPINESS	2216
741	角	ANGLE HORN	2047
742	標	MARK	1064
743	催	HOLD AN EVENT PRESS FOR	157
744	寺	BUDDHIST TEMPLE	2164
745	途	WAY	3107
746	岩	ROCK	2235
747	徒	FOLLOWER	416
748	賀	CONGRATULATE	2599
749	老	OLD	3197
750	属	BELONG TO	3145
751	夕	EVENING	3387
752	易	EASY EXCHANGE	2411
753	歴	PERSONAL HISTORY	3019
754	枚	COUNTER FOR FLAT THINGS	859
755	鈴	BELL	1710
756	益	BENEFIT PROFIT	2285
757	暴	VIOLENT	2515
758	督	SUPERVISE COMMANDER	2796

No.	Kanji	Meaning	Freq.
759	布	CLOTH	2973
		SPREAD	
760	短	SHORT	1182
761	旧	FORMER	14
762	沖	OFFING	262
763	節	JOINT	2691
		SEASON OF THE YEAR	
764	刑	PENALTY	830
765	豊	PLENTIFUL	2697
766	折	BREAK OFF	253
		FOLD	
767	固	SOLID	3086
		FIRM	
768	堂	HALL	2589
769	弱	WEAK	1167
770	永	ETERNAL	1937
771	未	NOT YET	3506
772	郡	COUNTY	1466
773	留	KEEP	2580
		STAY	
774	草	GRASS	2263
775	肉	FLESH	3200
776	背	BACK	2573
777	遠	DISTANT	3150
778	僚	COLLEAGUE	165
779	逆	REVERSE	3091
780	冷	COLD	80
781	婚	MARRY	470
782	被	BE SUBJECTED TO	1163
783	岸	SHORE	2236
784	禁	PROHIBIT	2795
785	頼	RELY ON	1615
		ASK	
786	素	ELEMENT	2458
		PLAIN	
787	喜	HAPPY	2308
788	博	EXTENSIVE	151
		DOCTOR	
789	採	PICK	499
		GATHER	
790	票	VOTE	2669
		SLIP	
791	困	BE IN TROUBLE	3070
792	便	CONVENIENT	95
		POST	
		EXCRETA	
793	系	SYSTEM	1944
		LINEAGE	
794	測	MEASURE	610
		CONJECTURE	
795	脳	BRAIN	975
796	陣	BATTLE FORMATION	455
		CAMP	
797	幕	CURTAIN	2335
		SHOGUNATE	
798	逃	ESCAPE	3095
799	逮	CATCH A CRIMINAL	3123
800	温	WARM	608
801	鮮	FRESH	1877
		VIVID	
802	希	RARE	2049
		ASPIRE	
803	札	TAG	817
804	房	CHAMBER	1946
805	街	CITY QUARTER	576
806	鋼	STEEL	1740
807	源	SOURCE	656
808	占	OCCUPY	2003
		DIVINE	
809	迫	PRESS	3074
810	倍	TIMES	108
		DOUBLE	
811	救	SAVE	1497
812	順	ORDER	18
		OBEY	
813	昇	ASCEND	2415
814	遅	SLOW	3133
		LATE	
815	絶	BREAK OFF	1353
		COME TO AN END	
816	奏	PLAY MUSIC	2577
817	避	AVOID	3179
818	曜	DAY OF THE WEEK	1096
819	志	AMBITION	2199
820	雑	MISCELLANEOUS	1385
		MIXED	
821	臨	BE PRESENT AT	1630
822	均	EVEN	235
823	換	EXCHANGE	587
824	亡	DECEASE	3402
825	竹	BAMBOO	228
826	秒	SECOND	1137
827	群	GROUP	1540
828	療	TREAT	3288

829	層	STRATUM	3161
830	措	DISPOSE	502
831	傾	INCLINE	154
832	栄	FLOURISH GLORY	2574
833	則	RULE	1444
834	緊	TIGHTEN EXIGENT	2838
835	衝	COLLIDE	725
836	御	GENERAL HONORIFIC TERM	577
837	列	ROW	824
838	混	MIX	519
839	脱	REMOVE ESCAPE FROM	973
840	戻	RETURN	1942
841	浦	SEASIDE	437
842	願	WISH ASK A FAVOR	1845
843	了	FINISH COMPREHEND	3350
844	徳	VIRTUE	684
845	承	AGREE TO	16
846	簡	SIMPLE	2721
847	星	STAR	2435
848	堅	FIRM	2823
849	慮	CONSIDER	3266
850	芝	LAWN GRASS	2180
851	郵	MAIL	1687
852	辞	WORD RESIGN	1364
853	縮	SHRINK	1414
854	密	CLOSE SECRET	2292
855	息	BREATH	2647
856	罪	CRIME	2610
857	扱	HANDLE	217
858	覚	PERCEIVE COMMIT TO MEMORY	2604
859	就	SET ABOUT	1694
860	笑	LAUGH	2646
861	築	CONSTRUCT	2715
862	弾	PROJECTILE SPRING BACK	572
863	丁	TOWN SUBSECTION MISCELLANEOUS COUNTER	3348
864	片	FRAGMENT ONE OF TWO	3461
865	曇	CLOUDY	2521
866	盗	STEAL	2670
867	荒	WILD	2260
868	略	ABRIDGED STRATEGY	1169
869	憲	CONSTITUTION	2368
870	絡	INTERLINK ENTWINE	1351
871	茶	TEA	2259
872	駐	STATIONED	1826
873	仲	INTERMEDIARY PERSONAL RELATIONS	43
874	互	RECIPROCAL	3437
875	欠	LACK	1987
876	塚	MOUND	556
877	盤	DISK BOARD	2851
878	維	FIBER	1370
879	皇	EMPEROR	2566
880	康	HEALTHY	3124
881	慶	FELICITATION	3173
882	拠	GROUNDS	312
883	雪	SNOW	2759
884	杉	CRYPTOMERIA	832
885	致	BRING ABOUT DO HUMBLY	1316
886	囲	ENCLOSE	3069
887	継	SUCCEED	1360
888	借	BORROW	122
889	渋	NOT GO SMOOTHLY ASTRINGENT	513
890	昼	DAYTIME	3097
891	恐	FEAR	2650
892	併	TOGETHER	83
893	堀	DITCH	467
894	薄	THIN	2370
895	奥	INNER PART	2824
896	旬	TEN-DAY PERIOD	2978
897	端	END	1221
898	鳥	BIRD	3312
899	跡	TRACE	1534
900	貸	LEND	2600
901	臣	RETAINER	3068
902	縄	ROPE	1388
903	酒	ALCOHOLIC DRINK	444
904	紅	CRIMSON	1277
905	騒	CLAMOR	1835

No.	Kanji	Meaning	Ref.
906	束	TIE UP BUNDLE	3554
907	廃	ABOLISH WASTE	3146
908	届	DELIVER REACH	3078
909	執	EXECUTE SEIZE	1680
910	需	DEMAND	2797
911	薬	DRUG	2375
912	項	CLAUSE	567
913	冬	WINTER	2157
914	吹	BLOW	231
915	躍	LEAP	1658
916	宙	SPACE MIDAIR	2221
917	射	SHOOT	1458
918	著	AUTHOR CONSPICUOUS	2300
919	香	SWEET SMELL	2568
920	季	SEASON	2554
921	稲	RICE PLANT	1219
922	更	RENEW	3541
923	納	PAY ACCEPT PUT AWAY	1300
924	炭	COAL CHARCOAL	2257
925	募	RAISE	2316
926	暮	DUSK LIVE	2354
927	械	MECHANICAL CONTRIVANCE	961
928	威	MIGHT THREATEN BY FORCE	3578
929	環	RING SURROUND	1090
930	翼	WING	2720
931	湾	BAY	613
932	徴	LEVY SYMPTOM	683
933	乳	MILK	1438
934	祭	FESTIVAL	2672
935	窓	WINDOW	2294
936	輪	WHEEL RING	1589
937	普	WIDESPREAD	2323
938	豆	BEAN	1943
939	鉱	ORE MINE	1709
940	巻	ROLL UP VOLUME	2645
941	痛	PAIN	3285
942	恵	FAVOR	2659
943	賛	APPROVE OF PRAISE	2809
944	充	FILL	2014
945	悩	SUFFER	421
946	荷	LOAD	2282
947	侵	INVADE	101
948	操	MANIPULATE	769
949	到	ARRIVE	1264
950	貿	TRADE	2601
951	瀬	SHALLOWS	806
952	秀	EXCELLENT	2545
953	柄	CHARACTER HANDLE	897
954	紹	INTRODUCE	1335
955	浅	SHALLOW	389
956	筆	BRUSH WRITING	2677
957	勉	ENDEAVOR	3318
958	貨	MONEY GOODS	2465
959	刺	STAB	1275
960	章	CHAPTER BADGE	2117
961	魚	FISH	2127
962	摘	PICK	694
963	像	IMAGE	166
964	娘	DAUGHTER GIRL	406
965	版	PRINTING PLATE PUBLISHING	872
966	宣	PROCLAIM	2252
967	刻	ENGRAVE POINT OF TIME	1267
968	紀	ERA	1276
969	邦	STATE JAPAN	847
970	聴	LISTEN	1418
971	巡	MAKE THE ROUNDS	3047
972	牛	CATTLE	3452
973	歓	JOYOUS	1867
974	兄	OLDER BROTHER	2154

No.	Kanji	Meaning	Freq.
975	敵	ENEMY	1864
976	訓	INSTRUCT	1454
977	奪	ROB	2343
978	販	ENGAGE IN SALES	1477
979	飲	DRINK	1692
980	徹	GO THROUGH	726
981	植	PLANT	990
982	律	LAW	363
		RHYTHM	
983	浮	FLOAT	435
984	唱	SING	462
985	踏	TREAD	1587
986	創	CREATE	1815
987	綿	COTTON	1373
988	揮	WIELD	589
989	皮	SKIN	3037
990	絵	PICTURE	1346
991	祝	CELEBRATE	913
992	袋	BAG	2588
993	華	MAGNIFICENT	2283
		CHINA	
994	看	WATCH	3220
		CARE FOR	
995	兼	CONCURRENTLY	2286
996	齢	AGE	1895
997	損	LOSS	651
998	棄	ABANDON	2137
999	贈	PRESENT A GIFT	1634
1000	帝	EMPEROR	2073
1001	暗	DARK	1010
1002	妙	MARVELOUS	239
1003	災	NATURAL CALAMITY	2206
1004	紛	CONFUSED	1296
1005	泉	SPRING	2567
1006	砂	SAND	1133
1007	飾	DECORATE	1717
1008	宗	RELIGIOUS SECT	2228
1009	舎	BUILDING	2060
1010	宝	TREASURE	2224
1011	快	PLEASANT	245
1012	描	DEPICT	488
1013	譲	CEDE	1649
1014	夢	DREAM	2336
1015	隣	NEIGHBOR	781
1016	弟	YOUNGER BROTHER	2044
1017	揚	RAISE HIGH	593
		EXALT	
1018	梅	JAPANESE APRICOT	925
1019	封	SEAL	1287
1020	複	COMPOUND	1222
1021	骨	BONE	2654
1022	秘	SECRET	1159
1023	慎	PRUDENT	643
1024	償	RECOMPENSE	176
1025	悲	SAD	2775
1026	塩	SALT	631
1027	促	HASTEN	103
1028	洗	WASH	388
1029	純	PURE	1297
1030	厳	SEVERE	3289
1031	壁	WALL	2895
1032	免	EXEMPT	2067
1033	至	COME TO	2182
1034	岳	HIGH MOUNTAIN	2557
1035	誤	MISTAKE	1542
1036	貫	PENETRATE	2460
1037	診	EXAMINE A PATIENT	1504
1038	幼	VERY YOUNG	191
1039	柳	WILLOW	899
1040	繊	FINE	1413
		FIBER	
1041	旨	PURPORT	2024
1042	陽	SUN	626
1043	潟	LAGOON	745
1044	敷	LAY	1870
1045	甲	SHELL	3481
		FIRST	
1046	霧	FOG	2817
1047	患	AFFECTED BY DISEASE	2747
1048	閉	CLOSE	3319
1049	為	DO	3577
		SAKE	
1050	刊	PUBLISH	190
1051	胸	CHEST	951
1052	銭	MONEY	1725
1053	献	OFFER	1785
1054	煙	SMOKE	1021
1055	豪	GREAT MAN	2140
		MAGNIFICENT	
1056	超	SURPASS	3313
1057	伴	ACCOMPANY	60
1058	勧	URGE	1857
1059	遭	MEET WITH	3159
1060	誌	MAGAZINE	1548

No.	Kanji	Meaning	Entry
1061	樹	STANDING TREE	1075
1062	忘	FORGET	2036
1063	杯	CUP	857
1064	郷	HOMETOWN	549
1065	欲	DESIRE	1475
1066	照	ILLUMINATE	2827
1067	童	CHILD	2130
1068	紡	SPIN	1295
1069	糖	SUGAR	1403
1070	還	RETURN	3180
1071	依	DEPEND ON	84
1072	遣	DISPATCH	3152
1073	預	DEPOSIT	1042
1074	里	COUNTRYSIDE	3542
		LEAGUE	
1075	菜	VEGETABLE	2305
1076	腕	ARM	1006
1077	双	SET OF TWO	25
1078	箱	BOX	2711
1079	礼	ETIQUETTE	818
		RITE	
1080	肩	SHOULDER	1947
1081	即	IMMEDIATE	1120
1082	湖	LAKE	604
1083	契	MAKE AN AGREEMENT	2639
1084	索	SEARCH FOR	2455
1085	摩	RUB AGAINST	3175
1086	飯	COOKED RICE	1691
		MEAL	
1087	竜	DRAGON	2099
1088	泳	SWIM	327
1089	寝	GO TO SLEEP	2329
1090	称	APPELLATION	1160
1091	戒	CAUTION	3204
1092	零	ZERO	2792
1093	詩	POETRY	1524
1094	包	WRAP	2966
		ENCOMPASS	
1095	浴	BATHE	445
1096	範	MODEL	2709
1097	粉	POWDER	1291
1098	枝	BRANCH	863
1099	惑	BEWILDERED	2786
1100	旗	FLAG	1047
1101	黄	YELLOW	2468
1102	燃	BURN	1081
1103	銃	GUN	1723
1104	倒	TOPPLE	124
1105	典	STANDARD WORK	2627
		CANON	
1106	菌	BACTERIA	2304
1107	忠	LOYALTY	2433
1108	驚	SURPRISE	2894
1109	滞	STAGNATE	663
		STAY	
1110	据	INSTALL	497
1111	繁	THRIVE	2853
1112	硬	HARD	1183
1113	帳	NOTEBOOK	473
1114	踊	DANCE	1558
1115	懇	EARNEST	2899
		FAMILIAR	
1116	貴	NOBLE	2606
		YOUR HONORABLE	
1117	泣	CRY	338
1118	拒	REFUSE	311
1119	雲	CLOUD	2773
1120	沼	MUDDY POND	339
1121	症	PATHOLOGICAL CONDITION	3280
1122	詰	REPRIMAND	1521
		STUFF	
1123	載	LOAD	3300
		PUT IN PRINT	
1124	矢	ARROW	2009
1125	桜	CHERRY	931
1126	勇	BRAVE	2089
1127	毒	POISON	2428
1128	誘	INDUCE	1550
1129	穴	HOLE	2159
1130	控	HOLD BACK	495
1131	湯	HOT WATER	612
1132	干	DRY	3379
1133	鳴	CRY	674
		SOUND	
1134	焦	SCORCH	2770
		BE IMPATIENT	
1135	綱	ESSENTIAL POINTS	1372
		ROPE	
1136	替	REPLACE	2783
1137	仙	IMMORTAL MOUNTAIN FAIRY	32
1138	銘	INSCRIPTION	1724
1139	殿	PALACE	1792
		FORMAL HONORIFIC TITLE	
1140	趣	FLAVOR	3317

		PURPOSE	
1141	畑	FIELD	905
1142	砲	HEAVY GUN	1151
1143	抱	HUG	306
1144	釣	ANGLE	1674
1145	麻	HEMP	3125
		BECOME NUMB	
1146	昔	FORMER TIMES	2432
1147	尊	HONOR	2324
1148	掲	PUT UP	494
1149	眼	EYE	1172
1150	寿	LONGEVITY	3557
		CONGRATULATIONS	
1151	染	DYE	2572
1152	捨	DISCARD	501
1153	甘	SWEET	3494
1154	晩	EVENING	979
1155	棋	SHOGI	987
1156	緩	SLACK	1389
1157	歯	TOOTH	2476
1158	菊	CHRYSANTHEMUM	2303
1159	撮	PHOTOGRAPH	737
1160	腰	WAIST	1036
1161	寒	COLD	2311
1162	釈	ELUCIDATE	1484
1163	掃	SWEEP	503
1164	獲	CATCH GAME	779
1165	触	TOUCH	1518
1166	句	PHRASE	2967
		HAIKU	
1167	繰	REEL	1427
		SHIFT ONWARD	
1168	壊	BREAK DOWN	756
1169	託	ENTRUST	1455
1170	緑	GREEN	1377
1171	排	EXCLUDE	490
		DISCHARGE	
1172	似	RESEMBLE	63
1173	軟	SOFT	1479
1174	邸	STATELY RESIDENCE	1131
1175	潮	TIDE	739
1176	露	DEW	2818
		EXPOSE	
1177	剣	SWORD	1672
1178	距	DISTANCE	1511
1179	卸	WHOLESALE	1447
1180	撤	WITHDRAW	738
1181	鬼	DEVIL	2657
1182	珍	RARE	909
1183	迷	PERPLEXED	3092
1184	襲	RAID	2917
1185	絹	SILK	1361
1186	微	SLIGHT	639
1187	牧	PASTURE	873
1188	謝	THANK	1620
		APOLOGIZE	
1189	暖	WARM	1011
1190	誇	BOAST	1522
1191	泊	STAY OVERNIGHT	331
1192	床	BED	3067
		FLOOR	
1193	脚	LEG	974
1194	臓	INTERNAL ORGAN	1102
1195	茂	GROW THICK	2245
1196	坊	SONNY	233
		COLLOQUIAL PERSON SUFFIX	
1197	鋭	SHARP	1730
1198	墜	DROP DOWN	2881
1199	誠	SINCERITY	1523
1200	敬	RESPECT	1701
1201	暑	SUMMER HEAT	2473
		HOT	
1202	慣	HABITUAL PRACTICE	685
1203	液	LIQUID	511
1204	妹	YOUNGER SISTER	278
1205	汚	DIRTY	222
1206	巣	NEST	2295
1207	俳	HAIKU	112
1208	掘	DIG	496
1209	貧	POOR	2123
1210	犠	SACRIFICE	1089
1211	虫	INSECT	3530
1212	濃	THICK	777
1213	氷	ICE	39
1214	荘	VILLA	2262
		DIGNIFIED	
1215	艦	WARSHIP	1435
1216	炎	FLAME	2420
		INFLAMMATION	
1217	挑	PROVOKE	372
1218	翌	THE FOLLOWING	2668
1219	儀	CEREMONY	169
1220	粛	PURGE	3581
1221	妥	COME TO TERMS	2400

No.	Kanji	Meaning	Ref.
1222	却	ELIMINATE	1118
1223	腹	BELLY	1034
1224	吸	SUCK BREATHE IN	202
1225	奇	UNUSUAL	2217
1226	懸	SUSPEND	2915
1227	勲	MERITORIOUS SERVICE	2869
1228	隆	PROSPER	545
1229	煮	BOIL	2785
1230	励	ENCOURAGE	1119
1231	衣	GARMENT	2013
1232	探	PROBE SEARCH	505
1233	軒	EAVES COUNTER FOR HOUSES	1459
1234	克	OVERCOME	2046
1235	潜	SUBMERGE LURK	746
1236	緒	OUTSET	1378
1237	彰	PROCLAIM MERITS	1860
1238	叫	SHOUT	201
1239	郊	SUBURB	1286
1240	訳	TRANSLATE SENSE	1473
1241	往	GO ON	292
1242	沈	SINK	261
1243	縫	SEW	1406
1244	亜	SUB- PHONETIC [a]	3540
1245	序	INTRODUCTORY PART ORDER	3065
1246	貯	LAY UP	1509
1247	恋	LOVE	2098
1248	紋	CREST	1299
1249	耐	WITHSTAND	1282
1250	柔	SOFT	2088
1251	廊	CORRIDOR	3147
1252	諮	CONSULT	1596
1253	阻	OBSTRUCT	348
1254	凍	FREEZE	129
1255	瞬	INSTANT	1247
1256	埋	BURY	403
1257	較	COMPARE	1536
1258	斎	OBSERVE RELIGIOUS ABSTINENCE	2115
1259	卵	EGG	849
1260	酸	ACID OXYGEN	1563
1261	灯	LAMP	825
1262	犬	DOG	3464
1263	貞	CHASTE	2083
1264	裂	SPLIT	2687
1265	疲	TIRED	3278
1266	礎	FOUNDATION STONE	1248
1267	陳	SET FORTH	540
1268	勘	CHECK INTUITIVE PERCEPTION	1777
1269	耳	EAR	3516
1270	祖	ANCESTOR	914
1271	涙	TEAR	440
1272	罰	PUNISHMENT	2613
1273	糧	FOOD PROVISIONS	1421
1274	孝	FILIAL PIETY	3205
1275	己	ONESELF	3380
1276	稿	MANUSCRIPT	1231
1277	抵	RESIST	319
1278	誉	HONOR	2502
1279	隻	ONE OF A PAIR COUNTER FOR SHIPS	2755
1280	奉	DEDICATE	2559
1281	網	NET	1374
1282	殊	SPECIAL	942
1283	縁	RELATION EDGE	1386
1284	猛	FIERCE	537
1285	壇	PLATFORM	754
1286	沿	ALONG	328
1287	肥	FATTEN	879
1288	忙	BUSY	214
1289	騰	RISE	1106
1290	魅	CHARM	3329
1291	丘	HILL	3495
1292	掛	SET HANG	493
1293	滝	WATERFALL	661
1294	眠	SLEEP	1147
1295	仮	TEMPORARY	50
1296	稚	CHILDISH	1206
1297	縦	VERTICAL	1408
1298	雇	EMPLOY	1956
1299	聖	HOLY SAINT	2830
1300	概	GENERAL	1048
1301	芳	FRAGRANT	2210
1302	墓	GRAVE	2332

No.	Kanji	Meaning	Frequency
1303	孫	GRANDCHILD	410
1304	怪	MYSTERIOUS	297
1305	抑	SUPPRESS	257
1306	麦	WHEAT	2408
1307	欄	COLUMN	1103
1308	脅	THREATEN	2109
1309	覧	LOOK OVER	2854
1310	頂	SUMMIT	145
		RECEIVE HUMBLY	
1311	狭	NARROW	396
1312	彫	CARVE	1683
1313	柱	PILLAR	896
1314	択	SELECT	255
1315	班	SQUAD	946
1316	魔	DEMON	3187
1317	是	RIGHT	2436
1318	圏	SPHERE	3148
1319	腐	ROT	3162
1320	拓	OPEN UP	317
1321	銅	COPPER	1721
1322	兆	OMEN	225
		TRILLION	
1323	哲	SAGACIOUS	2738
		PHILOSOPHY	
1324	俊	BRILLIANT PERSON	102
1325	裕	ABUNDANT	1195
1326	析	ANALYZE	862
1327	秩	ORDER	1158
1328	顧	LOOK BACK	1900
1329	既	ALREADY	1166
1330	携	CARRY IN HAND	648
1331	怒	GET ANGRY	2571
1332	僧	BONZE	159
1333	牲	SACRIFICE	907
1334	閥	CLIQUE	3325
1335	漫	RAMBLING	700
		COMIC	
1336	簿	RECORD BOOK	2727
1337	黙	SILENT	2865
1338	艇	BOAT	1365
1339	咲	BLOOM	349
1340	詐	SWINDLE	1502
1341	鑑	APPRAISE	1773
		REFERENCE VOLUME	
1342	仁	BENEVOLENCE	20
1343	随	FOLLOW	627
1344	忍	BEAR	2212

No.	Kanji	Meaning	Frequency
1345	敏	NIMBLE	1322
1346	滅	DESTROY	660
1347	飼	RAISE ANIMALS	1716
1348	謀	SCHEME	1593
1349	岐	DIVERGE	241
1350	籍	REGISTER	2731
1351	刷	PRINT	1273
1352	恩	GRACE	2655
		DEBT OF GRATITUDE	
1353	狂	CRAZY	269
1354	添	ADD TO	529
1355	陰	SHADE	541
1356	鐘	BELL	1769
1357	墨	INDIA INK	2753
1358	陛	IMPERIAL PALACE STEPS	453
1359	誕	BE BORN	1579
1360	姉	OLDER SISTER	280
1361	霊	SPIRIT	2805
1362	峰	PEAK	411
1363	恒	CONSTANT	367
1364	伏	PROSTRATE	45
1365	祉	BLESSEDNESS	876
1366	酔	BECOME INTOXICATED	1483
1367	塗	APPLY ON A SURFACE	2841
1368	彩	BEAUTIFUL COLORING	1681
1369	棒	ROD	983
1370	葬	FUNERAL	2320
1371	浪	BILLOW	439
		WANDER	
1372	削	CUT BY CHIPPING	1448
1373	握	GRASP	585
1374	滑	SLIDE	658
		SMOOTH	
1375	慰	CONSOLE	2867
1376	欺	DECEIVE	1703
1377	剤	PREPARATION	1669
1378	雅	ELEGANT	1197
1379	遇	TREAT	3135
		ENCOUNTER	
1380	舟	SMALL BOAT	3538
1381	烈	VEHEMENT	2652
1382	径	PATH	291
		DIAMETER	
1383	痢	DIARRHEA	3283
1384	輝	SHINE BRILLIANTLY	1402
1385	丈	STOUT	3419
		STATURE	

No.	Kanji	Meaning	Frequency
1386	髪	HAIR	2846
1387	我	SELF	3548
1388	遂	ACCOMPLISH	3138
1389	撲	DEAL A BLOW	733
1390	廷	COURT	3058
1391	泰	TRANQUIL	2583
1392	乾	DRY	1679
1393	漢	CHINESE	657
		FELLOW	
1394	喫	INGEST	551
1395	巧	SKILLFUL	188
1396	拝	WORSHIP	303
		HUMBLY	
1397	惨	MISERABLE	483
		CRUEL	
1398	悟	AWAKE TO	419
1399	丹	CINNABAR	3441
1400	孤	SOLITARY	356
1401	譜	SYSTEMATIC RECORD	1637
1402	朗	CHEERFUL	1325
		CLEAR	
1403	鼻	NOSE	2706
1404	妨	HINDER	238
1405	僕	I	164
		MANSERVANT	
1406	惜	REGRET	484
1407	拍	BEAT	304
1408	唯	ONLY	463
1409	潔	IMMACULATE	744
1410	披	OPEN OUT	305
1411	慢	ARROGANT	686
		SLUGGISH	
1412	泥	MUD	326
1413	俵	STRAW SACK	115
1414	藩	FEUDAL DOMAIN	2379
1415	抽	DRAW OUT	302
1416	汗	SWEAT	220
1417	刀	SWORD	2926
1418	脂	FAT	954
1419	偉	GREAT	148
1420	堤	EMBANKMENT	560
1421	升	*SHO*	3455
1422	詳	DETAILED	1526
1423	皆	ALL	2445
1424	呉	KINGDOM OF WU	2549
1425	盲	BLIND	2053
1426	穏	CALM	1235
		MILD	
1427	憩	TAKE A REST	2890
1428	碁	GO	2699
1429	豚	PIG	976
1430	没	SINK	260
1431	劣	INFERIOR	2395
1432	乏	SCANTY	1933
1433	桑	MULBERRY	2112
1434	壮	VIGOROUS	224
		GRAND	
1435	辻	CROSSROADS	3192
1436	琴	KOTO	2781
1437	硫	SULFUR	1184
1438	征	CONQUER	293
1439	斉	UNIFORM	2054
1440	唆	INSTIGATE	402
1441	啓	ENLIGHTEN	2763
1442	穂	SPIKE	1232
1443	汁	JUICE	195
		SOUP	
1444	寸	A BIT OF	2935
1445	輩	FELLOW	2807
1446	貢	TRIBUTE	2281
1447	嘆	SIGH	630
1448	屈	BEND	3079
1449	拾	PICK UP	379
1450	膨	EXPAND	1084
1451	剰	SURPLUS	1779
1452	尽	EXHAUST	3050
1453	祥	AUSPICIOUS	948
1454	肝	LIVER	841
1455	冒	RISK	2434
1456	奮	ROUSE UP	2367
1457	雷	THUNDER	2791
1458	謡	POPULAR SONG	1597
1459	如	AS	207
1460	胴	TRUNK	950
1461	俗	POPULAR	104
1462	帽	HEADGEAR	568
1463	叙	DESCRIBE	1446
1464	拘	ARREST	310
1465	穀	CEREAL	1824
1466	卓	TABLE	2064
		PROMINENT	
1467	扇	FAN	1950
1468	脈	VEIN	953
		PULSE	

1469	召	SUMMON	2001
1470	寛	LENIENT	2327
1471	亭	INN	2072
		PSEUDONYM SUFFIX	
1472	購	PURCHASE	1624
1473	玄	PROFOUND	1991
1474	耕	TILL	1308
1475	奨	ENCOURAGE	2842
1476	弊	EVIL PRACTICE	2884
1477	粗	COARSE	1329
1478	掌	PALM	2602
		TAKE CHARGE OF	
1479	懲	CHASTISE	2910
1480	軌	TRACK	1445
1481	冊	COUNTER FOR BOOKS	3483
1482	粧	APPLY MAKEUP	1345
1483	畳	TATAMI	2592
		FOLD UP	
1484	鏡	MIRROR	1766
		OPTICAL INSTRUMENT	
1485	薦	RECOMMEND	2373
1486	駆	DRIVE	1823
1487	淡	LIGHT	528
1488	熟	MATURE	2868
1489	塔	TOWER	561
1490	諭	ADMONISH	1598
1491	垣	FENCE	351
1492	祈	PRAY	875
1493	隔	APART	671
1494	喪	MOURNING	2825
1495	隠	HIDE	713
1496	浸	SOAK	442
1497	嫁	WED A MAN	635
		BRIDE	
1498	賢	WISE	2839
1499	粒	GRAIN	1328
1500	姫	DAUGHTER OF NOBLE BIRTH	407
1501	暇	FREE TIME	1012
1502	透	PASS THROUGH	3108
		TRANSPARENT	
1503	鎖	CHAIN	1761
1504	培	CULTIVATE	464
1505	覆	COVER	2726
		OVERTURN	
1506	擁	SUPPORT	770
1507	偏	ONE-SIDED	133
1508	款	ARTICLE	1700
1509	舶	OCEANGOING SHIP	1340
1510	浄	CLEAN	382
1511	怖	FEARFUL	296
1512	偽	FALSIFY	131
1513	覇	SUPREMACY	2730
1514	厘	*RIN*	3004
1515	寮	DORMITORY	2359
1516	湿	DAMP	609
1517	凡	COMMONPLACE	2938
1518	尿	URINE	3064
1519	冠	CROWN	2081
1520	貝	SHELLFISH	2543
1521	陶	POTTERY	546
1522	揺	SHAKE	594
1523	弦	STRING	287
1524	狩	HUNT	397
1525	紫	PURPLE	2688
1526	幻	PHANTOM	180
1527	衰	DECLINE	2100
1528	訂	REVISE	1442
1529	虚	VOID	3237
		FALSE	
1530	憂	BE ANXIOUS	2145
1531	戯	SPORT	1875
1532	閑	LEISURE	3322
		QUIET	
1533	訟	LITIGATE	1472
1534	臭	BAD SMELL	2633
1535	弓	BOW	3383
1536	尚	STILL	2233
		VALUE HIGHLY	
1537	符	SYMBOL	2661
1538	盾	SHIELD	3006
1539	架	LAY ACROSS	2569
1540	括	LUMP TOGETHER	376
1541	宴	BANQUET	2271
1542	獣	BEAST	1892
1543	匹	COUNTER FOR ANIMALS	2962
1544	燥	DRY UP	1087
1545	謙	HUMBLE	1617
1546	菓	CONFECTIONERY	2302
1547	娯	ENJOYMENT	405
1548	諾	CONSENT	1568
1549	虜	CAPTIVE	3255
1550	矛	HALBERD	2008
1551	陥	FALL IN	457
1552	坪	*TSUBO*	275

No.	Kanji	Meaning	Frequency
1553	又	AGAIN	3351
1554	涼	COOL	521
1555	鎮	QUELL	1759
1556	粋	REFINED	1293
1557	滋	NOURISH	602
1558	朴	SIMPLE	819
1559	旋	GYRATE	957
1560	芽	BUD	2240
1561	徐	SLOWLY	414
1562	緯	LATITUDE	1407
1563	胃	STOMACH	2561
1564	逸	LET SLIP	3120
1565	傑	OUTSTANDING PERSON	155
1566	机	DESK	820
1567	辛	PUNGENT HARD	2038
1568	酢	VINEGAR	1516
1569	仰	LOOK UP	48
1570	尼	BUDDHIST NUN	3033
1571	砕	CRUSH UP	1134
1572	匿	CONCEAL	3011
1573	偶	BY CHANCE COUPLE	132
1574	涯	OUTER LIMITS	512
1575	佳	FINE	86
1576	駄	GOOD FOR NOTHING	1821
1577	怠	REMISS	2085
1578	澄	LIMPID	740
1579	循	CIRCULATE	578
1580	傍	BESIDE	147
1581	鉛	LEAD	1707
1582	崩	CRUMBLE	2296
1583	軸	AXLE AXIS	1514
1584	衡	BALANCE	761
1585	曹	SERGEANT	2746
1586	暫	SHORT WHILE	2864
1587	刃	BLADE	2929
1588	詞	WORDS	1503
1589	殖	MULTIPLY	994
1590	胆	GALLBLADDER	919
1591	穫	HARVEST	1251
1592	栽	PLANT	3297
1593	舗	PAVE SHOP	1735
1594	紳	GENTLEMAN	1334
1595	禅	ZEN	1032
1596	嵐	STORM	2314
1597	噴	SPOUT	717
1598	獄	PRISON	712
1599	幾	HOW MANY SOME	3582
1600	顕	MANIFEST	1806
1601	鈍	DULL	1689
1602	隅	NOOK	623
1603	凶	BAD LUCK ATROCIOUS	2961
1604	糾	INQUIRE INTO	1278
1605	塾	PRIVATE SCHOOL	2860
1606	誓	VOW	2754
1607	酬	RECIPROCATE	1539
1608	冗	REDUNDANT	1976
1609	紺	DARK BLUE	1332
1610	漂	DRIFT	699
1611	桃	PEACH	936
1612	伯	OLDER SIBLING OF PARENT COUNT	59
1613	庶	MANIFOLD	3127
1614	晶	CRYSTAL	2474
1615	尻	BUTTOCKS	3032
1616	溝	CHANNEL	659
1617	碑	MONUMENT	1213
1618	禍	CALAMITY	1030
1619	賓	GUEST	2357
1620	蓄	STORE UP	2333
1621	腸	INTESTINES	1033
1622	筒	TUBE	2680
1623	霜	FROST	2815
1624	笛	FLUTE	2664
1625	悦	DELIGHTED	418
1626	恥	SHAME	1313
1627	畜	LIVESTOCK	2096
1628	恭	RESPECTFUL	2459
1629	扶	LEND SUPPORT TO	247
1630	斜	OBLIQUE	1486
1631	苗	SEEDLING	2237
1632	郭	OUTER ENCLOSURE	1678
1633	磨	POLISH	3181
1634	匠	CRAFTSMAN	2990
1635	珠	PEARL	947
1636	潤	MOIST	742
1637	魂	SOUL	1063
1638	溶	DISSOLVE MELT	664

No.	Kanji	Meaning	Ref.
1639	垂	HANG DOWN	3565
1640	刈	CLIP	28
1641	汽	STEAM	264
1642	騎	RIDE ON HORSEBACK	1834
1643	睡	SLEEP	1200
1644	峠	MOUNTAIN PASS	358
1645	尉	COMPANY OFFICER	1685
1646	肺	LUNG	916
1647	濁	TURBID	774
1648	姓	SURNAME	279
1649	某	A CERTAIN	2560
1650	轄	EXERCISE JURISDICTION OVER	1627
1651	憾	STRONGLY REGRET	764
1652	哀	SORROW	2068
		PITY	
1653	憶	SPECULATE	765
		REMEMBER	
1654	搬	CARRY	647
1655	猿	MONKEY	669
1656	篤	DEVOTED	2716
1657	吐	SPEW	203
1658	懐	BOSOM	763
		LONG FOR	
1659	灰	ASH	2979
1660	憤	INDIGNATION	730
1661	窮	BE IN EXTREMITY	2358
1662	閲	REVIEW	3330
1663	慨	DEPLORE	641
1664	猶	DELAY	619
1665	錠	LOCK	1737
		PILL	
1666	呈	PRESENT	2189
1667	賦	INSTALLMENT	1583
1668	麗	OF GRACEFUL BEAUTY	2151
1669	嬢	YOUNG LADY	758
1670	邪	EVIL	1124
1671	鶏	CHICKEN	1768
1672	唐	TANG DYNASTY	3115
1673	舌	TONGUE	2186
1674	酷	SEVERE	1562
1675	鍛	FORGE	1755
1676	后	EMPRESS	2981
1677	妃	PRINCESS	206
1678	暁	DAWN	980
1679	洞	CAVE	380
1680	枯	WITHER	898
1681	暦	CALENDAR	3018
1682	准	JUNIOR	127
1683	疎	SPARSE	1178
		ESTRANGE	
1684	践	IMPLEMENT	1535
1685	累	CUMULATE	2585
1686	賄	BRIBE	1529
1687	靴	SHOES	1781
1688	羊	SHEEP	2183
1689	朱	VERMILION	3531
1690	猟	HUNTING	538
1691	孔	OPEN HOLE	179
1692	羅	PHONETIC [ra]	2622
1693	摂	TAKE IN	650
		ACT AS REGENT	
1694	鯨	WHALE	1882
1695	炉	FURNACE	869
1696	拙	CLUMSY	315
1697	賠	COMPENSATE	1582
1698	該	CORRESPOND TO	1519
1699	礁	REEF	1243
1700	畔	WATERSIDE	1145
1701	租	LAND TAX	1161
1702	虐	CRUEL	3218
1703	漏	LEAK	701
1704	忌	MOURNING	2207
		ABHOR	
1705	慈	AFFECTIONATE	2339
1706	渓	RAVINE	516
1707	妊	BECOME PREGNANT	240
1708	乙	SECOND	3339
1709	愁	MELANCHOLY	2829
1710	薫	BALMY	2371
1711	蚊	MOSQUITO	1319
1712	膚	SKIN	3265
1713	侍	ATTEND UPON	85
		SAMURAI	
1714	岬	CAPE	284
1715	凝	CONGEAL	175
1716	疫	EPIDEMIC	3276
1717	鼓	DRUM	1786
1718	憎	HATE	687
1719	胞	MEMBRANOUS SAC	917
1720	翻	TURN OVER	1897
		RENDER	
1721	錯	MIXED UP	1743
1722	云	SUCH	1931
1723	枢	PIVOT	865

1724	帥	COMMANDER IN CHIEF	1290
1725	坑	PIT	236
1726	嗣	HEIR	1719
1727	酵	FERMENT	1561
1728	沸	BOIL	329
1729	裸	NAKED	1211
1730	疾	DISEASE	3279
1731	蒸	STEAM	2334
		EVAPORATE	
1732	倫	MORALS	120
1733	胎	FETUS	918
		WOMB	
1734	籠	BASKET	2734
1735	擬	IMITATE	788
1736	崇	REVERENCE	2297
1737	逓	RELAY	3106
1738	迭	ALTERNATE	3077
1739	殻	SHELL	1490
1740	褒	COMMEND	2144
1741	誰	WHO	1578
1742	猫	CAT	535
1743	吟	RECITE	230
1744	敢	BOLDLY	1706
1745	愉	PLEASED	582
1746	囚	PRISONER	3042
1747	幽	QUIET AND SECLUDED	3008
1748	酪	DAIRY PRODUCTS	1538
1749	剛	TOUGH	1673
1750	赴	PROCEED TO	3303
1751	寂	LONESOME	2290
1752	盆	TRAY	2079
		BON FESTIVAL	
1753	漸	GRADUALLY	706
1754	桟	PLANK BRIDGE	932
1755	鋳	CAST	1729
1756	嘱	CHARGE WITH	718
1757	奴	SLAVE	187
		GUY	
1758	鍋	POT	1752
1759	娠	CONCEIVE	408
1760	漠	DESERT	655
		OBSCURE	
1761	絞	STRANGLE	1349
		WRING	
1762	宰	PRESIDE	2275
1763	媒	INTERMEDIATE	564
1764	帆	SAIL	210
1765	偵	SPY	138
1766	愚	FOOLISH	2834
1767	棟	BLOCK	991
1768	戴	RECEIVE HUMBLY	3302
1769	頃	TIME	144
		ABOUT	
1770	肖	MODEL	2205
1771	鍵	KEY	1753
1772	尺	*SHAKU*	3440
1773	粘	STICKY	1327
1774	遍	ALL OVER	3136
1775	淑	GRACEFUL	527
1776	宜	RIGHT	2223
1777	蛮	BARBARIAN	2129
1778	壌	ARABLE SOIL	755
1779	醸	BREW	1654
1780	謹	RESPECTFULLY	1618
1781	朽	DECAY	821
1782	昆	INSECT	2413
1783	奔	RUSH	2218
1784	耗	WEAR AWAY	1309
1785	慕	ADORE	2353
1786	殉	DIE A MARTYR	941
1787	袖	SLEEVE	1164
1788	尋	INQUIRE	2322
1789	髄	MARROW	1842
1790	扉	HINGED DOOR	1955
1791	膜	MEMBRANE	1062
1792	稼	WORK	1230
1793	泡	BUBBLE	334
1794	肌	SKIN	827
1795	履	FULFILL	3171
1796	棚	SHELF	984
1797	滴	DROP	705
1798	炊	COOK	870
1799	斗	DIPPER	2953
		TO	
1800	腺	GLAND	1035
1801	雀	SPARROW	2469
		MAHJONG	
1802	眺	LOOK OUT OVER	1171
1803	俺	I	110
1804	悠	LEISURELY	2741
1805	廉	INCORRUPT	3153
		CHEAP	
1806	泌	SECRETE	332
1807	錬	REFINE	1741

No.	Kanji	Meaning	Freq.
1808	漬	PICKLE	702
1809	渦	WHIRLPOOL	603
1810	傘	UMBRELLA	2131
1811	但	PROVIDED THAT	72
1812	迄	UP TO	3201
1813	皿	PLATE	3474
1814	瓶	BOTTLE	1344
1815	缶	CAN	2033
1816	槽	TANK	1067
1817	宛	ADDRESS	2222
1818	濯	RINSE	793
1819	蚕	SILKWORM	2457
1820	壱	ONE	2197
1821	弐	TWO	3195
1822	伺	INQUIRE	69
1823	癖	HABIT	3290
1824	遷	TRANSFER	3170
1825	抄	EXCERPT	254
1826	堕	DEGENERATE	2822
1827	幣	CURRENCY	2885
1828	赦	AMNESTY	1478
1829	肪	ANIMAL FAT	877
1830	磁	MAGNETISM	1214
1831	窒	CHOKE NITROGEN	2288
1832	韻	RHYME	1811
1833	喚	CALL	550
1834	楼	TALL BUILDING	1019
1835	賊	BANDIT	1530
1836	寧	COURTEOUS	2345
1837	醜	UGLY	1629
1838	辱	HUMILIATE	2736
1839	飽	SATIATED	1715
1840	飢	STARVE	1668
1841	雌	FEMALE	1055
1842	弧	ARC	360
1843	逐	ONE BY ONE DRIVE OUT	3102
1844	峡	GORGE	357
1845	剖	DISSECT	1670
1846	伐	CUT DOWN	42
1847	痴	STUPID	3286
1848	縛	BIND	1405
1849	詠	RECITE POETRY	1500
1850	賜	DEIGN TO GIVE	1585
1851	悔	REPENT	365
1852	卑	MEAN	2642

No.	Kanji	Meaning	Freq.
1853	慌	FLURRIED	580
1854	殴	BEAT	886
1855	跳	JUMP	1532
1856	塊	LUMP	632
1857	擦	RUB	790
1858	繕	MEND	1423
1859	渇	RUN DRY THIRST	515
1860	恨	HOLD A GRUDGE	369
1861	茎	STEM	2242
1862	侮	INSULT	82
1863	搾	SQUEEZE	649
1864	悼	MOURN	485
1865	弔	CONDOLE	3432
1866	硝	NITER	1185
1867	惰	LAZY	579
1868	肯	ASSENT	2417
1869	芋	POTATO	2181
1870	餓	STARVED	1734
1871	倹	FRUGAL	116
1872	窃	STEAL	2253
1873	棺	COFFIN	985
1874	墳	TUMULUS	719
1875	漆	LACQUER	704
1876	墾	RECLAIM	2896
1877	姻	MARRIAGE	353
1878	窯	KILN	2361
1879	痘	SMALLPOX	3284
1880	吏	OFFICIAL	3536
1881	陪	ACCOMPANY A SUPERIOR	539
1882	塑	MODEL	2843
1883	謄	TRANSCRIBE	1093
1884	儒	CONFUCIANISM	174
1885	拷	TORTURE	373
1886	斥	EXPEL	2972
1887	婿	SON-IN-LAW	566
1888	享	ENJOY	2051
1889	倣	COPY AFTER	113
1890	陵	IMPERIAL MAUSOLEUM	544
1891	叔	YOUNGER SIBLING OF PARENT	1272
1892	庸	MEDIOCRE	3128
1893	嫡	LEGITIMATE CHILD	680
1894	衷	INNER HEART	2575
1895	勅	IMPERIAL DECREE	1451
1896	詔	IMPERIAL EDICT	1505
1897	繭	COCOON	2380
1898	丙	THIRD	3479

1899	斤	CATTY	2949
1900	宵	EARLY EVENING	2276
1901	矯	RECTIFY	1241
1902	厄	MISFORTUNE	2947
1903	酌	POUR WINE	1461
1904	俸	SALARY	114
1905	洪	FLOOD	386
1906	附	ATTACH	347
1907	罷	DISMISS	2617
1908	煩	VEXED	1022
1909	堪	ENDURE	559
1910	濫	EXCESSIVE	801
1911	謁	BE GRANTED AN AUDIENCE	1570
1912	寡	FEW	2344
1913	遵	OBEY	3167
1914	箇	COUNTER FOR ITEMS	2700
1915	迅	SWIFT	3046
1916	頒	DISTRIBUTE WIDELY	1043
1917	劾	EXPOSE CRIMES	1266
1918	璽	IMPERIAL SEAL	2911
1919	翁	OLD MAN	2108
1920	婆	OLD WOMAN	2762
1921	侯	FEUDAL LORD	98
1922	銑	PIG IRON	1726
1923	錘	SPINDLE	1744
1924	薪	FIREWOOD	2374
1925	匁	MOMME	3465
1926	勺	*SHAKU*	2933
1927	畝	*SE*	1465
1928	虞	FEARS	3254
1929	爵	RANK OF NOBILITY	2524
1930	隷	UNDERLING	1751
1931	嚇	INTIMIDATE	784
1932	脹	SWELL	1003
1933	朕	IMPERIAL WE	949
1934	且	AS WELL	3485
1935	甚	EXTREMELY	2643
1936	嫌	DISLIKE	636
1937	蛇	SNAKE	1343
1938	蛍	FIREFLY	2591
1939	頻	FREQUENTLY	1758
1940	唇	LIP	2737
1941	枠	FRAME	866
1942	遮	INTERRUPT	3158
1943	挿	INSERT	431
1944	襟	COLLAR	1252
1945	鉢	BOWL	1708
1946	栓	STOPPER	934
1947	挟	HOLD BETWEEN	377
1948	塀	FENCE	557
1949	搭	BOARD	592
1950	妄	RASH	2016
1951	頑	STUBBORN	1040
1952	肢	LIMB	882
1953	褐	BROWN	1210
1954	凹	CONCAVE	3482
1955	凸	CONVEX	3486
1956	把	GRIP	249
1957	抹	WIPE	313
1958	喝	SHOUT AT	461
1959	藻	ALGAE	2384
1960	逝	DEPART THIS LIFE	3104
1961	癒	HEAL	3291
1962	拐	KIDNAP	308
1963	雰	ATMOSPHERE	2772
1964	屯	STATION TROOPS	3457
1965	頁	PAGE	2086
1966	肛	ANUS	842
1967	揃	MAKE UNIFORM	590
1968	嬉	GLAD	722
1969	叱	SCOLD	182
1970	藤	WISTERIA	2382
1971	伊	PHONETIC [i] ITALY	49
1972	之	POSSESSIVE PARTICLE	3420
1973	奈	PHONETIC [na]	2219
1974	須	MUST	574
1975	熊	BEAR	2848
1976	鶴	CRANE	1850
1977	鹿	DEER	3126
1978	弘	DISSEMINATE	192
1979	旭	RISING SUN	2977
1980	駒	HORSE CHESSMAN	1827
1981	彦	MALE NAME ELEMENT	3295
1982	桂	AROMATIC TREE	928
1983	阿	PHONETIC [a]	346
1984	那	PHONETIC [na]	843
1985	乃	POSSESSIVE PARTICLE	2927
1986	鎌	SICKLE	1760
1987	弥	PHONETIC [mi]	288
1988	辰	THE DRAGON	2992
1989	亀	TURTLE	2128
1990	浩	VAST	438

1991	昌	PROSPERING	2414
1992	吾	I	2407
1993	也	CLASSICAL COPULA	3406
1994	栗	CHESTNUT	2649
1995	鷹	HAWK	3189
1996	梨	PEAR	2744
1997	磯	ROCKY BEACH	1242
1998	智	WISDOM	2784
1999	宏	GRAND	2202
2000	霞	MIST	2814
2001	嘉	HAPPY	2340
2002	李	PLUM	2398
2003	虎	TIGER	3212
2004	桐	PAULOWNIA	937
2005	錦	BROCADE	1738
2006	笹	BAMBOO GRASS	2663
2007	猪	WILD BOAR	536
2008	靖	PACIFY	1208
2009	綾	TWILL	1376
2010	庄	FEUDAL VILLAGE	3051
2011	蘭	ORCHID	2383
2012	淳	PUREHEARTED	514
2013	瑞	AUSPICIOUS OMEN	1027
2014	鳩	PIGEON	163
2015	輔	ASSIST	1559
2016	萩	*HAGI*	2319
2017	祐	DIVINE HELP	915
2018	駿	FLEET STEED	1832
2019	楠	CAMPHOR TREE	1018
2020	呂	PHONETIC [ro]	2187
2021	苑	IMPERIAL GARDEN	2239
2022	蝶	BUTTERFLY	1401
2023	哉	EXCLAMATORY PARTICLE	3294
2024	巳	THE SERPENT	3388
2025	亮	LUCID	2071
2026	稔	RIPEN	1207
2027	睦	FRIENDLY	1199
2028	朋	COMRADE	880
2029	斐	PHONETIC [i]	2776
2030	郁	AROMATIC	1288
2031	圭	SHARP CORNER	2165
2032	喬	TALL	2488
2033	毅	RESOLUTE	1866
2034	渥	GRACIOUS	600
2035	橘	MANDARIN	1077
2036	巌	CRAG	2386
2037	肇	ORIGINATE	2799
2038	瞳	PUPIL	1237
2039	甫	BARELY	3549
2040	旦	DAYBREAK	2389
2041	寅	THE TIGER	2289
2042	孟	MENCIUS	2220
2043	遼	FARAWAY	3168
2044	晃	DAZZLING	2450
2045	鯉	CARP	1879
2046	玲	TINKLING OF JADES	910
2047	聡	SHARP-WITTED	1384
2048	鯛	TAI	1881
2049	只	FREE OF CHARGE ORDINARY	2155
2050	艶	CHARMING ROMANCE	1908
2051	禄	RETAINER'S STIPEND	1002
2052	悌	BROTHERLY LOVE	424
2053	胤	PROGENY	17
2054	暢	FLUENT	1226
2055	欽	REVERE	1690
2056	欣	JOYFUL	852
2057	穣	YIELDING ABUNDANTLY	1250
2058	爾	THAT	3587
2059	晋	JIN DYNASTY	2656
2060	琢	POLISH	971
2061	敦	HONEST	1693
2062	匡	RECTIFY	2989
2063	亘	EXTEND OVER	1939
2064	亨	GO SMOOTHLY	2037
2065	馨	PERFUME	2879
2066	禎	PROPITIOUS OMEN	1031
2067	麿	CLASSICAL MALE NAME SUFFIX	3184
2068	丞	AIDE	2541
2069	蔦	JAPANESE IVY	2355
2070	酉	THE BIRD	3544
2071	卯	THE HARE	199
2072	亥	THE BOAR	2012
2073	惣	GENERAL	2780
2074	亦	ALSO	2011
2075	丑	THE OX	3433
2076	冴	CRISP AND CLEAR	79
2077	藍	INDIGO	2381
2078	梢	TIP OF A TWIG	963
2079	梓	CATALPA	962
2080	渚	STRAND	525
2081	杏	APRICOT	2397
2082	茜	MADDER	2261

2083	沙	SAND	266
2084	紗	GAUZE	1301
2085	鮎	AYU	1876
2086	隼	FALCON	2756
2087	葵	MALLOW	2317
2088	佑	HELP	74
2089	怜	CLEVER	298
2090	瑠	LAPIS LAZULI	1060
2091	芙	LOTUS	2208
2092	翠	JADE GREEN	2705
2093	絢	GORGEOUS	1347
2094	紘	WIDE-RANGING	1298
2095	耶	INTERROGATIVE PARTICLE	1283
2096	允	GIVE CONSENT	1982
2097	虹	RAINBOW	1285
2098	萌	GERMINATE	2301
2099	峻	STERN	412
2100	翔	SOAR	1357
2101	遥	FAR	3141
2102	嶺	RIDGE	2376
2103	伍	RANK	47
2104	巴	CIRCULAR COMMA PATTERN	3438
2105	昂	HIGH	2412
2106	碧	DEEP BLUE	2836
2107	汐	TIDE	223
2108	緋	SCARLET	1369
2109	諒	UNDERSTAND	1575
2110	矩	RULE	1148
2111	頌	EULOGIZE	1045
2112	眸	EYE	1170
2113	楓	MAPLE	1015
2114	慧	INTELLIGENT	2810
2115	皓	BRIGHT WHITE	1180
2116	惟	MEDITATE	481
2117	嵩	BULK	2331
2118	璃	GLASSY SUBSTANCE	1059
2119	蓉	COTTON ROSE	2337
2120	槙	PODOCARPUS	1051
2121	蕗	BUTTERBUR	2372
2122	脩	DRIED MEAT	136
2123	赳	VALIANT	3308
2124	茉	JASMINE	2244
2125	莉	JASMINE	2284
2126	尭	YAO	2063
2127	洸	VAST	387
2128	瑶	EXQUISITE	1026
2129	瑛	TRANSPARENT GEM	999
2130	惇	SINCERE	486
2131	伶	MUSICIAN	66
2132	洵	TRULY	383
2133	侑	URGE TO EAT	91
2134	彬	REFINED AND GENTLE	960
2135	迪	EDIFY	3076

APPENDIX 10

JŌYŌ KANJI LIST

The Japanese government has implemented various language reforms aimed at simplifying the Japanese writing system. The most important of these is the **Jōyō Kanji List**, an official list of 1945 characters widely used in general publications and education. Of these, the 1006 **Education Kanji** must be learned in the first six years of compulsory schooling[1] (see OUTLINE OF JAPANESE WRITING SYSTEM **§ 2.5 Language Reforms** for details).

This appendix lists the Jōyō Kanji classified by school grade for speedy reference. This enables the student to know the relative importance of each character, and could help the developer of teaching materials compile graded lessons (see FEATURES OF THIS DICTIONARY **§ 6.3 Character Importance**).

The characters are grouped under seven sections. The first six list the 1006 Education Kanji classified by school grade; the seventh lists the remaining 939 general-use characters. The number of characters for each section is indicated under the section heading. Within each section the characters are listed alphabetically by their principal readings, and further grouped by total stroke-count. The numerals to the right of the character column are the **entry numbers**.

GRADE 1

(80)

	Kanji	No.
B	貝	2543
	木	3450
	文	1962
C	竹	228
	町	1113
	中	3451
	虫	3530
D	大	3416
	男	2542
	田	3041
	土	3403
E	円	2955
G	学	2555
	月	2956
	五	3436
	玉	3477
H	八	3
	白	3493
	本	3502
	百	2026
I	一	3341
J	字	2172
	耳	3516
	人	3368
	女	3418
	上	3404
	十	3365
K	下	3378
	火	3463
	花	2211
	犬	3464
	見	2544
	気	3194
	金	2057
	口	3382
	校	929
	空	2227
	九	3369
	休	52
M	名	2169
	目	3043
N	年	2035
	二	1922
	日	3027
	入	3370
O	王	3439
	音	2070
R	林	861
	立	1992
	六	1965
	力	3371
S	左	2974
	三	1924
	山	2940
	正	3484
	生	3497
	青	2430
	夕	3387
	石	2971
	赤	2193
	千	3411
	川	6
	先	2394
	車	3552
	子	3390
	四	3044
	糸	2179
	七	3362
	森	2475
	小	7
	手	3456
	出	3498
	早	2390
	草	2263
	足	2188
	村	834
	水	10
T	天	3442
U	右	2975
	雨	3561

GRADE 2

(160)

	Kanji	No.
B	馬	3296
	売	2196
	買	2598
	麦	2408
	番	2748
	米	3529
	母	3475
	分	1972

1. A revised list of 1006 Education Kanji was promulgated on March 15, 1989. The dictionary underwent a final revision to incorporate the new list before it went to press. As a result, this is probably the first dictionary based on the new Education Kanji.

	Kanji	No.
	聞	3326
C	茶	2259
	地	204
	池	218
	知	1127
	長	2556
	鳥	3312
	朝	1695
	直	2932
	昼	3097
D	台	2005
	電	2790
	同	2987
	道	3134
	読	1541
E	遠	3150
	園	3156
F	父	1973
	風	3007
G	画	3000
	外	186
	楽	2826
	丸	3417
	岩	2235
	顔	1808
	元	1929
	言	1941
	原	3009
	午	1984
	後	361
	語	1543
	合	2019
	魚	2127
	牛	3452
H	半	3501
	歩	2416
	方	1963
	北	197
I	引	181
J	弱	1167
	寺	2164
	自	3525
	時	924
	場	558
K	何	65
	科	1138
	夏	2113
	家	2273
	歌	1825
	会	2020
	回	3055
	海	384
	絵	1346
	角	2047
	間	3323
	活	385
	兄	2154
	形	846
	計	1441
	汽	264
	帰	130
	記	1453
	近	3061
	戸	1930
	古	2002
	工	3381
	公	1974
	広	3035
	交	2015
	光	2391
	考	3196
	行	212
	高	2097
	黄	2468
	谷	2043
	国	3087
	黒	2740
	今	1968
	京	2052
	強	475
	教	1493
	弓	3383
M	毎	2034
	妹	278
	万	2936
	明	855
	鳴	674
	毛	3453
	門	888
N	内	3466
	南	2082
	肉	3200
R	来	3551
	里	3542
	理	970
S	才	3410
	細	1333
	作	68
	算	2702
	西	3520
	声	2198
	星	2435
	晴	981
	船	1341
	線	1392
	切	27
	雪	2759
	社	840
	止	2941
	市	1993
	矢	2009
	姉	280
	思	2564
	紙	1302
	心	11
	新	1784
	親	1799
	室	2254
	書	2658
	少	3467
	色	2029
	食	2075
	首	2265
	秋	1139
	週	3122
	春	2576
	組	1337
	走	2194
	数	1790
T	多	2170
	太	2152
	体	71
	弟	2044
	店	3085
	点	2084
	刀	2926
	冬	2157
	当	2177
	東	3568
	答	2681
	頭	1604
	通	3109
U	羽	226
	雲	2773
W	話	1527
Y	夜	2056
	野	1485
	用	2976
	曜	1096
	友	2952
Z	前	2266
	図	3071

GRADE 3
(200)

	Kanji	No.
A	悪	2745
	安	2171
	暗	1010
B	倍	108
	皿	3474
	勉	3318
	美	2264
	鼻	2706
	部	1676
	物	874
	秒	1137
	病	3277
C	着	3316
	丁	3348
	帳	473
	調	1567
	注	325
	柱	896
D	打	193
	代	30
	第	2660
	題	3337
	談	1569
	度	3100
	動	1778
	童	2130
E	泳	327
	駅	1822
F	夫	3460
	負	2091
	服	878
	福	1029
G	岸	2236
	銀	1722
	号	2153
	具	2552
	業	2612
H	波	330
	配	1460
	反	2945
	坂	234
	板	858
	畑	905
	発	2565
	平	3478
	返	3060
	皮	3037
	悲	2775
	品	2248
	筆	2677
	放	853
	氷	39
	表	2429
I	医	2993
	委	2553
	意	2136
	育	2050
	員	2269
	院	454
	飲	1692
J	次	54
	事	3567
	持	374
	実	2225
	助	1121
	乗	3576
	受	2421
	住	64
	重	3573
K	化	21
	荷	2282
	界	2563
	開	3321
	階	624
	寒	2311
	感	2835
	漢	657
	館	1748
	係	97
	軽	1515
	県	2641
	研	1132
	血	3526
	決	263
	起	3307
	期	1704
	庫	3112
	湖	604
	向	3052
	幸	2216
	港	605
	根	930
	区	2963
	苦	2243
	君	3206
	客	2250
	去	2156
	橋	1078
	曲	3527
	局	3063
	究	2203
	急	2092
	級	1279
	宮	2274
	球	969
M	命	2058
	面	2087
	味	274

問 3320
N 農 2698
O 横 1066
屋 3098
温 608
R 落 2318
礼 818
練 1375
列 824
路 1533
旅 922
両 3518
緑 1377
流 441
S 祭 2672
世 3496
整 2871
昔 2432
写 2000
者 3211
仕 34
死 3521
使 90
始 281
指 378
歯 2476
詩 1524
式 3049
申 3507
身 3553
神 912
真 2111
深 524
進 3121
所 851
暑 2473
昭 894
消 443
商 2116
章 2117
勝 1005
植 990
主 1938
守 2173
取 1262
酒 444
州 57
拾 379
終 1336
習 2667
集 2771
宿 2293
送 3093
相 900
想 2828
箱 2711
息 2647
速 3105
T 他 35
対 831
待 364
炭 2257
短 1182
定 2229
庭 3114
笛 2664
転 1480
鉄 1711
都 1686
投 256
豆 1943
島 3310
湯 612
登 2595
等 2682
追 3096
U 運 3140
W 和 1130
Y 役 244
薬 2375
予 1983
羊 2183
洋 392
葉 2321
陽 626
様 1052
由 3499
油 341
有 2983
遊 3142
Z 全 2022
族 958

GRADE 4
(200)

A 愛 2492
案 2270
B 梅 925
便 95
別 1117
望 2742
牧 873
C 置 2608
貯 1509
兆 225
腸 1033
仲 43
D 伝 44
努 2547
堂 2589
働 153
毒 2428
E 英 2238
栄 2574
塩 631
F 不 3434
付 31
府 3082
副 1776
粉 1291
G 芽 2240
害 2272
街 576
願 1845
芸 2209
議 1647
軍 2080
郡 1466
漁 698
H 敗 1476
博 151
飯 1691
兵 2551
辺 3029
変 2069
飛 3572
費 2607
必 15
包 2966
法 333
票 2669
標 1064
I 以 41
衣 2013
位 61
囲 3069
胃 2561
印 828
J 児 2546
治 335
辞 1364
順 18
K 加 38
果 3560
貨 2465
課 1573
改 243
械 961
各 2168
覚 2604
完 2201
官 2226
管 2701
関 3328
観 1880
径 291
型 2638
景 2470
建 3090
健 134
験 1833
欠 1987
結 1348
希 2049
季 2554
紀 1276
喜 2308
旗 1047
器 2713
機 1076
固 3086
功 189
好 208
候 119
航 1318
康 3124
告 2409
訓 1454
挙 2456
共 2393
協 93
鏡 1766
競 1847
極 1017
求 3550
泣 338
救 1497
給 1350
M 満 607
末 3505
未 3506
民 3036
無 2135
脈 953
N 念 2059
熱 2866
O 央 3509
億 170
R 令 1995
冷 80
例 89
歴 3019
連 3103
利 1114
陸 543
輪 1589
老 3197
労 2548
録 1742
類 1807
良 3558
料 1292
量 2471
S 差 3311
菜 2305
最 2472
昨 893
参 2066
産 3298
散 1702
札 817
刷 1273
殺 1324
察 2347
成 3537
省 2449
清 523
静 1728
席 3113
積 1236
浅 389
戦 1787
選 3169
折 253
節 2691
説 1547
借 122
士 3405
氏 2951
史 3510
司 2931
試 1525
臣 3068
信 100
失 3511
初 1116
松 864
笑 2646
唱 462
焼 997
象 2134
照 2827
賞 2618

種 1218
周 2998
祝 913
争 2030
倉 2104
巣 2295
束 3554
側 137
孫 410
卒 2055
T 帯 2582
隊 625
単 2256
達 3139
低 73
底 3084
停 139
的 1125
典 2627
徒 416
灯 825
特 945
得 477
Y 約 1280
要 2635
養 2365
浴 445
勇 2089
Z 材 836
残 943
然 2782
続 1362

GRADE 5
(185)

A 圧 2970
B 弁 2004
備 146
墓 2332
防 270
貿 2601
暴 2515
武 3210
仏 19
C 築 2715
張 474
D 団 3053
断 1492
銅 1721
導 2888
独 395
E 永 1937
営 2603
衛 760
易 2411
益 2285
液 511
演 697
F 布 2973
婦 469
富 2310
復 575
複 1222
G 賀 2599
額 1805
眼 1172
限 398
現 968
減 601
技 248
義 2338
護 1648
群 1540
逆 3091
H 破 1150
犯 196
判 1122
版 872
編 1387
比 26
肥 879
非 889
貧 2123
保 96
報 1698
豊 2697
俵 115
評 1501
I 移 1177
因 3054
J 示 1936
似 63
序 3065
条 2200
状 272
常 2590
情 482
授 492
準 2856
述 3075
術 476
K 可 2969
仮 50
価 87
河 336
過 3137
快 245
解 1517
格 926
確 1228
刊 190
幹 1718
慣 685
経 1331
件 51
券 2630
険 542
検 986
潔 744
基 2673
寄 2291
規 978
均 235
禁 2795
故 1141
個 117
効 1265
厚 3003
耕 1308
鉱 1709
構 1049
興 2909
講 1619
混 519
句 2967
居 3080
許 1470
境 676
久 3384
旧 14
M 迷 3092
綿 1373
務 1173
夢 2336
N 燃 1081
任 53
能 1323
O 応 3066
往 292
桜 931
恩 2655
R 略 1169
領 1224
留 2580
S 査 2437
再 3519
災 2206
妻 2558
採 499
際 714
酸 1563
賛 2809
制 1274
性 299
政 1142
勢 2857
精 1366
製 2803
責 2467
績 1412
銭 1725
接 500
設 1471
舎 2060
謝 1620
支 1979
志 2199
枝 863
師 1326
資 2695
飼 1716
識 1639
質 2808
承 16
招 316
証 1506
織 1422
職 1425
修 123
祖 914
素 2458
総 1379
則 1444
測 610
損 651
率 2118
T 退 3094
貸 2600
態 2847
提 591
程 1190
適 3160
敵 1864
統 1352
徳 684
Y 余 2042
預 1042
容 2277
輸 1607
Z 在 2984
財 1457
罪 2610
雑 1385
税 1191
舌 2186
絶 1353
造 3110
像 166
増 677
属 3145

GRADE 6
(181)

B 晩 979
暮 2354
亡 3402
忘 2036
棒 983
C 値 109
賃 2694
著 2300
庁 3034
頂 145
潮 739
宙 2221
忠 2433
D 段 1144
暖 1011
E 映 892
延 3073
沿 328
F 腹 1034
奮 2367
G 我 3548
劇 1904
激 776
源 656
厳 3289
疑 1565
誤 1542
H 派 381
拝 303
背 2573
肺 916
俳 112
班 946
並 2246
陛 453
閉 3319
片 3461
否 2406
批 250

秘 1159
補 1194
宝 2224
訪 1468
I 異 2584
遺 3166
域 465
J 若 2241
磁 1214
仁 20
除 456
城 352
蒸 2334
樹 1075
従 415
縦 1408
熟 2868
純 1297
K 灰 2979
届 3078
拡 309
革 2448
閣 3327
干 3379
巻 2645
看 3220
簡 2721
割 1816
系 1944
敬 1701
警 2893
絹 1361
権 1065
憲 2368
穴 2159
危 3199
机 820
揮 589
貴 2606
勤 1818
筋 2678
己 3380
呼 273
后 2981

孝 3205
皇 2566
紅 1277
降 458
鋼 1740
刻 1267
穀 1824
困 3070
骨 2654
供 88
胸 951
郷 549
吸 202
M 枚 859
幕 2335
盟 2794
密 2292
模 1050
N 難 1838
認 1546
納 1300
脳 975
乳 1438
R 乱 1260
卵 849
覧 2854
裏 2138
臨 1630
律 363
朗 1325
論 1574
S 砂 1133
済 522
裁 3299
策 2679
蚕 2457
冊 3483
盛 2675
聖 2830
誠 1523
宣 2252
専 2644
染 2572
泉 2567

洗 388
射 1458
捨 501
尺 3440
至 2182
私 1115
姿 2636
視 972
詞 1503
誌 1548
針 1666
処 3031
署 2609
諸 1577
将 460
傷 158
障 715
株 935
収 198
宗 2228
衆 2683
就 1694
縮 1414
奏 2577
窓 2294
創 1815
装 2685
層 3161
操 769
存 2982
尊 2324
垂 3565
推 504
寸 2935
T 宅 2174
担 318
探 505
誕 1579
展 3111
党 2581
討 1456
糖 1403
痛 3285
U 宇 2175

Y 訳 1473
幼 191
欲 1475
翌 2668
郵 1687
優 177
Z 座 3116
善 2325
蔵 2364
臓 1102

GENERAL-USE
(939)

A 亜 3540
哀 2068
握 585
B 婆 2762
培 464
陪 539
媒 564
賠 1582
漠 655
縛 1405
爆 1101
蛮 2129
盤 2851
伐 42
抜 246
罰 2613
閥 3325
尾 3062
微 639
敏 1322
瓶 1344
募 2316
慕 2353
簿 2727
乏 1933
忙 214
坊 233
妨 238
房 1946
肪 877

某 2560
冒 2434
剖 1670
畝 1465
紡 1295
傍 147
帽 568
膨 1084
謀 1593
朴 819
僕 164
墨 2753
撲 733
凡 2938
盆 2079
没 260
侮 82
舞 2146
蚊 1319
苗 2237
描 488
猫 535
C 嫡 680
恥 1313
致 1316
遅 3133
痴 3286
稚 1206
畜 2096
逐 3102
蓄 2333
沈 261
珍 909
朕 949
陳 540
鎮 1759
秩 1158
窒 2288
弔 3432
挑 372
彫 1683
眺 1171
釣 1674
塚 556

脹 1003
超 3313
跳 1532
徴 683
澄 740
聴 1418
懲 2910
勅 1451
沖 262
抽 302
衷 2575
鋳 1729
駐 1826
D 妥 2400
堕 2822
惰 579
駄 1821
諾 1568
濁 774
弾 572
壇 754
脱 973
奪 2343
泥 326
殿 1792
奴 187
怒 2571
洞 380
胴 950
鈍 1689
曇 2521
E 詠 1500
影 1889
鋭 1730
疫 3276
炎 2420
垣 351
宴 2271
援 586
煙 1021
猿 669
鉛 1707
縁 1386
悦 418

	Kanji	No.
	越	3314
	謁	1570
	閲	3330
F	扶	247
	怖	296
	附	347
	赴	3303
	浮	435
	符	2661
	普	2323
	腐	3162
	敷	1870
	膚	3265
	賦	1583
	譜	1637
	封	1287
	伏	45
	幅	569
	覆	2726
	紛	1296
	雰	2772
	噴	717
	墳	719
	憤	730
	払	194
	沸	329
G	雅	1197
	餓	1734
	刈	28
	劾	1266
	涯	512
	慨	641
	該	1519
	概	1048
	岳	2557
	含	2041
	頑	1040
	迎	3059
	鯨	1882
	撃	2863
	幻	180
	玄	1991
	弦	287
	宜	2223
	偽	131
	欺	1703
	儀	169
	戯	1875
	擬	788
	犠	1089
	吟	230
	互	3437
	呉	2549
	娯	405
	悟	419
	碁	2699
	拷	373
	剛	1673
	豪	2140
	獄	712
	懇	2834
	虞	3254
	偶	132
	遇	3135
	隅	623
	虐	3218
	御	577
	仰	48
	暁	980
	凝	175
H	把	249
	覇	2730
	鉢	1708
	杯	857
	排	490
	廃	3146
	輩	2807
	伯	59
	拍	304
	泊	331
	迫	3074
	舶	1340
	薄	2370
	帆	210
	伴	60
	畔	1145
	般	1317
	販	1477
	搬	647
	煩	1022
	頒	1043
	範	2709
	繁	2853
	藩	2379
	髪	2846
	丙	3479
	併	83
	坪	275
	柄	897
	塀	557
	幣	2885
	弊	2884
	壁	2895
	癖	3290
	偏	133
	遍	3136
	妃	206
	彼	290
	披	305
	卑	2642
	疲	3278
	被	1163
	扉	1955
	碑	1213
	罷	2617
	避	3179
	浜	436
	賓	2357
	頻	1758
	匹	2962
	泌	332
	捕	429
	浦	437
	舗	1735
	芳	2210
	邦	847
	奉	2559
	抱	306
	泡	334
	胞	917
	倣	113
	俸	114
	峰	411
	砲	1151
	崩	2296
	棚	984
	飽	1715
	褒	2144
	縫	1406
	奔	2218
	翻	1897
	漂	699
I	依	84
	威	3578
	為	3577
	尉	1685
	偉	148
	違	3151
	維	1370
	慰	2867
	緯	1407
	壱	2197
	姻	353
	陰	541
	隠	713
	韻	1811
	逸	3120
J	邪	1124
	蛇	1343
	寂	2290
	侍	85
	滋	602
	慈	2339
	璽	2911
	軸	1514
	刃	2929
	尽	3050
	迅	3046
	甚	2643
	陣	455
	尋	2322
	如	207
	叙	1446
	徐	414
	丈	3419
	冗	1976
	浄	382
	娘	406
	剰	1779
	畳	2592
	縄	1388
	壌	755
	嬢	758
	錠	1737
	譲	1649
	醸	1654
	辱	2736
	寿	3557
	需	2797
	儒	174
	汁	195
	充	2014
	柔	2088
	渋	513
	銃	1723
	獣	1892
	塾	2860
	巡	3047
	旬	2978
	盾	3006
	准	127
	殉	941
	循	578
	潤	742
	遵	3167
K	佳	86
	架	2569
	華	2283
	菓	2302
	渦	603
	嫁	635
	暇	1012
	禍	1030
	靴	1781
	寡	2344
	箇	2700
	稼	1230
	介	1967
	戒	3204
	怪	297
	拐	308
	悔	365
	皆	2445
	掛	493
	塊	632
	壊	756
	懐	763
	核	927
	殻	1490
	郭	1678
	較	1536
	隔	671
	獲	779
	嚇	784
	穫	1251
	甘	3494
	汗	220
	缶	2033
	肝	841
	冠	2081
	陥	457
	乾	1679
	勘	1777
	患	2747
	貫	2460
	喚	550
	堪	559
	換	587
	敢	1706
	棺	985
	款	1700
	閑	3322
	勧	1857
	寛	2327
	歓	1867
	監	2852
	緩	1389
	憾	764
	還	3180
	環	1090
	艦	1435
	鑑	1773
	括	376
	喝	461

渇 515
滑 658
褐 1210
轄 1627
刑 830
茎 2242
契 2639
恵 2659
啓 2763
掲 494
渓 516
蛍 2591
傾 154
携 648
継 1360
慶 3173
憩 2890
鶏 1768
肩 1947
兼 2286
倹 116
剣 1672
軒 1459
圏 3148
堅 2823
嫌 636
献 1785
遣 3152
賢 2839
謙 1617
繭 2380
顕 1806
懸 2915
傑 155
企 2021
肌 827
岐 241
忌 2207
奇 2217
祈 875
軌 1445
姫 407
既 1166
飢 1668
鬼 2657
崎 472
幾 3582
棋 987
棄 2137
輝 1402
騎 1834
吉 2167
菊 2303
斤 2949
菌 2304
琴 2781
緊 2838
謹 1618
襟 1252
喫 551
詰 1521
孤 356
弧 360
枯 898
雇 1956
誇 1522
鼓 1786
顧 1900
孔 179
巧 188
甲 3481
江 221
坑 236
抗 252
攻 242
更 3541
岬 284
拘 310
肯 2417
侯 98
恒 367
洪 386
荒 2260
郊 1286
香 2568
貢 2281
控 495
慌 580
硬 1183
絞 1349
項 567
溝 659
綱 1372
酵 1561
稿 1231
衡 761
購 1624
克 2046
酷 1562
込 3030
昆 2413
恨 369
婚 470
紺 1332
魂 1063
墾 2896
懇 2899
駆 1823
勲 2869
薫 2371
屈 3079
堀 467
掘 496
却 1118
脚 974
巨 3039
拠 312
拒 311
据 497
虚 3237
距 1511
凶 2961
叫 201
狂 269
享 2051
況 337
峡 357
挟 377
狭 396
恐 2650
恭 2459
脅 2109
矯 1241
響 2878
驚 2894
及 3385
丘 3495
朽 821
糾 1278
窮 2358

M

麻 3125
摩 3175
磨 3181
魔 3187
埋 403
膜 1062
慢 686
漫 700
抹 313
銘 1724
免 2067
滅 660
魅 3329
眠 1147
茂 2245
妄 2016
盲 2053
耗 1309
猛 537
網 1374
黙 2865
紋 1299
匁 3465
矛 2008
霧 2817
妙 239

N

軟 1479
寧 2345
粘 1327
尼 3033
弐 3195
妊 240
忍 2212
悩 421
濃 777
尿 3064

O

汚 222
凹 3482
押 314
欧 887
殴 886
翁 2108
奥 2824
憶 765
穏 1235
乙 3339

R

裸 1211
羅 2622
雷 2791
頼 1615
瀬 806
絡 1351
酪 1538
濫 801
欄 1103
励 1119
戻 1942
鈴 1710
零 2792
霊 2805
隷 1751
齢 1895
麗 2151
暦 3018
恋 2098
廉 3153
錬 1741
劣 2395
烈 2652
裂 2687
吏 3536
痢 3283
履 3171
離 1836
厘 3004
倫 120
隣 781
炉 869
露 2818
郎 1289
浪 439
廊 3147
楼 1019
滝 661
漏 701
涙 440
累 2585
塁 2593
虜 3255
慮 3266
了 3350
涼 521
猟 538
陵 544
僚 165
寮 2359
療 3288
糧 1421
柳 899
竜 2099
粒 1328
隆 545
硫 1184

S

佐 67
唆 402
詐 1502
鎖 1761
砕 1134
宰 2275
栽 3297
彩 1681
斎 2115
債 156
催 157
歳 2490
載 3300
削 1448
索 2455
酢 1516
搾 649
錯 1743
杉 832
桟 932
惨 483

傘 2131
撮 737
擦 790
井 3454
姓 279
征 293
斉 2054
牲 907
逝 3104
婿 566
誓 2754
請 1576
斥 2972
析 862
隻 2755
惜 484
跡 1534
潟 745
籍 2731
仙 32
占 2003
扇 1950
栓 934
旋 957
践 1535
銑 1726
潜 746
遷 3170
薦 2373
繊 1413
鮮 1877
拙 315
窃 2253
摂 650
卸 1447
斜 1486
赦 1478
煮 2785
遮 3158
勺 2933
酌 1461
釈 1484
爵 2524
旨 2024

芝 2180
伺 69
刺 1275
祉 876
肢 882
施 891
脂 954
紫 2688
嗣 1719
漬 702
雌 1055
賜 1585
諮 1596
伸 70
辛 2038
侵 101
津 390
唇 2737
娠 408
振 430
浸 442
紳 1334
診 1504
寝 2329
慎 643
審 2360
震 2806
薪 2374
疾 3279
執 1680
湿 609
漆 704
且 3485
庶 3127
緒 1378
升 3455
召 2001
匠 2990
扱 217
床 3067
抄 254
肖 2205
尚 2233
昇 2415

沼 339
咲 349
称 1160
宵 2276
症 3280
祥 948
渉 526
紹 1335
訟 1472
掌 2602
晶 2474
焦 2770
硝 1185
粧 1345
詔 1505
奨 2842
詳 1526
彰 1860
衝 725
償 176
礁 1243
鐘 1769
殖 994
触 1518
飾 1717
嘱 718
朱 3531
狩 397
殊 942
珠 947
趣 3317
囚 3042
舟 3538
秀 2545
臭 2633
愁 2829
酬 1539
醜 1629
襲 2917
叔 527
淑 1272
粛 3581
俊 102
瞬 1247

阻 348
租 1161
措 502
粗 1329
疎 1178
訴 1507
塑 2843
礎 1248
双 25
壮 224
荘 2262
捜 432
挿 431
桑 2112
掃 503
曹 2746
喪 2825
葬 2320
僧 159
遭 3159
槽 1067
燥 1087
霜 2815
騒 1835
繰 1427
藻 2384
即 1120
促 103
枢 865
崇 2297
吹 231
炊 870
帥 1290
粋 1293
衰 2100
酔 1483
遂 3138
睡 1200
穂 1232
錘 1744
T 怠 2085
耐 1282
胎 918
泰 2583

袋 2588
逮 3123
替 2783
滞 663
択 255
沢 267
卓 2064
拓 317
託 1455
濯 793
丹 3441
但 72
胆 919
淡 528
嘆 630
端 1221
鍛 1755
呈 2189
廷 3058
抵 319
邸 1131
亭 2072
帝 2073
訂 1442
貞 2083
逓 3106
偵 138
堤 560
艇 1365
締 1393
摘 694
滴 705
添 529
迭 3077
哲 2738
徹 726
撤 738
斗 2953
吐 203
途 3107
渡 611
塗 2841
到 1264
逃 3095

倒 124
凍 129
唐 3115
桃 936
透 3108
悼 485
盗 2670
陶 546
塔 561
搭 592
棟 991
痘 3284
筒 2680
稲 1219
踏 1587
謄 1093
闘 3334
騰 1106
峠 358
匿 3011
督 2796
篤 2716
屯 3457
豚 976
凸 3486
突 2230
墜 2881
U 芋 2181
W 賄 1529
惑 2786
枠 866
湾 613
腕 1006
Y 厄 2947
躍 1658
与 3421
誉 2502
庸 3128
揚 593
揺 594
溶 664
腰 1036
踊 1558
窯 2361

擁	770	諭	1598	猶	619	融	1831	禅	1032	俗	104
謡	1597	癒	3291	裕	1195	唯	463	漸	706	賊	1530
抑	257	又	3351	雄	1008	Z 剤	1669	繕	1423	随	627
翼	2720	幽	3008	誘	1550	暫	2864	憎	687	髄	1842
愉	582	悠	2741	憂	2145	是	2436	贈	1634		

APPENDIX 11

LIST OF KANJI SYNONYM GROUPS

This appendix classifies the characters into semantic categories called **synonym groups.** For quick reference, the groups are listed alphabetically by their **headwords,** a concise keyword that normally expresses the meaning shared by the group members. In the main part of the dictionary, synonym groups are given for the principal senses of each main entry character; here, the groups are brought together in one convenient listing.

1. **Benefits** This appendix could be useful in three principal ways:
   (*a*) It enables the learner to study the differences and similarities between closely-related characters together, rather than as isolated units, in an easy-to-read format.
   (*b*) It serves as a simple thesaurus that helps the student composing texts select the word most appropriate to the context.
   (*c*) It enables the user to look up an unknown character from its meaning, rather than from its form or reading.

   This appendix could be used in various other ways. Even browsing through it at random could be highly rewarding and provide much insight into the semantic relations between characters. For information on items (*a*) and (*b*) above, see **§ 5.1.2 Powerful Learning Aid** and **§ 5.1.3 Simple Kanji Thesaurus** in FEATURES OF THIS DICTIONARY beginning on p. 61a. Item (*c*) is described below.

2. **Format and Order** Each synonym group is headed by a headword in sanserif boldface type, and the groups are ordered alphabetically by their headwords. Each group lists the kanji synonyms roughly in order of semantic proximity. Each character is followed by its **synonym keyword** and **entry number.** Capitals distinguish keywords that are core meanings from those that are not. Cross-references, followed by an arrow ⇨, point to the headword where a desired group appears.

3. **Looking up by meaning** To a limited extent, it is possible to locate a character from its meaning by means of this appendix. Since this is merely a semantically classified list, not a real thesaurus, it is not particularly efficient as a lookup tool. Use it when you cannot recall the form or reading of your character but have some idea of what it looks like. Follow the procedure below:
   (*a*) Try to guess the headword under which your character may be classified. Think of general conceptual categories, rather than of specific terms. For example, for 'pear' try 'fruits'; for 'outstanding' try 'excellent', etc.
   (*b*) Look for your tentative headword in the listing. If it is there, there is a good chance that your character will be in that group. If it is not, repeat Step 1. The cross-references may help.
   (*c*) The number to the right of the synonym keyword is the entry number of your character.

A

abandon ⇨ DISCARD AND ABANDON

abnormal

変	ABNORMAL	2069
奇	UNUSUAL	2217
怪	MYSTERIOUS	297
妙	strange	239
異	not ordinary	2584
珍	curious	909

abridge

要	SUMMARIZE	2635
抄	EXCERPT	254
約	CONTRACT	1280
略	omit	1169

abstain ⇨ AVOID AND ABSTAIN

abstract thing

事	ABSTRACT THING	3567
物	THING	874

accompany

伴	ACCOMPANY	60
添	accompany	529
陪	ACCOMPANY A SUPERIOR	539
侍	ATTEND UPON	85
従	FOLLOW	415
随	FOLLOW	627

accomplish

達	ATTAIN	3139
遂	ACCOMPLISH	3138
成	ACHIEVE	3537
徹	GO THROUGH	726
破	carry through with	1150

accomplishment

績	ACHIEVEMENTS	1412
功	MERIT	189
勲	MERITORIOUS SERVICE	2869

accumulate

積	ACCUMULATE	1236
累	CUMULATE	2585
重	pile up	3573
盛る	heap up	2675

accuse ⇨ BLAME AND ACCUSE

a certain

某	A CERTAIN	2560
一	ONE	3341

act ⇨ DO AND ACT

acting arbitrarily

横	arbitrary	1066
独	act arbitrarily	395
専	arrogate to oneself	2644

active

活	ACTIVE	385
動	dynamic	1778

acts

行	ACT	212
挙	NOTEWORTHY ACT	2456
業	deed	2612

add

加	ADD	38
足す	add	2188

additional

追	additional	3096
補	supplementary	1194
副	accessory	1776

additionally

亦	ALSO	2011
又	also, and	3351
及び	and	3385
並びに	and also	2246
傍ら	besides	147
尚	STILL	2233
更に	furthermore	3541
且つ	AS WELL	3485
兼	CONCURRENTLY	2286

add to

付	ATTACH	31
附	ATTACH	347
加	ADD	38
追	add	3096
添	ADD TO	529

adhere to

執	adhere to	1680
着	stick to	3316

advance

進	ADVANCE	3121
興	cause to rise	2909
奨	ENCOURAGE	2842
勧	encourage	1857

advocate

唱	advocate	462
説	preach	1547

affair

事	AFFAIR	3567
儀	affair	169
件	MATTER	51

affairs

用	THINGS TO DO	2976
事	affairs	3567
務	affairs	1173

after

後	AFTER	361
余	after	2042

age

齢	AGE	1895
令	age	1995
年	years	2035
歳	AGE SUFFIX	2490
才	AGE SUFFIX	3410
寿	life span	3557

agents

使	ENVOY	90
偵	SPY	138

agree and approve

賛	APPROVE OF	2809
可	APPROVE	2969
認	RECOGNIZE	1546
諾	CONSENT	1568
承	AGREE TO	16
肯	ASSENT	2417
容	tolerate	2277

aircraft and spacecraft

機	AIRCRAFT	1076
空	aircraft	2227
船	spaceship	1341

all

皆	ALL	2445
都	all	1686
万	all	2936
全	WHOLE	2022
一	all in one	3341
満	FULL	607
丸	complete(ly)	3417
完	COMPLETE	2201
総	TOTAL	1379
諸	VARIOUS	1577
毎	EVERY	2034
各	EACH	2168

allot

充	allot	2014
当	assign	2177

alone

独	ALONE	395
孤	SOLITARY	356

alternate

迭	ALTERNATE	3077
交	INTERCHANGE	2015
輪	take turns	1589

anger

怒	GET ANGRY	2571
憤	INDIGNATION	730
慨	resent	641

angle and angular measure

角	ANGLE	2047
度	DEGREE	3100

angular measure ⇨ ANGLE AND ANGULAR MEASURE

animal

獣	BEAST	1892
畜	LIVESTOCK	2096
生	LIFE	3497
物	living thing	874

animals ⇨ COUNTERS FOR ANIMALS

answer

答	ANSWER	2681
解	solve	1517
返	reply	3060
応	RESPOND	3066

appear

現	APPEAR	968
出	come out	3498
顕	MANIFEST	1806

appearance

容	APPEARANCE	2277
姿	FIGURE	2636
相	PHASE	900
体	FORM (outer appearance)	71
色	COLOR	2029
風	air	3007

appoint

任	appoint	53
補	appoint	1194
挙	NOMINATE	2456

approach

寄る	DRAW NEAR	2291

迫	PRESS	3074
近	NEAR	3061
接	come close to	500

approve ⇨ AGREE AND APPROVE

approximately

約	APPROXIMATELY	1280
概	GENERAL	1048
大	in substance	3416
-頃	ABOUT	144
位	about	61
-方	about	1963
-程	...or thereabouts	1190
辺り	thereabouts	3029

areas and localities

地	PLACE	204
方	locality	1963
辺	VICINITY	3029
域	BOUNDED AREA	465
区	DISTRICT	2963
領	TERRITORY	1224
帯	BELT	2582
圏	SPHERE	3148

area units

坪	*TSUBO* (3.3 sq.m)	275
歩	*bu* (3.3 sq.m)	2416
畝	*SE* (0.99 ares)	1465
反	*tan* (9.9 ares)	2945
町	*cho* (99.2 ares)	1113

argue and discuss

議	DISCUSS	1647
争	CONTEND	2030
論	ARGUE	1574
弁	argue (for)	2004

arm ⇨ HAND AND ARM

armed forces

軍	ARMY	2080
兵	the military	2551
勢	forces	2857
隊	PARTY	625

arrange

並	LINE UP	2246
比	rank	26
列	arrange in a row	824
陳	lay out (for exhibit)	540
羅	spread out	2622
揃える	arrange properly	590
整	PUT IN ORDER	2871
理	put in order	970

arrive

着	ARRIVE	3316
到	ARRIVE	1264
至	COME TO	2182
及	REACH TO	3385
届く	REACH	3078
達	ATTAIN	3139

arrogance ⇨ BOASTING AND ARROGANCE

art

技	SKILL	248
術	PRACTICAL ART	476
芸	ART	2209
道	the way of an art	3134

ascend

昇	ASCEND	2415
上	go up	3404
騰	RISE (esp. in price)	1106
登	CLIMB	2595

Asian countries

日	JAPAN	3027
華	CHINA	2283
鮮	Korea	1877
泰	Thailand	2583
越	Vietnam	3314
印	India	828
比	Philippines	26

aspect

面	side	2087
上	from the viewpoint of	3404
柄	considering the character of	897

assembly

会	meeting	2020
集	gathering	2771

assistant

補	assistant	1194
丞	AIDE	2541

associates ⇨ FRIENDS AND ASSOCIATES

assume upright position

立	STAND	1992
起	RISE	3307

atmosphere

雰	ATMOSPHERE	2772
気	atmosphere	3194

atmospheric discharges

雷	THUNDER	2791
電	lightning	2790

atmospheric vapor ⇨KINDS OF ATMOSPHERIC VAPOR

attack

攻	ATTACK	242
撃	STRIKE	2863
襲	RAID	2917
侵	INVADE	101
爆	bomb	1101

attain proficiency

達	attain proficiency	3139
熟	become skilled	2868

attend

臨	BE PRESENT AT	1630
登	attend	2595
出	appear	3498

attention

気	care	3194
念	attention	2059

authority ⇨POWER AND AUTHORITY

avoid and abstain

避	AVOID	3179
逃	ESCAPE	3095
忌	shun	2207
禁	abstain from	2795

awake

悟	AWAKE TO	419
覚	awake	2604

B

bad

悪	BAD	2745
劣	INFERIOR	2395
下	of low grade	3378
弊	shabby	2884
粗	COARSE	1329
駄	GOOD FOR NOTHING	1821
廃	WASTE	3146

bags

俵	STRAW SACK	115
袋	BAG	2588
包	wrapper	2966
胞	MEMBRANOUS SAC	917

bamboo

竹	BAMBOO	228
笹	BAMBOO GRASS	2663

bank

銀	bank	1722
行	bank	212

barely

甫めて	BARELY	3549
辛い	bare	2038

bases ⇨BOTTOMS AND BASES

basis

基	BASE	2673
本	BASIS	3502
素	ELEMENT	2458
礎	foundation	1248
底	BOTTOM	3084
根	ROOT	930
拠	GROUNDS	312

baths

浴	bath	445
湯	hot bath	612
泉	hot spring	2567

bays ⇨INLETS AND BAYS

be ⇨EXIST AND BE

bear

負	BEAR (on the back)	2091
荷	carry on shoulder	2282
担	BEAR ON SHOULDER	318
支	SUPPORT	1979

bear and endure

堪	ENDURE	559
忍	BEAR	2212
耐	WITHSTAND	1282

beautiful

美	BEAUTIFUL	2264
佳	FINE	86
瑶	EXQUISITE	1026
麗	OF GRACEFUL BEAUTY	2151
艶	CHARMING	1908
妙	of marvelous beauty	239
華	MAGNIFICENT	2283
絢	GORGEOUS	1347
斐	florid	2776

become stupefied

酔	BECOME INTOXICATED	1483
麻	BECOME NUMB	3125

before

前	BEFORE	2266
先	AHEAD	2394
予	IN ADVANCE	1983

begin

始	BEGIN	281
-出す	begin to do	3498
-掛ける	start doing	493
発	START	2565
起	start	3307
就	SET ABOUT	1694
開	OPEN	3321
創	initiate	1815
肇	ORIGINATE	2799

beginnings

緒	OUTSET	1378
序	INTRODUCTORY PART	3065
端	start	1221
始	beginning	281
初	beginning	1116
元	ORIGIN	1929
本	origin	3502
根	ROOT	930
源	SOURCE	656

behavior

行	conduct	212
挙	deportment	2456
動	behavior	1778

be late and delay

遅	be late	3133
後	fall behind	361
滞	fall into arrears	663
延	POSTPONE	3073
猶	DELAY	619

bells

鈴	BELL (that jingles or rings)	1710
鐘	BELL (that tolls)	1769

bend

曲	CURVE	3527
屈	BEND	3079
折	bend	253

benefit

利	ADVANTAGE	1114
益	BENEFIT	2285
為	SAKE	3577
用	use(ful)	2976
役	SERVICE	244

be subjected to

被	BE SUBJECTED TO	1163
受	be subjected to	2421

between

中	MIDDLE	3451
仲	intermediate	43
間	BETWEEN	3323
際	inter-	714

bewildered

迷	PERPLEXED	3092
惑	BEWILDERED	2786

big and huge

大	BIG	3416
太	GREAT	2152
浩	VAST	438
巨	HUGE	3039

bird

鳥	BIRD	3312
酉	THE BIRD	3544

black colors

黒	BLACK	2740
漆	pitch-black	704

blame and accuse

責	BLAME	2467
叱	SCOLD	182
詰	REPRIMAND	1521
難	find fault with	1838
批	CRITICIZE	250
劾	EXPOSE CRIMES	1266
弾	impeach	572

bloom ⇨ SPROUT AND BLOOM

blow ⇨ BREATHE AND BLOW

blue and purple colors

青	BLUE	2430
碧	DEEP BLUE	2836
瑠	LAPIS LAZULI (bright blue)	1060
紺	DARK BLUE	1332
藍	INDIGO	2381
紫	PURPLE	2688

board games

局	board game	3063
棋	SHOGI	987
碁	GO	2699
雀	MAHJONG	2469

boards and plates

板	BOARD, PLATE	858
盤	BOARD	2851

boasting and arrogance

誇	BOAST	1522
慢	ARROGANT	686

boats and ships

船	SHIP	1341
舶	OCEANGOING SHIP	1340
艦	WARSHIP	1435
潜	submarine	746
舟	SMALL BOAT	3538
艇	BOAT	1365
隻	COUNTER FOR SHIPS	2755

bodies

体	BODY	71
塊	LUMP	632
球	BALL	969

bodily secretions

乳	MILK	1438
精	sperm	1366
汗	SWEAT	220
涙	TEAR	440

body

体	BODY	71
身	BODY (esp. vs. mind)	3553
肉	FLESH	3200

body projections

角	HORN	2047
尾	TAIL	3062

bombs ⇨ PROJECTILES AND BOMBS

bone

骨	BONE	2654
髄	MARROW	1842

books

本	BOOK	3502
書	BOOK	2658
冊	bound book	3483
籍	books	2731
著	literary work	2300
巻	VOLUME	2645
編	volume	1387
鑑	REFERENCE VOLUME	1773
典	STANDARD WORK	2627
経	religious classic	1331

books ⇨ COUNTERS FOR BOOKS

borrow ⇨ LEND AND BORROW

bottoms and bases

底	BOTTOM	3084
下	lower part	3378
基	BASE	2673
礎	FOUNDATION STONE	1248
盤	bedrock	2851
床	BED	3067

boundaries ⇨ EDGES AND BOUNDARIES

bow

礼	courtesy bow	818
拝	bow in veneration	303

bowed

凹	CONCAVE	3482
凸	CONVEX	3486

branch

支	BRANCH	1979
分	branch	1972

branches and twigs

枝	BRANCH	863
梢	TIP OF A TWIG	963

branch of study

科	SUBJECT OF STUDY	1138
学	branch of study	2555
門	field	888

brave

勇	BRAVE	2089
赳	VALIANT	3308
敢	bold	1706
豪	bold and unrestrained	2140
雄	HEROIC	1008
壮	heroic	224
義	chivalrous	2338

break

破	BREAK	1150
壊	BREAK DOWN	756
折	BREAK OFF	253
割る	crack	1816
裂	SPLIT	2687
砕	CRUSH UP	1134
崩	CRUMBLE	2296

break into small pieces

砕	CRUSH UP	1134
抹	pulverize	313

breathe and blow

息	BREATH	2647
気	breath	3194
吸	BREATHE IN	202
呼	breathe out	273
吹	BLOW	231

brew and ferment

醸	BREW	1654
酵	FERMENT	1561

bridges

橋 BRIDGE 1078
桟 PLANK BRIDGE 932

bright

明 BRIGHT 855
昭 LUMINOUS 894
蛍 fluorescent 2591
晃 DAZZLING 2450

brown colors

褐 BROWN 1210
茶 light brown 2259

Buddha

仏 BUDDHA 19
釈 Sakyamuni 1484

build

建 BUILD (a building) 3090
造 build (various structures) 3110
築 CONSTRUCT 2715
設 SET UP 1471

buildings

閣 TALL MAGNIFICENT BUILDING 3327
宇 large building 2175
殿 PALACE 1792
堂 HALL 2589
館 PUBLIC BUILDING 1748
舎 BUILDING 2060
棟 BLOCK 991

bundles and clusters

束 BUNDLE 3554
房 tuft 1946

burden

荷 LOAD 2282
貨 freight 2465

burn

焼 BURN 997
燃 BURN (undergo combustion) 1081
焦 SCORCH 2770

bury

埋 BURY 403
葬 bury (a corpse) 2320

business ⇨ INDUSTRY AND BUSINESS

busy

忙 BUSY 214
繁 bustling 2853
慌てる FLURRIED 580

buttocks

尻 BUTTOCKS 3032
肛 ANUS 842

buy

買 BUY 2598
購 PURCHASE 1624

C

calculate and count

算 CALCULATE 2702
計 COMPUTE 1441
数 count 1790

calendars

暦 CALENDAR 3018
新 new calendar 1784
旧 old calendar 14

call and invite

呼ぶ CALL 273
喚 CALL 550
召 SUMMON 2001
招 INVITE 316

calm and peaceful

安 PEACEFUL 2171
康 peaceful 3124
寧 peaceful 2345
泰 TRANQUIL 2583
静 QUIET 1728
平 CALM 3478
穏 CALM 1235

camps

陣 CAMP 455
営 BARRACKS 2603

capacity units

勺 *SHAKU* (0.018 liters) 2933
合 *go* (0.18 liters) 2019
立 liter 1992
升 *SHO* (1.8 liters) 3455
斗 *TO* (18 liters) 2953
石 *koku* (180 liters) 2971

cardinal points

東 EAST 3568
西 WEST 3520
北 NORTH 197
南 SOUTH 2082

careful

慎	PRUDENT	643
謹	carefully	1618
精	meticulous	1366

carry

運	CARRY	3140
搬	CARRY	647
輸	TRANSPORT	1607

carve ⇨ FORM AND CARVE

catch a criminal

捕	CATCH	429
逮	CATCH A CRIMINAL	3123
拘	ARREST	310

cattle

牛	CATTLE	3452
丑	THE OX	3433

cause

致	BRING ABOUT	1316
誘	INDUCE	1550

cause and reason

因	CAUSE	3054
由	REASON	3499
為	because	3577
故	reason	1141
訳	reason	1473

cavities ⇨ HOLES AND CAVITIES

celebrating and congratulating

祝	CELEBRATE	913
慶	FELICITATION	3173
賀	CONGRATULATE	2599
寿	CONGRATULATIONS	3557

central parts

核	NUCLEUS	927
仁	kernel	20
心	core	11

ceramics ware

陶	POTTERY	546
窯	ceramics	2361
磁	porcelain	1214

cereal

穀	CEREAL	1824
粉	flour	1291

cereals

米	RICE	3529
麦	WHEAT	2408
豆	BEAN	1943

ceremonies and festivities

式	CEREMONY	3049
儀	CEREMONY	169
典	formal ceremony	2627
礼	RITE	818
斎	religious ritual	2115
会	Buddhist ceremony	2020
祭	FESTIVAL	2672

certain

必	WITHOUT FAIL	15
確	CERTAIN	1228

certificates

証	CERTIFICATE	1506
券	CERTIFICATE	2630
状	official document	272
免	license	2067

change and replace

変	CHANGE	2069
更	change	3541
改	change	243
易	change	2411
化	CHANGE INTO, -ize	21
遷	undergo transition	3170
転	turn into	1480
換	EXCHANGE	587
交	INTERCHANGE	2015
替	REPLACE	2783
代	SUBSTITUTE	30
迭	ALTERNATE	3077

character ⇨ NATURE AND CHARACTER

characters

字	CHARACTER	2172
文	LETTER	1962
漢	kanji	657

charm

魅	CHARM	3329
幻	bewitch	180

chastity

貞	CHASTE	2083
操	chastity	769

chest

胸	CHEST	951
乳	breast	1438

child

児	CHILD (of any age)	2546
子	CHILD	3390
童	CHILD (young person)	2130

幼	young child	191
坊	SONNY	233

China

華	CHINA	2283
漢	CHINESE	657
支	China	1979
中	People's Republic of China	3451
台	Taiwan	2005
唐	Cathay	3115
呉	KINGDOM OF WU	2549

Chinese

漢	CHINESE (language)	657
中	Modern Chinese	3451

choose

選	CHOOSE	3169
択	SELECT	255
採	PICK	499
摘	pick out	694
抜	single out	246

circle

円	CIRCLE	2955
圏	circle	3148
丸	round or spherical shape	3417

circles

界	WORLD	2563
壇	circles	754

circular objects

環	RING	1090
輪	WHEEL, RING	1589
車	WHEEL	3552
盤	DISK	2851

cities and towns

都	METROPOLIS	1686
京	CAPITAL	2052
市	CITY	1993
町	TOWN	1113

class

級	GRADE	1279
段	grade	1144
位	RANK	61
階	RANK	624
身	social status	3553
格	STATUS	926
等	CLASS	2682
流	class	441
層	STRATUM	3161

classical particles

耶	INTERROGATIVE PARTICLE	1283
也	rhetorical particle	3406
哉	EXCLAMATORY PARTICLE	3294

class in school

組	class	1337
級	GRADE	1279

clean and purified

浄	CLEAN	382
清	clean	523
純	PURE	1297
潔	IMMACULATE	744
粋	REFINED (free from impurities)	1293
精	refined (purified)	1366

clean and wash

洗	WASH	388
濯	RINSE	793
浴	BATHE	445
浄	cleanse	382
粛	PURGE	3581
清	CLEAR	523
払	CLEAR AWAY	194
掃	SWEEP	503

clear

透	TRANSPARENT	3108
澄	LIMPID	740
清	CLEAR (liquid)	523
明	CLEAR (unclouded)	855
朗	CLEAR (sky)	1325
冴える	CRISP AND CLEAR	79

clergymen

僧	BONZE	159
坊	Buddhist priest	233
尼	BUDDHIST NUN	3033
父	FATHER	1973

close

閉	CLOSE	3319
鎖	lock up	1761
封	SEAL	1287

clothing

服	CLOTHES	878
-着	wear	3316
衣	GARMENT	2013
装	DRESS	2685

clusters ⇨ BUNDLES AND CLUSTERS
coagulate ⇨ SOLIDIFY AND COAGULATE
cold
冷 COLD 80
寒 COLD (weather) 2311
涼 COOL 521
cold seasons
冬 WINTER 2157
寒 coldest season 2311
秋 AUTUMN 1139
collapse
陥 FALL IN 457
落 FALL 2318
崩 CRUMBLE 2296
没 SINK 260
collected works
集 collection 2771
選 selection 3169
collide
衝 COLLIDE 725
突 DASH 2230
当たる HIT 2177
color
色 COLOR 2029
彩 BEAUTIFUL COLORING 1681
color
彩 color 1681
染 DYE 2572
combine
合 COMBINE 2019
結 TIE 1348
統 UNITE 1352
括 LUMP TOGETHER 376
総 integrate 1379
併 join together 83
come ⇨ GO AND COME
come off
脱 get out of place 973
外れる come off 186
come to an end
尽 be exhausted 3050
絶 COME TO AN END 1353
comfortable
楽 COMFORTABLE 2826
安 easy (without effort) 2171
comic
漫 COMIC 700

戯 sportive 1875
command
令 COMMAND 1995
命 ORDER 2058
comment upon
批 CRITICIZE 250
評 COMMENT 1501
commit
託 ENTRUST 1455
預 DEPOSIT 1042
委 COMMIT 2553
任 LEAVE TO 53
嘱 CHARGE WITH 718
communicate ⇨ INFORM AND COMMUNICATE
Communism
共 Communism 2393
左 the Left 2974
赤 RED 2193
compare
比 COMPARE 26
較 COMPARE 1536
校 COLLATE 929
照 check against 2827
対 OPPOSE (contrast) 831
参 refer 2066
compel and press
圧 PRESSURE 2970
迫 PRESS 3074
強 force 475
押す PUSH 314
compensate
償 RECOMPENSE 176
賠 COMPENSATE 1582
酬 RECIPROCATE 1539
報 REQUITE 1698
compete
競 COMPETE 1847
戦う contest 1787
闘 FIGHT 3334
争 CONTEND 2030
compile
編 COMPILE 1387
集 edit 2771
著 AUTHOR 2300
complex
繁 complicated 2853

煩	vexatious	1022
compose		
著	AUTHOR	2300
作	compose	68
書く	WRITE	2658
筆	write	2677
compound		
複	COMPOUND	1222
倍	DOUBLE	108
重	DUPLICATE	3573
compromise		
妥	COME TO TERMS	2400
譲	concede	1649
conceive		
妊	BECOME PREGNANT	240
娠	CONCEIVE	408
concentrate on		
注	CONCENTRATE	325
傾	devote oneself to	154
conditional conjunctions		
但し	PROVIDED THAT	72
然し	however	2782
confine ⇨ IMPRISON AND CONFINE		
Confucianists ⇨ CONFUCIUS AND CONFUCIANISTS		
Confucius and Confucianists		
孔	Confucius	179
子	the Master (Confucius)	3390
孟	MENCIUS	2220
congratulating ⇨ CELEBRATING AND CONGRATULATING		
conjecture		
推	INFER	504
憶	SPECULATE	765
測	CONJECTURE	610
察	GUESS	2347
conquer and suppress		
征	CONQUER	293
討	SUPPRESS BY ARMED FORCE	1456
伐	CUT DOWN	42
鎮	QUELL	1759
靖	PACIFY	1208
consider ⇨ THINK AND CONSIDER		
console		
慰	CONSOLE	2867
弔	CONDOLE	3432
conspicuous		
著	CONSPICUOUS	2300
顕	MANIFEST	1806
卓	PROMINENT	2064
傑	outstanding	155
constant		
定	fixed	2229
恒	CONSTANT	367
常	REGULAR	2590
例	regular	89
consume		
消	SPEND	443
費	expend	2607
尽	EXHAUST	3050
耗	WEAR AWAY	1309
contain and include		
含	CONTAIN (have as a part)	2041
容	CONTAIN (have within)	2277
包	ENCOMPASS	2966
挟	HOLD BETWEEN	377
containers		
箱	BOX	2711
籠	BASKET	2734
袋	BAG	2588
器	VESSEL	2713
瓶	BOTTLE	1344
缶	CAN	2033
槽	TANK	1067
棺	COFFIN	985
continents		
亜	Asia	3540
阿	Africa	346
欧	EUROPE	887
米	AMERICA	3529
豪	Australia	2140
continue		
続	CONTINUE	1362
継	SUCCEED	1360
連	IN SUCCESSION	3103
持	HOLD	374
contract and shrink		
縮	SHRINK	1414
約	CONTRACT	1280
cook		
煮	BOIL (cook by boiling)	2785
沸	BOIL (undergo boiling)	329
炊	COOK	870

蒸 STEAM 2334
焼く cook by fire 997
揚げる fry in deep fat 593

cooked dishes
-焼き roasted, baked or fried food 997
-揚げ fried food 593
-煮 boiled food 2785

cooperate
協 COOPERATE 93
携 join hands 648
調 harmonize 1567

copy
写 COPY 2000
謄 TRANSCRIBE 1093
複 duplicate 1222
拓 copy by rubbing 317

corners
角 corner 2047
圭 SHARP CORNER 2165
隅 NOOK 623

correct
正 RIGHT 3484
直す correct 2932
訂 REVISE 1442
改 REFORM 243
矯 RECTIFY 1241
匡 RECTIFY 2989

correspond to
該 CORRESPOND TO 1519
準 apply correspondingly 2856
当 be equivalent 2177

cosmetics
紅 rouge 1277
粉 face powder 1291

count ⇨ CALCULATE AND COUNT

counters for animals
匹 COUNTER FOR ANIMALS 2962
頭 counter for large animals 1604
羽 counter for birds 226

counters for books
冊 COUNTER FOR BOOKS 3483
巻 counter for volumes 2645
部 counter for copies 1676

counters for flat things
枚 COUNTER FOR FLAT THINGS 859
葉 counter for leaves 2321
丁 counter for sheets 3348
頁 counter for pages 2086
通 counter for letters 3109

counters for houses
軒 COUNTER FOR HOUSES 1459
戸 counter for households 1930
棟 counter for buildings 991

counters for long objects
本 counter for cylindrical objects 3502
筋 counter for slender objects 2678

counters for persons
人 counter for people 3368
名 counter for persons 2169

country
国 COUNTRY 3087
邦 STATE 847
土 land 3403

country ⇨ THE COUNTRY

courage
勇 bravery 2089
胆 pluck 919

court
廷 COURT 3058
裁 court 3299

courteous
寧 COURTEOUS 2345
丁 courteous 3348

cover and wrap
覆 COVER 2726
被 cover 1163
包 WRAP 2966

create
創 CREATE 1815
作 compose 68
生 produce 3497
発 START 2565
起 generate 3307

crimes and offenses
犯 OFFENSE 196
罪 CRIME 2610
凶 atrocious crime 2961

cross
渡 CROSS 611
渉 wade 526
越 GO BEYOND 3314

crowd
群 GROUP 1540
衆 MULTITUDE 2683

cruel

虐	CRUEL	3218
惨	CRUEL	483
酷	SEVERE	1562
残	RUTHLESS	943
凶	ATROCIOUS	2961

cry and sigh

泣	CRY	338
嘆	SIGH	630

cultivate

修	CULTIVATE	123
養	FOSTER (one's intellect)	2365
練	TRAIN	1375
錬	REFINE	1741
鍛	train	1755
磨	POLISH	3181
琢	POLISH	971

cultivated fields

畑	FIELD	905
牧	PASTURE	873
園	GARDEN	3156
田	RICE FIELD	3041
甫	vegetable garden	3549

cure and recover

療	TREAT	3288
治	CURE	335
医	cure	2993
癒	HEAL	3291
快	recover	245

curtain

幕	CURTAIN	2335
帳	drapery	473

custom

慣	HABITUAL PRACTICE	685
例	established practice	89
習	CUSTOM	2667
風	manners	3007
俗	popular custom	104
癖	HABIT	3290
弊	EVIL PRACTICE	2884

cut

切	CUT	27
断	CUT OFF	1492
裁	CUT OUT	3299
割	cut with a knife	1816
剖	DISSECT	1670
刈る	CLIP	28
伐	CUT DOWN	42
削	CUT BY CHIPPING	1448

cutting instruments

刀	SWORD (single-edged)	2926
剣	SWORD (double-edged)	1672
矛	HALBERD	2008
鎌	SICKLE	1760
刃	BLADE	2929

D

dairy products

酪	DAIRY PRODUCTS	1538
乳	MILK	1438

damage ⇨ **HARM AND DAMAGE**

dance

踊	DANCE (energetically)	1558
舞	DANCE (gracefully)	2146

danger

危	DANGEROUS	3199
険	DANGER	542

dark

暗	DARK	1010
黒	BLACK	2740
陰	shaded	541

dark-colored

暗	DARK	1010
濃	dark	777
深	DEEP	524

date

日	date	3027
忌	death anniversary	2207

dawn ⇨ **MORNING AND DAWN**

days

日	DAY	3027
曜	DAY OF THE WEEK	1096
昼	DAYTIME	3097
旦	first day	2389

days of the week

日	Sunday	3027
月	Monday	2956
火	Tuesday	3463
水	Wednesday	10
木	Thursday	3450
金	Friday	2057
土	Saturday	3403

dead
故 THE LATE 1141
亡 deceased 3402

deal with
扱う HANDLE 217
処 DEAL WITH 3031
措 dispose of 502
置 take proper steps 2608

decay
朽 DECAY 821
腐 ROT 3162
枯 WITHER 898

deceive
欺 DECEIVE 1703
詐 SWINDLE 1502
惑 mislead 2786
拐 defraud 308
偽 FALSIFY 131

decide
決 DECIDE 263
断 RESOLVE 1492
定 FIX 2229

decorate
飾 DECORATE 1717
粧 APPLY MAKEUP 1345
粉 apply face powder 1291
装 DRESS 2685

decrease
減 DECREASE 601
耗 WEAR AWAY 1309
削 cut down 1448
縮 SHRINK 1414
落 FALL 2318

degenerate
落 FALL 2318
衰 DECLINE 2100
堕 DEGENERATE 2822
破 break down 1150

degree
程 EXTENT 1190
度 DEGREE 3100
分 relative degree 1972

delay ⇨ BE LATE AND DELAY

deliver ⇨ TRANSMIT AND DELIVER

dense
濃 THICK (concentrated) 777
密 CLOSE 2292

depressed ⇨ SAD AND DEPRESSED

descend and fall
落 FALL 2318
墜 DROP DOWN 2881
降 DESCEND 458
下 go down 3378
倒 TOPPLE 124

descendant
孫 GRANDCHILD, descendant 410
胤 PROGENY 17
末 posterity 3505

describe
叙 DESCRIBE 1446
描 DEPICT 488
写 portray 2000

desire ⇨ WISH AND DESIRE

destroy
滅 DESTROY 660
亡 perish 3402
消 EXTINGUISH 443

detailed
詳 DETAILED 1526
細 MINUTE 1333
密 CLOSE 2292
精 meticulous 1366

detect
検 detect 986
感 SENSE 2835

deviate
逸 deviate 3120
外れる miss 186

diagram
表 TABLE 2429
図 DRAWING 3071

die
死 DIE 3521
没 die 260
亡 DECEASE 3402
殉 DIE A MARTYR 941
去 pass away 2156
逝 DEPART THIS LIFE 3104
枯 WITHER 898

difference ⇨ DIFFERING AND DIFFERENCE

differing and difference
違 DIFFER 3151
異 DIFFERENT 2584
差 DIFFERENCE 3311

dig
掘 DIG 496
削 excavate 1448
dignified
荘 DIGNIFIED 2262
威 dignified 3578
厳 solemn 3289
粛 solemnly 3581
direct and supervise
制 CONTROL 1274
管 EXERCISE CONTROL 2701
轄 EXERCISE JURISDICTION OVER 1627
掌 TAKE CHARGE OF 2602
監 OVERSEE 2852
督 SUPERVISE 2796
司 OFFICIATE 2931
宰 PRESIDE 2275
営 MANAGE 2603
理 manage 970
経 MANAGE 1331
direction
方 DIRECTION 1963
向 direction 3052
direction indicators
至 to 2182
-行き bound for 212
-向け (bound) for 3052
迄 UP TO 3201
以 TO THE...OF 41
自 from 3525
来 since 3551
dirty
汚 DIRTY 222
染 contaminate 2572
dirty
汚 DIRTY 222
濁 TURBID 774
disappear
消 disappear 443
没 disappear 260
disaster ⇨ MISFORTUNE AND DISASTER
discard and abandon
捨 DISCARD 501
棄 ABANDON 2137
discernment
識 power of discrimination 1639
眼 EYE 1172
discharge from mouth
吐 SPEW 203
吹 BLOW 231
discontinue
絶 BREAK OFF 1353
廃 ABOLISH 3146
断 CUT OFF 1492
止 STOP 2941
休 suspend 52
停 suspend 139
discriminate
識 DISCRIMINATE 1639
弁 distinguish 2004
分 tell apart 1972
discuss ⇨ ARGUE AND DISCUSS
disdain
侮 despise 82
軽 make light of 1515
disease
病 ILLNESS 3277
疾 DISEASE 3279
風 (infectious) disease 3007
症 PATHOLOGICAL CONDITION 3280
患 AFFECTED BY DISEASE 2747
疫 EPIDEMIC 3276
diseases and disease symptoms
痘 SMALLPOX 3284
熱 fever 2866
炎 INFLAMMATION 2420
痢 DIARRHEA 3283
下 diarrhea 3378
disease symptoms ⇨ DISEASES AND DISEASE SYMPTOMS
disgrace
恥 SHAME 1313
辱 HUMILIATE 2736
侮 INSULT 82
汚 defile 222
disguise
装 dress up 2685
化 change oneself into 21
dislike ⇨ HATE AND DISLIKE
dismiss
罷 DISMISS 2617
免 discharge 2067
解 release from office 1517

disordered

紛 CONFUSED 1296
乱 DISORDERED 1260
錯 MIXED UP 1743
混 mixed up 519
雑 mixed up 1385

disperse

解 DISSOLVE 1517
散 SCATTER 1702

display

展 DISPLAY 3111
陳 lay out (for exhibit) 540
掲 PUT UP 494

distance and interval

距 DISTANCE 1511
間 INTERVAL 3323
程 EXTENT 1190

distant

遠 DISTANT 3150
遥 FAR 3141
悠 far-off 2741
遼 FARAWAY 3168
隔 APART 671
離 separated 1836

distribute

配 DISTRIBUTE 1460
頒 DISTRIBUTE WIDELY 1043
分 DIVIDE 1972

diverge

岐 DIVERGE 241
分 branch off 1972

divide

除 divide 456
割る DIVIDE 1816

dividend ⇨INTEREST AND DIVIDEND

divine

占 DIVINE 2003
易 divination 2411

divisions of organizations

課 SECTION 1573
部 department 1676
局 BUREAU 3063

do and act

為 DO 3577
仕 DO 34
致す DO HUMBLY 1316
行 ACT 212

作 WORK 68

domesticated birds

鶏 CHICKEN 1768
鳩 PIGEON 163

domesticated mammals

牛 CATTLE 3452
馬 HORSE 3296
豚 PIG 976
羊 SHEEP 2183
犬 DOG 3464
猫 CAT 535

donate

施 give alms 891
恵む give charity 2659
寄 CONTRIBUTE 2291
献 donate 1785

doors

戸 DOOR 1930
扉 HINGED DOOR 1955
門 GATE 888
口 entrance (or exit) 3382

doubt

疑 DOUBT 1565
怪しむ suspect 297

dragon

竜 DRAGON 2099
辰 THE DRAGON 2992

draw

描 DEPICT 488
画 draw 3000

drinks

汁 JUICE, SOUP 195
乳 MILK 1438
酒 ALCOHOLIC DRINK 444
茶 TEA 2259

drip ⇨FLOW AND DRIP

drive out

斥 EXPEL 2972
排 EXCLUDE 490
追 chase away 3096
退 cause to retreat 3094
駆 drive away 1823
逐 DRIVE OUT 3102
払う clear out 194

dry

乾 DRY 1679
干 DRY 3379

燥 DRY UP 1087
渇 RUN DRY 515

during

間 for an interval of 3323
中 IN (the course of) 3451
内 within (a given period) 3466

E

eager

懇 EARNEST 2899
切 eager 27
篤 DEVOTED 2716
熱 HOT 2866

earlier Chinese dynasties

夏 Xia Dynasty 2113
商 Shang Dynasty 2116
周 Zhou Dynasty 2998
漢 Han Dynasty 657
晋 JIN DYNASTY 2656

early states of animal life

胎 FETUS 918
卵 EGG 849

early states of plant life

芽 BUD 2240
苗 SEEDLING 2237
種 SEED 1218

earnings ⇨ PAY AND EARNINGS

easy

易 EASY (without difficulty) 2411
安 easy (without effort) 2171
簡 SIMPLE 2721
軽 LIGHT 1515

economizing and economy

省 SAVE 2449
節 economize 2691
倹 FRUGAL 116

economy ⇨ ECONOMIZING AND ECONOMY

edges and boundaries

縁 EDGE 1386
端 edge 1221
辺 border 3029
境 BOUNDARY 676
界 BOUNDS 2563
際 VERGE 714
涯 OUTER LIMITS 512

editions

版 edition 872
刊 publication 190
訂 revision 1442
刷 printing 1273

elapse

過 PASS BY 3137
経 pass 1331
歴 pass 3019
去 pass away 2156

elated

高 high-spirited 2097
昂 high-spirited 2412
揚 exalted 593
奮 roused up 2367

election ⇨ VOTE AND ELECTION

electricity and magnetism

電 ELECTRICITY 2790
流 electric current 441
磁 MAGNETISM 1214

elegance ⇨ FLAVOR AND ELEGANCE

elegant

雅 ELEGANT 1197
淑 GRACEFUL 527
優 graceful 177
粋 REFINED 1293
彬 REFINED AND GENTLE 960

element

素 ELEMENT 2458
元 element 1929
単 unit 2256

elevations in water

島 ISLAND 3310
州 sandbar 57
礁 REEF 1243

eliminate

却 ELIMINATE 1118
削 cross out 1448
抹 wipe off 313
省 leave out 2449
脱 REMOVE 973
去 take away 2156
外す take off 186
除 RID OF 456
撤 WITHDRAW 738
排 EXCLUDE 490
払う CLEAR AWAY 194

embankment

堤	EMBANKMENT	560
防	dike	270

embrace

抱	HUG	306
擁	embrace	770

emit

出	PUT OUT	3498
発	EMIT	2565
放	radiate	853
排	DISCHARGE	490
射	SHOOT	1458
噴	SPOUT	717
吐	SPEW	203

employ

雇	EMPLOY	1956
用	EMPLOY	2976
使う	employ	90
役	press into service	244

employment ⇨ **WORK AND EMPLOYMENT**

emptiness and nothing

空	EMPTY	2227
白	WHITE (blank)	3493
虚	VOID	3237
無	NOTHING	2135
零	ZERO	2792

end

終	END	1336
絶	COME TO AN END	1353
閉	CLOSE	3319
了	FINISH	3350
済	SETTLE	522
-上げる	completion suffix	3404
完	COMPLETE	2201
結	CONCLUDE	1348

ends

末	LAST PART	3505
終	END	1336
尾	end	3062
局	close	3063

endure ⇨ **BEAR AND ENDURE**

energy and force

力	POWER, force	3371
勢	physical power	2857
気	energy	3194
圧	PRESSURE	2970

enlist

徴	LEVY	683
募	RAISE	2316

enter

入	ENTER	3370
-込む	MOVE INWARD	3030

equip and install

据える	INSTALL	497
敷	LAY	1870
架	LAY ACROSS	2569
装	FIT OUT	2685
設	SET UP	1471
備	PROVIDE	146

escape

逃	ESCAPE	3095
亡	flee	3402
走	run away	2194
脱	ESCAPE FROM	973

escort ⇨ **LEAD AND ESCORT**

essential content

実	substance	2225
体	substance	71
味	contents	274

essential part

精	ESSENCE (essential part)	1366
粋	essence (best part)	1293
髄	essence (vital part)	1842
枢	PIVOT	865
幹	TRUNK	1718
綱	ESSENTIAL POINTS	1372
旨	PURPORT	2024
要	summary	2635

estrange

疎	ESTRANGE	1178
離	separate from	1836
遠	DISTANT	3150

etiquette

礼	ETIQUETTE	818
儀	CEREMONY	169

European countries

英	ENGLAND	2238
独	GERMANY	395
仏	FRANCE	19
伊	ITALY	49
西	Spain	3520
蘭	Holland	2383
露	Russia	2818

evening and night

夜	NIGHT	2056
晩	EVENING	979
夕	EVENING	3387
宵	EARLY EVENING	2276
暮	DUSK	2354

evident

明	CLEAR	855
鮮	VIVID	1877
亮	LUCID	2071
顕	MANIFEST	1806

evil

邪	EVIL	1124
凶	ATROCIOUS	2961
悪	BAD	2745

evil ⇨ **WRONGDOING AND EVIL**

evil beings ⇨ **SUPERNATURAL AND EVIL BEINGS**

exact

確	CERTAIN	1228
正	RIGHT	3484
真-	right	2111

examination

検	examination	986
試	examination (school test)	1525

examine ⇨ **INVESTIGATE AND EXAMINE**

example

例	EXAMPLE	89
型	TYPE	2638

exceeding and excess

過	EXCEED	3137
超	SURPASS	3313
越	GO BEYOND	3314
濫	EXCESSIVE	801
余	EXCESS	2042
剰	SURPLUS	1779
冗	REDUNDANT	1976

excel

勝	EXCEL	1005
抜	STAND OUT	246
超	SURPASS	3313
越	GO BEYOND	3314

excellent and superior

優	SUPERIOR	177
秀	EXCELLENT	2545
英	DISTINGUISHED	2238
傑	outstanding	155
逸	exceptional	3120
名	first-rate	2169
上	of upper grade	3404
絶	without match	1353
卓	PROMINENT	2064
快	splendid	245
妙	MARVELOUS	239

excess ⇨ **EXCEEDING AND EXCESS**

excreta

便	EXCRETA	95
尿	URINE	3064
汗	SWEAT	220

execute

執	EXECUTE	1680
行	ACT	212
履	FULFILL	3171
施	CARRY OUT	891
践	IMPLEMENT	1535
果たす	effect	3560
遂	ACCOMPLISH	3138

exert oneself

努	EXERT	2547
勉	ENDEAVOR	3318
励	make efforts	1119
勤	work diligently	1818
尽	use all one's strength	3050
精	put one's heart into	1366

exist and be

在	BE	2984
存	EXIST	2982
有	exist	2983
居	be present	3080
臨	BE PRESENT AT	1630
也	CLASSICAL COPULA	3406

expand

脹	SWELL	1003
膨	EXPAND	1084
張	SPREAD	474
広げる	spread (out)	3035
拡	ENLARGE	309
伸	STRETCH	70
延	EXTEND	3073

expect

期	EXPECT	1704
待	wait for	364

expensive

貴	precious	2606

高 high-priced 2097

explain

説 EXPLAIN 1547
明 make clear 855
釈 ELUCIDATE 1484
講 expound 1619
解 CLARIFY 1517
注 annotate 325

explanatory remarks

注 annotation 325
評 COMMENT 1501

explode

爆 EXPLODE 1101
発 discharge 2565

express

表 EXPRESS 2429
揮 WIELD 589

expression

顔 FACE 1808
色 COLOR 2029

expressions ⇨ WORDS AND EXPRESSIONS

extend over

亘 EXTEND OVER 1939
及 REACH TO 3385

extensive ⇨ WIDE AND EXTENSIVE

extinguish

消 EXTINGUISH 443
滅 go out 660

extreme

極 EXTREME 1017
窮 extremity 2358
限 LIMIT 398
涯 OUTER LIMITS 512
果て end 3560

extreme in degree

酷 SEVERE 1562
厳 SEVERE 3289
激 intense 776
極 EXTREME 1017
痛 bitter(ly) 3285
切 keen 27
甚 EXTREMELY 2643
超 super- 3313
強 STRONG 475
重 HEAVY 3573
高 HIGH 2097
深 DEEP 524

大 BIG 3416

extreme in power

激 VIOLENT 776
荒 WILD 2260
狂 raging 269
烈 VEHEMENT 2652
猛 FIERCE 537

extremity

端 END 1221
末 end 3505
梢 tip 963
先 point 2394

eye

目 EYE 3043
眼 EYE 1172
眸 EYE 1170
瞳 PUPIL 1237

F

fabric

布 CLOTH 2973
地 fabric 204

fabrics

織 woven fabric 1422
紗 GAUZE 1301
絹 SILK 1361
綾 TWILL 1376
綿 COTTON 1373
麻 HEMP 3125
毛 wool 3453
錦 BROCADE 1738

face

向 TURN TOWARD 3052
面 FACE 2087
対 face (each other) 831

face orifices

口 MOUTH 3382
鼻 NOSE 2706
耳 EAR 3516
目 EYE 3043

fail

敗 fail 1476
落 fall through 2318
-損なう fail to (do) 651

fall ⇨ DESCEND AND FALL

false

虚	FALSE	3237
仮	fake	50
偽	sham	131
擬	imitation	788
義	artificial	2338

familiar and friendly

親	INTIMATE	1799
密	CLOSE	2292
近	NEAR	3061
睦	FRIENDLY	1199
懇	FAMILIAR	2899
和	HARMONIOUS	1130

family and relations

族	FAMILY	958
家	FAMILY	2273
門	family	888
氏	clan	2951
縁	RELATION	1386
姻	relative by marriage	353
親	RELATIVES	1799

farm and plant

植	PLANT	990
栽	PLANT (saplings)	3297
培	CULTIVATE	464
耕	TILL	1308
作	raise crops	68
農	farm, FARMING	2698

fast

速	QUICK	3105
早	QUICK	2390
疾	fast	3279
快	fast	245
急	rapid	2092
迅	SWIFT	3046
敏	NIMBLE	1322
即	IMMEDIATE	1120

fate and fortune

運	FORTUNE	3140
命	fate	2058
業	karma	2612
縁	karma relation	1386

fats and oils

油	OIL	341
脂	FAT	954
肪	ANIMAL FAT	877

fatten

肥	FATTEN	879
太る	grow fat	2152

faults and flaws

難	fault	1838
短	shortcoming	1182
陥	defect	457
欠	incompleteness	1987

favor

恵	FAVOR	2659
徳	act of kindness	684
恩	GRACE	2655

fear

怖	FEARFUL	296
恐	FEAR	2650

fee and price

料	FEE	1292
代	CHARGE	30
賃	CHARGES	2694
銭	money paid	1725
費	EXPENSE	2607
価	PRICE	87
値	price	109

feel deeply

感	feel deeply	2835
動	be moved	1778
嘆	sigh in admiration	630

feeling

感	SENSE (feeling)	2835
情	EMOTION	482
心	HEART	11
気	spirits	3194

fellow

奴	GUY	187
漢	FELLOW	657
輩	FELLOW (*belittling*)	2807
徒	fellows	416
棒	tough guy	983
坊	COLLOQUIAL PERSON SUFFIX	233
屋	colloquial person suffix	3098
物	character	874

fences and walls

壁	WALL	2895
塀	FENCE (for screening)	557
垣	FENCE (for partitioning)	351
囲い	enclosure	3069
欄	railing	1103

ferment ⇨ BREW AND FERMENT

festivities ⇨ CEREMONIES AND FESTIVITIES

feudal territorial divisions

藩 FEUDAL DOMAIN 2379
国 province (in former Japan) 3087
領 fief 1224
封 daimiate 1287
荘 manor (in feudal Japan) 2262

few

少 LITTLE 3467
寡 FEW 2344
乏 SCANTY 1933
薄 meager 2370
微 SLIGHT 639
寸 A BIT OF 2935

fiber-producing plants

麻 HEMP 3125
綿 COTTON 1373

fibers ⇨ THREADS AND FIBERS

fidelity

忠 LOYALTY 2433
義 faith 2338
孝 FILIAL PIETY 3205
悌 BROTHERLY LOVE 424
誠 SINCERITY 1523
実 faithfulness 2225
信 fidelity 100
操 constancy 769
節 moral integrity 2691

fight and war

闘 FIGHT 3334
戦 WAR 1787
征 go on a military expedition 293

fill

充 FILL 2014
満 fill 607
詰める STUFF 1521

fire

火 FIRE 3463
炎 FLAME 2420

firm and obstinate

堅 FIRM 2823
固 FIRM, stiff 3086
確 firm 1228
毅 RESOLUTE 1866
剛 TOUGH 1673
頑 STUBBORN 1040
硬 hard-line 1183

first

甲 FIRST 3481
初 FIRST 1116

first person pronouns

私 I (*polite*) 1115
僕 I (*familiar*) 164
俺 I (*intimate*) 110
吾 I (*elegant*) 2407
予 I (*pompous*) 1983
余 I (*pompous*) 2042
麿 I (*archaic*) 3184
朕 IMPERIAL WE 949
自 SELF 3525
我 SELF 3548
己 ONESELF 3380
身 ONE'S PERSON 3553

fish

魚 FISH 2127
貝 SHELLFISH 2543

fish ⇨ HUNT AND FISH

fishes

鯉 CARP 1879
鮎 AYU 1876
鯛 TAI 1881

fit

合 FIT 2019
適 suit 3160
揃える MAKE UNIFORM 590

five

五 FIVE 3436
伍 five (in legal documents) 47

flat supports

台 STAND 2005
座 SEAT 3116
壇 PLATFORM 754
棚 SHELF 984
架 rack 2569
床 BED 3067

flat things ⇨ COUNTERS FOR FLAT THINGS

flavor and elegance

趣 FLAVOR 3317
味 TASTE 274
風 elegance 3007
品 refinement 2248

flaws ⇨ FAULTS AND FLAWS

flesh
肉 FLESH 3200
筋 MUSCLE 2678
float
漂 DRIFT 699
浮 FLOAT 435
floor
階 FLOOR 624
層 story 3161
flourish
茂 GROW THICK 2245
繁 THRIVE 2853
flow and drip
流 FLOW 441
注 POUR 325
濫 overflow 801
漏 LEAK 701
滴 DROP 705
泌 SECRETE 332
flower
花 FLOWER 2211
華 flower 2283
flowering plants
菊 CHRYSANTHEMUM 2303
葵 MALLOW 2317
蓉 COTTON ROSE 2337
芙 LOTUS 2208
蘭 ORCHID 2383
萩 *HAGI* 2319
藤 WISTERIA 2382
桜 cherry blossom 931
梅 *ume blossom* 925
fly
飛 FLY 3572
翔 SOAR 1357
航 NAVIGATE 1318
fold
折 FOLD 253
畳む FOLD UP 2592
-fold
倍 TIMES 108
重 -fold 3573
follow and pursue
従 FOLLOW 415
随 FOLLOW 627
追 CHASE 3096

followers ⇨ STUDENTS AND FOLLOWERS
food
飯 MEAL 1691
食 FOOD, meal 2075
糧 FOOD PROVISIONS 1421
foolish
愚 FOOLISH 2834
暗 DARK 1010
痴 STUPID 3286
鈍 DULL 1689
foot
足 FOOT 2188
脚 LEG 974
footwear
靴 SHOES 1781
駄 clogs 1821
履 footwear 3171
足 counter for footwear 2188
force ⇨ ENERGY AND FORCE
force to move
推 propel 504
駆 DRIVE 1823
押す PUSH 314
foreign
外 foreign 186
異 foreign 2584
forest
林 FOREST, small woods 861
森 THICK WOODS 2475
forget
忘 FORGET 2036
遺 LEAVE BEHIND 3166
forgive
赦 AMNESTY 1478
免 EXEMPT 2067
許す forgive 1470
form
形 SHAPE 846
状 FORM (external) 272
体 FORM (characteristic) 71
姿 FIGURE 2636
form and carve
刻 ENGRAVE 1267
彫 CARVE 1683
塑 MODEL 2843
鋳 CAST 1729

former
旧 FORMER 14
元 former 1929
故 OLD (earlier time) 1141
前 previous 2266
先 former 2394
既 ALREADY 1166

fortune ⇨ FATE AND FORTUNE

found
立 ESTABLISH 1992
設 SET UP 1471
置 found 2608

fragrance ⇨ SMELL AND FRAGRANCE

frames
枠 FRAME 866
格 framework 926
額 picture frame 1805

friendly ⇨ FAMILIAR AND FRIENDLY

friends and associates
僚 COLLEAGUE 165
輩 FELLOW 2807
朋 COMRADE 880
友 FRIEND 2952

front
前 front 2266
面 FACE 2087
首 HEAD 2265

front parts of head
顔 FACE 1808
面 FACE 2087
額 forehead 1805

frozen water ⇨ KINDS OF FROZEN WATER

fruit
果 FRUIT 3560
実 fruit 2225

fruits and fruit trees
桃 PEACH 936
李 PLUM 2398
杏 APRICOT 2397
梅 JAPANESE APRICOT 925
橘 MANDARIN 1077
栗 CHESTNUT 2649
梨 PEAR 2744

fruit trees ⇨ FRUITS AND FRUIT TREES

fuel ⇨ KINDS OF FUEL

full
満 FULL 607
飽 SATIATED 1715

future
来 coming generations 3551
後 afteryears 361

G

game
技 game 248
戦 match 1787

gardens
園 GARDEN 3156
庭 GARDEN 3114
苑 IMPERIAL GARDEN 2239

garment parts
襟 COLLAR 1252
袖 SLEEVE 1164
懐 BOSOM 763

gas and vapor
気 GAS 3194
空 AIR 2227
汽 STEAM 264

gather
集 COLLECT 2771
収 collect 198
採 GATHER 499

general
総 GENERAL 1379
惣 GENERAL 2780

general counters
丁 MISCELLANEOUS COUNTER 3348
個 GENERAL COUNTER 117
箇 COUNTER FOR ITEMS 2700
点 counter for articles 2084
件 counter for cases 51

generation
代 GENERATION 30
世 generation 3496

genitals
陰 sex organ 541
胎 WOMB 918
恥 private parts 1313

gentle
優 gentle 177
穏 MILD 1235
柔 SOFT 2088

gentleman

紳	GENTLEMAN	1334
子	gentleman	3390
士	man of learning and virtue	3405

get

得	ACQUIRE	477
拾	PICK UP	379
獲	obtain	779
収	TAKE IN	198
取	TAKE	1262

get off

降	alight	458
下	get down	3378

get on

乗	GET ON	3576
搭	BOARD	592

give

与	GIVE	3421
上	give (to superior or others)	3404
下	give (to inferior or speaker)	3378
呉れる	give (to speaker)	2549
授	CONFER	492
賜	DEIGN TO GIVE	1585
贈	PRESENT A GIFT	1634
賄	BRIBE	1529
呈	PRESENT	2189
進	present to a superior	3121

give birth

生	BE BORN	3497
誕	BE BORN	1579
産	GIVE BIRTH	3298
殖	MULTIPLY	994

go and come

行	GO	212
往	GO ON	292
出	go to	3498
参	go somewhere	2066
来	COME	3551
通	go to and from	3109
向	head toward	3052
赴	PROCEED TO	3303

god

神	GOD	912
帝	the Supreme Being	2073
天	HEAVEN	3442
主	Lord	1938

good

良	GOOD	3558
善	GOOD	2325
好	FAVORABLE	208
順	favorable	18
佳	FINE	86
美	BEAUTIFUL	2264

good fortune

吉	LUCKY	2167
嘉	HAPPY	2340
祥	AUSPICIOUS	948
瑞	AUSPICIOUS OMEN	1027
禎	PROPITIOUS OMEN	1031
幸	GOOD FORTUNE	2216
福	FORTUNE	1029

govern

治	GOVERN	335
統	rule	1352

government

政	POLITICAL ADMINISTRATION	1142
治	government	335

governments

官	GOVERNMENT	2226
幕	SHOGUNATE	2335
廷	COURT	3058
朝	court	1695
宮	Imperial Court	2274

governments ⇨ **PARTS OF GOVERNMENTS**
grasses ⇨ **KINDS OF GRASSES**
gratitude ⇨ **THANKING AND GRATITUDE**

graves

墓	GRAVE	2332
墳	TUMULUS	719
陵	IMPERIAL MAUSOLEUM	544
塚	grave mound	556

great

偉	GREAT (of superior character)	148
大	BIG	3416
宏	GRAND (large in scale)	2202
壮	GRAND (having grandeur)	224
豪	MAGNIFICENT	2140
雄	HEROIC	1008

great persons

豪	GREAT MAN	2140
傑	OUTSTANDING PERSON	155
雄	hero	1008

匠	CRAFTSMAN	2990
聖	great master	2830
great respect		
栄	GLORY	2574
誉	HONOR	2502
光	honor	2391
green colors		
緑	GREEN	1377
青	GREEN	2430
翠	JADE GREEN	2705
grieve		
慨	DEPLORE	641
嘆	SIGH	630
悼	MOURN	485
傷	grieve	158
悲	feel sad	2775
groups		
群	GROUP (of any kind)	1540
組	group (of people)	1337
陣	lineup	455
連	set	3103
族	common-interest group (*slang*)	958
党	PARTY	2581
隊	PARTY (organized group)	625
団	BODY	3053
伍	ranks	47
班	SQUAD	946
軍	team	2080
grow		
成	grow up	3537
長	grow (up)	2556
生	grow	3497
育	grow	2050
発	develop	2565
伸	expand	70
展	UNFOLD	3111

H

hair		
毛	HAIR (of any kind)	3453
髪	HAIR (on the head)	2846
羽	FEATHER	226
hand and arm		
手	HAND	3456
腕	ARM	1006
掌	PALM	2602
指	FINGER	378
handle		
扱う	HANDLE	217
操	MANIPULATE	769
揮	WIELD	589
運	control movement skillfully	3140
handles		
柄	HANDLE	897
手	handle	3456
把	GRIP	249
hang		
掛ける	HANG	493
垂	HANG DOWN	3565
懸	SUSPEND	2915
釣り-	suspended	1674
happiness		
幸	HAPPINESS	2216
祉	BLESSEDNESS	876
福	FORTUNE	1029
hard		
硬	HARD	1183
堅	FIRM	2823
固	SOLID	3086
剛	TOUGH	1673
強	STRONG	475
harm and damage		
害	HARM, damage	2272
損	damage	651
傷	WOUND	158
harvest		
採	PICK	499
摘	PICK	694
穫	HARVEST	1251
刈る	reap	28
hate and dislike		
憎	HATE	687
悪	hate	2745
忌む	ABHOR	2207
嫌	DISLIKE	636
恨	HOLD A GRUDGE	369
head		
頭	HEAD	1604
首	HEAD, NECK	2265
脳	BRAIN	975

head ⇨ FRONT PARTS OF HEAD

headgear

帽	HEADGEAR	568
冠	CROWN	2081

healthy

康	HEALTHY	3124
健	ROBUST	134
生	health	3497

hear

聞	HEAR	3326
聴	LISTEN	1418

heat

熱	HEAT	2866
暑	SUMMER HEAT	2473

heating devices

炉	FURNACE	869
窯	KILN	2361
缶	steam boiler	2033

height

高	height	2097
丈	STATURE	3419
背	stature	2573

help

助	HELP	1121
佑	HELP (said esp. of God)	74
祐	DIVINE HELP	915
援	AID	586
佐	ASSIST	67
補	assist	1194
輔	ASSIST	1559
済	RELIEVE	522

hide

隠	HIDE	713
伏	lie in concealment	45
潜	LURK	746
匿	CONCEAL	3011
忍	perform by stealth	2212

high

高	HIGH	2097
喬	TALL	2488
峻	high and steep	412

high

高	HIGH	2097
上	upper	3404

high officials

相	MINISTER	900
宰	chief minister	2275

high parts of mountains

頂	SUMMIT	145
峰	PEAK	411
嶺	RIDGE	2376
峠	MOUNTAIN PASS	358

high-ranking

貴	NOBLE	2606
上	upper	3404
高	HIGH	2097
総	GENERAL	1379
太	of highest rank	2152

hills

丘	HILL	3495
岡	HILL	2997
台	heights	2005
坂	SLOPE	234
阪	slope	271
塚	MOUND	556
陵	high mound	544

hinder ⇨ OBSTRUCT AND HINDER

history

史	HISTORY	3510
伝	biography	44
歴	PERSONAL HISTORY	3019

hold

持	HOLD	374
提	carry in hand	591
携	CARRY IN HAND	648

hold an event

催	HOLD AN EVENT	157
挙	hold a function	2456

hold in the mind

持	HOLD	374
抱	HUG	306
懐	embosom	763

holes and cavities

穴	HOLE	2159
孔	OPEN HOLE	179
口	MOUTH	3382
坑	PIT	236
堀	DITCH	467
溝	CHANNEL	659
凹	concavity	3482
洞	CAVE	380

holiday

休	holiday	52
暇	leave of absence	1012

holy

聖	HOLY	2830
神	divine	912
霊	miraculous	2805

honorific prefixes

御	GENERAL HONORIFIC TERM	577
貴	YOUR HONORABLE	2606
尊	your honorable	2324
令	your honorable	1995

honorific suffixes

翁	honorific suffix	2108
老	honorific suffix	3197

horse

馬	HORSE	3296
駒	HORSE (*elegant*)	1827
駿	FLEET STEED	1832
午	the Horse	1984

hot

熱	HOT	2866
暑い	HOT (weather)	2473
炎	scorching	2420
温	WARM	608
暖	WARM (esp. weather)	1011

houses

家	HOUSE	2273
屋	HOUSE	3098
軒	house	1459
戸	HOUSEHOLD	1930
宅	DWELLING HOUSE	2174
居	residence	3080
邸	STATELY RESIDENCE	1131
住	housing	64

houses ⇨ COUNTERS FOR HOUSES

how many

幾	HOW MANY	3582
何-	HOW MANY	65

huge ⇨ BIG AND HUGE

humble

謙	HUMBLE	1617
拝	HUMBLY	303

humble prefixes

小	my little (*humble*)	7
弊	our [my] humble	2884
拙	my humble	315
愚	my foolish	2834

hunger and thirst

渇	THIRST	515
餓	STARVED	1734
飢	STARVE	1668

hunt and fish

猟	HUNTING	538
狩	HUNT	397
獲	CATCH GAME	779
漁	FISH	698
釣	ANGLE	1674

hurry

急	HURRY	2092
促	HASTEN	103

husband

夫	HUSBAND	3460
主	master of the house	1938

I

illusory mental images

夢	DREAM	2336
幻	PHANTOM	180

image

像	IMAGE	166
影	SHADOW	1889

images

像	IMAGE	166
仏	Buddhist image	19
偶	figure	132

imitate

擬	IMITATE	788
倣	COPY AFTER	113
模	pattern after	1050
肖	MODEL	2205
象	represent	2134

immediate

即	IMMEDIATE	1120
直	straight away	2932

impartial

公	impartial	1974
平	equal	3478

impatient

焦	BE IMPATIENT	2770
燥	restless	1087

imperial decree

勅	IMPERIAL DECREE	1451
詔	IMPERIAL EDICT	1505
宣	imperial proclamation	2252

important
要 IMPORTANT 2635
重 HEAVY 3573
impose
徴 LEVY 683
課 impose 1573
imprison and confine
拘 ARREST 310
禁 confine 2795
留 keep in custody 2580
置 place in custody 2608
incident
事 AFFAIR 3567
故 incident 1141
変 unexpected event 2069
incite
挑 PROVOKE 372
唆 INSTIGATE 402
扇 FAN 1950
激 excite 776
奮 ROUSE UP 2367
振 arouse to action 430
動 MOVE 1778
起 rise to action 3307
inclining ⇨OBLIQUENESS AND INCLINING
inclining toward
偏 ONE-SIDED 133
傾 incline toward 154
include ⇨CONTAIN AND INCLUDE
increase
加 add to 38
増 INCREASE 677
殖 MULTIPLY 994
倍 DOUBLE 108
indicate
指 POINT 378
示 SHOW 1936
標 MARK 1064
宛てる ADDRESS 2222
industry and business
業 BUSINESS, INDUSTRY 2612
商 TRADE 2116
産 industry 3298
工 manufacturing industry 3381
inexpensive
安 INEXPENSIVE 2171
廉 CHEAP 3153
低 low-priced 73
inform and communicate
報 INFORM 1698
通 COMMUNICATE 3109
告 NOTIFY 2409
届ける give notice 3078
達 issue a notice 3139
知 let know 1127
申 REPORT 3507
宣 PROCLAIM 2252
information
報 information 1698
信 MESSAGE 100
in front
前 BEFORE 2266
先 AHEAD 2394
ingest
喫 INGEST 551
服 take 878
食 EAT 2075
飲 DRINK 1692
inheritors
嫡 LEGITIMATE CHILD 680
嗣 HEIR 1719
injury
傷 WOUND 158
創 wound (cut) 1815
-擦れ sore 790
in-laws
婿 SON-IN-LAW 566
嫁 daughter-in-law 635
inlets and bays
江 INLET 221
浦 coastal indentation 437
湾 BAY 613
峡 narrows 357
inner
奥 inner 2824
深 DEEP 524
幽 QUIET AND SECLUDED 3008
inquire
問 QUESTION 3320
詰 question closely 1521
聞く ask 3326
質 query 2808
尋ねる INQUIRE 2322
伺う INQUIRE (*humble*) 69

諮	CONSULT	1596

insect

虫	INSECT	3530
昆	INSECT	2413
繭	COCOON	2380

insects

蚊	MOSQUITO	1319
蛍	FIREFLY	2591
蝶	BUTTERFLY	1401
蚕	SILKWORM	2457

inside

内	INSIDE	3466
裏	inside	2138
奥	INNER PART	2824
中	IN	3451

insignia

紋	CREST	1299
章	BADGE	2117

install ⇨ EQUIP AND INSTALL

instruct

訓	INSTRUCT	1454
指	direct	378

in succession

連	IN SUCCESSION	3103
歴	successive	3019
逐	ONE BY ONE	3102
逓	progressively	3106
漸	GRADUALLY	706

intelligent and wise

賢	WISE	2839
智	wise	2784
慧	INTELLIGENT	2810
怜	CLEVER	298
哲	SAGACIOUS	2738
明	clear-sighted	855
聡	SHARP-WITTED	1384
俊	brilliant	102
鋭	SHARP	1730
敏	NIMBLE	1322

intention ⇨ WILL AND INTENTION

intercross

交	intercross	2015
差	cross	3311

interest and dividend

利	interest	1114
子	interest	3390
配	dividend	1460

internal organs

心	HEART	11
肺	LUNG	916
胃	STOMACH	2561
腸	INTESTINES	1033
肝	LIVER	841
胆	GALLBLADDER	919

interrogatives

奈	interrogative forming element	2219
那	interrogative forming element	843
何	WHAT	65
誰	WHO	1578

interval ⇨ DISTANCE AND INTERVAL

investigate and examine

閲	REVIEW	3330
究	STUDY EXHAUSTIVELY	2203
察	INSPECT	2347
討	STUDY	1456
探	PROBE	505
検	EXAMINE	986
診	EXAMINE A PATIENT	1504
調	INVESTIGATE	1567
査	LOOK INTO	2437
審	EXAMINE CAREFULLY	2360
験	TEST	1833
勘	CHECK	1777
糾	INQUIRE INTO	1278

invite ⇨ CALL AND INVITE

iron and steel

鉄	IRON	1711
銑	PIG IRON	1726
鋼	STEEL	1740

J

Japan

日	JAPAN	3027
和	JAPAN	1130
邦	JAPAN	847
国	Japanese	3087

Japanese money denominations

文	*mon*	1962
両	*ryo*	3518
厘	*RIN*	3004
銭	sen	1725
円	YEN	2955

join

- 結 TIE 1348
- 縛 BIND 1405
- 束 TIE UP 3554
- 連 LINK 3103
- 係 CONNECT 97
- 接 join 500

join ⇨ PARTICIPATE AND JOIN

joint

- 節 JOINT 2691
- 関 connection 3328

journey

- 旅 TRAVEL 922
- 行 trip 212
- 遊 tour 3142
- 巡 tour around 3047

judge

- 判 JUDGE 1122
- 裁 JUDGE 3299
- 鑑 APPRAISE 1773
- 評 evaluate 1501
- 審 TRY 2360
- 決 DECIDE 263
- 視 REGARD 972

jump

- 跳 JUMP 1532
- 躍 LEAP 1658

K

Kansai cities

- 阪 OSAKA 271
- 神 Kobe 912
- 京 KYOTO 2052

Kanto cities

- 京 TOKYO 2052
- 東 Tokyo 3568
- 都 METROPOLIS OF TOKYO 1686
- 浜 Yokohama 436

keys ⇨ LOCKS AND KEYS

kill

- 殺 KILL 1324
- 刺 stab to death 1275
- 絞 STRANGLE 1349
- 窒 CHOKE 2288

kind

- 厚 KIND 3003
- 篤 cordial 2716
- 懇 cordial 2899
- 慈 AFFECTIONATE 2339
- 温 warmhearted 608
- 渥 GRACIOUS 600
- 優 kindly 177

kinds and types

- 型 TYPE 2638
- 類 KIND 1807
- 色 kind 2029
- 般 SORT 1317
- 属 genus 3145
- 品 category 2248
- 種 VARIETY 1218
- 様 variety 1052

kinds of atmospheric vapor

- 霧 FOG 2817
- 霞 MIST 2814
- 雲 CLOUD 2773

kinds of frozen water

- 氷 ICE 39
- 雪 SNOW 2759

kinds of fuel

- 炭 COAL, CHARCOAL 2257
- 薪 FIREWOOD 2374
- 油 OIL 341

kinds of grasses

- 草 GRASS 2263
- 芝 LAWN GRASS 2180
- 笹 BAMBOO GRASS 2663

kinds of numbers

- 数 NUMBER (mathematical unit) 1790
- 員 fixed number 2269
- 号 NUMBER (numerical designation) 2153
- 番 No. 2748
- 第 ORDINAL NUMBER PREFIX 2660
- -目 ordinal number suffix 3043
- 次 numerical order suffix 54

kinds of precipitation

- 雨 RAIN 3561
- 露 DEW 2818
- 霜 FROST 2815
- 雪 SNOW 2759

kinds of railway

鉄 railway 1711
電 electric railway 2790
車 railway car 3552
両 counter for railway cars 3518

kinds of skin

皮 SKIN (of any kind) 3037
膚 SKIN (of the human body) 3265
肌 SKIN (of the human body) 827
革 LEATHER 2448

kinds of sound

音 SOUND 2070
声 VOICE 2198
響 reverberation 2878
韻 melodious tone 1811
玲 TINKLING OF JADES 910

kinds of water

水 WATER 10
湯 HOT WATER 612
汽 STEAM 264
氷 ICE 39

kinds of wood

木 WOOD 3450
材 TIMBER 836
薪 FIREWOOD 2374

know and understand

知 KNOW 1127
通 know thoroughly 3109
得 gain understanding of 477
分かる understand 1972
解 understand 1517
諒 UNDERSTAND 1575
了 COMPREHEND 3350
悟 AWAKE TO 419

knowledge ⇨ LEARNING AND KNOWLEDGE

Korea

鮮 Korea 1877
朝 North Korea 1695
韓 SOUTH KOREA 1757

L

labels and slips

札 TAG 817
券 TICKET 2630
票 SLIP 2669

符 tally 2661
節 token 2691

lakes and marshes

沢 MARSH 267
沼 MUDDY POND 339
湖 LAKE 604
池 POND 218
潟 LAGOON 745

land and soil

土 SOIL 3403
地 GROUND 204
壌 ARABLE SOIL 755
泥 MUD 326
陸 LAND 543

language

語 LANGUAGE 1543
弁 dialect 2004

large numbers

百 HUNDRED 2026
千 THOUSAND 3411
万 TEN THOUSAND 2936
億 HUNDRED MILLION 170
兆 TRILLION 225
京 ten quadrillion 2052

last

末 last in time 3505
終 last 1336

late

遅 LATE (delayed) 3133
晩 late (advanced) 979

late ⇨ BE LATE AND DELAY

later Chinese dynasties

唐 TANG DYNASTY 3115
元 Yuan Dynasty 1929
明 Ming Dynasty 855
清 Qing Dynasty 523

latitude and longitude

緯 LATITUDE 1407
経 longitude 1331

laws and rules

法 LAW 333
律 LAW 363
典 CANON 2627
憲 CONSTITUTION 2368
令 ordinance 1995
則 RULE 1444
矩 RULE 1148

規 REGULATION 978
紀 discipline 1276

lazy

惰 LAZY 579
怠 REMISS 2085
慢 SLUGGISH 686

lead and escort

率 LEAD 2118
引 lead 181
導 GUIDE 2888
連 take along 3103

leaders

主 MASTER 1938
王 KING 3439
長 CHIEF 2556
頭 HEAD 1604
首 LEADER 2265
領 leader 1224

learn and study

学 STUDY 2555
考 study 3196
習 LEARN 2667
研 RESEARCH 1132
究 STUDY EXHAUSTIVELY 2203
攻 specialize 242

learning and knowledge

業 studies 2612
学 learning 2555
文 culture 1962
識 KNOWLEDGE 1639
知 knowledge 1127

leave

遺 LEAVE BEHIND 3166
残す leave 943

leave and set forth

去 GO AWAY 2156
離 leave 1836
発 START 2565
出 GO OUT 3498
退 RETREAT 3094
撤 WITHDRAW 738

left and right

右 RIGHT 2975
左 LEFT 2974

legislature

議 LEGISLATIVE BODY 1647
会 assembly 2020
院 House 454

leisure

暇 FREE TIME 1012
閑 LEISURE 3322

leisurely

悠 LEISURELY 2741
閑 idle 3322

lend and borrow

借 BORROW 122
債 DEBT 156
貸 LEND 2600
融 finance 1831

length units

寸 *sun* (3.03 cm) 2935
尺 *SHAKU* (30.3 cm) 3440
米 meter 3529
尋 fathom (1.8 m) 2322
間 *ken* (1.8 m) 3323
丈 *jo* (3.03 m) 3419
町 *cho* (109 m) 1113
里 LEAGUE, *ri* (3.4 km) 3542

less in degree

弱 WEAK 1167
軽 LIGHT 1515
微 SLIGHT 639
低 LOW 73
薄 THIN 2370
浅 SHALLOW 389

let do

放 LET GO 853
随 let do 627

lie down

伏 PROSTRATE 45
寝る lie down 2329

life

生 LIFE 3497
命 LIFE 2058
寿 LONGEVITY 3557

life energy

精 SPIRIT 1366
気 vital energy 3194

light

光 LIGHT 2391
明 light 855
灯 LAMP 825
照 sunlight 2827
虹 RAINBOW 1285

light-colored

淡	LIGHT	528
浅	light	389
薄い	pale	2370
鈍-	DULL	1689

lighter elements

水	hydrogen	10
酸	OXYGEN	1563
窒	NITROGEN	2288
塩	chlorine	631
臭	bromine	2633
硫	SULFUR	1184
炭	carbon	2257

like ⇨ LOVE AND LIKE

limbs

肢	LIMB	882
腕	ARM	1006
脚	LEG	974

line

線	LINE	1392
筋	THREADLIKE STRUCTURE	2678
条	strip	2200
脈	VEIN	953
棒	straight line	983
軸	AXIS	1514

lineage

系	LINEAGE	1944
血	BLOOD	3526

linear arrangements

伍	RANK	47
列	ROW	824
行	LINE (esp. of print)	212
欄	COLUMN	1103

lines ⇨ ROPES AND LINES

lines and line segments

線	LINE	1392
弧	ARC	360
弦	chord	287
径	DIAMETER	291
辺	side	3029

line segments ⇨ LINES AND LINE SEGMENTS

liquefy

溶	DISSOLVE, MELT	664
解	DISSOLVE	1517
融	FUSE	1831

liquid

液	LIQUID	511
汁	fluid	195
水	WATER	10

live

活	LIVE	385
暮らす	LIVE (pass one's life)	2354
生	live (be alive)	3497

load

載	LOAD	3300
積む	load	1236
搭	load on board	592

localities ⇨ AREAS AND LOCALITIES

locks and keys

鍵	KEY	1753
錠	LOCK	1737

longitude ⇨ LATITUDE AND LONGITUDE

long objects ⇨ COUNTERS FOR LONG OBJECTS

long time periods

時	TIME	924
代	age	30
紀	ERA	1276
世	AGE	3496
朝	dynastic period	1695
期	period	1704

look ⇨ SEE AND LOOK

lose

負	LOSE	2091
敗	BE DEFEATED	1476

losing and loss

失	LOSE	3511
喪	lose	2825
逸	LET SLIP	3120
損	LOSS, lose	651

loss ⇨ LOSING AND LOSS

loud

高い	loud	2097
朗	CLEAR (voice)	1325
騒	clamorous	1835

love

愛	LOVE	2492
情	love	482
恋	LOVE (for the opposite sex)	2098
艶	ROMANCE	1908

love and like

愛	LOVE	2492

恋 LOVE (the opposite sex) 2098
好 LIKE 208

low
低 LOW 73
下 lower 3378

lower
低 lower 73
下 bring down 3378

lowly
卑 MEAN 2642
下 of low rank 3378
低 LOW 73

luster
艶 gloss 1908
沢 luster 267

M

machines and tools
機 MACHINE 1076
械 MECHANICAL CONTRIVANCE 961
具 IMPLEMENT 2552
器 INSTRUMENT 2713
儀 measuring instrument 169
鏡 OPTICAL INSTRUMENT 1766

magnetism ⇨ELECTRICITY AND MAGNETISM

mail
郵 MAIL 1687
便 POST 95

main
主 MAIN 1938
正 chief 3484
本 head 3502
親- PARENT 1799
首 leading 2265

make
作 MAKE 68
造 MAKE 3110
成 FORM 3537
工 MANUFACTURE 3381
製 MANUFACTURE 2803
産 PRODUCE 3298
調 PREPARE 1567
組む ASSEMBLE 1337
構 CONSTRUCT 1049

make progress
進 ADVANCE 3121
亨 GO SMOOTHLY 2037

make sound or noise
鳴 SOUND 674
響 REVERBERATE 2878
騒 CLAMOR 1835

make widely known
布 SPREAD 2973
流 spread 441
伝 spread 44
広 spread 3035
弘 DISSEMINATE (esp. Buddhism) 192
及 REACH TO 3385

man
男 MAN 2542
郎 YOUNG MAN 1289
雄 MALE 1008
夫 male adult 3460
翁 OLD MAN 2108

mania and maniacs
痴 infatuated 3286
狂 maniac 269
魔 maniac 3187
熱 fever 2866

maniacs ⇨MANIA AND MANIACS

mansions
邸 STATELY RESIDENCE 1131
館 stately mansion 1748
荘 VILLA 2262

manuscript
稿 MANUSCRIPT 1231
草 draft 2263
案 draft 2270

many
百 numerous 2026
万 myriad 2936
多 MANY 2170
豊 PLENTIFUL 2697
沢 plentiful 267
穣 YIELDING ABUNDANTLY 1250
裕 ABUNDANT 1195
富 RICH 2310

mark
印 imprint 828
押 seal 314

画	mark off	3000

market

市	MARKET	1993
場	market	558

marks and signs

標	MARK (identifying sign)	1064
印	MARK (visible sign)	828
跡	TRACE	1534
紋	print	1299
符	SYMBOL	2661
号	SIGN	2153

marriage ⇨MARRYING AND MARRIAGE

marrying and marriage

嫁	WED A MAN	635
婚	MARRY	470
姻	MARRIAGE	353
縁	marriage relation	1386

marshes ⇨LAKES AND MARSHES

mathematical power

乗	power	3576
方	SQUARE	1963
平	square (measure)	3478

mats

畳	TATAMI	2592
薦	straw mat	2373
-敷き	underlay	1870

matter

質	MATTER	2808
物	substance	874
材	MATERIAL	836
料	MATERIALS	1292
資	material resources	2695

mature

熟	MATURE	2868
成	grow up	3537
稔	RIPEN	1207
実る	bear fruit	2225

meaning

義	MEANING	2338
意	MEANING	2136
訳	SENSE	1473
旨	PURPORT	2024
趣	PURPOSE	3317

means

策	MEASURE	2679
段	STEP	1144
手	means	3456

measure

測	MEASURE	610
量	measure	2471

measuring devices

尺	rule	3440
計	meter	1441
衡	scales	761

meat

肉	FLESH	3200
身	meat	3553
脩	DRIED MEAT	136

mediating and mediators

紹	INTRODUCE	1335
介	MEDIATE	1967
媒	INTERMEDIATE	564
仲	INTERMEDIARY	43

mediators ⇨MEDIATING AND MEDIATORS

medicines

薬	DRUG	2375
剤	PREPARATION	1669
錠	PILL	1737
丸	pill suffix	3417

meet

会	MEET	2020
遇	ENCOUNTER	3135
遭	MEET WITH	3159
見	SEE	2544
謁	BE GRANTED AN AUDIENCE	1570

merchandise

産	product	3298
品	ARTICLE (of merchandise)	2248
貨	GOODS	2465
物	commodity	874

merchant

屋	shopkeeper	3098
商	merchant	2116

metal

金	METAL	2057
鉱	ORE	1709

metals

金	GOLD	2057
銀	SILVER	1722
銅	COPPER	1721
鉄	IRON	1711
鉛	LEAD	1707

middle

中	MIDDLE	3451

央	CENTER	3509
心	HEART	11
核	NUCLEUS	927

military

武	MILITARY	3210
兵	military	2551

military officers and ranks

曹	SERGEANT	2746
尉	COMPANY OFFICER	1685
佐	FIELD OFFICER	67
将	GENERAL OFFICER	460
督	COMMANDER	2796
帥	COMMANDER IN CHIEF	1290

mine

坑	PIT	236
鉱	MINE	1709
山	mine	2940

miraculous

妙	MARVELOUS	239
魔	magic(al)	3187

misfortune and disaster

災	NATURAL CALAMITY	2206
難	DISASTER	1838
禍	CALAMITY	1030
厄	MISFORTUNE	2947
凶	BAD LUCK	2961

mistakes and mistaking

過	error	3137
失	SLIP	3511
誤	MISTAKE	1542
錯	mistaken	1743
-違える	mis-	3151

mistaking ⇨ **MISTAKES AND MISTAKING**

mix

混	MIX	519
交	intermingle	2015
雑	MIXED	1385
錯	MIXED UP	1743

model

範	MODEL	2709
典	CANON	2627
模	PATTERN	1050
程	ESTABLISHED FORM	1190
式	form	3049
準	STANDARD	2856
格	NORM	926

modifier suffixes

然	MODIFIER FORMING SUFFIX	2782
如	modifier suffix	207
爾	adjective suffix	3587
的	ADJECTIVAL SUFFIX	1125

moisten

潤	moisten	742
浸	SOAK	442
漬ける	immerse	702

monetary gifts

謝	monetary gift of thanks	1620
礼	monetary gift	818

money

金	MONEY	2057
銭	MONEY	1725
貨	MONEY (legal tender), coin	2465
幣	CURRENCY	2885
銀	SILVER	1722
財	finance	1457
資	RESOURCES	2695
-玉	coin suffix	3477
札	bill	817

monkey

猿	MONKEY	669
申	the Monkey	3507

months ⇨ **WEEKS AND MONTHS**

moon

月	MOON	2956
陰	moon	541

moral goodness

徳	VIRTUE	684
道	the way of moral conduct	3134
善	GOOD	2325
義	RIGHTEOUSNESS	2338

moral principles

倫	MORALS	120
道	the way of moral conduct	3134

morning and dawn

朝	MORNING	1695
暁	DAWN	980
旦	DAYBREAK	2389

most

最	MOST	2472
至	utmost	2182
極	EXTREME	1017

most recent

昨	LAST	893

去	last	2156
先	last	2394

motion

動	motion	1778
惰	inertia	579

motion picture

映	motion picture	892
画	film	3000

mountains

峰	PEAK	411
岳	HIGH MOUNTAIN	2557
山	MOUNTAIN	2940

mountains ⇨ HIGH PARTS OF MOUNTAINS

mourn and mourning

弔	CONDOLE	3432
悼	MOURN	485
喪	MOURNING	2825
忌	MOURNING	2207

mourning ⇨ MOURN AND MOURNING

mouth parts

唇	LIP	2737
歯	TOOTH	2476
舌	TONGUE	2186

move

動	MOVE	1778
運	MOVE	3140
滑	SLIDE	658
移	SHIFT	1177
転	remove	1480
遷	TRANSFER	3170
繰る	SHIFT ONWARD	1427

move forward

進	ADVANCE	3121
突	DASH	2230

move through water

泳	SWIM	327
渉	wade	526

multiply

乗	multiply	3576
掛ける	multiply	493

musical elements

韻	RHYME	1811
律	RHYTHM	363
拍	BEAT	304
調	TONE	1567
呂	ancient musical note	2187

musical instrument

管	wind instrument	2701
弦	string instrument	287

musical instruments

琴	KOTO	2781
鼓	DRUM	1786
笛	FLUTE	2664

music and songs

楽	MUSIC	2826
音	sound of music	2070
節	tune	2691
調べ	melody	1567
曲	MUSICAL COMPOSITION	3527
歌	SONG	1825
謡	POPULAR SONG	1597

mutual

相	MUTUAL	900
互	RECIPROCAL	3437

N

naked

裸	NAKED	1211
素	bare	2458

name

名	NAME	2169
銘	name (inscribed by maker)	1724
姓	SURNAME	279
氏	FAMILY NAME	2951
称	APPELLATION	1160
題	TITLE	3337
号	DESIGNATION	2153

name

呼	CALL	273
言う	call	1941
称	name	1160

name suffixes

郎	MALE NAME SUFFIX	1289
麿	CLASSICAL MALE NAME SUFFIX	3184
彦	MALE NAME ELEMENT	3295
-子	female name element	3390

national

国	national	3087
内	internal	3466

natural

地	natural	204
野	wild	1485
粗	crude	1329
原	in the original state	3009

nature and character

性	NATURE	299
気	temperament	3194
質	QUALITY	2808
品	grade of excellence	2248
柄	CHARACTER	897
格	(good) character	926

near

近	NEAR	3061
隣	neighboring	781
傍	BESIDE	147
沿	ALONG	328

necessity ⇨ **NEED AND NECESSITY**

neck

首	NECK	2265
項	nape	567

need and necessity

要	required	2635
必	must	15
須	MUST	574
需	DEMAND	2797
入	necessary	3370
用	needed for (a specific use)	2976

needle

針	NEEDLE	1666
刺	prickle	1275

negative

負	negative	2091
陰	negative	541

net

網	NET	1374
羅	bird net	2622

new

新	NEW	1784
鮮	FRESH	1877
生	raw	3497

next

次	NEXT	54
明	next	855
翌	THE FOLLOWING	2668
来	the coming	3551

night ⇨ **EVENING AND NIGHT**

nitrogen

窒	NITROGEN	2288
硝	NITER	1185

nobility

爵	RANK OF NOBILITY	2524
公	nobleman	1974
侯	FEUDAL LORD	98

noblemen

公	duke	1974
侯	marquis	98
伯	COUNT	59
子	viscount	3390
男	baron	2542

nominalizers

所	PARTICLE OF NOMINALIZATION	851
事	nominalization word	3567
子	NOUN SUFFIX	3390
性	-ITY	299

noon

午	NOON	1984
昼	midday	3097

North American countries

米	AMERICA	3529
加	Canada	38

notebook

帳	NOTEBOOK	473
簿	RECORD BOOK	2727
籍	REGISTER	2731

nothing ⇨ **EMPTINESS AND NOTHING**

not moving

固	FIRM	3086
定	fixed	2229
静	still	1728
止	still	2941

nourish ⇨ **RAISE AND NOURISH**

number ⇨ **QUANTITY AND NUMBER**

numbers ⇨ **KINDS OF NUMBERS**

O

obey

守	observe	2173
遵	OBEY	3167
順	OBEY	18

隷 be subordinate to 1751
従 FOLLOW 415

object

物 THING 874
品 ARTICLE 2248
体 BODY 71

obliqueness and inclining

斜 OBLIQUE 1486
傾 INCLINE 154

obstacle

障 HINDRANCE 715
関 BARRIER 3328

obstinate ⇨ **FIRM AND OBSTINATE**

obstruct and hinder

遮 INTERRUPT 3158
阻 OBSTRUCT 348
妨 HINDER 238
障 hinder 715
害 stand in the way 2272

occasions

際 OCCASION 714
折 occasion 253
時 timely occasion 924
機 OPPORTUNITY 1076
節 time 2691

occupy

占 OCCUPY 2003
拠 occupy 312
領 take possession of 1224
専 take exclusive possession of 2644

offenses ⇨ **CRIMES AND OFFENSES**

offer

供 OFFER (to a person or god) 88
献 OFFER (esp. to a superior) 1785
納 offer (as to a god) 1300
提 PRESENT 591
貢 offer tribute 2281
奉 DEDICATE 2559

offering

幣 offering 2885
貢 TRIBUTE 2281

offer wine

酌 POUR WINE 1461
献 offer wine 1785
酬 reciprocate wineglasses 1539

officials

官 GOVERNMENT OFFICIAL 2226
吏 OFFICIAL 3536
僚 official 165
司 officiator 2931
役 executive 244
事 officer 3567

offspring

子 CHILD 3390
孤 orphan 356
嫡 LEGITIMATE CHILD 680
息 son 2647
男 son 2542
惣 eldest son 2780
娘 DAUGHTER 406
女 daughter 3418
姫 DAUGHTER OF NOBLE BIRTH 407

of long duration

長 LONG 2556
永 ETERNAL 1937
久 OF LONG DURATION 3384
恒 permanent 367

oils ⇨ **FATS AND OILS**

old

古 OLD (not new) 2002
老 OLD (not young) 3197
故 OLD (of the past) 1141
旧 old 14

old persons

老 old person 3197
翁 OLD MAN 2108
婆 OLD WOMAN 2762

old times

昔 FORMER TIMES 2432
往 bygone days 292

omit

漏 omit 701
脱 leave out by mistake 973
抜く leave out 246
欠 missing 1987

one

一 ONE 3341
壱 ONE (in legal documents) 2197
片- ONE OF TWO 3461
隻 ONE OF A PAIR 2755
単 SINGLE 2256
個 INDIVIDUAL 117

one side

片-	one side	3461
偏	ONE-SIDED	133

only

唯	ONLY	463
一	one and only	3341

on the verge of

-掛かる	be on the verge of	493
将	on the verge of	460
-際	on the verge of	714
臨	on the point of	1630

open

開	OPEN	3321
展	UNFOLD	3111
披	open and read	305

opinion

見	view (personal opinion)	2544
観	VIEW (conception)	1880
説	opinion	1547
論	opinion	1574

opposite

対	OPPOSITE	831
反	COUNTER	2945
逆	REVERSE	3091
倒	upside-down	124

oppress ⇨ TORTURE AND OPPRESS

order

序	ORDER (sequence／arrangement)	3065
順	ORDER (sequence)	18
次	order (sequence)	54
番	NUMERICAL ORDER	2748
秩	ORDER (methodical arrangement)	1158

ordinary

常	NORMAL	2590
只-	ORDINARY	2155
並	ordinary	2246
平	common	3478
普	common	2323
庸	MEDIOCRE	3128
凡	COMMONPLACE	2938

organ

臓	INTERNAL ORGAN	1102
器	organ	2713
官	organ	2226

organize

組	ORGANIZE	1337
結	form	1348
編	put together	1387

organized bodies

会	SOCIETY	2020
協	association	93
団	BODY	3053
体	BODY	71
組	union	1337
労	workers' union	2548
連	federation	3103
講	fraternity	1619
院	INSTITUTION	454

original

素	primary	2458
原	ORIGINAL	3009
本	original	3502
初	FIRST	1116

other

他	OTHER	35
余	other	2042
別	ANOTHER	1117

outside

外	OUTSIDE	186
表	SURFACE	2429
面	FACE	2087

overturn

覆	OVERTURN	2726
翻	TURN OVER	1897
反	turn over	2945
転	turn [roll] over	1480
倒	TOPPLE	124

P

palace

宮	ROYAL PALACE	2274
殿	PALACE	1792

paper

紙	PAPER	1302
葉	LEAF	2321
丁	sheet	3348
頁	PAGE	2086
面	page (of a newspaper)	2087

parents

親 PARENT 1799
父 FATHER 1973
母 MOTHER 3475

part

分 PART 1972
部 SECTION 1676
局 LIMITED PART 3063
片 FRAGMENT 3461

part company

別 SEPARATE 1117
離 SEPARATE 1836

participate and join

参 PARTICIPATE 2066
与 take part in 3421
加 join 38
入 ENTER 3370

particle

粒 GRAIN 1328
子 particle suffix 3390
核 NUCLEUS 927

parties and sects

党 PARTY 2581
閥 CLIQUE 3325
流 school 441
派 SECT 381
翼 WING 2720
系 faction 1944
門 (religious) sect 888
宗 RELIGIOUS SECT (esp. Buddhist) 2228

parts of governments

閣 CABINET 3327
省 MINISTRY 2449

parts of periodicals

欄 COLUMN 1103
面 page (of a newspaper) 2087

parts of plays

幕 act 2335
場 scene 558

parts of towns

区 WARD 2963
街 CITY QUARTER 576
町 town section (*cho*) 1113
丁 TOWN SUBSECTION (*chome*) 3348
字 village or town section 2172

parts of writing

章 CHAPTER 2117
段 passage 1144
節 paragraph 2691
款 ARTICLE 1700
条 ARTICLE 2200
項 CLAUSE 567
目 ITEM 3043
箇 item 2700

pass

通 PASS 3109
過 PASS BY 3137
経 PASS THROUGH 1331

pattern

模 PATTERN (decorative design) 1050
文 decorative pattern 1962
柄 pattern (on cloth) 897
様 pattern 1052
紋 figure 1299

pawn

質 pawn 2808
当 pawn 2177

pay

払う PAY 194
納 PAY (to the authorities) 1300
済 settle accounts 522
支 pay out 1979
賦 INSTALLMENT 1583
償 RECOMPENSE 176

pay and earnings

給 PAY 1350
賃 WAGE 2694
料 FEE 1292
俸 SALARY 114
禄 RETAINER'S STIPEND 1002
収 income 198

peace

和 PEACE 1130
安 public peace 2171
治 public order 335

peaceful ⇨ CALM AND PEACEFUL

penetrate

透 PASS THROUGH 3108
貫 PENETRATE 2460
破 break through 1150

people

民 PEOPLE 3036

族 race 958

people ⇨ THE PEOPLE

perceive

覚 PERCEIVE 2604
知 KNOW 1127
感 FEEL 2835
認 RECOGNIZE 1546

performance

劇 DRAMA 1904
演 performance 697
芸 entertainment 2209

performers

優 ACTOR 177
俳 actor 112
伶 MUSICIAN 66

periodicals

誌 MAGAZINE 1548
紙 newspaper 1302
報 bulletin 1698

periodicals ⇨ PARTS OF PERIODICALS

periphery

周 PERIPHERY 2998
囲 circumference 3069
郭 OUTER ENCLOSURE 1678

permit

許 PERMIT 1470
免 license 2067
准 grant permission 127
允 GIVE CONSENT 1982

person

人 HUMAN BEING 3368
者 PERSON 3211
方 person (*honorific*) 1963
氏 person (*polite*) 2951

personal relations

縁 RELATION 1386
交 INTERCOURSE 2015
好 friendship 208
仲 PERSONAL RELATIONS 43

person in charge

係 PERSON IN CHARGE 97
-方 person in charge 1963
員 MEMBER (of a staff) 2269

persons ⇨ COUNTERS FOR PERSONS

phenomenon

象 PHENOMENON 2134
気 natural phenomenon 3194
物 physical phenomena 874

phonetic [a]

亜 PHONETIC [a] 3540
阿 PHONETIC [a] 346

phonetic [ha]

巴 phonetic [ha] 3438
波 phonetic [ha] 330

phonetic [i]

伊 PHONETIC [i] 49
斐 PHONETIC [i] 2776

phonetic [m]

弥 PHONETIC [mi] 288
摩 phonetic [ma] 3175

phonetic [na]

那 PHONETIC [na] 843
奈 PHONETIC [na] 2219

phonetic [r]

呂 PHONETIC [ro] 2187
路 phonetic [ru] 1533
羅 PHONETIC [ra] 2622

phonetic [s] / [sh]

沙 phonetic [sha] 266
遮 phonetic [sha] 3158
世 phonetic [se] 3496
須 phonetic [shu] 574
修 phonetic [shu] 123
西 phonetic [su] 3520
相 phonetic [sō] 900

photograph

撮 PHOTOGRAPH 737
写 shoot 2000

picture

絵 PICTURE 1346
画 PICTURE 3000
図 DRAWING 3071

pigments

墨 INDIA INK 2753
漆 LACQUER 704
藍 INDIGO 2381

places and positions

所 PLACE 851
処 place 3031
場 PLACE (for specific activity) 558
地 PLACE (particular location) 204
席 meeting place 3113
位 POSITION 61
点 POINT 2084

座	place	3116

places for landing or stopping

港	PORT	605
津	HARBOR (*elegant*)	390
駅	STATION	1822
停	stopping place	139

places of business

店	SHOP (of any kind)	3085
舗	SHOP (esp. traditional)	1735
屋	SMALL SHOP	3098
社	COMPANY	840

places of worship

堂	temple building	2589
塔	pagoda	561
寺	BUDDHIST TEMPLE	2164
社	Shinto shrine	840
宮	SHINTO SHRINE	2274
院	monastery	454
教	church	1493

plain and simple

素	PLAIN	2458
朴	SIMPLE (unadorned)	819
単	simple (uncomplicated)	2256

planning ⇨ PLANS AND PLANNING

plans and planning

計	PLAN	1441
画	DRAW UP A PLAN	3000
案	PROPOSAL	2270
企	PROJECT	2021
図	systematic plan	3071
謀	SCHEME	1593
策	SCHEME	2679
略	STRATEGY	1169

plant ⇨ FARM AND PLANT

plants

菜	VEGETABLE	2305
植	PLANT	990
栽	garden plant	3297

plants ⇨ SUPPORTING PARTS OF PLANTS

plates ⇨ BOARDS AND PLATES

play

遊	PLAY	3142
戯	SPORT	1875

play music

奏	PLAY MUSIC	2577
弾	play on (stringed instruments)	572

吹	BLOW	231

plays ⇨ PARTS OF PLAYS

pleasant ⇨ PLEASED AND PLEASANT

pleased and pleasant

楽	pleasurable	2826
快	PLEASANT	245
朗	CHEERFUL	1325
愉	PLEASED	582
悦	DELIGHTED	418
嬉しい	GLAD	722
喜	HAPPY	2308
歓	JOYOUS	1867
欣	JOYFUL	852

pleasure

楽	PLEASURE	2826
娯	ENJOYMENT	405
興	AMUSEMENT	2909

plural suffixes

-達	plural suffix	3139
-等	plural suffix	2682
衆	somewhat polite plural suffix	2683
-共	belittling plural suffix	2393
-方	polite plural suffix	1963

poetry

詩	POETRY	1524
歌	Japanese poetry	1825
俳	HAIKU	112
句	HAIKU	2967

points of land

岬	CAPE	284
崎	PROMONTORY	472

policy

策	policy	2679
是	policy	2436
綱	guiding principle	1372

polish and rub

磨	POLISH	3181
擦	RUB	790
摩	RUB AGAINST	3175
研	GRIND	1132
削	CUT BY CHIPPING	1448

poor

貧	POOR	2123
乏	poor	1933
窮	destitute	2358

positions ⇨ PLACES AND POSITIONS

positive

陽 positive 626
正 positive 3484

possess

有 HAVE 2983
蔵 own 2364
持 HOLD 374
属 BELONG TO 3145
享 ENJOY 2051
具 possess 2552

possessive particles

之 POSSESSIVE PARTICLE 3420
乃 POSSESSIVE PARTICLE 2927

possible

可 -ABLE 2969
能 possible 1323

posthumous worlds

天 HEAVEN 3442
幽 world of the dead 3008
獄 hell 712

post station

駅 relay station 1822
逓 RELAY 3106
宿 post station 2293

posture

姿 posture 2636
態 attitude 2847

potency

効 EFFECT 1265
験 efficacy 1833
能 action 1323
機 function 1076

powder

粉 POWDER 1291
末 powder 3505

power and authority

力 POWER 3371
威 MIGHT 3578
勢 POWER (to influence) 2857
権 POWER (to control) 1065
覇 SUPREMACY 2730

praise

賛 PRAISE 2809
美 regard as beautiful 2264
褒 COMMEND 2144
嘉 commend (esp. an inferior) 2340
彰 PROCLAIM MERITS 1860
称 acclaim 1160
賞 express admiration 2618
揚 EXALT 593
頌 EULOGIZE 1045

pray and worship

祈 PRAY 875
願 pray 1845
拝 WORSHIP 303
崇 REVERENCE 2297
斎 OBSERVE RELIGIOUS ABSTINENCE 2115

precept

戒 commandment 3204
訓 precept 1454

precious stones

玉 GEM 3477
珠 PEARL 947
瑛 TRANSPARENT GEM 999
瑠 LAPIS LAZULI 1060
璃 GLASSY SUBSTANCE 1059
晶 CRYSTAL 2474

precipitation ⇨ KINDS OF PRECIPITATION

prepare

備 PROVIDE 146
調 PREPARE 1567

present

今 PRESENT 1968
当 THE PRESENT 2177
現 ACTUAL 968

preservatize

漬ける PICKLE 702
薫 smoke 2371

preserve

留 KEEP 2580
保 PRESERVE 96
持 uphold 374

preserved foods

-漬け pickles 702
-干し dried food 3379

press ⇨ COMPEL AND PRESS

prevent

防 PREVENT 270
止 STOP 2941

price ⇨ FEE AND PRICE

principle

律 LAW 363

理 BASIC PRINCIPLE 970

print and publish

刷 PRINT 1273
印 print 828
植 typeset 990
刊 PUBLISH 190
版 PUBLISHING 872
載 PUT IN PRINT 3300
掲 display in writing 494

printing plate

版 PRINTING PLATE 872
梓 printing block 962

prison

獄 PRISON 712
監 prison 2852

prisoner

虜 CAPTIVE 3255
囚 PRISONER 3042

private ⇨ SECRET AND PRIVATE

prizes

賞 PRIZE 2618
杯 prize cup 857
章 decoration 2117

products of combustion

灰 ASH 2979
殻 cinders 1490
炭 CHARCOAL 2257
煙 SMOKE 1021

professionals ⇨ WORKERS AND PROFESSIONALS

profit

利 PROFIT 1114
益 PROFIT 2285
得 GAIN 477

profound

玄 PROFOUND 1991
幽 deep hidden 3008
奥 inmost 2824
深 DEEP 524

project

映 PROJECT 892
写 project 2000

projectiles and bombs

弾 PROJECTILE 572
丸 round projectile 3417
矢 ARROW 2009
爆 bomb 1101

雷 explosive device 2791

promise

約 PROMISE 1280
締 CONCLUDE (a treaty) 1393
協 reach an agreement 93
契 MAKE AN AGREEMENT 2639
盟 ALLIANCE 2794
誓 VOW 2754

prospering and prosperity

隆 PROSPER 545
振 rise 430
興 RISE TO PROSPERITY 2909
盛 PROSPEROUS 2675
昌 PROSPERING 2414
栄 FLOURISH 2574
繁 THRIVE 2853

prosperity ⇨ PROSPERING AND PROSPERITY

protect

守 PROTECT 2173
護 PROTECT 1648
衛 GUARD 760
警 GUARD AGAINST 2893
防 defend 270
番 WATCH 2748
保 PRESERVE 96
看 CARE FOR 3220

protective coverings

盾 SHIELD 3006
甲 armor 3481
面 mask 2087

prototype

型 TYPE 2638
儀 model 169

protrude and protruding

突 protruding 2230
凸 CONVEX 3486
隆 protuberant 545
起 RISE 3307
出る stick out 3498

protruding ⇨ PROTRUDE AND PROTRUDING

pseudonym suffixes

亭 PSEUDONYM SUFFIX 2072
屋 stage name suffix 3098

psyche

心 HEART 11
腹 heart 1034
衷 INNER HEART 2575

襟	inner mind	1252
胸	breast	951
懐	BOSOM	763
神	MIND	912
気	SPIRIT (consciousness)	3194
精	SPIRIT (mind)	1366
霊	SPIRIT (soul)	2805
魂	SOUL, spirit	1063

public

公	PUBLIC	1974
俗	POPULAR	104

public display

展	exhibition	3111
博	exposition	151

public offices

省	MINISTRY	2449
庁	GOVERNMENT AGENCY	3034
府	government office	3082
公	public office	1974
署	PUBLIC-SERVICE STATION	2609
局	public service office	3063
所	office	851

publish ⇨ **PRINT AND PUBLISH**

pull

引	DRAW	181
抽	DRAW OUT	302
抜	PULL OUT	246
控える	HOLD BACK	495
寄せる	DRAW NEAR	2291

punishment

刑	PENALTY	830
罰	PUNISHMENT	2613
懲	CHASTISE	2910
処	DEAL WITH (lawbreakers)	3031

purehearted

純	PURE	1297
淳	PUREHEARTED	514
清	clean	523
潔	IMMACULATE	744
廉	INCORRUPT	3153
敦	HONEST	1693
惇	SINCERE	486
直	straightforward	2932

purified ⇨ **CLEAN AND PURIFIED**

purple colors ⇨ **BLUE AND PURPLE COLORS**

pursue ⇨ **FOLLOW AND PURSUE**

push

押	PUSH	314
突く	THRUST	2230
圧	apply pressure	2970

put

据える	INSTALL	497
置	PLACE	2608
掛ける	SET	493
措	DISPOSE	502

put in

入	PUT IN	3370
挿	INSERT	431
-込む	cause to move inward	3030

put on ⇨ **WEAR AND PUT ON**

Q

quantity and number

量	QUANTITY	2471
嵩	BULK	2331
積	size	1236
額	AMOUNT	1805
分	content	1972
数	NUMBER	1790
勢	strength	2857

question

題	PROBLEM	3337
問	QUESTION (inquiry)	3320
論	question (issue)	1574

quiet

静	QUIET	1728
閑	QUIET	3322
寂	quiet	2290
幽	QUIET AND SECLUDED	3008
粛	still	3581
黙	SILENT	2865

quote

引	quote	181
挙	cite	2456

R

railway ⇨ **KINDS OF RAILWAY**

raise

揚	RAISE HIGH	593

掲	PUT UP	494
挙	RAISE	2456
上	raise	3404
起	raise up	3307
立てる	STAND	1992
拾う	PICK UP	379

raise and nourish

育	RAISE	2050
飼	RAISE ANIMALS	1716
養	FOSTER	2365
滋	NOURISH	602
牧	PASTURE	873

raise the temperature

暖	WARM (the air)	1011
温める	WARM (a thing)	608
熱	HEAT	2866

range

程	EXTENT	1190
範	range	2709
域	area	465
圏	SPHERE	3148
野	FIELD	1485
界	field (*phys*)	2563
場	field (*phys, psychol*)	558

ranks ⇨ **MILITARY OFFICERS AND RANKS**

rare

珍	RARE	909
希	RARE	2049

rare and sparse

薄い	THIN	2370
希	RARE	2049
疎	SPARSE	1178
粗	COARSE	1329

rash

滅	unreasonable	660
妄	RASH	2016
盲	BLIND	2053
暴	unrestrained	2515
荒	WILD	2260
濫	EXCESSIVE	801
乱	excessive	1260

rate

率	RATE	2118
割	rate	1816
比	ratio	26
歩	percentage	2416

rear

後	after-	361
背	BACK	2573
裏	REAR	2138
尻	tail end	3032
尾	TAIL	3062

reason

理	REASON	970
訳	SENSE	1473

reason ⇨ **CAUSE AND REASON**

reasoning

理	REASON	970
筋	thread	2678
脈	VEIN	953

rebellions ⇨ **WARFARE AND REBELLIONS**

receive

受	RECEIVE	2421
享	ENJOY	2051
領	receive	1224
収	TAKE IN	198
納	ACCEPT	1300
戴	RECEIVE HUMBLY	3302
頂	RECEIVE HUMBLY	145
拝	have the honor to receive	303

recent

近	RECENT	3061
新	NEW	1784

receptacles ⇨ **VESSELS AND RECEPTACLES**

recite

吟	RECITE	230
唱	chant	462
読	READ	1541
詠	RECITE POETRY	1500

reclaim

拓	OPEN UP	317
墾	RECLAIM	2896
開	OPEN	3321

recommend

薦	RECOMMEND	2373
推	recommend	504

records

記	written account	1453
録	RECORD	1742
譜	SYSTEMATIC RECORD	1637
誌	records	1548
史	HISTORY	3510
伝	biography	44

recover ⇨ CURE AND RECOVER

red colors

赤	RED	2193
紅	CRIMSON	1277
緋	SCARLET	1369
朱	VERMILION	3531
丹	CINNABAR	3441
茜	MADDER	2261

reduce the temperature

凍	FREEZE	129
冷	cool	80

refine

錬	REFINE (crude metals)	1741
精	REFINE (crude materials)	1366
留	distill	2580

reflect ⇨ SHINE AND REFLECT

reform

改	REFORM	243
革	REFORM	2448
更	RENEW	3541
新	make new	1784

refuse and reject

拒	REFUSE	311
断る	refuse	1492
否	SAY NO	2406
却	reject	1118

regret

惜	REGRET	484
恨	regret	369
憾	STRONGLY REGRET	764
悔	REPENT	365

regular

正	regular	3484
本	regular	3502

reject ⇨ REFUSE AND REJECT

relate

関	CONCERN	3328
係	CONNECT	97
絡	INTERLINK	1351
渉	HAVE RELATIONS WITH	526
連	LINK	3103

related by marriage

義	-in-law	2338
継	step-	1360

relations ⇨ FAMILY AND RELATIONS

release

放	LET GO	853
釈	release	1484

religion

教	RELIGION	1493
宗	religion	2228
道	the Way	3134

religions and sects

仏	Buddhism	19
法	Buddha's teachings	333
禅	ZEN	1032
儒	CONFUCIANISM	174
道	Taoism	3134

religious persons

聖	SAINT	2830
仙	IMMORTAL MOUNTAIN FAIRY	32

rely on

頼	RELY ON	1615
依	DEPEND ON	84

remain

残	REMAIN	943
余	REMAINING	2042
留	STAY	2580
滞	STAY	663

remember

憶	REMEMBER	765
覚える	COMMIT TO MEMORY	2604
記	commit to memory	1453
追	reminisce	3096
顧	LOOK BACK	1900

repair

直す	FIX	2932
修	REPAIR	123
繕	MEND	1423

repeating and repetition

再	ANOTHER TIME	3519
又	AGAIN	3351
復	repeat	575
重	DUPLICATE	3573
畳	reduplicate	2592
改	redo	243
-換える	redo	587
-直す	repetition suffix	2932
-返す	do over	3060

repetition ⇨ REPEATING AND REPETITION

replace ⇨ CHANGE AND REPLACE

reproductive cells

卵	ovum	849

精	sperm	1366

reptiles

亀	TURTLE	2128
蛇	SNAKE	1343
竜	DRAGON	2099

repute

声	reputation	2198
誉	HONOR	2502
名	NAME	2169
望	popularity	2742

request

請	REQUEST	1576
訴	APPEAL TO	1507
頼	ASK	1615
嘱	CHARGE WITH	718
要	REQUIRE	2635
願	ASK A FAVOR	1845
求	SEEK	3550

rescue

救	SAVE	1497
済	RELIEVE	522

resemble

似	RESEMBLE	63
類	be similar	1807

reside

住	LIVE	64
居	RESIDE	3080
生	inhabit	3497
植	colonize	990

resign

辞	RESIGN	1364
退	retire	3094

resist

抗	RESIST	252
抵	RESIST	319
耐	WITHSTAND	1282
対	OPPOSE	831
反	COUNTER	2945
逆	rebel	3091

resolutely

敢	BOLDLY	1706
断	resolutely	1492
決	decisively	263

respect

敬	RESPECT	1701
欽	REVERE	1690
仰	look up to	48
崇	REVERENCE	2297
尚	VALUE HIGHLY	2233
重	set value on	3573
拝	WORSHIP	303
慕	ADORE	2353
尊	HONOR	2324

respectful

恭	RESPECTFUL	2459
謹	RESPECTFULLY	1618
奉	reverentially	2559
拝	HUMBLY	303

responsibility

務	DUTY	1173
任	duty	53
責	RESPONSIBILITY	2467
分	one's part	1972

rest

休	REST	52
息	rest	2647
憩	TAKE A REST	2890

restaurant suffixes

亭	quality restaurant suffix	2072
閣	high-class restaurant suffix	3327
園	restaurant suffix	3156
苑	restaurant suffix	2239

restore ⇨ RETURN AND RESTORE

restrain

制	CONTROL (restrain)	1274
禁	PROHIBIT	2795
限	LIMIT	398
抑	SUPPRESS	257
束	TIE UP	3554
縛	BIND	1405
控える	HOLD BACK	495
渋る	hang [hold] back	513

return

帰	RETURN	130
還	RETURN	3180
回	turn back	3055
戻る	RETURN	1942
復	RETURN TO	575

return and restore

返	RETURN	3060
戻	RETURN	1942
還	RETURN	3180
復	RETURN TO	575

reveal
発 reveal 2565
露 EXPOSE 2818
暴 disclose 2515
披 OPEN OUT 305
顕 MANIFEST 1806
現 cause to appear 968

revise
訂 REVISE 1442
閲 REVIEW 3330
校 COLLATE 929

rice
米 RICE 3529
飯 COOKED RICE 1691
稲 RICE PLANT 1219

rich
富 RICH 2310
豪 wealthy 2140

right
正 RIGHT 3484
是 RIGHT 2436
端 correct 1221

right ⇨LEFT AND RIGHT

rise in rank
昇 ascend to a higher rank 2415
進 advance in rank 3121

risk
冒 RISK 2434
懸 stake 2915

rivers and streams
川 RIVER 6
河 RIVER 336
江 large river 221
渓 mountain stream 516
流 stream 441

rob ⇨STEAL AND ROB

rock and stone
石 STONE 2971
岩 ROCK 2235
巌 CRAG 2386

roof
屋 roof 3098
宇 roof 2175

roof parts
軒 EAVES 1459
棟 ridge 991

rooms
室 ROOM 2254
間 room 3323
房 CHAMBER 1946
斎 study 2115
堂 HALL 2589

ropes and lines
綱 ROPE (esp. of fiber) 1372
縄 ROPE (esp. of straw) 1388
緒 cord 1378
組 braid 1337
索 cable 2455
鎖 CHAIN 1761
線 LINE 1392
弦 STRING 287

round
丸い ROUND 3417
円 circular 2955

routes ⇨WAYS AND ROUTES

rub ⇨POLISH AND RUB

rulers
君 RULER 3206
王 KING 3439
帝 EMPEROR 2073
天 Heaven's messenger on earth 3442
皇 EMPEROR 2566

rules ⇨LAWS AND RULES

run
走 RUN 2194
奔 RUSH 2218
駆 gallop 1823

running water
流 CURRENT 441
潮 TIDE 739
汐 TIDE 223
瀬 rapids 806
滝 WATERFALL 661
洪 FLOOD 386
渦 WHIRLPOOL 603

S

sacrifice
犠 SACRIFICE 1089
牲 SACRIFICE 907

sad and depressed

悲 SAD 2775
哀 sorrowful 2068
愁 MELANCHOLY 2829
陰 gloomy 541
沈 depressed 261
寂 LONESOME 2290
惨 MISERABLE 483

same and uniform

等 EQUAL 2682
平 equal 3478
均 EVEN 235
斉 UNIFORM 2054
同 SAME 2987
一 same 3341

sand

砂 SAND (fine) 1133
沙 SAND (granular) 266

say ⇨ **SPEAK AND SAY**

schools

校 SCHOOL 929
学 EDUCATIONAL INSTITUTION 2555
院 INSTITUTION 454
塾 PRIVATE SCHOOL 2860
大 UNIVERSITY 3416
高 high school 2097
中 junior high school 3451
小 elementary school 7
園 kindergarten 3156

sea

海 SEA 384
洋 OCEAN 392
沖 OFFING 262

seals

印 SEAL 828
判 personal seal 1122
璽 IMPERIAL SEAL 2911

seasonings

糖 SUGAR 1403
塩 SALT 631
酢 VINEGAR 1516
油 OIL 341

seat

席 SEAT 3113
座 SEAT 3116

second

乙 SECOND 3339
次 second 54
後 AFTER (latter) 361
中 MIDDLE 3451

second person pronouns

君 YOU (*familiar*) 3206
爾 thou 3587
貴 you (*honorific*) 2606

secret and private

秘 SECRET 1159
密 SECRET 2292
暗 in the dark 1010
私 PRIVATE 1115
内 not public 3466
隠 hidden from view 713

sects ⇨ **RELIGIONS AND SECTS**

sects ⇨ **PARTIES AND SECTS**

securities

株 STOCK 935
債 BOND 156

see and look

見 SEE 2544
目 look 3043
観 VIEW 1880
覧 LOOK OVER 2854
眺 LOOK OUT OVER 1171
望 LOOK AFAR 2742
仰 LOOK UP 48
顧 LOOK BACK 1900
視 REGARD 972
看 WATCH 3220
察 INSPECT 2347

seek

探 SEARCH 505
索 SEARCH FOR 2455
捜 LOOK FOR 432
求 SEEK 3550
猟 hunt for 538

sell and trade

売 SELL 2196
卸す WHOLESALE 1447
販 ENGAGE IN SALES 1477
商 TRADE 2116
貿 TRADE 2601
易 EXCHANGE 2411

send

送 SEND 3093
投 SEND IN 256

回 send round 3055
遣 DISPATCH 3152
派 DISPATCH 381

sense

感 SENSE 2835
覚 sense 2604
勘 INTUITIVE PERCEPTION 1777

sentence and sentence parts

句 PHRASE 2967
文 sentence 1962
節 clause 2691

sentence parts ⇨ SENTENCE AND SENTENCE PARTS

separate

割 DIVIDE 1816
分 DIVIDE 1972
解 TAKE APART 1517
析 ANALYZE 862
別 SEPARATE 1117
離 SEPARATE 1836
隔 partition 671

servants

僕 MANSERVANT 164
奴 SLAVE 187
隷 UNDERLING 1751
臣 RETAINER 3068
従 follower 415
供 attendant 88

set forth ⇨ LEAVE AND SET FORTH

set in motion

動 MOVE 1778
駆 DRIVE 1823
掛ける set going 493

settle

着 settle (down) 3316
帰 settle in place 130
落 be concluded 2318

sew ⇨ WEAVE AND SEW

sex

性 SEX 299
情 (illicit) love 482
春 love 2576
色 lust 2029

shadow

影 SHADOW 1889
陰 SHADE 541

shafts

棒 ROD 983
桟 crosspiece 932
軸 AXLE 1514
錘 SPINDLE 1744

shake

振 SWING 430
震 QUAKE 2806
揺 SHAKE 594

sharp

鋭 SHARP 1730
先 pointed 2394

sheep

羊 SHEEP 2183
未 the Ram 3506

shells

殻 SHELL (of any kind) 1490
甲 SHELL (of animals) 3481
貝 seashell 2543

shine and reflect

輝 SHINE BRILLIANTLY 1402
光 shine 2391
照 ILLUMINATE 2827
映 REFLECT 892

ships ⇨ BOATS AND SHIPS

shoals

瀬 SHALLOWS 806
州 sandbar 57
礁 REEF 1243

shoot

射 SHOOT 1458
撃 fire 2863
発 discharge 2565

shores and watersides

畔 WATERSIDE 1145
-辺 -side 3029
浜 BEACH 436
岸 SHORE 2236
浦 SEASIDE 437
渚 STRAND 525
磯 ROCKY BEACH 1242

short and shortened

短 SHORT 1182
簡 simplified 2721
略 ABRIDGED 1169

shortened ⇨ SHORT AND SHORTENED

short time periods

頃 moment 144
瞬 INSTANT 1247
秒 SECOND 1137
分 MINUTE 1972
時 hour 924
暫 SHORT WHILE 2864

shout

叫 SHOUT 201
号 holler 2153
喝 SHOUT AT 461
喚 call out 550
呼 CALL 273
鳴 CRY 674

show

示 SHOW 1936
見せる show 2544
呈 PRESENT 2189

shrink ⇨ CONTRACT AND SHRINK

shrubs

藤 WISTERIA 2382
蔦 JAPANESE IVY 2355
萩 *HAGI* 2319
茉 JASMINE 2244
莉 JASMINE 2284

siblings

妹 YOUNGER SISTER 278
姉 OLDER SISTER 280
兄 OLDER BROTHER 2154
弟 YOUNGER BROTHER 2044

siblings of parents

叔 YOUNGER SIBLING OF PARENT 1272
伯 OLDER SIBLING OF PARENT 59

side

側 SIDE 137
方 side 1963
辺 -side 3029
面 side 2087
傍 BESIDE 147
横 SIDEWAYS 1066

sigh ⇨ CRY AND SIGH

signal

号 signal 2153
報 signal 1698

signs

候 indication 119
徴 SYMPTOM 683
症 symptom (of a disease) 3280
気 sign 3194
兆 OMEN 225

signs ⇨ MARKS AND SIGNS

similar

類 similar 1807
様 like 1052
如 AS 207
-通り as 3109
云 SUCH 1931

simple ⇨ PLAIN AND SIMPLE

sing

唱 SING 462
歌 sing 1825

sink

没 SINK 260
沈 SINK 261
潜 SUBMERGE 746

sit

座 SIT 3116
居 sit 3080

situations ⇨ STATES AND SITUATIONS

six

六 SIX 1965
陸 six (in legal documents) 543

size

寸 measurement 2935
大 size 3416

skill

力 POWER 3371
能 ABILITY 1323
技 SKILL 248
腕 skill 1006
才 TALENT 3410

skillful

巧 SKILLFUL 188
能 able 1323

skin ⇨ KINDS OF SKIN

sky

空 SKY 2227
天 HEAVEN 3442
宙 MIDAIR 2221

sleep

眠 SLEEP 1147

睡	SLEEP	1200
寝	GO TO SLEEP	2329

slips ⇨ LABELS AND SLIPS

slow

徐	SLOWLY	414
遅	SLOW	3133
緩	SLACK	1389
慢	SLUGGISH	686

small and tiny

小	SMALL	7
豆-	miniature	1943
微	SLIGHT	639
細	MINUTE	1333
寸	A BIT OF	2935

small numbers

一	ONE	3341
二	TWO	1922
三	THREE	1924
四	FOUR	3044
五	FIVE	3436
六	SIX	1965
七	SEVEN	3362
八	EIGHT	3
九	NINE	3369
十	TEN	3365

small water masses

滴	DROP	705
泡	BUBBLE	334

smell and fragrance

気	smell	3194
臭	BAD SMELL	2633
香	SWEET SMELL	2568
馨	PERFUME	2879
芳	FRAGRANT	2210
薫	BALMY	2371
郁	AROMATIC	1288

smooth

流	flowing	441
暢	FLUENT	1226
滑	SMOOTH	658

snake

蛇	SNAKE	1343
巳	THE SERPENT	3388

social gatherings

宴	BANQUET	2271
会	party	2020

society

社	SOCIETY	840
世	WORLD	3496
公	PUBLIC	1974

soft

柔	SOFT (supple and yielding)	2088
軟	SOFT (not hard)	1479
塑	plastic	2843

soil ⇨ LAND AND SOIL

soldiers and warriors

兵	SOLDIER	2551
卒	private	2055
士	MILITARY MAN	3405
武	warrior	3210
侍	SAMURAI	85

solidify and coagulate

固	solidify	3086
凝	CONGEAL	175
結	form into a mass	1348
凍	FREEZE	129

some

幾-	SOME	3582
何-	several	65
数	several	1790

songs ⇨ MUSIC AND SONGS

sorrow

哀	SORROW	2068
憂	grief	2145

sound ⇨ KINDS OF SOUND

sour substances

酢	VINEGAR	1516
酸	ACID	1563

space ⇨ UNIVERSE AND SPACE

spacecraft ⇨ AIRCRAFT AND SPACECRAFT

sparse ⇨ RARE AND SPARSE

speak and say

言	SAY	1941
云	say	1931
話	SPEAK	1527
口	give mouth to	3382
申す	SPEAK HUMBLY	3507
述	STATE	3075
陳	SET FORTH	540
弁	SPEAK ELOQUENTLY	2004
語る	TELL	1543
談	TALK	1569

speak humbly

申す	SPEAK HUMBLY	3507
啓	address respectfully	2763

speak in public

講	LECTURE	1619
演	make a speech	697

special

特	SPECIAL (distinct)	945
別	special (distinct)	1117
殊	SPECIAL (exceptional)	942
専	EXCLUSIVE	2644

speech

言	SPEECH	1941
談	TALK	1569
舌	TONGUE	2186
口	MOUTH	3382

spherical object

玉	spherical object	3477
球	BALL	969
丸	round body	3417

sports fields

場	ground(s)	558
庭	COURT	3114
野	baseball field	1485

spread

散	SCATTER	1702
布	SPREAD	2973
敷く	LAY	1870
舗	PAVE	1735
塗	APPLY ON A SURFACE	2841
抹	wipe over	313

spring back

弾	SPRING BACK	572
反	return in original direction	2945

sprout and bloom

萌	GERMINATE	2301
咲く	BLOOM	349

spy

偵	SPY	138
探	spy on	505

square

方	SQUARE	1963
角	square	2047

squeeze

搾	SQUEEZE	649
絞る	WRING	1349
圧	apply pressure	2970

stab

刺	STAB	1275
突く	THRUST	2230

stagnate

滞	STAGNATE	663
渋	NOT GO SMOOTHLY	513

standpoint

地	one's ground	204
立	standpoint	1992

stands ⇨TABLES AND STANDS

stars

星	STAR	2435
座	constellation	3116

states and situations

態	STATE	2847
状	CONDITION	272
況	CONDITIONS	337
景	business conditions	2470
勢	course of events	2857
境	SITUATION	676
局	current situation	3063
情	ACTUAL CONDITIONS	482
訳	circumstances	1473
調	TONE	1567
様	MODE	1052
相	PHASE	900

stay

滞	STAY	663
留	STAY	2580
駐	STATIONED	1826
屯	STATION TROOPS	3457
在	reside temporarily	2984
泊	STAY OVERNIGHT	331
宿	LODGE	2293

steal and rob

盗	STEAL	2670
窃	STEAL	2253
取	TAKE	1262
奪	ROB	2343
略	plunder	1169

steel ⇨IRON AND STEEL

steep

険	STEEP	542
急	steep	2092
峻	high and steep	412

steps

段	STEP	1144

階 stairs 624
陛 IMPERIAL PALACE STEPS 453

stick

着 STICK 3316
付 attach itself to 31
附 attach itself to 347

still

未 NOT YET 3506
尚 STILL 2233

stone ⇨ ROCK AND STONE

stop

止 STOP 2941
停 HALT 139
駐 park 1826

stoppers

栓 STOPPER 934
弁 VALVE 2004

store

蔵 STORE 2364
蓄 STORE UP 2333
貯 LAY UP 1509
納 PUT AWAY 1300

storehouse

倉 STOREHOUSE 2104
蔵 storehouse 2364
庫 STORAGE CHAMBER 3112

stories

話 story 1527
談 account 1569
語 tale 1543
説 narrative 1547

straight

直 STRAIGHT 2932
棒 straight 983

streams ⇨ RIVERS AND STREAMS

strict

厳 strict 3289
酷 SEVERE 1562
峻 STERN 412

strike

打 STRIKE 193
撃 STRIKE 2863
当てる HIT 2177
拍 BEAT (strike repeatedly) 304
撲 DEAL A BLOW 733
殴 BEAT (strike a person) 886

strong

強 STRONG 475
壮 VIGOROUS 224
丈 STOUT 3419
健 ROBUST 134
康 HEALTHY 3124

strongholds

城 CASTLE 352
塁 SMALL FORT 2593

structure

構 structure 1049
造り MAKE 3110

students and followers

生 STUDENT 3497
卒 graduate student 2055
学 scholar 2555
門 pupil 888
弟 disciple 2044
徒 FOLLOWER 416

study ⇨ LEARN AND STUDY
style ⇨ WAY AND STYLE
subjected to ⇨ BE SUBJECTED TO

submit and surrender

服 SUBMIT 878
伏 submit 45
屈 bend in submission 3079
降 surrender 458

subordinate

副 SECONDARY 1776
次 secondary 54
従 subordinate 415
亜 SUB– 3540
準 QUASI– 2856
半 semi– 3501
准 JUNIOR 127
助 assistant 1121

substitute

代 SUBSTITUTE 30
摂 ACT AS REGENT 650

subtract

減 subtract 601
引く subtract 181
控 HOLD BACK 495

succeed

継 SUCCEED 1360
承 succeed to 16
嗣 inherit 1719

sudden
急 SUDDEN 2092
激 sudden 776
暴 sudden 2515
突 abruptly 2230
sue
訴 SUE 1507
訟 LITIGATE 1472
告 accuse of 2409
控 accuse in court 495
suffering ⇨ TROUBLE AND SUFFERING
suffice
足 SUFFICE 2188
満 satisfied 607
suitable
適 SUITABLE 3160
当 proper 2177
宜 RIGHT 2223
便 CONVENIENT 95
sun
日 SUN 3027
陽 SUN 626
旭 RISING SUN 2977
superior ⇨ EXCELLENT AND SUPERIOR
supernatural and evil beings
鬼 DEVIL 2657
魔 DEMON 3187
怪 monster 297
霊 SPIRIT 2805
精 SPIRIT 1366
supervise ⇨ DIRECT AND SUPERVISE
supplement
補 SUPPLEMENT 1194
足 supplement 2188
給 SUPPLY 1350
充 fill up (a vacancy) 2014
supply
供 supply 88
給 SUPPLY 1350
納 deliver goods to a customer 1300
support
支 SUPPORT 1979
擁 SUPPORT 770
扶 LEND SUPPORT TO 247
賛 back up 2809
supporting parts of plants
根 ROOT 930
株 stump 935
幹 TRUNK 1718
茎 STEM 2242
supporting structures
柱 PILLAR 896
礎 FOUNDATION STONE 1248
suppress ⇨ CONQUER AND SUPPRESS
surrender ⇨ SUBMIT AND SURRENDER
surround
囲む ENCLOSE 3069
環 SURROUND 1090
包 ENCOMPASS 2966
swine
豚 PIG 976
猪 WILD BOAR 536
亥 THE BOAR 2012
system
系 SYSTEM 1944
制 SYSTEM 1274
統 INTERCONNECTED SYSTEM 1352
網 network 1374

T

tables and stands
卓 TABLE 2064
机 DESK 820
台 STAND 2005
take
把 GRIP 249
握 GRASP 585
執 SEIZE 1680
捕 CATCH 429
取 TAKE 1262
持 HOLD 374
take forcibly
奪 ROB 2343
拐 KIDNAP 308
収 take possession by force 198
take in
収 TAKE IN 198
摂 TAKE IN 650
喫 INGEST 551
吸 SUCK 202
take precautions
戒 take caution 3204

警 GUARD AGAINST 2893

talented persons ⇨ WISE AND TALENTED PERSONS

tall buildings

閣 TALL MAGNIFICENT BUILDING 3327
楼 TALL BUILDING 1019
塔 TOWER 561
台 observatory 2005

target

的 TARGET 1125
標 MARK 1064
目 aim 3043

tax

税 TAX 1191
租 LAND TAX 1161
貢 TRIBUTE 2281
賦 levy 1583

teach

教 TEACH 1493
授 teach 492
育 educate 2050
練 TRAIN 1375
訓 INSTRUCT 1454
諭 ADMONISH 1598
導 GUIDE 2888
迪 EDIFY 3076
啓 ENLIGHTEN 2763

temporary

仮 TEMPORARY 50
暫 for the time being 2864

temporary quarters

舎 temporary quarters 2060
寮 DORMITORY 2359
宿 lodging 2293
館 inn 1748
亭 INN 2072

ten

十 TEN 3365
拾 ten (in legal documents) 379

tendency

向 tendency 3052
性 NATURE 299
勢 trend 2857
傾 inclination 154
潮 TIDE 739
流 CURRENT 441

tender feelings for others

仁 BENEVOLENCE 20
慈 compassion 2339
情 sympathy 482
悲 mercy 2775
哀 PITY 2068

terms of assent

然 SO 2782
諾 yes 1568

terms of negation

不 NOT (negation) 3434
非 IS NOT (contrariety) 889
無 WITHOUT (nonexistence) 2135
没 lacking in 260
欠 LACK 1987
否 OR NOT 2406
未 NOT YET 3506

territorial divisions

州 STATE 57
県 PREFECTURE 2641
府 URBAN PREFECTURE 3082
道 district of Hokkaido 3134
都 METROPOLIS OF TOKYO 1686
省 province in China 2449
郡 COUNTY 1466

thanking and gratitude

謝 THANK 1620
礼 thanks 818
恩 DEBT OF GRATITUDE 2655

that ⇨ THIS AND THAT

the country

郊 SUBURB 1286
里 COUNTRYSIDE 3542
郷 the country 549
辺 BORDERLAND 3029

theory

論 THEORY (systematic knowledge) 1574
説 THEORY (proposed explanation) 1547

the people

民 PEOPLE 3036
衆 the multitude(s) 2683
庶 the masses 3127
公 PUBLIC 1974

thick

厚 THICK (great in depth) 3003

太 THICK (great in diameter) 2152

thieves

盗 thief 2670
泥 petty thief 326
賊 BANDIT 1530

thin

薄 THIN 2370
細 SLENDER 1333
繊 FINE 1413

think and consider

思 THINK 2564
考 THINK 3196
存 hold an opinion 2982
案 think out 2270
想 CONCEIVE 2828
慮 CONSIDER 3266
勘 take into consideration 1777
量 weigh 2471
惟 MEDITATE 481
省 INTROSPECT 2449

third person pronouns

彼 THIRD PERSON PRONOUN (*neutral*) 290
氏 third person pronoun (*polite*) 2951
奴 third person pronoun (*slang*) 187

thirst ⇨ HUNGER AND THIRST

this and that

本 THIS 3502
今 THIS (week, etc.) 1968
当 THE PRESENT 2177
該 the said 1519
同 the same 2987
之 this 3420
是 this 2436
爾 THAT 3587
彼 that 290

thought

念 THOUGHTS 2059
考え thought 3196
意 MIND 2136
想 conception 2828

threads and fibers

糸 THREAD 2179
緯 woof 1407
経 warp 1331
繊 FIBER 1413
維 FIBER 1370

threaten

脅 THREATEN 2109
威 THREATEN BY FORCE 3578
嚇 INTIMIDATE 784
喝 shout threats at 461

three

三 THREE 1924
参 three (in legal documents) 2066

throughout

通 through 3109
徹 all through 726
終 from beginning to end 1336
中 throughout 3451

throw

投 THROW 256
放 toss 853

tiger

虎 TIGER 3212
寅 THE TIGER 2289

tighten

締める TIGHTEN 1393
緊 TIGHTEN 2838
張 STRAIN 474

time and time counters

回 TIME 3055
度 TIME 3100
遍 counter for number of times 3136
返 counter for number of times 3060

time counters ⇨ TIME AND TIME COUNTERS

time periods

時 TIME 924
頃 TIME 144
暇 FREE TIME 1012
般 period of time 1317
刻 POINT OF TIME 1267
間 INTERVAL 3323
期 TERM 1704
節 SEASON OF THE YEAR 2691
季 SEASON (quarter) 2554
候 SEASON (time of year) 119

tiny ⇨ SMALL AND TINY

tire

疲 TIRED 3278
労 fatigue 2548

titles of address

氏 COURTESY TITLE 2951

兄 familiar title (seniors) 2154
君 FAMILIAR TITLE (peers) 3206
嬢 Miss 758
様 FORMAL TITLE 1052
殿 FORMAL HONORIFIC TITLE 1792
師 honorific title (clergymen) 1326
公 honorific title (noblemen) 1974

today ⇨ YESTERDAY AND TODAY

together
共 JOINT 2393
同 together 2987
併 TOGETHER 83
並 side by side 2246
兼 CONCURRENTLY 2286

tolerant
寛 LENIENT 2327
甘い indulgent 3494

tools ⇨ MACHINES AND TOOLS

tops
上 upper part 3404
頂 SUMMIT 145
頭 HEAD 1604

torture and oppress
拷 TORTURE 373
責める torture 2467
虐 treat cruelly 3218
迫 oppress 3074

total
総 TOTAL 1379
計 total 1441
和 sum 1130

touch
触 TOUCH 1518
接 CONTACT 500
当てる apply 2177

towns ⇨ PARTS OF TOWNS

towns ⇨ CITIES AND TOWNS

towns ⇨ VILLAGES AND TOWNS

trace
軌 TRACK 1445
跡 TRACE 1534

trade ⇨ SELL AND TRADE

transfer
譲 CEDE 1649
渡 hand over 611
付 deliver 31
附 deliver 347

translate
訳 TRANSLATE 1473
翻 RENDER 1897

transmit and deliver
伝 TRANSMIT 44
逓 RELAY 3106
届ける DELIVER 3078
達 deliver 3139

travel by vehicle
乗 RIDE 3576
走 travel by vehicle 2194
航 NAVIGATE 1318
騎 RIDE ON HORSEBACK 1834

treat and welcome
遇 TREAT 3135
待 treat 364
扱う HANDLE 217
款 treat cordially 1700
接 receive 500
迎 WELCOME 3059

tree
木 TREE 3450
樹 STANDING TREE 1075

trees
桜 CHERRY 931
柳 WILLOW 899
楓 MAPLE 1015
松 PINE 864
杉 CRYPTOMERIA 832
槙 PODOCARPUS 1051
楠 CAMPHOR TREE 1018
桐 PAULOWNIA 937
桂 AROMATIC TREE, katsura tree 928
梓 CATALPA 962
桑 MULBERRY 2112
漆 Japanese lacquer tree 704

trouble and suffering
困 BE IN TROUBLE 3070
窮 BE IN EXTREMITY 2358
悩 SUFFER 421
苦 SUFFERING 2243
痛 PAIN 3285
辛 HARD 2038
煩 VEXED 1022
難 DIFFICULT 1838

true

真	TRUE	2111
洵	TRULY	383
実	REAL	2225
本	real	3502
正	genuine	3484
現	ACTUAL	968

trunk parts

胸	CHEST	951
腹	BELLY	1034
胴	TRUNK	950
腰	WAIST	1036
背	BACK	2573
肩	SHOULDER	1947

try

試	TRY	1525
験	TEST	1833

tubular passages

管	PIPE	2701
筒	TUBE	2680
道	passage	3134
脈	VEIN	953

turn

旋	GYRATE	957
転	TURN	1480
回	TURN ROUND	3055
巡	MAKE THE ROUNDS	3047
循	CIRCULATE	578

twigs ⇨ BRANCHES AND TWIGS

twine ⇨ WIND AND TWINE

two

二	TWO	1922
弐	TWO (in legal documents)	3195
双	SET OF TWO	25
対	pair	831
偶	COUPLE	132
両	BOTH	3518

types ⇨ KINDS AND TYPES

U

uncultivated expanses of land

野	FIELD	1485
原	PLAIN	3009
漠	DESERT	655

understand ⇨ KNOW AND UNDERSTAND

undertake

負	BEAR	2091
担	UNDERTAKE	318

undomesticated mammals

虎	TIGER	3212
熊	BEAR	2848
象	ELEPHANT	2134
猪	WILD BOAR	536
鹿	DEER	3126
猿	MONKEY	669
鯨	WHALE	1882

uniform ⇨ SAME AND UNIFORM

unimportant

細	MINUTE	1333
微	SLIGHT	639
小	SMALL	7
末	last in importance	3505

units of learning

課	LESSON	1573
科	course	1138
講	LECTURE	1619

universe and space

宇	UNIVERSE	2175
宙	SPACE	2221

unrefined ⇨ VULGAR AND UNREFINED

unrestrained

漫	RAMBLING	700
散	unrestrained	1702

unsavory tastes

苦	BITTER	2243
辛	PUNGENT	2038
酸	sour	1563
渋い	ASTRINGENT	513

urge

勧	URGE	1857
催	PRESS FOR	157
促	HASTEN	103
誘	INDUCE	1550
励	ENCOURAGE	1119
侑	URGE TO EAT	91

urgent

急	URGENT	2092
緊	EXIGENT	2838
迫	pressing	3074

use

使	USE	90

用	EMPLOY	2976

V

vain

空	EMPTY	2227
虚	without substance	3237
徒	vain	416

valley

谷	VALLEY	2043
渓	RAVINE	516
峡	GORGE	357

value

値	VALUE	109
価	VALUE	87

vapor ⇨GAS AND VAPOR

vaporize

蒸	EVAPORATE	2334
留	distill	2580

various

諸	VARIOUS	1577
庶	MANIFOLD	3127
雑	MISCELLANEOUS	1385

vegetables

菜	greens	2305
芋	POTATO	2181
豆	BEAN	1943
蕗	BUTTERBUR	2372

vehicle

車	VEHICLE	3552
乗	vehicle	3576
輪	wheeled vehicle	1589
台	COUNTER FOR VEHICLES	2005

vertical

縦	VERTICAL	1408
垂	perpendicular	3565
立て-	standing	1992
直	STRAIGHT	2932

vessels and receptacles

盤	dish	2851
皿	PLATE	3474
盆	TRAY	2079
杯	CUP	857
鉢	BOWL	1708
鍋	POT	1752

view

景	SCENE	2470
風	(beautiful) scenery	3007
光	scenery	2391
観	VIEW	1880

villages and towns

町	TOWN	1113
村	VILLAGE	834
里	hamlet	3542
郷	HOMETOWN	549
庄	FEUDAL VILLAGE	3051

violate

違	VIOLATE	3151
破	BREAK	1150
犯	offend against	196
反	act contrary to	2945
背	go against	2573

violent

暴	VIOLENT	2515
猛	FIERCE	537
荒い	WILD	2260

virtuous

正	RIGHT	3484
義	righteous	2338
善	GOOD	2325
良	GOOD	3558

visit

訪	VISIT	1468
参	VISIT A HOLY PLACE	2066
寄	call at	2291
伺	call on	69

visitor

客	VISITOR	2250
賓	GUEST	2357

vivid

明	BRIGHT	855
鮮	VIVID	1877

vote and election

票	VOTE	2669
選	election	3169

vulgar and unrefined

俗	vulgar	104
卑	MEAN	2642
里	rural	3542
粗	COARSE	1329
野	rustic	1485
蛮	barbaric	2129

W

wait
- 待 WAIT 364
- 控える be in waiting 495

walk
- 歩 WALK 2416
- 徒 go on foot 416
- 脚 move on foot 974
- 足 travel on foot 2188
- 踏 TREAD 1587

walls ⇨ FENCES AND WALLS

wander
- 浪 WANDER 439
- 遊 move about freely 3142
- 漂 drift about 699
- 流 drift 441

war ⇨ FIGHT AND WAR

warfare and rebellions
- 戦 WAR 1787
- 軍 war 2080
- 役 war 244
- 陣 battle 455
- 乱 rebellion 1260
- 変 uprising 2069
- 闘 FIGHT 3334

warm seasons
- 春 SPRING 2576
- 夏 SUMMER 2113
- 暑 SUMMER HEAT 2473

warn
- 警 WARN 2893
- 戒 CAUTION 3204
- 諭 ADMONISH 1598
- 告 advise 2409

warriors ⇨ SOLDIERS AND WARRIORS

wash ⇨ CLEAN AND WASH

water ⇨ KINDS OF WATER

watersides ⇨ SHORES AND WATERSIDES

water sources
- 源 SOURCE 656
- 泉 SPRING 2567
- 井 WELL 3454

waves
- 波 WAVE 330
- 浪 BILLOW 439

way and style
- 風 MANNER 3007
- 様 MODE 1052
- 方 WAY 1963
- 途 WAY 3107
- 法 METHOD 333
- 流 STYLE 441
- 式 STYLE 3049
- 調 TONE 1567

ways and routes
- 道 WAY (path) 3134
- 途 WAY (route) 3107
- 路 ROAD 1533
- 筋 wayside 2678
- 通り street 3109
- 街 city street 576
- 辻 CROSSROADS 3192
- 岐 forked road 241
- 径 PATH 291
- 軌 TRACK 1445
- 線 LINE 1392

weak
- 弱 WEAK 1167
- 柔 SOFT 2088

weaken
- 衰 DECLINE 2100
- 弱 weaken 1167

wealth
- 財 WEALTH 1457
- 産 property 3298
- 富 riches 2310
- 宝 TREASURE 2224

weapons for shooting
- 銃 GUN (portable firearm) 1723
- 砲 HEAVY GUN 1151
- 火 firearms 3463
- 弓 BOW 3383

wear and put on
- 着 PUT ON 3316
- 装 DRESS 2685
- 帯 WEAR (esp. at the belt) 2582
- 履く put on footwear 3171
- 被る put on headgear 1163

weather
- 候 SEASONAL WEATHER 119
- 天 weather 3442

晴 FINE WEATHER 981

weave and sew

織 WEAVE 1422
紡 SPIN 1295
績 spin 1412
縫 SEW 1406
編 KNIT 1387
組 braid 1337

weeks and months

週 WEEK 3122
旬 TEN-DAY PERIOD 2978
月 MONTH 2956

weight

錘 weight 1744
鎮 weight 1759

weight units

匁 MOMME (3.75 g) 3465
斤 CATTY (600 g) 2949
貫 *kan* (3.75 kg) 2460
屯 ton 3457

welcome ⇨ TREAT AND WELCOME

west

洋 WESTERN 392
西 the West 3520

wet

湿 DAMP 609
潤 MOIST 742

white colors

白 WHITE 3493
皓 BRIGHT WHITE 1180
銀 SILVER 1722

wide and extensive

広 WIDE 3035
紘 WIDE-RANGING 1298
博 EXTENSIVE 151
浩 VAST 438
洸 VAST (expanse of water) 387

widespread

普 WIDESPREAD 2323
遍 ALL OVER 3136
通 common 3109
公 common (math) 1974

width

幅 WIDTH 569
員 girth 2269
径 DIAMETER 291

wild birds

鷹 HAWK 3189
隼 FALCON 2756
鶴 CRANE 1850
雀 SPARROW 2469

will and intention

志 AMBITION 2199
意 MIND 2136
図 intention 3071
気 mind to do something 3194
念 thought of doing something 2059
趣 PURPOSE 3317
欲 DESIRE 1475

win

勝 WIN 1005
克 OVERCOME 2046
征 CONQUER 293
破 BREAK 1150

wind

風 WIND 3007
嵐 STORM 2314
台 typhoon 2005

wind and twine

巻 ROLL UP 2645
繰る REEL 1427
絡 ENTWINE 1351

wings

翼 WING (of birds or aircraft) 2720
羽 WING (of birds or insects) 226
葉 plane 2321

wisdom

識 KNOWLEDGE 1639
知 knowledge 1127
智 WISDOM 2784
慧 prajna (transcendental wisdom) 2810
哲 PHILOSOPHY 2738

wise ⇨ INTELLIGENT AND WISE

wise and talented persons

哲 sage 2738
賢 wise man 2839
博 DOCTOR 151
秀 genius 2545
俊 BRILLIANT PERSON 102
才 person of talent 3410
通 well-informed person 3109

wish and desire

願	WISH	1845
望	HOPE	2742
希	ASPIRE	2049
懐	LONG FOR	763
慕	yearn for	2353
渇	thirst for	515
欲	DESIRE	1475
求	SEEK	3550

wives

妻	WIFE	2558
奥	wife	2824
内	wife	3466
室	wife (esp. of persons of rank)	2254
嫡	legitimate wife	680
婦	married woman	469
嫁	BRIDE	635
寡	widow	2344

wives of rulers

后	EMPRESS	2981
妃	PRINCESS	206
室	wife (esp. of persons of rank)	2254

woman

女	WOMAN	3418
婦	ADULT WOMAN	469
婆	OLD WOMAN	2762
嬢	YOUNG LADY	758
娘	GIRL	406
雌	FEMALE	1055

wood ⇨ KINDS OF WOOD

words and expressions

語	WORD	1543
辞	WORD	1364
詞	WORDS	1503
句	PHRASE	2967

work

働	WORK	153
稼	WORK (for a living)	1230
労	LABOR	2548
勤める	serve (in an office)	1818
仕	SERVE	34

work and employment

務	DUTY	1173
任	OFFICE	53
役	SERVICE (esp. public)	244
勤	SERVICE (employment)	1818
業	WORK	2612
職	EMPLOYMENT	1425
労	LABOR	2548

workers and professionals

家	professional	2273
客	skilled person	2250
士	PROFESSION SUFFIX	3405
師	profession suffix	1326
者	person who	3211
人	person of certain category	3368
員	MEMBER (of a staff)	2269
屋	colloquial occupation suffix	3098
手	OCCUPATION SUFFIX	3456
婦	woman worker	469
嬢	(unmarried) female worker	758
夫	MAN LABORER	3460
匠	CRAFTSMAN	2990
工	workman	3381

work metals

錬	REFINE (crude metals)	1741
鍛	FORGE	1755
鋳	CAST	1729
焼き	annealing	997

world

世	WORLD	3496
界	WORLD	2563

worldly

世	worldly	3496
俗	worldly	104

worry

憂	BE ANXIOUS	2145
配	concern oneself	1460
構う	MIND	1049
虞	FEARS (of undesirable event)	3254

worship ⇨ PRAY AND WORSHIP

wrap ⇨ COVER AND WRAP

write

書	WRITE	2658
筆	write	2677
写	COPY	2000
記	WRITE DOWN	1453
紀	record in writing	1276
控える	note down	495
録	RECORD	1742
登	register	2595

writing

文	WRITINGS	1962
筆	WRITING	2677
書	writing(s)	2658
銘	INSCRIPTION	1724

writing ⇨ **PARTS OF WRITING**

writing strips

簡	bamboo writing strips	2721
竹	bamboo writing tablets	228

written communications

状	LETTER	272
文	LETTER	1962
書	letter	2658
信	written communication	100
電	telegram	2790

wrongdoing and evil

罪	sin	2610
非	wrong(doing)	889
邪	wrong	1124
悪	evil (something bad)	2745
弊	evil(s) (something undesirable)	2884

Y

yang ⇨ **YIN AND YANG**

year

年	YEAR	2035
歳	YEAR	2490

yellow colors

黄	YELLOW	2468
金	golden	2057

yesterday and today

今	today	1968
昨	YESTERDAY	893

yin and yang

陰	yin	541
陽	yang	626

young

若	YOUNG	2241
弱	young	1167
少	young	3467
青	youthful	2430
幼	VERY YOUNG	191
稚	CHILDISH	1206

INDEXES

索引

ON–KUN INDEX

The **On–Kun Index** lists the characters alphabetically by their *on* (Chinese-derived) and *kun* (native Japanese) readings. It offers a quick way to look up a character from its reading, and is particularly useful for locating a character whose reading is known but whose exact form cannot be recalled.

1. **Scope** This index lists all the *on*, *kun*, and special readings appearing in the **entry-head data** for each character entry (see GUIDE **§4. Character Readings**). Readings identical in form (*ha*[1], *ha*[2]) or readings differing only in *okurigana* (*yu(ki)*, *yuki*) appear only once.

2. **Format** *On* readings are set in roman capitals; *kun* readings in roman lowercase. *Okurigana* endings are not shown in parentheses. The tiny numerals to the left of the character column indicate total stroke-count; the numerals to the right are the **entry numbers.**

3. **Order of Entries** The characters are listed alphabetically by the romanized transcriptions of their *on* and *kun* readings. They appear in the following order: (1) short vowels precede long vowels (o, ō), (2) *on* readings precede *kun* readings (AKU, aku), (3) ordinary readings precede prefixes and suffixes (ai, ai-, -ai). Characters having the same reading are listed in increasing order of their total stroke-counts, and further grouped by radical number.

4. **Hints for Speed** Since there are often many characters under a given *on* reading but only one or a few under the *kun* readings, it is usually faster to look up a character from its *kun* reading. When there are many entries under a given reading, you might save time by estimating the stroke-count of your character and using the tiny numerals as a rough guide for finding it more quickly.

— A —

Reading	Strokes	Character	Entry
A	7	亜	3540
	8	阿	346
	11	堊	2768
a	7	吾	2407
a-	7	吾	2407
abaku	9	発	2565
	15	暴	2515
abareru	15	暴	2515
abiru	10	浴	445
abiseru	10	浴	445
abunai	6	危	3199
abura	8	油	341
	10	脂	954
	14	膏	2141
ada	10	徒	416
adeyaka	19	艶	1908
aenai	12	敢	1706
aete	12	敢	1706
aezu	12	敢	1706
agameru	11	崇	2297
agari	3	上	3404
-agari	3	上	3404
agaru	3	上	3404
	10	挙	2456
	12	揚	593
-agaru	3	上	3404
-age	12	揚	593
ageru	3	上	3404
	10	挙	2456
	12	揚	593
-ageru	3	上	3404
AI	9	哀	2068
	13	愛	2492
ai	6	合	2019
	12	間	3323
	18	藍	2381
ai-	6	合	2019
	9	相	900
-ai	6	合	2019
aida	12	間	3323
aji	8	味	274
ajiwau	8	味	274
aka	7	赤	2193
aka-	7	赤	2193
akagane	14	銅	1721
akai	7	赤	2193
	9	紅	1277
akane	9	茜	2261
akarameru	7	赤	2193
akaramu	7	赤	2193
	8	明	855
akari	8	明	855
akarui	8	明	855
akarumu	8	明	855
akashi	12	証	1506
akasu	8	明	855
	13	飽	1715
akatsuki	12	暁	980
ake	6	朱	3531
	14	緋	1369

Reading	Strokes	Kanji	No.
-ake	8	明	855
akeru	8	明	855
		空	2227
	12	開	3321
aki	5	旦	2389
	6	旭	2977
	8	尭	2063
		昂	2412
		昌	2414
		空	2227
	9	亮	2071
		秋	1139
	10	晃	2450
	11	彬	960
	12	瑛	999
		皓	1180
	14	璃	1059
		聡	1384
	15	諒	1575
akinau	11	商	2116
akira	5	卯	199
		旦	2389
	6	旭	2977
	7	亨	2037
	8	昂	2412
		昌	2414
	9	亮	2071
		玲	910
	10	晃	2450
	11	彬	960
	12	瑛	999
		皓	1180
	14	翠	2705
		聡	1384
	15	慧	2810
	17	瞳	1237
akiraka	8	明	855
akiru	13	飽	1715
	14	厭	3017
AKU	11	堊	2768
		悪	2745
	12	握	585
		渥	600
aku	8	明	855
		空	2227
	12	開	3321
	13	飽	1715
akuru	8	明	855
ama	5	尼	3033
ama-	4	天	3442
	8	雨	3561
amaeru	5	甘	3494
amai	5	甘	3494
amaneku	12	普	2323
		遍	3136
amari	7	余	2042
amaru	7	余	2042
amasu	7	余	2042
amayakasu	5	甘	3494
ame	4	天	3442
	8	雨	3561
ami	14	網	1374
-ami	15	編	1387
amu	15	編	1387
AN	6	安	2171
		行	212
	7	杏	2397
	9	按	371
	10	案	2270
	13	暗	1010
	17	闇	3332
ana	4	孔	179
	5	穴	2159
anadoru	8	侮	82
ane	8	姉	280
ani	5	兄	2154
anzu	7	杏	2397
ao	8	青	2430
	14	碧	2836
ao-	8	青	2430
aogu	6	仰	48
aoi	8	青	2430
	12	葵	2317
	14	蒼	2507
aoru	14	煽	1056
ara-	9	荒	2260
	11	粗	1329
	13	新	1784
arai	9	荒	2260
	11	粗	1329
arakajime	4	予	1983
arashi	12	嵐	2314
-arashi	9	荒	2260
arasou	6	争	2030
arasu	9	荒	2260
arata	13	新	1784
aratamaru	7	改	243
aratameru	7	改	243
arau	9	洗	388
arawareru	8	表	2429
	11	現	968
arawasu	8	表	2429
	11	現	968
		著	2300
arazu	8	非	889
areru	9	荒	2260
aru	6	在	2984
		有	2983
aruji	5	主	1938
aruku	8	歩	2416
asa	5	旦	2389
	11	麻	3125
	12	朝	1695
asahi	6	旭	2977
asai	9	浅	389
asaru	14	漁	698
ase	6	汗	220
aseru	12	焦	2770
	15	褪	1234
ashi	7	足	2188
	11	悪	2745
		脚	974
asobasu	12	遊	3142
asobu	12	遊	3142
ataeru	3	与	3421
atai	8	価	87
	10	値	109
atakamo	8	宛	2222
	9	恰	368
atama	16	頭	1604
atarashii	13	新	1784
atari	5	辺	3029
	6	当	2177
ataru	4	中	3451
	6	当	2177
atataka	12	温	608
	13	暖	1011
atatakai	12	温	608
	13	暖	1011
atatamaru	12	温	608
	13	暖	1011
atatameru	12	温	608
	13	暖	1011
ate	6	当	2177
-ate	8	宛	2222
ateru	6	充	2014
		当	2177
	8	宛	2222
ato	9	後	361
	13	跡	1534
ATSU	5	圧	2970
atsu	11	惇	486
		淳	514
	12	敦	1693
		渥	600
atsui	9	厚	3003
	12	暑	2473
	15	熱	2866
	16	篤	2716
atsukai	6	扱	217
atsukau	6	扱	217
atsumaru	12	集	2771
atsumeru	12	集	2771
atsumu	6	伍	47
	8	侑	91
atsushi	11	惇	486
		淳	514
	12	敦	1693
		渥	600
au	6	会	2020
		合	2019
	12	遇	3135
	14	遭	3159
-au	6	合	2019
awa	8	泡	334
awai	11	淡	528
aware	9	哀	2068
awaremu	9	哀	2068
	15	憐	731
awaseru	6	会	2020
		合	2019
	8	併	83
	14	遭	3159
-awaseru	6	合	2019
awasu	6	合	2019
awatadashii	12	慌	580
awateru	12	慌	580
aya	4	文	1962
	9	郁	1288
	11	琢	971
	12	斐	2776
		絢	1347
	14	綾	1376
ayabumu	6	危	3199
ayamachi	12	過	3137
ayamaru	14	誤	1542
	17	謝	1620
	18	謬	1631
-ayamaru	14	誤	1542
ayamatsu	12	過	3137
ayashii	8	怪	297
ayashimu	8	怪	297
ayatsuru	16	操	769
ayaui	6	危	3199

D

E

F

furuu [10]振 430
[12]揮 589
[15]震 2806
[16]奮 2367
fusa [8]房 1946
[12]惣 2780
fusagu [13]塞 2330
fusegu [7]防 270
[16]禦 2870
fuseru [6]伏 45
[9]臥 1440
fushi [13]節 2691
fusu [6]伏 45
futa [2]二 1922
[4]双 25
[14]蓋 2503
futatabi [6]再 3519
futatsu [2]二 1922
futoi [4]太 2152
futokoro [16]懐 763
futoru [4]太 2152
[8]肥 879
FUTSU [4]仏 19
[5]払 194
[8]沸 329
fuyasu [12]殖 994
[14]増 677
fuyu [5]冬 2157

G

GA [4]牙 3435
[5]瓦 3476
[7]我 3548
[8]画 3000
芽 2240
[9]臥 1440
[12]賀 2599
[13]雅 1197
[15]餓 1734
-gachi [12]勝 1005
GAI [4]刈 28
[5]外 186
[6]亥 2012
[8]劾 1266
[10]害 2272
[11]涯 512
[12]街 576
[13]慨 641
碍 1201
該 1519
[14]概 1048
蓋 2503
-gakari [9]係 97
[11]掛 493
-gakaru [11]掛 493
-gake [11]掛 493
-gaki [10]書 2658
GAKU [8]学 2555
岳 2557
[13]楽 2826
[18]額 1805
gama [14]蒲 2504
GAN [3]丸 3417
[4]元 1929
[7]含 2041
[8]岩 2235
岸 2236
[11]眼 1172
[12]嵌 2313
[13]頑 1040
[18]顔 1808
[19]願 1845
[20]巌 2386
-gane [8]金 2057
gara [9]柄 897
[11]殻 1490
-gari [9]狩 397
-gashira [16]頭 1604
GAT- [6]合 2019
-gata [4]方 1963
[7]形 846
[9]型 2638
[15]潟 745
-gatai [12]堅 2823
[18]難 1838
GATSU [4]月 2956
gawa [11]側 137
-gawari [5]代 30
GE [3]下 3378
[4]牙 3435
[5]外 186
[10]夏 2113
[13]解 1517
[15]戯 1875
GEI [7]芸 2209
迎 3059
[19]鯨 1882
GEKI [9]逆 3091
[12]戟 1696
[13]隙 670
[15]劇 1904
撃 2863
[16]激 776
GEN [4]元 1929
幻 180
[5]玄 1991
[7]言 1941
[8]弦 287
[9]彦 3295
限 398
[10]原 3009
[11]現 968
眼 1172
絃 1330
[12]減 601
[13]嫌 636
源 656
[17]厳 3289
[18]験 1833
[22]儼 178
GETSU [4]月 2956
GI [6]伎 46
[7]岐 241
技 248
[8]宜 2223
[11]偽 131
[12]欺 1703
[13]義 2338
[14]疑 1565
[15]儀 169
戯 1875
誼 1571
[17]擬 788
犠 1089
[20]議 1647
-gi [6]衣 2013
[12]着 3316
-gime [7]決 263
[13]極 1017
-gimi [7]君 3206
GIN [7]吟 230
[14]銀 1722
-gire [4]切 27
[12]裂 2687
-giri [4]切 27
git- [4]牛 3452
-giwa [14]際 714
GO [4]五 3436
互 3437
午 1984
[6]伍 47
后 2981
[7]冴 79
吾 2407
呉 2549
[9]後 361
[10]娯 405
悟 419
[12]御 577
期 1704
[13]碁 2699
[14]誤 1542
語 1543
[20]護 1648
GŌ [5]号 2153
[6]合 2019
[9]拷 373
[10]剛 1673
格 926
降 458
[11]強 475
郷 549
[13]業 2612
[14]豪 2140
[17]濠 792
-goe [12]越 3314
-gokoro [4]心 11
GOKU [13]極 1017
[14]獄 712
GON [6]艮 3517
[7]言 1941
[8]欣 852
金 2057
[12]勤 1818
[15]権 1065
[17]厳 3289
goro [11]頃 144
-goro [11]頃 144
-goroshi [10]殺 1324
-goshi [12]越 3314
goto [6]毎 2034
-gotoni [6]毎 2034
gotoshi [6]如 207
GU [3]工 3381
[5]弘 192
[7]求 3550
[8]供 88
具 2552
[10]倶 111
[13]愚 2834
虞 3254
GŪ [10]宮 2274

Reading	Strokes	Kanji	No.
	11	偶	132
	12	遇	3135
		隅	623
-gumi	11	組	1337
-gumo	12	雲	2773
GUN	9	軍	2080
	10	郡	1466
	13	群	1540
gurai	7	位	61
guramu	5	瓦	3476
-gurushii	8	苦	2243
-gusa	9	草	2263
	14	種	1218
GYAKU	9	虐	3218
		逆	3091
GYO	11	魚	2127
	12	御	577
		馭	1814
	14	漁	698
	16	禦	2870
GYŌ	6	仰	48
		行	212
	7	形	846
	8	尭	2063
	12	暁	980
	13	業	2612
	16	凝	175
GYOKU	5	玉	3477
GYŪ	4	牛	3452

H

Reading	Strokes	Kanji	No.
HA	4	巴	3438
	7	把	249
	8	波	330
	9	派	381
	10	破	1150
	19	覇	2730
ha	3	刃	2929
	6	羽	226
	12	葉	2321
		歯	2476
	14	端	1221
haba	12	幅	569
habamu	8	阻	348
haberu	8	侍	85
habuku	9	省	2449
HACHI	2	八	3
	13	鉢	1708
hada	6	肌	827
	15	膚	3265
hadaka	13	裸	1211
hae	9	栄	2574
haeru	5	生	3497
	9	映	892
		栄	2574
hagane	16	鋼	1740
hagemasu	7	励	1119
hagemu	7	励	1119
hageshii	10	烈	2652
	16	激	776
hagi	12	萩	2319
hagukumu	8	育	2050
haha	5	母	3475
HAI	8	拝	303
		杯	857
	9	肺	916
		背	2573
	10	俳	112
		悖	420
		配	1460
	11	排	490
		敗	1476
	12	廃	3146
	15	誹	1572
		輩	2807
	17	癈	3287
hai	6	灰	2979
hairu	2	入	3370
haji	10	恥	1313
hajikeru	12	弾	572
hajiku	12	弾	572
hajimaru	8	始	281
hajime	7	初	1116
		甫	3549
	8	孟	2220
	9	哉	3294
	14	肇	2799
hajimeru	8	始	281
-hajimeru	8	始	281
hajimete	7	初	1116
		甫	3549
hajirau	10	恥	1313
hajiru	10	恥	1313
haka	13	墓	2332
hakarau	9	計	1441
hakarigoto	16	謀	1593
hakaru	7	図	3071
	9	計	1441
	12	測	610
		量	2471
	16	謀	1593
		諮	1596
hako	8	函	3001
	15	箱	2711
hakobu	12	運	3140
HAKU	5	白	3493
	7	伯	59
	8	拍	304
		泊	331
		迫	3074
	11	舶	1340
	12	博	151
	13	搏	646
	15	魄	1227
	16	薄	2370
haku	6	吐	203
	8	刷	1273
	9	穿	2251
	11	掃	503
	15	履	3171
hama	10	浜	436
hamaru	12	嵌	2313
hameru	12	嵌	2313
HAN	3	凡	2938
	4	反	2945
	5	半	3501
		犯	196
	6	帆	210
		汎	219
	7	伴	60
		判	1122
		坂	234
		阪	271
	8	板	858
		版	872
	9	叛	1143
	10	班	946
		畔	1145
		般	1317
	11	販	1477
	12	斑	1000
		飯	1691
	13	搬	647
		煩	1022
		頒	1043
	15	幡	723
		範	2709
	16	繁	2853
		蕃	2522
	18	藩	2379
hana	7	花	2211
	10	華	2283
	14	端	1221
		鼻	2706
hanabusa	8	英	2238
hanahada	9	甚	2643
hanahadashii	9	甚	2643
hanareru	8	放	853
	18	離	1836
hanashi	13	話	1527
hanasu	8	放	853
	13	話	1527
	18	離	1836
hanatsu	8	放	853
hane	6	羽	226
haneru	13	跳	1532
	15	撥	734
hara	10	原	3009
	13	腹	1034
-harai	5	払	194
haramu	7	妊	240
harasu	12	晴	981
harau	5	払	194
harawata	13	腸	1033
hare	12	晴	981
hare-	12	晴	981
hareru	12	晴	981
		脹	1003
hari	10	針	1666
	17	鍼	1754
-hari	11	張	474
haru	8	孟	2220
	9	春	2576
	11	張	474
		脩	136
	12	貼	1510
haruka	12	遥	3141
	15	遼	3168
hasamaru	9	挟	377
hasami	15	鋏	1731
hasamu	9	挟	377
	10	挿	431
	15	鋏	1731
hashi	14	端	1221
	15	箸	2708
	16	橋	1078
hashira	9	柱	896
hashiru	7	走	2194
hasu	7	芙	2208
	11	斜	1486
	13	蓉	2337
HAT-	8	法	333

Reading	Strokes	Kanji	No.
hata	9	畑	905
	10	畠	2578
	12	傍	147
	14	旗	1047
		端	1221
	15	幡	723
	16	機	1076
hatake	9	畑	905
	10	畠	2578
hataraku	13	働	153
hatasu	8	果	3560
	15	毅	1866
-hatasu	8	果	3560
hate	8	果	3560
hateru	8	果	3560
-hateru	8	果	3560
hato	13	鳩	163
HATSU	9	発	2565
	13	鉢	1708
	14	髪	2846
	15	撥	734
		潑	741
	19	醱	1645
hatsu	7	初	1116
	14	肇	2799
hatsu-	7	初	1116
haya	6	早	2390
	10	隼	2756
haya-	6	早	2390
	10	速	3105
hayabusa	10	隼	2756
hayai	6	早	2390
	10	速	3105
hayamaru	6	早	2390
hayameru	6	早	2390
	10	速	3105
hayashi	8	林	861
	17	駿	1832
hayasu	5	生	3497
hazukashii	10	恥	1313
hazukashimeru	10	辱	2736
hazumu	12	弾	572
hazureru	5	外	186
hazusu	5	外	186
hebi	11	蛇	1343
hedataru	13	隔	671
hedateru	13	隔	671
HEI	5	丙	3479
		平	3478
	7	兵	2551
	8	並	2246
		併	83
		坪	275
	9	柄	897
	10	病	3277
		陛	453
	11	閉	3319
	12	塀	557
	15	幣	2885
		弊	2884
	16	蔽	2523
	18	斃	2891
HEKI	14	碧	2836
	16	壁	2895
	18	癖	3290
HEN	4	片	3461
	5	辺	3029
	7	返	3060
	9	変	2069
		扁	3005
	11	偏	133
	12	遍	3136
	15	篇	2710
		編	1387
	19	騙	1841
herasu	12	減	601
heri	15	縁	1386
heru	11	経	1331
	12	減	601
HI	2	匕	2925
	4	比	26
	5	皮	3037
	6	妃	206
	7	否	2406
		批	250
	8	彼	290
		披	305
		泌	332
		肥	879
		非	889
	9	卑	2642
		飛	3572
	10	疲	3278
		秘	1159
		被	1163
	12	悲	2775
		扉	1955
		斐	2776
		費	2607
	14	碑	1213
		緋	1369
		蜚	2798
		鄙	1862
	15	罷	2617
		誹	1572
	16	避	3179
	20	譬	2903
hi	4	日	3027
		火	3463
	5	氷	39
	6	灯	825
	12	陽	626
hibiku	20	響	2878
hidari	5	左	2974
hidoi	14	酷	1562
hieru	7	冷	80
higashi	8	東	3568
hige	22	鬚	2855
hiideru	7	秀	2545
hijiri	13	聖	2830
hikae	11	控	495
hikaeru	11	控	495
hikari	6	光	2391
hikaru	6	光	2391
	10	晃	2450
hikeru	4	引	181
HIKI	5	疋	3480
hiki	4	匹	2962
		引	181
hiki-	4	引	181
	8	抽	302
-hiki	12	弾	572
hikiiru	11	率	2118
hiko	9	彦	3295
hiku	4	引	181
	9	退	3094
	10	挽	427
	12	弾	572
	13	惹	2493
	22	轢	1662
hikui	7	低	73
hikumaru	7	低	73
hikumeru	7	低	73
hima	13	暇	1012
hime	10	姫	407
hime-	10	姫	407
himeru	10	秘	1159
HIN	6	牝	826
	9	品	2248
	10	浜	436
	11	彬	960
		貧	2123
	15	賓	2357
	17	頻	1758
	19	瀕	805
hina	14	鄙	1862
hinabiru	14	鄙	1862
hinoe	5	丙	3479
hinoto	2	丁	3348
hira	5	平	3478
hira-	5	平	3478
hirakeru	12	開	3321
hiraki	12	開	3321
hiraku	8	拓	317
	11	啓	2763
	12	開	3321
hiro	4	丑	3433
	5	弘	192
	7	宏	2202
	9	洸	387
	10	浩	438
		紘	1298
	12	尋	2322
		皓	1180
	14	嘉	2340
hirogaru	5	広	3035
	8	拡	309
hirogeru	5	広	3035
	8	拡	309
hiroi	5	広	3035
hiromaru	5	広	3035
hiromeru	5	広	3035
hiromu	5	弘	192
hiroshi	5	弘	192
	7	宏	2202
	9	洸	387
	10	浩	438
		紘	1298
	12	皓	1180
hirou	9	拾	379
hiru	3	干	3379
	9	昼	3097
	11	乾	1679
hirugaeru	18	翻	1897
hirugaesu	18	翻	1897
hisa	8	弥	288
	10	桐	937
	11	亀	2128
hisashi	6	亘	1939
	8	弥	288
	11	亀	2128
hisashii	3	久	3384
hisomu	15	潜	746
hitai	18	額	1805

hitaru [10]浸 442
hitasu [10]浸 442
hito [2]人 3368
hito- [1]一 3341
hitomi [11]眸 1170
[17]瞳 1237
hitori [9]独 395
hitoshi [12]欽 1690
hitoshii [12]等 2682
hitotsu [1]一 3341
HITSU [4]匹 2962
[5]必 15
[8]泌 332
[12]筆 2677
hitsuji [5]未 3506
[6]羊 2183
hiya [7]冷 80
hiyakasu [7]冷 80
hiyasu [7]冷 80
hiyayaka [7]冷 80
HO [4]反 2945
[7]甫 3549
[8]歩 2416
[9]保 96
[10]哺 401
圃 3119
捕 429
浦 437
[12]堡 2821
補 1194
[14]蒲 2504
輔 1559
[15]舗 1735
ho [6]帆 210
[15]穂 1232
ho- [4]火 3463
[6]灯 825
HŌ [4]方 1963
[5]包 2966
[7]芳 2210
邦 847
[8]奉 2559
宝 2224
庖 3083
抱 306
抛 307
放 853
朋 880
法 333
泡 334
[9]保 96
封 1287
炮 906
胞 917
[10]倣 113
俸 114
峰 411
砲 1151
[11]崩 2296
捧 491
萌 2301
訪 1468
[12]報 1698
堡 2821
棚 984
[13]豊 2697
飽 1715
[15]褒 2144
[16]縫 1406
[17]繃 1411
hō [6]朴 819
hodo [12]程 1190
-hodo [12]程 1190
hodokosu [9]施 891
hodoku [13]解 1517
hogaraka [10]朗 1325
hoka [5]他 35
外 186
hoko [4]戈 3462
[5]矛 2008
[14]鉾 1720
hokoru [13]誇 1522
HOKU [5]北 197
homare [13]誉 2502
homeru [13]誉 2502
[15]褒 2144
賞 2618
hōmuru [12]葬 2320
HON [4]反 2945
[5]本 3502
[8]奔 2218
[9]叛 1143
品 2248
[18]翻 1897
hone [10]骨 2654
hono- [4]仄 2946
honō [8]炎 2420
[12]焔 996
honoka [4]仄 2946
honomekasu [4]仄 2946
honomeku [4]仄 2946
hora [9]洞 380
hori [11]堀 467
[17]濠 792
horobiru [3]亡 3402
[13]滅 660
horobosu [3]亡 3402
[13]滅 660
horobu [3]亡 3402
[13]滅 660
horu [11]彫 1683
掘 496
hōru [8]放 853
hoshi [9]星 2435
hoshi- [3]干 3379
hoshii [11]欲 1475
hoshiimama [16]擅 768
hosoi [11]細 1333
hosoru [11]細 1333
hossuru [11]欲 1475
hosu [3]干 3379
[11]乾 1679
HOT- [8]法 333
hotaru [11]蛍 2591
hotogi [6]缶 2032
hotoke [4]仏 19
HOTSU [9]発 2565
HYAKU [6]百 2026
HYŌ [5]平 3478
氷 39
[7]兵 2551
[8]拍 304
表 2429
[10]俵 115
[11]票 2669
[12]評 1501
[14]漂 699
[15]標 1064

— I —

I [3]已 3377
[5]以 41
[6]伊 49
衣 2013
[7]位 61
医 2993
囲 3069
[8]依 84
委 2553
易 2411
[9]威 3578
為 3577
畏 2562
胃 2561
韋 2268
[11]唯 463
尉 1685
惟 481
異 2584
移 1177
[12]偉 148
斐 2776
萎 2478
[13]意 2136
違 3151
[14]維 1370
[15]慰 2867
遺 3166
[16]緯 1407
謂 1595
i [4]井 3454
[6]亥 2012
[11]猪 536
-i [8]居 3080
iburu [18]燻 1098
ibusu [18]燻 1098
ICHI [1]一 3341
[7]壱 2197
ichi [5]市 1993
ichijirushii [11]著 2300
idaku [8]抱 306
idasu [5]出 3498
ideru [5]出 3498
idomu [9]挑 372
ie [10]家 2273
ieru [18]癒 3291
ii [6]好 208
[7]良 3558
-ii [7]良 3558
ikameshii [17]厳 3289
ikari [13]碇 1202
ikaru [9]怒 2571
ikasu [5]生 3497
[9]活 385
ike [6]池 218
ikeru [5]生 3497
[9]活 385
[10]埋 403
IKI [11]域 465
iki [10]息 2647
粋 1293
-iki [6]行 212

Reading	Strokes	Kanji	No.
ikidōru	15	憤	730
ikioi	13	勢	2857
ikiru	5	生	3497
	9	活	385
ikoi	16	憩	2890
ikou	16	憩	2890
IKU	8	育	2050
	9	郁	1288
iku	6	行	212
iku-	12	幾	3582
ikura	12	幾	3582
ikusa	13	戦	1787
ikutsu	12	幾	3582
ima	4	今	1968
imada	5	未	3506
imashimeru	7	戒	3204
	19	警	2893
imawashii	7	忌	2207
imi	7	忌	2207
imo	6	芋	2181
imōto	8	妹	278
imu	7	忌	2207
IN	4	允	1982
		引	181
	6	印	828
		因	3054
	9	姻	353
		胤	17
		音	2070
	10	員	2269
		院	454
	11	寅	2289
		陰	541
	12	飲	1692
	14	隠	713
	15	蔭	2517
	19	韻	1811
ina	7	否	2406
ina-	14	稲	1219
ine	14	稲	1219
inochi	8	命	2058
inoko	7	豕	3543
inoru	8	祈	875
	19	禱	1253
inoshishi	11	猪	536
inu	4	犬	3464
	6	戌	3535
	8	狗	345
inu-	4	犬	3464
inui	11	乾	1679
-ire	2	入	3370
ireru	2	入	3370
	10	容	2277
-iri	2	入	3370
iro	6	色	2029
irodoru	11	彩	1681
iru	2	入	3370
	8	居	3080
	9	要	2635
	10	射	1458
	15	鋳	1729
-iru	2	入	3370
isagiyoi	15	潔	744
isamu	9	勇	2089
isao	5	功	189
	15	勲	2869
ishi	5	石	2971
ishibumi	14	碑	1213
ishizue	18	礎	1248
iso	17	磯	1242
isogashii	6	忙	214
isogi	9	急	2092
isogu	9	急	2092
isoshimu	12	勤	1818
ita	8	板	858
itadaki	11	頂	145
itadaku	11	頂	145
	18	戴	3302
itai	12	痛	3285
itamashii	12	痛	3285
itameru	12	痛	3285
	13	傷	158
itamu	11	悼	485
	12	痛	3285
	13	傷	158
itaru	3	之	3420
	6	至	2182
	8	到	1264
	14	暢	1226
itasu	10	致	1316
itazura	10	徒	416
iteru	10	凍	129
ito	6	糸	2179
itoguchi	14	緒	1378
itoma	13	暇	1012
itonamu	12	営	2603
itoshii	13	愛	2492
itou	14	厭	3017
ITSU	1	一	3341
		乙	3339
	7	佚	62
	11	逸	3120
itsu	4	五	3436
itsukushimu	13	慈	2339
itsutsu	4	五	3436
itsuwaru	11	偽	131
	12	詐	1502
iu	4	云	1931
	7	言	1941
	16	謂	1595
iwa	8	岩	2235
	15	磐	2850
	20	巌	2386
iwaku	4	曰	3025
iwao	20	巌	2386
iwau	9	祝	913
iwaya	13	窟	2328
iya	7	否	2406
	8	弥	288
	13	嫌	636
	14	厭	3017
iyashii	9	卑	2642
	15	賤	1584
iyashimeru	9	卑	2642
	15	賤	1584
iyashimu	9	卑	2642
	15	賤	1584
iyasu	18	癒	3291
izanau	14	誘	1550
izumi	9	泉	2567

J

Reading	Strokes	Kanji	No.
JA	8	邪	1124
	11	蛇	1343
JAKU	8	若	2241
	10	弱	1167
	11	寂	2290
		雀	2469
	12	着	3316
	13	惹	2493
JAN	11	雀	2469
JI	5	仕	34
		示	1936
	6	地	204
		字	2172
		寺	2164
		次	54
		而	2027
		耳	3516
		自	3525
	7	似	63
		児	2546
	8	事	3567
		侍	85
		治	335
	9	持	374
	10	時	924
		除	456
	12	滋	602
	13	慈	2339
		辞	1364
	14	爾	3587
		磁	1214
	19	璽	2911
-ji	13	路	1533
JIKA	8	直	2932
JIKI	8	直	2932
	9	食	2075
JIKU	12	軸	1514
-jime	15	締	1393
-jimiru	9	染	2572
JIN	2	人	3368
	3	刃	2929
	4	仁	20
	6	尽	3050
		迅	3046
	7	沈	261
		臣	3068
	9	甚	2643
		神	912
	10	訊	1452
		陣	455
	12	尋	2322
	13	稔	1207
		腎	2832
-jirushi	6	印	828
JIT-	2	十	3365
JITSU	4	日	3027
	8	実	2225
JO	3	女	3418
	6	如	207
	7	助	1121
		序	3065
		抒	251
	9	叙	1446
	10	徐	414
		除	456
JŌ	3	上	3404
		丈	3419
	4	冗	1976
	6	丞	2541
		成	3537

7 条 2200
状 272
8 定 2229
帖 286
9 乗 3576
城 352
浄 382
10 娘 406
11 剰 1779
尉 1685
常 2590
情 482
盛 2675
12 場 558
畳 2592
13 蒸 2334
14 滌 696
静 1728
15 縄 1388
鄭 1888
16 壌 755
嬢 758
錠 1737
18 穣 1250
20 譲 1649
醸 1654
21 饒 1812
JOKU 10 辱 2736
16 濁 774
JU 7 寿 3557
8 受 2421
10 従 415
11 授 492
習 2667
12 就 1694
13 頌 1045
14 竪 2837
誦 1549
需 2797
16 儒 174
樹 1075
JŪ 2 十 3365
4 廿 3449
5 汁 195
6 充 2014
7 住 64
9 拾 379
柔 2088
重 3573
10 従 415
11 渋 513
14 銃 1723
16 獣 1892
縦 1408
JUKU 14 塾 2860
15 熟 2868
JUN 6 巡 3047
旬 2978
9 洵 383
盾 3006
10 准 127
殉 941
純 1297
11 淳 514
12 循 578
絢 1347
順 18
13 楯 1016
準 2856
馴 1820
15 潤 742
遵 3167
JUT- 2 十 3365
JUTSU 6 戌 3535
8 述 3075
11 術 476

— K —

KA 3 下 3378
4 化 21
戈 3462
火 3463
5 加 38
可 2969
瓜 3038
甲 3481
禾 3503
6 仮 50
7 何 65
花 2211
8 佳 86
価 87
果 3560
河 336
9 架 2569
科 1138
10 個 117
夏 2113
家 2273
荷 2282
華 2283
11 菓 2302
貨 2465
12 渦 603
過 3137
13 嫁 635
暇 1012
禍 1030
靴 1781
14 嘉 2340
寡 2344
歌 1825
箇 2700
15 稼 1230
課 1573
17 鍋 1752
霞 2814
ka 5 乎 3504
6 圭 2165
9 哉 3294
耶 1283
香 2568
10 蚊 1319
11 鹿 3126
19 蘭 2383
20 馨 2879
-ka 4 日 3027
kaba 14 蒲 2504
kabe 16 壁 2895
kabi 23 黴 814
kabiru 23 黴 814
kabu 10 株 935
kaburi 16 頭 1604
kaburu 10 被 1163
kabuseru 10 被 1163
kado 6 圭 2165
7 角 2047
8 門 888
kae- 12 替 2783
kaede 13 楓 1015
kaerimiru 9 省 2449
21 顧 1900
kaeru 4 反 2945
5 代 30
7 返 3060
9 変 2069
10 帰 130
12 換 587
替 2783
16 還 3180
-kaeru 4 反 2945
7 返 3060
12 換 587
kaesu 4 反 2945
7 返 3060
10 帰 130
-kaesu 7 返 3060
kaette 7 却 1118
kagameru 8 屈 3079
kagami 19 鏡 1766
23 鑑 1773
kagamu 8 屈 3079
kagayaku 15 輝 1402
kage 11 陰 541
15 影 1889
蔭 2517
kageri 17 翳 2874
kageru 11 陰 541
kagi 17 鍵 1753
kagiri 9 限 398
-kagiri 9 限 398
kagiru 9 限 398
kago 22 籠 2734
KAI 4 介 1967
刈 28
6 会 2020
回 3055
灰 2979
7 快 245
戒 3204
改 243
8 届 3078
怪 297
拐 308
9 廻 3089
徊 362
悔 365
恢 366
海 384
界 2563
皆 2445
11 掛 493
械 961
12 絵 1346
蛔 1359
街 576
開 3321
階 624
13 塊 632
解 1517
14 誨 1544
誡 1545

Reading	Kanji	No.
	希	2049
	忌	2207
	汽	264
	[8]其	2629
	奇	2217
	季	2554
	祈	875
	[9]紀	1276
	軌	1445
	[10]帰	130
	姫	407
	既	1166
	記	1453
	起	3307
	飢	1668
	鬼	2657
	[11]埼	466
	基	2673
	寄	2291
	崎	472
	規	978
	亀	2128
	[12]喜	2308
	幾	3582
	揆	588
	揮	589
	期	1704
	棋	987
	稀	1189
	葵	2317
	貴	2606
	[13]棄	2137
	毀	1791
	畸	1198
	詭	1520
	[14]旗	1047
	綺	1371
	[15]器	2713
	嬉	722
	毅	1866
	輝	1402
	麾	3174
	[16]機	1076
	[17]徽	787
	磯	1242
	[18]騎	1834
	[19]譏	1638
	[21]饑	1813
ki	[4]木	3450
	[5]生	3497
	[11]黄	2468
	[16]樹	1075
kiba	[4]牙	3435
kibi	[12]黍	2597
kibishii	[17]厳	3289
KICHI	[6]吉	2167
kieru	[10]消	443
kikoeru	[14]聞	3326
KIKU	[11]菊	2303
kiku	[7]利	1114
	[8]効	1265
	[10]訊	1452
	[14]聞	3326
	[17]聴	1418
kimaru	[7]決	263
	[13]極	1017
kimeru	[7]決	263
	[13]極	1017
kimi	[7]君	3206
kimo	[7]肝	841
KIN	[3]巾	3409
	[4]今	1968
	斤	2949
	[7]均	235
	近	3061
	[8]京	2052
	欣	852
	金	2057
	[9]衿	1140
	[11]菌	2304
	[12]勤	1818
	欽	1690
	琴	2781
	筋	2678
	[13]禁	2795
	[15]緊	2838
	[16]錦	1738
	[17]謹	1618
	[18]襟	1252
kinoe	[5]甲	3481
kinoto	[1]乙	3339
kinu	[6]衣	2013
	[13]絹	1361
kirai	[13]嫌	636
kirau	[13]嫌	636
kire	[4]切	27
-kire	[4]切	27
kireru	[4]切	27
-kireru	[4]切	27
kiri	[4]切	27
	[10]桐	937
	[19]霧	2817
-kiri	[4]切	27
kiru	[4]切	27
	[6]伐	42
	[11]剪	2306
	斬	1482
	[12]着	3316
	[14]截	3301
-kiru	[4]切	27
kisaki	[6]后	2981
-kise	[12]着	3316
kiseru	[12]着	3316
kishi	[8]岸	2236
kisou	[20]競	1847
kita	[5]北	197
kitaeru	[17]鍛	1755
kitanai	[6]汚	222
kitaru	[7]来	3551
kitasu	[7]来	3551
KITSU	[3]乞	1961
	[6]吃	200
	吉	2167
	[7]迄	3201
	[12]喫	551
	[13]詰	1521
	[16]橘	1077
kiwa	[14]際	714
kiwamari	[13]極	1017
	[15]窮	2358
kiwamaru	[7]谷	2043
	[13]極	1017
	[15]窮	2358
kiwameru	[7]究	2203
	[13]極	1017
	[15]窮	2358
kiwami	[13]極	1017
	[15]窮	2358
kiyo	[6]圭	2165
	[11]淳	514
	[20]馨	2879
kiyoi	[11]清	523
kiyomaru	[11]清	523
kiyomeru	[9]浄	382
	[11]清	523
kiyoshi	[6]圭	2165
	[11]淳	514
kizahashi	[12]階	624
kizami	[8]刻	1267
kizamu	[8]刻	1267
kizashi	[6]兆	225
	[11]萌	2301
kizasu	[6]兆	225
	[11]萌	2301
kizu	[11]疵	3282
	[13]傷	158
kizuku	[16]築	2715
-kko	[3]子	3390
	[7]児	2546
KO	[3]己	3380
	[4]戸	1930
	[5]乎	3504
	去	2156
	古	2002
	[8]呼	273
	固	3086
	拠	312
	股	881
	虎	3212
	[9]孤	356
	弧	360
	故	1141
	枯	898
	[10]個	117
	庫	3112
	[11]涸	517
	虚	3237
	[12]湖	604
	雇	1956
	[13]誇	1522
	鼓	1786
	[14]箇	2700
	[16]錮	1739
	[21]顧	1900
ko	[3]子	3390
	[5]仔	33
	[7]児	2546
	[10]娘	406
	粉	1291
	蚕	2457
ko-	[3]小	7
	[4]木	3450
	[11]黄	2468
-ko	[3]子	3390
	[5]処	3031
	[7]児	2546
KŌ	[3]口	3382
	工	3381
	[4]亢	1964
	公	1974
	勾	2942
	孔	179
	[5]功	189
	尻	3032

巧 188
広 3035
弘 192
甲 3481
6 亘 1939
交 2015
仰 48
光 2391
后 2981
向 3052
好 208
扣 216
江 221
考 3196
行 212
7 亨 2037
坑 236
孝 3205
宏 2202
抗 252
攻 242
更 3541
肛 842
8 劾 1265
岬 284
岡 2997
幸 2216
拘 310
昂 2412
肯 2417
9 侯 98
厚 3003
後 361
恒 367
恰 368
洪 386
洸 387
皇 2566
紅 1277
荒 2260
虹 1285
郊 1286
香 2568
10 倖 118
候 119
晃 2450
格 926
校 929
浩 438
紘 1298
耕 1308
耗 1309
航 1318
貢 2281
降 458
高 2097
11 康 3124
控 495
淆 518
黄 2468
12 慌 580
惶 581
港 605
甦 3315
皓 1180
硬 1183
絞 1349
項 567
13 媾 637
溝 659
較 1536
鉱 1709
14 構 1049
綱 1372
膏 2141
酵 1561
15 稿 1231
16 興 2909
衡 761
鋼 1740
17 講 1619
購 1624
18 鯁 1878
19 嚮 2901
曠 1100
20 礦 1256
kō- 9 神 912
kobamu 8 拒 311
kobiru 12 媚 565
kobotsu 13 毀 1791
koe 7 声 2198
8 肥 879
koeru 8 肥 879
12 超 3313
越 3314
kogareru 12 焦 2770
kogasu 12 焦 2770
kogeru 12 焦 2770
kogoeru 10 凍 129
koi 10 恋 2098
16 濃 777
18 鯉 1879
koishii 10 恋 2098
kokono 2 九 3369
kokonotsu 2 九 3369
kokoro 4 心 11
kokoromiru 13 試 1525
kokoroyoi 7 快 245
kokorozashi 7 志 2199
kokorozasu 7 志 2199
KOKU 5 石 2971
7 克 2046
告 2409
谷 2043
8 刻 1267
国 3087
9 剋 3305
11 黒 2740
14 穀 1824
酷 1562
koma 15 駒 1827
komaka 11 細 1333
komakai 11 細 1333
komaru 7 困 3070
kome 6 米 3529
komeru 5 込 3030
22 籠 2734
komi 5 込 3030
-komi 5 込 3030
komogomo 6 交 2015
komoru 22 籠 2734
komu 5 込 3030
11 混 519
-komu 5 込 3030
kōmuru 10 被 1163
14 蒙 2505
KON 4 今 1968
6 艮 3517
7 困 3070
近 3061
8 昆 2413
昏 2418
金 2057
9 建 3090
恨 369
10 根 930
11 婚 470
混 519
紺 1332
12 渾 606
13 献 1785
14 魂 1063
16 墾 2896
17 懇 2899
kona 10 粉 1291
kono 6 此 823
konomu 6 好 208
korashimeru 18 懲 2910
korasu 16 凝 175
18 懲 2910
kore 3 之 3420
6 伊 49
此 823
9 是 2436
11 惟 481
kōri 5 氷 39
10 郡 1466
koriru 18 懲 2910
koro 11 頃 144
korobu 11 転 1480
korogaru 11 転 1480
korogasu 11 転 1480
korogeru 11 転 1480
koromo 6 衣 2013
korosu 10 殺 1324
koru 16 凝 175
kōru 5 氷 39
10 凍 129
koshi 13 腰 1036
kosu 12 超 3313
越 3314
-kosu 12 越 3314
kosureru 17 擦 790
kosuru 17 擦 790
kotae 12 答 2681
kotaeru 7 応 3066
12 答 2681
koto 7 言 1941
8 事 3567
10 殊 942
11 異 2584
12 琴 2781
14 箏 2703
kotobuki 7 寿 3557
kotohogu 7 寿 3557
kotonaru 11 異 2584
kotowari 11 理 970
kotowaru 11 断 1492
KOTSU 3 乞 1961
10 骨 2654
13 滑 658
kou 3 乞 1961
10 恋 2098
15 請 1576

kowa- [7]声 2198
kowagaru [8]怖 296
[10]恐 2650
kowai [8]怖 296
[10]恐 2650
[11]強 475
kowareru [16]壊 756
kowashi [15]毅 1866
kowasu [16]壊 756
koyashi [8]肥 879
koyasu [8]肥 879
koyomi [14]暦 3018
kozue [11]梢 963
KU [2]九 3369
[3]久 3384
口 3382
工 3381
[4]公 1974
区 2963
[5]功 189
句 2967
[7]究 2203
[8]供 88
狗 345
苦 2243
[9]紅 1277
[10]倶 111
宮 2274
庫 3112
矩 1148
貢 2281
[14]駆 1823
[15]駒 1827
KŪ [8]供 88
空 2227
[10]宮 2274
kubaru [10]配 1460
kubi [9]首 2265
[16]頸 1611
kubiki [11]軛 1481
kubo [14]窪 2348
kubomaru [14]窪 2348
kubomu [5]凹 3482
[14]窪 2348
kuchi [3]口 3382
kuchibiru [10]唇 2737
kuchiru [6]朽 821
kuda [14]管 2701
kudakeru [9]砕 1134
kudaku [9]砕 1134
kudan [6]件 51
kudari [3]下 3378
kudaru [3]下 3378
[10]降 458
kudasaru [3]下 3378
kudasu [3]下 3378
[10]降 458
-kudasu [3]下 3378
kugi [10]釘 1667
kuiru [9]悔 365
kuji [23]籤 2735
kujira [19]鯨 1882
kuki [8]茎 2242
kukuru [9]括 376
kuma [14]熊 2848
kumi [6]伍 47
[11]組 1337
kumo [12]雲 2773
kumoru [16]曇 2521
kumu [7]汲 265
[10]酌 1461
[11]組 1337
KUN [7]君 3206
[10]訓 1454
[15]勲 2869
[16]薫 2371
[18]燻 1098
kuni [8]国 3087
kura [10]倉 2104
庫 3112
[15]蔵 2364
kuraberu [4]比 26
[13]較 1536
kurai [7]位 61
[13]暗 1010
kurasu [14]暮 2354
kurau [9]食 2075
[12]喰 552
kurenai [9]紅 1277
kureru [7]呉 2549
[14]暮 2354
kuri [10]栗 2649
kuro [11]黒 2740
kurogane [13]鉄 1711
kuroi [11]黒 2740
kuru [7]来 3551
[10]栗 2649
[19]繰 1427
kuruma [7]車 3552
kuruoshii [7]狂 269
kurushii [8]苦 2243
kurushimeru [8]苦 2243
kurushimu [8]苦 2243
kuruu [7]狂 269
kuruwa [11]郭 1678
[14]廓 3163
kusa [9]草 2263
kusa- [9]草 2263
kusai [9]臭 2633
-kusai [9]臭 2633
kusamura [18]叢 2621
kusarasu [14]腐 3162
kusare [14]腐 3162
kusareru [14]腐 3162
kusari [18]鎖 1761
kusaru [14]腐 3162
-kusaru [14]腐 3162
kusasu [14]腐 3162
kuse [18]癖 3290
kuseni [18]癖 3290
kushikezuru [11]梳 964
kushiki [8]奇 2217
kusu [13]楠 1018
kusuburu [18]燻 1098
kusunoki [13]楠 1018
kusuri [16]薬 2375
KUTSU [8]屈 3079
[11]堀 467
掘 496
[13]窟 2328
kutsu [8]沓 2419
[13]靴 1781
kutsugaeru [18]覆 2726
kutsugaesu [18]覆 2726
kutsurogu [13]寛 2327
kuu [9]食 2075
[12]喰 552
kuwa [10]桑 2112
kuwadateru [6]企 2021
kuwaeru [5]加 38
kuwashii [13]詳 1526
kuwawaru [5]加 38
kuyamu [9]悔 365
kuyashii [9]悔 365
kuyurasu [18]燻 1098
-kuzure [11]崩 2296
kuzureru [11]崩 2296
kuzusu [11]崩 2296
KYA [11]脚 974
KYAKU [7]却 1118
[9]客 2250
[10]格 926
[11]脚 974
KYO [5]巨 3039
去 2156
[8]居 3080
拒 311
拠 312
[10]挙 2456
[11]据 497
虚 3237
許 1470
[12]距 1511
[15]墟 720
[20]醵 1655
KYŌ [4]凶 2961
[5]兄 2154
[6]兇 2392
共 2393
匡 2989
叫 201
[7]亨 2037
孝 3205
杏 2397
狂 269
[8]享 2051
京 2052
供 88
協 93
況 337
[9]峡 357
挟 377
狭 396
香 2568
[10]恭 2459
恐 2650
校 929
胸 951
脇 952
脅 2109
[11]強 475
教 1493
経 1331
郷 549
[12]喬 2488
敬 1701
[14]兢 1566
境 676
[15]鋏 1731
鞏 2714
[16]橋 1078
興 2909
[17]矯 1241
[19]嚮 2901

Reading	Strokes	Kanji	No.
meguru	6	巡	3047
MEI	6	名	2169
	8	命	2058
		明	855
	9	迷	3092
	13	盟	2794
	14	銘	1724
		鳴	674
mekura	8	盲	2053
MEN	8	免	2067
	9	面	2087
	12	棉	988
	14	綿	1373
	15	緬	1390
men	6	牝	826
	14	雌	1055
meshi	12	飯	1691
mesu	5	召	2001
	6	牝	826
	14	雌	1055
MĒTORU	6	米	3529
METSU	13	滅	660
mezurashii	9	珍	909
MI	5	未	3506
	8	味	274
		弥	288
	9	美	2264
	15	魅	3329
mi	3	三	1924
		巳	3388
	7	身	3553
	8	実	2225
mi-	11	深	524
	12	御	577
michi	7	亨	2037
	8	迪	3076
	12	道	3134
	13	路	1533
michibiku	15	導	2888
michiru	12	満	607
midareru	7	乱	1260
midarini	6	妄	2016
midaru	7	乱	1260
midasu	7	乱	1260
midori	14	碧	2836
		緑	1377
		翠	2705
mieru	7	見	2544
migaku	16	磨	3181
migi	5	右	2975
mijikai	12	短	1182
mijime	11	惨	483
mikado	9	帝	2073
miki	13	幹	1718
mikotonori	12	詔	1505
mimi	6	耳	3516
MIN	5	民	3036
	8	明	855
	10	眠	1147
mina	9	皆	2445
minami	9	南	2082
minamoto	13	源	656
minato	12	港	605
mine	10	峰	411
	17	嶺	2376
minikui	17	醜	1629
minna	9	皆	2445
minoru	7	酉	3544
	8	実	2225
	13	稔	1207
	18	穣	1250
miru	7	見	2544
	9	看	3220
	12	診	1504
	18	観	1880
misaki	8	岬	284
misao	16	操	769
misasagi	11	陵	544
mise	8	店	3085
miseru	7	見	2544
mitasu	6	充	2014
	12	満	607
mitomeru	14	認	1546
MITSU	11	密	2292
mitsu	3	三	1924
	4	允	1982
	5	弘	192
	8	弥	288
	12	満	607
mitsugu	10	貢	2281
mittsu	3	三	1924
miya	10	宮	2274
miyabi	13	雅	1197
miyako	11	都	1686
mizo	13	溝	659
mizu	4	水	10
mizu-	4	水	10
	13	瑞	1027
mizukara	6	自	3525
mizuumi	12	湖	604
MO	8	茂	2245
	14	摸	691
		模	1050
mo	5	母	3475
	12	喪	2825
	14	裳	2615
	19	藻	2384
MŌ	3	亡	3402
	4	毛	3453
	6	妄	2016
	8	孟	2220
		盲	2053
	10	耗	1309
	11	望	2742
		猛	537
	14	摸	691
		網	1374
		蒙	2505
MOCHI	4	勿	2943
mochi	11	望	2742
-mochi	9	持	374
mochiiru	5	用	2976
modasu	15	黙	2865
modoru	7	戻	1942
modosu	7	戻	1942
moe	11	萌	2301
moeru	11	萌	2301
	16	燃	1081
moguru	15	潜	746
mōkeru	11	設	1471
MOKU	4	木	3450
	5	目	3043
	15	黙	2865
momo	6	百	2026
	7	李	2398
	10	桃	936
MON	4	文	1962
	8	門	888
	10	紋	1299
	11	問	3320
	14	聞	3326
monme	4	匁	3465
mono	8	物	874
		者	3211
mono-	8	物	874
moppara	9	専	2644
morasu	14	漏	701
moreru	14	漏	701
mori	6	守	2173
	7	杜	835
	12	森	2475
-mori	6	守	2173
moro	15	諸	1577
	19	艶	1908
moru	11	盛	2675
	14	漏	701
moshi	8	若	2241
mōshi-	5	申	3507
moshikuwa	8	若	2241
mosu	16	燃	1081
mōsu	5	申	3507
MOT-	4	勿	2943
motageru	17	擡	791
moteru	9	持	374
moto	3	下	3378
	4	元	1929
	5	本	3502
	10	素	2458
	11	基	2673
		許	1470
motoi	11	基	2673
motomeru	7	求	3550
motomu	12	須	574
motoru	10	悖	420
MOTSU	8	物	874
motsu	9	持	374
motte	5	以	41
mottomo	4	尤	3023
	12	最	2472
moyasu	16	燃	1081
moyōsu	13	催	157
MU	5	矛	2008
	8	武	3210
	11	務	1173
	12	無	2135
	13	夢	2336
	16	謀	1593
	19	霧	2817
mu	4	六	1965
mugi	7	麦	2408
mui	4	六	1965
mukaeru	7	迎	3059
mukashi	8	昔	2432
mukau	6	向	3052
-muke	6	向	3052
mukeru	6	向	3052
muki	6	向	3052
-muki	6	向	3052
muko	12	婿	566
mukō	6	向	3052
mukō-	6	向	3052
muku	6	向	3052
mukuiru	12	報	1698
	13	酬	1539

muna- [10]胸 951
[12]棟 991
munashii [8]空 2227
[11]虚 3237
mune [6]旨 2024
[8]宗 2228
[10]胸 951
[12]棟 991
mura [7]村 834
[13]群 1540
[18]叢 2621
muragaru [13]群 1540
[18]叢 2621
murasaki [12]紫 2688
murasu [13]蒸 2334
mure [13]群 1540
mureru [13]群 1540
蒸 2334
muro [9]室 2254
mushi [6]虫 3530
mushibamu [15]蝕 1796
mushiro [10]席 3113
[14]寧 2345
musu [5]生 3497
[11]産 3298
[13]蒸 2334
musubu [12]結 1348
musume [10]娘 406
mutsu [4]六 1965
[13]睦 1199
mutsumajii [13]睦 1199
mutsumu [13]睦 1199
muttsu [4]六 1965
muzukashii [18]難 1838
MYAKU [10]脈 953
MYŌ [6]名 2169
[7]妙 239
[8]命 2058
明 855
苗 2237

N

NA [7]那 843
[8]奈 2219
[9]南 2082
[10]納 1300
na [6]名 2169
[11]菜 2305
-na [6]名 2169
字 2172
nabe [17]鍋 1752
nado [12]等 2682
nae [8]苗 2237
naeru [12]萎 2478
naga [7]亨 2037
呂 2187
西 3544
[11]脩 136
[14]暢 1226
nagai [5]永 1937
[8]長 2556
nagameru [11]眺 1171
nagare [10]流 441
nagareru [10]流 441
nagasu [10]流 441
-nagasu [10]流 441
-nage [7]投 256
nagekawashii [13]嘆 630
nageku [13]嘆 630
[15]歎 1869
nageru [7]投 256
nageutsu [8]拋 307
nagisa [11]渚 525
nagomu [8]和 1130
nagoyaka [8]和 1130
naguru [8]殴 886
nagusameru [15]慰 2867
nagusamu [15]慰 2867
NAI [2]乃 2927
[4]内 3466
[8]奈 2219
nai [3]亡 3402
[12]無 2135
naka [4]中 3451
[6]仲 43
nakaba [5]半 3501
nakare [4]勿 2943
naki- [3]亡 3402
naku [8]泣 338
[14]鳴 674
nama [5]生 3497
nama- [5]生 3497
namakeru [9]怠 2085
namakura [12]鈍 1689
namamekashii [19]艶 1908
namari [13]鉛 1707
namaru [12]鈍 1689
nameraka [13]滑 658
nami [7]甫 3549
[8]並 2246
波 330
namida [10]涙 440
NAN [7]男 2542
[9]南 2082
[10]納 1300
[11]軟 1479
[13]楠 1018
[18]難 1838
nan [7]何 65
nan- [7]何 65
nana [2]七 3362
naname [11]斜 1486
nanatsu [2]七 3362
nani [7]何 65
nani- [7]何 65
nanigashi [9]某 2560
nano [2]七 3362
nao [8]尚 2233
[12]猶 619
naoki [8]直 2932
naoru [8]治 335
直 2932
naosu [8]治 335
直 2932
-naosu [8]直 2932
naraberu [8]並 2246
narabini [8]並 2246
narabu [8]並 2246
narai [11]習 2667
narasu [7]均 235
[13]馴 1820
[14]慣 685
鳴 674
narau [10]倣 113
[11]習 2667
nareru [13]馴 1820
[14]慣 685
nari [3]也 3406
[7]形 846
[13]稔 1207
naru [5]生 3497
[6]成 3537
[9]為 3577
[13]稔 1207
[14]鳴 674
nasake [11]情 482
nashi [11]梨 2744
nasu [5]生 3497
[6]成 3537
[9]為 3577
-nasu [6]成 3537
NAT- [10]納 1300
natsu [10]夏 2113
natsukashii [16]懐 763
natsukashimu [16]懐 763
natsukeru [16]懐 763
natsuku [16]懐 763
nawa [15]縄 1388
nawa- [8]苗 2237
nayamasu [10]悩 421
nayamu [10]悩 421
ne [3]子 3390
[9]音 2070
[10]値 109
根 930
[17]嶺 2376
-ne [10]根 930
nebaru [11]粘 1327
-negai [19]願 1845
negau [19]願 1845
NEI [14]寧 2345
[17]嚀 785
nekasu [13]寝 2329
neko [11]猫 535
nemui [10]眠 1147
nemuru [10]眠 1147
NEN [6]年 2035
[8]念 2059
[11]粘 1327
[12]然 2782
[13]稔 1207
[16]燃 1081
鮎 1876
-NEN [15]縁 1386
nengoro [17]懇 2899
neri- [14]練 1375
neru [13]寝 2329
煉 1023
[14]練 1375
[16]錬 1741
NETSU [15]熱 2866
nezu [13]鼠 2693
nezumi [13]鼠 2693
NI [2]二 1922
[4]仁 20
[5]尼 3033
[6]弐 3195
[7]児 2546
[14]爾 3587
ni [4]丹 3441
[10]荷 2282
-ni [12]煮 2785

nibu– 12 鈍 1689
nibui 12 鈍 1689
niburu 12 鈍 1689
NICHI 4 日 3027
nieru 12 煮 2785
nigai 8 苦 2243
nigaru 8 苦 2243
nigasu 9 逃 3095
nigeru 9 逃 3095
nigiru 12 握 585
nigoru 16 濁 774
nigosu 16 濁 774
nii– 13 新 1784
niji 9 虹 1285
nijimu 14 滲 703
nijū 4 廿 3449
NIKU 6 肉 3200
nikui 14 憎 687
–nikui 18 難 1838
nikumu 14 憎 687
nikurashii 14 憎 687
nikushimi 14 憎 687
NIN 2 人 3368
3 刃 2929
4 仁 20
6 任 53
7 妊 240
忍 2212
14 認 1546
ninau 8 担 318
nioi 4 匂 2944
9 臭 2633
niou 4 匂 2944
9 臭 2633
niowaseru 4 匂 2944
niru 7 似 63
12 煮 2785
nise 11 偽 131
nishi 6 西 3520
nishiki 16 錦 1738
NIT– 2 入 3370
niwa 10 庭 3114
niwatori 19 鶏 1768
niyasu 12 煮 2785
no 2 乃 2927
3 之 3420
11 野 1485
no– 11 野 1485
NŌ 10 悩 421
納 1300
能 1323
11 脳 975
13 農 2698
16 濃 777
–NŌ 4 王 3439
7 応 3066
nobasu 7 伸 70
8 延 3073
nobe 8 延 3073
noberu 7 伸 70
8 延 3073
述 3075
nobiru 7 伸 70
8 延 3073
nobori 3 上 3404
noboru 3 上 3404
8 昂 2412
昇 2415
12 登 2595
noboseru 3 上 3404
nobosu 3 上 3404
nobu 4 允 1982
6 亘 1939
7 辰 2992
9 洵 383
11 寅 2289
惟 481
脩 136
13 靖 1208
頌 1045
14 暢 1226
noburu 7 辰 2992
14 暢 1226
nochi 9 後 361
nogareru 9 逃 3095
nogasu 9 逃 3095
noki 10 軒 1459
nokoru 10 残 943
nokosu 10 残 943
nomi 28 鑿 2924
–nomi 12 飲 1692
nomu 7 呑 2410
12 飲 1692
NON 13 暖 1011
–NON 9 音 2070
nori 8 尭 2063
法 333
10 矩 1148
12 智 2784
–nori 9 乗 3576
noru 9 乗 3576
13 載 3300
noseru 9 乗 3576
13 載 3300
nosu 7 伸 70
notamau 9 宣 2252
notamawaku 4 曰 3025
9 宣 2252
notto 13 節 2691
nottoru 9 則 1444
nozoku 10 除 456
nozomu 11 望 2742
18 臨 1630
NU 9 怒 2571
nugeru 11 脱 973
nugu 11 脱 973
nukaru 7 抜 246
nukasu 7 抜 246
nukeru 7 抜 246
nuki 7 抜 246
11 貫 2460
16 緯 1407
nuku 7 抜 246
–nuku 7 抜 246
numa 8 沼 339
nuno 5 布 2973
nuri 13 塗 2841
nuru 13 塗 2841
nusa 15 幣 2885
nushi 5 主 1938
nusumu 11 盗 2670
nuu 16 縫 1406
NYA 8 若 2241
NYAKU 8 若 2241
NYO 3 女 3418
6 如 207
NYŌ 3 女 3418
7 尿 3064
NYŪ 2 入 3370
8 乳 1438
9 柔 2088

O

O 5 乎 3504
6 汚 222
8 和 1130
於 854
11 悪 2745
o 7 尾 3062
男 2542
14 緒 1378
o– 3 小 7
7 牡 839
8 阿 346
12 御 577
雄 1008
Ō 4 王 3439
5 凹 3482
央 3509
7 応 3066
8 往 292
押 314
欧 887
殴 886
9 皇 2566
10 桜 931
翁 2108
11 黄 2468
12 奥 2824
15 横 1066
18 謳 1632
24 鷹 3189
ō– 3 大 3416
obi 10 帯 2582
obiru 10 帯 2582
obiyakasu 10 脅 2109
oboeru 12 覚 2604
ochi 12 落 2318
ochiiru 10 陥 457
ochiru 12 落 2318
odateru 14 煽 1056
odayaka 16 穏 1235
odokasu 9 威 3578
10 脅 2109
17 嚇 784
odori 14 踊 1558
odorokasu 22 驚 2894
odoroku 22 驚 2894
odoru 14 踊 1558
21 躍 1658
odoshi 9 威 3578
15 縅 1391
odosu 9 威 3578
10 脅 2109
oeru 11 終 1336
ogamu 8 拝 303
ōgi 10 扇 1950
oginau 12 補 1194
ogosoka 17 厳 3289
ōi 6 多 2170
ōini 3 大 3416
oiru 6 老 3197

P

R

S

T

11 袋 2588
逮 3123
12 替 2783
貸 2600
隊 625
13 滞 663
14 態 2847
颱 3336
15 褪 1234
16 頽 1614
17 擡 791
18 戴 3302
tai 19 鯛 1881
-tai 9 度 3100
taira 5 平 3478
taka 8 尭 2063
昂 2412
10 峻 412
高 2097
11 琢 971
12 喬 2488
13 嵩 2331
24 鷹 3189
takai 10 高 2097
takamaru 10 高 2097
takameru 10 高 2097
takara 8 宝 2224
takashi 8 尭 2063
昂 2412
10 峻 412
12 喬 2488
13 嵩 2331
take 3 丈 3419
6 竹 228
8 孟 2220
岳 2557
虎 3212
10 赳 3308
13 嵩 2331
15 毅 1866
takeshi 8 孟 2220
9 洸 387
10 赳 3308
15 毅 1866
taki 13 滝 661
takigi 16 薪 2374
TAKU 6 宅 2174
7 択 255
沢 267
8 卓 2064
拓 317
9 度 3100
10 託 1455
11 琢 971
17 濯 793
taku 8 炊 870
12 焚 2778
takumi 5 巧 188
6 匠 2990
takumu 5 巧 188
takuwaeru 12 貯 1509
13 蓄 2333
tama 5 玉 3477
6 圭 2165
9 玲 910
10 珠 947
11 偶 132
球 969
12 弾 572
13 瑶 1026
瑞 1027
14 碧 2836
魂 1063
15 霊 2805
tama- 5 玉 3477
-tamae 12 給 1350
tamago 7 卵 849
tamaru 12 堪 559
13 溜 662
tamashii 14 魂 1063
tamau 12 給 1350
15 賜 1585
tamawaru 15 賜 1585
tame 9 為 3577
tameru 12 貯 1509
13 溜 662
17 矯 1241
tamesu 13 試 1525
tami 5 民 3036
tamotsu 9 保 96
tamou 12 給 1350
15 賜 1585
TAN 4 丹 3441
反 2945
5 旦 2389
7 但 72
8 担 318
9 単 2256
段 1144
炭 2257
胆 919
11 探 505
淡 528
12 堪 559
短 1182
13 嘆 630
14 端 1221
15 歎 1869
誕 1579
16 壇 754
17 鍛 1755
tana 8 店 3085
12 棚 984
tanagokoro 12 掌 2602
tane 9 胤 17
14 種 1218
tani 7 谷 2043
tanomoshii 16 頼 1615
tanomu 16 頼 1615
tanoshii 12 愉 582
13 楽 2826
tanoshimu 12 愉 582
13 楽 2826
taoreru 10 倒 124
18 斃 2891
taosu 10 倒 124
18 斃 2891
tarasu 8 垂 3565
tare 8 垂 3565
15 誰 1578
-tare 8 垂 3565
tareru 8 垂 3565
tariru 7 足 2188
taru 7 足 2188
tashika 15 確 1228
tashikameru 15 確 1228
tasu 7 足 2188
tasukaru 7 助 1121
tasukeru 7 助 1121
扶 247
tasuku 7 佑 74
9 祐 915
14 輔 1559
tataeru 10 称 1160
tatakau 13 戦 1787
18 闘 3334
tatami 12 畳 2592
tatami- 12 畳 2592
tatamu 12 畳 2592
tate 9 建 3090
盾 3006
13 楯 1016
14 竪 2837
16 縦 1408
館 1748
tate- 5 立 1992
-tate 5 立 1992
tateito 11 経 1331
tatematsuru 8 奉 2559
tateru 5 立 1992
9 建 3090
点 2084
11 閉 3319
-tateru 5 立 1992
tatoeru 8 例 89
12 喩 553
20 譬 2903
TATSU 12 達 3139
tatsu 5 立 1992
7 辰 2992
9 建 3090
発 2565
10 起 3307
竜 2099
11 断 1492
経 1331
12 絶 1353
裁 3299
14 蔦 2355
-tatsu 5 立 1992
tattobu 12 尊 2324
貴 2606
tattoi 12 尊 2324
貴 2606
tawamureru 15 戯 1875
tawara 10 俵 115
tayasu 12 絶 1353
tayori 9 便 95
tayoru 16 頼 1615
tazu 21 鶴 1850
tazuneru 11 訪 1468
12 尋 2322
tazusaeru 13 携 648
tazusawaru 13 携 648
te 4 手 3456
te- 4 手 3456
-te 4 手 3456
TEI 2 丁 3348
5 叮 183
7 体 71
低 73
呈 2189
廷 3058
弟 2044

Reading	Strokes	Kanji	No.
	8	定	2229
		底	3084
		低	294
		抵	319
		邸	1131
	9	亭	2072
		帝	2073
		柢	901
		牴	908
		訂	1442
		貞	2083
	10	庭	3114
		悌	424
		挺	428
		逓	3106
		釘	1667
	11	偵	138
		停	139
		第	2660
	12	堤	560
		幀	570
		提	591
		程	1190
		觝	1498
	13	碇	1202
		禎	1031
		艇	1365
		鼎	3585
	14	綴	1381
	15	締	1393
		鄭	1888
TEKI	8	的	1125
		迪	3076
	11	笛	2664
	14	嫡	680
		摘	694
		滌	696
		滴	705
		適	3160
	15	敵	1864
TEN	4	天	3442
	8	典	2627
		店	3085
	9	点	2084
	10	展	3111
	11	添	529
		転	1480
	12	奠	2132
		貼	1510
	13	殿	1792
	14	槙	1051
	19	顛	1843
	21	纏	1432
tenohira	12	掌	2602
tera	6	寺	2164
terasu	13	照	2827
tereru	13	照	2827
teru	6	旭	2977
	10	晃	2450
	12	瑛	999
		皓	1180
	13	照	2827
TETSU	8	迭	3077
	10	哲	2738
	13	鉄	1711
	14	綴	1381
	15	徹	726
		撤	738
TO	3	土	3403
	4	斗	2953
	6	吐	203
	7	図	3071
		杜	835
	9	度	3100
	10	徒	416
		途	3107
	11	都	1686
	12	渡	611
		登	2595
	13	塗	2841
	16	賭	1605
		頭	1604
to	2	十	3365
	4	戸	1930
to-	5	外	186
-to	2	人	3368
TŌ	2	刀	2926
	4	斗	2953
	5	冬	2157
	6	当	2177
		灯	825
	7	投	256
		杜	835
		豆	1943
	8	到	1264
		東	3568
		沓	2419
	9	逃	3095
	10	倒	124
		党	2581
		凍	129
		唐	3115
		島	3310
		桃	936
		桐	937
		納	1300
		討	1456
		透	3108
	11	悼	485
		盗	2670
		陶	546
	12	塔	561
		搭	592
		棟	991
		湯	612
		痘	3284
		登	2595
		筒	2680
		答	2681
		等	2682
		統	1352
		道	3134
	14	稲	1219
		読	1541
	15	踏	1587
	16	糖	1403
		頭	1604
	17	瞳	1237
		謄	1093
		蹈	1626
	18	藤	2382
		闘	3334
	19	禱	1253
	20	騰	1106
tō	2	十	3365
tobari	11	帳	473
tobasu	9	飛	3572
-tobasu	9	飛	3572
-tobi	13	跳	1532
tobira	12	扉	1955
toboshii	4	乏	1933
tobu	9	飛	3572
	12	翔	1357
	13	跳	1532
-todoke	8	届	3078
todokeru	8	届	3078
todokōru	13	滞	663
todoku	8	届	3078
todomaru	4	止	2941
	10	留	2580
todome	4	止	2941
todomeru	4	止	2941
	10	留	2580
togaru	6	尖	2176
toge	8	刺	1275
tōge	9	峠	358
togeru	12	遂	3138
togu	9	研	1132
toi	11	問	3320
tōi	13	遠	3150
tojiru	11	閉	3319
	14	綴	1381
tokasu	11	梳	964
	13	溶	664
		解	1517
	14	熔	1058
	16	融	1831
	18	鎔	1762
tokeru	13	溶	664
		解	1517
	14	熔	1058
	16	融	1831
	18	鎔	1762
toki	7	辰	2992
	9	秋	1139
	10	時	924
	11	斎	2115
toko	7	床	3067
	8	所	851
toko-	11	常	2590
tokoro	5	処	3031
	8	所	851
-tokoro	8	所	851
TOKU	10	匿	3011
		特	945
	11	得	477
	13	督	2796
	14	徳	684
		読	1541
	16	篤	2716
toku	11	梳	964
	13	溶	664
		解	1517
	14	説	1547
tomaru	4	止	2941
	8	泊	331
	10	留	2580
	11	停	139
tomeru	4	止	2941
	8	泊	331
	10	留	2580
	11	停	139
-tomeru	4	止	2941
	10	留	2580
tomi	12	富	2310

- 我 3548
- WAI [13]賄 1529
- waka- [8]若 2241
- wakai [8]若 2241
- wakareru [4]分 1972
  - [7]別 1117
- wakaru [4]分 1972
  - [7]判 1122
  - [13]解 1517
- wakasu [8]沸 329
- wakatsu [4]分 1972
  - [13]頒 1043
- wake [4]分 1972
  - [10]脇 952
  - [11]訳 1473
- wakeru [4]分 1972
  - [7]別 1117
- waki [10]脇 952
  - [12]傍 147
  - 腋 1004
- wakibasamu [9]挟 377
- wakimaeru [5]弁 2004
- WAKU [12]惑 2786
- waku [8]枠 866
  - 沸 329
  - [12]湧 615
- wameku [12]喚 550
- WAN [12]湾 613
  - 腕 1006
  - [22]彎 2918
- warabe [12]童 2130
- warau [10]笑 2646
- ware [7]吾 2407
  - 我 3548
- wareru [12]割 1816
- wari [12]割 1816
- waru [12]割 1816
- waru- [11]悪 2745
- warui [11]悪 2745
- wasureru [7]忘 2036
- wata [12]棉 988
  - [14]綿 1373
- watakushi [7]私 1115
- wataru [6]亘 1939
  - [8]弥 288
  - [12]渡 611
- -wataru [12]渡 611
- watashi [7]私 1115
- watasu [12]渡 611
- waza [7]技 248
  - [13]業 2612
- wazato [14]態 2847
- wazawai [7]災 2206
  - [13]禍 1030
- wazurau [11]患 2747
  - [13]煩 1022
- wazurawasu [13]煩 1022

Y

- YA [3]也 3406
  - [8]夜 2056
  - [9]耶 1283
  - [11]野 1485
- ya [2]八 3
  - [3]也 3406
  - [5]矢 2009
  - [8]弥 288
  - [9]哉 3294
  - 屋 3098
  - 耶 1283
  - [10]家 2273
- yabureru [10]破 1150
  - [11]敗 1476
- yaburu [10]破 1150
- yado [11]宿 2293
- yadoru [11]宿 2293
- yadosu [11]宿 2293
- yaiba [3]刃 2929
- yakara [15]輩 2807
- yakata [16]館 1748
- yakeru [12]焼 997
- yaki [12]焼 997
- yaki- [12]焼 997
- -yaki [12]焼 997
- yakko [5]奴 187
- YAKU [4]厄 2947
  - [7]役 244
  - [9]疫 3276
  - 約 1280
  - [10]益 2285
  - [11]訳 1473
  - 軛 1481
  - [16]薬 2375
  - [21]躍 1658
- yaku [12]焼 997
- yama [3]山 2940
- yamai [10]病 3277
- yameru [4]止 2941
  - [13]辞 1364
  - [15]罷 2617
- yami [17]闇 3332
- -yami [10]病 3277
- yamu [3]已 3377
  - [4]止 2941
  - [10]病 3277
- -yamu [4]止 2941
- yanagi [9]柳 899
- yaru [13]遣 3152
- yasashii [8]易 2411
  - [17]優 177
- yashiki [8]邸 1131
- yashinau [15]養 2365
- yashiro [7]社 840
- yasu [6]安 2171
  - [7]那 843
  - [10]悌 424
  - [13]靖 1208
  - 鳩 163
- yasui [6]安 2171
  - [8]易 2411
- yasumaru [6]休 52
  - 安 2171
- yasumeru [6]休 52
- yasumu [6]休 52
- yasuraka [6]安 2171
- yasushi [8]欣 852
  - [10]悌 424
  - [13]靖 1208
- yatou [12]雇 1956
  - [13]傭 160
- yatsu [2]八 3
  - [5]奴 187
- yattsu [2]八 3
- yawa [9]柔 2088
- yawara [9]柔 2088
- yawarageru [8]和 1130
- yawaragu [8]和 1130
- yawaraka [9]柔 2088
  - [11]軟 1479
- yawarakai [9]柔 2088
  - [11]軟 1479
- YO [3]与 3421
  - [4]予 1983
  - [7]余 2042
  - [13]誉 2502
  - 預 1042
- yo [5]世 3496
  - 代 30
  - 四 3044
  - [8]夜 2056
- YŌ [5]幼 191
  - 用 2976
  - [6]羊 2183
  - [9]洋 392
  - 要 2635
  - [10]容 2277
  - [11]庸 3128
  - [12]揚 593
  - 揺 594
  - 湧 615
  - 瑛 999
  - 葉 2321
  - 遥 3141
  - 陽 626
  - [13]傭 160
  - 溶 664
  - 瑶 1026
  - 腰 1036
  - 蓉 2337
  - [14]様 1052
  - 熔 1058
  - 踊 1558
  - [15]窯 2361
  - 養 2365
  - [16]擁 770
  - 謡 1597
  - [18]曜 1096
  - 鎔 1762
  - [24]鷹 3189
- yō [2]八 3
- yobu [8]呼 273
- yogoreru [6]汚 222
- yogosu [6]汚 222
- yoi [6]好 208
  - [7]良 3558
  - [10]宵 2276
  - [11]酔 1483
  - [12]善 2325
- -yoi [7]良 3558
- -yoke [10]除 456
- yokeru [16]避 3179
- yoko [15]横 1066
- yokoito [16]緯 1407
- yokoshima [8]邪 1124
- YOKU [3]弋 3422
  - [7]抑 257
  - [10]浴 445
  - [11]欲 1475
  - 翌 2668
  - [15]慾 2862
  - [17]翼 2720
- yome [13]嫁 635

-yomi [14]読 1541
yomigaeru [12]甦 3315
yomisuru [14]嘉 2340
yomu [12]詠 1500
[14]読 1541
yon [5]四 3044
yone [6]米 3529
-yori [11]寄 2291
yorokobasu [10]悦 418
[12]喜 2308
yorokobi [15]慶 3173
yorokobu [10]悦 418
[12]喜 2308
yoroshii [8]宜 2223
yoroshiku [8]宜 2223
yorozu [3]万 2936
yoru [5]由 3499
[6]因 3054
[8]依 84
夜 2056
拠 312
[11]寄 2291
yoseru [11]寄 2291
yoshi [4]允 1982
[5]由 3499
[6]伊 49
圭 2165
[7]甫 3549
[8]昌 2414
欣 852
[9]亮 2071
彦 3295
祐 915
[10]悌 424
桂 928
[11]彬 960
惟 481
[12]欽 1690
禄 1002
[13]睦 1199
禎 1031
[14]嘉 2340
[19]艶 1908
[20]厳 2386
馨 2879
yoshimi [14]嘉 2340
[15]誼 1571
yosoou [12]装 2685
yosu [4]止 2941
yotsu [5]四 3044
yottsu [5]四 3044

you [11]酔 1483
yowai [10]弱 1167
[17]齢 1895
yowamaru [10]弱 1167
yowameru [10]弱 1167
yowaru [10]弱 1167
YU [5]由 3499
[8]油 341
[12]喩 553
愉 582
猶 619
遊 3142
[16]諭 1598
輸 1607
[18]癒 3291
yu [12]湯 612
YŪ [2]又 3351
[4]友 2952
尤 3023
[5]右 2975
由 3499
[6]有 2983
[7]佑 74
邑 2190
酉 3544
[8]侑 91
油 341
[9]勇 2089
幽 3008
祐 915
[11]悠 2741
郵 1687
[12]游 614
湧 615
猶 619
裕 1195
遊 3142
雄 1008
[14]熊 2848
誘 1550
[15]憂 2145
[16]融 1831
[17]優 177
yū [3]夕 3387
yubi [9]指 378
yudaneru [8]委 2553
yue [9]故 1141
YUI [5]由 3499
[11]唯 463
惟 481
[15]遺 3166

yuka [7]床 3067
yuki [3]之 3420
[7]亨 2037
[8]侑 91
[10]晋 2656
[11]雪 2759
-yuki [6]行 212
yuku [6]行 212
[10]逝 3104
yume [13]夢 2336
yumi [3]弓 3383
yuragu [12]揺 594
yureru [12]揺 594
yuru [12]揺 594
yurugu [12]揺 594
yurui [15]緩 1389
yurumeru [15]緩 1389
yurumu [15]緩 1389
yurusu [11]許 1470
yuruyaka [15]緩 1389
yusaburu [12]揺 594
yusuburu [12]揺 594
yusuru [12]揺 594
yutaka [10]浩 438
[13]豊 2697
[18]穣 1250
yuu [12]結 1348
yuwaeru [12]結 1348
yuzuru [20]譲 1649

— Z —

ZA [7]坐 3547
[10]座 3116
ZAI [6]在 2984
[7]材 836
[10]剤 1669
財 1457
[13]罪 2610
-zakana [11]魚 2127
-zaki [9]咲 349
zama [14]様 1052
ZAN [10]残 943
[11]惨 483
斬 1482
[15]暫 2864
ZATSU [14]雑 1385
ZE [9]是 2436
ZEI [12]税 1191
[13]勢 2857
[14]説 1547
-zeki [14]関 3328
ZEN [6]全 2022
[9]前 2266
[12]善 2325
然 2782
[13]禅 1032
[14]漸 706
[18]繕 1423
zeni [14]銭 1725
zero [1]〇 3342
[13]零 2792
ZETSU [6]舌 2186
[12]絶 1353
ZŌ [10]造 3110
[11]曹 2746
[12]象 2134
[14]像 166
増 677
憎 687
雑 1385
[15]蔵 2364
[18]贈 1634
[19]臓 1102
-zoi [8]沿 328
ZOKU [9]俗 104
[11]族 958
[12]属 3145
[13]続 1362
賊 1530
[17]簇 2719
-zome [7]初 1116
[9]染 2572
ZON [6]存 2982
-zoroi [12]揃 590
ZU [4]手 3456
[7]図 3071
杜 835
豆 1943
[8]事 3567
[14]誦 1549
[16]頭 1604
zu [21]鶴 1850
ZUI [12]随 627
[13]瑞 1027
[19]髄 1842
-zuka [12]塚 556
-zukai [8]使 90
[13]遣 3152
-zukare [10]疲 3278
-zuke [5]付 31

RADICAL INDEX

HOW TO USE THE RADICAL INDEX

1. Format of Radical Index

For those familiar with the radical system, we have included the **Radical Index,** which lists the characters according to their traditional radicals and additional strokes. It is best not to use this index unless you are well acquainted with the traditional radical system. See **Appendix 6. The Radicals** for a description of the system and a detailed **Radical Chart.**

1. **Scope** The **Radical Index** lists all the main entry and reference entry characters. It does not list nonstandard forms, except for characters whose original radicals have been lost. To locate old or variant forms, use the **Pattern Index.**

2. **Format** The heading at the beginning of each section consists of the **radical number** and the **parent radical** in its full traditional form. **Variant forms** are given in parentheses only in cases where the difference between the parent and variant forms is so great as to be difficult to recognize. For example, Radical 64 手 (扌) includes the variant in parentheses but Radical 75 木, which has the very common left-side variant 木, does not since both forms are so similar that no confusion is likely to arise. The small numerals to the left of the character column indicate the stroke-count of the *nonradical* element; the numerals to the right are the **entry numbers.**

3. **Order of Entries** The radicals appear in order of increasing stroke-count and are numbered from 1 to 214 according to the traditional historical arrangement. The first character at the head of each section is always the parent radical in its traditional form. Characters sharing the same radical are listed in increasing order of the stroke-counts of their nonradical elements. The characters within a given stroke-count subsection are listed in alphabetical order of their principal *on* readings or, in cases where no *on* reading exists, their principal *kun* readings.

2. Instructions for Use

STEP 1	Determine the **radical** and **radical number** of your character: ⓐ Determine the radical. See **§ 4. How to Determine the Radical** below. ⓑ Determine the stroke-count of the radical. See **Appendix 2. How to Count Strokes.** ⓒ Determine the radical number using the **Quick Reference Radical Chart** on p. 1934. NOTE: If you have memorized the number of the radical in question, skip steps ①ⓑ and ①ⓒ.
STEP 2	Determine the stroke-count of the nonradical element. See **Appendix 2. How to Count Strokes.**
STEP 3	Turn to the section of the **Radical Index** which corresponds to your radical number.
STEP 4	Locate your character under the stroke-count of the nonradical element with the aid of the small numerals on the left of the character column. The main entry number appears to the right of the character.

Example: LOCATE THE CHARACTER ENTRY FOR 像.

STEP 1	Carrying out STEP 1 as described, we determine that the radical of 像 is the 2-stroke element 人 (亻), Radical No. 9.
STEP 2	Counting the strokes of the nonradical element 象 yields a stroke-count of 12.
STEP 3	Turn to the section headed "Radical 9 人 (亻)."
STEP 4	Under the nonradical stroke-count of 12 appears the character 像, entry number 166.

3. Cross-References

The simplification of characters that took place with the introduction of the Tōyō Kanji and Jōyō Kanji lists in the postwar period has resulted in the disappearance of the radical element from some characters. For example, 会 is traditionally classified under 日 (Radical 73) based on its old form 會, but 日 has completely disappeared from the simplified form 会. These "lost-radical" characters are listed under their traditional radicals, followed by the old form in parentheses. For example, the index entry for 会 appears at its traditional radical 日 (Radical 73):

会 (會) 2020°

In addition, the lost-radical characters are cross-referenced under another radical based on their simplified forms,[1] which is followed by the number of the traditional radical in square brackets. For example, 会 is cross-referenced under its new radical 人 (Radical 9), whereas traditionally it is classified under 日 (Radical 73):

会 [RAD. 73] 2020°

The entry numbers of all lost-radical characters, both at their traditional radicals and at their new radicals, are followed by a small superscript circle.

4. How to Determine the Radical

To determine which element of a character is the radical can be a laborious task. The following guidelines should be of help.

4.1 Radical Position The position of the radical within a character may be difficult to predict. A character may contain several radical elements, and to choose between them may require a knowledge of character etymology. 奮, for example, consists of 大, 隹, and 田, all of which are radicals. The general rule is: take the left radical in left-right characters (as 亻 in 休), the top radical in up-down characters (as 宀 in 完), and the enclosing radical in characters containing enclosures (as 广 in 広).

The **Important Radicals** chart below lists the most important radicals, classified by their position within the character. The radicals are shown in the form in which they occur most frequently. The position of many radicals is constant in relation to the rest of the character (though there are exceptions). These are classified in the chart below under the headings **left, right,** etc. The position of other radicals, classified under the heading **others,** is variable.

4.2 Important Radicals Memorizing the most important radicals and their numbers will greatly speed up the lookup process. Since most Japanese and Chinese character dictionaries follow the traditional radical system, users making extensive use of radical indexes will find it worthwhile to memorize the table below.

1. In selecting the new radical, we have followed 学研漢和大辞典 *gakken kanwa daijiten,* by 藤堂明保 *tōdō akiyasu,* and 常用漢和辞典 *jōyō kanwajiten,* by 石井庄司 *ishii shōji.*

Important Radicals

LEFT RADICALS ◧ 偏 *hen*

No.	Radical
9	亻
24	十
30	口
32	土
38	女
46	山
57	弓
60	彳
61	忄
64	扌
75	木
85	氵
86	火
93	牛
94	犭
96	王
112	石
113	礻
115	禾
119	米
120	糸
128	耳
130	月
137	舟
142	虫
145	衤
149	言
154	貝
157	足
159	車
164	酉
167	金
170	阝
184	食
187	馬
195	魚

RIGHT RADICALS ◨ 旁 *tsukuri*

No.	Radical
18	刂
26	卩
62	戈
66	攵
76	欠
163	阝
181	頁

TOP RADICALS ⬒ 冠 *kanmuri*

No.	Radical
8	亠
37	大
40	宀
46	山
116	穴
118	竹
122	罒
140	艹
173	雨

BOTTOM RADICALS ⬓ 脚 *ashi*

No.	Radical
10	儿
12	八
86	灬
154	貝

ENCLOSURES ◻ 囲い *kakoi*

No.	Radical
27	厂
31	囗
44	尸
53	广
104	疒
162	辶
169	門

OTHERS

No.	Radical
1	一
19	力
39	子
41	寸
50	巾
72	日
74	月
102	田
109	目
172	隹

4.3 Stroke Counting Since the characters within a given radical group are arranged in increasing order of the stroke-counts of their nonradical elements, it is important to learn how to count strokes accurately. Refer to **Appendix 2. How to Count Strokes** on p. 1734.

4.4 Variant Forms Radicals may occur in their unabbreviated traditional forms, or in an abbreviated form. For example, 人 (Radical 9) appears in its complete form in 仄, but in its abbreviated form of 亻 in 休. Some radicals, like 艸 (Radical 140) always appear in their abbreviated forms (in this case 艹 or 艹). To use the **Radical Index** effectively, one needs the ability to identify the parent radical from its variant forms. See the **Radical Chart** on p. 1772 for full information on standard forms and their variants.

4.5 Lost Radicals Since the radicals of some characters are based on their old forms, a knowledge of the latter may sometimes be necessary in order to identify the radical. See § 3. **Cross-References** above for details on how this problem is overcome in this dictionary.

4.6 Quick Reference Radical Chart This chart, which begins on the next page, helps you use the **Radical Index** more effectively by enabling you to quickly look up the radical number of your radical. If you have memorized the number of the radical in question, proceed to the **Radical Index** directly; otherwise, the quickest way to look up a character is to determine its radical number with the aid of this chart.

1. **Format** The left part of each column gives the **radical number** in boldface; the right part shows the **radical** in its **standard** or **parent form.**

2. **Order of Entries** The radicals and their variants are listed in order of increasing stroke-count of their standard forms. These are numbered consecutively from 1 to 214 according to the traditional historical arrangement. When a radical has more than one form, the standard form is given first, followed by all its variants.

3. **Cross-References** Some variants have a different stroke-count from their standard forms. Such variants are cross-referenced under their respective correct stroke-counts. The cross-references appear at the end of a given stroke-count section, and are distinguished by lightface radical numbers enclosed in square brackets. For example, Radical 162 has the six-stroke parent form 辵, one three-stroke variant 辶, and one four-stroke variant 辶. All three forms are listed together under 162, but the variants also appear at the end of the three- and four-stroke sections respectively.

QUICK REFERENCE RADICAL CHART

1 STROKE

1 一
2 丨
3 丶
4 丿 ノ
5 乙 乚
6 亅

2 STROKES

7 二
8 亠
9 人 亻 𠆢
10 儿
11 入
12 八 丷
13 冂
14 冖
15 冫
16 几 八
17 凵
18 刀 刂
19 力
20 勹
21 匕
22 匚
23 匸
24 十 ⺊
25 卜 ト
26 卩 㔾
27 厂
28 厶
29 又

3 STROKES

30 口 口
31 囗
32 土 士
33 士
34 夂
35 夊
36 夕
37 大
38 大 女 女
39 子
40 宀
41 寸
42 小 ⺌ ⺍
43 尢
44 尸
45 屮
46 山 山
47 巛 川
48 工 工
49 己 巳
50 巾
51 干
52 幺
53 广
54 廴 廴
55 廾
56 弋
57 弓
58 ヨ 彐 彑
59 彡
60 彳
[61] 忄
[64] 扌
[85] 氵
[94] 犭
[140] 艹
[162] 辶
[163] 阝
[170] 阝

4 STROKES

61 心 忄 ⺗
62 戈
63 戶 戸
64 手 扌
65 支 攴
66 攵 文
67 文
68 斗
69 斤
70 方
71 无 旡 旡
72 日 日
73 曰
74 月 月
75 木 木
76 欠
77 止
78 歹
79 殳
80 毋 毌 母
81 比
82 毛
83 氏
84 气
85 水 氵 氺
86 火 灬
87 爪 爫 爫
88 父
89 爻 爻
90 爿
91 片
92 牙 牙
93 牛 牜
94 犬 犭
[96] 王
[113] 礻
[122] 罒
[125] 耂
[130] 月
[140] 艹
[162] 辶

5 STROKES

95 玄
96 玉 王
97 瓜
98 瓦
99 甘
100 生
101 用
102 田
103 疋 ⺪
104 疒
105 癶
106 白
107 皮
108 皿
109 目
110 矛
111 矢 矢
112 石 石
113 示 礻 礻
114 禸
115 禾 禾
116 穴 穴
117 立 立
[71] 无
[80] 母
[85] 氺
[92] 牙
[122] 罒
[145] 衤

6 STROKES

118 竹 ⺮
119 米 米

No.	Radical
120	糸 糹
121	缶
122	网 罒 ⺳
123	羊 ⺶ ⺷
124	羽 羽
125	老 耂
126	而
127	耒 耒
128	耳 耳
129	聿
130	肉 月
131	臣 臣
132	自
133	至
134	臼 臼
135	舌 舌
136	舛 舛
137	舟 舟
138	艮 艮
139	色 色
140	艸 艹 艹 ⺾
141	虍
142	虫 虫
143	血 血
144	行 行
145	衣 衤
146	襾 覀 西
7 STROKES	
147	見
148	角 角
149	言 訁
150	谷 谷
151	豆 豆
152	豕 豕
153	豸
154	貝 貝
155	赤 赤
156	走 走
157	足 ⻊
158	身 身
159	車 車
160	辛 辛
161	辰
162	辵 ⻌ ⻌
163	邑 ⻏
164	酉 酉
165	釆 釆
166	里 里
[131]	臣
[134]	臼
[136]	舛
[168]	镸
[199]	麦
8 STROKES	
167	金 釒
168	長 镸
169	門
170	阜 ⻖
171	隶
172	隹
173	雨 ⻗
174	靑 青
175	非
[184]	飠
[210]	斉
9 STROKES	
176	面
177	革 革
178	韋 韋
179	韭
180	音 音
181	頁
182	風 風
183	飛
184	食 飠 食 食
185	首
186	香
10 STROKES	
187	馬 馬
188	骨 骨
189	高
190	髟
191	鬥
192	鬯
193	鬲 鬲
194	鬼 鬼
[178]	韋
[212]	竜
11 STROKES	
195	魚 魚
196	鳥 鳥
197	鹵
198	鹿
199	麥 麦 麦
200	麻 麻 麻 麻
[201]	黄
[203]	黒
[213]	亀
12 STROKES	
201	黃 黄
202	黍
203	黑 黒
204	黹
[211]	歯 歯
13 STROKES	
205	黽
206	鼎
207	鼓
208	鼠 鼠
14 STROKES	
209	鼻 鼻 鼻
210	齊 斉
15 STROKES	
211	齒 齒 齒 歯
16 STROKES	
212	龍 竜
213	龍 龜 龜 亀
17 STROKES	
214	龠
18 STROKES	
[213]	龜

RADICAL INDEX

1 STROKE

RADICAL 1 一

RADICAL 2 丨

RADICAL 3 丶

RADICAL 4 丿

RADICAL 5 乙(乚)

RADICAL 6 亅

2 STROKES

RADICAL 7 二

RADICAL 8 亠 lid

RADICAL 9 人(亻)

偏 133
健 134
偲 135
側 137
停 139
偵 138
10 備 146
傍 147
偉 148
傘 2131
11 働 153
傾 154
傑 155
債 156
催 157
傷 158
僧 159
傭 160
12 僕 164
僚 165
像 166
13 儀 169
舗 [RAD. 135] 1735°
億 170
14 儒 174
15 償 176
優 177
20 儼 178

RADICAL 10 儿

0 儿 4
2 元 1929
允 1982
3 兄 2154
4 兆 225
充 2014
光 2391
兇 2392
先 2394
5 児 2546
克 2046
6 免 2067
8 党 [RAD. 203] 2581°
12 兢 1566

RADICAL 11 入

0 入 3370
2 内(內) 3466°
4 全(全) 2022°
6 両(兩) 3518°

RADICAL 12 八(丷)

0 八 2928
八 3
丷 2
2 公 1974
六 1965
4 共 2393
5 兵 2551
6 具 2552
其 2629
典 2627
8 兼 2286

RADICAL 13 冂

0 冂 3352
2 円 [RAD. 31] 2955°
内 [RAD. 11] 3466°
3 冊 3483
4 再 3519
7 冒(冐) 2434°

RADICAL 14 冖

0 冖 3353
2 冗 1976
3 写 [RAD. 40] 2000°
7 冠 2081

RADICAL 15 冫

0 冫 1923
3 冬 2157
5 冴 79
冷 80
8 准 127
凌 128
凍 129
14 凝 175

RADICAL 16 几

0 几 3349
⺇ 3354
1 凡 2938
3 処 [RAD. 141] 3031°

RADICAL 17 凵

0 凵 3364
2 凶 2961
3 凹 3482
出 3498
凸 3486
6 函 3001

RADICAL 18 刀(刂)

0 刀 2926
刂 1
1 刃 2929
2 分 1972
刈 28
切 27
3 刊 190
4 刑 830
列 824
5 別 1117
判 1122
利 1114
初 1116
6 券 2630
刻 1267
刷 1273
制 1274
刺 1275
到 1264
7 剋 3305
削 1448
則 1444
前 2266
8 剖 1670
剛 1673
剣 1672
帰 [RAD. 77] 130°
剤 1669
9 副 1776
剰 1779
剪 2306
10 割 1816
創 1815
11 剿 1858
12 劃 1887
13 劇 1904

RADICAL 19 力

0 力 3371
3 加 38
功 189
4 劣 2395
5 努 2547
助 1121
励 1119
労 2548
6 劾 1266
効 1265
7 勅 1451
勇 2089
8 勉 3318
9 動 1778
勘 1777
務 1173
10 募 2316
勤 1818
勝 1005
11 勧 1857
勢 2857
13 勲 2869

RADICAL 20 勹

0 勹 3375
1 勺 2933
2 勾 2942
勿 2943
匁 3465
匂 2944
3 包 2966

RADICAL 21 匕

0 匕 2925
2 化 21
3 北 197

RADICAL 22 匚

0 匚 3355
4 匡 2989
匠 2990

RADICAL 23 匸

0 匸 3356
2 匹 2962
区 2963
5 医 [RAD. 164] 2993°
8 匿 3011

RADICAL 24 十

0 十 3365
十 3366
1 千 3411
2 午 1984
廿 3449
升 3455
3 半 3501
6 協 93
卒 2055
卓 2064
7 卑 2642
南 2082

4 STROKES

恰 368
恨 369
恐 2650
恭 2459
恩 2655
恋 2098
息 2647
7 悪 2745
悦 418
悟 419
悖 420
患 2747
悩 421
悧 422
悄 423
悌 424
悠 2741
8 悲 2775
惟 481
情 482
惨 483
惜 484
惣 2780
悼 485
惇 486
惑 2786
9 愛 2492
惰 579
愚 2834
意 2136
惹 2493
慈 2339
感 2835
慌 580
惶 581
愁 2829
想 2828
愉 582
10 慕 2353
慨 641
慄 642
慎 643
態 2847
11 慰 2867
慣 685
慶 3173
慧 2810
慢 686
慮 3266
慾 2862
憂 2145
憎 687
12 憤 730
憩 2890
憲 2368
憐 731
13 懐 763
憾 764
懇 2899
憶 765
14 懲 2910
16 懸 2915

RADICAL 62 戈

0 戈 3462
2 戌 3535
成 3537
3 我 3548
戒 3204
8 戟 1696
9 戦 1787
10 截 3301
11 戯 1875
14 戴 3302

RADICAL 63 戶

0 戶 2950
戸 1930
3 戻 1942
4 房 1946
所 851
5 扁 3005
6 扇 1950
8 扉 1955

RADICAL 64 手(扌)

0 手 3456
才 3410
扌 3414
2 打 193
払 194
3 扣 216
扱 217
4 抜 246
扶 247
技 248
把 249
批 250
抒 251
抗 252
折 253
承 16
抄 254
択 255
投 256
抑 257
5 拇 301
抽 302
拝 303
拍 304
披 305
抱 306
拋 307
拐 308
拡 309
拘 310
拗 312
拒 311
抹 313
押 314
拙 315
招 316
拓 317
担 318
抵 319
6 按 371
挑 372
拷 373
持 374
挌 375
括 376
挙 2456
挟 377
指 378
拾 379
7 挽 427
挺 428
捕 429
振 430
捜 432
挿 431
捉 433
8 描 488
掩 489
排 490
捧 491
授 492
掛 493
掲 494
控 495
掘 496
据 497
掠 498
採 499
接 500
捨 501
掌 2602
措 502
掃 503
推 504
探 505
9 握 585
援 586
換 587
揮 589
揆 588
揃 590
提 591
搭 592
揚 593
揺 594
10 搏 646
搬 647
携 648
搾 649
摂 650
損 651
11 撃 2863
摑 690
摩 3175
摸 691
摧 692
摺 693
摘 694
12 撲 733
撥 734
撈 735
撒 736
撮 737
撤 738
13 擅 768
操 769
擁 770
14 擬 788
擱 789
擦 790
擡 791
19 攣 2919

RADICAL 65 支

0 支 1980
支 1979

	棉	988
	棲	989
	森	2475
	植	990
	棟	991
9	楓	1015
	楽	2826
	業	2612
	楯	1016
	棄	2137
	極	1017
	楠	1018
	楼	1019
10	概	1048
	構	1049
	模	1050
	槙	1051
	様	1052
11	標	1064
	権	1065
	横	1066
	槽	1067
12	樹	1075
	機	1076
	橘	1077
	橋	1078
16	欄	1103

RADICAL 76 欠

0	欠	1987
2	次	54
4	欣	852
	欧	887
7	欲	1475
8	欺	1703
	款	1700
	欽	1690
9	歇	1788
10	歌	1825
11	歓	1867
	歎	1869

RADICAL 77 止

0	止	2941
1	正	3484
2	此	823
4	武	3210
	歩	2416
9	歳	2490
10	歴	3019
14	帰(歸)	130°

RADICAL 78 歹

0	歹	3445
2	死	3521
4	歿	868
6	殉	941
	殊	942
	残	943
8	殖	994

RADICAL 79 殳

0	殳	1978
4	殴	886
5	段	1144
6	殺	1324
7	殻	1490
9	殿	1792
	毀	1791
11	毅	1866

RADICAL 80 毋

0	毋	3446
	毌	3447
1	母	3475
2	毎	2034
4	毒	2428

RADICAL 81 比

0	比	26

RADICAL 82 毛

0	毛	3453

RADICAL 83 氏

0	氏	2951
1	民	3036

RADICAL 84 气

0	气	1986
2	気	3194

RADICAL 85 水(氵)

0	水	10
	氺	37
	氵	1925
1	永	1937
	氷	39
2	汁	195
	求	3550
3	池	218
	汎	219
	汗	220
	江	221
	汚	222
	汐	223
4	没	260
	沈	261
	沖	262
	決	263
	汽	264
	汲	265
	沙	266
	沢	267
	沓	2419
5	注	325
	泥	326
	泳	327
	沿	328
	沸	329
	波	330
	泊	331
	泌	332
	法	333
	泡	334
	治	335
	河	336
	況	337
	泣	338
	泉	2567
	沼	339
	沮	340
	泰	2583
	油	341
6	洞	380
	派	381
	浄	382
	洵	383
	海	384
	活	385
	洪	386
	洸	387
	浅	389
	洗	388
	津	390
	洲	391
	洋	392
7	浮	435
	浜	436
	浦	437
	浩	438
	浪	439
	涙	440
	流	441
	浸	442
	消	443
	浴	445
8	液	511
	涯	512
	渋	513
	淳	514
	渇	515
	渓	516
	涸	517
	淆	518
	混	519
	淋	520
	涼	521
	済	522
	清	523
	深	524
	渚	525
	渉	526
	淑	527
	淡	528
	添	529
9	渥	600
	減	601
	滋	602
	渦	603
	湖	604
	港	605
	渾	606
	満	607
	温	608
	湿	609
	測	610
	渡	611
	湯	612
	湾	613
	游	614
	湧	615
10	漠	655
	源	656
	準	2856
	漢	657
	滑	658
	溝	659
	滅	660
	滝	661
	溜	662
	滞	663
	溶	664
11	滌	696

RADICAL 103 疋

0 疋 3480
⺪ 3489
7 疎 1178
疏 1179
9 疑 1565

RADICAL 104 疒

0 疒 3512
4 疫 3276
5 病 3277
疲 3278
疾 3279
症 3280
6 疵 3282
7 痢 3283
痘 3284
痛 3285
8 痴 3286
12 癈 3287
療 3288
13 癖 3290
癒 3291

RADICAL 105 癶

0 癶 40
4 発 2565
7 登 2595

RADICAL 106 白

0 白 3493
1 百 2026
3 的 1125
4 皆 2445
皇 2566
7 皓 1180

RADICAL 107 皮

0 皮 3037

RADICAL 108 皿

0 皿 3474
4 盆 2079
5 益 2285
6 盛 2675
盗 2670
8 盟 2794
9 尽（盡） 3050°
10 盤 2851
監 2852

RADICAL 109 目

0 目 3043
3 直 2932
盲 2053
4 冒 [RAD. 13] 2434°
盾 3006
看 3220
県 [RAD. 120] 2641°
省 2449
相 900
5 眠 1147
真 2111
6 眸 1170
眺 1171
眼 1172
8 睦 1199
睡 1200
督 2796
12 瞳 1237
瞭 1238
13 瞬 1247

RADICAL 110 矛

0 矛 2008

RADICAL 111 矢

0 矢 2009
3 知 1127
5 矩 1148
7 短 1182
12 矯 1241

RADICAL 112 石

0 石 2971
4 研 1132
砂 1133
砕 1134
5 破 1150
砲 1151
6 砦 2671
7 硬 1183
硫 1184
硝 1185
8 碍 1201
碁 2699
碇 1202
9 碧 2836
碑 1213
磁 1214
10 磐 2850
確 1228
11 磨 3181
12 磯 1242
礁 1243
13 礎 1248
15 礦 1256

RADICAL 113 示（礻）

0 示 1936
礻 3469
1 礼 818
3 社 840
祀 1128
4 祈 875
祉 876
5 神 912
祝 913
祖 914
祐 915
6 票 2669
祭 2672
祥 948
8 禁 2795
禄 1002
9 福 1029
禍 1030
禎 1031
禅 1032
11 禦 2870
14 禱 1253

RADICAL 114 禸

0 禸 3470

RADICAL 115 禾

0 禾 3503
2 私 1115
秀 2545
4 秒 1137
科 1138
秋 1139
5 秩 1158
秘 1159
称 1160
租 1161
6 移 1177
7 稀 1189
程 1190
税 1191
8 稚 1206
稔 1207
9 穀 1824
種 1218
稲 1219
10 稼 1230
稿 1231
穂 1232
11 穎 1612
穏 1235
積 1236
13 穣 1250
穫 1251

RADICAL 116 穴

0 穴 2161
穴 2159
⺳ 2160
2 究 2203
3 空 2227
突 2230
4 穿 2251
窃 2253
6 窒 2288
窓 2294
8 窟 2328
9 窪 2348
10 窮 2358
窯 2361

RADICAL 117 立

0 立 1992
5 並（竝） 2246°
6 章 2117
7 童 2130
9 竪 2837
端 1221
15 競 1847

6 STROKES

RADICAL 118 竹（⺮）

0 竹 228
⺮ 229
4 笑 2646
5 第 2660
符 2661
笠 2662
笹 2663
笛 2664
6 筆 2677

- 裸 1211
- 製 2803
- 裳 2615
- 9 複 1222
- 褒 2144
- 10 褪 1234
- 13 襟 1252
- 15 襤 1257
- 16 襲 2917

RADICAL 146 襾

- 0 襾 3522
- 西 3520
- 覀 3523
- 3 要 2635
- 12 覆 2726
- 13 覇 2730

7 STROKES

RADICAL 147 見

- 0 見 2544
- 4 規 978
- 視 972
- 5 覚 2604
- 9 親 1799
- 10 覧 2854
- 11 観 1880

RADICAL 148 角

- 0 角 2047
- 5 觝 1498
- 6 解 1517
- 触 1518

RADICAL 149 言

- 0 言 1941
- 2 計 1441
- 訂 1442
- 3 訊 1452
- 記 1453
- 訓 1454
- 託 1455
- 討 1456
- 4 訪 1468
- 訣 1469
- 許 1470
- 設 1471
- 訟 1472
- 訳 1473
- 5 註 1499
- 詠 1500
- 評 1501
- 詐 1502
- 詞 1503
- 診 1504
- 証 1506
- 詔 1505
- 訴 1507
- 6 該 1519
- 詭 1520
- 詰 1521
- 誇 1522
- 誠 1523
- 試 1525
- 詩 1524
- 詳 1526
- 話 1527
- 誉 2502
- 7 読 1541
- 語 1543
- 誤 1542
- 誨 1544
- 誡 1545
- 認 1546
- 誓 2754
- 説 1547
- 誌 1548
- 誦 1549
- 誘 1550
- 8 調 1567
- 諾 1568
- 談 1569
- 謁 1570
- 誼 1571
- 誹 1572
- 課 1573
- 論 1574
- 諒 1575
- 請 1576
- 諸 1577
- 誰 1578
- 誕 1579
- 9 謀 1593
- 諷 1594
- 謂 1595
- 諮 1596
- 謡 1597
- 諭 1598
- 10 謙 1617
- 謹 1618
- 講 1619
- 謝 1620
- 謄 1093
- 11 謬 1631
- 謳 1632
- 12 譜 1637
- 警 2893
- 譏 1638
- 識 1639
- 13 議 1647
- 護 1648
- 譬 2903
- 譲 1649
- 16 変(變) 2069°
- 19 讃 1665

RADICAL 150 谷

- 0 谷 2043

RADICAL 151 豆

- 0 豆 1943
- 6 豊 2697

RADICAL 152 豕

- 0 豕 3543
- 4 豚 976
- 5 象 2134
- 7 豪 2140
- 9 予(豫) 1983°

RADICAL 153 豸

- 0 豸 2401
- 7 貌 1556

RADICAL 154 貝

- 0 貝 2543
- 2 負 2091
- 貞 2083
- 3 貢 2281
- 財 1457
- 4 販 1477
- 貧 2123
- 貨 2465
- 貫 2460
- 責 2467
- 5 買 2598
- 貿 2601
- 貯 1509
- 賀 2599
- 費 2607
- 貴 2606
- 弐(貳) 3195°
- 貸 2600
- 貼 1510
- 6 賃 2694
- 資 2695
- 賄 1529
- 賊 1530
- 8 売(賣) 2196°
- 賠 1582
- 賦 1583
- 賓 2357
- 賛 2809
- 賤 1584
- 賜 1585
- 質 2808
- 賞 2618
- 9 賢 2839
- 頼 1615
- 賭 1605
- 10 購 1624
- 11 贈 1634

RADICAL 155 赤

- 0 赤 2193
- 4 赦 1478
- 7 赫 1557

RADICAL 156 走

- 0 走 2194
- 赱 2195
- 2 赴 3303
- 3 起 3307
- 赳 3308
- 5 超 3313
- 越 3314
- 8 趣 3317

RADICAL 157 足

- 0 足 2188
- 𧾷 2191
- 5 距 1511
- 6 跳 1532
- 路 1533
- 跡 1534
- 践 1535
- 7 踊 1558
- 8 踏 1587
- 10 蹈 1626
- 11 蹟 1635
- 12 蹶 1643

13 躁 1652
14 躍 1658

RADICAL 158 身

0 身 3553

RADICAL 159 車

0 車 3552
2 軍 2080
軌 1445
3 軒 1459
4 軟 1479
転 1480
軛 1481
5 軸 1514
軽 1515
6 較 1536
載 3300
7 輔 1559
8 輩 2807
輝 1402
輪 1589
輛 1590
9 輯 1606
輸 1607
10 轄 1627
15 轢 1662

RADICAL 160 辛

0 辛 2038
6 辞 1364
9 辨 1609

RADICAL 161 辰

0 辰 2992
3 辱 2736
6 農 2698

RADICAL 162 辵(辶)

0 辵 1945
辶 1926
⻌ 1932
1 辷 3191
2 辺 3029
込 3030
辻 3192
3 迅 3046
迄 3201
4 迎 3059
返 3060
近 3061
5 迫 3074
述 3075
迪 3076
迭 3077
6 逆 3091
迷 3092
送 3093
退 3094
逃 3095
追 3096
7 逐 3102
連 3103
逝 3104
速 3105
逓 3106
途 3107
透 3108
通 3109
造 3110
8 逸 3120
進 3121
週 3122
逮 3123
9 遅 3133
道 3134
遇 3135
遍 3136
過 3137
遂 3138
達 3139
運 3140
遥 3141
遊 3142
10 遠 3150
違 3151
遣 3152
遡 3257
11 遮 3158
遭 3159
適 3160
12 遺 3166
遵 3167
遼 3168
選 3169
遷 3170
13 避 3179
還 3180

RADICAL 163 邑(阝)

0 邑 2190
阝 3398
4 邦 847
那 843
5 邪 1124
邸 1131
6 郁 1288
郊 1286
郎 1289
7 郡 1466
8 部 1676
郭 1678
郷 549
都 1686
郵 1687
11 鄙 1862
12 鄭 1888

RADICAL 164 西

0 酉 3544
3 配 1460
酌 1461
酒 444
4 酔 1483
5 酢 1516
6 酪 1538
酬 1539
7 酵 1561
酷 1562
酸 1563
8 醋 1591
10 醜 1629
11 医(醫) 2993°
12 醗 1645
13 醸 1654
醵 1655

RADICAL 165 釆

0 釆 3555
4 釈 1484

RADICAL 166 里

0 里 3542
2 重 3573
4 野 1485
5 量 2471

8 STROKES

RADICAL 167 金

0 金 2057
2 釜 2107
針 1666
釘 1667
3 釣 1674
4 鈑 1688
鈍 1689
5 鉛 1707
鉢 1708
鉱 1709
鈴 1710
鉄 1711
6 鉾 1720
銅 1721
銀 1722
銃 1723
銘 1724
銭 1725
銑 1726
銓 1727
7 鋳 1729
鋭 1730
鋏 1731
銷 1732
8 錠 1737
錦 1738
錮 1739
鋼 1740
錬 1741
録 1742
錯 1743
錘 1744
9 鍋 1752
鍵 1753
鍼 1754
鍛 1755
10 鎮 1759
鎌 1760
鎖 1761
鎔 1762
11 鏡 1766
12 鐘 1769
15 鑑 1773
20 鑿 2924

RADICAL 168 長

0 長 2556
镸 2550

RADICAL 169 門

0 門 888
3 閉 3319

PATTERN INDEX

The key to using this dictionary effectively is the **Pattern Index,** which allows you to quickly locate a character from its geometrical pattern. This index lists all the entries of the dictionary, including nonstandard forms and cross-reference entries.

The format of the index is described in detail in **§ 2.7 Pattern Index. Incorrect locations** are indicated by the superscript symbols ^{p}, ^{s}, and ^{ps} and are followed by cross-references to the correct locations (see **§ 2.6 Cross-References** for details). The order of entries is exactly the same as that of the character entries in the body of the dictionary (see **§ 2.5 Classification Scheme**).

Detailed instructions for using the index are given in **§ 3.1 SKIP Method.** The gist of the SKIP Method is as follows:

1. Determine the **SKIP number** of your character.
2. Determine the **entry number** by locating your character in the **Pattern Index**. Use the **subsection guides** and **subgroup guides.**
3. Locate your character entry from the entry number.

All section numbers above refer to SYSTEM OF KANJI INDEXING BY PATTERNS beginning on p. 106a.

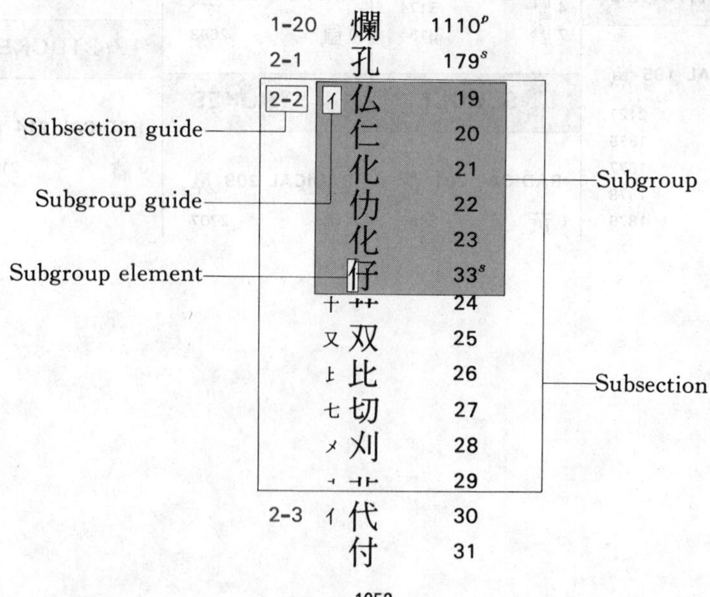

PATTERN INDEX

◧1 LEFT-RIGHT

		抗	252
		折	253
		抄	254
		択	255
		投	256
		抑	257
		技	258
		扱	259
		拒	311[s]
		扱	217[s]
	氵	没	260
		沈	261
		沖	262
		決	263
		汽	264
		汲	265
		沙	266
		沢	267
		没	268
		汚	222[s]
		注	342[s]
	犭	狂	269
	阝	防	270
		阪	271
	丬	状	272
3-5	口	呼	273
		味	274
	土	坪	275
		坪	276
	女	姆	277
		妹	278
		姓	279
		姉	280
		始	281
		姊	282
	子	孤	283
	山	岬	284
		岨	285
	巾	帖	286
	弓	弦	287
		弥	288
		弧	289
	彳	彼	290
		径	291
		往	292
		征	293
		彽	294
		往	295
	忄	怖	296
		怪	297
		怜	298
		性	299
		怜	300
	扌	拇	301
		抽	302
		拝	303
		拍	304
		披	305
		抱	306
		抛	307
		拐	308
		拡	309
		拘	310
		拒	311
		拠	312
		抹	313
		押	314
		拙	315
		招	316
		拓	317
		担	318
		抵	319
		抜	320
		拂	321
		抱	322
		拐	323
		拒	324
	氵	注	325
		泥	326
		泳	327
		沿	328
		沸	329
		波	330
		泊	331
		泌	332
		法	333
		泡	334
		治	335
		河	336
		況	337
		泣	338
		沼	339
		沮	340
		油	341
		注	342
		沿	343
		泡	344
	犭	狗	345
	阝	阿	346
		附	347
		阻	348
3-6	口	咲	349
		咲	350
	土	垣	351
		城	352
	女	姻	353
		姫	354
		姙	355
	子	孤	356
	山	峡	357
		峠	358
	干	形	359
	弓	弧	360
	彳	後	361

	埼	466
	堀	467
	培	468
女	婦	469
	婚	470
	婦	471
	娯	405^{s}
山	崎	472
巾	帳	473
弓	張	474
	強	475
彳	術	476
	得	477
	御	478
	従	479
	術	480
忄	惟	481
	情	482
	惨	483
	惜	484
	悼	485
	惇	486
	情	487
扌	描	488
	掩	489
	排	490
	捧	491
	授	492
	掛	493
	掲	494
	控	495
	掘	496
	据	497
	掠	498
	採	499
	接	500
	捨	501
	措	502

	掃	503
	推	504
	探	505
	控	506
	採	507
	接	508
	捨	509
	掃	510
	挽	427^{s}
	插	598^{s}
	揷	599^{s}
氵	液	511
	涯	512
	渋	513
	淳	514
	渇	515
	渓	516
	涸	517
	淆	518
	混	519
	淋	520
	涼	521
	済	522
	清	523
	深	524
	渚	525
	渉	526
	淑	527
	淡	528
	添	529
	淨	530
	涙	531
	清	532
	淺	533
	添	534
	渡	611^{s}
	游	614^{s}
犭	猫	535

	猪	536
	猛	537
	猟	538
阝	陪	539
	陳	540
	陰	541
	険	542
	陸	543
	陵	544
	隆	545
	陶	546
	陪	547
	陥	548
	隅	623^{s}
	随	627^{s}
亻	脩條	⇒◧2-9^{p}
亻	悠	2741^{p}
糸	郷	549
3-9 口	喚	550
	喫	551
	喰	552
	喩	553
	喝	554
	喫	555
土	塚	556
	塀	557
	場	558
	堪	559
	堤	560
	塔	561
	堺	562
	壻	563
女	媒	564
	媚	565
	婿	566
川	順	18^{p}
工	項	567
巾	帽	568

幅 569
幀 570
帽 571
弓 弾 572
强 573
彡 須 574
彳 復 575
街 576
御 577
循 578
忄 惰 579
慌 580
惶 581
愉 582
惱 583
愉 584
扌 握 585
援 586
換 587
揆 588
揮 589
揄 590
提 591
搭 592
揚 593
揺 594
描 595
援 596
掲 597
揷 598
插 599
捜 652[s]
氵 渥 600
減 601
滋 602
渦 603
湖 604
港 605

渾 606
満 607
温 608
湿 609
測 610
渡 611
湯 612
湾 613
游 614
湧 615
渇 616
港 617
渚 618
犭 猶 619
猫 620
猪 621
猶 622
阝 隅 623
階 624
隊 625
陽 626
随 627
隆 628
隊 629
纟 郷 673[s]
3-10 口 嘆 630
土 塩 631
塊 632
塚 633
塔 634
女 嫁 635
嫌 636
媾 637
嫌 638
彳 微 639
徴 640
忄 慨 641
慄 642

慎 643
慌 644
愼 645
扌 搏 646
搬 647
携 648
搾 649
摂 650
損 651
捜 652
搭 653
搖 654
摸 691[s]
止 雌 1055[s]
氵 漠 655
源 656
漢 657
滑 658
溝 659
滅 660
滝 661
溜 662
滞 663
溶 664
滋 665
渓 666
溝 667
溫 668
滿 709[s]
犭 猿 669
阝 隙 670
隔 671
隔 672
纟 郷 673
3-11 口 鳴 674
嘆 675
土 境 676
増 677

		擱	789
		擦	790
		擡	791
		擴	800[s]
	氵	濠	792
		濯	793
		濱	794
		濟	795
		濕	796
		濯	797
		濫	801[s]
	犭	獲	798
	阝	隱	799
3-15	扌	擴	800
	氵	濫	801
	犭	獵	802
3-16	土	壞	803
	忄	懷	804
	氵	瀕	805
		瀨	806
		瀝	807
		瀨	808
		瀧	809
3-17	土	壤	810
	女	孃	811
3-18	扌	攜	812
		攝	813
3-20		黴	814
3-21		囑	815
3-22		灣	816
4-1	木	札	817
	礻	礼	818
4-2	木	朴	819
		机	820
		朽	821
		杈	822
	止	此	823
	歹	列	824
	火	灯	825
	牙	邪	838[s]
	牛	牝	826
	月	肌	827
	冄	那	843[s]
	𠂎	印	828
	𠂎	印	829
	开	刑	830
	丰	邦	847[s]
4-3	文	対	831
	木	杉	832
		杓	833
		村	834
		杜	835
		材	836
		朽	821[s]
	爿	壯	837
	牙	邪	838
	牛	牡	839
	礻	社	840
	月	肝	841
		肛	842
	冄	那	843
	冊	那	844
	𠂎	臼	845
	开	形	846
	丰	邦	847
	丰	邦	848
	卯	卵	849
4-4	戶	所	850
	戸	所	851
	斤	欣	852
	方	放	853
		於	854
	日	明	855
		明	856
	木	杯	857
		板	858
		枚	859
		枅	860
		林	861
		析	862
		枝	863
		松	864
		枢	865
		枠	866
		松	867
		柱	902[s]
	歹	歿	868
	火	炉	869
		炊	870
	爿	狀	871
	片	版	872
	牛	牧	873
		物	874
	礻	祈	875
		祉	876
	月	肪	877
		服	878
		肥	879
		朋	880
		股	881
		肢	882
		肺	883
	月	服	884
		朋	885
	区	殴	886
		欧	887
	門	門	888
	非	非	889
4-5	手	拜	890
	方	施	891
	日	映	892
		昨	893
		昭	894
		旺	895

	木	柱	896
		柄	897
		枯	898
		柳	899
		相	900
		柢	901
		柱	902
		柄	903
		柨	904
	火	畑	905
		炮	906
	牛	牲	907
		牴	908
	王	珍	909
		玲	910
		玲	911
	礻	神	912
		祝	913
		祖	914
		祐	915
	月	肺	916
		胞	917
		胎	918
		胆	919
		胞	920
		脉	921
4-6	方	旅	922
		旅	923
	日	時	924
	木	梅	925
		格	926
		核	927
		桂	928
		校	929
		根	930
		桜	931
		桟	932
		栖	933

		栓	934
		株	935
		桃	936
		桐	937
		核	938
		校	939
		栓	940
	歹	殉	941
		殊	942
		残	943
	火	烟	944
	牛	特	945
	王	班	946
		珠	947
	礻	祥	948
	月	朕	949
		胴	950
		胸	951
		脇	952
		脈	953
		脂	954
		脈	955
	月	朕	956
4-7	方	旋	957
		族	958
	日	晩	959
	木	彬	960
		械	961
		梓	962
		梢	963
		梳	964
		梅	965
		梢	966
	火	焰	996[s]
	爿	將	967
	王	現	968
		球	969
		理	970

		琢	971
	𤴔	疎疏	⇒◧5-7[s]
	礻	視	972
	月	脱	973
		脚	974
		脳	975
		豚	976
		脫	977
	夫	規	978
4-8	日	晩	979
		暁	980
		晴	981
		晴	982
	木	棒	983
		棚	984
		棺	985
		検	986
		棋	987
		棉	988
		棲	989
		植	990
		棟	991
		棚	992
		桟	993
		極	1017[s]
	歹	殖	994
		殘	995
	火	焰	996
		焼	997
	片	牒	1025[s]
	牙	雅	998
	王	瑛	999
		斑	1000
		琢	1001
	礻	禄	1002
	月	脹	1003
		腋	1004
		勝	1005

Strokes	Radical	Character	No.
		腕	1006
	月	勝	1007
	厷	雄	1008
4-9	方	旒	1009
	日	暗	1010
		暖	1011
		暇	1012
		暗	1013
		暖	1014
	木	楓	1015
		楯	1016
		極	1017
		楠	1018
		楼	1019
	火	煖	1020
		煙	1021
		煩	1022
		煉	1023
		煙	1024
	片	牒	1025
	王	瑶	1026
		瑞	1027
		瑛	1028
	礻	福	1029
		禍	1030
		禎	1031
		禅	1032
	月	腸	1033
		腹	1034
		腺	1035
		腰	1036
		腳	1037
		腦	1038
		腰	1039
	元	頑	1040
	扌	瓶	1041
	予	預	1042
	分	頒	1043
	分	頒	1044
	公	頌	1045
	公	頌	1046
4-10	方	旗	1047
	木	概	1048
		構	1049
		模	1050
		楨	1051
		様	1052
		構	1053
		槙	1054
	止	雌	1055
	火	煽	1056
		熄	1057
		熔	1058
	王	璃	1059
		瑠	1060
		瑤	1061
	月	膜	1062
	云	魂	1063
4-11	木	標	1064
		権	1065
		横	1066
		槽	1067
		概	1068
		模	1069
		樓	1070
		樞	1071
		樣	1072
	王	璃	1059^{s}
	月	膜	1073
4-12	日	曉	1074
	木	樹	1075
		機	1076
		橘	1077
		橋	1078
		機	1079
		横	1080
	火	燃	1081
		燒	1082
		燈	1083
	月	膨	1084
	予	豫	1085
4-13	木	檢	1086
	火	燥	1087
	爿	牆	1088
	牛	犧	1089
	王	環	1090
		環	1091
	月	臆	1092
		謄	1093
		膽	1094
	月	謄	1095
4-14	日	曜	1096
		曜	1097
		曠	1100^{s}
	火	燻	1098
	月	臟	1102^{s}
4-15	日	曝	1099
		曠	1100
	火	爆	1101
	月	臟	1102
4-16	木	欄	1103
	火	爐	1104
	牛	犧	1105
	月	騰	1106
	月	騰	1107
4-17	木	櫻	1108
		欄	1109
	火	爛	1110
4-18	木	權	1111
	月	臟	1112^{s}
4-19		臟	1112
5-2	牙	邪	1124^{s}
	田	町	1113
	禾	利	1114

Group	Element	Character	No.
		私	1115
	衤	初	1116
	另	別	1117
	去	却	1118
	氐	邸	1131[s]
	厉	励	1119
	艮	即	1120
	且	助	1121
	半	判	1122
	半	判	1123
5-3	牙	邪	1124
	白	的	1125
		的	1126
	矢	知	1127
	示	祀	1128
		社	1129
	禾	和	1130
	氐	邸	1131
5-4	矢	矩	1148[s]
	石	研	1132
		砂	1133
		砕	1134
	示	祈	1135
		祉	1136
	禾	秒	1137
		科	1138
		秋	1139
	衤	衿	1140
	古	故	1141
	正	政	1142
	半	叛	1143
	𠂤	段	1144
5-5	田	畔	1145
		畔	1146
	目	眠	1147
	矢	矩	1148
		矩	1149
	石	破	1150
		砲	1151
		砲	1152
	示	祕	1153
		神	1154
		祝	1155
		祖	1156
		祐	1157
	禾	秩	1158
		秘	1159
		称	1160
		租	1161
	立	竝	1162
	衤	被	1163
		袖	1164
	門	門	1165
	艮	既	1166
	弓	弱	1167
	弓	弱	1168
5-6	田	略	1169
	目	眸	1170
		眺	1171
		眼	1172
	矛	務	1173
	石	研	1174
		硫	1175
	示	祥	1176
	禾	移	1177
5-7	正	疎	1178
		疏	1179
	白	皓	1180
		皓	1181
	矢	短	1182
	石	硬	1183
		硫	1184
		硝	1185
		硬	1186
		硝	1187
	示	視	1188
	禾	稀	1189
		程	1190
		税	1191
		程	1192
		税	1193
	衤	補	1194
		裕	1195
		裡	1196
5-8	牙	雅	1197
	田	畸	1198
	目	睦	1199
		睡	1200
	石	碍	1201
		碇	1202
		碑	1203
		碎	1204
	示	祿	1205
	禾	稚	1206
		稔	1207
	立	靖	1208
		靖	1209
	衤	褐	1210
		裸	1211
	号	號	1212
	此	雌	1055[ps]
5-9	石	碑	1213
		磁	1214
	示	福	1215
		禍	1216
		禎	1217
	禾	種	1218
		稲	1219
		稱	1220
		稻	1233[s]
	立	端	1221
	衤	複	1222
		褐	1223
		褪	1234[s]

Stroke	Component	Character	No.
	令	領	1224
	令	領	1225
	申	暢	1226
5-10	白	魄	1227
	石	確	1228
		磁	1229
	禾	稼	1230
		稿	1231
		穂	1232
		稲	1233
	衤	褪	1234
5-11	禾	穏	1235
		積	1236
5-12	目	瞳	1237
		瞭	1238
		瞳	1239
		瞬	1240
	矢	矯	1241
	石	磯	1242
		礁	1243
		磯	1244
	示	禪	1245
	禾	穗	1246
5-13	目	瞬	1247
	石	礎	1248
	示	禮	1249
	禾	穰	1250
		穫	1251
	衤	襟	1252
5-14	石	礦	1256[s]
	示	禱	1253
	禾	穫	1254
		穩	1255
	衤	襤	1257[s]
5-15	石	礦	1256
	衤	襤	1257
5-17		穰	1258
6-1	糸	糺	1259

Stroke	Component	Character	No.
	舌	乱	1260
	孚	乳	1438[s]
6-2	糸	糾	1261
	耳	取	1262
		耻	1263
		耶	1283[s]
	臣	臥	1440[s]
	至	到	1264
	交	効	1265
		郊	1286[s]
	亥	劾	1266
		刻	1267
	亥	劾	1268
		刻	1269
	虍	劇	1270
	缶	卸	1271
	朩	叔	1272
	有	郁	1288[s]
	吊	刷	1273
	良	郎	1289[s]
	制	制	1274
	朿	刺	1275
6-3	糸	紀	1276
		紅	1277
		糾	1278
		級	1279
		約	1280
		約	1281
	而	耐	1282
	耳	耶	1283
	至	致	1284
	虫	虹	1285
	开	形	359[p]
	交	郊	1286
	圭	封	1287
	有	郁	1288
	良	郎	1289
	自	帥	1290

Stroke	Component	Character	No.
6-4	米	粉	1291
		料	1292
		粋	1293
		粉	1294
	糸	紡	1295
		紛	1296
		純	1297
		紘	1298
		紋	1299
		納	1300
		紗	1301
		紙	1302
		紛	1303
		級	1304
		紋	1305
		納	1306
		級	1279[s]
	缶	缺	1307
	耒	耕	1308
		耗	1309
	耒	耘	1310
		耕	1311
		耗	1312
	耳	恥	1313
		耻	1314
		耺	1315
	至	致	1316
	舟	般	1317
		航	1318
	虫	蚊	1319
		蚊	1320
	交	效	1321
	毎	敏	1322
	自	能	1323
	杀	殺	1324
	良	朗	1325
	自	師	1326
	孝	教	1493[s]

Stroke	Radical	Character	No.
6-5	米	粘	1327
		粒	1328
		粗	1329
	糸	紘	1330
		経	1331
		紺	1332
		細	1333
		紳	1334
		紹	1335
		終	1336
		組	1337
		終	1338
		統	1339
	舟	舶	1340
		船	1341
		船	1342
	虫	蛇	1343
	并	瓶	1344
6-6	米	粧	1345
	糸	絵	1346
		絢	1347
		結	1348
		絞	1349
		給	1350
		絡	1351
		統	1352
		絶	1353
		絞	1354
		絲	1355
		絕	1356
	羊	翔	1357
		翔	1358
	舟	艇	1365^{s}
	虫	蛔	1359
6-7	糸	継	1360
		絹	1361
		続	1362
		經	1363
	舌	辞	1364
	舟	艇	1365
6-8	米	精	1366
		精	1367
		粹	1368
	糸	緋	1369
		維	1370
		綺	1371
		綱	1372
		綿	1373
		網	1374
		練	1375
		綾	1376
		緑	1377
		緒	1378
		総	1379
		綜	1380
		綴	1381
		網	1382
		綠	1383
	耳	聡	1384
	虫	蝶	1401^{s}
	号	號	1212^{s}
	此	雌	1055^{p}
	杂	雜	1385
6-9	糸	縁	1386
		編	1387
		縄	1388
		緩	1389
		緬	1390
		緘	1391
		線	1392
		締	1393
		緣	1394
		編	1395
		緯	1396
		緩	1397
		練	1398
		緒	1399
		締	1400
		縫	1406^{s}
	虫	蝶	1401
	光	輝	1402
6-10	米	糖	1403
		糖	1404
	糸	縛	1405
		縫	1406
		緯	1407
		縦	1408
		縛	1409
	舟	艙	1410
6-11	糸	繃	1411
		績	1412
		繊	1413
		縮	1414
		縫	1415
		縱	1416
		總	1417
	耳	聴	1418
		聯	1419
		聰	1420
	臣	臨	1630^{s}
6-12	米	糧	1421
	糸	織	1422
		繕	1423
		織	1424
		繩	1428^{s}
	耳	職	1425
		職	1426
6-13	糸	繰	1427
		繩	1428
		繪	1429
	弓	疆	1430
6-14	糸	繼	1431
	舟	艦	1435^{s}
6-15	糸	纏	1432

		織	1433
		績	1434
	舟	艦	1435
6-17		繊	1436
6-18		罐	1437
7-1	孚	乳	1438
	孚	乳	1439
7-2	臣	臥	1440
	言	計	1441
		訂	1442
	谷	卻	1443
	貝	則	1444
	車	軌	1445
	余	叙	1446
	缶	卸	1447
	肖	削	1448
	肖	削	1449
	皀	即	1450
	君	郡	1466[s]
	良	郎	1467[s]
	束	勅	1451
	享	郭	1678[s]
7-3	言	訊	1452
		記	1453
		訓	1454
		託	1455
		討	1456
	貝	財	1457
	身	射	1458
	車	軒	1459
	酉	配	1460
		酌	1461
		配	1462
		酌	1463
	镸	髟	1464
	亩	畝	1465
	君	郡	1466
	良	郎	1467
	享	郭	1678[s]
7-4	言	訪	1468
		訣	1469
		許	1470
		設	1471
		訟	1472
		訳	1473
		訟	1474
		註	1499[s]
	谷	欲	1475
	貝	敗	1476
		販	1477
	赤	赦	1478
	𧾷	距	1511[s]
	車	軟	1479
		転	1480
		軛	1481
		斬	1482
	酉	酔	1483
	釆	釈	1484
	里	野	1485
	余	斜	1486
		敍	1487
	杀	殺	1488
	毎	敏	1489
	声	殻	1490
	皀	既	1491
	㡭	断	1492
	孝	教	1493
	孝	敎	1494
	良	朗	1495
	束	敕	1496
	求	救	1497
	享	敦	1693[s]
7-5	角	觝	1498
	言	註	1499
		詠	1500
		評	1501
		詐	1502
		詞	1503
		診	1504
		詔	1505
		証	1506
		訴	1507
		評	1508
	貝	貯	1509
		貼	1510
	𧾷	距	1511
		距	1512
	身	躰	1513
	車	軸	1514
		軽	1515
	酉	酢	1516
7-6	角	解	1517
		触	1518
	言	該	1519
		詭	1520
		詰	1521
		誇	1522
		誠	1523
		詩	1524
		試	1525
		詳	1526
		話	1527
		該	1528
		誕	1579[s]
	貝	賄	1529
		賊	1530
		賊	1531
	𧾷	跳	1532
		路	1533
		跡	1534
		践	1535
	車	較	1536
		較	1537
	酉	酪	1538

Group	Element	Character	No.
		酬	1539
		酵	1561[s]
	君	群	1540
7-7	言	読	1541
		誤	1542
		語	1543
		誨	1544
		誡	1545
		認	1546
		説	1547
		誌	1548
		誦	1549
		誘	1550
		誤	1551
		認	1552
		誠	1553
		說	1554
		誕	1555
		誇	1522[s]
	豸	貌	1556
	貝	賦	1583[s]
	赤	赫	1557
	足	踊	1558
	車	輔	1559
		輕	1560
	酉	酵	1561
		酷	1562
		酸	1563
		酷	1564
	矣	疑	1565
	克	兢	1566
7-8	言	調	1567
		諾	1568
		談	1569
		謁	1570
		誼	1571
		誹	1572
		課	1573
		論	1574
		諒	1575
		請	1576
		諸	1577
		誰	1578
		誕	1579
		調	1580
		請	1581
		謀	1593[s]
		誤	1542[s]
		誘	1550[s]
	貝	賠	1582
		賦	1583
		賤	1584
		賜	1585
		賠	1586
	足	踏	1587
		踐	1588
	車	輪	1589
		輛	1590
	酉	醋	1591
		醉	1592
7-9	言	謀	1593
		諷	1594
		謂	1595
		諮	1596
		謡	1597
		諭	1598
		諾	1599
		謁	1600
		諮	1601
		諸	1602
		諡	1603
	豆	頭	1604
	貝	賭	1605
	足	蹈	1626[s]
	車	輯	1606
		輸	1607
		輸	1608
	辛	辦	1609
		辨	1610
	巠	頸	1611
	𥝢	頴	1612
	步	頻	1613
	禿	頽	1614
	束	頼	1615
		賴	1616
7-10	言	謙	1617
		謹	1618
		講	1619
		謝	1620
		謙	1621
		講	1622
		謠	1623
	貝	購	1624
		購	1625
	足	蹈	1626
	車	轄	1627
		轄	1628
	酉	醜	1629
7-11	臣	臨	1630
	言	謬	1631
		謳	1632
		謹	1633
	貝	贈	1634
	足	蹟	1635
	車	轉	1636
7-12	言	譜	1637
		譏	1638
		識	1639
		識	1640
		證	1641
	貝	贈	1642
	足	蹶	1643
	辛	瓣	1644
	酉	醱	1645

7-13	角	觸	1646
	言	議	1647
		護	1648
		譲	1649
		譜	1650
		譯	1651
	足	躁	1652
	辛	辦	1653
	酉	醸	1654
		醵	1655
	釆	釋	1656
7-14	言	護	1657
	足	躍	1658
		躍	1659
	辛	辯	1660
7-15	言	讀	1661
	車	轢	1662
7-17	言	讓	1663
	酉	釀	1664
7-19		讚	1665
8-2	金	針	1666
		釘	1667
	食	飢	1668
	斉	剤	1669
	音	剖	1670
		部	1676[s]
	音	剖	1671
	享	郭	1678[s]
	㑒	剣	1672
	岡	剛	1673
	者	都	1686[s]
	垂	郵	1687[s]
8-3	金	釣	1674
		鈎	1675
	林	彬	960[p]
	音	部	1676
	音	部	1677
	享	郭	1678

	車	乾	1679
	幸	執	1680
	采	彩	1681
	采	彩	1682
	周	彫	1683
	周	彫	1684
	尉	尉	1685
	者	都	1686
	垂	郵	1687
8-4	金	鈑	1688
		鈍	1689
		欽	1690
	革	靴	1781[s]
	食	飯	1691
		飲	1692
	享	敦	1693
	京	就	1694
	車	朝	1695
		戟	1696
		朝	1697
		乾	1679[s]
	幸	報	1698
	壳	殼	1699
	隶	款	1700
	苟	敬	1701
	昔	散	1702
	其	欺	1703
		期	1704
		期	1705
	耳	敢	1706
	𡋯	毀	1791[s]
8-5	金	鉛	1707
		鉢	1708
		鉱	1709
		鈴	1710
		鉄	1711
		鉛	1712
		銃	1713

		鈴	1714
	食	飽	1715
		飼	1716
		飾	1717
	并	瓶	1041[p]
	車	幹	1718
	冊	嗣	1719
8-6	金	鉾	1720
		銅	1721
		銀	1722
		銃	1723
		銘	1724
		銭	1725
		銑	1726
		銓	1727
	青	静	1728
8-7	金	鋳	1729
		鋭	1730
		鋏	1731
		銷	1732
		鋭	1733
	食	餓	1734
	舎	舗	1735
	舎	舖	1736
8-8	金	錠	1737
		錦	1738
		錮	1739
		鋼	1740
		錬	1741
		録	1742
		錯	1743
		錘	1744
		錄	1745
		錢	1746
		鍵	1753[s]
	青	靜	1747
	食	館	1748
	舎	舘	1749

Pattern	Element	Kanji	No.
	草	翰	1750
		隷	1751
8-9	金	鍋	1752
		鍵	1753
		鍼	1754
		鍛	1755
		錬	1756
	草	韓	1757
	歩	頻	1758
8-10	金	鎮	1759
		鎌	1760
		鎖	1761
		鎔	1762
		鎭	1763
		鐮	1764
		鎻	1765
8-11	金	鏡	1766
		鏡	1767
	奚	鶏	1768
8-12	金	鐘	1769
		鐘	1770
8-13		鐵	1771
8-14	金	鑄	1772
		鑑	1773[s]
		鑛	1774[s]
8-15	金	鑑	1773
		鑛	1774
9-2	食	飢	1775
	畐	副	1776
	甚	勘	1777
	者	都	1780[s]
	重	動	1778
	乗	剰	1779
9-3		都	1780
9-4	革	靴	1781
	食	飯	1782
		飲	1783
	亲	新	1784
	南	献	1785
	壴	鼓	1786
	単	戦	1787
	曷	歇	1788
	苟	敬	1789
	娄	数	1790
	皇	毀	1791
	展	殿	1792
9-5	食	飽	1793
		飼	1794
		飾	1795
9-6		蝕	1796
9-7	食	餓	1797
		餘	1798
	亲	親	1799
	育	龍	1800
	育	龍	1801
	県	縣	1802
9-8	食	館	1803
	柰	隸	1804
9-9	客	額	1805
	显	顕	1806
	类	類	1807
	彦	顔	1808
	彥	顏	1809
9-10	音	韻	1810
	音	韻	1811
	門	關	3335[p]
9-12	食	饒	1812
		饑	1813
10-2	馬	馭	1814
	倉	創	1815
	害	割	1816
	害	割	1817
	堇	勤	1818
	乘	剩	1819
10-3		馴	1820
10-4	馬	駄	1821
		駅	1822
		駆	1823
		駐	1828[s]
	𥞤	穀	1824
	哥	歌	1825
	𦰩	歎	1869[s]
10-5	馬	駐	1826
		駒	1827
		駐	1828
		駈	1829
10-6	骨	骼	1830
	鬲	融	1831
10-7	馬	駿	1832
	馬	翳	2874[p]
10-8	馬	験	1833
		騎	1834
		騒	1835
	骨	髄	1842[s]
	离	離	1836
	杂	雜	1837
	𦰩	難	1838
	奚	雞	1839
	𠂤	歸	1840
10-9	馬	騙	1841
	骨	髄	1842
	眞	顛	1843
	类	類	1844
	原	願	1845
10-10	馬	騷	1846
	竟	競	1847
10-11	馬	驅	1848
	奚	鷄	1849
	隺	鶴	1850
10-12	骨	髓	1855[s]
	髟	鬚	2855[p]
	耳	聽	1851
10-13	馬	驛	1852
		驗	1853

	骨	體	1854
		髓	1855
10-18		驢	1856
11-2	雀	勧	1857
	啚	鄙	1862s
	巢	剿	1858
	堇	勤	1859
11-3	章	彰	1860
	章	彰	1861
	啚	鄙	1862
	丵	對	1863
11-4	商	敵	1864
	商	敵	1865
	豙	毅	1866
	雀	歓	1867
	㱿	穀	1868
	菓	歎	1869
	専	敷	1870
	専	敷	1871
	婁	數	1872
	區	毆	1873
		歐	1874
	虚	戯	1875
11-5		鮎	1876
11-6		鮮	1877
11-7	魚	鯁	1878
		鯉	1879
	雀	観	1880
	鬥	鬪	3334p
11-8	魚	鯛	1881
		鯨	1882
		鯛	1883
	离	離	1836s
	菓	難	1884
11-9		鹹	1885
12-1		亂	1886
12-2	奠	鄭	1888s
	粦	鄰	1890s

	畫	劃	1887
12-3	奠	鄭	1888
	景	影	1889
	粦	鄰	1890
12-4	黑	默	1891
	兽	獣	1892
	單	戰	1893
12-5	黑	點	1894
	歯	齢	1895
		齡	1896
12-6	番	翻	1897
		飜	1898
12-7		辭	1899
12-9	雇	顧	1900
	雇	顧	1901
	番	飜	1902
13-2	僉	劍	1903
	豦	劇	1904
13-3	僉	劒	1905
		劔	1906
13-4		戲	1907
13-6		艶	1908
14-2	齊	劑	1909
	睿	叡	1910
	熏	勳	1911
14-4		斷	1912
14-9		顯	1913
15-2		勵	1914
15-4	嘼	獸	1915
15-5		齡	1916
16-4		獻	1917
18-2		勸	1918
18-4		歡	1919
18-6		艷	1920
18-7		觀	1921

▀2 UP-DOWN

1-1	一	二	1922
	丶	丫	1923
		辶	1926s
1-2	一	三	1924
	丶	丬	1925
		辶	1926
	ノ	彡	1927
		彳	1928
		乏	1933s
1-3	一	元	1929
		戸	1930
		云	1931
	丶	辶	1932
	ノ	乏	1933
		⺍	1934
		六	1935
		毛	3453p
		手	3456p
1-4	一	示	1936
	丶	永	1937
		主	1938
	ノ	禾	3503p
		乎	3504p
1-5	一	亘	1939
		亥	1940
	ノ	舌	2186p
1-6	一	言	1941
		戻	1942
		豆	1943
	ノ	系	1944
		乏	1945
		妥	2400p
		呑	2410p

秀 2545[p]
豸 2401[p]
釆 3555[p]
1-7 一 房 1946
肩 1947
ノ 受 2421[p]
秀 2545[ps]
垂 3565[p]
争 2422[p]
委季 ⇨▬5-3[p]
1-8 一 音 1948
帝 1949
ノ 重 3573[p]
香 2568[p]
1-9 一 扇 1950
鬲 1951
晉 1952
1-10 一 啇 1953
章 1954
1-11 一 扉 1955
屝 1956
童 1957
ノ 番 2748[p]
黍 2597[p]
爲 2477[p]
1-12 一 意 1958
ノ 愛 2492[p]
1-16 爵 2524[p]
2-1 亠 亡 3402[p]
ヘ 个 1959
个 1960
𠂉 乞 1961
ケ 3430[p]
ㇾ 乏 1933[ps]
2-2 亠 文 1962
方 1963
亢 1964
六 1965

文 1966
ヘ 介 1967
今 1968
仐 1969
八 分 1970
公 1971
八 分 1972
父 1973
公 1974
父 1975
冖 冗 1976
[illegible] 1977
几 殳 1978
十 支 1979
支 1980
ト 攴 1981
ム 允 1982
マ 予 1983
𠂉 午 1984
夂 1985
气 1986
乞 1961[s]
𠂉 欠 1987
ㇾ 乏 1933[p]
メ 爻 1988
㸚 1989
九 卆 1990
2-3 亠 玄 1991
立 1992
市 1993
主 1994
ヘ 令 1995
仝 1996
令 1997
令 1998
令 1999
冖 写 2000
刀 召 2001

十 古 2002
吉 2025[s]
ト 占 2003
ム 弁 2004
台 2005
又 圣 2006
圣 2007
亠 主 1938[p]
マ 矛 2008
𠂉 矢 2009
尔 2010
2-4 亠 亦 2011
亥 2012
衣 2013
充 2014
交 2015
妄 2016
[illegible] 2017
交 2018
亨 2037[s]
孛 2039[s]
ヘ 合 2019
会 2020
企 2021
全 2022
入 全 2023
ソ 羊 ⇨▬3-3[p]
冖 写 2000[s]
ヒ 旨 2024
十 吉 2025
一 百 2026
而 2027
七 乇 2028
𠂊 色 2029
争 2030
危 3199[p]
⺈ 危 2031
𠂉 缶 2032

		缶	2033
		毎	2034
		年	2035
		気	3194[p]
2-5	亠	忘	2036
		亨	2037
		辛	2038
		孛	2039
		言	2040
		享	2051[s]
	𠆢	含	2041
		余	2042
	八	谷	2043
	丷	弟	2044
	刀	兎	2045
	十	克	2046
	子	孟	2220[s]
	⺈	角	2047
	𠂉	毎	2048
	メ	希	2049
2-6	亠	育	2050
		享	2051
		京	2052
		盲	2053
		斉	2054
		卒	2055
		夜	2056
	𠆢	金	2057
		命	2058
		念	2059
		舎	2060
		𩙿	2061
		舍	2062
	八	劵巻	⇒⬒6-2[p]
	丷	並	2246[p]
	十	尭	2063
		直	2932[p]
	卜	卓	2064

		奌	2065
	ム	参	2066
	⺈	免	2067
2-7	亠	哀	2068
		変	2069
		音	2070
		亮	2071
		亭	2072
		帝	2073
		彥	2074
		彦	3295[p]
	𠆢	食	2075
		倉	2076
		食	2077
	八	盆	2078
	八	盆	2079
	丷	前首	etc⇒⬒3-6[p]
	冖	軍	2080
		冠	2081
	十	南	2082
	卜	貞	2083
		点	2084
	ム	怠	2085
	一	頁	2086
		面	2087
	マ	柔	2088
		勇	2089
		勇	2090
	⺈	負	2091
		急	2092
		急	2093
	⺈	負	2094
2-8	亠	旁	2095
		畜	2096
		高	2097
		恋	2098
		竜	2099
		衰	2100

		竟	2101
		离	2102
		衰	2103
		叀	2575[ps]
	𠆢	倉	2104
	八	益	2105
		翁	2106
	八	釜	2107
		翁	2108
	丷	差	3311[p]
		益兼	⇒⬒3-7[p]
	力	脅	2109
	匕	眞	2110
	十	真	2111
		索	2455[p]
	又	桑	2112
	一	夏	2113
	⺈	奂	2114
	𠂉	氣	3228[p]
2-9	亠	斎	2115
		商	2116
		章	2117
		率	2118
		高	2119
		産	2120
		率	2121
		産	3298[p]
	八	貧	2122
	八	貧	2123
	冖	冨	2124
	卜	鹵	2125
	ム	參	2126
	⺈	魚	2127
		亀	2128
2-10	亠	蛮	2129
		童	2130
		棄	2137[s]
	𠆢	傘	2131

Pattern		Kanji	No.
	八	奠	2132
		尊	2133
	丷	着	3316p
		善普 etc	⇨3-9p
	⺈	象	2134
	𠂉	無	2135
2-11	亠	意	2136
		棄	2137
		裏	2138
		喪	2825ps
	人	會	2139
	丷	義慈	⇨3-10p
2-12	亠	豪	2140
		膏	2141
		齊	2142
	一	福	1215p
	𠂉	舞	2143
2-13	亠	褒	2144
	丷	養	2365p
	一	憂	2145
	𠂉	舞	2146
2-14		龜	2147
2-15	亠	齋	2148
	人	龠	2149
2-16		龜	2150
2-17		麗	2151
3-1	大	太	2152
	龴	予	1983p
	亼	今	1968p
3-2	口	号	2153
		兄	2154
		只	2155
	土	去	2156
	夂	冬	2157
		冬	2158
	宀	穴	2159
		穴	2160
		穴	2161

Pattern		Kanji	No.
		字	2172s
	艹	芝	2180s
	龴	矛	2008p
	亼	令	1995p
		令	1998p
	𠫓	充	2162
3-3	口	吊	2163
		号	2153s
	土	寺	2164
		圭	2165
		吉	2166
	士	吉	2167
	夂	各	2168
	夕	名	2169
		多	2170
	宀	安	2171
		字	2172
		守	2173
		宅	2174
		宇	2175
	小	尖	2176
	⺌	当	2177
		光	2391p
	千	舌	2178
	幺	糸	2179
	艹	芝	2180
		芋	2181
		共	2393p
	𠫓	至	2182
	⺍	羊	2183
		羊	2184
	亡	妄	2185
	千	舌	2186
	亼	会合	⇨2-4p
3-4	口	呂	2187
		足	2188
		呈	2189
		邑	2190

Pattern		Kanji	No.
		𧾷	2191
		呈	2192
	土	赤	2193
		走	2194
		走	2195
	士	壳	2196
		壱	2197
		声	2198
		志	2199
	夂	条	2200
	宀	完	2201
		宏	2202
		究	2203
	小	肖	2204
	⺌	肖	2205
	⺍	学	2555ps
		労	2548p
	巛	災	2206
	己	忌	2207
	艹	芙	2208
		芸	2209
		芳	2210
		花	2211
	艹	芯	2423s
	𠂉	豸	2401p
	刃	忍	2212
	刃	忍	2213
	亡	忘	2214
	亼	含	2041p
	𠫓	育	2215
3-5	土	幸	2216
	大	奇	2217
	大	奔	2218
		奈	2219
	子	孟	2220
	宀	宙	2221
		宛	2222
		宜	2223

		宝	2224
		実	2225
		官	2226
		空	2227
		宗	2228
		定	2229
		突	2230
		空	2231
	小	尙	2232
	⺌	尚	2233
	⺍	當	2234
		学	2555^{p}
	山	岩	2235
		岸	2236
	艹	苗	2237
		英	2238
		苑	2239
		芽	2240
		若	2241
		茎	2242
		苦	2243
		茉	2244
		茂	2245
	䒑	並	2246
	亡	盲	2247
	亼	命念	⇨⬒2-6^{p}
	廿	革	2448^{s}
3-6	口	品	2248
	大	奔	2249
	宀	客	2250
		穿	2251
		宣	2252
		窃	2253
		室	2254
		突	2255
	⺍	単	2256
		栄	2574^{p}
	山	炭	2257
		炭	2258
	艹	茶	2259
		荒	2260
		茜	2261
		荘	2262
		草	2263
		革	2448^{p}
	䒑	美	2264
		首	2265
		前	2266
		前	2267
	土	韋	2268
	亼	食食	⇨⬒2-7^{p}
3-7	口	員	2269
	宀	案	2270
		宴	2271
		害	2272
		家	2273
		宮	2274
		宰	2275
		宵	2276
		容	2277
		害	2278
		宵	2279
	⺌	党	2581^{p}
	⺍	挙	2456^{p}
	山	峯	2280
	工	貢	2281
	艹	荷	2282
		華	2283
		莉	2284
		恭	2459^{p}
	䒑	益	2285
		兼	2286
		差	3311^{p}
	土	韋	2287
	亼	倉	2104^{p}
3-8	宀	窒	2288
		寅	2289
		寂	2290
		寄	2291
		密	2292
		宿	2293
		窓	2294
	⺌	常堂	⇨⬒5-6^{p}
	⺍	巣	2295
		蛍	2591^{p}
	山	崩	2296
		崇	2297
		崩	2298
		嵌	2313^{s}
	巛	巢	2299
	艹	著	2300
		萌	2301
		菓	2302
		菊	2303
		菌	2304
		菜	2305
		黄	2468^{p}
		葉	2321^{s}
	艹	萃萎	⇨⬒4-8^{s}
	䒑	剪	2306
	亼	棄	2326^{s}
	廿	黃	2487^{s}
3-9	土	堯	2307
	士	喜	2308
		壹	2309
	宀	富	2310
		寒	2311
		寒	2312
	⺌	掌	2602^{p}
	⺍	営覚	⇨⬒5-7^{p}
	山	嵌	2313
		嵐	2314
	⺕	尋	2315
	艹	募	2316

Section	Component	Character	Number
	爫	妥	2402
	牛	告	2403
	耂	孝	3205[p]
		考	3196[ps]
	艹	芝	2404
		芋	2405
	幺	系	1944[p]
	今	含	2041[p]
	不	否	2406
	五	吾	2407
	龶	麦	2408
	⺧	告	2409
	天	吞	2410
4-4	文	斉	2054[p]
	日	易	2411
		昂	2412
		昆	2413
		昌	2414
		昇	2415
	止	歩	2416
		肯	2417
	氏	昏	2418
	水	沓	2419
	火	炎	2420
	⺤	受	2421
	⺈	争	2422
	耂	者	3211[p]
	艹	芯	2423
		芙	2424
		芽	2425
		芳	2426
		花	2427
	今	念	2059[p]
	𠫓	育	2050[p]
	龶	毒	2428
		表	2429
		青	2430
		靑	2431

Section	Component	Character	Number
	龷	昔	2432
		芽	2240[p]
	中	忠	2433
	夳	奈	2219[p]
4-5	文	彥	2074[p]
	日	冒	2434
		星	2435
		是	2436
	木	査	2437
	耂	者	3217[p]
	艹	苗	2438
		英	2439
		苑	2440
		若	2441
		苦	2442
		茉	2443
		茂	2444
	分	盆	2079[p]
	比	皆	2445
	立	彦	3295[p]
	冃	冐	2446
	不	歪	2447
	廿	革	2448
	少	省	2449
	卌	帯	2582[s]
4-6	日	晃	2450
	父	釜	2107[p]
	艹	茶	2451
		荒	2452
		茜	2453
		草	2454
	公	翁	2108[p]
	𠙵	索	2455
	龸	挙	2456
	天	蚕	2457
	龶	素	2458
	龷	恭	2459
		華	2283[p]

Section	Component	Character	Number
4-7	文	斎	2115[p]
		產	2120[p]
	毌	貫	2460
	艹	荷	2461
		莖	2462
		莉	2463
		荘	2464
	化	貨	2465
	化	貨	2466
	分	貧	2123[p]
	立	産	3298[p]
		商	2116[p]
	龶	責	2467
	龷	黄	2468
	少	雀	2469
4-8	日	景	2470
		量	2471
		最	2472
		暑	2473
		晶	2474
	木	森	2475
	止	歯	2476
	爫	爲	2477
	艹	萎	2478
		萃	2479
		萌	2480
		萠	2481
		菓	2482
		華	2483
		菊	2484
		菌	2485
		菜	2486
	·	葉	2501[s]
	𠫓	棄	2137[ps]
	龷	葬	2320[p]
	廿	黃	2487
	中	貴	2606[p]
	天	喬	2488

4-9	日	暑	2489
	止	歳	2490
		歲	2491
	爫	愛	2492
	艹	惹	2493
		募	2494
		著	2495
		葵	2496
		萬	2497
		落	2498
		萩	2499
		葬	2500
		葉	2501
		蒸	2511[s]
	去	棄	2137[p]
	⺍	誉	2502
4-10	艹	蓋	2503
		蒲	2504
		蒙	2505
		蒐	2506
		蒼	2507
		墓	2508
		蓄	2509
		慈	2510
		蒸	2511
		幕	2512
		蓉	2513
		蔭	2517[s]
	卝	夢	2514
	比	態熊	⇨■10-4[p]
4-11	日	暴	2515
	止	齒	2516
	艹	蔭	2517
		慕	2518
		暮	2519
		蔦	2520
4-12	日	曇	2521
	艹	蕃	2522
		蔽	2523
4-13	爫	爵	2524
	艹	薄	2525
		蕗	2526
		薦	2527
		薪	2528
	卝	舊	2531[s]
4-14	艹	藉	2529
		薫	2530
		藍	2534[s]
		薦	2527[s]
		藏	2537[s]
	卝	舊	2531
4-15	艹	藝	2532
		藩	2533
		藍	2534
		藤	2535
		藥	2536
		藏	2537
	卝	繭	2538
4-16		藻	2539
4-17		蘭	2540
5-1		丞	2541
5-2	田	男	2542
	目	貝	2543
		見	2544
	禾	秀	2545
		季	2554[s]
	穴	究	2203[p]
	立	辛	2038[p]
	臼	兒	2625[s]
	旧	児	2546
	奴	努	2547
	古	克	2046[p]
	⺍	労	2548
		学	2555[s]
	吕	呉	2549
	巨	镸	2550
	丘	兵	2551
5-3	目	具	2552
	禾	委	2553
		季	2554
		秀	2545[s]
	穴	空突	⇨■3-5[p]
	襾	要	2634[s]
	占	桌	2065[p]
	⺍	学	2555
	巨	長	2556
	丘	岳	2557
	書	妻	2558
	夫	奉	2559
5-4	甘	某	2560
	田	胃	2561
		畏	2562
		界	2563
		思	2564
	癶	発	2565
	白	皇	2566
		泉	2567
	目	県	2641[p]
	禾	香	2568
	穴	窃穿	etc⇨■3-6[p]
	立	音	2070[p]
	加	架	2569
	夗	怨	2570
	奴	怒	2571
	氿	染	2572
	北	背	2573
	占	点	2084[p]
	⺈	急	2092[p]
	矛	柔	2088[p]
	⺍	栄	2574
	申	東	2575
	夫	春	2576
		奏	2577
	此	柴	2653[s]

5-5	玄	畜	2096p
	白	畠	2578
	立	竜	2099p
		竞	2101p
	⺊	监	2579
	卯	留	2580
	亞	晉	1952p
	八	益	2285p
	⺍	党	2581
	卌	帯	2582
	𡗗	泰	2583
	此	砦	2671s
	卌	帶	2676s
5-6	田	異	2584
		累	2585
		畧	2586
	穴	窓窒	⇨■3-8p
	立	章	2117p
	罒	罛	2587
	代	袋	2588
	⺍	堂	2589
		常	2590
	⺍	蛍	2591
	此	紫	2688s
5-7	田	畳	2592
		塁	2593
		異	2594
	癶	登	2595
		發	2596
	禾	黍	2597
	立	童	2130p
	罒	買	2598
	臼	鼠	2693s
	加	賀	2599
	代	貸	2600
	卯	貿	2601
	⺍	掌	2602
	⺍	営	2603
		覚	2604
	卌	黹	2605
	虫	貴	2606
	弗	費	2607
5-8	穴	窟	2328p
	立	意	2136p
	罒	置	2608
		署	2609
		罪	2610
	山	嵩	2331p
	⺍	當	2611
	业	業	2612
5-9	穴	窪	2348p
	罒	罰	2613
		署	2614
	⺍	裳	2615
	聿	盡	2616
5-10	穴	窮窯	⇨■3-12p
	罒	罷	2617
	⺍	賞	2618
5-11		罹	2619
5-12	西	覆	2725s
		聲	2872p
5-13	田	壘	2620
	业	叢	2621
5-14		羅	2622
5-15	声	馨	2879p
	⺍	黨	2623
5-17	田	疊	2624
	穴	竊	2387p
6-2	臼	兒	2625
	吕	呉	2549s
	卢	卓	2064p
	色	免	2067p
	垚	尭	2063p
	亠	卒	2055p
	爫	受	2421p
	且	具	2626
	曲	典	2627
	自	阜	2628
	甘	其	2629
	关	券	2630
	关	巻	2631
		劵	2632
6-3	羊	美	2264p
	自	臭	2633
	西	要	2634
	覀	要	2635
	次	姿	2636
		姿	2637
	刑	型	2638
	㓞	契	2639
	㓞	契	2640
	亦	変	2069p
	立	帝	2073p
	目	県	2641
	由	卑	2642
	甘	甚	2643
	叀	専	2644
	关	巻	2645
6-4	⺮	笑	2646
		笹	2663s
	羊	差	3311p
	自	息	2647
		臭	2648
	西	栗	2649
	巩	恐	2650
	巩	恐	2651
	列	烈	2652
	此	柴	2653
	亦	恋	2098p
	劦	脅	2109p
	叒	桑	2112p
	立	旁	2095p
	㐫	离	2102p
	兴	挙	2456p

	安	案	2270^p
	冎	骨	2654
	因	恩	2655
	亜	晋	2656
	由	鬼	2657
	聿	書	2658
		恵	2659
6-5	⺮	第	2660
		符	2661
		笠	2662
		笹	2663
		笛	2664
	羽	習	2665
		翌	2666
	羽	習	2667
		翌	2668
	覀	票	2669
	次	盗	2670
	此	砦	2671
	⺼	祭	2672
	厽	参	2126^p
	出	崇	2297^p
	其	基	2673
	聿	書	2674
	成	盛	2675
	卌	帯	2676
6-6	⺮	筆	2677
		筋	2678
		策	2679
		筒	2680
		答	2681
		等	2682
	羊	着	3316^p
	血	衆	2683
		衆	2684
	壮	装	2685
	吅	單	2686
	列	裂	2687

	此	紫	2688
	亦	蛮	2129^p
	⺈	象	2134^p
	旦	景	2470^p
	其	棊	2689
	聿	畫	2690
	癶	登	2595^p
6-7	⺮	節	2691
		⺮法	2692
	羊	義	2338^p
	臼	鼠	2693
	任	賃	2694
	次	資	2695
		資	2696
	兴	誉	2502^p
	艹	蓉	2337^p
	爫	愛	2492^p
	曲	豊	2697
		農	2698
	其	碁	2699
6-8	⺮	箇	2700
		管	2701
		算	2702
		箏	2703
	羽	翠	2704
	羽	翠	2705
	自	鼻	2706
		鼻	2707
		翬	2714^s
6-9	⺮	箸	2708
		範	2709
		篇	2710
		箱	2711
		節	2712
	羊	養	2365^p
	吅	器	2713
	巩	翬	2714
6-10	⺮	築	2715

		篤	2716
		築	2717
	吅	器	2718
6-11	⺮	簇	2719
	羽	翼	2720
6-12	⺮	簡	2721
		簡	2722
	羽	翼	2723
	虫	蟲	2724
	覀	覆	2725
	覀	覆	2726
		覇	2730^s
6-13	⺮	簿	2727
		簿	2728
	覀	覇	2729
	覀	覇	2730
6-14	⺮	籍	2731
		籍	2732
	吅	嚴	2733
6-16		籠	2734
6-17		籤	2735
7-2	卣	貞	2083^p
	百	頁	2086^p
	⺈	負	2091^p
	甬	勇	2089^p
7-3	辰	辱	2736
		唇	2737
	折	哲	2738
	直	真	2111^p
	百	夏	2113^p
	⺈	奐	2114^p
7-4	辰	脣	2739
	里	黒	2740
	攸	悠	2741
	𦣞	望	2742
	𦣞	望	2743
	利	梨	2744
	⺈	魚	2127^p

12-7	兟	贊	2892
	敬	警	2893
12-9	𦥑	譽	2880^{s}
	鄉	饗響	⇨▀13-9^{s}
12-10		驚	2894
13-2	晢	質	2808^{p}
	替	贊	2809^{p}
	𦥑	學	2898^{s}
13-3	辟	壁	2895
	貇	墾	2896
	道	導	2897
	𦥑	學	2898
13-4	貇	懇	2899
	毄	擊	2900
	與	舉	2875^{p}
13-6	鄉	嚮	2901
	毄	繫	2902
13-7	辟	譬	2903
	敬	警	2904
	與	譽	2880^{p}
	𦥑	覺	2905
13-9	鄉	饗	2906
		響	2907
13-10	敬	驚	2908
14-2		興	2909
14-4	與	擧	2875^{ps}
	徵	懲	2910
14-5		璽	2911
14-7	與	譽	2880^{ps}
	監	覽	2913^{s}
15-4		懲	2912
15-7		覽	2913
16-2		雙	2914
16-4		懸	2915
16-6	龍	襲	2916
	龍	襲	2917
19-3		彎	2918
19-4	䜌	攣	2919

		變	2920
		戀	2921
19-5		鹽	2923^{s}
19-6		蠻	2922
20-5		鹽	2923
20-8		鑿	2924

□3

ENCLOSURE

1-1	乚	匕	2925
	㇆	刀	2926
	㇌	乃	2927
	乀	八	2928
		入	3370^{p}
1-2	乚	巳	3388^{p}
	㇆	刃	2929
		刅	2930
1-3		巴	3438^{p}
1-4		司	2931
1-5		迅	3046^{p}
1-6		迅	3202^{p}
1-7		直	2932
1-12		置	2608^{p}
2-0		厂	3360^{p}
2-1	勹	勺	2933
		勻	2934
	㇌	乃	2927^{s}
	才	寸	2935
	丆	万	2936
	ナ	尤	2937
	几	凡	2938
		凡	2939
	凵	山	2940
2-2	辶	込辺	⇨□3-2^{s}
	丄	止	2941
	勹	勾	2942

		勿	2943
		匂	2944
	厂	反	2945
		仄	2946
		厄	2947
	丆	不	3434^{p}
	ア	及	2948
	厂	斤	2949
		戶	2950
	㇄	氏	2951
	ナ	友	2952
	十	斗	2953
		斗	2954
	冂	円	2955
		月	2956
		月	2957
		月	2958
		月	2959
	八	凢	2960
	凵	凶	2961
	匚	匹	2962
		区	2963
		巨	3039^{s}
	匚	匹	2964
	ユ	丑	2965
2-3	辶	巡迅	⇨□3-3^{s}
	勹	包	2966
		句	2967
		包	2968
	丁	可	2969
	厂	圧	2970
	丆	石	2971
	厂	斥	2972
	ナ	布	2973
		左	2974
		右	2975
		存	2982^{s}
	冂	用	2976

2-4	廴	廷	3058^{s}
	辶	近返	etc⇨□3-4^{s}
	九	旭	2977
	勹	旬	2978
	厂	灰	2979
		厎	2980
	厂	后	2981
	ナ	存	2982
		有	2983
		在	2984
		灰	2985
		有	2986
	冂	同	2987
		网	2988
		肉	3200^{p}
	匚	匡	2989
		匠	2990
	匚	臣	2991
2-5	廴	延	3073^{s}
	辶	述迫	etc⇨□3-5^{s}
	厂	辰	2992
	匚	医	2993
2-6	廴	建廻	⇨□3-6^{s}
	辶	送追	etc⇨□3-6^{s}
	厂	厚	3003^{s}
	厂	房	2994
		肩	2995
		戾	2996
	冂	罔	2997
		周	2998
		周	2999
	凵	画	3000
		函	3001
2-7	辶	通連	etc⇨□3-7^{s}
	厂	厖	3002
		厚	3003
		厘	3004
	厂	扁	3005
		盾	3006
	几	風	3007
	凵	幽	3008
		函	3001^{s}
2-8	辶	遇	3135^{s}
		遊	3142^{s}
		進週	etc⇨□3-8^{s}
	厂	原	3009
		辱唇	⇨▀7-3^{p}
	厂	扇	3010
	匚	匿	3011
2-9	辶	道運	etc⇨□3-9^{s}
	厂	脣	2739^{p}
	厂	盾	3012
	匚	區	3013
	匚	匿	3014
2-10	辶	違遠	etc⇨□3-10^{s}
	厂	扉	3015
		雇	3016
2-11		適遭	etc⇨□3-11^{s}
2-12	辶	選遺	etc⇨□3-12^{s}
	厂	厭	3017
		暦	3018
		歴	3019
2-13		避還	⇨□3-13^{s}
2-14	厂	曆	3020
		歷	3021
2-15		壓	3022
3-0	冂	冂	3431^{p}
	口	口	3382^{p}
	口	囗	3391^{p}
3-1	辶	辶	3191^{s}
	牙	牙	3435^{p}
	尸	尺	3440^{p}
	不	不	3434^{p}
	斤	斤	2949^{p}
	尢	尤	3023
	方	方	1963^{p}
	片	片	3461^{p}
	爪	爪	3024
	口	曰	3025
		曰	3026
	口	日	3027
		日	3028
3-2	辶	辺	3029
		込	3030
	辶	辻	3192^{s}
	夂	処	3031
	尸	尻	3032
		尼	3033
	广	庁	3034
		広	3035
	斤	斥	2972^{p}
	巳	民	3036
	皮	皮	3037
	才	存	2982^{ps}
	片	片	3514^{p}
	瓜	瓜	3038
	匚	巨	3039
		巨	3040
	口	田	3041
		囚	3042
	口	皿	3474^{p}
	口	目	3043
	且	且	3485^{p}
	口	四	3044
		罒	3045
3-3	辶	迅	3046
		巡	3047
		迄	3048
	弋	式	3049
	夕	名	2169^{p}
		多	2170^{p}
	尸	尽	3050
	广	庄	3051
	斤	后	2981^{p}

	ナ	衣	2013p
	亻	在存	⇒□2-4p
	冂	向	3052
	囗	団	3053
		因	3054
		回	3055
3-4	廴	延	3056
		廷	3057
	廴	廷	3058
	辶	迎	3059
		返	3060
		近	3061
		迄	3048s
	尸	尾	3062
		局	3063
		尿	3064
	广	序	3065
		応	3066
		床	3067
	亻冂	伺	69p
	匚	臣	3068
	囗	囲	3069
		困	3070
		図	3071
		囬	3072
3-5	廴	延	3073
	辶	迫	3074
		述	3075
		迪	3076
		迭	3077
	尸	届	3078
		屈	3079
		居	3080
		屆	3081
	广	府	3082
		庖	3083
		底	3084
		店	3085

		度	3100s
	亠	夜	2056p
	囗	固	3086
		国	3087
3-6	廴	建	3088
	廴	廻	3089
		建	3090
	辶	逆	3091
		迷	3092
		送	3093
		退	3094
		逃	3095
		追	3096
	⺄	飛	3572p
	尸	昼	3097
		屋	3098
		屍	3099
	广	度	3100
		席	3113s
		庭	3114s
	囗	圀	3101
3-7	辶	逐	3102
		連	3103
		逝	3104
		速	3105
		逓	3106
		途	3107
		透	3108
		通	3109
		造	3110
	匕	眞	2110p
	尸	展	3111
	广	庫	3112
		席	3113
		庭	3114
		唐	3115
		座	3116
		庭	3117

		唐	3118
		庶	3127s
	囗	圃	3119
3-8	辶	逸	3120
		進	3121
		週	3122
		逮	3123
		遇	3135s
		透	3108s
		遊	3142s
	广	康	3124
		麻	3125
		鹿	3126
		庶	3127
		庸	3128
		麻	3129
		[illegible]	3130
		廊	3147s
	囗	圏	3131
		國	3132
3-9	辶	遅	3133
		道	3134
		遇	3135
		遍	3136
		過	3137
		遂	3138
		達	3139
		運	3140
		遥	3141
		遊	3142
		迸	3143
	弋	貳	3144
	尸	属	3145
	广	廃	3146
		廊	3147
		廓	3163s
	囗	圏	3148
		圍	3149

Pattern	Element	Character	Number
3-10	⻌	遠	3150
		遑	3151
		遣	3152
		遮	3158[s]
	⻌	遡	3257[s]
	广	廉	3153
		廉	3154
		廊	3155
		廓	3163[s]
	口	園	3156
		圓	3157
3-11	⻌	遮	3158
		遭	3159
		適	3160
	尸	層	3161
	广	腐	3162
		廓	3163
		廣	3177[s]
	口	團	3164
		圖	3165
3-12	⻌	遺	3166
		遵	3167
		遼	3168
		選	3169
		遷	3170
	尸	履	3171
		層	3172
	广	慶	3173
		麼	3174
		摩	3175
		廢	3176
		廣	3177
		摩	3178
3-13	⻌	避	3179
		還	3180
	广	磨	3181
		磨	3182
3-14		應	3183

Pattern	Element	Character	Number
3-15	广	曆	3184
		曆	3185
3-16		願	1845[p]
3-18	尸	屬	3186
	广	魔	3187
		魔	3188
3-21		鷹	3189
3-22		廳	3190
4-1	⻌	辶	3191
	牙	牙	3488[p]
4-2	⻌	辻	3192
		込	3193
	气	気	3194
	弋	弐	3195
	耂	考	3196
		老	3197
		孝	3205[s]
	虍	虍	3198
	⺈	危	3199
	衣	衣	2013[p]
	艮	艮	3517[p]
	少	劣	2395[p]
	而	而	2027[p]
	尺	尽	3050[p]
	内	肉	3200
4-3	⻌	迄	3201
		迅	3202
		巡	3203
	呉	呉	2549[p]
	戈	戒	3204
	戸	戻	1942[p]
	耂	孝	3205
		考	3196[s]
	耂	希	2049[p]
	尹	君	3206
	亻	何	65[p]
	⺈	角	2047[p]
	尸	局	3063[p]

Pattern	Element	Character	Number
4-4	⻌	迎	3207
		返	3208
		近	3209
		迄	3201[s]
	弋	武	3210
	戸	房 戻	etc⇒□2-6[p]
	戸	房 肩	⇒■1-7[p]
	耂	者	3211
	虍	虎	3212
	亠	夜	2056[p]
4-5	⻌	迫	3213
		述	3214
		迪	3215
		迭	3216
	県	県	2641[p]
	戸	扁	3005[p]
	耂	者	3217
	虍	虐	3218
		虐	3219
		盾	3006[p]
	少	省	2449[p]
	手	看	3220
	冂	南	2082[p]
	尺	昼	3097[p]
4-6	⻌	逆	3221
		迷	3222
		迹	3223
		送	3224
		退	3225
		逃	3226
		追	3227
	气	氣	3228
	戸	扇	1950[p]
	虍	虐	3218[s]
4-7	⻌	逐	3229
		連	3230
		逝	3231
		速	3232